UNIVERSITY CASEBOOK SERIES®

CONSTITUTIONAL LAW

TWENTIETH EDITION

NOAH R. FELDMAN
Felix Frankfurter Professor of Law,
Harvard University

KATHLEEN M. SULLIVAN
Partner, Quinn Emanuel Urquhart & Sullivan, LLP
Former Professor of Law and Dean of the School of Law,
Stanford University
Former Professor of Law, Harvard University

FOUNDATION
PRESS

444 Cedar Street, Suite 700
St. Paul, MN 55101
1-877-888-1330

Printed in the United States of America

ISBN: 978-1-68328-787-2

For Mina Zipporah Feldman and Jaemin David Feldman

NRF

For my many students at Harvard and Stanford Law Schools,
who taught me as much as I taught them

KMS

PREFACE TO THE TWENTIETH EDITION

This edition of the casebook marks important changes in the composition of the Roberts Court. When the last edition went to press, Justice Antonin Scalia had died and a successor had not been confirmed. Subsequently, after the Republican Senate declined to vote on President Barack Obama's nominee, Judge Merrick Garland, President Donald Trump was elected and nominated Judge Neil Gorsuch, who was confirmed to fill the seat.

With the Court back at full strength, the October 2017 Term saw several consequential opinions that are featured in this edition. One, Masterpiece Cakeshop, Ltd. v. Colorado Civil Rights Commission, written by Justice Anthony Kennedy, was a much-anticipated followup to the landmark same-sex marriage decision, Obergefell v. Hodges. Although Masterpiece Cakeshop did not definitively address the potentially competing demands of equality and liberty, it arguably broke new doctrinal ground in the law of free exercise.

Another, Trump v. Hawaii, written by Chief Justice John Roberts, upheld President Trump's executive order banning immigration from five majority-Muslim countries. A dissent by Justice Sonia Sotomayor compared the Court's opinion to Korematsu v. United States. The Court's opinion rejected the comparison and for the first time repudiated Korematsu as "gravely wrong the day it was decided" and "overruled in the court of history."

The day after Trump v. Hawaii was handed down, Justice Kennedy retired, and President Trump nominated Judge Brett Kavanaugh, who was subsequently confirmed by the Senate. Justice Kennedy had emerged as the Court's swing vote after the retirement of Justice Sandra O'Connor. His replacement changes the balance of the Court and will likely lead to new trends in constitutional law.

As it has done since its first edition in 1937, the casebook aims to present constitutional law as a species of law, informed by history, politics, and ideas but also marked by a deep, if contested, internal structure. Our goal is that any student learning constitutional law from this book will be readily equipped to practice it. The casebook attempts to uncover and explicate the rules, standards, and methodologies that inform practice before the Court as much as it seeks to make sense of the Court's evolving doctrine.

In keeping with longstanding practice, deletions and alterations are marked by brackets rather than ellipses, and footnotes are renumbered from the original text opinions, with those from opinions by the Justices so designated.

This edition is the third since the most recent change in the authorship of the book. Beginning as Noel Dowling's Cases on Constitutional Law over three-quarters of a century ago, the book during the 1960s became Dowling and Gunther, then Gunther and Dowling. When the present authors studied from the book as students, it had become known as Gunther's Constitutional Law. The casebook became Gunther and Sullivan in 1997, and from 2001 to 2013 it was Sullivan and Gunther. After two editions as Sullivan and Feldman, it now becomes Feldman and Sullivan. The authors remain deeply committed to the book's unique place among constitutional law casebooks.

We are grateful to the many longtime faithful users of the casebook and to those who have joined their ranks with recent editions. Special thanks to

Judge Jeffrey Sutton for suggestions on state constitutional law; to Dan Coenen for very thoughtful detailed comments on the whole manuscript; and to Charles Fried, Martha Minow, and Laurence Tribe for many helpful suggestions over the years. Finally, we are thankful for excellent research assistance from Harleen Gambhir, Clare Duncan, Medha Gargeya, Sarah Grant, Victoria Hall-Palerm, Cate McCaffrey, Zach ZhenHe Tan and Grace Wallack.

We hope that you will enjoy teaching from this edition of the casebook, and that Gerald Gunther would continue to recognize his great presence in its pages.

NOAH FELDMAN
CAMBRIDGE, MASSACHUSETTS

KATHLEEN M. SULLIVAN
NEW YORK, NEW YORK

June 2019

SUMMARY OF CONTENTS

TABLE OF CONTENTS

TABLE OF CASES

The principal cases are in bold type.

TABLE OF AUTHORITIES

THE CONSTITUTION OF THE UNITED STATES OF AMERICA

We the People of the United States, in Order to form a more perfect Union, establish Justice, insure domestic Tranquility, provide for the common defence, promote the general Welfare, and secure the Blessings of Liberty to ourselves and our Posterity, do ordain and establish this Constitution for the United States of America.

ARTICLE I.

SECTION 1. All legislative Powers herein granted shall be vested in a Congress of the United States, which shall consist of a Senate and House of Representatives.

Congress / Leg. Branch

SECTION 2. The House of Representatives shall be composed of Members chosen every second Year by the People of the several States, and the Electors in each State shall have the Qualifications requisite for Electors of the most numerous Branch of the State Legislature.

House of Representatives

No Person shall be a Representative who shall not have attained to the Age of twenty five Years, and been seven Years a Citizen of the United States, and who shall not, when elected, be an Inhabitant of that State in which he shall be chosen.

Representatives and direct Taxes shall be apportioned among the several States which may be included within this Union, according to their respective Numbers, which shall be determined by adding to the whole Number of free Persons, including those bound to Service for a Term of Years, and excluding Indians not taxed, three fifths of all other Persons. The actual Enumeration shall be made within three Years after the first Meeting of the Congress of the United States, and within every subsequent Term of ten Years, in such Manner as they shall by Law direct. The Number of Representatives shall not exceed one for every thirty Thousand, but each State shall have at Least one Representative; and until such enumeration shall be made, the State of New Hampshire shall be entitled to chuse three, Massachusetts eight, Rhode Island and Providence Plantations one, Connecticut five, New-York six, New Jersey four, Pennsylvania eight, Delaware one, Maryland six, Virginia ten, North Carolina five, South Carolina five, and Georgia three.

When vacancies happen in the Representation from any State, the Executive Authority thereof shall issue Writs of Election to fill such Vacancies.

The House of Representatives shall chuse their Speaker and other Officers; and shall have the sole Power of Impeachment.

SECTION 3. The Senate of the United States shall be composed of two Senators from each State, chosen by the Legislature thereof, for six Years; and each Senator shall have one Vote.

Senate

Immediately after they shall be assembled in Consequence of the first Election, they shall be divided as equally as may be into three Classes. The Seats of the Senators of the first Class shall be vacated at the Expiration of the second Year, of the second Class at the Expiration of the fourth Year, and of the third Class at the Expiration of the sixth Year, so that one third may be chosen every second Year; and if Vacancies happen by Resignation, or otherwise, during the Recess of the Legislature of any State, the Executive thereof may make temporary Appointments until the next Meeting of the Legislature, which shall then fill such Vacancies.

No Person shall be a Senator who shall not have attained to the Age of thirty Years, and been nine Years a Citizen of the United States, and who shall not, when elected, be an Inhabitant of that State for which he shall be chosen.

The Vice President of the United States shall be President of the Senate, but shall have no Vote, unless they be equally divided.

The Senate shall chuse their other Officers, and also a President pro tempore, in the Absence of the Vice President, or when he shall exercise the Office of President of the United States.

The Senate shall have the sole Power to try all Impeachments. When sitting for that Purpose, they shall be on Oath or Affirmation. When the President of the United States is tried the Chief Justice shall preside: And no Person shall be convicted without the Concurrence of two thirds of the Members present.

Judgment in Cases of Impeachment shall not extend further than to removal from Office, and disqualification to hold and enjoy any Office of honor, Trust or Profit under the United States: but the Party convicted shall nevertheless be liable and subject to Indictment, Trial, Judgment and Punishment, according to Law.

SECTION 4. The Times, Places and Manner of holding Elections for Senators and Representatives, shall be prescribed in each State by the Legislature thereof; but the Congress may at any time by Law make or alter such Regulations, except as to the Places of chusing Senators.

The Congress shall assemble at least once in every Year, and such Meeting shall be on the first Monday in December, unless they shall by Law appoint a different Day.

SECTION 5. Each House shall be the Judge of the Elections, Returns and Qualifications of its own Members, and a Majority of each shall constitute a Quorum to do Business; but a smaller Number may adjourn from day to day, and may be authorized to compel the Attendance of absent Members, in such Manner, and under such Penalties as each House may provide.

Each House may determine the Rules of its Proceedings, punish its Members for disorderly Behaviour, and, with the Concurrence of two thirds, expel a Member.

Each House shall keep a Journal of its Proceedings, and from time to time publish the same, excepting such Parts as may in their Judgment require Secrecy; and the Yeas and Nays of the Members of either House on any question shall, at the Desire of one fifth of those Present, be entered on the Journal.

Neither House, during the Session of Congress, shall, without the Consent of the other, adjourn for more than three days, nor to any other Place than that in which the two Houses shall be sitting.

SECTION 6. The Senators and Representatives shall receive a Compensation for their Services, to be ascertained by Law, and paid out of the Treasury of the United States. They shall in all Cases, except Treason,

Felony and Breach of the Peace, be privileged from Arrest during their Attendance at the Session of their respective Houses, and in going to and returning from the same; and for any Speech or Debate in either House, they shall not be questioned in any other Place.

No Senator or Representative shall, during the Time for which he was elected, be appointed to any civil Office under the Authority of the United States, which shall have been created, or the Emoluments whereof shall have been encreased during such time; and no Person holding any Office under the United States, shall be a Member of either House during his Continuance in Office.

SECTION 7. All Bills for raising Revenue shall originate in the House of Representatives; but the Senate may propose or concur with amendments as on other Bills.

Every Bill which shall have passed the House of Representatives and the Senate, shall, before it become a Law, be presented to the President of the United States; If he approve he shall sign it, but if not he shall return it, with his Objections to that House in which it shall have originated, who shall enter the Objections at large on their Journal, and proceed to reconsider it. If after such Reconsideration two thirds of that House shall agree to pass the Bill, it shall be sent, together with the Objections, to the other House, by which it shall likewise be reconsidered, and if approved by two thirds of that House, it shall become a Law. But in all such Cases the Votes of both Houses shall be determined by Yeas and Nays, and the Names of the Persons voting for and against the Bill shall be entered on the Journal of each House respectively. If any Bill shall not be returned by the President within ten Days (Sunday excepted) after it shall have been presented to him, the Same shall be a Law, in like Manner as if he had signed it, unless the Congress by their Adjournment prevent its Return, in which Case it shall not be a Law.

Every Order, Resolution, or Vote to which the Concurrence of the Senate and House of Representatives may be necessary (except on a question of Adjournment) shall be presented to the President of the United States; and before the Same shall take Effect, shall be approved by him, or being disapproved by him, shall be repassed by two thirds of the Senate and House of Representatives, according to the Rules and Limitations prescribed in the Case of a Bill.

SECTION 8. The Congress shall have Power To lay and collect Taxes, Duties, Imposts and Excises, to pay the Debts and provide for the common Defence and general Welfare of the United States; but all Duties, Imposts and Excises shall be uniform throughout the United States;

To borrow Money on the credit of the United States;

To regulate Commerce with foreign Nations, and among the several States, and with the Indian Tribes;

To establish an uniform Rule of Naturalization, and uniform Laws on the subject of Bankruptcies throughout the United States;

To coin Money, regulate the Value thereof, and of foreign Coin, and fix the Standard of Weights and Measures;

To provide for the Punishment of counterfeiting the Securities and current Coin of the United States;

To establish Post Offices and post Roads;

To promote the Progress of Science and useful Arts, by securing for limited Times to Authors and Inventors the exclusive Right to their respective Writings and Discoveries;

To constitute Tribunals inferior to the supreme Court;

To define and punish Piracies and Felonies committed on the high Seas, and Offences against the Law of Nations;

To declare War, grant Letters of Marque and Reprisal, and make Rules concerning Captures on Land and Water;

To raise and support Armies, but no Appropriation of Money to that Use shall be for a longer Term than two Years;

To provide and maintain a Navy;

To make Rules for the Government and Regulation of the land and naval Forces;

To provide for calling forth the Militia to execute the Laws of the Union, suppress Insurrections and repel Invasions;

To provide for organizing, arming, and disciplining, the Militia, and for governing such Part of them as may be employed in the Service of the United States, reserving to the States respectively, the Appointment of the Officers, and the Authority of training the Militia according to the discipline prescribed by Congress;

To exercise exclusive Legislation in all Cases whatsoever, over such District (not exceeding ten Miles square) as may, by Cession of particular States, and the Acceptance of Congress, become the Seat of the Government of the United States, and to exercise like Authority over all Places purchased by the Consent of the Legislature of the State in which the Same shall be, for the Erection of Forts, Magazines, Arsenals, dock-Yards, and other needful Buildings;—And

To make all Laws which shall be necessary and proper for carrying into Execution the foregoing Powers, and all other Powers vested by this Constitution in the Government of the United States, or in any Department or Officer thereof.

SECTION 9. The Migration or Importation of such Persons as any of the States now existing shall think proper to admit, shall not be prohibited by the Congress prior to the Year one thousand eight hundred and eight, but a Tax or duty may be imposed on such Importation, not exceeding ten dollars for each Person.

The Privilege of the Writ of Habeas Corpus shall not be suspended, unless when in Cases of Rebellion or Invasion the public Safety may require it.

No Bill of Attainder or ex post facto Law shall be passed.

No Capitation, or other direct, Tax shall be laid, unless in Proportion to the Census or Enumeration herein before directed to be taken.

No Tax or Duty shall be laid on Articles exported from any State.

No Preference shall be given by any Regulation of Commerce or Revenue to the Ports of one State over those of another; nor shall Vessels bound to, or from, one State, be obliged to enter, clear or pay Duties in another.

No Money shall be drawn from the Treasury, but in Consequence of Appropriations made by Law; and a regular Statement and Account of the

Receipts and Expenditures of all public Money shall be published from time to time.

No Title of Nobility shall be granted by the United States: And no Person holding any Office of Profit or Trust under them, shall, without the Consent of the Congress, accept of any present, Emolument, Office, or Title, of any kind whatever, from any King, Prince or foreign State.

SECTION 10. No State shall enter into any Treaty, Alliance, or Confederation; grant Letters of Marque and Reprisal; coin Money; emit Bills of Credit; make any Thing but gold and silver Coin a Tender in Payment of Debts; pass any Bill of Attainder, ex post facto Law, or Law impairing the Obligation of Contracts, or grant any Title of Nobility.

states can't do things

No State shall, without the Consent of the Congress, lay any Imposts or Duties on Imports or Exports, except what may be absolutely necessary for executing its inspection Laws: and the net Produce of all Duties and Imposts, laid by any State on Imports or Exports, shall be for the Use of the Treasury of the United States; and all such Laws shall be subject to the Revision and Controul of the Congress.

No State shall, without the Consent of Congress, lay any Duty of Tonnage, keep Troops, or Ships of War in time of Peace, enter into any Agreement or Compact with another State, or with a foreign Power, or engage in War, unless actually invaded, or in such imminent Danger as will not admit of delay.

ARTICLE II.

SECTION 1. The executive Power shall be vested in a President of the United States of America. He shall hold his Office during the Term of four Years, and, together with the Vice President, chosen for the same Term, be elected, as follows

President / executive branch

Each State shall appoint, in such Manner as the Legislature thereof may direct, a Number of Electors, equal to the whole Number of Senators and Representatives to which the State may be entitled in the Congress: but no Senator or Representative, or Person holding an Office of Trust or Profit under the United States, shall be appointed an Elector.

The Electors shall meet in their respective States, and vote by Ballot for two Persons, of whom one at least shall not be an Inhabitant of the same State with themselves. And they shall make a List of all the Persons voted for, and of the Number of Votes for each; which List they shall sign and certify, and transmit sealed to the Seat of the Government of the United States, directed to the President of the Senate. The President of the Senate shall, in the Presence of the Senate and House of Representatives, open all the Certificates, and the Votes shall then be counted. The Person having the greatest Number of Votes shall be the President, if such Number be a Majority of the whole Number of Electors appointed; and if there be more than one who have such Majority, and have an equal Number of Votes, then the House of Representatives shall immediately chuse by Ballot one of them for President; and if no Person have a Majority, then from the five highest on the List the said House shall in like Manner chuse the President. But in chusing the President, the Votes shall be taken by States, the Representation from each State having one Vote; a quorum for this Purpose shall consist of a Member or Members from two thirds of the States, and a Majority of all the States shall be necessary to a Choice. In every Case, after the Choice of the President, the Person having the greatest Number of Votes of the

Electors shall be the Vice President. But if there should remain two or more who have equal Votes, the Senate shall chuse from them by Ballot the Vice President.

The Congress may determine the Time of chusing the Electors, and the Day on which they shall give their Votes; which Day shall be the same throughout the United States.

No Person except a natural born Citizen, or a Citizen of the United States, at the time of the Adoption of this Constitution, shall be eligible to the Office of President; neither shall any Person be eligible to that Office who shall not have attained to the Age of thirty five Years, and been fourteen Years a Resident within the United States.

In Case of the Removal of the President from Office, or of his Death, Resignation, or Inability to discharge the Powers and Duties of the said Office, the Same shall devolve on the Vice President, and the Congress may by Law provide for the Case of Removal, Death, Resignation or Inability, both of the President and Vice President, declaring what Officer shall then act as President, and such Officer shall act accordingly, until the Disability be removed, or a President shall be elected.

The President shall, at stated Times, receive for his Services, a Compensation, which shall neither be encreased nor diminished during the Period for which he shall have been elected, and he shall not receive within that Period any other Emolument from the United States, or any of them.

Before he enter on the Execution of his Office, he shall take the following Oath or Affirmation:—"I do solemnly swear (or affirm) that I will faithfully execute the Office of President of the United States, and will to the best of my Ability, preserve, protect and defend the Constitution of the United States."

SECTION 2. The President shall be Commander in Chief of the Army and Navy of the United States, and of the Militia of the several States, when called into the actual Service of the United States; he may require the Opinion, in writing, of the principal Officer in each of the executive Departments, upon any Subject relating to the Duties of their respective Offices, and he shall have Power to grant Reprieves and Pardons for Offences against the United States, except in Cases of Impeachment.

He shall have Power, by and with the Advice and Consent of the Senate, to make Treaties, provided two thirds of the Senators present concur; and he shall nominate, and by and with the Advice and Consent of the Senate, shall appoint Ambassadors, other public Ministers and Consuls, Judges of the supreme Court, and all other Officers of the United States, whose Appointments are not herein otherwise provided for, and which shall be established by Law: but the Congress may by Law vest the Appointment of such inferior Officers, as they think proper, in the President alone, in the Courts of Law, or in the Heads of Departments.

The President shall have Power to fill up all Vacancies that may happen during the Recess of the Senate, by granting Commissions which shall expire at the End of their next Session.

SECTION 3. He shall from time to time give to the Congress Information of the State of the Union, and recommend to their Consideration such Measures as he shall judge necessary and expedient; he may, on extraordinary Occasions, convene both Houses, or either of them, and in

Case of Disagreement between them, with Respect to the Time of Adjournment, he may adjourn them to such Time as he shall think proper; he shall receive Ambassadors and other public Ministers; he shall take Care that the Laws be faithfully executed, and shall Commission all the Officers of the United States.

SECTION 4. The President, Vice President and all Civil Officers of the United States, shall be removed from Office on Impeachment for, and Conviction of, Treason, Bribery, or other high Crimes and Misdemeanors.

ARTICLE III.

SECTION 1. The judicial Power of the United States, shall be vested in one supreme Court, and in such inferior Courts as the Congress may from time to time ordain and establish. The Judges, both of the supreme and inferior Courts, shall hold their Offices during good Behaviour, and shall, at stated Times, receive for their Services, a Compensation, which shall not be diminished during their Continuance in Office.

SECTION 2. The judicial Power shall extend to all Cases, in Law and Equity, arising under this Constitution, the Laws of the United States, and Treaties made, or which shall be made, under their Authority;—to all Cases affecting Ambassadors, other public Ministers and Consuls;—to all Cases of admiralty and maritime Jurisdiction;—to Controversies to which the United States shall be a Party;—to Controversies between two or more States;—between a State and Citizens of another State;—between Citizens of different States;—between Citizens of the same State claiming Lands under Grants of different States, and between a State, or the Citizens thereof, and foreign States, Citizens or Subjects.

In all Cases affecting Ambassadors, other public Ministers and Consuls, and those in which a State shall be Party, the Supreme Court shall have original Jurisdiction. In all the other Cases before mentioned, the supreme Court shall have appellate Jurisdiction, both as to Law and Fact, with such Exceptions, and under such Regulations as the Congress shall make.

The Trial of all Crimes, except in Cases of Impeachment, shall be by Jury; and such Trial shall be held in the State where the said Crimes shall have been committed; but when not committed within any State, the Trial shall be at such Place or Places as the Congress may by Law have directed.

SECTION 3. Treason against the United States, shall consist only in levying War against them, or in adhering to their Enemies, giving them Aid and Comfort. No Person shall be convicted of Treason unless on the Testimony of two Witnesses to the same overt Act, or on Confession in open Court.

The Congress shall have Power to declare the Punishment of Treason, but no Attainder of Treason shall work Corruption of Blood, or Forfeiture except during the Life of the Person attainted.

ARTICLE IV.

SECTION 1. Full Faith and Credit shall be given in each State to the public Acts, Records, and judicial Proceedings of every other State. And the Congress may by general Laws prescribe the Manner in which such Acts, Records and Proceedings shall be proved, and the Effect thereof.

SECTION 2. The Citizens of each State shall be entitled to all Privileges and Immunities of Citizens in the several States.

A Person charged in any State with Treason, Felony, or other Crime, who shall flee from Justice, and be found in another State, shall on Demand of the executive Authority of the State from which he fled, be delivered up, to be removed to the State having Jurisdiction of the Crime.

No Person held to Service or Labour in one State, under the Laws thereof, escaping into another, shall, in Consequence of any Law or Regulation therein, be discharged from such Service or Labour, but shall be delivered up on Claim of the Party to whom such Service or Labour may be due.

SECTION 3. New States may be admitted by the Congress into this Union; but no new State shall be formed or erected within the Jurisdiction of any other State; nor any State be formed by the Junction of two or more States, or Parts of States, without the Consent of the Legislatures of the States concerned as well as of the Congress.

The Congress shall have Power to dispose of and make all needful Rules and Regulations respecting the Territory or other Property belonging to the United States; and nothing in this Constitution shall be so construed as to Prejudice any Claims of the United States, or of any particular State.

SECTION 4. The United States shall guarantee to every State in this Union a Republican Form of Government, and shall protect each of them against Invasion; and on Application of the Legislature, or of the Executive (when the Legislature cannot be convened) against domestic Violence.

ARTICLE V.

The Congress, whenever two thirds of both Houses shall deem it necessary, shall propose Amendments to this Constitution, or, on the Application of the Legislatures of two thirds of the several States, shall call a Convention for proposing Amendments, which, in either Case, shall be valid to all Intents and Purposes, as Part of this Constitution, when ratified by the Legislatures of three fourths of the several States, or by Conventions in three fourths thereof, as the one or the other Mode of Ratification may be proposed by the Congress; Provided that no Amendment which may be made prior to the Year One thousand eight hundred and eight shall in any Manner affect the first and fourth Clauses in the Ninth Section of the first Article; and that no State, without its Consent, shall be deprived of its equal Suffrage in the Senate.

ARTICLE VI.

All Debts contracted and Engagements entered into, before the Adoption of this Constitution, shall be as valid against the United States under this Constitution, as under the Confederation.

This Constitution, and the Laws of the United States which shall be made in Pursuance thereof; and all Treaties made, or which shall be made, under the Authority of the United States, shall be the supreme Law of the Land; and the Judges in every State shall be bound thereby, any Thing in the Constitution or Laws of any State to the Contrary notwithstanding.

The Senators and Representatives before mentioned, and the Members of the several State Legislatures, and all executive and judicial Officers, both of the United States and of the several States, shall be bound by Oath or Affirmation, to support this Constitution; but no religious Test shall ever be required as a Qualification to any Office or public Trust under the United States.

ARTICLE VII.

The Ratification of the Conventions of nine States, shall be sufficient for the Establishment of this Constitution between the States so ratifying the Same.

* * *

ARTICLES IN ADDITION TO, AND AMENDMENT OF, THE CONSTITUTION OF THE UNITED STATES OF AMERICA, PROPOSED BY CONGRESS, AND RATIFIED BY THE SEVERAL STATES, PURSUANT TO THE FIFTH ARTICLE OF THE ORIGINAL CONSTITUTION.

AMENDMENT I [1791].

Congress shall make no law respecting an establishment of religion, or prohibiting the free exercise thereof; or abridging the freedom of speech, or of the press; or the right of the people peaceably to assemble, and to petition the Government for a redress of grievances.

AMENDMENT II [1791].

A well regulated Militia, being necessary to the security of a free State, the right of the people to keep and bear Arms, shall not be infringed.

AMENDMENT III [1791].

No Soldier shall, in time of peace be quartered in any house, without the consent of the Owner, nor in time of war, but in a manner to be prescribed by law.

AMENDMENT IV [1791].

The right of the people to be secure in their persons, houses, papers, and effects, against unreasonable searches and seizures, shall not be violated, and no Warrants shall issue, but upon probable cause, supported by Oath or affirmation, and particularly describing the place to be searched, and the persons or things to be seized.

AMENDMENT V [1791].

No person shall be held to answer for a capital, or otherwise infamous crime, unless on a presentment or indictment of a Grand Jury, except in cases arising in the land or naval forces, or in the Militia, when in actual service in time of War or public danger; nor shall any person be subject for the same offence to be twice put in jeopardy of life or limb; nor shall be compelled in any criminal case to be a witness against himself, nor be deprived of life, liberty, or property, without due process of law; nor shall private property be taken for public use, without just compensation.

AMENDMENT VI [1791].

In all criminal prosecutions, the accused shall enjoy the right to a speedy and public trial, by an impartial jury of the State and district wherein the crime shall have been committed, which district shall have been previously ascertained by law, and to be informed of the nature and cause of the accusation; to be confronted with the witnesses against him; to have compulsory process for obtaining Witnesses in his favor, and to have the Assistance of Counsel for his defence.

AMENDMENT VII [1791].

In Suits at common law, where the value in controversy shall exceed twenty dollars, the right of trial by jury shall be preserved, and no fact tried by a jury, shall be otherwise re-examined in any Court of the United States, than according to the rules of the common law.

AMENDMENT VIII [1791].

Excessive bail shall not be required, nor excessive fines imposed, nor cruel and unusual punishments inflicted.

AMENDMENT IX [1791].

The enumeration in the Constitution, of certain rights, shall not be construed to deny or disparage others retained by the people.

AMENDMENT X [1791].

The powers not delegated to the United States by the Constitution, nor prohibited by it to the States, are reserved to the States respectively, or to the people.

AMENDMENT XI [1798].

The Judicial power of the United States shall not be construed to extend to any suit in law or equity, commenced or prosecuted against one of the United States by Citizens of another State, or by Citizens or Subjects of any Foreign State.

AMENDMENT XII [1804].

The Electors shall meet in their respective states and vote by ballot for President and Vice-President, one of whom, at least, shall not be an inhabitant of the same state with themselves; they shall name in their ballots the person voted for as President, and in distinct ballots the person voted for as Vice-President, and they shall make distinct lists of all persons voted for as President, and of all persons voted for as Vice-President, and of the number of votes for each, which lists they shall sign and certify, and transmit sealed to the seat of the government of the United States, directed to the President of the Senate;—The President of the Senate shall, in the presence of the Senate and House of Representatives, open all the certificates and the votes shall then be counted;—The person having the greatest number of votes for President, shall be the President, if such number be a majority of the whole number of Electors appointed; and if no person have such majority, then from the persons having the highest numbers not exceeding three on the list of those voted for as President, the House of Representatives shall choose immediately, by ballot, the President. But in choosing the President, the votes shall be taken by states, the representation from each state having one vote; a quorum for this purpose shall consist of a member or members from two-thirds of the states, and a majority of all the states shall be necessary to a choice. And if the House of Representatives shall not choose a President whenever the right of choice shall devolve upon them, before the fourth day of March next following, then the Vice-President shall act as President, as in the case of the death or other constitutional disability of the President—The person having the greatest number of votes as Vice-President, shall be the Vice-President, if such number be a majority of the whole number of Electors appointed, and if no person have a majority, then from the two highest numbers on the list, the Senate shall choose the Vice-President; a quorum for the purpose shall consist of two-thirds of the whole number of Senators, and a majority of the whole number shall be necessary to a choice. But no person constitutionally ineligible to the office of President shall be eligible to that of Vice-President of the United States.

AMENDMENT XIII [1865].

SECTION 1. Neither slavery nor involuntary servitude, except as a punishment for crime whereof the party shall have been duly convicted, shall exist within the United States, or any place subject to their jurisdiction.

SECTION 2. Congress shall have power to enforce this article by appropriate legislation.

AMENDMENT XIV [1868].

SECTION 1. All persons born or naturalized in the United States and subject to the jurisdiction thereof, are citizens of the United States and of the State wherein they reside. No State shall make or enforce any law which shall abridge the privileges or immunities of citizens of the United States; nor shall any State deprive any person of life, liberty, or property, without due process of law; nor deny to any person within its jurisdiction the equal protection of the laws.

SECTION 2. Representatives shall be apportioned among the several States according to their respective numbers, counting the whole number of persons in each State, excluding Indians not taxed. But when the right to vote at any election for the choice of electors for President and Vice President of the United States, Representatives in Congress, the Executive and Judicial officers of a State, or the members of the Legislature thereof, is denied to any of the male inhabitants of such State, being twenty-one years of age, and citizens of the United States, or in any way abridged, except for participation in rebellion, or other crime, the basis of representation therein shall be reduced in the proportion which the number of such male citizens shall bear to the whole number of male citizens twenty-one years of age in such State.

SECTION 3. No person shall be a Senator or Representative in Congress, or elector of President and Vice President, or hold any office, civil or military, under the United States, or under any State, who, having previously taken an oath, as a member of Congress, or as an officer of the United States, or as a member of any State legislature, or as an executive or judicial officer of any State, to support the Constitution of the United States, shall have engaged in insurrection or rebellion against the same, or given aid or comfort to the enemies thereof. But Congress may by a vote of two-thirds of each House, remove such disability.

SECTION 4. The validity of the public debt of the United States, authorized by law, including debts incurred for payment of pensions and bounties for services in suppressing insurrection or rebellion, shall not be questioned. But neither the United States nor any State shall assume or pay any debt or obligation incurred in aid of insurrection or rebellion against the United States, or any claim for the loss or emancipation of any slave; but all such debts, obligations and claims shall be held illegal and void.

SECTION 5. The Congress shall have power to enforce, by appropriate legislation, the provisions of this article.

AMENDMENT XV [1870].

SECTION 1. The right of citizens of the United States to vote shall not be denied or abridged by the United States or by any State on account of race, color, or previous condition of servitude.

SECTION 2. The Congress shall have power to enforce this article by appropriate legislation.

AMENDMENT XVI [1913].

The Congress shall have power to lay and collect taxes on incomes, from whatever source derived, without apportionment among the several States, and without regard to any census or enumeration.

AMENDMENT XVII [1913].

The Senate of the United States shall be composed of two Senators from each State, elected by the people thereof, for six years; and each Senator shall have one vote. The electors in each State shall have the qualifications requisite for electors of the most numerous branch of the State legislatures.

When vacancies happen in the representation of any State in the Senate, the executive authority of such State shall issue writs of election to fill such vacancies: *Provided,* That the legislature of any State may empower the executive thereof to make temporary appointments until the people fill the vacancies by election as the legislature may direct.

This amendment shall not be so construed as to affect the election or term of any Senator chosen before it becomes valid as part of the Constitution.

AMENDMENT XVIII [1919].

SECTION 1. After one year from the ratification of this article the manufacture, sale, or transportation of intoxicating liquors within, the importation thereof into, or the exportation thereof from the United States and all territory subject to the jurisdiction thereof for beverage purposes is hereby prohibited.

SECTION 2. The Congress and the several States shall have concurrent power to enforce this article by appropriate legislation.

SECTION 3. This article shall be inoperative unless it shall have been ratified as an amendment to the Constitution by the legislatures of the several States, as provided in the Constitution, within seven years from the date of the submission hereof to the States by the Congress.

AMENDMENT XIX [1920].

The right of citizens of the United States to vote shall not be denied or abridged by the United States or by any State on account of sex.

Congress shall have power to enforce this article by appropriate legislation.

AMENDMENT XX [1933].

SECTION 1. The terms of the President and Vice President shall end at noon on the 20th day of January, and the terms of Senators and Representatives at noon on the 3d day of January, of the years in which such terms would have ended if this article had not been ratified; and the terms of their successors shall then begin.

SECTION 2. The Congress shall assemble at least once in every year, and such meeting shall begin at noon on the 3d day of January, unless they shall by law appoint a different day.

SECTION 3. If, at the time fixed for the beginning of the term of the President, the President elect shall have died, the Vice President elect shall become President. If a President shall not have been chosen before the time fixed for the beginning of his term, or if the President elect shall have failed to qualify, then the Vice President elect shall act as President until a

President shall have qualified; and the Congress may by law provide for the case wherein neither a President elect nor a Vice President elect shall have qualified, declaring who shall then act as President, or the manner in which one who is to act shall be selected, and such person shall act accordingly until a President or Vice President shall have qualified.

SECTION 4. The Congress may by law provide for the case of the death of any of the persons from whom the House of Representatives may choose a President whenever the right of choice shall have devolved upon them, and for the case of the death of any of the persons from whom the Senate may choose a Vice President whenever the right of choice shall have devolved upon them.

SECTION 5. Sections 1 and 2 shall take effect on the 15th day of October following the ratification of this article.

SECTION 6. This article shall be inoperative unless it shall have been ratified as an amendment to the Constitution by the legislatures of three-fourths of the several States within seven years from the date of its submission.

AMENDMENT XXI [1933].

SECTION 1. The eighteenth article of amendment to the Constitution of the United States is hereby repealed.

SECTION 2. The transportation or importation into any State, Territory, or possession of the United States for delivery or use therein of intoxicating liquors, in violation of the laws thereof, is hereby prohibited.

SECTION 3. This article shall be inoperative unless it shall have been ratified as an amendment to the Constitution by conventions in the several States, as provided in the Constitution, within seven years from the date of the submission hereof to the States by the Congress.

AMENDMENT XXII [1951].

SECTION 1. No person shall be elected to the office of the President more than twice, and no person who has held the office of President, or acted as President, for more than two years of a term to which some other person was elected President shall be elected to the office of the President more than once. But this Article shall not apply to any person holding the office of President when this Article was proposed by the Congress, and shall not prevent any person who may be holding the office of President, or acting as President, during the term within which this Article becomes operative from holding the office of President or acting as President during the remainder of such term.

SECTION 2. This article shall be inoperative unless it shall have been ratified as an amendment to the Constitution by the legislatures of three-fourths of the several States within seven years from the date of its submission to the States by the Congress.

AMENDMENT XXIII [1961].

SECTION 1. The District constituting the seat of Government of the United States shall appoint in such manner as the Congress may direct:

A number of electors of President and Vice President equal to the whole number of Senators and Representatives in Congress to which the District would be entitled if it were a State, but in no event more than the least populous State; they shall be in addition to those appointed by the States, but they shall be considered, for the purposes of the election of President and Vice President, to be electors appointed by a State; and they shall meet in the District and perform such duties as provided by the twelfth article of amendment.

SECTION 2. The Congress shall have power to enforce this article by appropriate legislation.

AMENDMENT XXIV [1964].

SECTION 1. The right of citizens of the United States to vote in any primary or other election for President or Vice President, for electors for President or Vice President, or for Senator or Representative in Congress, shall not be denied or abridged by the United States or any State by reason of failure to pay any poll tax or other tax.

SECTION 2. The Congress shall have power to enforce this article by appropriate legislation.

AMENDMENT XXV [1967].

SECTION 1. In case of the removal of the President from office or of his death or resignation, the Vice President shall become President.

SECTION 2. Whenever there is a vacancy in the office of the Vice President, the President shall nominate a Vice President who shall take office upon confirmation by a majority vote of both Houses of Congress.

SECTION 3. Whenever the President transmits to the President pro tempore of the Senate and the Speaker of the House of Representatives his written declaration that he is unable to discharge the powers and duties of his office, and until he transmits to them a written declaration to the contrary, such powers and duties shall be discharged by the Vice President as Acting President.

SECTION 4. Whenever the Vice President and a majority of either the principal officers of the executive departments or of such other body as Congress may by law provide, transmit to the President pro tempore of the Senate and the Speaker of the House of Representatives their written declaration that the President is unable to discharge the powers and duties of his office, the Vice President shall immediately assume the powers and duties of the office as Acting President.

Thereafter, when the President transmits to the President pro tempore of the Senate and the Speaker of the House of Representatives his written declaration that no inability exists, he shall resume the powers and duties of his office unless the Vice President and a majority of either the principal officers of the executive department or of such other body as Congress may by law provide, transmit within four days to the President pro tempore of the Senate and the Speaker of the House of Representatives their written declaration that the President is unable to discharge the powers and duties of his office. Thereupon Congress shall decide the issue, assembling within forty-eight hours for that purpose if not in session. If the Congress, within twenty-one days after receipt of the latter written declaration, or, if Congress is not in session, within twenty-one days after Congress is required to assemble, determines by two-thirds vote of both Houses that the President is unable to discharge the powers and duties of his office, the Vice President shall continue to discharge the same as Acting President; otherwise, the President shall resume the powers and duties of his office.

AMENDMENT XXVI [1971].

SECTION 1. The right of citizens of the United States, who are eighteen years of age or older, to vote shall not be denied or abridged by the United States or by any State on account of age.

SECTION 2. The Congress shall have power to enforce this article by appropriate legislation.

AMENDMENT XXVII [1992].

No law varying the compensation for the services of the Senators and Representatives shall take effect until an election of Representatives shall have intervened.

UNIVERSITY CASEBOOK SERIES®

CONSTITUTIONAL LAW

TWENTIETH EDITION

CHAPTER 1

THE SUPREME COURT'S AUTHORITY AND ROLE

It is traditional to begin the examination of American constitutional law with opinions from the Supreme Court presided over by Chief Justice John Marshall early in the nineteenth century. Attention to Marshall Court cases is more than a ritualistic bow to historical landmarks; key cases of this early period remain important today. In particular, Marbury v. Madison represents the Court's first and still most elaborate justification of its power of judicial review, and Martin v. Hunter's Lessee solidified federal supremacy over the states in the interpretation of federal law and the Constitution.

Although these and other Marshall Court decisions hold a sacrosanct position in the American legal canon today, it is important to remember that the outcome of each was far from inevitable. Today, we may take for granted that the Supreme Court's authority to determine the Constitution's meaning is final and exclusive of all other actors. As you read this chapter, consider the various steps in the development of this understanding, and the turning points that might have led to a different distribution of power. The purpose of the materials that follow is to develop this history and to explore the nature and scope of the Supreme Court's authority. Section 1 discusses Marbury v. Madison, its antecedents and its meaning. Section 2 examines Supreme Court review of state court judgments. Section 3 asks whether the Court's interpretive authority is exclusive or shared. And Section 4 sets forth the limits on constitutional adjudication adopted by the Court.

SECTION 1. THE POWER OF JUDICIAL REVIEW

Chief Justice Marshall's opinion in Marbury v. Madison represents the Court's foundational assertion of the power of judicial review. However, judicial review did not arise suddenly in 1803. Rather, Marbury reflected a variety of earlier practices and justifications. The interpretation of the case and its importance in its original historical context remain subject to debate. On one view, the decision is simply an incidental byproduct of the ordinary judicial function in deciding lawsuits: to look to the governing law, to consider the Constitution as one relevant source of law, and, in cases of conflicting legal statements, to give priority to the Constitution and to refuse enforcement of any contravening legal norm. On another view, the decision reads the Constitution as endowing the Court with the power to police the other branches, acting as the central guardian of constitutional principles and the special enforcer of constitutional norms.

Regardless of its origin, the case stands today at the forefront of the American constitutional canon, and many people around the world consider judicial review essential to the healthy functioning of democracy. Is Marbury's sanctified status justified? Does its reasoning grow logically out of the structure of constitutional democracy? What power, precisely, does the Court claim for itself?

Marbury v. Madison

1 Cranch (5 U.S.) 137, 2 L. Ed. 60 (1803).

[Before ceding power to the incoming Jefferson administration in March 1801, the outgoing Federalist administration of President John Adams made a rash of last-minute judicial appointments. William Marbury was one of those named a justice of the peace for the District of Columbia. Although he had received the nomination of the President and the advice and consent of the Senate, and although his commission had been signed by the President and sealed by outgoing Secretary of State John Marshall, his commission, like that of several others, was not delivered before the end of Adams's term. The Jefferson Administration chose to disregard the undelivered commissions.

Marbury and some disappointed colleagues decided to go directly to the Supreme Court to seek a writ of mandamus to compel Jefferson's Secretary of State, James Madison, to deliver their commissions. Their motion was supported by affidavits including one by John Marshall's brother, James, attesting to the circumstances under which the commissions had been signed and sealed but not timely delivered. Because the new Republican government cancelled two Supreme Court sittings, the Court did not announce a decision on this 1801 request until February 1803.]

■ The opinion of the Court was delivered by CHIEF JUSTICE [MARSHALL]:

At the last term on the affidavits then read and filed with the clerk, a rule was granted in this case, requiring the Secretary of State to show cause why a mandamus should not issue, directing him to deliver to William Marbury his commission as a justice of the peace for the county of Washington, in the district of Columbia.

No cause has been shown, and the present motion is for a mandamus. The peculiar delicacy of this case, the novelty of some of its circumstances, and the real difficulty attending the points which occur in it, require a complete exposition of the principles on which the opinion to be given by the court is [founded].

In the order in which the court has viewed this subject, the following questions have been considered and decided:

1st. Has the applicant a right to the commission he demands?

2d. If he has a right, and that right has been violated, do the laws of this country afford him a remedy?

3d. If they do afford him a remedy, is it a mandamus issuing from this court?

The first object of inquiry is—1st. Has the applicant a right to the commission he demands?

[It is] decidedly the opinion of the court, that when a commission has been signed by the president, the appointment is made; and that the commission is complete, when the seal of the United States has been affixed to it by the [secretary of state].

[To] withhold [Marbury's] commission, therefore, is an act deemed by the court not warranted by law, but violative of a vested legal right.

This brings us to the second inquiry; which is: If he has a right, and that right has been violated, do the laws of his country afford him a remedy?

The very essence of civil liberty certainly consists in the right of every individual to claim the protection of the laws, whenever he receives an injury. One of the first duties of government is to afford that protection. [The] government of the United States has been emphatically termed a government of laws, and not of men. It will certainly cease to deserve this high appellation, if the laws furnish no remedy for the violation of a vested legal right. If this obloquy is to be cast on the jurisprudence of our country, it must arise from the peculiar character of the case.

It behooves us then to enquire whether there be in its composition any ingredient which shall exempt it from legal investigation, or exclude the injured party from [legal redress].

Is it in the nature of the transaction? Is the act of delivering or withholding a commission to be considered as a mere political act, belonging to the executive department alone, for the performance of which entire confidence is placed by our constitution in the supreme executive; and for any misconduct respecting which, the injured individual has no remedy. That there may be such cases is not to be questioned; but that every act of duty, to be performed in any of the great departments of government, constitutes such a case, is not to be [admitted].

It follows, then, that the question, whether the legality of an act of the head of a department be examinable in a court of justice or not, must always depend on the nature of that [act].

By the constitution of the United States, the President is invested with certain important political powers, in the exercise of which he is to use his own discretion, and is accountable only to his country in his political character, and to his own conscience. To aid him in the performance of these duties, he is authorized to appoint certain officers, who act by his authority and in conformity with his orders. In such cases, their acts are his acts; and whatever opinion may be entertained of the manner in which executive discretion may be used, still there exists, and can exist, no power to control that discretion. The subjects are political. They respect the nation, not individual rights, and being entrusted to the executive, the decision of the executive is conclusive. The application of this remark will be perceived by adverting to the act of congress for establishing the department of foreign affairs. This officer, as his duties were prescribed by that act, is to conform precisely to the will of the President. He is the mere organ by whom that will is communicated. The acts of such an officer, as an officer, can never be examinable by the courts. But when the legislature proceeds to impose on that officer other duties; when he is directed peremptorily to perform certain acts; when the rights of individuals are dependent on the performance of those acts; he is so far the officer of the law; is amenable to the laws for his conduct; and cannot at his discretion sport away the vested rights of others.

The conclusion from this reasoning is, that where the heads of departments are the political or confidential agents of the executive, merely to execute the will of the President, or rather to act in cases in which the executive possesses a constitutional or legal discretion, nothing can be more perfectly clear than that their acts are only politically examinable. But where a specific duty is assigned by law, and individual rights depend upon the performance of that duty, it seems equally clear, that the individual who considers himself injured, has a right to resort to the laws of his country for a [remedy].

It is, then, the opinion of the Court [that Marbury has a] right to the commission; a refusal to deliver which is a plain violation of that right, for which the laws of his country afford him a remedy.

It remains to be inquired whether [he] is entitled to the remedy for which he applies. This depends on—1st. The nature of the writ applied for; and 2d. The power of this court.

1st. The nature of the writ. [This] writ, if awarded, would be directed to an officer of government, and its mandate to him would be, to use the words of Blackstone, "to do a particular thing therein specified, which appertains to his office and duty and which the court has previously determined, or at least supposes, to be consonant to right and justice." Or, in the words of Lord Mansfield, the applicant, in this case, has a right to execute an office of public concern, and is kept out of possession of that right. These circumstances certainly concur in this case.

Still, to render the mandamus a proper remedy, the officer to whom it is to be directed, must be one to whom, on legal principles, such writ may be directed; and the person applying for it must be without any other specific and legal remedy.

1st. With respect to the officer to whom it would be directed. The intimate political relation, subsisting between the president of the United States and the heads of departments, necessarily renders any legal investigation of the acts of one of those high officers peculiarly irksome, as well as delicate; and excites some hesitation with respect to the propriety of entering into such investigation. Impressions are often received without much reflection or examination, and it is not wonderful, that in such a case as this, the assertion, by an individual, of his legal claims in a court of justice, to which claims it is the duty of that court to attend, should at first view be considered by some, as an attempt to intrude into the cabinet, and to intermeddle with the prerogatives of the executive.

It is scarcely necessary for the court to disclaim all pretensions to such a jurisdiction. An extravagance, so absurd and excessive, could not have been entertained for a moment. The province of the court is, solely, to decide on the rights of individuals, not to enquire how the executive, or executive officers, perform duties in which they have a discretion. Questions, in their nature political, or which are, by the constitution and laws, submitted to the executive, can never be made in this court.

But, if this be not such a question; if so far from being an intrusion into the secrets of the cabinet, it respects a paper, which, according to law, is upon record, and to a copy of which the law gives a right, on the payment of ten cents; if it be no intermeddling with a subject, over which the executive can be considered as having exercised any control; what is there in the exalted station of the officer, which shall bar a citizen from asserting, in a court of justice, his legal rights, or shall forbid a court to listen to the claim; or to issue a mandamus, directing the performance of a duty, not depending on executive discretion, but on particular acts of congress and the general principles of law?

[Where the head of a department] is directed by law to do a certain act affecting the absolute rights of individuals, [it] is not perceived on what ground the courts of the country are further excused from the duty of giving [judgment].

This, then, is a plain case for a mandamus, either to deliver the commission, or a copy of it from the record; and it only remains to be enquired,

Whether it can issue from this court.

The act to establish the judicial courts of the United States authorizes the Supreme Court "to issue writs of mandamus in cases warranted by the principles and usages of law, to any courts appointed, or persons holding office, under the authority of the United States."[1]

The secretary of state, being a person holding an office under the authority of the United States, is precisely within the letter of the description; and if this court is not authorized to issue a writ of mandamus to such an officer, it must be because the law is unconstitutional, and therefore absolutely incapable of conferring the authority, and assigning the duties which its words purport to confer and assign.

The constitution vests the whole judicial power of the United States in one Supreme Court, and such inferior courts as congress shall, from time to time, ordain and establish. This power is expressly extended to all cases arising under the laws of the United States; and, consequently, in some form, may be exercised over the present case; because the right claimed is given by a law of the United States.

In the distribution of this power it is declared that "the Supreme Court shall have original jurisdiction in all cases affecting ambassadors, other public ministers and consuls, and those in which a state shall be a party. In all other cases, the Supreme Court shall have appellate jurisdiction."

It has been insisted, at the bar, that as the original grant of jurisdiction, to the supreme and inferior courts, is general, and the clause, assigning original jurisdiction to the Supreme Court, contains no negative or restrictive words, the power remains to the legislature, to assign original jurisdiction to that court in other cases than those specified in the article which has been recited; provided those cases belong to the judicial power of the United States.

---

[1] The full text of Section 13 of the Judiciary Act of 1789, 1 Stat. 73, reads: "And be it further enacted, That the Supreme Court shall have exclusive jurisdiction of all controversies of a civil nature, where a state is a party, except between a state and its citizens; and except also between a state and citizens of other states, or aliens, in which latter case it shall have original but not exclusive jurisdiction. And shall have exclusively all such jurisdiction of suits or proceedings against ambassadors, or other public ministers, or their domestics, or domestic servants, as a court of law can have or exercise consistently with the law of nations; and original, but not exclusive jurisdiction of all suits brought by ambassadors, or other public ministers, or in which a consul, or vice consul, shall be a party. And the trial of issues of fact in the Supreme Court, in all actions at law against citizens of the United States, shall be by jury. The Supreme Court shall also have appellate jurisdiction from the circuit courts and courts of the several states, in the cases herein after specially provided for; and shall have power to issue writs of prohibition to the district courts, when proceeding as courts of admiralty and maritime jurisdiction, and writs of mandamus, in cases warranted by the principles and usages of law, to any courts appointed, or persons holding office, under the authority of the United States."

If it had been intended to leave it in the discretion of the legislature to apportion the judicial power between the supreme and inferior courts according to the will of that body, it would certainly have been useless to have proceeded further than to have defined the judicial power, and the tribunals in which it should be vested. The subsequent part of the section is mere surplusage, is entirely without meaning, if such is to be the construction. If congress remains at liberty to give this court appellate jurisdiction, where the constitution has declared their jurisdiction shall be original; and original jurisdiction where the constitution has declared it shall be appellate; the distribution of jurisdiction, made in the constitution, is form without substance.

Affirmative words are often, in their operation, negative of other objects than those affirmed; and in this case, a negative or exclusive sense must be given to them or they have no operation at all.

It cannot be presumed that any clause in the constitution is intended to be without effect; and, therefore, such a construction is inadmissible, unless the words [require].

When an instrument organizing fundamentally a judicial system, divides it into one supreme, and so many inferior courts as the legislature may ordain and establish; then enumerates its powers, and proceeds so far to distribute them, as to define the jurisdiction of the supreme court by declaring the cases in which it shall take original jurisdiction, and that in others it shall take appellate jurisdiction; the plain import of the words seems to be, that in one class of cases its jurisdiction is original, and not appellate; in the other it is appellate, and not original. If any other construction would render the clause inoperative, that is an additional reason for rejecting such other construction, and for adhering to their obvious meaning.

To enable this court, then, to issue a mandamus, it must be shown to be an exercise of appellate jurisdiction, or to be necessary to enable them to exercise appellate jurisdiction.

It has been stated at the bar that the appellate jurisdiction may be exercised in a variety of forms, and that if it be the will of the legislature that a mandamus should be used for that purpose, that will must be obeyed. This is true, yet the jurisdiction must be appellate, not original.

It is the essential criterion of appellate jurisdiction, that it revises and corrects the proceedings in a cause already instituted, and does not create that cause. Although, therefore, a mandamus may be directed to courts, yet to issue such a writ to an officer for the delivery of a paper, is in effect the same as to sustain an original action for that paper, and, therefore, seems not to belong to appellate, but to original jurisdiction. Neither is it necessary in such a case as this, to enable the court to exercise its appellate jurisdiction.

The authority, therefore, given to the Supreme Court, by the act establishing the judicial courts of the United States, to issue writs of mandamus to public officers, appears not to be warranted by the constitution; and it becomes necessary to enquire whether a jurisdiction, so conferred, can be exercised.

The question, whether an act, repugnant to the constitution, can become the law of the land, is a question deeply interesting to the United States; but, happily, not of an intricacy proportioned to its interest. It seems only necessary to recognize certain principles, supposed to have been long and well established, to decide it.

That the people have an original right to establish, for their future government, such principles as, in their opinion, shall most conduce to their own happiness, is the basis on which the whole American fabric has been erected. The exercise of this original right is a very great exertion; nor can it, nor ought it, to be frequently repeated. The principles, therefore, so established, are deemed fundamental. And as the authority from which they proceed is supreme, and can seldom act, they are designed to be permanent.

This original and supreme will organizes the government, and assigns to different departments their respective powers. It may either stop here, or establish certain limits not to be transcended by those departments. The government of the United States is of the latter description. The powers of the legislature are defined and limited; and that those limits may not be mistaken, or forgotten, the constitution is written. To what purpose are powers limited, and to what purpose is that limitation committed to writing, if these limits may, at any time, be passed by those intended to be restrained? The distinction between a government with limited and unlimited powers is abolished, if those limits do not confine the persons on whom they are imposed, and if acts prohibited and acts allowed, are of equal obligation. It is a proposition too plain to be contested, that the constitution controls any legislative act repugnant to it; or, that the legislature may alter the constitution by an ordinary act.

Between these alternatives there is no middle ground. The constitution is either a superior, paramount law, unchangeable by ordinary means, or it is on a level with ordinary legislative acts, and, like other acts, is alterable when the legislature shall please to alter it.

If the former part of the alternative be true, then a legislative act contrary to the constitution is not law: if the latter part be true, then written constitutions are absurd attempts, on the part of the people, to limit a power in its own nature illimitable.

Certainly all those who have framed written constitutions contemplate them as forming the fundamental and paramount law of the nation, and consequently, the theory of every such government must be, that an act of the legislature, repugnant to the constitution, is void.

This theory is essentially attached to a written constitution, and is, consequently, to be considered, by this court, as one of the fundamental principles of our society. It is not therefore to be lost sight of in the further consideration of this subject.

If an act of the legislature, repugnant to the constitution, is void, does it, notwithstanding its invalidity, bind the courts, and oblige them to give it effect? Or, in other words, though it be not law, does it constitute a rule as operative as if it was a law? This would be to overthrow in fact what was established in theory; and would seem, at first view, an absurdity too gross to be insisted on. It shall, however, receive a more attentive consideration.

It is emphatically the province and duty of the judicial department to say what the law is. Those who apply the rule to particular cases, must of necessity expound and interpret that rule. If two laws conflict with each other, the courts must decide on the operation of each.

So if a law be in opposition to the constitution; if both the law and the constitution apply to a particular case, so that the court must either decide that case conformably to the law, disregarding the constitution; or conformably to the constitution, disregarding the law; the court must determine which of these conflicting rules governs the case. This is of the very essence of judicial duty.

If, then, the courts are to regard the constitution, and the constitution is superior to any ordinary act of the legislature, the constitution, and not such ordinary act, must govern the case to which they both apply.

Those then who controvert the principle that the constitution is to be considered, in court, as a paramount law, are reduced to the necessity of maintaining that courts must close their eyes on the constitution, and see only the law.

This doctrine would subvert the very foundation of all written constitutions. It would declare that an act which, according to the principles and theory of our government, is entirely void, is yet, in practice, completely obligatory. It would declare that if the legislature shall do what is expressly forbidden, such act, notwithstanding the express prohibition, is in reality effectual. It would be giving to the legislature a practical and real omnipotence, with the same breath which professes to restrict their powers within narrow limits. It is prescribing limits, and declaring that those limits may be passed at pleasure.

That it thus reduces to nothing what we have deemed the greatest improvement on political institutions—a written constitution—would of itself be sufficient, in America, where written constitutions have been viewed with so much reverence, for rejecting the construction. But the peculiar expressions of the constitution of the United States furnish additional arguments in favour of its rejection.

The judicial power of the United States is extended to all cases arising under the constitution. Could it be the intention of those who gave this power, to say that in using it the constitution should not be looked into? That a case arising under the constitution should be decided without examining the instrument under which it arises? This is too extravagant to be maintained.

In some cases, then, the constitution must be looked into by the judges. And if they can open it at all, what part of it are they forbidden to read or to obey?

There are many other parts of the constitution which serve to illustrate this subject. It is declared that "no tax or duty shall be laid on articles exported from any state." Suppose a duty on the export of cotton, of tobacco, or of flour; and a suit instituted to recover it. Ought judgment to be rendered in such a case? Ought the judges to close their eyes on the constitution, and only see the law?

The constitution declares that "no bill of attainder or ex post facto law shall be passed." If, however, such a bill should be passed, and a person should be prosecuted under it; must the court condemn to death those victims whom the constitution endeavors to preserve?

"No person," says the constitution, "shall be convicted of treason unless on the testimony of two witnesses to the same overt act, or on confession in open court." Here the language of the constitution is addressed especially to the courts. It prescribes, directly for them, a rule of evidence not to be departed from. If the legislature should change that rule, and declare *one* witness, or a confession *out* of court, sufficient for conviction, must the constitutional principle yield to the legislative act?

From these, and many other selections which might be made, it is apparent, that the framers of the constitution contemplated that instrument as a rule for the government of *courts*, as well as of the legislature.

Why otherwise does it direct the judges to take an oath to support it? This oath certainly applies, in an especial manner, to their conduct in their official character. How immoral to impose it on them, if they were to be used as the instruments, and the knowing instruments, for violating what they swear to support!

The oath of office, too, imposed by the legislature, is completely demonstrative of the legislative opinion on this subject. It is in these words: "I do solemnly swear that I will administer justice without respect to persons, and do equal right to the poor and to the rich; and that I will faithfully and impartially discharge all the duties incumbent on me as ______, according to the best of my abilities and understanding, agreeably to *the constitution*, and laws of the United States."

Why does a judge swear to discharge his duties agreeably to the constitution of the United States, if that constitution forms no rule for his government? If it is closed upon him, and cannot be inspected by him? If such be the real state of things, this is worse than solemn mockery. To prescribe, or to take this oath, becomes equally a crime.

It is also not entirely unworthy of observation that in declaring what shall be the *supreme* law of the land, the *constitution* itself is first mentioned; and not the laws of the United States generally, but those only which shall be made in *pursuance* of the constitution, have that rank. Thus, the particular phraseology of the constitution of the United States confirms and strengthens the principle, supposed to be essential to all written constitutions, that a law repugnant to the constitution is void; and that *courts*, as well as other departments, are bound by that instrument.

THE BACKGROUND AND MEANING OF MARBURY V. MADISON

1. ***The political and historical setting.*** The Marbury case represented just one clash between the Jeffersonian Republicans and the Marshall Court over the power of the federal judiciary. John Marshall, Secretary of State in the Cabinet of lame-duck Federalist President John Adams, was nominated as Chief Justice in January 1801 and took his oath of office on February 4, 1801. On February 17, the House of Representatives elected Thomas Jefferson President. Marshall continued to act as Secretary of State through March 3, 1801, the end of Adams's term. (Article I § 6 of the Constitution prohibits a member of Congress from serving simultaneously in "any civil office under the authority of the United States," but nothing in the Constitution expressly prohibited serving in the judiciary and the executive branch at once.) Indeed, on March 4, 1801—the day Marshall as Chief Justice administered the oath of office to new President Jefferson—Marshall agreed to comply with Jefferson's request "to perform the duties of Secretary

of State until a successor be appointed." James Madison, the defendant in Marbury, later became Marshall's successor as Secretary of State.

Four days before Jefferson's election, the Federalist Congress began efforts to maintain control of the federal judiciary. The Circuit Court Act of February 13, 1801, created sixteen Circuit Court judgeships that went to Federalists nominated during the last two weeks of Adams's term (the so-called "midnight judges"). Marbury and his co-petitioners were nominated to positions as justices of the peace created under the Organic Act of the District of Columbia passed February 27, 1801, less than a week before the end of Adams's term. Adams named 42 justices on March 2, 1801, and the Senate confirmed them on March 3, Adams's last day in office. The commissions of the petitioners in the Marbury case had been signed by Adams—as well as signed and sealed by Secretary of State Marshall—but not all of them had been delivered by the end of the day, and new President Jefferson chose to treat them as a "nullity." As Marshall wrote two weeks later, "I should [have] sent out the commissions which had been signed & sealed but for the extreme hurry of the time."

The Jeffersonians soon demonstrated that they would not complacently accept Federalist entrenchment in the judiciary: they made repeal of the Circuit Court Act of 1801 an early item of business in the new Congress. The 1801 Act was repealed on March 31, 1802, while the Marbury case was pending in the Supreme Court. During these congressional debates, a few Jeffersonians questioned the Court's authority to consider the constitutionality of congressional acts. In still another sign of mounting hostility to the Court, Congress abolished the June and December Terms of the Supreme Court created by the 1801 Act and provided that there would be only one Term, in February. Accordingly, there was no Court session in 1802; the Court that had received Marbury's petition in December 1801 could not reconvene until February 1803.

Wielding a still more potent weapon early in 1802, the Jeffersonian House voted to impeach Federalist District Judge John Pickering of New Hampshire, and many feared that impeachment of Supreme Court Justices would follow. The choice of Pickering as the first target, however, was a questionable one. Pickering, suffering from alcoholism and perhaps mental illness, was plainly incompetent to serve as a judge, but it took some stretching to convert this into "Treason, Bribery, or other high Crimes and Misdemeanors" as required by Art. II, § 4, of the Constitution. Nevertheless, the Senate voted to remove Pickering from office in March 1804.

On the day after Pickering's removal, Congress moved on to bigger game: the House impeached Supreme Court Justice Samuel Chase. To the Jeffersonians, Chase was a glaring example of Federalist abuse of judicial office: he had made electioneering statements from the bench in 1800, and he had conducted several vindictive sedition trials. A few months after the Marbury decision, he provided the immediate provocation for his impeachment: in May 1803, in a partisan charge to the federal grand jury in Baltimore, he criticized the Jeffersonians' repeal of the 1801 Circuit Court Act. The Senate tried Chase early in 1805. Were judges impeachable for conduct that did not constitute an indictable offense? The debate was lengthy and important: if the case against Chase succeeded, it was widely expected, Marshall and other federal judges would be next. But the Senate vote did not produce the constitutional majority necessary to convict Chase. The impeachment weapon was deflated—it was a "farce," "not even a scare-crow," as Jefferson reluctantly concluded. The Jefferson-Marshall dispute continued, but the Court had survived the most critical stage.

2. ***Was the question of judicial review avoidable?*** Could Marshall have decided Marbury's case in a way that obviated any need for its final pages establishing the power of judicial review of congressional enactments? Consider the following alternative routes by which Marshall might have avoided reaching the opinion's influential conclusion:

a. *Recusal.* Marshall was intimately acquainted with the facts of the Marbury controversy. As Secretary of State, he had signed and sealed Marbury's undelivered commission. An affidavit by his own brother James was introduced to prove the existence of some of the commissions. (James Marshall stated that he was to deliver a number of the commissions but that, "finding he could not conveniently carry the whole," he returned "several of them" to his brother's office.) In view of his involvement in the controversy, Marshall might have disqualified himself from participation in the decision.

b. *Common law.* The commission was a form of property, and Marshall determined that it vested when signed and sealed. He might have decided, however, that a commission does not vest as a matter of law until its delivery. In that case, Marbury would not have been entitled to the benefit of the commission despite the previous administration's signature and seal.

c. *Political question.* Marshall determined that Marbury's right to his commission was a legal, not political question, and thus a writ of mandamus would ordinarily be appropriate. He instead might have ruled the question whether Marbury's commission must be delivered a political question committed to the unreviewable discretion of the executive branch. He might also have ruled that, as a matter of prudence, cabinet officers should not be made subject to writs of mandamus.

d. *Statutory construction.* Marshall construed § 13 of the Judiciary Act of 1789 as expanding the original jurisdiction of the Supreme Court by authorizing it to issue writs of mandamus to executive officers. He might have found instead that the Act conferred mandamus power only apposite to appellate jurisdiction, and dismissed for lack of jurisdiction since this was not an appeal. Alternatively, he might have found that the Act conferred mandamus power apposite to one of the constitutionally authorized categories of original jurisdiction, and again dismissed for lack of jurisdiction since this case did not fall into any of those categories.

e. *Constitutional interpretation.* Marshall interpreted Art. III, § 2, cl. 2, as setting forth an exhaustive list of the categories of possible Supreme Court original jurisdiction. He might have interpreted the list instead as illustrative but not exhaustive, as setting a floor but not a ceiling. In this case, the statute would not have been unconstitutional even if it were interpreted as an expansion of the Court's original jurisdiction because Art. III would not have precluded such expansion.

3. ***Marshall's accomplishment in Marbury.*** Marshall's conspicuous avoidance of all the above escape hatches led Jefferson years later to complain that the "case of Marbury and Madison is continually cited by bench and bar, as if it were settled law, without any animadversion on its being merely an *obiter* dissertation of the Chief Justice." Letter from Thomas Jefferson to Justice William Johnson, June 12, 1823, 1 S. Car. His. & Gen. Mag. 1, 9–10 (1900). One influential account holds that "[t]he decision is a masterwork of indirection, a brilliant example of Marshall's capacity to

sidestep danger while seeming to court it, to advance in one direction while his opponents are looking in another." McCloskey, The American Supreme Court 25 (1960; 2d ed., Levinson, 1994). Faced with the unpalatable options of granting mandamus only to have his order defied, on one hand, and caving to the will of the Jeffersonians, on the other, Marshall found a third way. By construing § 13 of the Judiciary Act of 1789 broadly and Art. III, § 2, cl. 2 of the Constitution narrowly, Marshall discovered (some might say "invented") a constitutional conflict that robbed the Court of jurisdiction. This solution allowed Marshall not only to save the Court from embarrassment, but to present itself as a vindicator of the laws, a check on the other branches of government, and an institution mindful of the value of self-restraint. On this view, the denial of mandamus shrewdly avoided an immediate confrontation with the executive while providing a shield for the Court's assertion and exercise of the power of judicial review.

Scholars have debated just how intentional this subterfuge was, with some insisting that Marshall's interpretations of § 13 and Art. III were simply incorrect, see Van Alstyne, "A Critical Guide to Marbury v. Madison," 1969 Duke L.J. 1, while others find them "a good deal closer to certain features of his contemporaries' understanding of section 13 and Article III than the traditional account assumes," see Pfander, "Marbury, Original Jurisdiction, and the Supreme Court's Supervisory Powers," 101 Colum. L. Rev. 1515 (2001). Some have argued that any technical flaws in the opinion were aimed at accomplishing Marshall's larger goals. See Eskridge, "All About Words: Early Understandings of the 'Judicial Power' in Statutory Interpretation, 1776–1806," 101 Colum. L. Rev. 990 (2001) ("Although Marbury [is] counter-textual, [its] statutory sleight of hand was not a result of carelessness or inability, for the author was the most astute statutory analyst of the founding and consolidating periods.").

Marshall's opinion resonated with his fellow Federalists' position in their debate with Republicans over the federal judiciary's role: "The Republicans insisted that a judiciary armed with the authority to nullify acts of Congress, and both insulated and isolated from political responsibility, would become the tyrant, bending the nation to its will. [In] the Federalist lexicon, [by contrast,] the people were 'their own worst enemies.' They would be driven by their passions to the election of demagogues (such as Jefferson) who would lead an assault on the rights of the stable and virtuous members of the community (by undermining a national judiciary that was the best guarantor of these rights). Marshall's opinion in Marbury was loyal to this vision." O'Fallon, "Marbury," 44 Stan. L. Rev. 219 (1992).

A recent, comprehensive study of the pre-Marbury case law in both state and federal courts concludes that judicial invalidation of statutes for unconstitutionality was in fact surprisingly frequent, which "not only belies the notion that the institution of judicial review was created by Chief Justice Marshall in Marbury," but "also makes [Marshall's] often-criticized reasoning in the case understandable: what appears to be a puzzling, unconvincing and uniquely aggressive exercise of judicial review was fully consistent with prior judicial decisions in which courts had invalidated statutes that trenched on judicial authority and autonomy." Treanor, "Judicial Review Before Marbury," 58 Stan. L. Rev. 455 (2005).

4. ***Pre-constitutional antecedents of the power of judicial review.*** Lord Coke famously stated in Dr. Bonham's Case, 8 Rep. 118a (C.P. 1610), that "the common law will controul acts of Parliament, [and] adjudge

them to be utterly void" when the acts are "against common right and reason." But that was not truly descriptive of British practice in the seventeenth and eighteenth centuries. While the Privy Council had appellate jurisdiction over colonial courts, invalidation of legislation through that route was rare and unpopular.

A number of state court decisions in the years between independence and the federal constitutional convention involved judicial invalidation of state legislation. Scholars have debated the significance of these cases. While some have minimized their significance, see Crosskey, Politics and the Constitution In The History Of the United States (1953), more recent scholarship has increasingly found them to provide significant evidence of pre-constitutional acceptance of the power of courts to invalidate statutes on both written and unwritten constitutional grounds, see Sherry, "The Founders' Unwritten Constitution," 54 U. Chi. L. Rev. 1127 (1987); Treanor, "The Case of the Prisoners and the Origins of Judicial Review," 143 U. Pa. L. Rev. 491 (1994).

The spread of general ideas conducive to the acceptance of judicial review was perhaps more important than the existence of specific precedents. See Bailyn, The Ideological Origins of the American Revolution (1967), and Wood, The Creation of the American Republic, 1776–1787 (1969). Wood finds an especially hospitable climate for the development of judicial review in the evolving theories of the 1780s, particularly the replacement of traditional notions of legislative sovereignty by emphasis on popular sovereignty. For example, future Supreme Court Justice James Iredell developed, in the 1780s, the view that the will of the people as expressed in a constitution was superior to any legislative enactment. See Casto, "James Iredell and the American Origins of Judicial Review," 27 Conn. L. Rev. 329 (1995).

5. ***The Framers' understanding of judicial review.*** Did the Framers intend to grant the Court the power of judicial review? Some scholars argue that they did, and offer evidence from the debates surrounding the ratification of the Constitution. See Prakash & Yoo, "The Origins of Judicial Review," 70 U. Chi. L. Rev. 887 (2003). Others find little evidence of the framing generation's belief in judicial invalidation of statutes, especially of federal statutes. See Kramer, "The Supreme Court, 2000 Term—Foreword: We the Court," 115 Harv. L. Rev. 5 (2001). One historical study found a well-developed tradition in which British and colonial courts invalidated *corporate* bylaws for "repugnancy" to law, and concluded that "the court's ability to void repugnant legislation was simply assumed" by the framing generation "because of past corporate and colonial practices that limited legislation by the laws of the nation." Bilder, "The Corporate Origins of Judicial Review," 116 Yale L.J. 502 (2006). A more recent study has argued that litigation to interpret colonial corporate charters, such as that of the Massachusetts Bay Company, should be understood as a precursor to judicial review under the federal Constitution. Bowie, "Why the Constitution Was Written Down," 71 Stan. L. Rev. (2019).

In the Convention debates themselves, the most important statements regarding judicial power were made in discussion of a Council of Revision proposal that the Justices join with the President in the veto process. See generally Farrand, The Records of the Federal Convention of 1787 (1911). That provision was rejected, partly on grounds that assumed the existence of judicial review. Anti-Federalist Luther Martin, for example, thought "the association of the Judges with the Executive" a "dangerous innovation": "[The] Constitutionality of laws [will] come before the Judges in their proper official character. In this character they have a negative on the laws. Join them with the Executive in the Revision and they will have a double negative. It is necessary that the Supreme Judiciary should have the confidence of the people. This will soon be lost, if they are employed in the task of remonstrating [against] popular measures of the Legislature."

The Federalist Papers provide more explicit support for judicial review. These essays, which have become classic commentaries on the Constitution, were written by Alexander Hamilton, John Jay and James Madison, under the pseudonym Publius, and published in newspapers as campaign documents in defense of the proposed Constitution during the ratification proceedings in New York. The Federalist essays most directly concerned with the judiciary were five written by Alexander Hamilton, Nos. 78 through 82. The most famous is The Federalist, No. 78, in which Hamilton wrote: "[Whoever] attentively considers the different departments of power must perceive, that in a government in which they are separated from each other, the judiciary, from the nature of its functions, will always be the least dangerous to the political rights of the constitution; because it will be least in a capacity to annoy or injure them. The judiciary [has] no influence over either the sword or the purse, no direction either of the strength or of the wealth of the society, and can take no active resolution whatever. It may truly be said to have neither Force nor Will, but merely judgment.

"[Some] perplexity respecting the right of the courts to pronounce legislative acts void, because contrary to the constitution, has arisen from an imagination that the doctrine would imply a superiority of the judiciary to the legislative power. It is urged that the authority which can declare the acts of another void, must necessarily be superior to the one whose acts may be declared [void]. There is no position which depends on clearer principles, than that every act of a delegated authority, contrary to the tenor of the commission under which it is exercised, is void. No legislative act therefore contrary to the constitution can be valid. To deny this would be to affirm that the deputy is greater than his principal; that the servant is above his master; that the representatives of the people are superior to the people themselves; that men acting by virtue of powers may do not only what their powers do not authorise, but what they forbid.

"If it be said that the legislative body are themselves the constitutional judges of their own powers, and that the construction they put upon them is conclusive upon the other departments, it may be answered, that this cannot be the natural presumption, where it is not to be collected from any particular provisions in the constitution. It is not otherwise to be supposed that the constitution could intend to enable the representatives of the people to substitute their *will* to that of their constituents. It is far more rational to suppose that the courts were designed to be an intermediate body between the people and the legislature, in order, among other things, to keep the latter within the limits assigned to their authority. The interpretation of the laws is the proper and peculiar province of the courts. A constitution is in fact, and must be, regarded by the judges as a fundamental law. It therefore belongs to them to ascertain its meaning as well as the meaning of any particular act proceeding from the legislative body. If there should happen to be an irreconcilable variance between the two, that which has the superior obligation and validity ought of course to be preferred; or in other words, the constitution ought to be preferred to the statute, the intention of the people to the intention of their agents.

"Nor does this conclusion by any means suppose a superiority of the judicial to the legislative power. It only supposes that the power of the people is superior to both; and that where the will of the legislature declared in its statutes, stands in opposition to that of the people declared in the constitution, the judges ought to be governed by the latter, rather than the former. They ought to regulate their decisions by the fundamental laws, rather than by those which are not fundamental. [It] can be of no weight to say that the courts, on the pretence of a repugnancy, may substitute their own pleasure to the constitutional intentions of the legislature. This might as well happen in the case of two contradictory statutes; or it might as well happen in every adjudication upon any single statute. The courts must declare the sense of the law; and if they should be disposed to exercise WILL instead of JUDGMENT, the consequence would equally be the substitution of their pleasure to that of the legislative body. The observation, if it prove any thing, would prove that there ought to be no judges distinct from that body."

6. ***Modern perspectives on Marbury.*** Some two centuries after the Marbury decision was handed down, legal scholars are still debating the importance of Chief Justice Marshall's opinion. While the conventional understanding of Marbury as a brilliant doctrinal gambit continues to hold sway, some accounts suggest that the historical importance of the opinion has been overstated: "Marbury, it turns out, is a great deal less important than is commonly supposed. [Marbury] cannot have established the power of judicial review, since that power already was widely accepted before the Supreme Court's ruling. [If] judicial review had not already been well-established by the time of Marbury, that decision would not have convinced skeptics that the Constitution authorized the practice [because] Marbury's arguments in defense of judicial review are so thoroughly unpersuasive. [Marbury] declared the power of judicial review, but the early Marshall Court generally was too weak to exercise it." Klarman, "How Great Were the 'Great' Marshall Court Decisions?," 87 Va. L. Rev. 1111 (2001).

Other critics suggest that the historical importance of the case was trumped up in the late nineteenth century by those favoring aggressive judicial review: "[Proponents] of judicial review during the late nineteenth century [elevated] the Marbury decision—and Chief Justice John Marshall—to icon status to fend off attacks that the Court had acted in an unwarranted fashion. In the process, Marbury became, for the first time, a 'great case'—as measured by its treatment in judicial opinions, legal treatises, and casebooks—a moniker that would have been ill applied to the decision for most of the nineteenth century." Douglas, "The Rhetorical Uses of Marbury v. Madison: The Emergence of a 'Great Case,' " 38 Wake Forest L. Rev. 375 (2003). On this view, the Marbury of 1803 may be quite different from the modern Marbury. See Snowiss, Judicial Review and the Law of the Constitution (1990).

By contrast, other commentators express continued admiration for Marshall's institutional accomplishment in Marbury: "A reading of Marbury that cannot see its heroism is an obtuse reading. It was in the teeth of [a] massive assault on the judiciary that in Marbury, after all, Marshall took all the power for the courts that there was to take—power over the executive, the legislature, the works. And Marshall was not afraid to let Jefferson know what he thought of him. [In] Marbury, a great father of our country bequeathed to us his greatest legacy and our most precious inheritance—the inestimable treasure of an enforceable Constitution. [Perhaps] it is time to forgive ourselves for saying, ['This] is our greatest case.' " Weinberg, "Our Marbury," 89 Va. L. Rev. 1235 (2003).

At a minimum, say some commentators, Marbury is essential to understanding the Court's subsequent institutional role: "To understand Marbury is to understand the practice of constitutional law, or at least the judicial role; and to understand our constitutional practice is to understand Marbury. The two are too much interconnected in the constitutional mind for a perception of one not to color, or indeed sometimes determine, an understanding of the other." Fallon, "Marbury and the Constitutional Mind: A Bicentennial Essay on the Wages of Doctrinal Tension," 91 Calif. L. Rev. 1 (2003).

Finally, some suggest that critique is futile, as judicial review has become irreversibly embedded in the American psyche as a practical matter: "[A]ny organized attack on judicial review will encounter almost inevitable resistance, since Marbury is so firmly established in the constitutional system of a nation that is so profoundly conservative in preserving the continuity of its political institutions." Ross, "The Resilience of Marbury v. Madison: Why Judicial Review Has Survived So Many Attacks," 38 Wake Forest L. Rev. 733 (2003).

SECTION 2. SUPREME COURT AUTHORITY TO REVIEW STATE COURT JUDGMENTS

While Marbury established Supreme Court review of the constitutionality of actions of a coordinate branch of the federal government, a second major Marshall Court decision, Martin v. Hunter's Lessee, legitimated Supreme Court authority to review judgments of the state courts. As Justice Oliver Wendell Holmes famously observed, Supreme Court review of cases challenging state laws may in the long run have been the more important power: "I do not think the United States would come to an end if we lost our power to declare an Act of Congress void. I do think the Union would be imperiled if we could not make that declaration as to the laws of the several States." Holmes, Collected Legal Papers 295 (1920).

The Martin case involved a controversy over Section 25 of the Judiciary Act of 1789, which provided for Supreme Court review of final decisions of the highest state courts rejecting claims based on federal law—including federal constitutional law.[1] The Constitutional Convention debates had contemplated that federal questions could initially arise in state as well as

1 The full text of § 25 of the 1789 Judiciary Act provided: "That a final judgment or decree in any suit, in the highest court of law or equity of a State in which a decision in the suit could be had, where is drawn in question the validity of a treaty or statute of, or an authority exercised under the United States, and the decision is against their validity; or where is drawn in question the validity of a statute of, or an authority exercised under any State, on the ground of their being repugnant to the constitution, treaties or laws of the United States, and the decision is in favour of such their validity, or where is drawn in question the construction of any clause of the constitution, or of a treaty, or statute of, or commission held under the United States, and the decision is against the title, right, privilege or exemption specially set up or claimed by either party, under such clause of the said constitution, treaty, statute or commission, may be re-examined and reversed or affirmed in the Supreme Court of the United States upon a [writ of error]."

federal courts. Article III, which left the creation and jurisdiction of lower federal courts to the discretion of Congress, reflected a compromise between mandatory creation of lower federal courts and leaving initial application of federal law entirely to the state courts. This compromise, together with the Supremacy Clause of Art. VI, assumed that Supreme Court review would assure any necessary federal uniformity. That assumption would be tested in Martin.

Martin v. Hunter's Lessee

1 Wheat. (14 U.S.) 304, 4 L. Ed. 97 (1816).

[The case arose from the refusal by the Virginia Court of Appeals to obey the Supreme Court's mandate in Fairfax's Devisee v. Hunter's Lessee, 7 Cranch (11 U.S.) 603 (1813). That ruling resulted from a land dispute instituted in 1791 concerning the vast land holdings of Lord Fairfax. Virginia claimed that it had properly seized the Fairfax properties prior to 1783 as lands belonging to British loyalists during the Revolution and parceled out some of the land to its own citizens. Hunter claimed the land at issue under such a Virginia grant. Martin claimed title under a devise from Fairfax in 1781, claiming that title had not vested in Virginia prior to 1783 and, crucially, that his title was protected under various federal treaty provisions. Hunter's litigation was in abeyance for almost two decades.

In 1810, the Virginia Court of Appeals decided for Hunter, holding effective Virginia's seizure of the Fairfax lands. The United States Supreme Court reversed in 1813, siding with Martin and "instruct[ing]" the Virginia judges to enter judgment for Martin. The Virginia court issued a decision in 1815 declining to obey, concluding that "the appellate power of the Supreme Court of the United States does not extend to this court, under a sound construction of the constitution of the United States, 'and that § 25 was therefore unconstitutional.' " The Virginia judges claimed that the Constitution did not authorize federal courts to act directly upon, and reverse, state court rulings. The Virginia judges did not deny the supremacy of valid federal law under Art. VI of the Constitution. But they argued that if federal questions were permitted to arise in the state courts, then state courts must provide final adjudication. The Virginia court's challenge to § 25 elicited the following decision upholding that provision's constitutionality, authored for the Court by Justice Joseph Story, a Jeffersonian Republican from Massachusetts.]

■ JUSTICE STORY delivered the opinion of the Court:

[The] appellate power is not limited by the terms of the third article [of the Constitution] to any particular courts. The words are, "the judicial power (which includes appellate power) shall extend to all cases," & c., and "in all other cases before mentioned the supreme court shall have appellate jurisdiction." It is the case, then, and not the court, that gives the jurisdiction. If the judicial power extends to the case, it will be in vain to search in the letter of the constitution for any qualification as to the tribunal where it depends. [It] was foreseen that in the exercise of their ordinary jurisdiction, state courts would incidentally take cognizance of cases arising under the constitution, the laws, and treaties of the United States. Yet to all these cases the judicial power, by the very terms of the constitution, is to extend. It cannot extend by original jurisdiction if that was already rightfully and exclusively attached in the state courts; [it] must, therefore, extend by appellate jurisdiction, or not at all. It would seem to follow that the appellate power of the United States must, in such cases, extend to state tribunals.

[It] has been argued that such an appellate jurisdiction over state courts is inconsistent with the genius of our governments, and the spirit of the constitution. That the latter was never designed to act upon state sovereignties, but only upon the people, and that if the power exists, it will materially impair the sovereignty of the states, and the independence of their courts. We cannot yield to the force of this reasoning; it assumes principles which we cannot admit, and draws conclusions to which we do not yield our assent. It is a mistake [to believe] that the constitution was not designed to operate upon states, in their corporate capacities. It is crowded with provisions which restrain or annul the sovereignty of the states in some of the highest branches of their prerogatives.

[Nor] can [this] be deemed to impair the independence of state judges. It is assuming the very ground in controversy to assert that they possess an absolute independence of the United States. In respect to the powers granted to the United States, they are not independent; they are expressly bound to obedience, by the letter of the [constitution]. [The] argument urged from the possibility of the abuse of the revising power, is equally unsatisfactory. It is always a doubtful course, to argue against the use or existence of a power, from the possibility of its abuse. [From] the very nature of things, the absolute right of decision, in the last resort, must rest somewhere—wherever it may be vested, it is susceptible of abuse. [It] is further argued, that no great public mischief can result from a construction which shall limit the appellate power of the United States to cases in their own courts: first, because state judges are bound by an oath to support the constitution of the United States and must be presumed to be men of learning and integrity.

[A]dmitting that the judges of the state courts are, and always will be, of as much learning, integrity and wisdom as those of the courts of the United States (which we very cheerfully admit) [does] not aid the argument. [The] constitution has presumed [that] state attachments, state prejudices, state jealousies, and state interests, might sometimes obstruct, or control, or be supposed to obstruct or control, the regular administration of justice. [This] is not all. A motive of another kind, perfectly compatible with the most sincere respect for state tribunals, might induce the grant of appellate power over their decisions. That motive is the importance, and even necessity of *uniformity* of decisions throughout the whole United States, upon all subjects within the purview of the constitution. Judges of equal learning and integrity, in different states, might differently interpret a statute, or a treaty of the United States, or even the constitution itself: if there were no revising authority to control these jarring and discordant judgments, and harmonize them into uniformity, the laws, the treaties and the constitution of the United States would be different in different states. [The] public mischiefs that would attend such a state of things would be truly [deplorable].

FURTHER CLASHES BETWEEN SUPREME COURT AND STATE COURT AUTHORITY

1. ***Supreme Court review of state criminal cases.*** The Martin dispute was only the first of several states' rights attacks on § 25. In **Cohens v. Virginia**, 6 Wheat. (19 U.S.) 264 (1821), the Court sustained its jurisdiction to review the validity of state laws in criminal proceedings. That case arose from the conviction of the Cohen brothers in a Norfolk, Virginia court for selling District of Columbia lottery tickets in violation of Virginia law. The Cohens claimed that, under the Supremacy Clause, they were immune from state laws in selling congressionally authorized lottery tickets. The Supreme Court ultimately decided against them on the merits, reading the congressional statute as conferring no such immunity. But the major issue was jurisdictional: did the Supreme Court have constitutional authority to review such state judgments? Virginia's counsel reiterated the arguments advanced in Martin. They also emphasized that here, unlike in Martin, the State was a named party in the case. They argued that the grant of original jurisdiction to the Supreme Court of cases "in which a state shall be a party" precluded, by negative implication, the exercise of appellate jurisdiction in such a case.

Marshall did not participate in Martin v. Hunter's Lessee because he and his brother James had earlier contracted for the purchase of a large part of the Fairfax estate from the Fairfax heirs. The Cohens case gave Chief Justice MARSHALL the chance to have his say on § 25. Marshall's opinion reaffirmed and extended Story's defense of the constitutionality of § 25 and answered Virginia's new contentions by concluding "that the judicial [power] extends to all cases arising under the constitution or a law of the United States, whoever may be the parties." Marshall took a harsher view of the reliability of state judges than Story had expressed in Martin: "In many States, the judges are dependent for office and for salary on the will of the legislature. [When] we observe the importance which [the Constitution] attaches to the independence of judges, we are the less inclined to suppose that it can have intended to leave these constitutional questions to tribunals where this independence may not exist." Marshall's doubts about the capacity of state judges to interpret and enforce federal law adequately have persisted. For an argument in this vein, see, e.g., Neuborne, "The Myth of Parity," 90 Harv. L. Rev. 1105 (1977), emphasizing that federal judges are "as insulated from majoritarian pressures as is functionally possible" but that state judges "generally are elected for a fixed term, rendering them vulnerable to majoritarian pressure when deciding constitutional cases." But see Rubenstein, "The Myth of Superiority," 16 Const. Comment. 599 (1999).

2. ***Later state challenges to § 25.*** In the years before the Civil War, a number of states other than Virginia challenged the power of the Supreme Court to review state court decisions—often on grounds far broader than those advanced by Virginia in the Martin and Cohens cases. See Warren, "Legislative and Judicial Attacks on the Supreme Court of the United States—A History of the Twenty-Fifth Section of the Judiciary Act," 47 Am. L. Rev. 1 (1913). The courts of seven states issued challenges. And in Congress, there were several attempts to repeal § 25—the first major one in 1821, immediately after Cohens; the most serious one in 1831. These efforts failed. For a history of Congress's attempt to repeal § 25 in 1831, see Graber, "James Buchanan as Savior? Judicial Power, Political Fragmentation, and the Failed 1831 Repeal of Section 25," 88 Or. L. Rev. 95 (2009).

3. ***State interposition and nullification.*** More extreme positions asserted the states' right to "interpose" their own interpretations of the Constitution against federal decisions, based on the theory that the Constitution was merely a compact among the sovereign states. Such assertions varied in operative consequences. The Kentucky Resolutions of 1798, for example, urging congressional repeal of the Alien and Sedition Laws, denied that constitutional interpretations are exclusively the function of the federal courts or that federal court interpretations bind the nation. (The anonymous author of the Kentucky Resolutions was Thomas Jefferson.) The South Carolina Nullification Ordinance of 1832 asserted the claimed power of a state to block—at least temporarily, until the Constitution could be amended—enforcement of "unconstitutional" federal laws within the state.

SECTION 3. JUDICIAL EXCLUSIVITY IN CONSTITUTIONAL INTERPRETATION

Marbury v. Madison has often been said to have elided two separate questions:

First, is the Constitution the supreme law of the land?

Second, are the courts the ultimate or exclusive interpreters of the Constitution, or do other branches of government share in that authority?

To say that a government may not exceed its constitutional powers does not necessarily demonstrate *who* is to decide whether a law conflicts with the constitution: "The premise of a written Constitution would not be disserved, and legislative power would not necessarily be unbounded, if Congress itself judged the constitutionality of its enactments. Under such a system, courts would not ignore the Constitution; rather, they would simply treat the legislative interpretation as definitive, and thus leave to Congress the task of resolving apparent conflicts between statute and Constitution." Tribe, 1 American Constitutional Law § 3–2 (3d ed. 2000).

Marbury's position on the judiciary's role is itself ambiguous. On a narrow reading of Marbury, judicial review is simply a byproduct of a court's duty to decide cases within its jurisdiction in accordance with law, including the Constitution. Recall Marshall's modest statement that the Constitution is "a rule for the government of courts as well as the legislature" and thus that "courts, as well as other departments, are bound by that instrument." A broader reading of Marbury, however, regards the courts as having special competence to interpret law, including the Constitution, so that they are the ultimate, supreme interpreters of the Constitution. Recall Marshall's statement in Marbury that "[i]t is emphatically the province and duty of the judicial department to say what the law is," and the fact that much of his argument aimed to establish that courts are institutionally competent to consider issues of constitutionality. Recall too Hamilton's stronger statement in The Federalist, No. 78: "The interpretation of the laws is the proper and *peculiar* province of the courts." One famous statement of the second, broader interpretation of Marbury arose in the aftermath of Brown v. Board of Education, 347 U.S. 483 (1954), which held unconstitutional the racial segregation of the public schools.

Cooper v. Aaron

358 U.S. 1, 78 S. Ct. 1401, 3 L. Ed. 2d 5 (1958).

[Following Brown v. Board of Education, many southern jurisdictions resisted court orders mandating integration. An Arkansas federal district court, relying on Brown, directed desegregation of the Little Rock schools. The Little Rock school board, seeking to comply with that decree, was blocked in its efforts when Governor Orval Faubus placed Little Rock's Central High School "off limits" to African-American students and called out the National Guard. After a district court injunction against the Governor, the troops were withdrawn and African-American students were able to attend school under the protection of federally commanded troops, although resistance and protest continued. When the school board sought a postponement of the desegregation program, the district court granted that relief, noting the existence of "chaos, bedlam and turmoil" and finding the situation "intolerable." The court of appeals reversed; and that decision was affirmed by the Supreme Court, which in a highly unusual move, issued this jointly signed opinion.]

■ Opinion of the Court by CHIEF JUSTICE [WARREN and JUSTICES] BLACK, FRANKFURTER, DOUGLAS, BURTON, CLARK, HARLAN, BRENNAN, and WHITTAKER:

[This case] raises questions of the highest importance to the maintenance of our federal system of government. It [involves] a claim by the Governor and Legislature of a State that there is no duty on state officials to obey federal court orders resting on this Court's considered interpretation of the United States Constitution. Specifically it involves actions by the Governor and Legislature of Arkansas upon the premise that they are not bound by our holding in [Brown.]

[The] constitutional rights of respondents are not to be sacrificed or yielded to the violence and disorder which have followed upon the actions of the Governor and Legislature. [The] constitutional rights of children not to be discriminated against in school admission on grounds of race or color declared by this Court in [Brown] can neither be nullified openly and directly by state legislators or state executive or judicial officers, nor nullified indirectly by them through evasive schemes for segregation. [This] is enough to dispose of the case. However, we should answer the premise of the actions of the Governor and Legislature that they are not bound by our holding in the Brown case. It is necessary only to recall some basic constitutional propositions which are settled doctrine.

Article VI of the Constitution makes the Constitution the "supreme Law of the Land." In 1803, Chief Justice Marshall, speaking for a unanimous Court, referring to the Constitution as "the fundamental and paramount law of the nation," declared in the notable case of Marbury v. Madison that "It is emphatically the province and duty of the judicial department to say what the law is." This decision declared the basic principle that the federal judiciary is supreme in the exposition of the law of the Constitution, and that principle has ever since been respected by this Court and the Country as a permanent and indispensable feature of our constitutional system. It follows that the interpretation of the Fourteenth Amendment enunciated by this Court in the Brown case is the supreme law of the land, and Art. VI of the Constitution makes it of binding effect on the States "any Thing in the Constitution or Laws of any State to the Contrary notwithstanding." Every state legislator and executive and judicial officer is solemnly committed by oath taken pursuant to Art. VI, ¶ 3, "to support this Constitution." No state legislator or executive or judicial officer can war against the Constitution without violating his undertaking to support it.

[The] decision in Brown was unanimously reached by this Court only after the case had been briefed and twice argued and the issues had been given the most serious consideration. Since the first Brown opinion three new Justices have come to the Court. They are at one with the Justices still on the Court who participated in that basic decision as to its correctness, and that decision is now unanimously reaffirmed. The principles announced in that decision and the obedience of the States to them, according to the command of the Constitution, are indispensable for the protection of the freedoms guaranteed by our fundamental charter for all of us.

THE AUTHORITATIVENESS OF SUPREME COURT DECISIONS

1. ***The meaning of Cooper.*** Was Cooper truly a restatement of "settled doctrine" since Marbury, or was it a substantial expansion of the authority asserted by Chief Justice Marshall? Some commentators believe Cooper expanded Marbury by "confus[ing] Marshall's assertion of judicial authority to interpret the Constitution with judicial exclusiveness." Gunther, "The Subtle Vices of the 'Passive Virtues'—A Comment on Principle and Expediency in Judicial Review," 64 Colum. L. Rev. 1 (1964). Would the Court's opinion in Cooper have been more persuasive if it had urged the prudence of compliance with Brown rather than commanding adherence to that decision as supreme law? The Court might have stated that, although the Brown decision did not technically bind Arkansas because the state was not a party to the case, the Court was likely to continue to adhere to its unanimous ruling in Brown and thus state officials ought, in the interest of prudence and avoiding chaos in the legal system, to "obey" rather than resist Brown.

2. ***Critique of Cooper as asserting judicial hegemony.*** In a widely discussed 1987 speech, Edwin Meese, Attorney General in the Reagan administration, declared Cooper "at war with the Constitution, at war with the basic principles of democratic government, and at war with the very meaning of the rule of law." Meese distinguished the Constitution, which Article VI accords the status of "Supreme Law of the Land," from "what the Supreme Court says about the Constitution in its decisions." He wrote: "Obviously [a decision of the Supreme Court] does have binding quality: it binds the parties in a case and also the executive branch for whatever enforcement is necessary. But such a decision does not establish a supreme law of the land that is binding on all persons and parts of government henceforth and forevermore." Meese, "The Law of the Constitution," 61 Tul. L. Rev. 979 (1987).

Meese's article drew much critical commentary. Ramsey Clark, Attorney General during the Johnson administration and son of one of the signators to Brown, criticized Meese's speech as "a clumsy, vague assault on law. [If] the same issues in desegregation orders had to be litigated to the Supreme Court for every school district, [resistance to desegregation] would have prevailed outright." Clark, "Enduring Constitutional Issues," 61 Tul. L. Rev. 1093, 1094 (1987). But some commentators defended Meese's approach:

"[The] denunciation of Meese's speech [legitimates] government by legally trained elites, speaking an evermore esoteric language. [James] Madison's call in The Federalist for veneration of the Constitution has triumphed over Jefferson's plea for recurrent consideration of its utility and potential defects." Levinson, "Could Meese Be Right This Time?" 61 Tul. L. Rev. 1071, 1078 (1987).

3. ***Are Supreme Court interpretations binding on Congress?*** Article V provides that Congress may initiate an amendment to the Constitution, and the amendment process can be used to overturn a constitutional interpretation of the Supreme Court. But may Congress effect such an overruling by statute? **Dickerson v. United States**, 530 U.S. 428 (2000), answered that question no. Chief Justice REHNQUIST wrote for the Court: "In Miranda v. Arizona, [384 U.S. 436 (1966)], we held that certain warnings must be given before a suspect's statement made during custodial interrogation could be admitted in evidence. In the wake of that decision, Congress enacted 18 U.S.C. § 3501, which in essence laid down a rule that the admissibility of such statements should turn only on whether or not they were voluntarily made. We hold that Miranda, being a constitutional decision of this Court, may not be in effect overruled by an Act of Congress.

"[The] law in this area is clear. This Court has supervisory authority over the federal courts, and we may use that authority to prescribe rules of evidence and procedure that are binding in those tribunals, [although Congress] retains the ultimate authority to modify or set aside any judicially created rules of evidence and procedure that are not required by the Constitution. But Congress may not legislatively supersede our decisions interpreting and applying the Constitution. This case therefore turns on whether the Miranda Court announced a constitutional rule or merely exercised its supervisory authority to regulate evidence in the absence of congressional direction.

"[Miranda] is a constitutional decision [that Congress may not supersede legislatively.] [Both] Miranda and [its] companion cases applied the rule to proceedings in state courts—to wit, Arizona, California, and New York. [It] is beyond dispute that we do not hold a supervisory power over the courts of the several States. With respect to proceedings in state courts, our 'authority is limited to enforcing the commands of the United States Constitution.' [Moreover, the Miranda] opinion is replete with statements indicating that the majority thought it was announcing a constitutional rule. [Additional] support for our conclusion that Miranda is constitutionally based is found in the Miranda Court's invitation for legislative [solutions] that differed from the prescribed Miranda warnings but which were 'at least as effective in apprising accused persons of their right of silence and in assuring a continuous opportunity to exercise it.' "

"[Miranda] has become embedded in routine police practice to the point where the warnings have become part of our national culture. [While] we have overruled our precedents when subsequent cases have undermined their doctrinal underpinnings, [we] do not believe that this has happened to the Miranda decision. If anything, our subsequent cases have [reaffirmed] the decision's core ruling that unwarned statements may not be used as evidence in the prosecution's case in chief."

Justice SCALIA dissented, joined by Justice Thomas, disputing that Miranda had announced a constitutional rule in light of prior decisions that he read as concluding that "it is possible [for] the police to violate Miranda without also violating the Constitution." The dissent also took a narrow view of the Court's decision in Marbury: "[Marbury] held that an Act of Congress will not be enforced by the courts if what it prescribes violates the Constitution of the United States. [One] will search today's opinion in vain, however, for a statement [that] what 18 U.S.C. § 3501 prescribes [violates] the Constitution. [Section 3501] excludes from trial precisely what the Constitution excludes from trial, viz., compelled confessions. [And] so, to justify today's [result], the Court must adopt a significant new [principle that] statutes of Congress can be disregarded, not only when what they prescribe violates the Constitution, but when what they prescribe contradicts a decision of this Court that 'announced a constitutional rule.' [The] only thing that can possibly mean in the context of this case is that this Court has the power, not merely to apply the Constitution but to expand it, imposing what it regards as useful 'prophylactic' restrictions upon Congress and the States. That is an immense and frightening antidemocratic power, and it does not exist. [By] disregarding congressional action that concededly does not violate the Constitution, the Court [arrogates] to itself prerogatives reserved to the representatives of the people."

What is the role of the judiciary in relation to the legislative branch? Some commentators suggest that Marbury does not preclude a view of Congress as a co-equal protector of the Constitution: "Marshall, at least in Marbury, explicitly endorses judicial review, but he is silent on the legitimacy of legislative review and the relation between the two, and it is likely that he did not see them in conflict. It is at least a possible reading of Marbury that Marshall decided that the courts must consult the Constitution when deciding what the ordinary law is—that being the special province of the judiciary—just as the legislator must consult the Constitution when deciding what the ordinary law shall be—that, after all, being the province of the legislator." West, "Tom Paine's Constitution," 89 Va. L. Rev. 1413 (2003).

Could Congress circumvent a constitutional interpretation of the Supreme Court, without necessarily overruling it? Imagine that the Court invalidates a congressional statute because it is based on an impermissible purpose. May the legislature reenact the same law, defending it on the ground that the new enactment is not tainted by the previously identified impermissible purpose? See Coenen, "A Constitution of Collaboration: Protecting Fundamental Values with Second-Look Rules of Interbranch Dialogue," 42 Wm. & Mary L. Rev. 1575, 1755 (2001).

4. ***Are Supreme Court interpretations binding on the executive branch?*** Several of the nation's presidents, including the most venerated, have questioned the fidelity they must pay to judicial precedents interpreting the Constitution in a way they deemed wrong or unworkable:

a. *Jefferson.* Once in office, President Thomas Jefferson pardoned many convicted during the Adams administration under the Sedition Act of 1798, which criminalized defaming federal officials by bringing them into "contempt or disrepute," and which had been deployed by appointees of Adams's Federalist party against members of Jefferson's Republican party. In a letter, he explained: "You seem to think it devolved on the judges to decide on the validity of the sedition law. But nothing in the Constitution has given them a right to decide for the Executive, more than to the Executive to decide for them. Both magistracies are equally independent in the sphere of action assigned to them. The judges, believing the law constitutional, had a right to pass a sentence of fine and imprisonment; because that power was placed in their hands by the Constitution. But the Executive, believing the law to be unconstitutional, was bound to remit the execution of it; because that power has been confided to him by the Constitution. That instrument meant that its co-ordinate branches should be checks on each other. But the opinion which gives to the judges the right to decide what laws are constitutional, and what not, not only for themselves in their own sphere of action, but for the Legislature & Executive also, in their spheres, would make the judiciary a despotic branch." Jefferson, Letter to Abigail Adams, Sept. 11, 1804, 8 The Writings of Thomas Jefferson 310 (Ford ed. 1897).

judiciary can't choose what laws are constitutional

b. *Jackson*. President Andrew Jackson vetoed a bill to recharter the Bank of the United States in 1832, even though the Supreme Court in 1819 had held the establishment of the Bank within the constitutional authority of Congress. His veto message explained: "Mere precedent is a dangerous source of authority, and should not be regarded as deciding questions of constitutional power except where the acquiescence of the people and the States can be considered as well settled. [Even if] the opinion of the Supreme Court covered the whole ground of this act, it ought not to control the coordinate authorities of this Government. [It] is as much the duty of the House of Representatives, of the Senate, and of the President to decide upon the constitutionality of any bill or resolution which may be presented to them for passage or approval as it is of the supreme judges when it may be brought before them for judicial decision. The opinion of the judges has no more authority over Congress than the opinion of Congress has over the judges, and on that point the President is independent of both. The authority of the Supreme Court must not, therefore, be permitted to control the Congress or the Executive when acting in their legislative capacities, but to have only such influence as the force of their reasoning may deserve." Jackson, Veto Message, July 10, 1832, 2 Messages and Papers of the Presidents 576 (Richardson ed. 1896).

c. *Lincoln*. In Dred Scott v. Sandford, 19 How. (60 U.S.) 393 (1857), the Supreme Court infamously held that Scott, a man of African descent, was not a United States citizen and thus lacked the privilege to sue in federal court to assert his freedom from slavery. In campaigning for the Senate, Abraham Lincoln explained the nature of his opposition to the Dred Scott decision: "[We] do not propose that when Dred Scott has been decided to be a slave by the court, we, as a mob, will decide him to be free. We do not propose that, when any other one, or one thousand, shall be decided by that court to be slaves, we will in any violent way disturb the rights of property thus settled; but we nevertheless do oppose that decision as a political rule which shall be binding on the voter, to vote for nobody who thinks it wrong, which shall be binding on the members of Congress or the President to favor no measure that does not actually concur with the principles of that decision. [We] propose so resisting it as to have it reversed if we can, and a new judicial rule established upon this subject." Lincoln, Speech During Senatorial Campaign, October 1858, 3 The Collected Works of Abraham Lincoln 255 (Basler ed. 1953).

Once elected President, Lincoln further explained: "I do not forget the position assumed by some that constitutional questions are to be decided by the Supreme Court, nor do I deny that such decisions must be binding in any case upon the parties to a suit as to the object of that suit, while they are also entitled to very high respect and consideration in all parallel cases by all other departments of the Government. And while it is obviously possible that such decision may be erroneous in any given case, still the evil effect following it, being limited to that particular case, with the chance that it may be overruled and never become a precedent for other cases, can better be borne than could the evils of a different practice. At the same time, the candid citizen must confess that if the policy of the Government upon vital questions affecting the whole people is to be irrevocably fixed by decisions of the Supreme Court, the instant they are made in ordinary litigation between parties in personal actions, the people will have ceased to be their own rulers, having to that extent practically resigned their Government into the hands of that eminent tribunal." Lincoln, First Inaugural Address, March 4, 1861, 6 Messages and Papers of the Presidents 5 (Richardson ed. 1897).

d. *Roosevelt*. In Schechter Poultry Corp. v. United States, 295 U.S. 495 (1935), the Court narrowly construed national regulatory powers and invalidated the National Industrial Recovery Act, an important segment of New Deal emergency legislation. President Franklin D. Roosevelt nevertheless urged Congress to enact a law establishing a NIRA-like regulatory scheme for the bituminous coal industry: "Manifestly, no one is in a position to give assurance that the proposed act will withstand constitutional tests. [But] the situation is so urgent and the benefits of the legislation so evident that all doubts should be resolved in favor of the bill, leaving to the courts, in an orderly fashion, the ultimate question of constitutionality. A decision by the Supreme Court relative to this measure would be helpful as indicating [the] constitutional limits within which this Government must operate. [I] hope your committee will not permit doubts as to constitutionality, however reasonable, to block the suggested legislation." Roosevelt, Letter to Congressman Hill, July 6, 1935, 4 The Public Papers and Addresses of Franklin D. Roosevelt 297 (1938). Roosevelt expressed similar views in a draft speech prepared in the event that the Court were to decide it was unconstitutional for the Government to abrogate "gold clauses" in federal obligations (which in the end it did not): "[It] is the duty of the Congress and the President to protect the people of the United States to the best of their ability. [To] stand idly by and to permit the decision of the Supreme Court to be carried through to its logical, inescapable conclusion would so imperil the economic and political security of this nation that the legislative and executive officers of the Government must look beyond the narrow letter of contractual obligations, so that they may sustain the substance of the promise originally made in accord with the actual intention of the parties. [I] shall immediately take such steps as may be necessary, by proclamation and by message to [Congress]." Roosevelt, Proposed Speech on the Gold Clause Cases, Feb. 1935, 1 F.D.R.—His Personal Letters, 1928–1945, 459–60 (Elliott Roosevelt ed. 1950).

Should it matter whether the executive branch simply declines to act in ways the courts have held constitutionally permitted or instead acts in ways the courts have deemed constitutionally forbidden? The Supreme Court's decision in McCulloch v. Maryland would have permitted Jackson to sign a bank recharter bill, but Jackson emphasized the autonomy of "the Congress or the Executive when acting in their legislative capacities" to refuse to enact new legislation given their own constitutional doubts. Jefferson similarly defended the exercise of the pardon power as within his autonomy in his "own sphere of action." And Lincoln was careful to distinguish between direct interference with the Court decision in Dred Scott's case and acceptance of the constitutional interpretation of that case "as a political rule." All of these positions fell short of direct conflict with a court order. Only President Roosevelt's proposed speech on the "gold clause" issue contemplated direct defiance of the Supreme Court. What is the boundary between legitimate disagreement and improper defiance on the President's part?

5. ***Judicial review and democracy.*** Is judicial review consistent with democratic government? Especially on the broader interpretation of Marbury that sees judicial interpretation as authoritative? In declaring a law unconstitutional, an unelected court thwarts enforcement of a law that presumably reflects the will of the voters via the democratically elected Congress and President. This tension was famously labeled the "countermajoritarian difficulty" by Professor Alexander Bickel in his seminal work. See Bickel, The Least Dangerous Branch 16 (1962). For Bickel, who clerked for Justice Frankfurter when Brown v. Board of Education was pending before the Court, the countermajoritarian difficulty required an overarching commitment to judicial restraint. See generally Bickel, "The Supreme Court, 1960 Term—Foreword: The Passive Virtues," 75 Harv. L. Rev. 40 (1961). Can the tension Bickel identified be satisfactorily reconciled?

Judicial review also arguably makes the people lax toward enforcing constitutional norms themselves. Might overreliance on judicial review damage civic participation by allowing citizens and voters to exempt themselves from the task of constitutional deliberation? Consider the view that, when political actors avoid making constitutional judgments out of a reliance on the Court's ability to resolve these questions, "we evade our own responsibility as citizens in a democratic polity." Brest, "Constitutional Citizenship," 34 Clev. St. L. Rev. 175 (1986). For a classic account of judicial review as undemocratic and as undercutting popular responsibility, see Thayer, "The Origin and Scope of the American Doctrine of Constitutional Law," 7 Harv. L. Rev. 129 (1893). For a more recent argument against displacing "popular constitutionalism" with "judicial supremacy," see Kramer, The People Themselves: Popular Constitutionalism and Judicial Review (2004) ("Americans in the past always came to the same conclusion: that it was their right, and their responsibility, as republican citizens to say finally what the Constitution means. [Are] we still prepared to insist on our prerogative to control the meaning of our Constitution?"). Recall Lincoln's warning, above, against giving so much deference to Supreme Court decisions that "the people will have ceased to be their own rulers."

Scholars continue to debate the proper understanding of the countermajoritarian difficulty—and whether it is a difficulty at all. Can judicial enforcement of the Constitution be reconciled with democracy by conceiving of judges as enforcing rather than thwarting the people's will? Bruce Ackerman has argued for a "dualistic conception" of political life: during times of "normal politics," factions pursue narrow interests; during times of "constitutional politics," by contrast, the people speak, whether formally through constitutional amendments or informally through "constitutional moments" in which a "mobilized mass of American citizens express[ ] their assent through extraordinary institutional forms." Ackerman, "Discovering the Constitution," 93 Yale L.J. 1013 (1984). If constitutional norms are created by a uniquely participatory process, then might judicial review serve the function of "protecting them against erosion during more normal times, when the People are less involved in affairs of state"? Ackerman, "Constitutional Politics/Constitutional Law," 99 Yale L.J. 453 (1989).

Perhaps the criticisms of judicial review as undemocratic rest on an overly optimistic view of day-to-day representative government. Consider the view that "[Congress] is not us. The President is not us. ['We'] are not 'in' those bodies. Their determinations are not our self-government. Judges overriding those determinations do not, therefore, necessarily subtract anything from our freedom, although the judges, obviously, are not us." Michelman, "The Supreme Court, 1985 Term—Foreword: Traces of Self-Government," 100 Harv. L. Rev. 4 (1986).

If this is the case, should judicial review be limited to safeguarding the political process and maximizing citizens' participation in political decisionmaking, thereby ensuring that Congress and the executive *are*, in some sense, "us"? Professor John Hart Ely argued as much in Democracy and Distrust (1980): "[The] representation-reinforcing theory . . . bounds judicial review under the Constitution's open-ended provisions by insisting that it can appropriately concern itself only with questions of participation, and not with the substantive merits of the political choice under attack." Ely's theory was inspired by the famous fourth footnote in United States v. Carolene Products Co., 304 U.S. 144 (1938) (see p. 503, below), which introduced the idea of applying heightened judicial scrutiny to "legislation which restricts those political processes which can ordinarily be expected to bring about repeal of undesirable legislation" and statutes evincing "prejudice against discrete and insular minorities" with minimal political power.

Arguably, judicial review does not need to be reconciled with majoritarian democracy in the first place. Consider the argument that democratic theory "played no part in the consciousness of the framing generation," and that "[t]he judicial supremacy principle of Marbury was derived because the Framers' republic required a check on legislative and executive power, and thought that the savant status of judges, and disinterestedness would be its own check." White, "The Constitutional Journey of Marbury v. Madison," 89 Va. L. Rev. 1463 (2003).

Some defend judicial review against the charge that it is anti-democratic by noting that it has no practical substitute: "[J]udicial review thrives by default because none of the alternatives are palatable. By laying claim to the power to oversee the federal executive and the states, as well as Congress, the Marshall Court made possible the federal judiciary's control of constitutional arbitration. Thus, like the rest of the constitutional order, judicial review is a way of solving a practical problem of government." Farber, "Judicial Review and Its Alternatives: An American Tale," 38 Wake Forest L. Rev. 415, 449 (2003). Toward the end of his career, Judge Learned Hand made a similar pragmatic point. He insisted that there was "nothing in the United States Constitution that gave courts any authority to review the decisions of Congress" and indeed that such an authority was inconsistent with separation of powers, but found the Supreme Court's assumption of judicial review justified nonetheless by the practical need "to prevent the defeat of the venture at hand"—to keep the government from foundering. Hand, The Bill of Rights (1958).

The Supreme Court's decision in Obergefell v. Hodges (p. 583 below), mandating the recognition of same-sex marriage in all states, reinvigorated the debate over the relationship between judicial review and democracy. In one widely publicized case, a Kentucky county clerk who refused to issue marriage licenses to same-sex couples, citing her personal religious objections, was held in contempt of court and briefly jailed by a federal court. The clerk's supporters, including several major-party presidential candidates, maintained that the Obergefell decision was inconsistent with democratically-enacted legislation and was thus illegitimate. Does the addition of considerations of individual conscience strengthen the argument against judicial review? If President Lincoln had no authority to contravene Dred Scott, could individual judges have refused to enforce the ruling, on the grounds of their moral opposition to slavery? See generally Cover, Justice Accused (1975).

Beyond life tenure, what other mechanisms shield the judiciary from democratic pressures? Consider a recent exchange between President Donald Trump and Chief Justice John Roberts in late 2018. After President Trump referred to a district court judge who had issued an immigration-related ruling unfavorable to the administration as an "Obama judge," the Chief Justice took the highly unusual step of issuing an official statement through the Court's press office: "We do not have Obama judges or Trump judges, Bush judges or Clinton judges. [The] independent judiciary is something we should all be thankful for." Consider whether "democratic pressures" on the judiciary are distinguishable from partisan pressures.

6. ***Judicial review in other nations.*** The United States Constitution does not explicitly grant the judicial review power asserted in Marbury. Marshall relied instead on general principles and inferences from constitutional text and structure. Many other democratic nations, by contrast, have expressly vested the power of judicial review in ordinary courts or in special constitutional courts: "Canada, India, Ireland, and Japan have vested regular courts with interpretive power, while Civil-Law nations have tended to follow the model Hans Kelsen designed for Austria after World War I: a special tribunal exercising exclusive jurisdiction within the judiciary over constitutional interpretation." Murphy, "Constitutions, Constitutionalism, and Democracy," in Constitutionalism and Democracy: Transitions in the Contemporary World (Greenberg, Katz, Oliviero & Wheatley eds., 1993). And of the many constitutions drafted since 1989 in the former Communist nations of Eastern Europe and in post-apartheid South Africa, nearly all establish some explicit framework for judicial review, obviating the need for a Marbury-like case. See Hirschl, "The Political Origins of Judicial Empowerment Through Constitutionalization: Lessons from Four Constitutional Revolutions," 25 Law & Soc. Inquiry 91 (2000). Indeed, the story of judicial review has been one of steady expansion across the world, with the aftermath of World War II marking a watershed. More recently, "[t]he last two decades of the twentieth century witnessed [the] expansion of judicial review from the United States and Western Europe to democracies that had long resisted constitutionalized rights and to corners of the globe with troubled human rights records." Schor, "Mapping Comparative Judicial Review," 7 Wash. U. Global Stud. L. Rev. 257, 266 (2008).

The move towards judicial review has not been universal, and there are well-established democracies that do not subject political actors to judicial review. In Great Britain, for example, "[u]ntil recently, the law assumed that Parliament was omnicompetent and paramount. It could make or unmake law on any matter whatsoever. No court in the kingdom was competent to question the legal validity of any [statute]." Finer, Bogdanor & Rudden, "On the Constitution of the United Kingdom," in Comparing Constitutions (1995). Increasing enforcement of the European Convention on Human Rights, however, has subtly altered this parliamentary supremacy. The Supreme Court of the United Kingdom, operational since 2009, can declare legislation incompatible with the European Convention. International courts have increasingly made judicial review a source of domestic "constitutional" law within their member nations. For example, the law of employment discrimination in the United Kingdom has arisen largely from decisions of the European Union's court, and decisions of the European Court of Human Rights have overridden domestic policies in Britain and elsewhere. See, e.g., Dudgeon v. United Kingdom, 45 Eur. Ct. H.R. (1981) (invalidating criminal prohibition on consensual homosexual conduct in Northern Ireland). For a general comparative treatment of judicial review, see Jackson & Tushnet, Comparative Constitutional Law 455–708 (1999).

POLITICAL RESTRAINTS ON THE SUPREME COURT

Supreme Court decisions frequently stir popular opposition. Rulings on school desegregation, abortion, flag burning, and gay marriage are salient examples. What means are available to the executive and legislative branches to counter Supreme Court decisions, other than voicing their disapproval from the bully pulpit?

1. ***Judicial selection: the nomination and confirmation process.*** The President nominates Justices to the Supreme Court, but Art. II, § 2, cl. 2, provides that the appointment will not be effective unless the President obtains the "Advice and Consent of the Senate." It has long been accepted that the President may choose nominees who share his ideological views. But the proper role of the Senate in exercising its power to confirm or reject has been the subject of much dispute. The Senate rejected about twenty percent of presidential nominations for the Court in the nineteenth century, but most rejections were not based on ideological grounds. For several decades beginning with the New Deal era of the 1930s, the general view was that the Senate could reject a nominee only on grounds of incompetence or defects in character or temperament. Justice Antonin Scalia was confirmed by a vote of 98–0 in 1986. That attitude changed dramatically with President Ronald Reagan's nomination of Judge Robert Bork, then serving on the U.S. Court of Appeals for the D.C. Circuit, in 1987. The committee and floor debates were extensive and heated, much of the debate turned on ideological considerations, and the Bork nomination was rejected by a vote of 42 in favor and 58 against. Ever since, the Judiciary Committee has felt free to probe a nominee's constitutional views, though it is often stymied by nominees' refusal to discuss an issue on the ground that it might come before them. Moreover, the process of nomination and confirmation has come to include intense scrutiny of nominees' professional and private lives. In 1991, Professor Anita Hill testified during the confirmation of Justice Clarence Thomas regarding allegations of sexual harassment denied by Thomas. The 2018 hearings that preceded the confirmation of Justice Brett Kavanaugh included allegations by Dr. Christine Blasey Ford of sexual misconduct in the 1980s, allegations that Kavanaugh strenuously denied.

Is so active a senatorial role in the confirmation process appropriate and desirable? One writer has commented that "it is at least a *little* peculiar that we are told that scrutiny of 'judicial philosophy' is crucial to provide some democratic check on the Justices, but, at the same time, that the Court should not be responsive to political pressure or public protest." Carter, The Confirmation Mess 91 (1993). After his failed nomination, Bork remarked that "there is no possibility of an adequate judgment of judicial philosophy by a group of senators, nor is that fact surprising. [Senators], even the best of them, [simply] do not have much experience with constitutional law either as practitioners or as professors. The worst of them know only what they like and suppose that is the Constitution." Bork, The Tempting of America: The Political Seduction of the Law (1990).

Senators ≠ educated about Const.

2. ***Impeachment.*** Justices are appointed to the Court "to hold their Offices during good Behaviour," Art. III, § 1, which has long been understood to confer presumptive life tenure. Art. II, § 4, however, provides that any officer of the United States, including judges, may be removed from office "on Impeachment for, and Conviction of, Treason, Bribery, or other High Crimes and Misdemeanors." No Supreme Court Justice has ever been removed under that provision. Federalist Justice Samuel Chase was impeached by the House, but the Jeffersonians were unable to achieve the requisite two-thirds majority in the Senate to convict him. That episode established an important historical precedent that has not been violated since: an ideological disagreement with a sitting Justice is not a proper ground for impeachment. Still, that did not stop many "Impeach Earl Warren" signs from going up around the nation in the aftermath of the Court's decision in Brown.

3. ***Structural interference.*** Congress sets the size of and budget for the Court. While Justices' salaries "shall not be diminished during their Continuance in Office," Art. III, § 2, congressional power over the size and budget of the Court is a potential source of political checking power. President Franklin D. Roosevelt famously threatened in 1937 to "pack" or increase the size of the Court in order to ensure a majority of justices willing to uphold New Deal legislation. Even such relatively routine legislation as that of setting the time at which the Court meets can be used to serve political ends: recall the Jeffersonian legislation that caused the decision in Marbury to be postponed until 1803.

4. ***Jurisdiction-stripping.*** Art. III, § 2, gives Congress the power to make "Exceptions" to the Supreme Court's appellate jurisdiction. Does this power permit Congress to strip the Supreme Court of power over specific subject matters? During Reconstruction after the Civil War, the Court upheld one such selective withdrawal of jurisdiction. Under the Reconstruction Acts enacted in the aftermath of the Civil War, Congress imposed military government on former Confederate States. William McCardle was a Mississippi newspaper editor (and former sergeant in the Confederate army) in military custody on charges of publishing "incendiary and libelous articles." He brought a habeas corpus proceeding under the Act of Congress of February 5, 1867, which authorized federal courts to grant habeas corpus to anyone restrained "in violation of the Constitution" and also authorized appeals to the Supreme Court. He claimed that the Reconstruction Acts were beyond the constitutional power of Congress. After the lower court denied McCardle's habeas petition, he appealed to the Supreme Court. The Supreme Court sustained jurisdiction of that appeal, but after oral argument had been heard, Congress passed an Act of March 27, 1868, stating that so much of the 1867 Act "as authorized an appeal from

the judgment of the Circuit Court to the Supreme Court of the United States, or the exercise of any such jurisdiction by said Supreme Court, on appeals which have been, or may hereafter be taken, be, and the same is, hereby repealed."

In **Ex parte McCardle**, 7 Wall. (74 U.S.) 506 (1869), Justice CHASE wrote the opinion of the Court, holding that it lacked jurisdiction to entertain the petition: "[True,] the appellate jurisdiction of this Court is not derived from acts of Congress. It is, strictly speaking, conferred by the Constitution. But it is conferred 'with such exceptions and under such regulations as Congress shall make.' [The] provision of the act of 1867 affirming the appellate jurisdiction of this court in cases of habeas corpus is expressly repealed. It is hardly possible to imagine a plainer instance of positive exception. [It] is quite clear, therefore, that this court cannot proceed to pronounce judgment in this case, for it has no longer jurisdiction of the appeal; and judicial duty is not less fitly performed by declining ungranted jurisdiction than in exercising firmly that which the Constitution and the laws confer. Counsel seem to have supposed, if effect be given to the repealing act in question, that the whole appellate power of the court, in cases of habeas corpus, is denied. But this is an error. The act of 1868 does not except from that jurisdiction any cases but appeals from Circuit Courts under the act of 1867. It does not affect the jurisdiction which was previously exercised."

Assertions of broad congressional power to make exceptions to appellate jurisdiction have proved tempting to some critics of modern Court decisions, prompting recurrent congressional threats to curb the Court's power. Congressional proposals to eliminate the Court's appellate jurisdiction in such controversial areas as busing, abortion and school prayer, for example, failed in the 1970s and 1980s. In opposition to such proposals, some have argued that Art. III itself imposes "internal" limits on such congressional power. Henry M. Hart, Jr., argued that the "exceptions" power of Congress may not be exercised in a way that would interfere with the "essential" or "core" functions of the Court or "destroy the essential role of the Supreme Court in the constitutional plan." Hart, "The Power of Congress to Limit the Jurisdiction of Federal Courts: An Exercise in Dialectic," 66 Harv. L. Rev. 1362 (1953). Others have argued that "external" limitations in the Constitution, such as the provisions of the Bill of Rights, constrain Congress's court-stripping power. For example, Congress could not bar Supreme Court review by excluding certain litigants on the basis of race or political beliefs. But even if legislation singling out particular classes of *litigants* on the basis of their race or other suspect classifications is presumptively invalid, does it follow that singling out classes of *issues* for primary or exclusive adjudication in state rather than federal courts is similarly vulnerable to constitutional challenge? For an argument that it does, see Tribe, "Jurisdictional Gerrymandering: Zoning Disfavored Rights Out of the Federal Courts," 16 Harv. C.R.-C.L. L. Rev. 129 (1981); but see Tribe, I American Constitutional Law 274 n.28 (2000) (retreating from this argument). For a critique of such an argument, see Gunther, "Congressional Power to Curtail Federal Court Jurisdiction: An Opinionated Guide to the Ongoing Debate," 36 Stan. L. Rev. 895 (1984).

5. ***Constitutional amendment.*** Article V of the Constitution permits amendment of almost every provision. (Two slavery-related provisions of the Constitution were initially exempted from Article V, and

amendment of Article I's method of apportioning senators by state remains circumscribed by the requirement that "no State, without its Consent, shall be deprived of equal Suffrage in the Senate.") Article V specifies two methods for initiating the amendment process: Congress, by a two-thirds vote, may propose amendments for ratification by three-fourths of the states; or two-thirds of the states may apply to Congress to call a constitutional convention "for proposing Amendments." The first, congressionally initiated method has been traditionally used; the second, state-initiated convention method remains untried.

An amendment changing the text of the Constitution to reject a Supreme Court ruling, of course, binds the Court and supersedes its prior decision. But amendment of the Constitution under Article V has been exceedingly rare, and amendment to overturn the Court's constitutional decisions even rarer. Congress has considered over 11,000 amendments in the nation's history, but it has proposed only thirty-three with the requisite supermajority (a two-thirds vote of both houses); of those, only twenty-seven were eventually ratified by three-quarters of the states as Article V requires. Of those, almost half occurred in two concentrated and extraordinary historical circumstances: The first ten amendments, the Bill of Rights, were added in one fell swoop by the First Congress and ratified in 1791 as part of a grand political bargain to induce reluctant states to ratify the Constitution. And the Thirteenth, Fourteenth and Fifteenth Amendments, which abolished slavery and gave African-Americans rights of equal citizenship and the franchise, were imposed on the southern states by the Reconstruction Congress as a condition of readmission to the Union in the wake of the Civil War.

Amendments to overturn specific Supreme Court constitutional rulings have been ratified only four times since the founding. The Eleventh Amendment (adopted in 1798) overruled Chisholm v. Georgia (1793) and gave the states immunity against certain suits in federal court; the Fourteenth Amendment (1868) reversed the Dred Scott decision (1857) and granted national citizenship to former slaves; the Sixteenth Amendment (1913) was adopted to circumvent Pollock v. Farmers' Loan & Trust Corp. (1895) and permit a federal income tax; and the Twenty-Sixth Amendment (1971) overturned the Court's decision in Oregon v. Mitchell (1970) so as to require states to grant voting privileges to 18-year-olds.

The infrequency of constitutional amendment as a means of controlling the Supreme Court is no surprise. The supermajority provisions for amending the constitution, while less arduous than the unanimity that had been required to alter the Articles of Confederation, still require a degree of political and geographic consensus that is difficult to achieve. And a political culture of self-restraint has arisen toward altering the founding federal documents; as James Madison wrote in The Federalist No. 49, the amendment power is to be reserved "for certain great and extraordinary occasions." See Kyvig, Explicit and Authentic Acts: Amending the U.S. Constitution, 1776–1995 (1996). Moreover, the perceived need for amendment has been reduced by Supreme Court's manner of constitutional interpretation and judicial review. Reversals in constitutional doctrine have occurred frequently by judicial action rather than formal amendment: "[T]he Constitution changes in several ways, not just one. It has been changed by textual amendments, the Article V way; but changes in constitutional understandings have also occurred as a result of popular movements that altered not a single word in the text. And constitutional change can be led by judges, who produce new 'readings' of the Constitution when they resolve particular disputes." Sunstein, "Making Amends," New Republic 216:9, at 38 (Mar. 3, 1997).

To illustrate this point, consider the history of the Equal Rights Amendment (ERA), which would have amended the Constitution to bar expressly discrimination on the basis of sex. The ERA passed both houses of Congress in 1972 and fell three states short of ratification before the deadline lapsed on June 30, 1982. While the debate over ratification was fierce, the defeat of the ERA coincided with a series of cases in which the Supreme Court began to recognize equal protection for women as a robust constitutional principle and to subject statutes which discriminated on the basis of sex to heightened scrutiny. See Frontiero v. Richardson, 411 U.S. 677 (1973) (invalidating a federal law granting servicemen an automatic dependency allowance for their wives, but requiring servicewomen to demonstrate that their husbands were dependents); Craig v. Boren, 429 U.S. 190 (1976) (establishing that sex classifications are subject to intermediate scrutiny). The perceived need for the ERA may have been partially diminished by the Court's decisions in this arena and, as the Court's doctrine grew more protective of women, the issue lost political salience. At the same time, efforts to pass the ERA may have helped generate the results in Frontiero and Craig. See Mayeri, "A New E.R.A. or a New Era? Amendment Advocacy and the Reconstitution of Feminism," 103 Nw. U. L. Rev. 1223, 1224 (2009) ("[C]onstitutional law experts agree that feminists ultimately succeeded in achieving many, if not most, of their goals through litigation and legislation, despite the ERA's defeat.").

For arguments that there has been too much self-restraint in constitutional amendment practice, see the essays in Levinson, ed., Responding to Imperfection: The Theory and Practice of Constitutional Amendments (1995). For a further call for amending the existing text, see Levinson, Our Undemocratic Constitution: Where the Constitution Goes Wrong (and How We the People Can Correct It) (2006).

SECTION 4. CONSTITUTIONAL AND PRUDENTIAL LIMITS ON CONSTITUTIONAL ADJUDICATION: THE "CASE OR CONTROVERSY" REQUIREMENTS

A basic premise of Marbury v. Madison is that the Supreme Court plays a role in constitutional elaboration only because it is a *court*, a judicial body deciding *cases*. Article III, § 2, cl. 1 of the Constitution provides that the "judicial power shall extend" to a list of enumerated "cases" and "controversies." This affirmative grant of power has long been thought to imply a negative: that judicial power does not extend to anything but a case or controversy. To qualify as a case or controversy, a matter must be concrete and non-hypothetical, as affirmed by longstanding federal practice barring issuance of merely advisory opinions. It must also involve parties claiming an actual injury that is personal and concrete to them, as expressed in the law of standing, which has both constitutional and prudential elements. And the dispute must arise neither too late nor too soon for judicial resolution, as made clear in the doctrines of mootness and ripeness. Even if a case might otherwise appear concrete, it might still involve a nonjusticiable political question—one that is committed to the unreviewable discretion of another branch, or that is best left to another branch as a matter of prudence.

———

ADVISORY OPINIONS

1. ***Declining comment on Washington's war powers.*** The earliest of all nonjusticiability doctrines, first enforced well before Marbury v. Madison, stems from the Court's refusal to issue "advisory opinions"—opinions on the legality of executive or legislative action that do not involve an actual "case." In 1793, President Washington sought the advice of the Justices on some legal questions involving America's neutrality toward the ongoing war between England and France. Secretary of State Jefferson, on behalf of the President, wrote to the Justices: "These questions depend for their solution on the construction of our treaties, on the laws of nature and nations, and on the laws of the land, and are often presented under circumstances which do not give a cognizance of them to the tribunals of the country. Yet their decision is so little analogous to the ordinary functions of the executive, as to occasion much embarrassment and difficulty to them. The President therefore would be much relieved if he found himself free to refer questions of this description to the opinions of the judges of the [Court], whose knowledge of the subject would secure us against errors dangerous to the peace of the United States, and their authority insure the respect of all parties."

A few weeks later, the Justices firmly rejected that invitation: "[T]he three departments of the government [being] in certain respects checks upon each other, and our being judges of a court in the last resort, are considerations which afford strong arguments against the propriety of our extrajudicially deciding the questions alluded to, especially as the power given by the Constitution to the President, of calling on the heads of departments for opinions, seems to have been purposely as well as expressly united to the executive departments. We exceedingly regret every event that may cause embarrassment to your administration, but we derive consolation from the reflection that your judgment will discern what is [right]."

2. ***Advisory opinions and the political branches.*** Are there persuasive constitutional or policy arguments against advisory opinions? Early, authoritative resolution of constitutional doubts might well be desirable for legislative and executive officials. For example, just before the Court-packing crisis in 1937, President Roosevelt briefly considered a plan that would require the Court to give advisory opinions, "to say in advance of the passing of a law whether it was unconstitutional." See The Secret Diary of Harold L. Ickes—The First Thousand Days, 1933–1936 (1953).

Note that the policy against advisory opinions is not inevitable; some state supreme courts are authorized to issue advisory opinions. For instance, the Massachusetts Constitution, Mass. Const. Art. LXXXV, provides that "Each branch of the legislature, as well as the governor or council, shall have authority to require the opinions of the justices of the supreme judicial court upon important questions [and] solemn occasions." And the Michigan Constitution, Mich. Const. Art. 3, § 8, provides that "Either house of the legislature or the governor may request the opinion of the supreme court on important questions of law upon solemn occasions as to the constitutionality of legislation after it has been enacted into law but before its effective date."

These provisions are not merely theoretical: from 1990 to 2004, state supreme courts issued 143 responses to request for advisory opinions. See Persky, Comment, "'Ghosts That Slay': A Contemporary Look at State Advisory Opinions," 37 Conn. L. Rev. 1155, 1160 (2005) (providing a comprehensive evaluation of state advisory opinions and arguing that judicious use of them improves efficiency and accountability). Similarly, other nations that have modeled their constitutions after the United States Constitution have frequently chosen to diverge from the American example by granting an explicit advisory capacity to the courts.

3. ***Advisory opinions and judicial review.*** In **Rescue Army v. Municipal Court of Los Angeles**, 331 U.S. 549 (1947), the Court articulated some of the policy reasons underlying the refusal to issue advisory opinions. Justice RUTLEDGE stated: "[The] Court's refusal to render advisory opinions [and other nonjusticiability doctrines ensures that] constitutional issues affecting legislation will not be determined in friendly, nonadversary proceedings; in advance of the necessity of deciding them; in broader terms than are required by the precise facts to which the ruling is to be applied; [at] the instance of one who fails to show that he is injured by the statute's operation; [or] if a construction of the statute is fairly possible by which the question may be avoided. [Every] application [of these rules] has been an instance of reluctance, indeed, of refusal, to undertake the most important and the most delicate of the Court's functions [until] necessity compels it. [The] policy's ultimate foundations [lie] in all that goes to make up the unique place and character, in our scheme, of judicial review of governmental action for constitutionality. They are found in the delicacy of that function, particularly in view of possible consequences for others stemming also from constitutional routes; [the] necessity, if government is to function constitutionally, for each [branch of government] to keep within its power, including the courts; the inherent limitations of the judicial process, arising especially from its largely negative character and limited resources of enforcement."

Justice Frankfurter was also an impassioned opponent of advisory opinions: "Unless we are to embrace fatalism, legislation to a considerable extent must necessarily be based on probabilities, on hopes and fears, and not on demonstration. To meet the intricate, stubborn, and subtle problems of modern industrialism, the legislature must be given ample scope for putting its prophecies to the test of proof. But to submit legislative proposals to the judicial judgment, instead of the deliberate decision of the legislature, is to submit legislative doubts instead of legislative convictions. The whole focus of the judicial vision becomes thereby altered." Frankfurter, "A Note on Advisory Opinions," 37 Harv. L. Rev. 1002 (1924).

4. ***Nonadversary suits.*** Closely related to the prohibition on advisory opinions is the bar against nonadversary or "friendly" suits. A justiciable "controversy" only exists if the parties genuinely disagree about what the outcome of the lawsuit should be; otherwise, parties could obtain an advisory opinion by colluding to bring a lawsuit. As Justice BRANDEIS put it in **Ashwander v. Tennessee Valley Authority**, 297 U.S. 288 (1936), "The Court will not pass upon the constitutionality of legislation in a friendly, nonadversary, proceeding, declining because to decide such questions is legitimate only in the last resort, and as a necessity in the determination of real, earnest, and vital controversy between individuals. It never was the thought that, by means of a friendly suit, a party beaten in

the legislature could transfer to the courts an inquiry as to the constitutionality of the legislative act."

When the executive branch believes a law is unconstitutional and refuses to defend it in court, but continues to enforce it, is a suit against the government challenging that enforcement adversarial? The Court said yes in **United States v. Windsor**, 570 U.S. 744 (2013), in which it struck down Section 3 of the Defense of Marriage Act (DOMA) (see p. 575 below for the Court's opinion on the merits). The plaintiff, Edith Windsor, had won a lower-court judgment that § 3, which limited the definition of "marriage" to a union between one man and one woman for the purpose of all federal statutes, was unconstitutional. This would have entitled her to a refund of federal estate tax, paid on her wife's estate, that an opposite-sex spouse would not have owed. The Attorney General decided not to defend DOMA on appeal, but also declined to issue Windsor's tax refund. The Court allowed a group of House members (the Bipartisan Legal Advisory Group, or BLAG) to intervene and defend the law on its merits, and appointed an *amicus* to argue that no justiciable controversy existed.

Justice KENNEDY explained why, despite the government's agreement with the plaintiff on the merits, the case remained justiciable: "[The] Government's agreement with Windsor's position would not have deprived the District Court of jurisdiction to entertain and resolve the refund suit; for her injury (failure to obtain a refund allegedly required by law) was concrete, persisting, and unredressed. The Government's position—agreeing with Windsor's legal contention but refusing to give it effect—meant that there was a justiciable controversy between the parties. [An] order directing the Treasury to pay money is a real and immediate economic injury, indeed as real and immediate as an order directing an individual to pay a tax. That the Executive may welcome this order to pay the refund if it is accompanied by the constitutional ruling it wants does not eliminate the injury to the national Treasury if payment is made, or to the taxpayer if it is not.

"[One] consideration is the extent to which adversarial presentation of the issues is assured by the participation of *amici curiae* prepared to defend with vigor the constitutionality of the legislative act. [BLAG's] sharp adversarial presentation of the issues satisfies the prudential concerns that otherwise might counsel against hearing an appeal from a decision with which the principal parties agree. Were this Court to hold that prudential rules require it to dismiss the case, [extensive] litigation would ensue. The district courts in 94 districts throughout the Nation would be without precedential guidance not only in tax refund suits but also in cases involving the whole of DOMA's sweep involving over 1,000 federal statutes and a myriad of federal regulations. [Rights] and privileges of hundreds of thousands of persons would be adversely affected.

"[There] is no suggestion here that it is appropriate for the Executive as a matter of course to challenge statutes in the judicial forum rather than making the case to Congress for their amendment or repeal. The integrity of the political process would be at risk if difficult constitutional issues were simply referred to the Court as a routine exercise. But this case is not routine."

Justice SCALIA, in dissent, accused the majority of sweeping aside procedural obstacles due to its desire to reach DOMA's merits: "[The people] gave judges, in Article III, only the 'judicial Power,' a power to decide not abstract questions but real, concrete 'Cases' and 'Controversies.' Yet the plaintiff and the Government agree entirely on what should happen in this lawsuit. They agree that the court below got it right; and they agreed in the court below that the court below that one got it right as well. [We] are quite forbidden to say what the law is whenever (as today's opinion asserts) 'an Act of Congress is alleged to conflict with the Constitution.' We can do so only when that allegation will determine the outcome of a lawsuit, and is contradicted by the other party. The 'judicial Power' is not, as the majority believes, the power 'to say what the law is,' giving the Supreme Court the 'primary role in determining the constitutionality of laws.' The judicial power as Americans have understood it (and their English ancestors before them) is the power to adjudicate, with conclusive effect, disputed government claims (civil or criminal) against private persons, and disputed claims by private persons against the government or other private persons."

Do the justifications for forbidding advisory opinions (see note 3 above) still apply where, as in this case, there are zealous advocates for and against the constitutionality of the statute at issue? Is the separation of powers—the confinement of the judiciary to its proper role—the real value at stake here, as Justice Scalia maintains? Justice Kennedy's reasoning implies that the Court would not have been able to hear the case if the government had voluntarily refunded Ms. Windsor's taxes—does this logic grant the executive too much power to undermine the legislature?

STANDING

Lujan v. Defenders of Wildlife

504 U.S. 555, 112 S. Ct. 2130, 119 L. Ed. 2d 351 (1992).

■ JUSTICE SCALIA delivered the opinion of the Court with respect to Parts I, II, III–A, and IV, and an opinion with respect to Part III–B in which CHIEF JUSTICE [REHNQUIST] and JUSTICES WHITE and THOMAS join.

This case involves a challenge to a rule promulgated by the Secretary of the Interior interpreting § 7 of the Endangered Species Act of 1973 (ESA) in such fashion as to render it applicable only to actions within the United States or on the high seas. The preliminary issue, and the only one we reach, is whether the respondents here, plaintiffs below, have standing to seek judicial review of the rule.

I. The ESA seeks to protect species of animals against threats to their continuing existence caused by man. The ESA instructs the Secretary of the Interior to promulgate by regulation a list of those species which are either endangered or threatened under enumerated criteria, and to define the critical habitat of these species. Section 7(a)(2) of the Act then provides, in pertinent part: "Each Federal agency shall, in consultation with and with the assistance of the Secretary [of the Interior], insure that any action authorized, funded, or carried out by such agency [is] not likely to jeopardize the continued existence of any endangered species or threatened species or result in the destruction or adverse modification of habitat of such species which is determined by the Secretary, after consultation as appropriate with affected States, to be critical."

In 1978, the Fish and Wildlife Service (FWS) and the National Marine Fisheries Service (NMFS), on behalf of the Secretary of the Interior and the Secretary of Commerce respectively, promulgated a joint regulation stating that the obligations imposed by § 7(a)(2) extend to actions taken in foreign nations. The next year, however, the Interior Department began to reexamine its position. A revised joint regulation, reinterpreting § 7(a)(2) to require consultation only for actions taken in the United States or on the high seas, [was] promulgated in 1986. Shortly thereafter, [the plaintiffs], organizations dedicated to wildlife conservation and other environmental causes, filed this action against the Secretary of the Interior, seeking a declaratory judgment that the new regulation is in error as to the geographic scope of § 7(a)(2), and an injunction requiring the Secretary to promulgate a new regulation restoring the initial [interpretation]. [T]he Secretary moved for summary judgment on the standing issue, and [plaintiffs] moved for summary judgment on the merits. The District Court denied the Secretary's motion; it granted plaintiffs' merits motion, and ordered the Secretary to publish a revised regulation. The [Court of Appeals] affirmed.

II. Though some of [the] elements [of the doctrine of standing] express merely prudential considerations that are part of judicial self-government, the core component of standing is an essential and unchanging part of the case-or-controversy requirement of Article III. Over the years, our cases have established that the irreducible constitutional minimum of standing contains three elements: First, the plaintiff must have suffered an "injury in fact"—an invasion of a legally-protected interest which is (a) concrete and particularized, and (b) "actual or imminent, not 'conjectural' or 'hypothetical.'" Second, there must be a causal connection between the injury and the conduct complained of—the injury has to be "fairly [traceable] to the challenged action of the defendant, and [not] the result [of] the independent action of some third party not before the court." Third, it must be "likely," as opposed to merely "speculative," that the injury will be "redressed by a favorable decision."

III. [Plaintiffs have] not made the requisite demonstration of (at least) injury and redressability. A. [Plaintiffs'] claim to injury is that the lack of consultation with respect to certain funded activities abroad "increases the rate of extinction of endangered and threatened species." Of course, the desire to use or observe an animal species, even for purely aesthetic purposes, is undeniably a cognizable interest for purpose of standing. "But the 'injury in fact' test requires more than an injury to a cognizable interest. It requires that the party seeking review be himself among the injured." [With] respect to this aspect of the case, the Court of Appeals focused on the affidavits of two Defenders' members—Joyce Kelly and Amy Skilbred. Ms. Kelly stated that she traveled to Egypt in 1986 and "observed the traditional habitat of the endangered nile crocodile there and intends to do so again, and hopes to observe the crocodile directly," and that she "will suffer harm in fact as a result of [the] American [role] in overseeing the rehabilitation of the Aswan High Dam on the Nile [and in] developing [Egypt's] Master Water Plan." Ms. Skilbred averred that she traveled to Sri Lanka in 1981 and "observed the habitat" of "endangered species such as the Asian elephant and the leopard" at what is now the site of the Mahaweli Project funded by the Agency for International Development (AID), although she "was unable to see any of the endangered species"; "this development project," she continued, "will seriously reduce endangered, threatened, and endemic species habitat including areas that I visited, [which] may severely shorten the future of these species"; that threat, she concluded, harmed her because she "intends to return to Sri Lanka in the future and hopes to be more fortunate in spotting at least the endangered elephant and leopard." When Ms. Skilbred was asked at a subsequent deposition if and when she had any plans to return to Sri Lanka, she reiterated that "I intend to go back to Sri Lanka," but confessed that she had no current plans: "I don't know when. There is a civil war going on right now. I don't know. Not next year, I will say. In the future."

We shall assume for the sake of argument that these affidavits contain facts showing that certain agency-funded projects threaten listed species—though that is questionable. They plainly contain no facts, however, showing how damage to the species will produce "imminent" injury to Mss. Kelly and Skilbred. That the women "had visited" the areas of the projects before the projects commenced proves nothing. And the affiants' profession of an "intent" to return to the places they had visited before [is] simply not enough. Such "some day" intentions—without any description of concrete plans, or indeed even any specification of when the some day will be—do not support a finding of the "actual or imminent" injury that our cases require.

[Plaintiffs, besides relying on the Kelly and Skilbred affidavits,] propose a series of novel standing themes. [Among these are theories] called, alas, the "animal nexus" approach, whereby anyone who has an interest in studying or seeing the endangered animals anywhere on the globe has standing; and the "vocational nexus" approach, under which anyone with a professional interest in such animals can sue. Under these theories, anyone who goes to see Asian elephants in the Bronx Zoo, and anyone who is a keeper of Asian elephants in the Bronx Zoo, has standing to sue because the Director of AID did not consult with the Secretary regarding the AID-funded project in Sri Lanka. This is beyond all reason. Standing is not "an ingenious academic exercise in the conceivable," but as we have said requires, at the summary judgment stage, a factual showing of perceptible harm. It is clear that the person who observes or works with a particular animal threatened by a federal decision is facing perceptible harm, since the very subject of his interest will no longer exist. It is even plausible—though it goes to the outermost limit of plausibility—to think that a person who observes or works with animals of a particular species in the very area of the world where that species is threatened by a federal decision is facing such harm, since some animals that might have been the subject of his interest will no longer exist. It goes beyond the limit, however, and into pure speculation and fantasy, to say that anyone who observes or works with an endangered species, anywhere in the world, is appreciably harmed by a single project affecting some portion of that species with which he has no more specific connection.

B. Besides failing to show injury, [plaintiffs] failed to demonstrate redressability. [Since] the agencies funding the projects were not parties to the case, the District Court could accord relief only against the Secretary: He could be ordered to revise his regulation to require consultation for foreign projects. But this would not remedy respondents' alleged injury unless the funding agencies were bound by the Secretary's regulation, which is very much an open question. [Redress] of the only injury in fact respondents complain of requires action (termination of funding until consultation) by the individual funding agencies; and any relief the District Court could have provided in this suit against the Secretary was not likely to produce that action. [A] further impediment to redressability is the fact that the agencies generally supply only a fraction of the funding for a foreign project. Respondents have produced nothing to indicate that the projects they have named will either be suspended, or do less harm to listed species, if that fraction is eliminated. [It] is entirely conjectural whether the non-agency activity that affects respondents will be altered or affected by the agency activity they seek to achieve.

IV. The Court of Appeals found that respondents had standing for an additional reason: because they had suffered a "procedural injury." The so-called "citizen-suit" provision of the ESA provides, in pertinent part, that "any person may commence a civil suit on his own behalf (A) to enjoin any person, including the United States and any other governmental instrumentality or agency, [who] is alleged to be in violation of any provision of this chapter." The court held that, because § 7(a)(2) requires interagency consultation, the citizen-suit provision creates a "procedural right" to consultation in all "persons"—so that anyone can file suit in federal court to challenge the Secretary's (or presumably any other official's) failure to follow the assertedly correct consultative procedure, notwithstanding their inability to allege any discrete injury flowing from that failure. To understand the remarkable nature of this holding one must be clear about what it does not rest upon: This is not a case where plaintiffs are seeking to enforce a procedural requirement the disregard of which could impair a separate concrete interest of theirs (e.g., the procedural requirement for a hearing prior to denial of their license application, or the procedural requirement for an environmental impact statement before a federal facility is constructed next door to them). Nor is it simply a case where concrete injury has been suffered by many persons, as in mass fraud or mass tort situations. Nor, finally, is it the unusual case in which Congress has created a concrete private interest in the outcome of a suit against a private party for the government's benefit, by providing a cash bounty for the victorious plaintiff. Rather, the court held that the injury-in-fact requirement had been satisfied by congressional conferral upon all persons of an abstract, self-contained, noninstrumental "right" to have the Executive observe the procedures required by law. We reject this view.

reject the view that injury req. = satisfied by citizen-suit provision of ESA

We have consistently held that a plaintiff raising only a generally available grievance about government—claiming only harm to his and every citizen's interest in proper application of the Constitution and laws, and seeking relief that no more directly and tangibly benefits him than it does the public at large—does not state an Article III case or controversy. To be sure, our generalized-grievance cases have typically involved Government violation of procedures assertedly ordained by the Constitution rather than the Congress. But there is absolutely no basis for making the Article III inquiry turn on the source of the asserted right. Whether the courts were to act on their own, or at the invitation of Congress, in ignoring the concrete injury requirement described in our cases, they would be discarding a principle fundamental to the separate and distinct constitutional role of the Third Branch—one of the essential elements that identifies those "Cases" and "Controversies" that are the business of the courts rather than of the political branches. "The province of the court," as Chief Justice Marshall said in Marbury v. Madison, "is, solely, to decide on the rights of individuals." Vindicating the public interest (including the public interest in government observance of the Constitution and laws) is the function of Congress and the Chief Executive.

The question presented here is whether the public interest in proper administration of the laws (specifically, in agencies' observance of a particular, statutorily prescribed procedure) can be converted into an individual right by a statute that denominates it as such, and that permits all citizens (or, for that matter, a subclass of citizens who suffer no distinctive concrete harm) to sue. If the concrete injury requirement has the separation-of-powers significance we have always said, the answer must be obvious: To permit Congress to convert the undifferentiated public interest in executive officers' compliance with the law into an "individual right" vindicable in the courts is to permit Congress to transfer from the President to the courts the Chief Executive's most important constitutional duty, to "take Care that the Laws be faithfully executed." It would enable the courts, with the permission of Congress, "to assume a position of authority over the governmental acts of another and co-equal department," and to become " 'virtually continuing monitors of the wisdom and soundness of Executive action.' " We have always rejected that vision of our role: "[U]nder Article III, Congress established courts to adjudicate cases and controversies as to claims of infringement of individual rights whether by unlawful action of private persons or by the exertion of unauthorized administrative power." "Individual rights," within the meaning of this passage, do not mean public rights that have been legislatively pronounced to belong to each individual who forms part of the public. Nothing in this contradicts the principle that "[the] injury required by Art. III may exist solely by virtue of 'statutes creating legal rights, the invasion of which creates standing.' " [Warth v. Seldin.] [I]t is clear that in suits against the government, at least, the concrete injury requirement must remain. [We] hold that respondents lack standing to bring this action.

[Reversed.]

■ JUSTICE KENNEDY, with whom JUSTICE SOUTER joins, concurring in part and concurring in the judgment.

Although I agree with the essential parts of the Court's analysis, I write separately to make several observations. [I] join Part IV of the Court's opinion with the following observations. As government programs and policies become more complex and far-reaching, we must be sensitive to the articulation of new rights of action that do not have clear analogs in our common-law tradition. Modern litigation has progressed far from the paradigm of Marbury suing Madison to get his commission. [In] my view, Congress has the power to define injuries and articulate chains of causation that will give rise to a case or controversy where none existed before, and I do not read the Court's opinion to suggest a contrary view. In exercising this power, however, Congress must at the very least identify the injury it seeks to vindicate and relate the injury to the class of persons entitled to bring suit. The citizen-suit provision of the Endangered Species Act does not meet these minimal requirements, because while the statute purports to confer a right on "any person [to] enjoin [the] United States and any other governmental instrumentality or agency [who] is alleged to be in violation of any provision of this chapter," it does not of its own force establish that there is an injury in "any person" by virtue of any "violation."

The Court's holding that there is an outer limit to the power of Congress to confer rights of action is a direct and necessary consequence of the case and controversy limitations found in Article III. I agree that it would exceed those limitations if, at the behest of Congress and in the absence of any showing of concrete injury, we were to entertain citizen-suits to vindicate the public's nonconcrete interest in the proper administration of the laws. [The] party bringing suit must show that the action injures him in a concrete and personal way. This requirement is not just an empty formality. It preserves the vitality of the adversarial process by assuring both that the parties before the court have an actual, as opposed to professed, stake in the outcome, and that "the legal questions presented [will] be resolved [in] a concrete factual context conducive to a realistic appreciation of the consequences of judicial action." In addition, the requirement of concrete injury confines the Judicial Branch to its proper, limited role in the constitutional framework of [government].

■ JUSTICE STEVENS, concurring in the judgment.

Because I am not persuaded that Congress intended the consultation requirement in § 7(a)(2) [to] apply to activities in foreign countries, I concur in the judgment of reversal. I do not, however, agree with the Court's conclusion that [plaintiffs] lack standing because the threatened injury to their interest [is] not "imminent." Nor do I agree with the plurality's additional conclusion that respondents' injury is not "redressable" in this [litigation].

■ JUSTICE BLACKMUN, with whom JUSTICE O'CONNOR joins, dissenting.

I part company with the Court in this case in two respects. First, I believe that [plaintiffs] have raised genuine issues of fact—sufficient to survive summary judgment—both as to injury and as to redressability. Second, I question the Court's breadth of language in rejecting standing for "procedural" injuries. [To] prevent Congress from conferring standing for "procedural injuries" is another way of saying that Congress may not delegate to the courts authority deemed "executive" in nature. Here Congress seeks not to delegate "executive" power but only to strengthen the procedures it has legislatively mandated. [In] no sense is the Court's suggestion compelled by our "common understanding of what activities are appropriate to legislatures, to executives, and to courts." In my view, it reflects an unseemly solicitude for an expansion of power of the Executive Branch. [I] cannot join the Court on what amounts to a slash-and-burn expedition through the law of environmental standing.

Massachusetts v. Environmental Protection Agency

549 U.S. 497, 127 S. Ct. 1438, 167 L. Ed. 2d 248 (2007).

■ JUSTICE STEVENS delivered the opinion of the Court, in which JUSTICES KENNEDY, SOUTER, GINSBURG, and BREYER joined.

A well-documented rise in global temperatures has coincided with a significant increase in the concentration of carbon dioxide in the atmosphere. Respected scientists believe the two trends are related. For when carbon dioxide is released into the atmosphere, it acts like the ceiling of a greenhouse, trapping solar energy and retarding the escape of reflected heat. It is therefore a species-the most important species-of a "greenhouse gas." Calling global warming "the most pressing environmental challenge of our time," a group of States, local governments, and private organizations, alleged [that] the Environmental Protection Agency (EPA) has abdicated its responsibility under the Clean Air Act to regulate the emissions of four greenhouse gases, including carbon dioxide.

[Article III] of the Constitution limits federal-court jurisdiction to "Cases" and "Controversies." [No] justiciable "controversy" exists when parties seek adjudication of a political question, when they ask for an advisory opinion, or when the question sought to be adjudicated has been mooted by subsequent developments. This case suffers from none of these defects. The parties' dispute turns on the proper construction of a congressional statute, a question eminently suitable to resolution in federal court. Congress has moreover authorized this type of challenge to EPA action. [EPA] maintains that because greenhouse gas emissions inflict widespread harm, the doctrine of standing presents an insuperable jurisdictional obstacle. We do not agree. [Lujan] holds that a litigant must demonstrate that it has suffered a concrete and particularized injury that is either actual or imminent, that the injury is fairly traceable to the defendant, and that it is likely that a favorable decision will redress that injury. However, a litigant to whom Congress has "accorded a procedural right to protect his concrete interests"—here, the right to challenge agency action unlawfully withheld—"can assert that right without meeting all the normal standards for redressability and immediacy." Lujan. When a litigant is vested with a procedural right, that litigant has standing if there is some possibility that the requested relief will prompt the injury-causing party to reconsider the decision that allegedly harmed the litigant.

Only one of the petitioners needs to have standing to permit us to consider the petition for review. We stress here [the] special position and interest of Massachusetts. It is of considerable relevance that the party seeking review here is a sovereign State and not, as it was in Lujan, a private individual. Well before the creation of the modern administrative state, we recognized that States are not normal litigants for the purposes of invoking federal jurisdiction. As Justice Holmes explained in Georgia v. Tennessee Copper Co., 206 U.S. 230 (1907), a case in which Georgia sought to protect its citizens from air pollution originating outside its borders; "This is a suit by a State for an injury to it in its capacity of quasi-sovereign. In that capacity the State has an interest independent of and behind the titles of its citizens, in all the earth and air within its domain." [Just] as Georgia's independent interest "in all the earth and air within its domain" supported federal jurisdiction a century ago, so too does Massachusetts' well-founded desire to preserve its sovereign territory today.

[The Injury.] The harms associated with climate change are serious and well recognized. [That] these climate-change risks are "widely shared" does not minimize Massachusetts' interest in the outcome of this litigation. According to petitioners' unchallenged affidavits, global sea levels rose somewhere between 10 and 20 centimeters over the 20th century as a result of global warming. These rising seas have already begun to swallow Massachusetts' coastal land. Because the Commonwealth "owns a substantial portion of the state's coastal property," it has alleged a particularized injury in its capacity as a landowner.

[Causation.] EPA does not dispute the existence of a causal connection between man-made greenhouse gas emissions and global warming. At a minimum, therefore, EPA's refusal to regulate such emissions "contributes" to Massachusetts' injuries. EPA nevertheless maintains that its decision not to regulate greenhouse gas emissions from new motor vehicles contributes so insignificantly to petitioners' injuries that the agency cannot be haled into federal court to answer for them. For the same reason, EPA does not believe that any realistic possibility exists that the relief petitioners seek would mitigate global climate change and remedy their injuries. That is especially so because predicted increases in greenhouse gas emissions from developing nations, particularly China and India, are likely to offset any marginal domestic decrease.

But EPA overstates its case. Its argument rests on the erroneous assumption that a small incremental step, because it is incremental, can never be attacked in a federal judicial forum. Yet accepting that premise would doom most challenges to regulatory action. Agencies, like legislatures, do not generally resolve massive problems in one fell regulatory swoop. [That] a first step might be tentative does not by itself support the notion that federal courts lack jurisdiction to determine whether that step conforms to law. And reducing domestic automobile emissions is hardly a tentative step. [Considering] just emissions from the transportation sector, which represent less than one-third of this country's total carbon dioxide emissions, the United States would still rank as the third-largest emitter of carbon dioxide in the world, outpaced only by the European Union and China. Judged by any standard, U.S. motor-vehicle emissions make a meaningful contribution to greenhouse gas concentrations and hence, according to petitioners, to global warming.

The Remedy. While it may be true that regulating motor-vehicle emissions will not by itself reverse global warming, it by no means follows that we lack jurisdiction to decide whether EPA has a duty to take steps to slow or reduce it. Because of the enormity of the potential consequences associated with man-made climate change, the fact that the effectiveness of a remedy might be delayed during the (relatively short) time it takes for a new motor-vehicle fleet to replace an older one is essentially irrelevant. Nor is it dispositive that developing countries such as China and India are poised to increase greenhouse gas emissions substantially over the next century: A reduction in domestic emissions would slow the pace of global emissions increases, no matter what happens elsewhere.

In sum, [the] rise in sea levels associated with global warming has already harmed and will continue to harm Massachusetts. The risk of catastrophic harm, though remote, is nevertheless real. That risk would be reduced to some extent if petitioners received the relief they seek. We therefore hold that petitioners have standing to challenge the EPA's denial of their rulemaking petition.

■ CHIEF JUSTICE ROBERTS, with whom JUSTICES SCALIA, THOMAS, and ALITO join, dissenting.

[This] Court's standing jurisprudence [recognizes] that redress of grievances of the sort at issue here "is the function of Congress and the Chief Executive," not the federal courts. Lujan. [Petitioners] bear the burden of alleging an injury that is fairly traceable to the Environmental Protection Agency's failure to promulgate new motor vehicle greenhouse gas emission standards, and that is likely to be redressed by the prospective issuance of such standards. [Relaxing] Article III standing requirements because asserted injuries are pressed by a State [has] no basis in our jurisprudence. [Far] from being a substitute for Article III injury, parens patriae actions raise an additional hurdle for a state litigant: the articulation of a "quasi-sovereign interest" "apart from the interests of particular private parties." [In] the context of parens patriae standing, however, we have characterized state ownership of land as a "nonsovereign interes[t]" because a State "is likely to have the same interests as other similarly situated proprietors."

[The] status of Massachusetts as a State cannot compensate for petitioners' failure to demonstrate injury in fact, causation, and redressability. [If] petitioners rely on loss of land, [that] alleged injury must be "concrete and particularized." [The] very concept of global warming seems inconsistent with this particularization requirement. Global warming is a phenomenon "harmful to humanity at large," and the redress petitioners seek is focused no more on them than on the public generally—it is literally to change the atmosphere around the world. If petitioners' particularized injury is loss of coastal land, it is also that injury that must be "actual or imminent, not conjectural or hypothetical," "real and immediate," and "certainly impending." [But] aside from a single conclusory statement, there is nothing in petitioners' 43 standing declarations and accompanying exhibits to support an inference of actual loss of Massachusetts coastal land from 20th century global sea level increases. It is pure conjecture. [One] of petitioners' declarants predicts global warming will cause sea level to rise by 20 to 70 centimeters by the year 2100. [But] accepting a century-long time [renders] requirements of imminence and immediacy utterly toothless.

Petitioners' reliance on Massachusetts's loss of coastal land as their injury in fact for standing purposes creates insurmountable problems for them with respect to causation and redressability. [As] EPA explained in its denial of petitioners' request for rulemaking, "predicting future climate change necessarily involves a complex web of economic and physical factors." [Petitioners] are never able to trace their alleged injuries back through this complex web to the fractional amount of global emissions that might have been limited with EPA standards. In light of the bit-part domestic new motor vehicle greenhouse gas emissions have played in what petitioners describe as a 150-year global phenomenon, and the myriad additional factors bearing on petitioners' alleged injury—the loss of Massachusetts coastal land—the connection is far too speculative to establish causation.

Redressability is even more problematic. [Petitioners] cannot meaningfully predict what will come of the 80 percent of global greenhouse gas emissions that originate outside the United States. As the Court acknowledges, "developing countries such as China and India are poised to increase greenhouse gas emissions substantially over the next century," so the domestic emissions at issue here may become an increasingly marginal portion of global emissions, and any decreases produced by petitioners' desired standards are likely to be overwhelmed many times over by emissions increases elsewhere in the world.

Petitioners offer declarations attempting to address this uncertainty, contending that "[i]f the U.S. takes steps to reduce motor vehicle emissions, other countries are very likely to take similar actions regarding their own motor vehicles using technology developed in response to the U.S. program." [But] when the existence of an element of standing "depends on the unfettered choices made by independent actors not before the courts and whose exercise of broad and legitimate discretion the courts cannot presume either to control or to predict," a party must present facts supporting an assertion that the actor will proceed in such a manner. The declarations' conclusory (not to say fanciful) statements do not even come close. No matter, the Court reasons, because any decrease in domestic emissions will "slow the pace of global emissions increases, no matter what happens elsewhere." Every little bit helps, so Massachusetts can sue over any little bit.

[Today's] decision recalls the previous high-water mark of diluted standing requirements, United States v. Students Challenging Regulatory Agency Procedures (SCRAP), 412 U.S. 669 (1973). SCRAP involved "[p]robably the most attenuated injury conferring Art. III standing" and "surely went to the very outer limit of the law"—until today. In SCRAP, the Court based an environmental group's standing to challenge a railroad freight rate surcharge on the group's allegation that increases in railroad rates would cause an increase in the use of nonrecyclable goods, resulting in the increased need for natural resources to produce such goods. According to the group, some of these resources might be taken from the Washington area, resulting in increased refuse that might find its way into area parks, harming the group's members.

Over time, SCRAP became emblematic not of the looseness of Article III standing requirements, but of how utterly manipulable they are if not taken seriously as a matter of judicial self-restraint. SCRAP made standing seem a lawyer's game, rather than a fundamental limitation ensuring that courts function as courts and not intrude on the politically accountable branches. Today's decision is SCRAP for a new generation.

[The portions of the opinion of the Court and a dissent by Justice SCALIA going to the merits of the claim are omitted.]

THE CONSTITUTIONAL AND PRUDENTIAL ELEMENTS OF STANDING

1. ***Personal injury.*** Lujan and Massachusetts each reiterate the three irreducible, constitutionally required elements of standing: (1) personal injury, (2) causation, and (3) redressability. The first requirement, personal injury, requires an actual injury that is particularized and concrete, distinct and palpable. The most obvious examples are claims of material bodily or financial harm. But an injury need not be economic to confer standing. Such intangible, noneconomic injuries as vote dilution, loss of opportunity to participate in a racially neutral procedure, and aesthetic offense all have been found cognizable if sufficiently particular to the plaintiff. Note too that an organization may assert associational standing, claiming injury in fact so long as any of its members might have done so and the claim is germane to the organization's purpose.

Why require litigants to have an injury that is personal to them? To ensure zealous advocacy? To prevent officious intermeddling? To limit the floodgates of litigation? To ensure judicial restraint? The answer is not historical pedigree; most of the Court's standing cases are of relatively recent vintage, and the "injury in fact" requirement was never mentioned until 1970. Nor does the idea arise from historical practices at the founding: "[T]he English practice [did] not in fact demand injury to a personal interest, and [neither] the separation of powers nor advisory opinions doctrines as originally envisaged require insistence on a personal stake as the basic element of standing[ ]." Berger, "Standing to Sue in Public Actions: Is It a Constitutional Requirement?" 78 Yale L.J. 816, 827 (1969); see also Sunstein, "What's Standing After Lujan? Of Citizen Suits, Injuries, and

Article III," 91 Mich. L. Rev. 163 (1992) ("There is absolutely no affirmative evidence that Article III was intended to limit congressional power to create standing [or to require] a 'personal stake' or an 'injury in fact'—beyond the genuine requirement that some source of law confer a cause of action.").

Note that the Court gave special solicitude to the injury in fact asserted by Massachusetts because it is a sovereign state, suing in its parens patriae capacity. Should it have? Are states more or less likely to have a concrete stake in the outcome of such a case? Is it desirable to allow the states greater latitude than individuals in driving the national regulatory agenda? Consider the contrary view: "State attorneys general are political figures with political agendas and political aspirations. Their litigation decisions often reflect their political interests. [It] should come as no surprise that eleven of the twelve attorneys general suing in Mass. v. EPA were Democrats while the administration whose policies they challenged was Republican. Far from treating the states' participation as presumptively establishing standing, the Court should have seen the states' filing more as presumptive evidence that this was a political fight over national policy, just the sort of issue that traditionally would have been regarded as a political question." Cass, "Massachusetts v. EPA: The Inconvenient Truth About Precedent," 93 Va. L. Rev. In Brief 73 (2007).

"Personal injury" for standing purposes also has a timing component—the plaintiff's injury must be concrete, real and imminent as opposed to merely likely or probable. Does Massachusetts faithfully require the imminence requirement as set forth in Lujan? Could the plaintiffs in Lujan have cured their imminence problem by buying an airplane ticket to visit the endangered species habitats they were concerned about?

The Court recently reaffirmed standing's imminence requirement in **Clapper v. Amnesty International USA**, 568 U.S. 398 (2013), a constitutional challenge to Section 702 of the Foreign Intelligence Surveillance Act of 1978, 50 U.S.C. § 1881a, which allows the federal government, with the approval of the Foreign Intelligence Surveillance Court, to conduct surveillance of individuals outside the United States. The plaintiffs were a coalition of domestic advocacy groups and attorneys who anticipated that their overseas contacts would be targeted under Section 702, and that their own communications would be intercepted as a result. (This case was decided before Edward Snowden, a private contractor working for the National Security Agency, illegally leaked the existence of government programs, approved by the FISA court under the USA Patriot Act, that collected the metadata of all telecommunications initiating in or to the United States.) Justice ALITO, writing for the Court, explained why the plaintiffs lacked Article III standing: "[Respondents'] argument rests on their highly speculative fear that: (1) the Government will decide to target the communications of non-U.S. persons with whom they communicate; (2) in doing so, the Government will choose to invoke its authority under § 1881a rather than utilizing another method of surveillance; (3) the Article III judges who serve on the Foreign Intelligence Surveillance Court will conclude that the Government's proposed surveillance procedures satisfy § 1881a's many safeguards and are consistent with the Fourth Amendment; (4) the Government will succeed in intercepting the communications of respondents' contacts; and (5) respondents will be parties to the particular communications that the Government intercepts. [This] theory of standing, which relies on a highly attenuated chain of possibilities, does not satisfy the requirement that threatened injury must be certainly impending." The Court also rejected the alternative argument that the plaintiffs' burden of taking costly steps to secure their communications constituted a present injury: "[Respondents] cannot manufacture standing merely by inflicting harm on themselves based on their fears of hypothetical future harm that is not certainly impending. [If] the law were otherwise, an enterprising plaintiff would be able to secure a lower standard for Article III standing simply by making an expenditure based on a nonparanoid fear."

Justice BREYER, in dissent, argued that the harm faced by the plaintiffs "is as likely to take place as are most future events that commonsense inference and ordinary knowledge of human nature tell us will happen. [There] is a very high likelihood that Government, *acting under the authority of* § 1881a, will intercept at least some of the communications just described. First, the plaintiffs have engaged, and continue to engage, in electronic communications of a kind that the 2008 amendment, but not the prior Act, authorizes the Government to intercept. [Second], the plaintiffs have a strong *motive* to engage in, and the Government has a strong *motive* to listen to, conversations of the kind described. [Third], the Government's *past behavior* shows that it has sought, and hence will in all likelihood continue to seek, information about alleged terrorists and detainees through means that include surveillance of electronic communications. [Fourth], the Government has the *capacity* to conduct electronic surveillance of the kind at issue. To some degree this capacity rests upon technology available to the Government. [As] the majority appears to concede, *certainty* is not, and never has been, the touchstone of standing. The future is inherently uncertain. Yet federal courts frequently entertain actions for injunctions and for declaratory relief aimed at preventing future activities that are reasonably likely or highly likely, but not absolutely certain, to take place. And that degree of certainty is all that is needed to support standing here." Do the Snowden revelations vindicate Justice Breyer's position? Who would have standing to challenge the data collection now revealed?

Why restrict standing to claims of imminent or certainly impending injury? "Someone who feeds me a poison that increases my chances of dying next year has injured me, even if I am neither dead nor sure to die, and I may recover damages from him. [The] same reasoning establishes injury in fact when the government declines to enforce a law that was designed in part for my benefit. The court cannot know that any identified plaintiff will be better off if the law is enforced, but the law is about probabilities, not certainties." Easterbrook, "The Supreme Court, 1983 Term—Foreword: The Court and the Economic System," 98 Harv. L. Rev. 4 (1984).

2. ***Causation.*** Why require that the allegedly unlawful conduct caused plaintiff's injury in fact and that the injury is likely to be redressed by a favorable decision? The causation requirement puts the burden on a plaintiff to show that the harm alleged is "fairly traceable" to the government. Note the similarity of this issue to problems of causation in torts and criminal law, where similarly, not all actions that might be *empirical* causes of an injury are considered sufficiently proximate to that injury to be fairly attributable to a defendant as a *normative* matter.

The government's lack-of-causation defense will be stronger if standing "depends on the unfettered choices made by independent actors not before the courts and whose exercise of broad and legitimate discretion the courts cannot presume either to control or to predict." Lujan. For example, in **Allen**

v. Wright, 468 U.S. 737 (1984), the Court considered a claim by parents of black children attending public schools who asserted that the Internal Revenue Service had failed to fulfill its obligation to deny tax-exempt status to racially discriminatory or unbalanced private schools in their district. The parents claimed that by providing a subsidized alternative of segregated private schools, the IRS made the task of desegregating the public schools more difficult, injuring their own children by diminishing the quality of their education.

Writing for the Court, Justice O'CONNOR rejected this claim as lacking the causation required for standing: "[R]espondents allege harm to a concrete, personal interest that can support standing in some circumstances. The injury they identify—their children's diminished ability to receive an education in a racially integrated school—is, beyond any doubt, not only judicially cognizable but, as shown by cases [like Brown v. Board,] one of the most serious injuries recognized in our legal system. Despite the constitutional importance of curing the injury alleged by respondents, however, the federal judiciary may not redress it unless standing requirements are met. In this case, respondents' [claim] cannot support standing because the injury alleged is not fairly traceable to the Government conduct respondents challenge as unlawful.

"[The] illegal conduct challenged by respondents is the IRS's grant of tax exemptions to some racially discriminatory schools. The line of causation between that conduct and desegregation of respondents' schools is attenuated at best. From the perspective of the IRS, the injury to respondents is highly indirect and 'results from the independent action of some third party not before the court.' The diminished ability of respondents' children to receive a desegregated education would be fairly traceable to unlawful IRS grants of tax exemptions only if there were enough racially discriminatory private schools receiving tax exemptions in respondents' communities for withdrawal of those exemptions to make an appreciable difference in public school integration. [It] is, first, uncertain how many racially discriminatory private schools are in fact receiving tax exemptions. Moreover, it is entirely speculative [whether] withdrawal of a tax exemption from any particular school would lead the school to change its policies. It is just as speculative whether any given parent of a child attending such a private school would decide to transfer the child to public school as a result of any changes in educational or financial policy made by the private school once it was threatened with loss of tax-exempt status. It is also pure speculation whether, in a particular community, a large enough number of the numerous relevant school officials and parents would reach decisions that collectively would have a significant impact on the racial composition of the public schools. The links in the chain of causation between the challenged Government conduct and the asserted injury are far too weak for the chain as a whole to sustain respondents' standing."

Why did the Court reject a similar lack-of-causation defense in Massachusetts? The EPA argued, and the dissenters agreed, that foreign nations' greenhouse gas emissions, which are obviously beyond the EPA's control, represented independent intervening causes of global warming and its harms.

3. ***Redressability.*** What is the relationship between the causation and redressability requirements? Though related, the two categories are conceptually distinct. Redressability focuses more on remedy than liability.

While causation looks to the causal connection between the challenged conduct and the alleged injury, redressability looks to the causal connection between the alleged injury and the judicial relief requested. Note that partial redress may be sufficient; in Massachusetts, the majority found that, to satisfy the redressability requirement, petitioners need allege only that the harms caused to them by global warming would be reduced, not eliminated.

But as a practical matter, causation and redressability overlap; often, the lack of one will entail the lack of the other. If an independent actor breaks the chain of causation, that same independent actor may be an impediment to redress.

4. ***Prudential standing doctrines.*** In addition to the three constitutional requirements, the Court has imposed prudential limits on (1) third-party standing, (2) generalized grievances, and (3) suits outside a law's zone of interest. As then-Justice Rehnquist noted in Valley Forge Christian College v. Americans United for Separation of Church and State, 454 U.S. 464 (1982): "[Beyond] the constitutional requirements, the federal judiciary has also adhered to a set of prudential principles that bear on the question of standing. Thus, this Court has held that 'the plaintiff generally must assert his own legal rights and interests, and cannot rest his claim to relief on the legal rights or interests of third parties.' In addition, even when the plaintiff has alleged redressable injury sufficient to meet the requirements of Art. III, the Court has refrained from adjudicating 'abstract questions of wide public significance' which amount to 'generalized grievances,' pervasively shared and most appropriately addressed in the representative branches. Finally, the Court has required that the plaintiff's complaint fall within 'the zone of interests to be protected or regulated by the statute or constitutional guarantee in question.' "

5. ***Third-party standing.*** As a prudential matter, the Court generally restricts standing to the parties directly injured rather than allowing third parties, no matter how sympathetic, to assert their claims vicariously. There are, however, important exceptions. For example, in Craig v. Boren (1976; p. 761 below), a seller of beer was permitted to challenge as sex discrimination a state law imposing a higher age threshold on male than female beer buyers, based on reasoning that buyers and sellers had related economic interests. For another example, First Amendment overbreadth doctrine, see p. 1348 below, permits speakers whose own speech is unprotected to challenge laws that sweep in too much protected speech of others, reasoning that protected speakers might well be inhibited from challenging such laws. Third-party standing is thus more likely to be recognized the closer the relationship and the greater the unity of interest with the rightsholder, and the greater the unavoidable hindrance to the rightsholder's own assertion of rights.

6. ***Generalized grievances.*** The Court has long declined to adjudicate constitutional claims at the behest of a plaintiff who is merely one of millions of taxpayers or citizens interested in resolving constitutional doubts about governmental action. For example, in **Frothingham v. Mellon**, 262 U.S. 447 (1923), the Court refused to entertain a taxpayer's action to enjoin the Secretary of the Treasury from making conditional grants to state programs "to reduce maternal and infant mortality." The opinion stated that the interest of a federal taxpayer in the monies of the Treasury is "shared with millions of others; is comparatively minute and

indeterminable; and the effect upon future taxation, of any payment out of the funds, [too] remote, fluctuating and uncertain."

The Court made an exception to the ban on taxpayer standing in **Flast v. Cohen**, 392 U.S. 83 (1968), allowing taxpayers to challenge on Establishment Clause grounds a federal statute granting aid to religious schools. **Valley Forge Christian College v. Americans United**, 454 U.S. 464 (1982), however, limited Flast to government action under the Spending Clause holding it inapplicable to an in-kind transfer of property. And in **Hein v. Freedom From Religion Fdn.**, 551 U.S. 587 (2007), the Court further limited the Flast exception to challenges brought under the Establishment Clause against expenditures made "pursuant to an express congressional mandate and a specific congressional appropriation," holding the exception inapplicable to expenditures of executive branch funds on faith-based initiatives; a concurrence by Justices Scalia and Thomas would have overturned Flast altogether.

The Court likewise rejected as excessively generalized grievances the claims of citizens and taxpayers in **United States v. Richardson**, 418 U.S. 166 (1974), which held that a taxpayer did not have standing to claim that a law keeping CIA expenditures secret violated the Statement of Account Clause, Art. I, § 9, cl. 7, which requires that "a regular Statement of Account of the Receipts and Expenditures of all public Money shall be published from time to time," and in **Schlesinger v. Reservists Committee to Stop the War**, 418 U.S. 208 (1974), which held that past and present members of the armed forces Reserves lacked standing to challenge the membership of certain Members of Congress in the Reserves as violating the Incompatibility Clause, Art. I, § 6, cl. 2, which provides that "no Person holding any Office under the United States shall be a Member of either House during his continuance in the Office." If taxpayers or citizens cannot bring such suits, who can? On what basis? Does it matter if the answer is no one? Might some constitutional provisions be subject only to political, not legal enforcement?

The Court revisited the issue of taxpayer standing in **Arizona Christian School Tuition Org. v. Winn**, 563 U.S. 125 (2011), which held, by a vote of 5–4, that state taxpayers lack standing to challenge a state law giving tax credits for contributions to school tuition organizations (STOs) that are in turn used to provide scholarships to students attending private schools, including religious schools. Writing for the Court, Justice KENNEDY, joined by Chief Justice Roberts and Justices Scalia, Thomas and Alito, stated: "Even assuming the STO tax credit has an adverse effect on Arizona's annual budget, [to] conclude there is a particular injury in fact would require speculation that Arizona lawmakers react to revenue shortfalls by increasing respondents' tax liability. A finding of causation would depend on the additional determination that any tax increase would be traceable to the STO tax credits, as distinct from other governmental expenditures or other tax benefits. [Each] of the inferential steps to show causation and redressability depends on premises as to which there remains considerable doubt. [The] rule against taxpayer standing, a rule designed both to avoid speculation and to insist on particular injury, applies to respondents' lawsuit."

Rejecting the challengers' invocation of the Flast exception, he continued: "It is easy to see that tax credits and governmental expenditures can have similar economic consequences. [Yet] tax credits and governmental expenditures do not both implicate individual taxpayers in sectarian activities. A dissenter whose tax dollars are 'extracted and spent' knows that he has in some small measure been made to contribute to an establishment in violation of conscience. [When] Arizona taxpayers choose to contribute to STOs, they spend their own money, not money the State has collected from respondents or from other taxpayers."

Justice KAGAN, joined by Justices Ginsburg, Breyer and Sotomayor, dissented, objecting to the majority's "novel distinction in standing law between appropriations and tax expenditures": "Cash grants and targeted tax breaks are means of accomplishing the same government objective—to provide financial support to select individuals or organizations. [The] Court's arbitrary distinction threatens to eliminate *all* occasions for a taxpayer to contest the government's monetary support of religion. [From] now on, the government need follow just one simple rule—subsidize through the tax system—to preclude taxpayer challenges to state funding of religion."

If a citizen personally benefits from a law, but believes it to be invalid or improperly applied, does he or she have a personal stake in the case, or merely a generalized grievance? Consider **King v. Burwell**, 135 S. Ct. 2480 (2015). The plaintiffs in that case argued that they should not be required to purchase health insurance under the Patient Protection And Affordable Care Act of 2010 because the tax credit that would prevent their exemption from the Act's requirements was available only through health-care insurance exchanges "established by the State," whereas their states of residence all had federally-run health insurance exchanges. Should the plaintiffs have been allowed to bring a lawsuit to redress the "harm" of having a tax credit available to them? If their sole injury was that the government interpreted the law incorrectly, in what way was their harm specific to them? The Court in this high-profile case discussed standing at oral argument, but ultimately rejected the plaintiffs' argument on the merits without considering the question of standing.

7. ***Zone of interests.*** The "zone of interests" test was traditionally understood as a prudential standing doctrine that required plaintiffs' claims to fall within "the zone of interests to be protected or regulated by the statute or constitutional guarantee in question." The Court has recently cast doubt on this characterization, however. Writing for the Court in **Lexmark International, Inc. v. Static Control Components, Inc.**, 572 U.S. 118 (2014), Justice SCALIA suggested that the zone of interests inquiry is "not especially demanding," and in fact may be coextensive with the question of whether the plaintiff has a cause of action under the statute or constitutional provision in question. The Court further noted that prudential standing "is in some tension" with a federal courts' obligation to hear cases within its jurisdiction, but it stopped short of abandoning the category of prudential standing altogether.

8. ***Congressional power to confer standing.*** Congress has long authorized suits by "private attorneys general" to challenge governmental action. Lujan rejected the use of one such "citizen suit" provision in circumstances the Court deemed too far removed from any personal injury to the plaintiffs. Note, however, that the Court did not invalidate that provision on its face nor cast doubt on the validity of "citizen suit" provisions in general. Moreover, Justice Scalia did not obtain a majority for the portion of his opinion that seemingly would limit citizen suit standing to those who have suffered injuries that resemble interpersonal torts actionable at common law. The concurrence by Justices Kennedy and Souter took pains to

suggest that these Justices, crucial to the majority, would continue to uphold standing under citizen suit provisions even where the asserted injury is procedural or otherwise unlike a common law tort—so long as the statute is sufficiently specific about the nature of the interest and the injury. Citing that concurrence, Massachusetts reiterated that "Congress has the power to define injuries and articulate chains of causation that will give rise to a case or controversy where none existed before."

Nor did Lujan prevent the Court from upholding broad congressional conferrals of standing. In **FEC v. Akins**, 524 U.S. 11 (1998), for example, the Court, by a vote of 6–3, held that a group of voters had standing to challenge the failure of the Federal Election Commission to treat the American Israel Public Affairs Committee (AIPAC) as a "political committee" subject to certain reporting and disclosure requirements under federal election law, and to seek information about AIPAC's membership that they claimed would help them evaluate candidates for public office who had received AIPAC support. Justice BREYER's opinion for the Court rejected any claim that the lawsuit involved a nonjusticiable "generalized grievance": "[Often] the fact that an interest is abstract and the fact that it is widely shared go hand in hand. But their association is not invariable, and where a harm is concrete, though widely shared, the Court has found 'injury in fact.' [We] conclude that [the] informational injury at issue here, directly related to voting, the most basic of political rights, is sufficiently concrete and specific such that the fact that it is widely shared does not deprive Congress of constitutional power to authorize its vindication in the federal courts." Justice SCALIA dissented, joined by Justices O'Connor and Thomas. The dissent argued that the claimants here, like the challengers seeking to compel publication of CIA expenditures in Richardson, had merely a generalized grievance, " 'undifferentiated and common to all members of the public.' "

The Court also ruled that one variety of congressionally authorized privately initiated public action, the *qui tam* suit, does meet Article III's case and controversy requirements. **Vermont Agency of Natural Resources v. United States**, 529 U.S. 765 (2000), addressed the issue of suits under the federal False Claims Act, which permits a private party (the "relator") to sue fraudulent government contractors in the name of the federal government. The private party then maintains his or her own interest in the suit, and stands to win a personal payment if the government's claim is successful. In Vermont Agency, the Court ruled that, where the government's alleged injury in fact would meet Article III requirements, the Congress could legislatively *assign* the claim for that injury to a private plaintiff, who would then have standing according to "the doctrine that the assignee of a claim has standing to assert the injury in fact suffered by the assignor. [A] *qui tam* relator is, in effect, suing as a *partial* assignee of the United States."

9. ***Procedural violations and concreteness***. The plaintiffs in Lujan and Massachusetts v. EPA asserted a "procedural right," or a statutory-granted right to a certain governmental procedure. In **Spokeo, Inc. v. Robins**, 136 S. Ct. 1540 (2016),the Court held that a consumer could not satisfy the injury-in-fact requirements of Article III by alleging a bare procedural violation of the federal Fair Credit Reporting Act. Justice ALITO wrote the opinion: "[The] injury-in-fact requirement requires a plaintiff to allege an injury that is both concrete and particularized. [Congress'] role in identifying and elevating intangible harms does not mean that a plaintiff

automatically satisfies the injury-in-fact requirement whenever a statute grants a person a statutory right and purports to authorize that person to sue to vindicate that right. Article III standing requires a concrete injury even in the context of a statutory violation. [The] violation of a procedural right granted by statute can be sufficient in some circumstances to constitute injury in fact." The Court concluded that the plaintiff could not "satisfy the demands of Article III by alleging a bare procedural violation."

10. ***Standing and separation of powers.*** Note that in his Lujan opinion, Justice Scalia suggested that conferring standing on citizens to compel government enforcement action "unconstitutionally transfers from the Executive to the courts the responsibility to 'take Care that the Laws be faithfully executed,'" a position he reiterated in his Akins dissent. Does this argument suggest that excessively broad congressional conferrals of standing violate not only Article III but Article II as well? Is Justice Scalia's concern here that Congress and the courts will collude to reduce the prerogatives of the executive branch? In 1983, then-Judge Scalia delivered a lecture on standing that casts light upon his later opinions. He argued that standing is a "crucial and inseparable element" of the separation of powers, because "the law of standing roughly restricts courts to their traditional undemocratic role of protecting individuals and minorities against impositions of the majority, [while excluding courts] from the even more undemocratic role of prescribing how the other two branches should function in order to serve the interest of the majority itself." Scalia, "The Doctrine of Standing as an Essential Element in the Separation of Powers," 17 Suffolk U. L. Rev. 881 (1983).

11. ***Legislator standing.*** May legislators themselves assert standing to sue over deprivations of legislative prerogatives? Legislators plainly have standing to claim that they have been deprived of something to which they personally are entitled, such as their seat in the House or Senate, or that they have been unfairly singled out for special treatment. Legislator standing is a harder question when the assertion is based on loss of political power rather than private right. Are losers in the political process foreclosed from a second try in court?

The Court took up this question in **Raines v. Byrd**, 521 U.S. 811 (1997), which involved a challenge to the constitutionality of the Line Item Veto Act of 1996 by four Senators and two Congressmen who had voted against its passage in the 104th Congress. The Act provided that the President could "cancel" certain items appropriated for expenditure in enacted legislation, and that Congress could undo the cancellation only by passage of a "disapproval bill" signed by the President or reenacted by two thirds of each house over his veto. The Act specifically provided that "any Member of Congress" could bring an action alleging the unconstitutionality of any provision of the Act. In an opinion by Chief Justice REHNQUIST, the Court held that the legislators "have no standing to bring this suit. [Appellees] claim that [their] votes on future appropriations bills [will] be less 'effective' than before. [This alleged] institutional injury is wholly abstract and widely dispersed. [Our] conclusion neither deprives Members of Congress of an adequate remedy (since they may repeal the Act or exempt appropriations bills from its reach), nor forecloses the Act from constitutional challenge (by someone who suffers judicially cognizable injury as a result of the Act)." Justice SOUTER concurred in the judgment on the ground that, while it was "fairly debatable" whether the legislators' alleged deprivation of official voting power was sufficiently personal and concrete to give them standing, the Court ought nonetheless refrain from deciding such a politically sensitive question.

Justice STEVENS dissented: "[Appellees] articulated their claim as a combination of the diminished effect of their initial vote and the circumvention of their right to participate in the subsequent repeal. Whether one looks at the claim from this perspective, or as a simple denial of their right to vote on the precise text that will ultimately become law, [the] deprivation of this right 'essential to the legislator's office' constitutes a sufficient injury to provide every Member of Congress with standing to challenge the constitutionality of the statute."

Justice BREYER also dissented: "[The] Constitution does not draw an absolute line between disputes involving a 'personal' harm and those involving an 'official' harm. [The] lawmakers in this case complain of a lawmaking procedure that threatens the validity of many laws (for example, all appropriations laws) that Congress regularly and frequently enacts. The systematic nature of the harm immediately affects the legislators' ability to do their jobs." (The Line Item Veto Act was later successfully challenged by the City of New York and several hospital associations and health care employee unions aggrieved by President Clinton's cancellation of a Medicaid provision, and by an Idaho farmers' cooperative aggrieved by President Clinton's cancellation of the food processor capital gains provision. Both groups of litigants, unlike Senator Byrd et al., were held to have standing. See Clinton v. New York (1998; p. 401 below).)

12. ***Standing and federalism.*** Do "prudential" limits on Article III standing preclude standing for an individual indicted under a federal statute to challenge the indictment as exceeding Congress's powers by intruding upon the reserved autonomy of the States? In **Bond v. United States**, 564 U.S. 211 (2011), Justice KENNEDY wrote for a unanimous Court that they do not, holding that a woman indicted under the Chemical Weapons Convention Implementation Act of 1998 for placing chemicals on the mailbox of her husband's pregnant lover had Article III standing to challenge the indictment on federalism grounds even though no State was a party to the federal proceedings. Justice Kennedy also explained that her challenge was not precluded as an attempt to assert third-party standing: "An individual has a direct interest in objecting to laws that upset the constitutional balance between the National Government and the States when the enforcement of those laws causes injury that is concrete, particular, and redressable. Fidelity to principles of federalism is not for the States alone to vindicate." Justice GINSBURG, joined by Justice Breyer, filed a concurrence specifying that "Bond, like any other defendant, has a personal right not to be convicted under a constitutionally invalid law," and thus was asserting first-party, not third-party rights.

13. ***Standing and direct democracy.*** Ten states allow their citizens to enact laws and twenty allow them to amend the state constitution through the initiative process, gathering enough signatures to place a measure on the ballot, where it is then approved or rejected by the voters without the legislature's participation. If a measure enacted this way is challenged as unconstitutional, and the state government declines to defend it, should the original sponsors have standing on their initiative's behalf? The Court confronted this question in **Hollingsworth v. Perry**, 570 U.S. 693 (2013). In 2008, California's voters approved "Proposition 8," a ballot measure

overturning a state supreme court ruling that had legalized same-sex marriage in the state. Two same-sex couples filed a federal suit challenging Proposition 8, and when the state's governor and attorney general refused to defend it, the proposition's original proponents were allowed to intervene. The plaintiffs prevailed in both the district court and the court of appeals.

The Supreme Court held that Proposition 8's sponsors lacked standing to appeal the district court's original judgment invalidating Proposition 8, and thus vacated the court of appeals decision and effectively left the district court judgment in place. Chief Justice ROBERTS, writing for the Court, emphasized that the lower court "had not ordered [the sponsors] to do or refrain from doing anything. To have standing, a litigant must seek relief for an injury that affects him in a 'personal and individual way.' [Petitioners] had no 'direct stake' in the outcome of their appeal. Their only interest in having the District Court order reversed was to vindicate the constitutional validity of a generally applicable California law. We have repeatedly held that such a 'generalized grievance,' no matter how sincere, is insufficient to confer standing. [Lujan.] Petitioners argue that the California Constitution and its election laws give them a 'unique, special, and distinct role in the initiative process—one involving both authority and responsibilities that differ from other supporters of the measure.' True enough—but only when it comes to the process of enacting the law. [Petitioners] have no role—special or otherwise—in the enforcement of Proposition 8. [Unlike] California's elected officials, [petitioners] have taken no oath of office. [They] are free to pursue a purely ideological commitment to the law's constitutionality without the need to take cognizance of resource constraints, changes in public opinion, or potential ramifications for other state priorities. We have never before upheld the standing of a private party to defend the constitutionality of a state statute when state officials have chosen not to."

Justice KENNEDY dissented, pointing out that the state supreme court had already held that California law grants a special role to initiative sponsors, distinct from the general population, even after their ballot measure passes. He maintained that the Court should defer to the state court's position, and further that "[the] very object of the initiative system is to establish a lawmaking process that does not depend upon state officials. In California, the popular initiative is necessary to implement 'the theory that all power of government ultimately resides in the people.' The right to adopt initiatives has been described by the California courts as 'one of the most precious rights of [the State's] democratic process.' That historic role for the initiative system 'grew out of dissatisfaction with the then governing public officials and a widespread belief that the people had lost control of the political process.' The initiative's 'primary purpose,' then, 'was to afford the people the ability to propose and to adopt constitutional amendments or statutory provisions that their elected public officials had refused or declined to adopt.' The California Supreme Court has determined that this purpose is undermined if the very officials the initiative process seeks to circumvent are the only parties who can defend an enacted initiative when it is challenged in a legal proceeding. Giving the Governor and attorney general this *de facto* veto will erode one of the cornerstones of the State's governmental structure. And in light of the frequency with which initiatives' opponents resort to litigation, the impact of that veto could be substantial."

MOOTNESS AND RIPENESS

Mootness and ripeness limits on adjudication pertain to the timing of lawsuits. Mootness occurs when litigants who clearly had standing to sue at the outset of the litigation are deprived of a concrete stake in the outcome by changes in the facts or in the law occurring after the lawsuit has gotten under way. The ripeness doctrine seeks to prevent premature adjudication; it involves situations where the dispute is insufficiently developed and is instead too remote or speculative to warrant judicial action. In short, a case is not ripe when it is brought too soon, when the parties have not yet reached a concrete confrontation; a case is moot when changing circumstances developing after the initiation of the lawsuit have ended the controversy, so that the court no longer confronts a live dispute.

1. ***Mootness.*** The mootness doctrine requires that an actual controversy must be extant at all stages of review, not merely at the time the complaint is filed. The Court has treated the doctrine as an aspect of the Article III case or controversy requirement. Yet the Court has recurrently found a number of exceptions to the mootness barrier. One of the most important exceptions to mootness pertains to cases that are "capable of repetition yet evading review." For example, in Roe v. Wade, 410 U.S. 113 (1973), Roe's suit against the Texas abortion laws, brought in 1970, was not decided by the Court until 1973, when she obviously was no longer pregnant; yet the Court declined to dismiss the case as moot. Justice Blackmun explained: "[T]he normal 266-day human gestation period is so short that the pregnancy will come to term before the usual appellate process is complete. If that termination makes a case moot, pregnancy litigation seldom will survive much beyond the trial stage, and appellate review will be effectively denied. Our laws should not be that rigid. Pregnancy produces a classic justification for a conclusion of non-mootness. It truly could be 'capable of repetition, yet evading review.' "

Mootness doctrine seeks to reconcile Art. III requirements with the practical and equitable problem of preventing parties from manipulating the courts. " '[A] defendant's voluntary cessation of a challenged practice does not deprive a federal court of its power to determine the legality of the practice.' '[I]f it did, the courts would be compelled to leave "[t]he defendant [free] to return to his old ways." ['A] case might become moot [only] if subsequent events made it absolutely clear that the allegedly wrongful behavior could not reasonably be expected to recur.' " Friends of the Earth v. Laidlaw Environmental Services, 528 U.S. 167 (2000).

Like standing, mootness may be decided differently for different issues in a case. For example, the termination of past wrongful conduct might moot a claim for an injunction, but not a claim for damages. So long as the parties have a concrete interest, however small, in the outcome of the litigation, the case is not moot. See Ellis v. Brotherhood of Clerks, 466 U.S. 435 (1984).

2. ***Ripeness.*** How far along must a controversy be to present appropriate circumstances for adjudication? Federal courts will not render advisory opinions even though the litigants have intense curiosity about the answer. But courts normally adjudicate legal challenges where the relevant facts occurred in the past and are on the record. The typical problem of ripeness arises from situations in between, especially in requests for anticipatory relief. In such situations, the problems of contingencies and uncertainties as to the facts are most prominent, and the courts are most

likely to insist on a clearly defined record to assure informed and narrow decisionmaking. Ripeness rulings may rest on Art. III case or controversy grounds, but are sometimes based on discretionary, remedial or prudential grounds.

For an example of dismissal for nonripeness, consider United Public Workers v. Mitchell, 330 U.S. 75 (1947), involving an attack on a section of the Hatch Act of 1940 that prohibited federal executive branch employees from taking "any active part in political management or in political campaigns." The challengers sought a declaratory judgment that the provision was unconstitutional. The complaints of most of the challengers stated only that they desired to act contrary to the rule against political activity but not that the rule had been violated. The Court found such complaints premature. In the Court's view, the challenger's "generality of objection [was] really an attack on the political expediency of the [law], not the presentation of legal issues. It is beyond the competence of courts to render such a decision."

For another example of a dismissal for lack of ripeness, see Laird v. Tatum, 408 U.S. 1 (1972), a lawsuit seeking redress against allegedly unlawful "surveillance of lawful citizen political activity" by the U.S. Army. The majority, relying on Mitchell, held that the plaintiffs' claim did not present "a case for resolution by the courts because it rested mainly on the challengers' fear of future, punitive action"—action based on the results of the surveillance. According to the majority, the complaint rested largely on "speculative apprehensiveness that the Army might at some future date misuse the information in some way that would cause harm" to the plaintiffs, and such fears did not amount to "specific present objective harm" or "threat of specific future harm."

POLITICAL QUESTIONS

Recall Justice Marshall's statement in Marbury v. Madison that: "Questions, in their nature political, or which are, by the Constitution and laws, submitted to the executive can never be made in this court." Marbury thus disavowed the Court's authority to intervene with presidential decisions in which the President possessed "a Constitutional or legal discretion." Recall too Marbury's suggestion that certain "irksome" or "delicate" political matters ought be removed from the court's jurisdiction.

Even though in Marbury itself, the Court did not refrain from issuing its controversial ruling, Chief Justice Marshall thus anticipated the two strands of modern political question doctrine: first, that some matters are committed to the unreviewable discretion of the political branches, and second, that some otherwise legal questions ought to be left to the other branches as a matter of prudence. The first strand is an aspect of constitutional interpretation; it asks whether there has been "a textually demonstrable constitutional commitment of the issue to a coordinate political department." The second strand is an aspect of judicial discretion; it looks to the perception of "a lack of judicially discoverable and manageable standards for resolving an issue," enforcement problems or other institutional difficulties, including comity toward the other branches and danger to the legitimacy of the Court.

Some commentators doubt the very existence of any general discretionary political question doctrine. For example, Henkin, "Is There a 'Political Question' Doctrine?," 85 Yale L.J. 597 (1976), argues that all so-called political question cases involve the Court's either "accept[ing] decisions by the political branches [as being] within their constitutional authority" or "refus[ing] some (or all) remedies for reasons of equity": "The cases which are supposed to have established the political question doctrine required no [extraordinary] abstention from judicial review; they called only for the ordinary respect by the courts for the political domain. Having reviewed, the Court refused to invalidate the challenged actions because they were within the constitutional authority of President or Congress. In no case did the Court have to use the phrase 'political question.' "

Both the textual and prudential strands are summarized in the case that follows, Baker v. Carr, which involved an equal protection challenge to legislatures elected by districts with unequal populations. Before Baker, the Court had held nonjusticiable challenges to such malapportioned legislatures under the Republican Guarantee Clause. In Colegrove v. Green, 328 U.S. 549 (1946), for example, the Court declined to reach the merits of a challenge to the congressional districting scheme in Illinois. The challengers contended that the Illinois districting scheme was unconstitutional because the districts were not approximately equal in population. Justice Frankfurter stated: "[T]he petitioners ask of this Court what is beyond its competence to grant. [This] controversy concerns matters that bring courts into immediate and active relations with party contests. From the determination of such issues this Court has traditionally remained aloof. [T]he Constitution has conferred upon Congress exclusive authority to secure fair representation by the States in the popular [House of Representatives]. [Art. I, § 4.] Courts ought not to enter this political thicket." With Baker, the Court entered that thicket after all.

Baker v. Carr

369 U.S. 186, 82 S. Ct. 691, 7 L. Ed. 2d 663 (1962).

[Voters in Tennessee claimed that the apportionment of the Tennessee General Assembly violated their equal protection rights "by virtue of the debasement of their votes." They alleged that, although the state constitution allocated representation on a population basis, the Assembly had not been reapportioned since 1901, even though there had been substantial growth and redistribution of the population since then. They also claimed that, because of the malapportioned legislature, redress through changes in state law was difficult or impossible. They sought an injunction against further elections under the 1901 system and asked the federal trial court either to direct elections at large or to decree a reapportionment "by mathematical application of the Tennessee constitutional formulae to the most recent Federal Census figures." The lower court denied relief.]

■ JUSTICE BRENNAN delivered the opinion of the [Court].

[We] hold that this challenge to an apportionment presents no nonjusticiable "political question." [Of course] the mere fact that the suit seeks protection of a political right does not mean it presents a political question. Such an objection "is little more than a play upon words." Rather, it is argued that apportionment cases [can] involve no federal constitutional right except one resting on the guaranty of a republican form of government [Art. IV, § 4] and that complaints based on that clause have been held to present political questions which are nonjusticiable. We hold that the claim pleaded here neither rests upon nor implicates the Guaranty Clause. [To] show why we reject the argument based on the Guaranty Clause, we must examine the authorities under it. But because there appears to be some uncertainty as to why those cases did present political questions, and specifically as to whether this apportionment case is like those cases, we deem it necessary first to consider the contours of the "political question" doctrine.

Our discussion [requires] review of a number of political question cases, in order to expose the attributes of the doctrine—attributes which, in various settings, diverge, combine, appear, and disappear in seeming disorderliness. [That] review reveals that in the Guaranty Clause cases and in the other "political question" cases, it is the relationship between the judiciary and the coordinate branches of the Federal Government, and not the federal judiciary's relationship to the States, which gives rise to the "political question." We have said that "In determining whether a question falls within [the political question] category, the appropriateness under our system of government of attributing finality to the action of the political departments and also the lack of satisfactory criteria for a judicial determination are dominant considerations." The nonjusticiability of a political question is primarily a function of the separation of powers. Much confusion results from the capacity of the "political question" label to obscure the need for case-by-case inquiry. Deciding whether a matter has in any measure been committed by the Constitution to another branch of government, or whether the action of that branch exceeds whatever authority has been committed, is itself a delicate exercise in constitutional interpretation, and is a responsibility of this Court as ultimate interpreter of the [Constitution].

Foreign relations: There are sweeping statements to the effect that all questions touching foreign relations are political questions. Not only does resolution of such issues frequently turn on standards that defy judicial application, or involve the exercise of a discretion demonstrably committed to the executive or legislature; but many such questions uniquely demand single-voiced statement of the Government's views. Yet it is error to suppose that every case or controversy which touches foreign relations lies beyond judicial cognizance. Our cases in this field seem invariably to show a discriminating analysis of the particular question posed, in terms of the history of its management by the political branches, of its susceptibility to judicial handling in the light of its nature and posture in the specific case, and of the possible consequences of judicial [action].

Validity of enactments: In Coleman v. Miller, [307 U.S. 433 (1939)], this Court held that the questions of how long a proposed amendment to the Federal Constitution remained open to ratification, and what effect a prior rejection had on a subsequent ratification, were committed to congressional resolution and involved criteria of decision that necessarily escaped the judicial grasp. Similar considerations apply to the enacting process: "The respect due to coequal and independent departments," and the need for finality and certainty about the status of a statute contribute to judicial reluctance to inquire whether, as passed, it complied with all requisite [formalities].

It is apparent that several formulations which vary slightly according to the settings in which the questions arise may describe a political question, although each has one or more elements which identify it as essentially a function of the separation of powers. Prominent on the surface of any case held to involve a political question is found a textually demonstrable constitutional commitment of the issue to a coordinate political department; or a lack of judicially discoverable and manageable standards for resolving it; or the impossibility of deciding without an initial policy determination of a kind clearly for nonjudicial discretion; or the impossibility of a court's undertaking independent resolution without expressing lack of the respect due coordinate branches of government; or an unusual need for unquestioning adherence to a political decision already made; or the potentiality of embarrassment from multifarious pronouncements by various departments on one question. Unless one of these formulations is inextricable from the case at bar, there should be no dismissal for nonjusticiability on the ground of a political question's presence. The doctrine of which we treat is one of "political questions," not one of "political cases."

[But] it is argued that this case shares the characteristics of decisions that constitute a category not yet considered, cases concerning the Constitution's guaranty [of] a republican form of government. A conclusion as to whether the case at bar does present a political question cannot be confidently reached until we have considered those cases with special care. We shall discover that Guaranty Clause claims involve those elements which define a "political question," and for that reason and no other, they are nonjusticiable. In particular, [the] nonjusticiability of such claims has nothing to do with their touching upon matters of state governmental organization.

Republican form of government: Luther v. Borden, 7 How. 1 [1849], though in form simply an action for damages for trespass was, as Daniel Webster said in opening the argument for the defense, "an unusual case." The defendants, admitting an otherwise tortious breaking and entering, sought to justify their action on the ground that they were agents of the established lawful government of Rhode Island, which State was then under martial law to defend itself from active insurrection; that the plaintiff was engaged in that insurrection; and that they entered under orders to arrest the plaintiff. The case arose "out of the unfortunate political differences which agitated the people of Rhode Island in 1841 and 1842," and which had resulted in a situation wherein two groups laid competing claims to recognition as the lawful government. The plaintiff's right to recover depended upon which of the two groups was entitled to such recognition; but the lower court's refusal to receive evidence or hear argument on that issue, its charge to the jury that the earlier established or "charter" government was lawful, and the verdict for the defendants, were affirmed upon appeal to this Court.

Chief Justice TANEY's opinion for the Court reasoned as follows: (1) If a court were to hold the defendants' acts unjustified because the charter government had no legal existence during the period in question, it would follow that all of that government's actions—laws enacted, taxes collected, salaries paid, accounts settled, sentences passed—were of no effect; and that "the officers who carried their decisions into operation [were] answerable as trespassers, if not in some cases as criminals." [A] decision for the plaintiff would inevitably have produced some significant measure of chaos, a consequence to be avoided if it could be done without abnegation of the judicial duty to uphold the Constitution. (2) No state court had recognized as a judicial responsibility settlement of the issue of the locus of state governmental [authority]. (3) Since "the question relates, altogether, to the constitution and laws of [the] State," the courts of the United States had to follow the state courts' decisions unless there was a federal constitutional ground for overturning them. (4) No provision of the Constitution could be or had been invoked for this purpose except Art. IV, § 4, the Guaranty Clause. Having already noted the absence of standards whereby the choice between governments could be made by a court acting independently, Chief Justice Taney now found further textual and practical reasons for concluding that, if any department of the United States was empowered by the Guaranty Clause to resolve the issue, it was not the judiciary: "Under this article of the Constitution it rests with Congress to decide what government is the established one in a State. For as the United States guarantee to each State a republican government, Congress must necessarily decide what government is established in the State before it can determine whether it is republican or not. And when the senators and representatives of a State are admitted into the councils of the Union, the authority of the government under which they are appointed, as well as its republican character, is recognized by the proper constitutional authority. And its decision is binding on every other department of the government, and could not be questioned in a judicial tribunal. It is true that the contest in this case did not last long enough to bring the matter to this issue; and . . . Congress was not called upon to decide the controversy. Yet the right to decide is placed there, and not in the courts. So, too, as relates to the clause in the [Constitution, Art. IV, § 2] providing for cases of domestic violence. It rested with Congress, too, to determine upon the means proper to be adopted to fulfill this guarantee. [By] the act of February 28, 1795, [Congress] provided, that, 'in case of an insurrection in any State against the government thereof, it shall be lawful for the President of the United States, on application of the legislature of such State or of the executive (when the legislature cannot be convened), to call forth such number of the militia of any other State or States, as may be applied for, as he may judge sufficient to suppress such insurrection.' [It] is true that in this case the militia were not called out by the President. But upon the application of the governor under the charter government, the President recognized him as the executive power of the State, and took measures to call out the militia to support his authority if it should be found necessary for the general government to [interfere.]"

Clearly, several factors were thought by the Court in Luther to make the question there "political": the commitment to the other branches of the decision as to which is the lawful state government; the unambiguous action by the President, in recognizing the charter government as the lawful authority; the need for finality in the executive's decision; and the lack of criteria by which a court could determine which form of government was republican. But the only significance that Luther could have for our immediate purposes is in its holding that the Guaranty Clause is not a repository of judicially manageable standards which a court could utilize independently in order to identify a State's lawful government. The Court has since refused to resort to the Guaranty Clause—which alone had been invoked for the purpose—as the source of a constitutional standard for invalidating state action. See, [e.g.,] Pacific States Tel. & Telegraph Co. v.

Oregon, 223 U.S. 118 [1912] (claim that initiative and referendum negated republican government held nonjusticiable).

[We] come, finally, to the ultimate inquiry whether our precedents as to what constitutes a nonjusticiable "political question" bring the case before us under the umbrella of that doctrine. A natural beginning is to note whether any of the common characteristics which we have been able to identify and label descriptively are present. We find none: The question here is the consistency of state action with the Federal Constitution. We have no question decided, or to be decided, by a political branch of government coequal with this Court. Nor do we risk embarrassment of our government abroad, or grave disturbance at home, if we take issue with Tennessee as to the constitutionality of her action here challenged. Nor need the appellants, in order to succeed in this action, ask the Court to enter upon policy determinations for which judicially manageable standards are lacking. Judicial standards under the Equal Protection Clause are well developed and familiar, and it has been open to courts since the enactment of the Fourteenth Amendment to determine, if on the particular facts they must, that a discrimination reflects no policy, but simply arbitrary and capricious action. This case does, in one sense, involve the allocation of political power within a State, and the appellants might conceivably have added a claim under the Guaranty Clause. Of course, as we have seen, any reliance on that clause would be futile. But because any reliance on the Guaranty Clause could not have succeeded it does not follow that appellants may not be heard on the equal protection claim which in fact they tender. True, it must be clear that the Fourteenth Amendment claim is not so enmeshed with those political question elements which render Guaranty Clause claims nonjusticiable as actually to present a political question itself. But we have found that not to be the case [here].

Reversed and remanded.

■ JUSTICE FRANKFURTER, with whom JUSTICE HARLAN joins, [dissenting].

[From] its earliest opinions this Court has consistently recognized a class of controversies which do not lend themselves to judicial standards and judicial remedies. To classify the various instances as "political questions" is rather a form of stating this conclusion than revealing of analysis. Some of the cases so labeled have no relevance here. But from others emerge unifying considerations that are compelling.

1. The cases concerning war or foreign affairs, for example, are usually explained by the necessity of the country's speaking with one voice in such matters. While this concern alone undoubtedly accounts for many of the decisions, others do not fit the pattern. It would hardly embarrass the conduct of war were this Court to determine, in connection with private transactions between litigants, the date upon which war is to be deemed terminated. But the Court has refused to do so. [A] controlling factor in such cases is that, decision respecting these kinds of complex matters of policy being traditionally committed not to courts but to the political agencies of government for determination by criteria of political expediency, there exists no standard ascertainable by settled judicial experience or process by reference to which a political decision affecting the question at issue between the parties can be [judged].

2. The Court has been particularly unwilling to intervene in matters concerning the structure and organization of the political institutions of the

States. The abstention from judicial entry into such areas has been greater even than that which marks the Court's ordinary approach to issues of state power challenged under broad federal guarantees. [Where], however, state law has made particular federal questions determinative of relations within the structure of state government, not in challenge of it, the Court has resolved such narrow, legally defined questions in proper proceedings. In such instances there is no conflict between state policy and the exercise of federal judicial [power].

3. The cases involving Negro disfranchisement are no exception to the principle of avoiding federal judicial intervention into matters of state government in the absence of an explicit and clear constitutional imperative. For here the controlling command of Supreme Law is plain and unequivocal. An end of discrimination against the Negro was the compelling motive of the Civil War [Amendments].

4. The Court has refused to exercise its jurisdiction to pass on "abstract questions of political power, of sovereignty, of government." The "political question" doctrine, in this aspect, reflects the policies underlying the requirement of "standing": that the litigant who would challenge official action must claim infringement of an interest particular and personal to himself, as distinguished from a cause of dissatisfaction with the general frame and functioning of government—a complaint that the political institutions are awry. What renders cases of this kind non-justiciable is not necessarily the nature of the parties to them, for the Court has resolved other issues between similar parties; nor is it the nature of the legal question involved, for the same type of question has been adjudicated when presented in other forms of controversy. The crux of the matter is that courts are not fit instruments of decision where what is essentially at stake is the composition of those large contests of policy traditionally fought out in non-judicial forums, by which governments and the actions of governments are made and [unmade].

5. The influence of these converging considerations—the caution not to undertake decision where standards meet for judicial judgment are lacking, the reluctance to interfere with matters of state government in the absence of an unquestionable and effectively enforceable mandate, the unwillingness to make courts arbiters of the broad issues of political organization historically committed to other institutions and for whose adjustment the judicial process is ill-adapted—has been decisive of the settled line of cases, reaching back more than a century, which holds that Art. IV, § 4, of the Constitution, guaranteeing to the States "a Republican Form of Government," is not enforceable through the [courts].

The present case involves all of the elements that have made the Guarantee Clause cases non-justiciable. It is, in effect, a Guarantee Clause claim masquerading under a different label. But it cannot make the case more fit for judicial action that appellants invoke the Fourteenth Amendment rather than Art. IV, § 4, where, in fact, the gist of their complaint is the same—unless it can be found that the Fourteenth Amendment speaks with greater particularity to their situation. We have been admonished to avoid "the tyranny of labels." Art. IV, § 4, is not committed by express constitutional terms to Congress. It is the nature of the controversies arising under it, nothing else, which has made it judicially unenforceable. [W]here judicial competence is wanting, it cannot be created by invoking one clause of the Constitution rather than another.

What, then, is this question of legislative apportionment? Appellants invoke the right to vote and to have their votes counted. But they are permitted to vote and their votes are counted. [Their] complaint is simply that the representatives are not sufficiently numerous or powerful—in short, that Tennessee has adopted a basis of representation with which they are dissatisfied. Talk of "debasement" or "dilution" is circular talk. One cannot speak of "debasement" or "dilution" of the value of a vote until there is first defined a standard of reference as to what a vote should be worth. What is actually asked of the Court in this case is to choose among competing bases of representation—ultimately, really, among competing theories of political philosophy—in order to establish an appropriate frame of government for the State of Tennessee and thereby for all the States of the Union.

Once the electoral apportionment process is recognized for what it is—the product of legislative give-and-take and of compromise among policies that often conflict—the relevant constitutional principles at once put these appellants out of the federal courts. [Manifestly], the Equal Protection Clause supplies no clearer guide for judicial examination of apportionment methods than would the Guarantee Clause itself. Apportionment, by its character, is a subject of extraordinary complexity, involving—even after the fundamental theoretical issues concerning what is to be represented in a representative legislature have been fought out or compromised—considerations of geography, demography, electoral convenience, economic and social cohesions or divergences among particular local groups, communications, the practical effects of political institutions, ancient [traditions], respect for proven [incumbents], mathematical mechanics, [and] a host of others. [T]hese are not factors that lend themselves to evaluations of a nature that are the staple of judicial determinations or for which judges are equipped to adjudicate by legal training or experience or native wit. And this is the more so true because in every strand of this complicated, intricate web of values meet the contending forces of partisan politics. [Apportionment] battles are overwhelmingly party or intra-party contests. It will add a virulent source of friction and tension in federal-state relations to embroil the federal judiciary in them.

■ [JUSTICES DOUGLAS, CLARK, and STEWART each submitted separate concurring opinions, omitted here. A separate dissent by JUSTICE HARLAN is also omitted.]

DISTINGUISHING LEGAL FROM POLITICAL QUESTIONS

1. ***Congressional qualifications.*** **Powell v. McCormack**, 395 U.S. 486 (1969), arose from a challenge to the refusal of the House of Representatives in 1967 to seat Representative Adam Clayton Powell, Jr., based upon a House committee's finding that he had "wrongfully diverted House funds for the use of others and himself" and had made "false reports on expenditures of foreign currency" to a committee of the House. Powell argued that he had met all the formal requirements of Art. I, § 2, cl. 2, i.e., age, citizenship, and residence. McCormack, the Speaker of the House, argued in response that Art. I, § 5, cl. 1 (stating that "each House shall be the Judge of [the] Qualifications of its own Members") constituted an unreviewable textual commitment of the issue to Congress and that judicial

resolution of the issue would yield a "potentially embarrassing confrontation between coordinate branches."

The Court found Powell's claim of a wrongful basis for exclusion justiciable. Chief Justice WARREN's majority opinion concluded that Art. I, § 5, was "at most a 'textually demonstrable commitment' to Congress to judge only the qualifications expressly set forth in the Constitution." The Court also rejected McCormack's "embarrassing confrontation" argument, stating: "Our system of government requires that federal courts on occasion interpret the Constitution in a manner at variance with the construction given the document by another branch. The alleged conflict that such an adjudication may cause cannot justify the courts' avoiding their constitutional [responsibility]."

Note that Powell held justiciable the question what congressional qualifications consisted of but not the decision whether a member satisfied those qualifications. If the House determined that Powell could not be seated based on a false assertion that he was only 24 years old, would such a determination be unreviewable by any court?

2. ***Treaty abrogation.*** The Constitution sets forth procedures for the Senate to participate in treaty ratification but is silent as to any Senate role in treaty abrogation. In **Goldwater v. Carter**, 444 U.S. 996 (1979), the Court set aside lower court decisions on the merits of the question whether the President has authority to terminate a treaty unilaterally. Justice REHNQUIST's plurality opinion, joined by Chief Justice Burger and Justices Stewart and Stevens, insisted that the case presented a nonjusticiable political question because "it involves the authority of the President and the conduct of our country's foreign relations," and this was "a dispute between coequal branches of our government, each of which has resources available to protect and assert its interests, resources not available to private litigants outside the judicial forum."

Justice POWELL concurred in the judgment solely because he thought the dispute was not ripe for decision, strongly disagreeing with Justice Rehnquist as to justiciability. There was no "textually demonstrable constitutional commitment" of the treaty termination power to the President, nor was there any "lack of judicially discoverable and manageable standards: 'Resolution of the question may not be easy, but it only requires us to apply normal principles of [constitutional] interpretation. [The case] involves neither review of the President's activities as Commander-in-Chief nor impermissible interference in the field of foreign affairs.'" Justice Powell acknowledged that the political question doctrine does rest in part on "prudential concerns," but deemed those inhibitions inappropriate here: "Interpretation of the Constitution does not imply a lack of respect for a coordinate [branch]." Justice BRENNAN dissented, insisting that Justice Rehnquist's approach "profoundly misrepresents the political-question principle as it applies to matters of foreign relations." He would have found the case justiciable, but on the merits ruled that "the Constitution commits to the President alone the power to recognize, and withdraw recognition from, foreign regimes."

3. ***Impeachment proceedings.*** Article II, § 4 provides that the "The President, Vice President and all Civil Officers of the United States, shall be removed from Office on Impeachment for, and Conviction of Treason, Bribery, or other high Crimes and Misdemeanors." Article I sets forth specific procedures for Congress to follow when impeaching and convicting

officers. The House has the "sole Power of Impeachment," Art. I, § 2, cl. 5, and the "Senate shall have the sole Power to try all impeachments." Art. I, § 3, cl. 6. Does this mean the Senate may choose, by internal rule, to allow a committee of Senators, rather than the whole body, to hear and report upon evidence against an impeached officer?

In **Nixon v. United States**, 506 U.S. 224 (1993), the Court held this question nonjusticiable on both textual and prudential grounds. The case involved Walter L. Nixon, Jr., former Chief Judge of the United States District Court for the Southern District of Mississippi, who was convicted by a jury of making false statements before a federal grand jury and sentenced to prison. The House impeached, a committee of Senators heard evidence and presented briefs and arguments to the full body, and the Senate convicted Nixon and ordered him removed from office. Nixon challenged the trial by Senate committee as unconstitutional and argued he should have been tried by the body as a whole. Chief Justice REHNQUIST wrote the opinion of the Court dismissing Nixon's challenge as nonjusticiable: "[The] common sense meaning of the word 'sole' is that the Senate alone shall have authority to determine whether an individual should be acquitted or convicted. [The] history and contemporary understanding of the impeachment provisions support our reading of the constitutional language. The parties do not offer evidence of a single word in the history of the Constitutional Convention or in contemporary commentary that even alludes to the possibility of judicial review in the context of the impeachment powers.

"[In] addition to the textual commitment argument, we are persuaded that the lack of finality and the difficulty of fashioning relief counsel against justiciability. [Opening] the door of judicial review to the procedures used by the Senate in trying impeachments would 'expose the political life of the country to months, or perhaps years, of chaos.' [Equally] uncertain is the question of what relief a court may give other than simply setting aside the judgment of conviction. Could it order the reinstatement of a convicted federal judge, or order Congress to create an additional judgeship if the seat had been filled in the interim? [We] conclude [that] the word 'try' in the Impeachment Clause does not provide an identifiable textual limit on the authority which is committed to the Senate."

Justice WHITE, concurred only in the judgment, joined by Justice Blackmun: "That the word 'sole' is found only in the House and Senate Impeachment Clauses demonstrates that its purpose is to emphasize the distinct role of each in the impeachment process. [While] the majority is thus right to interpret the term 'sole' to indicate that the Senate ought to 'function independently and without assistance or interference,' it wrongly identifies the judiciary, rather than the House, as the source of potential interference with which the Framers were concerned. [The] historical evidence reveals above all else that the Framers were deeply concerned about placing in any branch the 'awful discretion, which a court of impeachments must necessarily have.' [In] a truly balanced system, impeachments tried by the Senate would serve as a means of controlling the largely unaccountable judiciary, even as judicial review would ensure that the Senate adhered to a minimal set of procedural standards in conducting impeachment trials." Reaching the merits, Justice White would have found the Senate's rule authorizing impeachment trial by committee a constitutional exercise of the Senate's authority.

Justice SOUTER likewise concurred in the judgment, but on different grounds: "I agree with the Court that this case presents a nonjusticiable political question. [It] seems fair to conclude that the [Impeachment Trial] Clause contemplates that the Senate may determine, within broad boundaries, such subsidiary issues as the procedures for receipt and consideration of evidence necessary to satisfy its duty to 'try' impeachments. [And as] the Court observes, judicial review of an impeachment trial would under the best of circumstances entail significant disruption of government. One can, nevertheless, envision different and unusual circumstances that might justify a more searching review of impeachment proceedings. If the Senate were to act in a manner seriously threatening the integrity of its results, convicting, say, upon a coin-toss, or upon a summary determination that an officer of the United States was simply 'a bad guy,' judicial interference might well be appropriate. In such circumstances, the Senate's action might be so far beyond the scope of its constitutional authority, and the consequent impact on the Republic so great, as to merit a judicial response despite the prudential concerns that would ordinarily counsel [silence]."

4. ***The constitutional amendment process.*** Coleman v. Miller held nonjusticiable the question of what is a reasonable period of time for ratification by the states of a constitutional amendment proposed by Congress under Article V. Is the best reason for such an outcome that the Court should not superintend the only constitutional procedure that allows for overrule of its own decisions? Note that Chief Justice Rehnquist gave a similar functional reason in Nixon for the Court to avoid ruling on the constitutionality of impeachment procedures—that "in our constitutional system, impeachment was designed to be the only check on the Judicial Branch by the Legislature."

The ratification debates in the late 1970s and early 1980s over the proposed Equal Rights Amendment (ERA), stirred renewed debate over the judicial reviewability of congressionally stipulated rules for governing the amendment process. During the ratification process for the ERA, there were disputes over the propriety of both some states' attempts to rescind their earlier ratification of the amendment and congressional attempts to extend the seven-year ratification period that the amendment had originally provided. Article V is notably silent on both issues. For the view that challenges to congressional decisions on such questions should be justiciable, see Dellinger, "The Legitimacy of Constitutional Change: Rethinking the Amendment Process," 97 Harv. L. Rev. 386 (1983); for the countervailing view, see Tribe, "A Constitution We Are Amending: In Defense of a Restrained Judicial Role," 97 Harv. L. Rev. 433, 436 (1983).

5. ***The presidential election process.*** When the 2000 election for President and Vice President was thrown into controversy because the vote in Florida resulted in a near statistical tie between the Gore-Lieberman and Bush-Cheney tickets, the matter was ultimately settled, at least as a practical matter, by the United States Supreme Court. Should it have been? Article II, § 1, cl. 2 provides: "Each State shall appoint, in such Manner as the Legislature thereof may direct, a Number of Electors" who in turn meet in their respective states to vote for the two top federal executive officers. Article II as modified by the Twelfth Amendment specifies in elaborate detail how Congress, which is entrusted with counting the states' electoral votes, shall resolve any inconclusive vote by the electors chosen by the states,

commonly referred to as "the electoral college." These procedures are further elaborated in provisions of federal election law under the Electoral Count Act of 1887, 3 U.S.C. §§ 5–7, 15–18, which was enacted in the wake of the contested and contentious Hayes-Tilden election of 1876 in order to ensure orderly handling of future disputes over the legitimacy of presidential electors.

In **Bush v. Gore**, 531 U.S. 98 (2000) (per curiam), the Court, having stayed certain recounts ordered by the Florida Supreme Court in state contest litigation brought by the Gore team, held that those recounts, because conducted under nonuniform standards, were unconstitutional under the Equal Protection Clause of the Fourteenth Amendment. The Court further ruled that no remedy for these violations was possible by December 12, the very date on which the Court issued its decision. December 12 was a significant date because 3 U.S.C. § 5 specifies that a state's selection of its electors "shall be conclusive, and shall govern in [Congress's] counting of the electoral votes," if completed six days prior to the electoral college vote, which under another federal law enacted pursuant to Art. II, § 1, cl. 4, takes place on December 18. The per curiam opinion read Florida law to have evinced the state's wish to take advantage of the December 12 "safe harbor" provision:

"The individual citizen has no federal constitutional right to vote for electors for the President of the United States unless and until the state legislature chooses a statewide election as the means to implement its power to appoint members of the electoral college. U.S. Const., Art. II, § 1. [When] the state legislature vests the right to vote for President in its people, the right to vote as the legislature has prescribed is fundamental; and one source of its fundamental nature lies in the equal weight accorded to each vote and the equal dignity owed to each voter. [The] right to vote is protected in more than the initial allocation of the franchise. Equal protection applies as well to the manner of its exercise. Having once granted the right to vote on equal terms, the State may not, by later arbitrary and disparate treatment, value one person's vote over that of another. [The] question before us [i]s whether the recount procedures the Florida Supreme Court has adopted are consistent with its obligation to avoid arbitrary and disparate treatment of the members of its electorate.

"[The] recount mechanisms implemented in response to the decisions of the Florida Supreme Court do not satisfy the minimum requirement for nonarbitrary treatment of voters necessary to secure the fundamental right. Florida's basic command for the count of legally cast votes is to consider the 'intent of the voter.' [As] seems to have been acknowledged at oral argument, the standards for accepting or rejecting contested ballots might vary not only from county to county but indeed within a single county from one recount team to another. [There] is no recount procedure in place under the State Supreme Court's order that comports with minimal constitutional standards. Because it is evident that any recount seeking to meet the December 12 date will be unconstitutional for the reasons we have discussed, we reverse the judgment of the Supreme Court of Florida ordering a recount to proceed."

The per curiam opinion also expressly disclaimed any precedential value the decision might hold: "Our consideration is limited to the present circumstances, for the problem of equal protection in election processes generally presents many complexities."

Justice STEVENS dissented, joined by Justices Ginsburg and Breyer: "The Constitution assigns to the States the primary responsibility for determining the manner of selecting the Presidential electors. See Art. II, § 1, cl. 2. When questions arise about the meaning of state laws, including election laws, it is our settled practice to accept the opinions of the highest courts of the States as providing the final answers. On rare occasions, however, either federal statutes or the Federal Constitution may require federal judicial intervention in state elections. This is not such an occasion. [Petitioners are not] correct in asserting that the failure of the Florida Supreme Court to specify in detail the precise manner in which the 'intent of the voter' [is] to be determined rises to the level of a constitutional violation. We found such a violation when individual votes within the same State were weighted unequally, [but] we have never before called into question the substantive standard by which a State determines that a vote has been legally cast.

"[Time] will one day heal the wound to that confidence that will be inflicted by today's decision. One thing, however, is certain. Although we may never know with complete certainty the identity of the winner of this year's Presidential election, the identity of the loser is perfectly clear. It is the Nation's confidence in the judge as an impartial guardian of the rule of law."

Justice SOUTER, joined by Justice Breyer, and joined in part by Justices Stevens and Ginsburg, also dissented. While Justice Souter agreed with the per curiam opinion that the disparate standards for determining voter intent were problematic under the Equal Protection Clause, he objected to the Court's remedy: "I would [remand] the case to the courts of Florida with instructions to establish uniform standards for evaluating the several types of ballots that have prompted differing treatments, to be applied within and among counties when passing on such identical ballots in any further recounting (or successive recounting) that the courts might order. Unlike the majority, I see no warrant for this Court to assume that Florida could not possibly comply with this requirement before the date set for the meeting of electors, December 18. [There] is no justification for denying the State the opportunity to try to count all disputed ballots now."

Justice GINSBURG, joined by Justice Stevens, and joined in part by Justices Souter and Breyer, also dissented: "[Petitioners] have not presented a substantial equal protection claim. Ideally, perfection would be the appropriate standard for judging the recount. But we live in an imperfect world, one in which thousands of votes have not been counted. I cannot agree that the recount adopted by the Florida court, flawed as it may be, would yield a result any less fair or precise than the certification that preceded that recount."

Justice BREYER, dissenting and joined in part by Justices Stevens, Souter, and Ginsburg, was troubled by the Court's having taken the case at all: "Despite the reminder that this case involves 'an election for the President of the United States,' [no] preeminent legal concern, or practical concern related to legal questions, required this Court to hear this case, let alone to issue a stay that stopped Florida's recount process in its tracks. [Of] course, the selection of the President is of fundamental national importance. But that importance is political, not legal. And this Court should resist the temptation unnecessarily to resolve tangential legal disputes, where doing so threatens to determine the outcome of the election.

"[The] decision by both the Constitution's Framers and the 1886 Congress to minimize this Court's role in resolving close federal Presidential elections is as wise as it is clear. However awkward or difficult it may be for Congress to resolve difficult electoral disputes, Congress, being a political body, expresses the people's will far more accurately than does an unelected Court. And the people's will is what elections are about. [Those] who caution judicial restraint in resolving political disputes have described the quintessential case for that restraint as a case marked, among other things, by the 'strangeness of the issue,' its 'intractability to principled resolution,' its 'sheer momentousness, . . . which tends to unbalance judicial judgment,' and 'the inner vulnerability, the self-doubt of an institution which is electorally irresponsible and has no earth to draw strength from.' [Those] characteristics mark this case.

"At the same time [the] Court is not acting to vindicate a fundamental constitutional principle, such as the need to protect a basic human liberty. No other strong reason to act is present. Congressional statutes tend to obviate the need. And, above all, in this highly politicized matter, the appearance of a split decision runs the risk of undermining the public's confidence in the Court itself. That confidence is a public treasure. It has been built slowly over many years, some of which were marked by a Civil War and the tragedy of segregation. It is a vitally necessary ingredient of any successful effort to protect basic liberty and, indeed, the rule of law itself.

"I fear that in order to bring this agonizingly long election process to a definitive conclusion, we have not adequately attended to that necessary 'check upon our own exercise of power,' 'our own sense of self-restraint.' [Justice] Brandeis once said of the Court, 'The most important thing we do is not doing.' [What] it does today, the Court should have left undone. I would repair the damage done as best we now can, by permitting the Florida recount to continue under uniform standards."

Should the Court have refrained from entering this "political thicket"? In some ways, the equal protection claim on which the per curiam opinion rested resembled the claim held justiciable in Baker v. Carr. But do Article II and the Twelfth Amendment reflect a textual commitment of the task of resolving contested presidential elections to Congress rather than the Court? Even if they do not, would it have been prudent for the Court to leave the matter to the interaction of the Florida political branches and the Congress? Or would a donnybrook in Congress over the identity of the new President, lasting well into January 2001 when the electoral votes were to be counted and the new President inaugurated, have been so undesirable for the nation that judicial intervention to settle the matter swiftly was appropriate?

The Court in Bush v. Gore recognized the implications of its intervention, but argued that it had no choice: "None are more conscious of the vital limits on judicial authority than are the Members of this Court, and none stand more in admiration of the Constitution's design to leave the selection of the President to the people, through their legislatures, and to the political sphere. When contending parties invoke the process of the courts, however, it becomes our unsought responsibility to resolve the federal and constitutional issues the judicial system has been forced to confront." Perhaps no other case could present in starker terms the tension between the democratic will of the people and the Court's role as guardian of the laws.

Consider the following view: The Court in Bush v. Gore "failed in the preservation of an institutional reticence to intercede in the political thicket when other institutional actors were amply well positioned to address the claimed harm. [The federal electoral count statute] carefully reserved to the political branches the key role in resolving contested presidential elections. [It] anticipates a potential role for state legislatures when a state 'has failed to make a choice of electors' [and] expressly anticipates that [if there are] rival sets of electors each claiming to represent their states [resolution] of such disputes is entrusted to independent determination by each branch of Congress. [This] was a considered judgment of Congress responding to the lessons of the stormy 1876 presidential election. [Congress] clearly concluded that such decisions would have an inevitable political cast and should therefore be kept clearly confined within the political branches." Issacharoff, "Political Judgments," 68 U. Chi. L. Rev. 637 (2001). On this view, what made this judicial intervention in the electoral process less appropriate than that in Baker v. Carr? Is the Court's intervention more appropriate to clear the channels of political change for political minorities than to ensure the vindication of majority political preferences? See generally Ely, Democracy and Distrust (1980). Who constituted the political minority and majority in Bush v. Gore? Separately, is there a difference between a judicial decree focused on the conduct of future elections, as opposed to determining the result in a presidential election that has already occurred?

6. ***Recognition of foreign sovereigns.*** Where Congress enacts a statute providing that Americans born in Jerusalem may elect to have "Israel" listed as the place of birth on their passports, but the State Department disagrees based on a policy not to take a position on the political status of Jerusalem, does a U.S. citizen's lawsuit seeking to vindicate his statutory right present a nonjusticiable political question? In **Zivotofsky v. Clinton**, 566 U.S. 189 (2012), the Court held that it does not, holding the case justiciable but declining to opine upon its merits. Section 214(d) of the 2002 Foreign Relations Authorization Act provides that, "[f]or purposes of the registration of birth, certification of nationality, or issuance of a passport of a United States citizen born in the city of Jerusalem, the Secretary [of State] shall, upon the request of the citizen or the citizen's legal guardian, record the place of birth as Israel." Petitioner Menachem Binyamin Zivotofsky, a U.S. citizen because both his parents were U.S. citizens, was born in Jerusalem in 2002, shortly after § 214(d) was enacted. His parents requested that his consular report of birth and U.S. passport list his place of birth as "Jerusalem, Israel," but U.S. officials declined, citing longstanding State Department policy to list the birthplace simply as "Jerusalem." Zivotofsky's parents filed a complaint on his behalf against the Secretary of State. The district court found that the case presented a nonjusticiable political question and the D.C. Circuit affirmed, reasoning that the Constitution gives the Executive the exclusive power to recognize foreign sovereigns, and that the exercise of this power cannot be reviewed by the courts.

In an 8–1 decision, the Supreme Court vacated and remanded, holding that the courts "are fully capable of determining whether this statute may be given effect, or instead must be struck down in light of authority conferred on the Executive by the Constitution." Because the Court found the sole issue to be the constitutionality of § 214(d), it found no textually demonstrable commitment of the issue exclusively to the Executive branch and no lack of judicially administrable standards. The Court acknowledged the clash on the merits but left the resolution of those questions for the lower courts to decide in the first instance.

Justice SOTOMAYOR wrote separately to clarify her view that she understood "the inquiry required by the political question doctrine to be more demanding than that suggested by the Court." Justice BREYER filed the lone dissent, arguing that the prudential considerations set forth in the Baker v. Carr factors should have led the Court "not to decide a case otherwise properly before it": "First, the issue before us arises in the field of foreign affairs. [The] Constitution primarily delegates the foreign affairs powers 'to the political departments of the government, Executive and Legislative,' not to the Judiciary. [Second,] if the courts must answer the constitutional question before us, they may well have to evaluate the foreign policy implications of foreign policy decisions. [In] the Middle East, administrative matters can have implications that extend far beyond the purely administrative. Political reactions in that region can prove uncertain. [Third,] the countervailing interests in obtaining judicial resolution of the constitutional determination are not particularly strong ones. Zivotofsky does not assert the kind of interest, e.g., an interest in property or bodily integrity, which courts have traditionally sought to protect. [The] interest that Zivotofsky asserts [is] akin to an ideological interest. [Fourth,] insofar as the controversy reflects different foreign policy views among the political branches of Government, those branches have nonjudicial methods of working out their differences[, which] minimizes the need for judicial intervention here."

Having resolved the justiciability issue, the Court later ruled on the merits in Zivotofsky v. Kerry, 135 S. Ct. 2076 (2015; p. 309 below).

CHAPTER 2

FEDERALISM: HISTORY AND PRINCIPLES

The Framers of the United States Constitution, meeting in convention behind closed doors in Philadelphia in 1787, aimed to remedy the perceived deficiencies of the post-revolutionary government organized under the Articles of Confederation. By the time of the Constitutional Convention, the formation of one national market had been impeded by a patchwork of mutually hostile state trade barriers. Depleted by the Revolutionary War, the state militias and small national army were perceived as too weak to defend states against insurrection, to say nothing of external attack. Most dangerous, the Confederation was dependent on funds from the states, which had the sole power to impose taxes. The states in turn had failed to pay off national war debts and to enforce some national treaty obligations. The Framers aimed to create a stronger national government to remedy these problems—but not one that was *too* powerful. Balancing power between the nation and the states was one of their central concerns. The government created under the Constitution came to be called "federal" to capture this balance between a mere federation and a genuinely national government.

The ARTICLES OF CONFEDERATION, Art. IX, had provided: "The United States in Congress assembled, shall have the sole and exclusive right and power of determining on peace and war—[of] sending and receiving ambassadors—entering into treaties and alliances, provided that no treaty of commerce shall be made whereby the legislative power of the respective States shall be restrained from imposing such imposts and duties on foreigners, as their own people are subjected to, or from prohibiting the exportation or importation of any species of goods or commodities whatsoever—[of] granting letters of marque and reprisal in times of peace—appointing courts for the trial of piracies and felonies committed on the high seas and establishing courts for receiving and determining finally appeals in all cases of captures. [The] United States in Congress assembled shall also have the sole and exclusive right and power of regulating the alloy and value of coin struck by their own authority, or by that of the respective States—fixing the standard of weights and measures throughout the United States—regulating the trade and managing all affairs with the Indians, not members of any of the States, provided that the legislative right of any State within its own limits be not infringed or violated—establishing or regulating post-offices from one State to another, throughout all the [United States]—making rules for the government and regulation of [the] land and naval forces, and directing their [operations]." But the Articles of Confederation emphasized the *limits* of those national powers: Article II stated that each State retained "every Power, Jurisdiction and right, which is not by this confederation *expressly* delegated to the United States."

The Framers agreed that the new Constitution should strengthen national powers, but there were several possible ways to do so. The

Convention at first considered a general, open-ended statement of congressional powers: the Virginia plan proposed "[t]hat the National Legislature ought to be empowered to enjoy the Legislative Rights vested in Congress by the Confederation; and moreover to legislate in all cases, to which the separate States are incompetent, or in which the harmony of the United States may be interrupted by exercise of individual legislation." The Convention delegates twice voted for such general formulations. Article I, § 8 of the new Constitution as finally adopted, however, took a different approach, setting forth a specifically enumerated list of granted powers—an approach that originated in the Convention's Committee of Detail. Article I, § 8 increased the range of Congress's powers over those conferred by the Articles. The most important new powers were the powers to levy taxes and to regulate interstate and foreign commerce. The lack of those powers had been widely blamed for the Articles' failure. Article I, § 8, cl. 18, the Necessary and Proper Clause, also gave Congress the power "To make all Laws which shall be necessary and proper for carrying into Execution the foregoing Powers, and all other Powers vested by this Constitution in the Government of the United States, or in any Department or Officer thereof."

To assuage fears of unlimited national power, the Tenth Amendment to the new Constitution later clarified that "[t]he powers not delegated to the United States by the Constitution, nor prohibited by it to the States, are reserved to the States respectively, or to the people." In contrast to the Articles of Confederation, however, the Tenth Amendment pointedly omitted the adverb "expressly" in assuring that the "powers not delegated to the United States" were so reserved.

The Tenth Amendment did little to clarify the exact nature of the vertical power structure established by the Framers, however. What boundaries did the Constitution establish between the respective powers of the national government and the states? How was each to be protected from incursions by the other? The text is sparse on these points: Articles I and II enumerate the affirmative powers of the federal government. They do not provide for specific state immunities. They merely suggest, by negative implication, that the national government would be incapable of aggrandizing itself at the expense of the states. In the other direction, Article I, § 10 expressly bars states from a short list of forbidden acts that might interfere with the national interest, including entering into treaties, coining money, granting titles of nobility, and requires congressional consent before states may impose customs duties, enter interstate compacts, or engage in war. Otherwise, the Constitution leaves intact what Madison in The Federalist No. 45 called the "numerous and indefinite" powers of the states. These ambiguities have given rise to controversy since the Founding.

This chapter explores the theoretical foundations and historical iterations of the controversies surrounding the location of the various powers in the federal system. Section 1 opens with McCulloch v. Maryland, the seminal Supreme Court decision which addressed both the limits of the Necessary and Proper Clause and the location of sovereignty in the constitutional system. Section 2 analyzes the ongoing debates surrounding the proper limits of federal power under the Necessary and Proper Clause. Section 3 discusses the question of where sovereignty resides in the constitutional system. Section 4 explores what values are promoted by the federal structure and the role of federalism in the contemporary context.

SECTION 1. ENUMERATED POWERS AND MCCULLOCH V. MARYLAND

There was virtually no discussion of the Necessary and Proper Clause at the Constitutional Convention. During the ratification debates in the states, however, some who feared a powerful central government focused on that Clause. Defenders of the Constitution—especially Alexander Hamilton and James Madison—insisted that the Clause was "harmless" and that objections to it were a "pretext." As Madison explained in The Federalist, No. 44: "Had the Constitution been silent on this head, there can be no doubt that all the particular powers requisite as means of executing the general powers would have resulted to the government, by unavoidable implication."

Almost immediately after ratification, it became clear that this debate had critical implications for establishing the limits of the power of the national government. In December 1790, Alexander Hamilton, Washington's Secretary of the Treasury, sent to the House of Representatives a report urging the incorporation of a national bank. He listed as among its principal advantages "[t]he augmentation of the active or productive capital," a greater "facility as to the government in obtaining pecuniary aids, especially in sudden emergencies," and the "facilitating of the payment of taxes." The issue was hotly debated. James Madison, then in Congress, argued that the incorporation of the bank would be unconstitutional because it would belie the Constitution's structure and purpose: "An interpretation that destroys the very characteristic of the Government cannot be just. Where a meaning is clear, the consequences, whatever they may be, are to be admitted—where doubtful, it is fairly triable by its consequences. In controverted cases, the meaning of the parties to the instrument, if it be collected by reasonable evidence, is a proper guide. [In] admitting or rejecting a constructive authority, not only the degree of its incidentality to the express authority is to be regarded, but the degree of its importance also; since on this will depend the probability or improbability of its being left to construction." Under Madison's interpretation, the Necessary and Proper Clause was essentially superfluous. If a given power was fully necessary to the exercise of an express power, that power had to be implied, with or without the Clause.

Further, Madison argued that incorporating the bank was not included among the powers enumerated in Article I, § 8, and that the Framers had intended to restrict the scope of the national government's implied powers to powers incidental to express powers. Defining powers that were independent ends and not incidental means—such as the power to form a national bank—as implied powers would eliminate the necessity of enumerated powers in the first instance. It has recently been argued that this was the first time the principle of enumerated powers was deployed in constitutional debate, and that Madison developed it as "an act of last-minute creativity" because he wanted to prevent the creation of the bank but lacked an affirmative prohibition supported by the text. Primus, " 'The Essential Characteristic': Enumerated Powers and the Bank of the United States" 117 Mich. L. Rev. 415 (2018).

Congress nevertheless passed the bill establishing the First Bank of the United States. While it sat on Washington's desk, the President requested opinions on its constitutionality from several of his Cabinet members—opinions that turned on the proper interpretation of the Clause.

Secretary of State Jefferson, following Madison, thought it unconstitutional. Invoking the Tenth Amendment, he insisted that the Necessary and Proper Clause did not justify the creation of the Bank: a bank was "not necessary, and consequently not authorized by this phrase." He added: "If such a latitude of construction be allowed to this phrase as to give any non-enumerated power, it will go to every one, for there is not one which ingenuity may not torture into a convenience in some instance or other, to some one of so long a list of enumerated powers. It would swallow up all the delegated powers. [Therefore] it was that the Constitution restrained them to the necessary means, that is to say, to those means without which the grant of power would be nugatory. [Can] it be thought that the Constitution intended that for a shade or two of convenience, more or less, Congress should be authorized to break down the most ancient and fundamental laws of the several States; such as [the] rules of descent, the acts of distribution, [etc.]?"

In response, Hamilton defended the constitutionality of the Bank. Taking specific issue with Jefferson's view of the Necessary and Proper Clause, he argued: "[N]either the grammatical nor popular sense of the term ['necessary'] requires [Jefferson's] construction. According to both, necessary often means no more than needful, requisite, incidental, useful or conducive to. [The] whole turn of the [clause] indicates, that it was the intent of the Convention [to] give a liberal latitude to the exercise of the specified powers. [Jefferson's] construction would beget endless uncertainty and embarrassment. The cases must be palpable and extreme, in which it could be pronounced, with certainty, that a measure was absolutely necessary, or one, without which the exercise of a given power would be nugatory. There are few measures of any government which would stand so severe a test." Hamilton added: "[W]hile on the one hand [Jefferson's construction] is deemed inadmissible, it will not be contended, on the other, that the clause in question gives any new or independent power. But it gives an explicit sanction to the doctrine of implied powers. [The] criterion is the end, to which the measure relates as a means. If the end be clearly comprehended within any of the specified powers, and if the measure have an obvious relation to that end, and is not forbidden by any particular provision of the Constitution, it may safely be deemed to come within the compass of the national authority. There is also this further criterion, which may materially assist the decision: Does the proposed measure abridge a pre-existing right of any State or of any individual? If it does not, there is a strong presumption in favor of its constitutionality." Hamilton concluded that the creation of the Bank "has a relation, more or less direct, to the power of collecting taxes, to that of borrowing money, to that of regulating trade between the States, and to those of raising and maintaining fleets and armies."

Two camps coalesced around these opposed positions and became the first political parties: the Federalists, led by Hamilton, and the Democratic-Republicans, led by Jefferson and Madison. It is worth noting that they relied on different frameworks of constitutional interpretation. Madison and Jefferson's strict or narrow constructionist view sought to limit the scope of the powers exercised by the national government as closely as possible to the powers enumerated in the Constitution, and urged a narrow reading of the Necessary and Proper Clause in the light of constitutional structure. Hamilton in contrast argued for broad constructionism and an accordingly broad reading of the Clause, thereby expanding the powers available to the national government.

The expiration of the charter of the First Bank of the United States in 1811 coincided with increasing national fiscal difficulties. Financial problems were aggravated during the War of 1812, and demands for a new national bank proliferated. By the end of the War, even President Madison—who had earlier argued the first Bank was unconstitutional—urged consideration of a successor institution. He explained that he now "waive[d]" the question of congressional power to incorporate a bank, "as being precluded in my judgment by repeated recognitions under varied circumstances of the validity of such an institution in acts of the legislative, executive, and judicial branches of the Government." (For a formalization of the argument that the Constitution may be given meaning through settled practice, or "liquidated", see Baude, "Constitutional Liquidation," 79 Stanford L. Rev. 1 (2019)). In 1816, Congress established the Second Bank.

The Bank flourished initially: the country was in a postwar economic boom; trade was active and prices were rising. The Bank liberally expanded credit, encouraging a speculative boom. But by the fall of 1818, a financial panic and depression shook the economy. The Bank, short of specie reserves, called in its excessive loans—and the debtors (state banks as well as private individuals) reacted with anger toward the central "monied power," the "monster" Bank. In October 1818, a congressional investigation of the Bank began, and there was considerable support for repeal of its charter. The January 1819 report of the investigating committee found that the Bank had indeed suffered from loose management under its first president, William Jones. But the charter-repeal move failed in February 1819; instead, Jones resigned and was succeeded by the more competent Langdon Cheves.

By 1819, the Bank issue was heated. Anti-Bank measures arose in several states. Indiana and Illinois prohibited banks not chartered by the state, while Maryland, Tennessee, Georgia, North Carolina, Kentucky and Ohio imposed taxes on "foreign" bank operations. The Baltimore branch of the Bank was especially controversial because its cashier James McCulloch and his accomplices were suspected of systematically looting the Bank by instigating unsecured loans and sanctioning unreported overdrafts. It was also the Bank's most active branch nationwide at the time the challenge to it was brought.

McCulloch v. Maryland

4 Wheat. (17 U.S.) 316, 4 L. Ed. 579 (1819).

[In April 1818, the Maryland legislature adopted "An Act to impose a Tax on all Banks or Branches thereof in the State of Maryland, not chartered by the Legislature." The law provided that any banks operating in Maryland "without authority from the State" could issue bank notes only on stamped paper, furnished by the State upon payment of a fee varying with the denomination of each note; but any bank subject to that requirement could "relieve itself" from it "by paying annually, in advance, [the] sum of fifteen thousand dollars." The Maryland statute also provided penalties for violators: the president, cashier and all other officers of the bank were to "forfeit" five hundred dollars "for each and every offense." The penalties were enforceable by indictment or by "action of debt, in the County Court," "one half to the informer, and the other half to the use of the State."

An action for the statutory penalty was brought in the County Court of Baltimore County by one John James, suing for himself and the State, against James McCulloch, the cashier of the Baltimore branch of the Bank of the United States. McCulloch admitted that the Bank was doing business without authority from Maryland and that he had issued bank notes without complying with the Maryland law. The case was decided against McCulloch on the basis of an agreed statement of facts, and the decision was affirmed by the Maryland Court of Appeals. From there, the case was taken by writ of error to the Supreme Court.]

lowered courts against D

■ CHIEF JUSTICE MARSHALL delivered the opinion of the Court.

In the case now to be determined, the defendant [in error], a sovereign state, denies the obligation of a law enacted by the legislature of the Union, and the plaintiff [in error], on his part, contests the validity of an act which has been passed by the legislature of that state. The constitution of our country, in its most interesting and vital parts, is to be considered; the conflicting powers of the government of the Union and of its members, as marked in that constitution, are to be discussed; and an opinion given, which may essentially influence the great operations of the government. No tribunal can approach such a question without a deep sense of its importance, and of the awful responsibility involved in its decision. But it must be decided peacefully, or remain a source of hostile legislation, perhaps of hostility of a still more serious nature; and if it is to be so decided, by this tribunal alone can the decision be made. On the Supreme Court of the United States has the constitution of our country devolved this important duty.

The first question made in the cause is, has Congress power to incorporate a bank? It has been truly said that this can scarcely be considered as an open question, entirely unprejudiced by the former proceedings of the nation respecting it. The principle now contested was introduced at a very early period of our history, has been recognized by many successive legislatures, and has been acted upon by the judicial department, in cases of peculiar delicacy, as a law of undoubted obligation. [The] power now contested was exercised by the first Congress elected under the present constitution. The bill for incorporating the bank of the United States did not steal upon an unsuspecting legislature, and pass unobserved. Its principle was completely understood, and was opposed with equal zeal and ability. After being resisted, first in the fair and open field of debate, and afterwards in the executive cabinet, with as much persevering talent as any measure has ever experienced, and being supported by arguments which convinced minds as pure and as intelligent as this country can boast, it became a law. The original act was permitted to expire; but a short experience of the embarrassments to which the refusal to revive it exposed the government, convinced those who were most prejudiced against the measure of its necessity, and induced the passage of the present law. It would require no ordinary share of intrepidity to assert that a measure adopted under these circumstances was a bold and plain usurpation, to which the constitution gave no countenance. These observations belong to the cause; but they are not made under the impression that, were the question entirely new, the law would be found irreconcilable with the constitution.

const. tested earlier on

In discussing this question, the counsel for the State of Maryland have deemed it of some importance, in the construction of the constitution, to consider that instrument not as emanating from the people, but as the act of sovereign and independent states. The powers of the general government, it has been said, are delegated by the states, who alone are truly sovereign; and must be exercised in subordination to the states, who alone possess supreme dominion.

It would be difficult to sustain this proposition. The Convention which framed the constitution was indeed elected by the state legislatures. But the instrument, when it came from their hands, was a mere proposal, without obligation, or pretensions to it. It was reported to the then existing Congress of the United States, with a request that it might "be submitted to a convention of delegates, chosen in each State by the people thereof, under the recommendation of its legislature, for their assent and ratification." This mode of proceeding was adopted; and by the convention, by Congress, and by the state legislatures, the instrument was submitted to the people. They acted upon it in the only manner in which they can act safely, effectively, and wisely, on such a subject, by assembling in convention. It is true, they assembled in their several states—and where else should they have assembled? No political dreamer was ever wild enough to think of breaking down the lines which separate the states, and of compounding the American people into one common mass. Of consequence, when they act, they act in their states. But the measures they adopt do not, on that account, cease to be the measures of the people themselves, or become the measures of the state governments.

From these conventions the constitution derives its whole authority. The government proceeds directly from the people; is "ordained and established" in the name of the people; and is declared to be ordained, "in order to form a more perfect union, establish justice, ensure domestic tranquility, and secure the blessings of liberty to themselves and to their posterity." The assent of the states, in their sovereign capacity, is implied in calling a convention, and thus submitting that instrument to the people. But the people were at perfect liberty to accept or reject it; and their act was final. It required not the affirmance, and could not be negatived, by the state governments. The constitution, when thus adopted, was of complete obligation, and bound the State sovereignties. [The] government of the Union, then (whatever may be the influence of this fact on the case), is, emphatically, and truly, a government of the people. In form and in substance it emanates from them. Its powers are granted by them, and are to be exercised directly on them, and for their benefit.

This government is acknowledged by all to be one of enumerated powers. The principle, that it can exercise only the powers granted to it, [is] now universally admitted. But the question respecting the extent of the powers actually granted, is perpetually arising, and will probably continue to arise, as long as our system shall exist. [If] any one proposition could command the universal assent of mankind, we might expect it would be this—that the government of the Union, though limited in its powers, is supreme within its sphere of action.

[Among] the enumerated powers, we do not find that of establishing a bank or creating a corporation. But there is no phrase in the instrument which, like the articles of confederation, excludes incidental or implied powers; and which requires that everything granted shall be expressly and minutely described. [The Articles of Confederation had provided that each state "retains" every power not "expressly delegated."] Even the 10th amendment, which was framed for the purpose of quieting the excessive jealousies which had been excited, omits the word "expressly," and declares only that the powers "not delegated to the United States, nor prohibited to the States, are reserved to the States or to the people"; thus leaving the question, whether the particular power which may become the subject of contest has been delegated to the one government, or prohibited to the other, to depend on a fair construction of the whole instrument. The men who drew and adopted this amendment had experienced the embarrassments resulting from the insertion of this word in the articles of confederation, and probably omitted it to avoid those embarrassments. A constitution, to contain an accurate detail of all the subdivisions of which its great powers will admit, and of all the means by which they may be carried into execution, would partake of the prolixity of a legal code, and could scarcely be embraced by the human mind. It would probably never be understood by the public. Its nature, therefore, requires, that only its great outlines should be marked, its important objects designated, and the minor ingredients which compose those objects be deduced from the nature of the objects themselves. That this idea was entertained by the framers of the American constitution, is not only to be inferred from the nature of the instrument, but from the language. Why else were some of the limitations, found in the ninth section of the 1st article, introduced? It is also, in some degree, warranted by their having omitted to use any restrictive term which might prevent its receiving a fair and just interpretation. In considering this question, then, we must never forget that it is *a constitution* we are expounding.

Although, among the enumerated powers of government, we do not find the word "bank," or "incorporation," we find the great powers to lay and collect taxes; to borrow money; to regulate commerce; to declare and conduct a war; and to raise and support armies and navies. The sword and the purse, all the external relations, and no inconsiderable portion of the industry of the nation, are entrusted to its government. It can never be pretended that these vast powers draw after them others of inferior importance, merely because they are inferior. [But] it may with great reason be contended, that a government, entrusted with such ample powers, on the due execution of which the happiness and prosperity of the nation so vitally depends, must also be entrusted with ample means for their execution. The power being given, it is the interest of the nation to facilitate its execution. It can never be their interest, and cannot be presumed to have been their intention, to clog and embarrass its execution by withholding the most appropriate means. Throughout this vast republic, from the St. Croix to the Gulf of Mexico, from the Atlantic to the Pacific, revenue is to be collected and expended, armies are to be marched and supported. The exigencies of the nation may require that the treasure raised in the north should be transported to the south, that raised in the east conveyed to the west, or that this order should be reversed. Is that construction of the constitution to be preferred which would render these operations difficult, hazardous, and expensive? Can we adopt that construction (unless the words imperiously require it) which would impute to the framers of that instrument, when granting these powers for the public good, the intention of impeding their exercise by withholding a choice of means? If, indeed, such be the mandate of the constitution, we have only to obey; but that instrument does not profess to enumerate the means by which the powers it confers may be executed; nor does it prohibit the creation of a corporation, if the existence of such a being be essential to the beneficial exercise of those powers. It is, then, the subject of fair inquiry, how far such means may be employed.

[The] government which has a right to do an act, and has imposed on it the duty of performing that act, must, according to the dictates of reason, be allowed to select the means; and those who contend that it may not select any appropriate means, that one particular mode of effecting the object is excepted, take upon themselves the burden of establishing that exception. [The] power of creating a corporation, though appertaining to sovereignty, is not, like the power of making war, or levying taxes, or of regulating commerce, a great substantive and independent power, which cannot be implied as incidental to other powers, or used as a means of executing them. It is never the end for which other powers are exercised, but a means by which other objects are accomplished. [The] power of creating a corporation is never used for its own sake, but for the purpose of effecting something else. No sufficient reason is, therefore, perceived, why it may not pass as incidental to those powers which are expressly given, if it be a direct mode of executing them.

But the constitution of the United States has not left the right of Congress to employ the necessary means, for the execution of the powers conferred on the government, to general reasoning. To its enumeration of powers is added that of making "all laws which shall be necessary and proper for carrying into execution the foregoing powers, and all other powers vested by this constitution, in the government of the United States, or in any department thereof." The counsel for the State of Maryland have urged various arguments, to prove that this clause, though in terms a grant of power, is not so in effect; but is really restrictive of the general right, which might otherwise be implied, of selecting means for executing the enumerated powers.

[The] argument on which most reliance is placed, is drawn from the peculiar language of this clause. Congress is not empowered by it to make all laws, which may have relation to the powers conferred on the government, but such only as may be *"necessary and proper"* for carrying them into execution. The word *"necessary"* is considered as controlling the whole sentence, and as limiting the right to pass laws for the execution of the granted powers, to such as are indispensable, and without which the power would be nugatory. That it excludes the choice of means, and leaves to Congress, in each case, that only which is most direct and simple.

Is it true, that this is the sense in which the word "necessary" is always used? Does it always import an absolute physical necessity, so strong, that one thing, to which another may be termed necessary, cannot exist without that other? We think it does not. If reference be had to its use, in the common affairs of the world, or in approved authors, we find that it frequently imports no more than that one thing is convenient, or useful, or essential to another. To employ the means necessary to an end, is generally understood as employing any means calculated to produce the end, and not as being confined to those single means, without which the end would be entirely unattainable. [It] is essential to just construction, that many words which import something excessive should be understood in a more mitigated sense—in that sense which common usage justifies. The word "necessary" is of this description. It has not a fixed character peculiar to itself. It admits of all degrees of comparison. [A] thing may be necessary, very necessary, absolutely or indispensably necessary. To no mind would the same idea be conveyed by these several phrases. This comment on the word is well illustrated by the passage cited at the bar, from the 10th section of the 1st article of the constitution. It is, we think, impossible to compare the sentence which prohibits a state from laying "imposts, or duties on imports or exports, except what may be *absolutely* necessary for executing its inspection laws," with that which authorizes Congress "to make all laws which shall be necessary and proper for carrying into execution" the powers of the general government, without feeling a conviction that the convention understood itself to change materially the meaning of the word "necessary," by prefixing the word "absolutely." This word, then, like others, is used in various senses; and, in its construction, the subject, the context, the intention of the person using them, are all to be taken into view.

Let this be done in the case under consideration. The subject is the execution of those great powers on which the welfare of a nation essentially depends. It must have been the intention of those who gave these powers, to insure, as far as human prudence could insure, their beneficial execution. This could not be done by confining the choice of means to such narrow limits as not to leave it in the power of Congress to adopt any which might be appropriate, and which were conducive to the end. This provision is made in a constitution intended to endure for ages to come, and, consequently, to be adapted to the various *crises* of human affairs. To have prescribed the means by which government should, in all future time, execute its powers, would have been to change, entirely, the character of the instrument, and give it the properties of a legal code. It would have been an unwise attempt to provide, by immutable rules, for exigencies which, if foreseen at all, must have been seen dimly, and which can be best provided for as they occur. To have declared that the best means shall not be used, but those alone without which the power given would be nugatory, would have been to deprive the legislature of the capacity to avail itself of experience, to exercise its reason, and to accommodate its legislation to circumstances. If we apply this principle of construction to any of the powers of the government, we shall find it so pernicious in its operation that we shall be compelled to discard it.

[Take], for example, the power "to establish post offices and post roads." This power is executed by the single act of making the establishment. But, from this has been inferred the power and duty of carrying the mail along the post road, from one post office to another. And, from this implied power, has again been inferred the right to punish those who steal letters from the post office, or rob the mail. It may be said, with some plausibility, that the right to carry the mail, and to punish those who rob it, is not indispensably necessary to the establishment of a post office and post road. This right is indeed essential to the beneficial exercise of the power, but not indispensably necessary to its existence. So, of the punishment of the crimes of stealing or falsifying a record or process of a Court of the United States, or of perjury in such Court. To punish these offences is certainly conducive to the due administration of justice. But courts may exist, and may decide the causes brought before them, though such crimes escape punishment.

[If a] limited construction of the word "necessary" must be abandoned in order to punish, whence is derived the rule which would reinstate it, when the government would carry its powers into execution by means not vindictive in their nature? If the word "necessary" means "needful," "requisite," "essential," "conducive to," in order to let in the power of punishment for the infraction of law; why is it not equally comprehensive when required to authorize the use of means which facilitate the execution of the powers of government without the infliction of punishment?

In ascertaining the sense in which the word "necessary" is used in this clause of the constitution, we may derive some aid from that with which it is associated. Congress shall have power "to make all laws which shall be necessary and *proper* to carry into execution" the powers of the government. If the word "necessary" was used in that strict and rigorous sense for which the counsel for the State of Maryland contend, it would be an extraordinary departure from the usual course of the human mind, as exhibited in composition, to add a word, the only possible effect of which is to qualify that strict and rigorous meaning; to present to the mind the idea of some choice of means of legislation not straitened and compressed within the narrow limits for which gentlemen contend.

But the argument which most conclusively demonstrates the error of the construction contended for by the counsel for the State of Maryland, is founded on the intention of the Convention, as manifested in the whole clause. To waste time and argument in proving that, without it, Congress might carry its powers into execution, would be not much less idle than to hold a lighted taper to the sun. As little can it be required to prove, that in the absence of this clause, Congress would have some choice of means. That it might employ those which, in its judgment, would most advantageously effect the object to be accomplished. That any means adapted to the end, any means which tended directly to the execution of the constitutional powers of the government, were in themselves constitutional. This clause, as construed by the State of Maryland, would abridge, and almost annihilate this useful and necessary right of the legislature to select its means. That this could not be intended, is, we should think, had it not been already controverted, too apparent for controversy. We think so for the following reasons: 1st. The clause is placed among the powers of Congress, not among the limitations on those powers. 2nd. Its terms purport to enlarge, not to diminish the powers vested in the government. It purports to be an additional power, not a restriction on those already granted. No reason has been, or can be assigned for thus concealing an intention to narrow the discretion of the national legislature under words which purport to enlarge it.

even w/out the clause, Congress would have this power anyways

[The] result of the most careful and attentive consideration bestowed upon this clause is, that if it does not enlarge, it cannot be construed to restrain the powers of Congress, or to impair the right of the legislature to exercise its best judgment in the selection of measures to carry into execution the constitutional powers of the government. If no other motive for its insertion can be suggested, a sufficient one is found in the desire to remove all doubts respecting the right to legislate on that vast mass of incidental powers which must be involved in the constitution, if that instrument be not a splendid bauble.

We admit, as all must admit, that the powers of the government are limited, and that its limits are not to be transcended. But we think the sound construction of the constitution must allow to the national legislature that discretion, with respect to the means by which the powers it confers are to be carried into execution, which will enable that body to perform the high duties assigned to it, in the manner most beneficial to the people. Let the end be legitimate, let it be within the scope of the constitution, and all means which are appropriate, which are plainly adapted to that end, which are not prohibited, but consist with the letter and spirit of the constitution, are constitutional.

[If] a corporation may be employed indiscriminately with other means to carry into execution the powers of the government, no particular reason can be assigned for excluding the use of a bank, if required for its fiscal operations. To use one, must be within the discretion of Congress, if it be an appropriate mode of executing the powers of government. That it is a convenient, a useful, and essential instrument in the prosecution of its fiscal operations, is not now a subject of controversy. All those who have been concerned in the administration of our finances, have concurred in representing its importance and necessity; and so strongly have they been felt, that statesmen of the first class, whose previous opinions against it had been confirmed by every circumstance which can fix the human judgment, have yielded those opinions to the exigencies of the nation. [But], were its necessity less apparent, none can deny its being an appropriate measure; and if it is, the degree of its necessity, as has been very justly observed, is to be discussed in another place. Should Congress, in the execution of its powers, adopt measures which are prohibited by the constitution; or should Congress, under the pretext of executing its powers, pass laws for the accomplishment of objects not entrusted to the government; it would become the painful duty of this tribunal, should a case requiring such a decision come before it, to say that such an act was not the law of the land. But where the law is not prohibited, and is really calculated to effect any of the objects entrusted to the government, to undertake here to inquire into the degree of its necessity, would be to pass the line which circumscribes the judicial department, and to tread on legislative ground. This court disclaims all pretensions to such a power.

After this declaration, it can scarcely be necessary to say that the existence of state banks can have no possible influence on the question. No trace is to be found in the constitution of an intention to create a dependence of the government of the Union on those of the states, for the execution of the great powers assigned to it. Its means are adequate to its ends; and on those means alone was it expected to rely for the accomplishment of its ends. To impose on it the necessity of resorting to means which it cannot control, which another government may furnish or withhold, would render its course precarious, the result of its measures uncertain, and create a dependence on other governments, which might disappoint its most important designs, and is incompatible with the language of the constitution. But were it otherwise, the choice of means implies a right to choose a national bank in preference to state banks, and Congress alone can make the election. [It] being the opinion of the Court, that the act incorporating the bank is constitutional; and that the power of establishing a branch in the State of Maryland might be properly exercised by the bank itself, we proceed to inquire—

2. Whether the State of Maryland may, without violating the constitution, tax that branch? That the power of taxation is one of vital importance; that it is retained by the states; that it is not abridged by the grant of a similar power to the government of the Union; that it is to be concurrently exercised by the two governments: are truths which have never been denied. But, such is the paramount character of the constitution, that its capacity to withdraw any subject from the action of even this power, is admitted. The states are expressly forbidden to lay any duties on imports or exports, except what may be absolutely necessary for executing their inspection laws. If the obligation of this prohibition must be conceded, [the] same paramount character would seem to restrain, as it certainly may restrain, a state from such other exercise of this power, as is in its nature

incompatible with, and repugnant to, the constitutional laws of the Union. A law, absolutely repugnant to another, as entirely repeals that other as if express terms of repeals were used. On this ground the counsel for the bank place its claim to be exempted from the power of a State to tax its operations. There is no express provision for the case, but the claim has been sustained on a principle which so entirely pervades the constitution, is so intermixed with the materials which compose it, so interwoven with its web, so blended with its texture, as to be incapable of being separated from it, without rending it into shreds. This great principle is, that the constitution and the laws made in pursuance thereof are supreme; that they control the constitution and laws of the respective States, and cannot be controlled by them. From this, which may be almost termed an axiom, other propositions are deduced as corollaries, on the truth or error of which, and on their application to this case, the cause has been supposed to depend. These are, 1st. That a power to create implies a power to preserve. 2d. That a power to destroy, if wielded by a different hand, is hostile to, and incompatible with these powers to create and to preserve. 3d. That where this repugnancy exists, that authority which is supreme must control, not yield to that over which it is supreme.

[That] the power of taxing [the bank] by the states may be exercised so as to destroy it, is too obvious to be denied. But taxation is said to be an absolute power, which acknowledges no other limits than those expressly prescribed in the constitution, and like sovereign power of every other description, is trusted to the discretion of those who use it. But the very terms of this argument admit, that the sovereignty of the state, in the article of taxation itself, is subordinate to, and may be controlled by the constitution of the United States. How far it has been controlled by that instrument must be a question of construction. In making this construction, no principle, not declared, can be admissible, which would defeat the legitimate operations of a supreme government. It is of the very essence of supremacy, to remove all obstacles to its action within its own sphere, and so to modify every power vested in subordinate governments, as to exempt its own operations from their own influence. This effect need not be stated in terms. It is so involved in the declaration of supremacy, so necessarily implied in it, that the expression of it could not make it more certain. We must, therefore, keep it in view, while construing the constitution.

The argument on the part of the State of Maryland is, not that the states may directly resist a law of Congress, but that they may exercise their acknowledged powers upon it, and that the constitution leaves them this right in the confidence that they will not abuse it. Before we proceed to examine this argument, and to subject it to the test of the constitution, we must be permitted to bestow a few considerations on the nature and extent of this original right of taxation, which is acknowledged to remain with the states. It is admitted that the power of taxing the people and their property is essential to the very existence of government, and may be legitimately exercised on the objects to which it is applicable, to the utmost extent to which the government may choose to carry it. The only security against the abuse of this power, is found in the structure of the government itself. In imposing a tax the legislature acts upon its constituents. This is in general a sufficient security against erroneous and oppressive taxation. [But] the means employed by the government of the Union have no such security, nor is the right of a state to tax them sustained by the same theory. Those means are not given by the people of a particular state, [but] by the people of all the states. They are given by all, for the benefit of all—and upon theory, should be subjected to that government only which belongs to all.

[We] find, then, on just theory, a total failure of this original right to tax the means employed by the government of the Union, for the execution of its powers. The right never existed, and the question whether it has been surrendered, cannot arise. But, waiving this theory for the present, let us resume the inquiry, whether this power can be exercised by the respective states, consistently with a fair construction of the constitution?

That the power to tax involves the power to destroy; that the power to destroy may defeat and render useless the power to create; that there is a plain repugnance, in conferring on one government a power to control the constitutional measures of another, which other, with respect to those very measures, is declared to be supreme over that which exerts the control, are propositions not to be denied. But all inconsistencies are to be reconciled by the magic of the word CONFIDENCE. Taxation, it is said, does not necessarily and unavoidably destroy. To carry it to the excess of destruction would be an abuse, to presume which, would banish that confidence which is essential to all government.

But is this a case of confidence? Would the people of any one state trust those of another with a power to control the most insignificant operations of their state government? We know they would not. Why, then, should we suppose that the people of any one state should be willing to trust those of another with a power to control the operations of a government to which they have confided their most important and most valuable interests? In the legislature of the Union alone, are all represented. The legislature of the Union alone, therefore, can be trusted by the people with the power of controlling measures which concern all, in the confidence that it will not be abused. This, then, is not a case of confidence, and we must consider it as it really is.

[If] we apply the principle for which the State of Maryland contends, to the constitution generally, we shall find it capable of changing totally the character of that instrument. We shall find it capable of arresting all the measures of the government, and of prostrating it at the foot of the states. [If] the states may tax one instrument, employed by the government in the execution of its powers, they may tax any and every other instrument. They may tax the mail; they may tax the mint; they may tax patent rights; they may tax the papers of the custom-house; they may tax judicial process; they may tax all the means employed by the government, to an excess which would defeat all the ends of government. [The American people] did not design to make their government dependent on the states.

[It] has also been insisted, that, as the power of taxation in the general and state governments is acknowledged to be concurrent, every argument which would sustain the right of the general government to tax banks chartered by the states, will equally sustain the right of the states to tax banks chartered by the general government. But the two cases are not on the same reason. The people of all the states have created the general government, and have conferred upon it the general power of taxation. The people of all the states, and the states themselves, are represented in Congress, and, by their representatives, exercise this power. When they tax the chartered institutions of the states, they tax their constituents; and these taxes must be uniform. But, when a state taxes the operations of the government of the United States, it acts upon institutions created, not by their own constituents, but by people over whom they claim no control. It acts upon the measures of a government created by others as well as themselves, for the benefit of others in common with themselves. The difference is that which always exists, and always must exist, between the action of the whole on a part, and the action of a part on the whole—between the laws of a government declared to be supreme, and those of a government which, when in opposition to those laws, is not supreme. But if the full application of this argument could be admitted, it might bring into question the right of Congress to tax the State banks, and could not prove the right of the States to tax the Bank of the United States.

[We conclude] that the states have no power, by taxation or otherwise, to retard, impede, burden, or in any manner control, the operations of the constitutional laws enacted by Congress to carry into execution the powers vested in the general government. [We] are unanimously of opinion, that the law passed by the legislature of Maryland, imposing a tax on the Bank of the United States, is unconstitutional and void. This opinion does not deprive the states of any resources which they originally possessed. It does not extend to a tax paid by the real property of the bank, in common with the other real property within the state, nor to a tax imposed on the interest which the citizens of Maryland may hold in this institution, in common with other property of the same description throughout the state. But this is a tax on the operations of the bank, and is, consequently, a tax on the operation of an instrument employed by the government of the Union to carry its powers into execution. Such a tax must be unconstitutional.

[Reversed.]

---

1. ***The Bank of the United States after McCulloch.*** By the decade following *McCulloch*, the Bank's difficulties had eased: it was managed more competently, and the nation had recovered from the depression. Not until the Jackson Administration did the Bank face another severe attack. The Jackson challenge proved fatal: the McCulloch decision was not an adequate shield against President Jackson's veto of the 1832 Bank recharter, and the Bank went out of existence in 1836.

As for the Baltimore branch cashier, James McCulloch: he was officially charged with misconduct a month after the Court decision, and in May, he was removed from office. Criminal proceedings against McCulloch and his associates were brought by Maryland and continued for several years. But Maryland lacked an embezzlement statute and the effort to obtain a common law conspiracy conviction failed.

2. ***Marshall's out-of-court defense of the McCulloch decision.*** A fierce ideological debate swiftly followed from the McCulloch decision in the newspapers of the day—with Judge Spencer Roane of Virginia writing as the chief critic in the Richmond Enquirer under the pseudonym "Hamden," and John Marshall himself as the chief defender, writing under the pseudonym "A Friend of the Constitution" in the Alexandria Gazette. These essays were unearthed in the 1960s, and reintroduced by Gerald Gunther. John Marshall's Defense of McCulloch v. Maryland (1969); Gunther, "Unearthing John Marshall's Major Out-of-Court Constitutional Commentary," 21 Stan. L. Rev. 449 (1969). In response to the critics who insisted that it was the sovereign states that had established the Constitution, Marshall explained that "the constitution is not the act of the state governments, but of the

people of the states." He noted that the people of the states had acted in their highest sovereign capacities to ratify the Constitution at their state conventions. He denied that he had described them in McCulloch as having acted as a single national populace. But he insisted that "the constitution of the United States is not an alliance or league between independent sovereigns." In other words, "Our constitution is not a compact. It is the act of a single party. It is the act of the people of the United States, assembling in their respective states, and adopting a government for the whole nation."

3. ***McCulloch's two holdings.*** In the McCulloch decision, Marshall rejected two arguments made by Maryland's counsel in favor of a state-centered view of the Constitution. First, Marshall took a broad view of Congress's implied powers in order to hold that Congress did have the power to charter a national bank. What were the sources of this holding? Marshall construed the Necessary and Proper Clause of Art. I, § 8, cl. 18, broadly. He also emphasized the broad and general nature of the document: "it is *a constitution* we are expounding" and "a constitution [is] intended to endure for ages to come, and, consequently, to be adapted to the various *crises* of human affairs." He held accordingly that Congress's own judgment deserved deference so long as it adopted means "which tended directly to the execution" of delegated powers, or were "appropriate" and "plainly adapted" to achieving legitimate ends. He rejected any more stringent requirement of necessity or indispensability.

Does this first holding leave in place any real judicially enforceable limits on the scope of congressional authority? Marshall insisted that the required means-ends relationship *was* judicially enforceable. In his 1819 "Friend of the Constitution" essays, for example, he denied "the unlimited power of congress to adopt any means whatever." He also insisted that the Court would invalidate laws enacted "under the pretext" of exercising granted powers. For example, "Congress certainly may not, under the pretext of collecting taxes, or of guaranteeing to each state a republican form of government, alter the law of descents." Should courts scrutinize the purity of legislative motives? For an argument that doing so is both imprudent and impossible, see Antonin Scalia, "Common Law Courts in a Civil-Law System: The Role of the Federal Courts in Interpreting the Constitution and Laws," in A Matter of Interpretation 16–23 (A. Gutmann ed. 1997).

The extent to which congressional authority has been actually limited has varied in the years since McCulloch. At the time of the case, the scope of Congress's implied powers was highly controversial. Yet because Jacksonian Democrats, who generally opposed an expansive federal government, maintained power through much of the antebellum nineteenth century, few cases evaluating the limits of Congress's powers came before the Court. Following the Civil War, the Reconstruction Amendments further expanded federal power, and as Congress began to pursue a more expansive regulatory agenda, the Court responded inconsistently, in some instances invalidating action it argued went too far beyond the enumerated powers. Starting with the New Deal, the boundaries of Congress's power, under the Commerce Clause in particular, appeared to expand. From 1937 to 1995, the federal government enjoyed what many viewed as almost unlimited legislative authority. See, e.g., Archibald Cox, The Court and the Constitution 166 (1987). Around the turn of the twenty-first century, the Supreme Court once again took some steps to curtail Congress's implied powers. See discussion of Commerce Clause power in Chapter 3.

The second holding in McCulloch was that Maryland lacked the power to tax the national bank. What was Marshall's source for that holding? No provision of the text specified that federal instrumentalities are immune from state taxation. Rather, as classically described in Charles Black, Jr., Structure and Relationship in Constitutional Law (1969), the second holding was an "inference from the structures and relationships created by the constitution." Black wrote: "Marshall's reasoning on this branch of the case is, as I read it, essentially structural. It has to do in great part with what he conceives to be the warranted relational proprieties between the national government and the government of the states, with the structural corollaries of national supremacy—and, at one point, of the mode of formation of the Union. [In] this, perhaps the greatest of our constitutional cases, judgment is reached not fundamentally on the basis of that kind of textual exegesis which we tend to regard as normal, but on the basis of reasoning from the total structure which the text has created."

Marshall's structural reasoning relied on the potentially destructive consequences of the power of taxation and the potentially self-interested motives of legislators to hoard benefits for their own constituents and export costs to others. When a legislature taxes its own constituents, he reasoned, the constituents' right to vote for or against their representatives is usually "a sufficient security against erroneous and oppressive taxation." In the national legislature "all [are] represented," so there is little reason to fear oppressive taxation of the states by the national government. When a state legislature taxes a national instrumentality, however, most of the nation's voters are excluded from representation. Therefore, the state has every incentive to soak the citizens of other states. Marshall suggested that judicial intervention is justified in such circumstances to prevent this predictable political result. John Hart Ely later generalized such a justification for judicial intervention in his masterwork, Democracy and Distrust (1980). He argued that democracy was the core goal of the Constitution and therefore that "representation-reinforcement" serves as a justification for judicial action. Under this view, a central role of the courts is to make up for flaws in the operation of representative government or breakdowns in the political process. Was this representation-reinforcing theme aptly applied in McCulloch? If Americans throughout the nation were truly oppressed by state taxation of the Bank, did not Congress have power to enact a law to bar state taxation? Especially in view of the Bank's powerful lobby in Washington, was this an appropriate case for judicial rather than congressional intervention on behalf of the Bank?

SECTION 2. THE LIMITS OF THE NECESSARY AND PROPER CLAUSE

Since McCulloch, the Supreme Court has repeatedly relied on Chief Justice Marshall's broad interpretation of the Necessary and Proper Clause in McCulloch v. Maryland, often in the context of similarly broad interpretations of Congress's commerce power. Nonetheless, as discussed in more depth in Chapter 3, in the twentieth century, the Supreme Court developed federalism-based limits to Congress's commerce power. Recent decisions have raised the question of whether the same limits should be applied to the Necessary and Proper Clause:

In United States v. Comstock, the Court considered the question whether the Necessary and Proper Clause grants authority to Congress to enact a statute, 18 U.S.C. § 4248, allowing federal district courts to order the civil commitment of mentally ill, sexually dangerous federal prisoners beyond the dates they would otherwise be released. The Court found, by a vote of 7–2, that the Clause does grant such authority. The dissent, however, criticized what it characterized as the Court's expansive interpretation of the Necessary and Proper Clause. In National Federation Of Independent Business v. Sebelius, 567 U.S. 519 (2012) ("NFIB"), by contrast, a 5–4 majority of the Court found the Necessary and Proper Clause an insufficient basis to sustain aspects of the Patient Protection and Affordable Care Act of 2010 that that same majority deemed to exceed the bounds of Congress's enumerated power under the Commerce Clause. The dissent would have found the invalidated provisions "an 'essential part of a larger regulation of economic activity' " valid under both clauses. In the 2018 case Ayestas v. Davis, the Supreme Court reiterated that "[t]he term 'necessary' in the Necessary and Proper Clause does not mean '*absolutely* necessary." 138 S. Ct. 1080, 1903 (2018) (emphasis in original).

United States v. Comstock

560 U.S. 126, 130 S. Ct. 1949 (2010).

■ JUSTICE BREYER delivered the opinion of the Court.

[Here] we ask whether the Federal Government has the authority under Article I of the Constitution to enact this federal civil-commitment program or whether its doing so falls beyond the reach of a government "of enumerated powers." McCulloch v. Maryland. [We] conclude that the Constitution grants Congress legislative power sufficient to enact § 4248. We base this conclusion on five considerations, taken together.

First, the Necessary and Proper Clause grants Congress broad authority to enact federal legislation [that is] "convenient, or useful" or "conducive" to the authority's "beneficial exercise." [McCulloch.] In determining whether the Necessary and Proper Clause grants Congress the legislative authority to enact a particular federal statute, we look to see whether the statute constitutes a means that is rationally related to the implementation of a constitutionally enumerated power. [Neither] Congress' power to criminalize conduct, nor its power to imprison individuals who engage in that conduct, nor its power to enact laws governing prisons and prisoners, is explicitly mentioned in the Constitution. But Congress nonetheless possesses broad authority to do each of those things in the course of "carrying into Execution" [its] enumerated powers.

Second, the civil-commitment statute before us constitutes a modest addition to a set of federal prison-related mental-health statutes that have existed [since] 1855. Third, Congress reasonably extended its longstanding civil-commitment system to cover mentally ill and sexually dangerous persons who are already in federal custody, even if doing so detains them beyond the termination of their criminal sentence. [The] Federal Government is the custodian of its prisoners [and] has the constitutional power to act in order to protect nearby (and other) communities from the danger federal prisoners may pose. [Moreover,] § 4248 is "reasonably adapted" to Congress' power to act as a responsible federal custodian. Congress could have reasonably concluded that federal inmates who suffer from a mental illness that causes them to "have serious difficulty in refraining from sexually violent conduct" would pose an especially high danger to the public if released. And Congress could also have reasonably concluded [that] a reasonable number of such individuals would likely not be detained by the States if released from federal custody.

Fourth, the statute properly accounts for state interests. [Section 4248 does not] invade state sovereignty [but rather] requires accommodation of state interests: [it] requires the Attorney General to encourage the relevant States to take custody of the individual without inquiring into the "suitability" of their intended care or treatment, and to relinquish federal authority whenever a State asserts its own. Fifth, the links between § 4248 and an enumerated Article I power are not too attenuated. [We need not] fear that our holding today confers on Congress a general "police power" [for] § 4248 is narrow in scope. It has been applied to only a small fraction of federal prisoners. And its reach is limited to individuals already "in the custody of the" Federal Government. [Taken] together, these considerations lead us to conclude that the statute is a "necessary and proper" means of exercising the federal authority that permits Congress to create federal criminal laws, to punish their violation, to imprison violators, to provide appropriately for those imprisoned, and to maintain the security of those who are not imprisoned but who may be affected by the federal imprisonment of others.

■ JUSTICE KENNEDY, joined by JUSTICE ALITO, concurring in the judgment.

[U]nder the Necessary and Proper Clause, application of a "rational basis" test should be at least as exacting as it has been in the Commerce Clause cases, if not more so. [Those] precedents require a tangible link to commerce, not a mere conceivable rational relation, as in [the due process cases]. The rational basis referred to in the Commerce Clause context is a demonstrated link in fact, based on empirical demonstration.

[It] is correct in one sense to say that if the National Government has the power to act under the Necessary and Proper Clause then that power is not one reserved to the States. But the precepts of federalism embodied in the Constitution inform which powers are properly exercised by the National Government in the first place. [It] is of fundamental importance to consider whether essential attributes of state sovereignty are compromised by the assertion of federal power under the Necessary and Proper Clause; if so, that is a factor suggesting that the power is not one properly within the reach of federal power.

■ JUSTICE ALITO, concurring in the judgment.

[It is] necessary and proper for Congress to protect the public from dangers created by the federal criminal justice and prison systems. [Just] as it is necessary and proper for Congress to provide for the apprehension of escaped federal prisoners, it is necessary and proper for Congress to provide for the civil commitment of dangerous federal prisoners who would otherwise escape civil commitment as a result of federal imprisonment.

■ JUSTICE THOMAS, joined in part by JUSTICE SCALIA, dissenting.

§ 4248 can be a valid exercise of congressional authority only if it is "necessary and proper for carrying into Execution" one or more of those federal powers actually enumerated in the Constitution. [The] Government identifies no specific enumerated power or powers as a constitutional predicate for § 4248, and none are readily discernable. Indeed, not even the Commerce Clause [can] justify federal civil detention of sex offenders [as sexual violence is a noneconomic activity]. [The] power to care for the mentally ill and, where necessary, the power "to protect the community from the dangerous tendencies of some" mentally ill persons, are among the numerous powers that remain with the States. [True,] 29 States appear as amici and argue that § 4248 is constitutional. They tell us that they do not object to Congress retaining custody of "sexually dangerous persons" after their criminal sentences expire because the cost of detaining such persons is "expensive" [and] these States would rather the Federal Government bear this expense. Congress' power, however, is fixed by the Constitution; it does not expand merely to suit the States' policy preferences, or to allow State officials to avoid difficult choices regarding the allocation of state funds. [Today's] opinion [comes] perilously close to transforming the Necessary and Proper Clause into a basis for [a] federal police power.

FEDERALISM-BASED LIMITS ON THE NECESSARY AND PROPER CLAUSE?

1. ***Determining the proper standard of review.*** In Comstock, the Court reiterated the principle that a federal statute must be "rationally related to the implementation of a constitutionally enumerated power" to be declared within Congress's power under the Necessary and Proper Clause. The Court proceeded, however, to set forth a five-factor test, under which it determined that the statute was necessary and proper. Is the Court's five-factor test compatible with its rational-basis test? With McCulloch? Justice Kennedy's concurrence argues for a more stringent version of rational-basis review in the context of the Necessary and Proper Clause than in the context of the Due Process Clause, analogizing the proper test to the more "exacting" form of rational-basis review applied under the Commerce Clause. Although he was not explicit on the point, he appeared to ground his demand for a stricter standard at least in part in federalism principles. In his dissent, Justice Thomas did not reach the question of the proper standard of review, as he could not identify an enumerated power for which the statute was necessary and proper, which he viewed as a prerequisite under McCulloch. Of the Court's opinions, which best accords with the principles and holding articulated in McCulloch?

2. ***"Proper federal action."*** In National Federation of Independent Business v. Sebelius (2012; p. 160), explored in further detail in Chapters 3 and 4, the Court addressed a challenge to a provision of the Patient Protection and Affordable Care Act of 2010 that required most individuals to obtain health insurance. One of the government's arguments for sustaining the constitutionality of the Act was that the mandate was an essential element of the Congress's power to regulate other aspects of the health care system under its Art. I § 8 commerce power, and could thus be sustained under the Necessary and Proper Clause. In his controlling opinion, Chief Justice ROBERTS rejected the government's argument, stressing that federal action must both be "necessary" and "proper" to be sustained under that provision: "[A]s our jurisprudence under the Necessary and Proper Clause has developed, we have been very deferential to Congress's

determination that a regulation is 'necessary.' We have thus upheld laws that are ' "convenient, or useful" or "conducive" to the authority's "beneficial exercise." ' [But] we have also carried out our responsibility to declare unconstitutional those laws that undermine the structure of government established by the Constitution. Such laws, which are not 'consist[ent] with the letter and spirit of the constitution,' [are] not '*proper* [means] for carrying into Execution' Congress's enumerated powers. [The] individual mandate cannot be sustained under the Necessary and Proper Clause as an essential component of the insurance reforms. Each of our prior cases upholding laws under that Clause involved exercises of authority derivative of, and in service to, a granted power. [The] individual mandate, by contrast, vests Congress with the extraordinary ability to create the necessary predicate to the exercise of an enumerated power. [Just] as the individual mandate cannot be sustained as a law regulating the substantial effects of the failure to purchase health insurance, neither can it be upheld as a 'necessary and proper' component of the insurance reforms."

Justice GINSBURG, joined by Justices Breyer, Sotomayor and Kagan, dissented with respect to the Chief Justice's rejection of the government's Necessary and Proper Clause argument: "When viewed as a component of the entire ACA, the provision's constitutionality becomes even plainer. The Necessary and Proper Clause 'empowers Congress to enact laws in effectuation of its [commerce] powe[r] that are not within its authority to enact in isolation.' [One] of Congress' goals in enacting the Affordable Care Act was to eliminate the insurance industry's practice of charging higher prices or denying coverage to individuals with preexisting medical conditions. The commerce power allows Congress to ban this practice, a point no one disputes. [Without] the individual mandate, Congress learned, guaranteed-issue and community-rating requirements would trigger an adverse-selection death-spiral in the health-insurance market: [The] minimum coverage provision is thus an 'essential par[t] of a larger regulation of economic activity'; without the provision, 'the regulatory scheme [w]ould be undercut.' "

In his opinion, the Chief Justice made no reference to Comstock's five-factor or rational-basis tests of what is "necessary and proper." He rather engaged in a rare in-depth analysis of "proper" as a distinct prong of the Necessary and Proper Clause. His opinion held that the individual mandate was not a "proper" exercise of power incidental to the commerce power under the Necessary and Proper Clause because it "undermine[d] the structure of government" by giving the federal government the "ability to create the necessary predicate to the exercise of an enumerated power" in compelling activity in the health insurance market. What is the scope of the "proper" requirement after NFIB? Is it likely to be read for the proposition that any law which, in the opinion of the Court, undermines the structure of government is invalid under the Necessary and Proper Clause? Or does it stand for the narrower proposition that Congress cannot use the Necessary and Proper Clause to create the necessary predicate for the exercise of an enumerated power? If the latter, where is the line between a "necessary predicate" and "an essential component"? To which of the three interpretive frameworks discussed above—strict constructionism, broad constructionism and structuralism—does the Chief Justice's opinion most closely adhere? Does his opinion represent a return to or a departure from the principles of McCulloch and broad constructionism? Is it consistent with Comstock?

3. In **United States v. Kebodeaux**, 570 U.S. 387 (2013), the Court addressed whether Congress has authority under the Necessary and Proper Clause to require a convicted member of the Air Force to register as a sex offender under the Sex Offender Registration and Notification Act (SORNA), enacted after his conviction. Justice BREYER, writing for the Court, explained that, "[at] the time of his offense and conviction Kebodeaux was subject to the federal Wetterling Act, an Act that imposed upon him registration requirements very similar to those that SORNA later mandated. [Like] SORNA, it imposed federal penalties upon federal sex offenders who failed to register in the States in which they lived, worked, and studied." Treating the registration requirement as a continuing obligation, he wrote of the former law: "[No] one here claims that the Wetterling Act [falls] outside the scope of the Necessary and Proper Clause. And it is difficult to see how anyone could persuasively do so. The Constitution explicitly grants Congress the power to 'make Rules for the . . . Regulation of the land and naval Forces.' Art. I, § 8, cl. 14. And, in the Necessary and Proper Clause itself, it grants Congress the power to 'make all Laws which shall be necessary and proper for carrying into Execution the foregoing Powers' and 'all other Powers' that the Constitution vests 'in the Government of the United States, or in any Department or Officer thereof.' [The] scope of the Necessary and Proper Clause is broad. [The] Constitution, for example, makes few explicit references to federal criminal law, but the Necessary and Proper Clause nonetheless authorizes Congress, in the implementation of other explicit powers, to create federal crimes, to confine offenders to prison, to hire guards and other prison personnel, to provide prisoners with medical care and educational training, to ensure the safety of those who may come into contact with prisoners, to ensure the public's safety through systems of parole and supervised release, and, where a federal prisoner's mental condition so requires, to confine that prisoner civilly after the expiration of his or her term of imprisonment. Comstock. Here, under the authority granted to it by the Military Regulation and Necessary and Proper Clauses, Congress could promulgate the Uniform Code of Military Justice. It could specify that the sex offense of which Kebodeaux was convicted was a military crime under that Code. It could punish that crime through imprisonment and by placing conditions upon Kebodeaux's release. And it could make the civil registration requirement at issue here a consequence of Kebodeaux's offense and conviction."

Chief Justice ROBERTS concurred, clarifying his view of the Court's invocation of public safety: "[Sandwiched] between [the majority's] discussion of the basis for Congress's power and its discussion of the inconsequential nature of the changes is a discussion of benefits from the registration system. [Those] consequences of the registration requirement are irrelevant for our purposes. Public safety benefits are neither necessary nor sufficient to a proper exercise of the power to regulate the military. What matters—all that matters—is that Congress could have rationally determined that 'mak[ing] the civil registration requirement at issue here a consequence of Kebodeaux's offense' would give force to the Uniform Code of Military Justice adopted pursuant to Congress's power to regulate the Armed Forces. Ordinarily such surplusage might not warrant a separate writing. Here, however, I worry that incautious readers will think they have found in the majority opinion something they would not find in either the Constitution or any prior decision of ours: a federal police power. [I] write separately to stress not only that a federal police power is immaterial to the result in this case, but also that such a power *could not* be material to the result in this case—because it does not exist. [In McCulloch v. Maryland], Chief Justice Marshall was emphatic that no 'great substantive and independent power' can be 'implied as incidental to other powers, or used as a means of executing them.' [It] is difficult to imagine a clearer example of such a 'great substantive and independent power' than the power to 'help protect the public . . . and alleviate public safety concerns,' I find it implausible to suppose—and impossible to support—that the Framers intended to confer such authority by implication rather than expression."

Justice ALITO also wrote separately concurring in the judgment.

Justice THOMAS, joined in part by Justice Scalia, dissented: "[It] is clear from the face of SORNA and from the Government's arguments that it is not directed at 'carrying into Execution' any of the federal powers enumerated in the Constitution, Art. I § 8, cl. 18, but is instead aimed at protecting society from sex offenders and violent child predators. The Government has failed to identify any enumerated power that [SORNA] 'carr[ies] into Execution' in this case." dissent

Kebodeaux was decided along the same seven-two split as was Comstock, with two justices writing separately to set out limiting principles to the Court's holding in each case. Do the breadth of the majority opinion and the fact that the holding commanded such a large majority suggest that the Necessary and Proper Clause will remain a significant source of federal legislative power, even as the Court interprets other of Congress's enumerated powers more narrowly?

4. In addition to asking whether the Court has correctly interpreted the scope of Congress's implied powers under the Necessary and Proper Clause, one might also ask whether the Court is the proper body to make that determination at all. John Manning argues that it is not. See Manning, "Foreword: The Means of Constitutional Power," 128 Harv. L. Rev. 1 (2014). He writes that "[t]he text of the Necessary and Proper Clause [delegates] to Congress broad and explicit (though not limitless) discretion to compose the government and prescribe the means of constitutional power." As a result, Manning argues, "[w]hen the Court asserts independent judgment to determine the content of 'necessary and proper' under vague criteria (as it does in structural constitutional cases), the judiciary substitutes itself for Congress as the people's delegatee contrary to the terms of the constitutional text." This view rejects the Rehnquist and Roberts Courts' interpretation of "proper" as "satisfy[ing] the Court's own conception of [principles] of federalism and separation of powers." See NFIB v. Sebelius, above and at p. 160. Is Manning correct that the Framers intended for the Court to defer to Congress's interpretation of its own power under the Necessary and Proper Clause? Is this reading tantamount to the fox guarding the hen house, or is there something unique about the Necessary and Proper Clause that warrants it being treated differently than other congressional powers?

SECTION 3. THE LOCATION OF SOVEREIGNTY IN THE FEDERAL SYSTEM

The Framers clearly intended for the Constitution to express the principle of popular sovereignty. The opening words of the preamble express as much: "We the People of the United States, in Order to form a more perfect Union, establish Justice, insure domestic Tranquility, provide for the common defence, promote the general Welfare, and secure the Blessings of Liberty to ourselves and our Posterity, do ordain and establish this Constitution for the United States of America." But whose sovereignty? Where does sovereignty reside in a system of vertically divided powers? Irreducibly in the States who joined together in a compact under the Constitution? In the peoples of the individual states that ratified the Constitution? Or in a single national populace that ordained the framing document as "We the People of the United States"? The Constitution never mentions the word "sovereign," and the location of sovereignty has proved divisive in the history of the nation, most crucially in the instance of Southern secession and Civil War. The decision by Chief Justice Marshall in McCulloch v. Maryland offered the Supreme Court's first extended discussion of the question. The Term Limits decision, which follows the discussion of McCulloch below, shows that the question remains controversial.

1. ***McCulloch and the location of sovereignty.*** Was the Constitution ratified by "We the People" of the United States as one national populace? Was it ratified by "We the States"? Or was it ratified by "We the Peoples" of the several States, acting as popular sovereigns in the conventions where ratification took place? Disagreement over these characterizations divided Marshall and his critics.

In upholding Congress's power to charter the Bank and rejecting Maryland's arguments for its power to tax the Bank, Chief Justice Marshall took what is often understood as a strong nationalist position—the position "Hampden" and other critics attributed to him in the newspaper debates of 1819. Does this mean that he located sovereignty in one national populace, "We the People of the United States"? This was the view taken, for example, by Justice Story in Martin v. Hunter's Lessee: "The constitution of the United States was ordained and established, not by the states in their sovereign capacities, but emphatically, as the preamble of the constitution declares, by 'the people of the united States.' " Marshall denies that he is taking this position in McCulloch, however, protesting that "[n]o political dreamer was ever wild enough to think of breaking down the lines which separate the states, and of compounding the American people into one common mass."

But Marshall also forcefully rejects the polar opposite view that the federal government is but a compact among the separate, sovereign States. As he wrote under his "Friend of the Constitution" moniker, "the constitution of the United States is not an alliance or league between independent sovereigns." Is it possible that the delegates to the state conventions, in ratifying the Constitution, were acting as *both* "We the People" and "We the Peoples" of the several states? Consider the interpretation that "[a] significant number of Americans simultaneously held—in varying mixtures and intensities—some concept of a 'We the People' of the United States and [some] concept of a 'We the People' of Delaware, and so on." Monaghan, "We the People[s], Original Understanding and Constitutional Amendment," 96 Colum. L. Rev. 121 (1996).

Is Marshall suggesting that sovereignty was located somewhere intermediate between these two poles? Consider the following argument: "Most often, state-oriented justices take a 'We the States' view, suggesting that the original popular sovereigns were the thirteen sovereign states themselves. At the opposite end of the spectrum is the 'We the People' position, in the sense that the Constitution's foundation rests on the assent of a single 'We the People of the United States.' Somewhere in the middle, though closer to the 'states' rights' end than the nationalist pole, comes the 'We the Peoples' account, a nuanced understanding that posits that the several discrete populaces of the states, rather than the states themselves, presided over the creation of the Constitution." Flaherty, "John Marshall, McCulloch v. Maryland, and 'We the People': Revisions in Need of Revising," 43 Wm. & Mary L. Rev. 1339 (2002). See also, Reese, "Or to the People: Popular Sovereignty and the Power to Choose a Government," 39 Cardozo L. Rev. 2051 (2018) (arguing that the Constitution established three sovereigns: the federal government, the state governments and the people).

The classic statement of this intermediate position is perhaps that of Madison in The Federalist, No. 39: "[I]t appears, on one hand, that the Constitution is to be founded on the assent and ratification of the people of America, given by deputies elected for the special purpose; but, on the other, that this assent and ratification is to be given by the people, not as individuals composing one entire nation, but as composing the distinct and independent States to which they respectively belong. It is to be the assent and ratification of the several States, derived from the supreme authority in each State—the authority of the people themselves. The act, therefore, establishing the Constitution will not be a *national* but a *federal* act."

With regard to sovereignty and the Constitution, consider also the skeptical view of Justice James Wilson, himself a Framer, in Chisholm v. Georgia, 2. U.S. (2 Dall.) 419, 454 (1793): "To the Constitution of the United States the term SOVEREIGN, is totally unknown. There is but one place where it could have been used with propriety. But, even in that place it would not, perhaps, have comported with the delicacy of those, who ordained and established the Constitution. They might have announced themselves 'SOVEREIGN' people of the United States: But serenely conscious of the fact, they avoided the ostentatious declaration."

2. ***The "compact theory" of sovereignty.*** In approving the Bank and rejecting Maryland's power to tax it, McCulloch demonstrates the real-world implications of the theoretical debate regarding the source of federal power in the constitutional system. Indeed, on the basis of the argument that national power emanates not from the people directly but from a compact among the states—commonly called "compact theory"—states have claimed some forms of power as against the federal government. Twenty years before McCulloch, the Virginia Resolutions of 1798, written by James Madison, and the Kentucky Resolutions of 1798, written by Thomas Jefferson, asserted that the states had the power to reject the controversial and much-criticized Alien and Sedition Acts. The Resolutions argued that because the states had compacted to grant limited power to a national government, they could determine that certain congressional acts passed pursuant to that power had exceeded their grant and thus declare those acts unconstitutional. The Virginia Resolution of 1798 stated: "[This] Assembly doth explicitly and peremptorily declare, that it views the powers of the federal government as resulting from the compact to which the states are parties, as limited by the plain sense and intention of the instrument constituting that compact, as no further valid than they are authorized by the grants enumerated in that compact; and that, in case of a deliberate, palpable, and dangerous exercise of other powers, not granted by the said compact, the states, who are parties thereto, have the right, and are in duty bound, to interpose, for arresting the progress of the evil, and for maintaining, within their respective limits, the

authorities, rights and liberties, appertaining to them." To what conclusion(s) does Virginia's position logically lead? Would such an interpretation result in anarchy? Does it follow from the argument that states have the right to secede? If so, is Virginia's argument necessarily flawed, or at least impractical? If Virginia's argument is flawed, does it follow that the Supreme Court is the right arbiter of constitutional questions?

Although a majority of states rejected the Resolutions at the time they were passed, and although the Supreme Court rejected in dicta in McCulloch the theory that the Resolutions espoused, South Carolina relied on the same line of argumentation during the Nullification Crisis of 1828 to 1833. In 1832, after Congress instituted tariffs that South Carolina deemed excessive and protectionist, the state called a convention that passed an Ordinance of Nullification, which declared the institution of the tariffs an unconstitutional expansion of Congress's taxing power. In response, Congress passed the Force Act of 1833, which authorized the executive to act to prevent nullification. President Jackson, who was otherwise a supporter of states' rights, issued a proclamation rejecting a nullification right as contrary to the Supremacy Clause of the Constitution and the continued existence of the United States. The crisis was averted by the adoption of a compromise tariff. But states continued to assert similar arguments up until the secession of the states of the Confederacy, which was justified partly by this theory.

The legitimacy of a right to secession was ultimately resolved by the Civil War itself, but states have occasionally continued to assert versions of compact theory to justify refusals to follow federal law. For example, immediately following the Supreme Court's 1954 decision Brown v. Board of Education, in which the Court declared public school segregation unconstitutional, a number of states adopted resolutions declaring the Supreme Court's decision null and void, relying, in part, on the Virginia and Kentucky Resolutions as well as arguments made during the Nullification Crisis. In Cooper v. Aaron (p. 21 above), the Supreme Court explicitly rejected the right of states to nullify the Court's decision. The Court's refusal to accept the theory has nonetheless failed to eliminate state reliance upon it. For example, before and after the Supreme Court decided NFIB v. Sebelius, discussed in greater detail below and in chapters 3 and 4, state legislators and officials asserted arguments grounded in compact theory as justifications for refusing to implement the Affordable Care Act of 2010. See John S. Adams, "U.S. Health Care Law Not Immune to Nullification," USA Today (Feb. 27, 2011).

RECENT CHALLENGES TO THE LOCATION OF SOVEREIGNTY IN THE CONSTITUTIONAL SYSTEM

The debate over the correct construction of the Constitution's creation—through agreement by the people or compact by the states—resurfaced in 1995, when the Court confronted an effort by the State of Arkansas to limit the number of terms of office any of its congressional representatives might serve. The narrow issue was whether a state may add non-incumbency to the age, citizenship and residence criteria for congressional eligibility set forth in the Qualifications Clause. But the closely divided 5–4 decision also elicited deep disagreement about relative power of the nation and the states:

U.S. Term Limits, Inc. v. Thornton

514 U.S. 779, 115 S. Ct. 1842, 131 L. Ed. 2d 881 (1995).

■ JUSTICE STEVENS delivered the opinion of the Court.

The Constitution sets forth qualifications for membership in the Congress of the United States[—the age, citizenship, and residence requirements of Art. I, § 2, cl. 2, and Art I, § 3, cl. 3]. Today's cases present a challenge to an amendment to the Arkansas State Constitution that prohibits the name of an otherwise-eligible candidate for Congress from appearing on the general election ballot if that candidate has already served three terms in the House of Representatives or two terms in the Senate. The Arkansas Supreme Court held that the amendment violates the Federal Constitution. We agree with that holding. Such a state-imposed restriction is contrary to the "fundamental principle of our representative democracy," embodied in the Constitution, that "the people should choose whom they please to govern them." Powell v. McCormack [1969; p. 66 above.] Allowing individual States to adopt their own qualifications for congressional service [also] would be inconsistent with the Framers' vision of a uniform National Legislature representing the people of the United States. If the qualifications set forth in the text of the Constitution are to be changed, that text must be amended.

[Our] holding in Powell, which involved the power of the House to exclude a member pursuant to Art. I, § 5, [depended on our] conclusion that Congress may not alter or add to the qualifications in the Constitution.[1] [But our] reaffirmation of Powell does not necessarily resolve the specific questions presented in these cases. For petitioners argue that whatever the constitutionality of additional qualifications for membership imposed by Congress, the historical and textual materials discussed in Powell do not support the conclusion that the Constitution prohibits additional qualifications imposed by States. In the absence of such a constitutional prohibition, petitioners argue, the Tenth Amendment and the principle of reserved powers require that States be allowed to add such qualifications.

[We] disagree. First, [the] power to add qualifications is not within the "original powers" of the States, and thus is not reserved to the States by the Tenth Amendment. Second, even if States possessed some original power in this area, we conclude that the Framers intended the Constitution to be the exclusive source of qualifications for members of Congress, and that the Framers thereby "divested" States of any power to add qualifications.

The "plan of the convention" [draws] a basic distinction between the powers of the newly created Federal Government and the powers retained

[1] The dissent treats Powell as simply an application of the "default rule" that if "the Constitution is silent about the exercise of a particular power—that is, where the Constitution does not speak either expressly or by necessary implication—the Federal Government lacks that power and the States enjoy it." [But] the Court has never treated the dissent's "default rule" as absolute. In McCulloch v. Maryland, for example, Chief Justice Marshall rejected the argument that the Constitution's silence on state power to tax federal instrumentalities requires that States have the power to do so. Under the dissent's unyielding approach, it would seem that McCulloch was wrongly decided. Similarly, the dissent's approach would invalidate our dormant Commerce Clause jurisprudence, because the Constitution is clearly silent on the subject of state legislation that discriminates against interstate commerce. [Footnote by Justice Stevens.]

by the pre-existing sovereign States. As Chief Justice Marshall explained, "it was neither necessary nor proper to define the powers retained by the States. These powers proceed, not from the people of America, but from the people of the several States; and remain, after the adoption of the constitution, what they were before, except so far as they may be abridged by that instrument." Sturges v. Crowninshield, 4 Wheat. (17 U.S.) 122 (1819). This classic statement by the Chief Justice endorsed Hamilton's reasoning in The Federalist No. 32 that the plan of the Constitutional Convention did not contemplate "an entire consolidation of the States into one complete national sovereignty," but only a partial consolidation in which "the State governments would clearly retain all the rights of sovereignty which they before had, and which were not, by that act, exclusively delegated to the United States." The text of the Tenth Amendment unambiguously confirms this [principle].

[But petitioners'] Tenth Amendment argument misconceives the nature of the right at issue because that Amendment could only "reserve" that which existed before. As Justice Story recognized, "the states can exercise no powers whatsoever, which exclusively spring out of the existence of the national government, which the constitution does not delegate to them. [No] state can say, that it has reserved, what it never possessed." 1 Story, [Commentaries on the Constitution of the United States] § 627 [(3d ed. 1858)]. Justice Story's position thus echoes that of Chief Justice Marshall in McCulloch, [which] rejected the argument that the Constitution's silence on the subject of state power to tax corporations chartered by Congress implies that the States have "reserved" power to tax such federal instrumentalities. As [Marshall] pointed out, an "original right to tax" such federal entities "never existed, and the question whether it has been surrendered, cannot arise."

[With] respect to setting qualifications for service in Congress, no such right existed before the Constitution was ratified. [T]he Framers envisioned a uniform national system, rejecting the notion that the Nation was a collection of States, and instead creating a direct link between the National Government and the people of the United States. In that National Government, representatives owe primary allegiance not to the people of a State, but to the people of the Nation. [In] short, as the Framers recognized, electing representatives to the National Legislature was a new right, arising from the Constitution itself. The Tenth Amendment thus provides no basis for concluding that the States possess reserved power to add qualifications to those that are fixed in the Constitution. [In] the absence of any constitutional delegation to the States of power to add qualifications to those enumerated in the Constitution, such a power does not exist.

[T]he Framers, in perhaps their most important contribution, conceived of a Federal Government directly responsible to the people, possessed of direct power over the people, and chosen directly, not by States, but by the people. [They] implemented this ideal most clearly in the provision [that] calls for the Members of the House of Representatives to be "chosen every second Year by the People of the several States." Art. I, § 2, cl. 1. Following the adoption of the 17th Amendment in 1913, this ideal was extended to elections for the Senate. The Congress of the United States, therefore, is not a confederation of nations in which separate sovereigns are represented by appointed delegates, but is instead a body composed of representatives of the people. [See] McCulloch v. Maryland. [Members] of Congress are chosen by separate constituencies, but [they] become, when elected, servants of the people of the United States. They are not merely delegates appointed by separate, sovereign States; they occupy offices that are integral and essential components of a single National Government. In the absence of a properly passed constitutional amendment, allowing individual States to craft their own qualifications for Congress would thus erode the structure envisioned by the Framers, a structure that was designed, in the words of the Preamble to our Constitution, to form a "more perfect Union."

[Affirmed.]

■ JUSTICE KENNEDY, concurring.

[Federalism] was our Nation's own discovery. The Framers split the atom of sovereignty. It was the genius of their idea that our citizens would have two political capacities, one state and one federal, each protected from incursion by the other. The resulting Constitution created a legal system unprecedented in form and design, establishing two orders of government, each with its own direct relationship, its own privity, its own set of mutual rights and obligations to the people who sustain it and are governed by it.

[A] distinctive character of the National Government, the mark of its legitimacy, is that it owes its existence to the act of the whole people who created it. [As] James Madison explained, the House of Representatives "derives its powers from the people of America," and "the operation of the government on the people in their individual capacities" makes it "a national government," not merely a federal one. The Federalist No. 39. The Court confirmed this principle in [McCulloch]. [I]t is true that "the people of each State retained their separate political identities," for the Constitution takes care both to preserve the States and to make use of their identities and structures at various points in organizing the federal union. It does not at all follow from this that the sole political identity of an American is with the State of his or her residence. It denies the dual character of the Federal Government which is its very foundation to assert that the people of the United States do not have a political identity as well, one independent of, though consistent with, their identity as citizens of the State of their residence.

[It] might be objected that because the States ratified the Constitution, the people can delegate power only through the States or by acting in their capacities as citizens of particular States. But in [McCulloch], the Court set forth its authoritative rejection of this idea. The political identity of the entire people of the Union is reinforced by the proposition, which I take to be beyond dispute, that, though limited as to its objects, the National Government is and must be controlled by the people without collateral interference by the States. McCulloch affirmed this proposition as well, when the Court rejected the suggestion that States could interfere with federal powers. The States have no power, reserved or otherwise, over the exercise of federal authority within its proper sphere. [T]here exists a federal right of citizenship, a relationship between the people of the Nation and their National Government, with which the States may not interfere. Because the Arkansas enactment intrudes upon this federal domain, it exceeds the boundaries of the Constitution.

■ JUSTICE THOMAS, with whom CHIEF JUSTICE REHNQUIST and JUSTICES O'CONNOR and SCALIA join, dissenting.

[Nothing] in the Constitution deprives the people of each State of the power to prescribe eligibility requirements for the candidates who seek to represent them in Congress. The Constitution is simply silent on this question. And where the Constitution is silent, it raises no bar to action by the States or the people. [Contrary] to the majority's suggestion, the people of the States need not point to any affirmative grant of power in the Constitution in order to prescribe qualifications for their representatives in Congress, or to authorize their elected state legislators to do so. [The] ultimate source of the Constitution's authority is the consent of the people of each individual State, not the consent of the undifferentiated people of the Nation as a whole. The ratification procedure erected by Article VII makes this point clear. The Constitution took effect once it had been ratified by the people gathered in convention in nine different States. But the Constitution went into effect only "between the States so ratifying the same." [In] Madison's words, the popular consent upon which the Constitution's authority rests was "given by the people, not as individuals composing one entire nation, but as composing the distinct and independent States to which they respectively belong." The Federalist No. 39.

When they adopted the Federal Constitution, of course, the people of each State surrendered some of their authority to the United States (and hence to entities accountable to the people of other States as well as to themselves). [Because] the people of the several States are the only true source of power, however, the Federal Government enjoys no authority beyond what the Constitution confers: the Federal Government's powers are limited and enumerated. [As] far as the Federal Constitution is concerned, [the] States can exercise all powers that the Constitution does not withhold from them. The Federal Government and the States thus face different default rules: where the Constitution is silent about the exercise of a particular power—that is, where the Constitution does not speak either expressly or by necessary implication—the Federal Government lacks that power and the States enjoy it. These basic principles are enshrined in the Tenth Amendment.

[To] be sure, when the Tenth Amendment uses the phrase "the people," it does not specify whether it is referring to the people of each State or the people of the Nation as a whole. But the latter interpretation would make the Amendment pointless: there would have been no reason to provide that where the Constitution is silent about whether a particular power resides at the state level, it might or might not do so. In addition, it would make no sense to speak of powers as being reserved to the undifferentiated people of the Nation as a whole, because the Constitution does not contemplate that those people will either exercise power or delegate it. The Constitution simply does not recognize any mechanism for action by the undifferentiated people of the Nation. In short, the notion of popular sovereignty that undergirds the Constitution does not erase state boundaries, but rather tracks them. The people of each State obviously did trust their fate to the people of the several States when they consented to the Constitution. At the same time, however, the people of each State retained their separate political identities.

[According] to the majority, the States possess only those powers that the Constitution affirmatively grants to them or that they enjoyed before the

Constitution was adopted; the Tenth Amendment "could only 'reserve' that which existed before." [The] majority [seeks] support for its view of the Tenth Amendment in [McCulloch]. But this effort is misplaced. McCulloch did make clear that a power need not be "expressly" delegated to the United States or prohibited to the States in order to fall outside the Tenth Amendment's reservation; delegations and prohibitions can also arise by necessary implication. True to the text of the Tenth Amendment, however, McCulloch indicated that all powers as to which the Constitution does not speak (whether expressly or by necessary implication) are "reserved" to the state level. [For] the past 175 years, McCulloch has been understood to rest on the proposition that the Constitution affirmatively barred Maryland from imposing its tax on the Bank's operations. For the majority, however, McCulloch apparently turned on the fact that before the Constitution was adopted, the States had possessed no power to tax the instrumentalities of the governmental institutions that the Constitution created. This understanding of McCulloch makes most of Chief Justice Marshall's opinion irrelevant; according to the majority, there was no need to inquire into whether federal law deprived Maryland of the power in question, because the power could not fall into the category of "reserved" powers anyway.

[T]he only true support for [the majority's] view of the Tenth Amendment comes from Joseph Story's 1833 treatise on constitutional law. Justice Story was a brilliant and accomplished man, and one cannot casually dismiss his views. On the other hand, he was not a member of the Founding generation, and his Commentaries on the Constitution were written a half century after the framing. Rather than representing the original understanding of the Constitution, they represent only his own understanding. In a range of cases concerning the federal/state relation, moreover, this Court has deemed positions taken in Story's commentaries to be more nationalist than the Constitution warrants. In this case too, Story's position that the only powers reserved to the States are those that the States enjoyed before the framing conflicts with both the plain language of the Tenth Amendment and the underlying theory of the Constitution.

[The] Constitution does not call for Members of Congress to be elected by the undifferentiated national citizenry; indeed, it does not recognize any mechanism at all (such as a national referendum) for action by the undifferentiated people of the Nation as a whole. [When] it comes to the selection of Members of Congress, the people of each State have retained their independent political identity. As a result, there is absolutely nothing strange about the notion that the people of the States or their state legislatures possess "reserved" powers in this [area].

TERM LIMITS AND MCCULLOCH

1. ***Opposing structural "default rules" for state and national power.*** In Term Limits, neither text nor historical evidence clearly resolved the issue whether states could impose term limits on congressional representatives. The opposing sides on the Court relied principally on opposite structural default rules to decide the case. In the view of the majority, the states have no reserved powers over the composition or operation of the federal government, because power may not be "reserved" over what does not yet exist. To the majority, the founding was the

constitutional equivalent of the Big Bang. Once it occurred, the states enjoyed only those powers over the federal government that the Constitution delegates to them. To the dissenters, by contrast, the states have all powers, including powers with respect to activities of the federal government, except those the Constitution withholds from them, either directly (e.g., by the express prohibitions in Art. I, § 9), or by necessary implication (as in McCulloch). In the dissenters' view, the states had not delegated to the national government the power to control term limits for federal officers, nor was an implied federal immunity a necessary implication of the federal structure as had been the case in McCulloch.

2. ***Term Limits and representation reinforcement.*** Which of the Term Limits opinions offers the better reading of McCulloch? McCulloch reasoned that a state should not be able to impose taxes on federal taxpayers, in part because residents of other states are not represented in the state's political process. The dissent tries to distinguish McCulloch, suggesting that even if the national government is necessarily immune from state taxation, it is not necessarily immune from state term limits.

But might it be argued that a state's imposition of term limits on its congressional representatives, like a state's taxation of a national bank, imposes negative externalities on citizens of other states, albeit intangible ones? For example, opponents of term limits argued that term limits would reduce the relative seniority of the congressional membership, in turn reducing legislative experience and thus the quality of the nation's governance. Might it be argued that judicial intervention here properly prevented Arkansas from "dumbing down Congress" in a way that rendered other states' representatives less effective? Or was this case in fact the inverse of McCulloch? While Maryland hoarded benefits and exported costs to citizens of other states by taxing the national bank, might it be argued that Arkansas only hurt its own citizens by imposing term limits, for it reduced the relative seniority and therefore power of its own state delegation in Congress? In any event, was judicial intervention truly needed here? If Congress believed it would be weakened by state-imposed term limits, why not enact legislation expressly prohibiting such measures? For discussion of these questions, see Sullivan, "Dueling Sovereignties: U.S. Term Limits, Inc. v. Thornton," 109 Harv. L. Rev. 78 (1995).

3. ***Reliance on the Federalist Papers.*** All three Term Limits opinions cite the Federalist Papers in support of their assertions of original understanding. Indeed, Justice Kennedy's concurrence and Justice Thomas's dissent both rely on The Federalist, No. 39, Justice Kennedy for the proposition that the " 'the operation of the government on the people in their individual capacities' makes [the government] 'a national government,' not merely a federal one," and Justice Thomas for the proposition that "the popular consent upon which the Constitution's authority rests was 'given by the people, not as individuals composing one entire nation, but as composing the distinct and independent States to which they respectively belong.' " As Term Limits demonstrates, reliance on the Federalist Papers has become an established form of constitutional interpretation. Should it be? Does it matter that constitutional historians disagree regarding the degree to which the delegates to the Constitutional Convention relied on the arguments advanced in the Federalist Papers? See, e.g., Kramer, "Madison's Audience," 112 Harv. L. Rev. 611 (1999) (arguing that James Madison's famous theory of factionalism, as expounded in The Federalist, No. 10, "played essentially

no role in shaping the Constitution or its ratification"). But see Coenen, "A Rhetoric for Ratification: The Argument of 'The Federalist' and its Impact on Constitutional Interpretation," 56 Duke L. J. 469 (2006) (arguing that despite its objective of advocacy, The Federalist has value for interpretation because it intended to set out "something akin to a consensus understanding of the Constitution").

SECTION 4. VALUES SERVED BY FEDERALISM

1. ***Federalism in the Framers' view.*** The Framers intended the vertical separation of powers between the national and state governments to serve the common good while preserving liberty. In The Federalist, No. 51, for example, Madison wrote that the vertical separation of powers between the nation and the states, along with the horizontal separation of powers among the federal branches, would give "double security" to the rights of the people by preventing the concentration of power: "In the compound republic of America, the power surrendered by the people is first divided between two distinct governments, and then the portion allotted to each subdivided among distinct and separate departments. Hence a double security arises to the rights of the people. The different governments will control each other, at the same time that each will be controlled by itself."

The framers also reasoned that each level of government, federal and state, had distinctive contributions to make to national welfare. They believed that some roles, such as national defense and the regulation of interstate commerce, were best allocated to the federal government because state regulation was unlikely to succeed. As Alexander Hamilton wrote in The Federalist, No. 25, for example, when enemies "encircle the union from Maine to Georgia," the common danger ought to be defended against by "a common treasury," lest "the security of all [be] subjected to the parsimony, improvidence or inability of a part." On the other hand, they expected state regulation of most aspects of public policy to be the default norm.

2. ***Structural changes in the federal system.*** The Civil War and its aftermath, the rise of national regulatory agencies in the early twentieth century and the acceleration of that development in the New Deal, however, resulted in limits to state power and a significant shift in power from the states to the national government, leading many to question the continuing viability of federalism as a check on national power. For example, the Fourteenth Amendment, already a major limit on state power, was eventually interpreted to apply virtually the entire Bill of Rights to the states. The Seventeenth Amendment, which provided for direct election of U.S. senators by the people instead of state legislatures, eliminated the most significant structural control the states had over the national legislature. And following the New Deal, Congress pursued and the Supreme Court approved a vast expansion in federal regulatory power over areas traditionally associated with the "police" powers of the states.

In light of these changes, do states have the capability to check federal tyranny in the twenty-first century? If so, following years of expansion of federal power, which powers should they choose to limit? Is there any principled way in which states can make this determination? Does federalism still serve the values set forth by the Framers? Responding to critiques of the continuing viability of federalism as a check on national power, both the Supreme Court and commentators have articulated various reasons why federal or state regulation might well have different comparative advantages. For general discussion of the institutional design of the federal system of government and the comparative merits of state and federal regulation, see Shapiro, Federalism—A Dialogue (1995); Merritt, "The Guarantee Clause and State Autonomy: Federalism for a Third Century," 88 Colum. L. Rev. 1 (1988); and McConnell, "Federalism: Evaluating the Founders' Design," 54 U. Chi. L. Rev. 1484 (1987).

3. ***Values promoted by state autonomy.*** Why might preserving some realm of state and local autonomy free of overriding national control be valuable as a matter of political and economic theory? Classic arguments include the following: First, state and local governments can deal with problems that vary geographically by tailoring policies to fit locally varying circumstances. See Tocqueville, Democracy in America ("In large centralized nations the lawgiver is bound to give the laws a uniform character which does not fit the diversity of places and of mores."). Second, state and local governments can compete for citizens and investment by offering varying policies to accommodate diverse preferences and ideologies, enabling citizens to "vote with their feet" by choosing the locale where they will be governed in the manner they prefer. Easterbrook, "Antitrust and the Economics of Federalism," 26 J.L. & Econ. 23, 33–35 (1983). Third, state experimentation in social policy can yield new practices later adopted elsewhere in the nation; as famously noted by Justice Brandeis, "It is one of the happy incidents of the federal system that a single courageous state may, if its citizens choose, serve as a laboratory; and try novel social and economic experiments without risk to the rest of the country." New State Ice Co. v. Liebmann, 285 U.S. 262 (1932) (Brandeis, J. dissenting). Fourth, the smaller scale of state and local government enables government to be closer to the citizenry, arguably making it more accessible and more responsive to citizen preferences and needs while allowing citizens greater opportunity to participate in and in turn to influence public policy. See Gregory v. Ashcroft, 501 U.S. 452, 458 (1991) (O'Connor, J.). Fifth, particular federal powers may prove especially dangerous at the national level because they are subject to particular abuse if one faction captures control: "For example, it might be better to have most policing done at the local level and avoid a national police force because of the dangers to civil liberties if there is a capture by autocratic rulers at the national level." Chemerinsky, "The Values of Federalism," 47 Fla. L. Rev. 499, 526 (1995) (discussing Rapaczynski, "From Sovereignty to Process: The Jurisprudence of Federalism After Garcia," 1985 Sup. Ct. Rev. 341, 388).

Taken together, to what degree do the above arguments apply to a specifically *federal* system? Are some of them founded in mere notions of decentralization, not federalism? Consider the following argument: "[M]any standard arguments advanced for federalism are clearly nothing more than policy arguments for decentralization. These are the claims that some nationally-defined policy is best achieved by permitting regional variation. [In] contrast, federalism allows the states to vary as they choose, pursuing their own policies instead of the national one. [Of] the standard arguments for federalism, four are really arguments that specific national policies are best implemented by decentralized decision-making; these are public participation, effectuating citizen choice through competition among jurisdictions, achieving economic efficiency through competition among jurisdictions, and encouraging experimentation." Rubin & Feeley, "Federalism: Some Notes on a National Neurosis," 41 UCLA L. Rev. 903, 925 (1994). See also, Fontana, "Federal Decentralization," 104 Va. L. Rev. 727

(2018) (arguing that though it currently lacks "a seat at the constitutional law table," federal decentralization "is emerging as one of the defining constitutional issues of our time").

4. ***Values promoted by national policymaking.*** When, by contrast, might the national government be a better source of regulation than the states? When might it be inefficient or otherwise undesirable to leave regulatory authority solely or principally with the states? Classic arguments for the expansive exercise of power at the national level counter those for decentralized state control outlined above: First, national regulation can respond to negative externalities (such as air pollution) by which activities in one state impose costs on those resident in another state. Second, the national government can provide certain "public goods" (such as a common defense against foreign enemies) that any state government, left to its own devices, will underproduce because it is subject to "free riders" and therefore cannot completely capture the benefits of its investment. Third, because of its larger scale and collective resources, the national government can provide better social insurance against catastrophes that occur unpredictably and vary geographically in their incidence (hurricanes for some; blizzards, earthquakes, tornadoes or floods for others). Fourth, the national government can redistribute resources (for example for education or health care) among the populations of different states whose citizens enjoy greatly unequal wealth and income. Fifth, national regulation can prevent the destructive aspects of competition among the states, for example where states seek to attract investment by allowing low-cost child labor or adult labor in sweatshop conditions; in such circumstances, arguably only national child-labor, minimum-wage and maximum-hour legislation can prevent "races to the bottom" among the states. Sixth, Justice Brandeis might have exaggerated the role of state experimentation in fomenting better solutions to universal problems, as "individual states will have no incentive to invest in experiments that involve any substantive or political risk, but will prefer to wait for other states to generate them." Rubin & Feeley, above.

Just as the above arguments counter the argument that efficiency will be best served by state regulation, other arguments counter the view that state regulation best serves liberty. According to one view, the animating principle behind a federal government of limited powers and a Bill of Rights that originally proscribed only federal government action is an expectation that states would serve as the primary protectors of individual liberty. It is therefore sometimes argued that states are better situated to protect individual rights than is the national government. See, e.g., Steven G. Calabresi, "A Government of Limited and Enumerated Powers: In Defense of United States v. Lopez," 94 Mich. L. Rev. 752, 787 (1995). In Bond v. United States, 564 U.S. 211 (2011) Justice Kennedy wrote for the Court: "Federalism secures the freedom of the individual. It allows States to respond, through the enactment of positive law, to the initiative of those who seek a voice in shaping the destiny of their own times without having to rely solely upon the political processes that control a remote central power." But what if the majority of a smaller polity holds a discriminatory view against a given minority? In such instances, might local responsiveness cause the very government tyranny federalism seeks to avoid? On this view, basic rights are best established and preserved at the more centralized level of government. James Madison argued in The Federalist, No. 10 and elsewhere that a local polity would be more easily captured by special interests than decisionmakers at the national level. This led to his famous prescription, which he considered the key to achieving the "great desideratum" of republican government that focused on protecting minorities: "Extend the sphere and you take in a greater variety of parties and interests; you make it less probable that a majority of the whole will have a common motive to invade the rights of other citizens." The adoption of the Fourteenth Amendment, and the incorporation of the majority of the Bill of Rights through its Due Process Clause, indicates a recognition that in certain instances, states may themselves be a threat to individual liberty. For an argument that federalism itself in fact endangers liberty, see Neuman, "Federalism and Freedom: A Critique," in The American Political Arena: Selected Readings 7 (J. Fiszman ed. 1966).

5. ***Who is the best guardian of federalism?*** Even if it is assumed that federalism should be promoted on the basis of these values, which institutional actor is best suited to ensure its vitality? Should the Supreme Court assume an activist role? Or should it channel responsibility for protecting state autonomy principally to the political process? The latter view is advanced in the classic article by Herbert Wechsler, "The Political Safeguards of Federalism—The Role of the States in the Composition and Selection of the National Government," 54 Colum. L. Rev. 543 (1954). In that article, Wechsler argued: "The actual extent of central intervention in the governance of our affairs is determined far less by the formal power distribution than by the sheer existence of the states and their political power to influence the action of the national authority. [National action has] always been regarded as exceptional in our polity, an intrusion to be justified by some necessity, the special rather than the ordinary case. [Even] when Congress acts, its tendency has been to frame enactments on an ad hoc basis to accomplish limited objectives, supplanting state-created norms only so far as may be necessary for the purpose. [Moreover, states play a] crucial role in the selection and the composition of the national authority. Representatives no less than Senators are allotted by the Constitution to the states, although their number varies with state population as determined by the census. [And] with the President, as with Congress, the crucial instrument of the selection—whether through electors, or, in the event of failure of majority, by the House voting as state units—is again the states. The consequence, of course, is that the states are the strategic yardsticks for the measurement of interest and opinion, the special centers of political activity, the separate geographical determinants of national as well as local politics. [If] this analysis is correct, the national political process in the United States—and especially the role of the states in the composition and selection of the central government—is intrinsically well adapted to retarding or restraining new intrusions by the center on the domain of the states."

For an argument that goes even further than Wechsler, concluding that the political safeguards of federalism are so adequate that the Court should "abstain from deciding constitutional questions of national power versus states' rights" altogether, see Choper, Judicial Review and the National Political Process (1980).

But, as noted above, are these arguments for the existence of political safeguards of federalism outdated and inadequate? As Justice Powell noted in dissent in Garcia v. San Antonio Metropolitan Transit Authority, 469 U.S. 528 (1985) (p. 170 below), which held that the federal government could extend the requirements of the Fair Labor Standards Act (FLSA) to state and local governments, many of the "political safeguards of federalism" noted by Wechsler have long since been eroded by structural change that has diminished the role of the states qua states in the national political process. For example, the 17th Amendment displaced state legislative control of the Senate by providing for the popular election of Senators, and the rise of national parties, national organized constituencies, and national media have greatly reduced the role of the electoral college in selecting Presidents.

How might political safeguards of federalism still operate despite these structural changes? Even if Wechsler overstated the formal political safeguards, might other, less formal features of the political process still protect a role for the states? Justice Blackmun noted in Garcia how effective the states had been as lobbyists for their own causes in federal policymaking. The political clout of lobbying organizations such as the National League of Cities, the National Governors Association, the U.S. Conference of Mayors and the National Association of Attorneys General is considerable. Indeed, after Garcia was decided, Congress amended the FLSA to reduce federal hour and wage requirements on the states. The FLSA Amendments of 1985 allowed state employers to substitute compensatory time off for mandatory overtime pay. Does this enactment suggest that the states can protect themselves in the political process without the help of the Supreme Court? Consider as well the fact that "states have remained the primary training ground for federal officials," while "the federal government depends on state administrators to oversee or implement so many of its programs." Kramer, "Putting the Politics Back in to the Political Safeguards of Federalism," 100 Colum. L. Rev. 215 (2000).

Might the rise of the political party system, about which Justice Powell worried, actually have helped preserve the political power of the states? Consider the following view: "The structural protections identified by Wechsler, Choper, and company are marginal at best. [Still,] it's hard to escape the feeling that [something] is acting to perpetuate the role of the states. [States] remain powerful and important institutions in American life [and] most of the law that really [matters] is still state law. So if the institutions relied on by the Framers don't do it, what are the mechanisms that make this happen? [Over] the course of American history, the principal institution in brokering state/federal relations [has] been the political party. Parties have done this by linking the fortunes of officeholders at state and federal levels, fostering a mutual dependency that protects state institutions by inducing federal lawmakers to take account of (at least some) desires of state officials." Kramer, "Understanding Federalism," 47 Vand. L. Rev. 1485 (1994).

Might there be yet another explanation for the continuing vitality of the states as institutional actors? Is it possible that federalism is being sustained, at least in part, by substantive constitutional commitments expressed by state officials on behalf of their constituents? See Joseph Blocher, "Popular Constitutionalism and the States Attorneys General," 122 Harv. L. Rev. F. 108 (2011) (arguing that the federalism arguments advanced by states attorneys general during Supreme Court litigation were rooted more in popular constitutionalism than in the interests of states as states).

Even if the political safeguards of federalism are weaker today than in previous eras, does it follow that judicial intervention to protect the states is required? Consider the view that judicial competence in this area is questionable because "it is not evident as a matter of constitutional law how significant a role the states must play, how important the functions they retain must be, in order for the constitutional minimum to be satisfied. It is obvious that today the significance of the states is considerably less in comparison to the federal government than it was at the time of the framers. It is also evident that the balance need not remain exactly what it was in 1789." Field, "Garcia v. San Antonio Metro. Transit Authority: The Demise of a Misguided Doctrine," 99 Harv. L. Rev. 84 (1985).

CHAPTER 3

THE COMMERCE POWER AND ITS FEDERALISM-BASED LIMITS

Creating effective national regulatory power over interstate commerce was a major motivation for the framing of the Constitution in place of the Articles of Confederation. Indeed, the poor condition of American commerce and the proliferating trade rivalries among the states were the immediate provocations for the calling of the Constitutional Convention. In response to those concerns, the Constitution, Art. I, § 8, cl. 3, granted Congress the power "To Regulate Commerce with foreign Nations, and among the Several States, and with the Indian Tribes." As Alexander Hamilton wrote in The Federalist, No. 22, a central purpose of that grant was to suppress the "interfering and unneighborly regulations of some States"—regulations which, "if not restrained by a national control," would prove to be ever more "serious sources of animosity and discord." The national commerce power, it was hoped, would help end hostile state restrictions, retaliatory trade regulations, and protective tariffs on imports from other states, promoting a national market and curbing the balkanization of the economy.

Since Chief Justice Marshall's day, the Court has often considered the scope and limits of the commerce power. The Commerce Clause has proved to be a central basis for the assertion of national regulatory authority. In the early decades of the twentieth century, the Court frequently struck down national regulatory laws as exceeding the proper scope of the commerce power. Beginning in 1937, however, the Court showed great deference to congressional action under the commerce power; indeed, no law was struck down as exceeding the reach of the commerce power for nearly six decades. The Court's 1995 decision in United States v. Lopez and its United States v. Morrison decision five years later marked a partial return to judicial intervention to prevent the Commerce Clause from becoming an unlimited national police power.

In examining these developments, consider both the substantive issue of the appropriate division of regulatory responsibility between the federal government and the states, and the institutional question of whether the courts are capable of setting workable boundaries to federal regulatory power. What are the relative merits of unified national regulation and diverse state regulation? Are the political restraints on Congress adequate to protect federalism-related values? Or is judicial intervention required because Congress has irreducible incentives to aggrandize its power at the expense of the states?

After examining the possibility of judicially enforced *internal* limits on the congressional commerce power, this chapter turns to judicial implication of additional *external* limits derived from the structural principles of federalism as reiterated in the Tenth and Eleventh Amendments. Even if

Congress otherwise might regulate a matter of interstate commerce, should a concern for state sovereignty and autonomy give rise to judicially enforceable defenses against regulation that would invade states' "traditional" or "integral" sovereign functions, "commandeer" their legislative processes, or abrogate their sovereign immunity against monetary damages? These cases raise similar concerns about central versus diverse legislation and about the desirability and administrability of the judicial role as the cases discussed earlier in the chapter.

Although this chapter focuses on the commerce power to explore limits on national regulation because congressional resort to that power has been such a prolific source of litigation, similar issues of restraint on national power have arisen in the context of the taxing and spending powers, which are explored below in Chapter 4. The flip side of the commerce power—its use by the Court as a negative source of implied restraint on *state* regulatory power that might interfere with free trade among the states—is explored below in Chapter 5.

SECTION 1. THE COMMERCE POWER BEFORE THE NEW DEAL

Chief Justice Marshall gave an expansive interpretation to the Commerce Clause early in the nineteenth century in a case involving a challenge to a state steamboat monopoly. The New York legislature granted to Robert Livingston and Robert Fulton the exclusive right to operate steamboats in New York waters, and Livingston and Fulton licensed Aaron Ogden to operate a ferry between New York City and Elizabethtown, New Jersey. Thomas Gibbons, once Ogden's partner, began operating a competing steamboat service in violation of Ogden's monopoly. Gibbons's ferries were licensed as "vessels to be employed in the coasting trade" under a federal statute enacted in 1793. Ogden obtained an injunction from the New York courts that ordered Gibbons, under New York law, to stop operating his ferries in New York waters. The Court interpreted the federal statute to preempt the New York monopoly law under Supremacy Clause of Article VI, and thus held Gibbons authorized to operate his ferry in New York waters. Chief Justice Marshall began his opinion with an examination of the scope of the commerce power underlying the federal statute, which entitled licensed ferry operators to "the privileges of ships or vessels employed in the coasting trade" and imposed fines for operating without a license:

Gibbons v. Ogden

9 Wheat. (22 U.S.) 1, 6 L. Ed. 23 (1824).

■ CHIEF JUSTICE MARSHALL delivered the opinion of the Court:

The subject to be regulated is commerce; and [to] ascertain the extent of the power, it becomes necessary to settle the meaning of the word. The counsel for the appellee would limit it to traffic, to buying and selling, or the interchange of commodities, and do not admit that it comprehends navigation. This would restrict a general term, applicable to many objects, to one of its significations. Commerce, undoubtedly, is traffic, but it is something more—it is intercourse. It describes the commercial intercourse between nations, and parts of nations, in all its branches, and is regulated by prescribing rules for carrying on that intercourse. [If] commerce does not include navigation, the government of the Union has no direct power over that subject, and can make no law prescribing what shall constitute American vessels, or requiring that they shall be navigated by American seamen. Yet this power has been exercised from the commencement of the government, has been exercised with the consent of all, and has been understood by all to be a commercial regulation. All America understands, and has uniformly understood, the word "commerce" to comprehend navigation.

The subject to which the power [is] applied [is] commerce "among the several states." The word "among" means intermingled with. A thing which is among others, is intermingled with them. Commerce among the states cannot stop at the external boundary line of each state, but may be introduced into the interior. It is not intended to say that these words comprehend that commerce which is completely internal, which is carried on between man and man in a state, or between different parts of the same state, and which does not extend to or affect other states. Such a power would be inconvenient, and is certainly unnecessary.

Comprehensive as the word "among" is, it may very properly be restricted to that commerce which concerns more states than one. The phrase is not one which would probably have been selected to indicate the completely interior traffic of a state, because it is not an apt phrase for that purpose; and the enumeration of the particular classes of commerce to which the power was to be extended, would not have been made, had the intention been to extend the power to every description. The enumeration presupposes something not enumerated; and that something, if we regard the language or the subject of the sentence, must be the exclusively internal commerce of a state. The genius and character of the whole government seem to be, that its action is to be applied to all the external concerns of the nation, and to those internal concerns which affect the states generally; but not to those which are completely within a particular state, which do not affect other states, and with which it is not necessary to interfere, for the purpose of executing some of the general powers of the government. The completely internal commerce of a state, then, may be considered as reserved for the state itself.

[The commerce power is] the power to regulate; that is, to prescribe the rule by which commerce is to be governed. This power, like all others vested in congress, is complete in itself, may be exercised to its utmost extent, and acknowledges no limitations, other than are prescribed in the constitution. [If], as has always been understood, the sovereignty of congress, though limited to specified objects, is plenary as to those objects, the power over [commerce] is vested in congress as absolutely as it would be in a single government, having in its constitution the same restrictions on the exercise of the power as are found in the constitution of the United States. The wisdom and the discretion of congress, their identity with the people, and the influence which their constituents possess at elections, are, in this, as in many other instances, as that, for example, of declaring war, the sole restraints on which they have relied, to secure them from its abuse. They are the restraints on which the people must often rely solely, in all representative governments.

JUDICIAL LIMITS ON THE COMMERCE POWER

1. ***The "direct vs. indirect" effects test.*** Affirmative exercise of the national commerce power was rare before 1887. For example, Congress enacted laws to improve water and land transportation, and laws prohibiting the importation of counterfeit money, see United States v. Marigold, 9 How. (50 U.S.) 560 (1850). Large-scale commercial regulation by Congress did not begin, however, until nineteenth century developments in industrialization, transportation, and communication gave rise to such legislation as the Interstate Commerce Act of 1887 and the Sherman Antitrust Act of 1890. Challenges to those statutes launched new judicial limitations on congressional authority over commerce.

Three principal judicial approaches emerged. Under the first, what mattered was whether the regulated activity had a "direct" or "indirect" effect on interstate commerce. In **United States v. E.C. Knight Co. [The Sugar Trust Case]**, 156 U.S. 1 (1895), for example, the Court affirmed the dismissal of a government civil action under the Sherman Act to set aside the acquisition by the American Sugar Refining Company of the stock of four other sugar refineries. Section 1 of the Sherman Act prohibited any contract, combination, or conspiracy "in restraint of trade or commerce among the several states." Section 2 provided penalties for any person "who shall monopolize, or combine or conspire [to] monopolize any part of the trade or commerce among the several states." The Government alleged that the acquired companies had produced about 33% of all sugar refined in the United States, and that American's acquisition gave it control of 98% of the nation's sugar refining capacity. The Court interpreted the statute not to extend to the challenged monopoly, based on the view that Congress could not constitutionally regulate "manufacture" under the Commerce Clause.

Chief Justice FULLER wrote for the Court: "Doubtless the power to control the manufacture of a given thing involves in a certain sense the control of its disposition, but this is a secondary and not the primary sense; and although the exercise of that power may result in bringing the operation of commerce into play, it does not control it, and affects it only incidentally and indirectly. Commerce succeeds to manufacture, and is not a part of it. [The] regulation of commerce applies to the subjects of commerce and not to matters of internal police. Contracts to buy, sell, or exchange goods to be transported among the several States, the transportation and its instrumentalities, and articles bought, sold, or exchanged for the purposes of such transit among the States, or put in the way of transit, may be regulated, but this is because they form part of interstate trade or commerce. The fact that an article is manufactured for export to another State does not of itself make it an article of interstate commerce, and the intent of the manufacturer does not determine the time when the article or product passes from the control of the State and belongs to commerce. [Contracts,] combinations, or conspiracies to control domestic enterprise in manufacture, agriculture, mining, production in all its forms, or to raise or lower prices or wages, might unquestionably tend to restrain external as well as domestic trade, but the restraint would be an indirect result, however inevitable and whatever its extent, and such result would not necessarily determine the object of the contract, combination, or conspiracy. [Slight] reflection will show that if the national power extends to all contracts and combinations in manufacture, agriculture, mining, and other productive industries, whose ultimate result may affect external commerce, comparatively little of business operations and affairs would be left for state control." As thus interpreted by the majority, the Sherman Act did not permit the suit against the Sugar Trust because the challenged actions "related exclusively to the acquisition of the Philadelphia refineries" and "bore no direct relation to commerce between the States."

Justice HARLAN dissented: "Any combination [that] disturbs or unreasonably obstructs freedom in buying and selling articles manufactured to be sold to persons in other States or to be carried to other States [affects] not incidentally, but directly, the people of all the States; and the remedy for such an evil is found only in the exercise of powers confided to [the national government.] While the opinion of the court in this case does not declare the act [to] be unconstitutional, it defeats the main object for which it was passed. For it is, in effect, held that the statute would be unconstitutional if interpreted as embracing such unlawful restraints upon the purchasing of goods in one State to be carried to another State as necessarily arise from the existence of combinations formed for the purpose and with the effect, not only of monopolizing the ownership of all such goods in every part of the country, but of controlling the prices for them in all the States. This view of the scope of the act leaves the public, so far as national power is concerned, entirely at the mercy of combinations which arbitrarily control the prices of articles purchased to be transported from one State to another State. [In] my judgment, the general government is not placed by the Constitution in such a condition of helplessness that it must fold its arms and remain inactive while capital combines, under the name of a corporation, to destroy competition, not in one State only, but throughout the entire country, in the buying and selling of articles—especially the necessaries of life—that go into commerce among the States."

2. ***The "substantial economic effects" test.*** Even while the formalistic "direct-indirect" distinction drawn in Knight remained on the books, an alternative approach arose, emphasizing instead the practical physical or economic effects of the regulated intrastate activities on interstate commerce. Under this approach, the Court upheld most congressional regulation of the railroad industry. In **Houston, East & West Texas Railway Co. v. United States [The Shreveport Rate Case]**, 234 U.S. 342 (1914), for example, the Court sustained congressional authority to regulate intrastate rail rates that discriminated against interstate railroad traffic. Several railroads had set rates for hauls between points within Texas lower than rates for hauls between points within Texas and Shreveport, Louisiana. The Interstate Commerce Commission (ICC) found that this rate structure "unjustly discriminated in favor of traffic within the state of Texas, and against similar traffic between Louisiana and Texas," and ordered the railroads to end the discrimination. The railroads challenged the ICC order, arguing that "Congress is impotent to control the intrastate charges of an interstate carrier."

Justice HUGHES's majority opinion rejected that challenge, holding that congressional authority, "extending to these interstate carriers as instruments of interstate commerce, necessarily embraces the right to control their operations in all matters having such a close and substantial relation to interstate traffic that the control is essential or appropriate to the security of that traffic, to the efficiency of the interstate service, and to the maintenance of conditions under which interstate commerce may be conducted upon fair terms and without molestation or hindrance. As it is competent for Congress to legislate to these ends, unquestionably it may seek their attainment by requiring that the agencies of interstate commerce shall not be used in such manner as to cripple, retard, or destroy it. The fact that carriers are instruments of intrastate commerce, as well as of interstate commerce, does not derogate from the complete and paramount authority of Congress over the latter, or preclude the Federal power from being exerted to prevent the intrastate operations of such carriers from being made a means of injury to that which has been confided to Federal care. Whenever the interstate and intrastate transactions of carriers are so related that the government of the one involves the control of the other, it is Congress, and not the State, that is entitled to prescribe the final and dominant rule, for otherwise Congress would be denied the exercise of its constitutional authority and the State, and not the Nation, would be supreme within the national field. [This] is not to say that Congress possesses the authority to regulate the internal commerce of a State, as such, but that it does possess the power to foster and protect interstate commerce, and to take all measures necessary or appropriate to that end, although intrastate transactions of interstate carriers may thereby be controlled." Justices Lurton and Pitney dissented.

3. ***The "stream of commerce" test.*** A third judicial approach suggested that some local activities could be regulated by Congress because they could be viewed as themselves "in" commerce or as an integral part of the "current of commerce." In sustaining a Sherman Act injunction against price fixing by meat dealers in **Swift & Co. v. United States**, 196 U.S. 375 (1905), for example, Justice HOLMES stated: "When cattle are sent for sale from a place in one State, with the expectation that they will end their transit, after purchase in another, and when in effect they do so, with only the interruption necessary to find a purchaser at the stockyard, and when this is a typical, constantly recurring course, the current thus existing is a current of commerce among the States, and the purchase of the cattle is a part and incident of such commerce. [Commerce] among the States is not a technical legal conception, but a practical one, drawn from the course of business."

4. ***National "police" regulation.*** Congress used the commerce power increasingly in the late nineteenth century not only to deal with the emerging problems of the national economy but also with problems of morality and criminality such as gambling, prostitution, and theft. Such legislation seemed to aim primarily at moral concerns rather than the economic concerns that had prompted the Commerce Clause. And while such congressional sanctions were imposed at the state line on interstate movements, the harm sought to be alleviated was primarily local. For a Progressive Era article advocating broad use of the Commerce Clause to exercise an "extensive national police power" to halt "objectionable commodities" or "objectionable transaction[s]," see Cushman, "The National Police Power Under the Commerce Clause of the Constitution," 3 Minn. L. Rev. 289, 381 (1919) ("[C]ongressional responsibility for the safe, free, uninterrupted flow of commerce between the states carries with it the constitutional authority to legislate on a wide range of problems, not commonly regarded as commercial in character, which vitally affect the national safety and welfare.").

In **Champion v. Ames [The Lottery Case]**, 188 U.S. 321 (1903), the Court upheld the Federal Lottery Act of 1895, which prohibited importing, mailing, or interstate transporting of lottery tickets, against constitutional challenge by a man indicted for shipping a box of Paraguayan lottery tickets from Texas to California. In a 5–4 ruling, Justice HARLAN wrote for that Court that "lottery tickets are subjects of traffic and therefore are subjects of commerce" and that the prohibition of commerce lay within the regulatory power of Congress. He continued: "[T]he suppression of nuisances injurious to public health or morality is among the most important duties of Government. [If] a State, when considering legislation for the suppression of lotteries within its own limits, may properly take into view the evils that inhere in the raising of money, in that mode, why may not Congress, invested with the power to regulate commerce among the several States, provide that such commerce shall not be polluted by the carrying of lottery tickets from one State to another? [As] a State may, for the purpose of guarding the morals of its own people, forbid all sales of lottery tickets within its limits, so Congress, for the purpose of guarding the people of the United States against the 'widespread pestilence of lotteries' and to protect the commerce which concerns all the States, may prohibit the carrying of lottery tickets from one State to another. In legislating upon the subject of the traffic in lottery tickets, as carried on through interstate commerce, Congress only supplemented the action of those States—perhaps all of them—which, for the protection of the public morals, prohibit the drawing of lotteries, as well as the sale or circulation of lottery tickets, within their respective limits.

"It is said, however, that if, in order to suppress lotteries carried on through interstate commerce, Congress may exclude lottery tickets from such commerce, that principle leads necessarily to the conclusion that Congress may arbitrarily exclude from commerce among the States any article, commodity or thing, of whatever kind or nature, or however useful or valuable, which it may choose, no matter with what motive. [It] will be time enough to consider the constitutionality of such legislation when we must do so. [It] would not be difficult to imagine legislation that [would be] hostile to the objects for the accomplishment of which Congress was invested with the general power to regulate commerce among the several States. But [the] possible abuse of a power is not an argument against its existence."

Chief Justice FULLER's dissent, joined by Justices Brewer, Shiras, and Peckham, responded: "That the purpose of Congress in this enactment was the suppression of lotteries cannot reasonably be denied. [Doubtless] an act prohibiting the carriage of lottery matter would be necessary and proper to the execution of a power to suppress lotteries; but that power belongs to the States and not to Congress. To hold that Congress has general police power would be to hold that it may accomplish objects not entrusted to the General Government, and to defeat the operation of the 10th Amendment. [To] transform a non-commercial article into a commercial one simply because it is transported [would take] a long step in the direction of wiping out all traces of state lines, and the creation of a centralized Government." The dissent distinguished cases involving the "power to prohibit the transportation of diseased animals and infected goods over railroads or on steamboats" as regulations of activities "in themselves injurious to the transaction of interstate commerce, and [essentially] commercial in their nature."

The Lottery Case precedent helped to sustain a wide variety of early-twentieth-century laws excluding from interstate commerce objects or persons claimed to be harmful. For example, in **Hipolite Egg Co. v. United States**, 220 U.S. 45 (1911), preserved eggs then located on the buyer's shelves had been confiscated under the Pure Food and Drugs Act of 1906 because the labels failed to disclose that they contained a "deleterious" ingredient. The action was challenged on the ground that "the shipment had passed out of interstate commerce before the seizure of the eggs." A unanimous Court rejected the attack. Justice McKENNA wrote: "The question here is whether articles which are outlaws of commerce may be seized wherever found. [Can] they escape the consequences of their illegal transportation by being mingled at the place of destination with other property? To give them such immunity would defeat, in many cases, the provision for their confiscation, and their confiscation or destruction is the especial concern of the law. The power to do so is certainly appropriate to the right to bar them from interstate commerce, and completes its purpose, which is not to prevent merely the physical movement of adulterated articles, but the use of them, or rather to prevent trade in them between the States by denying to them the facilities of interstate commerce. And appropriate means to that end, which we have seen is legitimate, are the seizure and condemnation of the articles at their point of destination. [McCulloch]."

In **Hoke v. United States**, 227 U.S. 308 (1913), the Court upheld the Mann Act, prohibiting the transportation of women in interstate commerce for immoral purposes. Again, Justice McKENNA wrote for a unanimous Court: "[Surely] if the facility of interstate transportation can be taken away from the demoralization of lotteries, the debasement of obscene literature, the contagion of diseased cattle or persons, the impurity of food and drugs, the like facility can be taken away from the systematic enticement to and the enslavement in prostitution and debauchery of women, and, more insistently, of girls. [The] principle established by the cases is the simple one, [that] Congress has power over transportation 'among the several States'; that the power is complete in itself, and that Congress, as an incident to it, may adopt not only means necessary but convenient to its exercise, and the means may have the quality of police regulations."

In contrast to the decisions upholding laws banning shipment of goods deemed to reflect harmful practices, however, the Court struck down a 1916 statute that excluded the products of child labor from interstate commerce.

Hammer v. Dagenhart [The Child Labor Case]

247 U.S. 251, 38 S. Ct. 529, 62 L. Ed. 1101 (1918).

[The challenged law barred the transportation in interstate commerce of goods produced in factories employing children under the age of fourteen or employing those between the ages of fourteen and sixteen for more than eight hours a day or six days a week or at night. The father of two children employed in a cotton mill in North Carolina obtained an injunction barring enforcement of the law on constitutional grounds.]

■ JUSTICE DAY delivered the opinion of the Court:

[The commerce power] is one to control the means by which commerce is carried on, which is directly the contrary of the assumed right to forbid commerce from moving and thus destroying it as to particular commodities. But it is insisted that [The Lottery Case, Hipolite Egg, and Hoke] establish the doctrine that the power to regulate given to Congress incidentally includes the authority to prohibit the movement of ordinary commodities. [These] cases demonstrate the contrary. They rest upon the character of the particular subjects dealt with and the fact that the scope of governmental authority, state or national, possessed over them is such that the authority to prohibit is as to them but the exertion of the power to regulate. [In each] of these instances the use of interstate transportation was necessary to the accomplishment of harmful results. In other words, although the power over interstate transportation was to regulate, that could only be accomplished by prohibiting the use of the facilities of interstate commerce to effect the evil intended.

This element is wanting in the present case. [The] act in its effect does not regulate transportation among the states, but aims to standardize the ages at which children may be employed in mining and manufacturing within the states. The goods shipped are of themselves harmless. [When] offered for shipment, and before transportation begins, the labor of their production is over, and the mere fact that they were intended for interstate commerce transportation does not make their production subject to federal control. [Over] interstate transportation, or its incidents, the regulatory power of Congress is ample, but the production of articles, intended for interstate commerce, is a matter of local regulation. [If] it were otherwise, all manufacture intended for interstate shipment would be brought under federal control to the practical exclusion of the authority of the States.

It is further contended that the authority of Congress may be exerted to control interstate commerce in the shipment of child-made goods because of the effect of the circulation of such goods in other States where the evil of this class of labor has been recognized by local legislation, and the right to thus employ child labor has been more rigorously restrained than in the State of production. In other words, that the unfair competition, thus engendered, may be controlled by closing the channels of interstate commerce to manufacturers in those States where the local laws do not meet what Congress deems to be the more just standard of other States. There is no power vested in Congress to require the States to exercise their police power so as to prevent possible unfair competition. Many causes may co-operate to give one State, by reason of local laws or conditions, an economic advantage over others. The Commerce Clause was not intended to give to Congress a general authority to equalize such conditions.

[We] have neither authority nor disposition to question the motives of Congress in enacting this legislation. [The] necessary effect of this act [is] to regulate the hours of labor of children in factories and mines within the States, a purely state authority. Thus the act in a two-fold sense is repugnant to the Constitution. It not only transcends the authority delegated to Congress over commerce but also exerts a power as to a purely local matter to which the federal authority does not extend. The far reaching result of upholding the act cannot be more plainly indicated than by pointing out that if Congress can thus regulate matters entrusted to local authority by prohibition of the movement of commodities in interstate commerce, all freedom of commerce will be at an end, and the power of the States over local matters may be eliminated, and thus our system of government be practically destroyed.

■ JUSTICE HOLMES, joined by JUSTICES MCKENNA, BRANDEIS, and CLARKE, dissenting.

[If] an act is within the powers specifically conferred upon Congress, it seems to me that it is not made any less constitutional because of the indirect effects that it may have, however obvious it may be that it will have those effects. [The] statute confines itself to prohibiting the carriage of certain goods in interstate or foreign commerce. Congress is given power to regulate such commerce in unqualified terms. It would not be argued today that the power to regulate does not include the power to prohibit. [The] question then is narrowed to whether the exercise of its otherwise constitutional power by Congress can be pronounced unconstitutional because of its possible reaction upon the conduct of the States in a matter upon which I have admitted that they are free from direct control. [I] should have thought that the most conspicuous decisions of this Court had made it clear that the power to regulate commerce [could] not be cut down or qualified by the fact that it might interfere with the carrying out of the domestic policy of any State.

[If] there is any matter upon which civilized countries have agreed [it] is the evil of premature and excessive child labor. I should have thought that if we were to introduce our own moral conceptions where in my opinion they do not belong, this was preeminently a case for upholding the exercise of all its powers by the United States. But I had thought that the propriety of the exercise of a power admitted to exist in some cases was for the consideration of Congress alone and that this Court always had disavowed the right to intrude its judgment upon questions of policy or morals. It is not for this Court to pronounce when prohibition is necessary to regulation if it ever may be necessary—to say that it is permissible as against strong drink but not as against the product of ruined lives. The act does not meddle with anything belonging to the States. They may regulate their internal affairs and their domestic commerce as they like. But when they seek to send their products across the state line they are no longer within their rights. [Congress] may carry out its views of public policy whatever indirect effect they may have upon the activities of the States.

SECTION 2. THE COMMERCE POWER AND THE NEW DEAL

1. ***The Supreme Court's invalidation of New Deal measures.*** President Franklin D. Roosevelt took office in 1933 in the midst of the Great Depression with a call for "action, and action now." The nation had experienced sharp drops in employment, production, and income, widespread business failures, and extensive home mortgage foreclosures. Congress enacted a dramatic set of remedial measures under FDR's "New Deal." The government sought to justify these measures under the Commerce Clause as based on the "substantially affecting commerce" rationale in Shreveport and the "in commerce" rationale in Swift, seeking to avoid invalidation on the rationales of cases like Knight and Hammer v. Dagenhart. But the Court increasingly rejected these efforts at justification under the Commerce Clause.

In the first test of major New Deal regulation under the commerce power, the Court invalidated a measure not central to the New Deal program, the Railroad Retirement Act of 1934. In **Railroad Retirement Board v. Alton Railroad Co.**, 295 U.S. 330 (1935), the Court decided by a

5–4 vote that Congress lacked the power to establish a compulsory retirement and pension plan for all carriers subject to the Interstate Commerce Act. Justice ROBERTS's majority opinion concluded that the law was "not in purpose or effect a regulation of interstate commerce within the meaning of the Constitution." He rejected the argument that pensions were "related to efficiency of transportation." Was it not "apparent," he asked, that such regulations "are really and essentially related solely to the social welfare of the worker, and therefore remote from any regulation of commerce as such?"

Other attempts to justify more vital New Deal laws under the commerce power soon failed as well. The National Industrial Recovery Act of 1933 authorized the President—ordinarily upon application by trade associations—to promulgate "codes of fair competition for the trade or industry." Several hundred codes were soon adopted. The typical code contained provisions regarding unfair trade practices, minimum wages and prices, maximum hours, and collective bargaining. Violation of any code provision "in any transaction in or affecting interstate commerce" was made punishable as a misdemeanor. The law was held unconstitutional in **Schechter Poultry Corp. v. United States**, 295 U.S. 495 (1935). The Schechter case (sometimes colloquially called "the sick chicken case") stemmed from convictions for violating the wage, hour, and trade practice provisions of the "Code of Fair Competition for the Live Poultry Industry of the Metropolitan [New York City] Area." The Court held both that the Act unconstitutionally delegated legislative power and that the application of the Act to intrastate activities exceeded the commerce power, and therefore that the wages and hours of employees at Schechter's Brooklyn slaughterhouse, which sold only to local poultry retailers, were not subject to federal control.

Chief Justice HUGHES's opinion for the Court rejected the government's attempted analogies to the "stream of commerce" rationale of Swift and the "affecting commerce" theory of Shreveport. These were not "transactions *'in'* interstate commerce," he insisted: the interstate transactions regarding poultry ended when the shipments reached the Brooklyn slaughterhouse. Nor did Schechter's transactions "directly *'affect'* interstate commerce." He rejected the government's argument "that hours and wages affect prices; that slaughterhouse men sell at a small margin above operating costs; that labor represents 50 to 60 per cent. of these costs; that a slaughterhouse operator paying lower wages or reducing his costs by exacting long hours of work, translates his saving into lower prices; that this results in demands for a cheaper grade of goods; and that the cutting of prices brings about a demoralization of the price structure." That argument, Chief Justice Hughes found, "proves too much": "If the federal government may determine the wages and hours of employees in the internal commerce of a State, because of their relation to cost and prices and their indirect effect upon interstate commerce, it would seem that a similar control might be exerted over other elements of cost, also affecting prices, such as the number of employees, rent, advertising, methods of doing business, etc. All the processes of production and distribution that enter into costs could likewise be controlled. If the cost of doing an intrastate business is in itself the permitted object of federal control, the extent of the regulation of cost would be a question of discretion and not of power." Finally, Chief Justice Hughes rejected an even broader argument "based upon the serious economic situation which led to the passage of the Recovery Act—the fall in prices, the decline in wages and employment, and the curtailment of the market for commodities." He found no constitutional justification in "the great importance of maintaining wage distributions which would provide the necessary stimulus in starting 'the cumulative forces making for expanding commercial activity.'" To that argument, he replied: "Without in any way disparaging this motive, it is enough to say that the recuperative efforts of the federal government must be made in a manner consistent with the authority granted by the Constitution."

Justice CARDOZO, joined by Justice Stone, submitted a brief concurring opinion, agreeing that the law was "delegation running riot" and that the commerce power objection was "far-reaching and incurable." On the latter, he elaborated: "There is a view of causation that would obliterate the distinction between what is national and what is local in the activities of commerce. Motion at the outer rim is communicated perceptibly, though minutely, to recording instruments at the center. [The] law is not indifferent to considerations of degree. Activities local in their immediacy do not become interstate and national because of distant repercussions. What is near and what is distant may at times be uncertain. [To] find immediacy or directness here is to find it almost everywhere. If centripetal forces are to be isolated to the exclusion of the forces that oppose and counteract them, there will be an end to our federal system."

In a press conference soon after Schechter, President Roosevelt expressed concern about the decision: "Does this decision mean that the United States Government has no control over any national economic problem?" The attempt to move the New Deal forward despite Schechter came immediately. For example, the National Labor Relations Act (Wagner Act) became law on July 5, 1935, guaranteeing the right of collective bargaining. And President Roosevelt quickly urged Congress to enact a law establishing an NIRA-like regulatory scheme for the bituminous coal industry. While that bill was pending in a House subcommittee, President Roosevelt wrote a controversial letter to Congressman Hill ending: "I hope your committee will not permit doubts as to constitutionality, however reasonable, to block the suggested legislation." The Bituminous Coal Conservation Act of 1935 was soon enacted, and a court challenge was filed immediately.

In **Carter v. Carter Coal Co.**, 298 U.S. 238 (1936), the Court invalidated the law. Among its objectives was the regulation of maximum hours and minimum wages in coal mines. Producers were to comply with a national bituminous coal code. The minimum wage and maximum hour provisions of the code, binding on all code members, were negotiated by a specified percentage of producers' and workers' representatives. The sanction imposed to make the provisions effective was, in effect, to levy a tax of 13.5% on all producers who did not accept the code. Carter brought a stockholder's suit against his company to enjoin it from paying the tax and complying with the code. Justice SUTHERLAND wrote the majority opinion: "Certain recitals [in] the act [suggest] that the distribution of bituminous coal is of national interest, affecting the health and comfort of the people and the general welfare of the nation. [The] proposition, often advanced and as often discredited, that the power of the federal government inherently extends to purposes affecting the nation as a whole with which the states severally [cannot] adequately deal, and the related notion that Congress, entirely apart from those powers delegated by the Constitution, may enact laws to promote the general welfare, have always definitely [been] rejected by this court. [The] general purposes which the act recites [are] beyond the power of Congress except so far, and only so far, as they may be realized by an exercise of some specific power granted by the Constitution. [W]e find no grant of power which authorizes Congress to legislate in respect of these general purposes unless it be found in the commerce clause—and this we now [consider].

"[T]he effect of the labor provisions of the [act] primarily falls upon production and not upon commerce. [P]roduction is a purely local activity. It follows that none of these essential antecedents of production constitutes a transaction in or forms any part of interstate commerce. [Schechter.] [The] local character of mining, of manufacturing and of crop growing is a fact, and remains a fact, whatever may be done with the products. [That] the production of every commodity intended for interstate sale and transportation has some effect upon interstate commerce may [be] freely granted; and we are brought to the final and decisive inquiry, whether here that effect is direct, as the 'preamble' recites, or indirect. The distinction is not formal, but substantial in the highest degree, as we pointed out in [Schechter].

"Whether the effect of a given activity or condition is direct or indirect is not always easy to determine. The word 'direct' implies that the activity or condition invoked or blamed shall operate proximately—not mediately, remotely, or collaterally—to produce the effect. It connotes the absence of an efficient intervening agency or condition. And the extent of the effect bears no logical relation to its character. The distinction between a direct and an indirect effect turns, not upon the magnitude of either the cause or the effect, but entirely upon the manner in which the effect has been brought about. If the production by one man of a single ton of coal intended for interstate sale and shipment, and actually so sold and shipped, affects interstate commerce indirectly, the effect does not become direct by multiplying the tonnage, or increasing the number of men employed, or adding to the expense or complexities of the business, or by all combined. It is quite true that rules of law are sometimes qualified by considerations of degree, as the government argues. But the matter of degree has no bearing upon the question here, since that question is not—What is the *extent* of the local activity or condition, or the *extent* of the effect produced upon interstate commerce? but—What is the *relation* between the activity or condition and the effect?

"Much stress is put upon the evils which come from the struggle between employers and employees over the matter of wages, working conditions, the right of collective bargaining, etc., and the resulting strikes, curtailment and irregularity of production and effect on prices; and it is insisted that interstate commerce is *greatly* affected thereby. But, [the] conclusive answer is that the evils are all local evils over which the federal government has no legislative control. [Such] effect as they may have upon commerce, however extensive it may be, is secondary and indirect. An increase in the greatness of the effect adds to its importance. It does not alter its character. [A] reading of the entire opinion [in Schechter] makes clear, what we now declare, that the want of power on the part of the federal government is the same whether the wages, hours of service, and working conditions, and the bargaining about them, are related to production before interstate commerce has begun, or to sale and distribution after it has [ended]."

In addition to the wage, hour, and other labor provisions, the code also had provided for minimum and maximum prices for sales of bituminous coal.

The majority opinion did not reach the constitutionality of the price provisions but found them inseverable from the labor provisions and hence invalid. By contrast, Justice CARDOZO's dissent, joined by Justices Brandeis and Stone, found the price provisions constitutional under the commerce power and argued that the suit was premature with respect to the labor provisions. Justice Cardozo wrote: "[I] am satisfied that the Act is within the power of the central government in so far as it provides for minimum and maximum prices. [Regulation] of prices being an exercise of the commerce power in respect of interstate transactions, the question remains whether it comes within that power as applied to intrastate sales where interstate prices are directly or intimately affected. Mining and agriculture and manufacture are not interstate commerce considered by themselves, yet their relation to that commerce may be such that for the protection of the one there is need to regulate the other. Sometimes it is said that the relation must be 'direct' to bring that power into play. In many circumstances such a description will be sufficiently precise to meet the needs of the occasion. [Always] the setting of the facts is to be viewed if one would know the closeness of the tie. Perhaps, if one group of adjectives is to be chosen in preference to another, 'intimate' and 'remote' will be found to be as good as any. At all events, 'direct' and 'indirect,' even if accepted as sufficient, must not be read too narrowly. [Shreveport shows] that the causal relation in such circumstances is so close and intimate and obvious as to permit it to be called direct without subjecting the word to an unfair or excessive strain. There is a like immediacy here. [The] prices for intrastate sales of coal have so inescapable a relation to those for interstate sales that a system of regulation for transactions of the one class is necessary to give adequate protection to the system of regulation adopted for the other." In a separate opinion, Chief Justice Hughes agreed with the majority that the labor provisions were invalid, but found the price provisions constitutional and severable.

2. ***Values underlying the pre-New Deal commerce power limitations.*** Why did the Court invalidate the early social programs of the New Deal on Commerce Clause grounds? One thread in the cases is the principle of enumerated powers: restricting the national power to those explicitly granted in the Constitution. The Court construed the commerce power narrowly, and explicitly rejected, in Schechter and Carter Coal, the functionalist argument that the necessity of a national power to solve national problems might inform the scope of the commerce power. Critics countered that the Court was reading a laissez faire economic ideology into the Constitution. For the view that these holdings represent the Court's longstanding privileging of personal property as "the core" constitutional value, see Feldman, Scorpions: The Battles and Triumphs of FDR's Great Supreme Court Justices 104–05 (2010).

3. ***FDR's Court-packing plan.*** The 1935 and 1936 decisions persuaded the Roosevelt Administration that strong measures were needed to save the New Deal from judicial invalidation. Several major New Deal laws had already been held unconstitutional; others—the National Labor Relations Act and the Social Security Act among them—might well have met a similar fate. Convictions hardened within the Administration that something had to be done about the Court. But President Roosevelt did not make Court reform an issue in his landslide 1936 reelection. Rather, he waited to propose changes in a Message to Congress on February 5, 1937: "[It is] one of the definite duties of the Congress constantly to maintain the

effective functioning of the Federal judiciary. [A]t the present time the Supreme Court is laboring under a heavy burden. [P]art of the problem of obtaining a sufficient number of judges to dispose of cases is the capacity of the judges themselves. This brings forward the question of aged or infirm judges—a subject of delicacy and yet one which requires frank discussion. [Modern] complexities call also for a constant infusion of new blood in the courts, just as it is needed in executive functions of the Government and in private business. [I], therefore, earnestly recommend that the necessity of an increase in the number of judges be supplied by legislation providing for the appointment of additional judges in all Federal courts, without exception, where there are incumbent judges of retirement age who do not choose to retire or to resign."

Six Justices were over seventy in 1937: Butler (71), Hughes (75), Sutherland (75), McReynolds (75), Van Devanter (78), and Brandeis (81). President Roosevelt's proposed bill would have provided: "When any judge of a court of the United States, appointed to hold his office during good behavior, has heretofore or hereafter attained the age of seventy years and has held a commission or commissions as judge of any such court or courts at least ten years, continuously or otherwise, and within six months thereafter has neither resigned nor retired, the President, for each such judge who has not so resigned or retired, shall nominate, and by and with the advice and consent of the Senate, shall appoint one additional judge to the court to which the former is commissioned. [No judge shall] be so appointed if such appointment would result [in] more than fifteen members of the Supreme Court of the United States."

In a radio address to the nation on March 9, 1937, the President challenged the Court more directly and defended his plan more forthrightly: "I want to talk with you very simply about the need for present action in this crisis—the need to meet the unanswered challenge of one-third of a nation ill-nourished, ill-clad, ill-housed. [When] the Congress has sought to stabilize national agriculture, to improve the conditions of labor, to safeguard business against unfair competition, to protect our national resources, and in many other ways to serve our clearly national needs, the majority of the Court has been assuming the power to pass on the wisdom of these acts of the Congress—and to approve or disapprove the public policy written into these laws. [We] have, therefore, reached the point as a Nation where we must take action to save the Constitution from the Court and the Court from itself. [This] plan will save our [Constitution] from hardening of the judicial arteries."

Chief Justice Charles Evans Hughes defended the Court against the plan in a letter to Senator Burton K. Wheeler, dated March 21, 1937 (previously read and approved by Justices Brandeis and Van Devanter), stating that "[t]he Supreme Court is fully abreast of its work," and that "[a]n increase in the number of Justices of the Supreme Court, apart from any question of policy, which I do not discuss, would not promote the efficiency of the Court. It is believed that it would impair that efficiency so long as the Court acts as a unit. There would be more judges to hear, more judges to confer, more judges to discuss, more judges to be convinced and to decide. The present number of Justices is thought to be large enough so far as the prompt, adequate, and efficient conduct of [our work] is concerned."

After extensive hearings, the Senate Judiciary Committee rejected the proposal in June 1937. While the controversy was raging, the Court seemed to change direction in a number of decisions sustaining regulatory statutes, and Justice Van Devanter retired. The final Senate debate was almost anti-climactic. Proposed amendments by the proponents failed to save the heart of the plan, and in late July it was in effect killed. The adverse committee report concluded: "We recommend the rejection of this bill as a needless, futile, and utterly dangerous abandonment of constitutional principle. [Under] the form of the Constitution it seeks to do that which is unconstitutional. [Its] practical operation would be to make the Constitution what the executive or legislative branches of the Government choose to say it is—an interpretation to be changed with each change of administration. It is a measure which should be so emphatically rejected that its parallel will never again be presented to the free representatives of the free people of America." Sen. Rep. No. 711, 75th Cong., 1st Sess. (1937).

Two years after his Court-packing plan was rejected, President Roosevelt claimed that he had lost the battle but won the war. Many contemporary observers, including Felix Frankfurter, who was not yet on the Court, believed Justice Roberts had changed his position in the face of the Court-packing plan—famously dubbed the "switch in time that saved the Nine." But a memorandum left by Justice Roberts and described by Justice Frankfurter after Justice Roberts's death suggests that the Court voted to uphold New Deal labor legislation in West Coast Hotel (p. 501 below) weeks before the judicial-reorganization plan was announced. See Frankfurter, "Mr. Justice Roberts," 104 U. Pa. L. Rev. 311, 313 (1955) (describing as "ludicrous" the charge "that a judge with the character of Roberts should have attributed to him a change of judicial views out of deference to political considerations"). For contrasting evaluations of the alleged "switch" by Justice Roberts, compare Ariens, "A Thrice-Told Tale, or Felix the Cat," 107 Harv. L. Rev. 620 (1994) (arguing that Justice Roberts's memorandum, as presented by Justice Frankfurter, fails adequately to reconcile Justice Roberts's votes, and arguing that archival evidence "cast[s] [doubt] on the significance, if not existence of the memorandum"), with Friedman, "A Reaffirmation: The Authenticity of the Roberts Memorandum, or Felix the Non-Forger," 142 U. Pa. L. Rev. 1985 (1994) (producing eyewitness testimony for the existence of, and arguing strongly for the authenticity of, the Roberts memorandum described by Frankfurter), and Friedman, "Switching Time and Other Thought Experiments: The Hughes Court and Constitutional Transformation," 142 U. Pa. L. Rev. 1891 (1994) (arguing that "Roberts had a conscientious change of mind, at least the substance of which, if not the timing, can be understood independent of political factors"). With respect to the broader question of why the Court abandoned its laissez faire jurisprudence, see Cushman, Rethinking the New Deal Court (1998), for an argument that the Court's ideological shift can be explained by the Court's coherent doctrinal development, independent of external political factors.

SECTION 3. THE COMMERCE POWER AFTER THE NEW DEAL

The Court's stance toward Congress's commerce power changed dramatically in 1937, beginning with a case testing the constitutionality of the National Labor Relations Act of 1935. The National Labor Relations Board (NLRB) had found that Jones & Laughlin, a major steel company, had engaged in "unfair labor practices" by discriminatory discharges of employees for union activity. (For a social history of the attempt to unionize

Jones & Laughlin's Aliquippa plant, see Casebeer, "Aliquippa: The Company Town and Contested Power in the Construction of Law," 43 Buff. L. Rev. 617 (1995).) The NLRB ordered the company to end discrimination and coercion. When the company failed to comply, the NLRB sought judicial enforcement of its order, but the court of appeals denied the Board's petition on the ground that "the order lay beyond the range of federal power." The Supreme Court reversed, upholding the NLRB order:

NLRB v. Jones & Laughlin Steel Corp.

301 U.S. 1, 57 S. Ct. 615, 81 L. Ed. 893 (1937).

■ CHIEF JUSTICE HUGHES delivered the opinion of the Court.

[Jones & Laughlin] is engaged in the business of manufacturing iron and steel in plants situated in Pittsburgh and nearby Aliquippa, Pennsylvania. It manufactures and distributes a widely diversified line of steel and pig iron, being the fourth largest producer of steel in the United States. With its subsidiaries—nineteen in number—it is a completely integrated enterprise, owning and operating ore, coal and limestone properties, lake and river transportation facilities and terminal railroads located at its manufacturing plants. It owns or controls mines in Michigan and Minnesota. It operates four ore steamships on the Great Lakes. It owns coal mines in Pennsylvania. It operates towboats and steam barges used in carrying coal to its factories. [It owns two railroads which connect its plants to major lines.] Much of its product is shipped to its warehouses in Chicago, Detroit, Cincinnati and Memphis—to the last two places by means of its own barges and transportation equipment. In Long Island City, New York, and in New Orleans it operates structural steel fabricating shops in connection with the warehousing of semi-finished materials sent from its works. [Approximately] 75 per cent. of its product is shipped out of Pennsylvania. Summarizing these operations, the Labor Board concluded that the works in Pittsburgh and Aliquippa "might be likened to the heart of a self-contained, highly integrated body. They draw in the raw materials from Michigan, Minnesota, West Virginia, Pennsylvania in part through arteries and by means controlled by the respondent; they transform the materials and then pump them out to all parts of the nation through the vast mechanism which the respondent has elaborated."

[The] Act is challenged in its entirety as an attempt to regulate all industry, thus invading the reserved powers of the States over their local concerns. It is asserted [that] the Act is not a true regulation [of] commerce or of matters which directly affect it but on the contrary has the fundamental object of placing under the compulsory supervision of the federal government all industrial labor relations within the nation. [We] think it clear that [the] Act may be construed so as to operate within the sphere of constitutional authority. The jurisdiction conferred upon the Board, and invoked in this instance, is found in § 10(a), which [provides]: "The Board is empowered [to] prevent any person from engaging in any [unfair labor practice] affecting commerce." [The Act] purports to reach only what may be deemed to burden or obstruct that commerce and, thus qualified, it must be construed as contemplating the exercise of control within constitutional bounds. It is a familiar principle that acts which directly burden or obstruct interstate or foreign commerce, or its free flow, are within the reach of the congressional power. Acts having that effect are not rendered immune because they grow out of labor disputes. [It] is the effect upon commerce, not the source of the injury, which is the criterion. [Whether] or not particular action does affect commerce in such a close and intimate fashion as to be subject to federal control [is] left by the statute to be determined as individual cases arise. We are thus to inquire whether in the instant case the constitutional boundary has been [passed].

[The] congressional authority to protect interstate commerce from burdens and obstructions is not limited to transactions which can be deemed to be an essential part of a "flow" of interstate or foreign commerce. [Although] activities may be intrastate in character when separately considered, if they have such a close and substantial relation to interstate commerce that their control is essential or appropriate to protect that commerce from burdens and obstructions, Congress cannot be denied the power to exercise that control. [Schechter.] Undoubtedly the scope of this power must be considered in the light of our dual system of government and may not be extended so as to embrace effects upon interstate commerce so indirect and remote that to embrace them, in view of our complex society, would effectually obliterate the distinction between what is national and what is local and create a completely centralized government. The question is necessarily one of degree. [The] close and intimate effect which brings the subject within the reach of federal power may be due to activities in relation to productive industry although the industry when separately viewed is local. [T]he fact that the employees here concerned were engaged in production is not determinative. The question remains as to the effect upon interstate commerce of the labor practice involved. [In Schechter], we found that the effect there was so remote as to be beyond the federal power. [In Carter], the Court was of the opinion that the provisions of the statute relating to production were invalid upon several grounds. [These] cases are not controlling here.

[It] is idle to say that the effect [of labor strife at respondent's manufacturing operations on interstate commerce] would be indirect or remote. It is obvious that it would be immediate and might be catastrophic. [When] industries organize themselves on a national scale, making their relation to interstate commerce the dominant factor in their activities, how can it be maintained that their industrial labor relations constitute a forbidden field into which Congress may not enter when it is necessary to protect interstate commerce from the paralyzing consequences of industrial war? We have often said that interstate commerce itself is a practical conception. It is equally true that interferences with that commerce must be appraised by a judgment that does not ignore actual experience. Experience has abundantly demonstrated that the recognition of the right of employees to self-organization and to have representatives of their own choosing for the purpose of collective bargaining is often an essential condition of industrial [peace]. [Reversed.]

■ JUSTICE MCREYNOLDS, joined by JUSTICES VAN DEVANTER, SUTHERLAND, and BUTLER, dissenting.

Any effect on interstate commerce by the discharge of employees shown here would be indirect and remote in the highest degree. In [Jones & Laughlin] ten men out of ten thousand were discharged; in the other cases only a few. The immediate effect in the factory may be to create discontent among all those employed and a strike may follow, which, in turn, may result in reducing production, which ultimately may reduce the volume of goods moving in interstate commerce. By this chain of indirect and progressively remote events we finally reach the evil with which it is said the legislation under consideration undertakes to deal. A more remote and indirect interference with interstate commerce or a more definite invasion of the powers reserved to the states is difficult, if not impossible, to imagine. [Whatever] effect any cause of [labor] discontent may ultimately have upon commerce is far too indirect to justify Congressional regulation. Almost anything—marriage, birth, death—may in some fashion affect [commerce].

United States v. Darby

312 U.S. 100, 61 S. Ct. 451, 85 L. Ed. 609 (1941).

[Darby, a Georgia lumber manufacturer, challenged an indictment charging him with violating the Fair Labor Standards Act of 1938. The District Court quashed the indictment, holding that the Act was unconstitutional because it sought to regulate hours and wages of employees in local manufacturing activities.]

■ JUSTICE STONE delivered the opinion of the Court.

[The] two principal questions [in] this case are, *first*, whether Congress has constitutional power to prohibit the shipment in interstate commerce of lumber manufactured by employees whose wages are less than a prescribed minimum or whose weekly hours of labor at that wage are greater than a prescribed maximum, and, *second*, whether it has power to prohibit the employment of workmen in the production of goods "for interstate commerce" at other than prescribed wages and hours. [The Act's purpose is] to exclude from interstate commerce goods produced for the commerce and to prevent their production for interstate commerce, under conditions detrimental to the maintenance of the minimum standards of living necessary for health and general well-being; and to prevent the use of interstate commerce as the means of competition in the distribution of goods so produced, and as the means of spreading and perpetuating such substandard labor conditions among the workers of the several [states].

The prohibition of shipment of the proscribed goods in interstate commerce [under § 15(a)(1)]. [While] manufacture is not of itself interstate commerce the shipment of manufactured goods interstate is such commerce and the prohibition of such shipment by Congress is indubitably a regulation of the commerce. The power to regulate commerce is the power "to prescribe the rule by which commerce is governed." [Gibbons.] It extends not only to those regulations which aid, foster and protect the commerce, but embraces those which prohibit it. It is conceded that the power of Congress to prohibit transportation in interstate commerce includes noxious articles, stolen articles, kidnapped persons, and articles such as intoxicating liquor or convict-made goods, traffic in which is forbidden or restricted by the laws of the state of destination. [But] it is said that the present prohibition falls within the scope of none of these categories; that while the prohibition is nominally a regulation of the commerce its motive or purpose is regulation of wages and hours of persons engaged in manufacture, the control of which has been reserved to the states and upon which Georgia and some of the states of destination have placed no [restriction]. The power of Congress over interstate commerce [can] neither be enlarged nor diminished by the exercise or non-exercise of state power. Congress, following its own conception of public policy concerning the restrictions which may appropriately be imposed on interstate commerce, is free to exclude from the commerce articles whose use in the states for which they are destined it may conceive to be injurious to the public health, morals or welfare, even though the state has not sought to regulate their use. [Lottery Case.]

[The] motive and purpose of the present regulation are plainly to make effective the Congressional conception of public policy that interstate commerce should not be made the instrument of competition in the distribution of goods produced under substandard labor conditions, which competition is injurious to the commerce and to the states from and to which the commerce flows. The motive and purpose of a regulation of interstate commerce are matters for the legislative judgment upon the exercise of which the Constitution places no restriction and over which the courts are given no control. [Whatever] their motive and purpose, regulations of commerce which do not infringe some constitutional prohibition are within the plenary power conferred on Congress by the Commerce Clause. Subject only to that limitation, [we] conclude that the prohibition of the shipment interstate of goods produced under the forbidden substandard labor conditions is within the constitutional authority of Congress.

[These] principles of constitutional interpretation have been so long and repeatedly recognized by this Court as applicable to the Commerce Clause, that there would be little occasion for repeating them now were it not for the decision of this Court twenty-two years ago in Hammer v. Dagenhart. In that case it was held by a bare majority of the Court over the powerful and now classic dissent of Justice Holmes [that] Congress was without power to exclude the products of child labor from interstate commerce. The reasoning and conclusion of the Court's opinion there cannot be reconciled with the conclusion which we have [reached]. Hammer v. Dagenhart has not been followed. The distinction on which the decision was rested that Congressional power to prohibit interstate commerce is limited to articles which in themselves have some harmful or deleterious property—a distinction which was novel when made and unsupported by any provision of the Constitution—has long since been abandoned. The thesis of the opinion that the motive of the prohibition or its effect to control in some measure the use or production within the states of the article thus excluded from the commerce can operate to deprive the regulation of its constitutional authority has long since ceased to have force. [The] conclusion is inescapable that Hammer v. Dagenhart was a departure from the principles which have prevailed in the interpretation of the Commerce Clause both before and since the decision and that such vitality, as a precedent, as it then had has long since been exhausted. It should be and now is overruled.

Validity of the wage and hour requirements. Section 15(a)(2) [requires] employers to conform to the wage and hour provisions with respect to all employees engaged in the production of goods for interstate commerce. As appellees' employees are not alleged to be "engaged in interstate commerce" the validity of the prohibition turns on the question whether the employment, under other than the prescribed labor standards, of employees engaged in the production of goods for interstate commerce is so related to the commerce and so affects it as to be within the reach of the power of Congress to regulate it.

[The] power of Congress [over] interstate commerce extends [to] activities intrastate which have a substantial effect on the commerce or the exercise of the Congressional power over it. [Congress,] having by the present Act adopted the policy of excluding from interstate commerce all goods produced for the commerce which do not conform to the specified labor standards, [may] choose the means reasonably adapted to the attainment of the permitted end, even though they involve control of intrastate activities. Such legislation has often been sustained with respect to powers, other than the commerce power, [when] the means chosen, although not themselves within the granted power, were nevertheless deemed appropriate aids to the accomplishment of some purpose within an admitted power of the national government. [A] familiar like exercise of power is the regulation of intrastate transactions which are so commingled with or related to interstate commerce that all must be regulated if the interstate commerce is to be effectively controlled. Shreveport.

[We] think also that § 15(a)(2), now under consideration, is sustainable independently of § 15(a)(1), which prohibits shipment or transportation of the proscribed goods. [T]he evils aimed at by the Act are the spread of substandard labor conditions through the use of the facilities of interstate commerce for competition by the goods so produced with those produced under the prescribed or better labor conditions; and the consequent dislocation of the commerce itself caused by the impairment or destruction of local businesses by competition made effective through interstate commerce. The Act is thus directed at the suppression of a method or kind of competition in interstate commerce which it has in effect condemned as "unfair." [The] means adopted by § 15(a)(2) for the protection of interstate commerce by the suppression of the production of the condemned goods for interstate commerce is so related to the commerce and so affects it as to be within the reach of the commerce power. Congress, to attain its objective in the suppression of nationwide competition in interstate commerce by goods produced under substandard labor conditions, has made no distinction as to the volume or amount of shipments in the commerce or of production for commerce by any particular shipper or producer. It recognized that in present day industry, competition by a small part may affect the whole and that the total effect of the competition of many small producers may be great. [So] far as [Carter] is inconsistent with this conclusion, its doctrine is limited in principle by the decisions under the Sherman Act and the National Labor Relations Act, which [we] follow. [Our] conclusion is unaffected by the Tenth Amendment, which [states] but a truism that all is retained which has not been surrendered. There is nothing in the history of its adoption to suggest that it was more than declaratory of the relationship between the national and state governments as it had been established by the Constitution before the amendment or that its purpose was other than to allay fears that the new national government might seek to exercise powers not granted, and that the states might not be able to exercise fully their [reserved powers]. [Reversed.]

Wickard v. Filburn

317 U.S. 111, 63 S. Ct. 82, 87 L. Ed. 122 (1942).

[Filburn, a dairy farmer in Ohio, sued Wickard, the Secretary of Agriculture, to enjoin enforcement of a marketing penalty imposed upon him under the Agricultural Adjustment Act of 1938 for exceeding a market quota for wheat that had been established for his farm. Filburn raised a small acreage of wheat to feed his livestock, use for seed, make flour for home consumption, and sell. Filburn's quota for 1941 was 223 bushels, but he harvested an excess of 239 bushels beyond his quota. As a result, he faced a penalty of $117 for the excess grown. Filburn challenged the marketing quota provisions of the Act as beyond the congressional commerce power.]

■ JUSTICE JACKSON delivered the opinion of the Court.

[It] is urged that under the Commerce [Clause], Congress does not possess the power it has in this instance sought to exercise. The question would merit little consideration since our decision in [Darby], except for the fact that this Act extends federal regulation to production not intended in any part for commerce but wholly for consumption on the farm. [At] the beginning Chief Justice Marshall described the federal commerce power with a breadth never yet exceeded. [Gibbons.] He made emphatic the embracing and penetrating nature of this power by warning that effective restraints on its exercise must proceed from political rather than from judicial processes. [The] Court's recognition of the relevance of the economic effects in the application of the Commerce Clause [has] made the mechanical application of legal formulas no longer feasible. Once an economic measure of the reach of the power granted to Congress in the Commerce Clause is accepted, questions of federal power cannot be decided simply by finding the activity in question to be "production" nor can consideration of its economic effects be foreclosed by calling them "indirect." [Even] if appellee's activity be local and though it may not be regarded as commerce, it may still, whatever its nature, be reached by Congress if it exerts a substantial economic effect on interstate commerce, and this irrespective of whether such effect is what might at some earlier time have been defined as "direct" or "indirect."

[The] parties have stipulated a summary of the economics of the wheat industry. Commerce among the states in wheat is large and important. Although wheat is raised in every state but one, production in most states is not equal to consumption. [The] wheat industry has been a problem industry for some years. [The] decline in the export trade has left a large surplus in production which, in connection with an abnormally large supply of wheat and other grains in recent years, caused congestion in a number of markets; tied up railroad cars; and caused elevators in some instances to turn away grains, and railroads to institute embargoes to prevent further congestion. [In] the absence of regulation the price of wheat in the United States would be much affected by world conditions. During 1941, producers who cooperated with the Agricultural Adjustment program received an average price on the farm of about $1.16 a bushel, as compared with the world market price of 40 cents a bushel. [The] maintenance by government regulation of a price for wheat undoubtedly can be accomplished as effectively by sustaining or increasing the demand as by limiting the supply. The effect of the statute before us is to restrict the amount which may be produced for market and the extent as well to which one may forestall resort to the market by producing to meet his own needs. That appellee's own contribution to the demand for wheat may be trivial by itself is not enough to remove him from the scope of federal regulation where, as here, his contribution, taken together with that of many others similarly situated, is far from trivial.

[One] of the primary purposes of the Act in question was to increase the market price of wheat, and to that end to limit the volume thereof that could affect the market. It can hardly be denied that a factor of such volume and variability as home-consumed wheat would have a substantial influence on price and market conditions. This may arise because being in marketable condition such [homegrown] wheat overhangs the market and, if induced by rising prices, tends to flow into the market and check price increases. But if we assume that it is never marketed, it supplies a need of the man who grew it which would otherwise be reflected by purchases in the open market. Home-grown wheat in this sense competes with wheat in commerce. The stimulation of commerce is a use of the regulatory function quite as definitely as prohibitions or restrictions thereon. This record leaves us in no doubt that Congress may properly have considered that wheat consumed on the farm where grown, if wholly outside the scheme of regulation, would have a substantial effect in defeating and obstructing its purpose to stimulate trade therein at increased [prices].

JUDICIAL DEFERENCE TOWARD EXERCISE OF THE COMMERCE POWER

1. ***The Court's shift toward deference to New Deal measures.*** There were rapid changes in the composition of the Court after Jones & Laughlin: by the time of the Darby decision, all four of the dissenters in Jones & Laughlin had left. Justice McReynolds was the last to go: he retired just a few days before Darby was announced. The decisions sustaining national power in Darby and Wickard, unlike that in Jones & Laughlin, were unanimous. From 1937 through 1941, President Roosevelt made seven appointments to the Court—Justices Black, Reed, Frankfurter, Douglas, Murphy, Byrnes, and Jackson—cementing the dominance of a deferential judicial stance toward Congress's commerce power.

2. ***The "in commerce" rationale.*** The first holding of Darby, overruling Dagenhart, permitted Congress to regulate the literal shipment of goods across state lines even if the motive of the regulation was to control aspects of local production. Was such a broad disavowal of judicial scrutiny necessary or justified? Did the disavowal in Darby signify a final rejection of the "pretext" limitation in McCulloch? May the regulation of local activities be upheld without any showing of the impact of the local activity on commerce, merely because the regulatory scheme includes a ban on interstate shipments?

3. ***The "substantially affecting commerce" rationale.*** Jones & Laughlin, Darby, and Wickard all relied on the substantial effects of local economic activity on interstate commerce as a basis for congressional authority. How significant must such predictive effects be? What evidence should Congress have considered and what findings should Congress have made before the Court may uphold legislation on such a basis? May the Court find such effects even in the absence of congressional findings? Need the

activity in question independently have such effects or is it sufficient that all like activities in the aggregate would do so?

4. ***Wickard's reach.*** Note that Wickard required a showing of "substantial economic effect on interstate commerce." But was any real substance left to that notion if the requirement was satisfied whenever the activity regulated, "taken together with that of many others similarly situated, is far from trivial"? Did this "aggregation" approach leave any local activity still unreachable? Did Wickard abandon all judicial concern with federalism-related limits on congressional power? Consider the view that federal regulation should be confined to protection against force and fraud in interstate transportation and sales: "[T]he power to protect interstate commerce against robbers and thieves is [not] sufficient warrant for the far more extensive social controls that treat competitive activities undertaken within different states. [The] ability to perceive the essential difference between violence and competition is all that is needed to respect the limitation on federal power that is implicit in the commerce clause." Epstein, "The Proper Scope of the Commerce Power," 73 Va. L. Rev. 1387 (1987).

5. ***The role of agriculture in shaping federal power.*** Consider the argument that the Court's expansive interpretation of the commerce power in Wickard should be understood in the context of the importance of agriculture in the Depression-era United States and the extent to which farmers were suffering from the effects of the Depression. Whereas prior post-Civil War political battles had often split the country along geographic lines, the effect of the Depression on agriculture meant that "North and South at last were united in mutual misery." Consequently, farmers across the country pushed to give the federal government sufficient power to alleviate their pain. The result was several Roosevelt administration agriculture relief laws, which, like the law at issue in Wickard, pushed the boundaries of the federal commerce power and gave the Court occasion to expand it. See Chen, "The Story of Wickard v. Filburn," in Constitutional Law Stories 69, 77 (Michael C. Dorf ed., 2004).

6. ***The commerce power and civil rights.*** Title II of the Civil Rights Act of 1964 prohibited discrimination "on the ground of race, color, religion, or national origin" in certain places of public accommodation. Under the law, a facility was covered "if its operations affect commerce, or if discrimination [is] supported by State action." The Act reached much private economic conduct that Congress lacked power to regulate under the civil rights enforcement power conferred by Section 5 of the Fourteenth Amendment because that power had previously been confined to remedies for state action (see the Civil Rights Cases, p. 856 below). Thus, both Congress and the administration focused on Congress's commerce power as the relevant source of congressional authority. Covered facilities under Title II included "any inn, hotel, motel [etc.]," "any restaurant, cafeteria, lunch room, lunch counter," and any "theater, concert hall, sports arena." The law defined establishments "affect[ing] commerce" as including any establishment that "offers to serve interstate travelers or a substantial portion of the food which it serves has moved in commerce."

Civil Rights Act ↑ reg. of private economic conduct based on commerce clause

In **Heart of Atlanta Motel v. United States**, 379 U.S. 241 (1964), the Court upheld the law against a Commerce Clause challenge by a motel located in downtown Atlanta that wished to continue its practice of refusing to offer rooms to African-Americans. The Court, in a unanimous opinion by Justice CLARK, stated: "While the Act as adopted carried no congressional findings, the record of its passage through each house is replete with evidence of the burdens that discrimination by race or color places upon interstate commerce. [This] testimony included the fact that our people have become increasingly mobile with millions of all races traveling from State to State; that Negroes in particular have been the subject of discrimination in transient accommodations, having to travel great distances to secure the same; that often they have been unable to obtain accommodations and have had to call upon friends to put them up overnight, [and] that these conditions had become so acute as to require the listing of available lodging for Negroes in a special guidebook which was itself 'dramatic testimony of the difficulties' Negroes encounter in travel. [We] shall not burden this opinion with further details since the voluminous testimony presents overwhelming evidence that discrimination by hotels and motels impedes interstate travel [both] in impairing 'the Negro traveler's pleasure and convenience' and in 'discouraging travel on the part of a substantial portion of the Negro community.'

"[The] determinative test of the exercise of power by the Congress under the Commerce Clause is simply whether the activity sought to be regulated is 'commerce which concerns more States than one' and has a real and substantial relation to the national interest. [In] framing [Title II] Congress was [dealing] with what it considered a moral problem. But that fact does not detract from the overwhelming evidence of the disruptive effect that racial discrimination has had on commercial intercourse. It was this burden which empowered Congress to enact appropriate legislation, and given this basis for the exercise of its power, Congress was not restricted by the fact that the particular obstruction to interstate commerce with which it was dealing was also deemed a moral and social wrong. It is said that the operation of the motel here is of a purely local character. [But] the power of Congress to promote interstate commerce also includes the power to regulate the local incidents thereof, including local activities in both the States of origin and destination, which might have a substantial and harmful effect upon that commerce. One need only examine the evidence which we have discussed above to see that Congress may—as it has—prohibit racial discrimination by motels serving travelers, however 'local' their operations may appear."

In a companion case to Heart of Atlanta, **Katzenbach v. McClung**, 379 U.S. 294 (1964), the Court likewise upheld the application of Title II to Ollie's Barbecue, a family restaurant in Birmingham, Alabama, with a seating capacity of 220 customers and located 11 blocks from an interstate highway. The barbecue catered to a family and white-collar trade with a take-out service for African-Americans. During the preceding year, the restaurant had purchased about $150,000 worth of food, 46% of which was meat bought from a local supplier who had purchased it out of state. The district court found "no demonstrable connection between food purchased in interstate commerce and sold in a restaurant and the conclusion of Congress that discrimination at the restaurant would affect that commerce." The Court reversed.

In his opinion for a unanimous Court, Justice CLARK relied on the evidence put forth in the congressional hearings: "The sole [question] narrows down to whether Title II, as applied to a restaurant receiving about $70,000 worth of food which has moved in commerce, is a valid exercise of the power of Congress. [Congress] conducted prolonged hearings on the Act.

[While] no formal findings were made, which of course is not necessary, it is well that we make mention of the testimony to determine whether the Act is a reasonable and appropriate means [to regulate commerce]. The record is replete with testimony of the burdens placed on interstate commerce by racial discrimination in restaurants. A comparison of per capita spending by Negroes in restaurants, theaters, and like establishments indicated less spending, after discounting income differences, in areas where discrimination is widely practiced. This condition, which was especially aggravated in the South, was attributed in the testimony [to] racial segregation. [This] diminutive spending springing from a refusal to serve Negroes and their total loss as customers has, regardless of the absence of direct evidence, a close connection to interstate commerce. [Moreover] there was an impressive array of testimony that discrimination in restaurants had a direct and highly restrictive effect upon interstate travel by Negroes. This resulted, it was said, because discriminatory practices prevent Negroes from buying prepared food served on the premises while on a trip, except in isolated and unkempt restaurants and under most unsatisfactory and often unpleasant conditions. This obviously discourages travel and obstructs interstate commerce for one can hardly travel without eating. Likewise, it was said that discrimination deterred professional, as well as skilled, people from moving into areas where such practices occurred and thereby caused industry to be reluctant to establish there. [We] believe that this testimony afforded ample basis for the conclusion that established restaurants in such areas sold less interstate goods because of the discrimination, that interstate travel was obstructed directly by it, that business in general suffered and that many new businesses refrained from establishing there as a result of it.

"The appellees contend that Congress has arbitrarily created a conclusive presumption that all restaurants meeting the criteria set out in the Act 'affect commerce.' Stated another way, they object to the omission of a provision for a case-by-case determination—judicial or administrative—that racial discrimination in a particular restaurant affects commerce. But[Congress'] action in framing this Act was not unprecedented. [See Darby.] Confronted as we are with the facts laid before Congress, we must conclude that it had a rational basis for finding that racial discrimination in restaurants had a direct and adverse effect on the free flow of interstate commerce. [We think] that Congress acted well within its power to protect and foster commerce in extending the coverage of Title II only to those restaurants offering to serve interstate travelers or serving food, a substantial portion of which has moved in interstate commerce. The absence of direct evidence connecting discriminatory restaurant service with the flow of interstate food, a factor on which the appellees place much reliance, is not, given the evidence as to the effect of such practices on other aspects of commerce, a crucial matter."

Justice BLACK's concurring opinion in Heart of Atlanta and McClung cautioned that not "every remote, possible, speculative effect on commerce" should be accepted "as an adequate constitutional ground to uproot and throw into the discard all our traditional distinctions between what is purely local [and] what affects the national interest," and that "some isolated and remote lunchroom which sells only to local people and buys almost all its supplies in the locality may possibly be beyond the reach of the [commerce] power of Congress." (In fact Justice Black, as the sole dissenter, did vote to treat the Lake Nixon Club near Little Rock, Arkansas, as outside the reach of the Commerce Clause because it was but a "little remote country place of recreation. Daniel v. Paul, 395 U.S. 298 (1969).) But relying on the "aggregation" theory of Wickard, he found the application of the Act to the Heart of Atlanta Motel and Ollie's Barbecue valid under the commerce power. Justice DOUGLAS's concurrence in Heart of Atlanta and McClung stated that he was "somewhat reluctant [to] rest solely on the Commerce Clause," and would have preferred to rest the judgment on the Fourteenth Amendment because of his belief that the right to be free from discriminatory state action occupied a more protected constitutional position than the movement of goods across state lines. Justice GOLDBERG's concurrence also joined the Court's opinions in both Heart of Atlanta and McClung but emphasized that the primary purpose of the Act was "the vindication of human dignity and not mere economics." In his view, Congress "clearly had authority under both § 5 of the Fourteenth Amendment and the Commerce Clause" to enact the law.

7. ***The commerce power and criminal law.*** The Constitution mentions few crimes explicitly. Art. I, § 8, authorizes Congress to punish the counterfeiting of money, piracies and felonies committed on the high seas, and offenses against the law of nations. But Congress has enacted a host of federal criminal laws under the authority of the commerce power. Some such laws contain explicit jurisdictional predicates requiring the passage of the defendant or the instruments of the crime across state lines. Others do not. What are the outer bounds of such authority? May Congress reach a solely intrastate crime based on interstate commercial effects? Need the crime be economic in nature for this rationale to apply?

In **Perez v. United States**, 402 U.S. 146 (1971), the Court appeared to reach the outer limits of the "affecting commerce" rationale for federal criminal laws. The decision upheld a federal prohibition of "extortionate credit transactions"—loansharking enforced by threats of violence. Perez had lent money to the owner of a butcher shop and threatened violence when the butcher insisted that he could not repay the loan in the amount of the agreed-upon weekly installments. In upholding Perez's conviction, Justice DOUGLAS's opinion cited the findings made by Congress after hearings that, " '[e]ven where extortionate credit transactions are purely intrastate in character, they nevertheless directly affect interstate and foreign commerce.' " He wrote: "[Perez] is clearly *a member of the class* which engages in 'extortionate credit transactions' as defined by Congress. [Extortionate] credit transactions, though purely intrastate, may in the judgment of Congress affect interstate commerce. [The] findings of Congress are quite adequate on that ground. [The hearings] supplied Congress with the knowledge that the loan shark racket provides organized crime with its second most lucrative source of revenue, exacts millions from the pockets of people, coerces its victims into the commission of crimes against property, and causes the takeover by racketeers of legitimate businesses. [We] relate the history of the Act [to] answer the impassioned plea of [Perez] that all that is involved in loan sharking is a traditionally local activity. It appears, instead, that loan sharking in its national setting is one way organized interstate crime holds its guns to the heads of the poor and the rich alike and syphons funds from numerous localities to finance its national operations."

SECTION 4. THE CONTEMPORARY COMMERCE POWER

For nearly sixty years after the New Deal, the Court did not strike down a single federal statute as exceeding Congress's power under the Commerce

Clause. The deferential judicial stance toward Congress exemplified in Darby, Wickard, Heart of Atlanta, and McClung continued, and it remained little challenge for the government to show "substantial effects on interstate commerce." In 1995, a decision invalidating a congressional gun control law broke that longstanding record:

United States v. Lopez

514 U.S. 549, 115 S. Ct. 1624, 131 L. Ed. 2d 626 (1995).

[In the Gun-Free School Zones Act of 1990, Congress made it a federal offense "for any individual knowingly to possess a firearm at a place that the individual knows, or has reasonable cause to believe, is a school zone." 18 U.S.C. § 922(q). Lopez, a twelfth-grade student, was convicted for knowingly possessing a concealed handgun and bullets at his San Antonio high school.]

■ CHIEF JUSTICE REHNQUIST delivered the opinion of the Court.

[Jones & Laughlin Steel, Darby, and Wickard] ushered in an era of Commerce Clause jurisprudence that greatly expanded the previously defined authority of Congress under that Clause. [But] even these modern-era precedents which have expanded congressional power under the Commerce Clause confirm that this power is subject to outer limits. [We] have identified three broad categories of activity that Congress may regulate under its commerce power. First, Congress may regulate the use of the channels of interstate commerce. Second, Congress is empowered to regulate and protect the instrumentalities of interstate commerce, or persons or things in interstate commerce, even though the threat may come only from intrastate activities. Finally, Congress' commerce authority includes the power to regulate those activities having a substantial relation to interstate commerce. Within this final category, admittedly, our case law has not been clear whether an activity must "affect" or "substantially affect" interstate commerce in order to be within Congress' power to regulate it under the Commerce Clause. We conclude, consistent with the great weight of our case law, that the proper test requires an analysis of whether the regulated activity "substantially affects" interstate commerce.

We now turn to consider the power of Congress, in the light of this framework, to enact § 922(q). The first two categories of authority may be quickly disposed of: § 922(q) is not a regulation of the use of the channels of interstate commerce, nor is it an attempt to prohibit the interstate transportation of a commodity through the channels of commerce; nor can § 922(q) be justified as a regulation by which Congress has sought to protect an instrumentality of interstate commerce or a thing in interstate commerce. Thus, if § 922(q) is to be sustained, it must be under the third category as a regulation of an activity that substantially affects interstate commerce.

[We] have upheld a wide variety of congressional Acts regulating intrastate economic activity where we have concluded that the activity substantially affected interstate commerce. Examples include the regulation of intrastate coal mining, intrastate extortionate credit transactions, restaurants utilizing substantial interstate supplies, inns and hotels catering to interstate guests, and production and consumption of home-grown wheat. These examples are by no means exhaustive, but the pattern is clear. Where economic activity substantially affects interstate commerce, legislation regulating that activity will be sustained. Even [Wickard], which is perhaps the most far reaching example of Commerce Clause authority over intrastate activity, involved economic activity in a way that the possession of a gun in a school zone does not. Section 922(q) is a criminal statute that by its terms has nothing to do with "commerce" or any sort of economic enterprise, however broadly one might define those terms. Section 922(q) is not an essential part of a larger regulation of economic activity, in which the regulatory scheme could be undercut unless the intrastate activity were regulated. It cannot, therefore, be sustained under our cases upholding regulations of activities that arise out of or are connected with a commercial transaction, which, viewed in the aggregate, substantially affects interstate commerce.

[Section] 922(q) contains no jurisdictional element which would ensure, through case-by-case inquiry, that the firearm possession in question affects interstate commerce. For example, in United States v. Bass, 404 U.S. 336 (1971), the Court interpreted [the possession component of] former 18 U.S.C. § 1202(a), which made it a crime for a felon to "receive, possess, or transport in commerce or affecting commerce [any] firearm," [to] require an additional nexus to interstate commerce. [Unlike] the statute in Bass, § 922(q) has no express jurisdictional element which might limit its reach to a discrete set of firearm possessions that additionally have an explicit connection with or effect on interstate commerce.

[The] Government concedes that "neither the statute nor its legislative history contains express congressional findings regarding the effects upon interstate commerce of gun possession in a school zone." [Congress] normally is not required to make formal findings as to the substantial burdens that an activity has on interstate commerce. But to the extent that congressional findings would enable us to evaluate the legislative judgment that the activity in question substantially affected interstate commerce, even though no such substantial effect was visible to the naked eye, they are lacking [here].

The Government's essential contention [is] that we may determine here that § 922(q) is valid because possession of a firearm in a local school zone does indeed substantially affect interstate commerce. The Government argues that possession of a firearm in a school zone may result in violent crime and that violent crime can be expected to affect the functioning of the national economy in two ways. First, the costs of violent crime are substantial, and, through the mechanism of insurance, those costs are spread throughout the population. Second, violent crime reduces the willingness of individuals to travel to areas within the country that are perceived to be unsafe. The Government also argues that the presence of guns in schools poses a substantial threat to the educational process by threatening the learning environment. A handicapped educational process, in turn, will result in a less productive citizenry. That, in turn, would have an adverse effect on the Nation's economic well-being. As a result, the Government argues that Congress could rationally have concluded that § 922(q) substantially affects interstate commerce.

We pause to consider the implications of the Government's arguments. The Government admits, under its "costs of crime" reasoning, that Congress could regulate not only all violent crime, but all activities that might lead to violent crime, regardless of how tenuously they relate to interstate commerce. Similarly, under the Government's "national productivity" reasoning, Congress could regulate any activity that it found was related to the economic productivity of individual citizens: family law (including marriage, divorce, and child custody), for example. Under the theories that the Government presents in support of § 922(q), it is difficult to perceive any limitation on federal power, even in areas such as criminal law enforcement or education where States historically have been sovereign. Thus, if we were to accept the Government's arguments, we are hard-pressed to posit any activity by an individual that Congress is without power to regulate.

[The] dissent reasons that (1) gun-related violence is a serious problem; (2) that problem, in turn, has an adverse effect on classroom learning; and (3) that adverse effect on classroom learning, in turn, represents a substantial threat to trade and commerce. [Justice] Breyer's rationale lacks any real limits because, depending on the level of generality, any activity can be looked upon as commercial. Under the dissent's rationale, Congress could just as easily look at child rearing as "falling on the commercial side of the line" because it provides a "valuable service—namely, to equip [children] with the skills they need to survive in life and, more specifically, in the workplace." We do not doubt that Congress has authority under the Commerce Clause to regulate numerous commercial activities that substantially affect interstate commerce and also affect the educational process. That authority, though broad, does not include the authority to regulate each and every aspect of local schools.

Admittedly, a determination whether an intrastate activity is commercial or noncommercial may in some cases result in legal uncertainty. [The] Constitution mandates this uncertainty by withholding from Congress a plenary police power that would authorize enactment of every type of legislation. [Any] possible benefit from eliminating this "legal uncertainty" would be at the expense of the Constitution's system of enumerated powers. [To] uphold the Government's contentions here, we would have to pile inference upon inference in a manner that would bid fair to convert congressional authority under the Commerce Clause to a general police power of the sort retained by the States. Admittedly, some of our prior cases have taken long steps down that road, giving great deference to congressional action. The broad language in these opinions has suggested the possibility of additional expansion, but we decline here to proceed any further. To do so would require us to conclude that the Constitution's enumeration of powers does not presuppose something not enumerated, and that there never will be a distinction between what is truly national and what is truly local. This we are unwilling to do. [Affirmed.]

■ JUSTICE KENNEDY, with whom JUSTICE O'CONNOR joins, concurring.

[The] history of our Commerce Clause decisions contains at least two lessons of relevance to this case. The first [is] the imprecision of content-based boundaries [such as the manufacture-commerce distinction] used without more to define the limits of the Commerce Clause. The second, related to the first but of even greater consequence, is that the Court as an institution and the legal system as a whole have an immense stake in the stability of our Commerce Clause jurisprudence as it has evolved to this point. [That] fundamental restraint on our power forecloses us from reverting to an understanding of commerce that would serve only an 18th-century [economy]; it also mandates against returning to the time when congressional authority to regulate undoubted commercial activities was limited by a judicial determination that those matters had an insufficient connection to an interstate system. Congress can regulate in the commercial sphere on the assumption that we have a single market and a unified purpose to build a stable national economy. [It] does not follow, however, that in every instance the Court lacks the authority and responsibility to review congressional attempts to alter the federal balance. This case requires us to consider our place in the design of the Government and to appreciate the significance of federalism in the whole structure of the Constitution.

Of the various structural elements in the Constitution, separation of powers, checks and balances, judicial review, and federalism, only concerning the last does there seem to be much uncertainty respecting the existence, and the content, of standards that allow the judiciary to play a significant role in maintaining the design contemplated by the Framers. [There] is irony in this, because of the four structural elements in the Constitution just mentioned, federalism was the unique contribution of the Framers to political science and political theory. Though on the surface the idea may seem counterintuitive, it was the insight of the Framers that freedom was enhanced by the creation of two governments, not one. The theory that two governments accord more liberty than one requires for its realization two distinct and discernable lines of political accountability: one between the citizens and the Federal Government; the second between the citizens and the States. If, as Madison expected, the federal and state governments are [to] hold each other in check by competing for the affections of the people, those citizens must have some means of knowing which of the two governments to hold accountable for the failure to perform a given function. Were the Federal Government to take over the regulation of entire areas of traditional state concern, areas having nothing to do with the regulation of commercial activities, the boundaries between the spheres of federal and state authority would blur and political responsibility would become illusory. The resultant inability to hold either branch of the government answerable to the citizens is more dangerous even than devolving too much authority to the remote central power.

To be sure, one conclusion that could be drawn from The Federalist Papers is that the balance between national and state power is entrusted in its entirety to the political process. [Whatever] the judicial role, it is axiomatic that Congress does have substantial discretion and control over the federal balance. [The] political branches of the Government must fulfill this grave constitutional obligation if democratic liberty and the federalism that secures it are to endure. At the same time, the absence of structural mechanisms to require those officials to undertake this principled task, and the momentary political convenience often attendant upon their failure to do so, argue against a complete renunciation of the judicial role. Although it is the obligation of all officers of the Government to respect the constitutional design, the federal balance is too essential a part of our constitutional structure and plays too vital a role in securing freedom for us to admit inability to intervene when one or the other level of Government has tipped the scales too far.

■ JUSTICE THOMAS, concurring.

[Although] I join the majority, I write separately to observe that our case law has drifted far from the original understanding of the Commerce Clause. [We] have said that Congress may regulate not only "Commerce [among] the several states," but also anything that has a "substantial effect" on such commerce. This test, if taken to its logical extreme, would give Congress a "police power" over all aspects of American life. [At] the time the original Constitution was ratified, "commerce" consisted of selling, buying, and bartering, as well as transporting for these purposes. As one would expect, the term "commerce" was used in contradistinction to productive activities such as manufacturing and agriculture.[If] Congress may regulate all matters that substantially affect commerce, there is no need for the Constitution to specify that Congress may enact bankruptcy laws, cl. 4, or coin money and fix the standard of weights and measures, cl. 5, or punish counterfeiters of United States coin and securities, cl. 6. [Much] if not all of Art. I, § 8 [would] be surplusage if Congress had been given authority over matters that substantially affect interstate commerce. An interpretation of cl. 3 that makes the rest of § 8 superfluous simply cannot be correct.

[From] the time of the ratification of the Constitution to the mid-1930's, it was widely understood that the Constitution granted Congress only limited powers, notwithstanding the Commerce Clause. Moreover, there was no question that activities wholly separated from business, such as gun possession, were beyond the reach of the commerce power. [Apart] from its recent vintage and its corresponding lack of any grounding in the original understanding of the Constitution, the substantial effects test suffers from the further flaw that it appears to grant Congress a police power over the Nation. When asked at oral argument if there were any limits to the Commerce Clause, the Government was at a loss for words. Likewise, the principal dissent insists that there are limits, but it cannot muster even one example.

[Discussion] of the original understanding and our first century and a half of case law does not necessarily require a wholesale abandonment of our more recent opinions. It simply reveals that our substantial effects test is far removed from both the Constitution and from our early case law and that the Court's opinion should not be viewed as "radical" or another "wrong turn" that must be corrected in the future. The analysis also suggests that we ought to temper our Commerce Clause jurisprudence. [If] we wish to be true to a Constitution that does not cede a police power to the Federal Government, our Commerce Clause's boundaries simply cannot be "defined" as being " 'commensurate with the national needs' " or self-consciously intended to let the Federal Government " 'defend itself against economic forces that Congress decrees inimical or destructive of the national economy.' " See Breyer, J., dissenting. Such a formulation of federal power is no test at all: it is a blank check.

■ JUSTICE BREYER, with whom JUSTICES STEVENS, SOUTER, and GINSBURG join, dissenting.

[The] power to "regulate Commerce [among] the several States" encompasses the power to regulate local activities insofar as they significantly affect interstate commerce. [I] use the word "significant" because the word "substantial" implies a somewhat narrower power than recent precedent suggests. But, to speak of "substantial effect" rather than "significant effect" would make no difference in this case. [In] determining whether a local activity will likely have a significant effect upon interstate commerce, a court must consider, not the effect of an individual act (a single instance of gun possession), but rather the cumulative effect of all similar instances (i.e., the effect of all guns possessed in or near schools). [The] Constitution requires us to judge the connection between a regulated activity and interstate commerce, not directly, but at one remove. Courts must give Congress a degree of leeway in determining the existence of a significant factual connection between the regulated activity and interstate commerce—both because the Constitution delegates the commerce power directly to Congress and because the determination requires an empirical judgment of a kind that a legislature is more likely than a court to make with accuracy. The traditional words "rational basis" capture this leeway. Thus, the specific question before us, as the Court recognizes, is not whether the "regulated activity sufficiently affected interstate commerce," but, rather, whether Congress could have had "a rational basis" for so concluding.

[Applying] these principles to the case at hand, we must ask whether Congress could have had a rational basis for finding a significant (or substantial) connection between gun-related school violence and interstate commerce. [As] long as one views the commerce connection, not as a "technical legal conception," but as "a practical one," the answer to this question must be yes. [Reports], hearings, and other readily available literature make clear that the problem of guns in and around schools is widespread and extremely serious. [Congress] obviously could have thought that guns and learning are mutually exclusive. And, Congress could therefore have found a substantial educational problem—teachers unable to teach, students unable to learn—and concluded that guns near schools contribute substantially to the size and scope of that problem.

Having found that guns in schools significantly undermine the quality of education in our Nation's classrooms, Congress could also have found, given the effect of education upon interstate and foreign commerce, that gun-related violence in and around schools is a commercial, as well as a human, problem. Education, although far more than a matter of economics, has long been inextricably intertwined with the Nation's economy. [The] evidence of (1) the extent of the gun-related violence problem, (2) the extent of the resulting negative effect on classroom learning, and (3) the extent of the consequent negative commercial effects, when taken together, indicate a threat to trade and commerce that is "substantial." At the very least, Congress could rationally have concluded that the links are "substantial." Specifically, Congress could have found that gun-related violence near the classroom poses a serious economic threat (1) to consequently inadequately educated workers who must endure low paying jobs, and (2) to communities and businesses that might (in today's "information society") otherwise gain, from a well-educated work force, an important commercial advantage. [In] sum, a holding that the particular statute before us falls within the commerce power would not expand the scope of that Clause. Rather, it simply would apply pre-existing law to changing economic circumstances. It would recognize that, in today's economic world, gun-related violence near the classroom makes a significant difference to our economic, as well as our social, well-being.

The majority's [holding] creates three serious legal problems. First, the majority's holding runs contrary to modern Supreme Court cases that have upheld congressional actions despite connections to interstate or foreign commerce that are less significant than the effect of school violence. The second legal problem the Court creates comes from its apparent belief that it can reconcile its holding with earlier cases by making a critical distinction between "commercial" and noncommercial "transactions." [This] approach fails to heed this Court's earlier warning not to turn "questions of the power of Congress" upon "formulas" that would give "controlling force to nomenclature such as 'production' and 'indirect' and foreclose consideration of the actual effects of the activity in question upon interstate commerce." Wickard. [If] a distinction between commercial and noncommercial activities is to be made, this is not the case in which to make it. [Congress] could rationally conclude that schools fall on the commercial side of the line. In 1990, the year Congress enacted the statute before us, primary and secondary schools spent $230 billion—that is, nearly a quarter of a trillion dollars—which accounts for a significant portion of our $5.5 trillion Gross Domestic Product for that year. [The] third legal problem created by the Court's holding is that it threatens legal uncertainty in an area of law that, until this case, seemed reasonably well settled. Congress has enacted many statutes (more than 100 sections of the United States Code), including criminal statutes (at least 25 sections), that use the words "affecting commerce" to define their scope, and other statutes that contain no jurisdictional language at all. [The] legal uncertainty now created will restrict Congress' ability to enact criminal laws aimed at criminal behavior that, considered problem by problem rather than instance by instance, seriously threatens the economic, as well as social, well-being of [Americans].

■ JUSTICE SOUTER, dissenting.

In reviewing congressional legislation under the Commerce Clause, we defer to what is often a merely implicit congressional judgment that its regulation addresses a subject substantially affecting interstate commerce "if there is any rational basis for such a finding." The practice of deferring to rationally based legislative judgments "is a paradigm of judicial restraint." In judicial review under the Commerce Clause, it reflects our respect for the institutional competence of the Congress on a subject expressly assigned to it by the Constitution and our appreciation of the legitimacy that comes from Congress's political accountability in dealing with matters open to a wide range of possible choices. It was not ever thus, however, as even a brief overview of Commerce Clause history during the past century reminds us. The modern respect for the competence and primacy of Congress in matters affecting commerce developed only after one of this Court's most chastening experiences, when it perforce repudiated an earlier and untenably expansive conception of judicial review in derogation of congressional commerce power. A look at history's sequence will serve to show how today's decision tugs the Court off course.

[The] period from the turn of the century to 1937 [is] noted for a series of cases applying highly formalistic notions of "commerce" to invalidate federal social and economic legislation. [See, e.g., Carter, Schechter, Hammer v. Dagenhart.] [The] distinction between what is patently commercial and what is not looks much like the old distinction between what directly affects commerce and what touches it only indirectly. [Thus,] it seems fair to ask whether the step taken by the Court today does anything but portend a return to the untenable jurisprudence from which the Court extricated itself almost 60 years ago.

■ JUSTICE STEVENS, dissenting.

Guns are both articles of commerce and articles that can be used to restrain commerce. Their possession is the consequence, either directly or indirectly, of commercial activity. In my judgment, Congress' power to regulate commerce in firearms includes the power to prohibit possession of guns at any location because of their potentially harmful use; it necessarily follows that Congress may also prohibit their possession in particular markets. The market for the possession of handguns by school-age children is, distressingly, substantial. Whether or not the national interest in eliminating that market would have justified federal legislation in 1789, it surely does today.

REHNQUIST-ERA RESTRICTIONS ON THE COMMERCE POWER

1. ***The role of congressional findings.*** In Katzenbach v. McClung, the Court considered the hearings that Congress had held on the commercial impacts of racial segregation, but noted that "formal findings" by Congress were "of course not necessary" to sustain legislation as rationally related to substantial effects on commerce. In Lopez, Chief Justice Rehnquist reiterated that "Congress normally is not required to make formal findings as to the substantial burdens that an activity has on interstate commerce," but found the absence of such findings unhelpful to the defense of § 922(q). Would explicit congressional findings of the effects described in Justice Breyer's dissent have helped to sustain the Act?

2. ***Jurisdictional nexus.*** In Lopez, Chief Justice Rehnquist noted that, unlike many federal statutes that expressly refer to and thus require proof of the interstate movement of persons or instruments of crime, "§ 922(q) contains no jurisdictional element which would ensure, through case-by-case inquiry, that the firearm possession in question affects interstate commerce." Would addition of such a requirement have been enough to uphold the statute? After the Lopez decision, Congress amended § 922(q) to read as follows: "It shall be unlawful for any individual knowingly to possess a firearm that has moved in or that otherwise affects interstate or foreign commerce at a place that the individual knows, or has reasonable cause to believe, is a school zone." Does this simple drafting fix cure the constitutional deficiency in the Act? The Supreme Court has not ruled on the constitutionality of the amended § 922(q), but it has been upheld at the court of appeals level. See, e.g., United States v. Dorsey, 418 F.3d 1038 (9th Cir. 2005); United States v. Danks, 221 F.3d 1037 (8th Cir. 1999). Does that make Lopez much ado about nothing? A mere lesson in congressional etiquette? Why should Congress put prosecutors to case-by-case proof of an interstate nexus? Can't Congress draw conclusive presumptions of interstate effects in the criminal context as it did in the civil rights acts? Most guns in the U.S. are manufactured in a few small New England states; why couldn't the government have presumed that a gun possessed in Texas necessarily would have traveled in interstate commerce?

congress added jurisdictional element

3. ***Areas of traditional state autonomy.*** Chief Justice Rehnquist expressed concern in Lopez that too broad an exercise of the commerce power could infringe upon "areas such as criminal law enforcement or education where States historically have been sovereign," and allow Congress to reach even "family law (including, marriage, divorce, and child custody)." How important to the decision in Lopez was the notion that the states bear historical responsibility for certain traditional areas of regulation? Are there some traditionally state-regulated activities that should be presumptively immune from congressional regulation under the commerce power, even if they have some genuine effect on interstate commerce? Numerous federal statutes—from marriage benefits in the tax code to the definition of marital

and survivor benefits in the Social Security laws—bear on what counts and does not count as a family relationship. For the view that Lopez was wrong to treat federal and state authority over families as mutually incompatible, see Dailey, "Federalism and Families," 143 U. Pa. L. Rev. 1787 (1995) ("State authority over family law need not be understood as inherently incompatible with either the complex workings of our modern industrial state nor with a national commitment to equality, toleration, and individual rights.").

4. ***Economic vs. noneconomic activities.*** Chief Justice Rehnquist distinguished the statute upheld in Wickard from that struck down in Lopez on the ground that Wickard "involved economic activity in a way that the possession of a gun in a school zone does not." What made the activity regulated in Lopez noneconomic? Since guns are rarely homemade, doesn't gun possession always entail a prior manufacture, purchase, and sale? How important to the decision in Lopez was the distinction between economic and noneconomic activity? This question is explored in the next case, in which the Court, in its first major elaboration of the commerce power after Lopez, invalidated civil damages provisions of the federal Violence Against Women Act (VAWA). The Court also deemed these provisions beyond Congress's civil rights enforcement power (for this part of the opinion, see p. 915 below).

United States v. Morrison

529 U.S. 598, 120 S. Ct. 1740, 146 L. Ed. 2d 658 (2000).

[Christy Brzonkala, a student at Virginia Polytechnic Institute, filed a rape charge against two football players also enrolled at the university. She dropped out of school and sued both men as well as Virginia Tech in federal district court under the Violence Against Women Act of 1994 (VAWA), 42 U.S.C. § 13981, which provided that: "A person (including a person who acts under color of any statute, ordinance, regulation, custom, or usage of any State) who commits a crime of violence motivated by gender . . . shall be liable to the party injured, in an action for the recovery of compensatory and punitive damages, injunctive and declaratory relief, and such other relief as a court may deem appropriate." The defendants challenged the constitutional power of Congress to apply this law to private acts of violence.]

■ CHIEF JUSTICE REHNQUIST delivered the opinion of the Court.

[Petitioners] seek to sustain § 13981 as a regulation of activity that substantially affects interstate commerce. Lopez [provides] the proper framework. [Lopez's] review of Commerce Clause case law demonstrates that in those cases where we have sustained federal regulation of intrastate activity based upon the activity's substantial effects on interstate commerce, the activity in question has been some sort of economic endeavor. [Gender-motivated] crimes of violence are not, in any sense of the phrase, economic activity. While we need not adopt a categorical rule against aggregating the effects of any noneconomic activity in order to decide these cases, thus far in our Nation's history our cases have upheld Commerce Clause regulation of intrastate activity only where that activity is economic in nature.

Like the Gun-Free School Zones Act at issue in Lopez, § 13981 contains no jurisdictional element establishing that the federal cause of action is in pursuance of Congress' power to regulate interstate commerce. Although

Lopez makes clear that such a jurisdictional element would lend support to the argument that § 13981 is sufficiently tied to interstate commerce, Congress elected to cast § 13981's remedy over a wider, and more purely intrastate, body of violent crime.

In contrast with the lack of congressional findings that we faced in Lopez, § 13981 is supported by numerous findings regarding the serious impact that gender-motivated violence has on victims and their families. But the existence of congressional findings is not sufficient, by itself, to sustain the constitutionality of Commerce Clause legislation. [Congress] found that gender-motivated violence affects interstate commerce "by deterring potential victims from traveling interstate, from engaging in employment in interstate business, and from transacting with business, and in places involved in interstate commerce; . . . by diminishing national productivity, increasing medical and other costs, and decreasing the supply of and the demand for interstate products." [The] reasoning that petitioners advance seeks to follow the but-for causal chain from the initial occurrence of violent crime (the suppression of which has always been the prime object of the States' police power) to every attenuated effect upon interstate commerce. If accepted, petitioners' reasoning would allow Congress to regulate any crime as long as the nationwide, aggregated impact of that crime has substantial effects on employment, production, transit, or consumption. [Petitioners'] reasoning, moreover, will not limit Congress to regulating violence but may [be] applied equally as well to family law and other areas of traditional state regulation since the aggregate effect of marriage, divorce, and childrearing on the national economy is undoubtedly significant.

We accordingly reject the argument that Congress may regulate noneconomic, violent criminal conduct based solely on that conduct's aggregate effect on interstate commerce. The Constitution requires a distinction between what is truly national and what is truly local. [The] regulation and punishment of intrastate violence that is not directed at the instrumentalities, channels, or goods involved in interstate commerce has always been the province of the States. Indeed, we can think of no better example of the police power, which the Founders denied the National Government and reposed in the States, than the suppression of violent crime and vindication of its victims.

■ JUSTICE THOMAS, concurring.

The majority opinion correctly applies our decision in [Lopez] and I join it in full. I write separately only to express my view that the very notion of a "substantial effects" test under the Commerce Clause is inconsistent with the original understanding of Congress' powers and with this Court's early Commerce Clause cases. [Until] this Court replaces its existing Commerce Clause jurisprudence with a standard more consistent with the original understanding, we will continue to see Congress appropriating state police powers under the guise of regulating commerce.

■ JUSTICE SOUTER, with whom JUSTICES STEVENS, GINSBURG, and BREYER join, dissenting.

[Congress] has the power to legislate with regard to activity that, in the aggregate, has a substantial effect on interstate commerce. The fact of such a substantial effect is not an issue for the courts in the first instance, but for the Congress, whose institutional capacity for gathering evidence and taking testimony far exceeds ours. By passing legislation, Congress indicates its conclusion, whether explicitly or not, that facts support its exercise of the commerce power. The business of the courts is to review the congressional assessment, not for soundness but simply for the rationality of concluding that a jurisdictional basis exists in fact. Any explicit findings that Congress chooses to make, though not dispositive of the question of rationality, may advance judicial review by identifying factual authority on which Congress relied.

[One] obvious difference from [Lopez] is the mountain of data assembled by Congress, here showing the effects of violence against women on interstate commerce. Passage of the Act in 1994 was preceded by four years of hearings, which included testimony from physicians and law professors; from survivors of rape and domestic violence; and from representatives of state law enforcement and private business. The record includes reports on gender bias from task forces in 21 States, and we have the benefit of specific factual findings in the eight separate Reports issued by Congress and its committees over the long course leading to enactment. [Congress] thereby explicitly stated the predicate for the exercise of its Commerce Clause power. [The] sufficiency of the evidence before Congress to provide a rational basis for the finding cannot seriously be questioned. Indeed, the legislative record here is far more voluminous than the record compiled by Congress and found sufficient in Heart of Atlanta Motel and Katzenbach v. McClung. [Gender-based] violence in the 1990's was shown to operate in a manner similar to racial discrimination in the 1960's in reducing the mobility of employees and their production and consumption of goods shipped in interstate commerce.

[The] Act would have passed muster at any time between Wickard in 1942 and Lopez in 1995, a period in which the law enjoyed a stable understanding that congressional power under the Commerce Clause [extended] to all activity that, when aggregated, has a substantial effect on interstate commerce. [The] fact that the Act does not pass muster before the Court today is therefore proof, to a degree that Lopez was not, that the Court's nominal adherence to the substantial effects test is merely that. [The] majority [rejects] the Founders' considered judgment that politics, not judicial review, should mediate between state and national interests as the strength and legislative jurisdiction of the National Government inevitably increased through the expected growth of the national economy.

[Today's] majority [also finds] no significance whatever in the state support for the Act based upon the States' acknowledged failure to deal adequately with gender-based violence in state courts, and the belief of their own law enforcement agencies that national action is essential. The National Association of Attorneys General supported the Act unanimously, and Attorneys General from 38 States urged Congress to enact the Civil Rights Remedy, [and] thirty-six [states] and the Commonwealth of Puerto Rico have filed an amicus brief in support of petitioners in these cases, and only one State has taken respondents' side. It is, then, not the least irony of these cases that the States will be forced to enjoy the new federalism whether they want it or not.

■ JUSTICE BREYER, with whom JUSTICE STEVENS joins, and with whom JUSTICES SOUTER and GINSBURG join as to Part I–A, dissenting.

I–A. [The] "economic/noneconomic" distinction is not easy to apply. Does the local street corner mugger engage in "economic" activity or "noneconomic" activity when he mugs for money? Would evidence that desire for economic domination underlies many brutal crimes against women save the present statute? [Why] should we give critical constitutional importance to the economic, or noneconomic, nature of an interstate-commerce-affecting cause? If chemical emanations through indirect environmental change cause identical, severe commercial harm outside a State, why should it matter whether local factories or home fireplaces release them? [The] Court's complex rules seem unlikely to help secure the very object that they seek, namely, the protection of "areas of traditional state regulation" from federal intrusion. [In] a world where most everyday products or their component parts cross interstate boundaries, Congress will frequently find it possible to redraft a statute using language that ties the regulation to the interstate movement of some relevant object, thereby regulating local criminal activity or, for that matter, family affairs. [How] much would be gained, for example, were Congress to reenact the present law in the form of "An Act Forbidding Violence Against Women Perpetrated at Public Accommodations or by Those Who Have Moved in, or through the Use of Items that Have Moved in, Interstate Commerce"?

[We] live in a Nation knit together by two centuries of scientific, technological, commercial, and environmental change. Those changes, taken together, mean that virtually every kind of activity, no matter how local, genuinely can affect commerce, or its conditions, outside the State—at least when considered in the aggregate. And that fact makes it close to impossible for courts to develop meaningful subject-matter categories that would exclude some kinds of local activities from ordinary Commerce Clause "aggregation" rules without, at the same time, depriving Congress of the power to regulate activities that have a genuine and important effect upon interstate commerce. Since judges cannot change the world, [Congress], not the courts, must remain primarily responsible for striking the appropriate state/federal balance.

THE COMMERCE POWER STRIKES BACK?

1. ***Was the Rehnquist-era "federalism revolution" overstated?*** After Lopez and Morrison (and the cases discussed in Section 5 below), many Court-watchers were ready to declare the resurgence of federalism the most profound constitutional shift by the Rehnquist Court. "When constitutional historians look back at the Rehnquist Court, they will say that its greatest changes in constitutional law were in the area of federalism." Chemerinsky, "Assessing Chief Justice William Rehnquist," 154 U. Pa. L. Rev. 1331 (2006).

While there is little doubt that the Rehnquist Court challenged the prevailing theory of federalism, the practical extent of the change remains less clear. Were the changes mere formalities or lasting limits on the power of Congress? Recall that, after Lopez, Congress reenacted the ban on gun possession in schools, this time simply being sure to include a jurisdictional nexus requirement. On the other hand, the provisions struck down in Morrison were not revived. Did it matter that the laws invalidated in Lopez and Morrison involved very specific subject matters that trenched upon areas traditionally reserved to the states?

2. ***The "aggregation" principle and general schemes of regulation.*** Wickard set forth the principle of "aggregation," which allows Congress to regulate activity that, taken in isolation, does not substantially affect interstate commerce, on the ground that multiple iterations of that

same activity would substantially affect interstate commerce. Note that Lopez and Morrison appeared to limit the aggregation principle to cases of "economic" or "commercial" activity. In Lopez, the government was unable to aggregate incidents of school gun violence, and in Morrison, the government was unable to aggregate incidents of gender-motivated violence. In both cases, the Court found it significant that the regulated activity was noneconomic or noncommercial.

Wickard's aggregation principle, however, was crucial to the majority's decision, five years after Morrison, to uphold the application of federal narcotics laws to state-authorized possession and use of homegrown marijuana for medicinal purposes. In the 6–3 decision, two justices who had been crucial to the Lopez and Morrison majorities, Justices Scalia and Kennedy, sided with the federal government, with only Chief Justice Rehnquist and Justices O'Connor and Thomas maintaining that Lopez and Morrison called for similar limits on congressional power here:

Gonzales v. Raich

545 U.S. 1, 125 S. Ct. 2195, 162 L. Ed. 2d 1 (2005).

■ JUSTICE STEVENS delivered the opinion of the Court[, in which JUSTICES KENNEDY, SOUTER, GINSBURG, and BREYER joined].

[The] question presented in this case is whether the [commerce] power includes the power to prohibit the local cultivation and use of marijuana in compliance with California law. California has been a pioneer in the regulation of marijuana. [In] 1996, California voters passed Proposition 215, now codified as the Compassionate Use Act of 1996. [The] Act creates an exemption from criminal prosecution for physicians, as well as for patients and primary caregivers who possess or cultivate marijuana for medicinal purposes with the recommendation or approval of a physician. Respondents Angel Raich and Diane Monson are California residents who suffer from a variety of serious medical conditions and have sought to avail themselves of medical marijuana pursuant to the terms of the Compassionate Use Act. [They] brought this action [seeking] injunctive and declaratory relief prohibiting the enforcement of the federal Controlled Substances Act (CSA), to the extent it prevents them from possessing, obtaining, or manufacturing cannabis for their personal medical use.

[Respondents] do not dispute that passage of the CSA [was] well within Congress' commerce power. Nor do they contend that any provision or section of the CSA amounts to an unconstitutional exercise of congressional authority. Rather, [they] argue that the CSA's categorical prohibition of the manufacture and possession of marijuana as applied to the intrastate manufacture and possession of marijuana for medical purposes pursuant to California law exceeds Congress' authority under the Commerce Clause.

[Our] case law firmly establishes Congress' power to regulate purely local activities that are part of an economic "class of activities" that have a substantial effect on interstate commerce. [Our] decision in Wickard is of particular relevance. [Wickard] establishes that Congress can regulate purely intrastate activity that is not itself "commercial," in that it is not produced for sale, if it concludes that failure to regulate that class of activity would undercut the regulation of the interstate market in that commodity. The similarities between this case and Wickard are striking. Like the farmer in Wickard, respondents are cultivating, for home consumption, a fungible commodity for which there is an established, albeit illegal, interstate market. Just as the Agricultural Adjustment Act was designed "to control the volume [of wheat] moving in interstate and foreign commerce in order to avoid surpluses . . . " and consequently control the market price, a primary purpose of the CSA is to control the supply and demand of controlled substances in both lawful and unlawful drug markets.

In Wickard, we had no difficulty concluding that Congress had a rational basis for believing that, when viewed in the aggregate, leaving home-consumed wheat outside the regulatory scheme would have a substantial influence on price and market conditions. Here too, Congress had a rational basis for concluding that leaving home-consumed marijuana outside federal control would similarly affect price and market conditions. [In] both cases, the regulation is squarely within Congress' commerce power because production of the commodity meant for home consumption, be it wheat or marijuana, has a substantial effect on supply and demand in the national market for that commodity. [Given] the enforcement difficulties that attend distinguishing between marijuana cultivated locally and marijuana grown elsewhere, and concerns about diversion into illicit channels, we have no difficulty concluding that Congress had a rational basis for believing that failure to regulate the intrastate manufacture and possession of marijuana would leave a gaping hole in the CSA. Thus, as in Wickard, when it enacted comprehensive legislation to regulate the interstate market in a fungible commodity, Congress was acting well within its [commerce authority.] That the regulation ensnares some purely intrastate activity is of no moment. As we have done many times before, we refuse to excise individual components of that larger scheme.

To support their contrary submission, respondents rely heavily on [Lopez and Morrison.] [They] read those cases far too broadly. [Here,] respondents ask us to excise individual applications of a concededly valid statutory scheme. In contrast, in both Lopez and Morrison, the parties asserted that a particular statute or provision fell outside Congress' commerce power in its entirety. This distinction is pivotal. [At] issue in Lopez was the validity of [a] brief, single-subject statute making it a crime for an individual to possess a gun in a school zone. The Act did not regulate any economic activity and did not contain any requirement that the possession of a gun have any connection to past interstate activity or a predictable impact on future commercial activity. [The] statutory scheme that the Government is defending in this litigation is at the opposite end of the regulatory spectrum. [The] CSA [was] a lengthy and detailed statute creating a comprehensive framework for regulating the production, distribution, and possession of five classes of "controlled substances." [Our] opinion in Lopez casts no doubt on the validity of such a program.

Nor does this Court's holding in Morrison. [VAWA] created a federal civil remedy for the victims of gender-motivated crimes of violence. [Despite] congressional findings that such crimes had an adverse impact on interstate commerce, we held the statute unconstitutional because, like the statute in Lopez, it did not regulate economic activity. [Unlike] those at issue in Lopez and Morrison, the activities regulated by the CSA are quintessentially economic. [The] CSA is a statute that regulates the production, distribution, and consumption of commodities for which there is an established, and lucrative, interstate market. Prohibiting the intrastate possession or manufacture of an article of commerce is a rational (and commonly utilized) means of regulating commerce in that product. [Because] the CSA is a statute that directly regulates economic, commercial activity, our opinion in Morrison casts no doubt on its constitutionality.

[The] case for the exemption comes down to the claim that a locally cultivated product that is used domestically rather than sold on the open market is not subject to federal regulation. Given the findings in the CSA and the undisputed magnitude of the commercial market for marijuana, our decisions in [Wickard] and the later cases endorsing its reasoning foreclose that claim. [Vacated and remanded.]

■ JUSTICE SCALIA, concurring in the judgment.

I agree with the Court's holding that the Controlled Substances Act (CSA) may validly be applied to respondents' cultivation, distribution, and possession of marijuana for personal, medicinal use. I write separately because my understanding of the doctrinal foundation on which that holding rests is, if not inconsistent with that of the Court, at least more nuanced. [Unlike] the channels, instrumentalities, and agents of interstate commerce, activities that substantially affect interstate commerce are not themselves part of interstate commerce, and thus the power to regulate them cannot come from the Commerce Clause alone. Rather, Congress's regulatory authority over [such] activities [derives] from the Necessary and Proper Clause. [The] authority to enact laws necessary and proper for the regulation of interstate commerce is not limited to laws governing intrastate activities that substantially affect interstate commerce. Where necessary to make a regulation of interstate commerce effective, Congress may regulate even those intrastate activities that do not themselves substantially affect interstate commerce. [Congress] may regulate even noneconomic local activity if that regulation is a necessary part of a more general regulation of interstate commerce. The relevant question is simply whether the means chosen are "reasonably adapted" to the attainment of a legitimate end under the commerce power.

[Justice O'Connor's] dissent objects that, by permitting Congress to regulate activities necessary to effective interstate regulation, the Court reduces Lopez and Morrison to "little more than a drafting guide." I think that criticism unjustified. Unlike the power to regulate activities that have a substantial effect on interstate commerce, the power to enact laws enabling effective regulation of interstate commerce can only be exercised in conjunction with congressional regulation of an interstate market, and it extends only to those measures necessary to make the interstate regulation effective. [This] is not a power that threatens to obliterate the line between "what is truly national and what is truly local." Lopez and Morrison affirm that Congress may not regulate certain "purely local" activity within the States based solely on the attenuated effect that such activity may have in the interstate market. But those decisions do not declare noneconomic intrastate activities to be categorically beyond the reach of the Federal Government.

[The] application of these principles to the case before us is straightforward. In the CSA, Congress has undertaken to extinguish the interstate market in Schedule I controlled substances, including marijuana. The Commerce Clause unquestionably permits this. [To] effectuate its objective, Congress has prohibited almost all intrastate activities related to Schedule I substances—both economic activities (manufacture, distribution, possession with the intent to distribute) and noneconomic activities (simple possession). That simple possession is a noneconomic activity is immaterial to whether it can be prohibited as a necessary part of a larger regulation. [By] this measure, I think the regulation must be sustained.

■ JUSTICE O'CONNOR, with whom CHIEF JUSTICE [REHNQUIST] and JUSTICE THOMAS join as to all but Part III, dissenting.

We enforce the "outer limits" of Congress' Commerce Clause authority not for their own sake, but to protect historic spheres of state sovereignty from excessive federal encroachment and thereby to maintain the distribution of power fundamental to our federalist system of government. One of federalism's chief virtues, of course, is that it promotes innovation by allowing for the possibility that "a single courageous State may, if its citizens choose, serve as a laboratory; and try novel social and economic experiments without risk to the rest of the country." New State Ice Co. v. Liebmann (1932) (Brandeis, J., dissenting).

This case exemplifies the role of States as laboratories. The States' core police powers have always included authority to define criminal law and to protect the health, safety, and welfare of their citizens. Exercising those powers, California (by ballot initiative and then by legislative codification) has come to its own conclusion about the difficult and sensitive question of whether marijuana should be available to relieve severe pain and suffering. Today the Court sanctions an application of the federal Controlled Substances Act that extinguishes that experiment, without any proof that the personal cultivation, possession, and use of marijuana for medicinal purposes, if economic activity in the first place, has a substantial effect on interstate commerce and is therefore an appropriate subject of federal regulation.

I. In Lopez, [our] decision about whether gun possession in school zones substantially affected interstate commerce turned on four considerations. First, we observed that our "substantial effects" cases generally have upheld federal regulation of economic activity that affected interstate commerce. [Second,] we noted that the statute contained no express jurisdictional requirement establishing its connection to interstate commerce. Third, we found telling the absence of legislative findings about the regulated conduct's impact on interstate commerce. [Finally,] we rejected as too attenuated the Government's argument that firearm possession in school zones could result in violent crime which in turn could adversely affect the national economy. [In] my view, the case before us is materially indistinguishable from Lopez and Morrison when the same considerations are taken into account.

II. [Today's] decision suggests that the federal regulation of local activity is immune to Commerce Clause challenge because Congress chose to act with an ambitious, all-encompassing statute, rather than piecemeal. [The] Court appears to reason that the placement of local activity in a comprehensive scheme confirms that it is essential to that scheme. If the Court is right, then Lopez stands for nothing more than a drafting guide: Congress should have described the relevant crime as "transfer or possession of a firearm anywhere in the nation" [or attached] the regulation of intrastate activity to a pre-existing comprehensive (or even not-so-comprehensive) scheme. [If] the Court always defers to Congress as it does today, little may be left to the notion of enumerated powers.

[The] Court's definition of economic activity is breathtaking [and] threatens to sweep all of productive human activity into federal regulatory reach. [It] will not do to say that Congress may regulate noncommercial activity simply because it may have an effect on the demand for commercial goods, or because the noncommercial endeavor can, in some sense, substitute for commercial activity. Most commercial goods or services have some sort of privately producible analogue. Home care substitutes for daycare. Charades games substitute for movie tickets. Backyard or windowsill gardening substitutes for going to the supermarket. To draw the line wherever private activity affects the demand for market goods is to draw no line at all, and to declare everything economic. [In] Lopez and Morrison, we suggested that economic activity usually relates directly to commercial activity. The homegrown cultivation and personal possession and use of marijuana for medicinal purposes has no apparent commercial character. Everyone agrees that the marijuana at issue in this case was never in the stream of commerce, and neither were the supplies for growing it. (Marijuana is highly unusual among the substances subject to the CSA in that it can be cultivated without any materials that have traveled in interstate commerce.) Lopez makes clear that possession is not itself commercial activity. And respondents have not come into possession by means of any commercial transaction; they have simply grown, in their own homes, marijuana for their own use, without acquiring, buying, selling, or bartering a thing of value.

The Court suggests that Wickard [established] federal regulatory power over any home consumption of a commodity for which a national market exists. I disagree. [In] contrast to the CSA's limitless assertion of power, Congress provided an exemption within the AAA for small producers. When Filburn planted the wheat at issue in Wickard, the statute exempted plantings less than 200 bushels (about six tons), and when he harvested his wheat it exempted plantings less than six acres. Wickard [did] not extend Commerce Clause authority to something as modest as the home cook's herb garden. [Wickard] did not hold or imply that small-scale production of commodities is always economic, and automatically within Congress' reach.

Even assuming that economic activity is at issue in this case, the Government has made no showing in fact that the possession and use of homegrown marijuana for medical purposes, in California or elsewhere, has a substantial effect on interstate commerce. [There] is simply no evidence that homegrown medicinal marijuana users constitute, in the aggregate, a sizable enough class to have a discernable, let alone substantial, impact on the national illicit drug market—or otherwise to threaten the CSA regime. [Common] sense suggests that medical marijuana users may be limited in number and that California's Compassionate Use Act and similar state legislation may well isolate activities relating to medicinal marijuana from the illicit market. In [Wickard,] the Court was able to consider "actual effects" because the parties had "stipulated a summary of the economics of the wheat industry." [The CSA's] bare declarations cannot be compared to the record before the Court in Wickard. [They] are asserted without any supporting evidence—descriptive, statistical, or otherwise. [Indeed,] if declarations like these suffice to justify federal regulation, and if the Court today is right about what passes rationality review before us, then our decision in Morrison should have come out the other way. In that case,

Congress had supplied numerous findings regarding the impact gender-motivated violence had on the national economy. [How] can it be that voluminous findings, documenting extensive hearings about the specific topic of violence against women, did not pass constitutional muster in Morrison, while the CSA's abstract, unsubstantiated, generalized findings about controlled substances do?

III. [Relying] on Congress' abstract assertions, the Court has endorsed making it a federal crime to grow small amounts of marijuana in one's own home for one's own medicinal use. This overreaching stifles an express choice by some States, concerned for the lives and liberties of their people, to regulate medical marijuana differently. If I were a California citizen, I would not have voted for the medical marijuana ballot initiative; if I were a California legislator I would not have supported the Compassionate Use Act. But whatever the wisdom of California's experiment with medical marijuana, the federalism principles that have driven our Commerce Clause cases require that room for experiment be protected in this case.

■ JUSTICE THOMAS, dissenting.

Respondents Diane Monson and Angel Raich use marijuana that has never been bought or sold, that has never crossed state lines, and that has had no demonstrable effect on the national market for marijuana. If Congress can regulate this under the Commerce Clause, then it can regulate virtually anything—and the Federal Government is no longer one of limited and enumerated powers. Respondents' local cultivation and consumption of marijuana is not "Commerce . . . among the several States." [No] evidence from the founding suggests that "commerce" included the mere possession of a good or some purely personal activity that did not involve trade or exchange for value. In the early days of the Republic, it would have been unthinkable that Congress could prohibit the local cultivation, possession, and consumption of marijuana.

[This] makes a mockery of Madison's assurance to the people of New York that the "powers delegated" to the Federal Government are "few and defined," while those of the States are "numerous and indefinite." The Federalist, No. 45.

COMMERCE CLAUSE REVIEW LEADING UP TO THE AFFORDABLE CARE ACT

1. ***Economic vs. noneconomic activity.*** Raich extended the economic-noneconomic distinction emphasized in Morrison. In Raich, the majority allowed the federal government to aggregate the effects of homegrown marijuana on the broader scheme of the CSA, even though the cultivation of marijuana at home for personal consumption is a noneconomic activity in itself, because the activities regulated by the CSA as a whole "are quintessentially economic"—namely, the "production, distribution, and consumption of commodities." Does Commerce Clause analysis now turn on the level of generality at which the Court assesses the activity being regulated? The Court considered marijuana regulation generally—not merely regulation of homegrown marijuana—as the proper level of analysis despite the fact that the respondents used only homegrown marijuana. If the Court had chosen homegrown marijuana as the proper level of analysis, then

could the Court have applied the Wickard aggregation principle? Lopez suggested that noneconomic activities like gun possession may *not* be aggregated to support an inference of substantial effect on commerce.

2. ***General vs. specific congressional schemes.*** The Raich majority distinguished the "comprehensive" narcotics regulation Congress had created in the CSA from the "single-subject" legislation struck down in Lopez. Does this mean Congress might have regulated Lopez's gun if it had done so as part of a general federal gun control law? Does the Raich majority thus draw a mere "drafting" distinction, as Justice O'Connor suggests? Or does its emphasis on the comprehensiveness of the federal scheme help to draw meaningful, substantive distinctions between Congress's proper regulation of national markets and improper displacement of state governments: "[T]here was insufficient political support for broad-based gun regulation. Congress could not pass the kind of law the Commerce Clause envisioned. It resorted to a brief single-subject statute because that was all it had the political support to do, and in doing so, passed the kind of law typical of local government." Althouse, "Why Not Heighten the Scrutiny of Congressional Power When the States Undertake Policy Experiments?," 9 Lewis & Clark L. Rev. 779 (2005).

3. ***States as "laboratories of experiment."*** In Lopez and Morrison, there was no stark conflict between state and federal policy: no state had actively allowed guns in schools, or encouraged violence against women; the goals of federal and state policies were shared, even if the policies were implemented differently. In Raich, by contrast, California's Compassionate Use Act, enacted by state voters in 1996, conflicted with federal narcotics law. It provided that state laws criminalizing small-scale possession and cultivation "shall not apply to a patient, or to a patient's primary caregiver, who possesses or cultivates marijuana for the personal medical purposes of the patient upon the written or oral recommendation or approval of a physician." (Twenty-two other states and the District of Columbia have since passed similar measures through ballot, statute, or constitutional amendment.) In Raich, however, the majority declined to defer to this exercise of the state's power to act as a "laboratory for experiment."

Should congressional commerce power be interpreted more restrictively in areas where the states are conducting such policy experiments? Consider the view that "recognition of the existence and capacity of state governments can and should occur through ['necessary and proper'] analysis. [Federal] action may well be necessary when failure to act would leave a regulatory void; it may well be less necessary when state regulation is taken into account." Young, "Just Blowing Smoke?," 2005 Sup. Ct. Rev. 1. Are such judicially administered limits to congressional power workable? Or does such a view allow the states to write their own exceptions to federal law?

Note that the dissenters in Raich made a point to suggest that their fidelity to federalism transcended their view of the wisdom of the state policy at stake; Justice O'Connor took pains to point out she would not have supported medicinal marijuana use if she were acting as a voter or a legislator. Does federalism predictably favor conservative or liberal substantive policies? Note that liberal state governments have invoked federalism principles to defend their own deviation from conservative federal policies on such issues as medical marijuana, assisted suicide, reproductive rights, stem cell research, and (before United States v. Windsor, p. 575 below) same-sex marriage. See Sullivan, "From States' Rights Blues to Blue

States' Rights: Federalism After the Rehnquist Court," 75 Fordham L. Rev. 799 (2006).

4. ***State efforts to legalize federal crimes.*** Raich differs from Lopez and Morrison in that a state law sought to carve out an exception from a federal regulatory regime; the federal laws struck down in Lopez and Morrison, by contrast, arguably duplicated rather than displaced state policies. Does this difference help explain the Court's greater deference to Congress in Raich? What are the implications for state efforts to legalize other activities that Congress has sought to proscribe, such as certain abortion procedures, physician-assisted suicide, needle exchange programs, possession of certain firearms, or online sports gambling? And why have states continued to legalize the use of medical marijuana despite the decision in Raich? One commentator suggests that the answer lies in the fact that the federal government depends upon the states as a practical matter to enforce marijuana prohibitions and other federal laws, but cannot require them to do so under the anticommandeering principle implicit in the federalist structure (see New York v. United States, p. 173 below): "[T]he federal government is only a two-bit player when it comes to marijuana enforcement. Only 1 percent of the roughly 800,000 marijuana cases generated every year are handled by federal authorities. [The] federal ban may be strict—and its penalties severe—but without the wholehearted cooperation of state law enforcement authorities its impact on private behavior will remain limited." Mikos, "On the Limits of Supremacy: Medical Marijuana and the States' Overlooked Power to Legalize Federal Crime," 62 Vand. L. Rev. 1421 (2009). Does this mean that judicial intervention is unnecessary in such cases to preserve the policy prerogatives of the states?

5. ***Federal protection for endangered species.*** Plaintiffs in several states have challenged the Endangered Species Act (ESA) as beyond the federal commerce power when applied to prohibit the taking of purely intrastate species. Four courts of appeal have rejected these challenges, citing the economic benefits of protecting endangered species generally and invoking Raich's "class of activities" principle: "Congress had a rational basis for believing that regulation of an intrastate activity was an essential part of a larger regulation of economic activity." Alabama-Tombigbee Rivers Coal. v. Kempthorne, 477 F.3d 1250 (11th Cir. 2007). But one federal district court decision invalidated an application of the ESA to the intrastate Utah prairie dog, finding the link to interstate commerce "too attenuated." PETPO v. U.S. Fish & Wildlife Serv., 57 F. Supp. 3d 1337 (D. Utah 2014).

6. ***The commerce power and the Affordable Care Act.*** The Patient Protection and Affordable Care Act of 2010 (ACA), a comprehensive overhaul of the nation's health care financing system enacted by Congress and signed into law by President Barack Obama, drew sharp constitutional challenge, especially to the provision popularly labeled the "individual mandate," which requires individuals who are not exempt and who do not receive health insurance through an employer or government program to purchase health insurance from a private insurer in order to maintain "minimum essential" health insurance coverage, on pain of a "penalty" to be paid to the Internal Revenue Service with an individual's taxes. In a sharply divided decision in National Federation of Independent Business v. Sebelius ("NFIB"), the Supreme Court upheld the minimum essential coverage provision by a 5–4 vote, but did so on the ground that it was within congressional authority as a tax, not as a regulation of commerce under the

Commerce Clause or Necessary and Proper Clause. (For the portion of the decision concerning the necessary and proper power, see above at p. 160; for the taxing power portion, see below p. 196.) Five Justices concluded that the mandate exceeded Congress's power under the Commerce Clause. Chief Justice Roberts provided the pivotal vote in both of these 5–4 lineups. The Commerce Clause ruling was as follows:

National Federation of Independent Business v. Sebelius

567 U.S. 519, 132 S. Ct. 2566, 183 L. Ed. 2d 450 (2012).

[In 2010, Congress enacted the Patient Protection and Affordable Care Act. The Act aims to increase the number of Americans covered by health insurance and decrease the cost of health care. The individual mandate requires most Americans to maintain "minimum essential" health insurance coverage. The mandate does not apply to some individuals, such as prisoners and undocumented aliens. Many individuals will receive the required coverage through their employer, or from a government program such as Medicaid or Medicare. But for individuals who are not exempt and do not receive health insurance through a third party, the means of satisfying the requirement is to purchase insurance from a private company. Those who do not comply with the mandate must make a "[s]hared responsibility payment" to the Federal Government. That payment, which the Act describes as a "penalty," is calculated as a percentage of household income, subject to a floor based on a specified dollar amount and a ceiling based on the average annual premium the individual would have to pay for qualifying private health insurance. The Act provides that the penalty will be paid to the Internal Revenue Service with an individual's taxes, and "shall be assessed and collected in the same manner" as tax penalties, such as the penalty for claiming too large an income tax refund.]

■ CHIEF JUSTICE ROBERTS announced the judgment of the Court and delivered an opinion with respect to Part III–A.

III. A. [The] Government's first argument is that the individual mandate is a valid exercise of Congress's power under the Commerce Clause and the Necessary and Proper Clause. According to the Government, the health care market is characterized by a significant cost-shifting problem. Everyone will eventually need health care at a time and to an extent they cannot predict, but if they do not have insurance, they often will not be able to pay for it. Because state and federal laws nonetheless require hospitals to provide a certain degree of care to individuals without regard to their ability to pay, hospitals end up receiving compensation for only a portion of the services they provide. To recoup the losses, hospitals pass on the cost to insurers through higher rates, and insurers, in turn, pass on the cost to policy holders in the form of higher premiums. Congress estimated that the cost of uncompensated care raises family health insurance premiums, on average, by over $1,000 per year.

In the Affordable Care Act, Congress addressed the problem of those who cannot obtain insurance coverage because of preexisting conditions or other health issues. It did so through the Act's "guaranteed-issue" and "community-rating" provisions. These provisions together prohibit insurance companies from denying coverage to those with such conditions or charging unhealthy individuals higher premiums than healthy individuals. The guaranteed-issue and community-rating reforms do not, however, address the issue of healthy individuals who choose not to purchase insurance to cover potential health care needs. In fact, the reforms sharply exacerbate that problem, by providing an incentive for individuals to delay purchasing health insurance until they become sick, relying on the promise of guaranteed and affordable coverage. The reforms also threaten to impose massive new costs on insurers, who are required to accept unhealthy individuals but prohibited from charging them rates necessary to pay for their coverage. This will lead insurers to significantly increase premiums on everyone. The individual mandate was Congress's solution to these problems. By requiring that individuals purchase health insurance, the mandate prevents cost-shifting by those who would otherwise go without it. In addition, the mandate forces into the insurance risk pool more healthy individuals, whose premiums on average will be higher than their health care expenses. This allows insurers to subsidize the costs of covering the unhealthy individuals the reforms require them to accept.

[The] Government contends that the individual mandate is within Congress's power because the failure to purchase insurance "has a substantial and deleterious effect on interstate commerce" by creating the cost-shifting problem. [Given] its expansive scope, it is no surprise that Congress has employed the commerce power in a wide variety of ways to address the pressing needs of the time. But Congress has never attempted to rely on that power to compel individuals not engaged in commerce to purchase an unwanted product.[1] [The] power to regulate commerce presupposes the existence of commercial activity to be regulated. If the power to "regulate" something included the power to create it, many of the provisions in the Constitution would be superfluous. [Our] precedent also reflects this understanding. As expansive as our cases construing the scope of the commerce power have been, they all have one thing in common: They uniformly describe the power as reaching "activity." [The] individual mandate, however, does not regulate existing commercial activity. It instead compels individuals to become active in commerce by purchasing a product, on the ground that their failure to do so affects interstate commerce. Construing the Commerce Clause to permit Congress to regulate individuals precisely because they are doing nothing would open a new and potentially vast domain to congressional authority.

[Applying] the Government's logic to the familiar case of Wickard v. Filburn shows how far that logic would carry us from the notion of a government of limited powers. [Wickard] has long been regarded as "perhaps the most far reaching example of Commerce Clause authority over intrastate activity," but the Government's theory in this case would go much further. [The] farmer in Wickard was at least actively engaged in the production of wheat, and the Government could regulate that activity because of its effect

---

[1] The examples of other congressional mandates cited by [Justice Ginsburg] are not to the contrary. Each of those mandates—to report for jury duty, to register for the draft, to purchase firearms in anticipation of militia service, to exchange gold currency for paper currency, and to file a tax return—are based on constitutional provisions other than the Commerce Clause. See Art. I, § 8, cl. 9 (to "constitute Tribunals inferior to the supreme Court"); id., cl. 12 (to "raise and support Armies"); id., cl. 16 (to "provide for organizing, arming, and disciplining, the Militia"); id., cl. 5 (to "coin Money"); id., cl. 1 (to "lay and collect Taxes"). [Footnote by Chief Justice Roberts.]

on commerce. The Government's theory here would effectively override that limitation, by establishing that individuals may be regulated under the Commerce Clause whenever enough of them are not doing something the Government would have them do.

Indeed, the Government's logic would justify a mandatory purchase to solve almost any problem. To consider a different example in the health care market, many Americans do not eat a balanced diet. That group makes up a larger percentage of the total population than those without health insurance. The failure of that group to have a healthy diet increases health care costs, to a greater extent than the failure of the uninsured to purchase insurance. Those increased costs are borne in part by other Americans who must pay more, just as the uninsured shift costs to the insured. Congress addressed the insurance problem by ordering everyone to buy insurance. Under the Government's theory, Congress could address the diet problem by ordering everyone to buy vegetables. People, for reasons of their own, often fail to do things that would be good for them or good for society. Those failures—joined with the similar failures of others—can readily have a substantial effect on interstate commerce. Under the Government's logic, that authorizes Congress to use its commerce power to compel citizens to act as the Government would have them act. That is not the country the Framers of our Constitution envisioned.

[The] Government [argues] that because sickness and injury are unpredictable but unavoidable, "the uninsured as a class are active in the market for health care, which they regularly seek and obtain." [But] we have never permitted Congress to anticipate that activity itself in order to regulate individuals not currently engaged in commerce. [Everyone] will likely participate in the markets for food, clothing, transportation, shelter, or energy; that does not authorize Congress to direct them to purchase particular products in those or other markets today. The Commerce Clause is not a general license to regulate an individual from cradle to grave, simply because he will predictably engage in particular transactions. Any police power to regulate individuals as such, as opposed to their activities, remains vested in the States. [The] individual mandate forces individuals into commerce precisely because they elected to refrain from commercial activity. Such a law cannot be sustained under a clause authorizing Congress to "regulate Commerce."

■ JUSTICES SCALIA, KENNEDY, THOMAS, and ALITO, dissenting.

[Whatever] may be the conceptual limits upon the Commerce Clause, [they] cannot be such as will enable the Federal Government to regulate all private conduct and to compel the States to function as administrators of federal programs. [The] striking case of Wickard v. Filburn, which held that the economic activity of growing wheat, even for one's own consumption, affected commerce sufficiently that it could be regulated, always has been regarded as the *ne plus ultra* of expansive Commerce Clause jurisprudence. To go beyond that, and to say the failure to grow wheat (which is not an economic activity, or any activity at all) nonetheless affects commerce and therefore can be federally regulated, is to make mere breathing in and out the basis for federal prescription and to extend federal power to virtually all human activity.

I. [The] Government offers two theories as to why the Individual Mandate is [constitutional.] Neither theory suffices to sustain its validity. A. [The] Government presents the Individual Mandate as a unique feature of a complicated regulatory scheme governing many parties with countervailing incentives that must be carefully balanced. Congress has imposed an extensive set of regulations on the health insurance industry, and compliance with those regulations will likely cost the industry a great deal. If the industry does not respond by increasing premiums, it is not likely to survive. And if the industry does increase premiums, then there is a serious risk that its products—insurance plans—will become economically undesirable for many and prohibitively expensive for the rest. This is not a dilemma unique to regulation of the health-insurance industry. Government regulation typically imposes costs on the regulated industry—especially regulation that prohibits economic behavior in which most market participants are already engaging. [Here,] however, Congress has impressed into service third parties, healthy individuals who could be but are not customers of the relevant industry, to offset the undesirable consequences of the regulation. Congress' desire to force these individuals to purchase insurance is motivated by the fact that they are further removed from the market than unhealthy individuals with pre-existing conditions, because they are less likely to need extensive care in the near future. If Congress can reach out and command even those furthest removed from an interstate market to participate in the market, then the Commerce Clause becomes a font of unlimited power.

[Gonzales v. Raich] is no precedent for what Congress has done here. That case's prohibition of growing and of possession [did] not represent the expansion of the federal power to direct into a broad new field. [Moreover, the] Court's opinion in Raich pointed out that the growing and possession prohibitions were the only practicable way of enabling the prohibition of interstate traffic in marijuana to be effectively enforced. [With] the present statute, by contrast, there are many ways other than this unprecedented Individual Mandate by which the regulatory scheme's goals of reducing insurance premiums and ensuring the profitability of insurers could be achieved. For instance, those who did not purchase insurance could be subjected to a surcharge when they do enter the health insurance system. Or they could be denied a full income tax credit given to those who do purchase the insurance.

B. The Government's second theory in support of the Individual Mandate is that [it] directs the manner in which individuals purchase health care services and related goods (directing that they be purchased through insurance) and is therefore a straightforward exercise of the commerce power. The primary problem with this argument is that [the Mandate] does not apply only to persons who purchase all, or most, or even any, of the health care services or goods that the mandated insurance covers. [The] decision to forgo participation in an interstate market is not itself commercial activity (or indeed any activity at all) within Congress' power to regulate. It is true that, at the end of the day, it is inevitable that each American will affect commerce and become a part of it, even if not by choice. But if every person comes within the Commerce Clause power of Congress to regulate by the simple reason that he will one day engage in commerce, the idea of a limited Government power is at an end.

C. [The] dissent dismisses the conclusion that the power to compel entry into the health-insurance market would include the power to compel entry into the new-car or broccoli markets. The latter purchasers, it says, "will be obliged to pay at the counter before receiving the vehicle or nourishment," whereas those refusing to purchase health-insurance will ultimately get treated anyway, at others' expense. But those differences do not show that the failure to enter the health-insurance market, unlike the failure to buy cars and broccoli, is an activity that Congress can "regulate."

■ JUSTICE GINSBURG, with whom JUSTICES BREYER, SOTOMAYOR, and KAGAN join, dissenting in part.

Unlike the Chief Justice, [I would hold] that the Commerce Clause authorizes Congress to enact the minimum coverage provision. In enacting the [ACA,] Congress comprehensively reformed the national market for healthcare products and services. By any measure, that market is immense. Collectively, Americans spent $2.5 trillion on health care in 2009, accounting for 17.6% of our Nation's economy. Within the next decade, it is anticipated, spending on health care will nearly double. [Unlike] the market for almost any other product or service, the market for medical care is one in which all individuals inevitably participate. Virtually every person residing in the United States, sooner or later, will visit a doctor or other health-care professional. When individuals make those visits, they face another reality of the current market for medical care: its high cost. In 2010, on average, an individual in the United States incurred over $7,000 in health-care expenses. Over a lifetime, costs mount to hundreds of thousands of dollars. When a person requires nonroutine care, the cost will generally exceed what he or she can afford to pay. [Although] every U.S. domiciliary will incur significant medical expenses during his or her lifetime, the time when care will be needed is often unpredictable. An accident, a heart attack, or a cancer diagnosis commonly occurs without warning. Inescapably, we are all at peril of needing medical care without a moment's notice.

To manage the risks associated with medical care—its high cost, its unpredictability, and its inevitability—most people in the United States obtain health insurance. [Not] all U.S. residents, however, have health insurance. In 2009, approximately 50 million people were uninsured, either by choice or, more likely, because they could not afford private insurance and did not qualify for government aid. [Unlike] markets for most products, however, the inability to pay for care does not mean that an uninsured individual will receive no care. Federal and state law, as well as professional obligations and embedded social norms, require hospitals and physicians to provide care when it is most needed, regardless of the patient's ability to pay. [As] a consequence, medical-care providers deliver significant amounts of care to the uninsured for which the providers receive no payment. Health-care providers do not absorb these bad debts. Instead, they raise their prices, passing along the cost of uncompensated care to those who do pay reliably: the government and private insurance companies. In response, private insurers increase their premiums, shifting the cost of the elevated bills from providers onto those who carry insurance. The net result: Those with health insurance subsidize the medical care of those without it. As economists would describe what happens, the uninsured "free ride" on those who pay for health insurance. The size of this subsidy is considerable. Congress found that the cost-shifting just described "increases family [insurance] premiums by on average over $1,000 a year."

States cannot resolve the problem of the uninsured on their own. [An] influx of unhealthy individuals into a State with universal health care would result in increased spending on medical services. To cover the increased costs, a State would have to raise taxes, and private health-insurance states can't solve this prob.

companies would have to increase premiums. Higher taxes and increased insurance costs would, in turn, encourage businesses and healthy individuals to leave the State. [Facing] that risk, individual States are unlikely to take the initiative in addressing the problem of the uninsured, even though solving that problem is in all States' best interests. Congress' intervention was needed to overcome this collective-action impasse.

Aware that a national solution was required, Congress could have taken over the health-insurance market by establishing a tax-and-spend federal program like Social Security. Such a program, commonly referred to as a single-payer system (where the sole payer is the Federal Government), would have left little, if any, room for private enterprise or the States. Instead of going this route, Congress enacted the ACA, a solution that retains a robust role for private insurers and state governments. [To] ensure that individuals with medical histories have access to affordable insurance, Congress [imposed] a "guaranteed issue" requirement, which bars insurers from denying coverage to any person on account of that person's medical condition or history [and required] insurers to use "community rating" to price their insurance policies, [barring] insurance companies from charging higher premiums to those with preexisting conditions. But these two provisions, Congress comprehended, could not work effectively unless individuals were given a powerful incentive to obtain insurance. [When] insurance companies are required to insure the sick at affordable prices, individuals can wait until they become ill to buy insurance. Pretty soon, those in need of immediate medical care [become] the insurance companies' main customers. This "adverse selection" problem leaves insurers with two choices: They can either raise premiums dramatically to cover their ever-increasing costs or they can exit the market. [Massachusetts,] Congress was told, cracked the adverse selection problem. By requiring most residents to obtain insurance, [Massachusetts] ensured that insurers would not be left with only the sick as customers. In coupling the minimum coverage provision with guaranteed-issue and community-rating prescriptions, Congress followed Massachusetts' lead.

[Consistent] with the Framers' intent, we have repeatedly emphasized that Congress' authority under the Commerce Clause is dependent upon "practical" considerations, including "actual experience." We afford Congress the leeway "to undertake to solve national problems directly and realistically." [Congress] had a rational basis for concluding that the uninsured, as a class, substantially affect interstate commerce [and that] their inability to pay for a significant portion of [their health care] consumption drives up market prices, foists costs on other consumers, and reduces market efficiency and stability. [The] minimum coverage provision, furthermore, bears a "reasonable connection" to Congress' goal of protecting the health-care market from the disruption caused by individuals who fail to obtain insurance. By requiring those who do not carry insurance to pay a toll, the minimum coverage provision gives individuals a strong incentive to insure. This incentive, Congress had good reason to believe, would reduce the number of uninsured and, correspondingly, mitigate the adverse impact the uninsured have on the national health-care market.

[The] inevitable yet unpredictable need for medical care and the guarantee that emergency care will be provided when required are conditions nonexistent in other markets. That is so of the market for cars, and of the market for broccoli as well. Although an individual might buy a car or a crown of broccoli one day, there is no certainty she will ever do so. And if she eventually wants a car or has a craving for broccoli, she will be obliged to pay at the counter before receiving the vehicle or nourishment. She will get no free ride or food, at the expense of another consumer forced to pay an inflated price. Upholding the minimum coverage provision on the ground that all are participants or will be participants in the health-care market would therefore carry no implication that Congress may justify under the Commerce Clause a mandate to buy other products and services.

NFIB AND THE COMMERCE POWER

1. ***The activity/inactivity distinction.*** Chief Justice Roberts's controlling opinion holds that the Commerce Clause permits the federal government to regulate only pre-existing economic activity. The federal government defended the Act by arguing that the decision to forgo health insurance constitutes economic activity because all persons will need medical care at some point in their lives and are inevitably active in the market for health care (as opposed to health insurance), but the Chief Justice's opinion rejected that argument. How much will the activity/inactivity distinction cabin the federal commerce power? How often does the federal government compel inactive persons to do something under its commerce power? Will the activity/inactivity Commerce Clause limitation change the scope of federal power or simply the form in which it is exercised? As Justice Ginsburg notes in dissent, "Congress could have taken over the health-insurance market by establishing a tax-and-spend federal program like Social Security." For an argument that NFIB is likely to limit the form more than the scope of federal regulation, see Metzger, Comment, "To Tax, To Spend, To Regulate," 126 Harv. L. Rev. 83 (2012).

2. ***Scope of the problem vs. the scope of the power.*** Should the scope of a problem and the states' inability to solve it on their own inform the scope of Congress's power under the Commerce Clause? Justice Ginsburg's dissent stresses that the Court in the past had "repeatedly emphasized that Congress' authority under the Commerce Clause is dependent upon 'practical' considerations [and that the Court] afford[ed] Congress the leeway 'to undertake to solve national problems directly and realistically.'" By contrast, do Chief Justice Roberts's opinion and Justice Scalia's dissent draw a formalist line between activity and inactivity without respect to the scope of the problem?

3. ***"We have never" Commerce Clause jurisprudence.*** A touchstone of Chief Justice Roberts's opinion and Justice Scalia's joint dissent is the purportedly unprecedented nature of the individual mandate. Rather than simply grounding the opinions in extrapolation from commerce power precedent, these opinions rely heavily on slippery-slope arguments stemming from the purportedly novel application of federal power at issue in the context of the individual mandate. Does the purportedly unique nature of the individual mandate in the Affordable Care Act limit the scope of this holding? Or does the Court's hostility to approving new categories of Commerce Clause power suggest future restrictions on the commerce power within other categories?

4. ***Values underlying NFIB's commerce power restriction.*** What values underlie the activity/inactivity distinction that the Court adopts to

define an outer limit of the commerce power? How much of the decision turns on the Court's textual reading of the word "regulate" as presupposing existing economic activity? How important is the Court's belief that the Constitution envisions a particular relationship between the citizen and the state, such that a country in which the federal government can compel a person to buy health insurance is, in Chief Justice Roberts's words, "not the country the Framers of our Constitution envisioned?" Is the citizen-state relationship rationale undercut by the fact that the states can compel identical conduct through their police powers? Is the Commerce Clause the proper constitutional avenue through which to define the citizen's relationship to the state by limiting federal power?

5. ***Shift in legal consensus leading up to NFIB.*** Upon passage of the Affordable Care Act in 2010, the general legal consensus seemed to be that the Act was a permissible exercise of the commerce power under precedents like Wickard and Raich. By the time the constitutional challenge reached the Supreme Court, that consensus had eroded. Randy Barnett, a principal advocate for invalidation of the ACA, proposed the new distinction between economic activity that the commerce power allowed Congress to regulate, and economic inactivity that Congress could not regulate. See Barnett, "Commandeering the People: Why the Individual Health Insurance Mandate Is Unconstitutional," 5 N.Y.U. J.L. & Liberty 581 (2010). That this activity/inactivity distinction eventually gained the approval of the Court demonstrates the capacity for seeming legal consensus to yield in the face of novel arguments. Compare Balkin, "From Off the Wall to On the Wall: How the Mandate Challenge Went Mainstream," The Atlantic (June 4, 2012) ("The history of American constitutional development, in large part, has been the history of formerly crazy arguments moving from off the wall to on the wall, and then being adopted by courts.").

SECTION 5. THE TENTH AMENDMENT AS AN EXTERNAL CONSTRAINT ON THE FEDERAL COMMERCE POWER

Lopez, Morrison, and NFIB revived *internal* restraints on the commerce power through heightened review of the scope of Congress's authority under Art. I, § 8. The Court has also developed several *external* restraints on the commerce power rooted in two textual sources, the Tenth and Eleventh Amendments, as well as in the general structural postulates of federalism. The Tenth Amendment provides: "The powers not delegated to the United States by the Constitution, nor prohibited by it to the States, are reserved to the States respectively, or to the people." As further discussed in Section 6 below, the Eleventh Amendment, enacted to overrule the Supreme Court decision in Chisholm v. Georgia, 2 U.S. (2 Dall.) 419 (1793) (allowing a suit by a South Carolina citizen against the state of Georgia), provides: "The judicial power of the United States shall not be construed to extend to any suit in law or equity, commenced or prosecuted against one of the United States by Citizens of another State, or by Citizens or Subjects of any Foreign State."

Does it make any difference whether state autonomy is protected by internal or external limits on Congress's power? By a decision that Congress has exceeded its authority or that, even though a congressional enactment was within Congress's authority, its application to the states is barred by an affirmative state privilege or immunity? Consider the following remark by

Justice O'Connor in the second New York v. United States decision, which follows below: "In the end, just as a cup may be half empty or half full, it makes no difference whether one views the question at issue in these cases as one of ascertaining the limits of the power delegated to the Federal Government under the affirmative provisions of the Constitution or one of discerning the core of sovereignty retained by the States under the Tenth Amendment. Either way, we must determine whether [any challenged provision] oversteps the boundary between federal and state authority." Are the two sorts of challenges always mirror images of one another, or are there some salient differences?

1. ***The rise and fall of state autonomy from federal regulation.*** The Court has never doubted that there must be *some* outer limits on federal power to interfere with the core functions implicit in state sovereignty. For example, **Coyle v. Oklahoma**, 221 U.S. 559 (1911), invalidated a condition in the federal enabling act for admission of Oklahoma to the union that had purported to specify the location of the state capital. The Court held that "[t]he power to locate its own seat of government [and] to change the same [are] essentially state powers beyond the control of Congress." Coyle has never been narrowed or overruled.

When states participate in economic activity alongside private actors, however, the question of whether they are exercising state sovereignty is more difficult. If states operate businesses or hire employees to provide public services, may they object to congressional exercises of the commerce power that reach those activities? Should they receive constitutionally compelled immunity from acts of Congress that private parties do not enjoy? Or are they simply participants in the marketplace that Congress may regulate on a par with private parties?

States sought such immunity unsuccessfully in several New Deal-era cases. In **United States v. California**, 297 U.S. 175 (1936), for example, the Court upheld a penalty imposed on a state-owned railroad for violation of the Federal Safety Appliance Act. Justice STONE's opinion found it unnecessary to rule upon California's argument that its operation of a railroad involved the exercise of "a public function in its sovereign capacity." "The sovereign power of the states," he wrote, "is necessarily diminished to the extent of the grants of power to the federal government in the Constitution." He also rejected California's argument that the State could claim immunity from federal regulation for "activities in which the States have traditionally engaged": "[T]here is no such limitation upon the plenary power to regulate commerce. The state can no more deny the power if its exercise has been authorized by Congress than can an individual."

In **New York v. United States**, 326 U.S. 572 (1946), the Court upheld against a similar state immunity claim the application of a federal tax to the State of New York's sale of bottled mineral water from state-owned springs. The vote was 6–2 (with Justice Jackson not participating), but the justices in the majority did not produce a united opinion. Justice FRANKFURTER wrote an opinion joined only by Justice Rutledge: "Surely the power of Congress to lay taxes has impliedly no less a reach than the power of Congress to regulate commerce. There are, of course, State activities and State-owned property that partake of uniqueness from the point of view of intergovernmental relations. These inherently constitute a class by themselves. Only a State can own a Statehouse; only a State can get income by taxing. These could not be included for purposes of federal taxation in any abstract category of taxpayers without taxing the State as a State. But so long as Congress generally taps a source of revenue by whomsoever earned and not uniquely capable of being earned only by a State, the Constitution of the United States does not forbid it merely because its incidence falls also on a State."

Chief Justice STONE wrote a separate opinion, joined by Justices Reed, Murphy, and Burton, that agreed with the result but cautioned: "[W]e are not prepared to say that the national government may constitutionally lay a non-discriminatory tax on every class of property and activities of States and individuals alike. Concededly a federal tax discriminating against a State would be an unconstitutional exertion of power over a coexisting sovereignty within the same framework of government. But [a] federal tax which is not discriminatory as to the subject matter may nevertheless so affect the State, merely because it is a State that is being taxed, as to interfere unduly with the State's performance of its sovereign functions of government. [A] State may, like a private individual, own real property and receive income. But [we] could hardly say that a general non-discriminatory real estate tax (apportioned), or an income tax laid upon citizens and States alike could be constitutionally applied to the State's capitol, its State-house, its public school houses, public parks, or its revenues from taxes or school lands, even though all real property and all income of the citizen is taxed."

Justice DOUGLAS dissented, joined by Justice Black: "A State's project is as much a legitimate governmental activity whether it is traditional, or akin to private enterprise, or conducted for profit. A State may deem it as essential to its economy that it own and operate a railroad, a mill, or an irrigation system as it does to own and operate bridges, street lights, or a sewage disposal plant. What might have been viewed in an earlier day as an improvident or even dangerous extension of state activities may today be deemed indispensable. [Here] a State is disposing of some of its natural resources. Tomorrow it may issue securities, sell power from its public power project, or manufacture fertilizer. Each is an exercise of its power of sovereignty. Must it pay the federal government for the privilege of exercising that inherent power?"

In **National League of Cities v. Usery**, 426 U.S. 833 (1976), a state-autonomy defense to otherwise valid federal regulation finally succeeded. That case involved amendments to the Fair Labor Standards Act (FLSA) that extended minimum wage and maximum hour provisions to employees of state and local governments. By a 5–4 decision, the Court held the extension within Congress's commerce authority, but nonetheless unconstitutional. Justice REHNQUIST wrote for the Court: "Appellants in no way challenge [the] breadth of authority granted Congress under the commerce power. Their contention, on the contrary, is that when Congress seeks to regulate directly the activities of States as public employers, it transgresses an affirmative limitation on the exercise of its power akin to other commerce power affirmative limitations contained in the Constitution. Congressional enactments which may be fully within the grant of legislative authority contained in the Commerce Clause may nonetheless be invalid because found to offend against the right to trial by jury contained in the Sixth Amendment, or the Due Process Clause of the Fifth Amendment. Appellants' essential contention is that the 1974 amendments to the Act, while undoubtedly within the scope of the Commerce Clause, encounter a similar constitutional barrier because they are to be applied directly to the States and subdivisions of States as employers.

"Our examination of the effect of the 1974 amendments, as sought to be extended to the States and their political subdivisions, satisfies us that both the minimum wage and the maximum hour provisions will impermissibly interfere with the integral governmental functions of these bodies, significantly alter[ing] or displac[ing] the States' abilities to structure employer-employee relationships in such areas as fire prevention, police protection, sanitation, public health, and parks and recreation. These activities are typical of those performed by state and local governments in discharging their dual functions of administering the public law and furnishing public services. Indeed, it is functions such as these which governments are created to provide, services such as these which the States have traditionally afforded their citizens. If Congress may withdraw from the States the authority to make those fundamental employment decisions upon which their systems for performance of these functions must rest, we think there would be little left of the States' 'separate and independent existence.' Coyle. Thus, [Congress] has attempted to exercise its Commerce Clause authority to prescribe minimum wages and maximum hours to be paid by the States in their capacities as sovereign governments. [This] exercise of congressional authority does not comport with the federal system of government embodied in the Constitution. We hold that insofar as the challenged amendments operate to directly displace the States' freedom to structure integral operations in areas of traditional governmental functions, they are not within the authority granted Congress by Art. I, § 8, cl. 3."

Justice BLACKMUN joined Justice Rehnquist's opinion, even though he was "not untroubled by certain possible implications of the Court's opinion." He viewed the prevailing opinion as adopting "a balancing approach" that permitted federal regulation "in areas such as environmental protection, where the federal interest is demonstrably greater and where state facility compliance with imposed federal standards would be essential." Justice BRENNAN's dissent, joined by Justices White and Marshall, charged that the prevailing opinion repudiated "principles governing judicial interpretation of our Constitution settled since the time of Chief Justice John Marshall, discarding his postulate that the Constitution contemplates that restraints upon exercise by Congress of its plenary commerce power lie in the political process and not in the judicial process." Justice Brennan urged "[j]udicial restraint" because "the political branches of our Government are structured to protect the interests of the States as well as the Nation as a whole, and that the States are fully able to protect their own interests."

Less than a decade after National League of Cities was decided, however, it was overruled, again by a vote of 5–4. In **Garcia v. San Antonio Metropolitan Transit Authority**, 469 U.S. 528 (1985), the Court held a municipal transit authority properly subject to the minimum wage and overtime requirements of the Fair Labor Standards Act. Justice BLACKMUN, who had concurred in National League of Cities in 1976, now wrote the majority opinion. Reviewing decisions of the Court and the lower courts in the aftermath of National League of Cities, he found that the effort to define "traditional governmental functions" that were immune from federal regulation had proved "unworkable" as courts divided over whether such novel state functions as transportation and sewage treatment were as "integral" to state sovereignty as police and fire protection. He then turned to the "more fundamental problem" that "no distinction that purports to separate out important governmental functions can be faithful to the role of federalism in a democratic society. [Any] rule of state immunity that looks to the 'traditional,' 'integral,' or 'necessary' nature of governmental functions inevitably invites an unelected federal judiciary to make decisions about which state policies it favors and which one it dislikes. [We] therefore now reject, as unsound in principle and unworkable in practice, a rule of state immunity from federal regulation that turns on a judicial appraisal of whether a particular governmental function is 'integral' or 'traditional.' [Apart] from the limitation of federal authority inherent in the delegated nature of Congress' Article I powers, the principal means chosen by the Framers to insure the role of the States in the federal system lies in the structure of the federal government itself. [States'] sovereign interests [are] more properly protected by procedural safeguards inherent in the structure of the federal system than by judicially created limitations on federal power. [Any] substantive restraint on the exercise of Commerce Clause powers [must] be tailored to compensate for possible failings in the national political process rather than to dictate a 'sacred province of state autonomy.'

"The political process insures that laws that unduly burden the States will not be promulgated. [The] Framers gave the States a role in the selection both of the Executive and the Legislative Branches of the Federal Government. The States were vested with indirect influence over the House of Representatives and the Presidency by their control of electoral qualifications and their role in Presidential elections. U.S. Const., Art. I, § 2, and Art. II, § 1. They were given more direct influence in the Senate, where each State received equal representation and each Senator was to be selected by the legislature of his State. Art. I, § 3. The significance attached to the States' equal representation in the Senate is underscored by the prohibition of any constitutional amendment divesting a State of equal representation without the State's consent. Art. V.

"The effectiveness of the federal political process in preserving the States' interests is apparent even today in the course of federal legislation. On the one hand, the States have been able to direct a substantial proportion of federal revenues into their own treasuries in the form of general and program-specific grants in aid. [As] a result, federal grants now account for about one-fifth of state and local government expenditures. [At] the same time that the States have exercised their influence to obtain federal support, they have been able to exempt themselves from a wide variety of obligations imposed by Congress under the Commerce Clause. The fact that some federal statutes such as the FLSA extend general obligations to the States cannot obscure the extent to which the political position of the States in the federal system has served to minimize the burdens that the States bear under the Commerce Clause."

Justice POWELL, joined by Chief Justice Burger and Justices Rehnquist and O'Connor, dissented: "The States' role in our system of government is a matter of constitutional law, not of legislative grace. [The decision] that federal political officials, invoking the Commerce Clause, are the sole judges of the limits of their own power [is] inconsistent with the fundamental principles of our constitutional system. Marbury." In a footnote, he took specific issue with whether the states' interests still had any meaningful political safeguards in Congress: "At one time in our history, the view that the structure of the Federal Government sufficed to protect the

States might have had a somewhat more practical basis. [Not] only is the premise of this view clearly at odds with the proliferation of national legislation over the past 30 years, but 'a variety of structural and political changes occurring in this century have combined to make Congress particularly insensitive to state and local values.' The adoption of the Seventeenth Amendment (providing for direct election of Senators), the weakening of political parties on the local level, and the rise of national media, among other things, have made Congress increasingly less representative of state and local interests, and more likely to be responsive to the demands of various national constituencies. [And] 'as Senators and members of the House develop independent constituencies among groups such as farmers, businessmen, laborers, environmentalists, and the poor, each of which generally supports certain national initiatives, their tendency to identify with state interests and the positions of state officials is reduced.' "

Justice Powell also stressed the importance of state and local autonomy to "principles of democratic self government": "[Federal] legislation is drafted primarily by the staffs of the congressional committees. [The] administration and enforcement of federal laws and regulations necessarily are largely in the hands of staff and civil service employees. These employees may have little or no knowledge of the States and localities that will be affected by the statutes and regulations for which they are responsible. In any case, they hardly are as accessible and responsive as those who occupy analogous positions in State and local governments. [Members] of the immense federal bureaucracy are not elected, know less about the services traditionally rendered by States and localities, and are inevitably less responsive to recipients of such services, than are state legislatures, city councils, boards of supervisors, and state and local commissions, boards, and agencies. It is at these state and local levels—not in Washington as the Court so mistakenly thinks—that 'democratic self-government' is best exemplified."

Justice O'CONNOR also dissented, joined by Justices Powell and Rehnquist: "In my view, federalism cannot be reduced to the weak 'essence' distilled by the majority today. [The] true 'essence' of federalism is that the States *as States* have legitimate interests which the National Government is bound to respect even though its laws are supreme. If federalism so conceived [is] to remain meaningful, this Court cannot abdicate its constitutional responsibility to oversee the Federal Government's compliance with its duty to respect the legitimate interests of the States. [The] last two decades have seen an unprecedented growth of federal regulatory activity. [The] political process has not protected against these encroachments on state activities even though they directly impinge on a State's ability to make and enforce its laws. With the abandonment of National League of Cities, all that stands between the remaining essentials of state sovereignty and Congress is the latter's underdeveloped capacity for self-restraint." Justice REHNQUIST's brief dissent stated: "I do not think it incumbent on those of us in dissent to spell out further the fine points of principle that will, I am confident, in time again command the support of the majority of this Court."

2. ***The scope of judicial protection of state autonomy from federal encroachment.*** The Garcia majority suggested that some judicial intervention might still be appropriate "to compensate for possible failings in the national political process." Does this procedural limit provide any judicially administrable protection for the states? The Court considered and

rejected application of such a limit in **South Carolina v. Baker**, 485 U.S. 505 (1988), which upheld removal of an exemption from federal income tax for interest from bearer bonds issued by the states. The law in effect forced states to switch to issuing tax-exempt registered bonds in order to raise debt capital. The Court rejected the State's argument that this was one of those situations in which state interests were impaired because of "extraordinary defects in the national political process." Justice BRENNAN's majority opinion held that "South Carolina has not even alleged that it was deprived of any right to participate in the national political process or that it was singled out in a way that left it politically isolated and powerless. Rather, South Carolina argues that the political process failed here because [the law] was 'imposed by a vote of an uninformed Congress relying upon incomplete information.' But nothing in Garcia or the Tenth Amendment authorizes courts to second-guess the substantive basis for congressional legislation. Where, as here, the national political *process* did not operate in a defective manner, the Tenth Amendment is not implicated."

3. ***"Commandeering" state governments.*** In several decisions that arose in the interim between National League of Cities and Garcia, the Court suggested in dicta that Congress might not be able to "commandeer[ ] the legislative processes of the States by directly compelling them to enact and enforce a federal regulatory program" or "conscript state [agencies] into the national bureaucratic army." The Rehnquist Court eventually issued two major decisions invalidating federal laws on such a ground—New York v. United States, which invalidated a federal law for commandeering state legislatures, and Printz v. United States, which invalidated a law for commandeering state executive officials. Note that unlike National League of Cities, which limited what subject matters Congress might regulate with respect to the states, these decisions merely limit the method by which Congress may regulate the states.

New York v. United States

505 U.S. 144, 112 S. Ct. 2408, 120 L. Ed. 2d 120 (1992).

[The Low-Level Radioactive Waste Policy Amendments Act of 1985 required states to provide for the disposal of such waste generated within their borders and provided three "incentives" to states to comply with that obligation: (1) "monetary" incentives, which allowed states with disposal sites to impose a surcharge on waste received from other states; (2) "access" incentives, which allowed states to increase the cost of access to their sites and then deny access altogether to waste generated in states that did not meet federal deadlines; and (3) a "take title" sanction, providing that a state that failed to provide for the disposal of all internally generated waste by a particular date must take title to the waste and become liable for all damages incurred by the waste's generator or owner. New York and two of its counties sought a declaratory judgment that all three provisions exceeded Congress's power and violated the Tenth Amendment. The Court upheld the first two incentives but held the third, "take title" provision unconstitutional.]

■ JUSTICE O'CONNOR delivered the opinion of the Court.

[The] constitutional question is as old as the Constitution: It consists of discerning the proper division of authority between the Federal Government and the States. We conclude that while Congress has substantial power under the Constitution to encourage the States to provide for the disposal of the radioactive waste generated within their borders, the Constitution does not confer upon Congress the ability simply to compel the States to do so.

[Federalism] questions can be viewed in either of two ways. In some cases the Court has inquired whether an Act of Congress is authorized by one of the powers delegated to Congress in Article I of the Constitution. In other cases the Court has sought to determine whether an Act of Congress invades the province of state sovereignty reserved by the Tenth Amendment. In a case like this one, [the] two inquiries are mirror images of each other. If a power is delegated to Congress in the Constitution, the Tenth Amendment expressly disclaims any reservation of that power to the States; if a power is an attribute of state sovereignty reserved by the Tenth Amendment, it is necessarily a power the Constitution has not conferred on Congress. [The] Tenth Amendment [thus] restrains the power of Congress, but this limit is not derived from the text of the Tenth Amendment itself, which [is] essentially a tautology. Instead, the Tenth Amendment confirms that the power of the Federal Government is subject to limits that may, in a given instance, reserve power to the States.

[Petitioners] do not contend that Congress lacks the power to regulate the disposal of low level radioactive waste. Regulation of [the] resulting interstate market in waste disposal [is] well within Congress' authority under the Commerce Clause. Petitioners likewise do not dispute that under the Supremacy Clause Congress could, if it wished, pre-empt state radioactive waste regulation. Petitioners contend only that the Tenth Amendment limits the power of Congress to regulate in the way it has chosen. Rather than addressing the problem of waste disposal by directly regulating the generators and disposers of waste, petitioners argue, Congress has impermissibly directed the States to regulate in this field. Most of our recent cases interpreting the Tenth Amendment have concerned the authority of Congress to subject state governments to generally applicable laws. This case presents no occasion to apply or revisit the holdings of any of these cases, as this is not a case in which Congress has subjected a State to the same legislation applicable to private parties. This case instead concerns the circumstances under which Congress may use the States as implements of regulation; that is, whether Congress may direct or otherwise motivate the States to regulate in a particular field or a particular way.

[Congress] may not simply "commandeer the legislative processes of the States by directly compelling them to enact and enforce a federal regulatory program." [T]he Constitution has never been understood to confer upon Congress the ability to require the States to govern according to Congress' instructions. Indeed, the question whether the Constitution should permit Congress to employ state governments as regulatory agencies was a topic of lively debate among the Framers. Under the Articles of Confederation, Congress lacked the authority in most respects to govern the people directly. [The] inadequacy of this governmental structure was responsible in part for the Constitutional Convention. Alexander Hamilton observed: "The great and radical vice in the construction of the existing Confederation is in the principle of LEGISLATION for STATES or GOVERNMENTS, in their CORPORATE or COLLECTIVE CAPACITIES, and as contradistinguished from the INDIVIDUALS of whom they consist." The Federalist, No. 15. As Hamilton saw it, "[we] must extend the authority of the Union to the persons of the citizens—the only proper objects of government." [The] Convention generated a great number of proposals for the structure of the new Government, but two quickly took center stage. Under the Virginia Plan, [Congress] would exercise legislative authority directly upon individuals, without employing the States as intermediaries. Under the New Jersey Plan, [Congress] would continue to require the approval of the States before legislating, as [under] the Articles of Confederation. [In] the end, the Convention opted for a Constitution in which Congress would exercise its legislative authority directly over individuals rather than [over States]. This choice was made clear to the subsequent state ratifying conventions.

[The] allocation of power contained in the Commerce Clause [thus authorizes] Congress to regulate interstate commerce directly; it does not authorize Congress to regulate state governments' regulation of interstate commerce. This is not to say that Congress lacks the ability to encourage a State to regulate in a particular way, or that Congress may not hold out incentives to the States as a method of influencing a State's policy choices. [First,] under Congress' spending power, "Congress may attach conditions on the receipt of federal funds." [Second,] where Congress has the authority to regulate private activity under the Commerce Clause, we have recognized Congress' power to offer States the choice of regulating that activity according to federal standards or having state law preempted by federal regulation. By either of these two methods, [the] residents of the State retain the ultimate decision as to whether or not the State will comply. [Where] Congress encourages state regulation rather than compelling it, state governments remain responsive to the local electorate's preferences; state officials remain accountable to the people.

By contrast, where the Federal Government compels States to regulate, the accountability of both state and federal officials is diminished. If the citizens of New York, for example, do not consider that making provision for the disposal of radioactive waste is in their best interest, they may elect state officials who share their view. That view can always be preempted under the Supremacy Clause if is contrary to the national view, but in such a case it is the Federal Government that makes the decision in full view of the public, and it will be federal officials that suffer the consequences if the decision turns out to be detrimental or unpopular. But where the Federal Government directs the States to regulate, it may be state officials who will bear the brunt of public disapproval, while the federal officials who devised the regulatory program may remain insulated from the electoral ramifications of their decision. Accountability is thus diminished when, due to federal coercion, elected state officials cannot regulate in accordance with the views of the local electorate in matters not preempted by federal regulation.

[The] take title provision [crosses] the line distinguishing encouragement from coercion. [The] take title provision offers state governments a "choice" of either accepting ownership of waste or regulating according to the instructions of Congress. [The] Constitution would not permit Congress simply to transfer radioactive waste from generators to state governments. Such a forced transfer, standing alone, would in principle be no different than a congressionally compelled subsidy from state governments to radioactive waste producers. The same is true of the provision requiring the States to become liable for the generators' damages. Standing alone, this provision would be indistinguishable from an Act of

Congress directing the States to assume the liabilities of certain state residents. Either type of federal action would "commandeer" state governments into the service of federal regulatory purposes, and would for this reason be inconsistent with the Constitution's division of authority between federal and state governments. [The] second alternative held out to state governments—regulating pursuant to Congress' direction—would, standing alone, present a simple command to state governments to implement legislation enacted by Congress. [The] Constitution does not empower Congress to subject state governments to this type of instruction.

Because an instruction to state governments to take title to waste, standing alone, would be beyond the authority of Congress, and because a direct order to regulate, standing alone, would also be beyond the authority of Congress, it follows that Congress lacks the power to offer the States a choice between the two. [A] choice between two unconstitutionally coercive regulatory techniques is no choice at all. [Whether] one views the take title provision as lying outside Congress' enumerated powers, or as infringing upon the core of state sovereignty reserved by the Tenth Amendment, the provision is inconsistent with the federal structure of our Government established by the Constitution.

[The State respondents] observe that [the] Act embodies a bargain among the sited and unsited States, a compromise to which New York was a willing participant and from which New York has reaped much benefit. [But] the Constitution does not protect the sovereignty of States for the benefit of the States or state governments as abstract political entities, or even for the benefit of the public officials governing the States. To the contrary, the Constitution divides authority between federal and state governments for the protection of individuals. State sovereignty is not just an end in itself: "Rather, federalism secures to citizens the liberties that derive from the diffusion of sovereign power." Where Congress exceeds its authority relative to the States, therefore, the departure from the constitutional plan cannot be ratified by the "consent" of state officials.

[States] are not mere political subdivisions of the United States. State governments are neither regional offices nor administrative agencies of the Federal Government. The positions occupied by state officials appear nowhere on the Federal Government's most detailed organizational chart. The Constitution instead "leaves to the several States a residuary and inviolable sovereignty," The Federalist No. 39, reserved explicitly to the States by the Tenth Amendment. Whatever the outer limits of that sovereignty may be, one thing is clear: The Federal Government may not compel the States to enact or administer a federal regulatory program. [Affirmed in part and reversed in part.]

■ JUSTICE WHITE, with whom JUSTICES BLACKMUN and STEVENS join, dissenting.

[The Act] resulted from the efforts of state leaders to achieve a state-based set of remedies to the waste problem. They sought not federal preemption or intervention, but rather congressional sanction of interstate compromises they had reached. [The] 1985 Act was very much the product of cooperative federalism, in which the States bargained among themselves to achieve compromises for Congress to sanction. [Unlike] legislation that directs action from the Federal Government to the States, the [congressional action] reflected hard-fought agreements among States as refereed by Congress. [New York's] actions subsequent to enactment of the [Act] fairly indicate its approval of the interstate agreement process embodied in those laws within the meaning of Art. I, § 10, cl. 3. [I] do not understand the principle of federalism to impede the National Government from acting as referee among the States to prohibit one from bullying another.

[The] Court tacitly concedes that a failing of the political process cannot be shown in this case because [the] States were well able to look after themselves in the legislative process that culminated in the 1985 Act's passage. The Court rejects this process-based argument by resorting to generalities and platitudes about the purpose of federalism being to protect individual rights. Ultimately, I suppose, the entire structure of our federal constitutional government can be traced to an interest in establishing checks and balances to prevent the exercise of tyranny against individuals. But these fears seem extremely far distant to me in a situation such as this. We face a crisis of national proportions in the disposal of low-level radioactive waste, and Congress has acceded to the wishes of the States by permitting local decisionmaking rather than imposing a solution from Washington. New York itself participated and supported passage of this legislation at both the gubernatorial and federal representative levels, and then enacted state laws specifically to comply with the deadlines and timetables agreed upon by the States in the 1985 Act. For me, the Court's civics lecture has a decidedly hollow ring at a time when action, rather than rhetoric, is needed to solve a national problem.

■ JUSTICE STEVENS, concurring in part and dissenting in part.

[The] notion that Congress does not have the power to issue "a simple command to state governments to implement legislation enacted by Congress" is incorrect and unsound. There is no such limitation in the Constitution. The Tenth Amendment surely does not impose any limit on Congress' exercise of the powers delegated to it by Article I. Nor does the structure of the constitutional order or the values of federalism mandate such a formal rule. To the contrary, the Federal Government directs state governments in many realms. The Government regulates state-operated railroads, state school systems, state prisons, state elections, and a host of other state functions. [I] see no reason why Congress may not also command the States to enforce federal water and air quality standards or federal standards for the disposition of low-level radioactive [wastes].

THE SCOPE AND LIMITS OF THE ANTICOMMANDEERING PRINCIPLE

1. ***Congressional alternatives to commandeering.*** Both the majority and the dissent in New York v. United States pointed out that Congress had available alternatives to commandeering for inducing state compliance with federal waste disposal goals. Indeed, the majority upheld the "monetary" and "access" provisions on the ground that they employed such permissible alternative methods. Consider the following alternatives:

a. *Spending power*. Under the Spending Clause (see Chapter 4 below), Congress may condition the payment of relevant federal funds on a state's agreement to take title to waste if it has not already provided a waste disposal facility.

b. *Commerce power*. Under the Commerce Clause, Congress may pass federal legislation directly regulating the private producers of low-level radioactive waste to limit their production of any more of it if disposal is unavailable. This would presumably induce them to pressure the states to act. Under the Commerce Clause, Congress also may authorize the states to burden out-of-state commerce (see Chapter 5 below); Justice O'Connor's opinion upheld the "monetary" and "access" incentives in New York v. United States as reflecting the permissible exercise of these powers.

c. *Conditional preemption*. Congress may threaten to pass federal legislation under the Commerce Clause unless states choose to regulate according to federal standards. In upholding the "access" incentives as involving such powers, Justice O'Connor noted that they were not impermissibly coercive "because any burden caused by a State's refusal to regulate will fall on those who generate waste and find no outlet for its disposal, rather than on the State as a sovereign."

Are these measures truly less intrusive upon state autonomy than laws that commandeer the states? Is state compliance with such laws truly more voluntary? Note that New York v. United States falls well short of reviving National League of Cities, as it limits merely the method by which the federal government may act upon the states—that is, through commandeering state legislatures—as opposed to exempting subject matter areas—such as state and local operation of police departments—from any form of federal control.

2. ***Commandeering state executive branch officials.*** Does the anticommandeering principle of New York v. United States extend to federal laws directed at state or local *executive* officials, as opposed to state legislatures? The Court reached this question in **Printz v. United States**, 521 U.S. 898 (1997), which held invalid, by a vote of 5–4, provisions of the Brady Handgun Violence Prevention Act that required state and local law enforcement officers (CLEOs) to conduct background checks on prospective handgun purchasers.

Justice SCALIA delivered the opinion of the Court, joined by Chief Justice Rehnquist and Justices O'Connor, Kennedy, and Thomas: "[The] Brady Act purports to direct state law enforcement officers to participate [in] the administration of a federally enacted regulatory scheme. [The] petitioners here object to being pressed into federal service, and contend that congressional action compelling state officers to execute federal laws is unconstitutional. [The] enactments of the early Congresses [contain] no evidence of an assumption that the Federal Government may command the States' executive power in the absence of a particularized constitutional authorization. [When] the First Congress enacted a law aimed at obtaining state assistance [in] holding [federal] prisoners in state jails at federal expense [it] issued not a command to the States' executive, but a recommendation to their legislatures.

"[The] Government also [points] to portions of The Federalist which [suggest] that Congress will probably 'make use of the State officers and State regulations, for collecting' federal taxes, The Federalist, No. 36 (A. Hamilton), and predicted that 'the eventual collection [of internal revenue] under the immediate authority of the Union, will generally be made by the officers, and according to the rules, appointed by the several States, The Federalist, No. 45 (J. Madison). The Government also invokes the Federalist's more general observations that the Constitution would 'enable the [national] government to employ the ordinary magistracy of each [State] in the execution of its laws,' The Federalist, No. 27 (A. Hamilton), and that it was 'extremely probable that in other instances, particularly in the organization of the judicial power, the officers of the States will be clothed in the correspondent authority of the Union,' The Federalist, No. 45 (J. Madison). But none of these statements necessarily implies—what is the critical point here—that Congress could impose these responsibilities without the consent of the States. They appear to rest on the natural assumption that the States would consent to allowing their officials to assist the Federal Government, an assumption proved correct by the extensive mutual assistance the States and Federal Government voluntarily provided one another in the early days of the Republic.

"[We] turn next to consideration of the structure of the Constitution, to see if we can discern among its 'essential postulates' a principle that controls the present cases. It is incontestable that the Constitution established a system of 'dual sovereignty.' Although the States surrendered many of their powers to the new Federal Government, they retained 'a residuary and inviolable sovereignty,' The Federalist, No. 39 (J. Madison). [The] Framers rejected the concept of a central government that would act upon and through the States [as had the Articles of Confederation], and instead designed a system in which the state and federal governments would exercise concurrent authority over the people—who were, in Hamilton's words, 'the only proper objects of government,' The Federalist, No. 15. [This] separation of the two spheres is one of the Constitution's structural protections of liberty. The Federalist, No. 51. The power of the Federal Government would be augmented immeasurably if it were able to impress into its service—and at no cost to itself—the police officers of the 50 States.

"[The] Government contends that New York is distinguishable [because] unlike the 'take title' provisions invalidated there, the background-check provision of the Brady Act does not require state legislative or executive officials to make policy, but instead issues a final directive to state CLEOs. [The] Government's distinction between 'making' law and merely 'enforcing' it [is] an interesting one. [But] executive action that has utterly no policymaking component is rare, particularly at an executive level as high as a jurisdiction's chief law-enforcement officer. [Even] assuming [that] the Brady Act leaves no 'policymaking' discretion with the States, we fail to see how that improves rather than worsens the intrusion upon state sovereignty. Preservation of the States as independent and autonomous political entities is arguably less undermined by requiring them to make policy in certain fields than by 'reducing [them] to puppets of a ventriloquist Congress.'

"[By] forcing state governments to absorb the financial burden of implementing a federal regulatory program, Members of Congress can take credit for 'solving' problems without having to ask their constituents to pay for the solutions with higher federal taxes. And even when the States are not forced to absorb the costs of implementing a federal program, they are still put in the position of taking the blame for its burdensomeness and for its defects. Under the present law, for example, it will be the CLEO and not some federal official who stands between the gun purchaser and immediate possession of his gun. [We] held in New York that Congress cannot compel the States to enact or enforce a federal regulatory program. Today we hold that Congress cannot circumvent that prohibition by conscripting the State's officers directly. The Federal Government may neither issue directives requiring the States to address particular problems, nor command the States' officers, or those of their political subdivisions, to administer or enforce a federal regulatory program." Justices O'Connor and Thomas filed separate concurrences.

Justice STEVENS filed a dissent joined by Justices Souter, Ginsburg, and Breyer: "[The] historical materials strongly suggest that the Founders intended to enhance the capacity of the federal government by empowering it—as a part of the new authority to make demands directly on individual citizens—to act through local officials. [Hamilton's] meaning [in The Federalist, No. 27] was unambiguous; the federal government was to have the power to demand that local officials implement national policy programs. [During] the debates concerning the ratification of the Constitution, it was assumed that state agents would act as tax collectors for the federal government. Opponents of the Constitution had repeatedly expressed fears that the new federal government's ability to impose taxes directly on the citizenry would result in an overbearing presence of federal tax collectors in the States. Federalists rejoined that this problem would not arise because, as Hamilton explained, 'the United States . . . will make use of the State officers and State regulations for collecting' certain taxes. The Federalist, No. 36. [Statutes] of the early Congresses required in mandatory terms that state judges and their clerks perform various executive duties with respect to applications for citizenship. [Similarly,] the First Congress enacted legislation requiring state courts to serve, functionally, like contemporary regulatory agencies in certifying the seaworthiness of vessels.

"[Perversely,] the majority's rule seems more likely to damage than to preserve the safeguards against tyranny provided by the existence of vital state governments. By limiting the ability of the Federal Government to enlist state officials in the implementation of its programs, the Court creates incentives for the National Government to aggrandize itself. In the name of State's rights, the majority would have the Federal Government create vast national bureaucracies to implement its policies. This is exactly the sort of thing that the early Federalists promised would not occur, in part as a result of the National Government's ability to rely on the magistracy of the states. [The] provision of the Brady Act that crosses the Court's newly defined constitutional threshold is more comparable to a statute requiring local police officers to report the identity of missing children to the Crime Control Center of the Department of Justice than to an offensive federal command to a sovereign state. If Congress believes that such a statute will benefit the people of the Nation, and serve the interests of cooperative federalism better than an enlarged federal bureaucracy, we should respect both its policy judgment and its appraisal of its constitutional power."

Justice SOUTER filed an additional dissent relying heavily on Hamilton's statement in The Federalist, No. 27, that "the Legislatures, Courts and Magistrates of the respective members will be incorporated into the operations of the national government, as far as its just and constitutional authority extends; and will be rendered auxiliary to the enforcement of its laws." Justice Souter concluded: "I cannot persuade myself that the statements from No. 27 speak of anything less than the authority of the National Government, when exercising an otherwise legitimate power (the commerce power, say), to require state 'auxiliaries' to take appropriate action. To be sure, it does not follow that any conceivable requirement may be imposed on any state official. I continue to agree, for example, [that] New York v. United States was rightly decided."

Justice BREYER likewise filed a dissent, joined by Justice Stevens: "[The] United States is not the only nation that seeks to reconcile the practical need for a central authority with the democratic virtues of more local control. At least some other countries, facing the same basic problem, have found that local control is better maintained through application of a principle that is the direct opposite of the principle the majority derives from the silence of our Constitution. The federal systems of Switzerland, Germany, and the European Union, for example, all provide that constituent states, not federal bureaucracies, will themselves implement many of the laws, rules, regulations, or decrees enacted by the central 'federal' body. They do so in part because they believe that such a system interferes less, not more, with the independent authority of the 'state,' member nation, or other subsidiary government, and helps to safeguard individual liberty as well. [As comparative] experience suggests, there is no need to interpret the Constitution as containing an absolute principle forbidding the assignment of virtually any federal duty to any state official."

3. ***States as objects of federal regulation vs. states as regulators.*** New York and Printz each rejected Congress's authority to dictate, through federal prescription, how the states regulate their own citizens. But neither decision questioned Congress's ability to regulate the states' own conduct under general laws that also regulate the similar conduct of private actors. Indeed, this is one of the greatest differences between New York and Printz on the one hand, and the overruled decision in National League of Cities on the other: National League not only invalidated laws that singled out the states for discriminatory treatment, but also required the exemption of the states from some otherwise valid, generally applicable federal laws, like laws regulating all employers' wages and hours. Recall the division among the justices in the *first* New York v. United States decision above.

The distinction between laws regulating the states and laws requiring the states to regulate their own citizens proved crucial in **Reno v. Condon**, 528 U.S. 141 (2000), in which a unanimous Court upheld a federal law limiting the commercial vending of personal data by the states. At issue were amendments to the federal Driver's Privacy Protection Act of 1994 (DPPA), which prohibited state motor vehicle departments (DMVs) from "knowingly disclos[ing] or otherwise mak[ing] available to any person or entity personal information about any individual obtained by the department in connection with a motor vehicle record" without that individual's consent. The DPPA also imposed extensive regulations on the resale or disclosure of DMV information obtained by private persons and entities. South Carolina filed a suit alleging that the DPPA violated principles of federalism.

Speaking for the unanimous Court, Chief Justice REHNQUIST rejected the state's claims of improper commandeering: "South Carolina contends that the DPPA violates the Tenth Amendment because it 'thrusts upon the States all of the day-to-day responsibility for administering its complex provisions,' [making] 'state officials the unwilling implements of federal policy.' [We] agree with South Carolina's assertion that the DPPA's provisions will require time and effort on the part of state employees, but reject the State's argument that the DPPA violates the principles laid down in either New York or Printz. We think, instead, that this case is governed by our decision in South Carolina v. Baker (1988[; p. 173 above]). In Baker, we upheld a statute that prohibited States from issuing unregistered bonds because the law 'regulate[d] state activities,' rather than 'seek[ing] to control or influence the manner in which States regulates private parties.' Like the statute at issue in Baker, the DPPA does not require the States in their sovereign capacity to regulate their own citizens. The DPPA regulates the States as the owners of databases. It does not require the South Carolina Legislature to enact any laws or regulations, and it does not require state officials to assist in the enforcement of federal statutes regulating private individuals. We accordingly conclude that the DPPA is consistent with the constitutional principles enunciated in New York and Printz." Chief Justice Rehnquist also rejected South Carolina's argument that the DPPA was unconstitutional because it regulates the states exclusively: "The essence of South Carolina's argument is that Congress may only regulate the States by means of 'generally applicable' laws, or laws that apply to individuals as well as States. But we need not address the question whether general applicability is a constitutional requirement for federal regulation of the States, because the DPPA is generally applicable. The DPPA regulates the universe of entities that participate as suppliers to the market for motor vehicle information—the States as initial suppliers of the information in interstate commerce and private resellers or redisclosers of that information in commerce."

Was the law upheld in Reno truly a generally applicable law? It was directed specifically at motor vehicle bureaus operated exclusively by state and local governments—and a private resale market that could not exist but for that uniquely state activity. Would a state's decisions as to how to handle motor vehicle records have qualified for mandatory immunity from federal regulation under the standard set forth in National League of Cities, later overruled in Garcia? If so, why did the Rehnquist Court not embrace Reno v. Condon as an opportunity to revive National League of Cities?

4. ***Anticommandeering as a limit to federal bars on state gambling laws.*** The Professional and Amateur Sports Protection Act (PASPA), enacted in 1992, makes it unlawful for states "to sponsor, operate, advertise, promote, license, or authorize by law or compact . . . a lottery, sweepstakes, or other betting, gambling, or wagering scheme based . . . on" competitive sporting events, 28 U.S.C. § 3702(1). As enacted, PASPA grandfathered in sports gambling in four states, and allowed New Jersey to set up sports gambling in Atlantic City within a year. New Jersey did not take advantage of the option at the time, but in 2012, its legislature authorized sports gambling in Atlantic City and at horseracing tracks. The lower courts held that the law violated PASPA, and the Supreme Court denied certiorari. So in 2014, the New Jersey legislature passed a new law that, instead of affirmatively authorizing sports gambling, repealed state-law provisions that prohibited such schemes. The lower courts again found a PASPA violation.

In **Murphy v. National Collegiate Athletic Ass'n**, 585 U.S. ___, 138 S. Ct. 1461 (2018), Justice ALITO wrote the opinion for a 6–3 Court, joined by Chief Justice Roberts and Justices Kennedy, Thomas, Kagan, and Gorsuch. The decision struck down the relevant PASPA provision as unconstitutional commandeering:

"The anticommandeering doctrine may sound arcane, but it is simply the expression of a fundamental structural decision incorporated into the Constitution, i.e., the decision to withhold from Congress the power to issue orders directly to the States. [The] PASPA provision at issue here—

prohibiting state authorization of sports gambling—violates the anticommandeering rule. [It] is as if federal officers were installed in state legislative chambers and were armed with the authority to stop legislators from voting on any offending proposals. A more direct affront to state sovereignty is not easy to imagine. Neither respondents nor the United States contends that Congress can compel a State to enact legislation, but they say that prohibiting a State from enacting new laws is another matter. [This] distinction is empty. It was a matter of happenstance that the laws challenged in New York and Printz commanded 'affirmative' action as opposed to imposing a prohibition. The basic principle—that Congress cannot issue direct orders to state legislatures—applies in either event. [Respondents] and the United States defend the anti-authorization prohibition on the ground that it constitutes a valid preemption provision, but it is no such thing. Preemption is based on the Supremacy Clause, and that Clause is not an independent grant of legislative power to Congress. [Therefore,] in order for the PASPA provision to preempt state law, it must [represent] the exercise of a power conferred on Congress by the Constitution; pointing to the Supremacy Clause will not do. [And] since the Constitution confers upon Congress the power to regulate individuals, not States, the PASPA provision at issue must be best read as one that regulates private actors.

"[It] is clear that the PASPA provision prohibiting state authorization of sports gambling is not a preemption provision because there is no way in which this provision can be understood as a regulation of private actors. It certainly does not confer any federal rights on private actors interested in conducting sports gambling operations. (It does not give them a federal right to engage in sports gambling.) Nor does it impose any federal restrictions on private actors. [Thus,] there is simply no way to understand the provision prohibiting state authorization as anything other than a direct command to the States."

SECTION 6. STATE SOVEREIGN IMMUNITY AND THE ELEVENTH AMENDMENT

The Eleventh Amendment states: "The judicial power of the United States shall not be construed to extend to any [suit] commenced or prosecuted against one of the United States by Citizens of another State, or by Citizens or Subjects of any Foreign States." It was adopted because of the uproar created by Chisholm v. Georgia, 2 U.S. (2 Dall.) 419 (1793), where the Court took original jurisdiction of a suit against Georgia by a South Carolina creditor seeking payment for goods purchased by Georgia during the Revolution. In Hans v. Louisiana, 134 U.S. 1 (1890), a much-criticized ruling, the Court held that the Eleventh Amendment applied not only to cases within federal diversity jurisdiction but also, its text notwithstanding, to cases within the federal question jurisdiction of the federal courts brought against a state by that state's own residents.

Later cases, however, made considerable inroads on the state sovereign immunity provided by the Eleventh Amendment. In Ex parte Young, 209 U.S. 123 (1908), the Court held that a federal court could issue a prohibitory injunction against state officials who sought to enforce an unconstitutional state law, on the ground that the defendant was not really the state but rather the official, acting beyond his constitutional authority. Moreover, in

Edelman v. Jordan, 415 U.S. 651 (1974), the Court ruled that the Eleventh Amendment permitted lawsuits for prospective injunctive relief against state officers, although not lawsuits for retrospective relief via a judgment for damages. In Fitzpatrick v. Bitzer, 427 U.S. 445 (1976), the Court held that Congress could abrogate the state's Eleventh Amendment immunity and allow states to be sued directly for retrospective damages pursuant to a proper exercise of its enforcement power under Section 5 of the Fourteenth Amendment. At the same time, the Court made some concession to federalism values by imposing a clear statement rule on Congress: "Congress may abrogate the States' constitutionally secured immunity from suit in federal court only by making its intention unmistakably clear in the language of the statute." Atascadero State Hosp. v. Scanlon, 473 U.S. 234, 242 (1985).

Fitzpatrick, however, left open the question whether Congress could also abrogate state sovereign immunity when it exercised its Art. I, § 8, powers, such as the commerce power, as opposed to its Fourteenth Amendment enforcement powers. In Pennsylvania v. Union Gas Co., 491 U.S. 1 (1989), a divided Court upheld the constitutionality of a federal environmental law that permitted suits for monetary damages against states in federal court; the Court held that "Congress has the authority to create such a course of action when legislating pursuant to the Commerce Clause." The majority in that case could not agree on a rationale for its holding.

1. ***The revival of state sovereign immunity in Seminole Tribe.*** Seven years later, in **Seminole Tribe of Florida v. Florida**, 517 U.S. 44 (1996), the Court overruled Pennsylvania v. Union Gas and held that Congress, when acting under its Art. I, § 8, commerce power, may not abrogate a state's sovereign immunity without the state's consent. The Seminole Tribe case arose under the Indian Gaming Regulatory Act, which provided that an Indian tribe may conduct certain gaming activities only in conformance with a valid compact between the tribe and the state in which the gaming activities are located. The Act, passed under the Indian Commerce Clause, imposed upon the states a duty to negotiate in good faith with an Indian tribe toward the formation of a compact, and authorized a tribe to sue the state in a federal court in order to compel performance of that duty.

Chief Justice REHNQUIST wrote for the majority, holding that, "notwithstanding Congress' clear attempt to abrogate the States' sovereign immunity, the Indian Commerce Clause does not grant Congress that power, and therefore [the law] cannot grant jurisdiction over a state that does not consent to be sued." The Court rejected the argument that a power to abrogate sovereign immunity should be recognized here because the Act authorized only prospective injunctive relief rather than retroactive monetary relief: "[W]e have often made it clear that the relief sought by a plaintiff suing a State is irrelevant to the question whether the suit is barred by the Eleventh Amendment." The Court stated that Pennsylvania v. Union Gas had "deviated sharply from our established federalism jurisprudence and essentially eviscerated our decision in Hans." But it upheld and distinguished Fitzpatrick v. Bitzer, since "the Fourteenth Amendment, adopted well after the adoption of the Eleventh Amendment and the ratification of the Constitution, operated to alter the preexisting balance between state and federal power achieved by Article III and the Eleventh Amendment." Chief Justice Rehnquist concluded: "[In] overruling Union Gas today, we can reconfirm that the background principle of state sovereign immunity embodied in the Eleventh Amendment is not so ephemeral as to dissipate when the subject of the suit is an area, like the regulation of Indian commerce, that is under the exclusive control of the Federal Government. [The] Eleventh Amendment restricts the judicial power under Article III, and Article I cannot be used to circumvent the constitutional limitations placed upon federal jurisdiction."

Justice STEVENS dissented: "The majority's opinion does not simply preclude Congress from establishing the rather curious statutory scheme under which the Indian tribes may seek the aid of a federal court to secure a State's good faith negotiations over gaming regulations. Rather, it prevents Congress from providing a federal forum for a broad range of actions against States, from those sounding in copyright and patent law to those concerning bankruptcy, environmental law, and the regulation of our vast national economy." In a separate dissent, Justice SOUTER, joined by Justices Ginsburg and Breyer, argued that judicial intervention to protect the states was unwarranted because the requirement that Congress make a plain statement of its intent to abrogate state sovereign immunity "is an adequate check on congressional overreaching."

What was the constitutional source of authority for the ruling in Seminole Tribe? Did its ruling follow from the text of the Eleventh Amendment? If not, was it rooted in structural principles of federalism? Would the states be at risk of losing their status as separate and independent sovereigns if they could be subjected to unlimited runs on their treasuries through money damages actions? Recall the principle in McCulloch that the power to tax is the power to destroy. Is the power to sue likewise the power to destroy? For the view that state sovereign immunity might have a common law but not a constitutional basis, see Jackson, "The Supreme Court, the Eleventh Amendment, and State Sovereign Immunity," 98 Yale. L.J. 1 (1988). For the view that "sovereign immunity is an anachronistic relic and the entire doctrine should be eliminated from American law," see Chemerinsky, "Against Sovereign Immunity," 53 Stan. L. Rev. 1201 (2001).

2. ***Extending state sovereign immunity from federal to state courts.*** Does the state sovereign immunity principle announced in Seminole Tribe extend even to federal lawsuits brought in state court? Such lawsuits do not implicate the literal text of the Eleventh Amendment, which refers only to a limit upon "the judicial power of the United States." In **Alden v. Maine**, 527 U.S. 706 (1999), the Court nonetheless extended the state sovereignty immunity bar announced in Seminole Tribe from lawsuits against states in federal court to lawsuits against states in state court. The sharply divided 5–4 decision affirmed the dismissal of a suit filed in a Maine state court by state probation officers seeking damages for the state's failure to pay them overtime compensation required by the federal Fair Labor Standards Act.

Justice KENNEDY wrote the opinion of the Court, acknowledging that this limitation on congressional power could not be derived from the text of the Eleventh Amendment, and rooting it instead in "the Constitution's structure, and its history." He stressed the "dignity" retained by the States in the federal system, even where their authority has been abrogated by the national power: "[Although] the Constitution establishes a National Government with broad, often plenary authority over matters within its recognized competence, the founding document 'specifically recognizes the

States as sovereign entities.' [Any] doubt regarding the constitutional role of the States as sovereign entities is removed by the Tenth Amendment. [The] federal system established by our Constitution preserves the sovereign status of the States, [together] with the dignity and essential attributes inhering in that status. [The] generation that designed and adopted our federal system considered immunity from private suits central to sovereign dignity. When the Constitution was ratified, it was well established in English law that the Crown could not be sued without consent in its own courts. [Although] the American people had rejected other aspects of English political theory, the doctrine that a sovereign could not be sued without its consent was universal in the States when the Constitution was drafted and ratified."

Having concluded that "sovereign immunity derives not from the Eleventh Amendment but from the structure of the original Constitution itself," Justice Kennedy turned to the specific question whether Congress may under Art. I subject nonconsenting states to private suits in their own courts: "Although the Constitution grants broad powers to Congress, our federalism requires that Congress treat the States in a manner consistent with their status as residuary sovereigns and joint participants in the governance of the Nation. [A] power to press a State's own courts into federal service to coerce the other branches of the State [is] the power [ultimately] to commandeer the entire political machinery of the State against its will. [Private] suits against nonconsenting States—especially suits for money damages—may threaten the financial integrity of the States. [An] unlimited congressional power to authorize suits in state court to levy upon the treasuries of the States for compensatory damages, attorney's fees, and even punitive damages could create staggering burdens, giving Congress a power and a leverage over the States that is not contemplated by our constitutional design." Justice Kennedy concluded that a decision the other way would be anomalous: "Congress cannot abrogate the States' sovereign immunity in federal court; were the rule to be different here, the National Government would wield greater power in the state courts than in its own judicial instrumentalities." Justice Kennedy took pains to insist that federal laws such as FLSA remained binding on the states, even if not enforceable through private lawsuits.

Justice SOUTER filed a dissent joined by Justices Stevens, Ginsburg, and Breyer. All four had dissented in Seminole Tribe. Justice Souter disagreed with the majority's arguments from history. He distinguished between two different conceptions of sovereign immunity: the first conception, which "[could] be traced to [its] origins in Roman sources [was] the 'natural law' view of sovereign immunity [and held that] the sovereign could not be sued by his subjects" and that Congress could not by statute abrogate this sovereignty. The second conception was a common law conception of sovereign immunity, derived from the notion that the king's writ did not run against himself; if "the source of sovereign immunity is the common law, [the] common law doctrine could be changed by Congress acting under the Commerce Clause." Justice Souter marshaled historical evidence to deny that the Founders adhered to a natural law conception of sovereign immunity: "[The] American Colonies did not enjoy sovereign immunity, that being a privilege understood in English law to be reserved for the Crown alone. [Despite] a tendency among the state constitutions to announce and declare certain inalienable and natural rights of men and even of the collective people of a State, no State declared that sovereign immunity was one of those rights. To the extent that States were thought to possess immunity, it was perceived as a prerogative of the sovereign under common law, [from] which it follows that it was subject to abrogation by Congress as to a matter within Congress's Article I authority. [There] is almost no evidence that the generation of the Framers thought sovereign immunity was fundamental in the sense of being unalterable. Whether one looks at the period before the framing, to the ratification controversies, or to the early republican era, the evidence is the same. Some Framers thought sovereign immunity was an obsolete royal prerogative inapplicable in a republic; some thought sovereign immunity was a common law power defeasible, like other common law rights, by statute; and perhaps a few thought, in keeping with a natural law view distinct from the common law conception, that immunity was inherent in a sovereign because the body that made a law could not logically be bound by it. Natural law thinking on the part of a doubtful few will not, however, support the Court's position."

Justice Souter also disputed the majority's arguments from the Constitution's structure: "The State of Maine is not sovereign with respect to the national objective of the FLSA. It is not the authority that promulgated the FLSA, on which the right of action in this case depends. That authority is the United States acting through the Congress, whose legislative power under Article I of the Constitution to extend FLSA coverage to state employees has already been decided, see Garcia, and is not contested here. [The] Court calls 'immunity from private suits central to sovereign dignity,' [but dignity is not] a quality easily translated from the person of the King to the participatory abstraction of a republican State. [It] would be hard to imagine anything more inimical to the republican conception, which rests on the understanding of its citizens precisely that the government is not above them, but of them, its actions being governed by law just like their own."

3. ***Extending state sovereign immunity to other federal laws.*** On the same day as Alden, the Court held state entities (such as public universities) immune from patent and trademark infringement actions brought against them in federal court. See Fla. Prepaid Postsecondary Educ. Expense Bd. v. Coll. Sav. Bank, 527 U.S. 627 (1999); Coll. Sav. Bank v. Fla. Prepaid Postsecondary Educ. Expense Bd., 527 U.S. 666 (1999). Soon afterward, the Court held the states immune from suits under the Age Discrimination in Employment Act of 1967 (ADEA), see **Kimel v. Fla. Bd. of Regents**, 528 U.S. 62 (2000), and Title I of the Americans with Disabilities Act (ADA), see **Bd. of Trs. of Univ. of Ala. v. Garrett**, 531 U.S. 356 (2001). In both cases, the Court reasoned that Congress lacked the power to abrogate state sovereign immunity insofar as these antidiscrimination laws were enacted under the commerce power; it also held that application of these laws to the states could not be justified under Section 5 of the Fourteenth Amendment (see p. 888 below for a discussion of that power). In each of these decisions, the Court split 5–4, with the justices following the same lineup as in Seminole Tribe and Alden.

4. ***Federal power vs. federal remedies.*** Note that the Seminole Tribe line of cases "enforce a vision of constitutional federalism not by restricting the reach of congressional authority to regulate the states, but rather by limiting the remedial means by which Congress may enforce regulation of the states that is otherwise within its substantive legislative power." Meltzer, "State Sovereign Immunity: Five Authors in Search of a Theory," 75 Notre Dame L. Rev. 1011 (2000). Thus, like New York and Printz

above, they do not overrule Garcia or revive National League of Cities by holding that federal statutes may not be applied to state employers or other sovereign state entities at all. Why did they not? Is adherence to stare decisis a sufficient explanation?

As Justice Kennedy noted in Alden, nothing in the state sovereign immunity decisions prevents federal laws from being enforced against the states through alternative mechanisms: Individuals may obtain injunctions against state officials under Ex parte Young; federal officials may enforce federal statutes through federal agencies at federal expense; Congress may condition federal spending programs on the states' agreement to waive sovereign immunity. From the federal government's perspective, are these enforcement routes adequate substitutes for private lawsuits? Are private suits a more effective enforcement mechanism because they do not require federal taxpayer funding and because plaintiffs who prevail in them can often recover attorney's fee awards?

For the view that "[t]aking a significant bite out of the enforcement apparatus for a vast range of federal statutes is every bit as significant as holding that one or two particular schemes may not be imposed against the states at all," see Meltzer, "Overcoming Immunity: the Case of Federal Regulation of Intellectual Property," 53 Stan. L. Rev. 1331 (2001). For contrary arguments that the Court's state sovereign immunity decisions do not deter litigation against the states so much as channel it into the form of injunction actions against state officials under Ex parte Young and 42 U.S.C. § 1983 that might still impose significant burdens on the states, see Monaghan, "The Sovereign Immunity 'Exception,'" 110 Harv. L. Rev. 102 (1996); Jeffries, "In Praise of the Eleventh Amendment and Section 1983," 84 Va. L. Rev. 47 (1998); and Jeffries, "The Right-Remedy Gap in Constitutional Law," 109 Yale L.J. 87 (1999).

5. ***Extending state sovereign immunity to federal agency proceedings.*** In **Federal Maritime Commission v. South Carolina State Ports Authority**, 535 U.S. 743 (2002), the Court extended the reach of state sovereign immunity from judicial proceedings to adjudications within federal administrative agencies. The case involved a cruise ship company's administrative complaint against a South Carolina port authority, heard before the Federal Maritime Commission (FMC), alleging that the state authority had violated the federal Shipping Act by disallowing berths in the state's ports for gambling vessels. Justice THOMAS's opinion for the Court rested upon structural principles extending beyond the Eleventh Amendment: "Dual sovereignty is a defining feature of our Nation's constitutional blueprint. States, upon ratification of the Constitution, did not consent to become mere appendages of the Federal Government." Justice Thomas reiterated the view from Alden that, while the Eleventh Amendment's text addressed the particular decision in Chisholm v. Georgia, it merely exemplified a much broader principle of state sovereign immunity. Even assuming that the FMC did not "exercise the judicial power of the United States" so as to trigger the Eleventh Amendment, Justice Thomas wrote, its adjudication of a private complaint offended "the sovereign immunity embedded in our constitutional structure and retained by the States when they joined the Union":

"The Framers, who envisioned a limited Federal Government, could not have anticipated the vast growth of the administrative state. [Formalized] administrative adjudications were all but unheard of in the late 18th century and early 19th century. [This] Court, however, has applied a presumption—first explicitly stated in Hans v. Louisiana—[that] the Constitution was not intended to 'rais[e] up' any proceedings against the States that were 'anomalous and unheard of when the Constitution was adopted.' [To] decide whether the Hans presumption applies here, [we] must examine FMC adjudications to determine whether they are the type of proceedings from which the Framers would have thought the States possessed immunity when they agreed to enter the Union. [FMC] administrative proceedings bear a remarkably strong resemblance to civil litigation in federal courts. [The] role of the [Administrative Law Judge] designated to hear a case is similar to that of an Article III judge. [In] short, the similarities between FMC proceedings and civil litigation are overwhelming. [The] preeminent purpose of state sovereign immunity is to accord States the dignity that is consistent with their status as sovereign entities. [Given] both this interest in protecting States' dignity and the strong similarities between FMC proceedings and civil litigation, we hold that state sovereign immunity bars the FMC from adjudicating complaints filed by a private party against a nonconsenting State. [The] Federal Government retains ample means of ensuring that state-run ports comply with the Shipping Act and other valid federal rules governing ocean-borne commerce. The FMC, for example, remains free to investigate alleged violations of the Shipping Act, either upon its own initiative or upon information supplied by a private party, and to institute its own administrative proceeding against a state-run port. Additionally, the Commission 'may bring suit in a district court of the United States to enjoin conduct in violation of [the Act].' "

Justice BREYER dissented, joined by Justices Stevens, Souter, and Ginsburg. While reiterating the view that Seminole Tribe, Alden, and Kimel were wrongly decided, he wrote they did not require the majority's result: "The legal body conducting the proceeding, the Federal Maritime Commission, is an 'independent' federal agency. Constitutionally speaking, an 'independent' agency belongs neither to the Legislative Branch nor to the Judicial Branch of Government. [The] agencies, even 'independent' agencies, are [appropriately] considered to be part of the Executive Branch. The President appoints their chief administrators, typically a Chairman and Commissioners, subject to confirmation by the Senate. The agencies derive their legal powers from congressionally enacted statutes. And the agencies enforce those statutes, *i.e.*, they 'execute' them, in part by making rules or by adjudicating matters in dispute. [In] exercising those powers, the agency is engaging in an Article II, Executive Branch activity. [Today's] decision, while permitting an agency to bring enforcement actions against States, forbids it to use agency adjudication in order to help decide whether to do so. Consequently the agency must rely more heavily upon its own informal staff investigations in order to decide whether a citizen's complaint has merit. The natural result is less agency flexibility, a larger federal bureaucracy, less fair procedure, and potentially less effective law enforcement. And at least one of these consequences, the forced growth of unnecessary federal bureaucracy, undermines the very constitutional objectives the Court's decision claims to serve."

6. ***State sovereign immunity and the Art. I bankruptcy power.*** Does the limitation announced in Seminole Tribe on Congress's power to abrogate state sovereign immunity extend to all congressional powers under Art. I, § 8? In **Central Virginia Community College v. Katz**, 546 U.S. 356 (2006), the Court considered that question with respect to Congress's

powers under the Bankruptcy Clause, Art. I, § 8, cl. 4, which provides that Congress shall have the power to establish "uniform Laws on the subject of Bankruptcies throughout the United States." By a vote of 5–4, the Court held that the federalism principles articulated in the state sovereign immunity line of cases did not bar Congress from subordinating a state entity to other creditors in a federal bankruptcy proceeding. The result depended upon Justice O'Connor, in her last term on the Court, joining the Seminole Tribe-Alden-Kimel-Garrett-FMC dissenters.

Justice STEVENS wrote for the Court, joined by Justices O'Connor, Souter, Ginsburg, and Breyer. He acknowledged "that statements in both the majority and the dissenting opinions in Seminole Tribe reflected an assumption that the holding in that case would apply to the Bankruptcy Clause," but noted that "[c]areful study and reflection have convinced us [that] that assumption was erroneous." Reviewing the law governing debt relief at the time of the Constitution's framing, Justice Stevens concluded that the Bankruptcy Clause had been "intended not just as a grant of legislative authority to Congress, but also to authorize limited subordination of state sovereign immunity in the bankruptcy arena." He continued: "Insofar as orders ancillary to the bankruptcy courts' *in rem* jurisdiction [implicate] States' sovereign immunity from suit, the States agreed in the plan of the Convention not to assert that immunity. [The] Framers, in adopting the Bankruptcy Clause, plainly intended to give Congress the power to redress the rampant injustice resulting from States' refusal to respect one another's [debtor] discharge orders." The majority also relied upon contemporaneous legislative enactments: "As demonstrated by the First Congress' immediate consideration and the Sixth Congress' enactment of a provision granting federal courts the authority to release debtors from state prisons, the power to enact bankruptcy legislation was understood to carry with it the power to subordinate state sovereignty." From this history, the majority inferred the States' consent: "In ratifying the Bankruptcy Clause, the States acquiesced in a subordination of whatever sovereign immunity they might otherwise have asserted in proceedings necessary to effectuate the *in rem* jurisdiction of the bankruptcy courts. [The] relevant 'abrogation' is the one effected in the plan of the Convention, not by statute."

Justice THOMAS dissented, joined by the newly appointed Chief Justice Roberts and Justices Scalia and Kennedy: "Under our Constitution, the States are not subject to suit by private parties for monetary relief absent their consent or a valid congressional abrogation, and it is 'settled doctrine' that nothing in Article I of the Constitution establishes those preconditions. [The] adoption of the Constitution merely established federal power to legislate in the area of bankruptcy law, and did not manifest an additional intention to waive the States' sovereign immunity against suit. [It] is difficult to discern an intention to abrogate state sovereign immunity through the Bankruptcy Clause when no such intention has been found in any of the other clauses in Article I."

CHAPTER 4

THE NATIONAL TAXING AND SPENDING POWERS AND THEIR FEDERALISM-BASED LIMITS

Apart from the commerce power, Congress's powers to tax and spend have also had significant impact on the allocation of authority within the federal system. The opening clause of Art. I, § 8 states: "The Congress shall have power To lay and collect Taxes, Duties, Imposts, and Excises, to pay the Debts and provide for the common Defense and general Welfare of the United States." Like the regulation of interstate commerce, the taxing and spending powers have been used to attempt to change state regulatory policy. Recently, the Court issued major holdings with respect to the federal taxing and spending regulatory powers in National Federation of Independent Business v. Sebelius, 567 U.S. 519 (2012). To what extent are the federalism-based limits upon taxing and spending regulations like and unlike those upon the commerce power? Are they more administrable by courts? Should Congress be able to bribe the states to do things it could not compel them to do? Note that the very important powers delegated to Congress by the Thirteenth, Fourteenth, and Fifteenth Amendments—each of which specifies that Congress may "enforce this article by appropriate legislation"—are discussed in Chapter 10 below. The war and treaty powers, though less frequently litigated, also have bearing on the federal structure. They are discussed in Chapter 6.

SECTION 1. THE TAXING POWER AS A REGULATORY DEVICE

To what extent may the congressional taxing power of Art. I, § 8, cl. 1 be used as a means of national regulation of arguably local affairs? Congress has sometimes invoked the taxing power when the commerce power seemed unusable. Has the Court been more successful in curbing "abuses" of the taxing power than of the commerce power? Is it easier to detect pretextual uses of the taxing power?

Child Labor Tax Case [Bailey v. Drexel Furniture Co.]

259 U.S. 20, 42 S. Ct. 449, 66 L. Ed. 817 (1922).

[In Hammer v. Dagenhart (p. 120 above), the Court held unconstitutional Congress's efforts to regulate child labor through exercise of the commerce power. A few months after the decision, Congress enacted the Child Labor Tax Law of 1919. That law imposed a federal excise tax of 10% of annual net profits on every employer of child labor in the covered businesses. The coverage provisions were similar to those in the law invalidated in Hammer v. Dagenhart. After paying a tax of over $6000, a company successfully brought a refund suit.]

■ CHIEF JUSTICE TAFT delivered the opinion of the Court.

[The child labor tax] law is attacked on the ground that it is a regulation of the employment of child labor in the States—an exclusively state function under the Federal Constitution and within the reservations of the Tenth Amendment. It is defended on the ground that it is a mere excise tax levied by the Congress of the United States under its broad power of taxation. [We] must construe the law and interpret the intent and meaning of Congress from the language of the act. [Does] this law impose a tax with only that incidental restraint and regulation which a tax must inevitably involve? Or does it regulate by the use of the so-called tax as a penalty? If a tax, it is clearly an excise. [But] this act is more. It provides a heavy exaction for a departure from a detailed and specified course of conduct in business: [that] employers shall employ in mines and quarries, children of an age greater than 16 years; in mills and factories, children of an age greater than 14 years, and shall prevent children of less than 16 years in mills and factories from working more than 8 hours a day or 6 days in a week. If an employer departs from its prescribed course of business, he is to pay the government one-tenth of his entire net income in the business for a full year. [A] court must be blind not to see that the so-called tax is imposed to stop the employment of children within the age limits prescribed. Its prohibitory and regulatory effect and purpose are palpable. All others can see and understand this. How can we properly shut our minds to it?

[Out of] a proper respect for the acts of a coordinate branch of the Government, this court has gone far to sustain taxing acts as such, even though there has been ground for suspecting from the weight of the tax it was intended to destroy its subject. But [here], the presumption of validity cannot prevail, because the proof of the contrary is found on the very face of the provisions. Grant the validity of this law, and all that Congress would need to do, hereafter, in seeking to take over to its control any one of the great number of subjects of public interest [reserved to the States] would be to enact a detailed measure of complete regulation of the subject and enforce it by a so-called tax upon departures from it. To give such magic to the word "tax" would be to break down all constitutional limitation of the powers of Congress and completely wipe out the sovereignty of the States.

The difference between a tax and a penalty is sometimes difficult to define and yet the consequences of the distinction in the required method of their collection often are important. Where the sovereign enacting the law has power to impose both tax and penalty the difference between revenue production and mere regulation may be immaterial, but not so when one sovereign can impose a tax only, and the power of regulation rests in another. Taxes are occasionally imposed in the discretion of the legislature on proper subjects with the primary motive of obtaining revenue from them and with the incidental motive of discouraging them by making their continuance onerous. They do not lose their character as taxes because of the incidental motive. But there comes a time in the extension of the penalizing features of the so-called tax when it loses its character as such and becomes a mere penalty with the characteristics of regulation and punishment. Such is the case [here]. The case before us can not be distinguished from that of Hammer v. Dagenhart. [This] case requires [the] application of the principle announced by Chief Justice Marshall in [McCulloch], in a much quoted passage [—the "pretext" passage].

But it is pressed upon us that this court has gone so far in sustaining taxing measures the effect or tendency of which was to accomplish purposes not directly within congressional power that we are bound by authority to maintain this law. The first of these is Veazie Bank v. Fenno, 8 Wall. 533 [1869]. In that case, [a] law which increased a tax on the circulating notes of persons and state banks from one per centum to ten per centum was [upheld]. It will be observed that the sole objection to the tax there was its excessive character. [There] were no elaborate specifications on the face of the act, as here, indicating the purpose to regulate matters of state concern and jurisdiction through an exaction so applied as to give it the qualities of a penalty for violation of law rather than a tax. [But] more than this, what was charged to be the object of the excessive tax was within the congressional [authority]. After having pointed out the legitimate means taken by Congress to secure a national medium or currency, the court said: "Having thus, in the exercise of undisputed constitutional powers, undertaken to provide a currency for the whole country, it cannot be questioned that Congress may, constitutionally, secure the benefit of it to the people by appropriate legislation. To this end, [Congress] may restrain, by suitable enactments, the circulation as money of any notes not issued under its own authority."

[The] next case is that of McCray v. United States, 195 U.S. 27 [1904]. That, like [Veazie], was the increase of an excise tax upon a subject properly taxable in which the taxpayers claimed that the tax had become invalid because the increase was excessive. It was a tax on oleomargarine, a substitute for butter. The tax on the white oleomargarine was one-quarter of a cent a pound, and on the yellow oleomargarine [was] ten cents per pound. This court [upheld the tax, applying] the same principle as that applied in [Veazie]. It was that Congress, in selecting its subjects for taxation, might impose the burden where and as it would and that a motive disclosed in its selection to discourage sale or manufacture of an article by a higher tax than on some other did not invalidate the tax.

[Finally], United States v. Doremus, 249 U.S. 86 [1919], involved the validity of the Narcotic Drug Act, which imposed a special tax on the manufacture, importation and sale or gift of opium or coca leaves or their compounds or derivatives. It required every person subject to the special tax to register with the Collector of Internal Revenue his name and place of business and forbade him to sell except upon the written order of the person to whom the sale was made on a form prescribed by the Commissioner of Internal Revenue. [The] validity of a special tax in the nature of an excise tax on the manufacture, importation and sale of such drugs was, of course, unquestioned. The provisions for subjecting the sale and distribution of the drugs to official supervision and inspection were held to have a reasonable relation to the enforcement of the tax and were therefore held valid. The court said that the act could not be declared invalid just because another motive than taxation, not shown on the face of the act, might have contributed to its [passage].

[Affirmed.] [Justice Clarke filed a lone dissent.]

upheld?

---

1. ***The scope of the taxing power in prior decisions.*** The important regulatory tax cases before the Child Labor Tax Case—Veazie, McCray, and Doremus—are described in Chief Justice Taft's opinion. Are the prior decisions distinguishable, or did the principal case manifest a significant shift in approach? Is the distinction between a "tax" and a "penalty"—between "revenue production" and "mere regulation"—persuasive? Judicially manageable?

2. ***The commerce power vs. the taxing power.*** Note that Justice Holmes was in the majority in the Child Labor Tax Case, just four years after his dissent in Hammer v. Dagenhart. In that dissent, he had insisted that the Court could *not* look to purposes and obvious collateral effects; here, by contrast, he joined in looking beyond the label Congress used to the forbidden purpose. Moreover, in Hammer v. Dagenhart, Holmes had relied on McCray, the oleomargarine tax case, to show that judicial inquiry into congressional purpose was improper. And the McCray tax decision of 1904, in turn, had relied on the Lottery Case of 1903 in rejecting the notion "that the judiciary may restrain the exercise of lawful power on the assumption that a wrongful purpose or motive has caused the power to be exerted." Thus, while Holmes earlier opposed judicial invalidation because of improper purpose in tax (McCray) as well as commerce (Lottery, Child Labor) cases, he declined to apply that position in the Child Labor Tax Case. Are Holmes's positions in these cases reconcilable? Are the uses of commerce and tax powers different? Is invalidation appropriate only where bad purpose is very clear?

Shortly after the Narcotics Act decision in Doremus in 1919, Justice Holmes wrote to Judge Learned Hand: "As to the [Drug Act case], (*between ourselves*) I am tickled at every case of that sort as they seem to me to confirm the ground of my dissent in the Child Labor case last term. Hammer v. Dagenhart. Also, I think the drug act cases rightly decided. In my opinion Congress may have what ulterior motives they please if the act passed in the immediate aspect is within their powers—though personally, were I a legislator I might think it dishonest to use powers in that way." Oliver Wendell Holmes to Learned Hand, April 3, 1919, quoted in Gunther, "Learned Hand and the Origins of Modern First Amendment Doctrine," 27 Stan. L. Rev. 719 (1975). Are Justice Holmes's positions in Doremus and the Child Labor Tax Case reconcilable? Are the cases distinguishable because the tax sanction in the child labor situation (10% of net profits for noncompliance) was more substantial than that in the narcotics situation ($1 a year)? Does calibration to the amount of taxed activity make one more justifiable as a regulatory device incidental to a revenue-raising measure?

3. ***Federal excise and license taxes.*** In United States v. Constantine, 296 U.S. 287 (1935), the defendant was convicted of conducting the business of retail dealer in malt liquor contrary to the laws of Alabama without having paid a special excise tax of $1000 imposed by Congress. He had paid the normal tax of $25 for conducting the business, and the question presented was "whether the exaction of $1000 in addition, by reason solely of his violation of state law, is a tax or penalty." Justice Roberts's opinion for the Court concluded that "the indicia which the section exhibits of an intent to prohibit and to punish violations of state law as such are too strong to be disregarded, remove all semblance of a revenue act and stamp the sum it exacts as a penalty. [T]he statute is a clear invasion of the police power,

inherent in the [states]." But Sonzinsky v. United States, 300 U.S. 506 (1937), sustained the National Firearms Act of 1934, which imposed a $200 annual license tax on dealers in firearms. Noting that the tax "is productive of some revenue," the Court said "we are not free to speculate as to the motives which moved Congress to impose it, or as to the extent to which it may operate to restrict the activities taxed. As it is not attended by an offensive regulation, and since it operates as a tax, it is within the national taxing power."

United States v. Kahriger, 345 U.S. 22 (1953), upheld the constitutionality of a federal occupational tax imposed on gambling. The 1951 Revenue Act levied a tax on persons engaged in the business of accepting wagers and required such persons to register with the Collector of Internal Revenue. The challenger claimed that Congress, "under the pretense of exercising its power to tax, has attempted to penalize illegal intrastate gambling through the regulatory features of the Act" and thus infringed "the police power which is reserved to the states." Justice REED's majority opinion rejected the challenge. He did not think that it was determinative that the legislative history suggested a congressional motive to suppress wagering. He responded: "[An] intent to curtail and hinder, as well as tax, was also manifest in the series of cases beginning with [Veazie], and in each of them the tax was [upheld]. [A] federal excise tax does not cease to be valid merely because it discourages or deters the activities taxed. Nor is the tax invalid because the revenue obtained is negligible. [The] instant tax has a regulatory effect. But regardless of [that], the wagering tax produces revenue [greater than] both the narcotics and firearms taxes which we have found valid." He added: "It is hard to understand why the power to tax should raise more doubts because of indirect effects than other federal powers. Unless there are [penalty] provisions extraneous to any tax need, courts are without authority to limit the exercise of the taxing power. All of the provisions of this [tax] are adapted to the collection of a valid tax. Nor do we find the registration requirements of the wagering tax offensive. [The] registration provisions make the tax simpler to collect."

Justice JACKSON's concurrence joined the majority opinion, "but with such doubts that if the minority agreed upon an opinion which did not impair legitimate use of the taxing power I probably would join it. [One] cannot formulate a revenue-raising plan that would not have economic and social consequences." But here, he noted, the purported tax law imposed tax and reporting obligations only on certain gamblers whose activities in most states were illegal. "This is difficult to regard as a rational or good-faith revenue measure. [On] the contrary, it seems to be a plan to tax out of existence a professional gambler whom it has been found impossible to prosecute out of existence. [The] evil that can come from this statute will probably soon make itself manifest to Congress. The evil of a judicial decision impairing the legitimate taxing power by extreme constitutional interpretations might not be transient. Even though this statute approaches the fair limits of constitutionality, I join the [decision]."

Justice FRANKFURTER, joined in large part by Justice Douglas, dissented: "[When] oblique use is made of the taxing power as to matters which substantively are not within the powers delegated to Congress, the Court cannot shut its eyes to orders obviously, because designedly, an attempt to control conduct which the Constitution left to the responsibility of the States, merely because Congress wrapped the legislation in the verbal cellophane of a revenue measure."

4. ***The taxing power after the New Deal.*** Hammer v. Dagenhart was overruled in Darby. Was there a parallel development regarding the taxing power? Is the majority approach in the Child Labor Tax Case (1922) more respectable today than the discredited Hammer v. Dagenhart (1918) position? Note that Justice Stone's opinion in Darby relied on McCray and Veazie (the early taxing power cases discussed in the Child Labor Tax Case) in support of his refusal to inquire into the motive and purpose of commerce regulation while Kahriger produced several opinions on the abuse of the taxing power issue from members of the post-1937 Court. Is the difference justifiable? Note that asking the question whether a tax is impermissibly regulatory depends upon there being an area of state autonomy in which it would be impermissible for the federal government to regulate—e.g., intrastate production in the pre-1937 conception of the Commerce Clause power. The more expansive the conception of permissible federal regulation, the more attenuated the area of impermissible regulatory intrusion through taxation.

Justice Reed in Kahriger thought it "hard to understand why the power to tax should raise more doubts because of indirect effects than other federal powers." What is the explanation of the difference? Is it because "ordinary," revenue-raising taxes are less likely to have "indirect effects" than "ordinary" commerce regulations? But see Justice Jackson's concurrence: "[One] cannot formulate a revenue-raising plan that would not have economic and social consequences." Is it because statutory schemes convey clearer implications about the primary purpose of taxation than of commerce legislation? But is there no historical guidance about the proper primary purpose of commerce regulations? And if some Justices are willing to distinguish between primary and ancillary objectives with respect to the taxing power, why do they decline to do so with respect to the commerce power?

5. ***Mandatory health insurance purchase as a tax.*** In upholding the "individual mandate" provision of the Patient Protection and Affordable Care Act of 2010 (ACA), a 5–4 majority of the Court relied upon the taxing power rather than the Commerce Clause or Necessary and Proper Clause as the proper source of Congress's authority to require individuals to maintain "minimum essential" health insurance coverage or pay a "penalty" to the Internal Revenue Service for failing to do so. Chief Justice Roberts wrote for the Court on the taxing power; for the opinions on the necessary and proper and commerce power holdings, in which he spoke for a different 5–4 lineup, see p. 107 and p. 160 above.

National Federation of Independent Business v. Sebelius

567 U.S. 519, 132 S. Ct. 2566, 183 L. Ed. 2d 450 (2012).

■ CHIEF JUSTICE ROBERTS announced the judgment of the Court and delivered the opinion of the Court with respect to Part III–C, in which

JUSTICES GINSBURG, BREYER, SOTOMAYOR, and KAGAN joined; and an opinion with respect to Parts III–B, and III–D.

III. B. Because the Commerce Clause does not support the individual mandate, it is necessary to turn to the Government's second argument: that the mandate may be upheld as within Congress's enumerated power to "lay and collect Taxes." Art. I, § 8, cl. 1. The Government's tax power argument asks us to view the statute differently than we did in considering its commerce power theory. In making its Commerce Clause argument, the Government defended the mandate as a regulation requiring individuals to purchase health insurance. The Government does not claim that the taxing power allows Congress to issue such a command. Instead, the Government asks us to read the mandate not as ordering individuals to buy insurance, but rather as imposing a tax on those who do not buy that product.

[Under] the mandate, if an individual does not maintain health insurance, the only consequence is that he must make an additional payment to the IRS when he pays his taxes. That, according to the Government, means the mandate can be regarded as establishing a condition—not owning health insurance—that triggers a tax—the required payment to the IRS. Under that theory, the mandate is not a legal command to buy insurance. Rather, it makes going without insurance just another thing the Government taxes, like buying gasoline or earning income. And if the mandate is in effect just a tax hike on certain taxpayers who do not have health insurance, it may be within Congress's constitutional power to tax.

C. [The] exaction the Affordable Care Act imposes on those without health insurance looks like a tax in many respects. The "[s]hared responsibility payment," as the statute entitles it, is paid into the Treasury by "taxpayer[s]" when they file their tax returns. [The] requirement to pay is found in the Internal Revenue Code and enforced by the IRS, which [must] assess and collect it "in the same manner as taxes." This process yields the essential feature of any tax: it produces at least some revenue for the Government. [It] is of course true that the Act describes the payment as a "penalty," not a "tax." [But] that label [does] not determine whether the payment may be viewed as an exercise of Congress's taxing power.

[In] Drexel Furniture, we focused on three practical characteristics of the so-called tax on employing child laborers that convinced us the "tax" was actually a penalty. First, the tax imposed an exceedingly heavy burden—10 percent of a company's net income—on those who employed children, no matter how small their infraction. Second, it imposed that exaction only on those who knowingly employed underage laborers. Such scienter requirements are typical of punitive statutes, because Congress often wishes to punish only those who intentionally break the law. Third, this "tax" was enforced in part by the Department of Labor, an agency responsible for punishing violations of labor laws, not collecting revenue. The same analysis here suggests that the shared responsibility payment may for constitutional purposes be considered a tax, not a penalty: First, for most Americans the amount due will be far less than the price of insurance, and, by statute, it can never be more. It may often be a reasonable financial decision to make the payment rather than purchase insurance, unlike the "prohibitory" financial punishment in Drexel Furniture. Second, the individual mandate contains no scienter requirement. Third, the payment is collected solely by the IRS through the normal means of taxation.

None of this is to say that the payment is not intended to affect individual conduct. Although the payment will raise considerable revenue, it is plainly designed to expand health insurance coverage. But taxes that seek to influence conduct are nothing new. [Today,] federal and state taxes can compose more than half the retail price of cigarettes, not just to raise more money, but to encourage people to quit smoking. [Indeed,] "[e]very tax is in some measure regulatory." That [the mandate] seeks to shape decisions about whether to buy health insurance does not mean that it cannot be a valid exercise of the taxing power. In distinguishing penalties from taxes, this Court has explained that "if the concept of penalty means anything, it means punishment for an unlawful act or omission." While the individual mandate clearly aims to induce the purchase of health insurance, it need not be read to declare that failing to do so is unlawful. Neither the Act nor any other law attaches negative legal consequences to not buying health insurance, beyond requiring a payment to the IRS.

[Congress's] ability to use its taxing power to influence conduct is not without limits. A few of our cases policed these limits aggressively, invalidating punitive exactions obviously designed to regulate behavior otherwise regarded at the time as beyond federal authority. See, e.g., Butler; Drexel Furniture. [We] have already explained that the shared responsibility payment's practical characteristics pass muster as a tax under our narrowest interpretations of the taxing power. Because the tax at hand is within even those strict limits, we need not here decide the precise point at which an exaction becomes so punitive that the taxing power does not authorize it.

[Although] the breadth of Congress's power to tax is greater than its power to regulate commerce, the taxing power does not give Congress the same degree of control over individual behavior. Once we recognize that Congress may regulate a particular decision under the Commerce Clause, the Federal Government can bring its full weight to bear. Congress may simply command individuals to do as it directs. [By] contrast, Congress's authority under the taxing power is limited to requiring an individual to pay money into the Federal Treasury, no more. [The] Affordable Care Act's requirement that certain individuals pay a financial penalty for not obtaining health insurance may reasonably be characterized as a tax. Because the Constitution permits such a tax, it is not our role to forbid it, or to pass upon its wisdom or fairness.

■ JUSTICES SCALIA, KENNEDY, THOMAS, and ALITO, dissenting.

[Our] cases establish a clear line between a tax and a penalty: " '[A] tax is an enforced contribution to provide for the support of government; a penalty . . . is an exaction imposed by statute as punishment for an unlawful act.' " [We] have never held [that] a penalty imposed for violation of the law was so trivial as to be in effect a tax. We have never held that *any* exaction imposed for violation of the law is an exercise of Congress' taxing power—even when the statute *calls* it a tax, much less when (as here) the statute repeatedly calls it a penalty. When an Act "adopt[s] the criteria of wrongdoing" and then imposes a monetary penalty as the "principal consequence on those who transgress its standard," it creates a regulatory penalty, not a tax. Child Labor Tax Case.

So the question is, quite simply, whether the exaction here is imposed for violation of the law. It unquestionably is. The minimum coverage provision is found in 26 U.S.C. § 5000A, entitled "*Requirement* to maintain minimum essential coverage." [It] commands that every "applicable individual *shall*" [have minimum coverage]. [And] several of Congress' legislative "findings" with regard to § 5000A confirm that it sets forth a legal requirement and constitutes the assertion of regulatory power, not mere taxing power. [The] fact that Congress (in its own words) "imposed . . . a penalty" for failure to buy insurance is alone sufficient to render that failure unlawful. [We] have never classified as a tax an exaction imposed for violation of the law.

[To] say that the Individual Mandate merely imposes a tax is not to interpret the statute but to rewrite it. Judicial tax-writing is particularly troubling. Taxes have never been popular, see, *e.g.,* Stamp Act of 1765, and in part for that reason, the Constitution requires tax increases to originate in the House of Representatives. See Art. I, § 7, cl. 1. That is to say, they must originate in the legislative body most accountable to the people, where legislators must weigh the need for the tax against the terrible price they might pay at their next election, which is never more than two years off. The Federalist No. 58 "defend[ed] the decision to give the origination power to the House on the ground that the Chamber that is more accountable to the people should have the primary role in raising revenue." [Imposing] a tax through judicial legislation inverts the constitutional scheme, and places the power to tax in the branch of government least accountable to the citizenry.

THE TAXING POWER AS A FEDERAL REGULATORY DEVICE AFTER NFIB

1. ***What are the limits of the federal taxing regulatory power?*** In upholding the individual mandate, Chief Justice Roberts wrote that the Court "need not here decide the precise point at which an exaction becomes so punitive that the taxing power does not authorize it." Does NFIB portend an expansion of federal regulation through the taxing power until the Court enforces limits? Might political resistance to taxes play a role in limiting federal power under this doctrine?

2. ***Institutionalism and doctrine.*** After the Chief Justice cast the deciding vote to sustain the individual mandate under the taxing power, some commentators suggested that the holding was motivated by a desire to protect the Court's institutional legitimacy and avoid a 5–4 holding along ideological lines striking down a signature legislative enactment of President Barack Obama's first term and one of the most important pieces of social legislation since President Lyndon Johnson's Great Society enactments. See Metzger, Comment, "To Tax, To Spend, To Regulate," 126 Harv. L. Rev. 83, 103 (2012). These commentators pointed to reports that the Chief Justice had initially indicated an inclination to strike down the individual mandate but changed his mind at some point, comparing him to an earlier Justice Roberts and his famous purported (though much disputed) "switch in time" to uphold President Roosevelt's New Deal legislation in West Coast Hotel. See Jan Crawford, "Roberts Switched Views to Uphold Health Care Law," CBS News (July 1, 2012). Other commentators disputed this account, arguing that the Chief Justice's opinion fit within the Court's taxing power jurisprudence and the decision could be seen "as one of law, not just of politics." Minow, "Affordable Convergence: 'Reasonable Interpretation' and the Affordable Care Act," 126 Harv. L. Rev. 126, 117 (2012). Is there room for both interpretations in explaining the outcome of the case?

3. ***A tax by any other name.*** Does it matter whether Congress labels a provision a tax or a penalty in analyzing whether the exercise of power may be sustained under the Taxing Clause? Justice Scalia's dissent points to Congress's decision to label the individual mandate's enforcement mechanism a penalty, rather than a tax. Chief Justice Roberts, by contrast, engages in a functionalist inquiry to hold that the exaction was an exercise of the taxing power, looking to (1) the relatively small monetary amount of the shared-responsibility exaction; (2) the fact that there was no scienter requirement to trigger it; and (3) the fact that the payments were made to the Internal Revenue Service. Did the Chief Justice adequately distinguish the exaction at issue here from the exaction in the Child Labor Tax Case that had been held an impermissible penalty? Is there any value to requiring Congress to comply with a clear statement rule of the sort Justice Scalia envisions? Or does such a formalist methodology unduly frustrate Congress's ability to pass legislation within its constitutional power simply because it has used the wrong labels?

4. ***The Court's inquiry into legislative purpose.*** Recall note 2 following the Child Labor Tax Case, p. 194 above. The Justices had previously been inconsistent as to whether a Court could look to congressional purpose to invalidate a tax that had a regulatory aim. In NFIB, by contrast, Chief Justice Roberts explicitly found that the Congress had a regulatory purpose, yet upheld the individual mandate on the ground that "every tax is in some measure regulatory." Does NFIB now indicate that a congressional regulatory purpose is irrelevant in determining whether a congressional action is valid under the tax power? Does the inquiry into constitutionality now turn on the manner in which a tax with a regulatory purpose is implemented?

SECTION 2. THE SPENDING POWER AS A REGULATORY DEVICE

The national spending power has an important impact on the actual functioning of the federal system. Federal funding of payments to individuals for old age or unemployment support; grants to states for education, crime control, highway construction or welfare payments; and the entrepreneurial operations of government-owned businesses such as the Tennessee Valley Authority, all involve policy choices with significant regulatory consequences. Litigation about the scope of the power has been rare, for restrictive doctrines regarding standing to sue have traditionally barred most taxpayer challenges to federal spending programs. But the constitutional questions are no less real for the sparsity of judicial decisions. The scope of the spending power has been a recurrent source of controversy ever since the early 19th century. What are the legitimate purposes of national spending? What is the proper role of courts in assessing legitimacy? What conditions may Congress impose on spending programs? What is constitutionally required with respect to the relationship between the condition, the particular program, and the "general welfare"? To what extent may Congress "coerce" state or individual behavior when it resorts to the carrot of federal funds rather than the stick of civil and criminal sanctions?

United States v. Butler

297 U.S. 1, 56 S. Ct. 312, 80 L. Ed. 477 (1936).

[The Agricultural Adjustment Act of 1933 sought to stabilize farm prices by curtailing agricultural production. It authorized the Secretary of Agriculture to make contracts with farmers to reduce their productive acreage in exchange for benefit payments. The payments were to be made out of a processing tax paid by the processor "upon the first domestic processing" of the particular commodity. The Butler case arose from imposition of a processing tax on cotton upon the Hoosac Mills Corporation. Butler and his co-receivers for the company successfully attacked the tax, claiming that it was an integral part of a program that unconstitutionally sought to control agricultural production—an activity that was the province of the states. The Court agreed, holding that the Act was not a valid exercise of the power to spend for the general welfare under Art. I § 8.]

■ JUSTICE ROBERTS delivered the opinion of the Court.

[The] clause thought to authorize the [Act] confers upon the Congress power "to lay and collect Taxes, Duties, Imposts and Excises, to pay the Debts and provide for the common Defense and general Welfare of the United States."

[Since] the foundation of the Nation, sharp differences of opinion have persisted as to the true interpretation of the phrase. Madison asserted it amounted to no more than a reference to the other powers enumerated in the subsequent clauses of the same section; that, as the United States is a government of limited and enumerated powers, the grant of power to tax and spend for the general national welfare must be confined to the enumerated legislative fields committed to the Congress. In this view the phrase is mere tautology, for taxation and appropriation are or may be necessary incidents of the exercise of any of the enumerated legislative powers. Hamilton, on the other hand, maintained the clause confers a power separate and distinct from those later enumerated, is not restricted in meaning by the grant of them, and Congress consequently has a substantive power to tax and to appropriate, limited only by the requirement that it shall be exercised to provide for the general welfare of the United States.

[We] conclude that the reading advocated by [Hamilton] is the correct one. While, therefore, the power to tax is not unlimited, its confines are set in the clause which confers it, and not in those of § 8 which bestow and define the legislative powers of the Congress. It results that the power of Congress to authorize expenditure of public moneys for public purposes is not limited by the direct grants of legislative power found in the Constitution. But the adoption of the broader construction leaves the power to spend subject to limitations. [We] are not now required to ascertain the scope of the phrase "general welfare of the United States" or to determine whether an appropriation in aid of agriculture falls within it. Wholly apart from that question, another principle embedded in our Constitution prohibits the enforcement of the [act]. The act invades the reserved rights of the states. It is a statutory plan to regulate and control agricultural production, a matter beyond the powers delegated to the federal government. The tax, the appropriation of the funds raised, and the direction for their disbursement, are but parts of the plan. They are but means to an unconstitutional end. [It] is an established principle that the attainment of a prohibited end may not be accomplished under the pretext of the exertion of powers which are granted [quoting Marshall's "pretext" statement in McCulloch].

[If] the taxing power may not be used as the instrument to enforce a regulation of matters of state concern with respect to which the Congress has no authority to interfere [e.g., Child Labor Tax Case], may it, as in the present case, be employed to raise the money necessary to purchase a compliance which the Congress is powerless to command? The Government asserts that whatever might be said against the validity of the plan if compulsory, it is constitutionally sound because the end is accomplished by voluntary co-operation. There are two sufficient answers to the contention. The regulation is not in fact voluntary. The farmer, of course, may refuse to comply, but the price of such refusal is the loss of benefits. The amount offered is intended to be sufficient to exert pressure on him to agree to the proposed regulation. The power to confer or withhold unlimited benefits is the power to coerce or destroy. If the cotton grower elects not to accept the benefits, he will receive less for his crops. [The] result may well be financial ruin. [This] is coercion by economic pressure. The asserted power of choice is illusory.

[But] if the plan were one for purely voluntary co-operation it would stand no better so far as federal power is concerned. At best, it is a scheme for purchasing with federal funds submission to federal regulation of a subject reserved to the states. It is said that Congress has the undoubted right to appropriate money to executive officers for expenditure under contracts between the government and individuals. [But] appropriations and expenditures under contracts for proper governmental purposes cannot justify contracts which are not within federal power. And contracts for the reduction of acreage and the control of production are outside the range of that power. An appropriation to be expended by the United States under contracts calling for violation of a state law clearly would offend the Constitution. Is a statute less objectionable which authorizes expenditure of federal moneys to induce action in a field in which the United States has no power to intermeddle? The Congress cannot invade state jurisdiction to compel individual action; no more can it purchase such action.

[We] are not here concerned with a conditional appropriation of money, nor with a provision that if certain conditions are not complied with the appropriation shall no longer be available. By the [Act] the amount of the tax is appropriated to be expended only in payment under contracts whereby the parties bind themselves to regulation by the Federal Government. There is an obvious difference between a statute stating the conditions upon which moneys shall be expended and one effective only upon assumption of a contractual obligation to submit to a regulation which otherwise could not be enforced. Many examples pointing the distinction might be cited. We are referred to appropriations in aid of education, and it is said that no one has doubted the power of Congress to stipulate the sort of education for which money shall be expended. But an appropriation to an educational institution which by its terms is to become available only if the beneficiary enters into a contract to teach doctrines subversive of the Constitution is clearly bad. An affirmance of the authority of Congress so to condition the expenditure of an appropriation would tend to nullify all constitutional limitations upon legislative power.

[Congress] has no power to enforce its commands on the farmer to the ends sought by the [Act]. It must follow that it may not indirectly accomplish those ends by taxing and spending to purchase compliance. The Constitution and the entire plan of our government negative any such use of the power to tax and to spend as the act undertakes to authorize. [If the Act is] a proper exercise of the federal taxing power, evidently the regulation of all industry throughout the United States may be accomplished by similar exercises of the same power. [The] sole premise [of the Government's argument] is that, though the makers of the Constitution, in erecting the federal government, intended sedulously to limit [its powers], they nevertheless by a single clause gave power to the Congress to tear down the barriers, to invade the states' jurisdiction, and to become a parliament of the whole people, subject to no restrictions save such as are self-imposed. The argument when seen in its true character and in the light of its inevitable results must be [rejected].

Affirmed.

■ JUSTICE STONE, dissenting, joined by JUSTICES BRANDEIS and CARDOZO.

[The majority's] suggestion of coercion finds no support in the record or in any data showing the actual operation of the act. Threat of loss, not hope of gain, is the essence of economic coercion. [It] is upon the contention that state power is infringed by purchased regulation of agricultural production that chief reliance is placed. [But the] Constitution requires that public funds shall be spent for a defined purpose, the promotion of the general welfare. Their expenditure usually involves payment on terms which will insure use by the selected recipients within the limits of the constitutional purpose. Expenditures would fail of their purpose and thus lose their constitutional sanction if the terms of payment were not such that by their influence on the action of the recipients the permitted end would be attained. The power of Congress to spend is inseparable from persuasion to action over which Congress has no legislative control. Congress may not command that the science of agriculture be taught in state universities. But if it would aid the teaching of that science by grants to state institutions, it is appropriate, if not necessary, that the grant be on the condition, incorporated in the Morrill Act, that it be used for the intended purpose. Similarly it would seem to be compliance with the Constitution, not violation of it, for the government to take and the university to give a contract that the grant would be so used. It makes no difference that there is a promise to do an act which the condition is calculated to induce. Condition and promise are alike valid since both are in furtherance of the national purpose for which the money is appropriated. [It] is a contradiction in terms to say that there is power to spend for the national welfare, while rejecting any power to impose conditions reasonably adapted to the attainment of the end which alone would justify the expenditure.

The limitation now sanctioned must lead to absurd consequences. The government may give seeds to farmers, but may not condition the gift upon their being planted in places where they are most needed or even planted at all. The government may give money to the unemployed, but may not ask that those who get it shall give labor in return, or even use it to support their families. [It] may support rural schools, [but] may not condition its grant by the requirement that certain standards be maintained. [Do] all its activities collapse because, in order to effect the permissible purpose, in myriad ways the money is paid out upon terms and conditions which influence action of the recipients within the states, which Congress cannot command? The answer would seem plain. If the expenditure is for a national public purpose, that purpose will not be thwarted because payment is on condition which will advance that purpose. The action which Congress induces by payments of money to promote the general welfare, but which it does not command or coerce, is but an incident to a specifically granted power, but a permissible means to a legitimate end. If appropriation in aid of a program of curtailment of agricultural production is constitutional, and it is not denied that it is, payment to farmers on condition that they reduce their crop acreage is constitutional. It is not any the less so because the farmer at his own option promises to fulfill the condition.

THE SPENDING POWER AFTER THE NEW DEAL

1. ***The 1937 Social Security cases.*** Butler was decided less than eight months after Schechter Poultry Corp. v. United States, p. 123 below, which struck down the National Industrial Recovery Act, the other key element of the so-called "first" New Deal. After the Butler case, New Dealers feared that the Social Security Act of 1935 was also at risk. But in companion cases in 1937, the Court upheld against state autonomy challenge the unemployment compensation and old age benefits schemes of the Social Security Act. The first of these cases, Steward Machine, involved a federal taxing structure designed to induce states to adopt laws complying with federal standards. The second case, Helvering v. Davis, did not try to enlist state legislatures but instead involved an exclusively federal spending scheme.

The 5–4 decision in **Charles C. Steward Machine Co. v. Davis**, 301 U.S. 548 (1937), sustained the unemployment compensation provisions of the Social Security Act. Title IX of the Act imposed a payroll tax on employers of eight or more. Unlike the tax in the Butler case, this tax was not earmarked but went into general funds. But a credit provision in the tax sought to induce the enactment of state laws that complied with federal standards. Under the scheme an employer was entitled to a credit of up to 90% of the federal tax for any contributions to a state unemployment fund certified by a federal agency as meeting the requirements of the Act. Steward Machine sought a refund of taxes paid to the federal government under Title IX.

Justice CARDOZO's majority opinion concluded that the scheme was "not void as involving the coercion of the States in contravention of the Tenth Amendment or of restrictions implicit in our federal form of government." He insisted that it had not been shown that "the tax and the credit in combination are weapons of coercion, destroying or impairing the autonomy of the states. [To] draw the line intelligently between duress and inducement there is no need to remind ourselves of facts as to the problem of unemployment that are now matters of common knowledge. [The] states were unable to give the requisite relief. [There] was need of help from the nation if the people were not to starve." He continued:

"[The] question is to be answered whether the [law] adopted has overleapt the bounds of power. The assailants of the statute say that its dominant end [is] to drive the state legislatures under the whip of economic pressure into the enactment of unemployment compensation laws at the bidding of the central government. Supporters of the statute say that its operation is not constraint, but the creation of a larger freedom, the states and the nation joining in a cooperative endeavor to avert a common evil. Before Congress acted, unemployment compensation insurance was still, for the most part, a project and no more. [Many states] held back through alarm lest, in laying such a toll upon their industries, they would place themselves in a position of economic disadvantage as compared with neighbors or competitors. [Two] consequences ensued. One was that the freedom of a state to contribute its fair share to the solution of a national problem was paralyzed by fear. The other was that in so far as there was failure by the states to contribute relief according to the measure of their capacity, a disproportionate burden, [was] laid upon the resources of the Government of the nation.

"The [Act] is an attempt to find a method by which all these public agencies may work together to a common end. Every dollar of the new taxes will continue in all likelihood to be used and needed by the nation as long as states are unwilling, whether through timidity or for other motives, to do what can be done at home. At least the inference is permissible that Congress so believed, though retaining undiminished freedom to spend the money as it pleased. On the other hand fulfillment of the home duty will be lightened and encouraged by crediting the [federal] taxpayer [to] the extent that his contributions under the laws of the locality have simplified or diminished the problem of relief and the probable demand upon the resources of the fisc. [Who] then is coerced through the operation of this statute? Not the taxpayer. He pays in fulfillment of the mandate of the local legislature. Not the state. Even now [Alabama] does not offer a suggestion that in passing the unemployment law she was affected by duress. [The] difficulty with petitioner's contention is that it confuses motive with coercion. [E]very rebate from a tax when conditioned upon conduct is in some measure a temptation. But to hold that motive or temptation is equivalent to coercion is to plunge the law in endless difficulties. The outcome of such a doctrine is the acceptance of a philosophical determinism by which choice becomes impossible. Till now the law has been guided by a robust common sense which assumes the freedom of the will as a working hypothesis in the solution of its problems. The wisdom of the hypothesis has illustration in this case. There would be a strange irony, indeed, if [Alabama's] choice were now to be annulled on the basis of an assumed duress in the enactment of a statute which her courts have accepted as a true expression of her will.

"[In] ruling as we do, we leave many questions open. We do not say that a tax is valid, when imposed by act of Congress, if it is laid upon the condition that a state may escape its operation through the adoption of a statute unrelated in subject matter to activities fairly within the scope of national policy and power. No such question is before us. The purpose of [Congress's] intervention, as we have shown, is to safeguard its own treasury and as an incident to that protection to place the states upon a footing of equal opportunity. [It] is one thing to impose a tax dependent upon the conduct of the taxpayers, or of the state in which they live, where the conduct to be stimulated or discouraged is unrelated to the fiscal need subserved by the tax in its normal operation, or to any other end legitimately national. The Child Labor Tax Case [was] decided in the belief that the [law] there condemned [was] exposed to that reproach. It is quite another thing to say that a tax will be abated upon the doing of an act that will satisfy the fiscal need, the tax and the alternative being approximate equivalents. In such circumstances, if in no others, inducement or persuasion does not go beyond the bounds of power.

"We do not fix the outermost line. Enough for present purposes that wherever the line may be, this statute is within it. Definition more precise must abide the wisdom of the future. The statute does not call for a surrender by the states of powers essential to their quasi-sovereign existence. [A] credit to taxpayers for payments made to a state under a state unemployment law will be manifestly futile in the absence of some assurance that the law leading to the credit is in truth what it professes to be. An unemployment law framed in such a way that the unemployed who look to it will be deprived of reasonable protection is one in name and nothing more. What is basic and essential may be assured by suitable conditions. The terms embodied in these sections are directed to that end. A wide range of judgment is given to the several states as to the particular type of statute to be spread upon their books. [What] they may not do, if they would earn the credit, is to depart from those standards which in the judgment of Congress are to be ranked as fundamental."

Justice Cardozo found the Butler decision distinguishable: "None of [the objections there] is applicable to the situation here developed. (a) The proceeds of the tax in controversy are not earmarked for a special group. (b) The unemployment compensation law which is a condition of the credit has had the approval of the state and could not be a law without it. (c) The condition is not linked to an irrevocable agreement, for the state at its pleasure may repeal its [law], terminate the credit, and place itself where it was before the credit was accepted. (d) The condition is not directed to the attainment of an unlawful end, but to an end, the relief of unemployment, for which nation and state may lawfully cooperate." Justices McReynolds, Sutherland, Van Devanter and Butler dissented.

In a companion case to Steward Machine, **Helvering v. Davis**, 301 U.S. 619 (1937), Justice CARDOZO again wrote for the majority, upholding the old age benefits provisions in Titles II and VIII of the Social Security Act of 1935, with only Justices McReynolds and Butler dissenting. The Act imposed federal taxes on covered employers and employees in order to provide for the payment of federal old age benefits. Relying on Butler's endorsement of the Hamiltonian position on the spending power, Justice Cardozo noted that, even when a broad view of the power to spend is accepted, "[t]he line must still be drawn" between general and local welfare but "[t]he discretion belongs to Congress, unless the choice is clearly wrong, a display of arbitrary power." He found no such abuse of power here: "Congress did not improvise a judgment when it was found that the award of old age benefits would be conducive to the general welfare. [The] problem is plainly national in area and dimensions. Moreover, laws of the separate states cannot deal with it effectively. Congress, at least, had a basis for that belief. [Apart] from the failure of resources, states and local governments are at times reluctant to increase so heavily the burden of taxation to be borne by their residents for fear of placing themselves in a position of economic disadvantage. A system of old age pensions has special dangers of its own, if put in force in one state and rejected in another. The existence of such a system is a bait to the needy and dependent elsewhere, encouraging them to migrate and seek a haven of repose. Only a power that is national can serve the interests of all."

2. ***The scope of the spending power.*** Note that Butler, Steward Machine and Helvering all endorse the Hamiltonian position that the power to spend for the "general Welfare" is not limited by the other grants of power in Art. I, § 8. Was the Butler majority's endorsement of the Hamiltonian

position on the spending power consistent with the result? Did the majority in effect adopt the Madisonian position that spending is confined to realizing the other powers enumerated in Art. I, § 8? If the Hamiltonian position is adopted, then why was it unconstitutional to spend for the purpose of reducing agricultural production, even if it is conceded that such production was not (under the law in 1936) directly reachable under the commerce or other powers? For an argument that Justice Roberts misapplied the Hamiltonian position, see Engdahl, "The Spending Power," 44 Duke L.J. 1 (1994). Or was the Court in effect drawing an external rather than an internal limit on the spending power, akin to the external Tenth Amendment limit drawn on Congress's commerce power during the brief reign of National League of Cities? Might it be saying that some otherwise valid exercises of the spending power invade the sovereign domain of the states?

3. ***Degrees of coercion.*** Note that the majority and dissent in Butler disagree about whether the AAA is coercive. Justice Stone asserts in dissent that "[t]hreat of loss, not hope of gain, is the essence of economic coercion" and Justice Cardozo takes a narrow view of coercion in Steward Machine, warning against confusing "motive" with "coercion." How workable is the test of coercion in this setting? Is the real question not the degree of coercion but how closely related the spending condition is to the appropriate exercise of federal power? Did Justice Cardozo persuasively distinguish Butler? Did Steward Machine involve an arguably greater "coercion" of the states than Butler because it aimed at getting the states themselves to change their laws?

4. ***The Rehnquist Court's deferential approach to regulatory conditions on spending.*** The size and range of federal spending programs have increased vastly in the post-New Deal United States, and detailed federal spending conditions have proliferated. See Rosenthal, "Conditional Federal Spending and the Constitution," 39 Stan. L. Rev. 1103 (1987). When, if ever, do such conditions run counter to "restrictions implicit in our federal form of government"? Despite the other enhanced judicial protections for federalism explored above in Chapter 3, the Rehnquist Court declined to impose similar judicially enforceable limits on federal spending conditions. The deference the Rehnquist-era Court showed to Congress in the spending context contrasted markedly with its contemporaneous decisions imposing heightened review upon Congress's exercise of its commerce power (see Chapter 3 above) and its civil rights enforcement powers (see Chapter 10 below). In contrast, in the spending-power portions of the NFIB v. Sebelius decision, see p. 212 below, the Roberts Court for the first time since the New Deal held a congressional measure invalid for amounting to regulation exceeding Congress's spending power.

South Dakota v. Dole

483 U.S. 203, 107 S. Ct. 2793, 97 L. Ed. 2d 171 (1987).

[The National Minimum Drinking Age Act, 23 U.S.C. § 158, enacted in 1984, directed the Secretary of Transportation to withhold 5% of the federal highway funds otherwise payable to states from any state that permitted purchase of alcoholic beverages by persons less than 21 years old. South Dakota, which permitted persons 19 years of age or older to purchase 3.2%

beer, sought a declaratory judgment that § 158 violated constitutional limits on the congressional spending power. Even in the post-New Deal Constitution, the Twenty-first Amendment gives states uniquely exclusive power to regulate the manufacture, transportation and consumption of alcohol. Nonetheless, the lower federal courts rejected South Dakota's claims that the spending condition exceeded the spending power or infringed state autonomy, and the Supreme Court affirmed.]

■ CHIEF JUSTICE REHNQUIST delivered the opinion of the Court.

[We] need not decide in this case whether [the Twenty-first Amendment] would prohibit an attempt by Congress to legislate directly a national minimum drinking age. Here, Congress has acted indirectly under its spending power to encourage uniformity in the States' drinking ages. [We] find this legislative effort within constitutional bounds even if Congress may not regulate drinking ages directly.

[Incident to the spending power], Congress may attach conditions on the receipt of federal funds, and has repeatedly employed the power "to further broad policy objectives by conditioning receipt of federal moneys upon compliance by the recipient with [federal] directives." The breadth of this power was made clear in [Butler]. Thus, objectives not thought to be within Article I's "enumerated legislative fields" may nevertheless be attained through the use of the spending power and the conditional grant of federal funds. The spending power is of course not unlimited. [The] first of these limitations is derived from the language of the Constitution itself: the exercise of the spending power must be in pursuit of "the general welfare." In considering whether a particular expenditure is intended to serve general public purposes, courts should defer substantially to the judgment of Congress. Second, we have required that if Congress desires to condition the States' receipt of federal funds, it "must do so unambiguously . . . enabl[ing] the States to exercise their choice knowingly, cognizant of the consequences of their participation." Third, our cases have suggested [that] conditions on federal grants might be illegitimate if they are unrelated "to the federal interest in particular national projects or programs." Finally, we have noted that other constitutional provisions may provide an independent bar to the conditional grant of federal funds.

South Dakota does not seriously claim that § 158 is inconsistent with any of the first three restrictions mentioned above. [The] State itself [admits] that it "has never contended that the congressional action [was] unrelated to a national concern in the absence of the Twenty-first Amendment." Indeed, the condition imposed by Congress is directly related to one of the main purposes for which highway funds are expended—safe interstate travel.[1] This goal of the interstate highway system had been frustrated by varying drinking ages among the States. A Presidential commission appointed to study alcohol-related accidents and fatalities on the Nation's highways concluded that the lack of uniformity in the States' drinking ages created "an

---

1 Our cases have not required that we define the outer bounds of the "germaneness" or "relatedness" limitation on the imposition of conditions under the spending power. *Amici* urge that we take this occasion to establish that a condition on federal funds is legitimate only if it relates directly to the purpose of the expenditure to which it is attached. See Brief for National Conference of State Legislatures et al. as *Amici Curiae*. Because petitioner has not sought such a restriction, and because we find any such limitation on conditional federal grants satisfied in this case in any event, we do not address whether conditions less directly related to the particular purpose of the expenditure might be outside the bounds of the spending power. [Footnote by Chief Justice Rehnquist.]

incentive to drink and drive" because "young persons commut[e] to border States where the drinking age is lower." By enacting § 158, Congress conditioned the receipt of federal funds in a way reasonably calculated to address this particular impediment to a purpose for which the funds are expended.

The remaining question about the validity of § 158 [is] whether the Twenty-first Amendment constitutes an "independent constitutional bar" to the conditional grant of federal funds. Petitioner, relying on its view that the Twenty-first Amendment prohibits *direct* regulation of drinking ages by Congress, asserts that "Congress may not use the spending power to regulate that which it is prohibited from regulating directly under the Twenty-first Amendment." But [the] "independent constitutional bar" limitation on the spending power is not, as petitioner suggests, a prohibition on the indirect achievement of objectives which Congress is not empowered to achieve directly. Instead, [the] power may not be used to induce the States to engage in activities that would themselves be unconstitutional. Thus, for example, a grant of federal funds conditioned on invidiously discriminatory state action or the infliction of cruel and unusual punishment would be an illegitimate exercise of the Congress' broad spending power. But no such claim can be or is made [here].

Our decisions have recognized that in some circumstances the financial inducement offered by Congress might be so coercive as to pass the point at which "pressure turns into compulsion." [Steward Machine.] Here, however, Congress has directed only that a State desiring to establish a minimum drinking age lower than 21 lose a relatively small percentage of certain federal highway funds. Petitioner contends that the coercive nature of this program is evident from the degree of success it has achieved. We cannot conclude, however, that a conditional grant of federal money of this sort is unconstitutional simply by reason of its success in achieving the congressional objective. When we consider, for a moment, that all South Dakota would lose if she adheres to her chosen course as to a suitable minimum drinking age is 5% of the funds otherwise obtainable under specified highway grant programs, the argument as to coercion is shown to be more rhetoric than [fact].

[Affirmed.]

■ JUSTICE O'CONNOR, dissenting.

[Sec. 158] is not a condition on spending reasonably related to the expenditure of federal funds and cannot be justified on that ground. Rather, it is an attempt to regulate the sale of liquor, an attempt that lies outside Congress' power to regulate commerce because it falls within the ambit of § 2 of the Twenty-first Amendment.[2] [The] Court's application of the requirement that the condition imposed be reasonably related to the purpose for which the funds are expended is cursory and unconvincing. [In] my view, establishment of a minimum drinking age of 21 is not sufficiently related to interstate highway construction to justify so conditioning funds appropriated for that purpose. [The] Court asserts the reasonableness of the relationship between the supposed purpose of the expenditure—"safe interstate travel"—and the drinking age condition. The Court reasons that Congress wishes that the roads it builds may be used safely, that drunken drivers threaten

[2] Justice BRENNAN submitted a separate dissent agreeing with Justice O'Connor on this issue.

highway safety, and that young people are more likely to drive while under the influence of alcohol under existing law than would be the case if there were a uniform national drinking age of 21. It hardly needs saying, however, that if the purpose of § 158 is to deter drunken driving, it is far too over- and under-inclusive. It is over-inclusive because it stops teenagers from drinking even when they are not about to drive on interstate highways. It is under-inclusive because teenagers pose only a small part of the drunken driving problem in this Nation.

When Congress appropriates money to build a highway, it is entitled to insist that the highway be a safe one. But it is not entitled to insist as a condition of the use of highway funds that the State impose or change regulations in other areas of the State's social and economic life because of an attenuated or tangential relationship to highway use or safety. Indeed, if the rules were otherwise, the Congress could effectively regulate almost any area of a State's social, political, or economic life on the theory that use of the interstate transportation system is somehow enhanced. If, for example, the United States were to condition highway moneys upon moving the state capital, I suppose it might argue that interstate transportation is facilitated by locating local governments in places easily accessible to interstate highways—or, conversely, that highways might become overburdened if they had to carry traffic to and from the state capital. In my mind, such a relationship is hardly more attenuated than the one which the Court finds supports § 158.

["The] appropriate inquiry [is] whether the spending requirement or prohibition is a condition on a grant or whether it is regulation. The difference turns on whether the requirement specifies in some way how the money should be spent, so that Congress' intent in making the grant will be effectuated. Congress has no power under the Spending Clause to impose requirements on a grant that go beyond specifying how the money should be spent. A requirement that is not such a specification is not a condition, but a regulation, which is valid only if it falls within one of Congress' delegated regulatory powers." This approach harks back to United States v. Butler. The Butler Court saw the Agricultural Adjustment Act for what it was—an exercise of regulatory, not spending, power. The error in Butler was not the Court's conclusion that the Act was essentially regulatory, but rather its crabbed view of the extent of Congress' regulatory power under the Commerce Clause. The Agricultural Adjustment Act was regulatory but it was regulation that today would likely be considered within Congress' commerce power. While Butler's authority is questionable insofar as it assumes that Congress has no regulatory power over farm production, its discussion of the spending power and its description of both the power's breadth and its limitations remain sound. [If] the spending power is to be limited only by Congress' notion of the general welfare, the reality, given the vast financial resources of the Federal Government, is that the Spending Clause gives "power to the Congress to tear down the barriers, to invade the states' jurisdiction, and to become a parliament of the whole people, subject to no restrictions save such as are self-imposed." [Butler.] This [was] not the Framers' plan.

THE SPENDING POWER BETWEEN DOLE AND NFIB

1. ***Dole's test.*** South Dakota v. Dole established a four-part test for a permissible exercise of the spending power. Most spending conditions will readily meet the first two requirements: namely, (1) that Congress has a purpose to serve the general welfare and (2) has made a clear statement of the funding condition. Thus, under Dole, the most important criteria are the latter two: whether federal grants to the states are (3) "unrelated" to the spending program or (4) "other constitutional provisions [provide] an independent bar to the conditional grant of federal funds." As to the third factor, why should a condition have to be "germane" to the purposes of the spending? Shouldn't factions be free to logroll in politics, putting together legislative compromises that reflect provisional coalitions and unprincipled tradeoffs? Or are unrelated conditions a form of legislative overreaching that wrongly divert social surplus to powerful factions at the expense of the public good? The majority in Dole took a broad view of relatedness. Justice O'Connor's dissent objected that the majority's deference to any conceivably rational relationship abdicated a judicial responsibility to ensure that a condition is "reasonably related to the expenditure of federal funds." What condition would be insufficiently germane to survive Dole review? A requirement that a state raise its drinking age in order to receive Medicaid funds? Money for community policing? Environmental cleanup funds?

Did Dole in effect impose a fifth, separate and additional requirement that a federal funding condition not be so coercive of the states as a practical matter as to amount to de facto commandeering? That issue arose in NFIB v. Sebelius. As later chapters will illustrate, similar questions about coercion and germaneness arise when government conditions grants of funds to *individuals* on their agreement to constrictions on their conduct that it would be unconstitutional for government to require by regulation. See generally Epstein, "The Supreme Court, 1987 Term—Foreword: Unconstitutional Conditions, State Power, and the Limits of Consent," 102 Harv. L. Rev. 4 (1988); and Sullivan, "Unconstitutional Conditions," 102 Harv. L. Rev. 1413 (1989). The classic early study is Hale, "Unconstitutional Conditions and Constitutional Rights," 35 Colum. L. Rev. 321 (1935).

2. ***The spending power and federalism.*** Recall the concern for state autonomy and the balance of state and federal power that animated the Rehnquist Court to revive constraints on Congress's commerce power, limit the federal government's power to "commandeer" the states, and cabin Congress's power to abrogate state sovereign immunity through Art. I legislation. See Chapter 3 above. Did Dole's more deferential approach to the spending power undermine these federalism decisions and afford Congress an end-run around Commerce Clause restraints?

Consider the view that the Court should presume invalid all "offers of federal funds to the states which, if accepted, would regulate the states in ways that Congress could not directly mandate under its other Article I powers." Baker, "Conditional Federal Spending After Lopez," 95 Colum. L. Rev. 1911 (1995).

Recall that Justice Cardozo stated in Helvering that "the discretion belongs to Congress" as to whether the spending power has invaded the province of the states. Dole likewise embraces the most deferential form of rationality review. Are there adequate "political safeguards of federalism" with respect to exercises of the spending power? Are those political safeguards greater for spending than overt regulation because legislators will have greater self-restraint in spending taxpayers' money than in regulating and imposing less visible costs? Consider the counterargument that broad latitude for regulatory spending conditions allows some states to aggrandize themselves "horizontally" at the expense of others: "Because Dole's interpretation of the spending power is so generous, it enhances Congress's authority to drive states toward a single nationwide policy. [Because] Congress need respond only to the preference of a majority of states in exercising its spending power, its action may well be at odds with the preferences of a dissenting minority of states." Baker & Berman, "Getting Off the Dole: Why the Court Should Abandon its Spending Doctrine," 78 Indiana L.J. 459 (2003).

3. ***The Affordable Care Act and the revival of limits on the spending power.*** In the twenty-five years following Dole, the Court never found that a condition on the expenditure of federal funds exceeded Congress's spending power by being impermissibly coercive or otherwise intruding upon the role of the States in the federalist system. That changed in the challenge to the Medicaid expansion provision of the Patient Protection and Affordable Care Act of 2010.

National Federation of Independent Business v. Sebelius

567 U.S. 519, 132 S. Ct. 2566, 183 L. Ed. 2d 450 (2012).

[The Medicaid program offers federal funding to States to assist pregnant women, children, needy families, the blind, the elderly, and the disabled in obtaining medical care. The Affordable Care Act (ACA) expanded the scope of the Medicaid program by requiring state programs to provide Medicaid coverage to all adults with an income up to 133 percent of the federal poverty level, many of whom various state programs had not previously covered. The ACA increased federal funding to cover the States' costs in expanding Medicaid coverage, but provided that, if a State did not comply with the Act's new coverage requirements, it might lose not only the federal funding for those requirements, but all of its federal Medicaid funds. In a challenge brought by twenty-six States led by Florida, Chief Justice Roberts wrote for seven Justices in holding that Congress had exceeded its spending power by providing that a State loses all Medicaid funding as the penalty for noncompliance with the new conditions.]

■ CHIEF JUSTICE ROBERTS announced the judgment of the Court and delivered an opinion with respect to Part IV, in which JUSTICES BREYER and KAGAN join.

IV. A. The States [contend] that the Medicaid expansion exceeds Congress's authority under the Spending Clause. They claim that Congress is coercing the States to adopt the changes it wants by threatening to withhold all of a State's Medicaid grants, unless the State accepts the new expanded funding and complies with the conditions that come with it. This, they argue, violates the basic principle that the "Federal Government may not compel the States to enact or administer a federal regulatory program." New York v. United States.

[The] Spending Clause grants Congress the power "to pay the Debts and provide for the . . . general Welfare of the United States." U.S. Const., Art. I, § 8, cl. 1. At the same time, our cases have recognized limits on Congress's power under the Spending Clause to secure state compliance with federal objectives. "We have repeatedly characterized . . . Spending Clause legislation as 'much in the nature of a contract.'" The legitimacy of Congress's exercise of the spending power "thus rests on whether the State voluntarily and knowingly accepts the terms of the 'contract.'" Respecting this limitation is critical to ensuring that Spending Clause legislation does not undermine the status of the States as independent sovereigns in our federal system.

That insight has led this Court [to] scrutinize Spending Clause legislation to ensure that Congress is not using financial inducements to exert a "power akin to undue influence." Steward Machine Co. v. Davis, [1937; p. 204]. [The States here] object that Congress has "crossed the line distinguishing encouragement from coercion" in the way it has structured the funding: Instead of simply refusing to grant the new funds to States that will not accept the new conditions, Congress has also threatened to withhold those States' existing Medicaid funds. The States claim that this threat serves no purpose other than to force unwilling States to sign up for the dramatic expansion in health care coverage effected by the Act. Given the nature of the threat and the programs at issue here, we must agree. We have upheld Congress's authority to condition the receipt of funds on the States' complying with restrictions on the use of those funds, because that is the means by which Congress ensures that the funds are spent according to its view of the "general Welfare." Conditions that do not here govern the use of the funds, however, cannot be justified on that basis. When, for example, such conditions take the form of threats to terminate other significant independent grants, the conditions are properly viewed as a means of pressuring the States to accept policy changes.

In South Dakota v. Dole, we considered a challenge to a federal law that threatened to withhold five percent of a State's federal highway funds if the State did not raise its drinking age to 21. [We] found that the inducement was not impermissibly coercive, because Congress was offering only "relatively mild encouragement to the States." [In] this case, the financial "inducement" Congress has chosen is much more than "relatively mild encouragement"—it is a gun to the head. Section 1396c of the Medicaid Act provides that if a State's Medicaid plan does not comply with the Act's requirements, the Secretary of Health and Human Services may declare that "further payments will not be made to the State." A State that opts out of the [ACA's] expansion in health care coverage thus stands to lose not merely "a relatively small percentage" of its existing Medicaid funding, but *all* of it. Medicaid spending accounts for over 20 percent of the average State's total budget, with federal funds covering 50 to 83 percent of those costs. [It] is easy to see how the Dole Court could conclude that the threatened loss of less than half of one percent of South Dakota's budget left that State with a "prerogative" to reject Congress's desired policy, "not merely in theory but in fact." The threatened loss of over 10 percent of a State's overall budget, in contrast, is economic dragooning that leaves the States with no real option but to acquiesce in the Medicaid expansion.

Here, the Government claims that the Medicaid expansion is properly viewed merely as a modification of the existing program because the States agreed that Congress could change the terms of Medicaid when they signed on in the first place. [The] Medicaid expansion, however, accomplishes a shift in kind, not merely degree. [It] is no longer a program to care for the neediest among us, but rather an element of a comprehensive national plan to provide universal health insurance coverage. "[Though] Congress' power to legislate under the spending power is broad, it does not include surprising participating States with postacceptance or 'retroactive' conditions." A State could hardly anticipate that Congress's reservation of the right to "alter" or "amend" the Medicaid program included the power to transform it so dramatically.

The Court in Steward Machine did not attempt to "fix the outermost line" where persuasion gives way to coercion. The Court found it "[e]nough for present purposes that wherever the line may be, this statute is within it." We have no need to fix a line either. It is enough for today that wherever that line may be, this statute is surely beyond it.

■ JUSTICE GINSBURG, joined by JUSTICE SOTOMAYOR, concurring in part, concurring in the judgment in part, and dissenting in part.

[The] Chief Justice [concludes] that the 2010 expansion is unduly coercive [because] the Medicaid expansion is [a] new grant program, not an addition to the Medicaid program existing before the ACA's enactment; [the] expansion was unforeseeable by the States when they first signed on to Medicaid; [and] the threatened loss of funding is so large that the States have no real choice but to participate in the Medicaid expansion. The Chief Justice therefore—for the first time ever—finds an exercise of Congress' spending power unconstitutionally coercive. Medicaid, as amended by the ACA, however, is not two spending programs; it is a single program with a constant aim—to enable poor persons to receive basic health care when they need it. Given past expansions, plus express statutory warning that Congress may change the requirements participating States must meet, there can be no tenable claim that the ACA fails for lack of notice. Moreover, States have no entitlement to receive any Medicaid funds; they enjoy only the opportunity to accept funds on Congress' terms.

A. Expansion has been characteristic of the Medicaid program. Akin to the ACA in 2010, the Medicaid Act as passed in 1965 augmented existing federal grant programs jointly administered with the States. States were not required to participate in Medicaid. But if they did, the Federal Government paid at least half the costs. [Since] 1965, Congress has amended the Medicaid program on more than 50 occasions, sometimes quite sizably, [adding] millions to the Medicaid-eligible population. [Nor] will the expansion exorbitantly increase state Medicaid spending. The Congressional Budget Office (CBO) projects that States will spend 0.8% more than they would have, absent the ACA. Whatever the increase in state obligations after the ACA, it will pale in comparison to the increase in federal funding.

[Any] fair appraisal of Medicaid would require acknowledgment of the considerable autonomy States enjoy under the Act. Far from "conscript[ing] state agencies into the national bureaucratic army," Medicaid "is designed to advance cooperative federalism." [States,] as first-line administrators, will continue to guide the distribution of substantial resources among their needy populations. [Congress could] have established Medicaid as an exclusively federal program. Instead, Congress gave the States the opportunity to partner in the program's administration and development. [Undoubtedly] the interests of federalism are better served when States retain a meaningful role in the implementation of a program of such importance.

B. [Prior] to today's decision, [the] Court has never ruled that the terms of any grant crossed the indistinct line between temptation and coercion. [This] case does not present the concerns that led the Court in Dole even to consider the prospect of coercion. In Dole, the condition—set 21 as the minimum drinking age—did not tell the States how to use funds Congress provided for highway construction. Further, in view of the Twenty-First Amendment, it was an open question whether Congress could directly impose a national minimum drinking age. The ACA, in contrast, relates solely to the federally funded Medicaid program; if States choose not to comply, Congress has not threatened to withhold funds earmarked for any other program. Nor does the ACA use Medicaid funding to induce States to take action Congress itself could not undertake. The Federal Government undoubtedly could operate its own health-care program for poor persons, just as it operates Medicare for seniors' health care.

C. [The] Chief Justice calls the ACA new, but in truth, it simply reaches more of America's poor than Congress originally covered. Medicaid was created to enable States to provide medical assistance to "needy persons." By bringing health care within the reach of a larger population of Americans unable to afford it, the Medicaid expansion is an extension of that basic aim. [Congress] has broad authority to construct or adjust spending programs to meet its contemporary understanding of "the general Welfare."

[The] Chief Justice finds the Medicaid expansion vulnerable because it took participating States by surprise. ["If] Congress intends to impose a condition on the grant of federal moneys, it must do so unambiguously." That requirement is met in this case. Section 2001 does not take effect until 2014. The ACA makes perfectly clear what will be required of States that accept Medicaid funding after that date: They must extend eligibility to adults with incomes no more than 133% of the federal poverty line. [Conditions] on federal funds [must] be unambiguously clear at the time a State receives and uses the money—not at the time, perhaps years earlier, when Congress passed the law establishing the program. In any event, from the start, the Medicaid Act put States on notice that the program could be changed: "The right to alter, amend, or repeal any provision of [Medicaid]," the statute has read since 1965, "is hereby reserved to the Congress." [Given] the enlargement of Medicaid in the years since 1965, a State would be hard put to complain that it lacked fair notice when, in 2010, Congress altered Medicaid to embrace a larger portion of the Nation's poor.

The Chief Justice sees no need to "fix the outermost line where persuasion gives way to coercion." Neither do the joint dissenters. [When] future Spending Clause challenges arrive, as they likely will in the wake of today's decision, how will litigants and judges assess whether "a State has a legitimate choice whether to accept the federal conditions in exchange for federal funds"? Are courts to measure the number of dollars the Federal Government might withhold for noncompliance? The portion of the State's budget at stake? And which State's—or States'—budget is determinative: the lead plaintiff, all challenging States (26 in this case, many with quite different fiscal situations), or some national median? Does it matter that Florida, unlike most States, imposes no state income tax, and therefore might be able to replace foregone federal funds with new state revenue? Or that the coercion state officials in fact fear is punishment at the ballot box for turning down a politically popular federal grant? [The] coercion inquiry, therefore, appears to involve political judgments that defy judicial calculation.

■ JUSTICES SCALIA, KENNEDY, THOMAS, and ALITO, dissenting.

IV. [The] ACA does not legally compel the States to participate in the expanded Medicaid program, but the Act authorizes a severe sanction for any State that refuses to go along: termination of all the State's Medicaid funding. For the average State, the annual federal Medicaid subsidy is equal to more than one-fifth of the State's expenditures. A State forced out of the program would not only lose this huge sum but would almost certainly find it necessary to increase its own health-care expenditures substantially, requiring either a drastic reduction in funding for other programs or a large increase in state taxes. And these new taxes would come on top of the federal taxes already paid by the State's citizens to fund the Medicaid program in other States.

[When] Congress makes grants to the States, it customarily attaches conditions. [This] practice of attaching conditions to federal funds greatly increases federal power. "[O]bjectives not thought to be within Article I's enumerated legislative fields, may nevertheless be attained through the use of the spending power and the conditional grant of federal funds." Dole. This formidable power, if not checked in any way, would present a grave threat to the system of federalism created by our Constitution. If Congress' "Spending Clause power to pursue objectives outside of Article I's enumerated legislative fields" is "limited only by Congress' notion of the general welfare, the reality, given the vast financial resources of the Federal Government, is that the Spending Clause gives 'power to the Congress to tear down the barriers, to invade the states' jurisdiction, and to become a parliament of the whole people, subject to no restrictions save such as are self-imposed,'" Dole (O'Connor, J., dissenting) (quoting Butler).

[The] legitimacy of attaching conditions to federal grants to the States depends on the voluntariness of the States' choice to accept or decline the offered package. Therefore, if States really have no choice other than to accept the package, the offer is coercive, and the conditions cannot be sustained under the spending power. And as our decision in South Dakota v. Dole makes clear, theoretical voluntariness is not enough. [When] a heavy federal tax is levied to support a federal program that offers large grants to the States, States may, as a practical matter, be unable to refuse to participate in the federal program and to substitute a state alternative.

[The] dimensions of the Medicaid program lend strong support to the petitioner States' argument that refusing to accede to the conditions set out in the ACA is not a realistic option. [The] States devote a larger percentage of their budgets to Medicaid than to any other item. Federal funds account for anywhere from 50% to 83% of each State's total Medicaid expenditures. [The] sheer size of this federal spending program in relation to state expenditures means that a State would be very hard pressed to compensate for the loss of federal funds by cutting other spending or raising additional revenue.

For these reasons, the offer that the ACA makes to the States—go along with a dramatic expansion of Medicaid or potentially lose all federal Medicaid funding—is quite unlike anything that we have seen in a prior spending-power case. In South Dakota v. Dole, the total amount that the

States would have lost if every single State had refused to comply with the 21-year-old drinking age was approximately $614 million—or about 0.19% of all state expenditures combined. South Dakota stood to lose, at most, funding that amounted to less than 1% of its annual state expenditures. Under the ACA, by contrast, the Federal Government has threatened to withhold 42.3% of all federal outlays to the states, or approximately $233 billion. South Dakota stands to lose federal funding equaling 28.9% of its annual state expenditures. Withholding $614.7 million, equaling only 0.19% of all state expenditures combined, is aptly characterized as "relatively mild encouragement," but threatening to withhold $233 billion, equaling 21.86% of all state expenditures combined, is a different matter.

What the statistics suggest is confirmed by the goal and structure of the ACA. In crafting the ACA, Congress clearly expressed its informed view that no State could possibly refuse the offer that the ACA extends. The stated goal of the ACA is near-universal health care coverage. [If] Congress had thought that States might actually refuse to go along with the expansion of Medicaid, Congress would surely have devised a backup scheme so that the most vulnerable groups in our society, those previously eligible for Medicaid, would not be left out in the cold. But nowhere in the over 900-page Act is such a scheme to be found. [In sum,] it is perfectly clear from the goal and structure of the ACA that the offer of the Medicaid Expansion was one that Congress understood no State could refuse. The Medicaid Expansion therefore exceeds Congress' spending power and cannot be implemented.

THE SPENDING POWER AFTER NFIB

1. ***The "gun to the head" standard.*** Chief Justice Roberts's opinion distinguishes permissible Spending Clause "encouragement" (as in Dole, where the federal threat to withdraw five percent of highway funding represented an "encouragement" for the state to raise its drinking age) from impermissible "gun-to-the head" coercion, defined to exist where the states lack a real choice as to whether to accept the federal funding and the corresponding conditions. In distinguishing the Medicaid expansion at issue in the Affordable Care Act from the highway funding in Dole, Chief Justice Roberts noted that (1) the ACA conditions did not limit how the states used the funds; (2) the federal threat at issue was the removal of an independent pre-existing grant, rather than the future denial of potential funding; (3) the threatened removal was of a large amount of funding; (4) the change in the Medicaid program was purportedly a change in kind, rather than degree, tying together previously separate programs into one package; and (5) the states were purportedly unable to predict the new conditions upon initially receiving the funds. Which of these characteristics are most important for distinguishing between the two categories of federal spending? For an argument that NFIB's Spending Clause holding should be read to restrict federal power only when several of these criteria are present at once, see Bagenstos, "The Anti-Leveraging Principle and the Spending Clause after NFIB," 101 Geo. L.J. 861 (2013). Recall Chief Justice Roberts's refusal elsewhere in NFIB, see p. 196 above, to define the point at which an exercise of the taxing power becomes impermissibly punitive. Do the two standards governing undue coercion in the taxing and spending contexts share doctrinal characteristics?

2. ***A 7–2 decision.*** In contrast to the Commerce Clause and Taxation Clause holdings, which were 5–4 decisions, the Spending Clause decision was a 7–2 decision. Is this lopsided outcome surprising in light of the fact that this was the first act of federal spending since the New Deal to be held impermissibly coercive by the Court? What might explain Justices Breyer and Kagan joining this but not the other part of Chief Justice Roberts's controlling opinion? Did they want to ensure a clear holding of the Court that the Medicaid expansion could be preserved absent the spending condition?

3. ***The future of cooperative federalism.*** In dissent, Justice Ginsburg argued that restrictions on federal ability to impose conditions on states in exchange for grants of federal funds will lead to less, not more state involvement in federal programs because the federal government will switch to purely national programs. Is this a likely outcome? Or do states have adequate alternative sources of power to pressure the federal government to include them in national programs notwithstanding the inability to impose some kinds of conditions on receipt of federal funding?

4. ***Judicial legislating?*** Having held that the Medicaid expansion violated the Spending Clause, Chief Justice Roberts's opinion imposed as a remedy the requirement that states be allowed to opt out of the expansion without losing their pre-existing federal Medicaid funding, severing the condition but leaving the remainder of the ACA Medicaid expansion intact. By contrast, Justice Scalia's dissent argued that "the most natural remedy would be to invalidate the Medicaid Expansion" in its entirety. Did the Chief Justice's resolution change the substance of the Medicaid expansion, unduly infringing Congress's Article I power? Or is it the judiciary's obligation to preserve as much of a law that has been approved by the political process as possible, consistent with the demands of the Constitution?

5. ***The ongoing saga of the ACA.*** Republicans opposed the ACA throughout the Obama administration and pledged to "repeal and replace" the law during the 2016 campaign. Upon taking control of both elected branches of government in 2017, Republicans introduced a bill that would eliminate the individual mandate and change several significant features of the health care market. But by that point the ACA—and particularly its requirement that insurers cover pre-existing conditions—had become increasingly popular, and Congress could not muster the votes for a repeal-and-replace measure. Instead, later in 2017 Republicans lowered the tax on those without insurance to $0, effectively eliminating the individual mandate.

Twenty states sued after the tax was zeroed out, claiming the individual mandate could no longer be justified under the tax power because there was no actual tax and that, without the individual mandate, the entire ACA must be struck down. In December 2018, a federal district judge in Texas agreed. The court ruled the mandate was now unconstitutional and was not severable from the rest of the ACA, reasoning that the mandate was the ACA's "keystone" and that Congress would not have wanted the ACA to stand without it. The judge stayed his decision, and the suit is pending appeal as this casebook goes to press.

In light of these developments, how important was the Supreme Court's intervention in 2012 to the political fate of the ACA? Many viewed Chief Justice Roberts's decision upholding the individual mandate as an effort to preserve the Court's institutional legitimacy and avoid accusations of partisanship. Could the result in NFIB have been a factor contributing to increasing acceptance of the ACA over the past few years? Does the lack of an actual tax affect the Court's reasoning at all?

CHAPTER 5

FEDERAL LIMITS ON STATE REGULATION OF INTERSTATE COMMERCE

The preceding three chapters examined the scope of national powers as limited by state concerns; this chapter explores the limits on state powers that flow from national concerns. On what basis, and to what extent, do the grants of enumerated powers to the national government, and the exercises of those powers, curtail state authority? Do the constraints arise from text? From history? From inferences based on the structure of the Constitution? This chapter explores those problems mainly in the context of the commerce power; but similar restrictions on state authority arise in connection with other national powers as well. See, e.g., as to bankruptcy, Sturges v. Crowninshield, 4 Wheat. (17 U.S.) 122 (1819), and Perez v. Campbell, 402 U.S. 637 (1971); as to foreign affairs, Zschernig v. Miller, 389 U.S. 429 (1968); as to copyright, Goldstein v. California, 412 U.S. 546 (1973); as to patents, Kewanee Oil Co. v. Bicron Corp., 416 U.S. 470 (1974).

Article I restraints on state regulation of commerce arise in two situations. In the first, which concerns the so-called "dormant commerce clause," Congress is silent: it has taken no action, express or implied, to make federal policy on a given subject matter. In that situation, the objection to state regulation rests entirely on the negative implications of the Commerce Clause of Art. I, § 8, cl. 3; on the unexercised commerce power itself; and the presumptive common-market, free trade values it embodies. See Section 1 below. In the second situation, Congress *has* exercised the commerce power, and the challenge to inconsistent state action rests on both the exercise of the commerce power under Art. I, § 8, cl. 3 and the preemptive effect of the federal legislation under the Supremacy Clause of Art. VI. See Section 3 below.

A further limit upon state regulation of interstate commerce arises from one of the rare rights-conferring provisions in the original Constitution: the Privileges and Immunities Clause of Article IV, § 2, which guarantees to the "Citizens of each State [all] Privileges and Immunities of Citizens in the several States." Like the judicially inferred dormant commerce clause, this provision bars certain state legislation that discriminates against out-of-state economic interests, but the two doctrines differ in important respects. See Section 2 below.

SECTION 1. THE DORMANT COMMERCE CLAUSE

Does a broad scope for the national commerce power itself imply limits on state power? The states regulate a great deal of economic activity that might affect interstate commerce in ways Congress has not specifically addressed. Should the courts invalidate such legislation even if Congress has not spoken? Under the so-called dormant commerce clause, the Court invalidates some "protectionist" state legislation, even in the absence of congressional preemption. The Constitution nowhere explicitly gives the Court this task. Article I, § 10 bars states from imposing duties on imports or exports in foreign commerce without the consent of Congress. And the Privileges and Immunities Clause of Article IV bars state discrimination against out-of-state citizens. But the text of the Constitution nowhere expressly divests the states of the power to regulate interstate commerce. Article I, § 8, cl. 3 provides, "The Congress shall have Power [to] regulate Commerce [among] the several States." Into that affirmative grant the Court has read judicially enforceable limits on state legislation when Congress has not acted. To justify these negative implications from the Commerce Clause, the Court has relied largely on history and on inferences from the federal structure.

THE NONDISCRIMINATION PRINCIPLE

1. ***The historical origins of the dormant commerce clause.*** The much-repeated story of the framing of the Constitution suggests that the Framers centralized the power to regulate interstate commerce in Congress in large part because they viewed destructive trade wars among the states as a major problem under the Articles of Confederation. Justice Jackson reviewed this history in his opinion for the Court in H.P. Hood & Sons v. Du Mond, 336 U.S. 525 (1949), see p. 255 below: "When victory relieved the Colonies from the pressure for solidarity that war had exerted, a drift toward anarchy and commercial warfare between states began. ['Each] State would legislate according to its estimate of its own interests, the importance of its own products, and the local advantages or disadvantages of its position in a political or commercial view.' This came 'to threaten at once the peace and safety of the Union.' The sole purpose for which Virginia initiated the movement which ultimately produced the Constitution was 'to take into consideration the trade of the United States; to examine the relative situations and trade of the said States; to consider how far a uniform system in their commercial regulations may be necessary to their common interest and their permanent harmony' [No] other federal power was so universally assumed to be necessary, no other state power was so readily relinquished. [As Madison] indicated, 'want of a general power over Commerce led to an exercise of this power separately, by the States, wch [sic] not only proved abortive, but engendered rival, conflicting and angry regulations.' The necessity of centralized regulation of commerce among the states was so obvious and so fully recognized that the few words of the Commerce Clause were little illuminated by debate."

While some historians have argued that such accounts of preconstitutional state trade wars are overstated, there can be little doubt that, during the Confederation period, at least some states, including Virginia, New York, Connecticut, Massachusetts, Rhode Island and South Carolina, imposed taxes, imposts, duties, and tonnage fees on imported goods that they did not impose on their own citizens. See Denning, "Confederation-Era Discrimination Against Interstate Commerce and the Legitimacy of the Dormant Commerce Clause," 94 Ky. L.J. 37 (2005–06) ("The men who drafted the Constitution were interested in arresting extant abuses of state commercial power that the Articles were powerless to stop."). Such discrimination led to fears of an escalating cycle of retaliation. As Alexander Hamilton wrote in The Federalist, No. 22, "interfering and unneighborly regulations of some States, contrary to the true spirit of the Union, have given just cause of umbrage and complaint to others. [Examples] of this nature, if not restrained by a national control, would be multiplied and extended till they became not less serious sources of animosity and discord than injurious impediments to the intercourse between the different parts of the Confederacy." Does this original history justify the expansion of the dormant commerce clause beyond tariffs, imposts, and duties imposed at the state border to state health, safety, and welfare regulations such as the one struck down in Philadelphia v. New Jersey?

Note that the Framers expressly adopted the Import-Export Clause of Art. I, § 10, cl. 2, which provides, "No State shall, without the Consent of the Congress, lay any Imposts or Duties on Imports or Exports, except what may be absolutely necessary for executing its inspection Laws." But the Supreme Court has interpreted that clause to apply only to goods coming from or going to nations outside the United States, not to imports or exports among the states. Woodruff v. Parham, 75 U.S. (8 Wall.) 123 (1869). Thus the dormant commerce clause, not the Import-Export Clause, has been the source of limitation on state tariffs and their regulatory equivalents. Justice Thomas has urged reinterpretation of the Import-Export Clause, suggesting that the original understanding of the terms "imports" and "exports" might have "encompassed not just trade with foreign nations, but trade with other States as well," and that Woodruff was wrongly decided. Camps Newfound/Owatonna, Inc. v. Town of Harrison, 520 U.S. 564 (1997) (Thomas, J., dissenting). More recently, Justice Scalia argued that the Import-Export Clause, not the dormant commerce clause, "addressed the evils of local impediments to commerce by prohibiting States from imposing certain especially burdensome taxes" and other tariffs. Comptroller of Treasury of Md. v. Wynne, ___ U.S. ___, 135 S. Ct. 1787 (2015) (Scalia, J., dissenting). Justice Alito, writing for the majority, also "noted the close relationship between the two provisions," but concluded that Justice Scalia's reading of the Import-Export Clause would not change the outcome in Wynne. Wynne is discussed fully at p. 292 below.

2. ***The political foundations of a presumption against discriminatory state laws.*** Philadelphia v. New Jersey (1978; p. 231 below) states a "virtually per se rule of invalidity" against state discrimination toward out-of-state commerce. What constitutional policies animate such a rule? Do state laws that protect local economic interests at the expense of out-of-state interests impair a *political* vision of national unity? Justice Cardozo famously wrote for the Court in Baldwin v. G.A.F. Seelig, Inc. (1935; p. 254 below), that "[t]he Constitution was framed upon the theory that the peoples of the several states must sink or swim together, and that in the long run prosperity and salvation are in union and not division." Does this suggest that dormant commerce clause cases reinforce a sense of national citizenship and political solidarity? Does a national common market reinforce a sense of national political identity? Conversely, are protectionist measures especially likely to spur retaliation that undermines national political unity? For the view that prevention of such destructive political conflict best explains dormant commerce clause review, see Denning, "Reconstructing the Dormant Commerce Clause Doctrine," 50 Wm. & Mary L. Rev. 417 (2008).

Alternatively, does dormant commerce clause enforcement correct the structural defect in the political process of states' incentives to export costs to unrepresented outsiders? For the general theory that judicial review can be best justified to correct such problems of underrepresentation and other impediments to the operation of democratic processes, see Ely, Democracy and Distrust (1980). Out-of-state interests are, by definition, formally unrepresented in a state's political process, and thus state lawmakers may be expected to advance the interests of in-state constituents who can vote for them at the expense of out-of-state residents who cannot. Thus discrimination against outsiders may be expected predictably to result from the normal operation of in-state politics. Chief Justice Stone captured this point in his opinion for the Court in Southern Pacific Co. v. Arizona, 325 U.S. 761 (1945), where he wrote that, "to the extent [the] burden of state regulation falls on interests outside the state, it is unlikely to be alleviated by the operation of those political restraints normally exerted when interests within the state are affected." On this view, judicial invalidation of facial discrimination against out-of-state interests reinforces democracy by supplying a kind of virtual representation for out-of-state citizens. Stated differently, such judicial review enforces a norm of "deliberative equality" by which states must give "equal regard to similarly situated in-state and out-of-state interests burdened by [a] regulation or tax." Williams, "The Foundations of the American Common Market," 84 Notre Dame L. Rev. 409 (2008). Should actual effects matter in such analysis? Consider the view that a state's structural incentives to act parochially to the disadvantage of outsiders are sufficient to render a discriminatory law suspect whether or not outsiders are actually harmed by it. See Tribe, American Constitutional Law § 6–5 (2d ed. 1988).

Are the assumptions underlying such representation-reinforcement theories correct? Do out-of-staters in fact wholly lack political influence in a state's political processes? Why can't in-state interests provide adequate virtual representation for out-of-staters to the extent they share mutual economic interests? For example, the New Jersey landfill operators arguably provided virtual representation in New Jersey's political process for out-of-state waste producers whose business they wanted. See Philadelphia v. New Jersey (p. 231 below). Should a court be permitted to invalidate a law on the theory that such virtual representation by proxy is inadequate? Moreover, voting is not the only form of political influence; out-of-state interests, for example, are generally free to lobby and donate campaign funds to in-state political representatives. Do such informal opportunities for political speech serve to offset the absence of formal political representation? For the view that the dormant commerce clause decisions do not serve national unity because they leave states free to prefer insiders in various ways and overprotect out-of-staters who can represent themselves through in-state allies and lobbying, see Heinzerling, "The Commercial Constitution," 1995 Sup. Ct. Rev. 217.

3. ***The economic foundations of a presumption against discriminatory state laws.*** Does the strong presumption against discriminatory state laws flow not so much from a political vision of national solidarity as from an economic vision of free trade? On this view goods, labor and investments can be allocated most efficiently if free to flow across state borders to the place where they are most highly valued. Such a view is parallel to arguments against protectionism at the national level. The early cases refer to such a social welfarist vision: Justice Cardozo's Baldwin

opinion, for example, noted that "prosperity" lies in "union and not division." And Justice Jackson's opinion in Hood & Sons v. Du Mond stated: "[The] principle that our economic unit is the Nation, which alone has the gamut of powers necessary to control of the economy, including the vital power of erecting customs barriers against foreign competition, has as its corollary that the states are not separable economic units. [The] material success that has come to inhabitants of the states which make up this federal free trade unit has been the most impressive in the history of commerce, but the established interdependence of the states only emphasizes the necessity of protecting interstate movement of goods against local burdens. [Our] system, fostered by the Commerce Clause, is that every farmer and every craftsman shall be encouraged to produce by the certainty that he will have free access to every market in the Nation, that no home embargoes will withhold his exports, and no foreign state will by customs duties or regulations exclude them. Likewise, every consumer may look to the free competition from every producing area in the Nation to protect him from exploitation by any."

4. ***Thinking about Europe.*** Some observers see an analogy between the states at the time that the Constitution was adopted and the European Union as it presently exists. The European Union is predicated on the theory that economic unity promotes political unity and vice versa. Does the strain of the post-2008 economic crisis on the European Union provide any lessons for American dormant commerce clause jurisprudence? Does the United Kingdom's 2016 referendum vote to exit the European Union change this understanding?

5. ***Erie and the political national unity justification for the dormant commerce clause.*** The national economic unity objective of the dormant commerce clause could be seen as connected to the goal of a single federal common law as announced by Swift v. Tyson, 41 U.S. (16 Pet.) 1 (1842). Did the elimination of a unified national common law in Erie Railroad Company v. Tompkins, 304 U.S. 64 (1938), strengthen or weaken the political national-unity justification for the dormant commerce clause?

THE HISTORY OF THE DORMANT COMMERCE CLAUSE

Chief Justice Marshall wrote several early decisions reflecting upon the limits the Commerce Clause might impose on state regulatory authority. Recall the case of the New York steamboat monopoly, Gibbons v. Ogden. In the first part of his opinion, see p. 114 above, Chief Justice Marshall set forth a broad reach for the congressional commerce power, opining that "[c]ommerce, undoubtedly, is traffic, but it is something more: it is intercourse," and that it reached into the interior of each state, allowing Congress to regulate intrastate activities that "affect the States generally." His decision ultimately rested on preemption grounds, holding that the Federal Navigation Act of 1793 barred New York's effort to restrict entry into New York waters under the Supremacy Clause of Article VI. As a result, Gibbons, the federal licensee, prevailed, and the injunction proceeding brought by Ogden, the holder of the New York monopoly, was dismissed. But Chief Justice Marshall also discussed, in dicta, the possibility that New York might not have authority to regulate interstate ship traffic in the first place, thus sketching his view of the negative implications of the Commerce Clause for state authority over commerce:

Gibbons v. Ogden

9 Wheat. (22 U.S.) 1, 6 L. Ed. 23 (1824).

■ CHIEF JUSTICE MARSHALL delivered the opinion of the Court.

[I]t has been urged, with great earnestness, that although the power of congress to regulate commerce with foreign nations, and among the several states, be co-extensive with the subject itself, and have no other limits than are prescribed in the constitution, yet the states may severally exercise the same power, within their respective jurisdictions. In support of this argument, it is said, that they possessed it as an inseparable attribute of sovereignty, before the formation of the constitution, and still retain it, except so far as they have surrendered it by that instrument; that this principle results from the nature of the government, and is secured by the tenth amendment; that an affirmative grant of power is not exclusive, unless in its own nature it be such that the continued exercise of it by the former possessor is inconsistent with the grant, and that this is not of that description. The appellant, conceding these postulates, except the last, contends that full power to regulate a particular subject, implies the whole power, and leaves no residuum; that a grant of the whole is incompatible with the existence of a right in another to any part of it.

[The] grant of the power to lay and collect taxes is, like the power to regulate commerce, made in general terms, and has never been understood to interfere with the exercise of the same power by the states; and hence has been drawn an argument which has been applied to the question under consideration. But the two grants are not, it is conceived, similar in their terms or their nature. [The] state governments remain, and constitute a most important part of our system. The power of taxation is indispensable to their existence, and is a power which, in its own nature, is capable of residing in, and being exercised by, different authorities at the same time. [When] each government exercises the power of taxation, neither is exercising the power of the other. But, when a state proceeds to regulate [interstate or foreign] commerce, it is exercising the very power that is granted to congress, and is doing the very thing which congress is authorized to do. There is no analogy, then, between the power of taxation and the power of regulating commerce.

[But] the inspection laws are said to be regulations of commerce, and are certainly recognised in the constitution, as being passed in the exercise of a power remaining with the states. That inspection laws may have a remote and considerable influence on commerce, will not be denied; but that a power to regulate commerce is the source from which the right to pass them is derived, cannot be admitted. The object of inspection laws, is to improve the quality of articles produced by the labour of a country; to fit them for exportation; or, it may be, for domestic use. They act upon the subject, before it becomes an article of [commerce], and prepare it for that purpose. They form a portion of that immense mass of legislation, which embraces every thing within the territory of a state, not surrendered to the general government; all which can be most advantageously exercised by the states themselves. Inspection laws, quarantine laws, health laws of every description, as well as laws for regulating the internal commerce of a state, and those which respect turnpike roads, ferries, & c., are component parts of this mass.

No direct general power over these objects is granted to congress; and, consequently, they remain subject to state legislation. If the legislative power of the Union can reach them, it must be for national purposes; it must be where the power is expressly given for a special purpose, or is clearly incidental to some power which is expressly given. It is obvious, that the government of the Union, in the exercise of its express powers, that, for example, of regulating [interstate commerce], may use means that may also be employed by a state, in the exercise of its acknowledged powers; that, for example, of regulating commerce within the state.

[If] a state, in passing laws on subjects acknowledged to be within its control, and with a view to those subjects, shall adopt a measure of the same character with one which congress may adopt, it does not derive its authority from the particular power which has been granted, but from some other, which remains with the state, and may be executed by the same means. All experience shows that the same measures, or measures scarcely distinguishable from each other, may flow from distinct powers; but this does not prove that the powers themselves are identical. Although the means used in their execution may sometimes approach each other so nearly as to be confounded, there are other situations in which they are sufficiently distinct, to establish their individuality. In our complex system, presenting the rare and difficult scheme of one general government, whose action extends over the whole, but which possesses only certain enumerated powers; and of numerous state governments, which retain and exercise all powers not delegated to the Union, contests respecting power must arise. Were it even otherwise, the measures taken by the respective governments to execute their acknowledged powers, would often be of the same description, and might, sometimes, interfere. This, however, does not prove that the one is exercising, or has a right to exercise, the powers of the other.

[It] has been contended by counsel for the appellant, that, as the word "to regulate" implies in its nature, full power over the thing to be regulated, it excludes, necessarily, the action of all others that would perform the same operation on the same thing. That regulation is designed for the entire result, applying in those parts which remain as they were, as well as to those which are altered. It produces a uniform whole, which is as much disturbed and deranged by changing what the regulating power designs to leave untouched, as that on which it has operated. There is great force in this argument, and the court is not satisfied that it has been refuted.

Since, however, in exercising the power of regulating their own purely internal affairs, whether of trading or police, the states may sometimes enact laws, the validity of which depends on their interfering with, and being contrary to, an act of congress passed in pursuance of the constitution, the court will enter upon the inquiry, whether the laws of New York [have], in their application to this case, come into collision with an act of congress, and deprived a citizen of a right to which that act entitles him. Should this collision exist, it will be immaterial, whether those laws were passed in virtue of a concurrent power "to regulate commerce with foreign nations and among the several states," or, in virtue of a power to regulate their domestic trade and police. In one case and the other, the acts of New York must yield to the law of congress; and the decision sustaining the privilege they confer, against a right given by a law of the Union, must be erroneous.

THE NASCENT DORMANT COMMERCE CLAUSE

1. ***Marshall's dormant commerce clause dicta.*** The above passage expresses Chief Justice Marshall's "tentative but unconsummated embrace of the Dormant Commerce Clause." Williams, "Gibbons," 79 N.Y.U. L. Rev. 1398 (2004). Marshall noted the "great force" in the argument for the exclusiveness of Congress's power over commerce and said that he was "not satisfied that it has been refuted." But he then made clear this was dicta, as he relied ultimately on preemption by federal statute under the Supremacy Clause. He also noted that even if the national commerce power was exclusive, it still coexisted with state power to enact legislation that might affect commerce—"[i]nspection laws, quarantine laws, health laws of every description." He thus outlined a division of power between Congress over interstate commercial regulation and the states over police regulations designed to protect the health, safety or welfare of their own citizens, distinguishing permissible state "police" regulations from impermissible state "commerce" regulations based on the purpose of the state regulation.

Why did Marshall articulate but then step back from the principle that the Commerce Clause, by negative implication, divested the states of power over interstate commerce? Consider the view that "Marshall's decision to eschew the Dormant Commerce Clause and rest the Gibbons decision on the preemptive effect of the Federal Navigation Act was an ingenious move on Marshall's part to find a way to protect interstate commerce yet avoid placing the judiciary at the forefront of the battle against state protectionist legislation." Williams, "Gibbons," supra. He thus helped deflect various contemporaneous efforts in Congress to weaken the Court's power to invalidate state legislation.

2. ***The Taney Court's search for formulations.*** After Marshall's death in 1835, the Court, under his successor, Roger Brooke Taney, searched for formulations of the negative implications of the Commerce Clause with little clarity or agreement. Some of the Justices sought to follow what they perceived to be Marshall's guidance: state regulations of "commerce" were prohibited because of the "exclusive" commerce power, but "police" regulations were constitutional. Chief Justice Taney himself took the polar opposite position: to Taney, state regulations of commerce were valid "unless they come in conflict with a law of Congress," and *no* implied prohibitions were enforceable.

A majority of the Taney Court, including the Chief Justice, finally converged on a single standard in Cooley v. Board of Wardens, 12 How. (53 U.S.) 299 (1851), a case arising from an 1803 Pennsylvania law that required ships entering or leaving the port of Philadelphia to engage a local pilot to guide them through the harbor. For failure to comply, the law imposed a penalty of half the pilotage fee, payable to the Board for a fund for retired pilots and their dependents. Cooley steered a middle course between the polar positions that had clashed in the earlier Taney Court cases. It rejected the view that the congressional commerce power was exclusive and that the states therefore lacked *all* power to regulate commerce. But it also rejected the view that the Commerce Clause, in the absence of national legislation, imposed *no* limits on the states at all. Cooley recognized *some* concurrent state regulatory power over commerce and adopted a position that has sometimes been called one of selective exclusiveness. The Court's continuously dominant position since Cooley has been that the Commerce Clause by its own force bars some, but not all, state regulation.

Cooley identified as the determinative factor the "subject" of regulation; it appeared to abandon Marshall's "purpose" inquiry. According to Cooley, some subjects are "of such a nature" as to require "a single uniform rule" by Congress; others, like the pilotage law at issue, are local, "imperatively demanding that diversity which alone can meet the local necessities." But Cooley left unanswered questions about how the "subjects" were to be identified and distinguished. For example, what was the "subject" found to be "local and not national" in Cooley itself? All pilotage regulation? Pilotage regulation with a certain purpose? Cooley seemed to assume that the pilotage rule was directed at the safety of local harbor traffic. Could it have been argued that an additional purpose was to assure the economic support of local pilots? Would the Cooley formula have permitted such an argument to be taken into account? Once a subject is recognized as "local" under Cooley, does every variety of state regulation become permissible? Or are there still limitations? For example, may a state give preference to local businesses when it regulates a "local" subject?

3. ***The aftermath of Cooley and the rise and fall of the "direct"-"indirect" distinction.*** In the late 19th century, the growth of a nationwide railroad system spurred demands for more extensive legislative controls. The early railroad regulation cases frequently cited Cooley, but it was difficult to square the course of the decisions with any simple application of the "national"-"local" distinction. Thus, Smith v. Alabama, 124 U.S. 465 (1888), justified the state regulation of railroad engineers on the ground that the law rested on safety considerations and that its impact on commerce was merely "indirect," not "direct." This "direct"-"indirect" distinction was increasingly invoked. Application of this test often turned as a practical matter, however, on an empirical showing of the burden on interstate commerce. Compare Southern Railway Co. v. King, 217 U.S. 524 (1910) (upholding, as imposing no "direct" burden on interstate commerce, a Georgia safety law requiring railroad trains to slow down and blow their whistles at set intervals) with Seaboard Air Line Ry. v. Blackwell, 244 U.S. 310 (1917) (invalidating as a "direct" burden on commerce the same law upon a showing that compliance with the law would have required a train to stop 124 times in 123 miles and thus more than doubled the duration of an Atlanta to South Carolina trip).

Justice (later Chief Justice) Stone, who joined the Court in 1926, soon took the lead in urging more useful and realistic criteria. In Di Santo v. Pennsylvania, 273 U.S. 34 (1927), the Court held unconstitutional as a "direct burden" on commerce a state law imposing a license fee of $50 on travel agents selling steamship tickets for foreign travel. In dissent, Justice Stone, joined by Justices Holmes and Brandeis, found the direct-indirect distinction "too mechanical, too uncertain in its application, and too remote from actualities, to be of value. [We] are doing little more than using labels to describe a result rather than any trustworthy formula by which it is reached. [It] seems clear that those interferences [with commerce that are] not deemed forbidden are to be sustained, not because the effect on commerce is nominally indirect, but because a consideration of all the facts and circumstances, such as the nature of the regulation, its function, the character of the business involved and the actual effect on the flow of commerce, lead to the conclusion that the regulation concerns interests peculiarly local and does not infringe the national interest in maintaining the freedom of commerce across state lines." Justice Stone's balancing formula anticipated the modern Court's approach.

4. ***Three modern categories of dormant commerce clause challenge.*** The Court's dormant commerce clause decisions increasingly abandoned any attempt to apply categorical distinctions between exercises of "police" and "commerce" powers, between "local" and "national" subject matters, or between "indirect" and "direct" effects. Instead the Court focused increasingly upon the form and purpose of state laws. Three lines of challenge have emerged, as the cases below demonstrate.

a. State laws that *facially discriminate* against out-of-state commerce are almost always struck down under a virtually per se rule of invalidity. Welton v. Missouri, 1 Otto (91 U.S.) 275 (1876), for example, invalidated a Missouri license requirement that applied to itinerant peddlers who sold merchandise "not the growth, produce, or manufacture of the State" but not to peddlers of Missouri goods. Justice Field stated for the Court that the "very object" of the Commerce Clause was to protect "against discriminating State legislation."

b. State laws that are facially neutral as between in-state and out-of-state interests but that have an *impermissibly protectionist purpose or effect* are also typically invalidated on the ground that they in fact favor local economic interests at the expense of out-of-state competitors. For example, in Buck v. Kuykendall, 267 U.S. 307 (1925), the Court held unconstitutional the state of Washington's denial of a certificate of convenience and necessity to an applicant seeking to operate an "auto stage line" to carry passengers and freight between Portland and Seattle. The denial relied on the ground that the territory was "already being adequately served by other carriers." Justice Brandeis noted that state regulations "adopted primarily to promote safety upon the highways and conservation in their use are not obnoxious to the Commerce Clause," but held that here the state's purpose was not safety but rather "the prohibition of competition."

c. State laws that are facially neutral but that have a *disproportionate adverse effect* on interstate commerce may also be struck down, under the balancing approach canonically set forth in Pike v. Bruce Church, Inc., 397 U.S. 137 (1970) (p. 261 below), where a unanimous Court stated: "Where the statute regulates evenhandedly to effectuate a legitimate local public interest, and its effects on interstate commerce are only incidental, it will be upheld unless the burden imposed on such commerce is clearly excessive in relation to the putative local benefits. [If] a legitimate local purpose is found, then the question becomes one of degree. And the extent of the burden that will be tolerated will of course depend on the nature of the local interest involved, and on whether it could be promoted as well with a lesser impact in interstate activities."

FACIAL DISCRIMINATION AGAINST OUT-OF-STATE COMMERCE

———

Philadelphia v. New Jersey

437 U.S. 617, 98 S. Ct. 2531, 57 L. Ed. 2d 475 (1978).

[A 1973 New Jersey law prohibited the importation of most "solid or liquid waste which originated or was collected outside the territorial limits of this State." The New Jersey waste ban was challenged by operators of private landfills in New Jersey and by several cities in other states that had agreements with these operators for waste disposal. A state trial judge declared the law unconstitutional because it discriminated against interstate commerce. The New Jersey Supreme Court reversed, holding that the law was designed to protect the State's health and environment, not its economy. The challengers claimed that the law, "while outwardly cloaked 'in the currently fashionable garb of environmental protection,' [is] actually no more than a legislative effort to suppress competition and stabilize the cost of solid waste disposal for New Jersey residents." In response, the state denied that the law was motivated by or economic protectionism, insisting that the state had denied its own private landfill operator an economic opportunity in order to protect the health, safety and welfare of the state's citizenry. The Supreme Court reversed, accepting the challengers' characterization and invalidating the New Jersey law.]

■ JUSTICE STEWART delivered the opinion of the Court.

The opinions of the Court through the years have reflected an alertness to the evils of "economic isolation" and protectionism, while at the same time recognizing that incidental burdens on interstate commerce may be unavoidable when a State legislates to safeguard the health and safety of its people. Thus, where simple economic protectionism is effected by state legislation, a virtually per se rule of invalidity has been erected. The clearest example of such legislation is a law that overtly blocks the flow of interstate commerce at a State's borders. Cf. Welton v. Missouri. But where other legislative objectives are credibly advanced and there is no patent discrimination against interstate trade, the Court has adopted a much more flexible approach, the general contours of which were outlined in [the Pike "balancing" formulation.] The crucial inquiry, therefore, must be directed to determining whether [the law] is basically a protectionist measure, or whether it can fairly be viewed as a law directed to legitimate local concerns, with effects upon interstate commerce that are only incidental.

[The parties'] dispute about ultimate legislative purpose need not be resolved, because its resolution would not be relevant to the constitutional issue to be decided in this case. Contrary to the evident assumption of the [state,] the evil of protectionism can reside in legislative means as well as legislative ends. Thus, it does not matter whether the ultimate aim of [the law] is to reduce the waste disposal costs of New Jersey residents or to save remaining open lands from pollution, for we assume New Jersey has every right to protect its residents' pocketbooks as well as their environment. And it may be assumed as well that New Jersey may pursue those ends by slowing the flow of *all* waste into the State's remaining landfills, even though interstate commerce may incidentally be affected. But whatever New Jersey's ultimate purpose, it may not be accomplished by discriminating against articles of commerce coming from outside the State unless there is some reason, apart from their origin, to treat them differently. Both on its face and in its plain effect, [the law] violates this principle of nondiscrimination.

The Court has consistently found parochial legislation of this kind to be constitutionally invalid, whether the ultimate aim of the legislation was to assure a steady supply of milk by erecting barriers to allegedly ruinous outside competition; or to create jobs by keeping industry within the State; or to preserve the State's financial resources from depletion by fencing out indigent immigrants. In each of these cases, a presumably legitimate goal was sought to be achieved by the illegitimate means of isolating the State from the national economy. [A] "State is without power to prevent privately owned articles of trade from being shipped and sold in interstate commerce on the ground that they are required to satisfy local demands or because they are needed by the people of the State."

The New Jersey law at issue in this case falls squarely within the area that the Commerce Clause puts off limits to state regulation. On its face, it imposes on out-of-state commercial interests the full burden of conserving the State's remaining landfill space. It is true that in our previous cases the scarce natural resource was itself the article of commerce, whereas here the scarce resource and the article of commerce are distinct. But that difference is without consequence. In both instances, the State has overtly moved to slow or freeze the flow of commerce for protectionist reasons. It does not matter that the State has shut the article of commerce inside the State in one case and outside the State in the other. What is crucial is the attempt by one State to isolate itself from a problem common to many by erecting a barrier against the movement of interstate trade.

The appellees argue that not all laws which facially discriminate against out-of-state commerce are forbidden protectionist regulations. In particular, they point to quarantine laws, which this Court has repeatedly upheld even though they appear to single out interstate commerce for special treatment. In the appellees' view, [this law] is analogous to such health-protective measures, since it reduces the exposure of New Jersey residents to the allegedly harmful effects of landfill sites. It is true that certain quarantine laws have not been considered forbidden protectionist measures, even though they were directed against out-of-state commerce. But those quarantine laws banned the importation of articles such as diseased livestock that required destruction as soon as possible because their very movement risked contagion and other evils. Those laws thus did not discriminate against interstate commerce as such, but simply prevented traffic in noxious articles, whatever their origin.

The New Jersey statute is not such a quarantine law. There has been no claim here that the very movement of waste into or through New Jersey endangers health, or that waste must be disposed of as soon and as close to its point of generation as possible. The harms caused by waste are said to arise after its disposal in landfill sites, and at that point, as New Jersey concedes, there is no basis to distinguish out-of-state waste from domestic waste. If one is inherently harmful, so is the other. Yet New Jersey has banned the former while leaving its landfill sites open to the latter. The New Jersey law blocks the importation of waste in an obvious effort to saddle those outside the State with the entire burden of slowing the flow of refuse into New Jersey's remaining landfill sites.

That legislative effort is clearly impermissible under the [Commerce Clause]. Today, cities in Pennsylvania and New York find it expedient or necessary to send their waste into New Jersey for disposal, and New Jersey claims the right to close its borders to such traffic. Tomorrow, cities in New Jersey may find it expedient or necessary to send their waste into Pennsylvania or New York for disposal, and those States might then claim the right to close their borders. The Commerce Clause will protect New Jersey in the future, just as it protects her neighbors now, from efforts by one State to isolate itself in the stream of interstate commerce from a problem shared by all. [Reversed.]

■ JUSTICE REHNQUIST, with whom CHIEF JUSTICE BURGER joins, dissenting.

[The cases sustaining quarantine laws] are dispositive of the present one. Under them, New Jersey may require germ-infected rags or diseased meat to be disposed of as best as possible within the State, but at the same time prohibit the *importation* of such items for disposal at the facilities that are set up within New Jersey for disposal of such material generated *within* the State. The physical fact of life that New Jersey must somehow dispose of its own noxious items does not mean that it must serve as a depository for those of every other State. Similarly, New Jersey should be free under our past precedents to prohibit the importation of solid waste because of the health and safety problems that such waste poses to its citizens. The fact that New Jersey continues to, and indeed must continue to, dispose of its own solid waste does not mean that New Jersey may not prohibit the importation of even more solid waste into the State. I simply see no way to distinguish solid waste, on the record of this case, from germ-infected rags, diseased meat, and other noxious items.

[The] Court implies that the challenged laws must be invalidated because New Jersey has left its landfills open to domestic waste. But, as the Court notes, this Court has repeatedly upheld quarantine laws "even though they appear to single out interstate commerce for special treatment." The fact that New Jersey has left its landfill sites open for domestic waste does not, of course, mean that solid waste is not innately harmful. Nor does it mean that New Jersey prohibits importation of solid waste for reasons other than the health and safety of its population. New Jersey must out of sheer necessity treat and dispose of its solid waste in some fashion, just as it must treat New Jersey cattle suffering from hoof-and-mouth disease. It does not follow that New Jersey must, under the Commerce Clause, accept solid waste or diseased cattle from outside its borders and thereby exacerbate its problems. [Because] I find no basis for distinguishing the [health] laws under challenge here from our past cases upholding state laws that prohibit the importation of items that could endanger the population of the State, I dissent.

---

1. ***Antidiscrimination and national prosperity.*** Recall the discussion above of the political and economic foundations of the presumption against discriminatory state laws embodied in the dormant commerce clause decisions. Do antidiscrimination rules actually help promote national "prosperity" or aggregate social welfare? In Philadelphia v. New Jersey, the Court assumes that a patchwork of mutually protectionist state laws will decrease national welfare because each state will have an incentive to hoard benefits and export costs, leading to mutually destructive

self-dealing by the states. On this view, even if state laws temporarily produce local benefits exceeding local costs, they nonetheless contribute to a situation in which national costs exceed national benefits. National social welfare will thus be increased by inhibiting each state's incentives to maximize its own welfare. From this it is supposed to follow that the Court should invalidate laws whose net effect is to export costs to other states.

Did Philadelphia v. New Jersey accurately analyze these relative costs and benefits and correctly determine that the law it invalidated involved a net decrease in social welfare? The Court suggested that that the New Jersey law "saddle[d] those outside the State with the entire burden of slowing the flow of refuse into New Jersey's remaining landfill sites." But did that fully describe the local and foreign costs and benefits involved? Consider the following:

a. *Local costs and benefits.* The New Jersey law benefited in-state landfill users (waste generators) by limiting demand for available landfill space, thus lowering the prices they would have to pay. But such benefits for New Jersey waste generators correlated with harms to other New Jersey residents: New Jersey landfill operators were arguably harmed by a law that, by limiting demand for their services, drove down the prices they could charge. Note that the plaintiffs challenging the law included New Jersey landfill operators as well as non-New Jersey waste producers.

b. *Foreign costs and benefits.* The Court assumed that New Jersey exported costs to out-of-state waste landfill users (waste generators), who faced higher prices for waste disposal in their own states or elsewhere. But such costs to non-New Jersey waste generators correlated with benefits to out-of-state landfill operators: By increasing demand for non-New Jersey landfill space, the law increased the prices out-of-state landfill operators could charge for available space.

Thus, whether New Jersey on balance exported costs to out-of-state interests depends upon whether the benefits to out-of-state landfill operators exceed the costs to out-of-state landfill users. And whether the law increases or decreases total social welfare depends on which is greater: aggregate benefits to in-state landfill users plus out-of-state landfill operators, or aggregate costs to in-state landfill operators plus out-of-state landfill users. The Court ignored both these questions, focusing solely on New Jersey's export of costs to out-of-state landfill users.

Are courts competent to assess the comparative costs and benefits of discriminatory state laws on a case-by-case basis? Are the economic predictions involved susceptible to manageable judicial standards? As a rule of thumb, should courts presume that facially discriminatory laws on balance export costs out-of state? Even if some facially discriminatory laws actually increase total social welfare? The Court often emphasizes the importance of long-term considerations, suggesting that "in the long run" mutual retaliation among the states will decrease national prosperity even if net social welfare is not decreased in the short run by any one state's barriers to trade. This assumes that one state's trade barriers will cause retaliatory trade barriers by other states. On this view, a presumption against facial discrimination represents the best protection for net social welfare over time. Is the presumption of mutual retaliation justified?

2. ***The role of governmental purpose.*** Some commentators argue that dormant commerce clause analysis aims centrally to block

protectionism, defined as "the purpose of improving the competitive position of local economic actors, just because they are local, vis-a-vis their foreign competitors," see Regan, "The Supreme Court and State Protectionism: Making Sense of the Dormant Commerce Clause," 84 Mich. L. Rev. 1091 (1986). Note, however, that Philadelphia v. New Jersey invalidated the New Jersey ban on waste originating out-of-state even though New Jersey claimed it was motivated by health, safety, and aesthetic considerations rather than economic favoritism. The Court declined to second-guess the good faith of that assertion, but subjected the law nonetheless to the "virtually per se rule of invalidity" for economic protectionism. Why? Should facial discrimination against outsiders give rise to a conclusive presumption of protectionist purpose, regardless of actual legislative motivation? Is that because actual protectionist purpose will rarely be made explicit, and will be difficult to smoke out? Does such a presumption give adequate weight to state autonomy?

3. ***The internet, facial discrimination and the dormant commerce clause.*** With the rise of internet shopping, the ability of customers in one state to easily purchase on the internet goods made in another state presents new issues in the application of the dormant commerce clause. While states have greater incentive to enact economic protectionist laws to protect in-state industries, they also have legitimate concerns in this context about their ability to enforce state laws against out of state companies. In **Granholm v. Heald**, 544 U.S. 460 (2005), the Court heard a dormant commerce clause challenge to Michigan and New York liquor-licensing schemes that imposed regulatory burdens on the abilities of out-of state wineries to sell wine directly to customers in those states, but exempted in-state wine distributors from those regulations. The out-of-state wineries and in-state consumers argued that this was impermissible facial discrimination. The states countered that Section 2 of the Twenty-First Amendment, which prohibited "transportation or importation into any State, Territory, or possession of the United States for delivery or use therein of intoxicating liquors, in violation of the laws thereof," allowed states to favor in-state wineries in a manner that the dormant commerce clause would otherwise prohibit. The states also argued that the licensing schemes advanced the legitimate local purposes of preventing minors from purchasing wine over the internet and facilitating tax collection. Justice KENNEDY's majority opinion rejected the states' arguments, holding that the discrimination violated the dormant commerce clause. Finding it "evident that the object and design of the Michigan and New York statutes [was] to grant in-state wineries a competitive advantage over wineries located beyond the States' borders," the majority held that "the laws in both States discriminate against interstate commerce in violation of the Commerce Clause, Art. I, § 8, cl. 3, and that the discrimination is neither authorized nor permitted by the Twenty-first Amendment." The Court also rejected the states' arguments that the discrimination was necessary to prevent minors from purchasing wine on the internet given the availability of nondiscriminatory alternatives. Justice STEVENS dissented, arguing that the framers of the Twenty-First Amendment regarded alcohol as a unique product, subject to greater state regulation than ordinary articles of commerce, and that Section 2 of the Amendment should be read to allow facial interstate discrimination that would otherwise not be permissible under the dormant commerce clause. As more commerce gets conducted over the internet in the future, might other state law enforcement needs justify

new state laws burdening interstate commerce? How is the Court likely to respond?

4. ***Permissible facial discrimination.*** Are state laws that facially discriminate against outsiders ever valid? Can the Philadelphia v. New Jersey strong presumption against overtly discriminatory statutes—a "virtually per se rule of invalidity"—ever be overcome? Justice Stewart found only very limited exceptions to the principle that "all laws which facially discriminate against out-of-state commerce are forbidden protectionist regulations": "certain quarantine laws" are permissible, but New Jersey's law was "not such a quarantine law." **Maine v. Taylor**, 477 U.S. 131 (1986), is another notable exception to the rule of "virtually per se invalidity." This 8–1 decision upheld a law banning the importation of out-of-state baitfish. Justice BLACKMUN's majority opinion, affording great deference to the findings of the district court, held that the ban had a legitimate environmental purpose stemming from "uncertainty about possible ecological effects on the possible presence of parasites and nonnative species" in shipments of out-of-state baitfish, and that that purpose "could not be served as well by available nondiscriminatory means." Only Justice STEVENS dissented: "If Maine wishes to rely on its interest in ecological preservation, it must show that interest, and the infeasibility of other alternatives, with far greater specificity. [The] State has not carried its substantial burden of proving why it cannot meet its environmental concerns in the same manner as other States with the same interest in the health of their fish and ecology."

5. ***Facially discriminatory taxes.*** Even if New Jersey may not exclude Philadelphia waste altogether, may it impose taxes upon only waste that originates out-of-state? In Chemical Waste Management, Inc. v. Hunt, 504 U.S. 334 (1992), the Court said no, invalidating an Alabama law imposing a hazardous waste disposal fee upon hazardous wastes generated outside Alabama and disposed of at a commercial facility in Alabama, but not upon identical wastes having a source in Alabama. Justice White's opinion for the Court found the discriminatory fee indistinguishable from the outright prohibition invalidated in Philadelphia v. New Jersey. May a state impose higher taxes on out-of-state waste than on in-state waste? In **Oregon Waste Systems, Inc. v. Department of Environmental Quality**, 511 U.S. 93 (1994), the Court again said no, invalidating an Oregon law imposing a $2.25 per ton surcharge on the disposal of out-of-state solid waste and a $0.85 surcharge on the disposal of identical solid waste generated in-state. Writing for the 7–2 majority, Justice Thomas found the differential surcharge facially discriminatory and thus subject to the "virtually per se rule of invalidity." He acknowledged that a differential tax might be permissible if it merely compensated for costs charged in other ways, such as by general taxation, to in-state waste producers: "[I]nterstate commerce may be made to 'pay its way.' [A] facially discriminatory tax that imposes on interstate commerce the rough equivalent of an identifiable and 'substantially similar' tax on intrastate commerce does not offend the negative Commerce Clause."[1] But he found no such compensatory feature in the Oregon law.

[1] This principle of permissible compensatory taxation was set forth in Henneford v. Silas Mason Co., 300 U.S. 577 (1937), where the Court had upheld a Washington use tax on goods bought in other states designed to compensate for the loss of the 2% tax on retail sales within Washington. As Justice Cardozo wrote for a unanimous Court, local retail sellers "will be helped

6. ***Facially discriminatory subsidies.*** A state may provide subsidies to in-state producers from general revenues without being required to provide them to out-of-state producers too. But what if the state taxes all producers of a product but then rebates part of the proceeds to in-state producers only, effectively lowering their costs? The Court found such a scheme impermissibly discriminatory, as the equivalent of a discriminatory tax, in **West Lynn Creamery, Inc. v. Healy**, 512 U.S. 186 (1994), which invalidated a Massachusetts law that imposed an assessment on all sales of milk to Massachusetts retailers, but rebated all proceeds from this assessment to Massachusetts dairy farmers. (Two thirds of Massachusetts milk sales involved milk from out of state.)

Justice STEVENS, writing for the Court, stated: "[Massachusetts'] pricing order is clearly unconstitutional. Its avowed purpose and its undisputed effect are to enable higher cost Massachusetts dairy farmers to compete with lower cost dairy farmers in other States. The 'premium payments' are effectively a tax which makes milk produced out of State more expensive. Although the tax also applies to milk produced in Massachusetts, its effect on Massachusetts producers is entirely (indeed more than) offset by the subsidy provided exclusively to Massachusetts dairy farmers. Like an ordinary tariff, the tax is thus effectively imposed only on out-of-state products." Justice Stevens rejected the state's argument that, because a nondiscriminatory tax is constitutional, and subsidies to in-state interests are generally constitutional, the program's combination of the two was constitutional: "A pure subsidy funded out of general revenue ordinarily imposes no burden on interstate commerce, but merely assists local business. The pricing order in this case, however, is funded principally from taxes on the sale of milk produced in other States. [The] pricing order thus violates the cardinal principle that a State may not 'benefit in-state economic interests by burdening out-of-state competitors.' "

Justice SCALIA, joined by Justice Thomas, concurred in the judgment. While a subsidy for the in-state members of the industry funded from the State's general revenues would have been constitutional, he reasoned, "a nondiscriminatory tax upon the industry, the revenues from which are placed into a segregated fund, which fund is disbursed as 'rebates' or 'subsidies' to in-state members of the industry," was not. Chief Justice REHNQUIST, joined by Justice Blackmun, dissented, arguing that the law provided merely for a permissible subsidy. He noted that political safeguards were sufficient, as "two strong interest groups opposed to the milk order—consumers and milk dealers" could protect out-of-staters in the political process, even if in-state milk producers were mollified by the rebate.

Should a discriminatory tax exemption be considered a permissible subsidy? The Court said no in **Camps Newfound/Owatonna, Inc. v. Town of Harrison**, 520 U.S. 564 (1997), which invalidated by a vote of 5–4 a Maine statute that provided a property tax exemption to "benevolent and charitable institutions incorporated" in the State, but denying the full exemption to any institution "conducted or operated principally for the benefit of persons who

---

to compete upon terms of equality with retail dealers in other states who are exempt from a sales tax"; local buyers will "no longer [be] tempted to place their orders in other states" to escape the local sales tax; and "the stranger from afar is subject to no greater burdens as a consequence of ownership than the dweller within the gates." Washington thus was permitted to require out-of-state sales to "share an equal burden with goods that have been purchased [in-state]."

are not residents of Maine." Justice Stevens wrote for the Court that the Maine statute "functionally serves as an export tariff that targets out-of-state consumers by taxing the businesses that principally serve them." He reasoned that since profit-making enterprises would be barred from such discrimination, not-for-profit entities should be too. And he rejected the argument that the tax exemption amounted to a permissible discriminatory subsidy.

Justice SCALIA dissented, joined by Chief Justice Rehnquist and Justices Thomas and Ginsburg. He argued that the Maine tax law did not constitute "facial discrimination" against interstate commerce: "The provision at issue here is a narrow tax exemption, designed merely to compensate or subsidize those organizations that contribute to the public fisc by dispensing public benefits the State might otherwise provide. [Disparate] treatment constitutes discrimination only if the objects of the disparate treatment are, for the relevant purposes, similarly situated. And for purposes of entitlement to a tax subsidy from the State, it is certainly reasonable to think that property gratuitously devoted to relieving the State of some of its welfare burden is not similarly situated to property used 'principally for the benefit of persons who are not residents of [the State].' "

Both West Lynn Creamery and Camps Newfound appeared to assume that straightforward cash state subsidies of in-state businesses would be permissible under the dormant commerce clause. Yet as Camps illustrates, the Court strikes down, as impermissible discrimination, differential tax benefits for in-staters and out-of-staters. For another illustration, consider New Energy Co. of Indiana v. Limbach, 486 U.S. 269 (1988), which invalidated an Ohio statute awarding a tax credit for sales of ethanol that was produced in Ohio, while distinguishing as permissible an Indiana subsidy for in-state ethanol. Thus, discriminatory subsidies are lawful even though discriminatory tax breaks are not. Yet isn't a tax benefit the functional economic equivalent of a cash subsidy? Consider the following argument that the two in fact differ in the political safeguards they entail: "[A] state's imposition of costs on its citizens is more visible when the state awards outright subsidies than when it doles out tax relief. [It] is easier for a legislator or a voter to see that a state is spending its money when it actually writes and sends out a check. And when state spending is more easily seen, it is more easily scrutinized, second-guessed, and blocked. [Tax] credits, exemptions, and the like are resistant to repeal because legislatures typically enact them as presumptively permanent features of state tax codes. In contrast, because subsidies involve the direct expenditure of funds, they routinely show up—and are subject to recurring reevaluation—as expense items in perennially controversial state budget bills." Coenen, "Business Subsidies and the Dormant Commerce Clause," 107 Yale L.J. 965 (1998).

HOME PROCESSING REQUIREMENTS

The Court has repeatedly invalidated state requirements that products be inspected, processed or treated inside the state before they may be shipped out-of-state. Such statutes generally single out by their terms in-state businesses and, on the basis of geographical location, give them a preference over potential out-of-state competitors. For example, Minnesota v. Barber, 136 U.S. 313 (1890), the Court struck down a Minnesota statute that required any meat sold within the state, whether originating within or without the State, to be examined by an inspector within the State. In Foster-Fountain Packing Co. v. Haydel, 278 U.S. 1 (1928), the Court struck down a Louisiana statute that forbade the exportation of shrimp unless the heads and hulls had first been removed within the State. Johnson v. Haydel, 278 U.S. 16 (1928), invalidated an analogous Louisiana statute for oysters. And in Toomer v. Witsell, 334 U.S. 385 (1948), the Court struck down South Carolina statute that required shrimp fishermen to unload, pack, and stamp their catch before shipping it to another State.

Are such laws best understood as facially discriminatory? Each of these laws draws a geographic boundary around permitted economic activities. And each can be described as categorically barring the import of the processing service—such as meat inspection or shrimp hulling—from another state, depriving out-of-state business of access to local demand for their services. Should a finding of discrimination require a further finding that the boundary has been drawn for the *purpose* of advantaging local businesses over out-of-state competitors? In Foster-Fountain Packing, Justice Butler looked behind the face of the law banning export of unhulled shrimp, and its asserted purpose (to keep shrimp hulls and heads in-state for use as fertilizer), to conclude: "The purpose [of the law] is not to retain the shrimp for the use of the people of Louisiana; it is to favor the canning of the meat and the manufacture of bran in Louisiana by withholding raw or unshelled shrimp from [Mississippi] plants. [The] practical operation and effect of the provisions complained of will be directly to obstruct and burden interstate commerce."

Do these cases turn on the availability of less discriminatory alternatives for serving the purported state goal? Such alternatives were an important factor in the Court's invalidation of a milk-processing ordinance in the case that follows.

Dean Milk Co. v. Madison

340 U.S. 349, 71 S. Ct. 295, 95 L. Ed. 329 (1951).

[A Madison, Wisconsin ordinance barred the sale of pasteurized milk unless it had been processed and bottled at an approved pasteurization plant within five miles of the central square of Madison. Five processing plants were within that five-mile area and there were 5,600 dairy farms within the county where Madison is located. The total raw milk production of these farms was more than ten times the requirements of Madison. Madison officials inspected the plants and farms every 30 days. Dean Milk, which challenged the ordinance, was based in Illinois, bought its milk from farms in northern Illinois and southern Wisconsin, and pasteurized it at its two Illinois plants, 65 and 85 miles from Madison. Dean Milk's farms and plants were licensed and inspected by Chicago public health authorities, and its milk was labeled "Grade A" under a Chicago ordinance which had adopted rating standards recommended by the U.S. Public Health Service. The Chicago ordinance, like Madison's, was patterned on the Model Milk Ordinance of the U.S. Public Health Service. Dean Milk was denied a license to sell its products in Madison solely because its plants were more than five miles away.]

■ JUSTICE CLARK delivered the opinion of the Court.

[There can be no] objection to the avowed purpose of this enactment. We assume that difficulties in sanitary regulation of milk and milk products originating in remote areas may present a situation in which "it appears that the matter is one which may appropriately be regulated in the interest of the safety, health and well-being of local communities." [But] this regulation [in] practical effect excludes from distribution in Madison wholesome milk produced and pasteurized in Illinois. [In] thus erecting an economic barrier protecting a major local industry against competition from without the State, Madison plainly discriminates against interstate commerce.[1] This it cannot do, even in the exercise of its unquestioned power to protect the health and safety of its people, if reasonable nondiscriminatory alternatives, adequate to conserve legitimate local interests, are available. A different view, that the ordinance is valid simply because it professes to be a health measure, would mean that the Commerce Clause of itself imposes no limitations on state action other than those laid down by the Due Process Clause, save for the rare instance where a state artlessly discloses an avowed purpose to discriminate against interstate goods. Our issue then is whether the discrimination inherent in the Madison ordinance can be justified in view of the character of the local interests and the available methods of protecting them.

[It] appears that reasonable and adequate alternatives are available. If [Madison] prefers to rely upon its own officials for inspection of distant milk sources, such inspection is readily open to it without hardship for it could charge the actual and reasonable cost of such inspection to the importing producers and processors. Moreover, appellee Health Commissioner of Madison testified that as proponent of the local milk ordinance he had submitted the provisions here in controversy and an alternative proposal based on § 11 of the Model Milk Ordinance recommended by the [U.S.] Public Health Service. The model provision imposes no geographical limitation on location of milk sources and processing plants but excludes from the municipality milk not produced and pasteurized conformably to standards as high as those enforced by the receiving city. In implementing such an ordinance, the importing city obtains milk ratings based on uniform standards and established by health authorities in the jurisdiction where production and processing occur. The receiving city may determine the extent of enforcement of sanitary standards in the exporting area by verifying the accuracy of safety ratings of specific plants or of the milkshed in the distant jurisdiction through the [U.S.] Public Health Service. The Commissioner testified that Madison consumers "would be safeguarded adequately" under either proposal, and that he had expressed no preference. [The Commissioner and a state official] agreed that a local health officer would be justified in relying upon the evaluation by the Public Health Service of enforcement conditions in remote producing areas.

To permit Madison to adopt a regulation not essential for the protection of local health interests and placing a discriminatory burden on interstate commerce would invite a multiplication of preferential trade areas destructive of the very purpose of the Commerce Clause. Under the circumstances here presented, the regulation must yield to the principle that

[1] It is immaterial that Wisconsin milk from outside the Madison area is subjected to the same proscription as that moving in interstate [commerce]. [Footnote by Justice Clark.]

"one state in its dealings with another may not place itself in a position of economic isolation." [Reversed.]

■ JUSTICE BLACK, with whom JUSTICES DOUGLAS and MINTON concur, dissenting.

[I] disagree with the Court's premises, reasoning, and judgment. (1) This ordinance does not exclude wholesome milk coming from Illinois or anywhere else. It does require that all milk sold in Madison must be pasteurized within five miles of the center of the city. But there was no finding in the state courts [that Dean] is unable to have its milk pasteurized within the defined geographical [area]. (2) Characterization of [the law] as a "discriminatory burden" on interstate commerce is merely a statement of the Court's result, which I think incorrect. [B]oth state courts below found that [the law] represents a good-faith attempt to safeguard public health by making adequate sanitation inspections possible. [The] fact that [the law], like all health regulations, imposes some burden on trade, does not mean that it "discriminates" against interstate commerce. (3) This health regulation should not be invalidated merely because the Court believes that alternative milk-inspection methods might insure the cleanliness and healthfulness of Dean's Illinois milk. [If] the principle announced today is to be followed, the Court should not strike down local health regulations unless satisfied beyond a reasonable doubt that the substitutes it proposes would not lower health standards. [I] do not think that either of the alternatives suggested by the Court would assure the people of Madison as pure a supply of milk as they receive under their own ordinance. On this record I would uphold the Madison law. At the very least, however, I would not invalidate it without giving the parties a chance to present evidence and get findings on the ultimate issues the Court thinks crucial—namely, the relative merits of the Madison ordinance and the alternatives suggested by the Court today.

C & A Carbone, Inc. v. Clarkstown

511 U.S. 383, 114 S. Ct. 1677, 128 L. Ed. 2d 399 (1994).

■ JUSTICE KENNEDY delivered the opinion of the Court.

The town of Clarkstown, New York [agreed] to close its landfill [and] build a new solid waste transfer station. [The] cost of building the transfer station was estimated at $1.4 million. A local private contractor agreed to construct the facility and operate it for five years, after which the town would buy it for $1. During those five years, the town guaranteed a minimum waste flow of 120,000 tons per year, for which the contractor could charge the hauler a so-called tipping fee of $81 per ton. [The] object of this arrangement was to amortize the cost of the transfer station: The town would finance its new facility with the income generated by the tipping fees. The problem [was] how to meet the yearly guarantee. [The] solution the town adopted was the flow control ordinance here in question, [which] requires all nonhazardous solid waste within the town to be deposited at the [transfer] station. [Carbone, a private recycler with a sorting facility in Clarkstown, sought to ship its nonrecyclable waste to cheaper processors outside the state rather than to the new facility as required.]

While the immediate effect of the ordinance is to direct local transport of solid waste to a designated site within the local jurisdiction, its economic effects are interstate in reach. [By] prevent[ing] everyone except the favored local operator from performing the initial processing step, [the] ordinance [deprives] out-of-state businesses of access to a local market. [The] ordinance is no less discriminatory because in-state or in-town processors are also covered by the prohibition. Dean Milk. [The] flow control ordinance is just one more instance of local processing requirements that we long have held invalid. The essential vice in laws of this sort is that they bar the import of the processing service. Out-of-state meat inspectors, or shrimp hullers, or milk pasteurizers, are deprived of access to local demand for their services. Put another way, the offending local laws hoard a local resource—be it meat, shrimp, or milk—for the benefit of local businesses that treat it.

The flow control ordinance has the same design and effect. It hoards solid waste, and the demand to get rid of it, for the benefit of the preferred processing facility. The only conceivable distinction from the cases cited above is that the flow control ordinance favors a single local proprietor. But this difference just makes the protectionist effect of the ordinance more acute. [Discrimination] against interstate commerce in favor of local business or investment is per se invalid, save in a narrow class of cases in which the municipality can demonstrate, under rigorous scrutiny, that it has no other means to advance a legitimate local interest. [Clarkstown] has any number of nondiscriminatory alternatives for addressing the health and environmental problems alleged to justify the ordinance in question. The most obvious would be uniform safety regulations enacted without the object to discriminate.

[The] flow control ordinance does serve a central purpose that a nonprotectionist regulation would not: It ensures that the town-sponsored facility will be profitable, so that the local contractor can build it and Clarkstown can buy it back at nominal cost in five years. In other words [the] flow control ordinance is a financing measure. [Revenue] generation is not a local interest that can justify discrimination against interstate commerce. Otherwise States could impose discriminatory taxes against solid waste originating outside the State. Clarkstown maintains that special financing is necessary to ensure the long-term survival of the designated facility. If so, the town may subsidize the facility through general taxes or municipal bonds. But having elected to use the open market to earn revenues for its project, the town may not employ discriminatory regulation to give that project an advantage over rival businesses from out of State. [State] and local governments may not use their regulatory power to favor local enterprise by prohibiting patronage of out-of-state competitors or their facilities.

■ JUSTICE SOUTER, joined by CHIEF JUSTICE REHNQUIST and JUSTICE BLACKMUN, dissenting.

[The] law does not differentiate between all local and all out-of-town providers of a service, but instead between the one entity responsible for ensuring that the job gets done and all other enterprises, regardless of their location. The ordinance thus falls outside that class of tariff or protectionist measures that the Commerce Clause has traditionally been thought to bar States from enacting against each other. [The] outstanding feature of the statutes or ordinances reviewed in the local processing cases is their distinction between two classes of private economic actors [according] to geography alone. [Local Law 9's] exclusion of outside capital is part of a broader exclusion of private capital, not a discrimination against out-of-state investors as such. [Subjecting] out-of-town investors and facilities to the same constraints as local ones is not economic protectionism.

Nor is the monopolist created by Local Law 9 just another private company successfully enlisting local government to protect the jobs and profits of local citizens. While our previous local processing cases have barred discrimination in markets served by private companies, Clarkstown's transfer station is essentially a municipal facility, built and operated under a contract with the municipality and soon to revert entirely to municipal ownership. This, of course, is no mere coincidence, since the facility performs a municipal function that tradition as well as state and federal law recognize as the domain of local government. The majority ignores this distinction between public and private enterprise, equating Local Law 9's "hoarding" of solid waste for the municipal transfer station with the design and effect of ordinances that restrict access to local markets for the benefit of local private firms. But private businesses, whether local or out of State, first serve the private interests of their owners, and there is therefore only rarely a reason other than economic protectionism for favoring local businesses over their out-of-town competitors. The local government itself occupies a very different market position, however, being the one entity that enters the market to serve the public interest of local citizens quite apart from private interest in private gain. Reasons other than economic protectionism are accordingly more likely to explain the design and effect of an ordinance that favors a public facility.

United Haulers Ass'n v. Oneida-Herkimer Solid Waste Management Authority

550 U.S. 330, 127 S. Ct. 1786, 167 L. Ed. 2d 655 (2007).

■ CHIEF JUSTICE ROBERTS delivered the opinion of the Court.

"Flow control" ordinances require trash haulers to deliver solid waste to a particular waste processing facility. In C & A Carbone, Inc. v. Clarkstown, this Court struck down under the Commerce Clause a flow control ordinance that forced haulers to deliver waste to a particular private processing facility. In this case, we face flow control ordinances quite similar to the one invalidated in Carbone. The only salient difference is that the laws at issue here require haulers to bring waste to facilities owned and operated by a state-created public benefit corporation. We find this difference constitutionally significant. Disposing of trash has been a traditional government activity for years, and laws that favor the government in such areas—but treat every private business, whether in-state or out-of-state, exactly the same—do not discriminate against interstate commerce for purposes of the Commerce Clause.

[The] flow control ordinances in this case benefit a clearly public facility, while treating all private companies exactly the same. Compelling reasons justify treating these laws differently from laws favoring particular private businesses over their competitors. [States] and municipalities are not private businesses—far from it. Unlike private enterprise, government is vested with the responsibility of protecting the health, safety, and welfare of its citizens. These important responsibilities set state and local government apart from a typical private business. Given these differences, it does not make sense to regard laws favoring local government and laws favoring private industry with equal skepticism. [Laws] favoring local government [may] be directed toward any number of legitimate goals unrelated to protectionism. [Treating] public and private entities the same under the dormant Commerce Clause would lead to unprecedented and unbounded interference by the courts with state and local government. [It] is not the office of the Commerce Clause to control the decision of the voters on whether government or the private sector should provide waste management services. [We] should be particularly hesitant to interfere with the Counties' efforts under the guise of the Commerce Clause because "waste disposal is both typically and traditionally a local government function."

Finally, it bears mentioning that the most palpable harm imposed by the ordinances—more expensive trash removal—is likely to fall upon the very people who voted for the laws. Our dormant Commerce Clause cases often find discrimination when a State shifts the costs of regulation to other States, because when "the burden of state regulation falls on interests outside the state, it is unlikely to be alleviated by the operation of those political restraints normally exerted when interests within the state are affected." Here, the citizens and businesses of the Counties bear the costs of the ordinances. There is no reason to step in and hand local businesses a victory they could not obtain through the political process. [Justice Scalia concurred in part; Justice Thomas concurred in the judgment, expressing regret for his vote with the majority in Carbone and stating his belief that the Court's entire dormant Commerce Clause jurisprudence should now be discarded.]

■ JUSTICE ALITO, with whom JUSTICES STEVENS and KENNEDY join, dissenting.

[The] fact that the flow control laws at issue discriminate in favor of a government-owned enterprise does not meaningfully distinguish this case from Carbone. The preferred facility in Carbone was [nominally] owned by a private contractor who had built the facility on the town's behalf, but it would be misleading to describe the facility as private. In exchange for the contractor's promise to build the facility for the town free of charge and then to sell it to the town five years later for $1, the town guaranteed that, during the first five years of the facility's existence, the contractor would receive "a minimum waste flow of 120,000 tons per year" and that the contractor could charge an above-market tipping fee. [The] only real difference between the facility at issue in Carbone and its counterpart in this case is that title to the former had not yet formally passed to the municipality. The Court exalts form over substance in adopting a test that turns on this technical distinction

[The] Court has long subjected discriminatory legislation to strict scrutiny, and has never, until today, recognized an exception for discrimination in favor of a state-owned entity. Nor has this Court ever suggested that discriminatory legislation favoring a state-owned enterprise is entitled to favorable treatment. To be sure, state-owned entities are accorded special status under the market-participant doctrine [see below]. But that doctrine is not applicable here. [Respondents] are doing exactly what the market-participant doctrine says they cannot: While acting as market participants by operating a fee-for-service business enterprise in an area in which there is an established interstate market, respondents are also regulating that market in a discriminatory manner and claiming that their special governmental status somehow insulates them from a dormant Commerce Clause challenge.

I see no basis for the [assumption] that discrimination in favor of an in-state facility owned by the government is likely to serve "legitimate goals unrelated to protectionism." Discrimination in favor of an in-state government facility serves " 'local economic interests,' " inuring to the benefit of local residents who are employed at the facility, local businesses that supply the facility with goods and services, and local workers employed by such businesses. Experience in other countries, where state ownership is more common than it is in this country, teaches that governments often discriminate in favor of state-owned businesses (by shielding them from international competition) precisely for the purpose of protecting those who derive economic benefits from those businesses, including their employees. Such discrimination amounts to economic protectionism in any realistic sense of the term. By the same token, discrimination in favor of an in-state, privately owned facility may serve legitimate ends, such as the promotion of public health and safety. For example, a State might enact legislation discriminating in favor of produce or livestock grown within the State, reasoning that the State's inspectors can more easily monitor the use of pesticides, fertilizers, and feed on farms within the State's borders. Such legislation would almost certainly be unconstitutional, notwithstanding its potential to promote public health and safety. See Philadelphia v. New Jersey. [If] the legislative means are themselves discriminatory, then regardless of how legitimate and nonprotectionist the underlying legislative goals may be, the legislation is subject to strict scrutiny. Dean Milk.

[Equally] unpersuasive is the Court's suggestion that the flow-control laws do not discriminate against interstate commerce because they "treat in-state private business interests exactly the same as out-of-state ones." [This] Court has long recognized that " 'a burden imposed by a State upon interstate commerce is not to be sustained simply because the statute imposing it applies alike to the people of all the States, including the people of the State enacting such statute.' "

THE DEAN MILK-CARBONE-UNITED HAULERS TRILOGY

1. ***Intrastate discrimination and interstate discrimination.*** The Court asserted in Dean Milk that "Madison plainly discriminates against interstate commerce," stating in footnote 2 that it is "immaterial" that Madison discriminates against Wisconsin milk from outside Madison as well as against Illinois milk. Should it be relevant that a local regulation burdens some intrastate as well as out-of-state producers? Arguably, the impact on intrastate businesses assures political checks upon potential abuses. Intrastate interests also burdened by the law might be thought to virtually represent out-of-state interests that are adversely affected. Might it be countered that other Wisconsin residents might tolerate Madison's protectionism if the state allows them to do the same, in which case they will not have any incentive to protect out-of-state interests? Unless the dormant commerce clause reached municipal as well as state discrimination, couldn't legislatures evade its force simply by making rules aimed at out-of-state businesses applicable to some intrastate businesses as well?

Carbone, like Dean Milk, treated as immaterial the fact that a town rather than the state had passed the flow control ordinance. Did the majority in United Haulers repudiate Dean Milk and Carbone when it emphasized that the county flow-control law there applied to in-state and out-of-state competitors alike? Or was the distinction Chief Justice Roberts drew one between public and private entities, not municipal and state laws?

2. ***"Reasonable nondiscriminatory alternatives."*** In Dean Milk, the Court inquired into whether Madison had "reasonable nondiscriminatory alternatives" for protecting milk safety. Carbone likewise suggested that the town had available nondiscriminatory alternatives, such as "uniform safety regulations." Note that this approach involves intensive judicial scrutiny. When a "rationality" standard of scrutiny prevails, by contrast, as it does for equal protection or due process review of economic laws, courts do *not* speculate about available alternatives; instead, they defer to the legislative choice if it is a conceivably rational method of promoting the state interest. Is judicial inquiry into less discriminatory alternative methods of regulation appropriate? Feasible? Does it amount to uninformed judicial intrusion into the legislative sphere? Or is it a neutral means by which the court can determine whether the asserted, legitimate purpose is a pretext for an illicit underlying purpose? In this regard, note that, in Dean Milk, while the majority did not charge that the Madison ordinance was enacted in bad faith, it did mention that milk production is a "major local industry" in the Madison area, hinting at possible protectionist motives. Did the availability to Madison of nondiscriminatory alternatives amount to circumstantial evidence that its purpose was more likely to protect local dairy farmers than to ensure healthful milk?

3. ***Traditional governmental function.*** Note that Chief Justice Roberts in United Haulers (like Justice Souter in his Carbone dissent), emphasized that waste hauling is a traditional function of municipal governments. What difference should this make to the constitutionality of an ordinance under the dormant commerce clause? Is this a resurrection of National League of Cities (1976; p. 169 above) by other means? Justice Alito pointed out in his United Haulers dissent that Garcia v. San Antonio Metro. Transit (1985; p. 170 above) had rejected any test of traditional or integral government functions as unsound and unworkable for Tenth Amendment purposes. Is it any more sound or workable here?

4. ***Differential taxation of municipal bonds.*** To what other public functions might United Haulers apply besides waste hauling? In **Department of Revenue of Kentucky v. Davis**, 553 U.S. 328 (2008), the Court considered a dormant commerce clause challenge to a differential scheme by which Kentucky exempted interest on its own public bonds from state income taxes but imposed such taxes on bond interest from other States. Billions of dollars of capital was at stake in the case, as 36 States took the same approach as Kentucky, five others took similar approaches, and all 49 other States filed an amicus curiae brief in its support.

A majority of the Court rejected the challenge and upheld the law, with Justice SOUTER delivering the judgment of the Court. In a portion of his opinion joined by Chief Justice Roberts and Justices Stevens, Scalia, Breyer and Ginsburg, he found the case governed by United Haulers: "In United Haulers, we explained that a government function is not susceptible to standard dormant commerce clause scrutiny owing to its likely motivation by legitimate objectives distinct from the simple economic protectionism the

Clause abhors. This logic applies with even greater force to laws favoring a State's municipal bonds, given that the issuance of debt securities to pay for public projects is a quintessentially public function, with [a] venerable history. [By] issuing bonds, state and local governments 'sprea[d] the costs of public projects over time,' much as one might buy a house with a loan subject to monthly payments. Bonds place the cost of a project on the citizens who benefit from it over the years, and they allow for public work beyond what current revenues could support. Bond proceeds are thus the way to shoulder the cardinal civic responsibilities listed in United Haulers: protecting the health, safety, and welfare of citizens. [Thus,] United Haulers provides a firm basis for reversal. Just like the ordinances upheld there, Kentucky's tax exemption favors a traditional government function without any differential treatment favoring local entities over substantially similar out-of-state interests."

Justice KENNEDY, joined by Justice Alito, filed a dissent, objecting to United Haulers as an "unfortunate recent exception" to the presumption against laws facially discriminating against out-of-state commerce: "The Court defends the Kentucky law by explaining that it serves a traditional government function and concerns the 'cardinal civic responsibilities' of protecting health, safety, and welfare. This is but a reformulation of the phrase 'police power,' long abandoned as a mere tautology. It is difficult to identify any state law that has come before us that would not meet the Court's description. [The] tax imposed here is an explicit discrimination against out-of-state issuances for admitted protectionist purposes. It cannot be sustained unless the Court disavows the discrimination principle, one of the most important protections we have elaborated for the Nation's interstate markets." Justice Kennedy objected that the majority "overlooks the argument that was central to the entire holding of United Haulers. There the Court concluded the ordinance applied equally to interstate and in-state commerce [because] the government had monopolized the waste processing industry. Nondiscrimination, not just state involvement, was central to the rationale. That justification cannot be invoked here, for discrimination against out-of-state bonds is the whole purpose of the law in question. Kentucky has not monopolized the bond market or the municipal bond market. Kentucky has entered a competitive, nonmonopolized market and, to give its bonds a market advantage, has taxed out-of-state municipal bonds at a higher rate. [This] case is not an extension of United Haulers; it is a rejection of its principal rationale—that in monopolizing the local market, the ordinance applied equally to interstate and local commerce."

In a portion of his opinion representing a plurality consisting only of himself and Justices Stevens and Breyer, Justice Souter defended the Kentucky law on the alternative ground that, in issuing the tax-exempt bonds in the first place, the State was acting as a market participant rather than a market regulator, and thus was entitled to prefer its own state residents—a theory based on the cases that follow. The dissent objected that bond interest taxation, not bond issuance, was the relevant event, and that the state was entitled to subsidize its own residents preferentially. Justice Thomas filed a concurrence in the judgment expressing his continued view that the Court generally lacks authority to invalidate state laws under the dormant commerce clause.

THE MARKET PARTICIPANT EXCEPTION

May a state or city discriminate in favor of its own residents when it functions not as a "regulator" of the market but rather as a "market participant"? A series of decisions has established such an exception, even for overt, facial discrimination, when government acts as a buyer or seller of goods or services or engages in a program of subsidies or other economic incentives to aid in-state businesses. The Court has limited the exception, as illustrated in the plurality opinion in South-Central Timber, which follows. Justice White's opinion in that case provides a useful review of the Alexandria Scrap, Reeves and Massachusetts Council cases that established the exception beginning in 1976. As Justice Alito noted in dissent in United Haulers, the market participant doctrine allows the state or municipality to favor its own residents in the course of its own dealings; it does not permit that government to regulate other private parties, including in their dealings with a state-owned entity.

South-Central Timber Development, Inc. v. Wunnicke

467 U.S. 82, 104 S. Ct. 2237, 81 L. Ed. 2d 71 (1984).

[In order to protect and promote the state's timber-processing industries, Alaska proposed to sell state-owned timber subject to the condition that the purchaser process the timber in Alaska before it was shipped out of state. South-Central was an Alaska corporation that purchased and logged timber and then shipped it elsewhere (primarily to Japan) for processing. South-Central claimed that the in-state processing requirement violated the dormant commerce clause. Alaska replied that its restriction on export of unprocessed timber was exempt from the Commerce Clause because of the "market participant" doctrine:]

■ Opinion of JUSTICE WHITE.

[Our] cases make clear that if a State is acting as a market participant, rather than as a market regulator, the dormant Commerce Clause places no limitation on its activities. See White v. Massachusetts Council of Construction Employers, Inc., 460 U.S. 204 (1983); Reeves, Inc. v. Stake, 447 U.S. 429 (1980); Hughes v. Alexandria Scrap Corp., 426 U.S. 794 (1976). The precise contours of the market-participant doctrine have yet to be established, however, the doctrine having been applied in only three cases of this Court to date.

The first of the cases, Alexandria Scrap, involved a Maryland program designed to reduce the number of junked automobiles in the State. A "bounty" was established on Maryland-licensed junk cars, and the State imposed more stringent documentation requirements on out-of-state scrap processors than on in-state ones. The Court rejected a Commerce Clause attack on the program, although it noted that under traditional Commerce Clause analysis the program might well be invalid because it had the effect of reducing the flow of goods in interstate commerce. The Court concluded that Maryland's action was not "the kind of action with which the Commerce Clause is concerned," because "[n]othing in the purposes animating the Commerce Clause prohibits a State, in the absence of congressional action, from participating in the market and exercising the right to favor its own citizens over others."

In Reeves, Inc. v. Stake, the Court upheld a South Dakota policy of restricting the sale of cement from a state-owned plant to state residents, declaring that "[t]he basic distinction drawn in Alexandria Scrap between States as market participants and States as market regulators makes good sense and sound law." The Court relied upon " 'the long recognized right of trader or manufacturer, engaged in an entirely private business, freely to exercise his own independent discretion as to parties with whom he will deal.' " In essence, the Court recognized the principle that the Commerce Clause places no limitations on a State's refusal to deal with particular parties when it is participating in the interstate market in goods.

The most recent of this Court's cases developing the market-participant doctrine is White v. Massachusetts Council of Construction Employers, Inc., in which the Court sustained against a Commerce Clause challenge an executive order of the Mayor of Boston that required all construction projects funded in whole or in part by city funds or city-administered funds to be performed by a work force of at least 50% city residents. The Court rejected the argument that the city was not entitled to the protection of the doctrine because the order had the effect of regulating employment contracts between public contractors and their employees. Recognizing that "there are some limits on a state or local government's ability to impose restrictions that reach beyond the immediate parties with which the government transacts business," the Court found it unnecessary to define those limits because "[e]veryone affected by the order [was], in a substantial if informal sense, 'working for the city.' " The fact that the employees were "working for the city" was "crucial" to the market-participant analysis in White.

The State of Alaska contends that its primary-manufacture requirement fits squarely within the market-participant doctrine, arguing that "Alaska's entry into the market may be viewed as precisely the same type of subsidy to local interests that the Court found unobjectionable in Alexandria Scrap." However, when Maryland became involved in the scrap market it was as a purchaser of scrap; Alaska, on the other hand, participates in the timber market, but imposes conditions downstream in the timber-processing market. Alaska is not merely subsidizing local timber processing in an amount "roughly equal to the difference between the price the timber would fetch in the absence of such a requirement and the amount the state actually receives." If the State directly subsidized the timber-processing industry by such an amount, the purchaser would retain the option of taking advantage of the subsidy by processing timber in the State or forgoing the benefits of the subsidy and exporting unprocessed timber. Under the Alaska requirement, however, the choice is made for him: if he buys timber from the State he is not free to take the timber out of state prior to processing.

The State also would have us find Reeves controlling. It states that "Reeves made it clear that the Commerce Clause imposes no limitation on Alaska's power to choose the terms on which it will sell its timber." Such an unrestrained reading of Reeves is unwarranted. Although the Court in Reeves did strongly endorse the right of a State to deal with whomever it chooses when it participates in the market, it did not—and did not purport to—sanction the imposition of any terms that the State might desire. For example, the Court expressly noted in Reeves that "Commerce Clause scrutiny may well be more rigorous when a restraint on foreign commerce is alleged"; that a natural resource "like coal, timber, wild game, or minerals," was not involved, but instead the cement was "the end product of a complex process whereby a costly physical plant and human labor act on raw materials;" and that South Dakota did not bar resale of South Dakota cement to out-of-state purchasers. In this case, all three of the elements that were not present in Reeves—foreign commerce, a natural resource, and restrictions on resale—are present.

Finally, Alaska argues that since the Court in White upheld a requirement that reached beyond "the boundary of formal privity of contract," then, a fortiori, the primary-manufacture requirement is permissible, because the State is not regulating contracts for resale of timber or regulating the buying and selling of timber, but is instead "a seller of timber, pure and simple." Yet it is clear that the State is more than merely a seller of timber. In the commercial context, the seller usually has no say over, and no interest in, how the product is to be used after sale; in this case, however, payment for the timber does not end the obligations of the purchaser, for, despite the fact that the purchaser has taken delivery of the timber and has paid for it, he cannot do with it as he pleases. Instead, he is obligated to deal with a stranger to the contract after completion of the sale.

That privity of contract is not always the outer boundary of permissible state activity does not necessarily mean that the Commerce Clause has no application within the boundary of formal privity. The market-participant doctrine permits a State to influence "a discrete, identifiable class of economic activity in which [it] is a major participant." [White.] Contrary to the State's contention, the doctrine is not *carte blanche* to impose any conditions that the State has the economic power to dictate, and does not validate any requirement merely because the State imposes it upon someone with whom it is in contractual privity.

The limit of the market-participant doctrine must be that it allows a State to impose burdens on commerce within the market in which it is a participant, but allows it to go no further. The State may not impose conditions, whether by statute, regulation, or contract, that have a substantial regulatory effect outside of that particular market.[1] Unless the "market" is relatively narrowly defined, the doctrine has the potential of swallowing up the rule that States may not impose substantial burdens on interstate commerce even if they act with the permissible state purpose of fostering local industry.

At the heart of the dispute in this case is disagreement over the definition of the market. Alaska contends that it is participating in the processed timber market, although it acknowledges that it participates in no way in the actual processing. South-Central argues, on the other hand, that although the State may be a participant in the timber market, it is using its leverage in that market to exert a regulatory effect in the processing market, in which it is not a participant. We agree with the latter position.

---

[1] The view of the market-participant doctrine expressed by Justice Rehnquist would validate under the Commerce Clause any contractual condition that the State had the economic power to impose, without regard to the relationship of the subject matter of the contract and the condition imposed. If that were the law, it would have been irrelevant that the employees in White were in effect "working for the city." If the only question were whether the condition is imposed by contract, a residency requirement could have been imposed with respect to the work force on all projects of any employer doing business with the city. [Footnote by Justice White.]

There are sound reasons for distinguishing between a State's preferring its own residents in the initial disposition of goods when it is a market participant and a State's attachment of restrictions on dispositions subsequent to the goods coming to rest in private hands. First, simply as a matter of intuition a state market participant has a greater interest as a "private trader" in the immediate transaction than it has in what its purchaser does with the goods after the State no longer has an interest in them. The common law recognized such a notion in the doctrine of restraints on alienation. Similarly, the antitrust laws place limits on vertical restraints. It is no defense in an action charging vertical trade restraints that the same end could be achieved through vertical integration; if it were, there would be virtually no antitrust scrutiny of vertical arrangements. We reject the contention that a State's action as a market regulator may be upheld against Commerce Clause challenge on the ground that the State could achieve the same end as a market participant. We therefore find it unimportant for present purposes that the State could support its processing industry by selling only to Alaska processors, by vertical integration, or by direct subsidy.

Second, downstream restrictions have a greater regulatory effect than do limitations on the immediate transaction. Instead of merely choosing its own trading partners, the State is attempting to govern the private, separate economic relationships of its trading partners; that is, it restricts the post-purchase activity of the purchaser, rather than merely the purchasing activity. In contrast to the situation in White, this restriction on private economic activity takes place after the completion of the parties' direct commercial obligations, rather than during the course of an ongoing commercial relationship in which the city retained a continuing proprietary interest in the subject of the contract.

In sum, the State may not avail itself of the market-participant doctrine to immunize its downstream regulation of the timber-processing market in which it is not a participant. [Because] of the protectionist nature of Alaska's local-processing requirement and the burden on commerce resulting therefrom, we conclude that it falls within the rule of virtual per se invalidity of laws that "bloc[k] the flow of interstate commerce at a State's borders." [Reversed and remanded.]

■ JUSTICE REHNQUIST, with whom JUSTICE O'CONNOR joins, dissenting.

In my view, the line of distinction drawn in the plurality opinion between the State as market participant and the State as market regulator is both artificial and unconvincing. [The] contractual term at issue here no more transforms Alaska's sale of timber into "regulation" of the processing industry than the resident-hiring preference imposed by the city of Boston in [White] constituted regulation of the construction industry. Alaska is merely paying the buyer of the timber indirectly, by means of a reduced price, to hire Alaska residents to process the timber. Under existing precedent, the State could accomplish that same result in any number of ways. For example, the State could choose to sell its timber only to those companies that maintain active primary-processing plants in Alaska. [Reeves.] Or the State could directly subsidize the primary-processing industry within the State. [Alexandria Scrap.] The State could even pay to have the logs processed and then enter the market only to sell processed logs. It seems to me unduly formalistic to conclude that the one path chosen by the State as best suited to promote its concerns is the path forbidden it by the Commerce Clause.

THE THEORY AND LIMITS OF THE MARKET PARTICIPANT EXCEPTION

1. ***Justifying state preferences for in-staters through subsidies rather than regulation.*** Is there any good reason to exempt states from the usual Commerce Clause restraints when they prefer their own residents over outsiders through the vehicle of subsidies rather than regulation? For varying defenses, see Wells & Hellerstein, "The Governmental-Proprietary Distinction in Constitutional Law," 66 Va. L. Rev. 1073 (1980); Varat, "State 'Citizenship' and Interstate Equality," 48 U. Chi. L. Rev. 487 (1981); Coenen, "Untangling the Market-Participant Exemption to the Dormant Commerce Clause," 88 Mich. L. Rev. 395 (1989). Consider the following possible defenses of the market participant exception:

a. *Text.* The Commerce Clause, Art. I, § 8, cl. 3, confers upon Congress the power to "regulate" commerce among the several states. Is the market participant exception adequately explained by the textual argument that subsidies are not "regulation"? Wouldn't such an argument also exempt discriminatory taxes on out-of-staters that have long been presumed invalid? And aren't subsidies sometimes "regulatory" when designed to induce changes in behavior?

b. *Economic effect.* Do preferential state expenditures cause less harm to national economic welfare than do discriminatory regulation or taxes? Consider the argument that discriminatory subsidies leave outsiders no worse off because such subsidies would not exist at all if the local preference were not allowed, and are self-limiting because, unlike regulation, they require the expenditure of general public funds and thus will face in-state political safeguards. See Regan, "The Supreme Court and State Protectionism: Making Sense of the Dormant Commerce Clause," 84 Mich. L. Rev. 1091 (1986). Given this rationale, should some state marketplace actions fall outside the exception because they harm the national marketplace too much? See generally Coenen, "State User Fees and the Dormant Commerce Clause," 50 Vanderbilt L. Rev. 795 (1997) (discussing, for example, state discrimination in affording access to state-owned roadways and airports).

c. *Parity with private actors.* Should a state government be immune from constitutional concerns when acting as a seller of cement or bidder for auto hulks or construction services because it can be expected to behave similarly to private actors, who are free contractually to pick and choose their counterparties? Or do state governments have very different incentives and constraints than private actors? Are states free from the cost constraints that discipline private economic actors because they possess unique coercive powers of taxation? And are state government officials more likely than private actors to discriminate in favor of local residents because the expected political benefits may offset the possible economic costs?

d. *Federalism.* Is exempting a state from judicial scrutiny when it acts as a market participant a means of respecting state sovereignty and the role of the states as laboratories for experiment? How could such a view be reconciled with the demise of National League of Cities (1976; p. 169 above), which carved out from affirmative federal commerce regulation certain state activities deemed integral to sovereignty, but was swiftly overruled? Is it backwards to exempt state proprietary but not sovereign activities from national market principles?

e. *Investment capture.* Is the best explanation for the market participant exception that it allows a state to capture the benefits of its citizens' tax investments? Consider the argument that "it is fair for [state] citizens to decide to restrict the benefits of state-created resources to state residents because they are the ones who paid for such benefits," and they will not engage in the "optimal degree of public investment" unless that can exclude out-of-state " 'free riders' " from "receiv[ing] the benefits of programs for which they have not paid." Williams, "Taking Care of Ourselves: State Citizenship, the Market, and the State," 69 Ohio St. L.J. 469 (2008). On this theory, should states ever be able to hoard natural resources whose control they enjoy by chance, not by their own tax effort?

2. ***Downstream effect.*** South-Central treated the requirement of in-state processing as amounting to an impermissibly discriminatory regulation rather than a permissibly preferential subsidy because it restricted economic activity beyond the market in which the state was a participant. Would the same argument apply if the condition were "upstream" of the market in which the state acts? Is the "downstream" restriction a meaningful constraint on Alaska's ability to prefer its own residents? Consider the dissent's arguments that Alaska could have conferred an economically identical subsidy on in-state processors by selling Alaska-owned timber only to Alaska timber processors, by vertically integrating its timber business with a state-owned processing plant, or by giving a cash subsidy to Alaska timber processors. Was the in-state processing requirement meaningfully distinguishable?

FACIALLY NEUTRAL LAWS WITH PROTECTIONIST PURPOSE OR EFFECT

Facial discrimination against interstate commerce is relatively rare, given the Court's readiness to invalidate such laws as "virtually per se invalid." As Justice Stevens observed in West Lynn Creamery, "tariffs against the products of other States are so patently unconstitutional that our cases reveal not a single attempt by any State to enact one. Instead, the cases are filled with state laws that aspire to reap some of the benefits of tariffs by other means." Yet the Court has treated as "protectionist," and thus as "virtually per se invalid," some laws that do not explicitly discriminate against outside commerce. What laws deserve such treatment? Only those with discriminatory *purpose*? Or should forbidden "discrimination" also include regulations whose *effect* is to favor local interests and disadvantage out-of-state interests? Discriminatory purpose may be difficult to discern from the text and history of a statute; the purpose to discriminate is often hidden rather than overt. But this difficulty may be overcome to the extent that proof of a forbidden purpose may be inferred from the effects of a state rule. Should discriminatory effects matter apart from providing evidence of purpose?

Consider the following cases, Baldwin v. Seelig and H.P. Hood v. Du Mond, which held invalid, as applied to out-of-state sellers or buyers, statutes that protected local economic interests by limiting access to local markets—even in the absence of any facial discrimination by the state.

Baldwin v. G.A.F. Seelig, Inc.

294 U.S. 511, 55 S. Ct. 497, 79 L. Ed. 1032 (1935).

[The New York Milk Control Act of 1933 set the minimum prices to be paid to milk producers by New York dealers. Baldwin held the law unconstitutional as applied to out-of-state milk producers. (The Nebbia v. New York decision, p. 500 below, had held the law permissible as to New York producers.) Seelig, a New York milk dealer, bought milk from Vermont milk producers at prices lower than the New York minimum. The law prohibited New York sales of out-of-state milk if the milk had been purchased below the price for similar purchases within New York. The State refused to license Seelig to sell milk in New York unless it agreed to conform to the state's price regulation regarding the sale of imported milk.]

■ JUSTICE CARDOZO delivered the opinion of the Court.

[New York] has no power to project its legislation into Vermont by regulating the price to be paid in that state for milk acquired there. So much is not disputed. New York is equally without power to prohibit the introduction within her territory of milk of wholesome quality acquired in Vermont, whether at high prices or at low ones. This again is not disputed. Accepting those postulates, New York asserts her power to outlaw milk so introduced by prohibiting its sale thereafter if the price that has been paid for it to the farmers of Vermont is less than would be owing in like circumstances to farmers in New York. The importer in that view may keep his milk or drink it, but sell it he may not.

Such a power, if exerted, will set a barrier to traffic between one state and another as effective as if customs duties, equal to the price differential, had been laid upon the thing transported. [Nice] distinctions have been made at times between direct and indirect burdens. They are irrelevant when the avowed purpose of the obstruction, as well as its necessary tendency, is to suppress or mitigate the consequences of competition between the states. Such an obstruction is direct by the very terms of the hypothesis. [A] chief occasion of the commerce clause was "the mutual jealousies and aggressions of the States, taking form in customs barriers and other economic retaliation." [If] New York, in order to promote the economic welfare of her farmers, may guard them against competition with the cheaper prices of Vermont, the door has been opened to rivalries and reprisals that were meant to be averted by subjecting commerce between the states to the power of the nation.

The argument is pressed upon us, however, that the end to be served by the Milk Control Act is something more than the economic welfare of the farmers or of any other class or classes. The end to be served is the maintenance of a regular and adequate supply of pure and wholesome milk, the supply being put in jeopardy when the farmers of the state are unable to earn a living income. Price security, we are told, is only a special form of sanitary security; the economic motive is secondary and subordinate; the state intervenes to make its inhabitants healthy, and not to make them rich.

On that assumption we are asked to say that intervention will be upheld as a valid exercise by the state of its internal police power, though there is an incidental obstruction to commerce between one state and another. This would be to eat up the rule under the guise of an exception. Economic welfare is always related to health, for there can be no health if men are starving. Let such an exception be admitted, and all that a state will have to do in times of stress and strain is to say that its farmers and merchants and workmen must be protected against competition from without, lest they go upon the poor relief lists or perish altogether. To give entrance to that excuse would be to invite a speedy end of our national solidarity. The Constitution was framed under the dominion of a political philosophy less parochial in range. It was framed upon the theory that the peoples of the several states must sink or swim together, and that in the long run prosperity and salvation are in union and not division.

[One] state in its dealings with another may not place itself in a position of economic isolation. Formulas and catchwords are subordinate to this overmastering requirement. [The] police power [may] not be used by the state of destination with the aim and effect of establishing an economic barrier against competition with the products of another [state]. Restrictions so contrived are an unreasonable clog on the mobility of commerce. They set up what is the equivalent of a rampart of customs duties designed to neutralize advantages belonging to the place of origin. They are thus hostile in conception as well as burdensome in result.

H.P. Hood & Sons v. Du Mond

336 U.S. 525, 69 S. Ct. 657, 93 L. Ed. 865 (1949).

[Hood was a Boston milk distributor who had long obtained milk from New York producers and had maintained three receiving depots there. Hood sought a New York license to establish a fourth depot but was denied the license on the basis of a New York law stating that licenses for new plants could not be issued unless the Commissioner was satisfied that "issuance of the license will not tend to a destructive competition in a market already adequately served, and that the issuance of the license is in the public interest."]

■ JUSTICE JACKSON delivered the opinion of the Court.

This case concerns the power of [New York] to deny additional facilities to acquire and ship milk in interstate commerce where the grounds of denial are that such limitation upon interstate business will protect and advance local economic interests. [New York's] regulations, designed to assure producers a fair price and a responsible purchaser, and consumers a sanitary and modernly equipped handler, are not challenged here but have been complied with. It is only additional restrictions, imposed for the avowed purpose and with the practical effect of curtailing the volume of interstate commerce to aid local economic interests, that are in question here.

[This] Court consistently has rebuffed attempts of states to advance their own commercial interests by curtailing the movement of articles of commerce, either into or out of the state, while generally supporting their right to impose even burdensome regulations in the interest of local health and safety. [The] principle that our economic unit is the Nation, which alone has the gamut of powers necessary to control of the economy, including the vital power of erecting customs barriers against foreign competition, has as its corollary that the states are not separable economic units.

[The] State, however, insists that denial of the license for a new plant does not restrict or obstruct interstate commerce, because petitioner has been licensed at its other plants without condition or limitation as to the quantities it may purchase. [In] the face of affirmative findings that the proposed plant would increase petitioner's supply, we can hardly be asked to assume that denial of the license will not deny petitioner access to such added supplies. While the state power is applied in this case to limit expansion by a handler of milk who already has been allowed some purchasing facilities, the argument for doing so, if sustained, would be equally effective to exclude an entirely new foreign handler from coming into the State to purchase. [Since] the statute as applied violates the Commerce Clause [it] cannot stand. [Reversed and remanded.]

■ JUSTICE BLACK, joined by JUSTICE MURPHY, dissenting.

Had a dealer supplying New York customers applied for a license to operate a new plant, the commissioner would have been compelled under the Act to protect petitioner's plants supplying Boston consumers in the same manner that this order would have protected New York consumers. [T]he Court cannot attribute to the commissioner an invidious purpose to [discriminate]. The language of this state Act is not discriminatory, the legislative history shows it was not so intended, and the commissioner has not administered it with a hostile eye. [The] basic question here is [whether] all local phases of interstate business are to be judicially immunized from state laws against destructive competitive business practices such as those prohibited by New York's law. [While] I have doubt about the wisdom of this New York law, I do not conceive it to be the function of this Court to revise that state's economic [judgments].

■ JUSTICE FRANKFURTER, joined by JUSTICE RUTLEDGE, dissenting.

[The effect of the Court's opinion] is to hold that no matter how important to the internal economy of a State may be the prevention of destructive competition, and no matter how unimportant the interstate commerce affected, a State cannot as a means of preventing such competition deny an applicant access to a market within the State if that applicant happens to intend the out-of-state shipment of the product that he buys.

IDENTIFYING PROTECTIONISM IN FACIALLY NEUTRAL LAWS

Baldwin and Hood involved the discriminatory application of facially neutral laws. May a statute ever be struck down on its face as de facto discrimination against interstate commerce? What if an apparently facially neutral statute actually exists solely in order to protect a particular in-state interest, or to target a particular out-of-state interest? Is such a law the equivalent of a commercial gerrymander? May a court smoke out a protectionist purpose from behind such an apparently neutral law? May it infer a protectionist purpose from a stark discriminatory effect? May it invalidate the law based solely on effect regardless of purpose?

In **Hunt v. Washington State Apple Advertising Comm'n**, 432 U.S. 333 (1977), the Court unanimously invalidated a North Carolina law requiring that closed containers of apples offered for sale or shipped into the State bear "no grade other than the applicable U.S. grade or standard." Washington State, the nation's largest producer of apples, was the source of half of all apples shipped in closed containers in interstate commerce. Washington had adopted strict inspection programs and required all apples shipped from the state to be graded in accordance with its quality standards. The Washington State grades were equivalent or superior to the comparable grades adopted by the U.S. Department of Agriculture (USDA). The North Carolina ban, which required the display of either the USDA grade or a "not graded" label, explicitly prohibited the display of any state grades. The Washington Commission, confronted with a serious obstacle to the marketing of its apples in North Carolina, prevailed in the district court, which found that the North Carolina law, while neutral on its face, discriminated against Washington growers in favor of their local counterparts and concluded that this discrimination was not justified by the asserted local interest in eliminating deception and confusion in the marketplace.

In affirming that result, the Court, while finding some aspects of the North Carolina law "somewhat suspect," found it unnecessary to "ascribe an economic protection motive to the North Carolina Legislature to resolve this case." Instead, Chief Justice BURGER concluded that the law could not stand in light of its discriminatory effect, "even if enacted for the declared purpose of protecting consumers. [A] finding that state legislation furthers matters of legitimate local concern, even in health and consumer protection areas, does not end the inquiry. [Dean Milk.] Rather, when such state legislation comes into conflict with the Commerce Clause's overriding requirement of a national 'common market,' we are confronted with the task of effecting an accommodation of the competing national and local interests.

"[Here, the law has] the practical effect of not only burdening interstate sales of Washington apples, but also discriminating against them. This discrimination takes various forms. The first, and most obvious, is the statute's consequence of raising the costs of doing business in the North Carolina market for Washington apple growers and dealers, while leaving those of their North Carolina counterparts unaffected. Second, the law had the effect of "stripping away from the Washington apple industry the competitive and economic advantages it has earned for itself through its expensive inspection and grading system." Third, the law had "a leveling effect which insidiously operates to the advantage of local apple producers," because "Washington apples which would otherwise qualify for and be sold under the superior Washington grades will now have to be marketed under their inferior USDA counterparts. Such 'downgrading' offers the North Carolina apple industry the very sort of protection against competing out-of-state products that the Commerce Clause was designed to prohibit." Chief Justice Burger noted that nondiscriminatory alternatives were "readily available—for example, North Carolina could effectuate its goal by permitting out-of-state growers to utilize state grades only if they also marked their shipments with the applicable USDA label."

In **Bacchus Imports, Ltd. v. Dias**, 468 U.S. 263 (1984), the Court had no trouble finding protectionist purpose *and* effect. The decision invalidated a Hawaii statute that exempted from the State's 20% wholesale liquor tax okolehao, a brandy distilled from the root of the ti plant, a shrub indigenous to Hawaii. The case also involved a tax exemption for fruit wine. Although this exemption was general in nature and did not specify an indigenous product, there was evidence that it was enacted to promote the local pineapple-wine industry. Writing for the Court, Justice WHITE found that the tax "violated the Commerce Clause because it had both the purpose and effect of discriminating in favor of local products." He explained: "[We] need not guess at the legislature's motivation, for it is undisputed that the purpose of the exemption was to aid Hawaiian industry. Likewise, the effect of the exemption is clearly discriminatory, in that it applies only to locally produced beverages, even though it does not apply to all such products." He rejected the State's efforts to defend the law as helping to promote a struggling local industry, holding that any effort to confer a benefit upon local industry not granted to out-of-state industry is presumptively invalid as discrimination under the Commerce Clause.

Can a law be considered protectionist in effect if there are no equivalent economic actors on either side of the state border? Compare Hunt and Bacchus with the following cases:

In **Exxon Corp. v. Governor of Maryland**, 437 U.S. 117 (1978), the Court upheld against dormant commerce clause challenge a law prohibiting producers or refiners of petroleum products from operating retail service stations in Maryland. Maryland acted in response to evidence that oil companies had favored their own gas stations over independent gas stations during the 1973 oil shortage. No gasoline was produced or refined in Maryland; all of its gasoline was imported from out-of-state refineries.

Justice STEVENS's majority opinion rejected Exxon's argument that the law discriminated against out-of-state commerce: "Plainly, the [law] does not discriminate against interstate goods, nor does it favor local producers and refiners. Since Maryland's entire gasoline supply flows in interstate commerce and since there are no local producers or refiners, such claims of disparate treatment between interstate and local commerce would be meritless." He also rejected Exxon's argument that the law protected in-state retail gas stations from competition by forcing only out-of-state oil companies to divest themselves of gas stations. "[The] divestiture requirements [fall] solely on interstate companies. But this fact does not lead, either logically or as a practical matter, to a conclusion that the State is discriminating against interstate commerce at the retail level. [There] are several major interstate marketers of petroleum that own and operate their own retail gasoline stations. These interstate dealers, who compete directly with the Maryland independent dealers, are not affected by the Act because they do not refine or produce gasoline. In fact, the Act creates no barriers whatsoever against interstate independent dealers: it does not prohibit the flow of interstate goods, place added costs upon them, or distinguish between in-state and out-of-state companies in the retail market. The absence of any of these factors fully distinguishes this case from those in which a State has been found to have discriminated against interstate commerce."[1]

[1] "If the effect of a state regulation is to cause local goods to constitute a larger share, and goods with an out-of-state source to constitute a smaller share, of the total sales in the market—as in Hunt and Dean Milk—the regulation may have a discriminatory effect on interstate commerce. But the Maryland statute has no impact on the relative proportions of local and out-of-state goods sold in Maryland and, indeed, no demonstrable effect whatsoever on the interstate

Justice BLACKMUN was the sole dissenter, taking the view that the Maryland law was discriminatory: "[It] is true that merely demonstrating a burden on some out-of-state actors does not prove unconstitutional discrimination. But when the burden is significant, when it falls on the most numerous and effective group of out-of-state competitors, when a similar burden does not fall on the class of protected in-state businessmen, and when the State cannot justify the resulting disparity by showing that its legislative interests cannot be vindicated by more evenhanded regulation, unconstitutional discrimination exists."

Similarly, in **Minnesota v. Clover Leaf Creamery Co.**, 449 U.S. 456 (1981), the Court, by a vote of 6–2, rejected a discriminatory effects claim, upholding a state law that banned the retail sale of milk products in plastic nonreturnable containers but permitted sales in nonreturnable containers made of pulpwood. In enacting the law, the legislature found that the use of nonreturnable containers "presents a solid waste management problem, [promotes] energy waste, and depletes natural resources." The resin used to make plastic containers originated out of state; pulpwood was a major Minnesota product. The challengers included a non-Minnesota company that manufactured equipment for producing plastic nonreturnable milk jugs, a non-Minnesota dairy that sold milk products in Minnesota in plastic nonreturnable milk jugs, a non-Minnesota manufacturer of polyethylene resin that sold such resin in many states, including Minnesota, and a plastics industry trade association.

Justice BRENNAN's majority opinion rejected an anti-protectionism challenge: "[The law here] does not effect 'simple protectionism,' but 'regulates evenhandedly' by prohibiting all milk retailers from selling their products in plastic, nonreturnable milk containers, without regard to whether the containers, or the sellers are from outside the State. [Pulpwood] producers are the only Minnesota industry likely to benefit significantly from the Act at the expense of out-of-state firms. Respondents point out that plastic resin, the raw material used for making plastic nonreturnable milk jugs, is produced entirely by non-Minnesota firms, while pulpwood, used for making paperboard, is a major Minnesota product. Nevertheless, it is clear that respondents exaggerate the degree of burden on out-of-state interests, both because plastics will continue to be used in the production of plastic pouches, plastic returnable bottles, and paperboard itself, and because out-of-state pulpwood producers will presumably absorb some of the business generated by the Act. Even granting that the out-of-state plastics industry is burdened relatively more heavily than the Minnesota pulpwood industry, we find that this burden is not 'clearly excessive' in light of the substantial state interest in promoting conservation of energy and other natural resources and easing solid waste disposal problems. [Pike.]

"In [Exxon], we upheld a Maryland statute barring producers and refiners of petroleum product—all of which were out-of-state businesses—from retailing gasoline in the State. We stressed that the Commerce Clause 'protects the interstate market, not particular interstate firms, from prohibitive or burdensome regulations.' A nondiscriminatory regulation serving substantial state purposes is not invalid simply because it causes some business to shift from a predominantly out-of-state industry to a predominantly in-state industry. Only if the burden on interstate commerce

flow of goods. The sales by independent retailers are just as much a part of the flow of [commerce] as the sales made by the refiner-operated stations." [Footnote by Justice Stevens.]

clearly outweighs the State's legitimate purposes does such a regulation violate the Commerce Clause." Justice POWELL dissented, urging that the case be remanded for the highest state court to "consider specifically whether the statute discriminated impermissibly against interstate commerce."

Are cases like Exxon and Clover Leaf distinguishable from cases like Hunt and Bacchus based on the presence or absence of protectionist legislative purpose? See Regan, "The Supreme Court and State Protectionism: Making Sense of the Dormant Commerce Clause," 84 Mich. L. Rev. 1091 (1986) (arguing that "the North Carolina legislature [in Hunt] was motivated by protectionist purpose, while the Maryland legislature [in Exxon] was not"). Arguably, the Maryland law was trying to combat the anticompetitive effects of vertical integration in the oil industry by the only means it could. Consider the alternative interpretation that "Exxon means that discriminatory effects claims can only be brought successfully when the burdens on the out-of-state economic actors are not borne by an in-state competitor, or when the market share lost as a result of the regulation inures to the benefit of in-state competitors. [In] both Exxon and Clover Leaf, the Court focused on the lack of harm to similarly-situated out-of-state entities in upholding the state laws" Denning & Lary, "Retail Store Size-Capping Ordinances and the Dormant Commerce Clause Doctrine," 37 Urb. Law. 907 (2005). On this view, in Exxon, "the Maryland statute left in-state and out-of-state independent gasoline dealers on the same competitive footing." Tribe, American Constitutional Law (3d ed. 2000).

Finally, consider two cases in the European Court of Justice addressing non-tariff barriers similar to those struck down in Hunt. Procureur du Roi v. Dassonville (1974), involved a challenge to a Belgian law that prevented the sale of certain products like Scotch whisky without a certificate of origin. As a result of the restriction, a trader wishing to sell Scotch whisky in Belgium needed to import directly from Scotland, but another trader selling the same whisky in France could sell whisky that was already in free circulation on the continent. The court struck down the law, holding that "[a]ll trading rules enacted by Member States which are capable of hindering . . . intra-Community trade are to be considered as measures having an effect equivalence to quantitative restrictions." Likewise, in Cassis de Dijon (1979), the European Union's high court considered a German law stipulating that products sold as fruit liqueur had to contain at least 25% alcohol by volume. An importer of French cassis, which traditionally contained an alcohol content of 15%, brought suit after a German authority prohibited the importation of the weaker French liqueur. The court concluded that there was no valid reason for the restriction of a product lawfully marketed in another Member State and thus ruled in favor of the importer.

BALANCING FACIALLY NEUTRAL LAWS WITH A DISPROPORTIONATE ADVERSE EFFECT ON COMMERCE

While the Court treats as "virtually per se invalid" laws that facially discriminate against interstate commerce and laws that are "protectionist" in purpose or effect, a law that is neither discriminatory nor protectionist still may be reviewed and struck down under the Court's residual balancing test. That balancing test has proven the most contested aspect of dormant commerce clause review. The Court's current formulation of the balancing test was stated in **Pike v. Bruce Church, Inc.**, 397 U.S. 137 (1970). That case involved a home processing requirement. An Arizona statute required that Arizona-grown cantaloupes advertise their State of origin on each package. Church was an Arizona grower of high quality cantaloupes. Instead of packing them in Arizona, it transported them to nearby California facilities; when packed in California, they were not identified as Arizona-grown. Arizona issued an order prohibiting Church from shipping uncrated cantaloupes from the company's Arizona ranch, and requiring that the cantaloupes be packed in Arizona and identified as coming from an Arizona packer. Compliance with the requirement would have required a capital outlay of $200,000 to pack Church's $700,000 cantaloupe crop.

In invalidating the requirement, Justice STEWART's opinion for a unanimous Court began with a restatement of the balancing test: "Where the statute regulates even-handedly to effectuate a legitimate local public interest, and its effects on interstate commerce are only incidental, it will be upheld unless the burden imposed on such commerce is clearly excessive in relation to the putative local benefits. [If] a legitimate local purpose is found, then the question becomes one of degree. And the extent of the burden that will be tolerated will of course depend on the nature of the local interest involved, and on whether it could be promoted as well with a lesser impact on interstate activities."

Turning to the Arizona requirement in light of this balancing formula, he noted that law did not have the "purpose and design" to promote safety or protect consumers from unfit goods, but instead was enacted "simply to protect and enhance the reputation of growers within the State. These are surely legitimate state interests. [But] application of the Act [to Church] has a far different impact, and quite a different purpose. [Arizona] is not complaining because the company is putting the good name of Arizona on an inferior or deceptively packaged product, but because it is not putting that name on a product that is superior and well packaged. [Although] it is not easy to see why the other growers of Arizona are entitled to benefit at the company's expense from the fact that it produces superior crops, we may assume that the asserted state interest is a legitimate one. But the State's tenuous interest in having the company's cantaloupes identified as originating in Arizona cannot constitutionally justify the requirement that the company build and operate an unneeded $200,000 packing plant in the State."

It is debatable whether Pike, having announced the influential balancing test, seriously applied it; portions of the opinion suggest that Arizona's order was invalid because, like other home-processing requirements, it was facially discriminatory: "The nature of [the] burden [on Church] is, constitutionally, more significant than its extent. For the Court has viewed with particular suspicion state statutes requiring business operations to be performed in the home State that could more efficiently be performed elsewhere. Even where the State is pursuing a clearly legitimate local interest, this particular burden on commerce has been declared to be virtually per se illegal." Nonetheless, Pike remains the canonical source for the balancing test.

Is balancing of state and national interests within the institutional competence of the courts? Are the relevant factual determinations within their administrative competence? Are the relevant judgments within their judicial competence? Or does balancing inevitably involve findings and judgments more suited to political resolution? Critics regard it as a form of lawless policymaking. Justice Scalia, for example, declines to participate in any Pike balancing. Concurring in the judgment in Bendix Autolite Corp. v. Midwesco Enterprises, Inc., 486 U.S. 888 (1988), he stated that "the scale analogy is not really appropriate, since the interests on both sides are incommensurate. It is more like judging whether a particular line is longer than a particular rock is heavy. [Weighing] the governmental interests of a State against the needs of interstate commerce is [a] task squarely within the responsibility of Congress. [I] would therefore abandon the 'balancing approach' to these negative commerce clause cases." Contrast the general defense of the Court's approach, including balancing, in Collins, "Economic Union as a Constitutional Value," 63 N.Y.U. L. Rev. 43 (1988)

In the case that follows, concerning a state truck-length regulation, the plurality opinion applied the Pike balancing test in upholding a district court finding that the harm to interstate commerce exceeded the safety benefit to the state. Note that the concurrence took a different approach to the same outcome:

Kassel v. Consolidated Freightways Corp.

450 U.S. 662, 101 S. Ct. 1309, 67 L. Ed. 2d 580 (1981).

■ JUSTICE POWELL announced the judgment of the Court and delivered an opinion in which JUSTICE WHITE, JUSTICE BLACKMUN, and JUSTICE STEVENS joined.

The question is whether an Iowa statute that prohibits the use of certain large trucks within the State unconstitutionally burdens interstate commerce.

I. [Consolidated Freightways] is one of the largest common carriers in the country. [Among] other routes, Consolidated carries commodities through Iowa on Interstate 80, the principal east-west route linking New York, Chicago, and the West Coast, and on Interstate 35, a major north-south route. Consolidated mainly uses two kinds of trucks. One consists of a three-axle tractor pulling a 40-foot two-axle trailer. This unit, commonly called a single, or "semi," is 55 feet in length overall. Such trucks have long been used on the Nation's highways. Consolidated also uses a two-axle tractor pulling a single-axle trailer which, in turn, pulls a single-axle dolly and a second single-axle trailer. This combination, known as a double, or twin, is 65 feet long overall. Many trucking companies, including Consolidated, increasingly prefer to use doubles to ship certain kinds of commodities. Doubles have larger capacities, and the trailers can be detached and routed separately if necessary. Consolidated would like to use 65-foot doubles on many of its trips through Iowa. [Iowa], however, by statute restricts the length of vehicles that may use its highways. Unlike all other States in the West and Midwest, Iowa generally prohibits the use of 65-foot doubles within its borders. Instead, most truck combinations are restricted to 55 feet in length. Doubles, mobile homes, trucks carrying vehicles such as tractors and other farm equipment, and singles hauling livestock, are permitted to be as long as 60 feet. Notwithstanding these restrictions, Iowa's statute permits cities abutting the state line by local ordinance to adopt the length limitations of the adjoining State.[1]

Because of Iowa's statutory scheme, Consolidated cannot use its 65-foot doubles to move commodities through the State. Instead, the company must do one of four things: (i) use 55-foot singles, (ii) use 60-foot doubles; (iii) detach the trailers of a 65-foot double and shuttle each through the State separately; or (iv) divert 65-foot doubles around Iowa. Dissatisfied with these options, Consolidated filed this suit in the District Court averring that Iowa's statutory scheme unconstitutionally burdens interstate commerce. Iowa defended the law as a reasonable safety measure enacted pursuant to its police power. The State asserted that 65-foot doubles are more dangerous than 55-foot singles and, in any event, that the law promotes safety and reduces road wear within the State by diverting much truck traffic to other States. In a 14-day trial, both sides adduced evidence on safety, and on the burden on interstate commerce imposed by Iowa's law. On the question of safety, the District Court found that the "evidence clearly establishes that the twin is as safe as the semi." [The] Court of Appeals agreed. [We] affirm.

II. [A] state's power to regulate commerce is never greater than in matters traditionally of local concern. For example, regulations that touch upon safety—especially highway safety—are those that "the Court has been most reluctant to invalidate." [But] the incantation of a purpose to promote the public health or safety does not insulate a state law from Commerce Clause attack. Regulations designed for that salutary purpose nevertheless may further the purpose so marginally, and interfere with commerce so substantially, as to be invalid under the Commerce Clause.

III. Applying these general principles, we conclude that the Iowa truck-length limitations unconstitutionally burden interstate commerce. [The] State failed to present any persuasive evidence that 65-foot doubles are less safe than 55-foot singles. Moreover, Iowa's law is now out of step with the laws of all other midwestern and western States. Iowa thus substantially burdens the interstate flow of goods by truck. In the absence of congressional action to set uniform standards, some burdens associated with state safety regulations must be tolerated. But where, as here, the State's safety interest has been found to be illusory, and its regulations impair significantly the federal interest in efficient and safe interstate transportation, the state law cannot be harmonized with the Commerce Clause.

A. The District Court found that the "evidence clearly establishes that the twin is as safe as the semi." The record supports this finding. The trial focused on a comparison of the performance of the two kinds of trucks in various safety categories. [The] District Court found [that] the 65-foot double was at least the equal of the 55-foot single in the ability to brake, turn, and maneuver. The double, because of its axle placement, produces less splash and spray in wet weather. And, because of its articulation in the middle, the

---

[1] Justice Powell also noted two other relevant Iowa exemptions: First, an Iowa truck manufacturer could obtain a permit to ship trucks as long as 70 feet. Second, permits were available to move oversized mobile homes if the unit was to be moved from a point within Iowa or delivered to an Iowa resident. In commenting on the second exemption, Justice Powell stated: "The parochial restrictions in the mobile home provision were enacted after Governor Ray vetoed a bill that would have permitted the interstate shipment of all mobile homes through Iowa. Governor Ray commented, in his [1972] veto message: 'This bill [would] make Iowa a bridge state as these oversized units are moved into Iowa after being manufactured in another state and sold in a third. None of the activity would be of particular economic benefit to Iowa.' "

double is less susceptible to dangerous "off-tracking," and to wind. None of these findings is seriously disputed by Iowa.

B. [Consolidated,] meanwhile, demonstrated that Iowa's law substantially burdens interstate commerce. Trucking companies that wish to continue to use 65-foot doubles must route them around Iowa or detach the trailers of the doubles and ship them through separately. Alternatively, trucking companies must use the smaller 55-foot singles or 60-foot doubles permitted under Iowa law. Each of these options engenders inefficiency and added expense. The record shows that Iowa's law added about $12.6 million each year to the costs of trucking companies. Consolidated alone incurred about $2 million per year in increased costs. In addition to increasing the costs of the trucking companies (and, indirectly, of the service to consumers), Iowa's law may aggravate, rather than ameliorate, the problem of highway accidents. Fifty-five foot singles carry less freight than 65-foot doubles. Either more small trucks must be used to carry the same quantity of goods through Iowa, or the same number of larger trucks must drive longer distances to bypass Iowa. In either case, [the] restriction requires more highway miles to be driven to transport the same quantity of goods. Other things being equal, accidents are proportional to distance traveled. Thus, if 65-foot doubles are as safe as 55-foot singles, Iowa's law tends to *increase* the number of accidents, and to shift the incidence of them from Iowa to other States.

IV. Perhaps recognizing the weakness of the evidence supporting its safety argument, and the substantial burden on commerce that its regulations create, Iowa urges the Court simply to "defer" to the safety judgment of the State. It argues that the length of trucks is generally, although perhaps imprecisely, related to safety. The task of drawing a line is one that Iowa contends should be left to its legislature. The Court normally does accord "special deference" to state highway safety regulations. [Less] deference to the legislative judgment is due, however, where the local regulation bears disproportionately on out-of-state residents and businesses. Such a disproportionate burden is apparent here. Iowa's scheme, although generally banning large doubles from the State, nevertheless has several exemptions that secure to Iowans many of the benefits of large trucks while shunting to neighboring States many of the costs associated with their use.

At the time of trial there were two particularly significant exemptions. First, singles hauling livestock or farm vehicles were permitted to be as long as 60 feet. [T]his provision undoubtedly was helpful to local interests. Second, cities abutting other States were permitted to enact local ordinances adopting the larger length limitation of the neighboring State. This exemption offered the benefits of longer trucks to individuals and businesses in important border cities without burdening Iowa's highways with interstate through traffic. The origin of the "border cities exemption" also suggests that Iowa's statute may not have been designed to ban dangerous trucks, but rather to discourage interstate truck traffic. In 1974, the legislature passed a bill that would have permitted 65-foot doubles in the State. Governor Ray vetoed the bill. He said: "I find sympathy with those who are doing business in our state and whose enterprises could gain from increased cargo carrying ability by trucks. However, with this bill, the Legislature has pursued a course that would benefit only a few Iowa-based companies while providing a great advantage for out-of-state trucking firms and competitors at the expense of our Iowa citizens."[2] After the veto, the "border cities exemption" was immediately enacted and signed by the Governor.

It is thus far from clear that Iowa was motivated primarily by a judgment that 65-foot doubles are less safe than 55-foot singles. Rather, Iowa seems to have hoped to limit the use of its highways by deflecting some through traffic. In the [lower courts], the State explicitly attempted to justify the law by its claimed interest in keeping trucks out of Iowa. The Court of Appeals correctly concluded that a State cannot constitutionally promote its own parochial interests by requiring safe vehicles to detour around it.

V. In sum, the statutory exemptions, their history, and the arguments Iowa has advanced in support of its law in this litigation, all suggest that the deference traditionally accorded a State's safety judgment is not warranted. The controlling factors thus are the findings of the District Court, accepted by the Court of Appeals, with respect to the relative safety of the types of trucks at issue, and the substantiality of the burden on interstate commerce. Because Iowa has imposed this burden without any significant countervailing safety interest, its statute violates the [Commerce Clause]. Affirmed.

■ JUSTICE BRENNAN, with whom JUSTICE MARSHALL joins, concurring in the judgment.

I. [The plurality and dissent are both] predicated upon the supposition that the constitutionality of a state regulation is determined by the factual record created by the State's lawyers in trial court. But that supposition cannot be correct, for it would make the constitutionality of state laws and regulations depend on the vagaries of litigation rather than on the judgments made by the State's lawmakers. In considering a Commerce Clause challenge to a state regulation, the judicial task is to balance the burden imposed on commerce against the local benefits sought to be achieved by the State's *lawmakers*. In determining those benefits, a court should focus ultimately on the regulatory purposes identified by the lawmakers and on the evidence before or available to them that might have supported their judgment. Since the court must confine its analysis to the purposes the lawmakers had for maintaining the regulation, the only relevant evidence concerns whether the lawmakers could rationally have believed that the challenged regulation would foster those purposes. It is not the function of the court to decide whether *in fact* the regulation promotes its intended purpose, so long as an examination of the evidence before or available to the lawmaker indicates that the regulation is not wholly irrational in light of its purposes.

II. [Justices] Powell and Rehnquist make the mistake of disregarding the intention of Iowa's lawmakers and assuming that resolution of the case must hinge upon the argument offered by Iowa's attorneys: that 65-foot doubles are more dangerous than shorter trucks. They then [reach] opposite conclusions as to whether the evidence adequately supports that empirical judgment. [Justices] Powell and Rehnquist have asked and answered the wrong question. For although Iowa's lawyers in this litigation have defended

[2] [E]xceptions also are available to benefit Iowa truck makers and Iowa mobile home manufacturers or purchasers. Although these exemptions are not directly relevant to the controversy over the safety of 65-foot doubles, they do contribute to the pattern of parochialism apparent in Iowa's statute. [Footnote by Justice Powell.]

the truck length regulation on the basis of the safety advantages of 55-foot singles and 60-foot doubles over 65-foot doubles, Iowa's actual rationale for maintaining the regulation had nothing to do with these purported differences. Rather, Iowa sought to discourage interstate truck traffic on Iowa's highways. Thus, the safety advantages and disadvantages of the types and lengths of trucks involved in this case are irrelevant to the [decision].

III. Though [Justice] Powell recognizes that the State's actual purpose in maintaining the truck length regulation was "to limit the use of its highways by deflecting some through traffic," he fails to recognize that this purpose, being *protectionist* in nature, is *impermissible* under the Commerce Clause. The Governor admitted that he blocked legislative efforts to raise the length of trucks because the change "would benefit only a few Iowa-based companies while providing a great advantage for out-of-state trucking firms and competitors at the expense of our Iowa citizens." Appellant Kassel, Director of the Iowa Department of Transportation, while admitting that the greater 65-foot length standard would be *safer* overall, defended the more restrictive regulations because of their benefits *within Iowa*.

[Iowa] may not shunt off its fair share of the burden of maintaining interstate truck routes, nor may it create increased hazards on the highways of neighboring States in order to decrease the hazards on Iowa highways. [The] decision of Iowa's lawmakers to promote *Iowa's* safety and other interests at the direct expense of the safety and other interests of neighboring States merits [no] deference. No special judicial acuity is demanded to perceive that this sort of parochial legislation violates the Commerce Clause.

■ JUSTICE REHNQUIST, with whom CHIEF JUSTICE BURGER and JUSTICE STEWART join, dissenting.

[The] safety benefits of a state law must be slight indeed before it will be struck down under the dormant Commerce Clause. [There] can be no doubt that the challenged statute is a valid highway safety regulation and thus entitled to the strongest presumption of validity against Commerce Clause challenges. [There] can also be no question that the particular limit chosen by Iowa [is] rationally related to Iowa's safety objective. [Iowa] adduced evidence supporting the relation between vehicle length and highway safety. [The] District Court approached the case as if the question were whether Consolidated's 65-foot trucks were as safe as others permitted on Iowa highways. [The] question, however, is whether the Iowa Legislature has acted rationally in regulating vehicle lengths and whether the safety benefits from this regulation are more than slight or problematical. The answering of the relevant question is not appreciably advanced by comparing trucks slightly over the length limit with those at the length limit. It is emphatically not our task to balance any incremental safety benefits from prohibiting 65-foot doubles as opposed to 60-foot doubles against the burden on interstate commerce. [Striking] down Iowa's law because Consolidated has made a voluntary business decision to employ 65-foot doubles, a decision based on the actions of other state legislatures, would essentially be compelling Iowa to yield to the policy choices of neighboring States. Under our Constitutional scheme, however, there is only one legislative body which can pre-empt the rational policy determination of the Iowa Legislature and that is Congress, [where] all the States are [represented].

[Justice] Brennan argues that the Court should consider only *the* purpose the Iowa legislators *actually* sought to achieve by the length limit, and not the purposes advanced by Iowa's lawyers in defense of the statute. This argument calls to mind what was said of the Roman Legions: that they may have lost battles, but they never lost a war, since they never let a war end until they had won it. [The] problems with a view such as that advanced in the concurring opinion are apparent. To name just a few, it assumes that individual legislators are motivated by one discernible "actual" purpose, and ignores the fact that different legislators may vote for a single piece of legislation for widely different reasons.

[The] effort in both the plurality and concurring opinions to portray the legislation involved here as protectionist is in error. Whenever a State enacts more stringent safety measures than its neighbors, in an area which affects commerce, the safety law will have the incidental effect of deflecting interstate commerce to the neighboring States. Indeed, the safety and protectionist motives cannot be separated: The whole purpose of safety regulation of vehicles is to *protect* the State from unsafe vehicles. If a neighboring State chooses *not* to protect its citizens from the danger discerned by the enacting State, that is its business, but the enacting State should not be penalized when the vehicles it considers unsafe travel through the neighboring State.

BALANCING INTERSTATE HARM AGAINST LOCAL BENEFIT

1. ***Deference to local safety concerns.*** Did Kassel pay insufficient attention to local safety concerns? Previous decisions had recognized some special state powers over safety in transportation. In **South Carolina State Highway Department v. Barnwell Bros.**, 303 U.S. 177 (1938), for example, the Court had upheld a 1933 South Carolina law prohibiting the use on state highways of trucks that were over 90 inches wide or that had a gross weight over 20,000 pounds. About 85 to 90% of the nation's trucks exceeded these limits. Justice STONE, writing for the Court, applied a deferential standard of review: "While the constitutional grant to Congress of power to regulate interstate commerce has been held to operate of its own force to curtail state power in some measure, it did not forestall all state action affecting interstate commerce. [Few] subjects of state regulation are so peculiarly of local concern as is the use of state highways. [Unlike] the railroads, local highways are built, owned and maintained by the state or its municipal subdivisions. The state has a primary and immediate concern in their safe and economical administration. [This] Court has often sustained the exercise of [state power over state highways] although it has burdened or impeded interstate commerce. [So] long as the state action does not discriminate, the burden is one which the Constitution permits because it is an inseparable incident of the exercise of a legislative authority, which, under the Constitution, has been left to the states."

By contrast, in **Southern Pacific Co. v. Arizona**, 325 U.S. 761 (1945), the Court had invalidated the Arizona Train Limit Law of 1912, which prohibited railroad trains of more than 14 passenger or 70 freight cars. Chief Justice STONE wrote for the Court: "[The] matters for ultimate determination here are the nature and extent of the burden which the state regulation of interstate trains, adopted as a safety measure, imposes on interstate commerce, and whether the relative weights of the state and national interests involved are such as to make inapplicable the rule, generally observed, that the free flow of interstate commerce and its freedom from local restraints in matters requiring uniformity of regulation are interests safeguarded by the commerce clause from state interference. [The] findings show that the operation of long trains [is] standard practice over the main lines of the railroads of the United States, and that, if the length of trains is to be regulated at all, national uniformity in the regulation adopted, such as only Congress can prescribe, is practically indispensable to the operation of an efficient and economical national railway [system].

"[The] decisive question is whether in the circumstances the total effect of the law as a safety measure in reducing accidents and casualties is so slight or problematical as not to outweigh the national interest in keeping interstate commerce free from interferences which seriously impede it and subject it to local regulation which does not have a uniform effect on the interstate train journey which it interrupts. [We] think, as the trial court found, that the Arizona Train Limit Law, viewed as a safety measure, affords at most slight and dubious advantage, if any, over unregulated train lengths [and] passes beyond what is plainly essential for safety. [Its] attempted regulation of the operation of interstate trains cannot establish nation-wide control such as is essential to the maintenance of an efficient transportation system, which Congress alone can prescribe."

Justice BLACK dissented, arguing: "[What] the Court today actually decides [is] this: [that] running shorter trains would increase the cost of railroad operations. [This] record in its entirety leaves me with no doubt whatever that many employees have been seriously injured and killed in the past, and that many more are likely to be so in the future, because of 'slack movement' in trains. [It] may be that offsetting dangers are possible in the operation of short trains. The balancing of these probabilities, however, is not in my judgment a matter for judicial determination, but one which calls for legislative consideration." Justice DOUGLAS also dissented, stating: "[My] view has been that the courts should intervene only where the state legislation discriminated against interstate commerce or was out of harmony with laws which Congress had enacted. [We] are dealing here with state legislation in the field of safety where the propriety of local regulation has long been recognized. Whether the question arises under the Commerce Clause or the Fourteenth Amendment, [the] legislation is entitled to a presumption of [validity]."

In **Bibb v. Navajo Freight Lines, Inc.**, 359 U.S. 520 (1959), the Court indicated that, even in trucking cases, it would invalidate facially neutral laws with a disproportionate effect on interstate commerce. An Illinois law requiring the use of contour mudguards on trucks and trailers operating on Illinois highways conflicted with an Arkansas rule requiring straight mudguards and forbidding contoured ones and was inconsistent with 45 states that authorized the use of straight mudguards. Justice DOUGLAS wrote for the Court: "Like any local law that conflicts with federal regulatory measures, [state] regulations that run afoul of the policy of free trade reflected in the Commerce Clause must also bow. This is one of those cases—few in number—where local safety measures that are nondiscriminatory place an unconstitutional burden on interstate commerce. [The] heavy burden which the Illinois mudguard law places on the interstate movement of trucks and trailers seems to us to pass the permissible limits even for safety regulations." Was Kassel simply an application of Bibb? If so, why did the decision so divide the Court?

2. ***State burdens on business entry.*** Pike balancing has also been used to invalidate state limits on business entry and regulation of corporate affairs. An early example was **Lewis v. BT Investment Managers, Inc.**, 447 U.S. 27 (1980). There, Justice BLACKMUN's opinion for a unanimous Court struck down a Florida law prohibiting ownership of local investment advisory businesses by out-of-state banks, bank holding companies and trust companies. The Court noted that the law "prevents competition in local markets by out-of-state firms with the kinds of resources and business interests that make them likely to attempt de novo entry" and found the law "parochial" in the sense that "it overtly prevents foreign enterprises from competing in local markets." Although Justice Blackmun noted that "on its face and in actual effect," the law displayed "a local favoritism or protectionism" that made it suspect under the Commerce Clause, he found it unnecessary to decide whether this was sufficient to render the law "per se invalid, for we are convinced that the disparate treatment of out-of-state bank holding companies cannot be justified as an incidental burden necessitated by legitimate local concerns."

The Court's attention shifted to state restraints on corporate takeover efforts in **Edgar v. Mite Corp.**, 457 U.S. 624 (1982). There, a sharply divided Court held unconstitutional the Illinois Business Take-Over Act, designed to regulate tender offers made to target companies that had certain specified business contacts with Illinois. Under the Act, takeover offers had to be registered with the Illinois Secretary of State 20 days before the offer became effective. During this 20-day period, the offeror could not communicate with shareholders, although the target company was free to disseminate information to them. The Secretary of State could refuse registration for lack of full and fair disclosure or where the offer was deemed inequitable or fraudulent. The only ground on which the majority could agree was the Pike balancing formula: the majority concluded that the Act imposed "a substantial burden on interstate commerce which outweighs its putative local benefits."

CTS Corp. v. Dynamics Corp. of America, 481 U.S. 69 (1987), involved a dormant commerce clause challenge to an Indiana law providing that a purchaser who acquired "control shares" in an Indiana corporation could acquire voting rights only to the extent approved by a majority vote of the prior disinterested stockholders. In addition to rejecting the argument that the Indiana law was preempted by the federal anti-takeover Williams Act, the Court rejected the Commerce Clause claim. Justice POWELL's majority opinion stated: "The principal objects of dormant Commerce Clause scrutiny are statutes that discriminate against interstate commerce. The Indiana Act is not such a statute. It has the same effects on tender offers whether or not the offeror is a domiciliary or resident of Indiana. [This] Court's recent Commerce Clause cases also have invalidated statutes that may adversely affect interstate commerce by subjecting activities to inconsistent regulations. The Indiana Act poses no such problem. So long as each State regulates voting rights only in the corporations it has created, each corporation will be subject to the law of only one State. [Every State] has enacted laws regulating corporate governance. By prohibiting certain transactions, and regulating others, such laws necessarily affect certain aspects of interstate commerce. [The] primary purpose of the Act is to protect the shareholders of Indiana corporations. It does this by affording shareholders, when a takeover offer is made, an opportunity to decide collectively whether the resulting change in voting control of the corporation, as they perceive it, would be desirable. A change of management may have important effects on the shareholders' interests; it is well within the State's role as overseer of corporate governance to offer this opportunity. The autonomy provided by allowing shareholders collectively to determine whether the takeover is advantageous to their interests may be especially beneficial where a hostile tender offer may coerce shareholders into tendering their shares.

"Appellee Dynamics responds to this concern by arguing that the prospect of coercive tender offers is illusory, and that tender offers generally should be favored because they reallocate corporate assets into the hands of management who can use them most effectively. [Indiana's] concern with tender offers is not groundless. Indeed, the potentially coercive aspects of tender offers have been recognized by the SEC and by a number of scholarly commentators. The Constitution does not require the States to subscribe to any particular economic theory. We are not inclined "to second-guess the empirical judgments of lawmakers concerning the utility of legislation" [Kassel (Brennan, J., concurring).] In our view, the possibility of coercion in some takeover bids offers additional justification for Indiana's decision to promote the autonomy of independent shareholders.

"Dynamics argues in any event that the State has 'no legitimate interest in protecting the nonresident shareholders.' [We] agree that Indiana has no interest in protecting nonresident shareholders *of nonresident corporations*. But this Act applies only to corporations incorporated in Indiana. [Indiana] has a substantial interest in preventing the corporate form from becoming a shield for unfair business dealing. Moreover, unlike the Illinois statute invalidated in MITE, the Indiana Act applies only to corporations that have a substantial number of shareholders in Indiana. Thus, every application of the Indiana Act will affect a substantial number of Indiana residents, whom Indiana indisputably has an interest in protecting. [On] its face, the Indiana [Act] evenhandedly determines the voting rights of shares of Indiana corporations. [To] the limited extent that the Act affects interstate commerce, this is justified by the State's interests in defining the attributes of shares in its corporations and in protecting shareholders."

Justice SCALIA concurred in part and in the judgment, rejecting the Pike balancing approach and suggesting that the Court limit itself to determining whether a state law "discriminates against interstate commerce" or "create[s] an impermissible risk of inconsistent regulation by different States": "[A] law can be both economic folly and constitutional. The Indiana [Act] is at least the latter." Justice WHITE's dissent, joined by Justices Blackmun and Stevens, concluded in part that the Act "directly inhibits interstate commerce, the very economic consequences the Commerce Clause was intended to prevent": "[It] is clear that Indiana is directly regulating the purchase and sale of shares of stock in interstate commerce. Appellant CTS' stock is traded on the New York Stock Exchange, and people from all over the country buy and sell CTS' shares daily. Yet, under Indiana's scheme, any prospective purchaser will be effectively precluded from purchasing CTS' shares if the purchaser crosses one of the Chapter's threshold ownership levels and a majority of CTS' shareholders refuse to give the purchaser voting rights. This Court should not countenance such a restraint on interstate trade."

Does the CTS case represent a de-emphasis on balancing? After CTS and Minnesota v. Clover Leaf, above, is there any genuine bite left to dormant commerce clause scrutiny of facially neutral laws that merely burden interstate commerce? Or does MITE, which applied the Pike balancing formula to a wholly nondiscriminatory state law, suggest that balancing still plays an important role even in the absence of hostile economic purposes?

SECTION 2. THE INTERSTATE PRIVILEGES AND IMMUNITIES CLAUSE OF ARTICLE IV

The Privileges and Immunities Clause of Art. IV, § 2, states: "The Citizens of each State shall be entitled to all Privileges and Immunities of Citizens in the several States." Like the dormant commerce clause, it serves as a restraint on state efforts to bar out-of-staters from access to local resources. As the Court noted in Hicklin v. Orbeck, 437 U.S. 518 (1978), there is a "mutually reinforcing relationship between the Privileges and Immunities Clause of Art. IV, § 2, and the Commerce Clause—a relationship that stems [in part from] their shared vision of federalism." And like the Fourteenth Amendment Equal Protection Clause, it protects citizens against discrimination—here, on the basis of state residency.

While related, Art. IV, § 2 and the dormant commerce clause have important differences: First, corporations enjoy no protection under the Privileges and Immunities Clause. Paul v. Virginia, 75 U.S. (8 Wall.) 168 (1869). Second, Congress may authorize, through affirmative exercise of its commerce power, state practices that would otherwise be impermissible under the dormant commerce clause; the Privileges and Immunities Clause, by contrast, is arguably a rights provision that Congress may not waive. Third, the Privileges and Immunities Clause safeguards only the exercise of "fundamental rights," unlike the dormant commerce clause. See Justice Bushrod Washington's classic statement in Corfield v. Coryell, 4 Wash.C.C. 371, 6 F.Cas. 546 (C.C.E.D.Pa.1823). And fourth, the Court has declined to recognize any "market participant" exception under the Privileges and Immunities Clause as it has under dormant commerce clause review.

The last difference is illustrated in the following case, which involved a challenge to a Camden, New Jersey, ordinance requiring that at least 40% of the employees of contractors and subcontractors working on city construction projects be Camden residents. This time, the Supreme Court found potential merit in the challenge, rejected a claim of market participant exemption, and remanded the case:

United Building & Construction Trades Council v. Mayor and Council of Camden

465 U.S. 208, 104 S. Ct. 1020, 79 L. Ed. 2d 249 (1984).

[The Camden ordinance required: "The developer/contractor, in hiring for jobs, shall make every effort to employ persons residing within the City of Camden but, in no event, shall less than forty percent (40%) of the entire labor force be residents of the City of Camden." The contractor was also obliged to ensure that any subcontractors working on such projects adhered to the same requirement. The United Building and Construction Trades Council of Camden challenged the ordinance as a violation of both the

Privileges and Immunities Clause of Art. IV and the dormant commerce clause. After the case was filed, the Supreme Court rejected the dormant commerce clause challenge to the substantially identical local jobs preference order in White v. Mass. Construction Council, discussed in South-Central Timber Development, Inc. v. Wunnicke, p. 248 above, but specifically declined to reach the merits of a privileges and immunities challenge to the Boston program because the Massachusetts court had not reached that issue. Accordingly, the Camden Council dropped its Commerce Clause challenge but pressed its privileges and immunities challenge.]

■ JUSTICE REHNQUIST delivered the opinion of the Court.

The Supreme Court of New Jersey "[declined] to apply the Privileges and Immunities Clause in the context of a municipal ordinance that has identical effects upon out-of-state citizens and New Jersey citizens not residing in the locality." [Two] separate contentions are advanced in support of this position: first, that the Clause only applies to laws passed by a *State* and, second, that the Clause only applies to laws that discriminate on the basis of *state* citizenship. The first argument can be quickly rejected. [It] is as true of the Privileges and Immunities Clause as of the Equal Protection Clause that what would be unconstitutional if done directly by the State can no more readily be accomplished by a city deriving its authority from the State. Thus, even if the ordinance had been adopted solely by Camden, and not pursuant to a state program or with state approval, the hiring preference would still have to comport with the [Clause].

The second argument merits more consideration. The New Jersey Supreme Court concluded that the [Clause] does not apply to an ordinance that discriminates solely on the basis of *municipal* residency. The Clause is phrased in terms of *state* [citizenship]. "The primary purpose of this clause [was] to help fuse into one Nation a collection of independent, sovereign States. It was designed to insure to a citizen of State A who ventures into State B the same privileges which the citizens of State B enjoy. For protection of such equality the citizen of State A was not to be restricted to the uncertain remedies afforded by diplomatic processes and official retaliation." Municipal residency classifications, it is argued, simply do not give rise to the same concerns.

We cannot accept this argument. We have never read the Clause so literally as to apply it only to distinctions based on state citizenship. [Despite] some initial uncertainty, it is now established that the terms "citizen" and "resident" are "essentially interchangeable" for purposes of analysis of most cases under the [clause]. A person who is not residing in a given State is ipso facto not residing in a city within that State. Thus, whether the exercise of a privilege is conditioned on state residency or on municipal residency, he will just as surely be excluded.

Given the Camden ordinance, an out-of-state citizen who ventures into New Jersey will not enjoy the same privileges as the New Jersey citizen residing in Camden. It is true that New Jersey citizens not residing in Camden will be affected by the ordinance as well as out-of-state citizens. And it is true that the disadvantaged New Jersey residents have no claim under the Privileges and Immunities Clause. But New Jersey residents at least have a chance to remedy at the polls any discrimination against them. Out-of-state citizens have no similar opportunity, and they must "not be restricted to the uncertain remedies afforded by diplomatic processes and official retaliation."[1] We conclude that Camden's ordinance is not immune from constitutional review at the behest of out-of-state residents merely because some in-state residents are similarly disadvantaged.

Application of the [Clause] to a particular instance of discrimination against out-of-state residents entails a two-step inquiry. As an initial matter, the court must decide whether the ordinance burdens one of those privileges and immunities protected by the Clause. [Baldwin].[2] Not all forms of discrimination against citizens of other States are constitutionally suspect. "Some distinctions between residents and nonresidents merely reflect the fact that this is a Nation composed of individual States, and are permitted; other distinctions are prohibited because they hinder the formation, the purpose, or the development of a single Union of those States. Only with respect to those 'privileges' and 'immunities' bearing upon the vitality of the Nation as a single entity must the State treat all citizens, resident and nonresident, equally."

As a threshold matter, then, we must determine whether an out-of-state resident's interest in employment on public works contracts in another State is sufficiently "fundamental" to the promotion of interstate harmony so as to "fall within the purview of the [Clause]." Certainly, the pursuit of a common calling is one of the most fundamental of those privileges protected by the Clause. [Public] employment, however, is qualitatively different from employment in the private sector; it is a subspecies of the broader opportunity to pursue a common calling. We have held that there is no fundamental right to government employment for purposes of the Equal Protection Clause. And in White we held that for purposes of the Commerce Clause everyone employed on a city public works project is, "in a substantial if informal sense, 'working for the city.' "

It can certainly be argued that for purposes of the Privileges and Immunities Clause everyone affected by the Camden ordinance is also

[1] The dissent suggests that New Jersey citizens not residing in Camden will adequately protect the interests of out-of-state residents and that the scope of the [Clause] should be measured in light of this political reality. What the dissent fails to appreciate is that the Camden ordinance at issue in this case was adopted pursuant to a comprehensive, state-wide program applicable in all New Jersey cities. The Camden resident-preference ordinance has already received state sanction and approval, and every New Jersey city is free to adopt a similar protectionist measure. Some have already done so. Thus, it is hard to see how New Jersey residents living outside Camden will protect the interests of out-of-state citizens.

More fundamentally, the dissent's proposed blanket exemption for all classifications that are less than state-wide would provide States with a simple means for evading the strictures of the [Clause]. Suppose, for example, that California wanted to guarantee that all employees of contractors and subcontractors working on construction projects funded in whole or in part by state funds are state residents. Under the dissent's analysis, the California legislature need merely divide the State in half, providing one resident-hiring preference for Northern Californians on all such projects taking place in Northern California, and one for Southern Californians on all projects taking place in Southern California. State residents generally would benefit from the law at the expense of out-of-state residents; yet, the law would be immune from scrutiny under the Clause simply because it was not phrased in terms of *state* citizenship or residency. Such a formalistic construction would effectively write the Clause out of the Constitution. [Footnote by Justice Rehnquist.]

[2] Baldwin v. Montana Fish and Game Comm'n, 436 U.S. 371 (1978), rejected an Art. IV challenge to a Montana elk-hunting license scheme imposing substantially higher fees on nonresidents than on residents. The majority opinion by Justice Blackmun (the dissenter in the Camden case) insisted that the precedents could best be understood in terms of the "fundamental rights" approach of Corfield v. Coryell, and concluded that, "[w]hatever rights or activities may be 'fundamental' " under Art. IV, "elk hunting by nonresidents in Montana is not one of them."

"working for the city" and, therefore, has no grounds for complaint when the city favors its own residents. But we decline to transfer mechanically into this context an analysis fashioned to fit the Commerce Clause. Our decision in White turned on a distinction between the city acting as a market participant and the city acting as a market regulator. The question whether employees of contractors and subcontractors on public works projects were or were not, in some sense, working for the city was crucial to that analysis. [But] the distinction between market participant and market regulator relied upon in White to dispose of the Commerce Clause challenge is not dispositive in this context. The two Clauses have different aims and set different standards for state conduct.

The Commerce Clause acts as an implied restraint upon state regulatory powers. Such powers must give way before the superior authority of Congress to legislate on (or leave unregulated) matters involving interstate commerce. When the State acts solely as a market participant, no conflict between state *regulation* and federal regulatory authority can arise. The Privileges and Immunities Clause, on the other hand, imposes a direct restraint on state action in the interests of interstate harmony. Hicklin v. Orbeck.[3] This concern with comity cuts across the market regulator-market participant distinction that is crucial under the Commerce Clause. It is discrimination against out-of-state residents on matters of fundamental concern which triggers the Clause, not regulation affecting interstate commerce. Thus, the fact that Camden is merely setting conditions on its expenditures for goods and services in the marketplace does not preclude the possibility that those conditions violate the Privileges and Immunities Clause. [The] fact that Camden is expending its own funds or funds it administers in accordance with the terms of a grant is certainly a factor—perhaps the crucial factor—to be considered in evaluating whether the statute's discrimination violates the [Clause]. But it does not remove the Camden ordinance completely from the purview of the Clause.

In sum, Camden may, without fear of violating the Commerce Clause, pressure private employers engaged in public works projects funded in whole or in part by the city to hire city residents. But that same exercise of power to bias the employment decisions of [contractors] against out-of-state residents may be called to account under the Privileges and Immunities Clause. A determination of whether a privilege is "fundamental" for purposes of that Clause does not depend on whether the employees of private contractors and subcontractors engaged in public works projects can or cannot be said to be "working for the city." The opportunity to seek employment with such private employers is "sufficiently basic to the livelihood of the Nation" [Baldwin] as to fall within the purview of the [Clause] even though the contractors and subcontractors are themselves engaged in projects funded in whole or part by the city.

[3] Hicklin v. Orbeck, 437 U.S. 518 (1978), was a unanimous decision invalidating an Alaska law requiring that residents be preferred over nonresidents in certain jobs. The "Alaska Hire" law was "an attempt to force virtually all businesses that benefit in some way from the economic ripple effect of Alaska's decision to develop its oil and gas resources to bias their employment practices in favor of the State's residents." Justice Brennan's opinion stated that Alaska had not demonstrated "that nonresidents were 'a peculiar source of the evil' [the law] was enacted to remedy, namely Alaska's 'uniquely high unemployment.' " He accordingly concluded that Alaska's discrimination against nonresidents did not "bear a substantial relationship to the particular 'evil' they [were] said to present."

The conclusion that Camden's ordinance discriminates against a protected privilege does not, of course, end the inquiry. We have stressed in prior cases that "[l]ike many other constitutional provisions, the privileges and immunities clause is not an absolute." It does not preclude discrimination against citizens of other States where there is a "substantial reason" for the difference in treatment. "[T]he inquiry in each case must be concerned with whether such reasons do exist and whether the degree of discrimination bears a close relation to them." Id. As part of any justification offered for the discriminatory law, nonresidents must somehow be shown to "constitute a peculiar source of the evil at which the statute is aimed."

[Camden] contends that its ordinance is necessary to counteract grave economic and social ills. Spiralling unemployment, a sharp decline in population, and a dramatic reduction in the number of businesses located in the city have eroded property values and depleted the city's tax base. The resident hiring preference is designed, the city contends, to increase the number of employed persons living in Camden and to arrest the "middle class flight" currently plaguing the city. The city also argues that all non-Camden residents employed on city public works projects, whether they reside in New Jersey or Pennsylvania, constitute a "source of the evil at which the statute is aimed." That is, they "live off" Camden without "living in" Camden. Camden contends that the scope of the discrimination practiced in the ordinance, with its municipal residency requirement, is carefully tailored to alleviate this evil without unreasonably harming nonresidents, who still have access to 60% of the available positions.

Every inquiry under the Privileges and Immunities Clause "must [be] conducted with due regard for the principle that the states should have considerable leeway in analyzing local evils and in prescribing appropriate cures." This caution is particularly appropriate when a government body is merely setting conditions on the expenditure of funds it controls. The Alaska Hire statute at issue in Hicklin v. Orbeck swept within its strictures not only contractors and subcontractors dealing directly with the State's oil and gas; it also covered suppliers who provided goods and services to those contractors and subcontractors. We invalidated the Act as "an attempt to force virtually all businesses that benefit in some way from the economic ripple effect of Alaska's decision to develop its oil and gas resources to bias their employment practices in favor of the State's residents." No similar "ripple effect" appears to infect the Camden ordinance. It is limited in scope to employees working directly on city public works projects. Nonetheless, we find it impossible to evaluate Camden's justification on the record as it now stands. No trial has ever been held in the case. No findings of fact have been made. The Supreme Court of New Jersey certified the case for direct appeal after the brief administrative proceedings that led to approval of the ordinance by the State Treasurer. It would not be appropriate for this Court either to make factual determinations as an initial matter or to take judicial notice of Camden's decay. We, therefore, deem it wise to remand the case to the [New Jersey Supreme Court to make the necessary findings]. [Reversed and remanded.]

■ JUSTICE BLACKMUN, dissenting.

For over a century the underlying meaning of the Privileges and Immunities Clause [has] been regarded as settled: at least absent some substantial noninvidious justification, a State may not discriminate between its own residents and residents of other States on the basis of state citizenship. Today, however, the Court casually extends the scope of the Clause by holding that it applies to laws that discriminate *among* state residents on the basis of *municipal* residence, simply because discrimination on the basis of municipal residence disadvantages citizens of other States "ipso facto." This novel interpretation arrives accompanied by little practical justification and no historical or textual support whatsoever. [Both] the text of the Clause and the historical record confirm that the Framers meant to foreclose any one State from denying citizens of other States the same "privileges and immunities" accorded its own citizens. [While] the Framers [conceived of the Clause] as an instrument for frustrating discrimination based on state citizenship, there is no evidence of any sort that they were concerned by intrastate discrimination based on municipal residence. The most obvious reason for this is also the most simple one: by the time the Constitution was enacted, such discrimination was rarely practiced and even more rarely successful.

[Finally,] the Court fails to attend to the functional considerations that underlie the [Clause]. The Clause has been a necessary limitation on state autonomy not simply because of the self-interest of individual States, but because state parochialism is likely to go unchecked by state political processes when those who are disadvantaged are by definition disenfranchised as well. The Clause remedies this breakdown in the representative process by requiring state residents to bear the same burdens that they choose to place on nonresidents; "by constitutionally tying the fate of outsiders to the fate of those possessing political power, the framers insured that their interests would be well looked after." Ely, Democracy and Distrust 83 (1980). As a practical matter, therefore, the scope of the Clause may be measured by asking whether failure to link the interests of those who are disadvantaged with the interests of those who are preferred will consign the former group to "the uncertain remedies afforded by diplomatic processes and official retaliation."

Contrary to the Court's tacit assumption, discrimination on the basis of municipal residence is substantially different in this regard from discrimination on the basis of state citizenship. The distinction is simple but fundamental: discrimination on the basis of municipal residence penalizes persons within the State's political community as well as those without. The Court itself points out that while New Jersey citizens who reside outside Camden are not protected by the [Clause], they may resort to the State's political processes to protect themselves. What the Court fails to appreciate is that this avenue of relief for New Jersey residents works to protect residents of other States as well; disadvantaged state residents who turn to the state legislature to displace ordinances like Camden's further the interests of nonresidents as well as their own. Nor is this mechanism for relief merely a theoretical one: in the past decade, several States [have] repealed or forbidden protectionist ordinances like the one at issue here. The Court [has] applied the [Clause] without regard for the political ills [that] it was designed to cure.[4]

[4] The Court raises the alternative prospect that a State might evade the [Clause] by dividing itself in half and granting the residents in each half of the State employment preferences over residents in the other half of the State. The Clause exists to protect against those classifications that a State's political process cannot be relied on to prevent, however, not those that it can, and there is no reason to believe that state residents will be willing to forgo access to employment in one half of a State merely to obtain privileged access to jobs in the other half. The fact that no State has attempted anything resembling the Court's proposed maneuver

---

THE SCOPE AND LIMITS OF INTERSTATE PRIVILEGES AND IMMUNITIES

1. ***The threshold requirement of an Art. IV "privilege."*** Note that not every activity that a state might regulate counts as a "privilege" of interstate citizenship. Only "fundamental" activities count. As Camden reiterated, private employment is sufficiently "fundamental" to constitute such a privilege. The Court did not reach the question whether public employment would count similarly. Does state-licensed employment count as such a privilege? In **Supreme Court of New Hampshire v. Piper**, 470 U.S. 274 (1985), the Court held that a state rule limiting bar admission to in-state residents violated the Privileges and Immunities Clause. The challenge was brought by a woman who lived in Vermont, 400 yards from the New Hampshire border, and took and passed the New Hampshire bar examination, but was denied admission to the bar because she was a nonresident.

Justice POWELL's majority opinion found that her claim involved a "privilege" under the Clause because, "[l]ike the occupations considered in our earlier cases, the practice of law is important to the national economy." He noted, moreover, the legal profession's role in representing "persons who raise unpopular federal claims." He found none of the state's asserted justifications for the discrimination sufficient under the standard of the Camden case. He pointed out: "The Clause does not preclude discrimination against nonresidents where: (i) there is a substantial reason for the difference in treatment; and (ii) the discrimination practiced against nonresidents bears a substantial relationship to the State's objective. [In] deciding whether the discrimination bears a close or substantial relationship to the State's objective, the Court has considered the availability of less restrictive means." Here, the State argued that nonresident members of the bar would be less likely "to become, and remain, familiar with local rules and procedures," to "behave ethically," to "be available for court proceedings," and to "do pro bono and other volunteer work in the State." Justice Powell concluded: "We find that none of these reasons meets the test of 'substantiality,' and that the means chosen do not bear the necessary relationship to the State's objectives."

Justice REHNQUIST's dissent argued that "the practice of law [is] fundamentally different from those other occupations that are practiced across state lines without significant deviation from State to State." He especially stressed the State's interest "in maximizing the number of resident lawyers, so as to increase the quality of the pool from which its lawmakers can be drawn." Moreover, he found the Court's "less restrictive means" analysis "both ill-advised and potentially unmanageable." He insisted that "such an analysis, when carried too far, will ultimately lead to striking down almost any statute on the ground that the Court could think of another 'less restrictive' way to write it," and that "the less-restrictive-

---

in the two centuries since the adoption of the Clause, despite the fact that none of this Court's precedents has foreclosed the option, strongly suggests that state political processes can be trusted to prevent this kind of Balkanization. The Court cannot justify deforming the Constitution's response to real problems by invoking imaginary and unrealistic ones. [Footnote by Justice Blackmun.]

means analysis, which is borrowed from our First Amendment jurisprudence," was "out of place in the context" of Art. IV.

2. ***Justifying differential treatment of outsiders under Art. IV.*** Note that the tests set forth in Camden and Piper employ intermediate rather than strict scrutiny. Unlike the dormant commerce clause, which permits facial discrimination only if the government has a compelling interest for which the law is the least restrictive means (recall Maine v. Taylor, the baitfish case), privileges and immunities review requires only a substantial interest to which the government's reason is closely related. Under that less demanding standard of review, should Camden's jobs preference program have survived privileges and immunities scrutiny upon remand? (The actual case was settled.) What facts and arguments would be relevant to this analysis? How could non-Camden residents be portrayed as a "peculiar source of the evil at which the statute is aimed"? Would the barrier in Piper survive dormant commerce clause scrutiny? Given its explicit prohibition of discrimination, is Art. IV a more legitimate vehicle than the dormant commerce clause for judicially created restraints on state burdens on interstate commerce? See Eule, "Laying the Dormant Commerce Clause to Rest," 91 Yale L.J. 425 (1982).

SECTION 3. CONGRESSIONAL ORDERING OF FEDERAL-STATE RELATIONSHIPS BY PREEMPTION AND CONSENT

CONGRESSIONAL PREEMPTION OF STATE REGULATION

The "dormant" Commerce Clause limits state regulatory power in the absence of congressional action. The Commerce Clause is not "dormant," however, when Congress affirmatively exercises that power. When Congress exercises a granted power, the federal law may supersede a contrary state law because of the operation of the Supremacy Clause of Article VI. When a valid federal statute explicitly bars certain types of state action, there is no difficulty in finding state laws preempted. But problems arise when the federal legislation does not clearly disclose its intended impact on state laws. In those situations, the claim is nevertheless often made that congressional action preempts state authority regarding the same subject matter. The Court's preemption rulings often turn on a determination of congressional intent in the setting of the particular text, history and purposes of the federal legislation involved. A classic analysis along these lines appears in the PG & E case that follows.

Pacific Gas & Elec. Co. v. State Energy Resources Conservation & Development Comm'n

461 U.S. 190, 103 S. Ct. 1713, 75 L. Ed. 2d 752 (1983).

[This case arose from a California law dealing with the problem of finding a long-term solution for disposing of nuclear waste. Sec. 25524.2 of the law, adopted in 1976, imposed a moratorium on the certification of nuclear energy plants until the State Energy Resources Conservation & Development Commission "finds that there has been developed and that the United States through its authorized agency has approved and there exists a demonstrated technology or means for the disposal of high-level nuclear waste." "Disposal" is defined as a "method for the permanent and terminal disposition" of such waste. PG & E sought a declaratory judgment that this provision was preempted by the federal Atomic Energy Act of 1954 as amended and therefore invalid under the Supremacy Clause. The Supreme Court rejected the preemption challenge and upheld the state law:

■ JUSTICE WHITE delivered the opinion of the Court.

The turning of swords into plowshares has symbolized the transformation of atomic power into a source of energy in American society. To facilitate this development the federal government relaxed its monopoly over fissionable materials and nuclear technology, and in its place, erected a complex scheme to promote the civilian development of nuclear energy, while seeking to safeguard the public and the environment from the unpredictable risks of a new technology. Early on, it was decided that the states would continue their traditional role in the regulation of electricity production. The interrelationship of federal and state authority in the nuclear energy field has not been simple. [This] case emerges from the intersection of the federal government's efforts to ensure that nuclear power is safe with the exercise of the historic state authority over the generation and sale of electricity.

[A] nuclear reactor must be periodically refueled and the "spent fuel" removed. This spent fuel is intensely radioactive and must be carefully stored. The general practice is to store the fuel in a water-filled pool at the reactor site. For many years, it was assumed that this fuel would be reprocessed; accordingly, the storage pools were designed as short-term holding facilities with limited storage capacities. As expectations for reprocessing remained unfulfilled, the spent fuel accumulated in the storage pools, creating the risk that nuclear reactors would have to be shut down. This could occur if there were insufficient room in the pool to store spent fuel and also if there were not enough space to hold the entire fuel core when certain inspections or emergencies required unloading of the reactor. In recent years, the problem has taken on special urgency. [Government] studies indicate that a number of reactors could be forced to shut down in the near future due to the inability to store spent fuel.

There is a second dimension to the problem. Even with water-pools adequate to store safely all the spent fuel produced during the working lifetime of the reactor, permanent disposal is needed because the wastes will remain radioactive for thousands of years. A number of long-term nuclear waste management strategies have been extensively examined. These range from sinking the wastes in stable deep seabeds, to placing the wastes beneath ice sheets in Greenland and Antarctica, to ejecting the wastes into space by rocket. The greatest attention has been focused on disposing of the wastes in subsurface geologic repositories such as salt deposits. Problems of how and where to store nuclear wastes [have] engendered considerable scientific, political, and public debate. There are both safety and economic aspects to the nuclear waste issue: first, if not properly stored, nuclear wastes might leak and endanger both the environment and human health; second, the lack of a long-term disposal option increases the risk that the insufficiency of interim storage space for spent fuel will lead to reactor-shutdowns, rendering nuclear energy an unpredictable and uneconomical adventure. The California [laws] at issue here are responses to these [concerns].

It is well-established that within Constitutional limits Congress may preempt state authority by so stating in express terms. Absent explicit preemptive language, Congress' intent to supersede state law altogether may be found from a "scheme of federal regulation so pervasive as to make reasonable the inference that Congress left no room to supplement it," "because the Act of Congress may touch a field in which the federal interest is so dominant that the federal system will be assumed to preclude enforcement of state laws on the same subject," or because "the object sought to be obtained by the federal law and the character of obligations imposed by it may reveal the same purpose." [Rice, below.] Even where Congress has not entirely displaced state regulation in a specific area, state law is preempted to the extent that it actually conflicts with federal law. Such a conflict arises when "compliance with both federal and state regulations is a physical impossibility" [Florida Lime, below], or where state law "stands as an obstacle to the accomplishment and execution of the full purposes and objectives of Congress." [Hines v. Davidowitz, below].

Petitioners [present] three major lines of argument as to why § 25524.2 is preempted. First, they submit that the statute—because it regulates construction of nuclear plants and because it is allegedly predicated on safety concerns—ignores the division between federal and state authority created by the Atomic Energy Act, and falls within the field that the federal government has preserved for its own exclusive control. Second, the statute, and the judgments that underlie it, conflict with decisions concerning the nuclear waste disposal issue made by Congress and the [federal] Nuclear Regulatory Commission. Third, the California statute frustrates the federal goal of developing nuclear technology as a source of energy. We consider each of these contentions in turn.

A. Even a brief perusal of the Atomic Energy Act reveals that, despite its comprehensiveness, it does not at any point expressly require the States to construct or authorize nuclear power plants or prohibit the States from deciding [not] to permit the construction of any further reactors. Instead, petitioners argue that the Act is intended to preserve the federal government as the sole regulator of all matters nuclear, and that § 25524.2 falls within the scope of this impliedly preempted field. But as we view the issue, Congress, in passing the 1954 Act and in subsequently amending it, intended that the federal government should regulate the radiological safety aspects involved in the construction and operation of a nuclear plant, but that the States retain their traditional responsibility in the field of regulating electrical utilities for determining questions of need, reliability, cost and other related state concerns. Need for new power facilities, their economic feasibility, and rates and services, are areas that have been characteristically governed by the States. [Thus], "Congress legislated here in a field which the States have traditionally occupied [so] we start with the assumption that the historic police powers of the States were not to be superseded by the Federal Act unless that was the clear and manifest purpose of Congress." [Rice.]

The Atomic Energy Act must be read, however, against another background. [Until 1954] the use, control and ownership of nuclear technology remained a federal monopoly. The Atomic Energy Act of 1954 grew out of Congress' determination that the national interest would be best served if the Government encouraged the private sector to become involved in the development of atomic energy for peaceful purposes under a program of federal regulation and licensing. The Act implemented this policy decision by providing for licensing of private construction, ownership, and operation of commercial nuclear power reactors. The AEC, however, was given exclusive jurisdiction to license the transfer, delivery, receipt, acquisition, possession and use of nuclear materials. Upon these subjects, no role was left for the states.

The Commission, however, was not given authority over the generation of electricity itself, or over the economic question whether a particular plant should be built. [The] Nuclear Regulatory Commission (NRC), which now exercises the AEC's regulatory authority, does not purport to exercise its authority based on economic considerations, [and] utility financial qualifications are only of concern to the NRC if related to the public health and safety. It is almost inconceivable that Congress would have left a regulatory vacuum; the only reasonable inference is that Congress intended the states to continue to make these judgments. Any doubt that ratemaking and plant-need questions were to remain in state hands was removed by § 271, which provided: "Nothing in this chapter shall be construed to affect the authority or regulations of any Federal, State or local agency with respect to the generation, sale, or transmission of electric power produced through the use of nuclear facilities licensed by the [Commission]." [This] account indicates that from the passage of the Atomic Energy Act in 1954 [to] the present day, Congress has preserved the dual regulation of nuclear-powered electricity generation: the federal government maintains complete control of the safety and "nuclear" aspects of energy generation; the states exercise their traditional authority over the need for additional generating capacity, the type of generating facilities to be licensed, land use, ratemaking, and the like.

The above is not particularly controversial. But deciding how § 25524.2 is to be construed and classified is a more difficult proposition. At the outset, we emphasize that the statute does not seek to regulate the construction or operation of a nuclear power plant. It would clearly be impermissible for California to attempt to do so, for such regulation, even if enacted out of non-safety concerns, would nevertheless directly conflict with the NRC's exclusive authority over plant construction and operation. Respondents appear to concede as much. Respondents do broadly argue, however, that although safety regulation of nuclear plants by states is forbidden, a state may completely prohibit new construction until its safety concerns are satisfied by the federal government. We reject this line of reasoning. State safety regulation is not preempted only when it conflicts with federal law. Rather, the federal government has occupied the entire field of nuclear safety concerns, except the limited powers expressly ceded to the states. When the federal government completely occupies a given field or an identifiable portion of it, as it has done here, the test of preemption is whether "the matter on which the state asserts the right to act is in any way regulated by the federal government." [Rice.] A state moratorium on nuclear construction grounded in safety concerns falls squarely within the prohibited field. Moreover, a state judgment that nuclear power is not safe enough to be further developed would conflict directly with the countervailing judgment of the NRC that nuclear construction may proceed notwithstanding extant uncertainties as to waste disposal. A state prohibition on nuclear construction for safety reasons would also be in the teeth of the Atomic

Energy Act's objective to insure that nuclear technology be safe enough for widespread development and use—and would be preempted for that reason.

That being the case, it is necessary to determine whether there is a nonsafety rationale for § 25524.2. [The California Assembly Committee which proposed the bill] reported that the waste disposal problem was "largely economic or the result of poor planning, *not* safety related." The Committee explained that the lack of a federally approved method of waste disposal created a "clog" in the nuclear fuel cycle. Storage space was limited while more nuclear wastes were continuously produced. Without a permanent means of disposal, the nuclear waste problem could become critical leading to unpredictably high costs to contain the problem or, worse, shutdowns in reactors. "Waste disposal *safety,*" the [Committee] notes, "is not directly addressed by the bills, which ask only that a method [of waste disposal] be chosen and accepted by the federal government." [Although specific] indicia of California's intent in enacting § 25524.2 are subject to varying interpretation, [we] should not become embroiled in attempting to ascertain California's true motive. First, inquiry into legislative motive is often an unsatisfactory venture. [Second], it would be particularly pointless for us to engage in such inquiry here when it is clear that the states have been allowed to retain authority over the need for electrical generating facilities easily sufficient to permit a state so inclined to halt the construction of new nuclear plants by refusing on economic grounds to issue certificates of public convenience in individual proceedings. In these circumstances, it should be up to Congress to determine whether a state has misused the authority left in its hands. Therefore, we accept California's avowed economic purpose as the rationale for enacting § 25524.2. Accordingly, the statute lies outside the occupied field of nuclear safety regulation.

B. Petitioners' second major argument concerns federal regulation aimed at the nuclear waste disposal problem itself. It is contended that § 25524.2 conflicts with federal regulation of nuclear waste disposal, with the NRC's decision that it is permissible to continue to license reactors, notwithstanding uncertainty surrounding the waste disposal problem, and with Congress' recent passage of legislation directed at that problem.

[The NRC has promulgated extensive and detailed regulations concerning the operation of nuclear facilities and the handling of nuclear materials. The regulations specify design and control requirements for fuel storage and handling of radioactive waste, both at the reactor site and away from the reactor. But no federal agency has yet licensed any permanent disposal facilities, and there is continued authorization of storage of spent fuel at reactor sites in pools of water. In 1977, the NRC refused to halt reactor licensing until a method of permanent disposal was certified.] The NRC's imprimatur, however, indicates only that it is safe to proceed with such plants, not that it is economically wise to do so. Because the NRC order does not and could not compel a utility to develop a nuclear plant, compliance with both it and § 25524.2 are possible. Moreover, because the NRC's regulations are aimed at insuring that plants are safe, not necessarily that they are economical, § 25524.2 does not interfere with the objective of the federal regulation. Nor has California sought through § 25524.2 to impose its own standards on nuclear waste disposal. The statute accepts that it is the federal responsibility to develop and license such technology. As there is no attempt on California's part to enter this field, one which is occupied by the federal government, we do not find § 25524.2 preempted any more by the NRC's obligations in the waste disposal field than by its licensing power over the plants [themselves].

C. Finally, it is strongly contended that § 25524.2 frustrates the Atomic Energy Act's purpose to develop the commercial use of nuclear power. It is well established that state law is preempted if it "stands as an obstacle to the accomplishment of the full purposes and objectives of Congress." [E.g., Hines; Florida Lime]. There is little doubt that a primary purpose of the Atomic Energy Act was, and continues to be, the promotion of nuclear power. [The] Court of Appeals is right, however, that the promotion of nuclear power is not to be accomplished "at all costs." The elaborate licensing and safety provisions and the continued preservation of state regulation in traditional areas belie that. Moreover, Congress has allowed the States to determine—as a matter of economics—whether a nuclear plant vis-a-vis a fossil fuel plant should be built. The decision of California to exercise that authority does not, in itself, constitute a basis for preemption. Therefore, while the argument of petitioners and the United States has considerable force, the legal reality remains that Congress has left sufficient authority in the states to allow the development of nuclear power to be slowed or even stopped for economic reasons. Given this statutory scheme, it is for Congress to rethink the division of regulatory authority in light of its possible exercise by the states to undercut a federal objective. The courts should not assume the role which our system assigns to Congress. [Affirmed.]

■ JUSTICE BLACKMUN, with whom JUSTICE STEVENS joins, concurring in part and concurring in the judgment.

I join the Court's opinion, except to the extent it suggests that a State may not prohibit the construction of nuclear power plants if the State is motivated by concerns about the safety of such plants. Since the Court finds that California was not so motivated, this suggestion is unnecessary to the Court's holding.

MODES OF PREEMPTION ANALYSIS

1. ***Types of preemption.*** As the Court acknowledged in PG&E, Congress may preempt state power to regulate in three ways: by express statement, by implied occupation of a regulatory field, or by implied preclusion of conflicting state regulations.

a. *Express preemption.* When preemption is *express,* the only issue is whether a state statute falls within the area preempted. The two types of implied preemption, however, require further analysis.

b. *Field preemption.* The Court requires a clear showing that Congress meant to occupy a field and so displace the states from regulation on that subject matter. In **Rice v. Santa Fe Elevator Corp.**, 331 U.S. 218 (1947), Justice DOUGLAS's majority opinion stated: "The question in each case is what the purpose of Congress was. Congress legislated here in a field which the States have traditionally occupied [grain warehousing practices]. So we start with the assumption that the historic police powers of the States were not to be superseded by the Federal Act unless that was the clear and manifest purpose of Congress. Such a purpose may be evidenced in several ways. The scheme of federal regulation may be so pervasive as to make reasonable the inference that Congress left no room for the States to supplement it. Or the Act of Congress may touch a field in which the federal interest is so dominant that the federal system will be assumed to preclude enforcement of state laws on the same subject." Why should the Court apply a strong presumption against field regulation in areas of traditionally local concern? Because field preemption creates at least a temporary regulatory vacuum, in which neither the states nor Congress are acting?

c. *Conflict preemption.* In **Hines v. Davidowitz**, 312 U.S. 52 (1941), the Court barred enforcement of Pennsylvania's Alien Registration Act of 1939 because of the federal Alien Registration Act of 1940. Justice BLACK's majority opinion stated: "[Where] the federal government, in the exercise of its superior authority in this field, has enacted a complete scheme of regulation and has therein provided a standard for the registration of aliens, states cannot, inconsistently with the purpose of Congress, conflict or interfere with, curtail or complement, the federal law, or enforce additional or auxiliary regulations. There is not—and from the very nature of the problem there cannot be—any rigid formula or rule which can be used as a universal pattern to determine the meaning and purpose of every act of Congress. This Court, in considering the validity of state laws in the light [of] federal laws touching the same subject, has made use of the following expressions: conflicting; contrary to; occupying the field; repugnance; difference; irreconcilability; inconsistency; violation; curtailment; and interference. But none of these expressions provides an infallible constitutional test or an exclusive constitutional yardstick. In the final analysis, there can be no one crystal clear distinctly marked formula. Our primary function is to determine whether, under the circumstances of [this] case, Pennsylvania's law stands as an obstacle to the accomplishment and execution of the full purposes and objectives of Congress."

In **Florida Lime & Avocado Growers, Inc. v. Paul**, 373 U.S. 132 (1963), the Court described a second strand of conflict preemption as applying in a situation where "compliance with both federal and state regulations is a physical impossibility." Florida Lime involved avocados certified as mature under the federal regulations but containing less than the minimum California oil content. Justice BRENNAN's majority opinion concluded that "there is neither such actual conflict between the two schemes of regulation that both cannot stand in the same area, nor evidence of a congressional design to pre-empt the field." He noted that there was no "physical impossibility" of complying with both standards and that the "maturity of avocados seems to be an inherently unlikely candidate for exclusive federal regulation. [Federal] regulation by means of minimum standards [of] agricultural commodities, however comprehensive *for those purposes* [of marketing] that regulation may be, does not of itself import displacement of state control over the distribution and retail sale of those commodities in the interests of the *consumers* of the commodities within the State." Nor could the Court find "an unambiguous congressional mandate" to exclude state regulation. The federal law here involved concerned "minimum" rather than "uniform" standards. The statutory scheme was "one of maturity regulations drafted and administered locally by the growers' own representatives, and designed to do no more than promote orderly competition among the South Florida growers."

Justice WHITE's dissent, joined by Justices Black, Douglas and Clark, concluded that the Supremacy Clause barred the application of California's "inconsistent and conflicting" legislation. The dissenters saw the federal scheme as a "comprehensive regulatory program" and insisted that California's interest was identical to the federal one. "There is no health interest here. The question is [a] purely economic one. [Despite] the repeated suggestions to this effect in the Court's opinion, there is no indication that the state regulatory scheme has any purpose other than protecting the good will of the avocado industry—such as protecting health or preventing deception of the public—unless as a purely incidental byproduct."

In **Gade v. National Solid Wastes Management Ass'n**, 505 U.S. 88 (1992), the Court found several Illinois provisions for licensing workers who handle hazardous waste preempted by federal Occupational Safety and Health Administration regulations, even though the federal regulations aimed only at worker safety and the state regulations aimed both at worker safety and public health. A plurality opinion by Justice O'CONNOR found conflict preemption, reading the federal scheme to forbid duplicative regulation. Both Justice KENNEDY, concurring in part and in the judgment because he found express preemption, and Justice SOUTER, dissenting along with Justices Blackmun, Stevens and Thomas, objected to the plurality's departure from the presumption that historic state powers may not be superseded without a clear showing of congressional intent.

How much deference should courts give to congressional or agency "purposes" or "objectives" when reviewing state laws challenged for implied conflict preemption? In **Wyeth v. Levine**, 555 U.S. 555 (2009), the Court upheld against implied conflict preemption challenge a state-law failure-to-warn judgment where an anti-nausea drug (Phenergan) bearing a label approved by the Food and Drug Administration was administered intravenously in a way that caused a musician to suffer amputation of her arm. Writing for the 6–3 majority upholding the state-law judgment, Justice STEVENS stated: "Impossibility pre-emption is a demanding defense. On the record before us, Wyeth has failed to demonstrate that it was impossible for it to comply with both federal and state requirements. The [regulation] permitted Wyeth to unilaterally strengthen its warning, and the mere fact that the FDA approved Phenergan's label does not establish that it would have prohibited such a change. Wyeth also argues that requiring it to comply with a state-law duty to provide a stronger warning about IV-push administration would obstruct the purposes and objectives of federal drug labeling regulation. Levine's tort claims, it maintains, are pre-empted because they interfere with 'Congress's purpose to entrust an expert agency to make drug labeling decisions that strike a balance between competing objectives.' We find no merit in this argument, which relies on an untenable interpretation of congressional intent and an overbroad view of an agency's power to pre-empt state law."

Justice THOMAS wrote separately, concurring in the judgment but expressing general skepticism toward the Court's implied conflict pre-emption jurisprudence, noting that it "routinely invalidates state laws based on perceived conflicts with broad federal policy objectives, legislative history, or generalized notions of congressional purposes that are not embodied within the text of federal law." In his view, the Supremacy Clause requires that "pre-emptive effect be given only those to federal standards and policies that are set forth in, or necessarily follow from, the statutory text that was produced through the constitutionally required bicameral and presentment procedures," a requirement that "Congressional and agency musings [do] not satisfy." He accordingly would not rely on such sources as prior regulatory history, comments, or agency litigating positions in order to discern a supposed conflict between state and federal law.

Justice ALITO, joined by Chief Justice Roberts and Scalia, dissented. On their view, a state tort jury could not be permitted to "countermand the FDA's considered judgment that Phenergan's FDA-mandated warning label renders its intravenous use 'safe.' [Federal law relies] on the FDA to make safety determinations like the one it made here. The FDA has long known about the risks associated with IV push in general and its use to administer Phenergan in particular. Whether wisely or not, the FDA has concluded—over the course of extensive, 54-year-long regulatory proceedings—that the drug is 'safe' [when] used in accordance with its FDA-mandated labeling. The unfortunate fact that respondent's healthcare providers ignored Phenergan's labeling may make this an ideal medical-malpractice case. But turning a common-law tort suit into a 'frontal assault' on the FDA's regulatory regime for drug labeling upsets the well-settled meaning of the Supremacy Clause and our conflict pre-emption jurisprudence."

2. ***Preemption and the foreign affairs power.*** In **Crosby v. National Foreign Trade Council**, 530 U.S. 363 (2000), the Court unanimously struck down a Massachusetts law barring state entities from buying goods or services from companies doing business with Burma (Myanmar). Delivering the opinion of the Court, Justice SOUTER held that Congress's passage of a federal law imposing mandatory and conditional sanctions on Burma preempted the Massachusetts law, since Massachusetts's more stringent and inflexible provisions presented "an obstacle to the accomplishment of Congress's full objectives under the federal Act." Justice Souter examined the legislative history of the Congressional act in great detail, and concluded that "the state law undermines the intended purpose and 'natural effect' of at least three provisions of the federal Act, that is, its delegation of effective discretion to the President to control economic sanctions against Burma, its limitation of sanctions solely to United States persons and new investment, and its directive to the President to proceed diplomatically in developing a comprehensive, multilateral strategy towards Burma."

He continued: "Congress manifestly intended to limit economic pressure against the Burmese Government to a specific range. [The] State [statute] conflicts with federal law at a number of points by penalizing individuals and conduct that Congress has explicitly exempted or excluded from sanctions. [The] conflicts are not rendered irrelevant by the State's argument that there is no real conflict between the statutes because they share the same goals and because some companies may comply with both sets of restrictions. The fact of a common end hardly neutralizes conflicting means, and the fact that some companies may be able to comply with both sets of sanctions does not mean that the state Act is not at odds with achievement of the federal decision. [Sanctions] are drawn not only to bar what they prohibit but to allow what they permit, and the inconsistency of sanctions here undermines the congressional calibration of force.

"[In addition], the state Act is at odds with the President's intended authority to speak for the United States among the world's nations in developing a 'comprehensive, multilateral strategy to bring democracy to and improve human rights practices [in] Burma.' Congress called for Presidential cooperation with [other] countries in developing such a strategy, directed the President to encourage a dialogue between the government of Burma and the democratic opposition, and required him to report to the Congress on the progress of his diplomatic efforts. [Congress's] express command to the President to take the initiative for the United States among the international community invested him with the maximum authority of the National Government, in harmony with the President's own constitutional powers. [This] clear mandate and invocation of exclusively national power belies any suggestion that Congress intended the President's effective voice to be obscured by state or local action. [T]he state Act undermines the President's capacity, in this instance for effective diplomacy. It is not merely that the differences between the state and federal Acts in scope and type of sanctions threaten to complicate discussions; they compromise the very capacity of the President to speak for the Nation with one voice in dealing with other governments. [The] President's maximum power to persuade rests on his capacity to bargain for the benefits of access to the entire national economy without exception for enclaves fenced off willy-nilly by inconsistent political tactics."

Justice Souter rejected the State's arguments that it should be free to act given Congress's failure to preempt the state law expressly: "A failure to provide for preemption expressly may reflect nothing more than the settled character of implied preemption doctrine, [and] in any event, the existence of conflict [under] the Supremacy Clause does not depend on express congressional recognition that federal and state law [conflict]. Because the state Act's provisions conflict with Congress's specific delegation to the President of flexible discretion, with limitation of sanctions to a limited scope of actions and actors, and with direction to develop a comprehensive, multilateral strategy under the federal Act, it is preempted, and its application is unconstitutional, under the Supremacy Clause."

CONGRESSIONAL CONSENT TO STATE REGULATION

May Congress, instead of precluding state action through preemption, validate state laws that, in the absence of such federal consent, would violate the dormant commerce clause? In Cooley, the Court suggested that Congress could not validate laws that were "unconstitutional" under the dormant commerce clause; yet a century later, it seemed clear to Justice Stone in Southern Pacific that the "undoubted" congressional "power to redefine the distribution of power over interstate commerce" included the authority "to permit the states to regulate the commerce in a manner which would otherwise not be permissible." What is the justification for that congressional authority? What is its scope?

1. ***The McCarran Act and state discrimination in insurance.*** In 1944, the Supreme Court found that the Sherman Anti-Trust Act of 1890 applied to the insurance business, even though the Court had held in 1868 that insurance was not commerce. United States v. South-Eastern Underwriters Ass'n, 322 U.S. 533 (1944). The Court concluded that "a nationwide business" such as insurance "is not deprived of its interstate character merely because it is built [upon] contracts which are local in nature." In response, Congress enacted the McCarran Act of 1945, which not only limited the applicability of antitrust laws to the business, but also sought to assure continued state authority over insurance. The Act contained a declaration "that the continued regulation and taxation by the several

States of the business of insurance is in the public interest, and that silence on the part of the Congress shall not be construed to impose any barrier to the regulation or taxation of such business by the several States." And Sec. 2 of the law provided: "(a) The business of insurance [shall] be subject to the laws of the several States which relate to the regulation or taxation of such business. (b) No Act of Congress shall be construed to invalidate, impair, or supersede any law enacted by any State for the purpose of regulating the business of insurance, or which imposes a fee or tax upon such business, unless such Act specifically relates to the business of insurance."

In **Prudential Insurance Co. v. Benjamin**, 328 U.S. 408 (1946), a New Jersey insurance corporation objected to the continued collection of a long-standing tax of 3% of the premiums received from all business done in South Carolina. No similar tax was required of South Carolina corporations. The Court assumed that the tax was "discriminatory" and hence invalid under Commerce Clause decisions. Nevertheless, the Court held that the McCarran Act validated the tax. Justice RUTLEDGE disagreed with the Company's contention that "Congress' declaration of policy adds nothing to the validity of what the states have done within the area covered by the declaration." To accept that claim "would ignore the very basis on which [the] Clark Distilling case [has] set the pattern of the law for governing situations like that now presented." He stated:

"Not yet has this Court held such a disclaimer [of a Commerce Clause prohibition] invalid. [On] the contrary, in each instance it has given effect to the congressional judgment contradicting its own previous one. It is true that rationalizations have differed concerning those decisions. [But] the results have been lasting and are at least as important, for the direction given to the process of accommodating federal and state authority, as the reasons stated for reaching them. [Apart from the] function of defining the outer boundary of its power, whenever Congress' judgment has been uttered affirmatively to contradict the Court's previously expressed view that specific action taken by the states in Congress' silence was forbidden by the commerce clause, this body has accommodated its previous judgment to Congress' expressed approval. Some part of this readjustment may be explained in ways acceptable on any theory of the commerce clause and the relations of Congress and the courts toward its functioning. Such explanations, however, hardly go to the root of the matter. For the fact remains that, in these instances, the sustaining of Congress' overriding action has involved something beyond correction of erroneous factual judgment in deference to Congress' presumably better-informed view of the facts, and also beyond giving due deference to its conception of the scope of its powers, when it repudiates, just as when its silence is thought to support, the inference that it has forbidden state action.

"[W]e would be going very far to rule that South Carolina no longer may collect her tax. To do so would flout the expressly declared policies of both Congress and the state. Moreover it would establish a ruling never heretofore made and in doing this would depart from the whole trend of decision in a great variety of situations most analogous to the one now presented. [The] power of Congress over commerce exercised entirely without reference to coordinated action of the states is not restricted, except as the Constitution expressly provides, by any limitation which forbids it to discriminate against interstate commerce and in favor of local trade. [This] broad authority Congress may exercise alone, subject to those limitations, or in conjunction with coordinated action by the states, in which case limitations imposed for the preservation of their powers become inoperative and only those designed to forbid action altogether by any power or combination of powers in our governmental system remain effective. Here both Congress and South Carolina have acted, and in complete co-ordination, to sustain the tax. It is therefore reinforced by the exercise of all the power of government residing in our scheme. Clear and gross must be the evil which would nullify such an exertion, one which could arise only by exceeding beyond cavil some explicit and compelling limitation imposed by a constitutional [provision] designed and intended to outlaw the action taken entirely from our constitutional framework." Note that the McCarran Act has been construed as exempting the insurance industry from Commerce Clause constrictions only, *not* from other constitutional restraints such as equal protection. See Metropolitan Life Ins. Co. v. Ward, 470 U.S. 869 (1985).

Justice Rutledge's conclusion regarding very broad congressional "consent" power is clearer than his reasoning. To the Cooley Court, congressional "consent" authority was questionable; to Justice Rutledge a century later, it was clear that Congress can "consent" to state laws the Court would otherwise consider "unconstitutional" under the dormant commerce clause. Why? Consider the following statement of a bright line for determining when congressional consent to otherwise unconstitutional state laws will be effective: Congress can validly consent to state laws when [the] constitutional limitation on state power is not matched by a similar or identical limitation on federal power. See Cohen, "Congressional Power to Validate Unconstitutional State Laws: A Forgotten Solution to an Old Enigma," 35 Stan. L. Rev. 387 (1983). Thus, for example, Congress may not ratify state equal protection violations, for equal protection guarantees bind the federal government and states alike (see Chapter 9). May Congress ratify state privileges and immunities violations? Is Art. IV more like the Commerce Clause or like equal protection?

2. ***Federal development grants and local-hire rules.*** In White v. Massachusetts Construction Council (discussed in South-Central Timber Development, Inc. v. Wunnicke, p. 248 above), the Court upheld a an executive order by the Mayor of Boston reserving 50% of jobs on public works projects to Boston residents. This facial discrimination was upheld against dormant commerce clause challenge as to *city*-funded projects under the market participant exception. The Court also noted that a significant percentage of the funds affected by the order were received from *federal* sources, including Urban Development Action Grants (UDAGs) and Community Development Block Grants (CDBGs) administered by federal agencies under the Housing and Community Development Acts of 1974 and 1977. In upholding this aspect of the City's order, the Court noted: "The Commerce Clause is a grant of authority to Congress, and not a restriction on the authority of that body. Congress, unlike a state legislature authorizing similar expenditures, is not limited by any negative implications of the Commerce Clause in the exercise of its spending power. Where state or local government action is specifically authorized by Congress, it is not subject to the Commerce Clause even if it interferes with interstate commerce. Southern Pacific. Thus, if the restrictions imposed by the city on construction projects financed in part by federal funds are directed by Congress then no dormant Commerce Clause issue is presented."

The Court observed that the regulations implementing the grant statutes specifically called for the maximum feasible training and employment of "lower-income *residents of the project area*," and concluded: "An examination of the applicable statutes reveals that these federal programs were intended to encourage economic revitalization, including improved opportunities for the poor, minorities, and unemployed. Examination of the regulations [indicates] that the Mayor's executive order sounds a harmonious note; the federal regulations for each program affirmatively permit the type of parochial favoritism expressed in the order."

SECTION 4. OTHER ASPECTS OF FEDERAL-STATE RELATIONSHIPS

STATE TAXATION OF INTERSTATE BUSINESS AND INCOME

States need tax revenues, and the Court has recognized that state tax bases would be unjustifiably curtailed if *all* interstate business were immunized from state tax obligations. Even interstate business arguably should bear its share of local tax burdens. Yet it would greatly disrupt the national economy if interstate business were subject to the multiple taxation, with most or all of its property or income being subjected to the tax scheme of each state in which it does business. The Court has sought to draw lines distinguishing between permissible and impermissible state taxation, balancing legitimate local needs against the interest in a national economy. The most commonly litigated taxes have been property taxes, sales and use taxes, net and gross receipts taxes, and license and franchise taxes. The typical subjects of taxation have been interstate transportation and interstate sales.

Congress has the authority to solve the problem, but what should the Court do in the absence of congressional guidance? The Court has imposed judicially enforced restraints on state taxes in the interest of the national economy under the dormant commerce clause. In **Complete Auto Transit, Inc. v. Brady**, 430 U.S. 274 (1977), the Court upheld against commerce challenge a Mississippi tax on a shipper of automobiles for the "privilege of doing business" in the state. Writing for a unanimous Court, Justice BLACKMUN reiterated that interstate commerce is not immune from state taxation and set forth the currently governing four-part test: he held that a state tax may be sustained against Commerce Clause challenge "when the tax is applied to an activity with a substantial nexus with the taxing State, is fairly apportioned, does not discriminate against interstate commerce, and is fairly related to the services provided by the State." In **Quill Corp. v. North Dakota**, 504 U.S. 298 (1992), the Court clarified that the substantial nexus with a state required under the Commerce Clause is greater than the minimum contacts with a state required under the Due Process Clause. In that case, a unanimous Court held it permissible under due process, but impermissible under the Auto Transit test, for a state to tax out-of-state businesses that had no physical presence in the state and whose only contacts with the state were by common carrier or the mails.

In **South Dakota v. Wayfair**, 584 U.S. ___, 138 S. Ct. 2080 (2018), the Court overruled Quill's physical presence rule by a 5–4 vote. Justice

KENNEDY wrote for the Court, joined by Justices Thomas, Ginsburg, Alito and Gorsuch:

"Quill created an inefficient 'online sales tax loophole' that gives out-of-state businesses an advantage. [Each] year, the physical presence rule becomes further removed from economic reality and results in significant revenue losses to the States. Quill is flawed on its own terms. First, the physical presence rule is not a necessary interpretation of the requirement that a state tax must be applied to an activity with a substantial nexus with the taxing State. Second, Quill creates rather than resolves market distortions. And third, Quill imposes the sort of arbitrary, formalistic distinction that the Court's modern Commerce Clause precedents disavow. [Quill] puts both local businesses and many interstate businesses with physical presence at a competitive disadvantage relative to remote sellers. Remote sellers can avoid the regulatory burdens of tax collection and can offer *de facto* lower prices caused by the widespread failure of consumers to pay the tax on their own. [In] effect, Quill has come to serve as a judicially created tax shelter for businesses that decide to limit their physical presence and still sell their goods and services to a State's consumers—something that has become easier and more prevalent as technology has advanced. Worse still, the rule produces an incentive to avoid physical presence in multiple States. Distortions caused by the desire of businesses to avoid tax collection mean that the market may currently lack storefronts, distribution points, and employment centers that otherwise would be efficient or desirable.

"[Here,] *stare decisis* can no longer support the Court's prohibition of a valid exercise of the States' sovereign power. [While] it can be conceded that Congress has the authority to change the physical presence rule, Congress cannot change the constitutional default rule. It is inconsistent with the Court's proper role to ask Congress to address a false constitutional premise of this Court's own creation. Courts have acted as the front line of review in this limited sphere; and hence it is important that their principles be accurate and logical, whether or not Congress can or will act in response. It is currently the Court, and not Congress, that is limiting the lawful prerogatives of the States. [*Stare decisis*] accommodates only legitimate reliance interests. Here, the tax distortion created by Quill exists in large part because consumers regularly fail to comply with lawful use taxes.

"[In] the absence of Quill, the first prong of the Complete Auto test simply asks whether the tax applies to an activity with a substantial nexus with the taxing State. [Here,] the nexus is clearly sufficient based on both the economic and virtual contacts respondents have with the State. The Act applies only to sellers that deliver more than $100,000 of goods or services into South Dakota or engage in 200 or more separate transactions for the delivery of goods and services into the State on an annual basis. S. B. 106, § 1. This quantity of business could not have occurred unless the seller availed itself of the substantial privilege of carrying on business in South Dakota. And respondents are large, national companies that undoubtedly maintain an extensive virtual presence."

Justice GORSUCH concurred and took the opportunity to cast doubt on the entirety of dormant commerce clause jurisprudence: "The Commerce Clause is found in Article I and authorizes *Congress* to regulate interstate commerce. Meanwhile our dormant commerce cases suggest Article III *courts* may invalidate state laws that offend no congressional statute. Whether and how much of this can be squared with the text of the Commerce

Clause, justified by *stare decisis*, or defended as misbranded products of federalism or antidiscrimination imperatives flowing from Article IV's Privileges and Immunities Clause are questions for another day."

■ CHIEF JUSTICE ROBERTS dissented, joined by JUSTICES BREYER, SOTOMAYOR, and KAGAN:

"E-commerce has grown into a significant and vibrant part of our national economy against the backdrop of established rules, including the physical-presence rule. Any alteration to those rules with the potential to disrupt the development of such a critical segment of the economy should be undertaken by Congress. The Court should not act on this important question of current economic policy, solely to expiate a mistake it made over 50 years ago. [Nothing] in today's decision precludes Congress from continuing to seek a legislative solution. But by suddenly changing the ground rules, the Court may have waylaid Congress's consideration of the issue. Armed with today's decision, state officials can be expected to redirect their attention from working with Congress on a national solution, to securing new tax revenue from remote retailers.

"[The] Court [breezily] disregards the costs that its decision will impose on retailers. Correctly calculating and remitting sales taxes on all e-commerce sales will likely prove baffling for many retailers. Over 10,000 jurisdictions levy sales taxes, each with 'different tax rates, different rules governing tax-exempt goods and services, different product category definitions, and different standards for determining whether an out-of-state seller has a substantial presence' in the jurisdiction. [The] burden will fall disproportionately on small businesses. One vitalizing effect of the Internet has been connecting small, even 'micro' businesses to potential buyers across the Nation. People starting a business selling their embroidered pillowcases or carved decoys can offer their wares throughout the country—but probably not if they have to figure out the tax due on every sale. And the software said to facilitate compliance is still in its infancy, and its capabilities and expense are subject to debate. The Court's decision today will surely have the effect of dampening opportunities for commerce in a broad range of new markets. A good reason to leave these matters to Congress is that legislators may more directly consider the competing interests at stake. Unlike this Court, Congress has the flexibility to address these questions in a wide variety of ways. [The] Court is of course correct that the Nation's economy has changed dramatically since the time that [Quill] roamed the earth. I fear the Court today is compounding its past error by trying to fix it in a totally different era. I would let Congress decide."

In **Comptroller of the Treasury of Maryland v. Wynne**, ___ U.S. ___, 135 S. Ct. 1787 (2015), the Court held for the first time that the dormant commerce clause's restrictions also applied to personal income tax. Writing for the majority, Justice ALITO found that Maryland's personal income tax scheme, which failed to give residents credit against their county tax for income taxes they had paid to other states, was not "fairly apportioned" under Complete Auto Transit. Because the internal logic of Maryland's tax scheme burdened interstate income with higher taxes than it did intrastate income, the Court concluded that the scheme was "inherently discriminatory and operates as a tariff. This identity between Maryland's tax and a tariff is fatal because tariffs are "the paradigmatic example of a law discriminating against interstate commerce."

INTERGOVERNMENTAL TAX IMMUNITIES

As McCulloch v. Maryland (p. 79 above) has already illustrated, one of the constitutional principles that governs relations between state and nation is that neither may destroy the autonomy of the other. In McCulloch, Chief Justice Marshall struck down Maryland's tax on the operations of a federal instrumentality, the Bank of the United States. For over a century after McCulloch, constitutional tax immunities expanded in a number of directions. Marshall in McCulloch had indicated that his views of federal immunity from state taxation did not necessarily imply a reciprocal immunity of state operations from federal taxes. Nevertheless, the post-Civil War Court held that state activities did enjoy a reciprocal immunity from federal taxation. Collector v. Day, 11 Wall. (78 U.S.) 113 (1871). Moreover, the Court expanded the circle of immunities from the primary immunity of the government itself to the derivative immunity of third persons—employees, lessees, patentees—in some ways related to governmental activities. In the late 1930s, that circle began to contract. For example, Helvering v. Gerhardt, 304 U.S. 405 (1938), and Graves v. New York ex rel. O'Keefe, 306 U.S. 466 (1939), held that the salaries of the employees of one government are not immune from income taxes imposed by the other. In recent years, intergovernmental tax immunities have continued to wane, although the Court continues to enforce a few constitutional tax immunities, as when states impose property taxes directly on federal property. See Rohr Aircraft Corp. v. San Diego County, 362 U.S. 628 (1960); see generally Massachusetts v. United States, 435 U.S. 444 (1978).

Increasingly, the scope of federal immunities depends upon Congress. Thus, when the specific McCulloch issue resurfaced in the Court a century and a half later, in **First Agric. Nat. Bank v. State Tax Comm'n**, 392 U.S. 339 (1968), the Court emphasized the dimensions of the *statutory* grant of immunity. Justice Marshall's dissent, joined by Justices Harlan and Stewart, argued that, in light of the "present functions and role of national banks," they should not be considered "constitutionally immune from nondiscriminatory state taxation." He suggested that McCulloch and other "hoary cases" could "and perhaps should" be read as banning only discriminatory taxes. That would "require a re-evaluation of the validity of the doctrine of intergovernmental tax immunities—a doctrine which does not rest upon any specific provisions of the Constitution, but rather upon this Court's concepts of federalism." Since Congress is able to provide statutory immunities, "there is little reason for this Court to cling to the view that the Constitution itself makes federal instrumentalities immune from state taxation in the absence of authorizing legislation."

For an effort to articulate "a narrow approach to governmental tax immunity," see United States v. New Mexico, 455 U.S. 720 (1982). There Justice Blackmun stated the basic principles as follows: "The one constant [is] simple enough to express: a State may not, consistent with the Supremacy Clause, lay a tax 'directly upon the United States.' [But] the limits on the immunity doctrine are [as] significant as the rule itself. [Tax] immunity is appropriate in only one circumstance: when the levy falls on the United States itself, or on an agency or instrumentality so closely connected to the Government that the two cannot realistically be viewed as separate entities. [This] view, we believe, comports with the principal purpose of the immunity doctrine, that of forestalling 'clashing sovereignty' [McCulloch], by preventing the States from laying demands directly on the Federal Government." But even under this "narrow approach," the Court continues to scrutinize closely those taxes alleged to discriminate against the federal government. See, e.g., Davis v. Michigan Dept. of Treasury, 489 U.S. 803 (1989).

INTERGOVERNMENTAL REGULATORY IMMUNITIES

Recall the discussion above of the state immunity from federal regulation that prevailed during the brief reign of National League of Cities v. Usery (1976; p. 169 above), later overruled in Garcia (1985; p. 170 above). To what extent is there an implied immunity of federal operations from state regulation? **Johnson v. Maryland**, 254 U.S. 51 (1920), relied on McCulloch in reversing the conviction of a post office employee for driving a truck without a state license. Justice Holmes's opinion for the Court concluded: "It seems to us that the immunity of the instruments of the United States from state control in the performance of their duties extends to a requirement that they desist from performance until they satisfy a state officer upon examination that they are competent for a necessary part of them and pay a fee for permission to go on." But he left the scope of the immunity somewhat unclear: "Of course an employee of the United States does not secure a general immunity from state law while acting in the course of his employment. [It] very well may be that, when the United States has not spoken, the subjection to local law would extend to general rules that might affect incidentally the mode of carrying out the employment—as, for instance, a [statute] regulating the mode of turning at the corners of streets."

The federal immunity from state regulation may at times be claimed by those in a close relationship with the government; as in the state tax area, the scope of the immunity turns largely on congressional policy. See, for example, Leslie Miller, Inc. v. Arkansas, 352 U.S. 187 (1956), barring application of a state licensing scheme to a federal contractor because of a "conflict" between the state requirement and federal regulations designed to ensure the reliability of contractors. As in the state tax area, again, the Court is particularly alert to state regulations based on hostility to federal law. For example, in North Dakota v. United States, 460 U.S. 300 (1983), several state laws were evidently enacted to slow down or control federal acquisition of easements pursuant to the Migratory Bird Conservation Act. Justice Blackmun's opinion found the state laws were "hostile to federal interests."

In addition to the above, Congress may employ other techniques in the ordering relations between the nation and the states. Other examples include: determining the scope of intergovernmental immunities; federal incorporation or adoption of state law either expressly or by implication, as in many areas of tax, copyright and bankruptcy law; and state administration of federal law, as in the unemployment compensation scheme of the Social Security Act or the distribution of Aid to Families with Dependent Children, or in the varied exercises of the federal spending power through conditional grants to the states.

MUTUAL OBLIGATIONS AMONG THE STATES

A number of constitutional provisions impose interstate obligations or facilitate interstate relationships. The major constitutional source of interstate obligations, Article IV, § 2, contains two important restraints: the interstate privileges and immunities clause (explored above), and the Extradition Clause, which obligates rendition of fugitives from justice. The Extradition Clause speaks in mandatory terms: a fugitive from justice "shall [be] delivered up" on "Demand of the executive Authority of the State from which he fled." A state's mandatory duty under the Extradition Clause was long held unenforceable by the federal courts, however, in the interest of avoiding confrontations between state and federal sovereignties. Kentucky v. Dennison, 24 How. (65 U.S.) 66 (1861). Dennison was overruled in Puerto Rico v. Branstad, 483 U.S. 219 (1987), which held that failure by a state to comply with its obligations under the Extradition Clause *may* be remedied by mandamus or injunctive relief in the federal courts. Congress has enacted legislation to deal with interstate fugitives from justice.

The major device for interstate collaboration recognized in the Constitution is the interstate compact. Article I, § 10 states that no state "shall, without the Consent of the Congress, [enter into] any Agreement or Compact with another State." Interstate compacts have been used to deal with a wide variety of interstate and regional problems, including boundaries, natural resources regulation and allocation, flood control, transportation, taxation, and crime control. Congress has at times encouraged compacts by giving advance consent, as with crime and flood control. But not all interstate agreements require congressional consent. Virginia v. Tennessee, 148 U.S. 503 (1893), stated that the Compact Clause is directed at the formation of any combination "which may tend to increase [the] political influence of the contracting States" so as to "impair the supremacy of the United States," and that there are "many matters upon which different States may agree that can in no respect concern the United States." The application of these criteria divided the Court in U.S. Steel Corp. v. Multistate Tax Commission, 434 U.S. 452 (1978), finding that the Multistate Tax Compact drafted in 1966 was not invalid for lack of congressional consent.

CHAPTER 6

SEPARATION OF POWERS

In addition to allocating power vertically between the federal government and the states, the Constitution allocates the legislative, executive and judicial powers of the federal government horizontally among the three branches described in Articles I, II and III.

The Framers, influenced not only by their own experiences but also by Enlightenment political theorists such as Montesquieu, sought to safeguard against tyranny by combating excessive concentration of power. They also intended to promote efficiency, for example by giving Congress power over the national market and placing executive power in the singular person of the President—although the tripartite scheme often produces more inefficiencies than, for example, a parliamentary system. Justice Brandeis recognized the inherent conflict between preventing tyranny and assuring efficiency in a well-known passage in his dissent in Myers v. United States, 272 U.S. 52 (1926) (p. 412 below), noting that "the doctrine of the separation of powers was adopted [not] to promote efficiency but to preclude the exercise of arbitrary power. The purpose was, not to avoid friction, but, by means of the inevitable friction incident to the distribution of the governmental powers among three departments, to save the people from autocracy." For a defense of the American separation of powers system against the critique of inefficiency, see Sargentich, "The Limits of the Parliamentary Critique of the Separation of Powers," 34 Wm. & Mary L. Rev. 679 (1993).

The constitutional provisions themselves reveal, however, that separation was not intended to be airtight. Repeatedly, powers are blended and intermixed. For example, the Congress legislates, but the President participates in the legislative process through the veto power. In diplomatic and military affairs, the President is Commander-in-Chief, makes treaties and appoints ambassadors, but treaties and ambassadorial appointments require the consent of the Senate, and the Congress has the power to raise and support the army and navy, to declare war and to make rules concerning prisoners of war. These areas of overlap and uncertainty have left ample room for competition among the branches—conflicts that are often resolved by tests of political strength. But they have also given rise to judicial interpretations of the textual and structural limits on executive and legislative action that oversteps its own authority or invades the authority of another branch.

Section 1 examines to what extent the constitutional grant of executive powers authorizes the President to fashion policy in the absence of congressional authority, or contrary to congressional prohibition. In what manner may Congress impose restraints on executive discretion? Are the boundaries between executive powers and legislative authority any different in the domestic sphere than with regard to the making of foreign policy and the use of military force? Section 2 discusses Congress's constitutional foreign affairs powers, including the authority to make war and ratify treaties. Does Congress's treaty power enable it to regulate in ways not otherwise permitted in accordance with its enumerated powers? What are the implications for both horizontal and vertical separation of powers? Section 3 looks at the political branches' power and discretion in times of national security emergency or terror, an issue that took on new urgency in the years after September 11, 2001. Section 4 turns to problems concerning the autonomy of each branch vis-à-vis the others. To what extent does the separation of powers protect each branch against interference by the others in performing its functions? Finally, Section 5 examines the degree to which, if at all, the executive and legislative branches are immune from judicial processes.

SECTION 1. EXECUTIVE ASSERTIONS OF POWER

Article II vests "[t]he executive power" in the President without qualification. In this respect, it differs from Article I, which delegates to Congress "[a]ll legislative powers herein granted." This disparity has given rise to arguments that the President has certain inherent powers beyond those specified in the Constitution. Because the President is the only elected official who both has a national constituency and leads his or her political party, the actual influence of the Presidency on national policy is obviously great. What is the President's constitutional authority to devise policy to deal with domestic problems? Are the President's policymaking powers justifiably greater in the sphere of foreign affairs? Does the Chief Executive have residual emergency powers? Do the specified executive powers in Article II or any inherent powers of the Presidency authorize the President to act when Congress has been silent? Are there any circumstances in which the President's powers take precedence even over conflicting congressional directives? Or is the President limited to the specific tasks assigned by Article II and to the execution of laws Congress enacts? Consider the following classic case:

Youngstown Sheet & Tube Co. v. Sawyer
[The Steel Seizure Case]

343 U.S. 579, 72 S. Ct. 863, 96 L. Ed. 1153 (1952).

■ JUSTICE BLACK delivered the opinion of the Court.

[We] are asked to decide whether [President Truman] was acting within his constitutional power when he issued an order directing the Secretary of Commerce [Sawyer] to take possession of and operate most of the Nation's steel mills. The mill owners argue that the President's order amounts to lawmaking, a legislative function which the Constitution has expressly confided to the Congress and not to the President. The Government's position is that the order was made on findings of the President that his action was necessary to avert a national catastrophe which would inevitably result from a stoppage of steel production, and that in meeting this grave emergency the President was acting within the aggregate of his constitutional powers as the Nation's Chief Executive and the Commander in Chief of the [Armed Forces]. The issue emerges here from the following series of events:

In the latter part of 1951 [during the Korean War], a dispute arose between the steel companies and their employees over terms and conditions

[for] new collective bargaining agreements. [Efforts to settle the dispute—including referral to the Federal Wage Stabilization Board—failed.] On April 4, 1952, the [Steelworkers'] Union gave notice of a nation-wide strike called to begin [on] April 9. The indispensability of steel as a component of substantially all weapons and other war materials led the President to believe that the proposed work stoppage would immediately jeopardize our national defense and that governmental seizure of the steel mills was necessary in order to assure the continued availability of steel. [Accordingly,] the President, a few hours before the strike was to begin, issued Executive Order 10340 [directing] the Secretary of Commerce to take possession of most of the steel mills and keep them running. The Secretary immediately issued his own possessory orders, calling upon the presidents of the various seized companies to serve as operating managers for the United States. [The] next morning the President sent a message to Congress reporting his [action]. Congress has taken no action. Obeying the Secretary's orders under protest, the companies brought proceedings against him in the District Court, [which] on April 30 issued a preliminary injunction restraining the Secretary from "continuing the seizure and possession of the plants [and] from acting under the purported authority of Executive Order No. 10340." On the same day the Court of Appeals stayed the District Court's injunction. Deeming it best that the issues raised be promptly decided by this Court, we granted certiorari on May 3 and set the cause for argument on May 12. [This decision was announced soon after, on June 2, 1952.]

The President's power, if any, to issue the order must stem either from an act of Congress or from the Constitution itself. There is no statute that expressly authorizes the President to take possession of property as he did here. Nor is there any act of Congress to which our attention has been directed from which such a power can fairly be implied. [There] are two statutes which do authorize the President to take both personal and real property under certain conditions, [the Selective Service Act of 1948 and the Defense Production Act of 1950]. However, the Government admits that these conditions were not met and that the President's order was not rooted in either of the statutes. The Government refers to the seizure provisions of one of these statutes [the 1950 Act] as "much too cumbersome, involved, and time-consuming for the crisis which was at hand." Moreover, the use of the seizure technique to solve labor disputes in order to prevent work stoppages was not only unauthorized by any congressional enactment; prior to this controversy, Congress had refused to adopt that method of settling labor disputes. When the Taft-Hartley Act was under consideration in 1947, Congress rejected an amendment which would have authorized such governmental seizures in cases of emergency.

President went against Cong. intent

It is clear that if the President had authority to issue the order he did, it must be found in some provision of the Constitution. And it is not claimed that express constitutional language grants this [power]. The contention is that presidential power should be implied from the aggregate of his powers under the Constitution. Particular reliance is placed on provisions in Article II which say that "The executive Power shall be vested in a President"; that "he shall take Care that the Laws be faithfully executed"; and that he "shall be Commander in Chief of the [Army and Navy]." The order cannot properly be sustained as an exercise of the President's military power as Commander in Chief of the Armed Forces. The Government attempts to do so by citing [cases] upholding broad powers in military commanders engaged in day-to-day fighting in a theater of war. Such cases need not concern us here. Even though "theater of war" be an expanding concept, we cannot with faithfulness to our constitutional system hold that the [Commander in Chief] has the ultimate power as such to take possession of private property in order to keep labor disputes from stopping production. This is a job for the Nation's lawmakers, not for its military authorities. Nor can the seizure order be sustained because of the several constitutional provisions that grant executive power to the President. In the framework of our Constitution, the President's power to see that the laws are faithfully executed refutes the idea that he is to be a lawmaker. The Constitution limits his functions in the law-making process to the recommending of laws he thinks wise and the vetoing of laws he thinks bad. And the Constitution is neither silent nor equivocal about who shall make laws which the President is to execute [quoting Art. I, § 1, and Art. I, § 8, cl. 18].

The President's order does not direct that a congressional policy be executed in a manner prescribed by Congress—it directs that a presidential policy be executed in a manner prescribed by the President. The preamble of the order itself, like that of many statutes, sets out reasons why the President believes certain policies should be adopted, proclaims these policies as rules of conduct to be followed, and again, like a statute, authorizes a government official to promulgate additional [regulations] consistent with the policy proclaimed and needed to carry that policy into execution. The power of Congress to adopt such public policies as those proclaimed by the order is beyond question. It can authorize the taking of private property for public use. It can make laws, [e.g.], those regulating the relationships between employers and [employees]. The Constitution does not subject this lawmaking power of Congress to presidential or military supervision or control.

It is said that other Presidents without congressional authority have taken possession of private business enterprises in order to settle labor disputes. But even if this be true, Congress has not thereby lost its exclusive constitutional authority to make laws necessary and proper to carry out the powers vested by the Constitution "in the Government of the United States, or any Department or Officer thereof." The Founders of this Nation entrusted the lawmaking power to the Congress alone in both good and bad times. It would do no good to recall the historical events, the fears of power and the hopes for freedom that lay behind their choice. Such a review would but confirm our holding that this seizure order cannot stand.

[Affirmed.]

■ JUSTICE FRANKFURTER, concurring.

Although the considerations relevant to the legal enforcement of the principle of separation of powers seem to me more complicated and flexible than may appear from what Justice Black has written, I join his opinion because I thoroughly agree with the application of the principle to the circumstances of this case. [The Framers] rested the structure of our central government on the system of checks and balances. [Not] so long ago it was fashionable to find [that system] obstructive to effective government. It was easy to ridicule that system as outmoded—too easy. The experience for which the world has passed in our own day has made vivid the realization that the [Framers] were not inexperienced doctrinaires. These long-headed statesmen had no illusion that our people enjoyed biological or psychological or sociological immunities from the hazards of concentrated power. [Marshall's admonition in McCulloch] that "it is *a constitution* we are expounding" is especially relevant when the Court is required to give legal sanction to an underlying principle of the Constitution—that of separation of powers. "The great ordinances of the Constitution do not establish and divide fields of black and white." The issue before us can be met, and therefore should be, without attempting to define the President's powers comprehensively. [We must] put to one side considerations of what powers a President would have had if there had been no legislation whatever bearing on the authority asserted by the seizure or if the seizure had been only for a short, explicitly temporary period, to be terminated automatically unless Congressional approval [were given].

It cannot be contended that the President would have had power to issue this order had Congress explicitly negated such authority in formal legislation. [In view of the Taft-Hartley Act of 1947], Congress has expressed its will to withhold this power from the President as though it had said so in so many words. [In effect], Congress said to the President, "You may not seize. Please report to us and ask for seizure power if you think it is needed in a specific situation." [The] content of the three authorities of government is not to be derived from an abstract analysis. The areas are partly interacting, not wholly disjointed. The Constitution is a framework for government. Therefore the way the framework has consistently operated fairly establishes that it has operated according to its true nature. Deeply embedded traditional ways of conducting government cannot supplant the Constitution or legislation, but they give meaning to the words of a text or supply them. It is an inadmissibly narrow conception of American constitutional law to confine it to the words of the Constitution and to disregard the gloss which life has written upon them. In short, a systematic, unbroken, executive practice, long pursued to the knowledge of the Congress and never before questioned, engaged in by Presidents who have also sworn to uphold the Constitution, making as it were such exercise of power part of the structure of our government, may be treated as a gloss on "executive Power" vested in the [President]. [Justice Frankfurter added an elaborate historical appendix to his opinion.] [But the] list of executive assertions of the power of seizure in circumstances comparable to the present reduces to three in the six-month period from June to December of 1941. [These] three isolated instances do not add up, either in number, scope, duration or contemporaneous legal justification, to the kind of executive construction of the Constitution [necessary to justify the actions here]. Nor do they come to us sanctioned by long-continued acquiescence of Congress giving decisive weight to a construction by the Executive of its [powers].

■ JUSTICE JACKSON, concurring.

[A] judge, like an executive advisor, may be surprised at the poverty of really useful and unambiguous authority applicable to concrete problems of executive power as they actually present themselves. Just what our forefathers did envision, or would have envisioned had they foreseen modern conditions, must be divined from materials almost as enigmatic as the dreams Joseph was called upon to interpret for Pharaoh. A century and a half of partisan debate and scholarly speculation yields no net result but only supplies more or less apt quotations from respected resources on each side of any question. They largely cancel each other. And court decisions are indecisive because of the judicial practice of dealing with the largest questions in the most narrow way. The actual art of governing under our Constitution does not and cannot conform to judicial definitions of the power of any of its branches based on isolated clauses or even single Articles torn from context. While the Constitution diffuses power the better to secure liberty, it also contemplates that practice will integrate the dispersed powers into a workable government. It enjoins upon its branches separateness but interdependence, autonomy but reciprocity. Presidential powers are not fixed but fluctuate, depending upon their disjunction or conjunction with those of Congress. We may well begin by a somewhat over-simplified grouping of practical situations in which a President may doubt, or others may challenge, his powers, and by distinguishing roughly the legal consequences of this factor of relativity.

1. When the President acts pursuant to an express or implied authorization of Congress, his authority is at its maximum, for it includes all that he possesses in his own right plus all that Congress can delegate. In these circumstances, and in these only, may he be said (for what it may be worth) to personify the federal sovereignty. If his act is held unconstitutional under these circumstances, it usually means that the Federal Government as an undivided whole lacks power. A seizure executed by the President pursuant to an Act of Congress would be supported by the strongest of presumptions and the widest latitude of judicial interpretation, and the burden of persuasion would rest heavily upon any who might attack it.

2. When the President acts in absence of either a congressional grant or denial of authority, he can only rely upon his own independent powers, but there is a zone of twilight in which he and Congress may have concurrent authority, or in which its distribution is uncertain. Therefore, congressional inertia, indifference or quiescence may sometimes, at least as a practical matter, enable, if not invite, measures of independent presidential responsibility. In this area, any actual test of power is likely to depend on the imperatives of events and contemporary imponderables rather than on abstract theories of law.

3. When the President takes measures incompatible with the expressed or implied will of Congress, his power is at its lowest ebb, for then he can rely only upon his own constitutional powers minus any constitutional powers of Congress over the matter. Courts can sustain exclusive presidential control in such a case only by disabling the Congress from acting upon the subject. Presidential claim to a power at once so conclusive and preclusive must be scrutinized with caution, for what is at stake is the equilibrium established by our constitutional system.

Into which of these classifications does this executive seizure of the steel industry fit? It is eliminated from the first by admission, for it is conceded that no congressional authorization exists for this seizure. [Can] it then be defended under flexible tests available to the second category? It seems clearly eliminated from that class because Congress has not left seizure of private property an open field but has covered it by three statutory policies inconsistent with this seizure. [This] leaves the current seizure to be justified only by the severe tests under the third grouping, where it can be supported only by any remainder of executive power after subtraction of such powers as Congress may have over the subject. In short, we can sustain the President only by holding that seizure of such strike-bound industries is within his domain and beyond control by [Congress].

The Solicitor General seeks the power of seizure in three clauses of the Executive Article, the first reading, "The executive Power shall be vested in a [President]." [The Government argues:] "In our view, this clause constitutes a grant of all the executive powers of which the Government is capable." If that be true, it is difficult to see why the forefathers bothered to add several specific items, including some trifling ones. [I] cannot accept the view that this clause is a grant in bulk of all conceivable executive power but regard it as an allocation to the presidential office of the generic powers thereafter stated. The clause on which the Government next relies is that "The President shall be Commander in Chief of the Army and Navy of the United States." [T]his loose appellation is sometimes advanced as support for any presidential action, internal or external, involving use of force, the idea being that it vests power to do anything, anywhere, that can be done with an army or navy. That seems to be the logic of an argument tendered at our bar—that the President having, on his own responsibility, sent American troops abroad derives from that act "affirmative power" to seize the means of producing a supply of steel for them. [No] doctrine that the Court could promulgate would seem to me more sinister and alarming than that a President whose conduct of foreign affairs is so largely uncontrolled, and often even is unknown, can vastly enlarge his mastery over the internal affairs of the country by his own commitment of the Nation's armed forces to some foreign venture. I do not, however, find it necessary or appropriate to consider the legal status of the Korean enterprise to discountenance argument based on it.

[The] Constitution expressly places in Congress power "to raise and *support* Armies" and "to *provide* and *maintain* a Navy." (Emphasis supplied.) This certainly lays upon Congress primary responsibility for supplying the armed forces. Congress alone controls the raising of revenues and their appropriation and may determine in what manner and by what means they shall be spent for military and naval procurement.

[There] are indications that the Constitution did not contemplate that the title Commander in Chief *of the Army and Navy* will constitute him also Commander in Chief of the country, its industries and its inhabitants. He has no monopoly of "war powers," whatever they are. [That] military powers of the Commander in Chief were not to supersede representative government of internal affairs seems obvious from the Constitution and from elementary American history. The third clause in which the Solicitor General finds seizure powers is that "he shall take Care that the Laws be faithfully executed." That authority must be matched against [the due process clause of the Fifth Amendment]. One gives a governmental authority that reaches so far as there is law, the other gives a private right that authority shall go no farther. These signify about all there is of the principle that ours is a government of laws, not of men, and that we submit ourselves to rulers only if under rules.

The Solicitor General lastly grounds support of the seizure upon nebulous, inherent powers never expressly granted but said to have accrued to the office from the customs and claims of preceding administrations. The plea is for a resulting power to deal with a crisis or an emergency according to the necessities of the case, the unarticulated assumption being that necessity knows no law. Loose and irresponsible use of adjectives colors all nonlegal and much legal discussion of presidential powers. "Inherent" powers, "implied" powers, "incidental" powers, "plenary" powers, "war" powers and "emergency" powers are used, often interchangeably and without fixed or ascertainable meanings. The vagueness and generality of the clauses that set forth presidential powers afford a plausible basis for pressures within and without an administration for presidential action beyond that supported by those whose responsibility it is to defend his actions in court. The claim of inherent and unrestricted presidential powers has long been a persuasive dialectical weapon in political controversy. While it is not surprising that counsel should grasp support from such unadjudicated claims of power, a judge cannot accept self-serving press statements of the attorney for one of the interested parties as authority in answering a constitutional question, even if the advocate was himself.[1] But prudence has counseled that actual reliance on such nebulous claims stop short of provoking a judicial [test].

In view of the ease, expedition and safety with which Congress can grant and has granted large emergency powers, certainly ample to embrace this crisis, I am quite unimpressed with the argument that we should affirm possession of them without statute. Such power either has no beginning or it has no end. If it exists, it need submit to no legal restraint. I am not alarmed that it would plunge us straightaway into dictatorship, but it is at least a step in that wrong direction. As to whether there is imperative necessity for such powers, it is relevant to note the gap that exists between the President's paper powers and his real powers. The Constitution does not disclose the measure of the actual controls wielded by the modern presidential [office]. Vast accretions of federal power, eroded from that reserved by the States, have magnified the scope of presidential [activity].

Executive power has the advantage of concentration in a single head in whose choice the whole Nation has a part, making him the focus of public hopes and expectations. No other personality in public life can begin to compete with him in access to the public mind through modern methods of communications. By his prestige as head of state and his influence upon public opinion he exerts a leverage upon those who are supposed to check and balance his power which often cancels their effectiveness. Moreover, rise of the party system has made a significant extra constitutional supplement to real executive power. [I] have no illusion that any decision by this Court can keep power in the hands of Congress if it is not wise and timely in meeting its problems. A crisis that challenges the President equally, or perhaps primarily, challenges Congress. If not good law, there was worldly wisdom in the maxim attributed to Napoleon that "The tools belong to the man who can use them." We may say that power to legislate for emergencies belongs in the hands of Congress, but only Congress itself can prevent power from slipping through its [fingers]. With all its defects, delays and inconveniences, men have discovered no technique for long preserving free government except that the Executive be under the law, and that the law be made by parliamentary deliberations. Such institutions may be destined to pass away. But it is the duty of the Court to be last, not first, to give them up.[2]

---

[1] Justice Jackson was the U.S. Attorney General when he was named to the Court in 1941.

[2] Each of the other Justices in the majority also wrote a separate opinion. Justice DOUGLAS concluded that the presidential seizure was legislative in nature; that it constituted "taking" in the constitutional sense, requiring just compensation under the Fifth Amendment; that the President has no power to raise revenues; and that the "branch of government that has the power to pay compensation for a seizure is the only one able to authorize a seizure." Justice BURTON concluded that the President's order "invaded the jurisdiction of Congress" because Congress had "prescribed for the President specific procedures, exclusive of seizure, for his use in meeting the present type of emergency." Justice CLARK, the only Justice in the majority who

■ CHIEF JUSTICE VINSON, with whom [JUSTICES REED and MINTON] join, dissenting.

The President has the duty to execute [legislative programs assuring financial support for the Korean War.] Their successful execution depends upon continued production of steel and stabilized prices for steel. Accordingly, [when] a strike shutting down the entire basic steel industry was threatened, the President acted to avert a complete shutdown of steel production. [One] is not here called upon even to consider the possibility of executive seizure of a farm, a corner grocery store or even a single industrial plant. Such considerations arise only when one ignores the central fact of this case—that the Nation's entire basic steel production would have shut down completely if there had been no Government seizure. [Accordingly], if the President has any power under the Constitution to meet a critical situation in the absence of express statutory authorization, there is no basis whatever for criticizing the exercise of such power in this case. [A] review of executive action demonstrates that our Presidents have on many occasions exhibited the leadership contemplated by the Framers when they made the President Commander in Chief, and imposed upon him the trust to "take Care that the Laws be faithfully executed." With or without explicit statutory authorization, Presidents have at such times dealt with national emergencies by acting promptly and resolutely to enforce legislative programs, at least to save those programs until Congress could act. Congress and the courts have responded to such executive initiative with consistent approval.

[Beginning] with the Bank Holiday Proclamation and continuing through World War II, executive leadership and initiative were characteristic of President Franklin D. Roosevelt's administration. [Six] months before Pearl Harbor, a dispute at a single aviation plant at Inglewood, California, interrupted a segment of the production of military [aircraft]. President Roosevelt ordered the seizure of the plant "pursuant to the powers vested in [him] by the Constitution and laws of the United States, as President [and] Commander in [Chief]." The Attorney General [i.e., future Justice Jackson] vigorously proclaimed that the President had the moral duty to keep this Nation's defense effort a "going concern." [Before and after Pearl Harbor], industrial concerns were seized to avert interruption of needed production. During the same period, the President directed seizure of the Nation's coal mines to remove an obstruction to the effective prosecution of the war. [This] amply demonstrates that Presidents have taken prompt action to enforce the laws and protect the country whether or not Congress happened to provide in advance for the particular method of execution. [T]he fact that Congress and the courts have consistently recognized and given their support to such executive action indicates that such a power of seizure has been accepted throughout our [history].

Much of the argument in this case has been directed at straw men. We do not now have before us the case of a President acting solely on the basis of his own notions of the public welfare. Nor is there any question of unlimited executive power in this case. The President himself closed the door to any such claim when he sent his Message to Congress stating his purpose

did not join Justice Black's opinion, similarly emphasized that Congress had prescribed methods to be followed by the President for emergencies such as this. He added, however, "that in the absence of such action by Congress, the President's independent power to act depends upon the gravity of the situation confronting the nation."

to abide by any action of Congress, whether approving or disapproving his seizure action. [The] absence of a specific statute authorizing seizure of the steel mills as a mode of executing the laws—both the military procurement program and the anti-inflation program—has not until today been thought to prevent the President from executing the laws. [Here], there is no statute prohibiting the action taken by the [President]. Executive inaction in [this] situation, courting national disaster, is foreign to the concept of energy and initiative in the Executive as created by the Founding Fathers. [The] broad executive power granted by Article II to an officer on duty 365 days a year cannot, it is said, be invoked to avert disaster. Instead, the President must confine himself to sending a message to Congress recommending action. Under this messenger-boy concept of the Office, the President cannot even act to preserve legislative programs from destruction so that Congress will have something left to act upon. [There is no question here that the possession] was other than temporary in character and subject to congressional direction—either approving, disapproving or regulating the manner in which the mills were to be administered and returned to the owners. [No] basis for claims of arbitrary action, unlimited powers or dictatorial usurpation of congressional power appears from the facts of this case. On the contrary, judicial, legislative and executive precedents throughout our history demonstrate that in this case the President acted in full conformity with his duties under the Constitution.

EXECUTIVE AUTHORITY TO MAKE NATIONAL DOMESTIC POLICY

1. ***The aftermath of Steel Seizure.*** In the wake of the decision, a 53-day steel strike ensued, there was a settlement, and no steel shortage occurred. President Truman, for whom organized labor was an important constituency, never did invoke his authority under the 1947 Taft-Hartley Act to enjoin the unions. President Truman was unrepentant about seizure of the mills, later writing: "Whatever the six justices of the Supreme Court meant by their differing opinions, [the President] must always act in a national emergency." Truman, II Memoirs: Years of Trial and Hope 475–78 (1956).

What difference did the Youngstown decision make? In order to legalize the steel seizure after the Youngstown decision, President Truman would have had to muster a majority of votes in both houses of Congress. If the Court had upheld the President's actions in Youngstown, opponents of the seizure would have had to raise a two-thirds majority in both Houses to pass a law invalidating the seizure over President Truman's likely veto. In other words, given the Court's decision, the votes of 51% of the members of either house were sufficient to stop the seizure; if Youngstown had been decided in favor of the Truman Administration, on the other hand, it would have required two-thirds votes of both Houses to end the seizure. Note that the elections of the 82nd Congress had given President Truman's Democratic Party only a 234–199 majority in the House of Representatives, and an even slimmer 48–47 advantage in the Senate; furthermore, Truman's support even within his own party was somewhat weak. Marcus, Truman and the Steel Seizure Case 36 (1977).

2. ***Separation of powers and individual rights.*** One of the chief justifications for separating national powers, as with the vertical separation of powers under federalism, is to preserve individual liberty. Were such individual liberties at stake in Steel Seizure? In a concurring opinion, Justice Douglas argued that because a taking of property was involved, Congress, which has the sole power of appropriation of funds, had the sole power to act. Is this persuasive? Even if the executive action had been sustained, couldn't the steel companies have sued for compensation under the Takings Clause of the Fifth Amendment and obtained judicial relief? Even if so, should the people have to pay for the costly actions of an improvident executive who acts without congressional authorization?

3. ***Formalism and functionalism.*** Justice Black's opinion, a product of his own text-oriented originalism, took a formalistic approach tending to categorize and rigidly separate legislative, executive and judicial functions. The authority for Truman's action, Black asserted, must derive from either a statute passed by Congress or from some specific provision of the Constitution. Truman's argument was based on the inherent authority of the executive under the Constitution—"that presidential power should be implied from the aggregate of his powers under the Constitution"—but Black was dismissive. The seizure had not taken place in a theater of war so Truman's Commander-in-Chief powers could not justify his conduct. While the Constitution vested "executive Power" in the President, that power was limited, in Black's view, to executing laws passed by Congress. The seizure did not rely on any congressional enactment, and the order was therefore beyond the President's power to execute.

Contrast the more flexible, functional approach emphasized by Justices Frankfurter and Jackson. Much scholarly commentary on separation of powers has endorsed the functional approach, arguing that the post-New Deal regulatory state—which requires a national government with the capacity to regulate complex industries—would be incompatible with a rigidly formalist separation-of-powers framework. Consider the following argument for the functional view: "When the Constitution confers power, it confers power on the three generalist political heads of authority, not on branches as such. [Its] silence about the shape of the inevitable, actual government was a product both of drafting compromises and of the explicit purpose to leave Congress free to make whatever arrangements it deemed 'necessary and proper' for the detailed pursuit of government purposes." Strauss, "Formal and Functional Approaches to Separation of Powers Questions—A Foolish Inconsistency?," 72 Cornell L. Rev. 488 (1987) (observing that "[v]irtually every part of the government Congress has created—the Department of Agriculture as well as the Securities and Exchange Commissions—exercises *all three* of the government functions the Constitution so carefully allocates among Congress, President and Court"). See also Sunstein, "Constitutionalism After the New Deal," 101 Harv. L. Rev. 421 (1987).

4. ***The Jackson opinion and its tripartite analysis.*** Of all the opinions in the Steel Seizure Case, Justice Jackson's has been the most influential and the most frequently cited in later decisions. Indeed, "[the] Supreme Court over the years has come to treat Jackson's concurrence as though it were the opinion of the Court." Feldman, Scorpions: The Battles and Triumphs of FDR's Great Supreme Court Justices 360 (2010).

What is the theory or method of constitutional interpretation, if any, underlying Jackson's three-part approach? Does Justice Jackson's distinction among three types of situations provide a useful general framework for the analysis of presidential power problems? To what extent do the other opinions accept that framework? To what extent do the various opinions accept Justice Frankfurter's view that unquestioned and continuous "executive practice" "may be treated as a gloss on 'Executive power'" granted by Article II? How persuasive should such "practice" be in constitutional interpretation? For an in-depth discussion of the role of historical practice in adjudicating separation-of-powers issues, see Bradley & Morrison, "Historical Gloss and the Separation of Powers," 126 Harv. L. Rev. 412 (2012).

Justice Jackson's first category—presidential action pursuant to congressional authority—refers to the most common variety of executive action. Justice Jackson's second category—presidential action in the context of congressional silence—presents greater difficulty. Justice Jackson suggests "a zone of twilight" in which President and Congress "may have concurrent authority." Note that Justice Jackson found that this case did not fall into this second category. Instead, he construed congressional silence—and refusals to grant the President statutory seizure authority—as a deliberate restraint on executive power; hence, the case fell into his third category, where executive authority is at its "lowest ebb." Was that a plausible reading of congressional silence? Congressional authority in the twilight zone typically stems from Article I, § 8, powers.[1] What are the "flexible tests" appropriate for that twilight zone? To what extent can congressional silence be attributed to mere inertia, or the desire to "pass the buck" to the President, for controversial decisions? What is the source of executive power in that twilight zone? For an argument for a narrow implied presidential power rooted in the nature of executive authority, see Monaghan, "The Protective Power of the Presidency," 93 Colum. L. Rev. 1 (1993) ("[T]he considerable debate on the issue of a presidential emergency power has obscured the existence of a narrower, inherent power [to] protect and defend the personnel, property, and instrumentalities of the United States from harm. [For] example, acting without statutory authority, the Executive has standing to enforce the contract or property rights of the United States."). Are there any situations in the domestic sphere that fall within Justice Jackson's third category: a presidential power to act even in the face of contrary congressional directions? Are any such powers in fact granted by Article II? In the following case, the Court answered that question in the affirmative, finding that Congress could not constitutionally interfere with the President's "recognition power."

---

[1] Note that congressional power under the Necessary and Proper Clause, Art. I, § 8, cl. 18, is not limited to implementation of powers specifically granted to Congress. Instead, it enables Congress to make all laws "necessary and proper for carrying into Execution the foregoing Powers, and *all other Powers* vested by this Constitution in the Government of the United States, or in any Department or Officer thereof." (Emphasis added.) Should this congressional implementation power be read as giving priority to congressional resolutions of conflicts between the legislative and executive branches in the "zone of twilight"? Van Alstyne, "The Role of Congress in Determining Incidental Powers of the President and of the Federal Courts: A Comment on the Horizontal Effect of The Sweeping Clause," 40 Law & Contemp. Probs. 102 (1976) (arguing that the Necessary and Proper Clause "assigns to Congress alone the responsibility to say by law what additional authority, if any, the executive and the courts are to have beyond that core of powers that are indispensable, rather than merely appropriate, or helpful, to the performance of their express duties under articles II and III of the Constitution").

Zivotofsky v. Kerry

576 U.S. ___, 135 S. Ct. 2076, 192 L. Ed. 2d 83 (2015).

■ JUSTICE KENNEDY delivered the opinion of the Court.

A delicate subject lies in the background of this case. That subject is Jerusalem. [Jerusalem's] political standing has long been, and remains, one of the most sensitive issues in American foreign policy, and indeed it is one of the most delicate issues in current international affairs. In 1948, President Truman formally recognized Israel in a signed statement of "recognition." [Yet], in contrast to a consistent policy of formal recognition of Israel, neither President Truman nor any later United States President has issued an official statement or declaration acknowledging any country's sovereignty over Jerusalem. [The] President's position on Jerusalem is reflected in State Department policy regarding passports and consular reports of birth abroad. Understanding that passports will be construed as reflections of American policy, the State Department's Foreign Affairs Manual instructs its employees, in general, to record the place of birth on a passport as the "country [having] present sovereignty over the actual area of birth." [Because] the United States does not recognize any country as having sovereignty over Jerusalem, the FAM instructs employees to record the place of birth for citizens born there as "Jerusalem."

In 2002, Congress passed the Act at issue here, the Foreign Relations Authorization Act, Fiscal Year 2003. Section 214 of the Act is titled "United States Policy with Respect to Jerusalem as the Capital of Israel." [That] subsection seeks to override the FAM by allowing citizens born in Jerusalem to list their place of birth as "Israel." Titled "Record of Place of Birth as Israel for Passport Purposes," § 214(d) states "[f]or purposes of the registration of birth, certification of nationality, or issuance of a passport of a United States citizen born in the city of Jerusalem, the Secretary shall, upon the request of the citizen or the citizen's legal guardian, record the place of birth as Israel."

In 2002, petitioner Menachem Binyamin Zivotofsky was born to United States citizens living in Jerusalem. [Pursuant] to § 214(d), Zivotofsky claims the right to have "Israel" recorded as his place of birth in his passport.

In considering claims of Presidential power this Court refers to Justice Jackson's familiar tripartite framework from *Youngstown Sheet & Tube Co. v. Sawyer*. [Because] the President's refusal to implement § 214(d) falls into Justice Jackson's third category, his claim must be "scrutinized with caution," and he may rely solely on powers the Constitution grants to him alone.

[Recognition] is a "formal acknowledgement" that a particular "entity possesses the qualifications for statehood" or "that a particular regime is the effective government of a state." Restatement (Third) of Foreign Relations Law of the United States § 203, Comment *a* (1986). [Legal] consequences follow formal recognition. Recognized sovereigns may sue in United States courts, and may benefit from sovereign immunity when they are sued. The actions of a recognized sovereign committed within its own territory also receive deference in domestic courts under the act of state doctrine. Recognition at international law, furthermore, is a precondition of regular diplomatic relations. Recognition is thus "useful, even necessary," to the existence of a state.

Despite the importance of the recognition power in foreign relations, the Constitution does not use the term "recognition," either in Article II or elsewhere. The Secretary asserts that the President exercises the recognition power based on the Reception Clause, which directs that the President "shall receive Ambassadors and other public Ministers." Art. II, § 3.

At the time of the founding, [prominent] international scholars suggested that receiving an ambassador was tantamount to recognizing the sovereignty of the sending state. It is a logical and proper inference, then, that a Clause directing the President alone to receive ambassadors would be understood to acknowledge his power to recognize other nations. This in fact occurred early in the Nation's history when President Washington recognized the French Revolutionary Government by receiving its ambassador.

[The] inference that the President exercises the recognition power is further supported by his additional Article II powers. It is for the President, "by and with the Advice and Consent of the Senate," to "make Treaties, provided two thirds of the Senators present concur." Art. II, § 2, cl. 2. In addition, "he shall nominate, and by and with the Advice and Consent of the Senate, shall appoint Ambassadors" as well as "other public Ministers and Consuls." *Ibid.*

As a matter of constitutional structure, these additional powers give the President control over recognition decisions. At international law, recognition may be effected by different means, but each means is dependent upon Presidential power. In addition to receiving an ambassador, recognition may occur on "the conclusion of a bilateral treaty," or the "formal initiation of diplomatic relations," including the dispatch of an ambassador. The President has the sole power to negotiate treaties, and the Senate may not conclude or ratify a treaty without Presidential action. The President, too, nominates the Nation's ambassadors and dispatches other diplomatic agents. Congress may not send an ambassador without his involvement. Beyond that, the President himself has the power to open diplomatic channels simply by engaging in direct diplomacy with foreign heads of state and their ministers. The Constitution thus assigns the President means to effect recognition on his own initiative. Congress, by contrast, has no constitutional power that would enable it to initiate diplomatic relations with a foreign nation. Because these specific Clauses confer the recognition power on the President, the Court need not consider whether or to what extent the Vesting Clause, which provides that the "executive Power" shall be vested in the President, provides further support for the President's action here.

The text and structure of the Constitution grant the President the power to recognize foreign nations and governments. The question then becomes whether that power is exclusive. The various ways in which the President may unilaterally effect recognition—and the lack of any similar power vested in Congress—suggest that it is. So, too, do functional considerations. Put simply, the Nation must have a single policy regarding which governments are legitimate in the eyes of the United States and which are not. Foreign countries need to know, before entering into diplomatic relations or commerce with the United States, whether their ambassadors will be received; whether their officials will be immune from suit in federal court;

and whether they may initiate lawsuits here to vindicate their rights. These assurances cannot be equivocal.

Recognition is a topic on which the Nation must "speak . . . with one voice." That voice must be the President's. Between the two political branches, only the Executive has the characteristic of unity at all times. And with unity comes the ability to exercise, to a greater degree, "[d]ecision, activity, secrecy, and dispatch." The Federalist No. 70 (A. Hamilton). The President is capable, in ways Congress is not, of engaging in the delicate and often secret diplomatic contacts that may lead to a decision on recognition. He is also better positioned to take the decisive, unequivocal action necessary to recognize other states at international law. These qualities explain why the Framers listed the traditional avenues of recognition—receiving ambassadors, making treaties, and sending ambassadors—as among the President's Article II powers.

[The] President since the founding has exercised this unilateral power to recognize new states—and the Court has endorsed the practice. Texts and treatises on international law treat the President's word as the final word on recognition.

It remains true, of course, that many decisions affecting foreign relations—including decisions that may determine the course of our relations with recognized countries—require congressional action. Congress may "regulate Commerce with foreign Nations," "establish an uniform Rule of Naturalization," "define and punish Piracies and Felonies committed on the high Seas, and Offences against the Law of Nations," "declare War," "grant Letters of Marque and Reprisal," and "make Rules for the Government and Regulation of the land and naval Forces." U. S. Const., Art. I, § 8. In addition, the President cannot make a treaty or appoint an ambassador without the approval of the Senate. Art. II, § 2, cl. 2. The President, furthermore, could not build an American Embassy abroad without congressional appropriation of the necessary funds. Art. I, § 8, cl. 1.

[Although] the President alone effects the formal act of recognition, Congress' powers, and its central role in making laws, give it substantial authority regarding many of the policy determinations that precede and follow the act of recognition itself. If Congress disagrees with the President's recognition policy, there may be consequences. Formal recognition may seem a hollow act if it is not accompanied by the dispatch of an ambassador, the easing of trade restrictions, and the conclusion of treaties. And those decisions require action by the Senate or the whole Congress. [In] this way ambition counters ambition, ensuring that the democratic will of the people is observed and respected in foreign affairs as in the domestic realm. See The Federalist No. 51 (J. Madison).

[In] support of his submission that the President has broad, undefined powers over foreign affairs, the Secretary quotes United States v. Curtiss-Wright Export Corp., which described the President as "the sole organ of the federal government in the field of international relations." This Court declines to acknowledge that unbounded power.

The Curtiss-Wright case does not extend so far as the Secretary suggests. [The] description of the President's exclusive power was not necessary to the holding of Curtiss-Wright—which, after all, dealt with congressionally authorized action, not a unilateral Presidential determination. Indeed, Curtiss-Wright did not hold that the President is free from Congress' lawmaking power in the field of international relations.

[As] the power to recognize foreign states resides in the President alone, the question becomes whether § 214(d) infringes on the Executive's consistent decision to withhold recognition with respect to Jerusalem.

[If] the power over recognition is to mean anything, it must mean that the President not only makes the initial, formal recognition determination but also that he may maintain that determination in his and his agent's statements. This conclusion is a matter of both common sense and necessity. If Congress could command the President to state a recognition position inconsistent with his own, Congress could override the President's recognition determination.

[This] is not to say Congress may not express its disagreement with the President in myriad ways. For example, it may enact an embargo, decline to confirm an ambassador, or even declare war. But [it] may not force the President himself to contradict his earlier statement.

■ JUSTICE THOMAS, concurring in the judgment in part and dissenting in part.

[The] Vesting Clause of Article II provides that "[t]he executive Power shall be vested in a President of the United States." Art. II, § 1. This Clause is notably different from the Vesting Clause of Article I, which provides only that "[a]ll legislative Powers *herein granted* shall be vested in a Congress of the United States," Art. I, § 1 (emphasis added). By omitting the words "herein granted" in Article II, the Constitution indicates that the "executive Power" vested in the President is not confined to those powers expressly identified in the document. Instead, it includes all powers originally understood as falling within the "executive Power" of the Federal Government.

Founding-era evidence reveals that the "executive Power" included the foreign affairs powers of a sovereign State. John Locke's 17th-century writings laid the groundwork for this understanding of executive power.

[William] Blackstone [described] the executive power in England as including foreign affairs powers, such as the "power of sending embassadors to foreign states, and receiving embassadors at home"; making "treaties, leagues, and alliances with foreign states and princes"; "making war and peace"; and "issu[ing] letters of marque and reprisal." 1 Commentaries on the Laws of England (1765).

[This] view of executive power was widespread at the time of the framing of the Constitution. [Given] this pervasive view of executive power, it is unsurprising that those who ratified the Constitution understood the "executive Power" vested by Article II to include those foreign affairs powers not otherwise allocated in the Constitution. James Iredell, for example, told the North Carolina ratifying convention that, under the new Constitution, the President would "regulate all intercourse with foreign powers" and act as the "primary agent" of the United States, though no specific allocation of foreign affairs powers in the document so provided.

[In] the Anglo-American legal tradition, passports have consistently been issued and controlled by the body exercising executive power—in England, by the King; in the colonies, by the Continental Congress; and in the United States, by President Washington and every President since.

[Justice Scalia] disapproves of my "assertion of broad, unenumerated 'residual powers' in the President," but offers no response to my interpretation of the words "executive Power" in the Constitution.

In the end, Justice Scalia characterizes my interpretation of the executive power, the naturalization power, and the Necessary and Proper Clause as producing "a presidency more reminiscent of George III than George Washington." But he offers no competing interpretation of either the Article II Vesting Clause or the Necessary and Proper Clause. And his decision about the Constitution's resolution of conflict among the branches could itself be criticized as creating a supreme legislative body more reminiscent of the Parliament in England than the Congress in America.

■ CHIEF JUSTICE ROBERTS, with whom JUSTICE ALITO joins, dissenting.

Today's decision is a first: Never before has this Court accepted a President's direct defiance of an Act of Congress in the field of foreign affairs. We have instead stressed that the President's power reaches "its lowest ebb" when he contravenes the express will of Congress, "for what is at stake is the equilibrium established by our constitutional system." *Youngstown Sheet & Tube Co.* v. *Sawyer*, (Jackson, J., concurring).

[I] write separately to underscore the stark nature of the Court's error on a basic question of separation of powers.

[The] majority places great weight on the Reception Clause, which directs that the Executive "shall receive Ambassadors and other public Ministers." Art. II, § 3. But that provision, framed as an obligation rather than an authorization, appears alongside the *duties* imposed on the President by Article II, Section 3, not the *powers* granted to him by Article II, Section 2. [The] majority's other asserted textual bases are even more tenuous. The President does have power to make treaties and appoint ambassadors. Art. II, § 2. But those authorities are *shared* with Congress, so they hardly support an inference that the recognition power is *exclusive*.

[As] for history, the majority admits that it too points in both directions. Some Presidents have claimed an exclusive recognition power, but others have expressed uncertainty about whether such preclusive authority exists. Those in the skeptical camp include Andrew Jackson and Abraham Lincoln, leaders not generally known for their cramped conceptions of Presidential power. Congress has also asserted its authority over recognition determinations at numerous points in history. The majority therefore falls short of demonstrating that "Congress has accepted" the President's exclusive recognition power. In any event, we have held that congressional acquiescence is only "pertinent" when the President acts in the absence of express congressional authorization, not when he asserts power to disregard a statute, as the Executive does here.

But even if the President does have exclusive recognition power, he still cannot prevail in this case, because the statute at issue *does not implicate recognition*. [Congress] has not disputed the Executive's assurances that § 214(d) does not alter the longstanding United States position on Jerusalem. And the annals of diplomatic history record no examples of official recognition accomplished via optional passport designation.

Ultimately, the only power that could support the President's position is the one the majority purports to reject: the "exclusive authority to conduct diplomatic relations." The Government offers a single citation for this allegedly exclusive power: Curtiss-Wright. But as the majority rightly acknowledges, Curtiss-Wright did not involve a claim that the Executive could contravene a statute; it held only that he could act pursuant to a legislative delegation.

■ JUSTICE SCALIA, with whom CHIEF JUSTICE [ROBERTS] and JUSTICE ALITO join, dissenting.

Before this country declared independence, the law of England entrusted the King with the exclusive care of his kingdom's foreign affairs. [The] People of the United States had other ideas when they organized our Government. They considered a sound structure of balanced powers essential to the preservation of just government, and international relations formed no exception to that principle.

[The] Constitution contemplates that the political branches will make policy about the territorial claims of foreign nations the same way they make policy about other international matters: The President will exercise his powers on the basis of his views, Congress its powers on the basis of its views. That is just what has happened here.

[Congress's] power to "establish an uniform Rule of Naturalization," Art. I, § 8, cl. 4, enables it to grant American citizenship to someone born abroad. The naturalization power also enables Congress to furnish the people it makes citizens with papers verifying their citizenship—say a consular report of birth abroad (which certifies citizenship of an American born outside the United States) or a passport (which certifies citizenship for purposes of international travel). [Even] on a miserly understanding of Congress's incidental authority, Congress may make grants of citizenship "effectual" by providing for the issuance of certificates authenticating them.

One would think that if Congress may grant Zivotofsky a passport and a birth report, it may also require these papers to record his birthplace as "Israel." The birthplace specification promotes the document's citizenship-authenticating function by identifying the bearer, distinguishing people with similar names but different birthplaces from each other, helping authorities uncover identity fraud, and facilitating retrieval of the Government's citizenship records. To be sure, recording Zivotofsky's birthplace as "Jerusalem" rather than "Israel" would fulfill these objectives, but when faced with alternative ways to carry its powers into execution, Congress has the "discretion" to choose the one it deems "most beneficial to the people." McCulloch v. Maryland [1819; p. 79, above]. It thus has the right to decide that recording birthplaces as "Israel" makes for better foreign policy. Or that regardless of international politics, a passport or birth report should respect its bearer's conscientious belief that Jerusalem belongs to Israel.

[§ 214(d)] has nothing to do with recognition. Section 214(d) does not require the Secretary to make a formal declaration about Israel's sovereignty over Jerusalem. And nobody suggests that international custom infers acceptance of sovereignty from the birthplace designation on a passport or birth report, as it does from bilateral treaties or exchanges of ambassadors.

[Section 214(d)] performs a more prosaic function than extending recognition. Just as foreign countries care about what our Government has to say about their borders, so too American citizens often care about what our Government has to say about their identities. [Even] if the Constitution gives the President sole power to extend recognition, it does not give him sole power to make all decisions relating to foreign disputes over sovereignty. To the contrary, a fair reading of Article I allows Congress to decide for itself how its laws should handle these controversies. Read naturally, power to "regulate Commerce with foreign Nations," § 8, cl. 3, includes power to regulate imports from Gibraltar as British goods or as Spanish goods. Read naturally, power to "regulate the Value . . . of foreign Coin," § 8, cl. 5, includes power to honor (or not) currency issued by Taiwan. And so on for the other enumerated powers.

[Recognition] is a type of legal act, not a type of statement. It is a leap worthy of the Mad Hatter to go from exclusive authority over making legal commitments about sovereignty to exclusive authority over making statements or issuing documents about national borders. The Court may as well jump from power over issuing declaratory judgments to a monopoly on writing law-review articles.

[That] brings me, in analytic crescendo, to [Justice Thomas's] suggestion that *even if* Congress's enumerated powers otherwise encompass § 214(d), and *even if* the President's power to regulate the contents of passports is not exclusive, the law might *still* violate the Constitution, because it conflicts with the President's passport policy. It turns the Constitution upside-down to suggest that in areas of shared authority, it is the executive policy that preempts the law, rather than the other way around. Congress *may* make laws necessary and proper for carrying into execution the President's powers, but the President *must* "take Care" that Congress's legislation "be faithfully executed." And Acts of Congress made in pursuance of the Constitution are the "supreme Law of the Land"; acts of the President (apart from treaties) are not. That [i]s why Justice Jackson was right to think that a President who "takes measures incompatible with the expressed or implied will of Congress" may "rely only upon his own constitutional powers *minus any constitutional powers of Congress over the matter*." Youngstown. And it is why Justice Thomas is wrong to think that even if § 214(d) operates in a field of shared authority the President might still prevail.

Whereas the Court's analysis threatens congressional power over foreign affairs with gradual erosion, [Justice Thomas's] approach shatters it in one stroke. The combination of (a) the concurrence's assertion of broad, unenumerated "residual powers" in the President, (b) its parsimonious interpretation of Congress's enumerated powers, and (c) its even more parsimonious interpretation of Congress's authority to enact laws "necessary and proper for carrying into Execution" the President's executive powers, produces (d) a presidency more reminiscent of George III than George Washington.

EXECUTIVE AUTHORITY OVER FOREIGN AND MILITARY AFFAIRS

1. ***Speaking with one voice.*** Should the President have more autonomous authority to act as to external affairs than domestic ones? Are there more explicit constitutional grants of such authority? Is there a greater practical need for the nation to "speak with one voice" in relation to foreign governments than in domestic affairs, conferring corresponding comparative advantage on the Presidency over the Congress? Does the President's greater ability to act with energy in moments of international crisis argue for greater independent executive authority in this sphere? How far does such authority extend—should it be time-limited pending congressional ratification in an

area, such as war, where authority is jointly distributed between the branches?

2. ***Executive agreements.*** Over the years, the executive branch has frequently resorted in foreign relations to unilateral executive agreements rather than treaties approved by the Senate according to the procedures set forth in Article II. Recurrent concerns have been voiced that such executive agreements, by bypassing treaty-making, might unduly intrude upon the Senate's role. (Fears have also been voiced that executive agreements may be on a par with treaties in terms of their legal force and may thus be able to supersede state legislation under the Supremacy Clause. See Missouri v. Holland (1920; p. 335 below).) Are such agreements supportable on the basis of inherent presidential authority? To what extent can executive agreements be justified as incidental to specified Article II powers? Must all executive agreements be made in pursuance of a statute?

In **United States v. Belmont**, 301 U.S. 324 (1937), the Court sustained the validity of an executive agreement and held that it took precedence over conflicting state policy. The agreement arose out of the American diplomatic recognition of the Soviet Union in 1933. At the same time as President Roosevelt recognized the USSR, an exchange of diplomatic correspondence between the President and Maxim Litvinov effected an assignment to the United States of all Soviet claims against Americans who held funds of Russian companies seized after the Revolution. The Belmont suit was brought by the United States in reliance upon that assignment, in order to recover funds deposited by a Russian corporation with a private New York banker. The lower courts dismissed the action on the ground that implementing the USSR's confiscation would violate the public policy of New York. Justice SUTHERLAND wrote for the majority, emphasizing that recognition, establishment of diplomatic relations and the assignment "were all parts of one transaction, resulting in an international compact between the two governments." He had no doubt that the negotiations and the agreements "were within the competence of the President": "in respect of what was done here, the Executive had authority to speak as the sole organ." And the assignment and agreement, unlike treaties, did not require the Senate's participation. He stated that "an international compact, as this was, is not always a treaty which requires the participation of the Senate. There are many such compacts, of which a protocol, a modus vivendi, a postal convention, and agreements like that now under consideration are illustrations." And the Supremacy Clause required that contrary state policies must give way. (The Litvinov Assignment resurfaced in the Court in United States v. Pink, 315 U.S. 203 (1942). Justice Douglas's opinion for the Court stated that the President "has the power to determine the policy [to] govern the question of recognition" and that, under the Supremacy Clause, such "international compacts and agreements as the Litvinov Assignment have a similar dignity" as treaties.)

Does Belmont support broad unilateral presidential authority to enter into executive agreements? Or is it important to distinguish among constitutional sources for particular agreements? Is it useful to invoke the three-pronged analysis of Justice Jackson's opinion in the Steel Seizure Case? Many executive agreements fall within his first category: they are adopted pursuant to statutory authority, as in trade agreements that authorize modification of tariffs through presidential agreements. The Litvinov agreement involved in Belmont, by contrast, rested on the constitutionally delegated presidential authority regarding diplomatic recognition, in Art. II, § 3 (stating that the President "shall receive Ambassadors and other public Ministers"). As to such agreements, it is arguable that Congress possesses *no* authority to interfere with executive power. Could Congress, under the Necessary and Proper Clause, enact guidelines for the negotiation of executive agreements? Consider the permissible scope of executive agreements outlined in the following case:

Dames & Moore v. Regan

453 U.S. 654, 101 S. Ct. 2972, 69 L. Ed. 2d 918 (1981).

■ JUSTICE REHNQUIST delivered the opinion of the Court.

[This] dispute involves various Executive Orders and regulations by which the President nullified attachments and liens on Iranian assets in the United States, directed that these assets be transferred to Iran, and suspended claims against Iran that may be presented to an International Claims Tribunal. This action was taken in an effort to comply with an Executive Agreement between the United States and Iran. [On] November 4, 1979, the American Embassy in Tehran was seized and our diplomatic personnel were captured and held hostage. In response to that crisis, President Carter, acting pursuant to the International Emergency Economic Powers Act [IEEPA], declared a national emergency on November 14, 1979, and blocked the removal or transfer of "all property and interests in property of the Government of Iran, its instrumentalities and controlled entities and the Central Bank of Iran which are or become subject to the jurisdiction of the [United States]." [On] November 15, 1979, the Treasury Department's Office of Foreign Assets Control issued a regulation providing that "[unless] licensed or authorized [any] attachment, judgment, decree, lien, execution, garnishment, or other judicial process is null and void with respect to any property in which on or since [November 14, 1979,] there existed an interest of Iran."

On December 19, 1979, petitioner Dames & Moore filed suit in the United States District Court [against] the Government of Iran, the Atomic Energy Organization of Iran, and a number of Iranian banks. In its complaint, petitioner alleged that its wholly owned subsidiary, Dames & Moore International, S. R. L., was a party to a written contract with the Atomic Energy Organization, and that the subsidiary's entire interest in the contract had been assigned to petitioner. [Petitioner] contended [that] it was owed $3,436,694.30 plus interest for services performed under the contract prior to the date of termination. The District Court issued orders of attachment directed against property of the defendants, and the property of certain Iranian banks was then attached to secure any judgment that might be entered against them.

On January 20, 1981, the Americans held hostage were released by Iran pursuant to an [Executive Agreement] entered into the day before. The Agreement stated that "[it] is the purpose of [the United States and Iran] [to] terminate all litigation as between the Government of each party and the nationals of the other, and to bring about the settlement and termination of all such claims through binding arbitration." In furtherance of this goal, the Agreement called for the establishment of an Iran-United States Claims

Tribunal which would arbitrate any claims not settled within six months. Awards of the Claims Tribunal are to be "final and binding" and "enforceable [in] the courts of any nation in accordance with its laws." Under the Agreement, the United States is obligated "to terminate all legal proceedings in United States courts involving claims of United States persons and institutions against Iran and its state enterprises, to nullify all attachments and judgments obtained therein, to prohibit all further litigation based on such claims, and to bring about the termination of such claims through binding arbitration." In addition, the United States must "act to bring about the transfer" by July 19, 1981, of all Iranian assets held in this country by American banks. One billion dollars of these assets will be deposited in a security account in the Bank of England, to the account of the Algerian Central Bank, and used to satisfy awards rendered against Iran by the Claims Tribunal. On January 19, 1981, President Carter issued a series of Executive Orders implementing the terms of the agreement. [On] February 24, 1981, President Reagan issued an Executive Order in which he "ratified" the January 19th Executive Orders. Moreover, he "suspended" all "claims which may be presented to [the] Tribunal" and provided that such claims "shall have no legal effect in any action now pending in any court of the United States." The suspension of any particular claim terminates if the Claims Tribunal determines that it has no jurisdiction over that claim; claims are discharged for all purposes when the Claims Tribunal either awards some recovery and that amount is paid, or determines that no recovery is [due].

[The] parties and the lower courts [have] all agreed that much relevant analysis is contained in [Youngstown]. Although we have in the past found and do today find Justice Jackson's classification of executive actions into three general categories analytically useful, [Jackson] himself recognized that his three categories represented "a somewhat over-simplified grouping," and it is doubtless the case that executive action in any particular instance falls, not neatly in one of three pigeonholes, but rather at some point along a spectrum running from explicit congressional authorization to explicit congressional prohibition. This is particularly true as respects cases such as the one before us, involving responses to international crises the nature of which Congress can hardly have been expected to anticipate in any detail.

[The Government] has principally relied on § 203 of the IEEPA as authorization for these actions. Section 1702 (a)(1) provides in part: "[T]he President may regulate, direct and compel; nullify, void, prevent or prohibit, any acquisition, holding, withholding, use, transfer, withdrawal, transportation, importation or exportation of, or dealing in, or exercising any right, power, or privilege with respect to, or transactions involving, any property in which any foreign country or a national thereof has any interest; by any person, or with respect to any property, subject to the jurisdiction of the United States." The Government contends that the acts of "nullifying" the attachments and ordering the "transfer" of the frozen assets are specifically authorized by the plain language of the above [statute]. Because the President's action in nullifying the attachments and ordering the transfer of the assets was taken pursuant to specific congressional authorization, it is "supported by the strongest of presumptions and the widest latitude of judicial interpretation, and the burden of persuasion would rest heavily upon any who might attack it." Youngstown (Jackson, J., concurring). Under the circumstances of this case, we cannot say that petitioner has sustained that heavy burden. A contrary ruling would mean that the Federal Government as a whole lacked the power exercised by the President and that we are not prepared to say.

[T]here remains the question of the President's authority to suspend claims pending in American courts. Such claims have, of course, an existence apart from the attachments which accompanied them. In terminating these claims, [the] President purported to act under authority of both the IEEPA and the so-called "Hostage Act" [of 1868]. [We conclude] that neither the IEEPA nor the Hostage Act constitutes specific authorization of the President's [action]. [However, this] is not to say that these statutory provisions are entirely irrelevant to the question of the validity of the President's action. We think both statutes highly relevant in the looser sense of indicating congressional acceptance of a broad scope for executive action in circumstances such as those presented in this case. [T]he IEEPA delegates broad authority to the President to act in times of national emergency with respect to property of a foreign country. The Hostage Act similarly indicates congressional willingness that the President have broad discretion when responding to the hostile acts of foreign sovereigns. [We] cannot ignore the general tenor of Congress' legislation in this area in trying to determine whether the President is acting alone or at least with the acceptance of Congress. [Congress] cannot anticipate and legislate with regard to every possible action the President may find it necessary to take or every possible situation in which he might act. Such failure of Congress specifically to delegate authority does not, "especially [in] the areas of foreign policy and national security," imply "congressional disapproval" of action taken by the Executive. On the contrary, the enactment of legislation closely related to the question of the President's authority in a particular case which evinces legislative intent to accord the President broad discretion may be considered to "invite" "measures on independent presidential responsibility," Youngstown (Jackson, J., concurring). At least this is so where there is no contrary indication of legislative intent and when, as here, there is a history of congressional acquiescence in conduct of the sort engaged in by the President. It is to that history which we now turn.

Not infrequently in affairs between nations, outstanding claims by nationals of one country against the government of another country are "sources of friction" between the two sovereigns. To resolve these difficulties, nations have often entered into agreements settling the claims of their respective nationals. As one treatise writer puts it, international agreements settling claims by nationals of one state against the government of another "are established international practice reflecting traditional international theory." L. Henkin, Foreign Affairs and the Constitution 262 (1972). Consistent with that principle, the United States has repeatedly exercised its sovereign authority to settle the claims of its nationals against foreign countries. Though those settlements have sometimes been made by treaty, there has also been a longstanding practice of settling such claims by executive agreement without the advice and consent of the Senate. Under such agreements, the President has agreed to renounce or extinguish claims of United States nationals against foreign governments in return for lump-sum payments or the establishment of arbitration procedures. [It] is clear that the practice of settling claims continues today. Since 1952, the President has entered into at least 10 binding settlements with foreign nations, including an $80 million settlement with the People's Republic of China.

Crucial to our decision today is the conclusion that Congress has implicitly approved the practice of claim settlement by executive agreement. This is best demonstrated by Congress' enactment of the International Claims Settlement Act of 1949. [Over] the years Congress has frequently amended the International Claims Settlement Act to provide for particular problems arising out of settlement agreements, thus demonstrating Congress' continuing acceptance of the President's claim settlement authority. [Finally,] the legislative history of the IEEPA further reveals that Congress has accepted the authority of the Executive to enter into settlement agreements. Though the IEEPA was enacted to provide for some limitation on the President's emergency powers, Congress stressed that "[nothing] in this act is intended [to] interfere with the authority of the President to [block assets], or to impede the settlement of claims of U.S. citizens against foreign countries."[1] In addition to congressional acquiescence in the President's power to settle claims, prior cases of this Court have also recognized that the President does have some measure of power to enter into executive agreements without obtaining the advice and consent of the Senate.

[In] light of all of the foregoing—the inferences to be drawn from the character of the legislation Congress has enacted in the area, such as the IEEPA and the Hostage Act, and from the history of acquiescence in executive claims settlement—we conclude that the President was authorized to suspend pending [claims]. As Justice Frankfurter pointed out in Youngstown, "a systematic, unbroken, executive practice, long pursued to the knowledge of the Congress and never before questioned [may] be treated as a gloss on 'Executive Power' vested in the President by § 1 of Art. II." Past practice does not, by itself, create power, but "long-continued practice, known to and acquiesced in by Congress, would raise a presumption that the [action] had been [taken] in pursuance of its [consent]." [In] light of the fact that Congress may be considered to have consented to the President's action in suspending claims, we cannot say that action exceeded the President's powers. Our conclusion is buttressed by the fact that the means chosen by the President to settle the claims of American nationals provided an alternative forum, the Claims Tribunal, which is capable of providing meaningful [relief]. [Just] as importantly, Congress has not disapproved of the action taken here. Though Congress has held hearings on the Iranian Agreement itself, Congress has not enacted legislation, or even passed a resolution, indicating its displeasure with the Agreement. Quite the contrary, the relevant Senate Committee has stated that the establishment of the Tribunal is "of vital importance to the United States." We are thus clearly not confronted with a situation in which Congress has in some way resisted the exercise of Presidential authority. Finally, we re-emphasize the narrowness of our decision. We do not decide that the President possesses plenary power to settle claims, even as against foreign governmental entities. [But] where, as here, the settlement of claims has been determined to be a necessary incident to the resolution of a major foreign policy dispute between our country and another, and where, as here, we can conclude that Congress acquiesced in the President's action, we are not prepared to say

---

1 Indeed, Congress has consistently failed to object to this longstanding practice of claim settlement by executive agreement, even when it has had an opportunity to do so. In 1972, Congress entertained legislation relating to congressional oversight of such agreements. But Congress took only limited [action]. [Footnote by Justice Rehnquist.]

that the President lacks the power to settle such claims. [Justices POWELL and STEVENS filed opinions concurring in part.]

DAMES & MOORE IN LIGHT OF YOUNGSTOWN

1. ***The use of Jackson's tripartite methodology.*** Is the approach of Dames & Moore reconcilable with that of Justice Black's opinion in Youngstown? William H. Rehnquist served a law clerk for Justice Jackson in the Term immediately following the Youngstown decision. In Dames & Moore, Justice Rehnquist seemingly followed Jackson's functional Youngstown approach more closely than Justice Black's—in retrospect a harbinger of the gradual transformation of the Jackson solo concurrence into the holding of Youngstown. Was Justice Rehnquist's view that Congress had given legislative approval to the executive agreement consistent with the implications drawn from congressional silence in Youngstown? Consider the view that the "Court should have demanded more specific legislative approval for the President's far-reaching measures," and that Dames & Moore "not only inverted the Steel Seizure holding" by construing failure of Congress to approve the Presidential Act as legislative disapproval, "but also condoned legislative inactivity at a time that demanded interbranch dialogue and bipartisan consensus." Koh, The National Security Constitution: Sharing Power after the Iran-Contra Affair 140 (1990).

2. ***Presidential authority over foreign relations.*** Does Dames & Moore (as well as the Court's upholding of every executive agreement it has confronted) suggest that presidential policymaking in foreign affairs stands on stronger footing than presidential policymaking in the domestic sphere? Is there adequate constitutional justification for that difference? For the historical argument that Article II does not grant the executive autonomous foreign affairs powers, and that the Washington presidency set the nation on a course of coordination between the President and Congress on such matters, see Casper, Separating Power (1997). For the historical argument that the President has broad, residual foreign affairs power from Article II, covering all matters except those allocated away from him, such as the war, treatymaking and commerce powers allocated to Congress, see Prakash & Ramsey, "The Executive Power Over Foreign Affairs," 111 Yale L.J. 231 (2001).

Is an executive agreement any more constitutionally acceptable if made effective through majority votes in both Houses of Congress? Even if such legislative ratification exists, it falls short of the two-thirds Senate vote the Constitution requires for treaty ratification. The question has resurfaced in connection with such important recent national policy debates as that over multilateral trade agreements such as the Trans-Pacific Partnership, the North American Free Trade Agreement and the 1994 World Trade Organization Agreement negotiated in the Uruguay Round of the GATT. For differing views on the constitutionality of such measures, compare Ackerman & Golove, "Is NAFTA Constitutional?," 108 Harv. L. Rev. 799 (1995), with Tribe, "Taking Text and Structure Seriously," 108 Harv. L. Rev. 1221 (1995). For a defense of the practice, see Yoo, "Laws as Treaties?: The Constitutionality of Congressional-Executive Agreements," 99 Mich. L. Rev. 757 (2001).

3. ***Executive power over the states pursuant to treaty power?*** Does the president or Congress have authority to direct the states to act in accordance with a treaty? In **Medellin v. Texas**, 552 U.S. 491 (2008), President George W. Bush issued a statement declaring that the United States would comply with its treaty obligations under the Vienna Convention on Consular Rights by means of states' respecting the judgment of the International Court of Justice [ICJ]. The ICJ judgment ordered the United States to cause states to re-review the death sentences of several Mexican nationals who had not been afforded the right to speak with a member of the Mexican consulate in violation of the Vienna Convention. Writing for the majority, Chief Justice ROBERTS stated that the President lacked the authority to direct the states to re-review the prisoners' death sentences, holding that unless a treaty is "self-executing" (i.e., not requiring any further congressional action in order to become domestic law), Congress, not the President has the power to make domestic laws in furtherance of carrying out treaty obligations:

"The United States marshals two principal arguments in favor of the President's authority 'to establish binding rules of decision that preempt contrary state law.' The Solicitor General first argues that the relevant treaties give the President the authority to implement the [ICJ] judgment and that Congress has acquiesced in the exercise of such authority. The United States also relies upon an 'independent' international dispute-resolution power wholly apart from the asserted authority based on the pertinent treaties. Medellín adds the additional argument that the President's Memorandum is a valid exercise of his power to take care that the laws be faithfully executed.

"We disagree. The President has an array of political and diplomatic means available to enforce international obligations, but unilaterally converting a non-self-executing treaty into a self-executing one is not among them. The responsibility for transforming an international obligation arising from a non-self-executing treaty into domestic law falls to Congress. As this Court has explained, when treaty stipulations are 'not self-executing they can only be enforced pursuant to legislation to carry them into effect.' Moreover, '[u]ntil such act shall be passed, the Court is not at liberty to disregard the existing laws on the subject.'

"The requirement that Congress, rather than the President, implement a non-self-executing treaty derives from the text of the Constitution, which divides the treaty-making power between the President and the Senate. The Constitution vests the President with the authority to 'make' a treaty. If the Executive determines that a treaty should have domestic effect of its own force, that determination may be implemented 'in mak[ing]' the treaty, by ensuring that it contains language plainly providing for domestic enforceability. If the treaty is to be self-executing in this respect, the Senate must consent to the treaty by the requisite two-thirds vote, consistent with all other constitutional restraints.

"Once a treaty is ratified without provisions clearly according it domestic effect, however, whether the treaty will ever have such effect is governed by the fundamental constitutional principle that '[t]he power to make the necessary laws is in Congress; the power to execute in the President.' As already noted, the terms of a non-self-executing treaty can become domestic law only in the same way as any other law—through passage of legislation by both Houses of Congress, combined with either the President's signature or a congressional override of a Presidential veto.

"[A] non-self-executing treaty, by definition, is one that was ratified with the understanding that it is not to have domestic effect of its own force. That understanding precludes the assertion that Congress has implicitly authorized the President—acting on his own—to achieve precisely the same result. We therefore conclude, given the absence of congressional legislation, that the non-self-executing treaties at issue here did not 'express[ly] or implied[ly]' vest the President with the unilateral authority to make them self-executing. Accordingly, the President's Memorandum does not fall within the first category of the Youngstown framework.

"Indeed, the preceding discussion should make clear that the non-self-executing character of the relevant treaties not only refutes the notion that the ratifying parties vested the President with the authority to unilaterally make treaty obligations binding on domestic courts, but also implicitly prohibits him from doing so. When the President asserts the power to 'enforce' a non-self-executing treaty by unilaterally creating domestic law, he acts in conflict with the implicit understanding of the ratifying Senate. His assertion of authority, insofar as it is based on the pertinent non-self-executing treaties, is therefore within Justice Jackson's third category, not the first or even the second.

"[We] thus turn to the United States' claim that—independent of the United States' treaty obligations—the Memorandum is a valid exercise of the President's foreign affairs authority to resolve claims disputes with foreign nations. The United States relies on a series of cases in which this Court has upheld the authority of the President to settle foreign claims pursuant to an executive agreement. In these cases this Court has explained that, if pervasive enough, a history of congressional acquiescence can be treated as a 'gloss on "Executive Power" vested in the President by § 1 of Art. II.'

"This argument is of a different nature than the one rejected above. Rather than relying on the United States' treaty obligations, the President relies on an independent source of authority in ordering Texas to put aside its procedural bar to successive habeas petitions. Nevertheless, we find that our claims-settlement cases do not support the authority that the President asserts in this case. The claims-settlement cases involve a narrow set of circumstances: the making of executive agreements to settle civil claims between American citizens and foreign governments or foreign nationals. They are based on the view that 'a systematic, unbroken, executive practice, long pursued to the knowledge of the Congress and never before questioned,' can 'raise a presumption that the [action] had been [taken] in pursuance of its consent.'

"[The] President's Memorandum is not supported by a 'particularly longstanding practice' of congressional acquiescence, but rather is what the United States itself has described as 'unprecedented action.' Indeed, the Government has not identified a single instance in which the President has attempted (or Congress has acquiesced in) a Presidential directive issued to state courts, much less one that reaches deep into the heart of the State's police powers and compels state courts to reopen final criminal judgments and set aside neutrally applicable state laws. The Executive's narrow and strictly limited authority to settle international claims disputes pursuant to an executive agreement cannot stretch so far as to support the current Presidential Memorandum.

"Medellín argues that the President's Memorandum is a valid exercise of his 'Take Care' power. The United States, however, does not rely upon the President's responsibility to 'take Care that the Laws be faithfully executed.' We think this a wise concession. This authority allows the President to execute the laws, not make them. For the reasons we have stated, the Avena judgment is not domestic law; accordingly, the President cannot rely on his Take Care powers here. [Affirmed.]"

Justice BREYER dissented: "Given the Court's comparative lack of expertise in foreign affairs; given the importance of the Nation's foreign relations; given the difficulty of finding the proper constitutional balance among state and federal, executive and legislative, powers in such matters; and given the likely future importance of this Court's efforts to do so, I would very much hesitate before concluding that the Constitution implicitly sets forth broad prohibitions (or permissions) in this area. I would thus be content to leave the matter in the constitutional shade from which it has emerged. Given my view of this case, I need not answer the question. And I shall not try to do so."

EXECUTIVE POWER, IMMIGRATION AND RELIGIOUS BIAS

On January 27, 2017, just after his inauguration, President Donald Trump signed Executive Order No. 13769, "Protecting the Nation from Foreign Terrorist Entry into the United States," 82 Fed. Reg. 8977. The order (EO-1) barred visitors from Iraq, Syria, Iran, Libya, Somalia, Sudan and Yemen from entering the United States for 90 days, suspended entry of Syrian refugees indefinitely and blocked any other refugees for 120 days. Volunteer lawyers flocked to airports to assist travelers who would be stopped as a result of the order. The American Civil Liberties Union, representing travelers, sued to block the operation of EO-1, alleging among other things that that it was motivated by anti-Muslim bias. The evidence came from statements by Trump as a candidate and by advisors including former New York mayor Rudolph Giuliani.

After a federal district in Washington State stayed the operation of EO-1, and the U.S. Court of Appeals for the Ninth Circuit upheld the ruling, Trump, on March 6, 2017, revoked the first order and signed a new, amended Executive Order No. 13780, 82 Fed. Reg. 13209. This second order (EO-2) allowed for case-by-case waivers, exempted travelers who already had visas and green cards and removed Iraq from the list of covered countries. It stated that the countries had been selected because each "is a state sponsor of terrorism, has been significantly compromised by terrorist organizations, or contains active conflict zones." EO-2 also mandated an executive-branch review of the adequacy of current practices of visa granting. Federal district courts in Hawaii and Maryland issued nationwide preliminary injunctions staying this order, and courts of appeals left those injunctions in place.

In **Trump v. International Refugee Assistance Project**, 582 U.S. ___, 137 S. Ct. 2080 (2017) (per curiam), the Supreme Court stayed the injunctions and allowed the travel ban to go into effect only with respect to foreign nationals who lacked a "credible claim of a bona fide relationship" with a person or entity in the United States. The court explained that denying entry to a foreign national "who [has] no connection to the United States at all" did "not burden any American party by reason of that party's relationship with the foreign national." It held that "[f]or individuals, a close familial relationship is required. [As] for entities, the relationship must be formal, documented, and formed in the ordinary course, rather than for the purpose of evading EO-2. The students from the designated countries who have been admitted to the University of Hawaii have such a relationship with an American entity. So too would a worker who accepted an offer of employment from an American company or a lecturer invited to address an American audience. Not so someone who enters into a relationship simply to avoid [EO-2]: For example, a nonprofit group devoted to immigration issues may not contact foreign nationals from the designated countries, add them to client lists, and then secure their entry by claiming injury from their exclusion."

On September 24, 2017, after the temporary order had expired, Trump issued a further Proclamation No. 9645, "Enhancing Vetting Capabilities and Processes for Detecting Attempted Entry Into the United States by Terrorists or Other Public-Safety Threats," 82 Fed. Reg. 45161. The Proclamation placed entry restrictions on certain nationals of Chad, Iran, Iraq, Libya, North Korea, Syria, Yemen and Venezuela, on the ground that those countries had inadequate systems in place for managing and sharing information about their nationals with the United States. The Proclamation stated that the Department of Homeland Security had made this determination after review in consultation with the State Department and intelligence agencies. The Proclamation suspended entry of all nationals from Iran, North Korea and Syria, except for Iranians seeking nonimmigrant student and exchange-visitor visas. For Somalia, it suspended entry of nationals seeking immigrant visas and required additional scrutiny of nationals seeking nonimmigrant visas. For Venezuela, the Proclamation limited entry only of certain government officials and their family members on nonimmigrant business or tourist visas. The Proclamation exempted lawful permanent residents and foreign nationals who had been granted asylum, and provided for case-by-case waivers when a foreign national demonstrates undue hardship, and that his entry is in the national interest and would not pose a threat to public safety. The Proclamation further directed DHS to assess on a continuing basis whether entry restrictions should be modified or continued.

The State of Hawaii, three individuals (Dr. Ismail Elshikh, John Doe #1 and John Doe #2) and the Muslim Association of Hawaii challenged the proclamation, and the district court granted a nationwide preliminary injunction barring its enforcement. The Ninth Circuit upheld the district court on statutory grounds and did not reach the plaintiffs' Establishment Clause claim.

In **Trump v. Hawaii**, 585 U.S. ___, 138 S. Ct. 2392 (2018), the Court reversed in an opinion by Chief Justice ROBERTS. First it addressed the statutory issues, holding that the president's actions were authorized by 8 U.S.C. §§ 1182(f), which "grants the President broad discretion to suspend the entry of aliens into the United States." The court held that "the President lawfully exercised that discretion based on his findings—following a worldwide, multi-agency review—that entry of the covered aliens would be detrimental to the national interest."

Turning to the constitutional issues, the Court first held that the plaintiffs had standing because "a person's interest in being united with his relatives is sufficiently concrete and particularized to form the basis of an

Article III injury in fact." The Court then rejected the plaintiffs' Establishment Clause claim that the Proclamation "singl[ed] out Muslims for disfavored treatment" and "operate[d] as a 'religious gerrymander,' in part because most of the countries covered by the Proclamation have Muslim-majority populations."

Chief Justice Roberts continued: "At the heart of plaintiffs' case is a series of statements by the President and his advisers casting doubt on the official objective of the Proclamation. For example, while a candidate on the campaign trail, the President published a 'Statement on Preventing Muslim Immigration' that called for a 'total and complete shutdown of Muslims entering the United States until our country's representatives can figure out what is going on.'" That statement remained on his campaign website until May 2017. Then-candidate Trump also stated that 'Islam hates us' and asserted that the United States was 'having problems with Muslims coming into the country.' Shortly after being elected, when asked whether violence in Europe had affected his plans to 'ban Muslim immigration,' the President replied, 'You know my plans. All along, I've been proven to be right.' One week after his inauguration, the President issued EO-1. In a television interview, one of the President's campaign advisers [editors' note: Rudy Giuliani] explained that when the President 'first announced it, he said, "Muslim ban." He called me up. He said, "Put a commission together. Show me the right way to do it legally."' The adviser said he assembled a group of Members of Congress and lawyers that 'focused on, instead of religion, danger. . . . [The order] is based on places where there [is] substantial evidence that people are sending terrorists into our country.'

"Plaintiffs also note that after issuing EO-2 to replace EO-1, the President expressed regret that his prior order had been 'watered down' and called for a 'much tougher version of his 'Travel Ban.' Shortly before the release of the Proclamation, he stated that the 'travel ban . . . should be far larger, tougher, and more specific,' but 'stupidly that would not be politically correct.' More recently, on November 29, 2017, the President retweeted links to three anti-Muslim propaganda videos. In response to questions about those videos, the President's deputy press secretary denied that the President thinks Muslims are a threat to the United States, explaining that 'the President has been talking about these security issues for years now, from the campaign trail to the White House' and 'has addressed these issues with the travel order that he issued earlier this year and the companion proclamation.'

"[The] issue before us is not whether to denounce the statements. It is instead the significance of those statements in reviewing a Presidential directive, neutral on its face, addressing a matter within the core of executive responsibility. In doing so, we must consider not only the statements of a particular President, but also the authority of the Presidency itself.

"The case before us differs in numerous respects from the conventional Establishment Clause claim. Unlike the typical suit involving religious displays or school prayer, plaintiffs seek to invalidate a national security directive regulating the entry of aliens abroad. Their claim accordingly raises a number of delicate issues regarding the scope of the constitutional right and the manner of proof. The Proclamation, moreover, is facially neutral toward religion. Plaintiffs therefore ask the Court to probe the sincerity of the stated justifications for the policy by reference to extrinsic statements—

many of which were made before the President took the oath of office. These various aspects of plaintiffs' challenge inform our standard of review.

"For more than a century, this Court has recognized that the admission and exclusion of foreign nationals is a fundamental sovereign attribute exercised by the Government's political departments largely immune from judicial control. Because decisions in these matters may implicate relations with foreign powers, or involve classifications defined in the light of changing political and economic circumstances, such judgments are frequently of a character more appropriate to either the Legislature or the Executive. Nonetheless, although foreign nationals seeking admission have no constitutional right to entry, this Court has engaged in a circumscribed judicial inquiry when the denial of a visa allegedly burdens the constitutional rights of a U.S. citizen.

"In Kleindienst v. Mandel, 408 U.S. 753 (1972), the Attorney General denied admission to a Belgian journalist and self-described 'revolutionary Marxist,' Ernest Mandel, who had been invited to speak at a conference at Stanford University. [We] held that 'when the Executive exercises this [delegated] power negatively on the basis of a facially legitimate and bona fide reason, the courts will neither look behind the exercise of that discretion, nor test it by balancing its justification' against the asserted constitutional interests of U.S. citizens. [Mandel's] narrow standard of review has particular force in admission and immigration cases that overlap with the area of national security.

"[A] conventional application of Mandel, asking only whether the policy is facially legitimate and bona fide, would put an end to our review. [For] our purposes today, we assume that we may look behind the face of the Proclamation to the extent of applying rational basis review. That standard of review considers whether the entry policy is plausibly related to the Government's stated objective to protect the country and improve vetting processes. As a result, we may consider plaintiffs' extrinsic evidence, but will uphold the policy so long as it can reasonably be understood to result from a justification independent of unconstitutional grounds.[1]

"[The] Court hardly ever strikes down a policy as illegitimate under rational basis scrutiny. On the few occasions where we have done so, a common thread has been that the laws at issue lack any purpose other than a bare [desire] to harm a politically unpopular group. In one case, we invalidated a local zoning ordinance that required a special permit for group homes for the intellectually disabled, but not for other facilities such as fraternity houses or hospitals. Cleburne v. Cleburne [p. 799]. And in another case, this Court overturned a state constitutional amendment that denied gays and lesbians access to the protection of antidiscrimination laws. The [amendment] seemed 'inexplicable by anything but animus.' Romer v. Evans [p. 553].

"The Proclamation does not fit this pattern. It cannot be said that it is impossible to discern a relationship to legitimate state interests or that the policy is 'inexplicable by anything but animus. [Because] there is persuasive evidence that the entry suspension has a legitimate grounding in national

[1] The dissent finds 'perplexing' the application of rational basis review in this context. But what is far more problematic is the dissent's assumption that courts should review immigration policies, diplomatic sanctions, and military actions under the *de novo* 'reasonable observer' inquiry applicable to cases involving holiday displays and graduation ceremonies.

security concerns, quite apart from any religious hostility, we must accept that independent justification.

"The Proclamation is expressly premised on legitimate purposes: preventing entry of nationals who cannot be adequately vetted and inducing other nations to improve their practices. The text says nothing about religion. [Five] of the seven nations currently included in the Proclamation have Muslim-majority populations. Yet that fact alone does not support an inference of religious hostility, given that the policy covers just 8% of the world's Muslim population and is limited to countries that were previously designated by Congress or prior administrations as posing national security risks. The Proclamation, moreover, reflects the results of a worldwide review process undertaken by multiple Cabinet officials and their agencies. Plaintiffs seek to discredit the findings of the review, pointing to deviations from the review's baseline criteria resulting in the inclusion of Somalia and omission of Iraq. But as the Proclamation explains, in each case the determinations were justified by the distinct conditions in each country.

"[More] fundamentally, plaintiffs and the dissent [suggest] that the policy is overbroad and does little to serve national security interests. But we cannot substitute our own assessment for the Executive's predictive judgments on such matters. [While] we of course 'do not defer to the Government's reading of the First Amendment,' the Executive's evaluation of the underlying facts is entitled to appropriate weight, particularly in the context of litigation involving 'sensitive and weighty interests of national security and foreign affairs.' Humanitarian Law Project [p. 1199].

"Finally, the dissent invokes Korematsu. Whatever rhetorical advantage the dissent may see in doing so, Korematsu has nothing to do with this case. The forcible relocation of U.S. citizens to concentration camps, solely and explicitly on the basis of race, is objectively unlawful and outside the scope of Presidential authority. But it is wholly inapt to liken that morally repugnant order to a facially neutral policy denying certain foreign nationals the privilege of admission. The entry suspension is an act that is well within executive authority and could have been taken by any other President—the only question is evaluating the actions of this particular President in promulgating an otherwise valid Proclamation.

"The dissent's reference to Korematsu, however, affords this Court the opportunity to make express what is already obvious: Korematsu was gravely wrong the day it was decided, has been overruled in the court of history, and—to be clear—'has no place in law under the Constitution.' Id. (Jackson, J., dissenting)."

Justice KENNEDY joined the opinion fully and concurred briefly in what would be his last opinion before announcing his retirement the following day: "There may be some common ground between the opinions in this case, in that the Court does acknowledge that in some instances, governmental action may be subject to judicial review to determine whether or not it is 'inexplicable by anything but animus,' Romer, which in this case would be animosity to a religion. Whether judicial proceedings may properly continue in this case, in light of the substantial deference that is and must be accorded to the Executive in the conduct of foreign affairs, and in light of today's decision, is a matter to be addressed in the first instance on remand. And even if further proceedings are permitted, it would be necessary to determine that any discovery and other preliminary matters would not themselves intrude on the foreign affairs power of the Executive.

"[There] are numerous instances in which the statements and actions of Government officials are not subject to judicial scrutiny or intervention. That does not mean those officials are free to disregard the Constitution and the rights it proclaims and protects. [The] very fact that an official may have broad discretion, discretion free from judicial scrutiny, makes it all the more imperative for him or her to adhere to the Constitution and to its meaning and its promise. [It] is an urgent necessity that officials adhere to [the First Amendment] in all their actions, even in the sphere of foreign affairs. An anxious world must know that our Government remains committed always to the liberties the Constitution seeks to preserve and protect, so that freedom extends outward, and lasts."

Justice BREYER, joined by Justice Kagan, dissented: "If [the Proclamation's] promulgation or content was significantly affected by religious animus against Muslims, it would violate the relevant statute or the First Amendment itself. If, however, its sole *ratio decidendi* was one of national security, then it would be unlikely to violate either the statute or the Constitution. [Members] of the Court principally disagree about the answer to this question, *i.e.*, about whether or the extent to which religious animus played a significant role in the Proclamation's promulgation or content. [The] Proclamation's elaborate system of exemptions and waivers can and should help us answer this question. [If] the Government is applying the exemption and waiver provisions as written, then its argument for the Proclamation's lawfulness is strengthened. [Since] the case-by-case exemptions and waivers apply without regard to the individual's religion, application of that system would help make clear that the Proclamation does not deny visas to numerous Muslim individuals (from those countries) who do not pose a security threat. [If] the Government is *not* applying the system of exemptions and waivers that the Proclamation contains, then its argument for the Proclamation's lawfulness becomes significantly weaker. [If] the Government is not applying the Proclamation's exemption and waiver system, the claim that the Proclamation is a 'Muslim ban,' rather than a 'security-based' ban, becomes much stronger. [Unfortunately] there is evidence that supports the second possibility, *i.e.*, that the Government is not applying the Proclamation as written. The Proclamation provides that the Secretary of State and the Secretary of Homeland Security 'shall coordinate to adopt guidance' for consular officers to follow when deciding whether to grant a waiver. Yet, to my knowledge, no guidance has issued. [The] State Department reported that during the Proclamation's first month, two waivers were approved out of 6,555 eligible applicants. [The] Government claims that number increased from 2 to 430 during the first four months of implementation. That number, 430, however, when compared with the number of pre-Proclamation visitors, accounts for a miniscule percentage of those likely eligible for visas, in such categories as persons requiring medical treatment, academic visitors, students, family members, and others belonging to groups that, when considered as a group (rather than case by case), would not seem to pose security threats. [The] Government has not had an opportunity to respond, and a court has not had an opportunity to decide. But, given the importance of the decision in this case, the need for assurance that the Proclamation does not rest upon a 'Muslim ban,' and the assistance in deciding the issue that answers to the exemption and waiver questions may provide, I would send this case back to the District Court for further proceedings. And, I would leave the injunction in effect while the matter is litigated. Regardless, the Court's decision today leaves the District

Court free to explore these issues on remand. If this Court must decide the question without this further litigation, I would, on balance, find the evidence of antireligious bias, including statements on a website taken down only after the President issued the two executive orders preceding the Proclamation, along with the other statements also set forth in Justice Sotomayor's opinion, a sufficient basis to set the Proclamation aside."

Justice SOTOMAYOR dissented, joined by Justice Ginsburg: "The United States of America is a Nation built upon the promise of religious liberty. [The] Court's decision today fails to safeguard that fundamental principle. It leaves undisturbed a policy first advertised openly and unequivocally as a 'total and complete shutdown of Muslims entering the United States' because the policy now masquerades behind a façade of national-security concerns. But this repackaging does little to cleanse [the] Proclamation of the appearance of discrimination that the President's words have created. [To] determine whether plaintiffs have proved an Establishment Clause violation, the Court asks whether a reasonable observer would view the government action as enacted for the purpose of disfavoring a religion. In answering that question, this Court has generally considered the text of the government policy, its operation, and any available evidence regarding the historical background of the decision under challenge, the specific series of events leading to the enactment or official policy in question, and the legislative or administrative history, including contemporaneous statements made by the decisionmaker. Lukumi. At the same time, however, courts must take care not to engage in "any judicial psychoanalysis of a drafter's heart of hearts. Although the majority briefly recounts a few of the statements and background events that form the basis of plaintiffs' constitutional challenge, that highly abridged account does not tell even half of the story. The full record paints a far more harrowing picture, from which a reasonable observer would readily conclude that the Proclamation was motivated by hostility and animus toward the Muslim faith.

"During his Presidential campaign, then-candidate Donald Trump pledged that, if elected, he would ban Muslims from entering the United States. [On] December 8, 2015, Trump justified his proposal during a television interview by noting that President Franklin D. Roosevelt 'did the same thing' with respect to the internment of Japanese Americans during World War II. In January 2016, during a Republican primary debate, Trump was asked whether he wanted to 'rethink [his] position' on 'banning Muslims from entering the country.' He answered, 'No.' A month later, at a rally in South Carolina, Trump told an apocryphal story about United States General John J. Pershing killing a large group of Muslim insurgents in the Philippines with bullets dipped in pigs' blood in the early 1900's. In March 2016, he expressed his belief that 'Islam hates us. . . . [W]e can't allow people coming into this country who have this hatred of the United States . . . [a]nd of people that are not Muslim.' That same month, Trump asserted that '[w]e're having problems with the Muslims, and we're having problems with Muslims coming into the country.' He therefore called for surveillance of mosques in the United States, blaming terrorist attacks on Muslims' lack of 'assimilation' and their commitment to 'sharia law.'

"[As] Trump's presidential campaign progressed, he began to describe his policy proposal in slightly different terms. In June 2016, for instance, he characterized the policy proposal as a suspension of immigration from countries 'where there's a proven history of terrorism.' [A] month before the 2016 election, Trump reiterated that his proposed 'Muslim ban' had 'morphed into a[n] extreme vetting from certain areas of the world.'

"On January 27, 2017, one week after taking office, President Trump signed [EO-1] As he signed it, President Trump read the title, looked up, and said "We all know what that means." That same day, President Trump explained to the media that, under EO-1, Christians would be given priority for entry as refugees into the United States. In particular, he bemoaned the fact that in the past, '[i]f you were a Muslim [refugee from Syria] you could come in, but if you were a Christian, it was almost impossible.' Considering that past policy "very unfair," President Trump explained that EO-1 was designed 'to help' the Christians in Syria. [After] EO-2 was issued, the White House Press Secretary told reporters that, by issuing EO-2, President Trump 'continue[d] to deliver on . . . his most significant campaign promises.' [While] litigation over EO-2 was ongoing, President Trump repeatedly made statements alluding to a desire to keep Muslims out of the country. [In] June 2017, the President [tweeted]: 'People, the lawyers and the courts can call it whatever they want, but I am calling it what we need and what it is, a TRAVEL BAN!' *Id.*, at 132–133. He added: 'That's right, we need a TRAVEL BAN for certain DANGEROUS countries, not some politically correct term that won't help us protect our people!' [On] November 29, 2017, President Trump retweeted three anti-Muslim videos. [Those] videos were initially tweeted by a British political party whose mission is to oppose 'all alien and destructive politic[al] or religious doctrines, including . . . Islam.' When asked about these videos, the White House Deputy Press Secretary connected them to the Proclamation, responding that the 'President has been talking about these security issues for years now, from the campaign trail to the White House' and 'has addressed these issues with the travel order that he issued earlier this year and the companion proclamation.'

"[Taking] all the relevant evidence together, a reasonable observer would conclude that the Proclamation was driven primarily by anti-Muslim animus, rather than by the Government's asserted national-security justifications. [Moreover,] despite several opportunities to do so, President Trump has never disavowed any of his prior statements about Islam. [Ultimately,] new window dressing cannot conceal an unassailable fact: the words of the President and his advisers create the strong perception that the Proclamation is contaminated by impermissible discriminatory animus against Islam and its followers.

"[The] majority rightly declines to apply Mandel's narrow standard of review. [In] doing so, however, the Court, without explanation or precedential support, limits its review of the Proclamation to rational-basis scrutiny. That approach is perplexing, given that in other Establishment Clause cases, including those involving claims of religious animus or discrimination, this Court has applied a more stringent standard of review. [But] even under rational-basis review, the Proclamation must fall [because it] is divorced from any factual context from which we could discern a relationship to legitimate state interests, and its sheer breadth is so discontinuous with the reasons offered for it that the policy is inexplicable by anything but animus. Romer. [It] is of no moment that the Proclamation also includes minor restrictions on two non-Muslim majority countries, North Korea and Venezuela, or that the Government has removed a few Muslim-majority countries from the list of covered countries since EO-1 was issued. [The] inclusion of North Korea and Venezuela, and the removal of other countries, simply reflect subtle efforts to start 'talking territory instead of Muslim,' precisely so the Executive Branch could evade criticism or legal consequences for the Proclamation's otherwise clear targeting of Muslims. The Proclamation's effect on North Korea and Venezuela, for example, is insubstantial, if not entirely symbolic. [The] worldwide review does little to break the clear connection between the Proclamation and the President's anti-Muslim statements. [The] majority empowers the President to hide behind an administrative review process that the Government refuses to disclose to the public. [Evidence] of which we can take judicial notice indicates that the multiagency review process could not have been very thorough. [The] September 2017 report the Government produced after its review process was a mere 17 pages. [That] the Government's analysis of the vetting practices of hundreds of countries boiled down to such a short document raises serious questions about the legitimacy of the President's proclaimed national-security rationale. [Congress also] has already erected a statutory scheme that fulfills the putative national-security interests the Government now puts forth to justify the Proclamation. [Several] former national-security officials from both political parties [have] advised that the Proclamation and its predecessor orders 'do not advance the national-security or foreign policy interests of the United States, and in fact do serious harm to those interests.' Brief for Former National Security Officials as *Amici Curiae*.

"[Just] weeks ago, the Court rendered its decision in Masterpiece Cakeshop [2018; p. 1576], which applied the bedrock principles of religious neutrality and tolerance in considering a First Amendment challenge to government action. [In] both instances, the question is whether a government actor exhibited tolerance and neutrality in reaching a decision that affects individuals' fundamental religious freedom. But unlike in Masterpiece, where a state civil rights commission was found to have acted without the neutrality that the Free Exercise Clause requires, the government actors in this case will not be held accountable for breaching the First Amendment's guarantee of religious neutrality and tolerance. Unlike in Masterpiece, where the majority considered the state commissioners' statements about religion to be persuasive evidence of unconstitutional government action, the majority here completely sets aside the President's charged statements about Muslims as irrelevant. That holding erodes the foundational principles of religious tolerance that the Court elsewhere has so emphatically protected, and it tells members of minority religions in our country 'that they are outsiders, not full members of the political community.'

"Today's holding is all the more troubling given the stark parallels between the reasoning of this case and that of *Korematsu*. [As] here, the Government invoked an ill-defined national-security threat to justify an exclusionary policy of sweeping proportion. As here, the exclusion order was rooted in dangerous stereotypes about, *inter alia*, a particular group's supposed inability to assimilate and desire to harm the United States. As here, the Government was unwilling to reveal its own intelligence agencies' views of the alleged security concerns to the very citizens it purported to protect. And as here, there was strong evidence that impermissible hostility and animus motivated the Government's policy.

"[Today,] the Court takes the important step of finally overruling Korematsu. [This] formal repudiation of a shameful precedent is laudable and long overdue. But it does not make the majority's decision here acceptable or right. By blindly accepting the Government's misguided invitation to sanction a discriminatory policy motivated by animosity toward a disfavored group, all in the name of a superficial claim of national security, the Court redeploys the same dangerous logic underlying Korematsu and merely replaces one gravely wrong decision with another."

SECTION 2. CONGRESSIONAL WAR AND TREATY POWERS, AND THE IMPLIED POWER OVER FOREIGN AFFAIRS

The Constitution grants Congress certain powers over war and treaty issues. These powers allow Congress to act in areas traditionally under executive control. In addition to separation of powers issues, federalism issues are often implicated when the exigencies of foreign affairs disrupt the balance of powers between the national and state governments.

Woods v. Cloyd W. Miller Co.

333 U.S. 138, 68 S. Ct. 421, 92 L. Ed. 596 (1948).

■ JUSTICE DOUGLAS delivered the opinion of the Court.

The case is here on a direct appeal [from] a judgment of the District Court holding unconstitutional Title II of the Housing and Rent Act of 1947. The District Court was of the view that the authority of Congress to regulate rents by virtue of the war power ended with the Presidential Proclamation terminating hostilities on December 31, 1946, since that proclamation inaugurated "peace-in-fact" though it did not mark termination of the war. It also concluded that, even if the war power continues, Congress did not act under it because it did not say [so]. [In our view, the] war power sustains this legislation. The Court said in Hamilton v. Kentucky Distilleries Co., 251 U.S. 146 [1919], that the war power includes the power "to remedy the evils which have arisen from its rise and progress" and continues for the duration of that emergency. Whatever may be the consequences when war is officially terminated, the war power does not necessarily end with the cessation of hostilities. [In Hamilton] and Ruppert v. Caffey, 251 U.S. 264 [1920], prohibition laws which were enacted after the Armistice in World War I were sustained as exercises of the war power because they conserved manpower and increased efficiency of production in the critical days during the period of demobilization, and helped to husband the supply of grains and cereals depleted by the war effort.

[The] constitutional validity of the present legislation follows a fortiori from those cases. The legislative history of the present Act makes abundantly clear that there has not yet been eliminated the deficit in housing which in considerable measure was caused by the heavy demobilization of veterans and by the cessation or reduction in residential construction during the period of hostilities due to the allocation of building materials to military projects. Since the war effort contributed heavily to that deficit, Congress has the power even after the cessation of hostilities to act to control the forces that a short supply of the needed article created. If that were not true, the Necessary and Proper Clause would be drastically limited in its application to the several war powers.

[We] recognize the force of the argument that the effects of war under modern conditions may be felt in the economy for years and years, and that if the war power can be used in days of peace to treat all the wounds which war inflicts on our society, it may not only swallow up all other powers of Congress but largely obliterate the Ninth and the Tenth Amendments as well. There are no such implications in today's decision. We deal here with the consequences of a housing deficit greatly intensified during the period of hostilities. [Any] power, of course, can be abused. But we cannot assume that Congress is not alert to its constitutional responsibilities. [The] question of the constitutionality of action taken by Congress does not depend on recitals of the power which it undertakes to exercise. Here it is plain from the legislative history that Congress was invoking its war power to cope with a current condition of which the war was a direct and immediate [cause].

Reversed.

■ JUSTICE JACKSON, concurring.

I agree with the result in this case, but the arguments that have been addressed to us lead me to utter more explicit misgivings about war powers than the Court has done. The Government asserts no constitutional basis for this legislation other than this vague, undefined and undefinable "war power." No one will question that this power is the most dangerous one to free government in the whole catalogue of powers. It usually is invoked in haste and excitement when calm legislative consideration of constitutional limitation is difficult. It is executed in a time of patriotic fervor that makes moderation unpopular. And, worst of all, it is interpreted by judges under the influence of the same passions and pressures. Always, as in this case, the Government urges hasty decision to forestall some emergency or serve some purpose and pleads that paralysis will result if its claims to power are denied or their confirmation delayed. Particularly when the war power is invoked to do things to the liberties of people, or to their property or economy that only indirectly affect conduct of the war and do not relate to the management of the war itself, the constitutional basis should be scrutinized with care.

I think we can hardly deny that the war power is as valid a ground for federal rent control now as it has been at any time. We still are technically in a state of war. I would not be willing to hold that war powers may be indefinitely prolonged merely by keeping legally alive a state of war that had in fact ended. I cannot accept the argument that war powers last as long as the effects and consequences of war, for if so they are permanent—as permanent as the war debts. But I find no reason to conclude that we could find fairly that the present state of war is merely technical. We have armies abroad exercising our war power and have made no peace terms with our allies, not to mention our principal enemies. I think the conclusion that the war power has been applicable during the lifetime of this legislation is unavoidable.

Missouri v. Holland

252 U.S. 416, 40 S. Ct. 382, 64 L. Ed. 641 (1920).

■ JUSTICE HOLMES delivered the opinion of the Court.

This is a bill in equity brought by the State of Missouri to prevent a game warden of the United States from attempting to enforce the [1918] Migratory Bird Treaty Act [on the ground] that the statute is an unconstitutional interference with the rights reserved to the States by the Tenth Amendment and that the [threatened] acts of the defendant [contravened] its will manifested in statutes. [The District Court held the Act constitutional.] On December 8, 1916, a treaty between the United States and Great Britain was proclaimed by the President. It recited that many species of birds in their annual migrations traversed certain parts of the United States and of Canada, that they were of great value as a source of food and in destroying insects injurious to vegetation, but were in danger of extermination through lack of adequate protection. It therefore provided for specified closed seasons and protection in other forms, and agreed that the two powers would take or propose to their law making bodies the necessary measures for carrying the treaty out. The [1918 Act] prohibited the killing, capturing or selling any of the migratory birds included in the terms of the treaty except as permitted by [federal] regulations compatible with those [terms].

To answer this question it is not enough to refer to the Tenth Amendment [because] by Article II, § 2, the power to make treaties is delegated expressly, and by Article VI treaties made under the authority of the United States [are] declared the supreme law of the land. If the treaty is valid there can be no dispute about the validity of the statute under Article I, § 8, as a necessary and proper means to execute the powers of the Government. It is said that a treaty cannot be valid if it infringes the Constitution, that there are limits, therefore, to the treaty-making power, and that one such limit is that what an act of Congress could not do unaided, in derogation of the powers reserved to the States, a treaty cannot do. [The fact that an] earlier act of Congress that attempted by itself and not in pursuance of a treaty to regulate the killing of migratory birds within the States had been held bad [in two lower court decisions] cannot be accepted as a test of the treaty power. Acts of Congress are the supreme law of the land only when made in pursuance of the Constitution, while treaties are declared to be so when made under the authority of the United States.

It is open to question whether the authority of the United States means more than the formal acts prescribed to make the convention. We do not mean to imply that there are no qualifications to the treaty-making power; but they must be ascertained in a different way. It is obvious that there may be matters of the sharpest exigency for the national well being that an act of Congress could not deal with but that a treaty followed by such an act could, and it is not lightly to be assumed that, in matters requiring national action, "a power which must belong to and somewhere reside in every civilized government" is not to be found. [W]hen we are dealing with words that also are a constituent act, like the [Constitution], we must realize that they have called into life a being the development of which could not have been foreseen completely by the most gifted of its begetters. It was enough for them to realize or to hope that they had created an organism; it has taken a century and has cost their successors much sweat and blood to prove that they created a nation. The case before us must be considered in the light of our whole experience and not merely in that of what was said a hundred years ago. The treaty in question does not contravene any prohibitory words to be found in the Constitution. The only question is whether it is forbidden by some invisible radiation from the general terms of the Tenth Amendment. We must consider what this country has become in deciding what that Amendment has reserved.

[Here] a national interest of very nearly the first magnitude is involved. It can be protected only by national action in concert with that of another power. The subject matter is only transitorily within the State and has no permanent habitat therein. But for the treaty and the statute there soon might be no birds for any powers to deal with. We see nothing in the Constitution that compels the Government to sit by while a food supply is cut off and the protectors of our forests and our crops are destroyed. It is not sufficient to rely upon the States. The reliance is vain, and were it otherwise, the question is whether the United States is forbidden to act. We are of opinion that the treaty and statute must be upheld.

[Affirmed.] [Justices Van Devanter and Pitney dissented.]

THE WAR AND TREATY POWERS

1. ***The duration of war.*** Woods v. Cloyd W. Miller Co. raises the question of when a war ends and what the consequences are of crossing the threshold from war back to peace. Justice Jackson's concurrence called the "vague, undefined and undefinable 'war power' " the "most dangerous one to free government in the whole catalogue of powers" because of the latitude it gives Congress and the executive to take extraordinary measures that implicate citizens' liberty and property rights. What, if any, limits are there on that power in a state of war with no clear end-point, such as the so-called "War on Terror" or "Long War"?

2. ***The living Constitution.*** Missouri v. Holland marks the invention of the metaphor of the Constitution as a living organism subject to the necessity of evolution. (The framers "called into life a being the development of which could not have been foreseen completely by the most gifted of its begetters. It was enough for them to realize or to hope that they had created an organism.") The metaphor has been developed into a full-throated theory of constitutional interpretation. See, e.g., Strauss, The Living Constitution (2010). What are the implications of Justice Holmes's formulation for originalism?

3. ***Justice Holmes's "sweat and blood."*** Justice Holmes's judicial pragmatism was informed by his experience as a Union soldier in the Civil War. In declaring that the Constitution was a living organism forged and maintained through "sweat and blood" Holmes surely had in mind his own wartime experience defending the Constitution. He was seriously wounded three times during the course of the war. After his death two days before his ninety-fourth birthday "two Civil War uniforms were found hanging in his closet with a note pinned to them. It read: 'These uniforms were worn by me in the Civil War and the stains upon them are my blood.' " Menand, The Metaphysical Club 61 (2001).

4. ***The treaty power and Congress's other powers.*** In Missouri v. Holland, Justice Holmes appeared to assume that Congress could regulate under the treaty power even on subjects beyond its otherwise enumerated powers. To what extent may a treaty authorize national regulation of local affairs not regulable under other grants of power? Whenever Art. I powers prove insufficient to reach a local problem, may the national government overcome that obstacle simply by making a treaty with a cooperating foreign government? Are there any judicially enforceable limits on the permissible subject matter of a treaty? Are there any traditionally local questions that cannot be "properly the subject of negotiation with a foreign country"? De Geofroy v. Riggs, 133 U.S. 258 (1890).

In the early 1950s, concerns that any and all constitutional limitations could be overridden via the treaty power spurred efforts to amend the Constitution. Justice Holmes's broad statements in Missouri v. Holland were frequently cited as justification. These fears generated popular support for the Bricker Amendment, which, as proposed by[1] the Senate Judiciary Committee in 1953, included the statement that "[a] provision of a treaty which conflicts with this Constitution shall not be of any force or effect," and that "[a] treaty shall become effective as internal law in the United States only through legislation which would be valid in the absence of treaty." The second section was directed against the principle that treaties can be self-executing. The Senate failed to enact a modified version stating, "A provision of a treaty or other international agreement which conflicts with this Constitution shall not be of any force or effect."

While the Bricker Amendment debate was still alive, the Supreme Court decided **Reid v. Covert**, 354 U.S. 1 (1957), which dealt with congressional power under Art. I, § 8, to provide for military jurisdiction over civilian dependents of American servicemen overseas. Executive agreements had been entered into with other nations permitting American military courts to exercise exclusive jurisdiction over offenses by American servicemen or their dependents overseas. The Government argued that the challenged statute could be sustained "as legislation which is necessary and proper to carry out the United States' obligations under the international agreements." Justice BLACK's plurality opinion replied: "The obvious and decisive answer to this, of course, is that no agreement with a foreign nation can confer power on the Congress, or on any other branch of Government, which is free from the restraints of the Constitution. [It] would be manifestly contrary to the objectives of those who created the Constitution, as well as those who were responsible for the Bill of Rights—let alone alien to our entire constitutional history and tradition—to construe Article VI as permitting the United States to exercise power under an international agreement without observing constitutional prohibitions. [There] is nothing in Missouri v. Holland which is contrary to the position taken here. There the Court carefully noted that the treaty involved was not inconsistent with any

[1] The concern was that the UN Charter or resolutions by UN agencies (e.g., the Draft Covenant on Civil and Political Rights) might undercut American constitutional guarantees. For example, Art. 55 of the UN Charter states that the UN shall promote "universal respect for, and observance of, human rights and fundamental freedoms without distinction as to race, sex, language, or religion." In Sei Fujii v. State, 217 P.2d 481 (1950), a California District Court of Appeal held an alien land law invalid on the ground that the UN Charter was self-executing. The California Supreme Court, however, rested its affirmance of the result on the 14th Amendment, 242 P.2d 617 (1952), after finding that the UN Charter provision was "not self-executing."

specific provision of the Constitution. The Court was concerned with the Tenth Amendment. To the extent that the United States can validly make treaties, the people and the States have delegated their power to the National Government and the Tenth Amendment is no barrier."

Justice Black's comments helped put to rest the concerns that treaties might be the basis for domestic action affecting individual rights beyond the limits governing other national powers. Did the decision give adequate reassurance on federalism-based concerns?

In recent years, American international commitments through treaties have vastly expanded. Does this development pose a new danger that the treaty power will be used as a bootstrap for domestic regulation, perhaps as an end-run around judicially-enforced constitutional limits on Congress's enumerated powers? Consider the argument that Missouri v. Holland was incorrect to assert that "the powers of Congress are not fixed by the Constitution, but rather may be expanded by treaty. [The] 'Power . . . to make Treaties' does not extend [to] the implementation of treaties already made. [Missouri v. Holland thus] permits evasion of the constitutional amendment mechanism specified in Article V. As a general rule, the subject matter of the legislative power can be increased only by constitutional amendment." Rosenkranz, "Executing the Treaty Power," 118 Harv. L. Rev. 1867 (2005).

The Court had a chance to revisit Missouri v. Holland in **Bond v. United States**, 572 U.S. 844 (2014), but declined to do so. The case arose from a criminal prosecution under the Chemical Weapons Convention Implementation Act, 18 U.S.C. § 229(a)(1), which forbids anyone "to develop, produce, otherwise acquire, transfer directly or indirectly, receive, stockpile, retain, own, possess, or use, or threaten to use, any chemical weapon," and defines chemical weapon very broadly to include essentially all toxic chemicals. Bond used two chemicals, an arsenic-based compound and potassium dichromate, in an extended attempt to give a rash to her erstwhile best-friend who had been having an affair with Bond's husband and was bearing his child. Bond managed to give her rival a rash on one thumb, and was charged with violating the statute. On appeal, the government disclaimed any commerce power to enact the statute, justifying it instead as a necessary and proper means to implement the Chemical Weapons Convention, an international treaty to which the U.S. is a signatory. The U.S. Court of Appeals for the Third Circuit upheld the conviction under Missouri v. Holland [1920; p. 335], relying on the statement in that case that "[i]f the treaty is valid there can be no dispute about the validity of the statute" that implements it "as a necessary and proper means to execute the powers of the Government."

In a 6–3 decision, the Court reversed. Chief Justice ROBERTS began by reciting the "well-established principle governing the prudent exercise of this Court's jurisdiction that normally the Court will not decide a constitutional question if there is some other ground upon which to dispose of the case." Because Bond argued that the law did not cover her conduct, the Court would consider that argument before reaching the constitutional question. Chief Justice Roberts next explained the background presumptions for the interpretation: "Among the background principles of construction that our cases have recognized are those grounded in the relationship between the Federal Government and the States under our Constitution. It has long been settled, for example, that we presume federal statutes do not abrogate state sovereign immunity, impose obligations on the States pursuant to section 5 of the Fourteenth Amendment, or preempt state law. Closely related to these is the well-established principle that it is incumbent upon the federal courts to be certain of Congress' intent before finding that federal law overrides the usual constitutional balance of federal and state powers. [It] is appropriate to refer to basic principles of federalism embodied in the Constitution to resolve ambiguity in a federal statute. In this case, the ambiguity derives from the improbably broad reach of the key statutory definition given the term—'chemical weapon'—being defined; the deeply serious consequences of adopting such a boundless reading; and the lack of any apparent need to do so in light of the context from which the statute arose—a treaty about chemical warfare and terrorism. We conclude that, in this curious case, we can insist on a clear indication that Congress meant to reach purely local crimes, before interpreting the statute's expansive language in a way that intrudes on the police power of the States."

The opinion went on to find that no such clear indication existed: "The Government would have us brush aside the ordinary meaning and adopt a reading of section 229 that would sweep in everything from the detergent under the kitchen sink to the stain remover in the laundry room. Yet no one would ordinarily describe those substances as 'chemical weapons.' [Any] parent would be guilty of a serious federal offense—possession of a chemical weapon—when, exasperated by the children's repeated failure to clean the goldfish tank, he considers poisoning the fish with a few drops of vinegar. We are reluctant to ignore the ordinary meaning of 'chemical weapon' when doing so would transform a statute passed to implement the international Convention on Chemical Weapons into one that also makes it a federal offense to poison goldfish." The government's approach, Chief Justice Roberts wrote, "would transform the statute from one whose core concerns are acts of war, assassination, and terrorism into a massive federal anti-poisoning regime that reaches the simplest of assaults."

Justice SCALIA, joined by Justice Thomas and in part by Justice Alito, concurred only in the judgment.[2] He would have reached the constitutional question and found that the treaty power did not extend to the statute—or indeed to any Congressional power to make laws. Justice Scalia accused the majority of "result-driven antitextualism," and concluded that the "unavoidable meaning" of the law covered Bond's conduct. Turning to the Necessary and Proper Clause and treaty-making clause, he rejected the validity of what he called the "ipse dixit" of Missouri v. Holland, according to which "If the treaty is valid there can be no dispute about the validity of the statute under Article I, § 8, as a necessary and proper means to execute the powers of the Government." Justice Scalia wrote: "It is obvious what the Clauses, read together, do not say. They do not authorize Congress to enact laws for carrying into execution 'Treaties,' even treaties that do not execute themselves, such as the Chemical Weapons Convention."

Justice Scalia then addressed the argument that Congress must have the power "to carry out the obligations to which the President and the Senate have committed the Nation." He maintained that the argument, "which makes no pretense of resting on text, unsurprisingly misconstrues it. [Because] the President and the Senate can enter into a non-self-executing compact with a foreign nation but can never by themselves (without the

[2] Justice Thomas also wrote a concurrence in the judgment, joined in full by Justice Scalia and in part by Justice Alito.

House) give that compact domestic effect through legislation, the power of the President and the Senate 'to make' a Treaty cannot possibly mean to 'enter into a compact with a foreign nation and then give that compact domestic legal effect.' Upon the President's agreement and the Senate's ratification, a treaty—no matter what kind—has been made and is not susceptible of any more making."

Justice Scalia went on to cite constitutional structure in support of the same conclusion: "Though Holland's change to the Constitution's text appears minor (the power to carry into execution the power to make treaties becomes the power to carry into execution treaties), the change to its structure is seismic. To see why vast expansion of congressional power is not just a remote possibility, consider two features of the modern practice of treaty making. In our Nation's early history, and extending through the time when Holland was written, treaties were typically bilateral, and addressed only a small range of topics relating to the obligations of each state to the other, and to citizens of the other—military neutrality, for example, or military alliance, or guarantee of most-favored-nation trade treatment. But beginning in the last half of the last century, many treaties were 'detailed multilateral instruments negotiated and drafted at international conferences,' and they sought to regulate states' treatment of their own citizens, or even 'the activities of individuals and private entities.' Consider also that, at least according to some scholars, the Treaty Clause comes with no implied subject-matter limitations. See, e.g., L. Henkin, Foreign Affairs and the United States Constitution (2d ed. 1996). On this view, '[t]he Tenth Amendment . . . does not limit the power to make treaties or other agreements,' Restatement (Third) of Foreign Relations Law of the United States § 302, Comment d (1986), and the treaty power can be used to regulate matters of strictly domestic concern, see id., at Comment c. If that is true, then the possibilities of what the Federal Government may accomplish, with the right treaty in hand, are endless and hardly farfetched."

5. ***Congressional power over "foreign affairs."*** The national government's treaty power is explicitly granted in the Constitution. Is there also an implicit foreign affairs power of Congress independent of authority to implement validly adopted treaties? Where in the Constitution is it found? Is it an inference from granted power or does it derive from extraconstitutional sources? The Court has recognized the power of Congress to regulate foreign affairs. See Perez v. Brownell, 356 U.S. 44, 57 (1958), sustaining a statutory provision regarding loss of citizenship: "Although there is in the Constitution no specific grant to Congress of power to enact legislation for the effective regulation of foreign affairs, there can be no doubt of the existence of this power in the law-making organ of the Nation. See, [e.g., United States v. Curtiss-Wright Export Corp., 299 U.S. 304 (1936); p. 392 above]. The States that joined together to form a single Nation and to create, through the Constitution, a Federal Government to conduct the affairs of that Nation must be held to have granted that Government the powers indispensable to its functioning effectively in the company of sovereign nations." In Zivotofsky, supra 309, the Court held that Congress had no power to make recognition determinations contrary to those of the President, but the majority noted that it "did not question the substantial powers of Congress over foreign affairs in general or passports in particular."

How extensive is the congressional power to enact legislation for the effective regulation of foreign affairs? Is it limited to the subject matter of foreign relations? Can the Court reexamine the factual basis of a congressional assertion that a problem *is* a foreign affairs concern?

6. ***Does the Constitution follow the flag?*** Is the government bound by the Constitution when it exercises jurisdiction outside of the United States? In **Downes v. Bidwell**, 182 U.S. 244 (1901), a fruit merchant brought a challenge to a U.S. law which enacted a duty on imports from the territory of Puerto Rico on the ground that it violated Article I, Section 8 of the Constitution, which provides that "all Duties, Imposts, and Excises shall be uniform throughout the United States." The Court held that the government was not always bound by every provision of the Constitution when it operated outside of the United States, finding that "[t]here is a clear distinction between such prohibitions as go to the very root of the power of Congress to act at all, irrespective of time of place, and such as are operative only 'throughout the United States' or among the several states." The Court held that the Revenue Clause of Article I, Section 8 of the Constitution was only operative within the United States and that the Puerto Rico duty was constitutionally permissible. The Court then "suggest[ed] without intending to decide, that there may be a distinction between certain natural rights enforced in the Constitution by prohibitions against interference with them [and which apply both within and outside of the United States], and what may be termed artificial or remedial rights which are peculiar to our own system of jurisprudence [and which apply only within the United States]. Of the former class are the rights to one's own religious opinions, [to] freedom of speech and of the press; to free access to courts of justice, to due process of law. [Of] the latter class are the rights to citizenship, to suffrage."

In its original context, the case reflected directly on the rise of the United States to what in dissent Justice Harlan called "world power" status in the wake of the Spanish-American War in which it had taken Puerto Rico, Guam and the Philippines from Spain. Justice Harlan's anti-imperial, anticolonial dissent argued that any territory acquired by the United States must be placed on the route to statehood, and that all constitutional rights must apply because Congress lacked the power to administer territory as a colony. The Court's holding to the contrary was widely read as an endorsement of the new expansion, which had been blessed by the public in the 1900 re-election of William McKinley. Downes, known as one of The Insular Cases, was treated as a historical curiosity by all but a few constitutional scholars until it became relevant to the question of detention abroad after September 11. It was cited by the Court in Boumediene, infra. For an account, see generally Burnett, "Untied States: American Expansion and Territorial Deannexation," 72 U. Chi. L. Rev. 797 (2005).

SECTION 3. EXECUTIVE AND CONGRESSIONAL DISCRETION IN TIMES OF WAR OR TERRORISM

THE PRESIDENT, CONGRESS AND WAR POWERS

The respective roles of President and Congress in decisions to commit military forces abroad are among the most contentious issues in American history. While the Constitution confers upon Congress the power to "declare war," Art. I, § 8, cl. 11, and to raise and support armies and navies, Art. I,

§ 8, cl. 12 & 13, it confers upon the President the authority to act as Commander in Chief of the armed forces, Art. II, § 2. The debates over the Constitution suggested that the President must have some inherent power to defend the nation against "sudden attack." Even if such defensive power exists, is there an inherent power in the Presidency to wage offensive strikes? Can the concept of defense be so broadly construed that it extends to foreign military actions to "defend" the nation's allies?

John Hart Ely argued that the constitutional assignment of the war declaration power to Congress was specifically designed to ensure that the decision to go to war would not be made lightly or quickly, or without public support adequate to sustain a full prosecution of the war. "What is at stake [is] the judgment that no single individual should be able to take the nation into war and thereby risk the lives of all of us, especially our young people." Ely further argued that this constitutional requirement serves to increase the effectiveness of the nation's military commitments: "Unless Congress has unequivocally authorized a war at the outset, it is a good deal more likely later to undercut the effort." Ely advocated a strong judicial role to rein in the executive in order to "induce" Congress "to discharge its constitutional responsibilities." Ely, War and Responsibility: Constitutional Lessons of Vietnam and Its Aftermath (1993).

A countervailing view is expressed by former legal adviser to the State Department Abraham Sofaer in "The Power over War," 50 U. Miami L. Rev. 33 (1995). Sofaer argues that efforts to have courts "pass on the legality of executive decisions to involve the nation in hostilities" would generally be "not only futile, but harmful to our national interests" because "judicial involvement in separation of powers conflict [tends] to create hard-and-fast rules in areas of overlapping authority [that] are intensely political and often require subtle handling." Sofaer further argues that the "President does not act irresponsibly merely because Congress has not specifically authorized the action taken" so long as he acts "in the absence of legislative direction to the contrary." Should courts resolve questions of whether there has been adequate congressional authorization of war? Should courts view such questions as justiciable?

If presidential war powers are to be restrained, is a greater assertion of congressional authority preferable to judicial intervention? In the wake of the Vietnam War (and the Watergate controversy), Congress sought to provide guidelines for the future use of armed forces. It adopted (overriding President Nixon's veto) a joint resolution, the WAR POWERS RESOLUTION OF 1973, an unusual, structural, quasi-constitutional law that focuses not on substantive policy but on processes and relationships. The War Powers Resolution provides that: "It is the purpose of this joint resolution to fulfill the intent of the framers of the Constitution of the United States and insure that the collective judgment of both the Congress and the President will apply to the introduction of United States Armed Forces into hostilities, or into situations where imminent involvement in hostilities is clearly indicated by the circumstances, and to the continued use of such forces in hostilities or in such situations." Its procedures specify that the President may introduce armed forces into hostilities pursuant only to "(1) a declaration of war, (2) specific statutory authorization, or (3) a national emergency created by attack upon the United States, its territories or possessions, or its armed forces"; that "[t]he President in every possible instance shall consult with Congress before introducing United States Armed Forces into hostilities" and during those hostilities; that when troops are introduced "into hostilities or into situations where imminent involvement in hostilities is clearly indicated by the circumstances," "the President shall submit within 48 hours to the Speaker of the House of Representatives and to the President pro tempore of the Senate a report, in writing," setting forth the circumstances necessitating the introduction of armed forces, the constitutional and legislative authority therefor, and such other information as the Congress may request; and that "[w]ithin sixty calendar days after a report is submitted or is required to be submitted, [the] President shall terminate any use of United States Armed Forces with respect to which such report was submitted (or required to be submitted), unless the Congress (1) has declared war or has enacted a specific authorization for such use of United States Armed Forces, (2) has extended by law such sixty-day period, or (3) is physically unable to meet as a result of an armed attack upon the United States," a period extendable for an additional thirty days in cases of "unavoidable military necessity"; and finally providing that at any time, forces abroad "shall be removed by the President if the Congress so directs by concurrent [resolution]."

Is it constitutional for one Congress to so restrict the President? In vetoing the War Powers Resolution, President Nixon rested heavily on alleged constitutional defects, arguing that the resolution "would attempt to take away, by a mere legislative act, authorities which the President has properly exercised under the Constitution for almost 200 years." He was "particularly disturbed by the fact that certain of the President's constitutional powers as Commander in Chief of the Armed Forces would terminate automatically" without "overt congressional action." Note too that the Resolution does not limit the use of armed forces to formal declarations of war but also mentions "specific statutory authorization," although it excludes mere congressional appropriations. Are the congressional "authorization[s]" recognized by the Resolution constitutionally adequate alternatives for formal declarations of war? For a defense of the Resolution arguing that it "is nothing more or less than a congressional definition of the word 'war' in article I [that] does not intrude on any presidential prerogative," see Carter, "The Constitutionality of the War Powers Resolution," 70 Va. L. Rev. 101 (1984). For the view that the War Powers Resolution should have been even more forceful, see Ely, War and Responsibility: Constitutional Lessons of Vietnam and Its Aftermath (1993), elaborating the argument in Ely, "Suppose Congress Wanted a War Powers Act That Worked," 88 Colum. L. Rev. 1379 (1988), that "[i]n large measure the tale of the [Resolution] has been a tale of congressional spinelessness" in the face of unanticipated presidential defiance, but that this "defect can be repaired, if Congress still has the will to be held accountable." For the view that the War Powers Resolution was unnecessary because Congress already possesses, especially through the appropriations power, ample authority to control and direct presidential conduct in war, see Sofaer, "The Presidency, War and Foreign Affairs: Practice Under the Framers," 40 Law & Contemp. Probs. 12 (1976). For the further view that the War Powers Resolution represents the inappropriate effort of one Congress to bind future Congresses to require a particular form of legislation before approval of presidential military action, and that any form of congressional approval is sufficient because "authorization is authorization," see Sofaer, "The War Powers Resolution and Kosovo," 34 Loy. L. Rev. 71 (2000).

Disputes over the meaning and scope of the War Powers Resolution have real-world implications. In February 2011 a revolt had begun in Libya against then-leader Muammar Qaddafi. On March 17, 2011, after several weeks of hand-wringing, the U.N. Security Council voted to authorize military action against Qaddafi's forces. Two days later, the United States and Europe commenced air strikes against Libyan targets. The North American Treaty Organization (NATO) assumed command of the action in early April and the United States shifted to what it termed a "supporting role," which involved providing refueling and surveillance services to allied aircraft and operating remotely piloted drones. Congress did not authorize the use of military force and the 60-day deadline came and went, sparking a separation-of-powers conflict. On June 3, 2011, the House passed a resolution calling on President Barack Obama's administration to explain its apparent violation of the War Powers Resolution. Just days before the War Powers Resolution's 90-day deadline for cessation of military action without congressional authorization, the Obama Administration took the position—in response to congressional demand for an explanation—that the War Powers Resolution did not apply because the United States was not engaged in "hostilities" in Libya under the meaning of the Resolution. The Administration argued that it was not engaged in "hostilities" because "U.S. operations [did] not involve sustained fighting or active exchanges of fire with hostile forces, nor [did] they involve U.S. ground troops." According to Harold H. Koh, then Legal Adviser to the Department of State, American forces had not been engaging in "hostilities" since at least the beginning of April when the U.S. shifted responsibility for the mission to NATO. Despite ongoing congressional opposition and what many saw as a strained legal interpretation, the Obama Administration continued to participate in the NATO-led operation until the Qaddafi regime was toppled several months later.

How should the viability of the War Powers Resolution be understood in light of the Libyan episode? On one view, the Obama Administration's arguably cavalier treatment of the Resolution demonstrated the law's futility as an enforceable check on the executive. On another view, while the Administration's interpretation of the Resolution functionally governed, the Resolution still drew attention to and thus meaningfully constrained the executive's conduct.

The Trump Administration similarly saw no need to seek congressional authorization prior to launching airstrikes three Syrian government chemical weapons facilities in April 2018. American forces had previously conducted airstrikes and ground operations against Islamic State targets under the purported authorization of the 2001 AUMF, but this was the first operation against a Syrian regime target. As required by the War Powers Resolution, President Trump notified Congress within 48 hours of launching the strike and said he "acted in the vital national security and foreign policy interests of the United States, pursuant to [his] constitutional authority to conduct foreign relations and as Commander in Chief and Chief Executive." Text of a Letter from the President to the Speaker of the House of Representatives and the President Pro Tempore of the Senate (April 8, 2017). In a memorandum opinion written after the strike, the Office of Legal Counsel provided its view that "[t]he President's direction was consistent with many others taken by prior Presidents, who have deployed our military forces in limited engagements without seeking the prior authorization of Congress. This deeply rooted historical practice, acknowledged by courts and

Congress, reflects the well-established division of war powers under our Constitution. [Before] the strikes occurred, we advised that the President could lawfully direct them because he had reasonably determined that the use of force would be in the national interest and that the anticipated hostilities would not rise to the level of a war in the constitutional sense." Memorandum from Steven Engel, Assistant Att'y Gen., Office of Legal Counsel, to Don McGahn, Counsel to the President (May 31, 2018). Some scholars have rejected this position, suggesting that it "the unilateral use of force here by the president, without congressional authorization, [is] premised on an astonishingly broad conception of the president's Article II powers" and "violate[s] international law." Goldsmith and Hathaway, "The Downsides of Bombing Syria," Lawfare, April 10, 2018.

Congress has been moderately more active in policing the use of force by the Trump Administration in its first two years, to only limited effect. In December 2018, the Senate, in a 56–41 vote, moved to check the President's authority to direct U.S. military assistance to Saudi Arabia for its war in Yemen. The measure died in the House of Representatives, which declined to take up a parallel bill. See Hirschfeld Davis and Schmitt, "Senate Votes to End Aid for Yemen Fight Over Khashoggi Killing and Saudis' War Aims," N.Y. Times (Dec. 13, 2018). The Senate also sought to constrain President Trump with regard to U.S. involvement in Syria, but in the opposite direction: it pushed back against a proposed troop withdrawal. See Edmondson, "Senate Rebukes Trump Over Troop Withdrawals From Syria and Afghanistan," N.Y. Times (Jan. 31, 2019). Does Congress have the power to force the President to keep U.S. forces engaged in operations abroad?

EMERGENCY CONSTITUTIONALISM

Is it reasonable to expect the government to behave within the same constitutional boundaries during periods of crisis as periods of calm? Should courts intervene during a national security crisis to determine whether or not the actions of the executive branch have violated the Constitution or infringed upon the powers of the legislative branch? Or should the judiciary wait until the crisis is resolved so as not to impede the political branches in their efforts to resolve it? And who defines the existence of a crisis? These questions, which have vexed the nation in periods of crisis from the Civil War to the present day, were cast in sharp relief following the terrorist attacks on American soil on September 11, 2001.

1. ***Emergencies and constitutional text.*** The constitutions of many nations include "state of emergency" or "state of siege" clauses providing mechanisms for suspension of certain provisions. The Suspension Clause of the United States Constitution, Article I, § 9, cl. 2, provides: "The privilege of the Writ of Habeas Corpus shall not be suspended, *unless when in Cases of Rebellion or Invasion the public Safety may require it.*" Habeas corpus is a protection of personal liberty inherited from English common law. It gives one who is arrested and detained by government the right to have a court direct the government official holding him in custody to produce him and provide good reason for "having the body"—or else release him. When it is suspended, a detainee ordinarily has no immediate legal recourse against the official who is holding him to demand his release, even if his detention is otherwise unlawful.

The Constitution also includes a few other specific and limited references to emergency circumstances: Article I § 8, cl. 15 provides, "The Congress shall have the Power . . . To provide for calling forth the Militia to execute the Laws of the Union, *suppress Insurrections, and repel Invasions*," and Article II, § 2, cl. 1 provides that the President shall be Commander in Chief of the state militias when they are so called. Art. I, § 10, cl.3, setting forth federal limits on the powers of the states, provides, "No State shall, without the Consent of Congress, lay any Duty of Tonnage, keep Troops or Ships of War in time of Peace, enter into any Agreement or Compact with another State, or with a foreign Power, or engage in War, *unless actually invaded, or in such imminent Danger as will not admit of delay*." Article IV, § 4 provides, "The Congress . . . shall protect each of [the states] *against Invasion*; and on Application of the Legislature, or of the Executive (when the Legislature cannot be convened) *against domestic violence*."

Among the rights provisions of the Constitution, the Third Amendment expressly limits executive discretion to conscript private property even in wartime by providing, "No Soldier shall, in time of peace, be quartered in any house, without the consent of the Owner, *nor in time of war, but in a manner to be prescribed by law*." But the Fifth Amendment's requirement of grand jury indictment is relaxed for martial law: "No person shall be held to answer for a capital, or otherwise infamous crime, unless on a presentment or indictment of a Grand Jury, *except in cases arising in the land or naval forces, or in the Militia, when in actual service in time of War or public danger*."

2. ***Lincoln's suspension of habeas corpus.*** President Abraham Lincoln took office on March 4, 1861, and on April 12, 1861, the first Battle of Fort Sumter began, initiating the Civil War. On April 27, 1861, after anti-Union mobs in Maryland had attacked Northern soldiers and destroyed railroad bridges along supply lines, Lincoln authorized military commanders to suspend the writ of habeas corpus between Philadelphia and Washington. Congress was not in session and Lincoln acted unilaterally, without congressional authority. The Suspension Clause, Article I, § 9, cl. 2, provides that "the privilege of the Writ of Habeas Corpus shall not be suspended, *unless* when in Cases of Rebellion or Invasion the public Safety may require it." Its placement in Article I, which enumerates the powers of Congress, suggests that such suspension requires legislative approval.

On May 25, 1861, Lincoln was severely rebuked by Chief Justice Roger Taney, who, riding circuit and sitting as trial judge, held illegal the detention by military authorities at Fort McHenry of one John Merryman, a Maryland farmer and prominent state legislator accused of participating in the Baltimore bridge-burnings. In Ex parte Merryman, 17 F. Cas. 144 (1861), Taney reasoned that only Congress could suspend the writ.

At the conclusion of his opinion, Taney squarely asserted that Lincoln had violated the rule of law by abrogating the Due Process Clause and the Fourth Amendment: "These great and fundamental laws, which Congress itself could not suspend, have been disregarded and suspended, like the writ of habeas corpus, by a military order, supported by force of arms. Such is the case now before me; and I can only say that if the authority which the Constitution has confided to the judiciary department and judicial officers may thus upon any pretext or under any circumstances be usurped by the military power at its discretion, the people of the United States are no longer living under a Government of laws, but every citizen holds life, liberty, and property at the will and pleasure of the army officer in whose military district he may happen to be found."

Conscious of his limited capacity as a judge to force Lincoln to reinstate habeas corpus, Taney described his role as declaring the law and leaving its execution to the President: "In such a case my duty was too plain to be mistaken. I have exercised all the power which the Constitution and laws confer on me, but that power has been resisted by a force too strong for me to overcome. It is possible that the officer who has incurred this grave responsibility may have misunderstood his instructions, and exceeded the authority intended to be given him. I shall, therefore, order all the proceedings in this case, with my opinion, to be filed and recorded in the Circuit Court of the United States for the District of Maryland, and direct the clerk to transmit a copy, under seal, to the President of the United States. It will then remain for that high officer, in fulfilment of his constitutional obligation to 'take care that the laws be faithfully executed,' to determine what measures he will take to cause the civil process of the United States to be respected and enforced."

In July of 1861, Congress convened and Lincoln sought retrospective authorization for his unilateral suspension of the writ. Addressing a special session of Congress on July 4, 1861, Lincoln asserted that he had authority to suspend, and that the textual location of the Suspension Clause in Article I was not a sufficient reason to restrict the power of suspension to Congress when a true emergency existed. At the same time, he advanced the argument that the end of preserving government in an emergency justified the means of suspension: "The whole of the laws which were required to be faithfully executed were being resisted and failing of execution in nearly one-third of the States. Must they be allowed to finally fail of execution, even had it been perfectly clear that by the use of the means necessary to their execution some single law, made in such extreme tenderness of the citizen's liberty that practically it relieves more of the guilty than of the innocent, should to a very limited extent be violated? To state the question more directly, are all the laws but one to go unexecuted and the Government itself go to pieces lest that one be violated? Even in such a case would not the official oath be broken if the Government should be overthrown, when it was believed that disregarding the single law would tend to preserve it?"

Senate Democrats blocked a bill that would have retrospectively approved suspension of the writ, and in February of 1862 Lincoln ordered most prisoners released. Nonetheless, on September 24, 1862, Lincoln unilaterally suspended the writ nationwide enabling indefinite military detention of draft resisters as well as ordinary criminals such as smugglers, blockade-runners and bootleggers selling liquor to soldiers. In all, over 13,000 civilians were arrested and detained by Union military forces. Congress eventually ratified the suspension of the writ by legislation enacted on March 3, 1863—nearly two years after Lincoln first suspended it.

3. ***Comparative emergency constitutionalism.*** Other nations have incorporated emergency provisions directly into their constitutions. The most famous example of a constitutional emergency provision was Article 48 of the German Weimar Constitution of 1919, which granted the President of the Reich power to intervene, with military assistance if necessary, should public order and security be seriously endangered. Article 48 expressly allowed for the temporary suspension of some fundamental rights; it also provided that any invocation of the emergency power must be reported to the

Reichstag, which had the power to overrule it. Invoked repeatedly between 1930 and 1932 by President Paul von Hindenburg at the request of various German Chancellors, Article 48 was also invoked by von Hindenburg on February, 28 1933, the day after the Reichstag fire, at the request of Chancellor Adolf Hitler. It arguably provided some legal cover for Hitler's rise to the position of Fuhrer under the terms of an enabling act passed by the Reichstag the following month in the form of a constitutional amendment.

Emergency provisions remain common in many modern constitutions. For example, the French Constitution allows the President to declare a "state of siege" in consultation with the two houses of the legislature, the Premier, and the Constitutional Council. This pronouncement vests greater authority in the executive, but forbids the President from dissolving the legislature. See Fitzpatrick, Human Rights in Crisis (1994).

The Constitution of India explicitly empowers the President to declare a "State of Emergency" in the event of "war or external aggression or armed rebellion." In that event, Parliament may vest the legislative power in the President, the President may suspend the judiciary's authority to enforce many of the Constitution's "fundamental rights," and the Parliament may provide for preventive detentions if necessary to protect "the security of the State, maintenance of public order, or maintenance of supplies and services essential to the community." See Jinks, "The Anatomy of an Institutionalized Emergency: Preventive Detention and Personal Liberty in India," 22 Mich. J. Int'l L. 311 (2001). This provision was invoked for a twenty-one month period known as "the Emergency" between June 1975 and March 1977, during which Prime Minister Indira Gandhi ruled by decree. The Emergency ended when Gandhi announced new elections, in which she was not reelected to Parliament and her Congress Party was turned out of government for the first time since Indian independence. The succeeding government arrested Gandhi and charged her with crimes committed during the Emergency; she was not convicted, and she and her party were returned to power by election in 1979.

Perhaps the most detailed constitutional provisions for emergency exceptions are set forth in the South African Constitution. Article 37 provides that Parliament may declare a state of emergency for 21 days, with one three-month extension by majority vote and subsequent extensions requiring a 60% supermajority. Unlike many other constitutions, South Africa's expressly provides for judicial review of the validity of declarations and extensions of states of emergency, and of any legislation or executive action taken under them. Legislation pursuant to a state of emergency "may derogate from the Bill of Rights only to the extent" that it is "strictly required by the emergency," and certain rights, including those to life, human dignity, and equality on the basis of race are expressly declared "non-derogable." While many ordinary rights of criminal procedure may be departed from under emergency legislation, the South African Constitution sets forth detailed requirements of publicity, visitation and access to counsel for those detained without trial, and provides for judicial review within 10 days and release unless "necessary to continue the detention to restore peace and order."

One recent survey of constitutional emergency powers in other advanced democracies emphasizes that there is nothing "inherent in the concept of an executive that entails plenary power in emergencies," noting that, while many foreign constitutions have explicit emergency provisions that expand executive authority, "they also subject the executive's power to limitations by the legislature and the courts, [define] what constitutes an emergency [and] impose time limits on the emergency and define the additional powers that executives may exercise. None of these other democracies permit[s] its executive to assume unchecked power, even in response to an emergency." Martinez, "Inherent Executive Power: A Comparative Perspective," 115 Yale L.J. 2480 (2006).

Would the United States Constitution be improved by the addition of explicit emergency procedures similar to those set forth in the French, Indian and South African Constitutions? In "The Emergency Constitution," 113 Yale L.J. 1029 (2004), Bruce Ackerman argues that indeed it might. Acknowledging that formal constitutional amendment might be prohibitively difficult, however, Ackerman suggests instead enactment of a "framework statute" providing the United States government with "the authority to detain suspects" for 45 to 60 days "without the kind of evidence normally required by liberal constitutions," but subject to limitation by principles of "supermajoritarianism, compensation, and decency": "Emergencies can be declared only after an actual attack; they can be continued for short intervals only by increasing supermajorities in the legislature and only after minority parties obtain privileged opportunities to inform themselves as to the real-world operation of the emergency regime and to publicize the facts as they see fit; [the] scope of emergency powers is limited to the needs for relief and prevention that justify them in the first place"; and individuals wrongly swept up in dragnets would receive liberal monetary compensation. Is Ackerman's legislative solution more promising than judicial elaboration of a constitutional common law of emergencies? For elaboration of this proposal, see Ackerman, Before the Next Attack: Preserving Civil Liberties in an Age of Terrorism (2006).

4. ***Two views of emergency constitutionalism.*** Consider two polar opposite views. The first is that the Constitution is continuous, invariant in its basic premises even in time of war or crisis. That is one reading of the disparate opinions that made up the majority in the Steel Seizure Case. That was also the view expressed in a famous dictum in **Ex parte Milligan**, 71 U.S. 2 (1866), (below p. 350). Although the case arose only after the Civil War, the Court in Milligan stated that "the Constitution of the United States is a law for rulers and people, equally in war and in peace, and covers with the shield of its protection all classes of men, at all times, and under all circumstances. No doctrine, involving more pernicious consequences, was ever invented by the wit of man than that any of its provisions can be suspended during any of the great exigencies of government. Such a doctrine leads directly to anarchy or despotism."

Contrast this view with the second, opposite view that in wartime, all usual constitutional bets are off and the executive must have the latitude to assume greater unilateral discretion. As the famous adage of Cicero has it, "Inter arma silent leges"—"*In the midst of arms the laws are silent.*" Arguably this may have been Lincoln's position when he unilaterally suspended habeas corpus.

It is possible to suppose an intermediate position. As Chief Justice Rehnquist wrote in 1998, "[t]he laws will not be silent in time of war, but they will speak with a somewhat different voice." Rehnquist, All the Laws But One: Civil Liberties in Wartime (1998). If such alternative approaches to interpreting constitutional protections prevail in wartime, how explicit should the Court be in specifying their limits? Will emergency exceptions, even if they merely interpret constitutional protections deferentially rather than abrogating them altogether, spill over into the peacetime order? How strict a separation should be maintained between periods of emergency and periods of normalcy? Should exceptions be allowed ex ante, so long as courts may invalidate them as unconstitutional ex post? Justice Jackson appeared to advocate for this view in his remarkable dissent in Korematsu v. United States (1944; p. 676 below), where he said that judicial ratification of otherwise extraconstitutional governmental conduct in wartime "lies about like a loaded weapon ready for the hand of any authority that can bring forward a plausible claim of an urgent need."

Proponents of a "strict" view of the Constitution during periods of emergency often argue that allowing a curtailment of liberties during those periods acts as a "one-way ratchet," reducing civil liberties permanently while increasing executive power. See Moe & Howell, "The Presidential Power of Unilateral Action," 15 J.L. Econ. & Org. 132 (1999). Critics of this view, however, argue that there is no reason to believe the ratchet works in only one direction, given the many precedents set during periods of tranquility that expand liberties: "Generally speaking, there is no reason to suppose that laws, policies and bureaucratic institutions created during an emergency systematically fail to change, or change back, after a crisis has passed because of institutional inertia and interest group pressure." E. Posner & Vermeule, "Accommodating Emergencies," 56 Stan. L. Rev. 605 (2003). Do these arguments assume a clear separation between periods of normalcy and emergency and the eventual resumption of normalcy?

Some scholars even suggest that emergency exceptions might benefit the constitutional order. One argues that if executive officials are allowed to act extra-constitutionally during a crisis, "provided that they openly and publicly acknowledge the nature of their actions," while the polity and courts decide after the crisis has passed whether or not executive actions went too far in curtailing civil liberties, stricter separation may be maintained between periods of emergency and periods of normalcy. See Gross, "Chaos and Rules: Should Responses to Violent Crises Always be Constitutional?," 112 Yale L.J. 1011 (2003). Others argue that ex post review and invalidation of the government's actions helps ensure a pattern of "social learning" in which citizens become increasingly dubious of the government's ex ante analysis of threats, and government as a result ratchets down its response with each successive emergency. See Tushnet, "Defending Korematsu?: Reflections on Civil Liberties in Wartime," 2003 Wis. L. Rev. 273 (2003) ("Knowing that government officials in the past have in fact exaggerated threats to national security or have taken actions that were ineffective with respect to the threats that actually were present, we have become increasingly skeptical about contemporary claims regarding those threats, with the effect that the scope of proposed government responses to threats has decreased.").

EXECUTIVE DETENTION AND TRIAL OF "ENEMY COMBATANTS"

Recall that President Lincoln and then Congress suspended habeas corpus rights for the duration of the Civil War. After the war ended, in **Ex**

parte Milligan, 71 U.S. 2 (1866), the Court ruled that, even though Lincoln's suspension of the writ with congressional authorization had been legal, such an emergency provision could not constitutionally authorize the trial and conviction of a civilian detained during the war by a military tribunal rather than by a civilian court. Milligan was a longtime citizen of Indiana, a non-rebellious state, and had never served in the armed forces. In 1864, Milligan was detained in Indiana by the U.S. military for allegedly participating in the rebellion and conspiring against the United States, and was convicted and sentenced to death by a military commission. After the war ended, a civilian grand jury was convened, and failed to indict Milligan for any offense. Still, the government intended to proceed with the execution. The Court issued a writ of habeas corpus.

Writing for the Court, Justice DAVIS suggested that if the government was worried about Milligan's rebellious activities, it should have indicted him under the criminal code and tried him in an Article III court of law. He stated: "Milligan, not a resident of one of the rebellious states, or a prisoner of war, but a citizen of Indiana for twenty years past, and never in the military or naval service, is, while at his home, arrested by the military power of the United States, imprisoned, and, on certain criminal charges preferred against him, tried, convicted, and sentenced to be hanged by a military commission, organized under the direction of the military commander of the military district of Indiana. Had this tribunal the legal power and authority to try and punish this man? No graver question was ever considered by this court, nor one which more nearly concerns the rights of the whole people; for it is the birthright of every American citizen when charged with crime, to be tried and punished according to law."

The Court rejected the government's argument that military jurisdiction was justified by "the 'laws and usages of war' ": "It can serve no useful purpose to inquire what those laws and usages are, whence they originated, where found, and on whom they operate; they can never be applied to citizens in states which have upheld the authority of the government, and where the courts are open and their process unobstructed. This court has judicial knowledge that in Indiana the Federal authority was always unopposed, and its courts always open to hear criminal accusations and redress grievances; and no usage of war could sanction a military trial there for any offence whatever of a citizen in civil life, in nowise connected with the military service. [One] of the plainest constitutional provisions was, therefore, infringed when Milligan was tried by a court not ordained and established by Congress, and not composed of judges appointed during good behavior. [Another] guarantee of freedom was broken when Milligan was denied a trial by jury. [This] right—one of the most valuable in a free country—is preserved to every one accused of crime who is not attached to the army, or navy, or militia in actual service. [The] discipline necessary to the efficiency of the army and navy, required other and swifter modes of trial than are furnished by the common law courts. [Every] one connected with these branches of the public service is amenable to the jurisdiction which Congress has created for their government, and, while thus serving, surrenders his right to be tried by the civil courts. All other persons, citizens of states where the courts are open, if charged with crime, are guaranteed the inestimable privilege of trial by jury.

"[It] is claimed that martial law covers with its broad mantle the proceedings of this military commission. The proposition is this: that in a time of war the commander of an armed force (if in his opinion the exigencies of the country demand it, and of which he is to judge), has the power, within the lines of his military district, to suspend all civil rights and their remedies, and subject citizens as well as soldiers to the rule of his will; and in the exercise of his lawful authority cannot be restrained, except by his superior officer or the President of the United States. If this position is sound to the extent claimed, then when war exists, foreign or domestic, and the country is subdivided into military departments for mere convenience, the commander of one of them can [substitute] military force for and to the exclusion of the laws. [Martial] law, established on such a basis, destroys every guarantee of the Constitution, and effectually renders the 'military independent of and superior to the civil power'—the attempt to do which by the King of Great Britain was deemed by our fathers such an offence, that they assigned it to the world as one of the causes which impelled them to declare their independence. Civil liberty and this kind of martial law cannot endure together; the antagonism is irreconcilable; and, in the conflict, one or the other must perish. [It] is essential to the safety of every government that, in a great crisis, like the one we have just passed through, there should be a power somewhere of suspending the writ of habeas corpus. [Unquestionably,] there is then an exigency which demands that the government, if it should see fit in the exercise of a proper discretion to make arrests, should not be required to produce the persons arrested in answer to a writ of habeas corpus. The Constitution goes no further. It does not say after a writ of habeas corpus is denied a citizen, that he shall be tried otherwise than by the course of the common law; if it had intended this result, it was easy by the use of direct words to have accomplished it.

"[It] is difficult to see how the safety of the country required martial law in Indiana. If any of her citizens were plotting treason, the power of arrest could secure them, until the government was prepared for their trial, when the courts were open and ready to try them. It was as easy to protect witnesses before a civil as a military tribunal; and as there could be no wish to convict, except on sufficient legal evidence, surely an ordained and established court was better able to judge of this than a military tribunal composed of gentlemen not trained to the profession of the law. [There] are occasions when martial rule can be properly applied. If, in foreign invasion or civil war, the courts are actually closed, and it is impossible to administer criminal justice according to law, then, on the theatre of active military operations, where war really prevails, there is a necessity to furnish a substitute for the civil authority, thus overthrown, to preserve the safety of the army and society; and as no power is left but the military, it is allowed to govern by martial rule until the laws can have their free course. As necessity creates the rule, so it limits its duration; for, if this government is continued after the courts are reinstated, it is a gross usurpation of power. Martial rule can never exist where the courts are open, and in the proper and unobstructed exercise of their jurisdiction."

What would the result have been if Milligan had been acting as a belligerent for the Confederate side? What if he had been deemed an unlawful belligerent working against the Union undercover? In the case that follows, arising from attempted acts of sabotage by a group of German nationals who landed from German submarines on American shores, the Court upheld their trial by military tribunal. (The Court permitted the trial by a brief per curiam opinion; the decision below setting forth the reasoning was actually published after the prisoners had been convicted by military tribunal and their death sentences executed.)

Ex parte Quirin

317 U.S. 1, 63 S. Ct. 2, 87 L. Ed. 3 (1942).

■ CHIEF JUSTICE STONE delivered the opinion of the Court.

[The] question for decision is whether the detention of petitioners by respondent for trial by Military Commission, appointed by Order of the President of July 2, 1942, on charges preferred against them purporting to set out their violations of the law of war and of the Articles of War, is in conformity to the laws and Constitution of the United States. After denial of their applications by the District Court, petitioners asked leave to file petitions for habeas corpus in this Court.

[The] following facts [except] as noted [are] undisputed. All the petitioners were born in Germany; all have lived in the United States. All returned to Germany between 1933 and 1941. All except petitioner Haupt are admittedly citizens of the German Reich, with which the United States is at war. Haupt came to this country with his parents when he was five years old [and claimed he was a naturalized US citizen]. [After] the declaration of war between the United States and the German Reich, petitioners received training at a sabotage school near Berlin, Germany, where they were instructed in the use of explosives and in methods of secret writing. Thereafter petitioners, with a German citizen, Dasch, proceeded from Germany to a seaport in Occupied France, where petitioners Burger, Heinck and Quirin, together with Dasch, boarded a German submarine which proceeded across the Atlantic to Amagansett Beach on Long Island, New York. The four were there landed from the submarine in the hours of darkness, on or about June 13, 1942, carrying with them a supply of explosives, fuses, and incendiary and timing devices. While landing they wore German Marine Infantry uniforms or parts of uniforms. Immediately after landing they buried their uniforms and the other articles mentioned, and proceeded in civilian dress to New York City. The remaining four petitioners [landing in Florida, took similar actions.] All were taken into custody in New York or Chicago by agents of the Federal Bureau of Investigation. All had received instructions in Germany from an officer of the German High Command to destroy war industries and war facilities in the United States, for which they or their relatives in Germany were to receive salary payments from the German Government.

[The] President, as President and Commander in Chief of the Army and Navy, by Order of July 2, 1942, appointed a Military Commission and directed it to try petitioners for offenses against the law of war and the Articles of War, and prescribed regulations for the procedure on the trial and for review of the record of the trial and of any judgment or sentence of the Commission. On the same day, by Proclamation, the President declared that "all persons who are subjects, citizens or residents of any nation at war with the United States or who give obedience to or act under the direction of any such nation, and who during time of war enter or attempt to enter the United States . . . through coastal or boundary defenses, and are charged with committing or attempting or preparing to commit sabotage, espionage, hostile or warlike acts, or violations of the law of war, shall be subject to the law of war and to the jurisdiction of military tribunals." The Proclamation also stated in terms that all such persons were denied access to the courts. [Petitioners'] main contention is that the President is without any statutory or constitutional authority to order the petitioners to be tried by military tribunal for offenses with which they are charged; that in consequence they are entitled to be tried in the civil courts with the safeguards, including trial by jury, which the Fifth and Sixth Amendments guarantee to all persons charged in such courts with criminal offenses. The Government [insists] that petitioners must be denied access to the courts [because] they are enemy aliens or have entered our territory as enemy belligerents.

[Constitutional] safeguards for the protection of all who are charged with offenses are not to be disregarded in order to inflict merited punishment on some who are guilty. Ex parte Milligan. But the detention and trial of petitioners—ordered by the President in the declared exercise of his powers as Commander in Chief of the Army in time of war and of grave public danger—are not to be set aside by the courts without the clear conviction that they are in conflict with the Constitution or laws of Congress constitutionally enacted.

[The] Constitution [invests] the President, as Commander in Chief, with the power to wage war which Congress has declared, and to carry into effect all laws passed by Congress for the conduct of war and for the government and regulation of the Armed Forces, and all laws defining and punishing offenses against the law of nations, including those which pertain to the conduct of war. [From] the very beginning of its history this Court has recognized and applied the law of war as including that part of the law of nations which prescribes, for the conduct of war, the status, rights and duties of enemy nations as well as of enemy individuals. By the Articles of War, Congress has explicitly provided, so far as it may constitutionally do so, that military tribunals shall have jurisdiction to try offenders or offenses against the law of war in appropriate cases. [It] is unnecessary for present purposes to determine to what extent the President as Commander in Chief has constitutional power to create military commissions without the support of Congressional legislation. For here Congress has authorized trial of offenses against the law of war before such commissions. We are concerned only with the question whether it is within the constitutional power of the National Government to place petitioners upon trial before a military commission for the offenses with which they are charged. [We] may assume that there are acts [which] would not be triable by military tribunal here, either because they are not recognized by our courts as violations of the law of war or because they are of that class of offenses constitutionally triable only by a jury. It was upon such grounds that the Court denied the right to proceed by military tribunal in Ex parte Milligan. But as we shall show, these petitioners were charged with an offense against the law of war which the Constitution does not require to be tried by jury.

[By] universal agreement and practice, the law of war draws a distinction between the armed forces and the peaceful populations of belligerent nations and also between those who are lawful and unlawful combatants. Lawful combatants are subject to capture and detention as prisoners of war by opposing military forces. Unlawful combatants are likewise subject to capture and detention, but in addition they are subject to trial and punishment by military tribunals for acts which render their belligerency unlawful. The spy who secretly and without uniform passes the military lines of a belligerent in time of war, seeking to gather military information and communicate it to the enemy, or an enemy combatant who without uniform comes secretly through the lines for the purpose of waging war by destruction of life or property, are familiar examples of belligerents who are generally deemed not to be entitled to the status of prisoners of war, but to be offenders against the law of war subject to trial and punishment by military tribunals. [Citizenship] in the United States of an enemy belligerent does not relieve him from the consequences of a belligerency which is unlawful because in violation of the law of war. [Nor] are petitioners any the less belligerents if, as they argue, they have not actually committed or attempted to commit any act of depredation or entered the theatre or zone of active military operations.

[Petitioners] insist that, even if the offenses with which they are charged are offenses against the law of war, their trial is subject to the requirement[s of the Fifth and Sixth Amendments.] We cannot say that Congress in preparing the Fifth and Sixth Amendments intended to extend trial by jury to the cases of alien or citizen offenders against the law of war otherwise triable by military commission, while withholding it from members of our own armed forces charged with infractions of the Articles of War punishable by death. [Petitioners], and especially petitioner Haupt, stress the pronouncement of this Court in the Milligan case that the law of war "can never be applied to citizens in states which have upheld the authority of the government, and where the courts are open and their process unobstructed." [But] the Court was at pains to point out that Milligan, a citizen twenty years resident in Indiana, who had never been a resident of any of the states in rebellion, was not an enemy belligerent either entitled to the status of a prisoner of war or subject to the penalties imposed upon unlawful belligerents. We construe the Court's statement as to the inapplicability of the law of war to Milligan's case as having particular reference to the facts before it. From them the Court concluded that Milligan, not being a part of or associated with the armed forces of the enemy, was a non-belligerent, not subject to the law of war save as—in circumstances found not there to be present and not involved here—martial law might be constitutionally established.

The Court's opinion is inapplicable to the case presented by the present record. We have no occasion now to define with meticulous care the ultimate boundaries of the jurisdiction of military tribunals to try persons according to the law of war. It is enough that petitioners here, upon the conceded facts, were plainly within those boundaries.

FROM QUIRIN TO THE 9/11 RESPONSE

1. ***The Court's motivations.*** The Court's opinion does not reveal a critical detail about the saboteurs' capture: the FBI learned about the plot from one of the co-conspirators. While on the train headed to New York City, Dasch told one of his co-conspirators, Burger, that he intended to turn himself in rather than carry out the orders. Dasch then proceeded to FBI headquarters in Washington, DC to do just that. The FBI, on his tip, was able to round up the other seven men. Once the saboteurs had been captured, President Roosevelt had no doubts as to their fate. The infiltrators would be

tried by court martial and executed immediately; the only question, Roosevelt told an aide, was whether they should die by gallows or firing squad. Roosevelt was equally clear regarding his intentions should he face an adverse court ruling: "I want one thing clearly understood," he told Attorney General Biddle. "I won't give them up. [I] won't hand them over to the United States marshal armed with a writ of habeas corpus." It was against this backdrop of a fait accompli that the Supreme Court scrambled to hear on an expedited basis (during its summer recess) the saboteurs' constitutional challenge to the trial by military commission. Note the odd circumstances of the Court's decision. On July 29, 1942, the Court heard argument in Quirin. Two days later, on July 31, 1942, the Court announced in a single unanimous order that the military commissions had the authority to try the saboteurs and did not violate the Fifth and Sixth Amendments. On August 8, 1942, six of the eight saboteurs were executed by electrocution. (The commission recommended that Dasch's sentence be commuted to thirty years' imprisonment and Burger's sentence commuted to life in prison because of their assistance in apprehending the others. The two men were ultimately pardoned by President Truman in 1948 and deported to Germany.) The Court did not issue an opinion explaining its decision until several months after the executions.

Consider the view that the Supreme Court rushed to rule on the constitutionality of the military commission in order to remain relevant in the face of the President's determination to swiftly execute the infiltrators. Did the Court succeed? Consider the fact that the Court's decision in Quirin undergirded much of the Bush Administration's legal strategy with respect to trying enemy combatants before military commissions. Assuming that the Court was troubled by the merits of its ruling in Quirin, would the Court have been better served by adopting Chief Justice Taney's posture in Merryman—in which Taney ruled the suspension of the writ of habeas corpus by any party other than Congress unconstitutional—and issuing an order that it knew would likely be ignored? Or should it have refrained from reviewing the case altogether, as Justice Jackson would have had the Court do in Korematsu?

2. ***Johnson v. Eisentrager.*** In **Johnson v. Eisentrager**, 339 U.S. 763 (1950), German radio men captured in the Pacific theater of war after Germany's surrender in World War II and designated as "enemy aliens" were accused of the war crime of continuing to fight after surrender because they were assisting Japanese forces (which were still at war). The men were tried and convicted by a U.S. military commission located in China. The prisoners were then repatriated to Germany to serve their sentences in Landsberg Prison, which was under the control of the American military, where they petitioned the district court of the District of Columbia for writs of habeas corpus. Justice JACKSON, writing for the Court, stressed that the aliens in that case could not be extended the privilege of litigation in U.S. courts:

"We are here confronted with a decision whose basic premise is that these prisoners are entitled, as a constitutional right, to sue in some court of the United States for a writ of habeas corpus. To support that assumption we must hold that a prisoner of our military authorities is constitutionally entitled to the writ, even though he (a) is an enemy alien; (b) has never been or resided in the United States; (c) was captured outside of our territory and there held in military custody as a prisoner of war; (d) was tried and convicted by a Military Commission sitting outside the United States; (e) for offenses against laws of war committed outside the United States; (f) and is at all times imprisoned outside the United States.

"We have pointed out that the privilege of litigation has been extended to aliens, whether friendly or enemy, only because permitting their presence in the country implied protection. No such basis can be invoked here, for these prisoners at no relevant time were within any territory over which the United States is sovereign, and the scenes of their offense, their capture, their trial and their punishment were all beyond the territorial jurisdiction of any court of the United States.

"Another reason for a limited opening of our courts to resident aliens is that among them are many of friendly personal disposition to whom the status of enemy is only one imputed by law. But these prisoners were actual enemies, active in the hostile service of an enemy power. There is no fiction about their enmity. Yet the decision below confers upon them a right to use our courts, free even of the limitation we have imposed upon resident alien enemies, to whom we deny any use of our courts that would hamper our war effort or aid the enemy.

"A basic consideration in habeas corpus practice is that the prisoner will be produced before the court. This is the crux of the statutory scheme established by the Congress; indeed, it is inherent in the very term 'habeas corpus.' [To] grant the writ to these prisoners might mean that our army must transport them across the seas for hearing. This would require allocation of shipping space, guarding personnel, billeting and rations. It might also require transportation for whatever witnesses the prisoners desired to call as well as transportation for those necessary to defend legality of the sentence. The writ, since it is held to be a matter of right, would be equally available to enemies during active hostilities as in the present twilight between war and peace. Such trials would hamper the war effort and bring aid and comfort to the enemy. They would diminish the prestige of our commanders, not only with enemies but with wavering neutrals. It would be difficult to devise more effective fettering of a field commander than to allow the very enemies he is ordered to reduce to submission to call him to account in his own civil courts and divert his efforts and attention from the military offensive abroad to the legal defensive at home. Nor is it unlikely that the result of such enemy litigiousness would be a conflict between judicial and military opinion highly comforting to enemies of the United States.

"Moreover, we could expect no reciprocity for placing the litigation weapon in unrestrained enemy hands."

3. ***The executive response to the events of 9/11.*** "On September 11, 2001, agents of the al Qaeda terrorist network hijacked four commercial airliners and used them as missiles to attack American targets. While one of the four attacks was foiled by the heroism of the plane's passengers, the other three killed approximately 3,000 innocent civilians, destroyed hundreds of millions of dollars of property, and severely damaged the U.S. economy." Rasul v. Bush, 542 U.S. 466 (2004). In response to the these terrorist attacks on New York City and Washington, D.C., Congress passed the JOINT RESOLUTION FOR THE AUTHORIZATION FOR USE OF MILITARY FORCE (AUMF), Pub. L. No. 107–40, 115 Stat. 224 § 2(a) (2001), which gave the President authority "to use all necessary and appropriate force against those nations, organizations, or persons he determines planned, authorized, committed, or aided the terrorist attacks that occurred on September 11,

2001, or harbored such organizations or persons, in order to prevent any future acts of international terrorism against the United States by such nations, organizations or persons." This congressional resolution was unusual because it permitted the President to engage the U.S. Armed Forces in hostilities without defining any particular nation against which the force should be directed. Section 2(b) of the Resolution explicitly states that the Resolution is supposed to constitute specific statutory authorization as defined by the War Powers Resolution, but is this the sort of open-ended Resolution envisioned by the War Powers Resolution? If it is, for how long is the authorization valid? Does the authorization have to be renewed, or does Congress have to explicitly revoke the authorization by concurrent resolution? Who has the power to decide whether the war has ended, and what are the criteria that should be used to make that determination?

Pursuant to the Joint Resolution, the President directed the United States Armed Forces to wage war against the Taliban government of Afghanistan, which was believed to have supported and harbored al-Qaeda terrorists. In the course of that campaign, several hundred foreign individuals thought to be fighters aligned against the United States were captured and eventually held in captivity as "enemy combatants" on a U.S. naval base in Guantanamo Bay, Cuba—a territory leased to and controlled by the U.S. military since 1903, even though "ultimate sovereignty" has continued to reside with Cuba. Several of these prisoners sought writs of habeas corpus in the federal district court of the District of Columbia, arguing for access to court, release from custody, access to counsel, freedom from interrogation and knowledge of the charges against them. The government argued that the federal courts had no jurisdiction over enemy aliens held outside the United States, relying upon Eisentrager.

In **Rasul v. Bush**, 542 U.S. 466 (2004), the Supreme Court rejected the government's argument, holding by a vote of 6–3 that the federal habeas statute, which authorized district courts, "within their respective jurisdictions," to entertain habeas applications by persons claiming to be held "in custody in violation of the . . . laws . . . of the United States," 28 U.S.C. § 2241, applied to petitions from Guantanamo detainees. Justice STEVENS wrote for the Court, joined by Justices O'Connor, Souter, Ginsburg and Breyer: "Consistent with the historic purpose of the writ [of habeas corpus], this Court has recognized the federal courts' power to review applications for habeas relief in a wide variety of cases involving Executive detention, in wartime as well as in times of peace. The Court has, for example, entertained the habeas petitions of an American citizen who plotted an attack on military installations during the Civil War, Ex parte Milligan, and of admitted enemy aliens convicted of war crimes during a declared war and held in the United States, Ex parte Quirin. [The] question now before us is whether the habeas statute confers a right to judicial review of the legality of Executive detention of aliens in a territory over which the United States exercises plenary and exclusive jurisdiction, but not 'ultimate sovereignty.' "

Justice Stevens distinguished the Guantanamo prisoners from those denied relief in Eisentrager on the ground that the Guantanamo prisoners "are not nationals of countries at war with the United States, and they deny that they have engaged in or plotted acts of aggression against the United States; they have never been afforded access to any tribunal, much less charged with and convicted of wrongdoing; and for more than two years they have been imprisoned in territory over which the United States exercises exclusive jurisdiction and control." Justice Stevens construed the habeas statute to reach those imprisoned in Guantanamo by U.S. custodians: "Whatever traction the presumption against extraterritoriality might have in other contexts, it certainly has no application to the operation of the habeas statute with respect to persons detained within 'the territorial jurisdiction' of the United States. By the express terms of its agreements with Cuba, the United States exercises 'complete jurisdiction and control' over the Guantanamo Bay Naval Base, and may continue to exercise such control permanently if it so chooses."

Justice KENNEDY concurred in the judgment, finding Eisentrager distinguishable because "Guantanamo Bay is in every practical respect a United States territory, and it is one far removed from any hostilities" and "the detainees at Guantanamo Bay are being held indefinitely, and without benefit of any legal proceeding to determine their status." Justice SCALIA dissented, joined by Chief Justice Rehnquist and Justice Thomas: "Today's opinion [overrules] Eisentrager [and] extends the habeas statute, for the first time, to aliens held beyond the sovereign territory of the United States and beyond the territorial jurisdiction of its courts. [In] abandoning the venerable statutory line drawn in Eisentrager, the Court boldly extends the scope of the habeas statute to the four corners of the earth. [Congress] is in session. If it wished to change federal judges' habeas jurisdiction from what this Court had previously held that to be, it could have done so. [For] this Court to create such a monstrous scheme in time of war, and in frustration of our military commanders' reliance upon clearly stated prior law, is judicial adventurism of the worst sort."

In addition to foreigners captured in Afghanistan, two American citizens were captured while allegedly fighting against American forces. One, John Walker Lindh, was tried and convicted by plea bargain through the civilian criminal justice system. See United States v. Lindh, 212 F. Supp. 2d 541 (E.D. Va. 2002) (denying motions for dismissal). The other, however, Yasir Esam Hamdi, a Louisiana-born Saudi-American, was detained by the U.S. military as an "enemy combatant" in naval brigs in Norfolk, Virginia and Charleston, South Carolina. Hamdi sought habeas relief in the Eastern District of Virginia. The government argued that Hamdi's status as an "enemy combatant" justified holding him in the United States indefinitely without formal charges or proceedings. The court of appeals held that, notwithstanding Hamdi's citizen status, deference to the military required denial of his requested habeas relief, and rejected Hamdi's argument that the NON-DETENTION ACT, passed by Congress in 1948, barred his indefinite detention. That Act states, "No citizen shall be imprisoned or otherwise detained by the United States except pursuant to an Act of Congress." 18 U.S.C. § 4001(a). The court of appeals expressed doubt that the Act applied in these circumstances but held that in any event the detention was congressionally authorized by the AUMF. In the Supreme Court ruling that follows, five justices agreed with that ruling as to congressional authorization, but the Court nonetheless vacated and remanded by a vote of 8–1:

Hamdi v. Rumsfeld

542 U.S. 507, 124 S. Ct. 2633, 159 L. Ed. 2d 578 (2004).

■ JUSTICE O'CONNOR announced the judgment of the Court and delivered an opinion, in which CHIEF JUSTICE REHNQUIST and JUSTICES KENNEDY and BREYER join.

At this difficult time in our nation's history, we are called upon to consider the legality of the Government's detention of a United States citizen on United States soil as an "enemy combatant" and to address the process that is constitutionally owed to one who seeks to challenge his classification as such. [We] hold that although Congress authorized the detention of combatants in the narrow circumstances alleged here, due process demands that a citizen held in the United States as an enemy combatant be given a meaningful opportunity to contest the factual basis for that detention before a neutral decisionmaker.

II. [The] threshold question before us is whether the Executive has the authority to detain citizens who qualify as "enemy combatants." There is some debate as to the proper scope of this term, and the Government has never provided any court with the full criteria that it uses in classifying individuals as such. It has made clear, however, that, for purposes of this case, the "enemy combatant" that it is seeking to detain is an individual who, it alleges, was " 'part of or supporting forces hostile to the United States or coalition partners' " in Afghanistan and who " 'engaged in an armed conflict against the United States' " there. We therefore answer only the narrow question before us: whether the detention of citizens falling within that definition is authorized.

The Government maintains that no explicit congressional authorization is required, because the Executive possesses plenary authority to detain pursuant to Article II of the Constitution. We do not reach the question whether Article II provides such authority, however, because we agree [that] Congress has in fact authorized Hamdi's detention, through the AUMF. [We] conclude that the AUMF is explicit congressional authorization for the detention of individuals in the narrow category we describe (assuming, without deciding, that such authorization is required), and that the AUMF satisfied [the Non-Detention Act's] requirement that a detention be "pursuant to an Act of Congress" (assuming, without deciding, that [the Act] applies to military detentions).

The AUMF authorizes the President to use "all necessary and appropriate force" against "nations, organizations, or persons" associated with the September 11, 2001, terrorist attacks. There can be no doubt that individuals who fought against the United States in Afghanistan as part of the Taliban, an organization known to have supported the al Qaeda terrorist network responsible for those attacks, are individuals Congress sought to target in passing the AUMF. We conclude that detention of individuals falling into the limited category we are considering, for the duration of the particular conflict in which they were captured, is so fundamental and accepted an incident to war as to be an exercise of the "necessary and appropriate force" Congress has authorized the President to use.

The capture and detention of lawful combatants and the capture, detention, and trial of unlawful combatants, by "universal agreement and practice," are "important incidents of war." Ex parte Quirin. The purpose of detention is to prevent captured individuals from returning to the field of battle and taking up arms once again. There is no bar to this Nation's holding one of its own citizens as an enemy combatant. In Quirin, one of the detainees, Haupt, alleged that he was a naturalized United States citizen. [It] is of no moment that the AUMF does not use specific language of detention. Because detention to prevent a combatant's return to the battlefield is a fundamental incident of waging war, in permitting the use of "necessary and appropriate force," Congress has clearly and unmistakably authorized detention in the narrow circumstances considered here.

Hamdi objects, nevertheless, that Congress has not authorized the indefinite detention to which he is now subject [and that he faces] the substantial prospect of perpetual detention. [The] prospect Hamdi raises is [not] far-fetched. If the Government does not consider this unconventional war won for two generations, and if it maintains during that time that Hamdi might, if released, rejoin forces fighting against the United States, then [Hamdi's] detention could last for the rest of his life. [Certainly], we agree that indefinite detention for the purpose of interrogation is not authorized. Further, we understand Congress' grant of authority for the use of "necessary and appropriate force" to include the authority to detain for the duration of the relevant conflict, and our understanding is based on longstanding law-of-war principles. [Active] combat operations against Taliban fighters apparently are ongoing in Afghanistan. The United States may detain, for the duration of these hostilities, individuals legitimately determined to be Taliban combatants who "engaged in an armed conflict against the United States."

Ex parte Milligan does not undermine our holding about the Government's authority to seize enemy combatants, as we define that term today. In that case, the Court made repeated reference to the fact that its inquiry into whether the military tribunal had jurisdiction to try and punish Milligan turned in large part on the fact that Milligan was not a prisoner of war, but a resident of Indiana arrested while at home there. That fact was central to its conclusion. Had Milligan been captured while he was assisting Confederate soldiers by carrying a rifle against Union troops on a Confederate battlefield, the holding of the Court might well have been different. The Court's repeated explanations that Milligan was not a prisoner of war suggest that had these different circumstances been present he could have been detained under military authority for the duration of the conflict, whether or not he was a citizen.

Moreover, as Justice Scalia acknowledges, the Court in Ex parte Quirin [dismissed] the language of Milligan that the petitioners had suggested prevented them from being subject to military process. Even accepting that [Milligan] once could have been viewed as standing for the sweeping proposition for which Justice Scalia cites [it]—that the military does not have authority to try an American citizen accused of spying against his country during wartime—Quirin makes undeniably clear that this is not the law today. Haupt [was] accused of being a spy. The Court in Quirin found him "subject to trial and punishment by [a] military tribuna[l]" for those acts, and held that his citizenship did not change this result.

Quirin was a unanimous opinion. It both postdates and clarifies Milligan, providing us with the most apposite precedent that we have on the question of whether citizens may be detained in such circumstances. Brushing aside such precedent—particularly when doing so gives rise to a host of new questions never dealt with by this Court—is unjustified and unwise.

To the extent that Justice Scalia accepts the precedential value of Quirin, he argues that it cannot guide our inquiry here because "[i]n Quirin it was uncontested that the petitioners were members of enemy forces," while Hamdi challenges his classification as an enemy combatant. [But] it is unclear why, in the paradigm outlined by Justice Scalia, such a concession should have any relevance. Justice Scalia envisions a system in which the only options are congressional suspension of the writ of habeas corpus or prosecution for treason or some other crime. He does not explain how his historical analysis supports the addition of a third option—detention under some other process after concession of enemy-combatant status—or why a concession should carry any different effect than proof of enemy-combatant status in a proceeding that comports with due process. To be clear, our opinion only finds legislative authority to detain under the AUMF once it is sufficiently clear that the individual is, in fact, an enemy combatant; whether that is established by concession or by some other process that verifies this fact with sufficient certainty seems beside the point.

Moreover, Justice Scalia presumably would come to a different result if Hamdi had been kept in Afghanistan or even Guantanamo Bay. This creates a perverse incentive. Military authorities faced with the stark choice of submitting to the full-blown criminal process or releasing a suspected enemy combatant captured on the battlefield will simply keep citizen-detainees abroad. Indeed, the Government transferred Hamdi from Guantanamo Bay to the United States naval brig only after it learned that he might be an American citizen. It is not at all clear why that should make a determinative constitutional difference.

III. Even in cases in which the detention of enemy combatants is legally authorized, there remains the question of what process is constitutionally due to a citizen who disputes his enemy-combatant status. [The] parties [agree] that, absent suspension, the writ of habeas corpus remains available to every individual detained within the United States. Only in the rarest of circumstances has Congress seen fit to suspend the writ. At all other times, it has remained a critical check on the Executive, ensuring that it does not detain individuals except in accordance with law. All agree suspension of the writ has not occurred here. Thus, it is undisputed that Hamdi was properly before an Article III court to challenge his detention under 28 U.S.C. § 2241.

[The] Government urges [that] because it is "undisputed" that Hamdi's seizure took place in a combat zone, the habeas determination can be made purely as a matter of law, with no further hearing or factfinding necessary. This argument is easily rejected. [The] circumstances surrounding Hamdi's seizure cannot in any way be characterized as "undisputed." [Under] the definition of enemy combatant that we accept today as falling within the scope of Congress' authorization, Hamdi would need to be "part of or supporting forces hostile to the United States or coalition partners" and "engaged in an armed conflict against the United States" to justify his detention in the United States for the duration of the relevant conflict. The habeas petition states only that "when seized by the United States Government, Mr. Hamdi resided in Afghanistan." [Accordingly,] we reject any argument that Hamdi has made concessions that eliminate any right to further process.

[The] Government [argues also] that further factual exploration is unwarranted and inappropriate in light of the extraordinary constitutional interests at stake. Under the Government's most extreme rendition of this argument, "respect for separation of powers and the limited institutional capabilities of courts in matters of military decision-making in connection with an ongoing conflict" ought to eliminate entirely any individual process, restricting the courts to investigating only whether legal authorization exists for the broader detention scheme. At most, the Government argues, courts should review its determination that a citizen is an enemy combatant under a very deferential "some evidence" standard. Under this review, a court would assume the accuracy of the Government's articulated basis for Hamdi's detention, as set forth in the [Defense department declaration], and assess only whether that articulated basis was a legitimate one. In response, Hamdi emphasizes that this Court consistently has recognized that an individual challenging his detention may not be held at the will of the Executive without recourse to some proceeding before a neutral tribunal to determine whether the Executive's asserted justifications for that detention have basis in fact and warrant in law.

Both of these positions highlight legitimate concerns. [The] ordinary mechanism that we use for balancing such serious competing interests, and for determining the procedures that are necessary to ensure that a citizen is not "deprived of life, liberty, or property, without due process of law," is the test that we articulated in Mathews v. Eldridge, 424 U.S. 319 (1976). Mathews dictates that the process due in any given instance is determined by weighing "the private interest that will be affected by the official action" against the Government's asserted interest, "including the function involved" and the burdens the Government would face in providing greater process.

[It] is beyond question that substantial interests lie on both sides of the scale in this case. Hamdi's "private interest . . . affected by the official action" is the most elemental of liberty interests—the interest in being free from physical detention by one's own government. [Nor] is the weight on this side of the Mathews scale offset by the circumstances of war or the accusation of treasonous behavior. [On] the other side of the scale are the weighty and sensitive governmental interests in ensuring that those who have in fact fought with the enemy during a war do not return to battle against the United States. [Our] Constitution recognizes that core strategic matters of warmaking belong in the hands of those who are best positioned and most politically accountable for making them. [Striking] the proper constitutional balance here is of great importance to the Nation during this period of ongoing combat. But it is equally vital that our calculus not give short shrift to the values that this country holds dear or to the privilege that is American citizenship. It is during our most challenging and uncertain moments that our Nation's commitment to due process is most severely tested; and it is in those times that we must preserve our commitment at home to the principles for which we fight abroad.

[We] hold that a citizen-detainee seeking to challenge his classification as an enemy combatant must receive notice of the factual basis for his classification, and a fair opportunity to rebut the Government's factual assertions before a neutral decisionmaker. [These] essential constitutional promises may not be eroded. At the same time, the exigencies of the circumstances may demand that, aside from these core elements, enemy combatant proceedings may be tailored to alleviate their uncommon potential to burden the Executive at a time of ongoing military conflict. Hearsay, for example, may need to be accepted as the most reliable available evidence from the Government in such a proceeding. Likewise, the Constitution would not be offended by a presumption in favor of the Government's evidence, so long as that presumption remained a rebuttable one and fair opportunity for rebuttal were provided. [We] think it unlikely that this basic process will have the dire impact on the central functions of warmaking that the Government forecasts. The parties agree that initial captures on the battlefield need not receive the process we have discussed here; that process is due only when the determination is made to continue to hold those who have been seized. [While] we accord the greatest respect and consideration to the judgments of military authorities in matters relating to the actual prosecution of a war, and recognize that the scope of that discretion necessarily is wide, it does not infringe on the core role of the military for the courts to exercise their own time-honored and constitutionally mandated roles of reviewing and resolving claims like those presented here.

[In] so holding, we necessarily reject the Government's assertion that separation of powers principles mandate a heavily circumscribed role for the courts in such circumstances. Indeed, the position that the courts must forgo any examination of the individual case and focus exclusively on the legality of the broader detention scheme cannot be mandated by any reasonable view of separation of powers, as this approach serves only to condense power into a single branch of government. We have long since made clear that a state of war is not a blank check for the President when it comes to the rights of the Nation's citizens. Youngstown. Whatever power the United States Constitution envisions for the Executive in its exchanges with other nations or with enemy organizations in times of conflict, it most assuredly envisions a role for all three branches when individual liberties are at stake.

Likewise, we have made clear that, unless Congress acts to suspend it, the Great Writ of habeas corpus allows the Judicial Branch to play a necessary role in maintaining this delicate balance of governance, serving as an important judicial check on the Executive's discretion in the realm of detentions. Thus, while we do not question that our due process assessment must pay keen attention to the particular burdens faced by the Executive in the context of military action, it would turn our system of checks and balances on its head to suggest that a citizen could not make his way to court with a challenge to the factual basis for his detention by his government, simply because the Executive opposes making available such a challenge. Absent suspension of the writ by Congress, a citizen detained as an enemy combatant is entitled to this process.

Because we conclude that due process demands some system for a citizen detainee to refute his classification, the proposed "some evidence" standard is inadequate. Any process in which the Executive's factual assertions go wholly unchallenged or are simply presumed correct without any opportunity for the alleged combatant to demonstrate otherwise falls constitutionally short. [An] interrogation by one's captor, however effective an intelligence-gathering tool, hardly constitutes a constitutionally adequate factfinding before a neutral decisionmaker. [Plainly,] the "process" Hamdi has received is not that to which he is entitled under the Due Process Clause. There remains the possibility that the standards we have articulated could be met by an appropriately authorized and properly constituted military tribunal. [In] the absence of such process, however, a court that receives a petition for a writ of habeas corpus from an alleged enemy combatant must itself ensure that the minimum requirements of due process are achieved. [Vacated and remanded.]

■ JUSTICE SOUTER, with whom JUSTICE GINSBURG joins, concurring in part, dissenting in part, and concurring in the judgment.

[The] Government has failed to demonstrate that the [AUMF] authorizes the detention complained of here even on the facts the Government claims. If the Government raises nothing further than the record now shows, the Non-Detention Act entitles Hamdi to be released. [In] requiring that any Executive detention be "pursuant to an Act of Congress," [Congress] necessarily meant to require a congressional enactment that clearly authorized detention or imprisonment. [The] defining character of American constitutional government is its constant tension between security and liberty, serving both by partial helpings of each. In a government of separated powers, deciding finally on what is a reasonable degree of guaranteed liberty whether in peace or war (or some condition in between) is not well entrusted to the Executive Branch of Government, whose particular responsibility is to maintain security. For reasons of inescapable human nature, the branch of the Government asked to counter a serious threat is not the branch on which to rest the Nation's entire reliance in striking the balance between the will to win and the cost in liberty on the way to victory; the responsibility for security will naturally amplify the claim that security legitimately raises. A reasonable balance is more likely to be reached on the judgment of a different branch. [Hence] the need for an assessment by Congress before citizens are subject to lockup, and likewise the need for a clearly expressed congressional resolution of the competing claims.

[Under] this principle of reading § 4001(a) [of the Non-Detention Act] robustly to require a clear statement of authorization to detain, none of the Government's arguments suffices to justify Hamdi's detention. [The AUMF's] focus is clear, and that is on the use of military power. It is fairly read to authorize the use of armies and weapons, whether against other armies or individual terrorists. But, [it] never so much as uses the word detention, and there is no reason to think Congress might have perceived any need to augment Executive power to deal with dangerous citizens within the United States, given the well-stocked statutory arsenal of defined criminal offenses covering the gamut of actions that a citizen sympathetic to terrorists might commit.

[In] a moment of genuine emergency, when the Government must act with no time for deliberation, the Executive may be able to detain a citizen if there is reason to fear he is an imminent threat to the safety of the Nation and its people. This case, however, does not present that question, because an emergency power of necessity must at least be limited by the emergency; Hamdi has been locked up for over two years. Because I find Hamdi's detention forbidden by § 4001(a) and unauthorized by the [AUMF], I would not reach any questions of what process he may be due in litigating disputed issues in a proceeding under the habeas statute or prior to the habeas enquiry itself. For me, it suffices that the Government has failed to justify holding him in the absence of a further Act of Congress, criminal charges, a showing that the detention conforms to the laws of war, or a demonstration that § 4001(a) is unconstitutional.

■ JUSTICE SCALIA, with whom JUSTICE STEVENS joins, dissenting.

[Where] the Government accuses a citizen of waging war against it, our constitutional tradition has been to prosecute him in federal court for treason or some other crime. Where the exigencies of war prevent that, the Constitution's Suspension Clause, Art. I, § 9, cl. 2, allows Congress to relax the usual protections temporarily. Absent suspension, however, the Executive's assertion of military exigency has not been thought sufficient to permit detention without charge. No one contends that the congressional Authorization for Use of Military Force, on which the Government relies to justify its actions here, is an implementation of the Suspension Clause. Accordingly, I would reverse the decision below.

The very core of liberty secured by our Anglo-Saxon system of separated powers has been freedom from indefinite imprisonment at the will of the Executive. [The] gist of the Due Process Clause, as understood at the founding and since, was to force the Government to follow those common-law procedures traditionally deemed necessary before depriving a person of life, liberty, or property. [These] due process rights have historically been vindicated by the writ of habeas corpus. In England before the founding, the writ developed into a tool for challenging executive confinement. [The] writ of habeas corpus was preserved in the Constitution—the only common-law writ to be explicitly mentioned. Hamilton lauded "the establishment of the writ of habeas corpus" in his Federalist defense as a means to protect against "the practice of arbitrary imprisonments . . . in all ages, [one of] the favourite and most formidable instruments of tyranny." The Federalist No. 84.

[The] reasoning and conclusion of Milligan logically cover the present case. The Government justifies imprisonment of Hamdi on principles of the law of war and admits that, absent the war, it would have no such authority. But if the law of war cannot be applied to citizens where courts are open, then Hamdi's imprisonment without criminal trial is no less unlawful than Milligan's trial by military tribunal.

[Except] for the actual command of military forces, all authorization for their maintenance and all explicit authorization for their use is placed in the control of Congress under Article I, rather than the President under Article II. As Hamilton explained, the President's military authority would be "much inferior" to that of the British King. The Federalist, No. 69. A view of the Constitution that gives the Executive authority to use military force rather than the force of law against citizens on American soil flies in the face of the mistrust that engendered these provisions.

The Government argues that our more recent jurisprudence ratifies its indefinite imprisonment of a citizen within the territorial jurisdiction of federal courts. It places primary reliance upon Ex parte Quirin, [a] World War II case upholding the trial by military commission of eight German saboteurs, one of whom, Herbert Haupt, was a U.S. citizen. The case was not this Court's finest hour. The Court upheld the commission and denied relief in a brief per curiam issued the day after oral argument concluded; [a] week later the Government carried out the commission's death sentence upon six saboteurs, including Haupt. The Court eventually explained its reasoning in a written opinion issued several months later.

Only three paragraphs of the Court's lengthy opinion dealt with the particular circumstances of Haupt's case. The Government argued that Haupt, like the other petitioners, could be tried by military commission under the laws of war. In agreeing with that contention, Quirin purported to interpret the language of Milligan ([that] the law of war "can never be applied to citizens in states which have upheld the authority of the government, and where the courts are open and their process unobstructed") in the following manner:

> "Elsewhere in its opinion . . . the Court was at pains to point out that Milligan, a citizen twenty years resident in Indiana, who had never been a resident of any of the states in rebellion, was not an enemy belligerent either entitled to the status of a prisoner of war or subject to the penalties imposed upon unlawful belligerents. We construe the Court's statement as to the inapplicability of the law of war to Milligan's case as having particular reference to the facts before it. From them the Court concluded that Milligan, not being a part of or associated with the armed forces of the enemy, was a non-belligerent, not subject to the law of war . . . ."

In my view this seeks to revise Milligan rather than describe it. [But] even if Quirin gave a correct description of Milligan, or made an irrevocable revision of it, Quirin would still not justify denial of the writ here. In Quirin it was uncontested that the petitioners were members of enemy forces. They were "admitted enemy invaders," and it was "undisputed" that they had landed in the United States in service of German forces. [Where] the petitioner insists that he is not a belligerent [Quirin] left the pre-existing law in place: Absent suspension of the writ, a citizen held where the courts are open is entitled either to criminal trial or to a judicial decree requiring his release. It follows [that] Hamdi is entitled to a habeas decree requiring his release unless (1) criminal proceedings are promptly brought, or (2) Congress has suspended the writ of habeas corpus. A suspension of the writ could, of course, lay down conditions for continued detention, similar to those that today's opinion prescribes under the Due Process Clause. But there is a world of difference between the people's representatives' determining the need for that suspension (and prescribing the conditions for it), and this Court's doing so.

The plurality finds justification for Hamdi's imprisonment in the [AUMF]. [This] is not remotely a congressional suspension of the writ, and no one claims that it is. Contrary to the plurality's view, I do not think this statute even authorizes detention of a citizen with the clarity necessary. [But] even if it did, I would not permit it to overcome Hamdi's entitlement to habeas corpus relief. The Suspension Clause of the Constitution, which carefully circumscribes the conditions under which the writ can be withheld, would be a sham if it could be evaded by congressional prescription of requirements other than the common-law requirement of committal for criminal prosecution that render the writ, though available, unavailing.

[Having] distorted the Suspension Clause, the plurality finishes up by transmogrifying the Great Writ—disposing of the present habeas petition by remanding for the District Court to "engage in a factfinding process that is both prudent and incremental." [This] judicial remediation of executive default is unheard of. The role of habeas corpus is to determine the legality of executive detention, not to supply the omitted process necessary to make it legal. It is not the habeas court's function to make illegal detention legal by supplying a process that the Government could have provided, but chose not to. If Hamdi is being imprisoned in violation of the Constitution (because without due process of law), then his habeas petition should be granted; the Executive may then hand him over to the criminal authorities, whose detention for the purpose of prosecution will be lawful, or else must release him.

[Where] the citizen is captured outside and held outside the United States, the constitutional requirements may be different. Cf. Eisentrager; Rasul v. Bush (Scalia, J., dissenting). Moreover, even within the United States, the accused citizen-enemy combatant may lawfully be detained once prosecution is in progress or in contemplation. [I] frankly do not know whether these tools are sufficient to meet the Government's security needs, including the need to obtain intelligence through interrogation. It is far beyond my competence, or the Court's competence, to determine that. But it is not beyond Congress's. If the situation demands it, the Executive can ask Congress to authorize suspension of the writ—which can be made subject to whatever conditions Congress deems appropriate, including even the procedural novelties invented by the plurality today. To be sure, suspension is limited by the Constitution to cases of rebellion or invasion. But whether the attacks of September 11, 2001, constitute an "invasion," and whether those attacks still justify suspension several years later, are questions for Congress rather than this Court. If civil rights are to be curtailed during wartime, it must be done openly and democratically, as the Constitution requires, rather than by silent erosion through an opinion of this Court.

Many think it not only inevitable but entirely proper that liberty give way to security in times of national crisis—that, at the extremes of military exigency, *inter arma silent leges*. Whatever the general merits of the view that war silences law or modulates its voice, that view has no place in the interpretation and application of a Constitution designed precisely to confront war and, in a manner that accords with democratic principles, to accommodate it. Because the Court has proceeded to meet the current emergency in a manner the Constitution does not envision, I respectfully dissent.

■ JUSTICE THOMAS, dissenting.

The Executive Branch, acting pursuant to the powers vested in the President by the Constitution and with explicit congressional approval, has determined that [Hamdi] is an enemy combatant and should be detained. This detention falls squarely within the Federal Government's war powers, and we lack the expertise and capacity to second-guess that decision. [Because] the Founders understood that they could not foresee the myriad potential threats to national security that might later arise, they chose to create a Federal Government that necessarily possesses sufficient power to handle any threat to the security of the Nation. [The] Founders intended that the President have primary responsibility—along with the necessary power—to protect the national security and to conduct the Nation's foreign relations. They did so principally because the structural advantages of a unitary Executive are essential in these domains. "Energy in the executive is a leading character in the definition of good government. It is essential to the protection of the community against foreign attacks." The Federalist, No. 70 (Hamilton). [Congress,] to be sure, has a substantial and essential role in both foreign affairs and national security. But it is crucial to recognize that judicial interference in these domains destroys the purpose of vesting primary responsibility in a unitary Executive.

[Although] the President very well may have inherent authority to detain those arrayed against our troops, I agree with the plurality that we need not decide that question because Congress has authorized the President to do so [under the AUMF.] Accordingly, the President's action here is "supported by the strongest of presumptions and the widest latitude of judicial interpretation." Dames & Moore. [In] this context, due process requires nothing more than a good-faith executive determination. [The] Executive's decision that a detention is necessary to protect the public need not and should not be subjected to judicial second-guessing. Indeed, at least in the context of enemy-combatant determinations, this would defeat the unity, secrecy, and dispatch that the Founders believed to be so important to the warmaking function.

THE SCOPE OF HAMDI

1. ***Application off the immediate battlefield.*** The plurality in Hamdi emphasized the context of the case, namely that Hamdi was a U.S. citizen who had been captured in an active combat zone on foreign soil. Would it make a difference if he had been apprehended on American soil? How far does an "active combat zone" extend, given the amorphous nature of terrorist activity by an international network of loosely affiliated covert substate actors? Does it include Yemen or Pakistan, where U.S. drone strikes are commonplace, and where troops are occasionally introduced, as they were when U.S. special forces killed Osama bin Laden on May 2, 2011? Was the U.S. an active combat zone after the events of 9/11? If Hamdi had been captured by a National Guardsman patrolling an airport in Chicago, would his indefinite detention be held authorized by the AUMF, as the majority in Hamdi said it was? Congress has in effect renewed the AUMF as recently as the National Defense Authorization Act of 2012. If the United States was an active combat zone after 2001, is it still?

2. ***The Mathews framework.*** In her plurality opinion, Justice O'Connor applied the Mathews v. Eldridge balancing framework to determine what process is due to citizen enemy combatants under the Constitution. An enemy combatant "must receive notice of the factual basis for his classification, and a fair opportunity to rebut the Government's factual assertions before a neutral decisionmaker," but hearsay evidence and a rebuttable presumption in favor of the government's evidence may be permitted. In Mathews, the Court held that the termination of statutorily conferred Social Security benefits implicates the Due Process Clause, but does not require a pre-termination hearing. The Court established a three-factor framework, which weighs the interests of the individual, the interests of and burdens on the government and the risk of error engendered by the procedures and the probable value of additional safeguards. The case is basic to the development of constitutional due process doctrine in the civil context, but Mathews seems an awkward fit for determining the process owed enemy combatants. Should the burdens on the government and the costs of additional process be relevant to this analysis? On one view, these considerations are even more important where the risks of false negatives (that is, the release of dangerous combatants) are so great. On another view,

the Mathews balancing approach is ill-suited—perhaps even inappropriate—to the context of confinement, where liberty is at stake.

3. ***Institutional competence.*** In wartime, which branch of the federal government is best suited to determine the appropriate balance between national security and civil liberties? Note the fundamentally opposed approaches of Justice Souter, in concurrence, and Justice Thomas, in dissent, on this point. In Justice Souter's view, the executive's special responsibility to maintain the nation's security may skew its judgment such that the other branches of government are better positioned to make these determinations. In Justice Thomas's view, however, it is the executive branch that is uniquely competent to balance sacrifices of liberty against necessities of security. Which Justice's view regarding the competence of the executive to make these determinations is more intuitive? If both Justice Souter and Justice Thomas are in some sense correct, how can these views be reconciled, if at all?

4. ***The Padilla case.*** Consider the case of Padilla v. Rumsfeld, in which a U.S. citizen was arrested by federal law enforcement officials in Chicago's O'Hare Airport for allegedly helping in a plot to detonate a "dirty bomb," and then turned over to the Department of Defense when he was declared an "enemy combatant" by the President. In Padilla v. Rumsfeld, 352 F.3d 695 (2d Cir. 2003), the court of appeals rejected the government's reliance on Quirin to justify Padilla's detention. Using Justice Jackson's tripartite framework from Youngstown, the court held that the Non-Detention Act constituted an explicit congressional prohibition against executive detentions absent congressional authorization, thereby placing President Bush's powers at their "lowest ebb." The court distinguished Quirin as a case in which the President's authority was "at a maximum" because Congress had explicitly authorized detentions as part of the Articles of War. The court held that the AUMF did not constitute the explicit congressional authorization required by the Non-Detention Act. President Bush, therefore, was left to "rely only upon his own constitutional powers minus any constitutional powers of Congress over the matter." The court found that the President's commander in chief powers under Article II were insufficient to authorize Padilla's detention.

On appeal, the Supreme Court did not reach the merits of these questions. In **Rumsfeld v. Padilla**, 542 U.S. 426 (2004), by a vote of 5–4, the Court reversed the decision on jurisdictional grounds, determining that Padilla had not properly filed his habeas petition against the Secretary of Defense in the Southern District of New York, and should instead have brought his action against the commander of the brig in the district of South Carolina where he was incarcerated. Chief Justice REHNQUIST wrote the opinion of the Court, joined by Justices O'Connor, Scalia, Kennedy and Thomas. Justice STEVENS, joined by Justices Souter, Ginsburg and Breyer, dissented, reasoning that jurisdiction should have been found based on existing exceptions to the rule that habeas is normally to be sought against the immediate physical custodian of the petitioner. He noted that "whether respondent is entitled to immediate release is a question that reasonable jurists may answer in different ways," but made clear that the four justices in the dissent would have found Padilla's detention to be unauthorized by Congress: "Consistent with the judgment of the Court of Appeals, I believe that the Non-Detention Act, 18 U.S.C. § 4001(a), prohibits—and the Authorization for Use of Military Force Joint Resolution does not authorize—

the protracted, incommunicado detention of American citizens arrested in the United States." Note that while Justices Stevens, Souter and Ginsburg took a similar position in Hamdi, Justice Breyer voted to uphold congressional authority in Hamdi but not Padilla. Is the circumstance of foreign versus domestic capture sufficient to support such different outcomes?

5. ***Military tribunals for enemy combatants.*** In addition to detaining enemy combatants at Guantanamo Bay, the U.S. government announced plans after 9/11 to try certain noncitizen enemy combatants by military tribunals. By an Executive Order issued in November 2001, concerning the DETENTION, TREATMENT, AND TRIAL OF CERTAIN NON-CITIZENS IN THE WAR AGAINST TERRORISM, President Bush announced that those alien detainees determined to have been engaged in unlawful acts of war including international terrorism would be tried before military commissions under the auspices of the Department of Defense. In announcing his authority to establish these tribunals, President Bush relied upon his Article II Commander-in-Chief powers as well as the AUMF and 10 U.S.C. §§ 821 and 836, both of which discuss military tribunals without specifically authorizing their use in this particular context.

The Executive took several steps to define the remedies available to unlawful combatant detainees in Guantanamo. On February 14, 2004, the government announced that it would review the status of these detainees once a year through three-member panels that would determine if a detainee still posed a threat to the United States. In July 2004, following the Supreme Court's decisions in Rasul and Hamdi, the Secretary of Defense issued the COMBAT STATUS REVIEW TRIBUNAL ORDER, formalizing a new review process allowing Guantanamo detainees to contest the basis for their designation as "enemy combatants" before military tribunals (CSRTs) comprised of three commissioned officers.

In the DETAINEE TREATMENT ACT (DTA), enacted in December 2005, Congress limited jurisdiction to review CSRT determinations to the court of appeals for the D.C. Circuit, which was permitted to review only whether the challenged determination complied with Defense Department procedures and, to the extent applicable, U.S. statutes and the Constitution. The DTA barred habeas petitions sought to be filed in other courts: "Except as provided in section 1005 of the [DTA], no court, justice, or judge shall have jurisdiction to hear or consider[ ] an application for a writ of habeas corpus filed by or on behalf of an alien detained by the Department of Defense at Guantanamo Bay, Cuba." In Hamdan v. Rumsfeld, the Court held that the DTA did not strip it of jurisdiction over existing appeals from denial of habeas in existing cases, and, on the merits of such an appeal, found the President's unilateral military tribunal procedures unauthorized by statute and contrary to international law:

Hamdan v. Rumsfeld

548 U.S. 557, 126 S. Ct. 2749, 165 L. Ed. 2d 723 (2006).

■ JUSTICE STEVENS announced the judgment of the Court and delivered the opinion of the Court [and an opinion with respect to Parts V and VI–D–iv, in which JUSTICES SOUTER, GINSBURG, and BREYER joined.]

Petitioner Salim Ahmed Hamdan, a Yemeni national, is in custody at an American prison in Guantanamo Bay, Cuba. In November 2001, during hostilities between the United States and the Taliban (which then governed Afghanistan), Hamdan was captured by militia forces and turned over to the U.S. military. In June 2002, he was transported to Guantanamo Bay. Over a year later, the President deemed him eligible for trial by military commission for then-unspecified crimes. After another year had passed, Hamdan was charged with one count of conspiracy "to commit . . . offenses triable by military commission." Hamdan [petitioned] for [a] writ of habeas corpus. [We] conclude that the military commission convened to try Hamdan lacks power to proceed because its structure and procedures violate both the Uniform Code of Military Justice (UCMJ) and the Geneva Conventions.

IV. [The] military commission, a tribunal neither mentioned in the Constitution nor created by statute, was born of military necessity. [Exigency] alone, of course, will not justify the establishment and use of penal tribunals not contemplated by Article I, § 8 and Article III, § 1 of the Constitution unless some other part of that document authorizes a response to the felt need. And that authority, if it exists, can derive only from the powers granted jointly to the President and Congress in time of war. The Constitution makes the President the "Commander in Chief" of the Armed Forces, Art. II, § 2, cl. 1, but vests in Congress the powers to "declare War . . . and make Rules concerning Captures on Land and Water," Art. I, § 8, cl. 11, to "raise and support Armies," cl. 12, to "define and punish . . . Offences against the Law of Nations," cl. 10, and "To make Rules for the Government and Regulation of the land and naval Forces," cl. 14.

[Whether] the President may constitutionally convene military commissions "without the sanction of Congress" in cases of "controlling necessity" is a question this Court has not answered definitively, and need not answer today. For we held in Quirin that Congress had, through Article of War 15 [adopted in 1916], sanctioned the use of military commissions in such circumstances. Article 21 of the UCMJ, the language of which is substantially identical to the old Article 15, [was] preserved by Congress after World War II. [But] even Quirin did not view the authorization as a sweeping mandate for the President to "invoke military commissions when he deems them necessary." Rather, [Quirin] recognized that Congress had simply preserved what power, under the Constitution and the common law of war, the President had had before 1916 to convene military commissions—with the express condition that the President and those under his command comply with the law of war.[1]

The Government would have us [find] in either the AUMF or the DTA specific, overriding authorization for the very commission that has been convened to try Hamdan. [There] is nothing in the text or legislative history

---

[1] Whether or not the President has independent power, absent congressional authorization, to convene military commissions, he may not disregard limitations that Congress has, in the proper exercise of its own war powers, placed on his powers. See Youngstown (Jackson, J., concurring). [Footnote by Justice Stevens.]

of the AUMF even hinting that Congress intended to expand or alter the authorization set forth in Article 21 of the UCMJ. [Although] the DTA, unlike either Article 21 or the AUMF, was enacted after the President had convened Hamdan's commission, it contains no language authorizing that tribunal or any other at Guantanamo Bay. [Together,] the UCMJ, the AUMF, and the DTA at most acknowledge a general Presidential authority to convene military commissions in circumstances where justified under the "Constitution and laws," including the law of war.

V. The common law governing military commissions may be gleaned from past practice and what sparse legal precedent exists. Commissions historically have been used in three situations. First, they have substituted for civilian courts at times and in places where martial law has been declared. [Second,] commissions have been established to try civilians "as part of a temporary military government over occupied enemy territory or territory regained from an enemy where civilian government cannot and does not function." The third type of commission, convened as an "incident to the conduct of war," [serves to] determine, typically on the battlefield itself, whether the defendant has violated the law of war. The last time the U.S. Armed Forces used the law-of-war military commission was during World War II. In Quirin, this Court sanctioned President Roosevelt's use of such a tribunal to try Nazi saboteurs captured on American soil during the War. [Since] Guantanamo Bay is neither enemy-occupied territory nor under martial law, the law-of-war commission is the only model available.

[The] charge against Hamdan [alleges] a conspiracy extending over a number of years, from 1996 to November 2001. [This offense] is not triable by law-of-war military commission. There is no suggestion that Congress has, in exercise of its constitutional authority to "define and punish . . . Offences against the Law of Nations," U.S. Const., Art. I, § 8, cl. 10, positively identified "conspiracy" as a war crime. [None] of the major treaties governing the law of war identifies conspiracy as a violation thereof. [The] International Military Tribunal at Nuremberg, over the prosecution's objections, pointedly refused to recognize as a violation of the law of war conspiracy to commit war crimes. [Hamdan] is charged not with an overt act for which he was caught redhanded in a theater of war and which military efficiency demands be tried expeditiously, but with an *agreement* the inception of which long predated the attacks of September 11, 2001 and the AUMF. That may well be a crime [prosecutable by court-martial or in federal court] but it is not an offense that "by the law of war may be tried by military commission."

VI. Whether or not the Government has charged Hamdan with an offense against the law of war cognizable by military commission, the commission lacks power to proceed. The UCMJ conditions the President's use of military commissions on compliance not only with the American common law of war, but also with the rest of the UCMJ itself [and] with the "rules and precepts of the law of nations," [including] the four Geneva Conventions signed in 1949. The procedures that the Government has decreed will govern Hamdan's trial by commission violate these laws.

A. [Every commission] must have a presiding officer and at least three other members, all of whom must be commissioned officers. [The] accused is entitled to appointed military counsel and may hire civilian counsel at his own expense. [The] accused also is entitled to a copy of the charge(s) against him, both in English and his own language (if different), to a presumption of innocence, and to certain other rights typically afforded criminal defendants in civilian courts and courts-martial. These rights are subject, however, to one glaring condition: The accused and his civilian counsel may be excluded from, and precluded from ever learning what evidence was presented during, any part of the proceeding that either the Appointing Authority or the presiding officer decides to "close." [The rules also] permit the admission of *any* evidence that, in the opinion of the presiding officer, "would have probative value to a reasonable person." Under this test, not only is testimonial hearsay and evidence obtained through coercion fully admissible, but neither live testimony nor witnesses' written statements need be sworn.

B. [Hamdan objects] that the procedures' admitted deviation from those governing courts-martial itself renders the commission illegal, [that] he may [be] convicted based on evidence he has not seen or heard, and that any evidence admitted against him need not comply with the admissibility or relevance rules typically applicable in criminal trials and court-martial proceedings.

C. [Article 36] of the UCMJ [provides that] the rules applied to military commissions must be the same as those applied to courts-martial unless such uniformity proves impracticable. [Nothing] in the record before us demonstrates that it would be impracticable to apply court-martial rules in this case. [The] only reason offered [is] the danger posed by international terrorism. Without for one moment underestimating that danger, it is not evident to us why it should require, in the case of Hamdan's trial, any variance from the rules that govern courts-martial. The absence of any showing of impracticability is particularly disturbing when considered in light of the clear and admitted failure to apply one of the most fundamental protections afforded not just by the Manual for Courts-Martial but also by the UCMJ itself: the right to be present. [Under] the circumstances, then, the rules applicable in courts-martial must apply.

D. [The] procedures adopted to try Hamdan also violate the Geneva Conventions. i. [The Geneva Conventions are part] of the law of war. And compliance with the law of war is the condition upon which the authority set forth in Article 21 is granted.

ii. [The] Geneva Conventions [apply] here even if the relevant conflict is not one between signatories. Article 3 [provides] that in a "conflict not of an international character occurring in the territory of one of the [signatories], each Party to the conflict shall be bound to apply, as a minimum," certain provisions [including one that] prohibits "the passing of sentences and the carrying out of executions [upon detainees] without previous judgment pronounced by a regularly constituted court affording all the judicial guarantees which are recognized as indispensable by civilized peoples."

iii. Common Article 3, then, is applicable here and [requires] that Hamdan be tried by a "regularly constituted court." ["The] regular military courts in our system are the courts-martial established by congressional statutes." At a minimum, a military commission "can be 'regularly constituted' by the standards of our military justice system only if some practical need explains deviations from court-martial practice." [No] such need has been demonstrated here.

iv. ["The] judicial guarantees which are recognized as indispensable by civilized peoples" [must] be understood to incorporate at least the barest of those trial protections that have been recognized by customary international law. Many of these are described in Article 75 of Protocol I to the Geneva Conventions of 1949, adopted in 1977. [Among] the rights set forth in Article 75 is the "right to be tried in [one's] presence." [The military commission procedures] dispense with the principles, articulated in Article 75 and indisputably part of the customary international law, that an accused must, absent disruptive conduct or consent, be present for his trial and must be privy to the evidence against him.

v. [Common Article 3] obviously tolerates a great degree of flexibility in trying individuals captured during armed conflict; its requirements are general ones, crafted to accommodate a wide variety of legal systems. But *requirements* they are nonetheless. The commission that the President has convened to try Hamdan does not meet those requirements.

VII. [It] bears emphasizing that Hamdan does not challenge, and we do not today address, the Government's power to detain him for the duration of active hostilities in order to prevent such harm. But in undertaking to try Hamdan and subject him to criminal punishment, the Executive is bound to comply with the Rule of Law that prevails in this jurisdiction.

[Reversed.]

■ JUSTICE BREYER, with whom JUSTICES KENNEDY, SOUTER, and GINSBURG join, concurring.

[The] Court's conclusion ultimately rests upon a single ground: Congress has not issued the Executive a "blank check." [Nothing] prevents the President from returning to Congress to seek the authority he believes necessary. Where, as here, no emergency prevents consultation with Congress, judicial insistence upon that consultation does not weaken our Nation's ability to deal with danger.

■ JUSTICE KENNEDY, with whom JUSTICES SOUTER, GINSBURG, and BREYER join as to Parts I and II, concurring in part.

I. [Trial] by military commission raises separation-of-powers concerns of the highest order. Located within a single branch, these courts carry the risk that offenses will be defined, prosecuted, and adjudicated by executive officials without independent review. Concentration of power puts personal liberty in peril of arbitrary action by officials, an incursion the Constitution's three-part system is designed to avoid. It is imperative, then, that when military tribunals are established, full and proper authority exists for the Presidential directive.

The proper framework for assessing whether Executive actions are authorized is the three-part scheme used by Justice Jackson in his opinion in Youngstown. In this case, [the] President has acted in a field with a history of congressional participation and regulation. In the [UCMJ], Congress has set forth governing principles for military courts. The UCMJ as a whole establishes an intricate system of military justice. It authorizes courts-martial in various forms; it regulates the organization and procedure of those courts; it defines offenses and rights for the accused; and it provides mechanisms for appellate review. [It] further recognizes that special military commissions may be convened to try war crimes. While these laws provide authority for certain forms of military courts, they also impose limitations. If the President has exceeded these limits, this becomes a case of conflict between Presidential and congressional action—a case within Justice Jackson's third category, not the second or first.

II. [The] Court is correct to conclude that the military commission the President has convened to try Hamdan is unauthorized. [Structural] differences between the military commissions and courts-martial—the concentration of functions, including legal decisionmaking, in a single executive official; the less rigorous standards for composition of the tribunal; and the creation of special review procedures in place of institutions created and regulated by Congress—remove safeguards that are important to the fairness of the proceedings and the independence of the court. Congress has prescribed these guarantees for courts-martial; and no evident practical need explains the departures here. For these reasons the commission cannot be considered regularly constituted under United States law and thus does not satisfy Congress' requirement that military commissions conform to the law of war. [Moreover,] the basic procedures for the commissions deviate from procedures for courts-martial, in violation of [UCMJ Article 36.] [The] Military Commission Order abandons the detailed Military Rules of Evidence [and] could permit admission of multiple hearsay and other forms of evidence generally prohibited on grounds of unreliability. [The] Government has made no demonstration of practical need for these special rules and procedures.

III. In light of the conclusion that the military commission here is unauthorized under the UCMJ, I see no need to consider several further issues addressed in the plurality opinion [and] dissent. [First,] I would not decide whether [Geneva Convention] Article 3's standard [necessarily] requires that the accused have the right to be present at all stages of a criminal trial. [I] likewise see no need to address the validity of the conspiracy charge against Hamdan. [Congress,] not the Court, is the branch in the better position to undertake the "sensitive task of establishing a principle not inconsistent with the national interest or international justice."

■ JUSTICE THOMAS, with whom JUSTICE SCALIA joins, and with whom JUSTICE ALITO joins in all but Parts I, II–C–1, and III–B–2, dissenting.[2]

[The] Court's evident belief that *it* is qualified to pass on the "military necessity" of the Commander in Chief's decision to employ a particular form of force against our enemies [is] antithetical to our constitutional structure.

I. [When] "the President acts pursuant to an express or implied authorization from Congress," his actions are "supported by the strongest of presumptions," Youngstown (Jackson, J., concurring). [Under] this framework, the President's decision to try Hamdan before a military commission for his involvement with al Qaeda is entitled to a heavy measure of deference. In the present conflict, Congress has authorized the President "to use all necessary and appropriate force against those nations, organizations, or persons *he determines* planned, authorized, committed, or aided the terrorist attacks that occurred on September 11, 2001 . . . in order to prevent any future acts of international terrorism against the United States by such nations, organizations or persons." [AUMF (emphasis added)]. As a plurality of the Court observed in Hamdi, the "capture, detention, and *trial* of unlawful combatants, by 'universal agreement and

---

[2] Justice SCALIA also filed a dissent objecting that the Court lacked jurisdiction under the DTA and should have abstained on comity grounds. Chief Justice ROBERTS, having sat on the D.C. Circuit panel below, took no part in the decision.

practice,' are 'important incidents of war.'" [Accordingly,] congressional authorization for military commissions pertaining to the instant conflict derives not only from Article 21 of the UCMJ, but also from the more recent, and broader, authorization contained in the AUMF. [In] such circumstances, [our] duty to defer to the Executive's military and foreign policy judgment is at its zenith; it does not countenance the kind of second-guessing the Court repeatedly engages in today.

II. A. [The] President's judgment—that the present conflict substantially predates the AUMF, extending at least as far back as al Qaeda's 1996 declaration of war on our Nation, and that the theater of war extends at least as far as the localities of al Qaeda's principal bases of operations—is beyond judicial reproach.

B. [Law-of-war] military commissions have jurisdiction over "'individuals of the enemy's army who have been guilty of illegitimate warfare or other offences in violation of the laws of war.'" [This] consideration is easily satisfied here, as Hamdan is an unlawful combatant charged with joining and conspiring with a terrorist network dedicated to flouting the laws of war.

C. [The] common law of war is [flexible] and evolutionary in nature, building upon the experience of the past and taking account of the exigencies of the present [and] affords a measure of respect for the judgment of military commanders. 1. [Hamdan] has been charged with conduct constituting two distinct violations of the law of war cognizable before a military commission: membership in a war-criminal enterprise and conspiracy to commit war crimes. 2. [Conspiracy] to violate the laws of war is [also] itself an offense cognizable before a law-of-war military commission. 3. [We] are not engaged in a traditional battle with a nation-state, but with a worldwide, hydra-headed enemy, who lurks in the shadows conspiring to reproduce the atrocities of September 11, 2001, and who has boasted of sending suicide bombers into civilian gatherings, has proudly distributed videotapes of beheadings of civilian workers, and has tortured and dismembered captured American soldiers. [The plurality's approach] would sorely hamper the President's ability to confront and defeat a new and deadly enemy.

III. A. [Far] from constraining the President's authority, Article 36 recognizes the President's prerogative to depart from the procedures applicable in criminal cases whenever *he alone* does not deem such procedures "practicable." [Nothing] in the text of Article 36 supports the Court's sweeping conclusion that it represents an unprecedented congressional effort to change the nature of military commissions from common-law war courts to tribunals that must presumptively function like courts-martial. [The] Court provides no explanation why the President's determination that employing court-martial procedures in the military commissions [would] hamper our war effort is in any way inadequate to satisfy its newly minted "practicability" requirement.

B. [Parts 1 and 2 of this section of the dissent argue that the Geneva Conventions are not judicially enforceable and do not apply to war with al Qaeda.] 3. [Even if] Article 3 were judicially enforceable and applicable to the present conflict, petitioner would not be entitled to relief. [Hamdan's] military commission [is] plainly "regularly constituted" because such commissions have been employed throughout our history to try unlawful combatants for crimes against the law of war. [Similarly,] the procedures to be employed by Hamdan's commission afford "all the judicial guarantees which are recognized as indispensable by civilized peoples." ["Civilized peoples"] would take into account the context of military commission trials against unlawful combatants in the war on terrorism, including the need to keep certain information secret in the interest of preventing future attacks on our Nation and its foreign installations so long as it did not deprive the accused of a fair trial.

■ JUSTICE ALITO, with whom JUSTICES SCALIA and THOMAS join, dissenting.

[I] cannot agree with the Court's conclusion that the military commission at issue here is not a "regularly constituted court" because its structure and composition differ from those of a court-martial. [Whatever] else may be said about the system that was created by Military Commission Order No. 1 and augmented by the [DTA], this system—which features formal trial procedures, multiple levels of administrative review, and the opportunity for review by a United States Court of Appeals and by this Court—does not dispense "summary justice."

THE AFTERMATH OF HAMDAN

1. ***Congressional response to Hamdan.*** After the decision in Hamdan, Congress enacted the MILITARY COMMISSIONS ACT of 2006 (MCA), Pub. L. No. 109–366, 120 Stat. 2600 (Oct. 17, 2006). The MCA states that it "shall apply to all cases, without exception, pending on or after the date of the enactment of this Act which relate to any aspect of the detention, transfer, treatment, trial, or conditions of detention of an alien detained by the United States since Sept. 11, 2001." The Act defines "unlawful combatant" as "a person who has engaged in hostilities or who has purposefully and materially supported hostilities against the United States or its co-belligerents who is not a lawful enemy combatant (including a person who is part of the Taliban, al Qaeda, or associated forces); or [ ] a person who, before, on, or after the date of the enactment of the [MCA], has been determined to be an unlawful enemy combatant by a [CSRT] or another competent tribunal established under the authority of the President or the Secretary of Defense."

The MCA provides the President with authority to try such alien unlawful enemy combatants by military commissions, for any offense made punishable by the law of war. The MCA also expanded the DTA's removal of habeas jurisdiction to all overseas enemy combatant detainees, regardless of where they were being held. Section 7, like the DTA, eliminated ordinary habeas review and limited review of the decisions of military tribunals to the U.S. Court of Appeals for the D.C. Circuit: "No court, justice, or judge shall have jurisdiction to hear or consider an application for a writ of habeas corpus filed by or on behalf of an alien detained by the United States who has been determined by the United States to have been properly detained as an enemy combatant or is awaiting such determination. Except as provided in [the DTA,] no court, justice, or judge shall have jurisdiction to hear or consider any other action against the United States or its agents relating to any aspect of the detention, transfer, treatment, trial, or conditions of confinement of an alien who is or was detained by the United States and has been determined by the United States to have been properly detained as an enemy combatant or is awaiting such determination."

Was Congress's enactment of the MCA sufficient to cure the lack of executive authority found by the Hamdan court? Note that Justice Breyer concurred separately, in an opinion joined by Justices Kennedy, Souter and Ginsburg, to emphasize that "[n]othing prevents the President from returning to Congress to seek the authority he believes necessary." Did the MCA provide that authority?

2. ***Enemy combatant habeas corpus rights after Hamdan.*** The Suspension Clause of Article I provides, "The Privilege of the Writ of Habeas Corpus shall not be suspended, unless when in Cases of Rebellion or Invasion the public Safety may require it." Art. I, § 9, cl. 2. Did the DTA and MCA unconstitutionally suspend the writ of habeas corpus, even if they otherwise provided the President's military tribunal procedures sufficient congressional authority to move them from Justice Jackson's Category 3 to Category 1? On remand, the district court in Hamdan's case found that the MCA had deprived it of statutory jurisdiction over Hamdan's habeas claims, and that, like the enemy combatants in Eisentrager, he lacked "the geographical and volitional predicates necessary to claim a constitutional entitlement to habeas corpus."

In February 2007, a divided panel of the Court of Appeals for the D.C. Circuit affirmed, finding that "the Constitution does not confer rights on aliens without property or presence within the United States." Boumediene v. Bush, 476 F.3d 981 (D.C. Cir. 2007). In 2008, the Supreme Court reversed that decision, holding that the DTA and MCA had unconstitutionally suspended the writ:

Boumediene v. Bush

553 U.S. 723, 128 S. Ct. 2229, 171 L. Ed. 2d 41 (2008).

■ JUSTICE KENNEDY delivered the opinion of the Court, in which JUSTICES STEVENS, SOUTER, GINSBURG, and BREYER joined.

Petitioners are aliens designated as enemy combatants and detained at the United States Naval Station at Guantanamo Bay, Cuba. [Petitioners] present a question not resolved by our earlier cases relating to the detention of aliens at Guantanamo: whether they have the constitutional privilege of habeas corpus, a privilege not to be withdrawn except in conformance with the Suspension Clause, Art. I, § 9, cl. 2. We hold these petitioners do have the habeas corpus privilege. [We] hold that [the DTA's] procedures are not an adequate and effective substitute for habeas corpus. Therefore § 7 of the Military Commissions Act of 2006 (MCA) operates as an unconstitutional suspension of the writ.

II. [As] a threshold matter, we must decide whether MCA § 7 denies the federal courts jurisdiction to hear habeas corpus actions pending at the time of its enactment. We hold the statute does deny that jurisdiction, so that, if the statute is valid, petitioners' cases must be dismissed.

III. A. [The] Framers viewed freedom from unlawful restraint as a fundamental precept of liberty, and they understood the writ of habeas corpus as a vital instrument to secure that freedom. Experience taught, however, that the common-law writ all too often had been insufficient to guard against the abuse of monarchial power. That history counseled the necessity for specific language in the Constitution to secure the writ and ensure its place in our legal system. [That] the Framers considered the writ a vital instrument for the protection of individual liberty is evident from the care taken to specify the limited grounds for its suspension. [The] Clause protects the rights of the detained by affirming the duty and authority of the Judiciary to call the jailer to account.

B. ["At] the absolute minimum" the Clause protects the writ as it existed when the Constitution was drafted and ratified. [The] Government argues the common-law writ ran only to those territories over which the Crown was sovereign. Petitioners argue that jurisdiction followed the King's officers. Diligent search by all parties reveals no certain conclusions. [The] Government points out there is no evidence that a court sitting in England granted habeas relief to an enemy alien detained abroad; petitioners respond there is no evidence that a court refused to do so for lack of jurisdiction. [We decline] to infer too much, one way or the other, from the lack of historical evidence on point.

IV. [Drawing] from its position that at common law the writ ran only to territories over which the Crown was sovereign, the Government says the Suspension Clause affords petitioners no rights because the United States does not claim sovereignty over the place of detention. Guantanamo Bay is not formally part of the United States. [We] accept the Government's position that Cuba, and not the United States, retains de jure sovereignty over Guantanamo Bay. As we did in Rasul, however, we take notice of the obvious and uncontested fact that the United States, by virtue of its complete jurisdiction and control over the base, maintains de facto sovereignty over this territory.

A. [The] Court has discussed the issue of the Constitution's extraterritorial application on many occasions. These decisions undermine the Government's argument that, at least as applied to noncitizens, the Constitution necessarily stops where de jure sovereignty ends.

[Practical] considerations weighed heavily [in] Johnson v. Eisentrager, where the Court addressed whether habeas corpus jurisdiction extended to enemy aliens who had been convicted of violating the laws of war. The prisoners were detained at Landsberg Prison in Germany during the Allied Powers' post-war occupation. The Court stressed the difficulties of ordering the Government to produce the prisoners in a habeas corpus proceeding. It "would require allocation of shipping space, guarding personnel, billeting and rations" and would damage the prestige of military commanders at a sensitive time. In considering these factors the Court sought to balance the constraints of military occupation with constitutional necessities.

True, the Court in Eisentrager denied access to the writ, and it noted the prisoners "at no relevant time were within any territory over which the United States is sovereign, and [that] the scenes of their offense, their capture, their trial and their punishment were all beyond the territorial jurisdiction of any court of the United States." The Government seizes upon this language as proof positive that the Eisentrager Court adopted a formalistic, sovereignty-based test for determining the reach of the Suspension Clause. We reject this reading for three reasons.

First, we do not accept the idea that the above-quoted passage from Eisentrager is the only authoritative language in the opinion and that all the rest is dicta. The Court's further determinations, based on practical considerations, were integral to Part II of its opinion and came before the decision announced its holding.

Second, because the United States lacked both de jure sovereignty and plenary control over Landsberg Prison, it is far from clear that the Eisentrager Court used the term sovereignty only in the narrow technical sense and not to connote the degree of control the military asserted over the facility. [That] the Court devoted a significant portion of Part II to a discussion of practical barriers to the running of the writ suggests that the Court was not concerned exclusively with the formal legal status of Landsberg Prison but also with the objective degree of control the United States asserted over it.

Third, [nothing] in Eisentrager says that de jure sovereignty is or has ever been the only relevant consideration in determining the geographic reach of the Constitution or of habeas corpus. [Questions] of extraterritoriality turn on objective factors and practical concerns, not formalism.

B. [The] United States has maintained complete and uninterrupted control of [Guantanamo] for over 100 years. [The] Government's view is that the Constitution had no effect there, at least as to noncitizens, because the United States disclaimed sovereignty in the formal sense of the term. The necessary implication of the argument is that by surrendering formal sovereignty over any unincorporated territory to a third party, while at the same time entering into a lease that grants total control over the territory back to the United States, it would be possible for the political branches to govern without legal constraint.

Our basic charter cannot be contracted away like this. The Constitution grants Congress and the President the power to acquire, dispose of, and govern territory, not the power to decide when and where its terms apply. Even when the United States acts outside its borders, its powers are not "absolute and unlimited" but are subject "to such restrictions as are expressed in the Constitution." Abstaining from questions involving formal sovereignty and territorial governance is one thing. To hold the political branches have the power to switch the Constitution on or off at will is quite another. The former position reflects this Court's recognition that certain matters requiring political judgments are best left to the political branches. The latter would permit a striking anomaly in our tripartite system of government, leading to a regime in which Congress and the President, not this Court, say "what the law is." Marbury.

C. [The] outlines of a framework for determining the reach of the Suspension Clause are suggested by the factors the Court relied upon in Eisentrager. In addition to the practical concerns discussed above, the Eisentrager Court found relevant that each petitioner:

> "(a) is an enemy alien; (b) has never been or resided in the United States; (c) was captured outside of our territory and there held in military custody as a prisoner of war; (d) was tried and convicted by a Military Commission sitting outside the United States; (e) for offenses against laws of war committed outside the United States; (f) and is at all times imprisoned outside the United States."

Based on this language from Eisentrager, and the reasoning in our other extraterritoriality opinions, we conclude that at least three factors are relevant in determining the reach of the Suspension Clause: (1) the citizenship and status of the detainee and the adequacy of the process through which that status determination was made; (2) the nature of the sites where apprehension and then detention took place; and (3) the practical obstacles inherent in resolving the prisoner's entitlement to the writ.

[The] petitioners, like those in Eisentrager, are not American citizens. But the petitioners in Eisentrager did not contest, it seems, the Court's assertion that they were "enemy alien[s]." In the instant cases, by contrast, the detainees deny they are enemy combatants. They have been afforded some process in CSRT proceedings to determine their status; but, unlike in Eisentrager [there] has been no trial by military commission for violations of the laws of war. The difference is not trivial. The records from the Eisentrager trials suggest that, well before the petitioners brought their case to this Court, there had been a rigorous adversarial process to test the legality of their detention. The Eisentrager petitioners were charged by a bill of particulars that made detailed factual allegations against them. To rebut the accusations, they were entitled to representation by counsel, allowed to introduce evidence on their own behalf, and permitted to cross-examine the prosecution's witnesses.

In comparison the procedural protections afforded to the detainees in the CSRT hearings are far more limited, and, we conclude, fall well short of the procedures and adversarial mechanisms that would eliminate the need for habeas corpus review. Although the detainee is assigned a "Personal Representative" to assist him during CSRT proceedings, the Secretary of the Navy's memorandum makes clear that person is not the detainee's lawyer or even his "advocate." The Government's evidence is accorded a presumption of validity. The detainee is allowed to present "reasonably available" evidence, but his ability to rebut the Government's evidence against him is limited by the circumstances of his confinement and his lack of counsel at this stage. And although the detainee can seek review of his status determination in the Court of Appeals, that review process cannot cure all defects in the earlier proceedings.

As to the second factor relevant to this analysis, the detainees here are similarly situated to the Eisentrager petitioners in that the sites of their apprehension and detention are technically outside the sovereign territory of the United States. [But] there are critical differences between Landsberg Prison, circa 1950, and the United States Naval Station at Guantanamo Bay in 2008. Unlike its present control over the naval station, the United States' control over the prison in Germany was neither absolute nor indefinite. Like all parts of occupied Germany, the prison was under the jurisdiction of the combined Allied Forces. The United States was therefore answerable to its Allies for all activities occurring there. [Guantanamo] Bay, on the other hand, is no transient possession. In every practical sense Guantanamo is not abroad; it is within the constant jurisdiction of the United States.

As to the third factor, we recognize, as the Court did in Eisentrager, that there are costs to holding the Suspension Clause applicable in a case of military detention abroad. Habeas corpus proceedings may require expenditure of funds by the Government and may divert the attention of military personnel from other pressing tasks. While we are sensitive to these concerns, we do not find them dispositive. Compliance with any judicial process requires some incremental expenditure of resources. [The] Government presents no credible arguments that the military mission at Guantanamo would be compromised if habeas corpus courts had jurisdiction to hear the detainees' claims. And in light of the plenary control the United States asserts over the base, none are apparent to us.

The situation in Eisentrager was far different, given the historical context and nature of the military's mission in post-War Germany. When hostilities in the European Theater came to an end, the United States became responsible for an occupation zone encompassing over 57,000 square miles with a population of 18 million. In addition to supervising massive reconstruction and aid efforts the American forces stationed in Germany faced potential security threats from a defeated enemy. In retrospect the post-War occupation may seem uneventful. But at the time Eisentrager was decided, the Court was right to be concerned about judicial interference with the military's efforts to contain "enemy elements, guerilla fighters, and 'werewolves.'"

Similar threats are not apparent here; nor does the Government argue that they are. The United States Naval Station at Guantanamo Bay consists of 45 square miles of land and water. The base has been used, at various points, to house migrants and refugees temporarily. At present, however, other than the detainees themselves, the only long-term residents are American military personnel, their families, and a small number of workers. The detainees have been deemed enemies of the United States. At present, dangerous as they may be if released, they are contained in a secure prison facility located on an isolated and heavily fortified military base.

[We] hold that Art. I, § 9, cl. 2, of the Constitution has full effect at Guantanamo Bay. If the privilege of habeas corpus is to be denied to the detainees now before us, Congress must act in accordance with the requirements of the Suspension Clause. [The] MCA does not purport to be a formal suspension of the writ; and the Government, in its submissions to us, has not argued that it is. Petitioners, therefore, are entitled to the privilege of habeas corpus to challenge the legality of their detention.

V. In light of this holding the question becomes whether the statute stripping jurisdiction to issue the writ avoids the Suspension Clause mandate because Congress has provided adequate substitute procedures for habeas corpus. [When] Congress has intended to replace traditional habeas corpus with habeas-like substitutes, [it] has granted to the courts broad remedial powers to secure the historic office of the writ. [In] contrast the DTA's jurisdictional grant is quite limited. The Court of Appeals has jurisdiction not to inquire into the legality of the detention generally but only to assess whether the CSRT complied with the "standards and procedures specified by the Secretary of Defense" and whether those standards and procedures are lawful.

B. [We] do not endeavor to offer a comprehensive summary of the requisites for an adequate substitute for habeas corpus. We do consider it uncontroversial, however, that the privilege of habeas corpus entitles the prisoner to a meaningful opportunity to demonstrate that he is being held pursuant to "the erroneous application or interpretation" of relevant law. [We hold] that when the judicial power to issue habeas corpus properly is invoked the judicial officer must have adequate authority to make a determination in light of the relevant law and facts and to formulate and issue appropriate orders for relief, including, if necessary, an order directing the prisoner's release.

C. [Even assuming] the DTA can be construed to allow the Court of Appeals to review or correct the CSRT's factual determinations, as opposed to merely certifying that the tribunal applied the correct standard of proof, we see no way to construe the statute to allow what is also constitutionally required in this context: an opportunity for the detainee to present relevant exculpatory evidence that was not made part of the record in the earlier proceedings. [This] evidence, however, may be critical to the detainee's argument that he is not an enemy combatant and there is no cause to detain him. [Petitioners] have met their burden of establishing that the DTA review process is, on its face, an inadequate substitute for habeas corpus.

IV.A. [The] question remains whether there are prudential barriers to habeas corpus review under these circumstances. [In] some of these cases six years have elapsed without the judicial oversight that habeas corpus or an adequate substitute demands. And there has been no showing that the Executive faces such onerous burdens that it cannot respond to habeas corpus actions. [While] some delay in fashioning new procedures is unavoidable, the costs of delay can no longer be borne by those who are held in custody. The detainees in these cases are entitled to a prompt habeas corpus hearing.

[Our] opinion does not undermine the Executive's powers as Commander in Chief. On the contrary, the exercise of those powers is vindicated, not eroded, when confirmed by the Judicial Branch. Within the Constitution's separation-of-powers structure, few exercises of judicial power are as legitimate or as necessary as the responsibility to hear challenges to the authority of the Executive to imprison a person.

■ JUSTICE SOUTER, with whom JUSTICES GINSBURG and BREYER join, concurring.

[A fact] insufficiently appreciated by the dissents is the length of the disputed imprisonments, some of the prisoners represented here today having been locked up for six years. Hence the hollow ring when the dissenters suggest that the Court is somehow precipitating the judiciary into reviewing claims that the military (subject to appeal to the Court of Appeals for the District of Columbia Circuit) could handle within some reasonable period of time. [After] six years of sustained executive detentions in Guantanamo, subject to habeas jurisdiction but without any actual habeas scrutiny, today's decision is no judicial victory, but an act of perseverance in trying to make habeas review, and the obligation of the courts to provide it, mean something of value both to prisoners and to the Nation.

■ CHIEF JUSTICE ROBERTS, with whom JUSTICES SCALIA, THOMAS, and ALITO join, dissenting.

[The] Court finds the DTA system an inadequate habeas substitute, for one central reason: Detainees are unable to introduce at the appeal stage exculpatory evidence discovered after the conclusion of their CSRT proceedings. [The] majority rests its decision on abstract and hypothetical concerns. Step back and consider what, in the real world, Congress and the Executive have actually granted aliens captured by our Armed Forces overseas and found to be enemy combatants:

> The right to hear the bases of the charges against them, including a summary of any classified evidence.
>
> The ability to challenge the bases of their detention before military tribunals modeled after Geneva Convention procedures.

> [The] right, before the CSRT, to testify, introduce evidence, call witnesses, question those the Government calls, and secure release, if and when appropriate.
>
> The right to the aid of a personal representative in arranging and presenting their cases before a CSRT.
>
> Before the D. C. Circuit, the right to employ counsel, challenge the factual record, contest the lower tribunal's legal determinations, ensure compliance with the Constitution and laws, and secure release, if any errors below establish their entitlement to such relief.

[This] statutory scheme provides the combatants held at Guantanamo greater procedural protections than have ever been afforded alleged enemy detainees—whether citizens or aliens—in our national history.

■ JUSTICE SCALIA, with whom THE CHIEF JUSTICE and JUSTICES THOMAS and ALITO join, dissenting.

Today, for the first time in our Nation's history, the Court confers a constitutional right to habeas corpus on alien enemies detained abroad by our military forces in the course of an ongoing war. The Chief Justice's dissent, which I join, shows that the procedures prescribed by Congress in the [DTA] provide the essential protections that habeas corpus guarantees; there has thus been no suspension of the writ, and no basis exists for judicial intervention beyond what the Act allows. My problem with today's opinion is more fundamental still: The writ of habeas corpus does not, and never has, run in favor of aliens abroad; the Suspension Clause thus has no application, and the Court's intervention in this military matter is entirely ultra vires.

[The] game of bait-and-switch that today's opinion plays upon the Nation's Commander in Chief will make the war harder on us. It will almost certainly cause more Americans to be killed. That consequence would be tolerable if necessary to preserve a time-honored legal principle vital to our constitutional Republic. But it is this Court's blatant *abandonment* of such a principle that produces the decision today. The President relied on our settled precedent in Johnson v. Eisentrager when he established the prison at Guantanamo Bay for enemy aliens. Citing that case, the President's Office of Legal Counsel advised him "that the great weight of legal authority indicates that a federal district court could not properly exercise habeas jurisdiction over an alien detained at [Guantanamo Bay]." Had the law been otherwise, the military surely would not have transported prisoners there, but would have kept them in Afghanistan, transferred them to another of our foreign military bases, or turned them over to allies for detention.

[The] Court purports to derive from our precedents a "functional" test for the extraterritorial reach of the writ, which shows that the [MCA] unconstitutionally restricts the scope of habeas. That is remarkable because the most pertinent of those precedents, Eisentrager, conclusively establishes the opposite. [Writing] for the Court, Justice Jackson held that American courts lacked habeas jurisdiction:

> "We are cited to *[sic]* no instance where a court, in this or any other country where the writ is known, has issued it on behalf of an alien enemy who, at no relevant time and in no stage of his captivity, has been within its territorial jurisdiction. Nothing in the text of the Constitution extends such a right, nor does anything in our statutes."

[The] Court would have us believe that Eisentrager rested on "[p]ractical considerations," such as the "difficulties of ordering the Government to produce the prisoners in a habeas corpus proceeding." Formal sovereignty, says the Court, is merely one consideration "that bears upon which constitutional guarantees apply" in a given location. This is a sheer rewriting of the case. Eisentrager mentioned practical concerns, to be sure—but not for the purpose of determining *under what circumstances* American courts could issue writs of habeas corpus for aliens abroad. It cited them to support *its holding* that the Constitution does not empower courts to issue writs of habeas corpus to aliens abroad *in any circumstances*.

The Court also tries to change Eisentrager into a "functional" test by quoting a paragraph that lists the characteristics of the German petitioners:

> "To support [the] assumption [of a constitutional right to habeas corpus] we must hold that a prisoner of our military authorities is constitutionally entitled to the writ, even though he (a) is an enemy alien; (b) has never been or resided in the United States; (c) was captured outside of our territory and there held in military custody as a prisoner of war; (d) was tried and convicted by a Military Commission sitting outside the United States; (e) for offenses against laws of war committed outside the United States; (f) and is at all times imprisoned outside the United States."

But that paragraph is introduced by a sentence stating that "[t]he foregoing demonstrates *how much further we must go* if we are to invest these enemy aliens, resident, captured and imprisoned abroad, with standing to demand access to our courts." How much further than *what*? Further than the rule set forth in the prior section of the opinion, which said that "in extending constitutional protections beyond the citizenry, the Court has been at pains to point out that it was the alien's presence within its territorial jurisdiction that gave the Judiciary power to act." In other words, the characteristics of the German prisoners were set forth, not in application of some "functional" test, but to show that the case before the Court represented an a fortiori application of the ordinary rule.

[After] transforming the a fortiori elements discussed above into a "functional" test, the Court is still left with the difficulty that most of those elements exist here as well with regard to all the detainees. To make the application of the newly crafted "functional" test produce a different result in the present cases, the Court must rely upon factors (d) and (e): The Germans had been tried by a military commission for violations of the laws of war; the present petitioners, by contrast, have been tried by a Combatant Status Review Tribunal (CSRT) whose procedural protections, according to the Court's ipse dixit, "fall well short of the procedures and adversarial mechanisms that would eliminate the need for habeas corpus review." But no one looking for "functional" equivalents would put Eisentrager and the present cases in the same category, much less place the present cases in a preferred category. The difference between them cries out for lesser procedures in the present cases. The prisoners in Eisentrager were *prosecuted* for crimes after the cessation of hostilities; the prisoners here are enemy combatants *detained* during an ongoing conflict.

[There] is simply no support for the Court's assertion that constitutional rights extend to aliens held outside U.S. sovereign territory, and Eisentrager could not be clearer that the privilege of habeas corpus does not extend to aliens abroad. By blatantly distorting Eisentrager, the Court avoids the difficulty of explaining why it should be overruled. The rule that aliens abroad are not constitutionally entitled to habeas corpus has not proved unworkable in practice; if anything, it is the Court's "functional" test that does not (and never will) provide clear guidance for the future.

[What] drives today's decision is neither the meaning of the Suspension Clause, nor the principles of our precedents, but rather an inflated notion of judicial supremacy. The Court says that if the extraterritorial applicability of the Suspension Clause turned on formal notions of sovereignty, "it would be possible for the political branches to govern without legal constraint" in areas beyond the sovereign territory of the United States. That cannot be, the Court says, because it is the duty of this Court to say what the law is. It would be difficult to imagine a more question-begging analysis. [Our] power "to say what the law is" is circumscribed by the limits of our statutorily and constitutionally conferred jurisdiction. And that is precisely the question in these cases: whether the Constitution confers habeas jurisdiction on federal courts to decide petitioners' claims. It is both irrational and arrogant to say that the answer must be yes, because otherwise we would not be supreme.

But so long as there are *some* places to which habeas does not run—so long as the Court's new "functional" test will not be satisfied *in every case*—then there will be circumstances in which "it would be possible for the political branches to govern without legal constraint." Or, to put it more impartially, areas in which the legal determinations of the *other* branches will be (shudder!) *supreme*. In other words, judicial supremacy is not really assured by the constitutional rule that the Court creates. The gap between rationale and rule leads me to conclude that the Court's ultimate, unexpressed goal is to preserve the power to review the confinement of enemy prisoners held by the Executive anywhere in the world. The "functional" test usefully evades the precedential landmine of Eisentrager but is so inherently subjective that it clears a wide path for the Court to traverse in the years to come.

[Putting] aside the conclusive precedent of Eisentrager, it is clear that the original understanding of the Suspension Clause was that habeas corpus was not available to aliens abroad. It is entirely clear that, at English common law, the writ of habeas corpus did not extend beyond the sovereign territory of the Crown. To be sure, the writ had an "extraordinary territorial ambit," because it was a so-called "prerogative writ," which, unlike other writs, could extend beyond the realm of England to other places where the Crown was sovereign. But prerogative writs could not issue to foreign countries, even for British subjects; they were confined to the King's dominions—those areas over which the Crown was sovereign. [What] history teaches is confirmed by the nature of the limitations that the Constitution places upon suspension of the common-law writ. It can be suspended only "in Cases of Rebellion or Invasion." Art. I, § 9, cl. 2. The latter case (invasion) is plainly limited to the territory of the United States; and while it is conceivable that a rebellion could be mounted by American citizens abroad, surely the overwhelming majority of its occurrences would be domestic. [The] text and history of the Suspension Clause provide no basis for our jurisdiction.

ASSESSING HAMDI, HAMDAN AND BOUMEDIENE

1. ***The interplay between the executive, legislative and judicial branches.*** Hamdi, Hamdan and Boumediene together represent a remarkable judicial response to executive action during a period of national security concern. Three times the President's new detention and trial procedures went before the Court, and three times the Court invalidated them—even after Congress expressly sought to confer its approval upon some aspects of those procedures. Note that the Court took different routes to these outcomes: Hamdi and Boumediene treated the President's actions as authorized by Congress, and thus within Justice Jackson's Youngstown Category 1, but nonetheless invalidated them as independently barred by the protections for individual rights reflected in the Due Process Clause (Hamdi) and the Suspension Clause (Boumediene). Only Hamdan found the President's actions within Justice Jackson's Category 3 because not only unauthorized by Congress but also in violation of affirmative limits that Congress had placed upon the President in the UCMJ. Which route reflects greater respect and comity for a coequal branch? Is it more of a slap to the President for the Court to find that his actions exceed his authority, as in Youngstown and Hamdan, or to find that they violate individual rights, as in Hamdi and Boumediene? Should a separation-of-powers claim be avoided if there is an available rights claim to resolve? Or does the canon favoring avoidance of constitutional issues require that statutory questions of executive authority be resolved prior to review of any rights claim?

Note that a finding of congressional authorization or congressional prohibition in effect remands the issue to Congress and invites further interbranch dialogue. If the Court reads "a broad legislative declaration as an endorsement of executive action," as it did the AUMF in Hamdi, "Congress can unmistakably legislate in a more pointed way that courts will then likely take as an effective bar to that executive action. [Thus,] the courts channel the issues back into the bilateral political process and keep open a critical congressional role." Issacharoff & Pildes, "Emergency Contexts Without Emergency Powers," 2 Int'l J. Const. Law 296 (2004). Is such a scenario realistic? Does Congress have the political will to stand up to the President in times of national security concern after the Court has upheld his challenged actions? And doesn't the likelihood of a presidential veto in effect require Congress to muster a two-thirds vote rather than a mere majority to stop a presidential initiative the Court has upheld? Conversely, if the Court reads a broad legislative declaration as a prohibition of executive action, as it did the UCMJ in Hamdan, Congress may respond by passing legislation approving and ratifying the executive's approach—and in this context may do so by mere majority vote. Did the Court, having invited such interbranch coordination in Hamdan, disregard its results in Boumediene? Consider the observation that Boumediene represents "the first time in its history [that] the Supreme Court declared unconstitutional a law enacted by Congress and signed by the president on an issue of military policy in a time of armed conflict, [upending] the joint decision of the political branches acting together." Cole, "Rights over Borders: Transnational Constitutionalism and Guantanamo Bay," 2007–2008 Cato Sup. Ct. Rev. 47. Is that fact cause for celebration or concern?

2. ***Inherent presidential authority in military affairs?*** In Youngstown, the Justices in the majority, after determining that President Truman's seizure order was contrary to congressional policy and thus within

Justice Jackson's Category 3, went on to decide the separate question whether that action was alternatively justified as within a domain reserved exclusively to the President and beyond Congress's control. The Youngstown majority found no such exclusive or preclusive authority conferred by the Vesting, Take Care, or Commander-in-Chief Clauses. As Justice Jackson put it, the fact that the President is Commander in Chief of the military does not make him "also Commander in Chief of the country, its industries and its inhabitants." Did the Court in Hamdan make the same effort to refute the possibility that the President has inherent authority to protect national security even in the face of the congressional prohibition it found in the UCMJ? Did Justice Souter's dissent Hamdi do so? Note that Justice Thomas, dissenting in Hamdi, suggested that "the President very well may have inherent authority to detain those arrayed against our troops," but found it unnecessary to decide that question because, in his view, the AUMF supplied sufficient statutory authority. If that question had been reached, how should it have been analyzed and answered? Consider the view that "the war powers issue that is now at the forefront of the most important clashes between the political branches" arises not when the President seeks to act without congressional authorization, but rather "when the chief executive acts contrary to congressional will," i.e., within Justice Jackson's Category 3. Barron & Lederman, "The Commander In Chief at the Lowest Ebb—Framing the Problem, Doctrine, and Original Understanding," 121 Harv. L. Rev. 689 (2008).

Does the President enjoy any exclusive authority in military affairs, precluding congressional enactments to the contrary, by virtue of the Commander in Chief Clause? In Ex parte Milligan (1866; p. 350 above), Chief Justice Chase suggested in concurrence that Congress may not "interfere[ ] with the command of the forces and the conduct of campaigns." The Office of Legal Counsel during the Administration of President George W. Bush similarly expressed the opinion that "Congress lacks authority under Article I to set the terms and conditions under which the President may exercise his authority as Commander in Chief to control the conduct of operations during a war," and construed the President's exclusive authority in this domain very broadly as extending beyond the battlefield to methods of interrogation (including torture), surveillance (including secret warrantless wiretapping), detention and trial. Memorandum from Jay S. Bybee, Assistant Att'y Gen., Office of Legal Counsel, to Alberto R. Gonzales, Counsel to the President (Aug. 1, 2002). The memorandum, substantially written by OLC attorney and law professor John Yoo, was later withdrawn by then-Assistant Attorney General (and also law professor) Jack Goldsmith. See Goldsmith, The Terror Presidency 142–62 (2007).

In one of the Supreme Court's earliest decisions on the interplay between congressional and executive power in wartime, the Supreme Court suggested at least some limits on the President's wartime power. In **Brown v. United States**, 12 U.S. 110 (1814), the Court confronted the question whether the Executive could constitutionally condemn British property seized during the War of 1812 absent congressional authorization. Writing for the Court, Chief Justice Marshall held it could not: "It is urged that, in executing the laws of war, the executive may seize and the Courts condemn all property which, according to the modern law of nations, is subject to confiscation, although it might require an act of the legislature to justify the condemnation of that property. [It] appears to the Court, that the power of confiscating enemy property is in the legislature, and that the legislature has not yet declared its will to confiscate property which was within our territory at the declaration of war." But, in dissent, Justice Story suggested that once Congress has declared war, the Executive enjoys all authority available to him under the law of nations, subject to congressional limitation: "The sovereignty, as to declaring war and limiting its effects, rests with the legislature. The sovereignty, as to its execution, rests with the president. If the legislature do not limit the nature of the war, all the regulations and rights of general war attach upon it."

Considerable scholarly commentary explores the textual, structural and historical basis for such arguments. For an account that concludes that "the President has a residual power over the military" but that Congress enjoys "horizontally concurrent power [that] may be used to trump any of the Commander in Chief's directives," see Prakash, "The Separation and Overlap of War and Military Powers," 87 Tex. L. Rev. 299 (2008) (noting, however, that numerous institutional restraints will prevent Congress from micromanaging military affairs). For an exhaustive review of the framing era that concludes that the Framers understood that "the legislature possessed the power to subject the Executive to control over all matters pertaining to warmaking, save those that would deprive him of superintendence," and that such power extended "even as to such clearly tactical matters as the movement of troops," see Barron & Lederman, supra; see also Barron & Lederman, "The Commander in Chief at the Lowest Ebb—A Constitutional History," 121 Harv. L. Rev. 944 (2008) (concluding based on an exhaustive review of post-framing history that "Congress has been an active participant in setting the terms of battle (and the conduct and organization of the armed forces and militia more generally)" and that presidents have rarely, until recently, claimed a preclusive power to defy congressional limitations in military affairs). Even if there were any such presidential power, how far would it extend into matters of domestic governance? Does the "war on terror" turn the entire nation into the "battlefield"?

3. ***The Vesting Clause and inherent executive power.*** Article II specifies some presidential powers, such as the power to issue pardons and the powers to make treaties and appointments, but unlike Article I, it does not limit presidential powers to any enumerated list. Instead, it simply "vests" the executive power in "a President of the United States." Does the Vesting Clause imply that, even apart from any Commander-in-Chief authority, the President possesses inherent, unenumerated executive power over matters related to national security? Is this reading supported by a functional argument that the President can act with greater energy and dispatch than the Congress? See Posner & Vermeule, "Accommodating Emergencies," 56 Stan. L. Rev. 605 (2003). For a comparative survey that concludes that "executives in other democracies generally seek some sort of legislative affirmation of their actions," even in the context of wartime, see Martinez, "Inherent Executive Power: A Comparative Perspective," 115 Yale L.J. 2480 (2006).

SECTION 4. CONGRESSIONAL AUTHORITY TO RESTRAIN AND ENABLE THE EXECUTIVE

The executive branch has burgeoned far beyond the imagination of the framers, to encompass a wide variety of executive and independent agencies, located not only within the Beltway of the nation's capital, but also across the land. How can Congress control the actions of such a greatly expanded executive branch? How can the executive branch be kept democratically accountable? It is unrealistic to suppose that Congress can concentrate power more closely in the modern President himself, as no one person can keep track of the vast modern federal bureaucracy. So Congress has two options: it can retain control over executive officers' actions, or it can retain control over executive officers' jobs.

CONGRESSIONAL CONTROL OVER THE ACTIONS OF THE EXECUTIVE BRANCH

One way for Congress to retain control over executive action is to be very specific and limiting in the delegation of power to agencies, so that the agencies' rulemaking power in turn will be limited. In principle, the constitutional grant of all legislative powers to Congress entails a principle of nondelegation—the theory that Congress may not constitutionally delegate its legislative power to another branch of government. But in practice, Congress has engaged frequently in broad delegations that in effect require agencies to make specific sub-rules—i.e., to exercise power much like that of a legislature—and the nondelegation doctrine has done little to stop the practice. As the Court put it in Touby v. United States, 500 U.S. 160 (1991), the doctrine "does not prevent Congress from seeking assistance, within proper limits, from the coordinate Branches. [Thus,] Congress does not violate the Constitution merely because it legislates in broad terms, leaving a certain degree of discretion to executive or judicial actors. So long as Congress 'lay[s] down by legislative act an intelligible principle to which the person or body authorized to [act] is directed to conform, such legislative action is not a forbidden delegation of legislative power.' " The rise of the modern state has made such broad delegations well-nigh unavoidable.

There are only two cases, both in 1935, in which the Court found a violation of the nondelegation doctrine. In Schechter Poultry (p. 123 above), the Court unanimously struck down the provision of the National Industrial Recovery Act that authorized the President to approve "codes of fair competition." (Recall that Justice Cardozo's separate opinion in that case commented: "This is delegation run riot.") And in Panama Ref. Co. v. Ryan, 293 U.S. 388 (1935), the Court struck down another provision of the NIRA on delegation grounds. But aside from those two decisions, the Court has consistently found that even the broadest congressional delegations are constitutionally permissible See, e.g., Yakus v. United States, 321 U.S. 414 (1944) (authorizing imposition of World War II price controls that "will be generally fair and equitable and will effectuate the purposes of this Act"). Only rarely have dissenters urged that the nondelegation doctrine be given sharper teeth. The Court accepted and heard argument on a nondelegation case, Gundy v. United States, No. 16-1829 (2d Cir. Jun. 22, 2017), during the 2018 term, but had not yet issued a decision as this casebook went to press. The question in Gundy was whether the federal Sex Offender Registration and Notification Act's delegation of authority to the attorney general to issue regulations under 42 U.S.C. § 16913 violates the nondelegation doctrine.

Is there a constitutional basis to support an effort to roll back the discretion granted to administrative agencies and executive departments?

Would aggressive application of the nondelegation doctrine be either workable or desirable? See Stewart, "The Reformation of American Administrative Law," 88 Harv. L. Rev. 1667 (1975). For an analysis of state courts' distinct approaches to nondelegation, see Rossi, "Institutional Design and the Lingering Legacy of Antifederalist Separation of Powers Ideals in the States," 52 Vand. L. Rev. (1999) (identifying twenty-three states as "moderate" nondelegation states and twenty states as "strong" nondelegation states in which state courts are significantly more likely to strike down statutes on nondelegation grounds). For a public choice theory analysis of the congressional incentives for delegating rulemaking authority, see Fiorina, "Legislative Choice of Regulatory Forms: Legal Process or Administrative Process," 39 Pub. Choice 33 (1982). For an argument that expansive delegation is not only unconstitutional but also dangerous to democracy, liberty and public welfare, see Schoenbrod, Power Without Responsibility: How Congress Abuses the People Through Delegation (1994) ("Some early [Court] opinions hold that the prohibition [on delegation] is total. [The] early cases were right and the modern cases wrong.").

Note that the nondelegation doctrine, very weak in the domestic sphere, is an even more toothless barrier in the context of foreign affairs. In **United States v. Curtiss-Wright Export Corp.**, 299 U.S. 304 (1936), Justice SUTHERLAND's opinion ended with an emphasis on "the unwisdom of requiring Congress in this field of governmental power to lay down narrowly definite standards by which the President is to be governed." Curtiss-Wright involved a Joint Resolution of Congress in 1934 authorizing the President to prohibit the sale of arms and munitions to Bolivia and Paraguay, which were involved in armed conflict. President Roosevelt immediately proclaimed an embargo. Curtiss-Wright was indicted for conspiracy to sell arms to Bolivia and challenged the Joint Resolution as an unconstitutional delegation of legislative power to the President. Justice Sutherland wrote: "In this vast external realm, with its important, complicated, delicate and manifold problems, the President alone has the power to speak or listen as a representative of a nation." Sutherland also wrote of "the very delicate, plenary and exclusive power of the President as the sole organ of the federal government in the field of international relations—a power which does not require as a basis for its exercise an act of Congress." According to oral tradition, the practice of citation to the decision is sometimes described in the Office of Legal Counsel at the Department of Justice as "Curtiss-Wright so I'm right." See Koh, The National Security Constitution, 94 (1990). In Zivotofsky, (p. 309 above), the Court claimed to reject Curtiss-Wright's sweeping dictum that the President has exclusive power to conduct international relations, but in dissent Justice Scalia accused the majority of replicating Curtiss-Wright's reasoning. For an extended argument from a former director of the Office of Legal Counsel that Zivotofsky will essentially replace Curtiss-Wright as a trump card for executive power in foreign affairs, see Jack Goldsmith, Zivotofsky II as Precedent in the Executive Branch, 129 Harv. L. Rev. 112 (2015).

Is the nondelegation principle especially weak with regard to Presidential regulation of the military? See, e.g., Loving v. United States, 517 U.S. 748 (1996) ("It is hard to deem lawless a delegation giving the President broad discretion to prescribe rules" governing factors to be considered when imposing the death penalty in courts-martial. "The delegated duty [is] interlinked with duties already assigned to the President by express terms of the Constitution.").

Even if the nondelegation doctrine is moribund or toothless, are there other techniques Congress might employ to try to maintain democratic control of the actions of the executive branch? For example, may Congress retain control over executive actions by reserving to itself or one of its houses the power to overrule them? The "one-House veto" was a technique adopted by Congress in a wide range of statutes to avoid the problem of agency "capture" by powerful private interests. If Congress had the power to delegate to the executive to begin with, did it also have the power to delegate subject to a reserved veto? The Chadha decision, which follows, gave a negative answer to that question:

INS v. Chadha

462 U.S. 919, 103 S. Ct. 2764, 77 L. Ed. 2d 317 (1983).

[Section 244(c)(2) of the Immigration and Nationality Act authorized one House of Congress, by resolution, to invalidate the decision of the Executive Branch to suspend deportation of a deportable alien if the alien met specified conditions and would suffer "extreme hardship" if deported. The Attorney General was required to report to Congress on each such suspension. Chadha was an Indian born in Kenya who had overstayed his student visa and was thus deportable. The Attorney General suspended his deportation pursuant to the Act and notified Congress of his action. The House of Representatives passed a resolution under § 244(c)(2) that the deportation "should not be suspended," based on a House committee recommendation. The House resolution was not submitted to the Senate or presented to the President. Chadha challenged the constitutionality of the one-House veto provision. Finding that the veto provision was severable from the rest of § 244 and that Chadha had standing to challenge the constitutionality of the one-House veto, and rejecting the argument that the veto issue presented a "nonjusticiable political question," Chief Justice Burger, writing for the Court, found the one-House veto unconstitutional on the merits.]

■ CHIEF JUSTICE BURGER delivered the opinion of the Court.

[The] fact that a given law or procedure is efficient, convenient, and useful in facilitating functions of government, standing alone, will not save it if it is contrary to the Constitution. Convenience and efficiency are not the primary objectives—or the hallmarks—of democratic government and our inquiry is sharpened rather than blunted by the fact that Congressional veto provisions are appearing with increasing frequency in statutes which delegate authority to executive and independent agencies. [Justice White] undertakes to make a case for the proposition that the one-House veto is a useful "political invention," and we need not challenge that assertion. [But] policy arguments supporting even useful "political inventions" are subject to the demands of the Constitution which defines powers and, with respect to this subject, sets out just how those powers are to be exercised. Explicit and unambiguous provisions of the Constitution prescribe and define the respective functions of the Congress and of the Executive in the legislative process. Since the precise terms of those familiar provisions are critical to the resolution of this case, we set them out verbatim.[1] [These] provisions of Art. I are integral parts of the constitutional design for the separation of powers. [We] find that the purposes underlying the Presentment Clauses, Art. I, § 7, cls. 2, 3, and the bicameral requirement of Art. I, § 1 and § 7, cl. 2, guide our resolution of the important question presented [here].

The Presentment Clauses. The records of the Constitutional Convention reveal that the requirement that all legislation be presented to the President before becoming law was uniformly accepted by the Framers. [During] the final debate on Art. I, § 7, cl. 2, James Madison expressed concern that it might easily be evaded by the simple expedient of calling a proposed law a "resolution" or "vote" rather than a "bill." As a consequence, Art. I, § 7, cl. 3 was added. [The] decision to provide the President with a limited and qualified power to nullify proposed legislation by veto was based on the profound conviction of the Framers that the powers conferred on Congress were the powers to be most carefully circumscribed. It is beyond doubt that lawmaking was a power to be shared by both Houses and the [President].

Bicameralism. The bicameral requirement of Art. I, §§ 1, 7 was of scarcely less concern to the Framers than was the Presidential veto and indeed the two concepts are interdependent. By providing that no law could take effect without the concurrence of the prescribed majority of the Members of both Houses, the Framers reemphasized their belief [that] legislation should not be enacted unless it has been carefully and fully considered by the Nation's elected officials. [After quoting from James Wilson, Alexander Hamilton, and Joseph Story, the Chief Justice continued:] We see therefore that the Framers were acutely conscious that the bicameral requirement and the Presentment Clauses would serve essential constitutional functions. The President's participation in the legislative process was to protect the Executive Branch from Congress and to protect the whole people from improvident laws. The division of the Congress into two distinctive bodies assures that the legislative power would be exercised only after opportunity for full study and debate in separate settings. The President's unilateral veto power, in turn, was limited by the power of two thirds of both Houses of Congress to overrule a veto thereby precluding final arbitrary action of one person. It emerges clearly that the prescription for legislative action in Art. I, §§ 1, 7 represents the Framers' decision that the legislative power of the Federal government be exercised in accord with a single, finely wrought and exhaustively considered, procedure.

[Although] not "hermetically" sealed from one another, the powers delegated to the three Branches are functionally identifiable. [When] the Executive acts, he presumptively acts in an executive or administrative capacity as defined in Art. II. And when, as here, one House of Congress purports to act, it is presumptively acting within its assigned sphere. Beginning with this presumption, we must nevertheless establish that the

---

1 Chief Justice Burger quoted the following provisions of Art. I: "All legislative Powers herein granted shall be vested in a Congress of the United States, which shall consist of a Senate *and* a House of Representatives." Art. I, § 1; "Every Bill which shall have passed the House of Representatives *and* the Senate, *shall*, before it become a Law, be presented to the [President]." Art. I, § 7, cl. 2; "*Every* Order, Resolution, or Vote to which the Concurrence of the Senate and House of Representatives may be necessary (except on a question of Adjournment) *shall be* presented to the President of the United States; and before the Same shall take Effect, *shall be* approved by him, or being disapproved by him, *shall be* repassed by two thirds of the Senate and House of Representatives, according to the Rules and Limitations prescribed in the Case of a Bill." Art. I, § 7, cl. 3. [Emphases by Chief Justice Burger.]

challenged action under [the law] is of the kind to which the procedural requirements of Art. I, § 7 apply. Not every action taken by either House is subject to the bicameralism and presentment requirements of Art. I. Whether actions taken by either House are, in law and fact, an exercise of legislative power depends not on their form but upon "whether they contain matter which is properly to be regarded as legislative in its character and effect." Examination of the action taken here by one House [reveals] that it was essentially legislative in purpose and effect. In purporting to exercise power defined in Art. I, § 8, cl. 4 to "establish an uniform Rule of Naturalization," the House took action that had the purpose and effect of altering the legal rights, duties and relations of persons, including the Attorney General, Executive Branch officials and Chadha, all outside the legislative branch. [The] one-House veto operated in this case to overrule the Attorney General and mandate Chadha's deportation; absent the House action, Chadha would remain in the United States. Congress has *acted* and its action has altered Chadha's status.

The legislative character of the one-House veto in this case is confirmed by the character of the Congressional action it supplants. Neither the House of Representatives nor the Senate contends that, absent the veto [provision] either of them, or both of them acting together, could effectively require the Attorney General to deport an alien once the Attorney General, in the exercise of legislatively delegated authority,[2] had determined the alien should remain in the United States. Without the challenged [provision], this could have been achieved, if at all, only by legislation requiring deportation.

[The] nature of the decision implemented by the one-House veto in this case further manifests its legislative character. After long experience with the clumsy, time consuming private bill procedure, Congress made a deliberate choice to delegate to the Executive Branch [the] authority to allow deportable aliens to remain in this country in certain specified circumstances. It is not disputed that this choice to delegate authority is precisely the kind of decision that can be implemented only in accordance with the procedures set out in Art. I. Disagreement with the Attorney General's decision on Chadha's deportation—that is, Congress' decision to deport Chadha—no less than Congress' original choice to delegate to the Attorney General the authority to make that decision, involves determinations of policy that Congress can implement in only one way: bicameral passage followed by presentment to the President. Congress must abide by its delegation of authority until that delegation is legislatively altered or revoked.

Finally, we see that when the Framers intended to authorize either House of Congress to act alone and outside of its prescribed bicameral

[2] Congress protests that affirming the Court of Appeals in this case will sanction "lawmaking by the [Attorney General]." [To] be sure, some administrative agency action—rule making, for example—may resemble "lawmaking." [But when] the Attorney General performs his duties pursuant to § 244, he does not exercise "legislative" power. The bicameral process is not necessary as a check on the Executive's administration of the laws because his administrative activity cannot reach beyond the limits of the statute that created [it]. The constitutionality of the Attorney General's execution of the authority delegated to him by § 244 involves only a question of delegation doctrine. [A] one-House veto is clearly legislative in both character and effect and is [not checked in the manner administrative actions are]; the need for the check provided by Art. I, §§ 1, 7 is therefore clear. Congress' authority to delegate portions of its power to administrative agencies provides no support for the argument that Congress can constitutionally control administration of the laws by way of a Congressional veto. [Footnote by Chief Justice Burger.]

legislative role, they narrowly and precisely defined the procedure for such action. There are but four provisions in the Constitution, explicit and unambiguous, by which one House may act alone with the unreviewable force of law, not subject to the President's veto: [The Chief Justice referred to the power of the House to initiate impeachments, the Senate's power to conduct trials on impeachment charges, the Senate's power over Presidential appointments, and the Senate's power to ratify treaties.] These carefully defined exceptions from presentment and bicameralism [provide] further support for the conclusion that Congressional authority is not to be [implied]. Since it is clear that the action by the House under § 244(c)(2) was not within any of the express constitutional exceptions authorizing one House to act alone, and equally clear that it was an exercise of legislative power, that action was subject to the standards prescribed in Article I.[3]

The choices we discern as having been made in the Constitutional Convention impose burdens on governmental processes that often seem clumsy, inefficient, even unworkable, but those hard choices were consciously made by men who had lived under a form of government that permitted arbitrary governmental acts to go unchecked. There is no support in the Constitution or decisions of this Court for the proposition that the cumbersomeness and delays often encountered in complying with explicit Constitutional standards may be avoided, either by the Congress or by the President. [Youngstown.] With all the obvious flaws of delay, untidiness, and potential for abuse, we have not yet found a better way to preserve freedom than by making the exercise of power subject to the carefully crafted restraints spelled out in the Constitution. We hold that the Congressional Veto [challenged here is unconstitutional].

[Affirmed.]

■ JUSTICE POWELL, concurring in the judgment.

[This] case may be decided on a narrower ground. When Congress finds that a particular person does not satisfy the statutory criteria for permanent residence in this country it has assumed a judicial function in violation of the principle of separation of powers. [The Framers were concerned] that trial by a legislature lacks the safeguards necessary to prevent the abuse of power. [On] its face, the House's action appears clearly adjudicatory. The House did not enact a general rule; rather it made its own determination that six specific persons did not comply with certain statutory criteria. It thus undertook the type of decision that traditionally has been left to other branches. [The] impropriety of the House's assumption of this function is

---

[3] Justice Powell's position is that the one-House veto in this case is a judicial act and therefore unconstitutional as beyond the authority vested in Congress by the Constitution. We agree that there is a sense in which one-House action pursuant to [this law] has a judicial cast, since it purports to "review" Executive action. [But] the attempted analogy between judicial action and the one-House veto is less than perfect. Federal courts do not enjoy a roving mandate to correct alleged excesses of administrative agencies; we are limited by Art. III [and] no justiciable case or controversy was presented by the Attorney General's decision to allow Chadha to remain in this country. We are aware of no decision [where] a federal court has reviewed a decision of the Attorney General suspending deportation [pursuant to the statute]. This is not surprising, given that no party to such action has either the motivation or the right to appeal from it. [Thus], Justice Powell's statement that the one-House veto in this case is "clearly adjudicatory" simply is not supported by his accompanying assertion that the House has "assumed a function ordinarily entrusted to the federal courts." We are satisfied that the one-House veto is legislative in purpose and effect and subject to the procedures set out in Art. I. [Footnote by Chief Justice Burger.]

confirmed by the fact that its action raises the very danger the Framers sought to avoid—the exercise of unchecked [power].

■ JUSTICE WHITE, dissenting.

Today the Court not only invalidates § 244(c)(2) of the [Act], but also sounds the death knell for nearly 200 other statutory provisions in which Congress has reserved a "legislative veto." For this reason, the Court's decision is of surpassing importance. And it is for this reason that the Court would have been well-advised to decide the case, if possible, on the narrower grounds of separation of powers, leaving for full consideration the constitutionality of other congressional review statutes operating on such varied matters as war powers and agency rulemaking, some of which concern the independent regulatory agencies. The prominence of the legislative veto mechanism in our contemporary political system and its importance to Congress can hardly be overstated. It has become a central means by which Congress secures the accountability of executive and independent agencies. Without the legislative veto, Congress is faced with a Hobson's choice: either to refrain from delegating the necessary authority, leaving itself with a hopeless task of writing laws with the requisite specificity to cover endless special circumstances across the entire policy landscape, or in the alternative, to abdicate its lawmaking function to the executive branch and independent agencies. To choose the former leaves major national problems unresolved; to opt for the latter risks unaccountable policymaking by those not elected to fill that role. Accordingly, over the past five decades, the legislative veto has been placed in nearly 200 statutes. The device is known in every field of governmental concern: reorganization, budgets, foreign affairs, war powers, and regulation of trade, safety, energy, the environment and the economy.

I. [Justice White reviewed the history of the legislative veto. He noted that it began as a "response to the problems of reorganizing the sprawling government structure" created after the Depression, that it "balanced delegations of statutory authority in new areas," and that it had been "important in resolving a series of major constitutional disputes between the President and Congress over claims of the President to broad impoundment, war, and national emergency powers." He continued:] Even this brief review [demonstrates] that the legislative veto [is] an important if not indispensable political invention that allows the President and Congress to resolve major constitutional and policy differences, assures the accountability of independent regulatory agencies, and preserves Congress' control over lawmaking. Perhaps there are other means of accommodation and accountability, but the increasing reliance of Congress upon the legislative veto suggests that the alternatives to which Congress must now turn are not entirely satisfactory.[4] [The] history of the legislative veto also makes clear that it has not been a sword with which Congress has struck out to aggrandize itself at the expense of the other branches—the concerns of Madison and Hamilton. Rather, the veto has been a means of defense, a reservation of ultimate authority necessary if Congress is to fulfill its

---

4 While Congress could write certain statutes with greater specificity, it is unlikely that this is a realistic or even desirable substitute for the legislative veto. [Oversight] hearings and congressional investigations have their purpose, but unless Congress is to be rendered a think tank or debating society, they are no substitute for the exercise of actual authority. [Finally], the passage of corrective legislation after agency regulations take effect or Executive Branch officials have acted entail the drawbacks endemic to a retroactive [response]. [Footnote by Justice White.]

designated role [as] the nation's lawmaker. [The] Executive has [often] agreed to legislative review as the price for a broad delegation of authority. To be sure, the President may have preferred unrestricted power, but that could be precisely why Congress thought it essential to retain a check on the exercise of delegated authority.

II. For all these reasons, the apparent sweep of the Court's decision today is regrettable. The Court's Article I analysis appears to invalidate all legislative vetoes irrespective of form or subject. Because the legislative veto is commonly found as a check upon rulemaking by administrative agencies and upon broad-based policy decisions of the Executive Branch, it is particularly unfortunate that the Court reaches its decision in a case involving the exercise of a veto over deportation decisions regarding particular individuals. [The] Constitution does not directly authorize or prohibit the legislative veto. Thus, our task should be to determine whether the legislative veto is consistent with the purposes of Art. I and the principles of Separation of [Powers]. We should not find the lack of a specific constitutional authorization for the legislative veto surprising, and I would not infer disapproval of the mechanism from its absence. From the summer of 1787 to the present the government of the United States has become an endeavor far beyond the contemplation of the Framers. Only within the last half century has the complexity and size of the Federal Government's responsibilities grown so greatly that the Congress must rely on the legislative veto as the most effective if not the only means to insure their role as the nation's lawmakers. But the wisdom of the Framers was to anticipate that the nation would grow and new problems of governance would require different solutions. Accordingly, our Federal Government was intentionally chartered with the flexibility to respond to contemporary needs without losing sight of fundamental democratic [principles].

III. [The bicameralism and presentment provisions of Art. I. do not answer] the constitutional question before us. The power to exercise a legislative veto is not the power to write new law without bicameral approval or presidential consideration. The veto must be authorized by statute and may only negative what an Executive department or independent agency has proposed. On its face, the legislative veto no more allows one House of Congress to make law than does the presidential veto confer such power upon the President.

[For] some time, the sheer amount of law—the substantive rules that regulate private conduct and direct the operation of government—made by the agencies has far outnumbered the lawmaking engaged in by Congress through the traditional process. There is no question but that agency rulemaking is lawmaking in any functional or realistic sense of the term. [If] Congress may delegate lawmaking power to independent and executive agencies, it is most difficult to understand Article I as forbidding Congress from also reserving a check on legislative power for itself. Absent the veto, the agencies receiving delegations of legislative or quasi-legislative power may issue regulations having the force of law without bicameral approval and without the President's signature. It is thus not apparent why the reservation of a veto over the exercise of that legislative power must be subject to a more exacting test. In both cases, it is enough that the initial statutory authorizations comply with the Article I requirements. [Under] the Court's analysis, the Executive Branch and the independent agencies may make rules with the effect of law while Congress, in whom the Framers confided the legislative power, may not exercise a veto which precludes such rules from having operative [force].

[However] resolutions of disapproval under [the law] are formally characterized, in reality, a departure from the status quo occurs only upon the concurrence of opinion among the House, Senate, and President. Reservations of legislative authority to be exercised by Congress should be upheld if the exercise of such reserved authority is consistent with the distribution of and limits upon legislative power that Article I provides. [The law] did not alter the division of actual authority between Congress and the Executive. At all times, whether through private bills, or through affirmative concurrent resolutions, or through the present one-House veto, a permanent change in a deportable alien's status could be accomplished only with the agreement of the Attorney General, the House, and the Senate. The central concern of the presentation and bicameralism requirements of Article I [is] fully satisfied by the operation of [this law].

IV. [The] history of the separation of powers doctrine is also a history of accommodation and practicality. Apprehensions of an overly powerful branch have not led to undue prophylactic measures that handicap the effective working of the national government as a whole. The Constitution does not contemplate total separation of the three branches of Government. [Our] decisions reflect this judgment. [The] veto provision does not "preven[t] the Executive Branch from accomplishing its constitutionally assigned functions." [Moreover], the Court believes that [this] legislative veto [is] best characterized as an exercise of legislative or quasi-legislative authority. Under this characterization, the practice does not, even on the surface, constitute an infringement of executive or judicial prerogative. [Nor] does § 244 infringe on the judicial power, as Justice Powell would [hold]. [I] do not suggest that all legislative vetoes are necessarily consistent with separation of powers principles. A legislative check on an inherently executive function, for example that of initiating prosecutions, poses an entirely different question. But the legislative veto device here—and in many other settings—is far from an instance of legislative tyranny over the Executive. It is a necessary check on the unavoidably expanding power of the agencies, both executive and independent, as they engage in exercising authority delegated by Congress.

V. [I] regret the destructive scope of the Court's holding. It reflects a profoundly different conception of the Constitution than that held by the Courts which sanctioned the modern administrative state. Today's decision strikes down in one fell swoop provisions in more laws enacted by Congress than the Court has cumulatively invalidated in its history. I fear it will now be more difficult "to insure that the fundamental policy decisions in our society will be made not by an appointed official but by the body immediately responsible to the people," Arizona v. California, 373 U.S. 546, 626 (1963) (Harlan, J., dissenting). I must dissent. [Justice REHNQUIST, joined by Justice White, submitted a separate dissent, expressing the view that the legislative veto provision was not severable.]

BICAMERALISM AND PRESENTMENT

1. ***The impact of Chadha.*** The Chadha ruling was the Court's first full encounter with the problem of legislative vetoes. Decisions in the wake

of Chadha demonstrated its broad impact. For example, summary decisions by the Supreme Court soon after Chadha struck down not only one-House veto provisions in regulatory statutes involving independent agencies but also two-House vetoes as in the Federal Trade Commission Improvements Act of 1980. Despite Chadha, Congress continued to enact legislative veto provisions in a number of statutes. Congress apparently assumed that fear of budgetary retaliation would assure that the executive branch would honor these provisions.

2. ***The rise of the administrative state.*** To what extent does increased governance via administrative agencies give rise to a new calculus for judging separation-of-powers claims? Has the division of powers changed because of congressional desire to hand off contentious decisions to the agencies? Or because the organization of contemporary society depends on tasks that actually are better handled by administrative agencies than by legislatures? Consider the following statement: "The legislative veto at issue in Chadha is not unconstitutional because it is an attempt by Congress to exercise legislative power without following the proper procedures for legislation, as the Court held, but because it is an attempt by Congress to exercise powers that can no longer be considered legislative. Whatever role the framers may have intended for private bills in immigration cases originally, today it has become an administrative function to say whether an individual case involves 'extreme hardship.' " Elliott, "INS v. Chadha: The Administrative Constitution, the Constitution, and the Legislative Veto," 1983 Sup. Ct. Rev. 125.

Given the rise of the administrative state, is it possible that congressional regulation of presidential action might *restore* checks and balances to a system that now gives the executive much more authority than could have been envisioned in the original plan of the Constitution? If the Framers probably could not have envisioned Chadha's legislative veto, is it any more likely that they would have envisioned an agency of the scale and power of the INS? Should Chadha be understood to place Congress under a special disability, through adoption of "a principle never explicitly articulated by the majority: 'that the legislature can delegate authority to others but not to itself' "? Tribe, "The Legislative Veto Decision: A Law by Any Other Name?" 21 Harv. J. on Legis. 1 (1984) (pointing to the Court's lack of concern with executive agencies entrusted with "quasi-legislative' powers").

3. ***Presidential vetoes.*** Do the bicameralism and presentment requirements operate as a check not only on innovations in the exercise of congressional power but also on innovations in the exercise of presidential power? Consider a law giving the President the power to disallow particular items of national spending without vetoing the entire bill. Does such a law aggrandize the power of the President to twist arms in the Congress by threat of vetoing items with special salience for particular members of Congress? Does a line item veto make members of Congress too dependent on presidential goodwill? Or does it rebalance the relationship between Congress and the President by enabling the President to prevent members of Congress from larding appropriations bills with special favors to their own individual states or districts? Does a line item veto help eliminate special interests from politics? Or does it simply allow a president to prefer his own special interests to those agreed upon by Congress through logrolling?

The analogy between the one-House legislative veto struck down in Chadha and a "line item veto" for the President led to the constitutional challenge in the following case:

Clinton v. New York

524 U.S. 417, 118 S. Ct. 2091, 141 L. Ed. 2d 393 (1998).

[Shortly after the decision in Raines v. Byrd, (p. 55 above) in which the Court held that legislators lacked standing to challenge the Line Item Veto Act of 1996, President Clinton exercised his authority under the Act by canceling a provision of the Balanced Budget Act of 1997 allowing New York to keep certain funds it would otherwise have had to repay to the federal government under the Medicaid program, and a provision of the Taxpayer Relief Act of 1997 giving a tax benefit to food processors acquired by farmers' cooperatives. Claiming that they would be adversely affected by two of these cancellations, New York City and several private organizations challenged the constitutionality of the Medicaid cancellation. The Snake River Potato Growers, a farmers' cooperative, challenged the constitutionality of the food processors' provision. Unlike the members of Congress who unsuccessfully filed suit in Raines, these challengers clearly met both Article III and prudential and standing requirements, enabling the Court to reach the merits of the line item veto's constitutionality.]

■ JUSTICE STEVENS delivered the opinion of the Court.

The Line Item Veto Act gives the President the power to "cancel in whole" three types of provisions that have been signed into law: "(1) any dollar amount of discretionary budget authority; (2) any item of new direct spending; or (3) any limited tax benefit." [In] identifying items for cancellation he must consider the legislative history, the purposes, and other relevant information about the items. He must determine, with respect to each cancellation, that it will "(i) reduce the Federal budget deficit; (ii) not impair any essential Government functions; and (iii) not harm the national interest." Moreover, he must transmit a special message to Congress notifying it of each cancellation within five calendar days (excluding Sundays) after the enactment of the canceled provision. [A] cancellation takes effect upon receipt by Congress of the special message from the President. If, however, a "disapproval bill" pertaining to a special message is enacted into law, the cancellations set forth in that message become "null and void." [A] majority vote of both Houses is sufficient to enact a disapproval bill. The Act does not grant the President the authority to cancel a disapproval bill, but he does, of course, retain his constitutional authority to veto such a bill.

[In] both legal and practical effect, the President has amended two Acts of Congress by repealing a portion of each. "Repeal of statutes, no less than enactment, must conform with Art. I." INS v. Chadha. There is no provision in the Constitution that authorizes the President to enact, to amend, or to repeal statutes [although] he may initiate and influence legislative proposals. Moreover, after a bill has passed both Houses of Congress, but "before it becomes a Law," it must be presented to the President. If he approves it, "he shall sign it, but if not he shall return it, with his Objections to that House in which it shall have originated, who shall enter the

Objections at large on their Journal, and proceed to reconsider it." Art. I, § 7, cl. 2. His "return" of a bill, which is usually described as a "veto," is subject to being overridden by a two-thirds vote in each House.

There are important differences between the President's "return" of a bill pursuant to Article I, § 7, and the exercise of the President's cancellation authority pursuant to the Line Item Veto Act. The constitutional return takes place before the bill becomes law; the statutory cancellation occurs after the bill becomes law. The constitutional return is of the entire bill; the statutory cancellation is of only a part. Although the Constitution expressly authorizes the President to play a role in the process of enacting statutes, it is silent on the subject of unilateral Presidential action that either repeals or amends parts of duly enacted statutes.

There are powerful reasons for construing constitutional silence on this profoundly important issue as equivalent to an express prohibition. The procedures governing the enactment of statutes set forth in the text of Article I were the product of the great debates and compromises that produced the Constitution itself. Familiar historical materials provide abundant support for the conclusion that the power to enact statutes may only "be exercised in accord with a single, finely wrought and exhaustively considered, procedure." [Chadha.] Our first President understood the text of the Presentment Clause as requiring that he either "approve all the parts of a Bill, or reject it in toto." What has emerged in these cases from the President's exercise of his statutory cancellation powers, however, are truncated versions of two bills that passed both Houses of Congress. They are not the product of the "finely wrought" procedure that the Framers designed.

[If] there is to be a new procedure in which the President will play a different role in determining the final text of what may "become a law," such change must come not by legislation but through the amendment procedures set forth in Article V of the Constitution.

[Affirmed.]

■ JUSTICE KENNEDY, concurring.

A nation cannot plunder its own treasury without putting its Constitution and its survival in peril. The statute before us, then, is of first importance, for it seems undeniable the Act will tend to restrain persistent excessive spending. Nevertheless, for the reasons given by Justice Stevens in the opinion for the Court, the statute must be found invalid. Failure of political will does not justify unconstitutional remedies. [I disagree with] Justice Breyer, who observes that the statute does not threaten the liberties of individual citizens. [Liberty] is always at stake when one or more of the branches seek to transgress the separation of powers. Separation of powers was designed to implement a fundamental insight: concentration of power in the hands of a single branch is a threat to liberty. [It] follows that if a citizen who is taxed has the measure of the tax or the decision to spend determined by the Executive alone, without adequate control by the citizen's Representatives in Congress, liberty is threatened.

■ JUSTICE BREYER, with whom JUSTICE O'CONNOR and JUSTICE SCALIA join as to Part III, dissenting.

III. The Court believes that the Act violates the literal text of the Constitution. A simple syllogism captures its basic reasoning: Major Premise: The Constitution sets forth an exclusive method for enacting, repealing, or amending laws. Minor Premise: The Act authorizes the

President to "repeal or amend" laws in a different way, namely by announcing a cancellation of a portion of a previously enacted law. Conclusion: The Act is inconsistent with the Constitution. I find this syllogism unconvincing, however, because its Minor Premise is faulty. When the President "canceled" the two appropriation measures now before us, he did not repeal any law nor did he amend any law. He simply followed the law, leaving the statutes, as they are literally written, intact.

[Imagine] that the canceled New York health care tax provision at issue here had [specifically provided] "that the President may prevent the just-mentioned provision from having legal force or effect if he determines x, y and z." [One] could not say that a President who "prevents" the [law] from "having legal force or effect," has either repealed or amended [it. He] has executed the law, not repealed it. It could make no significant difference to this linguistic point were the [proviso] to appear [at] the bottom of the statute page, say referenced by an asterisk, with a statement that it applies to every spending provision in the act next to which a similar asterisk appears. And that being so, it could make no difference if that proviso appeared, instead, in a different, earlier-enacted law, along with legal language that makes it applicable to every future spending provision picked out according to a specified formula. But, of course, this last-mentioned possibility is this very case.

[For] that reason, one cannot dispose of this case through a purely literal analysis as the majority does. Literally speaking, the President has not "repealed" or "amended" anything. He has simply executed a power conferred upon him by Congress, which power is contained in laws that were enacted in compliance with the exclusive method set forth in the Constitution. [Because] one cannot say that the President's exercise of the power the Act grants is, literally speaking, a "repeal" or "amendment," the fact that the Act's procedures differ from the Constitution's exclusive procedures for enacting (or repealing) legislation is beside the point. The Act itself was enacted in accordance with these procedures, and its failure to require the President to satisfy those procedures does not make the Act unconstitutional.

IV. Because I disagree with the Court's holding of literal violation, I must consider whether the Act nonetheless violates Separation of Powers principles. [There] are three relevant Separation of Powers questions here: (1) Has Congress given the President the wrong kind of power, i.e., "non-Executive" power? (2) Has Congress given the President the power to "encroach" upon Congress' own constitutionally reserved territory? (3) Has Congress given the President too much power, violating the doctrine of "nondelegation?" [The] answer to all these questions is "no."

[The] power the Act conveys [is] "executive." [It] closely resembles the kind of delegated authority—to spend or not to spend appropriations, to change or not to change tariff rates—that Congress has frequently granted the President, any differences being differences in degree, not kind. The fact that one could also characterize this kind of power as "legislative," say, if Congress itself (by amending the appropriations bill) prevented a provision from taking effect, is beside the point. This Court has frequently found that the exercise of a particular power [can] fall within the constitutional purview of more than one branch of Government, [for] the Constitution "blends" as well as "separates" powers in order to create a workable government.

[One] cannot say that the Act "encroaches" upon Congress' power, when Congress retained the power to insert, by simple majority, into any future appropriations bill, into any section of any such bill, or into any phrase of any section, a provision that says the Act will not apply. Congress also retained the power to "disapprove," and thereby reinstate, any of the President's cancellations. And it is Congress that drafts and enacts the appropriations statutes that are subject to the Act in the first place—and thereby defines the outer limits of the President's cancellation authority. [Nor] can one say the Act's grant of power "aggrandizes" the Presidential office. The grant is limited to the context of the budget. It is limited to the power to spend, or not to spend, particular appropriated items, and the power to permit, or not to permit, specific limited exemptions from generally applicable tax law from taking effect.

[While the] Constitution permits only those delegations where Congress "shall lay down by legislative act an intelligible principle to which the person or body authorized to [act] is directed to conform," [the] Court has only twice in its history found that a congressional delegation of power violated the "nondelegation" doctrine. [Panama Refining, Schechter Poultry.] [Unlike those cases,] the case before us does not involve [any] "roving commission," [or delegation] to private parties, nor does it bring all of American industry within its scope. It is limited to one area of government, the budget, and it seeks to give the President the power, in one portion of that budget, to tailor spending and special tax relief to what he concludes are the demands of fiscal responsibility. [Thus] the power the Act grants the President to prevent spending items from taking effect does not violate the "nondelegation" doctrine.

[I] recognize that the Act before us is novel. In a sense, it skirts a constitutional edge. But that edge has to do with means, not ends. The means chosen do not amount literally to the enactment, repeal, or amendment of a law [nor] violate any basic Separation of Powers principle. They do not improperly shift the constitutionally foreseen balance of power from Congress to the President. Nor, since they comply with Separation of Powers principles, do they threaten the liberties of individual citizens. They represent an experiment that may, or may not, help representative government work better. The Constitution, in my view, authorizes Congress and the President to try novel methods in this way.

CONGRESSIONAL CONSTRAINTS ON APPOINTMENT AND REMOVAL OF EXECUTIVE OFFICERS

1. ***Appointment of executive officers.*** An alternative to controlling what the executive does is to control who holds executive positions. Congressional efforts to curb presidential control of officials engaged in enforcing the law have produced recurrent constitutional disputes. What latitude does the President have to keep such a personnel function free from congressional control? Art. II, § 2, cl.2, the Appointments Clause, provides that the President "shall nominate, and by and with the Advice and Consent of the Senate, shall appoint [Ambassadors], Judges of the Supreme Court, and all other Officers of the United States, whose Appointments are not herein otherwise provided for, and which shall be established by Law: but the Congress may by Law vest the Appointment of such inferior Officers, as they think proper, in the President alone, in the Courts of Law, or in the Heads of Departments." In other words, this clause specifies that the

President shall appoint superior officers (such as cabinet heads) with the advice and consent of the Senate. But the clause allows Congress to vest appointment of inferior officers (i.e., those who report to some superior officer) in either the President acting solo, the heads of departments (e.g., cabinet officers), or the "Courts of Law."

The one body plainly excluded by that text from appointing executive officers is Congress. In **Buckley v. Valeo**, 424 U.S. 1 (1976), the Court's per curiam opinion relied on the Appointments Clause in holding unconstitutional, for most purposes, the composition of the Federal Election Commission [FEC] established by the Federal Election Campaign Act. Under the law, a majority of the FEC members was appointed by the President pro tempore of the Senate and the Speaker of the House. The FEC was given "direct and wide-ranging" enforcement power such as instituting civil actions against violations of the Act as well as "extensive rulemaking and adjudicative powers."

The Court held that such powers could be exercised only by "Officers of the United States" appointed in accordance with the Appointments Clause. According to the Court, an agency with a majority of congressionally named personnel could only exercise those powers that Congress might delegate to one of its own committees—e.g., investigatory and informative powers; since only "Officers" appointed in the constitutionally prescribed manner could undertake executive or quasi-judicial tasks, the FEC could not exercise such functions. The Court insisted that "any appointee exercising significant authority pursuant to the laws of the United States is an Officer of the United States, and must, therefore, be appointed in the manner prescribed by [the Appointments Clause]." Although Congress could vest appointment of "inferior Officers" in "Courts of Law" or "Heads of Departments" instead of the President, providing for the appointment of most FEC members by congressional officials was impermissible, since they could not be considered "Heads of Departments." The Court rejected the argument that, because of "the extraordinary authority reposed in Congress to regulate elections, this case stands on a different footing than if Congress had exercised its legislative authority in another field." The defenders of the FEC structure also argued that "Congress had good reason for not vesting in a Commission composed wholly of Presidential appointees the authority to administer the Act, since the administration of the Act would undoubtedly have a bearing on any incumbent President's campaign for reelection." To that argument, the Court responded that "such fears, however rational, do not by themselves warrant a distortion of the Framers' work." (Soon after the Buckley decision, Congress cured the constitutional flaw by reconstituting the FEC with a membership consisting entirely of presidential appointees.)

Lucia v. SEC, 585 U.S. ___, 138 S. Ct. 2044 (2018), involved a challenge to the constitutionality of SEC's appointment of its administrative law judges by staff decision rather than by the commissioners. The issue was whether the ALJs are "officers of the United States" who must by appointed by the President, a court of law, or a head of department under the Appointments Clause, Art. II, § 2, cl. 2, or merely employees, not subject to that Clause's requirement. Justice KAGAN, writing for the Court in a decision joined by Chief Justice Roberts and Justices Kennedy, Thomas, Alito and Gorsuch, held that the ALJs were officers under the clause and thus unconstitutionally appointed because not appointed by heads of department, which would include the commissioners but not their staff.

The decision relied upon the reasoning in a prior decision, Freytag v. Commissioner, 501 U.S. 868 (1991), which had held that special trial judges appointed by the Tax Court were officers subject to the Clause, but were constitutionally appointed because the Tax Court, although an Article I court and not an Article III court, is a court of law for Appointments Clause purposes: "[In] Freytag we applied the unadorned 'significant authority' test to adjudicative officials who are near-carbon copies of the Commission's ALJs [and] held that the Tax Court's special trial judges (STJs) are officers, not mere employees. [The] Court said: STJs 'take testimony, conduct trials, rule on the admissibility of evidence, and have the power to enforce compliance with discovery orders.' And the Court observed that STJs 'exercise significant discretion.' That fact meant they were officers, even when their decisions were not final." Justice Kagan observed that SEC ALJs have the same features, and "at the close of those proceedings, [issue] decisions much like that in Freytag—except with potentially more independent effect."

Justice THOMAS concurred, joined by Justice Gorsuch, to say that, "while precedents like Freytag discuss what is *sufficient* to make someone an officer of the United States, our precedents have never clearly defined what is *necessary*. I would resolve that question based on the original public meaning of 'Officers of the United States.' To the Founders, this term encompassed all federal civil officials with responsibility for an ongoing statutory duty [no] matter how important or significant the duty." Justice BREYER, joined by Justices Ginsburg and Sotomayor, concurred on statutory grounds only and dissented on the remedy: "I cannot answer the constitutional question that the majority answers without knowing the answer to a different, embedded constitutional question: [the] constitutionality of the statutory for cause removal protections that Congress provided for administrative law judges."

Justice SOTOMAYOR, joined by Justice Ginsburg, dissented: "To provide guidance to Congress and the Executive Branch, I would hold that one requisite component of 'significant authority' is the ability to make final, binding decisions on behalf of the Government. Accordingly, a person who merely advises and provides recommendations to an officer would not herself qualify as an officer." Under that standard, she would have held "that Commission ALJs are not officers because they lack final decisionmaking authority," as their decisions are always subject to the Commission's de novo review.

On July 10, 2018, just a few weeks after Lucia was decided, President Donald Trump issued an executive order placing all ALJs in the executive branch into the category of "excepted" civil service employees, meaning that ALJs would no longer be appointed on the basis of performance in competitive civil service examinations. The order explained the departure from historical practice with direct reference to Lucia: "Lucia may also raise questions about the method of appointing ALJs, including whether competitive examination and competitive service selection procedures are compatible with the discretion an agency head must possess under the Appointments Clause in selecting ALJs. Regardless of whether those procedures would violate the Appointments Clause as applied to certain ALJs, there are sound policy reasons to take steps to eliminate doubt regarding the constitutionality of the method of appointing officials who discharge such significant duties and exercise such significant discretion."

Does Lucia in fact support President Trump's order, even with the caveats the order includes?

2. ***Recess appointments.*** Article II, § 2 of the Constitution provides that "the President shall have power to fill up all vacancies that may happen during the recess of the Senate, by granting commissions which shall expire at the end of their next session." In **NLRB v. Noel Canning**, 573 U.S. 513 (2014), the Court for the first time considered the scope of the president's power to make recess appointments. The case arose from appointments to the National Labor Relations Board made by Pres. Barack Obama on January 4, 2012. At the time, "the Senate was in recess pursuant to a December 17, 2011, resolution providing for a series of brief recesses punctuated by 'pro forma session[s],' with 'no business . . . transacted,' every Tuesday and Friday through January 20, 2012." Justice BREYER wrote for Court joined by Justices Kennedy, Ginsburg, Kagan and Sotomayor, striking down the appointments because the recess was too short and the Senate preserved the capacity to transact business during the pro forma sessions. The opinion began by observing that, as a historical matter, "the Recess Appointments Clause reflects the tension between, on the one hand, the President's continuous need for the assistance of subordinates, and, on the other, the Senate's practice, particularly during the Republic's early years, of meeting for a single brief session each year." Justice Breyer then explained that historical precedent would be central to the opinion's reasoning: "We recognize, of course, that the separation of powers can serve to safeguard individual liberty, and that it is the 'duty of the judicial department'—in a separation-of-powers case as in any other—'to say what the law is,' Marbury v. Madison. But it is equally true that the longstanding 'practice of the government,' McCulloch, can inform our determination of 'what the law is,' Marbury. [Precedents] show that this Court has treated practice as an important interpretive factor even when the nature or longevity of that practice is subject to dispute, and even when that practice began after the founding era."

The Court then held, first, that the words "recess of the Senate" include both official recesses between Senate sessions and recesses that take place within sessions: "The constitutional text is . . . ambiguous. And we believe the Clause's purpose demands the broader interpretation. The Clause gives the President authority to make appointments during 'the recess of the Senate' so that the President can ensure the continued functioning of the Federal Government when the Senate is away. The Senate is equally away during both an inter-session and an intra-session recess, and its capacity to participate in the appointments process has nothing to do with the words it uses to signal its departure." Responding to the originalist argument that the only early recesses came between sessions, Justice Breyer wrote: "Indeed, from the founding until the Civil War inter-session recesses were the only kind of significant recesses that Congress took. The problem with this argument, however, is that it does not fully describe the relevant founding intent. The question is not: Did the Founders at the time think about intra-session recesses? Perhaps they did not. The question is: Did the Founders intend to restrict the scope of the Clause to the form of congressional recess then prevalent, or did they intend a broader scope permitting the Clause to apply, where appropriate, to somewhat changed circumstances? The Founders knew they were writing a document designed to apply to ever-changing circumstances over centuries."

The Court then suggested that a recess must be at least 10 days long to qualify. "The Recess Appointments Clause seeks to permit the Executive Branch to function smoothly when Congress is unavailable. And though Congress has taken short breaks for almost 200 years, and there have been many thousands of recess appointments in that time, we have not found a single example of a recess appointment made during an intra-session recess that was shorter than 10 days. [There] are a few historical examples of recess appointments made during inter-session recesses shorter than 10 days. [But] when considered against 200 years of settled practice, we regard these few scattered examples as anomalies. [We] therefore conclude, in light of historical practice, that a recess of more than 3 days but less than 10 days is presumptively too short to fall within the Clause. We add the word 'presumptively' to leave open the possibility that some very unusual circumstance—a national catastrophe, for instance, that renders the Senate unavailable but calls for an urgent response—could demand the exercise of the recess-appointment power during a shorter break."

The Court went on to hold that the words "vacancies that may happen" included both vacancies created before and during the recess. It noted that "Thomas Jefferson wrote that the Clause is 'certainly susceptible of [two] constructions.' [The] Clause's purpose strongly supports the broader interpretation. That purpose is to permit the President to obtain the assistance of subordinate officers when the Senate, due to its recess, cannot confirm them. [Historical] practice over the past 200 years strongly favors the broader interpretation."

Finally, the Court asked whether the relevant recess for the purposes of the case was the three-day recess between the Senate's pro forma sessions on January 3 and 6 or the longer recess that ran from December 20, 2011, to January 20, 2012. It concluded that "the pro forma sessions count as sessions, not as periods of recess. We hold that, for purposes of the Recess Appointments Clause, the Senate is in session when it says it is, provided that, under its own rules, it retains the capacity to transact Senate business. [The] standard we apply is consistent with the Constitution's broad delegation of authority to the Senate to determine how and when to conduct its business."

Justice SCALIA concurred only in the judgment, joined by Chief Justice Roberts, Justice Thomas and Justice Alito, arguing that the Court "sweeps away the key textual limitations on the recess-appointment power" and "justifies . . . atextual results on an adverse-possession theory of executive authority: Presidents have long claimed the powers in question, and the Senate has not disputed those claims with sufficient vigor, so the Court should not 'upset the compromises and working arrangements that the elected branches of Government themselves have reached.' " Justice Scalia would have read the recess appointments clause narrowly, according to "the plain, original meaning of the constitutional text" to include only recesses between sessions and only vacancies arising during the recess. "The Court's decision," Justice Scalia wrote, "transforms the recess-appointment power from a tool carefully designed to fill a narrow and specific need into a weapon to be wielded by future Presidents against future Senates. [The] majority's insistence on deferring to the Executive's untenably broad interpretation of the power is in clear conflict with our precedent and forebodes a diminution of this Court's role in controversies involving the separation of powers and the structure of government."

3. ***Removal of executive officers.*** The Appointments Clause is silent as to removal of executive appointees from office. The only explicit constitutional reference to the removal of executive personnel lies in the impeachment provisions. Nonetheless, from the outset, a power to remove subordinate executive officials by routes other than impeachment has been assumed. Is that power solely in the President? Or may Congress limit presidential removal authority? Should executive officers be removable by Congress through any means except impeachment under the procedures set forth in Art. I?

The following decision invalidated a scheme found to have impermissibly allowed removal of an executive officer by Congress. It involved a challenge to a statute, the Gramm-Rudman-Hollings Act, that aimed to achieve a balanced budget by establishing maximum annual permissible deficits. If needed to keep the deficit within the maximum, the Act required across-the-board cuts as follows: The Office of Management and Budget (OMB) and the Congressional Budget Office (CBO) would estimate the amount of the federal budget deficit for the next fiscal year. If the estimated deficit exceeded the target, OMB and the CBO would calculate the budget reductions required to meet the target and submit a joint report of their calculations to the Comptroller General. The Comptroller General would then, after exercising independent judgment in evaluating the estimates submitted to him, report his conclusions about the required budget reductions to the President. The President was required to put into effect the reductions submitted by the Comptroller General, unless Congress, within a specified time, met the deficit goal in other ways.

The constitutional challenge focused on the participation of the Comptroller General in this process. The office of the Comptroller General, the head of the General Accounting Office, was created by the Budget and Accounting Act of 1921. The Comptroller General is nominated by the President from a list of three persons recommended by the presiding officers of the House and the Senate, and is removable only by impeachment or by a Joint Resolution of Congress (which is subject to presidential veto) on the basis of reasons specified in the 1921 Act.

Bowsher v. Synar

478 U.S. 714, 106 S. Ct. 3181, 92 L. Ed. 2d 583 (1986).

■ CHIEF JUSTICE BURGER delivered the opinion of the Court.

The question presented by these appeals is whether the assignment by Congress to the Comptroller General of the United States of certain functions under the Balanced Budget and Emergency Deficit Control Act of 1985 [the Gramm-Rudman-Hollings Act] violates the doctrine of separation of powers.

[The] Constitution does not contemplate an active role for Congress in the supervision of officers charged with the execution of the laws it enacts. The President appoints "Officers of the United States" with the "Advice and Consent of the [Senate]." Article II, § 2. Once the appointment has been made and confirmed, however, the Constitution explicitly provides for removal of Officers of the United States by Congress only upon impeachment by the House of Representatives and conviction by the Senate.

[We] conclude that Congress cannot reserve for itself the power of removal of an officer charged with the execution of the laws except by impeachment. To permit the execution of the laws to be vested in an officer answerable only to Congress would, in practical terms, reserve in Congress control over the execution of the laws. [The] structure of the Constitution does not permit Congress to execute the laws; it follows that Congress cannot grant to an officer under its control what it does not possess.[1] Our decision in [Chadha] supports this conclusion. [To] permit an officer controlled by Congress to execute the laws would be, in essence, to permit a congressional veto. Congress could simply remove, or threaten to remove, an officer for executing the laws in any fashion found to be unsatisfactory to Congress.

[Appellants] urge that the Comptroller General performs his duties independently and is not subservient to Congress. [This] contention does not bear close scrutiny. [The 1921 Act] permits removal for "inefficiency," "neglect of duty," or "malfeasance." These terms are very broad and, as interpreted by Congress, could sustain removal of a Comptroller General for any number of actual or perceived transgressions of the legislative will. The Constitutional Convention chose to permit impeachment of executive officers only for "Treason, Bribery, or other high Crimes and Misdemeanors." It rejected language that would have permitted impeachment for "maladministration," with Madison arguing that "[s]o vague a term will be equivalent to a tenure during pleasure of the Senate." [Justice White] assures us [the] Comptroller General is unlikely to be removed by Congress. The separated powers of our government can not be permitted to turn on judicial assessment of whether an officer exercising executive power is on good terms with Congress. The Framers recognized that, in the long term, structural protections against abuse of power were critical to preserving liberty.

[Because] Congress had retained removal authority over the Comptroller General, he may not be entrusted with executive powers. The remaining question is whether the Comptroller General has been assigned such powers in the [1985 Act]. [Appellants] suggest that the duties assigned to the Comptroller General in the Act are essentially ministerial and mechanical so that their performance does not constitute "execution of the law" in a meaningful sense. On the contrary, we view these functions as plainly entailing execution of the law in constitutional terms. Interpreting a law enacted by Congress to implement the legislative mandate is the very essence of "execution" of the law. Under [the Act], the Comptroller General must exercise judgment concerning facts that affect the application of the Act. He must also interpret the provisions of the Act to determine precisely what budgetary calculations are required. Decisions of that kind are typically made by officers charged with executing a statute.

The executive nature of the Comptroller General's functions under the Act is revealed in § 252(a)(3), which gives the Comptroller General the ultimate authority to determine the budget cuts to be made. Indeed, the Comptroller General commands the President himself to carry out, [the]

[1] Appellants [are] wide of the mark in arguing that an affirmance in this case requires casting doubt on the status of "independent" agencies, because no issues involving such agencies are presented here. [This] case involves [a] statute that provides for direct congressional involvement over the decision to remove the Comptroller General. Appellants have referred us to no independent agency whose members are removable by the Congress for certain causes short of impeachable offenses, as is the Comptroller General. [Footnote by Chief Justice Burger.]

directive of the Comptroller General as to [budget reductions]. Congress of course initially determined the content of the [Act]; and undoubtedly the content of the Act determines the nature of the executive duty. However, as Chadha makes clear, once Congress makes its choice in enacting legislation, its participation ends. Congress can thereafter control the execution of its enactment only indirectly—by passing new legislation. By placing the responsibility for execution of the [Act] in the hands of an officer who is subject to removal only by itself, Congress in effect has retained control over the execution of the Act and has intruded into the executive function. The Constitution does not permit such [intrusion].

[Affirmed.][2]

■ JUSTICE WHITE, dissenting.

The Court, acting in the name of separation of powers, takes upon itself to strike down the Gramm-Rudman-Hollings Act, one of the most novel and far-reaching legislative responses to a national crisis since the New Deal. The basis of the Court's action is a solitary provision of another statute that was passed over sixty years ago and has lain dormant since that time. [The] Court's decision rests on a feature of the legislative scheme that is of minimal practical significance and that presents no substantial threat to the basic scheme of separation of powers.

[I] have no quarrel with the proposition that the powers exercised by the Comptroller under the Act may be characterized as "executive" in that they involve the interpretation and carrying out of the Act's mandate. I can also accept the general proposition that although Congress has considerable authority in designating the officers who are to execute legislation, the constitutional scheme of separated powers does prevent Congress from reserving an executive role for itself or for its "agents."

I cannot accept, however, that the exercise of authority by an officer removable for cause by a joint resolution of Congress is analogous to the impermissible execution of the law by Congress itself. [Because] the Comptroller is not an appointee of Congress but an officer of the United States appointed by the President with the advice and consent of the Senate, Buckley neither requires that he be characterized as an agent of the Congress nor in any other way calls into question his capacity to exercise "executive" authority. [And Congress] may remove the Comptroller only through a joint resolution, which by definition must be passed by both Houses and signed by the President. In other words, a removal of the Comptroller under the statute *satisfies the requirements of bicameralism and presentment laid down in* Chadha.

[Even] the results of the constitutional legislative process may be unconstitutional if those results are in fact destructive of the scheme of separation of powers. The question to be answered [is] whether there is a genuine threat of "encroachment or aggrandizement of one branch at the

[2] Justice STEVENS, joined by Justice Marshall, concurred in the judgment but disagreed with the majority's grounds: "It is not the dormant, carefully circumscribed congressional removal power that represents the primary constitutional evil. Nor do I agree [that] the analysis depends on a labeling of the functions assigned to the Comptroller General as 'executive powers.' Rather, I am convinced that the Comptroller General must be characterized as an agent of Congress [and] that the powers assigned to him under the [Act] require him to make policy that will bind the Nation. [Congress] may not exercise [its] power to formulate national policy by delegating that power [to] an individual agent of the Congress such as [the] Comptroller General."

expense of the other." Common sense indicates that the existence of the removal provision poses no such threat to the principle of separation of powers. [Action] taken in accordance with the "single, finely wrought, and exhaustively considered, procedure" established by Art. I [Chadha], should be presumptively viewed as a legitimate exercise of legislative power. That such action may represent a more or less successful attempt by Congress to "control" the actions of an officer of the United States surely does not in itself indicate that it is unconstitutional, for no one would dispute that Congress has the power to "control" administration through legislation imposing duties or substantive restraints on executive officers, through legislation increasing or decreasing the funds made available to such officers, or through legislation actually abolishing a particular office.

[The] practical result of the removal provision is not to render the Comptroller unduly dependent upon or subservient to Congress, but to render him one of the most independent officers in the entire federal establishment. Those who have studied the office agree that the procedural and substantive limits on the power of Congress and the President to remove the Comptroller make dislodging him against his will practically impossible. [Realistic] consideration of the nature of the Comptroller General's relation to Congress thus reveals that the threat to separation of powers conjured up by the majority is wholly chimerical. [The] majority's contrary conclusion rests on the rigid dogma that, outside of the impeachment process, any "direct congressional role in the removal of officers charged with the execution of the laws [is] inconsistent with separation of powers." Reliance on such an unyielding principle to strike down a statute posing no real danger of aggrandizement of congressional power is extremely misguided and insensitive to our constitutional [role].[3]

---

4. ***Fettering executive removal power.*** What if Congress does not seek to remove an executive officer by its own action, but seeks to limit the President's power of removal, for example by limiting removals to those for cause? Surely the President must be free to appoint and remove his or her own cabinet officers and confidential employees at will. But should other, inferior executive employees be allowed to be given greater protection from political reprisal?

In **Myers v. United States**, 272 U.S. 52 (1926), the Court held unconstitutional a statute providing that certain groups of postmasters could not be removed by the President without the consent of the Senate. Chief Justice TAFT's opinion rested on an expansive reading of executive powers under Art. II and found the statute an unconstitutional restriction on the President's control over executive personnel. Chief Justice Taft found that it was a "reasonable implication" from the President's power to execute the laws that "he should select those who were to act for him under his direction in the execution of the laws." And it was an additional plausible implication that "as his selection of administrative officers is essential to the execution

---

[3] In a separate dissent, Justice BLACKMUN argued that any constitutional problems "should be cured by refusing to allow congressional removal—if it ever is attempted—and not by striking down the central provisions of the [1985] Act. [I] cannot see the sense of invalidating legislation of this magnitude in order to preserve a cumbersome, 65-year-old removal power that has never been exercised and appears to have been all but forgotten until this litigation."

of the laws by him, so must be his power of removing those for whom he can not continue to be responsible."

Less than a decade after Myers, however, the Court curtailed some of its implications and distinguished Myers in holding that the President could *not* remove a member of an independent regulatory agency in defiance of restrictions in the statutory framework. In **Humphrey's Executor v. United States**, 295 U.S. 602 (1935), Justice SUTHERLAND's opinion for the Court found Congress *could* limit the President's power of removal of Federal Trade Commissioners to removal for cause and limited Myers to "purely executive officers." The FTC "cannot in any proper sense be characterized as an arm or an eye of the executive"; under the FTC Act, its duties were to be "free from executive control." Rather, it acted "in part quasi-legislatively and in part quasi-judicially." The Myers rule, then, stands simply for "the unrestrictable power of the President to remove purely executive officers." The Court applied the Humphrey's Executor rule rather than the Myers rule in **Wiener v. United States**, 357 U.S. 349 (1958), involving the removal of a member of the War Claims Commission. The statute establishing that Commission, unlike the one in Humphrey's Executor, did not specify permissible grounds for removal. But the Court emphasized that the Commission's function was of an "intrinsic judicial character" and held the removal illegal. As to officers who were not purely executive, power to remove existed "only if Congress may fairly be said to have conferred it." The Court noted: "This sharp differentiation derives from the difference in functions between those who are part of the Executive establishment and those whose tasks require absolute freedom from Executive interference."

Note that the Court in Humphrey's Executor glossed over the possible constitutional problems with having agencies with executive powers "independent" of the President in the first place. How does the Court's recognition of "independent" agencies square with separation of powers? Are "independent" agencies a fourth branch? Are they quasi-legislative or quasi-judicial? See generally Symposium, "The Independence of Independent Agencies," 1988 Duke L.J. 215; Strauss, "The Place of Agencies in Government: Separation of Powers and the Fourth Branch," 84 Colum. L. Rev. 573 (1984) (arguing that, at the agency level, "the rigid separation-of-powers compartmentalization of governmental functions should be abandoned in favor of analysis in terms of separation of functions and checks and balances," and advocating an analysis centered in "the formulation and specification of the controls that Congress, the Supreme Court, and the President may exercise over administration and regulation").

Does the vesting of executive power in the President alone create an argument for a "unitary executive" whose personnel decisions must be broadly discretionary? For an argument that the strong view of a unitary executive is not mandated by the text or history of the Constitution, see Lessig & Sunstein, "The President and the Administration," 94 Colum. L. Rev. 1 (1994). Lessig and Sunstein suggest that both the commitment to a unitary executive and the creation of substantially independent agencies in specific, limited areas where political interference would be especially detrimental, might be valid "[u]nder current circumstances," as "the best way of keeping faith with the most fundamental goals of the original scheme." For a response to Lessig and Sunstein, see Calabresi & Prakash, "The President's Power to Execute the Law," 104 Yale L.J. 541 (1994) ("The executive Power Clause actually does what it says it does, i.e., it vests (or grants) a power over law execution in the President, and it vests that power in him alone.")

5. ***The constitutionality of the independent counsel.*** Should the Humphrey's Executor principle extend beyond the independent agencies to any other office calling as a practical matter for independence from the President? What about an "independent counsel" to investigate alleged wrongdoing by the President or Vice President or their high-ranking appointees? Does the nation need someone to "guard the guardians," who must be politically insulated from presidential power? How insulated?

The Court addressed these questions in the case that follows, which involved the constitutionality of Congress's creation of "independent counsels" to investigate possible criminal wrongdoing by high-ranking executive officers:

Morrison v. Olson

487 U.S. 654, 108 S. Ct. 2597, 101 L. Ed. 2d 569 (1988).

[The Ethics in Government Act of 1978 required the Attorney General, upon "sufficient grounds" to investigate, to conduct a preliminary investigation of possible official violations of federal criminal law. The Attorney General then reported to a Special Division of the U.S. Court of Appeals for the District of Columbia Circuit, consisting of three Circuit Judges appointed by the Chief Justice for two-year terms, as to whether there were "reasonable grounds to believe that further investigation is warranted." If the Attorney General found such "reasonable grounds," she was required to apply to the Special Division for the appointment of an independent counsel, and the Special Division appointed such counsel and defined his or her jurisdiction.

Morrison v. Olson arose after independent counsel Alexia Morrison was appointed to investigate possible obstruction of congressional investigations, and a grand jury issued subpoenas to future Solicitor General Ted Olson, who moved to quash the subpoenas on the ground that the Act was unconstitutional. Chief Justice Rehnquist's majority opinion first rejected the claim that vesting the appointment of the independent counsel in the Special Division violated the literal text of the Appointments Clause of Art. 2, § 2, cl.2. He found the independent counsel to be an "inferior" officer for purposes of the Clause because she was removable by the Attorney General for "good cause," her duties were limited under the Act, and her tenure of office was "temporary." She was therefore not a "principal officer" who could be appointed only by the President with the advice and consent of the Senate.

Olson argued further that, even if the independent counsel was an "inferior" officer, the Appointments Clause did not permit Congress to place the power to appoint outside the Executive Branch. The Court, however, recognized a limited congressional power to provide for interbranch appointments. Vesting of the appointment power in the courts "would be improper if there was some 'incongruity' between the functions normally performed by the courts and the performance of their duty to appoint," but here there was not such incongruity. Finally, the Court turned to broader challenges resting on structural separation of powers principles.]

■ CHIEF JUSTICE REHNQUIST delivered the opinion of the Court.

V. [Two] related issues must be addressed: The first is whether the provision of the Act restricting the Attorney General's power to remove the independent counsel to only those instances in which he can show "good cause," taken by itself, impermissibly interferes with the President's exercise of his constitutionally appointed functions. The second is whether, taken as a whole, the Act violates the separation of powers by reducing the President's ability to control the prosecutorial powers wielded by the independent counsel.

A. [Unlike] Bowsher and Myers, this case does not involve an attempt by Congress itself to gain a role in the removal of executive officials other than its established powers of impeachment and conviction. The Act instead puts the removal power squarely in the hands of the Executive Branch; an independent counsel may be removed from office "only by the personal action of the Attorney General, and only for good cause." There is no requirement of congressional approval of the Attorney General's removal decision, though the decision is subject to judicial review. In our view, the removal provisions of the Act make this case more analogous to [Humphrey's Executor] and [Wiener] than to Myers or Bowsher.

[Appellees] contend that Humphrey's Executor and Wiener are distinguishable from this case because they did not involve officials who performed a "core executive function." They argue that our decision in Humphrey's Executor rests on a distinction between "purely executive" officials and officials who exercise "quasi-legislative" and "quasi-judicial" powers. [We] undoubtedly did rely on the terms "quasi-legislative" and "quasi-judicial" to distinguish the officials involved in Humphrey's Executor and Wiener from those in Myers, but our present considered view is that the determination of whether the Constitution allows Congress to impose a "good cause"-type restriction on the President's power to remove an official cannot be made to turn on whether or not that official is classified as "purely executive." The analysis contained in our removal cases is designed not to define rigid categories of those officials who may or may not be removed at will by the President, but to ensure that Congress does not interfere with the President's exercise of the "executive power" and his constitutionally appointed duty to "take care that the laws be faithfully executed" under Article II. [We] do not mean to suggest that an analysis of the functions served by the officials at issue is irrelevant. But the real question is whether the removal restrictions are of such a nature that they impede the President's ability to perform his constitutional duty, and the functions of the officials in question must be analyzed in that light.

[We] cannot say that the imposition of a "good cause" standard for removal by itself unduly trammels on executive authority. There is no real dispute that the functions performed by the independent counsel are "executive" in the sense that they are law enforcement functions that typically have been undertaken by officials within the Executive Branch. As we noted above, however, the independent counsel is an inferior officer under the Appointments Clause, with limited jurisdiction and tenure and lacking policymaking or significant administrative authority. Although the counsel exercises no small amount of discretion and judgment in deciding how to carry out his or her duties under the Act, we simply do not see how the

President's need to control the exercise of that discretion is so central to the functioning of the Executive Branch as to require as a matter of constitutional law that the counsel be terminable at will by the President.

Nor do we think that the "good cause" removal provision at issue here impermissibly burdens the President's power to control or supervise the independent counsel, as an executive official, in the execution of his or her duties under the Act. This is not a case in which the power to remove an executive official has been completely stripped from the [President]. Rather, because the independent counsel may be terminated for "good cause," the Executive, through the Attorney General, retains ample authority to assure that the counsel is competently performing his or her statutory responsibilities in a manner that comports with the provisions of the Act. Although we need not decide in this case exactly what is encompassed within the term "good cause" under the Act, the legislative history of the removal provision also makes clear that the Attorney General may remove an independent counsel for "misconduct." Here, [the] congressional determination to limit the removal power of the Attorney General was essential, in the view of Congress, to establish the necessary independence of the office. We do not think that this limitation as it presently stands sufficiently deprives the President of control over the independent counsel to interfere impermissibly with his constitutional obligation to ensure the faithful execution of the laws.

B. The final question to be addressed is whether the Act, taken as a whole, violates the principle of separation of powers by unduly interfering with the role of the Executive Branch. [We] observe first that this case does not involve an attempt by Congress to increase its own powers at the expense of the Executive Branch. Unlike some of our previous cases, most recently [Bowsher], this case simply does not pose a "dange[r] of congressional usurpation of Executive Branch functions." [Congress's] role under the Act is [largely] limited to receiving reports or other information and oversight of the independent counsel's activities, functions that we have recognized generally as being incidental to the legislative function of Congress.

Similarly, we do not think that the Act works any *judicial* usurpation of properly executive functions. [Once] the court has appointed a counsel and defined his or her jurisdiction, it has no power to supervise or control the activities of the counsel. [T]he various powers delegated by the statute to the [Special] Division are not supervisory or administrative, nor are they functions that the Constitution requires be performed by officials within the Executive Branch.

[Finally,] we do not think that the Act "impermissibly undermine[s]" the powers of the Executive Branch or "disrupts the proper balance between the coordinate branches [by] prevent[ing] the Executive Branch from accomplishing its constitutionally assigned functions." It is undeniable that the Act reduces the amount of control or supervision that the Attorney General and, through him, the President exercises over the investigation and prosecution of a certain class of alleged criminal activity. [Nonetheless], the Act does give the Attorney General several means of supervising or controlling the prosecutorial powers that may be wielded by an independent counsel. Most importantly, the Attorney General retains the power to remove the counsel for "good cause." [Notwithstanding] the fact that the counsel is to some degree "independent" and free from Executive supervision to a greater extent than other federal prosecutors, in our view [the] Act gives the

Executive Branch sufficient control over the independent counsel to ensure that the President is able to perform his constitutionally assigned [duties].

[Reversed.] [Justice Kennedy did not participate in the case.]

■ JUSTICE SCALIA, dissenting.

[If] to describe this case is not to decide it, the concept of a government of separate and coordinate powers no longer has meaning. [Art. II, § 1, cl. 1] of the Constitution provides: "The executive Power shall be vested in a President of the United States." [This] does not mean *some of* the executive power, but *all of* the executive power. It seems to me, therefore, that the decision [below] invalidating the present statute must be upheld on fundamental separation-of-powers principles if the following two questions are answered affirmatively: (1) Is the conduct of a criminal prosecution (and of an investigation to decide whether to prosecute) the exercise of purely executive power? (2) Does the statute deprive the President of the United States of exclusive control over the exercise of that power? [Governmental] investigation and prosecution of crimes is a quintessentially executive function. As for the second question, whether the statute before us deprives the President of exclusive control over that quintessentially executive activity: The Court does not, and could not possibly, assert that it does not. That is indeed the whole object of the statute. Instead, the Court points out that the President, through his Attorney General, has at least *some* control. That concession is alone enough to invalidate the statute. [It] is not for us to determine [how] much of the purely executive powers of government must be within the full control of the President. The Constitution prescribes that they *all* are.

[Is] it unthinkable that the President should have such exclusive power, even when alleged crimes by him or his close associates are at issue? No more so than that Congress should have the exclusive power of legislation, even when what is at issue is its own exemption from the burdens of certain laws. No more so than that this Court should have the exclusive power to pronounce the final decision on justiciable cases and controversies, even those pertaining to the constitutionality of a statute reducing the salaries of the Justices. A system of separate and coordinate powers necessarily involves an acceptance of exclusive power that can theoretically be abused. [The] Court has, nonetheless, replaced the clear constitutional prescription that the executive power belongs to the President with a "balancing test." What are the standards to determine how the balance is to be struck, that is, how much removal of presidential power is too much? Once we depart from the text of the Constitution, just where short of that do we stop?

[The] restrictions upon the removal of the independent counsel also violate our established precedent in dealing with that specific subject. [Before] the present decision it was [established] (1) that the President's power to remove principal officers who exercise purely executive powers could not be restricted [Myers], and (2) that his power to remove inferior officers who exercise purely executive powers, and whose appointment Congress had removed from the usual procedure of presidential appointment with Senate consent, could be restricted, at least where the appointment had been made by an officer of the Executive Branch. Since our 1935 decision in [Humphrey's Executor]—which was considered by many at the time the product of an activist, anti-New Deal court bent on reducing the power of President Franklin Roosevelt—it has been established that the line of permissible restriction upon removal of principal officers lies at the point at which the powers exercised by those officers are no longer purely executive. Thus, removal restrictions have been generally regarded as lawful for so-called "independent regulatory agencies." [It] has often been observed, correctly in my view, that the line between "purely executive" functions and "quasi-legislative" or "quasi-judicial" functions is not a clear one or even a rational one. But at least it permitted the identification of certain officers, and certain agencies, whose functions were entirely within the control of the President.

[Today,] however, Humphrey's Executor is swept into the dustbin of repudiated constitutional principles. [As] far as I can discern from the Court's opinion, it is now open season upon the President's removal power for all executive officers, with not even the superficially principled restriction of Humphrey's Executor as cover. The Court essentially says to the President "Trust us. We will make sure that you are able to accomplish your constitutional role." I think the Constitution gives the President—and the people—more protection than that.

The purpose of the separation and equilibration of powers in general, and of the unitary Executive in particular, was not merely to assure effective government but to preserve individual freedom. Those who hold or have held offices covered by the Ethics in Government Act are entitled to that protection as much as the rest of us, and I conclude my discussion by considering the effect of the Act upon the fairness of the process they receive. [Under] our system of government, the primary check against prosecutorial abuse is a political one. The prosecutors who exercise this awesome discretion are selected and can be removed by a President, whom the people have trusted enough to elect. Moreover, when crimes are not investigated and prosecuted fairly, nonselectively, with a reasonable sense of proportion, the President pays the cost in political damage to his administration. [That] is the system of justice the rest of us are entitled to, but what of that select class consisting of present or former high-level executive-branch officials? If an allegation is made against them of any violation of any federal criminal law, [the] Attorney General must give it his attention. That in itself is not objectionable. But if, after a 90-day investigation without the benefit of normal investigatory tools, the Attorney General is unable to say that there are "no reasonable grounds to believe" that further investigation is warranted, a process is set in motion that is *not* in the full control of persons "dependent on the people," and whose flaws cannot be blamed on the President. An independent counsel is selected, and the scope of his or her authority prescribed, by a panel of judges. What if they are politically partisan, as judges have been known to be, and select a prosecutor antagonistic to the [administration]? There is no remedy for that, not even a political one.

[The] ad hoc approach to constitutional adjudication has real attraction, even apart from its work-saving potential. It is guaranteed to produce a result, in every case, that will make a majority of the Court happy with the law. The law is, by definition, precisely what the majority thinks, taking all things into account, it *ought* to be. I prefer to rely upon the judgment of the wise men who constructed our system, and of the people who approved it, and of two centuries of history that have shown it to be sound. Like it or not, that judgment says, quite plainly, that "[t]he executive Power shall be vested in a President of the United States."

THE AFTERMATH OF MORRISON V. OLSON

1. ***The fate of the independent counsel.*** In the life of the Independent Counsel Act from its enactment in 1978 through the Clinton administration, every administration was investigated by independent counsel, with over sixteen investigations totaling well over $100 million in taxpayer expenditures. Ten of the sixteen produced no indictments. Controversy over the statute escalated during the Clinton administration, when independent counsels were appointed to investigate several cabinet officials and the President himself. A version of the statute authorizing appointment of independent prosecutors under the procedures discussed in Morrison v. Olson expired in 1999 and was not reauthorized. What checks on executive conflicts of interest exist without the statute? Is it an adequate check on executive wrongdoing in high office to allow the Attorney General to use ordinary conflict-of-interest principles to appoint his or her own special counsels in sensitive cases? Are congressional oversight and a vigilant free press an adequate backstop? For a critique of the independent counsel statute while it lasted, see Sunstein, "Bad Incentives and Bad Institutions," 86 Geo. L.J. 2267 (1998).

2. ***Other interbranch innovations.*** In **Mistretta v. United States**, 488 U.S. 361 (1989), the Court rejected both antidelegation and general separation-of-powers attacks on an unusually composed commission created to set federal guidelines for criminal sentences, the U.S. Sentencing Commission, established by the Sentencing Reform Act of 1984. The 8–1 ruling followed the flexible, functional approach of Morrison v. Olson rather than the more formal analysis of Bowsher and Chadha. The Commission was set up "as an independent commission in the judicial branch," consisting of seven voting members appointed by the President with the advice and consent of the Senate. At least three members were to be federal judges "selected after considering a list of six judges recommended to the President by the Judicial Conference of the United States." Members were removable from the Commission by the President for "good cause." The Act was a response to concern about "the great variation among sentences imposed by different judges upon similarly situated offenders" and "the uncertainty as to the time the offender would spend in prison." The law provided instead that the Commission would establish mandatory ranges of permissible sentences for different offenses that federal judges would have to apply in sentencing, unless downward departures were justified by substantial explanation.

Justice BLACKMUN's majority opinion began by rejecting the claim that Congress had granted the Commission "excessive legislative discretion in violation of the constitutionally based nondelegation doctrine." Applying the principle that Congress must lay down an "intelligible principle" to guide the agency exercising the congressionally delegated power, the Court noted that "our jurisprudence has been driven by a practical understanding that in our increasingly complex society, [Congress] simply cannot do its job absent an ability to delegate power under broad general directives." On this issue, he concluded that "we harbor no doubt that Congress' delegation of authority to the Sentencing Commission is sufficiently specific and detailed to meet constitutional requirements." He acknowledged that the Commission enjoyed "significant discretion in formulating guidelines," but added that "our cases do not at all suggest that delegations of this type may not carry with them the need to exercise judgment on matters of policy."

Justice Blackmun then turned to the broader claim that the Act violated separation of powers principles: "[T]he Framers did not require—and indeed rejected—the notion that the three Branches must be entirely separate and [distinct]. In adopting [a] flexible understanding of separation of powers [see Justice Jackson's opinion in Youngstown], we simply have recognized Madison's teaching that the greatest security against tyranny [lies] not in a hermetic division between the Branches, but in a carefully crafted system of checked and balanced power within each Branch. [The] Framers 'built into the tripartite Federal Government [a] self-executing safeguard against the encroachment or aggrandizement of one branch at the expense of the other.' It is this concern of encroachment and aggrandizement that has animated our separation-of-powers jurisprudence and aroused our vigilance against the 'hydraulic pressure inherent within each of the separate Branches to exceed the outer limits of its power.' [In] cases specifically involving the Judicial Branch, we have expressed our vigilance against two dangers: first, that the Judicial Branch neither be assigned nor allowed 'tasks that are more appropriately accomplished by [other] branches,' Morrison, and, second, that no provision of law 'impermissibly threatens the institutional integrity of the Judicial Branch.'

"[Petitioner] argues that the Act suffers from each of these constitutional infirmities. He argues that Congress [effected] an unconstitutional accumulation of power within the Judicial Branch while at the same time undermining the Judiciary's independence and integrity. Specifically, petitioner claims [that] Congress unconstitutionally has required the [Judicial] Branch, and individual Article III judges, to exercise not only their judicial authority, but legislative authority—the making of sentencing policy—as well. At the same time, petitioner asserts, Congress unconstitutionally eroded the integrity and independence of the Judiciary by requiring Article III judges to sit on the Commission, by requiring that those judges share their rulemaking authority with nonjudges, and by subjecting the Commission's members to appointment and removal by the President. [Although] the unique composition and responsibilities of the Sentencing Commission give rise to serious concerns about a disruption of the appropriate balance of governmental power among the coordinate Branches, we conclude [that] petitioner's fears for the fundamental structural protections of the Constitution prove, at least in this case, to be 'more smoke than fire,' and do not compel us to invalidate Congress' considered scheme for resolving the seemingly intractable dilemma of excessive disparity in criminal sentencing.

"[The] Sentencing Commission unquestionably is a peculiar institution within the framework of our Government. Our constitutional principles of separated powers are not violated, however, by mere anomaly or innovation. [Congress's] decision to create an independent rulemaking body to promulgate sentencing guidelines and to locate that body within the Judicial Branch is not unconstitutional unless Congress has vested in the Commission powers that are more appropriately performed by the other Branches or that undermine the integrity of the Judiciary. [As] a general principle, we stated [that] 'executive or administrative duties of a nonjudicial nature may not be imposed on judges holding office under Article III of the Constitution.' [Morrison.] Nonetheless, we have recognized significant exceptions to this general rule and have approved the assumption of some nonadjudicatory activities by the Judicial Branch. [That] judicial rulemaking, at least with respect to some subjects, falls within [a] twilight area is no longer an issue for dispute. None of our cases indicate that rulemaking per se is a function that may not be performed by an entity within the [Judicial Branch]. In light of this precedent and practice, we can discern no separation-of-powers impediment to the placement of the Sentencing Commission within the Judicial Branch.

"[Petitioner also] urges us to strike down the Act on the ground that its requirement of judicial participation on the Commission unconstitutionally conscripts individual federal judges for political service and thereby undermines the essential impartiality of the Judicial Branch. We find Congress' requirement of judicial service somewhat troublesome, but we do not believe that the Act impermissibly interferes with the functioning of the Judiciary. [The] principle of separation of powers does not absolutely prohibit Article III judges from serving on commissions such as that created by the Act. The judges serve on the Sentencing Commission not pursuant to their status and authority as Article III judges, but solely because of their appointment by the President as the Act directs. Such power as these judges wield as Commissioners is not judicial power; it is administrative power derived from the enabling legislation. [The] Constitution, at least as a per se matter, does not forbid judges from wearing two hats; it merely forbids them from wearing both hats at the same time. [That] the Constitution does not absolutely prohibit a federal judge from assuming extrajudicial duties does not mean that every extrajudicial service would be compatible with, or appropriate to, continuing service on the bench; nor does it mean that Congress may require a federal judge to assume extrajudicial duties as long as the judge is assigned those duties in an individual, not judicial, capacity. The ultimate inquiry remains whether a particular extrajudicial assignment undermines the integrity of the Judicial Branch. [We] cannot see how the service of federal judges on the Commission will have a constitutionally significant practical effect on the operation of the Judicial Branch."

In dissent, Justice SCALIA insisted that "I can find no place within our constitutional system for an agency created by Congress to exercise no governmental power other than the making of laws." Although he agreed with the Courts' rejection of the unconstitutional delegation attack, he added: "Precisely because the scope of delegation is largely uncontrollable by the courts, we must be particularly rigorous in preserving the Constitution's structural restrictions that deter excessive delegation. The major one [is] that the power to make law cannot be exercised by anyone other than Congress, except in conjunction with the lawful exercise of executive or judicial power. [A] pure delegation of legislative power is precisely what we have before us. It is irrelevant whether the standards are adequate, because they are not standards related to the exercise of executive or judicial powers; they are, plainly and simply, standards for further legislation. [Today's] decision may aptly be described as the Humphrey's Executor of the Judicial Branch, and I think we will live to regret it." He concluded with a more general criticism of "the regrettable tendency of our recent separation-of-powers jurisprudence to treat the Constitution as though it were no more than a generalized prescription that the functions of the Branches should not be commingled too much—how much is too much to be determined, case-by-case, by this Court. The Constitution is not that. Rather, [it] is a prescribed structure, a framework, for the conduct of government. [I] think the Court errs [not] so much because it mistakes the degree of commingling, but because it fails to recognize that this case is not about commingling, but about the creation of a new branch altogether, a sort of junior-varsity

Congress. [In] the long run the improvisation of a constitutional structure on the basis of currently perceived utility will be disastrous."

While the U.S. Sentencing Commission survived constitutional challenge in Mistretta, the Commission's ability to establish mandatory "Guidelines" ranges that bound federal judges ultimately would not. In **United States v. Booker**, 543 U.S. 220 (2005), the Court rendered the Guidelines advisory rather than mandatory in order to remedy the scheme's infringement of the Sixth Amendment right to a jury trial. The Guidelines continue to hold great sway, however, as sentencing judges are required to consider them, while appellate courts may apply a presumption of reasonableness to any within-Guidelines sentence. See Rita v. United States, 551 U.S. 338 (2007).

3. ***Multiple layers of tenure protection.*** In **Free Enterprise Fund v. Public Company Accounting Oversight Board**, 561 U.S. 477 (2010) the Court departed from the flexible, functionalist approach of Morrison and Mistretta and struck down a 'for cause' restriction on the presidential removal power for the first time. Established as part of a series of accounting reforms in the Sarbanes-Oxley Act of 2002, the Public Company Accounting Oversight Board is composed of five members appointed by the Securities and Exchange Commission (SEC), which is required by statute to be bipartisan. The Board has broad authority to inspect and investigate private accounting firms and impose sanctions against them. The SEC may remove Board members only for "good cause," and the President may remove SEC Commissioners only for "inefficiency, neglect of duty, or malfeasance in office."

In a 5–4 decision invalidating the removal provision as violating the separation of powers, Chief Justice ROBERTS wrote for the Court, joined by Justices Scalia, Kennedy, Thomas and Alito: "We have previously [e.g., in Humphrey's Executor and Morrison] upheld limited restrictions on the President's removal power. In those cases, however, only one level of protected tenure separated the President from an officer exercising executive power. It was the President—or a subordinate he could remove at will—who decided whether the officer's conduct merited removal under the good-cause standard. The Act before us does something quite different. It not only protects Board members from removal except for good cause, but withdraws from the President any decision on whether that good cause exists. That decision is vested instead in other tenured officers—the Commissioners—none of whom is subject to the President's direct control. The result is a Board that is not accountable to the President, and a President who is not responsible for the Board.

"The added layer of tenure protection makes a difference. Without a layer of insulation between the Commission and the Board, the Commission could remove a Board member at any time, and therefore would be fully responsible for what the Board does. The President could then hold the Commission to account for its supervision of the Board, to the same extent that he may hold the Commission to account for everything else it does. A second level of tenure protection changes the nature of the President's review. Now the Commission cannot remove a Board member at will. The President therefore cannot hold the Commission fully accountable for the Board's conduct, to the same extent that he may hold the Commission accountable for everything else that it does. The Commissioners are not responsible for the Board's actions. They are only responsible for their own determination of whether the Act's rigorous good-cause standard is met. And even if the President disagrees with their determination, he is powerless to intervene—unless that determination is so unreasonable as to constitute 'inefficiency, neglect of duty, or malfeasance in office.' This novel structure does not merely add to the Board's independence, but transforms it. Neither the President, nor anyone directly responsible to him, nor even an officer whose conduct he may review only for good cause, has full control over the Board. The President is stripped of the power our precedents have preserved, and his ability to execute the laws—by holding his subordinates accountable for their conduct—is impaired. That arrangement is contrary to Article II's vesting of the executive power in the President." The majority found the invalid removal provisions severable, excising them and leaving Board members removable by the SEC at will while leaving the rest of Sarbanes-Oxley intact.

Justice BREYER filed a dissent joined by Justices Stevens, Ginsburg and Sotomayor: "In Myers, the Court invalidated—for the first and only time—a congressional statute on the ground that it unduly limited the President's authority to remove an Executive Branch official. But soon thereafter the Court expressly disapproved most of Myers' broad reasoning. See Humphrey's Executor. [The] Court has since said that 'the essence of the decision in Myers' [was] the judgment that the Constitution prevents Congress from 'draw[ing] to itself . . . the power to remove or the right to participate in the exercise of that power.' Morrison. [Congress] has not granted itself any role in removing the members of the Accounting Board. [When] previously deciding this kind of nontextual question, the Court has emphasized the importance of examining how a particular provision, taken in context, is likely to function. [E.g., Steel Seizure.] It is not surprising that the Court in these circumstances has looked to function and context, and not to bright-line rules. For one thing, that approach embodies the intent of the Framers. As Chief Justice Marshall long ago observed, our Constitution is fashioned so as to allow the three coordinate branches, including this Court, to exercise practical judgment in response to changing conditions and 'exigencies.' McCulloch. For another, a functional approach permits Congress and the President the flexibility needed to adapt statutory law to changing circumstances.

"[The] 'for cause' restriction before us will not restrict presidential power significantly. For one thing, the restriction directly limits, not the President's power, but the power of an already independent agency. [The] statute provides the Commission with full authority and virtually comprehensive control over all of the Board's functions. [The] Commission's control over the Board's investigatory and legal functions is virtually absolute. Moreover, the Commission [controls] the Board's budget, [can] assign to the Board any 'duties or functions' that it 'determines are necessary or appropriate,' [and] has full 'oversight and enforcement authority over the Board,' including the authority to inspect the Board's activities whenever it believes it 'appropriate' to do so. [Everyone] concedes that the President's control over the Commission is constitutionally sufficient. See Humphrey's Executor. And if the President's control over the Commission is sufficient, and the Commission's control over the Board is virtually absolute, then, as a practical matter, the President's control over the Board should prove sufficient as well. [This] Court has long recognized the appropriateness of using 'for cause' provisions to protect the personal independence of those who [engage] in adjudicatory functions. Humphrey's Executor. Moreover, in addition to their adjudicative functions, the Accounting Board members supervise, and are themselves, technical professional experts. This Court has recognized [the] constitutional legitimacy of a justification that rests agency independence upon the need for technical expertise. Humphrey's Executor. [Congress] and the President could reasonably have thought it prudent to insulate the adjudicative Board members from fear of purely politically based removal."

4. ***Leadership structure of independent agencies.*** In **PHH Corp. v. Consumer Financial Protection Bureau**, 881 F.3d 75 (D.C. Cir. 2018) (en banc), the D.C. Circuit upheld, by a 7–3 vote, the single-director structure of the Consumer Financial Protection Bureau (CFPB), reversing a 3-judge panel that ruled it unconstitutional. The court determined that, consistent with Humphrey's Executor and its progeny, "shielding the Director of the CFPB from removal without cause is consistent with Article II." The fact that the CFPB, unique among independent agencies, is headed by a single director rather than a multi-member body was of no constitutional consequence. In dissent, then-Judge Kavanaugh, who authored the panel decision, wrote that the statutory structure was inconsistent with historical practice, posed a "serious threat to individual liberty" and substantially diminished presidential authority in violation of Article II. The en banc ruling in favor of the CFPB was not appealed to the Supreme Court.

SECTION 5. EXECUTIVE PRIVILEGES, IMMUNITIES AND CONGRESS'S POWER OF IMPEACHMENT

The text of Article I specifies that Members of Congress are "privileged from Arrest during their attendance at the Sessions of their respective Houses, and in going to and returning from the same," and that "for any speech or Debate in either House, they shall not be questioned in any Other Place," Art. I, § 6, cl.1. In contrast, the text of Article II specifies no privileges or immunities for the President or members of the Executive Branch. Nonetheless, the courts have developed implied executive privileges and immunities from the structure of the Constitution and analogies to common law.

A key statement of the scope and limits of executive privilege arose from the 1974 denouement of the Watergate controversy that grew out of a botched burglary at Democratic National Headquarters during the 1972 presidential campaign, by employees of President Nixon's re-election committee. After investigations by a Senate Select Committee disclosed White House involvement in the planning and cover-up of the burglary, President Nixon authorized the appointment of a Special Prosecutor. A federal grand jury indicted seven associates of President Nixon for conspiracy to obstruct justice and other offenses relating to the Watergate burglary and named the President as an unindicted co-conspirator. The District Court, upon motion of the Special Prosecutor, issued a subpoena to the President requiring him to produce certain tapes and documents. He released edited transcripts of some conversations but moved to quash the subpoena, claiming executive privilege. The District Court denied the motion, and the Supreme Court granted certiorari before judgment by the court of appeals. The Court granted and heard the case with exceptional speed, even though the House Judiciary Committee was considering Articles of Impeachment against President Nixon. (For criticism of the Court's haste, see Gunther, "Judicial Hegemony and Legislative Autonomy: The Nixon Case and the Impeachment Process," 22 UCLA L. Rev. 30 (1974).)

The Supreme Court upheld denial of the President's claim of executive privilege in an opinion by Nixon's own appointee, Chief Justice Warren Burger, that made President Nixon's resignation in August 1974 all but inevitable as the tape recordings he finally produced revealed damaging conversations:

United States v. Nixon

418 U.S. 683, 94 S. Ct. 3090, 41 L. Ed. 2d 1039 (1974).

■ CHIEF JUSTICE BURGER delivered the opinion of the Court.

This litigation presents for review the denial of a motion, filed [on] behalf of the [President] in the case of United States v. Mitchell et al., to quash a third-party subpoena duces tecum issued by the [District Court] pursuant to Fed. R. Crim. Proc. 17(c). The subpoena directed the President to produce certain tape recordings and documents relating to his conversations with aides and advisers. The court rejected the President's claims of absolute executive privilege, of lack of jurisdiction, and of failure to satisfy the requirements of [Rule 17(c)]. [W]e turn to the claim that the subpoena should be quashed because it demands "confidential conversations between a President and his close advisors that it would be inconsistent with the public interest to produce." [The] President's counsel [reads] the Constitution as providing an absolute privilege of confidentiality for all Presidential communications. [In] support of his claim of absolute privilege, the President's counsel urges two [grounds]: the need to protect the confidentiality of executive communications, and the implications of the separation of powers structure.

[After noting the importance of confidentiality, Chief Justice Burger continued:] [I]t is argued that the independence of the Executive Branch within its own sphere insulates a President from a judicial subpoena in an ongoing criminal prosecution, and thereby protects confidential Presidential communications. However, neither the doctrine of separation of powers, nor the need for confidentiality of high level communications, without more, can sustain an absolute, unqualified Presidential privilege of immunity from judicial process under all circumstances. The President's need for complete candor and objectivity from advisers calls for great deference from the courts. However, when the privilege depends solely on the broad, undifferentiated claim of public interest in the confidentiality of such conversations, a confrontation with other values arises. Absent a claim of need to protect military, diplomatic, or sensitive national security secrets, we find it difficult to accept the argument that even the very important interest in confidentiality of Presidential communications is significantly diminished by production of such material for in camera inspection with all the protection that a district court will be obliged to provide. [To] read the Art. II powers of the President as providing an absolute privilege as against a subpoena essential to enforcement of criminal statutes on no more than a generalized claim of the public interest in confidentiality of non-military and nondiplomatic discussions would upset the constitutional balance of "a workable government" and gravely impair the role of the courts under Art. III.

[After articulating justifications for a "presumptive privilege for Presidential communications," a privilege "inextricably rooted in the separation of powers," Chief Justice Burger continued:] But this presumptive privilege must be considered in light of our historic commitment to the rule of law. This is nowhere more profoundly manifest than in our view that "the twofold aim [of criminal justice] is that guilt shall not escape or innocence suffer." [The] need to develop all relevant facts in the adversary system is both fundamental and comprehensive. [To] ensure that justice is done, it is imperative to the function of courts that compulsory process be available for the production of evidence needed either by the prosecution or by the defense. [Evidentiary privileges] are designed to protect weighty and legitimate competing interests [e.g., self-incrimination, attorney, and priest privileges] [and] are not lightly created nor expansively construed, for they are in derogation of the search for truth.

In this case the President challenges a subpoena served on him as a third party requiring the production of materials for use in a criminal prosecution; he does so on the claim that he has a privilege against disclosure of confidential communications. He does not place his claim of privilege on the ground they are military or diplomatic secrets. As to these areas of Art. II duties the courts have traditionally shown the utmost deference to presidential responsibilities. [No] case of the Court, however, has extended this high degree of deference to a President's generalized interest in confidentiality. Nowhere in the Constitution [is] there any explicit reference to a privilege of confidentiality, yet to the extent this interest relates to the effective discharge of a President's powers, it is constitutionally based. The right to the production of all evidence at a criminal trial similarly has constitutional [dimensions].

In this case we must weigh the importance of the general privilege of confidentiality of Presidential communications in performance of his responsibilities against the inroads of such a privilege on the fair administration of criminal justice.[1] The interest in preserving confidentiality is weighty indeed and entitled to great respect. However, we cannot conclude that advisers will be moved to temper the candor of their remarks by the infrequent occasions of disclosure because of the possibility that such conversations will be called for in the context of a criminal prosecution. On the other hand, the allowance of the privilege to withhold evidence that is demonstrably relevant in a criminal trial would cut deeply into the guarantee of due process of law and gravely impair the basic function of the courts. A President's acknowledged need for confidentiality in the communications of his office is general in nature, whereas the constitutional need for production of relevant evidence in a criminal proceeding is specific and central to the fair adjudication of a particular criminal [case]. Without access to specific facts a criminal prosecution may be totally frustrated. The President's broad interest in confidentiality of communications will not be

1 We are not here concerned with the balance between the President's generalized interest in confidentiality and the need for relevant evidence in civil litigation, nor with that between the confidentiality interest and congressional demands for information, nor with the President's interest in preserving state secrets. We address only the conflict between the President's assertion of a generalized privilege of confidentiality against the constitutional need for relevant evidence in criminal trials. [Footnote by Chief Justice Burger.]

vitiated by disclosure of a limited number of conversations preliminarily shown to have some bearing on the pending criminal cases. We conclude that when the ground for asserting privilege as to subpoenaed materials sought for use in a criminal trial is based only on the generalized interest in confidentiality, it cannot prevail over the fundamental demands of due process of law in the fair administration of [criminal justice].

If a President concludes that compliance with a subpoena would be injurious to the public interest he may properly, as was done here, invoke a claim of privilege on the return of the subpoena. Upon receiving a claim of privilege from the Chief Executive, it became the further duty of the District Court to treat the subpoenaed material as presumptively privileged and to require the Special Prosecutor to demonstrate that the Presidential material was "essential to the justice of the [pending criminal] case."[2]

[We] affirm the order of the District Court.

THE SCOPE AND LIMITS OF EXECUTIVE PRIVILEGE

1. ***Presidential and other executive officials' amenability to judicial process.*** President Nixon claimed that the President was not amenable to judicial process and that impeachment and removal were preconditions to judicial proceedings against him. The decision clearly rejected Nixon's claim that he was immune from judicial process while in office. That question had long been in doubt, especially because of the Court's ruling in Mississippi v. Johnson, 71 U.S. (4 Wall.) 475 (1867), where the Court refused to entertain a suit attempting to enjoin President Andrew Johnson's enforcement of the Reconstruction Act, emphasizing the difficulties of enforcement and the availability of impeachment.

2. ***The scope of executive privilege.*** In the Nixon case, the Court ruled both that the President was subject to court orders issued in the course of a criminal proceeding and that his presumptive executive privilege did not bar compliance with the subpoena. Did the Court jump too quickly from its view that the President was amenable to judicial process to its conclusions that it was for the *courts* to decide the content of executive privilege? See Gunther, "Judicial Hegemony and Legislative Autonomy: The Nixon Case and the Impeachment Process," 22 UCLA L. Rev. 30 (1974) (arguing that it was possible to hold President Nixon amenable to judicial process but autonomous in determining the scope of executive privilege).

Note that assertions of presidential privilege may be subject to a strong political check. Relying on the privilege to shield communications from those investigating wrongdoing may cost the President significant political capital in Congress, and may negatively affect his public support. Does this suggest that judicial intervention to limit executive privilege claims is unnecessary?

Are claims of executive privilege stronger when asserted against congressional investigations than when asserted, as in Nixon, against subpoenas in criminal proceedings? Administrations since George Washington's have claimed that they may refuse to turn over information to

---

[2] Here and elsewhere in the opinion, Chief Justice Burger cited and quoted from the Aaron Burr treason trial in the early 19th century (in which John Marshall, sitting on the Circuit Court, issued a subpoena to President Thomas Jefferson). See United States v. Burr, 25 F. Cas. 187 (No. 14,694) (1807).

the legislative branch, and Congress has repeatedly denied the constitutional justifications for such a privilege. While the Nixon decision rejected the President's claim to an absolute privilege, it recognized a qualified "presumptive" privilege. Is congressional oversight power weighty enough to override an executive privilege claim? Is it comparable to the quasi-constitutional interest in the "fair administration of criminal justice"?

How widely should executive privilege extend? Does it shield only the President, or extend to those around him as well? To senior officers? How senior? To the First Lady? Can it be supplemented by other privileges? During the Clinton administration, claims of privilege for those around the President were litigated several times. See, e.g., In re Sealed Case, 148 F.3d 1073 (D.C.Cir.1998) (holding that federal evidence law does not support a "protective function privilege" for Secret Service agents assigned by law to protect the President). The Supreme Court denied certiorari in the case, but Justice Breyer's dissent from the denial of certiorari argued that the Supreme Court should have taken the case to decide whether the fact that "[t]he Constitution vests the entire 'Power' of one branch of Government in [the] 'President' " justifies a "special governmental privilege [needed] to help avert" the "national calamity" of "serious physical harm to the President." 525 U.S. 990 (1998) (Breyer, J. dissenting from denial of certiorari). Note one difficulty for those who would expand executive privilege: if the function of the privilege is to maintain the integrity of the executive branch, and if the negative effects of assertions of the privilege (such as denial or delay of due process to private citizens, or impediments to law enforcement, or constrictions on the investigatory functions of the legislature) are deemed necessary because of the importance of presidential privacy, then why not forbid the President and his inner circle from disclosing secrets even voluntarily?

3. ***Presidential immunity from civil damages liability for official actions.*** Eight years after the Nixon case, the Court announced an absolute presidential immunity from civil liability under some circumstances. The 5–4 decision in **Nixon v. Fitzgerald**, 457 U.S. 731 (1982), held that "the President is absolutely [rather than qualifiedly] immune from civil damages liability for his official acts"—at least "in the absence of explicit affirmative action by Congress." Fitzgerald, a widely publicized "whistle blower" of the late 1960s, lost his position with the Department of the Air Force in 1970. He was fired, he claimed, because of his widely publicized testimony before a congressional subcommittee. Fitzgerald's damage action claimed violation of his First Amendment and statutory rights, and the named defendants included former President Nixon as well as other officials.

In finding absolute civil damages immunity, Justice POWELL's majority opinion emphasized the President's "unique position in the constitutional scheme." He stressed that protecting the President from such suits would avoid rendering him "unduly cautious in the discharge of his official duties." He also suggested that, "[b]ecause of the singular importance of the President's duties, diversion of his energies by concern with private lawsuits would raise unique risks to the effective functioning of government. As is the case with prosecutors and judges—for whom absolute immunity now is established—a President must concern himself with matters likely to 'arouse the most intense feelings.' [In] view of the visibility of his office and the effect of his actions on countless people, the President would be an easily identifiable target for suits for civil damages. Cognizance of this personal vulnerability frequently could distract a President from his public duties, to the detriment not only of the President and his office but also the [Nation]."

Justice Powell added: "A rule of absolute immunity for the President will not leave the nation without sufficient protection against misconduct on the part of the chief executive. There remains the constitutional remedy of impeachment. In addition, there are formal and informal checks on Presidential action that do not apply with equal force to other executive officials. The President is subjected to constant scrutiny by the press. Vigilant oversight by Congress also may serve to deter Presidential abuses of [office]. Other incentives to avoid misconduct may include a desire to earn re-election, the need to maintain prestige as an element of Presidential influence, and a President's traditional concern for his historical stature. The existence of alternative remedies and deterrents establishes that absolute immunity will not place the President 'above the law.'"

Justice WHITE, joined by Justices Brennan, Marshall and Blackmun, dissented: "Attaching absolute immunity to the office of the President, rather than to particular activities that the President might perform, places the President above the law. It is a reversion to the old notion that the King can do no wrong." He would have held that the "scope of immunity is determined by function, not office. [The] only question that must be answered here is whether the dismissal of employees falls within a constitutionally assigned executive function, the performance of which would be substantially impaired by the possibility of a private action for damages. I believe it does not." (In a companion ruling, the Court refused to extend the absolute presidential immunity to the President's senior aides, although such persons are entitled to qualified immunity. Harlow v. Fitzgerald, 457 U.S. 800 (1982).)

4. ***Presidential immunity from civil damages liability for unofficial actions.*** Does the immunity provided to the President in Fitzgerald for official actions extend to lawsuits brought while he was in office but for his actions prior to assuming office? In the decision below, the Court refused to expand Nixon v. Fitzgerald to protect a sitting President, during his time in office, even temporarily from judicial process with respect to his unofficial acts:

Clinton v. Jones

520 U.S. 681, 117 S. Ct. 1636, 137 L. Ed. 2d 945 (1997).

■ JUSTICE STEVENS delivered the opinion of the Court.

This case raises a constitutional and a prudential question concerning the Office of the President of the United States. Respondent, a private citizen, seeks to recover damages from the current occupant of that office based on actions allegedly taken before his term began. The President submits that in all but the most exceptional cases the Constitution requires federal courts to defer such litigation until his term ends and that, in any event, respect for the office warrants such a stay. Despite the force of the arguments supporting the President's submissions, we conclude that they must be rejected.

Petitioner, William Jefferson Clinton, was elected to the Presidency in 1992, and re-elected in 1996. His term of office expires on January 20, 2001. In 1991 he was the Governor of the State of Arkansas. On May 6, 1994, [respondent Paula Corbin Jones] commenced this action in the United States District Court for the Eastern District of Arkansas by filing a complaint naming petitioner as [a] defendant. [As] the case comes to us, we are required to assume the truth of the detailed—but as yet untested—factual allegations in the complaint.

Those allegations principally describe events that are said to have occurred on the afternoon of May 8, 1991, during an official conference held at the Excelsior Hotel in Little Rock, Arkansas. The Governor delivered a speech at the conference; respondent—working as a state employee—staffed the registration desk. She alleges that [a state trooper also named in the complaint] persuaded her to leave her desk and to visit the Governor in a business suite at the hotel, where he made "abhorrent" sexual advances that she vehemently rejected. She further claims that her superiors at work subsequently dealt with her in a hostile and rude manner, and changed her duties to punish her for rejecting those advances. Respondent seeks actual damages of $75,000, and punitive damages of $100,000. Her complaint [alleges deprivation and conspiracy to deprive her of federal civil rights under color of state law, and state-law torts of intentional infliction of emotional distress and defamation.] Inasmuch as the legal sufficiency of the claims has not yet been challenged, we assume, without deciding, that each [count] states a cause of action as a matter of law. [Excepting defamation, the] alleged misconduct of petitioner was unrelated to any of his official duties as President of the United States and, indeed, occurred before he was elected to that office.

In response to the complaint, petitioner [filed] a motion to dismiss on grounds of Presidential immunity, and requested the court to defer all other pleadings and motions until after the immunity issue was resolved. [The] District Judge denied the motion to dismiss on immunity grounds and ruled that discovery in the case could go forward, but ordered any trial stayed until the end of petitioner's Presidency. [Both] parties appealed. A divided panel of the Court of Appeals affirmed the denial of the motion to dismiss, but because it regarded the order postponing the trial until the President leaves office as the "functional equivalent" of a grant of temporary immunity, it reversed that order.

[The President's] principal submission—that "in all but the most exceptional cases," the Constitution affords the President temporary immunity from civil damages litigation arising out of events that occurred before he took office—cannot be sustained on the basis of precedent. [The] principal rationale for affording certain public servants immunity from suits for money damages arising out of their official acts is inapplicable to unofficial conduct. In cases involving prosecutors, legislators, and judges we have repeatedly explained that the immunity serves the public interest in enabling such officials to perform their designated functions effectively without fear that a particular decision may give rise to personal liability. [That] rationale provided the principal basis for our holding that a former President of the United States was "entitled to absolute immunity from damages liability predicated on his official acts," Nixon v. Fitzgerald. Our central concern was to avoid rendering the President "unduly cautious in the discharge of his official duties."[1]

This reasoning provides no support for an immunity for unofficial conduct. As we explained in Fitzgerald, "the sphere of protected action must be related closely to the immunity's justifying purposes." Because of the President's broad responsibilities, we recognized in that case an immunity from damages claims arising out of official acts extending to the "outer perimeter of his authority." But we have never suggested that the President, or any other official, has an immunity that extends beyond the scope of any action taken in an official capacity. [As] our opinions have made clear, immunities are grounded in "the nature of the function performed, not the identity of the actor who performed it."

[The President's] strongest argument supporting his immunity claim is based on the text and structure of the Constitution. He does not contend that the occupant of the Office of the President is "above the law," in the sense that his conduct is entirely immune from judicial scrutiny. The President argues merely for a postponement of the judicial proceedings that will determine whether he violated any law. His argument is grounded in the character of the office that was created by Article II of the Constitution, and relies on separation of powers principles that have structured our constitutional arrangement since the founding. [The President] contends that he occupies a unique office with powers and responsibilities so vast and important that the public interest demands that he devote his undivided time and attention to his public duties. He submits that—given the nature of the office—the doctrine of separation of powers places limits on the authority of the Federal Judiciary to interfere with the Executive Branch that would be transgressed by allowing this action to proceed.

We have no dispute with the initial premise of the argument. [It] does not follow, however, that separation of powers principles would be violated by allowing this action to proceed. [There] is no suggestion that the Federal Judiciary is being asked to perform any function that might in some way be described as "executive." [Nor is there any] possibility that the decision will curtail the scope of the official powers of the Executive Branch. Rather [petitioner] contends that—as a by-product of an otherwise traditional exercise of judicial power—[this case] as well as the potential additional litigation that an affirmance [here] might spawn may impose an unacceptable burden on the President's time and energy, and thereby impair the effective performance of his office.

Petitioner's predictive judgment finds little support in either history or the relatively narrow compass of the issues raised in this particular case. [In] the more than 200-year history of the Republic, only three sitting Presidents

---

[1] [In] Fitzgerald [we noted] that "because of the singular importance of the President's duties, diversion of his energies by concern with private lawsuits would raise unique risks to the effective functioning of government," and suggested further that "cognizance of . . . personal vulnerability frequently could distract a President from his public duties." [The President] argues that in this aspect the Court's concern was parallel to the issue he suggests is of great importance in this case, the possibility that a sitting President might be distracted by the need to participate in litigation during the pendency of his office. In context, however, it is clear that our dominant concern was with the diversion of the President's attention during the decisionmaking process caused by needless worry as to the possibility of damages actions stemming from any particular official decision. [Footnote by Justice Stevens.]

have been subjected to suits for their private actions.[2] If the past is any indicator, it seems unlikely that a deluge of such litigation will ever engulf the Presidency. As for the case at hand, if properly managed by the District Court, it appears to us highly unlikely to occupy any substantial amount of petitioner's time.

[The] fact that a federal court's exercise of its traditional Article III jurisdiction may significantly burden the time and attention of the Chief Executive is not sufficient to establish a violation of the Constitution. [We] have long held that when the President takes official action, the Court has the authority to determine whether he has acted within the law. Perhaps the most dramatic example of such a case is our holding that President Truman exceeded his constitutional authority when he issued an order directing the Secretary of Commerce to take possession of and operate most of the Nation's steel mills in order to avert a national catastrophe. Youngstown. [It] is also settled that the President is subject to judicial process in appropriate circumstances. Although Thomas Jefferson apparently thought otherwise, Chief Justice Marshall, when presiding in the treason trial of Aaron Burr, ruled that a subpoena duces tecum could be directed to the President. United States v. Burr, 25 F. Cas. 30 (No. 14,692d) (CC Va. 1807). We unequivocally and emphatically endorsed Marshall's position when we held that President Nixon was obligated to comply with a subpoena commanding him to produce certain tape recordings of his conversations with his aides. United States v. Nixon.

[In] sum, "it is settled law that the separation-of-powers doctrine does not bar every exercise of jurisdiction over the President of the United States." Fitzgerald. If the Judiciary may severely burden the Executive Branch by reviewing the legality of the President's official conduct, and if it may direct appropriate process to the President himself, it must follow that the federal courts have power to determine the legality of his unofficial conduct. The burden on the President's time and energy that is a mere by-product of such review surely cannot be considered as onerous as the direct burden imposed by judicial review and the occasional invalidation of his official actions. We therefore hold that the doctrine of separation of powers does not require federal courts to stay all private actions against the President until he leaves office.

We add a final comment on [the] risk that our decision will generate a large volume of politically motivated harassing and frivolous litigation, and the danger that national security concerns might prevent the President from explaining a legitimate need for a continuance. We are not persuaded that either of these risks is serious. Most frivolous and vexatious litigation is terminated at the pleading stage or on summary judgment, with little if any personal involvement by the defendant. Moreover, the availability of sanctions provides a significant deterrent to litigation directed at the President in his unofficial capacity for purposes of political gain or harassment. History indicates that the likelihood that a significant number of such cases will be filed is remote. Although scheduling problems may arise, there is no reason to assume that the District Courts will be either unable to accommodate the President's needs or unfaithful to the tradition—especially

[2] Complaints against the pre-presidential conduct of Theodore Roosevelt and Harry Truman were dismissed before they took office, and two cases against John F. Kennedy involving an auto accident during the 1960 Presidential campaign were settled after he took office.

in matters involving national security—of giving "the utmost deference to Presidential responsibilities." Several Presidents, including petitioner, have given testimony without jeopardizing the Nation's security. In short, we have confidence in the ability of our federal judges to deal with both of these concerns. If Congress deems it appropriate to afford the President stronger protection, it may respond with appropriate legislation.

[The] Federal District Court has jurisdiction to decide this case. Like every other citizen who properly invokes that jurisdiction, respondent has a right to an orderly disposition of her claims. [Affirmed.]

■ JUSTICE BREYER, concurring in the judgment.

I agree with the majority that the Constitution does not automatically grant the President an immunity from civil lawsuits based upon his private conduct. Nor does the "doctrine of separation of powers . . . require federal courts to stay" virtually "all private actions against the President until he leaves office." [To] obtain a postponement the President must "bear the burden of establishing its need." In my view, however, once the President sets forth and explains a conflict between judicial proceeding and public duties, [the] Constitution permits a judge to schedule a trial in an ordinary civil damages action [only] within the constraints of a constitutional principle [that] forbids a federal judge in such a case to interfere with the President's discharge of his public duties. I have no doubt that the Constitution contains such a principle applicable to civil suits, based upon Article II's vesting of the entire "executive Power" in a single individual, implemented through the Constitution's structural separation of powers, and revealed both by history and case precedent.

[The] Constitution states that the "executive Power shall be vested in a President." Art. II, § 1. This constitutional delegation means that a sitting President is unusually busy, that his activities have an unusually important impact upon the lives of others, and that his conduct embodies an authority bestowed by the entire American electorate. He (along with his constitutionally subordinate Vice President) is the only official for whom the entire Nation votes, and is the only elected officer to represent the entire Nation both domestically and abroad. [Article] II makes a single President responsible for the actions of the Executive Branch in much the same way that the entire Congress is responsible for the actions of the Legislative Branch, or the entire Judiciary for those of the Judicial Branch. [The Founders decided] to vest Executive authority in one person rather than several [in order] to focus, rather than to spread, Executive responsibility thereby facilitating accountability. They also sought to encourage energetic, vigorous, decisive, and speedy execution of the laws by placing in the hands of a single, constitutionally indispensable, individual the ultimate authority that, in respect to the other branches, the Constitution divides among many.

[For] present purposes, this constitutional structure means that the President is not like Congress, for Congress can function as if it were whole, even when up to half of its members are absent, [and] that the President is not like the Judiciary, for judges often can designate other judges [to] sit even should an entire court be detained by personal litigation. It means that, unlike Congress, which is regularly out of session, the President never adjourns. More importantly, these constitutional objectives explain why a President, though able to delegate duties to others, cannot delegate ultimate responsibility or the active obligation to supervise that goes with it. And the related constitutional equivalence between President, Congress, and the

Judiciary, means that judicial scheduling orders in a private civil case must not only take reasonable account of, say, a particularly busy schedule, or a job on which others critically depend, or an underlying electoral mandate. They must also reflect the fact that interference with a President's ability to carry out his public responsibilities is constitutionally equivalent to interference with the ability of the entirety of Congress, or the Judicial Branch, to carry out their public obligations.

[It is true that in] several instances sitting Presidents have given depositions or testified at criminal trials, and [this] Court has twice authorized the enforcement of subpoenas seeking documents from a sitting President for use in a criminal case. I agree with the majority that these precedents reject any absolute Presidential immunity from all court process. But they do not cast doubt upon Justice Story's basic conclusion that "in civil cases," a sitting President "possesses an official inviolability" as necessary to permit him to "perform" the duties of his office without "obstruction or impediment." The first set of precedents tells us little about what the Constitution commands, for they amount to voluntary actions on the part of a sitting President. The second set of precedents amounts to a search for documents, rather than a direct call upon Presidential time. More important, both sets of precedents involve criminal proceedings in which the President participated as a witness. Criminal proceedings, unlike private civil proceedings, are public acts initiated and controlled by the Executive Branch, they are not normally subject to postponement, and ordinarily they put at risk, not a private citizen's hope for monetary compensation, but a private citizen's freedom from enforced confinement.

The remaining precedent to which the majority refers does not seem relevant in this case. That precedent, Youngstown, concerns official action. And any Presidential time spent dealing with, or action taken in response to, that kind of case is part of a President's official duties. Hence court review in such circumstances could not interfere with, or distract from, official duties. Insofar as a court orders a President, in any such a proceeding, to act or to refrain from action, it defines, or determines, or clarifies, the legal scope of an official duty. By definition (if the order itself is lawful), it cannot impede, or obstruct, or interfere with, the President's basic task—the lawful exercise of his Executive authority.

[Nixon v. Fitzgerald] strongly supports the principle that judges hearing a private civil damages action against a sitting President may not issue orders that could significantly distract a President from his official duties. [The] Court rested its conclusion in important part upon the fact that civil lawsuits "could distract a President from his public duties, to the detriment of not only the President and his office but also the Nation that the Presidency was designed to serve." [Fitzgerald's] key paragraph, explaining why the President enjoys an absolute immunity rather than a qualified immunity, contains seven sentences, four of which focus primarily upon time and energy distraction and three of which focus primarily upon official decision distortion. Indeed, that key paragraph begins by stating: "Because of the singular importance of the President's duties, diversion of his energies by concern with private lawsuits would raise unique risks to the effective functioning of government." Moreover, the Court, in numerous other cases, has found the problem of time and energy distraction a critically important consideration militating in favor of a grant of immunity.

just make sure it doesn't interfere w/ the presidents duties

[The] majority points to the fact that private plaintiffs have brought civil damage lawsuits against a sitting President only three times in our Nation's history; and it relies upon the threat of sanctions to discourage, and "the court's discretion" to manage, such actions so that "interference with the President's duties would not occur." I am less sanguine. Since 1960, when the last such suit was filed, the number of civil lawsuits filed annually in Federal District Courts has increased from under 60,000 to about 240,000; the number of federal district judges has increased from 233 to about 650; the time and expense associated with both discovery and trial have increased; an increasingly complex economy has led to increasingly complex sets of statutes, rules and regulations, that often create potential liability, with or without fault. And this Court has now made clear that such lawsuits may proceed against a sitting President. The consequence, as the Court warned in Fitzgerald, is that a sitting President, given "the visibility of his office," could well become "an easily identifiable target for suits for civil damages."

THE IMPLICATIONS AND AFTERMATH OF CLINTON V. JONES

1. ***Immunity for official vs. unofficial actions.*** Note that the immunity President Clinton sought in Jones was quite limited—the President was claiming temporary immunity from a civil action concerning unofficial conduct prior to assuming federal office, where speedy resolution of the case was of no particular exigency. To some degree, the Court's decision seems determined by the tyranny-preventing principle that the President cannot be placed "above the law." But might it be argued that the threat of tyranny (and therefore the argument for permitting judicial remedy against the President) is greater when the president's alleged violations concern abuse of official power (as in Nixon v. Fitzgerald, above) than when they involve private wrongdoing? Why, then, is the president immunized in the former case, but not in the latter?

2. ***The dangers of distortion vs. distraction.*** How can Clinton v. Jones be reconciled with Nixon v. Fitzgerald? Note that the case for presidential immunity relies on two very different types of concerns—first, the danger that fear of lawsuits will distort policymaking, and second, the concern that lawsuits will distract the president when he needs to conserve his energy and attention for matters of national importance. Suits regarding the president's private conduct obviously do not pose the danger of distortion. But don't they pose a threat of distraction from official duties? Was the Court correct to assume that the president's expenditure of time and energy on suits concerning his private conduct "surely cannot be [as] onerous as the [burden] imposed by judicial review [of] his official actions"? Does the fact that Jones's civil suit exposed the scandal that led to President Clinton's impeachment suggest that the Court was being unduly optimistic? What of Justice Breyer, who concurred despite expressing concerns that the decision might make the President a target for lawsuits?

Was the Court's decision in Clinton v. Jones justified as safeguarding the individual rights of those with private claims against the president, ensuring the principle that the president, unlike a king, is not above the law? How great a deprivation of this plaintiff's rights would it have been to have delayed her case until the president had left office? Is a categorical rule appropriate, or some sort of case-by-case analysis? Would it have been preferable to have explicitly balanced the plaintiff's interest in a speedy disposition against the president's interest (or the national interest) in avoiding distracting lawsuits? Is this what the decision in effect instructs the trial court to do? How should the plaintiff's individual right be balanced against separation of powers and presidential prerogatives?

3. ***May a sitting president be criminally indicted?*** Consider that, while the Court has immunized presidents and former presidents from personal liability in civil suits for official presidential actions, the Constitution clearly states that an impeached officer remains subject to criminal "Indictment, Trial, Judgment, and Punishment, according to Law." Art I, § 3. There is likewise general agreement that an unimpeached president is subject to prosecution after leaving office. Is the threat of eventual prosecution less constraining to a President than the threat of personal liability? Would this be because political considerations and informal norms can be soundly relied on to restrict criminal prosecution of former Presidents to the most egregious cases of malfeasance? Note that, one month after President Nixon's resignation, President Gerald Ford used his Art. II, § 2 "Power to grant Reprieves and Pardons" in pardoning Nixon for any crimes committed during the latter's Presidency.[1]

While there is widespread agreement that *former* presidents enjoy no special immunity from criminal prosecution, would it be constitutional to indict a *sitting* president? In connection with the independent counsel's investigation of and impeachment referral regarding President Clinton, there was some discussion of the possibility of criminal prosecution of the president, as either a substitute for or a supplement to the impeachment process. There are three possibilities for reducing the impact of indicting a sitting president: publicly indict the president but postpone trial until the expiration of his term; seal the indictment until after the president has left office; or wait to indict the president until after the term of office expires. How should the separation-of-powers concerns with an indictment of a sitting president be balanced against law-enforcement concerns? The office of the Independent Counsel investigating President Clinton apparently took the view that an indictment of a sitting president would be constitutional. See Memorandum from Ronald Rotunda to Kenneth Starr, Indep. Counsel, "Indictability of the President (May 13, 1988). The Office of Legal Counsel has disagreed, concluding in 1973 and reaffirming in 2000 that "the indictment and criminal prosecution of a sitting President would unduly interfere with the ability of the executive branch to perform its

---

[1] Another set of issues regarding control over President Nixon's papers remained in litigation for years. For a review of litigation concerning President Nixon's papers, including a discussion of the historical practices of former Presidents in controlling their papers, see Nixon v. United States, 978 F.2d 1269 (D.C.Cir.1992) (holding that, in restricting Nixon's rights to his presidential papers, the PRMPA effected a taking, for which the Fifth Amendment requires payment of "just compensation"). This litigation ended when the government agreed to pay Nixon's estate $18 million in 2000. The papers of Presidents since Ronald Reagan have been governed by the Presidential Records Act, 44 U.S.C. § 2201 et seq., passed by Congress in 1978, which gives complete "ownership, possession, and control" of presidential records to the United States, and regulates the president's maintenance and disposal of records during his term in office. When a president's term in office ends, the papers are put under the control of the Archivist of the United States. The Act provides for the public availability of most categories of presidential records. Does the Act comport with separation of powers concerns? Does it help to know that the Archivist is appointed by the President (with advice and consent of the Senate), and may be removed by the President with or without cause? See 44 U.S.C. § 2103.

constitutionally assigned duties, and would thus violate the constitutional separation of powers." Memorandum Opinion from Randolph Moss, Assistant Att'y Gen., Office of Legal Counsel, to Janet Reno, Att'y Gen. (Oct. 16, 2000). It is worth noting, however, that other federal officials have been indicted, and even convicted, prior to their impeachments. (See, e.g., the Walter Nixon case above at p. 68). So a president's immunity from indictment while in office would probably have to be founded on the specific needs of the executive branch, and not merely on a restrictive reading of Article I, § 3.

What are the functional differences between relying on *private citizens' civil suits* to punish executive malfeasance, and relying on *criminal trials*? Note that the criminal conviction of a former president would require the acquiescence of two branches of the federal government—the executive (in prosecuting), and the judiciary (in trying). The criminal trial might also involve the legislative branch, in the sense that the trial would be for violation of a law passed by Congress. On the other hand, if Nixon v. Fitzgerald had not granted immunity to the president, a civil suit against the president could be maintained by a private citizen, with the cooperation of the judicial, but neither the executive, nor (if suing under a common law or constitutional cause of action) the legislative branch. The executive branch authority over criminal proceedings exceeds that over civil proceedings in another way—any sitting president has the power to grant a reprieve or pardon to her predecessors, as in the Nixon case discussed above. There is no equivalent authority in the civil realm. Would the Art. II, § 2 power to grant pardons enable a sitting president to pardon himself?

4. ***Impeachment of the president.*** Art. II, § 4, states: "The President, Vice President and all civil Officers of the United States, shall be removed from Office on Impeachment for, and Conviction of, Treason, Bribery, or other high Crimes and Misdemeanors." American experience with presidential impeachments has been sparse. Only two presidents have ever been impeached—in both cases, the Senate then failed to convict. One other president narrowly escaped impeachment, by resigning before the House vote. Most impeachments voted by the House have involved federal judges.

a. *Andrew Johnson.* The nation's first presidential impeachment, was the 1868 impeachment of Andrew Johnson, who had become President on Abraham Lincoln's death. The immediate cause of Johnson's impeachment was his unilateral dismissal of Secretary of War Edwin Stanton, in violation of the Tenure of Office Act. (President Johnson had objected to the Act as an unconstitutional infringement on the executive power; the Act, which required Congressional assent for the President's removal of certain high-level federal officials, was similar to the law that was later struck down in Myers v. United States, p. 412 above.) Johnson was impeached in the House of Representatives by a vote of 126–47. In the Senate trial, presided over by Chief Justice Salmon Chase (in accordance with Art. I, § 3), Johnson escaped conviction and removal by only one vote. See generally Rehnquist, Grand Inquests: The Historical Impeachments of Justice Samuel Chase and President Andrew Johnson 143–248 (1992).

b. *Richard Nixon.* Recall from Nixon v. United States that the proceedings in the House Judiciary Committee during the spring and summer of 1974, considering the impeachment of President Nixon, provoked intense national attention. During consideration of the Nixon impeachment, as in other impeachments, the meaning of the "high Crimes and Misdemeanors" provision was a central source of controversy. What is the scope of that phrase? What presidential misconduct is properly the subject of impeachment proceedings? Must the conduct constitute a criminal offense? If the scope of impeachable offenses is not coextensive with criminality, what acceptable criteria can be stated? President Nixon's counsel claimed that "other high Crimes and Misdemeanors" is limited to serious acts which would be indictable as criminal offenses; the staff of the Judiciary Committee insisted that the impeachment route may reach serious abuses of office or breaches of trust even when they do not constitute criminal acts. The President relied on the text of the Constitution; the staff defended the broader position based on history—both English historical background and evidence regarding the intent of the Framers.

The three Articles of Impeachment adopted by the House Judiciary Committee in late July 1974 followed the approach of the impeachment inquiry staff. Article I, focusing on the Watergate cover-up, concluded that, "[in] all of this, Richard M. Nixon has acted in a manner contrary to his trust as President and subversive of constitutional government." Article II charged that Nixon had "repeatedly engaged in conduct violating the constitutional rights of citizens, impairing the due and proper administration of justice [or] contravening the laws governing the agencies of the executive branch." Article III charged that the President had "willfully disobeyed" (relying on executive privilege) a series of subpoenas issued by the Impeachment Committee. The Committee ultimately voted to impeach on all three Articles. Further proceedings—including a vote by the full House and a trial by the Senate—were abandoned when President Nixon resigned on August 9, 1974, after the release of the most incriminating Watergate tapes in the wake of the Court's ruling in United States v. Nixon.

c. *William Jefferson Clinton*. The only president other than Johnson to have been impeached is William Jefferson Clinton. On December 19, 1998, the House of Representatives passed two Articles of Impeachment, by votes of 228–206 and 221–212. (Two other proposed Articles of Impeachment failed to pass the House.) The Articles alleged that Clinton had "prevented, obstructed and impeded the administration of justice" in the course of discovery during the Clinton v. Jones civil suit, above, and that he had "willfully provided perjurious, false and misleading testimony to [a] grand jury," convened by the independent counsel investigating his conduct in the civil suit. As in previous impeachment controversies, there was extensive argument over the scope of offenses punishable by impeachment. In the end, the Senate vote on each article fell well short of the two-thirds needed to convict.

Once again, advocates on both sides pointed to the constitutional provision for removing the President for "Treason, Bribery, or other high Crimes and Misdemeanors." Art. II, § 4. Does the term "High Crimes and Misdemeanors" refer to a particular subset of criminal acts? Or to a subset of official, delegitimizing acts, whether criminal or not? The President's counsel took two defensive stances. First, they argued that Clinton's alleged misdeeds concerned private matters, not the discharge of his official duties—and that they were therefore not covered by an impeachment procedure that was intended to constrain the President's political misdeeds. Second, since Clinton's attorneys contested the criminality of his acts, some of the President's defenders argued that impeachment was inappropriate except in cases of *criminal* malfeasance. In short, the problem was in locating the term "High Crimes and Misdemeanors" somewhere within the universe of private vs. public acts, and criminal vs. noncriminal acts.

As a textual matter, the Impeachment Clause's explicit reference to "High Crimes and Misdemeanors" contains an implicit suggestion that not all crimes are impeachable. Does the term "High Crimes and Misdemeanors" refer to misdeeds relating solely to the President's official duties? Or relating to the office more broadly? Consider the view that "these words constitute technical terms of art that refer to political crimes. [Oftentimes], these offenses were characterized further as serious abuses of official power or serious breaches of the public trust." Gerhardt, "The Lessons of Impeachment History," 67 Geo. Wash. L. Rev. 603 (1999). Even if such a definition is accepted, is any presidential misconduct while in office truly private? Compare Rakove, "Statement on the Background and History of Impeachment," 67 Geo. Wash. L. Rev. 682 (1999) ("The central fact remains that the President's alleged misconduct remains tied to a legal suit that involves an incident occurring well before his election to office, and to behavior that was essentially private and non-official even if subsequent proceedings gave it a legal and public character."), with Presser, "Would George Washington Have Wanted Bill Clinton Impeached," 67 Geo. Wash. L. Rev. 666 (1999) ("These offenses, if true, would show that President Clinton engaged in a pattern of conduct that involved injury to the state and a betrayal of his constitutional duties [through abusing] his office for personal gain and [violating] his oath [to] uphold the Constitution and faithfully execute the laws.") Can virtually any presidential violation of the law while in office be characterized as an impeachable violation of the oath to "faithfully execute" his office and "preserve, protect, and defend the Constitution." Even a traffic violation?

Is criminality a prerequisite to impeachability? Can a president be impeached for failure to cooperate in a legislative investigation? One of the Articles of Impeachment rejected by the House would have impeached Clinton for "contraven[ing] the authority of the legislative branch and the truth-seeking purpose of a coordinate investigative proceeding [through] refus[ing] [to] respond to certain written [questions]." The rejected article charged that in so doing, Clinton had "assumed to himself functions and judgments necessary to the exercise of the sole power of impeachment vested by the Constitution in the House of Representatives and exhibited contempt for the inquiry, [undermining] the integrity of his office, [bringing] disrepute on the Presidency, [betraying] his trust as President, and [acting] in a manner subversive of the rule of law and justice, to the manifest injury of the people of the United States." Is it unfair to impeach a president for noncriminal actions taken in defense of executive independence? Even if so, are there other noncriminal actions that could warrant the impeachment remedy? Is impeachment a valid remedy for gross dereliction of duty? For self-dealing or violations of the Emoluments Clauses? For incompetence?

Do the two offenses specifically enumerated as impeachable in the Constitution—Treason and Bribery—help by analogy to delimit a clear boundary between impeachable and nonimpeachable crimes? The Constitution at least gives a definition of treason. See Art. III, § 3. But how should we interpret the Constitution's use of the term "bribery"? As including only what our contemporary statutes define as criminal acts of bribery? Or should we read bribery as encompassing any act where the President pays undue attention to his personal benefit at the expense of his public duty? As Madison's notes on the Constitutional Convention make clear, the Founders were aware of the difficulty of defining the impeachment power. Indeed, the term "high crimes and misdemeanors" was added to the Constitution in answer to Mason's suggestion that mere enumeration of treason and bribery would give inadequate scope to the impeachment power, because "[t]reason as defined in the Constitution will not reach many great and dangerous offenses. [Attempts] to subvert the Constitution may not be Treason as above defined." 2 Records of the Federal Convention 550 (Farrand, ed. 1923). The delegates chose to insert the term high crimes and misdemeanors as a substitute for Mason's initial suggestion of "maladministration"—a term which Madison objected to on the grounds that it would make the President's tenure too dependent on the "pleasure of the Senate."

d. *Impeachment as a political remedy*. Is the abstract attempt to differentiate impeachable acts from nonimpeachable ones a mere distraction? One commentator argues that "the categorical division of conduct into public or private areas is a mere artificiality in a process designed to deal with the perceived legitimacy of a President to govern." Turley, "Reflections on Murder, Misdemeanors, and Madison," 28 Hofstra L. Rev. 439 (1999). As an alternative, is it possible to see the impeachment question as less a matter of applying a clear-cut rule than as a question of implementing the structural design of the Constitution (via checks and balances), and of enabling governance to maintain its legitimacy (as an expression of popular sentiment)? One scholar argues against "constitutionalizing what is, in reality, a thoroughly political debate," on the grounds that excessively legalistic discussion of impeachment not only is inconclusive (given the inadequacy of legal criteria such as historical evidence and precedent), but also allows the impeachment's primary actors—Senators and Representatives—to evade responsibility for their decision. Klarman, "Constitutional Fetishism and the Clinton Impeachment Debate," 85 Va. L. Rev. 631 (1999). See also McGinnis, "Impeachment: The Structural Understanding," 67 Geo. Wash. L. Rev. 650 (1999) (arguing that the purpose of impeachment is to protect the public, rather than to punish a specific list of offenses; hence, both phases of impeachment are entrusted to the "prudential judgment" of the Congress, whose duty is "the evaluation of a range of offenses in relation to fitness for office").

Would such a view mean that the phrase "High Crimes and Misdemeanors" should be read more narrowly for presidential impeachments than for other impeachments? Should the bar for presidential impeachment be set uniquely high? Consider this view: "We might say that history has converged on the judgment that there is a lower threshold for judges than for presidents. Perhaps the theory is that judges cannot otherwise be removed from office; perhaps the theory is that it is uniquely destabilizing if presidents are too freely subject to removal from office." Sunstein, "Impeachment and Stability," 67 Geo. Wash. L. Rev. 699 (1999). Or should impeachment be more broadly applicable to the President to serve as "an active check on presidential conduct"—"a deterrent against presidential misconduct and [a way] to address factional disputes over the legitimacy to govern." Turley, "Congress as Grand Jury: The Role of the House of Representatives in the Impeachment of an American President," 67 Geo. Wash. L. Rev. 735 (1999). Is there a difference between impeaching someone who has been elected to the office of president (e.g., Clinton) and impeaching someone who was not (e.g., Johnson)? Does it make a difference whether the president's "crimes reflect character flaws that the people duly considered before voting for him, or [whether] the people continue to support him even after the facts come to light"? Amar, "On Impeaching Presidents," 28 Hofstra L. Rev. 291 (1999).

e. *The constitutionality of censure.* Did the Congress have other options for expressing their disapproval of the president, besides impeachment and removal from office? There are conflicting signs in the Constitution: Article I, § 7 provides that "Judgment in Cases of Impeachment shall not extend further than to removal from Office, and disqualification to hold and enjoy any Office of honor, Trust, or Profit under the United States." Article II, § 4 says that "The President . . . shall be removed from Office on Impeachment for, and Conviction of, Treason, Bribery, or other high Crimes and Misdemeanors." The former provision "seems to leave open the possibility of punishments that do not go as far as removal from office, such as censure. The latter seems to require removal from office for all impeachment convictions." Klarman, "Constitutional Fetishism and the Clinton Impeachment Debate," 85 Va. L. Rev. 631 (1999). Does the House of Representatives, because entrusted with the "sole Power of Impeachment," have discretion to engage in censure as a lesser included power? For an argument that censure would have been unconstitutional, see McDowell, " 'High Crimes and Misdemeanors': Recovering the Intentions of the Founders," 67 Geo. Wash. L. Rev. 626 (1999).

f. *Rethinking Morrison.* Should the example of the Clinton impeachment affect evaluation of the wisdom of the Morrison v. Olson decision? Is impeachment preferable to criminal prosecution by an independent counsel as a vehicle for addressing presidential misconduct? Consider the argument that impeachment has the advantages of being "national," "public and accountable," and "beautifully final" in its unappealability. Amar, "On Impeaching Presidents," 28 Hofstra L. Rev. 291 (1999). Should impeachment be unappealable? What if "the Senate were to act in a manner seriously threatening the integrity of its results, convicting, say, upon a coin-toss, or upon a summary determination that an officer of the United States was simply 'a bad guy' "? Recall Justice Souter's concurrence in (Walter) Nixon v. United States, p. 68 above.

CHAPTER 7

THE POST-CIVIL WAR AMENDMENTS AND THE "INCORPORATION" OF FUNDAMENTAL RIGHTS

The Bill of Rights originally guaranteed individual liberties only against the federal government. The proposal of the Bill of Rights was part of a political compromise designed to enlist support for ratification from Anti-Federalists who did not trust the enumeration of powers in the federal Constitution to serve as a sufficient check on the new national authority. Express checks on arbitrary exercises of authority were meant to add an external check to supplement the internal restraint that was expected to operate in a federal government of enumerated and thus limited powers. While Article I, § 10 imposed a handful of express prohibitions on state action, nothing in the first eight Amendments expressly constrained the states, and the 10th Amendment expressly reiterated that powers not delegated to the United States were reserved to the states.

The Reconstruction Amendments for the first time added to the original Constitution new express restraints upon the states. But these amendments did not specifically apply to the states all of the provisions of the Bill of Rights; rather, the Fourteenth Amendment, § 1 provided simply: "All persons born or naturalized in the United States and subject to the jurisdiction thereof, are citizens of the United States and of the State wherein they reside. No State shall make or enforce any law which shall abridge the privileges or immunities of citizens of the United States; nor shall any State deprive any person of life, liberty, or property, without due process of law; nor deny to any person within its jurisdiction the equal protection of the laws."

The Fourteenth Amendment's Due Process Clause, however, was later read to make applicable to state criminal proceedings virtually all of the procedural requirements that govern federal criminal law enforcement as a result of the Bill of Rights. Moreover, this process of "incorporating" Bill of Rights guarantees into the Fourteenth Amendment also came to reach other provisions of the original Bill of Rights, including the protection against uncompensated takings, the freedom of speech, and the right to free exercise of religion. The post-Civil War Amendments thus signified a major escalation in the national concern with the protection of individual rights from state governmental action. Why was it the Fourteenth Amendment's *Due Process Clause* that became the major vehicle for that nationalization of individual rights? Why not the *Privileges or Immunities Clause*, which would seem a more textually plausible home for substantive rights? The cases that follow help explain this history.

SECTION 1. INDIVIDUAL RIGHTS BEFORE THE CIVIL WAR

There were relatively few explicit references to individual rights in the original Constitution; its major concern was with governmental structure. The most litigated limitation on state power was the ban on state impairment of contracts in Article I, § 10. That section also prohibited state bills of attainder and ex post facto laws, and Article IV, § 4 provided that the "Citizens of each State shall be entitled to all Privileges and Immunities of Citizens in the several States." Few individual rights restrictions applied to the national government: Article I, § 9, stated that the "Privilege of the Writ of Habeas Corpus shall not be suspended, unless when in Cases of Rebellion or Invasion the public Safety may require it," and, paralleling the restrictions on the states, also prohibited ex post facto laws and bills of attainder. Article III defined the crime of treason narrowly and assured jury trials in criminal cases.

The ratification debates soon revealed demand for additional constitutional protection of individual rights. In response to these pressures, James Madison introduced proposals at the first session of Congress for a series of constitutional amendments that focused on protecting individual rights. Twelve amendments were proposed by Congress, and ten were ratified in 1791. For a useful documentary resource on the adoption of the Bill of Rights, see Cogan, ed., The Complete Bill of Rights: The Drafts, Debates, Sources, & Origins (1997).

In the Barron case, which follows, the Marshall Court held that the Bill of Rights restricted only the national government, not the states. The state courts of New York, Illinois and Mississippi had applied portions of the Bill of Rights against their states; similar approaches were advocated in Ohio and later Georgia. Yet Marshall—ordinarily not averse to nationalist interpretations—refused to find the amendments applicable to the states:

Barron v. Mayor and City Council of Baltimore

7 Pet. (32 U.S.) 243, 8 L. Ed. 672 (1833).

[Barron owned "an extensive and highly productive wharf, in the eastern section of Baltimore," which had "the deepest water in the harbor." The City diverted several streams in the course of street construction work; those streams deposited "large masses of sand and earth" near the wharf, making the water there too shallow for most vessels. Barron claimed that the state's action violated the Fifth Amendment's guarantee that private property shall not be "taken for public use, without just compensation." He argued that this provision "ought to be so construed as to restrain the legislative power of a state, as well as that of the United States."]

■ CHIEF JUSTICE MARSHALL delivered the opinion of the Court.

[The question is] of great importance, but not of much difficulty. The constitution was ordained and established by the people of the United States for themselves, for their own government, and not for the government of the individual states. Each state established a constitution for itself, and, in that constitution, provided such limitations and restrictions on the powers of its particular government as its judgment dictated. The people of the United States framed such a government for the United States as they supposed best adapted to their situation, and best calculated to promote their interests. The powers they conferred on this government were to be exercised by itself; and the limitations on power, if expressed in general terms, are naturally, and, we think, necessarily applicable to the government created by the instrument. They are limitations of power, granted in the instrument itself; not of distinct governments, framed by different persons and for different purposes. [If] these propositions be correct, the fifth amendment must be understood as restraining the power of the general government, not as applicable to the [states].

The ninth section [of Article I] having enumerated, in the nature of a bill of rights, the limitations intended to be imposed on the powers of the general government, the tenth proceeds to enumerate those which were to operate on the state legislatures. [If] the original constitution, in the ninth and tenth sections of the first article, draws this plain and marked line of discrimination between the limitations it imposes on the powers of the general government, and on those of the states; if in every inhibition intended to act on state power, words are employed which directly express that intent; some strong reason must be assigned for departing from this safe and judicious course in framing the amendments, before that departure can be assumed. We search in vain for that [reason]. Had the framers of these amendments intended them to be limitations on the powers of the state governments, they would have imitated the framers of the original constitution, and have expressed that [intention].

But it is universally understood, it is a part of the history of the day, that the great revolution which established the constitution of the United States, was not effected without immense opposition. Serious fears were extensively entertained that those powers which the patriot statesmen, who then watched over the interests of our country, deemed essential to union, and to the attainment of those invaluable objects for which union was sought, might be exercised in a manner dangerous to liberty. In almost every convention by which the constitution was adopted, amendments to guard against the abuse of power were recommended. These amendments demanded security against the apprehended encroachments of the general government—not against those of the local governments. In compliance with a sentiment thus generally expressed, to quiet fears thus extensively entertained, amendments were proposed by the required majority in congress, and adopted by the states. These amendments contain no expression indicating an intention to apply them to the state governments. This court cannot so apply them. We are of opinion that the [just compensation] provision in the fifth amendment [is] intended solely as a limitation on the exercise of power by the government of the United States, and is not applicable to the legislation of the states. We are therefore of opinion that there is no repugnancy between the [state's action] and the constitution of the United States. This court, therefore, has no jurisdiction of the cause; and it is dismissed.

While determining the scope of the Bill of Rights may not have been "of much difficulty," another issue in the early years of the Constitution proved much harder to resolve: slavery. Ever since Virginian colonists purchased nineteen African slaves from Dutch traders in 1619, a race-based slavery system had existed in North America. Over time, the institution of slavery became central to the economic livelihood of the Southern states. Although the Constitution itself never directly mentioned "slavery," the institution's marks were apparent throughout it: Article I, § 2 provided that slaves would be counted as three-fifths of a free person for apportionment and taxing purposes; Article I, § 9 prohibited Congress from closing the international slave trade until 1808 and from imposing taxes higher than ten dollars on each imported slave; and Article IV, § 2 declared that fugitive slaves remained subject to recapture and return even if they made it to a free state.

Although the Constitution implemented a number of compromises regarding slavery, the issue was far from settled. In 1820, Missouri's application to join the Union set off an unexpected political firestorm—which Thomas Jefferson famously called "a firebell in the night"—as antislavery northerners sought to use the occasion to prohibit the further expansion of slavery. Congress ultimately reached a deal, brokered by Henry Clay, to admit Missouri as a slave state but prohibit slavery in all territories north of Missouri's southern border and, to preserve the balance between slave states and free states in the Senate, to admit Maine as a free state. After the Missouri Compromise, the nation did not admit any new states for fifteen years; even then, it continued to follow the pattern of pairing slave and free states.

The Missouri settlement did not last long, and by 1850, slavery had become the key national issue again. Once more, Henry Clay helped craft a compromise that he hoped would hold the Union together. Under the Compromise of 1850, California would be admitted as a free state; in exchange, the slave states would receive a stronger fugitive slave law and the possibility of slavery in the Utah Territory, which was north of the Missouri Compromise line, through "popular sovereignty"—that is, the right of the people in the territory to adopt slavery through a popular vote. That compromise, however, left both sides unhappy, and the issue remained live. In 1854, the passage of the Kansas-Nebraska Act allowed popular sovereignty in Kansas and Nebraska, both north of the Missouri Compromise line. As a result, thousands of pro-and anti-slavery advocates streamed into Kansas to influence the vote; the factions soon began to collide in outright warfare. Perhaps realizing that there was no satisfactory political solution, the nation began to look to the courts to resolve the dispute. At his 1857 inauguration, President James Buchanan optimistically noted that the slavery question would soon be "speedily and finally settled" by the Court in the Dred Scott case. Days later, the Court released its opinion:

Dred Scott v. Sandford

19 How. (60 U.S.) 393, 15 L. Ed. 691 (1857).

[Dred Scott had been a slave belonging to Dr. Emerson, a U.S. army surgeon. Emerson brought Scott with him to postings in Illinois, a free state, and the Wisconsin Territory, a free territory under the Missouri Compromise, in 1836. Scott ultimately returned to Missouri in 1838 with his wife and Emerson's wife; Emerson died in the Iowa Territory in 1843. Scott attempted to purchase his and his wife's freedom from Emerson's widow,

Eliza Sanford; when she refused to accept his offer, Scott sued for a declaratory judgment, arguing that his two-year residence in the Wisconsin Territory—where Congress had prohibited slavery by law—had rendered him free. Scott sued in federal court under diversity jurisdiction; the Circuit Court of St. Louis County granted a directed verdict for Sanford, and Scott appealed.]

■ CHIEF JUSTICE TANEY delivered the opinion of the Court.

There are two leading questions presented by the record:

1. Had the Circuit Court of the United States jurisdiction to hear and determine the case between these parties? And

2. If it had jurisdiction, is the judgment it has given erroneous or not?

The [jurisdiction] question is simply this: Can a negro, whose ancestors were imported into this country, and sold as slaves, become a member of the political community formed and brought into existence by the Constitution of the United States, and as such become entitled to all the rights, and privileges, and immunities, guarantied by that instrument to the citizen? One of which rights is the privilege of suing in a court of the United States in the cases specified in the Constitution.

We think they [cannot], and that they are not included, and were not intended to be included, under the word 'citizens' in the Constitution, and can therefore claim none of the rights and privileges which that instrument provides for and secures to citizens of the United States.

[The Declaration of Independence states:] "We hold these truths to be self-evident: that all men are created equal; that they are endowed by their Creator with certain unalienable rights; that among them is life, liberty, and the pursuit of happiness; that to secure these rights, Governments are instituted, deriving their just powers from the consent of the governed."

The general words above quoted would seem to embrace the whole human family, and if they were used in a similar instrument at this day would be so understood. But it is too clear for dispute, that the enslaved African race were not intended to be included, and formed no part of the people who framed and adopted this declaration; for if the language, as understood in that day, would embrace them, the conduct of the distinguished men who framed the Declaration of Independence would have been utterly and flagrantly inconsistent with the principles they asserted; and instead of the sympathy of mankind, to which they so confidently appealed, they would have deserved and received universal rebuke and reprobation.

[The slave trade and fugitive slave] clauses in the Constitution point directly and specifically to the negro race as a separate class of persons, and show clearly that they were not regarded as a portion of the people or citizens of the Government then formed. [These] two provisions show, conclusively, that neither the description of persons therein referred to, nor their descendants, were embraced in any of the other provisions of the Constitution; for certainly these two clauses were not intended to confer on them or their posterity the blessings of liberty, or any of the personal rights so carefully provided for the citizen.

[If] anything in relation to the construction of the Constitution can be regarded as settled, it is that which we now give to the word 'citizen' and the word 'people.' [Therefore, the] court is of opinion, that, upon the facts stated in the plea in abatement, Dred Scott was not a citizen of Missouri within the meaning of the Constitution of the United States, and not entitled as such to sue in its courts.

[The Circuit Court also erred in its decision on the merits.] In considering this part of the controversy, two questions arise: 1. Was [Scott], together with his family, free in Missouri by reason of the stay in the territory of the United States hereinbefore mentioned? And 2. If they were not, is Scott himself free by reason of his removal to Rock Island, in the State of Illinois, as stated in the above admissions?

The act of Congress, upon which the plaintiff relies, declares that slavery and involuntary servitude, except as a punishment for crime, shall be forever prohibited in [the part of the Louisiana Territory], which lies north of thirty-six degrees thirty minutes north latitude, and not included within the limits of Missouri. [The Constitution] gives Congress the power 'to dispose of and make all needful rules and regulations respecting the territory or other property belonging to the United States.' [This clause] was intended for a specific purpose, [to] transfer to the new Government the property then held in common by the States, and to give to that Government power to apply it to the objects for which it had been destined by mutual agreement among the States before their league was dissolved. It applied only to the property which the States held in common at that time, and has no reference whatever to any territory or other property which the new sovereignty might afterwards itself acquire.

[It] may be safely assumed that citizens of the United States who migrate to a Territory belonging to the people of the United States, cannot be ruled as mere colonists. [They retain the rights guaranteed to them under the Constitution; Congress] could confer no power on any local Government, established by its authority, to violate the provisions of the Constitution. [The] act of Congress which prohibited a citizen from holding and owning property of this kind in the territory of the United States north of the line therein mentioned, is not warranted by the Constitution [because it deprives slaveholders of their property without due process of law, which is impermissible under the Fifth Amendment. It] is therefore void. [The judgment of the Circuit Court is affirmed.]

■ JUSTICE CURTIS, dissenting:

To determine whether any free persons, descended from Africans held in slavery, were citizens of the United States under the Confederation, and consequently at the time of the adoption of the Constitution of the United States, it is only necessary to know whether any such persons were citizens of either of the States under the Confederation, at the time of the adoption of the Constitution. Of this there can be no doubt. At the time of the ratification of the Articles of Confederation, all free native-born inhabitants of [five States], though descended from African slaves, were [citizens] of those States.

[Did] the Constitution of the United States deprive them or their descendants of citizenship? [It] would be strange, if we were to find in that instrument anything which deprived of their citizenship any part of the people of the United States who were among those by whom it was established. I can find nothing in the Constitution which, proprio vigore, deprives of their citizenship any class of persons who were citizens of the United States at the time of its adoption, or who should be native-born citizens of any State after its adoption; nor any power enabling Congress to disfranchise persons born on the soil of any State, and entitled to citizenship of such State by its Constitution and laws. And my opinion is, that, under the Constitution of the United States, every free person born on the soil of a State, who is a citizen of that State by force of its Constitution or laws, is also a citizen of the United States.

It is said [the territories clause] has no application to any territory save that then belonging to the United States. [But] when the Constitution was framed, a confident expectation was entertained, which was speedily realized, that North Carolina and Georgia would cede their claims to that great territory which lay west of those States. No doubt has been suggested that the first clause of this same article, which enabled Congress to admit new States, refers to and includes new States to be formed out of this territory, expected to be thereafter ceded by North Carolina and Georgia, as well as new States to be formed out of territory northwest of the Ohio, which then had been ceded by Virginia. It must have been seen, therefore, that the same necessity would exist for an authority to dispose of and make all needful regulations respecting this territory, when ceded, as existed for a like authority respecting territory which had been ceded.

[The institution of slavery must be created by positive laws. Is] it conceivable that the Constitution has conferred the right on every citizen to become a resident on the territory of the United States with his slaves, and there to hold them as such, but has neither made nor provided for any municipal regulations which are essential to the existence of slavery? Is it not more rational to conclude [that], being aware of these principles, and having said nothing to interfere with or displace them, and having empowered Congress to make all needful rules and regulations respecting the territory of the United States, it was [the Framers'] intention to leave to the discretion of Congress what regulations, if any, should be made concerning slavery therein? [In] my judgment, [the] position, that a prohibition to bring slaves into a Territory deprives any one of his property without due process of law, [will not] bear examination. [In] my opinion, the judgment of the Circuit Court should be reversed.

THE AFTERMATH OF DRED SCOTT

1. ***Dred Scott's error.*** The Dred Scott case is widely considered one of the greatest failures in the Supreme Court's history. But what exactly was wrong with the decision? Chief Justice Taney's methodology is much the same as in other cases: interpretation of the Constitution's text, consideration of its original meaning, and reasoning from its structure. What are the principled bases for rejecting Dred Scott's conclusions aside from simply deciding that it reached the "wrong" result?

2. ***Dred Scott and Marbury v. Madison.*** Dred Scott was just the second time in American history in which the Supreme Court struck down a federal law; the first occurred in 1803 in Marbury v. Madison. While the two cases have very different historical legacies, they may not have seemed so different to Chief Justice Taney. Like Marbury, Dred Scott invalidated an act of Congress and declared an issue beyond the reach of the political branches. Like Marshall in Marbury, Taney based his decision on the Court's lack of jurisdiction and placed the core of his holding in dicta. How can

Marbury's landmark statement of judicial authority be distinguished from Dred Scott's exemplification of judicial overreach?

3. ***Chief Justice Taney's aims.*** Commentators have often questioned why, after establishing that the lower court lacked jurisdiction, the Court proceeded to decide this case on merits. To answer this question, it is worth considering the broader aims of Chief Justice Roger Taney. Taney was a slaveholding unionist from Maryland who sought both to protect the interests of the Southern States and to prevent the dissolution of the union. He believed that if he could put an end to the recurring political controversy over the expansion of slavery, he could achieve both his aims. See Swisher, Roger B. Taney 504–05 (1935). Was Chief Justice Taney's strategy successful? (If you've heard of the Civil War, you may already know the answer to this question.)

4. ***The reception of Dred Scott.*** Despite Chief Justice Taney's intentions, Dred Scott proved to be anything but conciliatory. During his Senate campaign against Stephen Douglas, Abraham Lincoln denounced the decision, stating that the fledgling Republican Party "think[s] the Dred Scott decision is erroneous. We know the court that made it, has often over-ruled its own decisions, and we shall do what we can to have it over-rule this." The bulk of his famous "House Divided" speech was dedicated to Dred Scott. Lincoln cast the decision as part of a "slave power" conspiracy and warned that the Supreme Court would continue overreaching to expand the realm of slavery: "We shall lie down pleasantly dreaming that the people of Missouri are on the verge of making their State free, and we shall awake to the reality instead, that the Supreme Court has made Illinois a slave State."

Historians have debated how directly the Dred Scott decision led to Lincoln's election and the Civil War. But for at least some voters, a vote for the Republican Party was a vote against Dred Scott. As the Civil War progressed and its goals became entwined with abolition, it became clear that the President Lincoln and the Republican Party would also face certain legal obstacles to abolishing slavery. Specifically, the Dred Scott decision had held that blacks could never be full members of the American political union. The post-Civil War Amendments, and the Fourteenth Amendment in particular, sought to override that precedent.

The Dred Scott decision undercut Chief Justice Taney's reputation and marred his legacy. Upon his death in 1864, the Senate refused to allocate funds for a bust of Taney as they had done for previous chief justices. Senator Charles Sumner declared that the "name of Taney is to be hooted down the page of history" and that "judgment [would] fasten upon him the stigma which he deserves." Nine years later, when Chief Justice Salmon Chase died, Congress appropriated funding to commission busts of both Chase and Taney. See Swisher, Roger B. Taney 582 (1935) (quoting Congressional Globe, 38th Cong., 2nd Sess, p. 1012).

More recently, Justice Scalia, dissenting in Planned Parenthood v. Casey (1992; below p. 531), offered this reflection on Taney's legacy: "There comes vividly to mind a portrait by Emanuel Leutze that hangs in the Harvard Law School: Roger Brooke Taney, painted in 1859, the 82d year of his life, the 24th of his Chief Justiceship, the second after his opinion in Dred Scott. He is all in black, sitting in a shadowed red armchair, left hand resting upon a pad of paper in his lap, right hand hanging limply, almost lifelessly, beside the inner arm of the chair. He sits facing the viewer, and staring straight out. There seems to be on his face, and in his deep set eyes, an expression of profound sadness and disillusionment. Perhaps he always looked that way, even when dwelling upon the happiest of thoughts. But those of us who know how the lustre of his great Chief Justiceship came to be eclipsed by Dred Scott cannot help believing that he had that case—its already apparent consequences for the Court, and its soon to be played out consequences for the Nation—burning on his mind."

SECTION 2. THE POST-CIVIL WAR AMENDMENTS

In 1865, the Thirteenth Amendment gave constitutional sanction to President Lincoln's wartime Emancipation Proclamation, which applied only to areas in rebellion, by declaring that "[n]either slavery nor involuntary servitude . . . shall exist within the United States." But this amendment did not end the problems of ex-slaves: their rights continued to be severely limited by the "black codes" of many southern states. Congress accordingly adopted the Civil Rights Act of 1866—over President Andrew Johnson's veto, based on constitutional grounds—and immediately set the amendment process in motion to assure the constitutional validity of that law. The Fourteenth Amendment was ratified in 1868. The Fourteenth Amendment used more sweeping, general terms than the Act it was designed to sustain: the Amendment's language was not limited to the problems of race, color, or previous condition of servitude. It overruled Dred Scott, granting American citizenship to all persons "born . . . in the United States, and subject to the jurisdiction thereof," although it did so without making explicit mention of race. The Amendment's Privileges or Immunities, Due Process and Equal Protection Clauses also did not refer explicitly to race or previous legal status as a slave. In contrast, the Fifteenth Amendment, ratified two years later in 1870, did speak expressly about racial discrimination in voting. Each of the three post-Civil War Amendments ended with a section authorizing Congress to enact legislation to enforce its provisions. But for generations, delineation of the scope of the Amendments was left almost entirely to the Supreme Court.

The Court, however, soon gave a narrow reading to the Fourteenth Amendment in the Slaughter-House Cases, emphasizing that the Civil War Amendments had not been meant to expand radically the power of the Supreme Court to regulate the relationship of the states to their own citizens. The case arose from a challenge by would-be competitors to a state-conferred monopoly.

Slaughter-House Cases

16 Wall. (83 U.S.) 36, 21 L. Ed. 394 (1873).

[A Louisiana law of 1869 chartered a corporation—the Crescent City Live-Stock Landing and Slaughter-House Company—and granted to it a 25-year right "to maintain slaughterhouses, landings for cattle and stockyards" in an area that included the city of New Orleans. All competing facilities were required to close, but the corporation was required to permit independent butchers to slaughter cattle in its slaughterhouses at charges fixed by statute. Butchers not included in the monopoly claimed that the law deprived them of their right "to exercise their trade" and challenged it under the Fourteenth Amendment. The highest state court sustained the law.]

■ JUSTICE MILLER delivered the opinion of the Court.

[This Court is called] upon for the first time to give construction to the [Thirteenth and Fourteenth Amendments]. The most cursory glance [discloses] a unity of purpose, when taken in connection with the history of the times, which cannot fail to have an important bearing on any question of doubt concerning their true meaning. [The] overshadowing and efficient cause [of "the war of the rebellion"] was African slavery. In that struggle slavery, as a legalized social relation, perished. [Among] the first acts of legislation adopted by several of the States [were] laws which imposed upon the colored race onerous disabilities and burdens, and curtailed their rights in the pursuit of life, liberty, and property to such an extent that their freedom was of little value, while they had lost the protection which they had received from their former owners from motives both of interest and humanity. [These] circumstances [forced] upon the statesmen who had conducted the Federal government in safety through the crisis of the rebellion, and who supposed that by [the 13th Amendment] they had secured the result of their labors, the conviction that something more was necessary in the way of constitutional protection to the unfortunate race who had suffered so much. They accordingly [proposed the Fourteenth Amendment]. A few years' experience satisfied the thoughtful men who had been the authors of the other two amendments that [these] were inadequate for the protection of life, liberty, and property, without which freedom to the slave was no boon. They were in all those States denied the right of suffrage. [Hence] the 15th Amendment. [The] one pervading purpose found in [all three amendments], lying at the foundation of each, and without which none of them would have been even suggested [is] the freedom of the slave race, the security and firm establishment of that freedom, and the protection of the newly-made freeman and citizen from the oppressions of those who had formerly exercised unlimited dominion over him.

purpose of amendments

[The clause the plaintiffs rely most upon] speaks only of privileges and immunities of citizens of the United States, and does not speak of those of citizens of the several States. The argument, however, in favor of the plaintiffs rests wholly on the assumption that the citizenship is the same, and the privileges and immunities guaranteed by the clause are the same. The language is, "No State shall make or enforce any law which shall abridge the privileges or immunities of citizens of *the United States*." It is a little remarkable, if this clause was intended as a protection to the citizen of a State against the legislative power of his own State, that the word citizen of the State should be left out when it is so carefully used, and used in contradistinction to citizens of the United States, in the very sentence which precedes it. It is too clear for argument that the change in phraseology was adopted understandingly and with a purpose. Of the privileges and immunities of the citizen of the United States, and of the privileges and immunities of the citizen of the State, and what they respectively are, we will presently consider; but we wish to state here that it is only the former which are placed by this clause under the protection of the Federal Constitution, and that the latter, whatever they may be, are not intended to have any additional protection by this paragraph of the amendment. If, then, there is a difference between the privileges and immunities belonging to a citizen of the United States as such, and those belonging to the citizen of the

citizen of US v state

State as such, the latter must rest for their security and protection where they have heretofore rested; for they are not embraced by this paragraph of the amendment.

[The] Constitution, [Article IV, § 2, states]: "The citizens of each State shall be entitled to all the privileges and immunities of citizens of the several States." [The] first and the leading case on the subject is that of Corfield v. Coryell, decided by Mr. Justice Washington in the Circuit Court [in] 1823. "The inquiry," he says, "is, what are the privileges and immunities of citizens of the several States? We feel no hesitation in confining these expressions to those privileges and immunities which are *fundamental*, which belong of right to the citizens of all free governments, and which have at all times been enjoyed by citizens of the several States which compose this Union, from the time of their becoming free, independent, and sovereign. What these fundamental principles are, it would be more tedious than difficult to enumerate. They may all, however, be comprehended under the following general heads: protection by the government, with the right to acquire and possess property of every kind, and to pursue and obtain happiness and safety, subject, nevertheless, to such restraints as the government may prescribe for the general good of the whole." [This] description, when taken to include others not named, but which are of the same general character, embraces nearly every civil right for the establishment and protection of which organized government is instituted. They are, in the language of Judge Washington, those rights which are fundamental. [T]hey have always been held to be the class of rights which the State governments were created to establish and secure. [Article IV] did not create those rights, which it called privileges and immunities of citizens of the States. It threw around them in that clause no security for the citizen of the State in which they were claimed or exercised. Nor did it profess to control the power of the State governments over the rights of its own citizens. Its sole purpose was to declare to the several States, that whatever those rights, as you grant or establish them to your own citizens, or as you limit or qualify, or impose restrictions on their exercise, the same, neither more nor less, shall be the measure of the rights of citizens of other States within your jurisdiction.

[U]p to the adoption of the recent amendments, no claim or pretense was set up that those rights depended on the Federal government for their existence or protection, beyond the very few express limitations which the Federal Constitution imposed upon the [States]. But with the exception of these and a few other restrictions, the entire domain of the privileges and immunities of citizens of the [States] lay within the constitutional and legislative power of the States, and without that of the Federal government. Was it the purpose of the fourteenth amendment, by the simple declaration that no State should make or enforce any law which shall abridge the privileges and immunities of *citizens of the United States*, to transfer the security and protection of all the civil rights which we have mentioned, from the States to the Federal government?

[Such] a construction [would] constitute this court a perpetual censor upon all legislation of the States, on the civil rights of their own citizens, with authority to nullify such as it did not approve as consistent with those rights, as they existed at the time of the adoption of this amendment. [When,] as in the case before us, these consequences are so serious, so far-reaching and pervading, so great a departure from the structure and spirit of our institutions; when the effect is to fetter and degrade the State governments by subjecting them to the control of Congress, in the exercise of powers heretofore universally conceded to them of the most ordinary and fundamental character; when in fact it radically changes the whole theory of the relations of the State and Federal governments to each other and of both these governments to the people; the argument has a force that is irresistible, in the absence of language which expresses such a purpose too clearly to admit of doubt. We are convinced that no such results were intended by the Congress which proposed these amendments, nor by the legislatures of the States which ratified them.

Having shown that the privileges and immunities relied on in the argument are those which belong to citizens of the States as such, and that they are left to the State governments for security and protection, and not by this article placed under the special care of the Federal government, we may hold ourselves excused from defining the privileges and immunities of citizens of the United States which no State can abridge, until some case involving those privileges may make it necessary to do so. But lest it should be said that no such privileges and immunities are to be found if those we have been considering are excluded, we venture to suggest some which owe their existence to the Federal government, its National character, its Constitution, or its laws. One of these is well described in the case of Crandall v. Nevada [6 Wall. (73 U.S.) 35 (1868)]. It is said to be the right of the citizen of this great country, protected by implied guarantees of its Constitution, "to come to the seat of government to assert any claim he may have upon that government, to transact any business he may have with it, to seek its protection, to share its offices, to engage in administering its functions. He has the right of free access to its seaports, through which all operations of foreign commerce are conducted, to the subtreasuries, land offices, and courts of justice in the several States." Another privilege of a citizen of the United States is to demand the care and protection of the Federal government over his life, liberty, and property when on the high seas or within the jurisdiction of a foreign government. [The] right to peaceably assemble and petition for redress of grievances, the privilege of the writ of habeas corpus, are rights of the citizen guaranteed by the Federal Constitution. The right to use the navigable waters of the United States, however they may penetrate the territory of the several States, all rights secured to our citizens by treaties with foreign nations, are dependent upon citizenship of the United States, and not citizenship of a State.

[Justice Miller went on to opine that the slaughterhouse monopoly violated neither the Due Process Clause nor the Equal Protection Clause of the Fourteenth Amendment.]

[Affirmed.]

■ JUSTICE FIELD, joined by CHIEF JUSTICE CHASE and JUSTICES SWAYNE and BRADLEY, dissenting:

[The] question presented [is] one of the gravest [importance]. It is nothing less than the question whether the recent [Amendments] protect the citizens of the United States against the deprivation of their common rights by State legislation. In my judgment the fourteenth amendment does afford such [protection]. The amendment does not attempt to confer any new privileges or immunities upon citizens, or to enumerate or define those already existing. It assumes that there are such privileges and immunities which belong of right to citizens as such, and ordains that they shall not be abridged by State legislation. If this inhibition has no reference to privileges and immunities of this character, but only refers, as held by [the majority], to such privileges and immunities as were before its adoption specifically designated in the Constitution or necessarily implied as belonging to citizens of the United States, it was a vain and idle enactment, which accomplished [nothing]. With privileges and immunities thus designated or implied no State could ever have interfered by its laws, and no new constitutional provision was required to inhibit such interference. [But] if the amendment refers to the natural and inalienable rights which belong to all citizens, the inhibition has a profound [significance].

makes 14th amend. pointless

The terms, privileges and immunities, are not new in the amendment; they were in the Constitution before the amendment was adopted. [Corfield v. Coryell.] The privileges and immunities designated are those *which of right belong to the citizens of all free governments*. Clearly among these must be placed the right to pursue a lawful employment in a lawful manner, without other restraint than such as equally affects all persons. [What Article IV, § 2] did for the protection of the citizens of one State against hostile and discriminating legislation of other States, the fourteenth amendment does for the protection of every citizen of the United States against hostile and discriminating legislation against him in favor of others, whether they reside in the same or in different States. If under the fourth article of the Constitution equality of privileges and immunities is secured between citizens of different States, under the fourteenth amendment the same equality is secured between citizens of the [United States].

This equality of right, with exemption from all disparaging and partial enactments, in the lawful pursuits of life, throughout the whole country, is the distinguishing privilege of citizens of the United States. To them, everywhere, all pursuits, all professions, all avocations are open without other restrictions than such as are imposed equally upon all others of the same age, sex, and condition. The State may prescribe such regulations for every pursuit and calling of life as will promote the public health, secure the good order and advance the general prosperity of society, but when once prescribed, the pursuit or calling must be free to be followed by every citizen who is within the conditions designated, and will conform to the regulations. This is the fundamental idea upon which our institutions rest, and unless adhered to in the legislation of the country our government will be a republic only in name. The fourteenth amendment, in my judgment, makes it essential to the validity of the legislation of every State that this equality of right should be respected.

■ JUSTICE BRADLEY, dissenting:

[In] my judgment, it was the intention of the people of this country in adopting [the Fourteenth] amendment to provide National security against violation by the States of the fundamental rights of the citizen. [Any] law which establishes a sheer monopoly, depriving a large class of citizens of the privilege of pursuing a lawful employment, does abridge the privileges of those citizens.

THE MEANING OF THE SLAUGHTER-HOUSE CASES

1. ***The role of the Fourteenth Amendment in the balance of power between the nation and the states.*** Justice Miller was undoubtedly

correct that one of the central purposes of the Fourteenth Amendment was to protect "the newly-made freeman and citizen from the oppressions of those who had formerly exercised unlimited dominion over him." But the chief framers of the Fourteenth Amendment probably also intended to overrule Barron v. Baltimore by setting forth a baseline level of rights to constrain state governments. Given the historical experience of the Civil War, why did Justice Miller dismiss the proposition that the Amendment could have been meant to "radically change the whole theory of the relations of the State and Federal governments"? Might not that have been just what the framers of the Fourteenth Amendment had in mind? See Currie, "The Constitution in the Supreme Court: Limitations on State Power," 51 U. Chi. L. Rev. 329, 348 (1983); see also Aynes, "Constricting the Law of Freedom: Justice Miller, the Fourteenth Amendment, and the Slaughter-House Cases," 70 Chi-Kent L. Rev. 627, 686 (1994) (noting that "the gap between the intent of the amendment and Miller's ruling [is] so great, that many are willing, on that basis alone, to believe that Miller deliberately attempted to defeat the force of the amendment"). But see Lash, "Enforcing the Rights of Due Process: the Original Relationship Between the Fourteenth Amendment and the 1966 Civil Rights Act," 106 Geo. L. J. 1389 (2018) (arguing that "a closer look at [the legislative history] suggests that the 1866 Civil Rights Act is best understood as an attempt to protect the due process rights of all persons, and not the special privileges or immunities of United States citizens").

What light can be shed on these questions by the contemporaneous congressional debates over the Amendment? One of the Fourteenth Amendment's main architects, Congressman John Bingham, stated more than once that it was intended to reverse the Barron decision. And after the Amendment's ratification, Bingham explicitly pointed to the Bill of Rights as the main source of the Amendment's protected privileges and immunities: "[T]he privileges and immunities of citizens of the United States, as contradistinguished from citizens of a State, are chiefly defined in the first eight amendments to the Constitution of the United States. [These] eight articles I have shown never were limitations upon the power of the States, until made so by the fourteenth amendment." On the other hand, Charles Fairman's influential 1949 treatment of the debates discounted Bingham's statements, concluding that the Amendment was not proposed in order to apply against the states the restrictions set forth in the Bill of Rights. See Fairman, "Does the Fourteenth Amendment Incorporate the Bill of Rights? The Original Understanding," 2 Stan. L. Rev. 5 (1949). Fairman also took the lack of public comment over incorporation in the press and the lack of discussion in the state ratification debates of the changes that incorporation would involve for state law and government as evidence that the Amendment was not intended to incorporate new rights against the states. For criticism of Fairman, and a historical treatment of the Fourteenth Amendment "in light of the antislavery crusade that produced it," see Curtis, No State Shall Abridge: The Fourteenth Amendment and the Bill of Rights (1986).

2. ***The political legitimacy of the Fourteenth Amendment.*** After winning the Civil War, northern troops remained stationed throughout the South to oversee Reconstruction for over a decade. During that time, the North effectively controlled much of the South as occupied enemy territory—in fact, the Reconstruction-era military occupation originated with President Lincoln's appointment of military governors to manage occupied enemy territories during the Civil War in 1862. At the time Congress passed the Fourteenth Amendment, none of the former Confederate states was

represented in Congress. Congress then required that the occupied states, which had overwhelmingly rejected the Fourteenth Amendment, ratify the Amendment in order to gain readmission to the Union. See Act of March 2, 1867, 39 Stat. 428, 429 ("[W]hen [a rebel] State, by a vote of its legislature . . . , shall have adopted the [Fourteenth] amendment, . . . said State shall be declared entitled to representation in Congress . . . ."). Congress made clear that the South must choose between ratification and occupation. Tennessee, for example, was the only southern state excluded from the military occupation, because it had already ratified the Amendment.

Does the approach Congress took in securing the Fourteenth Amendment's ratification support Justice Miller's argument that pervasive federal control over the states was not "intended . . . by the legislatures of the States which ratified" it? Should the Court be willing to call into question the procedural legitimacy of laws or even constitutional amendments?

3. ***Privileges and immunities of national citizenship.*** Justice Miller's majority position in the Slaughter-House Cases has long been read to truncate the force of the Privileges or Immunities Clause of the Fourteenth Amendment, limiting it to a few structural rights of national (as distinct from state) citizenship—Justice Miller's potpourri of rights "which owe their existence to the Federal government, its National character, its Constitution, or its laws." Twining v. New Jersey, 211 U.S. 78 (1908). The clause has rarely been invoked to invalidate a state law, and when it has been, it has not had much shelf life; for example, Colgate v. Harvey, 296 U.S. 404 (1935), struck down a Vermont tax provision as a violation of federal privileges and immunities, but Colgate was overruled in Madden v. Kentucky, 309 U.S. 83 (1940), where the Court reiterated Justice Miller's position. Thus, although the language of the clause speaks to substantive matters more explicitly than do the companion clauses in the first section of the Fourteenth Amendment, use of the Privileges or Immunities Clause to expand substantive individual rights was precluded at the outset.

Is this a correct interpretation of the Slaughter-House opinion? Consider the following view: "[N]othing in Miller's opinion [negates] a role for the Privileges or Immunities Clause in the incorporation of Bill of Rights freedoms against the states, and [in fact], a more plausible reading of Miller's opinion specifically preserves such a role for the Clause." Newsome, "Setting Incorporationism Straight: A Reinterpretation of the Slaughter-House Cases," 109 Yale L.J. 643 (2000). See also Palmer, "The Parameters of Constitutional Reconstruction: Slaughter-House, Cruikshank, and the Fourteenth Amendment," 1984 U. Ill. L. Rev. 739 (arguing that the Slaughter-House Cases left substantial room for enforcement of the Bill of Rights through the Privileges or Immunities Clause, but that subsequent decisions misread Justice Miller's opinion).

Even if it is correct to read the Slaughter-House opinion as truncating the Privileges or Immunities Clause, is that a correct reading of the clause itself? Isn't "the most plausible interpretation of the [Clause] the one suggested by its language—that it was a delegation to future constitutional decision-makers to protect certain rights that the document neither lists, at least not exhaustively, nor even in any specific way gives directions for finding"? Ely, Democracy and Distrust (1980). Justice Field argued in dissent that the majority had rendered the Fourteenth Amendment's Privileges or Immunities Clause mere surplusage, because the rights in Justice Miller's list (such as the right to travel across state lines or petition the federal government for redress of grievances) were already protected either expressly or through the structural implications of the Constitution.

Even if the majority were correct, should the Slaughter-House opinion command contemporary adherence? Consider the following view: "[I]t seems doubtful that the 125-year-old Slaughter-House precedent should continue to command the respect that pre-1999 courts consistently accorded it." Tribe, 1 American Constitutional Law 1321 (3d ed., 2000) (arguing for revisiting the Slaughter-House decision and broadening the scope of Privileges or Immunities protections). See also Thomas, The Higher Law Background of the Privileges or Immunities Clause of the Fourteenth Amendment," 12 Harv. J.L. & Pub. Pol'y 63 (1989) (endorsing the contemporary use of the Privileges or Immunities Clause to reflect natural rights in the Constitution); Kurland, "The Privileges or Immunities Clause: 'Its Hour Come Round at Last'?" 1972 Wash. U. L.Q. 405 (suggesting that, "[w]ith government in control of so many essentials of our life" in the modern era, the Privileges and or Immunities Clause might serve as a "haven" for "privacy" and other protections against excessive legislative and executive discretion).

4. ***Resurrection of the privileges and immunities of national citizenship: the right to travel and durational residency requirements.*** One of the cases that Justice Miller cites to identify what rights are included in the "privileges and immunities" of national citizenship is **Crandall v. Nevada**, 6 Wall. (73 U.S.) 35 (1867). In Crandall, the Court invalidated a tax on passengers leaving the state via common carriers and emphasized the citizen's basic "right to come to the seat of [the national] government." That holding came to serve as the basis for later cases identifying a right to travel between states. In **Edwards v. California**, 314 U.S. 160 (1941), for example, the Court invalidated a law making it a misdemeanor to bring into California "any indigent person who is not a resident of the State, knowing him to be an indigent person." This so-called "anti-Okie law," famously the subject of John Steinbeck's novel, The Grapes of Wrath (1939), became especially controversial during the Great Depression. California argued "that the huge influx of migrants into California in recent years has resulted in problems of health, morals, and especially finance, the proportions of which are staggering." The Court was unanimous in striking down the law, but the Justices differed about the proper reasoning. Justice BYRNES's majority opinion relied solely on the Commerce Clause. Justice DOUGLAS's concurrence, joined by Justices Black and Murphy, argued that "the right of persons to move freely from State to State occupies a more protected position in our constitutional system than does the movement of cattle, fruit, steel and coal across state lines," and suggested that the right was an "incident of *national* citizenship protected by the privileges or immunities clause of the Fourteenth Amendment against state interference."

In 1999, the Court seemed to breathe new life into the Privileges or Immunities Clause of the Fourteenth Amendment with its decision in Saenz v. Roe, a case involving a challenge to a state law that distinguished among state residents in the distribution of welfare benefits according to the duration of their residence within the state:

Saenz v. Roe

526 U.S. 489, 119 S. Ct. 1518, 143 L. Ed. 2d 689 (1999).

[In 1992, California enacted a statute limiting the maximum welfare benefits available to newly arrived residents. The law limited the amount payable to a family that has resided in the State for less than 12 months to the amount payable by the State of the family's prior residence. In 1996, Congress enacted the Personal Responsibility and Work Opportunity Reconciliation Act of 1996, which among other things expressly authorized a state receiving federal welfare funds to "apply to a family the rules (including benefit amounts) of the [welfare] program . . . of another State if the family has moved to the State from the other State and has resided in the State for less than 12 months." Roe moved to California and was denied full welfare benefits under those two laws. Roe challenged the provisions, arguing that they violated the Privileges or Immunities Clause and the Citizenship Clause by interfering with the rights of U.S. citizens to travel freely between states.]

■ JUSTICE STEVENS delivered the opinion of the Court.

[The] word "travel" is not found in the text of the Constitution. Yet the "constitutional right to travel from one State to another" is firmly embedded in our jurisprudence. [The] "right to travel" discussed in our cases embraces at least three different components. It protects the right of a citizen of one State to enter and to leave another State, the right to be treated as a welcome visitor rather than an unfriendly alien when temporarily present in the second State, and, for those travelers who elect to become permanent residents, the right to be treated like other citizens of that State. [The] right to go from one place to another, including the right to cross state borders while en route, [was] vindicated in Edwards v. California, which invalidated a state law that impeded the free interstate passage of the indigent [and] reaffirmed [in] United States v. Guest, which afforded protection to the " 'right to travel freely to and from the State of Georgia and to use highway facilities and other instrumentalities of interstate commerce within the State of Georgia.' "

The second component of the right to travel is [expressly] protected by the text of the Constitution. The first sentence of Article IV, § 2, provides: "The Citizens of each State shall be entitled to all Privileges and Immunities of Citizens in the several States." Thus, by virtue of a person's state citizenship, a citizen of one State who travels in other States, intending to return home at the end of his journey, is entitled to enjoy the "Privileges and Immunities of Citizens in the several States" that he visits. This provision removes "from the citizens of each State the disabilities of alienage in the other States." Paul v. Virginia, 75 U.S. 168 (1869).

[What] is at issue in this case [is] this third aspect of the right to travel—the right of the newly arrived citizen to the same privileges and immunities enjoyed by other citizens of the same State. That right is protected not only by the new arrival's status as a state citizen, but also by her status as a citizen of the United States. [Despite] fundamentally differing views concerning the coverage of the Privileges or Immunities Clause of the Fourteenth Amendment, most notably expressed in the majority and dissenting opinions in the Slaughter-House Cases, it has always been common ground that this Clause protects the third component of the right to travel. Writing for the majority in the Slaughter-House Cases, Justice Miller explained that one of the privileges conferred by this Clause "is that a citizen of the United States can, of his own volition, become a citizen of any State of the Union by a bona fide residence therein, with the same rights as other citizens of that State."

[Neither] mere rationality nor some intermediate standard of review should be used to judge the constitutionality of a state rule that discriminates against some of its citizens because they have been domiciled in the State for less than a year. [It] is undisputed that respondents and the members of the class that they represent are citizens of California and that their need for welfare benefits is unrelated to the length of time that they have resided in California. We thus have no occasion to consider what weight might be given to a citizen's length of residence if the bona fides of her claim to state citizenship were questioned. Moreover, because whatever benefits they receive will be consumed while they remain in California, there is no danger that recognition of their claim will encourage citizens of other States to establish residency for just long enough to acquire some readily portable benefit, such as a divorce or a college education, that will be enjoyed after they return to their original domicile.

The classifications challenged in this case [may] not be justified by a purpose to deter welfare applicants from migrating to California. [Such] a purpose would be unequivocally impermissible. Disavowing any desire to fence out the indigent, California has instead advanced an entirely fiscal justification for its multi-tiered scheme. The enforcement of [the scheme] will save the State approximately $10.9 million a year. The question is not whether such saving is a legitimate purpose but whether the State may accomplish that end by the discriminatory means it has chosen. An evenhanded, across-the-board reduction of about 72 cents per month for every beneficiary would produce the same result. [The] Citizenship Clause of the Fourteenth Amendment expressly equates citizenship with residence: "That Clause does not provide for, and does not allow for, degrees of citizenship based on length of residence." It is equally clear that the Clause does not tolerate a hierarchy of 45 subclasses of similarly situated citizens based on the location of their prior residence.[1] [Neither] the duration of respondents' California residence, nor the identity of their prior States of residence, has any relevance to their need for benefits. [In] short, the State's legitimate interest in saving money provides no justification for its decision to discriminate among equally eligible citizens.

The question [remains] whether congressional approval of durational residency requirements in the 1996 [statute] somehow resuscitates the constitutionality of [the California law]. That question is readily answered, for we have consistently held that Congress may not authorize the States to violate the Fourteenth Amendment. Moreover, the protection afforded to the citizen by the Citizenship Clause of that Amendment is a limitation on the powers of the National Government as well as the States.

[Citizens] of the United States, whether rich or poor, have the right to choose to be citizens "of the State wherein they reside." U.S. Const., Amdt. 14, § 1. The States, however, do not have any right to select their citizens.

---

[1] See Cohen, Discrimination Against New State Citizens: An Update, 11 Const. Comm. 73, 79 (1994) ("Just as it would violate the Constitution to deny these new arrivals state citizenship, it would violate the Constitution to concede their citizenship in name only while treating them as if they were still citizens of other states"). [Footnote by Justice Stevens.]

[Affirmed.]

■ CHIEF JUSTICE REHNQUIST, with whom JUSTICE THOMAS joins, dissenting.

[This] Court has consistently recognized that while new citizens must have the same opportunity to enjoy the privileges of being a citizen of a State, the States retain the ability to use bona fide residence requirements to ferret out those who intend to take the privileges and run. [This] Court has repeatedly sanctioned the State's use of durational residence requirements before new residents receive in-state tuition rates at state universities. The Court has done the same in upholding a 1-year residence requirement for eligibility to obtain a divorce in state courts. [If] States can require individuals to reside in-state for a year before exercising the right to educational benefits, [and] the right to terminate a marriage, then States may surely do the same for welfare benefits. [The] welfare payment here and in-state tuition rates are cash subsidies provided to a limited class of people, and California's standard of living and higher education system make both subsidies quite attractive. [The] Court tries to distinguish education and divorce benefits by contending that the welfare payment here will be consumed in California, while a college education or a divorce produces benefits that are "portable" and can be enjoyed after individuals return to their original domicile. But this "you can't take it with you" distinction is more apparent than real. [A] welfare subsidy is [as] much an investment in human capital as is a tuition subsidy, and their attendant benefits are just as "portable." [I] therefore believe that the durational residence requirement challenged here is a permissible exercise of the State's power to "assure that services provided for its residents are enjoyed only by residents."

[Congress's] express approval of durational residence requirements for welfare recipients only goes to show the reasonableness of [the California] law. The National Legislature, where people from Mississippi as well as California are represented, has recognized the need to protect state resources in a time of experimentation and welfare reform. As States like California revamp their total welfare packages, they should have the authority and flexibility to ensure that their new programs are not exploited. Congress has decided that it makes good welfare policy to give the States this power. California has reasonably exercised it through an objective, narrowly tailored residence requirement. I see nothing in the Constitution that should prevent the enforcement of that requirement.

■ JUSTICE THOMAS, with whom CHIEF JUSTICE REHNQUIST joins, dissenting.

In my view, the majority attributes a meaning to the Privileges or Immunities Clause that likely was unintended when the Fourteenth Amendment was enacted and ratified. [At] the time the Fourteenth Amendment was adopted, people understood that "privileges or immunities of citizens" were fundamental rights, rather than every public benefit established by positive law. Accordingly, the majority's conclusion—that a State violates the Privileges or Immunities Clause when it "discriminates" against citizens who have been domiciled in the State for less than a year in the distribution of welfare benefits—appears contrary to the original understanding and is dubious at best. [Although] the majority appears to breathe new life into the [Privileges or Immunities] Clause today, it fails to address its historical underpinnings or its place in our constitutional jurisprudence. Because I believe that the demise of the Privileges or Immunities Clause has contributed in no small part to the current disarray of our Fourteenth Amendment jurisprudence, I would be open to reevaluating its meaning in an appropriate case. Before invoking the Clause, however, we should endeavor to understand what the framers of the Fourteenth Amendment thought that it meant.

SAENZ V. ROE AND THE "RIGHT TO TRAVEL"

1. ***The right to travel and the Equal Protection Clause.*** Prior to Saenz, in a line of cases beginning with **Shapiro v. Thompson**, 394 U.S. 618 (1969), the Court had temporarily found a home for the wandering right of interstate migration in the Equal Protection Clause of the Fourteenth Amendment. Viewing the right to travel as "fundamental" and thus as triggering strict scrutiny of classifications impinging on that right that would otherwise receive rationality review (see Chapter 9, Section 6 below), the Court struck down a number of durational residency requirements that were preconditions for receiving state benefits. Shapiro invalidated a state law similar to the one later struck down in Saenz, except that the law denied welfare benefits altogether to new state residents in the first year of residence.

In Shapiro, Justice BRENNAN wrote for the Court: "[There] is no dispute that the effect of the waiting-period requirement [is] to create two classes of needy resident families indistinguishable from each other except that one is composed of residents who have resided a year or more, and the second of residents who have resided less than a year, in the jurisdiction. [The] first class is granted and the second class is denied welfare aid upon which may depend the ability of the families to obtain the very means to subsist—food, shelter, and other necessities of life. [We] do not doubt that the one-year waiting-period device is well suited to discourage the influx of poor families in need of assistance. [But] the purpose of inhibiting migration by needy persons into the State is constitutionally impermissible. [We] recognize that a State has a valid interest in preserving the fiscal integrity of its programs. [But] a State may not accomplish such a purpose by invidious distinctions between classes of its citizens. [In] moving from State to State [appellees] were exercising a constitutional right, and any classification which serves to penalize the exercise of that right, unless shown to be necessary to promote a *compelling* governmental interest, is unconstitutional."

Shapiro gave rise to a line of cases in which the Court invalidated some, but not all, durational residency requirements as deterring or penalizing exercise of the fundamental right to interstate migration. In Dunn v. Blumstein, 405 U.S. 330 (1972), the Court invalidated Tennessee's requirement that a new state citizen reside in-state for one year before being eligible to vote. But the Court summarily affirmed a decision upholding state durational residency requirements for preferential in-state tuition rates at state universities. Starns v. Malkerson, 326 F. Supp. 234, aff'd, 401 U.S. 985 (1971); cf. Vlandis v. Kline, 412 U.S. 441 (1973) (holding that due process requires an opportunity for a student to show that "he is a bona fide resident entitled to the in-state rates," but not otherwise questioning such waiting periods). In Memorial Hospital v. Maricopa County, 415 U.S. 250 (1974), the Court invalidated an Arizona requirement of one year's residence in a county as a condition of an indigent's receiving free nonemergency hospitalization or medical care. Justice Marshall's majority opinion for the Court deemed medical care, like welfare, " 'a basic necessity of life' to an indigent," and held that "[Arizona's] durational residency requirement for free medical care penalizes indigents for exercising their right to migrate to and settle in that State." Justice Rehnquist was the sole dissenter. A year later, Justice Rehnquist wrote for the majority in Sosna v. Iowa, 419 U.S. 393 (1975), which upheld a requirement that a party reside in the state for one year before bringing a divorce action against a nonresident. He distinguished the prior cases: "Appellant was not irretrievably foreclosed from obtaining some part of what she sought, as was the case with the welfare recipients in Shapiro, the voters in Blumstein, or the indigent patient in Maricopa County. [Iowa's] requirement delayed her access to the courts, but, by fulfilling it, a plaintiff could ultimately obtain the same opportunity for adjudication which she asserts ought to be hers at an earlier point in time. [A] State such as Iowa may quite reasonably decide that it does not wish to become a divorce mill."

2. ***Saenz, Shapiro and Slaughter-House.*** Note that Saenz v. Roe achieves a result similar to that in Shapiro—both invalidate two-tier or multi-tier welfare schemes that distinguish among new and old state residents. Both decisions likewise treat a state's desire to avoid becoming a "welfare magnet" as reflecting impermissible discrimination against newcomers. But Saenz abandons the equal protection methodology of Shapiro and adopts new and different reasoning rooted in the structural postulates of federalism. Shapiro asked whether a benefit was important enough (akin to "necessities of life") that having to wait for as long as a year before receiving it would discourage would-be immigrants from moving into a new state, or penalize them if they did so. Under the Shapiro line of cases, the relative importance of the benefit thus helped determine whether the law impinged upon a fundamental right to travel in violation of equal protection. In Saenz, it was not clear that such an empirical deterrent or penalty effect existed, because new state residents would have received the same nominal dollar amount of welfare in California as in their prior states of residence—unlike in Shapiro, where new state residents received no welfare at all.

Saenz sidestepped that issue by abandoning the equal protection/fundamental rights methodology in favor of analysis under the Citizenship Clause and Privileges or Immunities Clause. Saenz treats *any* classification that treats new state citizens differently from longtime residents as presumptively unconstitutional, regardless of the importance or magnitude of the benefit and thus regardless of any hypothesized deterrent or penalty effect. After Saenz, it appears that a state may draw *no* distinction between classes of citizens based on length of residence without compelling justification. Should the right of new state residents against facially discriminatory laws extend to every state benefit? To public library cards, use of municipal parks and property tax exemptions? For the view that Saenz should have been limited to a right of *indigent* newcomers, and not all newcomers generally, because there is "nothing illegitimate about states' efforts to prevent other states from 'free riding' off of their redistributive tax efforts by limiting access to the fruits of that effort," see Hills, "Poverty, Residency, and Federalism: States' Duty of Impartiality Toward Newcomers," 1999 Sup. Ct. Rev. 277.

While Shapiro rested on a conception of individual liberty, Saenz rested more on the structure of the federal union. See Tribe, "Saenz Sans Prophecy: Does the Privileges or Immunities Revival Portend the Future—or Reveal the Structure of the Present?," 113 Harv. L. Rev. 110 (1999) (locating Saenz in "the Court's vision of governmental design in a federal union of equal states, and not primarily the Court's perception of a personal right ineluctably flowing from constitutional text or deeply rooted tradition"). Well before Saenz, some scholars had suggested that, for this reason, the right of interstate migration was better located in the Privileges or Immunities Clause than in the Equal Protection Clause. See Cohen, "Equal Treatment for Newcomers: The Core Meaning of National and State Citizenship," 1 Const. Comm. 9 (1984). If the right of interstate migration derives from structure rather than individual rights, however, then why did the Court disregard the fact that Congress had expressly approved California's approach? Congress of course may not abrogate individual rights, but isn't the national legislature, where all the states are represented, an adequate guardian of federal structure without judicial intervention?

Did Saenz repudiate the Slaughter-House Cases by recognizing that the Privileges or Immunities Clause does protect individual liberties against the states? Or did it merely clarify that interstate migration is a right peculiar to national citizenship, just like the other rights listed at the end of Justice Miller's majority opinion? Recall that Justice Miller cited the right of interstate travel protected in Crandall v. Nevada as a paradigmatic instance of rights "which owe their existence to the Federal government, its National character, its Constitution, or its laws." Is the right to migrate across state borders truly akin to the right upheld in Crandall to cross state borders without taxation?

3. ***Bona fide state residency.*** Note that Saenz declined to disturb the Sosna and Starns/Vlandis cases, which had permitted durational residency requirements for divorce and in-state public university tuition rates. Justice Stevens suggested these cases might still be valid, distinguishing welfare from "portable benefits, such as a divorce or a college education, that will be enjoyed after they return to their original domicile." What is the principle underlying this distinction? The answer requires recalling the Citizenship Clause of the Fourteenth Amendment, which provides: "All persons born or naturalized in the United States and subject to the jurisdiction thereof, are citizens of the United States and of the State wherein they reside." This clause suggests that a state may not discriminate against a national citizen simply because he or she is a new resident of the state. The state may inquire, however, into whether a person truly is a state resident. Justice Stevens' rationale thus may suggest the idea that some benefits (those that are portable, like a degree or decree) are more likely to attract fake residency claims than others, and where that is so, a durational residency requirement may be permissible to assure the bona fides of a claim of new state residency. Chief Justice Rehnquist's dissent ridiculed the distinction, suggesting that apparent newcomers might abscond with *any* state benefits, including welfare. Does Chief Justice Rehnquist's approach suggest that the state should have carte blanche to decide when a durational residency requirement is necessary to test for bona fide state residency? If so, what would be left of Saenz?

SECTION 3. THE "INCORPORATION" OF THE BILL OF RIGHTS THROUGH THE DUE PROCESS CLAUSE

"Due process of law" was not a wholly blank slate when the Fourteenth Amendment was added to the Constitution. The Court had already discussed the history and scope of due process in interpreting the Due Process Clause of the Fifth Amendment. The best known statement was by Justice Curtis in the course of considering the constitutionality of a distress warrant procedure in Murray's Lessee v. Hoboken Land & Improvement Co., 59 U.S. 272, 18 How. 272 (1856): "The words, 'due process of law,' were undoubtedly intended to convey the same meaning as the words, 'by the law of the land,' in Magna Carta. [The] constitution contains no description of those processes which it was intended to allow or forbid. It does not even declare what principles are to be applied to ascertain whether it be due process. [To] what principles, then, are we to resort to ascertain whether this process, enacted by congress, is due process? To this the answer must be twofold. We must examine the constitution itself, to see whether this process be in conflict with any of its provisions. If not found to be so, we must look to those settled usages and modes of proceeding existing in the common and statute law of England, before the emigration of our ancestors, and which are shown not to have been unsuited to their civil and political condition by having been acted on by them after the settlement of this country. [T]hough 'due process of law' generally implies and includes actor, reus, judex, regular allegations, opportunity to answer and a trial according to some settled course of judicial proceedings, [this] is not universally true." As Justice Curtis's last sentence suggests, concepts of notice and hearing have long been at the core of due process.

The Court has also long found that "fundamental fairness" as reflected in due process affords criminal defendants rights against the states that correspond to some of the guarantees in the Bill of Rights. As the Court recognized as early as 1908, in Twining v. New Jersey, 211 U.S. 78: "It is possible that some of the personal rights safeguarded by the first eight Amendments against National action may also be safeguarded against state action, because a denial of them would be a denial of due process of law. If this is so, it is not because those rights are enumerated in the first eight Amendments, but because they are of such a nature that they are included in the conception of due process."

While Twining recognized that some of the provisions in Bill of Rights were "incorporated" against the states by the Fourteenth Amendment, the question of precisely which rights were incorporated, and how a court could identify them, proved more difficult to resolve. In **Palko v. Connecticut**, 302 U.S. 319 (1937), Justice CARDOZO articulated the case for "selective" incorporation. Connecticut permitted the State to take appeals in criminal cases. Palko's second degree murder conviction had been set aside by the highest state court on an appeal taken by the State. On retrial, he was convicted of first degree murder. He claimed that such a retrial in the federal courts would have violated the Fifth Amendment's double jeopardy guarantee, and argued that "whatever is forbidden by the Fifth Amendment is forbidden by the Fourteenth also." Moreover, he argued that whatever would be "a violation of the original bill of rights [if] done by the federal government is now equally unlawful by force of the 14th Amendment if done by a state." Justice Cardozo replied: "There is no such general rule." He noted that, at that time, the Court had applied to the states some Bill of Rights guarantees (e.g., free speech and right to counsel) but not others (e.g., grand jury indictment, and the protection against self-incrimination). Explaining the difference, he stated: "The right to trial by jury and the immunity from prosecution except as the result of an indictment may have value and importance. Even so, they are not of the very essence of a scheme of ordered liberty. To abolish them is not to violate a 'principle of justice so rooted in the traditions and conscience of our people as to be ranked as fundamental.' Few would be so narrow or provincial as to maintain that a fair and enlightened system of justice would be impossible without them. What is true of jury trials and indictments is true also [of] the immunity from compulsory self-incrimination. This too might be lost, and justice still be [done]. We reach a different plane of social and moral values when we pass to [those guarantees of the Bill of Rights] brought within the [Fourteenth Amendment] by a process of absorption. These in their origin were effective against the federal government alone. If the [14th Amendment] has absorbed them, the process of absorption has had its source in the belief that neither liberty nor justice would exist if they were sacrificed. This is true, for illustration, of freedom of thought, and speech. Of that freedom one may say that it is the matrix, the indispensable condition, of nearly every other form of [freedom]. Fundamental too in the concept of due process, and so in that of liberty, is the thought that condemnation shall be rendered only after trial." Note that in subsequent years, the Court did incorporate additional constitutional guarantees such as the right to a jury trial, Duncan v. Louisiana, 391 U.S. 145 (1968), and the protection against double jeopardy, Benton v. Maryland, 395 U.S. 784 (1969). A few provisions of the Bill of Rights, like the right to a grand jury, remain unincorporated.

In **Adamson v. California**, 332 U.S. 46 (1947), a 5–4 majority adhered to Justice Cardozo's approach over the dissent of Justice Black. Adamson claimed that his murder conviction violated the Fourteenth Amendment because the prosecution had been permitted to comment on his failure to take the stand at his trial. Justice REED's majority opinion assumed that such a comment would violate the Fifth Amendment's self-incrimination privilege in a federal proceeding. He conceded, moreover, that the Fourteenth Amendment's Due Process Clause guaranteed a right to a "fair trial." But, under Palko, he concluded, not all Bill of Rights guarantees were protected by the Fourteenth Amendment, and he found no ground to make the self-incrimination privilege applicable to the states.

Justice BLACK's dissent, joined by Justice Douglas, contains the most famous exposition of the view that due process requires "total" incorporation of the Bill Rights. A landmark in the use of original historical research by a modern justice, the opinion extensively quoted debates in the Reconstruction congress, emphasizing statements made by Congressman John Bingham: "This decision reasserts a constitutional theory spelled out in [Twining], that this Court is endowed by the Constitution with boundless power under 'natural law' periodically to expand and contract constitutional standards to conform to the Court's conception of what at a particular time constitutes 'civilized decency' and 'fundamental liberty and justice.' [I] think that decision and the 'natural law' theory of the Constitution upon which it relies degrade the constitutional safeguards of the Bill of Rights and simultaneously appropriate for this Court a broad power which we are not authorized by the Constitution to exercise. [In my judgment] history conclusively demonstrates that the language of the first section of the Fourteenth Amendment, taken as a whole, was thought by those responsible for its submission to the people, and by those who opposed its submission, sufficiently explicit to guarantee that thereafter no state could deprive its citizens of the privileges and protections of the Bill of Rights. [I] would follow what I believe was the original purpose of the Fourteenth Amendment—to extend to all the people of the nation the complete protection of the [Bill of Rights].[1]

In a concurring opinion, Justice FRANKFURTER attacked Justice Black's "total incorporation" position, arguing that the Fourteenth Amendment's Due Process Clause "neither comprehends the specific provisions by which the founders deemed it appropriate to restrict the federal government nor is it confined to them. [A] construction which gives to due process no independent function but turns it into a summary of the specific provisions of the Bill of Rights [would] assume that no other abuses would reveal themselves in the course of time than those which had become manifest in 1791. [The issue here] is not whether an infraction of one of the specific provisions of the first eight Amendments is disclosed by the record [but] whether the criminal proceedings which resulted in conviction deprived the accused of the due process of [law]. Judicial review of that [guaranty] inescapably imposes upon this Court an exercise of judgment upon the whole course of the proceedings in order to ascertain whether they offend those canons of decency and fairness which express the notions of justice of English-speaking peoples even toward those charged with the most heinous offenses."[2]

Cardozo and Frankfurter defended their opposition to incorporating all of the Bill of Rights into the Fourteenth Amendment by arguing that such a position would unduly limit state autonomy in the enforcement of criminal law. Black's recurrent rejoinder was that the majority's "fundamental fairness"—"essence of a scheme of ordered liberty" approach was too vague and open-ended and left too much room for subjective views. Black insisted that his "total incorporation" view would curb excessive judicial discretion by relying on the allegedly clearer standards of the "specific" guarantees of the Bill of Rights. Respect for state policymakers permeates the majority positions from Palko to Adamson. But which approach better respected state autonomy in fact? Is the unpredictability of the flexible due process approach arguably more harmful to state concerns than a more rigid—possibly more interventionist, yet also more certain—interpretation that incorporated all the Bill of Rights?

Justice Frankfurter's flexible due process approach in Adamson insisted that due process interpretation "is not based on the idiosyncrasies of merely

[1] On this historical record, see Fairman, "Does the Fourteenth Amendment Incorporate the Bill of Rights? The Original Understanding," 2 Stan. L. Rev. 5 (1949), which disagreed with Justice Black's position; but see Crosskey, "Charles Fairman, 'Legislative History,' and the Constitutional Limitations on State Authority," 22 U. Chi. L. Rev. 1 (1954). See also Morrison, "Does the Fourteenth Amendment Incorporate the Bill of Rights? The Judicial Interpretation," 2 Stan. L. Rev. 140 (1949); Henkin, "Selective Incorporation' in the 14th Amendment," 73 Yale L.J. 74 (1963); Friendly, "The Bill of Rights as a Code of Criminal Procedure," 53 Cal. L. Rev. 929 (1965); and Aynes, "Charles Fairman, Felix Frankfurter, and the Fourteenth Amendment," 70 Chi-Kent L. Rev. 1197 (1995).

[2] The Court later held, in Malloy v. Hogan, 378 U.S. 1 (1964), that the Fifth Amendment's privilege against self-incrimination was applicable to the states under the 14th Amendment: "Decisions of the Court since Twining and Adamson have departed from the contrary view expressed in those cases." A year later, the Court overruled the specific holding in Adamson and found unconstitutional the California rule permitting comment on the defendant's failure to testify. Griffin v. California, 380 U.S. 609 (1965).

personal judgment." Yet can that approach be truly impersonal? What external criteria are available to give content to due process? As Justice Black commented a few years after Adamson in Rochin v. California, 342 U.S. 165 (1952), if "canons of decency and fairness which express the notions of justice of English-speaking peoples" are to govern, "one may well ask what avenues of investigation are open to discover 'canons' of conduct so universally favored that this Court should write them into the Constitution." Did Justice Black's position avoid judicial subjectivity any more effectively than the Palko-Adamson technique? Does incorporation of a "specific" Bill of Rights provision significantly curtail the range of judicial judgment? How specific are those guarantees? Contrast the guarantee of jury trial in civil cases involving more than 20 dollars with the considerably more open-ended dimensions of the protection against "unreasonable" searches and seizures and the assurance of "the Assistance of Counsel."

For a decade and a half after Adamson, the Court persisted in applying the flexible due process analysis articulated in Palko and Adamson. Beginning in the early 1960s, however, the Warren Court—without ever formally abandoning the "fundamental fairness" standard—began to look ever more to the Bill of Rights for guidance and began to apply ever more of those guarantees to the states via the 14th Amendment. Thus, while "selective" incorporation continued to govern in theory, Justice Black's position predominantly prevailed in fact. One by one, the Court found applicable to the states virtually all of the criminal procedure guarantees of the Bill of Rights. The Court's methodology shifted: while under Palko-Adamson, the Court looked at the facts of a case and asked whether the challenged state action violated the "fundamental fairness" requirement implicit in due process, the Court's later approach ascertained the relevant Bill of Rights provision and asked whether that *provision* is essential to "fundamental fairness" such that it should be made applicable to the states. The case that follows illustrates this new approach:

Duncan v. Louisiana

391 U.S. 145, 88 S. Ct. 1444, 20 L. Ed. 2d 491 (1968).

■ JUSTICE WHITE delivered the opinion of the Court.

[Duncan was convicted of battery, a misdemeanor punishable by a maximum of two years' imprisonment and a $300 fine. He sought trial by jury, but because the Louisiana Constitution grants jury trials only in cases in which capital punishment or imprisonment at hard labor might be imposed, the trial judge denied the request. He was convicted and sentenced to serve 60 days in the parish prison and pay a fine of $150. He argued on appeal that the Fourteenth Amendment's Due Process Clause incorporates the right to a jury trial in state criminal prosecutions where a sentence as long as two years may be imposed.]

[In] resolving conflicting claims concerning the meaning of this spacious language [of due process], the Court has looked increasingly to the Bill of Rights for guidance; many of the rights guaranteed by the first eight Amendments to the Constitution have been held to be protected against state action by the Due Process Clause of the [Fourteenth] Amendment. That clause now protects the right to compensation for property taken by the State

[Chicago, Burlington & Quincy R'wy Co. v. Chicago, 166 U.S. 226 (1897)]; the rights of speech, press, and religion covered by the First Amendment [Fiske v. Kansas, 274 U.S. 380 (1927)]; the Fourth Amendment rights to be free from unreasonable searches and seizures and to have excluded from criminal trials any evidence illegally seized [Mapp v. Ohio, 367 U.S. 643 (1961)]; the right guaranteed by the Fifth Amendment to be free of compelled self-incrimination [Malloy v. Hogan, 378 U.S. 1 (1964)]; and the Sixth Amendment rights to counsel [Gideon v. Wainwright, 372 U.S. 335 (1963)], to a speedy and public trial [Klopfer v. North Carolina, 386 U.S. 213 (1967); In re Oliver, 333 U.S. 257 (1948)], to confrontation of opposing witnesses [Pointer v. Texas, 380 U.S. 400 (1965)], and to compulsory process for obtaining witnesses [Washington v. Texas, 388 U.S. 14 (1967)].

The test for determining whether a right extended by the [Bill of Rights] is also protected against state action by the Fourteenth Amendment has been phrased in a variety of ways in the opinions of this Court. The question has been asked whether a right is among those "fundamental principles of liberty and justice which lie at the base of all our civil and political institutions," [Powell v. Alabama, 287 U.S. 45, 67 (1932)]; whether it is "basic in our system of jurisprudence," [In re Oliver, 333 U.S. 257, 273 (1948)]; and whether it is "a fundamental right, essential to a fair trial," [Gideon v. Wainwright, 372 U.S. 335, 343–344 (1963)]. Because we believe that trial by jury in criminal cases is fundamental to the American scheme of justice, we hold that the [Fourteenth] Amendment guarantees a right of jury trial in all criminal cases which—were they to be tried in a federal court—would come within the Sixth Amendment's guarantee. Since we consider the appeal before us to be such a case, we hold that the Constitution was violated when appellant's demand for jury trial was refused. [The] deep commitment of the Nation to the right of jury trial in serious criminal cases as a defense against arbitrary law enforcement qualifies for protection under the Due Process Clause of the [Fourteenth] Amendment, and must therefore be respected by the States.

Louisiana [contends] that even if it must grant jury trials in serious criminal cases, the conviction before us [is] constitutional because here the petitioner was tried for simple battery and was sentenced to only 60 days in the parish prison. We are not persuaded. It is doubtless true that there is a category of petty crimes or offenses which is not subject to the Sixth Amendment [and] should not be subject to the [Fourteenth Amendment]. Crimes carrying possible penalties up to six months do not require a jury trial if they otherwise qualify as petty offenses. [But here, the state] has made simple battery a criminal offense punishable by imprisonment for two years and a fine. The question [is] whether a crime carrying such a penalty is an offense which Louisiana may insist on trying without a jury. We think [not].

[Reversed and remanded.]

■ JUSTICE BLACK, with whom JUSTICE DOUGLAS joins, concurring.

[I agree with the holding] for reasons given by the Court. I also agree because of reasons given in my dissent in [Adamson]. I am very happy to support this selective process through which our Court has since the Adamson case held most of the specific Bill of Rights' protections applicable to the States to the same extent they are applicable to the [Federal Government]. All of these holdings making Bill of Rights' provisions applicable as such to the States mark, of course, a departure from the Twining doctrine. [The] dissent in this case, however, makes a spirited and forceful defense of that now discredited doctrine. [Justice] Harlan's objections to my Adamson dissent history, like that of most of the objectors, relies most heavily on a criticism written by Professor Charles Fairman and published in the Stanford Law Review. 2 Stan. L. Rev. 5 (1949). I have read and studied this article extensively, including the historical references, but am compelled to add that in my view it has completely failed to refute the inferences and arguments that I suggested in my Adamson [dissent].

[The dissent also] states that "the great words of the four clauses of the first section of the Fourteenth Amendment would have been an exceedingly peculiar way to say that 'The rights heretofore guaranteed against federal intrusion by the first eight Amendments are henceforth guaranteed against state intrusion as well.' " In response to this I can say only that the words "No State shall make or enforce any law which shall abridge the privileges or immunities of citizens of the United States" seem to me an eminently reasonable way of expressing the idea that henceforth the Bill of Rights shall apply to the States.[1] What more precious "privilege" of American citizenship could there be than that privilege to claim the protections of our great Bill of Rights? I suggest that any reading of "privileges or immunities of citizens of the United States" which excludes the Bill of Rights' safeguards renders the words of this section of the [Fourteenth] Amendment meaningless. [If] anything, it is "exceedingly peculiar" to read the [Fourteenth] Amendment differently from the way I do.

[Due] process, according to my Brother Harlan, is to be a phrase with no permanent meaning, but one which is found to shift from time to time in accordance with judges' predilections and understandings of what is best for the country. [It] is impossible for me to believe that such unconfined power is given to judges in our Constitution that is a written one in order to limit governmental power. Another tenet of the Twining doctrine as restated by my Brother Harlan is that "due process of law requires only fundamental fairness." But the "fundamental fairness" test is one on a par with that of shocking the conscience of the Court. Each of such tests depends entirely on the particular judge's idea of ethics and morals instead of requiring him to depend on the boundaries fixed by the written words of the Constitution.

■ JUSTICE HARLAN, with whom JUSTICE STEWART joins, dissenting.

[The] first section of the [Fourteenth] Amendment was meant neither to incorporate, nor to be limited to, the specific guarantees of the first eight Amendments. The overwhelming historical evidence marshalled by Professor Fairman demonstrates, to me conclusively, that the Congressmen and state legislators who wrote, debated, and ratified the [Fourteenth] Amendment did not think they were "incorporating" the Bill of Rights. [N]either history, nor sense, supports using the [Fourteenth] Amendment to put the States in a constitutional straitjacket with respect to their own development in the administration of criminal or civil law. Although [I] fundamentally disagree with the total incorporation view of the [Fourteenth] Amendment, it seems to me that such a position does at least have the virtue, lacking in the Court's selective incorporation approach, of internal consistency: we look to the Bill of Rights, word for word, clause for clause, precedent for precedent because, it is said, the men who wrote the Amendment wanted it that way. [Apart] from the approach taken by the

---

1 My view has been and is that the Fourteenth Amendment, *as a whole*, makes the Bill of Rights applicable to the States. This would certainly include the language of the Privileges and Immunities Clause, as well as the Due Process Clause. [Footnote by Justice Black.]

absolute incorporationists, I can see only one method of analysis that has any internal logic. That is to start with the words "liberty" and "due process of law" and attempt to define them in a way that accords with American traditions and our system of government.

[The] argument that jury trial is not a requisite of due process is quite simple. [If] due process of law requires only fundamental fairness, then the inquiry in each case must be whether a state trial process was a fair one. The Court has held, properly I think, that in an adversary process it is a requisite of fairness, for which there is no adequate substitute, that a criminal defendant be afforded a right to counsel and to cross-examine opposing witnesses. But it simply has not been demonstrated, nor, I think, can it be demonstrated, that trial by jury is the only fair means of resolving issues of fact. The jury is of course not without virtues. [The] jury system can also be said to have some inherent defects. [That] trial by jury is not the only fair way of adjudicating criminal guilt is well attested by the fact that it is not the prevailing way, either in England or in this country. [The] Court has chosen to impose upon every State one means of trying criminal cases; it is a good means, but it is not the only fair means, and it is not demonstrably better than the alternatives States might [devise].

INCORPORATION SINCE DUNCAN

1. ***The scope of incorporated rights.*** When a Bill of Rights guarantee is incorporated into the Fourteenth Amendment, does it apply to the states in precisely the same manner as it applies to the federal criminal process? Is every detail of the "incorporated" Bill of Rights provisions applicable "jot-for-jot" to the states? Under the Cardozo-Frankfurter approach, a finding that a right reflected in one of the Bill of Rights provisions was essential to "fundamental fairness" did not mean that all of the detailed interpretations of the relevant Bill of Rights provision necessarily were applicable to the states. For example, in Wolf v. Colorado, 338 U.S. 25 (1949), Justice Frankfurter wrote for the Court that the "core" of the Fourth Amendment guarantee was an ingredient of due process, but went on to find that the exclusionary rule applied in federal courts (barring the use of evidence obtained in violation of the Fourth Amendment) was not constitutionally required of the states. After more than a decade of controversy and confusion in the aftermath of Wolf, the Court reversed that ruling in Mapp v. Ohio, 367 U.S. 643 (1961), finding the exclusionary rule "an essential part of the right to privacy" recognized in Wolf. Incorporation thereafter meant not merely incorporating the "core" of the Bill of Rights guarantee, but applying to the states every detail of the contours of the guarantee. In Williams v. Florida, 399 U.S. 78 (1970), the petitioner sought reversal of a robbery conviction, claiming that he should have been tried by a 12-person jury rather than the six-person panel provided by Florida law in all but capital cases. Although earlier interpretations of the Sixth Amendment had assumed the 12-person panel to be constitutionally necessary, Justice White's majority opinion concluded that "the twelve-man panel is not a necessary ingredient of 'trial by jury,' " explaining that "that particular feature of the jury system appears to have been a historical accident, unrelated to the great purposes which gave rise to the jury in the first place." Justice Harlan concurred in the result under his fundamental

fairness approach, but objected that the majority, following incorporationist logic, had "diluted" Sixth Amendment guarantees: "The necessary consequence of this decision is that twelve-member juries are not constitutionally required in *federal* criminal trials either."

2. ***What rights have been incorporated?*** As a result of selective incorporation, all of the criminal process guarantees of the Bill of Rights have now been held applicable to the states, with the exception of the grand jury indictment provision of the Fifth Amendment and, arguably, the "excessive bail" provision of the Eighth Amendment. Thus the states are bound by the restrictions on search and seizure and warrants set forth in the Fourth Amendment; the rights against double jeopardy and compelled self-incrimination protected by the Fifth Amendment; the right in criminal cases to counsel, confrontation of witnesses and compulsory process, to speedy and public trial and to jury trial protected by the Sixth Amendment; and the ban on cruel and unusual punishment provided by the Eighth Amendment. Outside the criminal area, the Court has applied against the states as a matter of due process the freedom from establishment of religion and the rights to free exercise of religion, speech, press, assembly and petition for redress of grievances protected by the First Amendment, the right to possess firearms protected by the Second Amendment and the right against uncompensated takings protected by the Fifth Amendment. It has not applied to the states the protections of the Third Amendment, the right to jury trial for civil suits at common law for more than 20 dollars set forth in the Seventh Amendment, or the protection against excessive fines established by the Eighth Amendment. In 2019, in an opinion by Justice Ginsburg, the Court incorporated the Excessive Fines Clause of the Eighth Amendment, one of the few remaining provisions of the Bill of Rights that had yet to be incorporated. See Timbs v. Indiana, 139 S. Ct. 682 (2019). Justice Thomas concurred only in the judgment, reiterating his view that the Privileges and Immunities Clause, not the Due Process Clause, should be used to achieve incorporation. Justice Gorsuch concurred: "As an original matter, I acknowledge, the appropriate vehicle for incorporation may well be the Fourteenth Amendment's Privileges or Immunities Clause, rather than, as this Court has long assumed, the Due Process Clause." This marked the first time another justice had expressed agreement with Justice Thomas's view.

3. ***Incorporation and the right to keep and bear arms.*** The Second Amendment provides: "A well regulated Militia, being necessary to the security of a free State, the right of the people to keep and bear Arms, shall not be infringed." Is the Second Amendment one of the original Bill of Rights that ought to be incorporated against the States through the Fourteenth Amendment Due Process Clause? In **United States v. Cruikshank**, 92 U.S. 542 (1876), the Court vacated the convictions of members of a white mob for dispossessing African-Americans of their guns, holding that the Second Amendment did not apply except as against the federal government. In subsequent challenges to federal gun regulations, the Court, interpreting the Amendment narrowly in light of its preamble, declined to enforce the Amendment to protect gun possession or use unconnected to military purposes. In **United States v. Miller**, 307 U.S. 174 (1939), for example, the Court upheld a conviction under the National Firearms Act, holding that the regulated weapons lacked any "reasonable relationship to the preservation or efficiency of a well regulated militia."

In **District of Columbia v. Heller**, 554 U.S. 570 (2008), the Supreme Court for the first time enforced the Amendment expressly as a matter of individual right. Holding that Miller did not foreclose "adoption of the original understanding of the Second Amendment," the Court invalidated, by a vote of 5–4, a D.C. law that effectively banned the possession of handguns. Because D.C. is governed by the federal government, the Court did not need to reach the question whether the Second Amendment is incorporated under due process so as to apply to state or city gun ordinances. But the articulation of the right in Heller brought to the forefront a heated debate about whether the right to bear arms fits the criteria for other rights that have been incorporated against the states under the Due Process Clause or (as some gun rights advocates have suggested) under the Privileges or Immunities Clause.

Writing for the Court in Heller, Justice SCALIA, joined by Chief Justice Roberts and Justices Kennedy, Thomas and Alito, began by looking to the Second Amendment's text and history. "The Second Amendment is naturally divided into two parts: its prefatory clause [(A well regulated Militia, being necessary to the security of a free State,)] and its operative clause [(the right of the people to keep and bear Arms, shall not be infringed)]. The former does not limit the latter grammatically, but rather announces a purpose."

"The first salient feature of the operative clause is that it codifies a 'right of the people.' [Each time the Constitution uses this phrase, it] unambiguously refer[s] to individual rights, not "collective" rights, or rights that may be exercised only through participation in some corporate body. [We] start therefore with a strong presumption that the Second Amendment right is exercised individually and belongs to all Americans. [The] term ['keep and bear Arms'] was applied, then as now, to weapons that were not specifically designed for military use and were not employed in a military capacity[, as shown by contemporary dictionaries.] Although the phrase implies that the carrying of the weapon is for the purpose of "offensive or defensive action," it in no way connotes participation in a structured military organization.

"Putting all of these textual elements together, we find that they guarantee the individual right to possess and carry weapons in case of confrontation. This meaning is strongly confirmed by the historical background of the Second Amendment," which was in part a response to perceived abuses by the King during the Restoration and Revolutionary periods. Justice Scalia went on to ask: "Does the preface fit with an operative clause that creates an individual right to keep and bear arms? It fits perfectly, once one knows the history that the founding generation knew and that we have described above. That history showed that the way tyrants had eliminated a militia consisting of all the able-bodied men was not by banning the militia but simply by taking away the people's arms, enabling a select militia or standing army to suppress political opponents."

Justice Scalia then noted the limits of the holding. First, while distinguishing precedent on which the dissent relied, he conceded that "the Second Amendment does not protect those weapons not typically possessed by law-abiding citizens for lawful purposes, such as short-barreled shotguns." He then confirmed that other reasonable restrictions on firearm ownership could still be constitutional: "Like most rights, the right secured by the Second Amendment is not unlimited. [Although] we do not undertake an exhaustive historical analysis today of the full scope of the Second

Amendment, nothing in our opinion should be taken to cast doubt on longstanding prohibitions on the possession of firearms by felons and the mentally ill, or laws forbidding the carrying of firearms in sensitive places such as schools and government buildings, or laws imposing conditions and qualifications on the commercial sale of arms. [For these reasons,] we hold that the District's ban on handgun possession in the home violates the Second Amendment, as does its prohibition against rendering any lawful firearm in the home operable for the purpose of immediate self-defense."

Justice STEVENS dissented, joined by Justices Souter, Ginsburg and Breyer, taking a very different view of the founding text and history: "The question presented by this case is not whether the Second Amendment protects a 'collective right' or an 'individual right.' Surely it protects a right that can be enforced by individuals. But a conclusion that the Second Amendment protects an individual right does not tell us anything about the scope of that right. Guns are used to hunt, for self-defense, to commit crimes, for sporting activities, and to perform military duties. The Second Amendment plainly does not protect the right to use a gun to rob a bank; it is equally clear that it *does* encompass the right to use weapons for certain military purposes. Whether it also protects the right to possess and use guns for nonmilitary purposes like hunting and personal self-defense is the question presented by this case. The text of the Amendment, its history, and our decision in United States v. Miller (1939; p. 472 above) provide a clear answer to that question.

"The Second Amendment was adopted to protect the right of the people of each of the several States to maintain a well-regulated militia. It was a response to concerns raised during the ratification of the Constitution that the power of Congress to disarm the state militias and create a national standing army posed an intolerable threat to the sovereignty of the several States. Neither the text of the Amendment nor the arguments advanced by its proponents evidenced the slightest interest in limiting any legislature's authority to regulate private civilian uses of firearms. Specifically, there is no indication that the Framers of the Amendment intended to enshrine the common-law right of self-defense in the Constitution. [The] view of the Amendment we took in Miller—that it protects the right to keep and bear arms for certain military purposes, but that it does not curtail the Legislature's power to regulate the nonmilitary use and ownership of weapons—is both the most natural reading of the Amendment's text and the interpretation most faithful to the history of its adoption."

Justice BREYER filed a separate dissent, joined by Justices Stevens, Souter and Ginsburg. Justice Breyer, like Justice Stevens, argued that the Second Amendment does not protect an interest in individual self-defense, but also argued that D.C.'s regulation would survive the proper degree of scrutiny even assuming the Amendment did apply. Under an appropriate balancing of interests, "which focuses upon the presence of handguns in high-crime urban areas," Justice Breyer argued, the D.C. ordinance "represents a permissible legislative response to a serious, indeed life-threatening, problem," and is "tailored to" that problem because it "concerns one class of weapons, handguns, leaving residents free to possess shotguns and rifles." Justice Breyer found no evidence that the Framers of the Second Amendment viewed "handguns in particular" as central to the Second Amendment, much less that they would have extended the Amendment to the "right to keep loaded handguns in homes to confront intruders in urban settings."

How far does the right established in Heller extend? Does the Second Amendment bar regulations less restrictive than D.C.'s effective ban on possession of handguns? Consider Heller's possible application to laws that limit the type of weapons individuals may possess (e.g., a ban on personal possession of machine guns and automatic rifles but not handguns or shotguns); laws that restrict the classes of persons who may handle guns (e.g. a ban on gun possession by minors or persons with a history of criminal activity or mental illness); and laws that limit the manner in which guns are handled (e.g., a ban on concealed carry or carrying while intoxicated, or a requirement that guns be stored unloaded). After Heller, will the Court apply strict or more deferential scrutiny to such regulations? And will such laws be widely invalidated or broadly upheld? For discussion, see Volokh, "Implementing the Right to Keep and Bear Arms for Self-Defense: An Analytical Framework and a Research Agenda," 56 UCLA L. Rev. 1443 (2009); Tushnet, "Permissible Gun Regulations After Heller: Some Speculations About Method and Outcomes," 56 UCLA L. Rev. 1425 (2009).

Speculation about whether the Court would incorporate the newly defined Second Amendment right against the states through the Fourteenth Amendment arose quickly after Heller, but it did not have to continue for long. Two years after deciding Heller, the Court heard a challenge to gun control laws in Chicago. Plagued with some of the highest crime rates in the country, Chicago took a bold approach, effectively banning the possession of handguns for all private citizens in the city. A group of residents sued, arguing that the city's handgun ban violated the Second Amendment, as incorporated against the state government by the Fourteenth Amendment:

McDonald v. City of Chicago

561 U.S. 742, 130 S. Ct. 3020, 177 L. Ed. 2d 894 (2010).

■ JUSTICE ALITO announced the judgment of the Court and delivered the opinion of the Court [in] which CHIEF JUSTICE [ROBERTS], JUSTICE SCALIA and JUSTICE KENNEDY join [and in which JUSTICE THOMAS joins in part].

[Justice Alito wrote for the Court:] Two years ago, in District of Columbia v. Heller, we held that the Second Amendment protects the right to keep and bear arms for the purpose of self-defense, and we struck down a District of Columbia law that banned the possession of handguns in the home. [Chicago and its suburbs] have laws that are similar to the District of Columbia's, but [they] argue that their laws are constitutional because the Second Amendment has no application to the States. We have previously held that most of the provisions of the Bill of Rights apply with full force to both the Federal Government and the States. Applying the standard that is well established in our case law, we hold that the Second Amendment right is fully applicable to the States.

[In answering] the question whether the Second Amendment right to keep and bear arms is incorporated in the concept of due process, [we] must decide whether the right to keep and bear arms is fundamental to our scheme of ordered liberty, Duncan, or [whether] this right is "deeply rooted in this

Nation's history and tradition." [Our] decision in Heller points unmistakably to the answer. [Heller] makes it clear that this right is "deeply rooted in this Nation's history and tradition." Heller explored the right's origins, noting that the 1689 English Bill of Rights explicitly protected a right to keep arms for self-defense, and that by 1765, Blackstone was able to assert that the right to keep and bear arms was "one of the fundamental rights of Englishmen." Blackstone's assessment was shared by the American colonists. As we noted in Heller, King George III's attempt to disarm the colonists in the 1760's and 1770's "provoked polemical reactions by Americans invoking their rights as Englishmen to keep arms."

The right to keep and bear arms was considered no less fundamental by those who drafted and ratified the Bill of Rights. [Those] who were fearful that the new Federal Government would infringe traditional rights such as the right to keep and bear arms insisted on the adoption of the Bill of Rights as a condition for ratification of the Constitution. This is surely powerful evidence that the right was regarded as fundamental in the sense relevant here. This understanding persisted in the years immediately following the ratification of the Bill of Rights. In addition to the four States that had adopted Second Amendment analogues before ratification, nine more States adopted state constitutional provisions protecting an individual right to keep and bear arms between 1789 and 1820. Founding-era legal commentators confirmed the importance of the right to early Americans. [See] 3 J. Story, Commentaries on the Constitution of the United States § 1890, p. 746 (1833).

[After] the Civil War, many of the over 180,000 African Americans who served in the Union Army returned to the States of the old Confederacy, where systematic efforts were made to disarm them and other blacks. The laws of some States formally prohibited African Americans from possessing firearms. [Throughout] the South, armed parties, often consisting of ex-Confederate soldiers serving in the state militias, forcibly took firearms from newly freed slaves. [In response, both the Freedmen's Bureau Act and the Civil Rights Act of 1866 protected the right to bear arms, and Congress later reinforced the right by referring in the debates over the Fourteenth Amendment] to the right to keep and bear arms as a fundamental right deserving of protection.

[For the plurality only, Justice Alito continued:] [R]espondents' remaining arguments are at war with our central holding in Heller. [They] ask us to treat the right recognized in Heller as a second-class right, subject to an entirely different body of rules than the other Bill of Rights guarantees that we have held to be incorporated into the Due Process Clause. [Respondents argue that] if it is possible to imagine any civilized legal system that does not recognize a particular right, then the Due Process Clause does not make that right binding on the States. Therefore, [r]espondents continue, because such countries as England, Canada, Australia, Japan, Denmark, Finland, Luxembourg, and New Zealand either ban or severely limit handgun ownership, it must follow that no right to possess such weapons is protected by the Fourteenth Amendment. This line of argument is, of course, inconsistent with the long-established standard we apply in incorporation cases. [If] our understanding of the right to a jury trial, the right against self-incrimination, and the right to counsel were necessary attributes of any civilized country, it would follow that the United States is the only civilized Nation in the world.

[We] likewise reject [r]espondents' argument that we should depart from our established incorporation methodology on the ground that making the Second Amendment binding on the States and their subdivisions is inconsistent with principles of federalism and will stifle experimentation. [But unless] we turn back the clock or adopt a special incorporation test applicable only to the Second Amendment, [r]espondents' argument must be rejected. Under our precedents, if a Bill of Rights guarantee is fundamental from an American perspective, then, unless stare decisis counsels otherwise, that guarantee is fully binding on the States and thus limits (but by no means eliminates) their ability to devise solutions to social problems that suit local needs and values.

[Again for the Court, Justice Alito concluded:] In Heller, we held that the Second Amendment protects the right to possess a handgun in the home for the purpose of self-defense. Unless considerations of stare decisis counsel otherwise, a provision of the Bill of Rights that protects a right that is fundamental from an American perspective applies equally to the Federal Government and the States. We therefore hold that the Due Process Clause of the Fourteenth Amendment incorporates the Second Amendment right recognized in Heller. The judgment of the Court of Appeals is reversed, and the case is remanded for further proceedings.

■ JUSTICE SCALIA, concurring.

I join the Court's opinion. Despite my misgivings about Substantive Due Process as an original matter, I have acquiesced in the Court's incorporation of certain guarantees in the Bill of Rights "because it is both long established and narrowly limited." This case does not require me to reconsider that view, since straightforward application of settled doctrine suffices to decide it.

■ JUSTICE THOMAS, concurring in part and concurring in the judgment.

I agree with the Court that the Fourteenth Amendment makes the right to keep and bear arms set forth in the Second Amendment "fully applicable to the States." I write separately because I believe there is a more straightforward path to this conclusion, one that is more faithful to the Fourteenth Amendment's text and history.

Applying what is now a well-settled test, the plurality opinion concludes that the right to keep and bear arms applies to the States through the Fourteenth Amendment's Due Process Clause because it is "fundamental" to the American "scheme of ordered liberty," and " 'deeply rooted in this Nation's history and tradition.' " I agree with that description of the right. But I cannot agree that it is enforceable against the States through a clause that speaks only to "process." Instead, the right to keep and bear arms is a privilege of American citizenship that applies to the States through the Fourteenth Amendment's Privileges or Immunities Clause.

[After the Civil War], a series of constitutional amendments were adopted to repair the Nation from the damage slavery had caused. The provision at issue here, § 1 of the Fourteenth Amendment, [has] divided this Court for many years. That sentence begins with the command that "[n]o State shall make or enforce any law which shall abridge the privileges or immunities of citizens of the United States." On its face, this appears to grant the persons just made United States citizens a certain collection of rights—i.e., privileges or immunities—attributable to that status.

This Court's precedents accept that point, but define the relevant collection of rights quite narrowly. In the Slaughter-House Cases, decided just five years after the Fourteenth Amendment's adoption, the Court interpreted this text, now known as the Privileges or Immunities Clause, for the first time. In a closely divided decision, the Court drew a sharp distinction between the privileges and immunities of state citizenship and those of federal citizenship, and held that the Privileges or Immunities Clause protected only the latter category of rights from state abridgment. [As] a consequence of this Court's marginalization of the Clause, litigants seeking federal protection of fundamental rights turned to the remainder of § 1 in search of an alternative fount of such rights. They found one in a most curious place—that section's command that every State guarantee "due process" to any person before depriving him of "life, liberty, or property." [This] Court has determined that the Due Process Clause [even] applies rights against the States that are not mentioned in the Constitution at all, even without seriously arguing that the Clause was originally understood to protect such rights. See, e.g., Lochner v. New York; Roe v. Wade; Lawrence v. Texas.

All of this is a legal fiction. The notion that a constitutional provision that guarantees only "process" before a person is deprived of life, liberty, or property could define the substance of those rights strains credulity for even the most casual user of words. Moreover, this fiction is a particularly dangerous one. The one theme that links the Court's substantive due process precedents together is their lack of a guiding principle to distinguish "fundamental" rights that warrant protection from nonfundamental rights that do not.

[I] cannot accept a theory of constitutional interpretation that rests on such tenuous footing. This Court's substantive due process framework fails to account for both the text of the Fourteenth Amendment and the history that led to its adoption, filling that gap with a jurisprudence devoid of a guiding principle. I believe the original meaning of the Fourteenth Amendment offers a superior alternative, and that a return to that meaning would allow this Court to enforce the rights the Fourteenth Amendment is designed to protect with greater clarity and predictability than the substantive due process framework has so far [managed.]

"It cannot be presumed that any clause in the constitution is intended to be without effect." Marbury v. Madison. Because the Court's Privileges or Immunities Clause precedents have presumed just that, [they ought to be] set [a]side.

[The] evidence plainly shows that the ratifying public understood the Privileges or Immunities Clause to protect constitutionally enumerated rights, including the right to keep and bear arms. As the Court demonstrates, there can be no doubt that § 1 was understood to enforce the Second Amendment against the States. In my view, this is because the right to keep and bear arms was understood to be a privilege of American citizenship guaranteed by the Privileges or Immunities Clause.

[I] agree with the Court that the Second Amendment is fully applicable to the States. I do so because the right to keep and bear arms is guaranteed by the Fourteenth Amendment as a privilege of American citizenship.

■ JUSTICE STEVENS, dissenting.

This is a substantive due process case.

Section 1 of the Fourteenth Amendment decrees that no State shall "deprive any person of life, liberty, or property, without due process of law."

The Court has filled thousands of pages expounding that spare text. As I read the vast corpus of substantive due process opinions, they confirm several important principles that ought to guide our resolution of this case. The principal opinion's lengthy summary of our "incorporation" doctrine and its implicit (and untenable) effort to wall off that doctrine from the rest of our substantive due process jurisprudence, invite a fresh survey of this old terrain.

[The] Court hinges its entire decision on one mode of intellectual history, culling selected pronouncements and enactments from the 18th and 19th centuries to ascertain what Americans thought about firearms. [To] the extent the Court's opinion could be read to imply that the historical pedigree of a right is the exclusive or dispositive determinant of its status under the Due Process Clause, the opinion is seriously mistaken.

[A] rigid historical methodology is unfaithful to the Constitution's command. [Instead,] the liberty safeguarded by the Fourteenth Amendment is not merely preservative in nature but rather is a dynamic concept. [Because the judiciary is tasked with interpreting the Constitution, the] judge who would outsource the interpretation of "liberty" to historical sentiment has turned his back on a task the Constitution assigned to him and drained the document of its intended vitality.

The question in this case, then, is not whether the Second Amendment right to keep and bear arms (whatever that right's precise contours) applies to the States because the Amendment has been incorporated into the Fourteenth Amendment. It has not been. The question, rather, is whether the particular right asserted by petitioners applies to the States because of the Fourteenth Amendment itself, standing on its own bottom. And to answer that question, we need to determine, first, the nature of the right that has been asserted and, second, whether that right is an aspect of Fourteenth Amendment "liberty." [Understood] as a plea to keep their preferred type of firearm in the home, petitioners' argument has real force. The decision to keep a loaded handgun in the house is often motivated by the desire to protect life, liberty, and property. It is comparable, in some ways, to decisions about the education and upbringing of one's children. For it is the kind of decision that may have profound consequences for every member of the family, and for the world beyond. [And the] State's corresponding interest in regulation is somewhat weaker. The State generally has a lesser basis for regulating private as compared to public acts, and firearms kept inside the home generally pose a lesser threat to public welfare as compared to firearms taken outside.

[While] I agree with the Court that our substantive due process cases offer a principled basis for holding that petitioners have a constitutional right to possess a usable firearm in the home, I am ultimately persuaded that a better reading of our case law supports the city of Chicago. I would not foreclose the possibility that a particular plaintiff—say, an elderly widow who lives in a dangerous neighborhood and does not have the strength to operate a long gun—may have a cognizable liberty interest in possessing a handgun. But I cannot accept petitioners' broader submission. A number of factors, taken together, lead me to this conclusion.

First, firearms have a fundamentally ambivalent relationship to liberty. Just as they can help homeowners defend their families and property from intruders, they can help thugs and insurrectionists murder innocent victims. [Second,] the right to possess a firearm of one's choosing is different in kind from the liberty interests we have recognized under the Due Process Clause. [It] does not appear to be the case that the ability to own a handgun, or any particular type of firearm, is critical to leading a life of autonomy, dignity, or political equality. [Third,] the experience of other advanced democracies, including those that share our British heritage, undercuts the notion that an expansive right to keep and bear arms is intrinsic to ordered liberty. [Fourth,] the Second Amendment differs in kind from the Amendments that surround it, [in that it] was the States, not private persons, on whose immediate behalf the Second Amendment was adopted. Notwithstanding [Heller's] efforts to write the Second Amendment's preamble out of the Constitution, the Amendment still serves the structural function of protecting the States from encroachment by an overreaching Federal Government. [Fifth,] although it may be true that Americans' interest in firearm possession and state-law recognition of that interest are "deeply rooted" in some important senses, it is equally true that the States have a long and unbroken history of regulating firearms. The idea that States may place substantial restrictions on the right to keep and bear arms short of complete disarmament is, in fact, far more entrenched than the notion that the Federal Constitution protects any such right. [Finally,] this is a quintessential area in which federalism ought to be allowed to flourish without this Court's meddling. [States] and localities vary significantly in the patterns and problems of gun violence they face, as well as in the traditions and cultures of lawful gun use they claim. The city of Chicago, for example, faces a pressing challenge in combating criminal street gangs. Most rural areas do not.

[In conclusion, I] would proceed more cautiously. For the reasons set out at length above, I cannot accept either the methodology the Court employs or the conclusions it draws. Although impressively argued, the majority's decision to overturn more than a century of Supreme Court precedent and to unsettle a much longer tradition of state practice is not, in my judgment, built "upon respect for the teachings of history, solid recognition of the basic values that underlie our society, and wise appreciation of the great roles that the doctrines of federalism and separation of powers have played in establishing and preserving American freedoms."

■ JUSTICE BREYER, with whom JUSTICE GINSBURG and JUSTICE SOTOMAYOR join, dissenting.

In my view, Justice Stevens has demonstrated that the Fourteenth Amendment's guarantee of "substantive due process" does not include a general right to keep and bear firearms for purposes of private self-defense. [The] Court, however, does not expressly rest its opinion upon "substantive due process" concerns. Rather, it directs its attention to this Court's "incorporation" precedents and asks whether the Second Amendment right to private self-defense is "fundamental" so that it applies to the States through the Fourteenth Amendment. [I] shall therefore separately consider the question of "incorporation." I can find nothing in the Second Amendment's text, history, or underlying rationale that could warrant characterizing it as "fundamental" insofar as it seeks to protect the keeping and bearing of arms for private self-defense purposes. [The] majority here, like that in Heller, relies almost exclusively upon history to make the necessary showing. But to do so for incorporation purposes is both wrong and dangerous. [Where] history provides no clear answer, [it is proper] to look to other factors in considering whether a right is sufficiently "fundamental" to remove it from the political process in every State. I would include among those factors the nature of the right; any contemporary disagreement about whether the right is fundamental; the extent to which incorporation will further other, perhaps more basic, constitutional aims; and the extent to which incorporation will advance or hinder the Constitution's structural aims, including its division of powers among different governmental institutions (and the people as well). Is incorporation needed, for example, to further the Constitution's effort to ensure that the government treats each individual with equal respect? Will it help maintain the democratic form of government that the Constitution foresees?

[How] do these considerations apply here? [There] is no popular consensus that the private self-defense right described in Heller is fundamental. [One] side believes the right essential to protect the lives of those attacked in the home; the other side believes it essential to regulate the right in order to protect the lives of others attacked with guns. It seems unlikely that definitive evidence will develop one way or the other. [Moreover,] there is no reason here to believe that incorporation of the private self-defense right will further any other or broader constitutional objective. We are aware of no argument that gun-control regulations target or are passed with the purpose of targeting "discrete and insular minorities." Carolene Products. Nor will incorporation help to assure equal respect for individuals. Unlike the First Amendment's rights of free speech, free press, assembly, and petition, the private self-defense right does not comprise a necessary part of the democratic process that the Constitution seeks to establish. Unlike the First Amendment's religious protections, the Fourth Amendment's protection against unreasonable searches and seizures, the Fifth and Sixth Amendments' insistence upon fair criminal procedure, and the Eighth Amendment's protection against cruel and unusual punishments, the private self-defense right does not significantly seek to protect individuals who might otherwise suffer unfair or inhumane treatment at the hands of a majority. Unlike the protections offered by many of these same Amendments, it does not involve matters as to which judges possess a comparative expertise, by virtue of their close familiarity with the justice system and its operation. And, unlike the Fifth Amendment's insistence on just compensation, it does not involve a matter where a majority might unfairly seize for itself property belonging to a minority.

Finally, incorporation of the right will work a significant disruption in the constitutional allocation of decisionmaking authority, thereby interfering with the Constitution's ability to further its objectives. [First,] the incorporation of the right recognized in Heller would amount to a significant incursion on a traditional and important area of state concern, altering the constitutional relationship between the States and the Federal Government. Private gun regulation is the quintessential exercise of a State's "police power." [Second,] determining the constitutionality of a particular state gun law requires finding answers to complex empirically based questions of a kind that legislatures are better able than courts to make. [Third,] the ability of States to reflect local preferences and conditions—both key virtues of federalism—here has particular importance. The incidence of gun ownership varies substantially as between crowded cities and uncongested rural communities, as well as among the different geographic regions of the country. [The] nature of gun violence also varies as between rural communities and cities. Urban centers face significantly greater levels of firearm crime and homicide, while rural communities have proportionately greater problems with nonhomicide gun deaths, such as suicides and accidents. [Fourth,] incorporation of any right removes decisions from the democratic process, [and] the incorporation of this particular right does so without strong offsetting justification—as the example of [a Chicago suburb's] handgun ban helps to show. [The village] decided to ban handguns in 1983, after a local attorney was shot to death with a handgun that his assailant had smuggled into a courtroom in a blanket. A citizens committee spent months gathering information about handguns. It secured 6,000 signatures from community residents in support of a ban. And the village board enacted a ban into law. [A referendum approved the] ban by a vote of 8,031 to 6,368. And since that time, [c]rime has decreased and the community has seen no accidental handgun deaths.

Given the empirical and local value-laden nature of the questions that lie at the heart of the issue, why, in a Nation whose Constitution foresees democratic decisionmaking, is it so fundamental a matter as to require taking that power from the people? What is it here that the people did not know? What is it that a judge knows better?

[In] sum, the Framers did not write the Second Amendment in order to protect a private right of armed self-defense. There has been, and is, no consensus that the right is, or was, "fundamental." No broader constitutional interest or principle supports legal treatment of that right as fundamental. To the contrary, broader constitutional concerns of an institutional nature argue strongly against that treatment. Moreover, nothing in 18th-, 19th-, 20th-, or 21st-century history shows a consensus that the right to private armed self-defense, as described in Heller, is "deeply rooted in this Nation's history or tradition" or is otherwise "fundamental." Indeed, incorporating the right recognized in Heller may change the law in many of the 50 States. Read in the majority's favor, the historical evidence is at most ambiguous. And, in the absence of any other support for its conclusion, ambiguous history cannot show that the Fourteenth Amendment incorporates a private right of self-defense against the States.

THE MEANING AND IMPLICATIONS OF HELLER AND MCDONALD

1. ***History and incorporation.*** By the end of the Warren Court, many commentators assumed that incorporation had run its course. The 2010 decision in McDonald therefore came as something of a surprise for many. Does McDonald signify the beginning of a new era of incorporation, possibly driven by more politically conservative ideals, or is it simply a one-off case that was foreshadowed by earlier incorporation decisions? For a discussion of the competing ideologies, methodologies and historical trends leading to the McDonald decision, see Starger, "Exile on Main Street: Competing Traditions and Due Process Dissent," 95 Marq. L. Rev. 1253 (2012).

2. ***Guns and American history.*** Firearms and their regulation have long been part of the American legal tradition. In Heller, the majority and dissent exchanged competing visions of history. Justice Scalia's majority opinion recounted a story tracing back to the Restoration in England, when the monarch attempted to suppress dissenters by disarming them, leading to the 1689 Declaration of Right protecting the ability of (Protestant) Englishmen to possess weapons for self defense. It noted the same pattern of

attempting to disarm opponents during the late colonial period in the years leading to the Revolution, and focused as well on the treatment of gun possession in the early Republic, when the self-defense right was considered fundamental. More generally, guns have played an important role throughout American history. Colonists frequently brought their own guns when joining battles in the Revolutionary War; guns were a practical necessity for westward settlers who needed to hunt for their own food; and guns formed a fundamental part of America's "cowboy" ethos—a famous adage, dating from before the Civil War, links guns with American liberties by noting that "God may have made men, but Samuel Colt made them equal." Harcourt, "Introduction: Guns, Crime, and Punishment in America," 43 Ariz. L. Rev. 261 (2001).

As important as guns may have been in American history, another narrative exists, as illustrated by Justice Breyer's dissent in Heller. That narrative focuses on the long historical tradition of regulating firearms. Large colonial cities such as Boston sometimes went as far as to prohibit shooting any firearms within city limits. Later, several states in the early federal period banned certain types of firearms, such as concealed pistols. And as the majority itself recognized, there seems to be widespread historical consensus that states can prohibit convicted felons and the mentally insane from owning weapons. See also Churchill, "Gun Regulation, the Police Power, and the Right to Keep Arms in Early America: The Legal Context of the Second Amendment," 25 Law & Hist. Rev. 139 (2007).

How does Heller fit within these competing conceptions of firearms in American history? Does the recognition of a right unrelated to militia service effectively "lock in" the cowboy narrative of American gun ownership and shut down the regulation narrative?

3. ***The level of scrutiny for Second Amendment claims.*** Heller and McDonald left open the question of what standard of scrutiny to apply to Second Amendment claims. Once a federal or state law is found to intrude on the Second Amendment's guarantee, should courts subject it to strict scrutiny—which requires that the law be struck down unless it is narrowly tailored to serve a compelling government interest—or the more relaxed standard of intermediate scrutiny, which requires only that the statute have a substantial relationship to an important government interest? The distinction could have a huge impact on the permissible scope of firearms restrictions. For example, if we assume the government has a compelling interest in preventing mass shootings, a ban on assault weapons may very well be "substantially related" to that interest, but may not be "narrowly tailored"—in other words, the government could seek to prevent mass shootings via legislation that places less of a burden on the Second Amendment right. McDonald characterized the Second Amendment right as "fundamental," and invasions of fundamental rights are typically subject to strict scrutiny. However, lower courts have suggested that the proper level of scrutiny in Second Amendment cases depends on how close the challenged law comes to the "core" of the right to keep and bear arms. This approach would, in practice, cause the standard of review to turn on the type of firearm at issue and the breadth of the statute. See, e.g., New York State Rifle & Pistol Ass'n v. Cuomo, 804 F.3d 242 (2d Cir. 2015). Does this framework represent a commonsense approach to the wide variety of possible gun control measures? Or does it violate the McDonald plurality's prohibition

against treating the Second Amendment as "a second-class right, subject to an entirely different body of rules than the other Bill of Rights guarantees"?

In assessing the constitutionality of laws barring firearm possession, either due to age, mental illness, or criminal record, the courts of appeals have been unanimous finding intermediate scrutiny to be the appropriate level of scrutiny for these Second Amendment claims. See, e.g., Binderup v. Atty. Gen. U.S. of Am., 836 F.3d 336 (3d Cir. 2016) (felony conviction); Tyler v. Hillsdale Cty. Sheriff's Dep't, 837 F.3d 678 (6th Cir. 2015) (mental illness); United States v. Chovan, 735 F.3d 1127 (9th Cir. 2013) (felony conviction); NRA v. Bureau of Alcohol, Tobacco, Firearms & Explosives, 700 F.3d 185 (5th Cir. 2012) (persons under age 21). Other situations have not produced such consensus. Compare Kolbe v. Hogan, 849 F.3d 114 (4th Cir. 2017) (upholding a ban on assault weapons on the grounds that such firearms are not protected by the Second Amendment), with New York State Rifle & Pistol Ass'n v. Cuomo, 804 F.3d 242 (2d Cir. 2015) (finding that assault weapons are protected by the Second Amendment but upholding a statute banning them under intermediate scrutiny), and Heller v. District of Columbia ("Heller II"), 670 F.3d 1244 (D.C. Cir. 2011) (same).

CHAPTER 8

DUE PROCESS

The Due Process Clauses of the Fifth and Fourteenth Amendments by their terms might seem to refer only to the procedures required before any person is deprived of life, liberty or property. But in two lines of cases, one concerning economic liberties that prevailed early in the 20th century and one concerning personal privacy that is still governing early in the 21st, the Supreme Court has held that the clauses restrict the substance as well as the procedures of governmental regulation. Critics in both eras have objected that any notion of "substantive due process" lacks a textual foundation, with some charging that is a "contradiction in terms—sort of like 'green pastel redness.'" Ely, Democracy and Distrust 18 (1980). Defenders have sought to root this set of rights in the history and structure of the Constitution as well as in evolving social consensus. Critics have answered that such interpretive methods pose a risk of overly subjective judicial lawmaking.

The Court's encounters with substantive due process in the sphere of economic regulation in Section 1 of this chapter provide useful history and important background for assessment of later developments. Section 2 explores the revival of substantive due process to protect private decisions with respect to family, reproduction, sex and death. Section 3 briefly covers procedural due process cases with an emphasis on how "property" and "liberty" are defined. Section 4 serves to juxtapose economic substantive due process, which has been judicially implied, with two important protections of property rights that are express in constitutional text: the protection of contracts against "impairment" by the states and the protection of property against "taking" for "public use" without "just compensation."

SECTION 1. SUBSTANTIVE DUE PROCESS AND ECONOMIC LIBERTIES

An important strain of the natural law tradition, drawing on English antecedents, views a written constitution as merely reaffirming preexisting fundamental rights—such as life, liberty, and property—that are entitled to protection whether or not they are explicitly stated in the basic document. See generally Corwin, "The Basic Doctrine of American Constitutional Law," 12 Mich. L. Rev. 247 (1914); Corwin, "The 'Higher Law' Background of American Constitutional Law," 42 Harv. L. Rev. 149 (1928–29); Grey, "Do We Have an Unwritten Constitution?", 27 Stan. L. Rev. 703 (1975).

Some Justices on the early Supreme Court embraced this natural law approach. A notable example arose in **Calder v. Bull**, 3 Dall. (3 U.S.) 386 (1798). There, the Court rejected an attack on a Connecticut legislative act setting aside a probate court decree that had refused to approve a will. The legislation required a new hearing; at that second hearing, the will was approved. The challenge to the law came from the heirs who would have taken the property if the will had been ineffective. The Court rejected their claim that the Ex Post Facto Clause barred the Connecticut act: that clause was construed as being limited to criminal legislation. Calder v. Bull was handed down in the years before Chief Justice John Marshall persuaded his colleagues to abandon seriatim opinions. And of the several opinions, Justice Chase's most elaborately announced an inclination to invalidate legislation based on limitations not explicit in constitutional text. Justice CHASE stated (with emphasis in the original):

"I cannot subscribe to the *omnipotence* of a *State Legislature,* or that it is *absolute* and *without control;* although its authority should not be *expressly* restrained by the *Constitution,* or *fundamental law,* of the State. The people of the *United States* erected their Constitutions, or forms of governments, to establish justice, to promote the general welfare, to secure the blessings of liberty; and to protect their *persons* and *property* from violence. The purposes for which men enter into society will determine the *nature* and *terms* of the *social* compact; and as *they* are the foundation of the *legislative* power, *they* will decide what are the *proper* objects of it: The *nature,* and *ends* of *legislative* power will limit the *exercise* of it. This *fundamental* principle flows from the very nature of our free *Republican* governments, that no man should be compelled to do what the laws do *not* require; *nor to refrain from acts which the laws permit.* There are acts which the *Federal,* or *State,* Legislature cannot do, *without exceeding their authority.* There are certain *vital* principles in our *free Republican governments,* which will determine and over-rule an *apparent and flagrant* abuse of *legislative* power; as to authorize *manifest injustice by positive law;* or to take away that security for *personal liberty,* or *private property,* for the protection whereof the government was established. An ACT of the Legislature (for I cannot call it a *law*) contrary to the *great first principles* of the *social compact,* cannot be considered a *rightful exercise* of *legislative authority.* The obligation of a law in governments established on *express compact, and on republican principles,* must be determined by the *nature* of the *power,* on which it is founded. A few instances will suffice to explain what I mean. A law that punished a citizen for an *innocent* action, or, in other words, for an act, which, when done, was in violation of no *existing* law; a law that destroys, or impairs, the *lawful private* contracts of citizens; a law that makes a man *a Judge in his own cause;* or a law that takes *property* from A. and gives it to B. It is against all reason and justice, for a people to entrust a Legislature with SUCH powers; and, therefore, it cannot be presumed that they have done it. The *genius,* the *nature,* and the *spirit,* of our State Governments, amount to a prohibition of *such acts of legislation;* and the *general principles of law and reason* forbid them. The Legislature [cannot] change *innocence* into *guilt;* [or] violate the right of an *antecedent lawful private contract;* or the *right of private property.* To maintain that our Federal, or State, Legislature possesses *such powers,* if they had not been *expressly* restrained; would, in my opinion, be a *political heresy,* altogether inadmissible in our *free republican governments."* Justice Chase concluded that the Connecticut law had not exceeded legislative powers: since the initial invalidation of the will had not created any "vested" property rights in the heirs, the law was consistent with "natural justice."

Justice IREDELL's opinion challenged Justice Chase's natural law approach: "[S]ome speculative jurists have held, that a legislative act against natural justice must, in itself, be void; but I cannot think that, under [a constitutional scheme allocating powers without explicit limitations], any Court of Justice would possess a power to declare it so. Sir *William Blackstone,* having put the strong case of an act of Parliament, which should authorize a man to try his own cause, explicitly adds, that even in that case, 'there is no court that has power to defeat the intent of the Legislature.' In order, therefore, to guard against so great an evil, it has been the policy of all the *American* states, which have, individually, framed their state constitutions since the revolution, and of the people of the *United States*, when they framed the Federal Constitution, to define with precision the objects of the legislative power, and to restrain its exercise within marked and settled boundaries. If any act of Congress, or of the Legislature of a state, violates those constitutional provisions, it is unquestionably [void]. If, on the other hand, the Legislature of the Union, or the Legislature of any member of the Union, shall pass a law, within the general scope of their constitutional power, the Court cannot pronounce it to be void, merely because it is, in their judgment, contrary to the principles of natural justice. The ideas of natural justice are regulated by no fixed standard: the ablest and the purest men have differed upon the subject; and all that the Court could properly say, in such an event, would be, that the Legislature (possessed of an equal right of opinion) had passed an act which, in the opinion of the judges, was inconsistent with the abstract principles of natural justice."

In the early years of the Marshall Court, there were occasional echoes of Chase's natural law approach. For example, in **Fletcher v. Peck**, 6 Cranch (10 U.S.) 87 (1810), Chief Justice Marshall offered alternative routes for invalidating a Georgia effort to revoke a land grant "either by general principles which are common to our free institutions, or by the particular provisions of the constitution of the United States." Justice Johnson's concurrence relied not on the Contracts Clause but rather on "general principle, on the reason and nature of things." Although most pre-Civil War discussion of due process clauses in state constitutions and in the Fifth Amendment spoke of procedural implications of due process, there were some intimations that due process might also impose substantive restraints on legislation. Thus, in the infamous Dred Scott decision, p. 446 above, which held that "persons who are descendants of Africans [imported] into this country, and sold as slaves," are not United States citizens entitled to invoke the jurisdiction of a federal court, and thus rejected an enslaved man's suit seeking freedom, Chief Justice Taney's opinion commented, without elaboration: "An Act of Congress which deprives a citizen of the United States of his liberty or property, merely because he came himself or brought his property into a particular Territory of the United States, and who had committed no offense against the laws, could hardly be dignified with the name of due process of law." Dred Scott v. Sandford, 60 U.S. (19 How.) 393 (1857). Other substantive due process arguments before the Civil War came from anti-slavery lawyers, who argued, without success, that slavery was a deprivation of liberty without a proper basis in law (such as conviction for crime).

The growth of industrialization and corporate power in the post-Civil War years stirred popular demands for legislative responses. The new regulatory laws, opponents argued, contravened liberal, laissez-faire economic theory and the value of competition championed by social Darwinists like the English political theorist Herbert Spencer. The Slaughter-House Cases blocked use of the Fourteenth Amendment Privileges or Immunities Clause as a substantive restraint on state economic legislation. But lawyers soon pressed the Court to restrain economic regulation by other means. They frequently relied on Cooley, Constitutional Limitations (1868), a highly influential, largely libertarian treatise first published in the same year the Fourteenth Amendment was adopted. As Justice Miller noted, "the docket of this court is crowded with cases in which we are asked to hold that state courts and state legislatures have deprived their own citizens of life, liberty, or property without due process of law. There is here abundant evidence that there exists some strange misconception of the scope of this provision as found in the 14th Amendment." Davidson v. New Orleans, 96 U.S. 97 (1877).

Soon, substantive due process began to surface in majority opinions. In **Munn v. Illinois**, 94 U.S. 113 (1877), for example, the Court rejected an attack on a state law regulating the rates of grain elevators, but Chief Justice WAITE's majority opinion cautioned, "Undoubtedly, in mere private contracts, relating to matters in which the public has no interest, what is reasonable must be ascertained judicially." He emphasized that the police power included regulation of individual use of property that was "affected with a public interest," and found regulation of grain storage to fit that category because storage monopolies, like utilities, could exact monopoly prices. Chief Justice Waite took a similar stance in The Railroad Commission Cases, 116 U.S. 307 (1886), sustaining state regulation of railroad rates but, again, leaving the door open for greater judicial control in the future: "[It] is not to be inferred that this power [of] regulation [is] without limit. This power to regulate is not a power to destroy. Under pretense of regulating fares and freights, the State cannot require a railroad corporation to carry persons or property without reward; neither can it do that which in law amounts to a taking of private property for public use without just compensation, or without due process of law."

In the same year, in **Santa Clara County v. Southern Pac. Railroad**, 118 U.S. 394 (1886), the Court held, without discussion, that corporations were "persons" within the meaning of the Fourteenth Amendment. Chicago, M. & St. P. Ry. Co. v. Minnesota, 134 U.S. 418 (1890), was a significant turning point. That decision invalidated a state law authorizing administrative ratemaking without providing for judicial review. The immediate vice of the statute was the lack of adequate procedural protection for the railroads—the lack of judicial review. But the majority explanation suggested concern with substance as well as procedure: reasonableness of rates was found to be "eminently a question for judicial investigation"; depriving the railroad of the power to charge reasonable rates by administrative order would be, "in substance and effect," a deprivation of property without due process of law. By the end of the decade, the Court regularly scrutinized the substantive reasonableness of rates.

Substantive due process review soon ranged beyond rate regulation to encompass a wide variety of exercises of state police power. **Mugler v. Kansas**, 123 U.S. 623 (1887), sustained a law prohibiting intoxicating beverages, but the Court announced that it was prepared to examine the substantive reasonableness of state legislation. The first Justice HARLAN spoke for a Court whose composition had changed almost totally since the Slaughter-House Cases. He stated that not "every statute enacted ostensibly for the promotion" of "the public morals, the public health, or the public safety" would be accepted "as a legitimate exertion of the police powers of the State." The courts would not be "misled by mere pretenses": they were obligated "to look at the substance of things." Accordingly, if a purported exercise of the police power "has no real or substantial relation to those objects, or is a palpable invasion of rights secured by the fundamental law,

not just going to accept state police power → substantive due process it is the duty of the courts to so adjudge." And facts "within the knowledge of all" would be relied on in making that determination.

Ten years later, in **Allgeyer v. Louisiana**, 165 U.S. 578 (1897), the move toward substantive due process was complete: for the first time, the Court invalidated a state law on substantive due process grounds. Allgeyer involved a Louisiana law that prohibited obtaining insurance on Louisiana property "from any marine insurance company which has not complied in all respects" with Louisiana law. Allgeyer was convicted for mailing a letter advising an insurance company in New York of the shipment of goods, in accordance with a marine policy. The company was not licensed to do business in Louisiana. The Court reversed, holding the statute in violation of the Fourteenth Amendment "in that it deprives the defendants of their liberty without due process of law." Although Justice PECKHAM's opinion for a unanimous Court focused on state power over foreign corporations, his broad articulation of the "liberty of contract" advanced the development of substantive due process: "The liberty mentioned in that amendment means not only the right of the citizen to be free from the mere physical restraint of his person, as by incarceration, but the term is deemed to embrace the right of the citizen to be free in the enjoyment of all his faculties; to be free to use them in all lawful ways; to live and work where he will; to earn his livelihood by any lawful calling; to pursue any livelihood or avocation, and for that purpose to enter into all contracts which may be proper, necessary and essential to his carrying out to a successful conclusion the purposes above mentioned."

Soon after the turn of the century, this expansive conception of "liberty" bore fruit in more controversial contexts, as exemplified by the Lochner case, which follows. The case arose from a challenge to a New York labor law, and it eventually became famous as much for Justice Holmes's dissent as for the doctrine of the liberty of contract espoused by the Court:

Lochner v. New York

198 U.S. 45, 25 S. Ct. 539, 49 L. Ed. 937 (1905).

[Lochner was convicted and fined for permitting an employee to work in his Utica, N.Y., bakery for more than 60 hours in one week, or more than 10 hours in one day, in violation of a state maximum hours law. Lochner appealed, arguing that the law unconstitutionally burdened his right of contracting with employees in violation of the Fourteenth Amendment's Due Process Clause.]

■ JUSTICE PECKHAM delivered the opinion of the Court.

[The] statute necessarily interferes with the right of contract between the employer and [employees]. The general right to make a contract in relation to his business is part of the liberty of the individual protected by the 14th Amendment. [Allgeyer.] The right to purchase or to sell labor is part of the liberty protected by this amendment, unless there are circumstances which exclude the right. There are, however, [state police] powers [relating] to the safety, health, morals and general welfare of the public. [When] the [state legislature], in the assumed exercise of its police powers, has passed an act which seriously limits the right to labor or the right of contract in regard to their means of livelihood between persons who are sui juris (both employer and employee), it becomes of great importance to determine which shall prevail—the right of the individual to labor for such time as he may choose, or the right of the State to prevent the individual from laboring [beyond] a certain time prescribed by the State. This court [has] upheld the exercise of the police powers of the States in many cases which might fairly be considered as border ones, and it [has] been guided by rules of a very liberal nature, the application of which has resulted, in numerous instances, in upholding the validity of state statutes thus assailed. Among the later cases where the state law has been upheld [is] that of Holden v. Hardy.[1] [I]t was held that the kind of employment, mining, smelting, etc., and the character of the employees in such kinds of labor, were such as to make it reasonable and proper for the State to interfere to prevent the employees from being constrained by the rules laid down by the proprietors in regard to labor. [There] is nothing in Holden v. Hardy which covers the case now before [us].

It must, of course, be conceded that there is a limit to the valid exercise of the [police power]. Otherwise the 14th Amendment would have no efficacy and the legislatures of the States would have unbounded power, and it would be enough to say that any piece of legislation was enacted to conserve the morals, the health or the safety of the [people]. The claim of the police power would be a mere [pretext]. In every case that comes before this court, therefore, [the] question necessarily arises: Is this a fair, reasonable and appropriate exercise of the [police power], or is it an unreasonable, unnecessary and arbitrary interference with the right of the individual to his personal liberty or to enter into those contracts in relation to labor which may seem to him appropriate or necessary for the support of himself and his family? Of course the liberty of contract relating to labor includes both parties to it. The one has as much right to purchase as the other to sell labor. This is not a question of substituting the judgment of the court for that of the legislature. If the act be within the power of the State it is valid, although the judgment of the court might be totally opposed to the enactment of such a law. But the question would still remain: Is it within the police power of the State? and that question must be answered by the court.

The question whether this act is valid as a labor law, pure and simple, may be dismissed in a few words. There is no reasonable ground for interfering with the liberty of person or the right of free contract, by determining the hours of labor, in the occupation of a baker. There is no contention that bakers as a class are not equal in intelligence and capacity to men in other trades or manual occupations, or that they are not able to assert their rights and care for themselves without the protecting arm of the State, interfering with their independence of judgment and of action. They are in no sense wards of the State. Viewed in the light of a purely labor law, with no reference whatever to the question of health, we think that a law like the one before us involves neither the safety, the morals nor the welfare of the public, and that the interest of the public is not in the slightest degree affected by such an act. The law must be upheld, if at all, as a law pertaining to the health of the individual engaged in the occupation of a baker. [Clean] and wholesome bread does not depend upon whether the baker works but

[1] Holden v. Hardy, 169 U.S. 366 (1898), decided in the period between Allgeyer and Lochner, had upheld a Utah law limiting the employment of workers in underground mines to eight hours a day.

ten hours per day or only sixty hours a week. [The] mere assertion that the subject relates though but in a remote degree to the public health does not necessarily render the enactment valid. The act must have a more direct relation, as a means to an end, and the end itself must be appropriate and legitimate, before an act can be held to be valid which interferes with the general right of an individual to be free in his person and in his power to contract in relation to his own [labor].

We think the limit of the police power has been reached and passed in this case. There is, in our judgment, no reasonable foundation for holding this to be necessary or appropriate as a health law to safeguard the public health or the health of the individuals who are following the trade of a baker. If this statute be valid, [there] would seem to be no length to which legislation of this nature might not go. [We] think that there can be no fair doubt that the trade of a baker, in and of itself, is not an unhealthy one to that degree which would authorize the legislature to interfere with the right to labor, and with the right of free contract on the part of the individual, either as employer or employee. In looking through statistics regarding all trades and occupations, it may be true that the trade of a baker does not appear to be as healthy as some other trades, and is also vastly more healthy than still others. To the common understanding the trade of a baker has never been regarded as an unhealthy one. [It] might be safely affirmed that almost all occupations more or less affect the health. There must be more than the mere fact of the possible existence of some small amount of unhealthiness to warrant legislative interference with liberty. It is unfortunately true that labor, even in any department, may possibly carry with it the seeds of unhealthiness. But are we all, on that account, at the mercy of legislative majorities?

baker ≠ unhealthy to warrant police power

[It] is also urged [that] it is to the interest of the State that its population should be strong and robust, and therefore any legislation which may be said to tend to make people healthy must be valid as health laws, enacted under the police power. If this be a valid argument and a justification for this kind of legislation, it follows that the protection of the Federal Constitution from undue interference with liberty of person and freedom of contract is visionary, wherever the law is sought to be justified as a valid exercise of the police power. Scarcely any law but might find shelter under such [assumptions]. Not only the hours of employees, but the hours of employers, could be regulated, and doctors, lawyers, scientists, all professional men, as well as athletes and artisans, could be forbidden to fatigue their brains and bodies by prolonged hours of exercise, lest the fighting strength of the State be impaired. We mention these extreme cases because the contention is extreme. We do not believe in the soundness of the views which uphold this law. [The] act is not, within any fair meaning of the term, a health law, but is an illegal interference with the rights of individuals, both employers and employees, to make contracts regarding labor upon such terms as they may think best, or which they may agree upon with the other parties to such contracts. Statutes of the nature of that under review, limiting the hours in which grown and intelligent men may labor to earn their living, are mere meddlesome interferences with the rights of the individual, and they are not saved from condemnation by the claim that they are passed in the exercise of the police power and upon the subject of the health of the individual whose rights are interfered with, unless there be some fair ground, reasonable in and of itself, to say that there is material danger to the public health or to the health of the employees, if the hours of labor are not curtailed. [All that the State] could properly do has been done by it with regard to the conduct of bakeries, as provided for in the other sections of the act, [which] provide for the inspection of the premises where the bakery is carried on, with regard to furnishing proper wash-rooms and water-closets, [also] with regard to providing proper drainage, plumbing and painting [and] for other things of that [nature].

It was further urged [that] restricting the hours of labor in the case of bakers was valid because it tended to cleanliness on the part of the workers, as a man was more apt to be cleanly when not overworked, and if cleanly then his "output" was also more likely to be so. In our judgment it is not possible in fact to discover the connection between the number of hours a baker may work in the bakery and the healthful quality of the bread made by the workman. The connection, if any exists, is too shadowy and thin to build any argument for the interference of the legislature. If the man works ten hours a day it is all right, but if ten and a half or eleven his health is in danger and his bread may be unhealthful, and, therefore, he shall not be permitted to do it. This, we think, is unreasonable and entirely arbitrary. When assertions such as we have adverted to become necessary in order to give, if possible, a plausible foundation for the contention that the law is a "health law," it gives rise to at least a suspicion that there was some other motive dominating the legislature than the purpose to subserve the public health or welfare. This interference on the part of the legislatures of the several States with the ordinary trades and occupations of the people seems to be on the increase. [It] is impossible for us to shut our eyes to the fact that many of the laws of this character, while passed under what is claimed to be the police power for the purpose of protecting the public health or welfare, are, in reality, passed from other motives. We are justified in saying so when, from the character of the law and the subject upon which it legislates, it is apparent that the public health or welfare bears but the most remote relation to the law. The purpose of a statute must be determined from the natural and legal effect of the language employed; and whether it is or is not repugnant to the Constitution [must] be determined from the natural effect of such statutes when put into operation, and not from their proclaimed purpose.

[It] is manifest to us that the [law here] has no such direct relation to and no such substantial effect upon the health of the employee as to justify us in regarding the section as really a health law. It seems to us that the real object and purpose were simply to regulate the hours of labor between the master and his employees (all being men, sui juris), in a private business, not dangerous in any degree to morals or in any real and substantial degree, to the health of the employees. Under such circumstances the freedom of master and employee to contract with each other in relation to their [employment] cannot be prohibited or interfered with, without violating the Federal Constitution. [Reversed.]

■ JUSTICE HARLAN, with whom JUSTICES WHITE and DAY concurred, dissenting.

[There] is a liberty of contract which cannot be violated, [but] is subject to [reasonable police regulations]. It is plain that this statute was enacted in order to protect the physical well-being of those who work in [bakery] establishments. It may be that the statute had its origin in part, in the belief that employers and employees in such establishments were not upon an equal footing, and that the necessities of the latter often compelled them to submit to such exactions as unduly taxed their strength. Be this as it may, the statute must be taken as expressing the belief of the people of New York that, as a general rule, and in the case of the average man, labor in excess of sixty hours during a week in such establishments may endanger the health of those who thus labor. Whether or not this be wise legislation, it is not the province of the court to inquire. [The] courts are not concerned with the wisdom or policy of legislation. So that in determining the question of power to interfere with liberty of contract, the court may inquire whether the means devised by the State are germane to an end which may be lawfully accomplished and have a real or substantial relation to the protection of health, as involved in the daily work of the persons, male and female, engaged in [bakery] establishments. But when this inquiry is entered upon I find it impossible, in view of common experience, to say that there is here no real or substantial relation between the means employed by the State and the ends sought to be accomplished by its legislation. [Still] less can I say that the statute is, beyond question, a plain, not palpable invasion of rights secured by the fundamental [law].

Professor Hirt in his treatise on the "Diseases of the Workers" has said: "The labor of the bakers is among the hardest and most laborious imaginable, because it has to be performed under conditions injurious to the health of those engaged in it. It is hard, very hard work, not only because it requires a great deal of physical exertion in an overheated workshop and during unreasonably long hours, but more so because of the erratic demands of the public, compelling the baker to perform the greater part of his work at [night]." Another writer says: "The constant inhaling of flour dust causes inflammation of the lungs and of the bronchial tubes. The eyes also suffer through this [dust]. The long hours of toil to which all bakers are subjected produce rheumatism, cramps and swollen legs. [Nearly] all bakers are pale-faced and of more delicate health than the workers of other crafts, which is chiefly due to their hard work and their irregular and unnatural mode of living. [The] average age of a baker is below that of other workmen; they seldom live over their fiftieth [year]."

We judicially know that the question of the number of hours during which a workman should continuously labor has been, for a long period, and is yet, a subject of serious consideration among civilized peoples, and by those having special knowledge of the laws of health. [We] also judicially know that the number of hours that should constitute a day's labor in particular occupations involving the physical strength and safety of workmen has been the subject of enactments by Congress and by nearly all of the States. Many, if not most, of those enactments fix eight hours as the proper basis of a day's labor. I do not stop to consider whether any particular view of this economic question presents the sounder theory. [It] is enough for the determination of this case [that] the question is one about which there is room for debate and for an honest difference of opinion. There are many reasons of a weighty, substantial character, based upon the experience of mankind, in support of the theory that, all things considered, more than ten hours' steady work each day, from week to week, in a bakery or confectionery establishment, may endanger the health, and shorten the lives of the workmen, thereby diminishing their physical and mental capacity to serve the State, and to provide for those dependent upon them. If such reasons exist that ought to be the end of this case, for the State is not amenable to the judiciary, in respect of its legislative enactments, unless such enactments are plainly, palpably, beyond all question, inconsistent with the [Constitution]. A decision that the New York statute is void under the 14th Amendment will, in my opinion, involve consequences of a far-reaching and mischievous character; for such a decision would seriously cripple the inherent power of the States to care for the lives, health and well-being of their [citizens].

■ JUSTICE HOLMES, dissenting.

[This] case is decided upon an economic theory which a large part of the country does not entertain. If it were a question whether I agreed with that theory, I should desire to study it further and long before making up my mind. But I do not conceive that to be my duty, because I strongly believe that my agreement or disagreement has nothing to do with the right of a majority to embody their opinions in law. It is settled by various decisions of this court that [state laws] may regulate life in many ways which we as legislators might think as injudicious or if you like as tyrannical as this, and which equally with this interfere with the liberty to contract. Sunday laws and usury laws are ancient examples. A more modern one is the prohibition of lotteries. The liberty of the citizen to do as he likes so long as he does not interfere with the liberty of others to do the same, which has been a shibboleth for some well-known writers, is interfered with by school laws, by the Post Office, by every state or municipal institution which takes his money for purposes thought desirable, whether he likes it or not. The 14th Amendment does not enact Mr. Herbert Spencer's Social Statics. The other day we sustained the Massachusetts vaccination law. Jacobson v. Massachusetts, 197 U.S. 11 [1905]. United States and state statutes and decisions cutting down the liberty to contract by way of combination are familiar to this court. [The] decision sustaining an eight hour law for miners is still recent. Some of these laws embody convictions or prejudices which judges are likely to share. Some may not. But a constitution is not intended to embody a particular economic theory, whether of paternalism and the organic relation of the citizen to the State or of laissez faire. It is made for people of fundamentally differing views, and the accident of our finding certain opinions natural and familiar or novel and even shocking ought not to conclude our judgment upon the question whether statutes embodying them conflict with the [Constitution].

General propositions do not decide concrete cases. The decision will depend on a judgment or intuition more subtle than any articulate major premise. But I think that the proposition just stated, if it is accepted, will carry us far toward the end. Every opinion tends to become a law. I think that the word liberty in the 14th Amendment is perverted when it is held to prevent the natural outcome of a dominant opinion, unless it can be said that a rational and fair man necessarily would admit that the statute proposed would infringe fundamental principles as they have been understood by the traditions of our people and our law. It does not need research to show that no such sweeping condemnation can be passed upon the statute before us. A reasonable man might think it a proper measure on the score of health. Men whom I certainly could not pronounce unreasonable would uphold it as a first installment of a general regulation of the hours of work. Whether in the latter aspect it would be open to the charge of inequality I think it unnecessary to discuss.

______

THE MEANING AND IMPLICATIONS OF LOCHNER

The Court eventually repudiated Lochner and the related decisions it helped produce, and its very name later became synonymous with inappropriate judicial intervention in the legislative process. But what *were* the supposed evils of the Lochner decision? The Court has withdrawn from careful scrutiny of most economic regulations but has increased intervention as to laws infringing privacy and other noneconomic personal interests not explicitly protected by the Constitution. Can the two lines of cases be readily distinguished?

1. ***Lochner and the text of the Fourteenth Amendment.***

a. *"Liberty."* Justice Peckham read "liberty" broadly to include freedom of contract. If liberty at common law meant only freedom from physical restraint, could it mean more in the Due Process Clause? Should common law control the constitutional meaning of "liberty"? Even if liberty extends beyond bodily control, does it extend to contract? Why? Do contracts depend upon the existence of government? If so, are they properly subject to regulation?

b. *"Due process of law."* How do procedural limitations on government deprivations of liberty provide a basis for scrutiny of the substance of legislation? Recall the quip that "substantive due process" is a "contradiction in terms—sort of like 'green pastel redness.' " Ely, Democracy and Distrust 18 (1980). Does "due process of law" imply a substantive limitation on the conception of legitimate legislative process? Is a law that restrains economic liberty not properly understood as "law"? Does it exceed the expectations that underlay the social contract by which government was created in the first place?

2. ***Lochner and legislative ends.*** Justice Peckham's opinion in Lochner did not consider liberty of contract an absolute. He recognized that liberty of contract is subject to restraints under the police power in pursuit of proper governmental objectives. But what governmental objectives are legitimately within the police power? Justice Peckham recognized that "health" is a legitimate end of the police power, and most of his opinion considered whether New York's regulation could be justified as a health law designed to promote the health of bakers or of the consuming public. He was not satisfied that the means adequately promoted a "health" end.

Alternatively, the law might have been seen as promoting greater equality of bargaining power between employer and employee. But to Justice Peckham, such ends, unlike health, were illegitimate: "a labor law, pure and simple" was not within the permissible objectives contemplated by the police power. He condemned such legislative ends as impermissibly paternalistic or redistributive: "There is no contention that bakers as a class are not equal in intelligence and capacity to men in other trades or manual occupations. [They] are in no sense wards of the State." Could minimum wage or maximum hours laws be understood as not truly paternalistic or redistributive? What if such a law helped to solve a market failure? Suppose that all bakery workers would have preferred shorter hours and higher pay, but none of them individually had sufficient bargaining power to extract such conditions. May a state, under its police power, redress such a coordination problem in order to increase overall social welfare?

Even if such laws were understood as serving government ends of paternalism and redistribution, why are such ends not legitimate? Aren't legislatures entitled to choose among economic theories according to democratic will? Recall Holmes's statement in his Lochner dissent that a constitution "is not intended to embody a particular economic theory, whether of paternalism and the organic relation of the citizen to the State or of laissez faire." Did the Court err in Lochner in supposing that contract rights were prepolitical and thus beyond the reach of appropriate government intervention? If the existing distribution of wealth and income is the product of prior governmental action to allow the creation of markets and their protection through the laws of property and contract, then how can it be said that any existing distribution is irreducibly private and not amenable to redistribution in the public interest? See Tribe, American Constitutional Law 574–78 (2d ed. 1988); Sunstein, "Lochner's Legacy," 87 Colum. L. Rev. 873 (1987); Sunstein, "Naked Preferences and the Constitution," 84 Colum. L. Rev. 1689 (1984).

3. ***Lochner and the relationship between means and ends.*** Even as to ends, like health, that are conceded to be legitimate, Lochner demanded that there be "some fair ground, reasonable in and of itself, to say that there is material danger" to such an end. Justice Harlan's dissent likewise suggested that there must be a "real or substantial relation between the means employed by the State and the end sought to be accomplished by its legislation." Did the majority and the Harlan dissent apply the same standard but come to different results? Recall that Justice Harlan recited empirical data regarding the effect of long hours on the health of bakers, but the majority stated that the bakers' trade "is not an unhealthy one to that degree which would authorize the legislature to interfere."

Or did the Lochner majority in effect demand a stronger justification than Justice Harlan? The Harlan dissent argued that the state should prevail if "the question is one about which there is room for debate and for an honest difference of opinion." Did the majority demand more than that, based on the assumption that liberty of contract was a fundamental value warranting special judicial protection? On this view, it is not enough that a statute's means-ends relationship is minimally rational. When such stricter scrutiny is applied, does it inevitably rest on a judicial "balancing" of the competing public and private interests? Is that better left to legislatures? Or is the Court well equipped to scrutinize means-ends relationships even if it ought to defer to legislatures on the choice of ends?

4. ***Extensions of Lochner.*** From the Lochner decision in 1905 to the mid-1930s, the Court invalidated nearly 200 regulations on substantive due process grounds. Regulations of prices, wages and hours were especially vulnerable. Typically, as in Lochner, the invalidation of statutes provoked dissents, most often by Justice Holmes and, later, Justices Brandeis, Stone and Cardozo.

Following Lochner, the Court also invalidated many other sorts of labor laws, including those protecting the right to organize unions. In **Adair v. United States**, 208 U.S. 161 (1908), the Court held unconstitutional, under the Due Process Clause of the Fifth Amendment, a federal law prohibiting interstate railroad employers from requiring that employees agree as a condition of employment "not to join or become or remain a member of any labor organization" (so-called "yellow dog" contracts). The opinion in Adair was written by Justice HARLAN, one of the dissenters in Lochner. He stated that the "right of a person to sell his labor upon such terms as he deems proper [is] the same as the right of the purchaser of labor to prescribe the conditions. [The] employer and the employee have equality of right, and any legislation that disturbs that equality is an arbitrary interference with the liberty of contract."

Coppage v. Kansas, 236 U.S. 1 (1915), arose from the conviction of an employer under a similar yellow-dog-contract law, this time one enacted by Kansas. The Court, in an opinion by Justice PITNEY, held that the law violated due process: "Included in the right of personal liberty and the right of private property [is] the right to make contracts. [An] interference with this liberty so serious as that now under consideration, and so disturbing of equality of right, must be deemed to be arbitrary, unless it be supportable as a reasonable exercise of the police power of the State. [It] is said by the [state court] to be a matter of common knowledge that 'employees, as a rule, are not financially able to be as independent in making contracts for the sale of their labor as are employers in making contracts of purchase thereof.' No doubt, wherever the right of private property exists, there must and will be inequalities of fortune; and thus it naturally happens that parties negotiating about a contract are not equally unhampered by circumstances. [But it] is from the nature of things impossible to uphold freedom of contract and the right of private property without at the same time recognizing as legitimate those inequalities of fortune that are the necessary result of the exercise of those rights. [And since] a State may not strike them down directly it is clear that it may not do so indirectly, as by declaring in effect that the public good requires the removal of those inequalities that are but the normal and inevitable result of their exercise, and then invoking the police power in order to remove the inequalities, without other object in view."

Justice HOLMES dissented: "In present conditions a workman not unnaturally may believe that only by belonging to a union can he secure a contract that shall be fair to him. [If] that belief, whether right or wrong, may be held by a reasonable man, it seems to me that it may be enforced by law in order to establish the equality of position between the parties in which liberty of contract begins. Whether in the long run it is wise for the workingmen to enact legislation of this sort is not my concern, but I am strongly of opinion that there is nothing in the [Constitution] to prevent it."

The Court likewise invalidated a number of restraints on business entry. For example, in **New State Ice Co. v. Liebmann**, 285 U.S. 262 (1932), the Court invalidated an Oklahoma law that treated the manufacture of ice like a public utility, requiring a certificate of convenience and necessity as a prerequisite to entry into the business. See also Adams v. Tanner, 244 U.S. 590 (1917), striking down a law prohibiting employment agencies from collecting fees from workers. Justice Brandeis submitted extensive, data-laden dissents in both cases to demonstrate why reasonable legislators might think the restraints necessary.

Even during the Lochner era, however, many challenged laws withstood attack. In particular, the Court permitted legislatures to show solicitude for women workers. For example, **Muller v. Oregon**, 208 U.S. 412 (1908), sustained an Oregon law that provided that "no female" shall be employed in any factory or laundry for "more than ten hours during any one day." Justice BREWER stated that it was obvious that "woman's physical structure" placed her "at a disadvantage in the struggle for subsistence," and that, "as healthy mothers are essential to vigorous offspring, the physical well-being of woman becomes an object of public interest." Moreover, "woman has always been dependent upon man." Legislation to protect women "seems necessary to secure a real equality of right"; and such protective legislation is valid, "even when like legislation is not necessary for men and could not be sustained." The "inherent difference between the two sexes" justified "a difference in legislation" and "upholds that which is designed to compensate for some of the burdens which rest upon her."[1] In **Bunting v. Oregon**, 243 U.S. 426 (1917), the Court seemingly extended Muller and retrenched from Lochner by upholding a law establishing a maximum 10-hour work day for factory workers (male as well as female).

Any special solicitude for regulations protecting women disappeared, however, in **Adkins v. Children's Hospital**, 261 U.S. 525 (1923), which held that a District of Columbia law prescribing minimum *wages* for women violated due process. Justice SUTHERLAND noted that since Muller, the Nineteenth Amendment had been adopted, guaranteeing women the vote, and the civil inferiority of women was thus almost at a "vanishing point." Hence, liberty of contract could not be subjected to "a naked, arbitrary exercise" of legislative power over women any more than men. Justice HOLMES stated in dissent: "I confess that I do not understand the principle on which the power to fix a minimum for the wages of women can be denied by those who admit the power to fix a maximum for their hours of work. [The] bargain is equally affected whichever half you regulate. [It] will need more than the 19th Amendment to convince me that there are no differences between men and women, or that legislation cannot take those differences into account."

5. ***Lochner's flaws.*** By common consensus, Lochner was wrongly decided. Even constitutional courts abroad cite Lochner as a model of judicial overreach. But what, exactly, was wrong with the decision in Lochner? There are several plausible answers, each with its own implications. Perhaps Lochner was wrong because the Court stepped in to overturn a law passed with majority support. If so, how can Lochner be distinguished from any number of other individual rights cases, ranging from Roe v. Wade, p. 521 below, to McDonald v. City of Chicago, p. 475 above? Alternatively, it could be argued that Lochner was not wrong for overturning a popularly enacted law, but rather for overturning it on the basis of a right not explicitly stated in the Constitution. If so, can one distinguish cases such as Griswold v. Connecticut, p. 511 below, and Lawrence v. Texas, p. 563 below, which likewise overturned majoritarian laws on the basis of implied constitutional rights?

Another possibility is that Lochner's flaw lay neither in its countermajoritarian outcome nor its basing that outcome on an implied constitutional right, but rather in simply ascribing too much weight to that right. In other words, Lochner may have been correct to identify an implied

---

1 Muller was the first major case to resort to a fact-filled brief that came to be known as a "Brandeis brief," submitted by the defenders of the legislation. At the outset of its opinion, the Court noted: "In the brief filed by Mr. Louis D. Brandeis is a very copious collection of [expressions of opinion from other than judicial sources]. [The] legislation and opinions referred [to] may not be, technically speaking, authorities, [yet] they are significant of a widespread belief that woman's physical structure, and the functions she performs in consequence thereof, justify special legislation. [Constitutional] questions, it is true, are not settled by even a consensus of present public opinion. [At] the same time, when a question of fact is debated and debatable, and the extent to which a special constitutional limitation goes is affected by the truth in respect to that fact, a widespread and long continued belief concerning it is worthy of consideration. We take judicial cognizance of all matters of general knowledge."

freedom of contract sufficient to overturn some popular laws, but the Lochner Court erred in its balancing. See Strauss, "Why Was Lochner Wrong?", 70 U. Chi. L. Rev. 373 (2003). If so, is the conclusion that the Court "overvalued" the freedom of contract anything more than a bare statement of political preference? Can that conclusion be distinguished from arguing that the McDonald Court "overvalued" the right to keep and bear arms, or that the Roe Court "overvalued" the right to an abortion? Finally, Lochner may have been wrong just because it was decided in the realm of so-called "economic" rights rather personal liberty. If so, what is the constitutional basis for that distinction?

6. ***Constitutionalizing an economic theory.*** Justice Holmes famously declared in Lochner that "[This] case is decided upon an economic theory which a large part of the country does not entertain." Compare this admonition with the Thirteenth Amendment case of **Bailey v. Alabama**, 219 U.S. 219 (1911). Alabama had passed a law criminalizing any breach of a labor contract with intent to defraud; it also established a prima facie presumption that any breach had been carried out with fraudulent intent. The Supreme Court, per Justice HUGHES, held that compelling laborers to carry out contracts they otherwise wished to breach violated the Thirteenth Amendment's prohibition on "involuntary servitude."

Justice HOLMES dissented. He would have upheld the statute, writing that "[t]he 13th Amendment does not outlaw contracts for labor. That would be at least as great a misfortune for the laborer as for the man that employed him. For it certainly would affect the terms of the bargain unfavorably for the laboring man if it were understood that the employer could do nothing in case the laborer saw fit to break his word." Can Holmes's interpretation of the scope of the Thirteenth Amendment, derived at least in part from economic principles, be reconciled with his admonition in Lochner that economic theories should not be constitutionalized? Or is Holmes being consistent with his Lochner dissent in rejecting the majority's arguably economic-theory driven constitutional conclusion that a right to breach a contract was protected by the Constitution? Can both of these conclusions be true at once?

7. ***The economic climate of the Great Depression: Lochner and the New Deal.*** One reason for the Court's shift away from Lochner may have been the inability to square Lochner with remedial legislation passed during the Great Depression. Consider the economic circumstances following the stock market crash in 1929: unemployment rose from 3.2% before the Depression to 25.2% in 1933; GNP dropped nearly 30%, from over $700 billion to under $500 billion, in that same time; and housing construction in 1933 was at a mere 10% of its 1929 levels. For a discussion of the causes and effects of the Depression, see Ramirez, "The Law and Macroeconomics of the New Deal at 70," 62 Md. L. Rev. 515 (2003). Despite the brutal economic turn, during the early days of the Great Depression, the Court continued to apply Lochner's substantive due process doctrine to invalidate economic relief legislation. As the Depression went on, however, the Court began to retrench altogether from the premises on which Lochner had found economic regulation a violation of due process, ultimately expressly overruling Adkins. A key turning point was the following decision upholding a New York minimum price for the retail sale of milk:

Nebbia v. New York

291 U.S. 502, 54 S. Ct. 505, 78 L. Ed. 940 (1934).

■ JUSTICE ROBERTS delivered the opinion of the Court.

The Legislature of New York established [in 1933] a Milk Control Board with power [to] "fix minimum and maximum [retail] prices to be charged [by] stores to consumers for consumption off the premises where sold." The Board fixed nine cents as the price to be charged by a store for a quart of milk. Nebbia, the proprietor of a grocery store in Rochester, sold two quarts and a five cent loaf of bread for eighteen cents, and was convicted [of selling milk below the minimum price]. [The] question for decision is whether the [Constitution] prohibits a state from so fixing the selling price of milk. We first inquire as to the occasion for the legislation and its history. During 1932 the prices received by farmers for milk were much below the cost of production. [The] situation of the families of dairy producers had become desperate and called for state aid similar to that afforded the unemployed, if conditions should not improve. [Milk] is an essential item of diet. Failure of producers to receive a reasonable return [threatens] a relaxation of vigilance against contamination. The production and distribution of milk is a paramount industry of the state, and largely affects the health and prosperity of its people. [The] fluid milk industry is affected by factors of [price] instability peculiar to itself which call for special methods of control. [The] legislature adopted [this law] as a method of correcting the evils, which the report of the committee showed could not be expected to right themselves through the ordinary play of the forces of supply and demand, owing to the peculiar and uncontrollable factors affecting the industry.

[Under] our form of government the use of property and the making of contracts are normally matters of private and not a public concern. The general rule is that both shall be free of governmental interference. But neither property rights nor contract rights are absolute; for government cannot exist if the citizen may at will use his property to the detriment of his fellows, or exercise his freedom of contract to work them harm. Equally fundamental with the private right is that of the public to regulate it in the common interest.

[The] guaranty of due process [demands] only that the law shall not be unreasonable, arbitrary or capricious, and that the means selected shall have a real and substantial relation to the object sought to be attained. [But] we are told [that] the public control of rates or prices is per se unreasonable and unconstitutional, save as applied to business affected with a public interest. [There] is no closed class or category of businesses affected with a [public interest]. The phrase "affected with a public interest" can, in the nature of things, mean no more than that an industry, for adequate reason, is subject to control for the public good. [There] can be no doubt that upon proper occasion and by appropriate measures the state may regulate a business in any of its aspects, including the prices to be charged for the products or commodities it sells.

So far as the requirement of due process is concerned, [a] state is free to adopt whatever economic policy may reasonably be deemed to promote public welfare, and to enforce that policy by legislation adapted to its purpose. The courts are without authority either to declare such policy, or, when it is declared by the legislature, to override it. If the laws passed are seen to have a reasonable relation to a proper legislative purpose, and are neither arbitrary nor discriminatory, the requirements of due process are [satisfied]. Tested by these considerations we find no basis [for] condemning the provisions of the [law] here drawn into question. [Affirmed.]

■ JUSTICE MCREYNOLDS, joined by JUSTICES VAN DEVANTER, SUTHERLAND and BUTLER, dissenting.

[Interference] with guaranteed rights [is] defended upon the ground that the purpose was to promote the public welfare by increasing milk prices at the farm. [The court below has not] attempted to indicate how higher charges at stores to impoverished customers when the output is excessive and sale prices of producers are unrestrained, can possibly increase receipts at the farm. The Legislative Committee pointed out as the obvious cause of decreased consumption notwithstanding low prices, the consumers' reduced buying power. Higher store prices will not enlarge this power; nor will they decrease production. [It] appears to me wholly unreasonable to expect this legislation to accomplish the proposed end—increase of prices at the farm. [Not] only does the statute interfere arbitrarily with the rights of the little grocer to conduct his business according to standards long accepted; [it] takes away the liberty of twelve million consumers to buy a necessity of life in an [open market].

THE DEMISE OF LOCHNER AFTER THE NEW DEAL

1. ***Judicial deference to the means-ends relationship.*** Nebbia marked a significant shift from Lochner, suggesting a much-reduced judicial role in scrutinizing the means employed in economic regulations. While announcing that "the means selected shall have a real and substantial relation to the object sought to be attained," the decision undertook little independent examination of the economic rationality of the legislation, nor did it undertake to answer the dissent's critique of its economic premises.

2. ***Judicial deference to legislative ends.*** Other decisions retreated from the Lochner era's focus on impermissible legislative ends. A pivotal case was **West Coast Hotel Co. v. Parrish**, 300 U.S. 379 (1937), in which the Court, by a vote of 5–4, overruled Adkins v. Children's Hospital and upheld a state minimum wage law for women. Chief Justice HUGHES's majority opinion stated: "[T]he violation [of due process] alleged by those attacking minimum wage regulation for women is deprivation of freedom of contract. What is this freedom? The Constitution does not speak of freedom of contract. It speaks of liberty and prohibits the deprivation of liberty without due process of law. In prohibiting that deprivation the Constitution does not recognize an absolute and uncontrollable liberty. [Liberty] under the Constitution [is] necessarily subject to the restraints of due process, and regulation which is reasonable in relation to its subject and is adopted in the interests of the community is due process.

"[We] think that [Adkins] was a departure from the true application of the principles governing the regulation by the State of the relation of employer and employed. [What] can be closer to the public interest than the health of women and their protection from unscrupulous and overreaching employers? [The] legislature [was] clearly entitled to consider that [women] are in the class receiving the least pay, that their bargaining power is relatively weak, and that they are the ready victims of those who would take advantage of their necessitous circumstances. The legislature was entitled to adopt measures to reduce the evils of the 'sweating system,' the exploiting of workers at wages so low as to be insufficient to meet the bare cost of living, thus making their very helplessness the occasion of a most injurious competition. The legislature had the right to consider that its minimum wage requirements would be an important aid in carrying out its policy of protection. The adoption of similar requirements by many States evidences a deep-seated conviction both as to the presence of the evil and as to the means adapted to check it. Legislative response to that conviction cannot be regarded as arbitrary or capricious, and that is all we have to decide.

"[There] is an additional and compelling consideration which recent economic experience has brought into a strong light. The exploitation of a class of workers who are in an unequal position with respect to bargaining power and are thus relatively defenseless against the denial of a living wage is not only detrimental to their health and well being but casts a direct burden for their support upon the community. What these workers lose in wages the taxpayers are called upon to pay. [We] may take judicial notice of the unparalleled demands for relief which arose during the recent period of depression. [The] community is not bound to provide what is in effect a subsidy for unconscionable employers. The community may direct its law-making power to correct the abuse which springs from their selfish disregard of the public interest. [Adkins is] overruled."

Justice SUTHERLAND, joined by Justices Van Devanter, McReynolds and Butler, dissented, insisting that "the meaning of the Constitution does not change with the ebb and flow of economic events" and that the law had not "the slightest relation to the capacity or earning power of the employee, to the number of hours which constitute the day's work, the character of the place where the work is to be done, or the circumstances [of] the employment." To the extent that the minimum wage exceeded the fair value of the services rendered, the law amounted to "a compulsory exaction from the employer for the support of a partially indigent person, [and] therefore [arbitrarily] shifts to his shoulders a burden which, if it belongs to anybody, belongs to society as a whole."

Note West Coast Hotel's reversal of the distributive baseline assumed by Lochner: rather than viewing the regulation as a taking of property and windfall to employees, the Court suggested that *not* regulating would be a "subsidy to unconscionable employers" who would evade their fair share of the welfare costs they had imposed upon the community. On this view, regulation is not impermissible redistribution, but rather restoration of the balance of power between employer and employee to an appropriate baseline. If all income and wealth distributions result from government regulation of property and contract, then there is no natural baseline, and government inaction is as much a form of distribution as government action.

3. ***The impact of Nebbia and West Coast Hotel.*** Nebbia was decided in 1934, just before the Court struck down various New Deal laws as exceeding national power. See Chapters 3 & 4, supra. Relaxation of due process restraints was not smooth: two years after Nebbia, the Court seemed to adhere to Adkins rather than West Coast Hotel in Morehead v. New York ex rel. Tipaldo, 298 U.S. 587 (1936), which invalidated New York's minimum wage law for women. A few months after Morehead, President Roosevelt announced his Court-packing plan. While that controversy was raging, West Coast Hotel came down. Some viewed Justice Roberts's vote in West Coast

Hotel as "the switch in time that saved the Nine" from the Court-packing plan, which failed in the Senate soon afterward. Was it? Or was West Coast Hotel consistent with Justice Roberts's own earlier opinion in Nebbia, written prior to FDR's threat?

In 1938, in **United States v. Carolene Products Co.**, 304 U.S. 144, the Court rejected a due process challenge to a federal prohibition of the interstate shipment of "filled milk"—skimmed milk mixed with non-milk fats—as an "adulterated article of food" whose sale constituted a "fraud upon the public." Justice STONE's majority opinion made clear that challenging the "rational basis" of such economic legislation would be a difficult task. Legislative findings contributed to "informed judicial review," but were not essential: "Even in the absence of such aids, the existence of facts supporting the legislative judgment is to be presumed, for regulatory legislation affecting ordinary commercial transactions is not to be pronounced unconstitutional unless in the light of the facts made known or generally assumed it is of such a character as to preclude the assumption that it rests upon some rational basis within the knowledge and experience of the legislators. [It] is evident from all the considerations presented to Congress, and those of which we may take judicial notice, that the question is at least debatable whether commerce in filled milk should be left unregulated, or in some measure restricted, or wholly prohibited. [That] decision was for Congress, [and] neither the finding of a court derived by weighing the evidence nor the verdict of a jury can be substituted for it." Consider the view that the law upheld in the case was an "utterly unprincipled 'example of special interest legislation' " and that the claimed justifications for the ban were "patently bogus." Miller, "The True Story of Carolene Products," 1988 Sup. Ct. Rev. 397. Even if so, should the law have been struck down?

In the course of reaching the decision in Carolene Products, Justice Stone penned the famous Carolene Products Footnote 4, distinguishing cases warranting deference from those in which greater judicial scrutiny might be appropriate. After stating that, as to the filled milk statute, "the existence of facts supporting the legislative judgment is to be presumed," Justice Stone wrote: "There may be narrower scope for operation of the presumption of constitutionality when legislation appears on its face to be within a specific prohibition of the Constitution, such as those of the first ten Amendments, which are deemed equally specific when held to be embraced within the 14th. It is unnecessary to consider now whether legislation which restricts those political processes which can ordinarily be expected to bring about repeal of undesirable legislation, is to be subjected to more exacting judicial scrutiny under the general prohibitions of the 14th Amendment than are most other types of legislation [e.g.,] restrictions upon the right to vote; restraints upon the dissemination of information; interferences with political organizations; [and] prohibition of peaceable assembly. Nor need we enquire whether similar considerations enter into the review of statutes directed at particular religious, or national, or racial minorities; whether prejudice against discrete and insular minorities may be a special condition, which tends seriously to curtail the operation of those political processes ordinarily to be relied upon to protect minorities, and which may call for a correspondingly more searching judicial inquiry."

Justice Stone's "political process" rationale in footnote 4 suggests that judicial intervention is more appropriate the less political processes may be trusted to even out winners and losers over time. On this view, judicial intervention helps to reinforce democracy by clearing the channels of political change and preventing entrenched advantage or disadvantage in the political process. For an especially influential elaboration of this "political process" argument for heightened judicial scrutiny in some areas but not others, depending on whether it corrects political market failure, see Ely, Democracy and Distrust (1980). Note that the footnote seems to assume that rival economic factions (such as employers and employees, producers and retailers, truckers and railroads), unlike other factions (such as religious or racial minorities), will be able to compete fairly with one another in the political process, with no one economic faction becoming systematically disadvantaged. Is this assumption accurate? Consider the view that diffuse and unorganized interests such as consumers, nonunion workers, small businesses or the poor will be systematically disadvantaged in politics relative to focused and organized interests such as industry lobbies. Might some industries also gain entrenched advantage over others? If so, why isn't judicial intervention warranted to restore fair democratic competition?

MINIMUM RATIONALITY REVIEW OF ECONOMIC LEGISLATION

Carolene Products helped to introduce the minimum "rational basis" standard that continues to the present to govern due process review of economic legislation. Later decisions were even more deferential. Consider what techniques of deference to the legislature the Court employs in the following decision, which typifies minimum rationality review:

Williamson v. Lee Optical Co.

348 U.S. 483, 75 S. Ct. 461, 99 L. Ed. 563 (1955).

■ JUSTICE DOUGLAS delivered the opinion of the Court.

[The] District Court held unconstitutional [under] the Due Process Clause [the] portions of [a 1953 Oklahoma statute] § 2 which make it unlawful for any person not a licensed optometrist or ophthalmologist to fit lenses to a face or to duplicate or replace into frames lenses or other optical appliances, except upon written prescriptive authority of an Oklahoma licensed ophthalmologist or optometrist. An ophthalmologist is a duly licensed physician who specializes in the care of the eyes. An optometrist examines eyes for refractive error, recognizes (but does not treat) diseases of the eye, and fills prescriptions for eyeglasses. The optician is an artisan qualified to grind lenses, fill prescriptions, and fit frames. The effect of § 2 is to forbid the optician from fitting or duplicating lenses without a prescription from an ophthalmologist or optometrist. In practical effect, it means that no optician can fit old glasses into new frames or supply a lens, whether it be a new lens or one to duplicate a lost or broken lens, without a prescription. The [District Court] rebelled at the notion that a State could require a prescription [to] "take old lenses and place them in new frames and then fit the completed spectacles to the *face* of the eyeglass wearer." [The] court found that through mechanical devices and ordinary skills the optician could take a broken lens or a fragment thereof, measure its power, and reduce it to prescriptive terms. The court held that "Although [the legislature] was dealing with a matter of public interest, the particular means chosen are neither reasonably necessary nor reasonably related to the end sought to be achieved."

[The] Oklahoma law may exact a needless, wasteful requirement in many cases. But it is for the legislature, not the courts, to balance the advantages and disadvantages of the new requirement. It appears that in many cases the optician can easily supply the new frames or new lenses without reference to the old written prescription. It also appears that many written prescriptions contain no directive data in regard to fitting spectacles to the face. But in some cases the directions contained in the prescription are essential, if the glasses are to be fitted so as to correct the particular defects of vision or alleviate the eye condition. The legislature might have concluded that the frequency of occasions when a prescription is necessary was sufficient to justify this regulation of the fitting of eyeglasses. Likewise, when it is necessary to duplicate a lens, a written prescription may or may not be necessary. But the legislature might have concluded that one was needed often enough to require one in every case. Or the legislature may have concluded that eye examinations were so critical, not only for correction of vision but also for detection of latent ailments or diseases, that every change in frames and every duplication of a lens should be accompanied by a prescription from a medical expert. To be sure, the present law does not require a new examination of the eyes every time the frames are changed or the lenses duplicated. For if the old prescription is on file with the optician, he can go ahead and make the new fitting or duplicate the lenses. But the law need not be in every respect logically consistent with its aims to be constitutional. It is enough that there is an evil at hand for correction, and that it might be thought that the particular legislative measure was a rational way to correct it. The day is gone when this Court uses the Due Process Clause [to] strike down state laws, regulatory of business and industrial conditions, because they may be unwise, improvident, or out of harmony with a particular school of [thought].

[The] District Court [also held that] portion of § 3 which makes it unlawful "to solicit the sale [of] frames, mountings, [or] any other optical appliances" [to violate due process]. [R]egulation of the advertising of eyeglass frames was said to intrude "into a mercantile field only casually related to the visual care of the public" and restrict "an activity which in no way can detrimentally affect the people." [An] eyeglass frame, considered in isolation, is only a piece of merchandise. But an eyeglass frame is not used in isolation; [it] is used with lenses; and lenses, pertaining as they do to the human eye, enter the field of health. Therefore, the legislature might conclude that to regulate one effectively it would have to regulate the other. Or it might conclude that both the sellers of frames and the sellers of lenses were in a business where advertising should be limited or even abolished in the public interest. [The] advertiser of frames may be using his ads to bring in customers who will buy lenses. If the advertisement of lenses is to be abolished or controlled, the advertising of frames must come under the same restraints; or so the legislature might think. We see no constitutional reason why a State may not treat all who deal with the human eye as members of a profession who should use no merchandising methods for obtaining [customers]. [Reversed.]

———

CLOSER SCRUTINY OF ECONOMIC CLASSIFICATIONS?

1. ***Ex post justifications.*** Lee Optical exemplifies an extremely deferential judicial stance both to the legislature's selection of ends and its choice of means to those ends. Note the Court's willingness to accept a *conceivable* rational relationship to any legitimate end as sufficient—meaning that the challenged governmental actors can hypothesize reasons for the classification whether or not they contemplated those reasons at the time of enactment. For example, the Lee Optical decision refers to what the legislature "might" have found as the basis for the law. Does this allow too much justification by lawyers in litigation ex post, rather than by legislatures in deliberation ex ante?

How much does this deferential standard of review arise from concern about judicial competence to second-guess legislative motivations? Consider the Court's deference to legislative judgments in **Ferguson v. Skrupa**, 372 U.S. 726 (1963), which upheld a Kansas law prohibiting anyone from engaging "in the business of debt adjusting" except as an incident to "the lawful practice of law." Justice BLACK's opinion for the Court concluded that Kansas "was free to decide for itself that legislation was needed to deal with the business of debt adjusting." He reiterated that the Court had abandoned "the use of the 'vague contours' of the Due Process Clause to nullify laws which a majority of the Court believed to be economically unwise." And he added: "Unquestionably, there are arguments showing that the business of debt adjusting has social utility, but such arguments are properly addressed to the legislature, not to us. We refuse to sit as a 'super legislature to weigh the wisdom of legislation.' [Whether] the legislature takes for its textbook Adam Smith, Herbert Spencer, Lord Keynes or some other is no concern of ours." Justice HARLAN concurred briefly "on the ground that this state measure bears a rational relation to a constitutionally permissible objective. See [Lee Optical]."

Should minimal rationality review be applied with greater "bite"? Is this possible without resurrecting fears of Lochner-like judicial subjectivity? Suppose that courts tested the reasonableness of the means in terms of the actual purposes put forth by the defenders of the law, rather than purposes a legislature *might* have had, and required government to make some evidentiary showing that the means chosen actually promoted the proffered governmental purposes. Might such means-ends scrutiny avoid the dangers of judicial value judgments exemplified in the Lochner era?

2. ***Punitive damages and a partial revival of substantive due process.*** The one area in which the Court has revived heightened due process review in the area of economic liberty involves limitations on punitive damage awards in civil cases. Such awards are sometimes grossly disproportionate to actual or compensatory damages. Yet no independent textual provision limits such civil awards. The Excessive Fines Clause of the Eighth Amendment limits disproportionate criminal penalties, but has no civil analogue in the Constitution's text. Punitive damages awards have been challenged as violating due process. Do these challenges sound in substantive or procedural due process? What if they contend that a punitive damages verdict, if rendered by a jury without sufficiently clear and objective criteria, amounts to a naked wealth transfer or is not even properly described as "law"? Is such an argument reminiscent of the hypothesized natural law violations listed in Calder v. Bull?

After a series of decisions upholding challenged punitive damage awards but intimating that some constitutional limits might apply, see, e.g., Pacific Mutual Life Insurance Co. v. Haslip, 499 U.S. 1 (1991); TXO Production Corp. v. Alliance Resources Corp., 509 U.S. 443 (1993); Honda Motor Co., Ltd. v. Oberg, 512 U.S. 415 (1994), the Court invalidated an award as excessive in **BMW of North America, Inc. v. Gore**, 517 U.S. 559 (1996), which involved a $2 million punitive damages award for the concealed paint touch-up of a new car, compensatory damages for which were assessed at only $4000. The opinion of the Court, written by Justice STEVENS and joined by Justices O'Connor, Kennedy, Souter and Breyer, found the award "grossly excessive," resting this conclusion partly on notions of procedural due process—i.e., the requirement of fair notice to the defendant of potential legal liability. But as Justice BREYER clarified in his concurrence, joined by Justices O'Connor and Souter, such limits might also be seen as a matter of substantive due process: "This constitutional concern, itself harkening back to the Magna Carta, arises out of the basic unfairness of depriving citizens of life, liberty, or property, through the application, not of law and legal processes, but of arbitrary coercion. Requiring the application of law, rather than a decisionmaker's caprice, does more than simply provide citizens notice of what actions may subject them to punishment; it also helps to assure the uniform general treatment of similarly situated persons that is the essence of law itself." Justice SCALIA, joined by Justice Thomas, dissented: "I do not regard the Fourteenth Amendment's Due Process Clause as a secret repository of substantive guarantees against 'unfairness.'" Justice Ginsburg also dissented, joined by Chief Justice Rehnquist.

After Gore, it was uncertain how much was too much. The Gore opinion set forth several "guideposts": "the degree of reprehensibility; [the] disparity between the harm or potential harm suffered [and the] punitive damages award; and the difference between this remedy and the civil penalties authorized or imposed in comparable cases." In **State Farm Mut. Automobile Ins. Co. v. Campbell**, 538 U.S. 408 (2003), the Court applied the Gore guideposts to hold, by a vote of 6–3, that a $145 million punitive damages award, where full compensatory damages were only $1 million, was excessive in violation of the Due Process Clause. Justice KENNEDY wrote for the Court, joined by Chief Justice Rehnquist and Justices Stevens, O'Connor, Souter and Breyer: "While States possess discretion over the imposition of punitive damages, it is well established that there are procedural and substantive constitutional limitations on these awards. [To] the extent an award is grossly excessive, it furthers no legitimate purpose and constitutes an arbitrary deprivation of property." Justice Kennedy applied the Gore factors and concluded that the punitive damages award "was neither reasonable nor proportionate to the wrong committed, and it was an irrational and arbitrary deprivation of the property of the defendant." Justices Scalia, Thomas and Ginsburg dissented, adhering to the views they expressed in Gore.

In the next case involving a challenge to a punitive damages award after State Farm, the first to be considered by the new Roberts Court, the Court relied on the procedural aspects of due process without reaching the substantive aspects. In **Philip Morris USA v. Williams**, 549 U.S. 346 (2007), the Court split 5–4 in vacating a $79.5 million punitive damages award (as compared to $821,000 in compensatory damages) to the estate of a deceased smoker. Justice BREYER wrote the opinion of the Court, joined by Chief Justice Roberts and Justices Kennedy, Souter and Alito, vacating the award and remanding without reaching the question whether the award was in fact "grossly excessive." He focused on the trial court's failure to instruct the jury clearly not to punish Philip Morris for possible harm to persons other than Williams: "In our view, the Constitution's Due Process Clause forbids a State to use a punitive damages award to punish a defendant for injury that it inflicts upon nonparties [who are] strangers to the litigation. [To] permit punishment for injuring a nonparty victim would add a near standardless dimension to the punitive damages equation. [We] therefore conclude that the Due Process Clause requires States to provide assurance that juries are not asking the wrong question, i.e., seeking, not simply to determine reprehensibility, but also to punish for harm caused strangers." The Court remanded to the Oregon courts to fashion such safeguards in any new trial. Justice STEVENS dissented, reiterating his commitment to the limits imposed in Gore and State Farm but objecting to "the Court's imposition of a novel limit on the State's power to impose punishment in civil litigation." Justices Scalia, Thomas and Ginsburg also dissented.

In **Exxon Shipping Co. v. Baker**, 554 U.S. 471 (2008), the Court imposed a limit on punitive damages as a matter of federal common law rather than substantive due process, but commented on notions of proportionality derived from due process analysis. The case involved a $2.5 billion jury verdict against Exxon for the catastrophic oil spill in 1993 by the ship Exxon Valdez, which caused extensive damage to the Alaska coastline and fishing grounds. Under federal maritime law, the Court held, punitive damages could be awarded only at most in a one-to-one ratio to compensatory damages. It accordingly capped punitive damages in the case at the equivalent of the $507.5 million compensatory damages award.

In his opinion for the Court, Justice SOUTER alluded to its substantive due process precedents: "Today's enquiry differs from due process review because the case arises under federal maritime jurisdiction, and we are reviewing a jury award for conformity with maritime law. [Whatever] may be the constitutional significance of the unpredictability of high punitive awards, this feature of happenstance is in tension with the function of the awards as punitive, just because of the implication of unfairness that an eccentrically high punitive verdict carries in a system whose commonly held notion of law rests on a sense of fairness in dealing with one another. Thus, a penalty should be reasonably predictable in its severity, so that even Justice Holmes's 'bad man' can look ahead with some ability to know what the stakes are in choosing one course of action or another. [The] common sense of justice would surely bar penalties that reasonable people would think excessive for the harm caused in the circumstances." Justifying the 1:1 ratio after a detailed review of history, state law and empirical evidence, Justice Souter noted that "[w]hen compensatory damages are substantial, then a lesser ratio, perhaps only equal to compensatory damages, can reach the outermost limit of the due process guarantee." Justices Stevens, Ginsburg and Breyer dissented from the decision to overturn the particular award at issue, reasoning either that Congress should set the rules in this area or that this was a special case warranting an exception from any rigid ratio.

3. ***Economic Substantive Due Process in the States.*** Recently, in In **Patel v. Texas Department of Licensing and Regulation**, 469

S.W.3d 69 (Tex. 2015), the Texas Supreme Court heard a challenge to cosmetology licensing statutes and regulations The Court held that a 750-hour training requirement to become a licensed esthetician violated eyebrow threaders' right to "due course of law" (the Texas Constitution's analogue to the Due Process Clause), because the requirement was so burdensome as to be oppressive. Concurring, Justice Willett invoked not the economic burden on the threaders, but "the American Dream and the unalienable human right to pursue happiness without curtsying to government on bended knee." He wrote: "Occupational freedom, the right to earn a living as one chooses, is a nontrivial constitutional right entitled to nontrivial judicial protection. People are owed liberty by virtue of their very humanity—'endowed by their Creator,' as the Declaration affirms." Justice Willett (subsequently appointed to the U.S. Court of Appeals for the Fifth Circuit) thus appears to view invocation of natural law not as unwarranted Lochnerizing, but rather as expressing fidelity to the Framers' original intent.

SECTION 2. SUBSTANTIVE DUE PROCESS AND PRIVACY

May the Court invoke the Due Process Clause to protect fundamental values apart from economic liberties? The Court has maintained and expanded a line of cases applying heightened judicial scrutiny to laws threatening certain rights to "privacy." The concept of privacy referred to in these cases encompasses some aspects of individual decisionmaking deemed too personal to be regulated by the state—such as family formation, child-rearing, contraception, abortion, and sexual conduct. Do these cases revive the specter of Lochner and raise similar problems of interpretation and judicial competence? Or are they distinguishable from Lochner? Do they suggest that "Lochnerizing" is justifiable after all?

The Court's discussion of a fundamental right to privacy in Griswold v. Connecticut, p. 511 below, was not a sudden revival of substantive due process. In one sense, it built on an aspect of the Lochner tradition that never wholly died. For example, **Meyer v. Nebraska**, 262 U.S. 390 (1923), read "liberty" broadly to reverse the conviction of a teacher for teaching German and thus violating a state law prohibiting the teaching of foreign languages to young children. Justice McREYNOLDS, a devout Lochnerian, wrote for the Court: "Without doubt, [liberty] denotes not merely freedom from bodily restraint but also the right of the individual to contract, to engage in any of the common occupations of life, to acquire useful knowledge, to marry, establish a home and bring up children, to worship God according to the dictates of his own conscience, and generally to enjoy those privileges long recognized at common law as essential to the orderly pursuit of happiness by free men." He found that the Nebraska law "materially" interfered "with the calling of modern language teachers, with the opportunities of pupils to acquire knowledge, and with the power of parents to control the education of their own."

Two years later, in **Pierce v. Society of Sisters**, 268 U.S. 510 (1925), Justice McREYNOLDS wrote in a similar vein for a unanimous Court, sustaining a challenge by parochial and private schools to an Oregon law requiring children to attend public schools. Under the Meyer view of fundamental rights, the law interfered "with the liberty of parents and guardians to direct the upbringing and education of children under their control." There was no "general power of the State to standardize its children by forcing them to accept instruction from public teachers only. The child is not the mere creature of the State; those who nurture him and direct his destiny have the right, coupled with the high duty, to recognize and prepare him for additional obligations."

SUBSTANTIVE DUE PROCESS, CHILDBEARING AND CONTRACEPTION

In **Buck v. Bell**, 274 U.S. 200 (1927), Justice Holmes wrote for the Court to uphold a Virginia court's judgment ordering that Carrie Buck, "a feeble-minded" woman committed to a state mental institution, be sterilized at the age of eighteen. True to his repeated critiques of Lochner-style reasoning, Holmes wrote: "There can be no doubt that so far as procedure is concerned the rights of the patient are most carefully considered, and as every step in this case was taken in scrupulous compliance with the statute and after months of observation, there is no doubt that in that respect the plaintiff in error has had due process at law. The attack is not upon the procedure but upon the substantive law. [In] view of the general declarations of the Legislature and the specific findings of the Court obviously we cannot say as matter of law that the grounds do not exist, and if they exist they justify the result."

In a now infamous line, Justice Holmes concluded: "It is better for all the world, if instead of waiting to execute degenerate offspring for crime, or to let them starve for their imbecility, society can prevent those who are manifestly unfit from continuing their kind. The principle that sustains compulsory vaccination is broad enough to cover cutting the Fallopian tubes. [Three] generations of imbeciles are enough."

Justice Holmes did not mention that by the time the Supreme Court decided Buck, there was a robust consensus among the state courts that such eugenics laws were unconstitutional. In **Smith v. Board of Examiners of Feeble-Minded**, 88 A. 963 (N.J. 1913), for example, the New Jersey Supreme Court held that the law violated the Equal Protection Clause. The court recognized the conflict between a legislature's "inherent sovereignty to enact and enforce whatever regulations are in its judgment demanded for the welfare of society," on the one hand, and concern about "the forceable suppression of the constitutional rights of the individual," on the other. It concluded that the end—avoiding the procreation of epileptics—was not rationally tied to the means used—sterilizing those in institutions—and thus violated the Constitution. Other state courts agreed. See, e.g., Haynes v. Lapeer, Circuit Judge, 166 N.W. 938 (Mich. 1918); Osborn v. Thomson, 169 N.Y.S. 638 (Sup. Ct. 1918); Williams v. Smith, 131 N.E. 2 (Ind. 1921). For more on the history of state eugenics laws, see Sutton, 51 Imperfect Solutions: States and the Making of American Constitutional Law 84–132 (2018).

Justice Holmes likely would have considered these state supreme court decisions to be further examples of impermissible Lochernizing. But fifteen years after Buck, the Court reversed course. The Court's invalidation of a state eugenics law in **Skinner v. Oklahoma**, 316 U.S. 535 (1942), marked its first suggestion, after Lochner's demise, of a "basic liberty" not tied to a specific constitutional guarantee. Though the majority based its reasoning on the Equal Protection Clause, and thus avoided the question of substantive due process, Skinner's use of a heightened standard of scrutiny to protect a Court-defined "fundamental right" arguably presaged Griswold and Roe.

Oklahoma's Habitual Criminal Sterilization Act provided for compulsory sterilization after a third conviction for a felony involving "moral turpitude," but excluded some felonies—like embezzlement—to which the sterilization requirement would otherwise apply. Although state classifications among criminals would not ordinarily be overturned, Justice DOUGLAS explained for the Court, such usual deference to state police power legislation was not warranted here: "We are dealing here with legislation which involves one of the basic civil rights of man. Marriage and procreation are fundamental to the very existence and survival of the race. [There] is no redemption for the individual whom the law touches. Any experiment which the State conducts is to his irreparable injury. He is forever deprived of a basic liberty."

However, Justice Douglas stopped short of declaring compulsory sterilization inherently unconstitutional, and held that the law's true constitutional defect was its arbitrary application to some felonies but not others: "We mention these matters not to reexamine the scope of the police power of the States. We advert to them merely in emphasis of our view that *strict scrutiny* of the classification which a State makes in a sterilization law is essential, lest unwittingly, or otherwise, invidious discriminations are made against groups or types of individuals in violation of the constitutional guaranty of just and equal laws. [Sterilization] of those who have thrice committed grand larceny, with immunity for those who are embezzlers, is a clear, pointed, unmistakable discrimination."

Justice JACKSON, in a concurring opinion, came closer to opining that deprivation of the right to procreate was entirely outside the state's power: "There are limits to the extent to which a legislatively represented majority may conduct biological experiments at the expense of the dignity and personality and natural powers of a minority—even those who have been guilty of what the majority define as crimes."

Consider the scope of the "basic civil right" Justice Douglas discussed: should Skinner be read to apply only to freedom from sterilization, or does the opinion's reference to "marriage and procreation" as "fundamental" indicate a higher level of generality? Did Skinner help lay the groundwork for Roe v. Wade's right of reproductive autonomy, see p. 521, below, and Obergefell v. Hodges's right to same-sex marriage, see p. 583, below?

A more direct precursor to Roe and Obergefell was decided in 1965, with Justice Douglas again writing for the Court. Compare his 1942 methodology in Skinner to his reasoning in the opinion that follows:

Griswold v. Connecticut

381 U.S. 479, 85 S. Ct. 1678, 14 L. Ed. 2d 510 (1965).

■ JUSTICE DOUGLAS delivered the opinion of the Court.

[The] constitutionality [of two Connecticut provisions] is involved. [One] provides: "Any person who uses any drug, medicinal article or instrument for the purpose of preventing conception shall be fined not less than fifty dollars or imprisoned not less than sixty days nor more than one year or [both]."

[The other] provides: "Any person who assists, abets, counsels, causes, hires or commands another to commit any offense may be prosecuted and punished as if he were the principal offender." The appellants were found guilty as accessories and fined $100 each, against the claim that the accessory statute as so applied violated the 14th Amendment. [The state appellate courts affirmed.]

[We] are met with a wide range of questions that implicate the Due Process Clause of the 14th Amendment. Overtones of some arguments suggest that [Lochner] should be our guide. But we decline that invitation. [We] do not sit as a super-legislature to determine the wisdom, need, and propriety of laws that touch economic problems, business affairs, or social conditions. This law, however, operates directly on an intimate relation of husband and wife and their physician's role in one aspect of that relation. The association of people is not mentioned in the Constitution nor in the Bill of Rights. The right to educate a child in a school of the parents' choice—whether public or private or parochial—is also not mentioned. Nor is the right to study any particular subject or any foreign language. Yet the First Amendment has been construed to include certain of those rights. By [Pierce], the right to educate one's children as one chooses is made applicable to the States. [By Meyer], the same dignity is given the right to study the German language in a private school. [We] reaffirm the principle of the Pierce and the Meyer cases.

The foregoing cases suggest that specific guarantees in the Bill of Rights have penumbras, formed by emanations from those guarantees that help give them life and substance. Various guarantees create zones of privacy. The right of association contained in the penumbra of the First Amendment is one, as we have seen. The Third Amendment in its prohibition against the quartering of soldiers "in any house" in time of peace without the consent of the owner is another facet of that privacy. The Fourth Amendment explicitly affirms the "right of the people to be secure in their persons, houses, papers, and effects against unreasonable searches and seizures." The Fifth Amendment in its Self-Incrimination Clause enables the citizen to create a zone of privacy which government may not force him to surrender to his detriment. The Ninth Amendment provides: "The enumeration in the Constitution, of certain rights, shall not be construed to deny or disparage others retained by the people." The Fourth and Fifth Amendments were described in Boyd v. United States, 116 U.S. 616 [1886], as protection against all governmental invasions "of the sanctity of a man's home and the privacies of life." We recently referred [to] the Fourth Amendment as creating a "right to privacy, no less important than any other right carefully and particularly reserved to the people." We have had many controversies over these penumbral rights of "privacy and repose." These cases bear witness that the right of privacy which presses for recognition here is a legitimate one.

The present case [concerns] a relationship lying within the zone of privacy created by several fundamental constitutional guarantees. And it concerns a law which, in forbidding the *use* of contraceptives rather than regulating their manufacture or sale, seeks to achieve its goals by means having a maximum destructive impact upon that relationship. Such a law cannot stand in light of the familiar principle [that] a "governmental purpose to control or prevent activities constitutionally subject to state regulation may not be achieved by means which sweep unnecessarily broadly and thereby invade the area of protected freedoms." Would we allow the police to search the sacred precincts of marital bedrooms for telltale signs of the use of contraceptives? The very idea is repulsive to the notions of privacy surrounding the marriage relationship. We deal with a right of privacy older than the [Bill of Rights]. Marriage is a coming together for better or for worse, hopefully enduring, and intimate to the degree of being sacred. The association promotes a way of life, not causes; a harmony in living, not political faiths; a bilateral loyalty, not commercial or social projects. Yet it is an association for as noble a purpose as any involved in our prior decisions. [Reversed.]

■ JUSTICE GOLDBERG, whom CHIEF JUSTICE WARREN and JUSTICE BRENNAN join, concurring.

[Although] I have not accepted the view that "due process" as used in the 14th Amendment incorporates all of the first eight Amendments, [I] do agree that the concept of liberty protects those personal rights that are fundamental, and is not confined to the specific terms of the Bill of Rights. My conclusion [that liberty] embraces the right of marital privacy though that right is not mentioned explicitly in the Constitution is supported both by numerous decisions [and] by the language and history of the Ninth Amendment. [The] Ninth Amendment reads, "The enumeration in the Constitution, of certain rights, shall not be construed to deny or disparage others retained by the people." [It] was proffered to quiet expressed fears that a bill of specifically enumerated rights could not be sufficiently broad to cover all essential rights and that the specific mention of certain rights would be interpreted as a denial that others were protected.

[This] Court has had little occasion to interpret the Ninth Amendment, [but to] hold that a right so basic and fundamental and so deep-rooted in our society as the right of privacy in marriage may be infringed because that right is not guaranteed in so many words by the first eight amendments [is] to ignore the Ninth Amendment and to give it no effect whatsoever. [I] do not mean to imply that the Ninth Amendment is applied against the States by the Fourteenth [nor] that the Ninth Amendment constitutes an independent source of rights protected from infringement by either the States or Federal Government. [Rather,] the Ninth Amendment simply lends strong support to the view that the "liberty" protected by the Fifth and [14th] Amendments [is] not restricted to rights specifically mentioned in the first eight amendments. [I] believe that the right of privacy in the marital relation is fundamental and basic—a personal right "retained by the people" within the meaning of the Ninth Amendment, [a right] which is protected by the Fourteenth Amendment from infringement by the [States].

■ JUSTICE HARLAN, concurring in the judgment.

[I] find myself unable to join the Court's opinion [because] it seems to me to evince an approach [that] the Due Process Clause of the 14th Amendment does not touch this Connecticut statute unless the enactment is found to violate some right assured by the letter or penumbra of the Bill of Rights. [In] my view, the proper constitutional inquiry in this case is whether this Connecticut statute infringes the Due Process Clause of the 14th Amendment because the enactment violates basic values "implicit in the concept of ordered liberty." [The] Due Process Clause stands, in my opinion, on its own bottom. [Judicial self-restraint will be achieved] only by continual insistence upon respect for the teachings of history, solid recognition of the basic values that underlie our society, and wise application of the great roles that the doctrines of federalism and separation of powers have played [in] preserving American freedoms. Adherence to these principles will not, of course, obviate all constitutional differences of opinion among judges, nor should it. Their continued recognition will, however, go farther toward keeping most judges from roaming at large in the constitutional field than will the interpolation into the Constitution of an artificial and largely illusory restriction on the content of [due process].

[Justice HARLAN in Griswold relied expressly on his dissent in POE v. ULLMAN, 367 U.S. 497, 523 (1961), which had dismissed an appeal involving the Connecticut statute on justiciability grounds:

"[I] believe that a statute making it a criminal offense for *married couples* to use contraceptives is an intolerable and unjustifiable invasion of privacy in the conduct of the most intimate concerns of an individual's personal life. [Through] the course of this Court's decisions, [due process] has represented the balance which our Nation, built upon postulates of respect for the liberty of the individual, has struck between that liberty and the demands of organized society, [having] regard to what history teaches are the traditions from which it developed as well as the traditions from which it broke. That tradition is a living thing. [The] full scope of the liberty guaranteed by the Due Process Clause cannot be found in or limited by the precise terms of the specific guarantees elsewhere provided in the Constitution. This 'liberty' is not a series of isolated points pricked out in terms of [such specific guarantees as speech and religion]. It is a rational continuum which, broadly speaking, includes a freedom from all substantial arbitrary impositions and purposeless restraints, and which also recognizes [that] certain interests require particularly careful scrutiny of the state needs asserted to justify their abridgment.

"[Society] is not limited in its objects only to the physical well-being of the community, but has traditionally concerned itself with the moral soundness of its people as well. Indeed to attempt a line between public behavior and that which is purely consensual or solitary would be to withdraw from community concern a range of subjects with which every society in civilized times has found it necessary to deal. The laws regarding marriage which provide both when the sexual powers may be used and the legal and societal context in which children are born and brought up, as well as laws forbidding adultery, fornication and homosexual practices which express the negative of the proposition, confining sexuality to lawful marriage, form a pattern so deeply pressed into the substance of our social life that any Constitutional doctrine in this area must build upon that basis. [If] we had a case before us which required us to decide simply, and in abstraction, whether the moral judgment implicit in the application of the present statute to married couples was a sound one, the very controversial nature of these questions would, I think, require us to hesitate long before concluding that the Constitution precluded Connecticut from choosing as it has among these various views. [But we] are not presented simply with this moral judgment to be passed on as an abstract proposition. The secular state is not an examiner of consciences: it must operate in the realm of behavior, of overt actions, and where it does so operate, not only the underlying, moral purpose of its operations, but also the *choice of means* becomes relevant to any Constitutional judgment on what is done.

"[Here] the State is asserting the right to enforce its moral judgment by intruding upon the most intimate details of the marital relation with the full power of the criminal law. Potentially, this could allow the deployment of all the incidental machinery of the criminal law, arrests, searches and seizures; inevitably, it must mean at the very least the lodging of criminal charges, a public trial, and testimony as to the corpus delicti. [In] sum, the statute allows the State to enquire into, prove and punish married people for the private use of their marital intimacy. The statute must pass a more rigorous Constitutional test than that going merely to the plausibility of its underlying rationale. This enactment involves what, by common understanding throughout the English-speaking world, must be granted to be a most fundamental aspect of 'liberty,' the privacy of the home in its most basic sense, and it is this which requires that the statute be subjected to 'strict scrutiny.'

"That aspect of liberty which embraces the concept of the privacy of the home receives explicit Constitutional protection at two places only[—the Third and Fourth Amendments]. It is clear [that this] statute does not invade the privacy of the home in the usual sense, since the invasion involved [here] doubtless usually would [be] accomplished without any physical intrusion whatever into the home. What the statute undertakes to do, however, is to create a crime which is grossly offensive to this privacy. [The] home derives its pre-eminence as the seat of family life. And the integrity of that life is something so fundamental that it has been found to draw to its protection the principles of more than one explicitly granted Constitutional right. Of [the] whole 'private realm of family life' it is difficult to imagine what is more private or more intimate than a husband and wife's [marital relations].

"Of course, [there] are countervailing considerations. [It] would be an absurdity to suggest either that offenses may not be committed in the bosom of the family or that the home can be made a sanctuary for crime. The right of privacy [is] not an absolute. Thus, I would not suggest that adultery, homosexuality, fornication and incest are immune from criminal enquiry, however privately practiced. [Adultery,] homosexuality and the like are sexual intimacies which the State forbids altogether, but the intimacy of husband and wife is necessarily an essential and accepted feature of the institution of marriage, an institution which the State not only must allow, but which always it has fostered and protected. It is one thing when the State exerts its power either to forbid extra-marital sexuality altogether, or to say who may marry, but it is quite another when, having acknowledged a marriage and the intimacies inherent in it, it undertakes to regulate by means of the criminal law the details of that intimacy.

"[Since the law] marks an abridgment of important fundamental liberties, [it] will not do to urge in justification [that] the statute is rationally related to the effectuation of a proper state purpose. A closer scrutiny and stronger justification than that are required. Though the State has argued the Constitutional permissibility of the moral judgment underlying this statute, [its arguments do not] even remotely [suggest] a justification for the obnoxiously intrusive means it has chosen to effectuate that policy. [But] conclusive, in my view, is the utter novelty of this enactment. [No other State] has made the *use* of contraceptives a crime. [Though] undoubtedly the States [should] be allowed broad scope in experimenting, [I] must agree with [Justice Jackson's concurrence in Skinner] that 'There are limits to the extent to which a legislatively represented majority may [conduct] experiments at the expense of the dignity and personality' of the individual. In this instance these limits are, in my view, reached and passed."]

■ JUSTICE WHITE, concurring in the judgment.

In my view this Connecticut law as applied to married couples deprives them of "liberty" without [due process]. Surely the right invoked in this case, to be free of regulation of the intimacies of the marriage relationship, "come[s] to this Court with a momentum for respect lacking when appeal is made to liberties which derive merely from shifting economic arrangements." The Connecticut [law] deals rather substantially with this relationship. [A] statute with these effects bears a substantial burden of justification when attacked under the 14th Amendment. [An] examination of the justification offered, however, cannot be avoided by saying that the Connecticut anti-use statute invades a protected area of privacy and association or that it demeans the marriage relationship. The nature of the right invaded is pertinent, to be sure, for statutes regulating sensitive areas of liberty [do] require "strict scrutiny" and "must be viewed in light of less drastic means for achieving the same basic purpose." [But] such statutes, if reasonably necessary for the effectuation of a legitimate and substantial state interest, and not arbitrary or capricious in application, are not [invalid].

There is no serious contention that Connecticut thinks the use of artificial or external methods of contraception immoral or unwise in itself, or that the anti-use statute is founded upon any policy of promoting population expansion. Rather, the statute is said to serve the State's policy against all forms of promiscuous or illicit sexual relationships, be they premarital or extramarital, concededly a permissible and legitimate legislative goal. [But I] wholly fail to see how the ban on the use of contraceptives by married couples in any way reinforces the State's ban on illicit sexual relationships. [Perhaps] the theory is that the flat ban on use prevents married people from possessing contraceptives and without the ready availability of such devices for use in the marital relationship, there will be no or less temptation to use them in extramarital ones. This reasoning rests on the premises that married people will comply with the anti-use ban in regard to their marital relationship, notwithstanding total nonenforcement in this context and apparent nonenforcibility, but will not comply with criminal statutes prohibiting extramarital affairs and the anti-use statute in respect to illicit sexual relationships, a premise whose validity has not been demonstrated and whose intrinsic validity is not very evident. At most the broad ban is of marginal utility to the declared objective. A statute limiting its prohibition on use to persons engaging in the prohibited relationship would serve the end posited by Connecticut in the same way, and with the same effectiveness, or ineffectiveness, as the broad anti-use statute under attack in this case. I find nothing in this record justifying the sweeping scope of this statute, with its telling effect on the freedoms of [married persons].

■ JUSTICE BLACK, with whom JUSTICE STEWART joins, dissenting.

[The] law is every bit as offensive to me as it is to my Brethren [who], reciting reasons why it is offensive to them, hold it unconstitutional. [But] I cannot [join] their conclusion. [The] Court talks about a constitutional ["right of privacy"]. There are, of course, guarantees in certain specific constitutional provisions which are designed in part to protect privacy at certain times and places with respect to certain activities. Such, for example, is the [Fourth Amendment]. But I think it belittles that Amendment to talk about it as though it protects nothing but "privacy." One of the most effective ways of diluting or expanding a constitutionally guaranteed right is to substitute for the crucial word or words of a constitutional guarantee another word or words, more or less flexible and more or less restricted in [meaning]. "Privacy" is a broad, abstract and ambiguous concept which can easily be shrunken in meaning but which can [also] easily be interpreted as a constitutional ban against many things other than searches and seizures. [I] get nowhere in this case by talk about a constitutional "right of privacy" as an emanation from one or more constitutional provisions.[1] I like my privacy as well as the next one, but I am nevertheless compelled to admit that government has a right to invade it unless prohibited by some specific constitutional [provision].

This brings me to the arguments made by my Brothers Harlan, White and Goldberg. [I] discuss the due process and Ninth Amendment arguments together because on analysis they turn out to be the same thing—merely using different words to claim [the] power to invalidate any legislative act which the judges find irrational, unreasonable or offensive. [If] these formulas based on "natural justice" [are] to prevail, they require judges to determine what is or is not constitutional on the basis of their own appraisal of what laws are unwise or unnecessary. The power to make such decisions is of course that of a legislative body. [I] do not believe that we are granted [this power.] The two [cases they] cite and quote from, [Meyer] and [Pierce], were both decided in opinions by Justice McReynolds which elaborated the same natural law due process philosophy found in [Lochner]. [That was a] philosophy which many later opinions repudiated, and which I cannot [accept].

[Nor] does anything in the history of the [Ninth] Amendment offer any support for such a shocking doctrine. [That] Amendment was passed [to] assure the people that the [Constitution] was intended to limit the Federal Government to the powers granted expressly or by necessary implication. [This] fact is perhaps responsible for the peculiar phenomenon that for a period of a century and a half no serious suggestion was ever made that the Ninth Amendment, enacted to protect state powers against federal invasion, could be used as a weapon of federal power to prevent state legislatures from passing laws they consider appropriate to govern [local affairs].

■ JUSTICE STEWART, whom JUSTICE BLACK joins, dissenting.

[I] think this is an uncommonly silly law. [But] we are not asked in this case to say whether we think this law is unwise, or even asinine. We are asked to hold that it violates [the] Constitution. And that I cannot do. In the course of its opinion the Court refers to no less than six Amendments to the Constitution [but] does not say which of these Amendments, if any, it thinks is infringed by this Connecticut law. We *are* told that the Due Process Clause of the 14th Amendment is not, as such, the "guide" in this case. With that much I agree. [As] to the First, Third, Fourth, and Fifth Amendments, I can find nothing in any of them to invalidate this Connecticut [law]. [And to] say that the Ninth Amendment has anything to do with this case is to turn somersaults with history. The Ninth Amendment, like its companion the Tenth, [was] simply to make clear that the adoption of the Bill of Rights did not alter the plan that the *Federal* Government was to be a government of

---

1 The phrase "right to privacy" appears first to have gained currency from an article written by Messrs. Warren and (later Mr. Justice) Brandeis in 1890 which urged that States should give some form of tort relief to persons whose private affairs were exploited by others. The Right to Privacy, 4 Harv. L. Rev. 193. [Now, this Court exalts] a phrase which Warren and Brandeis used in discussing grounds for [common law] tort relief, to the level of a constitutional [rule]. [Footnote by Justice Black.]

express and limited powers. [What] provision of the Constitution, then, does make this state law invalid? The Court says it is the right of privacy "created by several fundamental constitutional guarantees." With all deference, I can find no such general right of privacy in the Bill of Rights, in any other part of the Constitution, or in any case ever before decided by this [Court].

THE MEANING AND IMPLICATIONS OF GRISWOLD

1. ***The constitutional basis of the privacy right in Griswold.*** Compare the different methods of constitutional interpretation by which the different opinions in Griswold arrive at the majority's conclusion that a right of privacy invalidates the Connecticut law. Justice Douglas disavows Lochner as a guide. He relies instead on the "penumbras" and "emanations" of several specific guarantees in the Bill of Rights. Does Justice Douglas's "penumbras" approach avoid extraconstitutional, "natural law" adjudication more effectively than the Lochner approach? Contrast with Justice Douglas's approach Justice Harlan's reliance on "basic values 'implicit in the concept of ordered liberty.'" Note his reference back to the issues faced in the incorporation controversy (see Chapter 7). What is added, if anything, by Justice Goldberg's reference to the Ninth Amendment, which provides that "The enumeration in the Constitution, of certain rights, shall not be construed to deny or disparage others retained by the people"? Is Justice Black right in charging that Griswold is of a piece with the free-wheeling substantive due process adjudication long discredited in the economic regulation area, or do these modes of reference to the Constitution's text offer more meaningful checks on judicial discretion? What checks on judicial discretion does Justice Harlan emphasize?

2. ***Lochner vs. Griswold.*** What, if anything, distinguishes the right to contract that the Court leaves interred with Lochner from the right to contraception that it embraces in Griswold? The answer cannot be that the favored rights of the Lochner era are distinguishable because they are not specifically mentioned in the Constitution. Liberty of contract surely could be seen as an emanation, or within the penumbra, of the Contracts Clause in Article I, section 10 of the Constitution. And a general protection of property could be seen as within the penumbra of the specific mention of "property" in the Takings Clause—not to mention the "specific" reference to property in the Fourteenth Amendment itself.

Does the difference thus turn on the nature of the right at stake? Is the use of contraception to control sexuality and reproduction closer to the core of personal identity and dignity than is work? Less dependent upon the existence of the law of property and contract? More likely to involve a breakdown of political processes in which factional gains and losses normally may be expected to even out over time? Recall Justice Stone's famous footnote four in Carolene Products (1938; p. 503 above), which called for special judicial solicitude toward rights of persons unlikely to be able to protect themselves in the "political process," and those of "discrete and insular minorities." Is Griswold best seen as a decision reinforcing the rights of groups especially likely to be systematically disadvantaged in the political process? Heterosexual couples would not seem to constitute a discrete and insular minority. Do pregnant women fit that description? Poor pregnant women? Did Griswold reflect the recognition of the entrenched political power of organized religious opposition to contraception? Note that the prohibition on contraception was enforced in practice not against doctors for the middle and upper classes but against birth control clinics used by indigent women. And it received strong support in heavily Catholic Connecticut from the leadership of the Catholic Church. On the social and political background of the case, see D. Garrow, Liberty and Sexuality (1994).

Or is any difference between Lochner and Griswold related more to the nature of the government interest than the nature of the individual right? Do contraception laws lack an objective justification comparable to justifications for labor laws such as avoiding races to the bottom among states competing for mobile labor and capital? Is any justification for a contraception law irreducibly moral and hence subjective? What's wrong with reflecting collective morality in law? For an argument that shifts the focus from the strength of the individual interest at stake to the impermissibility of the government's, see Rubenfeld, "The Right to Privacy," 102 Harv. L. Rev. 737 (1989) (arguing that the government many not justify enforcing orthodoxy in intimate life).

3. ***Griswold's divisiveness.*** Although all nine Justices agreed that Connecticut's law was poor policy, the basis for overruling (or, for the dissenters, upholding) the law was less clear. The decision ultimately generated six different opinions, each advocating a different approach. The disagreement over the constitutional roots of the right to privacy ultimately provoked a major rift between Justices Black and Douglas. Justice Black viewed Justice Douglas's majority opinion as a return to Lochner, and he criticized it harshly on that basis in his dissent. As a result, relations between the two became so strained that they did not speak to each other for several years, even though they had been close judicial allies who had stood together in the vast majority of their cases for nearly twenty-five years before Griswold, often against Justice Frankfurter.

4. ***The scope of "privacy" after Griswold.*** What is the scope of the "right of privacy" recognized in Griswold? Is it the interest in preventing intrusions into the home? The interest in avoiding disclosure of personal information? The interest in the protection of the "intimacies of the marriage relationship"? A broader interest in personal autonomy—in freedom from governmental regulation of a range of personal activities that do not harm others? The next contraception case to reach the Court helped answer that question only indirectly, because the Court premised its decision on equal protection rather than the bases outlined by the various opinions in Griswold. In **Eisenstadt v. Baird**, 405 U.S. 438 (1972), a short-staffed Court (Justices Powell and Rehnquist took no part) overturned a conviction under a law banning the distribution of contraceptives. Baird had distributed contraceptive foam, and the recipient was described by the state court as an *unmarried* person. The Court avoided explicit decision of the question whether the fundamental right recognized in Griswold extended beyond use to distribution and beyond married couples to unmarried persons. Instead, it purported to decide the case as a violation of equal protection even under a minimum rationality standard, even though its review was more searching than that standard usually entails. One important passage in Justice BRENNAN's opinion for the Court in Eisenstadt, however, clarified the nature of the right of privacy in a way that later was read to have expanded the arguably narrow ruling in Griswold to the unmistakably broader one in Roe v. Wade, below: "It is true that in Griswold the right of privacy in

question inhered in the marital relationship. Yet the marital couple is not an independent entity with a mind and heart of its own, but an association of two individuals each with a separate intellectual and emotional make-up. If the right of privacy means anything, it is the right of the *individual,* married or single, to be free from unwarranted governmental intrusion into matters so fundamentally affecting a person as the decision whether to bear or beget a child."

5. ***Access of minors to contraceptives.*** In **Carey v. Population Services, International**, 431 U.S. 678 (1977), a case decided after the 1973 decision in Roe v. Wade discussed below, a divided Court struck down a New York prohibition of the sale or distribution of contraceptives to minors under 16. Justice BRENNAN's plurality opinion, joined by Justices Stewart, Marshall and Blackmun, stated that strict scrutiny was required for restrictions on access to contraceptives, "because such access is essential to exercise of the constitutionally protected right of decision in matters of childbearing that is the underlying foundation of the holdings in Griswold, Eisenstadt, and Roe." He rejected the argument that the ban on distribution to persons under 16 could be justified "as a regulation of the morality of minors." He noted that minors have some constitutional rights, but that state power over children is greater than over adults. Against that background, he was unpersuaded that the state interest in discouraging sexual activity among the young were sufficiently "significant," and expressed "substantial reason for doubt [that] limiting access to contraceptives will in fact substantially discourage early sexual behavior." He added that, when a state "burdens the exercise of a fundamental right, its attempt to justify that burden as a rational means for the accomplishment of some significant state policy requires more than a bare assertion [that] the burden is connected to such a policy." Does the reference to "significant" state interests rather than the "compelling" state interests usually required to satisfy strict scrutiny suggest that a lesser standard of review applies to regulation of minors?

Justice WHITE concurred only in the result, on the ground that "the State has not demonstrated that the prohibition against distribution of contraceptives to minors measurably contributes to the deterrent purpose which the State advances." Justice STEVENS, in another separate opinion, concurred because of the irrationality of the means employed, objecting that the state should not be able to discourage underage sex by subjecting minors to increased risks of pregnancy and sexually transmitted disease. Justice POWELL's separate concurrence, while objecting to "extraordinary protection [of] all personal decisions in matters of sex," found the challenged restriction "defective" because it prohibited parents from distributing contraceptives to their children, "a restriction that unjustifiably interferes with parental interests in rearing their children." Justice REHNQUIST submitted a brief dissent; Chief Justice BURGER dissented without opinion.

SUBSTANTIVE DUE PROCESS AND ABORTION

Griswold, Eisenstadt and Carey protected a right to control reproductive choice using seemingly broad language attuned to personal decisionmaking rather than particular pharmaceutical devices. The Court in Eisenstadt, for example, spoke of heightened judicial solicitude for the right "to be free from unwarranted governmental intrusion into matters so fundamentally affecting a person as the decision whether to bear or beget a child." But these decisions were limited on their facts to the prevention of pregnancy through the use of contraception. Does the privacy calculus in reproductive decisionmaking alter once a pregnancy has begun? The Court finally reached that question in the following cases, which involved challenges to Texas abortion laws then typical of those adopted by most states:

Roe v. Wade

410 U.S. 113, 93 S. Ct. 705, 35 L. Ed. 2d 147 (1973).

[The challenged Texas law made it a crime to "procure an abortion" except "by medical advice for the purpose of saving the life of the mother." The challengers were a pregnant single woman (Jane Roe), a childless couple (John and Mary Doe), and a licensed physician (Dr. Hallford). The suits by Roe and the Does were class actions. A three-judge district court ruled the Does' complaint nonjusticiable, but granted declaratory relief to Roe and Dr. Hallford, holding the law unconstitutional under the Ninth Amendment.]

■ JUSTICE BLACKMUN delivered the opinion of the Court.

[The] Constitution does not explicitly mention any right of privacy. [But] the Court has recognized that a right of personal privacy, or a guarantee of certain areas or zones of privacy, does exist under the Constitution. In varying contexts, the Court or individual Justices have, indeed, found at least the roots of that right in the First Amendment; in the Fourth and Fifth Amendments; in the penumbras of the Bill of Rights [Griswold]; in the Ninth Amendment [id.]; or in the concept of liberty guaranteed [by] the 14th Amendment [Meyer]. These decisions make it clear that only personal rights that can be deemed "fundamental" or "implicit in the concept of ordered liberty" [Palko] are included in this guarantee of personal privacy. They also make it clear that the right has some extension to activities relating to marriage, procreation [Skinner], contraception [Eisenstadt], family relationships, and child rearing and education [Pierce; Meyer].

This right of privacy, whether it be founded in the 14th Amendment's concept of personal liberty [as] we feel it is, or, as the District Court determined, in the [Ninth Amendment], is broad enough to encompass a woman's decision whether or not to terminate her pregnancy. The detriment that the State would impose upon the pregnant woman by denying this choice altogether is apparent. Specific and direct harm medically diagnosable even in early pregnancy may be involved. Maternity, or additional offspring, may force upon the woman a distressful life and future. Psychological harm may be imminent. Mental and physical health may be taxed by child care. There is also the distress, for all concerned, associated with the unwanted child, and there is the problem of bringing a child into a family already unable, psychologically and otherwise, to care for it. In other cases, as in this one, the additional difficulties and continuing stigma of unwed motherhood may be involved. All these are factors the woman and her responsible physician necessarily will consider in consultation.

On the basis of elements such as these, appellants and some amici argue that the woman's right is absolute and that she is entitled to terminate her pregnancy at whatever time, in whatever way, and for whatever reason she alone chooses. With this we do not agree. [A] state may properly assert important interests in safeguarding health, in maintaining medical standards, and in protecting potential life. At some point in pregnancy, these respective interests become sufficiently compelling to sustain regulation of the factors that govern the abortion decision.

not an absolute right

[Texas argues] that the fetus is a "person" within the language and meaning of the 14th Amendment. [If so,] the appellant's case, of course, collapses, for the fetus' right to life is then guaranteed specifically by the Amendment. [The] Constitution does not define "person" in so many words. Section 1 of the 14th Amendment contains three references to "person." ["Person"] is used in other places in the Constitution. [But] in nearly all these instances, the use of the word is such that it has application only postnatally. None indicates, with any assurance, that it has any possible prenatal application.[1] All this, together with our observation [that] throughout the major portion of the 19th century prevailing legal abortion practices were far freer than they are today, persuades us that the word "person," as used in the 14th Amendment, does not include the unborn. [Texas] urges that, apart from the 14th Amendment, life begins at conception and is present throughout pregnancy, and that, therefore, the State has a compelling interest in protecting that life from and after conception. We need not resolve the difficult question of when life begins. When those trained [in] medicine, philosophy, and theology are unable to arrive at any consensus, the judiciary, at this point in the development of man's knowledge, is not in a position to speculate as to the answer. It should be sufficient to note [the] wide divergence of thinking on this most sensitive and difficult question. [The] unborn have never been recognized in the law as persons in the whole sense.

[The] State does have an important and legitimate interest in preserving and protecting the health of the pregnant woman [and] it has still *another* important and legitimate interest in protecting the potentiality of human life. These interests are separate and distinct. Each grows in substantiality as the woman approaches term and, at a point during pregnancy, each becomes "compelling." With respect to [the] interest in the health of the mother, the "compelling" point, in the light of present medical knowledge, is at approximately the end of the first trimester. This is so because of the now established medical fact [that] until the end of the first trimester mortality in abortion is less than mortality in normal childbirth. It follows that, from and after this point, a State may regulate the abortion procedure to the extent that the regulation reasonably relates to the preservation and protection of maternal health. Examples of permissible state regulation in this area are requirements as to the qualifications of the person who is to perform the abortion; [as] to the facility in which the procedure is to be performed; and the like. This means, on the other hand, that, for the period of pregnancy prior to this "compelling" point, the attending physician, in consultation with his patient, is free to determine, without regulation by the State, that, in his medical judgment, the patient's

[1] When Texas urges that a fetus is entitled to 14th Amendment protection as a person, it faces a dilemma. Neither in Texas nor in any other State are all abortions prohibited. Despite broad proscription, an exception always exists. The exception [in the Texas law], for an abortion procured or attempted by medical advice for the purpose of saving the life of the mother, is typical. But if the fetus is a person who is not to be deprived of life without due process of law, and if the mother's condition is the sole determinant, does not the Texas exception appear to be out of line with the Amendment's [command]? [Footnote by Justice Blackmun.]

pregnancy should be terminated. If that decision is reached, the judgment may be effectuated by an abortion free of interference by the State.

With respect to [the] interest in potential life, the "compelling" point is at viability. This is so because the fetus then presumably has the capability of meaningful life outside the mother's womb. State regulation protective of fetal life after viability thus has both logical and biological justifications. If the State is interested in protecting fetal life after viability, it may go so far as to proscribe abortion during that period, except when it is necessary to preserve the life or health of the mother. Measured against these standards, [the Texas law] sweeps too broadly [and] cannot survive the constitutional attack made upon it here.

To summarize: (a) [For] the stage prior to approximately the end of the first trimester, the abortion decision and its effectuation must be left to the medical judgment of the pregnant woman's attending physician. (b) For the stage subsequent to approximately the end of the first trimester, the State, in promoting its interest in the health of the mother, may, if it chooses, regulate the abortion procedure in ways that are reasonably related to maternal health. (c) For the stage subsequent to viability, the State in promoting its interest in the potentiality of human life may, if it chooses, regulate, and even proscribe, abortion except where it is necessary, in appropriate medical judgment, for the preservation of the life or health of the mother.

[This] decision leaves the State free to place increasing restrictions on abortion as the period of pregnancy lengthens, so long as those restrictions are tailored to the recognized state interests. The decision vindicates the right of the physician to administer medical treatment according to his professional judgment up to the points where important state interests provide compelling justifications for intervention. Up to those points, the abortion decision in all its aspects is inherently, and primarily, a medical decision, and basic responsibility for it must rest with the [physician].

■ JUSTICE STEWART, concurring.

In 1963, this Court, in [Ferguson v. Skrupa], purported to sound the death knell for the doctrine of substantive due process. Barely two years later, in [Griswold], the Court held a Connecticut birth control law unconstitutional. In view of what had been so recently said in Skrupa, the Court's opinion in Griswold understandably did its best to avoid reliance on [due process]. [Yet] the Connecticut law did not violate [any] specific provision of the Constitution. So it was clear to me then, and it is equally clear to me now, that the Griswold decision can be rationally understood only as a holding that the Connecticut statute substantively invaded ["liberty"]. As so understood Griswold stands as one in a long line of pre-Skrupa cases decided under the doctrine of substantive due process, and I now accept it as such. [T]he "liberty" protected by [due process] covers more than those freedoms explicitly named in the Bill of Rights. [In Eisenstadt], we recognized "the right of the *individual,* married or single, to be free from unwarranted governmental intrusion into matters so fundamentally affecting a person as the decision whether to bear or beget a child." That right necessarily includes the right of a woman to decide whether or not to terminate her [pregnancy]. [Justice Douglas and Chief Justice Burger also filed concurrences.]

■ JUSTICE WHITE, with whom JUSTICE REHNQUIST joins, dissenting.

[I] find nothing in the language or history of the Constitution to support the Court's judgment. The Court simply fashions and announces a new constitutional right for pregnant mothers and, with scarcely any reason or authority for its action, invests that right with sufficient substance to override most existing state abortion statutes. The upshot is that the people and the legislatures of the 50 States are constitutionally disentitled to weigh the relative importance of the continued existence and development of the fetus on the one hand against a spectrum of possible impacts on the mother on the other hand. As an exercise of raw judicial power, the Court perhaps has authority to do what it does today; but in my view its judgment is an improvident and extravagant exercise of the power of judicial review.

■ JUSTICE REHNQUIST, dissenting.

[I] have difficulty in concluding [that] the right of "privacy" is involved in this case. [Texas] bars the performance of a medical abortion by a licensed physician on a plaintiff such as Roe. A transaction resulting in an operation such as this is not "private" in the ordinary usage of that word. Nor is the "privacy" which the Court finds here even a distant relative of the [Fourth Amendment freedom from searches and seizures]. If the Court means by the term "privacy" no more than that the claim of a person to be free from unwanted state regulation of consensual transactions may be a form of "liberty" protected by the 14th Amendment, there is no doubt that similar claims have been upheld in our earlier decisions on the basis of that liberty. I agree [that "liberty"] embraces more than the rights found in the Bill of Rights. But that liberty is not guaranteed absolutely against deprivation, but only against deprivation without due process of law. The test traditionally applied in the area of social and economic legislation is whether or not a law such as that challenged has a rational relation to a valid state objective. [Lee Optical.] [If] the Texas statute were to prohibit an abortion even where the mother's life is in jeopardy, I have little doubt that such a statute would lack a rational relation to a valid state objective. [But] the Court's sweeping invalidation of any restrictions on abortion during the first trimester is impossible to justify under that standard. [As] in Lochner and similar cases applying substantive due process standards to economic and social welfare legislation, the adoption of the compelling state interest standard will inevitably require this Court to examine the legislative policies and pass on the wisdom of these policies in the very process of deciding whether a particular state interest put forward may or may not be "compelling."

THE MEANING AND IMPLICATIONS OF ROE

1. ***The protected privacy interest.*** Notice that Roe locates the privacy right in the liberty protected by the Fourteenth Amendment Due Process Clause, without invoking the approaches used by Justices Douglas (penumbras) and Goldberg (the Ninth Amendment) in Griswold. Justice Blackmun finds the right of privacy "broad enough to encompass a woman's decision whether or not to terminate her pregnancy." But what aspect of "privacy" explains this interest? The Court concedes that the situation here "is inherently different from marital intimacy [or] marriage, or procreation, or education" with which the cases from Meyer to Eisenstadt were concerned. Roe, unlike Griswold, involved no specter of government snooping into the

spatial privacy of the bedroom. Is the relevant privacy interest then one of bodily integrity? The right against battery is rooted in common law; is that a useful fact in this context? In what sense is a fetus involved in an unwanted touching? Does the answer depend on the circumstances of the pregnancy?

Alternatively, does Roe rest principally on an interest in personal "autonomy" in decisionmaking over certain critical life experiences? If so, what is the constitutional source of such a decisional autonomy interest? That procreative freedom is implicit in the concept of ordered liberty? Why? Because, in the 20th century, interference with procreation (either to facilitate it or to limit it) became associated with totalitarian regimes? Does Roe announce a presumptive right of decisional autonomy over the use of one's body for the life support of others even assuming that a countervailing life is at stake? See Thompson, "A Defense of Abortion," 1 Phil. & Pub. Aff. 47 (1971) (observing that tort law does not normally recognize good samaritan duties to rescue others in distress, and analogizing involuntary pregnancy to involuntary kidney support of an ailing violinist).

2. ***"Balancing" the competing government interests.*** The Court finds that the woman's prima facie right to end her pregnancy can be defeated only by "compelling" state interests. Justice Blackmun notes two relevant state interests: protecting the woman's health; and "protecting the potentiality of human life." At differing points in the trimester scheme, those interests become sufficiently "compelling" to justify state restraints. Consider how the Court determines when these interests become "compelling." Is it helpful to discuss whether the fetus is a "person" within the Fourteenth Amendment—or within any other provision of the Constitution? Is it accurate to say: "We need not resolve the difficult question of when life begins"? Must not the Court at least determine when "the potentiality of human life" represents a sufficiently strong moral claim to justify curtailment of the woman's interest in autonomy? Justice Blackmun states that Texas may not, "by adopting one theory of life," "override the rights of the pregnant woman that are at stake." Yet Justice Blackmun also notes that there is wide disagreement, in medicine and philosophy and law, about when life begins. Why should not that lack of consensus lead the Court to defer to, rather than invalidate, the state's judgment? Can the Court's judgment be supported by anything other than a judicial authority to infuse a particular set of moral values into the Constitution? For contrasting views, compare Tribe, Abortion: The Clash of Absolutes (1990), with McConnell, "How Not to Promote Serious Deliberation About Abortion," 58 U. Chi. L. Rev. 1181 (1991).

3. ***Roe vs. Lochner.*** Is the heightened scrutiny used in Roe v. Wade more justifiable than judicial interventions of the Lochner era? Consider the argument that Roe is even *less* defensible than Lochner because, rather than resting on the illegitimacy of the ends sought or the lack of a "plausible argument" that the legislative means further permissible ends, Roe simply announces that the "goal is not important enough to sustain the restriction." Ely, "The Wages of Crying Wolf: A Comment on Roe v. Wade," 82 Yale L.J. 920 (1973); see also Epstein, "Substantive Due Process by Any Other Name: The Abortion Cases," 1973 Sup. Ct. Rev. 159. Consider the countervailing argument that the Court was not choosing substantively between abortion and continued pregnancy, but rather "choosing among alternative allocations of decisionmaking authority," determining that "some types of choices ought to be remanded, on principle, to private decision-makers

unchecked by substantive governmental control." Tribe, "Foreword: Toward a Model of Roles in the Due Process of Life and Law," 87 Harv. L. Rev. 1 (1973). If so, why are decisions over reproduction more appropriately allocated to the private sphere than decisions over labor relations?

4. ***Roe and sex equality.*** Recall Justice Stone's Carolene Products footnote four, justifying special protection for "discrete and insular minorities" that do not receive adequate representation in the political process. Consider that the consequences of unwanted pregnancy fall, as a physical matter, entirely on women. Does that fact justify special judicial solicitude to protect pregnant women from restrictive abortion laws? See Siegel, "Reasoning from the Body: A Historical Perspective on Abortion Regulation and Questions of Equal Protection," 44 Stan. L. Rev. 261 (1992); Ginsburg, "Some Thoughts on Autonomy and Equality in Relation to Roe v. Wade," 63 N.C. L. Rev. 375 (1985); Law, "Rethinking Sex and the Constitution," 132 U. Pa. L. Rev. 955 (1984) (emphasizing that "laws governing reproduction implicate equality concerns" and noting that "restrictions on access to abortion plainly oppress women"); Karst, "Book Review," 89 Harv. L. Rev. 1028 (1976) (suggesting that the cases on contraception and abortion helped refashion "the roles women are to play in our society").

Are women a politically disadvantaged group warranting special judicial solicitude? Women are arguably neither discrete, nor insular, nor a minority, and in any event may enjoy consideration in the political process by the men with whom women live and become pregnant. Are "the unborn" a politically powerless group warranting judicial solicitude? Does the abortion right free women from subordination or merely increase men's sexual access to women under conditions of sex inequality? See MacKinnon, "Roe v. Wade: A Study in Male Ideology," in Abortion: Moral and Legal Perspectives 45 (Garfield & Hennessey eds. 1984). For sociological evidence that attitudes to abortion correlate closely with attitudes toward gender roles, see Luker, Abortion and the Politics of Motherhood (1984).

Even if sex equality provides an alternative ground for abortion rights, is such a ground an independently sufficient justification for abortion rights apart from privacy? In a world consisting solely of women (and sperm banks), would there be no justification for overturning a law that prohibited terminating a pregnancy once begun?

5. ***The political reaction to Roe.*** The litigation that led to Roe was not conducted by national pro-choice organizations, which did not yet exist, but by Sarah Weddington and Linda Coffee, aged twenty-six and twenty-seven, recent graduates of the Texas Law School. Nevertheless, Roe elicited fierce opposition and fueled strong efforts at political reversal. Opponents first sought to amend the Constitution to overturn the decision, for example by providing that nothing in the Constitution shall bar any State "from allowing, regulating, or prohibiting the practice of abortion," or that life begins "from the moment of conception." None proved successful. Efforts to curtail the force of Roe at the federal level then shifted from constitutional amendments to legislative initiatives under Congress's civil rights enforcement powers. For example, in 1981, some members of Congress proposed a Human Life Statute, relying on power under § 5 of the Fourteenth Amendment (see Chapter 10 below). Again, this effort failed, in part as a result of doubts about the constitutionality of trying to overturn a Supreme Court decision by statute.

According to some observers, opposition to Roe helped bring together Catholics and Protestant evangelicals, traditional religious opponents, in a common political cause. This alliance in turn became an important element of the conservative revival associated with the Moral Majority, the Christian Right, and the Presidencies of Ronald Reagan and George W. Bush. See Feldman, Divided By God 194–95 (2005). Roe certainly energized an anti-abortion movement and arguably antifeminist movements more broadly by giving citizens opposed to abortion rights a clear target and a reason to speak out. See, e.g., Post & Siegel, "Roe Rage: Democratic Constitutionalism and Backlash," 42 Harv. C.R.-C.L. L. Rev. 373 (2007); Klarman, "Fidelity, Indeterminacy, and the Problem of Constitutional Evil," 65 Fordham L. Rev. 1739 (1997) ("[Roe] actually spawned a right-to-life opposition which did not previously exist.").

6. ***The feminist implications of Roe.*** While Roe is popularly seen as a seminal development in American feminism, some scholars have observed that the decision is antifeminist in its approach. See, e.g., Siegel, "Reasoning from the Body: A Historical Perspective on Abortion Regulation and Questions of Equal Protection," 44 Stan. L. Rev. 261 (1992): "Because Roe and its progeny treat pregnancy as a physiological problem, they obscure the extent to which the community that would regulate a woman's reproductive choices is in fact implicated in them, responsible for defining motherhood in ways that impose material deprivations and dignitary injuries on those who perform its work." Likewise, the opinion could be understood to discount the pregnant woman's preferences in favor of the (implicitly male) doctor's: Justice Blackmun explained that "for the period of pregnancy prior to th[e] 'compelling' point, the attending physician, in consultation with *his* patient, is free to determine, without regulation by the State, that, in *his* medical judgment, the patient's pregnancy should be terminated" (emphasis added).

7. ***State regulation of abortion from Roe to Casey.*** Even if Roe barred states from prohibiting abortion before the third trimester, did it permit states to enact and enforce regulations that increased the difficulty or cost of obtaining an abortion? State legislatures passed a variety of such restrictions on abortion after Roe, and in the period between Roe and Casey, nearly all of them (with the exception of regulations of teenage abortion and limits on abortion funding) were struck down as impermissible under Roe:

a. *Regulations of medical procedures.* In **Doe v. Bolton**, 410 U.S. 179 (1973), the companion case to Roe v. Wade, the Court invalidated portions of a Georgia law requiring that abortions be performed in an accredited hospital, requiring prior approval of abortions by a hospital staff committee, and requiring the additional approval of an abortion by two doctors in addition to the attending doctor. The Court concluded that the attending physician's "best clinical judgment [should] be sufficient."

In **Akron v. Akron Center for Reproductive Health (Akron I)**, 462 U.S. 416 (1983), the Court invalidated a requirement that abortions performed after the first trimester be performed in a hospital rather than in outpatient facilities, which were typically less expensive. The Court struck down that provision as "a significant obstacle in the path of women seeking an abortion." The Court also invalidated a provision mandating a set of detailed guidelines regarding information the attending physician had to convey to the woman regarding the development of the fetus, the date of possible viability, and the complications that might result from an abortion.

Although the state said its interest was to insure that the "written consent of the pregnant woman" to an abortion would be "truly informed," Justice Powell's majority opinion found the information requirement unconstitutional, noting that much of the information required was "designed not to inform the woman's consent but rather to persuade her to withhold it altogether."

b. *Spousal and parental consent requirements.* In **Planned Parenthood of Central Missouri v. Danforth**, 428 U.S. 52 (1976), the Court struck down Missouri's requirement of a husband's written consent for an abortion during the first 12 weeks of pregnancy. The 6–3 decision, with Justice Blackmun writing for the majority, held that "the State cannot delegate authority [even to the spouse] to prevent abortion during the first trimester," since the woman "is the more directly and immediately affected by the pregnancy." In the same case, the majority struck down another provision requiring an unmarried woman under eighteen to obtain the consent of a parent as a prerequisite to obtaining an abortion. After holding that a state could not "give a third party an [absolute] veto" over the abortion decision, the Court added that this did not mean that "every minor, regardless of age or maturity, may give effective consent for termination of her pregnancy." Rather, as elaborated in a companion case, **Bellotti v. Baird (Bellotti I),** 428 U.S. 132 (1976), a blanket "parental veto" is "fundamentally different" from one permitting "a mature minor [to] obtain [an] order permitting the abortion without parental consultation." In short, a parental consent requirement was unconstitutional only if "it unduly burdens the right to seek an abortion." The Court clarified the extent to which parents could be involved in a minor's abortion decision in **Bellotti v. Baird (Bellotti II),** 443 U.S. 622 (1979). There, Justice Powell's plurality opinion announced that a state could involve a parent in a minor's abortion decision only if it also provided an alternative judicial bypass procedure so that the parental involvement would not amount to an "absolute, and possibly arbitrary, veto."

c. *Waiting period and reporting requirements.* In Akron I, supra, the Court struck down a mandatory 24-hour waiting period after the pregnant woman signed a consent form, a provision that increased the cost of obtaining an abortion by requiring two separate trips to a facility. And in Thornburgh v. American Coll. of Obst. & Gyn., 476 U.S. 747 (1986), the Court struck down several reporting requirements regarding the identities of the physician and the pregnant woman, noting that such provisions would "chill" the freedom to have an abortion.

d. *Abortion funding restrictions.* As to adult women, restrictions on public subsidies were the only abortion regulations upheld in the period between Roe and Casey. In **Maher v. Roe**, 432 U.S. 464 (1977), the Court by a vote of 6–3 upheld a Connecticut regulation granting Medicaid benefits for childbirth but not for medically unnecessary abortions. Justice POWELL's majority opinion held that strict scrutiny was not warranted because the unequal treatment of abortion and childbirth in the scheme did not interfere with the fundamental right recognized in Roe, and upheld the law under deferential "rationality" review. "[The] right [in Roe and its progeny] protects the woman from unduly burdensome interference with her freedom to decide whether to terminate her pregnancy. It implies no limitation on the authority of a State to make a value judgment favoring childbirth over abortion, and to implement that judgment by the allocation of public funds. [The] Connecticut regulation places no obstacles—absolute or otherwise—in the pregnant woman's path to an abortion. An indigent woman who desires an abortion suffers no disadvantage as a consequence of Connecticut's decision to fund childbirth; she continues as before to be dependent on private sources for the service she desires. The State may have made childbirth a more attractive alternative, thereby influencing the woman's decision, but it has imposed no restriction on access to abortions that was not already there. The indigency that may make it difficult—and in some cases, perhaps, impossible—for some women to have abortions is neither created nor in any way affected by the Connecticut regulation. [There] is a basic difference between direct state interference with a protected activity and state encouragement of an alternative [activity]." Justice BRENNAN's dissent, joined by Justices Marshall and Blackmun, argued that the distinction in state funding in effect coerced "indigent pregnant women to bear children they would not otherwise choose to have," unconstitutionally impinging upon the right of privacy.

Three years later, the Court in **Harris v. McRae**, 448 U.S. 297 (1980), rejected constitutional challenges to federal funding limitations in the so-called Hyde Amendment, which barred payments even for most medically necessary abortions (except for victims of rape or incest or where the mother's life was threatened), and thus went beyond the refusal to uphold medically "unnecessary" abortions upheld in Maher. In rejecting a substantive due process claim, Justice STEWART's majority opinion concluded that "it simply does not follow [from Roe] that a woman's freedom of choice carries with it a constitutional entitlement to the financial resources to avail herself of the full range of protected choices. The reason why was explained in Maher: although government may not place obstacles in the path of a woman's exercise of her freedom of choice, it need not remove those not of its own creation. Indigency falls in the latter category. The financial constraints that restrict an indigent woman's ability to enjoy the full range of constitutionally protected freedom of choice are the product not of governmental restrictions on access to abortions, but rather of her indigency. Although Congress has opted to subsidize medically necessary services generally [under Medicaid], but not certain medically necessary abortions, the fact remains that the Hyde Amendment leaves an indigent woman with at least the same range of choice in deciding whether to obtain a medically necessary abortion as she would have had if Congress had chosen to subsidize no health care costs at all. [Although] the liberty protected by the Due Process Clause affords protection against unwarranted governmental interference with freedom of choice in the context of certain personal decisions, it does not confer an entitlement to such funds as may be necessary to realize all the advantages of that freedom. To hold otherwise would mark a drastic change in our understanding of the Constitution. [To] translate the limitation on governmental power implicit in [due process] into an affirmative funding obligation would require Congress to subsidize the medically necessary abortion of an indigent woman even if Congress had not enacted a Medicaid program to subsidize other medically necessary services. Nothing in the Due Process Clause supports such an extraordinary result."

Justice BRENNAN, joined again by Justices Marshall and Blackmun in dissent, replied: "[It] is not simply the woman's indigency that interferes with her freedom of choice, but the combination of her own poverty and the government's unequal subsidization of abortion and childbirth. [The] fundamental flaw in the Court's due process analysis [is] its failure to acknowledge that the discriminatory distribution of the benefits of governmental largesse can discourage the exercise of fundamental liberties just as effectively as can an outright denial of those rights through criminal and regulatory sanctions." Justice STEVENS, a member of the Maher majority, dissented, insisting that this case was "fundamentally different" from Maher because the funding denial reached medically necessary abortions: "[The] Government must use neutral criteria in distributing benefits. [It] may not create exceptions for the sole purpose of furthering a governmental interest that is constitutionally subordinate to the individual interest that the entire program was designed to protect."

In **Rust v. Sullivan**, 500 U.S. 173 (1991), the Court extended the reasoning of Maher and McRae to a restriction on abortion counseling by any project receiving federal family planning funds. At issue were regulations promulgated by the Health and Human Services Department providing that a family planning project funded under Title X of the Public Health Service Act "may not provide counseling concerning the use of abortion as a method of family planning or provide referral for abortion as a method of family planning," may not "encourage, promote or advocate abortion as a method of family planning," and must be "physically and financially separate" from any abortion counseling or encouragement the recipient might otherwise conduct. The regulations permitted Title X projects to provide pregnant women with information about childbirth and prenatal care, but advised them to tell any pregnant woman who inquired about abortion that the project does not consider abortion an "appropriate method of family planning."

Chief Justice REHNQUIST, writing for the majority in the 5–4 decision, rejected a substantive due process challenge brought under the 5th Amendment by doctors and Title X grantees. "The Government has no constitutional duty to subsidize an activity merely because the activity is constitutionally protected and may validly choose to fund childbirth over abortion and 'implement that judgment by the allocation of public funds' for medical services relating to childbirth but not to those relating to abortion. [Government's] decision to fund childbirth but not abortion 'places no governmental obstacle in the path of a woman who chooses to terminate her pregnancy, but rather, by means of unequal subsidization of abortion and other medical services, encourages alternative activity deemed in the public interest.' [McRae.]"

Justice BLACKMUN dissented, joined on this point by Justices Marshall and Stevens: "By suppressing medically pertinent information and injecting a restrictive ideological message unrelated to considerations of maternal health, the Government places formidable obstacles in the path of Title X clients' freedom of choice and thereby violates their Fifth Amendment rights. [Although] her physician's words, in fact, are strictly controlled by the Government and wholly unrelated to her particular medical situation, the Title X client will reasonably construe them as professional advice to forgo her right to obtain an abortion. [In] view of the inevitable effect of the regulations, the majority's conclusion that [the regulations leave a woman in no worse a position than if the Government had not enacted Title X] is insensitive and contrary to common human experience. Both the purpose and result of the challenged regulations is to deny women the ability voluntarily to decide their procreative destiny. For these women, the Government will have obliterated the freedom to choose as surely as if it had banned abortions outright. The denial of this freedom is not a consequence of poverty but of the Government's ill-intentioned distortion of information it has chosen to provide." Justice O'Connor dissented separately on the ground that the regulations exceeded statutory authority. (The regulations did not go into effect for the duration of the litigation, and President Clinton rescinded them in 1993.) For more on the intersection of abortion-related disclosures and the First Amendment, see National Institute of Family and Life Advocates v. Becerra, infra, in Chapter 13's discussion of compelled speech.

In **Webster v. Reproductive Health Services**, 492 U.S. 490 (1989), the Court upheld provisions of a Missouri law barring state employees from performing abortions and the use of public facilities for abortions, even where the patient paid for the abortion herself. Chief Justice REHNQUIST, writing for a five-Justice majority, held these provisions constitutional in light of abortion-funding cases such as Harris v. McRae, noting that "our cases have recognized that the Due Process Clauses generally confer no affirmative right to governmental aid." Chief Justice Rehnquist noted that the case might be different if *all* health care was provided in state facilities, in which case, denial of public subsidies for abortion might have the same practical effect as regulation of abortion.

8. ***Roe and stare decisis.*** In the Court's abortion decisions following Roe, Justices Rehnquist and White maintained their view that the case was wrongly decided, Justices Scalia and Thomas expressed the same view, and Justice O'Connor expressed doubt about elaborations of the decision. Many commentators predicted Roe would be overruled. Others argued that Justice O'Connor was likely to reaffirm Roe at least in some form. See Estrich & Sullivan, "Abortion Politics: Writing for an Audience of One," 138 U. Pa. L. Rev. 119 (1989): "[N]otwithstanding the occasional strength of her rhetoric, Justice O'Connor has never questioned Roe's central premise that the liberty to choose abortion is fundamental, nor accepted [the] view that any state interest at any point in pregnancy may, if a state legislature chooses, outweigh a woman's right to choose. Quite to the contrary, she has sought to articulate a test which, again depending on how it is applied, could protect women as least against significant burdens on their privacy rights." That prediction proved correct, and Justice O'Connor's "undue burden" test became the prevailing one in the following decision, reviewing a set of abortion regulations from Pennsylvania:

Planned Parenthood of Southeastern Pa. v. Casey

505 U.S. 833, 112 S. Ct. 2791, 120 L. Ed. 2d 674 (1992).

[A Pennsylvania law placed various limits on the availability of abortions, such as imposing a mandatory 24-hour waiting period after a woman seeks an abortion before it could be performed, and requiring spousal notification absent a certification that such notice might cause physical injury. Petitioner argued that those conditions violated the holding of Roe v. Wade, which called for a broader protection of the abortion right than Pennsylvania granted. Respondent countered that the Court should overrule Roe entirely.]

■ JUSTICE O'CONNOR, JUSTICE KENNEDY, and JUSTICE SOUTER announced the judgment of the Court and delivered the opinion of the Court with respect to Parts I, II, III, V–A, V–C, and VI, an opinion with respect to Part V–E, in which JUSTICE STEVENS joins, and an opinion with respect to Parts IV, V–B, and V–D.

I. Liberty finds no refuge in a jurisprudence of doubt. [The] essential holding of [Roe] should be retained and once again reaffirmed.

II. [Constitutional] protection of the woman's decision to terminate her pregnancy derives from the Due Process Clause. [The] Clause has been understood to contain a substantive component. [It] is a promise of the Constitution that there is a realm of personal liberty which the government may not enter. [It] is settled now, as it was when the Court heard arguments in Roe, that the Constitution places limits on a State's right to interfere with a person's most basic decisions about family and parenthood, as well as bodily integrity. [Men] and women of good conscience can disagree [about] the profound moral and spiritual implications of terminating a pregnancy, even in its earliest stage. Some of us as individuals find abortion offensive to our most basic principles of morality, but that cannot control our decision. Our obligation is to define the liberty of all, not to mandate our own moral code. [Our] law affords constitutional protection to personal decisions relating to marriage, procreation, contraception, family relationships, child rearing, and education. [These] matters, involving the most intimate and personal choices a person may make in a lifetime, choices central to personal dignity and autonomy, are central to the liberty protected by the Fourteenth Amendment. At the heart of liberty is the right to define one's own concept of existence, of meaning, of the universe, and of the mystery of human life. Beliefs about these matters could not define the attributes of personhood were they formed under compulsion of the State.

[The] liberty of the woman is at stake in a sense unique to the human condition and so unique to the law. The mother who carries a child to full term is subject to anxieties, to physical constraints, to pain that only she must bear. That these sacrifices have from the beginning of the human race been endured by woman with a pride that ennobles her in the eyes of others and gives to the infant a bond of love cannot alone be grounds for the State to insist she make the sacrifice. Her suffering is too intimate and personal for the State to insist, without more, upon its own vision of the woman's role, however dominant that vision has been in the course of our history and our culture. The destiny of the woman must be shaped to a large extent on her own conception of her spiritual imperatives and her place in society. [Moreover, in] some critical respects the abortion decision is of the same character as the decision to use contraception, to which Griswold, Eisenstadt, and Carey afford constitutional protection. We have no doubt as to the correctness of those decisions. They support the reasoning in Roe relating to the woman's liberty because they involve personal decisions concerning not only the meaning of procreation but also human responsibility and respect for it.

III. A. [When] this Court reexamines a prior holding, its judgment is customarily informed by a series of prudential and pragmatic considerations designed to test the consistency of overruling a prior decision with the ideal of the rule of law, and to gauge the respective costs of reaffirming and overruling a prior case.

1. [Although] Roe has engendered opposition, it has in no sense proven "unworkable," representing as it does a simple limitation beyond which a state law is unenforceable. While Roe has [required] judicial assessment of [laws] affecting the exercise of the choice guaranteed against government infringement, and although the need for such review will remain as a consequence of today's decision, [these] determinations fall within judicial competence.

2. [Since] the classic case for weighing reliance heavily in favor of following the earlier rule occurs in the commercial context, where advance planning of great precision is most obviously a necessity, it is no cause for surprise that some would find no reliance worthy of consideration in support of Roe. [But] for two decades, [people] have organized intimate relationships and made choices that define their views of themselves and their places in society, in reliance on the availability of abortion in the event that contraception should fail. The ability of women to participate equally in the economic and social life of the Nation has been facilitated by their ability to control their reproductive lives. [While] the effect of reliance on Roe cannot be exactly measured, neither can the certain cost of overruling Roe for people who have ordered their thinking and living around that case be dismissed.

3. No evolution of legal principle has left Roe's doctrinal footings weaker than they were in 1973. [Roe] itself placed its holding in the succession of cases most prominently exemplified by Griswold. Roe [may also be seen] as a rule [of] personal autonomy and bodily integrity, with doctrinal affinity to cases recognizing limits on governmental power to mandate medical treatment or to bar its rejection.

4. [Time] has overtaken some of Roe's factual assumptions: advances in maternal health care allow for abortions safe to the mother later in pregnancy than was true in 1973, and advances in neonatal care have advanced viability to a point somewhat earlier. But these facts go only to the scheme of time limits on the realization of competing interests, and the divergences from the factual underpinnings of 1973 have no bearing on the validity of Roe's central holding that viability marks the earliest point at which the State's interest in fetal life is constitutionally adequate to justify a legislative ban on nontherapeutic abortions. [No] change in Roe's factual underpinning has left its central holding obsolete, and none supports an argument for overruling it.

B. [The] sustained and widespread debate Roe has provoked calls for some comparison between that case and others of comparable dimension that have responded to national controversies. The first example is that line of cases identified with [Lochner]. [West Coast Hotel] signaled the demise of Lochner by overruling Adkins. In the meantime, the Depression had come and, with it, the lesson that seemed unmistakable to most people by 1937, that the interpretation of contractual freedom protected in Adkins rested on fundamentally false factual assumptions about the capacity of a relatively unregulated market to satisfy minimal levels of human welfare.

[The] second comparison that 20th century history invites is with the cases employing the separate-but-equal rule. [They] began with Plessy v. Ferguson [1896; p. 657 below], holding that legislatively mandated racial segregation in public transportation works no denial of equal protection. [This rule was] repudiated in Brown v. Board of Education [1954; p. 661 below]. The Court in Brown [observed] that whatever may have been the understanding in Plessy's time of the power of segregation to stigmatize those who were segregated with a "badge of inferiority," it was clear by 1954 that legally sanctioned segregation had just such an effect, to the point that racially separate [facilities] were deemed inherently unequal. Society's understanding of the facts upon which a constitutional ruling was sought in 1954 was thus fundamentally different from the basis claimed for the decision in 1896. While we think Plessy was wrong the day it was decided, we must also recognize that the Plessy Court's explanation for its decision was so clearly at odds with the facts apparent to the Court in 1954 that the decision to reexamine Plessy was on this ground alone not only justified but required.

[Because] neither the factual underpinnings of Roe's central holding nor our understanding of it has changed, [the] Court could not pretend to be reexamining the prior law with any justification beyond a present doctrinal disposition to come out differently from the Court of 1973.

C. [Overruling] Roe's central holding would not only reach an unjustifiable result under principles of stare decisis, but would seriously weaken the Court's capacity to exercise the judicial power and to function as the Supreme Court of a Nation dedicated to the rule of law. [The] Court's power [lies] in its legitimacy, a product of substance and perception that shows itself in the people's acceptance of the Judiciary as fit to determine what the Nation's law means and to declare what it demands. [Where] the Court decides a case in such a way as to resolve the sort of intensely divisive controversy reflected in Roe and those rare, comparable cases, its decision has a dimension that the resolution of the normal case does not carry. [T]o overrule under fire in the absence of the most compelling reason to reexamine a watershed decision would subvert the Court's legitimacy beyond any serious question. [The] promise of constancy, once given, binds its maker for as long as the power to stand by the decision survives and the understanding of the issue has not changed so fundamentally as to render the commitment obsolete. [It] is therefore imperative to adhere to the essence of Roe's original decision, and we do so today.

IV. [We] conclude that the basic decision in Roe was based on a constitutional analysis which we cannot now repudiate. The woman's liberty is not so unlimited, however, that from the outset the State cannot show its concern for the life of the unborn, and at a later point in fetal development the State's interest in life has sufficient force so that the right of the woman to terminate the pregnancy can be restricted. [In] our view, the undue burden standard is the appropriate means of reconciling the State's interest with the woman's constitutionally protected liberty. [A] finding of an undue burden is a shorthand for the conclusion that a state regulation has the purpose or effect of placing a substantial obstacle in the path of a woman seeking an abortion of a nonviable fetus. A statute with this purpose is invalid because the means chosen by the State to further the interest in potential life must be calculated to inform the woman's free choice, not hinder it. [Regulations] which do no more than create a structural mechanism by which the State, or the parent or guardian of a minor, may express profound respect for the life of the unborn are permitted, if they are not a substantial obstacle to the woman's exercise of the right to choose. Unless it has that effect on her right of choice, a state measure designed to persuade her to choose childbirth over abortion will be upheld if reasonably related to that goal. Regulations designed to foster the health of a woman seeking an abortion are valid if they do not constitute an undue burden.

[We] now turn to [the] validity of [the] challenged provisions.

V. B. [Except] in a medical emergency, the [Pennsylvania] statute requires that at least 24 hours before performing an abortion a physician inform the woman of the nature of the procedure, the health risks of the abortion and of childbirth, and the "probable gestational age of the unborn child." [To] the extent Akron I and Thornburgh find a constitutional violation when the government requires, as it does here, the giving of [such] truthful, nonmisleading information, [those] cases go too far [and] are overruled. [A] State [may] further its legitimate goal of protecting the life of the unborn by enacting legislation aimed at ensuring a decision that is mature and informed, even when in so doing the State expresses a preference for childbirth over abortion.

[Whether] the mandatory 24-hour waiting period is nonetheless invalid because in practice it is a substantial obstacle to a woman's choice to terminate her pregnancy is a closer question. [For] those women who have the fewest financial resources, those who must travel long distances, and those who have difficulty explaining their whereabouts to husbands, employers, or others, the 24-hour waiting period will be "particularly burdensome." These findings are troubling in some respects, but they do not demonstrate that the waiting period constitutes an undue burden.

C. [Pennsylvania's] abortion law provides, except in cases of medical emergency, that no physician shall perform an abortion on a married woman without receiving a signed statement from the woman that she has notified her spouse that she is about to undergo an abortion. [In] well-functioning marriages, spouses discuss important intimate decisions such as whether to bear a child. But there are millions of women in this country who are the victims of regular physical and psychological abuse at the hands of their husbands. Should these women become pregnant, they may have very good reasons for not wishing to inform their husbands of their decision to obtain an abortion. [The] spousal notification requirement is thus likely to prevent a significant number of women from obtaining an abortion.

[For] the great many women who are victims of abuse inflicted by their husbands, or whose children are the victims of such abuse, a spousal notice requirement enables the husband to wield an effective veto over his wife's decision. [The] husband's interest in the life of the child [does] not permit the State to empower him with this troubling degree of authority over his wife. [Women] do not lose their constitutionally protected liberty when they marry.

D. [Pennsylvania also provides that, except] in a medical emergency, an unemancipated young woman under 18 may not obtain an abortion unless she and one of her parents (or guardian) provides informed consent as defined above. If neither a parent nor a guardian provides consent, a court may authorize the performance of an abortion upon a determination that the young woman is mature and capable of giving informed consent and has in fact given her informed consent, or that an abortion would be in her best interests. We have been over most of this ground before. [We] reaffirm today that a State may require a minor seeking an abortion to obtain the consent of a parent or guardian, provided there is an adequate judicial bypass [procedure].

E. [Every Pennsylvania] facility which performs abortions is required to file a [detailed report on the circumstances of the abortion]. Every abortion facility must also file quarterly reports showing the number of abortions performed broken down by trimester. In all events, the identity of each woman who has had an abortion remains confidential. [We] think [all these] provisions except that relating to spousal notice are constitutional. [The] collection of information with respect to actual patients is a vital element of medical research, and so it cannot be said that the requirements serve no purpose other than to make abortions more difficult. Nor do we find that the requirements impose a substantial obstacle to a woman's choice. At most they might increase the cost of some abortions by a slight amount. While at some point increased cost could become a substantial obstacle, there is no such showing [here].

■ JUSTICE STEVENS, concurring in part and dissenting in part.

The Court is unquestionably correct in concluding that the doctrine of stare decisis has controlling significance in a case of this kind. The societal costs of overruling Roe at this late date would be enormous. Roe is an integral part of a correct understanding of both the concept of liberty and the basic equality of men and women. [I] agree with the joint opinion that the State may "expres[s] a preference for normal childbirth," that the State may take steps to ensure that a woman's choice "is thoughtful and informed," and that "States are free to enact laws to provide a reasonable framework for a woman to make a decision that has such profound and lasting meaning." Serious questions arise, however, when a State attempts to "persuade the woman to choose childbirth over abortion." Decisional autonomy must limit the State's power to inject into a woman's most personal deliberations its own views of what is best.

■ JUSTICE BLACKMUN, concurring in part, concurring in the judgment in part, and dissenting in part.

Three years ago, [in Webster,] four Members of this Court appeared poised to "cas[t] into darkness the hopes and visions of every woman in this country" who had come to believe that the Constitution guaranteed her the right to reproductive choice. All that remained between the promise of Roe and the darkness of the plurality was a single, flickering flame. [But] now, just when so many expected the darkness to fall, the flame has grown bright. I do not underestimate the significance of today's joint opinion. Yet I remain steadfast [that] the right to reproductive choice is entitled to the full protection afforded [before] Webster. [The] Roe framework is far more administrable, and far less manipulable, than the "undue burden" standard. [Application] of [its strict scrutiny] results in the invalidation of all the challenged provisions. Indeed, as this Court has invalidated virtually identical provisions in prior cases, stare decisis requires that we again strike them down.

■ CHIEF JUSTICE REHNQUIST, with whom JUSTICE WHITE, JUSTICE SCALIA, and JUSTICE THOMAS join, concurring in the judgment in part and dissenting in part.

The joint opinion [retains] the outer shell of Roe, but beats a wholesale retreat from the substance of that case. We believe that Roe was wrongly decided, and that it can and should be overruled. [We] are now of the view that, in terming [the pregnant woman's] right fundamental, the Court in Roe read the earlier opinions upon which it based its decision much too broadly. Unlike marriage, procreation and contraception, abortion "involves the purposeful termination of potential life." [One] cannot ignore the fact that a woman is not isolated in her pregnancy, and that the decision to abort necessarily involves the destruction of a fetus. Nor do the historical traditions of the American people support the view that the right to terminate one's pregnancy is "fundamental." The common law which we inherited from England made abortion after "quickening" an offense. At the time of the adoption of the Fourteenth Amendment, statutory prohibitions or restrictions on abortion were commonplace. [By] the turn of the century virtually every State had a law prohibiting or restricting abortion on its books. By the middle of the present century, a liberalization trend had set in. But 21 of the restrictive abortion laws in effect in 1868 were still in effect in 1973 when Roe was decided, and an overwhelming majority of the States prohibited abortion unless necessary to preserve the life or health of the mother.

[The] joint opinion['s] discussion of the principle of stare decisis appears to be almost entirely dicta, because the joint opinion does not apply that principle in dealing with Roe. Roe decided that a woman had a fundamental right to an abortion. The joint opinion rejects that view. Roe decided that abortion regulations were to be subjected to "strict scrutiny." [The] joint opinion rejects that view. Roe analyzed abortion regulation under a rigid trimester framework. [The] joint opinion rejects that framework. [Decisions] following Roe, such as Akron I and Thornburgh are frankly overruled in part under the "undue burden" standard expounded in the joint opinion. [Authentic] principles of stare decisis do not require that any portion of [Roe] be kept intact. [Erroneous] decisions in [constitutional] cases are uniquely durable, because correction through legislative action, save for constitutional amendment, is impossible. [When] it becomes clear that a prior constitutional interpretation is unsound we are obliged to reexamine the question. [The] simple fact that a generation or more had grown used to [Plessy and Lochner] did not prevent the Court from correcting its errors in those cases, nor should it prevent us [here].

[The] opinion contends that the Court was entitled to overrule Plessy and Lochner in those cases, despite the existence of opposition to the original decisions, only because both the Nation and the Court had learned new lessons in the interim. This is at best a feebly supported, post hoc rationalization. [When] the Court finally recognized its error in West Coast Hotel, it did not [state] that Lochner had been based on an economic view that had fallen into disfavor, and that it therefore should be overruled. [And the] rule of Brown is not tied to popular opinion about the evils of segregation; it is a judgment that the Equal Protection Clause does not permit racial segregation. [The] Judicial Branch derives its legitimacy, not from following public opinion, but from deciding by its best lights whether legislative enactments [comport] with the Constitution. [The] sum of the joint opinion's labors in the name of stare decisis and "legitimacy" is this: Roe stands as a sort of judicial Potemkin Village, which may be pointed out to passers by as a monument to the importance of adhering to precedent. But behind the facade, an entirely new method of analysis [is] imported to decide the constitutionality of state laws regulating abortion. Neither stare decisis nor "legitimacy" are truly served by such an effort.

■ JUSTICE SCALIA, with whom CHIEF JUSTICE REHNQUIST, JUSTICE WHITE, and JUSTICE THOMAS join, concurring in the judgment in part and dissenting in part.

[Applying] the rational basis test, I would uphold the Pennsylvania statute in its entirety. I must, however, respond to a few of the more outrageous arguments in today's opinion, which it is beyond human nature to leave unanswered. [The] best the Court can do to explain how it is that the word "liberty" must be thought to include the right to destroy human fetuses is to rattle off a collection of adjectives that simply decorate a value judgment and conceal a political choice. [It] is not reasoned judgment that supports the Court's decision; only personal predilection. [The] Court's reliance upon stare decisis can best be described as contrived. [I] confess never to have heard of this new, keep-what-you-want-and-throw-away-the-rest version. [The] Court's description of the place of Roe in the social history of the United States is unrecognizable. Not only did Roe not [resolve] the deeply divisive issue of abortion; it did more than anything else to nourish it, by elevating it to the national level where it is infinitely more difficult to resolve. National politics were not plagued by abortion protests [or] abortion marches on Congress, before Roe was decided. Profound disagreement existed among our citizens over the issue [but] that disagreement was being worked out at the state level.

[I] am appalled by the Court's suggestion that the decision whether to stand by an erroneous constitutional decision must be strongly influenced—against overruling, no less—by the substantial and continuing public opposition the decision has generated. [In] my history-book, the Court was covered with dishonor and deprived of legitimacy by Dred Scott v. Sandford, an erroneous (and widely opposed) opinion that it did not abandon, rather than by West Coast Hotel, which produced the famous "switch in time" from the Court's erroneous (and widely opposed) constitutional opposition to the social measures of the New Deal. [Instead] of engaging in the hopeless task of predicting public perception—a job not for lawyers but for political campaign managers—the Justices should do what is legally right by asking two questions: (1) Was Roe correctly decided? (2) Has Roe succeeded in producing a settled body of law? If the answer to both questions is no, Roe should undoubtedly be overruled.

THE MEANING AND IMPLICATIONS OF CASEY

1. ***Casey's influence on substantive due process.*** The joint opinion promoted an expansive and philosophical definition of constitutionally protected liberty: "[Our] law affords constitutional protection to personal decisions relating to marriage, procreation, contraception, family relationships, child rearing, and education. [These] matters, involving the most intimate and personal choices a person may make in a lifetime, choices central to personal dignity and autonomy, are central to the liberty protected by the Fourteenth Amendment. At the heart of liberty is the right to define one's own concept of existence, of meaning, of the universe, and of the mystery of human life." Is this language merely a distillation of precedent—a restatement of the right to privacy underlying Griswold and Roe—or does it signify the expansion of substantive due process to protect other fundamental values? If not privacy, then what values was the Court

inferring from the Due Process Clause? The passage seems to suggest two, which are closely related: personal dignity and autonomy, in the sense of a person's right of self-definition. Does the joint opinion provide a standard for applying these values in particular cases, or does it, as Justice Scalia's dissent argued, merely "decorate a value judgment and conceal a political choice?"

The notion of personal dignity has had an especially powerful influence on Justice Kennedy's subsequent jurisprudence. Most notably, he cited Casey's "choices central to personal dignity" language verbatim in his 2003 opinion in Lawrence v. Texas, p. 563 below, holding that the Due Process Clause prohibits states from criminalizing consensual sodomy. He also repeatedly referenced "dignity" as a core constitutional value in two other major gay rights opinions: United States v. Windsor, p. 575 below, overturning the federal government's refusal to recognize state-sanctioned same-sex marriages, and Obergefell v. Hodges, p. 583 below, recognizing a constitutional right to marriage that cannot be denied to same-sex couples. By contrast, Justice Kennedy joined the opinion of the Court in Washington v. Glucksberg, p. 595 below, which rejected reliance on Casey's "personal dignity" language and upheld a state ban on physician-assisted suicide. He also explained that the Partial-Birth Abortion Ban Act "expresses respect for the dignity of human life" in Gonzales v. Carhart, p. 541 below, which, in sustaining federal abortion restrictions, arguably curtailed Casey's scope. Can these decisions be reconciled under a consistent definition of dignity, or do they illustrate that the concept is too malleable and subjective to serve as a constitutional standard?

2. ***Abortion and stare decisis.*** Casey surprised many observers with its strong emphasis on the need to adhere to Roe to protect the legitimacy of the judiciary. Was the joint opinion's homage to stare decisis convincing in light of the way it reaffirmed Roe but overruled Akron I and Thornburgh? Was the joint opinion's justification for a super-strong deference to precedent in controversial cases convincing? Was the joint opinion wise to emphasize the risks of "overrul[ing] under fire"? Do you agree with the joint opinion's view that the overruling of the Lochner line of cases and of Plessy v. Ferguson were justifiably based on changed "facts, or [society's] understanding of facts"? Is it arguable that the more important changes that explain West Coast Hotel and Brown were changes in values rather than facts? Note the comment in Fried, "Constitutional Doctrine," 107 Harv. L. Rev. 1140 (1994), that "paradoxically [the authors of the joint opinion in Casey] seem to give [continuity and stability] undue prominence relative to their conviction of the rightness of the actual [Roe] decision—almost as if the decision could not stand on its own and needed an apology."

3. ***Abortion regulation as sex discrimination.*** Note that all of the prevailing opinions in Casey refer to the relationship between the abortion right and gender equality. Consider the view that the Court in Casey addressed, "essentially for the first time," one of the issues central to the abortion debate, "the effect of abortion laws on the status of women" and "the danger that the political process will subordinate women." Strauss, "Abortion, Toleration, and Moral Uncertainty," 1993 Sup. Ct. Rev. 1. Did the joint opinion's discussion of the spousal notice provision in particular evince an understanding of abortion regulation as part of gender hierarchy? Why didn't the Court make an equal protection basis for the decision more explicit?

4. ***The "undue burden" standard and facial and as-applied challenges.*** Does the joint opinion's "undue burden" standard promise clarity and stability? What is its likely effect on restrictions on abortions of the sort litigated during the pre-Casey era but not considered in Casey? Note that the joint opinion, while finding the informed consent and waiting period requirements constitutional on their face, left open the question of whether they imposed undue burdens as applied. Does the test simply place a heavier burden on challengers to produce factual data of the sort relied on by the joint opinion in invalidating the spousal notice provision? Was the joint opinion consistent in striking down the spousal notification provision but upholding the 24-hour waiting period, despite acknowledging the prohibitive effect of both for some women?

Is facial invalidation always the right remedy for an abortion law containing a constitutional infirmity in some applications? **Ayotte v. Planned Parenthood of Northern New England**, 546 U.S. 320 (2006), answered that question in the negative, remanding for the lower courts' consideration of a more modest remedy a state abortion law that would have been unconstitutional in medical emergencies because it lacked an exception for the health of the mother. Justice O'CONNOR, in her final opinion on the Court, wrote for a unanimous Court: "New Hampshire does not dispute, and our precedents hold, that a State may not restrict access to abortions that are 'necessary, in appropriate medical judgment, for preservation of the life or health of the mother,' [nor that in] some very small percentage of cases, pregnant minors, like adult women, need immediate abortions to avert serious and often irreversible damage to their health. [When] a statute restricting access to abortion may be applied in a manner that harms women's health, what is the appropriate relief? In the case that is before us [we] agree with New Hampshire that the lower courts need not have invalidated the law wholesale. [Only] a few applications of New Hampshire's parental notification statute would present a constitutional problem. So long as they are faithful to legislative intent, then, in this case the lower courts can issue a declaratory judgment and an injunction prohibiting the statute's unconstitutional application." The Court remanded for determination whether the New Hampshire legislature would have viewed the law as so severable and for the choice of appropriate remedy.

5. ***"Partial birth" abortion.*** After Casey, abortion opponents escalated pressure to restrict certain procedures used to perform late-term abortions, labeling them "partial birth abortions." In **Stenberg v. Carhart**, 530 U.S. 914 (2000), the Court, applying Casey, struck down by a 5–4 vote a Nebraska law prohibiting late-term "dilation and extraction" (D & X) abortions without providing for exceptions to preserve the mother's health. Justice BREYER's majority opinion, joined by Justices Stevens, O'Connor, Souter, and Ginsburg, stated: "[Where] substantial medical authority supports the proposition that banning a particular abortion procedure could endanger women's health, Casey requires the statute to include a health exception when the procedure is 'necessary, in appropriate medical judgment, for the preservation of the life or health of the mother.'" Justice STEVENS, joined by Justice Ginsburg, concurred: "[D]uring the past 27 years, the central holding of Roe v. Wade has been endorsed by all but 4 of the 17 Justices who have addressed the issue. That holding—that the word 'liberty' in the Fourteenth Amendment includes a woman's right to make this difficult and extremely personal decision—makes it impossible for me to understand how a State has any legitimate interest in requiring a doctor to

follow any procedure other than the one that he or she reasonably believes will best protect the woman in her exercise of this constitutional liberty." Justice GINSBURG and Justice O'CONNOR filed separate concurrences.

Although he had been one of the authors of the Casey joint opinion, Justice KENNEDY dissented, joined by Chief Justice Rehnquist: "The Court's failure to accord any weight to Nebraska's interest in prohibiting partial-birth abortion is erroneous and undermines its discussion and holding. [Casey] is premised on the States having an important constitutional role in defining their interests in the abortion debate. [States] may take sides in the abortion debate and come down on the side of [life] in the unborn. [Nebraska] was entitled to conclude that its ban, while advancing important interests regarding the sanctity of life, deprived no woman of a safe abortion and therefore did not impose a substantial obstacle on the rights of any woman." Justice THOMAS also dissented, joined by Chief Justice Rehnquist and Justice Scalia: "[The] majority [fails] to distinguish between cases in which health concerns require a woman to obtain an abortion and cases in which health concerns cause a woman who desires an abortion (for whatever reason) to prefer one method over another. [Such] a health exception requirement eviscerates Casey's undue burden standard and imposes unfettered abortion-on-demand."

Seven years later, in the first full Term after Justice O'Connor's retirement from the Court and Justice Alito's succession to her seat, the Court came to the opposite conclusion with respect to the constitutionality of a *federal* ban on late-term abortions entitled the Partial-Birth Abortion Ban Act of 2003. This time, Justice Kennedy, who dissented in Stenberg, wrote for the Court. Does the Court succeed in distinguishing rather than overruling Stenberg?

Gonzales v. Carhart

550 U.S. 124, 127 S. Ct. 1610, 167 L. Ed. 2d 480 (2007).

■ JUSTICE KENNEDY delivered the opinion of the Court, in which CHIEF JUSTICE ROBERTS and JUSTICES SCALIA, THOMAS, and ALITO joined.

[The] surgical procedure referred to as "dilation and evacuation" or "D & E" is the usual abortion method in [the second] trimester. [In D & E, the] doctor, often guided by ultrasound, inserts grasping forceps through the woman's cervix and into the uterus to grab the fetus, [evacuating] the fetus piece by piece continues until it has been completely removed. A doctor may make 10 to 15 passes with the forceps to evacuate the fetus in its entirety. [The] abortion procedure that was the impetus for the numerous bans on "partial-birth abortion," including the Act, is a variation of this standard D & E. [In] an intact D & E procedure the doctor extracts the fetus in a way conducive to pulling out its entire body, instead of ripping it apart.

[The] Act departs in material ways from the statute in Stenberg. It adopts the phrase "delivers a living fetus," instead of " 'delivering . . . a living unborn child, or a substantial portion thereof.' " The Act's language, unlike the statute in Stenberg, expresses the usual meaning of "deliver" when used in connection with "fetus," namely, extraction of an entire fetus rather than removal of fetal pieces. [The] identification of specific anatomical landmarks [requires] the fetus to be delivered so that it is partially "outside the body of the mother," [unlike] the Nebraska statute. [Respondents] have not shown that requiring doctors to intend dismemberment before delivery to an anatomical landmark will prohibit the vast majority of D & E abortions. The Act, then, cannot be held invalid on its face on these grounds.

Under [Casey, the] question is whether the Act, measured by its text in this facial attack, imposes a substantial obstacle to late-term, but previability, abortions. The Act does not on its face impose a substantial obstacle. [The] Act proscribes a method of abortion in which a fetus is killed just inches before completion of the birth process. [The] Act expresses respect for the dignity of human life. [The] government may use its voice and its regulatory authority to show its profound respect for the life within the woman. [Casey's] premise that the State, from the inception of the pregnancy, maintains its own regulatory interest in protecting the life of the fetus that may become a child, cannot be set at naught by interpreting Casey's requirement of a health exception so it becomes tantamount to allowing a doctor to choose the abortion method he or she might prefer.

[The] Act's ban on abortions that involve partial delivery of a living fetus furthers the Government's objectives. [Congress] determined that the abortion methods it proscribed had a "disturbing similarity to the killing of a newborn infant," and thus it was concerned with "draw[ing] a bright line that clearly distinguishes abortion and infanticide." Respect for human life finds an ultimate expression in the bond of love the mother has for her child. [Whether] to have an abortion requires a difficult and painful moral decision. While we find no reliable data to measure the phenomenon, it seems unexceptionable to conclude some women come to regret their choice to abort the infant life they once created and sustained. Severe depression and loss of esteem can follow. [The] State has an interest in ensuring so grave a choice is well informed.

[The] prohibition in the Act would be unconstitutional [if] it "subject[ed] [women] to significant health risks." [The] evidence presented in the trial courts and before Congress demonstrates both sides have medical support for their position. [The] question becomes whether the Act can stand when this medical uncertainty persists. [The] Court has given state and federal legislatures wide discretion to pass legislation in areas where there is medical and scientific uncertainty. [The] Act is not invalid on its face where there is uncertainty over whether the barred procedure is ever necessary to preserve a woman's health, given the availability of other abortion procedures that are considered to be safe alternatives.

[In] these circumstances the proper means to consider exceptions is by as-applied challenge. [This] is the proper manner to protect the health of the woman if it can be shown that in discrete and well-defined instances a particular condition has or is likely to occur in which the procedure prohibited by the Act must be used. In an as-applied challenge the nature of the medical risk can be better quantified and balanced than in a facial attack. [Respondents] have not demonstrated that the Act would be unconstitutional in a large fraction of relevant cases. The Act is open to a proper as-applied challenge in a discrete case.

■ JUSTICE THOMAS, with whom JUSTICE SCALIA joins, concurring.

I join the Court's opinion because it accurately applies current jurisprudence, including Casey. I write separately to reiterate my view that the Court's abortion jurisprudence, including Casey and Roe, has no basis in the Constitution.

■ JUSTICE GINSBURG, with whom JUSTICES STEVENS, SOUTER, and BREYER join, dissenting.

[Today's] decision is alarming. [For] the first time since Roe, the Court blesses a prohibition with no exception safeguarding a woman's health.

[The] Court has consistently required that laws regulating abortion, at any stage of pregnancy and in all cases, safeguard a woman's health. We have thus ruled that a State must avoid subjecting women to health risks not only where the pregnancy itself creates danger, but also where state regulation forces women to resort to less safe methods of abortion. [Adolescents] and indigent women, research suggests, are more likely than other women to have difficulty obtaining an abortion during the first trimester of pregnancy. Minors may be unaware they are pregnant until relatively late in pregnancy, while poor women's financial constraints are an obstacle to timely receipt of services. Severe fetal anomalies and health problems confronting the pregnant woman are also causes of second-trimester abortions; many such conditions cannot be diagnosed or do not develop until the second trimester.

[The] Court offers flimsy and transparent justifications for upholding a nationwide ban on intact D & E sans any exception to safeguard a women's health. Today's ruling, the Court declares, advances "a premise central to [Casey's] conclusion"—i.e., the Government's "legitimate and substantial interest in preserving and promoting fetal life." But the Act scarcely furthers that interest: The law saves not a single fetus from destruction, for it targets only a method of performing abortion. And surely the statute was not designed to protect the lives or health of pregnant women. As another reason for upholding the ban, the Court emphasizes that the Act does not proscribe the nonintact D & E procedure. But why not, one might ask. Nonintact D & E could equally be characterized as "brutal," involving as it does "tear[ing] [a fetus] apart" and "ripp[ing] off" its limbs.

[Ultimately,] the Court admits that "moral concerns" are at work, concerns that could yield prohibitions on any abortion. [Revealing] in this regard, the Court invokes an antiabortion shibboleth for which it concededly has no reliable evidence: Women who have abortions come to regret their choices, and consequently suffer from "[s]evere depression and loss of esteem." Because of women's fragile emotional state and because of the "bond of love the mother has for her child," the Court worries, doctors may withhold information about the nature of the intact D & E procedure. The solution the Court approves, then, is not to require doctors to inform women, accurately and adequately, of the different procedures and their attendant risks. Instead, the Court deprives women of the right to make an autonomous choice, even at the expense of their safety. This way of thinking reflects ancient notions about women's place in the family and under the Constitution—ideas that have long since been discredited.

[Though] today's opinion does not go so far as to discard Roe or Casey, the Court, differently composed than it was when we last considered a restrictive abortion regulation, is hardly faithful to our earlier invocations of "the rule of law" and the "principles of stare decisis."

After Casey, the Supreme Court did not take up another case directly implicating its abortion jurisprudence for nearly twenty-five years. When it did, examining the constitutionality of a Texas abortion restriction, the Court invoked and interpreted Casey's undue-burden framework.

Whole Woman's Health et al. v. Hellerstedt, Commissioner, Texas Department of State Health Services, et al.

— U.S. —, 136 S. Ct. 2292, 195 L. Ed. 2d 665 (2016).

■ JUSTICE BREYER delivered the opinion of the Court, in which JUSTICES KENNEDY, GINSBURG, KAGAN, and SOTOMAYOR joined.

We must here decide whether two provisions of Texas' House Bill 2 violate the Federal Constitution as interpreted in Casey. The first provision, which we shall call the *"admitting-privileges requirement,"* says that "[a] physician performing or inducing an abortion must, on the date the abortion is performed or induced, have active admitting privileges at a hospital that is located not further than 30 miles from the location at which the abortion is performed or induced." [T]he second provision, which we shall call the *"surgical-center requirement,"* says that "the minimum standards for an abortion facility must be equivalent to the minimum standards adopted under [the Texas Health and Safety Code section] for ambulatory surgical centers."

We conclude that neither of these provisions confers medical benefits sufficient to justify the burdens upon access that each imposes.

The rule announced in Casey [requires] that courts consider the burdens a law imposes on abortion access together with the benefits.

[The] Court, when determining the constitutionality of laws regulating abortion procedures, has placed considerable weight upon evidence and argument presented in judicial proceedings. In Casey, for example, we relied heavily on the District Court's factual findings and the research-based submissions of *amici*. [And] Gonzales [said] that the "*Court retains an independent constitutional duty to review factual findings where constitutional rights are at stake*." *Ibid.* (emphasis added).

[The] relevant statute here does not set forth any legislative findings. Rather, one is left to infer that the legislature sought to further a constitutionally acceptable objective (namely, protecting women's health). For a district court to give significant weight to evidence in the judicial record in these circumstances is consistent with this Court's case law.

[The] purpose of the admitting-privileges requirement is to help ensure that women have easy access to a hospital should complications arise during an abortion procedure. But the District Court found that it brought about no such health-related benefit.

[We] have found nothing in Texas' record evidence that shows that, compared to prior law (which required a "working arrangement" with a doctor with admitting privileges), the new law advanced Texas' legitimate interest in protecting women's health.

[When] directly asked at oral argument whether Texas knew of a single instance in which the new requirement would have helped even one woman obtain better treatment, Texas admitted that there was no evidence in the record of such a case.

At the same time, the record evidence indicates that the admitting-privileges requirement places a "substantial obstacle in the path of a woman's choice." Casey. [As] of the time the admitting-privileges requirement began to be enforced, the number of facilities providing abortions dropped in half from about 40 to about 20. Eight abortion clinics closed in the months leading up to the requirement's effective date.

Eleven more closed on the day the admitting-privileges requirement took effect.

[In] our view, the record contains sufficient evidence that the admitting-privileges requirement led to the closure of half of Texas' clinics, or thereabouts. Those closures meant fewer doctors, longer waiting times, and increased crowding.

[There] is considerable evidence in the record supporting the District Court's findings indicating that the statutory provision requiring all abortion facilities to meet all surgical-center standards does not benefit patients and is not necessary.

[The] record makes clear that the surgical-center requirement provides no benefit when complications arise in the context of an abortion produced through medication. That is because, in such a case, complications would almost always arise only after the patient has left the facility. The record also contains evidence indicating that abortions taking place in an abortion facility are safe—indeed, safer than numerous procedures that take place outside hospitals and to which Texas does not apply its surgical-center requirements.

[Moreover,] many surgical-center requirements are inappropriate as applied to surgical abortions.

[The] record provides adequate evidentiary support for the District Court's conclusion that the surgical-center requirement places a substantial obstacle in the path of women seeking an abortion. The parties stipulated that the requirement would further reduce the number of abortion facilities available to seven or eight facilities, located in Houston, Austin, San Antonio, and Dallas/Fort Worth.

[Common] sense suggests that, more often than not, a physical facility that satisfies a certain physical demand will not be able to meet five times that demand without expanding or otherwise incurring significant costs.

[More] fundamentally, in the face of no threat to women's health, Texas seeks to force women to travel long distances to get abortions in crammed-to-capacity super-facilities. Patients seeking these services are less likely to get the kind of individualized attention, serious conversation, and emotional support that doctors at less taxed facilities may have offered.

■ JUSTICE GINSBURG, concurring.

The Texas law called H. B. 2 inevitably will reduce the number of clinics and doctors allowed to provide abortion services.

[Given] those realities, it is beyond rational belief that H. B. 2 could genuinely protect the health of women, and certain that the law would simply make it more difficult for them to obtain abortions." When a State severely limits access to safe and legal procedures, women in desperate circumstances may resort to unlicensed rogue practitioners, *faute de mieux*, at great risk to their health and safety. Targeted Regulation of Abortion Providers laws like H. B. 2 that do little or nothing for health, but rather strew impediments to abortion, cannot survive judicial inspection.

■ JUSTICE THOMAS, dissenting.

[Whatever] scrutiny the majority applies to Texas' law, it bears little resemblance to the undue-burden test the Court articulated in Casey.

First, today's decision requires courts to "consider the burdens a law imposes on abortion access together with the benefits those laws confer." Second, today's opinion tells the courts that, when the law's justifications are medically uncertain, they need not defer to the legislature, and must instead assess medical justifications for abortion restrictions by scrutinizing the record themselves. Finally, even if a law imposes no "substantial obstacle" to women's access to abortions, the law now must have more than a "reasonabl[e] relat[ion] to a legitimate state interest." These precepts are nowhere to be found in Casey or its successors, and transform the undue-burden test to something much more akin to strict scrutiny.

■ JUSTICE ALITO, with whom THE CHIEF JUSTICE and JUSTICE THOMAS join, dissenting.

[While] there can be no doubt that H. B. 2 caused some clinics to cease operation, the absence of proof regarding the reasons for particular closures is a problem because some clinics have or may have closed for [reasons] other than the two H. B. 2 requirements at issue here.

[Even] if the District Court had properly filtered out immaterial closures, its analysis would have been incomplete for a second reason. Petitioners offered scant evidence on the capacity of the clinics that are able to comply with the admitting privileges and ASC requirements, or on those clinics' geographic distribution. Reviewing the evidence in the record, it is far from clear that there has been a material impact on access to abortion.

[The] other potential obstacle to abortion access is the distribution of facilities throughout the State. [If] the only clinics in the State were those that would have remained open if the judgment of the Fifth Circuit had not been enjoined, roughly 95% of the women of reproductive age in the State would live within 150 miles of an open facility (or lived outside that range before H. B. 2).

[We] should decline to hold that these statistics justify the facial invalidation of the H. B. 2 requirements.

In the years since Whole Women's Health the composition of the Court has shifted. Justice Gorsuch filled the then-vacant seat left by Justice Scalia, and Justice Kavanaugh replaced Justice Kennedy, who joined the Court's opinion in Whole Women's Health. The consequences of these changes remain to be determined.

SUBSTANTIVE DUE PROCESS AND MARRIAGE AND FAMILY RELATIONSHIPS

Does substantive due process include a right to marry, divorce, retain relationships with one's children, or decide the composition of the household in which one lives? The Court has recognized some individual rights in the family context, including some not exercised in a traditional nuclear family unit. Is substantive due process an appropriate home for ground rules that constitutionalize family law? Recall the Meyer and Pierce cases of the Lochner era. Are such precedents more well-grounded than economic liberty precedents from the same era? The Court has extended these precedents considerably in developing the privacy line of substantive due process decisions.

1. ***Marriage.*** The state obviously regulates marriage and divorce extensively by setting forth the rules for entry and dissolution; may it also define the eligibility requirements so as to exclude some persons from the option to marry altogether? People of different races? People of different sexes? People in prison? People who have failed to pay past child support? The Court's 1967 decision in **Loving v. Virginia**, 388 U.S. 1 (1967), striking down Virginia's ban on interracial marriage, relied principally on equal protection, but Chief Justice WARREN's opinion for the Court also stated, as an alternative ground for the holding, "These statutes also deprive the Lovings of liberty without due process of law in violation of the Due Process Clause of the Fourteenth Amendment. The freedom to marry has long been recognized as one of the vital personal rights essential to the orderly pursuit of happiness by free men. Marriage is one of the 'basic civil rights of man,' fundamental to our very existence and survival. Skinner v. Oklahoma [1942; p. 510 above]. To deny this fundamental freedom on so unsupportable a basis as the racial classifications embodied in these statutes, classifications so directly subversive of the principle of equality at the heart of the Fourteenth Amendment, is surely to deprive all the State's citizens of liberty without due process of law. [Under] our Constitution, the freedom to marry, or not marry, a person of another race resides with the individual and cannot be infringed by the State."

In **Zablocki v. Redhail**, 434 U.S. 374 (1978), the Court again vindicated the right to marry, but via an equal protection route. The decision invalidated a Wisconsin law that provided that any resident "having minor issue not in his custody and which he is under an obligation to support by any court order" could not marry without obtaining court approval, which depended on proof that the applicant's support obligation had been met and that children covered by the support order "are not then and are not likely thereafter to become public charges." Redhail's application for a marriage license was denied because he had not obtained court permission, nor could he because he had not been paying court-ordered support for a daughter he had had in a previous unmarried relationship and the child had been receiving benefits under the AFDC program since her birth. He brought a class action challenging the law under the Equal Protection and Due Process Clauses. Although the majority ultimately analyzed the case in terms of the "fundamental rights" strand of equal protection, it was strongly influenced by substantive due process precedents treating the "right to marry" as "fundamental."

Justice MARSHALL's opinion for the Court stated that since "the right to marry is of fundamental importance, and since the classification at issue here significantly interferes with the exercise of that right, we believe that 'critical examination' of the state interests advanced [is] required." In explaining why "the right to marry is of fundamental importance for all individuals," he pointed to Loving and noted that the Griswold line of decisions had "established that the right to marry is part of the fundamental 'right of privacy' implicit in [the] Due Process Clause. [It] is not surprising that the decision to marry has been placed on the same level of importance as decisions relating to procreation, childbirth, child-rearing, and family relationships. [It] would make little sense to recognize a right of privacy with respect to other matters of family life and not with respect to the decision to enter the relationship that is the foundation of the family in our society. [If the] right to procreate means anything at all, it must imply some right to enter the only relationship in which [the State] allows sexual relations legally to take place." Where a law "interfere[d] directly and substantially with the right to marry," it cannot be upheld "unless it is supported by sufficiently important state interests and is closely tailored to effectuate only those interests." Even if "safeguarding the welfare of out-of-custody children," by providing an incentive to make support payments, was an important interest, the State had other, less intrusive means "for exacting compliance with support obligations," such as direct enforcement "via wage assignments, civil contempt proceedings, and criminal penalties."

Justice POWELL's concurrence in the judgment objected that "[a] 'compelling state purpose' inquiry would cast doubt on the network of restrictions that the States have fashioned to govern marriage and divorce," such as "bans on incest, bigamy, and homosexuality, as well as various preconditions to marriage, such as blood tests," but concluded that the law could not pass muster under even less exacting scrutiny. Justice STEVENS concurred, stating that the Constitution permits "direct and substantial" restraints on the right to marry, such as prohibitions on marriage to a child or close relative, but not, as in this case, "deliberate discrimination against the poor." Justice STEWART's opinion concurring in the judgment was the only one which found substantive due process the sole appropriate basis for decision, objecting that "to embrace the essence of that doctrine under the guise of equal protection serves no purpose but obfuscation." Justice REHNQUIST, the sole dissenter, found no basis for applying any "heightened standard of review," insisting on "the traditional presumption of validity" as expressed in such cases as Lee Optical.

The Court extended Zablocki in **Turner v. Safley**, 482 U.S. 78 (1987), to strike down a prison regulation that restricted prison inmates' right to marry by conditioning it on the prison superintendent's approval for "compelling reasons 'such as pregnancy or birth of a child.'" Justice O'CONNOR's opinion for the Court assumed that, under Loving and Zablocki "the decision to marry is a fundamental right," and ruled that it remained extant even in the prison context: "The right to marry, like many other rights, is subject to substantial restrictions as a result of incarceration. Many important attributes of marriage remain, however, after taking into account the limitations imposed by prison life. First, inmate marriages, like others, are expressions of emotional support and public commitment. These elements are an important and significant aspect of the marital relationship. In addition, many religions recognize marriage as having spiritual significance. Third, most inmates eventually will be released by parole or commutation, and therefore most inmate marriages are formed in the expectation that they ultimately will be fully consummated. Finally, marital status often is a pre-condition to the receipt of government benefits (e.g., Social Security benefits), property rights (e.g., tenancy by the entirety, inheritance rights), and other, less tangible benefits (e.g., legitimation of children born out of wedlock). [Taken] together, we conclude that these remaining elements are sufficient to form a constitutionally protected marital relationship in the prison context." The majority opinion proceeded to find this right violated by the prison regulation "even under the reasonable relationship test" as unjustified by legitimate rehabilitation or security concerns.

Does the line of cases from Loving to Zablocki and Turner support an argument on substantive due process grounds for the extension of marriage to gay and lesbian couples? Does due process forbid exclusion from marriage simply on the basis of the sex of one's partner?

2. ***Household composition and extended family relationships.*** In **Moore v. East Cleveland**, 431 U.S. 494 (1977), the Court invalidated a zoning ordinance limiting occupancy of a dwelling to members of a single "family," narrowly defined, as applied to a grandmother who shared her home with two grandsons who were first cousins rather than siblings. This relationship was not sufficiently close to constitute a "family" under the ordinance. According to the City's position, "any constitutional right to live together as a family extends only to the nuclear family—essentially a couple and their dependent children." The city government, which consisted predominantly of African-American lawmakers, sought to encourage middle-class residents living in nuclear family arrangements rather than in extended family arrangements prevalent in poorer urban communities.

Justice POWELL's plurality opinion gave substantive due process as the ground for invalidating the application of the ordinance to Mrs. Moore, suggesting that a scrutiny stricter than deferential rationality review was appropriate: "[W]hen the government intrudes on choices concerning family living arrangements, this Court must examine carefully the importance of the governmental interests advanced and the extent to which they are served by the challenged regulation." The ordinance could not survive that heightened scrutiny; although such articulated city interests as "preventing overcrowding" and "minimizing traffic and parking congestion" were "legitimate," the ordinance "serves them marginally, at best," and "has but a tenuous relation to them." Justice Powell held that the principles of the cases beginning with Meyer and Pierce covered "extended family" relationships such as Mrs. Moore's as well as "the nuclear family—essentially a couple and its dependent children."

Justice Powell acknowledged that "[s]ubstantive due process has at times been a treacherous field for this Court. There *are* risks when the judicial branch gives enhanced protection to certain substantive liberties without the guidance of the more specific provisions of the Bill of Rights. As the history of the Lochner era demonstrates, there is reason for concern lest the only limits to such judicial intervention become the predilections of those who happen at the time to be Members of this Court. That history counsels caution and restraint. But it does not counsel abandonment, nor does it require what the city urges here: cutting off any protection of family rights at the first convenient, if arbitrary boundary—the boundary of the nuclear family. [Appropriate] limits on substantive due process come not from drawing arbitrary lines but rather from 'careful respect for the teachings of history [and] solid recognition of the basic values that underlie our society.'

[Griswold, Harlan, J., concurring.] Our decisions establish that the Constitution protects the sanctity of the family precisely because the institution of the family is deeply rooted in this Nation's history and tradition. It is through the family that we inculcate and pass down many of our most cherished values, moral and cultural. Ours is by no means a tradition limited to respect for the bonds uniting the members of the nuclear family. The tradition of uncles, aunts, cousins, and especially grandparents sharing a household along with parents and children has roots equally venerable and equally deserving of constitutional recognition. [The] Constitution prevents East Cleveland from standardizing its children—and its adults—by forcing all to live in certain narrowly defined family patterns."

Justice STEVENS, whose vote was necessary for the 5–4 judgment, concurred only in the result, resting on a right to the enjoyment of property rather than on the liberty interest identified in Justice Powell's plurality opinion. Even applying the "limited standard of review" generally applicable in zoning cases, Justice Stevens found, the zoning ordinance was an unjustifiable restriction on Mrs. Moore's "right to use her own property as she sees fit."

Justice WHITE's dissent argued that Justice Powell's emphasis on history and tradition would "broaden enormously the horizons" of substantive due process: "[The] interest in residing with more than one set of grandchildren is [not] one that calls for any kind of heightened protection. [What] the deeply rooted traditions of the country are is arguable; which of them deserves the protection of the Due Process Clause is even more debatable." Justice STEWART's dissent, joined by Justice Rehnquist, likewise argued that Mrs. Moore's interest could not be considered "implicit in the concept of ordered liberty." He added: "To equate this interest with the fundamental decisions to marry and to bear and raise children is to extend the limited substantive contours of the Due Process Clause beyond recognition." Chief Justice BURGER dissented on procedural grounds.

Contrast with Moore the decision in **Village of Belle Terre v. Boraas**, 416 U.S. 1 (1974), where Justice Douglas's majority opinion, over Justice Marshall's dissent, found no privacy rights involved in a family-oriented zoning restriction excluding most *unrelated* groups from a village. Justice Douglas insisted the ordinance represented "economic and social legislation" and invoked the deferential judicial stance characteristic of zoning cases. In Moore, Justice Powell distinguished Belle Terre because it had affected "only *unrelated* individuals." Justice Marshall argued that strict scrutiny was appropriate: "The choice of household companions—of whether a person's 'intellectual and emotional' needs are best met by living with family, friends, professional associates or others—involves deeply personal considerations as to the kind and quality of intimate relationships within the home. That decision surely falls within the ambit of the right to privacy protected by the Constitution." Was the Court correct to draw the line at marital or blood ties? How important are marital or blood ties to the functions served by intimate relationships? Might the element of choice in forming such relationships deserve protection? See generally Karst, "The Freedom of Intimate Association," 89 Yale L.J. 624 (1980).

To what extent does a parent's right to control her child's upbringing, as recognized in Pierce v. Society of Sisters (p. 509, above), trump the state's ability to protect extended family relationships? In a 6–3 decision in **Troxel v. Granville**, 530 U.S. 57 (2000), the Court concluded that, when applying a Washington statute that granted "any person" the right to petition for child visitation rights "at any time," substantive due process required the state court to give "special weight" to the parent's preferences. The facts of the case involved a disagreement between the sole surviving parent of two children—a "fit, custodial mother"—and the children's paternal grandparents over how much visitation time the grandparents should receive. The trial court split the difference between their proposals, apparently based on a personal belief that children should spend time with their grandparents. The Supreme Court rejected this reasoning. Justice O'CONNOR, joined by Chief Justice Rehnquist and Justices Ginsburg and Breyer, stated that "it cannot now be doubted that the Due Process Clause of the Fourteenth Amendment protects the fundamental right of parents to make decisions concerning the care, custody, and control of their children. [So] long as a parent adequately cares for his or her children, [there] will normally be no reason for the State to inject itself into the private realm of the family [to contradict a parent's] decisions concerning [childrearing]. [If] a fit parent's decision of the kind at issue here becomes subject to judicial review, the court must accord at least some special weight to the parent's own determination. [The] Due Process Clause does not permit a State to infringe on the fundamental right of parents to make childrearing decisions simply because a state judge believes a 'better' decision could be made." Justice O'Connor declined to define "the precise scope" of parents' right to control their children's visitation, but concluded that, because the trial judge in this case had granted the visitation rights without according special weight to the mother's decision, the visitation order was an infringement on her due process right.

Justice STEVENS dissented: "[T]here are plainly any number of cases [in] which the 'person' [seeking] visitation is a once-custodial caregiver, an intimate relation, or even a genetic parent. Even the Court would seem to agree that in many circumstances, it would be constitutionally permissible for a court to award some visitation of a child to a parent or previous caregiver. [While the Constitution] certainly protects the parent-child relationship from arbitrary impairment by the State, we have never held that the parent's liberty interest in this relationship is so inflexible as to establish a rigid constitutional shield, protecting every arbitrary parental decision from any challenge absent a threshold finding of harm. [Cases] like this do not present a bipolar struggle between the parents and the State over who has final authority to determine what is in a child's best interests. There is at a minimum a third individual, whose interests are implicated in every case to which the statute applies—the child. [It] seems clear to me that the Due Process Clause of the Fourteenth Amendment leaves room for States to consider the impact on a child of possibly arbitrary parental decisions that neither serve nor are motivated by the best interests of the child."

Justice KENNEDY's dissent echoed Justice Stevens: "[T]he constitutionality of the application of the best interests standard depends on [specific] factors. [A] fit parent's right vis-a-vis a complete stranger is one thing; her right vis-a-vis another parent or a de facto parent may be another. [Family] courts in the 50 States confront these factual variations each day, and are best situated to consider the [issues] that arise." Justice SCALIA likewise dissented: "[W]hile I would think it entirely compatible with [representative] democracy [to] argue, in legislative chambers or in electoral campaigns, that the state has no power to interfere with parents' authority over the rearing of their children, I do not believe that the power which the Constitution confers upon me as a judge entitles me to deny legal effect to laws that (in my view) infringe upon what is (in my view) [an] unenumerated right."

3. ***Family relationships and the role of tradition.*** Can tradition and historical custom serve as useful checks upon judicial interpretation of "fundamental values" in substantive due process cases? Note the heavy reliance by Justice Powell in Moore on Justice Harlan's tradition-oriented approach. Is it easier for judges to discern that a value is deeply rooted in American tradition than to determine whether it arises from political philosophy or emerging social consensus? Or does reference to tradition straitjacket liberty into the past, perpetuating hidebound historical tendencies? Can a liberty be "fundamental" and yet inconsistent with prevailing tradition?

If tradition is to be a guide, what is the appropriate level of generality in defining the relevant tradition for substantive due process purposes? This was one of the issues that divided the Court in **Michael H. v. Gerald D.**, 491 U.S. 110 (1989), a case that arose from application of a California law establishing a presumption that a child born to the wife is legitimately a child of the marriage, a presumption rebuttable only under limited circumstances. Michael H., claiming to be the biological father of the child of Carole D. and Gerald D., a married couple, sought visitation and other rights with respect to the child. The California courts, relying on the presumption, rejected Michael H.'s claim of paternity, even though blood tests established a 98.07% probability that he was the child's father. Although there was no majority opinion, the Court upheld the California judgment.

Justice SCALIA, writing also for Chief Justice Rehnquist and in part for Justices O'Connor and Kennedy, concluded that none of Michael H.'s constitutional rights had been violated. He proceeded to analyze the case in substantive rather than procedural due process terms. In Justice Scalia's view, due process protection required "not merely that the interest denominated as a 'liberty' be 'fundamental' (a concept that, in isolation, is hard to objectify), but also that it be an interest traditionally protected by our society." Central to him was "the historic respect—indeed, sanctity would not be too strong a term—traditionally accorded to the relationships that develop within the unitary family. [Thus,] the legal issue [here] reduces to whether the relationship between the persons in the situation of Michael and Victoria [the child] has been treated as a protected family unit under the historic practices of our society, or whether on any other basis it has been accorded special protection. We think it impossible to find that it has. In fact, quite to the contrary, our traditions have protected the marital family (Gerald, Carole, and the child they acknowledge to be theirs) against the sort of claim Michael asserts."

In a lengthy footnote, Justice Scalia defended his position that resort to "tradition" required emphasis on the "most specific" level of generality at which the history and tradition could be perceived. Under this approach, the relevant historical tradition was that specifically relating adulterous natural fathers, not parents more generally. Justice Scalia stated: "We refer to the most specific level at which a relevant tradition protecting, or denying protection to, the asserted right can be identified. If [there] were no societal tradition, either way, regarding the rights of the natural father of a child adulterously conceived, we would have to consult, and [if possible] reason from, the traditions regarding natural fathers in general. But there is such a more specific tradition, and it unqualifiedly denies protection to such a parent. [Because] general traditions provide such imprecise guidance, they permit judges to dictate rather than discern the society's views. [Although] assuredly having the virtue (if it be that) of leaving judges free to decide as they think best when the unanticipated occurs, a rule of law that binds neither by text nor by any particular, identifiable tradition, is no rule of law at all."

Justice O'CONNOR, joined by Justice Kennedy, joined all of Justice Scalia's opinion *except* that footnote. Justice O'Connor commented: "This footnote sketches a mode of historical analysis [that] may be somewhat inconsistent with our past decisions in this area. See [Griswold; Eisenstadt]. On occasion the Court has characterized relevant traditions protecting asserted rights at levels of generality that might not be 'the most specific level' available. [See Loving v. Virginia.] I would not foreclose the unanticipated by the prior imposition of a single mode of historical analysis."

Justice BRENNAN's dissent, joined by Justices Marshall and Blackmun, included a strong objection to Justice Scalia's methodology: "Apparently oblivious to the fact that [the] concept [of tradition] can be as malleable and as elusive as 'liberty' itself, the plurality pretends that tradition places a discernible border around the Constitution. The pretense is seductive. [The] plurality has not found the objective boundary that it seeks. [If] we had looked to tradition with such specificity [as the plurality] in past cases, many a decision would have reached a different result. [E.g., Eisenstadt; Griswold.] The plurality's interpretive method [ignores] the good reasons for limiting the role of 'tradition' in interpreting the Constitution's deliberately capacious language. In the plurality's constitutional universe, we may not take notice of the fact that the original reasons for the conclusive presumption of paternity are out of place in a world in which blood tests can prove virtually beyond a shadow of a doubt who sired a particular child and in which the fact of illegitimacy no longer plays the burdensome and stigmatizing role it once did. [The] document that the plurality construes today is unfamiliar to me. It is not the living charter that I have taken to be our Constitution; it is instead a stagnant, archaic, hidebound document steeped in the prejudices and superstitions of a time long past."

After Michael H., how much turns on the level of generality with which the relevant right and the challenged practice are described? Was this a case about parental rights or the rights of adulterous fathers? For discussion, see Tribe & Dorf, "Levels of Generality in the Definition of Rights," 57 U. Chi. L. Rev. 1057, 1087, 1090 (1990).

SUBSTANTIVE DUE PROCESS, SEXUALITY AND HYBRID DUE PROCESS-EQUAL PROTECTION RIGHTS

The preceding sections have discussed the applicability of substantive due process principles to two related subjects: reproductive and sexual autonomy, and limitations on government intervention in family relationships—including certain "non-traditional" family relationships. The question of sexual orientation implicates both of these topics. What is the scope of constitutional protection for gay, lesbian, bisexual, and transgender people, both as individuals and in families? Does substantive due process protect only negative liberty—freedom from government interference in private decisions, such as consensual sexual behavior—or does it extend to positive liberty—the freedom to participate fully in all societal institutions, including marriage and child-rearing? If it extends to positive liberty, can the right really still be described as a privacy right, or does it rest on a different value—like the notion that all people should have "equal dignity"? To what extent do due-process arguments for LGBT rights complement, or overlap, arguments based on equal protection? These questions, and the Court's responses to them, are the subject of this sub-section.

Even in the decades during which the Court engaged in repeated review of contraception and abortion cases, it did not take up what might have been thought the antecedent issue of whether the Constitution protected sexual conduct itself from some forms of state regulation. See, e.g., Hollenbaugh v. Carnegie Free Library, 439 U.S. 1052 (1978), where the Court denied a petition for certiorari from a decision upholding the discharge of two public library employees for adulterous cohabitation, over Justices Marshall's and Brennan's dissent.

The Court's first consideration of the merits of a claimed right of privacy in sexual conduct occurred in **Bowers v. Hardwick**, 478 U.S. 186 (1986), a case involving a facial challenge to a Georgia law that defined sodomy as "committing or submitting to 'any sexual act involving the sex organs of one person and the mouth or anus of another,'" and made such an act a felony punishable by up to 20 years in prison. By a vote of 5–4, the Court upheld the statute as applied to "homosexual sodomy." Justice WHITE wrote the opinion of the Court, defining the issue narrowly as "whether the Federal Constitution confers a fundamental right upon homosexuals to engage in sodomy and hence invalidates the laws of the many States that still make such conduct illegal and have done so for a very long time." He found that so defined, the right was not fundamental within the meaning of the Court's precedents under the Due Process Clause: "[Pierce and Meyer] were described as dealing with child rearing and education; [Skinner] with procreation; [Loving] with marriage; [Griswold and Eisenstadt] with contraception; and [Roe] with abortion. The latter three cases were interpreted as construing [due process] to confer a fundamental individual right to decide whether or not to beget or bear a child. Accepting the decisions in these cases, [we] think it evident that none of the rights announced in those cases bears any resemblance to the claimed constitutional right of homosexuals to engage in acts of sodomy, that is asserted in this case. No connection between family, marriage, or procreation on the one hand and homosexual activity on the other has been demonstrated.

"Proscriptions against that conduct have ancient roots. Sodomy was a criminal offense at common law and was forbidden by the laws of the original thirteen States when they ratified the Bill of Rights. In 1868, when the Fourteenth Amendment was ratified, all but 5 of the 37 States in the Union had criminal sodomy laws. In fact, until 1961, all States outlawed sodomy, and today, 24 States and the District of Columbia continue to provide criminal penalties for sodomy performed in private and between consenting adults. Against this background, to claim that a right to engage in such conduct is 'deeply rooted in this Nation's history and tradition' or 'implicit in the concept of ordered liberty' is, at best, facetious.

"Nor are we inclined to take a more expansive view of our authority to discover new fundamental rights imbedded in the Due Process Clause. The Court is most vulnerable and comes nearest to illegitimacy when it deals with judge-made constitutional law having little or no cognizable roots in the language or design of the Constitution." Applying rationality review, the majority opinion upheld the law, rejecting the claim that morality alone was insufficient to provide a rational basis for a law: "The law is constantly based on notions of morality, and if all laws representing essentially moral choices are to be invalidated under the Due Process Clause, the courts will be very busy indeed."

Chief Justice BURGER filed a concurrence emphasizing that "proscriptions against sodomy have very 'ancient roots' " in "Judeo-Christian moral and ethical standards" and "millennia of moral teaching." Justice POWELL filed a concurrence suggesting that he might have regarded a 20-year prison sentence "for a single private, consensual act of sodomy" as creating "a serious Eighth Amendment issue" because it might amount to cruel and unusual punishment, but in view of the absence of any such prison sentence on the record in the case, found the law facially valid against substantive due process challenge.[1]

In dissent, Justice BLACKMUN, joined by Justices Brennan, Marshall and Stevens, argued that the right in question had been defined too narrowly: "[T]his case is about 'the most comprehensive of rights and the right most valued by civilized man,' namely, 'the right to be let alone.' [We] protect [privacy] rights not because they contribute, in some direct and material way, to the general public welfare, but because they form so central a part of an individual's life. Only the most willful blindness could obscure the fact that sexual intimacy is 'a sensitive, key relationship of human existence.' [The] fact that individuals define themselves in a significant way through their intimate sexual relationships with others suggests, in a Nation as diverse as ours, that there may be many 'right' ways of conducting those relationships, and that much of the richness of a relationship will come from the freedom an individual has to *choose* the form and nature of these intensely personal bonds. [The] Court claims that its decision today merely refuses to recognize a fundamental right to engage in homosexual sodomy; what the Court really has refused to recognize is the fundamental interest all individuals have in controlling the nature of their intimate associations with others."

Justice STEVENS too dissented, emphasizing that the Georgia sodomy law prohibited sodomy amongst all citizens, married or unmarried, heterosexual or homosexual. If the law could not be enforced as written, he argued, and was being used to target only a subset of the population, namely gay men, then the state must justify its application of the law under heightened scrutiny: "A policy of selective application must be supported by a neutral and legitimate interest—something more substantial than a habitual dislike for, or ignorance about, the disfavored group."

Well before the Supreme Court revisited its holding in Bowers, the Georgia Supreme Court invalidated its sodomy statute on state constitutional grounds. In **Powell v. State**, 510 S.E.2d 18 (Ga. 1998), that court held that "the 'right to be let alone' guaranteed by the Georgia Constitution is far more extensive that the right of privacy protected by the

[1] After his retirement, Justice Powell, who had cast the deciding vote in Bowers, stated that he "probably made a mistake" in voting as he did. He had initially voted with the majority but changed his vote. But he added that he still regarded the decision as "one of little or no importance" because no one had actually been prosecuted for homosexual conduct. See Jeffries, Justice Lewis F. Powell, Jr. 511–30 (1994).

U.S. Constitution." The court continued: "Adults who withdraw from the public gaze [to] engage in private unforced sexual behavior are exercising a right 'embraced within the right of personal liberty." The Kentucky Supreme Court distinguished Bowers inn **Commonwealth v. Wasson**, 842 S.W.2d 487 (Ky. 1992): "[State] constitutional jurisprudence in this area is not limited by the constraints inherent in federal due process analysis. Deviate sexual intercourse conducted in private by consenting adults is not beyond the protections of the guarantees of individual liberty in our Kentucky Constitution simply because 'proscriptions against that conduct have ancient roots.' [Bowers.] Kentucky constitutional guarantees against government intrusion address substantive rights." The court concluded, "Simply because the majority, speaking through the General Assembly, finds one type of extramarital intercourse more offensive than another, does not provide a rational basis for criminalizing the sexual preference of homosexuals."

After Bowers, the Court did not revisit the subject of sexual orientation for almost ten years. The case that follows was the Court's next major decision on the issue, and its first time invalidating a law that discriminated against gay and lesbian people. Note, however, that the Court's opinion did not refer to Bowers, and that it did not rely on substantive due process but on the Equal Protection Clause.

Romer v. Evans

517 U.S. 620, 116 S. Ct. 1620, 134 L. Ed. 2d 855 (1996).

■ JUSTICE KENNEDY delivered the opinion of the Court.

One century ago, the first Justice Harlan admonished this Court that the Constitution "neither knows nor tolerates classes among citizens." Plessy v. Ferguson (dissenting opinion). Unheeded then, those words now are understood to state a commitment to the law's neutrality where the rights of persons are at stake. The Equal Protection Clause enforces this principle and today requires us to hold invalid a provision of Colorado's Constitution.

I. [An] amendment to the [Colorado Constitution] adopted in a 1992 statewide referendum [as] "Amendment 2" [stemmed] in large part from ordinances that had been passed in various Colorado municipalities, [banning] discrimination in many transactions and activities, including housing, employment, education, public accommodations, and health and welfare services. What gave rise to the statewide controversy was the protection the ordinances afforded to persons discriminated against by reason of their sexual orientation. [Amendment 2], in explicit terms, does more than repeal or rescind these provisions. It prohibits all legislative, executive or judicial action at any level of state or local government designed to protect the named class, a class we shall refer to as homosexual persons or gays and lesbians. The amendment reads:

> "No Protected Status Based on Homosexual, Lesbian, or Bisexual Orientation. Neither the State of Colorado, through any of its branches or departments, nor any of its agencies, political subdivisions, municipalities or school districts, shall enact, adopt or enforce any statute, regulation, ordinance or policy whereby homosexual, lesbian or bisexual orientation, conduct, practices or

> relationships shall constitute or otherwise be the basis of or entitle any person or class of persons to have or claim any minority status, quota preferences, protected status or claim of discrimination. This Section of the Constitution shall be in all respects self-executing."

The State's principal argument in defense of Amendment 2 is that it puts gays and lesbians in the same position as all other persons. So, the State says, the measure does no more than deny homosexuals special rights. This reading of the amendment's language is implausible. We rely not upon our own interpretation of the amendment but upon the authoritative construction of Colorado's Supreme Court:

> ["The] immediate objective of Amendment 2 is, at a minimum, to repeal existing statutes, regulations, ordinances, and policies of state and local entities that barred discrimination based on sexual orientation; and various provisions prohibiting discrimination based on sexual orientation at state colleges. The 'ultimate effect' of Amendment 2 is to prohibit any governmental entity from adopting similar, or more protective statutes, regulations, ordinances, or policies in the future unless the state constitution is first amended to permit such measures."

Sweeping and comprehensive is the change in legal status effected by this law. So much is evident from the ordinances that the Colorado Supreme Court declared would be void by operation of Amendment 2. Homosexuals, by state decree, are put in a solitary class with respect to transactions and relations in both the private and governmental spheres. The amendment withdraws from homosexuals, but no others, specific legal protection from the injuries caused by discrimination, and it forbids reinstatement of these laws and policies.

The change that Amendment 2 works in the legal status of gays and lesbians in the private sphere is far-reaching, both on its own terms and when considered in light of the structure and operation of modern anti-discrimination laws. [Most] States have chosen to counter discrimination by enacting detailed statutory schemes. Colorado's state and municipal laws typify this emerging tradition of statutory protection and follow a consistent pattern. The laws first enumerate the persons or entities subject to a duty not to discriminate. The list goes well beyond the entities covered by the common law. The Boulder ordinance, for example, has a comprehensive definition of entities deemed places of "public accommodation." They include "any place of business engaged in any sales to the general public and any place that offers services, facilities, privileges, or advantages to the general public or that receives financial support through solicitation of the general public or through governmental subsidy of any kind." [These] statutes and ordinances also depart from the common law by enumerating the groups or persons within their ambit of protection. Enumeration is the essential device used to make the duty not to discriminate concrete and to provide guidance for those who must comply. In following this approach, Colorado's state and local governments have not limited anti-discrimination laws to groups that have so far been given the protection of heightened equal protection scrutiny under our cases. Rather, they set forth an extensive catalogue of traits which cannot be the basis for discrimination, including age, military status, marital status, pregnancy, parenthood, custody of a minor child, political affiliation, physical or mental disability of an individual or of his or her associates—and, in recent times, sexual orientation. Amendment 2 bars homosexuals from securing protection against the injuries that these public-accommodations laws address. That in itself is a severe consequence, but there is more. Amendment 2 [nullifies] specific legal protections for this targeted class in all transactions in housing, sale of real estate, insurance, health and welfare services, private education, and employment.

Not confined to the private sphere, Amendment 2 also operates to repeal and forbid all laws or policies providing specific protection for gays or lesbians from discrimination by every level of Colorado government. The State Supreme Court cited two examples of protections in the governmental sphere that are now rescinded and may not be reintroduced. The first is [the] Colorado Executive Order [which] forbids employment discrimination against " 'all state employees, classified and exempt' on the basis of sexual orientation." Also repealed, and now forbidden, are "various provisions prohibiting discrimination based on sexual orientation at state colleges." The repeal of these measures and the prohibition against their future reenactment demonstrates that Amendment 2 has the same force and effect in Colorado's governmental sector as it does elsewhere and that it applies to policies as well as ordinary legislation. Amendment 2's reach may not be limited to specific laws passed for the benefit of gays and lesbians.

It is a fair, if not necessary, inference from the broad language of the amendment that it deprives gays and lesbians even of the protection of general laws and policies that prohibit arbitrary discrimination in governmental and private settings. At some point in the systematic administration of these laws, an official must determine whether homosexuality is an arbitrary and thus forbidden basis for decision. Yet a decision to that effect would itself amount to a policy prohibiting discrimination on the basis of homosexuality, and so would appear to be no more valid under Amendment 2 than the specific prohibitions against discrimination the state court held invalid. If this consequence follows from Amendment 2, as its broad language suggests, it would compound the constitutional difficulties the law creates.

The state court did not decide whether the amendment has this effect, however, and neither need we. [Even] if, as we doubt, homosexuals could find some safe harbor in laws of general application, we cannot accept the view that Amendment 2's prohibition on specific legal protections does no more than deprive homosexuals of special rights. To the contrary, the amendment imposes a special disability upon those persons alone. Homosexuals are forbidden the safeguards that others enjoy or may seek without constraint. They can obtain specific protection against discrimination only by enlisting the citizenry of Colorado to amend the state constitution or perhaps, on the State's view, by trying to pass helpful laws of general applicability. This is so no matter how local or discrete the harm, no matter how public and widespread the injury. We find nothing special in the protections Amendment 2 withholds. These are protections taken for granted by most people either because they already have them or do not need them; these are protections against exclusion from an almost limitless number of transactions and endeavors that constitute ordinary civic life in a free society.

III. [The equal protection guarantee] must co-exist with the practical necessity that most legislation classifies for one purpose or another, with resulting disadvantage to various groups or persons. We have attempted to reconcile the principle with the reality by stating that, if a law neither burdens a fundamental right nor targets a suspect class, we will uphold the legislative classification so long as it bears a rational relation to some legitimate end. Amendment 2 fails, indeed defies, even this conventional inquiry. First, the amendment has the peculiar property of imposing a broad and undifferentiated disability on a single named group, an exceptional and, as we shall explain, invalid form of legislation. Second, its sheer breadth is so discontinuous with the reasons offered for it that the amendment seems inexplicable by anything but animus toward the class that it affects; it lacks a rational relationship to legitimate state interests.

Taking the first point, even in the ordinary equal protection case calling for the most deferential of standards, we insist on knowing the relation between the classification adopted and the object to be attained. The search for the link between classification and objective gives substance to the Equal Protection Clause; it provides guidance and discipline for the legislature, which is entitled to know what sorts of laws it can pass; and it marks the limits of our own authority. In the ordinary case, a law will be sustained if it can be said to advance a legitimate government interest, even if the law seems unwise or works to the disadvantage of a particular group, or if the rationale for it seems tenuous. The laws challenged in the cases just cited were narrow enough in scope and grounded in a sufficient factual context for us to ascertain that there existed some relation between the classification and the purpose it served. By requiring that the classification bear a rational relationship to an independent and legitimate legislative end, we ensure that classifications are not drawn for the purpose of disadvantaging the group burdened by the law.

Amendment 2 confounds this normal process of judicial review. It is at once too narrow and too broad. It identifies persons by a single trait and then denies them protection across the board. The resulting disqualification of a class of persons from the right to seek specific protection from the law is unprecedented in our jurisprudence. It is not within our constitutional tradition to enact laws of this sort. [Central] both to the idea of the rule of law and to our own Constitution's guarantee of equal protection is the principle that government and each of its parts remain open on impartial terms to all who seek its assistance. [Respect] for this principle explains why laws singling out a certain class of citizens for disfavored legal status or general hardships are rare. A law declaring that in general it shall be more difficult for one group of citizens than for all others to seek aid from the government is itself a denial of equal protection of the laws in the most literal sense.

[A] second and related point is that laws of the kind now before us raise the inevitable inference that the disadvantage imposed is born of animosity toward the class of persons affected. "[I]f the constitutional conception of 'equal protection of the laws' means anything, it must at the very least mean that a [bare] desire to harm a politically unpopular group cannot constitute a legitimate governmental interest." [Moreno]. Even laws enacted for broad and ambitious purposes often can be explained by reference to legitimate public policies which justify the incidental disadvantages they impose on certain persons. Amendment 2, however, in making a general announcement that gays and lesbians shall not have any particular protections from the law, inflicts on them immediate, continuing, and real injuries that outrun and belie any legitimate justifications that may be claimed for it. We conclude that, in addition to the far-reaching deficiencies of Amendment 2 that we have noted, the principles it offends, in another sense, are conventional and venerable; a law must bear a rational relationship to a legitimate governmental purpose and Amendment 2 does not.

The primary rationale the State offers for Amendment 2 is respect for other citizens' freedom of association, and in particular the liberties of landlords or employers who have personal or religious objections to homosexuality. Colorado also cites its interest in conserving resources to fight discrimination against other groups. The breadth of the Amendment is so far removed from these particular justifications that we find it impossible to credit them. We cannot say that Amendment 2 is directed to any identifiable legitimate purpose or discrete objective. It is a status-based enactment divorced from any factual context from which we could discern a relationship to legitimate state interests; it is a classification of persons undertaken for its own sake, something [equal protection] does not permit. [We] must conclude that Amendment 2 classifies homosexuals not to further a proper legislative end but to make them unequal to everyone else. This Colorado cannot do. A State cannot so deem a class of persons a stranger to its laws. Amendment 2 violates [equal protection], and the judgment of the Supreme Court of Colorado is affirmed.

■ JUSTICE SCALIA, with whom CHIEF JUSTICE REHNQUIST and JUSTICE THOMAS join, dissenting.

The Court has mistaken a Kulturkampf for a fit of spite. The constitutional amendment before us here is not the manifestation of a "bare [desire] to harm" homosexuals, but is rather a modest attempt by seemingly tolerant Coloradans to preserve traditional sexual mores against the efforts of a politically powerful minority to revise those mores through use of the laws. That objective, and the means chosen to achieve it, are not only unimpeachable under any constitutional doctrine hitherto pronounced (hence the opinion's heavy reliance upon principles of righteousness rather than judicial holdings); they have been specifically approved by [Congress] and by this Court. In holding that homosexuality cannot be singled out for disfavorable treatment, the Court contradicts a decision, unchallenged here, pronounced only 10 years ago, see Bowers, and places the prestige of this institution behind the proposition that opposition to homosexuality is as reprehensible as racial or religious bias. [Since] the Constitution of the United States says nothing about this subject, it is left to be resolved by normal democratic means, including the democratic adoption of provisions in state constitutions. This Court has no business imposing upon all Americans the resolution favored by the elite class from which the Members of this institution are selected, pronouncing that "animosity" toward homosexuality is evil.

[In] rejecting the State's arguments that Amendment 2 "puts gays and lesbians in the same position as all other persons," and "does no more than deny homosexuals special rights," the Court considers it unnecessary to decide the validity of the State's argument that Amendment 2 does not deprive homosexuals of the "protection [afforded by] general laws and policies that prohibit arbitrary discrimination in governmental and private settings." I agree that we need not resolve that dispute, because the Supreme Court of Colorado has resolved it for [us]: "[I]t is significant to note that Colorado law currently proscribes discrimination against persons who are not suspect classes, including discrimination based on age; marital or family status; veterans' status; and for any legal, off-duty conduct such as smoking tobacco. *Of course Amendment 2 is not intended to have any effect on this legislation, but seeks only to prevent the adoption of antidiscrimination laws intended to protect gays, lesbians, and bisexuals."* (Emphasis added.) The Court utterly fails to distinguish this portion of the Colorado court's opinion. [The] clear import of the Colorado court's conclusion [is] that "general laws and policies that prohibit arbitrary discrimination" would continue to prohibit discrimination on the basis of homosexual conduct as well. This analysis, which is fully in accord with (indeed, follows inescapably from) the text of the constitutional provision, lays to rest such [horribles] as the prospect that assaults upon homosexuals could not be prosecuted. The amendment prohibits special treatment of homosexuals, and nothing more. [The] only denial of equal treatment it contends homosexuals have suffered is this: They may not obtain *preferential* treatment without amending the state constitution.

[What Colorado] has done is not only unprohibited, but eminently reasonable. [The] Court's opinion contains grim, disapproving hints that Coloradans have been guilty of "animus" or "animosity" toward homosexuality, as though that has been established as Unamerican. Of course it is our moral heritage that one should not hate any human being or class of human beings. But I had thought that one could consider certain conduct reprehensible—murder, for example, or polygamy, or cruelty to animals—and could exhibit even "animus" toward such conduct. Surely that is the only sort of "animus" at issue here: moral disapproval of homosexual conduct, the same sort of moral disapproval that produced the centuries-old criminal laws that we held constitutional in Bowers. [Colorado] not only is one of the 25 States that have repealed their anti-sodomy laws, but was among the first to do so. But the society that eliminates criminal punishment for homosexual acts does not necessarily abandon the view that homosexuality is morally wrong and socially harmful; often, abolition simply reflects the view that enforcement of such criminal laws involves unseemly intrusion into the intimate lives of citizens. [Amendment 2] is designed to prevent piecemeal deterioration of the sexual morality favored by a majority of Coloradans, and is [an] appropriate means to that legitimate end.

THE MEANING AND IMPLICATIONS OF ROMER

1. ***Romer's rationale.*** As Chapter 9 explains in much greater detail, the Court has established three levels of review under the Equal Protection Clause for laws that treat different groups of people differently. The most demanding, known as strict scrutiny, applies to suspect classifications—discrimination against groups that the Court has held merit special protection, owing to their status as "discrete and insular minorities." Discrimination based on race and national origin are the paradigmatic suspect classifications. Strict scrutiny also applies when a particular group is singled out for deprivation of a fundamental right, as in Skinner v. Oklahoma, p. 510, above. Strict scrutiny invalidates a government action unless it is necessary to a compelling government interest. The next standard, intermediate scrutiny, is mainly used for classification on the basis of gender. Intermediate scrutiny requires that government action be substantially related to an important government interest. All other classifications are subject to deferential "rational basis review," meaning

they will be upheld if they are rationally related to some legitimate government interest.

Justice Kennedy's opinion in Romer purported to rely entirely on rational basis review in striking down Amendment 2. It gave no hint of applying strict scrutiny or even intermediate scrutiny to discrimination on the basis of sexual orientation. The Court relied on an amalgam of two arguments. The first was advanced in an amicus brief by a group of law professors (Tribe, Ely, Gunther, Kurland, and Sullivan) claiming that the Colorado provision was a rare example of a literal violation of equal protection by declaring gay persons alone ineligible for protection from discrimination. The Fourteenth Amendment by its terms guarantees equal *protection* of the law; in choosing that language, its Framers were concerned in part that Southern officials not look the other way when lynchings and other violence affected African-Americans. The second argument on which Justice Kennedy relied was that Amendment 2 could not survive even minimum rationality review, because Colorado's justifications of protecting the associational freedom of landlords and employers and of conserving law enforcement resources could not support the over- and underinclusive means invoked by Amendment 2 and thus revealed that Amendment 2 was solely based on animosity toward gay people.

Should the Court instead have declared discrimination against gay and lesbian people to be a suspect classification, or a quasi-suspect classification meriting intermediate scrutiny? Consider whether sexual orientation discrimination is analogous to race discrimination. A history of social opprobrium and legally imposed disadvantage applies in both contexts. Strict scrutiny is often justified as necessary to remedy the relative political powerlessness of "discrete and insular minorities." The closet, or socially reinforced secrecy about gay identity, has arguably imposed its own form of political powerlessness by creating a minority that could be construed variously as discrete and insular or diffuse and anonymous. But might it be argued to the contrary that sexual activity, unlike skin color, is wholly within the control of individuals, and hence the analogy falters? Does a distinction between sexual orientation and sexual activity make any sense? If it did, would it matter?

In only one case has any Justice ever argued that the analogy to race discrimination is sufficient to warrant formal heightened scrutiny of classifications based on sexual orientation: Justice Brennan, in a dissent from a denial of certiorari in Rowland v. Mad River School District, 470 U.S. 1009 (1985), wrote: "[H]omosexuals constitute a significant and insular minority of this country's population. Because of the immediate and severe opprobrium often manifested against homosexuals once so identified publicly, members of this group are particularly powerless to pursue their rights openly in the political arena. Moreover, homosexuals have historically been the object of [pernicious and sustained hostility, and it is fair to say that discrimination against homosexuals is likely to reflect deep-seated prejudice rather than rationality.]" Would such an equal-protection argument have provided stronger grounds for the challenge in Lawrence? What of the fact that the Georgia sodomy law upheld in Bowers was facially neutral as between same-sex and opposite-sex sexual activities?

2. ***Alternative justifications for Romer.*** Some commentators have suggested broader justifications for the Court's ruling. Farber & Sherry, "The Pariah Principle," 13 Const. Comment. 257 (1996), argues that the ruling

was justified because of the principle that "forbids the government from designating any societal group as untouchable, regardless of whether the group in question is generally entitled to some special degree of judicial protection, like blacks, or to no special protection, like left-handers (or, under current doctrine, homosexuals)." And Amar, "Attainder and Amendment 2: Romer's Rightness," 95 Mich. L. Rev. 203 (1996), argues that the text, history, and spirit of the Bill of Attainder Clause, Art. I, § 10, best justifies the majority ruling. But see Hills, "Is Amendment 2 Really a Bill of Attainder? Some Questions About Professor Amar's Analysis of Romer," 95 Mich. L. Rev. 236 (1996). For the view that Romer vindicated an "expressive" dimension of the Equal Protection Clause by vindicating the government's obligation to treat each person with equal concern, see Hellman, "The Expressive Dimension of Equal Protection," 85 Minn. L. Rev. 1 (2000).

As Justice Scalia pointed out in dissent, the Court's opinion in Romer—holding that the expression of society's disapproval of homosexuality is not a legitimate government interest—was in deep tension with Bowers. Seven years later, in another decision in which Justice Kennedy wrote the opinion of the Court, Bowers was formally overruled. The overruling occurred in a case involving a Texas law that, unlike the Georgia law in Bowers, prohibited only sodomy between persons of the same sex. The Court found the law invalid as a restriction on the right of privacy long rooted in substantive due process: "Bowers was not correct when it was decided, and it is not correct today. It ought not to remain binding precedent. Bowers v. Hardwick should be and now is overruled." Justice O'Connor provided a sixth vote, concurring in the judgment on equal protection grounds without repudiating her vote with the Bowers majority.

Lawrence v. Texas

539 U.S. 558, 123 S. Ct. 2472, 156 L. Ed. 2d 508 (2003).

■ JUSTICE KENNEDY delivered the opinion of the Court, in which JUSTICES STEVENS, SOUTER, GINSBURG, and BREYER joined.

Liberty protects the person from unwarranted government intrusions into a dwelling or other private places. In our tradition the State is not omnipresent in the home. And there are other spheres of our lives and existence, outside the home, where the State should not be a dominant presence. Freedom extends beyond spatial bounds. Liberty presumes an autonomy of self that includes freedom of thought, belief, expression, and certain intimate conduct. The instant case involves liberty of the person both in its spatial and more transcendent dimensions.

I. The question before the Court is the validity of a Texas statute making it a crime for two persons of the same sex to engage in certain intimate sexual conduct. In Houston, Texas, officers of the Harris County Police Department were dispatched to a private residence in response to a reported weapons disturbance. They entered an apartment where one of the petitioners, John Geddes Lawrence, resided. The right of the police to enter does not seem to have been questioned. The officers observed Lawrence and another man, Tyron Garner, engaging in a sexual act. The two petitioners were arrested, held in custody over night, and charged and convicted before a Justice of the Peace [of] "deviate sexual intercourse, namely anal sex, with a member of the same sex (man)," [under] Tex. Penal Code Ann. § 21.06(a) [which] provides: "A person commits an offense if he engages in deviate sexual intercourse with another individual of the same sex." The statute defines "[d]eviate sexual intercourse" as follows: "(A) any contact between any part of the genitals of one person and the mouth or anus of another person; or (B) the penetration of the genitals or the anus of another person with an object." § 21.01(1). The petitioners, having entered a plea of nolo contendere, were each fined $200 and assessed court costs of $141.25. [The] petitioners were adults at the time of the alleged offense. Their conduct was in private and consensual.

II. We conclude the case should be resolved by determining whether the petitioners were free as adults to engage in the private conduct in the exercise of their liberty under the Due Process Clause of the Fourteenth Amendment to the Constitution. For this inquiry we deem it necessary to reconsider the Court's holding in Bowers v. Hardwick. [The] most pertinent beginning point is our decision in Griswold. In Griswold the Court invalidated a state law prohibiting the use of drugs or devices of contraception and counseling or aiding and abetting the use of contraceptives. The Court described the protected interest as a right to privacy and placed emphasis on the marriage relation and the protected space of the marital bedroom. After Griswold it was established that the right to make certain decisions regarding sexual conduct extends beyond the marital relationship. Eisenstadt. [The] opinions in Griswold and Eisenstadt were part of the background for the decision in Roe v. Wade. [Both] Eisenstadt and Carey, as well as the holding and rationale in Roe, confirmed that the reasoning of Griswold could not be confined to the protection of rights of married adults. This was the state of the law with respect to some of the most relevant cases when the Court considered Bowers v. Hardwick.

[The] Court began its substantive discussion in Bowers as follows: "The issue presented is whether the Federal Constitution confers a fundamental right upon homosexuals to engage in sodomy and hence invalidates the laws of the many States that still make such conduct illegal and have done so for a very long time." That statement, we now conclude, discloses the Court's own failure to appreciate the extent of the liberty at stake. To say that the issue in Bowers was simply the right to engage in certain sexual conduct demeans the claim the individual put forward, just as it would demean a married couple were it to be said marriage is simply about the right to have sexual intercourse. The laws involved in Bowers and here are, to be sure, statutes that purport to do no more than prohibit a particular sexual act. Their penalties and purposes, though, have more far-reaching consequences, touching upon the most private human conduct, sexual behavior, and in the most private of places, the home. The statutes do seek to control a personal relationship that, whether or not entitled to formal recognition in the law, is within the liberty of persons to choose without being punished as criminals.

This, as a general rule, should counsel against attempts by the State, or a court, to define the meaning of the relationship or to set its boundaries absent injury to a person or abuse of an institution the law protects. It suffices for us to acknowledge that adults may choose to enter upon this relationship in the confines of their homes and their own private lives and still retain their dignity as free persons. When sexuality finds overt expression in intimate conduct with another person, the conduct can be but one element in a personal bond that is more enduring. The liberty protected by the Constitution allows homosexual persons the right to make this choice.

Having misapprehended the claim of liberty there presented to it, and thus stating the claim to be whether there is a fundamental right to engage in consensual sodomy, the Bowers Court said: "Proscriptions against that conduct have ancient roots." In academic writings, and in many of the scholarly amicus briefs filed to assist the Court in this case, there are fundamental criticisms of the historical premises relied upon by the majority and concurring opinions in Bowers [that] counsel against adopting the definitive conclusions upon which Bowers placed such reliance. [There] is no longstanding history in this country of laws directed at homosexual conduct as a distinct matter. Beginning in colonial times there were prohibitions of sodomy derived from the English criminal laws passed in the first instance by the Reformation Parliament of 1533. The English prohibition was understood to include relations between men and women as well as relations between men and men. Nineteenth-century commentators similarly read American sodomy, buggery, and crime-against-nature statutes as criminalizing certain relations between men and women and between men and men. The absence of legal prohibitions focusing on homosexual conduct may be explained in part by noting that according to some scholars the concept of the homosexual as a distinct category of person did not emerge until the late 19th century. Thus early American sodomy laws were not directed at homosexuals as such but instead sought to prohibit nonprocreative sexual activity more generally. This does not suggest approval of homosexual conduct. It does tend to show that this particular form of conduct was not thought of as a separate category from like conduct between heterosexual persons.

Laws prohibiting sodomy do not seem to have been enforced against consenting adults acting in private. A substantial number of sodomy prosecutions and convictions for which there are surviving records were for predatory acts against those who could not or did not consent, as in the case of a minor or the victim of an assault. As to these, one purpose for the prohibitions was to ensure there would be no lack of coverage if a predator committed a sexual assault that did not constitute rape as defined by the criminal law. [The] infrequency of these prosecutions [makes] it difficult to say that society approved of a rigorous and systematic punishment of the consensual acts committed in private and by adults. The longstanding criminal prohibition of homosexual sodomy upon which the Bowers decision placed such reliance is as consistent with a general condemnation of nonprocreative sex as it is with an established tradition of prosecuting acts because of their homosexual character. [Far] from possessing "ancient roots," American laws targeting same-sex couples did not develop until the last third of the 20th century. [It] was not until the 1970's that any State singled out same-sex relations for criminal prosecution, and only nine States have done so [Arkansas, Kansas, Kentucky, Missouri, Montana, Nevada, Oklahoma, Tennessee, Texas].

It must be acknowledged, of course, that the Court in Bowers was making the broader point that for centuries there have been powerful voices to condemn homosexual conduct as immoral. The condemnation has been shaped by religious beliefs, conceptions of right and acceptable behavior, and respect for the traditional family. For many persons these are not trivial concerns but profound and deep convictions accepted as ethical and moral principles to which they aspire and which thus determine the course of their lives. These considerations do not answer the question before us, however. The issue is whether the majority may use the power of the State to enforce these views on the whole society through operation of the criminal law.

[In] all events we think that our laws and traditions in the past half century are of most relevance here. These references show an emerging awareness that liberty gives substantial protection to adult persons in deciding how to conduct their private lives in matters pertaining to sex. This emerging recognition should have been apparent when Bowers was decided. In 1955 the American Law Institute promulgated the Model Penal Code and made clear that it did not recommend or provide for "criminal penalties for consensual sexual relations conducted in private." It justified its decision on three grounds: (1) The prohibitions undermined respect for the law by penalizing conduct many people engaged in; (2) the statutes regulated private conduct not harmful to others; and (3) the laws were arbitrarily enforced and thus invited the danger of blackmail. In 1961 Illinois changed its laws to conform to the Model Penal Code. Other States soon followed. [Likewise, a] committee advising the British Parliament recommended in 1957 repeal of laws punishing homosexual conduct. Parliament enacted the substance of those recommendations 10 years later. Of even more importance, almost five years before Bowers was decided the European Court of Human Rights considered a case with parallels to Bowers and to today's case. An adult male resident in Northern Ireland alleged he was a practicing homosexual who desired to engage in consensual homosexual conduct. The laws of Northern Ireland forbade him that right. He alleged that he had been questioned, his home had been searched, and he feared criminal prosecution. The court held that the laws proscribing the conduct were invalid under the European Convention on Human Rights. Dudgeon v. United Kingdom, 45 Eur. Ct. H.R. ¶ 52 (1981). Authoritative in all countries that are members of the Council of Europe (21 nations then, 45 nations now), the decision is at odds with the premise in Bowers that the claim put forward was insubstantial in our Western civilization.

In our own constitutional system the deficiencies in Bowers became even more apparent in the years following its announcement. The 25 States with laws prohibiting [sodomy] are reduced now to 13, of which 4 enforce their laws only against homosexual conduct. In those States where sodomy is still proscribed, whether for same-sex or heterosexual conduct, there is a pattern of nonenforcement with respect to consenting adults acting in private. The State of Texas admitted in 1994 that as of that date it had not prosecuted anyone under those circumstances.

Two principal cases decided after Bowers cast its holding into even more doubt. In [Planned Parenthood v.] Casey [1992; p. 531, above], the Court reaffirmed the substantive force of the liberty protected by the Due Process Clause. The Casey decision again confirmed that our laws and tradition afford constitutional protection to personal decisions relating to marriage, procreation, contraception, family relationships, child rearing, and education [involving "the] most intimate and personal choices a person may make in a lifetime, choices central to personal dignity and autonomy." Persons in a homosexual relationship may seek autonomy for these purposes, just as heterosexual persons do. The decision in Bowers would deny them this right.

The second post-Bowers case of principal relevance is Romer v. Evans [1996; p. 556 above]. There the Court struck down class-based legislation directed at homosexuals as a violation of the Equal Protection Clause. Romer invalidated an amendment to Colorado's constitution which named as a solitary class persons who were homosexuals, lesbians, or bisexual either by "orientation, conduct, practices or relationships." We concluded that the provision was "born of animosity toward the class of persons affected" and further that it had no rational relation to a legitimate governmental purpose. As an alternative argument in this case, counsel for the petitioners and some amici contend that Romer provides the basis for declaring the Texas statute invalid under the Equal Protection Clause. That is a tenable argument, but we conclude the instant case requires us to address whether Bowers itself has continuing validity. Were we to hold the statute invalid under the Equal Protection Clause some might question whether a prohibition would be valid if drawn differently, say, to prohibit the conduct both between same-sex and different-sex participants. Equality of treatment and the due process right to demand respect for conduct protected by the substantive guarantee of liberty are linked in important respects, and a decision on the latter point advances both interests. If protected conduct is made criminal and the law which does so remains unexamined for its substantive validity, its stigma might remain even if it were not enforceable as drawn for equal protection reasons. When homosexual conduct is made criminal by the law of the State, that declaration in and of itself is an invitation to subject homosexual persons to discrimination both in the public and in the private spheres. The central holding of Bowers has been brought in question by this case, and it should be addressed. Its continuance as precedent demeans the lives of homosexual persons.

prefer liberty arg.

[The] foundations of Bowers have sustained serious erosion from our recent decisions in Casey and Romer. When our precedent has been thus weakened, criticism from other sources is of greater significance. In the United States criticism of Bowers has been substantial and continuing, disapproving of its reasoning in all respects, not just as to its historical assumptions. The courts of five different States have declined to follow it in interpreting provisions in their own state constitutions parallel to the Due Process Clause of the Fourteenth Amendment. To the extent Bowers relied on values we share with a wider civilization, it should be noted that the reasoning and holding in Bowers have been rejected elsewhere. The European Court of Human Rights has followed not Bowers but its own decision in Dudgeon v. United Kingdom. Other nations, too, have taken action consistent with an affirmation of the protected right of homosexual adults to engage in intimate, consensual conduct. The right the petitioners seek in this case has been accepted as an integral part of human freedom in many other countries. There has been no showing that in this country the governmental interest in circumscribing personal choice is somehow more legitimate or urgent.

The doctrine of stare decisis is essential to the respect accorded to the judgments of the Court and to the stability of the law. It is not, however, an inexorable command. In Casey we noted that when a Court is asked to overrule a precedent recognizing a constitutional liberty interest, individual or societal reliance on the existence of that liberty cautions with particular strength against reversing course. The holding in Bowers, however, has not induced detrimental [individual] or societal reliance [of] the sort that could counsel against overturning its holding once there are compelling reasons to do so. Bowers itself causes uncertainty, for the precedents before and after its issuance contradict its central holding.

The rationale of Bowers does not withstand careful analysis. In his dissenting opinion in Bowers Justice Stevens came to these conclusions:

> "Our prior cases make two propositions abundantly clear. First, the fact that the governing majority in a State has traditionally viewed a particular practice as immoral is not a sufficient reason for upholding a law prohibiting the practice; neither history nor tradition could save a law prohibiting miscegenation from constitutional attack. Second, individual decisions by married persons, concerning the intimacies of their physical relationship, even when not intended to produce offspring, are a form of 'liberty' protected by the Due Process Clause of the Fourteenth Amendment. Moreover, this protection extends to intimate choices by unmarried as well as married persons."

Justice Stevens' analysis, in our view, should have been controlling in Bowers and should control here. Bowers was not correct when it was decided, and it is not correct today. It ought not to remain binding precedent. Bowers v. Hardwick should be and now is overruled.

The present case does not involve minors. It does not involve persons who might be injured or coerced or who are situated in relationships where consent might not easily be refused. It does not involve public conduct or prostitution. It does not involve whether the government must give formal recognition to any relationship that homosexual persons seek to enter. The case does involve two adults who, with full and mutual consent from each other, engaged in sexual practices common to a homosexual lifestyle. The petitioners are entitled to respect for their private lives. The State cannot demean their existence or control their destiny by making their private sexual conduct a crime. Their right to liberty under the Due Process Clause gives them the full right to engage in their conduct without intervention of the government. "It is a promise of the Constitution that there is a realm of personal liberty which the government may not enter." Casey. The Texas statute furthers no legitimate state interest which can justify its intrusion into the personal and private life of the individual.

Had those who drew and ratified the Due Process Clauses of the Fifth Amendment or the Fourteenth Amendment known the components of liberty in its manifold possibilities, they might have been more specific. They did not presume to have this insight. They knew times can blind us to certain truths and later generations can see that laws once thought necessary and proper in fact serve only to oppress. As the Constitution endures, persons in every generation can invoke its principles in their own search for greater freedom. [Reversed.]

■ JUSTICE O'CONNOR, concurring in the judgment.

The Court today overrules Bowers v. Hardwick. I joined Bowers, and do not join the Court in overruling it. Nevertheless, I agree with the Court that Texas' statute banning same-sex sodomy is unconstitutional. Rather than relying on the substantive component of the Fourteenth Amendment's Due Process Clause, as the Court does, I base my conclusion on the Fourteenth Amendment's Equal Protection Clause.

[We] have consistently held [that] some objectives, such as "a bare . . . desire to harm a politically unpopular group," are not legitimate state interests. When a law exhibits such a desire to harm a politically unpopular group, we have applied a more searching form of rational basis review to strike down such laws under the Equal Protection Clause. [The] statute at issue here makes sodomy a crime only if a person "engages in deviate sexual intercourse with another individual of the same sex." Sodomy between opposite-sex partners, however, is not a crime in Texas. [The] Texas statute makes homosexuals unequal in the eyes of the law by making particular conduct—and only that conduct—subject to criminal sanction. [And] the effect of Texas' sodomy law is not just limited to the threat of prosecution or consequence of conviction. Texas' sodomy law brands all homosexuals as criminals, thereby making it more difficult for homosexuals to be treated in the same manner as everyone else [including] in the areas of "employment, family issues, and housing."

Texas attempts to justify its law, and the effects of the law, by arguing that the statute satisfies rational basis review because it furthers the legitimate governmental interest of the promotion of morality. [This] case raises a different issue than Bowers: whether, under the Equal Protection Clause, moral disapproval is a legitimate state interest to justify by itself a statute that bans homosexual sodomy, but not heterosexual sodomy. It is not. Moral disapproval of this group, like a bare desire to harm the group, is an interest that is insufficient to satisfy rational basis review under the Equal Protection Clause. Indeed, we have never held that moral disapproval, without any other asserted state interest, is a sufficient rationale under the Equal Protection Clause to justify a law that discriminates among groups of persons.

Whether a sodomy law that is neutral both in effect and application would violate the substantive component of the Due Process Clause is an issue that need not be decided today. I am confident, however, that so long as the Equal Protection Clause requires a sodomy law to apply equally to the private consensual conduct of homosexuals and heterosexuals alike, such a law would not long stand in our democratic society.

■ JUSTICE SCALIA, with whom CHIEF JUSTICE REHNQUIST and JUSTICE THOMAS join, dissenting.

[Countless] judicial decisions and legislative enactments have relied on the ancient proposition that a governing majority's belief that certain sexual behavior is "immoral and unacceptable" constitutes a rational basis for regulation. [State] laws against bigamy, same-sex marriage, adult incest, prostitution, masturbation, adultery, fornication, bestiality, and obscenity are [sustainable] only in light of Bowers' validation of laws based on moral choices. Every single one of these laws is called into question by today's decision. [Section § 21.06(a)] undoubtedly imposes constraints on liberty. So do laws prohibiting prostitution, recreational use of heroin, and, for that matter, working more than 60 hours per week in a bakery. But there is no right to "liberty" under the Due Process Clause, though today's opinion repeatedly makes that claim. The Fourteenth Amendment expressly allows States to deprive their citizens of "liberty," so long as "due process of law" is provided. Our opinions applying the doctrine known as "substantive due process" hold that the Due Process Clause prohibits States from infringing fundamental liberty interests, unless the infringement is narrowly tailored to serve a compelling state interest. We have held repeatedly, in cases the Court today does not overrule, that only fundamental rights qualify for this so-called "heightened scrutiny" protection—that is, rights which are " 'deeply rooted in this Nation's history and tradition.' "

[Homosexual] sodomy is not a right "deeply rooted in our Nation's history and tradition." [An] "emerging awareness" is by definition not "deeply rooted in this Nation's history and tradition[s]." Constitutional entitlements do not spring into existence because some States choose to lessen or eliminate criminal sanctions on certain behavior. Much less do they spring into existence, as the Court seems to believe, because foreign nations decriminalize conduct. The Court's discussion of [foreign] views (ignoring, of course, the many countries that have retained criminal prohibitions on sodomy) is therefore meaningless dicta. Dangerous dicta, however, since "this Court . . . should not impose foreign moods, fads, or fashions on Americans."

[The] contention that there is no rational basis for the law here under attack [is] so out of accord with our jurisprudence—indeed, with the jurisprudence of any society we know—that it requires little discussion. The Texas statute undeniably seeks to further the belief of its citizens that certain forms of sexual behavior are "immoral and unacceptable"—the same interest furthered by criminal laws against fornication, bigamy, adultery, adult incest, bestiality, and obscenity. Bowers held that this was a legitimate state interest. The Court today reaches the opposite conclusion. [This] effectively decrees the end of all morals legislation. If, as the Court asserts, the promotion of majoritarian sexual morality is not even a legitimate state interest, none of the above-mentioned laws can survive rational-basis review.

[Today's] opinion is the product of a Court, which is the product of a law-profession culture, that has largely signed on to the so-called homosexual agenda, by which I mean the agenda promoted by some homosexual activists directed at eliminating the moral opprobrium that has traditionally attached to homosexual conduct. [It is clear] that the Court has taken sides in the culture war, departing from its role of assuring, as neutral observer, that the democratic rules of engagement are observed. Many Americans do not want persons who openly engage in homosexual conduct as partners in their business, as scoutmasters for their children, as teachers in their children's schools, or as boarders in their home. They view this as protecting themselves and their families from a lifestyle that they believe to be immoral and destructive.

[Let] me be clear that I have nothing against homosexuals, or any other group, promoting their agenda through normal democratic means. Social perceptions of sexual and other morality change over time, and every group has the right to persuade its fellow citizens that its view of such matters is the best. [But] it is the premise of our system that those judgments are to be made by the people, and not imposed by a governing caste that knows best.

■ JUSTICE THOMAS, dissenting.

I write separately to note that the law before the Court today "is . . . uncommonly silly." Griswold [(Stewart J., dissenting)]. If I were a member of the Texas Legislature, I would vote to repeal it. Punishing someone for expressing his sexual preference through noncommercial consensual conduct with another adult does not appear to be a worthy way to expend valuable law enforcement resources. Notwithstanding this, I recognize that as a member of this Court I am not empowered to help petitioners and others similarly situated [as] I "can find [neither in the Bill of Rights nor any other part of the Constitution a] general right of privacy," or as the Court terms it today, the "liberty of the person both in its spatial and more transcendent dimensions."

THE MEANING AND IMPLICATIONS OF LAWRENCE

1. ***The standard of scrutiny in Lawrence.*** Was the decision in Lawrence a logical extension of the privacy rights recognized in Griswold, Eisenstadt, Roe, Carey, and Casey, correcting a deviation from that logic in Bowers? Or did Lawrence take a broader view of the liberty interest at stake than had been taken in earlier decisions? Consider the view that "[p]art of the Court's response was simply to ratchet up the level of generality at which the liberty interest was described: rather than having a constitutional right to engage in oral or anal sex, individuals have a constitutionally protected interest in creating a 'personal relationship' in which 'sexuality finds overt expression in intimate conduct with another person.'" Karlan, "The Boundaries of Liberty After Lawrence v. Texas—Foreword: Loving Lawrence," 102 Mich. L. Rev. 1447 (2004). If that is so, then what are the implications of Lawrence for challenges to laws that continue to criminalize such private sexual practices as adultery, fornication, incest or bigamy? Was the singling out of gay oral or anal sexual conduct important to the result in Lawrence? Or if gay sex is protected against criminalization, is heterosexual sexual conduct likewise, by necessary implication, broadly protected from legal prohibition? The New Jersey Supreme Court held so as early as 1977, writing that "the conduct statutorily defined as fornication involves, by its very nature, a fundamental personal choice. Thus, the statute [barring fornication] infringes upon the right of privacy." State v. Saunders, 381 A.2d 333 (N.J. 1977); accord State v. Pilcher, 242 N.W.2d 348 (Iowa 1976).

What was the standard of scrutiny employed in Lawrence? Justice Kennedy never specifies one. Did the Court, in holding that the Texas law "furthers no legitimate state interest which can justify its intrusion into the personal and private life of the individual," simply strike down the Texas sodomy law under rational basis review, as Justice Scalia suggests disapprovingly in dissent? Or does the clause suggest heightened scrutiny and the lack of a sufficiently weighty interest to justify such an intrusion? Consider the view that, despite the lack of formulaic language, the Court must have been applying a form of strict scrutiny: "[The] strictness of the Court's standard in Lawrence, however articulated, could hardly have been more obvious. To search for the magic words proclaiming the right protected in Lawrence to be 'fundamental,' and to assume that in the absence of those words mere rationality review applied, is to universalize what is in fact only an occasional practice. Moreover, it requires overlooking passage after passage in which the Court's opinion indeed invoked the talismanic verbal formula of substantive due process." Tribe, "Lawrence v. Texas: The 'Fundamental Right' that Dare Not Speak Its Name," 117 Harv. L. Rev. 1893 (2004).

After Lawrence, is it necessary to demonstrate that a law infringes upon a "fundamental right" in order to win a claim under substantive due process? Justice Scalia noted in dissent that "nowhere does the Court's opinion declare that homosexual sodomy is a 'fundamental right' under the Due Process Clause." Did Lawrence announce a new, general presumption of liberty? Is a showing that a law implicates any aspect of liberty sufficient to shift the burden to the government to justify the law? Consider the view that "Lawrence ignores [any] sharp bifurcation between 'fundamental' liberty interests and other liberty interests. It instead focuses on the particular liberty interests endangered by the Texas statute, savoring their unique valence and exploring their particular significance." Post, "The Supreme Court, 2002 Term—Foreword: Fashioning the Legal Constitution: Culture, Courts, and Law," 117 Harv. L. Rev. 4 (2003). For an argument that the Court should abandon any effort to "distinguish[ ] those liberties that merit enhanced protection from those that do not," and should instead enforce a rebuttable presumption of liberty against all police power regulations, see Barnett, "Scrutiny Land," 106 Mich. L. Rev. 1479 (2008).

2. ***Due process vs. equal protection for claims of gay rights.*** Why did the Court use the Due Process Clause as the basis for striking down the Texas same-sex sodomy law, instead of the Equal Protection Clause, as in Romer? Justice O'Connor declined to repudiate her own vote with the majority in Bowers, opining in her concurrence that the Texas law, which targeted only same-sex sodomy, was properly reviewed under an equal protection analysis. But Justice Kennedy expressed concern that, should the law be struck down on that basis, the Texas legislature could simply reenact the law to prohibit all sodomy. Was this a realistic likelihood? Would the majority of Texas citizens support a law banning all sodomy, even in the context of heterosexual married couples, if the law was truly going to be enforced uniformly across the population? Would they be likely to support such a law only if they knew it would be enforced primarily or exclusively against gay people? Would this type of disparate enforcement present its own equal protection violation? Recall Justice Stevens's dissent in Bowers.

If Lawrence had been decided before Romer, how would the analysis in Romer have changed? The level of generality of the Lawrence right is, once again, a key inquiry here. If Lawrence established a fundamental right to engage in intimate personal relationships regardless of sexual orientation, then do all classifications on the basis of sexuality trigger strict scrutiny, the most difficult equal protection standard of review to satisfy? Could judicial nervousness regarding the far-reaching implications of such a decision explain the Lawrence Court's decision to employ substantive due process and to forego equal protection analysis?

The comparison of due process and equal protection, as a source of rights for gay and lesbian people, also turns on how sexual orientation is defined. Is sexual orientation predictive of conduct that should be protected from invasion under the Due Process Clause, or a status that should be protected against discrimination under the Equal Protection Clause? Consider the view that "[t]he situation of gay people provokes an 'analogical crisis,' because in some ways it involves regulation of particular acts in which gay people engage, and so seems most amenable to analysis under the liberty prong of the due process clause, while in other ways it involves regulation of a group of people who are defined not so much by what they *do* in the privacy of their bedrooms, but by who they *are* in the public sphere. [Homosexuality] straddles the line between conduct and status in ways that make it hard to apply conventional constitutional doctrine." Karlan, "Loving Lawrence," 102 Mich. L. Rev. 1447 (2004). See also Sunstein, "Sexual Orientation and the Constitution: A Note on the Relationship Between Due Process and Equal Protection," 55 U. Chi. L. Rev. 1161 (1988).

Alternatively, does the question of due process versus equal protection present a false dichotomy? The Court's opinion in Lawrence may reflect a recognition by Justice Kennedy that a narrow decision under the Equal

Protection Clause would have been inadequate without a substantive due process dimension, and that the two strands were intertwined like a double helix. Consider the view that "Lawrence, more than any other decision in the Supreme Court's history, both presupposed and advanced an explicitly equality-based and relationally situated theory of substantive liberty. The 'liberty' of which the Court spoke was as much about equal dignity and respect as it was about freedom of action—more so, in fact. And the Court left no doubt that it was protecting the equal liberty and dignity not of atomistic individuals torn from their social contexts, but of people as they relate to, and interact with, one another. [Because] the Bowers judgment and opinion (and their consequences) contributed to social and cultural construction of stigmatized gay and lesbian identities, the 'baby step' of holding the Texas ban on same-sex sodomy unconstitutional on purportedly narrower equal protection grounds, though logically available to the Lawrence Court, would have been woefully inadequate with respect to the twin constitutional commitments of equal respect and equal dignity." Tribe, "Lawrence v. Texas: The 'Fundamental Right' that Dare Not Speak Its Name," 117 Harv. L. Rev. 1893 (2004).

In both Romer and Lawrence, Justice Kennedy avoided the application of the conventional tiers of scrutiny, purporting to apply deferential standards of review while finding that the laws could not survive. Was the avoidance of the tiers of scrutiny simply a result of the thorny issues surrounding sexual orientation? Was it because both opinions shared the same author? Did it turn on the fact that sodomy laws had slipped into desuetude? See Sunstein, "Liberty After Lawrence," 65 Ohio St. L.J. 1059 (2004).

3. ***Lawrence and stare decisis.*** Justice Kennedy, the author of Lawrence, had no difficulty overruling the 17-year old decision in Bowers v. Hardwick, yet joined the joint opinion in Casey expressly declining to overrule Roe v. Wade. Can Lawrence's approach to stare decisis be reconciled with Casey's? Justice Scalia's dissent in Lawrence criticized the majority for inconsistency, suggesting that Roe and Casey had generated the same grounds for overrule that the Lawrence majority cited with respect to Bowers, including sustained public criticism, and that there was at least as much reason to uphold Bowers as to uphold Roe, including the long reliance society had had on morals laws. Can Roe and Bowers be persuasively distinguished with respect to their force as precedents?

4. ***Use of comparative constitutional law.*** Justice Kennedy's opinion in Lawrence, for the first time in a Supreme Court majority opinion, cited with approval an authority from European law. Twice in his opinion, Justice Kennedy referred to a decision by the European Court of Human Rights to protect private, consensual gay sexual conduct. In Dudgeon v. United Kingdom, 45 Eur. Ct. H.R. (1981), the European court held that laws penalizing homosexual conduct were invalid under the European Convention on Human Rights, and the decision became binding on all nations that are members of the Council of Europe. According to Justice Kennedy, it was important to take judicial notice of the laws throughout the larger Western civilization of which the United States is a part because there was nothing to suggest that the governmental interest in proscribing such conduct was more compelling in this country than in the others.

This was not the first time in recent years that the Court was influenced by comparison to foreign judicial opinions. In **Atkins v. Virginia**, 536 U.S.

304 (2002), a case reviewing the Eighth Amendment implications of executing convicted criminal defendants who are mentally retarded, the Court cited in a footnote an amicus brief by the European Union, stating that "within the world community, the imposition of the death penalty for crimes committed by mentally retarded offenders is overwhelmingly disapproved." Similarly, in a 2003 television interview, Justice Breyer stated that he "see[s] all the time how the world really—it's trite but it's true—is growing together. Through commerce, through globalization, through the spread of democratic institutions, through immigration to America, it's becoming more and more one world of many different kinds of people. And how they're going to live together across the world will be the challenge, and [how] our Constitution fits into the governing documents of other nations, I think will be a challenge for the next generations." Justice O'Connor has also been quoted as saying that "over time [the Court] will rely increasingly, or take notice at least increasingly, on international and foreign courts in examining domestic issues." Is the U.S. Supreme Court now engaged in a desirable trend toward taking into account other nations' decisions on the scope of human rights? Is the Court justifiably worried about the United States being an outlier in Western civilization? Should such concern carry over to other areas in which the United States is already an outlier, such as the death penalty and firearms regulation? Or should Americans be concerned, as Justice Scalia suggested in his Lawrence dissent, that the U.S. Constitution not be subverted by "foreign moods, fads, or fashions"? For the view that "[l]ooking beyond our borders came naturally to the Framers," and that Justice Kennedy was "clearly right that homosexual sodomy laws violate the modern understanding of human rights" as found by several foreign courts and other "respected international bodies," see Farber, "Constitutional Cadenzas," 56 Drake L. Rev. 833 (2008).

5. ***Lawrence and same-sex marriage.*** In Lawrence, Justice Kennedy pointedly noted that its decision invalidating a same-sex sodomy law on due process grounds "does not involve whether the government must give formal recognition to any relationship that homosexual persons seek to enter." Justice Scalia's dissent in Lawrence, however, warned that state laws against same-sex marriage were "called into question by today's decision." Indeed, just five months after Lawrence was handed down, the Supreme Judicial Court of Massachusetts held that the state's limitation of marriage to that between a man and a woman violated both the Due Process and Equal Protection Clauses of the state constitution, making Massachusetts the first state in the nation with legal same-sex marriage. Goodridge v. Department of Public Health, 798 N.E.2d 941 (Mass. 2003). Goodridge affirmed that "[whether] and whom to marry, how to express sexual intimacy, and whether and how to establish a family [are] among the most basic of every individual's liberty and due process rights," citing both Lawrence and Casey. Ten more states, plus the District of Columbia, followed over the next ten years, legalizing same-sex marriage via legislation, court ruling, or statewide referendum.

Consider whether there was something in particular about state courts that made them more receptive more quickly to these kinds of dignitary arguments for marriage equality. Professor William Rubenstein posited, long before the movement for same-sex marriage, that despite the general preference for federal court in civil rights litigation, state courts were for three reasons more promising sites for gay and lesbian activism: technical competence in family law and other related issues, greater familiarity with lesbian and gay people through run-of-the-mill legal and real-world encounters, and faster-acting majoritarian pressures. See Rubenstein, "The Myth of Superiority," 16 Const. Comment. 599 (1999). To what extent were these arguments borne out by subsequent developments?

Even in those states that recognized same-sex marriage, gay and lesbian couples faced a legal obstacle put in place by the federal government. In 1996, Congress had enacted, and President Clinton signed, the "Defense of Marriage Act" (DOMA), which defined marriage, for the purpose of all federal benefits, as "only a legal union between one man and one woman as husband and wife." After two federal courts of appeals invalidated this definition on equal protection grounds, the Supreme Court agreed to take up the question of DOMA's constitutionality, and invalidated its marriage definition under the equal protection principles that had long been found implicit as applicable to the federal government under the Due Process Clause of the 5th Amendment. See Bolling v. Sharpe [p. 663 below].

United States v. Windsor

570 U.S. 744, 133 S. Ct. 2675, 186 L. Ed. 2d 808 (2013).

■ JUSTICE KENNEDY delivered the opinion of the Court, in which JUSTICES GINSBURG, BREYER, SOTOMAYOR and KAGAN joined.

[In] 1996, as some States were beginning to consider the concept of same-sex marriage, and before any State had acted to permit it, Congress enacted the Defense of Marriage Act (DOMA). [Section] 3 of DOMA provides as follows: "In determining the meaning of any Act of Congress, or of any ruling, regulation, or interpretation of the various administrative bureaus and agencies of the United States, the word 'marriage' means only a legal union between one man and one woman as husband and wife, and the word 'spouse' refers only to a person of the opposite sex who is a husband or a wife." The definitional provision does not by its terms forbid States from enacting laws permitting same-sex marriages or civil unions or providing state benefits to residents in that status. The enactment's comprehensive definition of marriage for purposes of all federal statutes and other regulations or directives covered by its terms, however, does control over 1,000 federal laws in which marital or spousal status is addressed as a matter of federal law.

Edith Windsor and Thea Spyer met in New York City in 1963 and began a long-term relationship. Windsor and Spyer registered as domestic partners when New York City gave that right to same-sex couples in 1993. Concerned about Spyer's health, the couple made the 2007 trip to Canada for their marriage, but they continued to reside in New York City. The State of New York deems their Ontario marriage to be a valid one. Spyer died in February 2009, and left her entire estate to Windsor. Because DOMA denies federal recognition to same-sex spouses, Windsor did not qualify for the marital exemption from the federal estate tax, which excludes from taxation "any interest in property which passes or has passed from the decedent to his surviving spouse." 26 U.S.C. § 2056(a). Windsor paid $363,053 in estate taxes and sought a refund. The Internal Revenue Service denied the refund, concluding that, under DOMA, Windsor was not a "surviving spouse." Windsor commenced this refund suit. She contended that DOMA violates the guarantee of equal protection, as applied to the Federal Government through the Fifth Amendment.

III. [Until] recent years, many citizens had not even considered the possibility that two persons of the same sex might aspire to occupy the same status and dignity as that of a man and woman in lawful marriage. For marriage between a man and a woman no doubt had been thought of by most people as essential to the very definition of that term and to its role and function throughout the history of civilization. That belief, for many who long have held it, became even more urgent, more cherished when challenged. For others, however, came the beginnings of a new perspective, a new insight. The limitation of lawful marriage to heterosexual couples, which for centuries had been deemed both necessary and fundamental, came to be seen in New York and certain other States as an unjust exclusion.

Slowly at first and then in rapid course, the laws of New York came to acknowledge the urgency of this issue for same-sex couples who wanted to affirm their commitment to one another before their children, their family, their friends, and their community. And so New York recognized same-sex marriages performed elsewhere; and then it later amended its own marriage laws to permit same-sex marriage. New York, in common with, as of this writing, 11 other States and the District of Columbia, decided that same-sex couples should have the right to marry and so live with pride in themselves and their union and in a status of equality with all other married persons.

[By] history and tradition the definition and regulation of marriage, as will be discussed in more detail, has been treated as being within the authority and realm of the separate States. Yet it is further established that Congress, in enacting discrete statutes, can make determinations that bear on marital rights and privileges. Though [other federal statutes] establish the constitutionality of limited federal laws that regulate the meaning of marriage in order to further federal policy, DOMA has a far greater reach; for it enacts a directive applicable to over 1,000 federal statutes and the whole realm of federal regulations. And its operation is directed to a class of persons that the laws of New York, and of 11 other States, have sought to protect. [The] recognition of civil marriages is central to state domestic relations law applicable to its residents and citizens. The definition of marriage is the foundation of the State's broader authority to regulate the subject of domestic relations with respect to the "[protection] of offspring, property interests, and the enforcement of marital responsibilities." "[The] states, at the time of the adoption of the Constitution, possessed full power over the subject of marriage and divorce . . . [and] the Constitution delegated no authority to the Government of the United States on the subject of marriage and divorce." Haddock v. Haddock, 201 U.S. 562 (1906). [The] Federal Government, through our history, has deferred to state-law policy decisions with respect to domestic relations.

Against this background DOMA rejects the long-established precept that the incidents, benefits, and obligations of marriage are uniform for all married couples within each State, though they may vary, subject to constitutional guarantees, from one State to the next. Despite these considerations, it is unnecessary to decide whether this federal intrusion on state power is a violation of the Constitution because it disrupts the federal balance. The State's power in defining the marital relation is of central relevance in this case quite apart from principles of federalism. Here the State's decision to give this class of persons the right to marry conferred upon them a dignity and status of immense import. When the State used its historic and essential authority to define the marital relation in this way, its role and its power in making the decision enhanced the recognition, dignity, and protection of the class in their own community. DOMA, because of its reach and extent, departs from this history and tradition of reliance on state law to define marriage.

[New York's] actions were without doubt a proper exercise of its sovereign authority within our federal system, all in the way that the Framers of the Constitution intended. [The] States' interest in defining and regulating the marital relation, subject to constitutional guarantees, stems from the understanding that marriage is more than a routine classification for purposes of certain statutory benefits. Private, consensual sexual intimacy between two adult persons of the same sex may not be punished by the State, and it can form "but one element in a personal bond that is more enduring." [Lawrence.] By its recognition of the validity of same-sex marriages performed in other jurisdictions and then by authorizing same-sex unions and same-sex marriages, New York sought to give further protection and dignity to that bond. For same-sex couples who wished to be married, the State acted to give their lawful conduct a lawful status. This status is a far-reaching legal acknowledgment of the intimate relationship between two people, a relationship deemed by the State worthy of dignity in the community equal with all other marriages. It reflects both the community's considered perspective on the historical roots of the institution of marriage and its evolving understanding of the meaning of equality.

IV. DOMA seeks to injure the very class New York seeks to protect. By doing so it violates basic due process and equal protection principles applicable to the Federal Government. The Constitution's guarantee of equality "must at the very least mean that a bare congressional desire to harm a politically unpopular group cannot" justify disparate treatment of that group. Department of Agriculture v. Moreno, [p. 651 below]. In determining whether a law is motived by an improper animus or purpose, " '[discriminations] of an unusual character' " especially require careful consideration. [Romer.] DOMA cannot survive under these principles. The responsibility of the States for the regulation of domestic relations is an important indicator of the substantial societal impact the State's classifications have in the daily lives and customs of its people. DOMA's unusual deviation from the usual tradition of recognizing and accepting state definitions of marriage here operates to deprive same-sex couples of the benefits and responsibilities that come with the federal recognition of their marriages. This is strong evidence of a law having the purpose and effect of disapproval of that class. The avowed purpose and practical effect of the law here in question are to impose a disadvantage, a separate status, and so a stigma upon all who enter into same-sex marriages made lawful by the unquestioned authority of the States.

The history of DOMA's enactment and its own text demonstrate that interference with the equal dignity of same-sex marriages, a dignity conferred by the States in the exercise of their sovereign power, was more than an incidental effect of the federal statute. It was its essence. The House Report announced its conclusion that "it is both appropriate and necessary for Congress to do what it can to defend the institution of traditional heterosexual marriage. [The] effort to redefine 'marriage' to extend to homosexual couples is a truly radical proposal that would fundamentally alter the institution of marriage." The House concluded that DOMA expresses "both moral disapproval of homosexuality, and a moral conviction that heterosexuality better comports with traditional (especially Judeo-Christian) morality." The stated purpose of the law was to promote an "interest in protecting the traditional moral teachings reflected in heterosexual-only marriage laws." Were there any doubt of this far-reaching purpose, the title of the Act confirms it: The Defense of Marriage.

[DOMA's] operation in practice confirms this purpose. [DOMA's] principal purpose is to impose inequality, not for other reasons like governmental efficiency. [By] creating two contradictory marriage regimes within the same State, DOMA forces same-sex couples to live as married for the purpose of state law but unmarried for the purpose of federal law, thus diminishing the stability and predictability of basic personal relations the State has found it proper to acknowledge and protect. By this dynamic DOMA undermines both the public and private significance of state-sanctioned same-sex marriages; for it tells those couples, and all the world, that their otherwise valid marriages are unworthy of federal recognition. This places same-sex couples in an unstable position of being in a second-tier marriage. The differentiation demeans the couple, whose moral and sexual choices the Constitution protects, see Lawrence, and whose relationship the State has sought to dignify. And it humiliates tens of thousands of children now being raised by same-sex couples. The law in question makes it even more difficult for the children to understand the integrity and closeness of their own family and its concord with other families in their community and in their daily lives.

Under DOMA, same-sex married couples have their lives burdened, by reason of government decree, in visible and public ways. By its great reach, DOMA touches many aspects of married and family life, from the mundane to the profound. It prevents same-sex married couples from obtaining government healthcare benefits they would otherwise receive. It deprives them of the Bankruptcy Code's special protections for domestic-support obligations. It forces them to follow a complicated procedure to file their state and federal taxes jointly. It prohibits them from being buried together in veterans' cemeteries. For certain married couples, DOMA's unequal effects are even more serious. The federal penal code makes it a crime to "assaul[t], kidna[p], or murde[r] . . . a member of the immediate family" of "a United States official, a United States judge, [or] a Federal law enforcement officer," with the intent to influence or retaliate against that official. Although a "spouse" qualifies as a member of the officer's "immediate family," DOMA makes this protection inapplicable to same-sex spouses. DOMA also brings financial harm to children of same-sex couples. It raises the cost of health care for families by taxing health benefits provided by employers to their workers' same-sex spouses. And it denies or reduces benefits allowed to families upon the loss of a spouse and parent, benefits that are an integral part of family security.

[The] class to which DOMA directs its restrictions and restraints are those persons who are joined in same-sex marriages made lawful by the State. [The] federal statute is invalid, for no legitimate purpose overcomes the purpose and effect to disparage and to injure those whom the State, by its marriage laws, sought to protect in personhood and dignity. By seeking to displace this protection and treating those persons as living in marriages less respected than others, the federal statute is in violation of the Fifth

Amendment. This opinion and its holding are confined to those lawful marriages.

■ CHIEF JUSTICE ROBERTS, dissenting.

[Interests] in uniformity and stability amply justified Congress's decision to retain the definition of marriage that, at that point, had been adopted by every State in our Nation, and every nation in the world. The majority sees a more sinister motive, pointing out that the Federal Government has generally (though not uniformly) deferred to state definitions of marriage in the past. That is true, of course, but none of those prior state-by-state variations had involved differences over something—as the majority puts it—"thought of by most people as essential to the very definition of [marriage] and to its role and function throughout the history of civilization." That the Federal Government treated this fundamental question differently than it treated variations over consanguinity or minimum age is hardly surprising—and hardly enough to support a conclusion that the "principal purpose" of the 342 Representatives and 85 Senators who voted for it, and the President who signed it, was a bare desire to harm. Nor do the snippets of legislative history and the banal title of the Act to which the majority points suffice to make such a showing. At least without some more convincing evidence that the Act's principal purpose was to codify malice, and that it furthered *no* legitimate government interests, I would not tar the political branches with the brush of bigotry.

But while I disagree with the result to which the majority's analysis leads it in this case, I think it more important to point out that its analysis leads no further. The Court does not have before it, and the logic of its opinion does not decide, the distinct question whether the States, in the exercise of their "historic and essential authority to define the marital relation" may continue to utilize the traditional definition of marriage. [The] dominant theme of the majority opinion is that the Federal Government's intrusion into an area "central to state domestic relations law applicable to its residents and citizens" is sufficiently "unusual" to set off alarm bells. I think the majority goes off course, as I have said, but it is undeniable that its judgment is based on federalism.

■ JUSTICE SCALIA, with whom JUSTICE THOMAS joins, and with whom CHIEF JUSTICE ROBERTS joins as to Part I [on the issue of justiciability; see p. 36, above], dissenting.

II. [There] are many remarkable things about the majority's merits holding. The first is how rootless and shifting its justifications are. For example, the opinion starts with [discussion of] the traditional power of States to define domestic relations—initially fooling many readers, I am sure, into thinking that this is a federalism opinion. But we are eventually told that "it is unnecessary to decide whether this federal intrusion on state power is a violation of the Constitution," and that "[the] State's power in defining the marital relation is of central relevance in this case quite apart from principles of federalism" because "the State's decision to give this class of persons the right to marry conferred upon them a dignity and status of immense import."

[Equally] perplexing are the opinion's references to "the Constitution's guarantee of equality." [If] this is meant to be an equal-protection opinion, it is a confusing one. The opinion does not resolve and indeed does not even mention what had been the central question in this litigation: whether, under the Equal Protection Clause, laws restricting marriage to a man and a woman are reviewed for more than mere rationality. [In] accord with my previously expressed skepticism about the Court's "tiers of scrutiny" approach, I would review this classification only for its rationality. [The] majority never utters the dread words "substantive due process," perhaps sensing the disrepute into which that doctrine has fallen. [The] opinion does not argue that same-sex marriage is "deeply rooted in this Nation's history and tradition," a claim that would of course be quite absurd. So would the further suggestion (also necessary, under our substantive-due-process precedents) that a world in which DOMA exists is one bereft of " 'ordered liberty.' "

[As] I have observed before, the Constitution does not forbid the government to enforce traditional moral and sexual norms. [The] Constitution neither requires nor forbids our society to approve of same-sex marriage, much as it neither requires nor forbids us to approve of no-fault divorce, polygamy, or the consumption of alcohol. However, even setting aside traditional moral disapproval of same-sex marriage (or indeed same-sex sex), there are many perfectly valid—indeed, downright boring—justifying rationales for this legislation. Their existence ought to be the end of this case. For they give the lie to the Court's conclusion that only those with hateful hearts could have voted "aye" on this Act. And more importantly, they serve to make the contents of the legislators' hearts quite irrelevant.

[To] choose just one of these defenders' arguments, DOMA avoids difficult choice-of-law issues that will now arise absent a uniform federal definition of marriage. [DOMA] avoided [uncertainty] by specifying which marriages would be recognized for federal purposes. That is a classic purpose for a definitional provision. Further, DOMA preserves the intended effects of prior legislation against then-unforeseen changes in circumstance. [That] is not animus—just stabilizing prudence.

The penultimate sentence of the majority's opinion is a naked declaration that "[this] opinion and its holding are confined" to those couples "joined in same-sex marriages made lawful by the State." [In] my opinion, however, the view that *this* Court will take of state prohibition of same-sex marriage is indicated beyond mistaking by today's opinion. [By] formally declaring anyone opposed to same-sex marriage an enemy of human decency, the majority arms well every challenger to a state law restricting marriage to its traditional definition. [That] is why the language is there. The result will be a judicial distortion of our society's debate over marriage—a debate that can seem in need of our clumsy "help" only to a member of this institution. [We] might have covered ourselves with honor today, by promising all sides of this debate that it was theirs to settle and that we would respect their resolution. We might have let the People decide.

■ JUSTICE ALITO, with whom JUSTICE THOMAS joins as to Parts II and III, dissenting.

II. [The] family is an ancient and universal human institution. Family structure reflects the characteristics of a civilization, and changes in family structure and in the popular understanding of marriage and the family can have profound effects. Past changes in the understanding of marriage—for example, the gradual ascendance of the idea that romantic love is a prerequisite to marriage—have had far-reaching consequences. But the process by which such consequences come about is complex, involving the interaction of numerous factors, and tends to occur over an extended period of time. We can expect something similar to take place if same-sex marriage becomes widely accepted. The long-term consequences of this change are not now known and are unlikely to be ascertainable for some time to come. There are those who think that allowing same-sex marriage will seriously undermine the institution of marriage. At present, no one—including social scientists, philosophers, and historians—can predict with any certainty what the long-term ramifications of widespread acceptance of same-sex marriage will be. And judges are certainly not equipped to make such an assessment. The Members of this Court have the authority and the responsibility to interpret and apply the Constitution. [But] the Constitution simply does not speak to the issue of same-sex marriage. In our system of government, ultimate sovereignty rests with the people, and the people have the right to control their own destiny. Any change on a question so fundamental should be made by the people through their elected officials.

III. By asking the Court to strike down DOMA as not satisfying some form of heightened scrutiny, Windsor and the United States are really seeking to have the Court resolve a debate between two competing views of marriage. The first and older view, which I will call the "traditional" or "conjugal" view, sees marriage as an intrinsically opposite-sex institution. BLAG notes that virtually every culture, including many not influenced by the Abrahamic religions, has limited marriage to people of the opposite sex. [And] BLAG attempts to explain this phenomenon by arguing that the institution of marriage was created for the purpose of channeling heterosexual intercourse into a structure that supports child rearing. Others explain the basis for the institution in more philosophical terms. They argue that marriage is essentially the solemnizing of a comprehensive, exclusive, permanent union that is intrinsically ordered to producing new life, even if it does not always do so. While modern cultural changes have weakened the link between marriage and procreation in the popular mind, there is no doubt that, throughout human history and across many cultures, marriage has been viewed as an exclusively opposite-sex institution and as one inextricably linked to procreation and biological kinship.

The other, newer view is what I will call the "consent-based" vision of marriage, a vision that primarily defines marriage as the solemnization of mutual commitment—marked by strong emotional attachment and sexual attraction—between two persons. At least as it applies to heterosexual couples, this view of marriage now plays a very prominent role in the popular understanding of the institution. Indeed, our popular culture is infused with this understanding of marriage. Proponents of same-sex marriage argue that because gender differentiation is not relevant to this vision, the exclusion of same-sex couples from the institution of marriage is rank discrimination.

The Constitution does not codify either of these views of marriage (although I suspect it would have been hard at the time of the adoption of the Constitution or the Fifth Amendment to find Americans who did not take the traditional view for granted). The silence of the Constitution on this question should be enough to end the matter as far as the judiciary is concerned. Yet, Windsor and the United States implicitly ask us to endorse the consent-based view of marriage and to reject the traditional view, thereby arrogating to ourselves the power to decide a question that philosophers, historians, social scientists, and theologians are better qualified to explore. Because our constitutional order assigns the resolution of questions of this nature to the people, I would not presume to enshrine either vision of marriage in our constitutional jurisprudence.

THE MEANING AND IMPLICATIONS OF WINDSOR

1. ***Windsor's rationale.*** The Court's reasoning in Windsor rested on the fact that DOMA established separate and unequal federal treatment of couples that the state had chosen to treat alike. Why, then, did Justice Kennedy not base his analysis on equal protection alone? Would the principle the Court quoted from earlier equal protection decisions—that "a bare congressional desire to harm a politically unpopular group" cannot justify unequal treatment—have sufficed by itself to strike down DOMA's federal definition of marriage? Is it possible that the majority found some of the alternative justifications cited by the dissents and DOMA's defenders—such as the federal interest in uniform rules and the need to avoid complicated choice-of-law problems—reasonable enough to satisfy minimum rationality review?

Perhaps the idea that substantive due process protects dignity, not just privacy, rendered the traditional levels-of-scrutiny analysis inapplicable. The idea that the Constitution upholds a fundamental right to dignity implies that this right is held by all people equally; therefore, any statute that works a deprivation of dignity also infringes equality.

If this is so, could the Court have based the decision in Windsor on substantive due process alone? Was the opinion's inclusion of equal protection language an attempt to cabin the Court's holding and provide a limiting principle, leaving existing state bans on same-sex marriage unaffected? If stigmatizing same-sex relationships constitutes a deprivation of dignity, would a gradual approach, allowing state laws with the same effect to remain in place, have been consistent with this underlying premise?

2. ***Lawrence and Windsor: differing conceptions of dignity.*** Both Lawrence and Windsor cited individual dignity as a primary justification for striking down laws that burden gay and lesbian people, but the visions of dignity advanced by the two opinions differ in key respects. Lawrence conceptualized dignity as inherent in the individual, and explained that restricting a person's choice of sexual partner constitutes an invasion of that right by the state. Windsor, by contrast, understood dignity as a status conferred by the state on particular relationships; DOMA thus infringed a dignity interest that the state had created. Can these two definitions of dignity coexist? If the protection of equal dignity is a new constitutional principle—of the sort that typically develops gradually through multiple judicial decisions—is it necessary that the principle present perfect coherence right away? As you read the opinion in Obergefell v. Hodges, p. 583 below, recognizing a nationwide right to same-sex marriage even in states that do not choose to recognize such marriages, consider whether the Court adopted either Lawrence's or Windsor's idea of dignity, or whether it found a way to accommodate both.

3. ***Windsor and federalism.*** To what extent was Windsor's invocation of federalism principles relevant to the outcome? If DOMA deprived same-sex couples of dignity and the equal protection of the laws, does it matter whether the discrimination occurred in an area of law that the

states had traditionally regulated? Imagine that DOMA had included a provision specifically excluding sexual-orientation discrimination from the coverage of federal civil rights statutes. Would the lack of a tradition leaving such matters exclusively to the states have rendered this provision less vulnerable to Fifth Amendment-based equal protection challenge?

Windsor might be read as establishing a form of heightened equal protection scrutiny for laws that impinge on an area of law that has traditionally been reserved to the states. The Court once maintained that the Tenth Amendment outright forbade federal interference with the states' performance of "traditional governmental functions," but overruled that decision, see pp. 169–170, above, in part because of the difficulty of defining what should be considered "traditional governmental functions." Does Windsor present similar line-drawing problems? Could federal tort-reform legislation, capping punitive damages in some types of cases but not others, be challenged on the grounds that tort law has traditionally been reserved to the states? Or does domestic relations law have a unique status? The fact that federal courts abstain from family-law cases, even when they could properly be heard under diversity jurisdiction, supports the latter view.

4. ***Windsor and state recognition of same-sex marriage.*** The trend of expanding recognition of same-sex marriage that had begun in the years following Lawrence accelerated after Windsor. By the end of 2014, four federal courts of appeals had invalidated the state same-sex marriage bans within their jurisdiction. A contrary decision in the Sixth Circuit, upholding bans in four states, created a split in the circuits, and opened the way for the Supreme Court to determine, once and for all, whether the Constitution confers on same-sex couples a right of access to the institution of marriage. Justice Kennedy spoke for the Court once again in the following opinion:

Obergefell v. Hodges

576 U.S. ___, 135 S. Ct. 2584, 192 L. Ed. 2d 609 (2015).

■ JUSTICE KENNEDY delivered the opinion of the Court, in which JUSTICES GINSBURG, BREYER, SOTOMAYOR and KAGAN joined.

The Constitution promises liberty to all within its reach, a liberty that includes certain specific rights that allow persons, within a lawful realm, to define and express their identity. The petitioners in these cases seek to find that liberty by marrying someone of the same sex and having their marriages deemed lawful on the same terms and conditions as marriages between persons of the opposite sex.

[From] their beginning to their most recent page, the annals of human history reveal the transcendent importance of marriage. The lifelong union of a man and a woman always has promised nobility and dignity to all persons, without regard to their station in life. Marriage is sacred to those who live by their religions and offers unique fulfillment to those who find meaning in the secular realm. Its dynamic allows two people to find a life that could not be found alone, for a marriage becomes greater than just the two persons. Rising from the most basic human needs, marriage is essential to our most profound hopes and aspirations.

The centrality of marriage to the human condition makes it unsurprising that the institution has existed for millennia and across civilizations. Since the dawn of history, marriage has transformed strangers into relatives, binding families and societies together. [There] are untold references to the beauty of marriage in religious and philosophical texts spanning time, cultures, and faiths, as well as in art and literature in all their forms. It is fair and necessary to say these references were based on the understanding that marriage is a union between two persons of the opposite sex.

That history is the beginning of these cases. The respondents say it should be the end as well. To them, it would demean a timeless institution if the concept and lawful status of marriage were extended to two persons of the same sex. Marriage, in their view, is by its nature a gender-differentiated union of man and woman. This view long has been held and continues to be held in good faith by reasonable and sincere people here and throughout the world.

The petitioners acknowledge this history but contend that these cases cannot end there. Were their intent to demean the revered idea and reality of marriage, the petitioners' claims would be of a different order. But that is neither their purpose nor their submission. To the contrary, it is the enduring importance of marriage that underlies the petitioners' contentions. This, they say, is their whole point. Far from seeking to devalue marriage, the petitioners seek it for themselves because of their respect and need for its privileges and responsibilities. And their immutable nature dictates that same-sex marriage is their only real path to this profound commitment.

[The] ancient origins of marriage confirm its centrality, but it has not stood in isolation from developments in law and society. The history of marriage is one of both continuity and change. That institution even as confined to opposite-sex relations has evolved over time.

For example, marriage was once viewed as an arrangement by the couple's parents based on political, religious, and financial concerns; but by the time of the Nation's founding it was understood to be a voluntary contract between a man and a woman. As the role and status of women changed, the institution further evolved. Under the centuries-old doctrine of coverture, a married man and woman were treated by the State as a single, male-dominated legal entity. As women gained legal, political, and property rights, and as society began to understand that women have their own equal dignity, the law of coverture was abandoned. [These] new insights have strengthened, not weakened, the institution of marriage.

[The] Court has long held the right to marry is protected by the Constitution. In Loving v. Virginia (1967; 672 above), [a] unanimous Court held marriage is "one of the vital personal rights essential to the orderly pursuit of happiness by free men." [Over] time and in other contexts, the Court has reiterated that the right to marry is fundamental under the Due Process Clause. It cannot be denied that this Court's cases describing the right to marry presumed a relationship involving opposite-sex partners. The Court, like many institutions, has made assumptions defined by the world and time of which it is a part.

[Still, t]his Court's cases have expressed constitutional principles of broader reach. [And] in assessing whether the force and rationale of its cases apply to same-sex couples, the Court must respect the basic reasons why the right to marry has been long protected. This analysis compels the conclusion that same-sex couples may exercise the right to marry. The four principles and traditions to be discussed demonstrate that the reasons marriage is fundamental under the Constitution apply with equal force to same-sex couples.

A first premise of the Court's relevant precedents is that the right to personal choice regarding marriage is inherent in the concept of individual autonomy. This abiding connection between marriage and liberty is why Loving invalidated interracial marriage bans under the Due Process Clause. Like choices concerning contraception, family relationships, procreation, and childrearing, all of which are protected by the Constitution, decisions concerning marriage are among the most intimate that an individual can make.

[The] nature of marriage is that, through its enduring bond, two persons together can find other freedoms, such as expression, intimacy, and spirituality. This is true for all persons, whatever their sexual orientation. There is dignity in the bond between two men or two women who seek to marry and in their autonomy to make such profound choices.

A second principle in this Court's jurisprudence is that the right to marry is fundamental because it supports a two-person union unlike any other in its importance to the committed individuals. [Griswold.]

[Marriage] responds to the universal fear that a lonely person might call out only to find no one there. It offers the hope of companionship and understanding and assurance that while both still live there will be someone to care for the other. [While] *Lawrence* confirmed a dimension of freedom that allows individuals to engage in intimate association without criminal liability, it does not follow that freedom stops there. Outlaw to outcast may be a step forward, but it does not achieve the full promise of liberty.

A third basis for protecting the right to marry is that it safeguards children and families and thus draws meaning from related rights of childrearing, procreation, and education.

[As] all parties agree, many same-sex couples provide loving and nurturing homes to their children, whether biological or adopted. And hundreds of thousands of children are presently being raised by such couples. Most States have allowed gays and lesbians to adopt, either as individuals or as couples, and many adopted and foster children have same-sex parents. This provides powerful confirmation from the law itself that gays and lesbians can create loving, supportive families.

Excluding same-sex couples from marriage thus conflicts with a central premise of the right to marry. Without the recognition, stability, and predictability marriage offers, their children suffer the stigma of knowing their families are somehow lesser. They also suffer the significant material costs of being raised by unmarried parents, relegated through no fault of their own to a more difficult and uncertain family life. The marriage laws at issue here thus harm and humiliate the children of same-sex couples.

[Fourth] and finally, this Court's cases and the Nation's traditions make clear that marriage is a keystone of our social order. [For] that reason, just as a couple vows to support each other, so does society pledge to support the couple, offering symbolic recognition and material benefits to protect and nourish the union. Indeed, while the States are in general free to vary the benefits they confer on all married couples, they have throughout our history made marriage the basis for an expanding list of governmental rights, benefits, and responsibilities. These aspects of marital status include: taxation; inheritance and property rights; rules of intestate succession; spousal privilege in the law of evidence; hospital access; medical decisionmaking authority; adoption rights; the rights and benefits of survivors; birth and death certificates; professional ethics rules; campaign finance restrictions; workers' compensation benefits; health insurance; and child custody, support, and visitation rules. [There] is no difference between same- and opposite-sex couples with respect to this principle. Yet by virtue of their exclusion from that institution, same-sex couples are denied the constellation of benefits that the States have linked to marriage. This harm results in more than just material burdens. [It] demeans gays and lesbians for the State to lock them out of a central institution of the Nation's society. Same-sex couples, too, may aspire to the transcendent purposes of marriage and seek fulfillment in its highest meaning.

[The] right of same-sex couples to marry that is part of the liberty promised by the Fourteenth Amendment is derived, too, from that Amendment's guarantee of the equal protection of the laws. The Due Process Clause and the Equal Protection Clause are connected in a profound way, though they set forth independent principles. Rights implicit in liberty and rights secured by equal protection may rest on different precepts and are not always co-extensive, yet in some instances each may be instructive as to the meaning and reach of the other. In any particular case one Clause may be thought to capture the essence of the right in a more accurate and comprehensive way, even as the two Clauses may converge in the identification and definition of the right. This interrelation of the two principles furthers our understanding of what freedom is and must become. [Although] Lawrence elaborated its holding under the Due Process Clause, it acknowledged, and sought to remedy, the continuing inequality that resulted from laws making intimacy in the lives of gays and lesbians a crime against the State. Lawrence therefore drew upon principles of liberty and equality to define and protect the rights of gays and lesbians, holding the State "cannot demean their existence or control their destiny by making their private sexual conduct a crime."

This dynamic also applies to same-sex marriage. [The] marriage laws enforced by the respondents are in essence unequal: same-sex couples are denied all the benefits afforded to opposite-sex couples and are barred from exercising a fundamental right. Especially against a long history of disapproval of their relationships, this denial to same-sex couples of the right to marry works a grave and continuing harm. The imposition of this disability on gays and lesbians serves to disrespect and subordinate them. And the Equal Protection Clause, like the Due Process Clause, prohibits this unjustified infringement of the fundamental right to marry.

These considerations lead to the conclusion that the right to marry is a fundamental right inherent in the liberty of the person, and under the Due Process and Equal Protection Clauses of the Fourteenth Amendment couples of the same-sex may not be deprived of that right and that liberty. The Court now holds that same-sex couples may exercise the fundamental right to marry [and] the State laws challenged by Petitioners in these cases are now held invalid to the extent they exclude same-sex couples from civil marriage on the same terms and conditions as opposite-sex couples.

[No] union is more profound than marriage, for it embodies the highest ideals of love, fidelity, devotion, sacrifice, and family. In forming a marital union, two people become something greater than once they were. As some of the petitioners in these cases demonstrate, marriage embodies a love that may endure even past death. It would misunderstand these men and women to say they disrespect the idea of marriage. Their plea is that they do respect it, respect it so deeply that they seek to find its fulfillment for themselves. Their hope is not to be condemned to live in loneliness, excluded from one of civilization's oldest institutions. They ask for equal dignity in the eyes of the law. The Constitution grants them that right.

■ JUSTICE SCALIA, with whom JUSTICE THOMAS joins, dissenting.

[The] substance of today's decree is not of immense personal importance to me. The law can recognize as marriage whatever sexual attachments and living arrangements it wishes. [It] is of overwhelming importance, however, who it is that rules me. Today's decree says that my Ruler, and the Ruler of 320 million Americans coast-to-coast, is a majority of the nine lawyers on the Supreme Court. The opinion in these cases is the furthest extension in fact—and the furthest extension one can even imagine—of the Court's claimed power to create "liberties" that the Constitution and its Amendments neglect to mention. This practice of constitutional revision by an unelected committee of nine, always accompanied (as it is today) by extravagant praise of liberty, robs the People of the most important liberty they asserted in the Declaration of Independence and won in the Revolution of 1776: the freedom to govern themselves.

[Except] as limited by a constitutional prohibition agreed to by the People, the States are free to adopt whatever laws they like, even those that offend the esteemed Justices' "reasoned judgment." A system of government that makes the People subordinate to a committee of nine unelected lawyers does not deserve to be called a democracy.

Judges are selected precisely for their skill as lawyers; whether they reflect the policy views of a particular constituency is not (or should not be) relevant. Not surprisingly then, the Federal Judiciary is hardly a cross-section of America. Take, for example, this Court, which consists of only nine men and women, all of them successful lawyers who studied at Harvard or Yale Law School. Four of the nine are natives of New York City. Eight of them grew up in east- and west-coast States. Only one hails from the vast expanse in-between. Not a single Southwesterner or even, to tell the truth, a genuine Westerner (California does not count). Not a single evangelical Christian (a group that comprises about one quarter of Americans), or even a Protestant of any denomination. The strikingly unrepresentative character of the body voting on today's social upheaval would be irrelevant if they were functioning as *judges*, answering the legal question whether the American people had ever ratified a constitutional provision that was understood to proscribe the traditional definition of marriage. But of course the Justices in today's majority are not voting on that basis; *they say they are not*. And to allow the policy question of same-sex marriage to be considered and resolved by a select, patrician, highly unrepresentative panel of nine is to violate a principle even more fundamental than no taxation without representation: no social transformation without representation.

[The] opinion is couched in a style that is as pretentious as its content is egotistic. [The] opinion's showy profundities are often profoundly incoherent. [The] world does not expect logic and precision in poetry or inspirational pop-philosophy; it demands them in the law.

[With] each decision of ours that takes from the People a question properly left to them—with each decision that is unabashedly based not on law, but on the "reasoned judgment" of a bare majority of this Court—we move one step closer to being reminded of our impotence.

■ CHIEF JUSTICE ROBERTS, with whom JUSTICE SCALIA and JUSTICE THOMAS join, dissenting.

Petitioners make strong arguments rooted in social policy and considerations of fairness. They contend that same-sex couples should be allowed to affirm their love and commitment through marriage, just like opposite-sex couples. That position has undeniable appeal. [But] this Court is not a legislature. Whether same-sex marriage is a good idea should be of no concern to us. Under the Constitution, judges have power to say what the law is, not what it should be.

[Supporters] of same-sex marriage have achieved considerable success persuading their fellow citizens—through the democratic process—to adopt their view. That ends today. Five lawyers have closed the debate and enacted their own vision of marriage as a matter of constitutional law. Stealing this issue from the people will for many cast a cloud over same-sex marriage, making a dramatic social change that much more difficult to accept.

The majority's decision is an act of will, not legal judgment. The right it announces has no basis in the Constitution or this Court's precedent. [As] a result, the Court invalidates the marriage laws of more than half the States and orders the transformation of a social institution that has formed the basis of human society for millennia, for the Kalahari Bushmen and the Han Chinese, the Carthaginians and the Aztecs. Just who do we think we are?

[As] the majority notes, some aspects of marriage have changed over time. [These changes] did not, however, work any transformation in the core structure of marriage as the union between a man and a woman. If you had asked a person on the street how marriage was defined, no one would ever have said, "Marriage is the union of a man and a woman, where the woman is subject to coverture." The majority may be right that the "history of marriage is one of both continuity and change," but the core meaning of marriage has endured.

[The] majority's approach has no basis in principle or tradition, except for the unprincipled tradition of judicial policymaking that characterized discredited decisions such as Lochner.

[To] avoid repeating *Lochner*'s error of converting personal preferences into constitutional mandates, our modern substantive due process cases have stressed the need for judicial self-restraint. Our precedents have required that implied fundamental rights be "objectively, deeply rooted in this Nation's history and tradition," and "implicit in the concept of ordered liberty, such that neither liberty nor justice would exist if they were sacrificed." [Washington v. Glucksberg, p. 595 below.]

[Expanding] a right suddenly and dramatically is likely to require tearing it up from its roots. Even a sincere profession of "discipline" in identifying fundamental rights does not provide a meaningful constraint on a judge, for "what he is really likely to be 'discovering,' whether or not he is fully aware of it, are his own values," J. Ely, Democracy and Distrust (1980).

The only way to ensure restraint in this delicate enterprise is "continual insistence upon respect for the teachings of history, solid recognition of the basic values that underlie our society, and wise appreciation of the great roles [of] the doctrines of federalism and separation of powers." Griswold (Harlan, J., concurring in judgment).

[Neither] Lawrence nor any other precedent in the privacy line of cases supports the right that petitioners assert here. Unlike criminal laws banning contraceptives and sodomy, the marriage laws at issue here involve no government intrusion. They create no crime and impose no punishment. Same-sex couples remain free to live together, to engage in intimate conduct, and to raise their families as they see fit. No one is "condemned to live in loneliness" by the laws challenged in these cases—no one. At the same time, the laws in no way interfere with the "right to be let alone."

[One] immediate question invited by the majority's position is whether States may retain the definition of marriage as a union of two people. Although the majority randomly inserts the adjective "two" in various places, it offers no reason at all why the two-person element of the core definition of marriage may be preserved while the man-woman element may not. Indeed, from the standpoint of history and tradition, a leap from opposite-sex marriage to same-sex marriage is much greater than one from a two-person union to plural unions, which have deep roots in some cultures around the world.

[In] addition to their due process argument, petitioners contend that the Equal Protection Clause requires their States to license and recognize same-sex marriages. [Absent] from this portion of the opinion, however, is anything resembling our usual framework for deciding equal protection cases. [In] any event, the marriage laws at issue here do not violate the Equal Protection Clause, because distinguishing between opposite-sex and same-sex couples is rationally related to the States' legitimate state interest in preserving the traditional institution of marriage. [The] equal protection analysis might be different, in my view, if we were confronted with a more focused challenge to the denial of certain tangible benefits.

[If] you are among the many Americans—of whatever sexual orientation—who favor expanding same-sex marriage, by all means celebrate today's decision. Celebrate the achievement of a desired goal. Celebrate the opportunity for a new expression of commitment to a partner. Celebrate the availability of new benefits. But do not celebrate the Constitution. It had nothing to do with it.

■ JUSTICE THOMAS, with whom JUSTICE SCALIA joins, dissenting.

Even if the doctrine of substantive due process were somehow defensible—it is not—petitioners still would not have a claim. [The] majority claims these state laws deprive petitioners of "liberty," but the concept of "liberty" it conjures up bears no resemblance to any plausible meaning of that word as it is used in the Due Process Clauses.

[Both] of the Constitution's Due Process Clauses reach back to Magna Carta. [Although] the 1215 version of Magna Carta was in effect for only a few weeks, this provision was later reissued in 1225 with modest changes to its wording as follows: "No freeman shall be taken, or imprisoned, or be disseised of his freehold, or liberties, or free customs, or be outlawed, or exiled, or any otherwise destroyed; nor will we not pass upon him, nor condemn him, but by lawful judgment of his peers or by the law of the land."

In his influential commentary on the provision many years later, Sir Edward Coke interpreted the words "by the law of the land" to mean the same thing as "by due process of the common law."

After Magna Carta became subject to renewed interest in the 17th century, William Blackstone referred to this provision as protecting the "absolute rights of every Englishman." The Framers drew heavily upon Blackstone's formulation, adopting provisions in early State Constitutions that replicated Magna Carta's language, but were modified to refer specifically to "life, liberty, or property." State decisions interpreting these provisions between the founding and the ratification of the Fourteenth Amendment almost uniformly construed the word "liberty" to refer only to freedom from physical restraint. [Even] assuming that the "liberty" in those Clauses encompasses something more than freedom from physical restraint, it would not include the types of rights claimed by the majority. In the American legal tradition, liberty has long been understood as individual freedom *from* governmental action, not as a right *to* a particular governmental entitlement.

[To] the extent that the Framers would have recognized a natural right to marriage that fell within the broader definition of liberty, it would not have included a right to governmental recognition and benefits. Instead, it would have included a right to engage in the very same activities that petitioners have been left free to engage in—making vows, holding religious ceremonies celebrating those vows, raising children, and otherwise enjoying the society of one's spouse—without governmental interference.

[Perhaps] recognizing that these cases do not actually involve liberty as it has been understood, the majority goes to great lengths to assert that its decision will advance the "dignity" of same-sex couples. The flaw in that reasoning, of course, is that the Constitution contains no "dignity" Clause, and even if it did, the government would be incapable of bestowing dignity.

Human dignity has long been understood in this country to be innate. [Slaves] did not lose their dignity (any more than they lost their humanity) because the government allowed them to be enslaved. Those held in internment camps did not lose their dignity because the government confined them. And those denied governmental benefits certainly do not lose their dignity because the government denies them those benefits. The government cannot bestow dignity, and it cannot take it away. [Our] Constitution—like the Declaration of Independence before it—was predicated on a simple truth: One's liberty, not to mention one's dignity, was something to be shielded from—not provided by—the State. Today's decision casts that truth aside.

■ JUSTICE ALITO, with whom JUSTICES SCALIA and THOMAS join, dissenting.

[Today's] decision usurps the constitutional right of the people to decide whether to keep or alter the traditional understanding of marriage.

[The] system of federalism established by our Constitution provides a way for people with different beliefs to live together in a single nation. If the issue of same-sex marriage had been left to the people of the States, it is likely that some States would recognize same-sex marriage and others would not. It is also possible that some States would tie recognition to protection for conscience rights. The majority today makes that impossible. By imposing its own views on the entire country, the majority facilitates the marginalization of the many Americans who have traditional ideas.

Recalling the harsh treatment of gays and lesbians in the past, some may think that turnabout is fair play. But if that sentiment prevails, the Nation will experience bitter and lasting wounds.

THE MEANING AND IMPLICATIONS OF OBERGEFELL

1. ***Due process and equal protection: a "profound connection."*** Obergefell made explicit what Lawrence and Windsor implied: rights, and in particular rights for gay and lesbian people, can flow jointly from the Due Process Clause and Equal Protection Clause, with those two provisions acting in a synergistic way; such rights cannot be exclusively traced to one Clause or the other. As described in Obergefell, this conjunction of due process and equal protection comes into play when individual dignity is at stake. If a law treats different groups of people differently, and if the particular distinction at issue demeans the dignity of one group, then both equal protection and due process come into play to invalidate the law. How might this principle be applied in future cases? Do infringements on dignity act as a trigger for heightened judicial scrutiny under equal protection's established methodology? Notice, however, that the Court's opinion spends little time on the government interests at stake in same-sex marriage bans—ordinarily, evaluating the connection between the government's interest and the means used to implement that interest is key to equal protection analysis. As an alternative, is the notion of equality inherent in dignity itself, such that any deprivation of dignity also violates equality?

Could Obergefell have reached the same result by invoking equal protection alone? Justice Kennedy's opinion cites Loving for the proposition that marriage is a fundamental right; under the Equal Protection Clause, classifications that deny a fundamental right to some people but not others are subject to strict scrutiny (see Skinner v. Oklahoma, p. 510 above). What purpose is served by introducing the due process element?

For one possible response, see Yoshino, "A New Birth of Freedom? Obergefell v. Hodges," 129 Harv. L. Rev. 147 (2015). Consider the fact that a state can respond to a pure equal protection decision in one of two ways: by expanding access to the status or right at issue and providing it to both the formerly excluded group and the formerly included group, or by contracting access and denying the benefit to both groups. In Lawrence, Justice Kennedy worried that if the Court struck down Texas's ban on same-sex sodomy on equal-protection grounds alone, the state would respond by banning all sodomy, and the stigma imposed on gay and lesbian people would be unresolved, since the public would still see the ban as aimed primarily at homosexual sex. Using due process instead of equal protection compels a state to expand the right, not contract it. States thus cannot respond to Obergefell by exiting the marriage-licensing business entirely; they must instead open marriage to heterosexual and homosexual couples alike.

2. ***Dignity and the source of constitutional rights.*** At what level of generality does Obergefell's right operate? Does its holding apply exclusively to same-sex marriage, or does it instead promote a constitutional interest in dignity—similar to Griswold and Roe's interest in privacy—that might be applied to strike down laws in other areas? What principles might the Court use in the future to identify invasions of this dignity interest? Are the dissenters right to fear that Obergefell portends a return to the Lochner

era, where judicial understandings of how society should function underlay the invalidation of state law based on extratextual constitutional principles? Does the opinion's linkage of dignity and individual autonomy narrow the range of contexts in which the dignity right could be invoked? What would distinguish a state ban on polygamy, for instance, from a state ban on same-sex marriage under Obergefell's analysis? Does the answer depend on judges' moral reasoning, or on the fact that polygamous marriages, unlike same-sex marriages, may promote the subordination of one or more participants?

Does Obergefell reject an approach to substantive due process, that protects only those rights "deeply rooted in this Nation's history and tradition"? Can the Court place its constitutional imprimatur on a right that may not be "deeply rooted" but that has been accepted by an emerging consensus among the states? Among institutions?

3. ***The Court as educator.*** The Court's opinion places weight on the role that law and constitutional values play in educating the public. Justice Kennedy notes that "[as] the State itself makes marriage all the more precious by the significance it attaches to it, exclusion from that status has the effect of teaching that gays and lesbians are unequal in important respects." Should the Court consider the effect that its decisions as to rights will have on public opinion—is that a valid basis for judicial decisionmaking? Does it conflict with the formal notion that judges only adjudicate the controversies that are directly brought before them? With respect to a subject about which people are likely to have deeply-held preexisting convictions—such as same-sex marriage—is it realistic to think that the Court can change people's minds? For an argument that the opposite is true—that court decisions, on this issue in particular, have created public backlash against the newly-recognized right—see Klarman, From the Closet to the Altar (2013). Do political developments from Lawrence to Obergefell belie that thesis?

SUBSTANTIVE DUE PROCESS AND RIGHTS OVER THE TIMING AND CIRCUMSTANCES OF ONE'S DEATH

Does the Due Process Clause confer any substantive right to refuse unwanted medical treatment and nourishment? At any time or only near otherwise certain and imminent death? Even if there is some such right, does it extend to a right to a physician's assistance in terminating life more quickly and with less suffering? And even if there is such a right, do the risks of mistake and coercion, with such grave consequences, justify greater regulation than for other presumptive privacy rights? The Court considered these issues in the following decisions.

In **Cruzan v. Director, Missouri Dept. of Health**, 497 U.S. 261 (1990), the Court for the first time considered the question of a constitutional "right to die." The 5–4 majority held that on the facts of the case, discontinuation of life-sustaining procedures (here, artificial nutrition and hydration) was not constitutionally required. The case arose in the following context: Since 1983, when the then 25-year-old Nancy Beth Cruzan suffered severe injuries in an automobile accident, she had been in a persistent vegetative state, a state in which she exhibited some motor reflexes but no indications of significant cognitive functions. When it became apparent that

Cruzan had virtually no chance of regaining her cognitive faculties, her parents sought to discontinue tubal feeding. The Missouri trial court ordered the removal of the tube, finding that no state interest outweighed her "right to liberty." The trial court found that there was evidence suggesting that Cruzan "would not wish to continue on with her nutrition and hydration." However, she had neither executed a living will nor designated anyone to make health-care decisions for her in the event she became incompetent. The closely divided Missouri Supreme Court reversed the trial court ruling, finding Cruzan's remarks relied on by the trial judge so remote and general as to be "unreliable for the purposes of establishing her intent" and insisting that "clear and convincing evidence" of her wishes was lacking here.

Chief Justice REHNQUIST's opinion affirmed that ruling. He explained: "In this Court, the question is simply and starkly whether the Constitution prohibits Missouri from choosing the rule of decision which it did. [The] principle that a competent person has a constitutionally protected liberty interest in refusing unwanted medical treatment may be inferred from our prior decisions. [But] determining that a person has a 'liberty interest' under the Due Process Clause does not end the inquiry; 'whether respondent's constitutional rights have been violated must be determined by balancing his liberty interests against the relevant state interests.' [For] purposes of this case, we assume that the [Constitution] would grant a competent person a constitutionally protected right to refuse lifesaving hydration and nutrition. [But] an incompetent person is not able to make an informed and voluntary choice to exercise a hypothetical right to refuse treatment or any other right. Such a 'right' must be exercised for her, if at all, by some sort of surrogate. Here, Missouri has in effect recognized that under certain circumstances a surrogate may act for the patient in electing to have hydration and nutrition withdrawn in such a way as to cause death, but it has established a procedural safeguard to assure that the action of the surrogate conforms as best it may to the wishes expressed by the patient while competent. Missouri requires that evidence of the incompetent's wishes as to the withdrawal of treatment be proved by clear and convincing evidence. The question, then, is whether the United States Constitution forbids the establishment of this procedural requirement by the State. We hold that it does not.

"Whether or not Missouri's clear and convincing evidence requirement comports with the [Constitution] depends in part on what interests the State may properly seek to protect in this situation. Missouri relies on its interest in the protection and preservation of human life, and there can be no gainsaying this interest. [The] majority of States [have] laws imposing criminal penalties on one who assists another to commit suicide. We do not think a State is required to remain neutral in the face of an informed and voluntary decision by a physically-able adult to starve to death. But in the context presented here, a State has more particular interests at stake. The choice between life and death is a deeply personal decision of obvious and overwhelming finality. We believe Missouri may legitimately seek to safeguard the personal element of this choice through the imposition of heightened evidentiary requirements. It cannot be disputed that the Due Process Clause protects an interest in life as well as an interest in refusing life-sustaining medical treatment. Not all incompetent patients will have loved ones available to serve as surrogate decisionmakers. And even where family members are present, '[t]here will, of course, be some unfortunate situations in which family members will not act to protect a patient.' A State is entitled to guard against potential abuses in such situations. [Finally,] we think a State may properly decline to make judgments about the 'quality' of life that a particular individual may enjoy, and simply assert an unqualified interest in the preservation of human life to be weighed against the constitutionally protected interests of the individual.

"In our view, Missouri has permissibly sought to advance these interests through the adoption of a 'clear and convincing' standard of proof to govern such proceedings. [The] more stringent the burden of proof a party must bear, the more that party bears the risk of an erroneous decision. We believe that Missouri may permissibly place an increased risk of an erroneous decision on those seeking to terminate an incompetent individual's life-sustaining treatment. An erroneous decision not to terminate results in a maintenance of the status quo; the possibility of subsequent developments such as advancements in medical science, the discovery of new evidence regarding the patient's intent, changes in the law, or simply the unexpected death of the patient despite the administration of life-sustaining treatment, at least create the potential that a wrong decision will eventually be corrected or its impact mitigated. An erroneous decision to withdraw life-sustaining treatment, however, is not susceptible of correction. [In] sum, we conclude that a State may apply a clear and convincing evidence standard in proceedings where a guardian seeks to discontinue nutrition and hydration of a person diagnosed to be in a persistent vegetative state."

Justice O'CONNOR's concurrence "agree[d] that a protected liberty interest in refusing unwanted medical treatment may be inferred from our prior decisions, and that the refusal of artificially delivered food and water is encompassed within that liberty interest," but found no violation of that interest here. She emphasized that the Court "does not today decide the issue whether a State must also give effect to the decisions of a surrogate decisionmaker" and noted that such respect might well be constitutionally required in a future case. Justice SCALIA's concurrence, by contrast, argued that "the federal courts have no business in this field. [While] I agree with the Court's analysis today, and therefore join in its opinion, I would have preferred that we announce, clearly and promptly, that the federal courts have no business in this field; that American law has always accorded the State the power to prevent, by force if necessary, suicide—including suicide by refusing to take appropriate measures necessary to preserve one's life; that the point at which life becomes 'worthless,' and the point at which the means necessary to preserve it become 'extraordinary' or 'inappropriate,' are neither set forth in the Constitution nor known to the nine Justices of this Court any better than they are known to nine people picked at random from the Kansas City telephone directory; and hence, that even when it is demonstrated by clear and convincing evidence that a patient no longer wishes certain measures to be taken to preserve her life, it is up to the citizens of Missouri to decide, through their elected representatives, whether that wish will be honored."

Justice BRENNAN dissented, joined by Justices Marshall and Blackmun: "Nancy Cruzan is entitled to choose to die with dignity. [If] a competent person has a liberty interest to be free of unwanted medical treatment, [it] must be fundamental [and although such a right] may not be absolute, no State interest could outweigh the rights of an individual in Nancy Cruzan's position. [Missouri] does not claim, nor could it, that society as a whole will be benefited by Nancy's receiving medical treatment. No third party's situation will be improved and no harm to others will be averted. The only state interest asserted here is a general interest in the preservation of life. But the State has no legitimate general interest in someone's life, completely abstracted from the interest of the person living that life, that could outweigh the person's choice to avoid medical treatment."

Cruzan left open the question whether there was a liberty right or "interest" sufficient to invalidate a law with the effect of barring altogether the assistance of a physician in accelerating one's death. It also left open the question of what level of scrutiny might apply to such a claim. Those questions were squarely reached in the consolidated 1997 cases from Washington and New York that follow.

In reading these decisions, distinguish four different situations in which one might seek to accelerate one's death: (1) suicide when one is healthy or only temporarily ill; (2) withdrawal of life support when one is terminally ill; (3) physician-assisted suicide when one is terminally ill; (4) active euthanasia by a physician when one is terminally ill. Cruzan had addressed only the second situation. The cases that follow raised the third, and consider the difficulty of distinguishing the third and fourth. What are the similarities and differences among these four situations? Does it matter whether the strand of liberty that is emphasized is bodily integrity or, instead, decisional autonomy?

Washington v. Glucksberg

521 U.S. 702, 117 S. Ct. 2258, 138 L. Ed. 2d 772 (1997).

■ CHIEF JUSTICE REHNQUIST delivered the opinion of the Court.

[Washington] law provides: "A person is guilty of promoting a suicide attempt when he knowingly causes or aids another person to attempt suicide." "Promoting a suicide attempt" is a felony, punishable by up to five years' imprisonment and up to a $10,000 fine. At the same time, Washington's Natural Death Act, enacted in 1979, states that the "withholding or withdrawal of life-sustaining treatment" at a patient's direction "shall not, for any purpose, constitute a suicide."

[The en banc court of appeals held that] "the Constitution encompasses a due process liberty interest in controlling the time and manner of one's death" [and] that the State's assisted-suicide ban was unconstitutional "as applied to terminally ill competent adults who wish to hasten their deaths with medication prescribed by their physicians." [We] now reverse.

We begin, as we do in all due-process cases, by examining our Nation's history, legal traditions, and practices. In almost every State—indeed, in almost every western democracy—it is a crime to assist a suicide. The States' assisted-suicide bans are not innovations. Rather, they are longstanding expressions of the States' commitment to the protection and preservation of all human life. Indeed, opposition to and condemnation of suicide—and, therefore, of assisting suicide—are consistent and enduring themes of our philosophical, legal, and cultural heritages. [For] over 700 years, the Anglo-American common-law tradition has punished or otherwise disapproved of both suicide and assisting suicide. In the 13th century, Henry de Bracton, one of the first legal-treatise writers, observed that "just as a man may commit felony by slaying another so may he do so by slaying himself." [The criminal sanction for suicide was forfeiture of property to the king.] [Centuries] later, Sir William Blackstone, whose Commentaries on the Laws of England not only provided a definitive summary of the common law but was also a primary legal authority for 18th and 19th century American lawyers, [emphasized] that "the law has . . . ranked [suicide] among the highest crimes."

For the most part, the early American colonies adopted the common-law approach. [Over] time, however, the American colonies abolished [the] criminal-forfeiture sanction. [The] movement away from the common law's harsh sanctions did not represent an acceptance of suicide; rather, [it] reflected the growing consensus that it was unfair to punish the suicide's family for his wrongdoing. [Courts] continued to condemn it as a [grievous,] though nonfelonious, wrong. [Colonial] and early state legislatures and courts did not retreat from prohibiting assisting suicide. [And] the prohibitions against assisting suicide never contained exceptions for those who were near death. The earliest American statute explicitly to outlaw assisting suicide was enacted in New York in 1828, and many of the new States and Territories followed New York's example. [By] the time the Fourteenth Amendment was ratified, it was a crime in most States to assist a suicide. [In] this century, the Model Penal Code also prohibited "aiding" suicide, prompting many States to enact or revise their assisted-suicide bans.

[Though] deeply rooted, the States' assisted-suicide bans have in recent years been reexamined and, generally, reaffirmed. Because of advances in medicine and technology, Americans today are increasingly likely to die in institutions, from chronic illnesses. Public concern and democratic action are therefore sharply focused on how best to protect dignity and independence at the end of life, with the result that there have been many significant changes in state laws and in the attitudes these laws reflect. Many States, for example, now permit "living wills," surrogate health-care decisionmaking, and the withdrawal or refusal of life-sustaining medical treatment. At the same time, however, voters and legislators continue for the most part to reaffirm their States' prohibitions on assisting suicide.

[The] Due Process Clause guarantees more than fair process, and the "liberty" it protects includes more than the absence of physical restraint. [We] have also assumed, and strongly suggested, that the Due Process Clause protects the traditional right to refuse unwanted lifesaving medical treatment. Cruzan. But we "have always been reluctant to expand the concept of substantive due process because guideposts for responsible decisionmaking in this unchartered area are scarce and open-ended." By extending constitutional protection to an asserted right or liberty interest, we, to a great extent, place the matter outside the arena of public debate and legislative action. We must therefore "exercise the utmost care whenever we are asked to break new ground in this field," lest the liberty protected by the Due Process Clause be subtly transformed into the policy preferences of the members of this Court,

Our established method of substantive-due-process analysis has two primary features: First, we have regularly observed that the Due Process Clause specially protects those fundamental rights and liberties which are, objectively, "deeply rooted in this Nation's history and tradition," Moore v. East Cleveland (plurality opinion) and "implicit in the concept of ordered liberty," such that "neither liberty nor justice would exist if they were sacrificed," Palko v. Connecticut. Second, we have required in substantive-due-process cases a "careful description" of the asserted fundamental liberty interest. Our Nation's history, legal traditions, and practices thus provide the crucial "guideposts for responsible decisionmaking" that direct and restrain our exposition of the Due Process Clause. [This] approach tends to rein in the subjective elements that are necessarily present in due-process judicial review.

[The] question before us is whether the "liberty" specially protected by the Due Process Clause includes a right to commit suicide which itself includes a right to assistance in doing so. We now inquire whether this asserted right has any place in our Nation's traditions. Here [we] are confronted with a consistent and almost universal tradition that has long rejected the asserted right, and continues explicitly to reject it today, even for terminally ill, mentally competent adults. To hold for respondents, we would have to reverse centuries of legal doctrine and practice, and strike down the considered policy choice of almost every State. Respondents contend, however, that the liberty interest they assert is consistent with this Court's substantive-due-process line of cases, if not with this Nation's history and practice.

[Respondents] contend that in Cruzan we "acknowledged that competent, dying persons have the right to direct the removal of life-sustaining medical treatment and thus hasten death," and that "the constitutional principle behind recognizing the patient's liberty to direct the withdrawal of artificial life support applies at least as strongly to the choice to hasten impending death by consuming lethal medication." [The] right assumed in Cruzan, however, was not simply deduced from abstract concepts of personal autonomy. Given the common-law rule that forced medication was a battery, and the long legal tradition protecting the decision to refuse unwanted medical treatment, our assumption was entirely consistent with this Nation's history and constitutional traditions. The decision to commit suicide with the assistance of another may be just as personal and profound as the decision to refuse unwanted medical treatment, but it has never enjoyed similar legal protection. Respondents also rely on Casey. [But language in Casey suggesting that] many of the rights and liberties protected by the Due Process Clause sound in personal autonomy does not warrant the sweeping conclusion that any and all important, intimate, and personal decisions are so protected, and Casey did not suggest otherwise.

The history of the law's treatment of assisted suicide in this country has been and continues to be one of the rejection of nearly all efforts to permit it. That being the case, our decisions lead us to conclude that the asserted "right" to assistance in committing suicide is not a fundamental liberty interest protected by the Due Process Clause. The Constitution also requires, however, that Washington's assisted-suicide ban be rationally related to legitimate government interests. This requirement is unquestionably met here. Washington's assisted-suicide ban implicates a number of state interests.

First, Washington has an "unqualified interest in the preservation of human life." Cruzan. The State's prohibition on assisted suicide, like all homicide laws, both reflects and advances its commitment to this interest. This interest is symbolic and aspirational as well as practical. [Relatedly,] the State has an interest in preventing suicide, and in studying, identifying, and treating its causes. Those who attempt suicide—terminally ill or not—

often suffer from depression or other mental disorders. Research indicates, however, that many people who request physician-assisted suicide withdraw that request if their depression and pain are treated. [The] State also has an interest in protecting the integrity and ethics of the medical profession. [The] American Medical Association, like many other medical and physicians' groups, has concluded that "physician-assisted suicide is fundamentally incompatible with the physician's role as healer." And physician-assisted suicide could, it is argued, undermine the trust that is essential to the doctor-patient relationship by blurring the time-honored line between healing and harming. Next, the State has an interest in protecting vulnerable groups—including the poor, the elderly, and disabled persons—from abuse, neglect, and mistakes. [Finally,] the State may fear that permitting assisted suicide will start it down the path to voluntary and perhaps even involuntary euthanasia. [What] is couched as a limited right to "physician-assisted suicide" is likely, in effect, a much broader license, which could prove extremely difficult to police and contain.

We need not weigh exactingly the relative strengths of these various interests. They are unquestionably important and legitimate, and Washington's ban on assisted suicide is at least reasonably related to their promotion and protection. We therefore hold that [the Washington statute] does not violate the Fourteenth Amendment, either on its face or "as applied to competent, terminally ill adults who wish to hasten their deaths by obtaining medication prescribed by their doctors."[1] [Reversed.]

■ JUSTICE O'CONNOR, concurring.[2]

[I] join the Court's opinions because I agree that there is no generalized right to "commit suicide." But respondents urge us to address the narrower question whether a mentally competent person who is experiencing great suffering has a constitutionally cognizable interest in controlling the circumstances of his or her imminent death. I see no need to reach that question in the context of the facial challenges to the New York and Washington laws at issue here. The parties and amici agree that in these States a patient who is suffering from a terminal illness and who is experiencing great pain has no legal barriers to obtaining medication, from qualified physicians, to alleviate that suffering, even to the point of causing unconsciousness and hastening death. In this light, even assuming that we would recognize such an interest, I agree that the State's interests in protecting those who are not truly competent or facing imminent death, or those whose decisions to hasten death would not truly be voluntary, are sufficiently weighty to justify a prohibition against physician-assisted suicide.

---

[1] [We] emphasize that we today reject the Court of Appeals' specific holding that the statute is unconstitutional "as applied" to a particular class. Justice Stevens agrees with this holding, but would not "foreclose the possibility that an individual plaintiff seeking to hasten her death, or a doctor whose assistance was sought, could prevail in a more particularized challenge." Our opinion does not absolutely foreclose such a claim. However, given our holding that the Due Process Clause of the Fourteenth Amendment does not provide heightened protection to the asserted liberty interest in ending one's life with a physician's assistance, such a claim would have to be quite different from the ones advanced by respondents here. [Footnote by Chief Justice Rehnquist.]

[2] Justice GINSBURG concurs in the Court's judgments substantially for the reasons stated in this Opinion. Justice BREYER joins this opinion except insofar as it joins the opinions of the Court. [Footnote by Justice O'Connor.]

■ JUSTICE STEVENS, concurring in the judgments.

[Cruzan's] interest in refusing medical care was incidental to her more basic interest in controlling the manner and timing of her death. [The] source of [her] right to refuse treatment was not just a common-law rule. Rather, this right is an aspect of a far broader and more basic concept of freedom that is even older than the common law. This freedom embraces, not merely a person's right to refuse a particular kind of unwanted treatment, but also her interest in dignity, and in determining the character of the memories that will survive long after her death. [Avoiding] intolerable pain and the indignity of living one's final days incapacitated and in agony is certainly "at the heart of [the] liberty . . . to define one's own concept of existence, of meaning, of the universe, and of the mystery of human life." Casey. While I agree with the Court that Cruzan does not decide the issue presented by these cases, Cruzan did give recognition, not just to vague, unbridled notions of autonomy, but to the more specific interest in making decisions about how to confront an imminent death.

The state interests supporting a general rule banning the practice of physician-assisted suicide do not have the same force in all cases. [The] State's legitimate interest in preventing abuse does not apply to an individual who is not victimized by abuse, who is not suffering from depression, and who makes a rational and voluntary decision to seek assistance in dying. [Palliative care] cannot alleviate all pain and suffering [and an] individual adequately informed of the care alternatives thus might make a rational choice for assisted suicide. [For] some patients, it would be a physician's refusal to dispense medication to ease their suffering and make their death tolerable and dignified that would be inconsistent with the healing role.

[While] I would not say as a categorical matter that these state interests are invalid as to the entire class of terminally ill, mentally competent patients, I do not [foreclose] the possibility that an individual plaintiff seeking to hasten her death, or a doctor whose assistance was sought, could prevail in a more particularized challenge. Future cases will determine whether such a challenge may succeed.

■ JUSTICE SOUTER, concurring in the judgment.

[The] question [here] is whether the [Washington] statute sets up one of those "arbitrary impositions" or "purposeless restraints" at odds with the Due Process Clause of the Fourteenth Amendment. [Poe v. Ullman (Harlan, J., dissenting).] [My] understanding of unenumerated rights in the wake of the Poe dissent [begins] with a concept of "ordered liberty" comprising a continuum of rights to be free from "arbitrary impositions and purposeless restraints." [The] claims of arbitrariness that mark almost all instances of unenumerated substantive rights are those resting on interests in liberty sufficiently important to be judged "fundamental." In the face of an interest this powerful a State may not rest on threshold rationality or a presumption of constitutionality, but may prevail only on the ground of an interest sufficiently compelling to place within the realm of the reasonable a refusal to recognize the individual right asserted.

This approach calls for a court to assess the relative "weights" or dignities of the contending interests, and to this extent the judicial method is familiar to the common law. Common law method is subject, however, to two important constraints in the hands of a court engaged in substantive due process review. First, such a court is bound to confine the values that it recognizes to those truly deserving constitutional stature, either to those expressed in constitutional text, or those exemplified by "the traditions from which [the Nation] developed," or revealed by contrast with "the traditions from which it broke." [Second, it] is only when the legislation's justifying principle, critically valued, is so far from being commensurate with the individual interest as to be arbitrarily or pointlessly applied that the statute must give way. [The] "tradition is a living thing," albeit one that moves by moderate steps carefully taken.

[The] argument supporting respondents' position [progresses] through three steps of increasing forcefulness. First, it emphasizes the decriminalization of suicide. Reliance on this fact is sanctioned under the standard that looks not only to the tradition retained, but to society's occasional choices to reject traditions of the legal past. [The] second step in the argument is to emphasize that the State's own act of decriminalization gives a freedom of choice much like the individual's option in recognized instances of bodily autonomy. One of these, abortion, is a legal right to choose in spite of the interest a State may legitimately invoke in discouraging the practice, just as suicide is now subject to choice, despite a state interest in discouraging it. The third step is to emphasize that respondents [base] their claim on the traditional right to medical care and counsel, subject to the limiting conditions of informed, responsible choice when death is imminent, conditions that support a strong analogy to rights of care in other situations in which medical counsel and assistance have been available as a matter of course. There can be no stronger claim to a physician's assistance than at the time when death is imminent, a moral judgment implied by the State's own recognition of the legitimacy of medical procedures [such as the withdrawal of life-support or the administration of medication to alleviate pain] necessarily hastening the moment of impending death.

In my judgment, the importance of the individual interest here, as within that class of "certain interests" demanding careful scrutiny of the State's contrary claim, cannot be gainsaid. Whether that interest might in some circumstances, or at some time, be seen as "fundamental" to the degree entitled to prevail is not, however, a conclusion that I need draw here, for I am satisfied that the State's interests [are] sufficiently serious to defeat the present claim that its law is arbitrary or purposeless.

The State has put forward [interests] protecting life generally, discouraging suicide even if knowing and voluntary, and protecting terminally ill patients from involuntary suicide and euthanasia, both voluntary and nonvoluntary. [The] third is dispositive for me. [It] is different from the first two, for it addresses specific features of respondents' claim, and it opposes that claim not with a moral judgment contrary to respondents', but with a recognized state interest in the protection of nonresponsible individuals and those who do not stand in relation either to death or to their physicians as do the patients whom respondents describe. [The] argument is that a progression would occur, obscuring the line between the ill and the dying, and between the responsible and the unduly influenced, until ultimately doctors and perhaps others would abuse a limited freedom to aid suicides by yielding to the impulse to end another's suffering under conditions going beyond the narrow limits the respondents propose. [The] case for the slippery slope is fairly made out here, not because recognizing one due process right would leave a court with no principled basis to avoid recognizing another, but because there is a plausible case that the right claimed would not be readily containable by reference to facts about the mind that are matters of difficult judgment, or by gatekeepers who are subject to temptation, noble or not.

Respondents propose an answer to all this, the answer of state regulation with teeth. Legislation proposed in several States, for example, would authorize physician-assisted suicide but require two qualified physicians to confirm the patient's diagnosis, prognosis, and competence; and would mandate that the patient make repeated requests witnessed by at least two others over a specified time span; and would impose reporting requirements and criminal penalties for various acts of coercion. But at least at this moment there are reasons for caution in predicting the effectiveness of the teeth proposed. [While] I do not decide for all time that respondents' claim should not be recognized, I acknowledge the legislative institutional competence as the better one to deal with that claim at this time.

■ JUSTICE BREYER, concurring in the judgments.

I believe that Justice O'Connor's views, which I share, have greater legal significance than the Court's opinion suggests. I join her separate opinion, except insofar as it joins the majority. [I] do not agree [with] the Court's formulation of [the] claimed "liberty" interest. The Court describes it as a "right to commit suicide with another's assistance." But I would not reject the respondents' claim without considering a different formulation, for which our legal tradition may provide greater support. That formulation would use words roughly like a "right to die with dignity." But irrespective of the exact words used, at its core would lie personal control over the manner of death, professional medical assistance, and the avoidance of unnecessary and severe physical suffering—combined.

As Justice Souter points out, Justice Harlan's dissenting opinion in Poe offers some support for such a claim. In that opinion, Justice Harlan [recognized] that "certain interests require particularly careful scrutiny of the state needs asserted to justify their abridgment." [He] concluded that marital privacy was such a "special interest." He found in the Constitution a right of "privacy of the home"—with the home, the bedroom, and "intimate details of the marital relation" at its heart—by examining the protection that the law had earlier provided for related, but not identical, interests described by such words as "privacy," "home," and "family." The respondents here essentially ask us to do the same. They argue that one can find a "right to die with dignity" by examining the protection the law has provided for related, but not identical, interests relating to personal dignity, medical treatment, and freedom from state-inflicted pain.

I do not believe, however, that this Court need or now should decide whether or a not such a right is "fundamental." That is because, in my view, the avoidance of severe physical pain (connected with death) would have to comprise an essential part of any successful claim and because, as Justice O'Connor points out, the laws before us do not force a dying person to undergo that kind of pain. [State law here does] not prohibit doctors from providing patients with drugs sufficient to control pain despite the risk that those drugs themselves will kill. [Medical] technology [makes] the administration of pain-relieving drugs sufficient, except for a very few individuals for whom the ineffectiveness of pain control medicines can mean, not pain, but the need for sedation which can end in a coma. [This] legal circumstance means that the state laws before us do not infringe directly upon the (assumed) central interest (what I have called the core of the interest in dying with dignity). [Were] the legal circumstances different—for example, were state law to prevent the provision of palliative care, including the administration of drugs as needed to avoid pain at the end of life—then the law's impact upon serious and otherwise unavoidable physical pain (accompanying death) would be more directly at issue. And as Justice O'Connor suggests, the Court might have to revisit its conclusions in these cases.

THE MEANING AND IMPLICATIONS OF GLUCKSBERG

1. ***Due process methodology.*** Note the two competing approaches reflected in the Glucksberg opinions to discerning privacy rights implicit in substantive due process. Writing for the Court, Chief Justice Rehnquist takes a narrow positivist approach, emphasizing the need to ground any fundamental liberty interest or right in tradition narrowly defined. For example, he grounds the liberty interest in refusing unwanted medical care, as in Cruzan, in the common law right against battery, or unwanted touching. By contrast, Justice Souter's concurrence emphasizes a broader view of privacy as freedom from arbitrary restraint, and to the extent that view is guided by tradition, it relies on a broader view of tradition as exemplified by Justice Harlan's Poe dissent. Does Chief Justice Rehnquist have a majority for his approach? Note that five justices concurred separately to note their differences with the opinion of the Court.

2. ***The right to die and equal protection.*** In **Vacco v. Quill**, 521 U.S. 793 (1997), decided together with Glucksberg, the Court held that New York did not violate the Equal Protection Clause by prohibiting assisted suicide while permitting patients to refuse lifesaving medical treatment. Chief Justice REHNQUIST again wrote for the Court: "The Equal Protection Clause [embodies] a general rule that States must treat like cases alike but may treat unlike cases accordingly. [The] Court of Appeals concluded that some terminally ill people—those who are on life-support systems—are treated differently than those who are not, in that the former may 'hasten death' by ending treatment, but the latter may not 'hasten death' through physician-assisted suicide. This conclusion depends on the submission that ending or refusing lifesaving medical treatment 'is nothing more nor less than assisted suicide.' [We] think the distinction between assisting suicide and withdrawing life-sustaining treatment, a distinction widely recognized and endorsed in the medical profession and in our legal traditions, is both important and logical; it is certainly rational.

"The distinction comports with fundamental legal principles of causation and intent. First, when a patient refuses life-sustaining medical treatment, he dies from an underlying fatal disease or pathology; but if a patient ingests lethal medication prescribed by a physician, he is killed by that medication. Furthermore, a physician who withdraws, or honors a patient's refusal to begin, life-sustaining medical treatment purposefully intends, or may so intend, only to respect his patient's wishes and 'to cease doing useless and futile or degrading things to the patient when [the patient] no longer stands to benefit from them.' The same is true when a doctor provides aggressive palliative care; in some cases, painkilling drugs may hasten a patient's death, but the physician's purpose and intent is, or may be, only to ease his patient's pain. A doctor who assists a suicide, however, 'must, necessarily and indubitably, intend primarily that the patient be made dead.' Similarly, a patient who commits suicide with a doctor's aid necessarily has the specific intent to end his or her own life, while a patient who refuses or discontinues treatment might not. The law has long used actors' intent or purpose to distinguish between two acts that may have the same result.

"Given these general principles, it is not surprising that many courts, including New York courts, have carefully distinguished refusing life-sustaining treatment from suicide. [Similarly,] the overwhelming majority of state legislatures have drawn a clear line between assisting suicide and withdrawing or permitting the refusal of unwanted lifesaving medical treatment by prohibiting the former and permitting the latter. [This] Court has also recognized, at least implicitly, the distinction between letting a patient die and making that patient die. In Cruzan, we concluded that 'the principle that a competent person has a constitutionally protected liberty interest in refusing unwanted medical treatment may be inferred from our prior decisions,' and we assumed the existence of such a right for purposes of that case. But our assumption of a right to refuse treatment was grounded not, as the Court of Appeals supposed, on the proposition that patients have a general and abstract 'right to hasten death,' but on well established, traditional rights to bodily integrity and freedom from unwanted touching.

"For all these reasons, we disagree with respondents' claim that the distinction between refusing lifesaving medical treatment and assisted suicide is 'arbitrary' and 'irrational.' [By] permitting everyone to refuse unwanted medical treatment while prohibiting anyone from assisting a suicide, New York law follows a longstanding and rational distinction. [The] valid and important public interests [discussed in Glucksberg] easily satisfy the constitutional requirement that a legislative classification bear a rational relation to some legitimate end."

As they had in Glucksberg, Justice O'Connor concurred and Justices Stevens, Souter, Ginsburg and Breyer concurred in the judgment. Justice STEVENS noted: "[A]lthough the differences the majority notes in causation and intent between terminating life-support and assisting in suicide support the Court's rejection of the respondents' facial challenge, these distinctions may be inapplicable to particular terminally ill patients and their doctors. Our holding today does not foreclose the possibility that some applications of the New York statute may impose an intolerable intrusion on the patient's freedom." In a potentially significant footnote to the majority opinion, Chief Justice REHNQUIST expressly agreed with Justice Stevens (as he had in Glucksberg) that the holding did not foreclose possible as-applied challenges, but stated that "a particular plaintiff hoping to show that New York's assisted-suicide ban was unconstitutional in his particular case would need to present different and considerably stronger arguments than those advanced by respondents here." What might those arguments be?

3. ***Challenges left open by Glucksberg and Quill.*** What is the significance of the concurring opinions in Glucksberg and Vacco v. Quill? Only Justices Scalia, Kennedy and Thomas joined Chief Justice Rehnquist's opinion for the Court without qualification. The five concurring justices declined to join the opinion of the Court in its entirety. Justice O'Connor concurred only on the understanding that these cases did not involve dying in untreatable pain because both Washington and New York allowed

physicians to administer potentially lethal doses of painkilling medication. Does Justice O'Connor's opinion, together with the separate concurrences of Justices Stevens, Souter, Ginsburg and Breyer, comprise a majority for the proposition that the states are constitutionally required to permit such palliative practice? If so, what other forms of "active" assistance, if any, might be constitutionally protected? Does a ban on physician-assisted suicide give doctors an incentive to employ "terminal sedation," i.e., the practice of giving anesthesia to achieve pain reduction and then withdrawing food, water and medicine according to the interest established in Cruzan? Would swift physician-assisted suicide be preferable? Does the availability of such substitutes render the law ineffective at serving its supposed interests?

4. ***Distinguishing substantive due process cases.*** Recall Justice Stevens's dissent in McDonald v. City of Chicago, p. 475 above, arguing that McDonald was a substantive due process case. Likewise, in his dissent in Planned Parenthood v. Casey, p. 531 above, Justice Scalia characterized the Dred Scott decision as "rest[ing] upon the concept of 'substantive due process.' " Do you agree with those characterizations? Of the Court's most controversial substantive due process cases—such as Griswold, Roe, Lawrence, Glucksberg, and possibly McDonald and Dred Scott—how can you distinguish the "good" decisions from the "bad" ones?

SECTION 3. PROCEDURAL DUE PROCESS AND THE RIGHT TO A HEARING

While the cases discussed above concerned the implication of a substantive component in the Due Process Clauses of the Fifth and Fourteenth Amendments, the Court has also articulated the contours of the procedures required when government deprives persons of liberty or property. This often requires deciding at the threshold whether there was a preexisting right to liberty or property in the first place. This rich topic is largely left to civil procedure and administrative law courses and thus beyond the scope of this book. It is covered briefly here with a focus on how the Court identifies sources of "liberty" and "property" rights. What interests qualify as "liberty" or "property" rights, and what process must the government offer before depriving an individual of them?

DEFINING "PROPERTY" AND "LIBERTY"

Common law property rights may be defined in terms of tradition; in the welfare state, however, more and more rights come in the form of government entitlements. When might those more nebulous interests qualify as "property" under the Fifth and Fourteenth Amendments? The issue was first raised in Reich, "The New Property," 73 Yale L.J. 773 (1964). The seminal case guaranteeing due process even in the deprivation of government benefits, as opposed to traditional common law property, was **Goldberg v. Kelly**, 397 U.S. 254 (1970), which held that due process required that a welfare recipient be afforded "an evidentiary hearing *before* the termination of benefits." Justice BRENNAN's majority opinion stated: "Such benefits are a matter of statutory entitlement for persons qualified to receive them. [Termination] of aid pending resolution of the controversy over eligibility may deprive an *eligible* recipient of the very means by which to live while he waits." The opinion cited the Reich article in a footnote.

Later cases, however, cut back on the extension of due process hearing rights to all manner of government entitlements. In **Board of Regents v. Roth**, 408 U.S. 564 (1972), for example, the Court held that Roth, a nontenured teacher hired for one year at a campus of Wisconsin State University, had no constitutional right to a statement of reasons and a hearing before being denied rehire. Justice STEWART's opinion for the Court stated: "[The] range of interests protected by procedural due process is not infinite. [The] 14th Amendment's procedural protection of property is a safeguard of the security of interests that a person has already acquired in specific benefits. [The] terms of the respondent's appointment secured absolutely no interest in re-employment for the next year. [Nor,] significantly, was there any state statute or University rule or policy that secured his interest in re-employment or that created any legitimate claim to it. [The] respondent surely had an abstract concern in being rehired, but he did not have a *property* interest sufficient to require the University authorities to give him a hearing when they declined to renew his [contract]."

Judicial attentiveness to background state law in evaluating claimed constitutional entitlements was not always fatal to due process claims. For example, in **Perry v. Sindermann**, 408 U.S. 593 (1972), a companion case to Roth, a nontenured college avoided dismissal of his procedural due process claim by asserting that background state rules gave him an "entitlement to continued employment absent sufficient cause." Justice STEWART's majority opinion held that Sindermann's lack of a formal "tenure right to re-employment, taken alone, [did not defeat] his claim that the non-renewal of his contract violated due process," and ordered the case remanded. The Court observed: "A person's interest in a benefit is a 'property' interest for due process purposes if there are such rules or mutually explicit understandings that support his claim of entitlement to the benefit and that he may invoke at a hearing."

To what extent should the underlying statutory or common law from which the term "property" derives its content govern the question of whether a claimant is entitled to a hearing? May state law or federal legislation, in the process of delineating the existence of the property interest, include binding provisions barring hearings? An affirmative answer to the latter question was suggested by Justice REHNQUIST's plurality opinion in **Arnett v. Kennedy**, 416 U.S. 134 (1974), a decision rejecting a nonprobationary federal civil service employee's claim to a full hearing prior to dismissal. The governing federal law prescribed not only the grounds for removal but also removal procedures. The employee could be removed only for "cause," but the procedures did not provide for an adversary hearing. To Justice Rehnquist, those provisions were dispositive of the procedural due process claim. Although the law created a constitutionally protected property interest (an expectation of continued employment), "where the grant of a substantive right is inextricably intertwined with the limitations on the procedures which are to be employed in determining that right, a litigant [must] take the bitter with the sweet."

The "bitter with the sweet" principle espoused by Justice Rehnquist in Arnett, however, failed to command a majority of the Court. In **Bishop v. Wood**, 426 U.S. 341 (1976), a 5–4 majority concluded that the dismissal of a policeman did not implicate any "property" or "liberty" interest requiring a hearing to determine the sufficiency of the cause. In finding no constitutional "property" interest, Justice STEVENS's majority opinion emphasized that Bishop's claim had to be decided "by reference to state law" and relied on the lower courts' interpretation of the city ordinance to find that Bishop "held his position at the will and pleasure of the city." And in **Cleveland Board of Education v. Loudermill**, 470 U.S. 532 (1985), with only Justice Rehnquist dissenting on this issue, Justice WHITE for the other eight members of the Court made clear that state procedures contained in the law creating a property right are *not* the source of the constitutionally required procedures upon termination of that property right: "[It] is settled that the 'bitter with the sweet' approach [of the plurality in Arnett] misconceives the constitutional guarantee. If a clearer holding is needed, we provide it today. [The] Due Process Clause provides that certain substantive rights—life, liberty, and property—cannot be deprived except pursuant to constitutionally adequate procedures. The categories of substance and procedure are distinct. Were the rule otherwise, the Clause would be reduced to a mere tautology. 'Property' cannot be defined by the procedures provided for its deprivation any more than can life or liberty. [Once] it is determined that the Due Process Clause applies, 'the question remains what process is due.' The answer to that question is not to be found in [state law]."

The Roth line of cases established that the Due Process Clause does not protect against deprivation of all government benefits, but only of "entitlements" created by state law. Does a citizen of a state have an enforceable property interest for due process purposes in police enforcement of a restraining order? In **Town of Castle Rock v. Gonzales**, 545 U.S. 748 (2005), the Court answered that question negatively, by a vote of 7–2, in a case involving "horrible facts": an estranged husband who, in violation of a restraining order, abducted and killed his three children before being shot and killed by police upon whom he had opened fire. Justice SCALIA wrote for the Court, joined by Chief Justice Rehnquist and Justices O'Connor, Kennedy, Souter, Thomas and Breyer, rejecting a § 1983 claim by the children's mother, Theresa Gonzales: "Respondent claims [that] she had a property interest in police enforcement of the restraining order against her husband; and that the town deprived her of this property without due process by having a policy that tolerated nonenforcement of restraining orders. [Our] cases recognize that a benefit is not a protected entitlement if government officials may grant or deny it in their discretion. [We] do not believe that [Colorado law] made enforcement of restraining orders *mandatory*. [Even] if we were to think otherwise concerning the creation of an entitlement by Colorado, it is by no means clear that an individual entitlement to enforcement of a restraining order could constitute a 'property' interest for purposes of the Due Process Clause. Such a right would not, of course, resemble any traditional conception of property. Although that alone does not disqualify it from due process protection, as Roth and its progeny show, the right to have a restraining order enforced does not 'have some ascertainable monetary value,' as even our 'Roth-type property-as-entitlement' cases have implicitly required. Perhaps most radically, the alleged property interest here arises *incidentally,* not out of some new species of government benefit or service, but out of a function that government actors have always performed—to wit, arresting people who they have probable cause to believe have committed a criminal offense. [We] conclude, therefore, that respondent did not, for purposes of the Due Process Clause, have a property interest in police enforcement of the restraining order against her husband."

Justice STEVENS, joined by Justice Ginsburg, dissented: "Respondent certainly could have entered into a contract with a private security firm, obligating the firm to provide protection to respondent's family; respondent's interest in such a contract would unquestionably constitute 'property' within the meaning of the Due Process Clause. [Here,] Colorado undertook a comparable obligation, and respondent—with restraining order in hand—justifiably relied on that undertaking." Justice Souter filed a separate concurrence, joined by Justice Breyer.

The preceding cases make clear that the Court has often deferred to state law in delineating constitutionally protected *property* rights. To what extent has there been a parallel development regarding hearing rights triggered by alleged infringements of *liberty*? Can the Court narrow the reading of liberty in the procedural due process context without casting doubt on its very broad interpretations of liberty in the substantive due process cases from Meyer to Roe and beyond?

In **Paul v. Davis**, 424 U.S. 693 (1976), a sharply divided Court held, in a majority opinion by Justice REHNQUIST, that the plaintiff, whom the local police had named as an "active shoplifter" in flyers distributed to local merchants, had suffered no deprivation of liberty resulting from injury to his reputation. The plaintiff sued the local police under a federal civil rights law after the shoplifting charges were dismissed. Justice Rehnquist found that reputation alone was not a constitutionally protected interest: "[There] exists a variety of interests which are difficult of definition but are nevertheless comprehended within the meaning of either 'liberty' or 'property' as meant in the Due Process Clause. These interests attain this constitutional status by virtue of the fact that they have been initially recognized and protected by state law, and we have repeatedly ruled that the procedural guarantees of the 14th Amendment apply whenever the State seeks to remove or significantly alter that protected status. [In] each of these cases, as a result of the state action complained of, a right or status previously recognized by state law was distinctly altered or extinguished. It was this alteration, officially removing the interest from the recognition and protection previously afforded by the State, which we found sufficient to invoke the procedural guarantees contained in [due process]. But the interest in reputation alone [is] quite different from the 'liberty' or 'property' recognized in those decisions. Kentucky law does not extend to respondent any legal guarantee of present enjoyment of reputation which has been altered as a result of petitioners' actions. Rather his interest in reputation is simply one of a number which the State may protect against injury by virtue of its tort law, providing a forum for vindication of those interests by means of damages actions. And any harm or injury to that interest [does not] result in a deprivation of any 'liberty' or 'property' recognized by state or federal law, nor has it worked any change of respondent's status as theretofore recognized under the State's [laws]."

The restrictive reading of "liberty" in Paul v. Davis and its progeny evidently stemmed from a range of institutional concerns, including the fear of excessive Court interference in the administration of state programs and Justice Rehnquist's related fear about reading the Fourteenth Amendment as "a font of tort law to be superimposed upon whatever systems may already be administered by the States." Even assuming the substantiality of these concerns, were there no alternative routes to the result other than reading "liberty" more narrowly than its traditional broad reach? Would it have been possible to retain a more generous view of liberty and property and focus on the question of what procedural due process requires—and find that its requirements could be satisfied with informal hearings or no individualized hearings at all in many circumstances?

In **Kerry v. Din**, 576 U.S. ___, 135 S. Ct. 2128 (2015), a citizen alleged deprivation of a constitutional right to live in the United States with her spouse after denial of a visa application by her husband, a non-citizen, without adequate explanation of the reason for the visa denial. For a three-justice plurality eleven days before the Court decided Obergefell v. Hodges (p. 583, above), Justice SCALIA wrote that "[there] is no such constitutional right" for purposes of procedural due process analysis. "Unlike the States in Loving v. Virginia, the Federal Government here has not attempted to forbid a marriage." He dismissed Meyer, Pierce, and Griswold as irrelevant: "Nothing in the cases Din cites establishes a free-floating and categorical liberty interest in marriage [sufficient] to trigger constitutional protection whenever a regulation in any way touches upon an aspect of the marital relationship. [Here], a long practice of regulating spousal immigration precludes Din's claim that the denial of [her husband's] visa application has deprived her of a fundamental liberty interest."

Justice KENNEDY, joined by Justice Alito, concurred only in the judgment, and would have held that the government's explanation of the denial—invocation of "the statutory provision prohibiting the issuance of visas to persons who engage in terrorist activities"—sufficed as a matter of procedural due process.

Justice BREYER, joined by Justices Ginsburg, Sotomayor, and Kagan, dissented, and would have found a procedural due process interest in Din's "freedom to live together with her husband in the United States. [The] Due Process Clause entitles her to such procedural rights as long as (1) she seeks protection for a liberty interest sufficiently important for procedural protection to flow 'implicitly' from the design, object, and nature of the Due Process Clause, or (2) nonconstitutional law (a statute, for example) creates an expectation that a person will not be deprived of that kind of liberty without fair procedures. The liberty for which Ms. Din seeks protection easily satisfies both standards. As this Court has long recognized, the institution of marriage, which encompasses the right of spouses to live together and to raise a family, is central to human life, requires and enjoys community support, and plays a central role in most individuals' 'orderly pursuit of happiness.' At the same time, the law, including visa law, surrounds marriage with a host of legal protections to the point that it creates a strong expectation that government will not deprive married individuals of their freedom to live together without strong reasons and (in individual cases) without fair procedure. [How] exactly would it harm important security interests to give Ms. Din a better explanation?"

WHAT PROCESS IS "DUE"?

Assuming a government deprivation of constitutionally protected "liberty" and "property" has occurred, what procedural guarantees attach? The answer has largely been governed by the balancing approach of Justice

POWELL's majority opinion in **Mathews v. Eldridge**, 424 U.S. 319 (1976). There, the Court held that pretermination evidentiary hearings were not required in the context of disability benefits. Justice Powell stated: " '[Due process] is flexible and calls for such procedural protections as the particular situation demands.' Accordingly, resolution of the issue whether the administrative procedures provided here are constitutionally sufficient requires analysis of the governmental and private interests that are affected. More precisely, our prior decisions indicate that identification of the specific dictates of due process generally requires consideration of three distinct factors: First, the private interest that will be affected by the official action; second, the risk of an erroneous deprivation of such interest through the procedures used, and the probable value, if any, of additional or substitute procedural safeguards; and finally, the Government's interest, including the function involved and the fiscal and administrative burdens that the additional or substitute procedural requirement would entail." Do Justice Powell's three factors provide adequate guidance? The framework remains dominant in cases assessing due process requirements today.

Generally speaking, the additional process that is afforded to certain protected interests is an ex ante hearing: the individual to be deprived of liberty or property is given an opportunity to contest that decision before the deprivation actually occurs. Although decided well before Mathews, a foundational case in this field is **North American Cold Storage Co. v. Chicago**, 211 U.S. 306 (1908). There, the Court examined the weight of what Mathews would later label the government's interest in proceeding without additional process. A refrigeration company argued that a local ordinance allowing inspectors to destroy potentially contaminated meats without an ex ante hearing deprived the company of a property interest in its meats without due process. The Court held that circumstances demanding "the destruction of food which is not fit for human use" constituted an "emergency" such that the Court would defer to the "reasonable discretion of the legislature as to the necessity for a prior hearing."

At the other end of the spectrum, the Court examined a case involving little need for rapid government action and the distinctly important property interest in retaining one's job in **Perry v. Sindermann**, 408 U.S. 593 (1972), p. 605 above. Consider also **Ingraham v. Wright**, 430 U.S. 651 (1977), in which a student challenged a school's corporal punishment policy. Ingraham, a middle school student, had been paddled "[b]ecause he was slow to respond to his teacher's instructions." The paddling was so severe that it caused a hematoma "requiring medical attention and keeping him out of school for several days." Ingraham argued that the school's paddling policy deprived him of liberty—the right to be free from bodily harm—without due process. He urged in particular that the school should be required to provide some ex ante procedure before paddling students. Obviously, a full trial before each disciplinary measure would be unrealistic, but at a minimum, he argued, the school should give a student "prior notice and an opportunity to be heard" before paddling him.

Writing for the Court, Justice POWELL upheld the policy. Corporal punishment, Justice Powell explained, did implicate a "constitutionally protected liberty interest." Given the protected liberty interest, he asked, "what process is due?" Justice Powell began with the interest of the student. Because of the seriousness of corporal punishment and the risk that a teacher's punishment could erroneously be directed at the wrong student, "the child has a strong interest in procedural safeguards that minimize the risk of wrongful punishment and provide for the resolution of disputed questions of justification." On the other hand, he continued, the government's interest in maintaining order in classrooms was strong. Moreover, it was unclear whether requiring greater ex ante procedures would have anything more than an "incremental benefit," and that benefit was far outweighed by the costs of such an approach. Requiring greater procedure "would significantly burden the use of corporal punishment as a disciplinary measure. Hearings, even informal hearings, require time, personnel, and a diversion of attention from normal school pursuits. School authorities may well choose to abandon corporal punishment rather than incur the burdens of complying with the procedural requirements. Teachers, properly concerned with maintaining authority in the classroom, may well prefer to rely on other disciplinary measures which they may view as less effective rather than confront the possible disruption that prior notice and a hearing may entail." Therefore, Justice Powell concluded that "the Due Process Clause does not require notice and a hearing prior to the imposition of corporal punishment in the public schools, as that practice is authorized and limited by the common law." Rather, the opportunity to pursue relief in post-paddling tort proceedings sufficed for purposes of the Mathews standard.

Justice WHITE, joined by Justices Brennan, Marshall, and Stevens, dissented, explaining that "[t]he reason that the Constitution requires a State to provide 'due process of law' when it punishes an individual for misconduct is to protect the individual from erroneous or mistaken punishment that the State would not have inflicted had it found the facts in a more reliable way. [To] guard against [the] risk of punishing an innocent child, the Due Process Clause requires, not an "elaborate hearing" before a neutral party, but simply an informal give-and-take between student and disciplinarian which gives the student an opportunity to explain his version of the facts." Justice White went on to note that finding ex post remedies sufficient "rests on the novel theory that the State may punish an individual without giving him any opportunity to present his side of the story, as long as he can later recover damages from a state official if he is innocent. The logic of this theory would permit a State that punished speeding with a one-day jail sentence to make a driver serve his sentence first without a trial and then sue to recover damages for wrongful imprisonment." He therefore concluded that, in light of the seriousness of the interests involved and the risk of error, the school ought to be required to provide some ex ante process.

Justice STEVENS also dissented separately, agreeing with Justice White but further highlighting the notion that the type of deprivation might impact the process due to an individual. Property deprivations, he explained, are more likely to be remedied fully with ex post damages awards, whereas liberty deprivations may not be so easily corrected. Therefore, he argued, the Court ought to have special solicitude for liberty rights when litigants allege deprivations of due process.

SECTION 4. TEXTUAL GUARANTEES OF ECONOMIC LIBERTIES: THE TAKINGS CLAUSE AND THE CONTRACTS CLAUSE

Several explicit textual provisions in the Constitution protect property from government redistribution. Why, then, did economic liberties find a constitutional home in the Due Process Clause in Lochner and its progeny as explored in Section 1 above? Does the existence of those explicit clauses cut in favor or against judicial implication of unenumerated economic liberties? The Takings Clause of the Fifth Amendment provides that private property shall not "be taken for public use, without just compensation." Note that it does not forbid expropriation in the public interest, but merely requires that government pay for it. The Takings Clause has long been extended to the states as incorporated through the Due Process Clause of the Fourteenth Amendment. The Contracts Clause of Article I, § 10 provides that "No State shall [pass] any [Law] impairing the Obligation of Contracts." Note that the Constitution contains no similar limitation on the federal government. The Court's elaboration of these clauses is explored in the cases that follow.

THE TAKINGS CLAUSE

Among the earliest "specific" Bill of Rights guarantees absorbed into the Fourteenth Amendment's due process guarantee was the Fifth Amendment's command that private property shall not "be taken for public use, without just compensation." See Chicago, Burlington & Quincy Ry. Co. v. Chicago, 166 U.S. 226 (1897) (states are bound to pay just compensation), and Missouri Pac. Ry. v. Nebraska, 164 U.S. 403 (1896) (property may not be taken by the states for "private" rather than "public" use). The state and federal governments frequently resort to the power of eminent domain to "take" private land for public use. When property is "taken" through condemnation, the owner is entitled to "just compensation." Some aspects of takings law bear on issues similar to those raised by the economic due process cases described above in Section 1. First, does the "public use" clause impose any substantive limitation on takings? Second, should courts extend the compensation requirement to any government actions beyond formal takings under the government's power of eminent domain? Should courts enforce compensation requirements for so-called "regulatory takings"? If they do, are they as unmoored from text as are courts applying substantive due process?

Note that before just compensation can be considered, there must first be a taking. States possess the power of eminent domain as a traditional police power; but where does any such federal power come from? The Constitution never expressly confers the power to take property by eminent domain, but in **Kohl v. United States**, 91 U.S. 367 (1875), the Court held that federal government possessed the power as a matter of "political necessity" and called the taking power "inseparable from sovereignty, unless denied to it by its fundamental law." The Court explained the necessity in practical terms that called to mind the recent Civil War and Reconstruction, as well as increasing national communication and transportation: "The powers vested by the Constitution in the general government demand for their exercise the acquisition of lands in all the states. These are needed for forts, armories, and arsenals, for navy yards and lighthouses, for custom houses, post offices, and courthouses, and for other public uses. If the right to acquire property for such uses may be made a barren right by the unwillingness of propertyholders to sell, or by the action of a state prohibiting a sale to the federal government, the constitutional grants of power may be rendered nugatory, and the government is dependent for its practical existence upon the will of a state, or even upon that of a private citizen. This cannot be."

The Court also explained that the eminent domain power was implied by the Fifth Amendment, which "contains a provision that private property shall not be taken for public use without just compensation. What is that but an implied assertion that, on making just compensation, it may be taken?" It acknowledged that in the past the taking "power of the federal government has not heretofore been exercised adversely, but the nonuse of a power does not disprove its existence. In some instances the states, by virtue of their own right of eminent domain, have condemned lands for the use of the general government, and such condemnations have been sustained by their courts, without, however, denying the right of the United States to act independently of the states." Finally, the Court concluded that, given the necessity of the right, "[i]f the United States have the power, it must be complete in itself," not dependent on state approval.

It has recently been argued that the Framers did not intend that the federal government to have the power of eminent domain except in federally administered territories, and that early takings within states were made by states which then transferred the property to the federal government. Baude, "Rethinking the Federal Eminent Domain Power," 122 Yale L.J. (2013). If this were so, would it matter for Takings Clause analysis today? What does the answer tell you about originalism?

THE "PUBLIC USE" REQUIREMENT

1. ***Interpreting the Takings Clause.*** Should the Fifth Amendment be read to require not only "just compensation" for takings, but also an independent judicial demonstration that a taking will serve a "*public use*"? Why isn't the fact that the public will have to pay for the taking a sufficient guarantee that it will serve a public purpose? Won't the public decline to approve public expenditures for any mere private interest deal? Is there a danger that specific takings will disproportionately benefit organized special interests, but that the wide diffusion of costs among all taxpayers will lower any individual's motivation to protest and thus make public resistance through politics an insufficient check? Even if this may be so, are courts competent to police a line between truly public and excessively "private" takings? Don't even some "private" takings provide positive public benefits?

2. ***Judicial deference toward determinations of "public use."*** There is no issue of public use when government takes property in order to erect public property such as schools, city halls or roadways for actual use by the public. But is the public use requirement satisfied when government takes private property and then transfers it for development or use by other private parties? Despite some efforts by litigants to challenge such takings as excessively private in violation of the public use requirement, the

Supreme Court has extended the same deference toward legislative determinations of what constitutes "public use" as it does under economic due process scrutiny.

Such deference is illustrated by **Berman v. Parker**, 348 U.S. 26 (1954), which involved a challenge to a District of Columbia law authorizing the taking of private property for the purpose of redeveloping blighted urban areas. After condemnation, the government could lease or sell that property to private developers, who were required to conform to redevelopment plans adopted by a D.C. agency. Writing for a unanimous Court, Justice DOUGLAS sustained the scheme against challenge by an owner of a functioning store, stating: "The role of the judiciary in determining whether [the eminent domain power] is being exercised for a public purpose is an extremely narrow one. [The] concept of the public welfare is broad and inclusive. The values it represents are spiritual as well as physical, aesthetic as well as monetary. It is within the power of the legislature to determine that the community should be beautiful as well as healthy, spacious as well as clean, well-balanced as well as carefully patrolled. [If] those who govern the District of Columbia decide that the Nation's Capital should be beautiful as well as sanitary, there is nothing in the Fifth Amendment that stands in the way. [The] rights of these property owners are satisfied when they receive that just compensation which the Fifth Amendment exacts as the price of the taking."

This "extremely narrow" judicial role in determining the scope of "public use" was again demonstrated in the Court's unanimous decision in **Hawaii Housing Authority v. Midkiff**, 467 U.S. 229 (1984). The decision upheld Hawaii's use of eminent domain to solve the problem of concentrated land ownership, a problem traceable to Hawaii's early feudal land tenure system. In the 1960s, the legislature found that 72 private landowners owned 47% of the State's land and the state and federal governments 49%, leaving only 4% for other private owners. Moreover, on Oahu, the most urbanized island, 22 landowners owned 72.5% of the fee simple titles. The legislature concluded that "concentrated land ownership was responsible for skewing the State's residential fee simple market, inflating land prices, and injuring the public tranquility and welfare." The Hawaii Land Reform Act of 1967, designed to compel large landowners to break up their estates, created a mechanism to implement that purpose. Under the Act, tenants living on single-family residential lots under long-term leases from landowners were entitled to ask the State's Housing Authority to condemn the property on which they lived. After the state agency acquired the property by eminent domain, it could sell the land to tenants who had applied for fee simple ownership. The court of appeals for the Ninth Circuit ruled that such takings were invalid as for a private use—invoking Justice Chase's opinion in Calder v. Bull in suggesting that the Hawaii scheme effected naked transfers of property from A to B.

Writing for the Court in unanimously reversing the Ninth Circuit (Justice Marshall did not participate), Justice O'CONNOR rejected the claim that the purpose of the Hawaii scheme was redistribution for private rather than public benefit. After reviewing Berman, she noted that the "public use" requirement was "coterminous with the scope of a sovereign's police powers." She added: "[Where] the exercise of the eminent domain power is rationally related to a conceivable public purpose, the Court has never held a compensated taking to be proscribed by the Public Use Clause. On this basis, we have no trouble concluding that the Hawaii Act is constitutional.

[Regulating] oligopoly and the evils associated with it is a classic exercise of a State's police powers. We cannot disapprove of Hawaii's exercise of this power. Nor can we condemn as irrational the Act's approach to correcting the land oligopoly problem.

"[When] the legislature's purpose is legitimate and its means are not irrational, our cases make clear that empirical debates over the wisdom of takings—no less than debates over the wisdom of other kinds of socioeconomic legislation—are not to be carried out in the federal courts. [The] mere fact that property taken outright by eminent domain is transferred in the first instance to private beneficiaries does not condemn that taking as having only a private purpose. The Court long ago rejected any literal requirement that condemned property be put into use for the general public. [Government] does not itself have to use property to legitimate the taking; it is only the taking's purpose, and not its mechanics, that must pass scrutiny under the Public Use Clause. [The] State of Hawaii has never denied that the Constitution forbids even a compensated taking of property when executed for no reason other than to confer a private benefit on a particular private party. [But] no purely private taking is involved in these cases. The Hawaii Legislature enacted its Land Reform Act not to benefit a particular class of identifiable individuals but to attack certain perceived evils of concentrated property ownership in Hawaii—a legitimate public purpose."

Are there *any* circumstances in which courts should invoke public use as a limit on the government's taking power? If the mayor took land for his own residence? For a development project by his biggest campaign supporter? If the taking broke up a tightly knit community, or a racially or religiously identifiable voting bloc? How important was the antitrust dimension of the Court's reasoning in Midkiff, which spoke of the social interest in breaking up a land oligopoly? Would a different result have been likely in Midkiff if Hawaii's professed purpose had rested on a perception that concentrated land ownership was simply unjust? Consider the argument in the following case that a taking for private development violated the public use requirement. The Court again rejected the argument. But this time, the Court divided more closely, 5–4, on the question, with Justice O'Connor, the author of Midkiff, leading the dissenters:

Kelo v. City of New London

545 U.S. 469, 125 S. Ct. 2655, 162 L. Ed. 2d 439 (2005).

■ JUSTICE STEVENS delivered the opinion of the Court, in which JUSTICES KENNEDY, SOUTER, GINSBURG, and BREYER joined.

In 2000, the city of New London approved a development plan that [was] "projected to create in excess of 1,000 jobs, to increase tax and other revenues, and to revitalize an economically distressed city, including its downtown and waterfront areas." In assembling the land needed for this project, the city's development agent has purchased property from willing sellers and proposes to use the power of eminent domain to acquire the remainder of the property from unwilling owners in exchange for just compensation. The question presented is whether the city's proposed disposition of this property qualifies as a "public use" within the meaning of the Takings Clause of the Fifth Amendment to the Constitution.

I. The city of New London [suffered] decades of economic decline [that] led a state agency in 1990 to designate the City a "distressed municipality." [These] conditions prompted state and local officials to target New London, and particularly its Fort Trumbull area, for economic revitalization. To this end, respondent New London Development Corporation (NLDC), a private nonprofit entity established some years earlier to assist the City in planning economic development, was reactivated. [The] State authorized a $5.35 million bond issue to support the NLDC's planning activities and a $10 million bond issue toward the creation of a Fort Trumbull State Park. [The] pharmaceutical company Pfizer Inc. announced that it would build a $300 million research facility on a site immediately adjacent to Fort Trumbull; local planners hoped that Pfizer would draw new business to the area, thereby serving as a catalyst to the area's rejuvenation.

II. [In] all, the nine petitioners own 15 properties in Fort Trumbull. [There] is no allegation that any of these properties is blighted or otherwise in poor condition; rather, they were condemned only because they happen to be located in the development area. [The] Supreme Court of Connecticut [held] that all of the City's proposed takings were valid.

III. Two polar propositions are perfectly clear. On the one hand, it has long been accepted that the sovereign may not take the property of A for the sole purpose of transferring it to another private party B, even though A is paid just compensation. On the other hand, it is equally clear that a State may transfer property from one private party to another if future "use by the public" is the purpose of the taking; the condemnation of land for a railroad with common-carrier duties is a familiar example. Neither of these propositions, however, determines the disposition of this case. [The] City's development plan was not adopted "to benefit a particular class of identifiable individuals." [Then again], this is not a case in which the City is planning to open the condemned land—at least not in its entirety—to use by the general public.

[But] this "Court long ago rejected any literal requirement that condemned property be put into use for the general public." Indeed, while many state courts in the mid-19th century endorsed "use by the public" as the proper definition of public use, that narrow view steadily eroded over time. [When] this Court began applying the Fifth Amendment to the States at the close of the 19th century, it embraced the broader and more natural interpretation of public use as "public purpose."

[The] disposition of this case therefore turns on the question whether the City's development plan serves a "public purpose." Without exception, our cases have defined that concept broadly, reflecting our longstanding policy of deference to legislative judgments in this field. In Berman v. Parker, this Court upheld a redevelopment plan targeting a blighted area of Washington, D.C., in which most of the housing for the area's 5,000 inhabitants was beyond repair. [The] owner of a department store located in the area challenged the condemnation, pointing out that his store was not itself blighted. [Writing] for a unanimous Court, Justice Douglas refused to evaluate this claim in isolation, deferring instead to the legislative and agency judgment that the area "must be planned as a whole" for the plan to be successful.

In Hawaii Housing Authority v. Midkiff, the Court considered a Hawaii statute whereby fee title was taken from lessors and transferred to lessees (for just compensation) in order to reduce the concentration of land ownership. We unanimously upheld the statute and rejected the Ninth Circuit's view that it was "a naked attempt on the part of the state of Hawaii to take the property of A and transfer it to B solely for B's private use and benefit." [We] concluded that the State's purpose of eliminating the "social and economic evils of a land oligopoly" qualified as a valid public use. [Our] public use jurisprudence has wisely eschewed rigid formulas and intrusive scrutiny in favor of affording legislatures broad latitude in determining what public needs justify the use of the takings power.

IV. Those who govern the City were not confronted with the need to remove blight in the Fort Trumbull area, but their determination that the area was sufficiently distressed to justify a program of economic rejuvenation is entitled to our deference. The City has carefully formulated an economic development plan that it believes will provide appreciable benefits to the community, including—but by no means limited to—new jobs and increased tax revenue. [Given] the comprehensive character of the plan, the thorough deliberation that preceded its adoption, and the limited scope of our review, it is appropriate for us, as it was in Berman, to resolve the challenges of the individual owners, not on a piecemeal basis, but rather in light of the entire plan. Because that plan unquestionably serves a public purpose, the takings challenged here satisfy the public use requirement of the Fifth Amendment.

To avoid this result, petitioners urge us to adopt a new bright-line rule that economic development does not qualify as a public use. [Neither] precedent nor logic supports petitioners' proposal. Promoting economic development is a traditional and long accepted function of government. [Quite] simply, the government's pursuit of a public purpose will often benefit individual private parties. [It] is further argued that without a bright-line rule nothing would stop a city from transferring citizen A's property to citizen B for the sole reason that citizen B will put the property to a more productive use and thus pay more taxes. Such a one-to-one transfer of property, executed outside the confines of an integrated development plan, is not presented in this case. While such an unusual exercise of government power would certainly raise a suspicion that a private purpose was afoot, the hypothetical cases posited by petitioners can be confronted if and when they arise.

[In] affirming the City's authority to take petitioners' properties, we do not minimize the hardship that condemnations may entail, notwithstanding the payment of just compensation. We emphasize that nothing in our opinion precludes any State from placing further restrictions on its exercise of the takings power. [The] necessity and wisdom of using eminent domain to promote economic development are certainly matters of legitimate public debate. This Court's authority, however, extends only to determining whether the City's proposed condemnations are for a "public use" within the meaning of the Fifth Amendment to the Federal Constitution. Because over a century of our case law interpreting that provision dictates an affirmative answer to that question, we may not grant petitioners the relief that they seek. [Affirmed.]

■ JUSTICE KENNEDY, concurring.

[A] court applying rational-basis review under the Public Use Clause should strike down a taking that, by a clear showing, is intended to favor a particular private party, with only incidental or pretextual public benefits. [A] court confronted with a plausible accusation of impermissible favoritism to private parties should treat the objection as a serious one and review the record to see if it has merit, though with the presumption that the government's actions were reasonable and intended to serve a public purpose. Here, the trial court conducted a careful and extensive inquiry [and concluded] that benefiting Pfizer [or other private entities] was not "the primary motivation or effect of this development plan." [This] case, then, survives the meaningful rational basis review that in my view is required under the Public Use Clause.

[My] agreement with the Court that a presumption of invalidity is not warranted for economic development takings in general, or for the particular takings at issue in this case, does not foreclose the possibility that a more stringent standard of review than that announced in Berman and Midkiff might be appropriate for a more narrowly drawn category of takings. There may be private transfers in which the risk of undetected impermissible favoritism of private parties is so acute that a presumption (rebuttable or otherwise) of invalidity is warranted under the Public Use Clause. This demanding level of scrutiny, however, is not required simply because the purpose of the taking is economic development. [While] there may be categories of cases in which the transfers are so suspicious, or the procedures employed so prone to abuse, or the purported benefits are so trivial or implausible, that courts should presume an impermissible private purpose, no such circumstances are present in this case.

■ JUSTICE O'CONNOR, with whom CHIEF JUSTICE REHNQUIST and JUSTICES SCALIA and THOMAS join, dissenting.

[This] case returns us for the first time in over 20 years to the hard question of when a purportedly "public purpose" taking meets the public use requirement. It presents an issue of first impression: Are economic development takings constitutional? I would hold that they are not. In Berman and Midkiff, we emphasized the importance of deferring to legislative judgments about public purpose. [Yet] for all the emphasis on deference, Berman and Midkiff hewed to a bedrock principle without which our public use jurisprudence would collapse: "A purely private taking could not withstand the scrutiny of the public use requirement; it would serve no legitimate purpose of government and would thus be void." Midkiff. The Court's holdings in Berman and Midkiff were true to the principle underlying the Public Use Clause. In both those cases, the extraordinary, precondemnation use of the targeted property inflicted affirmative harm on society—in Berman through blight resulting from extreme poverty and in Midkiff through oligopoly resulting from extreme wealth. And in both cases, the relevant legislative body had found that eliminating the existing property use was necessary to remedy the harm. Thus a public purpose was realized when the harmful use was eliminated. Because each taking directly achieved a public benefit, it did not matter that the property was turned over to private use. Here, in contrast, New London does not claim that [petitioners'] well-maintained homes are the source of any social harm.

[In] moving away from our decisions sanctioning the condemnation of harmful property use, the Court today significantly expands the meaning of public use. It holds that the sovereign may take private property currently put to ordinary private use, and give it over for new, ordinary private use, so long as the new use is predicted to generate some secondary benefit for the public—such as increased tax revenue, more jobs, maybe even aesthetic pleasure. But nearly any lawful use of real private property can be said to generate some incidental benefit to the public. Thus, if predicted (or even guaranteed) positive side-effects are enough to render transfer from one private party to another constitutional, then the words "for public use" do not realistically exclude any takings, and thus do not exert any constraint on the eminent domain power.

[The] logic of today's decision is that eminent domain may only be used to upgrade—not downgrade—property. At best this makes the Public Use Clause redundant with the Due Process Clause, which already prohibits irrational government action. [In] any event, this constraint has no realistic import. For who among us can say she already makes the most productive or attractive possible use of her property? The specter of condemnation hangs over all property. Nothing is to prevent the State from replacing any Motel 6 with a Ritz-Carlton, any home with a shopping mall, or any farm with a factory. [Today] nearly all real property is susceptible to condemnation on the Court's theory. [The] fallout from this decision will not be random. The beneficiaries are likely to be those citizens with disproportionate influence and power in the political process, including large corporations and development firms. As for the victims, the government now has license to transfer property from those with fewer resources to those with more. The Founders cannot have intended this perverse result.

■ JUSTICE THOMAS, dissenting.

[The] Court replaces the Public Use Clause with a " 'Public Purpose' " Clause [that] enables the Court to hold, against all common sense, that a costly urban-renewal project whose stated purpose is a vague promise of new jobs and increased tax revenue, but which is also suspiciously agreeable to the Pfizer Corporation, is for a "public use." I cannot agree. [Our] cases have strayed from the Clause's original meaning, and I would reconsider them.

[The] Public Use Clause, like the Just Compensation Clause, [is] an express limit on the government's power of eminent domain. The most natural reading of the Clause is that it allows the government to take property only if the government owns, or the public has a legal right to use, the property, as opposed to taking it for any public purpose or necessity whatsoever. [Tellingly,] the phrase "public use" contrasts with the very different phrase "general Welfare" used elsewhere in the Constitution. The Framers would have used some such broader term if they had meant the Public Use Clause to have a similarly sweeping scope. [The Clause is] most naturally read to concern whether the property is used by the public or the government, not whether the purpose of the taking is legitimately public.

[There] is no justification [for] affording almost insurmountable deference to legislative conclusions that a use serves a "public use." [We] would not defer to a legislature's determination of the various circumstances that establish, for example, when a search of a home would be reasonable. [Yet] today the Court tells us that we are not to "second-guess the City's considered judgments," when the issue is, instead, whether the government may take the infinitely more intrusive step of tearing down petitioners' homes.

[Berman] and Midkiff erred by equating the eminent domain power with the police power of States. Traditional uses of that regulatory power, such as the power to abate a nuisance, required no compensation whatsoever, in sharp contrast to the takings power, which has always required compensation. The question whether the State can take property using the power of eminent domain is therefore distinct from the question whether it can regulate property pursuant to the police power. The "public purpose" test applied by Berman and Midkiff also cannot be applied in principled manner. [It] is far easier to analyze whether the government owns or the public has a legal right to use the taken property than to ask whether the taking has a "purely private purpose." For all these reasons, I would revisit our Public Use Clause cases and consider returning to the original meaning of the Public Use Clause: that the government may take property only if it actually uses or gives the public a legal right to use the property.

[Extending] the concept of public purpose to encompass any economically beneficial goal guarantees that these losses will fall disproportionately on poor communities. Those communities are not only systematically less likely to put their lands to the highest and best social use, but are also the least politically powerful. If ever there were justification for intrusive judicial review of constitutional provisions that protect "discrete and insular minorities," Carolene Products, surely that principle would apply with great force to the powerless groups and individuals the Public Use Clause protects. [Public] works projects in the 1950's and 1960's destroyed predominantly minority communities in St. Paul, Minnesota, and Baltimore, Maryland. In 1981, urban planners in Detroit, Michigan, uprooted the largely "lower-income and elderly" Poletown neighborhood for the benefit of the General Motors Corporation. Urban renewal projects have long been associated with the displacement of blacks. [Regrettably,] the predictable consequence of the Court's decision will be to exacerbate these effects.

THE MEANING AND IMPLICATIONS OF KELO

1. ***Broad reading of "public use."*** In taking an expansive view of what qualifies as a public use, did Kelo simply apply Berman and Midkiff, or did it extend those decisions' deference to the legislature one step further? After Kelo, are there any takings that will not satisfy the public use requirement so long as there is a conceivable public benefit, including job growth or increased tax base through future economic development? Note that Justice O'Connor wrote the Midkiff majority opinion upholding the Hawaii land reform act. Is her dissent in Kelo consistent with her position in Midkiff? Did she successfully distinguish Kelo from Berman and Midkiff on the basis that, in those cases, "precondemnation use of the targeted property inflicted affirmative harm on society—in Berman through blight resulting from extreme poverty and in Midkiff through oligopoly resulting from extreme wealth"? Why don't holdouts like New London homeowners Wright and Dey inflict similar "affirmative harm on society" by blocking development that cannot proceed around them? Recall that the particular property taken in Berman was not itself blighted.

2. ***The law and economics of takings for public use.*** Many extensions of eminent domain for uses beyond strictly government-run projects have focused on holdout problems. Private railroads, for example, have historically been beneficiaries of takings in eminent domain on the reasoning that a single landowner anywhere along the proposed track could

block the entire project by attempting to extract an exorbitant sum from the builder. Railroads cannot be situated just anywhere; they have to be continuous with existing track, and new tracks are limited as to how fast they can turn and what terrain they can cross. The entire social benefit of a railroad project would be lost if one landowner anywhere along the track could effectively veto the entire project. A taking in eminent domain for transfer to the railroad can solve the holdout problem without forcing the railroad to pay an exorbitant price.

In contrast, many private developments are not as sensitive to location. A developer of a housing project or an industrial park, for example, may have many possible locations. If one landowner threatens to demand an extreme sum then the developer might simply buy a different plot of land. But might holdout problems still adversely affect such private developments? Suppose a developer wants to build a business development like the one in Kelo. The local legislature has decided that it would bring social benefits such as economic development and increased tax base. Might there be something unique about one particular area (such as a waterfront view or access to transit) that makes it the only suitable location for such a project?

Justice Stevens in Kelo referred to Strickley v. Highland Boy Gold Mining Co., a case that illustrates why there might be social utility in allowing takings for private use but public benefit where a holdout problem would otherwise block economic productivity. There, the owner of a mine could transport his ore to market only by carrying it in aerial buckets over lands owned by other private parties. The landowner could have demanded an exorbitant fee for a trivial contribution to the mining venture. Strickley allowed the state to condemn the obstructing property for the mine owner's use upon payment of the landowner for his small losses.

Consider the view that both Midkiff and Kelo erred by extending "public use" beyond the context of genuine holdout problems: "One recurrent problem of social coordination arises when one party is in a position to blockade the productive ventures of another. [The] net gains from blocking the holdout are huge. The great intellectual blunder of the public use law over the past 50 or so years is that it has wrenched the public benefit language out of this narrow holdout context. [Any] comprehensive public project will produce some benefit for someone. [But] the slightest bit of reflection should have shown just how the new public use cases have migrated from the old mining cases, or even [the] Hawaii statute, which did not displace sitting tenants. Susette Kelo and her fellow plaintiffs have not tried to extract some unconscionable gain out of some sensible business venture. They have no desire to sell their homes at all. At the same time their subjective losses have been enormous. It was a perfectly sensible line for the court to say when subjective values are high, and holdout problems are nonexistent, the requisite public use is not present." Epstein, "Blind Justices: The Scandal of Kelo v. New London," Wall St. J., July 3, 2005. See generally Epstein, Takings: Private Property and Eminent Domain (1985).

3. ***Public response to Kelo.*** The Kelo decision elicited considerable and vocal public criticism. Public opinion polls indicated public disapproval of Kelo ranging from 65% to 97% of those surveyed. Groups ranging from the NAACP to the AARP publicly decried the opinion. One group of activists went as far as to propose the use of eminent domain to condemn the site of Justice Souter's home in the small town of Weare, New Hampshire in order to construct the so-called "Lost Liberty Hotel." President George W. Bush

issued an executive order instructing the federal government to limit its use of eminent domain in economic development cases. A number of bills were introduced in Congress by members of both parties seeking to limit the federal use of eminent domain power for economic development purposes. States too undertook legislative and constitutional responses, see note 4 below.

4. ***State constitutional interpretation of "public use."*** In deciding Kelo, the justices were aware of previous state controversies over whether takings for transfer to private parties were constitutional under the "public use" clauses of state constitutions. The most prominent took place in Michigan. Justice O'Connor's Kelo dissent expressly noted the Michigan Supreme Court's decision in **Poletown Neighborhood Council v. Detroit**, 410 Mich. 616, 304 N.W.2d 455 (1981), which had approved the taking of homes and small businesses in a working-class, immigrant community in Detroit for transfer to General Motors for construction of a planned automobile assembly plant. The Poletown dissent had warned that, "now that we have authorized local legislative bodies to decide that a different commercial or industrial use of property will produce greater public benefits than its present use, no homeowner's, merchant's or manufacturer's property, however productive or valuable to its owner, is immune from condemnation for the benefit of other private interests that will put it to a 'higher' use."

In **Wayne v. Hathcock**, 471 Mich. 445, 684 N.W.2d 765 (2004), the Michigan Supreme Court expressly overruled its prior holding in Poletown, as Justice O'Connor noted approvingly. In Hathcock, residents challenged a plan by a Michigan county to use eminent domain to acquire forty-six parcels required to create a business park with the goal of "creat[ing] thousands of jobs, and tens of millions of dollars in tax revenue." The Michigan court found the taking unconstitutional and held that Poletown had misconstrued the Michigan state constitution: "To justify the exercise of eminent domain solely on the basis of the fact that the use of that property by a private entity seeking its own profit might contribute to the economy's health is to render impotent our constitutional limitations on the government's power of eminent domain. Poletown's 'economic benefit' rationale would validate practically any exercise of the power of eminent domain on behalf of a private entity. After all, if one's ownership of private property is forever subject to the government's determination that another private party would put one's land to better use, then the ownership of real property is perpetually threatened by the expansion plans of any large discount retailer, 'megastore,' or the like."

Are there any grounds on which the Poletown taking might have been distinguished from the takings upheld in Midkiff and Kelo? What about the fact that the close-knit Polish immigrant community had developed social networks and business good will that could not be fairly compensated by cash payments to individual owners? Is it clear that such intangible costs can be factored into individual compensation payments?

In the wake of Kelo, nearly half the states have adopted statutory or constitutional restrictions on the use of eminent domain to transfer land to private developers. Michigan itself amended its state constitution in 2005 to add an express limitation that " 'public use' does not include the taking of private property for transfer to a private entity for the purpose of economic development or enhancement of tax revenues." Other states that have passed similar limitations include Alabama, Alaska, Colorado, Florida, Georgia, Idaho, Illinois, Indiana, Iowa, Kansas, Kentucky, Maine, Minnesota, Missouri, Nebraska, New Hampshire, North Carolina, Pennsylvania, South Dakota, Tennessee, Utah, Vermont, West Virginia and Wisconsin. The South Dakota bill, for example, provides that "No county, municipality, or housing and redevelopment commission [may] acquire private property by use of eminent domain [for] transfer to any private person, nongovernmental entity, or other public-private business entity [or] primarily for enhancement of tax revenue." Not every state attempt to restrict eminent domain has been successful. In both Arizona and New Mexico, for example, the governor vetoed bills passed by the state legislature. In 2006, California voters rejected Proposition 90, which would have amended the state constitution to provide that "private property may not be taken [for] private use" but only for occupation by a governmental agency or regulated entity such as a utility. And shortly after Kelo, some states interpreted their own constitutions' takings clauses in direct opposition to the Supreme Court's interpretation in Kelo. Ohio, for example, rejected the Supreme Court's public purpose rationale in **Norwood v. Horney**, 853 N.E.2d 1115 (Ohio 2006), expressing its disapproval of what it called an "almost unbridled expansion of the notion of public use," and ruling instead that a city's designation of certain areas as "deteriorating" was insufficient to justify a taking. It wrote: "[Although] economic factors may be considered in determining whether private property may be appropriated, the fact that the appropriation would provide an economic benefit to the government and community, standing alone, does not satisfy the public-use requirement of [the Ohio Constitution]."

5. ***Racial equality and eminent domain.*** Justice Thomas noted in his Kelo dissent that the use of eminent domain historically has had a disparate impact on minority communities. The public-interest law firm that represented the homeowners in Kelo analyzed over 10,000 threatened or actual eminent domain condemnations and concluded that the categories of residents are most at risk included "residents of older neighborhoods in locations that make them attractive for a supposedly higher and better use," "working-class and middle-income areas in general," and "neighborhoods with high concentrations of lower-income minority residents." Harney, "Court Ruling Leaves Poor at Greatest Risk," Wash. Post, July 2, 2005, at F1. Should courts consider such evidence when deciding public use challenges?

REGULATORY "TAKINGS"

Suppose government, rather than condemning property and formally transferring title to itself under the eminent domain power, merely "regulates" its use and thus substantially diminishes its value. Should such action obligate the government to pay the property owner "just compensation" for the loss under the Takings Clause? A series of Supreme Court decisions has held that it should, and "inverse condemnation" suits brought by property owners against regulations that are not formal takings have become commonplace. What is the constitutional authority for such extension of constitutional limitations from takings in eminent domain, which the framers of the 5th Amendment visualized, to modern land use, zoning, and environmental regulation, which they likely did not? Is regulatory takings law in effect a form of substantive due process, in which laws that diminish too much private value in relation to public benefit are not properly understood as duly enacted "law"? For examination of the comparative political economy of taking and regulation, see Kelman, Strategy or Principle? The Choice Between Regulation and Taxation (1999).

Justice Holmes stated the following "general rule" in the Pennsylvania Coal case, which follows: "[W]hile property may be regulated to a certain extent, if regulation goes too far it will be recognized as a taking." How far is "too far"? When does governmental action give rise to a duty to compensate? When may government impose property losses without paying compensation, through "the petty larceny of the police power"? In examining these materials, consider what criteria might best serve to draw the taking-regulation distinction: The magnitude of the harm to the private interest? The manner of imposing the harm? The degree to which the imposition interferes with legitimate private expectations? The nature and magnitude of the public interest?

Pennsylvania Coal Co. v. Mahon

260 U.S. 393, 43 S. Ct. 158, 67 L. Ed. 322 (1922).

■ JUSTICE HOLMES delivered the opinion of the court.

[The Pennsylvania Coal Company sought to mine under the plaintiffs' property, observing that the plaintiffs' deed to the property granted surface use only and reserved mining rights to the company. A 1921 state law, the Kohler Act,] forbids the mining of anthracite coal in such a way as to cause the subsidence of, among other things, any structure used as a human habitation. [The company argued that the law constituted an uncompensated taking of its property rights.] The question [here] is whether the police power can be stretched so far [as the Kohler Act attempts.]

Government hardly could go on if to some extent values incident to property could not be diminished without paying for every such change in the general law. As long recognized, some values are enjoyed under an implied limitation and must yield to the police power. But obviously the implied limitation must have its limits, or the contract and due process clauses are gone. One fact for consideration in determining such limits is the extent of the diminution. When it reaches a certain magnitude, in most if not in all cases there must be an exercise of eminent domain and compensation to sustain the act. So the question depends upon the particular facts.

[This] is the case of a single private house. No doubt there is a public interest even in this. [But] usually in ordinary private affairs the public interest does not warrant much of this kind of interference. A source of damage to such a house is not a public nuisance even if similar damage is inflicted on others in different places. The damage is not common or public. [The law] is not justified as a protection of personal safety. That could be provided for by notice. Indeed the very foundation of this bill is that the defendant gave timely notice of its intent to mine under the house. On the other hand the extent of the taking is great. It purports to abolish what is recognized in Pennsylvania as [a "very valuable" estate in land]. If we were called upon to deal with the plaintiffs' position alone, we should think it clear that the statute does not disclose a public interest sufficient to warrant so extensive a destruction of the defendant's constitutionally protected rights. But the case has been treated as one in which the general validity of the act should be discussed.

[It] is our opinion that the act cannot be sustained as an exercise of the police power, so far as it affects the mining of coal under streets or cities in places where the right to mine such coal has been reserved. [What] makes the right to mine coal valuable is that it can be exercised with profit. To make it commercially impracticable to mine certain coal has very nearly the same effect for constitutional purposes as appropriating or destroying it. This we think that we are warranted in assuming that the statute [does]. The rights of the public in a street purchased or laid out by eminent domain are those that it has paid for. If in any case its representatives have been so short sighted as to acquire only surface rights without the right of support, we see no more authority for supplying the latter without compensation than there was for taking the right of way in the first place and refusing to pay for it because the public wanted it very much. The protection of private property in the Fifth Amendment presupposes that it is wanted for public use, but provides that it shall not be taken for such use without compensation.

[When] this seemingly absolute protection is found to be qualified by the police power, the natural tendency of human nature is to extend the qualification more and more until at last private property disappears. But that cannot be accomplished in this way under the [Constitution]. The general rule at least is that while property may be regulated to a certain extent, if regulation goes too far it will be recognized as a taking. [A] strong public desire to improve the public condition is not enough to warrant achieving the desire by a shorter cut than the constitutional way of paying for the change. [It] is a question of degree. [This law goes beyond] any of the cases decided by this [Court]. We assume, of course, that the statute was passed upon the conviction that an exigency existed that would warrant it, and we assumed that an exigency exists that would warrant the exercise of eminent domain. But the question at bottom is upon whom the loss of the changes desired should fall. So far as private persons or communities have seen fit to take the risk of acquiring only surface rights, we cannot see that the fact that their risk has become a danger warrants the giving to them greater rights than they bought. [Reversed.]

■ JUSTICE BRANDEIS, dissenting.

[Every] restriction upon the use of property imposed in the exercise of the police power deprives the owner of some right theretofore enjoyed, and is, in that sense, an abridgment by the State of rights in property without making compensation. But a restriction imposed to protect the public health, safety or morals from dangers threatened is not a taking. The restriction here in question is merely the prohibition of a noxious use. The property so restricted remains in the possession of its owner. The State does not appropriate it or make any use of it. The State merely prevents the owner from making a use which interferes with paramount rights of the [public]. The restriction upon the use of this property can not, of course, be lawfully imposed, unless its purpose is to protect the public. [Furthermore], a restriction, though imposed for a public purpose, will not be lawful, unless the restriction is an appropriate means to the public end. But to keep coal in place is surely an appropriate means of preventing subsidence of the surface; and ordinarily it is the only available means. Restriction upon use does not become inappropriate as a means, merely because it deprives the owner of the only use to which the property can then be profitably put.

[It] is said that one fact for consideration in determining whether the limits of the police power have been exceeded is the extent of the resulting diminution in value, and that here the restriction destroys existing rights of property and contract. But values are relative. If we are to consider the value of the coal kept in place by the restriction, we should compare it with the value of all other parts of the land. [The law was] obviously enacted for a public purpose; and it seems, likewise, clear that mere notice of intention to mine would [not] secure the public safety. Yet it is said that [the law] cannot be sustained as an exercise of the police power where the right to mine such coal has been reserved. The conclusion seems to rest upon the assumption that in order to justify such exercise of the police power there must be "an average reciprocity of advantage" as between the owner of the property restricted and the rest of the community; and that here such reciprocity is absent. Reciprocity of advantage is an important consideration, and may even be essential, where the State's power is exercised for the purpose of conferring benefits upon the property of a neighborhood, as in drainage projects [or] upon adjoining owners, as by party wall provisions. But where the police power is exercised, not to confer benefits upon property owners but to protect the public from detriment and danger, there is in my opinion, no room for considering reciprocity of advantage [unless] it be the advantage of living and doing business in a civilized community.

THE MEANING AND IMPLICATIONS OF PENNSYLVANIA COAL

1. ***Distinguishing permissible regulations from regulatory takings.*** In contrast to the coal case, another decision a few years later reached the opposite conclusion on whether a regulation rose to the level of a taking requiring just compensation. In **Miller v. Schoene**, 276 U.S. 272 (1928), the Court upheld against takings challenge a Virginia law that provided for the destruction as a public nuisance of all ornamental red cedar trees that were or might be the source of a communicable plant disease known as cedar rust and that were growing within a prescribed radius of any apple orchard. Under the law, owners of the cedars were paid only the cost of removing their trees; they were not compensated for loss of the value of the standing cedars or the decrease in the value of their land caused by the destruction of the trees. The state courts upheld the state entomologist's order that a large number of cedars be cut down to protect nearby apple orchards. In affirming that decision and concluding that the cedars could be destroyed without paying compensation to their owners, Justice STONE's opinion for the unanimous Court stated:

"[Cedar rust] is destructive of the fruit and foliage of the apple, but without effect on the value of the cedar. [The] only practicable method of controlling the disease and protecting apple trees [is] the destruction of all red cedar trees, subject to the infection, located within two miles of apple orchards. The red cedar, aside from its ornamental use, has occasional use and value as lumber. It is indigenous to Virginia, is not cultivated or dealt in commercially on any substantial scale, and its value throughout the state is shown to be small as compared with that of the apple orchards of the state. Apple growing is one of the principal agricultural pursuits in Virginia.

[Many] millions of dollars are invested in the orchards, which furnish employment for a large portion of the population.

"[On] the evidence we may accept the conclusion of the [state court] that the state was under the necessity of making a choice between the preservation of one class of property and that of the other wherever both existed in dangerous proximity. It would have been none the less a choice if, instead of enacting the present statute, the state, by doing nothing, had permitted serious injury to the apple orchards within its borders to go on unchecked. When forced to such a choice the state does not exceed its constitutional powers by deciding upon the destruction of one class of property in order to save another which, in the judgment of the legislature, is of greater value to the public. It will not do to say that the case is merely one of a conflict of two private interests and that the misfortune of apple growers may not be shifted to cedar owners by ordering the destruction of their property; for it is obvious that there may be, and that here there is, a preponderant public concern in the preservation of the one interest over the other. [And] where the public interest is involved preferment of that interest over the property interest of the individual, to the extent even of its destruction, is one of the distinguishing characteristics of every exercise of the police power which affects property. [Where], as here, the choice is unavoidable, we cannot say that its exercise, controlled by considerations of social policy which are not unreasonable, involves any denial of due process."

What factors might distinguish Miller v. Schoene from Pennsylvania Coal v. Mahon? The essence of Holmes's opinion in the coal case would seem to be that a few should not bear all the cost of the public welfare; that cost should be spread through the compensation requirement. But why, then, was there no regulatory taking found in Miller? Conversely, why could the government not "shift the balance of misfortune" among private parties in the coal case as in the cedar case? If either government inaction or action amounts to a distributive choice, how can a court decide that the choice of action is unconstitutional? How reconcile the Holmes of Mahon with the Holmes of the Lochner dissent? Is there any greater textual basis for finding regulatory "takings" than violations of "substantive due process"? See Brauneis, "The Foundation of Our 'Regulatory Takings Jurisprudence': The Myth and Meaning of Justice Holmes's Opinion in Pennsylvania Coal Co. v. Mahon," 106 Yale L.J. 613 (1996).

The Court declined to follow the Mahon approach in a 1987 case on nearly identical facts. In **Keystone Bituminous Coal Ass'n v. Debenedictis**, 480 U.S. 470 (1987), the Court upheld, by a vote of 5–4, a modern day counterpart to the Kohler Act struck down in Pennsylvania Coal. At issue was a 1966 Pennsylvania law prohibiting coal mining that caused subsidence damage to preexisting public buildings, dwellings and cemeteries. Implementing administrative regulations required that 50% of the coal beneath such structures be kept in place as a means of providing surface support. Justice STEVENS's majority opinion distinguished Pennsylvania Coal without overruling it, holding that the restrictions in the 1966 law did *not* constitute a taking: First, he wrote, this law did not involve merely a balancing of private interests, but rather the protection of "the public interest in health, the environment, and the fiscal integrity of the area. That private individuals erred in taking a risk cannot estop the Commonwealth from exercising its police power to abate activity akin to a public nuisance." Second, there had been no showing here of a deprivation equivalent to that in Pennsylvania Coal, where certain mining was made "commercially impracticable" by the Kohler Act. The 27 million tons of coal that had to be left in place as a result of the law—less than 2% of the owners' total coal—did "not constitute a separate segment of property for takings purposes. Many zoning ordinances place limits on the property owner's right to make reasonable use of some segments of his property. A requirement that a building occupy no more than a specified percentage of the lot on which it is located could be characterized as a taking of the vacant area as readily as the requirement that coal pillars be left in place. [There] is no basis for treating the less than 2% of petitioners' coal as a separate parcel of property."

Chief Justice REHNQUIST, joined by Justices Powell, O'Connor and Scalia, dissented, insisting that both the language and the holding of Pennsylvania Coal dictated a similar "taking" finding here. He also objected to the majority's emphasis on the public purpose of the law: "[Public purpose] does not resolve the question of whether a taking has occurred; the existence of such a public purpose is merely a necessary prerequisite to the government's exercise of its taking power." The dissent also found the majority's reliance on the "public nuisance" theory misplaced, and its conclusion about the extent of the loss erroneous. With respect to the 27 million tons of coal to be left in place, "[t]here is no question that this coal is an identifiable and separate property interest. Unlike many property interests, the 'bundle' of rights in this coal is sparse. [From] the relevant perspective—that of the property owners—this interest has been destroyed every bit as much as if the government had proceeded to mine the coal for its own use."

Were the majority's distinctions persuasive? How should the numerator and denominator be selected in deciding how much of an owner's interest has been taken? Note that the majority saw the taking as involving a fraction of total resources owned, while the dissent engaged in a "conceptual severance" that treated the owners as losing 100% of the coal required to be left in place. How should a Court choose between these formulas? See Radin, "The Liberal Conception of Property: Cross Currents in the Jurisprudence of Takings," 88 Colum. L. Rev. 1667 (1988).

2. ***The scope of "property" under the Takings Clause.*** Note that the Court has not confined the notion of regulatory takings to real property in land. It has extended the concept to personal property. See Andrus v. Allard, 444 U.S. 51 (1979) (prohibition on sale of eagle feathers). It has extended it to intangible interests, requiring compensation for "takings," for example, by way of loss of repose from low-flying airplanes. See United States v. Causby, 328 U.S. 256 (1946); Griggs v. Allegheny County, 369 U.S. 84 (1962). It has extended it to other intangible interests, including intellectual property, see Ruckelshaus v. Monsanto Co., 467 U.S. 986 (1984) (trade secrets), and monetary interest generated from a fund into which a private individual has paid money, see Webb's Fabulous Pharmacies, Inc. v. Beckwith, 449 U.S. 155 (1980) ($100,000 in interest on a sum of $2 million that had been deposited in escrow in a fund with the registry of the court in an interpleader action); Phillips v. Washington Legal Foundation, 524 U.S. 156 (1998) (interest on clients' funds that lawyers are required to hold in trust in escrow accounts operated by state bars); but see Brown v. Legal Foundation of Washington, 538 U.S. 216 (2003) (holding by a vote of 5–4 that, despite Phillips, no compensation was required for a state's use of interest on lawyers' trust accounts to pay for legal services for the needy).

The Court has divided on when to extend the Takings Clause to regulations imposing new financial liability. Compare Connolly v. Pension Benefit Guaranty Corp., 475 U.S. 211 (1986) (holding that no compensable taking was imposed by amendments to the Employee Retirement Income Security Act of 1974 (ERISA) that require employers withdrawing from the program to pay their pro rata share of unfunded pension obligations) with Eastern Enterprises v. Apfel, 524 U.S. 498 (1998) (plurality opinion) (holding that provisions of the Coal Industry Retiree Health Benefit Act of 1992 that required companies formerly in the coal business to bear a significant share of retired miners' health care costs constituted a compensable taking because it "impose[d] severe retroactive liability on a limited class of parties that could not have anticipated the liability, and the extent of that liability is substantially disproportionate to the parties' experience").

3. ***The Penn Central balancing test.*** When may zoning, landmarking, or other environmental laws be challenged as being compensable "takings"? Even during the heyday of economic due process, a divided Court sustained a general zoning ordinance as a valid "police regulation," in Euclid v. Ambler Realty Co., 272 U.S. 365 (1926). But the Euclid Court emphasized that it was not passing on specific applications of zoning ordinances; and two years later, in Nectow v. Cambridge, 277 U.S. 183 (1928), an application of a zoning law was invalidated. By contrast, Goldblatt v. Hempstead, 369 U.S. 590 (1962), upheld a town "safety regulation"—resorted to after a state court had blocked an effort to deal with a local problem via zoning. Goldblatt owned a sand and gravel pit in a suburban area; the town had expanded rapidly. In the last of a series of local regulations of excavations, the town banned some types of mining and imposed a duty to refill some pits. Goldblatt claimed that the latest ordinance was "not regulatory" but rather amounted to confiscation of property without compensation. Justice Clark's opinion for the Court conceded that the regulation "completely prohibits a beneficial use to which the property has previously been devoted," but nevertheless found it justified as a "reasonable," noncompensable exercise of the police power.

In 1978, in an important and still governing test concerning the "taking-regulation" distinction, a divided Court held in **Penn Central Transportation Co. v. New York City**, 438 U.S. 104 (1978), that a New York City preservation law designating the Grand Central Terminal building a "landmark" constituted a permissible regulation, not a compensable taking. The law required the owner of a designated landmark to keep the building's exterior "in good repair" and to obtain approval from a city commission before making exterior alterations. A request for approval to build a multistory office building atop Grand Central Terminal was denied by the commission because, in its view, the office tower would impair the aesthetic quality of the Terminal's "flamboyant Beaux Arts facade." The owner of the Terminal brought suit claiming that the application of the law constituted a "taking." The 6–3 decision rejected that claim.

Justice BRENNAN's majority opinion concluded that a city may, as part of a comprehensive historic landmarks preservation program, "place restrictions on the development of individual historic landmarks [without] effecting a 'taking.'" He conceded that the inquiry involved "essentially ad hoc factual inquiries" rather than "any 'set formula,'" but set forth nonetheless an influential list of factors to consider in balancing public gain against private harm: "In engaging in these essentially ad hoc, factual inquiries, the Court's decisions have identified several factors that have particular significance. The economic impact of the regulation on the claimant and, particularly, the extent to which the regulation has interfered with distinct investment-backed expectations are, of course, relevant considerations. So, too, is the character of the governmental action. A 'taking' may more readily be found when the interference with property can be characterized as a physical invasion by government than when interference arises from some public program adjusting the benefits and burdens of economic life to promote the common good."

Distinguishing Pennsylvania Coal and analogizing to zoning cases, Justice Brennan held that "landmark laws are not like discriminatory, or 'reverse spot,' zoning: that is, a land use decision which arbitrarily singles out a particular parcel for different, less favorable treatment than the neighboring ones. In contrast to discriminatory zoning, [the law here] embodies a comprehensive plan to preserve structures of historic or aesthetic interest wherever they may be found in the city, [and] over 400 landmarks [have] been designated pursuant to this plan." Moreover, the interference with the owner's property was not so great as to fall within the Pennsylvania Coal principle. He emphasized that the owner's use of the air space had not been wholly banned and that the owner had exaggerated the economic effect of the law, since development rights on the restricted parcel were transferable to other nearby parcels. He concluded: "The restrictions imposed are substantially related to the promotion of the general welfare and not only permit reasonable beneficial use of the landmark site but afford [the owner] opportunities further to enhance not only the Terminal site proper but also other properties."

Justice REHNQUIST's dissent, joined by Chief Justice Burger and Justice Stevens, insisted that the severe impact of the law was not justified by either of two exceptions to the normal rule that "destruction of property" constitutes a compensable taking: there was no prohibition of "noxious uses," nor did the prohibition apply "over a broad cross section of land and thereby 'secure an average reciprocity of advantage.'" The dissent distinguished permissible zoning laws: "While zoning at times reduces *individual* property values, the burden is shared relatively evenly and it is reasonable to conclude that on the whole an individual who is harmed by one aspect of the zoning will be benefited by another. Here, however, a multimillion dollar loss has been imposed on [the owner]; it is uniquely felt and is not offset by any benefits flowing from the preservation of some 500 other 'Landmarks' in New York. [The City has] imposed a substantial cost on less than one-tenth of one percent of the buildings in New York for the general benefit of all its people. It is exactly this imposition of general costs on a few individuals at which the 'taking' protection is directed."

4. ***A per se rule for "permanent physical occupations."*** Are there any contexts in which no case-by-case Penn Central balancing is required, and there should instead be a categorical judgment that a type of regulation always constitutes a taking? The Court has set forth several categories of per se takings. In a 6–3 decision in **Loretto v. Teleprompter Manhattan CATV Corp.**, 458 U.S. 419 (1982), the Court held that, when the government authorizes a "permanent physical occupation" (even if a "minor" one) of an owner's property, there "is a taking without regard to the public interests that [the government action] may serve." It thus invalidated a New York law that provided that a landlord must permit a cable television

company to install cable wire upon a landlord's rental property. In defending the majority's per se rule, applicable to all "permanent physical occupations," Justice MARSHALL wrote that "a permanent physical occupation is a governmental action of such a unique character that it is a taking without regard to other factors that a court might ordinarily examine." Accordingly, "when the 'character of the governmental action' is a permanent physical occupation of property, our cases uniformly have found a taking to the extent of the occupation, without regard to whether the action achieves an important public benefit or has only minimal economic impact on the owner." In dissenting, Justice BLACKMUN, joined by Justices Brennan and White, condemned the decision as unduly formalistic. In his view, "history teaches that takings claims are properly evaluated under a multifactor balancing test."

5. ***A per se rule for regulations denying "all economically beneficial use."*** In **Lucas v. South Carolina Coastal Council**, 505 U.S. 1003 (1992), the Court set forth a virtually per se rule of invalidity for "confiscatory regulations, i.e., regulations that prohibit all economically beneficial use of land." Lucas had paid nearly $1 million for two lots on which he planned to build single family homes. In 1988, his plans were brought to "an abrupt end" with the enactment of South Carolina's Beachfront Management Act, an anti-erosion law, which had the effect of barring Lucas from erecting any permanent habitable structures on his two parcels. A state trial court found that this prohibition "deprive[d] Lucas of any reasonable economic use of the lots" and rendered his parcels "valueless." Finding a "taking," it ordered "just compensation" of more than $1 million. The highest state court reversed, ruling that when a regulation was designed "to prevent serious public harm," no compensation was owed, regardless of the regulation's effect on the property's value. The Court reversed and remanded the case.

Justice SCALIA's majority opinion stated that "regulatory action [is] compensable without case-specific inquiry into the public interest advanced in support of the restraint [where] regulation denies all economically beneficial or productive use of land. [We] have never set forth the justification for this rule. Perhaps it is simply [that] total deprivation of beneficial use is, from the landowner's point of view, the equivalent of a physical appropriation. [The] functional basis for permitting the government, by regulation, to affect property values without compensation—that 'Government hardly could go on if to some extent values incident to property could not be diminished without paying for every such change in the general law'—does not apply to the relatively rare situations where the government has deprived a landowner of all economically beneficial uses. On the other side of the balance, affirmatively supporting a compensation requirement, is the fact that regulations that leave the owner of land without economically beneficial or productive options for its use—typically, as here, by requiring land to be left substantially in its natural state—carry with them a heightened risk that private property is being pressed into some form of public service under the guise of mitigating serious public harm. [We think] that there are good reasons for our frequently expressed belief that when the owner of real property has been called upon to sacrifice all economically beneficial uses in the name of the common good, that is, to leave his property economically idle, he has suffered a taking.

"[Where] the State seeks to sustain regulation that deprives land of all economically beneficial use, we think it may resist compensation only if the logically antecedent inquiry into the nature of the owner's estate shows that the proscribed use interests were not part of his title to begin with. This accords, we think, with our 'takings' jurisprudence, which has traditionally been guided by the understandings of our citizens, regarding the content of, and the State's power over, the 'bundle of rights' that they acquire when they obtain title to property. [A] property owner necessarily expects the uses of his property to be restricted, from time to time, by various measures newly enacted by the State in legitimate exercise of its police powers. [In] the case of land, [the notion] that title is somehow held subject to the 'implied limitation' that the State may subsequently eliminate all economically valuable use is inconsistent with the historical compact recorded in the Takings Clause that has become part of our constitutional culture.

"[Confiscatory] regulations [cannot] be newly legislated or decreed (without compensation), but must inhere in the title itself, in the restrictions that background principles of the State's law of property and nuisance already place upon land ownership. A law or decree with such an effect must [do] no more than duplicate the result that could have been achieved [under] the State's law of private nuisance. [The] owner of a lake bed, for example, would not be entitled to compensation when he is denied the requisite permit to engage in a landfilling operation that would have the effect of flooding others' land. [Such] regulatory action may well have the effect of eliminating the land's only economically productive use, but it does not proscribe a productive use that was previously permissible under relevant property and nuisance principles. The use of these properties for what are now expressly prohibited purposes was always unlawful. [When], however, a regulation that declares "off-limits" all economically productive or beneficial uses of land goes beyond what the relevant background principles would dictate, compensation must be paid to sustain it. [To] win its case South Carolina must do more than proffer the legislature's declaration that the uses Lucas desires are inconsistent with the public interest. [Instead,] as it would be required to do if it sought to restrain Lucas in a common-law action for public nuisance, South Carolina must identify background principles of nuisance and property law that prohibit the uses he now intends in the circumstances in which the property is presently found."

Justice KENNEDY concurred in the judgment but cautioned that "coastal property may present such unique concerns for a fragile land system that the State can go further in regulating its development and use than the common law of nuisance might otherwise permit." Justice BLACKMUN dissented, criticizing the majority's adoption of a per se rule and its refusal to engage in a case-specific inquiry. Another dissent by Justice STEVENS criticized the holding for "effectively freezing the State's common-law, denying the legislature much of its traditional power to revise the law governing the rights and uses of property." Justice SOUTER would have dismissed certiorari as improperly granted because a later amendment to the South Carolina Act permitted some building on beachfront property after obtaining a special permit, mooting Lucas's claim that he had been deprived of all beneficial use.

On remand in Lucas, the South Carolina Supreme Court held that common law principles of property and nuisance would not have prohibited the planned development and thus that Lucas was entitled to compensation.

Other state court decisions following Lucas, however, have relief on this background-principles exception in allowing states to stop, without payment or compensation, real estate developments alleged to cause a total diminution of value of the regulated land.

On what constitutional source did Justice Scalia predicate the right he found entitled to categorical protection in Lucas? If the text of the Constitution does not furnish it, nor the intent of the founding generation, may this absence be cured by the subsequent "understandings of our citizens, regarding the content of, and the State's power over, the 'bundle of rights' that they acquire when they obtain title to property"? By our "constitutional culture"? Are these the sorts of authority normally relied upon by Justice Scalia, who usually favors reliance on text and the original history of the relevant constitutional provision?

6. ***Regulatory takings and the timing of government action.*** The takings cases so far deal with property owners whose interests were affected by a government regulation imposed upon their property after they had acquired it. Should a property owner be able to pursue a regulatory takings claim even after the government has repealed the regulation? Should a property owner be able to pursue a regulatory takings claim even if the challenged regulation was already in force when he purchased the property? These questions were addressed in the following cases:

In **First English Evangelical Lutheran Church v. Los Angeles County**, 482 U.S. 304 (1987), Chief Justice REHNQUIST's 6–3 majority opinion concluded that mere invalidation of the regulation restricting the use of the property was a constitutionally insufficient remedy when government regulation proves sufficiently burdensome to constitute a taking; the State was also required to pay damages for the temporary taking in effect during the period before the ordinance was struck down. The State could "elect to abandon its intrusion or discontinue regulations," yet it had to pay compensation "for the period of time during which regulations deny a landowner all use of his land." He wrote: "where the government's activities have already worked a taking of all use of property, no subsequent action by the government can relieve it of the duty to provide compensation for the period during which the taking was effective." He recognized that this holding would "undoubtedly lessen" the flexibility of land-use planners, but "such consequences necessarily flow from any decision upholding a claim of constitutional right." Justice Stevens, joined in part by Justices Blackmun and O'Connor, dissented.

In **Palazzolo v. Rhode Island**, 533 U.S. 606 (2001), the Court held that a property owner could challenge as a regulatory taking restrictions on his property that had originally been imposed prior to his acquisition of that property. The State of Rhode Island had argued that the inverse condemnation action should automatically fail where the landowner had acquired property already restricted under state law; on the State's theory, the acquirer's property rights—and, under Penn Central, his reasonable investment-backed expectations—were defined by the property's pre-acquisition restrictions. In an opinion written by Justice KENNEDY and joined by Chief Justice Rehnquist and Justices O'Connor, Scalia, and Thomas, the Court disagreed: "The State may not put so potent a Hobbesian stick into the Lockean bundle." The fact that restrictions on land use predated a landowner's acquisition of title could not be dispositive, because "future generations, too, have a right to challenge unreasonable limitations on the use and value of land." Having held that claims based on pre-acquisition regulations were not automatically barred, the Court remanded for consideration under Penn Central.

In **Tahoe-Sierra Preservation Council, Inc. v. Tahoe Regional Planning Agency**, 535 U.S. 302 (2002), the Court held by a vote of 6–3 that a temporary development ban would have to be evaluated case by case under the Penn Central test, rather than treated categorically as a taking under the per se rule of Lucas. Speaking for the Court, Justice STEVENS wrote: "The ultimate constitutional question is whether the concepts of 'fairness and justice' that underlie the Takings Clause will be better served [by] categorical rules or by a Penn Central inquiry into all the relevant circumstances in particular cases. [The] extreme categorical rule that any deprivation of all economic use, no matter how brief, constitutes a compensable taking surely cannot be sustained. [Such a] broad submission would apply to numerous 'normal delays in obtaining building permits, changes in zoning ordinances, variances, and the like,' as well as to orders temporarily prohibiting access to crime scenes, businesses that violate health codes, [and] fire-damaged buildings. [Such] a rule would [require] changes in [practices] that have long been considered permissible exercises of the police power. [In] rejecting petitioners' per se rule, we do not hold that the temporary nature of a land-use restriction precludes finding that it effects a taking; we simply recognize that it should not be given exclusive significance one way or the other." Justice Stevens therefore concluded that temporary development bans must be assessed case by case in light of their durations, owners' expectations, and other factors.

Chief Justice REHNQUIST, joined by Justices Scalia and Thomas, dissented: "[The] 'temporary' prohibition in this case that the Court finds is not a taking lasted almost six years. The 'permanent' prohibition that the Court held to be a taking in Lucas lasted less than two years, [because] the law, as it often does, changed. [Land-use] regulations are not irrevocable. [Under] the Court's decision today, the takings question turns entirely on the initial label given a regulation, a label that is often without much meaning. There is every incentive for government to simply label any prohibition on development 'temporary,' or to fix a set number of years. [Because] the rationale for the Lucas rule applies just as strongly in this case, the 'temporary' denial of all viable use of land for six years is a taking [that] requires compensation." Justice THOMAS wrote an additional dissent, joined by Justice Scalia: "[The majority's] 'logical' assurance that a 'temporary restriction . . . merely causes a diminution in value,' is cold comfort to the property owners in this case or any other. After all, '*[i]n the long run* we are all dead.' John Maynard Keynes, Monetary Reform (1924). I would hold that regulations prohibiting all productive uses of property are subject to Lucas' per se rule, regardless of whether the property so burdened retains theoretical useful life and value if, and when, the 'temporary' moratorium is lifted. [Such] potential future value bears on the amount of compensation due and has nothing to do with the question whether there was a taking in the first place."

7. ***Conditions on development permits as "takings."*** May the government exact a physical occupation that would otherwise constitute a taking as a condition of granting permission to develop one's land? The government is not obliged to allow such development in the first place under an otherwise permissible zoning scheme. Does the greater power to deny a

permit include the lesser power to grant it on such a condition? Or is this an overreaching use of the zoning power to exact an impermissible taking? The Court answered these questions in the following cases:

In **Nollan v. California Coastal Comm'n**, 483 U.S. 825 (1987), the Court found a condition on a beachfront building permit to constitute a compensable taking. The Nollans were owners of beachfront property in California who sought permission to replace their small bungalow with a larger house. The Commission conditioned its grant of permission on the Nollans' agreement to allow the public to pass across their beachfront land, which was located between two public beaches. The Nollans claimed that this requirement constituted a taking, and the Court agreed. Justice SCALIA's majority opinion in the 5–4 decision began by noting that there clearly would have been a taking if the state regulation had directly imposed such an easement of access, because it would have amounted to "a 'permanent physical occupation'" as in Loretto. He acknowledged that California could have denied the permit entirely, or imposed any number of other restrictions that "substantially advanced" the purpose behind denying the permit—namely, the preservation of public views of the coastline past houses near the beach. But he found the relationship between the State's professed interest in preserving sightlines to the beach insufficiently close to the easement required of the Nollans, concluding that "[it] is quite impossible to understand how a requirement that people already on the public beaches be able to walk across the Nollans' property reduces any obstacles to viewing the beach created by the new house. [If California] wants an easement across the Nollans' property, it must pay for it." He concluded: "In short, unless the permit condition serves the same governmental purpose as the development ban, the building restriction is not a valid regulation of land use but 'an out-and-out plan of extortion.'" In finding no adequate nexus between the condition and the purpose of the building restriction, he applied a kind of heightened scrutiny of the means-ends relationship between the development condition and the state's regulatory purpose. Although he did not detail precisely the appropriate level of scrutiny, he did indicate that the standard is more rigorous than the deferential approach of the minimum rationality required for due process.

Justice BRENNAN, joined by Justice Marshall, dissented, objecting to the majority's imposition of "a standard of precision for the exercise of a State's police power that has been discredited for the better part of this century. [The] Court demands a degree of exactitude that is inconsistent with our standard for reviewing the rationality of a State's exercise of its police power for the welfare of its citizens. [The] Nollans' development blocks visual access, the Court tells us, while the Commission seeks to preserve lateral access along the coastline. Thus, it concludes, the State acted irrationally. Such a narrow conception of rationality, however, has long since been discredited as a judicial arrogation of legislative authority." What were the majority's and the dissent's competing conceptions of the latitude the California government should have had for advancing the recreational use of its coastline? See Radin, "Evaluating Government Reasons for Changing Property Regimes," 55 Alb. L. Rev. 587 (1992).

Two years after Nollan, the Court clarified the degree of scrutiny applicable to conditional development exactions under the Takings Clause. In **Dolan v. City of Tigard**, 512 U.S. 374 (1994), Dolan had sought a permit to increase the size of her plumbing and electrical supply store. The store was located on one side of her nearly two-acre lot; on the other side of the lot lay the flood plain of Fanno Creek, which flowed along the west side of the property. The City conditioned the approval of a building permit on the dedication of a portion of her property for flood control and traffic improvements. With respect to flood control, the City's condition required her to dedicate the flood plain portion of her lot to permit improvement of the drainage system along the creek. With respect to traffic concerns, she was required to dedicate a 15-foot strip adjoining the flood plain for a public pedestrian/bicycle path. Dolan challenged the City's dedication conditions on the ground that they were not sufficiently related to the interest in curbing harmful effects of the development and that they therefore constituted an uncompensated taking of her property.

Chief Justice REHNQUIST's majority opinion held the conditions unconstitutional: "Under the well-settled doctrine of 'unconstitutional conditions,' the government may not require a person to give up a constitutional right—here the right to receive just compensation when property is taken for a public use—in exchange for a discretionary benefit conferred by the government where the property sought has little or no relationship to the benefit. [We] must first determine whether the 'essential nexus' exists between the 'legitimate state interests' and the permit condition exacted by the City. Nollan. If we find that a nexus exists, we must then decide the required degree of connection between the exactions and the projected impact of the proposed development. We were not required to reach this question in Nollan, because we concluded that the connection did not meet even the loosest standard." Unlike Nollan, the "essential nexus" requirement was easily met here. But the conditions failed the second inquiry into "whether the degree of the exactions demanded by the city's permit conditions bear the required relationship to the projected impact of petitioner's proposed development."

In analyzing this second question, the Court noted that the Oregon Supreme Court had deferred "to what it termed the 'city's unchallenged factual findings' supporting the dedication conditions and found them to be reasonably related to the impact of the expansion of petitioner's business." In determining whether these findings were constitutionally sufficient, the Court examined decisions of other state courts, which had been "dealing with this question a good deal longer than we have." Chief Justice Rehnquist noted that some state courts accepted "very generalized statements as to the necessary connection between the required dedication and the proposed development." This approach, Chief Justice Rehnquist concluded, was "too lax to adequately protect" the property owner. Other state courts required "a very exacting correspondence, described as the 'specifi[c] and uniquely attributable' test." This too was unacceptable to the majority: "We do not think the Federal Constitution requires such exacting scrutiny given the nature of the interests involved." Chief Justice Rehnquist continued: "A number of state courts have taken an intermediate position, requiring the municipality to show a 'reasonable relationship' between the required dedication and the impact of the proposed development. [We] think the ['rough proportionality'] test adopted by a majority of the state courts is closer to the federal constitutional norm than either of those previously discussed. No precise mathematical calculation is required, but the City must make some sort of individualized determination that the required dedication is related both in nature and extent to the impact of the proposed development." Applying that standard to this case, Chief Justice Rehnquist explained that flood control was a valid interest, but that "the city has never said why a public greenway, as opposed to a private one, was required in the interest of flood control. [It] is difficult to see why a recreational visitor's trampling along petitioner's floodplain easement are sufficiently related to the city's legitimate interest in reducing flooding problems along Fanno Creek. [Moreover,] the city must make some effort to quantify its findings in support of the dedication for the pedestrian/bicycle pathway beyond the conclusory statement that it would offset some of the traffic demand generated. [The] city's goals [are] laudable, but there are outer limits to how this may be done."

Justice STEVENS, joined by Justices Blackmun and Ginsburg, dissented: "Under the Court's approach, a city must not only 'quantify its findings,' and make 'individualized determination[s]' with respect to the nature and extent of the relationship between the conditions and the impact, but also demonstrate 'proportionality.' The correct inquiry should instead concentrate on whether the required nexus is present and venture beyond considerations of a condition's nature or germaneness only if the developer establishes that a concededly germane condition is so grossly disproportionate to the proposed development's adverse effects that it manifests motives other than land use regulation on the part of the city. [The] so-called 'regulatory takings' doctrine that the Holmes dictum [in Pennsylvania Coal] kindled has an obvious kinship with the line of substantive due process cases that Lochner exemplified. Besides having similar ancestry, both doctrines are potentially open-ended sources of judicial power to invalidate state economic regulations that Members of this Court view as unwise or unfair."

Why should a state and local government be constrained to keep development exactions "germane" to the purpose for which permission to build might have been denied altogether? Is the problem one of government overreaching, or to use Justice Scalia's term in Nollan, government extortion? See generally Sullivan, "Unconstitutional Conditions," 102 Harv. L. Rev. 1413 (1989). What are the outer limits of judicially enforceable germaneness and proportionality? May a developer of an office building be required to provide a new subway station? A new public park? A new day care center? A public museum? May a private university be required to keep its undeveloped lands undeveloped as parkland indefinitely as a price of adding new buildings to its academic center?

THE CONTRACTS CLAUSE

The Contracts Clause prohibits any state "Law impairing the Obligation of Contracts." Art. I, § 10. The major purpose of the clause originally was to restrain state laws affording debtor relief—e.g., laws postponing payments of debts and laws authorizing payments in installments or in commodities. Yet the Court first interpreted the clause in cases involving public grants rather than private contracts. In Fletcher v. Peck, 6 Cranch (10 U.S.) 87 (1810), a contract dispute arose from a 1795 grant of land from the Georgia legislature. There were charges of bribery, and a new legislature annulled the grant in 1796. The grantees had in the meanwhile sold their lands to investors. The Court held the 1796 law invalid: according to Chief Justice Marshall, the law was barred "either by general principles which are common to our free institutions, or by the particular provisions" of the Constitution. And in Dartmouth College v. Woodward, 4 Wheat. (17 U.S.) 518 (1819), the Court struck down New Hampshire's effort to "pack" the College Board of Trustees by increasing its size, finding that the law violated the 1769 charter of the College that had given the trustees the power to fill all Board vacancies. As Marshall said in Dartmouth College: "It is more than possible that the preservation of rights of this description was not particularly in the view of the framers of the Constitution. [It] is probable that interferences of more frequent recurrence, [of] which the mischief was more extensive, constituted the great motive for imposing this restriction on the State legislatures." But that, he found, was no reason for limiting the scope of the clause to private contracts. A few weeks after Dartmouth College, the Marshall Court applied the Contracts Clause to a law closer to the "mischief" which had motivated the Framers: in Sturges v. Crowninshield, 4 Wheat. (17 U.S.) 122 (1819), the Court held unconstitutional a New York insolvency law discharging debtors of their obligations upon surrender of their property.

From the beginning, however, the Court's interpretations assured that the Contracts Clause would not be an inflexible barrier to public regulation. Thus, just a few years after Dartmouth College, a divided Court stated that the Contracts Clause did not prohibit *all* state insolvency laws: Ogden v. Saunders, 12 Wheat. (25 U.S.) 213 (1827), held that such laws could be validly applied to contracts made *after* the law was enacted; the earlier decision in Sturges, the Court made clear, applied only to retroactive insolvency laws. Moreover, the Court soon elaborated a distinction stated in Sturges: that the constitutional ban on the impairment of contractual "obligations" did not prohibit legislative changes in "remedies." Thus, in Bronson v. Kinzie, 1 How. (42 U.S.) 311 (1843), the Court stated that the permissible scope of remedial changes depended on their "reasonableness," provided "no substantial right" was impaired. The early Court also safeguarded against excessively broad interpretations of publicly granted privileges. In Providence Bank v. Billings, 4 Pet. (29 U.S.) 514 (1830), for example, Marshall refused to read an implied immunity from taxation into a bank's charter.

Chief Justice Taney, Marshall's successor, quickly developed that approach in the better-known Charles River Bridge Case in 1837. Charles River Bridge v. Warren Bridge, 11 Pet. (36 U.S.) 420 (1837). There, the company's charter to operate a toll bridge did not prevent the state from authorizing the construction of a competing, free bridge: "[Any] ambiguity in the terms of the contract must operate against the adventurers, and in favour of the public." Moreover, certain powers of the state were held to be inalienable. Legislative assurance that the power of eminent domain would not be exercised could not prevent action later taking corporate property upon payment of just compensation. See West River Bridge Co. v. Dix, 6 How. (47 U.S.) 507 (1848). So with at least some exercises of the police power: a state grant of a charter to operate a lottery did not bar the enforcement of a later law prohibiting lotteries. Stone v. Mississippi, 101 U.S. 814 (1880).

Would the Court also sustain legislation provoked by twentieth-century economic crises—the modern versions of the debtor relief laws that had motivated the adoption of the clause? Blaisdell, which follows, addresses that question. The case arose from a challenge to a Depression-era Minnesota law, which sought to respond to the crisis by authorizing relief from mortgage foreclosures and other loan remedies. The highest state court sustained the law as an "emergency" measure, and the Supreme Court affirmed.

Home Building & Loan Ass'n v. Blaisdell

290 U.S. 398, 54 S. Ct. 231, 78 L. Ed. 413 (1934).

[The Minnesota Mortgage Moratorium Law of 1933, enacted during the Depression, granted temporary relief from foreclosures and permitted local courts to extend the period of redemption from foreclosure sales "for such additional time as the court may deem just and equitable," but not beyond May 1, 1935. Extensions were to be conditioned upon an order requiring the mortgagor to "pay all or a reasonable part" of the fair income or rental value of the property toward the payment of taxes, insurance, interest and principal. No action for a deficiency judgment could be brought during such a court-extended period of redemption. The Blaisdells obtained a court order under the Act extending the period of redemption on condition that they pay the Association $40 per month. This extension clearly modified the lender's contractual right to foreclose.]

■ CHIEF JUSTICE HUGHES delivered the opinion of the Court.

[In] determining whether the provision for this temporary and conditional relief exceeds the power of the State by reason of the [Contracts Clause], we must consider the relation of emergency to constitutional power, the historical setting of [the] clause, the development of the jurisprudence of this Court in the construction of that clause, and the principles of construction which we may consider to be established. Emergency does not create power. Emergency does not increase granted power [or] diminish the restrictions imposed upon power [granted]. While emergency does not create power, emergency may furnish the occasion for the exercise of power. [T]he reasons which led to the adoption of [the clause have] frequently been described. The widespread distress following the revolutionary period, and the plight of debtors, had called forth in the States an ignoble array of legislative schemes for the defeat of creditors and the invasion of contractual obligations. Legislative interferences had been so numerous and extreme that the confidence essential to prosperous trade had been undermined and the utter destruction of credit was threatened. [It] was necessary to interpose the restraining power of a central authority in order to secure the foundations even of "private faith." But full recognition of the occasion and general purposes of the clause does not suffice to fix its precise scope. [To] ascertain the scope of the [clause] we examine the course of judicial decisions in its application. These put it beyond question that the prohibition is not an absolute one and is not to be read with literal exactness like a mathematical formula. [The] inescapable problems of construction have been: What is a contract? What are the obligations of contracts? What constitutes impairment of these obligations? What residuum of power is there still in the States [to] protect the vital interests of the [community]?

Not only is the [Contracts Clause] qualified by the measure of control which the State retains over remedial processes, but the State also continues to possess authority to safeguard the vital interests of its people. [The] reservation of essential attributes of sovereign power [is] read into contracts as a postulate of the legal order. The policy of protecting contracts against impairment presupposes the maintenance of a government by virtue of which contractual relations are worth while. [The] protective power of the State, its police power, may be exercised [in] directly preventing the immediate and literal enforcement of contractual obligations by a temporary and conditional restraint, where vital public interests would otherwise suffer. [If] state power exists to give temporary relief from the enforcement of contracts in the presence of disasters due to physical causes such as fire, flood, or earthquake, that power cannot be said to be nonexistent when the urgent public need demanding such relief is produced [by] economic causes. [It] is manifest from [our] decisions that there has been a growing appreciation of public needs and of the necessity of finding ground for a rational compromise between individual rights and public welfare. [The] question is no longer merely that of one party to a contract as against another, but of the use of reasonable means to safeguard the economic structure upon which the good of all depends.

It is no answer to say that this public need was not apprehended a century ago, or to insist that what the provision of the Constitution meant to the vision of that day it must mean to the vision of our time. If by the statement that what the Constitution meant at the time of its adoption it means today, it is intended to say that the great clauses of the Constitution must be confined to the interpretation which the framers, with the conditions and outlook of their time, would have placed upon them, the statement carries its own refutation. [With] a growing recognition of public needs and the relation of individual right to public security, the Court has sought to prevent the perversion of the clause through its use as an instrument to throttle the capacity of the States to protect their fundamental [interests].

Applying the criteria established by our decisions, we conclude: [The] conditions upon which the period of redemption is extended do not appear to be unreasonable. [The] integrity of the mortgage indebtedness is not impaired; interest continues to run; the validity of the sale and the right of a mortgagee-purchaser to title or to obtain a deficiency judgment, if the mortgagor fails to redeem within the extended period, are maintained; and the conditions of redemption, if redemption there be, stand as they were under the prior law. [The] legislation is temporary in operation. It is limited to the exigency which called it forth. [T]he operation of the statute itself could not validly outlast the emergency or be so extended as virtually to destroy the contracts. We are of the opinion that the Minnesota statute as here applied does not violate the [Contracts Clause]. [Affirmed.]

■ JUSTICE SUTHERLAND, with whom JUSTICES VAN DEVANTER, MCREYNOLDS, and BUTLER join, dissenting.

[The Contracts Clause] was meant to foreclose state action impairing the obligation of contracts *primarily and especially* in respect of such action aimed at giving relief to debtors *in time of emergency*. [A] statute which materially delays enforcement of the mortgagee's contractual right of ownership and possession does not modify the remedy merely; it destroys, for the period of delay, *all* remedy so far as the enforcement of that right is concerned. The phrase "obligation of a contract" in the constitutional sense imports a legal duty to perform the specified obligation of *that* contract, not to substitute and perform, against the will of one of the parties, a different [obligation]. And a state [has] no more power to accomplish such a substitution than has one of the parties to the contract against the will of the other.

THE SCOPE AND LIMITS OF BLAISDELL

1. ***Contracts Clause cases after Blaisdell.*** Although most cases in the four decades after Blaisdell rejected Contracts Clause attacks on state laws, Blaisdell did not assure the validity of all state measures. Soon after Blaisdell, for example, Worthen Co. v. Thomas, 292 U.S. 426 (1934), struck down an Arkansas law exempting most payments under life insurance policies from garnishment. Nevertheless, by the late 1960s, the restraints imposed by the Contracts Clause seemed minor. El Paso v. Simmons, 379 U.S. 497 (1965), was typical, holding 8–1 that Texas could eliminate the rights of purchasers of certain public lands to reinstate their interests in the lands by payment of delinquent interest.

2. ***Impairment of public contracts.*** Should courts inspect more closely a state's decision to retrench from its own contractual obligations? After four decades of deference to state laws impairing private contracts after Blaisdell, the Court invalidated a state law as violating the Contracts Clause when it revoked its own obligations. In **United States Trust Co. v. New Jersey**, 431 U.S. 1 (1977), the Court decided by a vote of 4–3 that a law impairing a state's *own* obligations was subject to greater scrutiny than legislation interfering with private contracts. The suit challenged a 1974 repeal of a statutory covenant made by New Jersey and New York in 1962—a covenant that had limited the ability of the Port Authority of New York and New Jersey to subsidize rail passenger transportation from revenues and reserves. The Port Authority was established by a bi-state compact between New York and New Jersey; its activities (including the provision of transportation facilities) were largely financed by bonds sold to the public. The covenant was designed in part to assure bondholders that bond revenues would not be used to any great extent to finance the predictably unprofitable rail operations.

Justice BLACKMUN wrote for the Court: "[As] with laws impairing the obligations of private contracts, an impairment [of state obligations] may be constitutional if it is reasonable and necessary to serve an important public purpose. In applying this standard, however, complete deference to a legislative assessment of reasonableness and necessity is not appropriate because the State's self-interest is at stake. [If] a State could reduce its financial obligations whenever it wanted to spend the money for what it regarded as an important public purpose, the Contract Clause would provide no protection at all."

Justice Blackmun conceded the importance of "mass transportation, energy conservation, and environmental protection" as legislative goals. But he rejected New Jersey's contention that "these goals are so important that any harm to bondholders from repeal of the 1962 covenant is greatly outweighed by the public benefit. [A] State cannot refuse to meet its legitimate financial obligations simply because it would prefer to spend the money to promote the [public good]." The States argued that the 1974 repeal was justified by "the States' plan for encouraging users of private automobiles to shift to public transportation" by raising bridge and tunnel tolls and using the extra revenue from those tolls to subsidize improved commuter rail service. Repeal of the 1962 covenant was supposedly necessary to implement this plan "because the new mass transit facilities could not possibly be self-supporting and the covenant's 'permitted deficits' level had already been exceeded." But that argument proved unpersuasive: "We reject this justification because the repeal was neither necessary to achievement of the plan nor reasonable in light of the circumstances."

Justice BRENNAN dissented, joined by Justices White and Marshall, stating that the majority "remolds the Contract Clause into a potent instrument for overseeing important policy determinations of the state legislature." The Court's "reasonable and necessary" standard of review, he objected, "stands the Contract Clause completely on its head and both formulates and strictly applies a novel standard for reviewing a State's attempt to relieve its citizens from unduly harsh contracts entered into by earlier legislators. [This] Court should have learned long ago that the Constitution—be it through the Contract or Due Process Clause—can actively intrude into such economic and policy matters only if my Brethren are prepared to bear enormous institutional and social costs." Justices Stewart and Powell did not participate.

3. ***The Contracts Clause and private obligations.*** The Court reinvigorated the Contracts Clause as applied to private contracts in **Allied Structural Steel Co. v. Spannaus**, 438 U.S. 234 (1978). The 5–3 decision invalidated the application of Minnesota's Private Pension Benefits Protection Act, which required employers who had established an employee pension plan and who terminated the plan or closed a Minnesota office to pay a "pension funding charge" if their pension funds were insufficient to finance full pensions for all employees who had worked at least 10 years. When the Company closed its Minnesota office in 1975, it was subjected to a charge of about $185,000 because some discharged workers, who had no vested rights under the pension plan, had been employed for more than 10 years.

Justice STEWART's majority opinion held that the Act's imposition of a new obligation on the employer violated the Contracts Clause: "[The company] had no reason to anticipate that its employees' pension rights could become vested except in accordance with the terms of the plan. It relied heavily, and reasonably, on this legitimate contractual expectation in calculating its annual contributions to the pension fund. [The law nullifies the] express terms of the company's contractual obligations and imposes a completely unexpected liability in potentially disabling amounts. [This] law simply does not possess the attributes of those state laws that in the past have survived challenge. [It] did not effect simply a temporary alteration of the contractual relationships of those within its coverage, but worked a severe, permanent, and immediate change in those relationships—irrevocably and retroactively. And its narrow aim was leveled not at every Minnesota employer, not even at every Minnesota employer who left the State, but only at those who had in the past been sufficiently enlightened as voluntarily to agree to establish pension plans for their employees."

Justice BRENNAN's dissent, joined by Justices White and Marshall, insisted that the clause was applicable only to laws that "diminished or nullified" private contractual obligations. Here, the law, "like all positive social legislation," simply imposed "new, additional obligations on a particular class of persons." The only relevant constitutional limitation in the case was due process, and that guarantee had not been violated.

4. ***The Contracts Clause and state pension reform.*** With state government budgets stretched in the wake of the 2008 financial crisis and subsequent economic downturn, states have sought to restructure public employee pension plans, in the process modifying state statutes that typically establish the plans and the benefits under them. Pension recipients, individually and as members of unions, have argued that such modifications to pension benefits specified by statute violate the Contracts Clause, as well as similar state constitutional obligations. The Supreme Court has not ruled directly on this question, and no appellate court has yet blocked a restructuring. Typically, the courts that have adjudicated the question have first asked whether the new state law has "operated as a substantial impairment of a contractual relationship" under Spannaus, which requires determining whether the language of the relevant statute reflects an intent to create contractual rights. If so, the next question is whether the state's action is reasonable and necessary under United States Trust Co. v. New Jersey.

Should the ordinary Contracts Clause standards apply when the state is acting as an employer administering a pension fund? If so, is the state in a stronger position vis-à-vis its employees than a private employer? Would applying the Contracts Clause more rigorously leave the state in a worse position than a private employer?

5. ***The Contracts Clause and originalism.*** In 2002, Minnesota enacted a law specifying that on divorce, a spouse designated as the revocable beneficiary of a life insurance policy or similar asset would cease to be the beneficiary unless the other spouse specifically re-named him or her. A spouse who was married in 1997 and divorced in 2007, and who would not have collected under the statute after her spouse's 2011 death, claimed that she should collect the life insurance because the state law impaired the life-insurance contract. Citing Spannaus, the Court in **Sveen v. Melin**, ___ U.S. ___, 138 S. Ct. 1815 (2018), rejected the claim and upheld the law. Justice KAGAN wrote for an 8–1 Court: "Minnesota's revocation-on-divorce statute does not substantially impair pre-existing contractual arrangements. True enough that in revoking a beneficiary designation, the law makes a significant change. As Melin says, the whole point of buying life insurance is to provide the proceeds to the named beneficiary. But three aspects of Minnesota's law, taken together, defeat Melin's argument that the change it effected severely impaired her ex-husband's contract. First, the statute is designed to reflect a policyholder's intent—and so to support, rather than impair, the contractual scheme. Second, the law is unlikely to disturb any policyholder's expectations because it does no more than a divorce court could always have done. And third, the statute supplies a mere default rule, which the policyholder can undo in a moment. Indeed, Minnesota's revocation statute stacks up well against laws that this Court upheld against Contracts Clause challenges as far back as the early 1800s."

Justice GORSUCH dissented: "Because legislation often disrupts existing social arrangements, it usually applies only prospectively. [When] it comes to legislation affecting contracts, the Constitution hardens the presumption of prospectivity into a mandate. [In] the Contracts Clause the framers were absolute. [When] some delegates at the Constitutional Convention sought softer language, James Madison acknowledged the 'inconvenience' a categorical rule could sometimes entail 'but thought on the whole it would be overbalanced by the utility of it.' Kmiec & McGinnis, The

Contract Clause: A Return to the Original Understanding, 14 Hastings Const. L. Q. 525, 529–530 (1987). For much of its history, this Court construed the Contracts Clause in this light. [More] recently, though, the Court has charted a different course. Our modern cases permit a state to substantially impair a contractual obligation in pursuit of a significant and legitimate public purpose so long as the impairment is reasonable. That test seems hard to square with the Constitution's original public meaning. After all, the Constitution does not speak of 'substantial' impairments—it bars 'any' impairment. Under a balancing approach, too, how are the people to know today whether their lawful contracts will be enforced tomorrow, or instead undone by a legislative majority with different sympathies? Should we worry that a balancing test risks investing judges with discretion to choose which contracts to enforce—a discretion that might be exercised with an eye to the identity (and popularity) of the parties or contracts at hand? How are judges supposed to balance the often radically incommensurate goods found in contracts and legislation? [Many] critics have raised serious objections along these and other lines. They deserve a thoughtful reply, if not in this case then in another."

CHAPTER 9

EQUAL PROTECTION

The Fourteenth Amendment provides that no State shall "deny to any person within its jurisdiction the equal protection of the laws." The Court has also interpreted this guarantee to apply to the federal government, as an aspect of Fifth Amendment due process, and generally treats equal protection claims the same against the states as against the federal government. This command cannot literally require equal treatment of all persons, since almost all laws classify in some way by imposing burdens on or granting benefits to some people and not others. The Court therefore has subjected all classifications to some kind of requirement of a rational relationship to a legitimate governmental purpose, but has interpreted equal protection to presume some classifications more likely than others to lack such a justifying relationship.

In its historical origins, the Equal Protection Clause was directed at racial discrimination against African-Americans. In the earliest interpretation of the Fourteenth Amendment, in the Slaughter-House Cases (p. 451 above), the Court suggested that concern with racial classifications exhausted the meaning of the clause. In later cases, however, equal protection has never been so cabined. The Warren Court extended heightened equal protection scrutiny to classifications ranging beyond race, including sex, alienage and illegitimacy; and to burdens on "fundamental interests" such as voting and court access (but not to food, housing or education).

For nonracial classifications, the Court has ordinarily read the command of equal protection to require only that differences in treatment have some minimally rational basis, though some formulations have interpreted this reasonableness requirement with more bite than others. Economic legislation was struck down on equal protection grounds as early as 1897, when, in Gulf, C. & S. F. Ry. v. Ellis, 165 U.S. 150, the Court relied on equal protection to strike down a regulation requiring railroads (but not other defendants) to pay attorneys' fees to successful plaintiffs in certain cases. The Lochner-era Court, however, rarely used equal protection to strike down economic laws, using due process instead. And the post-Lochner Court has treated regulation in the economic area with deference against due process and equal protection claims alike.

While some justices have claimed that a single standard should apply to all equal protection cases as there is but one Equal Protection Clause, the Court in recent decades has employed roughly three tiers of review: strict scrutiny of race discrimination and its analogues (which the Court deems inherently suspect), intermediate scrutiny of sex discrimination (which is in many respects like but in some respects unlike race discrimination), and mere rational relationship review for other classifications (including all socioeconomic laws and laws classifying along lines like age and disability that the Court does not see as inherently suspect). Because rationality review is sometimes heightened (especially if some inappropriate ground of "animus" is at work), and strict scrutiny is sometimes relaxed (as for "affirmative action"), it may be more accurate to speak of a spectrum of standards in reviewing equal protection challenges than of three fixed tiers.

Strict scrutiny requires that regulation serve *compelling* governmental interests and be *essential* to those interests—i.e., the least restrictive means. Intermediate scrutiny requires that a regulation serve *important* governmental objectives and be *substantially* related to achievement of those objectives. Rationality review requires only a *rational* relationship to *legitimate* ends. The Court has required that for heightened levels of scrutiny a law be measured by its actual government purposes, but has allowed rationality review to be satisfied by conceivable government purposes even if hypothesized after the fact.

The sections that follow explore first, in Section 1, the prevailing deferential rationality review of economic regulations; next, in Section 2, the origins and applications of strict scrutiny with respect to race discrimination; next, in Sections 3 and 4, the extension of heightened scrutiny to other classifications, principally determined by reference to analogies or disanalogies to the paradigm case of race discrimination; finally, in Section 5, the rise and plateau of heightened scrutiny of laws not simply because they classify but also because the grounds for classification impinge upon fundamental interests. An earlier section, "Substantive Due Process, Sexuality, and Hybrid Due-Process-Equal Protection Rights." (see Chapter 8, p. 553, above), addresses equal protection issues in relation to sexual orientation.

SECTION 1. MINIMUM RATIONALITY REVIEW OF ECONOMIC REGULATION

Though enacted to address race discrimination, the Equal Protection Clause has been invoked to challenge laws and regulations that appear to have no racially discriminatory effect. After all, many laws treat individuals unequally in a formal sense: for example, tax provisions treat different earners differently, and businesses are regulated differently based on their products and means of production. For regulations that do not involve racial classification or other classifications held to warrant heightened scrutiny, the Court has applied minimal rationality review to determine whether there the regulation bears a rational relationship to a legitimate government interest. Such review does not demand anything approaching a perfect fit to an actual governmental purpose; any rational basis is enough.

Why should a court apply even this minimal level of review? Linde, "Due Process of Lawmaking," 55 Neb. L. Rev. 197 (1976), for example, argues that "the dogma that [the Constitution] requires every law to be a rational means to a legislative end [is] not a rational premise for judicial review [and is] even less plausible as a constitutional command to lawmakers." But would abandonment of rationality review render an equal protection claim a political question, thus rendering the legislature and executive self-policing? Assuming rationality review is applied to avoid such a result, why not apply more stringent review to the many economic classifications that pervade the regulatory state? Would demands for greater or perfect congruence make effective legislative action impossible? Are courts fulfilling their constitutional duty when they act so deferentially?

Note that the Court has considered more demanding forms of the means-ends fit requirement under rationality review. In one influential early formulation, for example, the Court stated that "the classification must be reasonable, not arbitrary, and must rest upon some ground of difference having *a fair and substantial relation* to the object of the legislation, so that all persons similarly circumstanced shall be treated alike." F.S. Royster Guano Co. v. Virginia, 253 U.S. 412 (1920) (emphasis added). Under another, earlier formulation, the Court set forth a more permissive standard that is closer to the predominant standard employed today: "When the classification [is] called in question, if any state of facts *reasonably can be conceived* that would sustain it, the existence of that state of facts at the time the law was enacted must be assumed." Lindsley v. Natural Carbonic Gas Co., 220 U.S. 61 (1911). Which of these formulations is at work in the various opinions in the case that follows, upholding against equal protection challenge a municipal regulation that banned advertising on trucks for hire but not on trucks advertising the goods carried by the truck's owner?

Railway Express Agency v. New York

336 U.S. 106, 69 S. Ct. 463, 93 L. Ed. 533 (1949).

■ JUSTICE DOUGLAS delivered the opinion of the Court.

Section 124 of the [New York City Traffic Regulations] provides: "No person shall operate [on] any street an advertising vehicle; provided that nothing herein contained shall prevent the putting of business notices upon business delivery vehicles, so long as such vehicles are engaged in the usual business [of] the owner and not used merely or mainly for advertising." Appellant is engaged in a nationwide express business. It operates about 1,900 trucks in New York City and sells the space on the exterior sides of these trucks for advertising[, for] the most part unconnected with its own business. It was [convicted]. [The state court] concluded that advertising on [vehicles] constitutes a distraction to vehicle drivers and to pedestrians alike and therefore affects the safety of the public in the use of the streets. We do not sit to weigh evidence on the due process issue in order to determine whether the regulation is sound or appropriate; nor is it our function to pass judgment on its [wisdom].

The question of equal protection of the laws is pressed more strenuously on us. It is pointed out that the regulation draws the line between advertisements of products sold by the owner of the truck and general advertisements. It is argued that unequal treatment on the basis of such a distinction is not justified by the aim and purpose of the regulation. It is said, for example, that one of appellant's trucks carrying the advertisement of a commercial house would not cause any greater distraction of pedestrians and vehicle drivers than if the commercial house carried the same advertisement on its own truck. Yet the regulation allows the latter to do what the former is forbidden from doing. It is therefore contended that the classification which the regulation makes has no relation to the traffic problem since a violation turns not on what kind of advertisements are carried on trucks but on whose trucks they are carried. That, however, is a superficial way of analyzing the problem. [The] local authorities may well have concluded that those who advertise their own wares on their trucks do not present the same traffic problem in view of the nature or extent of the advertising which they use. It would take a degree of omniscience which we lack to say that such is not the case. [We] cannot say that that judgment is not an allowable one. Yet if it is, the classification has relation to the purpose for which it is made and does not contain the kind of discrimination against which [equal protection] affords protection. It is by such practical considerations based on experience rather than by theoretical inconsistencies that the question of equal protection is to be answered. And the fact that New York City sees fit to eliminate from traffic this kind of distraction but does not touch what may be even greater ones in a different category, such as the vivid displays on Times Square, is immaterial. It is no requirement of equal protection that all evils of the same genus be eradicated or none at [all]. Affirmed.

[Justice RUTLEDGE "acquiesced" in the Court's opinion, noting that he was "dubitante" on the equal protection question.]

■ JUSTICE JACKSON, concurring.

[My] philosophy as to the relative readiness with which we should resort to [the due process and equal protection] clauses is almost diametrically opposed to the philosophy which prevails on this Court. While claims of denial of equal protection are frequently asserted, they are rarely sustained. But the Court frequently uses the due process clause to strike down measures taken by municipalities to deal with activities in their streets and public places which the local authorities consider as creating hazards, annoyances or discomforts to their inhabitants. [The] burden should rest heavily upon one who would persuade us to use the due process clause to strike down a substantive law or ordinance. [Invalidation] of a statute or an ordinance on due process grounds leaves ungoverned and ungovernable conduct which many people find objectionable. Invocation of the equal protection clause, on the other hand, does not disable any governmental body from dealing with the subject at hand. It merely means that the prohibition or regulation must have a broader impact. I regard it as a salutary doctrine that [governments] must exercise their powers so as not to discriminate between their inhabitants except upon some reasonable differentiation fairly related to the object of regulation. This equality is not merely abstract justice. [There] is no more effective practical guaranty against arbitrary and unreasonable government than to require that the principles of law which officials would impose upon a minority must be imposed generally. Conversely, nothing opens the door to arbitrary action so effectively as to allow those officials to pick and choose only a few to whom they will apply legislation and thus to escape the political retribution that might be visited upon them if larger numbers were [affected].

This case affords an illustration. Even casual observations from the sidewalks of New York will show that an ordinance which would forbid all advertising on vehicles would run into conflict with many interests, including some, if not all, of the great metropolitan newspapers, which use that advertising extensively. Their blandishment of the latest sensations is not less a cause of diverted attention and traffic hazard than the commonplace cigarette advertisement which this truckowner is forbidden to display. But any regulation applicable to all such advertising would require much clearer justification in local conditions to enable its enactment than does some regulation applicable to a few. I do not mention this to criticize the motives of those who enacted this ordinance, but it dramatizes the point that we are much more likely to find arbitrariness in the regulation of the few than of the [many]. In this case, if [New York] should assume that display of any advertising on vehicles tends and intends to distract the attention of persons using the highways and to increase the dangers of its traffic, I should think it fully within its constitutional powers to forbid it all. [Instead, however,] the City seeks to reduce the hazard only by saying that while some may, others may not exhibit such appeals. The same display, for example, advertising cigarettes, which this appellant is forbidden to carry on its trucks, may be carried on the trucks of a cigarette dealer. [The] courts of New York have declared that the sole nature and purpose of the regulation before us is to reduce traffic hazards. There is not even a pretense here that the traffic hazard created by the advertising which is forbidden is in any manner or degree more hazardous than that which is [permitted]. I do not think differences of treatment under law should be approved on classification because of differences unrelated to the legislative purpose. The equal protection clause ceases to assure either equality or protection if it is avoided by any conceivable difference that can be pointed out between those bound and those left free. This Court has often announced the principle that the differentiation must have an appropriate relation to the object of the [legislation].

The question in my mind comes to this. Where individuals contribute to an evil or danger in the same way and to the same degree, may those who do so for hire be prohibited, while those who do so for their own commercial ends but not for hire be allowed to continue? I think the answer has to be that the hireling may be put in a class by himself and may be dealt with differently than those who act on their own. But this is not merely because such a discrimination will enable the lawmaker to diminish the evil. That might be done by many classifications, which I should think wholly unsustainable. It is rather because there is a real difference between doing in self-interest and doing for hire, so that it is one thing to tolerate action from those who act on their own and it is another thing to permit the same action to be promoted for a price. [It] is not difficult to see that, in a day of extravagant advertising[, the] rental of truck space could become an obnoxious enterprise. [In] view of the control I would concede to cities to protect citizens in quiet and orderly use for their proper purposes of the highways and public places, I think the judgment below must be affirmed.

JUDICIAL DEFERENCE TO ECONOMIC REGULATION

1. ***Deference to governmental ends.*** Railway Express is typical of the Court's deferential approach to legislation challenged under the Equal Protection Clause in the late 1940s. Is there any limit to the deference shown here? Consider **Kotch v. Board of River Port Pilot Commissioners**, 330 U.S. 552 (1947), which upheld by a 5–4 vote Louisiana's nepotistic pilotage laws granting state certificates only to relatives and friends of incumbents. Was there any conceivably rational relationship here to any genuine public end? Was this not patronage pure and simple? Justice Black's majority opinion relied on the "entirely unique" nature of pilotage "in the light of its history in Louisiana" and the alleged rationale of the need to preserve a close-knit community. Does this amount to a purely post hoc rationalization?

To what extent should the government be required to defend the actual purpose of the statute, as opposed to any post-hoc rationalization of the impugned legislation? In **U.S. Railroad Retirement Board v. Fritz**, 449 U.S. 166 (1980), the Court rejected an equal protection challenge to Congress's restructuring of the railroad retirement system and a distinction Congress drew to deny certain classes of workers entitlement to dual benefits. In practical operation, the workers that benefitted from this reform were certain incumbent union members, at the expense of other railroad workers.

Upholding the legislation, the Court relied on the fact that "plausible reasons" for the distinction existed, based on the relative equities of these workers. To the Court, it was "constitutionally irrelevant whether this reasoning in fact underlay the legislative decision." This was especially so given that "the legislature must necessarily engage in a process of line drawing."

Should this highly deferential standard be limited to cases where the government is engaging in a necessary line-drawing exercise to distribute benefits and entitlements? Or should deference be granted regardless of the type of economic legislation that is being challenged?

2. ***Deference to means-ends relationships.*** In applying minimal rationality review, the Court allows legislatures to act underinclusively, or "one step at a time." In **Williamson v. Lee Optical Co.**, 348 U.S. 483 (1955) for example, the Court rejected an equal protection as well as a due process challenge to Oklahoma's scheme for the regulation of opticians. Justice DOUGLAS stated for a unanimous Court: "[T]he District Court held that it violated [equal protection to] subject opticians to this regulatory system and to exempt [all] sellers of ready-to-wear glasses. The problem of legislative classification is a perennial one, admitting of no doctrinaire definition. Evils in the same field may be of different dimensions and proportions, requiring different remedies. Or so the legislature may think. Or the reform may take one step at a time, addressing itself to the phase of the problem which seems most acute to the legislative mind. The legislature may select one phase of one field and apply a remedy there, neglecting the others. The prohibition of [equal protection] goes no further than invidious discrimination. We cannot say that that point has been reached here. For all this record shows, the ready-to-wear branch of this business may not loom large in Oklahoma or may present problems of regulation distinct from the other branch."

Should the Court scrutinize such underinclusive schemes more closely when a law is challenged as an unwarranted preference for a favored group? Should Justice Jackson's Railway Express concerns have been heeded in Lee Optical? Did Lee Optical simply protect professional rent-seeking by optical professionals? Should the Court have insisted that the regulations "must have a broader impact," to safeguard against arbitrariness? See Klarman, "An Interpretive History of Modern Equal Protection," 90 Mich. L. Rev. 213 (1991). Should the Court have done less to hypothesize rationales that *might* have influenced a legislature? Should it have tested the fit between means and ends on the basis of actual rather than conceivable purposes, and on the basis of demonstrated rather than conceivable contributions of classifications to purposes? Is the "one step at a time" rationale ultimately subversive of *any* real judicial scrutiny of "special interest" legislation? What limits might the Court impose on justifying laws via the "one step at a time" rationale?

In one decision, Morey v. Doud, 354 U.S. 457 (1957), the Court invalidated an exemption by name of a particular company from a general regulatory scheme. The challenged Illinois law had imposed financial responsibility requirements on businesses issuing money orders but had explicitly exempted the American Express Company. The 6–3 decision held the exemption unconstitutional. Justice Burton's majority opinion emphasized that the exemption created "a closed class," and that this grant of an economic advantage to a named company bore "no reasonable relation" to the purposes of the law.

But in **New Orleans v. Dukes**, 427 U.S. 297 (1976) (per curiam), the Court overruled Morey as aberrational and returned to a highly deferential stance toward economic preferences, stating that Morey had "so far depart[ed] from proper equal protection analysis in cases of exclusively economic regulation that it should be, and it is, overruled." Dukes in turn upheld against equal protection challenge a 1972 New Orleans provision that exempted pushcart food vendors who had "continually operated the same business for eight years prior to January 1, 1972" from a prohibition against such vendors in the French Quarter (Vieux Carré). The ordinance was challenged by a vendor barred from continuing her business because she had been in business in the French Quarter for only two years at the time the provision was adopted. The Court emphasized that the grandfather clause was "solely an economic regulation aimed at enhancing the vital role of the French Quarter's tourist-oriented charm in the economy of New Orleans." Noting that "rational distinctions [in economic regulations] may be made with substantially less than mathematical exactitude," the Court rejected the lower court's holding that the grandfather provision "failed even the rationality test" and found instead that "the city's classification rationally furthers the purpose which [the] city had identified as its objective in enacting the provisions, that is, '[preserving] the appearance and custom valued by the Quarter's residents and attractive to tourists.' " The Court suggested that the exempted vendors might have had a greater reliance interest and might have "themselves become part of the distinctive character and charm that distinguishes the Vieux Carré.' "

3. ***Exception for classifications based on "animus."*** The 7–2 decision in **U.S. Dept. of Agriculture v. Moreno**, 413 U.S. 528 (1973), departed from this deferential trend. Purporting to apply a rationality standard, the Court in Moreno struck down a provision of the federal food stamp program limiting assistance to "households" defined as groups of *related* persons. This provision was challenged as discriminatory against otherwise qualifying group living arrangements. The law recited the congressional purpose as "rais[ing] levels of nutrition among low-income households" and increasing consumption of food so as to "strengthen our agricultural economy." Justice BRENNAN's majority opinion found the exclusion of "unrelated persons" to be "clearly irrelevant" to these purposes and thus "wholly without any rational basis." He noted that the limited legislative history indicated "that the amendment was intended to prevent so-called 'hippies' and 'hippie communes' from participating in the food stamp program." This purpose did not justify the classification, in his view: "For if the constitutional conception of 'equal protection of the laws' means anything, it must at the very least mean that a bare congressional desire to harm a politically unpopular group cannot constitute a *legitimate* governmental interest." (Compare the similar grounds for invalidation of laws found to embody "animus" on purportedly rational-basis review in Cleburne Living Center, p. 799 below, and Romer v. Evans, p. 556.)

But the Court found no similarly disqualifying animus in the law upheld in **New York City Transit Auth. v. Beazer**, 440 U.S. 568 (1979). Justice STEVENS's majority opinion in Beazer upheld the exclusion of all methadone users from any Transit Authority (TA) employment. The lower court had concluded that, because about 75% of patients who have been on methadone treatment for at least a year were free of illicit drug use and because the exclusion applied to jobs that were not safety-sensitive, the exclusion had "no rational relation to the demands of the job to be performed." Reversing, Justice Stevens viewed the exclusionary policy as "supported by the legitimate inference that as long as a treatment program (or other drug use) continues, a degree of uncertainty persists." Justice WHITE's dissent, joined by Justice Marshall, insisted that, given the facts in the record, "[the] rule's classification of successfully maintained persons as dispositively different from the general population is left without any justification and, with its irrationality and invidiousness thus uncovered, must fall before the Equal Protection Clause." He commented that the TA had stipulated that one of the reasons for the drug policy was that the TA believed that "an adverse public reaction would result if it were generally known that [TA] employed persons with a prior history of drug abuse, including persons participating in methadone maintenance programs." He found it hard "to reconcile that stipulation of animus against former addicts with our past holdings that 'a bare [desire] to harm a politically unpopular group cannot constitute a *legitimate* governmental interest,' [Moreno]."

4. ***Rationality review with bite.*** May a court ever invalidate an economic regulation on rationality review in the absence of animus (i.e., an impermissible end) toward a particular disfavored group? Is the fit between means and ends ever subject to heightened scrutiny even if the end is legitimate? **Allegheny Pittsburgh Coal v. Webster County**, 488 U.S. 336 (1989), presented the rare case in which the Court could find no real connection between a classification and its purposes, even under rational-basis review. In this case, a unanimous Court struck down aspects of the West Virginia property tax system. The West Virginia Constitution establishes a general principle of uniform taxation so that all property is to be taxed in proportion to its value. For the years beginning in 1975, the County tax assessor valued Allegheny Pittsburgh's real property on the basis of its recent purchase price. Other properties not recently transferred were assessed on the basis of their previous assessments, with minor modifications. The system resulted in gross disparities in the assessed value of comparable properties. Thus, for several years beginning in 1975, the Company was assessed "at roughly 8 to 35 times more than comparable neighboring property, and these discrepancies [continued] for more than ten years." The Court concluded that the assessment system violated equal protection.

Chief Justice REHNQUIST's opinion for the Court held: "[West Virginia's] Constitution and laws provide that all property [shall] be taxed at a rate uniform throughout the state according to its estimated market value. There is no suggestion [that] the State may have adopted a different system in practice from that specified by statute. [We] have no doubt that [the Company has] suffered [from] 'intentional systematic undervaluation by state officials' of comparable property in Webster County. [The] fairness of one's allocable share of the total property tax burden can only be meaningfully evaluated by comparison with the share of others similarly situated relative to their property holdings. The relative undervaluation of comparable property in Webster County over time therefore denies petitioner the equal protection of law."[1]

This exception to means-ends deference, however, was a narrow one; three years later, in **Nordlinger v. Hahn**, 505 U.S. 1 (1992), the Court upheld California's Proposition 13, imposing property taxation rates based on the price of property at the time of acquisition. Such a system in effect discriminated among classes of property owners based on the duration of their property ownership, a factor not obviously related to relevant grounds for property taxation. In rejecting the equal protection claim that longer-term property owners were unduly benefitting at the expense of newer property owners, Justice BLACKMUN's majority opinion distinguished Allegheny Pittsburgh, suggesting that California had an adequate factual basis for its acquisition-value taxation scheme. He stated that "the Equal Protection Clause does not demand for purposes of rational-basis review that a legislature or governing decisionmaker actually articulate at any time the purpose or rationale supporting its classification. Fritz [p. 654 below]. Nevertheless, this Court's review does require that a purpose may conceivably or may reasonably have been the purpose and policy of the relevant governmental decisionmaker. Allegheny Pittsburgh was the rare case where the facts precluded any plausible inference that the reason for the unequal assessment practice was to achieve the benefits of an acquisition-value tax scheme. By contrast, [Proposition 13] was enacted precisely to achieve the benefits of an acquisition-value system." Justice THOMAS concurred in the result, but was unpersuaded that Allegheny Pittsburgh was distinguishable and urged that it be overruled. Justice STEVENS, the sole dissenter, stated: "Similarly situated neighbors have an equal right to share in the benefits of local government. It would obviously be unconstitutional to provide one with more or better fire or police protection than the other; it is just as plainly unconstitutional to require one to pay five times as much in property taxes as the other for the same government services. [The] severe inequalities created by Proposition 13 are arbitrary and unreasonable and do not rationally further a legitimate state interest."

But for a recent decision permitting an equal protection challenge to proceed under rationality review, see **Village of Willowbrook v. Olech**, 528 U.S. 562 (2000) (per curiam). Olech, a homeowner, sued the Village of Willowbrook alleging a violation of Equal Protection: the Village had demanded a 33-foot easement as a condition of connecting her house to the municipal water supply, when the Village had only required a 15-foot easement from other property-owners seeking similar access. Although the complainant had alleged that the Village's discriminatory treatment was "motivated by ill will resulting from the Olechs' previous filing of an unrelated, successful lawsuit against the Village," the Court addressed the Village's actions simply as an instance of irrationality, without regard to motive or animus: "Our cases have recognized successful equal protection claims brought by 'a class of one,' where the plaintiff alleges that she has been intentionally treated differently from others similarly situated and there is no rational basis for the difference in treatment. In doing so, we have

[1] For differing comments on Allegheny Pittsburgh Coal, see Cohen, "State Law in Equality Clothing: A Comment on [Allegheny]," 38 UCLA L. Rev. 87 (1990); Ely, "Another Spin on [Allegheny]," 38 UCLA L. Rev. 107 (1990); and Glennon, "Taxation and Equal Protection," 58 Geo. Wash. L. Rev. 261 (1990).

explained that '[t]he purpose of the equal protection clause of the Fourteenth Amendment is to secure every person within the State's jurisdiction against intentional and arbitrary discrimination, whether occasioned by express terms of a statute or by its improper execution through duly constituted agents. That reasoning is applicable to this case. Olech's complaint can fairly be construed as alleging that the Village intentionally demanded a 33-foot easement as a condition of connecting her property to the municipal water supply where the Village only required a 15-foot easement from other similarly situated property owners. The complaint also alleged that the Village's demand was 'irrational and wholly arbitrary' and that the Village ultimately connected her property after receiving a clearly adequate 15-foot easement. These allegations, quite apart from the Village's subjective motivation, are sufficient to state a claim for relief under traditional equal protection analysis."

Justice BREYER concurred separately to emphasize Olech's allegations about the Village's motive, and to allay concerns that the ruling would "transform [ordinary] violations of city or state law into violations of the Constitution. It might be thought that a rule that looks only to an intentional difference in treatment and a lack of a rational basis for that different treatment would work such a transformation. Zoning decisions, for example, will often, perhaps almost always, treat one landowner differently from another. [This] case, however, does not directly raise the question of whether the simple and common instance of a faulty zoning decision would violate the Equal Protection Clause. That is because [Olech has] alleged an extra factor as well—'[illegitimate] animus or ill will.' [In] my view, the presence of that added factor in this case is sufficient to minimize any concern about transforming run-of-the-mill zoning cases into cases of constitutional right."

SHOULD RATIONALITY REVIEW BE STRICTER?

Three theories offer potential bases for greater scrutiny within the framework of rationality standards. The first suggests heightened judicial concern for all minorities who have an inadequate say in the governmental process whether or not a classification disadvantaging them is suspect. The second theory emphasizes the Constitution's roots in civic republicanism and associated notions of civic virtue and argues that it is impermissible to award opportunities to one group rather than another simply on the basis of "naked preferences," so that legislation must be justified by public values rather than merely as compromises among private interests. The third argues that the Court should engage in more serious, less deferential review in order to discipline legislatures and assure that the legislative means *genuinely* promote *articulated* governmental purposes.

1. ***Judicial solicitude for economic minorities?*** Recall Carolene Products footnote four, which suggested a greater basis for judicial scrutiny where there might be "prejudice against discrete and insular minorities"—prejudice which "tends seriously to curtail the operation of those political processes ordinarily to be relied upon to protect minorities." That consideration clearly underlies some of the expansions of strict scrutiny for suspect and quasi-suspect classifications, considered in Sections 2–5 below. But can that rationale be applied as well to losing minorities that are not identified by "suspect" criteria—including losing *economic* minorities? Can

economic minorities be protected without a return to the interventionism of the Lochner era?

For example, should the losing opticians in Oklahoma have received more careful scrutiny of their complaint than Lee Optical afforded? Consider the response that, even if some economic minorities should be protected, "the losers in the legislature were not permanently disadvantaged minorities." The opticians might well have anticipated new legislative alliances. On this view, Carolene Products footnote four makes "the legitimacy of judicial protection of the losers in the legislative process turn on the losers' long-term chances of becoming winners." Karst, "Invidious Discrimination: Justice Douglas and the Return of the 'Natural-Law-Due-Process Formula,'" 16 UCLA L. Rev. 716 (1969). What groups are unlikely to have such reversal of fortune over time? Is any economic faction a systematic and permanent political loser?

Note that when the Court employs deferential rationality review, its implicit model of socioeconomic legislation is that economic factions will not become entrenched over time, and that gains and losses will even out. Is this an accurate view? Much modern political theory supposes, to the contrary, that some small, well-organized and intensely focused groups (e.g., industrial lobbies or single-issue advocacy groups) may have success in the political process quite disproportionate to their numbers, while large but unorganized and diffuse groups (e.g., consumers or working people) may lack influence proportionate to their numbers. See generally Olson, The Logic of Collective Action (1965). Should judicial solicitude be extended beyond "discrete and insular minorities" to other politically disadvantaged groups? To diffuse and non-discrete majorities like consumers? To minorities like gay men and lesbians, who are harder to classify along the axes of discreteness and insularity? For elaboration of such ideas, see Ackerman, "Beyond Carolene Products," 98 Harv. L. Rev. 713 (1985).

2. ***Civic republicanism and "naked preferences."*** According to the pluralist conception of democracy, a key function of government is to distribute resources to competing interest groups based on their political strength, so that an open preference by the legislature for one group over another is ordinarily unproblematic. On a civic republican conception of democratic government, by contrast, legitimate governmental action must respond to something other than "naked preferences"; the task of legislators "is not to respond to private pressure but instead to select [public] values through deliberation and debate." Accordingly, government action can only be justified on the basis of "some public value" rather than the mere "raw exercise of political power." This approach would use rationality review "to ensure that classifications rest on something other than a naked preference for one person or group over another. Thus, [in Lee Optical, the] Court upheld deferential treatment of optometrists and opticians on the ground not that [equal protection] tolerated an unprincipled distribution of wealth to one rather than to the other—though there is a plausible argument that such a naked preference was indeed taking place—but that the deferential treatment was a means of protecting consumers. The Court has made clear in rationality cases that the government must be able to invoke some public value that the classification at issue can be said to serve." Sunstein, "Naked Preferences and the Constitution," 84 Colum. L. Rev. 1689 (1984). See also Sunstein, "Public Values, Private Interests, and the Equal Protection

Clause," 1982 Sup. Ct. Rev. 127; Sunstein, "Interest Groups in American Public Law," 38 Stan. L. Rev. 29 (1985).

Can Sunstein's approach be implemented without a return to the skeptical scrutiny of government ends akin to that of the Lochner era? Is his reading of Lee Optical persuasive? Does the civic republican position rest on a plausible understanding of American politics, or would it encourage an excessive intrusion of judicial notions of desirable policy into political reality? Don't laws often mix private and public purposes? Compare Posner, "[The] Constitutionality of Preferential Treatment of Racial Minorities," 1974 Sup. Ct. Rev. 1: "The Court's expressed view [is] that the political process is one of honestly attempting to promote efficiency or justice, or some other equally general conception of the public good. [But many] public policies are better explained as the outcome of the pure power struggle—clothed in a rhetoric of public interest that is a mere fig leaf—among narrow interest or pressure groups. [The] real 'justification' for most legislation is simply that it is a product of the constitutionally created political process of our society."

3. ***Rationality review "with bite."*** Can the Lochnerian dangers of heightened scrutiny of economic and social regulation be averted by intensified scrutiny of legislative *means* rather than ends? See Gunther, "The Supreme Court, 1971 Term—Foreword: In Search of Evolving Doctrine on a Changing Court: A Model for a Newer Equal Protection," 86 Harv. L. Rev. 1 (1972), suggesting that more serious scrutiny under the "mere rationality" standard could be achieved by viewing equal protection "as a means-focused, relatively narrow, preferred ground of decision in a broad range of cases." It would have the Court "less willing to supply justifying rationales by exercising its imagination. It would have the Court assess the means in terms of legislative purposes that have substantial basis in actuality, not merely in conjecture. Moreover, it would have the Justices gauge the reasonableness of questionable means on the basis of materials that are offered to the Court, rather than resorting to rationalizations created by perfunctory judicial hypothesizing." See also Gunther, "Commentary," 71 Chi.-Kent L. Rev. 813 (1996).

SECTION 2. RACE DISCRIMINATION

THE UNCONSTITUTIONALITY OF RACIAL SEGREGATION

1. ***Early interpretation of the 14th Amendment.*** The Fourteenth Amendment guarantee of equal protection was expected by its framers to be enforced primarily by Congress. Recall that the Slaughter-House Cases (1872; p. 451 above) emphasized racial discrimination as the central concern of the Fourteenth Amendment. Seven years after that decision, the Court developed that theme in **Strauder v. West Virginia**, 100 U.S. 303 (1880). Strauder, an African-American defendant, was convicted of murder by a jury from which African-Americans had been excluded because of an explicit command of a state law providing that "all white male persons who are twenty-one years of age and who are citizens of this State shall be liable to serve as [jurors]." Strauder unsuccessfully sought to remove his case to a federal court. The Court held that removal should have been granted and found the law unconstitutional.

Justice STRONG's majority opinion emphasized that the "common purpose" of the post-Civil War Amendments was the "securing to a race recently emancipated [all] the civil rights the superior race enjoy." He added: "[What is equal protection] but declaring, [in] regard to the colored race, for whose protection the amendment was primarily designed, that no discrimination shall be made against them by law because of their color? [That] the West Virginia statute respecting juries [is] such a discrimination ought not to be doubted. Nor would it be if the persons excluded by it were white men. If in those States where the colored people constitute a majority of the entire population a law should be enacted excluding all white men from jury service, [we] apprehend no one would be heard to claim that it would not be a denial to white men of [equal protection]. Nor if a law should be passed excluding all naturalized Celtic Irishmen, would there be any doubt of its inconsistency with the spirit of the amendment. The very fact that colored people are singled out and expressly denied by a statute all right to participate in the administration of the law, as jurors, because of their color, [is] practically a brand upon them, affixed by the law, an assertion of their inferiority, and a stimulant to that race prejudice which is an impediment to securing to individuals of the race that [equal justice]. We do not say [that] a State may not prescribe the qualifications of its jurors, and in so doing make discriminations. It may confine the selection to males, to freeholders, to citizens, to persons within certain ages, or to persons having educational qualifications. We do not believe the 14th Amendment was ever intended to prohibit this. Looking at its history, it is clear it had no such purpose. Its aim was against discrimination because of race or color. [We] are not now called upon to affirm or deny that it had other purposes."

2. ***"Separate but equal."*** Strauder applied to jury trials. In other areas of social life outside such core civic functions, equal treatment for the newly freed slaves and their descendants was harder to enforce. The Civil Rights Cases (1883; p. 856 below) barred application of civil rights laws to purely private action. "Black codes" and other devices for racial segregation arose in the South. And in areas of publicly regulated activity that were further from the core of government than jury service, the Court eventually approved segregationist laws as consistent with equal protection under the fiction of "separate but equal."

In **Plessy v. Ferguson**, 163 U.S. 537 (1896), for example, the Court sustained an 1890 Louisiana law that required "equal but separate accommodations" for "white" and "colored" railroad passengers. Plessy, the challenger, alleged that he was "seven-eighths Caucasian and one-eighth African blood; that the mixture of colored blood was not discernible in him; and that he was entitled to every right [of] the white race." He was arrested for refusing to leave a seat in a coach for whites. Justice BROWN's majority opinion, after finding the 13th Amendment inapplicable, stated: "The object of the [14th] Amendment was undoubtedly to enforce the absolute equality of the two races before the law, but in the nature of things it could not have been intended to abolish distinctions based upon color, or to enforce social, as distinguished from political equality, or a commingling of the two races upon terms unsatisfactory to either. Laws [requiring] their separation in places where they are liable to be brought into contact do not necessarily imply the inferiority of either race to the other, and have been generally, if not universally, recognized as within the competency of the state legislatures in the exercise of their police power. The most common instance of this is connected with the establishment of separate schools for white and colored children, which have been [upheld] even by courts of States where the political rights of the colored race have been longest and most earnestly enforced. [Laws] forbidding the intermarriage of the two races may be said in a technical sense to interfere with the freedom of contract, and yet have been universally recognized as within the police power of the state. [The] distinction between laws interfering with the political equality of the negro and those requiring the separation of the two races in schools, theaters, and railway carriages has been frequently drawn by this Court." [E.g., Strauder.]

"[It is suggested] that the same argument that will justify the state legislature in requiring railways to provide separate accommodations for the two races will also authorize them to require separate cars to be provided for people whose hair is of a certain color, or who are aliens, or who belong to certain nationalities, or to enact laws requiring colored people to walk upon one side of the street, and white people upon the other, or requiring white men's houses to be painted white, and colored men's black, or their vehicles or business signs to be of different colors, upon the theory that one side of the street is as good as the other, or that a house or vehicle of one color is as good as one of another color. The reply to all this is that every exercise of the police power must be reasonable, and extend only to such laws as are enacted in good faith for the promotion of the public good, and not for the annoyance or oppression of a particular class. [In] determining the question of reasonableness, [the legislature] is at liberty to act with reference to the established usages, customs, and traditions of the people, and with a view to the promotion of their comfort, and the preservation of the public peace and good order. Gauged by this standard, we cannot say that [this law] is unreasonable, or more obnoxious to the [14th Amendment] than the [laws] requiring separate schools for colored children, [the] constitutionality of which does not seem to have been [questioned].

"We consider the underlying fallacy of the plaintiff's argument to consist in the assumption that the enforced separation of the two races stamps the colored race with a badge of inferiority. If this be so, it is not by reason of anything found in the act, but solely because the colored race chooses to put that construction upon it. [The argument] assumes that social prejudices may be overcome by legislation, and that equal rights cannot be secured to the negro except by an enforced commingling of the two races. We cannot accept this proposition. If the two races are to meet upon terms of social equality, it must be the result of natural affinities, a mutual appreciation of each other's merits, and a voluntary consent of individuals. [Legislation] is powerless to eradicate racial instincts or to abolish distinctions based upon physical differences, and the attempt to do so can only result in accentuating the difficulties of the present situation. If the civil and political rights of both races be equal, one cannot be inferior to the other civilly or politically. If one race be inferior to the other socially, the [Constitution] cannot put them upon the same plane."

The first Justice HARLAN dissented: "[I] deny that any legislative body or judicial tribunal may have regard to the race of citizens when the civil rights of those citizens are involved. [It] was said in argument that the [law] does not discriminate against either race, but prescribes a rule applicable alike to white and colored citizens. But [every one] knows that [the law] had its origin in the purpose, not so much to exclude white persons from railroad cars occupied by blacks, as to exclude colored people from coaches [assigned] to white persons. [The] fundamental objection, therefore, to the statute is that it interferes with the personal freedom of citizens. The white race deems itself to be the dominant race in this country. And so it is, in prestige, in achievements, in education, in wealth and in power. So, I doubt not, it will continue to be for all time, if it remains true to its great heritage and holds fast to the principles of constitutional liberty. But in view of the Constitution, in the eye of the law, there is in this country no superior, dominant, ruling class of citizens. There is no caste here. Our Constitution is color-blind, and neither knows nor tolerates classes among citizens.

"[It] is, therefore, to be regretted that this high tribunal [has] reached the conclusion that it is competent for a State to regulate the enjoyment by citizens of their civil rights solely upon the basis of race. In my opinion, the judgment this day rendered will, in time, prove to be quite as pernicious as the decision made [in] the Dred Scott case. [The] present decision [will] encourage the belief that it is possible, by means of state enactments, to defeat the beneficent purposes which the [people] had in view when they adopted the recent amendments of the [Constitution]. Sixty millions of whites are in no danger from the presence here of eight millions of blacks. The destinies of the two races [are] indissolubly linked together, and the interests of both require that the common government of all shall not permit the seeds of race hate to be planted under the sanction of law. What can more certainly arouse race hate, what more certainly create and perpetuate a feeling of distrust between these races, than state enactments, which, in fact, proceed on the ground that colored citizens are so inferior and degraded that they cannot be allowed to sit in public coaches occupied by white citizens? [We] boast of the freedom enjoyed by our people above all other peoples. But it is difficult to reconcile that boast with a state of the law which, practically, puts the brand of servitude and degradation upon a large class of our fellow citizens,—our equals before the law. The thin disguise of 'equal' accommodations [will] not mislead any one, nor atone for the wrong this day done."

Justice Harlan's ringing dissent is as renowned as Justice Brown's majority opinion is infamous. But note Justice Harlan's insistence that the white race "deems itself," and is, dominant "in prestige, in achievements, in education, in wealth and in power"? Or of his prediction that "it will continue to be for all time, if it remains true to its great heritage and holds fast to the principles of constitutional liberty"?

Justice Harlan also wrote in Plessy that "[t]here is a race so different from our own that we do not permit those belonging to it to become citizens of the United States. Persons belonging to it are, with few exceptions, absolutely excluded from our country. I allude to the Chinese race. But by the statute in question, a Chinaman can ride in the same passenger coach with white citizens of the United States, while citizens of the black race [cannot]." Justice Harlan was not merely reporting a fact. He joined a series of decisions by the court upholding the permanent exclusion of Chinese immigrants from citizenship. See Gabriel J. Chin, "The Plessy Myth: Justice Harlan and the Chinese Cases," 82 Iowa L. Rev. 151 (1996). What do you make of Justice Harlan's views in Plessy compared to his apparent views on Chinese immigrants?

3. ***Segregation in public education.*** Led by the NAACP Legal Defense Fund and in particular by Thurgood Marshall, later Justice Marshall, legal challenges to officially mandated segregation began with efforts to show that the "separate but equal" doctrine of Plessy was

vulnerable in the context of education. A methodical and masterly litigation strategy eventually culminated in Brown v. Board of Education in 1954, holding that segregated public schools violated equal protection. The litigation strategy initially postponed challenging "separate but equal" outright, and sought to pressure segregated institutions by demanding adherence to the "equal" part of "separate but equal," challenging the lack of material equality between predominantly black and white schools. The initial challenges did not focus on K–12 but rather on the education provided for black students seeking graduate and professional school training. For the history of the litigation, see Kluger, Simple Justice (1976; reissued 2004).

The first in the sequence of school segregation cases that culminated in Brown was Missouri ex rel. Gaines v. Canada, 305 U.S. 337 (1938). Gaines, a black applicant, had been refused admission to the University of Missouri Law School because of his race. Missouri's defense to his suit for admission was that, pending the establishment of a black law school in the state, it would pay Gaines's tuition in an out-of-state school. Chief Justice Hughes's majority opinion concluded that the State was obligated to furnish Gaines "within its borders facilities for legal education substantially equal to those which the State there offered for persons of the white race, whether or not other Negroes sought the same opportunity." In the absence of such facilities, Gaines was entitled to be admitted to the existing state law school. In Sipuel v. Oklahoma, 332 U.S. 631 (1948), the Court reaffirmed the principles of Gaines.

Sweatt v. Painter, 339 U.S. 629 (1950), required the admission of blacks to the University of Texas Law School even though the state had recently established a law school for blacks. Chief Justice Vinson's opinion for the Court found no "substantial equality in the educational opportunities offered white and Negro law students by the State. In terms of number of the faculty, variety of courses and opportunity for specialization, size of the student body, scope of the library, availability of law review and similar activities, the University of Texas Law School is superior. What is more important, the University of Texas Law School possesses to a far greater degree those qualities which are incapable of objective measurement but which make for greatness in a law school. Such qualities, to name but a few, include reputation of the faculty, experience of the administration, position and influence of the alumni, standing in the community, traditions and prestige." He added that a law school "cannot be effective in isolation from the individuals and institutions with which the law interacts," and he noted that the newly established black law school "excludes from its student body members of the racial groups which number 85% of the population of the state and include most of the lawyers, witnesses, jurors, judges and other officials with whom petitioner would inevitably be dealing when he becomes a member of the Texas Bar."

McLaurin v. Oklahoma State Regents, 339 U.S. 637 (1950), involved a black student who had been admitted to a state university's graduate program not offered at the state's black school, but had been required to sit in separate sections in or adjoining the classrooms, library and cafeteria facilities. Chief Justice Vinson's opinion found that the restrictions impaired the "ability to study, to engage in discussions and exchange views with other students and, in general, to learn his profession." Finally, in Brown v. Board, the Court confronted a head-on challenge to the notion of "separate but equal."

Brown v. Board of Education [Brown I]

347 U.S. 483, 74 S. Ct. 686, 98 L. Ed. 873 (1954).

■ CHIEF JUSTICE WARREN delivered the opinion of the Court.

These cases come to us from the States of Kansas, South Carolina, Virginia, and Delaware. [In] each of the cases, minors of the Negro race [seek] the aid of the courts in obtaining admission to the public schools of their community on a nonsegregated basis. In each instance, they had been denied admission to schools attended by white children under laws requiring or permitting segregation according to race. [In most of the cases, the courts below denied relief, relying on] the so-called "separate but equal" doctrine announced by this Court in Plessy. [The] plaintiffs contend that segregated public schools are not "equal" and cannot be made "equal," and that hence they are deprived of the equal protection of the laws. [Argument] was heard in the 1952 Term, and reargument was heard this Term on certain questions propounded by the Court. Reargument was largely devoted to the circumstances surrounding the adoption of the 14th Amendment in 1868. It covered exhaustively consideration of the Amendment in Congress, ratification by the states, then existing practices in racial segregation, and the views of proponents and opponents of the Amendment. This discussion and our own investigation convince us that, although these sources cast some light, it is not enough to resolve the problem with which we are faced. At best, they are inconclusive. The most avid proponents of the post-War Amendments undoubtedly intended them to remove all legal distinctions among "all persons born or naturalized in the United States." Their opponents, just as certainly, were antagonistic to both the letter and the spirit of the Amendments and wished them to have the most limited effect. What others in Congress and the state legislatures had in mind cannot be determined with any degree of certainty.

An additional reason for the inconclusive nature of the Amendment's history, with respect to segregated schools, is the status of public education at that time. In the South, the movement toward free common schools, supported by general taxation, had not yet taken hold. Education of white children was largely in the hands of private groups. Education of Negroes was almost nonexistent, and practically all of the race were illiterate. In fact, any education of Negroes was forbidden by law in some states. Today, in contrast, many Negroes have achieved outstanding success in the arts and sciences as well as in the business and professional world. It is true that public school education [had] advanced further in the North, but the effect of the Amendment on Northern States was generally ignored in the congressional debates. Even in the North, the conditions of public education did not approximate those existing today. The curriculum was usually rudimentary; ungraded schools were common in rural areas; [and] compulsory school attendance was virtually unknown. As a consequence, it is not surprising that there should be so little in the history of the 14th Amendment relating to its intended effect on public education.

In the first cases in this Court construing the 14th Amendment, decided shortly after its adoption, the Court interpreted it as proscribing all state-imposed discriminations against the Negro race. [Slaughter-House Cases.]

The doctrine of "separate but equal" did not make its appearance in this Court until 1896 in [Plessy], involving not education but transportation. [In] recent cases, all on the graduate school level, inequality was found in that specific benefits enjoyed by white students were denied to Negro students of the same educational qualifications. Gaines; Sipuel; Sweatt; McLaurin. In none of these cases was it necessary to reexamine the doctrine to grant relief to the Negro plaintiff. And in [Sweatt], the Court expressly reserved decision on the question whether [Plessy] should be held inapplicable to public education. In the instant cases, that question is directly presented. Here, unlike [Sweatt], there are findings below that the Negro and white schools involved have been equalized or are being equalized, with respect to buildings, curricula, qualifications and salaries of teachers, and other "tangible" factors. Our decision, therefore, cannot turn on merely a comparison of these tangible factors in the Negro and white schools involved in each of the cases. We must look instead to the effect of segregation itself on public education.

In approaching this problem, we cannot turn the clock back to 1868 when the Amendment was adopted, or even to 1896 when Plessy was written. We must consider public education in the light of its full development and its present place in American life throughout the Nation. Only in this way can it be determined if segregation in public schools deprives these plaintiffs of [equal protection]. Today, education is perhaps the most important function of state and local governments. Compulsory school attendance laws and the great expenditures for education both demonstrate our recognition of the importance of education to our democratic society. It is required in the performance of our most basic public responsibilities, even service in the armed forces. It is the very foundation of good citizenship. Today it is a principal instrument in awakening the child to cultural values, in preparing him for later professional training, and in helping him to adjust normally to his environment. In these days, it is doubtful that any child may reasonably be expected to succeed in life if he is denied the opportunity of an education. Such an opportunity, where the state has undertaken to provide it, is a right which must be made available to all on equal terms.

We come then to the question presented: Does segregation of children in public schools solely on the basis of race, even though the physical facilities and other "tangible" factors may be equal, deprive the children of the minority group of equal educational opportunities? We believe that it does. In [Sweatt], this Court relied in large part on "those qualities which are incapable of objective measurement but which make for greatness in a law school." In McLaurin, the Court [again] resorted to intangible considerations: "[the] ability to study, to engage in discussions and exchange views with other students, and, in general, to learn [the] profession." Such considerations apply with added force to children in grade and high schools. To separate them from others of similar age and qualifications solely because of their race generates a feeling of inferiority as to their status in the community that may affect their hearts and minds in a way unlikely ever to be undone. The effect of this separation on their educational opportunities was well stated by a finding in the Kansas case by a court which nevertheless felt compelled to rule against the Negro plaintiffs: "Segregation of white and colored children in public schools has a detrimental effect upon the colored children. The impact is greater when it has the sanction of the law; for the policy of separating the races is usually interpreted as denoting the inferiority of the negro group. A sense of inferiority affects the motivation of a child to learn. Segregation with the sanction of law, therefore, has a tendency to [retard] the educational and mental development of negro children and to deprive them of some of the benefits they would receive in a [racially] integrated school system." Whatever may have been the extent of psychological knowledge at the time of [Plessy], this finding is amply supported by modern authority.[1] Any language in [Plessy] contrary to this finding is rejected.

We conclude that in the field of public education the doctrine of "separate but equal" has no place. Separate educational facilities are inherently unequal. Therefore, we hold that the plaintiffs and others similarly situated for whom the actions have been brought are, by reason of the segregation complained of, deprived of [equal protection]. This disposition makes unnecessary any discussion whether such segregation also violates [due process]. Because these are class actions, because of the wide applicability of this decision, and because of the great variety of local conditions, the formulation of decrees in these cases presents problems of considerable complexity. On reargument, the consideration of appropriate relief was necessarily subordinated to the primary question—the constitutionality of segregation in public education. We have now announced that such segregation is a denial of [equal protection]. In order that we may have the full assistance of the parties in formulating decrees, the cases will be restored to the docket, and the parties are requested to present further argument [see Brown II, below].

THE MEANING AND IMPLICATIONS OF BROWN V. BOARD

1. ***Extension of desegregation to the federal government.*** In **Bolling v. Sharpe**, 347 U.S. 497 (1954), decided on the same day as Brown I, the Court held that racial segregation in the District of Columbia public schools violated the Due Process Clause of the Fifth Amendment. Chief Justice WARREN's opinion stated: "The Fifth Amendment [does] not contain an equal protection clause. [But] the concepts of equal protection and due process, both stemming from our American ideal of fairness, are not mutually exclusive. The 'equal protection of the laws' is a more explicit safeguard of prohibited unfairness than 'due process of law,' and, therefore, we do not imply that the two are always interchangeable phrases. But, as this Court has recognized, discrimination may be so unjustifiable as to be violative of due process. Classifications based solely upon race must be scrutinized with particular care, since they are contrary to our traditions and hence constitutionally suspect. Although the Court has not assumed to define 'liberty' with any great precision, that term is not confined to mere freedom from bodily restraint. Liberty under law extends to the full range of

---

[1] K.B. Clark, Effect of Prejudice and Discrimination on Personality Development (Midcentury White House Conference on Children and Youth, 1950); Witmer and Kotinsky, Personality in the Making (1952), c. VI; Deutscher and Chein, The Psychological Effects of Enforced Segregation: A Survey of Social Science Opinion, 26 J. Psychol. 259 (1948); Chein, What are the Psychological Effects of Segregation Under Conditions of Equal Facilities?, 3 Int. J. Opinion and Attitude Res. 229 (1949); Brameld, Educational Costs, in Discrimination and National Welfare (McIver, ed., 1949), 44–48; Frazier, The Negro in the United States (1949), 674–681. And see generally Myrdal, An American Dilemma (1944). [Footnote by Chief Justice Warren; number eleven in the original.]

conduct which the individual is free to pursue, and it cannot be restricted except for a proper governmental objective. Segregation in public education is not reasonably related to any proper governmental objective, and thus it imposes on Negro children of the District of Columbia a burden that constitutes an arbitrary deprivation of their liberty in violation of [due process]. In view of our decision that the Constitution prohibits the states from maintaining racially segregated public schools, it would be unthinkable that the same Constitution would impose a lesser duty on the Federal Government."

2. ***Segregation in other public facilities.*** Soon after the 1954 decision in Brown, the Court found legally mandated segregation in public facilities unconstitutional in contexts other than education. Despite the Court's emphasis on the school context in Brown, its results in the later cases were reached in brief per curiam orders, most simply citing Brown. See, e.g., Mayor of Baltimore v. Dawson, 350 U.S. 877 (1955) (beaches); Gayle v. Browder, 352 U.S. 903 (1956) (buses); Holmes v. Atlanta, 350 U.S. 879 (1955) (golf courses); New Orleans City Park Improvement Association v. Detiege, 358 U.S. 54 (1958) (parks); cf. Turner v. Memphis, 369 U.S. 350 (1962) (municipal airport restaurant). Not until Johnson v. Virginia, 373 U.S. 61 (1963), reversing a contempt conviction for refusal to comply with a state judge's order to move to a section of a courtroom reserved for blacks, did the Court state: "[It] is no longer open to question that a State may not constitutionally require segregation of public facilities."

3. ***The theory of Brown v. Board.*** What are the bases and justifications for Brown? Consider the following four possible interpretations of Chief Justice Warren's oracular opinion:

a. *Color-blindness.* Race is never a permissible basis on which to distribute public benefits or burdens. Is this the implication of the famous concluding passage stating, "Separate educational facilities are inherently unequal"? Recall Justice Harlan's insistence in his Plessy dissent that "Our Constitution is color-blind."

b. *Caste.* Race is an impermissible basis for distributing public benefits and burdens when it has the social and psychological effect of stigmatizing or subordinating a racial group. Recall the passage stating that to separate black and white schoolchildren on the basis of race generates in the black children "a feeling of inferiority as to their status in the community that may affect their hearts and minds in a way unlikely ever to be undone." Under this interpretation, Brown does not prohibit all us of race, but only the imposition of racial hierarchy or caste. As Justice Harlan wrote in his Plessy dissent, "there is in this country no superior, dominant, ruling class of citizens. There is no caste here." Note that, while the caste and color-blindness views reinforce one another in Brown, the choice between them might have differing implications for the constitutionality of race-based affirmative action.

c. *White supremacy.* Segregation laws were the impermissibly tainted products of white supremacy, i.e., legislative processes in which white voters predominated and blacks were largely disenfranchised. Under this interpretation, would all-black schools be permissible if they were voluntarily created by predominantly black political bodies?

d. *Integration.* Recall Chief Justice Warren's emphasis on "the importance of education to our democratic society." Was Brown based on an empirical supposition that integrated schools would produce better educational results for black schoolchildren? That integration is a desirable social policy that is likely to increase social welfare? That educational integration would help decrease racial separation more broadly in society?

4. ***Brown and the Court's internal drama.*** Having heard the case argued in 1952, the Court was unable to reach consensus, thought to be desirable before a decision of such moment. Four sitting justices, including Chief Justice Fred Vinson, were from segregated states, and all four of those indicated at conference that they were not prepared to strike down segregation. The Court set the case for reargument in October Term 1953. In September 1953, Vinson died, prompting Justice Frankfurter to comment, "This is the first indication I have ever had that there is a God." President Eisenhower appointed former California governor Earl Warren as Chief Justice, and Warren, who as Attorney General of California had supported the internment of Japanese-Americans during World War II, set his considerable political skills to convincing the other justices to reach a unanimous result in Brown. For the detailed story, see Kluger, Simple Justice (1977), and Klarman, From Jim Crow to Civil Rights (2004).

5. ***Brown and history.*** Do the history and "central purpose" of the Fourteenth Amendment justify the Brown decision? In the end, the Court considered the historical materials inconclusive. Was that accurate? Consider the observation that the history of the Fourteenth Amendment "rather clearly" demonstrates "that it was not expected in 1866 to apply to segregation," and therefore that "the record of history, properly understood, left the way open to, in fact invited, a decision based on the moral and material state of the nation in 1954, not 1866." Bickel, "The Original Understanding and the Segregation Decision," 69 Harv. L. Rev. 1 (1955). (This article grew out of Bickel's research for Justice Frankfurter as his law clerk in 1952–53.) Is the Brown opinion best explained, then, as reflecting "an awareness on the part of [the Framers of the 14th Amendment] that it was *a constitution* they were writing, which led to a choice of language capable of growth"? For further exploration of this history, compare McConnell, "Originalism and the Desegregation Decision," 81 Va. L. Rev. 947 (1995), with Klarman, "Brown, Originalism and Constitutional Theory," 81 Va. L. Rev. 1881 (1995).

6. ***Brown and sociology and psychology.*** Was the Brown Court correct to consider social science data in order to find that state-imposed segregation "generates a feeling of inferiority" and thus "has a tendency to retard the educational and mental development of Negro children"? Were empirical data central to the Court's holding? The Brown opinion's reliance on social science evidence in the famous footnote 11 has been the focus of considerable controversy. See K.B. Clark, "The Desegregation Cases," 5 Vill. L. Rev. 224 (1959); see also Stell v. Savannah-Chatham Bd. of Ed., 220 F. Supp. 667 (S.D. Ga.1963), rev'd, 333 F.2d 55 (5th Cir. 1964) (where the District Judge, after an extensive hearing to survey the social science data nearly a decade after Brown, unsuccessfully tried in effect to "reverse" Brown). Consider the comment that "I would not have the constitutional rights of Negroes—or of other Americans—rest on any such flimsy foundation as some of the scientific demonstrations in these records. [Behavioral science findings] have an uncertain expectancy of life." Cahn, "Jurisprudence," 30 NYU L. Rev. 150 (1955). Consider the comment of Justice Thomas in his concurring opinion in Jenkins v. Missouri, 515 U.S. 70

(1995): "Segregation was not unconstitutional because it might have caused psychological feelings of inferiority. [Psychological] injury is irrelevant to the question whether [state actors] have engaged in intentional discrimination—the critical question for ascertaining violations of [equal protection]."

In Parents Involved in Cmty. Sch. v. Seattle Sch. Dist. No. 1 (2007; below p. 736), Justice Thomas expressed skepticism about the educational value of school integration: "Add to the inconclusive social science the fact of black achievement in 'racially isolated' environments. [Before] *Brown,* the most prominent example of an exemplary black school was Dunbar High School. Sowell, Education: Assumptions Versus History, at 29 ('[I]n the period 1918–1923, Dunbar graduates earned fifteen degrees from Ivy League colleges, and ten degrees from Amherst, Williams, and Wesleyan'). [Dunbar] is by no means an isolated example. [Even] after *Brown,* some schools with predominantly black enrollments have achieved outstanding educational results. [There] is also evidence that black students attending historically black colleges achieve better academic results than those attending predominantly white colleges. Given this tenuous relationship between forced racial mixing and improved educational results for black children, the dissent cannot plausibly maintain that an educational element supports the integration interest, let alone makes it compelling."

7. ***Brown and the social meaning of segregation.*** A prominent article shortly after Brown questioned whether the decision, however desirable its outcome, was based on neutral principles, given that segregation symmetrically affected blacks and whites alike. See Wechsler, "Toward Neutral Principles of Constitutional Law," 73 Harv. L. Rev. 1 (1959). Charles Black, a Southerner by origin, replied that the "purpose and impact of segregation in the southern regional culture" were "matters of common notoriety, matters not so much for judicial notice as for the background knowledge of educated men who live in the world," and stated: "[I]f a whole race of people finds itself confined within a system which is set up and continued for the very purpose of keeping it in an inferior station, and if the question is then solemnly propounded whether such a race is being treated 'equally,' I think we ought to exercise one of the sovereign prerogatives of philosophers—that of laughter. [Segregation] is historically and contemporaneously associated in a functioning complex with practices which are indisputably and grossly discriminatory." Black, "The Lawfulness of the Segregation Decisions," 69 Yale L.J. 421 (1960).

Contrast Wechsler's argument: "For me, assuming equal facilities, the question posed by state-enforced segregation is not one of discrimination at all. Its human and its constitutional dimensions lie entirely elsewhere, in the denial by the state of freedom to associate, a denial that impinges in the same way on any groups or races that may be involved." He asked: "Given a situation where the state must practically choose between denying the association to those individuals who wish it or imposing it on those who would avoid it, is there a basis in neutral principles for holding that the Constitution demands that the claims for association should prevail?"

8. ***A former Ku Klux Klan member as a leading voice for desegregation.*** In the run-up to the Court's decision in Brown II, the Justices of the Supreme Court were aware of the importance of the issue before the Court and hotly debated how to proceed. Justice Hugo Black, who had joined the Ku Klux Klan as a young, ambitious politician, became the unlikely leading voice for desegregation. Black's "Klan membership was a

terrible stain on his reputation and a crushing blow to a man jealous of his honor. [With] this weight upon him, Black could not let his own dishonor stand unaddressed. In the end, there was one way for Black to prove, once and for all, that he was not a racist: to vote definitively to end segregation." As a result, Black became "the strongest internal voice on the Supreme Court calling for a unilateral end to segregation." Southern reaction was so hostile to Black's desegregation vote that his son was ultimately forced to resign his law firm partnership in Alabama and move to Miami, Florida. Feldman, Scorpions: The Battles and Triumphs of FDR's Great Supreme Court Justices 376, 380–81 (2010).

IMPLEMENTING BROWN V. BOARD

1. ***Brown's remedial aftermath.*** Eager to unite the Court behind a single opinion, Chief Justice Warren postponed until the 1954 Term arguments over the specific remedies that would implement school desegregation. The decision in **Brown v. Board of Education [Brown II]**, 349 U.S. 294 (1955), recognizing the possibility of resistance, allowed remedies to proceed "with all deliberate speed."

Chief Justice WARREN delivered the opinion of the Court: "These cases were decided on May 17, 1954. [Full] implementation of these constitutional principles may require solution of varied local school problems. School authorities have the primary responsibility for elucidating, assessing, and solving these problems; courts will have to consider whether the action of school authorities constitutes good faith implementation of the governing constitutional principles. Because of their proximity to local conditions and the possible need for further hearings, the courts which originally heard these cases can best perform this judicial appraisal. Accordingly, we believe it appropriate to remand the cases to those courts. In fashioning and effectuating the decrees, the courts will be guided by equitable principles. Traditionally, equity has been characterized by a practical flexibility in shaping its remedies and by a facility for adjusting and reconciling public and private needs. These cases call for the exercise of these traditional attributes of equity power. At stake is the personal interest of the plaintiffs in admission to public schools as soon as practicable on a nondiscriminatory basis. To effectuate this interest may call for elimination of a variety of obstacles in making the transition to school systems operated in accordance with the constitutional principles set forth in [Brown I]. Courts of equity may properly take into account the public interest in the elimination of such obstacles in a systematic and effective manner. But it should go without saying that the vitality of these constitutional principles cannot be allowed to yield simply because of disagreement with them.

"While giving weight to these public and private considerations, the courts will require that the defendants make a prompt and reasonable start toward full compliance with [Brown I]. Once such a start has been made, the courts may find that additional time is necessary to carry out the ruling in an effective manner. The burden rests upon the defendants to establish that such time is necessary in the public interest and is consistent with good faith compliance at the earliest practicable date. To that end, the courts may consider problems related to administration, arising from the physical condition of the school plant, the school transportation system, personnel, revision of school districts and attendance areas into compact units to achieve a system of determining admission to the public schools on a nonracial basis, and revision of local laws and regulations which may be necessary in solving the foregoing problems. They will also consider the adequacy of any plans the defendants may propose to meet these problems and to effectuate a transition to a racially nondiscriminatory school system. During this period of transition, the courts will retain jurisdiction of these cases. The [cases are accordingly remanded to the lower courts] to take such proceedings and enter such orders and decrees consistent with this opinion as are necessary and proper to admit to public schools on a racially nondiscriminatory basis with all deliberate speed the parties to these [cases]."

After its promulgation of general guidelines in Brown II, the Court remained silent about implementation for several years. Enforcement of the desegregation requirement was left largely to lower court litigation and to the political arena. The decision indeed met with massive resistance, often violent, which the Court condemned in Cooper v. Aaron (1958; see p. 21 above), signing an opinion reaffirming the Brown principle in the face of official resistance in Little Rock, Arkansas. Integration of the public schools did not meaningfully accelerate until after the enactment of the Civil Rights Act of 1964, which conditioned the receipt of federal funds for education on states' compliance with desegregation. After Brown had been accepted by the other branches of the national government, the Court ruled frequently on implementation questions.

2. ***Eliminating the vestiges of de jure segregation.*** In **Green v. County School Board**, 391 U.S. 430 (1968), for the first time since Brown II, the Court issued a detailed opinion on the question of remedies. The school district argued that good faith "freedom of choice" plans adequately complied with the Brown mandate, even though, after three years of operation, no white child had chosen to attend the former black school and about 85% of the black children remained in the all-black school. The unanimous Court found the plan inadequate in complying with desegregation requirements. Justice BRENNAN's opinion emphasized that "[r]acial identification of the system's schools" remained "complete" and that "the transition to a unitary, nonracial system of public education was and is the ultimate end to be brought about. [What] is involved here is the question whether the Board has achieved the 'racially nondiscriminatory school system' Brown II held must be effectuated. [School] boards [then] operating state-compelled dual systems [were] clearly charged with the affirmative duty to take whatever steps might be necessary to convert to a unitary system in which racial discrimination would be eliminated root and branch." School officials were required to "fashion steps which promise realistically to convert promptly to a system without a 'white' school and a 'Negro' school, but just schools."

In rural and small town areas with no significant residential segregation, the elimination of "freedom of choice" plans and their variants and the adoption of geographic zoning largely eliminated racially identifiable schools. But in large Southern cities with substantial residential segregation—as in the North—geographic zoning alone could not substantially alter the racial composition of schools. In 1971, the Court turned to the problem of metropolitan areas in the South. **Swann v. Charlotte-Mecklenburg Board of Education**, 402 U.S. 1 (1971), arose in the school district covering the Charlotte, North Carolina, metropolitan area, which had been wholly segregated, de jure, at the time of Brown in 1954. In 1965, the district adopted a court-approved desegregation plan including geographic zoning and free transfers. By 1969, about half of the black students were in formerly white schools, but the remainder attended virtually all-black schools. After Green, the district court ordered the school authorities to prepare a more effective plan. Ultimately, the lower court appointed its own expert and accepted his plan, which involved some redrawing of district lines as well as some busing of elementary school students in both directions.

The Court, in a unanimous decision by Chief Justice BURGER, affirmed the district court's order. "Once a right and a violation have been shown, the scope of a district court's equitable powers to remedy past wrongs is broad. [The] constitutional command to desegregate schools does not mean that every school in every community must always reflect the racial composition of the school system as a whole. [But] in a system with a history of segregation the need for remedial criteria of sufficient specificity to assure a school authority's compliance with its constitutional duty warrants a presumption against schools that are substantially disproportionate in their racial composition." In order to produce a unitary system, courts had broad discretion to use "frank—and sometimes drastic—gerrymandering of school districts and attendance zones."

3. ***Desegregation outside the South.*** In **Keyes v. School District**, 413 U.S. 189 (1973), the Court's first decision on school desegregation in a Northern or Western district that had not had a background of state-mandated segregation, Justice BRENNAN's majority opinion purported to adhere to the de jure-de facto distinction. But he set forth criteria that would facilitate a finding of purposeful discrimination in Northern districts and that would permit court orders for district-wide remedies to rest on findings of intentional discrimination in only *part* of the district "where plaintiffs prove that the school authorities have carried out a systematic program of segregation affecting a substantial proportion of the students, schools, teachers and facilities," or where a showing of intentional segregation in one area was probative as to intentional segregation in other areas. Justice REHNQUIST was the only member of the Court in total disagreement with the majority. He concluded: "To require that a genuinely 'dual' system be disestablished, in the sense of the assignment of a child to a particular school is not made to depend on his race, is one thing. To require that school boards affirmatively undertake to achieve racial mixing in schools where such mixing is not achieved in sufficient degree by neutrally drawn boundary lines is quite obviously something else."

4. ***Limiting interdistrict remedies.*** In **Milliken v. Bradley**, 418 U.S. 717 (1974), the Court reversed lower court orders that had directed busing across district lines between the city of Detroit, where de jure segregation had been found, and suburban areas, where it had not. The 5–4 ruling concluded "that absent an inter-district violation there is no basis for an inter-district remedy." Chief Justice BURGER's majority opinion concluded: "[The] notion that school district lines may be casually ignored or treated as a mere administrative convenience is contrary to the history of public education in our country. [Before] the boundaries of separate and autonomous school districts may be set aside by consolidating the separate units for remedial purposes or by imposing a cross-district remedy, it must first be shown [that] racially discriminatory acts of the state or local school

districts, or of a single school district, have been a substantial cause of inter-district segregation. Thus an inter-district remedy might be in order where the racially discriminatory acts of one or more school districts caused racial segregation in an adjacent district, or where district lines have been deliberately drawn on the basis of race." Justice WHITE's dissent, joined by Justices Douglas, Brennan and Marshall, objected to the Court's protection of the state from mere "undue administrative inconvenience": "[Michigan] has successfully insulated itself from its duty to provide effective desegregation remedies by vesting sufficient power over its public schools in its local school districts."

5. ***Limiting the federal courts' remedial powers.*** In **Missouri v. Jenkins**, 495 U.S. 33 (1990), the Court limited the power of the federal courts, in implementing desegregation, to impose fiscal burdens on states and localities. Missouri and the Kansas City, Missouri, School District were found to have operated a segregated school system. Under a desegregation plan approved by the district court, expenditures of over $450 million were necessary. Various state law provisions prevented the school district from raising taxes to finance the 25% share of desegregation costs for which the district court held it liable. The district court ordered a significant increase in the district's property tax rates, despite the state law limitations. Justice WHITE's majority opinion found that the district court's order "contravened the principles of [federal/state] comity that must govern the exercise of the [court's] equitable discretion in this area." The trial court should not have ordered the tax increase "directly," but "could have authorized or required [the district] to levy property taxes at a rate adequate to fund the desegregation remedy and could have enjoined the operation of state laws that would have prevented [this]."

In 1995, the Kansas City case returned to the Supreme Court once more. In **Missouri v. Jenkins**, 515 U.S. 70 (1995), the 5–4 decision of the Court held that a federal court could not order salary increases and remedial education programs on the ground that "student achievement levels were still at or below the national norms at many grade levels." Chief Justice REHNQUIST's majority opinion reiterated that "the nature and scope of the remedy are to be determined by the violation, [which] means that federal-court decrees must directly address and relate to the constitutional violation itself." He noted that, while "a mandate for significant educational improvement, both in teaching and in facilities, may have been justified originally, its indefinite extension is not." He concluded that the lower court's remedy "results in so many imponderables and is so far removed from the task of eliminating the racial identifiability of the [Kansas City] schools that we believe it is beyond the admittedly broad discretion of the District Court."

6. ***Terminating long-standing decrees.*** At what point is it possible to say that a decree, originally entered to remedy de jure segregation, is no longer necessary? Does compliance with a decree bring judicial involvement to an end unless there is evidence of new de jure segregation? These questions came to the Court in **Board of Ed. of Oklahoma City v. Dowell**, 498 U.S. 237 (1991). Oklahoma City had at the time of Brown operated an explicitly segregated school system. In 1972 the District Court ordered system-wide busing. That plan produced substantial integration in the public schools, and in 1977 the court entered an order terminating the case and ending its jurisdiction. In part because of demographic changes that had "led to greater burdens on young black children," the school board in 1984

reintroduced a neighborhood school system for grades K–4. Challengers argued that the new plan would reinstitute segregation. The court of appeals held that the 1972 decree remained in force and imposed an "affirmative duty [not] to take any action that would impede the process of disestablishing the dual system and its effects."

The Supreme Court reversed, with Chief Justice REHNQUIST writing for the majority: "From the very first, federal supervision of local school systems was intended as a temporary measure to remedy past discrimination. [Injunctions] entered in school desegregation cases [are] not intended to operate in perpetuity. [Dissolving] a desegregation decree after the local authorities have operated in compliance with it for a reasonable period of time recognizes that 'necessary concern for the important values of local control of public school systems' dictates that a federal court's regulatory control of such systems not extend beyond the time required to remedy the effects of past intentional discrimination." Justice MARSHALL, joined by Justices Blackmun and Stevens, dissented, chastising the majority for suggesting that after 65 years of official segregation, "13 years of desegregation was enough. [The] majority's standard ignores how the stigmatic harm identified in Brown I can persist even after the State ceases actively to enforce segregation. [Our] school-desegregation jurisprudence establishes that the *effects* of past discrimination remain chargeable to the school district regardless of its lack of continued enforcement of segregation, and the remedial decree is required until those effects have been finally eliminated."

ELIMINATING OTHER VESTIGES OF SEGREGATION

1. ***Interracial cohabitation.*** Even as desegregation proceeded in public schools and other public institutions, segregation in the regulation of private relationships continued. In **McLaughlin v. Florida**, 379 U.S. 184 (1964), the Court invalidated a criminal adultery and fornication statute prohibiting cohabitation by interracial unmarried couples. Justice WHITE's majority opinion emphasized: "[We] deal here with a classification based upon the race of the participants, which must be viewed in light of the historical fact that the central purpose of the 14th Amendment was to eliminate racial discrimination emanating from official sources in the States. This strong policy renders racial classifications 'constitutionally suspect' and subject to the 'most rigid scrutiny,' and 'in most circumstances irrelevant' to any constitutionally acceptable legislative purpose. [We] deal here with a racial classification embodied in a criminal statute. [Our] inquiry, therefore, is whether there clearly appears in the relevant materials some overriding statutory purpose requiring the proscription of the specified conduct when engaged in by a white person and a Negro, but not otherwise. Without such justification the racial classification [here] is reduced to an invidious discrimination forbidden by [equal protection]."

2. ***Antimiscegenation statutes.*** Bans on interracial marriage persisted in most Southern states up until the following 1967 decision, aptly named Loving v. Virginia. As in Brown, Loving presented the Court with the problem of a statute that was facially symmetrical in the barrier it posed to racial integration. With which of the rationales in Brown is Loving most consistent?

Loving v. Virginia

388 U.S. 1, 87 S. Ct. 1817, 18 L. Ed. 2d 1010 (1967).

[Mildred Loving, an African-American woman, married Richard Loving, a white man. Married in the District of Columbia, they returned to Virginia, where they were convicted of violating Virginia's criminal ban on miscegenation. The trial judge suspended their one-year jail sentences on the condition that they leave the state and not return to Virginia together for 25 years.]

■ CHIEF JUSTICE WARREN delivered the opinion of the Court.

This case presents a constitutional question never addressed by this Court: whether a statutory scheme adopted by [Virginia] to prevent marriages between persons solely on the basis of racial classifications violates [the] 14th Amendment. For reasons which seem to us to reflect the central meaning of those constitutional commands, we conclude that these statutes cannot stand.

Virginia is now one of 16 States which prohibit and punish marriages on the basis of racial classifications. Penalties for miscegenation arose as an incident to slavery and have been common in Virginia since the colonial period. [T]he State does not contend [that] its powers to regulate marriage are unlimited notwithstanding the commands of the 14th Amendment, [but] argues that the meaning of [equal protection] is only that state penal laws containing an interracial element as part of the definition of the offense must apply equally to whites and Negroes in the sense that members of each race are punished to the same degree. Thus, the State contends that, because its miscegenation statutes punish equally both the white and the Negro participants in an interracial marriage, these statutes, despite their reliance on racial classifications, do not constitute an invidious discrimination based upon [race]. Because we reject the notion that the mere "equal application" of a statute containing racial classifications is enough to remove the classifications from the 14th Amendment's proscription of all invidious racial discriminations, we do not accept the State's contention that these statutes should be upheld if there is any possible basis for concluding that they serve a rational purpose. [W]e deal with statutes containing racial classifications, and the fact of equal application does not immunize the statute from the very heavy burden of justification which the 14th Amendment has traditionally required of state statutes drawn according to race.

The State argues that statements [in] Congress about the time of the passage of the 14th Amendment indicate that the Framers did not intend the Amendment to make unconstitutional state miscegenation laws. [W]e have said in connection with a related problem that although these historical sources "cast some light" they are not sufficient to resolve the problem; "[a]t best, they are inconclusive." Brown v. Board. We have rejected the proposition that the debates in the Thirty-ninth Congress or in the State legislatures which ratified the 14th Amendment supported the theory [that] the requirement of equal protection of the laws is satisfied by penal laws defining offenses based on racial classifications so long as white and Negro participants in the offense were similarly punished.

[The] clear and central purpose of the 14th Amendment was to eliminate all official state sources of invidious racial discrimination in the States. [E.g., Slaughter-House Cases; Strauder.] There can be no question but that Virginia's miscegenation statutes rest solely upon distinctions drawn according to race. The statutes proscribe generally accepted conduct if engaged in by members of different races. At the very least, [equal protection] demands that racial classifications, especially suspect in criminal statutes, be subjected to the "most rigid scrutiny," and, if they are ever to be upheld, they must be shown to be necessary to the accomplishment of some permissible state objective, independent of the racial discrimination which it was the object of the 14th Amendment to eliminate. [There] is patently no legitimate overriding purpose independent of invidious racial discrimination which justifies this classification. The fact that Virginia prohibits only interracial marriages involving white persons demonstrates that the racial classifications must stand on their own justification, as measures designed to maintain White Supremacy.[1] We have consistently denied the constitutionality of measures which restrict the rights of citizens on account of race. There can be no doubt that restricting the freedom to marry solely because of racial classifications violates the central meaning of [equal protection]. Reversed.

---

3. ***Interracial remarriage and child custody.*** In **Palmore v. Sidoti**, 466 U.S. 429 (1984), the Court faced the question whether the "best interests of the child" standard could ever permit a custody allocation to prefer a same-race to an interracial remarriage by the child's parents. The case arose from a custody battle after Palmore and Sidoti (both white) were divorced. Initially, Palmore, the mother, was awarded custody of their three-year-old daughter. When the mother entered a second marriage, to an African-American man, the state court awarded custody to the father as in "the best interest" of the child. The trial court found that, "despite the strides that had been made in bettering relations between the races in this country, it is inevitable that [the daughter] will, if allowed to remain in the present [situation], suffer from the social stigmatization that is sure to come." The Court unanimously reversed that ruling.

Chief Justice BURGER noted that the custody ruling had rested wholly on race, since it was "clear that the outcome would have been different had [Palmore] married a Caucasian male." He wrote for the Court: "A core purpose of the [14th Amendment] was to do away with all governmentally imposed discrimination based on race. Classifying persons according to their race is more likely to reflect racial prejudice than legitimate public concerns; the race, not the person, dictates the category. Such classifications are subject to the most exacting scrutiny; to pass constitutional muster, they

---

1 Appellants point out that the State's concern in these statutes, as expressed in the words of the 1924 Act's title, "An Act to Preserve Racial Integrity," extends only to the integrity of the white race. While Virginia prohibits whites from marrying any nonwhite (subject to the exception for the descendants of Pocahontas), Negroes, Orientals, and any other racial class may intermarry without statutory interference. Appellants contend that this distinction renders Virginia's miscegenation statutes arbitrary and unreasonable even assuming the constitutional validity of an official purpose to preserve "racial integrity." We need not reach this contention because we find the racial classifications in these statutes repugnant to the 14th Amendment, even assuming an even-handed state purpose to protect the "integrity" of all races. [Footnote by Chief Justice Warren.]

must be justified by a compelling governmental interest and must be 'necessary [to] the accomplishment' of its legitimate purpose. [McLaughlin; see Loving.] The goal of granting custody based on the best interests of the child is indisputably a substantial governmental interest for purposes of [equal protection]. It would ignore reality to suggest that racial and ethnic prejudices do not exist or that all manifestations of those prejudices have been eliminated. There is a risk that a child living with a step-parent of a different race may be subject to a variety of pressures and stresses not present if the child were living with parents of the same racial or ethnic origin. The question, however, is whether the reality of private biases and the possible injury they might inflict are permissible considerations for removal of an infant child from the custody of its natural mother. We have little difficulty concluding that they are not. The Constitution cannot control such prejudices but neither can it tolerate them. Private biases may be outside the reach of the law, but the law cannot, directly or indirectly, give them effect. [The] effects of racial prejudice, however real, cannot justify a racial classification removing an infant child from the custody of its natural mother found to be an appropriate person to have such custody."

After Palmore, may race ever be taken into account in state-supervised family arrangements? May a child placed by the state for adoption be matched with adoptive parents of the same race? In order to help the child avoid difficulty or embarrassment in encounters with others? In order to ensure the children's enculturation in race-specific traditions? In order to enhance the parents' sense of cohesion within the adoptive family? For discussion, see Banks, "The Color of Desire: Fulfilling Adoptive Parents' Racial Preference Through Discriminatory State Action," 107 Yale L.J. 875 (1998); Bartholet, "Where Do Black Children Belong? The Politics of Race Matching in Adoption," 139 U. Pa. L. Rev. 1163 (1991).

4. ***The problem of facially symmetrical race-based laws.*** Note that the laws struck down in Brown and Loving did not contain racial classifications explicitly disadvantaging racial minorities. On their face, the segregationist laws applied equally to blacks and whites. Nevertheless, the Court applied strict scrutiny and struck down the laws. Why? Is the reason that all governmental advertence to race is impermissible? Palmore v. Sidoti stated: "Classifying persons according to their race is more likely to reflect racial prejudice than legitimate public concerns; the race, not the person, dictates the category." And "our Constitution is color-blind," insisted the first Justice Harlan's dissent in Plessy v. Ferguson. Is *all* racial discrimination "illegal, immoral, unconstitutional"? Bickel, The Morality of Consent (1975). Over the years, some Justices have suggested a per se rule invalidating all governmental distinctions among individuals made because of race. But, as the preceding cases illustrate, the Court has not stated so comprehensive a prohibition; rather, disadvantaging racial classifications are ordinarily "suspect," must be subjected to "the most rigid scrutiny," and bear a "very heavy burden of justification." Would a flat rule banning all racial classifications that disadvantage minorities be preferable to the Court's approach? Or is the reason instead for invalidation in Loving that the facial symmetry of the prohibition was a mirage, and the law in fact embodied the subordinating inequality of what the Court called "White Supremacy"? Does this require a background examination of history and sociology not apparent on the face of the law? For an argument that, while Brown conceived equal protection as eliminating racial *subordination*, decisions like McLaughlin and Loving began treating racial *classification* as presumptively

unconstitutional, see Siegel, "Equality Talk: Antisubordination and Anticlassification Values in Constitutional Struggles Over Brown," 117 Harv. L. Rev. 1470 (2004).

5. ***Permissible uses of racial criteria?*** Is the use of racial criteria for segregatory purposes ever constitutionally permissible? Is any justification for racial classification strong enough to survive the strict scrutiny avowed by the Court in Loving and Palmore? In **Johnson v. California**, 543 U.S. 499 (2005), the Court, by a vote of 5–3, held that strict scrutiny must be applied to a state policy of segregating prisoners by race even where preventing racial gang violence was the justification. Justice O'CONNOR wrote for the Court, joined by Justices Kennedy, Souter, Ginsburg, and Breyer:

"The California Department of Corrections (CDC) has an unwritten policy of racially segregating prisoners in double cells in reception centers for up to 60 days each time they enter a new correctional facility. [The] CDC's asserted rationale for this practice is that it is necessary to prevent violence caused by racial gangs. [We] have held that '*all* racial classifications [imposed by government] . . . must be analyzed by a reviewing court under strict scrutiny.' [The] CDC claims that its policy should be exempt from our categorical rule because it is 'neutral'—that is, [all] prisoners are 'equally' segregated. The CDC's argument ignores our repeated command that 'racial classifications receive close scrutiny even when they may be said to burden or benefit the races equally.' Indeed, we rejected the notion that separate can ever be equal—or 'neutral'—50 years ago in Brown v. Board. [The] need for strict scrutiny is no less important [where] prison officials cite racial violence as the reason for their policy. [Indeed,] by insisting that inmates be housed only with other inmates of the same race, it is possible that prison officials will breed further hostility among prisoners and reinforce racial and ethnic divisions. [When] government officials are permitted to use race as a proxy for gang membership and violence without demonstrating a compelling government interest and proving that their means are narrowly tailored, society as a whole suffers. [In] the prison context, when the government's power is at its apex, we think that searching judicial review of racial classifications is necessary to guard against invidious discrimination. [Strict] scrutiny does not preclude the ability of prison officials to address the compelling interest in prison safety. Prison administrators, however, will have to demonstrate that any race-based policies are narrowly tailored to that end. [Prisons] are dangerous places, and the special circumstances they present may justify racial classifications in some contexts. Such circumstances can be considered in applying strict scrutiny, which is designed to take relevant differences into account." Because the lower courts had reviewed the prison segregation policy under a deferential standard of review derived from challenges to prison regulations in other contexts, the Court remanded for determination of whether California could satisfy strict scrutiny.

Justice STEVENS dissented, arguing that the prison's policy was unconstitutional as an equal protection violation on the record before the Court without need for remand for further fact finding. Justice THOMAS, joined by Justice Scalia, also dissented but in the opposite direction, arguing that strict scrutiny should not apply: "The Constitution has always demanded less within the prison walls. Time and again, even when faced with constitutional rights no less 'fundamental' than the right to be free from state-sponsored racial discrimination, we have deferred to the reasonable judgments of officials experienced in running this Nation's prisons. There is good reason for such deference in this case. California oversees roughly 160,000 inmates, in prisons that have been a breeding ground for some of the most violent prison gangs in America—all of them organized along racial lines. In that atmosphere, California racially segregates a portion of its inmates, in a part of its prisons, for brief periods of up to 60 days, until the State can arrange permanent housing. The majority is concerned with sparing inmates the indignity and stigma of racial discrimination. California is concerned with their safety and saving their lives." In 2008, pursuant to a settlement agreement between the plaintiffs and the state, California began to implement a plan to desegregate the California prisons.

FACIAL DISCRIMINATION AGAINST RACIAL MINORITIES

1. ***Strict scrutiny of racially discriminatory laws.*** While Brown, Loving and Palmore involved facially symmetrical or neutral laws, they applied a standard of strict scrutiny first announced in Korematsu v. United States, where the government's discrimination against a minority based on race or ancestry was overt. While announcing this demanding standard, **Korematsu v. United States**, 323 U.S. 214 (1944), was one of the very rare cases in which a classification imposing disadvantage based on race *survived* strict scrutiny. The case arose because of the notorious internment of more than one hundred thousand Americans and non-citizens of Japanese origin in camps during World War II. Although there was no evidence of disloyalty on the part of persons of Japanese origin in the United States, soon after the attack on Pearl Harbor of December 7, 1941, President Roosevelt issued an Executive Order purporting to safeguard "against espionage [and] against sabotage." The order provided that certain military commanders on the West Coast might designate "military areas" in the United States "from which any or all persons may be excluded, and with respect to which the right of any person to enter, remain in, or leave shall be subject to whatever restrictions" the "Military Commander may impose in his discretion." As framed, the resulting military orders nominally required first curfews and then exclusion from the West Coast area. In reality, by requiring persons of Japanese ancestry on the West Coast to report to relocation centers from which they were deported to camps, the orders effectively mandated internment. Many Japanese-Americans lost property during the resulting decoration and internment. The conditions in the camps, which Roosevelt several times publicly called "concentration camps," were brutal.

In Hirabayashi v. United States, 320 U.S. 81 (1943), the Court unanimously upheld the curfew orders. Then, in 1944, in Korematsu, the Court sustained, against challenge under the equal protection requirement implied in the Fifth Amendment Due Process Clause, a conviction for violating a military order during World War II excluding all persons of Japanese ancestry from designated West Coast areas.

Early in his majority opinion, Justice BLACK stated the governing standard: "[All] legal restrictions which curtail the civil rights of a single racial group are immediately suspect. That is not to say that all such restrictions are unconstitutional. It is to say that courts must subject them to the most rigid scrutiny. Pressing public necessity may sometimes justify the existence of such restrictions; racial antagonism never can." But here, the requisite "pressing public necessity" was found. He explained: "Like curfew, exclusion of those of Japanese origin was deemed necessary by the [military authorities] because of the presence of an unascertained number of disloyal members of the group, most of whom we have no doubt were loyal to this country." The military authorities had found "that it was impossible to bring about an immediate segregation of the disloyal from the loyal." The judgment that "exclusion of the whole group [was] a military imperative answers the contention that the exclusion was in the nature of group punishment based on antagonism to those of Japanese origin." In a closing passage, Justice Black reiterated that the Court had not endorsed racial discrimination: "To cast this case into outlines of racial prejudice, without reference to the real military dangers which were presented, merely confuses the issue." Korematsu was excluded, he insisted, "because we are at war with the Japanese Empire, because the properly constituted military authorities feared an invasion of our West Coast and felt constrained to take proper security measures, because they decided that the military urgency of the situation demanded that all citizens of Japanese ancestry be segregated from the West Coast temporarily and finally, because Congress, reposing its confidence in this time of war in our military leaders—as inevitably it must—determined that they should have the power to do just this. There was evidence of disloyalty on the part of some, the military authorities considered that the need for action was great, and time was short. We cannot—by availing ourselves of the calm perspective of hindsight—now say that at that time these actions were unjustified."

Justice FRANKFURTER concurred, citing the Court's decision upholding the curfew in Hirabayashi as providing precedent sufficient to sustain the government's action against Korematsu. Frankfurter also laid out some principles regarding the executive and legislative wartime powers, specifically responding to Justice Jackson's argument in dissent (below) that the courts should not clothe an unconstitutional government wartime action in legitimacy by upholding it, but rather should step aside: "The provisions of the Constitution which confer on the Congress and the President powers to enable this country to wage war are as much part of the Constitution as provisions looking to a nation at peace. [The] war power of the Government is 'the power to wage war successfully.' [Therefore] the validity of action under the war power must be judged wholly in the context of war. That action is not to be stigmatized as lawless because like action in times of peace would be lawless. [The] respective spheres of action of military authorities and of judges are of course very different. But within their sphere, military authorities are no more outside the bounds of obedience to the Constitution than are judges within theirs. 'The war power of the United States, like its other powers [is] subject to applicable constitutional limitations.' [To] recognize that military orders are 'reasonably expedient military precautions' in time of war and yet to deny them constitutional legitimacy makes of the Constitution an instrument for dialetic subtleties not reasonably to be attributed to the hard-headed Framers, of whom a majority had had actual participation in war. [Being] an exercise of the war power explicitly granted by the Constitution for safeguarding the national life by prosecuting war effectively, I find nothing in the Constitution which denies to Congress the power to enforce such a valid military order by making its violation an offense triable in the civil courts. [To] find that the Constitution does not forbid the military measures now complained of does not carry with it approval of that which Congress and the Executive did. That is their business, not ours."

Justice MURPHY wrote the strongest dissent—even though he did not invoke the "suspect classification"-"strict scrutiny" test and purported to apply the "reasonableness" standard. He acknowledged that, while "great respect" for military judgment in wartime was "appropriate," "the military claim must subject itself to the judicial process of having its reasonableness determined." He was not persuaded that the deprivation of individual rights here was "reasonably related to a public danger that is so 'immediate, imminent, and impending' as not to admit of delay and not to permit the intervention of ordinary constitutional processes to alleviate the danger." The exclusion order applicable to "all persons of Japanese ancestry" seemed to him "an obvious racial discrimination" and hence a denial of equal protection. He conceded that there was "a very real fear of invasion," sabotage, and espionage on the West Coast in 1942. But he insisted that "the exclusion, either temporarily or permanently, of all persons with Japanese blood in their veins has [no] reasonable relation" to the "removal of the dangers." He explained: "[T]hat relation is lacking because the exclusion order necessarily must rely for its reasonableness upon the assumption that *all* persons of Japanese ancestry may have a dangerous tendency to commit sabotage and espionage." He found it "difficult to believe that reason, logic or experience could be marshaled in support of such an assumption." He argued that the "forced exclusion was the result in good measure of [an] erroneous assumption of racial guilt rather than bona fide military necessity." The justification for exclusion rested "mainly upon questionable racial and sociological grounds" not charged or proved—"an accumulation of much of the misinformation, half-truths and insinuations that for years have been directed against Japanese Americans by people with racial and economic prejudices—the same people who have been among the foremost advocates of the evacuation. A military judgment based upon such racial and sociological considerations is not entitled to the great weight ordinarily given the judgments based upon strictly military considerations." He accordingly dissented from "this legalization of racism."

In a separate dissent, Justice JACKSON stated that the military orders may or may not have been "expedient military precautions," but they should not be enforced by civil courts committed to the Constitution. He elaborated: "[A] judicial construction of the due process clause that will sustain this order is a far more subtle blow to liberty than the promulgation of the order itself. A military order, however unconstitutional, is not apt to last longer than the military emergency. [But] once a judicial opinion [rationalizes] the Constitution to show that the Constitution sanctions such an order, the Court for all time has validated the principle of racial discrimination in criminal procedure and of transplanting American citizens. The principle then lies about like a loaded weapon ready for the hand of any authority that can bring forward a plausible claim of an urgent need. [A] military commander may overstep the bounds of constitutionality, and it is an incident. But if we review and approve, that passing incident becomes a doctrine of the Constitution." Earlier he had noted: "[I]f we cannot confine military expedients by the Constitution, neither would I distort the Constitution to approve all that the military may deem expedient."

Justice ROBERTS also dissented. He rejected the government's reliance on the Hirabayashi Court's upholding of the curfew order and stressed that

Korematsu faced much more than a temporary exclusion from his home (the constitutional validity of which would have been more likely): "This is not a case of keeping people off the streets at night as was [Hirabayashi] nor a case of temporary exclusion of a citizen from an area for his own safety or that of the community, nor a case of offering him an opportunity to go temporarily out of an area where his presence might cause danger to himself or to his fellows. On the contrary, it is the case of convicting a citizen as a punishment for not submitting to imprisonment in a concentration camp, based on his ancestry, and solely because of his ancestry, without evidence or inquiry concerning his loyalty and good disposition towards the United States. [The] Government's argument, and the opinion of the court, in my judgment, erroneously divide that which is single and indivisible and thus make the case appear as if the petitioner violated a Military Order, sanctioned by Act of Congress, which excluded him from his home.

[The] predicament in which the petitioner thus found himself was this: He was forbidden, by Military Order, to leave the zone in which he lived; he was forbidden, by Military Order, after a date fixed, to be found within that zone unless he were in an Assembly Center located in that zone. [This] case cannot, therefore, be decided on any such narrow ground as the possible validity of a Temporary Exclusion Order under which the residents of an area are given an opportunity to leave and go elsewhere in their native land outside the boundaries of a military area. To make the case turn on any such assumption is to shut our eyes to reality."

2. ***Scope of racial classifications.*** Discrimination against African-Americans was the historical focus of the Fourteenth Amendment, but as Korematsu illustrates, the Court has found that classifications resting on *any* advertence to race, national origin, ancestry or ethnicity are suspect. Recall that in Strauder, the first case invalidating racial discrimination under the Fourteenth Amendment, the Court mentioned laws directed at "all naturalized Celtic Irishmen" as falling within "the spirit of the amendment." Without much discussion, later Courts have treated discrimination based on national origin and ancestry the same as discrimination against blacks. See, e.g., Yick Wo v. Hopkins, below (invalidating discriminatory application of health ordinance against Chinese-Americans); Hernandez v. Texas, 347 U.S. 475 (1954) (striking struck down discrimination against Mexican-Americans in jury selection, noting that "community prejudices are not static, and from time to time other differences [than 'differences in race and color'] from the community norm may define other groups which need the same protection"); Rice v. Cayetano, 528 U.S. 495 (2000) (invalidating voting classification limiting certain elections to native Hawaiians defined as descendants of the peoples inhabiting the Hawaiian Islands in 1778) (stating that "ancestral inquiry [implicates] the same grave concerns as a classification specifying a particular race by name").

3. ***Aftermath of Korematsu.*** Korematsu is a case that has come to live in infamy. For contemporaneous criticism, see, e.g., Rostow, "The Japanese American Cases—A Disaster," 54 Yale L.J. 489 (1945). For later criticism, see Irons, Justice at War (1983). In 1984, a district court in San Francisco issued a writ of coram nobis vacating Korematsu's conviction, Korematsu v. United States, 584 F. Supp. 1406 (N.D. Cal. 1984), on the grounds of governmental misconduct in the submission of false information to the Supreme Court in the 1940s. One of Korematsu's co-counsel stated

that the 1984 ruling "sucked away the factual underpinnings" of the Court decision.

In **Trump v. Hawaii**, 585 U.S. ___, 138 S. Ct. 2392 (2018), discussed in full earlier at p. 325, the Court insisted it was formally overruling Korematsu, albeit in the context of upholding an executive order that plaintiffs contended functioned as a broad exclusion of Muslims from travel into the United States. Chief Justice ROBERTS, citing Justice Jackson's Korematsu dissent, wrote: "Korematsu was gravely wrong the day it was decided, has been overruled in the court of history, and—to be clear—'has no place in law under the Constitution.'"

In dissent, Justice SOTOMAYOR noted that the formal overruling was "laudable" but argued that the majority, by "blindly accepting the Government's misguided invitation to sanction discriminatory policy motivated by animosity toward a disfavored group, all in the name of a superficial claim to national security, [ ] redeploys the same dangerous logic underlying Korematsu and merely replaces one 'gravely wrong' decision with another."

Who has the better of this argument? Moreover, if Chief Justice Roberts is correct in arguing that President Trump's executive order was factually and legally different from the one in Korematsu, was it actually open for the Court to overrule a precedent that had allegedly little to do with the facts of the case before it? For a possible answer, see Greene, "Is Korematsu Good Law?," 128 Yale L.J. F. 629 (2019).

4. ***The Chinese Exclusion Act of 1882.*** The Chinese Exclusion Act was a law passed by Congress banning "laborers" of Chinese dissent from entry into the United States for a period of ten years. The law also banned Chinese persons who came as laborers from becoming citizens. This was explicit discrimination against Chinese persons on racial grounds, given that the government allowed laborers of other ethnicities to immigrate without extra restriction during that time. The Supreme Court affirmed the Act against a number of challenges in **Chae Chan Ping v. United States**, 130 U.S. 581 (1889). There, the Court held that the United States had the sovereign power to exclude aliens for any reason it judged sufficient. Later, in Fong Yue Ting v. United States, 142 U.S. 698 (1893), the Court held that it was constitutionally permissible to deport Chinese persons on racial grounds. For an overview of the caselaw during the period surrounding the Chinese Exclusion Act see Chin, "Segregation's Last Stronghold: Race Discrimination and the Constitutional Law of Immigration," 46 UCLA L. Rev. 1, 1–6 (1998). Would the government have the power to exclude aliens from immigration on facially racial grounds today, notwithstanding the Equal Protection Clause?

RACIALLY DISCRIMINATORY PURPOSE AND EFFECT

1. ***Racially discriminatory application of facially neutral laws.*** Cases like Strauder and Korematsu involved explicit disadvantaging racial classifications on the face of the law; cases like Brown and Loving involved explicit advertence to race on the face of the law. Can a law that is racially neutral on its face ever give rise to a finding of racially discriminatory purpose and therefore to strict scrutiny?

The Court has answered that question in the affirmative in several circumstances. One such circumstance arises when a facially neutral law receives racially discriminatory application. Equal protection binds all branches of state government—executive and judicial as well as legislative (recall Palmore, applying equal protection to a judicial decision). Yick Wo is the leading early case illustrating that a facially neutral law may impose purposeful discrimination because of the manner of its administration. A San Francisco ordinance prohibited operating a laundry (except in a brick or stone building) without the consent of the Board of Supervisors. Of 320 laundries, 310 were in wooden buildings. The Board granted permits to operate laundries in wooden buildings to all but one of the non-Chinese applicants, but to none of those among the 240 Chinese laundry operators who applied for permits. A Chinese alien who had operated a laundry for many years was refused a permit, convicted of a misdemeanor for illegally operating his laundry, and imprisoned.

In **Yick Wo v. Hopkins**, 118 U.S. 356 (1886), the Court, in a habeas corpus proceeding, held the challenger's imprisonment unjustified. Justice MATTHEWS's opinion found discrimination in the *administration* of the law: "[T]he facts shown establish an administration directed so exclusively against a particular class of persons as [to] require the conclusion, that, whatever may have been the intent of the ordinances as adopted, they are applied by the public authorities charged with their administration [with] a mind so unequal and oppressive as to amount to a practical denial by the State of [equal protection]. Though the law itself be fair on its face and impartial in appearance, yet, if it is applied and administered by public authority with an evil eye and an unequal hand, so as practically to make unjust and illegal discriminations between persons in similar circumstances, [the] denial of equal justice is still within the prohibition of the Constitution. The present cases [are] within this class. [While the] consent of the supervisors is withheld from [petitioners] and from two hundred others who have also petitioned, all of whom happen to be Chinese subjects, eighty others, not Chinese subjects, are permitted to carry on the same business under similar conditions. The fact of this discrimination is admitted. No reason for it is shown, and the conclusion cannot be resisted, that no reason for it exists except hostility to the race and nationality to which the petitioners belong, and which in the eye of the law is not justified."

Note that while Yick Wo is frequently cited for the proposition that the racially selective enforcement of a facially neutral law presumptively violates the Equal Protection Clause, the case has lacked exact progeny; it has not led to frequent dismissals of criminal prosecutions on the ground that the prosecution acted in a racially selective manner. For an historical account that suggests that this may be so because the decision rested less on racial equality than on "the conclusion that the laundrymen had been arbitrarily deprived of a constitutionally protected property interest," see Chin, "Unexplainable on Grounds of Race: Doubts About Yick Wo," 2008 U. Ill. L. Rev. 1359. For the counterargument that the case did have a significant racial dimension because it extended the Fourteenth Amendment for the first time beyond anti-black discrimination and held that "arbitrary denials of fundamental economic rights [include] those based on racial discrimination," see Joo, "Yick Wo Re-Revisited: Nonblack Nonwhites and Fourteenth Amendment History," 2008 U. Ill. L. Rev. 1427.

2. ***Racially discriminatory purpose underlying facially neutral laws.*** The Court has declined to find race discrimination in facially neutral laws with a racially disproportionate effect. But if the racially disproportionate effect is extreme enough, may a racially discriminatory purpose be inferred? For an example of an inference of discriminatory motive from circumstantial evidence of extreme racially disparate impact, see **Gomillion v. Lightfoot**, 364 U.S. 339 (1960), finding that an Alabama law redefining the city boundaries of Tuskegee was a device to disenfranchise blacks in violation of the 15th Amendment. The statute, which altered "the shape of Tuskegee from a square to an uncouth twenty-eight-sided figure," was alleged to result in removing from the city "all save only four or five of its 400 Negro voters while not removing a single white voter or resident." Justice Frankfurter's opinion found that, if the allegations were proved, "the conclusion would be irresistible, tantamount for all practical purposes to a mathematical demonstration, that the legislation is solely concerned with segregating white and colored voters by fencing Negro citizens out of town so as to deprive them of their preexisting municipal vote."

In **Griffin v. County School Board of Prince Edward County**, 377 U.S. 218 (1964), the Court likewise discerned racially discriminatory purpose in a law that made no facial advertence to race. The decision found the closing of public schools unconstitutional in one of the counties involved in the first group of school desegregation cases decided together with Brown v. Board of Education. The public school closing scheme included grants of public funds to white children to attend private schools. Justice Black emphasized that "public schools were closed and private schools operated in their place with state and county assistance, for one reason, and one reason only: to ensure [that] white and colored children in Prince Edward County would not, under any circumstances, go to the same school. Whatever nonracial grounds might support a State's allowing a county to abandon public schools, the object must be a constitutional one, and grounds of race and opposition to desegregation do not qualify as constitutional."

Why, then, did the Court decline to find racially discriminatory purpose in the 5–4 decision in **Palmer v. Thompson**, 403 U.S. 217 (1971), holding that the city of Jackson, Mississippi, had *not* acted unconstitutionally in closing its public swimming pools after they had been ordered desegregated? Justice BLACK's majority opinion, after noting that there was no "affirmative duty" to operate swimming pools, rejected the argument that the closing was unconstitutional because it "was motivated by a desire to avoid integration." He asserted that "no case in this Court had held that a legislative act may violate equal protection solely because of the motivations of the men who voted for it." Ascertaining motivation was "extremely difficult." Though there was some evidence that the city had acted in part because of "ideological opposition to racial integration," there was also substantial evidence that the city had thought that the pools "could not be operated safely and economically on an integrated basis." He added that it was "difficult or impossible for any court to determine the 'sole' or 'dominant' motivation behind the choices of a group of legislators. Furthermore, there is an element of futility in a judicial attempt to invalidate a law because of the bad motives of its supporters. If the law is struck down for this reason, rather than because of its facial content or effect, it would presumably be valid as soon as the legislature or relevant governing body repassed it for different reasons." He conceded that there was "language in some of our cases" suggesting "that the motive or purpose behind a law is relevant to its constitutionality." "But," he added, "the focus in those cases was on the actual effect of the enactments, not upon the motivation which led the States to behave as they did," and the record here showed "no state action affecting blacks differently from whites."

Justice WHITE's dissent insisted that whites and blacks were not being treated alike when both were denied use of public services: "The fact is that closing the pools is an expression of official policy that Negroes are unfit to associate with whites." He asserted that forbidden "racial motive or animus" was a common focus of judicial inquiry—in the context of federal civil rights legislation, for example. He found that here "desegregation, and desegregation alone," was the cause of the closing.

In Palmer, Justice Black distinguished Gomillion as resting "on the actual effect" of the law, "not upon the motivation" underlying it. But was not the "effect" relevant in Gomillion only because it amounted to a "mathematical demonstration" of discriminatory purpose? Was the improper purpose clearer in Gomillion than in Palmer? Why, if the pool closing was an obvious response to a desegregation order? Was the difference that the effect was symmetrical on blacks and whites? How square that with Loving, above? In Palmer, Justice Black distinguished Griffin on the ground that, "unlike the 'private schools' in [Griffin], there is nothing here to show the city is directly or indirectly involved the funding or operation" of the private swimming pools that remained in the wake of the municipal pool closing. Was this distinction persuasive? See Brest, "Palmer v. Thompson: An Approach to the Problem of Unconstitutional Legislative Motive," 1971 Sup. Ct. Rev. 95; Ely, "Legislative and Administrative Motivation in Constitutional Law," 79 Yale L.J. 1205 (1970).

3. ***Facially neutral laws with racially discriminatory effect.*** If no purposeful discrimination appears on the face of a statute or can be inferred from the manner in which it is administered, and there is insufficient evidence of racially hostile motivation by lawmakers or administrators, may the statute be held unconstitutional nonetheless because it has a disproportionately adverse impact on racial minorities? Might some facially neutral laws with such effects reflect unconscious racial prejudice? See Lawrence, "The Id, the Ego, and Equal Protection: Reckoning With Unconscious Racism," 39 Stan. L. Rev. 317 (1987), arguing that racism "is a malady that we all share, because we all have been scarred by a common history," and adding that "unconscious prejudice presents [a problem] in that it is not subject to self-correction within the political process." Should courts enforcing equal protection invalidate laws based only upon a finding of a flawed *process* reflecting racial animus, or should they strive to assure greater racial equality in *result*? Compare Brest, "The Supreme Court, 1975 Term—Foreword: In Defense of the Antidiscrimination Principle," 90 Harv. L. Rev. 1 (1976), with Fiss, "Groups and the Equal Protection Clause," 5 Phil. & Pub. Affairs 107 (1976). Should de facto "discrimination" be treated like de jure, purposeful discrimination? The following case answered that question in the negative:

Washington v. Davis

426 U.S. 229, 96 S. Ct. 2040, 48 L. Ed. 2d 597 (1976).

[This case arose from an equal protection challenge by African-American applicants to the District of Columbia Metropolitan Police Department who were rejected for failing to perform satisfactorily on a written test measuring verbal ability, vocabulary, reading and comprehension. The examination was one generally used throughout the federal service and originally developed by the U.S. Civil Service Commission. The district court found that a higher percentage of African-Americans than whites had failed the examination and that the test had not been validated to establish its reliability for measuring subsequent job performance, but denied relief, finding that the test was reasonably related to the requirements of the police recruit training program and that it was not designed or operated "to discriminate against otherwise qualified blacks." The court of appeals found the lack of discriminatory intent regarding the test irrelevant and emphasized its disproportionate impact, finding such impact alone sufficient to establish a constitutional violation, absent proof by petitioners that the test was an adequate measure of job performance.]

■ JUSTICE WHITE delivered the opinion of the Court.

[The] central purpose of [equal protection is] the prevention of official conduct discriminating on the basis of race. [But] our cases have not embraced the proposition that a law or other official act, without regard to whether it reflects a racially discriminatory purpose, is unconstitutional *solely* because it has a racially disproportionate impact. Almost 100 years ago, [Strauder] established that the exclusion of Negroes from grand and petit juries in criminal proceedings violated [equal protection], but the fact that a particular jury or a series of juries does not statistically reflect the racial composition of the community does not in itself make out an invidious discrimination forbidden by the Clause. [The] school desegregation cases have also adhered to the basic equal protection principle that the invidious quality of a law claimed to be racially discriminatory must ultimately be traced to a racially discriminatory purpose. That there are both predominantly black and predominantly white schools in a community is not alone violative of [equal protection]. The essential element of de jure segregation is "a current condition of segregation resulting from intentional state action. [The] differentiating factor between de jure segregation and so-called de facto segregation [is] *purpose* or *intent* to segregate."

This is not to say that the necessary discriminatory racial purpose must be express or appear on the face of the statute, or that a law's disproportionate impact is irrelevant in cases involving Constitution-based claims of racial discrimination. A statute, otherwise neutral on its face, must not be applied so as invidiously to discriminate on the basis of race. [Yick Wo.] It is also clear from the cases dealing with racial discrimination in the selection of juries that the systematic exclusion of Negroes is itself such an "unequal application of the law [as] to show intentional discrimination." A prima facie case of discriminatory purpose may be proved as well by the absence of Negroes on a particular jury combined with the failure of the jury commissioners to be informed of eligible Negro jurors in a community or with racially nonneutral selection procedures. With a prima facie case made out, "the burden of proof shifts to the State to rebut the presumption of unconstitutional action by showing that permissible racially neutral selection criteria and procedures have produced the monochromatic result."

Necessarily, an invidious discriminatory purpose may often be inferred from the totality of the relevant facts, including the fact, if it is true, that the law bears more heavily on one race than another. It is also not infrequently true that the discriminatory impact—in the jury cases for example, the total or seriously disproportionate exclusion of Negroes from jury venires—may for all practical purposes demonstrate unconstitutionality because in various circumstances the discrimination is very difficult to explain on nonracial grounds. Nevertheless, we have not held that a law, neutral on its face and serving ends otherwise within the power of government to pursue, is invalid under [equal protection] simply because it may affect a greater proportion of one race than of another. Disproportionate impact is not irrelevant, but it is not the sole touchstone of an invidious racial discrimination forbidden by the Constitution. Standing alone, it does not trigger the rule that racial classifications are to be subjected to the strictest scrutiny and are justifiable only by the weightiest of considerations.

There are some indications to the contrary in our cases. [See Palmer v. Thompson.] [Palmer] warned against grounding decision on legislative purpose or motivation, thereby lending support for the proposition that the operative effect of the law rather than its purpose is the paramount factor. But the holding of the case was that the legitimate purposes of the ordinance—to preserve peace and avoid deficits—were not open to impeachment by evidence that the councilmen were actually motivated by racial considerations. Whatever dicta the opinion may contain, the decision did not involve, much less invalidate, a statute or ordinance having neutral purposes but disproportionate racial consequences.

[We] have difficulty understanding how a law establishing a racially neutral qualification for employment is nevertheless racially discriminatory and denies "any person [equal protection]" simply because a greater proportion of Negroes fail to qualify than members of other racial or ethnic groups. [The test,] which is administered generally to prospective government employees, concededly seeks to ascertain whether those who take it have acquired a particular level of verbal skill; and it is untenable that the Constitution prevents the Government from seeking modestly to upgrade the communicative abilities of its employees rather than to be satisfied with some lower level of competence, particularly where the job requires special ability to communicate orally and in writing. Respondents, as Negroes, could no more successfully claim that the test denied them equal protection than could white applicants who also failed. The conclusion would not be different in the face of proof that more Negroes than whites had been disqualified by [the test]. That other Negroes also failed to score well would, alone, not demonstrate that respondents individually were being denied [equal protection] by the application of an otherwise valid qualifying test being administered to prospective police recruits.

Nor on the facts of the case before us would the disproportionate impact of [the test] warrant the conclusion that it is a purposeful device to discriminate against Negroes. [The] test is neutral on its face and rationally may be said to serve a purpose the Government is constitutionally empowered to pursue. Even agreeing with the District Court that the differential racial effect of [the test] called for further inquiry, we think the District Court correctly held that the affirmative efforts of the [Police

Department] to recruit black officers, the changing racial composition of the recruit classes and of the force in general, and the relationship of the test to the training program negated any inference that the Department discriminated on the basis of [race].

Under [Title VII of the Civil Rights Act of 1964], Congress provided that when hiring and promotion practices disqualifying substantially disproportionate numbers of blacks are challenged, discriminatory purpose need not be proved, and that it is an insufficient response to demonstrate some rational basis for the challenged practices. It is necessary, in addition, that they be "validated" in terms of job performance in any one of several [ways]. However this process proceeds, it involves a more probing judicial review of, and less deference to, the seemingly reasonable acts of [administrators] than is appropriate under the Constitution where special racial impact, without discriminatory purpose, is claimed. We are not disposed to adopt this more rigorous standard for the purposes of applying the Fifth and the 14th Amendments in cases such as this. A rule that a statute designed to serve neutral ends is nevertheless invalid, absent compelling justification, if in practice it benefits or burdens one race more than another would be far reaching and would raise serious questions about, and perhaps invalidate, a whole range of tax, welfare, public service, regulatory, and licensing statutes that may be more burdensome to the poor and to the average black than to the more affluent white. [In] our view, extension of the rule beyond those areas where it is already applicable by reason of statute [should] await legislative prescription.[1]

■ JUSTICE STEVENS, concurring.

[The] requirement of purposeful discrimination is a common thread running through the cases summarized [by the Court]. Although it may be proper to use the same language to describe the constitutional claim in each of [the] contexts, the burden of proving a prima facie case may well involve differing evidentiary considerations. The extent of deference that one pays to the trial court's determination of the factual issue [will] vary in different contexts. Frequently the most probative evidence of intent will be objective evidence of what actually happened rather than evidence describing the subjective state of mind of the actor. For normally the actor is presumed to have intended the natural consequences of his deeds. This is particularly true in the case of governmental action which is frequently the product of compromise, of collective decisionmaking, and of mixed motivation. It is unrealistic, on the one hand, to require the victim of alleged discrimination to uncover the actual subjective intent of the decisionmaker or, conversely, to invalidate otherwise legitimate action simply because an improper motive affected the deliberation of a participant in the decisional process. A law conscripting clerics should not be invalidated because an atheist voted for it. My point in making this observation is to suggest that the line between discriminatory purpose and discriminatory impact is not nearly as bright, and perhaps not quite as critical, as the reader of the Court's opinion might assume.

I agree, of course, that a constitutional issue does not arise every time some disproportionate impact is shown. On the other hand, when the disproportion is as dramatic as in Gomillion or Yick Wo, it really does not

[1] Justice White also rejected the statutory claim. Justice STEWART joined the constitutional part of Justice White's opinion. Justice BRENNAN, joined by Justice Marshall, dissented on the statutory issue and did not reach the constitutional claim.

matter whether the standard is phrased in terms of purpose or effect. Therefore, although I accept the statement of the general rule in the Court's opinion, I am not yet prepared to indicate how that standard should be applied in the many cases which have formulated the governing standard in different language. My agreement with the [Court's conclusion] rests on a ground narrower than the Court describes. There are two reasons why I am convinced that the challenge to [the test] is insufficient. First, the test serves the neutral and legitimate purpose of requiring all applicants to meet a uniform minimum standard of literacy. Second, the same test is used throughout the federal service. The applicants for employment in the [D.C.] Police Department represent such a small fraction of the total number of persons who have taken the test that their experience is of minimal probative value in assessing the neutrality of the [test].

THE MEANING AND IMPLICATIONS OF WASHINGTON V. DAVIS

1. ***Circumstantial evidence of discriminatory purpose.*** While Washington v. Davis rejected heightened scrutiny of a civil service exam that had not been adopted for racially discriminatory reasons, nothing in the decision retreated from the earlier decisions in cases like Yick Wo, Gomillion and Griffin suggesting that racially discriminatory purpose may sometimes be smoked out from behind apparently racially neutral laws. Decisions following Washington v. Davis confirmed that racially discriminatory purpose may still be inferred even absent the stark statistical disparities involved in those cases. For example, **Arlington Heights v. Metropolitan Housing Corp.**, 429 U.S. 252 (1977), reaffirmed that "official action will not be held unconstitutional solely because it results in a racially disproportionate impact" but elaborated on the "subjects of proper inquiry" in determining whether an unconstitutional discriminatory purpose exists. The case involved a challenge to a Chicago suburb's refusal to grant a request to rezone certain property from a single-family to a multiple-family classification. A nonprofit developer planned to build federally subsidized townhouse units in the largely white suburb, so that low and moderate income tenants, including members of racial minorities, might live there. Although the lower federal courts found that the suburb's officials were motivated by a concern for the integrity of the zoning plan rather than by racial hostility, the court of appeals held the denial of the rezoning request unconstitutional because its "ultimate effect" was racially discriminatory.

In reversing that decision, Justice POWELL's majority stated: "Davis does not require a plaintiff to prove that the challenged action rested solely on racially discriminatory purposes. Rarely can it be said that a legislature or administrative body operating under a broad mandate made a decision motivated solely by a single concern, or even that a particular purpose was the 'dominant' or 'primary' one." It was enough to show "that a discriminatory purpose has been a motivating factor in the decision. [Determining] whether invidious discriminatory purpose was a motivating factor demands a sensitive inquiry into such circumstantial and direct evidence of intent as may be available. The impact of the official action [may] provide an important starting point. Sometimes a clear pattern, unexplainable on grounds other than race, emerges from the effect of the state action even when the governing legislation appears neutral on its face.

[E.g., Yick Wo; Gomillion.] The evidentiary inquiry is then relatively easy. But such cases are rare. Absent a pattern as stark as that in Gomillion or Yick Wo, impact alone is not determinative, and the Court must look to other evidence.

"The historical background of the decision is one evidentiary source, particularly if it reveals a series of official actions taken for invidious purposes. The specific sequence of events leading up to the challenged decision also may shed some light on the decisionmaker's purposes. For example, if the property involved here always had been zoned [for multiple-family housing] but suddenly was changed to [a single-family classification] when the town learned of [the developer's] plans to erect integrated housing, we would have a far different case. Departures from the normal procedural sequence also might afford evidence that improper purposes are playing a role. Substantive departures too may be relevant, particularly if the factors usually considered important by the decisionmaker strongly favor a decision contrary to the one reached. The legislative or administrative history may be highly relevant, especially where there are contemporary statements by members of the decisionmaking body, minutes of its meetings, or reports."

Justice Powell clarified the effect of a finding of racial motive: "Proof that the decision by the Village was motivated in part by a racially discriminatory purpose would not necessarily have required invalidation of the challenged decision. Such proof would, however, have shifted to the Village the burden of establishing that the same decision would have resulted even had the impermissible purpose not been considered. If this were established, the complaining party in a case of this kind no longer fairly could attribute the injury complained of to improper consideration of a discriminatory purpose. In such circumstances, there would be no justification for judicial interference with the challenged decision. But in this case respondents failed to make the required threshold showing." Justice Powell found precedent for this burden-shifting scheme in a First Amendment case, Mt. Healthy City School Dist. Bd. of Educ. v. Doyle, 429 U.S. 274 (1977).

After summarizing the list of factors that might give rise to a finding of "racially discriminatory intent" sufficient to shift the burden to the government, Justice Powell found no basis for such a finding on the facts here. Specifically, while the refusal to rezone "arguably" bore more heavily on racial minorities, there was "little about the sequence of events leading up to the decision that would spark suspicion." The area in which the tract lay had long been zoned for single family use, and the rezoning request was handled according to the usual procedures. He concluded that the challengers had "simply failed to carry their burden of proving that discriminatory purpose was a motivating factor in the Village's decision." Justices Marshall, Brennan and White disagreed with the case's disposition (Justice Stevens did not participate). Justice WHITE's dissent objected to the majority's "failure to follow our usual practice in this situation" by remanding for reconsideration in light of Davis and to the Court's "lengthy discussion of the standards for proving the racially discriminatory purpose required by Davis [in] light of the lower courts' findings that the suburb's decision rested on legitimate grounds."

Why shouldn't proof of discriminatory purpose produce an immediate invalidation of the law, instead of merely shifting the burden of justification to the government? If the discriminatory purpose inquiry is largely designed to cleanse or purify the decisionmaking process, what justifies ever validating a governmental decision once it has been found to have been discriminatorily motivated? Arguably, the reason is similar to that often given to avoid *any* motivation inquiries—the futility of invalidating a law when the lawmakers could enact the very same law if their motives were pure. But would not full adherence to the process-cleansing rationale—the rationale that in part underlies the modern Court's emphasis on "purpose" rather than "effect"—warrant in effect a remand of the issue to the lawmakers for reconsideration on the basis of purely legitimate factors? Some legislators, "after being informed that they initially acted unconstitutionally, may refuse to vote for reenactment. [And] if a statute is invalidated on judicial review, the legislature often will decline or fail to consider a new law. In many situations, therefore, judicial action on the basis of motive results in an effective, not a futile, invalidation." Eisenberg, "Disproportionate Impact and Illicit Motive: Theories of Constitutional Adjudication," 52 N.Y.U. L. Rev. 36 (1977).

2. ***Proving discriminatory purpose after Arlington Heights.*** How difficult is it to make a record of purposeful discrimination? What is the role of circumstantial and historical evidence of the kind described in Arlington Heights? In **Rogers v. Lodge**, 458 U.S. 613 (1982), the Court by a vote of 6–3 affirmed lower court findings of racially discriminatory vote dilution from circumstantial evidence surrounding an at-large election system in Burke County, Georgia, and upheld an order mandating a switch to single-member districts. Justice WHITE wrote for the Court: "Burke County had a total population of 19,349, of whom 10,385, or 53.6%, were black. [W]hites constitute a slight majority of the voting age population. As of 1978, 6,373 persons were registered to vote in Burke County, of whom 38% were black. The Burke County Board of Commissioners governs the county. It was created in 1911 [under state law] and consists of five members elected at large to concurrent 4-year terms by all qualified voters in the county. [We are] unconvinced that we should disturb the District Court's finding that the at-large system in Burke County was being maintained for the invidious purpose of diluting the voting strength of the black population. [The] District Court found that blacks have always made up a substantial majority of the population in Burke County, but that they are a distinct minority of the registered voters. There was also overwhelming evidence of bloc voting along racial lines. Hence, although there had been black candidates, no black had ever been elected to the Burke County Commission. These facts bear heavily on the issue of purposeful discrimination."

Justice POWELL dissented, joined by Justice Rehnquist. They protested that the case was indistinguishable from a prior case, Mobile v. Bolden, 446 U.S. 55 (1980), in which an at-large voting system had been upheld: "There are some variances in the largely sociological evidence presented in the two cases. But Mobile held that this *kind* of evidence was not enough." In the dissenters' view, the majority was inviting federal courts "to engage in deeply subjective inquiries into the motivations of local officials in structuring local governments." Justice STEVENS's separate dissent emphasized, "I do not believe that [subjective intent] can [determine] constitutionality."

Hunter v. Underwood, 471 U.S. 222 (1985), likewise struck down a facially neutral law found in fact to reflect racially discriminatory purpose. The decision relied both on evidence of starkly disparate impact and on circumstantial historical evidence from which discriminatory intent could be inferred. The decision invalidated a section of the Alabama Constitution, adopted in 1901, disenfranchising all persons convicted of crimes involving "moral turpitude." Underwood, a white person, and Edwards, a black person, were blocked from the voter rolls because each had been convicted of presenting a worthless check. They brought suit claiming that the misdemeanors included within the provision were intentionally adopted to disenfranchise blacks on account of their race. The federal district court rejected their claim, but the court of appeals reversed. Following the approach of Arlington Heights, the court of appeals, after finding that discriminatory intent was a motivating factor for the provision, concluded that it would not have been enacted in the absence of the racially discriminatory motivation.

In affirming that ruling, Justice REHNQUIST's opinion noted that, even though the section "on its face is racially neutral," it clearly had a "racially discriminatory impact," because, as the Court of Appeals had noted, it had "disfranchised approximately ten times as many blacks as whites." Justice Rehnquist recognized "the difficulties in determining the actual motivations of the various legislators that produced a given decision," but found that the usual difficulties in identifying motivation did "not obtain in this case." He noted that, at the Alabama Constitutional Convention of 1901, a "zeal for white supremacy ran rampant." Appellants argued that "the existence of a permissible motive for [the section], namely the disenfranchisement of poor whites, trumps any proof of a parallel impermissible motive." Justice Rehnquist rejected that argument: "Whether or not intentional disenfranchisement of poor whites would qualify as a 'permissible motive,' [it] is clear that where both impermissible racial motivation and racially discriminatory impact are demonstrated, Arlington Heights and Mt. Healthy supply the proper analysis. [An] additional purpose to discriminate against poor whites would not render nugatory the purpose to discriminate against all blacks, and it is beyond peradventure that the latter was a 'but-for' motivation for the enactment of the [section]." The Court also rejected the claim that here there was a "legitimate interest" in denying the franchise to those convicted of crimes involving moral turpitude, pointing out that the 1901 Convention had "selected such crimes as vagrancy, living in adultery, and wife beating that were thought to be more commonly committed by blacks."

3. ***Disparate impact in statutory non-discrimination law.*** In the statutory context, the Court has accepted that non-discrimination statutes can go further than the Equal Protection Clause in providing for disparate impact liability. One relatively recent example is **Texas Dept. of Housing and Community Affairs v. Inclusive Communities Project**, 576 U.S. ___, 135 S. Ct. 2507 (2015), where the Court held that disparate impact claims were cognizable under the Fair Housing Act. Yet, in recognizing such claims, the majority opinion by Justice KENNEDY warned that a disparate impact claim that "relies on a statistical disparity must fail if the plaintiff cannot point to a defendant's policy or policies causing that disparity." Such a "robust causality requirement" was necessary to prevent situations where disparate-impact liability causes "race to be used and considered in a pervasive way" such that "serious constitutional questions" arise.

This view appears to endorse concerns raised by Justice SCALIA in the earlier case of **Ricci v. DeStefano**, 557 U.S. 557 (2009). There, the Court, in a case brought by white and Hispanic firefighers, ruled that the New Haven Fire Department had violated Title VII of the Civil Rights Act when it discarded test results because black firefighters had not performed well enough to qualify for promotions. In doing so, the Court rejected the Fire Department's defence that it chose to invalidate the results to avoid disparate impact liability. In his concurrence, Justice Scalia cited approvingly to Primus, "Equal Protection and Disparate Impact: Round Three," 117 Harv. L. Rev. 493 (2003), and argued that statutory disparate impact liability was inconsistent with the Equal Protection Clause. In particular, Justice Scalia reasoned: "If the Federal Government is prohibited from discriminating on the basis of race, [then] surely it is also prohibited from enacting laws mandating that [employers] discriminate on the basis of race. [As] the facts of these cases illustrate, Title VII's disparate-impact provisions place a racial thumb on the scales, often requiring employers to evaluate the racial outcomes of their policies, and to make decisions based on (because of) those racial outcomes. That type of racial decisionmaking is, as the Court explains, discriminatory."

Is Justice Scalia correct that statutory disparate impact liability is at odds with the Equal Protection Clause? Even if so, is Justice Kennedy's adoption of a robust causality requirement sufficient to mitigate these concerns?

AFFIRMATIVE ACTION AND RACE PREFERENCES

To what extent may racial classifications be used to aid rather than disadvantage minorities? As seen above, racial classifications disadvantaging minorities are "suspect" and are permissible only for "compelling" justifications. Is a level of scrutiny lower than "strict" appropriate when the racial objective is "benign"? Can courts adequately distinguish between benign purposes and hostile ones masquerading behind a "benign" facade? May race preferences be used to remedy the effects of past purposeful state discrimination? May they also be used to compensate for past societal injustices? May they be future-oriented? Can less-than-strict scrutiny of benign racial classifications be defended on the ground that the Fourteenth Amendment's original purpose was directed at hostile legislation subordinating a disadvantaged minority? Or does the evolution of equal protection criteria since Reconstruction warrant a broader suspicion of *all* racial classifications? Should the courts, on political process grounds, defer to any political process in which such a politically dominant racial group gives preferences to racial minorities and so disadvantages itself? For an argument for deference on this political process ground, see Ely, "The Constitutionality of Reverse Racial Discrimination," 41 U. Chi. L. Rev. 723 (1974). Should the context in which race preferences are employed matter to the constitutional analysis? The Court first faced these questions in reviewing challenges to preferential admissions programs in higher education.

Regents of Univ. of California v. Bakke

438 U.S. 265, 98 S. Ct. 2733, 57 L. Ed. 2d 750 (1978).

[The University of California at Davis Medical School reserved 16 out of 100 places in its entering class for members of minority groups: "Blacks," "Chicanos," "Asians," and "American Indians." A separate committee was established to administer this special admissions program. This admissions procedure was challenged by Allan Bakke, a white applicant who was rejected even though applicants were admitted under the special program with grade point averages, MCAT scores, and benchmark scores significantly lower than Bakke's.]

■ JUSTICE POWELL announced the judgment of the Court.

This case presents a challenge to the special admissions program of the petitioner, the Medical School of the University of California at Davis, which is designed to assure the admission of a specified number of students from certain minority groups. [The Supreme Court of California held] the special admissions program unlawful, [enjoined] petitioner from considering the race of any applicant, [and ordered Bakke's] admission. For the reasons stated in the following opinion, I believe that so much of the judgment of the California court as holds petitioner's special admissions program unlawful and directs that respondent be admitted to the Medical School must be affirmed. For the reasons expressed in a separate opinion, [Chief Justice Burger and Justices Stewart, Rehnquist and Stevens] concur in this judgment. I also conclude for the reasons stated in the following opinion that the portion of the court's judgment enjoining petitioner from according any consideration to race in its admissions process must be reversed. For reasons expressed in separate opinions, [Justices Brennan, White, Marshall and Blackmun] concur in this judgment and join Parts I and V–C of this opinion.]

II. [Justice Powell first considered Title VI of the Civil Rights Act of 1964, which provides: "No person in the United States shall, on the ground of race, color, or national origin, be excluded from participation in, be denied the benefits of, or be subjected to discrimination under any program or activity receiving Federal financial assistance."] [We] assume only for the purposes of this case that respondent has a right of action under Title VI. [In] view of the clear legislative intent, Title VI must be held to proscribe only those racial classifications that would violate [equal protection].

III. A. [The parties] disagree as to the level of judicial scrutiny to be applied to the special admissions program. [Petitioner] argues that the court below erred in applying strict scrutiny [because white males] are not a "discrete and insular minority" requiring extraordinary protection from the majoritarian political process. [Carolene Products, fn. 4.] [These] characteristics may be relevant in deciding whether or not to add new types of classifications to the list of "suspect" categories or whether a particular classification survives close examination. Racial and ethnic classifications, however, are subject to stringent examination without regard to these additional characteristics. Racial and ethnic distinctions of any sort are inherently suspect and thus call for the most exacting judicial examination.

B. [Although] many of the Framers of the 14th Amendment conceived of its primary function as bridging the vast distance between members of the Negro race and the white "majority," the Amendment itself was framed in universal [terms]. "[This] Court consistently repudiated '[d]istinctions between citizens solely because of their ancestry' as being 'odious to a free people whose institutions are founded upon the doctrine of equality.' " Petitioner urges us to adopt for the first time a more restrictive view of [equal protection] and hold that discrimination against members of the white "majority" cannot be suspect if its purpose can be characterized as "benign." The clock of our liberties, however, cannot be turned back to 1868. It is far too late to argue that the guarantee of equal protection to *all* persons permits the recognition of special wards entitled to a degree of protection greater than that accorded [others].

Once the artificial line of a "two-class theory" of the 14th Amendment is put aside, the difficulties entailed in varying the level of judicial review according to a perceived "preferred" status of a particular racial or ethnic minority are intractable. [The] white "majority" itself is composed of various minority groups, most of which can lay claim to a history of prior discrimination at the hands of the state and private individuals. [There] is no principled basis for deciding which groups would merit "heightened judicial solicitude" and which would not. [Moreover,] there are serious problems of justice connected with the idea of preference itself. First, it may not always be clear that a so-called preference is in fact benign. [Second,] preferential programs may only reinforce common stereotypes holding that certain groups are unable to achieve success without special protection based on a factor having no relationship to individual worth. Third, there is a measure of inequity in forcing innocent persons in respondent's position to bear the burdens of redressing grievances not of their making [When classifications] touch upon an individual's race or ethnic background, he is entitled to a judicial determination that the burden he is asked to bear on that basis is precisely tailored to serve a compelling governmental [interest].

IV. [The] special admissions program purports to serve the purposes of: (i) "reducing the historic deficit of traditionally disfavored minorities in medical schools and the medical profession"; (ii) countering the effects of societal discrimination; (iii) increasing the number of physicians who will practice in communities currently underserved; and (iv) obtaining the educational benefits that flow from an ethnically diverse student body.

A. [If] petitioner's purpose is to assure within its student body some specified percentage of a particular group merely because of its race or ethnic origin, such a preferential purpose must be rejected not as insubstantial but as facially invalid. Preferring members of any one group for no reason other than race or ethnic origin is discrimination for its own sake. This the Constitution forbids.

B. The State certainly has a legitimate and substantial interest in ameliorating, or eliminating where feasible, the disabling effects of identified discrimination. [The] school desegregation cases [attest] to the importance of this state goal, [which is] far more focused than the remedying of the effects of "societal discrimination," an amorphous concept of injury that may be ageless in its reach into the past. We have never approved a classification that aids persons perceived as members of relatively victimized groups at the expense of other innocent individuals in the absence of judicial, legislative, or administrative findings of constitutional or statutory violations. [Without] such findings of constitutional or statutory violations, it cannot be said that the government has any greater interest in helping one individual than in refraining from harming another. [Petitioner] does not purport to have made, and is in no position to make, such findings. Its broad mission is education, not the formulation of any legislative policy or the adjudication of particular claims of illegality.

C. [Petitioner] identifies, as another purpose of its program, improving the delivery of health care services to communities currently underserved. [There] is virtually no evidence in the record indicating that petitioner's special admissions program is either needed or geared to promote that goal. [Petitioner] simply has not carried its burden of demonstrating that it must prefer members of particular ethnic groups over all other individuals in order to promote better health care delivery to deprived citizens.

D. The fourth goal asserted by petitioner is the attainment of a diverse student body. This clearly is a constitutionally permissible goal for an institution of higher education. Academic freedom, though not a specifically enumerated constitutional right, long has been viewed as a special concern of the First Amendment. The freedom of a university to make its own judgments as to education includes the selection of its student body. [Thus,] in arguing that its universities must be accorded the right to select those students who will contribute the most to the "robust exchange of ideas," petitioner invokes a countervailing constitutional interest, that of the First Amendment[, and] must be viewed as seeking to achieve a goal that is of paramount importance in the fulfillment of its mission. An otherwise qualified medical student with a particular background [may] bring to a professional school of medicine experiences, outlooks and ideas that enrich the training of its student body and better equip its graduates to render with understanding their vital service to humanity. [As] the interest of diversity is compelling in the context of a university's admissions program, the question remains whether the program's racial classification is necessary to promote this interest.

V. A. It may be assumed that the reservation of a specified number of seats in each class for individuals from the preferred ethnic groups would contribute to the attainment of considerable ethnic diversity in the student body. But petitioner's argument that this is the only effective means of serving the interest of diversity is seriously flawed. [The] diversity that furthers a compelling state interest encompasses a far broader array of qualifications and characteristics of which racial or ethnic origin is but a single though important element. Petitioner's special admissions program, focused *solely* on ethnic diversity, would hinder rather than further attainment of genuine [diversity].

The experience of other university admissions programs, which take race into account in achieving the educational diversity valued by the First Amendment, demonstrates that the assignment of a fixed number of places to a minority group is not a necessary means toward that end. An illuminating example is found in the Harvard College program: "In recent years Harvard College has expanded the concept of diversity to include students from disadvantaged economic, racial and ethnic groups. [In] practice, this new definition of diversity has meant that race has been a factor in some admission decisions. When the Committee on Admissions reviews the large middle group of applicants who are 'admissible' and deemed capable of doing good work in their courses, the race of an applicant may tip the balance in his favor just as geographic origin or a life spent on a farm may tip the balance in other candidates' cases. A farm boy from Idaho can bring something to Harvard College that a Bostonian cannot offer.

Similarly, a black student can usually bring something that a white person cannot offer. In Harvard college admissions the Committee has not set target-quotas for the number of blacks, or of musicians, football players, physicists or Californians to be admitted in a given year. [But in] choosing among thousands of applicants who are not only 'admissible' academically but have other strong qualities, the Committee, with a number of criteria in mind, pays some attention to distribution among many types and categories of students."

In such an admissions program, race or ethnic background may be deemed a "plus" in a particular applicant's file, yet it does not insulate the individual from comparison with all other candidates for the available seats. [This] kind of program treats each applicant as an individual in the admissions process. [It] has been suggested that an admissions program which considers race only as one factor is simply a subtle and more sophisticated—but no less effective—means of according racial preference than the Davis program. A facial intent to discriminate, however, is evident in petitioner's preference program and not denied in this case. No such facial infirmity exists in an admissions program where race or ethnic background is simply one element—to be weighed fairly against other elements—in the selection process. [A court] would not assume that a university, professing to employ a facially nondiscriminatory admissions policy, would operate it as a cover for the functional equivalent of a quota system.

B. [In] summary, it is evident that the Davis special admissions program involves the use of an explicit racial classification never before countenanced by this Court. [W]hen a State's distribution of benefits or imposition of burdens hinges on the color of a person's skin or ancestry, that individual is entitled to a demonstration that the challenged classification is necessary to promote a substantial state interest. Petitioner has failed to carry this burden. For this reason, that portion of the California court's judgment holding petitioner's special admissions program invalid under the 14th Amendment must be affirmed.

C. In enjoining petitioner from ever considering the race of any applicant, however, the courts below failed to recognize that the State has a substantial interest that legitimately may be served by a properly devised admissions program involving the competitive consideration of race and ethnic origin. For this reason, so much of the judgment as enjoins petitioner from any consideration of the race of any applicant must be reversed.

VI. With respect to respondent's entitlement to an injunction directing his admission to the Medical School, petitioner has conceded that it could not carry its burden of proving that, but for the existence of its unlawful special admissions program, respondent still would not have been admitted. Hence, respondent is entitled to the injunction, and that portion of the judgment must be affirmed.

■ Opinion of JUSTICES BRENNAN, WHITE, MARSHALL, and BLACKMUN, concurring in the judgment in part and dissenting.

[Unquestionably] a government practice or statute [which] contains "suspect classifications" is to be subjected to "strict scrutiny." [But] whites as a class [do not have] any of the "traditional indicia of [suspectness]." [Nor] has anyone suggested that the University's purposes contravene the cardinal principle that racial classifications that stigmatize—because they are drawn on the presumption that one race is inferior to another or because they put the weight of government behind racial hatred and separatism—are invalid without more. On the other hand, the fact that this case does not fit neatly into our prior analytic framework for race cases does not mean that it should be analyzed by applying the very loose rational-basis [standard]. Instead, a number of considerations—developed in gender discrimination cases but which carry even more force when applied to racial classifications—lead us to conclude that racial classifications designed to further remedial purposes "must serve important governmental objectives and must be substantially related to achievement of those objectives."

standard of review

First, race, like "gender-based classifications, too often [has] been inexcusably utilized to stereotype and stigmatize politically powerless segments of society." While a carefully tailored statute designed to remedy past discrimination could avoid these vices, we nonetheless have recognized that the line between honest and thoughtful appraisal of the effects of past discrimination and paternalistic stereotyping is not so clear and that a statute based on the latter is patently capable of stigmatizing all women with a badge of inferiority. State programs designed ostensibly to ameliorate the effects of past racial discrimination obviously create the same hazard of stigma, since they may promote racial separatism and reinforce the views of those who believe that members of racial minorities are inherently incapable of succeeding on their own.

Second, race, like gender and illegitimacy, is an immutable characteristic which its possessors are powerless to escape or set aside. [Such] divisions are contrary to our deep belief that "legal burdens should bear some relationship to individual responsibility or wrongdoing" and that advancement sanctioned, sponsored, or approved by the State should ideally be based on individual merit or achievement, or at the least on factors within the control of an individual. Because this principle is so deeply rooted it might be supposed that it would be considered in the legislative process and weighed against the benefits of programs preferring individuals because of their race. But this is not necessarily so: The "natural consequence of our governing processes [may well be] that the most 'discrete and insular' of whites [will] be called upon to bear the immediate, direct costs of benign discrimination."

[In] sum, because of the significant risk that racial classifications established for ostensibly benign purposes can be misused, causing effects not unlike those created by invidious classifications, it is inappropriate to inquire only whether there is any conceivable basis that might sustain such a classification. Instead, to justify such a classification an important and articulated purpose for its use must be shown. In addition, any statute must be stricken that stigmatizes any group or that singles out those least well represented in the political process to bear the brunt of a benign program. Thus our review under the 14th Amendment should be strict—not " 'strict' in theory and fatal in fact," because it is stigma that causes fatality—but strict and searching [nonetheless].

Davis' articulated purpose of remedying the effects of past societal discrimination [is] sufficiently important to justify the use of race-conscious admissions programs where there is a sound basis for concluding that minority underrepresentation is substantial and chronic, and that the handicap of past discrimination is impeding access of minorities to the medical school. [A] state government may adopt race-conscious programs if the purpose of such programs is to remove the disparate racial impact its actions might otherwise have and if there is reason to believe that the disparate impact is itself the product of past discrimination, whether its own or that of society at large. There is no question that Davis' program is valid under this test. [Davis] had a sound basis for believing that the problem of underrepresentation of minorities was substantial and chronic and that the problem was attributable to handicaps imposed on minority applicants by past and present racial [discrimination]. Davis clearly could conclude that the serious and persistent underrepresentation of minorities in medicine [is] the result of handicaps under which minority applicants labor as a consequence of a background of deliberate, purposeful discrimination against minorities in education and in society generally, as well as in the medical [profession].

[The] second prong of our test—whether the Davis program stigmatizes any discrete group or individual and whether race is reasonably used in light of the program's objectives—is clearly satisfied by the Davis [program]. Bakke [was not] in any sense stamped as inferior by the Medical School's [rejection]. Moreover, there is absolutely no basis for concluding that Bakke's rejection [will] affect him throughout his life in the same way as the segregation of the Negro school children in Brown I would have affected them. [In] addition, there is simply no evidence that the Davis program discriminates intentionally or unintentionally against any minority group which it purports to benefit. The program does not establish a quota in the invidious sense of a ceiling on the number of minority applicants to be admitted. Nor can the program reasonably be regarded as stigmatizing the program's beneficiaries or their race as inferior. The Davis program does not simply advance less qualified applicants; rather it compensates applicants, whom it is uncontested are fully qualified to study medicine, for educational disadvantage which it was reasonable to conclude was a product of state-fostered discrimination. Once admitted, these students must satisfy the same degree requirements as regularly admitted students; and their performance is evaluated by the same standards by which regularly admitted students are judged. Under these circumstances, [there] is no reasonable basis to conclude that minority graduates [would] be stigmatized as inferior by the existence of such programs.

Finally, Davis' special admissions program cannot be said to violate the Constitution simply because it has set aside a predetermined number of places for qualified minority applicants rather than using minority status as a positive factor to be considered in evaluating the applications of disadvantaged minority applicants. For purposes of constitutional adjudication, there is no difference between the two approaches. In any admissions program which accords special consideration to disadvantaged racial minorities, a determination of the degree of preference to be given is unavoidable, and any given preference that results in the exclusion of a white candidate is no more or less constitutionally acceptable than a program such as that at Davis. [That] the Harvard approach does [not] make public the extent of the preference and the precise workings of the system while the Davis program employs a specific, openly stated number, does not condemn the latter plan for purposes of 14th Amendment adjudication. It may be that the Harvard plan is more acceptable to the public than is the Davis "quota." If it is, any State [is] free to adopt it in preference to a less acceptable [alternative]. But there is no basis for preferring a particular preference program simply because in achieving the same goals that [Davis] is pursuing, it proceeds in a manner that is not immediately apparent to the [public].

■ JUSTICE MARSHALL.

[It] must be remembered that, during most of the past 200 years, the Constitution as interpreted by this Court did not prohibit the most ingenious and pervasive forms of discrimination against the Negro. Now, when a State acts to remedy the effects of that legacy of discrimination, I cannot believe that this same Constitution stands as a barrier.

■ JUSTICE BLACKMUN.

[I] yield to no one in my earnest hope that the time will come when an "affirmative action" program is unnecessary and is, in truth, only a relic of the past. [At] some time, [the] United States must and will reach a stage of maturity where action along this line is no longer necessary. Then persons will be regarded as persons, and discrimination of the type we address today will be an ugly feature of history that is instructive but that is behind [us]. It is somewhat ironic to have us so deeply disturbed over a program where race is an element of consciousness, and yet to be aware of the fact, as we are, that institutions of higher learning, albeit more on the undergraduate than the graduate level, have given conceded preferences up to a point to those possessed of athletic skills, to the children of alumni, to the affluent who may bestow their largess on the institutions, and to those having connections with celebrities, the famous, and the powerful. [That] the 14th Amendment has expanded beyond its original 1868 [conception] does not mean for me that [it] has broken away from [its] original intended purposes. Those original aims persist. [I] suspect that it would be impossible to arrange an affirmative action program in a racially neutral way and have it successful. To ask that this be so is to demand the impossible. In order to get beyond racism, we must first take account of race. There is no other way.

■ JUSTICE STEVENS, with whom CHIEF JUSTICE BURGER and JUSTICES STEWART and REHNQUIST join, concurring in the judgment in part and dissenting in part.

If the state court was correct in its view that the University's special program was illegal, and that Bakke was therefore unlawfully excluded from the medical school because of his race, we should affirm its judgment, regardless of our views about the legality of admissions programs that are not now before the Court. [The] question whether race can ever be used as a factor in an admissions decision is not an issue in this case, and that discussion of that issue is inappropriate. [Title VI contains a "crystal clear" meaning:] "Race cannot be the basis of excluding anyone from participation in a federally funded program."

BAKKE AND AMICUS BRIEFS

At the time of *Bakke*, the Justices had been debating to what extent the Court should rely on amicus briefs submitted by third parties when making decisions. "Justices Hugo Black, William J. Brennan Jr., Thurgood Marshall, and William O. Douglas [appreciated] the briefs: They [believed that the amicus briefs] kept the brethren in touch with the views and attitudes of many dozens of groups. [Black wrote in one memo] that 'most of the cases before this Court involve matters that affect far more people than the immediate record parties. I think the public interest would be better served [by allowing for greater amicus participation.]" Justice Black's nemesis on the Court, Justice Frankfurter, however, had objected to the use of amicus briefs as allowing "the Court [to be] exploited as a soap box or as an advertising medium." Ball, The Bakke Case, 79–80 (2000). In Bakke, Black's perspective prevailed, and amicus briefs attained new importance in shaping the Court's opinion. In describing a permissible model for an affirmative action program, Justice Powell's opinion for the Court relied heavily on Harvard University's amicus brief explaining its use of racial categories as non-quota "plus factors." Id. Powell, a Virginian educated at Washington & Lee University, had earned a master of laws degree from Harvard Law School.

RACE PREFERENCES IN EMPLOYMENT AND CONTRACTING

Are the reasons for giving some deference to public officials for the use of race preferences in the education context absent in the context of government employment and contracting? Is the contribution of racial diversity to the educational mission irrelevant to the composition of work crews? To the ownership of small businesses receiving government contracts? Consider these questions in the following series of cases:

1. ***Race preferences in public employment.*** In **Wygant v. Jackson Board of Education**, 476 U.S. 267 (1986), the Court held unconstitutional a minority preference in teacher layoffs. The case arose from a collective bargaining agreement that provided that, when layoffs were required for fiscal reasons, teachers with the most seniority would be retained, "except that at no time will there be a greater percentage of minority personnel laid off than the current percentage of minority personnel employed at the time of the layoff." In consequence, some white teachers were laid off, even though they had more seniority than blacks who were retained. Some of the laid-off teachers brought an action alleging that the layoffs violated their equal protection rights. The district court dismissed the claim, holding that racial preferences need not be grounded on a finding of past purposeful discrimination but may attempt to remedy societal discrimination by providing "role models" for minority schoolchildren. The court of appeals affirmed, but the Supreme Court reversed by a 5–4 vote.

Justice POWELL's plurality opinion, joined by Chief Justice Burger and Justice Rehnquist, applied strict scrutiny, as he had in Bakke. He held that the goal of providing "minority role models" in order to overcome societal discrimination was not "compelling," stating: "This Court never has held that societal discrimination alone is sufficient to justify a racial classification. Rather, the Court has insisted upon some showing of prior discrimination by the governmental unit involved before allowing limited use of racial classifications in order to remedy such discrimination. [The] role model theory employed by the District Court has no logical stopping point. [It] allows the Board to engage in discriminatory hiring and layoff practices long past the point required by any legitimate remedial purpose." Even if the layoff provision were justified by a compelling interest in remedying prior employment discrimination, the layoff provision was "not sufficiently narrowly tailored" to achieving it: "While hiring goals impose a diffuse burden, [layoffs] impose the entire burden of achieving racial equality on particular individuals. [That] burden is too intrusive."

Justice WHITE concurred in the judgment: "Whatever the legitimacy of hiring goals or quotas may be, the discharge of white teachers to make room for blacks, none of whom has been shown to be a victim of any racial discrimination, is quite a different matter." Justice O'CONNOR also concurred only in the judgment, agreeing with the plurality's rejection of the "role model" and "societal discrimination" rationales. On the "remedial" justification, however, she insisted that she would not require (and would read the plurality opinion as not requiring) "a contemporaneous antecedent finding of past discrimination by a court or other competent body [as] a constitutional prerequisite to a public employer's voluntary agreement to an affirmative action plan." She elaborated: "A violation of [constitutional] requirements does not arise with the making of a finding; it arises when the wrong is committed. [The] imposition of a requirement that public employers make findings that they have engaged in illegal discrimination before they engage in affirmative action programs would severely undermine public employers' incentive to meet voluntarily their civil rights obligations."

Justice MARSHALL's dissent, joined by Justices Brennan and Blackmun, stated: "Because I believe that a public employer, with the full agreement of its employees, should be permitted to preserve the benefits of a legitimate and constitutional affirmative-action hiring plan even while reducing its workforce, I dissent." In a separate dissent, Justices STEVENS argued that there was no need to rely on the remedial rationale to justify the program. Instead, he focused on "whether the Board's action advances the public interest in educating children for the future" and accordingly defended the "role model" justification for the provision: "In the context of public education, it is quite obvious that a school board may reasonably conclude that an integrated faculty will be able to provide benefits to the student body that could not be provided by an all white, or nearly all white, faculty."

2. ***Race preferences in public contracting.*** In **Fullilove v. Klutznick**, 448 U.S. 448 (1980), the Court rejected a facial constitutional challenge to a requirement in a congressional spending program that, absent an administrative waiver, 10% of federal funds granted for local public works projects must be used by the state or local grantee to procure services from businesses controlled by members of specified minority groups—Negroes, Spanish-speaking, Orientals, Eskimos and Aleuts. This "minority set-aside" program was challenged on equal protection grounds by nonminority contractors. Although the Court upheld the program's constitutionality, there was no majority opinion: Chief Justice BURGER's opinion announcing the judgment of the Court, joined by Justices White and Powell, concluded: "This opinion does not adopt, either expressly or implicitly, the formulas of analysis articulated in such cases as Bakke. However, our analysis demonstrates that the MBE provision would survive judicial review under either 'test' articulated in the several Bakke [opinions]." Surveying the relevant congressional powers under Art. I, § 8, and § 5 of the 14th Amendment, he emphasized that Congress "may legislate without compiling the kind of 'record' appropriate with respect to judicial or administrative proceedings. [We] are satisfied that Congress had abundant historical basis from which it could conclude that traditional procurement practices, when applied to minority businesses, could perpetuate the effects of prior discrimination. Accordingly, Congress reasonably determined that the

prospective elimination of these barriers to minority firm access to public contracting opportunities generated by the 1977 Act was appropriate to ensure that those businesses were not denied equal opportunity to participate in [federal grants]."

Justice POWELL's concurrence reasoned that, under the analysis set forth in his Bakke opinion, the provision was "justified as a remedy that serves the compelling governmental interest in eradicating the continuing effects of past discrimination identified by Congress." Justice MARSHALL, joined by Justices Brennan and Blackmun, concurred in the judgment, finding, under the test they articulated in Bakke, that "the racial classifications employed [here] are substantially related to the achievement of the important and congressionally articulated goal of remedying the present effects of past racial discrimination." Justice STEWART's dissent, joined by Justice Rehnquist, stated: "I think today's decision is wrong for the same reason that [Plessy] was wrong. [Equal protection] absolutely prohibits invidious discrimination by government. [Racial] discrimination is by definition invidious discrimination. The rule cannot be any different when the persons injured by a racially biased law are not members of a racial minority." Justice STEVENS's distinctive dissent objected to the lax congressional procedures used in arriving at its 10% set-aside figure and in delineating the eligible minority groups after only perfunctory floor debate.

When the City of Richmond, Virginia sought to employ a minority business set-aside modeled on the congressional set-aside upheld in Fullilove, however, the Court found it an equal protection violation under the Fourteenth Amendment. The Court's composition had changed by then, with Reagan appointees Justices O'Connor and Kennedy replacing Justices Stewart and Powell. At issue in the Richmond case was a 1983 program that required prime contractors on city projects to subcontract at least 30% of the dollar amount of the contract to Minority Business Enterprises (MBEs) defined as "[a] business at least [51%] of which is owned and controlled [by] minority group members" and identified eligible minority groups as "Blacks, Spanish-speaking, Orientals, Indians, Eskimos, or Aleuts." In enacting the plan, the City Council had noted that, while the general population of Richmond was 50% black, only 0.67% of the city's prime construction contracts had been awarded to minority businesses in the five-year period from 1978 to 1983, and that a variety of contractors' associations had virtually no minority businesses within their membership. The case was brought by a contractor whose low bid on a city project was not accepted because of failure to comply with the plan's requirements.

In **Richmond v. J.A. Croson Co.**, 488 U.S. 469 (1989), the Court invalidated the plan. Justice O'CONNOR wrote for the Court. In a portion of the opinion joined only by Chief Justice Rehnquist and Justices White, she distinguished Fullilove: "[That] Congress may identify and redress the effects of society-wide discrimination does not mean that [the] States and their political subdivision are free to decide that such remedies are appropriate. Section 1 of the Fourteenth Amendment [stemmed] from a distrust of state legislative enactments based on race; § 5 [is] " 'a *positive* grant of legislative power' " to Congress. Thus, our treatment of an exercise of congressional power in Fullilove cannot be dispositive here." In a portion of the opinion joined only by Chief Justice Rehnquist and Justices White and Kennedy, she wrote that even race preferences required strict scrutiny: "Absent searching judicial inquiry into the justification for such race-based measures, there is simply no way of determining what classifications are 'benign' or 'remedial' and what classifications are in fact motivated by illegitimate notions of racial inferiority or simple racial politics. Indeed, the purpose of strict scrutiny is to 'smoke out' illegitimate uses of race by assuring that the legislative body is pursuing a goal important enough to warrant use of a highly suspect tool." She argued against applying here any argument for deference to race preferences where the majority merely disadvantages itself (recall Carolene Products footnote four, p. 503 above), suggesting that the need for judicial vigilance persisted where "blacks comprise approximately 50% of the population of the city of Richmond. Five of the nine seats on the City Council are held by blacks."

Writing for the Court, Justice O'Connor held: "While there is no doubt that the sorry history of both private and public discrimination in this country has contributed to a lack of opportunities for black entrepreneurs, this observation, standing alone, cannot justify a rigid racial quota in the awarding of public contracts in [Richmond]. It is sheer speculation how many minority firms there would be in Richmond absent past societal discrimination. [There] is nothing approaching a prima facie case of a constitutional or statutory violation by *anyone* in the Richmond construction industry. [While] the States and their subdivisions may take remedial action when they possess evidence that their own spending practices are exacerbating a pattern of prior discrimination, they must identify that discrimination, public or private, with some specificity before they may use race-conscious relief. [None] of the evidence presented by the city points to any identified discrimination in the Richmond construction industry. We therefore hold that the city has failed to demonstrate a compelling interest in apportioning public contracting opportunities on the basis of race.

"To accept Richmond's claim that past societal discrimination alone can serve as the basis for rigid racial preferences would be to open the door to competing claims for 'remedial relief' for every disadvantaged group. The dream of a Nation of equal citizens in a society where race is irrelevant to personal opportunity and achievement would be lost in a mosaic of shifting preferences based on inherently unmeasurable claims of past wrongs. [The City's] analysis applies only to the inclusion of blacks within the Richmond set-aside program. There is *absolutely no evidence* of past discrimination against Spanish-speaking, Oriental, Indian, Eskimo, or Aleut persons in any aspect of the Richmond construction industry. [It] may well be that Richmond has never had an Aleut or Eskimo citizen. [The] gross overinclusiveness of Richmond's racial preference strongly impugns the city's claim of remedial motivation." Finding it "obvious that such a program is not narrowly tailored to remedy the effects of prior discrimination," Justice O'Connor's opinion for the Court noted that "there does not appear to have been any consideration of the use of race-neutral means to increase minority business participation in city contracting [such as] a race-neutral program of city financing for small firms," and that under Richmond's program, "there is no inquiry into whether or not the particular MBE seeking a racial preference has suffered from the effects of past discrimination by the city or prime contractors."

In a concluding portion of the opinion again joined only by Chief Justice Rehnquist and Justices White and Kennedy, Justice O'Connor qualified the holding to leave some latitude for race-conscious contracting measures: "Nothing we say today precludes a state or local entity from taking action to rectify the effects of identified discrimination within its jurisdiction. If [Richmond] had evidence before it that nonminority contractors were systematically excluding minority businesses from subcontracting opportunities it could take action to end the discriminatory exclusion. Where there is a significant statistical disparity between the number of qualified minority contractors willing and able to perform a particular service and the number of such contractors actually engaged by the locality or the locality's prime contractors, an inference of discriminatory exclusion could arise. Under such circumstances, the city could act to dismantle the closed business system by taking appropriate measures against those who discriminate on the basis of race or other illegitimate criteria. In the extreme case, some form of narrowly tailored racial preference might be necessary to break down patterns of deliberate exclusion." But she emphasized the availability of "race-neutral devices to increase the accessibility of city contracting opportunities to small entrepreneurs of all races. Simplification of bidding procedures, relaxation of bonding requirements, and training and financial aid for disadvantaged entrepreneurs of all races would open the public contracting market to all those who have suffered the effects of past societal discrimination or neglect."

Justice STEVENS concurred in part and in the judgment, disagreeing with "the premise that seems to underlie today's decision [that] a governmental decision that rests on a racial classification is never permissible except as a remedy for a past wrong," but agreeing that "the Richmond ordinance cannot be justified as a remedy for past discrimination. [Instead] of carefully identifying the characteristics of the two classes of contractors that are respectively favored and disfavored by its ordinance, [Richmond] has merely engaged in the type of stereotypical analysis that is a hallmark of violations of [equal protection]." Justice KENNEDY likewise concurred in part and in the judgment, rejecting "a rule of automatic invalidity for racial preferences in almost every case" in favor of "the proposition that any racial preference must face the most rigorous scrutiny by the courts." Applying that standard, he found here "an ordinance and a legislative record open to the fair charge that it is not a remedy but is itself a preference which will cause the same corrosive animosities that the Constitution [forbids]."

Justice SCALIA concurred only in the judgment, agreeing with the Court's "conclusion that strict scrutiny must be applied to all governmental classification by race," but not with its suggestion that "state and local governments may in some circumstances discriminate on the basis of race in order (in a broad sense) 'to ameliorate the effects of past discrimination.' [In] my view there is only one circumstance in which the States may act *by race* to 'undo the effects of past discrimination': where that is necessary to eliminate their own maintenance of a system of unlawful racial classification. [This] distinction explains our school desegregation cases, in which we have made plain that States and localities sometimes have an obligation to adopt race-conscious remedies. [Nothing] prevents Richmond from according a contracting preference to identified victims of discrimination. While most of the beneficiaries might be black, neither the beneficiaries nor those disadvantaged by the preference would be identified *on the basis of their race.* [When] we depart from this American principle [of color-blindness] we play with fire, and much more than an occasional DeFunis [or] Croson burns."

Justice MARSHALL dissented, joined by Justices Brennan and Blackmun: "It is a welcome symbol of racial progress when the former capital of the Confederacy acts forthrightly to confront the effects of racial discrimination in its midst. In my view, nothing in the Constitution can be construed to prevent [Richmond] from allocating a portion of its contracting dollars for businesses owned or controlled by members of minority groups. [Richmond] has two powerful interests in setting aside a portion of public contracting funds for minority-owned enterprises. The first is the city's interest in eradicating the effects of past racial discrimination. [The second] is the prospective one of preventing the city's own spending decisions from reinforcing and perpetuating the exclusionary effects of past discrimination. [In] my judgment, Richmond's set-aside plan also [is] substantially related to the interests it seeks to serve in remedying past discrimination and in ensuring that municipal contract procurement does not perpetuate that discrimination. [Richmond's] 30% figure was patterned directly on the Fullilove precedent. Congress' 10% figure fell 'roughly halfway between the present percentage of minority contractors and the percentage of minority group members in the Nation.'

"[Today,] for the first time, a majority of this Court has adopted strict scrutiny as its standard of [equal protection] review of race-conscious remedial measures. This is an unwelcome development. A profound difference separates governmental actions that themselves are racist, and governmental actions that seek to remedy the effects of prior racism or to prevent neutral governmental activity from perpetuating the effects of such racism. Racial classifications 'drawn on the presumption that one race is inferior to another or because they put the weight of government behind racial hatred and separatism' warrant the strictest judicial scrutiny because of the very irrelevance of these rationales. By contrast, racial classifications drawn for the purpose of remedying the effects of discrimination that itself was race-based have a highly pertinent basis: the tragic and indelible fact that discrimination against blacks and other racial minorities in this Nation has pervaded our Nation's history and continues to scar our society." Justice BLACKMUN also filed a dissent joined by Justice Brennan.

Croson distinguished rather than overruled Fullilove, suggesting for the time being that the federal government might enjoy more deference than the states with respect to challenged race preferences. But in the following case—decided after Justice Souter had succeeded Justice Brennan, Justice Thomas had succeeded Justice Marshall, Justice Ginsburg had succeeded Justice White, and Justice Breyer had succeeded Justice Blackmun—the Court explicitly disavowed Fullilove's deferential standard, adopting strict scrutiny for race preferences in federal and state contracting alike:

Adarand Constructors, Inc. v. Pena

515 U.S. 200, 115 S. Ct. 2097, 132 L. Ed. 2d 158 (1995).

■ JUSTICE O'CONNOR announced the judgment of the Court and delivered an opinion with respect to Parts I, II, III–A, III–B, III–D, and IV, which is for the Court except insofar as it might be inconsistent with the views expressed in JUSTICE SCALIA's concurrence, and an opinion with respect to Part III–C in which JUSTICE KENNEDY joins.

Petitioner Adarand Constructors, Inc., claims that the Federal Government's practice of giving general contractors on government projects a financial incentive to hire subcontractors controlled by "socially and economically disadvantaged individuals," and in particular, the Government's use of race-based presumptions in identifying such individuals, violates the equal protection component of the Fifth Amendment's Due Process Clause. The Court of Appeals rejected Adarand's claim. We [vacate] the Court of Appeals' judgment and remand the case for further proceedings.

I. In 1989, the Central Federal Lands Highway Division (CFLHD), which is part of the United States Department of Transportation (DOT), awarded the prime contract for a highway construction project in Colorado to Mountain Gravel & Construction Company. Mountain Gravel then solicited bids from subcontractors for the guardrail portion of the contract. Adarand, a Colorado-based highway construction company specializing in guardrail work, submitted the low bid. Gonzales Construction Company also submitted a bid. The prime contract's terms provide that Mountain Gravel would receive additional compensation if it hired subcontractors certified as small businesses controlled by "socially and economically disadvantaged individuals." Gonzales is certified as such a business; Adarand is not. Mountain Gravel awarded the subcontract to Gonzales, despite Adarand's low bid, and Mountain Gravel's Chief Estimator has submitted an affidavit stating that Mountain Gravel would have accepted Adarand's bid, had it not been for the additional payment it received by hiring Gonzales instead. Federal law requires that a subcontracting clause similar to the one used here must appear in most federal agency contracts, and it also requires the clause to state that "[t]he contractor shall presume that socially and economically disadvantaged individuals include Black Americans, Hispanic Americans, Native Americans, Asian Pacific Americans, and other minorities, or any other individual found to be disadvantaged by the [Small Business] Administration pursuant to section 8(a) of the Small Business Act." Adarand claims that the presumption [discriminates] on the basis of race in violation of the Fifth Amendment obligation not to deny anyone [equal protection].

II. [The Court held that Adarand had standing not only to sue for damages for a contract it had lost in the past, but also to seek forward-looking injunctive and declaratory relief against future use of the subcontracting compensation clause.]

III. The Government [concedes] that "the race-based rebuttable presumption used in some certification determinations under the Subcontracting Compensation Clause" is subject to some heightened level of scrutiny. The parties disagree as to what that level should be. [With Croson], the Court finally agreed that the Fourteenth Amendment requires strict scrutiny of all race-based action by state and local governments. But Croson of course had no occasion to declare what standard of review the Fifth Amendment requires for such action taken by the Federal Government. Croson observed simply that the Court's "treatment of an exercise of congressional power in Fullilove cannot be dispositive here," because [the case] did not implicate Congress' broad power under § 5 of the Fourteenth

Amendment. [Thus,] some uncertainty persisted with respect to the standard of review for federal racial classifications.

Despite lingering uncertainty in the details, however, the Court's cases through Croson had established three general propositions with respect to governmental racial classifications. First, skepticism: " '[a]ny preference based on racial or ethnic criteria must necessarily receive a most searching examination' " Wygant (plurality opinion of Powell, J.). Second, consistency: "the standard of review under the Equal Protection Clause is not dependent on the race of those burdened or benefited by a particular classification" [Croson], i.e., all racial classifications reviewable under the Equal Protection Clause must be strictly scrutinized. And third, congruence: "[e]qual protection analysis in the Fifth Amendment area is the same as that under the Fourteenth Amendment." Taken together, these three propositions lead to the conclusion that any person, of whatever race, has the right to demand that any governmental actor subject to the Constitution justify any racial classification subjecting that person to unequal treatment under the strictest judicial scrutiny.[1] [We] hold today that all racial classifications, imposed by whatever federal, state, or local governmental actor, must be analyzed by a reviewing court under strict scrutiny. In other words, such classifications are constitutional only if they are narrowly tailored measures that further compelling governmental interests.

Justice Stevens chides us for our "supposed inability to differentiate between 'invidious' and 'benign' discrimination." [To him,] our view of consistency "equate[s] remedial preferences with invidious discrimination," and ignores the difference between "an engine of oppression" and an effort "to foster equality in society," or, more colorfully, "between a 'No Trespassing' sign and a welcome mat." It does nothing of the kind. The principle of consistency simply means that whenever the government treats any person unequally because of his or her race, that person has suffered an injury that falls squarely within the language and spirit of the Constitution's guarantee of equal protection. It says nothing about the ultimate validity of any particular law; that determination is the job of the court applying strict scrutiny.

D. Our action today makes explicit [that] federal racial classifications, like those of a State, must serve a compelling governmental interest, and must be narrowly tailored to further that interest. [It] follows that to the

[1] Justice O'Connor here diminished the force of Court's intervening decision in **Metro Broadcasting, Inc. v. FCC**, 497 U.S. 547 (1990), as a "surprising turn" and "a significant departure from much of what had come before it." In Metro Broadcasting, the Court, by a vote of 5–4, had upheld two "minority preference policies" employed by the FCC, one "awarding an enhancement for minority ownership in comparative proceedings" for new broadcast licenses; the other, a "minority 'distress sale' program," permitting "a limited category of existing radio and television broadcast stations to be transferred only to minority-controlled firms." Justice BRENNAN's majority opinion had applied intermediate scrutiny and found the policies closely tailored to "serve the important governmental objective of broadcast diversity." Justice STEVENS in concurrence had "endorse[d] this focus on the future benefit, rather than the remedial justification, of such decisions," analogizing the public interest in broadcast diversity to a legitimate "interest in an integrated police force, diversity in the composition of a public school faculty or diversity in the student body of a professional school." Justice O'Connor in Adarand criticized Metro Broadcasting, from which she had dissented along with Chief Justice Rehnquist and Justices Scalia and Kennedy, for "turn[ing] its back on Croson's explanation of why strict scrutiny of all governmental racial classifications is [essential]" and for rejecting "congruence between the standards applicable to federal and state racial classifications." She stated that,"[t]o the extent that Metro Broadcasting is inconsistent with [Adarand's] holding, it is [overruled]."

extent (if any) that Fullilove held federal racial classifications to be subject to a less rigorous standard, it is no longer controlling. [We] think that requiring strict scrutiny is the best way to ensure that courts will consistently give racial classifications [detailed] examination, both as to ends and as to means. [Finally,] we wish to dispel the notion that strict scrutiny is "strict in theory, but fatal in fact." The unhappy persistence of both the practice and the lingering effects of racial discrimination against minority groups in this country is an unfortunate reality, and government is not disqualified from acting in response to it. [When] race-based action is necessary to further a compelling interest, such action is within constitutional constraints if it satisfies the "narrow tailoring" test this Court has set out in previous cases.

IV. Because our decision today alters the playing field in some important respects, we think it best to remand the case to the lower courts for further consideration in light of the principles we have announced. [Vacated and remanded.]

■ JUSTICE SCALIA, concurring in part and concurring in the judgment.

[In] my view, government can never have a "compelling interest" in discriminating on the basis of race in order to "make up" for past racial discrimination in the opposite direction. Individuals who have been wronged by unlawful racial discrimination should be made whole; but under our Constitution there can be no such thing as either a creditor or a debtor race. That concept is alien to the Constitution's focus upon the individual, and its rejection of dispositions based on [race]. [In] the eyes of government, we are just one race here. It is American.

■ JUSTICE THOMAS, concurring in part and concurring in the judgment.

I agree with the majority's conclusion that strict scrutiny applies to all government classifications based on race. I write separately, however, to express my disagreement with the premise underlying Justice Stevens' and Justice Ginsburg's dissents: that there is a racial paternalism exception to the principle of equal protection. I believe that there is a "moral [and] constitutional equivalence" between laws designed to subjugate a race and those that distribute benefits on the basis of race in order to foster some current notion of equality. Government cannot make us equal; it can only recognize, respect, and protect us as equal before the law. That these programs may have been motivated, in part, by good intentions cannot provide refuge from the principle that under our Constitution, the government may not make distinctions on the basis of race. As far as the Constitution is concerned, it is irrelevant whether a government's racial classifications are drawn by those who wish to oppress a race or by those who have a sincere desire to help those thought to be disadvantaged. There can be no doubt that the paternalism that appears to lie at the heart of this program is at war with the principle of inherent equality that underlies and infuses our Constitution.

These programs not only raise grave constitutional questions, they also undermine the moral basis of the equal protection principle. Purchased at the price of immeasurable human suffering, the equal protection principle reflects our Nation's understanding that such classifications ultimately have a destructive impact on the individual and our society. [T]here can be no doubt that racial paternalism and its unintended consequences can be as poisonous and pernicious as any other form of discrimination. So-called "benign" discrimination teaches many that because of chronic and apparently immutable handicaps, minorities cannot compete with them without their patronizing indulgence. Inevitably, such programs engender attitudes of superiority or, alternatively, provoke resentment among those who believe that they have been wronged by the government's use of race. These programs stamp minorities with a badge of inferiority and may cause them to develop dependencies or to adopt an attitude that they are "entitled" to preferences. [In] my mind, government-sponsored racial discrimination based on benign prejudice is just as noxious as discrimination inspired by malicious prejudice. In each instance, it is racial discrimination, plain and simple.

■ JUSTICE STEVENS, with whom JUSTICE GINSBURG joins, dissenting.

[The] Court's concept of "consistency" assumes that there is no significant difference between a decision by the majority to impose a special burden on the members of a minority race and a decision by the majority to provide a benefit to certain members of that minority notwithstanding its incidental burden on some members of the majority. In my opinion that assumption is untenable. There is no moral or constitutional equivalence between a policy that is designed to perpetuate a caste system and one that seeks to eradicate racial subordination. Invidious discrimination is an engine of oppression, subjugating a disfavored group to enhance or maintain the power of the majority. Remedial race-based preferences reflect the opposite impulse: a desire to foster equality in society. No sensible conception of the Government's constitutional obligation to "govern impartially" should ignore this distinction. The consistency that the Court espouses would disregard the difference between a "No Trespassing" sign and a welcome mat.

[The] Court's concept of "congruence" assumes that there is no significant difference between a decision by the Congress of the United States to adopt an affirmative-action program and such a decision by a State or a municipality. [Federal] affirmative-action programs represent the will of our entire Nation's elected representatives, whereas a state or local program may have an impact on nonresident entities who played no part in the decision to enact it. Thus, in the state or local context, individuals who were unable to vote for the local representatives who enacted a race-conscious program may nonetheless feel the effects of that program. [Congressional] deliberations about a matter as important as affirmative action should be accorded far greater deference than those of a State or [municipality].

■ JUSTICE GINSBURG, with whom JUSTICE BREYER joins, dissenting.

[The] divisions in this difficult case should not obscure the Court's recognition of the persistence of racial inequality and a majority's acknowledgment of Congress' authority to act affirmatively, not only to end discrimination, but also to counteract discrimination's lingering effects. Those effects, reflective of a system of racial caste only recently ended, are evident in our workplaces, markets, and neighborhoods. Job applicants with identical resumes, qualifications, and interview styles still experience different receptions, depending on their race. White and African-American consumers still encounter different deals. People of color looking for housing still face discriminatory treatment by landlords, real estate agents, and mortgage lenders. Minority entrepreneurs sometimes fail to gain contracts though they are the low bidders, and they are sometimes refused work even after winning contracts. Bias both conscious and unconscious, reflecting traditional and unexamined habits of thought, keeps up barriers that must come down if equal opportunity and nondiscrimination are ever genuinely to become this country's law and practice. Given this history and its practical consequences, Congress surely can conclude that a carefully designed affirmative action program may help to realize, finally, the "equal protection of the laws" the Fourteenth Amendment has promised since 1868.

[The] lead opinion uses one term, "strict scrutiny," to describe the standard of judicial review for all governmental classifications by race. [The] strict standard announced is indeed "fatal" for classifications burdening groups that have suffered discrimination in our society. [For] a classification made to hasten the day when "we are just one race," however, the lead opinion has dispelled the notion that "strict scrutiny" is "fatal in fact." [While] I would not disturb the programs challenged in this case, and would leave their improvement to the political branches, I see today's decision as one that allows our precedent to evolve, still to be informed by and responsive to changing conditions.

■ [Another dissent, by JUSTICE SOUTER, joined by JUSTICE GINSBURG and JUSTICE BREYER, is omitted].

AFFIRMATIVE ACTION AFTER CROSON AND ADARAND

1. ***Justifications for affirmative action.*** Note that Bakke approved diversity in the classroom as a compelling interest, but found the UC Davis admissions policy not narrowly tailored to such an end. Croson and Adarand, by contrast, appeared to view only remedial justifications as sufficient in the contracting context. Remedial justifications may be broad or narrow; Justice Scalia would confine permissible racial remedies to the identified victims of specific past acts of discrimination while Wygant considered (and rejected) an argument for correcting broader societal prejudice. Croson and Adarand seemed to settle somewhere in between: on remedies for identified past discrimination, but not limited to particularized victims. Was Justice Stevens correct to observe in Metro Broadcasting that forward-looking justifications are preferable to backward-looking ones? For an argument that remedial justifications are over- and underinclusive in ways that distributive or utilitarian justifications are not, see Sullivan, "The Supreme Court—1985 Term—Comment: Sins of Discrimination," 100 Harv. L. Rev. 78 (1986).

2. ***"Strict in theory but not fatal in fact."*** Gerald Gunther wrote in an oft-quoted phrase in 1972 that strict scrutiny, for example of racial classifications, is "strict in theory and fatal in fact." Gunther, "The Supreme Court, 1971 Term—Foreword: In Search of Evolving Doctrine on a Changing Court: A Model for a Newer Equal Protection," 86 Harv. L. Rev. 1 (1972). Justice O'Connor took pains in Adarand, however, to dispel the notion that this is inevitably so, suggesting that some race-conscious measures might survive strict scrutiny in the affirmative action context, even though few laws outside of wartime (recall Korematsu) could survive such scrutiny when directed against racial minorities. Was this a signal that the Court was creating in effect a new tier of review, a kind of "strict scrutiny minus," applicable to race preferences? In the lower courts after Croson and Adarand, many race preferences were upheld under this new standard, including those in which the government had merely "passively participated" in private

discrimination. One important empirical study of federal judicial applications of strict scrutiny in the equal protection and other contexts from 1990 to 2003 suggests that "30 percent of all applications of strict scrutiny—nearly one in three—result in the challenged law being upheld," and thus concludes that "strict scrutiny is far from the inevitably deadly test imagined by the Gunther myth and more closely resembles the context-sensitive tool described by O'Connor." Winkler, "Fatal in Theory and Strict in Fact: An Empirical Analysis of Strict Scrutiny in the Federal Courts," 59 Vand. L. Rev. 793 (2006). For an historical argument that strict scrutiny was a late arrival in racial equal protection cases in any event, having originated decades earlier in free speech cases, see Siegel, "The Origin of the Compelling State Interest Test and Strict Scrutiny," 48 Am. J. Leg. Hist. 355 (2006).

3. ***The implications of Croson and Adarand for the vitality of Bakke.*** For the 25 years following the Bakke decision, many public and private universities and colleges followed Bakke's guidance in continuing to use race preferences in admissions, but to fashion them along the Harvard rather than the UC Davis model. During that period, however, the Court reviewed with increasing strictness and skepticism race preferences in employment and contracting, as illustrated by Croson and Adarand. These cases led to speculation that race preferences in education would eventually meet the same fate. They also raised questions whether any nonremedial justifications (such as diversity) could continue to justify affirmative action.

In a pair of 2003 decisions involving equal protection challenges to the use of race preferences in admissions at the University of Michigan, however, the Court reaffirmed and elaborated upon Justice Powell's opinion for the Court in Bakke finding diversity a compelling interest justifying race preferences in the context of university admissions. Applying that standard, the Court issued split judgments, upholding the use of race preferences by the Michigan Law School on the ground that it was part of individualized review of files that was narrowly tailored to produce diversity, but invalidating the use of race preferences in Michigan undergraduate admissions on the ground that it involved too mechanical a procedure for taking race into account.

Grutter v. Bollinger

539 U.S. 306, 123 S. Ct. 2325, 156 L. Ed. 2d 304 (2003).

■ JUSTICE O'CONNOR delivered the opinion of the Court, [in which JUSTICES STEVENS, SOUTER, GINSBURG, and BREYER joined].

This case requires us to decide whether the use of race as a factor in student admissions by the University of Michigan Law School (Law School) is unlawful.

I. A. The Law School ranks among the Nation's top law schools. It receives more than 3,500 applications each year for a class of around 350 students. Seeking to "admit a group of students who individually and collectively are among the most capable," the Law School looks for individuals with "substantial promise for success in law school" and "a strong likelihood of succeeding in the practice of law and contributing in diverse ways to the well-being of others." [The Law School's admissions policy also] aspires to "achieve that diversity which has the potential to enrich everyone's education and thus make a law school class stronger than the sum of its parts." The policy does not restrict the types of diversity contributions eligible for "substantial weight" in the admissions process, but instead recognizes "many possible bases for diversity admissions." The policy does, however, reaffirm the Law School's longstanding commitment to "one particular type of diversity," that is, "racial and ethnic diversity with special reference to the inclusion of students from groups which have been historically discriminated against, like African-Americans, Hispanics and Native Americans, who without this commitment might not be represented in our student body in meaningful numbers." By enrolling a " 'critical mass' of [underrepresented] minority students," the Law School seeks to "ensur[e] their ability to make unique contributions to the character of the Law School." The policy does not define diversity "solely in terms of racial and ethnic status."

B. Petitioner Barbara Grutter is a white Michigan resident who applied to the Law School in 1996 with a 3.8 grade point average and 161 LSAT score. The Law School initially placed petitioner on a waiting list, but subsequently rejected her application. In December 1997, petitioner filed suit [alleging] that respondents discriminated against her on the basis of race in violation of the Fourteenth Amendment. [After a 15-day bench trial,] the District Court concluded that the Law School's use of race as a factor in admissions decisions was unlawful. [Sitting] en banc, the Court of Appeals reversed.

II. A. We last addressed the use of race in public higher education over 25 years ago. In the landmark Bakke case we reviewed a racial set-aside program that reserved 16 out of 100 seats in a medical school class for members of certain minority groups. [Since] this Court's splintered decision in Bakke, Justice Powell's opinion announcing the judgment of the Court has served as the touchstone for constitutional analysis of race-conscious admissions policies. Public and private universities across the Nation have modeled their own admissions programs on Justice Powell's views on permissible race-conscious policies. [Today] we endorse Justice Powell's view that student body diversity is a compelling state interest that can justify the use of race in university admissions.

B. [We] have held that all racial classifications imposed by government "must be analyzed by a reviewing court under strict scrutiny." This means that such classifications are constitutional only if they are narrowly tailored to further compelling governmental interests. [Strict] scrutiny is not "strict in theory, but fatal in fact." Although all governmental uses of race are subject to strict scrutiny, not all are invalidated by it. [Context] matters when reviewing race-based governmental action under the Equal Protection Clause. [Not] every decision influenced by race is equally objectionable and strict scrutiny is designed to provide a framework for carefully examining the importance and the sincerity of the reasons advanced by the governmental decisionmaker for the use of race in that particular context.

III. A. With these principles in mind, we turn to the question whether the Law School's use of race is justified by a compelling state interest. Before this Court, as they have throughout this litigation, respondents assert only one justification for their use of race in the admissions process: obtaining "the educational benefits that flow from a diverse student body."

We first wish to dispel the notion that the Law School's argument has been foreclosed, either expressly or implicitly, by our affirmative-action cases decided since Bakke. It is true that some language in those opinions might be read to suggest that remedying past discrimination is the only permissible justification for race-based governmental action. See, e.g., Croson. But we have never held that the only governmental use of race that can survive strict scrutiny is remedying past discrimination. Nor, since Bakke, have we directly addressed the use of race in the context of public higher education. Today, we hold that the Law School has a compelling interest in attaining a diverse student body.

The Law School's educational judgment that such diversity is essential to its educational mission is one to which we defer. [Our] scrutiny of the interest asserted by the Law School is no less strict for taking into account complex educational judgments in an area that lies primarily within the expertise of the university. Our holding today is in keeping with our tradition of giving a degree of deference to a university's academic decisions. [We] have long recognized that, given the important purpose of public education and the expansive freedoms of speech and thought associated with the university environment, universities occupy a special niche in our constitutional tradition. [Our] conclusion that the Law School has a compelling interest in a diverse student body is informed by our view that attaining a diverse student body is at the heart of the Law School's proper institutional mission.

[The] Law School seeks to "enroll a 'critical mass' of minority students." The Law School's interest is not simply "to assure within its student body some specified percentage of a particular group merely because of its race or ethnic origin." That would amount to outright racial balancing, which is patently unconstitutional. Rather, the Law School's concept of critical mass is defined by reference to the educational benefits that diversity is designed to produce. These benefits are substantial. [The] Law School's admissions policy promotes "cross-racial understanding," helps to break down racial stereotypes, and "enables [students] to better understand persons of different races." These benefits are "important and laudable," because "classroom discussion is livelier, more spirited, and simply more enlightening and interesting" when the students have "the greatest possible variety of backgrounds." [Student] body diversity promotes learning outcomes, and "better prepares students for an increasingly diverse workforce and society, and better prepares them as professionals." These benefits are not theoretical but real, as major American businesses have made clear [in their amicus briefs in support of the University] that the skills needed in today's increasingly global marketplace can only be developed through exposure to widely diverse people, cultures, ideas, and viewpoints. What is more, high-ranking retired officers and civilian leaders of the United States military assert [in their amicus brief] that, "[b]ased on [their] decades of experience," a "highly qualified, racially diverse officer corps . . . is essential to the military's ability to fulfill its princip[al] mission to provide national security." [At] present, "the military cannot achieve an officer corps that is both highly qualified and racially diverse unless the service academies and the ROTC used limited race-conscious recruiting and admissions policies." [We] agree that "[i]t requires only a small step from this analysis to conclude that our country's other most selective institutions must remain both diverse and selective."

[Moreover,] universities, and in particular, law schools, represent the training ground for a large number of our Nation's leaders. Individuals with law degrees occupy roughly half the state governorships, more than half the seats in the United States Senate, and more than a third of the seats in the United States House of Representatives. The pattern is even more striking when it comes to highly selective law schools. A handful of these schools accounts for 25 of the 100 United States Senators, 74 United States Courts of Appeals judges, and nearly 200 of the more than 600 United States District Court judges. In order to cultivate a set of leaders with legitimacy in the eyes of the citizenry, it is necessary that the path to leadership be visibly open to talented and qualified individuals of every race and ethnicity.

B. [Even] in the limited circumstance when drawing racial distinctions is permissible to further a compelling state interest, [the means] must be specifically and narrowly framed. [We] find that the Law School's admissions program bears the hallmarks of a narrowly tailored plan. As Justice Powell made clear in Bakke, truly individualized consideration demands that race be used in a flexible, nonmechanical way. It follows from this mandate that universities cannot establish quotas for members of certain racial groups or put members of those groups on separate admissions tracks. Nor can universities insulate applicants who belong to certain racial or ethnic groups from the competition for admission. Universities can, however, consider race or ethnicity more flexibly as a "plus" factor in the context of individualized consideration of each and every applicant. We are satisfied that the Law School's admissions program, like the Harvard plan described by Justice Powell, does not operate as a quota. [The] Law School's goal of attaining a critical mass of underrepresented minority students does not transform its program into a quota.

[That] a race-conscious admissions program does not operate as a quota does not, by itself, satisfy the requirement of individualized consideration. When using race as a "plus" factor in university admissions, a university's admissions program must remain flexible enough to ensure that each applicant is evaluated as an individual and not in a way that makes an applicant's race or ethnicity the defining feature of his or her application. The importance of this individualized consideration in the context of a race-conscious admissions program is paramount. Here, the Law School engages in a highly individualized, holistic review of each applicant's file, giving serious consideration to all the ways an applicant might contribute to a diverse educational environment. The Law School affords this individualized consideration to applicants of all races. [We] also find that [the] Law School's race-conscious admissions program adequately ensures that all factors that may contribute to student body diversity are meaningfully considered alongside race in admissions decisions. The Law School does not [limit] in any way the broad range of qualities and experiences that may be considered valuable contributions to student body diversity. To the contrary, the [admissions] policy makes clear "[t]here are many possible bases for diversity admissions," and provides examples of admittees who have lived or traveled widely abroad, are fluent in several languages, have overcome personal adversity and family hardship, have exceptional records of extensive community service, and have had successful careers in other fields. The Law School seriously considers each "applicant's promise of making a notable contribution to the class by way of a particular strength, attainment, or characteristic—e.g., an unusual intellectual achievement, employment experience, nonacademic performance, or personal background." All applicants have the opportunity to highlight their own potential diversity contributions through the submission of a personal statement, letters of recommendation, and an essay describing the ways in which the applicant will contribute to the life and diversity of the Law School.

[Petitioner] and the United States argue that the Law School's plan is not narrowly tailored because race-neutral means exist to obtain the educational benefits of student body diversity that the Law School seeks. We disagree. Narrow tailoring does not require exhaustion of every conceivable race-neutral alternative. Nor does it require a university to choose between maintaining a reputation for excellence or fulfilling a commitment to provide educational opportunities to members of all racial groups. Narrow tailoring does, however, require serious, good faith consideration of workable race-neutral alternatives that will achieve the diversity the university seeks.

We agree with the Court of Appeals that the Law School sufficiently considered workable race-neutral alternatives. The District Court took the Law School to task for failing to consider race-neutral alternatives such as "using a lottery system" or "decreasing the emphasis for all applicants on undergraduate GPA and LSAT scores." But these alternatives would require a dramatic sacrifice of diversity, the academic quality of all admitted students, or both. [The] United States advocates "percentage plans," recently adopted by public undergraduate institutions in Texas, Florida, and California to guarantee admission to all students above a certain class-rank threshold in every high school in the State. The United States does not, however, explain how such plans could work for graduate and professional schools. Moreover, even assuming such plans are race-neutral, they may preclude the university from conducting the individualized assessments necessary to assemble a student body that is not just racially diverse, but diverse along all the qualities valued by the university. We are satisfied that the Law School adequately considered race-neutral alternatives currently capable of producing a critical mass without forcing the Law School to abandon the academic selectivity that is the cornerstone of its educational mission.

[To] be narrowly tailored, a race-conscious admissions program [also] must not "unduly burden individuals who are not members of the favored racial and ethnic groups." We are satisfied that the Law School's admissions program does not. Because the Law School considers "all pertinent elements of diversity," it can (and does) select nonminority applicants who have greater potential to enhance student body diversity over underrepresented minority applicants.

[We] are mindful, however, that "[a] core purpose of the Fourteenth Amendment was to do away with all governmentally imposed discrimination based on race." Accordingly, race-conscious admissions policies must be limited in time. [We] see no reason to exempt race-conscious admissions programs from the requirement that all governmental use of race must have a logical end point. [We] take the Law School at its word that it would "like nothing better than to find a race-neutral admissions formula" and will terminate its race-conscious admissions program as soon as practicable. It has been 25 years since Justice Powell first approved the use of race to further an interest in student body diversity in the context of public higher education. Since that time, the number of minority applicants with high grades and test scores has indeed increased. We expect that 25 years from now, the use of racial preferences will no longer be necessary to further the interest approved today.

IV. In summary, the Equal Protection Clause does not prohibit the Law School's narrowly tailored use of race in admissions decisions to further a compelling interest in obtaining the educational benefits that flow from a diverse student body. [Affirmed.]

■ JUSTICE GINSBURG, with whom JUSTICE BREYER joins, concurring.

[It] is well documented that conscious and unconscious race bias, even rank discrimination based on race, remain alive in our land, impeding realization of our highest values and ideals. As to public education, data for the years 2000–2001 show that 71.6% of African-American children and 76.3% of Hispanic children attended a school in which minorities made up a majority of the student body. And schools in predominantly minority communities lag far behind others measured by the educational resources available to them. However strong the public's desire for improved education systems may be, it remains the current reality that many minority students encounter markedly inadequate and unequal educational opportunities. [As] lower school education in minority communities improves, an increase in the number of such students may be anticipated. From today's vantage point, one may hope, but not firmly forecast, that over the next generation's span, progress toward nondiscrimination and genuinely equal opportunity will make it safe to sunset affirmative action.

■ JUSTICE SCALIA, with whom JUSTICE THOMAS joins, concurring in part and dissenting in part.

[Unlike] a clear constitutional holding that racial preferences in state educational institutions are impermissible, or even a clear anticonstitutional holding that racial preferences in state educational institutions are OK, today's Grutter-Gratz split double header [see Gratz v. Bollinger, the undergraduate admissions decision, below] seems perversely designed to prolong the controversy and the litigation. Some future lawsuits will presumably focus on whether the discriminatory scheme in question contains enough evaluation of the applicant "as an individual," and sufficiently avoids "separate admissions tracks" to fall under Grutter rather than Gratz. Some will focus on whether a university has gone beyond the bounds of a " 'good faith effort' " and has so zealously pursued its "critical mass" as to make it an unconstitutional de facto quota system, rather than merely " 'a permissible goal.' " Other lawsuits may focus on whether, in the particular setting at issue, any educational benefits flow from racial diversity. Still other suits may challenge the bona fides of the institution's expressed commitment to the educational benefits of diversity that immunize the discriminatory scheme in Grutter. (Tempting targets, one would suppose, will be those universities that talk the talk of multiculturalism and racial diversity in the courts but walk the walk of tribalism and racial segregation on their campuses—through minority-only student organizations, separate minority housing opportunities, separate minority student centers, even separate minority-only graduation ceremonies.) And still other suits may claim that the institution's racial preferences have gone below or above the mystical Grutter-approved "critical mass." Finally, litigation can be expected on behalf of minority groups intentionally short changed in the institution's composition of its generic minority "critical mass." I do not look forward to any of these cases. The

Constitution proscribes government discrimination on the basis of race, and state-provided education is no exception.

■ JUSTICE THOMAS, with whom JUSTICE SCALIA joins as to Parts I–VII, concurring in part and dissenting in part.

Frederick Douglass, speaking to a group of abolitionists almost 140 years ago, delivered a message lost on today's majority:

> "[I]n regard to the colored people, there is always more that is benevolent, I perceive, than just, manifested towards us. What I ask for the negro is not benevolence, not pity, not sympathy, but simply justice. The American people have always been anxious to know what they shall do with us. . . . I have had but one answer from the beginning. Do nothing with us! [All] I ask is, give him a chance to stand on his own legs! Let him alone! . . . [Y]our interference is doing him positive injury."

Like Douglass, I believe blacks can achieve in every avenue of American life without the meddling of university administrators. Because I wish to see all students succeed whatever their color, I share, in some respect, the sympathies of those who sponsor the type of discrimination advanced by the University of Michigan Law School (Law School). The Constitution does not, however, tolerate institutional devotion to the status quo in admissions policies when such devotion ripens into racial discrimination. Nor does the Constitution countenance the unprecedented deference the Court gives to the Law School, an approach inconsistent with the very concept of "strict scrutiny."

I. [The] Constitution abhors classifications based on race, not only because those classifications can harm favored races or are based on illegitimate motives, but also because every time the government places citizens on racial registers and makes race relevant to the provision of burdens or benefits, it demeans us all.

II. [Unlike] the majority, I seek to define with precision the interest being asserted by the Law School before determining whether that interest is so compelling as to justify racial discrimination. The Law School maintains that it wishes to obtain "educational benefits that flow from student body diversity." [But attaining] "diversity," whatever it means,[1] is the mechanism by which the Law School obtains educational benefits, not an end of itself. [It] is the educational benefits that are the end, or allegedly compelling state interest, not "diversity." [But the] Law School [refuses] to entertain changes to its current admissions system that might produce the same educational benefits. The Law School adamantly disclaims any race-neutral alternative that would reduce "academic selectivity." [Instead] the Court upholds the use of racial discrimination as a tool to advance the Law School's interest in offering a marginally superior education while maintaining an elite institution.

---

1 "[D]iversity," for all of its devotees, is more a fashionable catchphrase than it is a useful term, especially when something as serious as racial discrimination is at issue. Because the Equal Protection Clause renders the color of one's skin constitutionally irrelevant to the Law School's mission, I refer to the Law School's interest as an "aesthetic." That is, the Law School wants to have a certain appearance, from the shape of the desks and tables in its classrooms to the color of the students sitting at them. [It] must be remembered that the Law School's racial discrimination does nothing for those too poor or uneducated to participate in elite higher education and therefore presents only an illusory solution to the challenges facing our Nation. [Footnote by Justice Thomas.]

III. [Under] the proper standard, there is no pressing public necessity in maintaining a public law school at all and, it follows, certainly not an elite law school. [While] legal education at a public university may be good policy or otherwise laudable, it is obviously not a pressing public necessity.

IV. [The] Court never explicitly holds that the Law School's desire to retain the status quo in "academic selectivity" is itself a compelling state interest. [Therefore], the Law School should be forced to choose between its classroom aesthetic and its exclusionary admissions system—it cannot have it both ways. With the adoption of different admissions methods, such as accepting all students who meet minimum qualifications, the Law School could achieve its vision of the racially aesthetic student body without the use of racial discrimination. [The] Court ignores the fact that other top law schools have succeeded in meeting their aesthetic demands without racial discrimination. [The] sky has not fallen at Boalt Hall at the University of California, Berkeley, for example. Prior to Proposition 209's adoption of Cal. Const., Art. 1, § 31(a), which bars the State from "grant[ing] preferential treatment . . . on the basis of race . . . in the operation of . . . public education," Boalt Hall enrolled 20 blacks and 28 Hispanics in its first-year class for 1996. In 2002, without deploying express racial discrimination in admissions, Boalt's entering class enrolled 14 blacks and 36 Hispanics. Total underrepresented minority student enrollment at Boalt Hall now exceeds 1996 levels. [The] Court will not even deign to make the Law School try other methods, however, preferring instead to grant a 25-year license to violate the Constitution.

V. [The] rallying cry that in the absence of racial discrimination in admissions there would be a true meritocracy ignores the fact that the entire process is poisoned by numerous exceptions to "merit." For example, in the national debate on racial discrimination in higher education admissions, much has been made of the fact that elite institutions utilize a so-called "legacy" preference to give the children of alumni an advantage in admissions. This, and other, exceptions to a "true" meritocracy give the lie to protestations that merit admissions are in fact the order of the day at the Nation's universities. The Equal Protection Clause does not, however, prohibit the use of unseemly legacy preferences or many other kinds of arbitrary admissions procedures. What the Equal Protection Clause does prohibit are classifications made on the basis of race. So while legacy preferences can stand under the Constitution, racial discrimination cannot.[2]

VI. [I must also] contest the notion that the Law School's discrimination benefits those admitted as a result of it. [The] Law School tantalizes unprepared students with the promise of a University of Michigan degree and all of the opportunities that it offers. These overmatched students take the bait, only to find that they cannot succeed in the cauldron of competition. [To] cover the tracks of the aestheticists, this cruel farce of racial discrimination must continue—in selection for the Michigan Law Review, and in hiring at law firms and for judicial clerkships—until the "beneficiaries" are no longer tolerated. While these students may graduate with law degrees, there is no evidence that they have received a qualitatively

[2] Were this Court to have the courage to forbid the use of racial discrimination in admissions, legacy preferences (and similar practices) might quickly become less popular—a possibility not lost, I am certain, on the elites (both individual and institutional) supporting the Law School in this case. [Footnote by Justice Thomas.]

better legal education (or become better lawyers) than if they had gone to a less "elite" law school for which they were better prepared.

[Beyond] the harm the Law School's racial discrimination visits upon its test subjects, no social science has disproved the notion that this discrimination "engender[s] attitudes of superiority or, alternatively, provoke[s] resentment among those who believe that they have been wronged by the government's use of race." "These programs stamp minorities with a badge of inferiority and may cause them to develop dependencies or to adopt an attitude that they are 'entitled' to preferences." It is uncontested that each year, the Law School admits a handful of blacks who would be admitted in the absence of racial discrimination. Who can differentiate between those who belong and those who do not? The majority of blacks are admitted to the Law School because of discrimination, and because of this policy all are tarred as undeserving. This problem of stigma does not depend on determinacy as to whether those stigmatized are actually the "beneficiaries" of racial discrimination. When blacks take positions in the highest places of government, industry, or academia, it is an open question today whether their skin color played a part in their advancement. The question itself is the stigma—because either racial discrimination did play a role, in which case the person may be deemed "otherwise unqualified," or it did not, in which case asking the question itself unfairly marks those blacks who would succeed without discrimination.

■ CHIEF JUSTICE REHNQUIST, with whom JUSTICE SCALIA, JUSTICE KENNEDY, and JUSTICE THOMAS join, dissenting.[3]

[The] Law School claims it must take the steps it does to achieve a " 'critical mass' " of underrepresented minority students. But its actual program bears no relation to this asserted goal. [From] 1995 through 2000, the Law School admitted between 1,130 and 1,310 students. Of those, between 13 and 19 were Native American, between 91 and 108 were African-Americans, and between 47 and 56 were Hispanic. If the Law School is admitting between 91 and 108 African-Americans in order to achieve "critical mass," thereby preventing African-American students from feeling "isolated or like spokespersons for their race," one would think that a number of the same order of magnitude would be necessary to accomplish the same purpose for Hispanics and Native Americans. [But] respondents offer no race-specific reasons for such disparities.

[The] Court recognizes that ["outright] racial balancing [is] patently unconstitutional." The Court concludes [that] the Law School's use of race in admissions [only] pays " '[s]ome attention to numbers.' " But the correlation between the percentage of the Law School's pool of applicants who are members of the three minority groups and the percentage of the admitted applicants who are members of these same groups is far too precise to be dismissed as merely the result of the school paying "some attention to [the] numbers." [From] 1995 through 2000 the percentage of admitted applicants who were members of these minority groups closely tracked the percentage of individuals in the school's applicant pool who were from the same groups. [For] example, in 1995, when 9.7% of the applicant pool was African-American, 9.4% of the admitted class was African-American. By 2000, only 7.5% of the applicant pool was African-American, and 7.3% of the admitted

[3] Justice KENNEDY also filed a separate dissent, agreeing with the District Court that an inference could be drawn from the record "that the Law School's pursuit of critical mass mutated into the equivalent of a quota."

class was African-American. This correlation is striking. [The] tight correlation between the percentage of applicants and admittees of a given race [must] result from careful race based planning by the Law School. [But] this is precisely the type of racial balancing that the Court itself calls "patently unconstitutional."

Gratz v. Bollinger

539 U.S. 244, 123 S. Ct. 2411, 156 L. Ed. 2d 257 (2003).

[This case, like Grutter, involved a challenge by white students to an admissions policy of the University of Michigan, this time by the undergraduate College of Literature, Science, and the Arts (LSA). Although the college considered the challengers "qualified," they were ultimately denied admission. The college considered a number of factors in making admissions decisions, including high school grades, standardized test scores, high school quality, curriculum strength, geography, alumni relationships, leadership, and race. The college used a selection method under which every applicant from an underrepresented racial or ethnic minority group—namely, African-Americans, Hispanics, and Native Americans—was automatically awarded 20 points of the 100 needed to guarantee admission. It was undisputed that the University admitted virtually every qualified applicant from these groups. The majority opinion began by dismissing the dissenters' objections that the challengers lacked standing. Chief Justice Rehnquist proceeded:]

■ CHIEF JUSTICE REHNQUIST delivered the opinion of the Court, in which JUSTICES O'CONNOR, SCALIA, KENNEDY, and THOMAS, joined.

Petitioners argue [that] the University's use of race in undergraduate admissions violates the Fourteenth Amendment [because] this Court has only sanctioned the use of racial classifications to remedy identified discrimination, a justification on which respondents have never relied, [and that] "diversity as a basis for employing racial preferences is simply too open-ended, ill-defined, and indefinite to constitute a compelling interest capable of supporting narrowly-tailored means." [For] the reasons set forth today in Grutter v. Bollinger [above] the Court has rejected these arguments. [But we] find that the University's policy, which automatically distributes 20 points, or one-fifth of the points needed to guarantee admission, to every single "underrepresented minority" applicant solely because of race, is not narrowly tailored to achieve the interest in educational diversity that respondents claim justifies their program.

[Justice] Powell's opinion in Bakke emphasized the importance of considering each particular applicant as an individual, assessing all of the qualities that individual possesses, and in turn, evaluating that individual's ability to contribute to the unique setting of higher education. The admissions program Justice Powell described, however, did not contemplate that any single characteristic automatically ensured a specific and identifiable contribution to a university's diversity. [The] current LSA policy does not provide such individualized consideration. The LSA's policy automatically distributes 20 points to every single applicant from an "underrepresented minority" group, as defined by the University. The only consideration that accompanies this distribution of points is a factual review of an application to determine whether an individual is a member of one of these minority groups. [Even if a student's] "extraordinary artistic talent" rivaled that of Monet or Picasso, the applicant would receive, at most, five points under the LSA's system. At the same time, every single underrepresented minority applicant [would] automatically receive 20 points for submitting an application. Clearly, the LSA's system does not offer applicants the individualized selection process.

[We] conclude, therefore, that because the University's use of race in its current freshman admissions policy is not narrowly tailored to achieve respondents' asserted compelling interest in diversity, the admissions policy violates the Equal Protection Clause of the Fourteenth Amendment.

■ JUSTICE O'CONNOR, concurring.[1]

Unlike the law school admissions policy the Court upholds today in Grutter, the procedures employed by the University of Michigan's Office of Undergraduate Admissions do not provide for a meaningful individualized review of applicants. The law school considers the various diversity qualifications of each applicant, including race, on a case-by-case basis. By contrast, the Office of Undergraduate Admissions relies on the selection index to assign every underrepresented minority applicant the same, automatic 20-point bonus without consideration of the particular background, experiences, or qualities of each individual applicant. [Although] the Office of Undergraduate Admissions does assign 20 points to some "soft" variables other than race, the points available for other diversity contributions, such as leadership and service, personal achievement, and geographic diversity, are capped at much lower levels. Even the most outstanding national high school leader could never receive more than five points for his or her accomplishments—a mere quarter of the points automatically assigned to an underrepresented minority solely based on the fact of his or her race. [The] selection index, by setting up automatic, predetermined point allocations for the soft variables, ensures that the diversity contributions of applicants cannot be individually assessed. This policy stands in sharp contrast to the law school's admissions plan, which enables admissions officers to make nuanced judgments with respect to the contributions each applicant is likely to make to the diversity of the incoming class.

■ JUSTICE THOMAS, concurring.

I join the Court's opinion because I believe it correctly applies our precedents, including today's decision in Grutter v. Bollinger. For similar reasons to those given in my separate opinion in that case, however, I would hold that a State's use of racial discrimination in higher education admissions is categorically prohibited by the Equal Protection Clause.

■ JUSTICE SOUTER, dissenting.[2]

[Although] the freshman admissions system here is subject to argument on the merits, I think it is closer to what Grutter approves than to what Bakke condemns, and should not be held unconstitutional on the current

[1] Justice BREYER concurred in the judgment, and joined Justice O'Connor's concurring opinion except insofar as it joined that of the Court, and Justice Ginsburg's dissent except insofar as it found no constitutional violation.

[2] Justice STEVENS, joined by Justice Souter, filed a separate dissent on the ground that the named petitioners lacked standing. Justice Ginsburg joined Justice Souter's dissent on the merits.

record. The record does not describe a system with a quota like the one struck down in Bakke, which "insulate[d]" all nonminority candidates from competition from certain seats. [The] plan here, in contrast, lets all applicants compete for all places and values an applicant's offering for any place not only on grounds of race, but on grades, test scores, strength of high school, quality of course of study, residence, alumni relationships, leadership, personal character, socioeconomic disadvantage, athletic ability, and quality of a personal essay. [Since] college admission is not left entirely to inarticulate intuition, it is hard to see what is inappropriate in assigning some stated value to a relevant characteristic, whether it be reasoning ability, writing style, running speed, or minority race.

[It] seems especially unfair to treat the candor of the admissions plan as an Achilles' heel. In contrast to the college's forthrightness in saying just what plus factor it gives for membership in an underrepresented minority, it is worth considering the character of one alternative thrown up as preferable, because supposedly not based on race. Drawing on admissions systems used at public universities in California, Florida, and Texas, the United States contends that Michigan could get student diversity in satisfaction of its compelling interest by guaranteeing admission to a fixed percentage of the top students from each high school in Michigan. While there is nothing unconstitutional about such a practice, it nonetheless suffers from a serious disadvantage. It is the disadvantage of deliberate obfuscation. The "percentage plans" are just as race conscious as the point scheme (and fairly so), but they get their racially diverse results without saying directly what they are doing or why they are doing it. In contrast, Michigan states its purpose directly and, if this were a doubtful case for me, I would be tempted to give Michigan an extra point of its own for its frankness. Equal protection cannot become an exercise in which the winners are the ones who hide the ball.

■ JUSTICE GINSBURG, with whom JUSTICE SOUTER joins, dissenting.

[The] Court once again maintains that the same standard of review controls judicial inspection of all official race classifications. This insistence on "consistency" would be fitting were our Nation free of the vestiges of rank discrimination long reinforced by law. But we are not far distant from an overtly discriminatory past, and the effects of centuries of law-sanctioned inequality remain painfully evident in our communities and schools. [Unemployment], poverty, and access to health care vary disproportionately by race. Neighborhoods and schools remain racially divided. African-American and Hispanic children are all too often educated in poverty-stricken and underperforming institutions. Adult African-Americans and Hispanics generally earn less than whites with equivalent levels of education. Equally credentialed job applicants receive different receptions depending on their race. Irrational prejudice is still encountered in real estate markets and consumer transactions. [Actions] designed to burden groups long denied full citizenship stature are not sensibly ranked with measures taken to hasten the day when entrenched discrimination and its after effects have been extirpated. [Where] race is considered "for the purpose of achieving equality," no automatic proscription is in order.

[The] stain of generations of racial oppression is still visible in our society, and the determination to hasten its removal remains vital. One can reasonably anticipate, therefore, that colleges and universities will seek to maintain their minority enrollment—and the networks and opportunities thereby opened to minority graduates—whether or not they can do so in full candor through adoption of affirmative action plans of the kind here at issue. Without recourse to such plans, institutions of higher education may resort to camouflage. For example, schools may encourage applicants to write of their cultural traditions in the essays they submit, or to indicate whether English is their second language. Seeking to improve their chances for admission, applicants may highlight the minority group associations to which they belong, or the Hispanic surnames of their mothers or grandparents. [If] honesty is the best policy, surely Michigan's accurately described, fully disclosed College affirmative action program is preferable to achieving similar numbers through winks, nods, and disguises.

THE MEANING AND IMPLICATIONS OF GRUTTER AND GRATZ

1. ***Bakke vs. Grutter and Gratz.*** After Grutter and Gratz, Bakke remained good law insofar as achieving diversity in higher education remained a compelling state interest sufficient to justify at least some race preferences in higher education. Was the diversity interest that was upheld in Grutter, however, the same as that upheld in Bakke? Is Grutter simply a reaffirmance of Powell's opinion in Bakke, or does it have more far-reaching implications? Did Grutter replace Bakke's emphasis on diversity in educational inputs with a new emphasis on diversity in educational outputs? Consider the view that, "[a]lthough Grutter casts itself as merely endorsing Justice Powell's opinion in Bakke, Grutter's analysis of diversity actually differs quite dramatically from Powell's. Powell conceptualizes diversity as a value intrinsic to the educational process itself [because] education was a practice of enlightenment [that] thrived on the 'robust exchange of ideas' characteristically provoked by confrontation between persons of distinct life experiences. [Grutter instead] conceives of education as instrumental for the achievement of extrinsic social goods like professionalism, citizenship, or leadership. [Grutter's] justifications for diversity thus potentially reach far more widely than do Powell's." Post, "The Supreme Court, 2002 Term—Foreword: Fashioning the Legal Constitution: Culture, Courts, and the Law," 117 Harv. L. Rev. 4 (2003).

Other scholars agree that "Justice O'Connor championed diversity not only in the classroom but beyond. After noting that higher education 'must be accessible to all individuals regardless of race or ethnicity,' she linked education to leadership. [It] may be possible to confine [her] words to law schools or to higher education generally, but it may also be that diversity has now been writ large to include all public institutions. [The] debate has shifted from whether Bakke would be overruled to how far it should be extended." Jeffries, "Bakke Revisited," 2003 Sup. Ct. Rev. 1. If Grutter's conception of diversity "depends on minority participation in leadership for satisfaction," then it might be argued that "in Grutter, the Court endorsed a subtly, but importantly, different claim [than in Bakke]: diverse discourse on campus and its societal reverberations notwithstanding, student body diversity at a particular educational institution is sought to produce, and in fact produces, not just racial-majority leaders who are open to diverse perspectives, but actual and substantial racial diversity in the leadership ranks of important non-educational institutions." Lee, "University Dons and

Warrior Chieftains: Two Concepts of Diversity," 72 Fordham L. Rev. 2301 (2004).

2. ***The Court's rationale—epistemic, distributive, compensatory, or something else?*** Despite upholding one affirmative action program and striking down another, the Court assumed in both Grutter and Gratz that seeking diversity in higher education is a compelling state interest; Gratz simply found the undergraduate admissions program not sufficiently narrowly tailored to that goal. Why is diversity a compelling interest? Because it improves the quality of higher education? Distributes the benefits of higher education to a broader cross-section of the population? Or compensates those segments of society that have been harmed by racial discrimination in the past? Many observers see the rationale as epistemic or distributive, not compensatory: "The goal articulated in Grutter—integrating the leadership of major American institutions—does not look back to catalogue all the multifold harms of slavery and Jim Crow, and offer a remedy. Rather the opinion places us in the Here and Now, and looks to our national future. The nation needs integration of our leading institutions, not to compensate victims of past iniquities, but to serve the whole nation's present vital purposes at home and overseas. The mission, the bottom line, the production line: The military, businesses, and union leaders who offered those three briefs as amici curiae regarded the need for integration at all levels of their institutions as virtually self-evident." Karst, "The Revival of Forward-Looking Affirmative Action," 104 Colum. L. Rev. 60 (2004).

Is the desire to create a more integrated political and social leadership a cognizable interest under the Equal Protection Clause? Is such a concern in tension with the understanding that the Fourteenth Amendment "protects persons, not groups"? Consider the following view: "Both the rhetoric and the doctrine of Grutter—and Gratz—are committed to individualism as the dominant understanding of equal protection. [To] whatever degree individualism tolerates race-conscious decisionmaking, it may incorporate within itself some of the concerns with racial hierarchy that a strictly colorblind regime would reject. But even so, it is individualism rather than hierarchy that operates as the dominant meaning of equal protection." Primus, "Equal Protection and Disparate Impact: Round Three," 117 Harv. L. Rev. 493 (2003).

Others question whether the Court is truly concerned with the diversity in higher education for epistemic or distributive purposes: "If students and faculty are benefited by 'diversity' to the point that it qualifies as a compelling interest justifying discrimination that would otherwise be unconstitutional, why the lack of concern about the absence at virtually all elite institutions of a 'critical mass' of faculty who are Evangelical Protestants, devout Catholics, social conservatives, Republicans, etc.? [Few] people who shape university policy notice, much less care about, the absence of diversity of political and religious viewpoint and affiliation in institutions that allegedly prize the engagement of ideas. It is therefore difficult to credit the claim that a desire for the intellectual benefits of diversity really motivates the defense of preference schemes." George, "Gratz and Grutter: Some Hard Questions," 103 Colum. L. Rev. 1634 (2003).

But consider the countervailing view: "Critics argue that the schools are inconsistent: Diversity policy does not discount admissions criteria for members of different political, religious, and other groups. [The] reason for focusing on African Americans, however, is central to Justice O'Connor's path-breaking perception in Grutter that there is something special and important for society, in the world outside the university, about admitting blacks. Blacks occupy a unique place in American society, with their background of slavery, state-enforced segregation, and widespread discrimination." Greenberg, "Diversity, the University, and the World Outside," 103 Colum. L. Rev. 1610 (2003). Does this reasoning convert the diversity rationale back into a compensatory one?

Justice O'Connor wrote near the end of her opinion in Grutter: "We expect that 25 years from now, the use of racial preferences will no longer be necessary to further the interest approved today." Does this suggest that there is still a compensatory underpinning to the decision? If affirmative action is compensatory in nature, then diversity in education as a compelling interest should decrease in importance over time. Does this language create a presumption of invalidity for affirmative action come the year 2028? Was it Justice O'Connor's intention to place a definitive temporal limit to affirmative action? Or was she simply stating an aspiration that affirmative action will no longer be needed two or three decades in the future? What theory of constitutional interpretation would justify introducing such a pragmatic, temporal dimension to a holding? Is a generational reevaluation of affirmative action healthy for the nation?

Some observers argue that the Court has supported affirmative action only where it has benefited the white majority: "To rest the case for affirmative action on diversity because it contributes to learning incorporates an irony. It argues that admitting blacks is good because it helps whites. Otherwise they would suffer from being alone with only white classmates." Greenberg, above. "It was diversity in the classroom, on the work floor, and in the military, not the need to address past and continuing racial barriers, that gained O'Connor's vote. Once again, blacks and Hispanics are the fortuitous beneficiaries of a ruling motivated by other interests that can and likely will change when different priorities assert themselves. [In] addition, it was a boost to a wide range of corporate and institutional entities with which she identifies." Bell, "Diversity's Distractions," 103 Colum. L. Rev. 1622 (2003).

3. ***The extent of harm to nonminority applicants.*** Are the plaintiffs in reverse-discrimination cases such as Bakke, Grutter, and Gratz justified in seeking admission to the university as relief? Isn't it probable that in many cases, even in the absence of affirmative action, their applications would have been rejected? In Bakke, there were many other white applicants who had been denied admission despite better entrance exam scores and grades than Allan Bakke. The university only stipulated that Bakke would have been admitted in the absence of affirmative action in order to ensure that the case would not be dismissed on standing grounds. If a plaintiff cannot demonstrate that he would have been admitted in the absence of an unconstitutional racial preference program, is it enough for standing for the plaintiff to claim he had the right to compete on an equal footing?

An article that predated the 2003 decisions presented a statistical model showing that a nonminority applicant's chance of being admitted under a race-neutral admissions process is not significantly greater than the same person's chance of being admitted under a race-conscious process: "[T]here is no doubt that receiving a rejection letter from a selective institution is a considerable disappointment. But the reflexive tendency to blame affirmative action runs counter to basic reasoning and empirical evidence. In any highly selective competition where white applicants greatly outnumber minority applicants, and where multiple objective and nonobjective criteria are relevant, the average white applicant will not fare significantly worse under a selection process that is race-conscious than under a process that is race-neutral." Liu, "The Causation Fallacy: Bakke and the Basic Arithmetic of Selective Admissions," 100 Mich. L. Rev. 1045 (2002).

4. ***Narrow tailoring and means-ends fit.*** Given the Court's concern with creating diversity both in higher education and in the nation's leadership ranks, why did the Court uphold the law school's preference system but strike down the undergraduate program? Are the two really distinguishable? The Court treated the point system in Gratz as more problematic than the individualized file review in Grutter, despite the fact that each made determinative use of race in some cases. Are the dissenters in both cases right to ask, "How can it be constitutionally permissible to do 'through winks, nods, and disguises' what it is unconstitutional to do honestly and above board?" George, note 2 above (suggesting that "the answer offered by Justice O'Connor—that the Law School was doing something fundamentally or essentially different from what the college was doing, something free of the discriminatory element she found in the college's awarding of points—just isn't persuasive").

5. ***Race-neutral alternatives.*** Before Grutter was announced, some states that had already eliminated affirmative action programs began experimenting with "alternative action" programs: race-neutral alternatives for achieving racial diversity at universities. These plans were often a reaction to the decline in minority acceptance and enrollment after race preferences had been prohibited in a jurisdiction. Texas, for example, enacted a so-called "Ten Percent Plan" in response to the Fifth Circuit's 2000 decision in Hopwood v. Texas striking down racial preferences. The plan guaranteed admission at one of the University of Texas campuses to anyone graduating in the top ten percent of his or her high school class. This plan was designed to enhance minority enrollment at the university level based on the assumption that residential communities in Texas, and therefore Texas's high schools, are largely racially segregated de facto. Some opponents of affirmative action support this type of race-neutral program, but critics point out that it reinforces segregation and argue that admission of minorities in the top 10% of their classes reduces the number of spots available to students from other schools who placed lower relative to their classes but may have had superior overall records of achievement. Other jurisdictions have experimented with increasing the use of socioeconomic disadvantage as a basis for preference in admissions on the assumption that it would have the by-product of increasing racial diversity in admissions. For example, the University of California law schools tried class-based affirmative action after, first, the state Regents, and later, a state constitutional amendment passed by initiative forbade race preferences in public institutions. See Sander, "Experimenting with Class-Based Affirmative Action," 47 J. Legal Educ. 472, 484 (1997); Malamud, "A Response to Professor Sander," 47 J. Legal Educ. 504 (1997).

Does the Court imply in Grutter and Gratz that such a facially neutral program would be constitutional? Even if there were direct evidence that it was intended as a partial substitute for affirmative action? Why would such a facially neutral program be considered less constitutionally suspect than a race-conscious one if it is conceded that it is racially motivated? Isn't this at odds with the Court's decisions in Washington v. Davis and Arlington Heights, which stressed that the Court will look to race-based purpose as the touchstone of equal protection scrutiny? For arguments suggesting that such race-neutral alternatives should not trigger strict scrutiny, see Forde-Mazrui, "The Constitutional Implications of Race-Neutral Affirmative Action," 88 Geo. L.J. 2331 (2000); Sullivan, "After Affirmative Action," 59 Ohio St. L.J. 1039 (1998) (concluding that race-conscious programs remain more transparent and efficient).

6. ***The role of amicus briefs.*** Over one hundred amicus briefs were filed in support of the parties in both Grutter and Gratz. In the Court's opinions, a surprising amount of attention was paid to amicus briefs, especially the arguments of a group of retired military officers and of several major corporations who argued that the Court should find a compelling interest in maintaining racial preferences. In one amicus brief, for example, a group of well-known retired senior military officers, including General Wesley Clark and former Secretary of Defense William Cohen, stated that "a highly qualified, racially diverse officer corps educated and trained to command our nation's racially diverse enlisted ranks is essential to the military's ability to fulfill its principal mission to provide national security. The primary sources for the nation's officer corps are the service academies and the ROTC, the latter comprised of students already admitted to participating colleges and universities. At present, the military cannot achieve an officer corps that is both highly qualified and racially diverse unless the service academies and the ROTC use limited race-conscious recruiting and admissions policies." The military officials pointed to the Vietnam era and the undermining effects of a racial hierarchy on the military: "In the 1960s and 1970s, while integration increased the percentage of African Americans in the enlisted ranks, the percentage of minority officers remained extremely low, and perceptions of discrimination were pervasive. This deficiency in the officer corps and the discrimination perceived to be its cause led to low morale and heightened racial tension." Therefore, they concluded, "the government's compelling interest in promoting racial diversity in higher education is buttressed by its compelling national security interest in a cohesive military."

Is the Court justified in comparing access to leadership positions in the military to access to leadership positions in civilian society? Consider the view that "the military service academies and officer training programs are unique gate-keeping institutions insofar as they are a sufficient condition for direct entry into leadership of an important public institution—the officer corps of the nation's armed forces. [No] civilian institution of higher learning, however prestigious, can claim to be a true gate-keeper [in this sense]. There is no such thing as a State Governors' School, a U.S. Congress academy, a federal judge academy, or a corporate chief executive officer (CEO) academy, to which anyone with qualifications can apply and acceptance to which guarantees a gubernatorial mansion, a Senate or House seat, a federal judgeship, or a CEO job upon graduation." Lee, note 1 above.

American corporations expressed views similar to those in the military brief. An amicus brief filed by sixty-five of the nation's leading corporations, ranging from American Express to Xerox, argued that "[t]he existence of racial and ethnic diversity in institutions of higher education is vital to amici's efforts to hire and maintain a diverse workforce, and to employ individuals of all backgrounds who have been educated and trained in a diverse environment. [Such] a workforce is important to amici's continued success in the global marketplace. [First,] a diverse group of individuals educated in a cross-cultural environment has the ability to facilitate unique and creative approaches to problem-solving arising from the integration of different perspectives. Second, such individuals are better able to develop products and services that appeal to a variety of consumers and to market offerings in ways that appeal to those consumers. Third, a racially diverse group of managers with cross-cultural experience is better able to work with business partners, employees, and clientele in the United States and around the world. Fourth, individuals who have been educated in a diverse setting are likely to contribute to a positive work environment, by decreasing incidents of discrimination and stereotyping." General Motors, in an amicus brief it filed on its own, further explained how a diverse workforce enhances profitability: "Racial minorities in the United States presently wield an impressive $600 billion in annual purchasing power. Moreover, with the global expansion of many businesses and the advent of internet shopping, the customer bases of many businesses now include people from many races and diverse cultures around the world. Having high-level employees who possess cross-cultural competence is essential for a business to profit from these vast market opportunities." "Instead of finding that the consideration of diversity leads to racial tension and stigmatization," General Motors concluded, "businesses have discovered just the opposite: valuing diversity has helped their bottom line."

7. ***Education vs. hiring and procurement.*** Consider the Court's different approaches in upholding race preferences in Grutter while invalidating them in Croson and Adarand. The Court in Grutter proved that its admonition in Adarand was not just empty words—the application of strict scrutiny does not necessarily mean "fatal in fact." But why does it seem to be less "fatal" in the education context than in the hiring and procurement contexts analyzed in Croson and Adarand? Some observers do not believe the Court adequately explained the difference: "Justice O'Connor structures her argument [in Grutter] so that preparation for the world beyond graduation has the constitutional protection of being a subset of academic freedom. [But] if affirmative action in the university is constitutional because it prepares students to become military officers, public servants, members of the bar, and civic leaders, why is not affirmative action constitutional in commissioning army officers, appointing public servants, and so forth?" Greenberg, note 2 above.

Is the Court assuming that once affirmative action enhances the opportunities available to minority applicants at the university level, the playing field is therefore level in the post-university world? Is it assuming that education and contracting reflect different structural values? Consider the view that "[i]nherent in the concept of diversity-based affirmative action is a recognition of the positive educational value of race and life experience. This differs dramatically from contracting cases involving guardrails and urinals, where affirmative action has no such theory of value." Amar & Katyal, "Bakke's Fate," 43 UCLA L. Rev. 1745 (1996).

Or is the Court giving special deference to educational institutions that it does not give to employers and contractors because the university enjoys academic freedom that other institutions in society do not? Does the Court implicitly "trust" educators to use affirmative action wisely and fairly in a way that it does not trust others? In other contexts, the Court gives special deference to university educators in allowing them to define and implement their educational mission. For example, in Board of Regents of the University of Wisconsin System v. Southworth, below, p. 1445 (2000), the Court analyzed the constitutionality under the First Amendment of a mandatory "activities fee" charged to the students by the university to promote extracurricular activities. Students who objected to some of the groups that the fee was being used to fund claimed that the University must grant them the choice not to fund such groups, as they were offensive to their personal beliefs. The Court upheld the fee, however, giving great deference to the University's determination of its own educational mission: "[The] University may determine that its mission is well served if students have the means to engage in dynamic discussions of philosophical, religious, scientific, social, and political subjects in their extracurricular campus life outside the lecture hall. If the University reaches this conclusion, it is entitled to impose a mandatory fee to sustain an open dialogue to these ends." Is composition of a student body similarly a core aspect of such academic freedom?

Must a university's "mission" be clearly defined prior to litigation in order to receive deference from the Court, or is post hoc rationalization permissible once litigation has begun? In Grutter and Gratz, the Court seems to ascribe to universities a "mission" of training their students for leadership roles in American civic society, despite the fact that many universities do not include such a goal in their mission statements. Does it matter whether such a goal is included explicitly in a university's mission statement? Compare, for example, the University of Michigan's mission statement ("The mission of the University of Michigan is to serve the people of Michigan and the world through preeminence in creating, communicating, preserving and applying knowledge, art, and academic values, and in developing leaders and citizens who will challenge the present and enrich the future.") with the mission statement of Brown University ("The mission of Brown University is to serve the community, the nation, and the world by discovering, communicating, and preserving knowledge and understanding in a spirit of free inquiry, and by educating and preparing students to discharge the offices of life with usefulness and reputation."). What if a university has no predefined "mission" at all?

8. ***Challenges to race-based admissions preferences after Grutter.*** Though Justice O'Connor predicted in Grutter that racial preferences in university admissions might no longer be necessary in 25 years, the Court granted review a mere 9 years after the decision in Grutter in a challenge to race-conscious aspects of the affirmative action admissions policy of the University of Texas at Austin. In particular, Texas had previously adopted a "Ten Percent Plan" that increased the racial diversity of its public university classes by admitting for a portion of each class the top ten percent of graduates from every Texas high school. In practical operation, the effects of residential racial segregation meant that the top ten percent of many schools were mostly minority students. In **Fisher v. University of Texas (Fisher I)**, 570 U.S. 297 (2013), Justice KENNEDY wrote an opinion for the Court, joined by Chief Justice Roberts and Justices Scalia, Thomas, Breyer, Alito and Sotomayor, declining to strike down the use of race preferences in higher education admissions under the regime established in Grutter and Gratz but remanding for closer analysis of a Texas plan for its narrow tailoring to the goal of diversity.

On remand, the Fifth Circuit (2–1) upheld the University of Texas's affirmative action plan, without sending the case to the district court for further fact-finding. Fisher appealed.

Fisher v. University of Texas at Austin et al.

576 U.S. ___, 136 S. Ct. 2198, 195 L. Ed. 2d 511 (2016).

■ JUSTICE KENNEDY delivered the opinion of the Court.

The Court is asked once again to consider whether the race-conscious admissions program at the University of Texas is lawful under the Equal Protection Clause. [Although] the University's new admissions policy was a direct result of Grutter, it is not identical to the policy this Court approved in that case. Instead, consistent with the State's legislative directive, the University continues to fill a significant majority of its class through the Top Ten Percent Plan (or Plan). Today, up to 75 percent of the places in the freshman class are filled through the Plan. As a practical matter, this 75 percent cap, which has now been fixed by statute, means that, while the Plan continues to be referenced as a "Top Ten Percent Plan," a student actually needs to finish in the top seven or eight percent of his or her class in order to be admitted under this category.

The University did adopt an approach similar to the one in *Grutter* for the remaining 25 percent or so of the incoming class. This portion of the class continues to be admitted based on a combination of their AI and PAI scores. Now, however, race is given weight as a sub-factor within the Personal Achievement Index.

[Therefore], although admissions officers can consider race as a positive feature of a minority student's application, there is no dispute that race is but a "factor of a factor of a factor" in the holistic-review calculus.

[The] University's program is *sui generis*. Unlike other approaches to college admissions considered by this Court, it combines holistic review with a percentage plan. This approach gave rise to an unusual consequence in this case: The component of the University's admissions policy that had the largest impact on petitioner's chances of admission was not the school's consideration of race under its holistic-review process but rather the Top Ten Percent Plan. Because petitioner did not graduate in the top 10 percent of her high school class, she was categorically ineligible for more than three-fourths of the slots in the incoming freshman class. It seems quite plausible, then, to think that petitioner would have had a better chance of being admitted to the University if the school used race-conscious holistic review to select its entire incoming class, as was the case in Grutter.

Despite the Top Ten Percent Plan's outsized effect on petitioner's chances of admission, she has not challenged it. For that reason, throughout this litigation, the Top Ten Percent Plan has been taken, somewhat artificially, as a given premise.

Petitioner's acceptance of the Top Ten Percent Plan complicates this Court's review. In particular, it has led to a record that is almost devoid of information about the students who secured admission to the University through the Plan. The Court thus cannot know how students admitted solely based on their class rank differ in their contribution to diversity from students admitted through holistic review.

[The] fact that this case has been litigated on a somewhat artificial basis, furthermore, may limit its value for prospective guidance. The Texas Legislature, in enacting the Top Ten Percent Plan, cannot much be criticized, for it was responding to Hopwood, which at the time was binding law in the State of Texas. That legislative response, in turn, circumscribed the University's discretion in crafting its admissions policy.

[That] does not diminish, however, the University's continuing obligation to satisfy the burden of strict scrutiny in light of changing circumstances. The University engages in periodic reassessment of the constitutionality, and efficacy, of its admissions program. Going forward, that assessment must be undertaken in light of the experience the school has accumulated and the data it has gathered since the adoption of its admissions plan.

As the University examines this data, it should remain mindful that diversity takes many forms. Formalistic racial classifications may sometimes fail to capture diversity in all of its dimensions and, when used in a divisive manner, could undermine the educational benefits the University values. Through regular evaluation of data and consideration of student experience, the University must tailor its approach in light of changing circumstances, ensuring that race plays no greater role than is necessary to meet its compelling interest. The University's examination of the data it has acquired in the years since petitioner's application, for these reasons, must proceed with full respect for the constraints imposed by the Equal Protection Clause. The type of data collected, and the manner in which it is considered, will have a significant bearing on how the University must shape its admissions policy to satisfy strict scrutiny in the years to come.

[As] this Court's cases have made clear, however, the compelling interest that justifies consideration of race in college admissions is not an interest in enrolling a certain number of minority students. Rather, a university may institute a race-conscious admissions program as a means of obtaining "the educational benefits that flow from student body diversity." Fisher I, see also Grutter. As this Court has said, enrolling a diverse student body "promotes cross-racial understanding, helps to break down racial stereotypes, and enables students to better understand persons of different races." Id. Equally important, "student body diversity promotes learning outcomes, and better prepares students for an increasingly diverse workforce and society." *Id.*

Increasing minority enrollment may be instrumental to these educational benefits, but it is not [a] goal that can or should be reduced to pure numbers. Indeed, since the University is prohibited from seeking a particular number or quota of minority students, it cannot be faulted for failing to specify the particular level of minority enrollment at which it believes the educational benefits of diversity will be obtained.

On the other hand, asserting an interest in the educational benefits of diversity writ large is insufficient. A university's goals cannot be elusory or amorphous—they must be sufficiently measurable to permit judicial scrutiny of the policies adopted to reach them.

The record reveals that in first setting forth its current admissions policy, the University articulated concrete and precise goals. [The]

University identifies the educational values it seeks to realize through its admissions process: the destruction of stereotypes, the " 'promot[ion of] cross-racial understanding,' " the preparation of a student body " 'for an increasingly diverse workforce and society,' " and the " 'cultivat[ion of] a set of leaders with legitimacy in the eyes of the citizenry.' " Later in the proposal, the University explains that it strives to provide an "academic environment" that offers a "robust exchange of ideas, exposure to differing cultures, preparation for the challenges of an increasingly diverse workforce, and acquisition of competencies required of future leaders." All of these objectives, as a general matter, mirror the "compelling interest" this Court has approved in its prior cases.

The University has provided in addition a "reasoned, principled explanation" for its decision to pursue these goals. The University's 39-page proposal was written following a year-long study, which concluded that "[t]he use of race-neutral policies and programs ha[d] not been successful" in "provid[ing] an educational setting that fosters cross-racial understanding, provid[ing] enlightened discussion and learning, [or] prepar[ing] students to function in an increasingly diverse workforce and society."

[A] university bears a heavy burden in showing that it had not obtained the educational benefits of diversity before it turned to a race-conscious plan. The record reveals, however, that, at the time of petitioner's application, the University could not be faulted on this score. [The] demographic data the University has submitted show consistent stagnation in terms of the percentage of minority students enrolling at the University from 1996 to 2002. In 1996, for example, 266 African-American freshmen enrolled, a total that constituted 4.1 percent of the incoming class. In 2003, the year Grutter was decided, 267 African-American students enrolled—again, 4.1 percent of the incoming class. The numbers for Hispanic and Asian-American students tell a similar story. Although demographics alone are by no means dispositive, they do have some value as a gauge of the University's ability to enroll students who can offer underrepresented perspectives.

In addition to this broad demographic data, the University put forward evidence that minority students admitted under the Hopwood regime experienced feelings of loneliness and isolation.

This anecdotal evidence is, in turn, bolstered by further, more nuanced quantitative data. In 2002, 52 percent of undergraduate classes with at least five students had no African-American students enrolled in them, and 27 percent had only one African-American student. In other words, only 21 percent of undergraduate classes with five or more students in them had more than one African-American student enrolled. Twelve percent of these classes had no Hispanic students, as compared to 10 percent in 1996.

[Petitioner] argues that considering race was not necessary because such consideration has had only a " 'minimal impact' in advancing the [University's] compelling interest." [It] is not a failure of narrow tailoring for the impact of racial consideration to be minor. The fact that race consciousness played a role in only a small portion of admissions decisions should be a hallmark of narrow tailoring, not evidence of unconstitutionality.

[Petitioner] suggests that the University could intensify its outreach efforts to African-American and Hispanic applicants. But the University submitted extensive evidence of the many ways in which it already had intensified its outreach efforts to those students. The University has created three new scholarship programs, opened new regional admissions centers, increased its recruitment budget by half-a-million dollars, and organized over 1,000 recruitment events. Perhaps more significantly, in the wake of Hopwood, the University spent seven years attempting to achieve its compelling interest using race-neutral holistic review. None of these efforts succeeded, and petitioner fails to offer any meaningful way in which the University could have improved upon them at the time of her application.

Petitioner also suggests altering the weight given to academic and socioeconomic factors in the University's admissions calculus. This proposal ignores the fact that the University tried, and failed, to increase diversity through enhanced consideration of socioeconomic and other factors. And it further ignores this Court's precedent making clear that the Equal Protection Clause does not force universities to choose between a diverse student body and a reputation for academic excellence. Grutter.

Petitioner's final suggestion is to uncap the Top Ten Percent Plan, and admit more—if not all—the University's students through a percentage plan. As an initial matter, petitioner overlooks the fact that the Top Ten Percent Plan, though facially neutral, cannot be understood apart from its basic purpose, which is to boost minority enrollment.

[Even] if, as a matter of raw numbers, minority enrollment would increase under such a regime, petitioner would be hard-pressed to find convincing support for the proposition that college admissions would be improved if they were a function of class rank alone. That approach would sacrifice all other aspects of diversity in pursuit of enrolling a higher number of minority students. [Class] rank is a single metric, and like any single metric, it will capture certain types of people and miss others. This does not imply that students admitted through holistic review are necessarily more capable or more desirable than those admitted through the Top Ten Percent Plan. It merely reflects the fact that privileging one characteristic above all others does not lead to a diverse student body. Indeed, to compel universities to admit students based on class rank alone is in deep tension with the goal of educational diversity as this Court's cases have defined it.

■ JUSTICE ALITO, with whom THE CHIEF JUSTICE and JUSTICE THOMAS join, dissenting.

Something strange has happened since our prior decision in this case. In that decision, we held that strict scrutiny requires the University of Texas at Austin (UT or University) to show that its use of race and ethnicity in making admissions decisions serves compelling interests and that its plan is narrowly tailored to achieve those ends. [On] remand, UT failed to do what our prior decision demanded. The University has still not identified with any degree of specificity the interests that its use of race and ethnicity is supposed to serve. Its primary argument is that merely invoking "the educational benefits of diversity" is sufficient and that it need not identify any metric that would allow a court to determine whether its plan is needed to serve, or is actually serving, those interests. This is nothing less than the plea for deference that we emphatically rejected in our prior decision. Today, however, the Court inexplicably grants that request.

[It] is important to understand what is and what is not at stake in this case. *What is not at stake* is whether UT or any other university may adopt an admissions plan that results in a student body with a broad representation of students from all racial and ethnic groups.

[*What is at stake*] is whether university administrators may justify systematic racial discrimination simply by asserting that such discrimination is necessary to achieve "the educational benefits of diversity," without explaining—much less proving—why the discrimination is needed or how the discriminatory plan is well crafted to serve its objectives. Even though UT has never provided any coherent explanation for its asserted need to discriminate on the basis of race, and even though UT's position relies on a series of unsupported and noxious racial assumptions, the majority concludes that UT has met its heavy burden. This conclusion is remarkable—and remarkably wrong.

---

9. ***Asian-Americans and the future of affirmative action.*** In his Fisher II dissent, Justice ALITO highlighted the alleged harms that he believed Texas's affirmative action policy imposed on Asian-American students. Specifically, Justice Alito charged the Texas plan with discriminating "*against* Asian-American students," accused the majority of "act[ing] almost as if Asian-American students do not exist," and argued that Texas relied on "crude, overly simplistic racial and ethnic categories" at the expense of recognizing intra-Asian-American diversity.

Since Fisher II, Asian-American plaintiffs brought a suit, **Students for Fair Admissions, Inc. v. President & Fellows of Harvard College**, Case No. 1:2014cv14176, alleging that Harvard College's use of race in its admissions process violates the Equal Protection Clause and Title IX of the Civil Rights Act. Notably, the Harvard College admissions system at issue in this case is the direct descendant of the one that Justice Powell cited as an exemplar for constitutional, race-conscious admissions in Bakke.

As this casebook goes to press, the suit has undergone a bench trial in the District of Massachusetts, and the judgment has yet to be issued. Should the case or another like it ultimately reach the Supreme Court, and with Justice Kennedy now replaced by Justice Kavanaugh, what might that mean for the future of affirmative action in higher education?

10. ***Race-based preferences and the political process.*** In the aftermath of Gratz and Grutter, the State of Michigan by referendum adopted a constitutional amendment prohibiting the state from using race-conscious affirmative action. In **Schuette v. Coalition to Defend Affirmative Action**, 572 U.S. 291 (2014), a splintered Court held that the amendment did not violate equal protection. The relevant equal protection precedents were Hunter v. Erickson, 393 U.S. 385 (1969), in which the Court had struck down a voter initiative in Akron, Ohio overturning a municipal fair housing ordinance and requiring that any new fair housing ordinance be approved by referendum; and Washington v. Seattle, 458 U.S. 457 (1982), in which the Court struck down a statewide referendum reversing a mandatory desegregation busing plan enacted by the Seattle School Board. Hunter and Seattle had recognized an equal-protection right against differential access to the political process, prohibiting "plac[ing] special burdens on racial minorities within the governmental process" that "mak[e] it more difficult for certain . . . minorities than for other members of the community to achieve legislation that is in their interest." Seattle. Each case thus held that fair housing or desegregation advocates should not have to resort to referenda rather than ordinary legislation to achieve their goals. In

Schuette, the governing opinion distinguished but declined to overrule those decisions.

Justice KENNEDY wrote a plurality opinion joined by Chief Justice Roberts and Justice Alito. Distinguishing the precedents, the opinion said that "those cases were ones in which the political restriction in question was designed to be used, or was likely to be used, to encourage infliction of injury by reason of race. What is at stake here is not whether injury will be inflicted but whether government can be instructed not to follow a course that entails, first, the definition of racial categories and, second, the grant of favored status to persons in some racial categories and not others. The electorate's instruction to governmental entities not to embark upon the course of race-defined and race-based preferences was adopted, we must assume, because the voters deemed a preference system to be unwise, on account of what voters may deem its latent potential to become itself a source of the very resentments and hostilities based on race that this Nation seeks to put behind it. Whether those adverse results would follow is, and should be, the subject of debate. Voters might likewise consider, after debate and reflection, that programs designed to increase diversity—consistent with the Constitution—are a necessary part of progress to transcend the stigma of past racism. [There] is no authority in the Constitution of the United States or in this Court's precedents for the Judiciary to set aside Michigan laws that commit this policy determination to the voters."

Justice SCALIA, joined by Justice Thomas, concurred separately to say that Gratz and Grutter were wrongly decided: "It has come to this. Called upon to explore the jurisprudential twilight zone between two errant lines of precedent, we confront a frighteningly bizarre question: Does the Equal Protection Clause of the Fourteenth Amendment forbid what its text plainly requires? Needless to say (except that this case obliges us to say it), the question answers itself." Justice BREYER also concurred separately, expressing the view that "I continue to believe that the Constitution permits, though it does not require, the use of the kind of race-conscious programs that are now barred by the Michigan Constitution." Justice Breyer saw the issue as appropriate for democratic determination: "The Constitution allows local, state, and national communities to adopt narrowly tailored race-conscious programs designed to bring about greater inclusion and diversity. But the Constitution foresees the ballot box, not the courts, as the normal instrument for resolving differences and debates about the merits of these programs."

Justice SOTOMAYOR, joined by Justice Ginsburg, wrote a lengthy dissent. The case involved, she wrote, the "last chapter of discrimination: A majority of the Michigan electorate changed the basic rules of the political process in that State in a manner that uniquely disadvantaged racial minorities. [Hunter] and Seattle vindicated a principle that is as elementary to our equal protection jurisprudence as it is essential: The majority may not suppress the minority's right to participate on equal terms in the political process."

Justice Sotomayor then offered a substantive defense of why race should be taken into account: "My colleagues are of the view that we should leave race out of the picture entirely and let the voters sort it out. We have seen this reasoning before. It is a sentiment out of touch with reality, one not required by our Constitution, and one that has properly been rejected as 'not sufficient' to resolve cases of this nature. [Race] matters. Race matters in part because of the long history of racial minorities' being denied access to the political process. And although we have made great strides, voting discrimination still exists; no one doubts that. Race also matters because of persistent racial inequality in society—inequality that cannot be ignored and that has produced stark socioeconomic disparities. And race matters for reasons that really are only skin deep, that cannot be discussed any other way, and that cannot be wished away. Race matters to a young man's view of society when he spends his teenage years watching others tense up as he passes, no matter the neighborhood where he grew up. Race matters to a young woman's sense of self when she states her hometown, and then is pressed, 'No, where are you really from?', regardless of how many generations her family has been in the country. Race matters to a young person addressed by a stranger in a foreign language, which he does not understand because only English was spoken at home. Race matters because of the slights, the snickers, the silent judgments that reinforce that most crippling of thoughts: 'I do not belong here.'

"In my colleagues' view, examining the racial impact of legislation only perpetuates racial discrimination. This refusal to accept the stark reality that race matters is regrettable. The way to stop discrimination on the basis of race is to speak openly and candidly on the subject of race, and to apply the Constitution with eyes open to the unfortunate effects of centuries of racial discrimination. As members of the judiciary tasked with intervening to carry out the guarantee of equal protection, we ought not sit back and wish away, rather than confront, the racial inequality that exists in our society. It is this view that works harm, by perpetuating the facile notion that what makes race matter is acknowledging the simple truth that race does matter."

Justice Kennedy distinguished Schuette from Hunter and Seattle by asserting that the Michigan referendum was not designed "to encourage infliction of injury by reason of race." In other words, because the referendum in Schuette sought to preclude certain forms of racial categorization and preference, it did not fall under the political process precedents. Is that distinction convincing? Recall Carolene Products footnote four; Ely, Democracy and Distrust (1980). Consider also Romer v. Evans (p. 556), in which Justice Kennedy wrote for the Court invalidating an amendment to the Colorado Constitution that excluded sexual orientation as a ground for state antidiscrimination prohibitions. Can Schuette and Romer be reconciled?

RACIAL DIVERSITY IN K–12 PUBLIC EDUCATION

Do the principles of Grutter and Gratz control when a public school district uses racial identity as one basis on which to assign students to schools within a district? Does diversity constitute a compelling interest in this context? Even if it does, are there more race-neutral means for achieving it? Does the K–12 context differ from the university context because all students are included and school assignments are a zero-sum game, as opposed to a selective process? These and related questions were raised in a pair of consolidated cases decided as the first major pronouncement by the new Roberts Court on issues of race and equal protection, with Chief Justice Roberts having succeeded Chief Justice Rehnquist and Justice Alito having succeeded Justice O'Connor, whose vote had pivotally determined the outcomes in Grutter and Gratz. The Court held that both Seattle's and Louisville's efforts at racial mixing of their K–12 school populations violated equal protection:

Parents Involved in Community Schools v. Seattle School District

551 U.S. 701, 127 S. Ct. 2738, 168 L. Ed. 2d 508 (2007).

▪ CHIEF JUSTICE ROBERTS announced the judgment of the Court, and delivered the opinion of the Court with respect to Parts I, II, III–A, and III–C, and an opinion with respect to Parts III–B and IV, in which JUSTICES SCALIA, THOMAS, and ALITO join.

The school districts in these cases voluntarily adopted student assignment plans that rely upon race to determine which public schools certain children may attend. The Seattle school district classifies children as white or nonwhite; the Jefferson County school district as black or "other." In Seattle, this racial classification is used to allocate slots in oversubscribed high schools. In Jefferson County, it is used to make certain elementary school assignments and to rule on transfer requests. In each case, the school district relies upon an individual student's race in assigning that student to a particular school, so that the racial balance at the school falls within a predetermined range based on the racial composition of the school district as a whole. Parents of students denied assignment to particular schools under these plans solely because of their race brought suit, contending that allocating children to different public schools on the basis of race violated the Fourteenth Amendment guarantee of equal protection. The Courts of Appeals below upheld the plans. We [reverse].

I. Both cases present the same underlying legal question—whether a public school that had not operated legally segregated schools or has been found to be unitary may choose to classify students by race and rely upon that classification in making school assignments. Although we examine the plans under the same legal framework, the specifics of the two plans, and the circumstances surrounding their adoption, are in some respects quite different.

Seattle School District operates 10 regular public high schools. In 1998, it adopted the plan at issue in this case for assigning students to these schools. The plan allows incoming ninth graders to choose from among any of the district's high schools, ranking however many schools they wish in order of preference. Some schools are more popular than others. If too many students list the same school as their first choice, the district employs a series of "tiebreakers" to determine who will fill the open slots at the oversubscribed school. The first tiebreaker selects for admission students who have a sibling currently enrolled in the chosen school. The next tiebreaker depends upon the racial composition of the particular school and the race of the individual student. In the district's public schools approximately 41 percent of enrolled students are white; the remaining 59 percent, comprising all other racial groups, are classified by Seattle for assignment purposes as nonwhite. If an oversubscribed school is not within 10 percentage points of the district's overall white/nonwhite racial balance, it is what the district calls "integration positive," and the district employs a tiebreaker that selects for assignment students whose race "will serve to bring the school into balance." [Seattle] has never operated segregated schools—legally separate schools for students of different races—nor has it ever been subject to court-ordered desegregation.

[Jefferson] County Public Schools operates the public school system in metropolitan Louisville, Kentucky. In 1973 a federal court found that Jefferson County had maintained a segregated school system, and in 1975 the District Court entered a desegregation decree. Jefferson County operated under this decree until 2000, when the District Court dissolved the decree after finding that the district had achieved unitary status by eliminating "to the greatest extent practicable" the vestiges of its prior policy of segregation. In 2001, after the decree had been dissolved, Jefferson County adopted the voluntary student assignment plan at issue in this case. Approximately 34 percent of the district's 97,000 students are black; most of the remaining 66 percent are white. The plan requires all nonmagnet schools to maintain a minimum black enrollment of 15 percent, and a maximum black enrollment of 50 percent.

III. A. [It] is well established that when the government distributes burdens or benefits on the basis of individual racial classifications, that action is reviewed under strict scrutiny. [In] order to satisfy this searching standard of review, the school districts must demonstrate that the use of individual racial classifications in the assignment plans here under review is "narrowly tailored" to achieve a "compelling" government interest. [Our] prior cases, in evaluating the use of racial classifications in the school context, have recognized two interests that qualify as compelling. The first is the compelling interest of remedying the effects of past intentional discrimination. Yet the Seattle public schools have not shown that they were ever segregated by law, and were not subject to court-ordered desegregation decrees. The Jefferson County public schools were previously segregated by law and were subject to a desegregation decree [but it has since] achieved "unitary" status.

[The] second government interest we have recognized as compelling for purposes of strict scrutiny is the interest in diversity in higher education upheld in Grutter. The entire gist of the analysis in Grutter was that the admissions program at issue there focused on each applicant as an individual, and not simply as a member of a particular racial group. [The] point of the narrow tailoring analysis in which the Grutter Court engaged was to ensure that the use of racial classifications was indeed part of a broader assessment of diversity, and not simply an effort to achieve racial balance, which the Court explained would be "patently unconstitutional." In the present cases, by contrast, race is not considered as part of a broader effort to achieve "exposure to widely diverse people, cultures, ideas, and viewpoints"; race, for some students, is determinative standing alone. The districts argue that other factors, such as student preferences, affect assignment decisions under their plans, but under each plan when race comes into play, it is decisive by itself. It is not simply one factor weighed with others in reaching a decision, as in Grutter; it is *the* factor. Like the University of Michigan undergraduate plan struck down in Gratz, the plans here "do not provide for a meaningful individualized review of applicants" but instead rely on racial classifications in a "nonindividualized, mechanical" way. [In] upholding the admissions plan in Grutter, [this] Court relied upon considerations unique to institutions of higher education. The present cases are not governed by Grutter.

B. Perhaps recognizing that reliance on Grutter cannot sustain their plans, both school districts assert additional interests, distinct from the interest upheld in Grutter, to justify their race-based assignments. [Seattle] contends that its use of race helps to reduce racial concentration in schools and to ensure that racially concentrated housing patterns do not prevent nonwhite students from having access to the most desirable schools. Jefferson County has articulated a similar goal, phrasing its interest in terms of educating its students "in a racially integrated environment." Each school district argues that educational and broader socialization benefits flow from a racially diverse learning environment, and each contends that because the diversity they seek is racial diversity—not the broader diversity at issue in Grutter—it makes sense to promote that interest directly by relying on race alone.

The parties and their amici dispute whether racial diversity in schools in fact has a marked impact on test scores and other objective yardsticks or achieves intangible socialization benefits. The debate is not one we need to resolve, however, because it is clear that the racial classifications employed by the districts are not narrowly tailored to the goal of achieving the educational and social benefits asserted to flow from racial diversity. In design and operation, the plans are directed only to racial balance, pure and simple, an objective this Court has repeatedly condemned as illegitimate.

The plans are tied to each district's specific racial demographics, rather than to any pedagogic concept of the level of diversity needed to obtain the asserted educational benefits. [The] districts offer no evidence that the level of racial diversity necessary to achieve the asserted educational benefits happens to coincide with the racial demographics of the respective school districts. [Seattle did not] demonstrate in any way how the educational and social benefits of racial diversity or avoidance of racial isolation are more likely to be achieved at a school that is 50 percent white and 50 percent Asian-American, which would qualify as diverse under Seattle's plan, than at a school that is 30 percent Asian-American, 25 percent African-American, 25 percent Latino, and 20 percent white, which under Seattle's definition would be racially concentrated.

[This] working backward to achieve a particular type of racial balance, rather than working forward from some demonstration of the level of diversity that provides the purported benefits, is a fatal flaw under our existing precedent. [The] principle that racial balancing is not permitted is one of substance, not semantics. Racial balancing is not transformed from "patently unconstitutional" to a compelling state interest simply by relabeling it "racial diversity." While the school districts use various verbal formulations to describe the interest they seek to promote—racial diversity, avoidance of racial isolation, racial integration—they offer no definition of the interest that suggests it differs from racial balance.

C. The districts assert, as they must, that the way in which they have employed individual racial classifications is necessary to achieve their stated ends. The minimal effect these classifications have on student assignments, however, suggests that other means would be effective. Seattle's racial tiebreaker results, in the end, only in shifting a small number of students between schools. [Similarly,] Jefferson County's use of racial classifications has only a minimal effect on the assignment of students. [While] we do not suggest that *greater* use of race would be preferable, the minimal impact of the districts' racial classifications on school enrollment casts doubt on the necessity of using racial classifications. [The] districts have also failed to show that they considered methods other than explicit racial classifications to achieve their stated goals. Narrow tailoring requires "serious, good faith consideration of workable race-neutral alternatives."

IV. [Justice Breyer's dissent] asserts that these cases are controlled by Grutter, claiming that the existence of a compelling interest in these cases "follows a fortiori" from Grutter, and accusing us of tacitly overruling that case. The dissent overreads Grutter, however. [The] Court was exceedingly careful in describing the interest furthered in Grutter as "not an interest in simple ethnic diversity" but rather a "far broader array of qualifications and characteristics" in which race was but a single element. We take the Grutter Court at its word.

[The] parties and their amici debate which side is more faithful to the heritage of Brown, but the position of the plaintiffs in Brown was spelled out in their brief and could not have been clearer: "The Fourteenth Amendment prevents states from according differential treatment to American children on the basis of their color or race." What do the racial classifications at issue here do, if not accord differential treatment on the basis of race? As counsel who appeared before this Court for the plaintiffs in Brown put it: "We have one fundamental contention which we will seek to develop in the course of this argument, and that contention is that no State has any authority under the equal-protection clause of the Fourteenth Amendment to use race as a factor in affording educational opportunities among its citizens." There is no ambiguity in that statement. And it was that position that prevailed in this Court. [What] do the racial classifications do in these cases, if not determine admission to a public school on a racial basis? [Before] Brown, schoolchildren were told where they could and could not go to school based on the color of their skin. The school districts in these cases have not carried the heavy burden of demonstrating that we should allow this once again—even for very different reasons. For schools that never segregated on the basis of race, such as Seattle, or that have removed the vestiges of past segregation, such as Jefferson County, the way "to achieve a system of determining admission to the public schools on a nonracial basis," is to stop assigning students on a racial basis. The way to stop discrimination on the basis of race is to stop discriminating on the basis of race.

■ JUSTICE THOMAS, concurring.

[The dissent] claims that the school districts are threatened with resegregation and that they will succumb to that threat if these plans are declared unconstitutional. It also argues that these plans can be justified as part of the school boards' attempts to "eradicate earlier school segregation." Contrary to the dissent's rhetoric, neither of these school districts is threatened with resegregation, and neither is constitutionally compelled or permitted to undertake race-based remediation. Racial imbalance is not segregation. [In] the context of public schooling, segregation is the deliberate operation of a school system to "carry out a governmental policy to separate pupils in schools solely on the basis of race." Racial imbalance is the failure of a school district's individual schools to match or approximate the demographic makeup of the student population at large. [Although] presently observed racial imbalance might result from past *de jure* segregation, racial imbalance can also result from any number of innocent private decisions, including voluntary housing choices. Because racial imbalance is not inevitably linked to unconstitutional segregation, it is not unconstitutional in and of itself. [Although] there is arguably a danger of racial imbalance in schools in Seattle and Louisville, there is no danger of resegregation. No one contends that Seattle has established or that Louisville has reestablished a dual school system that separates students on the basis of race.

[It] is far from apparent that coerced racial mixing has any educational benefits, much less that integration is necessary to black achievement. [Even] after Brown, some schools with predominantly black enrollments have achieved outstanding educational results. There is also evidence that black students attending historically black colleges achieve better academic results than those attending predominantly white colleges. [Given] this tenuous relationship between forced racial mixing and improved educational results for black children, the dissent cannot plausibly maintain that an educational element supports the integration interest, let alone makes it compelling.

[Most] of the dissent's criticisms of today's result can be traced to its rejection of the color-blind Constitution. [But] I am quite comfortable in the company I keep. My view of the Constitution is Justice Harlan's view in Plessy: "Our Constitution is color-blind, and neither knows nor tolerates classes among citizens." And my view was the rallying cry for the lawyers who litigated Brown ("That the Constitution is color blind is our dedicated belief"). [What] was wrong in 1954 cannot be right today.

■ JUSTICE KENNEDY, concurring in part and concurring in the judgment.

[Parts] of the opinion by the Chief Justice imply an all-too-unyielding insistence that race cannot be a factor in instances when, in my view, it may be taken into account. The plurality opinion is too dismissive of the legitimate interest government has in ensuring all people have equal opportunity regardless of their race. The plurality's postulate that "the way to stop discrimination on the basis of race is to stop discriminating on the basis of race," is not sufficient to decide these cases. Fifty years of experience since Brown should teach us that the problem before us defies so easy a solution. School districts can seek to reach Brown's objective of equal educational opportunity. The plurality opinion is at least open to the interpretation that the Constitution requires school districts to ignore the problem of *de facto* resegregation in schooling. I cannot endorse that conclusion. To the extent the plurality opinion suggests the Constitution mandates that state and local school authorities must accept the status quo of racial isolation in schools, it is, in my view, profoundly mistaken.

[In] the administration of public schools by the state and local authorities it is permissible to consider the racial makeup of schools and to adopt general policies to encourage a diverse student body, one aspect of which is its racial composition.

[School] boards may pursue the goal of bringing together students of diverse backgrounds and races through other means, including strategic site selection of new schools; drawing attendance zones with general recognition of the demographics of neighborhoods; allocating resources for special programs; recruiting students and faculty in a targeted fashion; and tracking enrollments, performance, and other statistics by race. These mechanisms are race conscious but do not lead to different treatment based on a classification that tells each student he or she is to be defined by race, so it is unlikely any of them would demand strict scrutiny to be found permissible. Executive and legislative branches, which for generations now have considered these types of policies and procedures, should be permitted to employ them with candor and with confidence that a constitutional violation does not occur whenever a decisionmaker considers the impact a given approach might have on students of different races. Assigning to each student a personal designation according to a crude system of individual racial classifications is quite a different matter; and the legal analysis changes accordingly.

[In] the cases before us it is noteworthy that the number of students whose assignment depends on express racial classifications is limited. I join Part III–C of the Court's opinion because I agree that in the context of these plans, the small number of assignments affected suggests that the schools could have achieved their stated ends through different means. These include the facially race-neutral means set forth above or, if necessary, a more nuanced, individual evaluation of school needs and student characteristics that might include race as a component. The latter approach would be informed by Grutter, though of course the criteria relevant to student placement would differ based on the age of the students, the needs of the parents, and the role of the schools.

[If] it is legitimate for school authorities to work to avoid racial isolation in their schools, must they do so only by indirection and general policies? Does the Constitution mandate this inefficient result? Why may the authorities not recognize the problem in candid fashion and solve it altogether through resort to direct assignments based on student racial classifications? So, the argument proceeds, if race is the problem, then perhaps race is the solution.

The argument ignores the dangers presented by individual classifications, dangers that are not as pressing when the same ends are achieved by more indirect means. When the government classifies an individual by race, it must first define what it means to be of a race. Who exactly is white and who is nonwhite? To be forced to live under a state-mandated racial label is inconsistent with the dignity of individuals in our society. And it is a label that an individual is powerless to change. Governmental classifications that command people to march in different directions based on racial typologies can cause a new divisiveness. The practice can lead to corrosive discourse, where race serves not as an element of our diverse heritage but instead as a bargaining chip in the political process. On the other hand race-conscious measures that do not rely on differential treatment based on individual classifications present these problems to a lesser degree.

[This] Nation has a moral and ethical obligation to fulfill its historic commitment to creating an integrated society that ensures equal opportunity for all of its children. A compelling interest exists in avoiding racial isolation, an interest that a school district, in its discretion and expertise, may choose to pursue. Likewise, a district may consider it a compelling interest to achieve a diverse student population. Race may be one component of that diversity, but other demographic factors, plus special talents and needs, should also be considered. What the government is not permitted to do, absent a showing of necessity not made here, is to classify every student on the basis of race and to assign each of them to schools based on that classification. Crude measures of this sort threaten to reduce children to racial chits valued and traded according to one school's supply and another's demand.

■ JUSTICE STEVENS, dissenting.

There is a cruel irony in the Chief Justice's reliance on our decision in Brown. [He] states: "Before Brown, schoolchildren were told where they could and could not go to school based on the color of their skin." This sentence reminds me of Anatole France's observation: "The majestic equality of the law, forbids rich and poor alike to sleep under bridges, to beg in the streets, and to steal their bread." The Chief Justice fails to note that it was only black schoolchildren who were so ordered; indeed, the history books do not tell stories of white children struggling to attend black schools. In this and other ways, the Chief Justice rewrites the history of one of this Court's most important decisions.

■ JUSTICE BREYER, with whom JUSTICES STEVENS, SOUTER, and GINSBURG join, dissenting.

These cases consider the longstanding efforts of two local school boards to integrate their public schools. The school board plans before us resemble many others adopted in the last 50 years by primary and secondary schools throughout the Nation. All of those plans represent local efforts to bring about the kind of racially integrated education that Brown long ago promised—efforts that this Court has repeatedly required, permitted, and encouraged local authorities to undertake. This Court has recognized that the public interests at stake in such cases are "compelling." We have approved of "narrowly tailored" plans that are no less race-conscious than the plans before us. And we have understood that the Constitution *permits* local communities to adopt desegregation plans even where it does not *require* them to do so.

[A] longstanding and unbroken line of legal authority tells us that the Equal Protection Clause permits local school boards to use race-conscious criteria to achieve positive race-related goals. Swann. [The principle] that the government may voluntarily adopt race-conscious measures to improve conditions of race even when it is not under a constitutional obligation to do so [has] been accepted by every branch of government and is rooted in the history of the Equal Protection Clause itself. [The] basic objective of those who wrote the Equal Protection Clause [was] forbidding practices that lead to racial exclusion. The Amendment sought to bring into American society as full members those whom the Nation had previously held in slavery. There is reason to believe that those who drafted an Amendment with this basic purpose in mind would have understood the legal and practical difference between the use of race-conscious criteria in defiance of that purpose, namely to keep the races apart, and the use of race-conscious criteria to further that purpose, namely to bring the races together.

[No] case—not Adarand, Gratz, Grutter, or any other—has ever held that the test of "strict scrutiny" means that all racial classifications—no matter whether they seek to include or exclude—*must* in practice be treated the same. [Rather,] they apply the strict scrutiny test in a manner that is "fatal in fact" only to racial classifications that harmfully *exclude;* they apply the test in a manner that is *not* fatal in fact to racial classifications that seek to *include*.

[Here,] the context is one in which school districts seek to advance or to maintain racial integration in primary and secondary schools. [This] context is *not* a context that involves the use of race to decide who will receive goods or services that are normally distributed on the basis of merit and which are in short supply. It is not one in which race-conscious limits stigmatize or exclude; the limits at issue do not pit the races against each other or otherwise significantly exacerbate racial tensions. They do not impose burdens unfairly upon members of one race alone but instead seek benefits for members of all races alike. The context here is one of racial limits that seek, not to keep the races apart, but to bring them together. In my view, this contextual approach to scrutiny is altogether fitting. I believe that the law requires application here of a standard of review that is not "strict" in the traditional sense of that word. [Apparently] Justice Kennedy also agrees that strict scrutiny would not apply in respect to certain "race-conscious" school board policies.

[The] interest at stake possesses three essential elements. First, there is a historical and remedial element: an interest in setting right the consequences of prior conditions of segregation. [Second,] there is an educational element: an interest in overcoming the adverse educational effects produced by and associated with highly segregated schools. Third, there is a democratic element: an interest in producing an educational environment that reflects the "pluralistic society" in which our children will live. It is an interest in helping our children learn to work and play together with children of different racial backgrounds. It is an interest in teaching children to engage in the kind of cooperation among Americans of all races that is necessary to make a land of three hundred million people one Nation. [In] light of this Court's conclusions in Grutter, the "compelling" nature of these interests in the context of primary and secondary public education follows here *a fortiori*.

[Several factors] lead me to conclude that the boards' use of race-conscious criteria in these plans passes even the strictest "tailoring" test. First, the race-conscious criteria at issue only help set the outer bounds of *broad* ranges. They constitute but one part of plans that depend primarily upon other, nonracial elements. To use race in this way is not to set a forbidden "quota." In fact, the defining feature of both plans is greater emphasis upon student choice. [Second,] broad-range limits on voluntary school choice plans are less burdensome, and [hence] *more narrowly tailored* than the race-conscious admission plans that this Court approved in Grutter. Here, race becomes a factor only in a fraction of students' non-merit-based assignments—not in large numbers of students' merit-based applications. Moreover, the effect of applying race-conscious criteria here affects potentially disadvantaged students *less severely,* not more severely, than the criteria at issue in Grutter. Disappointed students are not rejected from a State's flagship graduate program; they simply attend a different one of the district's many public schools. Third, [the] school boards' widespread consultation, their experimentation with numerous other plans, [make] clear that plans that are less explicitly race-based are unlikely to achieve the board's "compelling" objectives. [Giving] some degree of weight to a local school board's knowledge, expertise, and concerns in these particular matters is not inconsistent with rigorous judicial scrutiny. It simply recognizes that judges are not well suited to act as school administrators. [In] sum, the districts' race-conscious plans satisfy "strict scrutiny" and are therefore lawful.

THE MEANING AND IMPLICATIONS OF PARENTS INVOLVED

1. ***Parents Involved and the Court's interpretation of Brown.*** Chief Justice Roberts imputes to the lawyers who argued Brown v. Board an interpretation of the Constitution that bars any use of race to classify or differential treatment on the basis of race. Was that truly consistent with the Brown advocates' position? Consider the view that the Chief Justice committed a "contextual fallacy" because the Brown counsel he quoted (Robert Carter, later a district judge for the Southern District of New York) was arguing that "racial classifications were impermissible to *segregate* schools," but that did "not mean that he thought they could not be used to *integrate* schools." Goldstein, "Not Hearing History: A Critique of Chief Justice Roberts's Reinterpretation of Brown," 69 Ohio St. L.J. 791 (2008) (noting that "the 'feeling of inferiority' language in Brown only had meaning in 1954 when applied to black children"). See also Liu, "'History Will Be Heard': An Appraisal of the Seattle/Louisville Decision," 2 Harv. L. & Pol'y Rev. 53 (2008) (noting that Brown "nowhere used the term 'colorblind' ").

2. ***Judicial intervention in democratic decisionmaking.*** Note that Justice Breyer's dissent emphasizes the voluntary nature of the two cities' integration plans and argues that judicial restraint is appropriate out of respect for the democratic processes that generated them and the importance of local control over education. As one prominent federal judge noted, these arguments are typically associated with "conservative arguments against race-based decisionmaking," but in his view, they "fail ultimately to persuade" because, "[w]ithout the prospect of strict judicial scrutiny of race-based classifications, it is anything but certain that racial proportionality would not become more prevalent," and "racial allocation" would not "start rolling downhill." Wilkinson, "The Seattle and Louisville School Cases: There is No Other Way," 121 Harv. L. Rev. 158 (2007). Is this argument persuasive? Or are there political safeguards against such results even in the absence of strict judicial review?

RACE PREFERENCES IN ELECTORAL DISTRICTING

What latitude does equal protection permit government in using race as a factor in the composition of the population of electoral districts? District lines are drawn by state legislatures, under a constitutional requirement that federal districts be equipopulous under the principle of "one person, one vote." When populations shift, new lines must be drawn. Are such districts consistent with equal protection if drawn deliberately to achieve a certain level of racial minority voting population? May race be used in this context to get beyond race, as Justice Blackmun suggested in Bakke? Does such districting enable black majorities to vindicate their suppressed preferences to elect black representatives? Or does the use of race in districting invidiously entrench racial stereotyping in political representation?

In an early case addressing these questions, **United Jewish Organizations v. Carey**, 430 U.S. 144 (1977) (UJO), the Court was willing to apply deferential review to racial preferences in electoral districting. New York had redrawn districts in Brooklyn in order to maintain black representation in the state legislature, in an attempt to comply with the Voting Rights Act. The redistricting affected an area where about 30,000 Hasidic Jews lived. In order to create substantial nonwhite majorities in a few districts, New York's revision split the Hasidic community into several districts. The Hasidic Jewish residents challenged the redistricting as unconstitutional racial reapportionment under the 14th and 15th Amendments. In rejecting that challenge, Justice White's opinion (entirely joined by Justice Stevens and partly joined by Justices Brennan, Blackmun and Rehnquist) held that New York had done no more than the Attorney General was authorized to require under the Voting Rights Act.

In a portion of the opinion joined only by Justices Stevens and Rehnquist, Justice WHITE stated: "[W]hether or not the plan was authorized [by] the Voting Rights Act, New York was entitled to consider racial factors in redistricting under the Constitution." He noted that New York's plan "represented no racial slur or stigma with respect to whites or any other race." Although black representatives were more likely to be elected in the redrawn districts, "as long as whites in [Brooklyn], as a group, were provided with fair representation, we cannot conclude that there was a cognizable discrimination against whites." Chief Justice Burger's dissent concluded: "While petitioners may have no constitutional right to remain unified within a single political district, they do have [the] constitutional right not to be carved up so as to create a voting bloc composed of some other ethnic or racial group through [this] kind of racial [gerrymandering]."

After the decennial census of 1990, population shifts required many states to draw new state and congressional electoral district boundaries. The U.S. Department of Justice, acting pursuant to §§ 2 and 5 of the Voting Rights Act, strongly encouraged the creation of the number of "majority-minority districts"—districts delineated to contain a majority of members of racial groups that constituted a minority within the state. The creation of such "majority-minority" districts promptly engendered legal challenges that have repeatedly reached the Supreme Court:

Shaw v. Reno [Shaw I]

509 U.S. 630, 113 S. Ct. 2816, 125 L. Ed. 2d 511 (1993).

■ JUSTICE O'CONNOR delivered the opinion of the Court.

This case involves two of the most complex and sensitive issues this Court has faced in recent years: the meaning of the constitutional "right" to vote, and the propriety of race-based state legislation designed to benefit members of historically disadvantaged racial minority groups. As a result of the 1990 census, North Carolina became entitled to a twelfth seat in the United States House of Representatives. The General Assembly enacted a reapportionment plan that included one majority-black congressional district. After the Attorney General of the United States objected to the plan pursuant to [§ 5] of the Voting Rights Act, the General Assembly passed new legislation creating a second majority-black district. Appellants allege that the revised plan, which contains district boundary lines of dramatically irregular shape, constitutes an unconstitutional racial gerrymander. The question before us is whether appellants have stated a cognizable claim.

[The] voting age population of North Carolina is approximately 78% white, 20% black, and 1% Native American; the remaining 1% is predominantly Asian. The black population is relatively dispersed; blacks constitute a majority of the general population in only 5 of the State's 100 counties. [The] largest concentrations of black citizens live in the Coastal Plain, primarily in the northern part. The General Assembly's first redistricting plan contained one majority-black district centered in that area of the State. [This district] is somewhat hook shaped. Centered in the northeast portion of the State, it moves southward until it tapers to a narrow band; then, with finger-like extensions, it reaches far into the southern-most part of the State near the South Carolina border. District 1 has been compared to a "Rorschach ink-blot test" and a "bug splattered on a windshield." The second majority-black district, District 12, is even more unusually shaped. It is approximately 160 miles long and, for much of its length, no wider than the I-85 corridor. It winds in snake-like fashion through tobacco country, financial centers, and manufacturing areas "until it gobbles in enough enclaves of black neighborhoods." [Of] the 10 counties through which District 12 passes, five are cut into three different districts; even towns are divided. [One] state legislator has remarked that "[i]f you drove down the interstate with both car doors open, you'd kill most of the people in the district."

[Appellants] alleged that the deliberate segregation of voters into separate districts on the basis of race violated their constitutional right to participate in a "color-blind" electoral process. [This] Court never has held that race-conscious state decisionmaking is impermissible in all circumstances. What appellants object to is redistricting legislation that is so extremely irregular on its face that it rationally can be viewed only as an effort to segregate the races for purposes of voting, without regard for traditional districting principles and without sufficiently compelling justification. [We] conclude that appellants have stated a claim upon which relief can be granted under [equal protection].

[Appellants] contend that redistricting legislation that is so bizarre on its face that it is "unexplainable on grounds other than race," demands the same close scrutiny that we give other state laws that classify citizens by race. Our voting rights precedents support that conclusion. [Redistricting] differs from other kinds of state decisionmaking in that the legislature always is aware of race when it draws district lines, just as it is aware of age, economic status, religious and political persuasion, and a variety of other demographic factors. That sort of race consciousness does not lead inevitably to impermissible race discrimination. [When] members of a racial group live together in one community, a reapportionment plan that concentrates members of the group in one district and excludes them from others may reflect wholly legitimate purposes. The district lines may be drawn, for example, to provide for compact districts of contiguous territory, or to maintain the integrity of political subdivisions. The difficulty of proof, of course, does not mean that a racial gerrymander, once established, should receive less scrutiny [than] other state legislation classifying citizens by race. Moreover, it seems clear to us that proof sometimes will not be difficult at all. In some exceptional cases, a reapportionment plan may be so highly irregular that, on its face, it rationally cannot be understood as anything other than an effort to "segregat[e] [voters]" on the basis of race. Gomillion [was] such a case. So, too, would be a case in which a State concentrated a dispersed minority population in a single district by disregarding traditional districting principles such as compactness, contiguity, and respect for political subdivisions. We emphasize that these criteria are important not because they are constitutionally required—they are not—but because they are objective factors that may serve to defeat a claim that a district has been gerrymandered on racial lines.

Put differently, we believe that reapportionment is one area in which appearances do matter. A reapportionment plan that includes in one district individuals who belong to the same race, but who are otherwise widely separated by geographical and political boundaries, and who may have little in common with one another but the color of their skin, bears an uncomfortable resemblance to political apartheid. It reinforces the perception that members of the same racial group—regardless of their age, education, economic status, or the community in which the live—think alike, share the same political interests, and will prefer the same candidates at the polls. We have rejected such perceptions elsewhere as impermissible racial stereotypes. By perpetuating such notions, a racial gerrymander may exacerbate the very patterns of racial bloc voting that majority-minority districting is sometimes said to counteract. The message that such districting sends to elected representatives is equally pernicious. When a district obviously is created solely to effectuate the perceived common interests of one racial group, elected officials are more likely to believe that their primary obligation is to represent only the members of that group, rather than their constituency as a whole. This is altogether antithetical to our system of representative democracy. [For] these reasons, we conclude that a plaintiff challenging a reapportionment statute under [equal protection] may state a claim by alleging that the legislation, though race-neutral on its face, rationally cannot be understood as anything other than an effort to separate voters into different districts on the basis of race, and that the separation lacks sufficient [justification].

[The] state appellees suggest that a covered jurisdiction may have a compelling interest in creating majority-minority districts in order to comply with the Voting Rights Act. The States certainly have a very strong interest in complying with federal antidiscrimination laws that are constitutionally valid as interpreted and as applied. But in the context of a Fourteenth Amendment challenge, courts must bear in mind the difference between what the law permits, and what it requires. [The] state appellees alternatively argue that the General Assembly's plan advanced a compelling interest entirely distinct from the Voting Rights Act. We previously have recognized a significant state interest in eradicating the effects of past racial discrimination. But the State must have a "strong basis in evidence for [concluding] that remedial action [is necessary]." [Croson]

[Racial] classifications of any sort pose the risk of lasting harm to our society. They reinforce the belief, held by too many for too much of our history, that individuals should be judged by the color of their skin. Racial classifications with respect to voting carry particular dangers. Racial gerrymandering, even for remedial purposes, may balkanize us into competing racial factions; it threatens to carry us further from the goal of a political system in which race no longer [matters]. It is for these reasons that race-based districting by our state legislatures demands close judicial scrutiny. [We] hold [that] appellants have stated a claim under [equal protection] by alleging that the North Carolina General Assembly adopted a reapportionment scheme so irrational on its face that it can be understood only as an effort to segregate voters into separate voting districts because of their race, and that the separation lacks sufficient [justification]. [Reversed and remanded.]

■ JUSTICE WHITE, with whom JUSTICES BLACKMUN and STEVENS join, dissenting.

The facts of this case mirror those presented in [UJO], where the Court rejected a claim that creation of a majority-minority district violated the Constitution. [Of] particular relevance, five of the Justices reasoned that members of the white majority could not plausibly argue that their influence over the political process had been unfairly canceled. [The] Court today chooses not to overrule, but rather to sidestep, UJO. It does so by glossing over the striking similarities, focusing on surface differences, most notably the (admittedly unusual) shape of the newly created district, and imagining an entirely new cause of action.

[The] majority attempts to distinguish UJO by imagining a heretofore unknown type of constitutional claim. [The] logic of its theory appears to be that race-conscious redistricting that "segregates" by drawing odd-shaped lines is qualitatively different from race-conscious redistricting that affects groups in some other way. The distinction is without foundation. [As] I understand the [majority's] theory, a redistricting plan that uses race to "segregate" voters by drawing "uncouth" lines is harmful in a way that a plan that uses race to distribute voters differently is not, for the former "bears an uncomfortable resemblance to political apartheid." The distinction is [untenable]. Given two districts drawn on similar, race-based grounds, the one does not become more injurious than the other simply by virtue of being snake-like. [By] focusing on looks rather than impact, the majority [in its approach] will unnecessarily hinder to some extent a State's voluntary effort to ensure a modicum of minority representation [where] the minority population is geographically dispersed. [When the] creation of a majority-minority district does not unfairly minimize the voting power of any other group, the Constitution does not justify, much less mandate, such obstruction.

[I] have no doubt that a State's compliance with the Voting Rights Act clearly constitutes a compelling interest. [The] Court [warns] that the State's redistricting effort must be "narrowly tailored" to further its interest in complying with the law. It is evident to me, however, that what North Carolina did was precisely tailored to meet the objection of the Attorney General to its prior plan. Hence, I see no need for a remand at all, even accepting the majority's basic approach. Furthermore, how it intends to manage this standard, I do not know. Is it more "narrowly tailored" to create an irregular majority-minority district as opposed to one that is compact but harms other State interests such as incumbency protection or the representation of rural interests? Of the following two options—creation of two minority influence districts or of a single majority-minority district—is one "narrowly tailored" and the other not? [State] efforts to remedy minority vote dilution are wholly unlike what typically has been labeled "affirmative action." To the extent that no other racial group is injured, remedying a Voting Rights Act violation does not involve preferential treatment. It involves, instead, an attempt to equalize treatment, and to provide minority voters with an effective voice in the political process. [Equal protection] surely, does not stand in the [way].

■ JUSTICE BLACKMUN, dissenting.

I join Justice White's dissenting opinion. [It] is particularly ironic that the case in which today's majority chooses to abandon settled law and to recognize for the first time this "analytically distinct" constitutional claim, is a challenge by white voters to the plan under which North Carolina has sent black representatives to Congress for the first time since [Reconstruction].

■ JUSTICE STEVENS, dissenting.

[I] believe that [equal protection] is violated when the State creates the kind of uncouth district boundaries seen in Gomillion and this case for the sole purpose of making it more difficult for members of a minority group to win an election. [However, it] is not violated when the majority acts to facilitate the election of a member of a group that lacks such power because it remains underrepresented in the state legislature—whether that group is defined by political affiliation, by common economic interests, or by religious, ethnic, or racial characteristics. The difference between constitutional and unconstitutional gerrymanders has nothing to do with whether they are based on assumptions about the groups they affect, but whether their purpose is to enhance the power of the group in control of the districting process at the expense of any minority group, and thereby to strengthen the unequal distribution of electoral power. When an assumption that people in particular a minority group (whether they are defined by the political party, religion, ethnic group, or race to which they belong) will vote in a particular way is used to *benefit* that group, no constitutional violation occurs. Politicians have always relied on assumptions that people in particular groups are likely to vote in a particular way when they draw new district lines, and I cannot believe that anything in today's opinion will stop them from doing so in the future. [If] it is permissible to draw boundaries to provide adequate representation for rural voters, for union members, for Hasidic Jews, for Polish Americans, or for Republicans, it necessarily follows that it is permissible to do the same thing for members of the very minority group whose history in the United States gave birth to [equal protection]. A contrary conclusion could only be described as [perverse].

■ JUSTICE SOUTER, dissenting.

[Until] today, the Court has analyzed equal protection claims involving race in electoral districting differently from equal protection claims involving other forms of governmental conduct. [Unlike] other contexts in which we have addressed the State's conscious use of race, electoral districting calls for decisions that nearly always require some consideration of race for legitimate reasons where there is a racially mixed population. As long as members of racial groups have the commonality of interest implicit in our ability to talk about concepts like "minority voting strength," and "dilution of minority votes," and as long as racial bloc voting takes place, legislators will have to take race into account in order to avoid dilution of minority voting strength in the districting plans they adopt. [A] second distinction between districting and most other governmental decisions in which race has figured is that those other decisions using racial criteria characteristically occur in circumstances in which the use of race to the advantage of one person is necessarily at the obvious expense of a member of a different race. Thus, for example, [when] race is used to supplant seniority in layoffs, someone is laid off who would not be otherwise. [In] districting, by contrast, the mere placement of an individual in one district instead of another denies no one a right or benefit provided to [others]. I would not respond to the seeming egregiousness of the redistricting now before us by untethering the concept of racial gerrymander in such a case from the concept of harm exemplified by [vote dilution].

THE AFTERMATH OF SHAW I

1. ***The role of a district's irregular shape.*** A significant question remaining open after Shaw I was whether the existence of a bizarrely shaped district was a necessary prerequisite for a finding of unconstitutionality. Two years later, in **Miller v. Johnson**, 515 U.S. 900 (1995), the Court answered that question in the negative. As in Shaw, the case concerned a congressional district, in this case the newly created Eleventh District in Georgia. After two previous attempts at congressional redistricting had failed to receive Department of Justice preclearance under the Voting Rights Act, largely for failure to locate certain concentrations of black citizens within a majority-black district and for failure to take the opportunity to create three rather than two majority-black districts, Georgia responded by creating three majority-black districts, including the Eleventh. The Justice Department gave clearance, but suit was filed by white voters in the District, claiming the existence of a racially gerrymandered district.

With Justice KENNEDY writing for the majority, the Court held the districting unconstitutional, largely on the authority of Shaw, and confronted directly the question of the relevance of the shape of the District: "The essence of the equal protection claim recognized in Shaw is that the State has used race as a basis for separating voters into districts. Just as the State may not, absent extraordinary justification, segregate citizens on the basis of race in its public parks, buses, golf courses, beaches, and schools, so did we recognize in Shaw that it may not separate its citizens into different voting districts on the basis of race. [Our] observation in Shaw of the consequences of racial stereotyping was not meant to suggest that a district must be bizarre on its face before there is a constitutional violation. Nor was our conclusion in Shaw that in certain instances a district's appearance [can] give rise to an equal protection claim, a holding that bizarreness was a threshold showing. [Shape] is relevant not because bizarreness is a necessary element of the constitutional wrong or a threshold requirement of proof, but because it may be persuasive circumstantial evidence that race for its own sake, and not other districting principles, was the legislature's dominant and controlling rationale in drawing its district lines. The logical implication [is] that parties may rely on evidence other than bizarreness to establish race-based districting."

Justice Kennedy went on to specify the standard to be applied to make out a claim after Shaw: "Parties alleging that a State has assigned voters on the basis of race are neither confined in their proof to evidence regarding the district's geometry and makeup nor required to make a threshold showing of bizarreness. Although race-based decisionmaking is inherently suspect [Adarand], until a claimant makes a showing sufficient to support that allegation the good faith of a state legislature must be presumed. [Redistricting] legislatures will, for example, almost always be aware of racial demographics, but it does not follow that race predominates in the redistricting process. [The] plaintiff's burden is to show, either through circumstantial evidence of a district's shape and demographics or more direct evidence going to legislative purpose, that race was the predominant factor motivating the legislature's decision to place a significant number of voters within or without a particular district. To make this showing, a plaintiff must prove that the legislature subordinated traditional race-neutral districting principles, including but not limited to compactness, contiguity, respect for political subdivisions or communities defined by actual shared interests, to racial considerations. [Although] by comparison with other districts the geometric shape of the Eleventh District may not seem bizarre on its face, when shape is considered in conjunction with its racial and population densities, [and in conjunction with] evidence showing that the General Assembly was motivated by a predominant, overriding desire to assign black populations to the Eleventh District and thereby permit the creation of a third majority-black district[, Georgia's] congressional redistricting plan cannot be upheld unless it satisfies strict scrutiny, our most rigorous and exacting standard of constitutional review." Finding that standard satisfied neither by Georgia's desire to comply with the views of the Department of Justice, nor by any other interest, the Court upheld the judgment of unconstitutionality.

Justice O'CONNOR issued a brief concurring opinion, explaining the evidentiary importance of "substantial disregard of customary and traditional districting practices." Consequently, she argued, "application of the Court's standard does not throw into doubt the vast majority of the Nation's 435 congressional districts [even] though race may well have been considered in the redistricting process." Justice STEVENS dissented on the grounds that in his view the plaintiffs had no standing to sue, and in addition he, along with Justices Breyer and Souter (in part), joined the dissenting opinion of Justice GINSBURG. Her dissent was based largely on disagreement with what she described as the majority's new "race-as-predominant-factor" standard: "[That] ethnicity defines some [voting] groups is a political reality. Until now, no constitutional infirmity has been seen in districting Irish or Italian voters together, for example, so long as the delineation does not abandon traditional apportionment practices. If Chinese-Americans and Russian-Americans may seek and secure group recognition in the delineation of voting districts, then African-Americans should not be dissimilarly treated."

2. ***The role of compliance with the Voting Rights Act.*** A year after the decision in Miller, the Court was called upon to decide, after remand, the litigation that had produced Shaw v. Reno (Shaw I). In **Shaw v. Hunt (Shaw II)**, 517 U.S. 899 (1996), the Court was called upon to decide whether the trial court had correctly determined that, although the North Carolina redistricting plan had been significantly based on race, the justifications were sufficiently compelling to satisfy strict scrutiny. Writing for the Court, Chief Justice REHNQUIST followed Shaw I and Miller in agreeing that strict scrutiny was the appropriate standard, but disagreed that a compelling interest supported the use of race in this case. The Court took issue with the Department of Justice's expansive determination of what was required by sections 2 and 5 of the Voting Rights Act. Since neither the race-based redistricting nor the actual shape of the district were required by the Voting Rights Act, the redistricting could not be said to serve a compelling interest through narrowly tailored means. Thus, the Court "once again" did not reach the question "whether under the proper circumstances compliance with the Voting Rights Act, on its own, could be a compelling state interest." Justice STEVENS, joined (on the merits, but not as to Justice

Stevens's objection to the standing of the plaintiffs) by Justices Ginsburg and Breyer, dissented, echoing many of the themes in his dissents in the earlier cases. For Justice Stevens strict scrutiny was inappropriate and, even if it were, he would have found it satisfied here: "[S]ome legislators felt that the sorry history of race relations in North Carolina in past decades was a sufficient reason for making it easier for more black leaders to participate in the legislative process and to represent the State in the Congress of the United States. Even if that history does not provide the kind of precise guidance that will justify certain specific affirmative action programs in particular industries, it surely provides an adequate basis for a decision to facilitate the election of representatives of the previously disadvantaged minority."

On the same day as Shaw II, the Court also decided **Bush v. Vera**, 517 U.S. 952 (1996), presenting many of the same issues in the context of a recent Texas redistricting. Justice O'CONNOR wrote a plurality opinion, representing her views as well as those of Chief Justice Rehnquist and Justice Kennedy. She reiterated that "[s]trict scrutiny does not apply merely because redistricting is performed with consciousness of race. Nor does it apply to all cases of intentional creation of majority-minority districts. [For] strict scrutiny to apply, the plaintiffs must prove that other, legitimate districting principles were 'subordinated' to race. [Miller.] By that, we mean that race must be 'the predominant factor motivating the legislature's [redistricting] decision.' [Miller.]" Applying this standard, especially in light of the evidence that the legislature had focused on race and had "substantially neglected traditional districting criteria such as compactness," Justice O'Connor agreed with the district court that race had been the predominant factor and that strict scrutiny must therefore apply. And in applying strict scrutiny, she concluded, as the Court had in Shaw II, that the racially based districting was not necessary to ameliorate the effects of past discrimination and thus could not satisfy a strict scrutiny standard.

In addition to writing a plurality opinion, Justice O'CONNOR wrote her own concurrence, emphasizing that compliance with the Voting Rights Act might constitute a compelling interest sufficient to withstand strict scrutiny, although that was not a situation presented by this record. Justice KENNEDY also wrote his own concurring opinion, largely to make clear that for him the question of when the creation of a majority-minority district would trigger strict scrutiny was more open than it seemed from the plurality opinion. Justice THOMAS, joined by Justice Scalia, concurred in the judgment, but emphasized that for him strict scrutiny was applicable in any case involving the intentional creation of a majority-minority district, and that race necessarily "predominated" in any case in which a majority-minority district was created because of "racial demographics."

Justice STEVENS, joined by Justices Ginsburg and Breyer, dissented, largely to question whether it was plausible for the Court to substitute its judgment for that of political officials about the likelihood of minority candidates prevailing in districts that were not majority-minority: "Perhaps minority candidates, forced to run in majority-white districts, will be able to overcome the long history of stereotyping and discrimination that has heretofore led the vast majority of majority-white districts to reject minority candidates. Perhaps not. I am certain only that bodies of elected federal and state officials are in a far better position than anyone on this Court to assess whether the Nation's long history of discrimination has been overcome, and that nothing in the Constitution requires this unnecessary intrusion into the ability of States to negotiate solutions to political differences while providing long-excluded groups the opportunity to participate effectively in the democratic process." Justice SOUTER, joined by Justices Ginsburg and Breyer, also dissented, in an opinion applicable both to Bush v. Vera and Shaw II. He objected to the entire line of cases starting with Shaw I, finding that they had erected an unworkable and unpredictable standard.

3. ***A district satisfying strict scrutiny under Shaw.*** In **Lawyer v. Department of Justice**, 521 U.S. 567 (1997), a 5–4 majority of the Court upheld against equal protection challenge a Florida redistricting plan for state legislative districts. After the 1990 census, the Florida state legislature had devised a districting plan, the Justice Department had refused to preclear it under § 5 of the Voting Rights Act, the legislature reached an impasse in devising a new plan, and the Florida Supreme Court had devised its own plan. The state court's plan called for an irregularly shaped senate district with a voting-age population that was 45.8% black and that comprised portions of four counties in the Tampa Bay area. That plan was challenged in federal district court as violating the equal protection rights of white voters, and a different plan was fashioned in a settlement of that lawsuit joined by all parties except appellant, who was one of the several plaintiffs in the suit. The district court approved the plan in the settlement without formally adjudicating the state supreme court's earlier plan unconstitutional. In an opinion by Justice SOUTER joined by all the dissenters in the Shaw line of cases plus Chief Justice Rehnquist, the Court found no procedural problem in the settlement, and found no clear error (the appropriate standard of review after Miller) in the district court's finding that the plan reached in the settlement did not subordinate traditional districting principles to race:

"The District Court looked to the shape and composition of [the challenged state senate district] as redrawn in [the settlement plan] and found them 'demonstrably benign and satisfactorily tidy.' The district is located entirely in the Tampa Bay area, has an end-to-end distance no greater than that of most Florida Senate districts. [The] District Court found that the residents of [the district] 'regard themselves as a community.' Evidence indicated that [the district] comprises a predominantly urban, low-income population, the poorest of the nine districts in the Tampa Bay region and among the poorest districts in the State, whose white and black members alike share a similarly depressed economic condition, and interests that reflect it. The fact that [the district] is not a majority black district, the black voting-age population being 36.2%, supports the District Court's finding that the district is not a 'safe' one for black-preferred candidates, but one that 'offers to any candidate, without regard to race, the opportunity' to seek and be elected to office."

In answer to appellant's objection that the percentage of black voters in the district was higher than that in any of the three counties it drew from, Justice Souter wrote: "[W]e have never suggested that the percentage of black residents in a district may not exceed the percentage of black residents in any of the counties from which the district is created, and have never recognized similar racial composition of different political districts as being necessary to avoid an inference of racial gerrymandering in any one of them."

Justice SCALIA dissented, joined by Justices O'Connor, Kennedy and Thomas. The dissent did not reach the constitutionality of the district but objected that the settlement was an "unprecedented intrusion upon state sovereignty." In the dissent's view, the district court should not have approved the settlement without first finding the state supreme court's plan unconstitutional and giving "the State an opportunity to do its own redrawing of the district to remedy whatever unconstitutional features it contained."

4. ***The North Carolina district—again.*** In **Easley v. Cromartie**, 532 U.S. 234 (2001), the Court dealt again with the North Carolina congressional district whose first 1992 rendition had been the subject of Shaw I (1993) and Shaw II (1996). On remand after an earlier decision invalidating summary judgment for the challengers, Hunt v. Cromartie, 526 U.S. 541 (1999) the district court had allowed discovery and held a three-day trial, finding that the district had been drawn for predominantly racial, not political motives and was unconstitutional. In a decision written by Justice BREYER, the Supreme Court reversed. Reviewing the district court's factual findings for clear error, he stated: "[Those] who claim that a legislature has improperly used race as a criterion [must] show at a minimum that the 'legislature subordinated traditional race-neutral districting principles [to] racial considerations.' [Miller v. Johnson.] Race must not simply have been '*a* motivation for the drawing of a majority minority district,' [Bush v. Vera, O'Connor, J. concurring], but 'the *predominant* factor motivating the legislature's districting decision.'" Plaintiffs must show that a facially neutral law 'is unexplainable on grounds other than race.' [The] underlying districting decision is one that ordinarily falls within a legislature's sphere of competence. [Miller.] Hence, [courts] must 'exercise *extraordinary caution* in adjudicating claims that a State has drawn district lines on the basis of race.' Caution is especially appropriate [where] the State has articulated a legitimate political explanation for its [decision], and the voting population is one in which race and political affiliation are highly correlated."

The Court examined the record in detail, including both sides' expert testimony. The fact that the district "excluded heavily white precincts with high Democratic Party *registration,* while including heavily African-American precincts with equivalent, or lower, Democratic Party registration" was inconclusive, because the legislature might well have expected the "voting behavior" of the precincts to differ from their "party registration." "[White] voters registered as Democrats 'cross-over' to vote for a Republican candidate more often than do African Americans. [Hence], a legislature may, by [choosing] reliable Democratic precincts [without] regard to race, end up with a district containing more heavily African-American precincts, but the reasons would be political rather than racial." The Court credited one legislator's contemporaneous statement about the plan's "geographic, racial, and partisan balance" to show only "that the legislature considered race, along with other considerations," and to say "little or nothing about whether race played a *predominant* role." And the Court discounted as inconclusive a legislative staffer's private email about having "moved the Greensboro Black community" into the district, because the email did not point to an obvious racial motive. Finally, the Court found unavailing the plaintiffs' claim that the purely political objective of creating a safe Democratic seat could have been obtained under a slightly different map. "A showing that the legislature might have 'swapped' a handful of precincts out of a total of 154 precincts, involving a population of a few hundred out of a total population of about half a million, cannot significantly strengthen appellees' case. [In] a case such as this one where majority-minority districts (or the approximate equivalent) are at issue and where racial identification correlates highly with political affiliation, the party attacking the legislatively drawn boundaries must show at the least that the legislature could have achieved its legitimate political objectives in alternative ways that are comparably consistent with traditional districting principles[, and that] those districting alternatives would have brought about significantly greater racial balance."

Justice THOMAS dissented, joined by Chief Justice REHNQUIST and Justices SCALIA and KENNEDY, saying that "the District Court's view of the evidence was [not] impermissible," that "racial gerrymandering offends the Constitution whether the motivation is malicious or benign," and that it was "not a defense that the legislature merely may have drawn the district based on the stereotype that blacks are reliable Democratic voters."

Consider the observation that Easley illustrates that "the Supreme Court has been unwilling to apply strict scrutiny strictly" where to do so might eliminate consideration of race in districting, thus "permitting race to be taken into account when it is one factor among many and its inclusion produces districts that do not deviate too obviously from the sorts of districts created for other groups." Karlan, "Easing the Spring: Strict Scrutiny and Affirmative Action After the Redistricting Cases," 43 Wm. & Mary L. Rev. 1569 (2002).

SECTION 3. SEX DISCRIMINATION

If the history and contemporaneous purpose of the Fourteenth Amendment were all that counted, only racial classifications directed against African-Americans would be suspect. But the Court has not confined the categories of "suspect" classifications to race. The following three sections turn to efforts to establish new categories of "suspect" or "quasi-suspect" classifications warranting heightened or strict scrutiny. Identification of additional classifications warranting heightened scrutiny has typically extrapolated from the characteristics that have elicited strict scrutiny of governmental use of racial criteria. Is the critical element the possession of an immutable trait that distinguishes the possessor from the majority? A trait relied on by the classifier for the purpose—or the effect—of stigmatizing those possessing it? A trait relied upon by the majority to signify its superiority vis-à-vis those possessing the trait? A trait rarely relevant to legitimate governmental objectives yet traditionally used to disadvantage those who possess it? A trait traditionally used and readily usable for "we-they" generalizations? See Ely, "The Wages of Crying Wolf," Yale L.J. 920 (1973) ("The danger is [greater] in we-they situations that we will overestimate the validity of the proposed stereotypical classification by seizing upon the positive myths about our own class and the negative myths about theirs [and] too readily assuming that virtually the entire membership of the two classes fit the stereotypes and therefore that not many of 'them' will be unfairly deprived, nor many of 'us' unfairly benefitted, by the proposed classification."). Should it matter whether the trait has been used to denominate a class that is "relegated to such a position of political powerlessness as to command extraordinary protection from the majoritarian political process"? Recall Carolene Products footnote four; Ely, Democracy and Distrust (1980). Does it matter how much a trait used to classify persons resembles race? How is sex like race? How is it unlike race? What of the other characteristics considered in Sections 4 and 5?

In addition to these conceptual and doctrinal concerns, consider the ways in which underlying social movements may have affected the outcomes in particular cases and the ways in which case outcomes may, themselves, have affected the shape of social movements. For example, how does the history of the civil rights movement and its impact on the cases discussed in Section 2 compare to the history of the feminist movement or the movement for gay and lesbian equality? For discussion of social movements and their relationships to constitutional cases and arguments, see Balkin & Siegel, "Principles, Practices, and Social Movements," 154 U. Pa. L. Rev. 927 (2006).

DISCRIMINATING ON THE BASIS OF SEX

1. ***Constitutional sources of sex equality.*** The U.S. Constitution is the only major Western Constitution with a bill of rights that lacks a provision explicitly declaring the equality of the sexes. For example, the French Constitution since 1946 has provided that "The law guarantees to the woman, in all spheres, rights equal to those of the man." Article 3 of the German Basic Law provides that "Men and women shall have equal rights," and that "No one may be disadvantaged or favored because of his [sex.]." The Constitution of India provides that "the State shall not discriminate against any citizen on grounds of [sex.]." Among newer constitutions, Canada's provides that "Every individual is equal before and under the law and has the right to the equal protection and equal benefit of the law without discrimination and, in particular, without discrimination based on [sex.]" And South Africa's provides that neither the state nor any person may "unfairly discriminate directly or indirectly against anyone on [grounds] including [gender], sex, pregnancy, or marital status." For a comparison between such constitutional approaches to sex discrimination and the U.S. approach, see Sullivan, "Constitutionalizing Women's Equality," 90 Cal. L. Rev. 735 (2002).

In contrast, the U.S. Constitution, in its original text, never referred to women at all. The only known use of the pronoun "she" in the framing deliberations concerned a later-rejected clause that would have referred to the rendition of fugitive slaves. Of course some clauses governing the rights of individuals must have applied implicitly to women (e.g., habeas corpus, ex post facto, bills of attainder). But the Constitution provided no federal protection against laws explicitly treating women differently from men. Did the Fourteenth Amendment Equal Protection and Privileges or Immunities Clauses contemplate equality for women? While suffragists participated in the fight for abolition, the text of the Fourteenth Amendment did not reflect their struggle; indeed, the second section of the Amendment introduced the word "male" into the Constitution and linked it to the franchise, providing for the apportionment of representatives among states by population but penalizing states that limited the vote of noncriminal "male" inhabitants.

The Supreme Court soon confirmed that the guarantees of the Fourteenth Amendment did not apply to sex discrimination, even when that discrimination was explicit. In 1873, the Court denied that federal privileges and immunities included the right of Myra Bradwell to practice law in Illinois. **Bradwell v. State**, 16 Wall. (83 U.S.) 130 (1873). Even Justice Bradley, who had a day earlier dissented from the decision in the Slaughter-House Cases (p. 451 above)—there arguing, contrary to the Court, that federal privileges and immunities should include the right to pursue an occupation—wrote in a concurring opinion in Bradwell that such privileges would apply to men only: "[I]t certainly cannot be affirmed, as an historical fact [that] it is one of the privileges and immunities of women as citizens to engage in any and every profession, occupation, or employment in civil life. [Man] is, or should be, woman's protector and defender. The natural and proper timidity and delicacy which belongs to the female sex evidently unfits it for many of the occupations of civil life. The constitution of the family organization, which is founded in the divine ordinance, as well as in the nature of things, indicates the domestic sphere as that which properly belongs to the domain and functions of womanhood. [The] paramount destiny and mission of woman are to fulfill the noble and benign offices of wife and mother. This is the law of the Creator."

The next year, in **Minor v. Happersett**, 88 U.S. 162, 21 Wall. 162 (1874), the Court denied that federal privileges and immunities included the right of women to vote in state elections, suggesting that women may be persons within the meaning of the 14th Amendment, and even citizens, but that they were not thereby entitled to participate in a political or professional realm reserved to men.

Only the Nineteenth Amendment addresses expressly any aspect of women's equality, providing that "the right of citizens of the United States to vote shall not be denied or abridged by the United States or by any state on account of sex." The provision has been construed narrowly to apply only to the formal franchise; in the aftermath of its 1920 passage, the Court failed to find in it any implied right against sex discrimination in, for example, jury service or state-licensed occupations. See Brown, Note, "The Nineteenth Amendment and Women's Equality," 102 Yale L.J. 2175 (1993). The Nineteenth Amendment bears analogy to the guarantee against race discrimination in the Fifteenth Amendment, but no text explicitly specifies an equal protection guarantee for the sexes comparable to the general guarantee in the Fourteenth Amendment.

An Equal Rights Amendment, debated in successive Congresses since 1923 and proposed by both houses in 1971–72, would have provided that "[e]quality of rights under the law shall not be denied or abridged by the United States or by any State on account of sex," and would have authorized Congress to enact implementing legislation. See Brown et al., "The Equal Rights Amendment: A Constitutional Basis for Equal Rights for Women," 80 Yale L.J. 871 (1971). Although Congress submitted that proposed amendment to the states early in 1972 and about half the necessary number of states ratified it within a few months, the ratification effort ran into substantial obstacles thereafter. In 1978, Congress extended the period for ratification until 1982. On June 30, 1982, that extension period expired and the proposed amendment accordingly failed of ratification, one of only six amendment proposals in our history to have passed Congress but failed ratification in the states. Thirty-five states had ratified it, but the additional three required states could not be mustered. What would have been the impact of the proposed amendment? To what extent would it have changed the results in the cases considered below? Is it possible that, though the Equal Rights Amendment was never ratified, the strength of the social movement advocating for the amendment had considerable effects on the constitutional outcomes discussed below? See Mayeri, "Constitutional

Choices: Legal Feminism and the Historical Dynamics of Change," 92 Cal. L. Rev. 755 (2004).

While the battle for the ratification of the proposed Equal Rights Amendment was under way in the early 1970s, the Court considered a growing number of cases challenging sex classifications under the Equal Protection Clause of the Fourteenth Amendment, several litigated by Ruth Bader Ginsburg, who would later become an appellate judge and then Justice. For her own reflections on the history of this litigation, see Ginsburg & Flagg, "Some Reflections on the Feminist Thought of the 1970s," 1989 U. Chi. L. F. 9; Ginsburg, "Constitutional Adjudication in the United States as a Means of Advancing the Equal Stature of Men and Women Under the Law," 26 Hofstra L. Rev. 263 (1997). Some of these challenges succeeded, even though the Court at the outset purported to apply the rationality standard and even though the Court never did assimilate sex criteria to the fully "suspect" status of racial ones. By the mid-1970s, in Craig v. Boren (1976; p. 761 below), a consensus was reached at last: the majority applied a heightened but only intermediate, not strict, level of scrutiny.

It is also interesting to note that the Court often refers to discrimination on the basis of "gender," rather than the potentially more accurate description of discrimination on the basis of "sex." This tendency to use the term "gender" in place of "sex" may be the product of a conscious, strategic choice by Ginsburg, then a professor and chief litigator for the Women's Rights Project at the American Civil Liberties Union, to use the word "gender" in her briefs and articles. Ginsburg credits her secretary at Columbia Law School for giving her the idea to switch the terms, telling Ginsburg, "I'm typing all these briefs and articles for you and the word sex, sex, sex is on every page." Ginsburg's secretary continued, "Don't you know that those nine men (on the Supreme Court)—they hear that word, and their first association is not the way you want them to be thinking? Why don't you use the word gender? It is a grammatical term and it will ward off distracting associations." Crocker, "Ginsburg Explains Origin of Sex, Gender," L.A. Times, Nov. 21, 1993.

2. ***Deference to laws maintaining "separate spheres."*** For the Court's characteristic stance toward sex discrimination claims in an earlier era, see **Goesaert v. Cleary**, 335 U.S. 464 (1948), rejecting an attack on a Michigan law which provided that no woman could obtain a bartender's license unless she was "the wife or daughter of the male owner" of a licensed liquor establishment. Justice FRANKFURTER stated: "Michigan could, beyond question, forbid all women from working behind a bar. This is so despite the vast changes in the social and legal position of women. The fact that women may now have achieved the virtues that men have long claimed as their prerogatives and now indulge in vices that men have long practiced, does not preclude the States from drawing a sharp line between the sexes, certainly in such matters as the regulation of the liquor traffic. [The] Constitution does not require legislatures to reflect sociological insight, or shifting social standards, any more than it requires them to keep abreast of the latest scientific standards. [Michigan] evidently believes that the oversight assured through ownership of a bar by a barmaid's husband or father minimizes hazards that may confront a barmaid without such protecting oversight. This Court is certainly not in a position to gainsay such belief by the Michigan legislature. [Since the line drawn] is not without a basis in reason, we cannot give ear to the suggestion that the real impulse

behind this legislation was an unchivalrous desire of male bartenders to try to monopolize the calling." Justice RUTLEDGE, joined by Justices Douglas and Murphy, dissented without challenging the majority's assumptions; instead, he focused on the inadequate fit between means and ends. The dissenters, like the majority, assumed that "benign," "protective" legislation regarding women was clearly constitutional. Recall that, during the Lochner era, one of the few types of laws regulating working conditions readily sustained by the Court was the setting of maximum working hours for women.

3. ***Heightened scrutiny under rationality review.*** In **Reed v. Reed**, 404 U.S. 71 (1971), the appellant's brief urged the Court to find sex a suspect classification. The Court declined. Yet the unanimous Court invalidated the challenged law under the Equal Protection Clause while purporting to apply a traditional "rationality" standard. The state courts had sustained a preference for men over women in the appointment of administrators of estates as a rational method "to resolve an issue that would otherwise require a hearing as to the relative merits" of the petitioning relatives. Chief Justice BURGER stated the question as "whether a difference in the sex of competing applicants for letters of administration bears a rational relationship to a state objective that is sought to be advanced by the operation of [the law]." The majority answered no: "Clearly the objective of reducing the work load on probate courts by eliminating one class of contests is not without some legitimacy." But giving "a mandatory preference to members of either sex over members of the other, merely to accomplish the elimination of hearings on the merits, is to make the very kind of arbitrary legislative choice forbidden by [equal protection]; and whatever may be said as to the positive values of avoiding intrafamily controversy, the choice in this contest may not lawfully be mandated solely on the basis of sex." Shouldn't this law have survived scrutiny under conventional rationality review? If a "stereotype" bears a basis in fact (e.g., men, on average, have more years of formal education than women), why isn't it a permissible basis for a statutory presumption? In a world where women are unequal, aren't preferences for men "rational," and indeed the more unequal women are, the more rational the discrimination against them? Did Reed therefore necessarily import some suspicion of sex-based laws?

4. ***The failure to adopt strict scrutiny.*** In **Frontiero v. Richardson**, 411 U.S. 677 (1973), the Court sustained an equal protection challenge to a federal law affording male members of the armed forces an automatic dependency allowance for their wives, but requiring servicewomen to prove that their husbands were dependent. Justice BRENNAN's opinion advocated treating gender as a suspect classification, but he obtained only a plurality, not a majority of votes for this analysis. Joined by Justices Douglas, White and Marshall, he concluded that "classifications based upon sex, like [those] upon race, alienage, and national origin, are inherently suspect and must therefore be subjected to close judicial scrutiny." He found implicit support for that position in Reed's "departure from 'traditional' rational-basis analysis." He elaborated:

"[Our] Nation has had a long and unfortunate history of sex discrimination. Traditionally, such discrimination was rationalized by an attitude of 'romantic paternalism' which, in practical effect, put women, not on a pedestal, but in a cage. As a result of notions such as these, our statute books gradually became laden with gross, stereotyped distinctions between the sexes and, indeed, throughout much of the 19th century the position of women in our society was, in many respects, comparable to that of blacks under the pre-Civil War slave codes. Neither slaves nor women could hold office, serve on juries, or bring suit in their own names, and married women traditionally were denied the legal capacity to hold or convey property or to serve as legal guardians of their own children. And although blacks were guaranteed the right to vote in 1870, women were denied even that right [until the] adoption of the 19th Amendment half a century later. It is true, of course, that the position of women in America has improved markedly in recent decades. Nevertheless, it can hardly be doubted that, in part because of the high visibility of the sex characteristic, women still face pervasive, although at times more subtle, discrimination in our educational institutions, in the job market and, perhaps most conspicuously, in the political arena.[1]

"Moreover, since sex, like race and national origin, is an immutable characteristic, the imposition of special disabilities upon the members of a particular sex because of their sex would seem to violate 'the basic concept of our system that legal burdens should bear some relationship to individual responsibility.' And what differentiates sex from such nonsuspect statuses as intelligence or physical disability, and aligns it with the recognized suspect criteria, is that the sex characteristic frequently bears no relation to ability to perform or contribute to society. As a result, statutory distinctions between the sexes often have the effect of invidiously relegating the entire class of females to inferior legal status without regard to the actual capabilities of its individual members." Applying the "strict judicial scrutiny" he found appropriate, Justice Brennan found it "clear" that the law was unconstitutional. The Government had relied on promoting "administrative convenience:" "[It] maintains that, as an empirical matter, wives [frequently] are dependent upon their husbands, while husbands rarely are dependent upon their wives. Thus, the Government argues that [Congress] might reasonably have concluded that it would be both cheaper and easier simply conclusively to presume that wives of male members are financially dependent upon their husbands, while burdening female members with the task of establishing dependency in fact. The Government offers no concrete evidence [tending] to support its view that such differential treatment in fact saves the Government any money. [Moreover], any statutory scheme which draws a sharp line between the sexes, *solely* for the purpose of achieving administrative convenience, [violates equal protection]. [Reed.]"

Justice POWELL, joined by Chief Justice Burger and Justice Blackmun, concurred only in the judgment, arguing that it was unnecessary "in this case to characterize sex as a suspect classification" because the case could and should be decided "on the authority of Reed" and "any expansion of its rationale" should be reserved for the future. Moreover, any general categorization of sex classifications as suspect should be postponed because of the pending Equal Rights Amendment ("which if adopted will resolve the substance of this precise question"): "[This] reaching out to pre-empt by judicial action a major political decision which is currently in process of resolution does not reflect appropriate respect for duly prescribed legislative

[1] "It is true, of course, that when viewed in the abstract, women do not constitute a small and powerless minority. Nevertheless, in part because of past discrimination, women are vastly underrepresented in this Nation's decisionmaking [councils]." [Footnote by Justice Brennan.]

processes." Justice STEWART, who also concurred solely in the judgment, stated merely that the law worked "an invidious discrimination in violation of the Constitution. [Reed.]" Justice REHNQUIST dissented.

Justice Brennan never did get that elusive fifth vote for his proposed strict scrutiny standard, and sex equality claims were thereafter litigated under the intermediate scrutiny standard articulated in Craig and Virginia Military, below. Should he have? Note Justice Brennan's analogy of women to discrete and insular minorities warranting special judicial solicitude under Carolene Products footnote four. Is the assumption of women's entrenched political powerlessness accurate? Might it be argued that women are neither discrete, insular, nor a minority? Consider the view that the Court should strike down sex classifications only if they were enacted while women's access to the political process was blocked, and that the passage of the 19th Amendment and the enfranchisement of women means that "if women don't protect themselves from sex discrimination in the future, it [will be] because for one reason or another—substantive disagreement or more likely the assignment of a low priority to the issue—they don't choose to." Ely, Democracy and Distrust (1980).

5. ***Convergence upon intermediate scrutiny, or an "exceedingly persuasive justification."*** Faced with the analogical challenge that sex is neither just like race nor just another garden-variety basis for presumptively permissible distinctions, as in the case of socioeconomic classifications, the Court settled on the approach of a third standard of scrutiny, intermediate between strict scrutiny and rationality review. The standard was announced in 1976 in Craig v. Boren, below, which required "important" ends and "substantially related" means.

Craig v. Boren

429 U.S. 190, 97 S. Ct. 451, 50 L. Ed. 2d 397 (1976).

■ JUSTICE BRENNAN delivered the opinion of the Court.

The interaction of two sections of an Oklahoma statute prohibits the sale of "non-intoxicating" 3.2% beer to males under the age of 21 and to females under the age of 18. The question [is] whether such a gender-based differential constitutes a denial to males 18–20 years of age of [equal protection]. [To] withstand constitutional challenge, previous cases establish that classifications by gender must serve important governmental objectives and must be substantially related to achievement of those objectives. [Reed and subsequent decisions (e.g., Frontiero)] have rejected administrative ease and convenience as sufficiently important objectives to justify gender-based classifications. Reed has also provided the underpinning for decisions that have invalidated statutes employing gender as an inaccurate proxy for other, more germane bases of classification. Hence, "archaic and overbroad" generalizations concerning the financial position of servicewomen, Frontiero, and working women, could not justify use of a gender line in determining eligibility for certain governmental entitlements. Similarly, increasingly outdated misconceptions concerning the role of females in the home rather than in the "marketplace and world of ideas" were rejected as loose-fitting characterizations incapable of supporting state statutory schemes that were premised upon their accuracy. In light of the weak congruence between gender and the characteristic or trait that gender purported to represent, it was necessary that the legislatures choose either to realign their substantive laws in a gender-neutral fashion, or to adopt procedures for identifying those instances where the sex-centered generalization actually comported to fact. In this case, too, "Reed, we feel, is controlling."

We turn then to the question whether, under Reed, the difference between males and females with respect to the purchase of 3.2% beer warrants the differential in age drawn by the Oklahoma statute. We conclude that it [does not]. We accept for purposes of discussion the District Court's identification of the objective underlying [the law] as the enhancement of traffic safety. [But] appellees' statistics in our view cannot support the conclusion that the gender-based distinction closely serves to achieve that objective and therefore the distinction cannot under Reed withstand equal protection challenge. [Even] were this statistical evidence accepted as accurate, it nevertheless offers only a weak answer to the equal protection question presented here. The most focused and relevant of the statistical surveys, arrests of 18–20-year-olds for alcohol-related driving offenses, exemplifies the ultimate unpersuasiveness of this evidentiary record. Viewed in terms of the correlation between sex and the actual activity that Oklahoma seeks to regulate—driving while under the influence of alcohol—the statistics broadly establish that .18% of females and 2% of males in that age group were arrested for that offense. While such a disparity is not trivial in a statistical sense, it hardly can form the basis for employment of a gender line as a classifying device. Certainly if maleness is to serve as a proxy for drinking and driving, a correlation of 2% must be considered an unduly tenuous "fit." Indeed, prior cases have consistently rejected the use of sex as a decisionmaking factor even though the statutes in question certainly rested on far more predictive empirical relationships than this. Moreover, the statistics exhibit a variety of other shortcomings that seriously impugn their value to equal protection analysis. Setting aside the obvious methodological problems,[1] the surveys do not adequately justify the salient features of Oklahoma's gender-based traffic-safety law. None purports to measure the use and dangerousness of 3.2% beer as opposed to alcohol generally, a detail that is of particular importance since, in light of its low alcohol level, Oklahoma apparently considers the 3.2% beverage to be "nonintoxicating."

[The] showing offered by the appellees does not satisfy us that sex represents a legitimate, accurate proxy for the regulation of drinking and driving. In fact, when it is further recognized that Oklahoma's statute prohibits only the selling of 3.2% beer to young males and not their drinking the beverage once acquired (even after purchase by their 18–20-year-old female companions), the relationship between gender and traffic safety becomes far too tenuous to satisfy Reed's requirement that the gender-based difference be substantially related to achievement of the [statutory objective]. [In] sum, the principles embodied in [equal protection] are not to be rendered inapplicable by statistically measured but loose-fitting generalities concerning the drinking tendencies of aggregate groups. We

[1] The very social stereotypes that find reflection in age differential laws are likely substantially to distort the accuracy of these comparative statistics. Hence "reckless" young men who drink and drive are transformed into arrest statistics, whereas their female counterparts are chivalrously escorted [home]. [Footnote by Justice Brennan.]

conclude that [this] gender-based differential [is] a denial of [equal protection to males aged 18–20].[2] [Reversed.]

■ JUSTICE POWELL, concurring.

[Reed] and subsequent cases involving gender-based classifications make clear that the Court subjects such classifications to a more critical examination than is normally applied when "fundamental" constitutional rights and "suspect classes" are not present. I view this as a relatively easy case. [The] decision [turns] on whether the [state] has adopted a means that bears a "fair and substantial relation" to this objective. Reed. It seems to me that the statistics offered by the [state] do tend generally to support the [classification]. Even so, I am not persuaded that these facts and the inferences fairly drawn from them justify this classification based on a three-year age differential between the sexes, and especially one that is so easily circumvented as to be virtually meaningless. [This] gender-based classification does not bear a fair and substantial relation to the object of the legislation.

■ JUSTICE STEVENS, concurring.

There is only one Equal Protection Clause. [I] am inclined to believe that what has become known as the two-tiered analysis of equal protection claims does not describe a completely logical method of deciding cases, but rather is a method the Court has employed to explain decisions that actually apply a single standard in a reasonably consistent fashion. [In] this case, the classification [is] objectionable because it is based on an accident at birth, because it is a mere remnant of the now almost universally rejected tradition of discriminating against males in this age bracket, and because, to the extent it reflects any physical difference between males and females, it is actually perverse.[3]

The question then is whether the traffic safety justification put forward by the State is sufficient to make an otherwise offensive classification acceptable. The classification is not totally irrational. For the evidence does indicate that there are more males than females in this age bracket who drive and also more who drink. Nevertheless, [it] is difficult to believe that the statute was actually intended to cope with the problem of traffic safety, since it has only a minimal effect on access to a not-very-intoxicating beverage and does not prohibit its consumption. Moreover, [the] legislation imposes a restraint on [100%] of the males in the class allegedly because about 2% of them have probably violated one or more laws relating to the consumption of alcoholic beverages. It is unlikely that this law will have a significant deterrent effect either on that 2% or on the law-abiding 98%. But even assuming some such slight benefit, it does not seem to me that an insult to all of the young men of the State can be justified by visiting the sins of the 2% on the 98%.

■ [JUSTICE STEWART, concurring in the judgment, stated that the law "amounts to total irrationality" and to "invidious discrimination. See [Reed]."]

---

[2] Insofar as Goesaert v. Cleary may be inconsistent, that decision is [disapproved]. [Footnote by Justice Brennan.]

[3] Because males are generally heavier than females, they have a greater capacity to consume alcohol without impairing their driving ability than do females. [Footnote by Justice Stevens.]

■ JUSTICE REHNQUIST, dissenting.

The Court's disposition of this case is objectionable on two grounds. First is its conclusion that *men* challenging a gender-based statute which treats them less favorably than women may invoke a more stringent standard of judicial review than pertains to most other types of classifications. Second is the Court's enunciation of this standard, without citation to any source, as being that "classifications by gender must serve *important* governmental objectives and must be *substantially* related to achievement of those objectives." [I] think the [law] challenged here need pass only the "rational basis" equal protection analysis expounded in cases such as [Lee Optical], and I believe that it is constitutional under that analysis.

I. [There] is no suggestion in the Court's opinion that males in this age group are in any way peculiarly disadvantaged, subject to systematic discriminatory treatment, or otherwise in need of special solicitude from the courts. [It] is true that a number of our opinions contain broadly phrased dicta implying that the same test should be applied to all classifications based on sex, whether affecting females or males. [E.g., Frontiero; Reed.] However, before today, no decision of this Court has applied an elevated level of scrutiny to invalidate a statutory discrimination harmful to [males]. [There] being no plausible argument that this is a discrimination against females, the Court's reliance on our previous sex-discrimination cases is ill-founded. [The] Court's [standard of review] apparently comes out of thin air. How is this Court to define what objectives are important? How is it to determine whether a particular law is "substantially" related to the achievement of such objective, rather than related in some other way to its achievement? Both of the phrases used are so diaphanous and elastic as to invite subjective judicial preferences or prejudices relating to particular types of legislation, masquerading as judgments whether such legislation is directed at "important" objectives or whether the relationship to those objectives is "substantial" [enough].

II. [Under the] applicable rational basis test, [legislatures] are entitled to draw factual conclusions on the basis of the determination of probable cause which an arrest by a police officer normally represents. In this situation, they could reasonably infer that the incidence of drunk driving is a good deal higher than the incidence of arrest. And while [such] statistics may be distorted as a result of stereotyping, the legislature is not required to prove before a court that its statistics are perfect. In any event, if stereotypes are as pervasive as the Court suggests, they may in turn influence the conduct of the men and women in question, and cause the young men to conform to the wild and reckless image which is their stereotype. [The statistical] evidence suggests clear differences between the drinking and driving habits of young men and women. Those differences are grounds enough for the State reasonably to conclude that young males pose by far the greater drunk driving hazard, both in terms of sheer numbers and in terms of hazard on a per-driver basis. The gender-based difference in treatment in this case is therefore not [irrational].

■ [CHIEF JUSTICE BURGER dissented, stating that he was "in general agreement" with Justice Rehnquist.]

SEX EQUALITY AFTER CRAIG V. BOREN

1. ***Toward stricter scrutiny?*** The 1982 ruling in Mississippi University for Women v. Hogan, which follows below, reiterated the Craig standard but added that defenders of a gender-classifying law "must carry the burden of showing an '*exceedingly persuasive justification*' for the classification." Was this a mere restatement of Craig, or did it suggest a move toward a level of scrutiny more intensive than "intermediate"? The "exceedingly persuasive" formulation proved central in the 1994 decision in J.E.B. and in the 1996 ruling in United States v. Virginia, which follow below. In the Virginia case, Justice Scalia's dissent charged that Justice Ginsburg's resort to that "amorphous" phrase in her majority opinion was in effect an endorsement of strict rather than intermediate scrutiny, thereby "drastically revis[ing] our established standards for reviewing sex-based classifications." Is there merit in his charge? Or did the majority merely apply Craig's intermediate standard with special care?

2. ***All-female nursing schools.*** What implications did the intermediate review adopted in Craig have for single-sex schools? In **Mississippi University for Women v. Hogan**, 458 U.S. 718 (1982), the first sex discrimination case the Court considered after Justice O'Connor was appointed the first woman justice in its history, sustained by a vote of 5–4 a male applicant's challenge to the State's policy of excluding men from the Mississippi University for Women (MUW) School of Nursing. MUW, founded in 1884 (to provide for the "Education of White Girls"), was the oldest state-supported all-female university in the nation. Its School of Nursing was established in 1971. Hogan, a male registered nurse in Columbus, Mississippi, where MUW is located, was denied admission to the School's baccalaureate program. He was told he could only audit courses and would have to go to one of the State's coeducational nursing schools elsewhere in Mississippi to obtain credits toward a degree. In invalidating the School of Nursing's single-sex admissions policy, Justice O'CONNOR's majority opinion applied and restated the Craig standard and rejected the State's effort to justify its system as "benign" and "compensatory." She sketched the framework for her analysis by stating "several firmly-established principles": "That this statute discriminates against males rather than against females does not exempt it from scrutiny or reduce the standard of review. [Moreover,] the party seeking to uphold a statute that classifies individuals on the basis of their gender must carry the burden of showing an 'exceedingly persuasive justification' for the classification. The burden is met only by showing that the classification serves 'important governmental objectives and that the discriminatory means employed' are 'substantially related to the achievement of those objectives.'

"[Although] the test for determining the validity of a gender-based classification is straightforward, it must be applied free of fixed notions concerning the roles and abilities of males and females. Care must be taken in ascertaining whether the statutory objective itself reflects archaic and stereotypic notions. Thus, if the statutory objective is to exclude or 'protect' members of one gender because they are presumed to suffer from an inherent handicap or to be innately inferior, the objective itself is illegitimate. If the State's objective is legitimate and important, we must next determine whether the requisite direct, substantial relationship between objective and means is present. The purpose of requiring that close relationship is to assure that the validity of a classification is determined through reasoned

SoR

analysis rather than through the mechanical application of traditional, often inaccurate, assumptions about the proper roles of men and women. The need for the requirement is amply revealed by reference to the broad range of statutes already invalidated by this Court, statutes that relied upon the simplistic, outdated assumption that gender could be used as a 'proxy for other, more germane bases of classification' [Craig] to establish a link between objective and classification."

Justice O'Connor found that the MUW scheme could not survive scrutiny under this analysis. She rejected the State's primary justification, that the single-sex admissions policy "compensates for discrimination against women and, therefore, constitutes educational affirmative action." She acknowledged that, in "limited circumstances, a gender-based classification favoring one sex can be justified if it intentionally and directly assists members of the sex that is disproportionately burdened." But such a "benign" justification requires "searching analysis." A state may establish a "compensatory" justification "only if members of the gender benefited by the classification actually suffer a disadvantage related to the classification." Here, however, the State had made "no showing that women lacked opportunities to obtain training in the field of nursing or to attain positions of leadership in that field when the MUW School of Nursing opened its doors or that women currently are deprived of such opportunities." She noted, for example, that, in 1970, "women earned 94 percent of the nursing baccalaureate degrees conferred in Mississippi and 98.6 percent of the degrees earned nationwide. [Accordingly, rather] than compensate for discriminatory barriers faced by women, MUW's policy of excluding males [tends] to perpetuate the stereotyped view of nursing as an exclusively woman's job. [MUW's] admissions policy lends credibility to the old view that women, not men, should become nurses, and makes the assumption that nursing is a field for women a self-fulfilling prophecy. Thus, we conclude that, although the State recited a 'benign, compensatory purpose,' it failed to establish that the alleged objective is the actual purpose underlying the discriminatory classification."

Moreover, MUW's policy failed "the second part of the equal protection test, for the State has made no showing that the gender-based classification is substantially and directly related to its proposed compensatory objective. To the contrary, MUW's policy of permitting men to attend classes as auditors fatally undermines its claim that women, at least those in the School of Nursing, are adversely affected by the presence of men. [The] record in this case is flatly inconsistent with the claim that excluding men from the School of Nursing is necessary to reach any of MUW's educational goals. Thus, [we] conclude that the State has fallen far short of establishing the 'exceedingly persuasive justification' needed to sustain the gender-based classification."

Justice POWELL dissented, joined by Justice Rehnquist, objecting to the Court's heightened scrutiny of a State's effort "to provide women with a traditionally popular and respected choice of educational environment," and to the Court's "applying a heightened equal protection standard, developed in cases of genuine sexual stereotyping, to a narrowly utilized state classification that provides an *additional* choice for women: [In] no previous case have we applied it to invalidate state efforts to *expand* women's choices.[1]

[1] Justice Powell added in a footnote: "Sexual segregation in education differs from the tradition typified by [Plessy v. Ferguson], of 'separate but equal' *racial* segregation. It was

[Mississippi's] accommodation [of] student choices is legitimate because it is completely consensual and is important because it permits students to decide for themselves the type of college education they think will benefit them most." Chief Justice BURGER and Justice BLACKMUN submitted separate dissenting notations.

3. ***Sex-based peremptory strikes.*** In **J.E.B. v. Alabama ex rel. T.B.**, 511 U.S. 127 (1994), the Court held that peremptory challenges to jurors on the basis of their gender are unconstitutional. Alabama sued J.E.B. to establish paternity and award child support on behalf of T.B., the mother of a minor child. The state used most of its peremptory challenges to strike male jurors. (J.E.B., the defendant, in turn used most of his peremptory strikes to remove female jurors, but that issue was not before the Court). As a result, an all-woman jury was empaneled. Justice BLACKMUN's opinion for the Court held the state's gender-based peremptory challenges unconstitutional, explaining: "Under our equal protection jurisprudence, gender-based classifications require 'an exceedingly persuasive justification' in order to survive constitutional scrutiny. [Far] from proffering an exceptionally persuasive justification for its gender-based peremptory challenges, respondent maintains that its decision to strike virtually all males from the [jury] 'may reasonably have been based upon the perception, supported by history, that men otherwise totally qualified to serve on a jury might be more sympathetic and receptive to the arguments of a man alleged in a paternity action to be the father of an out-of-wedlock child, while women equally qualified to serve on an jury might be more sympathetic and receptive to the arguments of the complaining witness who bore the child.' We shall not accept as a defense to gender-based peremptory challenges 'the very stereotype the law condemns.' [Respondent] offers virtually no support for the conclusion that gender alone is an accurate predictor of jurors' attitudes; yet it urges this Court to condone the same stereotypes that justified the wholesale exclusion of women from juries and the ballot box."

In a brief dissent, Chief Justice REHNQUIST stated that "the two sexes differ, both biologically and, to a diminishing extent, in experience. It is not merely 'stereotyping' to say that these differences may produce a difference in outlook which is brought into the jury room. Accordingly, use of peremptory challenges on the basis of sex is generally not the sort of derogatory and invidious act which peremptory challenges directed at black jurors may be." In another dissent, Justice SCALIA, joined by Chief Justice Rehnquist and Justice Thomas, remarked: "Today's opinion is an inspiring demonstration of how thoroughly up-to-date and right-thinking we Justices are in matters pertaining to the sexes (or as the Court would have it, genders), and how sternly we disapprove [of] the male chauvinist attitudes of our predecessors. [Peremptory] challenges coexisted with the Equal Protection Clause for 120 years. This case is a perfect example of how the system as a whole is even-handed. [For] every man struck by the government, petitioner's own lawyer struck a woman. To say that men were singled out for discriminatory treatment in this process is preposterous."

---

characteristic of racial segregation that segregated facilities were offered, not as alternatives to increase the choices available to blacks, but as the *sole* alternative. MUW stands in sharp contrast. Of Mississippi's eight public universities and 16 public junior colleges, only MUW considers sex as a criterion for admission. Women consequently are free to select a coeducational education environment for themselves if they so desire; their attendance at MUW is not a matter of coercion."

4. ***All-male public military academies.*** Hogan had held single-sex education unconstitutional when an all-female nursing school excluded a male applicant. Would the Court rule the same way if an all-male school excluded a female applicant? Would it do so a fortiori? In the case that follows, the Court applied the "exceedingly persuasive justification" standard to hold unconstitutional a state's decision to rectify the exclusion of young women from a public military academy by providing a separate, young women's training academy using different methods in a different location:

United States v. Virginia

518 U.S. 515, 116 S. Ct. 2264, 135 L. Ed. 2d 735 (1996).

■ JUSTICE GINSBURG delivered the opinion of the Court.

Virginia's public institutions of higher learning include an incomparable military college, Virginia Military Institute (VMI). The United States maintains that the Constitution's equal protection guarantee precludes Virginia from reserving exclusively to men the unique educational opportunities VMI affords. We agree.

I. Founded in 1839, VMI is today the sole single-sex school among Virginia's 15 public institutions of higher learning. VMI's distinctive mission is to produce "citizen-soldiers," men prepared for leadership in civilian life and in military service. VMI pursues this mission through pervasive training of a kind not available anywhere else in Virginia, an "adversative method" [that] constantly endeavors to instill physical and mental discipline in its cadets and impart to them a strong moral code. [Neither] the goal of producing citizen-soldiers nor VMI's implementing methodology is inherently unsuitable to women. And the school's impressive record in producing leaders has made admission desirable to some women. Nevertheless, Virginia has elected to preserve exclusively for men the advantages and opportunities a VMI education affords.

II. From its establishment in 1839, [VMI] has remained financially supported by Virginia. [Today, it] enrolls about 1300 men as cadets. [Its] "adversative, or doubting, model of education" [features] "physical rigor, mental stress, absolute equality of treatment, absence of privacy, minute regulation of behavior, and indoctrination in desirable values." [VMI] cadets live in spartan barracks where surveillance is constant and privacy nonexistent; they wear uniforms, eat together in the mess hall, and regularly participate in drills. Entering students are incessantly exposed to the rat line, "an extreme form of the adversative model," comparable in intensity to Marine Corps boot camp. Tormenting and punishing, the rat line bonds new cadets to their fellow sufferers and, when they have completed the 7-month experience, to their former [tormentors].

In 1990, prompted by a complaint filed [by] a female high-school student seeking admission to VMI, the United States sued, [alleging] that VMI's exclusively male admission policy violated [equal protection]. The District Court ruled in favor of VMI, [but the Court of Appeals reversed and remanded, suggesting] these options for the State: Admit women to VMI; establish parallel institutions or programs; or abandon state support, leaving VMI free to pursue its policies as a private institution. [In response,] Virginia proposed a parallel program for women: Virginia Women's Institute for Leadership (VWIL). The 4-year, state-sponsored undergraduate program would be located at Mary Baldwin College, a private liberal arts school for women, and would be open, initially, to about 25 to 30 students. Although VWIL would share VMI's mission—to produce "citizen-soldiers"—the VWIL program would differ, as does Mary Baldwin College, from VMI in academic offerings, methods of education, and financial resources. [The] District Court [decided] the plan met the requirements of [equal protection]. [A] divided Court of Appeals [affirmed].

III. The cross-petitions in this case present two ultimate issues. First, does Virginia's exclusion of women from the educational opportunities provided by VMI—extraordinary opportunities for military training and civilian leadership development—deny to women "capable of all of the individual activities required of VMI cadets" the equal protection of the [laws]? Second, if VMI's "unique" situation—as Virginia's sole single-sex public institution of higher education—offends the Constitution's equal protection principle, what is the remedial requirement?

IV. We note, once again, the core instruction of this Court's pathmarking decisions in [J.E.B.] and [Hogan]: Parties who seek to defend gender-based government action must demonstrate an "exceedingly persuasive justification" for that action. Today's skeptical scrutiny of official action denying rights or opportunities based on sex responds to volumes of history. [Since] Reed, the Court has repeatedly recognized that neither federal nor state government acts compatibly with the equal protection principle when a law or official policy denies to women, simply because they are women, full citizenship stature—equal opportunity to aspire, achieve, participate in and contribute to society based on their individual talents and capacities. Without equating gender classifications, for all purposes, to classifications based on race or national origin, the Court, in post-Reed decisions, has carefully inspected official action that closes a door or denies opportunity to women (or to men). To summarize the Court's current directions for cases of official classification based on gender: Focusing on the differential treatment or denial of opportunity for which relief is sought, the reviewing court must determine whether the proffered justification is "exceedingly persuasive." The burden of justification is demanding and it rests entirely on the State. The State must show "at least that the [challenged] classification serves 'important governmental objectives and that the discriminatory means employed' are 'substantially related to the achievement of those objectives.'" The justification must be genuine, not hypothesized or invented post hoc in response to litigation. And it must not rely on overbroad generalizations about the different talents, capacities, or preferences of males and females.

The heightened review standard our precedent establishes does not make sex a proscribed classification. Supposed "inherent differences" are no longer accepted as a ground for race or national origin classifications. Physical differences between men and women, however, are enduring: "The two sexes are not fungible; a community made up exclusively of one [sex] is different from a community composed of both." "Inherent differences" between men and women, we have come to appreciate, remain cause for celebration, but not for denigration of the members of either sex or for artificial constraints on an individual's opportunity.[1] [Such] classifications may not be used, as they once were, to create or perpetuate the legal, social, and economic inferiority of women. Measuring the record in this case against the review standard just described, we conclude that Virginia has shown no "exceedingly persuasive justification" for excluding all women from the citizen-soldier training afforded by VMI and the remedy proffered by Virginia—the Mary Baldwin VWIL program—does not cure the constitutional violation.

V. [Virginia] asserts two justifications in defense of VMI's exclusion of women. First, "[single-sex] education provides important educational benefits," and the option of single-sex education contributes to "diversity in educational approaches." Second, "[the] unique VMI method of character development and leadership training," the school's adversative approach, would have to be modified were VMI to admit women. We consider these [in] turn.

A. Single-sex education affords pedagogical benefits to at least some students, Virginia emphasizes, and that reality is uncontested in this litigation. Similarly, it is not disputed that diversity among public educational institutions can serve the public good. But Virginia has not shown that VMI was established, or has been maintained, with a view to diversifying, by its categorical exclusion of women, educational opportunities within the State. In cases of this genre, our precedent instructs that "benign" justifications proffered in defense of categorical exclusions will not be accepted automatically; a tenable justification must describe actual state purposes, not rationalizations for actions in fact differently grounded. [Neither] recent nor distant history bears out Virginia's alleged pursuit of diversity through single-sex educational options. In 1839, when the State established VMI, a range of educational opportunities for men and women was scarcely contemplated. Higher education at the time was considered dangerous for women; reflecting widely held views about women's proper place, the Nation's first universities and colleges [admitted] only men. [A VMI committee] studied the problem from 1983 until 1986 and [counseled] against "change of VMI's status as a single-sex college." Whatever internal purpose the Mission Study Committee served, [we] can hardly extract from that effort any state policy evenhandedly to advance diverse educational options. [In] sum, we find no persuasive evidence in this record that VMI's male-only admission policy "is in furtherance of a state policy of 'diversity.'" [However] "liberally" this plan serves the State's sons, it makes no provision whatever for her daughters.

B. Virginia next argues that VMI's adversative method of training provides educational benefits that cannot be made available, unmodified, to women. Alterations to accommodate women would necessarily be [so] "drastic," Virginia asserts, as to transform, indeed "destroy," [at] least these three aspects of VMI's program—physical training, the absence of privacy,

---

1 Several amici have urged that diversity in educational opportunities is an altogether appropriate governmental pursuit and that single-sex schools can contribute importantly to such diversity. Indeed, it is the mission of some single-sex schools "to dissipate, rather than perpetuate, traditional gender classifications." See Brief for Twenty-Six Private Women's [Colleges]. We do not question the State's prerogative evenhandedly to support diverse educational opportunities. We address specifically and only an educational opportunity recognized by the [lower courts] as "unique," an opportunity available only at Virginia's premier military institute, the State's sole single-sex public university or college. [Footnote by Justice Ginsburg.]

and the adversative approach. And it is uncontested that women's admission would require accommodations, primarily in arranging housing assignments and physical training programs for female cadets. It is also undisputed, however, that "the VMI methodology could be used to educate women." The District Court even allowed that some women may prefer it to the methodology a women's college might pursue. The parties, furthermore, agree that "some women can meet the physical standards [VMI] now imposes on men." [In] support of its initial judgment for Virginia, [the] District Court made "findings" on "gender-based developmental differences" [that] restate the opinions of Virginia's expert witnesses, opinions about typically male or typically female "tendencies." For example, "males tend to need an atmosphere of adversativeness," while "females tend to thrive in a cooperative atmosphere." [The] United States emphasizes that [we] have cautioned reviewing courts to take a "hard look" at generalizations or "tendencies" of the kind pressed by [Virginia]. State actors controlling gates to opportunity [may] not exclude qualified individuals based on "fixed notions concerning the roles and abilities of males and females."

It may be assumed [that] most women would not choose VMI's adversative method. [However,] it is also probable that "many men would not want to be educated in such an environment." (On that point, even our dissenting colleague might agree.) [The] issue, however, is not whether "women—or men—should be forced to attend VMI" [but] whether the State can constitutionally deny to women who have the will and capacity, the training and attendant opportunities that VMI uniquely affords. The notion that admission of women would downgrade VMI's stature, destroy the adversative system and, with it, even the school, is a judgment hardly proved, a prediction hardly different from other "self-fulfilling prophecies" once routinely used to deny rights or opportunities. When women first sought admission to the bar and access to legal education, concerns of the same order were [expressed]. Medical faculties similarly resisted men and women as partners in the study of medicine. [Surely,] the State's great goal [of producing citizen-soldiers] is not substantially advanced by women's categorical exclusion, in total disregard of their individual merit, from the State's premier "citizen-soldier" corps. Virginia, in sum, "has fallen far short of establishing the 'exceedingly persuasive justification' " that must be the solid base for any gender-defined classification.

VI. In the second phase of the litigation, Virginia presented its remedial plan—maintain VMI as a male-only college and create VWIL as a separate program for women. [The lower courts approved the plan.] [The] United States challenges this "remedial" ruling as pervasively misguided. A. A remedial decree [must] closely fit the constitutional violation; it must be shaped to place persons unconstitutionally denied an opportunity or advantage in "the position they would have occupied in the absence of [discrimination]."

[VWIL] affords women no opportunity to experience the rigorous military training for which VMI is famed. Instead, the VWIL program "deemphasizes" military education, and uses a "cooperative method" of education "which reinforces self-esteem." VWIL students participate in ROTC and a "largely ceremonial" Virginia Corps of Cadets, but Virginia deliberately did not make VWIL a military institute. The VWIL House is not a military-style residence and VWIL students need not live together throughout the 4-year program, eat meals together, or wear uniforms during the school day. VWIL students thus do not experience the "barracks" life "crucial to the VMI experience," the spartan living arrangements designed to foster an "egalitarian ethic." [VWIL] students receive their "leadership training" in seminars [etc.] lacking the "physical rigor, mental stress, [minute] regulation of behavior, and indoctrination in desirable values" made hallmarks of VMI's citizen-soldier training. Kept away from the pressures, hazards, and psychological bonding characteristic of VMI's adversative training, VWIL students will not know the "feeling of tremendous accomplishment" commonly experienced by VMI's successful cadets.

Virginia maintains that these methodological differences are "justified pedagogically," based on "important differences between men and women in learning and developmental needs," "psychological and sociological differences" [that] Virginia describes as "real" and "not stereotypes." [Generalizations] about "the way women are," estimates of what is appropriate for most women, no longer justify denying opportunity to women whose talent and capacity place them outside the average description. [In] contrast to the generalizations about women on which Virginia rests, we note again these dispositive realities: VMI's "implementing methodology" is not "inherently unsuitable to women," "some women [do] well under [the] adversative model," "some women, at least, would want to attend [VMI] if they had the opportunity," "some women are capable of all of the individual activities required of VMI cadets," and "can meet the physical standards [VMI] now imposes on men." It is on behalf of these women that the United States has instituted this suit, and it is for them that a remedy must be crafted, a remedy that will end their exclusion from a state-supplied educational opportunity for which they are [fit].

B. In myriad respects other than military training, VWIL does not qualify as VMI's equal. VWIL's student body, faculty, course offerings, and facilities hardly match VMI's. Nor can the VWIL graduate anticipate the benefits associated with VMI's 157-year history, the school's prestige, and its influential alumni network. Virginia, in sum, while maintaining VMI for men only, has failed to provide any "comparable single-gender women's institution." Instead, the Commonwealth has created a VWIL program fairly appraised as a "pale shadow" of VMI in terms of the range of curricular choices and faculty stature, funding, prestige, alumni support and influence. Virginia's VWIL solution is reminiscent [of] Sweatt v. Painter. [More] important than the tangible features, the Court emphasized [in Sweatt] are "those qualities which are incapable of objective measurement but which make for greatness" in a school, including "reputation of the faculty, experience of the administration, position and influence of the alumni, standing in the community, traditions and prestige." [In] line with Sweatt, we rule here that Virginia has not shown substantial equality in the separate educational opportunities the State supports at VWIL and VMI.

C. Valuable as VWIL may prove for students who seek the program offered, Virginia's remedy affords no cure at all for the opportunities and advantages withheld from women who want a VMI education and can make the grade. In sum, Virginia's remedy does not match the constitutional violation; the State has shown no "exceedingly persuasive justification" for withholding from women qualified for the experience premier training of the kind VMI affords. [Remanded.]

■ CHIEF JUSTICE REHNQUIST, concurring in the judgment.

[Not until Hogan in 1982 was Virginia placed] on notice that VMI's men-only admissions policy was open to serious question. [Before] this Court, Virginia has sought to justify VMI's single-sex admissions policy primarily on the basis that diversity in education is desirable, and that while most of the public institutions of higher learning in the State are coeducational, there should also be room for single-sex institutions. I agree with the Court that there is scant evidence in the record that this was the real reason that Virginia decided to maintain VMI as men only. But, unlike the majority, I would consider only evidence that postdates [Hogan], and would draw no negative inferences from the State's actions before that time. [After] Hogan, the State was entitled to reconsider its policy with respect to VMI, and to not have earlier justifications, or lack thereof, held against it.

Even if diversity in educational opportunity were the State's actual objective, the State's position would still be problematic. The difficulty with its position is that the diversity benefited only one sex; there was single-sex public education available for men at VMI, but no corresponding single-sex public education available for women. When Hogan placed Virginia on notice that VMI's admissions policy possibly was unconstitutional, VMI could have dealt with the problem by admitting [women]. Was there something else the State could have done to avoid an equal protection violation? I do not think [that] the State's options were as limited as the majority may imply. [Had] Virginia made a genuine effort to devote comparable public resources to a facility for women, and followed through on such a plan, it might well have avoided an equal protection violation. I do not believe the State was faced with the stark choice of either admitting women to VMI [or] abandoning VMI and starting from scratch for both men and [women]. [It] is not the "exclusion of women" that violates the Equal Protection Clause, but the maintenance of an all-men school without providing any—much less a comparable—institution for women. Accordingly, the remedy should not necessarily require either the admission of women to VMI, or the creation of a VMI clone for women. An adequate remedy [might] be a demonstration by Virginia that its interest in educating men in a single-sex environment is matched by its interest in educating women in a single-sex institution. To demonstrate such, the State does not need to create two institutions with the same number of faculty PhD's, similar SAT scores, or comparable athletic fields. Nor would it necessarily require that the women's institution offer the same curriculum as the [men's]. It would be sufficient [if] the two institutions offered the same quality of education and were of the same overall caliber. [But] the state should avoid assuming demand based on stereotypes; it must not assume a priori, without evidence, that there would be no interest in a women's school of civil engineering, or in a men's school of nursing. In the end, the women's institution Virginia proposes, VWIL, fails as a remedy, because it is distinctly inferior to the existing men's institution and will continue to be for the foreseeable future. [I] therefore ultimately agree [that] Virginia has not provided an adequate remedy.

■ JUSTICE SCALIA, dissenting.

Today the Court shuts down an institution that has served the people of [Virginia] with pride and distinction for over a century and a half. [The] tradition of having government-funded military schools for men is as well rooted in the traditions of this country as the tradition of sending only men into military combat. The people may decide to change the one tradition, like the other, through democratic processes; but the assertion that either tradition has been unconstitutional through the centuries is not law, but politics-smuggled-into-law. And the same applies, more broadly, to single-sex education in general which [is] threatened by today's decision with the cut-off of all state and federal support. Today, however, change is forced upon Virginia, and reversion to single-sex education is prohibited nationwide, not by democratic processes but by order of this Court.

[The] United States urged us to hold in this case "that strict scrutiny is the correct constitutional standard for evaluating classifications that deny opportunities to individuals based on their sex." [The Court] effectively accepts [this]. Although the Court in two places recites the test as stated in Hogan, [the] Court proceeds to interpret "exceedingly persuasive justification" in a fashion that contradicts the reasoning of Hogan and our other precedents. [Only] the amorphous "exceedingly persuasive justification" phrase, and not the standard elaboration of intermediate scrutiny, can be made to yield this conclusion that VMI's single-sex composition is unconstitutional because there exist several women (or, one would have to conclude under the Court's reasoning, a single woman) willing and able to undertake VMI's program. Intermediate scrutiny has never required a least-restrictive-means analysis, but only a "substantial relation" between the classification and the state interests that it serves. [There] is simply no support in our cases for the notion that a sex-based classification is invalid unless it relates to characteristics that hold true in every instance.

Not content to execute a de facto abandonment of the intermediate [scrutiny test], the Court purports to reserve the question whether, even in principle, a higher standard (i.e., strict scrutiny) should apply. [If] the question of the applicable standard of review for sex-based classifications were to be [reconsidered], the stronger argument would be not for elevating the standard to strict scrutiny, but for reducing it to rational-basis review. [Normal,] rational-basis review of sex-based classifications would be much more in accord with the genesis of heightened standards of judicial review, the famous footnote [four in Carolene Products]. It is hard to consider women a "discrete and insular minority" unable to employ the "political processes ordinarily to be relied upon," when they constitute a majority of the electorate. And the suggestion that they are incapable of exerting that political power smacks of the same paternalism that the Court so roundly condemns. Moreover, a long list of legislation proves the proposition false.

[It] is beyond question that Virginia has an important state interest in providing effective college education for its citizens. That single-sex instruction is an approach substantially related to that interest should be evident enough from the long and continuing history in this country of men's and women's colleges. [But] besides its single-sex constitution, VMI is different from other colleges [in employing] a "distinctive educational method." [A] State's decision to maintain within its system one school that provides the adversative method is "substantially related" to its goal of good education. [Virginia's] election to fund one public all-male institution and one on the adversative model—and to concentrate its resources in a single entity that serves both these interests in diversity—is substantially related to the State's important educational interests.

[The] Court suggests that Virginia's [asserted] interest in promoting diversity of educational options [is] not "genuine," but is a pretext for discriminating against women. [The] relevance of [the 1980s Study

Committee] is that its very creation, its sober 3-year study, and the analysis it produced, utterly refute the claim that VMI has elected to maintain its all-male student-body composition for some misogynistic [reason]. [That] VMI would not have to change very much if it were to admit women [is] irrelevant: If VMI's single-sex status is substantially related to the government's important educational objectives, [that] concludes the inquiry. There should be no debate in the federal judiciary over "how much" VMI would be required to change if it admitted women and whether that would constitute "too much" change.

[Under] the constitutional principles announced and applied today, single-sex public education is unconstitutional. By going through the motions of applying a balancing test—asking whether the State has adduced an "exceedingly persuasive justification" for its sex-based classification—the Court creates the illusion that government officials in some future case will have a clear shot at justifying some sort of single-sex public education. [But] the Court indicates that if any program restricted to one sex is "unique," it must be opened to members of the opposite sex "who have the will and capacity" to participate in it. [The] enemies of single-sex education have won. [There] are few extant single-sex public educational programs. The potential of today's decision for widespread disruption of existing institutions lies in its application to *private* single-sex education. Government support is immensely important to private educational institutions. Charitable status under the tax law is also highly significant for private [colleges,] and it is certainly not beyond the Court that rendered today's decision to hold that a donation to a single-sex college should be deemed contrary to [public policy]. [The] only hope for state-assisted single-sex private schools is that the Court will not apply in the future the principles of law it has applied today. That is a substantial hope, I am happy and ashamed to say. [It] will certainly be possible for this Court to write a future opinion that ignores the broad principles of law set forth today, and that characterizes as utterly dispositive the opinion's perceptions that VMI was a uniquely prestigious all-male institution, conceived in chauvinism, etc., etc. I will not join that [opinion].[2]

SEX EQUALITY, SEX DIFFERENCES AND THE QUESTION OF GENDER

1. ***Is single-sex education ever constitutional?*** Does the rejection of the VWIL remedy in the Virginia case cast doubt on the constitutionality of all public single-sex education? Note that, while Justice Scalia objects that this is the necessary implication of the decision, Justice Ginsburg denies as much, suggesting in a footnote that the state might run single-sex schools as part of a state program designed "evenhandedly to support diverse educational opportunities." What kinds of single-sex schools might pass muster under this test? Is separate but equal sometimes permissible for sex in public education, even though separate but equal is flatly impermissible for race?

---

[2] Justice THOMAS, whose son was attending VMI, did not participate in this case. Immediately after the Court's decision was announced, the Citadel, the only other state-supported military academy in the nation, announced that it would comply with the "letter and spirit" of the Virginia ruling, and that women would be in attendance by August 1996. VMI, after unsuccessfully exploring the possibility of privatization, also ultimately announced that it would admit women (and did so in late 1996).

After Virginia, what legitimate differences in pedagogy or educational opportunities could possibly justify separating students by sex? Consider the following variations: Most lower courts have upheld sex-segregated athletic programs in public education. See Note, "Boys Muscling in on Girls' Sports," 53 Ohio St. L.J. 891 (1992). Is athletic sex segregation justified as reflecting real physical differences between the sexes? Is this conditional on a school's providing women athletes opportunities equal to those of men? If so, must every sport have both a girls' and boys' team? Or should such separate teams be held unconstitutional as reinforcing stereotypes about women athletes? Might self-defense classes be limited to women on the ground that women are more vulnerable than men to physical and sexual attack? Even if sex-based segregation is permissible in such settings, may it ever be justified for classroom learning on the ground that women speak in a "different voice" than men? An influential book on moral reasoning by Carol Gilligan, In a Different Voice (1982), suggested that girls on average engage in different forms of moral reasoning than boys, evincing more concern than boys do about caring for others and about preserving relationships and less concern than boys about establishing hierarchy or clear winners. For example, while a boy might advise stealing a drug to save an ill family member, a girl might suggest bargaining with the pharmacist to postpone payment. What would be the constitutional consequences of recognizing sex differences in "voice"? Are the differences Gilligan real? If so, are they natural differences or artifacts of women's relatively more powerless position in social and economic life? If the latter, should they ever be grounds for sex segregation in education? Note that Virginia sought to rely on Gilligan's "different voice" argument as justifying the educational differences between VMI and VWIL, but Gilligan signed an amicus brief on the side of the challengers, protesting that Virginia had misconstrued her work.

Interest in single-sex public schools has increased since the mid-1990s among educators as a response to continuing different rates of performance by boys and girls on various educational measures. One study noted that, while only three single-sex public schools existed nation-wide in 1995, over 44 existed by the 2005–06 school year in over one-third of the states. See Jenkins, "Constitutional Lessons for the Next Generation of Public Single-Sex Elementary and Secondary Schools," 47 Wm. & Mary L. Rev. 1953 (2006). The federal government signaled willingness to support experimentation with single-sex education in the funding provisions of the No Child Left Behind Act of 2001. Should such schools be deemed more permissible if a school district provides dual academies, one for girls and one for boys, which students can elect on a voluntary basis? Even if some standalone same-sex academies are allowed, should they have to prove a strong causal link to better educational outcomes? For such arguments, see Jenkins, supra.

2. ***"Real" differences?*** Note that Virginia sought to rely on the physical incompatibility of most women with the adversative method as a basis for prediction that too few women would join the program to make it sustainable. The Court rejected this reasoning as too close to stereotyping that failed to take account of the exceptional woman. Are there any differences between men and women, however, that are "real" and not stereotypical, and that therefore may be taken into account in law?

What about laws that discriminate with respect to biologically sex-related characteristics like pregnancy or the capacity to become pregnant?

Traditional equal protection principles require that only those who are similarly situated should be treated alike. Differences in treatment can be justified when they correspond to relevant differences. Are there any "real" biological differences besides the capacity or incapacity to gestate and bear children? Is that difference, even if real, one that may be accounted for in law? Do average differences between the sexes in height, weight, strength, speed or stamina also count as real differences? What about vulnerability to sexual coercion or torture, for example by enemies at war? Are all differences between the sexes other than reproductive capacities simply socially constructed? Does some legislative action allegedly relying on "real" differences in fact reflect overbroad, archaic generalizations and stereotypes? What if a "stereotype" reflects measurable differences in average behavior? Is the goal of constitutionalizing sex equality to deemphasize the impact of sexual differences in order to achieve a gender-"neutral" society? Can society ever be gender-neutral in the same way some have aspired to make it color-blind? The following cases consider such questions.

3. ***Pregnancy classifications.*** In **Geduldig v. Aiello**, 417 U.S. 484 (1974), the Court held that exclusion of "disability that accompanies normal pregnancy and childbirth" from California's disability insurance system did not constitute "invidious discrimination" under the Equal Protection Clause. Justice STEWART's majority opinion claimed that the challenged classification was not "based upon gender as such" and therefore applied a very deferential standard of review. He argued in a footnote: "The California insurance program does not exclude anyone from benefit eligibility because of gender but merely removes one physical condition—pregnancy—from the list of compensable disabilities. While it is true that only women can become pregnant, it does not follow that every legislative classification concerning pregnancy is a sex-based classification like those considered in Reed and Frontiero. Normal pregnancy is an objectively identifiable physical condition with unique characteristics. Absent a showing that distinctions involving pregnancy are mere pretexts designed to effect an invidious discrimination against the members of one sex or the other, lawmakers are constitutionally free to include or exclude pregnancy from the coverage of legislation such as this on any reasonable basis, just as with respect to any other physical condition. [The] program divides potential recipients into two groups—pregnant women and nonpregnant persons. While the first group is exclusively female, the second includes members of both sexes. The fiscal and actuarial benefits of the program thus accrue to members of both sexes." Moreover, Justice Stewart noted in the text of his opinion: "There is no evidence in the record [that the selection of the risks] work to discriminate against any definable group or class in terms of the aggregate risk protection derived by that group or class from the program. There is no risk from which men are protected and women are not. Likewise, there is no risk from which women are protected and men are not."

Justice BRENNAN's dissent, joined by Justices Douglas and Marshall, concluded that there had been sex discrimination in California's "singling out for less favorable treatment a gender-linked disability peculiar to women [even while] men receive full compensation for all disabilities suffered, including those that affect only or primarily their sex, such as prostatectomies, circumcision, hemophilia, and gout. In effect, one set of rules is applied to females and another to males. Such dissimilar treatment of men and women, on the basis of physical characteristics inextricably limited to one sex, inevitably constitutes sex discrimination." And the state's interest in preserving the fiscal integrity of its program could not justify this discrimination.[1]

4. ***Gender-specific statutory rape laws.*** In **Michael M. v. Superior Court**, 450 U.S. 464 (1981), the Court upheld California's "statutory rape" law, which punished the male, but not the female, participant in sexual intercourse when the female was under 18 and not the male's wife. The challenger, at the time of the alleged statutory rape, was a 17-year-old male who had engaged in intercourse with a 16-year-old female. Justice REHNQUIST's plurality opinion, joined by Chief Justice Burger and Justices Stewart and Powell, stated (five years after Craig v. Boren) that "[We have held] that the traditional minimum rationality test takes on a somewhat 'sharper focus' when gender-based classifications are challenged. See [Craig; Reed]. [Underlying] these decisions is the principle that a legislature may not 'make overbroad generalizations based on sex which are entirely unrelated to any differences between men and women or which demean the ability or social status of the affected class.' But because [equal protection] does not [require] 'things which are different in fact [to] be treated in law as though they were the same,' this Court has consistently upheld statutes where the gender classification is not invidious, but rather realistically reflects the fact that the sexes are not similarly situated in certain circumstances. As the Court has stated, a legislature may 'provide for the special problems of women.'

"We are satisfied not only that the prevention of illegitimate pregnancy is at least one of the 'purposes' of the statute, but also that the State has a strong interest in preventing such pregnancy.[2] Because virtually all of the significant harmful and inescapably identifiable consequences of teenage pregnancy fall on the young female, a legislature acts well within its authority when it elects to punish only the participant who, by nature, suffers few of the consequences of his conduct. It is hardly unreasonable for a legislature acting to protect minor females to exclude them from punishment. Moreover, the risk of pregnancy itself constitutes a substantial deterrence to young females. No similar natural sanctions deter males. A criminal sanction imposed solely on males thus serves to roughly 'equalize' the deterrents on the sexes.

"We are unable to accept the contention that the statute is impermissibly underinclusive and must [be] *broadened* so as to hold the female as criminally liable as the male. It is argued that this statute is not *necessary* to deter teenage pregnancy because a gender-neutral statute [would] serve that goal equally well. The relevant inquiry, however, is not

[1] Title VII of the 1964 Civil Rights Act, barring employment discrimination based on sex, was similarly interpreted not to extend to the exclusion of pregnancies from private disability plans in General Electric Co. v. Gilbert, 429 U.S. 125 (1976). The Gilbert ruling was mooted by Congress when it amended Title VII in 1978 to expressly forbid discrimination on the basis not only of sex but also of pregnancy.

[2] "Although petitioner concedes that the State has a 'compelling' interest in preventing teenage pregnancy, he contends that the 'true' purpose of [the law] is to protect the virtue and chastity of young women. As such, the statute is unjustifiable because it rests on archaic stereotypes. [But the only] question for us [is] whether the legislation violates [equal protection], not whether its supporters may have endorsed it for reasons no longer generally accepted. Even if the preservation of female chastity were one of the motives of the statute, and even if that motive be impermissible, petitioner's argument must fail because '[i]t is a familiar practice of constitutional law that this Court will not strike down an otherwise constitutional statute on the basis of an allegedly illicit legislative motive.' United States v. O'Brien, 391 U.S. 367 (1968)." [Footnote by Justice Rehnquist.]

whether the statute is drawn as precisely as it might have been, but whether the line chosen by the [State] is within constitutional limitations. In any event, we cannot say that a gender-neutral statute would be as effective as the statute California has chosen to enact. The State persuasively contends that a gender-neutral statute would frustrate its interest in effective enforcement [because] a female is surely less likely to report violations of the statute if she herself would be subject to criminal prosecution. [In] upholding the [law] we also recognize [that] the statute places a burden on males which is not shared by females. But we find nothing to suggest that men, because of past discrimination or peculiar disadvantages, are in need of the special solicitude of the courts. Nor is this a case where the gender classification is made 'solely [for] administrative convenience,' [or] rests on 'the baggage of sexual stereotypes.' As we have held, the statute instead reasonably reflects the fact that the consequences of sexual intercourse and pregnancy fall more heavily on the female than on the male." Justice STEWART, who joined Justice Rehnquist's opinion, also submitted a separate opinion. Justice BLACKMUN concurred in the judgment, stating that he voted to uphold the gender-based classification on the basis of the Reed and Craig tests.

Justice BRENNAN's dissent, joined by Justices White and Marshall, objected that none of the three opinions comprising the majority "fairly applies the equal protection analysis this Court has so carefully developed since [Craig]." He added that it was "perhaps because the gender classification in California's statutory rape law was initially designed to [further] outmoded sexual stereotypes [regarding the special need to protect young women's chastity], rather than to reduce the incidence of teenage pregnancies, that the State has been unable to demonstrate a substantial relationship between the classification and its newly asserted goal." In arguing that this relationship had not been shown, he rejected, for example, the State's assertion that law enforcement problems created by a gender-neutral statutory rape law would make such a law less effective than a gender-based statute in deterring sexual activity: "Even if fewer persons were prosecuted under the gender-neutral law, as the State suggests, it would still be true that twice as many persons would be *subject* to arrest."

A separate dissent by Justice STEVENS stated that a statute such as this, "applicable to only half of the joint participants in the risk-creating conduct," was impermissible sex discrimination—even though he agreed with the plurality's assumption "that the joint act that this law seeks to prohibit creates a greater risk of harm for the female than for the male." He stated: "The argument that a special need for protection provides a rational explanation for an exemption is one I simply do not comprehend." The fact that a female confronted a greater risk of harm than a male was "a reason for applying the prohibition to her," not for exempting her. "Surely, if we examine the problem from the point of view of society's interest in preventing the risk-creating conduct from occurring at all, it is irrational to exempt 50% of the potential violators." He added: "Finally, even if my logic is faulty and there actually is some speculative basis for treating equally guilty males and females differently, I still believe that any such speculative justification would be outweighed by the paramount interest in even-handed enforcement of the law. A rule that authorizes punishment of only one of two equally guilty wrongdoers violates the essence of the constitutional requirement that the sovereign must govern impartially."

Recall Justice Rehnquist's objections in dissent in Craig to the Court's extension of judicial solicitude to male as opposed to female litigants. Did his Michael M. opinion vindicate that view sub rosa? Or did it carve out only a limited exception to heightened scrutiny of laws nominally protective of females? Note that most of the cases brought to the Court between Reed and Frontiero and Virginia were brought by men, not women. For criticisms of Michael M., see Williams, "The Equality Crisis: Some Reflections on Culture, Courts and Feminism," 7 Women's Rts. L. Rep. 175 (1982) ("If we can't have it both ways, we have to decide which way we want to have it."), and Olsen, "Statutory Rape: A Feminist Critique of Rights Analysis," 63 Tex. L. Rev. 387 (1984).

5. ***Exclusion of women from the military draft.*** In **Rostker v. Goldberg**, 453 U.S. 57 (1981), the Court by a vote of 6–3 rejected a claim, under the equal protection aspect of Fifth Amendment due process, that the Military Selective Service Act (MSSA) was unconstitutional in "authorizing the President to require the registration of males and not females." Emphasizing that the purpose of draft registration was "to facilitate any eventual conscription," Justice REHNQUIST's majority opinion noted: "The case arises in the context of Congress' authority over national defense and military affairs, and perhaps in no other area has the Court accorded Congress greater deference. [The] tests and limitations to be applied may differ because of the military context. [In] deciding the question before us we must be particularly careful not to substitute our judgment of what is desirable for that of Congress, or our own evaluation of evidence for a reasonable evaluation by the Legislative Branch. [No] one could deny that under the test of [Craig], the Government's interest in raising and supporting armies is an 'important governmental interest.' Congress and its Committees carefully considered and debated two alternative means of furthering that interest: the first was to register only males for potential conscription, and the other was to register both sexes. Congress chose the former alternative. [Congress] determined that any future draft, which would be facilitated by the registration scheme, would be characterized by a need for combat troops. [Since] women are [by statute] excluded from combat, Congress concluded that they would not be needed in the event of a draft, and therefore decided [not to register them]. [This] is not a case of Congress arbitrarily choosing to burden one of two similarly situated [groups]. Men and women, because of the combat restrictions on women, are simply not similarly situated for purposes of a draft or registration for a draft. [The] exemption of women from registration is not only sufficiently but closely related to Congress' purpose in authorizing registration. [The] Constitution requires that Congress treat similarly situated persons similarly, not that it engage in gestures of superficial equality."

Justice MARSHALL's dissent, joined by Justice Brennan, stated: "The Court today places its imprimatur on one of the most potent remaining public expressions of 'ancient canards about the proper role of women.' [In] my judgment, there simply is no basis for concluding in this case that excluding women from registration is substantially related to the achievement of a concededly important governmental interest in maintaining an effective defense. [In] this case, the Government makes no claim that preparing for a draft of combat troops cannot be accomplished just as effectively by *registering* both men and women but *drafting* only men if only men turn out to be needed. Nor can the Government argue that this alternative entails the additional cost and administrative inconvenience of registering women. This

Court has repeatedly stated that the administrative convenience of employing a sex classification is not an adequate constitutional justification under the [Craig] test. [Testimony] about personnel requirements in the event of a draft established that women could fill at least 80,000 of the 650,000 positions for which conscripts would be inducted. Thus, with respect to these 80,000 or more positions, the statutes and policies barring women from combat do not provide a reason for distinguishing between male and female potential conscripts; the two groups are, in the majority's parlance, 'similarly situated.'" Justice WHITE also dissented, in an opinion joined by Justice Brennan.

Note that Rostker, unlike Michael M., does not involve a physical, biological difference between men and women. In Michael M., the majority emphasized that most of the harmful consequences of teenage pregnancy fall on the young female; in Rostker, the majority emphasized that women are ineligible for combat duty. But that "disability" of women was the product not of biological factors but rather of a legal construct, the congressionally imposed barrier to women's combat service. And the barrier to women's combat service was not challenged in the case. Should it have been?

Are men and women relevantly different with respect to the capacity to engage in combat? Since Rostker, women's presence in the U.S. armed forces has risen from 8.4 percent to nearly 15 percent, and Congress has repealed the statutory bar on women's eligibility for combat positions. Several branches of the U.S. Armed Forces continue to exclude women by regulation from some combat positions, however, even as women's presence in the military has expanded. Suppose that such remaining combat exclusions were directly challenged as violations of equal protection. Do any real differences justify such exclusions? Consider the arguments, advanced in some amicus briefs in Rostker, that the exclusion of women from combat is justified because women are more likely to be pregnant or the primary caretakers of young children, and more vulnerable than men to rape and sexual coercion as prisoners of war. What of the argument that the presence of women in combat will undermine the command structure, either by introducing heterosexual sexual interactions or confusing male soldiers who have been enculturated to be chivalrous toward the opposite sex? What of the argument, especially as to those in infantry or other physically arduous roles, that women are on average physically smaller and weaker than men? For the argument that "[t]oday, women serve—and die—in combat, as the present war in Iraq has amply demonstrated," and that this "extrajudicial transformation in women's military status" has "undermined Rostker's status as constitutional interpretation," see Hasday, "Fighting Women: The Military, Sex, and Extrajudicial Constitutional Change," 93 Minn. L. Rev. 96 (2008).

6. ***Discrimination against unmarried fathers.*** Many aspects of family law have disfavored fathers of children born out of wedlock as compared with mothers of such children. (Recall Michael H. (1989; p. 552 above.)) The Court has applied intermediate scrutiny to some such laws on the ground that they involved sex discrimination. The 5–4 decision in **Caban v. Mohammed**, 441 U.S. 380 (1979), invalidated a New York law granting the mother but not the father of an illegitimate child the right to block the child's adoption by withholding consent. This provision was challenged by a father who had lived with his children and their mother as a family for several years. Justice POWELL's majority opinion concluded that the law

was "another example of 'overbroad generalizations' in gender-based classifications" and that "no showing has been made that the [distinction bears] a substantial relationship to the proclaimed interests of the State in promoting the adoption of illegitimate children." He rejected the argument that the distinction could be justified "by a fundamental difference between maternal and paternal relations," insisting that there was no "universal difference [at] every phase of a child's development," "even if unwed mothers as a class were closer than unwed fathers to their newborn infants." The facts in this case, he added, demonstrated that "an unwed father may have a relationship with his children fully comparable to that of a mother." Justice STEVENS's dissent, joined by Chief Justice Burger and Justice Rehnquist, argued that the real differences between the male and female, especially during the child's infancy, were "significant, and that these 'natural differences between unmarried fathers and mothers made it probable that the mother, and not the father or both parents, would have custody of the newborn infant.' "

Contrast the Court's more recent decision, in **Nguyen v. INS**, 533 U.S. 53 (2001), upholding a law that treated children born outside of wedlock to one parent who was a citizen and one parent who was a noncitizen differently depending on whether it was the mother or the father who was the citizen. Under 8 U.S.C. § 1409, children with citizen-mothers are automatically considered citizens at birth, provided the mother has met certain minimal residency requirements. But children with citizen-fathers must meet three conditions to be considered citizens at birth: establishment of the "blood relationship" by "clear and convincing evidence," the father's written promise of financial support, and fulfillment before the child's eighteenth birthday of one of three formal recognitions of paternity—legal legitimation, the father's declaration of paternity under oath, or a court order of paternity.

In an opinion by Justice KENNEDY, the Court upheld the distinction as "based on the significant difference between [a mother's and a father's] relationships to the potential citizen at the time of birth," and "substantially related to the achievement" of "two important governmental objectives: [assuring] that a biological parent-child relationship exists [and ensuring] that the child and [citizen] parent have [an] opportunity [to] develop [a] relationship [providing] a connection between child and citizen parent and, in turn, the United States. In the case of a citizen mother and a child born overseas, the opportunity for a meaningful relationship [inheres] in the very event of birth. [The] mother knows that the child is in being and is hers and has an initial point of contact with him. [The] same opportunity [is not biologically inevitable] in the case of the unwed father. [It] is not always certain that a father will know that a child was conceived, nor is it always clear that even the mother will be sure of the father's identity[, particularly] in the case of a child born overseas and out of wedlock. [To] fail to acknowledge even our most basic biological differences—such as the fact that a mother must be present at birth but the father need not be—risks making the guarantee of equal protection superficial. [The statute] at issue is not marked by misconception and prejudice, nor does it show disrespect for either class. [Equal] protection does not forbid Congress to address the problem at hand in a manner specific to each gender." In a concurrence joined by Justice Thomas, Justice SCALIA wrote that, even if Nguyen had stated an Equal Protection claim, the Court would "lack[ ] power to provide [conferral] of citizenship on a basis other than that prescribed by Congress."

Justice O'CONNOR dissented, joined by Justices Souter, Ginsburg, and Breyer. She found the law not narrowly tailored to the goal of verifying the parent-child biological relationship, given the "efficacy and availability of modern technology" such as DNA testing. She further criticized the majority both for ignoring "the availability of sex-neutral alternatives," and for overstating the evidentiary difference between proof of maternity and proof of paternity: "[A] mother will not always have formal legal documentation of birth because a birth certificate may not issue or may subsequently be lost. Conversely, a father's name may well appear on a birth certificate. While it is doubtless true that a mother's blood relation to a child is uniquely 'verifiable from the birth itself' to those present at birth, the majority has not shown that a mother's birth relation is uniquely verifiable *by the INS,* much less that any greater verifiability warrants a sex-based, rather than a sex-neutral, statute. [If] rational basis scrutiny were appropriate in this case, then the claim that '[t]he Constitution [does] not require that Congress elect one particular mechanism from among many possible methods [ ]' would have much greater force. [But equal] protection demands more when a facially sex-based classification is at issue."

Pointing out that the petitioner had, in fact, been raised since age five by his citizen-father in Texas, Justice O'Connor charged that the law was based "not in biological differences but instead in a stereotype—i.e., 'the generalization that mothers are significantly more likely than fathers [to] develop caring relationships with their children.' Such a claim relies on 'the very stereotype the law condemns,' [J.E.B.], 'lends credibility' to the generalization, [Hogan], and helps to convert that 'assumption' into 'a self-fulfilling prophecy,' [I] trust that the depth and vitality of [our] precedents will ensure that today's error remains an aberration."

In **Sessions v. Morales-Santana**, 579 U.S. ___, 137 S. Ct. 1678 (2017), Justice GINSBURG, writing for six justices, applied intermediate scrutiny to invalidate, under the equal protection principle implicit in the Fifth Amendment, a federal statutory immigration scheme that differentiated between fathers and mothers. The law allowed an unwed U.S.-citizen mother to transmit citizenship to her child born abroad if she had lived continuously in the United States for one year prior to the child's birth. Yet, for unwed U.S. citizen fathers or married couples, this physical presence requirement was lengthened to ten years, of which five must have occurred after the parent reached age eighteen. The scheme traced to amendments to the Immigration and Nationality Act enacted in 1940 and 1952. Justice Ginsburg wrote: "History reveals what lurks behind § 1409. [During] this era, two once habitual, but now untenable, assumptions pervaded our Nation's citizenship laws and underpinned judicial and administrative rulings: In marriage, husband is dominant, wife subordinate; unwed mother is the natural and sole guardian of a non-marital child. [For] unwed parents, the father-controls tradition never held sway. Instead, the mother was regarded as the child's natural and sole guardian. [In] the 1940 Act, Congress discarded the father-controls assumption concerning married parents, but codified the mother-as-sole-guardian perception regarding unmarried parents. [Concern] about the attachment of foreign-born children to the United States explains the treatment of unwed citizen fathers, who, according to the familiar stereotype, would care little about, and have scant contact with, their nonmarital children. For unwed citizen mothers, however, there was no need for a prolonged residency prophylactic: The alien father, who might transmit foreign ways, was presumptively out of the picture. [Overbroad] generalizations of that order, the Court has come to comprehend, have a constraining impact, descriptive though they may be of the way many people still order their lives. Laws according or denying benefits in reliance on '[s]tereotypes about women's domestic roles,' the Court has observed, may 'creat[e] a self-fulfilling cycle of discrimination that force[s] women to continue to assume the role of primary family caregiver.' Nevada Dept. of Human Resources v. Hibbs. Correspondingly, such laws may disserve men who exercise responsibility for raising their children. In light of the equal protection jurisprudence this Court has developed, [the law's] discrete duration-of-residence requirements for unwed mothers and fathers who have accepted parental responsibility is stunningly anachronistic."

Yet having struck down the disparity in treatment, the Court that held that the remedy was not to shorten the residency for fathers but to eliminate the favorable treatment of unwed mothers. Justice Ginsburg wrote: "The choice between these outcomes is governed by the legislature's intent, as revealed by the statute at hand. Ordinarily, we have reiterated, 'extension, rather than nullification, is the proper course.' [Here,] however, the discriminatory exception consists of favorable treatment for a discrete group (a shorter physical-presence requirement for unwed U.S.-citizen mothers giving birth abroad). [The] residual policy here, the longer physical-presence requirement, [evidences] Congress' recognition of the importance of residence in this country as the talisman of dedicated attachment. And the potential for disruption of the statutory scheme is large. For if § 1409(c)'s one-year dispensation were extended to unwed citizen fathers, would it not be irrational to retain the longer term when the U.S.-citizen parent is married? Disadvantageous treatment of marital children in comparison to nonmarital children is scarcely a purpose one can sensibly attribute to Congress. [Put] to the choice, Congress, we believe, would have abrogated § 1409(c)'s exception, preferring preservation of the general rule." Justice THOMAS, joined by Justice Alito, concurred only in the judgment, stating that, in light of the remedy, the constitutional issue should not have been reached. Justice Gorsuch did not participate.

Note that this is the first instance in which the Court, having found unconstitutional gender-stereotyping favoring women, chose to remedy the inequality by levelling down rather than levelling up. Is this remedy the correct one? If the Court may not strip citizenship retroactively from children born abroad to unwed U.S.-citizen mothers who had already benefited from the favorable U.S.-residency requirement, doesn't this result leave intact unequal treatment of existing children born abroad to similarly-situated unwed U.S.-citizen fathers?

7. ***The role of "real" differences.*** Are women better off with a constitutional jurisprudence that denies "real" differences or one that acknowledges them? Can "real" or biological differences be acknowledged for purposes of benefiting women (e.g., longer employment leaves for pregnancy than for disability) but not burdening them (e.g., barring pregnant women from some workplaces)? Does it matter whether the reason for the exclusion is biological (e.g., safety of fetuses) or symbolic (e.g., concern for the sensibilities of schoolchildren viewing a pregnant teacher's swollen girth)? If women can't have it both ways, must they decide which way they want to have it?

Some commentators have argued that the Court's general insistence on formal equality—on an essentially gender-blind Constitution—in fact causes material harm to women by ignoring important sex-based differences, or by holding women to standards that have been established principally by men in a sexually unequal past. Thus, Sex Equality, Sex Differences, and the Supreme Court," 92 Yale L.J. 913 (1983), criticized the dissenters in Michael M. and Rostker for focusing on a means-ends analysis and on "irrationality," and urged instead an "explicitly normative theory of sex equality that identifies with some particularity the dynamics and harmful consequences of sexism." Law, "Rethinking Sex and the Constitution," 132 U. Pa. L. Rev. 955 (1984), argued that sexual equality doctrine must confront squarely the reality of categorical biological differences between men and women: "To reconcile the ideal of human equality with the reality of biological difference we must (1) begin to distinguish clearly between laws that classify on the basis of sex and laws that govern reproduction; (2) recognize that laws governing reproduction implicate equality concerns; and (3) establish a test that can determine when laws governing reproduction violate constitutional equality norms." And Karst, "Woman's Constitution," 1984 Duke L.J. 447, claimed that the "male conception of society underlies the very constitutional doctrine that women seek to use in effecting a reconstructed order of male-female relations," suggesting an alternative constitutional approach resting on the premise that women as a group "do tend to have a different perception of social relations and a different approach to moral issues," emphasizing the individual "as part of a network of relationships" that finds "security in connection rather than separation and the competitive pursuit of individual power."

8. ***Discrimination against transgender and gender-nonconforming individuals.*** Should discrimination against transgender or gender-nonconforming plaintiffs be seen as a form of sex discrimination? If this equation is possible, should the same standard of intermediate scrutiny traditionally applied in sex discrimination cases also apply in cases brought by transgender or gender-nonconforming plaintiffs?

Transgender plaintiffs forwarding sex discrimination claims typically make two arguments. First, that because someone discriminating based on gender identity must invariably take into account the gender of the victim, the two forms of discrimination are inextricably linked. Second, that discrimination on the basis of gender identity is a form of sex stereotyping that the Court in **Price Waterhouse v. Hopkins**, 490 U.S. 228 (1989) has recognized as prohibited sex discrimination.

It might only be a matter of time before the Court has to address this question, although likely first in the context of statutory interpretation. In the 2016–2017 Term, the Court was scheduled to hear the appeal of **Gloucester County School Board v. G.G.**, 822 F.3d 709 (4th Cir. 2016), wherein which the Fourth Circuit held that Title IX's prohibition of discrimination "on the basis of sex" applied to a school's restroom policy that restricted transgender students from using the restroom congruent with their gender identity. However, because the Fourth Circuit, in reaching its decision, relied on a 2015 opinion letter from the Obama Administration's Department of Education's Office of Civil Rights, the Court ultimately remanded the case, prior to oral arguments, when that same letter was revoked by the Trump Administration. As this casebook goes to press, there are pending petitions for certiorari on the question of whether the prohibition of employment discrimination "because of" sex in Title VII of the Civil Rights Act ought to be similarly interpreted to include gender identity discrimination.

In the constitutional context, the question also may be proceeding towards eventual adjudication by the Court. In particular, in challenging the Pentagon's policy to disqualify from military service, subject to certain exceptions, "transgender persons who require or have undergone gender transition" and "transgender persons with a history or diagnosis of gender dysphoria, plaintiffs have argued that this exclusion ought to seen as a form of sex discrimination subject to intermediate scrutiny. The Court, in a 5–4 decision that tracked the usual ideological divide, has stayed the preliminary injunctions issued by various district courts against the executive order, allowing the order to go into full effect pending final resolution by the Court.

SEX-BASED PURPOSE AND EFFECT

Should purpose and effect of statutes or policies alleged to discriminate on the basis of sex be analyzed similarly to purpose and effect in race discrimination claims? In **Personnel Administrator of Mass. v. Feeney**, 442 U.S. 256 (1979), the Court relied on the reasoning in the racial disparate impact cases Washington v. Davis and Arlington Heights, p. 684 above, to reject a sex discrimination challenge to a Massachusetts law granting "absolute lifetime" preference to veterans for state civil service positions, even though "the preference operates overwhelmingly to the advantage of males." Under the law, "all veterans who qualify for state civil service positions must be considered for appointment ahead of any qualifying nonveterans." (Over 98% of the veterans in Massachusetts were male; only 1.8% were female.) Challenger Helen B. Feeney, who was not a veteran, claimed that the law denied equal protection to women. In rejecting her challenge, Justice STEWART's majority opinion stated that the principles of Washington v. Davis and Arlington Heights "apply with equal force to a case involving alleged gender discrimination. When a statute gender-neutral on its face is challenged on the ground that its effects upon women are disproportionately adverse, a two-fold inquiry is thus appropriate. The first question is whether the statutory classification is indeed neutral in the sense that it is not gender-based. If the classification itself, covert or overt, is not based upon gender, the second question is whether the adverse effect reflects invidious gender-based discrimination. In this second inquiry, impact provides an 'important starting point' [Arlington Heights], but purposeful discrimination is 'the condition that offends the Constitution.'"

Engaging in the first step of that inquiry, Justice Stewart noted that Feeney had "acknowledged that state hiring preferences for veterans are not per se invalid, for she has limited her challenge to the absolute lifetime preference." He continued: "The District Court made two central findings that are relevant here: first, that [the law] serves legitimate and worthy purposes; second, that the absolute preference was not established for the purpose of discriminating against women. [Thus,] the distinction between veterans and nonveterans [here] is not a pretext for gender discrimination. [If] the impact of this statute could not be plausibly explained on a neutral ground, impact itself would signal that the real classification made by the law was in fact not neutral. [But this] is not a law that can plausibly be explained only as a gender-based classification. Indeed, it is not a law that can rationally be explained on that ground. Veteran status is not uniquely male. Although few women benefit from the preference, the nonveteran class is not substantially all-female. To the contrary, significant numbers of nonveterans are men, and all nonveterans—male as well as female—are placed at a disadvantage. Too many men are affected by [the law] to permit the inference that the statute is but a pretext for preferring men over women. [The] distinction made by [the law is] quite simply between veterans and nonveterans, not between men and women."

On the second part of the inquiry, Justice Stewart stated: "The dispositive question [is] whether the appellee has shown that a gender-based discriminatory purpose has, at least in some measure, shaped the Massachusetts veterans' preference legislation. [She] points to two basic factors which in her view distinguish [the law] from the neutral rules at issue in [Davis and Arlington Heights]. The first is the nature of the preference, which is said to be demonstrably gender-biased in the sense that it favors a status reserved under federal military policy primarily to men. The second concerns the impact of the absolute lifetime preference upon the employment opportunities of women, an impact claimed to be too inevitable to have been unintended. The appellee contends that these factors, coupled with the fact that the preference itself has little if any relevance to actual job performance, more than suffice [to prove discriminatory intent]. The contention that [the law] is 'inherently non-neutral' or 'gender-biased' presumes that the State, by favoring veterans, intentionally incorporated into its public employment policies the panoply of sex-based and assertedly discriminatory federal laws that have prevented all but a handful of women from becoming veterans. There are two serious difficulties with this argument. First, it is wholly at odds with the District Court's central finding that Massachusetts has not [acted] for the purpose of discriminating against women. Second, it cannot be reconciled with the assumption made by both the appellee and the District Court that a more limited hiring preference for veterans could be sustained. Taken together, these difficulties are fatal. To the extent that the status of veteran is one that few women have been enabled to achieve, every hiring preference for veterans, however modest or extreme, is inherently gender-biased. [Invidious] discrimination does not become less so because the discrimination accomplished is of a lesser magnitude. Discriminatory intent [either] is a factor that has influenced the legislative choice or it is not. The District Court's conclusion that the [law] was not originally enacted or subsequently reaffirmed for the purpose of giving an advantage to males as such necessarily compels the conclusion that the State intended nothing more than to prefer 'veterans.' Given this finding, simple logic suggests that an intent to exclude women from significant public jobs was not at work in this law. To reason that it was [is] merely to restate the fact of impact, not to answer the question of intent.

"To be sure, this case is unusual in that it involves a law that by design is not neutral. The law overtly prefers veterans as such. As opposed to the written test at issue in Davis, it does not purport to define a job related characteristic. To the contrary, it confers upon a specifically described group—perceived to be particularly deserving—a competitive head start. But the District Court found, and the appellee has not disputed, that this legislative choice was legitimate. The basic distinction between veterans and nonveterans having been found not gender-based, and the goals of the preference having been found worthy, [the law] must be analyzed as is any other neutral law that casts a greater burden upon women as a group than upon men as a group. The enlistment policies of the armed services may well have discriminated on the basis of sex. But the history of discrimination against women in the military is not on trial in this case. The appellee's ultimate argument rests upon the presumption, common to the criminal and civil law, that a person intends the natural and foreseeable consequences of his voluntary actions. [It] would [be] disingenuous to say that the adverse consequences of this legislation for women were unintended, in the sense that they were not volitional or in the sense that they were not foreseeable. 'Discriminatory purpose,' however, implies more than intent as volition or intent as awareness of consequences. It implies that the decisionmaker, in this case a state legislature, selected or reaffirmed a particular course of action at least in part 'because of,' not merely 'in spite of,' its adverse effects upon an identifiable group.[1] Yet nothing in the record demonstrates that this preference for veterans was originally devised or subsequently re-enacted because it would accomplish the collateral goal of keeping women in a stereotypic and predefined place in the Massachusetts Civil Service. [When] the totality of legislative actions establishing and extending the Massachusetts veterans' preference are considered, the law remains what it purports to be: a preference for veterans of either sex over nonveterans of either sex, not for men over women."

Justice STEVENS, joined by Justice White, concurred in the opinion and added: "I confess that I am not at all sure that there is any difference between the two questions [posed]. If a classification is not overtly based on gender, I am inclined to believe the question whether it is covertly gender-based is the same as the question whether its adverse effects 'reflect invidious gender-based discrimination.' However the question is phrased, for me the answer is largely provided by the fact that the number of males disadvantaged by [the law] (1,867,000) is sufficiently large—and sufficiently close to the number of disadvantaged females (2,954,000)—to refute the claim that the rule was intended to benefit males as a class over females as a class."

Justice MARSHALL, joined by Justice Brennan, dissented: "In my judgment, [the law] evinces purposeful gender-based discrimination. [The] absolute preference formula has rendered desirable state civil service employment an almost exclusively male prerogative. [This] consequence followed foreseeably, indeed inexorably, from the long history of policies severely limiting women's participation in the military. Although neutral in form, the statute is anything but neutral in application. [Where] the foreseeable impact of a facially neutral policy is so disproportionate, the burden should rest on the State to establish that sex-based considerations played no part in the choice of the particular legislative scheme. Clearly, that burden was not sustained here. The legislative history of the statute reflects the Commonwealth's patent appreciation of the impact the preference

[1] "This is not to say that the inevitability or foreseeability of consequences of a neutral rule has no bearing upon the existence of discriminatory intent. Certainly, when the adverse consequences of a law upon an identifiable group are as inevitable as the gender-based consequences of [this law], a strong inference that the adverse effects were desired can reasonably be drawn. But in this inquiry—made as it is under the Constitution—an inference is a working tool, not a synonym for proof. When as here, the impact is essentially an unavoidable consequence of a legislative policy that has in itself always been deemed to be legitimate, and when, as here, the statutory history and all of the available evidence affirmatively demonstrate the opposite, the inference simply fails to ripen into proof." [Footnote by Justice Stewart.]

system would have on women, and an equally evident desire to mitigate that impact only with respect to certain traditionally female occupations. Until 1971, the statute and implementing [regulations] exempted from operation of the preference any job requisitions 'especially calling for women.' In practice, this exemption, coupled with the absolute preference for veterans, has created a gender-based civil service hierarchy, with women occupying low grade clerical and secretarial jobs and men holding more responsible and remunerative positions. [Such] a statutory scheme both reflects and perpetuates precisely the kind of archaic assumptions about women's roles which we have previously held invalid. Particularly when viewed against the range of less discriminatory alternatives available to assist veterans, Massachusetts' choice of a formula that so severely restricts public employment opportunities for women cannot reasonably be thought gender-neutral."

SEX-BASED PREFERENCES: AFFIRMATIVE ACTION FOR WOMEN

As the cases so far make clear, sex classifications disadvantaging *women* evoke intermediate scrutiny. But as Craig, Hogan, and other cases make clear, so do many sex classifications that disadvantage *men*—including laws that give females a benefit, such as the ability to purchase near beer at 18 or to attend a nearby nursing school, not available to men. What explained those decisions? The idea that the supposed "preference" for females was rooted in archaic and overbroad generalizations about appropriate roles for men and women? Recall Justice Brennan's description in his Frontiero opinion of the tradition of "romantic paternalism" in which the "pedestal" on which women were placed could all too often become a "cage." Does this suggest that the male litigants in those cases were also representing women's interest in rendering gender roles more fluid between the sexes? What about the near-term losses suffered by the women who lost their previous privileges? Does equal protection for women mean deprivations for ladies—those women likely to conform to the archaic stereotypes of physical fragility or financial dependence upon men? And what, if any, explicit preferences for women might still be allowed? Can you sort out a pattern in the cases that follow?

1. ***Property tax exemptions.*** In **Kahn v. Shevin**, 416 U.S. 351 (1974)—decided two years before Craig mandated intermediate scrutiny for sex classifications—the Court applied a deferential standard of review to uphold a state property tax exemption for widows (but not for widowers). Justice DOUGLAS's majority opinion held that the distinction rested " 'upon some ground of difference having a fair and substantial relation to the subject of the legislation.' Reed." Justice Douglas stated that the state tax law was "reasonably designed to further the state policy of cushioning the financial impact of spousal loss upon the sex for which that loss imposes a disproportionately heavy burden"; thus, laws "designed to rectify the effects of past discrimination against women" readily passed muster. Justice BRENNAN's dissent, joined by Justice Marshall, urged "close judicial scrutiny" of gender-based classifications, even benign ones. He thought the law served a "compelling governmental interest," but found the statute invalid because it had not resorted to the most narrowly available means. Although "this country's history of pervasive sex discrimination against

women" justified "remedial measures to correct the resulting economic imbalances," "less drastic means" were available to achieve that objective, since the property tax exemption was granted to all widows, whatever their financial status: "[The] State could readily narrow the class of beneficiaries to those widows for whom the effects of past economic discrimination against women have been a practical reality." Justice White also dissented.

2. ***Alimony after divorce.*** In **Orr v. Orr**, 440 U.S. 268 (1979), the Court struck down laws that authorized the Alabama courts to impose alimony obligations on husbands but not on wives. Justice BRENNAN's majority opinion, applying the Craig v. Boren standard, found Alabama's scheme unconstitutional. In examining the "benign" justification, Justice Brennan stated that helping needy spouses and "compensating women for past discrimination during marriage" were "legitimate and important" objectives. But the "means" aspect of that test had not been satisfied: "even if sex were a reliable proxy for need, and even if the institution of marriage did discriminate against women, these factors still would not 'adequately justify the salient features of' Alabama's statutory scheme. Under the statute, individualized hearings at which the parties' relative financial circumstances are considered *already* occur. [Since these] hearings can determine which women were in fact discriminated against vis-à-vis their husbands, as well as which family units defied the stereotype and left the husband dependent on the wife, Alabama's alleged compensatory purpose may be effectuated without placing burdens solely on husbands. Progress toward fulfilling such a purpose would not be hampered, and it would cost the State nothing more, if it were to treat men and women equally by making alimony burdens independent of sex." Here, moreover, Alabama's "use of a gender classification actually produces perverse results," by giving "an advantage only to the financially secure wife whose husband is in need." Such a scheme was clearly irrational since nondependent wives are "precisely those who are not 'needy spouses' and who are 'least likely to have been victims [of] discrimination' by the institution of marriage." Finally, Justice Brennan commented generally on the dangers latent in "benign" gender classifications: "[Even] statutes purportedly designed to compensate for and ameliorate the effects of past discrimination must be carefully tailored," since they "carry the inherent risk of reinforcing stereotypes about the 'proper place' of women and their need for special protection."

3. ***Social security benefits.*** The social security system produced many challenges in the 1970s. Ruth Bader Ginsburg, later Justice Ginsburg, was the lead lawyer in most of these, and the plaintiff was typically male (here as in other settings in which the early sex equality precedents were established; Sharon Frontiero, p. 759 above, was an exception). Thus, **Weinberger v. Wiesenfeld**, 420 U.S. 636 (1975), invalidated a Social Security provision applicable when a covered wage earner dies. In the case of a deceased husband and father, benefits were payable both to the widow and to the couple's minor children in her care. But in the case of a deceased wife and mother, benefits were payable only to the minor children and not to the widower. The Court sustained the widower's challenge, finding an unjustifiable discrimination against covered female wage earners by affording them less protection for their survivors than that provided for survivors of male wage earners. The Court rejected the effort to defend the classification as a benign one because that had not been the actual purpose of Congress.

And **Califano v. Goldfarb**, 430 U.S. 199 (1977), set aside a gender-based distinction in a federal benefits program under which survivors' benefits based on the earnings of a deceased husband covered by the Act were payable to his widow, but benefits on the basis of the earnings of a deceased wife were payable to a widower only if he "was receiving at least one-half of his support" from his deceased wife. Justice BRENNAN's plurality opinion found the scheme, "burdening a widower but not a widow with the task of proving dependency upon the deceased spouse," indistinguishable from that struck down in Wiesenfeld. He found the discrimination to be directed against female workers, whose Social Security taxes produced less protection for their spouses than was produced by the efforts of men. He insisted that Wiesenfeld was inconsistent with Kahn and thought the later, Wiesenfeld analysis should govern. Justice STEVENS's concurrence insisted that the relevant discrimination here was "against surviving male spouses, rather than against deceased female wage earners." Justice REHNQUIST's dissent, joined by Chief Justice Burger and Justices Stewart and Blackmun, argued, inter alia, that the deferential approach of Kahn should be followed with respect to benign sex classifications, that discrimination against men should not be treated as an "invidious discrimination," and that heightened scrutiny of sex distinctions should apply only when they disadvantaged women, because it was women who had "in the past been the victims of unfair treatment."

Contrast **Califano v. Webster**, 430 U.S. 313 (1977) (per curiam), which sustained, as a valid gender preference, the Social Security Act's formula for computing old age benefits. Under the challenged statutory formula, a female wage earner could exclude from the computation of her "average monthly wage" three more lower-earning years than a similarly situated male wage earner could exclude. This resulted in a slightly higher "average monthly wage" and a correspondingly higher level of monthly old-age benefits for the retired female wage earner. (In this case, for example, the male challenger was awarded a monthly benefit of $185.70, but a similarly situated female wage earner would have been awarded $240 per month.) In sustaining that scheme, the Court reiterated the Craig standard and stated:

"Reduction of the disparity in economic condition between men and women caused by the long history of discrimination against women has been recognized as [an] important governmental objective. [Kahn]. But 'the mere recitation of a benign, compensatory purpose is not an automatic shield that protects against any inquiry into the actual purposes underlying a legislative scheme.' [Wiesenfeld.] Accordingly, we have rejected attempts to justify gender classifications as compensation for past discrimination against women when the classifications in fact penalized women wage earners, or when its legislative history revealed that the classification was not enacted as compensation for past discrimination. [Goldfarb; Wiesenfeld.]

"The statutory scheme involved here is more analogous to those upheld in Kahn and Ballard than to those struck down in Wiesenfeld and Goldfarb. The more favorable treatment of the female wage earner enacted here was not a result of 'archaic and overbroad generalizations' about women or of 'the role-typing society has long imposed' upon women, such as casual assumptions that women are 'the weaker sex' or are more likely to be child-rearers or dependents. Rather, 'the only discernible purpose of [the law's more favorable treatment is] the permissible one of redressing our society's longstanding disparate treatment of women.' The challenged statute operated directly to compensate women for past economic discrimination. [Allowing] women, who as such have been unfairly hindered from earning as much as men, to eliminate additional low-earning years from the calculation of their retirement benefits works directly to remedy some part of the effect of past discrimination. The legislative history [also] reveals that [Congress] purposely enacted the more favorable treatment for female wage earners to compensate for past employment discrimination against women."

But in **Wengler v. Druggists Mutual Ins. Co.**, 446 U.S. 142 (1980), the Court struck down a Missouri workers' compensation law providing that a widow qualified for death benefits without having to prove actual dependence on her husband's earnings, but that a widower was not entitled to death benefits unless he demonstrated actual dependence on his wife's earnings or mental or physical incapacity to earn wages. Justice WHITE's opinion found that "the statute discriminates against both men and women"—against women because the benefits that the working woman could expect to be paid to a spouse in case of her work-related death were less than those payable to the spouse of the deceased male wage earner, and against men because a widower, unlike a widow, had to prove his incapacity or dependency. Justice White rejected the claim that, regarding women, this was "benign" discrimination and, applying the Craig standard, found that the discriminatory means employed did not substantially serve the statutory end of providing for needy spouses. He also rejected the argument that the discrimination was justified because "most women are dependent on male wage earners and that it is more efficient to presume dependency in the case of women than to engage in case-to-case determination." The burden of making that "benign" justification was not met "simply by noting that in 1925 the state legislature thought widows to be more in need of prompt help than men or that today 'the substantive difference in the economic standing of working men and women justifies the advantage given to widows.'" Justice STEVENS concurred, stating that "[n]othing has happened since the decision in [Goldfarb] to persuade me that this kind of gender-based classification can simultaneously disfavor the male class and the female class." He agreed, however, that the state had "failed to justify the disparate treatment of persons who have as strong a claim to equal treatment as to similarly situated surviving spouses." The sole dissenter was Justice REHNQUIST, who stated that he continued to believe that Goldfarb was "wrongly decided."

4. ***Military promotions.*** **Schlesinger v. Ballard**, 419 U.S. 498 (1975), rejected a male officer's challenge to sex distinctions in the Navy's promotion system. The system accorded to women officers a 13-year tenure before mandatory discharge for want of promotion; males, by contrast, had to be discharged if they had been twice passed over for promotion, even though they might have had less than 13 years of commissioned service. Justice STEWART's majority opinion applied the deferential rationality standard. Justice BRENNAN's dissent, joined by Justices Douglas and Marshall, insisted that strict scrutiny was applicable, but argued further that the scheme could not survive even rationality review. Justice Stewart insisted that the different treatment of men and women officers reflected "not archaic and overbroad generalizations, but, instead, the demonstrable fact that male and female line officers in the Navy are *not* similarly situated with respect to opportunities for professional service." Justice Brennan's dissent insisted that the majority had conjured up a legislative purpose: "I find nothing in the statutory scheme or the legislative history to support the

supposition that Congress intended [to] compensate women for other forms of disadvantage visited upon them by the Navy."

5. ***Affirmative action for women or ladies?*** Is it fair to characterize the pattern in these cases as holding that affirmative action for women is permissible but affirmative action for ladies is not? The Court invalidates preferences for females that reinforce traditional "archaic or overbroad stereotypes" that women are typically more fragile or financially dependent on men, but upholds those preferences for females that compensate women who have undertaken traditionally male roles for past disadvantage—including societal disadvantage such as differential average pay to women and men in the private sector. Note that such compensation for past societal discrimination receives only intermediate scrutiny in the sex discrimination context. Would such a loose compensatory justification survive the strict scrutiny employed in Croson and Adarand in the context of race preferences? What of the suggestion in the race preference cases that societal discrimination is never a sufficient predicate? Is sustaining affirmative action for women more readily than affirmative action for African-Americans consistent with the original purpose of the Fourteenth Amendment? Does the "exceedingly persuasive" standard the Court used in VMI require better justifications than those upheld in Webster and Ballard? Did the lawyers arguing for the United States as amicus in VMI make a strategic blunder in arguing (unsuccessfully) for strict scrutiny of sex classifications? If they had succeeded, would they have undermined the constitutionality of affirmative action for women?

SECTION 4. DISCRIMINATION BASED ON OTHER POTENTIALLY "SUSPECT" CLASSIFICATIONS

Are there other classifications beyond those based on race or sex that may warrant heightened judicial scrutiny under the Equal Protection Clause? What criteria are appropriate in evaluating the claims of other groups to heightened scrutiny? Is the appropriate approach assessing the degree to which these groups have experiences analogous to those of racial minority groups? To women? Which aspects matter most: the immutability of a characteristic, the imposition of political disadvantage based on that characteristic, or social prejudice and subordination, stereotyping and stigma based on that characteristic?

SEXUAL ORIENTATION

While classifications based on sexual orientation have not been formally acknowledged as suspect, the Court has struck down state sodomy laws, a state constitutional amendment excluding sexual orientation from the reach of state antidiscrimination laws, and laws defining marriage so as to preclude official recognition of same-sex marriage in both federal and state laws. Because these decisions involve an intertwined discussion of both substantive due process and equal protection principles, they are discussed in Chapter 8, p. 553 above, but may be reconsidered here in light of the areas discussed below.

ALIENAGE

The Equal Protection Clause holds that "no *person* shall be deprived of equal protection of the law." It does not condition equal protection on citizenship. Is alienage thus a "suspect" classification? Alienage is not an "unalterable" trait since noncitizens may become naturalized citizens. Aliens are legitimately excluded from voting, as the Court has always recognized; citizenship is the defining prerequisite of political participation. Does the justification for heightened scrutiny of alienage classifications rest solely, then, on the "political powerlessness" rationale and on the history of discrimination against many groups of aliens? And if heightened scrutiny for alienage classifications *is* justified, may some activities with civic aspects akin to voting be reserved for citizens? The following cases trace the escalation of scrutiny of most but not all *state* discrimination against noncitizens. Note that the federal government has considerably greater latitude, under the immigration and naturalization power, to discriminate against and among noncitizens given the predominant federal interest in immigration.

Note that the cases that follow involve *legally* resident aliens. Undocumented aliens—those who are not legally resident in the country—have not been accorded heightened equal protection scrutiny, with the exception of undocumented children barred from attending public school, see Plyler v. Doe (1982; p. 849 below). In Plyler, the Court explicitly rejected "the claim that 'illegal aliens' are a 'suspect class.'" Noting that "undocumented status is not irrelevant to any proper legislative goal," the Court also pointed out that status was not "an absolutely immutable characteristic since it is the product of conscious, indeed unlawful, action."

1. ***Strict scrutiny of state alienage classifications.***

a. *Welfare benefits.* In **Graham v. Richardson**, 403 U.S. 365 (1971), the Court held that states could not deny welfare benefits to noncitizens. Justice BLACKMUN's opinion announced: "[The] Court's decisions have established that classifications based on alienage, like those based on nationality or race, are inherently suspect and subject to close judicial scrutiny. Aliens as a class are a prime example of a 'discrete and insular' minority (see Carolene Products footnote four) for whom such heightened judicial solicitude is appropriate. Accordingly, it was said in [Takahashi v. Fish & Game Comm'n, 334 U.S. 410 (1948),[1] that] 'the power of a state to apply its laws exclusively to its alien inhabitants as a class is confined within narrow limits.'" He also offered a significant "additional" reason for the invalidation of the restriction: the "area of federal-state relations." Noting that "Congress has not seen fit to impose any burden or restriction on aliens who become indigent after their entry into the United States," he concluded that "state laws that restrict the eligibility of aliens for welfare benefits merely because of their alienage conflict with these overriding national policies in an area constitutionally entrusted to the Federal Government."

b. *Bar admission.* Two years after Graham, a divided Court applied the strict scrutiny prescribed by Graham to invalidate Connecticut's exclusion of resident aliens from law practice, **In re Griffiths**, 413 U.S. 717 (1973). Justice POWELL's majority opinion found none of the asserted state

---

1 Takahashi held that California's purported ownership of fish in its off-shore waters did not justify denying commercial fishing licenses to noncitizens. The case rested largely on preemption, federal supremacy grounds.

interests sufficiently substantial: neither the "undoubted interest in high professional standards" nor the role of lawyers in protecting clients' interests and serving as "officers of the Court" established that the State "must exclude all aliens from the practice of law."

c. *Civil service jobs.* The Court likewise invalidated New York's law providing that only American citizens might hold permanent positions in the competitive classified civil service. In **Sugarman v. Dougall**, 413 U.S. 634 (1973), Justice BLACKMUN's majority opinion emphasized that the state barrier did not cover all high policymaking positions but covered a number of menial ones. Accordingly, the restriction had "little, if any, relationship" to the State's "substantial" interest "in having an employee of undivided loyalty." Justice Blackmun cautioned, however, that the Court had not held "that a State may not, in an appropriately defined class of positions, require citizenship as a qualification for office. [Such] power inheres in the State by virtue of its obligation [to] 'preserve the basic conception of a political community.' And this power and responsibility of the State applies, not only to the qualifications of voters, but also to persons holding state elective or important non-elective executive, legislative and judicial positions, for officers who participate directly in the formulation, execution, or review of broad public policy perform functions that go to the heart of representative government. [Such] state action [is] not wholly immune from scrutiny under [equal protection]. But our scrutiny will not be so demanding where we deal with matters resting firmly within a State's constitutional prerogatives. This is no more than a recognition of a State's historical power to exclude aliens from participation in its democratic political institutions."

Justice REHNQUIST's dissent, applicable to both Griffiths and Dougall, questioned any extension of suspect classification analysis beyond the race area. And, as noted earlier, he objected to the reliance in Graham on the Carolene Products footnote rationale. He also thought any "immutable trait" analysis inapplicable: "[There] is a marked difference between a status or condition such as illegitimacy, national origin, or race, which cannot be altered by an individual, and the 'status' of the [challengers here]."

2. ***The "governmental function" exception.*** Justice Blackmun's dicta in Dougall regarding greater deference to exclusion of noncitizens from "public policy functions that go to the heart of representative government" bore fruit in a series of cases rejecting equal protection claims by noncitizens. In these cases, the Court upheld alienage-based exclusions from public employment by exercising deferential review rather than strict scrutiny.

a. *Police officers.* In **Foley v. Connelie**, 435 U.S. 291 (1978), Chief Justice BURGER's majority opinion held that New York *could* bar employment of aliens as state troopers. He argued that "to require every statutory exclusion of aliens to clear the high hurdle of 'strict scrutiny' [would] 'obliterate all the distinctions between citizens and aliens, and thus depreciate the historic values of citizenship.' [The] practical consequence [is] that 'our scrutiny will not be so demanding where we deal with matters firmly within a State's constitutional prerogatives.' Dougall. The State need only justify its classification by a showing of some rational relationship between the interests sought to be protected and the limiting qualification." He found that the state police force fell within the Dougall exception: "Police officers in the ranks do not formulate policy, per se, but they are clothed with authority to exercise an almost infinite variety of discretionary powers. [Clearly] the exercise of police authority calls for a very high degree of judgment and discretion." He concluded: "In the enforcement and execution of the laws the police function is one where citizenship bears a rational relationship to the special demands of the particular position."

b. *Public school teachers.* **Ambach v. Norwick**, 441 U.S. 68 (1979), applied the public function exception to hold that a state may refuse to employ as elementary and secondary school teachers aliens who are eligible for citizenship but who refuse to seek naturalization. Justice POWELL, writing for a 5–4 majority, emphasized that a less demanding scrutiny was required when aliens were excluded from "state functions" that were "bound up with the operation of the State as a governmental entity." He explained: "[The] assumption of [citizenship status] denotes an association with a polity which, in a democratic republic, exercises the powers of governance. [It] is because of this special significance of citizenship that governmental entities [have] wider latitude in limiting the participation of noncitizens." He stressed the importance of public schools in preparing individuals for participation as citizens and in "the preservation of the values on which our society rests," and he noted a teacher's "opportunity to influence the attitudes of students toward government, the political process, and a citizen's social responsibilities." Accordingly, it was "clear that public school teachers come well within the 'governmental function' principle recognized in [Dougall] and Foley."

c. *Notaries public.* **Bernal v. Fainter**, 467 U.S. 216 (1984), however, identified a limit to the public function exception: the Court's 8–1 decision found that the exception could not justify the Texas barrier to aliens becoming notaries public. Justice MARSHALL (who had dissented from all applications of the Dougall exception to strict scrutiny) wrote for the majority and applied strict scrutiny. He stated: "We emphasize, as we have in the past, that the political-function exception must be narrowly construed; otherwise the exception will swallow the rule and depreciate the significance that should attach to the designation of a group as a 'discrete and insular' minority for whom heightened judicial solicitude is appropriate." In finding the Dougall exception inapplicable to notaries public, he relied on the fact that their duties, although important, were "essentially clerical and ministerial." In the absence of either policymaking responsibilities or broad discretion of the type exercised by teachers and other public employees, the duties would not be deemed to be within the "governmental function" exception. Justice Rehnquist was the sole dissenter.

3. ***Alienage restrictions and federal preemption.*** Are the decisions above better explained by federalism concerns than equal protection concerns? Do the Court's opinions in this area follow an unarticulated theory of preemption in which the states are implicitly barred from altering the immigration scheme established by the federal government? See Note, "The Equal Treatment of Aliens: Preemption or Equal Protection?", 31 Stan. L. Rev. 1069 (1979) (adding that "since the federal government does not admit resident aliens to the *political* community—admission does not confer citizenship—the states may exclude resident aliens from state [political] functions without offending federal power").

For a rare decision striking down a state alienage restriction on federalism-related rather than equal protection grounds, see **Toll v. Moreno**, 458 U.S. 1 (1982), which struck down the University of Maryland's policy of granting preferential tuition and fees treatment to students with "in-state" status. "Nonimmigrant aliens" were not eligible for such status even if they were domiciled in Maryland. Justice BRENNAN's opinion relied entirely on federal preemption: "In light of Congress' explicit decision not to bar [such] aliens from acquiring domicile, the State's decision to deny 'in-state' status to [them], *solely* on account of [their] federal immigration status, surely amounts to an ancillary 'burden not contemplated by Congress' in admitting these aliens to the United States. [The] University's policy violates the Supremacy Clause." In the course of his opinion, Justice Brennan stated: "Commentators have noted [that] many of the Court's decisions concerning alienage classifications, such as Takahashi, are better explained in preemption than equal protection terms. Takahashi and Graham stand for the broad principle that 'state regulation not congressionally sanctioned that discriminates against aliens lawfully admitted to the country is impermissible if it imposes additional burdens not contemplated by Congress.'"

4. ***Federal restrictions on aliens.*** Congress has broad latitude to control the flow of immigrants across the nation's borders. Indeed, the national immigration and naturalization power has often been read as virtually plenary. Entry to the nation is often understood as a matter of privilege or grace. Are there any constitutional limits on the power of the federal government to discriminate against and among aliens? Consider the following cases:

a. *Public employment.* In **Hampton v. Mow Sun Wong**, 426 U.S. 88 (1976), the Court invalidated a Civil Service Commission (CSC) regulation barring resident aliens from employment in the federal competitive civil service—even while recognizing that "overriding national interests may provide a justification for a citizenship requirement in the federal service [though] an identical requirement may not be enforced by a State." Justice STEVENS's opinion found that the national interests offered in defense of the ban either (a) were not properly the concern of the CSC and had not explicitly emanated from Congress or the President, or (b) to the extent that they were within CSC competence, had not been evaluated fully by the CSC. Justice Stevens found it unnecessary to determine the substantive validity of the alien ban under the equal protection component of Fifth Amendment due process and rested instead on the "narrower" ground that "essential procedures" had not been followed—"procedures" involving the source and the deliberativeness of the regulation: "Since these residents were admitted as a result of decisions made by the Congress and the President, [due process] requires that the decision to impose [the] deprivation of an important liberty be made either at a comparable level of government or, if it is to be permitted to be made by the [CSC], that it be justified by reasons which are properly the concern of that agency." And these "structural due process" requirements had not been satisfied here. Justice Stevens explained that when "an overriding national interest" is asserted as a justification for a discriminatory rule which would be barred by equal protection if adopted by a state, "due process requires that there be a legitimate basis for presuming that the [federal] rule was actually intended to serve that interest." Here, there was no basis for such a presumption. He was willing to assume "that if the Congress or the President had expressly imposed the citizenship requirement, it would be justified by the national interest in providing an incentive for aliens to become naturalized, or possibly even as providing the President with an expendable token for treaty negotiating purposes." But those were not interests "which can reasonably be assumed to have influenced the CSC": "we are not willing to presume that the [agency] was deliberately fostering an interest so far removed from [its] normal responsibilities."

Justice REHNQUIST's dissent, joined by Chief Justice Burger and Justices White and Blackmun, charged the majority with enunciating "a novel conception" that "inexplicably melds together the concepts of equal protection, procedural and substantive due process." Justice Rehnquist argued that the majority had implicitly found "faulty" delegation of power to the CSC. The "overriding national interest" involved here, he insisted, was not any "specific interest in excluding these particular aliens from the civil service, but a general interest in formulating policies toward aliens."

b. *Medical benefits.* In **Mathews v. Diaz**, 426 U.S. 67 (1976), decided on the same day as Hampton, the Court held that Congress may condition an alien's eligibility for participation in a federal Medicare program on (a) admission for permanent residence and (b) continuous residence in the United States for five years. Justice STEVENS once again wrote the prevailing opinion, but this time for a unanimous Court, applying a deferential standard of review. He reasoned that Congress, under its "broad power over naturalization and immigration," regularly made rules that would be unacceptable if applied to citizens; disparate treatment of aliens and citizens did not demonstrate invidiousness. Turning to the welfare area, he insisted that congressional provision of some benefits to citizens "does not require it to provide like benefits for *all aliens*." The "real question" was "not whether discrimination between citizens and aliens is permissible" but "whether the statutory discrimination *within* the class of aliens—allowing benefits to some aliens but not to others—" was valid. Justice Stevens's scrutiny was extremely deferential: "The reasons that preclude judicial review of political questions also dictate a narrow standard of review of decisions made by the Congress or the President in the area of immigration and naturalization."

DISABILITY, AGE, POVERTY

Age is immutable in the sense that one is powerless to change the date one is born; disability is often incapable of medical correction; poverty often imposes conditions of relative political powerlessness that than become entrenched over generations. Are classifications based on these characteristics therefore subject to heightened scrutiny? Or are such classifications inescapable in social regulation? Typically relevant to the legitimate interests of government? "Real" rather than stereotypical bases for legally enforced distinctions?

In the Cleburne case, which follows, the Court rejected the argument that heightened scrutiny was appropriate in a case involving exclusion of a group home for the mentally disabled, yet struck down the classification while purporting to apply deferential rationality review:

Cleburne v. Cleburne Living Center, Inc.

473 U.S. 432, 105 S. Ct. 3249, 87 L. Ed. 2d 313 (1985).

■ JUSTICE WHITE delivered the opinion of the Court.

A Texas city denied a special use permit for the operation of a group home for the mentally retarded, acting pursuant to a municipal zoning ordinance requiring permits for such homes. The Court of Appeals for the Fifth Circuit held that mental retardation is a "quasi-suspect" classification and that the ordinance violated [equal protection] because it did not substantially further an important governmental purpose. We hold that a lesser standard of scrutiny is appropriate, but conclude that under that standard the ordinance is invalid as applied in this case.

I. In July, 1980, respondent Jan Hannah purchased a building [in] the city of Cleburne, Texas, with the intention of leasing it to Cleburne Living Centers, Inc. (CLC), for the operation of a group home for the mentally retarded. [After] holding a public hearing on CLC's application, the city council voted three to one to deny a [special use permit].

II. [The] general rule [under equal protection] is that legislation is presumed to be valid and will be sustained if the classification drawn by the statute is rationally related to a legitimate state interest. When social or economic legislation is at issue, [equal protection] allows the states wide [latitude]. The general rule gives way, however, when a statute classifies by race, alienage or national origin. These factors are so seldom relevant to the achievement of any legitimate state interest that laws grounded in such considerations are deemed to reflect prejudice and antipathy—a view that those in the burdened class are not as worthy or deserving as others. For these reasons and because such discrimination is unlikely to be soon rectified by legislative means, these laws are subjected to [strict scrutiny]. Legislative classifications based on gender also call for a heightened standard of review. That factor generally provides no sensible ground for differential treatment. [Because] illegitimacy is beyond the individual's control and bears "no relation to the individual's ability to participate in and contribute to society," official discriminations resting on that characteristic are also subject to somewhat heightened review. We have declined, however, to extend heightened review to differential treatment based on age. [The] lesson of Murgia [below] is that where individuals in the group affected by a law have distinguishing characteristics relevant to interests the state has the authority to implement, the courts have been very reluctant [to] closely scrutinize legislative choices as to whether, how and to what extent those interests should be pursued. In such cases, [equal protection] requires only a rational means to serve a legitimate end.

III. Against this background, we conclude [that] the Court of Appeals erred in holding mental retardation a quasi-suspect [classification]. First, it is undeniable [that] those who are mentally retarded have a reduced ability to cope with and function in the everyday world. Nor are they all cut from the same pattern: [they] range from those whose disability is not immediately evident to those who must be constantly cared for. They are thus different, immutably so, in relevant respects, and the states' interest in dealing with and providing for them is plainly a legitimate one. How this large and diversified group is to be treated under the law is a difficult and often a technical matter, very much a task for legislators guided by qualified professionals and not by the perhaps ill-informed opinions of the judiciary.

Heightened scrutiny inevitably involves substantive judgments about legislative decisions, and we doubt that the predicate for such judicial oversight is present where the classification deals with mental retardation.

Second, [both] national and state [lawmakers] have been addressing [the] difficulties [of the mentally retarded] in a manner that belies a continuing antipathy or prejudice and a corresponding need for more intrusive oversight by the judiciary. Thus, the federal government has not only outlawed discrimination against the mentally retarded in federally funded programs but it has also provided the retarded with the right to receive "appropriate treatment, services, and habilitation" in a setting that is "least restrictive of [their] personal liberty." [Texas] has similarly enacted [such legislation.] [It] may be, as CLC contends, that legislation designed to benefit, rather than disadvantage, the retarded would generally withstand examination under a test of heightened scrutiny. The relevant inquiry, however, is whether heightened scrutiny is constitutionally mandated in the first instance. Even assuming that many of these laws [would survive scrutiny], merely requiring the legislature to justify its efforts in these terms may lead it to refrain from acting at all. Much recent legislation intended to benefit the retarded also assumes the need for measures that might be perceived to disadvantage them. The Education of the Handicapped Act, for example, requires an "appropriate" education, not one that is equal in all respects to the education of non-retarded children; clearly, admission to a class that exceeded the abilities of a retarded child would not be appropriate. [Given] the wide variation in the abilities and needs of the retarded themselves, governmental bodies must have a certain amount of flexibility and freedom from judicial oversight in shaping and limiting their remedial efforts.

Third, the legislative response, which could hardly have occurred and survived without public support, negates any claim that the mentally retarded are politically powerless in the sense that they have no ability to attract the attention of the lawmakers. [Fourth,] if the large and amorphous class of the mentally retarded were deemed quasi-suspect[, it] would be difficult to find a principled way to distinguish a variety of other groups who have perhaps immutable disabilities setting them off from others, who cannot themselves mandate the desired legislative responses, and who can claim some degree of prejudice from at least part of the public at large. One need mention in this respect only the aging, the disabled, the mentally ill, and the infirm. We are reluctant to set out on that course, and we decline to do so.

Doubtless, there have been and there will continue to be instances of discrimination against the retarded that are in fact invidious, and that are properly subject to judicial correction under constitutional norms. But the appropriate method of reaching such instances is not to create a new quasi-suspect classification [but to] look to the likelihood that governmental action premised on a particular classification is valid as a general matter, not merely to the specifics of the case before us. Because mental retardation is a characteristic that the government may legitimately take into account in a wide range of decisions, and because both state and federal governments have recently committed themselves to assisting the retarded, we will not presume that any given legislative action, even one that disadvantages retarded individuals, is rooted in considerations that the Constitution will not tolerate. Our refusal to recognize the retarded as a quasi-suspect class does not leave them entirely unprotected from invidious discrimination. To withstand equal protection review, legislation that distinguishes between the mentally retarded and others must be rationally related to a legitimate governmental purpose. This standard, we believe, affords government the latitude necessary both to pursue policies designed to assist the retarded in realizing their full potential, and to freely and efficiently engage in activities that burden the retarded in what is essentially an incidental manner. The State may not rely on a classification whose relationship to an asserted goal is so attenuated as to render the distinction arbitrary and irrational. See, [e.g., Moreno]. Furthermore, some objectives—such as "a [bare] desire to harm politically unpopular group," [ibid.]—are not legitimate state [interests].

IV. [The] constitutional issue is clearly posed. The City does not require a special use permit in an R-3 zone for apartment houses, multiple dwellings, boarding and lodging houses, fraternity or sorority houses, dormitories, apartment hotels, hospitals, sanitariums, nursing homes for convalescents or the aged (other than for the insane or feeble-minded or alcoholics or drug addicts), private clubs or fraternal orders, and other specified uses. It does, however, insist on a special permit for [the group home here] and it does so [because] it would be a facility for the mentally retarded. May the city require the permit for this facility when other care and multiple dwelling facilities are freely permitted? [In] our view the record does not reveal any rational basis for believing that [the] home would pose any special threat to the city's legitimate [interests].

no

The District Court found that the City Council's insistence on the permit rested on several factors. First, the Council was concerned with the negative attitude of the majority of property owners located within 200 feet of [the group home], as well as with the fears of elderly residents of the neighborhood. But mere negative attitudes, or fear, unsubstantiated by factors which are properly cognizable in a zoning proceeding, are not permissible bases for treating a home for the mentally retarded differently from apartment houses, multiple dwellings, and the [like].

Second, the Council [was] concerned that the facility was across the street from a junior high school, and feared that the students might harass the occupants of [the] home. But the school itself is attended by about 30 mentally retarded students, and denying a permit based on such vague, undifferentiated fears is again permitting some portion of the community to validate what would otherwise be an equal protection violation. The [third] objection to the home's location was that it was located on "a five hundred year flood plain." This concern with the possibility of a flood, however, can hardly be based on a distinction between [the] home and, for example, nursing homes, homes for convalescents or the aged, or sanitariums or hospitals, any of which could be located on [the] site without obtaining a special use permit. The same may be said of another concern of the Council—doubts about the legal responsibility for actions which the mentally retarded might take. If there is no concern about legal responsibility with respect to other uses that would be permitted in the area, such as boarding and fraternity houses, it is difficult to believe that the groups of mildly or moderately mentally retarded individuals who would live at [the home] would present any different or special hazard.

Fourth, the Council was concerned with the size of the home and the number of people that would occupy it. [But] there would be no restrictions on the number of people who could occupy this home as a boarding house, nursing home, family dwelling, fraternity house, or dormitory. [At] least this record does not clarify [how] the characteristics of the intended occupants of [the] home rationally justify denying to those occupants what would be permitted to groups occupying the same site for different purposes. [The] short of it is that requiring the permit in this case appears to us to rest on an irrational prejudice against the mentally retarded.

■ JUSTICE STEVENS, with whom CHIEF JUSTICE BURGER joins, concurring.

The Court of Appeals disposed of this case as if a critical question to be decided were which of three clearly defined standards of equal protection review should be applied to a legislative classification discriminating against the mentally retarded. [But] our cases reflect a continuum of judgmental responses to differing classifications which have been explained in opinions by terms ranging from "strict scrutiny" at one extreme to "rational basis" at the other. I have never been persuaded that these so called "standards" adequately explain the decisional process. Cases involving classifications based on alienage, illegal residency, illegitimacy, gender, age, or—as in this case—mental retardation, do not fit well into sharply defined classifications. [I] have always asked myself whether I could find a "rational basis" for the classification at issue. The term "rational," of course, includes a requirement that an impartial lawmaker could logically believe that the classification would serve a legitimate public purpose that transcends the harm to the members of the disadvantaged class. Thus, the word "rational"—for me at least—includes elements of legitimacy and neutrality that must always characterize the performance of the sovereign's duty to govern impartially. [In] every equal protection case, we have to ask certain basic questions. What class is harmed by the legislation, and has it been subjected to a "tradition of disfavor" by our laws? What is the public purpose that is being served by the law? What is the characteristic of the disadvantaged class that justifies the disparate treatment? In most cases the answer to these questions will tell us whether the statute has a "rational basis." The answers will result in the virtually automatic invalidation of racial classifications and in the validation of most economic classifications, but they will provide differing results in cases involving classifications based on alienage, gender, or illegitimacy. But that is not because we apply an "intermediate standard of review" in these cases; rather it is because the characteristics of these groups are sometimes relevant and sometimes irrelevant to a valid public purpose, or, more specifically, to the purpose that the challenged laws purportedly intended to serve.

Every law that places the mentally retarded in a special class is not presumptively irrational. The differences between mentally retarded persons and those with greater mental capacity are obviously relevant to certain legislative decisions. [Even so,] the Court of Appeals correctly observed [that] the mentally retarded "have been subjected to a history of unfair and often grotesque mistreatment." [The record] convinces me that this permit was required because of the irrational fears of neighboring property owners, rather than for the protection of the mentally retarded persons who would reside in respondent's home.

■ JUSTICE MARSHALL, with whom JUSTICES BRENNAN and BLACKMUN join, concurring in the judgment in part and dissenting in part.

[The] Court's heightened scrutiny discussion is [puzzling] given that Cleburne's ordinance is invalidated only after being subjected to precisely the sort of probing inquiry associated with heightened scrutiny. [The] rational basis test invoked today is most assuredly not the rational basis test of [Lee Optical]. [The] Court, for example, concludes that legitimate concerns for fire hazards or the serenity of the neighborhood do not justify singling out respondents to bear the burdens of these concerns, for analogous permitted uses appear to pose similar threats. Yet under the traditional and most minimal version of the rational basis test, "reform may take one step at a time." [Lee Optical.]

[When] a zoning ordinance works to exclude the retarded from all residential districts in a community, these two considerations require that the ordinance be convincingly justified as substantially furthering legitimate and important purposes. First, the interest [in] establishing group homes is substantial. [Second,] the mentally retarded have been subject to a "lengthy and tragic history" of segregation and discrimination that can only be called grotesque. [In] light of the importance of the interest at stake and the history of discrimination the retarded have suffered, [equal protection] requires us to do more than review the distinctions drawn by Cleburne's zoning ordinance as if they appeared in a taxing statute or in economic or commercial legislation. The searching scrutiny I would give to restrictions on the ability of the retarded to establish community group homes leads me to conclude that Cleburne's vague generalizations for classifying the "feeble minded" with drug addicts, alcoholics, and the insane, and excluding them where the elderly, the ill, the boarder, and the transient are allowed, are not substantial or important enough to overcome the suspicion that the ordinance rests on impermissible assumptions or outmoded and perhaps invidious [stereotypes]. [In] light of the scrutiny that should be applied here, Cleburne's ordinance sweeps too broadly to dispel the suspicion that it rests on a bare desire to treat the retarded as outsiders, pariahs who do not belong in the community. The Court, while disclaiming that special scrutiny is necessary or warranted, reaches the same [conclusion].

THE CABINING OF SUSPECT CLASSIFICATIONS

1. ***Age classifications.*** Cleburne was not the first case in which the Court rejected an attempted claim to heightened equal protection scrutiny of allegedly irrational classifications. An attempt to establish heightened scrutiny for age-based classifications failed in **Massachusetts Bd. of Retirement v. Murgia**, 427 U.S. 307 (1976), in which the per curiam opinion applied rationality standards in sustaining a mandatory retirement law for uniformed state police officers. Before applying its deferential criteria, the majority rejected a suspect classification claim: "[The] class of uniformed State Police Officers over 50 [does not] constitute a suspect class for purposes of equal protection analysis. [While] the treatment of the aged in this Nation has not been wholly free of discrimination, such persons, unlike, say, those who have been discriminated against on the basis of race or national origin, have not experienced a 'history of purposeful unequal treatment' or been subjected to unique disabilities on the basis of stereotyped characteristics not truly indicative of their abilities. The class subject to the compulsory retirement feature of the Massachusetts statute consists of uniformed state police officers over the age of 50. It cannot be said to discriminate only against the elderly. Rather, it draws the line at a certain

age in middle life. But even old age does not define a 'discrete and insular' group in need of 'extraordinary protection from the majoritarian political process.' Instead, it marks a stage that each of us will reach if we live out our normal span."

Justice MARSHALL's dissent observed: "[The] Court is quite right in suggesting that distinctions exist between the elderly and traditional suspect classes such as Negroes, and between the elderly and 'quasi-suspect' classes such as women or illegitimates. [E.g.,] the elderly are not isolated in society, and discrimination against them is not pervasive but is centered primarily in employment. [But the] elderly are undoubtedly discriminated against, and when legislation denies them an important benefit—employment—I conclude that to sustain the legislation [here, the State] must show a reasonably substantial interest and a scheme reasonably closely tailored to achieving that interest."

2. ***Poverty and wealth classifications.*** Should governmental action that has a differential impact dependent upon economic condition receive heightened scrutiny? Consider the following comment on the difficulty of considering de facto wealth classifications suspect: "The trouble is that, unlike a de facto racial classification which usually must seek its justifications in purposes completely distinct from its race-related impacts, a de facto pecuniary classification typically carries a highly persuasive justification inseparable from [the] hard choices it forces upon the financially straitened. For the typical form assumed by such a classification is simply the charging of a price, reasonably approximating cost, for some good or service which the complaining person may freely choose to purchase or not to purchase. [But] the risk of exposure to markets and their 'decisions' is not normally deemed objectionable, to say the least, in our society. Not only do we not inveigh generally against unequal distribution of income or full-cost pricing for most goods. We usually regard it as both the fairest and most efficient arrangement to require each consumer to pay the full market price of what he consumes." Michelman, "Supreme Court, 1968 Term—Foreword: On Protecting the Poor Through the Fourteenth Amendment," 83 Harv. L. Rev. 7 (1969). For contrary views, see Winter, "Poverty, Economic Equality, and the Equal Protection Clause," 1972 Sup. Ct. Rev. 41; Bork, "The Impossibility of Finding Welfare Rights in the Constitution," 1979 Wash. U. L.Q 695.

The Court in fact has repeatedly declined to find wealth classifications alone sufficient to trigger strict scrutiny (although wealth classifications coupled with a burden on a fundamental interest are a different matter, see Section 5 below) In **James v. Valtierra**, 402 U.S. 137 (1971), for example, Justice BLACK's majority opinion rejected an equal protection challenge to a California constitutional requirement that "[n]o low rent housing project shall hereafter be developed [by] any state public body" without prior approval in a local referendum. The provision defined "low rent housing project" as any development "for persons of low income"—"persons or families who lack the amount of income which is necessary [to] enable them, without financial assistance, to live in decent, safe and sanitary dwellings, without overcrowding." He emphasized that the provision did not involve "distinctions based on race," and rejected the contention that the provision "singled out" advocates of low-income housing by mandating a referendum while many other referenda only took place upon citizen initiative. Justice MARSHALL's dissent, joined by Justices Brennan and Blackmun, insisted that the provision "on its face constitutes invidious discrimination": it was "an explicit classification on the basis of poverty—a suspect classification which demands exacting judicial scrutiny." The majority, he objected, had treated the provision "as if it contained a totally benign, technical economic classification." He insisted that "singling out the poor to bear a burden not placed on any other class of citizens tramples the values the 14th Amendment was designed to protect."

SECTION 5. THE "FUNDAMENTAL INTERESTS" BRANCH OF EQUAL PROTECTION

Do classifications that would otherwise receive rational basis review sometimes require closer scrutiny because they bear upon fundamental rights or interests? Recall Skinner v. Oklahoma (1942; p. 510 above), which invalidated on equal protection grounds a law requiring sterilization of some recidivist thieves but not others, on the ground that procreation is a "fundamental right." Such interests that are capable of escalating review are not rooted in any independent source of protection elsewhere in the Constitution; if they were, there would be no need for litigants to resort to equal protection in order to protect them indirectly. The Warren Court's implication of fundamental interests under equal protection raised institutional and interpretive difficulties similar to those that marked the history of substantive due process; indeed, the search for "fundamental values" that inhered in this strand of equal protection analysis led some to refer to it as "substantive equal protection." In fact, however, the Court has developed this line of cases in only a very few areas.

This section focuses on the two principal strands of fundamental interests equal protection analysis that have survived since the Warren Court—the fundamental interest in voting, which has allowed equal protection claims to succeed against denials and "dilutions" of voting rights, and the fundamental interest in access to court or to some aspects of the judicial process. Note that a third strand of fundamental interest/equal protection analysis developed by the Warren Court, concerning the right of interstate migration upheld in Shapiro v. Thompson (1969; p. 462 above), is still good law but was given a whole new rationale by the Rehnquist Court in Saenz v. Roe (1999; p. 459 above), which reconceptualized this right under the Privileges or Immunities Clause rather than the Equal Protection Clause of the Fourteenth Amendment. This section ends with some major decisions *declining* to extend the fundamental interest branch of equal protection analysis to education, welfare benefits, and housing.

FUNDAMENTAL INTEREST IN VOTING

The original Constitution contains no "right" to vote. It explicitly left to the states the determination of qualifications of voters for both national and state elections. See Art. I, § 2 and Art. II, § 1. A number of constitutional amendments (the Fourteenth, Nineteenth, Twenty-fourth and Twenty-sixth) have expanded the franchise so as to limit that state power. Should courts scrutinize state voting schemes under the Equal Protection Clause apart from these express constitutional restrictions? Recall Justice Stone's footnote four in Carolene Products, mentioning "restrictions upon the right to vote" as a specific illustration of restrictions on "political processes" that warrant special judicial vigilance. Are there adequate constitutional justifications for the Court to move beyond specific language in the Constitution to guarantee broad access to the political process based on general principles of democracy? Is denial of the vote the "quintessential stoppage" in the democratic process, justifying active judicial supervision? See generally Ely, Democracy and Distrust (1980). Are political safeguards self-evidently insufficient in this area because the in-groups will always seek to choke off access by the out-groups? Consider first the district court's review of state denials of the right to vote as in the Harper and Kramer cases and then its decisions concerning state laws that "dilute" the right to vote without denying it altogether.

Harper v. Virginia State Board of Elections

383 U.S. 663, 86 S. Ct. 1079, 16 L. Ed. 2d 169 (1966).

[This case, establishing that voting in state elections is fundamental for equal protection purposes even in the absence of any textual right, arose from a challenge to Virginia's annual $1.50 poll tax on all residents over 21. The State made payment of the poll taxes a precondition for voting. Appellants' suit to have the poll tax declared unconstitutional was dismissed by a three-judge district court on the authority of Breedlove v. Suttles, 302 U.S. 277 (1937), where the Court had unanimously rejected an equal protection attack on the Georgia poll tax. The Supreme Court reversed.]

■ JUSTICE DOUGLAS delivered the opinion of the [Court].

[The] right to vote in state elections is nowhere expressly mentioned [in the Constitution]. [But] once the franchise is granted to the electorate, lines may not be drawn which are inconsistent with [equal protection]. [We] conclude that a State violates [equal protection] whenever it makes the affluence of the voter or payment of any fee an electoral standard. Voter qualifications have no relation to wealth nor to paying or not paying this or any other tax. Our cases demonstrate that [equal protection] restrains the States from fixing voter qualifications which invidiously discriminate. Long ago in [Yick Wo,] the Court referred to "the political franchise of voting" as a "fundamental political right, because preservative of all rights."

[It] is argued that a State may exact fees from citizens for many different kinds of licenses; that if it can demand from all an equal fee for a driver's license, it can demand from all an equal poll tax for voting. But we must remember that the interest of the State, when it comes to voting, is limited to the power to fix qualifications. Wealth, like race, creed, or color, is not germane to one's ability to participate intelligently in the electoral process. Lines drawn on the basis of wealth or property, like those of race, are traditionally disfavored. To introduce wealth or payment of a fee as a measure of a voter's qualifications is to introduce a capricious or irrelevant factor. [In] this context—that is, as a condition of obtaining a ballot—the requirement of fee paying causes an "invidious" discrimination [that] runs afoul of [equal protection]. [Breedlove v. Suttles sanctioned the use of a poll tax] as "a prerequisite of voting." To that extent [it] is overruled.

We agree, of course, with Mr. Justice Holmes that the Due Process Clause of the 14th Amendment "does not enact Mr. Herbert Spencer's Social Statistics." [Lochner.] Likewise, the Equal Protection Clause is not shackled to the political theory of a particular era. In determining what lines are unconstitutionally discriminatory, we have never been confined to historic notions of equality, any more than we have restricted due process to a fixed catalogue of what was at a given time deemed to be the limits of fundamental rights. Notions of what constitutes equal treatment for purposes of [equal protection] *do* change. [Compare Plessy with Brown.] Our conclusion [is] founded not on what we think governmental policy should be, but on what [equal protection] requires. We have long been mindful that where fundamental rights and liberties are asserted under [equal protection], classifications which might invade or restrain them must be closely scrutinized and carefully confined. See [e.g., Skinner]. Those principles apply here. For to repeat, wealth or fee paying [has] no relation to voting qualifications; the right to vote is too precious, too fundamental to be so burdened or conditioned. Reversed.

■ JUSTICE BLACK, dissenting.

[Poll tax] legislation can "reasonably," "rationally" and without an "invidious" or evil purpose to injure anyone be found to rest on a number of state policies including (1) the State's desire to collect its revenue, and (2) its belief that voters who pay a poll tax will be interested in furthering the State's welfare when they vote. [And] history is on the side of "rationality" of the State's poll tax policy. [Another] reason for my dissent [is] that it seems to be using the old "natural-law-due-process formula" to justify striking down state laws as violations of [equal protection]. There is no more constitutional support for this Court to use [equal protection than to use due process] to write into the Constitution its notions of what it thinks is good governmental [policy].

■ JUSTICE HARLAN, whom JUSTICE STEWART joins, dissenting.

[The Court uses] captivating phrases, but they are wholly inadequate to satisfy the standard governing adjudication of the equal protection issue: Is there a rational basis for Virginia's poll tax as a voting qualification? I think the answer to that question is undoubtedly "yes." Property qualifications and poll taxes have been a traditional part of our political structure. [It] is certainly a rational argument that payment of some minimal poll tax promotes civic responsibility, weeding out those who do not care enough about public affairs to pay $1.50 or thereabouts a year for the exercise of the franchise. It is also arguable, indeed it was probably accepted as sound political theory by a large percentage of Americans through most of our history, that people with some property have a deeper stake in community affairs, and are consequently more responsible, more educated, more knowledgeable, more worthy of confidence, than those without means, and that the community and Nation would be better managed if the franchise were restricted to such citizens. Property and poll-tax qualifications [are] not in accord with current egalitarian notions of how a modern democracy should be organized. [But] it is all wrong [for] the Court to adopt the political doctrines popularly accepted at a particular moment of our history and to declare all others to be irrational and [invidious]. It was not too long ago that Mr. Justice Holmes felt impelled to remind the Court that [due process] does not enact the laissez-faire theory of society. [Lochner.] The times have changed, and perhaps it is appropriate to observe that neither does [equal protection] of that Amendment rigidly impose upon America an ideology of unrestrained [egalitarianism].

Kramer v. Union Free School District No. 15

395 U.S. 621, 89 S. Ct. 1886, 23 L. Ed. 2d 583 (1969).

■ CHIEF JUSTICE WARREN delivered the opinion of the Court.

[Sec. 2012 of the New York Education Law] provides that in certain New York school districts residents [may] vote in the school district election only if they (1) own (or lease) taxable real property within the district, or (2) are parents (or have custody of) children enrolled in the local public schools. [The law was unsuccessfully challenged in the lower court by "a bachelor who neither owns nor leases taxable real property": appellant was "a thirty-one-year-old college-educated stockbroker who lives in his parents' home."]

[We] must give the statute a close and exacting examination. This is necessary because statutes distributing the franchise constitute the foundation of our representative society. Any unjustified discrimination in determining who may participate in political affairs or in the selection of public officials undermines the legitimacy of representative government. [Laws] granting the franchise to residents on a selective basis always pose the danger of denying some citizens any effective voice in the governmental affairs which substantially affect their lives. Therefore, if a challenged [law] grants the right to vote to some bona fide residents of requisite age and citizenship and denies the franchise to others, the Court must determine whether the conclusions are necessary to promote a compelling state interest. [The] presumption of constitutionality and the approval given "rational" classifications in other types of enactments are based on an assumption that the institutions of state government are structured so as to represent fairly all the people. However, when the challenge to the statute is in effect a challenge of this basic assumption, the assumption can no longer serve as the basis for presuming constitutionality.

[We turn] to [the] question whether the exclusion is necessary to promote a compelling state interest. [Appellees] argue that the State has a legitimate interest in limiting the franchise in school district elections [to] those "primarily interested in such elections" [and] that the State may reasonably and permissibly conclude that "property taxpayers" [and] parents of the children enrolled in the district's schools are those "primarily interested" in school affairs. [We] need express no opinion as to whether the State in some circumstances might limit the exercise of the franchise to those "primarily interested" or "primarily affected." [For], assuming, arguendo, that New York legitimately might limit the franchise in these school district elections to those "primarily interested in school affairs," [§ 2012] does not meet the exacting standard of precision we require of statutes which selectively distribute the franchise. [Its] classifications [permit] inclusion of many persons who have, at best, a remote and indirect interest in school affairs and, on the other hand, exclude others who have a distinct and direct interest in the school meeting [decisions].[1] Reversed.

---

[1] For example, appellant resides with his parents in the school district, pays state and federal taxes and is interested in and affected by school board decisions; however, he has no

■ JUSTICE STEWART, with whom JUSTICES BLACK and HARLAN join, dissenting.

[Clearly] a State may reasonably assume that its residents have a greater stake in the outcome of elections held within its boundaries than do other persons [and] that residents, being generally better informed regarding state affairs than are nonresidents, will be more likely [to] vote responsibly. And the same may be said of legislative assumptions regarding the electoral competence of adults and literate persons on the one hand, and of minors and illiterates on the other. [So] long as the classification is rationally related to a permissible legislative end, [there] is no denial of equal protection. Thus judged, the statutory classification involved here seems to me clearly to be valid [and the] Court does not really argue the contrary. [The] Court's asserted justification for applying [its strict] standard cannot withstand analysis. [In] any event, it seems to me that under *any* equal protection standard, short of a doctrinaire insistence that universal suffrage is somehow mandated by the Constitution, the appellant's claim must be [rejected].

STRICT SCRUTINY OF VOTE DENIALS

Kramer sought to explain more clearly than Harper had why "equal" participation in the electoral process is a "fundamental interest" triggering equal protection strict scrutiny, even though there is no constitutional "right" to vote. In examining the post-Kramer cases which follow, consider especially what state interests are sufficiently "compelling" to survive strict scrutiny in this area, and what means are sufficiently narrowly tailored. Note that in this area, unlike most other spheres of strict scrutiny, some laws *do* survive judicial review.

1. ***Limited purpose elections and special purpose governmental units.*** In **Cipriano v. Houma**, 395 U.S. 701 (1969), decided on the same day as Kramer, the unanimous Court invalidated a Louisiana law permitting only property owners to vote in elections regarding the issuance of municipal utility bonds. The Court noted that the bonds were to be paid entirely from the operations of the utilities and not from property taxes. A year later, in **Phoenix v. Kolodziejski**, 399 U.S. 204 (1970), the majority extended Cipriano, holding that the restriction of the franchise to property owners was no more valid in elections on general obligation bonds (which looked largely to property tax revenues for servicing) than in elections on revenue bonds. Justice WHITE's majority opinion concluded that the differences between the interests of those who did and did not own property were not "sufficiently substantial to justify excluding the latter from the franchise."

Three years later, however, the majority found the Kramer-Cipriano-Kolodziejski line of cases inapplicable and sustained an election scheme for a water storage district under which only landowners were permitted to vote and in which votes were proportioned according to the assessed valuation of the land. **Salyer Land Co. v. Tulare Lake Basin Water Storage Dist.**, 410 U.S. 719 (1973). Justice REHNQUIST's majority opinion noted that the district's main purpose was to assure water for farming, and that project

vote. On the other hand, an uninterested unemployed young man who pays no state or federal taxes, but who rents an apartment in the district, can [vote]. [Footnote by Chief Justice Warren.]

costs were assessed upon the land in proportion to benefits received. He found the demanding requirements of such cases as Kramer inapplicable to the district "by reason of its special limited purpose and of the disproportionate effect of its activities on landowners as a group." Accordingly, the details of the election scheme were subjected only to the minimal scrutiny, and those details—the exclusion of mere residents and lessees, and weighting the votes according to the value of the land—easily survived that scrutiny. Justice DOUGLAS, joined by Justices Brennan and Marshall dissented, objecting that voting by the large landowning corporations that farmed 85% of the land in the district created "a corporate political kingdom undreamed of by those who wrote our Constitution."

2. ***Disenfranchisement of felons.*** Many states disenfranchise convicted felons even if they have served their sentences and completed their parole. In **Richardson v. Ramirez**, 418 U.S. 24 (1974), the California Supreme Court had struck down such a barrier under the assumed compulsion of the higher decree of scrutiny demanded by voting cases. But the Court reversed, finding an exception to the usual equal protection standard in the recognition of ex-felons' disenfranchisement in the rarely invoked § 2 of the 14th Amendment. The reduced representation sanction of § 2 is specifically inapplicable to denials of the vote "for participation in rebellion, or other crime." Justice REHNQUIST's majority opinion drew on the language and history of that provision to conclude "that those who framed and adopted the 14th Amendment could not have intended to prohibit outright in § 1 of that Amendment that which was expressly exempted from the lesser sanction of reduced representation imposed by § 2 of the Amendment." He accordingly concluded that "the exclusion of felons from the vote has an affirmative sanction [which] was not present in the case of the other restrictions on the franchise" invalidated in the Harper-Kramer line of cases. Justice MARSHALL, joined by Justice Brennan, dissented on the merits, urging strict scrutiny.

3. ***Voter ID requirements.*** What level of scrutiny should apply to a state law requiring voters to present specified forms of identification at the polls in order to vote? Are such requirements subject to facial challenge on the ground that they have the same de facto discriminatory effect as a poll tax? In **Crawford v. Marion County Election Board**, 553 U.S. 181 (2008), the Supreme Court rejected a challenge to an Indiana law (SEA 483) requiring citizens voting in person to present government-issued photo identification. Justice STEVENS, writing for a plurality in an opinion joined by Chief Justice Roberts and Justice Kennedy, declined to apply the strict scrutiny applied in Harper and instead engaged in a balancing of interests: "The State has identified several state interests that arguably justify the burdens that SEA 483 imposes on voters and potential voters. [Each] is unquestionably relevant to the State's interest in protecting the integrity and reliability of the electoral process. The first is the interest in deterring and detecting voter fraud. [The] only kind of voter fraud that SEA 483 addresses is in-person voter impersonation at polling places. The record contains no evidence of any such fraud actually occurring in Indiana at any time in its history. Moreover, petitioners argue that provisions of the Indiana Criminal Code punishing such conduct as a felony provide adequate protection against the risk that such conduct will occur in the future. It remains true, however, that flagrant examples of such fraud in other parts of the country have been documented throughout this Nation's history. [Not]

only is the risk of voter fraud real but [it] could affect the outcome of a close election.

"[The] burdens that are relevant to the issue before us are those imposed on persons who are eligible to vote but do not possess a current photo identification that complies with the requirements of SEA 483. The fact that most voters already possess a valid driver's license, or some other form of acceptable identification, would not save the statute under our reasoning in Harper, if the State required voters to pay a tax or a fee to obtain a new photo identification. But [the] photo identification cards issued by Indiana's BMV [are] free. For most voters who need them, the inconvenience of making a trip to the BMV, gathering the required documents, and posing for a photograph surely does not qualify as a substantial burden on the right to vote, or even represent a significant increase over the usual burdens of voting. [The] severity of that burden is [mitigated] by the fact that, if eligible, voters without photo identification may cast provisional ballots that will ultimately be counted. To do so, however, they must travel to the circuit court clerk's office within 10 days to execute the required affidavit. It is unlikely that such a requirement would pose a constitutional problem unless it is wholly unjustified. And even assuming that the burden may not be justified as to a few voters, that conclusion is by no means sufficient to establish petitioners' right to [facial invalidation]."

Justice Stevens thus declined to rely on record evidence that SEA 483 had been particularly burdensome for some voters such as the disabled and the elderly. Nor did he take account of the fact that "all of the Republicans in the General Assembly voted in favor of SEA 483 and the Democrats were unanimous in opposing it," reasoning that, "if a nondiscriminatory law is supported by valid neutral justifications, those justifications should not be disregarded simply because partisan interests may have provided one motivation for the votes of individual legislators."

Justice SCALIA filed a concurrence in the judgment, joined by Justices Thomas and Alito, stressing that "the burden at issue is minimal and justified" and that strict scrutiny under Harper should not be employed, even in as-applied challenges, for "nonsevere, nondiscriminatory restrictions" on the right to vote—a possibility he believed the plurality had left open. He concluded that "the Indiana photo-identification law is a generally applicable, nondiscriminatory voting regulation, and our precedents refute the view that individual impacts are relevant to determining the severity of the burden it imposes. [The] Fourteenth Amendment does not regard neutral laws as invidious ones, even when their burdens purportedly fall disproportionately on a protected class. A fortiori it does not do so when, as here, the classes complaining of disparate impact are not even protected."

Justice SOUTER dissented, joined by Justice Ginsburg. Finding that "Indiana's 'Voter ID Law' threatens to impose nontrivial burdens on the voting right of tens of thousands of the State's citizens, and a significant percentage of those individuals are likely to be deterred from voting," he would have found the law unconstitutional even on a balancing analysis. Justice Souter explained: "Voting-rights cases raise two competing interests, the one side being the fundamental right to vote. The Judiciary is obliged to train a skeptical eye on any qualification of that right. [The] travel costs and fees necessary to get one of the limited variety of federal or state photo identifications needed to cast a regular ballot under the Voter ID Law [will] affect voters according to their circumstances, with the average person probably viewing it as nothing more than an inconvenience. Poor, old, and disabled voters who do not drive a car, however, may find the trip prohibitive. [The] burden of traveling to a more distant BMV office rather than a conveniently located polling place is probably serious for many of the individuals who lack photo identification. They almost certainly will not own cars, and public transportation in Indiana is fairly limited.

"For those voters who can afford the roundtrip, a second financial hurdle appears: in order to get photo identification for the first time, they need to present 'a birth certificate, a certificate of naturalization, U.S. veterans photo identification, U.S. military photo identification, or a U.S. passport.' [Indiana] counties charge anywhere from $3 to $12 for a birth certificate, and that same price must usually be paid for a first-time passport, since a birth certificate is required to prove U.S. citizenship by birth. The total fees for a passport, moreover, are up to about $100. So most voters must pay at least one fee to get the ID necessary to cast a regular ballot. [Both] the travel costs and the fees are disproportionately heavy for, and thus disproportionately likely to deter, the poor, the old, and the immobile." The dissent found "that provisional ballots do not obviate the burdens of getting photo identification" because the "need to travel to the county seat each election amounts to a high hurdle." And finding that these burdens would deter or discourage a substantial number of Indiana voters, Justice Souter stated that Indiana's purported interests must withstand "a rigorous assessment."

Applying such review, Justice Souter's dissent found SEA 483 wanting, for even if preventing voter fraud is an important interest in the abstract, "the State has not come across a single instance of in-person voter impersonation fraud in all of Indiana's history." He concluded: "the Indiana statute crosses a line when it targets the poor and the weak. If the Court's decision in Harper v. Virginia Bd. of Elections stands for anything, it is that being poor has nothing to do with being qualified to vote. Harper made clear that '[t]o introduce wealth or payment of a fee as a measure of a voter's qualifications is to introduce a capricious or irrelevant factor.' The State's requirements here, that people without cars travel to a motor vehicle registry and that the poor who fail to do that get to their county seats within 10 days of every election, likewise translate into unjustified economic burdens uncomfortably close to the outright $1.50 fee we struck down 42 years ago. Like that fee, the onus of the Indiana law is illegitimate just because it correlates with no state interest so well as it does with the object of deterring poorer residents from exercising the franchise."

Justice BREYER filed a separate dissent, comparing the burden imposed by the Indiana statute to the poll tax struck down in Harper: "[A]n Indiana nondriver, most likely to be poor, elderly, or disabled, will find it difficult and expensive to travel to the Bureau of Motor Vehicles, particularly if he or she resides in one of the many Indiana counties lacking a public transportation system. [Many] of these individuals may be uncertain about how to obtain the underlying documentation, usually a passport or a birth certificate, upon which the statute insists. And some may find the costs associated with these documents unduly burdensome (up to $12 for a copy of a birth certificate; up to $100 for a passport). By way of comparison, this Court previously found unconstitutionally burdensome a poll tax of $1.50 (less than $10 today, inflation-adjusted). See Harper." He concluded that, "while the Constitution does not in general forbid Indiana from enacting a photo ID requirement, this statute imposes a disproportionate burden upon those without valid photo IDs."

4. ***Counting and recounting votes.*** In **Bush v. Gore**, 531 U.S. 98 (2000), the Court addressed an equal protection challenge to the recount procedures ordered by the Florida Supreme Court in the 2000 presidential election. Democrat Al Gore, who initially trailed Republican George W. Bush by a narrow vote margin, had requested a recount. On appeal from a lower court ruling, the Florida Supreme Court ordered a manual recount of "undervotes"—ballots which failed to record a presidential choice in machine counts—in all Florida counties. In a per curiam decision, from which Justices Breyer, Ginsburg, Souter, and Stevens dissented, the Court found that the Florida Supreme Court's recount order constituted an equal protection violation because, *inter alia*, the order to recount only the "undervotes" and the failure to establish uniform standards for accepting or rejecting contested ballots did not equally protect the "fundamental right of each voter." By halting the recount, the Court's decision allowed Florida Secretary of State Katherine Harris's previous certification of Bush as the winner of the state's electoral votes to stand, giving Bush the requisite number of electoral votes to win the presidency.

Though the Court emphasized that its "consideration" was "limited to the present circumstances," and though it has been said that "Bush v. Gore is dead" as a precedent, Hasen, "The Untimely Death of Bush v. Gore," 60 Stan. L. Rev. 1 (2007), the case played a role in the 2012 Ohio presidential election between Democratic incumbent Barack Obama and Republican Mitt Romney. In the summer of 2012, Obama's campaign brought an equal protection challenge to Ohio's allegedly conflicting and different deadlines for in-person early voting. An Ohio federal district court agreed that the Ohio system violated the Equal Protection Clause and entered a preliminary injunction against Ohio's enacting the different early voting deadlines. In doing so, the district court relied on Bush, particularly the Court's admonition that "[h]aving once granted the right to vote on equal terms, the State may not, by later and arbitrary and disparate treatment, value one person's vote over that of another." Obama for America v. Husted, 888 F.Supp.2d 897 (S.D. Ohio 2012). Given the values of the rule of law in a precedent-based system, is it coherent for a court to assert that a given decision should not have precedential weight?

VOTE "DILUTION": REAPPORTIONMENT AND GERRYMANDERING

Before 1962, legislative districting controversies were thought to be nonjusticiable. The prevailing attitude about the justiciability of districting disputes was reflected in Justice Frankfurter's opinion in **Colegrove v. Green**, 328 U.S. 549 (1946). There, the majority refused to reach the merits of a federal court challenge to the congressional districting scheme in Illinois. The challengers contended that the Illinois law delineating congressional districts was unconstitutional because the districts were not approximately equal in population. Justice FRANKFURTER's plurality opinion affirming the dismissal of the complaint stated: "[T]he petitioners ask of this Court what is beyond its competence to grant. [This] controversy concerns matters that bring courts into immediate and active relations with party contests. From the determination of such issues this Court has traditionally remained aloof. [Courts] ought not to enter this political thicket." But in 1962, in Baker v. Carr, a divided Court held equal protection challenges to legislative apportionments justiciable, expressing optimism that judicially manageable standards could be formulated. Soon, suits challenging state legislative apportionment schemes were instituted in over 30 states.

The formulation of standards began two years later, with the "one person, one vote" decision in Reynolds v. Sims, which follows. With Reynolds, the Court moved from a concern with absolute denials of the franchise, as in Harper and Kramer, to the question of dilution of voting rights, in view of the Reynolds emphasis on the right of each voter to "an equally effective voice in the election of [members of the] state legislature."

Reynolds v. Sims

377 U.S. 533, 84 S. Ct. 1362, 12 L. Ed. 2d 506 (1964).

[This case arose from a challenge to the malapportionment of the Alabama legislature. The challengers claimed that the existing districting scheme, based on the 1900 census, discriminated against voters in counties whose populations had grown proportionately far more than others since the 1900 census. The lower federal court found that the old apportionment as well as two new ones devised by the legislature violated equal protection.]

■ CHIEF JUSTICE WARREN delivered the opinion of the [Court].

[Undoubtedly,] the right of suffrage is a fundamental matter in a free and democratic society. Especially since the right to exercise the franchise in a free and unimpaired manner is preservative of other basic civil and political rights, any alleged infringement of the right of citizens to vote must be carefully and meticulously [scrutinized].

Legislators represent people, not trees or acres. Legislators are elected by voters, not farms or cities or economic interests. As long as ours is a representative form of government, [the] right to elect legislators in a free and unimpaired fashion is a bedrock of our political system. It could hardly be gainsaid that a constitutional claim had been asserted by an allegation that certain otherwise qualified voters had been entirely prohibited from voting for members of their state legislature. And, if a State should provide that the votes of citizens in one part of the State should be given two times, or five times, or 10 times the weight of votes of citizens in another part of the State, it could hardly be contended that the right to vote of those residing in the disfavored areas had not been effectively diluted. [Of] course, the effect of state legislative districting schemes which give the same number of representatives to unequal numbers of constituents is [identical]. Weighting the votes of citizens differently, by any method or means, merely because of where they happen to reside, hardly seems [justifiable].

Logically, in a society ostensibly grounded on representative government, it would seem reasonable that a majority of the people of a State could elect a majority of that State's legislators. [To] sanction minority control of state legislative bodies would appear to deny majority rights in a way that far surpasses any possible denial of minority rights that might otherwise be thought to result. [And] the concept of equal protection has been traditionally viewed as requiring the uniform treatment of persons standing in the same relation to the governmental action questioned or challenged. With respect to the allocation of legislative representation, all voters, as citizens of a State, stand in the same relation regardless of where they live. Any suggested criteria for the differentiation of citizens are insufficient to justify any discrimination as to the weight of their votes, unless relevant to the permissible purposes of legislative apportionment. Since the achieving of fair and effective representation for all citizens is concededly the basic aim of legislative apportionment, we conclude that [equal protection] guarantees the opportunity for equal participation by all voters in the election of state legislators. Diluting the weight of votes because of place of residence impairs basic constitutional rights under the 14th Amendment just as much as invidious discriminations based upon factors such as race [or] economic status. Our constitutional system amply provides for the protection of minorities by means other than giving them majority control of state legislatures.

[We] are told that the matter of apportioning representation in a state legislature is a complex and many-faceted one. We are advised that States can rationally consider factors other than population. [We] are admonished not to restrict the power of the States to impose differing views as to political philosophy on their citizens. We are cautioned about the dangers of entering into political thickets and mathematical quagmires. Our answer is this: a denial of constitutionally protected rights demands judicial protection; our oath and our office require no less of us. [To] the extent that a citizen's right to vote is debased, he is that much less a citizen. [The] weight of a citizen's vote cannot be made to depend on where he lives. Population is, of necessity, the starting point for consideration and the controlling criterion for judgment in legislative apportionment controversies. A citizen, a qualified voter, is no more nor no less so because he lives in the city or on the farm. This is the clear and strong command of [equal protection]. [We] hold that, as a basic constitutional standard, [equal protection] requires that the seats in both houses of a bicameral state legislature must be apportioned on a population basis. Simply stated, an individual's right to vote for state legislators is unconstitutionally impaired when its weight is in a substantial fashion diluted when compared with votes of citizens living in other parts of the [State].

[We] find the federal analogy inapposite and irrelevant to state legislative districting schemes. [The] system of representation in the two Houses [of Congress] is one conceived out of compromise and concession indispensable to the establishment of our federal republic [and] is based on the consideration that in establishing our type of federalism a group of formerly independent States bound themselves together under one national government. [Political] subdivisions of States—counties, cities, or whatever—never were and never have been considered as sovereign entities. Rather, they have been traditionally regarded as subordinate governmental instrumentalities created by the [State]. [The] relationship of the States to the Federal Government could hardly be less analogous.

[Equal protection] requires that a State make an honest and good faith effort to construct districts, in both houses of its legislature, as nearly of equal population as is practicable. We realize that it is a practical impossibility to arrange legislative districts so that each one has an identical number of residents, or citizens, or voters. Mathematical exactness or precision is hardly a workable constitutional requirement. [So] long as the divergences from a strict population standard are based on legitimate considerations incident to the effectuation of a rational state policy, some deviations from the equal-population principle are constitutionally permissible, [but] neither history alone, nor economic or other sorts of group interests, are permissible factors in attempting to justify disparities from population-based representation. Citizens, not history or economic interests, cast votes. Considerations of area alone provide an insufficient justification for deviations from the equal-population principle. Again, people, not land or trees or pastures, vote. [A] consideration that appears to be of more substance in justifying some deviations from population-based representation in state legislatures is that of insuring some voice to political subdivisions, as political subdivisions. [In] many States much of the legislature's activity involves the enactment of so-called local legislation, directed only to the concerns of particular political subdivisions. And a State may legitimately desire to construct districts along political subdivision lines to deter the possibilities of gerrymandering. [But] if, even as a result of a clearly rational state policy of according some legislative representation to political subdivisions, population is submerged as the controlling consideration, [the] right of all of the State's citizens to cast an effective and adequately weighted vote would be unconstitutionally [impaired]. [Affirmed.]

[In five companion cases to Reynolds v. Sims, the Court relied on its principles to invalidate apportionment schemes in Colorado, New York, Maryland, Virginia, and Delaware. The Colorado case, **Lucas v. Forty-Fourth Gen. Assembly**, 377 U.S. 713 (1964), warrants special mention, because the defenders of the districting there argued that it should be sustained because it had been approved by the voters of the state by a statewide referendum. Moreover, the voters had rejected a plan to apportion both houses on the basis of population. Chief Justice WARREN's opinion concluded that this background did not justify deviation from the Reynolds requirement. He stated: "An individual's constitutionally protected right to cast an equally weighted vote cannot be denied even by a vote of a majority of a State's electorate, if the apportionment scheme adopted by the voters fails to measure up to the requirements of [equal protection]. Manifestly, the fact that an apportionment plan is adopted in a popular referendum is insufficient to sustain its constitutionality or to induce a court of equity to refuse to act. [A] citizen's constitutional rights can hardly be infringed simply because a majority of the people choose that it be. We hold that the fact that a challenged legislative apportionment plan was approved by the electorate is without federal constitutional significance, if the scheme adopted fails to satisfy the basic requirements of [equal protection], as delineated [in Reynolds]."]

■ JUSTICE HARLAN, dissenting [in all six cases].

The Court's constitutional discussion [is] remarkable [for] its failure to address itself at all to the 14th Amendment as a whole or to the legislative history of the Amendment pertinent to the matter at hand. Stripped of aphorisms, the Court's argument boils down to the assertion that petitioners' right to vote has been invidiously "debased" or "diluted" by systems of apportionment which entitle them to vote for fewer legislators than other voters, an assertion which is tied to [equal protection] only by the constitutionally frail tautology that "equal" means "equal." [The] history of the adoption of the 14th Amendment provides conclusive evidence that neither those who proposed nor those who ratified the Amendment believed that [equal protection] limited the power of the States to apportion their legislatures as they saw fit. Moreover, the history demonstrates that the intention to leave this power undisturbed was deliberate and was widely believed to be essential to the adoption of the Amendment. [See also § 2 of the 14th Amendment. An extensive review of the history is omitted.]

Although [the Court] provides only generalities in elaboration of its main thesis, its opinion nevertheless fully demonstrates how far removed these problems are from fields of judicial competence. [In] one or another of today's opinions, the Court declares it unconstitutional for a State to give consideration to any of the following in establishing legislative districts: (1) history; (2) "economic or other sorts of group interests"; (3) area; (4) geographical considerations; (5) a desire "to insure effective representation for sparsely settled areas"; (6) "availability of access of citizens to their representatives"; (7) theories of bicameralism (except those approved by the Court); (8) occupation; (9) "an attempt to balance urban and rural power"; (10) the preference of a majority of voters in the State. So far as presently appears, the *only* factor which a state may consider, apart from numbers, is political subdivisions. But even "a clearly rational state policy" recognizing this factor is unconstitutional if "population is submerged as the controlling consideration." [I] know of no principle of logic or practical or theoretical politics, still less any constitutional principle, which establishes all or any of these exclusions. [The Court] says only that "legislators represent people, not trees or acres." [This] may be conceded. But it is surely equally obvious, and, in the context of elections, more meaningful to note that people are not ciphers and that legislators can represent their electors only by speaking for their interests—economic, social, political—many of which do reflect the place where the electors live. The Court does not establish, or indeed even attempt to make a case for the proposition that conflicting interests within a State can only be adjusted by disregarding them when voters are grouped for purposes of [representation].

▪ JUSTICE STEWART, whom JUSTICE CLARK joins, dissenting [in the Colorado and New York cases].

[My] own understanding of the various theories of representative government is that no one theory has ever commanded unanimous assent. [But] even if it were thought that the rule announced today by the Court is, as a matter of political theory, the most desirable general rule which can be devised, [I] could not join in the fabrication of a constitutional mandate which imports and forever freezes one theory of political thought into our [Constitution]. Representative government is a process of accommodating group interests through democratic institutional arrangements. [Appropriate] legislative apportionment, therefore, should ideally be designed to insure effective representation in the State's legislature, in cooperation with other organs for political power, of the various groups and interests making up the electorate. [Population] factors must often to some degree be subordinated in devising a legislative apportionment plan which is to achieve the important goal of ensuring a fair, effective, and balanced representation of the regional, social, and economic interests within a State. [What] constitutes a rational plan reasonably designed to achieve this objective will vary from State to State, [but] so long as a State's apportionment plan reasonably achieves, in the light of the State's own characteristics, effective and balanced representation of all substantial interests, without sacrificing the principle of effective majority rule, that plan cannot be considered irrational.

In **Evenwel v. Abbott**, 578 U.S. ___, 136 S. Ct. 1120 (2016), a group of Texas voters argued that the principle of one person, one vote should be understood as requiring one voter, one-vote. They challenged Texas's population-based districting on the ground that it produces unequal districts when measured by voter-eligible population. The Court rejected the claim that only the population of eligible voters could be used in determining districts. Justice GINSBURG wrote: "We hold, based on constitutional history, this Court's decisions, and longstanding practice, that a State may draw its legislative districts based on total population. [James] Madison explained in the Federalist Papers, 'that as the aggregate number of representatives allotted to the several states, is to be . . . founded on the aggregate number of inhabitants; so, the right of choosing this allotted number in each state, is to be exercised by such part of the inhabitants, as the state itself may designate.' The Federalist No. 54. In other words, the basis of *representation* in the House was to include all inhabitants—although slaves were counted as only three-fifths of a person—even though States remained free to deny many of those inhabitants the right to participate in the selection of their representatives. [The] Framers of the Fourteenth Amendment considered at length the possibility of allocating House seats to States on the basis of voter population. [Supporters] of apportionment based on voter population employed the same voter-equality reasoning that appellants now echo. [Voter-based] apportionment proponents encountered fierce resistance from proponents of total-population apportionment. Much of the opposition was grounded in the principle of representational equality. [The] product of these debates was § 2 of the Fourteenth Amendment, which retained total population as the congressional apportionment base. See U.S. Const., Amdt. 14, § 2 ("Representatives shall be apportioned among the several States according to their respective numbers, counting the whole number of persons in each State, excluding Indians not taxed."). Appellants ask us to find in the Fourteenth Amendment's Equal Protection Clause a rule inconsistent with this "theory of the Constitution." But [this] theory underlies not just the method of allocating House seats to States; it applies as well to the method of apportioning legislative seats within States. [Reynolds] involved features of the federal electoral system that contravene the principles of both voter *and* representational equality to favor interests that have no relevance outside the federal context. Senate seats were allocated to States on an equal basis to respect state sovereignty and increase the odds that the smaller States would ratify the Constitution. [The] Framers' answer to the apportionment question in the congressional context therefore undermines appellants' contention that districts must be based on voter population.

Justice THOMAS concurred but wrote separately to say that "this Court has never provided a sound basis for the one-person, one-vote principle." Justice ALITO also concurred, joined by Justice Thomas, to reject the "meretricious argument" that "the one-person, one-vote principle requires districts that are equal in total population. [First], the allocation of congressional representation sheds little light on the question [because] that allocation plainly violates one person, one vote. This is obviously true with respect to the Senate. [Second], Reynolds v. Sims squarely rejected the argument that the Constitution's allocation of congressional representation establishes the test for the constitutionality of a state legislative districting plan. [Third], reliance on the Constitution's allocation of congressional representation is profoundly ahistorical. When the formula for allocating House seats was first devised in 1787 and reconsidered at the time of the adoption of the Fourteenth Amendment in 1868, the overwhelming concern was far removed from any abstract theory about the nature of representation. Instead, the dominant consideration was the distribution of political power among the States."

JUDICIAL SCRUTINY OF POLITICAL GERRYMANDERS

There are many ways to draw equipopulous districts within a given state to satisfy the requirements of Reynolds v. Sims. If the lines are drawn in a deliberate effort to maximize the voting strength of members of political parties, has equal protection been violated? Such a practice is often referred to as "gerrymandering," a phrase coined in 1812 in response to a law signed by Massachusetts Governor Elbridge Gerry that produced a district whose shape resembled a lizard or a salamander, and which a critic therefore dubbed a "gerrymander."

In **Gaffney v. Cummings**, 412 U.S. 735 (1973), the Court rejected a challenge to a districting plan the challengers characterized "as nothing less than a gigantic political gerrymander, invidiously discriminatory under the 14th Amendment." Justice WHITE's majority opinion held political considerations permissible: "Politics [is] inseparable from districting and apportionment. [It] is not only obvious, but absolutely unavoidable, that the location and shape of districts may well determine the political complexion of the area. [The] reality is that districting inevitably has and is intended to have substantial political consequences. [Judicial] interest should be at its lowest ebb when a State purports fairly to allocate political power to the parties in accordance with their voting strength. [We do not] have a constitutional warrant to invalidate a state plan, otherwise within tolerable population limits, because it undertakes, not to minimize or eliminate the political strength of any group or party, but to recognize it and, through districting, provide a rough sort of proportional representation in the legislative halls of the State."

The Court's unwillingness to consider purely political gerrymandering as constituting a possible equal protection violation was relaxed somewhat in the following decision. The challenged apportionment plan, adopted by the Republican-controlled Indiana legislature, provided for state senate and house districts of substantially equal population. The Democrats nonetheless claimed that, by using a mix of single and multi-membered districts and gerrymandering district lines, the plan substantially understated Democratic voting strength. In elections held under the plan in 1982, the Democrats received 51.9 percent of the total house vote and 53.1 percent of the total senate vote, yet won only forty-three of 100 house seats and only thirteen of twenty-five senate seats. The Court held the political gerrymandering claim justiciable under the Equal Protection Clause but declined to agree with the challengers on the merits:

Davis v. Bandemer

478 U.S. 109, 106 S. Ct. 2797, 92 L. Ed. 2d 85 (1986).

■ JUSTICE WHITE announced the judgment of the Court and delivered an opinion in which JUSTICES BRENNAN, MARSHALL, and BLACKMUN joined as to Parts III, and IV.

III. [In] order to succeed the [plaintiffs] were required to prove both intentional discrimination against an identifiable political group and an actual discriminatory effect on that group. [We] are confident that if the law challenged here had discriminatory effects on Democrats, this record would support a finding that the discrimination was intentional. Thus, we decline to overturn the District Court's finding of discriminatory intent as clearly erroneous. Indeed, quite aside from the anecdotal evidence, the shape of the House and Senate Districts, and the alleged disregard for political boundaries, we think it most likely that whenever a legislature redistricts, those responsible for the legislation will know the likely political composition of the new districts and will have a prediction as to whether a particular district is a safe one for a Democratic or Republican candidate or is a competitive district that either candidate might win. [As] long as redistricting is done by a legislature, it would not be very difficult to prove that the likely political consequences of the reapportionment were intended.

[We] do not accept, however, the District Court's legal and factual bases for concluding that the 1981 Act visited a sufficiently adverse effect on the appellees' constitutionally protected rights to make out a violation of [equal protection]. The District Court held that because any apportionment scheme that purposely prevents proportional representation is unconstitutional, Democratic voters need only show that their proportionate voting influence has been adversely affected. Our cases, however, clearly foreclose any claim that the Constitution requires proportional representation or that legislatures in reapportioning must draw district lines to come as near as possible to allocating seats to the contending parties in proportion to what their anticipated statewide vote will be.

The typical election for legislative seats in the United States is conducted in described geographical districts, with the candidate receiving the most votes in each district winning the seat allocated to that district. If all or most of the districts are competitive—defined by the District Court in this case as districts in which the anticipated split in the party vote is within the range of 45% to 55%—even a narrow statewide preference for either party would produce an overwhelming majority for the winning party in the state legislature. This consequence, however, is inherent in winner-take-all, district-based elections, and we cannot hold that such a reapportionment law would violate [equal protection] because the voters in the losing party do not have representation in the legislature in proportion to the statewide vote received by their party candidates. [The] mere fact that a particular apportionment scheme makes it more difficult for a particular group in a particular district to elect the representatives of its choice does not render that scheme constitutionally infirm. [An] individual or a group of individuals who votes for a losing candidate is usually deemed to be adequately represented by the winning candidate and to have as much opportunity to influence that candidate as other voters in the district. We cannot presume in such a situation, without actual proof to the contrary, that the candidate elected will entirely ignore the interests of those voters. This is true even in a safe district where the losing group loses election after election. Thus, a group's electoral power is not unconstitutionally diminished by the simple fact of an apportionment scheme that makes winning elections more difficult, and a failure of proportional representation alone does not constitute impermissible discrimination under [equal protection].

[Unconstitutional] discrimination occurs only when the electoral system is arranged in a manner that will consistently degrade a voter's or a group of voters' influence on the political process as a whole. [Such] a finding of unconstitutionality must be supported by evidence of continued frustration of the will of a majority of the voters or effective denial to a minority of voters of a fair chance to influence the political process. [District-based elections] hardly ever produce a perfect fit between votes and representation. The one-person, one-vote imperative often mandates departure from this [result]. [Inviting] attack on minor departures from some supposed norm would too much embroil the judiciary in second-guessing what has consistently been referred to as a political task for the legislature, a task that should not be monitored too closely unless the express or tacit goal is to effect its removal from legislative halls. We decline to take a major step toward that end, [so] much at odds with our history and experience.

The District Court's findings do not satisfy this threshold condition to stating and proving a cause of action. In reaching its conclusion, the District Court relied primarily on the results of the 1982 elections. Relying on a single election to prove unconstitutional discrimination is unsatisfactory. The District Court observed, and the parties do not disagree, that Indiana is a swing State. Voters sometimes prefer Democratic candidates, and sometimes Republican. The District Court did not find that because of the 1981 Act the Democrats could not in one of the next few elections secure a sufficient vote to take control of the assembly.

[We] recognize that our own view may be difficult of application. Determining when an electoral system has been "arranged in a manner that will consistently degrade a voter's or a group of voters' influence on the political process as a whole" is of necessity a difficult inquiry. Nevertheless, we believe that it recognizes the delicacy of intruding on this most political of legislative functions and is at the same time consistent with our prior cases regarding individual multi-member districts, which have formulated a parallel standard.

IV. In sum, we hold that political gerrymandering cases are properly justiciable under the Equal Protection Clause. We also conclude, however, that a threshold showing of discriminatory vote dilution is required for a prima facie case of an equal protection violation. In this case, the findings made by the District Court of an adverse effect on the appellees do not surmount the threshold [requirement].

[JUSTICE O'CONNOR's opinion concurring in the judgment, joined by CHIEF JUSTICE BURGER and JUSTICE REHNQUIST, insisted that political gerrymandering poses a nonjusticiable political question. In claiming that there were no judicially manageable standards to resolve the issue, Justice O'Connor accused the plurality of moving toward mandating a system of proportional representation for political parties. She acknowledged that "the plurality has qualified its use of a *standard* of proportional representation in a variety of ways so as to avoid a *requirement* of proportional representation. The question is whether these qualifications are likely to be enduring in the face of the tremendous political pressures that courts will confront when called on to decide political gerrymandering claims. Because the most easily measured indicia of political power relate solely to winning and losing elections, there is a grave risk that the plurality's various attempts to qualify and condition the group right the Court has created will gradually pale in importance. What is likely to remain is a loose form of proportionality, under which *some* deviations from proportionality are permissible, but any significant, persistent deviations from proportionality are suspect."]

■ JUSTICE POWELL, with whom JUSTICE STEVENS joins, dissenting.

Gerrymandering is "the deliberate and arbitrary distortion of district boundaries and populations for partisan or personal political purposes." [The] term "gerrymandering," however, is also used loosely to describe the common practice of the party in power to choose the redistricting plan that gives it an advantage at the polls. An intent to discriminate in this sense may be present whenever redistricting occurs. [Consequently,] only a sensitive and searching inquiry can distinguish gerrymandering in the "loose" sense from gerrymandering that amounts to unconstitutional discrimination. Because it is difficult to develop and apply standards that will identify the unconstitutional gerrymander, courts may seek to avoid their responsibility to enforce [equal protection] by finding that a claim of gerrymandering is nonjusticiable. I agree with the plurality that such a course is mistaken. [Moreover,] I am convinced that appropriate judicial standards can and should be developed.

[Defining] unconstitutional gerrymandering properly focuses on whether the boundaries of the voting districts have been distorted deliberately and arbitrarily to achieve illegitimate ends. Under this definition, the merits of a gerrymandering claim must be determined by reference to the configurations of the districts, the observance of political subdivision lines, and other criteria that have independent relevance to the fairness of [redistricting]. The most important [criteria] are the shapes of voting districts and adherence to established political subdivision boundaries. Other relevant considerations include the nature of the legislative procedures by which the apportionment law was adopted and legislative history reflecting contemporaneous legislative goals. To make out a case of unconstitutional partisan gerrymandering, the plaintiff should be required to offer proof concerning these factors, which bear directly on the fairness of a redistricting plan, as well as evidence concerning population disparities and statistics tending to show vote dilution. No one factor should be [dispositive].

POLITICAL GERRYMANDERS AFTER DAVIS

1. ***The continuing question of justiciability.*** In **Vieth v. Jubelirer**, 541 U.S. 267 (2004), there were four votes but not quite five to treat all political gerrymandering claims as nonjusticiable political questions. The case involved a challenge to a Pennsylvania redistricting scheme drawn in the wake of the 2000 census that state Democrats contended had unfairly advantaged Republican candidates. Justice SCALIA, joined by Chief Justice Rehnquist and Justices O'Connor and Thomas, would have concluded that political gerrymandering claims are nonjusticiable because no judicially discernible and manageable standards for adjudicating such claims exist. They would therefore have overruled Davis v. Bandemer

entirely. But Justice KENNEDY, while providing a fifth vote to reject the challenge in this case, declined to take the courts out of judicial review of political gerrymanders altogether: "A decision ordering the correction of all election district lines drawn for partisan reasons would commit federal and state courts to unprecedented intervention in the American political process. The Court is correct to refrain from directing this substantial intrusion into the Nation's political life. While agreeing with the plurality that the complaint the appellants filed in the District Court must be dismissed, and while understanding that great caution is necessary when approaching this subject, I would not foreclose all possibility of judicial relief if some limited and precise rationale were found to correct an established violation of the Constitution in some redistricting cases. [A] determination that a gerrymander violates the law must rest on something more than the conclusion that political classifications were applied. It must rest instead on a conclusion that the classifications, though generally permissible, were applied in an invidious manner or in a way unrelated to any legitimate legislative objective." Dissents were filed by Justices Stevens, Souter, and Breyer, each venturing different accounts of how political gerrymanders might be reviewable under judicially manageable standards. Justice STEVENS, for example, wrote that "in evaluating a challenge to a specific district, I would [ask] whether the legislature allowed partisan considerations to dominate and control the lines drawn, forsaking all neutral principles."

Two Terms later, in **League of United Latin American Citizens v. Perry**, 548 U.S. 399 (2006), the Court declined to revisit the justiciability issue as no party relied upon it. Even though redistricting normally awaited the decennial census, Texas had redrawn district lines in 2003 after the Republican Party took control of both houses of the state legislature, and there was no question that it did so for the purpose of conferring partisan advantage. The Court nonetheless upheld the redistricting, with Justice Kennedy suggesting in a portion of his opinion that a congressional plan that reflects state political party power is not invalid partisan discrimination even if its purpose is avowedly partisan.

Was the majority' decision in Vieth to refrain from engaging in "unprecedented intervention in the American political process" an example of the Court exercising the "passive virtues" championed by Professor Bickel and discussed in Chapter 1? Is the countermajoritarian difficulty particularly acute in cases that are so closely connected to partisan electoral politics, making judicial restraint and the passive virtues particularly important? Or might such cases provide a situation in which judicial review and oversight are particularly necessary to protect important democratic values? Is the desire to prevent the Court from unduly interfering with the American political process consistent with the result and reasoning of Bush v. Gore?

2. ***What is the harm in partisan gerrymandering*?** Davis permits challenges to partisan gerrymanders if "the electoral system is arranged in a manner that will consistently degrade a voter's or a group of voters' influence on the political process as a whole." What is the theory of this remaining cause of action, difficult as it has been to vindicate through constitutional adjudication? Consider the argument that that voters are entitled to the opportunity for competitive elections, and that even bipartisan gerrymandering that divides up a state into safe districts for

Republicans and Democrats inhibits such competition, just like a cartel among business competitors to divide up sales territories. See Issacharoff, "Gerrymandering and Political Cartels," 116 Harv. L. Rev. 593 (2002). But see Persily, "In Defense of Foxes Guarding the Henhouses: The Case for Judicial Acquiescence to Incumbent-Protecting Gerrymanders," 116 Harv. L. Rev. 649 (2002) (arguing that competitive primaries offset the anticompetitive effects of districting and that the high rate of incumbency in the Senate shows that electoral districting is not the chief cause of incumbent safety). Or consider the view that districting along party lines fosters an excessive partisanship that "subverts popular sovereignty" by allowing legislators rather than the people to choose their representatives. See Briffault, "Defining the Constitutional Question in Partisan Gerrymandering," 14 Corn. J.L. & Pub. Pol'y 397 (2005). Consider the countervailing argument that the "electorate divides along a multitude of different lines" and that nothing in the Constitution presupposes any particular "ideal mix of legislators" along any such lines, including those of party affiliation. See Alexander & Prakash, "Tempest in an Empty Teapot: Why the Constitution Does Not Regulate Gerrymandering," 50 Wm. & Mary L. Rev. 1 (2008) (concluding that "there is no standard available in theory, much less in practice, for declaring partisan gerrymandering [to]be unconstitutional").

In **Gill v. Whitford**, 585 U.S. ___, 137 S. Ct. 2268 (2018), Democratic voters in Wisconsin alleged that a state redistricting plan harmed their party's ability to convert Democratic votes into Democratic seats in the legislature through "cracking" Democratic voters among different districts in which those voters fail to achieve electoral majorities and "packing" other Democratic voters in a few districts in which Democratic candidates win by large margins. To address justiciability, they offered the theory of an "efficiency gap" that compares each party's respective "wasted" votes—*i.e.*, votes cast for a losing candidate or for a winning candidate in excess of what that candidate needs to win—across all legislative districts. In an opinion by Chief Justice ROBERTS, the Court held that the voters lacked standing because they had not demonstrated particularized injury: "To the extent the plaintiffs' alleged harm is the dilution of their votes, that injury is district specific. [The] boundaries of the district, and the composition of its voters, determine whether and to what extent a particular voter is packed or cracked. [Remedying] the individual voter's harm, therefore, does not necessarily require restructuring all of the State's legislative districts. It requires revising only such districts as are necessary to reshape the voter's district—so that the voter may be unpacked or uncracked, as the case may be. [In] cases where a plaintiff fails to demonstrate Article III standing, we usually direct the dismissal of the plaintiff's claims. This is not the usual case. It concerns an unsettled kind of claim this Court has not agreed upon, the contours and justiciability of which are unresolved. Under the circumstances, [we] decline to direct dismissal."

In concurrence, Justice KAGAN, joined by Justices Ginsburg, Breyer, and Sotomayor, agreed with the remand for lack of standing, but introduced an "associational theory" of harm based on Justice Kennedy's concurrence in Vieth v. Jubelirer to show how "partisan gerrymanders may infringe the First Amendment rights of association held by parties, other political organizations, and their members." Such an associational claim, she wrote, "would occasion a different standing inquiry" because "the gerrymander has burdened the ability of like-minded people across the State to affiliate in a political party and carry out that organization's activities and objects." She acknowledged that partisan gerrymandering was an old practice, but explained that "technology makes today's gerrymandering altogether different from the crude linedrawing of the past. New redistricting software enables pinpoint precision in designing districts. With such tools, mapmakers can capture every last bit of partisan advantage, while still meeting traditional districting requirements (compactness, contiguity, and the like). Gerrymanders have thus become ever more extreme and durable, insulating officeholders against all but the most titanic shifts in the political tides. [Courts] have a critical role to play in curbing partisan gerrymandering. [This Court] will again be called on to redress extreme partisan gerrymanders. I am hopeful we will then step up to our responsibility to vindicate the Constitution against a contrary law."

Justice Kagan's concurrence was widely read as a call to Justice Kennedy to adopt his Vieth theory in a future case. But Justice Kennedy resigned just ten days after the opinion appeared. What does that say about Justice Kagan's call, if that is what it was?

3. ***Options for a "workable standard."*** In Vieth v. Jubelirer, Justice KENNEDY left the door open to the potential justiciability of gerrymandering claims should a "workable standard" emerge that allows the Court to measure "a gerrymander's burden on representational rights." Since then, observers have taken up that invitation to find such a workable standard.

In the lead-up to Gil v. Whitford, it appeared that a candidate for such a workable standard had emerged. The "efficiency gap," proposed in Stephanopoulos & McGhee, "Partisan Gerrymandering and the Efficiency Gap," 82 U. Chi. L. Rev. 831 (2015), was a quantitative measure of gerrymandering that rested on the concept of wasted votes. These wasted votes were defined as votes that were unnecessary for a candidate's victory or defeat beyond the 50–50 baseline. Put simply, the efficiency gap was the difference in the number of these wasted votes per party, divided by the total number of votes in each state. Notably, the lower court in Gil v. Whitford relied in part on these measures to find the existence of unconstitutional gerrymandering.

Yet, given the Court's punt in Gil v. Whitford, the question of whether the efficiency gap could provide a workable standard was left unanswered. With Justice Kavanaugh replacing Justice Kennedy, is the search for a workable standard still a worthwhile inquiry?

4. ***Independent commissions.*** One solution to political gerrymanders is to place redistricting authority in an independent, non-partisan commission. Art. I, § 4, cl. 1 provides that "The Times, Places and Manner of holding Elections for Senators and Representatives, shall be prescribed in each State by the Legislature thereof; but the Congress may at any time by Law make or alter such Regulations." Does a commission count as "the legislature"?

The Court considered this issue in **Arizona State Legislature v. Arizona Independent Redistricting Commission**, 576 U.S. ___, 135 S. Ct. 2652 (2015), and split 5–4. In an opinion for the Court, Justice GINSBURG upheld the placing of redistricting authority in the Arizona Independent Redistricting Commission. The opinion acknowledged that government-by-initiative is a product of the Progressive era and that "[direct] lawmaking by the people was virtually unknown when the Constitution of 1787 was drafted." But Justice Ginsburg wrote that "our precedent teaches that redistricting is a legislative function, to be performed in accordance with the State's prescriptions for lawmaking, which may include the referendum and the Governor's veto. [We] see no constitutional barrier to a State's empowerment of its people by embracing that form of lawmaking. [The] history and purpose of the Clause weigh heavily against such preclusion, as does the animating principle of our Constitution that the people themselves are the originating source of all the powers of government. [The] dominant purpose of the Elections Clause, the historical record bears out, was to empower Congress to override state election rules, not to restrict the way States enact legislation. [The] Clause was the Framers' insurance against the possibility that a State would refuse to provide for the election of representatives to the Federal Congress. (See The Federalist No. 59 (A. Hamilton)). The Clause was also intended to act as a safeguard against manipulation of electoral rules by politicians and factions in the States to entrench themselves or place their interests over those of the electorate."

Ginsburg explained that "it is characteristic of our federal system that States retain autonomy to establish their own governmental processes," and invoked "the role of the States as laboratories for devising solutions to difficult legal problems." She went on to address political philosophy, invoking Madison, John Locke, and the Declaration of Independence: "The Framers may not have imagined the modern initiative process in which the people of a State exercise legislative power coextensive with the authority of an institutional legislature. But the invention of the initiative was in full harmony with the Constitution's conception of the people as the font of governmental power." Practically, "[banning] lawmaking by initiative to direct a State's method of apportioning congressional districts would do more than stymie attempts to curb partisan gerrymandering, by which the majority in the legislature draws district lines to their party's advantage. It would also cast doubt on numerous other election laws adopted by the initiative method of legislating. [The] list of endangered state elections laws, were we to sustain the position of the Arizona Legislature, would not stop with popular initiatives. Almost all state constitutions were adopted by conventions and ratified by voters at the ballot box, without involvement or approval by 'the Legislature.' [The] Clause surely was not adopted to diminish a State's authority to determine its own lawmaking processes."

Chief Justice ROBERTS dissented: "Just over a century ago, Arizona became the second State in the Union to ratify the Seventeenth Amendment. That Amendment transferred power to choose United States Senators from 'the Legislature' of each State, Art. I, § 3, to 'the people thereof.' [What] chumps! Didn't they realize that all they had to do was interpret the constitutional term 'the Legislature' to mean 'the people'? The Court today performs just such a magic trick with the Elections Clause. Art. I, § 4. [The] Court's position has no basis in the text, structure, or history of the Constitution, and it contradicts precedents from both Congress and this Court. The Constitution contains seventeen provisions referring to the 'Legislature' of a State, many of which cannot possibly be read to mean 'the people.' [The] majority largely ignores this evidence, relying instead on disconnected observations about direct democracy, a contorted interpretation of an irrelevant statute, and naked appeals to public policy. [No] matter how concerned we may be about partisanship in redistricting, this Court has no power to gerrymander the Constitution."

The Chief Justice concluded that the "constitutional text, structure, history, and precedent establish a straightforward rule: Under the Elections Clause, 'the Legislature' is a representative body that, when it prescribes election regulations, may be required to do so within the ordinary lawmaking process, but may not be cut out of that process. Put simply, the state legislature need not be exclusive in congressional districting, but neither may it be excluded. [Several] constitutional amendments over the past century have involved modifications of the electoral process. Amendments 19, 22, 24, 26. Unfortunately, today's decision will only discourage this democratic method of change. Why go through the hassle of writing a new provision into the Constitution when it is so much easier to write an old one out?"

Justice SCALIA, joined by Justice Thomas, would have dismissed the case as not constituting a case or controversy. Justice THOMAS, joined by Justice Scalia, dismissed the majority's decision as "faux federalism."

5. ***Political gerrymandering under state constitutions***. Another potential solution to political gerrymanders might be to seek redress under state constitutions. In such cases, should gerrymandering plaintiffs rely primarily on state equal protection guarantees? Or might plaintiffs be able to find more specific clauses in state constitutions that govern redistricting?

In **League of Women Voters v. Pennsylvania**, 178 A.3d 737 (Pa. 2018), the Supreme Court of Pennsylvania held that the Commonwealth's 2011 Redistricting Plan violated the Free and Equal Elections Clause of the Pennsylvania Constitution. Specifically, the court held that when "neutral criteria of compactness, contiguity, minimization of the division of political subdivisions, and maintenance of popular equality" are "subordinated, in whole or in part, to extraneous considerations such as gerrymandering for unfair partisan political advantage," a congressional redistricting plan violates the Pennsylvania Constitution. Notably, the majority opinion expressly distinguished its decision from federal gerrymandering jurisprudence: "While federal courts have, to date, been unable to settle on a workable standard by which to assess such claims under the federal Constitution, we find no such barriers under our great Pennsylvania charter. The people of this Commonwealth should never lose sight of the fact that, in its protection of essential rights, our founding document is the ancestor, not the offspring, of the federal Constitution. We conclude that, in this matter, it provides a constitutional standard, and remedy, even if the federal charter does not."

In issuing its remedial plan, the Supreme Court of Pennsylvania ordered that, should the legislative and executive branches fail to come up with a constitutionally satisfactory redistricting plan, "this Court shall proceed expeditiously to adopt a plan based on the evidentiary record." Given the division of power in Pennsylvania, the court ultimately took on this task of redistricting. Does this result implicate a similar set of concerns regarding Art. I, § 4, cl. 1 of the Constitution as was raised in Arizona State Legislature v. Arizona Independent Redistricting Commission? Republican lawmakers attempted to rely on such arguments in seeking a stay of the Pennsylvania's Supreme Court redistricting plan. However, Justice ALITO, sitting by designation, summarily denied the stay application.

FUNDAMENTAL RIGHT OF ACCESS TO COURTS

In the cases that follow, the Court carefully scrutinizes and frequently invalidates economic barriers impeding access to the criminal and civil processes. What is the proper constitutional basis for this line of cases? The Court has repeatedly divided on the issue of whether procedural due process or equal protection provides the appropriate analytical framework. Justice Harlan was long the leading advocate of the due process approach. The majority has most commonly emphasized the relevance of the fundamental interest branch of equal protection. Since wealth has not been accepted as a suspect classification, something more than the mere existence of economic barriers must be involved to explain the Court interventions. What is that "something more"? Is the stricter scrutiny triggered by the existence of a "fundamental interest" in these cases? Is there a "fundamental interest," for example, in effective participation in the criminal appellate process—even though there is no constitutional "right" to a criminal appeal? What are the plausible limits on the principles implicit in these cases?

ECONOMIC BARRIERS AND THE CRIMINAL PROCESS

1. ***Transcripts on appeal.*** **Griffin v. Illinois**, 351 U.S. 12 (1956), launched the "access to courts" strand of equal protection. Griffin held that a state must provide a trial transcript or its equivalent to an indigent criminal defendant appealing a conviction on nonfederal grounds. (The state ordinarily required that, in order to obtain review, appellants must furnish transcripts to the appellate court.) The challengers in Griffin attacked the failure to provide them free transcripts and claimed that the resulting "refusal to afford appellate reviews solely because of poverty" was unconstitutional. Justice BLACK's plurality opinion, joined by Chief Justice Warren and Justices Douglas and Clark, stated: "[D]ue process and equal protection both call for procedures in criminal trials which allow no invidious discriminations. [In] criminal trials a State can no more discriminate on account of poverty than on account of religion, race, or color. Plainly the ability to pay costs in advance bears no rational relationship to a defendant's guilt or innocence and could not be used as an excuse to deprive a defendant of a fair trial. [There] is no meaningful distinction between a rule which would deny the poor the right to defend themselves in a trial court and one which effectively denies the poor an adequate appellate review accorded to all who have money enough to pay the costs in advance. It is true that a State is not required by the [Constitution] to provide appellate courts or a right to appellate review at all. But that is not to say that a State that does grant appellate review can do so in a way that discriminates against some convicted defendants on account of their poverty. [All] States now provide some method of appeal from criminal convictions. [To] deny adequate review to the poor means that many of them may lose their life, liberty or property because of unjust convictions which appellate courts would set aside. [There] can be no equal justice where the kind of trial a man gets depends on the amount of money he has. Destitute defendants must be afforded as adequate appellate review as defendants who have money enough to buy transcripts." Justice FRANKFURTER concurred in the result.

Justice HARLAN's dissent sketched an approach he elaborated in a number of later cases. He thought the equal protection emphasis misplaced and found no violation of due process. On equal protection, he noted: "All that Illinois has done is to fail to alleviate the consequences of differences in economic circumstances that exist wholly apart from any state action. The Court thus holds that, at least in this area of criminal appeals, [equal protection] imposes on the States an affirmative duty to lift the handicaps flowing from differences in economic circumstances. That holding produces the anomalous result that a constitutional admonition to the States to treat all persons equally means in this instance that Illinois must give to some what it requires others to pay for. [T]he issue here is not the typical equal protection question of the reasonableness of a 'classification' on the basis of which the State has imposed legal disabilities, but rather the reasonableness of the State's failure to remove natural disabilities. [I] submit that the basis for that holding is simply an unarticulated conclusion that it violates 'fundamental fairness' for a State which provides for appellate review [not] to see to it that such appeals are in fact available to those it would imprison for serious crimes. That of course is the traditional language of due process." Turning to due process, he asked: "Can it be that, while it was not unconstitutional for Illinois to afford no appeals, its steady progress in increasing the safeguards against erroneous convictions has resulted in a constitutional decline?" He insisted that the only due process guarantee was "simply the right not to be denied an appeal for arbitrary or capricious reasons," and "[n]othing of that kind" appeared here.

2. ***Counsel on appeal.*** **Douglas v. California**, 372 U.S. 353 (1963), extended Griffin by holding that a state must appoint counsel for an indigent defendant for "the *first appeal,* granted as a matter of [statutory right], from a criminal conviction." It rejected California's system of appointing counsel only after "an independent investigation of the record" and a determination that "it would be of advantage to the defendant or helpful to the appellate court to have counsel appointed." Justice DOUGLAS's opinion in this 6–3 decision stated that denial of counsel on appeal to an indigent "would seem to be a discrimination at least as invidious as that condemned in Griffin." Justice Douglas elaborated: "We are dealing only with the *first appeal.* [Where] the merits of *the one and only appeal* an indigent has as a right are decided without benefit of counsel, we think an unconstitutional line has been drawn between rich and poor. When an indigent is forced to run this gauntlet of a preliminary showing of merit, the right to appeal does not comport with fair procedure. [The] discrimination is not between 'possibly good and obviously bad cases,' but between cases where the rich man can require the court to listen to argument of counsel before deciding on the merits, but a poor man cannot. There is lacking that equality demanded by the [14th Amendment] where the rich man [enjoys] the benefit of [counsel] while the indigent [is] forced to shift for himself."

Justice HARLAN, joined by Justice Stewart, dissented: "[Equal protection] is not apposite. [This] should be judged solely under [due process]. [As to equal protection, the] States, of course, are prohibited [from] discriminating between 'rich' and 'poor' *as such* in the formulation and application of their laws. But it is a far different thing to suggest that [this] prevents the State from adopting a law of general applicability that may affect the poor more harshly than it does the [rich]. Every financial exaction which the State imposes on a uniform basis is more easily satisfied by the well-to-do than by the indigent. Yet I take it that no one would dispute the constitutional power of the State to levy a uniform sales tax, to charge tuition at a state university, to fix rates for the purchase of water from a municipal corporation, [or] to establish minimum bail for various categories of offenses. [Laws] such as these do not deny equal protection to the less fortunate for one essential reason: [equal protection] does not impose on the States 'an affirmative duty to lift the handicaps flowing from differences in economic circumstances.' To so construe it would be to read into the Constitution a philosophy of leveling that would be foreign to many of our basic concepts of the proper relations between government and society. The State may have a moral obligation to eliminate the evils of poverty, but it is not required by [equal protection] to give to some whatever others can afford.

"[As to due process,] appellate review is in itself not required by the 14th Amendment [and] thus the question presented is the narrow one whether the State's rules with respect to the appointment of counsel are so arbitrary or unreasonable, *in the context of the particular appellate procedure that it has established,* as to require their invalidation. [What] the Court finds constitutionally offensive here bears a striking resemblance to the rules of this Court and many state courts of last resort on petitions for certiorari or for leave to appeal filed by indigent defendants pro se. [I] cannot agree that the Constitution prohibits a State, in seeking to redress economic imbalances at its bar of justice and to provide indigents with full review, from taking reasonable steps to guard against needless expense. This is all that California has [done]." Justice CLARK also submitted a dissent.

Ross v. Moffitt, 417 U.S. 600 (1974), refused to extend Douglas to require provision of counsel in discretionary appeals. Justice REHNQUIST's majority opinion reviewed the Griffin-Douglas line of cases and noted that their "precise rationale" had "never been explicitly stated, some support being derived from [equal protection], and some from [due process]." Justice Rehnquist added: "Neither clause by itself provides an entirely satisfactory basis for the result reached." Turning to the clauses separately, he disposed of the due process contention in a brief passage. He emphasized the "significant differences between the trial and appellate stages." Defendants were entitled to a trial, but there was no right to an appeal: "Unfairness results only if indigents are singled out by the State and denied meaningful access to the appellate system because of their poverty. That question is more profitably considered under an equal protection analysis." Turning to equal protection, he emphasized that the guarantee "does not require absolute equality" but merely assurance that "indigents have an adequate opportunity to present their claims fairly within the adversarial system." Not providing counsel to assist in seeking discretionary review did not deny indigents "meaningful access" to the highest state court. "[The] fact that a particular service might be of benefit to an indigent defendant does not mean that the service is constitutionally required. The duty of the State under our cases [is] only to assure the indigent defendant an adequate opportunity to present his claims fairly in the context of the State's appellate process."

Justice DOUGLAS's dissent, joined by Justices Brennan and Marshall, drew on due process as well as equal protection. Can the Griffin-Douglas principle, developed in the context of expenses on appeals, be extended to the often larger expenditures required to mount a major defense at trial? A defendant who can pay for extensive scientific tests, expert witnesses, and a private investigator, for example, will often be better off than one who cannot afford these. Is the state obligated to minimize the comparative advantage of the well-to-do criminal defendant?

In **Halbert v. Michigan**, 545 U.S. 605 (2005), the Court revisited the line distinguishing Douglas from Ross. Holding unconstitutional, by a vote of 6–3, Michigan's practice of denying appointed appellate counsel to indigents convicted by guilty or nolo contendere pleas, the Court applied Douglas and distinguished Ross. Justice GINSBURG, joined by Justices Stevens, O'Connor, Kennedy, Souter and Breyer, wrote for the Court: "We hold that Douglas provides the controlling instruction. [A] defendant who pleads guilty or *nolo contendere* in a Michigan court does not thereby forfeit all opportunity for appellate review. Although he relinquishes access to an appeal as of right, he is entitled to apply for leave to appeal, and that entitlement is officially conveyed to him. [Whether] formally categorized as the decision of an appeal or the disposal of a leave application, the Court of Appeals' ruling on a plea-convicted defendant's claims provides the first, and likely the only, direct review the defendant's conviction and sentence will receive. Parties like Halbert, however, are disarmed in their endeavor to gain first-tier review. As the Court in Ross emphasized, a defendant seeking State Supreme Court review following a first-tier appeal as of right earlier had the assistance of appellate counsel [and] may also be armed with an opinion of the intermediate appellate court addressing the issues counsel raised. A first-tier review applicant, forced to act *pro se*, will face a record unreviewed by appellate counsel, and will be equipped with no attorney's brief prepared for, or reasoned opinion by, a court of review. Persons in Halbert's situation are particularly handicapped as self-representatives. [Navigating] the appellate process without a lawyer's assistance is a perilous endeavor for a layperson, and well beyond the competence of individuals, like Halbert, who have little education, learning disabilities, and mental impairments." She concluded that the Due Process and Equal Protection Clauses require the appointment of counsel for defendants seeking first-tier review from convictions on pleas.

Justice THOMAS, joined by Chief Justice Rehnquist and Scalia, dissented: "Douglas [does] not support extending the right to counsel to any form of discretionary review, as Ross v. Moffitt, and later cases make clear. Moreover, Michigan has not engaged in the sort of invidious discrimination against indigent defendants that Douglas condemns. Michigan has done no more than recognize the undeniable difference between defendants who plead guilty and those who maintain their innocence, in an attempt to divert resources from largely frivolous appeals to more meritorious ones. The majority substitutes its own policy preference for that of Michigan voters, and it does so based on an untenable reading of Douglas.

"[Admittedly,] the precise rationale for the Griffin/Douglas line of cases has never been made explicit. Those cases, however, have a common theme. States may not impose financial barriers that preclude indigent defendants from securing appellate review altogether. Nor may States create 'unreasoned distinctions' among defendants that 'arbitrarily cut off appeal rights for indigents while leaving open avenues of appeals for more affluent persons.' Far from being an 'arbitrary' or 'unreasoned' distinction, Michigan's differentiation between defendants convicted at trial and defendants convicted by plea is sensible. [Lacking] support in this Court's cases, the majority effects a not-so-subtle shift from whether the record is adequate to enable discretionary review to whether plea-convicted defendants are generally able to 'naviga[te] the appellate process without a lawyer's assistance.' This rationale lacks any stopping point. *Pro se* defendants may have difficulty navigating discretionary direct appeals and collateral proceedings, but this Court has never extended the right to counsel beyond first appeals as of right."

ECONOMIC BARRIERS AND CIVIL LITIGATION

1. ***Divorce.*** The appellants in **Boddie v. Connecticut**, 401 U.S. 371 (1971), were indigent welfare recipients who sought to file divorce actions in the state courts but were unable to pay the required court fees and costs for services of process. (The amount involved was $60.) They claimed that this financial barrier unconstitutionally restricted their access to the courts. Justice HARLAN's majority opinion sustained that claim, relying entirely on due process rather than equal protection. He concluded "that, given the basic position of the marriage relationship in this society's hierarchy of values and the concomitant state monopolization of the means for legally dissolving this relationship, due process [prohibits] a State from denying, solely because of inability to pay, access to its courts to individuals who seek judicial dissolution of their marriages." He noted that "this Court has seldom been asked to view access to the courts as an element of due process," but that was because "resort to the courts is not usually the only available, legitimate means of resolving private disputes." Here, however, the claims asserted by would-be plaintiffs were "akin to that of defendants faced with exclusion from the only forum effectively empowered to settle their disputes." Accordingly, the applicable principles were those stated "in our due process decisions that delimit rights of defendants compelled to litigate their differences in the judicial forum." He emphasized one of these "settled principles": "due process requires, at a minimum, that absent a countervailing state interest of overriding significance, persons forced to settle their claims of right and duty through the judicial process must be given a meaningful opportunity to be heard."

Justice Harlan concluded with an attempt to limit the scope of the decision: "We do not decide that access for all individuals to the courts is a right that is, in all circumstances, guaranteed [by due process, for] in the case before us this right is the exclusive precondition to the adjustment of the fundamental human relationship. The requirement that these appellants resort to the judicial process is entirely a state-created matter." Justice DOUGLAS's concurring opinion insisted that the equal protection principle of the Griffin line of cases, not due process, was the appropriate ground of decision. Justice BLACK was the only dissenter, emphasizing that his opinion in Griffin did not suggest that its requirements for criminal defendants were applicable to "the quite different field of civil cases."

2. ***Welfare and bankruptcy.*** Two months after Boddie, Justice Black, who had dissented there, found broad implications in the case. He argued that if Boddie were to continue to be the law, it should be "expanded to all civil cases." Meltzer v. C. Buck LeCraw & Co., 402 U.S. 954 (1971). Lower courts, too, read Boddie broadly. But when the issue of the applicability of Boddie in other civil contexts finally reached the Court, the majority called a halt. In the first post-Boddie ruling, the Court refused to extend "the principle of Boddie to the no-asset bankruptcy proceeding."

In **United States v. Kras**, 409 U.S. 434 (1973), an indigent had challenged the $50 filing fee requirement in voluntary bankruptcy proceedings. Justice BLACKMUN's majority opinion emphasized that

Boddie "obviously stopped short of an unlimited rule that an indigent at all times and in all cases has the right to relief without the payment of fees." And the bankruptcy situation was sufficiently distinguishable from divorce: Boddie involved the "fundamental" marital relationship; the interest in discharge in bankruptcy did "not rise to the same constitutional level." Moreover, Boddie had emphasized the "utter exclusiveness" of a court remedy; governmental control over debts is not "nearly so exclusive."

Justice STEWART's dissent, joined by Justices Douglas, Brennan, and Marshall, would have found the Boddie due process rationale "equally" applicable here. In a separate dissent, Justice MARSHALL went further: "I view [Boddie] as involving the right of access to the courts [and] not just the right to a discharge in bankruptcy. When a person raises a claim of right or entitlement under the laws, the only forum in our legal system empowered to determine that claim is a court." In another dissent, Justice DOUGLAS, joined by Justice Brennan, emphasized that "discrimination based on wealth" is "particularly 'invidious.' "

In **Ortwein v. Schwab**, 410 U.S. 656 (1973), the same 5–4 majority found Kras rather than Boddie applicable in rejecting an attack by indigents on Oregon's $25 filing fee prerequisite to judicial review of administrative denials of welfare benefits. The Court noted, per curiam, that the interest in welfare payments, like that in a bankruptcy discharge, "has far less constitutional significance than the interest of the Boddie appellants." Moreover, the claim of discrimination against the poor had to fail because welfare payments are "in the area of economics and social welfare" and no suspect classification was involved. Are the distinctions between Boddie and the later cases justifiable?

3. ***Paternity.*** In the 1980s, however, Boddie was followed and Kras and Ortwein distinguished in the unanimous decision in **Little v. Streater**, 452 U.S. 1 (1981), holding that due process entitled an indigent defendant in a paternity action to state-subsidized blood grouping tests. Chief Justice BURGER emphasized the unique quality of blood grouping tests as a "source of exculpatory evidence" and "the State's prominent role in litigation." Moreover, paternity proceedings in Connecticut in fact had "quasi-criminal" overtones, even though they were characterized as "civil" by the State. Accordingly, "an indigent defendant, who faces the State as an adversary [and] who must overcome the evidentiary burden Connecticut imposes, lacks 'a meaningful opportunity to be heard' [Boddie]." Thus, the "fundamental fairness" requirement of due process had not been satisfied. According to Chief Justice Burger, because defendant had "no choice of an alternative forum and his interests, as well as those of the child, are constitutionally significant [because the creation of a parent-child relationship was at stake], this case is comparable to Boddie rather than to Kras and Ortwein." Compare with Little the divided Court's decision on the same day in Lassiter v. Department of Social Services, 452 U.S. 18 (1981), rejecting the claim of an indigent mother involved in a state court parental status determination proceeding that she was entitled to counsel.

Consider the application of the foregoing line of cases in the following case, which revived the Court's attention to de facto wealth discrimination in the judicial process and raised again questions of why equal protection should extend to nonpurposeful deprivations of opportunities the state was not required to provide in the first place:

M.L.B. v. S.L.J.

519 U.S. 102, 117 S. Ct. 555, 136 L. Ed. 2d 473 (1996).

■ JUSTICE GINSBURG delivered the opinion of the Court.

By order of a Mississippi Chancery Court, petitioner M.L.B.'s parental rights to her two minor children were forever terminated. M.L.B. sought to appeal from the termination decree, but Mississippi required that she pay in advance record preparation fees estimated at $2,352.36. Because M.L.B. lacked funds to pay the fees, her appeal was dismissed. [We] agreed to hear and decide [the following question]: May a State, consistent with the Due Process and Equal Protection Clauses of the Fourteenth Amendment, condition appeals from trial court decrees terminating parental rights on the affected parent's ability to pay record preparation fees? We hold that [it may not.]

[Courts] have confronted, in diverse settings, the "age-old problem" of "providing equal justice for poor and rich, weak and powerful alike." Griffin v. Illinois. Concerning access to appeal in general, and transcripts needed to pursue appeals in particular, Griffin is the foundation case. Griffin involved an Illinois rule that effectively conditioned thoroughgoing appeals from criminal convictions on the defendant's procurement of a transcript of trial proceedings. Indigent defendants, other than those sentenced to death, were not excepted from the rule, so in most cases, defendants without means to pay for a transcript had no access to appellate review at all. Although the Federal Constitution guarantees no right to appellate review, once a State affords that right, Griffin held, the State may not "bolt the door to equal justice."

[In] contrast to the "flat prohibition" of "bolted doors" that the Griffin line of cases securely established, the right to counsel at state expense, as delineated in our decisions, is less encompassing. A State must provide trial counsel for an indigent defendant charged with a felony, Gideon v. Wainwright, but that right does not extend to nonfelony trials if no term of imprisonment is actually imposed, Scott v. Illinois. A State's obligation to provide appellate counsel to poor defendants faced with incarceration applies to appeals of right. Douglas v. California. In Ross v. Moffitt, however, we held that neither the Due Process Clause nor the Equal Protection Clause requires a State to provide counsel at state expense to an indigent prisoner pursuing a discretionary appeal in the state system or petitioning for review in this Court.

We have also recognized a narrow category of civil cases in which the State must provide access to its judicial processes without regard to a party's ability to pay court fees. In Boddie v. Connecticut, we held that the State could not deny a divorce to a married couple based on their inability to pay approximately $60 in court costs. Crucial to our decision in Boddie was the fundamental interest at stake. "Given the basic position of the marriage relationship in this society's hierarchy of values and the concomitant state monopolization of the means for legally dissolving this relationship," we said, due process "prohibits a State from denying, solely because of inability to pay, access to its courts to individuals who seek judicial dissolution of their marriages." [In] United States v. Kras, the Court clarified that a constitutional requirement to waive court fees in civil cases is the exception, not the general rule. Kras concerned fees, totaling $50, required to secure a discharge in bankruptcy. The Court recalled in Kras that "on many occasions we have recognized the fundamental importance . . . under our Constitution" of "the associational interests that surround the establishment and dissolution of the [marital] relationship." But bankruptcy discharge entails no "fundamental interest," we said. Although "obtaining [a] desired new start in life [is] important," that interest, the Court explained, "does not rise to the same constitutional level" as the interest in establishing or dissolving a marriage. Nor is resort to court the sole path to securing debt forgiveness, we stressed; in contrast, termination of a marriage, we reiterated, requires access to the State's judicial machinery.

[In] sum, this Court has not extended Griffin to the broad array of civil cases. But tellingly, the Court has consistently set apart from the mine run of cases those involving state controls or intrusions on family relationships. In that domain, to guard against undue official intrusion, the Court has examined closely and contextually the importance of the governmental interest advanced in defense of the intrusion.

[Does] the Fourteenth Amendment require Mississippi to accord M.L.B. access to an appeal—available but for her inability to advance required costs—before she is forever branded unfit for affiliation with her children? Respondents urge us to classify M.L.B.'s case with the generality of civil cases, in which indigent persons have no constitutional right to proceed in forma pauperis. M.L.B., on the other hand, maintains that the accusatory state action she is trying to fend off is barely distinguishable from criminal condemnation in view of the magnitude and permanence of the loss she faces. [We] agree [with M.L.B.]

[We] observe first that the Court's decisions concerning access to judicial processes, commencing with Griffin, [reflect] both equal protection and due process concerns. [The] equal protection concern relates to the legitimacy of fencing out would-be appellants based solely on their inability to pay core costs. The due process concern homes in on the essential fairness of the state-ordered proceedings anterior to adverse state action. ["Most] decisions in this area," we have recognized, "rest on an equal protection framework," [because] due process does not independently require that the State provide a right to appeal.

[In Mayer v. Chicago, 404 U.S. 189 (1971), we] applied Griffin to a petty offender, fined a total of $500, who sought to appeal from the trial court's judgment. An "impecunious medical student," the defendant in Mayer could not pay for a transcript. We held that the State must afford him a record complete enough to allow fair appellate consideration of his claims. The defendant in Mayer faced no term of confinement, but the conviction, we observed, could affect his professional prospects and, possibly, even bar him from the practice of medicine. The State's pocketbook interest in advance payment for a transcript, we concluded, was unimpressive when measured against the stakes for the defendant.

Similarly here, the stakes for petitioner M.L.B.—forced dissolution of her parental rights—are large, " 'more substantial than mere loss of money.' " In contrast to loss of custody, which does not sever the parent-child bond, parental status termination is "irretrievably destructive" of the most fundamental family relationship. And the risk of error, Mississippi's experience shows, is considerable. [The] countervailing government interest, as in Mayer, is financial. Mississippi urges, as the justification for its appeal cost prepayment requirement, the State's legitimate interest in offsetting the costs of its court system. But in the tightly circumscribed category of parental status termination cases, appeals are few, and not likely to impose an undue burden on the State.

[In] aligning M.L.B.'s case and Mayer—parental status termination decrees and criminal convictions that carry no jail time—for appeal access purposes, we do not question the general rule, stated in Ortwein, that fee requirements ordinarily are examined only for rationality. The State's need for revenue to offset costs, in the mine run of cases, satisfies the rationality requirement; States are not forced by the Constitution to adjust all tolls to account for "disparity in material circumstances." But our cases solidly establish two exceptions to that general rule. The basic right to participate in political processes as voters and candidates cannot be limited to those who can pay for a license. Nor may access to judicial processes in cases criminal or "quasi criminal in nature," turn on ability to pay. [We] place decrees forever terminating parental rights in the category of cases in which the State may not "bolt the door to equal justice."

[In] numerous cases, respondents point out, the Court has held that government "need not provide funds so that people can exercise even fundamental rights." [See, e.g., Harris v. McRae (1980); Chapter 8 above.] A decision for M.L.B., respondents contend, would dishonor our cases recognizing that the Constitution "generally confers no affirmative right to governmental aid, even where such aid may be necessary to secure life, liberty, or property interests of which the government itself may not deprive the individual." DeShaney v. Winnebago County Dept. of Social Servs. [(1989); Chapter 10 below.] Complainants in the cases on which respondents rely sought state aid to subsidize their privately initiated action or to alleviate the consequences of differences in economic circumstances that existed apart from state action. M.L.B.'s complaint is of a different order. She is endeavoring to defend against the State's destruction of her family bonds, and to resist the brand associated with a parental unfitness adjudication. Like a defendant resisting criminal conviction, she seeks to be spared from the State's devastatingly adverse action.

[Respondents] and the dissenters urge that we will open floodgates if we do not rigidly restrict Griffin to cases typed "criminal." But [termination] decrees "work a unique kind of deprivation." In contrast to matters modifiable at the parties' will or based on changed circumstances, termination adjudications involve the awesome authority of the State "to destroy permanently all legal recognition of the parental relationship." [We] are therefore satisfied that the label "civil" should not entice us to leave undisturbed the Mississippi courts' disposition of this case. For the reasons stated, we hold that Mississippi may not withhold from M.L.B. "a 'record of sufficient completeness' to permit proper [appellate] consideration of [her] claims." [Reversed.]

■ JUSTICE KENNEDY, concurring in the judgment.

In my view the cases most on point, and the ones which persuade me we must reverse the judgment now reviewed, are the decisions addressing procedures involving the rights and privileges inherent in family and personal relations. [E.g., Boddie; Lassiter,] cases resting exclusively upon the Due Process Clause. Here, due process is quite a sufficient basis for our holding.

■ JUSTICE THOMAS, with whom JUSTICE SCALIA joins, and with whom CHIEF JUSTICE REHNQUIST joins except as to Part II, dissenting.

Today the majority holds that the Fourteenth Amendment requires Mississippi to afford petitioner a free transcript because her civil case involves a "fundamental" right. The majority seeks to limit the reach of its holding to the type of case we confront here, one involving the termination of parental rights. I do not think, however, that the new-found constitutional right to free transcripts in civil appeals can be effectively restricted to this case. The inevitable consequence will be greater demands on the States to provide free assistance to would-be appellants in all manner of civil cases involving interests that cannot, based on the test established by the majority, be distinguished from the admittedly important interest at issue here. The cases on which the majority relies, primarily cases requiring appellate assistance for indigent criminal defendants, were questionable when decided, and have, in my view, been undermined since. Even accepting those cases, however, I am of the view that the majority takes them too far. I therefore dissent.

I. Petitioner requests relief under both the Due Process and Equal Protection Clauses, though she does not specify how either clause affords it. The majority accedes to petitioner's request. But, carrying forward the ambiguity in the cases on which it relies, the majority does not specify the source of the relief it grants.

[Assuming] that petitioner's interest may not be impinged without due process of law, I do not think that the Due Process Clause requires the result the majority reaches. Petitioner's largest obstacle to a due process appeal gratis is our oft-affirmed view that due process does not oblige States to provide for any appeal, even from a criminal conviction. [The] majority reaffirms that due process does not require an appeal. [Unlike in] Boddie, [where the concern] was that indigent persons were deprived of "fundamental rights" with no hearing whatsoever, [Petitioner] received not merely a hearing, but in fact enjoyed procedural protections above and beyond what our parental termination cases have required. She received both notice and a hearing before a neutral, legally trained decisionmaker. She was represented by counsel—even though due process does not in every case require the appointment of counsel. Through her attorney, petitioner was able to confront the evidence and witnesses against her. And [the] Chancery Court was required to find that petitioner's parental unfitness was proved by clear and convincing evidence. [There] seems, then, no place in the Due Process Clause—certainly as an original matter, and even as construed by this Court—for the constitutional "right" crafted by the majority today.

[I] do not think that the equal protection theory underlying the Griffin line of cases remains viable. [In] Griffin, the State of Illinois required all criminal appellants whose claims on appeal required review of a trial transcript to obtain it themselves. The plurality thought that this "discriminated against some convicted defendants on account of their poverty." Justice Harlan, in dissent, perceived a troubling shift in this Court's equal protection jurisprudence. Disputing [the Court's] early manifestation of the "disparate impact" theory of equal protection, Justice Harlan argued: "No economic burden attendant upon the exercise of a privilege bears equally upon all, and in other circumstances the resulting differentiation is not treated as an invidious classification by the State, even though discrimination against 'indigents' by name would be unconstitutional." Justice Harlan offered the example of a state university that conditions an education on the payment of tuition. If charging tuition did not create a discriminatory classification, then, Justice Harlan wondered, how did any other reasonable exaction by a State for a service it provides?

[Justice] Harlan's views were accepted by the Court in Washington v. Davis [1976; sec. 1 above] in which we rejected a disparate impact theory of the Equal Protection Clause altogether. We spurned the claim that "a law, neutral on its face and serving ends otherwise within the power of government to pursue, is invalid under the Equal Protection Clause simply because it may affect a greater proportion of one race than of another." Absent proof of discriminatory purpose, official action did not violate the Fourteenth Amendment "solely because it has a racially disparate impact." [The] lesson of Davis is that the Equal Protection Clause shields only against purposeful discrimination: A disparate impact, even upon members of a racial minority, the classification of which we have been most suspect, does not violate equal protection. The Clause is not a panacea for perceived social or economic inequity; it seeks to "guarantee equal laws, not equal results." [I] see no principled difference between a facially neutral rule that serves in some cases to prevent persons from availing themselves of state employment, or a state-funded education, or a state-funded abortion—each of which the State may, but is not required to, provide—and a facially neutral rule that prevents a person from taking an appeal that is available only because the State chooses to provide it.

[The] Griffin line of cases ascribed to—one might say announced—an equalizing notion of the Equal Protection Clause that would, I think, have startled the Fourteenth Amendment's Framers. In those cases, the Court did not find, nor did it seek, any purposeful discrimination on the part of the state defendants. That their statutes had disproportionate effect on poor persons was sufficient for us to find a constitutional violation. In Davis, among other cases, we began to recognize the potential mischief of a disparate impact theory writ large, and endeavored to contain it. In this case, I would continue that enterprise. Mississippi's requirement of prepaid transcripts in civil appeals seeking to contest the sufficiency of the evidence adduced at trial is facially neutral; it creates no classification. The transcript rule reasonably obliges would-be appellants to bear the costs of availing themselves of a service that the State chooses, but is not constitutionally required, to provide. Any adverse impact that the transcript requirement has on any person seeking to appeal arises not out of the State's action, but out of factors entirely unrelated to it.

II. [If] this case squarely presented the question, I would be inclined to vote to overrule Griffin and its progeny. Even were I convinced that the cases on which the majority today relies ought to be retained, I could not agree with the majority's extension of them. The interest at stake in this case differs in several important respects from that at issue in cases such as Griffin. Petitioner's interest in maintaining a relationship with her children is the subject of a civil, not criminal, action. [Taking] the Griffin line as a given, [I] would restrict it to the criminal appeals to which its authors, see Boddie v. Connecticut (Black, J., dissenting), sought to limit it.

NO FUNDAMENTAL INTEREST IN FOOD, SHELTER, EDUCATION

The fundamental interest line of cases prompted academic speculation and advocacy about potential constitutional protections for "necessities" such as welfare, housing and education, and possible equal protection challenges to classifications impinging on access to such goods. Some commentators advocated such expansion. See Michelman, "The Supreme Court, 1968 Term—Foreword: On Protecting the Poor Through the Fourteenth Amendment," 83 Harv. L. Rev. 7 (1969), which argued that even in a market economy persons were entitled to "minimum protection" against economic deprivations in certain areas. The Court, however, declined to extend the fundamental interests branch of equal protection from the narrow areas of voting and court access (and during the life of Shapiro v. Thompson, interstate travel). The following cases illustrate the cabining of this branch of equal protection:

1. ***Welfare benefits.*** In **Dandridge v. Williams**, 397 U.S. 471 (1970), the Court rejected a challenge to Maryland's implementation of the Aid to Families with Dependent Children (AFDC) program, jointly financed by the state and federal governments. Maryland granted most eligible families their "standard of need," but imposed a "maximum grant" limit of $250 per month per family, regardless of the family size or computed standard of need. In rejecting the equal protection attack on that limitation, Justice STEWART's majority opinion stated: "[Here] we deal with state regulation in the social and economic field, [claimed] to violate the 14th Amendment only because the regulation results in some disparity in grants of welfare payments to the largest AFDC families. For this Court to approve the invalidation of state economic or social regulation [here] would be far too reminiscent of an era when the Court thought the 14th Amendment gave it power to strike down state laws 'because they may be unwise, improvident, or out of harmony with a particular school of thought.' [Lee Optical]. That era long ago passed into history. In the area of economics and social welfare, a State does not violate [equal protection] merely because the classifications made by its laws are imperfect. If the classification has some 'reasonable basis,' it does not offend the Constitution.

"To be sure, [the cases] enunciating this fundamental standard under [equal protection] have in the main involved state regulation of business or industry. The administration of public welfare assistance, by contrast, involves the most basic economic needs of impoverished human beings. We recognize the dramatically real factual difference between the cited cases and this one, but we can find no basis for applying a different constitutional standard. It is a standard that has consistently been applied to state legislation restricting the availability of employment opportunities. And it is a standard that is true to the principle that the 14th Amendment gives the federal courts no power to impose upon the States their views of what constitutes wise economic or social policy. [The] intractable economic, social, and even philosophical problems presented by public welfare assistance programs are not the business of this Court. The Constitution may impose certain procedural safeguards upon systems of welfare administration. But the Constitution does not empower this Court to second-guess state officials charged with the difficult responsibility of allocating limited public welfare funds among the myriad of potential recipients." (Justice Stewart readily found a "reasonable basis" for the challenged regulation "in the State's legitimate interest in encouraging employment and in avoiding discrimination between welfare families and the families of the working poor.")

Justice MARSHALL's dissent, joined by Justice Brennan, insisted that the Maryland regulation could not be sustained even under the majority's "reasonableness" test. But he devoted most of his opinion to advocating a stricter standard of review, even while finding the Warren Court's rigid two-tier analysis inappropriate here. He criticized the majority for "focusing upon the abstract dichotomy between two different approaches to equal protection problems that have been utilized by this Court": "This case simply defies easy characterization in terms of one or the other of these 'tests.' The cases relied on by the Court, in which a 'mere rationality' [rather than 'compelling interest'] test was actually used, are most accurately described as involving the application of equal protection reasoning to the regulation of [business interests]. This case, involving the literally vital interests of a powerless minority—poor families without breadwinners—is far removed from the area of business regulation, as the Court concedes. Why then is the standard used in those cases imposed here? In my view, equal protection analysis of this case is not appreciably advanced by the a priori definition of a 'right,' fundamental or otherwise. Rather, concentration must be placed upon the character of the classification in question, the relative importance to individuals in the class discriminated against of the governmental benefits that they do not receive, and the asserted state interests in support of the classification. [It] is the individual interests here at stake that [most] clearly distinguish this case from the 'business regulation' equal protection cases. AFDC support to needy dependent children provides the stuff that sustains those children's lives: food, clothing, shelter. And this Court has already recognized several times that when a benefit, even a 'gratuitous' benefit, is necessary to sustain life, stricter constitutional standards, both procedural and substantive, are applied to the deprivation of that benefit."

2. ***Housing.*** An effort to establish a "fundamental interest" in "decent shelter" and "possession of one's home" failed in **Lindsey v. Normet**, 405 U.S. 56 (1972). That 5–2 decision sustained Oregon's summary "forcible entry and wrongful detainer" procedure for the eviction of tenants after alleged nonpayment of rent. Justice WHITE's majority opinion rejected the argument "that a more stringent standard than mere rationality should be applied both to the challenged classification and its stated purpose." One of the rejected contentions was that "the 'need for decent shelter' and the 'right to retain peaceful possession of one's home' are fundamental interests which are particularly important to the poor and which may be trenched upon only after the State demonstrates some superior interest."

Justice White replied: "We do not denigrate the importance of decent, safe and sanitary housing. But the Constitution does not provide judicial remedies for every social and economic ill. We are unable to perceive in that document any constitutional guarantee of access to dwellings of a particular quality or any recognition of the right of a tenant to occupy the real property of his landlord beyond the term of his lease, without the payment of [rent]. Absent constitutional mandate, the assurance of adequate housing and the definition of landlord-tenant relationships is a legislative not a judicial function." Exercising deferential review, he found no constitutional flaw in the fact that eviction actions "differ substantially from other litigation, where the time between complaint and trial is substantially longer, and where a broader range of issues may be considered." Here, there were "unique factual and legal characteristics of the landlord-tenant relationship that justify special statutory treatment." Accordingly, such features as limiting the issue at trial to that of the tenant's default and barring such defenses as the landlord's failure to maintain the premises were found rational.

3. ***Education.*** Education might be thought to be a material precondition for exercise of other rights, both those explicitly protected in the Constitution, such as speech, or those, such as voting. deemed fundamental by the Court in other equal protection decisions. But the Court declined to extend the fundamental interests branch of equal protection to a state financing scheme for public schools that created large effective disparities in the amount of tax funds available per child in different school districts in Texas, and thus rejected the equal protection claims in Rodriguez, which follows.

Traditionally, public school education has been financed mainly through property taxes imposed by local school districts. The Rodriguez case involved a challenge to the Texas system of financing public education, which relied heavily on local property taxes. The claim alleged that the system violated equal protection because it produced substantial interdistrict disparities in per-pupil expenditures, stemming from the differences in taxable property values among the districts. The challengers in this class action were Mexican-American parents of children in the Edgewood school district in San Antonio, suing on behalf of children of poor families residing in districts having a low property tax base. Although contributions from a statewide "minimum foundation school program" served to reduce interdistrict disparities, district spending continued to vary considerably on the basis of local property wealth. For example, during the 1967–68 school year, Edgewood had an average assessed property value per pupil of $5960. By taxing itself at a rate of 1.05%—the highest rate in the metropolitan area—the district raised $26 for the education of each child. State and federal support brought Edgewood per pupil expenditures to $356. By contrast, the affluent Alamo Heights district had a property tax base of more than $49,000 per pupil. By taxing itself at only .85%, it raised $333 per pupil. State and federal support brought Alamo Heights spending to $594 per pupil. The district court, applying strict scrutiny, held that such disparities in spending despite comparable tax effort violated equal protection. The Supreme Court reversed:

San Antonio Independent School Dist. v. Rodriguez

411 U.S. 1, 93 S. Ct. 1278, 36 L. Ed. 2d 16 (1973).

■ JUSTICE POWELL delivered the opinion of the [Court].

I. [We] must decide, first whether the Texas system of financing public education operates to the disadvantage of some suspect class or impinges upon a fundamental right explicitly or implicitly protected by the Constitution, thereby requiring strict judicial scrutiny. If so, the judgment of the District Court [which had found wealth a "suspect" classification and education a "fundamental interest"] should be affirmed. If not, the Texas scheme must still be examined to determine whether it rationally furthers some legitimate, articulated state purpose and therefore does not constitute an invidious discrimination in violation of [equal protection].

II. [We] find neither the suspect-classification nor the fundamental-interest analysis persuasive. A. The wealth discrimination discovered by the District Court, [and] by several other courts that have recently struck down school financing laws in other States, is quite unlike any of the forms of wealth discrimination heretofore reviewed by this Court. [The] individuals or groups of individuals who constituted the class discriminated against in our prior cases shared two distinguishing characteristics: because of their impecunity they were completely unable to pay for some desired benefit, and as a consequence, they sustained an absolute deprivation of a meaningful opportunity to enjoy that benefit. [E.g. Griffin, Douglas.] [Even] a cursory examination, however, demonstrates that neither of the two distinguishing characteristics of wealth classifications can be found here.

First, [there] is reason to believe that the poorest families are not necessarily clustered in the poorest property districts. [A recent] Connecticut study found that the poor were clustered around commercial and industrial areas—those same areas that provide the most attractive sources of property tax income for school districts. [T]here is no basis on the record [for] assuming that the poorest people [are] concentrated in the poorest districts [in Texas].

[Second], lack of personal resources has not occasioned an absolute deprivation of the desired benefit. The argument here is not that the children [are] receiving no public education; rather, it is that they are receiving a poorer quality education [than] children in districts having more assessable wealth. Apart from the unsettled and disputed question whether the quality of education may be determined by the amount of money expended for it, a sufficient answer to appellees' argument is that, at least where wealth is involved, [equal protection] does not require absolute equality or precisely equal advantages. Nor, indeed, in view of the infinite variables affecting the educational process, can any system assure equal quality of education except in the most relative sense. [For] these two reasons[, the] disadvantaged class is not susceptible of identification in traditional terms.[1]

[This] brings us [to] the third way in which the classification scheme might be defined—*district* wealth discrimination. Since the only correlation indicated by the evidence is between district property wealth and expenditures, it may be argued that discrimination might be found without regard to the individual income characteristics of district residents. [However] described, it is clear that appellees' suit asks this Court to extend its most exacting scrutiny to review a system that allegedly discriminates against a large, diverse, and amorphous class, unified only by the common factor of residence in districts that happen to have less taxable wealth than other districts. The system of alleged discrimination and the class it defines have none of the traditional indicia of suspectness: the class is not saddled

1 An educational system might be hypothesized, however, in which the analogy to the wealth discrimination cases would be considerably closer. If elementary and secondary education were made available by the State only to those able to pay a [tuition], there would be a clearly defined class of "poor" people—definable in terms of their inability to pay the prescribed sum—who would be absolutely precluded from receiving an education. That case would present a far more compelling set of circumstances for judicial assistance than the case before us today. [But] Texas [has] provided what it considers to be an adequate base education for all children [and no proof was offered at trial persuasively discrediting the State's assertion]. [Footnote by Justice Powell.]

with such disabilities, or subjected to such a history of purposeful unequal treatment, or relegated to such a position of political powerlessness as to command extraordinary protection from the majoritarian political process. We thus conclude that the Texas system does not operate to the peculiar disadvantage of any suspect class.

[Recognizing] that this Court has never heretofore held that wealth discrimination alone provides an adequate basis for invoking strict scrutiny, appellees [also] assert that the State's system impermissibly interferes with the exercise of a "fundamental" right [requiring] the strict standard of judicial [review].

B. In [Brown v. Board of Education], a unanimous Court recognized that "education is perhaps the most important function of state and local governments." [Nothing] this Court holds today in any way detracts from our historic dedication to public education. [But] the importance of a service performed by the State does not determine whether it must be regarded as fundamental for purposes of examination under [equal protection]. [The] key to discovering whether education is "fundamental" is not to be found in comparisons of the relative societal significance of education as opposed to subsistence or housing. Nor is it to be found by weighing whether education is as important as the right to travel. Rather, the answer lies in assessing whether there is a right to education explicitly or implicitly guaranteed by the Constitution.

Education, of course, is not among the rights afforded explicit protection under our Federal Constitution. Nor do we find any basis for saying it is implicitly so protected. [It] is appellees' contention, however, that education is distinguishable from other services and benefits provided by the State because it bears a peculiarly close relationship to other rights and liberties accorded protection under the Constitution. Specifically, they insist that education is itself a fundamental personal right because it is essential to the effective exercise of First Amendment freedoms and to intelligent utilization of the right to vote. In asserting a nexus between speech and education, appellees urge that the right to speak is meaningless unless the speaker is capable of articulating his thoughts intelligently and persuasively. The "marketplace of ideas" is an empty forum for those lacking basic communicative tools. [A] similar line of reasoning is pursued with respect to the right to vote. Exercise of the franchise, it is contended, cannot be divorced from the educational foundation of the voter. [We] need not dispute any of these propositions. [Yet] we have never presumed to possess either the ability or the authority to guarantee to the citizenry the most *effective* speech or the most *informed* electoral choice. That these may be desirable goals [is] not to be doubted. [But] they are not values to be implemented by judicial intrusion into otherwise legitimate state activities.

[Whatever] merit appellees' argument might have if a State's financing system occasioned an absolute denial of educational opportunities to any of its children, that argument provides no basis for finding an interference with fundamental rights where only relative differences in spending levels are involved and where—as is true in the present case—no charge fairly could be made that the system fails to provide each child with an opportunity to acquire the basic minimal skills necessary for the enjoyment of the rights of speech and a full participation in the political process. [Furthermore,] the logical limitations on appellees' nexus theory are difficult to perceive. How, for instance, is education to be distinguished from the significant personal interests in the basics of decent food and shelter? Empirical examination might well buttress an assumption that the ill-fed, ill-clothed, and ill-housed are among the most ineffective participants in the political process and that they derive the least enjoyment from the benefits of the First Amendment. If so, appellees' thesis would cast serious doubt on the authority of Dandridge v. Williams and Lindsey v. Normet.

[The] present case, in another basic sense, is significantly different from any of the cases in which [we have] applied strict scrutiny [to] legislation touching upon constitutionally protected rights. Each of our prior cases involved legislation which "deprived," "infringed," or "interfered" with the free exercise of some such fundamental personal right or liberty. A critical distinction between those cases and the one now before us lies in what Texas is endeavoring to do with respect to education. [Every] step leading to the establishment of the system Texas utilizes today [was] implemented in an effort to *extend* [public education]. [We] think it plain that [the] thrust of the Texas system is affirmative and reformatory and, therefore, should be scrutinized under judicial principles sensitive to the nature of the State's efforts and to the rights reserved to the States under the Constitution.

C. [We] need not rest our decision, however, solely on the inappropriateness of the strict scrutiny test. A century [of] adjudication under [equal protection] affirmatively supports the application of the traditional standard of review, which requires only that the State's system be shown to bear some rational relationship to legitimate state purposes. [We] have here nothing less than a direct attack on the way in which Texas has chosen to raise and disburse state and local tax revenues. [A]ppellees would have the Court intrude in an area in which it has traditionally deferred to state legislatures. [Thus] we stand on familiar ground when we continue to acknowledge that the Justices of this Court lack both the expertise and the familiarity with local problems so necessary to the making of wise decisions with respect to the raising and disposition of public revenues. [No] scheme of taxation [has] yet been devised which is free of all discriminatory impact. [And] this case also involves the most persistent and difficult questions of educational policy, another area in which this Court's lack of specialized knowledge and experience counsels against premature interference with the informed judgments made at the state and local levels. Education, perhaps even more than welfare assistance, presents a myriad of "intractable economic, social, and even philosophical problems." [Dandridge v. Williams.] [In] such circumstances, the judiciary is well advised to refrain from imposing on the States inflexible constitutional restraints that could circumscribe [continued research and experimentation].

III. [The] Texas system of school finance, [w]hile assuring a basic education for every child in the State, [encourages] a large measure of participation in and control of each district's schools at the local level. [Appellees] suggest that local control could be preserved and promoted under other financing systems that resulted in more equality in educational expenditures. While it is no doubt true that reliance on local property taxation for school revenues provides less freedom of choice with respect to expenditures for some districts than for others, the existence of "some inequality" in the manner in which the State's rationale is achieved is not alone a sufficient basis for striking down the entire system. [Nor] must the financing system fail because, as appellees suggest, other methods of satisfying the State's interest, which occasion "less drastic" disparities in expenditures, might be conceived. Only where state action impinges on the exercise of fundamental constitutional rights or liberties must it be found to have chosen the least restrictive alternative. It is also well to remember that even those districts that have reduced ability to make free decisions with respect to how much they spend on education still retain under the present system a large measure of authority as to how available funds will be allocated. They further enjoy the power to make numerous other decisions with respect to the operation of the schools. The people of Texas may be justified in believing [that] along with increased control of the purse strings at the State level will go increased control over local policies. Appellees further urge that the Texas system is unconstitutionally arbitrary because it allows the availability of local taxable resources to turn on "happenstance." [But] any scheme of local taxation—indeed the very existence of identifiable local governmental units—requires the establishment of jurisdictional boundaries that are inevitably arbitrary. It is equally inevitable that some localities are going to be blessed with more taxable assets than others. Nor is local wealth a static quantity. [In] sum, [we] cannot say that [the Texas interdistrict] disparities are the product of a system that is so irrational as to be invidiously discriminatory. [The equal protection standard] is whether the challenged state action rationally furthers a legitimate state purpose or interest. [We] hold that the Texas plan abundantly satisfies this standard.

IV. [A] cautionary postscript seems appropriate. [Affirmance here] would occasion in Texas and elsewhere an unprecedented upheaval in public education. [The] complexity of [the] problems is demonstrated by the lack of consensus with respect to whether it may be said with any assurance that the poor, the racial minorities, or the children in overburdened core-city school districts would be benefitted by abrogation of traditional modes of financing education. [We] hardly need add that this Court's action today is not to be viewed as placing its judicial imprimatur on the status quo. The need is apparent for reform in tax systems which may well have relied too long and too heavily on the local property tax. [But] the ultimate solutions must come from the lawmakers and from the democratic pressures of those who elect them. Reversed.

■ JUSTICE STEWART, concurring.

[I] join the opinion [because] I am convinced that any other course would mark an extraordinary departure from principled adjudication under [equal protection]. The uncharted directions of such a departure are suggested, I think, by [Justice Marshall's] imaginative [dissent]. Unlike other provisions of the Constitution, [equal protection] confers no substantive rights and creates no substantive liberties. The function of [equal protection], rather, is simply to measure the validity of *classifications* created by state laws. [Quite] apart from [equal protection], a state law that impinges upon a substantive right or liberty created or conferred by the Constitution is, of course, presumptively invalid, whether or not the law's purpose or effect is to create any classifications. [Numerous] cases in this Court illustrate this principle. In refusing to invalidate the Texas system of financing its public schools, the Court today applies with thoughtfulness and understanding the basic principles [of equal protection].

■ JUSTICE WHITE, with whom JUSTICES DOUGLAS and BRENNAN join, dissenting.

[T]his case would be quite different if it were true that the Texas system, while insuring minimum educational expenditures in every district through state funding, extended a meaningful option to all local districts to increase their per-pupil [expenditures]. But for districts with a low per-pupil real estate tax base, [the] Texas system utterly fails to extend a realistic choice to parents because the property tax, which is the only revenue-raising mechanism extended to school districts, is practically and legally unavailable. [Requiring] the State to establish only that unequal treatment is in furtherance of a permissible goal, without also requiring the State to show that the means chosen to effectuate that goal are rationally related to its achievement, makes equal protection analysis no more than an empty [gesture].

■ JUSTICE MARSHALL, with whom JUSTICE DOUGLAS concurs, dissenting.

[I] must once more voice my disagreement with the Court's rigidified approach to equal protection analysis. [The] Court apparently seeks to establish today that equal protection cases fall into one of two neat categories which dictate the appropriate standard of review—strict scrutiny or mere rationality. But this Court's [decisions] defy such easy categorization. A principled reading of what this Court has done reveals that it has applied a spectrum of standards in reviewing discrimination allegedly violative of [equal protection]. This spectrum clearly comprehends variations in the degree of care with which the Court will scrutinize particular classifications, depending, I believe, on the constitutional and societal importance of the interest adversely affected and the recognized invidiousness of the basis upon which the particular classification is drawn.

[I] therefore cannot accept the majority's labored efforts to demonstrate that fundamental interests, which call for [strict scrutiny], encompass only established rights which we are somehow bound to recognize from the text of the Constitution itself. [It] will not do to suggest that the "answer" to whether an interest is fundamental for purposes of equal protection analysis is *always* determined by whether that interest "is a [right] explicitly or implicitly guaranteed by the Constitution." I would like to know where the Constitution guarantees the right to procreate [Skinner v. Oklahoma], or the right to vote in state elections [e.g., Reynolds v. Sims], or the right to an appeal from a criminal conviction [e.g., Griffin v. Illinois]. These are instances in which, due to the importance of the interests at stake, the Court has displayed a strong concern with the existence of discriminatory state treatment. But the Court has never said or indicated that these are interests which independently enjoy full-blown constitutional [protection].

The majority is, of course, correct when it suggests that the process of determining which interests are fundamental is a difficult one. But I do not think the problem is insurmountable. And I certainly do not accept the view that the process need necessarily degenerate into an unprincipled, subjective "picking-and-choosing" between various interests or that it must involve this Court in creating "substantive constitutional rights in the name of guaranteeing equal protection of the laws." Although not all fundamental interests are constitutionally guaranteed, the determination of which interests are fundamental should be firmly rooted in the text of the Constitution. The task in every case should be to determine the extent to which constitutionally guaranteed rights are dependent on interests not mentioned in the Constitution. As the nexus between the specific constitutional guarantee and the nonconstitutional interest draws closer, the nonconstitutional interest becomes more fundamental and the degree of judicial scrutiny applied when the interest is infringed on a discriminatory basis must be adjusted accordingly. Thus, it cannot be denied that interests such as procreation, the exercise of the state franchise, and access to criminal appellate processes are not fully guaranteed to the citizen by our Constitution. But these interests have nonetheless been afforded special judicial consideration in the face of discrimination because they are, to some extent, interrelated with constitutional guarantees. Procreation is now understood to be important because of its interaction with the established constitutional right of privacy. The exercise of the state franchise is closely tied to basic civil and political rights inherent in the First Amendment. And access to criminal appellate processes enhances the integrity of the range of rights implicit in the [guarantee of due process]. Only if we closely protect the related interests from state discrimination do we ultimately ensure the integrity of the constitutional guarantee itself. This is the real lesson that must be taken from our previous decisions involving interests deemed to be fundamental.

[It] is true that this Court has never deemed the provision of free public education to be required by the Constitution. [But] education directly affects the ability of a child to exercise his First Amendment [interests]. [Of] particular importance is the relationship between education and the political process and the demonstrated effect of education on the exercise of the franchise by the electorate. [It] is this very sort of intimate relationship between a particular personal interest and specific constitutional guarantees that has heretofore caused the Court to attach special significance, for purposes of equal protection analysis, to individual interests such as procreation and the exercise of the state franchise.[2] [These factors] compel us to recognize the fundamentality of education and to scrutinize with appropriate care the bases for state discrimination affecting equality of educational opportunity in Texas school districts—a conclusion which is only strengthened when we consider the character of the classification in this [case].

[We] are told that in every prior case involving a wealth classification, the members of the disadvantaged class have "shared two distinguishing characteristics: because of their impecunity they were completely unable to pay for some desired benefit, and as a consequence, they sustained an absolute deprivation of a meaningful opportunity to enjoy that benefit." I cannot agree. [Harper, Griffin and Douglas] refute the majority's contention that we have in the past required an absolute deprivation before subjecting wealth classifications to strict scrutiny. [This] is not to say that the form of wealth classification in this case does not differ significantly from those recognized [in previous decisions]. Here, the children [are] being

[2] I believe that the close nexus between education and our established constitutional values with respect to freedom of speech and participation in the political process makes this a different case than our prior decisions concerning discrimination affecting public welfare, see, e.g., [Dandridge v. Williams], or housing, see, e.g., [Lindsey v. Normet]. There can be no question that, as the majority suggests, constitutional rights may be less meaningful for someone without enough to eat or without decent housing. But the crucial difference lies in the closeness of the relationship. Whatever the severity of the impact of insufficient food or inadequate housing on a person's life, they have never been considered to bear the same direct and immediate relationship to constitutional concerns for free speech and for our political processes as education has long been recognized to bear. Perhaps the best evidence of this fact is the unique status which has been accorded public education as the single public service nearly unanimously guaranteed in the constitutions of our States. Education, in terms of constitutional values, is much more analogous, in my judgment, to the right to vote in state elections than to public welfare or [public housing]. [Footnote by Justice Marshall.]

discriminated against not necessarily because of their personal wealth or the wealth of their families, but because of the taxable property wealth of the residents of the district in which they happen to live. The appropriate question, then, is whether the same degree of judicial [scrutiny] that has previously been afforded wealth classifications is warranted here. [That] wealth classifications alone have not necessarily been considered to bear the same high degree of suspectness as have classifications based on, for instance, race or alienage may be explainable on a number of grounds. The "poor" may not be seen as politically powerless as certain discrete and insular minority groups. Personal poverty may entail much the same social stigma as historically attached to certain racial or ethnic groups [but it] is not a permanent disability; its shackles may be escaped. Perhaps, most importantly, though, personal wealth may not necessarily share the general irrelevance as a basis for legislative action that race or nationality is recognized to have. While the "poor" have frequently been a legally disadvantaged group, it cannot be ignored that social legislation must frequently take cognizance of the economic status of our citizens. Thus, we have generally gauged the invidiousness of wealth classifications with an awareness of the importance of the interests being affected and the relevance of personal wealth to those interests.

[Here], both the nature of the interest and the classification dictate close judicial scrutiny of the purposes which Texas seeks to serve with its present educational financing scheme and of the means it has selected to serve that purpose. [I] need not now decide how I might ultimately strike the balance were we confronted with a situation where the State's sincere concern for local control inevitably produced educational inequality. For on this record, it is apparent that the State's purported concern with local control is offered primarily as an excuse rather than as a justification for interdistrict inequality. [School districts] cannot choose to have the best education in the State by imposing the highest tax rate. Instead, the quality of the educational opportunity offered by any particular district is largely determined by the amount of taxable property located in the district—a factor over which local voters can exercise no [control]. In my judgment, any substantial degree of scrutiny [reveals] that the State has selected means wholly inappropriate to secure its purported interest in assuring its school districts local fiscal control.

Given its rejection of a strict scrutiny standard of review for disparities in education funding, Rodriguez is typically seen as a loss for those advocating for education equity. However, some, including Judge Jeffrey S. Sutton of the Sixth Circuit, seek to tell a different story. In Sutton, "51 Imperfect Solutions: States and the Making of American Constitutional Law," (2018), Judge Sutton "prompts a provocative question: Is it possible that the Rodriguez plaintiffs ultimately won by losing?" In particular, Judge Sutton observes that the loss in Rodriquez channeled energy to both state legislatures and state courts. In the latter forum, plaintiffs relied on state constitutional guarantees of "a thorough and efficient system of common schools," apparent in some form in all state constitutions, to argue that states had a positive obligation to equalize educational funding. Moreover, Judge Sutton argues that these state-level solutions were preferable given that they could be better tailored to the needs and context in individual states, as opposed to a one-size-fits-all approach imposed by the Court.

How convincing is this narrative of the fight for school funding equality? Did the Rodriguez plaintiffs really lose by winning? If so, can a similar strategy be pursued for issues like political gerrymandering, discussed above at pp. 820–825? How can a state-focussed strategy be reconciled with prevailing fears that there will always be hold out states resistant to change on any given issue?

In **Plyler v. Doe**, 457 U.S. 202 (1982), in contrast, the Court applied heightened scrutiny to hold that the exclusion of undocumented children altogether from Texas public schools violated equal protection. The decision, which divided sharply 5–4, did not rest squarely on either the illegal alien status of the children or on a view of education as a fundamental interest, but rather on an unusual and perhaps unique amalgam of the two. The case arose from class action on behalf of certain school-age children of Mexican origin residing in Smith County, Texas, who could not establish that they had been legally admitted into the United States. The suit attacked the exclusion of the children from the public schools of the Tyler Independent School District. Since 1977, the District had required "undocumented" children to pay a "full tuition fee" in order to enroll. The lower federal courts held that the exclusion of the children from free public education violated equal protection. The Court affirmed. Justice BRENNAN wrote the opinion of the Court: "The question presented by these cases is whether, consistent with [equal protection], Texas may deny to undocumented school-age children the free public education that it provides to children who are citizens of the United States or legally admitted aliens. [Sheer] incapability or lax enforcement of the laws barring entry into this country [has] resulted in the creation of a substantial 'shadow population' of illegal migrants—numbering in the millions—within our borders. This situation raises the specter of a permanent caste of undocumented resident aliens, encouraged by some to remain here as a source of cheap labor, but nevertheless denied the benefits that our society makes available to citizens and lawful residents. The existence of such an underclass presents most difficult problems for a Nation that prides itself in adherence to principles of equality under law."[1]

"The children who are plaintiffs in these cases are special members of this underclass. Persuasive arguments support the view that a State may withhold its beneficence from those whose very presence within the United States is the product of their own unlawful conduct. These arguments do not apply with the same force to classifications imposing disabilities on the minor *children* of such illegal entrants. [Of] course, undocumented status is not irrelevant to any proper legislative goal. Nor is undocumented status an absolutely immutable characteristic since it is the product of conscious, indeed unlawful, action. But [the Texas law] is directed against children, and imposes its discriminatory burden on the basis of a legal characteristic over which children can have little control. It is thus difficult to conceive of a rational justification for penalizing these children for their presence within the United States.

[1] "We reject the claim that 'illegal aliens' are a 'suspect class.' No case in which we have attempted to define a suspect class has addressed the status of persons unlawfully in our country. Unlike most of the classifications that we have recognized as suspect, entry into this class, by virtue of entry into this country, is the product of voluntary action. Indeed, entry into the class is itself a crime. In addition, it could hardly be suggested that undocumented status is a 'constitutional irrelevancy'." [Footnote by Justice Brennan.]

"Public education is not a 'right' granted to individuals by the Constitution. [Rodriguez.] But neither is it merely some governmental 'benefit' indistinguishable from other forms of social welfare legislation. Both the importance of education in maintaining our basic institutions, and the lasting impact of its deprivation on the life of the child, mark the distinction. [In] addition, education provides the basic tools by which individuals might lead economically productive lives to the benefit of us all. In sum, education has a fundamental role in maintaining the fabric of our society. We cannot ignore the significant social costs borne by our Nation when select groups are denied the means to absorb the values and skills upon which our social order rests. In addition to the pivotal role of education in sustaining our political and cultural heritage, denial of education to some isolated group of children poses an affront to one of the goals of [equal protection]: the abolition of governmental barriers presenting unreasonable obstacles to advancement on the basis of individual merit. [Undocumented] aliens [are not] a suspect class [and] education [is not] a fundamental [right]. But more is involved in this case than the abstract question whether [this law] discriminates against a suspect class, or whether education is a fundamental right. [This law] imposes a lifetime hardship on a discrete class of children not accountable for their disabling status. [In] determining the rationality of [this law], we may appropriately take into account its costs to the Nation and to the innocent children who are its victims. In light of these countervailing costs, the discrimination contained in [this law] can hardly be considered rational unless it furthers some substantial goal of the State." Under this heightened standard, Justice Brennan found inadequate the state's proffered interests in discouraging illegal immigration, avoiding burdens on public schools, and reserving public education for those likely to reside later within the state. He concluded: "If the State is to deny a discrete group of innocent children the free public education that it offers to other children residing within its borders, that denial must be justified by a showing that it furthers some substantial state interest. No such showing was made here."

Justice BLACKMUN, who had joined Justice Powell's Rodriguez opinion, concurred in Plyler: "Other benefits provided by the State, such as housing and public assistance, are of course [important]. But classifications involving the complete denial of education are in a sense unique, for they strike at the heart of equal protection values by involving the State in the creation of permanent class distinctions. In a sense, then, denial of an education is the analogue of denial of the right to vote: the former relegates the individual to second-class social status; the latter places him at a permanent political disadvantage. [In] such circumstances, the voting decisions suggest that the State must offer something more than a rational basis for its classification. [Given] the extraordinary nature of the interest involved, this makes the classification here fatally [imprecise]."

Justice POWELL, the author of Rodriguez, likewise concurred: "[I] agree with the Court that their children should not be left on the streets uneducated. [Texas] effectively denies to the school age children of illegal aliens the opportunity to attend the free public schools that the State makes available to all residents. They are excluded only because of a status resulting from the violation by parents or guardians of our immigration laws and the fact that they remain in our country unlawfully. The respondent children are innocent in this respect. [Our] review in a case such as this is properly heightened. Cf. Craig v. Boren. [These] children [have] been singled out for a lifelong penalty and stigma. A legislative classification that threatens the creation of an underclass of future citizens and residents cannot be reconciled with one of the fundamental purposes of the 14th Amendment. In these unique circumstances, the Court properly may require that the State's interests be substantial and that the means bear a fair and substantial relation to these interests. [The] State's denial of education to these children bears no substantial relation to any substantial state interest. [The] exclusion of [these] children from state-provided education is a type of punitive discrimination based on status that is impermissible under [equal protection]."

Chief Justice BURGER, joined by Justices White, Rehnquist, and O'Connor dissented: "Were it our business to set the Nation's social policy, I would agree without hesitation that it is senseless for an enlightened society to deprive any children—including illegal aliens—of an elementary education. [However, we] trespass on the assigned function of the political branches [when] we assume a policymaking role as the Court does today.[The] Court [correctly] rejects any suggestion that illegal aliens are a suspect class or that education is a fundamental right. Yet by patching together bits and pieces of what might be termed quasi-suspect-class and quasi-fundamental-rights analysis, the Court spins out a theory custom-tailored to the facts of these cases. [If] ever a court was guilty of an unabashedly result-oriented approach, this case is a prime example." He concluded: "Once it is conceded [that] illegal aliens are not a suspect class, and that education is not a fundamental right, our inquiry should focus on and be limited to whether the legislative classification at issue bears a rational relationship to a legitimate state purpose. [It] simply is not 'irrational' for a State to conclude that it does not have the same responsibility to provide benefits for persons whose very presence in the State and this country is illegal as it does to provide for persons lawfully present." Is Plyler limited to education? After Plyler, could a state enact a law barring access for the children of undocumented immigrants to public hospitals or other state-financed medical services?

Can Plyler be extended even to other wealth-related classifications within the context of education? Contrast with Plyler the decision a year later in Martinez v. Bynum, 461 U.S. 321 (1983), rejecting a facial challenge to a Texas law authorizing a school district to deny tuition-free education to minors who live apart from their parents and whose presence in the district was "for the primary purpose of attending the public free schools." Justice Powell's majority opinion found this a valid "bona fide residence requirement." Note also the Court's decision in Kadrmas v. Dickinson Public Schools, 487 U.S. 450 (1988), holding by a vote of 5–4 that a state may permit local school boards to assess a user fee for transporting students to and from public schools, relying on Rodriguez and rejecting any analogy to Plyler: "Unlike the children in [Plyler], Sarita Kadrmas has not been penalized by the government for illegal conduct by her parents."

CHAPTER 10

CONGRESS'S CIVIL RIGHTS ENFORCEMENT POWERS

The preceding chapters considered challenges before courts on due process and equal protection grounds to actions by an arm of government. This chapter broadens the focus beyond limits on governmental action to restraints on seemingly private conduct, and beyond the Court's role to that of Congress in enforcing the guarantees of the post-Civil War Amendments.

The first theme—the applicability of constitutional guarantees to seemingly private conduct—reflects the fact that the Fourteenth and Fifteenth Amendments, like most limits in the Constitution, are addressed to government action, not to private behavior. For example, the central prohibitions of § 1 of the Fourteenth Amendment begin with "No State shall." From the beginning, the Court's interpretations of that Amendment have reiterated "the essential dichotomy set forth in that Amendment between deprivation by the State, subject to scrutiny under its provisions, and private conduct, 'however discriminatory and wrongful,' against which the 14th Amendment offers no shield." But the state-private distinction is deceptively simple. As governmental involvement in the private sector has become more pervasive, traditional notions as to what activity constitutes "state action" have become blurred. Under what circumstances is arguably private behavior subject to such restraints as those in the Fourteenth Amendment? When may a challenger relying on the Fourteenth Amendment insist that the Court impose constitutional restraints on a seemingly "private" actor—or at least require that government withdraw from involvement with "private" actors' conduct? See Section 2 below.

The second theme—the role of Congress—reflects the fact that each of the three post-Civil War amendments grants Congress authority to protect civil rights. The final sections of the Thirteenth, Fourteenth and Fifteenth Amendments each give Congress the "power to enforce" such amendment "by appropriate legislation." These are not the only sources of congressional power to enact civil rights laws: the commerce power has been invoked as a source for civil rights legislation forbidding private racial discrimination. But the post-Civil War additions, unlike the original grants, were born of a special concern with racial discrimination; and the civil rights powers they confer are potentially the most far-reaching. See Sections 3 and 4 below. A brief introduction to the statutory framework follows in Section 1.

SECTION 1. THE CIVIL RIGHTS STATUTES OF THE RECONSTRUCTION ERA

The adoption of the Thirteenth, Fourteenth and Fifteenth Amendments, and the enactment of the Civil Rights Acts of 1866, 1870, 1871 and 1875, aimed to fulfill the "one pervading purpose" underlying all of these amendments: "the freedom of the slave race, the security and firm establishment of that freedom, and the protection of the newly-made freeman and citizen from the oppressions of those who had formerly exercised unlimited dominion over him." Slaughter-House Cases. Each of the initial civil rights statutes derived authority from the new enforcement powers granted Congress by the Reconstruction Amendments:

1. ***The 1866 Act.*** The Thirteenth Amendment, ratified in 1865, gave constitutional support to the wartime Emancipation Proclamation. Congress, however, considered additional protection of the newly freed slaves necessary—partly because of the "black codes" enacted in several states, which imposed severe legal restrictions just short of formal slavery. The Civil Rights Act of 1866 sought to end these restrictions. Section 1 stated that all persons born in the United States were "citizens of the United States" and proceeded to list certain rights of "such citizens, of every race and color, without regard to any previous condition of slavery"—such as the right to contract and own property. Its modern counterparts remain codified as 42 U.S.C. §§ 1981 & 1982. A criminal enforcement provision followed in § 2, codified today as 18 U.S.C. § 242. During the debates on the 1866 Act, constitutional doubts were raised about the adequacy of the Thirteenth Amendment to support the constitutionality of the law. These doubts were reflected in President Johnson's veto: "[W]here can we find a Federal prohibition against the power of any State to discriminate?" Congress overrode the veto, but in light of the constitutional concerns raised by President Johnson and other opponents, the machinery was put in motion nonetheless to enact a new amendment designed in part to validate the 1866 Act. The result of the process was the Fourteenth Amendment, which was ratified in 1868.

2. ***The 1870 Act.*** In 1870, the Fifteenth Amendment was ratified, prohibiting denial of the franchise "on account of race, color, or previous condition of servitude." Unlike the Fourteenth Amendment, it explicitly mentions race. Congress promptly passed enforcement legislation. The 1870 Enforcement Act dealt primarily with state denials of voting rights. Section 6, however, went further: it provided criminal sanctions for private conspiracies to violate federal rights. The current version of this criminal provision is 18 U.S.C. § 241.

3. ***The 1871 and 1875 Acts.*** In 1871, Congress not only amended the 1870 Act, but also enacted a new law, the Civil Rights Act of 1871. The 1871 Act, known as the Ku Klux Klan Act, established civil liabilities together with parallel criminal liabilities. The substance of these civil provisions has been preserved. For example, 42 U.S.C. § 1983 creates a cause of action for deprivations, under color of state law, of rights secured by the Constitution and federal laws. And 42 U.S.C. § 1985(3) provides for civil actions for certain private conspiracies to interfere with civil rights. The Civil Rights Act of 1875, which contained, inter alia, "public accommodations" provisions, was in large part held unconstitutional as exceeding Congress's power in the 1883 Civil Rights Cases, see below.

4. ***Civil rights laws that survive from Reconstruction.*** As outlined above, many of Congress's earliest statutes enforcing civil rights still remain in force today, including the following:

a. *Criminal provisions:* 18 U.S.C. § 241 (derived from § 6 of the 1870 Act): "*Conspiracy against rights.* If two or more persons conspire to injure, oppress, threaten, or intimidate any inhabitant of any State, Territory or District in the free exercise or enjoyment of any right or privilege secured to him by the Constitution or laws of the United States, or because of his having so exercised the same; or [i]f two or more persons go in disguise on the highway, or on the premises of another, with intent to prevent or hinder his free exercise or enjoyment of any right or privilege so secured—They shall be fined not more than $10,000 or imprisoned not more than ten years, or both; and if death results, they shall be subject to imprisonment for any term of years or for life."

18 U.S.C. § 242 (derived from § 2 of the 1866 Act): "*Deprivation of rights under color of law.* Whoever, under color of any law, statute, ordinance, regulation, or custom, willfully subjects any inhabitant of any State, Territory, or District to the deprivation of any rights, privileges, or immunities secured or protected by the [Constitution or laws], or to different punishments, pains, or penalties, on account of such inhabitant being an alien, or by reason of his color, or race, than are prescribed for the punishment of citizens, shall be fined not more than $1,000 or imprisoned not more than one year, or both; and if bodily injury results shall [be] imprisoned not more than ten [years]; and if death results shall be subject to imprisonment for any term of years or for life."

b. *Civil provisions:* 42 U.S.C. § 1981 (derived from the 1866 and 1870 Acts): "*Equal rights under the law.* All persons within the jurisdiction of the United States shall have the same right in every State and Territory to make and enforce contracts, to sue, be parties, give evidence, and to the full and equal benefit of all laws and proceedings for the security of persons and property as is enjoyed by white citizens, and shall be subject to like punishment, pains, penalties, taxes, licenses, and exactions of every kind, and to no other."

42 U.S.C. § 1982 (derived from the 1866 Act): "*Property rights of citizens.* All citizens of the United States shall have the same right, in every State and Territory, as is enjoyed by white citizens thereof to inherit, purchase, lease, sell, hold, and convey real and personal property."

42 U.S.C. § 1983 (derived from § 1 of the Civil Rights Act of 1871): "*Civil action for deprivation of rights.* Every person who, under color of any statute, ordinance, regulation, custom, or usage, of any State or Territory or the District of Columbia, subjects, or causes to be subjected, any citizen of the United States or other person within the jurisdiction thereof to the deprivation of any rights, privileges or immunities secured by the Constitution and laws, shall be liable to the party injured in an action at law, suit in equity, or other proper proceedings for redress."

42 U.S.C. § 1985(3) (derived from Civil Rights Act of 1871): "*Conspiracy to interfere with civil rights.* [If] two or more persons in any State or Territory conspire or go in disguise on the highway or on the premises of another, for the purpose of depriving, either directly or indirectly, any person or class of persons of the equal protection of the laws, or of equal privileges and immunities under the laws; [the] party so injured or deprived may have an action for the recovery of damages occasioned by such injury or deprivation, against any one or more of the conspirators."

5. ***The second wave of civil rights legislation in the 1960s.*** Renewed congressional efforts at civil rights enforcement began with the Civil Rights Act of 1957, which, like the Civil Rights Act of 1960, primarily expanded remedies against racial discrimination in voting. The Civil Rights Act of 1964 moved substantially beyond the area of voting rights. The 1964

provisions based primarily on the Article I powers of Congress have already been considered in Chapter 3. In addition, the 1964 Act included several provisions primarily rooted in the post-Civil War Amendments. Thus, Titles I and VIII contained new voting rights provisions, and Titles III and IV dealt with desegregation of schools and other public facilities. After the Voting Rights Act of 1965 was adopted (see Section 4 below), Johnson administration proposals for additional omnibus civil rights laws were repeatedly blocked in the Senate. In 1968, however—after the assassination in April 1968 of Rev. Dr. Martin Luther King, Jr.—new legislation was enacted, adding new federal criminal laws against violent deprivations of civil rights in 18 U.S.C. § 245.

One question underlying the laws passed both during Reconstruction and during the civil rights movement of the 1960s (sometimes called the Second Reconstruction) was how far they could extend under the Constitution. Since the Fourteenth Amendment gives Congress the power to enforce a provision prohibiting "State[s]" from depriving individuals of certain rights, when, if ever, could Congress reach the actions of entities other than states? The following sections address that question.

SECTION 2. THE REQUIREMENT OF STATE ACTION

Civil Rights Cases

109 U.S. 3, 3 S. Ct. 18, 27 L. Ed. 835 (1883).

[Sec. 1 of the Civil Rights Act of 1875 provided: "[A]ll persons within the jurisdiction of the United States shall be entitled to the full and equal enjoyment of the accommodations, advantages, facilities, and privileges of inns, public conveyances on land or water, theatres, and other places of public amusement; subject only to the conditions and limitations established by law, and applicable alike to citizens of every race and color, regardless of any previous condition of servitude." Sec. 2 made violation a misdemeanor and also authorized aggrieved persons to recover $500 "for every such offense." This decision involved five cases, from Kansas, California, Missouri, New York and Tennessee. Four of the cases were criminal indictments; the fifth, an action for the civil penalty. The cases grew out of exclusions of African-Americans from hotels, theaters and railroads.]

■ JUSTICE BRADLEY delivered the opinion of the Court.

Has Congress constitutional power to make such a law? [The] power is sought, first, in the 14th Amendment. [It] is State action of a particular character that is prohibited [by the first section of the 14th Amendment]. Individual invasion of individual rights is not the subject-matter of the amendment. [The] last section of the amendment invests Congress with power to enforce it by appropriate legislation. To enforce what? To enforce the prohibition. To adopt appropriate legislation for correcting the effects of such prohibited State laws and State acts, and thus to render them effectually null, void, and innocuous. This is the legislative power conferred upon Congress, and this is the whole of it. It does not invest Congress with power to legislate upon subjects which are within the domain of State legislation; but to provide modes of relief against State legislation, or State action, of the kind referred to.

[But this law declares] that certain acts committed by individuals shall be deemed offences, and shall be prosecuted and punished by proceedings in the federal courts. It does not profess to be corrective of any constitutional wrong committed by the States; [it] applies equally to cases arising in States which have the justest laws respecting the personal rights of citizens, and whose authorities are ever ready to enforce such laws, as to those which arise in States that may have violated the prohibition of the amendment. In other words, it steps into the domain of local jurisprudence, and lays down rules for the conduct of individuals in society towards each [other], without referring in any manner to any supposed action of the State or its authorities.

[Civil rights,] such as are guaranteed by the Constitution against State aggression, cannot be impaired by the wrongful acts of individuals, unsupported by State authority in the shape of laws, customs, or judicial or executive proceedings. The wrongful act of an individual, unsupported by any such authority, is simply a private wrong, or a crime of that individual. [If] not sanctioned in some way by the State, or not done under State authority, [the injured party's] rights remain in full force, and may presumably be vindicated by resort to the laws of the State for redress. An individual cannot deprive a man of his right to vote, to hold property, to buy and sell, to sue in the courts, or to be a witness or a juror; he may, by force or fraud, interfere with the enjoyment of the right in a particular case; he may commit an assault against the person, or commit murder, or use ruffian violence at the polls, or slander the good name of a fellow citizen; but, unless protected in these wrongful acts by some shield of State law or State authority, he cannot destroy or injure the right; he will only render himself amenable to satisfaction or punishment; and amenable therefor to the laws of the State where the wrongful acts are committed.

[The] abrogation and denial of rights, for which the States alone were or could be responsible, was the great seminal and fundamental wrong which was intended to be remedied. And the remedy to be provided must necessarily be predicated upon that wrong. [It] is clear that the law in question cannot be sustained by any grant of legislative power made to Congress by the 14th Amendment. [Whether] Congress, in the exercise of its power to regulate commerce amongst the several States, might or might not pass a law regulating rights in public conveyances passing from one State to another, [is] a question which is not now before us, as the sections in question are not conceived in any such view.

[Justification for the law is also] sought [in] the 13th Amendment. [Such] legislation may be primary and direct in its character; for the amendment is not a mere prohibition of State laws establishing or upholding slavery, but an absolute declaration that slavery or involuntary servitude shall not exist in any part of the United States. [It] is assumed that the power vested in Congress to enforce the article by appropriate legislation, clothes Congress with power to pass all laws necessary and proper for abolishing all badges and incidents of slavery in the United States: and upon this assumption it is claimed, that this is sufficient authority for [enacting this law]; the argument being, that the denial of such equal accommodations and privileges is, in itself, a subjection to a species of servitude within the meaning of the amendment. [W]e are forced to the conclusion that such an act of refusal has nothing to do with slavery or involuntary servitude, and that if it is violative of any right of the party, his redress is to be sought under the laws of the State; or if those laws are adverse to his rights and do not protect him, his remedy will be found in the corrective legislation which Congress has adopted, or may adopt, for counteracting the effect of State laws, or State action, prohibited by the 14th Amendment.

It would be running the slavery argument into the ground to make it apply to every act of discrimination which a person may see fit to make as to the guests he will entertain, or as to the people he will take into his coach or cab or car, or admit to his concert or theatre, or deal with in other matters of intercourse or business. Innkeepers and public carriers, by the laws of all the States, so far as we are aware, are bound, to the extent of their facilities, to furnish proper accommodation to all unobjectionable persons who in good faith apply for them. If the laws themselves make any unjust discrimination, amenable to the prohibitions of the 14th Amendment, Congress has full power to afford a remedy under that amendment and in accordance with it. When a man has emerged from slavery, and by the aid of beneficent legislation has shaken off the inseparable concomitants of that state, there must be some stage in the progress of his elevation when he takes the rank of a mere citizen, and ceases to be the special favorite of the laws.

■ JUSTICE HARLAN, dissenting.

The opinion in these cases proceeds, it seems to me, upon grounds entirely too narrow and artificial. I cannot resist the conclusion that the substance and spirit of the recent amendments of the Constitution have been sacrificed by a subtle and ingenious verbal criticism. [Was] it the purpose of the [13th Amendment] simply to destroy the institution [of slavery], and then remit the race, theretofore held in bondage, to the several States for such protection, in their civil rights, [as] those States, in their discretion, might choose to provide? [That] there are burdens and disabilities which constitute badges of slavery and servitude, and that the power to enforce by appropriate legislation the 13th Amendment may be exerted by legislation of a direct and primary character, for the eradication, not simply of the institution, but of its badges and incidents, are propositions which ought to be deemed indisputable.

[I] do not contend that the 13th Amendment invests Congress with authority, by legislation, to define and regulate the entire body of the civil rights which citizens enjoy, or may enjoy, in the several States. But I hold that since slavery [was] the moving or principal cause of the adoption of that amendment, and since that institution rested wholly upon the inferiority, as a race, of those held in bondage, their freedom necessarily involved immunity from, and protection against, all discrimination against them, because of their race, in respect of such civil rights as belong to freemen of other races. Congress, therefore, [may] enact laws to protect that people against the deprivation, *because of their race,* of any civil rights granted to other freemen in the same State; and such legislation may be of a direct and primary character operating upon States, their officers and agents, and, also, upon, at least, such individuals and corporations as exercise public functions and wield power and authority under the [State].

It remains now to inquire what are the legal rights of colored persons in respect of the accommodations, privileges and facilities of public conveyances, inns and places of public amusement? *First,* as to public conveyances on land and water. [The] sum of the adjudged cases is that a railroad corporation is a governmental agency, created primarily for public purposes, and subject to be controlled for the public benefit. [Such] being the relations these corporations hold to the public, it would seem that the right of a colored person to use an improved public highway, upon the terms accorded to freemen of other races, is as fundamental [as] are any of the rights which my brethren concede to be so far fundamental as to be deemed the essence of civil [freedom]. *Second,* as to inns. [A] keeper of an inn is in the exercise of a quasi-public employment. [The] public nature of his employment forbids him from discriminating against any person asking admission as a guest on account of the race or color of that person. *Third.* As to places of public amusement. [Within] the meaning of the act of 1875, [they] are such as are established and maintained under direct license of the law. [The] local government granting the license represents [the colored race] as well as all other races within its jurisdiction. A license from the public to establish a place of public amusement, imports, in law, equality of right, at such places, among all the members of that public. [I] am of the opinion that [racial] discrimination practiced by corporations and individuals in the exercise of their public or quasi-public functions is a badge of servitude the imposition of which Congress may prevent under its power, by appropriate legislation, to enforce the [13th Amendment].

[The] assumption that [the 14th] amendment consists wholly of prohibitions upon State laws and State proceedings in hostility to its provisions, is unauthorized by its language. The first clause of the first section [is] of a distinctly affirmative character. [The] citizenship thus acquired by [the colored] race [may] be protected, not alone by the [judiciary], but by congressional legislation of a primary, direct character; this, because the power of Congress is not restricted to the enforcement of prohibitions upon State laws or State action. It is, in terms distinct and positive, to enforce "the *provisions of this article*" [i.e., the amendment]—*all* of the provisions—affirmative and prohibitive. But what was secured to colored citizens of the United States—as between them and their respective States—by the national grant to them of State citizenship? With what rights, privileges, or immunities did this grant invest them? There is one, if there be no other—exemption from race discrimination in respect of any civil right belonging to citizens of the white race in the same State.

[But] if it were conceded that the power of Congress could not be brought into activity until the rights specified in the act of 1875 had been abridged or denied by some State law or State action, I maintain that the decision of the court is erroneous. [In] every material sense applicable to the practical enforcement of the 14th Amendment, railroad corporations, keepers of inns, and managers of places of public amusement are agents or instrumentalities of the State, because they are charged with duties to the public, and are amenable, in respect of their duties and functions, to governmental regulation. [I] agree that if one citizen chooses not to hold social intercourse with another, he is not and cannot be made amenable to the [law]. [But the] rights which Congress [endeavored] to secure and protect [here] are legal, not social rights. [Today,] it is the colored race which is denied, by corporations and individuals wielding public authority, rights fundamental in their freedom and citizenship. At some future time, it may be that some other race will fall under the ban of race discrimination. If the constitutional amendments be enforced, according to the intent with which [they] were adopted, there cannot be, in this republic, any class of human beings in practical subjection to another class.

THE SCOPE AND LIMITS OF STATE ACTION AFTER THE CIVIL RIGHTS CASES

1. ***The policies underlying the state action requirement.*** The Civil Rights Cases invalidated Congress's regulation of private parties—railroads, innkeepers, theater operators and the like—for the purpose of preventing race discrimination. While the Framers of the Reconstruction Amendments envisioned Congress as the chief enforcer of civil rights, judicial enforcement of the Equal Protection Clause assumed much greater importance in later decades. Yet the same state action limitation that the Civil Rights Cases imposed upon Congress's exercise of powers under § 5 of the Fourteenth Amendment also applies to the federal courts when adjudicating individual causes of action brought directly under § 1 of the Fourteenth Amendment.

What purposes are served by such a requirement? The Civil Rights Cases mention two: federalism or the importance of respecting state prerogatives to govern their own citizens; and liberty, or the importance of a sphere of individual liberty to act free of constitutional norms. As to federalism, was Justice Bradley assuming that most states would in fact police against race discrimination by enacting common carrier laws and enforcing other tort and criminal laws? If states failed to enact such laws, would such an omission justify congressional enforcement? If so, against whom—private actors or only state officials? As to liberty, is it desirable to maintain a sphere of private behavior in which individuals are free from constitutional norms? Are there internal limits upon constitutional claims even if they do not independently violate constitutional rights to privacy or association?

2. ***"Public function" as a basis for state action.*** Can a private entity's performance of traditionally "public functions" make 14th Amendment restraints applicable? In **Marsh v. Alabama**, 326 U.S. 501 (1946), the Court held that a "company town" may not limit speech through restrictions that would violate the First Amendment (incorporated against the states through the Fourteenth Amendment) if imposed by a municipality. Chickasaw, Alabama, was owned by the Gulf Shipbuilding Corporation. Except for its private ownership, it had "all the characteristics of any other American town." Marsh, a Jehovah's Witness, was convicted under the state criminal trespass law because she distributed religious literature without permission. Justice BLACK's majority opinion held that a state may not "impose criminal punishment on a person who undertakes to distribute religious literature on the premises of a company-owned town contrary to the wishes of the town's management." He noted that an ordinary town could not constitutionally have prohibited her activities under the First Amendment. That a corporation owned title to the town could not justify impairing the public's interest "in the functioning of the community in such a manner that the channels of communication remain free. [Since its] facilities are built and operated primarily to benefit the public and since their operation is essentially a public function, it is subject to state regulation."

The Court later considered whether shopping centers, which were replacing downtown business areas throughout the nation, should be subjected to First Amendment constitutional restraints, just as the company town had been in Marsh. In Amalgamated Food Employees Union v. Logan Valley Plaza, Inc., 391 U.S. 308 (1968), Justice Marshall, writing for the Court, concluded that a shopping center was "clearly the functional equivalent to the business district of Chickasaw involved in Marsh." Four years later, in Lloyd Corp. v. Tanner, 407 U.S. 551 (1972), the majority tried to distinguish Logan Valley in permitting a shopping center to exclude anti-war leafleters. But in Hudgens v. NLRB, 424 U.S. 507 (1976), the Court made clear that Logan Valley was no longer the law and that shopping center owners were not engaged in "state action."

The public function test was relied on as an alternative ground in **Evans v. Newton**, 382 U.S. 296 (1966), which held invalid under the Equal Protection Clause the operation of a park in Macon, Georgia, for "whites only" pursuant to a trust established in Senator Bacon's 1911 will—even after the city trustee was replaced by private trustees. Justice Douglas's majority opinion explained: "The service rendered even by a private park of this character is municipal in nature. [Golf clubs,] social centers, luncheon clubs, schools [and] other like organizations in the private sector are often racially oriented. A park, on the other hand, is more like a fire department or police department that traditionally serves the community. Mass recreation through the use of parks is plainly in the public domain; and state courts that aid private parties to perform that public function on a segregated basis implicate the State in conduct proscribed by the 14th Amendment. Like the streets of the company town in [Marsh], the predominant character and purpose of this park are municipal."

The White Primary Cases applied the public function concept in holding that Democratic Party groups in Southern one-party states could not exclude African-Americans from candidate selection processes prior to general elections, despite repeated efforts to eliminate all formal indicia of state involvement from such primary schemes. Nixon v. Herndon, 273 U.S. 536 (1927), held unconstitutional under the 14th Amendment a Texas law that, on its face, excluded blacks from Democratic primaries. When Texas responded by granting to party executive committees the power to prescribe membership qualifications, the resulting racial exclusion was again found unconstitutional under the 14th Amendment, in Nixon v. Condon, 286 U.S. 73 (1932), on the ground that the law had made the committee an agent of the state. This time, Texas enacted no new law. Instead, a third round of racial exclusions stemmed from action of the state party convention. That exclusion survived constitutional attack in Grovey v. Townsend, 295 U.S. 45 (1935), which found the convention an organ of a voluntary, private group, not of the state.

But Grovey v. Townsend was overruled nine years later, in **Smith v. Allwright**, 321 U.S. 649 (1944), which found that the white primary established by the state convention violated the 15th Amendment. The Smith Court pointed to an intervening decision, United States v. Classic, 313 U.S. 299 (1941), which had held that Art. I, § 4, authorized congressional control of primaries "where the primary is by law made part of the election machinery." Classic was relevant in Smith, according to Justice REED's majority opinion, "because the recognition of the place of the primary in the electoral scheme makes clear that state delegation to a party of the power to fix the qualifications of primary elections is delegation of a state function that may make the party's action the action of the State. [We] think that this statutory system for the selection of party nominees for inclusion on the general election ballot makes the party which is required to follow these legislative directions an agency of the State in so far as it determines the participants in a primary election."

Terry v. Adams, 345 U.S. 461 (1953), found the 15th Amendment violated by the exclusion of African-American voters from the "pre-primary" elections of the Jaybird Democratic Association, a "voluntary club" of white Democrats. Candidates who won the Jaybird elections typically ran unopposed in the Democratic primaries. There was no opinion on which a majority could agree, but only Justice Minton dissented from the result. Justice BLACK, joined by Justices Douglas and Burton, found that, although the Amendment "excludes social or business clubs," it barred race discrimination in "any election" in which public officials are chosen. Justice FRANKFURTER stated that the "vital requirement" was "State responsibility—that somewhere, somehow, to some extent, there be an infusion by conduct by officials [into] any scheme" denying the franchise because of race, but found here that, here, county election officials were in effect "participants in the scheme." Justice CLARK, joined by Chief Justice Vinson and Justices Reed and Jackson, concurred on the ground that the Jaybirds operated "as an auxiliary of the local Party" and were therefore subject to the principles of Smith v. Allwright. He emphasized the Jaybirds' "decisive power" in the county's electoral process and concluded that "when a state structures its electoral apparatus in a form which devolves upon a political organization the uncontested choice of public officials, that organization itself, in whatever disguise, takes on those attributes of government which draw the Constitution's safeguards into play."

The "public function" analysis launched by Marsh was later cabined in a significant way. In Jackson v. Metropolitan Edison Co., 419 U.S. 345 (1974), Justice Rehnquist's majority opinion noted that the Court had "found state action present in the exercise by a private entity of powers traditionally *exclusively* reserved to the State." He found no state action in a public utility's cutoff of service, because "the supplying of utility service is not traditionally the exclusive prerogative of the State." Justice Marshall's dissent argued that utility service was a public function since "the State invariably either provides the service itself or permits private companies to act as state surrogates in providing it." For the full opinions, see p. 870 below. The Court likewise emphasized the "carefully confined bounds" of the public function test in Flagg Bros., Inc. v. Brooks, 436 U.S. 149 (1978), holding that a warehouseman's proposed sale of goods entrusted to him for storage to satisfy a warehousemen's lien under the Uniform Commercial Code did not constitute state action. Writing again for the Court, Justice Rehnquist rejected the plaintiff's claim that the State had delegated to the warehouseman "a power 'traditionally exclusively reserved to the State' ": "[Creditors] and debtors have had available to them historically a far wider number of choices than has one who would be an elected public official, or a member of Jehovah's Witnesses who wished to distribute literature in Chickasaw." Justice Stevens's dissent, joined by Justices White and Marshall disagreed: "Whether termed 'traditional,' 'exclusive,' or 'significant,' the state power to order binding, nonconsensual resolution of a conflict between debtor and creditor is exactly the sort of power with which [due process] is concerned." Some scholars have speculated that the public function doctrine could be rejuvenated to enable judicial supervision of social media platforms. How viable is this option in the light of existing doctrine? See Jonathan Peters, "The 'Sovereigns of Cyberspace' and State Action: The

First Amendment's Application—or Lack Thereof—to Third-Party Platforms," 32 Berkeley Tech. L.J. 989 (2017).

3. ***State enforcement of private agreements.*** Contrast with the public function analysis the reasoning in the decision that follows, finding state action in the enforcement of a racially restrictive covenant entered into by private property owners. The decision arose from challenges to judicial enforcement in Missouri and Michigan of agreements among property owners to exclude persons of designated races. In the Missouri case, for example, a 1911 agreement signed by 30 out of 39 property owners in the area restricted occupancy for 50 years to persons of "the Caucasian race" and excluded "people of the Negro or Mongolian race." The petitioners in these cases were African-Americans who had purchased houses from white owners despite the racially restrictive covenants. Respondents, owners of other properties subject to the terms of the covenants, sued to enjoin the black purchasers from occupying the property. The state courts granted the relief. The Supreme Court reversed:

Shelley v. Kraemer

334 U.S. 1, 68 S. Ct. 836, 92 L. Ed. 1161 (1948).

[Petitioners, African-Americans, attempted to purchase property subject to racially restrictive covenants. Respondents sought to enjoin their use of the property, and petitioners argued that the covenants were unenforceable under the Equal Protection Clause.]

■ CHIEF JUSTICE VINSON delivered the opinion of the [Court].

Whether the equal protection clause [inhibits] judicial enforcement by state courts of restrictive [real estate] covenants based on race or color is a question which this Court has not heretofore been called upon to consider. [It] cannot be doubted that among the civil rights intended to be protected from discriminatory state action by the 14th Amendment are the rights to acquire, enjoy, own and dispose of property. Equality in the enjoyment of property rights was regarded by the framers of that Amendment as an essential precondition to the realization of other basic civil rights and liberties which the Amendment was intended to guarantee. [Restrictions] on the right of occupancy of the sort sought to be created by the private agreements in these cases could not be squared with the requirements of the 14th Amendment if imposed by state statute or local ordinance. [But] the present cases [do] not involve action by state legislatures or city councils. Here the particular patterns of discrimination and the areas in which the restrictions are to operate, are determined, in the first instance, by the terms of agreements among private individuals. Participation of the State consists in the enforcement of the restrictions so defined. The crucial issue [is] whether this distinction removes these cases from [the 14th Amendment].

Since [the] Civil Rights Cases, the principle has become firmly [established] that the action inhibited by the first section of the 14th Amendment is only such action as may fairly be said to be that of the States. That Amendment erects no shield against merely private conduct, however discriminatory or wrongful. We conclude, therefore, that the restrictive agreements standing alone cannot be regarded as violative of any rights guaranteed to petitioners by the 14th Amendment. So long as the purposes of those agreements are effectuated by voluntary adherence to their terms, it would appear clear that there has been no action by the State and the provisions of the Amendment have not been violated. But here there was more. These are cases in which the purposes of the agreements were secured only by judicial enforcement by state courts of the restrictive terms of the agreements. The respondents urge that judicial enforcement of private agreements does not amount to state action; or, in any event, the participation of the State is so attenuated in character as not to amount to state action within the meaning of the 14th Amendment.

[That] the action of state courts and judicial officers in their official capacities is to be regarded as action of the State within the meaning of the 14th Amendment, is a proposition which has long been established by decisions of this Court. [We] have no doubt that there has been state action in these cases in the full and complete sense of the phrase. The undisputed facts disclose that petitioners were willing purchasers of properties upon which they desired to establish homes. The owners of the properties were willing sellers; and contracts of sale were accordingly consummated. It is clear that but for the active intervention of the state courts, supported by the full panoply of state power, petitioners would have been free to occupy the properties in question without restraint. These are not cases, as has been suggested, in which the States have merely abstained from action, leaving private individuals free to impose such discriminations as they see fit. Rather, these are cases in which the States have made available to such individuals the full coercive power of government to deny to petitioners, on the grounds of race or color, the enjoyment of property rights in premises which petitioners are willing and financially able to acquire and which the grantors are willing to sell. The difference between judicial enforcement and non-enforcement of the restrictive covenants is the difference to petitioners between being denied rights of property available to other members of the community and being accorded full enjoyment of those rights on an equal footing.

The enforcement of the restrictive agreements by the state courts in these cases was directed pursuant to the common-law policy of the States as formulated by those courts in earlier decisions. [The] judicial action in each case bears the clear and unmistakable imprimatur of the State. We have noted that previous decisions of this Court have established the proposition that judicial action is not immunized from the operation of the 14th Amendment simply because it is taken pursuant to the state's common-law policy. Nor is the Amendment ineffective simply because the particular pattern of discrimination, which the State has enforced, was defined initially by the terms of a private agreement. State action, as that phrase is understood for the purposes of the 14th Amendment, refers to exertions of state power in all forms. And when the effect of that action is to deny rights subject to the protection of the 14th Amendment, it is the obligation of this Court to enforce the constitutional commands.

We hold that in granting judicial enforcement of the restrictive agreements in these cases, the States have denied petitioners the equal protection of the laws and that, therefore, the action of the state courts cannot stand. [That] discrimination has occurred in these cases is [clear]. Respondents urge, however, that since the state courts stand ready to enforce restrictive covenants excluding white [persons], enforcement of covenants excluding colored persons may not be deemed a denial of equal protection of the laws to the colored persons who are thereby affected. This contention does not bear scrutiny. The parties have directed our attention to no case in which a court, state or federal, has been called upon to enforce a covenant excluding members of the white majority from ownership or occupancy of real property on grounds of race or color. But there are more fundamental considerations. The rights created by the first section of the 14th Amendment are, by its terms, guaranteed to the individual. The rights established are personal rights. It is, therefore, no answer to these petitioners to say that the courts may also be induced to deny white persons rights of ownership and occupancy on grounds of race or color. Equal protection of the laws is not achieved through indiscriminate imposition of [inequalities]. Reversed.[1]

STATE ACTION AFTER SHELLEY V. KRAEMER

1. ***The scope of Shelley.*** Does Shelley bar all enforcement of private racially restrictive actions? Five years later, the Court extended Shelley to block damages suits to enforce racially restrictive covenants in Barrows v. Jackson, 346 U.S. 249 (1953). But in **Evans v. Abney**, 396 U.S. 435 (1970), the Court's 5–2 decision upholding a reverter demonstrated that Shelley had not barred all state involvement in enforcing racial restrictions on private property. Senator Bacon's will had conveyed property in trust to Macon, Georgia, for use as a park "for white people only." After Evans v. Newton had held that the park could not be operated on a racially discriminatory basis, the state court ruled that "Senator Bacon's intention to provide a park for whites only had become impossible to fulfill and that accordingly the trust had failed and the parkland and other trust property had reverted by operation of Georgia law to the heirs of the Senator." The Court, in a majority opinion by Justice BLACK, held that this ruling did not constitute state discrimination under the Fourteenth Amendment: "[A]ny harshness that may have resulted from the State court's decision can be attributed solely to its intention to effectuate as nearly as possible the explicit terms of Senator Bacon's will." He found the case "easily distinguishable from [Shelley], where we held unconstitutional state judicial action which had affirmatively enforced a private scheme of discrimination against Negroes. Here the effect of the Georgia decision eliminated all discrimination against Negroes in the park by eliminating the park itself, and the termination of the park was a loss shared equally by the white and Negro citizens of Macon."

After Evans v. Abney, may a court enforce a racially restrictive testamentary provision? In **Pennsylvania v. Board of Directors of Trusts**, 353 U.S. 230 (1957), the Court found state action in the denial of admission of nonwhite students to Girard College, established by Stephen Girard's 1831 will setting up a trust for a school solely for "poor white male

[1] Justices Reed, Jackson and Rutledge did not participate in the case. In a companion case to Shelley, Hurd v. Hodge, 334 U.S. 24 (1948), the Court held that the courts in the District of Columbia could not enforce restrictive covenants even though the Fourteenth Amendment is not applicable to the federal government. Chief Justice Vinson stated that such action would deny "rights [protected] by the Civil Rights Act"; moreover, it would be contrary to the public policy of the United States to allow a federal court to enforce an agreement constitutionally unenforceable in state courts.

orphans." Because the will had named the City of Philadelphia as trustee and the board of trustees was composed of city officials and persons named by local courts, the Court found that "[t]he Board which operates Girard College is an agency of the State" and its refusal to admit petitioners "discrimination by the State." After that ruling, the state court substituted private trustees to carry out Girard's will but a federal court of appeals decision held that this substitution was unconstitutional state action. Does Evans v. Abney dictate the opposite result? Or are the cases distinguishable?

2. ***Examples in state law.*** Some states have taken a broader approach to determining when a state's enforcement of a racially restrictive provision would be invalid under state constitutional provisions barring race discrimination. Consider, for instance, a trust established to benefit a local medical center if it promised to use the funds only for white patients, or, if the medical center refused the funds because of that restriction, to benefit a local state university (with no racial limit). Some states have held that the university cannot legally take the money in such cases, because doing so would use the machinery of the state, in the form of judicial decisions and property recognition, to perpetuate a racial distinction. Instead, because the courts will not enforce the racial provision, the medical center is free to use the money without the racial limitation. See Home for Incurables of Baltimore City v. Univ. of Md. Med. Sys. Corp., 797 A.2d 746 (Md. 2002). Is this model better or worse than the current federal doctrine?

3. ***Significant state involvement in racially discriminatory action.*** How significant must the state involvement in racially discriminatory action be? In **Burton v. Wilmington Parking Authority**, 365 U.S. 715 (1961), the Court reversed a Delaware decision upholding the exclusion of an African-American customer from a private restaurant located in a public parking building under a provision of state law. Justice CLARK, writing for the Court, noted: "The parking building is owned and operated by the Wilmington Parking Authority, an agency of the State of Delaware, and the restaurant is the Authority's lessee. [The Supreme Court of Delaware] held that Eagle was acting in 'a purely private capacity' under its lease; that its action was not that of the Authority and was not, therefore, state action.

"[We conclude] that the exclusion of appellant [was] discriminatory state action. [The] land and building were publicly owned. As an entity, the building was dedicated to 'public uses' in performance of the Authority's 'essential governmental functions.' [It] cannot be doubted that the peculiar relationship of the restaurant to the parking facility in which it is located confers on each an incidental variety of mutual benefits. [Neither] can it be ignored, especially in view of Eagle's affirmative allegation that for it to serve Negroes would injure its business, that profits earned by discrimination not only contribute to, but are indispensable elements in, the financial success of a governmental agency. [The] benefits mutually conferred, together with the obvious fact that the restaurant is operated as an integral part of a public building devoted to a public parking service, indicates that degree of state participation and involvement in discriminatory action which it was the design of the 14th Amendment to condemn. [By] its inaction, the Authority, and through it the State, has not only made itself a party to the refusal of service, but has elected to place its power, property and prestige behind the admitted discrimination. [When] a State leases public property in the manner and for the purpose shown to have been the case here, the proscriptions of the 14th Amendment must be complied with by the lessee as certainly as though they were binding covenants written into the agreement [itself]."

Justice STEWART concurred separately, rejecting the majority's "interdependence" theory in favor of an alternative theory emphasizing the Delaware Supreme Court's creation of a rule of law permitting race to be equated with "offensiveness." He observed that, although the state law allowed restaurants to exclude patrons whose presence would be "offensive" to most other customers, the state court did not inquire whether the plaintiff would actually have been offensive, but simply assumed that he was due to his race. "The [state court] has thus construed this legislative enactment as authorizing discriminatory classification based exclusively on color. Such a law seems to me clearly violative of the [14th Amendment]." Justices Harlan and Frankfurter dissented, urging that the case be sent back to the state court to see whether Justice Stewart's reading was correct.

What is the difference between the majority's approach in Burton and Justice Stewart's concurrence? Does the majority focus on state actors while Justice Stewart focuses on state action? Does the Burton majority retreat from the broadest implications of Shelley, by insisting that the state must be involved "to some significant extent" to bring private conduct under the Fourteenth Amendment? Under Burton, it is not enough to find merely *some* nexus between the state and the private discriminator. Does Burton provide adequate guidance for evaluating the "significance" of state involvement? Note the concurrence's emphasis instead on the state rule of law involved. Would Justice Stewart have decided differently if there had been no definitive state court ruling on the state law right of businesses to exclude customers on the basis of race? Which approach is more easily administered?

4. ***State "encouragement" of private discrimination.*** In **Reitman v. Mulkey**, 387 U.S. 369 (1967), the Court found state action in a state's repeal of fair housing laws barring racial discrimination in the sale or rental of private dwellings. California enacted fair housing laws in 1957 and 1963. In 1964, California voters, acting through the initiative process, adopted Proposition 14, amending the state constitution to prohibit the state from denying "the right of any person [to] decline to sell, lease or rent [real property] to such person or persons as he, in his absolute discretion, chooses." The Mulkeys sued in a state court on the basis of previously enacted fair housing laws, claiming that Reitman had refused to rent them an apartment because of their race. They claimed that Proposition 14, which in effect repealed the antidiscrimination laws, violated equal protection, and they prevailed in the California Supreme Court. The state court found the case "undeniably analogous" to the "authorizing" of racial discrimination found by Justice Stewart's concurrence in Burton. The Court affirmed the state judgment.

Justice WHITE's majority opinion in the 5–4 decision acknowledged that mere repeal of an antidiscrimination law did not establish unconstitutional state action. But as the state court here had held, "the intent of [Proposition 14] was to authorize private racial discrimination in the housing market, to repeal the [fair housing laws], and to create a constitutional right to discriminate on racial grounds. [Moreover,] the court assessed the ultimate impact of [Proposition 14] in the California environment and concluded that [it] would encourage and significantly involve the State in private racial [discrimination]. Private discriminations in housing were now not only free from [fair housing laws] but they also enjoyed a far different status than was true before the passage of those [laws]. The right to discriminate [was] now embodied in the State's basic charter, immune from legislative, executive, or judicial regulation at any level of the state government. Those practicing racial discriminations need no longer rely solely on their personal choice. They could now invoke express constitutional [authority]."

Justice HARLAN's dissent, joined by Justices Black, Clark and Stewart, insisted: "[All] that has happened is that California has effected a pro tanto repeal of its prior statutes forbidding private discrimination. This runs no more afoul of the 14th Amendment than would have California's failure to pass any such antidiscrimination statutes in the first instance." Justice Harlan objected to the majority's emphasis on the notion that Proposition 14 "*encourages* private discrimination": "By focusing on 'encouragement' the Court, I fear, is forging a slippery and unfortunate criterion by which to measure the constitutionality of a statute simply permissive in purpose and effect, and inoffensive on its face. [Every] act of private discrimination is either forbidden by state law or permitted by it. [Under] this theory 'state action' in the form of laws that do nothing more than passively permit private discrimination could be said to tinge *all* private discrimination with the taint of unconstitutional state encouragement."

What is the reach of the "encouragement" theme of Reitman? Was Proposition 14 truly distinguishable from a mere repeal of an antidiscrimination law? Was there a significant difference here because California did not merely repeal antidiscrimination laws but incorporated that repeal into a constitutional provision? Why should that make a difference? Does Reitman ultimately rest on the notion that a state simply may not intentionally "authorize" racial discrimination? Is "authorization" distinct from failure to prohibit what the state has power to prohibit? Is the "authorization" rationale tantamount to imposing an affirmative duty on the state to prevent private discrimination?

5. ***State involvement through licensing.*** Does governmental licensing of a private actor constitute sufficient governmental involvement to warrant the application of constitutional restraints? In **Moose Lodge No. 107 v. Irvis**, 407 U.S. 163 (1972), the Court, by a vote of 6–3, rejected a claim that a private club's racial discrimination was unconstitutional because the club held a state liquor license. It found that, with one exception, the operation of the state liquor regulation scheme did "not sufficiently implicate the State in the discriminatory guest policies of Moose Lodge so as to make the latter 'State action.'"

Writing for the Court, Justice REHNQUIST, citing Shelley, conceded that "the impetus for the forbidden discrimination need not originate with the State if it is state action that enforces privately originated discrimination." But that did not mean "that discrimination by an otherwise private entity would be violative of [equal protection] if the private entity receives any sort of benefit or service at all from the state, or if it is subject to state regulation in any degree whatever. Since state-furnished services include such necessities of life as electricity, water, and police and fire protection, such a holding would utterly emasculate the distinction between private as distinguished from State conduct." To find unconstitutional state action in situations "where the impetus for the discrimination is private, the State must have 'significantly involved itself with invidious discriminations,' Reitman." He found here "nothing approaching the symbiotic relationship between lessor and lessee" in Burton. The lower court had emphasized that the liquor regulations were "pervasive." Justice Rehnquist responded: "However detailed this type of regulation may be in some particulars, it cannot be said to in any way foster or encourage racial discrimination." And that conclusion was not undercut by the fact that Pennsylvania limited the number of liquor licenses in each city, since that fell "far short of conferring upon club licensees a monopoly in the dispensing of liquor."

Justice DOUGLAS's dissent explained that, while he would not apply constitutional restrictions to private clubs simply because they had a state license of some kind, there were "special circumstances" warranting a state action finding here because a fraternal organization desiring to form a nondiscriminatory club would have to "purchase a license held by an existing club, which can exact a monopoly price for the transfer." Justice BRENNAN's dissent stressed the "pervasive regulatory schemes under which the State dictates and continually supervises virtually every detail of the operation of a licensee's business."

Might the plaintiff, Mr. Irvis, have employed an alternative litigation strategy to obtain relief similar to that obtained by Mr. Burton in the Wilmington parking authority case? Note that Burton arose from a decision by the highest state court, while Irvis was litigated in federal court. Might Mr. Irvis instead have sued the Pennsylvania Liquor Authority in state court contesting his exclusion on racial grounds as a violation of the implied conditions of a liquor license? If he had done so and lost, he might have appealed that state court ruling to the U.S. Supreme Court on the same theory Justice Stewart employed in his Burton concurrence—namely, that the state had adopted a racially discriminatory rule of law. Soon after the Irvis decision, Mr. Irvis in fact won his battle on the basis of state law. The Pennsylvania Supreme Court sustained an administrative ruling under the state public accommodations law ordering the Lodge to end its ban on black guests.

6. ***State action in light of changing societal circumstances.*** From its beginnings in the Civil Rights Cases, the state action requirement was fundamentally linked to redressing racial injustice. Much of the motivation for the state action decisions of the Warren and Burger Courts may likewise have been racial justice. For example, recall Evans v. Abney (p. 865 above). After the Warren Court's early desegregation decisions, many southern states attempted to preserve segregation by transferring public goods like parks and golf courses to private control, on the theory that the new private owners could continue perpetuating discriminatory policies even if the state could not. Had the Court declined to find state action in cases like Evans v. Abney, it effectively would have handed a blueprint to southern states showing how to preserve segregation for all time.

Beginning in the early 1970s, however, it became clear that resistance to formal integration had largely evaporated. A new generation of state action cases testing the limits of the civil rights era decisions began to arise. In the new cases, plaintiffs sought to obtain relief from private actions other than race discrimination. One such case arose from a federal civil rights action under 42 U.S.C. § 1983 against Metropolitan Edison Co.:

Jackson v. Metropolitan Edison Co.

419 U.S. 345, 95 S. Ct. 449, 42 L. Ed. 2d 477 (1974).

■ JUSTICE REHNQUIST delivered the opinion of the Court.

[In this case, the petitioner sought damages and injunctive relief against a private company regulated by the Pennsylvania Public Utilities Commission (PUC) for terminating electric service for alleged nonpayment without notice, hearing and an opportunity to pay any amounts found due. The petitioner claimed that this termination violated her right to procedural due process. The lower courts dismissed her complaint and the Court affirmed.]

[The] mere fact that a business is subject to state regulation does not by itself convert its action into that of the State for purposes of the 14th Amendment. [Moose Lodge.] Nor does the fact that the regulation is extensive and detailed, as in the case of most public utilities, do so. It may well be that acts of a heavily regulated utility with at least something of a governmentally protected monopoly will more readily be found to be "state" acts than will the acts of an entity lacking these characteristics. But the inquiry must be whether there is a sufficiently close nexus between the State and the challenged action of the regulated entity so that the action of the latter may be fairly treated as that of the State itself.

Petitioner advances a series of contentions which, in her view, lead to the conclusion that this case should fall on the Burton side of the line drawn in the Civil Rights Cases, rather than on the Moose Lodge side of that line. We find none of them persuasive. Petitioner first argues that "state action" is present because of the monopoly status allegedly conferred upon [Metropolitan]. As a factual matter, it may well be doubted that the State ever granted or guaranteed Metropolitan a monopoly.[1] But assuming that it had, this fact is not determinative in considering whether Metropolitan's termination of service to petitioner was "state action." [Although] certain monopoly aspects were presented in [Moose Lodge], we found that the lodge's action was not subject to the provisions of the 14th Amendment. In each of those cases, there was insufficient relationship between the challenged actions of the entities involved and their monopoly status. There is no indication of any greater connection here.

[We] also reject the notion that Metropolitan's termination is state action because the State "has specifically authorized and approved" the termination practice. [Metropolitan] filed with the [PUC] a general tariff—a provision of which states Metropolitan's right to terminate service for nonpayment. This provision has appeared in Metropolitan's previously filed tariffs for many years and has never been the subject of a hearing or other scrutiny by the [PUC]. Although the Commission did hold hearings on portions of Metropolitan's general tariff relating to a general rate increase, it never even considered the reinsertion of this provision in the newly filed general tariff. [The] nature of governmental regulation of private utilities is such that a utility may frequently be required by the state regulatory scheme to obtain approval for practices a business regulated in less detail would be free to institute without any approval from a regulatory body. Approval by a

---

1 [Such] public utility companies are natural monopolies created by the economic forces of high threshold capital requirements and virtually unlimited economy of scale. Regulation was superimposed on such natural monopolies as a substitute for competition and not to eliminate [it]. [Footnote by Justice Rehnquist.]

state utility commission of such a request from a regulated utility, where the Commission has not put its own weight on the side of the proposed practice by ordering it, does not transmute a practice initiated by the utility and approved by the Commission into "state action." At most, the Commission's failure to overturn this practice amounted to no more than a determination that [the] utility was authorized to employ such a practice if it so desired.

Respondent's exercise of the choice allowed by state law, where the initiative comes from it and not from the State, does not make its action in doing so "state action" for purposes of the 14th Amendment. We also find absent in the instant case the symbiotic relationship presented in [Burton]. All of petitioner's arguments taken together show no more than that Metropolitan was a heavily regulated private utility, enjoying at least a partial monopoly in the providing of electrical service within its territory, and that it elected to terminate service to petitioner in a manner which the [PUC] found permissible under state law. Under our decision this is not sufficient to connect the [State] with respondent's action so as to make the latter's conduct attributable to the State for purposes of the 14th [Amendment]. Affirmed.

■ JUSTICE MARSHALL, dissenting.[2]

[Our] state action cases have repeatedly relied on several factors clearly presented by this case: a state-sanctioned monopoly; an extensive pattern of cooperation between the "private" entity and the state; and a service uniquely public in nature. Today the Court takes a major step in repudiating this line of [authority]. When the State confers a monopoly on a group or organization, this Court has held that the organization assumes many of the obligations of the State. Even when the Court has not found state action based solely on the State's conferral of a monopoly, it has suggested that the monopoly factor weighs heavily in determining whether constitutional obligations can be imposed on formally private entities.

[The] majority distinguishes [prior] cases with a cryptic assertion that public utility companies are "natural monopolies." The theory behind the distinction appears to be that since the State's purpose in regulating a natural monopoly is not to aid the company but to prevent its charging monopoly prices, the State's involvement is somehow less significant for state action purposes. I cannot agree that so much should turn on so narrow a distinction. [The] difficulty inherent [in] economic analysis counsels against excusing natural monopolies from the reach of state action principles.

[The] suggestion that the State would have to "put its own weight on the side of the proposed practice by ordering it" seems to me to mark a sharp departure from our previous state action cases. From the Civil Rights Cases to Moose Lodge, we have consistently indicated that state authorization and approval of "private" conduct would support a finding of state action. [Moreover,] I question the wisdom of giving such short shrift to the extensive interaction between the company and the State, and focusing solely on the extent of state support for the particular activity under challenge. In cases where the State's only significant involvement is through financial support or limited regulation of the private entity, it may be well to inquire whether

[2] A separate dissent by Justice DOUGLAS argued that in the aggregate, Metropolitan's actions were "sufficiently intertwined with those of the State [to] warrant a holding [of] 'state action.'" Justice BRENNAN also submitted a dissent.

the State's involvement suggests state approval of the objectionable conduct. But where the State has so thoroughly insinuated itself into the operations of the enterprise, it should not be fatal if the State has not affirmatively sanctioned the particular practice in question.

[What] is perhaps most troubling about the Court's opinion is that it would appear to apply to a broad range of claimed constitutional violations by the company. The Court has not adopted the notion [that] different standards should apply to state action analysis when different constitutional claims are presented. Thus, the majority's analysis would seemingly apply as well to a company that refused to extend service to Negroes, welfare recipients, or any other group that the company preferred, for its own reasons, not to serve. I cannot believe that this Court would hold that the State's involvement with the utility company was not sufficient to impose upon the company an obligation to meet the constitutional mandate of nondiscrimination. Yet nothing in the analysis of the majority opinion suggests otherwise.

THE STATE ACTION DOCTRINE AFTER MOOSE LODGE AND JACKSON

1. ***The insufficiency of state acquiescence.*** In **Flagg Bros., Inc. v. Brooks**, 436 U.S. 149 (1978), the Court held that a warehouseman's sale of bailed goods to satisfy a warehouseman's lien under the Uniform Commercial Code (UCC) was not state action. Justice REHNQUIST's majority opinion rejected the claim that the warehouseman's proposed sale was "properly attributable to the State because the State has authorized and encouraged it in enacting [the UCC]. [This] Court [has] never held that a State's mere acquiescence in a private action converts that action into that of the State. The Court rejected a similar argument in [Jackson]. The clearest demonstration of this distinction appears in [Moose Lodge]. These cases clearly rejected the notion that our prior cases permitted the imposition of 14th Amendment restraints on private action by the simple device of characterizing the State's inaction as 'authorization' or 'encouragement.'

"It is quite immaterial that the State has embodied its decision not to act in statutory form. If New York had no commercial statutes at all, its courts would still be faced with the decision whether to prohibit or permit the sort of sale threatened here the first time an aggrieved bailor came before them for relief. A judicial decision to deny relief would be no less an 'authorization' or 'encouragement' of that sale than the legislature's decision embodied in this statute. [If] the mere denial of judicial relief is considered sufficient encouragement to make the State responsible for those private acts, all private deprivations of property would be converted into public acts whenever the State, for whatever reason, denies relief sought by the putative property owner. [New York] is in no way responsible for [the warehouseman's] decision, a decision which the [state] permits but does not compel, to threaten to sell these respondents' belongings."

Justice STEVENS's dissent, joined by Justices White and Marshall, criticized the "permission"-"compulsion" distinction: "Under this approach a State could enact laws authorizing private citizens to use self-help in countless situations without any possibility of federal challenge. A state statute could authorize the warehouseman to retain all proceeds of the lien sale, even if they far exceeded the amount of the alleged debt; it could authorize finance companies to enter private homes to repossess merchandise; or indeed, it could authorize 'any person with sufficient physical power' to acquire and sell the property of his weaker neighbor. An attempt to challenge the validity of any such outrageous statute would be defeated by the reasoning the Court uses today: The Court's rationale would characterize action pursuant to such a statute as purely private action, which the State permits but does not compel."

2. ***The insufficiency of state regulation or subsidies.*** In **Blum v. Yaretsky**, 457 U.S. 991 (1982), the Court held that certain privately owned nursing homes receiving reimbursements from the state for caring for Medicaid patients were not state actors for purposes of a claim by a class of Medicaid patients that their procedural due process rights had been violated when they were transferred (by decisions of the physicians and administrators in the nursing homes) from "skilled nursing facilities" to less expensive "health related facilities." The transfer decisions resulted in lower Medicaid benefits for the patients. In turning down the claim that the transfer decision triggered the 14th Amendment's procedural due process requirements, Justice REHNQUIST's majority opinion held that the decisions turned "on medical judgments made by private parties according to professional standards that are not established by the State." The mere fact of extensive state regulation of the nursing homes did not trigger 14th Amendment guarantees. Citing Jackson, Justice Rehnquist stated that "constitutional standards are invoked only when it can be said that the State is *responsible* for the specific conduct of which the plaintiff complains"; here, by contrast, "the complaining party seeks to hold the State liable for the actions of private parties." He added that a state "normally can be held responsible for a private decision only when it has exercised a coercive power or has provided such significant encouragement, either overt or covert, that the choice must in law be deemed to be that of the State. Mere approval of or acquiescence in the initiatives of a private party is not sufficient to justify holding the State responsible." Nor was the Burton standard satisfied here simply because the State subsidized the operating and capital costs of the facilities, licensed them, and paid the medical expenses of more than 90% of the patients: "[Privately] owned enterprises providing services that the State would not necessarily provide, even though they are extensively regulated, do not fall within the ambit of Burton." Justice BRENNAN dissented, joined by Justice Marshall; he argued that the nursing home's operations were so closely tied to state fiscal interests and state regulations that they ought to be considered interdependent under the Burton standard.

In **Rendell-Baker v. Kohn**, 457 U.S. 830 (1982), the majority, closely tracking Justice Rehnquist's approach in Blum, held that "a private school, whose income is derived primarily from public sources and which is regulated by public authorities," could not be considered as engaging in state action when it discharged certain employees. The employees had brought a federal civil rights action claiming that school officials, in firing them from the staff of a small private school for "maladjusted" students, had violated their constitutional rights to free speech and procedural due process. After examining all of the alleged indicia of state action, Chief Justice BURGER's majority opinion concluded that the school's action did not fall within the 14th Amendment. He noted that, even though public funds accounted for almost all of the school's operating budget, the school was "not fundamentally different from many private corporations whose business depends primarily on contracts [with] the government. Acts of such private contractors do not become acts of the government by reason of their significant or even total engagement in performing public contracts." Justices Marshall and Brennan dissented in Rendell-Baker as they had in Blum.

3. ***The insufficiency of state inaction.*** In **DeShaney v. Winnebago County Social Services Department**, 489 U.S. 189 (1989), the Court, by a vote of 6–3, found that a State's *failure* to act to protect a boy from a violent father did not trigger Fourteenth Amendment protections. Petitioner Joshua DeShaney was a boy who was beaten and permanently injured by his father, with whom he lived. When he was one year old, a Wyoming court granted his parents a divorce and awarded custody to his father. Soon after, the father moved to Winnebago County, Wisconsin. Two years later, county social workers received recurrent reports that the father was physically abusing Joshua. The caseworkers noted each of these reports as well as the boy's suspicious injuries, but took no action to remove him from his father's custody. When Joshua was four years old, his father beat him so severely that he suffered permanent brain injuries that left him profoundly retarded and confined to an institution for life. (The father was later convicted of child abuse.) This action was brought by Joshua and his mother claiming that the *State* had deprived him of his liberty in violation of due process.

Chief Justice REHNQUIST's majority opinion rejected that claim: "[Nothing] in the language of the Due Process Clause itself requires the State to protect the life, liberty, and property of its citizens against invasion by private actors. The Clause is phrased as a limitation on the State's power to act, not as a guarantee of certain minimal levels of safety and security. [Its] language cannot fairly be extended to impose an affirmative obligation on the State to ensure that those interests do not come to harm through other means. [Its] purpose was to protect the people from the State, not to ensure that the State [protect] them from each other.

"[Petitioners] contend, however, that even if [due process] imposes no affirmative obligation on the State to provide [adequate] protective services, such a duty may arise out of certain 'special relationships' created or assumed by the State with respect to particular individuals. [They] argue that such a 'special relationship' existed here because the State knew that Joshua faced a special danger of abuse [and] specifically proclaimed, by word and by deed, its intention to protect him against that danger. [Accordingly,] the State acquired an affirmative 'duty,' enforceable through [due process], to do so in a reasonably competent fashion. We reject this argument. It is true that in certain limited circumstances the Constitution imposes upon the State affirmative duties of care and protection with respect to particular individuals. [But such cases] stand only for the proposition that when the State takes a person into its custody and holds him there against his will, the Constitution imposes upon it a corresponding duty to assume some responsibility for his safety and general well-being. [The] affirmative duty to protect arises not from the State's knowledge of the individual's predicament or from its expressions of intent to help him, but from the limitation which it has imposed on his freedom to act on his own behalf.

"Judges and lawyers, like other humans, are moved by natural sympathy in a case like this to find a way for Joshua and his mother to receive adequate compensation for the grievous harm inflicted upon them. But before yielding to that impulse, it is well to remember once again that the harm was inflicted not by [the State], but by Joshua's father. The most that can be said of the state functionaries in this case is that they stood by and did nothing when suspicious circumstances dictated a more active role for them."

Justice BRENNAN, joined by Justices Marshall and Blackmun, dissented: "It may well be [that due process] creates no general right to basic governmental services. That, however, is not the question presented here. [I] would focus first on the action that Wisconsin *has* taken with respect to Joshua and children like him, rather than on the actions that the State failed to take. [Through] its child-protection program, the State actively intervened in Joshua's life and, by virtue of this intervention, acquired ever more certain knowledge that Joshua was in grave danger. [Inaction] can be every bit as abusive of power as action, [and] oppression can result when a State undertakes a vital duty and then ignores it." Justice BLACKMUN's separate dissent insisted that the facts here involved "not mere passivity, but active state intervention in the life of [Joshua]—intervention that triggered a fundamental duty to aid the boy once the State learned of the severe danger to which he was exposed. The Court fails to recognize this duty because it attempts to draw a sharp and rigid line between action and inaction. But such formalistic reasoning has no place in the interpretation of the broad and stirring Clauses of the 14th Amendment." In a passage sometimes considered emblematic of Justice Blackmun's jurisprudence, he ended: "Poor Joshua! [It] is a sad commentary upon American life, and constitutional principles, [that he] now is assigned to live out the remainder of his life profoundly retarded."

4. ***Decisions finding state action to be present.*** The set of cases including Moose Lodge, Jackson, Blum, Rendell-Baker and DeShaney declined to expand the state action doctrine into new areas, but it did not necessarily mark an unbroken trend; in several decisions during this period, a majority of the Court still found state action in cases involving claimed violations by private parties. Consider what theories of state action succeeded in the cases that follow.

In **Lugar v. Edmondson Oil Co.**, 457 U.S. 922 (1982), the Court found the state action requirement satisfied when a creditor, pursuant to a state law, attached the debtor's property in an ex parte proceeding, alleging that the debtor might dispose of the property to defeat creditors. The attachment writ was issued by a state clerk, and the writ was executed by the Sheriff. In a later hearing, a state judge dismissed the attachment. The debtor brought suit against the creditor under § 1983 for denial of due process. Justice WHITE's majority opinion stated: "The [central] question is whether, under the facts of this case, [the creditors], who are private parties, may be appropriately characterized as 'state actors.' [We] have consistently held that a private party's joint participation with state officials in the seizure of disputed property is sufficient to characterize that party as a 'state actor' for purposes of the 14th Amendment. [The lower court] erred in holding that in this context 'joint participation' required something more than invoking the aid of state officials to take advantage of state-created attachment procedures. [Whatever] may be true in other contexts, this is sufficient when the State has created a system whereby state officials will attach property on the ex parte application of one party to a private dispute." In finding Flagg

Bros. distinguishable, Justice White relied in part on the fact that the creditor's remedy involved in Flagg Bros. (a warehouseman's sale pursuant to a statutory warehouseman's lien) could be exercised without the intervention of a state official, and simply pursuant to state procedures. Here, by contrast, the issuance and execution of the writ of attachment pursuant to the creditor's suit was undertaken by state officials.

Chief Justice BURGER dissented, insisting that the creditor "did no more than invoke a presumptively valid state prejudgment attachment procedure available to all. [This] case is no different from the situation in which a private party commences a lawsuit and secures injunctive relief which, even if temporary, may cause significant injury to the defendant. Invoking a judicial process, of course, implicates the State and its officers but does not transform essentially private conduct into actions of the State." Justice POWELL also dissented, joined by Justices Rehnquist and O'Connor, stating: "[This] decision is as unprecedented as it is unjust. [Our] cases do not establish that a private party's mere invocation of state legal procedures constitutes 'joint participation.' "

Relying on the analytical approach of Lugar, the Court in **Edmonson v. Leesville Concrete Co.**, 500 U.S. 614 (1991), held that use by a private litigant in a civil proceeding of peremptory challenges to exclude jurors on the basis of race constituted state action for Fourteenth Amendment equal protection purposes. Justice KENNEDY's opinion for the Court found that peremptory challenges in civil litigation were the creatures of "statutory authorization" and that very idea of a peremptory challenge has "no significance outside a court of law." Relying on the "overt, significant participation of the government" in both the peremptory challenge system and civil litigation generally; on the pervasive statutory regulation of the jury system; and on the active involvement of the judge in voir dire examination of jurors and in administering the system, he concluded: "The peremptory challenge is used in selecting an entity that is a quintessential governmental body, having no attributes of a private actor. [If] the government confers on a private body the power to choose the government's employees or officials, the private body will be bound by the constitutional mandate of race-neutrality. [Finally,] we note that the injury caused by the discrimination is made more severe because the government permits it to occur within the courthouse itself. [To] permit racial exclusion in this official forum compounds the racial insult inherent in judging a citizen by the color of his or her skin."

Justice O'CONNOR, joined by Chief Justice Rehnquist and Justice Scalia, dissented, maintaining that, in view of Jackson and Blum, it was necessary to show that the government was involved in the specific decision challenged, a showing not made here. She emphasized that "[i]t is the nature of a peremptory that its exercise is left wholly within the discretion of the litigant. [T]he peremptory is, by design, an enclave of private action in a government-managed proceeding." Justice SCALIA's separate dissent, echoing earlier criticisms of Shelley and Burton, chastised the majority for distorting state action doctrine where race was at issue: "To overhaul the doctrine of state action in this fashion—what a magnificent demonstration of this institution's hostility to race-based judgments, even by private actors! The price of the demonstration is, alas, high, and much of it will be paid by the minority litigants who use our courts."

And in **Brentwood Academy v. Tennessee Secondary School Athletic Ass'n**, 531 U.S. 288 (2001), the Court held a statewide interscholastic athletics association comprised of public and private schools to be a state actor because of "public entwinement" in its management and control, notwithstanding the Association's nominally private status under state law. 84% of the Association's member schools were public schools, which relied on the Association to adopt and enforce rules for interscholastic athletic competition. Justice SOUTER wrote for the Court: "The nominally private character of the Association is overborne by the pervasive entwinement of public institutions and public officials in its composition and workings. [To] the extent of 84% of its membership, the Association is an organization of public schools represented by their officials acting in their official capacity to provide an integral element of secondary public schooling. There would be no recognizable Association, legal or tangible, without the public school officials, who do not merely control but overwhelmingly perform all but the purely ministerial acts by which the Association exists and functions in practical terms." The Court also noted that Association employees were even "eligible for membership in the state employee retirement system," and that members of the state board of education were assigned ex officio roles in the Association.

In dissent, Justice Thomas, joined by Chief Justice Rehnquist and Justices Scalia and Kennedy, objected that the Court had never before "found state action based on mere 'entwinement.' [Until] today, we have found a private organization's acts to constitute state action only when the organization performed a public function; was created, coerced, or encouraged by the government; or acted in a symbiotic relationship with the government. [I] am not prepared to say that any private organization that permits public entities and public officials to participate acts as the State in anything or everything it does, and our state-action jurisprudence has never reached that far."

5. ***Other nations' approaches to the problem of state action.*** The United States has principally adopted what comparativists call a "vertical" approach to constitutional rights, regulating through constitutional law only conduct that involves some degree of state action (with some notable exceptions, like slavery). In contrast, other nations (like some U.S. states with respect to certain rights) have embraced various "horizontal" positions that apply constitutional rights provisions to relations between purely private individuals. In Ireland, courts have developed constitutional tort actions that accord a variety of individual rights, including freedom of association, freedom from sex discrimination, and the right to earn a livelihood. See Stephen Gardbaum, "The 'Horizontal Effect' of Constitutional Rights," 102 Mich. L. Rev. 387, 396–97 (2003). Similarly, the South African Constitution stipulates that "[a] provision of the Bill of Rights binds a natural or juristic person if, and to the extent that, it is applicable, taking account of the nature of the right and the nature of any duty imposed by the right," Section 8(2), and that "[n]o person may unfairly discriminate directly or indirectly against anyone on one or more grounds [that apply to the state]," Section 9(4). What concerns or values might animate the decision to adopt a horizontal approach to constitutional rights? For a sense of how some foreign judiciaries have grappled with the "horizontal effects" problem, see Mark Tushnet, "The Issue of State Action/Horizontal Effect in Comparative Constitutional Law," 1 Int'l J. Const. L. 79, 80–84 (2003) (detailing notable cases from Canada, South Africa, Germany and the Czech Republic).

SECTION 3. CONGRESSIONAL POWER TO REACH PRIVATE INTERFERENCE WITH CONSTITUTIONAL RIGHTS

To what extent may Congress provide criminal and civil sanctions against private interferences with constitutional rights? Recall that the modern counterparts of post-Civil War civil rights laws contain both criminal and civil provisions and that they fall into two groups: one reaches only action "under color" of law; the other reaches private conspiracies, without any state nexus requirement on the face of the statutes. On the criminal side, 18 U.S.C. § 242 covers action "under color" of law, while § 241 is directed at private conspiracies. On the civil side, 42 U.S.C. § 1983 provides for remedies against state action; § 1985(3) is the civil conspiracy provision. What persons are covered by these provisions? What rights are protected by them? What is the power of Congress to safeguard Fourteenth Amendment rights against interferences by seemingly private actors?

Due process and equal protection rights under the Fourteenth Amendment, as well as Fifteenth Amendment voting rights, apply only to *state* interferences. Under the Court's interpretations of the state action concept, some seemingly private behavior is reachable under the 14th and 15th Amendments. But may Congress go beyond the Court's view of "state action" and reach additional private actors? For example, may the private conspiracy provisions, §§ 241 and 1985(3), be applied to private actors who interfere with Fourteenth Amendment rights? That problem is discussed, but not resolved, in Guest, below. The other post-Civil War Amendment, the Thirteenth Amendment, is *not* limited to state action; it applies to private interferences generally. Jones v. Mayer, below, found that Congress, may, under § 2 of the Thirteenth Amendment, deal broadly with private acts of racial discrimination. The Thirteenth Amendment, then, provides an independent constitutional basis for congressional sanctions against private interferences with rights, but it may be seen as limited to addressing racial discrimination.

These materials emphasize federal *constitutional* rights. But note that the rights-protecting statutes considered in this section typically speak not only of rights under the Constitution but also of rights under the "laws of the United States." To the extent that Congress acts under powers applicable to private individuals—e.g., the commerce and spending powers—Congress may protect the statutory rights it has created against private interferences. Recall, e.g., the public accommodations provisions of the 1964 Civil Rights Act, enacted under the commerce power.

United States v. Guest

383 U.S. 745, 86 S. Ct. 1170, 16 L. Ed. 2d 239 (1966).

■ JUSTICE STEWART delivered the opinion of the Court.

The six defendants [were indicted] for criminal conspiracy in violation of 18 U.S.C. § 241. [The] indictment alleged a single conspiracy by the defendants to deprive Negro citizens of the free exercise and enjoyment of several specified rights secured by the Constitution and laws of the United

States. [The charge involved the killing of Lemuel Penn, a black reserve officer returning from active duty to Washington, D.C. in 1964. The Penn shooting was one of the widely publicized incidents of civil rights violence in the South in the 1960s. The federal indictment was brought after the defendants had been acquitted of murder in a Georgia court.] The defendants [successfully] moved to dismiss the indictment on the ground that it did not charge an offense under the laws of the United States. [We] reverse. [W]e deal here with issues of statutory construction, not with issues of constitutional [power].

II. The second numbered paragraph of the indictment alleged that the defendants conspired to injure, oppress, threaten, and intimidate Negro citizens of the United States in the free exercise and enjoyment of: "The right to the equal utilization, without discrimination upon the basis of race, of public facilities in the vicinity of Athens, Georgia, owned, operated or managed by or on behalf of the State of Georgia or any subdivision thereof." Correctly characterizing this paragraph as embracing rights protected by [equal protection, the] District Court held as a matter of statutory construction that § 241 does not encompass any 14th Amendment rights. [The] argument is therefore made that, since there exist no [equal protection] rights against wholly private action, the judgment [on] this branch of the case must be affirmed.

On its face, the argument is unexceptionable. [Equal protection] speaks to the State or to those acting under the color of its authority. [But here,] the indictment in fact contains an express allegation of state involvement sufficient at least to require the denial of a motion to dismiss. One of the means of accomplishing the object of the conspiracy, according to the indictment, was "By causing the arrest of Negroes by means of false reports that such Negroes had committed criminal acts." [The] allegation of the extent of official involvement [here] is not clear. [But it] is broad enough to cover a charge of active connivance by agents of the State in the making of the "false reports," or other conduct amounting to official discrimination clearly sufficient to constitute denial of rights protected by [equal protection]. Reversed and remanded.

▪ JUSTICE CLARK, with whom JUSTICE BLACK and JUSTICE FORTAS join, concurring.

I join the opinion of the Court in this case, but believe it worthwhile to comment on its Part II. [The] Court's interpretation of the indictment clearly avoids the question whether Congress, by appropriate legislation, has the power to punish private conspiracies that interfere with 14th Amendment rights. My Brother Brennan, however, [suggests] that the Court indicates sub silentio that Congress does not have the power to outlaw such conspiracies. Although the Court specifically rejects any such connotation, it is, I believe, both appropriate and necessary under the circumstances here to say that there now can be no doubt that the specific language of § 5 empowers the Congress to enact laws punishing all conspiracies—with or without state action—that interfere with 14th Amendment rights.

▪ JUSTICE BRENNAN, with whom CHIEF JUSTICE WARREN and JUSTICE DOUGLAS join, concurring in part and dissenting in part.

I agree with so much of Part II as construes § 241 to encompass conspiracies to injure, oppress, threaten or intimidate citizens in the free exercise or enjoyment of 14th Amendment rights. [I] do not agree with [that portion] of Part II which holds [that] a conspiracy to interfere with the exercise of the right to equal utilization of state facilities is not within the meaning of § 241 [unless] discriminatory conduct by state officers is involved in the alleged conspiracy. [I] believe that § 241 reaches such a private conspiracy, not because the 14th Amendment of its own force prohibits such a conspiracy, but because § 241, as an exercise of congressional power under § 5 of that Amendment, prohibits *all* conspiracies to interfere with the exercise of a "right [secured] by the Constitution." [For] me, the right to use state facilities without discrimination on the basis of race is, within the meaning of § 241, a right created by, arising under and dependent upon the 14th Amendment and hence is a right "secured" by that Amendment. [The] 14th Amendment commands the State to provide the members of all races with equal access to the public facilities it owns or manages, and the right of a citizen to use those facilities without discrimination on the basis of race is a basic corollary of this command. [Whatever] may be the status of the right to equal utilization of privately owned facilities, it must be emphasized that we are here concerned with the right to equal utilization of public facilities owned or operated by or on behalf of the [State].

[My] view as to the scope of § 241 requires that I reach the question of constitutional power—whether § 241 or legislation indubitably designed to punish entirely private conspiracies to interfere with the exercise of 14th Amendment rights constitutes a permissible exercise of the power granted to Congress by § 5 of the 14th Amendment. [A] majority of the members of the Court expresses the view today that § 5 empowers Congress to enact laws punishing *all* conspiracies to interfere with the exercise of 14th Amendment rights, whether or not state officers or others acting under the color of state law are implicated in the conspiracy. [§ 5] authorizes Congress to make laws that it concludes are reasonably necessary to protect a right created by and arising under that Amendment; and Congress is thus fully empowered to determine that punishment of private conspiracies interfering with the exercise of such a right is necessary to its full protection. [I] acknowledge that some of the decisions of this Court, most notably an aspect of the Civil Rights Cases, have declared that Congress' power under § 5 is confined to the adoption of "appropriate legislation for correcting the effects [of] prohibited State laws and State [acts]." I do not accept—and a majority of the Court today rejects—this interpretation of § 5. It reduces the legislative power to enforce the provisions of the Amendment to that of the judiciary; and it attributes a far too limited objective to the Amendment's sponsors.

Viewed in its proper perspective, [§ 5] appears as a positive grant of legislative power, authorizing Congress to exercise its discretion in fashioning remedies to achieve civil and political equality for all citizens. No one would deny that Congress could enact legislation directing state officials to provide Negroes with equal access to state schools, parks and other [state] facilities. [Nor] could it be denied that Congress has the power to punish state officers who [conspire] to threaten, harass and murder Negroes for attempting to use these facilities. And I can find no principle of federalism nor word of the Constitution that denies Congress power to determine that in order adequately to protect the right to equal utilization of state facilities, it is also appropriate to punish other individuals—not state officers themselves and not acting in concert with state officers—who engage in the same brutal conduct for the same misguided purpose.

CRIMINAL SANCTIONS FOR PRIVATE INTERFERENCE WITH FOURTEENTH AMENDMENT RIGHTS

1. ***Degree of state involvement.*** Justice Stewart's opinion in Guest sustained the portion of the indictment covering interference with Fourteenth Amendment rights, without reaching the question whether § 5 of the Fourteenth Amendment may reach purely private actors, by finding the allegation "broad enough to cover a charge of active connivance by agents of the State." Under this theory, "private" defendants may be reached if they are sufficiently involved with state officials. This approach thus relies on the Court's interpretations of § 1 of the Fourteenth Amendment (e.g., Burton), considered above in Section 2 of this chapter, without asserting any independent congressional power to expand the reach of the Fourteenth Amendment. But even this rationale of reaching private actors because of state "involvement" is not without difficulty. How much state involvement with the private actors must be shown? Does such a reading introduce vagueness, or lack of fair warning, into §§ 241 and 242?

United States v. Price, 383 U.S. 787 (1966), the companion case to Guest, arose out of the widely publicized murder of civil rights workers Schwerner, Chaney and Goodman, near Philadelphia, Mississippi, in 1964. The defendants were three local law enforcement officials and 15 private individuals, all allegedly involved in the killing. There were two indictments against the 18 defendants: one based on 18 U.S.C. § 242; the other on § 241. The alleged conspiracy involved releasing the victims from jail at night, intercepting and killing them, and disposing of their bodies—all with the purpose to "punish" the victims summarily and thus to deprive them of their 14th Amendment right "not to be summarily punished without [due process of law]." The District Court dismissed most of the charges.

Justice FORTAS wrote for the Court, reinstating the dismissed charges. The first indictment charged violations of 18 U.S.C. § 242, which required that the "person indicted has acted 'under color' of law." But that did not bar reaching private individuals: "Private persons, jointly engaged with state officials in the prohibited action, are acting 'under color' of law for purposes of the statute. It is enough that [the accused] is a willful participant in joint activity with the State or its agents." Justice Fortas particularly emphasized the Burton analysis. Here, he noted, "state officers participated in every phase of the alleged [joint adventure]: the release from jail, the interception, assault and murder. [Those] who took advantage of participation by state officers in accomplishment of the foul purpose alleged must suffer the consequences of that participation." The second indictment charged all 18 defendants with a conspiracy under 18 U.S.C. § 241, the "private conspiracy" section. [The] Court had no difficulty in holding that § 241 did apply, and that its reach in this context presented no constitutional difficulty because of the presence of state action: "[Section 241] extends to conspiracies otherwise within the scope of the section, participated in by officials alone or in collaboration with private persons."

Do the broad references in 18 U.S.C. §§ 241 and 242 to rights "secured" by the Constitution give adequate notice of what is prohibited? Or are they void for vagueness? **Screws v. United States**, 325 U.S. 91 (1945), rejected such concerns by reading a strict scienter requirement into these criminal provisions. The case involved a "shocking and revolting episode in law enforcement." The defendants were police officers (Screws was a sheriff in Georgia) who arrested the black victim for theft and beat him "with their fists and with a solid-bar blackjack" after he allegedly reached for a gun and used insulting language. The victim was knocked on the ground and beaten until he was unconscious. He died soon after. "There was evidence that Screws held a grudge against [the victim] and had threatened to 'get' him." The defendants were convicted under 18 U.S.C. § 242 for "willfully" and "under color of law" depriving the victim of his 14th Amendment rights, including "the right not to be deprived of life without due process of law."

Justice DOUGLAS's opinion, joined by Chief Justice Stone and Justices Black and Reed, conceded that there would be a serious vagueness problem if "a local law enforcement officer violates [§ 242] if he does an act which some court later holds deprives a person of due process of law." But he found it possible to read § 242 "more narrowly" to avoid the vagueness difficulty: "[I]f we construe 'willfully' in [§ 242] as connoting a purpose to deprive a person of a specific constitutional right, we would introduce no innovation. [W]here the punishment imposed is only for an act knowingly done with the purpose of doing that which the statute prohibits, the accused cannot be said to suffer from lack of warning or knowledge that the act which he does is a violation of law. [The] presence of a bad purpose or evil intent alone may not be sufficient. [But] a requirement of a specific intent to deprive a person of a federal right made definite by decision or other rule of law saves the Act from any charge of unconstitutionality on the grounds of [vagueness]. [The] specific intent required by the Act is an intent to deprive a person of a right which has been made specific either by the express terms of the Constitution or laws of the United States or by decisions interpreting them." But in this case, the trial judge had not instructed the jury properly on the question of intent, and the conviction was accordingly reversed.

2. ***Congressional power to reach private actors under § 5 of the Fourteenth Amendment.*** Price and Screws involved applications of the criminal sanctions of the civil rights laws to actors reachable under the Court's own interpretations of the state action concept. But Justice Brennan's opinion in Guest suggested that Congress under § 5 of the Fourteenth Amendment may go further in reaching private behavior than the Court would under § 1. How far-reaching is that congressional power? Note that the Brennan and Clark opinions in Guest continue to assume that Fourteenth Amendment rights are rights against the state. Thus, Justice Brennan notes that the Fourteenth Amendment "commands the State to provide the members of all races with equal access" to public facilities. He draws from this obligation a "basic corollary": "the right of a citizen to use those facilities without discrimination on the basis of race." What kinds of private interferences with the relationship between the state and the individual *are* reachable under this view of § 5? Are the private interferences limited to those directly aimed at state officials, in order to hamper them from carrying out their Fourteenth Amendment obligations? Or may Congress also reach private interferences directed against the private citizen who has a "corollary" right against the state? May Congress go even further than that?

The Brennan theory in Guest is most readily applicable where the private interference is directed against the state officials themselves. But Justice Brennan was clearly willing to give that theory a broader reach in Guest: he was prepared to sustain the application of § 241 to a private interference with a private citizen who had a right of access to public facilities. In short, he found power to reach the private actor interfering with the state-victim relationship by intimidations directed not against the state official but against the victim. Under that theory, is it essential that the defendant *intends* to interfere with the victim's access to state facilities? Or is it enough that murder of the victim has the *effect* of interfering with the victim's use of state facilities? Is the theory even more far-reaching than that? May Congress act directly under § 5 to prevent private interferences with access to *private* facilities as well? May Congress bar private interferences with access to *private* housing, on the theory that that is appropriate legislation to protect access to *public* housing? The Guest rationale presumably does not go that far.

CIVIL SANCTIONS FOR PRIVATE INTERFERENCE WITH FOURTEENTH AMENDMENT RIGHTS

1. ***Civil remedies against private conspiracies.*** 42 U.S.C. § 1983, the civil counterpart of 18 U.S.C. § 242, provides civil remedies for deprivations of rights "under color of law." And 42 U.S.C. § 1985(3) [formerly designated § 1985(c)] grants civil remedies for certain private conspiracies to deny "the equal protection of the laws, or of equal privileges and immunities under the laws," as does 18 U.S.C. § 241 in the criminal sphere. In Collins v. Hardyman, 341 U.S. 651 (1951), the Court in effect construed § 1985(c) as reaching only conspiracies under color of state law, finding no cause of action under § 1985(c) where plaintiffs, members of a political club, alleged that defendants broke up their meeting (held to adopt a resolution opposing the Marshall Plan) and thus interfered with their rights to petition the national government for redress of grievances. Justice Jackson's majority opinion concluded: "[Such] private discrimination is not inequality before the law unless there is some manipulation of the law or its agencies."

But in **Griffin v. Breckenridge**, 403 U.S. 88 (1971), a unanimous Court discarded that interpretation and held § 1985(c) applicable to certain purely private conspiracies to deprive persons of civil rights. The Court found it unnecessary to reach the question whether Congress had power under the Fourteenth Amendment to enact the provision. Instead, Justice Stewart relied on Congress's power to reach private conduct under the Thirteenth Amendment. The petitioners in Griffin were African-Americans who charged that white individuals had conspired to detain, assault and beat them for the purpose of preventing them "from seeking the equal protection of the laws and from enjoying the equal rights, privileges and immunities of citizens." They claimed that the respondents, mistakenly believing the driver to be a civil rights worker, blocked the car, forced the inhabitants to get out of it, and threatened and clubbed them. The lower federal courts dismissed the complaint on the authority of Collins.

Justice STEWART's opinion concluded that § 1985(c) covered "private conspiracies." Reading the law to cover private action did not mean that it would apply "to all tortious, conspiratorial interferences with the rights of others," but only those with an "invidiously discriminatory motivation." He added: "The language requiring intent to deprive of *equal* protection, or *equal* privileges and immunities, means that there must be some racial, or perhaps otherwise class-based, invidiously discriminatory animus behind the conspirators' action." After finding that petitioners' complaint easily fell within this new construction of § 1985(c), Justice Stewart turned to the question of congressional power to reach this private conspiracy and found adequate constitutional basis in § 2 of the Thirteenth Amendment, concluding "that Congress was wholly within its powers under § 2 of [that] Amendment in creating a statutory cause of action for Negro citizens who have been the victims of conspiratorial, racially discriminatory private action aimed at depriving them of the basic rights that the law secures to all free men."

What is the constitutionally permissible scope of 42 U.S.C. § 1985(3)? To what extent may Congress reach "invidiously discriminatory intent other than racial bias"? To what extent may Congress reach private interferences with Fourteenth Amendment rights—an issue not reached in Griffin? In **United Brotherhood of Carpenters v. Scott**, 463 U.S. 825 (1983), the Court held by a vote of 5–4 that no cause of action under § 1985(3) was stated by a claim that a union had violently interfered with nonunion workers' First Amendment rights not to associate with a union. Justice WHITE's majority opinion concluded that an alleged conspiracy to infringe First Amendment rights is not a violation of § 1985(3) unless it is proved that "the state is involved in the conspiracy or that the aim of the conspiracy is to influence the activity of the state." He refused to construe the section to "reach conspiracies motivated by economic or commercial animus." Justice BLACKMUN's dissent, joined by Justices Brennan, Marshall and O'Connor, read the legislative history quite differently and found "no basis for the Court's crabbed and uninformed reading of the words of § 1985(3)."

In the 1990s, blockades of abortion clinics served as an arena for disputes about the ability of the federal civil rights laws to reach private conspiracies. In the wake of repeated obstructions of access to abortion clinics by groups such as Operation Rescue, a group of abortion clinics and supporting organizations brought suit under § 1985(3) seeking a federal court injunction against those who would obstruct access to abortion clinics. The plaintiffs prevailed in the lower federal courts, but in **Bray v. Alexandria Women's Health Clinic**, 506 U.S. 263 (1993), the Court reversed, holding that animus toward abortion did not constitute a class-based animus towards women, and thus that the animus required by section 1985(3) was not present. Writing for the majority, Justice SCALIA echoed Carpenters in refusing either to affirm or to reject the suggestion in Griffin that forms of class-based animus other than race-based animus could fall within the domain of § 1985(3). He insisted that § 1985(3) did not include within the notion of a "class" those whose connections lay only in a common "desire to engage in conduct that the section 1985(3) defendant disfavors. [This] definitional ploy would convert the statute into the 'general federal tort law' it was the very purpose of the animus requirement to avoid. [The] record in this case does not indicate that petitioners' demonstrations are motivated by a purpose [directed] specifically to women as a class." Thus no conspiracy with intent to interfere with a right protected against private action could be shown. Justice STEVENS, joined by Justice Blackmun, dissented, objecting to the majority's "parsimonious construction" of the statute and claiming that § 1985 covered "a large-scale conspiracy that violates the victims' constitutional rights by overwhelming the local authorities." The Court's Bray decision was largely superseded by the Freedom of Access to Clinic Entrances Act of 1994.

2. ***Civil remedies against actions "under color" of state law.*** 42 U.S.C. § 1983—like its criminal counterpart, 18 U.S.C. § 242—provides

remedies against actions "under color" of law. What is the scope of this provision? In Monroe v. Pape, 365 U.S. 167 (1961), the Court permitted a damage action against police officers for unlawful invasion of petitioners' home and for illegal search, seizure and detention. Justice Douglas's majority opinion emphasized that the "specific intent" requirement of Screws for criminal cases was not applicable here: "[§ 1983] should be read against the background of tort liability that makes a man responsible for the natural consequences of his actions."

The language of § 1983 covers not only action "under color" of state law, but refers also to "custom, or usage, of any State." In the Court's first extensive consideration of that phrase, in Adickes v. S.H. Kress & Co., 398 U.S. 144 (1970), Justice Harlan's majority opinion concluded that this "requires state involvement [and] not simply a practice that reflects longstanding social habit." "Custom," he insisted, "must have the force of law by virtue of the persistent practices of state officials." Justice Brennan's dissent argued that "custom" means "custom of the people of a State, not custom of state officials"—"a widespread and longstanding practice," not necessarily "backed by the force of the State."

CONGRESSIONAL POWER TO REACH PRIVATE CONDUCT UNDER THE THIRTEENTH AMENDMENT

Jones v. Alfred H. Mayer Co.

392 U.S. 409, 88 S. Ct. 2186, 20 L. Ed. 2d 1189 (1968).

■ JUSTICE STEWART delivered the opinion of the Court.

In this case we are called upon to determine the scope and the constitutionality [of] 42 U.S.C. § 1982.[1] [P]etitioners filed a complaint [that] respondents had refused to sell them a home [for] the sole reason that petitioner [is] a Negro. Relying in part upon [§ 1982], the petitioners sought injunctive and other relief. [The lower federal courts dismissed the complaint], concluding that § 1982 applies only to state action and does not reach private refusals to sell. [We] reverse. [We] hold that § 1982 bars *all* racial discrimination, private as well as public, in the sale or rental of property, and that the statute, thus construed, is a valid exercise of the power of Congress to enforce the 13th Amendment.

[On] its face, [§ 1982] appears to prohibit *all* discrimination against Negroes in the sale or rental of property—discrimination by private owners as well as discrimination by public authorities. [Our] examination of the relevant history [persuades] us that Congress meant exactly what it said. In its original form, § 1982 was part [of] the Civil Rights Act of 1866. [It] is quite true that some members of Congress supported the 14th Amendment "in order to eliminate doubt as to the constitutional validity of the Civil Rights Act as applied to the States." But it certainly does not follow that the

[1] As noted above, § 1982 states: "All citizens of the United States shall have the same right, in every State and Territory, as is enjoyed by white citizens thereof to inherit, purchase, lease, sell, hold, and convey real and personal property."

adoption of the 14th Amendment or the subsequent readoption of the Civil Rights Act were meant somehow to *limit* its application to state action.

[The] remaining question is whether Congress has power under the Constitution to do what § 1982 purports to do: to prohibit all racial discrimination, private and public, in the sale and rental of property. [Does] the authority of Congress to enforce the 13th Amendment "by appropriate legislation" include the power to eliminate all racial barriers to the acquisition of real and personal property? We think the answer to that question is plainly yes. "By its own unaided force and effect," the 13th Amendment "abolished slavery, and established universal freedom." Civil Rights Cases. Whether or not the Amendment *itself* did any more than that—a question not involved in this case—it is at least clear that the Enabling Clause of that Amendment empowered Congress to do much more. For that clause clothed "Congress with power to pass *all laws necessary and proper for abolishing all badges and incidents of slavery in the United States.*" [Surely] Congress has the power under the 13th Amendment rationally to determine what are the badges and the incidents of slavery, and the authority to translate that determination into effective legislation.

Nor can we say that the determination Congress has made is an irrational one. For this Court recognized long ago that, whatever else they may have encompassed, the badges and incidents of slavery—its "burdens and disabilities"—included restraints upon "those fundamental rights which are the essence of civil freedom, namely, the same right [to] inherit, purchase, lease, sell and convey property, as is enjoyed by white citizens." Just as the Black Codes, enacted after the Civil War to restrict the free exercise of those rights, were substitutes for the slave system, so the exclusion of Negroes from white communities became a substitute for the Black Codes. And when racial discrimination herds men into ghettos and makes their ability to buy property turn on the color of their skin, then it too is a relic of slavery. [At] the very least, the freedom that Congress is empowered to secure under the 13th Amendment includes the freedom to buy whatever a white man can buy, the right to live wherever a white man can live. If Congress cannot say that being a free man means at least this much, then the 13th Amendment made a promise the Nation cannot [keep]. Reversed.

■ JUSTICE HARLAN, whom JUSTICE WHITE joins, dissenting.

[The Court] finds it "plain and unambiguous" [that the language of § 1982] forbids purely private as well as state-authorized discrimination. [I] do not find it so. For me, there is an inherent ambiguity in the term "right," as used in § 1982. The "right" referred to may either be a right to equal status under the law, in which case the statute operates only against state-sanctioned discrimination, or it may be an "absolute" right enforceable against private individuals. To me, the words of the statute, taken alone, suggest the former interpretation, not the latter.

THIRTEENTH AMENDMENT POWERS AND THE 1866 CIVIL RIGHTS ACT

1. ***The scope of congressional power after the Jones case.*** How far-reaching is the 13th Amendment power recognized in Jones? Did it in

effect make the public accommodations and employment discrimination provisions of the 1964 Civil Rights Act, enacted under the commerce power, superfluous? Did it have that effect especially in view of § 1981, another legacy of the Civil Rights Act of 1866? Section 1981 guarantees all persons "the same right [to] make and enforce contracts, to sue, be parties, give evidence, and to the full and equal benefits of all laws and proceedings for the security of persons and property as is enjoyed by white citizens." Is there any law against racial discrimination that Congress may not consider a remedy for the "badges of servitude"? May Congress deal with discrimination against groups other than African-Americans?

2. ***Later interpretations of the 1866 Act.*** The Court applied the 1866 Civil Rights Act—and expanded its broad interpretation—in **Sullivan v. Little Hunting Park, Inc.**, 396 U.S. 229 (1969). There, a residents' association operated a community park and playground facilities. Subject to the board's approval, a member who rented his house could assign his share to his tenant. Sullivan leased his house to Freeman and assigned his membership share to him. The board "refused to approve the assignment, because Freeman was a Negro." Sullivan was expelled for protesting that decision. The Court found that Sullivan and Freeman could sue under § 1982 for damages and injunctive relief. Justice DOUGLAS's majority opinion found the corporation's refusal an interference with the right to "lease" within the terms of the 1866 Act. He rejected the state court's finding that the case involved a private social club: "There was no plan or purpose of exclusiveness. It is open to every white person within the geographic area, there being no selective element other than race." Justice HARLAN dissented: "[Lurking] in the background are grave constitutional issues should § 1982 be extended too far into some types of private discrimination." He cited the Civil Rights Cases. What are those "grave constitutional issues"? Which concerns of the Civil Rights Cases are relevant to 13th Amendment legislation? Note that there is no state action limitation under the 13th Amendment.

In **Runyon v. McCrary**, 427 U.S. 160 (1976), the Court held that § 1981 (derived from the 1866 Act) "prohibits private, commercially operated, nonsectarian schools from denying admission to prospective students because they are Negroes" and that as so applied, § 1981 was constitutional. The decision thus enabled direct suits against private all-white academies that had arisen as an end run around the integration of the public schools ordered after Brown v. Board. Justice STEWART's majority opinion relied on his approach in Jones for the statutory interpretation, and he found no violation of "constitutionally protected rights of free association and privacy, or a parent's right to direct the education of his children."

Justice WHITE's dissent, joined by Justice Rehnquist, argued that, despite the broad reading of § 1982 in Jones, § 1981 ought not to be given the majority's construction. He argued that the legislative history of § 1981 "confirms that the statute means what it says and no more, i.e., that it outlaws any legal rule disabling any person from making or enforcing a contract, but does not prohibit private racially motivated refusals to contract." The holding, he added, "threatens to embark the judiciary on a treacherous course. [Whites] and blacks will undoubtedly choose to form a variety of associational relationships pursuant to [racially exclusionary contracts]. Social clubs, black and white, and associations designed to further the interests of blacks or whites are but two examples. [As] the associational or contractual relationships become more private, the pressures to hold § 1981 inapplicable to them will increase. Imaginative judicial construction of the word 'contract' is foreseeable; [13th Amendment] limitations on Congress' power to ban 'badges and incidents of slavery' may be discovered; the doctrine of the right to association may be bent to cover a given situation. [Courts] will be called upon to balance sensitive policy considerations against each other, [all] under the guise of 'construing' a statute. This is a task appropriate for the legislature, not for the judiciary."

Congress later codified the majority's interpretation in the 1991 reenactment of § 1981.

SECTION 4. CONGRESSIONAL POWER TO ENFORCE CIVIL RIGHTS UNDER THE 14TH AND 15TH AMENDMENTS

Historically, most of the laws enacted by Congress under its powers to "enforce" the Fourteenth and Fifteenth Amendments were quite narrowly "remedial": Congress simply provided enforcement mechanisms to implement judicially declared rights. For example, the post-Civil War "under color" of law provisions afforded remedies for the deprivation of rights by the state as secured by the Constitution and interpreted by the Court. The Guest case suggested a potentially broader congressional power: the authority to extend the reach of the Fourteenth Amendment to cover some private behavior. But even there, Congress did not purport to modify the substantive *content* of the rights it protected.

Other laws, however, relied on a broader understanding than Guest contemplated of the enforcement power conferred by § 5 of the Fourteenth Amendment and § 2 of the Fifteenth Amendment, which the Court has interpreted identically. Specifically, Congress attempted to justify several civil rights laws, most prominently during the civil rights era of the 1960s, on the basis of "prophylactic" authority. Under that theory, Congress need not wait to find specific violations of civil rights, as the remedial theory would require; instead, it may pass proactive, broad, and sometimes creatively structured laws that prevent potential civil rights violations in the future. This section of the chapter examines the interaction of these theories and the scope of congressional authority to enforce the provisions of the Fourteenth and Fifteenth Amendments.

CONGRESSIONAL PROTECTION OF VOTING RIGHTS

1. ***Historical background.*** Prior to the Voting Rights Act of 1965, congressional legislation directed against racial discrimination in voting was quite clearly remedial. Congress merely provided enforcement mechanisms; the rights guaranteed were stated in the very general terms of the Constitution. Delineation of the content of the rights was left to the courts; and implementation was left to litigation resting on the congressionally prescribed remedies. Frustration with that case-by-case approach led to the enactment of the 1965 Act. Chief Justice WARREN's opinion in South Carolina v. Katzenbach, 383 U.S. 301 (1966), contained a summary of the "historical experience" that led Congress to two basic conclusions: "First: Congress felt itself confronted by an insidious and pervasive evil which had been perpetuated in certain parts of our country through unremitting and

ingenious defiance of the Constitution. Second: Congress concluded that the unsuccessful remedies which it had prescribed in the past would have to be replaced by sterner and more elaborate measures in order to satisfy the clear commands of the 15th Amendment." Excerpts from Chief Justice Warren's account of the historical background follow:

"The 15th Amendment [was] ratified in 1870. Promptly thereafter Congress passed the Enforcement Act of 1870, which made it a crime for public officers and private persons to obstruct exercise of the right to vote. [E]nforcement of the laws became spotty and ineffective, and most of their provisions were repealed in 1894. [Meanwhile,] beginning in 1890, [Alabama,] Georgia, Louisiana, Mississippi, North Carolina, South Carolina, and Virginia enacted tests still in use which were specifically designed to prevent Negroes from voting. Typically, they made the ability to read and write a registration qualification. [These] laws were based on the fact that as of 1890 in each of the named States, more than two-thirds of the adult Negroes were illiterate while less than one-quarter of the adult whites were unable to read or write. At the same time, alternate tests were prescribed in all of [the] States to assure that white illiterates would not be deprived of the franchise. These included grandfather clauses, property qualifications, 'good character' tests, and the requirement that registrants 'understand' or 'interpret' certain matter.

"The course of subsequent 15th Amendment litigation [demonstrates] the variety and persistence of these and similar institutions designed to deprive Negroes of the right to vote. [According to] the evidence in recent Justice Department voting suits, [discriminatory enforcement of voting qualifications] is now the principal method used to bar Negroes from the polls. [White] applicants for registration have often been excused altogether from the literacy and understanding tests or have been given easy versions, have received extensive help from voting officials, and have been registered despite serious errors in their answers. Negroes, on the other hand, have typically been required to pass difficult versions of all the [tests]. The good-morals requirement is so vague and subjective that it has constituted an open invitation to abuse at the hands of voting officials. [In recent years,] Congress has repeatedly tried to cope with the problem by facilitating case-by-case litigation against voting discrimination. The Civil Rights Act of 1957 authorized the Attorney General to seek injunctions against public and private interference with the right to vote on racial grounds. Perfecting amendments in the Civil Rights Act of 1960 permitted the joinder of States as parties defendant, gave the Attorney General access to local voting records, and authorized courts to register voters in areas of systematic discrimination. Title I of the Civil Rights Act of 1964 expedited the hearing of voting cases before three-judge courts and outlawed some of the tactics used to disqualify Negroes from voting in federal elections. [This] legislation has proved ineffective for a number of reasons. Voting suits are unusually onerous to prepare. [Litigation] has been exceedingly slow. [Even when] favorable decisions have finally been obtained, some of the States affected have merely switched to discriminatory devices not covered by the federal decrees or have enacted difficult new tests. [Alternatively,] certain local officials have defied and evaded court orders or have simply closed their registration offices to freeze the voting rolls."

2. ***The constitutional status of literacy tests before the 1965 Act.*** It was against that background that Congress enacted the Voting Rights Act

of 1965 "to rid the country of racial discrimination in voting." One controversial provision of that "complex scheme of stringent remedies aimed at areas where voting discrimination has been most flagrant" suspended literacy tests in covered localities—including many localities where there had been no judicial finding of discriminatory practices. In that sense, Congress moved beyond where the courts had gone. A few years earlier, moreover, the Court had refused to strike down literacy tests on their face. In **Lassiter v. Northampton County Election Bd.**, 360 U.S. 45 (1959), Justice DOUGLAS, for a unanimous Court, rejected a black citizen's attack on North Carolina's literacy test. The operative part of the state provision stated: "Every person presenting himself for registration shall be able to read and write any section of the [North Carolina] Constitution in the English language." Justice Douglas stated: "The States have long been held to have broad powers to determine the conditions under which the right of suffrage may be exercised, absent of course the discrimination which the Constitution condemns. [Residence] requirements, age, previous criminal record are obvious examples indicating factors which a State may take into consideration in determining the qualifications of voters. The ability to read and write likewise has some relation to standards designed to promote intelligent use of the ballot. Literacy and illiteracy are neutral on race, creed, color, and [sex]. Literacy and intelligence are obviously not synonymous. [Yet] in our society where newspapers, periodicals, books, and other printed matter canvass and debate campaign issues, a State might conclude that only those who are literate should exercise the franchise. [We] do not sit in judgment on the wisdom of [the State's] policy. We cannot say [that] it is not an allowable [one]. Of course a literacy test, fair on its face, may be employed to perpetuate that discrimination which the 15th Amendment was designed to uproot. No such influence is charged here."

3. ***Section 5 of the Voting Rights Act.*** **South Carolina v. Katzenbach**, 383 U.S. 301 (1966), sustained § 5 of the Voting Rights Act of 1965, largely directed at racial discrimination in the South, as a proper exercise of congressional power under § 2 of the 15th Amendment. In covered areas, the Act suspended literacy tests and other devices for five years from the last occurrence of substantial voting discrimination. Moreover, § 5 barred any new "standard, practice, or procedure with respect to voting" pending scrutiny by federal authorities to determine whether their use would violate the 15th Amendment. Covered areas were those states or political subdivisions determined by the Attorney General to use a test or device discouraging voting and having recently had less than 50% of their residents vote. The areas that had been brought under coverage by the Act by the time this case reached the Court were the states of South Carolina, Alabama, Alaska, Georgia, Louisiana, Mississippi, and Virginia, 26 counties in North Carolina, three counties in Arizona, one county in Hawaii, and one county in Idaho.

Chief Justice WARREN stated for the Court: "Congress may use any rational means to effectuate the constitutional prohibition of racial discrimination in voting. The basic test to be applied [under § 2] is the same as in all cases concerning the express powers of Congress with relation to the reserved powers of the States. McCulloch. [We] reject South Carolina's argument that Congress may appropriately do no more than to forbid violations of the 15th Amendment in general terms—that the task of fashioning specific remedies or of applying them to particular localities must necessarily be left entirely to the courts. Congress is not circumscribed by any such artificial rules." Prescribing remedies for voting discrimination "which go into effect without any need for prior adjudication" was "clearly a legitimate response to the problem, for which there is ample precedent under other constitutional provisions. [See McClung; Darby.]" Congress "had found that case-by-case litigation was inadequate to combat widespread and persistent discrimination in voting"; accordingly, it "might well decide to shift the advantage of time and inertia from the perpetrators of the evil to its victims." And the "specific remedies" in the Act were "appropriate means of combating the evil."

Chief Justice Warren found that the areas covered by the Act "were an appropriate target for the new remedies," noting that the law "intentionally confines these remedies to a small number of States and political subdivisions which in most instances were familiar to Congress by name. [Congress] began work with reliable evidence [in judicial proceedings and in findings by the Justice Department and the Civil Rights Commission] of actual voting discrimination in a great majority of the [areas] affected by the new remedies of the Act. The formula eventually evolved to describe these areas was relevant to the problem of voting discrimination, and Congress was therefore entitled to infer a significant danger of the evil in the few remaining States and political subdivisions covered. [Tests] and devices are relevant to voting discrimination because of their long history as a tool for perpetrating the evil; a low voting rate is pertinent for the obvious reason that widespread disenfranchisement must inevitably affect the number of actual voters. Accordingly, the coverage formula is rational in both practice and theory. [In] most of the States [covered], various tests and devices have been instituted with the purpose of disenfranchising Negroes, have been framed in such a way as to facilitate this aim, and have been administered in a discriminatory fashion for many years. Under these circumstances, the 15th Amendment has clearly been violated."

4. ***Later extensions of the Voting Rights Act.*** The Voting Rights Act Amendments of 1970 not only extended the 1965 Act for five years but added a number of new provisions. In one of the 1970 provisions, Congress suspended the use of literacy tests on a *nationwide* basis, not just in the areas subject to the coverage formula of the 1965 Act. In 1975, the Voting Rights Act was once again amended, and extended for 7 years, until 1982. One of its provisions was to make permanent the nationwide ban on literacy tests. The 1970 Act produced another major Court decision on congressional powers. In Oregon v. Mitchell (1970; p. 898 below), although the Court divided on all other provisions of the 1970 Act, it was unanimous in one respect: every Justice found the nationwide literacy test suspension constitutional. Some Justices accepted the 1970 extension on the basis of the congressional interest in nationwide uniformity and in "this country's history of discriminatory educational opportunities in both the North and the South." Even Justice Harlan, the member of the Warren Court who took the most restrictive view of congressional powers under the 14th and 15th Amendments, agreed that the expanded reach of the literacy test provision fell within the "remedial" powers of Congress. He explained: "Despite the lack of evidence of specific instances of discriminatory application or effect, Congress could have determined that racial prejudice is prevalent throughout the Nation, and that literacy tests unduly lend themselves to discriminatory application, either conscious or unconscious. The danger of violation of § 1 of the [15th Amendment] was sufficient to authorize the exercise of congressional power under § 2. [While] a less sweeping approach

in this delicate area might well have been appropriate, the choice which Congress made was within the range of the reasonable."

The Voting Rights Act was extended again several times, most recently in 2006. Two challenges to this expansion reached the Supreme Court. The first, Northwest Austin Municipal Utility District No. One v. Holder, 557 U.S. 193 (2009) [p. 908, below], resulted in the Court expressing "serious doubts" about the extension's constitutionality. In the second, Shelby County v. Holder, 570 U.S. 529 (2013) [p. 909, below], the Court invalidated the § 4(b) coverage formula of the Voting Rights Act, rendering § 5 and its preclearance provisions inoperable.

5. ***The scope of congressional power to enforce civil rights.*** Do the decisions upholding the Voting Rights Act of 1965 suggest that Congress may go beyond the previous decisions of the Court in protecting citizens against deprivation of voting or other civil rights? If so, on what is such power based—Congress's superior fact-finding competence regarding systemic harms, or Congress's independent power and duty to interpret the Constitution apart from any decision by the Court? The following decision read congressional civil rights enforcement power broadly, but was ambiguous as to its theoretical basis:

Katzenbach v. Morgan

384 U.S. 641, 86 S. Ct. 1717, 16 L. Ed. 2d 828 (1966).

■ JUSTICE BRENNAN delivered the opinion of the Court.

[Section 4(e)] of the Voting Rights Act of 1965 [provides] that no person who has successfully completed the sixth primary grade in [an accredited school in] Puerto Rico in which the language of instruction was other than English shall be denied the right to vote in any election because of his inability to read or write English. Appellees, registered voters in New York City, brought this suit to challenge the constitutionality of § 4(e) insofar as it pro tanto prohibits the enforcement of the election laws of New York requiring an ability to read and write English. [We hold that] § 4(e) is a proper exercise of the powers granted to Congress by § 5 of the 14th Amendment.

[New York] argues that an exercise of congressional power under § 5 of the 14th Amendment that prohibits the enforcement of a state law can only be sustained if the judicial branch determines that the state law is prohibited by the provisions of the Amendment that Congress sought to enforce. More specifically, [it] urges that § 4(e) cannot be sustained as appropriate legislation to enforce [equal protection] unless the judiciary decides—even with the guidance of a congressional judgment—that the application of the English literacy requirement prohibited by § 4(e) is forbidden by [equal protection] itself. We disagree. Neither the language nor history of § 5 supports such a construction. [A] construction [that] would require a judicial determination that the enforcement of the state law precluded by Congress violated the Amendment, as a condition of sustaining the congressional enactment, [would] confine the legislative power in this context to the insignificant role of abrogating only those state laws that the judicial branch was prepared to adjudge unconstitutional, or of merely informing the judgment of the judiciary by particularizing the "majestic generalities" of § 1 of the Amendment.

Thus our task in this case is not to determine whether the New York English literacy requirement as applied [violates equal protection]. Accordingly, our decision in [Lassiter] is inapposite. Lassiter did not present the question before us here: Without regard to whether the judiciary would find that [equal protection] itself nullifies New York's English literacy requirement [as] applied, could Congress prohibit the enforcement of the state law by legislating under § 5 of the 14th Amendment? In answering this question, our task is limited to determining whether such legislation is, as required by § 5, appropriate legislation to enforce [equal protection]. By including § 5 the draftsmen sought to grant to Congress, by a specific provision applicable to the 14th Amendment, the same broad powers expressed in the Necessary and Proper Clause. The classic formulation of the reach of those powers was established [in McCulloch]. Section 2 of the 15th Amendment grants Congress a similar [power]. Correctly viewed, § 5 is a positive grant of legislative power authorizing Congress to exercise its discretion in determining whether and what legislation is needed to secure the guarantees of the 14th Amendment. We therefore proceed to the consideration whether § 4(e) is "appropriate legislation" to enforce [equal protection], that is, under the [McCulloch] standard, whether § 4(e) may be regarded as an enactment to enforce [equal protection], whether it is "plainly adapted to that end" and whether it is not prohibited by but is consistent with "the letter and spirit of the Constitution."[1]

There can be no doubt that § 4(e) may be regarded as an enactment to enforce [equal protection]. [Specifically,] § 4(e) may be viewed as a measure to secure for the Puerto Rican community residing in New York nondiscriminatory treatment by government—both in the imposition of voting qualifications and the provision or administration of governmental services, such as public schools, public housing and law enforcement. Section 4(e) may be readily seen as "plainly adapted" to furthering these aims of [equal protection]. The practical effect of § 4(e) is to prohibit New York from denying the right to vote to large segments of its Puerto Rican community. [This] enhanced political power will be helpful in gaining nondiscriminatory treatment in public services for the entire Puerto Rican community. Section 4(e) thereby enables the Puerto Rican minority better to obtain "perfect equality of civil rights and equal protection of the laws." It was well within congressional authority to say that this need of the Puerto Rican minority for the vote warranted federal intrusion upon any state interests served by the English literacy requirement. It was for Congress, as the branch that made this judgment, to assess and weigh the various conflicting considerations—the risk or pervasiveness of the discrimination in governmental services, the effectiveness of eliminating the state restriction on the right to vote as a means of dealing with the evil, the adequacy or availability of alternative remedies, and the nature and significance of the

---

[1] Contrary to the suggestion of the dissent, § 5 does not grant Congress power to exercise discretion in the other direction and to enact "statutes so as in effect to dilute equal protection and due process decisions of this Court." We emphasize that Congress' power under § 5 is limited to adopting measures to enforce the guarantees of the Amendment; § 5 grants Congress no power to restrict, abrogate, or dilute these guarantees. Thus, for example, an enactment authorizing the States to establish racially segregated systems of education would not be—as required by § 5—a measure "to enforce" the Equal Protection Clause since that clause of its own force prohibits such state laws. [Footnote by Justice Brennan.]

state interest that would be affected by the nullification of the English literacy requirement as applied to residents who have successfully completed the sixth grade in a Puerto Rican school. It is not for us to review the congressional resolution of these factors. It is enough that we be able to perceive a basis upon which the Congress might resolve the conflict as it did. There plainly was such a basis [here]. Any contrary conclusion would require us to be blind to the realities familiar to the legislators.

The result is no different if we confine our inquiry to the question whether § 4(e) was merely legislation aimed at the elimination of an invidious discrimination in establishing voter qualifications. We are told that New York's English literacy requirement originated in the desire to provide an incentive for non-English speaking immigrants to learn the English language and in order to assure the intelligent exercise of the franchise. Yet Congress might well have questioned, in light of the many exemptions provided, and some evidence suggesting that prejudice played a prominent role in the enactment of the requirement, whether these were actually the interests being served. Congress might have also questioned whether denial of a right deemed so precious and fundamental in our society was a necessary or appropriate means of encouraging persons to learn English, or of furthering the goal of an intelligent exercise of the franchise. Finally, Congress might well have concluded that as a means of furthering the intelligent exercise of the franchise, an ability to read or understand Spanish is as effective as ability to read English for those to whom Spanish-language newspapers and Spanish-language radio and television programs are available to inform them of election issues and governmental affairs. Since Congress undertook to legislate so as to preclude the enforcement of the state law, and did so in the context of a general appraisal of literacy requirements for voting, to which it brought a specially informed legislative competence, it was Congress' prerogative to weigh these competing considerations. Here again, it is enough that we perceive a basis upon which Congress might predicate a judgment that the application of New York's [requirement] constituted an invidious discrimination in violation of [equal protection].

There remains the question whether the congressional remedies adopted in § 4(e) constitute means which are not prohibited by, but are consistent "with the letter and spirit of the constitution." [Appellees claim that § 4(e)] works an invidious discrimination in violation of the Fifth Amendment by prohibiting the enforcement of the English literacy requirement only for those educated in American-flag schools [in] which the language of instruction was other than English, and not for those educated in schools beyond the territorial limits of the United States in which the language of instruction was also other than English. [This argument] falls on the merits. Section 4(e) does not restrict or deny the franchise but in effect extends the franchise to persons who otherwise would be denied it by state law. Thus we need not decide whether a state literacy law conditioning the right to vote on achieving a certain level of education in an American-flag school [discriminates] invidiously against those educated in non-American-flag schools. We need only decide whether the challenged limitation on the relief effected in § 4(e) was permissible. In deciding that question, the principle that calls for the closest scrutiny of distinctions in laws *denying* fundamental rights [is] inapplicable; for the distinction challenged [here] is presented only as a limitation on a reform measure aimed at eliminating an existing barrier to the exercise of the franchise. Rather, in deciding the constitutional propriety of the limitations in such a reform measure we are guided by the familiar [principle that] "reform may take one step at a time" [Lee Optical]. [The] congressional choice to limit the relief effected in § 4(e) may, for example, reflect Congress' greater familiarity with the quality of instruction in American-flag schools, a recognition of the unique historic relationship between the Congress and the Commonwealth of Puerto Rico, an awareness of the Federal Government's acceptance of the desirability of the use of Spanish as the language of instruction in Commonwealth schools, and the fact that Congress has fostered policies encouraging migration from the Commonwealth to the States. We have no occasion to determine in this case whether such factors would justify a similar distinction embodied in a voting-qualification law that denied the franchise to persons educated in non-American-flag schools. We hold only that the limitation on relief effected in § 4(e) does not constitute a forbidden discrimination since these factors might well have been the basis for the decision of Congress to go "no farther than it [did]." Reversed.

■ JUSTICE HARLAN, whom JUSTICE STEWART joins, dissenting.

Worthy as its purposes may be thought by many, I do not see how § 4(e) can be sustained except at the sacrifice of fundamentals in the American constitutional system—the separation between the legislative and judicial function and the boundaries between federal and state political authority. By the same token I think that the validity of New York's literacy test, a question which the Court considers *only* in the context of the federal statute, must be upheld. It will conduce to analytical clarity if I discuss the second issue first. I. [Applying] the basic equal protection standard, the issue in [Cardona v. Power][2] is whether New York has shown that its English-language literacy test is reasonably designed to serve a legitimate state interest. I think that it has. [The] same interests recounted in [Lassiter] indubitably point toward upholding the rationality of the New York voting test. [The] range of material available to a resident of New York literate only in Spanish is much more limited than what is available to an English-speaking resident [and] the business [of] government is conducted in English. [The] ballot [is] likewise in English. It is also true that most candidates [make] their speeches in English. New York may justifiably want its voters to be able to understand candidates directly, rather than through possibly imprecise translations or summaries reported in a limited number of Spanish news media. [Given] the State's legitimate concern with promoting and safeguarding the intelligent use of the ballot, and given also New York's long experience with the process of integrating non-English-speaking residents into the mainstream of American life, I do not see how it can be said that this [requirement] is unconstitutional. I would uphold the validity of the [law], unless the federal statute prevents that result, the question to which I now turn.

---

[2] **Cardona v. Power**, 384 U.S. 672 (1966), a companion case to Morgan, was an appeal from an unsuccessful state court equal protection challenge to the New York literacy requirement. The plaintiff was a New York resident educated in Puerto Rico who did not allege that she had completed sixth grade education—the minimum under § 4(e). The state courts, prior to the enactment of § 4(e), rejected her equal protection attack. Justice Brennan's majority opinion vacated that judgment and remanded the case: appellant might be covered by § 4(e) and her case "might therefore be moot"; even if she were not so covered, the state court should determine whether "in light of this federal enactment, those applications of the New York English literacy requirement not in terms prohibited by § 4(e) have continuing validity." Justice Douglas, joined by Justice Fortas, reached the merits of the equal protection claim and dissented, arguing that the requirement could not survive the strict scrutiny mandated in voting cases by Harper v. Virginia Bd. of Elections, 383 U.S. 663 (1966).

II. [The] pivotal question in [Morgan] is what effect the added factor of a congressional enactment has on the straight equal protection [argument]. The Court declares that [under § 5] the test for judicial review [is] simply one of rationality; that is, in effect, was Congress acting rationally in declaring that the New York statute is irrational? [The] Court has confused the issue of how much enforcement power Congress possesses under § 5 with the distinct issue of what questions are appropriate for congressional determination and what questions are essentially judicial in nature. When recognized state violations of federal constitutional standards have occurred, Congress is of course empowered by § 5 to take appropriate remedial measures to redress and prevent the wrongs. But it is a judicial question whether the condition with which Congress has thus sought to deal is in truth an infringement of the Constitution, something that is the necessary prerequisite to bringing the § 5 power into play at all. [The] question here is not whether the statute is appropriate remedial legislation to cure an established violation of a constitutional command, but whether there has in fact been an infringement of that constitutional command, that is, whether a particular state practice or, as here, a statute is so arbitrary or irrational as to offend [equal protection]. That question is one for the judicial branch ultimately to determine. [In] effect the Court reads § 5 of the 14th Amendment as giving Congress the power to define the *substantive* scope of the Amendment. If that indeed be the true reach of § 5, then I do not see why Congress should not be able as well to exercise its § 5 "discretion" by enacting statutes so as in effect to dilute equal protection and due process decisions of this Court.

I do not mean to suggest [that] a legislative judgment of the type incorporated in § 4(e) is without any force whatsoever. Decisions on questions of equal protection and due process are based not on abstract logic, but on empirical foundations. To the extent "legislative facts" are relevant to a judicial determination, Congress is well equipped to investigate them, and such determinations are of course entitled to due respect. In [South Carolina], such legislative findings were made to show that racial discrimination in voting was actually occurring. Similarly, in [Heart of Atlanta Motel and McClung (Chapter 3 above)], the congressional determination that racial discrimination in a clearly defined group of public accommodations did effectively impede interstate commerce was based on "voluminous testimony" [before Congress] and in the context of which it passed remedial legislation. But no such factual data provide a legislative record supporting § 4(e)[3] by way of showing that Spanish-speaking citizens are fully as capable of making informed decisions in a New York election as are English-speaking citizens. Nor was there any showing whatever to support the Court's alternative argument that § 4(e) should be viewed as but a remedial measure designed to cure or assure against unconstitutional discrimination of other varieties, e.g., in "public schools, public housing and law enforcement." [There] is simply no legislative record supporting such hypothesized discrimination of the sort we have hitherto insisted upon when congressional power is brought to bear on constitutionally reserved state concerns. [Thus], we have here not a matter of giving deference to a congressional estimate, based on its determination of legislative facts, bearing upon the validity *vel non* of a statute, but rather what can at most

[3] There were no committee hearings or reports referring to this section, which was introduced from the floor during debate on the full Voting Rights Act. [Footnote by Justice Harlan.]

be called a legislative announcement that Congress believes a state law to entail an unconstitutional deprivation of equal protection. Although this kind of declaration is of course entitled to the most respectful consideration, I do not believe it lessens our responsibility to decide the fundamental issue of whether in fact the state enactment violates federal constitutional rights.

THE MEANING AND AFTERMATH OF KATZENBACH V. MORGAN

1. ***Congressional power: substantive or remedial?*** Note that the majority opinion in Morgan rested on alternative rationales. First, Justice Brennan found § 4(e) rationally related to securing for Puerto Ricans in New York nondiscriminatory treatment in the "provision or administration of governmental services." Second, he suggested, Congress could reasonably have thought § 4(e) would eliminate "an invidious discrimination in establishing voter qualifications." Discrimination against Puerto Ricans in providing public services was already clearly unconstitutional under Court-developed interpretations of equal protection that barred discrimination on the basis of race or national origin; under the first theory, then, Congress could have been viewed as implementing judicially determined constitutional rights. Was the second theory, in contrast, a substantive reinterpretation of the Constitution that exceeded Congress's merely "remedial" powers? The Court had not held that requiring English literacy tests of Puerto Ricans literate in Spanish was itself unconstitutional discrimination in voting—although it had noted in Lassiter that some applications of literacy tests might violate equal protection if a proxy for race discrimination.

Under the second theory, then, Congress arguably was making the initial determination that an English literacy test in these circumstances was unconstitutional, and thus determining the substantive content of rights under § 1 of the Fourteenth Amendment. Was such a substantive reinterpretation permissible under the text of § 5 of the Fourteenth Amendment, which speaks of the power to "enforce," not the power to interpret? Was it permissible under the separation of powers set forth in Marbury v. Madison and broadly interpreted in Cooper v. Aaron? Did it confuse the role of the legislative and judicial branches, as Justice Harlan charged? Commentators after Morgan vigorously debated this point. One prominent theory defended the decision as *not* authorizing substantive reinterpretation but rather simply acknowledging Congress's special institutional competence to find facts pertaining to remedies of Court-declared constitutional rights. See Cox, "Foreword—Constitutional Adjudication and the Promotion of Human Rights," 80 Harv. L. Rev. 91 (1966); Cox, "The Role of Congress in Constitutional Determinations," 40 U. Cinn. L. Rev. 199 (1971) ("[T]he Morgan decision follows logically from the basic principles determining the respective functions of the legislative and judicial branches outside the field of preferred constitutional rights. Whether a state law denies equal protection depends to a large extent upon the finding and appraisal of the practical importance of relevant facts."). For the Court's ultimately negative answer to the question whether Congress has any substantive interpretive competence under the 14th Amendment, and expressly disavowing any such interpretation of Morgan in favor of a purely remedial interpretation, see the City of Boerne decision below.

May the Court recognize a congressional remedial power that in effect expands civil rights beyond Court-announced contours and yet avoid deference to congressional judgments diluting or contracting such rights? Justice Brennan's important "one-way ratchet" footnote in Morgan tried to safeguard against the risk of dilution: Justice Brennan insisted that § 5 "grants Congress no power to restrict, abrogate, or dilute these guarantees." Is that because the Fifth Amendment would bar such action by its own force because it binds Congress itself not to violate due process or, after Bolling v. Sharpe, equal protection? Even if Justice Brennan's distinction between "dilution" and "expansion" in the Morgan footnote is persuasive, how is it to be applied? Recall the Court's disposition (in the last part of Morgan) of the claim that § 4(e) of the 1965 Act unfairly discriminated against those literate in foreign languages who were not covered by § 4(e). Justice Brennan's scrutiny of that claim was very deferential, supposedly because § 4(e) was viewed as "a reform measure" rather than a restriction on existing rights.

2. ***Application of Morgan to other voting rights provisions.*** **Oregon v. Mitchell**, 400 U.S. 112 (1970), involved constitutional challenges by several states to several provisions of the Voting Rights Act Amendments of 1970. Section 302 prohibited denying to any citizen the right to vote in any election "on account of age if such citizen is eighteen years of age or older." That provision provoked a division on the Court over the scope of the Morgan decision. By a 5–4 vote, the voting age provision was upheld for federal elections; but another 5–4 division held the 18-year-old vote provision unconstitutional as applied to state elections. Justices Douglas, Brennan, White and Marshall thought the provision valid as applied to all elections, state as well as federal; Chief Justice Burger and Justices Harlan, Stewart and Blackmun thought the provision exceeded congressional power as applied to any election, federal or state; Justice Black cast the deciding vote—he thought it constitutional as applied to federal elections but not to state elections. (With far more consensus, the Court also upheld challenged provisions expanding the ban on literacy tests for voting and easing state standards for registration and absentee ballots.)

Justice BLACK, in announcing the judgment of the Court, conceded Congress's power under Art. I to override state regulations of the time, place or manner of federal elections, but emphasized that "[no] function is more essential to the separate and independent existence of the States [than] the power to determine within the limits of the Constitution the qualifications of their own voters for state, county, and municipal [offices]." He conceded too that where Congress "attempts to remedy racial discrimination under its enforcement powers, its authority is enhanced by the avowed intention of the Framers of the 13th, 14th, and 15th Amendments," but found that, in enacting the 18-year-old vote provisions, "Congress made no legislative findings that the 21-year-old vote requirement was used by the States to disenfranchise voters on account of race" and expressed "doubt that such a finding, if made, could be supported by substantial evidence."

Justice BRENNAN, joined by Justices White and Marshall, dissented from the judgment insofar as it declared § 302 unconstitutional as applied to state and local elections: "[We] believe there is serious question whether a statute [denying the franchise to citizens] between the ages of 18 and 21 [could] withstand present scrutiny under [equal protection]. But there is no reason for us to decide whether, in a proper case, we would be compelled to hold this restriction a violation of [equal protection]. [The only question here is] whether Congress could rationally have concluded that denial of the franchise to citizens between the ages of 18 and 21 was unnecessary to promote any legitimate interests of the States in assuring intelligent and responsible [voting]. [Congress] had ample evidence upon which it could have based the conclusion that exclusion of citizens 18 to 21 years of age from the franchise is wholly unnecessary to promote any legitimate interest the States may have in assuring intelligent and responsible voting. [Morgan.] If discrimination is unnecessary to promote any legitimate state interest, it is plainly unconstitutional under [equal protection], and Congress has ample power to forbid it under [§ 5]."

Justice STEWART, who had joined the dissent in Morgan, concurred in part and dissented in part, joined by Chief Justice Burger and Justice Blackmun. He read Morgan to hold "that Congress could impose on the States a remedy for the denial of equal protection that elaborated upon the direct command of the Constitution, and that it could override state laws on the ground that they were in fact used as instruments of invidious discrimination even though a court in an individual lawsuit might not have reached that factual conclusion," but argued that it would be "necessary to go much further to sustain § 302. The state laws that it invalidates do not invidiously discriminate against any discrete and insular minority. Unlike the statute considered in Morgan, § 302 is valid only if Congress has the power not only to provide the means of eradicating situations that amount to a violation of [equal protection], but also to determine as a matter of substantive constitutional law what situations fall within the ambit of the clause, and what state interests are 'compelling.' "

Justice HARLAN, who wrote the Morgan dissent, also concurred in part and dissented in part, arguing as a historical matter that § 1 of the 14th Amendment could not have been intended to "reach discriminatory voting qualifications." He suggested that "the very fact that constitutional amendments were deemed necessary to bring about federal abolition of state restrictions on voting by reason of race, sex, and [the] failure to pay state poll taxes, is itself forceful evidence of the common understanding in 1869, 1919, and 1962, respectively, that the 14th Amendment did not empower Congress to legislate in these respects." He reiterated his view that "[a]lthough Congress' expression of the view that it does have power to alter state suffrage qualifications is entitled to the most respectful consideration, [this] cannot displace the duty of this Court to make an independent determination whether Congress has exceeded its powers," and suggested that deferring to Congress's "substitut[ion of] its own judgment for those of the States" would be especially objectionable in the area of establishing voter qualifications: "[In] this area, to rely on Congress would make that body a judge in its own cause. The role of final arbiter belongs to this [Court]."

The decision was handed down on December 21, 1970. Three months later, on March 23, 1971, Congress submitted the 26th Amendment to the states for ratification and on June 30, 1971, the ratification process was completed. The 26th Amendment provides that the federal and state governments may not deny the vote "on account of age" to citizens "eighteen years of age or older."

In **Rome v. United States**, 446 U.S. 156 (1980), the Court considered the constitutionality of § 5 of the Voting Rights Act of 1965 as applied to changes in election procedures by Rome, Georgia. The city, which had determined that city commissioners would be elected at large, made a number of annexations to its territory. Because Georgia had been designated a covered jurisdiction under the 1965 Act, the State and its municipalities were required to comply with the preclearance provisions of § 5 of the Act. The Attorney General refused to approve the electoral changes, concluding that in a city such as Rome, with a predominantly white population and a norm of racial bloc voting, the changes would deprive black voters of the opportunity to elect a candidate of their choice. Under § 5, the Attorney General could approve a change in voting practice only if it "does not have the purpose and will not have the effect of denying or abridging the right to vote on account of race or color." In the Rome case, the Attorney General found no forbidden "purpose" but relied on the "effect" provision. The Attorney General also refused to preclear 13 of the annexations for purposes of city commission elections, finding that Rome had not carried its burden of proving that these annexations would not dilute the black vote. The city then sought declaratory relief in a three-judge district court. That court rejected all of the city's challenges, finding that the disapproved changes and annexations, while not adopted for any discriminatory purpose, did have a discriminatory effect. The Supreme Court affirmed.

Justice MARSHALL wrote for the Court, affirming the findings as to discriminatory effect, holding that Rome could not bail out of the preclearance requirement so long as the state was subject to it, and reiterating that § 5 was within Congress's enforcement power under the 15th Amendment: "Congress passed the Act under [the 15th Amendment]. [The city claims] that § 1 of the Amendment prohibits only purposeful racial discrimination in voting, and that in enforcing that provision, [Congress] may not prohibit voting practices lacking discriminatory intent even if they are discriminatory in effect. We hold that, even if § 1 of the Amendment prohibits only purposeful discrimination, the prior decisions of this Court foreclose any argument that Congress may not, pursuant to § 2, outlaw voting practices that are discriminatory in effect. The [city is] asking us to do nothing less than overrule our decision in [South Carolina]. [South Carolina] makes clear that Congress may, under the authority of § 2 of the 15th Amendment, prohibit state action that, though in itself not violative of § 1, perpetuates the effects of past discrimination. Other decisions of this Court also recognize Congress' broad power to enforce the Civil War Amendments. [See Katzenbach v. Morgan and Oregon v. Mitchell.] [In] the present case, we hold that the Act's ban on electoral changes that are discriminatory in effect is an appropriate method of promoting the purposes of the 15th Amendment, even if it is assumed that § 1 of the Amendment prohibits only intentional discrimination in voting. Congress could rationally have concluded that, because electoral changes by jurisdictions with a demonstrable history of intentional racial discrimination in voting create the risk of purposeful discrimination, it was proper to prohibit changes that have a discriminatory [impact]."

Justice POWELL dissented: "Under § 2 of the 15th Amendment Congress may impose such constitutional deprivations only if it is acting to remedy violations of voting rights. In view of the District Court finding that Rome has not denied [the] voting rights of blacks, the 15th Amendment provides no authority for continuing those deprivations until the entire State of Georgia satisfies the bailout standards. [South Carolina] upheld the imposition of preclearance as a prophylactic measure based on the remedial power of Congress to enforce the 15th Amendment. But the Court emphasized that preclearance, like any remedial device, can be imposed only in response to some harm."

Justice REHNQUIST, joined by Justice Stewart, also dissented: "Congress is granted only the power to 'enforce' by 'appropriate' legislation the limitations on state action embodied in those Amendments. While the presumption of constitutionality is due to any act of a coordinate branch of the Federal Government or of one of the States, it is this Court which is ultimately responsible for deciding challenges to the exercise of power by those entities. [Marbury; Nixon.] Today's decision is nothing less than a total abdication of that authority, rather than an exercise of the deference due to a coordinate branch of the [government]. [I] do not believe that prohibition of these changes can genuinely be characterized as a remedial exercise of congressional enforcement powers. Thus, the result of the Court's holding is that Congress effectively has the power to determine for itself that this conduct violates the Constitution. [To] permit congressional power to prohibit the conduct challenged in this case requires state and local governments to cede far more of their powers to the Federal Government than the Civil War Amendments ever envisioned; and it requires the judiciary to cede far more of its power to interpret and enforce the Constitution than ever envisioned."

3. ***Confining Congress's civil rights enforcement power.*** Recall the discussion in Chapter 3, p. 147 above, of the Rehnquist Court decisions cabining the commerce power in order to respect values of federalism. The following decision in City of Boerne v. Flores similarly established judicially enforceable limits on Congress's civil rights enforcement power. The decision put to rest any doubt lingering after Morgan over whether Congress has substantive power to reinterpret the Constitution by statute rather than constitutional amendment—it held that the power to "enforce" civil rights is strictly remedial and that Congress lacks any power to set forth new substantive interpretations of the Fourteenth Amendment so as to overrule prior interpretations of the Court. It also required closer judicial scrutiny than had Morgan's deferential McCulloch test of the means used to effect such a remedy. Here the question was whether Congress had exceeded its powers under § 5 of the Fourteenth Amendment to remedy violations of the Free Exercise Clause, incorporated against the States by the Due Process Clause of § 1 of the Fourteenth Amendment. That question has significant federalism implications. Recall that under the Court's 1996 holding in Seminole Tribe v. Florida (1996; p. 184 above), Congress may not enact legislation under its Article I powers that abrogates a state's immunity to suits for monetary damages without its consent. But recall as well that Seminole Tribe and its progeny did not disturb the Court's earlier holdings that Congress *may* subject nonconsenting states to lawsuits pursuant to its powers under § 5 of the Fourteenth Amendment. The Court in Boerne addressed the interplay of these considerations by describing the limits on Congress's § 5 powers:

City of Boerne v. Flores

521 U.S. 507, 117 S. Ct. 2157, 138 L. Ed. 2d 624 (1997).

■ JUSTICE KENNEDY delivered the opinion of the Court.

A decision by local zoning authorities to deny a church a building permit was challenged under the Religious Freedom Restoration Act of 1993 (RFRA). The case calls into question the authority of Congress to enact RFRA. We conclude the statute exceeds Congress' power.

[Congress] enacted RFRA in direct response to the Court's decision in Employment Div., Dept. of Human Resources of Ore. v. Smith [1990; p. 1593, below]. There we considered a Free Exercise Clause claim brought by members of the Native American Church who were denied unemployment benefits when they lost their jobs because they had used peyote. Their practice was to ingest peyote for sacramental purposes, and they challenged an Oregon statute of general applicability which made use of the drug criminal. In evaluating the claim, we declined to apply the balancing test set forth in Sherbert v. Verner [1963; p. 1583 below], under which we would have asked whether Oregon's prohibition substantially burdened a religious practice and, if it did, whether the burden was justified by a compelling government interest. [Smith] held that neutral, generally applicable laws may be applied to religious practices even when not supported by a compelling governmental interest.

[The Court's] constitutional interpretation [was] debated by Members of Congress in hearings and floor debates. Many criticized the Court's reasoning, and this disagreement resulted in the passage of RFRA. [The] Act's stated purposes are: "(1) to restore the compelling interest test as set forth in [Sherbert] and to guarantee its application in all cases where free exercise of religion is substantially burdened; and (2) to provide a claim or defense to persons whose religious exercise is substantially burdened by government." RFRA prohibits "government" from "substantially burdening" a person's exercise of religion even if the burden results from a rule of general applicability unless the government can demonstrate the burden "(1) is in furtherance of a compelling governmental interest; and (2) is the least restrictive means of furthering that compelling governmental interest." The Act's mandate applies to any "branch, department, agency, instrumentality, and official (or other person acting under color of law) of the United States," as well as to any "State, or . . . subdivision of a State."

Congress relied on its Fourteenth Amendment enforcement power in enacting the most far reaching and substantial of RFRA's provisions, those which impose its requirements on the States. [All] must acknowledge that § 5 is "a positive grant of legislative power" to Congress. Katzenbach v. Morgan. [Legislation] which deters or remedies constitutional violations can fall within the sweep of Congress' enforcement power even if in the process it prohibits conduct which is not itself unconstitutional and intrudes into "legislative spheres of autonomy previously reserved to the States." [Congress'] power under § 5, however, extends only to "enforcing" the provisions of the Fourteenth Amendment. The Court has described this power as "remedial," South Carolina v. Katzenbach. The design of the Amendment and the text of § 5 are inconsistent with the suggestion that Congress has the power to decree the substance of the Fourteenth Amendment's restrictions on the States. Legislation which alters the meaning of the Free Exercise Clause cannot be said to be enforcing the

Clause. Congress does not enforce a constitutional right by changing what the right is. It has been given the power "to enforce," not the power to determine what constitutes a constitutional violation.

[While] the line between measures that remedy or prevent unconstitutional actions and measures that make a substantive change in the governing law is not easy to discern, and Congress must have wide latitude in determining where it lies, the distinction exists and must be observed. There must be a congruence and proportionality between the injury to be prevented or remedied and the means adopted to that end. Lacking such a connection, legislation may become substantive in operation and effect. History and our case law support drawing the distinction, one apparent from the text of the Amendment.

The Fourteenth Amendment's history[1] confirms the remedial, rather than substantive, nature of the Enforcement Clause. The Joint Committee on Reconstruction of the 39th Congress began drafting what would become the Fourteenth Amendment in January 1866. [In] February, Republican Representative John Bingham of Ohio reported the following draft amendment to the House of Representatives on behalf of the Joint Committee: "The Congress shall have power to make all laws which shall be necessary and proper to secure to the citizens of each State all privileges and immunities of citizens in the several States, and to all persons in the several States equal protection in the rights of life, liberty, and property."

The proposal encountered immediate opposition. [The] criticisms had a common theme: The proposed Amendment gave Congress too much legislative power at the expense of the existing constitutional structure. [The] Amendment in its early form was not again considered. Instead, the Joint Committee began drafting a new article of Amendment, which it reported to Congress on April 30, 1866. Section 1 of the new draft Amendment imposed self-executing limits on the States. Section 5 prescribed that "the Congress shall have power to enforce, by appropriate legislation, the provisions of this article." Under the revised Amendment, Congress' power was no longer plenary but remedial. Congress was granted the power to make the substantive constitutional prohibitions against the States effective. [The] revised Amendment proposal did not raise the concerns expressed earlier regarding broad congressional power to prescribe uniform national laws with respect to life, liberty, and property. After revisions not relevant here, the new measure passed both Houses and was ratified in July 1868 as the Fourteenth Amendment. The significance of the defeat of the Bingham proposal was apparent even then. During the debates over the Ku Klux Klan Act only a few years after the Amendment's ratification, Representative James Garfield argued there were limits on Congress' enforcement power, saying "unless we ignore both the history and the language of these clauses we cannot, by any reasonable interpretation, give to [§ 5] the force and effect of the rejected [Bingham] clause." Scholars of successive generations have agreed with this assessment. [As] enacted, the Fourteenth Amendment confers substantive rights against the States which, like the provisions of the Bill of Rights, are self-executing. The power to interpret the Constitution in a case or controversy remains in the Judiciary.

---

[1] Justice Scalia, while joining the rest of Justice Kennedy's opinion for the Court, did not join this account of 14th Amendment's legislative history in the Reconstruction Congress.

The remedial and preventive nature of Congress' enforcement power, and the limitation inherent in the power, were confirmed in our earliest cases on the Fourteenth Amendment. In the Civil Rights Cases, the Court invalidated sections of the Civil Rights Act of 1875 which prescribed criminal penalties for denying to any person "the full enjoyment of" public accommodations and conveyances, on the grounds that it exceeded Congress' power by seeking to regulate private conduct. The Enforcement Clause, the Court said, did not authorize Congress to pass "general legislation upon the rights of the citizen, but corrective legislation; that is, such as may be necessary and proper for counteracting such laws as the States may adopt or enforce, and which, by the amendment, they are prohibited from making or enforcing. . . ."

[Recent] cases have continued to revolve around the question of whether § 5 legislation can be considered remedial. In South Carolina v. Katzenbach [we] upheld various provisions of the Voting Rights Act of 1965, finding them to be "remedies aimed at areas where voting discrimination has been most flagrant," and necessary to "banish the blight of racial discrimination in voting, which has infected the electoral process in parts of our country for nearly a century." We noted evidence in the record reflecting the subsisting and pervasive discriminatory—and therefore unconstitutional—use of literacy tests. The Act's new remedies, includ[ing] the suspension of [literacy tests,] were deemed necessary given the ineffectiveness of the existing voting rights laws and the slow costly character of case-by-case litigation. After South Carolina v. Katzenbach, the Court continued to acknowledge the necessity of using strong remedial and preventive measures to respond to the widespread and persisting deprivation of constitutional rights resulting from this country's history of racial discrimination. See Oregon v. Mitchell; City of Rome; Katzenbach v. Morgan.

Any suggestion that Congress has a substantive, non-remedial power under the Fourteenth Amendment is not supported by our case law. In Oregon v. Mitchell, a majority of the Court concluded Congress had exceeded its enforcement powers by enacting legislation lowering the minimum age of voters from 21 to 18 in state and local elections. The five Members of the Court who reached this conclusion explained that the legislation intruded into an area reserved by the Constitution to the States. Four of these five [all but Justice Black] were explicit in rejecting the position that § 5 endowed Congress with the power to establish the meaning of constitutional provisions.

There is language in our opinion in Katzenbach v. Morgan which could be interpreted as acknowledging a power in Congress to enact legislation that expands the rights contained in § 1 of the Fourteenth Amendment. This is not a necessary interpretation, however, or even the best one. In Morgan, the Court considered the constitutionality of § 4(e) of the Voting Rights Act of 1965, which provided that no person who had successfully completed the sixth primary grade in a public school in, or a private school accredited by, the Commonwealth of Puerto Rico in which the language of instruction was other than English could be denied the right to vote because of an inability to read or write English. New York's Constitution, on the other hand, required voters to be able to read and write English. The Court provided two related rationales for its conclusion that § 4(e) could "be viewed as a measure to secure for the Puerto Rican community residing in New York nondiscriminatory treatment by government." Under the first rationale,

Congress could prohibit New York from denying the right to vote to large segments of its Puerto Rican community, in order to give Puerto Ricans "enhanced political power" that would be "helpful in gaining nondiscriminatory treatment in public services for the entire Puerto Rican community." Section 4(e) thus could be justified as a remedial measure to deal with "discrimination in governmental services." The second rationale, an alternative holding, did not address discrimination in the provision of public services but "discrimination in establishing voter qualifications." The Court perceived a factual basis on which Congress could have concluded that New York's literacy requirement "constituted an invidious discrimination in violation of the Equal Protection Clause." Both rationales for upholding § 4(e) rested on unconstitutional discrimination by New York and Congress' reasonable attempt to combat it.

[If] Congress could define its own powers by altering the Fourteenth Amendment's meaning, no longer would the Constitution be "superior paramount law, unchangeable by ordinary means." It would be "on a level with ordinary legislative acts, and, like other acts, . . . alterable when the legislature shall please to alter it." Marbury v. Madison. Under this approach, it is difficult to conceive of a principle that would limit congressional power. Shifting legislative majorities could change the Constitution and effectively circumvent the difficult and detailed amendment process contained in Article V.

We now turn to consider whether RFRA can be considered enforcement legislation under § 5 of the Fourteenth Amendment. Respondent contends that RFRA is a proper exercise of Congress' remedial or preventive power [because] it prevents and remedies laws which are enacted with the unconstitutional object of targeting religious beliefs and practices. To avoid the difficulty of proving such violations, it is said, Congress can simply invalidate any law which imposes a substantial burden on a religious practice unless it is justified by a compelling interest and is the least restrictive means of accomplishing that interest. If Congress can prohibit laws with discriminatory effects in order to prevent racial discrimination in violation of the Equal Protection Clause, then it can do the same, respondent argues, to promote religious liberty.

While preventive rules are sometimes appropriate remedial measures, there must be a congruence between the means used and the ends to be achieved. The appropriateness of remedial measures must be considered in light of the evil presented. [In] contrast to the record which confronted Congress and the judiciary in the voting rights cases, RFRA's legislative record lacks examples of modern instances of generally applicable laws passed because of religious bigotry. The history of persecution in this country detailed in the hearings mentions no episodes occurring in the past 40 years. Rather, the emphasis of the hearings was on laws of general applicability which place incidental burdens on religion.

[This] lack of support in the legislative record, however, is not RFRA's most serious shortcoming. [As] a general matter, it is for Congress to determine the method by which it will reach a decision. Regardless of the state of the legislative record, RFRA cannot be considered remedial, preventive legislation, if those terms are to have any meaning. RFRA is so out of proportion to a supposed remedial or preventive object that it cannot be understood as responsive to, or designed to prevent, unconstitutional behavior. It appears, instead, to attempt a substantive change in constitutional protections. Preventive measures prohibiting certain types of laws may be appropriate when there is reason to believe that many of the laws affected by the congressional enactment have a significant likelihood of being unconstitutional. Remedial legislation under § 5 "should be adapted to the mischief and wrong which the [Fourteenth] Amendment was intended to provide against." Civil Rights Cases.

RFRA is not so confined. Sweeping coverage ensures its intrusion at every level of government, displacing laws and prohibiting official actions of almost every description and regardless of subject matter. [The] reach and scope of RFRA distinguish it from other measures passed under Congress' enforcement power, even in the area of voting rights. In South Carolina v. Katzenbach, the challenged provisions were confined to those regions of the country where voting discrimination had been most flagrant, and affected a discrete class of state laws, i.e., state voting laws. [The] provisions restricting and banning literacy tests upheld in Katzenbach v. Morgan and Oregon v. Mitchell attacked a particular type of voting qualification. [In] City of Rome, the Court rejected a challenge to the constitutionality of a Voting Rights Act provision [imposed] only on jurisdictions with a history of intentional racial discrimination in voting. [This] is not to say, of course, that § 5 legislation requires termination dates, geographic restrictions or egregious predicates. Where, however, a congressional enactment pervasively prohibits constitutional state action in an effort to remedy or to prevent unconstitutional state action, limitations of this kind tend to ensure Congress' means are proportionate to ends legitimate under § 5.

The stringent test RFRA demands of state laws reflects a lack of proportionality or congruence between the means adopted and the legitimate end to be achieved. If an objector can show a substantial burden on his free exercise, the State must demonstrate a compelling governmental interest and show that the law is the least restrictive means of furthering its interest. Claims that a law substantially burdens someone's exercise of religion will often be difficult to contest. Requiring a State to demonstrate a compelling interest and show that it has adopted the least restrictive means of achieving that interest is the most demanding test known to constitutional law. [Laws] valid under Smith would fall under RFRA without regard to whether they had the object of stifling or punishing free exercise. We make these observations not to reargue the position of the majority in Smith but to illustrate the substantive alteration of its holding attempted by RFRA. Even assuming RFRA would be interpreted in effect to mandate some lesser test, say one equivalent to intermediate scrutiny, the statute nevertheless would require searching judicial scrutiny of state law with the attendant likelihood of invalidation. This is a considerable congressional intrusion into the States' traditional prerogatives and general authority to regulate for the health and welfare of their citizens.

The substantial costs RFRA exacts, both in practical terms of imposing a heavy litigation burden on the States and in terms of curtailing their traditional general regulatory power, far exceed any pattern or practice of unconstitutional conduct under the Free Exercise Clause as interpreted in Smith. Simply put, RFRA is not designed to identify and counteract state laws likely to be unconstitutional because of their treatment of religion. [In] addition, the Act imposes in every case a least restrictive means requirement [which] also indicates that the legislation is broader than is appropriate if the goal is to prevent and remedy constitutional violations.

[Our] national experience teaches that the Constitution is preserved best when each part of the government respects both the Constitution and the proper actions and determinations of the other branches. [It] is for Congress in the first instance to "determine whether and what legislation is needed to secure the guarantees of the Fourteenth Amendment," and its conclusions are entitled to much deference. Katzenbach v. Morgan. Congress' discretion is not unlimited, however, and the courts retain the power, as they have since Marbury v. Madison, to determine if Congress has exceeded its authority under the Constitution. Broad as the power of Congress is under the Enforcement Clause of the Fourteenth Amendment, RFRA contradicts vital principles necessary to maintain separation of powers and the federal balance. [Reversed.]

THE MEANING AND SCOPE OF BOERNE

1. ***Boerne and Marbury.*** Did Boerne simply repudiate an unusually flagrant attempt by Congress to overturn the substance of one of the Court's own decisions by means of statute rather than constitutional amendment? Was the ruling more about the horizontal separation of powers than about federalism? Or did the decision announce a new, stricter standard of scrutiny for all statutes claimed to enforce the civil rights guaranteed by the Fourteenth Amendment? Note that Boerne invalidated RFRA only insofar as it applied to the states; RFRA's strict scrutiny of the denial of religious exemptions from general laws has continued to be applied to the federal government. Does this suggest that, however irritated the Court might have been at Congress's disregard for its decision in Smith, Boerne sounded in federalism and not the separation of powers?

2. ***Boerne and Morgan.*** The Boerne decision did not overrule Morgan, but clarified that it was justifiable only as an exercise of Congress's remedial power. The decision plainly disavowed any power of Congress to confer new substantive rights not derived from prior decisions of the Court interpreting the Fourteenth Amendment. But Boerne also purported to reaffirm the specific holdings of the prior decisions in South Carolina, Morgan and Rome upholding a congressional remedial power that extended beyond mere embodiment of prior Court holdings. How can one reconcile these aspects of Boerne with its repudiation of Congress's power to "expand" Fourteenth Amendment rights? What remaining prophylactic power does Congress have to forestall state violations of rights the Court has found in the Fourteenth Amendment? And what remaining factfinding power does Congress have to identify systemic violations of such rights? How specific must its findings be to justify the exercise of civil rights enforcement power? Note that Justice Kennedy's opinion for the Court suggests that "[p]reventive measures prohibiting certain types of laws may be appropriate when there is reason to believe that many [such laws] have a significant likelihood of being unconstitutional." How many are enough to pass that threshold and make a law remedial rather than substantive?

Note that by requiring Congress to follow the Court's own prior substantive definitions of rights, Boerne may have inverted the roles of each branch anticipated by the Framers of the Fourteenth Amendment. On one historical view, the members of the 39th Congress, who enacted a series of civil rights laws in addition to proposing the Fourteenth Amendment, were seeking to assert their own "legislative centrality" in the civil rights enforcement process, both "reclaiming [Congress's] prerogatives against overreaching" by President Andrew Johnson, who had vetoed civil rights legislation because of Congress's failure to seat the former Confederate States, and expressing "little reason to trust or cede authority to the federal courts," which had rendered "the grotesquely pro-slavery decision in Dred Scott v. Sandford" during their lifetimes. Epps, "Interpreting the Fourteenth Amendment: Two Don'ts and Three Dos," 16 Wm. & Mary Bill of Rts. J. 433 (2007); see generally Epps, Democracy Reborn: The Fourteenth Amendment and the Fight for Equal Rights in Post-Civil War America (2006). For further criticism of the "court-centered model of constitutional interpretation" set forth in Boerne (and progeny), see Post & Siegel, "Equal Protection by Law: Federal Antidiscrimination Legislation After Morrison and Kimel," 110 Yale L.J. 441 (2000).

3. ***Congruent and proportional.*** Assuming that Congress is acting remedially, what kind of means-end test is the requirement that a congressional civil rights remedy be "congruent and proportional" to the state violations Congress has identified? The phrase, drawn from the language of equity used to limit the scope of injunctions, suggests that remedies must be both related to (congruent with) and not too over- or underinclusive in relation to (proportional to) the underlying violations. Does this in effect ratchet up the scrutiny applicable to the exercise of § 5 power from the rationality review employed in McCulloch to a kind of intermediate scrutiny? For an argument that Boerne's congruence and proportionality test is unjustified by either the text or history of the Fourteenth Amendment, and that § 5 legislation should be evaluated by the rational relationship test set forth in McCulloch v. Maryland, see Caminker, " 'Appropriate' Means-Ends Constraints on Section Five Powers," 53 Stan. L. Rev. 1127 (2001).

4. ***Congruence and proportionality and the Voting Rights Act.*** In Boerne, Justice Kennedy took pains not to question Congress's authority to enact, as civil rights remedies, the provisions of the Voting Rights Act of 1965 (VRA) as reauthorized in 1970 and 1982. In 2006, Congress extended for another 25 years the preclearance provisions of § 5 of the Voting Right Act, which require certain covered jurisdictions to obtain federal approval for changes in election procedures in order to ensure that those procedures do not discriminate on the basis of race. A Texas utility district sought to avail itself of the "bailout" provision of the extension law, which releases a "political subdivision" from the preclearance requirement if it can show it has not used any forbidden voting test for 10 years; the district argued in the alternative that the 2006 extension of the VRA preclearance provisions unconstitutionally exceeded Congress's civil rights enforcement authority under Boerne.

In **Northwest Austin Municipal Utility District No. One v. Holder**, 557 U.S. 193 (2009), the Supreme Court avoided the constitutional question, which had been extensively briefed on both sides, through the use of the canon of constitutional avoidance: it interpreted the term "political subdivision" to include the utility district and thus allowed the district to invoke the bailout provision. In writing for the unanimous Court, Chief Justice ROBERTS noted that there were serious "constitutional concerns" with the law.

Although the Court gave Congress a warning shot by identifying its "concerns" with the law but deciding the case on other grounds, Congress declined to amend § 5 of the Voting Rights Act. Three years later, the Court granted certiorari to consider the provision's constitutionality in Shelby County v. Holder.

Shelby County v. Holder

570 U.S. 529, 133 S. Ct. 2612, 186 L. Ed. 2d 651 (2013).

■ CHIEF JUSTICE ROBERTS delivered the opinion of the Court.

The Voting Rights Act of 1965 employed extraordinary measures to address an extraordinary problem. Section 5 of the Act required States to obtain federal permission before enacting any law related to voting—a drastic departure from basic principles of federalism. And § 4 of the Act applied that requirement only to some States—an equally dramatic departure from the principle that all States enjoy equal sovereignty. This was strong medicine, but Congress determined it was needed to address entrenched racial discrimination in voting, "[Nearly] 50 years later, they are still in effect; indeed, they have been made more stringent, and are now scheduled to last until 2031. There is no denying, however, that the conditions that originally justified these measures no longer characterize voting in the covered jurisdictions. By 2009, "the racial gap in voter registration and turnout [was] lower in the States originally covered by § 5 than it [was] nationwide." Since that time, Census Bureau data indicate that African-American voter turnout has come to exceed white voter turnout in five of the six States originally covered by § 5, with a gap in the sixth State of less than one half of one percent. At the same time, voting discrimination still exists; no one doubts that. The question is whether the Act's extraordinary measures, including its disparate treatment of the States, continue to satisfy constitutional requirements.

I. A. The Fifteenth Amendment was ratified in 1870, in the wake of the Civil War. "[The] first century of congressional enforcement of the Amendment, however, can only be regarded as a failure." In the 1890s, Alabama, Georgia, Louisiana, Mississippi, North Carolina, South Carolina, and Virginia began to enact literacy tests for voter registration and to employ other methods designed to prevent African-Americans from voting. Congress passed statutes outlawing some of these practices and facilitating litigation against them, but litigation remained slow and expensive, and the States came up with new ways to discriminate as soon as existing ones were struck down. Voter registration of African-Americans barely improved. Inspired to action by the civil rights movement, Congress responded in 1965 with the Voting Rights Act. Section 2 was enacted to forbid, in all 50 States, any "standard, practice, or procedure . . . imposed or applied . . . to deny or abridge the right of any citizen of the United States to vote on account of race or color." [Other] sections targeted only some parts of the country. At the time of the Act's passage, these "covered" jurisdictions were those States or political subdivisions that had maintained a test or device as a prerequisite to voting as of November 1, 1964, and had less than 50 percent voter registration or turnout in the 1964 Presidential election. Such tests or devices included literacy and knowledge tests, good moral character requirements, the need for vouchers from registered voters, and the like. A covered jurisdiction could "bail out" of coverage if it had not used a test or device in the preceding five years "for the purpose or with the effect of denying or abridging the right to vote on account of race or color." In 1965, the covered States included Alabama, Georgia, Louisiana, Mississippi, South Carolina, and Virginia. The additional covered subdivisions included 39 counties in North Carolina and one in Arizona. In those jurisdictions, § 4 of the Act banned all such tests or devices. Section 5 provided that no change in voting procedures could take effect until it was approved by federal authorities in Washington, D. C.—either the Attorney General or a court of three judges. A jurisdiction could obtain such "preclearance" only by proving that the change had neither "the purpose [nor] the effect of denying or abridging the right to vote on account of race or color."

II. A. "[The] Framers of the Constitution intended the States to keep for themselves, as provided in the Tenth Amendment, the power to regulate elections.' " [Not] only do States retain sovereignty under the Constitution, there is also a "fundamental principle of *equal* sovereignty" among the States.

[The] Voting Rights Act sharply departs from these basic principles. It suspends "*all* changes to state election law—however innocuous—until they have been precleared by federal authorities in Washington, D. C." [And] despite the tradition of equal sovereignty, the [preclearance requirement] applies to only nine States (and several additional counties).

B. [In] 1966, we found these departures from the basic features of our system of government justified. Katzenbach. Several States had enacted a variety of requirements and tests "specifically designed to prevent" African-Americans from voting. Case-by-case litigation had proved inadequate to prevent such racial discrimination in voting.

C. [Nearly] 50 years later, things have changed dramatically. [In] the covered jurisdictions, "[voter] turnout and registration rates now approach parity. Blatantly discriminatory evasions of federal decrees are rare. And minority candidates hold office at unprecedented levels." Northwest Austin. The tests and devices that blocked access to the ballot have been forbidden nationwide for over 40 years.

[There] is no doubt that these improvements are in large part *because of* the Voting Rights Act. Yet the Act has not eased the restrictions in § 5 or narrowed the scope of the coverage formula in § 4(b) along the way. Those extraordinary and unprecedented features were reauthorized—as if nothing had changed.

[Respondents] do not deny that there have been improvements on the ground, but argue that much of this can be attributed to the deterrent effect of § 5, which dissuades covered jurisdictions from engaging in discrimination that they would resume should § 5 be struck down. Under this theory, however, § 5 would be effectively immune from scrutiny; no matter how "clean" the record of covered jurisdictions, the argument could always be made that it was deterrence that accounted for the good behavior.

III. [Coverage] today is based on decades-old data and eradicated practices. The formula captures States by reference to literacy tests and low voter registration and turnout in the 1960s and early 1970s. But such tests have been banned nationwide for over 40 years. [The] Fifteenth Amendment [is] not designed to punish for the past; its purpose is to ensure a better future. To serve that purpose, Congress—if it is to divide the States—must identify those jurisdictions to be singled out on a basis that makes sense in light of current conditions. It cannot rely simply on the past.

[In] defending the coverage formula, the Government, the intervenors, and the dissent also [rely] heavily on data from the record that they claim justify disparate coverage. [But] Congress did not use the record it compiled to shape a coverage formula grounded in current conditions. It instead reenacted a formula based on 40-year-old facts having no logical relation to the present day. [If] Congress had started from scratch in 2006, it plainly could not have enacted the present coverage formula. It would have been irrational for Congress to distinguish between States in such a fundamental way based on 40-year-old data, when today's statistics tell an entirely different story.

[Striking] down an Act of Congress "is the gravest and most delicate duty that this Court is called on to perform." We do not do so lightly. Congress could have updated the coverage formula [after Northwest Austin], but did not do so. Its failure to act leaves us today with no choice but to declare § 4(b) unconstitutional. [Our] decision in no way affects the permanent, nationwide ban on racial discrimination in voting found in § 2. We issue no holding on § 5 itself, only on the coverage formula. Congress may draft another formula based on current conditions. Such a formula is an initial prerequisite to a determination that exceptional conditions still exist justifying such an "extraordinary departure from the traditional course of relations between the States and the Federal Government." Our country has changed, and while any racial discrimination in voting is too much, Congress must ensure that the legislation it passes to remedy that problem speaks to current conditions.

■ JUSTICE THOMAS, concurring.

I join the Court's opinion in full but write separately to explain that I would find § 5 of the Voting Rights Act unconstitutional as well. The Court's opinion sets forth the reasons. While the Court claims to "issue no holding on § 5 itself," its own opinion compellingly demonstrates that Congress has failed to justify " 'current burdens' " with a record demonstrating " 'current needs.' " By leaving the inevitable conclusion unstated, the Court needlessly prolongs the demise of that provision. For the reasons stated in the Court's opinion, I would find § 5 unconstitutional.

■ JUSTICE GINSBURG, with whom [JUSTICES] BREYER, SOTOMAYOR, and KAGAN join, dissenting.

In the Court's view, the very success of § 5 of the Voting Rights Act demands its dormancy. Congress was of another mind. Recognizing that large progress has been made, Congress determined, based on a voluminous record, that the scourge of discrimination was not yet extirpated. The question this case presents is who decides whether, as currently operative, § 5 remains justifiable, this Court, or a Congress charged with the obligation to enforce the post-Civil War Amendments "by appropriate legislation.

I. "[Voting] discrimination still exists; no one doubts that." But the Court today terminates the remedy that proved to be best suited to block that discrimination. The VRA has worked to combat voting discrimination where other remedies had been tried and failed. Particularly effective is the VRA's requirement of federal preclearance for all changes to voting laws in the regions of the country with the most aggravated records of rank discrimination against minority voting rights. [Although] the VRA wrought dramatic changes in the realization of minority voting rights, the Act, to date, surely has not eliminated all vestiges of discrimination against the exercise of the franchise by minority citizens. [Congress] found that as "registration and voting of minority citizens increas[ed], other measures may be resorted to which would dilute increasing minority voting strength." Efforts to reduce the impact of minority votes, in contrast to direct attempts to block access to the ballot, are aptly described as "second-generation barriers" to minority voting.

Second-generation barriers come in various forms. One of the blockages is racial gerrymandering, the redrawing of legislative districts in an "effort to segregate the races for purposes of voting." Another is adoption of a system of at-large voting in lieu of district-by-district voting in a city with a sizable black minority. By switching to at-large voting, the overall majority could control the election of each city council member, effectively eliminating the potency of the minority's votes. A similar effect could be achieved if the city engaged in discriminatory annexation by incorporating majority-white areas into city limits, thereby decreasing the effect of VRA-occasioned increases in black voting.

[In] the long course of the legislative [reauthorization] process, Congress "amassed a sizable record." The House and Senate Judiciary Committees held 21 hearings, heard from scores of witnesses, received a number of investigative reports and other written documentation of continuing discrimination in covered jurisdictions. In all, the legislative record Congress compiled filled more than 15,000 pages. [After] considering the full legislative record, Congress made the following findings[found]: The VRA has directly caused significant progress in eliminating first-generation barriers to ballot access, leading to a marked increase in minority voter registration and turnout and the number of minority elected officials. But despite this progress, "second generation barriers constructed to prevent minority voters from fully participating in the electoral process" continued to exist, as well as racially polarized voting in the covered jurisdictions, which increased the political vulnerability of racial and language minorities in those jurisdictions.

II. [It] is well established that Congress' judgment regarding exercise of its power to enforce the Fourteenth and Fifteenth Amendments warrants substantial deference. The VRA addresses the combination of race discrimination and the right to vote, which is "preservative of all rights." When confronting the most constitutionally invidious form of discrimination, and the most fundamental right in our democratic system, Congress' power to act is at its height. [The] stated purpose of the Civil War Amendments was to arm Congress with the power and authority to protect all persons within the Nation from violations of their rights by the States. In exercising that power, then, Congress may use "all means which are appropriate, which are plainly adapted" to the constitutional ends declared by these Amendments. McCulloch [p. 79 above]. So when Congress acts to enforce the right to vote free from racial discrimination, we ask not whether Congress has chosen the means most wise, but whether Congress has rationally selected means appropriate to a legitimate end.

III. A. [The] surest way to evaluate whether that remedy remains in order is to see if preclearance is still effectively preventing discriminatory changes to voting laws. On that score, the record before Congress was huge. In fact, Congress found there were *more* DOJ objections between 1982 and

2004 (626) than there were between 1965 and the 1982 reauthorization (490). [Congress] also received evidence that litigation under § 2 of the VRA was an inadequate substitute for preclearance in the covered jurisdictions. Litigation occurs only after the fact, when the illegal voting scheme has already been put in place and individuals have been elected pursuant to it, thereby gaining the advantages of incumbency. [And] litigation places a heavy financial burden on minority voters. [The] number of discriminatory changes blocked or deterred by the preclearance requirement suggests that the state of voting rights in the covered jurisdictions would have been significantly different absent this remedy.

B. [There] is no question [that] the covered jurisdictions have a unique history of problems with racial discrimination in voting. Consideration of this long history, still in living memory, was altogether appropriate.

[Congress] might have been charged with rigidity had it afforded covered jurisdictions no way out or ignored jurisdictions that needed superintendence. Congress, however, responded to this concern [e.g., by] allowing [a] jurisdiction[ ] to "bail out" of preclearance [by] showing that it has complied with the Act for ten years,

IV. B. [The] Court stops any application of § 5 by holding that § 4(b)'s coverage formula is unconstitutional. It pins this result, in large measure, to "the fundamental principle of equal sovereignty." In Katzenbach, however, the Court held, in no uncertain terms, that the principle "*applies only to the terms upon which States are admitted to the Union,* and not to the remedies for local evils which have subsequently appeared." [Today's] unprecedented extension of the equal sovereignty principle outside its proper domain—the admission of new States—is capable of much mischief.

THE VOTING RIGHTS ACT AFTER SHELBY COUNTY

1. ***Implications for Section 5.*** Shelby County invalidated § 4(b) of the Voting Rights Act—the coverage formula used to determine which state and local governments had to adhere to § 5's preclearance requirement—but not § 5 itself. In theory, Congress could enact a new statute with a coverage formula consistent with the Court's requirements, but proposals to do so, like the Voting Rights Amendment Act of 2014 (VRAA), have yet to succeed. Unless they do, § 5 of Voting Rights Act remains effectively inoperable. In the wake of Shelby, states such as Texas, North Carolina, Alabama, and Mississippi began to implement strict voter identification laws of the sort that had previously stalled at preclearance. Critics predicted that the new laws would disproportionately affect the rights of poor and minority voters. For more on the constitutionality of voter identification laws, see Chapter 9, p. 810.

2. ***State sovereign immunity decisions and § 5 of the Fourteenth Amendment.*** Since Boerne, the Court has held states immune from suits directed against them under various federal statutes on the ground that Congress lacked power to abrogate state sovereign immunity under its commerce power or other Article I authority, and that Congress also lacked power to impose such liability under its Fourteenth Amendment, § 5 authority unless it could demonstrate that application of the statute to the

states served to remedy state constitutional violations under the standards set forth in Boerne.

The leading case arose from two statutes enacted by Congress in order to expressly abrogate state sovereign immunity against patent and trademark suits. In the absence of Article I authority for Congress to impose liability on the states, the constitutionality of the patent and trademark statutes as applied to the states as potential infringers turned on whether those statutes were validly enacted against the states pursuant to Congress' powers under § 5 of the Fourteenth Amendment. In both cases, the Court concluded that they were not. In **Florida Prepaid Postsecondary Education Expense Board v. College Savings Bank**, 527 U.S. 627 (1999), the Court, by a 5–4 vote, invalidated the Patent and Plant Variety Protection Remedy Clarification Act, which had expressly abrogated the states' sovereign immunity from claims of patent infringement. The case arose from a patent infringement claim brought under the Act by a New Jersey bank against a Florida agency that had allegedly copied the bank's patented college tuition savings program. The bank and the United States defended the statute as an exercise of Congress's power to prevent state deprivations of property, here in the form of patent rights, without due process of law.

Chief Justice REHNQUIST, writing for the Court, reiterated that " 'appropriate' legislation pursuant to the Enforcement Clause of the Fourteenth Amendment could abrogate state sovereignty," and that "the 'provisions of this article,' to which § 5 refers, include the Due Process Clause of the Fourteenth Amendment." Turning to the question whether the Patent Remedy Act could be viewed as permissibly remedial or preventive legislation within the meaning of Boerne, Chief Justice Rehnquist continued: "The underlying conduct at issue here is state infringement of patents and the use of sovereign immunity to deny patent owners compensation for the invasion of their patent rights. [In] enacting the Patent Remedy Act, however, Congress identified no pattern of patent infringement by the States, let alone a pattern of constitutional [due process] violations. Unlike the undisputed record of racial discrimination confronting Congress in the voting rights cases, Congress came up with little evidence of infringing conduct on the part of the States. [Moreover, Congress] barely considered the availability of state remedies for patent infringement and hence whether the States' conduct might have amounted to a constitutional violation under the Fourteenth Amendment. [The] legislative record thus suggests that the Patent Remedy Act does not respond to a history of 'widespread and persisting deprivation of constitutional rights' of the sort Congress has faced in enacting proper prophylactic § 5 legislation. Boerne. [Though] the lack of support in the legislative record is not determinative, identifying the targeted constitutional wrong or evil is still a critical part of our § 5 calculus. [Here], the record at best offers scant support for Congress' conclusion that States were depriving patent owners of property without due process of law by pleading sovereign immunity in federal-court patent actions.

"Because of this lack, the provisions of the Patent Remedy Act are 'so out of proportion to a supposed remedial or preventive object that [they] cannot be understood as responsive to, or designed to prevent, unconstitutional behavior.' [Despite] subjecting States to this expansive liability, Congress did nothing to limit the coverage of the Act to cases involving arguable constitutional violations, such as where a State refuses to offer any state-court remedy for patent owners whose patents it had infringed. Nor did it make any attempt to confine the reach of the Act by limiting the remedy to certain types of infringement, such as nonnegligent infringement or infringement authorized pursuant to state policy; or providing for suits only against States with questionable remedies or a high incidence of infringement. Instead, Congress made all States immediately amenable to suit in federal court for all kinds of possible patent infringement and for an indefinite duration. [The] historical record and the scope of coverage therefore make it clear that the Patent Remedy Act cannot be sustained under § 5 of the Fourteenth Amendment."

Justice STEVENS dissented, joined by Justices Souter, Ginsburg and Breyer. Emphasizing the need for federal uniformity in patent law, he argued that it was "appropriate" under Boerne for Congress to conclude that state remedies would be inadequate to "guarantee patentees due process in infringement actions against state defendants," and thus appropriate to pass the Patent Remedy Act as a preventive measure. Asserting that the Court had gone beyond the limits set forth in Boerne, he warned that "[t]he Court's opinion today threatens to read Congress' power to pass prophylactic legislation out of § 5 altogether."

3. ***Boerne and the role of congressional findings.*** Did Boerne suggest that Congress could legislate prophylactically against civil rights violations so long as it compiled a better evidentiary record and findings of state misconduct or indifference? In the following decision, the Court found even a voluminous congressional record insufficient to uphold the civil damages provisions of the Violence Against Women Act of 1994 (VAWA).

United States v. Morrison

529 U.S. 598, 120 S. Ct. 1740, 146 L. Ed. 2d 658 (2000).

[The case arose from rape charge brought by Christy Brzonkala, a student at Virginia Polytechnic Institute, against two football players also enrolled at the university. She filed a complaint under the Virginia Tech disciplinary system, but one of the accused was not punished and the other's punishment was eventually suspended. She dropped out of school and sued both men and Virginia Tech in federal district court for damages under the civil damages provisions of VAWA. The Court found that those provisions exceeded Congress's power to enforce the Equal Protection Clause against gender discrimination. (For the portion of the opinion holding that the VAWA civil damages provisions also exceeded Congress's power under the Commerce Clause, see p. 148 above.)]

■ CHIEF JUSTICE REHNQUIST delivered the opinion of the Court.

In these cases we consider the constitutionality of 42 U.S.C. § 13981, which provides a federal civil remedy for the victims of gender-motivated violence. [Section 13981] was part of the Violence Against Women Act of 1994, [which] states that "[a]ll persons within the United States shall have the right to be free from crimes of violence motivated by gender." To enforce that right, [the law] declares: "A person (including a person who acts under color of any statute, ordinance, regulation, custom, or usage of any State) who commits a crime of violence motivated by gender and thus deprives another of the right [to be free of such crimes] shall be liable to the party injured, in an action for the recovery of compensatory and punitive damages, injunctive and declaratory relief, and such other relief as a court may deem appropriate."

[Petitioners'] § 5 argument is founded on an assertion that there is pervasive bias in various state justice systems against victims of gender-motivated violence. This assertion is supported by a voluminous congressional record. Specifically, Congress received evidence that many participants in state justice systems are perpetuating an array of erroneous stereotypes and assumptions. Congress concluded that these discriminatory stereotypes often result in insufficient investigation and prosecution of gender-motivated crime, inappropriate focus on the behavior and credibility of the victims of that crime, and unacceptably lenient punishments for those who are actually convicted of gender-motivated violence. Petitioners contend that this bias denies victims of gender-motivated violence the equal protection of the laws and that Congress therefore acted appropriately in enacting a private civil remedy against the perpetrators of gender-motivated violence to both remedy the States' bias and deter future instances of discrimination in the state courts.

[However,] the language and purpose of the Fourteenth Amendment place certain limitations on the manner in which Congress may attack discriminatory conduct. These limitations are necessary to prevent the Fourteenth Amendment from obliterating the Framers' carefully crafted balance of power between the States and the National Government. Foremost among these limitations is the time-honored principle that the Fourteenth Amendment, by its very terms, prohibits only state action.

Shortly after the Fourteenth Amendment was adopted, we decided two cases interpreting the Amendment's provisions, United States v. Harris, 106 U.S. 629 (1883), and the Civil Rights Cases, [1883; p. 856 above]. In Harris, the Court considered a challenge to § 2 of the Civil Rights Act of 1871. That section sought to punish "private persons" for "conspiring to deprive any one of the equal protection of the laws enacted by the State." We concluded that this law exceeded Congress' § 5 power because the law was "directed exclusively against the action of private persons, without reference to the laws of the State, or their administration by her officers." [We] reached a similar conclusion in the Civil Rights Cases. In those consolidated cases, we held that the public accommodation provisions of the Civil Rights Act of 1875, which applied to purely private conduct, were beyond the scope of the § 5 enforcement power.

[Petitioners] argue that, unlike the situation in the Civil Rights Cases, here there has been gender-based disparate treatment by state authorities, whereas in those cases there was no indication of such state action. There is abundant evidence, however, to show that the Congresses that enacted the Civil Rights Acts of 1871 and 1875 had a purpose similar to that of Congress in enacting § 13981: There were state laws on the books bespeaking equality of treatment, but in the administration of these laws there was discrimination against newly freed slaves. [But] even if that distinction were valid, we do not believe it would save § 13981's civil remedy. For the remedy is simply not "corrective in its character, adapted to counteract and redress the operation of such prohibited [s]tate laws or proceedings of [s]tate officers." Civil Rights Cases. Or, as we have phrased it in more recent cases, prophylactic legislation under § 5 must have a "congruence and proportionality between the injury to be prevented or remedied and the means adopted to that end." Florida Prepaid; Boerne. [Section] 13981 is not aimed at proscribing discrimination by officials which the Fourteenth Amendment might not itself proscribe; it is directed not at any State or state actor, but at individuals who have committed criminal acts motivated by gender bias.

In the present cases, for example, § 13981 visits no consequence whatever on any Virginia public official involved in investigating or prosecuting Brzonkala's assault. The section is, therefore, unlike any of the § 5 remedies that we have previously upheld. [Section 13981] is also different from these previously upheld remedies in that it applies uniformly throughout the Nation. Congress' findings indicate that the problem of discrimination against the victims of gender-motivated crimes does not exist in all States, or even most States. [For] these reasons, we conclude that Congress' power under § 5 does not extend to the enactment of § 13981. [Affirmed.]

■ JUSTICE BREYER, with whom JUSTICE STEVENS joins, dissenting.

[Petitioners claim] that Congress used § 5 to remedy the actions of state actors, namely, those States which, through discriminatory design or the discriminatory conduct of their officials, failed to provide adequate (or any) state remedies for women injured by gender-motivated violence—a failure that the States, and Congress, documented in depth. [This] Court has held that Congress at least sometimes can enact remedial "[l]egislation . . . [that] prohibits conduct which is not itself unconstitutional." Boerne. The statutory remedy does not in any sense purport to "determine what constitutes a constitutional violation." It intrudes little upon either States or private parties. It may lead state actors to improve their own remedial systems, primarily through example. It restricts private actors only by imposing liability for private conduct that is, in the main, already forbidden by state law. Why is the remedy "disproportionate"? And given the relation between remedy and violation—the creation of a federal remedy to substitute for constitutionally inadequate state remedies—where is the lack of "congruence"?

The majority adds that Congress found that the problem of inadequacy of state remedies "does not exist in all States, or even most States." But Congress had before it the task force reports of at least 21 States documenting constitutional violations. And it made its own findings about pervasive gender-based stereotypes hampering many state legal systems, sometimes unconstitutionally so. The record nowhere reveals a congressional finding that the problem "does not exist" elsewhere. Why can Congress not take the evidence before it as evidence of a national problem? This Court has not previously held that Congress must document the existence of a problem in every State prior to proposing a national solution. And the deference this Court gives to Congress' chosen remedy under § 5, suggests that any such requirement would be inappropriate.

THE MEANING AND SCOPE OF MORRISON

1. ***The problem of state omissions to act.*** What authority does Morrison leave Congress to legislate to correct state *omissions* to protect civil

rights clearly protected by prior judicial interpretations of the Fourteenth Amendment? Was the problem in Morrison that Congress had not documented such failures with respect to sex bias in state criminal justice systems? That it had not demonstrated it nationwide, nor limited the law to specific jurisdictions found to be backwaters of sexism? Or was the problem instead that no matter how lax the states had been shown to be, the civil damages remedy was directed at private actors—here the alleged date rapists—and not against state officials as such? How does Congress's authority to correct inaction by states compare to its authority to correct inaction by individuals under NFIB v. Sebelius (p. 160 above)?

2. ***Section 5 authority for antidiscrimination statutes outside the area of race.*** Even if Boerne reaffirmed the Voting Rights Act cases, implicitly grandfathering them and shielding them from the new heightened scrutiny, did it portend new limits on Congress's power to include the state governments within the reach of other antidiscrimination statutes? What about those antidiscrimination statutes aimed at classifications that the Court has subjected to less than strict scrutiny, such as statutes aimed at discrimination on the basis of age or disability? The following decisions, applying the tests set forth in Boerne and Morrison, uphold some but strike down other federal antidiscrimination laws as applied against the states. (Note that these statutes are not questioned on their face or as applied to private actors; as against private actors, these laws are generally permissible exercises of Congress's commerce power. Commerce Clause authority is insufficient to uphold these laws as against the states, however, insofar as these laws create causes of action that abrogate state sovereign immunity.)

In the cases below, consider whether the Court is more likely to defer to Congress's exercise of civil rights enforcement power in areas where the Court has applied heightened scrutiny under § 1 of the Fourteenth Amendment. Is a statute more likely to receive deference the more suspect the classification against which the remedy is directed? Or does Morrison demonstrate that heightened scrutiny of a characteristic under § 1 (there, gender) is no guarantee of success under § 5?

a. *Age discrimination.* In **Kimel v. Florida Board of Regents**, 528 U.S. 62 (2000), the Court ruled by a vote of 5–4 that Congress had exceeded its Fourteenth Amendment remedial authority in allowing state employees to sue the states for violations of the Age Discrimination in Employment Act (ADEA). After noting that the Fourteenth Amendment was the sole source of possible congressional authority to abrogate sovereign immunity here under the Seminole Tribe line of cases, the Court examined the ADEA under the test announced in Boerne. Because the ADEA failed the "congruence and proportionality test," the majority held, Congress's attempt to abrogate the states' sovereign immunity was unconstitutional.

Justice O'CONNOR, joined by Chief Justice Rehnquist and Justices Scalia, Kennedy, and Thomas, noted that the antidiscrimination protections of the ADEA for state employees far exceeded the requirements of equal protection: "Applying [the] 'congruence and proportionality' test, [we] conclude that the ADEA is not 'appropriate legislation' under § 5 of the Fourteenth Amendment. [The] substantive requirements the ADEA imposes on state and local governments are disproportionate to any unconstitutional conduct that conceivably could be targeted by the Act. We have considered claims of unconstitutional age discrimination under the Equal Protection Clause three times. In all three cases, we held that the age classifications at issue did not violate the Equal Protection Clause. [Our] Constitution permits States to draw lines on the basis of age when they have a rational basis for doing so at a class-based level, even if it 'is probably not true' that those reasons are valid in the majority of cases.

"[The ADEA], through its broad restriction on the use of age as a discriminating factor, prohibits substantially more state employment decisions and practices than would likely be held unconstitutional under the applicable equal protection [standard]. [Congress], through the ADEA, has effectively elevated the standard for analyzing age discrimination to heightened scrutiny. [Congress] never identified any pattern of age discrimination by the States, much less any discrimination whatsoever that rose to the level of constitutional violation. [Congress] had virtually no reason to believe that state and local governments were unconstitutionally discriminating against their employees on the basis of age. [In] light of the indiscriminate scope of the Act's substantive requirements, and the lack of evidence of widespread and unconstitutional age discrimination by the States, we hold that the ADEA is not a valid exercise of Congress' power under § 5 of the Fourteenth Amendment. The ADEA's purported abrogation of the States' sovereign immunity is accordingly invalid."

Justice THOMAS, joined by Justice Kennedy, concurred with the Court's Fourteenth Amendment analysis, but deemed the constitutional question unnecessary to reach because the ADEA did not evince an unmistakable intention to abrogate the states' sovereign immunity. In dissent, Justice STEVENS, joined by Justices Souter, Ginsburg, and Breyer, did not reach the Fourteenth Amendment issue, since, consistent with the dissenters' views in prior cases, he deemed the ADEA's abrogation of sovereign immunity justified under the Commerce Power.

b. *Disability discrimination.* One term after the Kimel decision, the Court once again found Congress to have exceeded its § 5 enforcement power in providing a damages remedy against state employers for discrimination based on a nonsuspect classification. In **Board of Trustees of The University of Alabama v. Garrett**, 531 U.S. 356 (2001), the Court held invalid Congress's attempt to abrogate sovereign immunity for state-employer violations of Title I of the Americans with Disabilities Act of 1990 (ADA), 42 U.S.C. §§ 12111–12117. Title I prohibits covered employers from "discriminat[ing] against a qualified individual" on account of the disability, requires covered employers to "mak[e] reasonable accommodations to the [physical] or mental limitations of [otherwise] qualified" disabled workers except in cases of "undue hardship," and makes available money damages for violations. As in Kimel, because application of the ADA damages provision against state employers required abrogation of the states' sovereign immunity, the provision could be sustained only if it was within Congress's Fourteenth Amendment powers.

Writing for the Court, Chief Justice REHNQUIST reiterated that "it is the responsibility of this Court, not Congress, to define the substance of constitutional guarantees." Following the Court's prior decisions such as City of Cleburne, Tex. v. Cleburne Living Center, 473 U.S. 432 (1985), Rehnquist identified the substantive equal protection guarantee as requiring a mere rational relationship between classifications based on disability and legitimate legislative ends. He then found that Congress had failed to identify "a history and pattern of unconstitutional employment discrimination by the States against the disabled" adequate to show that the states had engaged in irrational discrimination. Although the dissent compiled several appendices listing reports and discriminatory incidents purported to support the law, Rehnquist expressed doubt about this record, questioning the force of "unexamined, anecdotal accounts" submitted to a task force but "not [to] Congress." Additionally, he noted that the record primarily detailed discrimination not by states but by "units of local governments, such as cities and counties" that do not enjoy Eleventh Amendment immunity and therefore could not provide a rational basis for abrogating that immunity.

Moreover, according to Rehnquist, those incidents that were attributable to states may not have risen to the level of *unconstitutional* discrimination in the first place, and were not sufficiently pervasive to support this drastic a remedy: "[Even] if it were to be determined that each incident [showed] unconstitutional action on the part of the State, [these few] incidents taken together fall far short of even suggesting the pattern of unconstitutional discrimination on which § 5 legislation must be based." Rehnquist found it "telling [that Congress] assembled only such minimal evidence of unconstitutional state discrimination" given the large numbers of both state employees and disabled Americans. Finally, the majority opinion held, the ADA's reasonable accommodation provision required far more than was necessary to vindicate the particular rights at issue and effectively shifted the burden of proof to state employers: "[Whereas] it would be entirely rational (and therefore constitutional) for a state employer to conserve scarce financial resources by hiring employees who are able to use existing facilities, the ADA requires employers to 'mak[e] existing facilities used by employees readily accessible to and usable by individuals with disabilities.' [The] accommodation duty far exceeds what is constitutionally required in that it makes unlawful a range of alternate responses that would be reasonable but would fall short of imposing an 'undue burden' upon the employer. The Act also makes it the employer's duty to prove that it would suffer such a burden, instead of requiring (as the Constitution does) that the complaining party negate reasonable bases for the employer's decision."

Justice KENNEDY's concurrence, joined by Justice O'CONNOR, called the ADA "a milestone on the path to a more decent, tolerant, progressive society," but nevertheless found inadequate evidence of constitutional violations to sustain it as an exercise of § 5 power: "If the States had been transgressing the Fourteenth Amendment by their mistreatment or lack of concern for those with impairments, one would have expected to find in decisions of the courts of the States and also the courts of the United States extensive litigation and discussion of the constitutional violations. This confirming judicial documentation does not exist."

Justice BREYER dissented, joined by Justices Stevens, Souter, and Ginsburg: "In my view, Congress reasonably could have concluded that the remedy before us constitutes an 'appropriate' way to enforce [the] equal protection requirement. And that is all the Constitution requires. [Congress] compiled a vast legislative record documenting 'massive, society-wide discrimination' against persons with disabilities. In addition to the information presented at 13 congressional hearings, and its own prior experience gathered over 40 years during which it contemplated and enacted considerable similar legislation, Congress created a special task force [that] held hearings in every State, attended by more than 30,000 people, including thousands who had experienced discrimination first hand."

For Justice Breyer, discriminatory state practices could be inferred from general societal practices: "The powerful evidence of discriminatory treatment throughout society in general, including discrimination by private persons and local governments, implicates state governments as well, for state agencies form part of that same larger society." And, unlike the majority, Justice Breyer also considered evidence of municipal government violations to be probative, because "[local] governments often work closely with, and under the supervision of, state officials, and in general, state and local government employers are similarly situated." Criticizing the majority's "decision to hold Congress to a strict judicially created evidentiary standard," Justice Breyer also argued that there was an ample record of discrimination by the states themselves: "There are roughly 300 examples of discrimination by state governments themselves in the legislative record. [Those] who presented instances of discrimination rarely provided additional, independent evidence sufficient to prove in court that, in each instance, the discrimination they suffered lacked justification from a judicial standpoint. [But] a legislature is not a court of law. And Congress, unlike courts, must, and does, routinely draw general conclusions [from] anecdotal and opinion-based evidence of this kind, particularly when the evidence lacks strong refutation. [Unlike] courts, Congress directly reflects public attitudes and beliefs, enabling Congress better to understand where, and to what extent, refusals to accommodate a disability amount to behavior that is callous or unreasonable to the point of lacking constitutional justification. Unlike judges, Members of Congress can directly obtain information from constituents who have first-hand experience with discrimination and related issues."

The decision in Garrett, which dealt only with Title I of the ADA, left open the question whether the Fourteenth Amendment, § 5 authorizes Congress, in the face of the otherwise applicable sovereign immunity bar, to permit suits against the states for money damages under Title II of the ADA, which provides: "No qualified individual with a disability shall, by reason of such disability, be excluded from participation or denied the benefits of the services, programs or activities of a public entity, or be subjected to discrimination by any such entity." In **Tennessee v. Lane**, 541 U.S. 509 (2004), Justice O'Connor moved over to join the Garrett dissenters in answering that question affirmatively, with the majority now holding Title II a permissible exercise of Congress's civil rights enforcement power, at least as applied to cases involving access to the courts. The case involved a challenge by a paraplegic who objected to the lack of an elevator in a county courthouse, alleging that he had had to crawl up two flights of stairs in order to appear to answer a set of criminal charges.

Justice STEVENS wrote for the 5–4 majority, joined by Justices O'Connor, Souter, Ginsburg and Breyer. He emphasized that Title II's purpose extended beyond protection against simple unequal treatment to also protecting against deprivations of certain fundamental interests: "In Garrett we identified Title I's purpose as enforcement of the Fourteenth Amendment's command that 'all persons similarly situated should be treated alike.' As we observed, classifications based on disability violate that constitutional command if they lack a rational relationship to a legitimate governmental purpose. Title II, like Title I, seeks to enforce this prohibition on irrational disability discrimination. But it also seeks to enforce a variety of other basic constitutional guarantees, infringements of which are subject to more searching judicial review. These rights include some, like the right of access to the courts at issue in this case, that are protected by the Due Process Clause of the Fourteenth Amendment. The Due Process Clause and the Confrontation Clause of the Sixth Amendment, as applied to the States via the Fourteenth Amendment, both guarantee to a criminal defendant such as respondent Lane the 'right to be present at all stages of the trial where his absence might frustrate the fairness of the proceedings.' The Due Process Clause also requires the States to afford certain civil litigants a 'meaningful opportunity to be heard' by removing obstacles to their full participation in judicial proceedings. We have held that the Sixth Amendment guarantees to criminal defendants the right to trial by a jury composed of a fair cross section of the community. [And,] finally, we have recognized that members of the public have a right of access to criminal proceedings secured by the First Amendment.

"[While] § 5 authorizes Congress to enact reasonably prophylactic remedial legislation, the appropriateness of the remedy depends on the gravity of the harm it seeks to prevent. [It] is not difficult to perceive the harm that Title II is designed to address. Congress enacted Title II against a backdrop of pervasive unequal treatment in the administration of state services and programs, including systematic deprivations of fundamental rights. For example, 'as of 1979, most States . . . categorically disqualified "idiots" from voting, without regard to individual capacity.' The majority of these laws remain on the books. [A] number of States have prohibited and continue to prohibit persons with disabilities from engaging in activities such as marrying and serving as jurors. The historical experience that Title II reflects is also documented in this Court's cases, which have identified unconstitutional treatment of disabled persons by state agencies in a variety of settings, including unjustified commitment, the abuse and neglect of persons committed to state mental health hospitals, and irrational discrimination in zoning decisions, [see] Cleburne. This pattern of disability discrimination persisted despite several federal and state legislative efforts to address it [that Congress identified in its deliberations over the ADA]. In the deliberations that led up to the enactment of the ADA, Congress identified important shortcomings in existing laws that rendered them 'inadequate to address the pervasive problems of discrimination that people with disabilities are facing.' As the Court's opinion in Garrett observed, the 'overwhelming majority' of these examples concerned discrimination in the administration of public programs and services. With respect to the particular services at issue in this case, Congress learned that many individuals, in many States across the country, were being excluded from courthouses and court proceedings by reason of their disabilities. [The] conclusion that Congress drew from this body of evidence is set forth in the text of the ADA itself: 'Discrimination against individuals with disabilities persists in such critical areas as . . . education, transportation, communication, recreation, institutionalization, health services, voting, and access to public services.' This finding, together with the extensive record of disability discrimination that underlies it, makes clear beyond peradventure that inadequate provision of public services and access to public facilities was an appropriate subject for prophylactic legislation.

"The only question that remains is whether Title II is an appropriate response to this history and pattern of unequal treatment. Whatever might be said about Title II's other applications, the question presented in this case is whether Congress had the power under § 5 to enforce the constitutional right of access to the courts. Because we find that Title II unquestionably is valid § 5 legislation as it applies to the class of cases implicating the accessibility of judicial services, we need go no further.

"Congress' chosen remedy for the pattern of exclusion and discrimination described above, Title II's requirement of program accessibility, is congruent and proportional to its object of enforcing the right of access to the courts. Recognizing that failure to accommodate persons with disabilities will often have the same practical effect as outright exclusion, Congress required the States to take reasonable measures to remove architectural and other barriers to accessibility. But Title II does not require States to employ any and all means to make judicial services accessible to persons with disabilities, and it does not require States to compromise their essential eligibility criteria for public programs. It requires only 'reasonable modifications' that would not fundamentally alter the nature of the service provided, and only when the individual seeking modification is otherwise eligible for the service. This duty to accommodate is perfectly consistent with the well-established due process principle that, "within the limits of practicability, a State must afford to all individuals a meaningful opportunity to be heard" in its courts. [Judged] against this backdrop, Title II's affirmative obligation to accommodate persons with disabilities in the administration of justice cannot be said to be 'so out of proportion to a supposed remedial or preventive object that it cannot be understood as responsive to, or designed to prevent, unconstitutional behavior.' It is, rather, a reasonable prophylactic measure, reasonably targeted to a legitimate end."

Chief Justice REHNQUIST, joined by Justices Kennedy and Thomas, filed a dissent: "[T]he majority identifies nothing in the legislative record that shows Congress was responding to widespread violations of the due process rights of disabled persons. Rather than limiting its discussion of constitutional violations to the due process rights on which it ultimately relies, the majority sets out on a wide-ranging account of societal discrimination against the disabled. Some of this evidence would be relevant if the Court were considering the constitutionality of the statute as a whole; but the Court rejects that approach in favor of a narrower 'as-applied' inquiry. We discounted much the same type of outdated, generalized evidence in Garrett as unsupportive of Title I's ban on employment discrimination. [Even] if the anecdotal evidence and conclusory statements relied on by the majority could be properly considered, the mere existence of an architecturally 'inaccessible' courthouse—i.e., one a disabled person cannot utilize without assistance—does not state a violation of due process. Nor does an "inaccessible" courthouse violate the Equal Protection Clause, unless it is irrational for the State not to alter the courthouse to make it 'accessible.' But financial considerations almost always furnish a rational basis for a State to decline to make those alterations. Garrett." Chief Justice Rehnquist also objected to the majority's use of an "as-applied" approach in the § 5 context: "The effect is to rig the congruence-and-proportionality test by artificially constricting the scope of the statute to closely mirror a recognized constitutional right."

Justice SCALIA filed a separate dissent, expressing regret that he had earlier signed onto the "congruence and proportionality" test, which he said, "like all such flabby tests, is a standing invitation to judicial arbitrariness and policy-driven decisionmaking. Worse still, it casts this Court in the role of Congress's taskmaster. Under it, the courts (and ultimately this Court) must regularly check Congress's homework to make sure that it has identified sufficient constitutional violations to make its remedy congruent and proportional." He would have limited Congress under § 5 to remedying conduct that itself violates a provision of the 14th Amendment, but grandfathered "prophylactic legislation," like the Voting Rights Act, in the area of race discrimination.

In **United States v. Georgia**, 546 U.S. 151 (2006), the Court considered whether a disabled inmate in a Georgia prison could sue the State under Title II of the ADA. In a unanimous opinion by Justice SCALIA, the Court assumed that a paraplegic prisoner, in alleging that prison officials had deliberately refused to accommodate his disability-related needs in such fundamentals as mobility, hygiene and medical care, had stated claims based on conduct that independently violated § 1 of the Fourteenth Amendment, which incorporates the Eighth Amendment's guarantee against cruel and unusual punishment. Distinguishing the case from prior cases in which states asserted sovereign immunity against federal civil rights laws, Justice Scalia wrote: "While the Members of this Court have disagreed regarding the scope of Congress's 'prophylactic' enforcement powers under § 5 of the Fourteenth Amendment, no one doubts that § 5 grants Congress the power to 'enforce . . . the provisions of the Amendment' by creating private remedies against the States for *actual* violations of those provisions. [Thus,] insofar as Title II creates a private cause of action for damages against the States for conduct that *actually* violates the Fourteenth Amendment, Title II validly abrogates state sovereign immunity." What explains the Court's unanimity in Georgia as compared with the divisions in Garrett and Lane?

c. *Family leave and gender discrimination*. The Court again rejected a claim of state sovereign immunity to suit under a federal antidiscrimination statute, finding adequate Fourteenth Amendment, § 5 authority, in **Nevada Department of Human Resources v. Hibbs**, 538 U.S. 721 (2003). In that decision, the Court distinguished Kimel and Garrett, upholding Congress's power to apply the family-care provision of the Family Medical Leave Act of 1993 (FMLA) to the states under § 5. One goal of the FMLA was to prevent gender discrimination by making it possible for parents of either gender to take a leave of absence to care for a sick family member; the rationale was that without such a provision, women would most frequently be forced to leave work and would be more likely than men to suffer adverse employment consequences as a result. Writing for the Court, Chief Justice REHNQUIST, joined by Justices O'Connor, Souter, Ginsburg and Breyer, reasoned that the FMLA was appropriately tailored to preventing gender discrimination in the workplace: "Congress may enact so-called prophylactic legislation that proscribes facially constitutional conduct, in order to prevent and deter unconstitutional conduct. [The] FMLA aims to protect the right to be free from gender-based discrimination in the workplace. We have held that statutory classifications that distinguish between males and females are subject to heightened scrutiny. [We] now inquire whether Congress had evidence of a pattern of constitutional violations on the part of the States in this area.

"The history of the many state laws limiting women's employment opportunities is chronicled in—and, until relatively recently, was sanctioned by—this Court's own opinions. For example, in Bradwell v. Illinois and Goesaert v. Cleary, the Court upheld state laws prohibiting women from practicing law and tending bar, respectively. State laws frequently subjected women to distinctive restrictions, terms, conditions, and benefits for those jobs they could take. [Congress] responded to this history of discrimination by abrogating States' sovereign immunity in Title VII of the Civil Rights Act of 1964. [But] state gender discrimination did not cease. [According] to evidence that was before Congress when it enacted the FMLA, States continue to rely on invalid gender stereotypes in the employment context, specifically in the administration of leave benefits. Reliance on such stereotypes cannot justify the States' gender discrimination in this area. [The] persistence of such unconstitutional discrimination by the States justifies Congress' passage of prophylactic § 5 legislation."

Chief Justice Rehnquist distinguished prior cases holding that other federal causes of action against the states had exceeded Congress's civil rights enforcement power: "We reached the opposite conclusion in Garrett and Kimel. In those cases, the § 5 legislation under review responded to a purported tendency of state officials to make age- or disability-based distinctions. Under our equal protection case law, discrimination on the basis of such characteristics is not judged under a heightened review standard, and passes muster if there is 'a rational basis for doing so.' [Thus,] in order to impugn the constitutionality of state discrimination against the disabled or the elderly, Congress must identify, not just the existence of age- or disability-based state decisions, but a 'widespread pattern' of irrational reliance on such criteria. We found no such showing with respect to the ADEA and Title I of the Americans with Disabilities Act of 1990 (ADA). Here, however, Congress directed its attention to state gender discrimination, which triggers a heightened level of scrutiny. Because the standard for demonstrating the constitutionality of a gender-based classification is more difficult to meet than our rational-basis test [it] was easier for Congress to show a pattern of state constitutional violations."

Noting that the "impact of the discrimination targeted by the FMLA is significant," that "[s]tereotypes about women's domestic roles are reinforced by parallel stereotypes presuming a lack of domestic responsibilities for men," and that such perceptions "lead to subtle discrimination that may be difficult to detect on a case-by-case basis," Chief Justice Rehnquist concluded that "Congress' chosen remedy, the family-care leave provision of the FMLA, is 'congruent and proportional to the targeted violation.'" He rejected the argument that Congress had exceeded its authority by creating a new substantive entitlement to a floor of 12 weeks' leave, rather than simply outlawing gender-based discrimination by the States in the provision of leave benefits: "Congress 'is not confined to the enactment of legislation that merely parrots the precise wording of the Fourteenth Amendment,' but may prohibit 'a somewhat broader swath of conduct, including that which is not itself forbidden by the Amendment's text.'" He also noted that, "[u]nlike the statutes at issue in City of Boerne, Kimel, and Garrett, which applied broadly to every aspect of state employers' operations, the FMLA is narrowly targeted at the fault line between work and family—precisely where sex-based overgeneralization has been and remains strongest—and affects only one aspect of the employment relationship."

Justice SCALIA dissented: "There is no guilt by association, enabling the sovereignty of one State to be abridged under § 5 of the Fourteenth Amendment because of violations by another State, or by most other States, or even by 49 other States. [Today's] opinion for the Court does not even attempt to demonstrate that each one of the 50 States covered by [the FMLA] was in violation of the Fourteenth Amendment." Justice KENNEDY, joined by Justices Scalia and Thomas, dissented as well, arguing that the FMLA was not a congruent and proportional remedy to any demonstrated gender discrimination by the states: "The Court is unable to show that States have engaged in a pattern of unlawful conduct which warrants the remedy of opening state treasuries to private suits. [All] would agree that women historically have been subjected to conditions in which their employment opportunities are more limited than those available to men. [But the FMLA] seeks to ensure that eligible employees, irrespective of gender, can take a minimum amount of leave time to care for an ill relative. The relevant question, as the Court seems to acknowledge, is whether, notwithstanding the passage of Title VII and similar state legislation, the States continued to engage in widespread discrimination on the basis of gender in the provision of family leave benefits. If such a pattern were shown, the Eleventh Amendment would not bar Congress from devising a congruent and proportional remedy. The evidence to substantiate this charge must be far more specific, however, than a simple recitation of a general history of employment discrimination against women." He continued: "Our concern with gender discrimination, which is subjected to heightened scrutiny, as opposed to age- or disability-based distinctions, which are reviewed under rational standard, does not alter this conclusion. The application of heightened scrutiny is designed to ensure gender-based classifications are not based on the entrenched and pervasive stereotypes which inhibit women's progress in the workplace. This consideration does not divest respondents of their burden to show that 'Congress identified a history and pattern of unconstitutional employment discrimination by the States.' "

Nine years later, the Court considered a different challenge to the FMLA on state sovereign immunity grounds. While Hibbs had approved the FMLA's family-care provision, **Coleman v. Court of Appeals of Maryland**, 566 U.S. 30 (2012), featured a challenge to the FMLA's self-care provision, which allowed employees to take a leave of absence from work to treat their own illnesses. The Court reached the opposite result that it had in Hibbs, finding that the provision invalidly abrogated state sovereign immunity. Writing for a plurality, Justice KENNEDY, joined by Chief Justice Roberts and Justices Thomas and Alito, explained that "[w]hether a congressional Act passed under § 5 can impose monetary liability upon States requires an assessment of both the 'evil or wrong that Congress intended to remedy,' [Hibbs], and the means Congress adopted to address that evil, see Boerne. Legislation enacted under § 5 must be targeted at 'conduct transgressing the Fourteenth Amendment's substantive provisions.' [Florida Prepaid; see also Kimel; Boerne]." And "[t]here must be a congruence and proportionality between the injury to be prevented or remedied and the means adopted to that end. [Florida Prepaid]."

Justice Kennedy distinguished the self-care provision here from the family care provisions in Hibbs: " [What] the family-care provisions have to support them, the self-care provision lacks, namely evidence of a pattern of state constitutional violations accompanied by a remedy drawn in narrow terms to address or prevent [alleged constitutional] violations." While some of the facially neutral policies the self-care provision targeted had a disparate impact on women, the provision was too blunt and forceful to address that problem properly. It was therefore "out of proportion" to the harms it sought to address and hence was unconstitutional.

Justice THOMAS wrote a separate concurrence, noting that he fully endorsed the plurality's opinion but that he believed Hibbs had been wrongly decided, and that even there Congress's response had been disproportionate to the evil it sought to address. Justice SCALIA concurred in the judgment, admitting that the plurality's application of the "congruence and proportionality" test was correct but challenging the validity of the test itself: "This grading of Congress's homework is a task we are ill suited to perform and ill advised to undertake. [As] I have explained in greater detail [in Lane, p. 921 above], outside of the context of racial discrimination (which is different for *stare decisis* reasons), I would limit Congress's § 5 power to the regulation of conduct that *itself* violates the Fourteenth Amendment. Failing to grant state employees leave for the purpose of self-care—or any other purpose, for that matter—does not come close."

In dissent, Justice GINSBURG, joined by Justice Breyer and joined in relevant part by Justices Sotomayor and Kagan, argued that the self-care provision "validly enforces the right to be free from gender discrimination in the workplace." Citing the history of the FMLA and of gender discrimination in the workplace, Justice Ginsburg explained that, as Congress found, the examples of gender discrimination in the congressional record "were hardly isolated incidents." Noting that the self-care provision was particularly relevant for pregnancy and maternity leave, which is a gender-based concern, she explained that "Congress' concern was solidly grounded in workplace realities" and therefore provided a legitimate interest to support the legislation. The response, moreover, was properly proportionate to that problem, because the legislation had to be considered holistically. Congress deliberately "avoided a legislative package that, overall, was or would be seen as geared to women only," a policy choice that Congress believed necessary to promote its aims and to which the Court should thus defer. That legislative package operated, Justice Ginsburg continued, by "reduc[ing] employers' incentives to prefer men over women, advanc[ing] women's economic opportunities, and la[ying] the foundation for a more egalitarian relationship at home and at work. [Because t]he self-care provision is a key part of that endeavor, [it was] a valid exercise of congressional power under § 5 of the Fourteenth Amendment."

How do Hibbs and Coleman relate? Was the only flaw with the self-care provision in Coleman an underdeveloped congressional record? Or does Coleman suggest that the Court may enforce limits on creative approaches to remedial legislation if the remedy operates too indirectly on its face? What does that mean for remedial laws that might not be able to pass in Congress if they are explicitly tailored to a particular protected group, such as female employees?

3. ***The relative roles of Congress and the Court in antidiscrimination law.*** Note that Kimel and Garrett suggest that Congress may not remedy state discrimination on the basis of characteristics like age or disability that are subject to the very deferential test of rationality review. Does this mean that Congress is virtually powerless against such discrimination by the states, since it could correct only wholly irrational discrimination? Should Congress have greater freedom than courts to identify the factual basis for deeming a form of discrimination irrational? For an argument, cited in Justice Breyer's dissent in Garrett, that courts must apply deferential review to state judgments because of "restraints on the institutional competence of courts to review democratic lawmaking," but that

Congress should not be fettered by similar constraints when identifying patterns of irrational state discrimination, see Post & Siegel, "Equal Protection By Law: Federal Antidiscrimination Legislation After Morrison and Kimel," 110 Yale L.J. 441 (2000).

Boerne suggested that the Court enjoys primacy over Congress as the expositor of the substantive scope of Fourteenth Amendment rights. It thus limited Congress's powers under § 5 of the Fourteenth Amendment to "enforcing" Fourteenth Amendment rights already identified by the Court, rather than "interpreting" the Fourteenth Amendment in the first instance. Did Hibbs suggest a newly expansive view of § 5 of the Fourteenth Amendment? Or was the Court just reinforcing its intention to limit § 5 legislation to remedying discrimination against suspect or quasi-suspect groups already identified by the Court? After Hibbs, will the Court uphold the application to the states of any law passed by Congress under § 5 of the Fourteenth Amendment as long as it deals with an already-identified suspect or quasi-suspect classification, such as gender or race? If the fact that gender discrimination is subject to heightened scrutiny is what distinguishes Hibbs from Kimel and Garrett, how does one explain the Court's decision in Morrison to invalidate civil damages suits under VAWA and in Coleman to invalidate the self-care provision? See Post & Siegel, "Legislative Constitutionalism and Section Five Power: Policentric Interpretation of the Family and Medical Leave Act," 112 Yale L.J. 1943 (2003).

Should the level of scrutiny that the Court would apply to a group classification have any bearing on the type of evidence on which Congress must base antidiscrimination legislation? Just because the FMLA sought to target gender discrimination, as opposed to age or disability discrimination, doesn't mean that gender discrimination by states was actually more prevalent than age or disability discrimination, or that the remedy Congress enacted was a better fit for remedying such discrimination. When a suspect or quasi-suspect classification is at issue, does Hibbs stand for the proposition that Congress's remedy does not have to be quite as "congruent and proportional" as the Court has previously demanded? Or does Coleman suggest that the § 1 and § 5 inquiries are wholly distinct?

Does the Court's remedial focus in these cases mean that Congress's enforcement powers are only temporary? The Court in Shelby County declined to strike down the VRA's preclearance regime, but it made clear its view that "Congress [cannot] rely simply on the past" in exercising its enforcement power. Justice Thomas would have gone further and struck down the preclearance regime on the ground that "circumstances in the covered jurisdictions can no longer be characterized as 'exceptional' or 'unique' [and] the extensive pattern of discrimination that led the Court to previously uphold § 5 as enforcing the Fifteenth Amendment no longer exists."

4. ***The limits of the Boerne line of cases as a protection of federalism.*** The Boerne line of cases, like the Lopez line of cases noted above in Chapter 3 (see p. 140), constitutes a limit on the power of Congress relative to the states. And the Kimel line of cases applies that limit in the context of state sovereign immunity, further protecting the states against the prospect that Congress will impose crippling liability upon their treasuries. But how significant is such a limit? Most of these cases protect the states in the realm of employment law, but less than 4 percent of the workforce is employed by the states. Moreover, individual state officers may be sued for prospective

injunctive relief under Ex parte Young, 209 U.S. 123 (1908), even if the States may not be sued in their own names. And the federal government may bring enforcement actions against the States under federal antidiscrimination laws, even if Congress may not subject the States to suits by private individuals. Are these alternatives likely to be equally effective deterrents to state discrimination? Or are private causes of action for money damages, coupled with the prospect of attorneys' fees if successful, the most effective means of vindicating federal antidiscrimination laws?

CHAPTER 11

FREEDOM OF SPEECH— CATEGORIES OF SPEECH— DEGREES OF PROTECTED EXPRESSION

SECTION 1. FREE SPEECH: AN OVERVIEW

The First Amendment to the United States Constitution provides: "Congress shall make no law abridging the freedom of speech, or of the press." As written, the First Amendment is simple and unqualified. But there has been a broad consensus that not all expression or communication is included within "the freedom of speech." The Court's first major encounters with free speech claims did not arise until after World War I. In the decades since, claimed infringements of First Amendment rights have become a source of frequent controversy and a staple of Court business.

Are some types of speech clearly covered by the First Amendment, while others are entitled to less protection, or excluded from protection altogether? What government interests are sufficient to justify lesser or no protection for speech? Chapter 11 explores these questions after this overview. It begins by reviewing the speech that the Court has deemed *not* protected by the First Amendment. Of course many speech acts receive no First Amendment protection: bribery, perjury, antitrust conspiracies and solicitation to murder are not considered protected speech, and such traditional exclusions are so uncontroversial as to go unlitigated. But the Court has debated extensively whether several other categories of speech should be held outside First Amendment protection: in particular, the categories of incitement, fighting words, libel, obscenity, and child pornography. The Court continues to hold such categories nominally unprotected, but the story of Chapter 11 is largely one of the shrinking of these categories' boundaries to avoid trenching upon speech that is considered clearly within the First Amendment, especially "political" speech and speech critical of governmental policies and officials. The Court has also grappled with the question whether to treat some speech as protected, but not fully protected. It has upheld various regulations of sexually explicit but nonobscene speech, and it has treated commercial speech (i.e., advertising) as explicitly enjoying lesser First Amendment protection. Chapter 11 concludes by exploring these "lower value" categories.

Chapter 12 turns from the question of the categories of speech to the modes or techniques of abridgement, and to their influence on the relevant standard of review. Chapter 13, the last of the free expression chapters, turns to several rights derived from the right of free speech, including the right to association and the right against being compelled to speak.

FIRST AMENDMENT HISTORY

In Palko v. Connecticut, 302 U.S. 319 (1937), Justice Cardozo characterized protection of speech as a "fundamental" liberty in part because "our history, political and legal," recognized "freedom of thought and speech" as "the indispensable condition of nearly every other form of freedom." Does history in fact support special protection of First Amendment rights? What is the scope of "the freedom of speech" enshrined by the Framers of the Bill of Rights? What evils of pre-Constitution history was the Amendment designed to avert?

1. ***Prior restraints.*** A prominent technique of restraint in English law after invention of the printing press had been the licensing of printers—the submission of publications to royal officials with the power to give or withhold an imprimatur of approval. It was this practice that the great poet, scholar, and political theorist John Milton protested in a tract called Areopagitica—A Speech for the Liberty of Unlicensed Printing (1664). As William Blackstone described the evils of the practice: "[To] subject the press to the restrictive power of a licenser [is] to subject all freedom of sentiment to the prejudices of one man, and make him the arbitrary and infallible judge of all controverted points in learning, religion, and government." 4 Blackstone, Commentaries on the Laws of England *151–52.

Prior restraint through licensing was abandoned in England a century before the adoption of the American Bill of Rights. Nevertheless, a barrier to licensing was at one time viewed as the major thrust of the First Amendment. Blackstone had expressed the view that "[t]he liberty of the press [consists] in laying no *previous* restraints upon publication, and not in freedom from censure for criminal matter when published." Justice Holmes, a great legal historian as author of The Common Law (1881), initially embraced the Blackstonian view that freedom of expression was protected solely against prior restraints. See, e.g., Patterson v. Colorado, 205 U.S. 454 (1907). Compare his grudging recognition 12 years later, in Schenck, below, that "[i]t well may be that the prohibition of laws abridging the freedom of speech is not confined to previous restraints, although to prevent them may have been the main purpose."

2. ***Seditious libel.*** In pre-Revolutionary England, hundreds of people were prosecuted and convicted for seditious libel—"the intentional publication, without lawful excuse or justification, of written blame of any public man, or of the law, or of any institution established by law." Viewing treason laws as too cumbersome to use against critics of government, the Stuart monarchs used seditious libel instead. The English judges held, on the question of what was "intentional publication," that it was sufficient to show that the defendant had intended to publish writings having a seditious tendency; the Crown did not have to prove that the defendant maliciously intended to cause sedition. Moreover, under English law it was the judge, not the jury, who decided whether the writing had a seditious tendency. Truth was not a defense.

In the colonies, trials for seditious libel were extremely rare. The best known was the prosecution of John Peter Zenger in New York in 1735. Zenger was tried for criticizing the Governor General of the colony in his weekly publication. The judge refused the pleas of Zenger's counsel that the truth of the alleged libel was an absolute defense and that the jury, not the judge, should decide the issues of seditious tendency and intent. The jury, disregarding the judge's instructions, found Zenger not guilty.

The English Bill of Rights of 1689 provided that "the freedom of speech and debates or proceedings in Parliament ought not to be impeached or questioned in any court or place out of Parliament." Although this provision only applied to speech and debate in Parliament, it provided some protection for members against seditious libel charges. Its language ("the freedom of speech") clearly influenced the drafting of the First Amendment.

The question whether the First Amendment embodied a general principle against the suppression of seditious libel has divided historians. Zechariah Chafee, Jr.'s influential work on free speech argued that the Framers of the First Amendment had more in mind than the banning of the long-gone censorship through licensing: he insisted that they "intended to wipe out the common law of sedition and make further prosecutions for criticism of the government, without any incitement to law-breaking, forever impossible." Chafee, Free Speech in the United States (1941) (revising Freedom of Speech (1920)). Compare, however, Leonard Levy's historical study denying that the First Amendment was "intended to wipe out the common law of sedition." Levy, Legacy of Suppression (1960). Levy's "revisionist interpretation" (which he later revised and softened in The Emergence of a Free Press (1985)), claimed that 18th century Americans "did not believe in a broad scope for freedom of expression, particularly in the realm of politics." He concluded that "libertarian theory from the time of Milton to the ratification of the First Amendment substantially accepted the right of the state to suppress seditious libel." For Levy, the First Amendment Framers' main concern was with states' rights and the fear of national power rather than with individual liberty, and he argued that a "broad libertarian theory of freedom of speech and press did not emerge in the United States" until the Jeffersonian battle against the Sedition Act of 1798.

3. ***The Sedition Act of 1798.*** The Sedition Act of 1798, enacted by the Federalists, barred the publication of "false, scandalous, and malicious writing [against] the Government of the United States, or either House of [Congress], or the President, [with] intent to defame [them]; or to bring them [into] contempt or disrepute; or to excite against them [the] hatred of the good people of the United States, or to stir up sedition within the United States. . . . " In order to eliminate the most criticized procedural aspects of English law, the Act provided that truth *would* be a defense, that malicious intent *was* an element of the crime, and that the jury *would* decide such issues as the seditious tendency of the publication. The Act was rigorously enforced, entirely against Jeffersonian Republicans, including their leading newspapers. The federal courts applying the act imprisoned publishers and writers and assessed large fines against them. Although the Supreme Court did not rule on the Act's constitutionality, it was upheld by several lower federal courts, in decisions written in some cases by Supreme Court Justices riding circuit. The Act was a major factor in the defeat of the Federalists by the Jeffersonian Republicans in the 1800 election. It expired of its own force in March 1801, and Jefferson, the new President, pardoned all of those convicted under it. Levy notes, however, that the Jeffersonians in power "were not much more tolerant of their political critics than the Federalists had been."

How did Congress pass such a speech restrictive law in the immediate aftermath of the enactment of the First Amendment? Historical context sheds some light: "[To] understand the [Sedition Act of 1798] we must appreciate the Federalists' view of 'the freedom of speech, or of the press.' In short, the Federalists had little faith in free and open debate. [The] Federalists believed that the common man could easily be manipulated and misled. [After] witnessing the violent aftershocks of the French Revolution, the Federalists had no doubt of both the power and danger of public opinion." Stone, The Story of Sedition Act of 1798, 14–17 *in* First Amendment Stories (Garnett & Koppelman eds., 2012). Following French aggression toward U.S. shipping vessels, Federalists were able to capitalize on the public's fear and resulting enthusiasm for war abroad. President Adams acted to further foment distrust of French sympathizers, warning in his public speeches that "the United States of America are at present placed in a hazardous and afflictive situation, by the unfriendly disposition, conduct and demands of a foreign power . . . ." It was the presence, whether real or imagined, of an external threat that permitted Congress to pass its first major restriction on civil liberties and free speech.

To Republicans, the Sedition Act was a flagrant violation of the Constitution and evidenced Adams' "appetite for tyranny." Jefferson, Madison, and other Republicans of the time rejected the English conception of freedom of speech, believing the First Amendment to prohibit more than merely prior restraints. Their hopes that the Court would intervene by finding the Act unconstitutional, however, were not realized. Justice James Iredell, while riding circuit only a few years earlier, had charged a Virginia grand jury to issue a presentment against several Republican Congressmen who had written public letters that attempted "at a time of real public danger, to disseminate unfounded calumnies against the happy government of the United States," articulating the British understanding of the Free Speech Clause in his opinion. See Thomas Jefferson to James Madison, Aug. 3, 1797, 17 Papers of James Madison 33 (quoting Richmond Gazette, May 24, 1797). Quoting Blackstone, Iredell had articulated the British understanding of the Free Speech Clause in his order: "The liberty of the press is indeed essential to the nature of a free state. And this consists in laying no previous restraints upon publications, and not in freedom from censure for criminal matter when published." To argue for their alternative interpretation, Jefferson and Madison turned to state legislatures: Jefferson to Kentucky and Madison to Virginia. Each drafted and submitted a set of resolutions to the respective states' legislatures. Madison's Virginia Resolutions asserted that the state legislature believed the Sedition Act to be unconstitutional and called on other states to make similar declarations, while Jefferson's Kentucky Resolutions would have had the states declare the law null and void. Yet other states ultimately rejected the resolutions and the Act went into effect.

4. ***Later history.*** The century after the Sedition Act controversy witnessed efforts to suppress abolitionist literature during the slavery controversy, and attempts to suppress seditious publications during the Civil War, see Randall, Constitutional Problems Under Lincoln (rev. ed. 1951). But not until the World War I era did major free speech issues reach the Supreme Court. Why that was so constitutes a historical puzzle. For exploration of the antecedents of modern free speech jurisprudence in the years before World War I, see Rabban, "The First Amendment in Its Forgotten Years," 90 Yale L.J. 514 (1981); Rabban, "The Free Speech League, the ACLU, and Changing Conceptions of Free Speech in American History," 45 Stan. L. Rev. 47 (1992); Rabban, "The IWW Free Speech Fights and

Popular Conceptions of Free Expression Before World War I," 80 Va. L. Rev. 1055 (1994). For discussion on the relationship between labor organizing in the interwar period and the development of First Amendment rights, see Weinrib, The Taming of Free Speech: America's Civil Liberties Compromise (2016). Weinrib argues the concept of civil liberties was born as an adjunct to, and in service of, the radical labor movement after the First World War. However the ACLU began to reorient their agenda away from the rights of labor organizers towards a neutral vision of personal freedom of expression. Weinrib argues this latter vision, unhooked from its redistributive origins, became the modern conception of civil liberties we know today.

5. ***The right to petition.*** At a minimum, the Petition Clause ("Congress shall make no law . . . abridging . . . the right of the people . . . to petition the Government for a redress of grievances") protected an exception for speech critical of government that was formally presented to government officials. This provision had roots in Magna Carta, and a similar provision was codified in the English Bill of Rights of 1689. See Krotoszynski & Carpenter, "The Return of Seditious Libel," 55 UCLA L. Rev. 1239 (2008).

FIRST AMENDMENT THEORY

Philosophical justifications for the protection of free speech supplement the uncertain light cast by history. Free speech has been thought to serve three principal values: advancing knowledge and "truth" in the "marketplace of ideas," facilitating representative democracy and self-government, and promoting individual autonomy, self-expression and self-fulfillment. See Emerson, The System of Freedom of Expression (1970). Protection of free speech has also been defended based on a negative theory of government power, questioning both the competence and the incentives of state officials to regulate the flow of ideas among citizens. See Sullivan, "Two Concepts of Freedom of Speech," 124 Harv. L. Rev. 143 (2010). These values have animated much of the Court's reasoning in free speech cases, though not always articulately and not always consistently. What is the consequence of one emphasis or another for the implementation of First Amendment values in the decisions that follow?

1. ***Truth.*** The classic statements of the value of speech in the search for truth are those of John Milton and John Stuart Mill. John Milton wrote in 1644, protesting a licensing scheme for books: "And though all the winds of doctrine were let loose to play upon the earth, so Truth be in the field, we do injuriously, by licensing and prohibiting, to misdoubt her strength. Let her and Falsehood grapple; who ever knew Truth put to the worst, in a free and open encounter?" Milton, Areopagitica—A Speech for the Liberty of Unlicensed Printing (1644). John Stuart Mill's classic libertarian argument came two centuries after Milton's, in On Liberty (1859). Mill's central argument was that the suppression of opinion is wrong, whether or not the opinion is true: if it is true, society is denied the truth; if it is false, society is denied the fuller understanding of truth which comes from its conflict with error; and when the received opinion is part truth and part error, society can know the whole truth only by allowing the airing of competing views.

As Mill summarized his argument in Chapter II of On Liberty: "First, if any opinion is compelled to silence, that opinion may, for aught we can certainly know, be true. To deny this is to assume our own infallibility.

Secondly, though the silenced opinion be in error, it may, and very commonly does, contain a portion of the truth; and since the general or prevailing opinion on any subject is rarely or never the whole truth, it is only by the collision of adverse opinions that the remainder of the truth has any chance of being supplied. Thirdly, even if the received opinion be not only true, but the whole truth; unless it is suffered to be, and actually is, vigorously and earnestly contested, it will, by most of those who receive it, be held in the manner of a prejudice, with little comprehension or feeling of its rational grounds. And not only this, but, fourthly, the meaning of the doctrine itself will be in danger of being lost, or enfeebled."

Justice Brandeis echoed these truth-based rationales for speech protection in his concurrence in Whitney v. California, below: "freedom to think as you will and to speak as you think are means indispensable to the discovery and spread of political truth." Justice Holmes did so in a different, pragmatist vein in his dissent in Abrams v. United States, below: "[W]hen men have realized that time has upset many fighting faiths, they may come to believe even more than they believe the very foundations of their own conduct that the ultimate good desired is better reached by free trade in ideas—that the best test of truth is the power of the thought to get itself accepted in the competition of the market and that truth is the only ground upon which their wishes safely can be carried out. That at any rate is the theory of our constitution." Is there reason to expect truth to emerge through the self-regulating operation of a free "marketplace of ideas"? Any more than to expect the commercial marketplace always to be efficient or just? Recall from the Lochner materials that Justice Holmes would have allowed government considerable latitude to regulate the economic marketplace. Why would he tie government's hands and insist on laissez-faire when it comes to the marketplace of ideas?

A number of commentators have criticized the "marketplace" rationale on the ground that its assumptions do not fit the realities of a contemporary society in which certain political and economic interest groups wield disproportionate resources and power. See e.g., Barron, "Access to the Press—A New First Amendment Right," 80 Harv. L. Rev. 1641 (1967) (arguing that the notion of a "self-operating marketplace of ideas [has] long ceased to exist" and insisting that a "realistic view of the first amendment requires recognition that a right of expression is somewhat thin if it can be exercised only at the sufferance of the managers of mass communications"); Wellington, "On Freedom of Expression," 88 Yale L.J. 1105 (1979) ("In the long run, true ideas do tend to drive out false ones. The problem is that the short run may be very long."); Ingber, "The Marketplace of Ideas: A Legitimizing Myth," 1984 Duke L.J. 1 ("[T]he market is strongly biased in favor of positions that support entrenched ideas."); MacKinnon, Only Words (1993) ("These days, censorship occurs less through explicit state policy than through official and unofficial privileging of powerful groups and viewpoints. This is accomplished through silencing in many forms and enforced by the refusal of publishers and editors to publish [expressions] of dissent."). Note also Herbert Marcuse's assertion that, "[u]nder the rule of monopolistic media—themselves the mere instruments of economic and political power—a mentality is created for which right and wrong, true and false are predefined wherever they affect the vital interests of the society." Marcuse, "Repressive Tolerance," in Robert Wolff et al., A Critique of Pure Tolerance 95 (1965).

2. ***Self-government.*** Some emphasize that speech is essential to representative government. Brandeis made this argument in Whitney v. California (1927; p. 965 below), when he claimed that the Framers believed "that without free speech and assembly discussion would be futile; that with them, discussion affords ordinarily adequate protection against the dissemination of noxious doctrine; that the greatest menace to freedom is an inert people; that public discussion is a political duty; and that this should be a fundamental principle of the American government." Various justices have also emphasized the political function of free speech. For example, Justice Brennan, in New York Times Co. v. Sullivan (1967; p. 1006 below), invoked "a profound national commitment to the principle that debate on public issues should be uninhibited, robust, and wide-open, and that it may well include vehement, caustic, and sometimes unpleasantly sharp attacks on government and public officials." And Justice Black, in Mills v. Alabama, 384 U.S. 214 (1966), stated that "there is practically universal agreement that a major purpose of [the First Amendment] was to protect the free discussion of governmental affairs."

Alexander Meiklejohn argued that "public" speech—speech on public issues affecting "self-government"—must be wholly immune from regulation, while "private" speech is entitled to less complete protection. See Meiklejohn, Free Speech and Its Relation to Self-Government (1948). He analogized public speech to a town meeting in which all viewpoints should be presented in order to arrive at wise public policy.

Zechariah Chafee, Jr., an important free-speech advocate who almost lost his Harvard professorship after criticizing the result in Abrams v. United States (1919; p. 950 below), criticized Meiklejohn's theory of public speech for taking too narrow a view of the First Amendment, finding it "shocking" that Meiklejohn would apparently omit to protect art and literature. See Chafee, "Book Review," 62 Harv. L. Rev. 891 (1949). Meiklejohn replied that art, literature, philosophy and the sciences should indeed be included in First Amendment protection, as they help "voters acquire the intelligence, integrity, sensitivity, and generous devotion to the general welfare that, in theory, casting a ballot is assumed to express." Meiklejohn, "The First Amendment Is an Absolute," 1961 Sup. Ct. Rev. 245. Judge and scholar Robert Bork (whose Supreme Court nomination was later rejected by the Senate) disagreed with Meiklejohn's concession: many activities beyond art and literature inform voting, but if there is not to be "an analogical stampede, the protection of the first amendment must be cut off when it reaches the outer limits of political speech." Bork, "Neutral Principles and Some First Amendment Problems," 47 Ind. L.J. 1 (1971). For contemporary discussion of the argument that the First Amendment is principally about political deliberation, compare Sunstein, Democracy and the Problem of Free Speech (1993); Sunstein, "Free Speech Now," 59 U. Chi. L. Rev. 255 (1992) and BeVier, "The First Amendment and Political Speech: An Inquiry Into the Substance and Limits of Principle," 30 Stan. L. Rev. 299 (1978) with Schauer, "The Boundaries of the First Amendment," 117 Harv. L. Rev. 1765 (2004) ("Theories based on self-government of democratic deliberation have a hard time explaining why . . . the doctrine now covers pornography, commercial advertising, and art, [none] of which has much to do with political deliberation or self-governance, except under such an attenuated definition of 'political' that the justification's core loses much of its power.").

Free speech in the political conception arguably serves at least four different functions. First, as Meiklejohn's town meeting analogy suggests, broad debate informs and improves the making of public policy. Second, free speech prevents government from entrenching itself indefinitely—it keeps clear the "channels of political change." Ely, Democracy and Distrust (1980). Third, free speech prevents government abuse of power. See Blasi, "The Checking Value in First Amendment Theory," 1977 A.B.F. Res. J. 521 (emphasizing "the value that free speech, a free press, and free assembly can serve in checking the abuse of power by public officials," and arguing that "the role of the ordinary citizen is not so much to contribute on a continuing basis to the formation of public policy as to retain a veto power to be employed when the decisions of officials pass certain bounds"). Fourth, free speech promotes political stability by providing a safety valve for dissent. As Justice Brandeis cautioned in his Whitney concurrence, "Those who won our independence [knew] that fear breeds repression; that repression breeds hate; that hate menaces stable government [and] that the path of safety lies in the opportunity to discuss freely supposed grievances and proposed remedies." See also Emerson, The System of Freedom of Expression (1970) (arguing that freedom of expression "provides a framework in which the conflict necessary to the progress of a society can take place without destroying the society").

If the principal purpose of speech is to further democracy, may government intervene in the marketplace of ideas in order to improve the deliberative quality of the discussion? For arguments along these lines, see Sunstein, supra; Fiss, "Free Speech and Social Structure," 71 Iowa L. Rev. 1405 (1986). Robert Post criticizes such "collectivist" political speech theories for assuming that there is some proper conception of good political discourse that stands outside of political debate itself. See Post, Constitutional Domains (1995).

While Meiklejohn's conception of free speech as facilitating democratic self-government focuses largely on the listener, and the capacity of free speech to inform and enlighten those who hear public debate, is there also a democratic benefit to the speaker? Consider the view that the speaker has an interest in participating in public debate in order to lend democratic legitimacy to the political process. See Post, "Participatory Democracy and Free Speech," 97 Va. L. Rev. 477 (2011); Weinstein, "Participatory Democracy as the Central Value of Free Speech Doctrine," 97 Va. L. Rev. 491 (2011).

3. ***Autonomy.*** A third rationale for protecting speech emphasizes the values of individual liberty, autonomy, and self-fulfillment. Unlike the truth and self-government theories, which view speech as instrumental to desired social consequences, autonomy theories emphasize the intrinsic worth of speech to individual speakers and listeners. Justice Brandeis echoed this theme, too, in his Whitney concurrence, suggesting that "[t]hose who won our independence believed that the final end of the State was to make men free to develop their faculties; [they] valued liberty both as an end and as a means." In one view, this concept of individual self-realization encompasses both "development of the individual's powers and abilities—an individual 'realizes' his or her own full potential—[and] the individual's control of his or her own destiny through making life-affecting decisions—an individual 'realizes' the goals in life that he or she has set." Redish, The Value of Free Speech, 130 U. Penn. L. Rev. 591 (1982). An emphasis on individual self-

realization extends First Amendment protection beyond the political realm to art, literature and even entertainment and advertising. See id. (arguing that democratic self-government is not an end in itself but a means to "the much broader value of individual self-realization," and thus that the First Amendment is "much broader than Bork or Meiklejohn would have it").

Some autonomy-based theories of free speech emphasize the affirmative value of speech in the development of rational human capacities. See Baker, Human Liberty and Freedom of Speech (1989); Richards, "Free Speech and Obscenity Law: Toward a Moral Theory of the First Amendment," 123 U. Pa. L. Rev. 45 (1974); Baker, "Scope of the First Amendment Freedom of Speech," 25 UCLA L. Rev. 964 (1978); Emerson, Toward a General Theory of the First Amendment (1963). On this theory, freedom of expression is necessary to an individual's right to self-fulfillment through use of the "powers of imagination, insight and feeling." Others emphasize the obverse: the inconsistency of censorship with human autonomy, and the impropriety of paternalism as a ground for interference with speech. See Strauss, "Persuasion, Autonomy, and Freedom of Expression," 91 Colum. L. Rev. 334 (1991) (arguing that a central principle of the First Amendment is that government may not stop speech for reason of its power to persuade the listener, and that "[v]iolating the persuasion principle is wrong for some of the reasons that lies [are] wrong: both involve a denial of autonomy in the sense that they interfere with a person's control over her own reasoning processes"). See also Scanlon, "A Theory of Freedom of Expression," 1 Phil. & Pub. Aff. 204 (1972) (arguing that "an autonomous person cannot accept without independent consideration the judgment of others as to what he should believe or what he should do," including the judgment of the state expressed through the suppression of dissent). But see Scanlon, "Freedom of Expression and Categories of Expression," 40 U. Pitt. L. Rev. 519 (1979) (retreating from autonomy-centered view of speech).

Autonomy theories of speech have been criticized as being too broad. See Bork, supra (arguing that self-fulfillment is not a principle that can "distinguish speech from any other human activity," for "an individual may develop his faculties or derive pleasure from trading on the stock market [or] engaging in sexual activities," and there is no neutral way to rank speech ahead of these alternative forms of "personal gratification"). Consider as a potential response the argument that the First Amendment's meaning is premised on the preservation of dissent. On this idea, its purpose is "to protect the romantics—those who would break out of classical forms: the dissenters, the unorthodox, the outcasts" and to "sponsor the individualism, the rebelliousness, the antiauthoritarianism, the spirit of nonconformity within us all." Shiffrin, The First Amendment, Democracy, and Romance (1993). If the protection of autonomy serves to encourage dissent, does speech necessarily rank above other forms of autonomous human activity in its importance to achieving that goal? Is the autonomy rationale of the First Amendment then inextricably tied with notions of democracy and social contribution?

4. ***Negative theories.*** Some theories of speech protection focus less on the affirmative instrumental or intrinsic value of speech than on the special reasons to distrust government in the realm of speech regulation. Frederick Schauer thus defends free speech on the basis of an "argument from governmental incompetence"—an emphasis on "a distrust of the ability of government to make the necessary distinctions, a distrust of governmental

determinations of truth and falsity." Schauer, Free Speech: A Philosophical Enquiry (1982). Schauer states: "Even if there is nothing especially good about speech compared to other conduct, the state may have less ability to regulate speech than it has to regulate other forms of conduct, or the attempt to regulate speech may entail special harms or special dangers not present in regulation of other conduct. [Throughout] history the process of regulating speech has been marked with what we now see to be fairly plain errors"—including "the banning of numerous admittedly great works of art because someone thought them obscene." He adds that "acts of suppression that have been proved erroneous seem to represent a disproportionate percentage of the governmental mistakes of the past. [Experience] arguably shows that governments are particularly bad at censorship." He concludes: "Freedom of speech is based in large part on a distrust of the ability of government to make the necessary distinctions, a distrust of governmental determinations of truth and falsity, an appreciation of the fallibility of political leaders, and of somewhat deeper distrust of governmental power in a more general sense." See also Schauer, "The Second-Best First Amendment," 31 Wm. & Mary L. Rev. 1 (1989).

For a related argument that free speech protection should assume government is prone to pathological reactions to speech, see Blasi, "The Pathological Perspective and the First Amendment," 85 Colum. L. Rev. 449 (1985) (arguing that "the overriding objective at all times should be to equip the first amendment to do maximum service in those historical periods when intolerance of unorthodox ideas is most prevalent. [The] first amendment, in other words, should be targeted for the worst of times.").

Why might government regulation of speech be more suspect than governmental regulation of other activities? With respect to political speech, the answer is that the incumbent regime will be biased in its own favor against dissidents and challengers. Can this argument be broadened to reach cultural or social dissent as well? See Justice Jackson's opinion in the second flag salute case, West Virginia Board of Education v. Barnette (1943; p. 1392 below): "If there is any fixed star in our constitutional constellation, it is that no official, high or petty, can prescribe what shall be orthodox in politics, nationalism, religion, or other matters of opinion or force citizens to confess by word or act their faith therein."

5. ***Eclectic theories.*** Are these varying rationales better considered jointly than separately? The Court itself often relies upon an amalgam of the above theories. Some commentators argue that any adequate protection of free speech must rely upon "several strands of theory in order to protect a rich variety of expressional modes." Tribe, American Constitutional Law 789 (2d ed. 1988). See also Bloustein, "The Origin, Validity, and Interrelationships of the Political Values Served by Freedom of Expression," 33 Rutgers L. Rev. 372 (1981); Shiffrin, "The First Amendment and Economic Regulation: Away From a General Theory of the First Amendment," 78 Nw. U. L. Rev. 1212 (1983).

FIRST AMENDMENT JURISPRUDENCE

Assuming that freedom of expression warrants protection because of its value to society and the individual, what is the appropriate judicial responsibility for protecting it? Should speech have a preferred position to other liberties in the Constitution, and thus receive greater protection from regulation than other activities? The Court has long shown special judicial solicitude for free speech, meaning that governmental action directed at expression must satisfy a greater burden of justification than governmental action directed at most other forms of behavior. What justifies this special protection of freedom of expression? Assuming that speech is to be specially protected, what judicial techniques best implement that protection? Should protection be absolute? If not, are exceptions to protection better made through categorization of types of speech as more or less valuable and of types of regulation as more or less permissible? Or is it better to uphold a speech regulation only by explicit balancing of speech values against countervailing governmental interests in each case? Do categories reflect implicit balancing in any event?

1. ***Justifying special protection for speech.*** Since the New Deal, the Court has deferred to government in the economic sphere, upholding a wide range of regulation against equal protection and substantive due process challenge. In speech cases, by contrast, the Court treats speech as enjoying strong presumptive protection, and frequently intervenes to strike down government regulation. Thus, the Court has declined to read the Fourteenth Amendment as mandating laissez-faire in economic markets. But it has read the First Amendment to require a considerable amount of laissez-faire in the marketplace of ideas. Justice Holmes himself expressed both positions: in his dissent in Lochner v. New York, 198 U.S. 45 (1905), he wrote that labor regulation is permissible because the liberty clause "does not enact Mr. Herbert Spencer's Social Statics," nor does it "embody a particular economic theory" of free trade. But in his dissent in Abrams v. United States (1919; p. 950 below), he argued that regulation of dissident speech is impermissible because the Free Speech Clause recognizes that "the ultimate good desired is better reached by free trade in ideas—that the best test of truth is the power of the thought to get itself accepted in the competition of the market."

What explains this asymmetrical approach? Is it a sufficient answer that the First Amendment explicitly mentions freedom of speech while the text of the Fourteenth Amendment is framed abstractly? One of the most influential statements of the modern Court's double standard occurs in footnote four in Justice Stone's opinion in United States v. Carolene Products Co., 304 U.S. 144 (1938). Stone spoke of a "narrower scope for operation of the presumption of constitutionality when legislation appears on its face to be within a specific prohibition of the Constitution, such as those of the first ten amendments, which are deemed equally specific when held to be embraced within the 14th." Are First Amendment rights truly more "specific" than, for example, the Contracts Clause and other protections of "property"? He also suggested, more tentatively, a "more exacting judicial scrutiny" of legislation restricting the "political processes," listing "restraints upon the dissemination of information" among his examples. But the Court's special solicitude has extended well beyond political speech.

Does the explanation lie instead in the difference between the practical functions of that speech and economic transactions play in the development of civil society? Justice Frankfurter—though he objected to the view that free speech was entitled to a "preferred position" and was often willing to defer to government speech regulation himself—suggested as much in explicating Holmes' asymmetrical opinions: "The ideas now governing the constitutional protection of freedom of speech derive essentially from the opinions of Mr. Justice Holmes, [who] seldom felt justified in opposing his own opinion to economic views which the legislature embodied in law. But since he also realized that the progress of civilization is to a considerable extent the displacement of error which once held sway as official truth by beliefs which in turn have yielded to other beliefs, for him the right to search for truth was of a different order than some transient economic dogma. And without freedom of expression, thought becomes checked and atrophied. Therefore, in considering what interests are so fundamental as to be enshrined in the Due Process Clause, those liberties of the individual which history has attested as the indispensable conditions of an open as against a closed society come to this Court with a momentum for respect lacking when appeal is made to liberties which derive merely from shifting economic arrangements." Kovacs v. Cooper, 336 U.S. 77 (1949) (Frankfurter, J., concurring).

Might it be argued that economic markets and the marketplace of ideas should be treated the same? Arguments for symmetry have been made from both directions. For an overview of these arguments, see Sullivan, "Free Speech and Unfree Markets," 42 UCLA L. Rev. 949 (1995). Some have suggested that constitutional guarantees should be rigorously enforced against regulation of both speech and economic markets. See, e.g., R.H. Coase, "The Economics of the First Amendment: The Market for Goods and the Market for Ideas," 64 Am. Econ. Rev. Proc. 384 (1974); Epstein, "Property, Speech, and the Politics of Distrust," 59 U. Chi. L. Rev. 41 (1992). For a reply to Epstein, see Michelman, "Liberties, Fair Values, and Constitutional Method," 59 U. Chi. L. Rev. 91 (1992). For criticism of the export of market metaphors to the area of speech, see Radin, Contested Commodities, Ch. 12 (1996).

Others have suggested a symmetrical move in the opposite direction: that there should be no more presumptive protection for speech against government regulation than for economic activities. On this view, there are imperfections in the marketplace of ideas, just as there are in the economic marketplace. If speech has negative external effects, if some persons or entities have monopoly power over speech, or if the distribution of speech is skewed by unequal speaking power, say these commentators, then regulation may be justified in the interest of speech itself just as regulation in the economic markets is sometimes justified in the interest of efficiency or distribution. For variations on such views, see Sunstein, Democracy and the Problem of Free Speech (1993); Schauer, "The Political Incidence of the Free Speech Principle," 64 U. Colo. L. Rev. 935 (1993); Balkin, "Some Realism About Pluralism: Legal Realist Approaches to the First Amendment," 1990 Duke L.J. 375. Neither of these arguments for symmetry has made headway with the contemporary Supreme Court, which continues to accord heightened protection to speech.

2. ***Absolutes versus balancing.*** An important debate in First Amendment adjudication in the 1960s was over whether First Amendment rights are "absolute" or subject to the "balancing" of competing interests. Justice Black was the principal advocate of the former position. Justice Black wrote, "I do not subscribe to ['the doctrine that permits constitutionally protected rights to be "balanced" away when a majority of the Court thinks that a State might have interest sufficient to justify abridgment of those freedoms'] for I believe that the First Amendment's unequivocal command that there shall be no abridgment of the rights of free speech and assembly

shows that the men who drafted our Bill of Rights did all the 'balancing' that was to be [done]. [I] fear that the creation of 'tests' by which speech is left unprotected under certain circumstances is a standing invitation to abridge [it]." Konigsberg v. State Bar of California, 366 U.S. 36 (1961) (Black, J., dissenting). See also Black, "The Bill of Rights," 35 N.Y.U. L. Rev. 865 (1960), and Black, A Constitutional Faith (1968).

Justices Frankfurter and Harlan rejected Black's approach and advocated explicit balancing instead. For example, Justice Harlan wrote for the majority in Konigsberg, supra, which upheld a denial of bar admission to an applicant who had refused to answer questions about Communist Party membership, as follows: "[W]e reject the view that freedom of speech and association [are] 'absolutes,' not only in the undoubted sense that where the constitutional protection exists it must prevail, but also in the sense that the scope of that protection must be gathered solely from a literal reading of the First Amendment. Throughout its history this Court has consistently recognized [that] constitutionally protected freedom of speech is narrower than an unlimited license to talk. [When] constitutional protections are asserted against the exercise of valid governmental powers a reconciliation must be effected, and that perforce requires an appropriate weighing of the respective interests involved." Similarly, Justice Frankfurter defended balancing: "Absolute rules would inevitably lead to absolute exceptions, and such exceptions would eventually corrode the rules. The demands of free speech in a democratic society as well as [countervailing governmental interests] are better served by candid and informed weighing of the competing interests, within the confines of the judicial process, than by announcing dogmas too inflexible for the non-Euclidean problems to be solved." Dennis v. United States, p. 970 below.

There may be somewhat less to the "absolutes"-"balancing" debate than meets the eye. See, e.g., Kalven, "Upon Rereading Mr. Justice Black on the First Amendment," 14 UCLA L. Rev. 428 (1967) (commenting that the "absolutes"-"balancing" controversy "seems to me on the whole to have been an unfortunate, misleading, and unnecessary one"). Justice Black, for example, did not support every freedom of expression claim. Justice Harlan's "balancing," on the other hand, was not necessarily deferential. In one of the flag burning cases, Street v. New York (1969; p. 1184 below), for example, he wrote the majority opinion sustaining the First Amendment challenge while Justice Black dissented on the ground that the prosecution was not for "spoken words," but for speech "used as an integral part of conduct" in burning the flag in public. Similarly, in Cohen v. California (1971; p. 998 below), the "Fuck the Draft" case, Justice Harlan's statement for the majority was one of the most speech-protective (albeit largely "balancing" in approach), while Justice Black was once again in dissent.

The relative merits of absolute and balancing approaches were explored in an extended debate between Laurent Frantz and Wallace Mendelson. Frantz favored rules and argued that balancing would tend inevitably to be too deferential to government judgments or to the prejudices of the predominant political culture, and would provide inadequate guidance to decisionmakers. See Frantz, "The First Amendment in the Balance," 71 Yale L.J. 1424 (1962); Frantz, "Is the First Amendment Law? A Reply to Professor Mendelson," 51 Calif. L. Rev. 729 (1963). See also Ely, "Flag Desecration: A Case Study in the Roles of Categorization and Balancing in First Amendment Analysis," 88 Harv. L. Rev. 1482 (1975) ("[W]here messages are proscribed because they are dangerous, balancing tests inevitably become intertwined with the ideological predispositions of those doing the balancing—or if not that, at least with the relative confidence or paranoia of the age in which they are doing it."). Mendelson, in contrast, favored balancing: "Balancing seems to me the essence of the judicial process—the nexus between abstract law and concrete [life]. Surely the choice is simply this: shall the balancing be done 'intuitively' or rationally; covertly or out in the open?" Mendelson, "The First Amendment and the Judicial Process: A Reply to Mr. Frantz," 17 Vand. L. Rev. 479 (1964). For a discussion of "First Amendment balancing in the Harlan manner," see Gunther, "In Search of Judicial Quality on a Changing Court: The Case of Justice Powell," 24 Stan. L. Rev. 1001 (1972).

3. ***Categorization versus balancing.*** Even if it is conceded that the First Amendment is *not* absolute, a pervasive question of judicial methodology remains: should any reduced protection for speech be analyzed in terms of "categorization" or of "balancing"? Categorization strives for "bright-line" rules. Categorization along a spectrum of relatively more or less "protected speech" distinguishes what kind of expression does or does not trigger the First Amendment's demands for special government justification before it may be regulated. Categorization of speech as protected or unprotected forecloses free-form balancing of interests in a particular case. It sorts cases into those presumptively won either by government or by the speaker. Balancing approaches, in contrast, could go either way depending on the particular facts and interests at issue. See generally Sullivan, "The Supreme Court—1991 Term—Foreword: The Justices of Rules and Standards," 106 Harv. L. Rev. 22 (1992); Sullivan, "Post-Liberal Judging: The Roles of Categorization and Balancing," 63 U. Colo. L. Rev. 293 (1992).

Categorization of types of speech finds certain varieties of speech unprotected on a wholesale basis because the claim simply does not belong in the First Amendment ballpark—either because some "utterances are no essential part of any exposition of ideas, and are of such slight social value as a step to truth," or because, as is often suggested implicitly, there are such powerful state interests justifying restrictions that the type of expression can be wholly excluded from "the freedom of speech." Chaplinsky v. New Hampshire (1942; p. 986 below). See generally, on this "two-level" theory of speech, Kalven, "The Metaphysics of the Law of Obscenity," 1960 Sup. Ct. Rev. 1. As noted in Farber, "The Categorical Approach to Protecting Speech in American Constitutional Law," 84 Ind. L.J. 917 (2009), in some cases "the categorical approach functions as a prepackaged form of strict scrutiny" that gives "clearer notice to speakers, as well as governments, about the boundaries of permissible regulation," and in others it signals a "perceived lack of First Amendment value." The balancing approach, by contrast, asserts that a very broad range of expression is presumptively within the First Amendment and may be found unprotected only after the restrictions are shown to be outweighed by the governmental interest in a particular case. A balancing approach, in short, permits judicial evaluations only on the state interest side of the balance, and would not shortcut the balancing process by encouraging judicial evaluations of the relative merit of the speech on the other side of the balance.

Categorization has the attraction of clarity and of providing guidance to judges and other government officials. Categorization is also defended as a recognition of the diversity of the types of speech, and a welcome alternative to the excessive flexibility of balancing. By avoiding the weighing of every allegedly protected speech manifestation against all relevant state interests, the argument goes, categorization curtails the manipulative, result-oriented uses of balancing and yields more uniform results across cases. Finally, by drawing sharp distinctions between protected and unprotected classes of speech, categorization might actually be speech-protective after all. A unitary theory of the First Amendment that would extend similarly strong protection to all varieties of communication might ultimately dilute First Amendment protections, because some types of speech will inevitably receive less protection, with the result that even the protection of core political speech will suffer. "It is inconceivable that we will ignore such well-established governmental concerns as safety, reputation, protection against fraud, and protection of children. [Certain] state interests are inevitably going to be recognized, and the alternatives then are diluting those tests that are valuable precisely because of their strength, or formulating new tests and categories that leave existing standards strong within their narrower range. [A] narrow but strong First Amendment, with its strong principle universally available for all speech covered by the First Amendment, has much to be said for it. First Amendment protection can be like an oil spill, thinning out as it broadens." Schauer, "Codifying the First Amendment: New York v. Ferber," 1982 Sup. Ct. Rev. 285. See also Sunstein, Democracy and the Problem of Free Speech (1993).

But categorization also may cast entire classes of speech outside the First Amendment on a wholesale basis, without adequate examination of the bases for the conclusion. It may also, in its striving for general and bright-line rules, unduly slight the distinctions among types of speech within the category and the differences in contexts (and competing state interests) that particular examples of excluded speech may in fact present. Finally, variation in the levels of protection for speech may result ultimately in a myriad, increasingly ad hoc range of First Amendment rules and an excessive codification harmful to long range protection of First Amendment values. For additional classic commentary on categorization and balancing in the context of free speech, see Scanlon, "Freedom of Expression and Categories of Expression," 40 U. Pitt. L. Rev. 519 (1979); and Ely, "Flag Desecration: A Case Study in the Roles of Categorization and Balancing in First Amendment Analysis," 88 Harv. L. Rev. 1482 (1975).

Ultimately, then, categorization and balancing may run together. Balancing can function effectively as a rule if it is given a sufficiently speech-protective form. When regulations are subject to strict judicial scrutiny, which requires both a showing of "compelling" state ends and the unavailability of less restrictive means, the government virtually always loses and the speaker virtually always wins. Strict scrutiny thus functions more like categorization than balancing. Likewise, minimum rationality review amounts in practice to a category in the government's favor. True balancing continues to operate only when the Court applies intermediate scrutiny to speech.

Conversely, categorization itself often reflects a prior or implicit balancing process. As Melville Nimmer argued, the Court's established categories of unprotected speech commonly emerge from "definitional balancing," a "third approach which avoids the all or nothing implications of absolutism versus ad hoc balancing." If the Court holds, for example, that knowingly or recklessly false and defamatory statements of fact are unprotected by the First Amendment, it must do so based on an implicit assumption that any individual's free speech interests involved in defamatory speech are trumped by the government's competing interests in suppressing the class of defamatory speech altogether. Thus, definitional balancing in the Court's earlier decisions generates per se rules or categories for future cases in which the balance is certain to come out the same way. Nimmer, "The Right to Speak from Times to Time: First Amendment Theory Applied to Libel and Misapplied to Privacy," 56 Cal. L. Rev. 935 (1968).

SECTION 2. INCITEMENT TO VIOLENCE OR SUBVERSION

Should the First Amendment protect incitement to engage in lawless or violent activities? Even to exhortations to overthrow government? Speech that advocates genocide or glorifies terrorism? Consider John Stuart Mill, the English philosopher, writing in On Liberty (1859): "No one pretends that actions should be as free as opinions. On the contrary, even opinions lose immunity, when the circumstances in which they are expressed are such as to constitute their expression a positive instigation to some mischievous act. An opinion that corn-dealers are starvers of the poor, or that private property is robbery, ought to be unmolested when simply circulated through the press, but may justly incur punishment when delivered orally to an excited mob assembled before the house of a corn-dealer, or when handed about among the same mob in the form of a placard."

The Court has grappled repeatedly with the line between "opinion" and "instigation," as illustrated first by a series of cases involving agitation against the war and the draft during World War I. Typically in these cases, the speaker presented claims at the core of First Amendment concerns: expression critical of government policies. The government asserted especially strong interests for restraining speech: protecting governmental operations, even assuring the survival of government. Moreover, the government's restrictions often resembled the traditional curbs on seditious libel.

Should subversive speech be regulated only when it presents a "clear and present danger" of severe harms such as violence? The Court developed such a test in cases reviewing prosecutions under section 3 of Title I of the 1917 Espionage Act and its 1918 amendments. The 1917 Act, while largely directed at espionage and disclosure of military secrets, also created three new offenses: "[1] Whoever, when the United States is at war, shall willfully make or convey false reports or false statements with intent to interfere with the operation or success of the military or naval forces of the United States or to promote the success of its enemies, and [2] whoever, when the United States is at war, shall willfully cause or attempt to cause insubordination, disloyalty, mutiny, or refusal of duty, in the military or naval forces of the United States, or [3] shall willfully obstruct the recruiting or enlistment service of the United States, to the injury of the service or of the United States, shall be punished by a fine of not more than $10,000 or imprisonment for not more than twenty years, or both." There were over 2,000 prosecutions and over 1,000 convictions in the lower federal courts under the 1917 and 1918 laws. Stone, "The Origins of the 'Bad Tendency' Test: Free Speech in Wartime," 2002 Sup. Ct. Rev. 411. Very few such cases reached the Supreme Court. In the following case, the Court rejected a First Amendment challenge to such a conviction, in a unanimous opinion by Justice Holmes.

Schenck v. United States

249 U.S. 47, 39 S. Ct. 247, 63 L. Ed. 470 (1919).

■ JUSTICE HOLMES delivered the opinion of the Court.

This is an indictment in three counts. The first charges a conspiracy to violate the Espionage Act of June 15, 1917, by causing and attempting to cause insubordination, & c., in the military and naval forces of the United States, and to obstruct the recruiting and enlistment service of the United States, when the United States was at war with the German Empire, to-wit, that the defendants wilfully conspired to have printed and circulated to men who had been called and accepted for military service [a document] alleged to be calculated to cause such insubordination and obstruction. [The] second count alleges a conspiracy to commit an offence against the United States, to-wit, to use the mails for the transmission of matter declared to be non-mailable by [the 1917 Espionage Act], to-wit, the above mentioned document. [The] third count charges an unlawful use of the mails for the transmission of the same matter. [The] defendants were found guilty on all the counts. They set up the First Amendment to the Constitution, [and] bringing the case here on that ground have argued some other points [also].

The document in question upon its first printed side recited the first section of the 13th Amendment, said that the idea embodied in it was violated by the Conscription Act and that a conscript is little better than a convict. In impassioned language it intimated that conscription was despotism in its worst form and a monstrous wrong against humanity in the interest of Wall Street's chosen few. It said "Do not submit to intimidation," but in form at least confined itself to peaceful measures such as a petition for the repeal of the act. The other and later printed side of the sheet was headed "Assert Your Rights." It stated reasons for alleging that any one violated the Constitution when he refused to recognize "your right to assert your opposition to the draft," and went on, "If you do not assert and support your rights, you are helping to deny or disparage rights which it is the solemn duty of all citizens and residents of the United States to retain." It described the arguments on the other side as coming from cunning politicians and a mercenary capitalist press, and even silent consent to the conscription law as helping to support an infamous conspiracy. It denied the power to send our citizens away to foreign shores to shoot up the people of other lands, and added that words could not express the condemnation such cold-blooded ruthlessness deserves, & c., & c., winding up, "You must do your share to maintain, support and uphold the rights of the people of this country." Of course the document would not have been sent unless it had been intended to have some effect, and we do not see what effect it could be expected to have upon persons subject to the draft except to influence them to obstruct the carrying of it out. The defendants do not deny that the jury might find against them on [this].

But it is said, suppose that that was the tendency of this circular, it is protected by the [First Amendment]. Two of the strongest expressions are said to be quoted respectively from well-known public men. It well may be that the prohibition of laws abridging the freedom of speech is not confined to previous restraints, although to prevent them may have been the main purpose, as intimated in Patterson v. Colorado, 205 U.S. 454 [1907]. We admit that in many places and in ordinary times the defendants in saying all that was said in the circular would have been within their constitutional rights. But the character of every act depends upon the circumstances in which it is done. The most stringent protection of free speech would not protect a man in falsely shouting fire in a theatre and causing a panic. [The] question in every case is whether the words used are used in such circumstances and are of such a nature as to create a clear and present danger that they will bring about the substantive evils that Congress has a right to prevent. It is a question of proximity and degree. When a nation is at war many things that might be said in time of peace are such a hindrance to its effort that their utterance will not be endured so long as men fight, and that no Court could regard them as protected by any constitutional right. It seems to be admitted that if an actual obstruction of the recruiting service were proved, liability for words that produced that effect might be enforced. [The 1917 law] punishes conspiracies to obstruct as well as actual obstruction. If the act (speaking, or circulating a paper), its tendency and the intent with which it is done are the same, we perceive no ground for saying that success alone warrants making the act a [crime]. Affirmed.

THE "CLEAR AND PRESENT DANGER" TEST

1. ***Holmes's formulation.*** What is the meaning of "clear and present danger" as used in Schenck? Holmes had made important contributions to the law of criminal attempt when he sat on the Massachusetts Supreme Judicial Court. See, e.g., Commonwealth v. Peaslee, 59 N.E. 55 (Mass. 1901) (Holmes, J.), which involved the attempted arson conviction of a defendant who had gathered flammable materials but had not ignited them: "The question on the evidence [is] whether the defendant's acts come near enough to the accomplishment of the substantive offense to be punishable. [It] is a question of degree. [The] degree of proximity held sufficient may vary with [circumstances]." Is the clear and present danger test simply a common law-like test for determining when speech comes close enough to causing a crime to be punished? Should mere speech ever count as preparation for crime outside the narrow case of direct solicitation of an accomplice?

2. ***Early application of the test to uphold convictions.*** Schenck was followed within a week by two other unanimous decisions authored by Justice Holmes, Frohwerk and Debs, which purported to follow Schenck. In **Frohwerk v. United States**, 249 U.S. 204 (1919), Justice HOLMES again spoke for the Court in affirming convictions under the 1917 Act for conspiracy and attempt to cause disloyalty, mutiny and refusal of duty in the military and naval forces of the United States—all on account of publishing and circulating twelve newspaper articles: "We think it necessary to add to what has been said in [Schenck] only that the First Amendment while prohibiting legislation against free speech as such cannot have been, and obviously was not, intended to give immunity for every possible use of language. [We] venture to believe that neither Hamilton nor Madison, nor any other competent person then or later, ever supposed that to make criminal the counseling of a murder within the jurisdiction of Congress would be an unconstitutional interference with free speech. [We] have

decided in [Schenck] that a person may be convicted of a conspiracy to obstruct recruiting by words of persuasion.

"[S]o far as the language of the articles goes there is not much to choose between expressions to be found in them and those before us in [Schenck]. The first begins by declaring it a monumental and inexcusable mistake to send our soldiers to France, says that it comes no doubt from the great trusts, and later that it appears to be outright murder without serving anything practical; speaks of the unconquerable spirit and undiminished strength of the German nation, and characterizes its own discourse as words of warning to the American people. [There] is much more to the general effect that we are in the wrong and are giving false and hypocritical reasons for our course, but the foregoing is enough to indicate the kind of matter with which we have to deal. [On] this record it is impossible to say that it might not have been found that the circulation of the paper was in quarters where a little breath would be enough to kindle a flame and that the fact was known and relied upon by those who sent the paper out."

In **Debs v. United States**, 249 U.S. 211 (1919), a companion case to Frohwerk, the defendant was Eugene V. Debs, the longtime leader and frequent presidential candidate of the Socialist Party. In 1912, Debs had gotten over 900,000 votes, nearly 6% of the total. In 1920 (while Debs was in jail because of the conviction affirmed in this case) he again received over 900,000 votes, 3.4% of the total vote. Debs did not serve the full ten-year term to which he was sentenced: in 1921, he was released, on order of President Harding. The Court considered two counts of the indictment concerning Debs's delivery of a speech at the state convention of the Ohio Socialist Party. The first alleged that, in June 1918, Debs had "caused and incited and attempted to cause and incite insubordination, disloyalty, mutiny and refusal of duty in the [armed] forces" and "with intent so to do delivered, to an assembly of people, a public speech." The second alleged that he "obstructed and attempted to obstruct the recruiting and enlistment service" of the U.S. and "to that end and with that intent delivered the same speech." In affirming the conviction, Justice HOLMES wrote:

"The main theme of the speech was socialism, its growth, and a prophecy of its ultimate success. With that we have nothing to do, but if a part or the manifest intent of the more general utterances was to encourage those present to obstruct the recruiting service and if in passages such encouragement was directly given, the immunity of the general theme may not be enough to protect the speech. The speaker began by saying that he had just returned from a visit to the workhouse in the neighborhood where three of their most loyal comrades were paying the penalty for their devotion to the working class—[persons] who had been convicted of aiding and abetting another in failing to register for the draft. He said that he had to be prudent and might not be able to say all that he thought, thus intimating to his hearers that they might infer that he meant more, but he did say that those persons were paying the penalty for standing erect and for seeking to pave the way to better conditions for all mankind. Later he added further eulogies and said that he was proud of them. [There] followed personal experiences and illustrations of the growth of socialism, a glorification of minorities, and a prophecy of the success of the international socialist crusade, with the interjection that 'you need to know that you are fit for something better than slavery and cannon fodder.' The rest of the discourse had only the indirect though not necessarily ineffective bearing on the offences alleged that is to be found in the usual contrasts between capitalists and laboring men, sneers at the advice to cultivate war gardens, attribution to plutocrats of the high price of coal, & c. [The] defendant addressed the jury himself, and while contending that his speech did not warrant the charges said 'I have been accused of obstructing the war. I admit it. Gentlemen, I abhor war. I would oppose the war if I stood alone.' The statement was not necessary to warrant the jury in finding that one purpose of the speech, whether incidental or not does not matter, was to oppose not only war in general but this war, and that the opposition was so expressed that its natural and intended effect would be to obstruct recruiting. If that was intended and if, in all the circumstances, that would be its probable effect it would not be protected by reason of its being part of a general program and expressions of a general and conscientious belief.

"[The chief defense] based upon the First Amendment [was disposed of in Schenck]. There was introduced [in evidence] an 'Anti-war Proclamation and Program' adopted at St. Louis in April, 1917, coupled with testimony that about an hour before his speech the defendant had stated that he approved of that platform in spirit and in substance. [Counsel] argued against its admissibility, at some length. This document contained the usual suggestion that capitalism was the cause of the war and that our entrance into it 'was instigated by the predatory capitalists in the United States.' [Its] first recommendation was, 'continuous, active, and public opposition to the war, through demonstrations, mass petitions, and all other means within our power.' Evidence that the defendant accepted this view and this declaration of his duties at the time that he made his speech is evidence that if in that speech he used words tending to obstruct the recruiting service he meant that they should have that effect. [We] should add that the jury were most carefully instructed that they could not find the defendant guilty for advocacy of any of his opinions unless the words used had as their natural tendency and reasonably probable effect to obstruct the recruiting service, & c., and unless the defendant had the specific intent to do so in his mind. Without going into further particulars we are of opinion that the verdict on the fourth count, for obstructing and attempting to obstruct the recruiting service of the United States, must be sustained. Therefore it is less important to consider whether that upon the third count, for causing and attempting to cause insubordination, & c., in the military and naval forces, is equally impregnable. The jury were instructed that for the purposes of the statute the persons designated by the Act of May 18, 1917, registered and enrolled under it, and thus subject to be called into the active service, were a part of the military forces of the United States. The Government presents a strong argument from the history of the statutes that the instruction was correct and in accordance with established legislative usage. We see no sufficient reason for differing from the [conclusion]."

Abrams v. United States

250 U.S. 616, 40 S. Ct. 17, 63 L. Ed. 1173 (1919).

[After seizing power during the Russian Revolution of 1917, the revolutionary government in the Soviet Union signed a peace treaty with Germany; the overthrown Czarist government of Russia had been an ally of the United States in the war against Germany. In 1918, the United States sent military forces to cities in the northern part of the Soviet Union. The Abrams defendants were Russian immigrants and, according to their own testimony, "revolutionists" and "anarchists." Perceiving the American military expedition as an attempt to "crush the Russian revolution," they wrote and distributed thousands of circulars on New York City streets advocating a general strike and appealing to workers in ammunitions factories to stop producing weapons to be used against the Russian revolutionaries. They were charged under the 1918 amendments to the Espionage Act for committing actions "intended to incite, provoke and encourage resistance to the United States" during World War I, and of conspiring "to urge, incite and advocate curtailment of production [of] ordnance and ammunition, necessary [to] the prosecution of the war."]

■ JUSTICE CLARKE delivered the opinion of the Court.

It will not do to say [that] the only intent of these defendants was to prevent injury to the Russian cause. Men must be held to have intended, and to be accountable for, the effects which their acts were likely to produce. Even if their primary purpose and intent was to aid the cause of the Russian Revolution, the plan of action which they adopted necessarily involved, before it could be realized, defeat of the war program of the United States, for the obvious effect of this appeal, if it should become effective, as they hoped it might, would be to persuade persons of character such as those whom they regarded themselves as addressing not to aid government loans and not to work in ammunition factories where their work would produce 'bullets, bayonets, cannon' and other munitions of war, the use of which would cause the 'murder' of Germans and [Russians]. [The] interpretation we have put upon these articles circulated in the greatest port of our land, from which great numbers of soldiers were at the time taking ship daily, and in which great quantities of war supplies of every kind were at the time being manufactured for transportation overseas, is [the] fair interpretation of [them]. [The writings] sufficiently show, that while the immediate occasion for this particular outbreak of lawlessness, on the part of the defendant alien anarchists, may have been resentment caused by our Government sending troops into Russia as a strategic operation against the Germans on the eastern battle front, yet the plain purpose of their propaganda was to excite, at the supreme crisis of the war, disaffection, sedition, riots, and, as they hoped, revolution, in this country for the purpose of embarrassing and if possible defeating the military plans of the Government in Europe.

■ JUSTICE HOLMES, joined by JUSTICE BRANDEIS, dissenting.

This indictment is founded wholly upon the publication of two leaflets which I shall describe in a moment. [There were four counts; the majority found sufficient evidence to justify conviction under the third and fourth.] The third count alleges a conspiracy to encourage resistance to the United States in the [war with Germany] and to attempt to effectuate the purpose by publishing the [two] leaflets. The fourth count lays a conspiracy to incite curtailment of production of things necessary to the prosecution of the war and to attempt to accomplish it by publishing the second [leaflet]. The first of these leaflets says that the President's cowardly silence about the intervention in Russia reveals the hypocrisy of the plutocratic gang in Washington. It intimates that "German militarism combined with allied capitalism to crush the Russian revolution"; goes on that the tyrants of the world fight each other until they see a common enemy—working class enlightenment, when they combine to crush it; and that now militarism and capitalism combined, though not openly, to crush the Russian revolution. It says that there is only one enemy of the workers of the world and that is capitalism; that it is a crime for workers of America, & c., to fight the workers' republic of Russia, and ends "Awake! Awake, you Workers of the World! Revolutionists." A note adds "It is absurd to call us pro-German. We hate and despise German militarism more than do you hypocritical tyrants. We have more reasons for denouncing German militarism than has the coward of the White House."

The other leaflet, headed "Workers Wake Up," with abusive language says that America together with the Allies will march for Russia to help the Czecho-Slovaks in their struggle against the Bolsheviki, and that this time the hypocrites shall not fool the Russian emigrants and friends of Russia in America. It tells the Russian emigrants that they now must spit in the face of the false military propaganda by which their sympathy and help to the prosecution of the war have been called forth and says that with the money they have lent or are going to lend "they will make bullets not only for the Germans but also for the Workers Soviets of Russia," and further, "Workers in the ammunition factories, you are producing bullets, bayonets, cannon, to murder not only the Germans, but also your dearest, best, who are in Russia and are fighting for freedom." It then appeals to the same Russian emigrants at some length not to consent to the "inquisitionary expedition to Russia," and says that the destruction of the Russian revolution is "the politics of the march to Russia." The leaflet winds up by saying "Workers, our reply to this barbaric intervention has to be a general strike!," and after a few words on the spirit of revolution, exhortations not to be afraid, and some usual tall talk ends "Woe unto those who will be in the way of progress. Let solidarity live! The Rebels."

[With regard to the fourth count] it seems too plain to be denied that the suggestion to workers in the ammunition factories that they are producing bullets to murder their dearest, and the further advocacy of a general strike, both in the second leaflet, do urge curtailment of production of things necessary to the prosecution of the war within the meaning of [the 1918 amendments of the] Act of 1917. But to make the conduct criminal that statute requires that it should be "with intent by such curtailment to cripple or hinder the United States in the prosecution of the war [with Germany]." It seems to me that no such intent is proved. I am aware of course that the word intent as vaguely used in ordinary legal discussion means no more than knowledge at the time of the act that the consequences said to be intended will ensue. Even less than that will satisfy the general principle of civil and criminal liability. But, when words are used exactly, a deed is not done with intent to produce a consequence unless that consequence is the aim of the deed. It may be obvious, and obvious to the actor, that the consequence will follow, and he may be liable for it even if he regrets it, but he does not do the act with intent to produce it unless the aim to produce it is the proximate motive of the specific act, although there may be some deeper motive behind. It seems to me that this statute must be taken to use its words in a strict and accurate sense. They would be absurd in any other. A patriot might think that we were wasting money on aeroplanes, or making more cannon of a certain kind than we needed, and might advocate curtailment with success, yet even if it turned out that the curtailment hindered and was thought by other minds to have been obviously likely to hinder the United States in the prosecution of the war, no one would hold such conduct a crime. I admit that my illustration does not answer all that might be said but it is enough to show what I think and to let me pass to a more important aspect of the case. I refer to the [First Amendment].

I never have seen any reason to doubt that the questions of law that alone were before this Court in the cases of [Schenck, Frohwerk, and Debs] were rightly decided. I do not doubt for a moment that by the same reasoning that would justify punishing persuasion to murder, the United States constitutionally may punish speech that produces or is intended to produce a clear and imminent danger that it will bring about forthwith certain substantive evils that the United States constitutionally may seek to prevent. The power undoubtedly is greater in time of war than in time of peace because war opens dangers that do not exist at other times. But as against dangers peculiar to war, as against others, the principle of the right to free speech is always the same. It is only the present danger of immediate evil or an intent to bring it about that warrants Congress in setting a limit to the expression of opinion where private rights are not concerned. Congress certainly cannot forbid all effort to change the mind of the country. Now nobody can suppose that the surreptitious publishing of a silly leaflet by an unknown man, without more, would present any immediate danger that its opinions would hinder the success of the government arms or have any appreciable tendency to do so. Publishing those opinions for the very purpose of obstructing, however, might indicate a greater danger and at any rate would have the quality of an attempt. So I assume that the second leaflet if published for the purposes alleged in the fourth count might be punishable. [But] I do not see how anyone can find the intent required by the statute in any of the defendants' words. The second leaflet is the only one that affords even a foundation for the charge, and there, without invoking the hatred of German militarism expressed in the former one, it is evident from the beginning to the end that the only object of the paper is to help Russia and stop American intervention there against the popular government—not to impede the United States in the war that it was carrying on. To say that two phrases taken literally might import a suggestion of conduct that would have interference with the war as an indirect and probably undesired effect seems to me by no means enough to show an attempt to produce that effect.

In this case sentences of twenty years imprisonment have been imposed for the publishing of two leaflets that I believe the defendants had as much right to publish as the Government has to publish the Constitution of the United States now vainly invoked by them. Even if I am technically wrong and enough can be squeezed from these poor and puny anonymities to turn the color of legal litmus paper; I will add, even if what I think the necessary intent were shown; the most nominal punishment seems to me all that possibly could be inflicted, unless the defendants are to be made to suffer not for what the indictment alleges but for the creed that they avow—a creed that I believe to be the creed of ignorance and immaturity when honestly held, as I see no reason to doubt that it was held here, but which, although made the subject of examination at the trial, no one has a right even to consider in dealing with the charges before the Court.

Persecution for the expression of opinions seems to me perfectly logical. If you have no doubt of your premises or your power and want a certain result with all your heart you naturally express your wishes in law and sweep away all opposition. To allow opposition by speech seems to indicate that you think the speech impotent, as when a man says that he has squared the circle, or that you do not care whole-heartedly for the result, or that you doubt either your power or your premises. But when men have realized that time has upset many fighting faiths, they may come to believe even more than they believe the very foundations of their own conduct that the ultimate good desired is better reached by free trade in ideas—that the best test of truth is the power of the thought to get itself accepted in the competition of the market, and that truth is the only ground upon which their wishes safely can be carried out. That at any rate is the theory of our Constitution. It is an experiment, as all life is an experiment. Every year if not every day we have to wager our salvation upon some prophecy based upon imperfect knowledge. While that experiment is part of our system I think that we should be eternally vigilant against attempts to check the expression of opinions that we loathe and believe to be fraught with death, unless they so imminently threaten immediate interference with the lawful and pressing purposes of the law that an immediate check is required to save the country. I wholly disagree with the argument of the Government that the First Amendment left the common law as to seditious libel in force. History seems to me against the notion. I had conceived that the United States through many years had shown its repentance for the Sedition Act of 1798, by repaying fines that it imposed. Only the emergency that makes it immediately dangerous to leave the correction of evil counsels to time warrants making any exception to the sweeping command, "Congress shall make no [law] abridging the freedom of speech." Of course I am speaking only of expressions of opinion and exhortations, which were all that were uttered here, but I regret that I cannot put into more impressive words my belief that in their conviction upon this indictment the defendants were deprived of their rights under the [Constitution].

ALTERNATIVES TO CLEAR AND PRESENT DANGER

1. ***An intermediate, consequentialist approach.*** The "clear and present danger" test set forth by Justice Holmes in Schenck and applied in Frohwerk, Debs, and (over Holmes's dissent) in Abrams, steers between two poles: one pole of the debate holds that restriction on speech, at least political speech, is *never* legitimate to prevent subversion, violence, or other types of law violation—that punishment must be limited to illegal action, even if the speech directly "incites" that action. Holmes rejected that "perfect immunity" for speech. At the other pole, it has been argued that "[t]here [should] be no constitutional protection for any speech advocating the violation of law." Bork, "Neutral Principles and Some First Amendment Problems," 47 Ind. L.J. 1 (1971). On this view, a democracy need not tolerate speech that would reject its own commitment to liberal toleration and peaceful electoral change. Holmes likewise rejected that approach; "clear and present danger" purports to draw the line between these poles, with special emphasis on consequences of speech. But Holmes also rejected a more restrictive intermediate solution: the "bad tendency" test widely applied by the lower courts at the time, which held that "any tendency in speech to produce bad acts, no matter how remote, would suffice to validate a repressive statute." Chafee, "Book Review," 62 Harv. L. Rev. 891 (1949).

2. ***Tightening the requirements of clear and present danger.*** Holmes's Schenck opinion appeared to reject the "bad tendency" test in favor

of a test of "clear and present" immediacy, assuring special attention to the immediate risk of an evil. But note the reference to "the act, [its] tendency and the intent" at the end of the opinion. What is the relevance of "intent" to immediate risk of harm? Is the "shouting fire" analogy relevant to political speech? What if the speaker believes that there is a fire? Was Holmes's approach in Frohwerk more protective of speech than the "bad tendency" test? The Frohwerk opinion refers to "language that might be taken to convey an innuendo of a different sort," and to "a little breath" that might "kindle a flame." Did Holmes persuasively demonstrate the "clear and present danger" of Debs's speech? Did he deprecate the "general theme" unduly? Did he unduly emphasize what "his hearers [might] infer"? Was a "natural tendency and reasonably probable effect" enough to send Debs to jail? Should the speech of a national candidate for President be treated the same as a cry of "fire" in a crowded theater?

The Abrams dissent emphasizes immediacy more than its predecessors. Does it concentrate adequately on immediate proximity of speech to danger? Note the comment about a "silly leaflet" that would not present "any immediate danger" *or* "have any appreciable tendency to do so." Is "tendency" enough? Note also the reference to "the present danger of immediate evil" *or* "an intent to bring it about." Should "intent" be enough? Are "tendency" and "intent" reliable indicia of immediacy of danger? Is Holmes's approach applicable only in contexts (as with the 1917 Act) where the law is mainly directed at an evil other than speech (e.g., obstruction of military recruiting), and where speech is evidence of the risk of that evil? Or is it also useful when the legislature proscribes speech directly? Does Holmes accept the legislative statement of the evil? Must speech create immediate risk of causing the legislatively determined evil—e.g., interference with recruiting? Or does the Court define the evil? Note the reference to "an immediate [check] required to save the country," in Holmes's last paragraph. Is Holmes concerned with the gravity of the evil? Do immediacy requirements vary with gravity?

3. ***The evolution of Holmes's Abrams dissent.*** The Abrams dissent, with its genuine immediacy requirement, arguably made the clear and present danger test more speech-protective than did Schenck-Frohwerk-Debs. Did Justice Holmes change his mind about free speech in the period between the Schenck trilogy of cases in the spring of 1919 and the Abrams dissent in the fall of that year? Some of Justice Holmes's correspondence suggests as much. Gerald Gunther concluded "that Holmes was [at the time of Schenck] quite insensitive to any claim for special judicial protection of free speech; that the Schenck standard was not truly speech-protective; and that it was not until the fall of 1919, with his famous dissent in [Abrams], that Holmes put some teeth into the clear and present danger formula, at least partly as a result of probing criticism by acquaintances such as Learned Hand." Gunther, "Learned Hand and the Origins of Modern First Amendment Doctrine: Some Fragments of History," 27 Stan. L. Rev. 719 (1975); see also Gunther, Learned Hand: the Man and the Judge 161–70 (1994). In the summer of 1918, for example, Holmes, in a letter to Hand, espoused the "natural right" to silence "the other fellow when he disagrees": free speech, he insisted, "stands no differently than freedom from vaccination"—a freedom that the state could legitimately curtail, as demonstrated in Jacobson v. Massachusetts, 197 U.S. 11 (1905), a decision consistent with Justice Holmes's generally deferential due process philosophy. In 1918, Holmes seemed impervious to Hand's arguments that

the "natural right" to silence dissenters must be curbed by the law in the interests of democratic presuppositions and the search for truth.

Debs provoked criticism of Holmes both by Hand in correspondence and by Ernst Freund in an article in The New Republic. Freund wrote that "to be permitted to agitate at your own peril, subject to a jury's guessing at motive, tendency and possible effect, makes the right of free speech a precarious gift." Freund, "The Debs Case and Freedom of Speech," The New Republic, May 3, 1919, reprinted at 40 U. Chi. L. Rev. 239 (1973). And in the spring of 1919, Hand insisted to Holmes that liability for speech should not rest on guesses about the future impact of the words (but only "when the words [are] directly an incitement." Holmes wrote back, "I don't quite get your point." Hand wrote to Freund, "I have so far been unable to make [Holmes] see that he and we have any real differences." The Abrams dissent may have indicated some eventual responsiveness on Holmes's part to these criticisms. See Gunther, Learned Hand: the Man and the Judge, at 164–66. For further argument that Holmes's attitude toward free speech did shift significantly in 1919, see White, "Justice Holmes and the Modernization of Free Speech Jurisprudence: The Human Dimension," 80 Calif. L. Rev. 391 (1992).

For the contrary view that Holmes's views were consistent but that he was simply "biding his time until the Court should have before it a conviction so clearly wrong as to let him speak out his deepest thoughts about the First Amendment," see Chafee, Free Speech in the United States 86 (1941). For further argument that Holmes's views did not undergo a conversion, see Novick, Honorable Justice 473–74 (1989); Novick, "The Unrevised Holmes and Freedom of Expression," 1991 Sup. Ct. Rev. 303.

4. ***An alternative approach: Learned Hand and the Masses case.*** Two years before the issue reached the Court in Schenck, the problem of interpreting the Espionage Act of 1917 arose in a case before Learned Hand, then a District Judge for the Southern District of New York. Hand's opinion in Masses plainly reveals considerable solicitude for speech, but it does so without mentioning clear and present danger. Although the opinion was technically only an interpretation of the Act, Hand's private correspondence makes clear that it was designed as a carefully considered alternative to the prevalent constitutional analyses of free speech issues. See Gunther, Learned Hand: the Man and the Judge, at 151–61, 168–69. Consider the advantages and disadvantages of Hand's approach in the World War I context. How would Schenck, Debs, or Abrams have gone under that standard? Would Hand's approach have avoided some of the difficulties of the clear and present danger test?

Masses Publishing Co. v. Patten

244 Fed. 535 (S.D.N.Y.1917).

■ LEARNED HAND, DISTRICT JUDGE.

The plaintiff applies for a preliminary injunction against the postmaster of New York to forbid his refusal to accept its magazine in the mails under the following circumstances: The plaintiff is a publishing company in the city of New York engaged in the production of a monthly revolutionary journal called "The Masses," containing both text and cartoons. [In] July, 1917, the postmaster of New York, acting upon the direction of the Postmaster General, advised the plaintiff that the August [issue] to which he had had access would be denied the mails under the Espionage Act of June 15, 1917. [T]he defendant, while objecting generally that the whole purport of the [issue] was in violation of the law, since it tended to produce a violation of the law, to encourage the enemies of the United States, and to hamper the government in the conduct of the war, specified four cartoons and four pieces of text as especially falling within [the 1917 Act]. [In] this case there is no dispute of fact which the plaintiff can successfully challenge except the meaning of the words and pictures in the magazine.

Coming to the act itself, [I] turn directly to section 3 of title 1, which the plaintiff is said to violate. That section contains three provisions. The first is, in substance, that no one shall make any false statements with intent to interfere with the operation or success of the military or naval forces of the United States or to promote the success of its enemies. The defendant says that the cartoons and text of the magazine, constituting, as they certainly do, a virulent attack upon the war, [may] interfere with the success of the military forces of the United States. That such utterances may have the effect so ascribed to them is unhappily true. [Dissension] within a country is a high source of comfort and assistance to its [enemies]. All this, however, is beside the question whether such an attack is a willfully false statement. That phrase properly includes only a statement of fact which the utterer knows to be false, and it cannot be maintained that any of these statements are of fact, or that the plaintiff believes them to be false. They are all within the range of opinion and of criticism; they are all certainly believed to be true by the utterer. As such they fall within the scope of that right to criticise either by temperate reasoning, or by immoderate and indecent invective, which is normally the privilege of the individual in countries dependent upon the free expression of opinion as the ultimate source of authority.

The next phrase relied upon is that which forbids any one from willfully causing insubordination, disloyalty, mutiny, or refusal of duty in the military or naval forces of the United States. The defendant's position is that to arouse discontent and disaffection among the people with the prosecution of the war and with the draft tends to promote a mutinous and insubordinate temper among the troops. This, too, is true; men who become satisfied that they are engaged in an enterprise dictated by the unconscionable selfishness of the rich, and effectuated by a tyrannous disregard for the will of those who must suffer and die, will be more prone to insubordination than those who have faith in the cause and acquiesce in the means. Yet to interpret the word "cause" so broadly would, as before, involve necessarily as a consequence the suppression of all hostile criticism, and of all opinion except what encouraged and supported the existing policies, or which fell within the range of temperate argument. It would contradict the normal assumption of democratic government that the suppression of hostile criticism does not turn upon the justice of its substance or the decency and propriety of its temper.

The defendant's position, therefore, in so far as it involves the suppression of the free utterance of abuse and criticism of the existing law, or of the policies of the war, is not, in my judgment, supported by the language of the statute. Yet there has always been a recognized limit to such expressions, incident indeed to the existence of any compulsive power of the state itself. One may not counsel or advise others to violate the law as it stands. Words are not only the keys of persuasion, but the triggers of action, and those which have no purport but to counsel the violation of law cannot by any latitude of interpretation be a part of that public opinion which is the final source of government in a democratic state. To counsel or advise a man to an act is to urge upon him either that it is his interest or his duty to do it. While, of course, this may be accomplished as well by indirection as expressly, since words carry the meaning that they impart, the definition is exhaustive, I think, and I shall use it. Political agitation, by the passions it arouses or the convictions it engenders, may in fact stimulate men to the violation of law. Detestation of existing policies is easily transformed into forcible resistance of the authority which puts them in execution, and it would be folly to disregard the causal relation between the two. Yet to assimilate agitation, legitimate as such, with direct incitement to violent resistance, is to disregard the tolerance of all methods of political agitation which in normal times is a safeguard of free government. The distinction is not a scholastic subterfuge, but a hard-bought acquisition in the fight for freedom, and the purpose to disregard it must be evident when the power exists. If one stops short of urging upon others that it is their duty or their interest to resist the law, it seems to me one should not be held to have attempted to cause its violation.

It seems to me, however, quite plain that none of the language and none of the cartoons in this paper can be thought directly to counsel or advise insubordination or mutiny, without a violation of their meaning quite beyond any tolerable understanding. I come, therefore, to the third phrase of the section, which forbids any one from willfully obstructing the recruiting or enlistment service of the United States. [Here] again, [since] the question is of the expression of opinion, I construe the sentence, so far as it restrains public utterance, as I have construed the other two, and as therefore limited to the direct advocacy of resistance to the recruiting and enlistment service. If so, the inquiry is narrowed to the question whether any of the challenged matter may be said to advocate resistance to the draft, taking the meaning of the words with the utmost latitude which they can bear. As to the cartoons it seems to me quite clear that they do not fall within such a test.

The text offers more embarrassment. The poem to Emma Goldman and Alexander Berkman, at most, goes no further than to say that they are martyrs in the cause of love among nations. Such a sentiment holds them up to admiration, and hence their conduct to possible emulation. [The] paragraphs upon conscientious objectors are of the same kind. [It] is plain enough that the paper has the fullest sympathy for these people, that it admires their courage, and that it presumptively approves their conduct. [Moreover], these passages [occur] in a magazine which attacks with the utmost violence the draft and the war. That such comments have a tendency to arouse emulation in others is clear enough but that they counsel others to follow these examples is not so plain. Literally at least they do not, and while, as I have said, the words are to be taken, not literally, but according to their full import, the literal meaning is the starting point for interpretation. One may admire and approve the course of a hero without feeling any duty to follow him. There is not the least implied intimation in these words that others are under a duty to follow. The most that can be said is that, if others do follow, they will get the same admiration and the same approval. Now, there is surely an appreciable distance between esteem and emulation; and unless there is here some advocacy of such emulation, I cannot see how the passages can be said to fall within [the law]. The question before me is quite the same as what would arise upon a motion to dismiss an indictment at the close of the proof: Could any reasonable man say, not that the indirect result of the language might be to arouse a seditious disposition, for that would not be enough, but that the language directly advocated resistance to the draft? I cannot think that upon such language any verdict would [stand].

COMPARING THE HOLMES AND HAND APPROACHES

1. ***The aftermath of Masses.*** District Judge Hand's decision granting the preliminary injunction was swiftly reversed on appeal. Masses Publishing Co. v. Patten, 246 Fed. 24 (2d Cir.1917). The Circuit not only emphasized the broad administrative discretion of the Postmaster General, but also disagreed with Hand's incitement test: "This court does not agree that such is the law. If the natural and reasonable effect of what is said is to encourage resistance to a law, and the words are used in an endeavor to persuade to resistance, it is immaterial that the duty to resist is not mentioned, or the interest of the persons addressed in resistance is not suggested." As Hand wrote in one of his letters, his opinion "seemed to meet with practically no professional approval whatever." Gunther, Learned Hand: the Man and the Judge 160 (1994). He was passed over at the time for promotion to the Second Circuit. Without the ability to use the mails, The Masses could not reach its intended audience. Its editors were soon indicted and tried for Espionage Act violations, though several juries hung and failed to convict. The Masses soon went out of business.

2. ***Masses and statutory construction.*** Note that Hand casts his opinion in terms of statutory construction, suggesting that Congress should not be assumed to have passed a broadly speech-suppressive law without a clear statement. A reexamination of the legislative history suggests that Congress did not in fact intend to prohibit broadly all criticism of the war effort: "Although Congress's stance in enacting the Espionage Act could hardly be characterized as civil libertarian, its elimination of [a proposed] press censorship provision (over the strong objections of the President)," and its "abandonment of [proposed] 'treasonable or anarchistic' language in the 'nonmailability' provision" arguably "reflected a genuine concern for the potential impact of the legislation on the freedoms of speech and press." Stone, "Judge Learned Hand and the Espionage Act of 1917: a Mystery Unraveled," 70 U. Chi. L. Rev. 335 (2003). Does this suggest that Hand was correct that federal prosecutors were stretching the Espionage Act beyond its intended limits in pursuing publications like The Masses?

3. ***The strengths and weaknesses of Hand's incitement test.*** How does the Masses "incitement" standard differ from "clear and present danger"? Hand's test focused less on forecasts about the likelihood that the speech would produce danger (e.g., draft obstruction) and focused more on the speaker's words. Does the shift in focus from proximity of danger to content of speech promote greater protection of speech? How would Eugene Debs have fared under the Masses approach? Are courts more competent to use traditional judicial tools to scrutinize words for evidence of incitement than they are to assess risks and hazard guesses about the possible future impact of words in complex contexts? Or does the Masses approach underestimate the importance of context in discerning incitement? How would it deal with the indirect but purposeful incitement of Marc Anthony's

oration over the body of Caesar? How would it deal with the problem of the harmless inciter, the speaker explicitly urging law violation but with little realistic hope of success? Should even express incitement sometimes be protected? See Scanlon, "A Theory of Freedom of Expression," 1 Phil. & Pub. Aff. 204 (1972) (arguing that speech may not be restricted on the ground that it will lead listeners to believe "subsequent harmful acts [to] be worth performing").

4. ***The historical background of the Hand-Holmes contrast.*** Learned Hand's correspondence reveals that he perceived a considerable difference between his Masses approach and Holmes's clear and present danger test, even as refined in the Abrams dissent, which he welcomed. In a series of letters from 1919 to 1921 to Professor Zechariah Chafee, Jr., the period's most prominent commentator on First Amendment problems, Hand elaborated the differences between the Masses analysis and the alternatives. See Gunther, Learned Hand: the Man and the Judge 167–70 (1994). As Hand wrote to Chafee, soon after Abrams: "I do not altogether like the way Justice Holmes put the limitation. I myself think it is a little more manageable and quite adequate a distinction to say that there is an absolute and objective test to language. [I] still prefer that which I attempted to state in my first 'Masses' opinion, rather than to say that the connection between the words used and the evil aimed at should be 'immediate and direct.' " He elaborated later: "I prefer a test based upon the nature of the utterance itself. If, taken in its setting, the effect upon the hearers is only to counsel them to violate the law, it is unconditionally illegal. [As] to other utterances, it appears to me that regardless of their tendency they should be permitted."

Hand's major objection to formulations such as "clear and present danger" or "natural and reasonable tendency" was that they were too slippery in "practical administration": "I think it is precisely at those times when alone the freedom of speech becomes important as an institution, that the protection of a jury on such an issue is illusory." And, as he said in another letter, "I am not wholly in love with Holmesy's test and the reason is this. Once you admit that the matter is one of degree, [you] give to Tomdickandharry, D.J., so much latitude that the jig is at once up. [Even] the Nine Elder Statesmen have not shown themselves wholly immune from the 'herd instinct' and what seem 'immediate and direct' to-day may seem very remote next year even though the circumstances surrounding the utterance be unchanged. I own I should prefer a qualitative formula, hard, conventional, difficult to evade." See generally Gunther, "Learned Hand and the Origins of Modern First Amendment Doctrine: Some Fragments of History," 27 Stan. L. Rev. 719 (1975).

5. ***Reversion to the bad tendency test: the Red Scare cases.*** In the wake of World War I and the Russian Revolution, the United States entered the "Red Scare" era, a period of feverish anti-radicalism that lasted from the 1920s to the 1930s. In addition to mass deportations of aliens by the federal government, two-thirds of the states enacted laws prohibiting the advocacy of criminal anarchy and criminal syndicalism. Soon, such laws came before the Court in the following cases:

Gitlow v. New York

268 U.S. 652, 45 S. Ct. 625, 69 L. Ed. 1138 (1925).

■ JUSTICE SANFORD delivered the opinion of the Court.

Benjamin Gitlow was indicted [and convicted] for the statutory crime of criminal anarchy. New York Penal Law, §§ 160, 161.[1] [The] contention here is that the statute, by its terms and as applied in this case, is repugnant to the due process clause of the [14th Amendment]. The indictment was in two counts. The first charged that the defendant had advocated, advised and taught the duty, necessity and propriety of overthrowing and overturning organized government by force, violence and unlawful means, by certain writings therein set forth entitled "The Left Wing Manifesto"; the second that he had printed, published and knowingly circulated and distributed a certain paper called "The Revolutionary Age," containing the writings set forth in the [first count].

The defendant is a member of the Left Wing Section of the Socialist Party, a dissenting branch or faction of that party formed [in 1919] in opposition to its dominant policy of "moderate Socialism." [He] arranged for the printing [and publication of 16,000 copies of the first issue of the paper, which contained the Left Wing Manifesto]. It was admitted that the defendant signed a card subscribing to the Manifesto and Program of the [Left Wing]. There was no evidence of any effect resulting from the publication and circulation of the Manifesto. [The Manifesto] condemned the dominant "moderate Socialism" for its recognition of the necessity of the democratic parliamentary state [and] advocated [the] necessity of accomplishing the "Communist Revolution" by a militant and "revolutionary Socialism," based on "the class struggle" and mobilizing the "power of the proletariat in action," through mass industrial revolts developing into mass political strikes and "revolutionary mass action," for the purpose of conquering and destroying the parliamentary state and establishing in its place, through a "revolutionary dictatorship of the proletariat," the system of [Communist Socialism].

The court [charged] the jury, in substance, that they must determine what was the intent, purpose and fair meaning of the Manifesto; [that] a mere statement or analysis of social and economic facts and historical incidents, in the nature of an essay, accompanied by prophecy as to the future course of events, but with no teaching, advice or advocacy of action, would not constitute the advocacy, advice or teaching of a doctrine for the overthrow of government within the meaning of the statute; that a mere statement that unlawful acts might accomplish such a purpose would be insufficient, unless there was a teaching, advising and advocacy of employing

[1] The New York statute (enacted well before the Red Scare, in 1902, after the assassination of President McKinley) provided: "§ 160. *Criminal anarchy defined.* Criminal anarchy is the doctrine that organized government should be overthrown by force or violence, or by assassination of the executive head or of any of the executive officials of government, or by any unlawful means. The advocacy of such doctrine either by word of mouth or writing is a felony; § 161. *Advocacy of criminal anarchy.* Any person who: 1. By word of mouth or writing advocates, advises or teaches the duty, necessity or propriety of overthrowing or overturning organized government by force or violence, or by assassination of the executive head or of any of the executive officials of government, or by any unlawful means; or, 2. Prints, publishes, edits, issues or knowingly circulates, sells, distributes or publicly displays any book, paper, document, or written or printed matter in any form, containing or advocating, advising or teaching the doctrine that organized government should be overthrown by force, violence or any unlawful [means], [i]s guilty of a [felony]."

such unlawful acts for the purpose of overthrowing [government]. [The] sole contention here [is] that as there was no evidence of any concrete result flowing from the publication of the Manifesto or of circumstances showing the likelihood of such result, the statute as construed and [applied] penalizes the mere utterance, as such, of "doctrine" having no quality of incitement, without regard either to the circumstances of its utterance or to the likelihood of unlawful consequences; [and thus] contravenes [due process].

The statute does not penalize the utterance or publication of abstract "doctrine" or academic discussion having no quality of incitement to any concrete action. It is not aimed against mere historical or philosophical essays. It does not restrain the advocacy of changes in the form of government by constitutional and lawful means. What it prohibits is language advocating, advising or teaching the overthrow of organized government by unlawful means. These words imply urging to [action]. The Manifesto, plainly, is neither the statement of abstract doctrine [nor] mere prediction that industrial disturbances and revolutionary mass strikes will result spontaneously in an inevitable process of evolution in the economic system. It advocates and urges in fervent language mass action which shall progressively foment industrial disturbances and through political mass strikes and revolutionary mass action overthrow and destroy organized parliamentary government. It concludes with a call to action in these words: "The proletarian revolution and the Communist reconstruction of society—*the struggle for these*—is now indispensable. [The] Communist International calls the proletariat of the world to the final struggle!" This is not the expression of philosophical abstraction, the mere prediction of future events; it is the language of direct incitement. The means advocated for bringing about the destruction of organized parliamentary government, namely, mass industrial revolts usurping the functions of municipal government, political mass strikes directed against the parliamentary state, and revolutionary mass action for its final destruction, necessarily imply the use of force and violence, and in their essential nature are inherently unlawful in a constitutional government of law and order. That the jury were warranted in finding that the Manifesto advocated not merely the abstract doctrine of overthrowing organized government by force, violence and unlawful means, but action to that end, is clear.

For present purposes we may and do assume that freedom of speech and of the press—which are protected by the First Amendment from abridgment by Congress—are among the fundamental personal rights and "liberties" protected by the due process clause of the 14th Amendment from impairment by the States.[2] [It] is a fundamental principle, long established, that the freedom of speech and of the press which is secured by the Constitution, does not confer an absolute right to speak or publish, without responsibility, whatever one may choose. [A] State may punish utterances endangering the foundations of organized government and threatening its overthrow by unlawful means. [In] short this freedom does not deprive a State of the primary and essential right of [self preservation]. By enacting the present statute the State has determined, through its legislative body, that utterances advocating the overthrow of organized government by force, violence and unlawful means, are so inimical to the general welfare and

[2] This dicta was the Court's first indication that First Amendment guarantees are "incorporated" as against the States through the Due Process Clause of the Fourteenth Amendment.

involve such danger of substantive evil that they may be penalized in the exercise of its police power. That determination must be given great weight. Every presumption is to be indulged in favor of the validity of the statute. That utterances inciting to the overthrow of organized government by unlawful means, present a sufficient danger of substantive evil to bring their punishment within the range of legislative discretion, is clear. Such utterances, by their very nature, involve danger to the public peace and to the security of the State. They threaten breaches of the peace and ultimate revolution. And the immediate danger is none the less real and substantial, because the effect of a given utterance cannot be accurately foreseen. The State cannot reasonably be required to measure the danger from every such utterance in the nice balance of a jeweler's scale. A single revolutionary spark may kindle a fire that, smouldering for a time, may burst into a sweeping and destructive conflagration. It cannot be said that the State is acting arbitrarily or unreasonably when in the exercise of its judgment as to the measures necessary to protect the public peace and safety, it seeks to extinguish the spark without waiting until it has enkindled the flame or blazed into the conflagration. It cannot reasonably be required to defer the adoption of measures for its own peace and safety until the revolutionary utterances lead to actual disturbances of the public peace or imminent and immediate danger of its own destruction; but it may, in the exercise of its judgment, suppress the threatened danger in its incipiency. [We] cannot hold that the present statute is an arbitrary or unreasonable exercise of the police power of the State unwarrantably infringing the freedom of speech or press; and we must and do sustain its constitutionality.

This being so it may be applied to every utterance—not too trivial to be beneath the notice of the law—which is of such a character and used with such intent and purpose as to bring it within the prohibition of the statute. [In] other words, when the legislative body has determined generally, in the constitutional exercise of its discretion, that utterances of a certain kind involve such danger of substantive evil that they may be punished, the question whether any specific utterance coming within the prohibited class is likely, in and of itself, to bring about the substantive evil, is not open to consideration. It is sufficient that the statute itself be constitutional and that the use of the language comes within its prohibition. It is clear that the question in such cases is entirely different from that involved in those cases where the statute merely prohibits certain acts involving the danger of substantive evil, without any reference to language itself, and it is sought to apply its provisions to language used by the defendant for the purpose of bringing about the prohibited results. There, if it be contended that the statute cannot be applied to the language used by the defendant because of its protection by the freedom of speech or press, it must necessarily be found, as an original question, without any previous determination by the legislative body whether the specific language used involved such likelihood of bringing about the substantive evil as to deprive it of the constitutional protection. In such cases it has been held that the general provisions of the statute may be constitutionally applied to the specific utterance of the defendant if its natural tendency and probable effect was to bring about the substantive evil which the legislative body might prevent. [Schenck; Debs.] And the ["clear and present danger" passage in Schenck]—upon which great reliance is placed in the defendant's argument—was manifestly intended, as shown by the context, to apply only in cases of this class, and has no application to those like the present, where the legislative body itself has previously determined the danger of substantive evil arising from utterances of a specified character. [It] was not necessary, within the meaning of the statute, that the defendant should have advocated "some definite or immediate act or acts" of force, violence or unlawfulness. It was sufficient if such acts were advocated in general terms; and it was not essential that their immediate execution should have been advocated. Nor was it necessary that the language should have been "reasonably and ordinarily calculated to incite certain persons" to acts of force, violence or unlawfulness. The advocacy need not be addressed to specific persons. Thus, the publication and circulation of a newspaper article may be an encouragement or endeavor to persuade to murder, although not addressed to any person in [particular]. Affirmed.

■ JUSTICE HOLMES, dissenting.

[Justice] Brandeis and I are of opinion that this judgment should be reversed. The general principle of free speech, it seems to me, must be taken to be included in the 14th Amendment, in view of the scope that has been given to the word "liberty" as there used, although perhaps it may be accepted with a somewhat larger latitude of interpretation than is allowed to Congress by the sweeping language that governs or ought to govern the laws of the United States. If I am right, then I think that the criterion sanctioned by the full Court in [Schenck] applies. [It] is true that in my opinion this criterion was departed from in [Abrams], but the convictions that I expressed in that case are too deep for it to be possible for me as yet to believe that it [has] settled the law. If what I think the correct test is applied, it is manifest that there was no present danger of an attempt to overthrow the government by force on the part of the admittedly small minority who shared the defendant's views. It is said that this manifesto was more than a theory, that it was an incitement. Every idea is an incitement. It offers itself for belief and if believed it is acted on unless some other belief outweighs it or some failure of energy stifles the movement at its birth. The only difference between the expression of an opinion and an incitement in the narrower sense is the speaker's enthusiasm for the result. Eloquence may set fire to reason. But whatever may be thought of the redundant discourse before us it had no chance of starting a present conflagration. If in the long run the beliefs expressed in proletarian dictatorship are destined to be accepted by the dominant forces of the community, the only meaning of free speech is that they should be given their chance and have their way. If the publication of this document had been laid as an attempt to induce an uprising against government at once and not at some indefinite time in the future it would have presented a different question. The object would have been one with which the law might deal, subject to the doubt whether there was any danger that the publication could produce any result, or in other words, whether it was not futile and too remote from possible consequences. But the indictment alleges the publication and nothing more.

Whitney v. California

274 U.S. 357, 47 S. Ct. 641, 71 L. Ed. 1095 (1927).

[Anita Whitney was convicted under the Criminal Syndicalism Act of California, enacted in 1919.[1] The charge was that she "did [organize] and assist in organizing, and was, is, and knowingly became a member of an organization [organized] to advocate, teach, aid and abet criminal syndicalism." She had attended the 1919 national convention of the Socialist Party as a delegate from the Oakland branch. The convention split between the "radicals" and the old-line democratic Socialists. The "radicals"—including Whitney—went to another hall and formed the Communist Labor Party [CLP], adopting a platform similar to the Left Wing Manifesto involved in Gitlow. Later in 1919, she was a branch delegate to a convention called to organize a California unit of the CLP. As a member of that convention's resolutions committee, she supported a moderate resolution proposing the achievement of the CLP's goals through traditional political processes. The proposed resolution was defeated on the floor and a more militant program was adopted. Whitney remained a member of the Party and testified at the trial "that it was not her intention that the [CLP] of California should be an instrument of terrorism or violence."]

■ JUSTICE SANFORD delivered the opinion of the Court.

While it is not denied that the evidence warranted the jury in finding that the defendant became a member of and assisted in organizing the [CLP] of California, and that this was organized to [advocate] criminal syndicalism as defined by the Act, it is urged that the Act, as here construed and applied, deprived the defendant of her liberty without due process of law. [The] argument is, in effect, that the character of the state organization could not be forecast when she attended the convention; that she had no purpose of helping to create an instrument of terrorism and violence; that she "took part in formulating and presenting to the convention a resolution which, if adopted, would have committed the new organization to a legitimate policy of political reform by the use of the ballot"; that it was not until after the majority of the convention turned out to be "contrary-minded, and other less temperate policies prevailed" that the convention could have taken on the character of criminal syndicalism; and that as this was done over her protest, her mere presence in the convention, however violent the opinions expressed therein, could not thereby become a crime. This contention, while advanced in the form of a constitutional objection to the Act, is in effect nothing more than an effort to review the weight of the evidence for the purpose of showing that the defendant did not join and assist in organizing the [CLP] with a knowledge of its unlawful character and purpose. This question, which is foreclosed by the verdict of the jury, [is] one of fact merely which is not open to review in this Court, involving as it does no constitutional question [whatever].

[1] The pertinent provisions of the Act stated: "Section 1. The term 'criminal syndicalism' as used in this act is hereby defined as any doctrine or precept advocating, teaching or aiding and abetting the commission of crime, sabotage, [or] unlawful acts of force and violence or unlawful methods of terrorism as a means of accomplishing a change in industrial ownership or control, or effecting any political change. Sec. 2. Any person who: . . . [4.] Organizes or assists in organizing, or is or knowingly becomes a member of, any organization, society, group or assemblage of persons organized or assembled to advocate, teach or aid and abet [criminal syndicalism]; [i]s guilty of a [felony]."

[The Act] as applied in this case [is not] repugnant to the due process clause as a restraint of the rights of free speech, assembly, and association. That [a state] may punish those who abuse [freedom of speech] by utterances inimical to the public welfare, tending to incite to crime, disturb the public peace, or endanger the foundations of organized government and threaten its overthrow by unlawful means, is not open to question. [Gitlow.] [The legislative] determination must be given great weight. [The] essence of the offense [is] the combining with others in an association for the accomplishment of the desired ends through the advocacy and use of criminal and unlawful methods. It partakes of the nature of a criminal conspiracy. [That] such [united] action involves even greater danger to the public peace and security than the isolated utterances and acts of individuals, is clear. We cannot hold that, as here applied, the Act is an unreasonable or arbitrary exercise of the police power of the State, unwarrantably infringing any right of free speech, assembly or association, or that those persons are protected from punishment by [due process] who abuse such rights by joining and furthering an organization thus menacing the peace and welfare of the [State]. Affirmed.

■ JUSTICE BRANDEIS, joined by JUSTICE HOLMES, concurring.

The felony which the statute created is a crime very unlike the old felony of conspiracy or the old misdemeanor of unlawful assembly. The mere act of assisting in forming a society for teaching syndicalism, of becoming a member of it, or of assembling with others for that purpose is given the dynamic quality of crime. There is guilt although the society may not contemplate immediate promulgation of the doctrine. Thus the accused is to be punished, not for attempt, incitement or conspiracy, but for a step in preparation, which, if it threatens the public order at all, does so only remotely. The novelty in the prohibition introduced is that the statute aims, not at the practice of criminal syndicalism, nor even directly at the preaching of it, but at association with those who propose to preach it.

Despite arguments to the contrary which had seemed to me persuasive, it is settled that the due process clause of the 14th Amendment applies to matters of substantive law as well as to matters of procedure. Thus all fundamental rights comprised within the term liberty are protected by the [Constitution] from invasion by the States. The right of free speech, the right to teach and the right of assembly are, of course, fundamental rights. These may not be denied or abridged. But, although the rights of free speech and assembly are fundamental, they are not in their nature absolute. Their exercise is subject to restriction, if the particular restriction proposed is required in order to protect the State from destruction or from serious injury, political, economic or moral. That the necessity which is essential to a valid restriction does not exist unless speech would produce, or is intended to produce, a clear and imminent danger of some substantive evil which the State constitutionally may seek to prevent has been settled. See [Schenck].

It is said to be the function of the legislature to determine whether at a particular time and under the particular circumstances the formation of, or assembly with, a society organized to advocate criminal syndicalism constitutes a clear and present danger of substantive evil; and that by enacting the law here in question the legislature of California determined that question in the affirmative. Compare [Gitlow]. The legislature must obviously decide, in the first instance, whether a danger exists which calls for a particular protective measure. But where a statute is valid only in case certain conditions exist, the enactment of the statute cannot alone establish the facts which are essential to its validity. Prohibitory legislation has repeatedly been held invalid because unnecessary, where the denial of liberty involved was that of engaging in a particular business. The power of the courts to strike down an offending law is no less when the interests involved are not property rights, but the fundamental personal rights of free speech and assembly.

This Court has not yet fixed the standard by which to determine when a danger shall be deemed clear; how remote the danger may be and yet be deemed present; and what degree of evil shall be deemed sufficiently substantial to justify resort to abridgment of free speech and assembly as the means of protection. To reach sound conclusions on these matters, we must bear in mind why a State is, ordinarily, denied the power to prohibit dissemination of social, economic and political doctrine which a vast majority of its citizens believes to be false and fraught with evil consequence.

Those who won our independence believed that the final end of the State was to make men free to develop their faculties; and that in its government the deliberative forces should prevail over the arbitrary. They valued liberty both as an end and as a means. They believed liberty to be the secret of happiness and courage to be the secret of liberty. They believed that freedom to think as you will and to speak as you think are means indispensable to the discovery and spread of political truth; that without free speech and assembly discussion would be futile; that with them, discussion affords ordinarily adequate protection against the dissemination of noxious doctrine; that the greatest menace to freedom is an inert people; that public discussion is a political duty; and that this should be a fundamental principle of the American government. They recognized the risks to which all human institutions are subject. But they knew that order cannot be secured merely through fear of punishment for its infraction; that it is hazardous to discourage thought, hope and imagination; that fear breeds repression; that repression breeds hate; that hate menaces stable government; that the path of safety lies in the opportunity to discuss freely supposed grievances and proposed remedies; and that the fitting remedy for evil counsels is good ones. Believing in the power of reason as applied through public discussion, they eschewed silence coerced by law—the argument of force in its worst form. Recognizing the occasional tyrannies of governing majorities, they amended the Constitution so that free speech and assembly should be guaranteed.

Fear of serious injury cannot alone justify suppression of free speech and assembly. Men feared witches and burned women. It is the function of speech to free men from the bondage of irrational fears. To justify suppression of free speech there must be reasonable ground to fear that serious evil will result if free speech is practiced. There must be reasonable ground to believe that the danger apprehended is imminent. There must be reasonable ground to believe that the evil to be prevented is a serious one. Every denunciation of existing law tends in some measure to increase the probability that there will be violation of it. Condonation of a breach enhances the probability. Expressions of approval add to the probability. Propagation of the criminal state of mind by teaching syndicalism increases it. Advocacy of law-breaking heightens it still further. But even advocacy of violation, however reprehensible morally, is not a justification for denying free speech where the advocacy falls short of incitement and there is nothing to indicate that the advocacy would be immediately acted on. The wide difference between advocacy and incitement, between preparation and attempt, between assembling and conspiracy, must be borne in mind. In order to support a finding of clear and present danger it must be shown either that immediate serious violence was to be expected or was advocated, or that the past conduct furnished reason to believe that such advocacy was then contemplated.

Those who won our independence by revolution were not cowards. They did not fear political change. They did not exalt order at the cost of liberty. To courageous, self-reliant men, with confidence in the power of free and fearless reasoning applied through the processes of popular government, no danger flowing from speech can be deemed clear and present, unless the incidence of the evil apprehended is so imminent that it may befall before there is opportunity for full discussion. If there be time to expose through discussion the falsehood and fallacies, to avert the evil by the processes of education, the remedy to be applied is more speech, not enforced silence. Only an emergency can justify repression. Such must be the rule if authority is to be reconciled with freedom. Such, in my opinion, is the command of the Constitution. It is therefore always open to Americans to challenge a law abridging free speech and assembly by showing that there was no emergency justifying it.

Moreover, even imminent danger cannot justify resort to prohibition of these functions essential to effective democracy, unless the evil apprehended is relatively serious. Prohibition of free speech and assembly is a measure so stringent that it would be inappropriate as the means for averting a relatively trivial harm to society. A police measure may be unconstitutional merely because the remedy, although effective as a means of protection, is unduly harsh or oppressive. Thus, a State might, in the exercise of its police power, make any trespass upon the land of another a crime, regardless of the results or of the intent or purpose of the trespasser. It might, also, punish an attempt, a conspiracy, or an incitement to commit the trespass. But it is hardly conceivable that this Court would hold constitutional a statute which punished as a felony the mere voluntary assembly with a society formed to teach that pedestrians had the moral right to cross unenclosed, unposted, waste lands and to advocate their doing so, even if there was imminent danger that advocacy would lead to a trespass. The fact that speech is likely to result in some violence or in destruction of property is not enough to justify its suppression. There must be the probability of serious injury to the State. Among free men, the deterrents ordinarily to be applied to prevent crime are education and punishment for violations of the law, not abridgment of the rights of free speech and assembly.

[The California] legislative declaration [stating that the Act was "necessary to the immediate preservation of the public peace and safety," because many people were going "from place to place in this state" advocating criminal syndicalism] satisfies the requirement of the constitution of the State concerning emergency legislation. [But] it does not preclude enquiry into the question whether, at the time and under the circumstances, the conditions existed which are essential to validity under the Federal Constitution. As a statute, even if not void on its face, may be challenged because invalid as applied, the result of such an inquiry may depend upon the specific facts of the particular case. Whenever the fundamental rights of free speech and assembly are alleged to have been invaded, it must remain open to a defendant to present the issue whether there actually did exist at the time a clear danger; whether the danger, if any, was imminent; and whether the evil apprehended was one so substantial as to justify the stringent restriction interposed by the legislature. The legislative [declaration] creates merely a rebuttable presumption that these conditions have been satisfied.

Whether in 1919, when Miss Whitney did the things complained of, there was in California such clear and present danger of serious evil, might have been made the important issue in the case. She might have required that the issue be determined either by the court or the jury. She claimed below that the statute as applied to her violated the [Constitution]; but she did not claim that it was void because there was no clear and present danger of serious evil, nor did she request that the existence of these conditions of a valid measure thus restricting the rights of free speech and assembly be passed upon by the court or a jury. On the other hand, there was evidence on which the court or jury might have found that such danger existed. I am unable to assent to the suggestion in the opinion of the Court that assembling with a political party, formed to advocate the desirability of a proletarian revolution by mass action at some date necessarily far in the future, is not a right within the protection of the 14th Amendment. In the present case, however, there was other testimony which tended to establish the existence of a conspiracy, on the part of members of the International Workers of the World, to commit present serious crimes; and likewise to show that such a conspiracy would be furthered by the activity of the society of which Miss Whitney was a member. Under these circumstances the judgment of the state court cannot be disturbed. Our power of review in this case [from a state court] is limited [to] the particular claims duly made below, and denied. [We] lack here the power occasionally exercised on review of judgments of lower federal courts to correct in criminal cases vital errors, although the objection was not taken in the trial court. Because we may not enquire into the errors now alleged, I concur in affirming the judgment of the state court.

CRIMINAL ANARCHY AND SYNDICALISM LAWS

1. ***Legislative presumptions of harm from speech.*** In Gitlow and Whitney, unlike the Schenck trilogy and Abrams, the Court was faced with a prior legislative determination that certain classes of speech caused an intolerable risk of serious harm. Is the "clear and present danger" standard applicable in such cases? Arguably, the clear and present danger test made it inherently difficult for judges to confront and set aside a legislative judgment that a particular variety of speech is dangerous. The clear and present danger test puts great emphasis on context and guesses about future harm; to the extent that this involves an empirical judgment, judges may feel particularly incompetent to second-guess legislative judgments. Recall that, in his dissents from Court invalidations of state economic regulations on substantive due process grounds, Holmes repeatedly urged deference to legislative judgments, in cases beginning with Lochner. What explains his abandonment of such deference here? Should it matter that the Gitlow law was enacted in 1902, long before the evolution of the post-World War I radicalism that gave rise to the Gitlow prosecution? In contrast, Whitney involved prosecution for 1919 behavior under a 1919 law. On these questions, see Rogat, "Mr. Justice Holmes, Some Modern Views—The Judge as

Spectator," 31 U. Chi. L. Rev. 213 (1964), and Linde, " 'Clear and Present Danger' Reexamined: Dissonance in the Brandenburg Concerto," 22 Stan. L. Rev. 1163 (1970).

2. ***An alternative approach: the Masses test.*** Would adoption of the Masses "incitement" test have alleviated the judicial difficulty in Gitlow and Whitney? By emphasizing what speech is protected (and the speaker's words rather than guesses about future harms), would courts have been in a better position to protect speech without direct confrontations with legislative judgments that particular types of speech present a "clear and present danger" of an especially grave evil?

3. ***Comparing the Holmes and Brandeis approaches.*** Was Brandeis more successful than Holmes in confronting the Gitlow-Whitney problem? In what respects do Brandeis's justifications for the clear and present danger test differ from Holmes's? Brandeis, like Holmes, was deferential to legislative judgments underlying economic regulations during the Lochner era. Note how his Whitney concurrence sidesteps direct confrontation with the California legislature by considering Whitney's challenge to the law only "as applied." Might Brandeis have justified lessened deference to the legislature here by emphasizing that the legislators, by curtailing expressions of speech and opinions, had undercut the basis for the usual reliance on the processes of representation? Recall the Carolene Products footnote, above. Note also that Brandeis' version adds an additional variable to the "immediacy of harm" emphasis of Holmes: Brandeis also speaks of the "gravity of the evil." On the Whitney litigation and the Brandeis opinion, see Blasi, "The First Amendment and the Ideal of Civic Courage: The Brandeis Opinion in Whitney v. California," 29 Wm. & Mary L. Rev. 653 (1988). For a close reading and comparative interpretation of Holmes's and Brandeis's approaches, see Lahav, "Holmes and Brandeis: Libertarian and Republican Justifications for Free Speech," 4 J.L. & Pol. 451 (1987).

Dennis v. United States

341 U.S. 494, 71 S. Ct. 857, 95 L. Ed. 1137 (1951).

[After World War II, fears mounted of threats to national security posed by the Soviet Union and China, and anticommunist sentiment generated a number of restrictions on subversive speech. Former State Department official Alger Hiss was convicted of perjury in connection with a congressional inquiry into his alleged spying activities for the Soviet Union. Senator Joseph McCarthy conducted a series of hearings accusing government officials of communist activities. Against this backdrop, national leaders of the Communist Party were prosecuted under the Smith Act of 1940, a federal law quite similar to the New York criminal anarchy statute sustained in Gitlow.]

■ CHIEF JUSTICE VINSON announced the judgment of the Court and an opinion in which JUSTICES REED, BURTON and MINTON join.

Petitioners were indicted in July, 1948, for violation of the conspiracy provisions of the Smith Act[1] during the period of April, 1945, to July, 1948, [and convicted after jury trial. The] indictment charged the petitioners with willfully and knowingly conspiring (1) to organize as the Communist Party of the United States of America a society, group and assembly of persons who teach and advocate the overthrow and destruction of the Government of the United States by force and violence, and (2) knowingly and willfully to advocate and teach the duty and necessity of overthrowing and destroying the Government of the United States by force and [violence]. The trial of the case extended over nine months, [resulting] in a record of 16,000 pages. Our limited grant of the writ of certiorari has removed from our consideration any question as to the sufficiency of the [evidence]. [T]he Court of Appeals held that the record supports the following broad conclusion: [that] the Communist Party is a highly disciplined organization, adept at infiltration into strategic positions, use of aliases, and double-meaning language; that the Party is rigidly controlled; that Communists, unlike other political parties, tolerate no dissension from the policy laid down by the guiding forces; [that] the literature of the Party and the statements and activities of its leaders, petitioners here, advocate, and the general goal of the Party was, during the period in question, to achieve a successful overthrow of the existing order by force and [violence].

[No] one could conceive that it is not within the power of Congress to prohibit acts intended to overthrow the Government by force and violence. The question with which we are concerned here is not whether Congress has such *power*, but whether the *means* which it has employed conflict with [the] Constitution. [Petitioners attack] the statute on the grounds that by its terms it prohibits academic discussion of the merits of Marxism-Leninism, that it stifles ideas and is contrary to all concepts of a free speech and a free press. [The] very language of the Smith Act negates [this] interpretation. [The Act] is directed at advocacy, not discussion. Thus, the trial judge properly charged the jury that they could not convict if they found that petitioners did "no more than pursue peaceful studies and discussions or teaching and advocacy in the realm of ideas." [But the application of the Act] in this case has resulted in convictions for the teaching and advocacy of the overthrow of the Government by force and violence, which, even though coupled with the intent to accomplish that overthrow, contains an element of speech. For this reason, we must pay special heed to the demands of the First Amendment marking out the boundaries of speech.

[Although] no case subsequent to Whitney and Gitlow has expressly overruled the majority opinions in those cases, there is little doubt that subsequent opinions have inclined toward the Holmes-Brandeis rationale. [In] this case we are [therefore] squarely presented with the application of

1 "Sec. 2. (a) It shall be unlawful for any person—(1) to knowingly or willfully advocate, abet, advise, or teach the duty, necessity, desirability, or propriety of overthrowing or destroying any government in the United States by force or violence, or by the assassination of any officer of any such [government]; (3) to organize or help to organize any society, group, or assembly of persons who teach, advocate, or encourage the overthrow or destruction of any government in the United States by force or violence; or to be or become a member of, or affiliate with, any such society, group, or assembly of persons, knowing the purposes [thereof]. Sec. 3. It shall be unlawful for any person to attempt to commit, or to conspire to commit, any of the acts prohibited [by] this title."

the "clear and present danger" test, and must decide what that phrase imports. [Overthrow] of the Government by force and violence is certainly a substantial enough interest for the Government to limit speech. [If], then, this interest may be protected, the literal problem which is presented is what has been meant by the use of the phrase ["clear and present danger"]. Obviously, the words cannot mean that before the Government may act, it must wait until the putsch is about to be executed, the plans have been laid and the signal is awaited. If Government is aware that a group aiming at its overthrow is attempting to indoctrinate its members and to commit them to a course whereby they will strike when the leaders feel the circumstances permit, action by the Government is required. The argument that there is no need for Government to concern itself, for Government is strong, it possesses ample powers to put down a rebellion, it may defeat the revolution with ease needs no answer. For that is not the question. Certainly an attempt to overthrow the Government by force, even though doomed from the outset because of inadequate numbers or power of the revolutionists, is a sufficient evil for Congress to prevent. The damage which such attempts create both physically and politically to a nation makes it impossible to measure the validity in terms of the probability of success, or the immediacy of a successful attempt. [We] must therefore reject the contention that success or probability of success is the criterion.

The situation with which Justices Holmes and Brandeis were concerned in Gitlow was a comparatively isolated event, bearing little relation in their minds to any substantial threat to the safety of the community. [They] were not confronted with any situation comparable to the instant one—the development of an apparatus designed and dedicated to the overthrow of the Government, in the context of world crisis after crisis. Chief Judge Learned Hand, writing for the majority [of the Second Circuit] below, interpreted the phrase as follows: "In each case [courts] must ask whether the gravity of the 'evil,' discounted by its improbability, justifies such invasion of free speech as is necessary to avoid the danger." We adopt this statement of the rule. As articulated by Chief Judge Hand, it is as succinct and inclusive as any other we might devise at this [time]. Likewise, we are in accord with the court below, which affirmed the trial court's finding that the requisite danger existed. The mere fact that from the period 1945 to 1948 petitioners' activities did not result in an attempt to overthrow the Government by force and violence is of course no answer to the fact that there was a group that was ready to make the attempt. The formation by petitioners of such a highly organized conspiracy, with rigidly disciplined members subject to call when the leaders, these petitioners, felt that the time had come for action, coupled with the inflammable nature of world conditions, similar uprisings in other countries, and the touch-and-go nature of our relations with countries with whom petitioners were in the very least ideologically attuned, convince us that their convictions were justified on this score. And this analysis disposes of the contention that a conspiracy to advocate, as distinguished from the advocacy itself, cannot be constitutionally restrained, because it comprises only the preparation. It is the existence of the conspiracy which creates the danger. [If] the ingredients of the reaction are present, we cannot bind the Government to wait until the catalyst is added.

[Petitioners] intended to overthrow the Government of the United States as speedily as the circumstances would permit. Their conspiracy to organize the Communist Party and to teach and advocate the overthrow of the [Government] by force and violence created a "clear and present danger" of an attempt to overthrow the Government by force and [violence]. Affirmed.

■ JUSTICE FRANKFURTER, concurring in affirmance of the judgment.

[The] historic antecedents of the First Amendment preclude the notion that its purpose was to give unqualified immunity to every expression that touched on matters within the range of political interest. [Absolute] rules would inevitably lead to absolute exceptions, and such exceptions would eventually corrode the rules. The demands of free speech in a democratic society as well as the interest in national security are better served by candid and informed weighing of the competing interests, within the confines of the judicial process, than by announcing dogmas too inflexible for the non-Euclidean problems to be solved. But how are competing interests to be assessed? Since they are not subject to quantitative ascertainment, the issue necessarily resolves itself into asking, who is to make the adjustments?—who is to balance[?] Full responsibility for the choice cannot be given to the courts. Courts are not representative bodies. [Their] judgment is best informed, and therefore most dependable, within narrow limits. Their essential quality is detachment, founded on independence. History teaches that the independence of the judiciary is jeopardized when courts become embroiled in the passions of the day and assume primary responsibility in choosing between competing political, economic and social pressures. Primary responsibility for adjusting the interests which compete in the situation before us of necessity belongs to the Congress. [We] are to set aside the judgment [of legislators] only if there is no reasonable basis for [it].

[These] general considerations underlie decision of the case before us. On the one hand is the interest in security. The Communist Party was not designed by these defendants as an ordinary political party. For the circumstances of its organization, its aims and methods, and the relation of the defendants to its organization and aims we are concluded by the jury's verdict. [In] finding that the defendants violated [the statute,] we may not treat as established fact that the Communist Party in this country is of significant size, well-organized, well-disciplined, conditioned to embark on unlawful activity when given the command. But in determining whether application of the statute to the defendants is within the constitutional powers of Congress, we are not limited to the facts found by the jury. We must view such a question in the light of whatever is relevant to a legislative judgment. We may take judicial notice that the Communist doctrines which these defendants have conspired to advocate are in the ascendency in powerful nations who cannot be acquitted of unfriendliness to the institutions of this country. We may take account of evidence brought forward at this trial and elsewhere, much of which has long been common knowledge. In sum, it would amply justify a legislature in concluding that recruitment of additional members for the Party would create a substantial danger to national security.

On the other hand is the interest in free speech. The right to exert all governmental powers in aid of maintaining our institutions and resisting their physical overthrow does not include intolerance of opinions and speech that cannot do harm although opposed and perhaps alien to dominant, traditional opinion. [And a] public interest is not wanting in granting freedom to speak their minds even to those who advocate the overthrow of the Government by force. For, as the evidence in this case abundantly illustrates, coupled with such advocacy is criticism of defects in our society.

[Moreover, suppressing] advocates of overthrow inevitably will also silence critics who do not advocate overthrow but fear that their criticism may be so construed. [It] is self-delusion to think that we can punish [the defendants] for their advocacy without adding to the risks run by loyal citizens who honestly believe in some of the reforms these defendants advance. It is a sobering fact that in sustaining the convictions before us we can hardly escape restriction on the interchange of [ideas].

[But it] is not for us to decide how we would adjust the clash of interests which this case presents were the primary responsibility for reconciling it ours. Congress has determined that the danger created by advocacy of overthrow justifies the ensuing restriction on freedom of speech. [To] make validity of legislation depend on judicial reading of events still in the womb of time—a forecast, that is, of the outcome of forces at best appreciated only with knowledge of the topmost secrets of nations—is to charge the judiciary with duties beyond its [equipment].

■ JUSTICE JACKSON, concurring.

[The] "clear and present danger" test was an innovation by [Justice] Holmes in [Schenck, refined] in later cases, all arising before the era of World War II revealed the subtlety and efficacy of modernized revolutionary techniques used by totalitarian parties. [I] would save it, unmodified, for application as a "rule of reason" in the kind of case for which it was devised. When the issue is criminality of a hotheaded speech on a street corner, or circulation of a few incendiary pamphlets, or parading by some zealots behind a red flag, or refusal of a handful of school children to salute our flag, it is not beyond the capacity of the judicial process to gather, comprehend, and weigh the necessary materials for decision whether it is a clear and present danger of substantive evil or a harmless letting off of steam. It is not a prophecy, for the danger in such cases has matured by the time of trial or it was never present. The test applies and has meaning where a conviction is sought to be based on a speech or writing which does not directly or explicitly advocate a crime but to which such tendency is sought to be attributed by construction or by implication from external circumstances. The formula in such cases favors freedoms that are vital to our society, and, even if sometimes applied too generously, the consequences cannot be grave.

[I] think reason is lacking for applying that test to this case. If we must decide that this Act and its application are constitutional only if we are convinced that petitioner's conduct creates a "clear and present danger" of violent overthrow, we must appraise imponderables, including international and national phenomena which baffle the best informed foreign offices and our most experienced politicians. [No] doctrine can be sound whose application requires us to make a prophecy of that sort in the guise of a legal decision. The judicial process simply is not adequate to a trial of such far-flung issues. The answers given would reflect our own political predilections and nothing more. The authors of the clear and present danger test never applied it to a case like this, nor would I. If applied as it is proposed here, it means that the Communist plotting is protected during its period of incubation; its preliminary stages of organization and preparation are immune from the law; the Government can move only after imminent action is manifest, when it would, of course, be too [late].

■ JUSTICE BLACK, dissenting.

[The] only way to affirm these convictions is to repudiate directly or indirectly the established "clear and present danger" rule. This the Court does in a way which greatly restricts the protections afforded by the First Amendment. [I] cannot agree that the First Amendment permits us to sustain laws suppressing freedom of speech and press on the basis of Congress' or our own notions of mere "reasonableness." [The] Amendment as so construed is not likely to protect any but those "safe" or orthodox views which rarely need its protection. I must also express my objection to the holding [because] it sanctions the determination of a crucial issue of fact by the judge rather than by the [jury]. Public opinion being what it now is, few will protest the conviction of these Communist petitioners. There is hope, however, that in calmer times, when present pressures, passions and fears subside, this or some later Court will restore the First Amendment liberties to the high preferred place where they belong in a free society.

■ JUSTICE DOUGLAS, dissenting.

If this were a case where those who claimed protection under the First Amendment were teaching the techniques of sabotage, the assassination of the President, the filching of documents from public files, the planting of bombs, the art of street warfare, and the like, I would have no doubts. The freedom to speak is not absolute; the teaching of methods of terror and other seditious conduct should be beyond the pale along with obscenity and immorality. This case was argued as if those were the facts. The argument imported much seditious conduct into the record. That is easy and it has popular appeal, for the activities of Communists in plotting and scheming against the free world are common knowledge. But the fact is that no such evidence was introduced at the trial. There is a statute which makes a seditious conspiracy unlawful. Petitioners, however, were not charged with a "conspiracy to overthrow" the Government. They were charged with a conspiracy to form a party and groups and assemblies of people who teach and advocate the overthrow of our Government by force or violence and with a conspiracy to advocate and teach its overthrow by force and violence. It may well be that indoctrination in the techniques of terror to destroy the Government would be indictable under either statute. But the teaching which is condemned here is of a different character.

So far as the present record is concerned, what petitioners did was to organize people to teach and themselves teach the Marxist-Leninist doctrine contained chiefly in four books: Foundations of Leninism by Stalin (1924), The Communist Manifesto by Marx and Engels (1848), State and Revolution by Lenin (1917), History of the Communist Party of the Soviet Union (B) (1939). Those books are to Soviet Communism what Mein Kampf was to Nazism. If they are understood, the ugliness of Communism is revealed, its deceit and cunning are exposed, the nature of its activities becomes apparent, and the chances of its success less likely. That is not, of course, the reason why petitioners chose these books for their classrooms. They are fervent Communists to whom these volumes are gospel. They preached the creed with the hope that some day it would be acted upon. The opinion of the Court does not outlaw these texts nor condemn them to the fire, as the Communists do literature offensive to their creed. But if the books themselves are not outlawed, if they can lawfully remain on library shelves, by what reasoning does their use in a classroom become a crime? [The] Act, as construed, requires the element of intent—that those who teach the creed believe in it. The crime then depends not on what is taught but on who the teacher is. That is to make freedom of speech turn not on *what is said,* but on the *intent* with which it is said. Once we start down that road we enter territory dangerous to the liberties of every [citizen].

There comes a time when even speech loses its constitutional immunity. Speech innocuous one year may at another time fan such destructive flames that it must be halted in the interests of the safety of the Republic. That is the meaning of the clear and present danger test. When conditions are so critical that there will be no time to avoid the evil that the speech threatens, it is time to call a halt. Otherwise, free speech which is the strength of the Nation will be the cause of its destruction. Yet free speech is the rule, not the exception. The restraint to be constitutional must be based on more than fear, on more than passionate opposition against the speech, on more than a revolted dislike for its contents. There must be some immediate injury to society that is likely if speech is [allowed].

[If] we are to take judicial notice of the threat of Communists within the nation, it should not be difficult to conclude that *as a political party* they are of little consequence. [Communism] in the world scene is no bogeyman; but Communism as a political faction or party in this country plainly is. Communism has been so thoroughly exposed in this country that it has been crippled as a political force. Free speech has destroyed it as an effective political party. [How] it can be said that there is a clear and present danger that this advocacy will succeed is, therefore, a mystery. [I]n America [Communists] are miserable merchants of unwanted ideas; their wares remain unsold. [But] the mere statement of the opposing views indicates how important it is that we know the facts before we act. Neither prejudice nor hate nor senseless fear should be the basis of this solemn act. Free speech [should] not be sacrificed on anything less than plain and objective proof of danger that the evil advocated is [imminent]. [Justice CLARK did not participate in the decision.]

"CLEAR AND PRESENT DANGER" AFTER DENNIS

1. ***The Dennis formulation.*** Did Dennis ignore clear and present danger or fall prey to the inherent weaknesses of clear and present danger? What, if anything, did the Holmes standard say about the Dennis problem? What "substantive evil" was relevant? Did Dennis abandon the focus on immediacy in the Abrams dissent and the Whitney concurrence? What degree of deference to the legislative judgment was appropriate in Dennis? Should the legislative judgment have been assessed in terms of the 1940 circumstances, when the Smith Act became law or the circumstances in 1948, when the Dennis indictment was brought? See Linde, " 'Clear and Present Danger' Reexamined: Dissonance in the Brandenburg Concerto," 22 Stan. L. Rev. 1163 (1970) (arguing that, in view of the interval of more than a decade between the enactment of the Smith Act and the Dennis decision, it was effectively impossible to point to any particular "legislative judgment that would deserve deference for its assessment of the danger from revolutionary speech"). For the view that the Dennis formulation is a "powerful formula" for resolving a variety of speech issues, see Van Alstyne, "A Graphic Review of the Free Speech Clause," 70 Calif. L. Rev. 107, 128 (1982).

2. ***Clear and present danger and Learned Hand.*** In Dennis, the Court adopted the clear and present danger formulation set forth by Chief Judge Learned Hand in the decision of the court of appeals for the Second Circuit affirming the convictions below: "[Courts] must ask whether the gravity of the 'evil,' discounted by its improbability, justifies such invasion of free speech as is necessary to avoid the danger." How could Hand, the author of the Masses opinion, have adopted the clear and present danger test he had long criticized and interpreted it in a relatively speech-restrictive way? The answer, suggests Gerald Gunther, is that he was "a judge of a lower court who took seriously his obligation to follow Supreme Court precedents," and that his Masses test had sunk "into oblivion in the years between World War I and World War II," while the Supreme Court "had adhered to and struggled to clarify its 'clear and present danger' test." Gunther, Learned Hand: the Man and the Judge 600 (1994). Privately, Hand said at the time that he would still have preferred to rely on the Masses test, id. at 604, and that he personally would never have prosecuted the Communist leaders, for " '[t]he blood of martyrs is the seed of the church,' " id. at 603. Consider, however, how Hand transformed the clear and present danger test into a measure of gravity discounted by probability. Recall Hand's famous test for negligence liability expressed in United States v. Carroll Towing Co., 159 F.2d 169 (2d. Cir. 1947) ("Possibly it serves to bring this notion into relief to state it in algebraic terms: if the probability be called P; the injury, L; and the burden, B; liability depends upon whether B is less than L multiplied by P: i.e., whether $B < PL$.") Is there a relation between these two formulations?

In his last years, Judge Hand repudiated the view that rights such as speech should receive special judicial protection, suggesting that he viewed the Bill of Rights primarily as merely "admonitory or hortatory, not definite enough to be guides on concrete occasions." Hand, The Bill of Rights (1958).

3. ***Free speech theory and advocacy of totalitarian government.*** Dennis, even more sharply than the earlier subversive speech cases, raises the question why the First Amendment should protect those who, were they in power, would deny free speech rights to others. Some have argued it should not: "Speech advocating violent overthrow [of government is] not 'political speech' as that term must be defined by a Madisonian system of government [because] it violates constitutional truths about processes and because it is not aimed at a new definition of political truth by a legislative majority. Violent overthrow of government breaks the premises of our system concerning the ways in which truth is defined, and yet those premises are the only reasons for protecting political speech." Bork, "Neutral Principles and Some First Amendment Problems," 47 Ind. L.J. 1 (1971).

For arguments to the contrary, finding First Amendment value in protecting radically subversive speech, see Emerson, The System of Freedom of Expression (1970) (arguing that "democratic society should tolerate opinion which attacks the fundamental institutions of democracy for much the same reasons that it tolerates other opinion," and that "suppression of any group in a society destroys the atmosphere of freedom essential to the life and progress of a healthy community. [It] is not possible for a society to practice both freedom of expression and suppression of expression at the same time."); Meiklejohn, Free Speech and Its Relation to Self-Government 48 (1948) (arguing that the First Amendment "means that certain substantive evils which, in principle, Congress has a right to prevent, must be endured if the only way of avoiding them is by the abridging of that freedom of speech upon which the entire structure of our free institutions rests"); Smith, "Radically Subversive Speech and the Authority of Law," 94 Mich. L. Rev. 348 (1995) (arguing that radically subversive speech is valuable because a democracy, unlike an authoritarian regime, requires recognition of the possibility that the existing state might be illegitimate).

4. ***Vietnam era loosening of clear and present danger.*** Issues parallel to those in the World War I Espionage Act cases arose in connection with opposition to United States policy in the Vietnam war. In **Bond v. Floyd**, 385 U.S. 116 (1966), the Court held that the First Amendment barred Georgia from refusing to seat Julian Bond, a duly elected representative, in the state legislature. The State's justification was that Bond could not conscientiously take the required oath to "support the Constitution of this State and of the United States" in light of statements he had made or subscribed to that were critical of the draft and of Vietnam policy. Bond was an official of the Student Nonviolent Coordinating Committee (SNCC), which issued a statement that "We are in sympathy with, and support, the men in this country who are unwilling to respond to a military draft." Chief Justice WARREN's opinion for a unanimous Court held that Bond could not have been constitutionally convicted for counseling, aiding, or abetting the refusal or evasion of draft registration. The SNCC statement alone "cannot be interpreted as a call to unlawful refusal to be drafted." Nor could Bond's own statement that he admired the courage of people who burned their draft cards. "No useful purpose would be served by discussing the many decisions of this Court which establish that Bond could not have been convicted for these statements consistently with the First Amendment." And Bond's position as an elected legislator did not change the situation: "[W]hile the State has an interest in requiring its legislators to swear to a belief in constitutional processes of government, surely the oath gives it no interest in limiting its legislators' capacity to discuss their views of local or national policy."

5. ***The modern incitement test and the Court's repudiation of Whitney.*** By the 1960s, the Court had become more protective of speech in connection with the civil rights movement, and the fear of domestic communism had abated politically. In a case arising from a prosecution under a state syndicalism statute much like the one upheld in Whitney, the Court overruled that decision, retaining a form of the clear and present danger test but making that test much more difficult for the government to satisfy:

Brandenburg v. Ohio

395 U.S. 444, 89 S. Ct. 1827, 23 L. Ed. 2d 430 (1969).

■ PER CURIAM.

The appellant, a leader of a Ku Klux Klan group, was convicted under the Ohio Criminal Syndicalism statute for "advocat[ing] the duty, necessity, or propriety of crime, sabotage, violence, or unlawful methods of terrorism as a means of accomplishing industrial or political reform" and for "voluntarily assembl[ing] with any society, group, or assemblage of persons formed to teach or advocate the doctrines of criminal syndicalism." He was fined $1,000 and sentenced to one to 10 years' imprisonment.

The record shows that a man, identified at trial as the appellant, telephoned an announcer-reporter on the staff of a Cincinnati television station and invited him to come to a Ku Klux Klan "rally" to be held at a [farm]. With the cooperation of the organizers, the reporter and a cameraman attended the meeting and filmed the events. Portions of the films were later broadcast on the local station and on a national network. The prosecution's case rested on the films and on testimony identifying the appellant as the person who communicated with the reporter and who spoke at the [rally]. One film showed 12 hooded figures, some of whom carried firearms. They were gathered around a large wooden cross, which they burned. No one was present other than the participants and the newsmen who made the film. Most of the words uttered during the scene were incomprehensible when the film was projected, but scattered phrases could be understood that were derogatory of Negroes and, in one instance, of Jews.[1] Another scene on the same film showed the appellant, in Klan regalia, making a speech. The speech, in full, was as follows: "This is an organizers' meeting. We have had quite a few members here today which are—we have hundreds, hundreds of members throughout [Ohio]. I can quote from a newspaper clipping from the Columbus, Ohio Dispatch, five weeks ago Sunday morning. The Klan has more members in [Ohio] than does any other organization. We're not a revengent organization, but if our President, our Congress, our Supreme Court, continues to suppress the white, Caucasian race, it's possible that there might have to be some revengeance taken. We are marching on Congress July the Fourth, four hundred thousand strong. From there we are dividing into two groups, one group to march on St. Augustine, Florida, the other group to march into Mississippi. Thank you." The second film showed six hooded figures one of whom, later identified as the appellant, repeated a speech very similar to that recorded on the first film. The reference to the possibility of "revengeance" was omitted, and one sentence was added: "Personally, I believe the nigger should be returned to Africa, the Jew returned to Israel." Though some of the figures in the films carried weapons, the speaker did not.

The Ohio [law] was enacted in 1919. From 1917 to 1920, identical or quite similar laws were adopted by 20 States and two territories. [In 1927,] this Court sustained the constitutionality of California's Criminal Syndicalism Act, the text of which is quite similar to that of the laws of Ohio. [Whitney.] The Court upheld the statute on the ground that, without more, "advocating" violent means to effect political and economic change involves such danger to the security of the State that the State may outlaw it. But Whitney has been thoroughly discredited by later decisions. See [Dennis]. These later decisions have fashioned the principle that the constitutional guarantees of free speech and free press do not permit a State to forbid or proscribe advocacy of the use of force or of law violation except where such advocacy is directed to inciting or producing imminent lawless action and is likely to incite or produce such action. "[The] mere abstract teaching [of] the moral propriety or even moral necessity for a resort to force and violence, is not the same as preparing a group for violent action and steeling it to such

[1] The significant portions that could be understood were: "How far is the nigger going to—yeah"; "This is what we are going to do to the niggers"; "A dirty nigger"; "Send the Jews back to Israel"; "Let's give them back to the dark garden"; "Save America"; "Let's go back to constitutional betterment"; "Bury the niggers"; "We intend to do our part"; "Give us our state rights"; "Freedom for the whites"; "Nigger will have to fight for every inch he gets from now on." [Footnote by the Court.]

action." A statute which fails to draw this distinction impermissibly intrudes upon the freedoms guaranteed by the First and 14th Amendments. It sweeps within its condemnation speech which our Constitution has immunized from governmental control.

Measured by this test, Ohio's [law] cannot be sustained. The Act punishes persons who "advocate or teach the duty, necessity, or propriety" of violence "as a means of accomplishing industrial or political reform"; or who publish or circulate or display any book or paper containing such advocacy; or who "justify" the commission of violent acts "with intent to exemplify, spread or advocate the propriety of the doctrines of criminal syndicalism"; or who "voluntarily assemble" with a group formed "to teach or advocate the doctrines of criminal syndicalism." Neither the indictment nor the trial judge's instructions to the jury in any way refined the statute's bald definition of the crime in terms of mere advocacy not distinguished from incitement to imminent lawless action. Accordingly, we are here confronted with a statute which, by its own words and as applied, purports to punish mere advocacy and to forbid, on pain of criminal punishment, assembly with others merely to advocate the described type of action.[2] Such a statute falls within the condemnation of the First and 14th Amendments. The contrary teaching of [Whitney] cannot be supported, and that decision is therefore overruled. Reversed.

■ JUSTICE BLACK, concurring.

I agree with [Justice Douglas] that the "clear and present danger" doctrine should have no place in the interpretation of the First Amendment. I join the Court's opinion, which, as I understand it, simply cites [Dennis] but does not indicate any agreement [with] the "clear and present danger" doctrine on which Dennis purported to rely.

■ JUSTICE DOUGLAS, concurring.

[Though] I doubt if the "clear and present danger" test is congenial to the First Amendment in time of a declared war, I am certain it is not reconcilable with the First Amendment in days of peace. [I] see no place in the regime of the First Amendment for any "clear and present danger" test, whether strict and tight as some would make it, or free-wheeling as the Court in Dennis rephrased it. When one reads the opinions closely and sees when and how the "clear and present danger" test has been applied, great misgivings are aroused. First, the threats were often loud but always puny and made serious only by judges so wedded to the status quo that critical analysis made them nervous. Second, the test was so twisted and perverted in Dennis as to make the trial of those teachers of Marxism an all-out political trial which was part and parcel of the cold war that has eroded substantial parts of the First Amendment. [The] line between what is permissible and not subject to control and what may be made impermissible and subject to regulation is the line between ideas and overt acts. The example usually given by those who would punish speech is the case of one who falsely shouts fire in a crowded theatre. This is, however, a classic case where speech is brigaded with action.

---

[2] Statutes affecting the right of assembly, like those touching on freedom of speech, must observe the established distinctions between mere advocacy and incitement to imminent lawless action, for "[the] right of peaceable assembly is a right cognate to those of free speech and free press and is equally fundamental." [Footnote by the Court.]

THE MEANING AND IMPLICATIONS OF BRANDENBURG

1. ***The best of Hand and Holmes?*** Can Brandenburg be viewed as combining Hand's incitement emphasis in Masses with the consequentialism of Holmes's clear and present danger test? Consider the following comment: "The incitement emphasis is Hand's; the reference to 'imminent' reflects a limited influence of Holmes, combined with later experience; and 'the likely to incite or produce such action' addition in the Brandenburg standard is the only reference to the need to guess about future consequences of speech, so central to the Schenck approach. Under Brandenburg, probability of harm is no longer the central criterion for speech limitations. The inciting language of the speaker—the Hand focus on 'objective' words—is the major consideration. And punishment of the harmless inciter is prevented by the Schenck-derived requirement of a likelihood of dangerous consequences." Gunther, "Learned Hand and the Origins of Modern First Amendment Doctrine," 27 Stan. L. Rev. 719 (1975).

2. ***Later applications of Brandenburg: antiwar protests, civil rights boycotts, antiabortion websites.*** The Brandenburg standard was the primary ground for reversal of a disorderly conduct conviction in **Hess v. Indiana**, 414 U.S. 105 (1973). After a campus antiwar demonstration during which there had been arrests, over 100 demonstrators blocked the street until they were moved to the curb by the police. Hess, standing off the street, said: "We'll take the fucking street later (or again)." The state court relied primarily on a finding that this statement was "intended to incite further lawless action on the part of the crowd in the vicinity of appellant and was likely to produce such action." The Court summarily reversed: "At best, [the] statement could be taken as counsel for present moderation; at worst, it amounted to nothing more than advocacy of illegal action at some indefinite future time." The Court added that "since there was no evidence, or rational inference from the import of the language, that his words were intended to produce, and likely to produce, *imminent* disorder, those words could not be punished by the State on the ground that they had 'a tendency to lead to violence.' "

In **NAACP v. Claiborne Hardware Co.**, 458 U.S. 886 (1982), the Court set aside, on First Amendment grounds, a large damages award against alleged participants in an economic boycott of white merchants by civil rights activists in a Mississippi county. The boycott sought to secure compliance with a list of demands for racial justice. One of the defendants was Charles Evers, the Field Secretary of the NAACP, who took a leading role in the boycott. One of the arguments advanced to defend the imposition of liability on Evers was that "a finding that his public speeches were likely to incite lawless action could justify holding him liable for unlawful conduct that in fact followed within a reasonable period." In one speech, Evers had stated that boycott violators would be "disciplined" by their own people. Justice STEVENS's opinion rejected the incitement rationale for imposing liability on Evers:

"While many of the comments in Evers' speeches might have contemplated 'discipline' in the permissible form of social ostracism, it cannot be denied that references [e.g.] to the possibility that necks would be [broken] implicitly conveyed a sterner message. In the passionate atmosphere in which the speeches were delivered, they might have been understood as inviting an unlawful form of discipline or, at least, as intending to create a fear of violence whether or not improper discipline was specifically intended. [This] Court has made clear, however, that mere *advocacy* of the use of force or violence does not remove speech from the protection of the First Amendment. [The] emotionally charged rhetoric of Charles Evers' speeches did not transcend the bounds of protected speech set forth in Brandenburg. The lengthy addresses generally contained an impassioned plea for black citizens to unify, to support and respect each other, and to realize the political and economic power available to them. In the course of those pleas, strong language was used. If that language had been followed by acts of violence, a substantial question would be presented whether Evers could be held liable for the consequences of that unlawful conduct. In this case, however, [almost all] acts of violence identified in 1966 occurred weeks or months after the April 1, 1966 speech; the chancellor made no finding of any violence after the challenged 1969 speech. [When an advocate's] appeals do not incite lawless action, they must be regarded as protected speech."

Does a true threat against particular individuals take speech outside any consideration of the associated political message under Brandenburg? Does the speech protection set forth in Claiborne Hardware attenuate when antiabortion activists, on a website on the Internet, display "WANTED" posters identifying physicians who perform abortions, with lines drawn through the names of those doctors who provided abortion services who had been killed or wounded by persons opposing abortion through violence? In **Planned Parenthood v. American Coalition of Life Activists**, 290 F.3d 1058 (9th Cir. 2002) (en banc), a sharply divided court of appeals upheld the application of civil liability to such speech under the Freedom of Access to Clinics Entrances Act (FACE), which provides a right of action against whoever by "threat of force [intentionally] intimidates [any] person because that person is or has been [providing] reproductive health services." 18 U.S.C. § 248(a)(1) & (c)(1)(A). The majority opinion stated that, "while advocating violence is protected, threatening a person with violence is not. [We] disagree that Claiborne is closely analogous. Claiborne, of course, did not arise under a threats statute. [As] the opinion points out, there was no context to give the speeches (including the expression 'break your neck') the implication of authorizing or directly threatening unlawful conduct. [No] specific individuals were targeted. For all that appears, 'the break your neck' comments were hyperbolic vernacular." The court held that the First Amendment did not bar submission to a jury of the question whether the "wanted" posters and similar expression constituted "true threats" under FACE. The dissenters objected that, while "the statements could reasonably be interpreted as an effort to intimidate plaintiffs into ceasing their abortion-related activities, [the] Supreme Court has told us that 'speech does not lose its protected character . . . simply because it may embarrass others or coerce them into action.' Claiborne Hardware. In other words, some forms of intimidation enjoy constitutional protection. [To] the extent Claiborne Hardware differs from our case, the difference makes ours a far weaker case for the imposition of liability." Which side had the better of the argument? For discussion of the case, see Karst, "Threats and Meanings: How the Facts Govern First Amendment Doctrine," 58 Stan. L. Rev. 1337 (2006).

3. ***The scope of Brandenburg: factual data and torts.*** The "incitement" and "advocacy" language of Brandenburg describes speech that

in some way *urges* people to action. Does Brandenburg apply as well to the communication of *information* that may facilitate criminal acts but does not advocate the law violation? For example, consider instructions on the chemical procedures manufacturing illegal drugs, a manual on how to be a "hit man," plans for the security system at Fort Knox, or information allegedly endangering national security because it relates to the construction of illegal (in private hands) bombs or weapons. Do the dangers involved in the dissemination of this type of information fit the Brandenburg model?

Moreover, consider whether Brandenburg should apply in the absence of any "political" component to the speech. For example, does Brandenburg have any application to speech facilitating purely private, interpersonal crimes, and lacking in any broader ideological aim or context? Consider the definition of criminal solicitation in the ALI Model Penal Code, § 5.02(1): "A person is guilty of solicitation to commit a crime if with the purpose of promoting or facilitating its commission he commands, encourages, or requests another person to engage in specific conduct which would constitute such crime or an attempt to commit such crime or which would establish his complicity in its commission or attempted commission." See also the definitions of attempt and conspiracy in Model Penal Code §§ 5.01(1)(c) and 5.03(1). See generally Greenawalt, Speech, Crime, and the Uses of Language (1989).

As the incitement cases illustrate, many instances of speech that make it easier for listeners or readers to commit crimes also have valuable uses: a manual on contract assassination may also be useful to mystery writers and executives seeking to instruct security details. Should the valuable element immunize the dangerous element? Consider the proposed rule "that crime-facilitating speech ought to be constitutionally protected unless (1) it's said to a person or a small group of people when the speaker knows these few listeners are likely to use the information for criminal purposes, (2) it's within one of the few classes of speech that has almost no noncriminal value, or (3) it can cause extraordinarily serious harm (on the order of a nuclear attack or a plague) even when it's also valuable for lawful purposes." Volokh, "Crime-Facilitating Speech," 57 Stan. L. Rev. 1095 (2005). Does such a rule adequately limit the scope of Brandenburg?

Should the First Amendment protect a mass-market trade book whose topic is crime facilitation? Would Volokh's test require as much? A suit for civil liability for wrongful death was permitted to proceed against the book Hit Man: A Technical Manual for Independent Contractors. The publisher stipulated that it knew the book would be read by would-be murderers for hire. The court of appeals reversed dismissal of the suit, stating that the publisher's "astonishing stipulations, coupled with the extraordinary comprehensiveness, detail, and clarity of Hit Man's instructions for criminal activity and murder in particular, the boldness of its palpable exhortation to murder, the alarming power and effectiveness of its peculiar form of instruction, the notable absence from its text of the kind of ideas for the protection of which the First Amendment exists, and the book's evident lack of any even arguably legitimate purpose beyond the promotion and teaching of murder, render this case unique in the law. In at least these circumstances, we are confident that the First Amendment does not erect the absolute bar to the imposition of civil liability." **Rice v. Paladin Enters.**, 128 F.3d 233 (4th Cir. 1997). Would the case have been permissible absent the publisher's stipulation?

Finally, is the incitement deemed punishable by Brandenburg limited to face-to-face encounters? Can lawless action be directed over television, radio, cable or the internet? Does use of such communications media preclude a finding of imminence? In an age of instantaneous global communication over the internet and social media, does an imminence requirement make it too difficult for government to take adequate preventive measures in the face of terrorist threats?

4. ***Brandenburg and new threats of terrorism.*** Acts of domestic and international terrorism have inspired new political efforts to curtail speech that might incite violence. For example, in the wake of the 1995 Oklahoma City bombing of a federal building and day care center, members of Congress considered amending federal law to prohibit dissemination of bombmaking information. In 1999, after extensive study by the DOJ of possible free speech objections, Congress enacted a law making it an offense "to teach or demonstrate the making or use of an explosive, a destructive device, or a weapon of mass destruction, or to distribute by any means information pertaining to, in whole or in part, the manufacture or use of an explosive, destructive device, or weapon of mass destruction" either knowing or intending "that the teaching, demonstration, or information be used for, or in furtherance of, an activity that constitutes a Federal crime of violence." Pub. L. No. 106–54, 113 Stat. 398. Does the intent requirement conform the statute to Brandenburg? Even without an imminence requirement?

The bombing of the World Trade Center and the Pentagon on September 11, 2001, and the fear of further terrorist activity by al Qaeda and other groups, have led to renewed initiatives to limit the circulation of information related to terrorist methods. "Are we entering an age where the clear and present danger will push back on the Brandenburg standard? [When] the law feels the full force of the [chemical, biological, nuclear, and radiological weapons] threat, the decision may well be made that that this test no longer fits the times we face." Donohue, "Terrorist Speech and the Future of Free Expression," 27 Cardozo L. Rev. 233 (2005). Does pure technological information stripped of any political advocacy even trigger Brandenburg at all?

In an age of proliferating terrorist incidents, should Brandenburg be relaxed to permit regulation of speech that inspires conversion to terrorist causes? Other nations do not enforce such stringent protections of speech. For example, the British Terrorism Act of 2006, passed in the wake of the July 7, 2005 bombings in London, prohibits publishing "a statement that is likely to be understood by some or all of the members of the public to whom it is published as a direct or indirect encouragement or other inducement to them to the commission, preparation or instigation of acts of terrorism." Indirect encouragement includes a statement that "glorifies the commission or preparation (whether in the past, in the future or generally) of such acts or offences; and is a statement from which those members of the public could reasonably be expected to infer that what is being glorified is being glorified as conduct that should be emulated by them in existing circumstances." 2006 Terrorism Act, Chapter 11. The Act requires intent or recklessness toward such encouragement. Would Brandenburg forbid a similar law in the United States? If so, should U.S. law be changed to emulate British law? For further consideration of Brandenburg's application to modern terrorist threats, see Healy, "Brandenburg in a Time of Terror," 84 Notre Dame L. Rev. 655 (2009).

In practice, speech in support of terrorism has been prosecuted under the so-called "material support" statute, 18 U.S.C. § 2339B. The statute criminalizes the knowing provision of "material support or resources to [an organization the entity knows to have been designated as] a foreign terrorist organization." Material support is defined as "any property, tangible or intangible, or service, including currency or monetary instruments or financial securities, financial services, lodging, training, expert advice or assistance." The Court addressed the constitutionality of this approach in Holder v. Humanitarian Law Project (2010; p. 1195 below), in an opinion that did not mention Brandenburg at all. In that case, several U.S. citizens and organizations, including the Humanitarian Law Project, sought to facilitate the humanitarian and political activities of two groups—the Partiya Karkeran Kurdistan and the Liberation Tigers of Tamil Eelam—that had been designated by the Secretary of State as foreign terrorist organizations. HLP challenged application of the material support statute to that conduct, arguing that the prohibition was a violation of their right to freedom of speech and association under the First Amendment. HLP argued that the Government should have had to prove that plaintiffs had specific intent to further the organization's unlawful, violent activities. The Court upheld the law as applied to HLP, however, giving Congress and the executive deference in determining the types of activities that could further a terrorist threat. It held that the Government was prohibiting material support in the form of speech, but that the suppression was justified to achieve a compelling interest in preventing terrorism. Does the definition of such speech as material support render Brandenburg irrelevant for contemporary speech? Does the fact that the Court gave the Government deference on the severity of the threat posed by the communications do so? In addition to the deference argument, the Court also argued that "[m]aterial support meant to 'promot[e] peaceable, lawful conduct,' can further terrorism by [lending] legitimacy to foreign terrorist groups [which] makes it easier for those groups to persist, to recruit members, and to raise funds—all of which facilitate more terrorist attacks, [and because] money is fungible, and [may be used to support terrorist activities.]" Should the Court have required additional proof that these types of "material support" actually posed a threat? For discussion of Holder's likely impact on Brandenburg, see Cole, "The First Amendment's Borders," 6. Harv. L. & Pol'y Rev. 147 (2012) (exploring potential implications of the decision and possibilities for narrowing its application in future cases).

SECTION 3. FIGHTING WORDS AND HOSTILE AUDIENCES

Like the cases covered above in section 2, the cases that follow involve the problem of speech that induces violence or potential violence on the part of listeners. But here the violence is directed against the speaker rather than undertaken in sympathy with the speaker's cause. The typical claim is that a speaker's provocative message so outrages the audience that some listeners are likely to resort to violence in response. The state seeks to stop the speaker in order to promote the interest in assuring order and avoiding violence. The problem has arisen both in the context of one-on-one encounters between individuals, which has given rise to the doctrine of "fighting words," and in the context of encounters between speakers and hostile audiences, which has given rise to judicial concern over the problem of the "heckler's veto."

Does the apprehension of hostile listener reaction justify restricting the speaker? Should speakers be punished for provoking listeners to punch or want to punch them in the nose? Only if the speaker uses extremely provocative words? Even if the audience is very easily provoked? Does the First Amendment impose an obligation on the government to protect the speaker from the violent listener or the angry crowd? Or may government stop the speaker, simply by showing that his words created an immediate danger of disorder? Would recognition of that justification legitimate a "heckler's veto"? Assuming that law enforcement's capacity to prevent violent listener reaction will never be perfect, must society tolerate occasional brawls as a price of free speech?

FIGHTING WORDS

Chaplinsky v. New Hampshire

315 U.S. 568, 62 S. Ct. 766, 86 L. Ed. 1031 (1942).

[Chaplinsky, a Jehovah's Witness engaged in distributing literature on the streets of Rochester, New Hampshire, had allegedly attracted a "restless" crowd by denouncing all religion as a "racket." When a disturbance broke out, a police officer escorted Chaplinsky away. The police officer and Chaplinsky encountered the City Marshal. In the ensuing argument between Chaplinsky and the City Marshal, Chaplinsky called the Marshal a "God damned racketeer" and "a damned Fascist," adding that "the whole government of Rochester are Fascists or agents of Fascists"). Chaplinsky was subsequently convicted under a state law stating that no person "shall address any offensive, derisive or annoying word to any other person who is lawfully in any street or other public place, nor call him by any offensive or derisive name."]

■ JUSTICE MURPHY delivered the opinion of the Court.

It is now clear that "Freedom of speech and freedom of the press, which are protected by the First Amendment from infringement by Congress, are among the fundamental personal rights and liberties which are protected by the Fourteenth Amendment from invasion by state action." Allowing the broadest scope to the language and purpose of the Fourteenth Amendment, it is well understood that the right of free speech is not absolute at all times and under all circumstances. There are certain well-defined and narrowly limited classes of speech, the prevention and punishment of which have never been thought to raise any Constitutional problem. These include the lewd and obscene, the profane, the libelous, and the insulting or "fighting" words—those which by their very utterance inflict injury or tend to incite an immediate breach of the peace. It has been well observed that such utterances are no essential part of any exposition of ideas, and are of such slight social value as a step to truth that any benefit that may be derived from them is clearly outweighed by the social interest in order and morality. "Resort to epithets or personal abuse is not in any proper sense communication of information or opinion safeguarded by the Constitution, and its punishment as a criminal act would raise no question under that instrument."

The state statute here challenged comes to us authoritatively construed by the highest court of New Hampshire. On the authority of its earlier decisions, the state court declared that the statute's purpose was to preserve the public peace, no words being "forbidden except such as have a direct tendency to cause acts of violence by the person to whom, individually, the remark is addressed." It was further said: "The word 'offensive' is not to be defined in terms of what a particular addressee thinks. The test is what men of common intelligence would understand would be words likely to cause an average addressee to fight. The English language has a number of words and expressions which by general consent are 'fighting words' when said without a disarming smile. Such words, as ordinary men know, are likely to cause a fight. So are threatening, profane or obscene revilings. Derisive and annoying words can be taken as coming within the purview of the statute as heretofore interpreted only when they have this characteristic of plainly tending to excite the addressee to a breach of the peace. The statute, as construed, does no more than prohibit the face-to-face words plainly likely to cause a breach of the peace by the addressee, words whose speaking constitute a breach of the peace by the speaker—including 'classical fighting words', words in current use less 'classical' but equally likely to cause violence, and other disorderly words, including profanity, obscenity and threats."

We are unable to say that the limited scope of the statute as thus construed contravenes the constitutional right of free expression. It is a statute narrowly drawn and limited to define and punish specific conduct lying within the domain of state power, the use in a public place of words likely to cause a breach of the peace. Nor can we say that the application of the statute to the facts disclosed by the record substantially or unreasonably impinges upon the privilege of free speech. Argument is unnecessary to demonstrate that the appellations 'damn racketeer' and 'damn Fascist' are epithets likely to provoke the average person to retaliation, and thereby cause a breach of the peace.

Affirmed.

FIGHTING WORDS SINCE CHAPLINSKY

1. ***The Court's methodology in excluding "fighting words" from First Amendment protection.*** The Chaplinsky opinion illustrates the intersection of the categorization and balancing approaches to free speech analysis. In describing "fighting words" as one of the "classes of speech, the prevention and punishment of which have never been thought to raise any Constitutional problem," the decision categorized such speech as wholly outside of First Amendment coverage. But in reaching that categorical holding, Justice Murphy engaged in balancing: he attached a low value to the speech claiming protection ("no essential part of any exposition of ideas"; "slight social value as a step to truth"), and measured that weak variety of "speech" against the competing state interests ("any benefit that may be derived [is] clearly outweighed by the social interest in order and morality"). Such balancing took place, however, at the general, wholesale or definitional

level, producing a total exclusion of a class of speech from First Amendment coverage and avoiding any more particularized inquiry.

2. ***The contemporary vitality of the "fighting words" exception.*** The Court has never overruled Chaplinsky's holding that "fighting words" are excluded from free speech protection, but it has not sustained a conviction on the basis of the fighting words doctrine since Chaplinsky. Does this mean that the fighting words doctrine is "nothing more than a quaint remnant of an earlier morality that has no place in a democratic society dedicated to the principle of free expression"? Gard, "Fighting Words as Free Speech," 58 Wash. U. L.Q. 531, 535–36 (1980). Consider the view that, especially in light of later Supreme Court decisions upholding the right to use profane language in many settings, "the entire treatment of the First Amendment in Chaplinsky is based upon some moralistic aberration in free speech jurisprudence that infects the entire fighting words thesis and deserves to be extirpated as a poisonous weed in the field of the First Amendment." Caine, "The Trouble with 'Fighting Words': Chaplinsky v. New Hampshire Is a Threat to First Amendment Values and Should Be Overruled," 88 Marq. L. Rev. 441 (2004). For a contrary view, see Greenawalt, "Insults and Epithets, Are They Protected Speech?", 42 Rutgers L. Rev. 287 (1990) (arguing that fighting words should not be protected because they are intended to inflict harm rather than communicate ideas).

Is there any danger to freedom of speech even in a precedent that has atrophied from misuse? Does it still lie around like a loaded weapon? One comprehensive study of fighting words cases from 1996–2001 found that Chaplinsky remains an ongoing justification for state punishment of provocative speech, especially in cases involving punishment "of racial minorities for talking back to the police." Caine, supra. Should there be special reason to refrain from punishing speech directed at public officials?

3. ***The limitation of the "fighting words" exception.*** Justice Murphy's opinion in Chaplinsky defined fighting words as *either* those "which by their very utterance inflict injury" *or* those which "tend to incite an immediate breach of the peace." He also suggested that their suppression was justified by the social interest in "order *and* morality." Later cases, however, have focused only on the breach-of-peace and order rationales. As John Ely put it, later cases made clear that the "fighting words" exception "was no longer to be understood as a euphemism for controversial or dirty talk but was to require instead a quite unambiguous invitation to a brawl." Ely, Democracy and Distrust 114 (1980).

Supreme Court cases since Chaplinsky have repeatedly declined to find such factual support for fighting words convictions. In **Gooding v. Wilson**, 405 U.S. 518 (1972), for example, the Court reversed a conviction under a Georgia statute providing that any person "who shall, without provocation, use to or of [another], opprobrious words or abusive language, tending to cause a breach of the peace," was guilty of a misdemeanor. Antiwar picketers at an Army building refused a police request to stop blocking access to inductees. In the ensuing scuffle, appellee said to a police officer, "White son of a bitch, I'll kill you," "You son of a bitch, I'll choke you to death," and "You son of a bitch, if you ever put your hands on me again, I'll cut you all to pieces." Justice BRENNAN's majority opinion found that statute void on its face because it swept in protected speech ranging beyond the "fighting words" punishable under Chaplinsky: "We have [made] our own examination of the Georgia cases [and conclude that] Georgia appellate decisions have not construed [the statute] to be limited in application, as in Chaplinsky, to words that 'have a direct tendency to cause acts of violence by the person to whom, individually, the remark is addressed.' " See also Rosenfeld v. New Jersey, 408 U.S. 901 (1972) (vacating the conviction of a defendant who used the word "motherfucker" to describe teachers at a school board meeting, holding that in the context of such a meeting, these are not fighting words because they would not have the effect of inciting an immediate breach of the peace.)

Later cases have also tended to limit fighting words to those directed face-to-face to an individual, rather than generally at a group. See Terminiello v. Chicago (1949; p. 991 below), which reversed the breach-of-peace conviction of a speaker who had condemned an angry crowd outside the auditorium as "snakes," "slimy snakes," "slimy scum." For another example, in **Texas v. Johnson**, 491 U.S. 397 (1989), the Court invalidated on free speech grounds the conviction of a political protestor who burned an American flag. The statute under which he was convicted prohibited desecration of a flag in a manner the defendant "knows will seriously offend one or more persons likely to observe or discover [such] action." The Court rejected the government's argument that Johnson's conduct fell within the exception for fighting words as defined in Chaplinsky. Justice BRENNAN wrote for the Court: "No reasonable onlooker would have regarded Johnson's generalized expression of dissatisfaction with the policies of the Federal Government as a direct personal insult or an invitation to exchange fisticuffs. We thus conclude that the State's interest in maintaining order is not implicated on these facts." For the complete holding in Texas v. Johnson, see p. 1186 below.

Does the "fighting words" exception as narrowed to words that are invitations to breaches of the peace give too much protection to listeners who threaten to respond to provocation by fighting? Is it based on an outdated and gendered honor culture? Does it wrongly reinforce a macho code of barroom brawls? Does it give too little protection to those who respond to insulting epithets by flight rather than fight? Does it permit greater insult to be leveled at the average woman than the average man? Consider whether it would be constitutional to outlaw "street harassment," defined as occurring when a man addresses to a woman in a public place unwelcome "references to male or female genitalia or to female body parts or to sexual activities, solicitation of sex, [or] similar words that by their very utterance inflict injury or naturally tend to provoke violent resentment, even if the woman did not herself react with violence." See Bowman, "Street Harassment and the Informal Ghettoization of Women," 106 Harv. L. Rev. 517, 575 (1993).

4. ***Jehovah's Witness religious persecution revisited.*** Like the many Jehovah's Witnesses who were subject to religiously motivated abuse for refusing to salute the flag in the period surrounding the Court's decision in Gobitis (1940; p. 1390 above), Chaplinsky, also a Jehovah's Witness, was subject to abuse on account of his religion. On the day of the altercation, "Walter Chaplinsky [was] surrounded by a group of men who scornfully invited him to salute the flag. While one veteran attempted to pummel Chaplinsky, the town marshal looked on, warned the [Jehovah's] Witness that things were turning ugly, but refused to arrest the assailant. After the marshal left, the assailant returned with a flag and attempted to impale Chaplinsky on the flagpole, eventually pinning him onto a car while other

members of the crowd began to beat him. A police officer then arrived, not to detain or disperse members of the mob but to escort Chaplinsky to the police station. En route, the officer and others who joined the escort directed epithets at the hapless Witness. When Chaplinsky responded in kind [he was convicted of the offense at issue in the case]." Blasi & Shiffrin, The Story of W. Virginia State Bd. of Educ. v. Barnette *in* First Amendment Stories (Garnett & Koppelman eds., 2012). The Court in Chaplinsky omitted the details of the altercation leading up to the "fighting words" for which Walter Chaplinsky was convicted. Does the abuse that Chaplinsky was subjected to prior to his altercation with the police officer have any effect on whether his insults were properly considered fighting words?

HOSTILE AUDIENCES AND THE HECKLER'S VETO

The hostile audience cases that follow are similar to the fighting words cases in that they involve speech that provokes unsympathetic listeners to violence or threats of violence. But they differ in three respects. First, unlike fighting words cases, hostile audience cases need not involve speech specifically directed at the listener. Second, fighting words are treated as offensive because of the form their message takes; Chaplinsky would not likely have been convicted if he had said, "with all due respect, I find the incumbent government less than honorable." Hostile audience cases arise when an audience is provoked either by the form of the message or by the message itself. Third, and in part because it is not the form of speech that is pivotal, the hostile audience decisions have addressed the problem through balancing rather than categorization.

Do the "heckler's veto" cases that follow give adequate weight to the First Amendment interests of the abrasive speaker in the public forum, or do they give undue weight to audience reactions as justifications for curtailment of speech? Does the First Amendment impose responsibility on the state to restrain the hostile audience, or does the speaker bear the risk of having his provocative words stopped by the hecklers' response? By what standards can the competing interests best be reconciled? By what mechanisms? Subsequent punishment? Permit systems? Protective custody but not punishment of the speaker in violent situations?

EARLY HOSTILE AUDIENCES CASES

1. ***Cantwell and "abusive remarks" not "directed to the person of the hearer."*** Jesse Cantwell, a Jehovah's Witness, was arrested while proselytizing on the streets of New Haven, Connecticut, and convicted of the common law offense of inciting a breach of the peace. In **Cantwell v. Connecticut**, 310 U.S. 296 (1940), the Court invalidated the conviction. Justice ROBERTS wrote for the Court: "[We] must determine whether the alleged protection of the State's interest [in 'peace and good order'] has been pressed, in this instance, to a point where it has come into fatal collision with the overriding interest protected by [the First Amendment]. [No] one would have the hardihood to suggest that the principle of freedom of speech sanctions incitement to riot or that religious liberty connotes the privilege to

exhort others to physical attack upon those belonging to another sect. When clear and present danger of riot, disorder, interference with traffic upon the public streets, or other immediate threat to public safety, peace, or order appears, the power of the State to prevent or punish is obvious.

"[Having] these considerations in mind, we note that Jesse Cantwell, on April 26, 1938, was upon a public street, where he had a right to be, and where he had a right peacefully to impart his views to others. There is no showing that his deportment was noisy, truculent, overbearing or offensive. [It] is not claimed that he intended to insult or affront the hearers by playing the record. It is plain that he wished only to interest them in his propaganda. The sound of the phonograph is not shown to have disturbed residents of the street, to have drawn a crowd, or to have impeded traffic.

"The record played by Cantwell embodies a general attack on all organized religious systems as instruments of Satan and injurious to man; it then singles out the Roman Catholic Church for strictures couched in terms which naturally would offend not only persons of that persuasion, but all others who respect the honestly held religious faith of their fellows. The hearers were in fact highly offended. One of them said he felt like hitting Cantwell and the other that he was tempted to throw Cantwell off the street. The one who testified he felt like hitting Cantwell said, in answer to the question 'Did you do anything else or have any other reaction?' 'No, sir, because he said he would take the victrola and he went.' The other witness testified that he told Cantwell he had better get off the street before something happened to him and that was the end of the matter as Cantwell picked up his books and walked up the street. Cantwell's conduct, in the view of the court below, considered apart from the effect of his communication upon his hearers, did not amount to a breach of the peace. One may, however, be guilty of the offense if he commit acts or make statements likely to provoke violence and disturbance of good order, even though no such eventuality be intended. [But in practically all such cases], the provocative language which was held to amount to a breach of the peace consisted of profane, indecent, or abusive remarks directed to the person of the hearer.

"We find in the instant case no assault or threatening of bodily harm, no truculent bearing, no intentional discourtesy, no personal abuse. On the contrary, we find only an effort to persuade a willing listener to buy a book or to contribute money in the interest of what Cantwell, however misguided others may think him, conceived to be true religion. [Although] the contents of the record not unnaturally aroused animosity, we think that, in the absence of a statute narrowly drawn to define and punish specific conduct as constituting a clear and present danger to a substantial interest of the State, the petitioner's communication, considered in the light of the constitutional guarantees, raised no such clear and present menace to public peace and order as to render him liable to conviction of the common law offense [in question]."

2. ***Terminiello and "provocative" speech that "invites dispute."*** In **Terminiello v. Chicago**, 337 U.S. 1 (1949), the Court reversed the breach of the peace conviction of an abrasive speaker, but on the basis of an improper charge to the jury and without directly reaching the "hostile audience" issue. The speaker was Father Arthur Terminiello, sometimes called "the Father Coughlin of the South," a well-known national personality whose speeches and writings warned that the United States must be saved from communists and Jews. Terminiello's speech viciously denounced

various political and racial groups. Even before he spoke at an auditorium in the predominantly Jewish Chicago neighborhood of Albany Park, an angry anti-Terminiello crowd had gathered outside the auditorium. Inside, the speaker condemned the crowd as "snakes," "slimy scum," and other epithets. The crowd on the street threw bottles, stink bombs, and brickbats, breaking about twenty-eight windows in the hall. After the disturbance, Terminiello was convicted under a breach of the peace statute construed by the trial judge to include speech which "stirs the public to anger, invites dispute, brings about a condition of unrest, or creates a disturbance." Justice DOUGLAS's majority opinion found that standard unconstitutional: "[A] function of free speech under our system of government is to invite dispute. It may indeed best serve its high purpose when it induces a condition of unrest, creates dissatisfaction with conditions as they are, or even stirs people to anger. Speech is often provocative and challenging. It may strike at prejudices and preconceptions and have profound unsettling effects as it presses for acceptance of an idea. That is why freedom of speech, though not absolute [Chaplinsky], is nevertheless protected against censorship or punishment, unless shown likely to produce a clear and present danger of a serious substantive evil that rises far above public inconvenience, annoyance, or unrest."

Writing in dissent, Justice JACKSON emphasized what he saw as a direct continuity with the struggle between Fascism and Communism in pre-World War II Europe: "As this case declares a nation-wide rule that disables local and state authorities from punishing conduct which produces conflicts of this kind, it is unrealistic not to take account of the nature, methods and objectives of the forces involved. This was not an isolated, spontaneous and unintended collision of political, racial or ideological adversaries. It was a local manifestation of a world-wide and standing conflict between two organized groups of revolutionary fanatics, each of which has imported to this country the strong-arm technique developed in the struggle by which their kind has devastated Europe. Increasingly, American cities have to cope with it. One faction organizes a mass meeting, the other organizes pickets to harass it; each organizes squads to counteract the other's pickets; parade is met with counterparade. Each of these mass demonstrations has the potentiality, and more than a few the purpose, of disorder and violence. [H]itler summed up the strategy of the mass demonstration as used by both fascism and communism: 'We should not work in secret conventicles but in mighty mass demonstrations, and it is not by dagger and poison or pistol that the road can be cleared for the movement but *by the conquest of the streets*. We must teach the Marxists that the future is National Socialism, just as it will some day be the master of the state.' (Emphasis supplied.) 1 Nazi Conspiracy & Aggression (GPO, 1946) 204, 2 id. 140, Docs. 2760–PS, 404–PS, from 'Mein Kampf.' First laughed at as an extravagant figure of speech, the battle for the streets became a tragic reality when an organized Sturmabteilung [ed. note: Storm Detachment or Brownshirts, a Nazi paramilitary force] began to give practical effect to its slogan that 'possession of the streets is the key to power in the state.' Ibid., also Doc. 2168–PS."

Justice Jackson then pointed to the apparent disparity between the Court's opinions in Terminiello and Chaplinsky: "Only recently this Court held that a state could punish as a breach of the peace use of epithets such as 'damned racketeer' and 'damned fascists,' addressed to only one person, an official, because likely to provoke the average person to retaliation. But these are mild in comparison to the epithets 'slimy scum,' 'snakes,' 'bedbugs,' and the like, which Terminiello hurled at an already inflamed mob of his adversaries. How this present decision, denying state power to punish civilly one who precipitated a public riot involving hundreds of fanatic fighters in a most violent melee, can be squared with [Chaplinsky], is incomprehensible to me. [W]e must bear in mind also that no serious outbreak of mob violence, race rioting, lynching or public disorder is likely to get going without help of some speech-making to some mass of people."

In the light of the failures of liberalism in the Weimar Republic, how seriously do you take Jackson's argument from the Nazi precedent about the need for state control of the streets? As a matter of consequentialist logic, can Terminiello be squared with Chaplinsky? Should "fighting words" doctrine be applicable to speech that provokes a mob? In September of 2012, protests broke out world-wide in response to an anti-Muslim film produced in the United States and viewable on the internet. Should insults to a religion, such as Islam, that are highly likely to provoke violence, count as fighting words?

3. ***Focus on the nature of the speech or of the audience?*** To what extent should protection of speech turn on the response of the particular audience? To what extent should it turn on the words and content of the speech? Can the Court delineate the protected area by holding that words short of "fighting words" are protected, no matter what their probable impact, or should the boundaries of protection depend on the context and environment?

Feiner v. New York

340 U.S. 315, 71 S. Ct. 303, 95 L. Ed. 295 (1951).

[Irving Feiner was a young veteran who had returned from three years of service in the armed forces in World War II and was attending university in Syracuse, New York, on the G.I. Bill. In March 1949, Feiner addressed a crowd of 75 to 80 persons, black and white, on a street corner in a predominantly black residential section of Syracuse. Soon after he began, two policemen, summoned by a telephone complaint, arrived to investigate and found the crowd filling the sidewalk and spreading into the street. Feiner's speech made derogatory remarks about President Truman and the Mayor of Syracuse (calling them both "bums") and about the American Legion ("a Nazi Gestapo"). He also said: "The Negroes don't have equal rights; they should rise up in arms and fight for them." Feiner's statements "stirred up a little excitement," and there was "some pushing, shoving and milling around" in the crowd. After Feiner had been speaking about 20 minutes, one of the onlookers said to the arresting policeman: "If you don't get that son of a bitch off, I will go over and get him off there myself." After Feiner ignored two police requests to stop speaking, he was arrested. The disorderly conduct charge stated the grounds as "ignoring and refusing to heed and obey reasonable police orders issued [to] regulate and control said crowd and to prevent a breach [of] the peace and to prevent injuries to pedestrians attempting to use said walk."]

■ CHIEF JUSTICE VINSON delivered the opinion of the Court.

We are not faced here with blind condonation by a state court of arbitrary police action. [The state courts] found that the officers in making the arrest were motivated solely by a proper concern for the preservation of order and protection of the general welfare, and that there was no evidence which could lend color to a claim that the acts of the police were a cover for suppression of petitioner's views and opinions. Petitioner was thus neither arrested nor convicted for the making or the content of his speech. Rather, it was the reaction which it actually engendered. [Cantwell.] [The] findings of the New York courts as to the condition of the crowd and the refusal of petitioner to obey the police requests, supported as they are by the record of this case, are persuasive that the conviction of petitioner for violation of public peace, order and authority does not exceed the bounds of proper state police action. This Court respects, as it must, the interests of the community in maintaining peace and order on its streets. [We] cannot say that the preservation of that interest here encroaches on the constitutional rights of this petitioner.

We are well aware that the ordinary murmurings and objections of a hostile audience cannot be allowed to silence a speaker, and are also mindful of the possible danger of giving overzealous police officials complete discretion to break up otherwise lawful public meetings. [But] we are not faced here with such a situation. It is one thing to say that the police cannot be used as an instrument for the suppression of unpopular views, and another to say that, when as here the speaker passes the bounds of argument or persuasion and undertakes incitement to riot, they are powerless to prevent a breach of the peace. Nor in this case can we condemn the considered judgment of three New York courts approving the means which the police, faced with a crisis, used in the exercise of their power and duty to preserve peace and order. The findings [below] as to [the] imminence of greater disorder coupled with petitioner's deliberate defiance of the police officers convince us that we should not reverse this conviction in the name of free speech.

Affirmed.

■ JUSTICE BLACK, dissenting.

The record before us convinces me that petitioner, a young college student, has been sentenced to the penitentiary for the unpopular views he expressed on matters of public interest while lawfully making a street-corner speech. [It] seems far-fetched to suggest that the "facts" show any imminent threat of riot or uncontrollable disorder. [Nor] does one isolated threat to assault the speaker forebode disorder. [Moreover], assuming that the "facts" did indicate a critical situation, I reject the implication of the Court's opinion that the police had no obligation to protect petitioner's constitutional right to talk. The police of course have power to prevent breaches of the peace. But if, in the name of preserving order, they ever can interfere with a lawful public speaker, they first must make all reasonable efforts to protect him. Here the policemen did not even pretend to try to protect petitioner. According to the officers' testimony, the crowd was restless but there is no showing of any attempt to quiet it; pedestrians were forced to walk into the street, but there was no effort to clear a path on the sidewalk; one person threatened to assault petitioner but the officers did nothing to discourage this when even a word might have sufficed. Their duty was to protect petitioner's right to talk, even to the extent of arresting the man who threatened to interfere. Instead, they shirked that duty and acted only to suppress the right to speak.

Finally, I cannot agree with the Court's statement that petitioner's disregard of the policeman's unexplained request amounted to such "deliberate defiance" as would justify an arrest or conviction for disorderly conduct. On the contrary, I think that the policeman's action was a "deliberate defiance" of ordinary official duty as well as of the constitutional right of free speech. For at least where time allows, courtesy and explanation of commands are basic elements of good official conduct in a democratic society. [Today's] holding means that as a practical matter, minority speakers can be silenced in any city.

DISTINGUISHING FEINER IN LATER CASES

1. ***Street demonstrations.*** Contrast the holding in Feiner with the holdings of several later cases involving street demonstrations that attracted hostile crowds. In **Edwards v. South Carolina**, 372 U.S. 229 (1963), the Court reversed breach of peace convictions of 187 black student demonstrators who had walked along the South Carolina State House grounds to protest against racial discrimination. They carried placards with such messages as "Down with segregation." After a large crowd of onlookers gathered, the marchers were ordered to disperse within 15 minutes; when they did not do so, they were arrested. The Court, in an opinion by Justice STEWART, held that "South Carolina infringed the petitioners' constitutionally protected rights." He added: "The 14th Amendment does not permit a State to make criminal the peaceful expression of unpopular views. [Terminiello.]" He noted that there had been no violence by the demonstrators or the onlookers; that there was no evidence of "fighting words"; and that the circumstances were "a far cry from the situation" in Feiner. Justice CLARK's lone dissent viewed the record differently. To him, there was a "much greater danger of riot and disorder" here than in Feiner. "[This] was by no means the passive demonstration which this Court relates. [It] is my belief that anyone conversant with the almost spontaneous combustion in some Southern communities in such a situation will agree that the City Manager's action may well have averted a major catastrophe."

Why was the protest march in Edwards held "a far cry" from Feiner? Does the difference lie in the fact that the onlookers in Edwards in fact remained peaceful and that ample police were at hand? Should the focus be on the reasonable audience's reaction, or on the actual audience's response? Would an outbreak of disorder simply show police failure to protect "peaceful" speech?

In **Cox v. Louisiana**, 379 U.S. 536 (1965), the Court likewise invalidated a breach of peace conviction of a civil rights demonstrator who had attracted the attention of a hostile crowd. In December, 1961, 23 students from a black college were arrested in Baton Rouge, Louisiana, and jailed for picketing stores that maintained segregated lunch counters. The next day, appellant Cox, an ordained minister, led about 2,000 students in a peaceful march toward the courthouse in order to protest the jailing. As Cox approached the vicinity of the courthouse, he was met by the police chief, who, according to Cox, permitted the demonstration but insisted that it must be confined to the west side of the street, across from the courthouse. The students lined up on the sidewalk 101 feet from the courthouse steps. About 100 to 300 whites gathered on the opposite sidewalk. About 75 policemen were stationed on the street between the two groups. Some demonstrators carried picket signs advocating boycotts of "unfair" stores and the group sang songs and hymns, including "We Shall Overcome" and "God Bless America." The jailed students, out of sight of the demonstrators, responded by singing, and this in turn was greeted by cheers from the demonstrators. Cox gave a speech protesting the "illegal arrest" of the jailed students and urged the demonstrators to sit at segregated lunch counters. This evoked some "muttering" and "grumbling" from the white onlookers across the street. The sheriff viewed Cox's appeal to sit in at lunch counters as "inflammatory" and ordered the demonstration "broken up immediately." When the demonstrators did not disperse, policemen exploded tear gas shells. The demonstrators ran away. The next day, Cox was arrested and charged with several offenses.

Justice GOLDBERG, writing for the Court, invalidated Cox's conviction for "disturbing the peace" by failing to disperse when ordered to do so by a law enforcement officer: "It is clear to us that on the facts of this case, which are strikingly similar to those present in [Edwards], Louisiana infringed appellant's rights of free speech and free assembly by convicting him under this statute. [Our] independent examination of the [record] shows no conduct which the State had a right to prohibit as a breach of the peace. [The State argues] that while the demonstrators started out to be orderly, the loud cheering and clapping by the students in response to the singing from the jail converted the peaceful assembly into a riotous one. The record, however, does not support this assertion. [The] State contends that the conviction should be sustained because of fear expressed [that] 'violence was about to erupt' because of the demonstration. [But] the students themselves were not violent and threatened no violence. [There] is no indication [that] any member of the white group threatened violence. And [the] policemen [could] have handled the crowd. This situation, like that in Edwards, is 'a far cry from the situation in [Feiner].' "

2. ***Permit requirements as an alternative approach.*** Would a prior permit scheme be a more speech-protective mechanism to deal with the hostile audience problem than the use of on-the-spot police discretion? See generally Blasi, "Prior Restraints on Demonstrations," 68 Mich. L. Rev. 1481 (1970).

In **Kunz v. New York**, 340 U.S. 290 (1951), decided the same day as Feiner, the Court reversed a conviction for violating a New York City ordinance which prohibited public worship meetings in the street "without first obtaining a permit" from the police commissioner. The ordinance also made it unlawful "to ridicule or denounce any form of religious belief" or to "expound atheism or agnosticism [in] any street." Kunz, a Baptist minister, was convicted for holding a meeting in 1948 without a permit. Two years earlier, he had obtained a permit, but that had been revoked in the same year after an administrative hearing: there had been complaints that Kunz had engaged in "scurrilous attacks on Catholics and Jews," and the revocation was based on "evidence that he had ridiculed and denounced other religious beliefs in his meetings." Kunz's application for permits in 1947 and 1948 were "disapproved," without stated reasons. Chief Justice VINSON's majority opinion condemned the permit system as involving impermissibly standardless discretion: "Disapproval of the 1948 permit application by the police commissioner was justified by the New York courts on the ground that a permit had previously been revoked 'for good reasons.' It is noteworthy that there is no mention in the ordinance of reasons for which such a permit application can be refused. [We] have here, then, an ordinance which gives an administrative official discretionary power to control in advance the right of citizens to speak on religious matters on the streets of New York. As such, the ordinance is clearly invalid as a prior restraint on the exercise of First Amendment rights."

Justice JACKSON dissented: "[I]f the Court conceives, as Feiner indicates, that upon uttering insulting, provocative or inciting words the policeman on the beat may stop the meeting, then its assurance of free speech in this decision is 'a promise to the ear to be broken to the hope,' if the patrolman on the beat happens to have prejudices of his own. [It] seems to me that this [permit] procedure better protects freedom of speech than to let everyone speak without leave, but subject to surveillance and to being ordered to stop in the discretion of the police."

3. ***Permit fees.*** Should it be permissible to deny a permit for a meeting or parade due to a lack of police resources to handle the anticipated hostile audience reactions? If not, may government charge demonstrators a fee based on such anticipated reactions? In **Forsyth County, Georgia v. Nationalist Movement**, 505 U.S. 123 (1992), the Court invalidated a county ordinance requiring demonstrators on public property to pay a fee of up to $1000 a day to cover any public cost that "exceeds the usual and normal cost of law enforcement." The county administrator was authorized to vary the fee depending on "the expense incident . . . to the maintenance of public order." The ordinance was passed in response to 1987 civil rights marches in Forsyth County, which had billed itself as "the whitest county in America." After a march by a group of 90 civil rights demonstrators was forced to halt by a crowd of 400 counter-demonstrators, a second march was held in which 20,000 civil rights demonstrators, including several senators and an assistant attorney general, marched successfully past a crowd of 1000 counter-demonstrators, who in turn were contained by 3000 state and local police and national guardsmen. The cost of police protection on that occasion was $670,000. This case arose when a group called the Nationalist Movement proposed to demonstrate in opposition to the federal holiday commemorating the birthday of Martin Luther King, Jr., and was assessed a $100 fee by the county.

The Court, in an opinion by Justice BLACKMUN, held the ordinance facially invalid, reasoning that it left impermissibly standardless discretion in the hands of the county administrator. "There are no articulated standards either in the ordinance or in the county's established practice. The administrator is not required to rely on any objective factors. He need not provide any explanation for his decision, and that decision is unreviewable. Nothing in the law or its application prevents the official from encouraging some views and discouraging others through the arbitrary application of fees. The First Amendment prohibits the vesting of such unbridled discretion in a government official." Justice Blackmun also noted that imposing such a fee legitimated a heckler's veto: "The fee assessed will depend on the administrator's measure of the amount of hostility likely to be created by the speech based on its content. Those wishing to express views unpopular with bottle-throwers, for example, may have to pay more for their permit. [Speech] cannot be financially burdened, any more than it can be punished or banned, simply because it might offend a hostile mob." Nor could the ordinance be saved by the $1000 fee cap, for "a tax based on the content of speech does not become more constitutional because it is a small tax." Chief Justice REHNQUIST, joined by Justices White, Scalia and Thomas, dissented.

Forsyth County suggests that the public should bear the cost of protecting a speaker who is likely to provoke a hostile audience (although it does not rule out the permissibility of a flat user fee for speech in public spaces without regard to whether the audience is likely to be hostile). Is this the proper allocation of the cost, as the public is broadly speaking the beneficiary of free speech? If so, should there be a government-funded victims compensation fund to compensate bystanders injured in a riot caused by a speaker? See generally Schauer, "Uncoupling Free Speech," 92 Colum. L. Rev. 1321 (1992).

Cohen v. California

403 U.S. 15, 91 S. Ct. 1780, 29 L. Ed. 2d 284 (1971).

■ JUSTICE HARLAN delivered the opinion of the Court.

This case may seem at first blush too inconsequential to find its way into our books, but the issue it presents is of no small constitutional significance. [Cohen] was convicted [of violating a California law] which prohibits "maliciously and willfully disturb[ing] the peace or quiet of any neighborhood or person [by] offensive conduct." He was given 30 days' imprisonment. The facts upon which his conviction rests are detailed in the opinion of the [state court] "On April 26, 1968, the defendant was observed in the Los Angeles County Courthouse in the corridor outside [of] the Municipal Court wearing a jacket bearing the words 'Fuck the Draft.' [There] were women and children present in the corridor. The defendant was arrested. The defendant testified that he wore the jacket as a means of informing the public of the depth of his feelings against the Vietnam War and the draft. The defendant did not engage in, nor threaten to engage in, nor did anyone as the result of his conduct in fact commit or threaten to commit any act of violence." In affirming the conviction the [state court] held that "offensive conduct" means "behavior which has a tendency to provoke *others* to acts of violence or to in turn disturb the peace," and that the State had proved this element because, on the facts of this case, "[i]t was certainly reasonably foreseeable that such conduct might cause others to rise up to commit a violent act against the person of the defendant or attempt to forceably remove his jacket." [We reverse.]

I. In order to lay hands on the precise issue which this case involves, it is useful first to canvass various matters which this record does *not* present. The conviction quite clearly rests upon the asserted offensiveness of the *words* Cohen used to convey his message to the public. The only "conduct" which the State sought to punish is the fact of communication. Thus, we deal here with a conviction resting solely upon "speech," not upon any separately identifiable conduct which allegedly was intended by Cohen to be perceived by others as expressive of particular views but which, on its face, does not necessarily convey any message and hence arguably could be regulated without effectively repressing Cohen's ability to express himself. Cf. [United States v. O'Brien]. Further, the State certainly lacks power to punish Cohen for the underlying content of the message the inscription conveyed. At least so long as there is no showing of an intent to incite disobedience to or disruption of the draft, Cohen [could not] be punished for asserting the evident position on the inutility or immorality of the draft his jacket reflected. [Cohen's] conviction, then, rests squarely upon his exercise of the "freedom of speech" [and] can be justified, if at all, only as a valid regulation of the manner in which he exercised that freedom, not as a permissible prohibition on the substantive message it conveys. This does not end the inquiry, of course, for the [First Amendment has] never been thought to give absolute protection to every individual to speak whenever or wherever he pleases, or to use any form of address in any circumstances that he chooses. In this vein, too, however, we think it important to note that several issues typically associated with such problems are not presented here.

In the first place, Cohen was tried under a statute applicable throughout the entire State. Any attempt to support this conviction on the ground that the statute seeks to preserve an appropriately decorous atmosphere in the courthouse where Cohen was arrested must fail in the absence of any language in the statute that would have put appellant on notice that certain kinds of otherwise permissible speech or conduct would nevertheless [not] be tolerated in certain places. No fair reading of the phrase "offensive conduct" can be said sufficiently to inform the ordinary person that distinctions between certain locations are thereby created.

In the second place, as it comes to us, this case cannot be said to fall within those relatively few categories of instances where prior decisions have established the power of government to deal more comprehensively with certain forms of individual expression simply upon a showing that such a form was employed. This is not, for example, an obscenity case. Whatever else may be necessary to give rise to the States' broader power to prohibit obscene expression, such expression must be, in some significant way, erotic. [Roth.] It cannot plausibly be maintained that this vulgar allusion to the [draft] would conjure up such psychic stimulation in anyone likely to be confronted with Cohen's crudely defaced jacket.

This Court has also held that the States are free to ban the simple use, without a demonstration of additional justifying circumstances, of so-called "fighting words," those personally abusive epithets which, when addressed to the ordinary citizen, are, as a matter of common knowledge, inherently likely to provoke violent reaction. [Chaplinsky.] While the four-letter word displayed by Cohen in relation to the draft is not uncommonly employed in a personally provocative fashion, in this instance it was clearly not "directed to the person of the hearer." No individual actually or likely to be present could reasonably have regarded the words on appellant's jacket as a direct personal insult. Nor do we have here an instance of the exercise of the State's police power to prevent a speaker from intentionally provoking a given group to hostile reaction. There is, as noted above, no showing that anyone who saw Cohen was in fact violently aroused or that [Cohen] intended such a result.

Finally, [much] has been made of the claim that Cohen's distasteful mode of expression was thrust upon unwilling or unsuspecting viewers, and that the State might therefore legitimately act as it did in order to protect the sensitive from otherwise unavoidable exposure to appellant's crude form of protest. Of course, the mere presumed presence of unwilling listeners or viewers does not serve automatically to justify curtailing all speech capable of giving offense. While this Court has recognized that government may properly act in many situations to prohibit intrusion into the privacy of the home of unwelcome views and ideas which cannot be totally banned from the public dialogue, we have at the same time consistently stressed that "we are often 'captives' outside the sanctuary of the home and subject to objectionable speech." The ability of government, consonant with the Constitution, to shut off discourse solely to protect others from hearing it is, in other words, dependent upon a showing that substantial privacy interests are being invaded in an essentially intolerable manner. Any broader view of this authority would effectively empower a majority to silence dissidents simply as a matter of personal predilections.

In this regard, persons confronted with Cohen's jacket were in a quite different posture than, say, those subjected to the raucous emissions of sound trucks blaring outside their residences. Those in the Los Angeles courthouse could effectively avoid further bombardment of their sensibilities simply by averting their eyes. And, while it may be that one has a more substantial claim to a recognizable privacy interest when walking through a courthouse corridor than, for example, strolling through Central Park, surely it is nothing like the interest in being free from unwanted expression in the confines of one's own home. Given the subtlety and complexity of the factors involved, if Cohen's "speech" was otherwise entitled to constitutional protection, we do not think the fact that some unwilling "listeners" in a public building may have been briefly exposed to it can serve to justify this breach of the peace conviction where, as here, there was no evidence that persons powerless to avoid appellant's conduct did in fact object to it, and where [the statute] evinces no concern [with] the special plight of the captive auditor, but, instead, indiscriminately sweeps within its prohibitions all "offensive conduct" that disturbs "any neighborhood or person."

II. Against this background, the issue flushed by this case stands out in bold relief. It is whether California can excise, as "offensive conduct," one particular scurrilous epithet from the public discourse, either upon the theory of the court below that its use is inherently likely to cause violent reaction or upon a more general assertion that the States, acting as guardians of public morality, may properly remove this offensive word from the public vocabulary. The rationale of the California court is plainly untenable. At most it reflects an "undifferentiated fear or apprehension of disturbance [which] is not enough to overcome the right to freedom of expression." We have been shown no evidence that substantial numbers of citizens are standing ready to strike out physically at whoever may assault their sensibilities with execrations like that uttered by Cohen. There may be some persons about with such lawless and violent proclivities, but that is an insufficient base upon which to erect, consistently with constitutional values, a governmental power to force persons who wish to ventilate their dissident views into avoiding particular forms of expression. The argument amounts to little more than the self-defeating proposition that to avoid physical censorship of one who has not sought to provoke such a response by a hypothetical coterie of the violent and lawless, the States may more appropriately effectuate that censorship themselves.

Admittedly, it is not so obvious that the [First Amendment] must be taken to disable the States from punishing public utterance of this unseemly expletive in order to maintain what they regard as a suitable level of discourse within the body politic. We think, however, that examination and reflection will reveal the shortcomings of a contrary viewpoint. At the outset, we cannot overemphasize that, in our judgment, most situations where the State has a justifiable interest in regulating speech will fall within one or more of the various established exceptions, discussed above but not applicable here, to the usual rule that governmental bodies may not prescribe the form or content of individual expression. Equally important to our conclusion is the constitutional backdrop against which our decision must be made. The constitutional right of free expression is powerful medicine in a society as diverse and populous as ours. It is designed and intended to remove governmental restraints from the arena of public discussion, putting the decision as to what views shall be voiced largely into the hands of each of us, in the hope that use of such freedom will ultimately produce a more capable citizenry and more perfect polity and in the belief that no other approach would comport with the premise of individual dignity and choice upon which our political system rests. See [Whitney concurrence].

To many, the immediate consequence of this freedom may often appear to be only verbal tumult, discord, and even offensive utterance. These are, however, within established limits, in truth necessary side effects of the broader enduring values which the process of open debate permits us to achieve. That the air may at times seem filled with verbal cacophony is, in this sense, not a sign of weakness but of strength. We cannot lose sight of the fact that, in what otherwise might seem a trifling and annoying instance of individual distasteful abuse of a privilege, these fundamental societal values are truly [implicated].

Against this perception of the constitutional policies involved, we discern certain more particularized considerations that peculiarly call for reversal of this conviction. First, the principle contended for by the State seems inherently boundless. How is one to distinguish this from any other offensive word? Surely the State has no right to cleanse public debate to the point where it is grammatically palatable to the most squeamish among us. Yet no readily ascertainable general principle exists for stopping short of that result were we to affirm the judgment below. For, while the particular four-letter word being litigated here is perhaps more distasteful than most others of its genre, it is nevertheless often true that one man's vulgarity is another's lyric. Indeed, we think it is largely because governmental officials cannot make principled distinctions in this area that the Constitution leaves matters of taste and style so largely to the individual.

Additionally, we cannot overlook the fact, because it is well illustrated by the episode involved here, that much linguistic expression serves a dual communicative function: it conveys not only ideas capable of relatively precise, detached explication, but otherwise inexpressible emotions as well. In fact, words are often chosen as much for their emotive as their cognitive force. We cannot sanction the view that the Constitution, while solicitous of the cognitive content of individual speech, has little or no regard for that emotive function which, practically speaking, may often be the more important element of the overall message sought to be [communicated]. Finally, and in the same vein, we cannot indulge the facile assumption that one can forbid particular words without also running a substantial risk of suppressing ideas in the process. Indeed, governments might soon seize upon the censorship of particular words as a convenient guise for banning the expression of unpopular views. [It] is, in sum, our judgment that, absent a more particularized and compelling reason for its actions, the State may not, consistently with the [First Amendment], make the simple public display here involved of this single four-letter expletive a [criminal offense]. Reversed.

■ JUSTICE BLACKMUN, with whom CHIEF JUSTICE BURGER and JUSTICE BLACK join, dissenting.

I dissent, and I do so for two reasons: Cohen's absurd and immature antic, in my view, was mainly conduct and little speech. Further, the case appears to me to be well within the sphere of [Chaplinsky]. As a consequence, this Court's agonizing over First Amendment values seems misplaced and unnecessary.

■ [JUSTICE WHITE dissented on other grounds.]

OFFENSIVE SPEECH

1. ***Cohen and Chaplinsky.*** The Court's decision in Cohen highlighted three limitations on the holding of Chaplinsky. First, Chaplinsky had included "the lewd" and "the profane" as categories of speech not entitled to First Amendment protection. Cohen made clear, however, that profanity was at least sometimes protected speech. Second, Cohen reiterated that the fighting words exception is limited to statements "directed to the person of the hearer," not addressed generally to the world at large. Third, Cohen undermined the notion that there is any unprotected category of "words that by their very utterance inflict injury." It emphasized the emotive power of words and suggested that preventing psychic offense was not, at least in this case, a sufficient justification for punishing speech.

2. ***Offensive words and free speech theory.*** Under which theory of the free speech protections does the Court's holding Cohen fall? Did Cohen's inflammatory choice of words serve the interests of the search for truth through discourse? Of self-government? Of personal autonomy? Or did the Court's holding defer to a skepticism of the government's competence in censoring the aesthetics of speech in the public sphere? For an argument that profanity does not contribute to the rational public discourse at the heart of the First Amendment, see Bickel, The Morality of Consent (1975); Cox, The Role of the Supreme Court in American Government (1976).

3. ***Speech thrust on the unwary.*** Justice Harlan asserted that those offended by the message on Cohen's jacket were in a public place. Should it matter that some people (jurors and defendants, for instance) may not be in the courthouse willingly, but under legal compulsion? Harlan also suggested that those in the courthouse who did not like the message could look away and avoid seeing it further. Is this a satisfactory response to speech that breaks decorum?

SECTION 4. INJURY TO REPUTATION, SENSIBILITY, DIGNITY, EQUALITY

While the previous section dealt with speech that provokes violence against the speaker, the following cases involve government regulations of speech that causes harm other than from physical violence to the subjects of his or her speech. The harm at issue in these cases may involve either direct psychological harm to the listener from hearing the hurtful speech or the more indirect harm to reputation or social relations caused by propagating harmful messages to third parties. Consider the decisions below applying the First Amendment increasingly to limit the scope of the unprotected category of libel, to impose similar limits on non-defamation torts, and to define the possible scope of new limits on speech directed at the expression of hatred or contempt toward individuals based on their racial or other group status.

LIBEL

The Court in Chaplinsky (1942; p. 986 above) readily categorized libel—the tortious assertion as facts of defamatory statements about an individual—as a category of speech undeserving of any First Amendment protection. Over time, the Court has considered constitutional challenges to libel laws and judgments and narrowed the category of libel unprotected by the First Amendment. In more recent decades, the Court has also considered First Amendment limits on non-defamation torts such as the invasion of privacy and the intentional infliction of emotional distress.

Such cases are explored below with respect to injury to individuals, but the Court's first major libel decision after Chaplinsky, in Beauharnais, involved the context of a statute aimed not at the protection of individuals but rather directed at false and injurious statements about racial or other social groups:

Beauharnais v. Illinois

343 U.S. 250, 72 S. Ct. 725, 96 L. Ed. 919 (1956).

[Beauharnais, president of the White Circle League in Illinois, had organized the circulation of a leaflet setting forth a petition calling on Chicago officials "to halt the further encroachment, harassment and invasion of white people, their property, neighborhoods and persons, by the Negro." The leaflet called on Chicago's white people to unite and warned that if "persuasion and the need to prevent the white race from becoming mongrelized by the negro will not unite us, then the [aggressions], rapes, robberies, knives, guns and marijuana of the negro surely will." He was convicted under an Illinois criminal group libel law prohibiting the publishing, selling, or exhibiting in any public place of any publication which "portrays depravity, criminality, unchastity, or lack of virtue of a class of citizens, of any race, color, creed or religion, [or which] exposes the citizens of any race, color, creed or religion to contempt, derision, or obloquy, or which is productive of breach of the peace or riots." The trial court had refused to give a "clear and present danger" charge requested by petitioner.]

■ JUSTICE FRANKFURTER delivered the opinion of the Court.

The statute before us is not a catchall enactment left at large by the State court which applied it. [It] is a law specifically directed at a defined evil, its language drawing from history and practice in Illinois and in more than a score of other jurisdictions a meaning confirmed by the Supreme Court of that State in upholding this conviction.

No one will gainsay that it is libelous falsely to charge another with being a rapist, robber, carrier of knives and guns, and user of marijuana. The precise question before us, then, is whether [the 14th Amendment] prevents a State from punishing such libels—as criminal libel has been defined, limited and constitutionally recognized time out of mind—directed at designated collectivities and flagrantly disseminated. [If] an utterance directed at an individual may be the object of criminal sanctions, we cannot deny to a State power to punish the same utterance directed at a defined group, unless we can say that this is a wilful and purposeless restriction unrelated to the peace and well-being of the State.

Illinois [could conclude, from the State's own experience,] that wilful purveyors of falsehood concerning racial and religious groups promote strife and tend powerfully to obstruct the manifold adjustments required for free, ordered life in a metropolitan, polyglot community. From the murder of the abolitionist Lovejoy in 1837 to the Cicero riots of 1951, Illinois has been the scene of exacerbated tension between races, often flaring into violence and destruction. In many of these outbreaks, utterances of the character here in question, so the Illinois legislature could conclude, played a significant part. [In] the face of this history and its frequent obligato of extreme racial and religious propaganda, we would deny experience to say that the Illinois legislature was without reason in seeking ways to curb false or malicious defamation of racial and religious groups, made in public places and by means calculated to have a powerful emotional impact on those to whom it was presented. [It] may be argued, and weightily, that this legislation will not help matters. [But it] is not within our competence to confirm or deny claims of social scientists as to the dependence of the individual on the position of his racial or religious group in the community. [W]e are precluded from saying that speech concededly punishable when immediately directed at individuals cannot be outlawed if directed at groups with whose position and esteem in society the affiliated individual may be inextricably involved. [Libelous] utterances not being within the area of constitutionally protected speech, it is unnecessary, either for us or for the State courts, to consider the issues behind the phrase 'clear and present danger.' [We] find no warrant in the Constitution for denying to Illinois the power to pass the law here under attack.

■ JUSTICE BLACK, with whom JUSTICE DOUGLAS joins, dissenting.

[Reliance upon the 'group libel law'] label may make the Court's holding more palatable for those who sustain it, but the sugar-coating does not make the censorship less deadly. However tagged, the Illinois law is not that criminal libel which has been 'defined, limited and constitutionally recognized time out of mind.' For as 'constitutionally recognized' that crime has provided for punishment of false, malicious, scurrilous charges against individuals, not against huge groups. This limited scope of the law of criminal libel [has] confined state punishment of speech and expression to the narrowest of areas involving nothing more than purely private feuds. Every expansion of the law of criminal libel so as to punish discussion of matters of public concern means a corresponding invasion of the area dedicated to free expression by the First Amendment. [I] think the [First Amendment] 'absolutely' forbids such laws without any 'ifs' or 'buts' or 'whereases.' [If] there be minority groups who hail this holding as their victory, they might consider the possible relevancy of this ancient remark: 'Another such victory and I am undone.' "

■ [JUSTICES DOUGLAS, REED, and JACKSON filed separate dissents.]

THE LEGACY OF BEAUHARNAIS

1. ***Debate over Beauharnais.*** Was Beauharnais correct to subordinate "individualistic liberalism" to prevention of the social harms of group libel? See Riesman, "Democracy and Defamation: Control of Group Libel," 42 Colum. L. Rev. 727 (1942), cited by both majority and minority. Or are group libel laws, as Justice Black suggested, likely to curtail valuable discussion and hurt the very minority groups they seek to protect? See Tanenhaus, "Group Libel," 35 Cornell L.Q. 261 (1950); Beth, "Group Libel and Free Speech," 39 Minn. L. Rev. 167 (1955).

2. ***The vitality of Beauharnais.*** Have the First Amendment developments of recent decades drained Beauharnais of all vitality? Some of the measures adopted by Skokie, Illinois, in the late 1970s to block planned demonstrations by American neo-Nazis relied on the approach sustained in Beauharnais. As noted in the fuller treatment of the Skokie controversy at p. 1033 below, state and lower federal courts struck down all of the ordinances designed to block the Nazi marchers, including one that prohibited the "dissemination of any materials within [Skokie] which [intentionally] promotes and incites hatred against persons by reasons of their race, national origin, or religion." Most of the judges found Beauharnais no longer controlling. The Seventh Circuit, for example, stated: "It may be questioned, after cases such as Cohen v. California, Gooding v. Wilson, and Brandenburg v. Ohio, whether the *tendency to induce violence* approach sanctioned implicitly in Beauharnais would pass constitutional muster today." Collin v. Smith, 578 F.2d 1197 (7th Cir.1978). But note Justice Blackmun's dissent, joined by Justice Rehnquist, from a denial of a stay of the Court of Appeals order: "Beauharnais has never been overruled or formally limited in any way." Smith v. Collin, 436 U.S. 953 (1978). For examples of later efforts to resuscitate and extend the reasoning of Beauharnais, see the materials below at p. 1033 on hate speech as well as the materials below on the regulation of pornography as the subordination of women at p. 1076. For an argument that state efforts to regulate group libel are not only desirable, but also might be constitutional, see Waldron, The Harm in Hate Speech (2012). Can dicta by a lower court contribute to a Supreme Court case being regarded as no longer good law? Or is Beauharnais still good law?

3. ***Broader "fundamentals" of reputation.*** In his Beauharnais dissent, Justice Black argued that criminal libel "has provided for punishment of false, malicious, scurrilous charges against individuals, not against huge groups. This limited scope of the law of criminal libel is of no small importance. It has confined state punishment of speech and expression to the narrowest of areas involving nothing more than purely private feuds." But is this true? Consider the view that Justice Black's claim ignores a key difference between the personal reputation concerns that animate civil libel cases and the "broader social concern for the *fundamentals* of anyone's reputation or civic dignity as a member of society in good standing" that has served as the focus of criminal libel law. See Waldron, "Dignity and Defamation: The Visibility of Hate," 123 Harv. L. Rev. 1596 (2010). According to Waldron, past cases demonstrate that criminal libel law was

actually intended to address defamation on a wider scale. Does this view rehabilitate Beauharnais as a basis for regulating hate speech?

FIRST AMENDMENT LIMITS ON LIBEL

Chaplinsky and Beauharnais did not question that libel counted as a category of speech outside the boundaries of First Amendment protection. Subsequently, however, the Court has curtailed the boundaries of libel law to reduce the chilling effect that libel actions can have on the freedom of speech and the freedom of the press.

With some exceptions, most of the cases in this section arose as civil actions brought by private plaintiffs against defendants who then raised the freedom of speech as an affirmative defense. In these cases, the First Amendment is implicated not when the state itself prohibits or punishes speech directly, but only when the state enforces private causes of action that have the effect of chilling speech by imposing civil damages liability.

New York Times Co. v. Sullivan

376 U.S. 254, 84 S. Ct. 710, 11 L. Ed. 2d 686 (1964).

[This libel action stemmed from a paid, full-page, fundraising advertisement in the New York Times in March 1960 by the Committee to Defend Martin Luther King and the Struggle for Freedom in the South. The ad, headed "Heed Their Rising Voices," charged the existence of "an unprecedented wave of terror" against blacks engaged in nonviolent demonstrations in the South. Sullivan, the Montgomery, Ala., police commissioner, sued the Times and several black clergymen who had signed the ad. Sullivan objected especially to the claim that "truckloads of police armed with shotguns and tear-gas ringed the Alabama State College Campus" in Montgomery and complained about inaccuracies such as the statement that Dr. King had been arrested seven times when he was only arrested four times. Sullivan's witnesses testified that they took the charges to implicate Sullivan, and that he did not participate in the events regarding Dr. King. Sullivan offered no proof that he had suffered actual pecuniary loss. He recovered a judgment for $500,000 under Alabama libel law.]

■ JUSTICE BRENNAN delivered the opinion of the Court.

We are required in this case to determine for the first time the extent to which the constitutional protections for speech and press limit a State's power to award damages in a libel action brought by a public official against critics of his official conduct. [We] hold that the rule of law applied by the Alabama courts is constitutionally deficient for failure to provide the safeguards for freedom of speech and of the press that are required by the [First Amendment] in a libel action brought by a public official against critics of his official conduct. We further hold that under the proper safeguards the evidence presented in this case is constitutionally insufficient to support the judgment." In explaining that conclusion, Justice Brennan stated:]

Under Alabama law, [a] publication is "libelous per se" if the words "tend to injure a person [in] his reputation" or to "bring [him] into public contempt." [Once] "libel per se" has been established, the defendant has no defense as to stated facts unless he can persuade the jury that they were true in all their particulars. [Unless] he can discharge the burden of proving truth, general damages are presumed, and may be awarded without proof of pecuniary injury. The question before us is whether this rule of liability, as applied to an action brought by a public official against critics of his official conduct, abridges the freedom of speech and of the [press].

Respondent [and] the Alabama courts [rely heavily] on statements of this Court to the effect that the Constitution does not protect libelous publications. Those statements do not foreclose our inquiry here. None of the cases sustained the use of libel laws to impose sanctions upon expression critical of the official conduct of public officials. [Like] insurrection, contempt, advocacy of unlawful acts, breach of the peace, obscenity, solicitation of legal business, and the various other formulae for the repression of expression that have been challenged in this Court, libel can claim no talismanic immunity from constitutional limitations. It must be measured by standards that satisfy the [First Amendment].

[W]e consider this case against the background of a profound national commitment to the principle that debate on public issues should be uninhibited, robust, and wide-open, and that it may well include vehement, caustic, and sometimes unpleasantly sharp attacks on government and public officials. The present advertisement, as an expression of grievance and protest on one of the major public issues of our time, would seem clearly to qualify for the constitutional protection. The question is whether it forfeits that protection by the falsity of some of its factual statements and by its alleged defamation of respondent. Authoritative interpretations of the First Amendment guarantees have consistently refused to recognize an exception for any test of truth—whether administered by judges, juries, or administrative officials—and especially not one that puts the burden of proving truth on the speaker. "The constitutional protection does not turn upon the truth, popularity, or social utility of the ideas and beliefs which are offered." [E]rroneous statement is inevitable in free debate and [must] be protected if the freedoms of expression are to have the "breathing space" that they "need [to] survive." [Injury] to official reputation affords no more warrant for repressing speech that would otherwise be free than does factual error. [If] judges are to be treated as "men of fortitude, able to thrive in a hardy climate," surely the same must be true of other government officials, such as elected city commissioners. Criticism of their official conduct does not lose its constitutional protection merely because it is effective criticism and hence diminishes their official reputations.

If neither factual error nor defamatory content suffices to remove the constitutional shield from criticism of official conduct, the combination of the two elements is no less inadequate. This is the lesson to be drawn from the great controversy over the Sedition Act of 1798, which first crystallized a national awareness of the central meaning of the First Amendment. [Although] the Sedition Act was never tested in this Court, the attack upon its validity has carried the day in the court of history. Fines levied in its prosecution were repaid by Act of Congress on the ground that it was unconstitutional. [President Jefferson] pardoned those who had been convicted and sentenced under the Act and remitted their fines. [Its] invalidity [has] also been assumed by Justices of this Court. [These] views reflect a broad consensus that the Act, because of the restraint it imposed upon criticism of government and public officials, was inconsistent with the [First Amendment].

What a State may not constitutionally bring about by means of a criminal statute is likewise beyond the reach of its civil law of libel. The fear of damage awards under a rule such as that invoked by the Alabama courts here may be markedly more inhibiting than the fear of prosecution under a criminal statute. [The] judgment awarded in this case—without the need for any proof of actual pecuniary loss—was [1,000] times greater than that provided by the Sedition Act. And since there is no double jeopardy limitation applicable to civil lawsuits, this is not the only judgment that may be awarded against petitioners for the same publication. Whether or not a newspaper can survive a succession of such judgments, the pall of fear and timidity imposed upon those who would give voice to public criticism is an atmosphere in which the First Amendment freedoms cannot [survive].

The state rule of law is not saved by its allowance of the defense of truth. A defense for erroneous statements honestly made is no less essential here than was the requirement of proof of guilty knowledge which [we have] held indispensable to a valid conviction of a bookseller for possessing obscene writings for sale. [A] rule compelling the critic of official conduct to guarantee the truth of all his factual assertions—and to do so on pain of libel judgments virtually unlimited in amount—leads to a comparable "self-censorship." Allowance of the defense of truth, with the burden of proving it on the defendant, does not mean that only false speech will be deterred.[1] [Under] such a rule, would-be critics of official conduct may be deterred from voicing their criticism, even though it is believed to be true and even though it is in fact true, because of doubt whether it can be proved in court or fear of the expense of having to do so. They tend to make only statements which "steer far wider of the unlawful zone." The rule thus dampens the vigor and limits the variety of public debate. It is inconsistent with the [First Amendment].

The constitutional guarantees require, we think, a federal rule that prohibits a public official from recovering damages for a defamatory falsehood relating to his official conduct unless he proves that the statement was made with "actual malice"—that is, with knowledge that it was false or with reckless disregard of whether it was false or not. [We] consider that the proof presented to show actual malice lacks the convincing clarity which the constitutional standard demands, and hence that it would not constitutionally sustain the judgment for respondent under the proper rule of law. [E.g., we] think the evidence against the Times supports at most a finding of negligence in failing to discover the misstatements, and is constitutionally insufficient to show the recklessness that is required for a finding of actual malice. We also think the evidence was constitutionally defective in another respect: it was incapable of supporting the jury's finding that the allegedly libelous statements were made "of and concerning" respondent. [There] was no reference to respondent in the advertisement, either by name or official position. [As the highest state court made clear, reliance was placed solely] on the bare fact of respondent's official position. [This] has disquieting implications for criticism of governmental conduct. [It raises] the possibility that a good-faith critic of government will be penalized

1 Even a false statement may be deemed to make a valuable contribution to public debate, since it brings about "the clearer perception and livelier impression of truth, produced by its collision with error." Mill, On Liberty; see also Milton, Areopagitica. [Footnote by Justice Brennan.]

for his criticism [and] strikes at the very center of the constitutionally protected area of free expression. We hold that such a proposition may not constitutionally be utilized to establish that an otherwise impersonal attack on governmental operations was a libel of an official responsible for those operations. Since it was relied on exclusively, [the] evidence was constitutionally insufficient to support a finding that the statements referred to [respondent]. Reversed and remanded.

■ JUSTICE BLACK, with whom JUSTICE DOUGLAS joins, concurring.

[I] base my vote to reverse on the belief that the First and 14th Amendments not merely "delimit" a State's power to award damages to "public officials against critics of their official conduct" but completely prohibit a State from exercising such a [power]. "Malice," even as defined by the Court, is an elusive, abstract concept, hard to prove and hard to disprove. The requirement that malice be proved provides at best an evanescent protection for the right critically to discuss public affairs. [Therefore], I vote to reverse exclusively on the ground that the [defendants] had an absolute, unconditional constitutional right to publish in the Times advertisement their criticisms of the Montgomery agencies and [officials].

[In another concurrence, Justice GOLDBERG, joined by Justice Douglas, stated that the Constitution afforded "an absolute, unconditional privilege to criticize official conduct" of public officials, but did not protect "defamatory statements directed against the private conduct of a public official or private citizen."]

THE MEANING AND IMPLICATIONS OF NEW YORK TIMES

1. ***New York Times and the civil rights movement.*** By saving the New York Times and other newspapers from potentially crippling damage judgments, the New York Times decision arguably made possible important coverage of and advertisement by the civil rights movement in the South at a time of crucial activity against racial segregation. For an account of the events leading up to the decision and the stakes involved, see Lewis, Make No Law (1991).

2. ***The First Amendment interest in false statements of fact.*** What is the First Amendment value in the false statements of fact inherent in defamatory statements? Did New York Times overrule the Chaplinsky dictum that libel was a category of speech wholly outside First Amendment protection? Justice Brennan, relying on John Stuart Mill, suggested in New York Times that "[e]ven a false statement may be deemed to make a valuable contribution to public [debate]." But a decade later, Justice Powell wrote for the Court in Gertz v. Welch (1974; p. 1015 below) that, although "[u]nder the First Amendment there is no such thing as a false idea, [there] is no constitutional value in false statements of fact."

Is the better view of New York Times not that it held libel intrinsically valuable, but that it held the protection of negligent libels instrumentally necessary to afford adequate "breathing room" for truth? Consider Justice Powell's acknowledgement in Gertz that "some falsehood" needs to be protected "in order to protect speech that matters." On this view, New York Times continued to treat some libel as wholly unprotected; it simply limited that category to knowingly or recklessly false statements. Consider Justice

Brennan's statement soon after New York Times, in Garrison v. Louisiana, 379 U.S. 64 (1964), which extended the New York Times principle to state *criminal* libel cases: "Although honest utterance, even if inaccurate, may further the fruitful exercise of the right of free speech, it does not follow that the lie, knowingly and deliberately published about a public official, should enjoy a like immunity. [For] the use of the known lie as a tool is at once at odds with the premises of democratic government and with the orderly manner in which economic, social, or political change is to be effected. Calculated falsehood falls into that class of utterances [which are excluded under Chaplinsky]. Hence the knowingly false statement and the false statement made with reckless disregard of the truth do not enjoy constitutional protection."

Note that, despite Justice Powell's statement that "there is no such thing as a false idea," the Court has rejected the idea that the First Amendment requires any separate threshold inquiry into whether an allegedly defamatory statement is one of fact or opinion. See Milkovich v. Lorain Journal Co., 497 U.S. 1 (1990). Writing for the Court, Chief Justice Rehnquist explained that any statement that "does not contain a provably false factual connotation will receive full constitutional protection," but that a false statement of fact gains no constitutional immunity if the speaker simply adds "the words 'I think.' "

3. ***The Court's methodology in New York Times.*** Soon after the New York Times decision, Harry Kalven reported that Alexander Meiklejohn viewed it as " 'an occasion for dancing in the streets.' " Kalven, "The New York Times Case: A Note on 'The Central Meaning of the First Amendment,' " 1964 Sup. Ct. Rev. 191. In their view, the "central meaning of the [First] Amendment is that seditious libel cannot be made the subject of government sanction," and New York Times got that principle "right side up for the first time." Kalven added "that the effect of the Times opinion," by effectively guaranteeing freedom to criticize the government, "is necessarily to discard or diminish in importance the clear-and-present danger test, the balancing formula, [and] the two-level speech theory of Beauharnais."

Did the Times opinion truly eschew balancing? There was no "ad hoc balancing": no resort to the view "that the court, in each case, balance the individual and social interest in freedom of expression against the social interest sought by the regulation." Emerson, "Toward a General Theory of the First Amendment," 72 Yale L.J. 877 (1963). But as Kalven himself recognized, there was, "of course, a sense in which the Court did indulge in balancing. It did not go the whole way and give an absolute privilege to the 'citizen-critic' "; it did balance "two obvious conflicting interests." As Melville Nimmer described New York Times, it was a case of "definitional balancing": the derivation, through a balancing process, of a series of categorical rules for differing problems of free speech. Nimmer, "The Right to Speak from Times to [Time]," 56 Calif. L. Rev. 935 (1968). On this view, a category of unprotected speech simply represents a per se rule for an implicit balancing that would always come out the same way if engaged in case by case. For a critical analysis of definitional balancing, see Aleinikoff, "Constitutional Law in the Age of Balancing," 96 Yale L.J. 943 (1987).

4. ***Criticism of New York Times.*** There have been recurrent attacks on New York Times on the ground that it gives inadequate protection to the reputation interests of defamation plaintiffs. See, e.g., Nagel, "How Useful is Judicial Review in Free Speech Cases?," 69 Cornell L. Rev. 302 (1984);

Monaghan, "Of 'Liberty' and 'Property,'" 62 Cornell L. Rev. 405 (1977). For a critical analysis of the reputation interest, see Post, "The Social Foundations of Defamation Law: Reputation and the Constitution," 74 Calif. L. Rev. 691 (1986). There have also been complaints from the other side: that the actual malice test gives inadequate protection to defamation defendants because cases can still get to a jury and incur large verdicts causing litigation costs even in cases where defendants ultimately prevail on appeal. See, e.g., Anderson, "Libel and Press Self-Censorship," 53 Tex. L. Rev. 422 (1975); Lewis, "New York Times v. Sullivan [Reconsidered]," 83 Colum. L. Rev. 602 (1983); Smolla, "[The] Rejuvenation of the American Law of Libel," 132 U. Pa. L. Rev. 1 (1984).

Would any alternative approach better reconcile the competing interests in speech and reputation? Consider Justice White's argument in dissent in Dun & Bradstreet v. Greenmoss Builders (1985; p. 1019 below), that the "necessary breathing room for speakers can be ensured by limitations on recoverable damages; it does not also require depriving many public figures of any room to vindicate their reputations sullied by false statements of fact." For the view that a return to the common law of defamation, with strict liability but relatively low damage awards, would be preferable, see Epstein, "Was New York Times v. Sullivan Wrong?," 53 U. Chi. L. Rev. 782 (1986). For the proposal that plaintiffs ought to be able to obtain a declaration of falsity (requiring no showing of fault and including no damage awards) as an alternative to libel suits, see Leval, "The No-Money, No-Fault Libel Suit: Keeping Sullivan in Its Proper Place," 101 Harv. L. Rev. 1287 (1988); and Franklin, "A Declaratory Judgment Alternative to Current Libel Law," 74 Calif. L. Rev. 809 (1986).

5. ***Procedural developments after New York Times.*** The Court has given plaintiffs one significant procedural victory since New York Times: In Herbert v. Lando, 441 U.S. 153 (1979), the Court rejected a television producer's claim to a broad First Amendment-based editorial privilege that would have precluded questions in pretrial discovery proceedings pertaining to his liability under the Times "actual malice" standard. Lando leaves members of the press open to wide-ranging inquiries on the issue of whether they were guilty of knowing or reckless falsity, and thus to the costs of defending against extensive discovery. Although the press vehemently criticized that ruling, none of the Justices was prepared to uphold all of the broad media claims; even Justices Marshall and Brennan were willing to grant only a limited privilege.

Most other procedural rulings in this area since New York Times, however, have benefited defendants. In Philadelphia Newspapers, Inc. v. Hepps, 475 U.S. 767 (1986), the Court held, by a 5–4 vote, that the plaintiff was required to bear the burden of proof in establishing the falsity of the allegedly defamatory statement in cases governed by New York Times, as those decisions had displaced the common law rule presuming falsity. New York Times itself required that evidence of actual malice be clear and convincing; a preponderance of evidence was not enough. Anderson v. Liberty Lobby, Inc., 477 U.S. 242 (1986), required lower courts to inquire into the convincing clarity of actual malice evidence at the summary judgment stage. And in Bose Corp. v. Consumers Union, 466 U.S. 485 (1984), the Court held that appellate courts "must exercise independent judgment and determine [de novo] whether the record establishes actual malice with convincing clarity," rather than review the judgment below only for clear error. See generally Matheson, "Procedure in Public Person Defamation Cases: The Impact of the First Amendment," 66 Tex. L. Rev. 215 (1987).

6. ***False statements of fact outside the libel context.*** In a case that arose outside of the libel context, the Supreme Court has found the First Amendment to forbid the criminalization of false statements of fact. The Stolen Valor Act, 18 U.S.C. § 704 (b), (c), made it a crime to falsely claim receipt of military decorations or medals, and provided an enhanced penalty if the Congressional Medal of Honor was involved. After Xavier Alvarez falsely stated at a California public hearing that he was a retired marine who had been wounded in combat and had been awarded the Congressional Medal of Honor, he was convicted under the Act. The Supreme Court reversed his conviction in **United States v. Alvarez**, 567 U.S. 709 (2012). The Court rejected the argument that false statements were completely outside First Amendment protection and held that counter-speech was sufficient to achieve the government's asserted interest in preserving the integrity and purpose of the Medal.

Writing for a plurality joined by Chief Justice Roberts and Justices Ginsburg and Sotomayor, Justice KENNEDY applied the "exacting scrutiny" he deemed appropriate to such a content-based restriction even in the context of regulating falsity, emphasizing that the Court's libel precedents had never said false statements deserve *no* protection, and explaining that "[o]ur constitutional tradition stands against the idea that we need Oceania's Ministry of Truth. [The] mere potential for the exercise of [governmental] power [to compile a list of subjects about which false statements are punishable] casts a chill, a chill the First Amendment cannot permit if free speech, thought, and discourse are to remain a foundation of our freedom. [The] remedy for speech that is false is speech that is true. [The] response to the unreasoned is the rational; to the uninformed, the enlightened; to the straightout lie, the simple truth. [See Whitney.]"

Justice BREYER, joined by Justice Kagan, concurred only in the judgment, noting that "[f]alse factual statements can serve useful human objectives, for example: in social contexts, where they may prevent embarrassment, protect privacy, shield a person from prejudice, provide the sick with comfort, or preserve a child's innocence; in public contexts, where they may stop a panic or otherwise preserve calm in the face of danger; and even in technical, philosophical, and scientific contexts, where (as Socrates' methods suggest) examination of a false statement (even if made deliberately to mislead) can promote a form of thought that ultimately helps realize the truth." The concurrence nonetheless treated regulation of false statements as undeserving of strict scrutiny, and thus, applying only potentially more deferential "intermediate scrutiny," found that the Act swept too broadly, creating "a significant risk of First Amendment harm" while the government could have served its important interests by enacting a "similar but more finely tailored statute"

Justice ALITO, in a dissent joined by Justices Scalia and Thomas, argued that the Court had "repeatedly endorsed the principle that false statements of fact do not merit First Amendment protection for their own sake," and that "the Stolen Valor Act presents no risk at all that valuable speech will be suppressed. The speech punished by the Act is not only verifiably false and entirely lacking in intrinsic value, but it also fails to serve any instrumental purpose that the First Amendment might protect."

THE SCOPE OF NEW YORK TIMES

The Court has considered three variables in deciding how far to extend New York Times' substantive limits on liability to other settings: (1) the identity of the plaintiff (public official, public figure or private figure), (2) the identity of the defendant (media or nonmedia), and (3) the nature of the issue discussed (matter of public or private concern). It has also considered whether to vary the available remedies in various settings.

1. ***Public figures v. public officials.*** In **Curtis Publishing Co. v. Butts** and **Associated Press v. Walker**, decided together at 388 U.S. 130 (1967), the Court applied the New York Times rule to libel actions "instituted by persons who are not public officials, but who are 'public figures' and involved in issues in which the public has a justified and important interest." Butts grew out of a Saturday Evening Post article that claimed that the University of Georgia athletic director (and former football coach) had fixed a football game. In Walker, a retired general challenged an AP report that he had led a violent crowd in opposition to the enforcement of a desegregation decree at the University of Mississippi. The Court was sharply divided in its reasoning. Four of the Justices (Harlan, Clark, Stewart and Fortas) opposed extending the New York Times rule; three (Chief Justice Warren, and Justices Brennan and White) urged application of New York Times to public figures; the remaining two (Black and Douglas) urged a broader press immunity, as they had in New York Times. But the result was that the New York Times rule was extended to "public figures" cases.

In announcing the view that became the Court position, Chief Justice WARREN stated that "differentiation between 'public figures' and 'public officials' and adoption of separate standards of proof for each have no basis in law, logic, or First Amendment policy. Increasingly in this country, the distinctions between governmental and private sectors are blurred. [It] is plain that although they are not subject to the restraints of the political process, 'public figures,' like 'public officials,' often play an influential role in ordering society. And surely as a class these 'public figures' have as ready access as 'public officials' to mass media, [both] to influence policy and to counter criticism of their views and activities. Our citizenry has a legitimate and substantial interest in the conduct of such persons, and freedom of the press to engage in uninhibited debate about their involvement in public issues and events is as crucial as it is in the case of 'public officials.'"

In announcing the position of the four Justices who opposed extension of the New York Times rule, Justice HARLAN examined the similarities and differences between "public officials" and other "public figures," agreed that "public figure" actions "cannot be left entirely to state libel laws," but insisted that "the rigorous federal requirements of New York Times are not the only appropriate accommodation of the conflicting interests at stake." He concluded: "We [would] hold that a 'public figure' who is not a public official may also recover damages for a defamatory falsehood whose substance makes substantial danger to reputation apparent, on a showing of highly unreasonable conduct constituting an extreme departure from the standards of investigation and reporting ordinarily adhered to by responsible publishers."

2. ***Defining "public figures."*** Despite the broad holdings in Butts and Walker, however, in other cases the Court has construed the "public figure" category quite narrowly. In the Gertz case that follows, for example, the Court found that a lawyer who had "long been active in community and professional affairs," and was "well-known in some circles," was nonetheless a private figure because "he had achieved no general fame or notoriety in the community [or] pervasive involvement in the affairs of society." In Time, Inc. v. Firestone, 424 U.S. 448 (1976), the Court held that a wealthy divorcee whose divorce was mischaracterized in Time was not a public figure because she had not assumed "any role of especial prominence in the affairs of society, other than perhaps Palm Beach society." In Hutchinson v. Proxmire, 443 U.S. 111 (1979), the Court held that a scientist whose federally funded research on monkey behavior had been characterized by the defendant Senator as an egregious example of wasteful government spending was not a public figure, as he had not "thrust himself or his views into public controversy to influence others." And in Wolston v. Reader's Digest Ass'n, Inc., 443 U.S. 157 (1979), the Court held that Wolston's brief stint in the public eye in 1958, after a criminal contempt conviction for failure to appear before a grand jury investigating Soviet espionage, did not make him a public figure for purposes of a 1974 allegation that he was a "Soviet agent." The majority emphasized that Wolston had not "voluntarily thrust" or "injected" himself into the controversy.

3. ***Private figures.*** After extending the New York Times standard to "public figures," the divided Court's balancing approach encountered new challenges when publishers claimed First Amendment defenses to defamation suits by *private* individuals. Justice Brennan's plurality opinion in **Rosenbloom v. Metromedia, Inc.**, 403 U.S. 29 (1971) extended New York Times to a "private" plaintiff's action claiming defamation in a report "about the individual's involvement in an event of public or general interest." Rosenbloom arose from a libel action by a distributor of nudist magazines, based on radio reports about police action against his allegedly obscene books, about his lawsuit, and about police interference with his business. Some of the news reports referred to "girlie book peddlers" and the "smut literature racket." Justice BRENNAN's plurality opinion, joined by Chief Justice Burger and Justice Blackmun, argued that the critical criterion should be the *subject matter* of the allegedly defamatory report rather than the status of the plaintiff. He insisted that experience since New York Times had "disclosed the artificiality, in terms of the public's interest, of a simple distinction between 'public' and 'private' individuals" and concluded: "If a matter is a subject of public or general interest, it cannot suddenly become less so merely because a private individual is involved, or because in some sense the individual did not 'voluntarily' choose to become involved. The public's primary interest is in the event; the public focus is on the conduct of the participant and the content, effect, and significance of the conduct, not the participant's prior anonymity or notoriety. [We] honor the commitment to robust debate on public issues [by] extending constitutional protection to all discussion and communication involving matters of public or general concern without regard to whether the persons involved are famous or anonymous."

Gertz v. Robert Welch, Inc.

418 U.S. 323, 94 S. Ct. 2997, 41 L. Ed. 2d 789 (1974).

[Elmer Gertz, a Chicago lawyer, initiated a libel action against the publisher of "American Opinion," an "outlet for the views of the John Birch Society." Gertz had been retained by a victim's family in a civil suit against a Chicago policeman who had been convicted of murder. The magazine charged Gertz with being an architect of the "frame-up" of the policeman in the murder trial and called Gertz, inter alia, a "Communist-fronter." Despite a jury verdict for the plaintiff, the district court entered a judgment notwithstanding the verdict on the grounds that the public nature of the case brought it within the ambit of New York Times and that Gertz had not demonstrated that the American Opinion had requisite awareness of falsity.]

■ JUSTICE POWELL delivered the opinion of the Court.

The principal issue in this case is whether a newspaper or broadcaster that publishes defamatory falsehoods about an individual who is neither a public official nor a public figure may claim a constitutional privilege against liability for the injury inflicted by those statements.

[Under] the First Amendment there is no such thing as a false idea. However pernicious an opinion may seem, we depend for its correction not on the conscience of judges and juries but on the competition of other ideas. But there is no constitutional value in false statements of fact. Neither the intentional lie nor the careless error materially advances society's interest in "uninhibited, robust, and wide-open" debate on public issues. [They] belong to that category of utterances which "are no essential part of any exposition of ideas, and are of such slight social value as a step to truth that any benefit that may be derived from them is clearly outweighed by the social interest in order and morality."

[Although] the erroneous statement of fact is not worthy of constitutional protection, it is nevertheless inevitable in free debate. [And] punishment of error runs the risk of inducing a cautious and restrictive exercise of the constitutionally guaranteed freedoms of speech and press. Our decisions recognize that a rule of strict liability that compels a publisher or broadcaster to guarantee the accuracy of his factual assertions may lead to intolerable self-censorship. [The] First Amendment requires that we protect some falsehood in order to protect speech that matters.

The need to avoid self-censorship by the news media is, however, not the only societal value at issue. If it were, this Court would have embraced long ago the view that publishers and broadcasters enjoy an unconditional and indefeasible immunity from liability for defamation. [Such] a rule would, indeed, obviate the fear that the prospect of civil liability for injurious falsehood might dissuade a timorous press from the effective exercise of First Amendment freedoms. Yet absolute protection for the communications media requires a total sacrifice of the competing value served by the law of defamation.

The legitimate state interest underlying the law of libel is the compensation of individuals for the harm inflicted on them by defamatory falsehood. We would not lightly require the State to abandon this purpose, for, as [Justice] Stewart has reminded us, the individual's right to the protection of his own good name "reflects no more than our basic concept of the essential dignity and worth of every human being—a concept at the root of any decent system of ordered liberty. The protection of private personality, like the protection of life itself, is left primarily to the individual States under the Ninth and Tenth Amendments. But this does not mean that the right is entitled to any less recognition by this Court as a basic of our constitutional system."

[Some] tension necessarily exists between the need for a vigorous and uninhibited press and the legitimate interest in redressing wrongful injury. [In] our continuing effort to define the proper accommodation between these competing concerns, we have been especially anxious to assure to the freedoms of speech and press that "breathing space" essential to their fruitful exercise. [To] that end this Court has extended a measure of strategic protection to defamatory falsehood.

The New York Times standard defines the level of constitutional protection appropriate to the context of defamation of a public person. Those who, by reason of the notoriety of their achievements or the vigor and success with which they seek the public's attention, are properly classed as public figures and those who hold governmental office may recover for injury to reputation only on clear and convincing proof that the defamatory falsehood was made with knowledge of its falsity or with reckless disregard for the truth. [Plainly] many deserving plaintiffs, including some intentionally subjected to injury, will be unable to surmount the barrier of the New York Times test. Despite this substantial abridgment of the state law right to compensation for wrongful hurt to one's reputation, the Court has concluded that the protection of the New York Times privilege should be available to publishers and broadcasters of defamatory falsehood concerning public officials and public figures. [For] the reasons stated below, we conclude that the state interest in compensating injury to the reputation of private individuals requires that a different rule should obtain with respect to them.

[We] have no difficulty in distinguishing among defamation plaintiffs. The first remedy of any victim of defamation is self-help—using available opportunities to contradict the lie or correct the error and thereby to minimize its adverse impact on reputation. Public officials and public figures usually enjoy significantly greater access to the channels of effective communication and hence have a more realistic opportunity to counteract false statements then private individuals normally enjoy. Private individuals are therefore more vulnerable to injury, and the state interest in protecting them is correspondingly greater.

More important than the likelihood that private individuals will lack effective opportunities for rebuttal, there is a compelling normative consideration underlying the distinction between public and private defamation plaintiffs. An individual who decides to seek governmental office must accept certain necessary consequences of that involvement in public affairs. He runs the risk of closer public scrutiny than might otherwise be the case. And society's interest in the officers of government is not strictly limited to the formal discharge of official duties. [Those] classed as public figures stand in a similar position. Hypothetically, it may be possible for someone to become a public figure through no purposeful action of his own, but the instances of truly involuntary public figures must be exceedingly rare. For the most part those who attain this status have assumed roles of especial prominence in the affairs of society. [More] commonly, those classed as public figures have thrust themselves to the forefront of particular public controversies in order to influence the resolution of the issues involved. In either event, they invite attention and comment.

[For] these reasons we conclude that the States should retain substantial latitude in their efforts to enforce a legal remedy for defamatory falsehood injurious to the reputation of a private individual. The extension of the New York Times test proposed by the Rosenbloom plurality would abridge this legitimate state interest to a degree that we find unacceptable. [Nor] does the Constitution require us to draw so thin a line between the drastic alternatives of the New York Times privilege and the common law of strict liability for defamatory error. The "public or general interest" test for determining the applicability of the New York Times standard to private defamation actions inadequately serves both of the competing values at stake. On the one hand, a private individual whose reputation is injured by defamatory falsehood that does concern an issue of public or general interest has no recourse unless he can meet the rigorous requirements of New York Times.

[We] hold that, so long as they do not impose liability without fault, the States may define for themselves the appropriate standard of liability for a publisher or broadcaster of defamatory falsehood injurious to a private individual. This approach provides a more equitable boundary between the competing concerns involved here. It recognizes the strength of the legitimate state interest in compensating private individuals for wrongful injury to reputation, yet shields the press and broadcast media from the rigors of strict liability for defamation.

[This] conclusion is not based on a belief that the considerations which prompted the adoption of the New York Times privilege for defamation of public officials and its extension to public figures are wholly inapplicable to the context of private individuals. Rather, we endorse this approach in recognition of the strong and legitimate state interest in compensating private individuals for injury to reputation. But this countervailing state interest extends no further than compensation for actual injury. [It] is therefore appropriate to require that state remedies for defamatory falsehood reach no farther than is necessary to protect the legitimate interest involved. It is necessary to restrict defamation plaintiffs who do not prove knowledge of falsity or reckless disregard for the truth to compensation for actual injury. We need not define 'actual injury,' as trial courts have wide experience in framing appropriate jury instructions in tort actions. Suffice it to say that actual injury is not limited to out-of-pocket loss. Indeed, the more customary types of actual harm inflicted by defamatory falsehood include impairment of reputation and standing in the community, personal humiliation, and mental anguish and suffering.

■ JUSTICE BRENNAN, dissenting.

While [the majority's] arguments are forcefully and eloquently presented, I cannot accept them, for the reasons I stated in Rosenbloom: 'The New York Times standard was applied to libel of a public official or public figure to give effect to the (First) Amendment's function to encourage ventilation of public issues, not because the public official has any less interest in protecting his reputation than an individual in private life. [In] the vast majority of libels involving public officials or public figures, the ability to respond through the media will depend on the same complex factor on which the ability of a private individual depends: the unpredictable event of the media's continuing interest in the story. Thus the unproved, and highly improbable, generalization that an as yet (not fully defined) class of "public figures" involved in matters of public concern will be better able to respond through the media than private individuals also involved in such matters seems too insubstantial a reed on which to rest a constitutional distinction.'

We recognized in [New York Times] that a rule requiring a critic of official conduct to guarantee the truth of all of his factual contentions would inevitably lead to self-censorship when publishers, fearful of being unable to prove truth or unable to bear the expense of attempting to do so, simply eschewed printing controversial articles. Adoption, by many States, of a reasonable-care standard in cases where private individuals are involved in matters of public interest—the probable result of today's decision—will likewise lead to self-censorship since publishers will be required carefully to weigh a myriad of uncertain factors before publication. [Most] hazardous, the flexibility which inheres in the reasonable-care standard will create the danger that a jury will convert it into "an instrument for the suppression of those 'vehement, caustic, and sometimes unpleasantly sharp attacks,' . . . which must be protected if the guarantees of the First and Fourteenth Amendments are to prevail."

[I] reject the argument that my Rosenbloom view improperly commits to judges the task of determining what is and what is not an issue of "general or public interest." I noted in Rosenbloom that performance of this task would not always be easy. [B]ut surely the courts, the ultimate arbiters of all disputes concerning clashes of constitutional values, would only be performing one of their traditional functions in undertaking this duty.

■ JUSTICE WHITE, dissenting.

[The] Court does not contend, and it could hardly do so, that those who wrote the First Amendment intended to prohibit the Federal Government, within its sphere of influence in the Territories and the District of Columbia, from providing the private citizen a peaceful remedy for damaging falsehood. [The] central meaning of New York Times, and for me the First Amendment as it relates to libel laws, is that seditious libel—criticism of government and public officials—falls beyond the police power of the State. [In] a democratic society such as ours, the citizen has the privilege of criticizing his government and its officials. But neither New York Times nor its progeny suggests that the First Amendment intended in all circumstances to deprive the private citizen of his historic recourse to redress published falsehoods damaging to reputation or that, contrary to history and precedent, the Amendment should now be so interpreted. Simply put, the First Amendment did not confer a "license to defame the citizen."

[It] is difficult for me to understand why the ordinary citizen should himself carry the risk of damage and suffer the injury in order to vindicate First Amendment values by protecting the press and others from liability for circulating false information. This is particularly true because such statements serve no purpose whatsoever in furthering the public interest or the search for truth but, on the contrary, may frustrate that search and at the same time inflict great injury on the defenseless individual.

[In] disagreeing with the Court on the First Amendment's reach in the area of state libel laws protecting nonpublic persons, I do not repudiate the principle that the First Amendment "rests on the assumption that the widest possible dissemination of information from diverse and antagonistic sources is essential to the welfare of the public, that a free press is a condition of a free society." [I] fail to see how the quality or quantity of public debate will be promoted by further emasculation of state libel laws for the benefit of the news media. If anything, this trend may provoke a new and radical imbalance in the communications process. [It] is not at all inconceivable that virtually unrestrained defamatory remarks about private citizens will discourage them from speaking out and concerning themselves with social problems. This would turn the First Amendment on its head.

[Freedom] and human dignity and decency are not antithetical. Indeed, they cannot survive without each other. Both exist side-by-side in precarious balance, one always threatening to over-whelm the other. Our experience as a Nation testifies to the ability of our democratic institutions to harness this dynamic tension.

DEFAMATION OF PRIVATE PARTIES AFTER GERTZ

In the years following Gertz, the constitutional limits on defamation claims for private individuals continued to divide the court. In **Dun & Bradstreet, Inc. v. Greenmoss Builders**, 472 U.S. 749 (1985), the alleged defamation involved a private credit report given by Dun & Bradstreet to a bank regarding Greenmoss, a construction contractor. The report erroneously claimed that Greenmoss had filed for voluntary bankruptcy. A Vermont jury, instructed that it need not consider "actual malice," returned a verdict for the builder and awarded $50,000 in compensatory and $300,000 in punitive damages. The Vermont Supreme Court found the Gertz standard inapplicable, holding that the operations of credit reporting agencies were not the type of activities encompassed by New York Times and its progeny. A divided Supreme Court affirmed this holding, but not on the ground that nonmedia defendants were excluded from New York Times. Rather, a majority of the Court—Justice White in concurrence plus the four dissenters—found no relevant distinction between the institutional media and other forms of communication. The plurality declined to reach any such distinction, emphasizing a different distinction between speech on matters of public and private concern.

Justice POWELL, writing for himself and Justices Rehnquist and O'Connor, began with the proposition that "not all speech is of equal First Amendment importance." He distinguished speech "on matters of public concern" from speech "on matters of purely private concern" far from the core of the First Amendment. "[In] light of the reduced constitutional value of speech involving no matters of public concern, we hold that the state interest adequately supports awards of presumed and punitive damages—even absent a showing of 'actual malice.' " Applying this approach, Justice Powell found that credit reports such as the one at issue here—involving nothing that "concerns a public matter"—were outside the Gertz principles. The credit report, he wrote, contained "speech solely in the individual interest of the speaker and its specific business audience. [Moreover,] since the credit report was made available to only five subscribers, who, under the terms of the subscription agreement, could not disseminate it further, it cannot be said that the report involves any 'strong interest in the free flow of commercial information.' "

Chief Justice BURGER and Justice WHITE separately concurred in the judgment, each urging that Gertz itself be overruled. Justice White also urged that the entire constitutionalization of the law of defamation, going back to New York Times, be reevaluated: "I remain convinced that Gertz was erroneously decided. I have also become convinced that the Court struck an improvident balance in [New York Times]. In a country like ours, [adequate] information about their government is of transcendent importance [to the people]. That flow of intelligence deserves full First Amendment protection. Criticism and assessment of the performance of public officials and of government in general are not subject to penalties imposed by law. But these First Amendment values are not at all served by circulating false statements of fact about public officials. On the contrary, erroneous information frustrates these values. They are even more disserved when the statements falsely impugn the honesty of those men and women and hence lessen the confidence in government. [It] is difficult to argue that the United States did not have a free and vigorous press before the rule in New York Times was announced."

Justice BRENNAN, joined by Justices Marshall, Blackmun and Stevens, dissented. He rejected the claim that the relevant distinction was between the media and other forms of communication. But rejecting the media/nonmedia distinction did not for the dissenters compel the conclusion reached by the Court. Rather, Justice Brennan objected to the distinction between matters of public and private concern. And even if there were such a distinction, he viewed Justice Powell's delineation as "impoverished": "[This] Court has consistently rejected the argument that speech is entitled to diminished First Amendment protection simply because it concerns economic matters. [Even] if the subject matter of credit reporting were properly considered [as] purely a matter of private discourse, this speech would fall well within the range of valuable expression for which the First Amendment demands protection. Much expression that does not directly involve public issues receives significant protection."

PRIVACY TORTS

States have recognized numerous torts protecting individuals from injury by speech for reasons other than defamation. Among these are various privacy torts elaborated since publication of an article on the subject by Samuel D. Warren and later Justice Brandeis, "The Right to Privacy," 4 Harv. L. Rev. 193 (1890). Four distinct types of privacy invasion have emerged: intrusion into the plaintiff's private affairs, public disclosure of non-newsworthy facts the plaintiff would have preferred to keep secret, publicity placing the plaintiff in a false light, and appropriation of the plaintiff's name or likeness. Some protection for individual privacy has been deemed necessary to preserve human dignity and individuality. Preserving privacy, however, by definition often impedes the free flow of information. Should the First Amendment be read to limit the reach of privacy torts? The Supreme Court has reached this question only with respect to "false light" invasion of privacy claims, claims against disclosure of facts already in the public record, and appropriation claims. It has yet to confront a case involving public disclosure of truly private facts.

For an argument in support of legal protections for individual privacy, see Edelman, "Free Press v. Privacy: Haunted by the Ghost of Justice Black," 68 Tex. L. Rev. 1195 (1990). For criticism of privacy torts on free speech grounds, see Kalven, "Privacy in Tort Law—Were Warren and Brandeis Wrong?," 31 Law & Contemp. Prob. 326 (1966); Zimmerman, "Requiem for a Heavyweight: a Farewell to Warren and Brandeis's Privacy Tort," 68 Cornell L. Rev. 291 (1983); Posner, "The Right to Privacy," 12 Ga. L. Rev. 393 (1978).

1. ***"False light" invasion of privacy.*** In "false light" privacy cases, the claim is that the disclosure not only invaded privacy but was also false—though not necessarily injurious to reputation, the gist of defamation actions. The Supreme Court's decision in **Time, Inc. v. Hill**, 385 U.S. 374 (1967), focused primarily on "false light" privacy actions, and the decision by a divided Court was that the New York Times standard should be applicable to such actions.

In 1952, the Hill family had been held hostage by three escaped convicts for 19 hours but was released unharmed. Three years later, a play portrayed the incident as involving considerable violence, though in fact there had been none. Life magazine's story on the play posed the actors in the original Hill home and indicated that the play accurately portrayed the actual incident. The original incident had been widely reported, but the Hills had tried to stay out of the public eye thereafter. Though the Life magazine report that was the subject of the action did not substantially damage the Hills' reputation—they were portrayed as courageous—they ultimately recovered a $30,000 judgment under New York law.

The Hill suit was based on a New York "right of privacy" statute prohibiting anyone from using "for advertising purposes, or for the purposes of trade, the name, portrait or picture of any living person without having first obtained the written consent of such person." Under the statute, truth was a defense in actions "based upon newsworthy people or events," but a "newsworthy person" could recover when he or she was the subject of a "fictitious" report—a report involving "material and substantial falsification." Justice BRENNAN's opinion for the Court concluded that "the constitutional protections for speech and press preclude the application of the New York statute to redress false reports of matters of public interest in the absence of proof that the defendant published the report with knowledge of its falsity or in reckless disregard of the truth." Justice Brennan went on to indicate, in a much-debated dictum, that "newsworthiness" would offer similar protection even in a "true" privacy action.

Does the Hill principle, announced in 1967, survive the Court's 1974 retreat in Gertz from Justice Brennan's position that the New York Times principle applies to all "newsworthy" matters? Does Hill move well beyond the seditious libel emphasis that was seen as the "central meaning" of the First Amendment in New York Times? Nimmer criticized the Court for failing to "pierce the superficial similarity between false light invasion of privacy and defamation" and urged that disclosure of nondefamatory matters interfering with privacy not be afforded First Amendment protection. He noted, for example, that, unlike "injury arising from defamation, 'more speech' is irrelevant in mitigating the injury due to an invasion of privacy." See Nimmer, "The Right to Speak From Times to Time: First Amendment Theory Applied to Libel and Misapplied to Privacy," 56 Calif. L. Rev. 935 (1968). On the other hand, is New York Times even more obviously applicable in the nondefamation setting because only true speech is involved, not false statements of fact? See Kalven, "The Reasonable Man and the First Amendment: Hill, Butts, and Walker," 1967 Sup. Ct. Rev. 267, suggesting that "the logic of New York Times and Hill taken together grants the press some measure of constitutional protection for anything the press thinks is a matter of public interest."

2. ***Disclosure of rape victims' names.*** In **Cox Broadcasting Corp. v. Cohn**, 420 U.S. 469 (1975), a father had sued because of the broadcasting of the fact that his daughter had been a rape victim. Barring liability, the Court relied especially on "the public interest in a vigorous press." The decision did not reach the question of whether Hill and its dictum had survived Gertz. The Court held merely that civil liability in a "true" privacy action could not be imposed upon a broadcaster for accurately publishing information released to the public in official court records. Justice WHITE's opinion for the Court commented: "In this sphere of collision between claims of privacy and those of the free press, the interests on both sides are plainly rooted in the traditions and significant concerns of our society." But he found it unnecessary to decide "the broader question whether truthful publication may ever be subjected to civil or criminal liability," or "whether the State may ever define and protect an area of privacy free from unwanted publicity in the press." However, he recognized the "impressive credentials for a right of privacy" and claimed that earlier cases had "carefully left open the question" whether the Constitution requires "that truth be recognized as a defense in a defamation action brought by a private person," as well as "the question whether truthful publication of very private matters unrelated to public affairs could be constitutionally proscribed."

Cox Broadcasting's prohibition on the restriction of lawfully obtained truthful information, including the identities of juveniles and victims of sexual offenses, has been applied in a number of subsequent cases. In **Florida Star v. B.J.F.**, 491 U.S. 524 (1989), a newspaper published the name of a victim of a sexual offense obtained from a police report made available in the police department's press room. Justice Marshall's majority opinion overturned a judgment based on a state law barring the publication of the names of such victims. Although again declining "to hold broadly that truthful publication may never be punished consistent with the First Amendment," Justice Marshall found the law unacceptable. Justice Scalia concurred in part and in the judgment. Justice White, the author of Cox Broadcasting, dissented, joined by Chief Justice Rehnquist and Justice O'Connor, distinguishing Cox as involving judicial records. He also raised doubts about the entire line of privacy cases beginning with Time, Inc. v. Hill. Questioning whether privacy was being unduly sacrificed in all of them, he observed that "[t]oday, we have hit the bottom of the slippery slope. I would find a place to draw the line higher on the hillside: a spot high enough to protect B.J.F.'s desire for privacy and peace-of-mind in the wake of a horrible personal tragedy."

3. ***Appropriation torts.*** **Zacchini v. Scripps-Howard Broadcasting Co.**, 433 U.S. 562 (1977), dealt with a suit based on the plaintiff's "right of publicity" rather than an interest in privacy per se. The Court distinguished Time and held that the First Amendment does not "immunize the media [from liability for damages] when they broadcast a performer's entire act without his consent."

Zacchini had performed a "human cannonball" act in which he was shot from a cannon into a net some 200 feet away. The defendant filmed Zacchini's performance at a county fair and showed the entire 15-second act on a television news program. In allowing recovery, Justice White distinguished this case from the 'false light' privacy claim in Hill. Hill was not a case involving 'intrusion'" or "private details" about a non-newsworthy person. And neither did Hill involve a claim of a "right of publicity" as here; this kind of claim was a "discrete kind of 'appropriation.'" Unlike "false light" cases designed to protect the interest in reputation, suits such as this one rested on the state interest "in protecting the proprietary interest of the individual in his act in part to encourage such entertainment," an interest "closely analogous to those of patent and copyright law." Moreover, a "right of publicity" case did not significantly intrude on dissemination of information to the public: "the only question is who gets to do the publishing." Accordingly, Justice White found the performer's claim a strong one, and the media arguments weak. Justice Powell, joined by Justices Brennan and Marshall, dissented.

Issues similar to those in Zacchini are presented by the inherent tensions between copyright law and First Amendment principles. See Harper & Row v. Nation Enterprises, 471 U.S. 539 (1985), where The Nation magazine published an article containing 300 to 400 words from former President Ford's yet-to-be published memoirs. Justice O'Connor's majority opinion rejected the argument that the "fair use" defense under the copyright laws had to be interpreted in light of the First Amendment when the words of an important public figure were involved. She stated that, in view of the First Amendment protections already embodied in copyright law, and the latitude the fair use defense traditionally afforded to scholarship and comment, there was no warrant for expanding the doctrine of fair use to create what amounted to a public figure exception to copyright. Justice Brennan, joined by Justices White and Marshall, dissented.

4. ***Public disclosure of illegally intercepted information.*** Should the First Amendment protect the dissemination of a private conversation that is illegally obtained? Does it matter what the topic of the conversation is? Who the disseminator is? The Supreme Court addressed this issue in the following case involving a civil damages suit under a federal statute protecting the privacy of electronic communications:

Bartnicki v. Vopper

532 U.S. 514, 121 S. Ct. 1753, 149 L. Ed, 2d 787 (2001).

[Bartnicki was the chief negotiator for the Pennsylvania State Education Association, a teacher's union, during a high-profile collective-bargaining negotiation with the school board. While preparing for a possible strike, Bartnicki had a heated phone conversation regarding the school board with Kane, the president of the local union, who said, among other things, that "'If they're not gonna move for three percent, we're gonna have to go to their, their homes. . . . To blow off their front porches, we'll have to do some work on some of those guys.'" The call was secretly intercepted and taped by an unidentified person who turned the tape over to a local citizen who opposed the union's demands, who in turn gave the tape to a local radio talk show host who then played the tape on air. The union negotiators filed complaint for damages against the radio broadcasters and their local citizen informant under 18 U.S.C. § 2511(1)(c), which provides that any person who "intentionally discloses, or endeavors to disclose, to any other person the contents of any wire, oral, or electronic communication, knowing or having reason to know that the information was obtained through the interception of a wire, oral, or electronic communication in violation of this subsection; . . . shall be punished."]

■ JUSTICE STEVENS delivered the opinion of the Court.

These cases raise an important question concerning what degree of protection, if any, the First Amendment provides to speech that discloses the contents of an illegally intercepted communication.

[The] persons who made the disclosures did not participate in the interception, but they did know—or at least had reason to know—that the interception was unlawful. Accordingly, these cases present a conflict between interests of the highest order—on the one hand, the interest in the full and free dissemination of information concerning public issues, and, on the other hand, the interest in individual privacy and, more specifically, in fostering private speech.

[We] accept respondents' submission on three factual matters that serve to distinguish most of the cases that have arisen under § 2511. First, respondents played no part in the illegal interception. Rather, they found out about the interception only after it occurred, and in fact never learned the identity of the person or persons who made the interception. Second, their access to the information on the tapes was obtained lawfully, even though the information itself was intercepted unlawfully by someone else. [Florida Star] Third, the subject matter of the conversation was a matter of public concern. If the statements about the labor negotiations had been made in a public arena—during a bargaining session, for example—they would have been newsworthy. This would also be true if a third party had inadvertently overheard Bartnicki making the same statements to Kane when the two thought they were alone.

In this suit, the basic purpose of the statute at issue is to "protec[t] the privacy of wire[, electronic,] and oral communications." [The] statute does not distinguish based on the content of the intercepted conversations, nor is it justified by reference to the content of those conversations. Rather, the communications at issue are singled out by virtue of the fact that they were illegally intercepted—by virtue of the source, rather than the subject matter. On the other hand, the naked prohibition against disclosures is fairly characterized as a regulation of pure speech.

[In the Pentagon Papers case], the Court upheld the right of the press to publish information of great public concern obtained from documents stolen by a third party. In so doing, that decision resolved a conflict between the basic rule against prior restraints on publication and the interest in preserving the secrecy of information that, if disclosed, might seriously impair the security of the Nation. [However], [we] did not resolv[e] the question "whether, in cases where information has been acquired unlawfully by a newspaper or by a source, government may ever punish not only the unlawful acquisition, but the ensuing publication as well." [Florida Star.] The question here, however, is a narrower version of that still-open question. Simply put, the issue here is this: "Where the punished publisher of information has obtained the information in question in a manner lawful in itself but from a source who has obtained it unlawfully, may the government punish the ensuing publication of that information based on the defect in a chain?"

[The] Government identifies two interests served by the statute—first, the interest in removing an incentive for parties to intercept private conversations, and second, the interest in minimizing the harm to persons whose conversations have been illegally intercepted. We assume that those interests adequately justify the prohibition in § 2511(1)(d) against the interceptor's own use of information that he or she acquired by violating § 2511(1)(a), but it by no means follows that punishing disclosures of lawfully obtained information of public interest by one not involved in the initial illegality is an acceptable means of serving those ends.

The normal method of deterring unlawful conduct is to impose an appropriate punishment on the person who engages in it. If the sanctions that presently attach to a violation of § 2511(1)(a) do not provide sufficient deterrence, perhaps those sanctions should be made more severe. But it would be quite remarkable to hold that speech by a law-abiding possessor of information can be suppressed in order to deter conduct by a non-law-abiding third party. [With] only a handful of exceptions, the violations of § 2511(1)(a) that have been described in litigated cases have been motivated by either financial gain or domestic disputes. In virtually all of those cases, the identity of the person or persons intercepting the communication has been known.

[The] Government's second argument, however, is considerably stronger. Privacy of communication is an important interest. Moreover, the fear of public disclosure of private conversations might well have a chilling effect on private speech. "In a democratic society privacy of communication is essential if citizens are to think and act creatively and constructively. Fear or suspicion that one's speech is being monitored by a stranger, even without the reality of such activity, can have a seriously inhibiting effect upon the willingness to voice critical and constructive ideas." [We] need not decide whether that interest is strong enough to justify the application of § 2511(c) to disclosures of trade secrets or domestic gossip or other information of purely private concern. [Hill.]

[The] enforcement of that provision in these cases, however, implicates the core purposes of the First Amendment because it imposes sanctions on the publication of truthful information of public concern. [Privacy] concerns give way when balanced against the interest in publishing matters of public importance. [A] stranger's illegal conduct does not suffice to remove the First Amendment shield from speech about a matter of public concern. The months of negotiations over the proper level of compensation for teachers at the Wyoming Valley West High School were unquestionably a matter of public concern, and respondents were clearly engaged in debate about that concern. That debate may be more mundane than the Communist rhetoric that inspired Justice Brandeis' classic opinion in [Whitney], but it is no less worthy of constitutional protection.

■ JUSTICE BREYER, with whom JUSTICE O'CONNOR joins, concurring.

I join the Court's opinion because I agree with its "narrow" holding, limited to the special circumstances present here: (1) the radio broadcasters acted lawfully (up to the time of final public disclosure); and (2) the information publicized involved a matter of unusual public concern, namely a threat of potential physical harm to others. I write separately to explain why, in my view, the Court's holding does not imply a significantly broader constitutional immunity for the media. As the Court recognizes, the question before us—a question of immunity from statutorily imposed civil liability—implicates competing constitutional concerns. [The] statutes directly interfere with free expression in that they prevent the media from publishing information. At the same time, they help to protect personal privacy—an interest here that includes not only the "right to be let alone," [but] also "the interest . . . in fostering private speech."

[I] would ask whether the statutes strike a reasonable balance between their speech-restricting and speech-enhancing consequences. Or do they instead impose restrictions on speech that are disproportionate when measured against their corresponding privacy and speech-related benefits, taking into account the kind, the importance, and the extent of these benefits, as well as the need for the restrictions in order to secure those benefits? What this Court has called "strict scrutiny"—with its strong presumption against constitutionality—is normally out of place where, as here, important competing constitutional interests are implicated.

[The] statutory restrictions before us directly enhance private speech. The statutes ensure the privacy of telephone conversations much as a trespass statute ensures privacy within the home. [At] the same time, these statutes restrict public speech directly, deliberately, and of necessity. [They] resemble laws that would award damages caused through publication of information obtained by theft from a private bedroom. [Rather] than broadly forbid this kind of legislative enactment, the Constitution demands legislative efforts to tailor the laws in order reasonably to reconcile media freedom with personal, speech-related privacy.

Nonetheless, looked at more specifically, the statutes, as applied in these circumstances, do not reasonably reconcile the competing constitutional objectives. Rather, they disproportionately interfere with media freedom. [The] broadcasters here engaged in no unlawful activity other than the ultimate publication of the information another had previously obtained. [The] speakers had little or no legitimate interest in maintaining the privacy of the particular conversation. [Where] publication of private information constitutes a wrongful act, the law recognizes a privilege allowing the reporting of threats to public safety. [Further], the speakers themselves, the president of a teacher's union and the union's chief negotiator, were "limited public figures," for they voluntarily engaged in a public controversy. They thereby subjected themselves to somewhat greater public scrutiny and had a lesser interest in privacy than an individual engaged in purely private affairs.

[I] emphasize the particular circumstances before us because, in my view, the Constitution permits legislatures to respond flexibly to the challenges future technology may pose to the individual's interest in basic personal privacy. Clandestine and pervasive invasions of privacy, unlike the simple theft of documents from a bedroom, are genuine possibilities as a result of continuously advancing technologies. Eavesdropping on ordinary cellular phone conversations in the street (which many callers seem to tolerate) is a very different matter from eavesdropping on encrypted cellular phone conversations or those carried on in the bedroom. But the technologies that allow the former may come to permit the latter. [For] these reasons, we should avoid adopting overly broad or rigid constitutional rules, which would unnecessarily restrict legislative flexibility.

■ CHIEF JUSTICE REHNQUIST, with whom JUSTICE SCALIA and JUSTICE THOMAS join, dissenting.

Technology now permits millions of important and confidential conversations to occur through a vast system of electronic networks. These advances, however, raise significant privacy concerns. [To] effectuate these important privacy and speech interests, Congress and the vast majority of States have proscribed the intentional interception and knowing disclosure of the contents of electronic communications.

[The] "dry-up-the-market" theory, which posits that it is possible to deter an illegal act that is difficult to police by preventing the wrongdoer from enjoying the fruits of the crime, is neither novel nor implausible. It is a time-tested theory that undergirds numerous laws, such as the prohibition of the knowing possession of stolen goods. [The] same logic applies here and demonstrates that the incidental restriction on alleged First Amendment freedoms is no greater than essential to further the interest of protecting the privacy of individual communications.

These statutes also protect the important interests of deterring clandestine invasions of privacy and preventing the involuntary broadcast of private communications. [They] further the First Amendment rights of the parties to the conversation. "At the heart of the First Amendment lies the principle that each person should decide for himself or herself the ideas and beliefs deserving of expression, consideration, and adherence." [The] chilling effect of the Court's decision upon these private conversations will surely be [great].

The Court concludes that the private conversation between Gloria Bartnicki and Anthony Kane is somehow a "debate .... worthy of constitutional protection." [The] point, however, is that Bartnicki and Kane had no intention of contributing to a public "debate" at all, and it is perverse to hold that another's unlawful interception and knowing disclosure of their conversation is speech "worthy of constitutional protection." [The] Constitution should not protect the involuntary broadcast of personal conversations. Even where the communications involve public figures or concern public matters, the conversations are nonetheless private and worthy of protection. Although public persons may have forgone the right to live their lives screened from public scrutiny in some areas, it does not and should not follow that they also have abandoned their right to have a private conversation without fear of it being intentionally intercepted and knowingly disclosed.

Surely "the interest in individual privacy," at its narrowest, must embrace the right to be free from surreptitious eavesdropping on, and involuntary broadcast of, our cellular telephone conversations. The Court subordinates that right, not to the claims of those who themselves wish to speak, but to the claims of those who wish to publish the intercepted conversations of others. Congress' effort to balance the above claim to privacy against a marginal claim to speak freely is thereby set at naught.

INTENTIONAL INFLICTION OF EMOTIONAL DISTRESS

Another common-law non-defamation tort, the tort of intentional infliction of emotional distress, provides a private cause of action against a defendant who intentionally or recklessly causes a plaintiff severe emotional injury through extreme or outrageous conduct. Traditionally, a plaintiff can sue for civil damages even when the sole source of the distress is a speech act. A series of Supreme Court decisions, however, has suggested that the tort may be limited on First Amendment grounds for both public and private defendants.

Hustler Magazine v. Falwell

485 U.S. 46, 108 S. Ct. 876, 99 L. Ed. 2d 41 (1988).

[In 1983, Hustler Magazine ran a "parody" of an advertisement for Campari Liqueur entitled "Jerry Falwell Talks About His First Time." The parody was modeled after actual Campari ads that included interviews with various celebrities about their "first times." Although it was clear by the end of each interview that this meant the first time they had sampled Campari, the ads clearly played on a sexual double entendre. Copying the form and layout of these Campari ads, Hustler chose Falwell, a nationally known minister and commentator on public affairs, as its featured celebrity and printed an alleged "interview" revealing that his "first time" was during a drunken incestuous rendezvous with his mother in an outhouse. The parody suggested that Falwell was a hypocrite who preached only when he was drunk. In small print at the bottom of the page, the ad contained the disclaimer, "Ad parody—not to be taken seriously." The magazine's table of contents also listed the ad as "Fiction; Ad and Personality Parody." Falwell sought damages against the magazine for invasion of privacy, libel, and intentional infliction of emotional distress. The jury found for him only on the last claim.]

■ CHIEF JUSTICE REHNQUIST delivered the opinion of the Court.

This case presents us with a novel [question]. We must decide whether a public figure may recover damages for emotional harm caused by the publication of an ad parody offensive to him, and doubtless gross and repugnant in the eyes of most. Respondent would have us find that a State's interest in protecting public figures from emotional distress is sufficient to deny First Amendment protection to speech that is patently offensive and is intended to inflict emotional injury, even when that speech could not reasonably have been interpreted as stating actual facts about the public figure involved. This we decline to do.

[The] sort of robust political debate encouraged by the First Amendment is bound to produce speech that is critical of those who hold public office or those public figures who are "intimately involved in the resolution of important public [questions]." Such criticism, inevitably, will not always be reasoned or moderate; public figures as well as public officials will be subject to "vehement, caustic, and sometimes unpleasantly sharp attacks." [In Falwell's view,] so long as the utterance was intended to inflict emotional distress, was outrageous, and did in fact inflict serious emotional distress, it is of no constitutional import whether the statement was a fact or an opinion, or whether it was true or false. It is the intent to cause injury that is the gravamen of the tort, and the State's interest in preventing emotional harm simply outweighs whatever interest a speaker may have in speech of this type.

Generally speaking the law does not regard the intent to inflict emotional distress as one which should receive much solicitude, and it is quite understandable that most if not all jurisdictions have chosen to make it civilly culpable where the conduct in question is sufficiently "outrageous." But in the world of debate about public affairs, many things done with motives that are less than admirable are protected by the First Amendment. In Garrison v. Louisiana, we held that even when a speaker or writer is motivated by hatred or ill-will his expression was protected by the First Amendment. [Thus,] while such a bad motive may be deemed controlling for purposes of tort liability in other areas of the law, we think the First Amendment prohibits such a result in the area of public debate about public figures.

Were we to hold otherwise, there can be little doubt that political cartoonists and satirists would be subjected to damages awards without any showing that their work falsely defamed its subject. [The] appeal of the political cartoon or caricature is often based on exploration of unfortunate physical traits or politically embarrassing events—an exploration often calculated to injure the feelings of the subject of the portrayal. The art of the cartoonist is often not reasoned or even-handed, but slashing and one-sided. [But from] the viewpoint of history it is clear that our political discourse would have been considerably poorer without [cartoonists]. [Falwell] contends, however, that the caricature in question here was so "outrageous" as to distinguish it from more traditional political cartoons. There is no doubt that the caricature of [Falwell] and his mother published in Hustler is at best a distant cousin of [traditional] political cartoons, [and] a rather poor relation at that. If it were possible by laying down a principled standard to separate the one from the other, public discourse would probably suffer little or no harm. But we doubt that there is any such standard, and we are quite sure that the pejorative description "outrageous" does not supply one. "Outrageousness" in the area of political and social discourse has an inherent subjectiveness about it which would allow a jury to impose liability on the basis of the jurors' tastes or views, or perhaps on the basis of their dislike of a particular expression. An "outrageousness" standard thus runs afoul of our longstanding refusal to allow damages to be awarded because the speech in question may have an adverse emotional impact on the audience. Admittedly, these oft-repeated First Amendment principles, like other principles, are subject to limitations. [But] the sort of expression involved in this case does not seem to us to be governed by any exception to the general First Amendment principles stated above.

We conclude that public figures and public officials may not recover for the tort of intentional infliction of emotional distress by reason of publications such as the one here at issue without showing in addition that the publication contains a false statement of fact which was made with "actual malice," i.e., with knowledge that the statement was false or with reckless disregard as to whether or not it was true. This is not merely a "blind application" of the New York Times standard, it reflects our considered judgment that such a standard is necessary to give adequate "breathing space" to the freedoms protected by the First Amendment.

Reversed.

■ [JUSTICE WHITE concurred, but stated that New York Times had "little to do with this case, for here the jury found that the ad contained no assertion of fact."]

Snyder v. Phelps

562 U.S. 443, 131 S. Ct. 1207, 179 L. Ed. 2d 172 (2011).

[The Westboro Baptist Church is a religious organization known for its members' public protests of homosexuality in the United States. For 20 years, Westboro members have traveled to military funerals to express their belief that God hates the United States for its tolerance of homosexuality and that God is killing American soldiers as punishment for the Nation's sinful policies. In 2006, Westboro staged a picket outside the funeral of a Marine killed in the line of duty in Iraq. The picketing was peaceful and took place on public land 1,000 feet from the funeral. A Maryland jury held Westboro liable for $2.9 million in compensatory damages and $8 million in punitive damages for the torts of intentional infliction of emotional distress, intrusion upon seclusion and civil conspiracy; the trial court remitted the punitives.]

■ CHIEF JUSTICE ROBERTS delivered the opinion of the Court.

Whether the First Amendment prohibits holding Westboro liable for its speech in this case turns largely on whether that speech is of public or private concern, as determined by all the circumstances of the case. [The] First Amendment reflects "a profound national commitment to the principle that debate on public issues should be uninhibited, robust, and wide-open." [New York Times.] However, where matters of purely private significance are at issue, First Amendment protections are often less rigorous. [See Hustler.] That is because restricting speech on purely private matters does not implicate the same constitutional concerns as limiting speech on matters of public interest.

[Speech] deals with matters of public concern when it can 'be fairly considered as relating to any matter of political, social, or other concern to the community,' or when it 'is a subject of legitimate news interest; that is, a subject of general interest and of value and concern to the public.' [Deciding] whether speech is of public or private concern requires us to examine the 'content, form, and context' of that speech, 'as revealed by the whole record.' [In] considering content, form, and context, no factor is dispositive, and it is necessary to evaluate all the circumstances of the speech, including what was said, where it was said, and how it was said.

[The] "content" of Westboro's signs plainly relates to broad issues of interest to society at large, rather than matters of "purely private concern." The placards read "God Hates the USA/Thank God for 9/11," "America is Doomed," "Don't Pray for the USA," "Thank God for IEDs," "Fag Troops," "Semper Fi Fags," "God Hates Fags," "Maryland Taliban," "Fags Doom Nations," "Not Blessed Just Cursed," "Thank God for Dead Soldiers," "Pope in Hell," "Priests Rape Boys," "You're Going to Hell," and "God Hates You." While these messages may fall short of refined social or political commentary, the issues they highlight—the political and moral conduct of the United States and its citizens, the fate of our Nation, homosexuality in the military, and scandals involving the Catholic clergy—are matters of public import. The signs certainly convey Westboro's position on those issues, in a manner designed [to] reach as broad a public audience as possible. And even if a few of the signs—such as "You're Going to Hell" and "God Hates

You"—were viewed as containing messages related to Matthew Snyder or the Snyders specifically, that would not change the fact that the overall thrust and dominant theme of Westboro's demonstration spoke to broader public issues.

Apart from the content of Westboro's signs, Snyder contends that the "context" of the speech—its connection with his son's funeral—makes the speech a matter of private rather than public concern. The fact that Westboro spoke in connection with a funeral, however, cannot by itself transform the nature of Westboro's speech. Westboro's signs, displayed on public land next to a public street, [are] "fairly characterized as constituting speech on a matter of public concern," and the funeral setting does not alter that conclusion.

[Snyder] goes on to argue that Westboro's speech should be afforded less than full First Amendment protection "not only because of the words" but also because the church members exploited the funeral "as a platform to bring their message to a broader audience." There is no doubt that Westboro chose to stage its picketing at the Naval Academy, the Maryland State House, and Matthew Snyder's funeral to increase publicity for its views and because of the relation between those sites and its [views regarding homosexuality]. Westboro's choice to convey its views in conjunction with Matthew Snyder's funeral made the expression of those views particularly hurtful to many, especially to Matthew's father. The record makes clear that the applicable legal term—"emotional distress"—fails to capture fully the anguish Westboro's choice added to Mr. Snyder's already incalculable grief. But Westboro conducted its picketing peacefully on matters of public concern at a public place adjacent to a public street.

[Westboro's] choice of where and when to conduct its picketing is not beyond the Government's regulatory reach—it is "subject to reasonable time, place, or manner restrictions" that are consistent with the standards announced in this Court's precedents. Maryland now has a law imposing restrictions on funeral picketing, as do 43 other States and the Federal Government. To the extent these laws are content neutral, they raise very different questions from the tort verdict at issue in this case. [The] record confirms that any distress occasioned by Westboro's picketing turned on the content and viewpoint of the message conveyed, rather than any interference with the funeral itself. A group of parishioners standing at the very spot where Westboro stood, holding signs that said "God Bless America" and "God Loves You," would not have been subjected to liability. It was what Westboro said that exposed it to tort damages. Given that Westboro's speech was at a public place on a matter of public concern, that speech is entitled to "special protection" under the First Amendment. Such speech cannot be restricted simply because it is upsetting or arouses contempt.

The jury here was instructed that it could hold Westboro liable for intentional infliction of emotional distress based on a finding that Westboro's picketing was "outrageous." "Outrageousness," however, is a highly malleable standard with "an inherent subjectiveness about it which would allow a jury to impose liability on the basis of the jurors' tastes or views, or perhaps on the basis of their dislike of a particular expression." [Hustler] [Such] a risk is unacceptable; "in public debate [we] must tolerate insulting, and even outrageous, speech in order to provide adequate 'breathing space' to the freedoms protected by the First Amendment."

[Speech] is powerful. It can stir people to action, move them to tears of both joy and sorrow, and—as it did here—inflict great pain. On the facts before us, we cannot react to that pain by punishing the speaker. As a Nation we have chosen a different course—to protect even hurtful speech on public issues to ensure that we do not stifle public debate. That choice requires that we shield Westboro from tort liability for its picketing in this case.

■ JUSTICE BREYER, concurring.

While I agree with the Court's conclusion that the picketing addressed matters of public concern, I do not believe that our First Amendment analysis can stop at that point. A State can sometimes regulate picketing, even picketing on matters of public concern. [As] I understand the Court's opinion, it does not hold or imply that the State is always powerless to provide private individuals with necessary protection. Rather, the Court has reviewed the underlying facts in detail, as will sometimes prove necessary where First Amendment values and state-protected (say, privacy-related) interests seriously conflict. That review makes clear that Westboro's means of communicating its views consisted of picketing in a place where picketing was lawful and in compliance with all police directions. The picketing could not be seen or heard from the funeral ceremony itself. And Snyder testified that he saw no more than the tops of the picketers' signs as he drove to the funeral. To uphold the application of state law in these circumstances would punish Westboro for seeking to communicate its views on matters of public concern without proportionately advancing the State's interest in protecting its citizens against severe emotional harm.

■ JUSTICE ALITO, dissenting.

Our profound national commitment to free and open debate is not a license for the vicious verbal assault that occurred in this case.

[It] is well established that a claim for the intentional infliction of emotional distress can be satisfied by speech. [And] although this Court has not decided the question, I think it is clear that the First Amendment does not entirely preclude liability for the intentional infliction of emotional distress by means of speech. [This] Court has recognized that words may "by their very utterance inflict injury" and that the First Amendment does not shield utterances that form "no essential part of any exposition of ideas, and are of such slight social value as a step to truth that any benefit that may be derived from them is clearly outweighed by the social interest in order and morality." [Chaplinsky.] When grave injury is intentionally inflicted by means of an attack like the one at issue here, the First Amendment should not interfere with recovery.

In this case, respondents brutally attacked Matthew Snyder, and this attack, which was almost certain to inflict injury, was central to respondents' well-practiced strategy for attracting public attention. [This] strategy works because it is expected that respondents' verbal assaults will wound the family and friends of the deceased and because the media is irresistibly drawn to the sight of persons who are visibly in grief. The more outrageous the funeral protest, the more publicity the Westboro Baptist Church is able to obtain.

[It] is abundantly clear that respondents, going far beyond commentary on matters of public concern, specifically attacked Matthew Snyder because (1) he was a Catholic and (2) he was a member of the United States military. Both Matthew and petitioner were private figures, and this attack was not speech on a matter of public concern. While commentary on the Catholic Church or the United States military constitutes speech on matters of public concern, speech regarding Matthew Snyder's purely private conduct does not.

[Respondents'] outrageous conduct caused petitioner great injury, and the Court now compounds that injury by depriving petitioner of a judgment that acknowledges the wrong he suffered. In order to have a society in which public issues can be openly and vigorously debated, it is not necessary to allow the brutalization of innocent victims like petitioner. I therefore respectfully dissent.

Intentional infliction of emotional distress after Snyder. What facts were essential to the holding in Snyder? That the speech took place in public setting? That the speech implicated matters of public concern? Consider whether Snyder has any effect on a purely interpersonal assertion of the tort concerning statements made in a private setting, or unaffected by references to matters of public debate. What might a state or local government do after Snyder to prevent similar harms at funerals in the future? Impose "buffer zones" around funerals barring any speech within a certain time and place in relation to any funeral?

HATE SPEECH

While the preceding section considered First Amendment limits on traditional torts protecting individual reputation, sensibility and dignity, should the First Amendment limit efforts to curb speech perceived as harmful and offensive to racial or religious minorities or other historically disempowered groups, apart from the tendency of that speech to incite immediate violence or provoke an immediate fight? Recall that Chaplinsky included among the categories of unprotected speech those words that "by their very utterance inflict injury." And recall that Beauharnais upheld a group libel law, treating false statements about racial or other groups as categorically unprotected. Should these precedents inform challenges to new efforts to regulate abusive or denigrating words directed at racial or other groups? Should the Chaplinsky list of unprotected categories be expanded to cover a new category for such hate speech? Consider the strength of the government justifications for such regulation in the following cases:

Collin v. Smith

578 F.2d 1197 (7th Cir. 1978).

[In the late 1970s, the National Socialist Party of America attempted to organize a march through the town of Skokie, Illinois. The NSPA chose Skokie for their demonstration largely because the town included a large Jewish population, including thousands of survivors of the Nazi holocaust in Europe during World War II. In response, the village of Skokie enacted three ordinances to prohibit demonstrations such as the one the NSPA contemplated. The first established a comprehensive permit system for parades and public assemblies; the second prohibited the "dissemination of any materials within [Skokie] which [intentionally] promotes and incites hatred against persons by reason of their race, national origin, or religion"; the third prohibited public demonstrations by members of political parties while wearing "military-style" uniforms. The NSPA applied for a permit application for a half-hour march that would involve 30 to 50 demonstrators wearing uniforms including swastikas and carrying a party banners featuring statements such as "White Free Speech," "Free Speech for the White Man," and "Free Speech for White America." Represented by a Jewish ACLU attorney, the NSPA and its leader at that time, Frank Collin, brought a federal court action to challenge the Skokie ordinances on First Amendment grounds.]

■ JUDGE PELL delivered the opinion of the court.

[The] conflict underlying this litigation has commanded substantial public attention, and engendered considerable and understandable emotion. We would hopefully surprise no one by confessing personal views that NSPA's beliefs and goals are repugnant to the core values held generally by residents of this country, and, indeed, to much of what we cherish in civilization. As judges sworn to defend the Constitution, however, we cannot decide this or any case on that basis. Ideological tyranny, no matter how worthy its motivation, is forbidden as much to appointed judges as to elected legislators.

[Our] task here is to decide whether the First Amendment protects the activity in which appellees wish to engage, not to render moral judgment on their views or tactics. No authorities need be cited to establish the proposition, which the Village does not dispute, that First Amendment rights are truly precious and fundamental to our national life. Nor is this truth without relevance to the saddening historical images this case inevitably arouses. It is, after all, in part the fact that our constitutional system protects minorities unpopular at a particular time or place from governmental harassment and intimidation, that distinguishes life in this country from life under the Third Reich.

[Above] all else, the First Amendment means that government has no power to restrict expression because of its message, its ideas, its subject matter, or its content. To permit the continued building of our politics and culture, and to assure self-fulfillment for each individual, our people are guaranteed the right to express any thought, free from government censorship. [This] is not to say, of course, that content legislation is per se invalid. [But] analysis of content restrictions must begin with a healthy respect for the truth that they are the most direct threat to the vitality of First Amendment rights.

[This] ordinance cannot be sustained on the basis of some of the more obvious exceptions to the rule against content control. While some would no doubt be willing to label appellees' views and symbols obscene, the constitutional rule that obscenity is unprotected applies only to material with erotic content. Furthermore, [the] Village tells us that it does not rely on a fear of responsive violence to justify the ordinance, and does not even suggest that there will be any physical violence if the march is held. The concession also eliminates any argument based on the fighting words doctrine of Chaplinsky v. New Hampshire.

Four basic arguments are advanced by the Village to justify the content [restrictions]. First, it is said that the content criminalized by [the ordinance] is "totally lacking in social content," and that it consists of "false statements of fact" in which there is "no constitutional value." [Gertz v. Robert Welch.] To the degree that the symbols in question can be said to assert anything specific, it must be the Nazi ideology, which cannot be treated as a mere false "fact." Under the First Amendment there is no such thing as a false idea. However pernicious an opinion may seem, we depend for its correction not on the conscience of judges and juries but on the competition of other ideas.

The Village's second argument [centers] on Beauharnais v. Illinois. [It] may be questioned, after cases such as [Cohen v. California] and [Brandenburg v. Ohio], whether the tendency to induce violence approach sanctioned implicitly in Beauharnais would pass constitutional muster today. Assuming that it would, however, it does not support [the ordinance], because the Village, as we have indicated, does not assert appellees' possible violence, an audience's possible responsive violence, or possible violence against third parties by those incited by appellees, as justifications for [it].

The Village's third argument is that it has a policy of fair housing, which the dissemination of racially defamatory material could undercut. We reject this argument without extended discussion. That the effective exercise of First Amendment rights may undercut a given government's policy on some issue is, indeed, one of the purposes of those rights.

The Village's fourth argument is that the Nazi march, involving as it does the display of uniforms and swastikas, will create a substantive evil that it has a right to prohibit: the infliction of psychic trauma on resident holocaust survivors and other Jewish residents. Assuming that specific individuals could proceed in tort under this theory to recover damages provably occasioned by the proposed march, and that a First Amendment defense would not bar the action, it is nonetheless quite a different matter to criminalize protected First Amendment conduct in anticipation of such results.

It would be grossly insensitive to deny, as we do not, that the proposed demonstration would seriously disturb, emotionally and mentally, at least some, and probably many of the Village's residents. The problem with engrafting an exception on the First Amendment for such situations is that they are indistinguishable in principle from speech that "invite(s) dispute." Terminiello v. Chicago. Yet these are among the "high purposes" of the First Amendment. It is perfectly clear that a state many not "make criminal the peaceful expression of unpopular views."

[The] preparation and issuance of this opinion has not been an easy task, or one which we have relished. Recognizing the implication that often seems to follow over-protestation, we nevertheless feel compelled once again to express our repugnance at the doctrines which the appellees desire to profess publicly. [Yet] our Regret at the use appellees plan to make of their rights is not in any sense an Apology for upholding the First Amendment. The result we have reached is dictated by the fundamental proposition that if these civil rights are to remain vital for all, they must protect not only those society deems acceptable, but also those whose ideas it quite justifiably rejects and despises.

---

1. ***The fallout of Skokie.*** Collin and the NSPA cancelled the planned demonstration three days before it was to take place. Relying on the rulings in the Skokie litigation, the Nazis had obtained a federal court order setting aside the Chicago Park District's $60,000 liability insurance requirement which had previously blocked Nazi demonstrations in city parks there. Collin explained that the aim of the Nazis' Skokie efforts had been "pure agitation to restore our right to free speech." He stated that "he had used the threat of the Skokie march to win the right to rally in [Chicago]." No serious violence occurred when about 25 Nazis held a rally in a Chicago park on July 9, 1978.

2. ***Skokie at the Supreme Court.*** The dispute over the NSPA march in Skokie reached the U.S. Supreme Court three times. The first time, the NSPA sought a stay of an injunction against the march upheld by Illinois state courts. The Supreme Court treated the stay petition as a petition for certiorari, granted the writ, and summarily reversed the highest state court's denial of the stay. In its 5–4 per curiam disposition in **National Socialist Party v. Skokie**, 432 U.S. 43 (1977), the Court emphasized the need for "strict procedural safeguards" in the First Amendment area, including immediate appellate review. The ruling led the Illinois courts to set aside the injunction.

The case reached the Supreme Court a second time following the Seventh Circuit's decision in Collin. With the Nazi demonstration scheduled for June 25, 1978, Skokie sought a Supreme Court stay of the Court of Appeals ruling, pending review. On June 12, 1978, the Supreme Court denied the stay. Justice Blackmun, joined by Justice Rehnquist, dissented from that order, stating that the Court of Appeals decision "is in some tension with this Court's decision, 25 years ago, in Beauharnais," and noting that "Beauharnais has never been overruled or formally limited in any way." Smith v. Collin, 436 U.S. 953.

The final scene in the Skokie drama took place in October 1978, when the Supreme Court declined to review the Seventh Circuit decision invalidating the Skokie ordinances. **Smith v. Collin**, 439 U.S. 916 (1978). Justice BLACKMUN, joined by Justice White, dissented, urging that certiorari be granted "in order to resolve any possible conflict that may exist between the ruling of the Seventh Circuit here and Beauharnais." He added: "I also feel that the present case affords the Court an opportunity to consider whether, in the context of the facts that this record appears to present, there is no limit whatsoever to the exercise of free speech. There indeed may be no such limit, but when citizens assert, not casually but with deep conviction, that the proposed demonstration is scheduled at a place and in a manner that is taunting and overwhelmingly offensive to the citizens of that place, that assertion, uncomfortable though it may be for judges, deserves to be examined. It just might fall into the same category as one's 'right' to cry 'fire' in a crowded theater, for 'the character of every act depends upon the circumstances in which it is done.' Schenck."

For the view that permitting the Nazi march served the value of mastering pervasive social tendencies toward intolerance, and that it makes sense to carve out free speech as an arena of "extraordinary self-restraint" in order to promote self-restraint in other arenas, see Bollinger, The Tolerant Society (1986).

3. ***Regulating racist and other discriminatory speech on campus.*** Beginning in the late 1980s, a number of colleges and universities around the nation, responding to reports of racially tense exchanges on

campuses, considered or adopted regulations to curb speech expressing hatred or bias toward members of racial, religious, or other groups. These regulations provoked extensive debates on campuses, in the media, and in the academic literature about the permissibility under the First Amendment of such rules.

In April 1988, for example, the University of Michigan adopted a regulation subjecting individuals to discipline for "[any] behavior, verbal or physical, that stigmatizes or victimizes an individual on the basis of race, ethnicity, religion, sex, sexual orientation, creed, national origin, ancestry, age, marital status, handicap or Vietnam-era veteran status" which "has the purpose or reasonably foreseeable effect of interfering with an individual's academic efforts, employment, participation in University sponsored extra-curricular activities or personal safety." A federal district court held the regulation unconstitutional under the First Amendment as overbroad and impermissibly vague. Doe v. University of Mich., 721 F. Supp. 852 (E.D. Mich. 1989).

In June 1990, Stanford University added to its "fundamental standard" of conduct for members of the university community a prohibition of "discriminatory harassment": "Speech or other expression constitutes harassment by personal vilification if it: (a) is intended to insult or stigmatize an individual or small group of individuals on the basis of their sex, race, color, handicap, religion, sexual orientation, or national and ethnic origin; and (b) is addressed directly to the individual or individuals whom it insults or stigmatizes; and (c) makes use of insulting or 'fighting' words or non-verbal symbols. In [this context], insulting or 'fighting' words or non-verbal symbols are [those] 'which by their very utterance inflict injury or tend to incite to an immediate breach of the peace,' and which are commonly understood to convey direct and visceral hatred or contempt for human beings on the basis of their sex, race, color, handicap, religion, sexual orientation, or national and ethnic origin."

In 1995, a California state court struck down the Stanford standard under a California statute providing that a private university may not impose limitations on speech that would violate the First Amendment if imposed by a public university. The decision, Corry v. Stanford, No. 740309 (Cal. Super. Ct. Santa Clara Co. 1995), held that the Stanford standard was overbroad under Chaplinsky because it reached insults that did not threaten to provoke immediate violence, and was impermissibly content-discriminatory under R.A.V. v. St. Paul, which follows, because it focused on bigoted insults while leaving other insults alone. The University did not appeal. For an account of the history of the Stanford standard by its author, and an argument for its constitutionality even in the wake of R.A.V., see Grey, "How to Write a Speech Code Without Really Trying: Reflections on the Stanford Experience," 29 U.C. Davis L. Rev. 891 (1996).

R.A.V. v. City of St. Paul

505 U.S. 377, 112 S. Ct. 2538, 120 L. Ed. 2d 305 (1992).

■ JUSTICE SCALIA delivered the opinion of the Court.

In the predawn hours of June 21, 1990, petitioner and several other teenagers allegedly assembled a crudely-made cross by taping together broken chair legs. They then allegedly burned the cross inside the fenced yard of a black family that lived across the street from the house where petitioner was staying. Although this conduct could have been punished under any of a number of laws [including laws against terroristic threats, arson, and criminal damage to property], one of the two provisions under which [St. Paul] chose to charge petitioner (then a juvenile) was the St. Paul Bias-Motivated Crime Ordinance which provides:

> "Whoever places on public or private property a symbol, object, appellation, characterization or graffiti, including, but not limited to, a burning cross or Nazi swastika, which one knows or has reasonable grounds to know arouses anger, alarm or resentment in others on the basis of race, color, creed, religion or gender commits disorderly conduct and shall be guilty of a misdemeanor."

Petitioner moved to dismiss this count on the ground that the St. Paul ordinance was substantially overbroad and impermissibly content-based and therefore facially invalid under the First Amendment. The trial court granted this motion, but the Minnesota Supreme Court reversed.

I. [Assuming,] arguendo, that all of the expression reached by the ordinance is proscribable under the "fighting words" doctrine, we nonetheless conclude that the ordinance is facially unconstitutional in that it prohibits otherwise permitted speech solely on the basis of the subjects the speech addresses. The First Amendment generally prevents government from proscribing speech, or even expressive conduct, because of disapproval of the ideas expressed. Content-based regulations are presumptively invalid. From 1791 to the present, however, our society, like other free but civilized societies, has permitted restrictions upon the content of speech in a few limited areas, which are "of such slight social value as a step to truth that any benefit that may be derived from them is clearly outweighed by the social interest in order and morality." Chaplinsky. [Our] decisions since the 1960's have narrowed the scope of the traditional categorical exceptions for defamation and for obscenity, but a limited categorical approach has remained an important part of our First Amendment jurisprudence.

We have sometimes said that these categories of expression are "not within the area of constitutionally protected speech," or that the "protection of the First Amendment does not extend" to them. Such statements must be taken in context, however. [What] they mean is that these areas of speech can, consistently with the First Amendment, be regulated because of their constitutionally proscribable content (obscenity, defamation, etc.)—not that they are categories of speech entirely invisible to the Constitution, so that they may be made the vehicles for content discrimination unrelated to their distinctively proscribable content. Thus, the government may proscribe libel; but it may not make the further content discrimination of proscribing only libel critical of the government. [Nor could a] city council [enact] an ordinance prohibiting only those legally obscene works that contain criticism of the city government or, indeed, that do not include endorsement of the city government. Such a simplistic, all-or-nothing-at-all approach to First

Amendment protection is at odds with common sense and with our jurisprudence as well.

The proposition that a particular instance of speech can be proscribable on the basis of one feature (e.g., obscenity) but not on the basis of another (e.g., opposition to the city government) is commonplace, and has found application in many contexts. We have long held, for example, that nonverbal expressive activity can be banned because of the action it entails, but not because of the ideas it expresses—so that burning a flag in violation of an ordinance against outdoor fires could be punishable, whereas burning a flag in violation of an ordinance against dishonoring the flag is not.

[Thus], the exclusion of "fighting words" from the scope of the First Amendment simply means that, for purposes of that Amendment, the unprotected features of the words are, despite their verbal character, essentially a "nonspeech" element of communication. Fighting words are thus analogous to a noisy sound truck: [both] can be used to convey an idea; but neither has, in and of itself, a claim upon the First Amendment. As with the sound truck, however, so also with fighting words: The government may not regulate use based on hostility—or favoritism—towards the underlying message expressed.

The concurrences describe us as setting forth a new First Amendment principle that prohibition of constitutionally proscribable speech cannot be "underinclusive" [so that] "a government must either proscribe all speech or no speech at all." That easy target is of the concurrences' own invention. In our view, the First Amendment imposes not an "underinclusiveness" limitation but a "content discrimination" limitation upon a State's prohibition of proscribable speech. There is no problem whatever, for example, with a State's prohibiting obscenity (and other forms of proscribable expression) only in certain media or markets, for although that prohibition would be "underinclusive," it would not discriminate on the basis of content.

Even the prohibition against content discrimination that we assert the First Amendment requires is not absolute. [When] the basis for the content discrimination consists entirely of the very reason the entire class of speech at issue is proscribable, no significant danger of idea or viewpoint discrimination exists. [Thus, a state] might choose to prohibit only that obscenity which is the most patently offensive in its prurience—i.e., that which involves the most lascivious displays of sexual activity. But it may not prohibit, for example, only that obscenity which includes offensive political messages. And the Federal Government can criminalize only those threats of violence that are directed against the President, since the reasons why threats of violence are outside the First Amendment (protecting individuals from the fear of violence, from the disruption that fear engenders, and from the possibility that the threatened violence will occur) have special force when applied to the person of the President. But the Federal Government may not criminalize only those threats against the President that mention his policy on aid to inner cities. [And a state] may choose to regulate price advertising in one industry but not in others, because the risk of fraud [is] in its view greater there. But a State may not prohibit only that commercial advertising that depicts men in a demeaning fashion.

Another valid basis for according differential treatment to even a content-defined subclass of proscribable speech is that the subclass happens to be associated with particular "secondary effects" of the speech, so that the regulation is "justified without reference to the content of the . . . speech." A State could, for example, permit all obscene live performances except those involving minors. Moreover, since words can in some circumstances violate laws directed not against speech but against conduct (a law against treason, for example, is violated by telling the enemy the nation's defense secrets), a particular content-based subcategory of a proscribable class of speech can be swept up incidentally within the reach of a statute directed at conduct rather than speech. Thus, for example, sexually derogatory "fighting words," among other words, may produce a violation of Title VII's general prohibition against sexual discrimination in employment practices. Where the government does not target conduct on the basis of its expressive content, acts are not shielded from regulation merely because they express a discriminatory idea or philosophy. [Finally,] it may not even be necessary to identify any particular "neutral" basis, so long as the nature of the content discrimination is such that there is no realistic possibility that official suppression of ideas is afoot. (We cannot think of any First Amendment interest that would stand in the way of a State's prohibiting only those obscene motion pictures with blue-eyed actresses.)

II. Applying these principles to the St. Paul ordinance, we conclude that, even as narrowly construed by the Minnesota Supreme Court [to apply only to] "fighting words," the remaining, unmodified terms make clear that the ordinance applies only to "fighting words" that insult, or provoke violence, "on the basis of race, color, creed, religion or gender." Displays containing abusive invective, no matter how vicious or severe, are permissible unless they are addressed to one of the specified disfavored topics. Those who wish to use "fighting words" in connection with other ideas—to express hostility, for example, on the basis of political affiliation, union membership, or homosexuality—are not covered. The First Amendment does not permit St. Paul to impose special prohibitions on those speakers who express views on disfavored subjects.

In its practical operation, moreover, the ordinance goes even beyond mere content discrimination, to actual viewpoint discrimination. Displays containing some words—odious racial epithets, for example—would be prohibited to proponents of all views. But "fighting words" that do not themselves invoke race, color, creed, religion, or gender—aspersions upon a person's mother, for example—would seemingly be usable ad libitum in the placards of those arguing in favor of racial, color, etc. tolerance and equality, but could not be used by that speaker's opponents. One could hold up a sign saying, for example, that all "anti-Catholic bigots" are misbegotten; but not that all "papists" are, for that would insult and provoke violence "on the basis of religion." St. Paul has no such authority to license one side of a debate to fight freestyle, while requiring the other to follow Marquis of Queensbury Rules.

[The] content-based discrimination reflected in the St. Paul ordinance comes within neither any of the specific exceptions to the First Amendment prohibition we discussed earlier, nor within a more general exception for content discrimination that does not threaten censorship of ideas. It assuredly does not fall within the exception for content discrimination based on the very reasons why the particular class of speech at issue (here, fighting words) is proscribable. [St. Paul] has not singled out an especially offensive mode of expression—it has not, for example, selected for prohibition only those fighting words that communicate ideas in a threatening (as opposed to a merely obnoxious) manner. Rather, it has proscribed fighting words of whatever manner that communicate messages of racial, gender, or religious intolerance.

Finally, St. Paul [argues] that, even if the ordinance regulates expression based on hostility towards its protected ideological content, this discrimination is nonetheless justified because it is narrowly tailored to serve compelling state interests [in protecting the] rights of members of groups that have historically been subjected to discrimination, including the right of such group members to live in peace where they wish. We do not doubt that these interests are compelling, and that the ordinance can be said to promote them. [The] dispositive question in this case, [however,] is whether content discrimination is reasonably necessary to achieve St. Paul's compelling interests; it plainly is not. An ordinance not limited to the favored topics, for example, would have precisely the same beneficial effect. In fact the only interest distinctively served by the content limitation is that of displaying the city council's special hostility towards the particular biases thus singled out. That is precisely what the First Amendment forbids. The politicians of St. Paul are entitled to express that hostility—but not through the means of imposing unique limitations upon speakers who (however benightedly) disagree.

Let there be no mistake about our belief that burning a cross in someone's front yard is reprehensible. But St. Paul has sufficient means at its disposal to prevent such behavior without adding the First Amendment to the fire. Reversed.

■ JUSTICE WHITE, with whom JUSTICES BLACKMUN and O'CONNOR join, and with whom JUSTICE STEVENS joins except as to Part I(A), concurring in the judgment.

I agree with the majority that the judgment of the Minnesota Supreme Court should be reversed. However, our agreement ends there. This case could easily be decided within the contours of established First Amendment law by holding, as petitioner argues, that the St. Paul ordinance is fatally overbroad because it criminalizes not only unprotected expression but expression protected by the First Amendment.

I. A. This Court's decisions have plainly stated that expression falling within certain limited categories so lacks the values the First Amendment was designed to protect that the Constitution affords no protection to that expression. Chaplinsky. [Thus,] this Court has long held certain discrete categories of expression [e.g., child pornography, obscenity and most libel] to be proscribable on the basis of their content. All of these categories are content based. But the Court has held that First Amendment does not apply to them because their expressive content is worthless or of de minimis value to society. [It] is inconsistent to hold that the government may proscribe an entire category of speech because the content of that speech is evil, but that the government may not treat a subset of that category differently without violating the First Amendment; the content of the subset is by definition worthless and undeserving of constitutional protection. [A] ban on all fighting words or on a subset of the fighting words category would restrict only the social evil of hate speech, without creating the danger of driving viewpoints from the marketplace. [By] characterizing fighting words as a form of "debate," the majority legitimates hate speech as a form of public discussion.

B. In a second break with precedent, the Court refuses to sustain the ordinance even though it would survive under the strict scrutiny applicable to other protected expression. [The] Court expressly concedes that [the government interest in ensuring the rights of members of groups that have historically been subject to discrimination] is compelling and is promoted by the ordinance, [but holds that such a law] could never pass constitutional muster if [its object] could be accomplished by banning a wider category of speech. This appears to be a general renunciation of strict scrutiny review, a fundamental tool of First Amendment analysis.

C. The Court has patched up its argument with an apparently nonexhaustive list of ad hoc exceptions, in what can be viewed either as an attempt to confine the effects of its decision to the facts of this case, or as an effort to anticipate some of the questions that will arise from its radical revision of First Amendment law. [For example,] Title VII makes it unlawful to discriminate "because of [an] individual's race, color, religion, sex, or national origin," and the regulations covering hostile workplace claims forbid "sexual harassment," which includes "unwelcome sexual advances, requests for sexual favors, and other verbal or physical conduct of a sexual nature" which creates "an intimidating, hostile, or offensive working environment." [Hence,] the majority's second exception, which the Court indicates would insulate a Title VII hostile work environment claim from an underinclusiveness challenge because "sexually derogatory 'fighting words' . . . may produce a violation of Title VII's general prohibition against sexual discrimination in employment practices." [But if] the relationship between the broader statute and specific regulation is sufficient to bring the Title VII regulation within [this exception], then all St. Paul need do to bring its ordinance within [it] is to add some prefatory language concerning discrimination generally.

II. Although I disagree with the Court's analysis, I do agree with its conclusion: The St. Paul ordinance is unconstitutional. However, I would decide the case on overbreadth grounds. [Although] the ordinance as construed reaches categories of speech that are constitutionally unprotected, it also criminalizes a substantial amount of expression that—however repugnant—is shielded by the First Amendment. [I] understand the [Minnesota Supreme Court] to have ruled that St. Paul may constitutionally prohibit expression that "by its very utterance" causes "anger, alarm or resentment." Our fighting words cases have made clear, however, that such generalized reactions are not sufficient to strip expression of its constitutional protection. The mere fact that expressive activity causes hurt feelings, offense, or resentment does not render the expression unprotected. The ordinance is therefore fatally overbroad and invalid on its face. [I] join the judgment, but not the folly of the opinion.

■ JUSTICE BLACKMUN, concurring in the judgment.

[I] fear that the Court has been distracted from its proper mission by the temptation to decide the issue over "politically correct speech" and "cultural diversity," neither of which is presented here. [I] see no First Amendment values that are compromised by a law that prohibits hoodlums from driving minorities out of their homes by burning crosses on their lawns, but I see great harm in preventing the people of Saint Paul from specifically punishing the race-based fighting words that so prejudice their community.

■ JUSTICE STEVENS, with whom JUSTICES WHITE and BLACKMUN join as to Part I, concurring in the judgment.

I. [The] Court [applies] the prohibition on content-based regulation to speech that the Court had until today considered wholly "unprotected" by the First Amendment—namely, fighting words. This new absolutism in the prohibition of content-based regulations severely contorts the fabric of settled First Amendment law. Our First Amendment decisions have created a rough hierarchy in the constitutional protection of speech. Core political speech occupies the highest, most protected position; commercial speech and nonobscene, sexually explicit speech are regarded as a sort of second-class expression; obscenity and fighting words receive the least protection of all. Assuming that the Court is correct that this last class of speech is not wholly "unprotected," it certainly does not follow that fighting words and obscenity receive the same sort of protection afforded core political speech. Yet in ruling that proscribable speech cannot be regulated based on subject matter, the Court does just that.

[Perhaps] because the Court recognizes these perversities, it quickly offers some ad hoc limitations on its newly extended prohibition on content-based regulations. [For example, the Court concedes that] "the Federal Government can criminalize only those physical threats that are directed against the President." [Precisely] this same reasoning, however, compels the conclusion that St. Paul's ordinance is constitutional. Just as Congress may determine that threats against the President entail more severe consequences than other threats, so [St. Paul] may determine that threats based on the target's race, religion, or gender cause more severe harm to both the target and to society than other threats.

II. Although I agree with much of Justice White's analysis, I do not join Part I–A of his opinion because I have reservations about the "categorical approach" to the First Amendment. Admittedly, the categorical approach to the First Amendment has some appeal: either expression is protected or it is not—the categories create safe harbors for governments and speakers alike. But this approach sacrifices subtlety for clarity and is, I am convinced, ultimately unsound. As an initial matter, the concept of "categories" fits poorly with the complex reality of expression. Few dividing lines in First Amendment law are straight and unwavering, and efforts at categorization inevitably give rise only to fuzzy boundaries. [Moreover,] the categorical approach does not take seriously the importance of context. The meaning of any expression and the legitimacy of its regulation can only be determined in context. [The] history of the categorical approach is largely the history of narrowing the categories of unprotected speech. This evolution, I believe, indicates that the categorical approach is unworkable and the quest for absolute categories of "protected" and "unprotected" speech ultimately futile.

III. As the foregoing suggests, I disagree with both the Court's and part of Justice White's analysis of the constitutionality St. Paul ordinance. Unlike the Court, I do not believe that all content-based regulations are equally infirm and presumptively invalid; unlike Justice White, I do not believe that fighting words are wholly unprotected by the First Amendment. To the contrary, I believe our decisions establish a more complex and subtle analysis, one that considers the content and context of the regulated speech, and the nature and scope of the restriction on speech. Applying this analysis and assuming arguendo (as the Court does) that the St. Paul ordinance is not overbroad, I conclude that such a selective, subject-matter regulation on proscribable speech is constitutional.

[Looking] to the content and character of the regulated activity, two things are clear. First, by hypothesis the ordinance bars only low-value speech, namely, fighting words. [Second,] the ordinance regulates "expressive conduct [rather] than . . . the written or spoken word." Looking to the context of the regulated activity, it is again significant that the statute (by hypothesis) regulates only fighting words. [By] hypothesis, then, the St. Paul ordinance restricts speech in confrontational and potentially violent situations. [The] St. Paul ordinance regulates speech not on the basis of its subject matter or the viewpoint expressed, but rather on the basis of the harm the speech causes. [Contrary] to the Court's suggestion, the ordinance regulates only a subcategory of expression that causes injuries based on "race, color, creed, religion or gender," not a subcategory that involves discussions that concern those characteristics. [Contrary] to the suggestion of the majority, the St. Paul ordinance does not regulate expression based on viewpoint. [Just] as the ordinance would prohibit a Muslim from hoisting a sign claiming that all Catholics were misbegotten, so the ordinance would bar a Catholic from hoisting a similar sign attacking Muslims. The St. Paul ordinance is evenhanded. [To] extend the Court's pugilistic metaphor, the St. Paul ordinance simply bans punches "below the belt"—by either party. It does not, therefore, favor one side of any debate.

Finally, it is noteworthy that the St. Paul ordinance is, as construed by the Court today, quite narrow. The St. Paul ordinance does not ban all "hate speech," nor does it ban, say, all cross-burnings or all swastika displays. [Petitioner] is free to burn a cross to announce a rally or to express his views about racial supremacy, he may do so on private property or public land, at day or at night, so long as the burning is not so threatening and so directed at an individual as to "by its very [execution] inflict injury." Taken together, these several considerations persuade me that the St. Paul ordinance is not an unconstitutional content-based regulation of speech. Thus, were the ordinance not overbroad, I would vote to uphold it.

THE MEANING AND IMPLICATIONS OF R.A.V.

1. ***The hate speech debate.*** Did the Supreme Court in R.A.V. wrongly discourage efforts to control hate speech? Should existing exceptions to First Amendment protection have been analogized or expanded? Recall that in Beauharnais v. Illinois (1952; p. 1003 above), the Court found no First Amendment bar against a law prohibiting "expos[ure of] the citizens of any race, color, creed or religion to contempt, derision, or obloquy," reasoning that libel, whether individual or group, lies outside the First Amendment altogether. Beauharnais has never been overruled. Is this decision a basis for laws like St. Paul's? Later decisions have unsettled its foundations. New York Times v. Sullivan assumed libel limited to a provably false statements of fact and to speech "of and concerning" an individual, not the government in general. Does this undermine the notion that group libel is unprotected? Might it be countered that a verbal attack on a group of private individuals on the basis of their race is a far cry from seditious libel, and thus implicates lesser First Amendment concern than the verdict in New York Times?

The R.A.V. concurrences found the St. Paul ordinance overbroad if viewed as a fighting words ordinance because it encompassed non-violent responses. Could a narrower hate speech law than St. Paul's survive First Amendment review under Chaplinsky? Alternatively, should St. Paul's law (or Stanford's) have survived even as written under the forgotten branch of Chaplinsky that included words that "by their very utterance inflict injury" in addition to words that tend to incite immediate breaches of the peace? On this view, racist or other bigoted epithets should be no more protected when they cause fright or flight than when they cause fights, for in either case they are "no essential part of any exposition of ideas." For an argument that this strand of Chaplinsky is still extant or worth reviving, see Grey, "Responding to Abusive Speech on Campus: A Model Statute," Reconstruction 50, Winter 1990 (arguing against protection for any "words that would justify imposition of tort liability for intentional infliction of emotional distress"); Grey, "Civil Rights vs. Civil Liberties: The Case of Discriminatory Verbal Harassment," 8 Soc. Phil. & Pol. 81 (1991). Are the unprotected categories enumerated in Chaplinsky a nonexhaustive list that may be extended to hate speech as a new category of speech that is "of such slight social value as a step to truth" that any benefit that may be derived from them is clearly outweighed by social interests? For such arguments, see Delgado, "Words that Wound: A Tort Action for Racial Insults, Epithets, and Name-Calling," 17 Harv. C.R.-C.L. L. Rev. 133 (1982); Matsuda, "Public Response to Racist Speech: Considering the Victim's Story," 87 Mich. L. Rev. 2320 (1989); Waldron, The Harm in Hate Speech (2012).

Those opposing such initiatives object that hate speech regulation "would endanger fundamental free speech values," "violate the cardinal principles that speech restrictions must be content-and viewpoint-neutral," and go well beyond the narrow bounds the Court has imposed on the "fighting words" exception. Strossen, "Regulating Racist Speech on Campus: A Modest Proposal?" 1990 Duke L.J. 484; see also Fried, "A New First Amendment Jurisprudence: A Threat to Liberty," 59 U. Chi. L. Rev. 225 (1992) (assailing "those who promulgate these regulations [for] assign[ing] to themselves the authority to determine which ideas are false and which false ideas people may not express as they choose"); Weinstein, "A Constitutional Roadmap to the Regulation of Campus Hate Speech," 38 Wayne L. Rev. 163 (1991) (condemning as "thought control" the purpose "to combat racism by preventing its contagion from infecting the hearts and minds of a new generation of potential racists and sexists"); Lewis, Freedom for the Thought That We Hate (2007) (arguing that hate speech regulations may be overenforced, resulting in the suppression of unpopular ideas).

Other opponents suggest that such regulations are unduly paternalistic as well as misguided because articulate diatribe about racial inferiority, which is not proscribable as hate speech, might well be more hurtful to an individual and contribute more to the social construction of racism than do vulgar racial epithets, which are disfavored under conventional social norms and thus more easily discounted or ignored. See Henry Louis Gates, Jr., "Let Them Talk," The New Republic, Sept. 20, 1993; Karst, "Boundaries and Reasons: Freedom of Expression and the Subordination of Groups," 1990 Ill. L. Rev. 95 (arguing that "for women and for the members of racial and ethnic minorities a first amendment doctrine that offers less protection to 'low value' speech is not just unhelpful; it is dangerous" because a subordinated group's "escape from subordinate status is accomplished primarily though persuasion," and "precisely because an important part of a group's subordination consists in silencing, their emancipation requires a generously defined freedom of expression"). For an argument that grassroots organization of minority voices is preferable to top-down disciplinary solutions to racist speech, see Calleros, "Paternalism, Counterspeech, and Campus Hate-Speech [Codes]," 27 Ariz. St. L.J. 1249 (1995). For a reply to these various inefficacy arguments, see Delgado & Yun, " 'The Speech We Hate': First Amendment Totalism, The ACLU and the Principle of Dialogic Politics," 27 Ariz. St. L.J. 1281 (1995).

In Matal v. Tam (2017; p. 1343 below), Simon Tam challenged the denial of trademark registration for his band name "The Slants." Tam argued in that by reclaiming a racial slur as the name of the rock band, he would "help to 'reclaim' the term and drain it of its denigrating force." The Court did not engage with this argument directly, but reemphasized that speech may not be banned merely because it "expressed ideas that offend," even if the government's intent is to protect marginalized groups.

2. ***Hate speech: a comparative perspective.*** Does R.A.V. make it too difficult to prosecute or regulate speech directed at expressing hatred on the basis of race or any other group characteristic that is protected against discriminatory conduct? In contrast to the U.S. approach, in which racist hate speech is protected unless it constitutes a threat (see note 6 below), nations like Great Britain, Northern Ireland, Israel and Australia regulate racist hate speech "based on the idea that hate speech that vilifies a group poses a more serious threat to the public order than insults directed at a person for his or her personal characteristics," and nations like Canada, Denmark, France, Germany, and the Netherlands have laws against racist hate speech "premised on the need to protect human dignity 'quite apart from any interest in safeguarding public order.' " Bell, "Restraining the Heartless: Racist Speech and Minority Rights," 84 Ind. L.J. 963 (2009). Note too that the International Covenant on Civil and Political Rights, Art. 20(2), provides that "any advocacy of national, racial or religious hatred that constitutes incitement to discrimination, hostility or violence shall be prohibited by law." Why might the United States be an outlier among comparable nations in its robust protection of such speech?

3. ***Distinguishing the regulation of hate speech from the regulation of hate crimes.*** One term after R.A.V., the Court confronted a First Amendment challenge to a state law enhancing the sentence for bias-motivated assault. Two state supreme courts—Wisconsin and Ohio—had reasoned that aggravating the penalty for racially motivated hate crimes violated the principle of viewpoint neutrality set forth in R.A.V. Just as government may not selectively regulate unprotected speech such as fighting words on the basis of the viewpoint of the speaker, these state courts reasoned, so government may not regulate conduct based solely on the viewpoint of an actor. For an articulation of this position, see Gellman, "Sticks and Stones Can Put You in Jail, But Can Words Increase Your Sentence?," 39 UCLA L. Rev. 333 (1991).

In **Wisconsin v. Mitchell**, 508 U.S. 476 (1993), the Supreme Court unanimously rejected that argument, drawing a sharp distinction between the regulation of speech and conduct. The effect of Mitchell was to limit the holding of R.A.V. to viewpoint-selective laws aimed expressly at otherwise unprotected words or symbols. Chief Justice REHNQUIST delivered the opinion of the Court: "On the evening of October 7, 1989, a group of young black men and boys, including Mitchell, gathered at an apartment complex in Kenosha, Wisconsin. Several members of the group discussed a scene from the motion picture 'Mississippi Burning,' in which a white man beat a young black boy who was praying. The group moved outside and Mitchell asked them: 'Do you all feel hyped up to move on some white people?' Shortly thereafter, a young white boy approached the group on the opposite side of the street where they were standing. As the boy walked by, Mitchell said: 'You all want to fuck somebody up? There goes a white boy; go get him.' Mitchell counted to three and pointed in the boy's direction. The group ran towards the boy, beat him severely, and stole his tennis shoes. The boy was rendered unconscious and remained in a coma for four days.

"[Mitchell] was convicted of aggravated battery. That offense ordinarily carries a maximum sentence of two years' imprisonment. But because the jury found that Mitchell had intentionally selected his victim because of the boy's race, the maximum sentence for Mitchell's offense was increased to seven years under [a Wisconsin] provision [that] enhances the maximum penalty for an offense whenever the defendant 'intentionally selects the person against whom the crime . . . is committed . . . because of the race, religion, color, disability, sexual orientation, national origin or ancestry of that person. . . .'

"[Mitchell] argues that the Wisconsin penalty-enhancement statute is invalid because it punishes the defendant's discriminatory motive, or reason, for acting. But [a defendant's motive for committing an offense is traditionally a factor considered by a judge at sentencing, and] motive plays the same role under the Wisconsin statute as it does under federal and state antidiscrimination laws, which we have previously upheld against constitutional challenge. Title VII, for example, makes it unlawful for an employer to discriminate against an employee 'because of such individual's race, color, religion, sex, or national origin.' [In] R.A.V. v. St. Paul, we cited Title VII [as] an example of a permissible content-neutral regulation of conduct.

"Nothing in our decision last Term in R.A.V. compels a different result here. [W]hereas the ordinance struck down in R.A.V. was explicitly directed at expression (i.e., 'speech' or 'messages'), the statute in this case is aimed at conduct unprotected by the First Amendment. Moreover, the Wisconsin statute singles out for enhancement bias-inspired conduct because this conduct is thought to inflict greater individual and societal harm. For example, according to the State and its amici, bias-motivated crimes are more likely to provoke retaliatory crimes, inflict distinct emotional harms on their victims, and incite community unrest. The State's desire to redress these perceived harms provides an adequate explanation for its penalty-enhancement provision over and above mere disagreement with offenders' beliefs or biases. As Blackstone said long ago, 'it is but reasonable that among crimes of different natures those should be most severely punished, which are the most destructive of the public safety and happiness.' 4 W. Blackstone, Commentaries *16. [Reversed.]"

4. ***The role of motive in R.A.V. and Mitchell.*** Mitchell permitted the state to enhance punishment for a crime motivated by the victim's race. In so doing, the Court focused heavily on the material consequences of such conduct: it assumed that such violence has greater in terrorem and incendiary effects on society than ordinary violence. What if the state instead enhanced punishment for a crime "motivated by the defendant's beliefs about race," or by "the defendant's attempt to communicate a racist message"?

Such crimes might have similar effects to those described in Mitchell. But for the view that such laws might violate the First Amendment, even though Mitchell was correctly decided, see Tribe, "The Mystery of Motive, Private and [Public]," 1993 Sup. Ct. Rev. 1. To what extent was the debate between the majority and the concurring opinions in R.A.V. really about St. Paul's true motive in enacting the ordinance? As a law professor, now-Supreme Court Justice Elena Kagan argued that "half hidden beneath a swirl of doctrinal formulations," the Justices disagreed about whether the hate-crime law was "purely censorial—a simple desire to blot out ideas" or "an effort by the government, divorced from mere hostility toward ideas, to counter a severe and objectively ascertainable harm." Kagan, "Private Speech, Public Purpose: The Role of Governmental Motive in First Amendment Doctrine," 63 U. Chi. L. Rev. 413, 422 (1996). Was the law in Mitchell devoid of censorial motive?

5. ***Hostile environment sexual or racial harassment.*** Federal civil rights statutes barring employment discrimination have been construed to bar sexual or racial harassment in the workplace, including by the creation of a racially or sexually hostile environment that adversely affects working conditions. After R.A.V. and Mitchell, are such laws constitutional? For the argument that such laws raise serious First Amendment questions, see Browne, "Title VII as Censorship: Hostile-Environment Harassment and the First Amendment," 52 Ohio State L.J. 481 (1991); Volokh, "Freedom of Speech and Workplace Harassment," 39 UCLA L. Rev. 1791 (1992). For a defense based partly on the notion that employees in the workplace context are effectively a captive audience, see Fallon, "Sexual Harassment, Content-Neutrality, and the First Amendment Dog That Didn't Bark," 1994 S. Ct. Rev. 1. See also Strossen, "Regulating Workplace Sexual Harassment and Upholding the First Amendment—Avoiding a Collision," 37 Vill. L. Rev. 757 (1992).

Analogous issues arise on university campuses under Title VI's protection against a racially hostile educational environment and Title IX's protection against a hostile educational environment based on sex discrimination. See, e.g., Department of Education, Office for Civil Rights, "Racial Incidents and Harassment Against Students at Educational Institutions; Investigative Guidance," 59 Federal Register 47 (1994). Thus, in one highly publicized incident, the University of Oklahoma expelled two students who led fellow fraternity-members in a racist chant stating a commitment to exclude African-Americans from the fraternity and alluding to lynching. Some commentators deemed the expulsion unconstitutional, noting that "racist speech is constitutionally protected, just as is expression of other contemptible ideas; and universities may not discipline students based on their speech." Volokh, "No, It's Not Constitutional for the University of Oklahoma to Expel Students for Racist Speech," March 10, 2015, available at https://www.washingtonpost.com/news/volokh-conspiracy/wp/2015/03/10/no-a-public-university-may-not-expel-students-for-racist-speech/. Consider the contrary view that the students "are being expelled not for their opinions per se, but because their speech was a form of discriminatory conduct that would create a hostile educational environment for black students" because it "was literally designed to inculcate the value of racial discrimination by making pledges recite their commitment never to admit a black member to the fraternity." Feldman, "Oklahoma's Right to Expel Frat Boys," March 11, 2015, available at http://www.bloombergview.com/articles/2015-03-11/oklahoma-s-right-to-expel-frat-boys.

6. ***The problem of true threats.*** When does racist or other hateful speech escalate to a threat to cause bodily injury? In dicta in R.A.V., Justice Scalia assumed that threats are an unprotected category of speech and that threats of violence against the President are a permissibly proscribable subcategory of that category of unprotected speech. Are true threats always proscribable? Recall the discussion of threats in NAACP v. Claiborne Hardware and Planned Parenthood v. ACLA at pp. 981 and 982 above.

In **Watts v. United States**, 394 U.S. 705 (1969), the Court reversed, per curiam, a conviction under a 1917 law making it a felony "knowingly and willfully" to make "any threat to take the life" of the President. Petitioner had said at a public rally, "Now I have already received my draft classification as 1–A and I have got to report for my physical this Monday coming. I am not going. If they ever make me carry a rifle, the first man I want to get in my sights is L.B.J. They are not going to make me kill my black brothers." The opinion stated: "What is a threat must be distinguished from what is constitutionally protected speech. [We] do not believe that the kind of political hyperbole indulged in by petitioner fits within that statutory term. [We] agree with petitioner that his only offense [was] 'a kind of very crude offensive method of stating a political opposition to the President.' Taken in context, and regarding the expressly conditional nature of the statement and the reaction of the listeners [laughter], we do not see how it could be interpreted otherwise."

Would the cross-burning in R.A.V. have been subject to prosecution under a statute aimed at true threats generally? At threats based on race? Is a statute that focuses on cross-burning as a threat of violence more likely to satisfy the First Amendment than was the ordinance invalidated in R.A.V.? Is a ban on cross-burning intended to intimidate analogous to the ban on death threats against the President? Consider these questions in light of the following case:

Virginia v. Black

538 U.S. 343, 123 S. Ct. 1536, 155 L. Ed. 2d 535 (2003).

■ JUSTICE O'CONNOR announced the judgment of the Court and delivered the opinion of the Court with respect to Parts I, II, and III, and an opinion with respect to Parts IV and V, in which CHIEF JUSTICE REHNQUIST, and JUSTICES STEVENS and BREYER join.

In this case we consider whether the Commonwealth of Virginia's statute banning cross burning with "an intent to intimidate a person or group of persons" violates the First Amendment. Va. Code Ann. § 18.2–423 (1996). We conclude that while a State, consistent with the First Amendment, may ban cross burning carried out with the intent to intimidate, the provision in the Virginia statute treating any cross burning as prima facie evidence of intent to intimidate renders the statute unconstitutional in its current form.

I. Respondents [were convicted] of violating Virginia's cross-burning statute, § 18.2–423. That statute provides:

"It shall be unlawful for any person or persons, with the intent of intimidating any person or group of persons, to burn, or cause to be burned, a cross on the property of another, a highway or other public place. Any person who shall violate any provision of this section shall be guilty of a Class 6 felony.

"Any such burning of a cross shall be prima facie evidence of an intent to intimidate a person or group of persons."

[Black was convicted under the statute after a jury trial in which the jury was instructed that "the burning of a cross by itself is sufficient evidence from which you may infer the required intent" to intimidate. The Supreme Court of Virginia reversed the conviction, holding that the Virginia cross-burning statute "is analytically indistinguishable from the ordinance found unconstitutional in R.A.V."]

II. Cross burning originated in the 14th century as a means for Scottish tribes to signal each other. [Cross] burning in this country, however, long ago became unmoored from its Scottish ancestry. Burning a cross in the United States is inextricably intertwined with the history of the Ku Klux Klan. The first Ku Klux Klan [fought] Reconstruction and the corresponding drive to allow freed blacks to participate in the political process, [imposing] "a veritable reign of terror" throughout the South. [In] response, Congress passed what is now known as the Ku Klux Klan Act. [By] the end of Reconstruction in 1877, the first Klan no longer existed. The genesis of the second Klan began in 1905. [From] the inception of the second Klan, cross burnings have been used to communicate both threats of violence and messages of shared ideology. [Often,] the Klan used cross burnings as a tool of intimidation and a threat of impending violence. [The] decision of this Court in Brown v. Board of Education, along with the civil rights movement of the 1950's and 1960's, sparked another outbreak of Klan violence. These acts of violence included bombings, beatings, shootings, stabbings, and mutilations. Members of the Klan burned crosses on the lawns of those associated with the civil rights movement, assaulted the Freedom Riders, bombed churches, and murdered blacks as well as whites whom the Klan viewed as sympathetic toward the civil rights movement.

Throughout the history of the Klan, cross burnings have also remained potent symbols of shared group identity and ideology. The burning cross became a symbol of the Klan itself and a central feature of Klan gatherings. [At] Klan gatherings across the country, cross burning became the climax of the rally or the initiation. [Throughout] the Klan's history, the Klan continued to use the burning cross in their ritual ceremonies. For its own members, the cross was a sign of celebration and ceremony. [And] cross burnings featured prominently in Klan rallies when the Klan attempted to move toward more nonviolent tactics to stop integration. In short, a burning cross has remained a symbol of Klan ideology and of Klan unity.

To this day, regardless of whether the message is a political one or whether the message is also meant to intimidate, the burning of a cross is a "symbol of hate." And while cross burning sometimes carries no intimidating message, at other times the intimidating message is the only message conveyed. For example, when a cross burning is directed at a particular person not affiliated with the Klan, the burning cross often serves as a message of intimidation, designed to inspire in the victim a fear of bodily harm. Moreover, the history of violence associated with the Klan shows that the possibility of injury or death is not just hypothetical. The person who burns a cross directed at a particular person often is making a serious threat, meant to coerce the victim to comply with the Klan's wishes unless the victim is willing to risk the wrath of the Klan. [In] sum, while a burning cross does not inevitably convey a message of intimidation, often the cross burner intends that the recipients of the message fear for their lives. And when a cross burning is used to intimidate, few if any messages are more powerful.

III. A. [We] have long recognized that the government may regulate certain categories of expression consistent with the Constitution [such as fighting words and incitement. Chaplinsky; Brandenburg]. And the First Amendment also permits a State to ban a "true threat." Watts. "True threats" encompass those statements where the speaker means to communicate a serious expression of an intent to commit an act of unlawful violence to a particular individual or group of individuals. The speaker need not actually intend to carry out the threat. Rather, a prohibition on true threats "protect[s] individuals from the fear of violence" and "from the disruption that fear engenders," in addition to protecting people "from the possibility that the threatened violence will occur." Intimidation in the constitutionally proscribable sense of the word is a type of true threat, where a speaker directs a threat to a person or group of persons with the intent of placing the victim in fear of bodily harm or death. [Some] cross burnings fit within this meaning of intimidating speech.

B. The Supreme Court of Virginia ruled that in light of R.A.V. v. City of St. Paul, even if it is constitutional to ban cross burning in a content-neutral manner, the Virginia cross-burning statute is unconstitutional because it discriminates on the basis of content and viewpoint. [We] disagree. [We] did not hold in R.A.V. that the First Amendment prohibits all forms of content-based discrimination within a proscribable area of speech. [Indeed,] we noted that it would be constitutional to ban only a particular type of threat [such as] "those threats of violence that are directed against the President." [Similarly,] Virginia's statute does not run afoul of the First Amendment insofar as it bans cross burning with intent to intimidate. Unlike the statute at issue in R.A.V., the Virginia statute does not single out for opprobrium only that speech directed toward "one of the specified disfavored topics." It does not matter whether an individual burns a cross with intent to intimidate because of the victim's race, gender, or religion, or because of the victim's "political affiliation, union membership, or homosexuality." Moreover, as a factual matter it is not true that cross burners direct their intimidating conduct solely to racial or religious minorities.

The First Amendment permits Virginia to outlaw cross burnings done with the intent to intimidate because burning a cross is a particularly virulent form of intimidation. Instead of prohibiting all intimidating messages, Virginia may choose to regulate this subset of intimidating messages in light of cross burning's long and pernicious history as a signal of impending violence.

IV. The Supreme Court of Virginia ruled in the alternative that Virginia's cross-burning statute was unconstitutionally overbroad due to its provision stating that "[a]ny such burning of a cross shall be prima facie evidence of an intent to intimidate a person or group of persons." [Respondents] contend that the provision is unconstitutional on its face. [The] prima facie evidence provision, as interpreted by the jury instruction [in Black's case], renders the statute unconstitutional. As construed by the jury instruction, the prima facie provision strips away the very reason why a State may ban cross burning with the intent to intimidate. The prima facie evidence provision permits a jury to convict in every cross-burning case in which defendants exercise their constitutional right not to put on a defense [and] the Commonwealth to arrest, prosecute, and convict a person based solely on the fact of cross burning itself.

It is apparent that the provision as so interpreted " 'would create an unacceptable risk of the suppression of ideas.' " The act of burning a cross may mean that a person is engaging in constitutionally proscribable intimidation. But that same act may mean only that the person is engaged in core political speech. [The] prima facie provision makes no effort to distinguish among these different types of cross burnings. [It] may be true that a cross burning, even at a political rally, arouses a sense of anger or hatred among the vast majority of citizens who see a burning cross. But this sense of anger or hatred is not sufficient to ban all cross burnings. As Gerald Gunther has stated, " 'The lesson I have drawn from my childhood in Nazi Germany and my happier adult life in this country is the need to walk the sometimes difficult path of denouncing the bigot's hateful ideas with all my power, yet at the same time challenging any community's attempt to suppress hateful ideas by force of law.' " Casper, "Gerry," 55 Stan. L. Rev. 647, 649 (2002). The prima facie evidence provision in this case ignores all of the contextual factors that are necessary to decide whether a particular cross burning is intended to intimidate. The First Amendment does not permit such a shortcut. For these reasons, the prima facie evidence provision, as interpreted through the jury instruction and as applied in [Black's] case, is unconstitutional on its face.

■ JUSTICE STEVENS, concurring.

Cross burning with "an intent to intimidate" unquestionably qualifies as the kind of threat that is unprotected by the First Amendment. For the reasons stated in the separate opinions that Justice White and I wrote in R.A.V., that simple proposition provides a sufficient basis for upholding the basic prohibition in the Virginia statute even though it does not cover other types of threatening expressive conduct.

■ JUSTICE SCALIA, with whom JUSTICE THOMAS joins, concurring in part, concurring in the judgment in part, and dissenting in part.

I agree with the Court that, under our decision in R.A.V., a State may, without infringing the First Amendment, prohibit cross burning carried out with the intent to intimidate. [But] I believe there is no justification for the plurality's apparent decision to invalidate [the prima-facie-evidence] provision on its face.

I. ["Prima] facie evidence" [is] evidence that suffices, on its own, to establish a particular fact. But it is hornbook law that this is true only to the extent that the evidence goes unrebutted. [Presentation] of evidence that a defendant burned a cross in public view is automatically sufficient, on its own, to support an inference that the defendant intended to intimidate only until the defendant comes forward with some evidence in rebuttal.

II. The question presented, then, is whether, given this understanding of the term "prima facie evidence," the cross-burning statute is constitutional. [The] plurality is correct [that] some individuals who engage in protected speech may, because of the prima-facie-evidence provision, be subject to conviction. [But the] class of persons that the plurality contemplates could impermissibly be convicted under § 18.2–423 includes only those individuals who (1) burn a cross in public view, (2) do not intend to intimidate, (3) are nonetheless charged and prosecuted, and (4) refuse to present a defense. Conceding (quite generously, in my view) that this class of persons exists, it cannot possibly give rise to a viable facial challenge, not even with the aid of our First Amendment overbreadth doctrine. [The] notion that the set of cases identified by the plurality in which convictions might improperly be obtained is sufficiently large to render the statute substantially overbroad is fanciful.

■ JUSTICE SOUTER, with whom JUSTICE KENNEDY and JUSTICE GINSBURG join, concurring in the judgment in part and dissenting in part.

I agree with the majority that the Virginia statute makes a content-based distinction within the category of punishable intimidating or threatening expression, the very type of distinction we considered in R.A.V. I disagree that any exception should save Virginia's law from unconstitutionality under the holding in R.A.V. or any acceptable variation of it.

[R.A.V.] defines the special virulence exception to the rule barring content-based subclasses of categorically proscribable expression this way: prohibition by subcategory is nonetheless constitutional if it is made "entirely" on the "basis" of "the very reason" that "the entire class of speech at issue is proscribable" at all. The Court explained that when the subcategory is confined to the most obviously proscribable instances, "no significant danger of idea or viewpoint discrimination exists," and the explanation was rounded out with some illustrative examples. None of them, however, resembles the case before us. [This] case [does not] present any analogy to the statute prohibiting threats against the President. The content discrimination in that statute relates to the addressee of the threat and reflects the special risks and costs associated with threatening the President. Again, however, threats against the President are not generally identified by reference to the content of any message that may accompany the threat, let alone any viewpoint, and there is no obvious correlation in fact between victim and message. Millions of statements are made about the President every day on every subject and from every standpoint; threats of violence are not an integral feature of any one subject or viewpoint as distinct from others. Differential treatment of threats against the President, then, selects nothing but special risks, not special messages. A content-based proscription of cross burning, on the other hand, may be a subtle effort to ban not only the intensity of the intimidation cross burning causes when done to threaten, but also the particular message of white supremacy that is broadcast even by nonthreatening cross burning.

[No] content-based statute should survive [under] R.A.V. without a high probability that no "official suppression of ideas is afoot." I believe the prima facie evidence provision stands in the way of any finding of such a high probability here. [As] I see the likely significance of the evidence provision, its primary effect is to skew jury deliberations toward conviction in cases where the evidence of intent to intimidate is relatively weak and arguably consistent with a solely ideological reason for burning. [To] the extent the prima facie evidence provision skews prosecutions, then, it skews the statute toward suppressing ideas. [Since] no R.A.V. exception can save the statute as content based, it can only survive if narrowly tailored to serve a compelling state interest, a stringent test the statute cannot pass; a content-neutral statute banning intimidation would achieve the same object without singling out particular content.

■ JUSTICE THOMAS, dissenting.

In every culture, certain things acquire meaning well beyond what outsiders can comprehend. That goes for both the sacred and the profane. I believe that cross burning is the paradigmatic example of the latter. Although I agree with the majority's conclusion that it is constitutionally permissible to "ban . . . cross burning carried out with intent to intimidate," I believe that the majority errs in imputing an expressive component to the activity in question. [In] our culture, cross burning has almost invariably meant lawlessness and understandably instills in its victims well-grounded fear of physical violence.

Virginia's experience has been no exception. [In] the early 1950s the people of Virginia viewed cross burning as creating an intolerable atmosphere of terror. [At] the time the statute was enacted, racial segregation was not only the prevailing practice, but also the law in Virginia. [It] strains credulity to suggest that a state legislature that adopted a litany of segregationist laws self-contradictorily intended to squelch the segregationist message. Even for segregationists, violent and terroristic conduct, the Siamese twin of cross burning, was intolerable. [Accordingly], this statute prohibits only conduct, not expression. And, just as one cannot burn down someone's house to make a political point and then seek refuge in the First Amendment, those who hate cannot terrorize and intimidate to make their point. In light of my conclusion that the statute here addresses only conduct, there is no need to analyze it under any of our First Amendment tests.

Are apparent threats protected if posted in social media? If they emulate an artistic form like rap? In **Elonis v. United States**, 575 U.S. ___, 135 S. Ct. 2001 (2015), a man who was angry that his wife had left him was convicted for posting apparently threatening statements about his former wife in rap-lyric form on Facebook (e.g., "Did you know that it's illegal for me to say I want to kill my wife? . . . It's one of the only sentences that I'm not allowed to say. . . .") under 18 U.S.C. § 875(c), which makes it a crime to transmit in interstate commerce "any communication containing any threat . . . to injure the person of another." The Court overturned the conviction on the non-constitutional ground that the statute implicitly required a showing of purpose to make a threat or knowledge that the communication will be viewed as a threat, which had not been charged to the jury.

Justice ALITO, concurring in part and dissenting in part, would have added that a finding of recklessness was sufficient to convict. He argued that conviction on recklessness grounds would not violate the First Amendment: "It is settled that the Constitution does not protect true threats. See Virginia v. Black; R. A. V. And there are good reasons for that rule: True threats inflict great harm and have little if any social value. A threat may cause serious emotional stress for the person threatened and those who care about that person, and a threat may lead to a violent confrontation. It is true that a communication containing a threat may include other statements that have value and are entitled to protection. But that does not justify constitutional protection for the threat itself.

"Elonis argues that the First Amendment protects a threat if the person making the statement does not actually intend to cause harm. [But] whether or not the person making a threat intends to cause harm, the damage is the same. And the fact that making a threat may have a therapeutic or cathartic effect for the speaker is not sufficient to justify constitutional protection. [Elonis] also claims his threats were constitutionally protected works of art. Words like his, he contends, are shielded by the First Amendment because they are similar to words uttered by rappers and singers in public performances and recordings. To make this point, his brief includes a lengthy excerpt from the lyrics of a rap song in which a very well-compensated rapper imagines killing his ex-wife and dumping her body in a lake. If this celebrity can utter such words, Elonis pleads, amateurs like him should be able to post similar things on social media. But context matters. Taken in context, lyrics in songs that are performed for an audience or sold in recorded form are unlikely to be interpreted as a real threat to a real person. Statements on social media that are pointedly directed at their victims, by contrast, are much more likely to be taken seriously. To hold otherwise would grant a license to anyone who is clever enough to dress up a real threat in the guise of rap lyrics, a parody, or something similar."

For suppression of a threat to be permissible, does the First Amendment require subjective intent on the part of the threatener, or would an objective test pass muster? Because the Court decided the Elonis case on statutory grounds, the question remains open. Is a negligent threat any less harmful to the threatened individual than is a threat made with intent to cause harm? What about a threat made recklessly? Is Justice Alito correct that the fact that threatening communication might include other statements of value does not justify constitutional protection for the threat itself? Should it matter that the threat was made over the internet? That it was made as part of an artistic expression? Should the fact that threats have become more commonplace in new media forums and in popular music affect the analysis? For an argument that online harassment causes serious psychological and physical harm and that its trivialization, particularly in the context of threats of violence against female writers online, entrenches gender inequality, see Citron, Hate Crimes in Cyberspace (2014).

SECTION 5. SEXUALLY EXPLICIT EXPRESSION

In Chaplinsky, the Court categorized "obscenity" as expression outside of First Amendment protection, because it is "of such slight social value as a step to truth that any benefit that may be derived from [it] is outweighed by the social interest in order and morality." The Court has continued to regard obscenity as an unprotected category of speech, although it has struggled mightily with the question of how to define that category—how to delineate the area excluded from constitutional protection so that properly protected speech would not also be curtailed. The Court has added an additional category of sexually explicit speech to the Chaplinsky list by holding that child pornography is unprotected speech. If speech is sexually explicit but is not obscene and does not constitute child pornography, it is within the realm of First Amendment protection, but the Court has wrestled with the question whether it should occupy a subordinate position as "lower value" speech. A majority of the Court has never agreed with the creation of such a formal low-value category for sexually explicit speech, but the Court has nonetheless upheld a number of restrictions on such speech through balancing analysis. These developments are examined in turn in this section.

What justifications might there be for restraining sexually explicit speech? To safeguard against the violent or antisocial conduct that it might cause? Under clear and present danger or under an incitement test? To avoid the "corrupting" of individual morals and character by the "sin of obscenity"—whether or not improper behavior results? To protect the sensibilities of the audience by safeguarding against the risk of shock from offensive sexual materials? To protect children against exposure to sexual materials because of the greater susceptibility of the immature to their harmful effects? To protect society's moral standards against erosion? To preserve or improve the quality of life or the tone of the community?

Questions such as these assume that obscenity may belong in the First Amendment ballpark, thus triggering a requirement of some justification. But are sexually explicit materials properly considered a variety of "speech"? Are they more aptly described as aids to sexual arousal or sexual activity itself? Do they communicate ideas and appeal to the intellectual process, or do they simply induce a purely physical effect? Which if any of the values underlying First Amendment protection justify the imposition of First Amendment scrutiny here? The arguments from self-government and democracy seem largely directed at political speech. The arguments from the marketplace of ideas and the search for truth are broader and seem to include scientific debate as well. But do they also extend to artistic and literary communication? Note that the Court's definitions of obscenity in the cases that follow protect materials of certain "literary, artistic, political, or scientific value" and that the obscenity category typically focuses on hard-core pornography. Can such materials nevertheless claim First Amendment protection? Do they serve the autonomy rationale for protecting speech?

OBSCENITY

The Court's first direct encounter with the constitutionality of obscenity control took place fifteen years after Chaplinsky, in Roth. The Warren Court's attempt to define unprotected obscenity in Roth spawned a tortuous period of divided rulings, until a new definition of obscenity was agreed upon in 1973 by the Burger Court in Miller and Paris Adult, below. The Miller test continues to define unprotected obscenity today.

Roth v. United States; Alberts v. California

354 U.S. 476, 77 S. Ct. 1304, 1 L. Ed. 2d 1498 (1957).

[In these cases, the Court sustained the validity of federal and state obscenity laws without reaching the question of whether any particular materials to which the laws were applied were obscene. Roth, a New York publisher and seller, was convicted of mailing obscene advertising and an obscene book in violation of a federal statute barring the mailing of "obscenity." Alberts, engaged in the mail order business, was convicted under a California law for "lewdly keeping for sale obscene and indecent books" and "publishing an obscene advertisement of them."]

■ JUSTICE BRENNAN delivered the opinion of the Court.

The dispositive question is whether obscenity is utterance within the area of protected speech and press. Although this is the first time the question has been squarely presented [here], expressions found in numerous opinions indicate that this Court has always assumed that obscenity is not protected by the freedoms of speech and press. In light [of] history, it is apparent that the unconditional phrasing of the First Amendment was not intended to protect every utterance. [T]here is sufficiently contemporaneous evidence to show that obscenity [like libel, see Beauharnais] was outside the protection intended for speech and [press]. All ideas having even the slightest redeeming social importance—unorthodox ideas, controversial ideas, even ideas hateful to the prevailing climate of opinion—have the full protection of the guaranties, unless excludable because they encroach upon the limited area of more important interests. But implicit in the history of the First Amendment is the rejection of obscenity as utterly without redeeming social importance. This rejection for that reason is mirrored in the universal judgment that obscenity should be restrained, reflected in the international agreement of over 50 nations, in the obscenity laws of all of the 48 States, and in the 20 obscenity laws enacted by the Congress from 1842 to 1956. This is the same judgment expressed [in Chaplinsky]. [We] hold that obscenity is not within the area of constitutionally protected speech or press.

It is strenuously urged that these obscenity statutes offend the constitutional guaranties because they punish incitation to impure sexual *thoughts,* not shown to be related to any overt antisocial conduct which is or may be incited in the persons stimulated to such *thoughts.* [It] is insisted that the constitutional guaranties are violated because convictions may be had without proof either that obscene material will perceptibly create a clear and present danger of antisocial conduct, or will probably induce its recipients to such conduct. But, in light of our holding that obscenity is not protected speech, the complete answer to this argument is [in Beauharnais].

However, sex and obscenity are not synonymous. Obscene material is material which deals with sex in a manner appealing to prurient interest.[1] The portrayal of sex, e.g., in art, literature and scientific works, is not itself sufficient reason to deny material the constitutional protection of freedom of speech and press. Sex, a great and mysterious motive force in human life, has indisputably been a subject of absorbing interest to mankind through the ages; it is one of the vital problems of human interest and public [concern]. The fundamental freedoms of speech and press [are] indispensable to [our free society's] continued growth. [It] is therefore vital that the standards for judging obscenity safeguard the protection of freedom of speech and press for material which does not treat sex in a manner appealing to prurient interest.

The early leading standard of obscenity allowed material to be judged merely by the effect of an isolated excerpt upon particularly susceptible persons. Regina v. Hicklin, [1868] L.R. 3 Q.B. 360 [which defined obscenity as material tending "to deprave and corrupt those whose minds are open to

[1] I.e., material having a tendency to excite lustful thoughts. Webster's New International Dictionary (Unabridged, 2d ed., 1949) defines *prurient,* in pertinent part, as follows: "Itching; longing; uneasy with desire or longing; of persons, having itching, morbid, or lascivious longings; of desire, curiosity or propensity, lewd."

[We] perceive no significant difference between the meaning of obscenity developed in the case law and the definition of the A.L.I., Model Penal Code (Tent. Draft No. 6, 1957): "[A] thing is obscene if, considered as a whole, its predominant appeal is to prurient interest, i.e., a shameful or morbid interest in nudity, sex, or excretion, and if it goes substantially beyond customary limits of candor in description or representation of such matters." [Footnote by the Court.]

such immoral influences"]. Some American courts adopted this standard but later decisions have rejected it and substituted this test: whether to the average person, applying contemporary community standards, the dominant theme of the material taken as a whole appeals to prurient interest. The Hicklin test, judging obscenity by the effect of isolated passages upon the most susceptible persons, might well encompass material legitimately treating with sex, and so it must be rejected as unconstitutionally restrictive of the freedoms of speech and press. On the other hand, the substituted standard provides safeguards adequate to withstand the charge of constitutional infirmity. Both trial courts below sufficiently followed the proper [standard]. [W]e hold that these statutes, applied according to the proper standard for judging obscenity, do not offend constitutional safeguards against convictions based upon protected material, or fail to give men in acting adequate notice of what is [prohibited]. Affirmed.

■ JUSTICE DOUGLAS, joined by JUSTICE BLACK, dissenting.

When we sustain these convictions, we make the legality of a publication turn on the purity of thought which a book or tract instills in the mind of the reader. I do not think we can approve that standard and be faithful to the command of the First Amendment. [I] reject too the implication that problems of freedom of speech and of the press are to be resolved by weighing against the values of free expression, the judgment of the Court that a particular form of that expression has 'no redeeming social importance.' I would give the broad sweep of the First Amendment full support. I have the same confidence in the ability of our people to reject noxious literature as I have in their capacity to sort out the true from the false in theology, economics, politics, or any other field.

OBSCENITY BETWEEN ROTH AND MILLER

1. ***Defining obscenity after Roth.*** The Supreme Court's holding in Roth left the Court with no consensus on the precise definition of "obscenity." As Justice Brennan's dissent in Paris Adult Theatre I v. Slaton, 413 U.S. 49, 73 (1973), aptly summarized, a decade after Roth four different approaches had emerged on the Court. "[Justices] Black and Douglas consistently maintained that government is wholly powerless to regulate any sexually oriented matter on the ground of its obscenity. [Justice] Harlan [believed] that the Federal Government [could] control the distribution of 'hard core' pornography, while the States [could ban] 'any material which, taken as a whole, has been reasonably found in state judicial proceedings to treat with sex in a fundamentally offensive manner, under rationally established criteria for judging such material.' Jacobellis v. Ohio, [378 U.S. 184 (1964)]. [Justice] Stewart regarded 'hard core' pornography as the limit of both federal and state power. See, e.g., Ginzburg v. United States, 383 U.S. 463 (1966) (dissenting opinion); [Jacobellis] (concurring opinion). [Justice Stewart's concurrence in Jacobellis said of 'hard-core pornography': 'I shall not today attempt further to define the kinds of material I understand to be embraced within that shorthand description; and perhaps I could never succeed in intelligibly doing so. But I know it when I see it, and the motion picture involved in this case is not that.']

"The view that, [in this period,] enjoyed the most, but not majority, support was an interpretation of Roth adopted by [Chief Justice Warren and

Justices Fortas and Brennan] in Memoirs v. Massachusetts, 383 U.S. 413 (1966). We expressed the view that Federal or State Governments could control the distribution of material where 'three [elements] coalesce: it must be established that (a) the dominant theme of the material taken as a whole appeals to a prurient interest in sex; (b) the material is patently offensive because it affronts contemporary community standards relating to the description or representation of sexual matters; and (c) the material is utterly without redeeming social value.' Even this formulation, however, concealed differences of opinion.[1] Moreover, it did not provide a definition covering all situations.[2] Nor, finally, did it ever command a majority of the [Court]."

As Justice Brennan noted, beginning in Redrup v. New York, 386 U.S. 767 (1967), the Court essentially treated obscenity cases as a numbers game. "The Court began the practice [of] per curiam reversals of convictions for the dissemination of materials that at least five members of the Court, applying their separate tests, deemed not to be obscene. [The] Redrup approach [resolves] cases as between the parties, but offers only the most obscure guidance to legislation, adjudication by other courts, and primary conduct. By disposing of cases through summary reversal or denial of certiorari we have deliberately and effectively obscured the rationale underlying the decisions. It comes as no surprise that judicial attempts to follow our lead conscientiously have often ended in hopeless [confusion]." "Redrupping" involved the justices in a regular practice of privately screening putatively obscene films in the Supreme Court to determine whether each of the individual justices considered them obscene according to his own standard. See Woodward & Armstrong, The Brethren (1979). How might Redrupping help explain why the Court revisited the issue of obscenity in Miller, below?

2. ***Limiting portrayals of sexual immorality.*** Most obscenity rulings in this period, treating obscenity as simply wholly outside the First Amendment, were conspicuously silent about the interests thought to justify control of expression pertaining to sex. One case in the post-Roth years—though not dealing directly with an "obscenity" law—spoke more explicitly about such justifications. **Kingsley Int'l Pictures Corp. v. Regents**, 360 U.S. 684 (1959), invalidated a New York motion picture licensing law. The law banned any "immoral" film, defined as a film that "portrays acts of sexual immorality [or] which expressly or impliedly presents such acts as desirable, acceptable, or proper patterns of behavior." The state denied a license to the film "Lady Chatterley's Lover" under this law because "its subject matter is adultery presented as being right and desirable for certain people under certain circumstances." The Court invalidated the State's action. Justice STEWART's opinion emphasized that "sexual immorality" under the New York scheme was "entirely different from" concepts like "obscenity" or "pornography," and that New York had not claimed that "the film would itself operate as an incitement to illegal action." He concluded that the state had prevented the exhibition of the film "because that picture advocates an idea—that adultery under certain circumstances may be proper behavior.

---

[1] In supporting this statement, Justice Brennan noted: "Compare Jacobellis v. Ohio, supra, at 192–195 (Brennan, J., joined by Goldberg, J.) (community standards national), with id., at 200–201 (Warren, C.J., joined by Clark, J., dissenting) (community standards local)."

[2] In supporting this comment, Justice Brennan stated: "See Mishkin v. New York, 383 U.S. 502 (1966) (prurient appeal defined in terms of a deviant sexual group); Ginzburg v. United States, supra ('pandering' probative evidence of obscenity in close cases). See also Ginsberg v. New York, 390 U.S. 629 (1968) (obscenity for juveniles)."

Yet the First Amendment's basic guarantee is of freedom to advocate ideas. The State, quite simply, has thus struck at the very heart of constitutionally protected liberty. [The constitutional] guarantee is not confined to the expression of ideas that are conventional or shared by a majority. It protects advocacy of the opinion that adultery may sometimes be proper, no less than advocacy of socialism or the single tax."

3. ***Possession of obscene materials.*** In **Stanley v. Georgia**, 394 U.S. 557 (1969), the Court reversed a conviction for knowing "possession of obscene matter," holding that the First Amendment prohibits "making the private possession of obscene material a crime."

In Stanley, a search of a home for bookmaking evidence had uncovered obscene films. Georgia defended its law on the basis of Roth and with the argument: "If the State can protect the body of the citizen, may it [not] protect his mind?" In striking contrast to the approach of the earlier obscenity cases, Justice MARSHALL's opinion systematically canvassed the asserted state justifications. Justice MARSHALL held: "[The constitutional] right to receive information and ideas, regardless of their social worth, [is] fundamental to our free society. Moreover, in the context of this case—a prosecution for mere possession [in] the privacy of a person's own home—that right takes on an added dimension. For also fundamental is the right to be free, except in very limited circumstances, from unwanted governmental intrusions into one's privacy. [W]e think that mere categorization of these films as 'obscene' is insufficient justification for such a drastic invasion of personal liberties guaranteed by the First and Fourteenth Amendments. Whatever may be the justifications for other statutes regulating obscenity, we do not think they reach into the privacy of one's own home. If the First Amendment means anything, it means that a State has no business telling a man, sitting alone in his own house, what books he may read or what films he may watch.

"[In] the face of these traditional notions of individual liberty, Georgia asserts the right to protect the individual's mind from the effects of obscenity. We are not certain that this argument amounts to anything more than the assertion that the State has the right to control the moral content of a person's thoughts.[3] To some, this may be a noble purpose, but it is wholly inconsistent with the philosophy of the First Amendment. [Kingsley Pictures.] Whatever the power of the state to control public dissemination of ideas inimical to the public morality, it cannot constitutionally premise legislation on the desirability of controlling a person's private thoughts. Perhaps recognizing this, Georgia asserts that exposure to obscenity may lead to deviant sexual behavior or crimes of sexual violence. [Given] the present state of knowledge, the State may no more prohibit mere possession of [obscenity] on the ground that it may lead to antisocial conduct than it may prohibit possession of chemistry books on the ground that they may lead to the manufacture of homemade spirits. It is true that in Roth this Court rejected the necessity of proving that exposure to obscene material would create a clear and present danger of antisocial [conduct]. But that case dealt

[3] " 'Communities believe, and act on the belief, that obscenity is immoral, is wrong for the individual, and has no place in a decent society. They believe, too, that adults as well as children are corruptible in morals and character, and that obscenity is a source of corruption that should be eliminated. Obscenity is not suppressed primarily for the protection of others. Much of it is suppressed for the purity of the community and for the salvation and welfare of the "consumer." Obscenity, at bottom, is not crime. Obscenity is sin.' Henkin, Morals and the Constitution: The Sin of Obscenity, 63 Colum. L. Rev. 391, 395 (1963)." [Footnote by Justice Marshall.]

with public distribution of obscene materials and such distribution is subject to different objections. For example, there is always the danger that obscene material might fall into the hands of children or that it might intrude upon the sensibilities or privacy of the general public. No such dangers are present in this case. Finally, we are faced with the argument that prohibition of possession of [obscenity] is a necessary incident to statutory schemes prohibiting distribution. That argument is based on alleged difficulties of proving an intent to distribute or in producing evidence of actual distribution. We are not convinced that such difficulties exist, but even if they did we do not think that they would justify infringement of the individual's right to read or observe what he pleases. Because that right is so fundamental to our scheme of individual liberty, its restriction may not be justified by the need to ease the administration of otherwise valid criminal laws."

Justice STEWART, joined by Justices Brennan and White, concurred only in the result, solely on the ground that the films were seized in violation of the Fourth Amendment. Justice Brennan later, in his Paris Adult dissent, said he was "now inclined to agree" with much of the principal Stanley opinion.

Miller v. California

413 U.S. 15, 93 S. Ct. 2607, 37 L. Ed. 2d 419 (1973).

[The Miller case arose from a conviction under California Penal Code § 311.2(a), for knowingly distributing obscene matter by causing five unsolicited advertising brochures for "adult" material to be sent through the mail. The State charged that the brochures consisted mostly of "pictures and drawings very explicitly depicting men and women in groups of two or more engaging in a variety of sexual activities with genitals often prominently displayed."]

■ CHIEF JUSTICE BURGER delivered the opinion of the Court.

This is one of a group of "obscenity-pornography" cases being reviewed [in] a re-examination of standards enunciated in earlier cases involving what [Justice] Harlan called "the intractable obscenity problem." [This] case involves the application of a State's criminal obscenity statute to a situation in which sexually explicit materials have been thrust by aggressive sales action upon unwilling recipients who had in no way indicated any desire to receive such materials. This Court has recognized that the States have a legitimate interest in prohibiting dissemination or exhibition of obscene material when the mode of dissemination carries with it a significant danger of offending the sensibilities of unwilling recipients or of exposure to juveniles. [Stanley.] It is in this context that we are called on to define the standards which must be used to identify obscene material that a State may regulate.

Obscene material is unprotected by the First Amendment. [Roth.] [However, state] statutes designed to regulate obscene materials must be carefully limited. As a result, we now confine the permissible scope of such regulation to works which depict or describe sexual conduct. That conduct must be specifically defined by the applicable state law, as written or authoritatively construed. [The] basic guidelines for the trier of fact must be: (a) whether "the average person, applying contemporary community standards" would find that the work, taken as a whole, appeals to the prurient interest [Roth], (b) whether the work depicts or describes, in a patently offensive way, sexual conduct specifically defined by the applicable state law, and (c) whether the work, taken as a whole, lacks serious literary, artistic, political, or scientific value. We do not adopt as a constitutional standard the "*utterly* without redeeming social value" test of [Memoirs]. If a state law that regulates obscene material is thus limited, as written or construed, [First Amendment values] are adequately protected by the ultimate power of appellate courts to conduct an independent review of constitutional claims when necessary.

We emphasize that it is not our function to propose regulatory schemes for the States. [It] is possible, however, to give a few plain examples of what a state statute could define for regulation under [part] (b) of the standard announced in this opinion: (a) Patently offensive representations or descriptions of ultimate sexual acts, normal or perverted, actual or simulated. (b) Patently offensive representations or descriptions of masturbation, excretory functions, and lewd exhibition of the genitals.

Sex and nudity may not be exploited without limit by films or pictures exhibited or sold in places of public accommodation any more than live sex and nudity can be exhibited or sold without limit in such public places. At a minimum, prurient, patently offensive depiction or description of sexual conduct must have serious literary, artistic, political, or scientific value to merit First Amendment protection. For example, medical books [necessarily] use graphic illustrations and descriptions of human anatomy. In resolving the inevitably sensitive questions of fact and law, we must continue to rely on the jury system, accompanied by the safeguards that judges, rules of evidence, presumption of innocence and other protective features provide, as we do with [other] offenses against society and its individual members.

[Justice] Brennan [has] abandoned his former position and now maintains that no formulation of this Court, the Congress, or the States can adequately distinguish obscene material unprotected by the First Amendment from protected expression. [Paris, below.] Paradoxically, [he] indicates that suppression of unprotected obscene material is permissible to avoid exposure to unconsenting adults, as in this case, and to juveniles, although he gives no indication of how the division between protected and nonprotected materials may be drawn with greater precision for these purposes than for regulation of commercial exposure to consenting adults only. Nor does he indicate where in the Constitution he finds the authority to distinguish between a willing "adult" one month past the state law age of majority and a willing "juvenile" one month younger.

Under the holdings announced today, no one will be subject to prosecution for the sale or exposure of obscene materials unless these materials depict or describe patently offensive "hard core" sexual conduct specifically defined by the regulating state law, as written or construed. We are satisfied that these specific prerequisites will provide fair notice to a dealer in such materials that his public and commercial activities may bring prosecution. If the inability to define regulated materials with ultimate, god-like precision altogether removes the power of the States or the Congress to regulate, then "hard core" pornography may be exposed without limit to the juvenile, the passerby, and the consenting adult alike, as, indeed, Mr. Justice

Douglas contends. [In] this belief, however, [he] now stands alone. [Today,] for the first time since [Roth], a majority of this Court has agreed on concrete guidelines to isolate "hard core" pornography from expression protected by the First Amendment. Now we may abandon the casual practice of [Redrup] and attempt to provide positive guidance to the federal and state courts [alike].

Under a National Constitution, fundamental First Amendment limitations on the powers of the States do not vary from community to community, but this does not mean that there are, or should or can be, fixed, uniform national standards of precisely what appeals to the "prurient interest" or is "patently offensive." These are essentially questions of fact, and our nation is simply too big and too diverse for this Court to reasonably expect that such standards could be articulated for all 50 States in a single formulation, even assuming the prerequisite consensus exists. [It] is neither realistic nor constitutionally sound to read the First Amendment as requiring that the people of Maine or Mississippi accept public depiction of conduct found tolerable in Las Vegas, or New York City. [People] in different States vary in their tastes and attitudes, and this diversity is not to be strangled by the absolutism of imposed uniformity. [We] hold that the requirement that the jury evaluate the materials with reference to "contemporary standards of the State of California" [is] constitutionally adequate.

The dissenting Justices sound the alarm of repression. But, in our view, to equate the free and robust exchange of ideas and political debate with commercial exploitation of obscene material demeans the grand conception of the First Amendment and its high purposes in the historic struggle for freedom. [The] First Amendment protects works which, taken as a whole, have serious literary, artistic, political, or scientific value, regardless of whether the government or a majority of the people approve of the ideas these works represent. [But] the public portrayal of hard core sexual conduct for its own sake, and for the ensuing commercial gain, is a different matter. There is no evidence, empirical or historical, that the stern 19th century American censorship of public distribution and display of material relating to sex in any way limited or affected expression of serious literary, artistic, political, or scientific ideas. [We] do not see the harsh hand of censorship of ideas [and] "repression" of political liberty lurking in every state regulation of commercial exploitation of human interest in sex. [In] sum, we (a) reaffirm the Roth holding that obscene material is not protected by the First Amendment; (b) hold that such material can be regulated by the States, subject to the specific safeguards enunciated above, without a showing that the material is "*utterly* without redeeming social value"; and (c) hold that obscenity is to be determined by applying "contemporary community standards," [not "national standards"]. Vacated and remanded.

■ JUSTICE DOUGLAS, dissenting.

[Until] a civil proceeding has placed a tract beyond the pale, no criminal prosecution should be sustained. For no more vivid illustration of vague and uncertain laws could be designed than those we have fashioned. [If] a specific book [has] in a civil proceeding been condemned as obscene [and] thereafter a person publishes [it], then a vague law has been made specific. There would remain the underlying question whether the First Amendment allows an implied exception in the case of obscenity. I do not think it does and my views on the issue have been stated over and over again. But at least a criminal prosecution brought at that juncture would not violate [the] void-for-vagueness test. No such protective procedure has been designed by California in this case. Obscenity—which even we cannot define with precision—is a hodge-podge. To send men to jail for violating standards they cannot understand, construe, and apply is a monstrous thing to do in a Nation dedicated to fair trials and due process.

■ JUSTICE BRENNAN, with whom JUSTICES STEWART and MARSHALL join, dissenting.

In my dissent in [Paris, below], I noted that I had no occasion to consider the extent of state power to regulate the distribution of sexually oriented material to juveniles or the offensive exposure of such material to unconsenting adults. [I] need not now decide whether a statute might be drawn to impose, within the requirements of the First Amendment, criminal penalties for the precise conduct at issue here [—mailing unsolicited brochures]. For it is clear that under my dissent in [Paris], the statute [here] is unconstitutionally overbroad, and therefore invalid on its [face].

Paris Adult Theatre I v. Slaton

413 U.S. 49, 93 S. Ct. 2628, 37 L. Ed. 2d 446 (1973).

[This case arose from a Georgia civil proceeding to enjoin the showing of two allegedly obscene films at two "adult" theaters. At a trial before a judge, the evidence consisted primarily of the films and of photographs of the entrance to the theaters, with signs indicating that the theatres exhibit "Atlanta's Finest Mature Feature Films" and warning "Adult Theatre—You must be 21 and able to prove it. If viewing the nude body offends you, Please Do Not Enter." Two state investigators who saw the films testified that the signs did not indicate "the full nature of what was shown. In particular, nothing indicated that the films depicted—as they did—scenes of simulated fellatio, cunnilingus, and group sex intercourse." The trial judge dismissed the complaint. He held the showing of obscene films permissible where there was "requisite notice to the public" and "reasonable protection against the exposure of these films to minors." The Georgia Supreme Court reversed. The Supreme Court vacated and remanded for reconsideration in light of Miller, but noted that "nothing precludes the State of Georgia from the regulation of the allegedly obscene material exhibited in Paris Adult Theatre I provided that the applicable Georgia law, as written or authoritatively interpreted by the Georgia courts, meets the First Amendment standards set forth in Miller."]

■ CHIEF JUSTICE BURGER delivered the opinion of the Court.

We categorically disapprove the theory [that] obscene, pornographic films acquire constitutional immunity from state regulation simply because they are exhibited for consenting adults only. [Although] we have often pointedly recognized the high importance of the state interest in regulating the exposure of obscene materials to juveniles and unconsenting adults, this Court has never declared these to be the only legitimate state interests permitting regulation of obscene material. [In] particular, we hold that there are legitimate state interests at stake in stemming the tide of commercialized obscenity, even assuming it is feasible to enforce effective safeguards against exposure to juveniles and to passersby.[1] [These] include the interest of the public in the quality of life and the total community environment, the tone of commerce in the great city centers, and, possibly, the public safety itself. The Hill-Link Minority Report of the Commission on Obscenity and Pornography [1970] indicates that there is at least an arguable correlation between obscene material and crime. Quite apart from sex crimes, however, there remains one problem of large proportions aptly described by Professor Bickel: "It concerns the tone of the society, the mode, or to use terms that have perhaps greater currency, the style and quality of life, now and in the future. A man may be entitled to read an obscene book in his room, or expose himself indecently there. [We] should protect his privacy. But if he demands a right to obtain the books and pictures he wants in the market, and to foregather in public places—discreet, if you will, but accessible to all—with others who share his tastes, *then to grant him his right is to affect the world about the rest of us, and to impinge on other privacies*. Even supposing that each of us can, if he wishes, effectively avert the eye and stop the ear (which, in truth, we cannot), what is commonly read and seen and heard and done intrudes upon us all, want it or not." 22 The Public Interest 25–26 (Winter, 1971). (Emphasis added.) As [Chief] Justice Warren stated, there is a "right of the Nation and of the States to maintain a decent society" [Jacobellis dissent].

But, it is argued, there is no scientific data which conclusively demonstrate that exposure to obscene materials adversely affects men and women or their society. It is [urged] that, absent such a demonstration, any kind of state regulation is "impermissible." We reject this argument. It is not for us to resolve empirical uncertainties underlying state legislation, save in the exceptional case where that legislation plainly impinges upon rights protected by the Constitution itself. [Although] there is no conclusive proof of a connection between antisocial behavior and obscene material, the legislature of Georgia could quite reasonably determine that such a connection does or might exist. In deciding Roth, this Court implicitly accepted that a legislature could legitimately act on such a conclusion to protect "*the social interest in order and morality*."

From the beginning of civilized societies, legislators and judges have acted on various unprovable assumptions. [If] we accept the unprovable assumption that a complete education requires certain books and the well nigh universal belief that good books, plays, and art lift the spirit, improve the mind, enrich the human personality and develop character, can we then say that a state legislature may not act on the corollary assumption that commerce in obscene books, or public exhibitions focused on obscene conduct, have a tendency to exert a corrupting and debasing impact leading to antisocial behavior? [The sum of experience] affords an ample basis for legislatures to conclude that a sensitive, key relationship of human existence, central to family life, community welfare, and the development of human personality, can be debased and distorted by crass commercial exploitation of sex. Nothing in the Constitution prohibits a State from

[1] It is conceivable that an "adult" theatre can—if it really insists—prevent the exposure of its obscene wares to juveniles. An "adult" bookstore, dealing in obscene books, magazines, and pictures, cannot realistically make this claim. [The] legitimate interest in preventing exposure of juveniles to obscene materials cannot be fully served by simply barring juveniles from the immediate physical premises of "adult" bookstores, when there is a flourishing "outside business" in these materials. [Footnote by the Court.]

reaching such a conclusion and acting on it legislatively simply because there is no conclusive evidence or empirical [data].

It is asserted, however, that standards for evaluating state commercial regulations are inapposite in the present context, as state regulation of access by consenting adults to obscene material violates the constitutionally protected right to privacy enjoyed by petitioners' customers. [I]t is unavailing to compare a theater open to the public for a fee, with the private home of [Stanley] and the marital bedroom of [Griswold]. [Nothing] in this Court's decisions intimates that there is any "fundamental" privacy right "implicit in the concept of ordered liberty" to watch obscene movies in places of public accommodation. [The] idea of a "privacy" right and a place of public accommodation are, in this context, mutually exclusive. Conduct or depictions of conduct that the state police power can prohibit on a public street do not become automatically protected by the Constitution merely because the conduct is moved to a bar or a "live" theatre stage, any more than a "live" performance of a man and woman locked in a sexual embrace at high noon in Times Square is protected by the Constitution because they simultaneously engage in a valid political dialogue. [We also] reject the claim that [Georgia] is here attempting to control the minds or thoughts of those who patronize theaters. [Where] communication of ideas, protected by the First Amendment, is not involved, or the particular privacy of the home protected by Stanley, or any of the other "areas or zones" of constitutionally protected privacy, the mere fact that, as a consequence, some human "utterances" or "thoughts" may be incidentally affected does not bar the State from acting to protect legitimate state interests. Cf. [Roth; Beauharnais]. [Finally, for] us to say that our Constitution incorporates the proposition that conduct involving consenting adults only is always beyond state regulation, is a step we are unable to take. [W]e hold that the States have a legitimate interest in regulating commerce in obscene material and in regulating exhibition of obscene material in places of public accommodation, including so-called "adult" theaters from which minors are [excluded]. Vacated and remanded.

■ JUSTICE BRENNAN, with whom JUSTICES STEWART and MARSHALL join, dissenting.

[I] am convinced that the approach initiated 16 years ago in [Roth], and culminating in the Court's decision today, cannot bring stability to this area of the law without jeopardizing fundamental First Amendment values, and I have concluded that the time has come to make a significant departure from that approach. [The] essence of our problem in the obscenity area is that we have been unable to provide "sensitive tools" to separate obscenity from other sexually oriented but constitutionally protected speech, so that efforts to suppress the former do not spill over into the suppression of the latter. [I] am reluctantly forced to the conclusion that none of the available formulas, including the one announced today, can reduce the vagueness [of] our obscenity standards to a tolerable level. The vagueness of the standards in the obscenity area produces a number of separate problems, [including a] lack of fair notice, [a] chill on protected expression, and [a severe] stress [on] the state and federal judicial machinery. [These problems] persuade me that a significant change in direction is urgently required. I turn, therefore, to the alternatives that are now open.

1. The approach requiring the smallest deviation from our present course would be to draw a new line between protected and unprotected

speech, still permitting the States to suppress all material on the unprotected side of the line. In my view, clarity cannot be obtained pursuant to this approach except by drawing a line that resolves all doubt in favor of state [power]. We could hold, for example, that any depiction or description of human sexual organs [is] outside the protection of the First Amendment. [That] formula would [reduce the vagueness problems. But it] would be appallingly [overbroad].

2. The alternative adopted by the Court today [embodies] a restatement of the Roth-Memoirs definition of obscenity. [In] my view, the restatement leaves unresolved the very difficulties that compel our rejection of the underlying Roth approach, while at the same time contributing substantial difficulties of its own. [T]he Court today permits suppression if the government can prove that the materials lack "*serious* literary, artistic, political or scientific value." But [Roth] held that certain expression is obscene, and thus outside the protection of the First Amendment, precisely *because* it lacks even the slightest redeeming social value. The Court's approach necessarily assumes that some works will be deemed obscene—even though they clearly have *some* social value—because the State was able to prove that the value, measured by some unspecified standard, was not sufficiently "serious" to warrant constitutional protection. That result [is] nothing less than a rejection of the fundamental First Amendment premises and rationale of the Roth opinion and an invitation to widespread suppression of sexually oriented speech.

3. [I] have also considered the possibility of reducing our own role, and the role of appellate courts generally, in determining whether particular matter is obscene. Thus, [we] might adopt the position that where a lower federal or state court has conscientiously applied the constitutional standard, its finding of obscenity will be no more vulnerable to reversal by this Court than any finding of fact. [But] it is implicit in [Redrup] that the First Amendment requires an independent review by appellate courts of the constitutional fact of obscenity. [In any event, while this approach would mitigate institutional stress,] it would neither offer nor produce any cure for the other vices of vagueness. [Plainly], the institutional gain would be more than offset by the unprecedented infringement of First Amendment rights.

4. Finally, I have considered the view, urged so forcefully since 1957 by our Brothers Black and Douglas, that the First Amendment bars the suppression of any sexually oriented expression. [But that would strip] the States of power to an extent that cannot be justified by the commands of the Constitution, at least so long as there is available an alternative approach that strikes a better balance between the guarantee of free expression and the States' legitimate interests.

[Given the] inevitable side-effects of state efforts to suppress what is assumed to be *unprotected* speech, we must scrutinize with care the state interest that is asserted to justify the suppression. For in the absence of some very substantial interest in suppressing such speech, we can hardly condone the ill-effects that seem to flow inevitably from the [effort]. Because we assumed—incorrectly, as experience has proven—that obscenity could be separated from other sexually oriented expression without significant costs, [we] had no occasion in Roth to prove the asserted state interest in curtailing unprotected, sexually oriented speech. Yet, as we have increasingly come to appreciate the vagueness of the concept of obscenity, we have begun to recognize and articulate the state interests at stake. [The] opinions in

Redrup and [Stanley] reflected our emerging view that the state interests in protecting children and in protecting unconsenting adults may stand on a different footing from the other asserted state interests. It may well be, as one commentator has argued, that "exposure to [erotic material] is for some persons an intense emotional experience. A communication of this nature, imposed upon a person contrary to his wishes, has all the characteristics of a physical assault. [It] constitutes an invasion of his privacy." [T. Emerson, The System of Freedom of Expression 496 (1970).] But cf. [Cohen]. Similarly, if children are "not possessed of that full capacity for individual choice which is the presupposition of First Amendment guarantees," [the] State may have a substantial interest in precluding the flow of obscene materials even to consenting juveniles. [But whatever the strength of those interests, they] cannot be asserted in defense of the holding of the Georgia Supreme Court. [The justification here] must be found [in] some independent interest in regulating the reading and viewing habits of consenting adults.

[Of course, a State need not] remain utterly indifferent to—and take no action bearing on—the morality of the community. The traditional description of state police power does embrace the regulation of morals as well as health, safety, and general welfare of the citizenry. And much legislation—compulsory public education laws, civil rights laws, even the abolition of capital punishment—is grounded, at least in part, on a concern with the morality of the community. But the State's interest in regulating morality by suppressing obscenity, while often asserted, remains essentially unfocused and ill-defined. And, since the attempt to curtail unprotected speech necessarily spills over into the area of protected speech, the effort to serve this speculative interest through the suppression of obscene material must tread heavily on rights protected by the First Amendment.

[In] short, while I cannot say that the interests of the State—apart from the question of juveniles and unconsenting adults—are trivial or nonexistent, I am compelled to conclude that these interests cannot justify the substantial damage to constitutional rights and to this Nation's judicial machinery that inevitably results from state efforts to bar the distribution even of unprotected material to consenting adults. I would hold, therefore, that at least in the absence of distribution to juveniles or obtrusive exposure to unconsenting adults, the [First Amendment prohibits governments] from attempting wholly to suppress sexually oriented materials on the basis of their allegedly "obscene" contents. Nothing in this approach precludes [governments] from taking action to serve what may be strong and legitimate interests through regulation of the manner of distribution of sexually oriented material. [I] do not pretend to have found a complete and infallible [answer]. Difficult questions must still be faced, notably in the areas of distribution to juveniles and offensive exposure to unconsenting adults. Whatever the extent of state power to regulate in those areas, it should be clear that the view I espouse today would introduce a large measure of clarity to this troubled area, would reduce the institutional pressure on this Court and the rest of the State and Federal Judiciary, and would guarantee fuller freedom of expression while leaving room for the protection of legitimate governmental [interests].

———

OBSCENITY LAW AFTER MILLER AND PARIS

1. ***Justifications for obscenity regulation.*** What government interests do the preceding cases suggest are served by suppressing obscene speech? Consider the following:

a. *Corruption.* The Hicklin test held the harm of obscenity to be the "depravity and corruption" it induced in the mind of its consumer. This frankly paternalistic rationale seeks to protect the consumer from his own worst impulses. See Henkin, "Morals and the Constitution: The Sin of Obscenity," 63 Colum. L. Rev. 391 (1963). But this rationale was undermined by Stanley, which held that the choice to consume obscene materials was up to the consumer, at least in his own home. The opinions in Miller and Paris make little reference to this rationale; Chief Justice Burger mentions the "corrupting and debasing impact" of obscenity only insofar as it leads to "antisocial behavior."

b. *Offense to unwilling onlookers.* Exposure to obscenity can be shocking to the sensibilities of many adults, who would not willingly view it. Children are presumed incapable of consenting to such exposure. All the justices appear to agree that obscenity may be regulated to prevent unwilling exposure to these audiences. Even Justice Brennan, dissenting in Paris, notes that he might uphold laws aimed at "distribution to juveniles or obtrusive exposure to unconsenting adults." Should this narrow range of state interests be the only ones tolerable in the obscenity sphere, as Justice Brennan suggested? Or do even these interests clash with the Court's approach in Cohen v. California, which read the First Amendment to require that those offended by Cohen's jacket simply avert their eyes?

c. *Inducement of criminal conduct.* Chief Justice Burger, writing for the Court in Paris, noted that there is "at least an arguable correlation between obscene material and [sex] crimes." This rationale supposes that readers and viewers of obscene materials will be induced to imitate their depictions of adultery, fornication, prostitution, sexual assault, rape, oral or anal sex, bestiality or other activities made criminal by many states. But note the absence in this reasoning of any requirement of tight causation or "clear and present danger" that these results will follow from obscenity consumption, or of intent on the part of the obscenity disseminator to bring them about. In this respect, Miller and Paris differ from Brandenburg in the incitement context.

d. *Eroding moral standards.* Chief Justice Burger in Paris notes that "crass commercial exploitation of sex" can undermine "a sensitive, key relationship of human existence, central to family life." May government suppress speech to uphold a particular moral view of sex, in particular that it is appropriately practiced only in private and in heterosexual monogamous marriages? Does Kingsley Pictures undermine this rationale for regulating obscenity by holding that speech may not be suppressed on the ground that it expresses immoral ideas? Can the interest in public morality be accepted as a justification to bar obscenity without undercutting Justice Harlan's protective approach to offensive speech in Cohen?

e. *Harming the social fabric.* Writing for the Court in Paris Adult, Chief Justice Burger notes that commercial distribution of obscenity causes harm to "the quality of life and the total community environment" even if it is consumed only by willing adults. Quoting Bickel, he takes a communitarian rather than an individualist view of speech: "'what is commonly read and seen and heard and done intrudes upon us all, want it or not.' " On this view, the Stanleys of the world are never truly home alone consuming pornography in a purely self-regarding way. Obscenity distribution and consumption affects even non-observing bystanders. Is this view consistent with the rhetoric of the "marketplace of ideas"? Contrast this view with the highly individualistic and relativistic approach the Court took to offensive speech in Cohen and Hustler.

2. ***The value of obscenity as "speech"?*** Given the tensions between these government interests and other areas of First Amendment law, is the assertedly low value of sexually explicit materials doing most of the work in the Court's obscenity cases? Chaplinsky spoke of unprotected speech as that which has so little value as a step to truth that it is "clearly outweighed" by social interests. If obscenity is sufficiently low-value speech, then even vague or problematic social interests might be sufficient to justify its regulation. What features of obscenity might render it of low value?

a. *Nonpolitical*. Are art and literature subordinate to political speech? If so, then perhaps obscenity is unprotected because it is nonpolitical. But if that is so, "the novel, the poem, the painting, the drama, or the piece of sculpture" would likewise be unprotected. Kalven, "The Metaphysics of the Law of Obscenity," 1960 Sup. Ct. Rev. 1 The self-expression or autonomy rationale certainly brings literature and art within the First Amendment. But even Alexander Meiklejohn, a strong defender of the political conception of the First Amendment, eventually viewed literature and art as part of political discourse broadly construed: they educate voters and so give them "the knowledge, intelligence, sensitivity to human values [and] capacity for sane and objective judgment which, so far as possible, a ballot should express." Meiklejohn, "The First Amendment Is an Absolute," 1961 Sup. Ct. Rev. 245. For an exploration of the values of artistic expression, see Nahmod, "Artistic Expression and Aesthetic Theory: The Beautiful, The Sublime and the First Amendment," 1987 Wis. L. Rev. 221.

b. *Noncognitive*. Is obscenity more like conduct than speech because it "bypasses the brain for the groin," as one court stated in an obscenity trial involving the lyrics of 2 Live Crew? Frederick Schauer, for example, argues that the First Amendment should be read to protect speech that appeals to cognitive and emotive processes. In contrast, hard-core pornography is "designed to produce a purely physical effect": "The concept fundamental to the Miller test is that material appealing to the prurient interest *is* sex, and not merely describing or advocating sex. Material that appeals to the prurient interest is material that turns you on. Period." Schauer, "Speech and 'Speech'—Obscenity and 'Obscenity': An Exercise in the Interpretation of Constitutional Language," 67 Geo. L.J. 899 (1979). See also Sunstein, "Words, Conduct, Caste," 60 U. Chi. L. Rev. 795 (1993) ("Many forms of pornography are not an appeal to the exchange of ideas, political or otherwise; they operate as masturbatory aids and do not qualify for top-tier First Amendment protection"). Might such a view undermine protection for other speech that operates in both rational and irrational ways? Is there *any* communication that is purely cognitive or purely non-cognitive? Are the categories meaningful?

c. *Not susceptible to counterspeech*. The premise of much speech protection is that more speech is a better remedy than state suppression. Can anyone really talk back to obscene materials? Or do they act by an insidious conditioning mechanism that undermines the possibility of counterspeech? Consider Clor, Obscenity and Public Morality (1969): Obscene materials "do not make arguments which are to be met by intelligent defense," but rather have an effect upon "a delicate network of moral and aesthetic feelings, sensibilities, [and] tastes." Thus those "whose sensibilities are frequently assaulted by prurient and lurid impressions may become desensitized." Might the same argument apply to other areas of speech, such as commercial or political advertising?

3. ***Critiques of obscenity law after Miller.*** In addition to questioning the above justifications, critics of Miller have suggested that it privileges one conception of sex over others in violation of the usual First Amendment norm of viewpoint neutrality. On this view, Miller in effect permits government to punish sexual dissent. For example, see Richards, "Free Speech and Obscenity Law: Toward a Moral Theory of the First Amendment," 123 U. Pa. L. Rev. 45 (1974) (arguing that pornography can be seen to embody the "idea of [sexuality] as a profound and shattering ecstasy," or "a view of sensual delight in the erotic celebration of the body," in opposition to more repressive "Victorian" or "Catholic" views); Scanlon, "Freedom of Expression and Categories of Expression," 40 U. Pitt. L. Rev. 519 (1979) (describing "partisans of pornography" as seeking "a fair opportunity to influence the sexual mores of the society" through "informal politics"); Gey, "The Apologetics of Suppression: The Regulation of Pornography as Act and Idea," 86 Mich. L. Rev. 1564 (1988) (arguing that "the suppression of pornography [permits] the state [to] certify and enforce a moral code that reinforces and justifies the political status quo"); Cole, "Playing by Pornography's Rules: The Regulation of Sexual Expression," 143 U. Pa. L. Rev. 111 (1994).

If pornography is a form of sexual dissent, should its distribution be permitted only when the speaker has such a purpose, while speakers may be "forbid[en from] distributing the same material with no intent to influence people's views but merely to provide sexual stimulation"? For an argument drawing such a distinction, see Weinstein, "Democracy, Sex and the First Amendment," 31 NYU Rev. L. & Soc. Change 865 (2007); for the counterargument, see Koppelman, "Free Speech and Pornography: A Response to James Weinstein," 31 NYU Rev. L. & Soc. Change 899 (2007).

4. ***Post-Miller decisions.*** Although the number of obscenity cases decided by the Court has diminished dramatically since the 1973 rulings, the Miller-Paris standards have not wholly extricated the Court from the unwelcome task of case-by-case review in obscenity cases. In **Jenkins v. Georgia**, 418 U.S. 153 (1974), for example, the Court unanimously reversed a state conviction for showing the film "Carnal Knowledge." The state court had mistakenly assumed that, under the new standards, a jury verdict virtually precluded further review regarding most elements of obscenity. Justice REHNQUIST countered: "Even though questions of appeal to the 'prurient interest' or of patent offensiveness are 'essentially questions of fact,' it would be a serious misreading of Miller to conclude that juries have unbridled discretion in determining what is 'patently offensive.' [While the Miller illustrations] did not purport to be an exhaustive catalog of what juries might find patently offensive, [they were] certainly intended to fix substantive constitutional limitations [on] the type of material subject to such a determination." He concluded that, under Miller, "Carnal Knowledge" "could not be found to depict sexual conduct in a patently offensive way. [While] the subject matter of the picture is, in a broader sense, sex, and there

are scenes in which sexual conduct including 'ultimate sexual acts' is to be understood to be taking place, the camera does not focus on the bodies of the actors at such time. There is no exhibition whatever of the actors' genitals, lewd or otherwise, during these scenes. There are occasional scenes of nudity, but nudity alone is not enough to make material legally obscene under the Miller standards." The Court relied in part on the fact that the film starred prominent actors (including Jack Nicholson) and had been nominated for Academy Awards. Jenkins thus implicitly concluded that the obscenity laws could not be easily extended to "mainstream" materials, regardless of local views. Justice BRENNAN, joined by Justices Stewart and Marshall, and Justice DOUGLAS concurred separately in the result.

5. ***Community standards.*** Whose standards are to govern in determination of "prurient interest," "patent offensiveness," and "serious literary, artistic, political or scientific value": those of the locality, the state or the nation? Chief Justice Burger wrote in Miller that the "people of Maine or Mississippi" need not tolerate depictions that might be "tolerable in Las Vegas, or New York City." In **Hamling v. United States**, 418 U.S. 87 (1974), the Court opted for local rather than statewide or national standards in federal obscenity prosecutions and rejected the argument that application of local standards would unduly inhibit producers of materials for a national market. The Hamling ruling was again by a 5–4 vote. (In Jenkins, the Court had similarly refused to require that statewide standards be applied in state prosecutions, even though a statewide standard had been used in Miller.) And in **Smith v. United States**, 431 U.S. 291 (1977), the majority held that determination of local "community standards" in federal obscenity prosecutions was for the jury, even where the defendant had mailed the allegedly obscene materials solely intrastate, in a state which had no law prohibiting sales to adults. Justice BLACKMUN's majority opinion concluded that state law, although relevant, "is not conclusive as to the issue of contemporary community standards for appeal to the prurient interest and patent offensiveness." Justice STEVENS dissented: "The question of offensiveness to community standards, whether national or local, is not one that the average juror can be expected to answer with evenhanded consistency. [In] the final analysis, the guilt or innocence of a criminal defendant in an obscenity trial is determined primarily by individual jurors' subjective reactions to the materials in question rather than by the predictable application of rules of law. As [Justice] Harlan noted: '[It is] often true that one man's vulgarity is another's lyric [and that is why] the Constitution leaves matters of taste and style [to] the individual' [Cohen]."

Smith also made clear, however, that the "literary, artistic, political, or scientific value" factor of the Miller test was *not* to be measured by local community standards. This point was elaborated in **Pope v. Illinois**, 481 U.S. 497 (1987), where Justice WHITE's majority opinion stated: "Just as the ideas a work represents need not obtain majority approval to merit protection, neither [does] the value of the work vary from community to community based on the degree of local acceptance it has won. The proper inquiry is not whether an ordinary member of any given community would find serious [value] in allegedly obscene material, but whether a reasonable person would find such value in the material, taken as a whole." Justice SCALIA's concurrence argued that it was "quite impossible" to come to an objective assessment of (at least) literary or artistic value: "Just as there is no use arguing about taste, there is no use litigating about it." He suggested "the need for reexamination of Miller," but offered no alternative to it. Justice

STEVENS's dissent, joined by Justice Marshall, attacked the majority's "reasonable person" standard, insisting that "communicative material of this sort is entitled to the protection of the First Amendment if *some reasonable persons* could consider it as having serious [value]."

Is the notion of "community standards" still meaningful in the era of the internet? It is intriguing to note that some online platforms use "community standards" as a term to describe their own rules for regulating content. With more than 2 billion users worldwide on Facebook, for example, what does it mean for the word "community" to be used in this way? Does it change the meaning of the phrase "community standards" as it relates to definitions of obscenity?

6. ***Serious value.*** Is "serious value" a magic bullet that allows mainstream publishers and producers to escape obscenity charges, confining the practical reach of Miller to hard-core pornography? Publishers have often called expert witnesses to testify to serious artistic value in obscenity trials. See generally de Grazia, Girls Lean Back Everywhere (1992). Similar testimony was offered in two prominent obscenity trials in the early 1990s. An art gallery and its directors were tried in Cincinnati for obscenity violations as a result of displaying an exhibit of photographs by Robert Mapplethorpe containing explicit depictions of homoerotic and sadomasochistic activities. The curator of the exhibit testified to the artistic value of the photographs. Asked repeatedly by prosecutors whether she would describe particular photographs as depicting male genitalia, she demurred, answering that she saw instead, for example, examples of "classical line and form." The Cincinnati jury found the defendants not guilty. Expert testimony on the antecedents of rap in early African-American oral traditions was less successful in averting an obscenity conviction in Broward County, Florida, for sellers of the sexually graphic lyrics in the musical recording "As Nasty As They Wanna Be" by the rap group 2 Live Crew. A federal trial judge in Fort Lauderdale found the lyrics album obscene in a civil proceeding. The judgment was reversed by the Court of Appeals. Luke Records, Inc. v. Navarro, 960 F.2d 134 (11th Cir. 1992). Does expert testimony that describes art or music in terms of its artistic value take an unduly formalist view of art, underestimating its controversial moral and political content and its emotive impact upon its audience? See Adler, Note, "Post-Modern Art and the Death of Obscenity Law," 99 Yale L.J. 1359 (1990).

7. ***Pornography as a cause of antisocial conduct.*** A Commission appointed by Attorney General Edwin Meese in 1986 concluded that some forms of obscenity *could* cause violent antisocial conduct. In assessing the effects of sexually explicit materials, the Commission emphasized distinctions among the content of such materials, distinguishing between (a) materials portraying sexual violence; (b) materials that contained no explicit violence but were plainly degrading, usually to women; and (c) materials, that, while sexually explicit, contained neither violence nor degradation.

With respect to sexually violent materials, the Commission concluded that the "scientific findings and ultimate conclusions of [a prior] 1970 Commission are least reliable for today, [because] material of this variety was largely absent from that Commission's inquiries. [The] research [shows] a causal relationship between exposure to [sexually violent material] and aggressive behavior towards women." The Commission relied not solely on "experimental evidence" but also on "clinical evidence" and on "less scientific evidence [as well as] our own common sense." Turning to materials containing no violence but depicting women "as existing solely for the sexual satisfaction of [men]," the Commission found the evidence "more tentative" but inclined somewhat in the same direction as with sexually violent material. But with regard to material containing neither violence nor degradation, "we are on the current state of the evidence persuaded that material of this type does not bear a causal relationship to rape or other acts of sexual violence."

With respect to the framing and enforcement of legal restraints, the Commission found that the type of material currently designated as legally obscene was properly considered outside the coverage of the First Amendment. But its recommendations about law enforcement started with the assumption that the constitutional permissibility of regulation did not address the advisability of regulation. It rejected all proposals for expanding the scope of existing obscenity laws, recommended that enforcement of existing obscenity laws take into account as priorities the subdivisions recommended by the Commission, and urged that enforcement of existing obscenity laws against sexually violent materials be increased substantially. It divided on the issue whether there should be any enforcement at all regarding materials neither violent nor degrading. Noting that the category of sexually violent material is dominated by material "unquestionably protected by the First Amendment," the Commission nevertheless urged enforcement of existing laws with respect to the segment of that material that was legally obscene, even though such regulation "would likely address little more than the tip of the iceberg." In reaching this conclusion, the Commission emphasized that "law serves an important symbolic function [even through] strikingly underinclusive regulation. Conversely, we are aware of the message conveyed by repeal or non-enforcement of existing laws with respect to certain kinds of materials. [We] are unwilling to have the law send out the wrong signal." The Commission's report prompted immediate controversy and considerable criticism.

For further discussion of the "causation" problem, see an article by one member of the Commission. Schauer, "Causation Theory and the Causes of Sexual Violence," 1987 A.B.F.Res. J. 737. Schauer argues that "the claim of [the Report], put accurately, is that sexually violent material, some but not much of which happens to be sexually explicit and some but even less of which is legally obscene, bears a causal relationship, taken probabilistically, to the incidence of sexual violence," and that, since the causal relationship is independent of sexual explicitness, government regulation under existing First Amendment doctrine is both "strikingly underinclusive" and "a false cut at the problem." For criticism of the Commission's Report, see Hawkins & Zimring, Pornography in a Free Society (1988).

SEXUALLY EXPLICIT BUT NONOBSCENE EXPRESSION

The Court has considered a number of free speech challenges to laws regulating sexual expression that falls short of any of the definitions of obscenity considered above. In these cases, the Court has wrestled with the question whether such speech ought to be understood to occupy a subordinate position under the First Amendment, even if it does not comprise a wholly unprotected category of speech. Justice Stevens was a leading advocate of such a "lower value" approach: for example, in American Mini Theatres, below, he suggested that "few of us would march our sons and daughters off to war to preserve the citizen's right to see 'Specified Sexual Activities' exhibited in the theaters of our choice." In several plurality opinions, Justice Stevens supported content regulation of sexually offensive displays and speech under an approach that falls short of categorical exclusion of that type of communication from the First Amendment, but that treats such expression as less valuable than core, political speech and accordingly more readily restrainable.

By and large, however, that view has not prevailed on the Court, at least not explicitly. As the cases that follow illustrate, the Court has invalidated bans on misogynistic pornography, nudity in drive-in theaters, nude dancing, and "dial-a-porn" telephone services. In each of these decisions, the Court proceeded from the assumption that indecent or sexually explicit speech that does not amount to obscenity is protected speech and that severe restrictions or total bans of such speech will be subject to strict scrutiny.

At the same time, the Court has upheld a number of less severe restrictions on modes of disseminating sexually explicit but non-obscene expression. As one commentator put it, restrictions on sexual expression "will be permitted so long as those restrictions do not have the effect of a de facto prohibition on dissemination." Schauer, "Categories and the First Amendment," 34 Vand. L. Rev. 265 (1981). In particular, the Court has upheld zoning laws that disperse or concentrate establishments that specialize in materials of specified sexual content in order to serve goals related to property values or ancillary activities in the vicinity of such speech.

Would similar restrictions be tolerated if applied to speech of specified political content? Speech of specified political content likewise could not be channeled to another time or place merely because it was not totally banned. By deferring to content-specific regulations of sexual expression in these circumstances, has the Court implicitly, if not explicitly, treated sexually explicit speech as a subordinate species of speech?

Alternatively, can the zoning cases be explained by virtue of the secondary effects of so-called red-light districts that once occupied a prominent place in American cities, and that often featured adult movie theaters and bookstores as their anchor businesses? If so, would these cases still make sense now that the internet has reduced demand for such brick-and-mortar businesses and most have been relegated to exurban highway exits?

In examining the materials that follow, consider whether it is better to embrace openly Justice Stevens's "lower value" methodology, which treats the First Amendment as covering widely differing varieties of speech that must be aligned in a hierarchy with differing degrees of protection, or to maintain a unitary approach to the value of speech. Can the "lower value" approach be defended as enabling the Justices to deal sensibly with relatively insignificant speech without risking dilution of the protection for "political" expression at the core of the First Amendment? Or does the "lower value" approach show the weakness of judicial efforts to check majoritarian repression, by defining speech as "less valuable" in exactly those situations where it most sharply attacks majoritarian values?

REGULATING PORNOGRAPHY AS SUBORDINATION OF WOMEN

Beginning in the 1980s, opponents of sexually explicit materials advocated a novel theory for restrictive legislation that treated pornography as subject to regulation not for reason of its obscenity but rather on the ground that it constitutes sex discrimination, or the subordination of women to men. The argument was reflected in a model ordinance drafted in 1983 by two feminist theorists, Catharine MacKinnon and Andrea Dworkin, for the city of Minneapolis.

MacKinnon and Dworkin argued that pornography posed a problem not of immorality but of power: "Pornography sexualizes rape, battery, sexual harassment, prostitution, and child sexual abuse. [It] eroticizes the dominance and submission that is the dynamic common to them all." MacKinnon, "Pornography, Civil Rights, and Speech," 20 Harv. C.R.-C.L. L. Rev. 1 (1985). "Pornography, unlike obscenity, is a discrete, identifiable system of sexual exploitation that hurts women as a class by creating inequality and abuse." Dworkin, "Against the Male Flood: Censorship, Pornography, and Equality," 8 Harv. Women's L.J. 1 (1985).

The MacKinnon-Dworkin ordinance was adopted by the Minneapolis City Council at the end of 1983, but vetoed by the city's mayor on the ground that the "remedy sought [is] neither appropriate nor enforceable within our cherished tradition and constitutionally protected right of free speech." It was enacted in revised form, however, by Indianapolis in 1984. The Indianapolis ordinance was struck down by U.S. District Judge Sarah Evans Barker as overbroad, sweeping in protected speech as well as unprotected obscenity.

American Booksellers Ass'n v. Hudnut

771 F.2d 323 (7th Cir.1985), aff'd mem., 475 U.S. 1001 (1986).

■ EASTERBROOK, CIRCUIT JUDGE.

Indianapolis enacted an ordinance defining "pornography" as a practice that discriminates against women. [The] City's definition of "pornography" is considerably different from "obscenity," [which] is not protected by the [First Amendment].

> "Pornography" under the ordinance is "the graphic sexually explicit subordination of women, whether in pictures or in words, that also includes one or more of the following: (1) Women are presented as sexual objects who enjoy pain or humiliation; or (2) Women are presented as sexual objects who experience sexual pleasure in being raped; or (3) Women are presented as sexual objects tied up or cut up or mutilated or bruised or physically hurt, or as dismembered or truncated or fragmented or severed into body parts; or (4) Women are presented as being penetrated by objects or animals; or (5) Women are presented in scenarios of degradation, injury, abasement, torture, shown as filthy or inferior, bleeding, bruised, or hurt in a context that makes these conditions sexual; or (6) Women are presented as sexual objects for domination, conquest, violation, exploitation, possession, or use, or through postures or positions of servility or submission or display."

The statute provides that the "use of men, children, or transsexuals in the place of women in [provisions] (1) through (6) above shall also constitute pornography under this section." The ordinance as passed in April 1984 defined "sexually explicit" to mean actual or simulated intercourse or the uncovered exhibition of the genitals, buttocks or anus. An amendment in June 1984 deleted this provision, leaving the term undefined.

The Indianapolis ordinance [unlike the obscenity standard] does not refer to the prurient interest, to offensiveness, or to the standards of the community. It demands attention to particular depictions, not to the work judged as a whole. It is irrelevant under the ordinance whether the work has literary, artistic, political, or scientific value. The City and many amici point to these omissions as virtues. They maintain that pornography influences attitudes, and the statute is a way to alter the socialization of men and women rather than to vindicate community standards of offensiveness. And as one of the principal drafters of the ordinance has asserted, "if a woman is subjected, why should it matter that the work has other value?" [MacKinnon, "Pornography, Civil Rights, and Speech," above.] [Those] supporting the ordinance say that it will play an important role in reducing the tendency of men to view women as sexual objects, a tendency that leads to both unacceptable attitudes and discrimination in the workplace and violence away from it. Those opposing the ordinance point out that much radical feminist literature is explicit and depicts women in ways forbidden by the ordinance and that the ordinance would reopen old battles.

[We] do not try to balance the arguments for and against [the ordinance]. The ordinance discriminates on the ground of the content of the speech. Speech treating women in the approved way—in sexual encounters "premised on equality"—is lawful no matter how sexually explicit. Speech treating women in the disapproved way—as submissive in matters sexual or as enjoying humiliation—is unlawful no matter how significant the literary, artistic, or political qualities of the work taken as a whole. The state may not ordain preferred viewpoints in this way. The Constitution forbids the state to declare one perspective right and silence opponents.

[Under] the First Amendment the government must leave to the people the evaluation of ideas. Bold or subtle, an idea is as powerful as the audience allows it to be. A belief may be pernicious—the beliefs of Nazis led to the death of millions, those of the Klan to the repression of millions. A pernicious belief may prevail. Totalitarian governments today rule much of the planet, practicing suppression of billions and spreading dogma that may enslave others. One of the things that separates our society from theirs is our absolute right to propagate opinions that the government finds wrong or even hateful. The ideas of the Klan may be propagated. [Brandenburg]. Communists may speak freely and run for office. [The] Nazi Party may march through a city with a large Jewish population. [Collin v. Smith]. People may teach religions that others despise. People may seek to repeal laws guaranteeing equal opportunity in employment or to revoke the constitutional amendments granting the vote to blacks and women. They may do this because "above all else, the First Amendment means that government has no power to restrict expression because of its message [or] its [ideas]."

Under the ordinance graphic sexually explicit speech is "pornography" or not depending on the perspective the author adopts. Speech that "subordinates" women and [even] simply presents women in "positions of servility or submission or display" is forbidden, no matter how great the literary or political value of the work taken as a whole. Speech that portrays women in positions of equality is lawful, no matter how graphic the sexual content. This is thought control. It establishes an "approved" view of women, of how they may react to sexual encounters, of how the sexes may relate to each other. Those who espouse the approved view may use sexual images; those who do not, may not.

Indianapolis justifies the ordinance on the ground that pornography affects thoughts. Men who see women depicted as subordinate are more likely to treat them so. Pornography is an aspect of dominance. It does not persuade people so much as change them. It works by socializing, by establishing the expected and the permissible. In this view pornography is not an idea; pornography is the injury. There is much to this perspective. Beliefs are also facts. People often act in accordance with the images and patterns they find around them. [People] taught from birth that black people are fit only for slavery rarely rebelled against that creed; beliefs coupled with the self-interest of the masters established a social structure that inflicted great harm while enduring for centuries. Words and images act at the level of the subconscious before they persuade at the level of the conscious. Even the truth has little chance unless a statement fits within the framework of beliefs that may never have been subjected to rational study.

Therefore we accept the premises of this legislation. Depictions of subordination tend to perpetuate subordination. The subordinate status of women in turn leads to affront and lower pay at work, insult and injury at home, battery and rape on the streets.[1] In the language of the legislature, "[p]ornography is central in creating and maintaining sex as a basis of discrimination. Pornography is a systematic practice of exploitation and subordination based on sex which differentially harms women.]"

Yet this simply demonstrates the power of pornography as speech. All of these unhappy effects depend on mental intermediation. Pornography affects how people see the world, their fellows, and social relations. If pornography is what pornography does, so is other speech. Hitler's orations affected how some Germans saw Jews. Communism is a world view, not simply a Manifesto by Marx and Engels or a set of speeches. The Alien and Sedition Acts [rested] on a sincerely held belief that disrespect for the government leads to social collapse and revolution—a belief with support in the history of many nations. Most governments of the world act on this empirical regularity, suppressing critical speech. In the United States, however, the strength of the support for this belief is irrelevant. Seditious libel is protected speech unless the danger is not only grave but also imminent.

Racial bigotry, anti-semitism, violence on television, reporters' biases—these and many more influence the culture and shape our socialization. None is directly answerable by more speech, unless that speech too finds its place in the popular culture. Yet all is protected as speech, however insidious. Any other answer leaves the government in control of all of the institutions of culture, the great censor and director of which thoughts are good for us. Sexual responses often are unthinking responses, and the association of

1 [In] saying that we accept the finding that pornography as the ordinance defines it leads to unhappy consequences, we mean only that there is evidence to this effect, that this evidence is consistent with much human experience, and that as judges we must accept the legislative resolution of such disputed empirical [questions]. [Footnote by Judge Easterbrook.]

sexual arousal with the subordination of women therefore may have a substantial effect. But almost all cultural stimuli provoke unconscious responses. Religious ceremonies condition their participants. Teachers convey messages by selecting what not to [cover]. People may be conditioned in subtle ways. If the fact that speech plays a role in a process of conditioning were enough to permit governmental regulation, that would be the end of freedom of speech.

It is possible to interpret the claim that the pornography is the harm in a different way. Indianapolis emphasizes the injury that models in pornographic films and pictures may suffer. The record contains materials depicting sexual torture, penetration of women by red-hot irons and the like. These concerns have nothing to do with written materials subject to the statute, and physical injury can occur with or without the "subordination" of women. [A] state may make injury in the course of producing a film unlawful independent of the viewpoint expressed in the film. The more immediate point, however, is that the image of pain is not necessarily pain. [The film] Body Double is sexually explicit and a murder occurs—yet no one believes that the actress suffered pain or died. [No one] believes that [Jane Fonda in Barbarella] was actually tortured to make the film. In Carnal Knowledge a woman grovels to please the sexual whims of a character played by Jack Nicholson; no one believes that there was a real sexual submission, and the Supreme Court held the film protected by the First Amendment. And this works both ways. The description of women's sexual domination of men in Lysistrata was not real dominance. Depictions may affect slavery, war, or sexual roles, but a book about slavery is not itself slavery, or a book about death by poison a murder.

[Much] of Indianapolis's argument rests on the belief that when speech is "unanswerable," and the metaphor that there is a "marketplace of ideas" does not apply, the First Amendment does not apply either. The metaphor is honored; Milton's Aeropagitica and Mill's On Liberty defend freedom of speech on the ground that the truth will prevail, and many of the most important cases under the First Amendment recite this position. The Framers undoubtedly believed it. As a general matter it is true. But the Constitution does not make the dominance of truth a necessary condition of freedom of speech. To say that it does would be to confuse an outcome of free speech with a necessary condition for the application of the amendment. A power to limit speech on the ground that truth has not yet prevailed and is not likely to prevail implies the power to declare truth. At some point the government must be able to say (as Indianapolis has said): "We know what the truth is, yet a free exchange of speech has not driven out falsity, so that we must now prohibit falsity." If the government may declare the truth, why wait for the failure of speech? Under the First Amendment, however, there is no such thing as a false idea [Gertz], so the government may not restrict speech on the ground that in a free exchange truth is not yet dominant. At any time, some speech is ahead in the game; the more numerous speakers prevail. Supporters of minority candidates may be forever "excluded" from the political process because their candidates never win, because few people believe their positions. This does not mean that freedom of speech has failed.

We come, finally, to the argument that pornography is "low value" speech, that it is enough like obscenity that Indianapolis may prohibit it. Some cases hold that speech far removed from politics and other subjects at the core of the Framers' concerns may be subjected to special regulation. E.g.,

Chaplinsky. These cases do not sustain statutes that select among viewpoints, however. [At] all events, "pornography" is not low value speech within the meaning of these cases. Indianapolis seeks to prohibit certain speech because it believes [it] influences social relations and politics on a grand scale, that it controls attitudes at home and in the legislature. This precludes a characterization of the speech as low value. True, pornography and obscenity have sex in common. But Indianapolis left out of its definition any reference to literary, artistic, political, or scientific value. The ordinance applies to graphic sexually explicit subordination in works great and small. The Court sometimes balances the value of speech against the costs of its restriction, but it does this by category of speech and not by the content of particular works. [Indianapolis] has created an approved point of view and so loses the support of these cases.

Any rationale we could imagine in support of this ordinance could not be limited to sex discrimination. Free speech has been on balance an ally of those seeking change. Governments that want stasis start by restricting speech. [Change] in any complex system ultimately depends on the ability of outsiders to challenge accepted views and the reigning institutions. Without a strong guarantee of freedom of speech, there is no effective right to challenge what is. [The] definition of "pornography" is unconstitutional. No construction or excision of particular terms could save [it]. Affirmed.

[The Supreme Court summarily affirmed the Seventh Circuit's decision. Chief Justice Burger and Justices Rehnquist and O'Connor dissented, urging that the case be set for oral argument.]

HUDNUT AND THE SOCIAL HARMS OF PORNOGRAPHY

1. ***Regulating viewpoint or preventing harm?*** Is Hudnut correctly decided? For a negative answer, see Sunstein, "Pornography and the First Amendment," 1986 Duke L.J. 589 (1986), arguing that anti-pornography legislation is "directed at harm rather than at viewpoint" and that because of its "focus on harm, antipornography legislation [does] not pose the dangers associated with viewpoint-based restrictions." For a contrary view, see Tribe, American Constitutional Law 925 (2d ed. 1988): "*All* viewpoint-based regulations are targeted at some supposed harm, whether it be linked to an unsettling ideology like Communism [or] to socially shunned practices like adultery." Noting that government may outlaw incitements of sexual violence against women, as it may other incitements of crimes, Tribe adds that it is "altogether different, and far more constitutionally tenuous, for a government to outlaw [the] incitement of violence against women *only* when such incitement is caused by words or pictures that express a particular point of view: that women are meant for domination." Sunstein replies that the First Amendment permits a variety of nonneutral speech regulations to prevent serious harms: for example, banning employers during unionization periods from engaging in anti-union speech. In such cases, "the partisanship of the regulation is not apparent because there is so firm a consensus on the presence of real-world harms that the objection from neutrality does not even register." For further commentary, see Stone, "Anti-Pornography Legislation As Viewpoint Discrimination," 9 Harv. J. L. & Pub.Pol'y. 701 (1986), Kagan, "Regulation of Hate Speech and Pornography After R.A.V.," 60 U. Chi. L. Rev. 873 (1993).

2. ***Pornography and maintaining a decent society.*** Note that the MacKinnon-Dworkin argument, like Chief Justice Burger's argument for the majority in Paris Adult Theatre, views sexual speech as shaping the community rather than as merely gratifying individual consumers. But Chief Justice Burger treated obscenity as a minority practice deviating from governing norms of privacy and monogamous heterosexual marriage, while MacKinnon and Dworkin view pornography as the expression of existing majority practice.

3. ***Feminist arguments against pornography regulation.*** Many feminists opposed the MacKinnon-Dworkin argument: "[F]or many women (perhaps most), pornography is primarily victimizing, threatening and oppressive, [but] for others, [it] is on occasion liberating and transformative, [a] healthy attack on a stifling and oppressive societal denial of female sexuality," and a defiance of oppression by "marital, familial, productive, and reproductive values." West, "The Feminist-Conservative Anti-Pornography [Alliance]," 1987 A.B.F. Res. J. 681. "By defining sexually explicit images of women as subordinating and degrading to them, the [MacKinnon-Dworkin] ordinance reinforces the stereotypical view that 'good' women do not seek and enjoy sex [and] perpetuates a stereotype of women as helpless victims, incapable of consent, and in need of protection." Hunter & Law, "Brief Amici Curiae of Feminist Anti-Censorship Task Force," 21 U. Mich. J.L. Ref. 69 (1987–88). See also, Strossen, Defending Pornography: Free Speech, Sex, and the Fight for Women's Rights (1995); Meyer, "Sex, Sin, and Women's Liberation: Against Porn-Suppression," 72 Tex. L. Rev. 1097 (1994).

4. ***Gay pornography.*** Does the MacKinnon-Dworkin argument apply to pornography depicting gay sex? How can pornography subordinate women if only men are depicted or if only women are depicted? The Supreme Court of Canada has held that violent gay pornography, like violent straight pornography, constitutes sex discrimination under the Canadian Constitution. See Little Sisters Book and Art Emporium v. Canada, 2000 SCC 69. For support of this position, see also Christopher N. Kendall, Violent Gay Pornography: An Issue of Sex Discrimination (2004). For an argument that gay male pornography both liberates and helps build community among gay men and that feminist anti-pornography arguments should not apply to it, see Sherman, "Love Speech: The Social Utility of Pornography," 47 Stan. L. Rev. 661 (1995).

NUDITY BANS

The following cases involve local attempts to regulate nudity in the entertainment industry, both in broadcast media and on the live stage. While the Court has upheld limitations on where or when adult material may be broadcast, see American Mini Theatres, below, it has consistently invalidated total bans on nudity. Consider which philosophy of free speech is implicated in these cases: can commercial nudity be defended under any cognizable theory of the First Amendment? Is the Court concerned primarily with the speaker's right to express him or herself through nudity or with the listener's right to access nudity? Do First Amendment protections for commercial nudity recognize the value of commercial nudity as speech or are they a buffer against chilling more valuable forms of expression?

Erznoznik v. Jacksonville

422 U.S. 205, 95 S. Ct. 2268, 45 L. Ed. 2d 125 (1975).

[Erznoznik concerned a challenge to the facial validity of an ordinance prohibiting drive-in movie theaters with screens visible from public streets from showing films containing nudity. The ordinance prohibited exhibitions of "the human male or female bare buttocks, human female bare breasts, or human bare pubic areas." Concededly, the ban applied to nonobscene films. The city's major defense was that "it may protect its citizens against unwilling exposure to materials that may be offensive."]

■ JUSTICE POWELL delivered the opinion of the Court.

This Court has considered analogous issues—pitting the First Amendment rights of speakers against the privacy rights of those who may be unwilling viewers or auditors—in a variety of contexts. Such cases demand delicate balancing. [Although] each case ultimately must depend on its own specific facts, some general principles have emerged. A State or municipality may protect individual privacy by enacting reasonable time, place, and manner regulations applicable to all speech irrespective of content. But when the government, acting as censor, undertakes selectively to shield the public from some kinds of speech on the ground that they are more offensive than others, the First Amendment strictly limits its power. Such selective restrictions have been upheld only when the speaker intrudes on the privacy of the home or the degree of captivity makes it impractical for the unwilling viewer or auditor to avoid exposure. The plain, if at times disquieting, truth is that in our pluralistic society, [with] constantly proliferating new and ingenious forms of expression, "we are inescapably captive audiences for many purposes." Much that we encounter offends our esthetic, if not our political and moral, sensibilities. Nevertheless, the Constitution does not permit government to decide which types of otherwise protected speech are sufficiently offensive to require protection for the unwilling listener or viewer. Rather, absent the narrow circumstances described above, the burden normally falls upon the viewer to "avoid further bombardment of [his] sensibilities simply by averting [his] eyes." [Cohen.]

The Jacksonville ordinance discriminates among movies solely on the basis of content. Its effect is to deter drive-in theaters from showing movies containing any nudity, however innocent or even educational. This discrimination cannot be justified as a means of preventing significant intrusions on privacy. The ordinance seeks only to keep these films from being seen from public streets and places where the offended viewer readily can avert his eyes. In short, the screen of a drive-in theater is not "so obtrusive as to make it impossible for an unwilling individual to avoid exposure to it." Thus, we conclude that the limited privacy interest of persons on the public streets cannot justify this censorship of otherwise protected speech on the basis of its content.

[Appellee] attempts to support the ordinance as an exercise of the city's undoubted police power to protect children. [Assuming] the ordinance is aimed at prohibiting youths from viewing the films, the restriction is broader than permissible. The ordinance is not directed against sexually explicit nudity, nor is it otherwise limited. Rather, it sweepingly forbids display of all films containing any uncovered buttocks or breasts, irrespective of context or pervasiveness. Thus it would bar a film containing a picture of a baby's buttocks, the nude body of a war victim, or scenes from a culture in which nudity is indigenous. [Clearly] all nudity cannot be deemed obscene even as to minors. Nor can such a broad restriction be justified by any other governmental interest pertaining to minors. Speech that is neither obscene as to youths nor subject to some other legitimate proscription cannot be suppressed solely to protect the young from ideas or images that a legislative body thinks unsuitable for them.

[Appellee also] claimed that nudity on a drive-in movie screen distracts passing motorists, thus slowing the flow of traffic and increasing the likelihood of accidents. Nothing in the record or in the text of the ordinance suggests that it is aimed at traffic regulation. [By] singling out movies containing even the most fleeting and innocent glimpses of nudity the legislative classification is strikingly underinclusive. There is no reason to think that a wide variety of other scenes in the customary screen diet, ranging from soap opera to violence, would be any less distracting to the passing motorist. [Even] a traffic regulation cannot discriminate on the basis of content unless there are clear reasons for the distinctions.

[In] concluding that this ordinance is invalid we do not deprecate the legitimate interests asserted by the city of Jacksonville. We hold only that the present ordinance does not satisfy the rigorous constitutional standards that apply when government attempts to regulate expression. Where First Amendment freedoms are at stake we have repeatedly emphasized that precision of drafting and clarity of purpose are essential. These prerequisites are absent here. Accordingly the judgment below is reversed.

■ CHIEF JUSTICE BURGER, with whom JUSTICE REHNQUIST joins, dissenting.

The Court's analysis seems to begin and end with the sweeping proposition that, regardless of the circumstances, government may not regulate any form of "communicative" activity on the basis of its content. [None] of the cases upon which the Court relies remotely implies that the Court ever intended to establish inexorable limitations upon state power in this area.

[A] careful consideration of the diverse interests involved in this case illustrates, for me, the inadequacy of the Court's rigidly simplistic approach. Whatever validity the notion that passersby may protect their sensibilities by averting their eyes may have when applied to words printed on an individual's jacket, see [Cohen], it distorts reality to apply that notion to the outsize screen of a drive-in movie theater. Such screens [are] designed to [attract and hold] the attention of all observers. [It is] not unreasonable for lawmakers to believe that public nudity on a giant screen [may] have a tendency to divert attention from [the driver's] task and cause accidents. [Moreover,] those persons who legitimately desire to [view the films] are not foreclosed from doing so. [The films] may be exhibited [in] indoor theaters [and in any] drive-in movie theater [with a] screen [shielded] from public view. Thus, [the ordinance is] not a restriction on any "message." [The] First Amendment interests involved in this case are trivial at best.

[The] Jacksonville ordinance involved in this case, although no model of draftsmanship, is narrowly drawn to regulate only certain unique public exhibitions of nudity; it would be absurd to suggest that it operates to suppress expression of ideas.

NUDITY BANS AFTER ERZNOZNIK

Six years later, even after the Court upheld a zoning ordinance directed at adult theaters, see American Mini Theatres, below, **Schad v. Mount Ephraim**, 452 U.S. 61 (1981), reiterated that a total ban on displays of nudity is impermissible. The challenge was brought by the operators of a store selling "adult" materials who had added a coin-operated mechanism permitting customers to watch a live, nude dancer performing behind a glass panel. The ordinance of the Borough of Mt. Ephraim, New Jersey, described the "permitted uses" in the small community's commercial zone and barred all other uses. As construed by the state courts, the ban covered all "live entertainment." Justice WHITE's majority opinion stated: "By excluding live entertainment throughout [the] Borough, [the ordinance] prohibits a wide range of expression that has long been held to be within the protections of the [First Amendment]. Entertainment, as well as political and ideological speech, is protected. [Nor] may an entertainment program be prohibited solely because it displays the nude human figure. 'Nudity alone' does not place otherwise protected material outside the mantle of the First Amendment. [When] a zoning law infringes upon a protected liberty, it must be narrowly drawn and must further a sufficiently substantial government interest.

"[In] this case, however, Mount Ephraim has not adequately justified its substantial restriction of protected activity. [The] Borough has presented no evidence, and it is not immediately apparent as a matter of experience, that live entertainment poses problems [more] significant than those associated with various permitted uses; nor does it appear that the Borough's zoning authority has arrived at a defensible conclusion that unusual problems are presented by live entertainment. [Mount] Ephraim asserts that it could have chosen to eliminate all commercial uses within its boundaries. Yet we must assess the exclusion of live entertainment in light of the commercial uses Mount Ephraim allows, not in light of what the Borough might have done.[1] [The] Borough [contends] that live entertainment in general and nude dancing in particular are amply available in close-by areas outside the limits of the Borough. [But] there is no evidence in this record to support the proposition that the kind of entertainment appellants wish to provide is available in reasonably nearby [areas]."

Chief Justice BURGER, joined by Justice Rehnquist, dissented: "[Even] assuming that the 'expression' manifested in the nude dancing that is involved here is somehow protected speech under the First Amendment, [Mt. Ephraim] is entitled to regulate it. [The] zoning ordinance imposes a minimal intrusion on genuine rights of expression; only by contortions of logic can it be made [otherwise]. [To] invoke the First Amendment to protect the activity involved in this case trivializes and demeans that great Amendment."

---

1 "Thus, our decision today does not establish that every unit of local government entrusted with zoning responsibilities must provide a commercial zone in which live entertainment is permitted." [Footnote by Justice White.]

ZONING COMMERCIAL SEXUAL EXPRESSION

While the Court has invalidated total bans on nudity, it has indicated a willingness to allow legislatures to impose substantial regulations on where sexual commercial activity, including sexually explicit expression, may be carried out. In each of the following three cases, the Court upheld a local government's zoning regulation of adult entertainment. In doing so, the Court increasingly looked to the purported "secondary effects" of the speech in question rather than to the social value of the speech.

Young v. American Mini Theatres

427 U.S. 50, 96 S. Ct. 2440, 49 L. Ed. 2d 310 (1976).

[A Detroit "Anti-Skid Row Ordinance" differentiated between motion picture theaters that exhibited sexually explicit "adult movies" and those that showed other fare. The Detroit ordinance required dispersal of "adult" theaters and bookstores: it stated that an "adult" theater may not be located within 1,000 feet of any two other "regulated uses" (such as bars, billiard halls, hotels and cabarets) or within 500 feet of a residential area. Theaters are classified as "adult" on the basis of the character of the motion pictures they exhibit. If a theater presented "material distinguished or characterized by emphasis on matters depicting, describing or relating to 'specified sexual activities' or 'specified anatomical areas,' "[1] it was an "adult" establishment. The impact of the classification was to channel the display of the sexually explicit (but not necessarily obscene) materials into limited portions of the city, not to ban the display from the city entirely. The ordinance was challenged by the operators of two adult motion picture theaters located within 1,000 feet of two other "regulated uses." The city argued that the ordinance was a zoning law needed because the location of several "regulated uses" in the same neighborhood tended to attract undesirable transients, adversely affected property values, and caused an increase in crime.]

■ JUSTICE STEVENS delivered the opinion of the Court.

[The following portion of Justice Stevens's opinion was joined only by Chief Justice Burger and Justices White and Rehnquist:] A remark attributed to Voltaire characterizes our zealous adherence to the principle that the Government may not tell the citizen what he may or may not say. Referring to a suggestion that the violent overthrow of tyranny might be legitimate, he said: "I disapprove of what you say, but I will defend to the death your right to say it." The essence of that comment has been repeated time after time in our decisions invalidating attempts [to] impose selective controls upon the dissemination of ideas. [Some of our statements], read literally and without regard for the facts of the case in which [they were] made, would absolutely preclude any regulation of expressive activity predicated in whole or in part on the content of the communication. [But

---

[1] The ordinance defined these terms as follows: "Specified Sexual Activities" were defined as: "1. Human Genitals in a state of sexual stimulation or arousal; 2. Acts of human masturbation, sexual intercourse or sodomy; 3. Fondling or other erotic touching of human genitals, pubic region, buttock or female breast." "Specified Anatomical Areas" were defined as: "1. Less than completely and opaquely covered: (a) human genitals, pubic region, (b) buttock, and (c) female breast below a point immediately above the top of the areola; and 2. Human male genitals in a discernibly turgid state, even if completely and opaquely covered."

under our decisions the] question whether speech is, or is not, protected by the First Amendment often depends on the content of the speech. [E.g., incitement, fighting words, private-figure defamation, and obscenity.] [The Detroit ordinances draw a line] on the basis of content without violating the Government's paramount obligation of neutrality in its regulation of protected communication. For the regulation of the places where sexually explicit films may be exhibited is unaffected by whatever social, political, or philosophical message the film may be intended to communicate; whether the motion picture ridicules or characterizes one point of view or another, the effect of the ordinances is exactly the same.

Moreover, even though we recognize that the First Amendment will not tolerate the total suppression of erotic materials that have some arguably artistic value, it is manifest that society's interest in protecting this type of expression is of a wholly different, and lesser, magnitude than the interest in untrammeled political debate that inspired Voltaire's immortal comment. Whether political oratory or philosophical discussion moves us to applaud or to despise what is said, every schoolchild can understand why our duty to defend the right to speak remains the same. But few of us would march our sons and daughters off to war to preserve the citizen's right to see "Specified Sexual Activities" exhibited in the theaters of our choice. Even though the First Amendment protects communication in this area from total suppression, we hold that the State may legitimately use the content of these materials as the basis for placing them in a different classification from other motion pictures.

The remaining question is whether the line drawn by these ordinances is justified by the city's interest in preserving the character of its neighborhoods. [The] record discloses a factual basis for the [Council's] conclusion that this kind of restriction will have the desired effect.[2] It is not our function to appraise the wisdom of its decision to require adult theaters to be separated rather than concentrated in the same areas. In either event, the city's interest in attempting to preserve the quality of urban life is one that must be accorded high respect. Moreover, the city must be allowed a reasonable opportunity to experiment with solutions to admittedly serious problems. Since what is ultimately at stake is nothing more than a limitation on the place where adult films may be exhibited,[3] even though the determination of whether a particular film fits that characterization turns on the nature of its content, we conclude that the city's interest in the present and future character of its neighborhoods adequately supports its classification of [motion pictures].

---

[2] The Common Council's determination was that a concentration of "adult" movie theaters causes the area to deteriorate and become a focus of crime, effects which are not attributable to theaters showing other types of films. It is this secondary effect which this zoning ordinance attempts to avoid, not the dissemination of "offensive" speech. In contrast, in Erznoznik, the justifications offered by the city rested primarily on the city's interest in protecting its citizens from exposure to unwanted, "offensive" speech. The only secondary effect relied on to support that ordinance was the impact on traffic—an effect which might be caused by a distracting open-air movie even if it did not exhibit nudity.

[3] The situation would be quite different if the ordinance had the effect of suppressing, or greatly restricting access to, lawful speech. Here, however, the District Court [found]: 'There are myriad locations in the City of Detroit which must be over 1,000 feet from existing regulated establishments. This burden on First Amendment rights is [slight].

■ JUSTICE POWELL, concurring in the judgment and in portions of the opinion.

[My] approach to the resolution of this case is sufficiently different [from Justice Stevens'] to prompt me to write separately.[4] I view the case as presenting an example of innovative land-use regulation, implicating First Amendment concerns only incidentally and to a limited [extent]. [This zoning] situation is not analogous [to] any other prior case. The unique situation presented by this ordinance calls [for] a careful inquiry into the competing concerns of the State and the interests protected by the guaranty of free expression. Because a substantial burden rests upon the State when it would limit in any way First Amendment rights, it is necessary to identify with specificity the nature of the infringement in each [case].

The inquiry for First Amendment purposes [looks] only to the effect of this ordinance upon freedom of expression. This prompts essentially two inquiries: (i) does the ordinance impose any content limitation on the creators of adult movies or their ability to make them available to whom they desire, and (ii) does it restrict in any significant way the viewing of these movies by those who desire to see them? On the record in this case, these inquiries must be answered in the negative. At most the impact of the ordinance on these interests is incidental and minimal. [The] ordinance is addressed only to the places at which this type of expression may be presented, a restriction that does not interfere with content. Nor is there any significant overall curtailment of adult movie presentations, or the opportunity for a message to reach an audience. [In] these circumstances, it is appropriate to analyze the permissibility of Detroit's action under the four-part test of United States v. O'Brien [1968; p. 1176 below]. Under that test, a governmental regulation is sufficiently justified, despite its incidental impact upon First Amendment interests, "if it is within the constitutional power of the Government; if it furthers an important or substantial governmental interest; if the governmental interest is unrelated to the suppression of free expression; and if the incidental restriction [on] First Amendment freedoms is no greater than is essential to the furtherance of that interest."

[There is] no question that the Ordinance was within the power of the Detroit Common Council to enact. Nor is there doubt that the interests furthered by this Ordinance are both important and substantial. The third and fourth tests of O'Brien also are met on this record. It is clear [that] Detroit has not embarked on an effort to suppress free expression. The Ordinance was already in existence, and its purposes clearly set out, for a full decade before adult establishments were brought under it. When this occurred, it is clear [that] the governmental interest prompting the inclusion in the ordinance of adult establishments was wholly unrelated to any suppression of free expression.[5] Nor is there reason to question that the

---

[4] I do not think we need reach, nor am I inclined to agree with, the [holding] that nonobscene, erotic materials may be treated differently under First Amendment principles from other forms of protected [expression].

[5] [The Council] simply acted to protect the economic integrity of large areas of its city against the effects of a predictable interaction between a concentration of certain businesses and the responses of people in the area. If it had been concerned with restricting the message purveyed by adult theaters, it would have tried to close them or restrict their number rather than circumscribe their choice as to location.

degree of incidental encroachment upon such expression was the minimum necessary to further the purpose of the [ordinance].[6]

The dissent perceives support for its position in [Erznoznik]. I believe this perception is a clouded one. [T]he ordinance in Erznoznik was a misconceived attempt directly to regulate content of expression. The Detroit zoning ordinance, in contrast, affects expression only incidentally and in furtherance of governmental interests wholly unrelated to the regulation of expression. [Although] courts must be alert to the possibility of direct rather than incidental effects of zoning on expression, and especially to the possibility of pretextual use of the power to zone as a means of suppressing expression, it is clear that this is not such a case."

■ JUSTICE STEWART, joined by JUSTICES BRENNAN, MARSHALL and BLACKMUN, dissenting.

[This] case does not involve a simple zoning ordinance, or a content-neutral time, place, and manner restriction, or a regulation of obscene expression or other speech that is entitled to less than the full protection of the First Amendment. The kind of expression at issue here is no doubt objectionable to some, but that fact does not diminish its protected status any more than did the particular content of the "offensive" expression in [Erznoznik or Cohen]. What this case does involve is the constitutional permissibility of selective interference with protected speech whose content is thought to produce distasteful effects. It is elementary that a prime function of the First Amendment is to guard against just such interference. By refusing to invalidate Detroit's ordinance the Court rides roughshod over cardinal principles of First Amendment law, which require that time, place and manner regulations that affect protected expression be content-neutral except in the limited context of a captive or juvenile audience. In place of these principles the Court invokes a concept wholly alien to the First Amendment. [The Court] stands "Voltaire's immortal comment" on its head. For if the guarantees of the First Amendment were reserved for expression that more than a "few of us" would take up arms to defend, then the right of free expression would be defined and circumscribed by current popular [opinion].

The fact that the "offensive" speech here may not address "important" topics—"ideas of social and political significance," in the Court's terminology—does not mean that it is less worthy of constitutional protection [e.g., Cohen]. Moreover, in the absence of a judicial determination of obscenity, it is by no means clear that the speech is not "important" even on the Court's terms. I can only interpret today's decision as an aberration. The Court is undoubtedly sympathetic, as am I, to the well-intentioned efforts of Detroit to "clean up" its streets and prevent the proliferation of "skid rows." But it is in those instances where protected speech grates most unpleasantly against the sensibilities that judicial vigilance must be at its height. [The] factual parallels between [Erznoznik] and this [case] are [striking]. The Court must never forget that the consequences of rigorously enforcing the guarantees of the First Amendment are frequently unpleasant. Much speech that seems to be of little or no value will enter the marketplace of ideas, threatening the quality of our social discourse and, more generally, the

[6] In my view [the] dissent misconceives the issue in this case by insisting that it involves an impermissible time, place and manner restriction based on the content of expression. It involves nothing of the kind. We have here merely a decision by the city to treat certain movie theaters differently because they have markedly different effects upon their [surroundings].

serenity of our lives. But that is the price to be paid for constitutional freedom.

Renton v. Playtime Theatres, Inc.

475 U.S. 41, 106 S. Ct. 925, 89 L. Ed. 2d 29 (1986).

[Unlike the Detroit ordinance at issue in Mini Theatres, the zoning ordinance at issue in Renton attempted to regulate the location of adult theaters by concentrating them rather than by dispersing them. Drawing on the findings of a zoning study conducted in the city of Seattle, the ordinance provided that such establishments "may not be located within 1,000 feet of any residential zone, single- or multiple-family dwelling, church, park, or school."]

■ JUSTICE REHNQUIST delivered the opinion of the Court.

This Court has long held that regulations enacted for the purpose of restraining speech on the basis of its content presumptively violate the First Amendment. On the other hand, so-called "content-neutral" time, place, and manner regulations are acceptable so long as they are designed to serve a substantial governmental interest and do not unreasonably limit alternative avenues of communication. [At] first glance, the Renton ordinance, like the ordinance in American Mini Theatres, does not appear to fit neatly into either the "content-based" or the "content-neutral" category. To be sure, the ordinance treats theaters that specialize in adult films differently from other kinds of theaters. Nevertheless, [the] Renton ordinance is aimed not at the *content* of the films shown at "adult motion picture theatres," but rather at the *secondary effects* of such theaters on the surrounding community. [The] District Court's finding as to "predominate" intent [is] more than adequate to establish that the city's pursuit of its zoning interests here was unrelated to the suppression of free expression. The ordinance by its terms is designed to prevent crime, protect the city's retail trade, maintain property values, and generally "protec[t] and preserv[e] the quality of [the city's] neighborhoods, commercial districts, and the quality of urban life," not to suppress the expression of unpopular views.

The appropriate inquiry in this case, then, is whether the Renton ordinance is designed to serve a substantial governmental interest and allows for reasonable alternative avenues of communication. [We] hold that Renton was entitled to rely on the experiences of Seattle and other cities, and in particular on the "detailed findings" summarized in the Washington Supreme Court's Northend Cinema opinion, in enacting its adult theater zoning ordinance. The First Amendment does not require a city, before enacting such an ordinance, to conduct new studies or produce evidence independent of that already generated by other cities, so long as whatever evidence the city relies upon is reasonably believed to be relevant to the problem that the city addresses. That was the case here.

[Finally], turning to the question whether the Renton ordinance allows for reasonable alternative avenues of communication, we note that the ordinance leaves some 520 acres, or more than five percent of the entire land area of Renton, open to use as adult theater sites. [Respondents] argue, however, that some of the land in question is already occupied by existing businesses, that "practically none" of the undeveloped land is currently for sale or lease, and that in general there are no "commercially viable" adult theater sites within the 520 acres left open by the Renton ordinance. [That] respondents must fend for themselves in the real estate market, on an equal footing with other prospective purchasers and lessees, does not give rise to a First Amendment violation. [In] our view, the First Amendment requires only that Renton refrain from effectively denying respondents a reasonable opportunity to open and operate an adult theater within the city, and the ordinance before us easily meets this requirement.

■ JUSTICE BRENNAN, joined by JUSTICE MARSHALL, dissenting.

[Renton] was interested not in controlling the "secondary effects" associated with adult businesses, but in discriminating against adult theaters based on the content of the films they exhibit. [That] some residents may be offended by the content of the films shown at adult movie theaters cannot form the basis for state regulation of speech.

[The] Court holds that Renton was entitled to rely on the experiences of cities like Detroit and Seattle, which had enacted special zoning regulations for adult entertainment businesses after studying the adverse effects caused by such establishments. However, even assuming that Renton was concerned with the same problems as Seattle and Detroit, it never actually reviewed any of the studies conducted by those cities. [The] Court's approach largely immunizes such measures from judicial scrutiny, since a municipality can readily find other municipal ordinances to rely upon, thus always retrospectively justifying special zoning regulations for adult theaters.

Even assuming that the ordinance should be treated like a content-neutral time, place, and manner restriction, I would still find it unconstitutional. [The] Renton Council was aware only that some residents had complained about adult movie theaters, and that other localities had adopted special zoning restrictions for such establishments. These are not "facts" sufficient to justify the burdens the ordinance imposed upon constitutionally protected expression.

Finally, the ordinance is invalid because it does not provide for reasonable alternative avenues of communication. The District Court found that the ordinance left 520 acres in Renton available for adult theater sites, an area comprising about five percent of the city. [Respondents] do not ask Renton to guarantee low-price sites for their businesses, but seek only a reasonable opportunity to operate adult theaters in the city. By denying them this opportunity, Renton can effectively ban a form of protected speech from its borders.

City of Los Angeles v. Alameda Books, Inc.

535 U.S. 425, 122 S. Ct. 1728, 152 L. Ed. 2d 670 (2002).

[In 1978, the City of Los Angeles, responding to a 1977 city study that had concluded that "concentrations of adult businesses are associated with higher rates of prostitution, robbery, assaults, and thefts in surrounding communities," enacted a law that, like the law in Young v. American Mini Theatres, imposed density limits on adult "establishments," restricting their placement near preexisting adult stores, or near schools, parks and religious institutions. Several years later, realizing that the density limits on adult "establishments" had "allow[ed] concentration of multiple adult enterprises in a single structure," and concerned that independent adult establishments could be replaced by "an adult-oriented department store," the city amended its law to also prohibit "the establishment or maintenance of more than one adult entertainment business in the same building, structure or portion thereof," defining an "Adult Entertainment Business" as an "adult arcade, bookstore, cabaret, motel, theater, or massage parlor or a place for sexual encounters." Under the amendment, any type of adult activity at an establishment was considered to "constitute a separate adult entertainment business even if operated in conjunction with another adult entertainment business at the same establishment."]

■ JUSTICE O'CONNOR announced the judgment of the Court and delivered an opinion in which CHIEF JUSTICE REHNQUIST and JUSTICES SCALIA and THOMAS join.

The central component of the 1977 study is a report on city crime patterns provided by the Los Angeles Police Department. [While] the study reveals that areas with high concentrations of adult establishments are associated with high crime rates, areas with high concentrations of adult establishments are also areas with high concentrations of adult operations, albeit each in separate establishments. It was therefore consistent with the findings of the 1977 study, and thus reasonable, for Los Angeles to suppose that a concentration of adult establishments is correlated with high crime rates because a concentration of operations in one locale draws, for example, a greater concentration of adult consumers to the neighborhood, and a high density of such consumers either attracts or generates criminal activity. [It] is rational for the city to infer that reducing the concentration of adult operations in a neighborhood, whether within separate establishments or in one large establishment, will reduce crime rates.[1]

[While] the city certainly bears the burden of providing evidence that supports a link between concentrations of adult operations and asserted secondary effects, it does not bear the burden of providing evidence that rules out every theory for the link between concentrations of adult establishments that is inconsistent with its own. [In] Renton, we specifically refused to set such a high bar, [holding instead that] a municipality may rely on any evidence that is "reasonably believed to be relevant" for demonstrating a connection between speech and a substantial, independent government interest. This is not to say that a municipality can get away with shoddy data or reasoning. The municipality's evidence must fairly support the municipality's rationale for its ordinance. If plaintiffs fail to cast direct doubt on this rationale, either by demonstrating that the municipality's evidence does not support its rationale or by furnishing evidence that disputes the municipality's factual findings, the municipality meets the standard set forth in Renton. If plaintiffs succeed in casting doubt on a municipality's rationale

[1] The plurality left open the separate question whether Los Angeles could justify its ordinance based on another jurisdiction's finding of secondary effects where the municipality had not explicitly considered that study at the time of enacting the ordinance: "Unlike the city of Renton, the city of Los Angeles conducted its own study of adult businesses. We have concluded that the Los Angeles study provides evidence to support the city's theory that a concentration of adult operations in one locale attracts crime, and can be reasonably relied upon to demonstrate that [the ordinance] is designed to promote the city's interest in reducing crime. Therefore, the city need not present foreign studies to overcome the summary judgment against it."

in either manner, the burden shifts back to the municipality to supplement the record with evidence renewing support for a theory that justifies its ordinance.

Justice Souter faults the city for relying on the 1977 study not because the study fails to support the city's theory that adult department stores, like adult minimalls, attract customers and thus crime, but because the city does not demonstrate that free-standing single-use adult establishments reduce crime. In effect, Justice Souter asks the city to demonstrate, not merely by appeal to common sense, but also with empirical data, that its ordinance will successfully lower crime. Our cases have never required that municipalities make such a showing, certainly not without actual and convincing evidence from plaintiffs to the contrary.[2]

■ JUSTICE KENNEDY, concurring.

The fiction that this sort of ordinance is content neutral [is] perhaps more confusing than helpful. [These] ordinances are content based and we should call them so. Nevertheless, [the] central holding of Renton is sound: A zoning restriction that is designed to decrease secondary effects and not speech should be subject to intermediate rather than strict scrutiny. [Zoning] regulations do not automatically raise the specter of impermissible content discrimination, even if they are content based, because they have a prima facie legitimate purpose: to limit the negative externalities of land use. [The] zoning context provides a built-in legitimate rationale, which rebuts the usual presumption that content-based restrictions are unconstitutional.

[The] plurality's analysis does not address how speech will fare under the city's ordinance. As discussed, the necessary rationale for applying intermediate scrutiny is the promise that zoning ordinances like this one may reduce the costs of secondary effects without substantially reducing speech. [If] two adult businesses are under the same roof, an ordinance requiring them to separate will have one of two results: One business will either move elsewhere or close. The city's premise cannot be the latter. It is true that cutting adult speech in half would probably reduce secondary effects proportionately. But again, a promised proportional reduction does not suffice. Content-based taxes could achieve that, yet these are impermissible. The premise, therefore, must be that businesses—even those that have always been under one roof—will for the most part disperse rather than shut down." Applying this approach, Justice Kennedy found that the city's justification was credible enough to survive summary judgment: "The city may next infer—from its study and from its own experience—that two adult businesses under the same roof are no better than two next door. The city could reach the reasonable conclusion that knocking down the wall between two adult businesses does not ameliorate any undesirable secondary effects of their proximity to one another. If the city's first ordinance was justified, therefore, then the second is too. Dispersing two adult businesses under one roof is reasonably likely to cause a substantial reduction in secondary effects while reducing speech very little.

[2] Justice SCALIA joined the plurality's decision, but wrote a brief concurrence reiterating his view that, "[a]s I have said elsewhere, [in] a case such as this [a] 'secondary effects' analysis [is] quite unnecessary. The Constitution does not prevent those communities that wish to do so from regulating, or indeed entirely suppressing, the business of pandering sex."

■ JUSTICE SOUTER, with whom JUSTICES STEVENS, and GINSBURG join, dissenting.

[Z]oning of businesses based on their sales of expressive adult material receives mid-level scrutiny, even though it raises a risk of content-based restriction. [Adult] speech refers not merely to sexually explicit content, but to speech reflecting a favorable view of being explicit about sex and a favorable view of the practices it depicts; a restriction on adult content is thus also a restriction turning on a particular viewpoint, of which the government may disapprove. This risk of viewpoint discrimination is subject to a relatively simple safeguard, however. If combating secondary effects of property devaluation and crime is truly the reason for the regulation, it is possible to show by empirical evidence that the effects exist, that they are caused by the expressive activity subject to the zoning, and that the zoning can be expected either to ameliorate them or to enhance the capacity of the government to combat them, [without] suppressing the expressive activity itself. [The] weaker the demonstration of facts distinct from disapproval of the "adult" viewpoint, the greater the likelihood that nothing more than condemnation of the viewpoint drives the regulation.

[Requiring] empirical justification of claims about property value or crime is not demanding anything Herculean. [These] harms can be shown by police reports, crime statistics, and studies of market value, all of which are within a municipality's capacity or available from the distilled experiences of comparable communities. [And] precisely because this sort of evidence is readily available, reviewing courts need to be wary when the government appeals, not to evidence, but to an uncritical common sense [to] justify such a zoning restriction. [Common] sense is [not] always illegitimate in First Amendment demonstration. [But] we must be careful about substituting common assumptions for evidence, when the evidence is as readily available as public statistics and municipal property valuations, lest we find out when the evidence is gathered that the assumptions are highly debatable. [In] this case [the] government has not shown that bookstores containing viewing booths, isolated from other adult establishments, increase crime or produce other negative secondary effects in surrounding neighborhoods, and we are thus left without substantial justification for viewing the city's First Amendment restriction as [not] simply content based. By the same token, the city has failed to show any causal relationship between the breakup policy and elimination or regulation of secondary effects.

[Justice Breyer also joined the following portion of the dissent:] [The] plurality overlooks a key distinction between the zoning regulations at issue in Renton and Young [and those at issue in Los Angeles'] breakup requirement. In [Renton and Young],[the] limitations on location required no further support than the factual basis tying location to secondary effects; the zoning approved in those two cases had no effect on the way the owners of the stores carried on their adult businesses beyond controlling location. [The] Los Angeles ordinance, however, does impose a heavier burden, and one lacking any demonstrable connection to the interest in crime control. The city no longer accepts businesses as their owners choose to conduct them within their own four walls, but bars a video arcade in a bookstore, a combination shown by the record to be commercially natural, if not universal. [Since] the city presumably does not wish merely to multiply adult establishments, it makes sense to ask what offsetting gain the city may obtain from its new breakup policy. The answer may lie in the fact that two establishments in place of one will entail two business overheads in place of one: two monthly rents, two electricity bills, two payrolls. Every month business will be more expensive than it used to be, perhaps even twice as much. That sounds like a good strategy for driving out expressive adult businesses. It sounds, in other words, like a policy of content-based regulation.

ZONING LAWS AND SECONDARY EFFECTS

1. ***Is sexually explicit speech different?*** Is the "secondary effects" reasoning the Supreme Court embraced in Renton confined to laws regulating sexually explicit materials? If so, is that because, as Justice Stevens insisted all along, they involve a "lower value" kind of speech? Consider the implications of the distinction between content regulation and secondary effects regulation as it might pertain to "full value" communication. May a city, in order to preserve tranquility in the park, restrict all "inflammatory" speeches, regardless of the point of view expressed? May a state, in order to prevent bodily injury, restrict all discussions of violence? May a city bar all political rallies to prevent the accumulation of litter? Are these content regulations or secondary effects regulations? Does it matter whether the effects the law aims at depend upon the listener's cognitive response or are distinct from listener response? Are not most content regulations premised ultimately on "secondary effects" of the communication in the sense of listener response? For a case limiting the "secondary effects" reasoning of Renton by declining to extend it in the context of political speech, see Boos v. Barry, p. 1172 below.

2. ***Empirical evidence of secondary effects.*** What level of specificity is needed for the empirical evidence by which a government justifies its finding of adverse secondary effects resulting from adult businesses? In Alameda Books, the Court failed to reach a majority consensus on the standard for determining whether an ordinance serves a substantial government interest under Renton. Must a city provide conclusive empirical proof that crime or other social harms emanate from adult establishments? Must it prove that such harms are attributable solely to those establishments? Should legislatures be able to rely on the experiences of other similarly situated governments?

CHILD PORNOGRAPHY

Although the Supreme Court has invalidated substantial bans on adult pornography, it has been much more deferential to legislators' attempts to regulate pornography involving minors. The Court has held that the state's unique interest in protecting children from sexual abuse justifies prohibitions against both the actual production of child pornography and the possession of it by consumers, whether or not the pornography is technically "obscene." While Chaplinsky listed a series of traditionally protected speech categories, such as libel or fighting words, child pornography stands out as a rare instance in the last several decades in which the Supreme Court has recognized a new category of unprotected speech.

New York v. Ferber

458 U.S. 747, 102 S. Ct. 3348, 73 L. Ed. 2d 1113 (1982).

[Ferber, the owner of a bookstore specializing in sexually oriented products, was convicted under § 263.15 of the New York Penal Law for selling two films devoted almost exclusively to depicting young boys masturbating. The provision stated: "A person is guilty of promoting a sexual performance by a child when, knowing the character and content thereof, he produces, directs or promotes any performance which includes sexual conduct by a child less than sixteen years of age." Another section of the law defined "sexual conduct" as "actual or simulated sexual intercourse, deviate sexual intercourse, sexual bestiality, masturbation, sadomasochistic abuse, or lewd exhibition of the genitals." The law prohibited the distribution of material depicting children engaged in sexual conduct; it did not require that the material be legally obscene.]

■ JUSTICE WHITE delivered the opinion of the Court.

This case [constitutes] our first examination of a statute directed at and limited to depictions of sexual activity involving children.[1] We believe our inquiry should begin with the question of whether a State has somewhat more freedom in proscribing works which portray sexual acts or lewd exhibitions of genitalia by children [than in regulating obscenity].

In Chaplinsky v. New Hampshire, the Court laid the foundation for the excision of obscenity from the realm of constitutionally protected expression. [Embracing] this judgment, the Court squarely held in [Roth] that "obscenity is not within the area of constitutionally protected speech or press." Throughout this period, we recognized "the inherent dangers of undertaking to regulate any form of expression." [Miller.] The Miller standard, like its predecessors, was an accommodation between the State's interests in protecting the "sensibilities of unwilling recipients" from exposure to pornographic material and the dangers of censorship inherent in unabashedly content-based laws. Like obscenity statutes, laws directed at the dissemination of child pornography run the risk of suppressing protected expression by allowing the hand of the censor to become unduly heavy. For the following reasons, however, we are persuaded that the States are entitled to greater leeway in the regulation of pornographic depictions of children.

First. It is evident [that] a state's interest in safeguarding the physical and psychological well being of a minor" is "compelling." The prevention of sexual exploitation and abuse of children constitutes a government objective of surpassing importance. [The] legislative judgment [is] that the use of

---

[1] Justice White had noted earlier that, "[i]n recent years, the exploitive use of children in the production of pornography has become a serious national problem." The federal government and 47 states had enacted statutes "specifically directed at the production of child pornography." At least half of these did not require "that the materials produced be legally obscene." Moreover, 35 states and Congress had passed legislation prohibiting the distribution of such materials. Twenty of these states prohibited the distribution of material depicting children engaged in sexual conduct without requiring that the material be legally obscene. New York was one of these 20 states. (The laws in the other 15 states, as well as the federal law, prohibited the dissemination of such material only if it was obscene.)

children as subjects of pornographic materials is harmful to the physiological, emotional, and mental health of the [child].

Second. The distribution of photographs and films depicting sexual activity by juveniles is intrinsically related to the sexual abuse of children in at least two ways. First, the materials produced are a permanent record of the children's participation and the harm to the child is exacerbated by their circulation. Second, the distribution network for child pornography must be closed if the production of material which requires the sexual exploitation of children is to be effectively controlled. [Ferber argues] that it is enough for the State to prohibit the distribution of materials that are legally obscene under the Miller test. While some States may find that this approach properly accommodates [their interests], it does not follow that the First Amendment prohibits a State from going further. The Miller [standard] does not reflect the State's particular and more compelling interest in prosecuting those who promote the sexual exploitation of children. [E.g.,] a work which, taken on the whole, contains serious literary, artistic, political, or scientific value may nevertheless embody the hardest core of child pornography. "It is irrelevant to the child [who has been abused] whether or not the material has a literary, artistic, political, or [social value]."

Third. The advertising and selling of child pornography provides an economic motive for and is thus an integral part of the production of such materials, an activity illegal throughout the nation. "It rarely has been suggested that the constitutional freedom for speech and press extends its immunity to speech or writing used as an integral part of conduct in violation of a valid criminal statute." We note that were the statutes outlawing the employment of children in these films and photographs fully effective, and the constitutionality of these laws have not been questioned, the First Amendment implications would be no greater than that presented by laws against distribution: enforceable production laws would leave no child pornography to be marketed.

Fourth. The value of permitting live performances and photographic reproductions of children engaged in lewd sexual conduct is exceedingly modest, if not de minimis. We consider it unlikely that visual depictions of children performing sexual acts or lewdly exhibiting their genitals would often constitute an important and necessary part of a literary performance or scientific or educational work. [If] it were necessary for literary or artistic value, a person over the statutory age who perhaps looked younger could be utilized. Simulation outside of the prohibition of the statute could provide another alternative. Nor is there any question here of censoring a particular literary theme or portrayal of sexual activity. The First Amendment interest is limited to that of rendering the portrayal somewhat more 'realistic' by utilizing or photographing children.

Fifth. Recognizing and classifying child pornography as a category of material outside the protection of the First Amendment is not incompatible with our earlier decisions. [See American Mini Theatres and, e.g., Chaplinsky; Beauharnais.] [Thus], it is not rare that a content-based classification of speech has been accepted because it may be appropriately generalized that within the confines of the given classification, the evil to be restricted so overwhelmingly outweighs the expressive interests, if any, at stake, that no process of case-by-case adjudication is [required].

There are, of course, limits on the category of child pornography which, like obscenity, is unprotected by the First Amendment. As with all legislation in this sensitive area, the conduct to be prohibited must be adequately defined by the applicable state law, as written or authoritatively construed. [The] test for child pornography is separate from the obscenity standard enunciated in Miller, but may be compared to it for purpose of clarity. The Miller formulation is adjusted in the following respects: A trier of fact need not find that the material appeals to the prurient interest of the average person; it is not required that sexual conduct portrayed be done so in a patently offensive manner; and the material at issue need not be considered as a whole.

[The law's] prohibition incorporates a definition of sexual conduct that comports with the above-stated principles. [We] hold that § 263.15 sufficiently describes a category of material the production and distribution of which is not entitled to First Amendment protection. It is therefore clear that there is nothing unconstitutionally "underinclusive" about a statute that singles out this category of material for proscription. It also follows that the State is not barred by the First Amendment from prohibiting the distribution of unprotected materials produced outside the State.

■ JUSTICE O'CONNOR, concurring.

Although I join the Court's opinion, I write separately to stress that the Court does not hold that New York must except "material with serious literary, scientific, or educational value" from its statute. The Court merely holds that, even if the First Amendment shelters such material, New York's current statute is not sufficiently overbroad to support respondent's facial attack. The compelling interests identified in today's opinion suggest that the Constitution might in fact permit New York to ban knowing distribution of works depicting minors engaged in explicit sexual conduct, regardless of the social value of the depictions. For example, a 12-year-old child photographed while masturbating surely suffers the same psychological harm whether the community labels the photograph "edifying" or "tasteless." The audience's appreciation of the depiction is simply irrelevant to New York's asserted interest in protecting children from psychological, emotional, and mental harm.

■ JUSTICE BRENNAN, joined by JUSTICE MARSHALL, concurring in the judgment.

I agree with much of what is said in the Court's opinion. [But] in my view application of § 263.15 or any similar statute to depictions of children that in themselves do have serious literary, artistic, scientific, or medical value, would violate the First Amendment. As the Court recognizes, the limited classes of speech, the suppression of which does not raise serious First Amendment concerns, have two attributes. They are of exceedingly "slight social value," and the State has a compelling interest in their regulation. See [Chaplinsky v. New Hampshire]. The First Amendment value of depictions of children that are in themselves serious contributions to art, literature, or science, is, by definition, simply not "de minimis." At the same time, the State's interest in suppression of such materials is likely to be far less compelling. For the Court's assumption of harm to the child resulting from the "permanent record" and "circulation" of the child's "participation" lacks much of its force where the depiction is a serious contribution to art or science. [In] short, it is inconceivable how a depiction of a child that is itself a serious contribution to the world of art or literature or science can be deemed "material outside the protection of the First Amendment."

■ [JUSTICE STEVENS submitted a separate opinion concurring only in the judgment and JUSTICE BLACKMUN simply noted his concurrence in the result.]

CHILD PORNOGRAPHY AS UNPROTECTED SPEECH

1. ***The Court's methodology in Ferber.*** On its face, the majority's analysis suggests that Ferber is a rare modern case in the tradition of the Chaplinsky exclusionary categorization approach: the majority simply casts outside the First Amendment the entire class of child pornography, even though the class concededly includes materials not "obscene." But that technique produces vastly more discussion in this case than it had in Chaplinsky, and the Court also draws on a variety of other First Amendment techniques. In contrast to the Chaplinsky approach, the majority speaks at length not only about the limited social value of the communication involved but also, and most notably, about the state interests justifying restraint. So seen, Ferber is a core example of the "definitional balancing" technique involved in New York Times v. Sullivan. See Schauer, "Codifying the First Amendment: New York v. Ferber," 1982 Sup. Ct. Rev. 285 (noting that "Ferber can be viewed as partially relying on [a] 'covered but outweighed' path to nonprotection" and adds that defamation cases provide one of the closest parallels to the Ferber methodology). Note too that Justice White, in examining the First Amendment side of the balance, finds the value of child pornography "exceedingly modest, if not de minimis" by stating that child pornography does not constitute "an important and necessary part of a literary performance or scientific or educational work." Does that mark a departure from prior analyses? Does a work have to be "necessary" to literary expression to qualify for First Amendment protection?

2. ***Possession of child pornography.*** In **Osborne v. Ohio**, 495 U.S. 103 (1990), Stanley v. Georgia was held inapplicable to child pornography, with the effect of allowing the mere possession of child pornography to be made unlawful. Justice WHITE's majority opinion concluded that the same interests in eliminating the entire chain of distribution that justified the result in Ferber also justified eliminating the demand by criminalizing possession of child pornography. The Court also rejected Osborne's overbreadth challenge to the Ohio law. Although the law on its face barred the possession of "nude" photographs and although simple depictions of nudity cannot be proscribed, Justice White relied on the fact that the state courts had limited the reach of the law to cases in which "such nudity constitutes a lewd exhibition or involves a graphic focus on the genitals, and where the person depicted is neither the child nor the ward of the person charged." Because of the lack of instructions on lewdness at trial, however, the conviction was reversed on due process grounds and remanded for a new trial. Justice BRENNAN dissented, joined by Justices Marshall and Stevens. The dissent emphasized the statute's overbreadth and suggested that the narrowing state court construction was an insufficient guarantee that the law would not be applied to material as innocuous as the "well-known commercial advertisement for a suntan lotion show[ing] a dog pulling the bottom half of a young girl's bikini." The dissent also objected to the failure to extend Stanley to child pornography.

3. ***Virtual child pornography and proximate harm.*** In **Ashcroft v. Free Speech Coalition**, 535 U.S. 234 (2002), below at p. 1354 the Supreme Court clarified that the harm justifying a flat ban on child pornography is the direct harm to children in the production of pornographic materials, rather than the more attenuated harm to children from subsequent actions by consumers. The case involved a challenge to the Child Pornography Prevention Act of 1996, which extended the federal prohibition against child pornography to sexually explicit images that appear to depict minors but are produced without using any real children, either by using adults who look like minors or by using computer imaging. Justice KENNEDY's majority opinion noted that Ferber had upheld a total ban on child pornography only "[w]here the images are themselves the product of child sexual abuse. [The] production of the work, not its content, was the target of the statute. In contrast to the speech in Ferber, speech that itself is the record of sexual abuse, the CPPA prohibits speech that records no crime and creates no victims by its production. Virtual child pornography is not 'intrinsically related' to the sexual abuse of children, as were the materials in Ferber. While the Government asserts that the images can lead to actual instances of child abuse, the causal link is contingent and indirect. The harm does not necessarily follow from the speech, but depends upon some unquantified potential for subsequent criminal acts. [Without] a significantly stronger, more direct connection, the Government may not prohibit speech on the ground that it may encourage pedophiles to engage in illegal conduct." Concurring, Justice THOMAS kept open the possibility that bans on virtual child pornography may become legitimate once advancing imaging technologies rendered virtual pornography so indistinguishable from live pornography that protected status would make it "impossible to enforce actual child pornography laws."

SECTION 6. SPEECH IN NEW MEDIA

In several key cases, the Court has addressed the special First Amendment concerns raised by successive advances in communications technology, from broadcast radio to cable to the internet. Technological advances have opened up a number of new possibilities for both self-expression and for the consumption of speech. Mass communication media like radio and television have allowed speakers to reach broader audiences than ever before. Cheap and private communication technologies, from home videos to the internet, have proliferated niche markets for expression and entertainment. Digital imaging tools have allowed artists and filmmakers to create ever more convincing simulations of reality without encountering the many legal and practical hurdles faced by traditional producers. Finally, potentially anonymous communications tools like the internet have allowed speakers to engage in increasingly controversial speech without fear of attribution or detection.

Do the new expressive possibilities of technology today require a new approach to the freedom of speech? How much weight should we attach to the unprecedented power of communications media to reach unsuspecting audiences or to harm listeners? Is there a place for something like a secondary effects doctrine for online speech? Should the Court protect community moral standards against the intrusions of new communications media or will moral standards change to accommodate the new possibilities for expression today?

INDECENT AND SEXUAL SPEECH IN NEW MEDIA

The Court has considered several restrictions on sexually explicit but not obscene communications over communications media that have vastly expanded the power of such expressions to reach broader and sometimes unwilling audiences—both minors and adults. These decisions follow a pattern similar to that in the zoning cases: outright bans are invalidated but some partial regulations are upheld. In the decisions that follow, note that Justice Stevens's theory that indecent speech should explicitly be assigned low First Amendment value again falls short of capturing a majority of the Court. What is the alternative rationale for regulation in these cases?

FCC v. Pacifica Foundation

438 U.S. 726, 98 S. Ct. 3026, 57 L. Ed. 2d 1073 (1978).

[Pacifica arose from a mid-afternoon weekday broadcast by a New York radio station of a twelve-minute monologue called "Filthy Words" by comedian George Carlin. Carlin satirized "the words you couldn't say on the public, ah, airwaves, um, the ones you definitely wouldn't say, ever," especially the "original" seven dirty words: "shit, piss, fuck, cunt, cocksucker, motherfucker, and tits." Carlin repeated these words in a variety of colloquialisms. The monologue was aired as part of a program on contemporary attitudes toward the use of language. Immediately before the broadcast, the station had advised listeners that it would include "sensitive language which might be regarded as offensive to some." The FCC received a complaint from a man who stated that he had heard the broadcast while driving with his young son. In response, the FCC issued a Declaratory Order granting the complaint and holding that Pacifica could be subject to future administrative sanctions. The FCC explained that Carlin's "patently offensive," though not obscene, language should be regulated by principles analogous to those found in the law of nuisance where the "law generally speaks to *channeling* behavior more than actually prohibiting it." Later, the FCC explained that its regulation of certain words depicting sexual and excretory activity was designed to channel them "to times of day when children most likely would not be exposed." The Court of Appeals overturned the FCC Order.

Justice STEVENS, writing for the majority, found that the governing statute's prohibition of "censorship" by the FCC did not limit the Commission's authority to impose sanctions "on licensees who engage in obscene, indecent, or profane broadcasting," found Carlin's monologue "indecent" within the meaning of the statute, and rejected Pacifica's argument that "indecent" broadcasts should be limited to those that were "obscene." He also wrote for the majority in part IV(C) of his opinion, below, noting the special problems of the broadcast medium. But in part IV(B) of his opinion, below, Justice Stevens wrote only for himself, Chief Justice Burger and Justice Rehnquist.]

IV(B). [The] question in this case is whether a broadcast of patently offensive words dealing with sex and excretion may be regulated because of its content. [T]he fact that society may find speech offensive is not a sufficient reason for suppressing it. Indeed, if it is the speaker's opinion that gives offense, that consequence is a reason for according it constitutional protection. [If] there were any reason to believe that the Commission's characterization of the Carlin monologue as offensive could be traced to its political content—or even to the fact that it satirized contemporary attitudes about four letter words[1]—First Amendment protection might be required. But that is simply not this case. These words offend for the same reasons that obscenity offends. Their place in the hierarchy of First Amendment values was aptly sketched by Mr. Justice Murphy [in Chaplinsky].

Although these words ordinarily lack literary, political, or scientific value, they are not entirely outside the protection of the First Amendment. Some uses of even the most offensive words are unquestionably protected. Indeed, we may assume, arguendo, that this monologue would be protected in other contexts. Nonetheless, the constitutional protection accorded to a communication containing such patently offensive sexual and excretory language need not be the same in every context. It is a characteristic of speech such as this that both its capacity to offend and its "social value" [Chaplinsky] [vary] with the circumstances. Words that are commonplace in one setting are shocking in another. To paraphrase [Justice] Harlan, one occasion's lyric is another's vulgarity. Cf. [Cohen]. In this case it is undisputed that the content of Pacifica's broadcast was "vulgar," "offensive," and "shocking." Because content of that character is not entitled to absolute constitutional protection under all circumstances, we must consider its context in order to determine whether the Commission's action was constitutionally permissible.

IV(C). We have long recognized that each medium of expression presents special First Amendment problems. And of all forms of communication, it is broadcasting that has received the most limited First Amendment protection. [The] reasons for these distinctions are complex, but two have relevance to the present case. First, the broadcast media have established a uniquely pervasive presence in the lives of all Americans. Patently offensive, indecent material presented over the airwaves confronts the citizen, not only in public, but also in the privacy of the home, where the individual's right to be let alone plainly outweighs the First Amendment rights of an intruder. Because the broadcast audience is constantly tuning in and out, prior warnings cannot completely protect the listener or viewer from unexpected program content. To say that one may avoid further offense by turning off the radio when he hears indecent language is like saying that the remedy for an assault is to run away after the first blow. One may hang up on an indecent phone call, but that option does not give the caller a constitutional immunity or avoid a harm that has already taken place.[2]

---

[1] The monologue does present a point of view; it attempts to show that the words it uses are "harmless" and that our attitudes toward them are "essentially silly." The Commission objects, not to this point of view, but to the way in which it is expressed. The belief that these words are harmless does not necessarily confer a First Amendment privilege to use them while proselytizing, just as the conviction that obscenity is harmless does not license one to communicate that conviction by the indiscriminate distribution of an obscene leaflet. [Footnote by Justice Stevens.]

[2] Outside the home, the balance between the offensive speaker and the unwilling audience may sometimes tip in favor of the speaker, requiring the offended listener to turn away. See [Erznoznik and Cohen]. [Footnote by Justice Stevens.]

Second, broadcasting is uniquely accessible to children, even those too young to read. Although Cohen's written message might have been incomprehensible to a first grader, Pacifica's broadcast could have enlarged a child's vocabulary in an instant. Other forms of offensive expression may be withheld from the young without restricting the expression at its source. Bookstores and motion picture theaters, for example, may be prohibited from making indecent material available to children. [Ginsberg v. New York, 390 U.S. 676 (1968)[3]]. The ease with which children may obtain access to broadcast material, coupled with the concerns recognized in Ginsberg, amply justify special treatment of indecent broadcasting.

It is appropriate [to] emphasize the narrowness of our holding. This case does not involve a two-way radio conversation between a cab driver and a dispatcher, or a telecast of an Elizabethan comedy. We have not decided that an occasional expletive in either setting would justify any sanction or, indeed, that this broadcast would justify a criminal prosecution. The [FCC's] decision rested entirely on a nuisance rationale under which context is all-important. The concept requires consideration of a host of variables. The time of day was emphasized by the [FCC]. The content of the program in which the language is used will also affect the composition of the audience, and differences between radio, television, and perhaps closed-circuit transmissions, may also be relevant. As [Justice] Sutherland wrote, a "nuisance may be merely a right thing in the wrong place—like a pig in the parlor instead of the barnyard." Euclid v. Ambler Realty Co. We simply hold that when the Commission finds that a pig has entered the parlor, the exercise of its regulatory power does not depend on proof that the pig is obscene. Reversed.

■ [JUSTICE POWELL, joined by JUSTICE BLACKMUN, wrote a separate concurrence, declining to join part IV(B) of JUSTICE STEVENS's opinion:]

[T]he Commission sought to "channel" the monologue to hours when the fewest unsupervised children would be exposed to it. [This] consideration provides strong support for the Commission's holding. The Court has recognized society's right to "adopt more stringent controls on communicative materials available to youths than on those available to adults." [The] Commission properly held that [the] language involved in this case is as potentially degrading and harmful to children as representations of many erotic acts. In most instances, the dissemination of this kind of speech to children may be limited without also limiting willing adults' access to it. [The] difficulty is that such a physical separation of the audience cannot be accomplished in the broadcast media. During most of the broadcast hours [the] broadcaster cannot reach willing adults without also reaching children. This [is] one of the distinctions between the broadcast and other media. [The] Commission was entitled to give substantial weight to this [difference].

A second difference [is] that broadcasting [comes] directly into the home, the one place where people ordinarily have the right not to be assaulted by

---

[3] In Ginsberg, the Court upheld against First Amendment challenge a New York statute prohibiting a person from knowingly selling to a minor material "harmful to minors" where that phrase was defined to cover any description or representation of nudity, or sexual conduct that (1) predominantly appealed to the prurient interest of minors, (2) was patently offensive to prevailing standards in the adult community as a whole with respect to what is suitable material for minors, and (3) was utterly without redeeming social importance for minors. Justice BRENNAN, writing for the Court, held that it was constitutional for a state "to accord minors under 17 a more restricted right than that assured to adults."

uninvited and offensive sights and sounds. Although the First Amendment may require unwilling adults to absorb the first blow of offensive but protected speech when they are in public before they turn away, a different order of values obtains in the home. [This] is not to say, however, that the Commission has an unrestricted license to decide what speech, protected in other media, may be banned from the airwaves in order to protect unwilling adults from momentary exposure to it in their homes. Making the sensitive judgments required in these cases is not easy. But this responsibility has been reposed initially in the Commission, and its judgment is entitled to respect. [It] is said that this ruling will have the effect of "reduc[ing] the adult population [to hearing] only what is fit for children." [Butler v. Michigan, 352 U.S. 380 (1957)]. This argument is not without force. [But the] Commission's holding does not prevent willing adults from purchasing Carlin's record, from attending his performances, or indeed, from reading the transcript reprinted as an appendix to the Court's opinion. On its face, it does not prevent respondent from broadcasting the monologue during late evening hours. [On] the facts of this case, the Commission's order did not violate respondent's First Amendment rights.

[I] do not join Part IV(B), however, because I do not subscribe to the theory that the Justices of this Court are free generally to decide on the basis of its content which speech protected by the First Amendment is most "valuable" and hence deserving of the most protection, and which is less "valuable" and hence deserving of less protection. In my view, the result in this case does not turn on whether Carlin's monologue, viewed as a whole, or the words that comprise it, have more or less "value" than a candidate's campaign speech. This is a judgment for each person to make, not one for the judges to impose upon him. The result turns instead on the unique characteristics of the broadcast media, combined with society's right to protect its children from speech generally agreed to be inappropriate for their years, and with the interest of unwilling adults in not being assaulted by such offensive speech in their homes. Moreover, I doubt whether today's decision will prevent any adult who wishes to receive Carlin's message in Carlin's own words from doing so, and from making for himself a value judgment as to the merit of the message and words.

■ JUSTICE BRENNAN, with whom JUSTICE MARSHALL joins, dissenting:

For the second time in two years, see [American Mini Theatres], the Court refuses to embrace the notion, completely antithetical to basic First Amendment values, that the degree of protection the First Amendment affords protected speech varies with the social value ascribed to that speech by five Members of this Court. [Despite] our unanimous agreement that the Carlin monologue is protected speech, a majority of the Court [finds] that, on the facts of this case, the FCC is not constitutionally barred from imposing sanctions on Pacifica for its airing of the Carlin monologue. This majority apparently believes that the FCC's disapproval of Pacifica's afternoon broadcast of Carlin's "Dirty Words" recording is a permissible time, place, and manner [regulation].

"The ability of government, consonant with the Constitution, to shut off discourse solely to protect others from hearing it [is] dependent upon a showing that substantial privacy interests are being invaded in an essentially intolerable manner." [Cohen.] [But an] individual's actions in switching on and listening to communications transmitted over the public airways and directed to the public at large do not implicate fundamental privacy interests, even when engaged in within the home. Instead, [these] actions are more properly viewed as a decision to take part, if only as a listener, in an ongoing public discourse [through] communication he voluntarily admits into his home. [Moreover,] the very fact that those interests are threatened only by a radio broadcast precludes any intolerable invasion of privacy; for unlike other intrusive modes of communication, such as sound trucks, "[t]he radio can be turned off"—and with a minimum of effort. Whatever the minimal discomfort suffered by a listener who inadvertently tunes into a program he finds offensive during the brief interval before he can simply extend his arm and switch stations, [it] is surely worth the candle to preserve the broadcaster's right to send, and the right of those interested to receive, a message entitled to full First Amendment protection. To reach a contrary balance [is] clearly, to follow [Justice] Stevens' reliance on animal metaphors, "to burn the house to roast the pig."

[The] government unquestionably has a special interest in the well-being of children. [But here] the Court, for the first time, allows the government to prevent minors from gaining access to materials that are not obscene, and are therefore protected, as to them. [This] result violates [the] principle of Butler v. Michigan [that government may not] "reduce the adult population [to] reading only what is fit for children." [Taken] to their logical extreme, the [majority's] rationales would support the cleansing of public radio of any "four-letter words" whatsoever, regardless of their context. The rationales could justify the banning from radio of a myriad of literary works, novels, poems, and plays by the likes of Shakespeare, Joyce, Hemingway, Ben Jonson, Henry Fielding, Robert Burns, and Chaucer; they could support the suppression of a good deal of political speech, such as the Nixon tapes; and they could even provide the basis for imposing sanctions for the broadcast of certain portions of the Bible. [I] would place the responsibility and the right to weed worthless and offensive communications from the public airways where it belongs and where, until today, it resided: in a public free to choose those communications worthy of its attention from a marketplace unsullied by the censor's hand.

[It is no answer to suggest that] "[t]here are few, if any, thoughts that cannot be expressed by the use of less offensive language." [For a] given word may have a unique capacity to capsule an idea, evoke an emotion, or conjure up an image. Cohen. [Nor is it sufficient to suggest alternatives to hearing the broadcast, such as buying Carlin's record, for] in many cases, the medium may well be the message. [There] runs throughout the opinions of my Brothers Powell and Stevens [a] depressing inability to appreciate that in our land of cultural pluralism, there are many who think, act, and talk differently from the Members of this Court, and who do not share their fragile sensibilities. [Today's] decision will thus have its greatest impact [on] persons who do not share the Court's view as to which words or expressions are acceptable and who, for a variety of reasons, including a conscious desire to flout majoritarian conventions, express themselves using words that may be regarded as offensive by those from different socio-economic backgrounds. [The Court] confirm[s] Carlin's prescience as a social commentator by the result it reaches today.

THE LIMITS OF PACIFICA

1. ***Pacifica and "fleeting expletives."*** How important to the free speech ruling in Pacifica was the fact that Carlin's monologue made deliberate, repeated, and pervasive use of sexual and excretory terms? Should the First Amendment protect the use, even in the broadcasting context, of isolated utterances of "the F- and S-words" where those words are not repeated? After U2 leader Bono used the F-word at the Golden Globe awards as an intensifier to say how "brilliant" he found his award, the FCC issued an order stating that any prior interpretations exempting the use of fleeting expletives from its indecency regulations were "no longer good law." After celebrities Cher and Nicole Richie used the F- and S-words on other live broadcasts, the FCC issued sanction orders finding those utterances indecent. The Commission reasoned that any "dichotomy between 'expletives' and 'descriptions or depictions of sexual or excretory functions' is artificial," and that "granting an automatic exemption for 'isolated or fleeting' expletives unfairly forces viewers (including children)" to take " 'the first blow.' "

In **Federal Communications Commission v. Fox Television Stations, Inc.**, 556 U.S. 502 (2009), the Supreme Court, without reaching the question of whether such an application of the statutory ban on indecent broadcasts was constitutional under the Free Speech Clause, found by a vote of 5–4 that the FCC had not acted arbitrarily or capriciously in violation of the Administrative Procedure Act by changing its policy to extend to fleeting expletives. Justice SCALIA wrote the opinion of the Court, finding the FCC's policy change neither arbitrary nor capricious despite its exemptions for some uses of fleeting expletives such as those in the broadcast movie Saving Private Ryan. The majority opinion declined to rule on the constitutionality of the FCC's orders but noted that "any chilled references to excretory and sexual material 'surely lie at the periphery of First Amendment concern.' Pacifica."

Justice THOMAS filed a concurrence joining the Court's opinion but noting "the questionable viability" of Pacifica in light of "technological advances" that had undermined its factual assumptions: "[T]raditional broadcast television and radio are no longer the 'uniquely pervasive' media forms they once were. For most consumers, traditional broadcast media programming is now bundled with cable or satellite services. Broadcast and other video programming is also widely available over the Internet. And like radio and television broadcasts, Internet access is now often freely available over the airwaves and can be accessed by portable computer, cell phones, and other wireless devices." Justice Thomas stated that he was "open to reconsideration" of Pacifica in a future case.

Justices Stevens and Ginsburg filed dissents and Justice Breyer filed a dissent joined by Justices Stevens, Souter and Ginsburg. Justice STEVENS, the author of Pacifica, denied that Pacifica "permits the FCC to punish the broadcast of *any* expletive that has a sexual or excretory origin. [There] is a critical distinction between the use of an expletive to describe a sexual or excretory function and the use of such a word for an entirely different purpose, such as to express an emotion. [Those] words may not be polite, but that does not mean they are necessarily 'indecent.' " Justice GINSBURG wrote that "there is no way to hide the long shadow the First Amendment casts over what the Commission has done," and emphasized that "the unscripted fleeting expletives at issue here," unlike the " 'verbal shock treatment' " in the Carlin monologue in Pacifica, "are neither deliberate nor relentlessly repetitive." Justice BREYER would have found the FCC's change of policy arbitrary and capricious, and in particular faulted the FCC for failing to take into account the significant risk that local broadcasters would reduce live coverage because they were unable to afford "bleeping" technology or other costly means of complying with the FCC's new policy.

2. ***Captive audiences: Pacifica's privacy invasion rationale.*** Recall that in Cohen v. California (1971; p. 998 above), Justice Harlan's opinion rejected any "captive audience" rationale for restricting Cohen's speech, reasoning that government may not shield listeners from offensive speech in the public square—they must simply avert their eyes and ears. But, as Pacifica illustrates, the Court *has* allowed government to rely upon such "captive audience" rationales when applied to the home. Pacifica relied upon prior decisions including **Rowan v. U.S. Post Office Department**, 397 U.S. 728 (1970), which upheld against First Amendment challenge a federal law permitting recipients of a "pandering advertisement" that offered for sale "matter which the addressee in his sole discretion believes to be erotically arousing or sexually provocative" to request a post office order requiring the mailer to remove his or her name from his mailing list and to stop all future mailings. The law was enacted in response to concern "with use of mail facilities to distribute unsolicited advertisements that recipients found to be offensive because of their lewd and salacious character." A mail order business claimed that the federal law violated its right to communicate.

Chief Justice BURGER's opinion found the constitutional challenge unpersuasive: "[T]he right of every person 'to be let alone' must be placed in the scales with the right of others to communicate. In today's complex society we are inescapably captive audiences for many purposes, but a sufficient measure of individual autonomy must survive to permit every householder to exercise control over unwanted mail. [Weighing] the highly important right to communicate [against] the very basic right to be free from sights, sounds and tangible matter we do not want, it seems to us that a mailer's right to communicate must stop at the mailbox of an unreceptive addressee. [In] effect the power of a householder under the statute is unlimited; he may prohibit the mailing of a dry goods catalog because he objects to the contents—or indeed the text of the language touting the merchandise. Congress provided the sweeping power not only to protect privacy but to avoid possible constitutional questions that might arise from vesting the power to make any discretionary evaluation of the material in a governmental official." Chief Justice Burger added: "If this prohibition operates to impede the flow of even valid ideas, the answer is that no one has a right to press even 'good' ideas on an unwilling recipient. That we are often 'captives' outside the sanctuary of the home and subject to objectionable speech and other sound does not mean we must be captives everywhere."

Does it matter who controls the right to opt out: government or the householder? Consider the development of the so-called "V-chip" for television. Such a device would enable parents to block selected channels or shows based on their violent content. Would a law mandating that television sets contain V-chips provide a closer analogy to Rowan than did the law in Pacifica? What if the V-chip screened out only programs rated excessively violent by a government official?

Does the "captive audience" rationale for broadcasting or cable restrictions extend beyond sexually explicit speech? Could government ban, on grounds of offensiveness or harm to children, the broadcast of political advertisements for an anti-abortion candidate that contained photographs of aborted fetuses? See Levi, "The FCC, Indecency, and Anti-Abortion Political Advertising," III Villanova Sports & Ent. L.J. 85 (1996).

The Court limited Rowan's "captive audience" rationale in Consolidated Edison [Con Ed.] v. Public Service Comm'n [PSC], 447 U.S. 530 (1980), which invalidated an order of the New York PSC prohibiting the inclusion in monthly electric bills of inserts that discussed controversial issues of public policy. The PSC order had barred "utilities from using bill inserts to discuss political matters, including the desirability of future development of nuclear power." The highest state court had sustained the order as protecting the privacy of the utility's customers, reasoning that they "have no choice whether to receive the insert and the views expressed in the insert may inflame their sensibilities." The Court reversed. Justice POWELL's majority opinion explained: "Even if a short exposure to Consolidated Edison's views may offend the sensibilities of some consumers, [they may] escape exposure to objectionable material simply by transferring the bill insert from envelope to wastebasket." Justice STEVENS concurred in the judgment, reiterating his "lower value speech" theory of American Mini Theatres and Pacifica, but limiting it to cases of offensiveness that is "independent[ ] of the message the speaker intends to convey."

Does the Con Ed. principle apply only to political speech? Or does it extend to sexual materials? In **Bolger v. Youngs Drug Products Corp.**, 463 U.S. 60 (1983), the Court invalidated a federal law barring the mailing of unsolicited advertisements for contraceptive products, especially condoms. One of the proffered justifications was to protect recipients from offense. The Court rejected that argument. Writing for the Court, Justice MARSHALL observed: "[We] have never held that [government] can shut off the flow of mailings to protect those recipients who might potentially be offended. The First Amendment 'does not permit the government to prohibit speech as intrusive unless the "captive" audience cannot avoid objectionable speech.' [The] 'short, regular, journey from mail box to trash can [is] an acceptable burden [so] far as the Constitution is concerned.' " Any interest in protecting children's sensibilities, he suggested, could be adequately served by parental self-help: "We can reasonably assume that parents already exercise substantial control over the disposition of mail once it enters their mailbox. [And parents] must already cope with a multitude of external stimuli that color their children's perception of sensitive subjects." The advertisements were "entirely suitable for adults. [The] level of discourse reaching a mailbox cannot be limited to that which would be suitable for a sandbox." Pacifica was distinguished on the ground that the receipt of mail is "far less intrusive and uncontrollable" than are radio and television broadcasts.

Justice REHNQUIST, joined by Justice O'Connor, concurred in the judgment. He noted the substantial governmental interest in preventing intrusion into the home, but argued that the statute here imposed an unduly large restriction in view of the extent of the intrusion. Justice STEVENS, also concurring in the judgment, took issue with the majority's "virtually complete rejection of offensiveness as a possibly legitimate justification for the suppression of speech." But he found the statute nonetheless objectionable because it prohibits "ideas, not style": by limiting information about contraception but not conception, it excluded "one advocate from a forum to which adversaries have unlimited access."

Sable Communications, Inc. v. FCC

492 U.S. 115, 117, 109 S. Ct. 2829, 2832, 106 L. Ed. 2d 93 (1989).

[Sable involved a challenge to congressional control of "sexually-oriented pre-recorded telephone messages" ("dial-a-porn" services), available on a pay-per-message basis by a telephone call initiated by the listener. In 1988, Congress amended the Communications Act of 1934 to target such services, criminally prohibiting telephone messages that were either obscene or indecent.]

■ JUSTICE WHITE delivered the opinion of the Court.

The District Court upheld the prohibition against obscene interstate telephone communications for commercial purposes, but enjoined the enforcement of the statute insofar as it applied to indecent messages. We affirm the District Court in both respects.

[Sexual] expression which is indecent but not obscene is protected by the First Amendment; and the federal parties do not submit that the sale of such materials to adults could be criminalized solely because they are indecent. The Government may, however, regulate the content of constitutionally protected speech in order to promote a compelling interest if it chooses the least restrictive means to further the articulated interest. We have recognized that there is a compelling interest in protecting the physical and psychological well-being of minors.

[In] attempting to justify the complete ban and criminalization of the indecent commercial telephone communications with adults as well as minors, the federal parties rely on FCC v. Pacifica. [Pacifica] is readily distinguishable from these cases, most obviously because it did not involve a total ban on broadcasting indecent material. [Pacifica] also relied on the "unique" attributes of broadcasting, noting that broadcasting is "uniquely pervasive," can intrude on the privacy of the home without prior warning as to program content, and is "uniquely accessible to children, even those too young to read." The private commercial telephone communications at issue here are substantially different from the public radio broadcast at issue in Pacifica. In contrast to public displays, unsolicited mailings and other means of expression which the recipient has no meaningful opportunity to avoid, the dial-it medium requires the listener to take affirmative steps to receive the communication. There is no "captive audience" problem here; callers will generally not be unwilling listeners. The context of dial-in services, where a caller seeks and is willing to pay for the communication, is manifestly different from a situation in which a listener does not want the received message. Placing a telephone call is not the same as turning on a radio and being taken by surprise by an indecent message. Unlike an unexpected outburst on a radio broadcast, the message received by one who places a call to a dial-a-porn service is not so invasive or surprising that it prevents an unwilling listener from avoiding exposure to it.

[The] federal parties nevertheless argue that the total ban on indecent commercial telephone communications is justified because nothing less could prevent children from gaining access to such messages. We find the argument quite unpersuasive. The FCC, after lengthy proceedings, determined that its credit card, access code, and scrambling rules were a satisfactory solution to the problem of keeping indecent dial-a-porn messages out of the reach of minors. [For] all we know from this record, the FCC's technological approach to restricting dial-a-porn messages to adults who seek them would be extremely effective, and only a few of the most enterprising and disobedient young people would manage to secure access to such messages.

Under our precedents, § 223(b), in its present form, has the invalid effect of limiting the content of adult telephone conversations to that which is suitable for children to hear. [Because] the statute's denial of adult access to telephone messages which are indecent but not obscene far exceeds that which is necessary to limit the access of minors to such messages, we hold that the ban does not survive constitutional scrutiny.

■ JUSTICE SCALIA, concurring.

I join the Court's opinion because I think it correct that a wholesale prohibition upon adult access to indecent speech cannot be adopted merely because the FCC's alternate proposal could be circumvented by as few children as the evidence suggests. But where a reasonable person draws the line in this balancing process—that is, how few children render the risk unacceptable—depends in part upon what mere "indecency" (as opposed to "obscenity") includes. The more narrow the understanding of what is "obscene," and hence the more pornographic what is embraced within the residual category of "indecency," the more reasonable it becomes to insist upon greater assurance of insulation from minors. [Finally,] I note that while we hold the Constitution prevents Congress from banning indecent speech in this fashion, we do not hold that the Constitution requires public utilities to carry it.

■ JUSTICE BRENNAN, with whom JUSTICES MARSHALL and STEVENS join, concurring in part and dissenting in part.

[I] have long been convinced that the exaction of criminal penalties for the distribution of obscene materials to consenting adults is constitutionally intolerable. [The] very evidence the Court adduces to show that denying adults access to all indecent commercial messages "far exceeds that which is necessary to limit the access of minors to such messages," also demonstrates that forbidding the transmission of all obscene messages is unduly heavyhanded. Because this criminal statute curtails freedom of speech far more radically than the Government's interest in preventing harm to minors could possibly license on the record before us, I would [strike] down the statute on its face.

TOTAL BANS ON INDECENT SPEECH ON CABLE AND ONLINE

1. ***Indecent sexual speech and cable programming.*** In light of Sable, Congress could not simply ban sexually explicit but non-obscene programming on cable television. But in **Denver Area Educational Telecommunications Consortium v. FCC**, 518 U.S. 727 (1996), the Court, in an opinion by Justice BREYER, held it lawful for the federal government, under the Cable Television Consumer Protection and

Competition Act of 1992, to authorize "a cable operator to enforce prospectively a written and published policy of prohibiting programming that the cable operator reasonably believes describes or depicts sexual or excretory activities or organs in a patently offensive manner as measured by contemporary community standards." Justice Breyer reasoned that the importance of the interest in "protecting children from exposure to patently offensive depictions of sex" and "the similarity of the problem and its solution to those at issue in Pacifica" justified such a grant of discretion to cable operators. Like broadcasting, he suggested, cable programs are highly accessible to children, pervasive, and likely to confront citizens in the privacy of their homes without prior warning. Justice Breyer also distinguished Sable: "The ban at issue in Sable [was] not only a total governmentally imposed ban on a category of communications, but also involved a communications medium, telephone service, that was significantly less likely to expose children to the banned material, was less intrusive, and allowed for significantly more control over what comes into the home than either broadcasting or the cable transmission system before us." (This portion of Justice Breyer's plurality opinion was joined by Justices Stevens, Souter, and O'Connor plus Chief Justice Rehnquist and Justices Scalia and Thomas writing separately.) In other portions of Denver Area, however, the Court invalidated provisions of the Cable Act that gave cable operators discretion over indecent programming on "leased access channels," which federal law requires cable operators to reserve for commercial use by cable programmers who are unaffiliated with the operator, and "public access channels," which federal law permits municipalities to reserve for their own public, educational, or governmental use.

2. ***Distinguishing cable from broadcasting.*** Did Denver Area mean that cable would be treated like broadcasting in subsequent cases? A negative answer to that question issued in **United States v. Playboy Entertainment Group**, 529 U.S. 803 (2000), where the Court for the first time struck down, under strict scrutiny, a law that regulated indecency on a non-broadcast medium even while falling short of a total ban. By a vote of 5–4, the Court invalidated provisions of a federal telecommunications law that required cable operators either to fully scramble sexually explicit programming or, if they were unable to do so because of "signal bleed," to confine such programming to late-night hours when children were unlikely to view it. Writing for the Court, Justice KENNEDY, joined by Justices Stevens, Souter, Thomas and Ginsburg, held the law subject to strict scrutiny on the grounds that it was content-based, and that its time-channeling requirement significantly restricted cable operators' speech even though it did not impose a complete prohibition: "The distinction between laws burdening and laws banning speech is but a matter of degree. The Government's content-based burdens must satisfy the same rigorous scrutiny as its content-based bans." He distinguished zoning cases as "irrelevant," writing that "the lesser scrutiny afforded regulations targeting the secondary effects of crime or declining property values has no application to content-based regulations targeting the primary effects of protected speech." He likewise distinguished broadcasting cases, reasoning that cable systems, unlike broadcasters, "have the capacity to block unwanted channels on a household-by-household basis," and that "targeted blocking is less restrictive than banning."

Applying strict scrutiny, Justice Kennedy wrote: "When a plausible, less restrictive alternative is offered to a content-based speech restriction, it is the Government's obligation to prove that the alternative will be ineffective to achieve its goals. The Government has not met that burden here." He found such an alternative in a different provision of the law requiring cable operators to block undesired channels at individual households upon request, and rejected, at least without a better record, a variety of government arguments as to why such voluntary blocking might be ineffective.

Justice THOMAS concurred separately to express the view that the government might regulate much sexual cable programming as obscene under the Miller test, but that its attempt to regulate merely indecent sexual speech on cable was not defensible. Justice SCALIA dissented on the ground that lesser scrutiny should apply to regulation of commercial trafficking in sexual speech, a proposition that Justice STEVENS disputed in a separate concurrence. Justice BREYER dissented, joined by Chief Justice Rehnquist and Justices O'Connor and Scalia. He concluded that the voluntary opt-out provision was not a "*similarly* practical and *effective* way to accomplish [the time channeling provision's] child-protecting objective," and argued for applying a First Amendment narrow tailoring standard that would afford "a degree of leeway [for] the legislature when it chooses among possible alternatives in light of predicted comparative effects."

3. ***Sexually explicit speech and the internet.*** The decisions allowing regulation of sexual speech on the broadcast media relied heavily on the assumption that television and radio broadcast technology invade privacy and repose, "pushing" unwanted sounds or images upon unwitting audiences. What is the implication of such decisions for the new medium of the internet, in which text, sounds, and images are "pulled" from their sources through the volition of the user rather than broadcast en masse? What latitude does government have to seek to prevent children from having too-ready access to sexually explicit material over the internet?

Reno v. American Civil Liberties Union

521 U.S. 844, 117 S. Ct. 2329, 138 L. Ed. 2d 874 (1997).

■ JUSTICE STEVENS delivered the opinion of the Court.

At issue is the constitutionality of two statutory provisions enacted to protect minors from "indecent" and "patently offensive" communications on the Internet. Notwithstanding the legitimacy and importance of the congressional goal of protecting children from harmful materials, we [agree] that the statute abridges "the freedom of speech" protected by the First Amendment.

[Two provisions of] the "Communications Decency Act of 1996" (CDA) [are] challenged in this case. [The "indecent transmission" provision, 47 U.S.C. § 223(a),] prohibits the knowing transmission of obscene or indecent messages to any recipient under 18 years of age. It provides in pertinent part: "(a) Whoever (1) in interstate or foreign communications . . . (B) by means of a telecommunications device knowingly (i) makes, creates, or solicits, and (ii) initiates the transmission of, any comment, request, suggestion, proposal, image, or other communication which is obscene or indecent, knowing that the recipient of the communication is under 18 years of age, regardless of whether the maker of such communication placed the call or initiated the communication; . . . [or] (2) knowingly permits any telecommunications facility under his control to be used for any activity prohibited by paragraph (1) with the intent that it be used for such activity, shall be fined [or] imprisoned not more than two years, or both."

The ["patently offensive display" provision, 47 U.S.C. § 223(d),] prohibits the knowing sending or displaying of patently offensive messages in a manner that is available to a person under 18 years of age. It provides: "(d) Whoever (1) in interstate or foreign communications knowingly (A) uses an interactive computer service to send to a specific person or persons under 18 years of age, or (B) uses any interactive computer service to display in a manner available to a person under 18 years of age, any comment, request, suggestion, proposal, image, or other communication that, in context, depicts or describes, in terms patently offensive as measured by contemporary community standards, sexual or excretory activities or organs, regardless of whether the user of such service placed the call or initiated the communication; or (2) knowingly permits any telecommunications facility under such person's control to be used for an activity prohibited by paragraph (1) with the intent that it be used for such activity, shall be fined [or] imprisoned not more than two years, or both." The breadth of these prohibitions is qualified by two affirmative defenses.[1]

The judgment of the District Court enjoins the Government from enforcing the prohibitions in § 223(a)(1)(B) insofar as they relate to "indecent" communications, but expressly preserves the Government's right to investigate and prosecute the obscenity or child pornography activities prohibited therein. The injunction against enforcement of §§ 223(d)(1) and (2) is unqualified because those provisions contain no separate reference to obscenity or child pornography. [We] conclude that the judgment should be affirmed.

In arguing for reversal, the Government [relies upon] Ginsberg v. New York, 390 U.S. 629 (1968); Pacifica; Renton. A close look at these cases, however, raises—rather than relieves—doubts concerning the constitutionality of the CDA. In Ginsberg, we upheld the constitutionality of a New York statute that prohibited selling to minors under 17 years of age material that was considered obscene as to them even if not obscene as to adults. [But] the statute upheld in Ginsberg was narrower than the CDA. First, we noted in Ginsberg that "the prohibition against sales to minors does not bar parents who so desire from purchasing the magazines for their children." Under the CDA, by contrast, neither the parents' consent—nor even their participation—in the communication would avoid the application of the statute. Second, the New York statute applied only to commercial transactions, whereas the CDA contains no such limitation. Third, the New York statute cabined its definition of material that is harmful to minors with the requirement that it be "utterly without redeeming social importance for

---

1 [47 U.S.C.] § 223(e)(5) provides: (5) It is a defense to a prosecution under subsection (a)(1)(B) or (d) of this section, or under subsection (a)(2) of this section with respect to the use of a facility for an activity under subsection (a)(1)(B) of this section that a person (A) has taken, in good faith, reasonable, effective, and appropriate actions under the circumstances to restrict or prevent access by minors to a communication specified in such subsections, which may involve any appropriate measures to restrict minors from such communications, including any method which is feasible under available technology; or (B) has restricted access to such communication by requiring use of a verified credit card, debit account, adult access code, or adult personal identification number. [Footnote by Justice Stevens.]

minors." The CDA fails to provide us with any definition of the term "indecent" [and] omits any requirement that the "patently offensive" material covered by § 223(d) lack serious literary, artistic, political, or scientific value. Fourth, the New York statute defined a minor as a person under the age of 17, whereas the CDA, in applying to all those under 18 years, includes an additional year of those nearest majority.

[There] are significant differences between the order upheld in Pacifica and the CDA. First, the order in Pacifica, issued by an agency that had been regulating radio stations for decades, targeted a specific broadcast that represented a rather dramatic departure from traditional program content in order to designate when—rather than whether—it would be permissible to air such a program in that particular medium. The CDA's broad categorical prohibitions are not limited to particular times and are not dependent on any evaluation by an agency familiar with the unique characteristics of the Internet. Second, unlike the CDA, the Commission's declaratory order was not punitive; we expressly refused to decide whether the indecent broadcast "would justify a criminal prosecution." Finally, the Commission's order applied to a medium which as a matter of history had "received the most limited First Amendment protection," in large part because warnings could not adequately protect the listener from unexpected program content. The Internet, however, has no comparable history. Moreover, the District Court found that the risk of encountering indecent material by accident is remote because a series of affirmative steps is required to access specific material.

In Renton, we upheld a zoning ordinance that kept adult movie theatres out of residential neighborhoods. The ordinance was aimed, not at the content of the films shown in the theaters, but rather at the "secondary effects"—such as crime and deteriorating property values—that these theaters fostered. [According] to the Government, the CDA is constitutional because it constitutes a sort of "cyberzoning" on the Internet. But the CDA applies broadly to the entire universe of cyberspace. And the purpose of the CDA is to protect children from the primary effects of "indecent" and "patently offensive" speech, rather than any "secondary" effect of such speech. Thus, the CDA is a content-based blanket restriction on speech, and, as such, cannot be "properly analyzed as a form of time, place, and manner regulation." These precedents, then, surely do not require us to uphold the CDA and are fully consistent with the application of the most stringent review of its provisions.

[Some] of our cases have recognized special justifications for regulation of the broadcast media that are not applicable to other speakers, see Red Lion Broadcasting Co. v. FCC [1969; Chapter 13 below]; Pacifica. In these cases, the Court relied on the history of extensive government regulation of the broadcast medium; the scarcity of available frequencies at its inception; and its "invasive" nature, see Sable. Those factors are not present in cyberspace. Neither before nor after the enactment of the CDA have the vast democratic fora of the Internet been subject to the type of government supervision and regulation that has attended the broadcast industry. Moreover, the Internet is not as "invasive" as radio or television. The District Court specifically found that "communications over the Internet do not 'invade' an individual's home or appear on one's computer screen unbidden. Users seldom encounter content 'by accident.'" It also found that "almost all sexually explicit images are preceded by warnings as to the content." We distinguished Pacifica in Sable on just this basis, [explaining that the "dial-a-porn medium] requires the listener to take affirmative steps to receive the communication."

[Finally,] unlike the conditions that prevailed when Congress first authorized regulation of the broadcast spectrum, the Internet can hardly be considered a "scarce" expressive commodity. It provides relatively unlimited, low-cost capacity for communication of all kinds, [including] not only traditional print and news services, but also audio, video, and still images, as well as interactive, real-time dialogue. Through the use of chat rooms, any person with a phone line can become a town crier with a voice that resonates farther than it could from any soapbox. Through the use of Web pages, mail exploders, and newsgroups, the same individual can become a pamphleteer. As the District Court found, "the content on the Internet is as diverse as human thought." We agree with its conclusion that our cases provide no basis for qualifying the level of First Amendment scrutiny that should be applied to this medium.

[The] Government argues that the statute is no more vague than the obscenity standard this Court established in Miller v. California. But that is not so. [The] Miller test [contains] a critical requirement that is omitted from the CDA: that the proscribed ["patently offensive"] material be "specifically defined by the applicable state law." [Moreover,] the Miller definition is limited to "sexual conduct," whereas the CDA extends also to include "excretory activities" as well as "organs" of both a sexual and excretory nature. [Each] of Miller's additional two prongs—that, taken as a whole, the material appeal to the "prurient" interest, and that it "lack serious literary, artistic, political, or scientific value"—critically limits the uncertain sweep of the obscenity definition. The [latter] requirement is particularly important because, unlike the "patently offensive" and "prurient interest" criteria, it is not judged by contemporary community standards. This "societal value" requirement, absent in the CDA, allows appellate courts to impose some limitations and regularity on the definition by setting, as a matter of law, a national floor for socially redeeming value. [In] contrast to Miller and our other previous cases, the CDA thus presents a greater threat of censoring speech that, in fact, falls outside the statute's scope. [That] danger provides further reason for insisting that the statute not be overly broad.

We are persuaded that the CDA lacks the precision that the First Amendment requires when a statute regulates the content of speech. In order to deny minors access to potentially harmful speech, the CDA effectively suppresses a large amount of speech that adults have a constitutional right to receive and to address to one another. That burden on adult speech is unacceptable if less restrictive alternatives would be at least as effective in achieving the legitimate purpose that the statute was enacted to serve.

[It] is true that we have repeatedly recognized the governmental interest in protecting children from harmful materials. But that interest does not justify an unnecessarily broad suppression of speech addressed to adults. [In] arguing that the CDA does not so diminish adult communication, the Government relies on the incorrect factual premise that prohibiting a transmission whenever it is known that one of its recipients is a minor would not interfere with adult-to-adult communication. The findings of the District Court make clear that this premise is untenable. Given the size of the potential audience for most messages, in the absence of a viable age verification process, the sender must be charged with knowing that one or more minors will likely view it.

[The] District Court found that at the time of trial existing technology did not include any effective method for a sender to prevent minors from obtaining access to its communications on the Internet without also denying access to adults. The Court found no effective way to determine the age of a user who is accessing material through e-mail, mail exploders, newsgroups, or chat rooms. As a practical matter, the Court also found that it would be prohibitively expensive for noncommercial—as well as some commercial—speakers who have Web sites to verify that their users are adults. These limitations must inevitably curtail a significant amount of adult communication on the Internet. By contrast, the District Court found that "despite its limitations, currently available user-based software suggests that a reasonably effective method by which parents can prevent their children from accessing sexually explicit and other material which parents may believe is inappropriate for their children will soon be widely available."

The breadth of the CDA's coverage is wholly unprecedented. [It] is not limited to commercial speech or commercial entities. Its open-ended prohibitions embrace all nonprofit entities and individuals posting indecent messages or displaying them on their own computers in the presence of minors. The general, undefined terms "indecent" and "patently offensive" cover large amounts of nonpornographic material with serious educational or other value. Moreover, the "community standards" criterion as applied to the Internet means that any communication available to a nation-wide audience will be judged by the standards of the community most likely to be offended by the message. [The] breadth of this content-based restriction of speech imposes an especially heavy burden on the Government to explain why a less restrictive provision would not be as effective as the CDA. It has not done so. The arguments in this Court have referred to possible alternatives such as requiring that indecent material be "tagged" in a way that facilitates parental control of material coming into their homes, making exceptions for messages with artistic or educational value, providing some tolerance for parental choice, and regulating some portions of the Internet—such as commercial web sites—differently than others, such as chat rooms. Particularly in the light of the absence of any detailed findings by the Congress, or even hearings addressing the special problems of the CDA, we are persuaded that the CDA is not narrowly tailored if that requirement has any meaning at all.

[We] agree with the District Court's conclusion that the CDA places an unacceptably heavy burden on protected speech, and that the defenses do not constitute the sort of "narrow tailoring" that will save an otherwise patently invalid unconstitutional provision. In Sable, we remarked that the speech restriction at issue there amounted to " 'burning the house to roast the pig.' " The CDA, casting a far darker shadow over free speech, threatens to torch a large segment of the Internet community.

[Finally,] the Government [argues that an] interest in fostering the growth of the Internet provides an independent basis for upholding the constitutionality of the CDA. The Government apparently assumes that the unregulated availability of "indecent" and "patently offensive" material on the Internet is driving countless citizens away from the medium because of the risk of exposing themselves or their children to harmful material. We find this argument singularly unpersuasive. [The] record demonstrates that the growth of the Internet has been and continues to be phenomenal. As a matter of constitutional tradition, in the absence of evidence to the contrary, we presume that governmental regulation of the content of speech is more likely to interfere with the free exchange of ideas than to encourage it. The interest in encouraging freedom of expression in a democratic society outweighs any theoretical but unproven benefit of censorship. [Affirmed.]

■ JUSTICE O'CONNOR, with whom CHIEF JUSTICE REHNQUIST joins, concurring in the judgment in part and dissenting in part.

I write separately to explain why I view the CDA as little more than an attempt by Congress to create "adult zones" on the Internet. [The] creation of "adult zones" is by no means a novel concept. States have long denied minors access to certain establishments frequented by adults. States have also denied minors access to speech deemed to be "harmful to minors." The Court has previously sustained such zoning laws, but only if they [succeed] in preserving adults' access while denying minors' access to the regulated speech. [The] Court has previously only considered laws that operated in the physical world, a world that with two characteristics that make it possible to create "adult zones": geography and identity. See Lessig, Reading the Constitution in Cyberspace, 45 Emory L. J. 869, 886 (1996). A minor can see an adult dance show only if he enters an establishment that provides such entertainment. And should he attempt to do so, the minor will not be able to conceal completely his identity (or, consequently, his age). Thus, the twin characteristics of geography and identity enable the establishment's proprietor to prevent children from entering the establishment, but to let adults inside.

The electronic world is fundamentally different. Because it is no more than the interconnection of electronic pathways, cyberspace allows speakers and listeners to mask their identities. [Cyberspace is also] malleable. Thus, it is possible to construct barriers in cyberspace and use them to screen for identity, making cyberspace more like the physical world and, consequently, more amenable to zoning laws. This transformation of cyberspace is already underway. Internet speakers (users who post material on the Internet) have begun to zone cyberspace itself through the use of "gateway" technology. Such technology requires Internet users to enter information about themselves—perhaps an adult identification number or a credit card number—before they can access certain areas of cyberspace, much like a bouncer checks a person's driver's license before admitting him to a nightclub. Internet users who access information have not attempted to zone cyberspace itself, but have tried to limit their own power to access information in cyberspace, much as a parent controls what her children watch on television by installing a lock box. This user-based zoning is accomplished through the use of screening software [or] browsers with screening capabilities, both of which search addresses and text for keywords that are associated with "adult" sites and, if the user wishes, blocks access to such sites. [Despite] this progress, the transformation of cyberspace is not complete. [Gateway] technology is not ubiquitous in cyberspace, and because without it "there is no means of age verification," cyberspace still remains largely unzoned—and unzoneable. User-based zoning is also in its infancy. Although the prospects for the eventual zoning of the Internet appear promising, [given] the present state of cyberspace, I agree with the Court that the "display" provision cannot pass muster. Until gateway technology is available throughout cyberspace, [a] speaker cannot be reasonably assured that the speech he displays will reach only adults because it is impossible to confine speech to an "adult zone." Thus, the only way for a speaker to avoid liability under the CDA is to refrain completely from using indecent speech. But this forced silence impinges on the First Amendment right of adults to make and obtain this speech and, for all intents and purposes, "reduces the adult population [on the internet] to reading only what is fit for children." [I thus] agree with the Court that the provisions are overbroad in that they cover any and all communications between adults and minors, regardless of how many adults might be part of the audience to the communication. [But I would] therefore sustain the "indecency transmission" and "specific person" provisions to the extent they apply to the transmission of Internet communications where the party initiating the communication knows that all of the recipients are minors.

ONLINE REGULATIONS AFTER RENO

1. ***Child Online Protection Act.*** In response to the Court's invalidation of the CDA, Congress made a second attempt to protect children from sexually explicit internet speech by enacting the Child Online Protection Act of 1998 ("COPA"), 112 Stat. 2681–736, codified at 47 U.S.C. § 231. COPA prohibits any person from "knowingly and with knowledge of the character of the material, in interstate or foreign commerce by means of the World Wide Web, mak[ing] any communication for commercial purposes that is available to any minor and that includes any material that is harmful to minors," which in turn is defined in § 231(a)(1) as:

> "any communication, picture, image, graphic image file, article, recording, writing, or other matter of any kind that is obscene or that (A) the average person, applying contemporary community standards, would find, taking the material as a whole and with respect to minors, is designed to appeal to, or is designed to pander to, the prurient interest; (B) depicts, describes, or represents, in a manner patently offensive with respect to minors, an actual or simulated sexual act or sexual contact, an actual or simulated normal or perverted sexual act, or a lewd exhibition of the genitals or post-pubescent female breast; and (C) taken as a whole, lacks serious literary, artistic, political, or scientific value for minors."

The statute also provides affirmative defenses: one may escape conviction by demonstrating that he "has restricted access by minors to material that is harmful to minors (A) by requiring use of a credit card, debit account, adult access code, or adult personal identification number; (B) by accepting a digital certificate that verifies age, or (C) by any other reasonable measures that are feasible under available technology." § 231(c)(1).

2. ***Ashcroft v. American Civil Liberties Union I.*** In **Ashcroft v. American Civil Liberties Union**, 535 U.S. 564 (2002), the Court rejected the argument that COPA was unconstitutional on its face simply by virtue of its use of "community standards" to identify "material that is harmful to minors." The challengers claimed that COPA's "community standards" component would effectively force all speakers on the Web to abide by the "most puritan" community's standards. Justice THOMAS wrote for a plurality of the Court, joined by Chief Justice Rehnquist, Justice Scalia and in part by Justice O'Connor. He stated that, even though Web publishers

cannot control the geographic scope of the recipients of their communications, the use of "community standards" did not *by itself* "render[ ] COPA's reliance on community standards constitutionally infirm. [It] is sufficient to note that community standards need not be defined by reference to a precise geographic area. [Absent] geographic specification, a juror applying community standards will inevitably draw upon personal 'knowledge of the community or vicinage from which he comes.' [When] the scope of an obscenity statute's coverage is sufficiently narrowed by a 'serious value' prong and a 'prurient interest' prong, we have held that requiring a speaker disseminating material to a national audience to observe varying community standards does not violate the First Amendment. [Sable.] [We] do not believe that the [internet's] 'unique characteristics' justify adopting a different approach than that set forth in Hamling and Sable. If a publisher chooses to send its material into a particular community, [then] it is the publisher's responsibility to abide by that community's standards. [If] a publisher wishes for its material to be judged only by the standards of particular communities, then it need only take the simple step of utilizing a medium that enables it to target the release of its material into those communities."

Justice O'CONNOR, concurred in part and in the judgment, stating that, given "Internet speakers' inability to control the geographic location of their audience, [adoption] of a national standard is necessary in my view for any reasonable regulation of Internet obscenity." Justice BREYER concurred in part and in the judgment, suggesting that "Congress intended the statutory word 'community' to refer to the Nation's adult community taken as a whole, not to geographically separate local areas. [To] read the statute as adopting the community standards of every locality in the United States would provide the most puritan of communities with a heckler's Internet veto affecting the rest of the Nation." Justice KENNEDY, joined by Justices Souter and Ginsburg, concurred only in the judgment: "[The] economics and technology of Internet communication differ in important ways from those of telephones and mail. Paradoxically, [it] is easy and cheap to reach a worldwide audience on the Internet, but expensive if not impossible to reach a geographic subset. A Web publisher in a community where avant garde culture is the norm may have no desire to reach a national market; he may wish only to speak to his neighbors; nevertheless, if an eavesdropper in a more traditional, rural community chooses to listen in, there is nothing the publisher can do. As a practical matter, COPA makes the eavesdropper the arbiter of propriety on the Web. [The] national variation in community standards constitutes a particular burden on Internet speech. [But] this observation '*by itself* [does not suffice] to enjoin the Act."

Justice STEVENS dissented: "[In] its original form, the community standard provided a shield for communications that are offensive only to the least tolerant members of society. [In] the context of the Internet, however, community standards become a sword, rather than a shield. If a prurient appeal is offensive in a puritan village, it may be a crime to post it on the World Wide Web. [By] approving the use of community standards in this context, [the majority] endorses a construction of COPA that has 'the intolerable consequence of denying some sections of the country access to material, there deemed acceptable, which in others might be considered offensive to prevailing community standards of decency.' [If] the material were forwarded through the mails, as in Hamling, or over the telephone, as in Sable, the sender could avoid destinations with the most restrictive standards. [A] provider who posts material on the Internet cannot prevent it from entering any geographic community. [In] light of this fundamental difference in technologies, the rules applicable to the mass mailing of an obscene montage or to obscene dial-a-porn should not be used to judge the legality of messages on the World Wide Web."

3. ***Ashcroft v. American Civil Liberties Union II.*** On remand in the case, the court of appeals affirmed on the merits the district court's previous issuance of a preliminary injunction barring enforcement of COPA pending trial on grounds of likely invalidity under the First Amendment.

This time, a 5–4 majority of the Supreme Court affirmed. In **Ashcroft v. American Civil Liberties Union**, 542 U.S. 656 (2004), Justice KENNEDY, joined by Justices Stevens, Souter, Thomas, and Ginsburg, wrote for the Court: "As the Government bears the burden of proof on the ultimate question of COPA's constitutionality, respondents must be deemed likely to prevail unless the Government has shown that respondents' proposed less restrictive alternatives are less effective than COPA. Applying that analysis, the District Court concluded that respondents were likely to prevail. That conclusion was not an abuse of discretion, because on this record there are a number of plausible, less restrictive alternatives to the statute.

"The primary alternative considered by the District Court was blocking and filtering software. Blocking and filtering software is an alternative that is less restrictive than COPA, and, in addition, likely more effective as a means of restricting children's access to materials harmful to them. [Filters] impose selective restrictions on speech at the receiving end, not universal restrictions at the source. Under a filtering regime, adults without children may gain access to speech they have a right to see without having to identify themselves or provide their credit card information. Even adults with children may obtain access to the same speech on the same terms simply by turning off the filter on their home computers. Above all, promoting the use of filters does not condemn as criminal any category of speech, and so the potential chilling effect is eliminated, or at least much diminished.

"[Filters] also may well be more effective than COPA. First, a filter can prevent minors from seeing all pornography, not just pornography posted to the Web from [the U.S.] COPA does not prevent minors from having access to [foreign] materials. [In] addition, [verification] systems may be subject to evasion and circumvention, for example by minors who have their own credit cards. Finally, filters also may be more effective because they can be applied to all forms of Internet communication, including e-mail, not just communications available via the World Wide Web. [Filtering] software, of course, is not a perfect solution to the problem of children gaining access to harmful-to-minors materials. It may block some materials that are not harmful to minors and fail to catch some that are. Whatever the deficiencies of filters, however, the Government failed to introduce specific evidence proving that existing technologies are less effective than the restrictions in COPA. In the absence of a showing as to the relative effectiveness of COPA and the alternatives proposed by respondents, it was not an abuse of discretion for the District Court to grant the preliminary injunction.

"The closest precedent on the general point is our decision in Playboy Entertainment Group, [which,] like this case, involved a content-based restriction designed to protect minors from viewing harmful materials. The choice was between a blanket speech restriction and a more specific technological solution that was available to parents who chose to implement it. Absent a showing that the proposed less restrictive alternative would not be as effective, we concluded, the more restrictive option preferred by Congress could not survive strict scrutiny. [Here] too, the Government has failed to show, at this point, that the proposed less restrictive alternative will be less effective."

Justice BREYER, joined by Chief Justice Rehnquist and Justice O'Connor, dissented, arguing that, even if strict scrutiny applied, the government had satisfied its burden of showing that no less restrictive means was available to serve the concededly compelling interest in preventing child access to sexually explicit speech on the internet: "Conceptually speaking, the presence of filtering software is not an alternative legislative approach to the problem of protecting children from exposure to commercial pornography. Rather, it is part of the status quo, i.e., the backdrop against which Congress enacted the present statute. It is always true, by definition, that the status quo is less restrictive than a new regulatory law. It is always less restrictive to do nothing than to do something. But 'doing nothing' does not address the problem Congress sought to address—namely that, despite the availability of filtering software, children were still being exposed to harmful material on the Internet.

"[Given] the existence of filtering software, does the problem Congress identified remain significant? Does the Act help to address it? [The] answers to [these] questions are clear: Filtering software, as presently available, does not solve the 'child protection' problem. It suffers from four serious inadequacies that prompted Congress to pass legislation instead of relying on its voluntary use. First, its filtering is faulty, allowing some pornographic material to pass through without hindrance. [Second,] filtering software costs money. Not every family has the $40 or so necessary to install it. Third, filtering software depends upon parents willing to decide where their children will surf the Web and able to enforce that decision. As to millions of American families, that is not a reasonable possibility. [Fourth,] software blocking lacks precision, with the result that those who wish to use it to screen out pornography find that it blocks a great deal of material that is valuable. [Thus,] Congress could reasonably conclude that a system that relies entirely upon the use of such software is not an effective system. And a law that adds to that system an age-verification screen requirement significantly increases the system's efficacy. [It thus] significantly helps to achieve a compelling congressional goal, protecting children from exposure to commercial pornography. There is no serious, practically available 'less restrictive' way similarly to further this compelling interest." Justice Scalia filed a separate dissent reiterating his view that regulation of commercial pornography ought not be subjected to strict scrutiny.

4. ***Child pornography and digital simulation of reality.*** Digital imaging technology today allows speakers to create ever more realistic depictions of fictional characters, scenes, and events. These technological tools can mitigate the risks involved in more traditional forms of speech, for example by avoiding the harms of producing violent, sexual, or otherwise graphic content. Yet they may also create greater harms in the reception of speech, by proliferating previously impractical levels of graphic expression. Consider how digital simulation affects the permissible scope of regulation of child pornography in the following case:

———

Ashcroft v. Free Speech Coalition

535 U.S. 234, 122 S. Ct. 1389, 152 L. Ed. 2d 403 (2002).

[The Child Pornography Prevention Act of 1996 (CPPA), 18 U.S.C. § 2251, extended the federal prohibition against child pornography to sexually explicit images that appear to depict minors but are produced without using any real children, either by using adults who look like minors or by using computer imaging. Section § 2256(8)(B) prohibited "any visual depiction, including any photograph, film, video, picture, or computer or computer-generated image or picture' that 'is, or appears to be, of a minor engaging in sexually explicit conduct." Section 2256(8)(D) prohibited possession of films containing no child pornography, "if they had, at any time anywhere in the chain of distribution, been promoted or sold in a manner erroneously suggesting the presence of child pornography." The government argued that the consumption and use of even simulated child pornography could increase the incidence of sexual abuse of children.]

■ JUSTICE KENNEDY delivered the opinion of the Court.

By prohibiting child pornography that does not depict an actual child, the [CPPA] goes beyond Ferber, which distinguished child pornography from other sexually explicit speech because of the State's interest in protecting the children exploited by the production process. The CPPA [prohibits] "any visual depiction, including any photograph, film, video, picture, or computer or computer-generated image or picture," that "is, or appears to be, of a minor engaging in sexually explicit conduct." The section captures a range of depictions, sometimes called "virtual child pornography," which include computer-generated images, as well as images produced by more traditional means.

[These] images do not involve, let alone harm, any children in the production process; but Congress decided the materials threaten children in other, less direct, ways. Pedophiles might use the materials to encourage children to participate in sexual activity. [Furthermore], pedophiles might "whet their own sexual appetites" with the pornographic images, "thereby increasing the creation and distribution of child pornography and the sexual abuse and exploitation of actual children." [The] sexual abuse of a child is a most serious crime and an act repugnant to the moral instincts of a decent people. The prospect of crime, however, by itself does not justify laws suppressing protected speech. It is also well established that speech may not be prohibited because it concerns subjects offending our sensibilities. See [FCC v. Pacifica].

The CPPA prohibits speech despite its serious literary, artistic, political, or scientific value. The statute proscribes the visual depiction of an idea—that of teenagers engaging in sexual activity—that is a fact of modern society and has been a theme in art and literature throughout the ages. [William] Shakespeare created the most famous pair of teenage lovers, one of whom is just 13 years of age. See Romeo and Juliet. [Contemporary] movies pursue similar themes. [If] these films, or hundreds of others of lesser note that explore those subjects, contain a single graphic depiction of sexual activity within the statutory definition, the possessor of the film would be subject to severe punishment without inquiry into the work's redeeming value. This is inconsistent with an essential First Amendment rule: The artistic merit of a work does not depend on the presence of a single explicit scene.

Where the images are themselves the product of child sexual abuse, Ferber recognized that the State had an interest in stamping it out without regard to any judgment about its content. The production of the work, not its content, was the target of the statute. In contrast to the speech in Ferber, speech that itself is the record of sexual abuse, the CPPA prohibits speech that records no crime and creates no victims by its production. [While] the Government asserts that the images can lead to actual instances of child abuse, the causal link is contingent and indirect. The harm does not necessarily follow from the speech, but depends upon some unquantified potential for subsequent criminal acts.

[The Government] argues that the CPPA is necessary because pedophiles may use virtual child pornography to seduce children. The Government, of course, may punish adults who provide unsuitable materials to children, and it may enforce criminal penalties for unlawful solicitation. The precedents establish, however, that speech within the rights of adults to hear may not be silenced completely in an attempt to shield children from it. [The] Government cannot ban speech fit for adults simply because it may fall into the hands of children.

The Government submits further that virtual child pornography whets the appetites of pedophiles and encourages them to engage in illegal conduct. This rationale cannot sustain the provision in question. [The] government "cannot constitutionally premise legislation on the desirability of controlling a person's private thoughts." [Without] a significantly stronger, more direct connection, the Government may not prohibit speech on the ground that it may encourage pedophiles to engage in illegal conduct.

The Government next argues that its objective of eliminating the market for pornography produced using real children necessitates a prohibition on virtual images as well. [The] hypothesis is somewhat implausible. If virtual images were identical to illegal child pornography, the illegal images would be driven from the market by the indistinguishable substitutes. Few pornographers would risk prosecution by abusing real children if fictional, computerized images would suffice.

Finally, the Government says that the possibility of producing images by using computer imaging makes it very difficult for it to prosecute those who produce pornography by using real children. Experts, we are told, may have difficulty in saying whether the pictures were made by using real children or by using computer imaging. [The] argument, in essence, is that protected speech may be banned as a means to ban unprotected speech. This analysis turns the First Amendment upside down. The Government may not suppress lawful speech as the means to suppress unlawful speech. [The] Constitution requires the reverse.

[The] Government relies on an affirmative defense under the statute, which allows a defendant to avoid conviction for nonpossession offenses by showing that the materials were produced using only adults and were not otherwise distributed in a manner conveying the impression that they depicted real children. The Government raises serious constitutional difficulties by seeking to impose on the defendant the burden of proving his speech is not unlawful.

Respondents challenge § 2256(8)(D) as well. This provision bans depictions of sexually explicit conduct that are "advertised, promoted, presented, described, or distributed in such a manner that conveys the impression that the material is or contains a visual depiction of a minor engaging in sexually explicit conduct." [Even] if a film contains no sexually explicit scenes involving minors, it could be treated as child pornography if the title and trailers convey the impression that the scenes would be found in the movie. [The] Court has recognized that pandering may be relevant, as an evidentiary matter, to the question whether particular materials are obscene. Section 2256(8)(D), however, prohibits a substantial amount of speech that falls outside [the Court's previously recognized] rationale. Materials falling within the proscription are tainted and unlawful in the hands of all who receive it, though they bear no responsibility for how it was marketed, sold, or described. [Possession] is a crime even when the possessor knows the movie was mislabeled. The First Amendment requires a more precise restriction.

■ JUSTICE THOMAS, concurring in the judgment.

In my view, the Government's most persuasive [justification for CPPA] is the prosecution rationale—that persons who possess and disseminate pornographic images of real children may escape conviction by claiming that the images are computer-generated, thereby raising a reasonable doubt as to their guilt. At this time, however, the Government['s assertion of the problem is not supported by any examples of defendants] acquitted [in this fashion]. [Technology] may evolve to the point where it becomes impossible to enforce actual child pornography laws because the Government cannot prove that certain pornographic images are of real children. In the event this occurs, the Government should not be foreclosed from enacting a regulation of virtual child pornography that contains an appropriate affirmative defense or some other narrowly drawn restriction.

■ CHIEF JUSTICE REHNQUIST, joined by JUSTICE SCALIA, dissenting.

Congress has a compelling interest in ensuring the ability to enforce prohibitions of actual child pornography, and we should defer to its findings that rapidly advancing technology soon will make it all but impossible to do so. [I agree] that serious First Amendment concerns would arise were the Government ever to prosecute someone for simple distribution or possession of a film with literary or artistic value. [But the CPPA] need not be construed to reach such materials. [The statute's definition of] "sexually explicit conduct" [only] reaches "visual depictions" of: "actual or simulated . . . sexual intercourse, including genital-genital, oral-genital, anal-genital, or oral-anal, whether between persons of the same or opposite sex; . . . bestiality; . . . masturbation; . . . sadistic or masochistic abuse; . . . or lascivious exhibition of the genitals or pubic area of any person." [I] think the definition reaches only the sort of "hard core of child pornography" that we found without protection in Ferber.

---

5. ***Deep fakes.*** Since Ashcroft, new technology for creating "deep fakes" has come into existence. Such technology allows a virtually seamless merger of images of one person's face and another person's body to be created and distributed on the internet. It also allows for the manipulation of moving images so that a person can be shown to say words he or she did not in fact say. What does this suggest for the future of pornography regulation going forward? What about regulation of faked moving images, regardless of sexual content?

6. ***Social media bans.*** In **Packingham v. North Carolina**, 581 U.S. ___, 137 S. Ct. 1730 (2017), the Court considered a state law that made it a felony for a registered sex offender "to access a commercial social networking Web site where the sex offender knows that the site permits minor children to become members or to create or maintain personal Web pages." North Carolina had prosecuted over 1,000 people for violating this law, including petitioner, who was indicted after posting a statement on his personal Facebook profile about a positive experience in traffic court. Finding the law invalid on its face, Justice KENNEDY, joined by Justices Ginsburg, Breyer, Sotomayor, and Kagan, wrote: "A fundamental principle of the First Amendment is that all persons have access to places where they can speak and listen, and then, after reflection, speak and listen once more. The Court has sought to protect the right to speak in this spatial context. A basic rule, for example, is that a street or a park is a quintessential forum for the exercise of First Amendment rights. Even in the modern era, these places are still essential venues for public gatherings to celebrate some views, to protest others, or simply to learn and inquire. While in the past there may have been difficulty in identifying the most important places (in a spatial sense) for the exchange of views, today the answer is clear. It is cyberspace—the 'vast democratic forums of the Internet' in general, Reno v. American Civil Liberties Union, and social media in particular. Seven in ten American adults use at least one Internet social networking service. One of the most popular of these sites is Facebook, the site used by petitioner leading to his conviction in this case. According to sources cited to the Court in this case, Facebook has 1.79 billion active users. This is about three times the population of North America. Social media offers relatively unlimited, low-cost capacity for communication of all kinds. On Facebook, for example, users can debate religion and politics with their friends and neighbors or share vacation photos. On LinkedIn, users can look for work, advertise for employees, or review tips on entrepreneurship. And on Twitter, users can petition their elected representatives and otherwise engage with them in a direct manner. Indeed, Governors in all 50 States and almost every Member of Congress have set up accounts for this purpose. In short, social media users employ these websites to engage in a wide array of protected First Amendment activity on topics as diverse as human thought. [The] forces and directions of the Internet are so new, so protean, and so far reaching that courts must be conscious that what they say today might be obsolete tomorrow.

"[This] case is one of the first this Court has taken to address the relationship between the First Amendment and the modern Internet. As a result, the Court must exercise extreme caution before suggesting that the First Amendment provides scant protection for access to vast networks in that medium. [Even] making the assumption that the statute is content neutral and thus subject to intermediate scrutiny, the provision cannot stand. [For] centuries now, inventions heralded as advances in human progress have been exploited by the criminal mind. [So] it will be with the Internet and social media. [The] statute here enacts a prohibition unprecedented in the scope of First Amendment speech it burdens. [By] prohibiting sex offenders from using those websites, North Carolina with one broad stroke bars access to what for many are the principal sources for knowing current events, checking ads for employment, speaking and listening in the modern public square, and otherwise exploring the vast realms of human thought and knowledge. These websites can provide perhaps the most powerful mechanisms available to a private citizen to make his or her voice heard. [It] is unsettling to suggest that only a limited set of websites can be used even by persons who have completed their sentences. Even convicted criminals—and in some instances especially convicted criminals—might receive legitimate benefits from these means for access to the world of ideas, in particular if they seek to reform and to pursue lawful and rewarding lives."

Justice ALITO, joined by Chief Justice Roberts and Justice Thomas, concurred only in the judgment: "[I] agree with the Court that [the law] violates the Free Speech Clause of the First Amendment. I cannot join the opinion of the Court, however, because of its undisciplined dicta. The Court is unable to resist musings that seem to equate the entirety of the internet with public streets and parks. And this language is bound to be interpreted by some to mean that the States are largely powerless to restrict even the most dangerous sexual predators from visiting any internet sites, including, for example, teenage dating sites and sites designed to permit minors to discuss personal problems with their peers. [The] State's interest in protecting children from recidivist sex offenders plainly applies to internet use. [It] is not enough, however, that the law before us is designed to serve a compelling state interest; it also must not 'burden substantially more speech than is necessary to further the government's legitimate interests.' The North Carolina law fails this requirement." Justice Gorsuch did not participate.

7. ***Newer media***. Further questions are raised by the emergence of highly-regulated social media platforms. Does the existence of private content regulation reduce the need for government regulation? Is it all the more necessary for the government to not regulate alternative platforms? In general, how does the advent of social media, also called Internet 3.0, change your understanding of the First Amendment? Does the more active regulation by European states, which tends to require platforms to respect privacy to a greater degree, influence that understanding?

A doctrinal problem not yet resolved involves private users blocking others from accessing social media accounts or channels they control. In **Knight First Amendment Inst. at Columbia Univ. v. Trump**, 302 F. Supp. 3d 541 (S.D.N.Y. 2018), Judge Buchwald ruled that President Donald Trump's blocking of Twitter users from his feed violated the First Amendment. Buchwald held that the Twitter feed constituted a designated public forum because it was an " 'interactive space' where users may directly engage with the content of the President's tweets." Blocking users because their tweets disagreed with or criticized the president thus "constitute[d] viewpoint discrimination that violates the First Amendment." The question of whether Twitter is a limited public forum is discussed further at p. 1269 below.

Further issues arise with regard to a private media platform's regulation of its own user base. Following the "Unite the Right" rally that took place in August 2017, Twitter banned a number of high-profile white-supremacist accounts from the platform. One such banned user sued Twitter, raising a free speech claim, among others. See Johnson v. Twitter, Inc., No. 18CECG00078 (Cal. Super. Ct. June 6, 2018). In Johnson, the district court granted Twitter's motion to dismiss. As a private sector company, the court reasoned, Twitter's "choice not to allow certain speech is a right protected by the First Amendment." [Note that the issue of compelled access to other's private property for speech purposes is discussed at p. 1402, below.]

In **Sandvig v. Sessions**, 315 F. Supp. 3d 1 (D.D.C. 2018), the D.C. District Court considered whether researchers can be prosecuted under the Computer Fraud and Abuse Act (CFAA) for violating a platform's terms of service when the researchers test whether the platform discriminates based on various legally-protected traits. While dismissing plaintiffs claims that the statute was facially overbroad or impermissibly vague, the court held the plaintiffs had stated a valid First Amendment claim against the law as applied to them. The court viewed receiving information from the websites and as well as publishing the results as protected First Amendment activity.

VIOLENT SPEECH IN NEW MEDIA

The proliferation of cheap and private communications technology has led to the rise of increasingly specialized, clandestine markets for speech. Many of these markets involve violence, cruelty, or other behavior considered offensive by more mainstream audiences. The Court has not designated any category of speech "unprotected" since Ferber placed child pornography outside the reach of the First Amendment in 1982. Are there other categories of speech so presumptively injurious and lacking in social value that they may be deemed similarly unprotected?

United States v. Stevens

559 U.S. 460, 130 S. Ct. 1577, 176 L. Ed. 2d 435 (2010).

[18 U.S.C. § 48 criminalized the commercial creation, sale, or possession of any visual or auditory depiction "in which a living animal is intentionally maimed, mutilated, tortured, wounded, or killed," if that conduct violates federal or state law where "the creation, sale, or possession takes place," unless the depiction has "serious religious, political, scientific, educational, journalistic, historical, or artistic value." While the legislative history focused primarily on "crush videos," which show torture and killing of helpless animals to appeal to a sexual fetish, the statute's text was not limited to such videos. Stevens challenged his indictment for distributing videos of dogfighting, which is unlawful in all 50 States and the District of Columbia.]

■ CHIEF JUSTICE ROBERTS delivered the opinion of the Court.

From 1791 to the present, [this Court has recognized several] "well-defined and narrowly limited classes of speech, the prevention and punishment of which have never been thought to raise any Constitutional problem." Chaplinsky.

The Government argues that "depictions of animal cruelty" should be added to the list. [We] are unaware of any [tradition] excluding depictions of animal cruelty from "the freedom of speech" codified in the First Amendment, and the Government points us to none. The Government contends [that] categories of speech may be exempted from the First Amendment's protection without any long-settled tradition of subjecting that speech to regulation. [The] Government thus proposes that a claim of categorical exclusion should be considered under a simple balancing test: "Whether a given category of speech enjoys First Amendment protection depends upon a categorical balancing of the value of the speech against its societal costs."

As a free-floating test for First Amendment coverage, that sentence is startling and dangerous. The First Amendment's guarantee of free speech does not extend only to categories of speech that survive an ad hoc balancing of relative social costs and benefits. The First Amendment itself reflects a judgment by the American people that the benefits of its restrictions on the Government outweigh the costs.

In Ferber, for example, we [noted] that the State of New York had a compelling interest in protecting children from abuse, and that the value of using children in these works (as opposed to simulated conduct or adult actors) was de minimis. But our decision did not rest on this "balance of competing interests" alone. We made clear that Ferber presented a special case: The market for child pornography was "intrinsically related" to the underlying abuse, and was therefore "an integral part of the production of such materials, an activity illegal throughout the Nation." [Our] decisions in Ferber and other cases cannot be taken as establishing a freewheeling authority to declare new categories of speech outside the scope of the First Amendment.

[The] Government makes no effort to defend the constitutionality of § 48 as applied beyond crush videos and depictions of animal fighting. It argues that those particular depictions are intrinsically related to criminal conduct or are analogous to obscenity (if not themselves obscene), and that the ban on such speech is narrowly tailored to reinforce restrictions on the underlying conduct, prevent additional crime arising from the depictions, or safeguard public mores. [Nor] does the Government seriously contest that the presumptively impermissible applications of § 48 (properly construed) far outnumber any permissible ones. However "growing" and "lucrative" the markets for crush videos and dogfighting depictions might be, they are dwarfed by the market for other depictions, such as hunting magazines and videos, that we have determined to be within the scope of § 48. We therefore need not and do not decide whether a statute limited to crush videos or other depictions of extreme animal cruelty would be constitutional. We hold only that § 48 is not so limited but is instead substantially overbroad, and therefore invalid under the First Amendment.

■ JUSTICE ALITO, dissenting.

The First Amendment protects freedom of speech, but it most certainly does not protect violent criminal conduct, even if engaged in for expressive purposes. Crush videos [record] the commission of violent criminal acts, and it appears that these crimes are committed for the sole purpose of creating the videos. [Congress] was presented with compelling evidence that the only way of preventing these crimes was to target the sale of the videos. Under these circumstances, I cannot believe that the First Amendment commands Congress to step aside and allow the underlying crimes to continue. [The] most relevant of our prior decisions is Ferber. [The] Court there held that child pornography is not protected speech, and I believe that Ferber's reasoning dictates a similar conclusion here.

[The core characteristics of Ferber] are shared by § 48, as applied to crush videos. First, the conduct depicted in crush videos is criminal in every State and the District of Columbia. Thus, any crush video made in this country records the actual commission of a criminal act that inflicts severe physical injury and excruciating pain and ultimately results in death. [Second], the criminal acts shown in crush videos cannot be prevented without targeting the conduct prohibited by § 48—the creation, sale, and possession for sale of depictions of animal torture with the intention of realizing a commercial profit. [Finally], the harm caused by the underlying crimes vastly outweighs any minimal value that the depictions might conceivably be thought to possess.

REGULATING VIOLENT SPEECH IN NEW MEDIA AFTER STEVENS

1. ***Subcultures and online speech.*** Is there a way in which advancing communications technologies might actually limit the expressive possibilities of underground cultures? In Ashcroft v. American Civil Liberties Union I, p. 1117 above, a plurality of the Court insisted that communications on the internet may constitutionally be judged for obscenity under the "community standards" of any audience those communications reach. Yet four Justices countered that submitting online speech to the community standards of any potential audience, rather than its *intended* audience, might impermissibly chill communications among fringe subcultures. Concurring only in the judgment, Justice Kennedy, joined by Justices Souter and Ginsburg, wrote: "[The] economics and technology of Internet communication differ in important ways from those of telephones and mail. [A] Web publisher in a community where avant garde culture is the norm may have no desire to reach a national market; he may wish only to speak to his neighbors; nevertheless, if an eavesdropper in a more traditional, rural community chooses to listen in, there is nothing the publisher can do. [The plurality's holding] makes the eavesdropper the arbiter of propriety on the Web." Justice Stevens noted: "[In] its original form, the community standard provided a shield for communications that are offensive only to the least tolerant members of society. [In] the context of the Internet, however, community standards become a sword, rather than a shield. If a prurient appeal is offensive in a puritan village, it may be a crime to post it on the World Wide Web. [By] approving the use of community standards in this context, [the plurality] endorses a construction of COPA that has 'the intolerable consequence of denying some sections of the country access to material, there deemed acceptable, which in others might be considered offensive to prevailing community standards of decency.' "

2. ***Violent video games.*** Do the Court's decisions on sexually explicit speech in new media leave any latitude to regulate speech embodying violent activities? Even if the protection is directed specifically at minors? The Court considered these issues in the following case:

Brown v. Entertainment Merchants Ass'n

564 U.S. 786, 131 S. Ct. 2729, 180 L. Ed. 2d 708 (2011).

[A California statute prohibited the sale or rental to minors of violent video games, defined as any games "in which the range of options available to a player includes killing, maiming, dismembering, or sexually assaulting an image of a human being" in a depiction that "appeals to a deviant or morbid interest of minors," is "patently offensive to prevailing standards in the community as to what is suitable for minors," and "causes the game, as a whole, to lack serious literary, artistic, political, or scientific value for minors."]

■ JUSTICE SCALIA delivered the opinion of the Court.

California correctly acknowledges that video games qualify for First Amendment protection. The Free Speech Clause exists principally to protect discourse on public matters, but we have long recognized that it is difficult to distinguish politics from entertainment, and dangerous to try. Like the protected books, plays, and movies that preceded them, video games communicate ideas—and even social messages—through many familiar literary devices (such as characters, dialogue, plot, and music) and through features distinctive to the medium (such as the player's interaction with the virtual world). That suffices to confer First Amendment protection.

[Last Term], in Stevens, we held that new categories of unprotected speech may not be added to the list by a legislature that concludes certain speech is too harmful to be tolerated. [That] holding controls this case. As in Stevens, California has tried to make violent-speech regulation look like obscenity regulation by appending a saving clause required for the latter. That does not suffice. Our cases have been clear that the obscenity exception to the First Amendment does not cover whatever a legislature finds shocking, but only depictions of "sexual conduct," Miller.

California does not argue that it is empowered to prohibit selling offensively violent works to adults—and it is wise not to, since that is but a hair's breadth from the argument rejected in Stevens. Instead, it wishes to create a wholly new category of content-based regulation that is permissible only for speech directed at children.

That is unprecedented and mistaken. "[M]inors are entitled to a significant measure of First Amendment protection, and only in relatively narrow and well-defined circumstances may government bar public dissemination of protected materials to them." Erznoznik v. Jacksonville. No doubt a State possesses legitimate power to protect children from harm, but that does not include a free-floating power to restrict the ideas to which children may be exposed.

California's argument would fare better if there were a longstanding tradition in this country of specially restricting children's access to depictions of violence, but there is none. Certainly the books we give children to read—or read to them when they are younger—contain no shortage of gore. Grimm's Fairy Tales, for example, are grim indeed. As her just deserts for trying to poison Snow White, the wicked queen is made to dance in red hot slippers "till she fell dead on the floor, a sad example of envy and jealousy." Cinderella's evil stepsisters have their eyes pecked out by doves. And Hansel and Gretel (children!) kill their captor by baking her in an oven.

Because the Act imposes a restriction on the content of protected speech, it is invalid unless California can demonstrate that it passes strict scrutiny—that is, unless it is justified by a compelling government interest and is narrowly drawn to serve that interest. [California] cannot meet that standard. [It] acknowledges that it cannot show a direct causal link between violent video games and harm to minors. [California's studies] do not prove that violent video games cause minors to act aggressively. [And] California has (wisely) declined to restrict Saturday morning cartoons, the sale of games rated for young children, or the distribution of pictures of guns. The consequence is that its regulation is wildly underinclusive when judged against its asserted justification, which in our view is alone enough to defeat it. Underinclusiveness raises serious doubts about whether the government is in fact pursuing the interest it invokes, rather than disfavoring a particular speaker or viewpoint. [Moreover,] California cannot show that the Act's restrictions meet a substantial need of parents who wish to restrict their children's access to violent video games but cannot do so. The video-game industry has in place a voluntary rating system designed to inform consumers about the content of games. [And] finally, the Act's purported aid to parental authority is vastly overinclusive. Not all of the children who are forbidden to purchase violent video games on their own have parents who care whether they purchase violent video games. [This] is not the narrow tailoring to 'assisting parents' that restriction of First Amendment rights requires.

California's effort to regulate violent video games is the latest episode in a long series of failed attempts to censor violent entertainment for minors. While we have pointed out above that some of the evidence brought forward to support the harmfulness of video games is unpersuasive, we do not mean to demean or disparage the concerns that underlie the attempt to regulate them—concerns that may and doubtless do prompt a good deal of parental oversight. [But e]ven where the protection of children is the object, the constitutional limits on governmental action apply.

■ JUSTICE ALITO, with whom CHIEF JUSTICE ROBERTS joins, concurring in the judgment.

Respondents in this case, representing the video-game industry, ask us to strike down the California law on [the] narrower ground that the law's definition of "violent video game" is impermissibly vague. [I] agree with the latter argument[.] [The] California violent video game law fails to provide the fair notice that the Constitution requires. And I would go no further.

[In resolving the First Amendment claim], the Court is far too quick to dismiss the possibility that the experience of playing video games (and the effects on minors of playing violent video games) may be very different from anything that we have seen before. [Today's] most advanced video games create realistic alternative worlds in which millions of players immerse themselves for hours on end. These games feature visual imagery and sounds that are strikingly realistic, and in the near future video-game graphics may be virtually indistinguishable from actual video footage. Many of the games already on the market can produce high definition images, and it is predicted that it will not be long before video-game images will be seen in three dimensions. [Some] amici who support respondents foresee the day when " 'virtual-reality shoot-'em-ups' " will allow children to " 'actually feel the splatting blood from the blown-off head' " of a victim.

[In] some of these games, the violence is astounding. Victims by the dozens are killed with every imaginable implement, including machine guns, shotguns, clubs, hammers, axes, swords, and chainsaws. [The] objective of one game is to rape a mother and her daughters; in another, the goal is to rape Native American women. There is a game in which players engage in "ethnic cleansing" and can choose to gun down African-Americans, Latinos, or Jews. In still another game, players attempt to fire a rifle shot into the head of President Kennedy as his motorcade passes by the Texas School Book Depository.

If the technological characteristics of the sophisticated games that are likely to be available in the near future are combined with the characteristics of the most violent games already marketed, the result will be games that allow troubled teens to experience in an extraordinarily personal and vivid way what it would be like to carry out unspeakable acts of violence. [When] all of the characteristics of video games are taken into account, there is certainly a reasonable basis for thinking that the experience of playing a video game may be quite different from the experience of reading a book, listening to a radio broadcast, or viewing a movie. And if this is so, then for at least some minors, the effects of playing violent video games may also be quite different. The Court acts prematurely in dismissing this possibility out of hand.

■ JUSTICE THOMAS, dissenting.

The practices and beliefs of the founding generation establish that "the freedom of speech," as originally understood, does not include a right to speak to minors (or a right of minors to access speech) without going through the minors' parents or guardians. [T]he founding generation understood parents to have a right and duty to govern their children's growth. Parents were expected to direct the development and education of their children and ensure that bad habits did not take root. [In] light of this history, the Framers could not possibly have understood 'the freedom of speech' to include an unqualified right to speak to minors.

■ JUSTICE BREYER, dissenting.

California's law imposes no more than a modest restriction on expression. The statute prevents no one from playing a video game, it prevents no adult from buying a video game, and it prevents no child or adolescent from obtaining a game provided a parent is willing to help. [There] is considerable evidence that California's statute significantly furthers [a] compelling interest. Unlike the majority, I would find sufficient grounds in [the state's psychological] studies and expert opinions for this Court to defer to an elected legislature's conclusion that the video games in question are particularly likely to harm children. This Court has always thought it owed an elected legislature some degree of deference in respect to legislative facts of this kind, particularly when they involve technical matters that are beyond our competence, and even in First Amendment cases.

---

3. ***The role of history in categories of unprotected or less protected speech.*** In Stevens, the Court asserted that historical evidence of a "long-settled tradition of subjecting [certain categories of] speech to regulation" is required for those categories to receive an exemption from First Amendment protection. This holding was reiterated in Entertainment

Merchants. Is history the proper basis upon which to determine the value of a category of speech? One scholar has argued that even the categories of speech traditionally recognized as having always been excepted from the First Amendment—obscenity, libel, profanity, and fighting words—have in fact only been treated this way since the New Deal. Lakier, "Inventing Low-Value Speech," 128 Harv. L. Rev. 2166 (2015). If this analysis is correct, is there good reason for history to serve as a limit to regulation of new types of speech?

SECTION 7. COMMERCIAL SPEECH

This section considers one last category of speech—commercial advertising, or speech that merely proposes a commercial transaction—that, because of its content, was once treated as wholly outside the First Amendment. Since 1976, commercial speech has been held to be protected, but not fully protected speech. It thus operates as a category of "lower value" speech not entitled to the high degree of protection afforded to "core" speech. A number of justices have questioned this categorization approach, urging that commercial speech instead be protected just like other speech unless it poses distinctively commercial harms, such as the danger of deception or overreaching. Their approach would substitute balancing for categorization. But they have not yet commanded a majority of the Court. Thus, commercial speech continues to stand as the lone formal exception to the two-level approach to speech set forth in Chaplinsky: unlike incitement, fighting words, malicious libel, obscenity, or child pornography, it enjoys First Amendment protection, but not as much First Amendment protection as other speech.

Before 1976, the Court assumed that most types of commercial speech fell wholly outside the First Amendment. In **Valentine v. Chrestensen**, 316 U.S. 52 (1942), the Court stated that the First Amendment imposed no "restraint on government as respects purely commercial advertising." Valentine sustained a ban on distribution of a handbill advertisement soliciting customers to pay admission to tour a privately owned submarine. The entrepreneur in Valentine printed his advertising message on one side of the circular; on the other side, he published a protest against the city's denial of permission to use a municipal pier for his exhibit. The Court viewed the ban as a regulation of business activity rather than protected political speech and considered the political protest merely an attempt to evade the city regulation forbidding distribution of advertisements in the streets.

The Valentine approach did not mean that First Amendment protection was denied simply because the speaker had a commercial motive. Recall that New York Times v. Sullivan rejected the argument that the First Amendment did not apply to a "paid 'commercial' advertisement": "That the Times was paid for publishing the advertisement is as immaterial [as] is the fact that newspapers and books are sold." In similar fashion, movies have long enjoyed First Amendment protections even though they are produced and distributed for profit.

Virginia Pharmacy Board v. Virginia Citizens Consumer Council

425 U.S. 748, 96 S. Ct. 1817, 48 L. Ed. 2d 346 (1976).

[A Virginia law provided that pharmacists were guilty of "unprofessional conduct" if they advertised the prices of prescription drugs. Since only pharmacists were authorized to dispense such drugs, the law effectively prevented the dissemination of prescription drug price information in the State. About 95% of all prescription drugs were prepared by pharmaceutical manufacturers rather than by the pharmacists themselves. A lower court invalidated the law on First Amendment grounds.]

■ JUSTICE BLACKMUN delivered the opinion of the Court.

[Justice Blackmun began by noting that the challenge to the law came not from a pharmacist but from prescription drug consumers who claimed that the First Amendment entitled them to drug price information, but found that the audience for drug price information could assert a First Amendment interest: "[W]here a speaker exists [as here], the protection afforded [by the First Amendment] is to the communication, to its source and to its recipients both. [If] there is a right to advertise, there is a reciprocal right to receive the advertising, and it may be asserted by [the consumers here]."]

IV. The appellants contend that the advertisement of prescription drug prices is outside the protection of the First Amendment because it is "commercial speech." There can be no question that in past decisions the Court has given some indication that commercial speech is unprotected. [Last] Term, in Bigelow v. Virginia, 421 U.S. 809 (1975), the notion of unprotected "commercial speech" all but passed from the scene. We reversed a conviction for violation of a Virginia statute that made the circulation of any publication to encourage or promote the processing of an abortion in Virginia a misdemeanor. The defendant had published in his newspaper the availability of abortions in New York. We rejected the contention that the publication was unprotected because it was commercial. [We] noted that [the] advertisement "did more than simply propose a commercial transaction. It contained factual material of clear 'public interest.' " [Here,] in contrast, the question whether there is a First Amendment exception for "commercial speech" is squarely before us. Our pharmacist does not wish to editorialize on any subject, cultural, philosophical, or political. He does not wish to report any particularly newsworthy fact, or to make generalized observations even about commercial matters. The "idea" he wishes to communicate is simply this: "I will sell you the X prescription drug at the Y price." Our question, then, is whether this communication is wholly outside the protection of the First Amendment.

V. [It] is clear [that] speech does not lose its First Amendment protection because money is spent to project it, as in a paid [advertisement]. [E.g., New York Times.] [Our] question is whether speech which does "no more than propose a commercial transaction" is so removed from any "exposition of ideas" [Chaplinsky] and from "truth, science, morality, and arts in general, in its diffusion of liberal sentiments on the administration of Government" [Roth] that it lacks all protection. Our answer is that it is not. Focusing first on the individual parties to the transaction that is proposed in the commercial advertisement, we may assume that the advertiser's interest is a purely economic one. That hardly disqualifies him for protection under the First Amendment. The interests of the contestants in a labor dispute are primarily economic, but it has long been settled that both the employee and the employer are protected by the First Amendment where they express themselves on the merits of the dispute in order to influence its outcome. [As] to the particular consumer's interest in the free flow of commercial information, that interest may be as keen, if not keener by far, than his interest in the day's most urgent political debate. [Those] whom the suppression of prescription drug price information hits the hardest are the poor, the sick, and particularly the aged. [When] drug prices vary as strikingly as they do, information as to who is charging what becomes more than a convenience. It could mean the alleviation of physical pain or the enjoyment of basic necessities.

Advertising, however tasteless and excessive it sometimes may seem, is nonetheless dissemination of information as to who is producing and selling what product, for what reason, and at what price. So long as we preserve a predominantly free enterprise economy, the allocation of our resources in large measure will be made through numerous private economic decisions. It is a matter of public interest that those decisions, in the aggregate, be intelligent and well informed. To this end, the free flow of commercial information is indispensable. And if it is indispensable to the proper allocation of resources in a free enterprise system, it is also indispensable to the formation of intelligent opinions as to how that system ought to be regulated or altered. Therefore, even if the First Amendment were thought to be primarily an instrument to enlighten public decisionmaking in a democracy, we could not say that the free flow of information does not serve that goal.

Arrayed against these substantial individual and societal interests are a number of justifications for the advertising ban. These have to do principally with maintaining a high degree of professionalism on the part of licensed pharmacists. Indisputably, the State has a strong interest in maintaining that professionalism. [Price] advertising, it is argued, will place in jeopardy the pharmacist's expertise and, with it, the customer's health. It is claimed that the aggressive price competition that will result from unlimited advertising will make it impossible for the pharmacist to supply professional services in the compounding, handling, and dispensing of prescription drugs. [The] strength of these proffered justifications is greatly undermined by the fact that high professional standards, to a substantial extent, are guaranteed by the close regulation to which pharmacists in Virginia are subject. [At] the same time, we cannot discount the Board's justifications entirely. The Court regarded justifications of this type sufficient to sustain [such advertising bans] on due process and equal protection grounds.

The challenge now made, however, is based on the First Amendment. This casts the Board's justifications in a different light, for on close inspection it is seen that the State's protectiveness of its citizens rests in large measure on the advantages of their being kept in ignorance. The advertising ban does not directly affect professional standards one way or the other. It affects them only through the reactions it is assumed people will have to the free flow of drug price information. [It] appears to be feared that if the pharmacist who wishes to provide low cost, and assertedly low quality, services is permitted to advertise, he will be taken up on his offer by too many unwitting customers. They will choose the low-cost, low-quality service and drive the "professional" pharmacist out of business. They will [destroy] the pharmacist-customer relationship. [There] is, of course, an alternative to this highly paternalistic approach. That alternative is to assume that this information is not in itself harmful, that people will perceive their own best interests if only they are well enough informed, and that the best means to that end is to open the channels of communication rather than to close them. [It] is precisely this kind of choice, between the dangers of suppressing information, and the dangers of its misuse if it is freely available, that the First Amendment makes for us. Virginia is free to require whatever professional standards it wishes of its pharmacists. [But] it may not do so by keeping the public in ignorance of the entirely lawful terms that competing pharmacists are [offering].

VI. In concluding that commercial speech, like other varieties, is protected, we of course do not hold that it can never be regulated in any way. Some forms of commercial speech regulation are surely permissible. [There] is no claim, for example, that the prohibition on prescription drug price advertising is a mere time, place, and manner restriction. We have often approved restrictions of that kind provided that they are justified without reference to the content of the regulated speech, that they serve a significant governmental interest, and that in so doing they leave open ample alternative channels for communication of the information. [But this law] singles out speech of a particular content and seeks to prevent its dissemination completely. Nor is there any claim that prescription drug price advertisements are forbidden because they are false or misleading in any way. Untruthful speech, commercial or otherwise, has never been protected for its own sake. [E.g., Gertz.] Obviously, much commercial speech is not provably false, or even wholly false, but only deceptive or misleading. We foresee no obstacle to a State's dealing effectively with this problem.[1] The First Amendment, as we construe it today, does not prohibit the State from insuring that the stream of commercial information flows cleanly as well as freely. Also, there is no claim that the transactions proposed in the forbidden advertisements are themselves illegal in any way. [Cf., e.g., Pittsburgh Press.] Finally, the special problems of the electronic broadcast media are likewise not in this case. What is at issue is whether a State may completely suppress the dissemination of concededly truthful information about entirely lawful activity, fearful of that information's effect upon its disseminators and

---

1 In concluding that commercial speech enjoys First Amendment protection, we have not held that it is wholly undifferentiable from other forms. There are commonsense differences between speech that does "no more than propose a commercial transaction" and other varieties. Even if the differences do not justify the conclusion that commercial speech is valueless, and thus subject to complete suppression by the State, they nonetheless suggest that a different degree of protection is necessary to insure that the flow of truthful and legitimate commercial information is unimpaired. The truth of commercial speech, for example, may be more easily verifiable by its disseminator than, let us say, news reporting or political commentary, in that ordinarily the advertiser seeks to disseminate information about a specific product or service that he himself provides and presumably knows more about than anyone else. Also, commercial speech may be more durable than other kinds. Since advertising is the sine qua non of commercial profits, there is little likelihood of its being chilled by proper regulation and foregone entirely.

Attributes such as these, the greater objectivity and hardiness of commercial speech, may make it less necessary to tolerate inaccurate statements for fear of silencing the speaker. They may also make it appropriate to require that a commercial message appear in such a form, or include such additional information, warnings and disclaimers as are necessary to prevent its being deceptive. They also make inapplicable the prohibition against [prior restraints]. [Footnote by Justice Blackmun.]

its recipients. Reserving other questions, we conclude that the answer to this one is in the negative. Affirmed.

■ JUSTICE REHNQUIST, dissenting.

The logical consequences of the Court's decision in this case, a decision which elevates commercial intercourse between a seller hawking his wares and a buyer seeking to strike a bargain to the same plane as has been previously reserved for the free marketplace of ideas, are far reaching indeed. Under the Court's opinion the way will be open not only for dissemination of price information but for active promotion of prescription drugs, liquor, cigarettes and other products the use of which it has previously been thought desirable to discourage.

The Court speaks of the consumer's interest in the free flow of commercial [information]. [It] speaks of the importance in a "predominantly free enterprise economy" of intelligent and well-informed decisions as to allocation of resources. While there is again much to be said for [this] as a matter of desirable public policy, there is certainly nothing in the [Constitution] which requires [Virginia] to hew to the teachings of Adam Smith in its legislative decisions regulating the pharmacy profession. [I]f the sole limitation on permissible state proscription of advertising is that it may not be false or misleading, surely the difference between pharmacists' advertising and lawyers' and doctors' advertising can be only one of degree and not of [kind].

The Court insists that the rule it lays down is consistent even with the view that the First Amendment is "primarily an instrument to enlighten public decisionmaking in a democracy." I had understood this view to relate to public decisionmaking as to political, social, and other public issues, rather than the decision of a particular individual as to whether to purchase one or another kind of shampoo. It is undoubtedly arguable that many people in the country regard the choice of shampoo as just as important as who may be elected to local, state, or national political office, but that does not automatically bring information about competing shampoos within the protection of the First Amendment.[It] is one thing to say that the line between strictly ideological and political commentaries and other kinds of commentary is difficult to [draw]. But it is another thing to say that because that line is difficult to draw, we will stand at the other end of the [spectrum].

In the case of "our" hypothetical pharmacist, he may now presumably advertise not only the prices of prescription drugs, but may attempt to energetically promote their sale so long as he does so truthfully. But such a line simply makes no allowance whatever for what appears to have been a considered legislative judgment in most States that while prescription drugs are a necessary and vital part of medical care and treatment, there are sufficient dangers attending their widespread use that they simply may not be promoted in the same manner as hair creams, deodorants, and toothpaste. The very real dangers that general advertising for such drugs might create in terms of encouraging, even though not sanctioning, illicit use of them by individuals for whom they have not been prescribed, or by generating patient pressure upon physicians to prescribe them, are simply not dealt with in the Court's [opinion].

I do not believe that the First Amendment mandates the Court's "open door policy" toward such commercial advertising.

COMMERCIAL SPEECH AND FIRST AMENDMENT THEORY

1. ***Advertising as "speech."*** Is commercial speech "speech" or merely an aspect of the conduct of commercial sales? For an argument that advertising is merely a first step in contracts or exchanges that are fully regulable, see Farber, "Commercial Speech and First Amendment Theory," 74 Nw. U. L. Rev. 372 (1979). See also Posner, "Free Speech in an Economic Perspective," 20 Suffolk L. Rev. 1 (1986) (suggesting that unlike most speech, which will be underproduced because speakers cannot fully capture its benefits once it is disseminated, the benefits of commercial speech "are more readily captured by its producer through sale of the underlying product," reducing the need for free speech protection); Cass, "Commercial Speech, Constitutionalism, Collective Choice," 56 U. Cin. L. Rev. 1317 (1988).

2. ***Advertising and the rationales for freedom of speech.*** Recall the varying rationales for protecting expression under the First Amendment discussed at pp. 935–940 above. Does speech that does "no more than propose a commercial transaction" warrant protection under any of these rationales? Does commercial advertising contribute to better decisionmaking in a representative form of government (recall the Meiklejohn rationale)? Is it a part of the free marketplace of ideas (recall the Holmes rationale)? Is protection of advertising justifiable only under an individual self-realization, autonomy rationale? If the primary purpose of commercial advertising is to contribute to a more efficient operation of the free *economic* market, is that a quality relevant to First Amendment theory? Can protection of the economic market under the First Amendment be reconciled with the modern Court's "hands-off" attitude in economic regulation cases? For a general discussion of these questions, see Collins, Shiffrin, Chemerinsky & Sullivan, "Symposium: Thoughts On Commercial Speech: A Roundtable Discussion," 41 Loy. L.A. L. Rev. 333 (2007); Brudney, "The First Amendment and Commercial Speech," 53 B.C. L. Rev. 1153 (2012).

In light of Virginia Board, consider the following possible defenses and critiques of the proposition that commercial speech should be protected under the First Amendment:

a. *Self-government.* Justice Rehnquist dissented from Virginia Pharmacy and progeny on the ground that "in a democracy, the economic is subordinate to the political." Central Hudson, (1980; p. 1142 below). On this view, advertising is subordinate to expressions of political ideology and dissent, for it does not inform public deliberation or contribute to representative government. For elaborations of this critique of protection for commercial speech, see Jackson & Jeffries, "Commercial Speech: Economic Due Process and the First Amendment," 65 Va. L. Rev. 1 (1979); Sunstein, Democracy and the Problem of Free Speech 130–44 (1993).

In Virginia Pharmacy, Justice Blackmun answers such arguments by suggesting that "public decisionmaking" should be viewed broadly, and that the free flow of commercial information contributes to that process by making the "numerous private economic decisions" that drive our "free enterprise economy" more "intelligent and well informed." Jackson & Jeffries reply: this is "a non sequitur. [In] terms of relevance to political decisionmaking, advertising is neither more nor less significant than a host of other market activities that legislatures concededly may regulate." For a contrary view, see Shiffrin, "The First Amendment and Economic Regulation: Away from a General Theory of the First Amendment," 78 Nw.

U. L. Rev. 1212 (1983). For discussion of the relationship between commercial speech and democratic values and the proper limits of commercial speech protection in a democracy, see Post, "The Constitutional Status of Commercial Speech," 48 UCLA L. Rev. 1 (2000).

b. *Truth.* The Millian notion that the unregulated clash of individual expression will produce truth in the long run might seem unrelated to pitches for sales for short-run profit. But Justice Blackmun's opinion likens the clash between advertisers to other clashes of opinion: if the discount drug retailer advertises his low prices, "nothing prevents the 'professional' pharmacist from marketing his own assertedly superior product." Individuals, he suggests, may be relied on to choose between them. See Coase, "Advertising and Free Speech," 6 J. Legal Studies 1 (1977) (arguing for parallel treatment of markets and the marketplace of ideas). Jackson & Jeffries, supra, argue that this argument confuses economic values—"the opportunity of the individual producer or consumer to maximize his own economic utility" and "the aggregate economic efficiency of a free market economy"—with free speech values, effectively resurrecting Lochner under the guise of the First Amendment.

c. *Autonomy.* Some proponents of autonomy as a central value underlying the Free Speech Clause reject protection for commercial speech because it is generally engaged in by corporations, which lack a human personality or capacity for self-fulfillment. See Jackson & Jeffries, supra ("[w]hatever else it may mean, the concept of a first amendment right of speaker autonomy in matters of belief and expression stops short of a seller hawking his wares"); Baker, Human Liberty and Freedom of Speech 194–224 (1989); Baker, "Commercial [Speech]," 62 Iowa L. Rev. 1 (1976) ("commercial speech is not a manifestation of individual freedom or choice," and "lacks the crucial connections with individual liberty and self-realization which exist for speech generally").

Justice Blackmun's opinion suggests, however, that it is not the speaker's but rather the *listener's* autonomy that matters here: the alternative to "paternalistic" speech regulation is to assume that *consumers* "will perceive their own best interests if only they are well enough informed." For the view that such listener autonomy is a central free speech value that helps justify protection of commercial speech, see Strauss, "Persuasion, Autonomy and Freedom of Expression," 91 Colum. L. Rev. 334 (1991); Neuborne, "The First Amendment and Government Regulation of Capital Markets," 55 Brooklyn L. Rev. 5 (1989); Redish, "The First Amendment in the Marketplace: Commercial Speech and the Values of Free Expression," 39 Geo. Wash. L. Rev. 429 (1971) (choosing among "the relative merits of competing products" promotes "the intangible goal of rational self-fulfillment"). But are consumers truly choosing freely when they respond to advertising? Is not a goal of advertising to create demands and alter tastes? Might the listener's autonomy be impaired by lack of relevant information or by addiction to a product? See Fallon, "Two Senses of Autonomy," 46 Stan. L. Rev. 875 (1994); Law, "Addiction, Autonomy and Advertising," 77 Iowa L. Rev. 909 (1992) (arguing that advertising for psychoactive products that cause physiological dependence may be regulated).

d. *Negative First Amendment theory.* Some theories rely less on the affirmative values of free speech than on the premise that there is special reason to distrust government when it regulates speech. For example, incumbents have an incentive to suppress challengers and dissidents. But is there any reason to fear that government will suppress commercial speech for ideologically partisan reasons? See Scanlon, "Freedom of Expression and Categories of Expression," 40 U. Pitt. L. Rev. 519 (1979) (arguing that commercial speech should not get full protection because government is less partisan in the competition between firms than in the struggle between political views). What if government is captured by powerful private interest groups, such as the pharmacy profession in Virginia Pharmacy? If bias against a competitor of such a group justifies First Amendment protection of the competitor's advertising, should it also justify protection of the competitor's production and sales under the Equal Protection or Due Process Clauses? See Jackson & Jeffries, supra ("Exactly the same values that are impaired by Virginia's ban against drug price advertising are also invaded by [most] other instances of governmental regulation of the economy.").

3. ***"Commonsense differences" between commercial and other speech.*** In dicta in Virginia Pharmacy, the Court set forth three important limitations on protection for commercial speech: First, free speech protection does not extend to advertisements for illegal transactions. Second, free speech protection does not extend to factually false or misleading advertisements. Third, commercial speech does not enjoy the special procedural protections other speech does against the ban on prior restraint or the presumption against laws that are overbroad, even if aimed at an unprotected category. Justice Blackmun explained this "different degree of protection" by reference to two "commonsense differences": that commercial speech is hardier than other speech because profit-driven, and more objectively verifiable than other speech. Are these distinctions persuasive? Consider the following comments:

a. *Hardiness.* "It might just as easily be said that we need not fear that commercial magazines and newspapers will cease publication for fear of governmental regulation, because they are in business for profit." Redish, "The Value of Free Speech," 130 U. Pa. L. Rev. 591 (1982). "[O]ther interests can be just as strong as economics, sometimes stronger. [Speech] backed by religious feeling can persist in extraordinarily hostile climates; [a]rtistic impulses can also cause expression to persist in the face of hostile government regulation." Kozinski & Banner, "Who's Afraid of Commercial Speech?," 76 Va. L. Rev. 627 (1990).

b. *Verifiability.* "[T]he seller can check his facts more easily than can a third party. However so can certain politicians who make false and deceptive political statements regarding facts within their knowledge." Alexander, "Speech in the Local [Marketplace]," 14 San Diego L. Rev. 357 (1977). "It is certainly easier to determine the truth of the claim 'Cucumbers cost sixty-nine cents' than the claim 'Republicans will govern more effectively.' But not all commercial speech is so objective. What about the statement 'America is turning 7-Up'?" Kozinski & Banner, supra. "[M]uch scientific speech can easily be labeled true or false, but we would be shocked at the suggestion that it is therefore entitled to a lesser degree of protection." Id.

4. ***Defining commercial speech.*** Virginia Board defined commercial speech as that which "does no more than propose a commercial transaction," and made clear that it did *not* include all speech produced for profit. Later in Central Hudson, below, the Court referred to commercial speech as "expression related solely to the economic interests of the speaker and its audience." Justice Stevens, in concurrence, objected that such a

definition "is unquestionably too broad." Later decisions would appear to agree with him. It is settled that corporate speech can amount to political or other fully protected speech, even when engaged in out of commercial self-interest. The fact of economic motivation does not automatically ratchet down the level of scrutiny. Thus the definition of commercial speech would appear to be the narrower one set forth in Virginia Board.

What if an advertisement contains a mixture of promotional and informational content? In **Bolger v. Youngs Drug Products Corp.**, 463 U.S. 60 (1983), the Court invalidated a federal statute prohibiting the mailing of unsolicited advertisements for contraceptives. At issue were a "drug store flyer" as well as two informational pamphlets, "Condoms and Human Sexuality" and "Plain Talk about Venereal Disease." Justice MARSHALL's opinion for the Court reasoned that the materials amounted to commercial rather than fully protected speech: "The mailings constitute commercial speech notwithstanding the fact that they contain discussions of important public issues such as venereal disease and family planning. A company has the full panoply of protections available [for] its direct comments on public issues, so there is no reason for providing similar constitutional protection when such statements are made in the context of commercial transactions."

COMMERCIAL SPEECH AFTER VIRGINIA PHARMACY

1. ***Real estate "For Sale" signs as protected speech.*** In **Linmark Associates, Inc. v. Town of Willingboro**, 431 U.S. 85 (1977), the Court relied in part on Virginia Pharmacy to strike down an ordinance prohibiting the posting of real estate "For Sale" and "Sold" signs. The town's objective was to stem the flight of white homeowners from a racially integrated community through "panic selling." Justice MARSHALL wrote for the Court: "The [town here, like the State in Virginia Pharmacy,] acted to prevent its residents from obtaining certain information. That information [is] of vital interest to Willingboro residents, since it may bear on one of the most important decisions they have a right to make: where to live and raise their families. The [town] has sought to restrict the free flow of this data because it fears that otherwise, homeowners will make decisions inimical to what the [town] views as the homeowners' self-interest and the corporate interest of the township: they will choose to leave town. The [town's] concern, then, was not with any commercial aspect of 'For Sale' signs—with offerors communicating offers to offerees—but with the substance of the information communicated to Willingboro citizens. If dissemination of this information can be restricted, then every locality in the country can suppress any facts that reflect poorly on the locality, so long as a plausible claim can be made that disclosure would cause the recipients of the information to act 'irrationally.' Virginia Pharmacy denies government such sweeping powers [to deny its citizens] information that is neither false nor misleading."

2. ***Contraceptive advertising.*** The Court relied on Virginia Pharmacy in **Carey v. Population Services, International**, 431 U.S. 678 (1977), which invalidated a New York ban on the advertising or display of nonprescription contraceptives. Justice Brennan noted that here, as in Virginia Pharmacy, there were "substantial individual and societal interests in the free flow of commercial information," and, as in Bigelow, the

information suppressed "related to activity with which, at least in some respects, the State could not interfere."

3. ***Regulating lawyer advertising.*** Virginia Pharmacy had left some doubt about whether it would apply to commercial communications by lawyers. But the Court soon made it clear that the Virginia Pharmacy principles would apply to lawyers' advertising as well. The course of decisions began with the 5–4 ruling in **Bates v. State Bar of Arizona**, 433 U.S. 350 (1977), holding that states could not prohibit lawyers from price advertising of "routine legal services." Justice BLACKMUN's majority opinion rejected a variety of justifications for the restraint, including "adverse effect on professionalism" and the claim that attorney advertising was "inherently misleading."

A year later, two cases involving lawyers' solicitation of clients came to the Court. In these cases, the distinction between commercial and noncommercial speech proved critical. In **Ohralik v. Ohio State Bar Association**, 436 U.S. 447 (1978), involving "classic examples of 'ambulance chasing,'" the Court sustained a lawyer's suspension from law practice for violating anti-solicitation rules. Justice POWELL's majority opinion stated that "the State may proscribe in-person solicitation for pecuniary gain under circumstances likely to result in adverse consequences" without a showing of actual harm and with some leeway for prophylactic rules. But in **In re Primus**, 436 U.S. 412 (1978), the Court set aside disciplinary action in a case involving an attorney who did volunteer work for the ACLU. She had been reprimanded for writing a letter asking a woman who had been sterilized whether she wanted to become a plaintiff in a lawsuit against a doctor who had allegedly participated in a program of sterilizing pregnant mothers as a condition of continued receipt of Medicaid benefits. Justice Powell's majority opinion there emphasized that the attorney's letter fell within "the generous zone of First Amendment protection reserved for associational freedoms" and concluded that a state may not punish a lawyer "who, seeking to further political and ideological goals through associational activity, including litigation, advises a lay person of her legal rights and discloses in a subsequent letter that free legal assistance is available from a nonprofit organization." Bates and its progeny were explored and applied in a number of cases over the ensuing decade. In **Zauderer v. Office of Disciplinary Counsel**, 471 U.S. 626 (1985), an Ohio attorney had been reprimanded for advertising his availability to represent women who had suffered injuries in connection with the use of the Dalkon Shield intrauterine device. The ad contained a line drawing of the device and stated: "If there is no recovery, no legal fees are owed by our clients." The State objected in part because the ad solicited clients with respect to a specific legal problem and contained an illustration. Justice WHITE's opinion for the Court struck down the restriction on illustrations: "[W]e are unsure that the State's desire that attorneys maintain their dignity in their communications with the public is an interest substantial enough to justify the abridgment of their First Amendment rights."

The Zauderer ruling in turn provided a major basis for the Court's decision in **Shapero v. Kentucky Bar Ass'n**, 486 U.S. 466 (1988), striking down a flat ban on direct-mail solicitation by lawyers that was "targeted" to specific recipients known to need legal services of a particular kind. Kentucky claimed that it was needed to prevent potential clients from feeling "overwhelmed." Justice BRENNAN's majority opinion distinguished Ohralik as dealing with the special dangers of face-to-face solicitation and found the flat ban too broad a remedy for a mere possibility of abuse: "The State can regulate [any] abuses and minimize mistakes through far less restrictive and more precise means."

Two years later, **Peel v. Attorney Registration and Disciplinary Comm'n of Ill.**, 496 U.S. 91 (1990), followed both Zauderer and Shapero in invalidating a disciplinary sanction for an attorney's representation on his letterhead that he was "certified as a civil trial specialist by the National Board of Trial Advocacy." Justice STEVENS' plurality opinion concluded that truthful representation of certification by a legitimate organization with "rigorous requirements" could not be deemed misleading under the First Amendment just because some readers might think the organization was governmentally affiliated.

The Court, however, remains willing to uphold some restrictions on lawyer advertising. In **Florida Bar v. Went For It, Inc.**, 515 U.S. 618 (1995), the Court upheld, by a vote of 5–4, a Florida Bar rule prohibiting personal injury lawyers from sending targeted direct-mail solicitations to victims and their relatives for 30 days following an accident or disaster, and from receiving referrals from anyone who made such a contact. Justice O'CONNOR, writing for the Court, held that the bar rule served substantial state interests in "protecting the privacy and tranquility of personal injury victims and their loved ones against intrusive, unsolicited contact by lawyers," and in "protecting the flagging reputations of Florida lawyers by preventing them from engaging in conduct that, the Bar maintains, 'is universally regarded as deplorable and beneath common decency because of its intrusion upon the special vulnerability and private grief of victims or their families.'" Justice KENNEDY wrote a pointed dissent, joined by Justices Stevens, Souter and Ginsburg: "I take it to be uncontroverted that when an accident results in death or injury, it is often urgent at once to investigate the occurrence, identify witnesses, and preserve evidence."

Justice Kennedy rejected the state's arguments "that victims or their families will be offended by receiving a solicitation during their grief and trauma. [We] do not allow restrictions on speech to be justified on the ground that the expression might offend the listener."

Central Hudson Gas v. Public Service Comm'n

447 U.S. 557, 100 S. Ct. 2343, 65 L. Ed. 2d 341 (1980).

[The New York Public Service Commission (PSC) prohibited electrical utilities from engaging in promotional advertising designed to stimulate demand for electricity. The ban continued a policy begun at a time of severe fuel shortage, even though the shortage had eased. The PSC permitted "institutional and informational" advertising not intended to promote sales. The Court invalidated the promotional advertising restriction.]

■ JUSTICE POWELL delivered the opinion of the Court.

The Commission's order restricts only commercial speech, that is, expression related solely to the economic interests of the speaker and its audience. [In previous] commercial speech cases, a four-part analysis has developed. At the outset, we must determine whether the expression is protected by the First Amendment. For commercial speech to come within that provision, it at least must concern lawful activity and not be misleading. Next, we ask whether the asserted governmental interest is substantial. If both inquiries yield positive answers, we must determine whether the regulation directly advances the governmental interest asserted, and whether it is not more extensive than is necessary to serve that interest.

[The] Commission does not claim that the expression at issue either is inaccurate or relates to unlawful activity. [The] Commission [argues that] the State's interest in conserving energy is sufficient to support suppression of advertising designed to increase consumption of electricity. In view of our country's dependence on energy resources beyond our control, no one can doubt the importance of energy conservation. Plainly, therefore, the state interest asserted is substantial. [Moreover,] the State's interest in energy conservation is directly advanced by the Commission order at issue here. There is an immediate connection between advertising and demand for electricity. Central Hudson would not contest the advertising ban unless it believed that promotion would increase its sales. Thus, we find a direct link between the state interest in conservation and the Commission's order.

[The] critical inquiry in this case [is] whether the Commission's complete suppression of speech ordinarily protected by the First Amendment is no more extensive than necessary to further the State's interest in energy conservation. The Commission's order reaches all promotional advertising, regardless of the impact of the touted service on overall energy use. [The] Commission's order prevents appellant from promoting electric services [such as the "heat pump" and the use of electric heat as a "backup" to solar and other heat sources] that would reduce energy use by diverting demand from less efficient sources, or that would consume roughly the same amount of energy as do alternative sources. In neither situation would the utility's advertising endanger conservation or mislead the public. To the extent that the Commission's order suppresses speech that in no way impairs the State's interest in energy conservation, the Commission's order violates the [First Amendment]. The Commission also has not demonstrated that its interest in conservation cannot be protected adequately by more limited regulation of appellant's commercial expression. To further its policy of conservation, the Commission could attempt to restrict the format and content of Central Hudson's advertising. It might, for example, require that the advertisements include information about the relative efficiency and expense of the offered service. In the absence of a showing that more limited speech regulation would be ineffective, we cannot approve the complete suppression of Central Hudson's [advertising]. Reversed.

■ JUSTICE BLACKMUN, with whom JUSTICE BRENNAN joins, concurring.

[I] concur only in the Court's judgment, [because] I believe the test now evolved and applied by the Court is not consistent with our prior cases and does not provide adequate protection for truthful, nonmisleading, noncoercive commercial speech. I agree with the Court that [its] level of intermediate scrutiny is appropriate for a restraint on commercial speech designed to protect consumers from misleading or coercive speech, or a regulation related to the time, place, or manner of commercial speech. I do not agree, however, that the Court's four-part test is the proper one to be applied when a State seeks to suppress information about a product in order to manipulate a private economic decision that the State cannot or has not regulated or outlawed directly. [I] disagree with the Court [when] it says that suppression of speech may be a permissible means to achieve [energy conservation]. [I] seriously doubt whether suppression of information concerning the availability and price of a legally offered product is ever a permissible way for the State to "dampen" demand for or use of the product. Even though "commercial" speech is involved, such a regulatory measure strikes at the heart of the First Amendment. This is because it is a covert attempt by the State to manipulate the choices of its citizens, not by persuasion or direct regulation, but by depriving the public of the information needed to make a free choice.

■ JUSTICE STEVENS, with whom JUSTICE BRENNAN joins, concurring in the judgment.

This case involves a governmental regulation that completely bans promotional advertising by an electric utility. This ban encompasses a great deal more than mere proposals to engage in certain kinds of commercial transactions. It prohibits all advocacy of the immediate or future use of electricity. It curtails expression by an informed and interested group of persons of their point of view on questions relating to the production and consumption of electrical energy—questions frequently discussed and debated by our political leaders. [I] concur in the result because I do not consider this to be a "commercial speech" case. Accordingly, I see no need to decide whether the Court's four-part analysis adequately protects commercial speech—as properly defined—in the face of a blanket ban of the sort involved in this case.

■ JUSTICE REHNQUIST, dissenting.

The Court's analysis [is] wrong in several respects. Initially, I disagree with the Court's conclusion that the speech of a state-created monopoly, which is the subject of a comprehensive regulatory scheme, is entitled to protection under the First Amendment. [The] extensive regulations governing decisionmaking by public utilities suggest that for purposes of First Amendment analysis, a utility is far closer to a state-controlled enterprise than is an ordinary corporation. Accordingly, I think a State has broad discretion in determining the statements that a utility may make in that such statements emanate from the entity created by the State to provide important and unique public services. [I] also think New York's ban on such advertising falls within the scope of permissible state regulation of an economic activity by an entity that could not exist in corporate form, say nothing of enjoy monopoly status, were it not for the laws of New York.

[The] Court's decision today fails to give due deference to [the] subordinate position of commercial speech. [The] test adopted by the [Court] elevates the protection accorded commercial speech that falls within the scope of the First Amendment to a level that is virtually indistinguishable from that of noncommercial speech. I think [that] by labeling economic regulation of business conduct as a restraint on "free speech," [the Court has] gone far to resurrect the discredited doctrine of cases such as [Lochner]. [Identification] of speech that falls within [the First Amendment's] protection is not aided by the metaphorical reference to a "marketplace of ideas." There is no reason for believing that the marketplace of ideas is free from market imperfections any more than there is to believe that the invisible hand will always lead to optimum economic decisions in the commercial market. [Even] if I were to agree that commercial speech is entitled to some First Amendment protection, I would hold here that the

State's decision to ban promotional advertising, in light of the substantial state interest at stake, [is] constitutionally [permissible].

The plethora of opinions filed in this case highlights the doctrinal difficulties that emerge from this Court's decisions granting First Amendment protection to commercial speech. [I] remain of the view that the Court unleashed a Pandora's box when it "elevated" commercial speech to the level of traditional political speech by according it First Amendment protection. [The] notion that more speech is the remedy to expose falsehood and fallacies is wholly out of place in the commercial [bazaar]. [In] a democracy, the economic is subordinate to the [political].

[The] final part of the Court's [test] leaves room for so many hypothetical "better" ways that any ingenious lawyer will surely seize on one of them to secure the invalidation of what the state agency actually did. [It] is in my view inappropriate for the Court to invalidate the State's ban on commercial advertising here based on its speculation that in some cases the advertising may result in a net savings in electrical energy [use].

COMMERCIAL SPEECH REGULATION AFTER CENTRAL HUDSON

1. ***Commercial speech and "least restrictive alternative" analysis.*** Central Hudson stated that commercial speech regulations must be "no more extensive than necessary" to serve a substantial government interest. In **Board of Trustees, State Univ. of New York v. Fox**, 492 U.S. 469 (1989), the Court explicitly clarified that this did *not* mean that government must employ the "least restrictive alternative." The case involved a regulation by the University restricting the operation of commercial enterprises on its campuses. The effect of the regulation was to bar a company from selling its housewares in dormitories through the use of "Tupperware parties." Justice SCALIA's majority opinion rejected the constitutional challenge. He first concluded that the speech involved was commercial, and that the Central Hudson analysis was applicable. Turning to that analysis, he noted that the speech proposed a lawful transaction and was not misleading. He found, however, that the state interests in promoting an educational rather than a commercial atmosphere on campuses, insuring the security of students, and preventing their exploitation were sufficiently substantial to satisfy that prong of the Central Hudson test.

Justice Scalia acknowledged that the Court's own prior statements in Central Hudson and in cases such as Zauderer, above, supported the impression that the use of the word "necessary" in Central Hudson could be read as incorporating a "least restrictive alternative" requirement. Nevertheless, he rejected that interpretation, concluding: "[O]ur decisions require [a] 'fit between the legislature's ends and the means chosen to accomplish those ends,'—a fit that is not necessarily perfect, but reasonable; that represents not necessarily the single best disposition but one whose scope is 'in proportion to the interest served'; that employs not necessarily the least restrictive means but [a] means narrowly tailored to achieve the desired objective. Within those bounds we leave it to governmental decisionmakers to judge what manner of regulation may best be employed."

2. ***Differential treatment of commercial speech.*** In **Metromedia, Inc. v. San Diego**, 453 U.S. 490 (1981), the Court struck down an ordinance

regulating the placement of *non*commercial billboards, but made clear that portions of the ordinance banning offsite commercial billboards would be permissible. Applying the Central Hudson test, Justice WHITE's plurality opinion found that the ban on offsite commercial billboards satisfied its first, second, and fourth criteria, but found more problematic the question of whether such a ban "directly advanced" the acknowledged governmental interests "in traffic safety and the appearance of the city." Finding no ulterior motives, the plurality reviewed deferentially the determinations made by San Diego, especially those relating to traffic safety, and suggested that the ban on commercial billboards satisfied all aspects of the Central Hudson test. Because the dissenting opinions of Chief Justice Burger and Justices Rehnquist and Stevens would have upheld the restriction in its entirety, a majority of the Court agreed that restrictions on *commercial* billboards for both aesthetic and traffic safety reasons satisfy the Central Hudson standard.

In **City of Cincinnati v. Discovery Network, Inc.**, 507 U.S. 410 (1993), however, the Court held that commercial speech may not be treated differently from noncommercial speech for aesthetic or safety purposes in the absence of some distinctive harm from commercial speech. Cincinnati barred respondents from placing 62 newsracks on public property to dispense free advertisements for adult education classes and real estate sales, treating such materials as "commercial handbills" whose distribution on public property was prohibited. But the city permitted the placement on public property of between 1500 and 2000 newsracks distributing general circulation newspapers. The city defended the selective commercial newsrack ban as "motivated by its interest in the safety and attractive appearance of its streets and sidewalks" and as justified by the lower value of commercial speech. The Court invalidated the ban.

Justice STEVENS, writing for the Court, noted: "[In] this case, the distinction bears no relationship whatsoever to the particular interests that the city has asserted. [The] city has asserted an interest in esthetics, but respondent publishers' newsracks are no greater an eyesore than the newsracks permitted to remain on Cincinnati's sidewalks. Each newsrack, whether containing 'newspapers' or 'commercial handbills,' is equally unattractive. [The] city's primary concern [is] with the aggregate number of newsracks on its streets. On that score, however, all newsracks, regardless of whether they contain commercial or noncommercial publications, are equally at fault. [Cincinnati] has not asserted an interest in preventing commercial harms by regulating the information distributed by respondent publishers' newsracks. [In] the absence of some basis for distinguishing between 'newspapers' and 'commercial handbills' that is relevant to an interest asserted by the city, we are unwilling to recognize Cincinnati's bare assertion that the 'low value' of commercial speech is a sufficient justification for its selective and categorical ban on newsracks dispensing 'commercial handbills.' "

In a later decision, the Court declined to find a First Amendment violation in the differential treatment of speech intended to be used for commercial purposes. In **Los Angeles Police Department v. United Reporting**, 528 U.S. 32 (1999), the Court rejected a facial attack on a state law that permitted arrest records to be disclosed for "scholarly, journalistic, political, or governmental" purposes, but not in order "to sell a product or service." The opinion of the Court by Chief Justice REHNQUIST found that "the section in question is not an abridgment of anyone's right to engage in speech, be it commercial or otherwise, but simply a law regulating access to information in the hands of the police department."

3. ***The rise and fall of the "vice" exception.*** Virginia Board and Central Hudson made clear that the limited protection of commercial advertising does not extend to advertising of illegal activity. But what of restrictions on the advertising of products or services that are legal but are widely viewed as harmful, such as cigarettes, alcohol, and gambling? Virginia Board suggested that paternalism is an invalid basis for speech regulation. But Central Hudson suggested that advertising restrictions are directly related to suppressing demand. Assuming that suppressing demand for vice is a substantial government end, should suppression of advertisements for vice-related activities always be upheld, even if paternalistic?

In **Posadas de Puerto Rico Assocs. v. Tourism Company of Puerto Rico**, 478 U.S. 328 (1986), the Court upheld, by a vote of 5–4, a Puerto Rico law prohibiting gambling casinos from advertising their facilities to residents of Puerto Rico. Justice REHNQUIST's majority opinion stated: "The particular kind of commercial speech at issue here [concerns] a lawful activity and is not misleading or fraudulent, at least in the abstract. We must therefore proceed to the three remaining steps of the Central Hudson analysis. [The] first [involves] an assessment of the strength of the government's interest in restricting the speech. The interest at stake in this case [is] the reduction of demand for casino gambling by the residents of Puerto Rico." Justice Rehnquist found that the legislative determination that excess gambling would impair the health, safety, and welfare of Puerto Rico residents, "some of the very same concerns [that] have motivated the vast majority of the 50 States to prohibit casino gambling," were sufficient to qualify as a "substantial" governmental interest. Turning to the remaining steps of the Central Hudson analysis, Justice Rehnquist noted that the law directly advanced the government's asserted interest: "[Puerto Rico] obviously believed [that] advertising of casino gambling aimed at [its residents] would serve to increase the demand for the product advertised. We think the legislature's belief is [reasonable]." Finally, he found the law "no more extensive than necessary to serve the government's interest," noting that the law had been construed to permit advertising of casino gambling aimed at tourists, and rejecting the challengers' argument that Puerto Rico ought employ "a 'counterspeech' policy" as a less restrictive means.

The Court's deferential approach to the regulation of gambling advertising in Posadas led many observers to conclude that there was an implicit "vice" exception to the protection of commercial speech. The Court reinforced such an impression in **United States v. Edge Broadcasting Co.**, 509 U.S. 418 (1993), which upheld a federal statute prohibiting the broadcast of lottery advertisements except by stations licensed to states that conduct lotteries. Edge Broadcasting operated a radio station in North Carolina, a nonlottery state, but over 90% of its listeners were in neighboring Virginia, a lottery state. North Carolina listeners could also hear a number of Virginia radio stations that broadcast lottery ads. The Court rejected Edge's claim that it had a First Amendment right to broadcast advertisements for the Virginia lottery. Justice WHITE wrote the opinion for the Court. Upholding the law both on its face and as applied to Edge, he wrote: "We have no doubt that the statutes directly advanced the governmental interest at stake in this case. [Instead] of favoring either the lottery or the nonlottery State, Congress opted to support the antigambling policy of a State like North Carolina by forbidding stations in such a State from airing lottery advertising. At the same time it sought not to unduly interfere with the policy of a lottery sponsoring State such as Virginia. [This] congressional policy of balancing the interests of lottery and nonlottery States is the substantial governmental interest that satisfies Central Hudson. [It] is also the interest that is directly served by applying the statutory restriction to all stations in North Carolina." He noted that here, "as in Posadas de Puerto Rico, the Government obviously legislated on the premise that the advertising of gambling serves to increase the demand for the advertised product. See also Central Hudson. Congress clearly was entitled to determine that broadcast of promotional advertising of lotteries undermines North Carolina's policy against gambling, even if the North Carolina audience is not wholly unaware of the lottery's existence."

But in **Rubin v. Coors Brewing Co.**, 514 U.S. 476 (1995), and 44 Liquormart, Inc. v. Rhode Island, which follows, the Court decisively rejected any notion that there is a "vice" exception to the protection of commercial speech. In Coors, the Court unanimously invalidated a provision of the federal Alcohol Administration Act that prohibited beer labels from displaying alcohol content. The government defended the provision as necessary to preventing "strength wars" among brewers who would seek to compete in the marketplace based on the potency of their beer. Writing for the Court, Justice THOMAS rejected the government's suggestion "that legislatures have broader latitude to regulate speech that promotes socially harmful activities, such as alcohol consumption, than they have to regulate other types of speech." Rather, the Central Hudson test applied to commercial advertising of vice and other activities alike. Applying that test, he found that the government had asserted "a significant interest in protecting the health, safety, and welfare of its citizens by preventing brewers from competing on the basis of alcohol strength, which could lead to greater alcoholism and its attendant social costs."

Justice Thomas found, however, that the provision did not directly advance that interest, "given the overall irrationality of the Government's regulatory scheme." Furthermore, Justice Thomas concluded that the ban was "more extensive than necessary" because the government had alternative options, "such as directly limiting the alcohol content of beers, prohibiting marketing efforts emphasizing high alcohol strength (which is apparently the policy in some other Western nations), or limiting the labeling ban only to malt liquors, [all] of which could advance the Government's asserted interest in a manner less intrusive to respondent's First Amendment rights."

---

44 Liquormart, Inc. v. Rhode Island

517 U.S. 484, 116 S. Ct. 1495, 134 L. Ed. 2d 711 (1996).

[Rhode Island law prohibited advertisement of the price of alcoholic beverages "in any manner whatsoever," except by tags or signs inside liquor stores. The state courts had several times upheld the law against First

Amendment challenge, finding that the law reasonably served the state goal of promoting "temperance." Two high-volume discount liquor retailers challenged the law under the Free Speech Clause in federal court. The Rhode Island Liquor Stores Association intervened on behalf of the state. The district court invalidated the law, finding "that Rhode Island's off-premises liquor price advertising ban has no significant impact on levels of alcohol consumption in Rhode Island." The court of appeals reversed, finding "inherent merit" in Rhode Island's argument that competitive price advertising would lower prices and that lower prices would produce more sales, increasing the consumption of alcohol.

[The Supreme Court unanimously reversed, invalidating the Rhode Island law. But it divided into several camps on the reasoning. Justice Stevens announced the judgment of the Court and wrote a plurality opinion joined at different points by Justices Kennedy, Souter, Thomas and Ginsburg. Joined by Justices Kennedy and Ginsburg only, he wrote that bars against "dissemination of truthful, nonmisleading commercial messages for reasons unrelated to the preservation of a fair bargaining process" should receive strict scrutiny, which the Rhode Island law failed. In the alternative, Justice Stevens wrote, joined on this point by Justices Kennedy, Souter and Ginsburg, the Rhode Island law in any event failed the Central Hudson test. Justice Thomas concurred but would have held that a ban on truthful price information is per se illegitimate. Justice O'Connor, joined by Chief Justice Rehnquist and Justices Souter and Breyer, concurred in the judgment, reasoning simply that the Rhode Island law failed the Central Hudson test. Justice Scalia concurred in the judgment.]

■ JUSTICE STEVENS [joined by JUSTICES KENNEDY and GINSBURG].

[Not] all commercial speech regulations are subject to a similar form of constitutional review. [When] a State regulates commercial messages to protect consumers from misleading, deceptive, or aggressive sales practices, or requires the disclosure of beneficial consumer information, the purpose of its regulation is consistent with the reasons for according [less than full] constitutional protection to commercial speech and therefore justifies less than strict review. However, when a State entirely prohibits the dissemination of truthful, nonmisleading commercial messages for reasons unrelated to the preservation of a fair bargaining process, there is far less reason to depart from the rigorous review that the First Amendment generally demands. [Complete] speech bans, unlike content-neutral restrictions on the time, place, or manner of expression, are particularly dangerous because they all but foreclose alternative means of disseminating certain information.

[The] special dangers that attend complete bans on truthful, nonmisleading commercial speech cannot be explained away by appeals to the "commonsense distinctions" that exist between commercial and noncommercial speech. [It] is the State's interest in protecting consumers from "commercial harms" [such as deception and overreaching] that provides "the typical reason why commercial speech can be subject to greater governmental regulation than noncommercial speech." Discovery Network. Yet bans that target truthful, nonmisleading commercial messages rarely protect consumers from such harms. Instead, [bans] against truthful, nonmisleading commercial speech [usually] rest solely on the offensive assumption that the public will respond "irrationally" to the truth. Linmark. The First Amendment directs us to be especially skeptical of regulations that seek to keep people in the dark for what the government perceives to be their own good. That teaching applies equally to state attempts to deprive consumers of accurate information about their chosen products.

■ JUSTICE STEVENS [joined by JUSTICES KENNEDY, SOUTER and GINSBURG].

The State argues that the price advertising prohibition should [be] upheld because it directly advances the State's substantial interest in promoting temperance, and because it is no more extensive than necessary. Central Hudson. [The] State bears the burden of showing not merely that its regulation will advance its interest, but also that it will do so "to a material degree." Edenfield. We can agree that common sense supports the conclusion that a prohibition against price advertising [will] tend to mitigate competition and maintain prices at a higher level than would prevail in a completely free market. [We] can even agree [that] demand, and hence consumption throughout the market, is somewhat lower whenever a higher, noncompetitive price level prevails. However, [we] cannot agree [that] the price advertising ban will significantly advance the State's interest in promoting temperance. [The] State has presented no evidence to suggest that its speech prohibition will significantly reduce market-wide consumption. Indeed, the District Court's considered and uncontradicted finding on this point is directly to the contrary. [In] addition, [the] State has not identified what price level would lead to a significant reduction in alcohol consumption, nor has it identified the amount that it believes prices would decrease without the ban. Thus, [any] connection between the ban and a significant change in alcohol consumption would be purely fortuitous. [Any] conclusion that elimination of the ban would significantly increase alcohol consumption would [rest on] "speculation or conjecture."

[The] State also cannot satisfy the requirement that its restriction on speech be no more extensive than necessary. It is perfectly obvious that alternative forms of regulation that would not involve any restriction on speech would be more likely to achieve the State's goal of promoting temperance. [Higher] prices can be maintained either by direct regulation or by increased taxation. Per capita purchases could be limited as is the case with prescription drugs. Even educational campaigns focused on the problems of excessive, or even moderate, drinking might prove to be more effective. As a result, even under the less than strict standard that generally applies in commercial speech cases, the State has failed to establish a "reasonable fit" between its abridgment of speech and its temperance goal. Fox, Coors, Linmark. It necessarily follows that the price advertising ban cannot survive the more stringent constitutional review that Central Hudson itself concluded was appropriate for the complete suppression of truthful, nonmisleading commercial speech.

■ JUSTICE STEVENS [joined by JUSTICES KENNEDY, THOMAS, and GINSBURG].

[Relying] on the Central Hudson analysis set forth in Posadas and Edge Broadcasting, Rhode Island [argues] that, because expert opinions as to the effectiveness of the price advertising ban "go both ways," the Court of Appeals correctly concluded that the ban constituted a "reasonable choice" by the legislature. [The] reasoning in Posadas does support the State's argument, but, on reflection, we are now persuaded that Posadas [clearly] erred in concluding that it was "up to the legislature" to choose suppression over a less speech-restrictive policy. The Posadas majority's conclusion on that point cannot be reconciled with the unbroken line of prior cases striking down similarly broad regulations on truthful, nonmisleading advertising when non-speech-related alternatives were available. [We] also cannot accept the State's [contention that it may ban liquor price advertising because it may ban the sale of alcoholic beverages outright. Such] "greater-includes-the-lesser" reasoning, [which was] endorsed toward the end of the majority's opinion in Posadas, [is] inconsistent with both logic and well-settled doctrine. [Contrary] to the assumption made in Posadas, we think it quite clear that banning speech may sometimes prove far more intrusive than banning conduct. [Finally,] we find unpersuasive the State's contention that, under Posadas and Edge, the price advertising ban should be upheld because it targets commercial speech that pertains to a "vice" activity. [Our] decision last Term striking down an alcohol-related advertising restriction effectively rejected the very contention respondents now make. See Coors Brewing. Moreover, the scope of any "vice" exception to the protection afforded by the First Amendment would be difficult, if not impossible, to define.

■ JUSTICE SCALIA, concurring in part and concurring in the judgment.

[The] briefs and arguments of the parties in the present case provide no illumination on [state legislative practices toward advertising regulation at the time the First and Fourteenth Amendments were adopted.] [Since] I do not believe we have before us the wherewithal to declare Central Hudson wrong—or at least the wherewithal to say what ought to replace it—I must resolve this case in accord with our existing jurisprudence, which all except Justice Thomas agree would prohibit the challenged regulation. I am not disposed to develop new law, or reinforce old, on this issue, and accordingly I merely concur in the judgment of the Court.

■ JUSTICE THOMAS, concurring in part and concurring in the judgment.

In cases such as this, in which the government's asserted interest is to keep legal users of a product or service ignorant in order to manipulate their choices in the marketplace, the balancing test adopted in Central Hudson should not be applied, in my view. Rather, such an "interest" is per se illegitimate and can no more justify regulation of "commercial" speech than it can justify regulation of "noncommercial" speech. [Where,] as here, the asserted interest is one that is to be achieved through keeping would-be recipients of the speech in the dark, [a]pplication of the advancement-of-state-interest prong of Central Hudson makes little sense. [Faulting] the State for failing to show that its price advertising ban decreases alcohol consumption "significantly," as Justice Stevens does, seems to imply that if the State had been more successful at keeping consumers ignorant and thereby decreasing their consumption, then the restriction might have been upheld. This contradicts Virginia Pharmacy Board's rationale for protecting "commercial" speech in the first instance.

[In] their application of [Central Hudson,] both Justice Stevens and Justice O'Connor hold that because the State can ban the sale of lower priced alcohol altogether by instituting minimum prices or levying taxes, it cannot ban advertising regarding lower priced liquor. [Their] opinions would appear to commit the courts to striking down restrictions on speech whenever a direct regulation (i.e., a regulation involving no restriction on speech regarding lawful activity at all) would be an equally effective method of dampening demand by legal users. But it would seem that directly banning a product (or rationing it, taxing it, controlling its price, or otherwise restricting its sale in specific ways) would virtually always be at least as effective in discouraging consumption as merely restricting advertising regarding the product would be, and thus virtually all restrictions with such a purpose would fail the fourth prong of the Central Hudson test. [I] welcome this outcome; but, rather than "applying" the fourth prong of Central Hudson to reach the inevitable result that all or most such advertising restrictions must be struck down, I would adhere to the doctrine adopted in Virginia Pharmacy Board, and in Justice Blackmun's Central Hudson concurrence, that all attempts to dissuade legal choices by citizens by keeping them ignorant are impermissible.

■ JUSTICE O'CONNOR, with whom CHIEF JUSTICE REHNQUIST and JUSTICES SOUTER and BREYER join, concurring in the judgment.

[I] agree with the Court that Rhode Island's price-advertising ban is invalid. I would resolve this case more narrowly, however, by applying our established Central Hudson test to determine whether this commercial-speech regulation survives First Amendment scrutiny. Under that test, [our] conclusion is plain: Rhode Island's regulation fails First Amendment scrutiny. Both parties agree that the first two prongs of the Central Hudson test are met. Even if we assume arguendo that Rhode Island's regulation also satisfies the requirement that it directly advance the governmental interest, Rhode Island's regulation fails the final prong; that is, its ban is more extensive than necessary to serve the State's interest.

Rhode Island offers [one] justification for its ban on price advertising: [to] keep alcohol prices high as a way to keep consumption low. By preventing sellers from informing customers of prices, the regulation prevents competition from driving prices down and requires consumers to spend more time to find the best price for alcohol. The higher cost of obtaining alcohol, Rhode Island argues, will lead to reduced consumption. The fit between Rhode Island's method and this particular goal is not reasonable. [The] State has other methods at its disposal [that] would more directly accomplish this stated goal without intruding on sellers' ability to provide truthful, nonmisleading information to customers. [A sales] tax, for example, is not normally very difficult to administer and would have a far more certain and direct effect on prices, without any restriction on speech. The principal opinion suggests further alternatives, such as limiting per capita purchases or conducting an educational campaign about the dangers of alcohol consumption. The ready availability of such alternatives—at least some of which would far more effectively achieve Rhode Island's only professed goal, at comparatively small additional administrative cost—demonstrates that the fit between ends and means is not narrowly tailored. [Because] Rhode Island's regulation fails even the less stringent standard set out in Central Hudson, nothing here requires adoption of a new analysis for the evaluation of commercial speech regulation.

COMMERCIAL SPEECH REGULATION AFTER LIQUORMART

1. ***What standard of scrutiny?*** Central Hudson clearly set forth a standard of intermediate scrutiny for review of regulations of commercial speech, even where content-based. A number of justices have advocated full strict scrutiny for at least some regulations of commercial speech: Justices Brennan, Marshall, Blackmun and Stevens did so in pre-Liquormart concurrences or dissents, and Justices Stevens, Kennedy, Ginsburg and Thomas did so in Liquormart. But never have five of them sat on the Court

at the same time or on the same case. Thus, even after Liquormart, Central Hudson remains the governing test for reviewing commercial speech regulations.

But what does Central Hudson mean after Liquormart? Arguably, the stringency of a standard of review depends more on its application than its verbal formulation: it is a function of the factors that must be examined, the strength of the state justifications required, and the rigor with which an appellate court will in fact examine legislative or lower court determinations with respect to those justifications. Does Liquormart subject the Rhode Island regulation to the practical equivalent of strict scrutiny? Is its emphasis on the availability of less restrictive regulatory alternatives such as price floors and taxes consistent with the holding in Fox that the government need not employ the least restrictive alternative? Is Justice Thomas correct to predict that, after Liquormart, no ban on truthful price advertising may be upheld? Even if that is so, does the stringent application of Central Hudson in Liquormart have any application beyond the context of a total ban on truthful price data? For discussion of such questions, see Sullivan, "Cheap Spirits, Cigarettes and Free Speech," 1996 Sup. Ct. Rev. 123.

In **Lorillard Tobacco Co. v. Reilly**, 533 U.S. 525 (2001), the Court found the Central Hudson test "an adequate basis for decision" for striking down a set of tobacco advertising regulations. Massachusetts, seeking to protect children from seeing tobacco advertising, had sought to prohibit outdoor advertising of cigarettes, smokeless tobacco, and cigars within 1,000 feet of a school or playground, and to require that indoor point-of-sale advertising of such products be placed no lower than five feet from the floor. A 6–3 majority of the Court found these regulations as to cigarettes preempted by the Federal Cigarette Labeling and Advertising Act, which requires specific warning labels on cigarette packages and expressly prohibits state regulations requiring different labels and any other state law "with respect to the advertising or promotion of any cigarettes" whose packages do bear the specified labels. That ruling left for consideration whether the same regulations with respect to smokeless tobacco and cigars violated the First Amendment.

A majority found that they did, with Justice O'CONNOR writing the opinion of the Court. Neither of the first two parts of the Central Hudson test was in issue: the State had conceded for purposes of litigation that the advertising was not unlawful or misleading, and the tobacco advertisers did not contest that the government had an important interest in preventing tobacco use by minors. Six justices—Justice O'Connor, joined in this part of her opinion by Chief Justice Rehnquist and Justices Stevens, Souter, Ginsburg and Breyer—concluded that the outdoor advertising regulations would have satisfied the third part of the Central Hudson test by directly and materially advancing the state interest in preventing harms from underage use of smokeless tobacco or cigars that they believed the state had adequately empirically documented.

But a different 5–4 majority—Justice O'Connor, joined in this part of her opinion by Chief Justice Rehnquist and Justices Scalia, Kennedy and Thomas—found that the outdoor advertising regulations were not sufficiently narrowly tailored to satisfy the fourth part of Central Hudson: "In some geographical areas, these regulations would constitute nearly a complete ban on the communication of truthful information about smokeless tobacco and cigars to adult consumers. [The] uniformly broad sweep of the geographical limitation demonstrates a lack of tailoring. [In] addition, the range of communications restricted seems unduly broad. For instance, [a] ban on all signs of any size seems ill suited to target the problem of highly visible billboards, as opposed to smaller signs. [The] State's interest in preventing underage tobacco use is substantial, and even compelling, but it is no less true that the sale and use of tobacco products by adults is a legal activity. We must consider that tobacco retailers and manufacturers have an interest in conveying truthful information about their products to adults, and adults have a corresponding interest in receiving truthful information about tobacco products. In a case involving indecent speech on the Internet we explained that 'the governmental interest in protecting children from harmful materials . . . does not justify an unnecessarily broad suppression of speech addressed to adults.' Reno v. ACLU." The same five justices picked up a sixth vote from Justice Souter in concluding that the indoor advertising height regulations failed both the third and fourth steps of Central Hudson analysis: "Not all children are less than 5 feet tall, and those who are certainly have the ability to look up and take in their surroundings."

Justices KENNEDY, joined by Justice Scalia, and Justice THOMAS each wrote separate concurrences in part and in the judgment that raised questions about the adequacy of the Central Hudson test. Justice Kennedy stated his "continuing concerns that the test gives insufficient protection to truthful, nonmisleading commercial speech," and Justice Thomas restated his view that "when the government seeks to restrict truthful speech in order to suppress the ideas it conveys, strict scrutiny is appropriate, whether or not the speech in question may be characterized as 'commercial.' " Justice STEVENS, joined by Justices Ginsburg, Breyer and Souter, would have remanded for further factfinding on whether the 1000-foot outdoor advertising ban was narrowly tailored to the important state interest in preventing underage tobacco use, and joined by Justices Ginsburg and Breyer only, would have upheld the sales display regulations as a mere adjunct to the regulation of conduct.

Note that in 2009, Congress passed the Family Smoking Prevention and Tobacco Control Act, which included several significant restrictions on tobacco advertising. Tobacco manufacturers challenged the restrictions on First Amendment grounds. Applying the Central Hudson test, the Sixth Circuit upheld a majority of the regulations, finding that the government had significant interest in preventing juvenile smoking, and that the bans on free samples, non-tobacco merchandise, and event sponsorship were sufficiently tailored to achieving that interest. See Discount Tobacco City & Lottery, Inc. v. U.S., 674 F.3d 509 (2012). The panel held, however, that the Act's ban on distribution of free gifts with tobacco purchases was insufficiently tailored to achieving a substantial governmental interest and thus violated the First Amendment. It also rejected a ban on color imagery in tobacco advertising. The Supreme Court denied certiorari.

Another case in which the Supreme Court applied the Central Hudson test was **Thompson v. Western States Medical Center**, 535 U.S. 357 (2002). There, the Court struck down a provision of the Food and Drug Modernization Act of 1997 that conditioned an exemption from FDA approval requirements for makers of "compounded drugs" on their not "advertis[ing] or promot[ing] the compounding of any particular drug, class of drug, or type of drug." The Act did, however, allow providers to advertise and promote the compounding *service* without losing their exemption. Writing for the Court, Justice O'CONNOR found the government's ends important but its means insufficiently narrowly tailored to them: "Preserving the effectiveness and integrity of the FDCA's new drug approval process is clearly an important governmental interest, and the Government has every reason to want as many drugs as possible to be subject to that approval process. The Government also has an important interest [in] permitting the continuation of the practice of compounding so that patients with particular needs may obtain medications suited to those needs.

"[But] the Government has failed to demonstrate that the speech restrictions are 'not more extensive than is necessary to serve [those] interest[s].' [Several] non-speech-related means of drawing a line between compounding and large-scale manufacturing might be possible here. [Even] if the Government had argued that the [speech-related] restrictions were motivated by a fear that advertising compounded drugs would put people who do not need such drugs at risk by causing them to convince their doctors to prescribe the drugs anyway, [this] concern amounts to a fear that people would make bad decisions if given truthful information about compounded drugs. [We] have previously rejected the notion that the Government has an interest in preventing the dissemination of truthful commercial information in order to prevent members of the public from making bad decisions with the information. [Virginia Board.]"

Justice BREYER dissented, joined by Chief Justice Rehnquist and Justices Stevens and Ginsburg: "[The] Court seriously undervalues the importance of the Government's interest in protecting the health and safety of the American public." Endorsing a "lenient" interpretation of the First Amendment in the commercial speech context, he concluded: "[An] overly rigid 'commercial speech' doctrine will transform what ought to be a legislative or regulatory decision about the best way to protect the health and safety of the American public into a constitutional decision prohibiting the legislature from enacting necessary protections. As history in respect to the Due Process Clause shows, any such transformation would involve a tragic constitutional misunderstanding."

2. ***Paternalism and commercial speech.*** The opinions of Justices Stevens and Thomas in Liquormart emphasized the illegitimacy of any government interest in keeping consumers ignorant of truthful and nonmisleading commercial information. Tracking the reasoning of Virginia Pharmacy, they suggested that government may not suppress truthful price data out of fear that consumers will act on it in ways that are harmful to their self-interest. How far does this anti-paternalism rationale extend? May the state ban tobacco ads that depict smokers as rugged and healthy or as socially and financially successful, on the ground that such positive images of smoking will induce consumers to act against their own self-interest in health? For an argument that such regulation should be permissible, see Blasi & Monaghan, "The First Amendment and Cigarette Advertising," 250 JAMA 502 (1986). For an argument that such regulation is unconstitutional, see Redish, "Tobacco Advertising and the First Amendment," 81 Iowa L. Rev. 589 (1996).

3. ***Commercial speech fault lines on the Roberts Court.*** May a State restrict the sale, disclosure, and use of pharmacy records for the purpose of revealing to pharmaceutical manufacturers the prescribing practices of individual doctors? In **Sorrell v. IMS Health Co.**, 564 U.S. 552

(2011), the Court considered a free speech challenge to § 4631(d) of Vermont's Prescription Confidentiality Law, which attempted to limit the practice of pharmaceutical "detailing" by providing that, unless the prescriber consents, health insurers and pharmacies "shall not sell, license, or exchange for value regulated records containing prescriber-identifiable information, nor permit the use of regulated records containing prescriber-identifiable information for marketing or promoting a prescription drug" and that "[p]harmaceutical manufacturers and pharmaceutical marketers shall not use prescriber-identifiable information for marketing or promoting a prescription drug." The law contained exceptions allowing sale of the same information to other users, such as private or academic researchers. By a vote of 6–3 in which the Justices diverged sharply into two camps on commercial speech methodology, the Court ruled that Vermont's law violated the First Amendment even if reviewed under the heightened scrutiny applicable to commercial speech rather than the strict scrutiny applicable to other content-and speaker-based restrictions.

Justice KENNEDY wrote for the Court, joined by Chief Justice Roberts and Justices Scalia, Thomas, Alito, and Sotomayor: "Vermont's law enacts content-and speaker-based restrictions on the sale, disclosure, and use of prescriber-identifying information. [As] a result of these content-and speaker-based rules, detailers cannot obtain prescriber-identifying information, even though the information may be purchased or acquired by other speakers with diverse purposes and viewpoints. Detailers are likewise barred from using the information for marketing, even though the information may be used by a wide range of other speakers. [The] law on its face burdens disfavored speech by disfavored speakers." Justice Kennedy observed that the law even discriminated on the basis of viewpoint because it sought to restrict promotional efforts for brand-name drugs at the expense of generic drugs favored by state policy.

Justice Kennedy continued: "It follows that heightened judicial scrutiny is warranted. Commercial speech is no exception. A 'consumer's concern for the free flow of commercial speech often may be far keener than his concern for urgent political dialogue.' That reality has great relevance in the fields of medicine and public health, where information can save lives." The majority opinion rejected the State's arguments that "heightened judicial scrutiny is unwarranted because its law is a mere commercial regulation" or "because sales, transfer, and use of prescriber-identifying information are conduct, not speech." To the contrary, Justice Kennedy wrote, "the creation and dissemination of information are speech within the meaning of the First Amendment." Turning to the standard of scrutiny, he continued: "In the ordinary case it is all but dispositive to conclude that a law is content-based and, in practice, viewpoint-discriminatory. [The] outcome is the same whether a special commercial speech inquiry or a stricter form of judicial scrutiny is applied.

"[The] State seeks to achieve its policy objectives through the indirect means of restraining certain speech by certain speakers—that is, by diminishing detailers' ability to influence prescription decisions. Those who seek to censor or burden free expression often assert that disfavored speech has adverse effects. But the 'fear that people would make bad decisions if given truthful information' cannot justify content-based burdens on speech. Thompson; Virginia Bd. of Pharmacy; 44 Liquormart."

Justice BREYER filed a dissent, joined by Justices Ginsburg and Kagan. He argued that the Court should have applied a "more lenient" standard of scrutiny than Central Hudson because Vermont's law was part of a broader scheme of "ordinary commercial or regulatory legislation that affects speech in less direct ways" than a simple ban on advertising. Echoing then-Justice Rehnquist's dissent in Central Hudson, he suggested that the majority's approach portended a " 'retur[n] to the bygone era of Lochner v. New York, in which it was common practice for this Court to strike down economic regulations adopted by a State based on the Court's own notions of the most appropriate means for the State to implement its considered policies.' " Because the Vermont statute's "requirements form part of a traditional, comprehensive regulatory regime" to ensure that pharmaceutical products are both safe and effective, and because "Vermont's statute is directed toward information that exists only by virtue of government regulation," the dissenters would have applied the mere rational-basis review applicable to ordinary economic regulations. Even under Central Hudson, however, Justice Breyer concluded, the Vermont anti-detailing law should have been upheld as narrowly tailored to a substantial state interest in protecting public health by ensuring more "fair and balanced" prescribing practices by physicians.

In Matal v. Tam (2017; p. 1343 below), the Court focused its attention on government speech doctrine but also noted that, even if the commercial speech doctrine applied, the Lanham Act's disparagement clause "cannot withstand even Central Hudson review." Justice Alito delivered the opinion of the Court in Part IV, which the Chief Justice, Justice Thomas, and Justice Breyer joined:

"It is claimed that the disparagement clause serves two interests. The first is [that] Government has an interest in preventing speech expressing ideas that offend. [That] idea strikes at the heart of the First Amendment. Speech that demeans on the basis of race, ethnicity, gender, religion, age, disability, or any other similar ground is hateful; but the proudest boast of our free speech jurisprudence is that we protect the freedom to express 'the thought that we hate.'

The second interest asserted is protecting the orderly flow of commerce. [A] simple answer [is] that the disparagement clause is not 'narrowly drawn' to drive out trademarks that support invidious discrimination. [It] applies to trademarks like the following: 'Down with racists,' 'Down with sexists,' 'Down with homophobes.' It is not an anti-discrimination clause; it is a happy-talk clause.

[There] is also a deeper problem with the argument that commercial speech may be cleansed of any expression likely to cause offense. The commercial market is well stocked with merchandise that disparages prominent figures and groups, and the line between commercial and non-commercial speech is not always clear. [If] affixing the commercial label permits the suppression of any speech that may lead to political or social 'volatility,' free speech would be endangered."

CHAPTER 12

FREEDOM OF SPEECH—MODES OF REGULATION AND STANDARDS OF REVIEW

Chapter 11 explored the distinction between protected and unprotected or less protected forms of expression. In Chapter 12, the focus shifts from the nature of the speech involved to the nature of the government regulation involved. Section 1 of this chapter examines a key distinction: that between regulations that aim at the content of speech and regulations that aim at some other, content-neutral interest, such as peace and quiet, the orderly movement of crowds, the aesthetic attractiveness of public spaces, or the economic competitiveness of an industry. Outside the area of unprotected categories of speech, the Court has scrutinized content-based distinctions more carefully than those it considers content-neutral, although it still subjects most content-neutral regulations of speech or symbolic conduct to heightened rather than minimum rationality review. Section 2 turns to the problem of speech-restrictive laws that the government enacts or enforces in its capacity as proprietor, educator, employer, or patron. The discussion there begins with the law governing public forums and ends with the problem of unconstitutional conditions on government subsidies. Finally, Section 3 turns to a set of special procedural restrictions on how government regulates speech—the strong presumptions against overbreadth, vagueness and prior restraint—that seek to prevent government from restricting speech too broadly, too unclearly or too soon, even if it could restrict the very same speech under a law that was written or applied in a different way.

SECTION 1. CONTENT-BASED AND CONTENT-NEUTRAL REGULATIONS

Does it matter for First Amendment purposes if a law is written with reference to the ideas, message or communicative impact of expression? If the effect is the suppression of speech, why should it matter how government accomplishes that suppression? The Court has paid close attention to the distinction between content-based and content-neutral laws. Why might that be so?

To introduce the problem, suppose that a municipality enacted laws prohibiting the construction or maintenance, even on private property, of:

1. any billboard
2. any political billboard
3. any billboard supporting a Republican candidate
4. any billboard tending to arouse political anger or hostility

5. any message on a billboard during the three weeks preceding a general election

6. any billboard in any area zoned for residential use

7. any billboard larger than 12 by 40 feet

Every one of these laws would alike prohibit a Republican proprietor from erecting, in a residential neighborhood, a 20- by 50-foot billboard urging election of a Republican candidate in a close race in the weeks just before the election. Yet while each of these laws would have the identical effect on such proposed speech, the Court would scrutinize them differently. Which of these laws appear content-neutral? Which ones appear content-based? Which ones, if any, do not appear to aim at speech at all? Which, if any, of these laws more troubling than others under First Amendment principles? Why? The Supreme Court has addressed this issue most prominently in the following case, Reed v. Town of Gilbert, 576 U.S. ___, 135 S. Ct. 2218 (2015).

THE DISTINCTION BETWEEN CONTENT-BASED AND CONTENT-NEUTRAL LAWS

For some time, the Court treated the distinction between content-based and content-neutral regulations as crucial in First Amendment law. In Reed, the Court drew a bright line. See Genevieve Lakier, "Reed v. Town of Gilbert, Arizona, and the Rise of the Anticlassificatory First Amendment," 2016 Sup. Ct. Rev. 223 (2016).

Reed v. Town of Gilbert

576 U.S. ___, 135 S. Ct. 2218, 192 L. Ed. 2d 236 (2015).

■ JUSTICE THOMAS delivered the opinion of the Court.

The town of Gilbert, Arizona, has adopted a comprehensive code governing the manner in which people may display outdoor signs. [The] Sign Code prohibits the display of outdoor signs anywhere within the Town without a permit, but it then exempts 23 categories of signs from that requirement. These exemptions include everything from bazaar signs to flying banners. Three categories of exempt signs are particularly relevant here.

The first is "Ideological Sign[s]." This category includes any "sign communicating a message or ideas for noncommercial purposes that is not a Construction Sign, Directional Sign, Temporary Directional Sign Relating to a Qualifying Event, Political Sign, Garage Sale Sign, or a sign owned or required by a governmental agency." Of the three categories discussed here, the Code treats ideological signs most favorably, allowing them to be up to 20 square feet in area and to be placed in all "zoning districts" without time limits.

The second category is "Political Sign[s]." This includes any "temporary sign designed to influence the outcome of an election called by a public body." The Code treats these signs less favorably than ideological signs. The Code allows the placement of political signs up to 16 square feet on residential property and up to 32 square feet on nonresidential property, undeveloped municipal property, and "rights-of-way." These signs may be displayed up to 60 days before a primary election and up to 15 days following a general election.

The third category is "Temporary Directional Signs Relating to a Qualifying Event." This includes any "Temporary Sign intended to direct pedestrians, motorists, and other passersby to a 'qualifying event.'" A "qualifying event" is defined as any "assembly, gathering, activity, or meeting sponsored, arranged, or promoted by a religious, charitable, community service, educational, or other similar non-profit organization." The Code treats temporary directional signs even less favorably than political signs. Temporary directional signs may be no larger than six square feet. They may be placed on private property or on a public right-of-way, but no more than four signs may be placed on a single property at any time. And, they may be displayed no more than 12 hours before the "qualifying event" and no more than 1 hour afterward.

Petitioners Good News Community Church (Church) and its pastor, Clyde Reed, wish to advertise the time and location of their Sunday church services. The Church is a small, cash-strapped entity that owns no building, so it holds its services at elementary schools or other locations in or near the Town. In order to inform the public about its services, which are held in a variety of different locations, the Church began placing 15 to 20 temporary signs around the Town, frequently in the public right-of-way abutting the street. The signs typically displayed the Church's name, along with the time and location of the upcoming service. Church members would post the signs early in the day on Saturday and then remove them around midday on Sunday.

[This] practice caught the attention of the Town's Sign Code compliance manager, who twice cited the Church for violating the Code.

[Content-based] laws—those that target speech based on its communicative content—are presumptively unconstitutional and may be justified only if the government proves that they are narrowly tailored to serve compelling state interests. Government regulation of speech is content based if a law applies to particular speech because of the topic discussed or the idea or message expressed.

[The] Town's Sign Code is content based on its face. [The] restrictions in the Sign Code that apply to any given sign [depend] entirely on the communicative content of the sign. If a sign informs its reader of the time and place a book club will discuss John Locke's Two Treatises of Government, that sign will be treated differently from a sign expressing the view that one should vote for one of Locke's followers in an upcoming election, and both signs will be treated differently from a sign expressing an ideological view rooted in Locke's theory of government. More to the point, the Church's signs inviting people to attend its worship services are treated differently from signs conveying other types of ideas. [A] law that is content based on its face is subject to strict scrutiny regardless of the government's benign motive, content-neutral justification, or lack of animus toward the ideas contained in the regulated speech.

[The] Court of Appeals [reasoned] that the Sign Code was content neutral because it "does not mention any idea or viewpoint, let alone single one out for differential treatment." This analysis conflates two distinct but related limitations that the First Amendment places on government regulation of speech. [A] speech regulation targeted at specific subject matter is content based even if it does not discriminate among viewpoints within that subject matter. For example, a law banning the use of sound trucks for political speech—and only political speech—would be a content-based regulation, even if it imposed no limits on the political viewpoints that could be expressed. The Town's Sign Code likewise singles out specific subject matter for differential treatment, even if it does not target viewpoints within that subject matter. [That] is a paradigmatic example of content-based discrimination.

[The] Sign Code's distinctions are [also] not speaker based. The restrictions for political, ideological, and temporary event signs apply equally no matter who sponsors them. [But] the fact that a distinction is speaker based does not [automatically] render the distinction content neutral. [A] law limiting the content of newspapers, but only newspapers, could not evade strict scrutiny simply because it could be characterized as speaker based.

Nor do the Sign Code's distinctions hinge on whether and when an event is occurring. The Code does not permit citizens to post signs on any topic whatsoever within a set period leading up to an election, for example. Instead, come election time, it requires Town officials to determine whether a sign is "designed to influence the outcome of an election" (and thus "political") or merely "communicating a message or ideas for noncommercial purposes" (and thus "ideological"). That obvious content-based inquiry does not evade strict scrutiny review simply because an event (*i.e.*, an election) is involved.

[It] is the Town's burden to demonstrate that the Code's differentiation between temporary directional signs and other types of signs [furthers] a compelling governmental interest and is narrowly tailored to that end.

The Town [has] offered only two governmental interests in support of the distinctions the Sign Code draws: preserving the Town's aesthetic appeal and traffic safety. Assuming for the sake of argument that those are compelling governmental interests, the Code's distinctions fail as hopelessly underinclusive. [The] Town cannot claim that placing strict limits on temporary directional signs is necessary to beautify the Town while at the same time allowing unlimited numbers of other types of signs that create the same problem.

The Town similarly has not shown that limiting temporary directional signs is necessary to eliminate threats to traffic safety, but that limiting other types of signs is not.

The Town has ample content-neutral options available to resolve problems with safety and aesthetics.

[At] the same time, the presence of certain signs may be essential, both for vehicles and pedestrians, to guide traffic or to identify hazards and ensure safety. A sign ordinance narrowly tailored to the challenges of protecting the safety of pedestrians, drivers, and passengers—such as warning signs marking hazards on private property, signs directing traffic, or street numbers associated with private houses—well might survive strict scrutiny.

■ JUSTICE ALITO, with whom JUSTICE KENNEDY and JUSTICE SOTOMAYOR join, concurring.

[As] the Court shows, the regulations at issue in this case are replete with content-based distinctions, and as a result they must satisfy strict scrutiny. This does not mean, however, that municipalities are powerless to enact and enforce reasonable sign regulations. I will not attempt to provide anything like a comprehensive list, but here are some rules that would not be content based:

> Rules regulating the size of signs. These rules may distinguish among signs based on any content-neutral criteria, including any relevant criteria listed below.
>
> Rules regulating the locations in which signs may be placed. These rules may distinguish between free-standing signs and those attached to buildings.
>
> Rules distinguishing between lighted and unlighted signs.
>
> Rules distinguishing between signs with fixed messages and electronic signs with messages that change.
>
> Rules that distinguish between the placement of signs on private and public property.
>
> Rules distinguishing between the placement of signs on commercial and residential property.
>
> Rules distinguishing between on-premises and off-premises signs.
>
> Rules restricting the total number of signs allowed per mile of roadway.
>
> Rules imposing time restrictions on signs advertising a one-time event. Rules of this nature do not discriminate based on topic or subject and are akin to rules restricting the times within which oral speech or music is allowed.

Properly understood, today's decision will not prevent cities from regulating signs in a way that fully protects public safety and serves legitimate esthetic objectives.

■ JUSTICE KAGAN, with whom JUSTICE GINSBURG and JUSTICE BREYER join, concurring in the judgment.

Countless cities and towns across America have adopted ordinances regulating the posting of signs, while exempting certain categories of signs based on their subject matter.

[Given] the Court's analysis, many sign ordinances of that kind are now in jeopardy. [On] the majority's view, courts would have to determine that a town has a compelling interest in informing passersby where George Washington slept. [The] consequence—unless courts water down strict scrutiny to something unrecognizable—is that our communities will find themselves in an unenviable bind: They will have to either repeal the exemptions that allow for helpful signs on streets and sidewalks, or else lift their sign restrictions altogether and resign themselves to the resulting clutter.

Although the majority insists that applying strict scrutiny to all such ordinances is "essential" to protecting First Amendment freedoms, I find it challenging to understand why that is so. [We] apply strict scrutiny to facially content-based regulations of speech [when] there is any realistic possibility that official suppression of ideas is afoot. That is always the case when the regulation facially differentiates on the basis of viewpoint.

[Subject-matter] regulation [may] have the intent or effect of favoring some ideas over others. When that is realistically possible [we] insist that the law pass the most demanding constitutional test. But when that is not realistically possible, we may do well to relax our guard so that "entirely reasonable" laws imperiled by strict scrutiny can survive.

[The] Town of Gilbert's defense of its sign ordinance—most notably, the law's distinctions between directional signs and others—does not pass strict scrutiny, or intermediate scrutiny, or even the laugh test. [Accordingly,] there is no need to decide in this case whether strict scrutiny applies to every sign ordinance in every town across this country containing a subject-matter exemption

---

1. ***Viewpoint restrictions.*** Well before the Supreme Court squarely ruled that content-based restrictions always invoke strict scrutiny, the Court used discrimination against certain ideas or viewpoints as its archetypal model for triggering strict scrutiny. Several of the decisions already explored in Chapter 11 are illustrative. For example, Kingsley International Pictures Corp. v. Regents (1959; p. 1059 above) held that a state may not deny a license to a film "because that picture advocates an idea—that adultery under certain circumstances may be proper behavior. [The] First Amendment's basic guarantee is of freedom to advocate ideas." Brandenburg v. Ohio (1969; p. 978 above) made clear that, in the absence of incitement to imminent lawless action, the "mere advocacy" of violent overthrow of democracy or capitalism could not be made a crime. Justice Scalia's opinion for the Court in R.A.V. v. St. Paul (1992; p. 1038 above), suggested that the St. Paul ordinance prohibiting symbols that tend to arouse racial anger or alarm was invalid in part as "viewpoint discrimination" because it prohibited fighting words by bigots but not against them: "St. Paul has no [authority] to license one side of a debate to fight freestyle, while requiring the other to follow Marquis of Queensbury rules." And Judge Easterbrook's decision in American Booksellers Ass'n v. Hudnut (1985; p. 1076 above) invalidated a feminist-inspired anti-pornography ordinance as "thought control" because "speech that 'subordinates' women [is] forbidden" while speech "that portrays women in positions of equality is lawful, no matter how graphic the sexual content."

After Reed v. Gilbert, the emphasis on viewpoint discrimination may well have become secondary, because every case of viewpoint discrimination necessarily appears to involve content-based discrimination. (Can you think of any exceptions?)

2. ***Subject matter restrictions.*** Is content discrimination suspect in the absence of viewpoint discrimination? What if government eliminates expression on an entire topic? The Court has generally scrutinized subject matter restrictions strictly. Recall that Justice Scalia's opinion for the Court subjected the St. Paul ordinance in R.A.V. to strict scrutiny not only because it involved viewpoint discrimination but also because it forbade only those fighting words that were "addressed to one of the specified disfavored topics" of race, color, creed, religion or gender. Recall too the Court's invalidation of

a ban on the display of all nudity on drive-in theater screens in Erznoznik v. Jacksonville (1975; p. 1082 above). Consider the following cases involving other restrictions on the subject matter of speech.

In **Police Department v. Mosley**, 408 U.S. 92 (1972), the Court invalidated a Chicago disorderly conduct ordinance which barred picketing within 150 feet of a school while the school was in session, but exempted "peaceful picketing of any school involved in a labor dispute." Mosley had conducted a solitary picket outside a Chicago high school, carrying a sign saying "Jones High School practices black discrimination." Justice MARSHALL's opinion for the Court found the law's "selective exclusion [of speech] from a public place" unconstitutional. He stated: "The central problem with Chicago's ordinance is that it describes the permissible picketing in terms of its subject matter. [The] operative distinction is the message on a picket sign. [Above] all else, the First Amendment means that government has no power to restrict expression because of its message, its ideas, its subject matter, or its content. To permit the continued building of our politics and culture, and to assure self-fulfillment for each individual, our people are guaranteed the right to express any thought, free from government censorship. The essence of this forbidden censorship is content control. [Necessarily], then, under [equal protection], not to mention the First Amendment itself, government may not grant the use of a forum to people whose views it finds acceptable, but deny use to those wishing to express less favored or more controversial views. And it may not select which issues are worth discussing or debating in public facilities. There is an 'equality of status in the field of ideas,' and government must afford all points of view an equal opportunity to be heard."

Justice Marshall noted that "reasonable 'time, place, and manner' " regulations of picketing may be necessary to further significant governmental interests." But this was not a time, place, and manner regulation, as it defined the prohibited speech "in terms of subject matter," which was "never permitted." He rejected the argument that preventing school disruption justified the ordinance: "If peaceful labor picketing is permitted, there is no justification for prohibiting all nonlabor picketing, both peaceful and nonpeaceful. 'Peaceful' nonlabor picketing [is] obviously no more disruptive than 'peaceful' labor picketing. But Chicago's ordinance permits the latter and prohibits the former." Moreover, he rejected the argument that a city could prohibit all nonlabor picketing "because, as a class, nonlabor picketing is more prone to produce violence than labor picketing": "Predictions about imminent disruption from picketing involve judgments appropriately made on an individualized basis, not by means of broad classifications, especially those based on subject matter."

Technically, Justice Marshall rested the Mosley judgment on the Equal Protection Clause of the Fourteenth Amendment. But he noted: "Of course, the equal protection claim in this case is closely intertwined with First Amendment interests: the Chicago ordinance affects picketing, which is expressive conduct; moreover, it does so by classifications formulated in terms of the subject of the picketing." Later cases have assimilated the Mosley holding into First Amendment analysis.

In **Carey v. Brown**, 447 U.S. 455 (1980), the Court found another picketing restriction unconstitutional under Mosley. The case involved a peaceful picket outside the mayor's home advocating racial integration of the schools through busing. The picketers were convicted under a state law that generally barred picketing outside residences or dwellings, but exempted "the peaceful picketing of a place of employment involved in a labor dispute." Justice BRENNAN, writing for the majority, held that the law impermissibly "accords preferential treatment to the expression of views on one particular subject; information about labor disputes may be freely disseminated, but discussion of all other issues is restricted." It was thus "constitutionally indistinguishable" from Mosley. Justice REHNQUIST, joined by Chief Justice Burger and Justice Blackmun, dissented, arguing that the basis for distinction in the law was "not content, [but] rather the character of the residence sought to be picketed."

Simon & Schuster, Inc. v. Members of New York State Crime Victims Board, 502 U.S. 105 (1991), involved a challenge to New York's "Son of Sam" law, enacted to prevent a serial murderer and other criminals from profiting at the expense of their victims from books about their crimes. The law required payment to the Crime Victims Board of any proceeds due to a person accused of, convicted of, or admitting to a crime, for the production of a book or other work describing the crime. The Board was to place these funds in escrow for five years so that they would be available to satisfy any damage judgments that victims of the defendant's crimes might obtain. The law was challenged by the publisher of a book entitled "Wiseguy: Life in a Mafia Family." A principal source for the book was a former organized crime operative, Henry Hill, who, in exchange for compensation, had recounted his participation in various robberies, extortions, drug dealing and frauds. New York sought payment from the publisher and the publisher challenged the statute under the First Amendment. The Court unanimously invalidated the statute. Justice O'CONNOR, writing for the Court, stated: "[T]he Government's ability to impose content-based burdens on speech raises the specter that the Government may effectively drive certain ideas or viewpoints from the marketplace. The Son of Sam law is a such a content-based statute. It singles out income derived from expressive activity for a burden the State places on no other income, and it is directed only at works with a specified content. Whether the First Amendment 'speaker' is considered to be Henry Hill, whose income the statute places in escrow because of the story he has told, or Simon & Schuster, which can publish books about crime with the assistance of only those criminals willing to forgo remuneration for at least five years, the statute plainly imposes a financial disincentive only on speech of a particular content."

Because the statute was content-based, Justice O'Connor subjected it to strict scrutiny, and found it not narrowly tailored to the state's "undisputed compelling interest in ensuring that criminals do not profit from their crimes." She found that the State had not shown "any greater interest in compensating victims from the proceeds of such 'storytelling' than from any of the criminal's other assets." She also found the law "significantly overinclusive" as it would potentially sweep in "such works as The Autobiography of Malcolm X, which describes crimes committed by the civil rights leader before he became a public figure; Civil Disobedience, in which Thoreau acknowledges his refusal to pay taxes and recalls his experience in jail; and even the Confessions of Saint Augustine, in which the author laments 'my past foulness and the carnal corruptions of my soul,' one instance of which involved the theft of pears from a neighboring vineyard." Justice KENNEDY, concurring in the judgment, would not have applied strict scrutiny but would have found the law invalid per se: "Here a law is directed to speech alone where the speech in question is not obscene, not defamatory, not words tantamount to an act otherwise criminal, not an impairment of some other constitutional right, not an incitement to lawless action, and not calculated or likely to bring about imminent harm the State has the substantive power to prevent. No further inquiry is necessary to reject the State's argument that the statute should be upheld. [The] New York statute amounts to raw censorship based on content. [That] ought to end the matter."

Could the defect of the laws struck down in Mosley and Carey be cured by an ordinance barring *all* picketing outside a school or home? Would such a law be less restrictive of speech? How? Could New York pass a new law requiring the escrow of *all* proceeds from crime and apply it to Henry Hill's book proceeds? What is the difference between that law and the law struck down in Simon & Schuster? The above cases indicate that the Court will accord subject matter restrictions strict scrutiny, which is almost always fatal. But as the next case suggests, there might be occasional exceptions.

In **Burson v. Freeman**, 504 U.S. 191 (1992), the Court upheld against a First Amendment challenge a state law prohibiting the solicitation of votes, the display of political posters or signs, and the distribution of political campaign materials within 100 feet of the entrance to a polling place. Justice BLACKMUN announced the judgment of the Court and wrote for a plurality joined by Chief Justice Rehnquist and Justices White and Kennedy: "This Court has held that the First Amendment's hostility to content-based regulation extends not only to a restriction on a particular viewpoint, but also to a prohibition of public discussion of an entire topic. [As] a facially content-based restriction on political speech in a public forum, [the ban on campaign materials] must be subjected to exacting scrutiny. Tennessee asserts [that] its regulation protect[s] the right of its citizens to vote freely for the candidates of their choice [and] protects the right to vote in an election conducted with integrity and reliability. [These interests] obviously are compelling ones. [To] survive strict scrutiny, however, a State must do more than assert a compelling state interest—it must demonstrate that its law is necessary to serve the asserted interest. [An] examination of the evolution of election reform, both in this country and abroad, demonstrates the necessity of restricted areas in or around polling places. [That history] reveals a persistent battle against two evils: voter intimidation and election fraud. After an unsuccessful experiment with an unofficial ballot system, all 50 States, together with numerous other Western democracies, settled on the same solution: a secret ballot secured in part by a restricted zone around the voting compartments. [It] is the rare case in which we have held that a law survives strict scrutiny. This, however, is such a rare case. [The] State [has] asserted that the exercise of free speech rights conflicts with another fundamental right, the right to cast a ballot in an election free from the taint of intimidation and fraud. A long history, a substantial consensus, and simple common sense show that some restricted zone around polling places is necessary to protect that fundamental right. Given the conflict between these two rights, we hold that requiring solicitors to stand 100 feet from the entrances to polling places does not constitute an unconstitutional compromise."

Justice KENNEDY wrote a separate concurrence, stating that, despite the preference he expressed in Simon & Schuster for a per se rule against content discrimination rather than case-by-case strict scrutiny, "there is a narrow area in which the First Amendment permits freedom of expression to yield to the extent necessary for the accommodation of another constitutional right. That principle can apply here without danger that the general rule permitting no content restriction will be engulfed by the analysis." Justice Scalia concurred in the judgment, finding that the vicinity of the polling place was not a traditional public forum and therefore that viewpoint neutrality was all that was required. Justice STEVENS dissented, joined by Justices O'Connor and Souter: "Tennessee's statutory 'campaign-free zone' raises constitutional concerns of the first magnitude. The statute directly regulates political expression and thus implicates a core concern of the First Amendment. Moreover, it targets only a specific subject matter (campaign speech) and a defined class of speakers (campaign workers) and thus regulates expression based on its content. [Within] the zone, [the law] silences all campaign-related expression, but allows expression on any other subject: religious, artistic, commercial speech, even political debate and solicitation concerning issues or candidates not on the day's ballot. [This] discriminatory feature of the statute severely undercuts the credibility of its purported law-and-order justification. Tennessee's content-based discrimination is particularly problematic because such a regulation will inevitably favor certain groups of candidates. [Candidates] with fewer resources, candidates for lower visibility offices, and 'grassroots' candidates benefit disproportionately from last-minute campaigning near the polling place." Accordingly, the dissenters concluded, the law could not survive the applicable strict scrutiny.

In another election context, that of *judicial* elections, the Court by contrast struck down as impermissibly content-based a restriction on the subject matter of speech, this time by judicial candidates. In **Republican Party of Minnesota v. White**, 536 U.S. 765 (2002), the Court invalidated by a vote of 5–4 a provision of the Minnesota code of judicial conduct that stated that a "candidate for a judicial office, including an incumbent judge," shall not "announce his or her views on disputed legal or political issues." The provision—known as the "announce clause"—was challenged by a candidate who sought to distribute literature criticizing Minnesota Supreme Court decisions on crime, welfare, and abortion. In his opinion for the Court, Justice SCALIA wrote: "[The] announce clause both prohibits speech on the basis of its content and burdens a category of speech that is 'at the core of our First Amendment freedoms'—speech about the qualifications of candidates for public office. [The] proper test to be applied to determine the constitutionality of such a restriction is what our cases have called strict scrutiny. [Under] the strict-scrutiny test, respondents have the burden to prove that the announce clause is (1) narrowly tailored, to serve (2) a compelling state interest. In order for respondents to show that the announce clause is narrowly tailored, they must demonstrate that it does not 'unnecessarily circumscribe protected expression.' "

Justice Scalia rejected the state's arguments that its interests in preserving the impartiality or the appearance of the impartiality of the state judiciary were sufficiently compelling to justify the announce clause: "One meaning of 'impartiality' in the judicial context—and of course its root meaning—is the lack of bias for or against either *party* to the proceeding. Impartiality in this sense assures equal application of the law. [We] think it plain that the announce clause is not narrowly tailored to serve impartiality (or the appearance of impartiality) in this sense. Indeed, the clause is barely tailored to serve that interest *at all*, inasmuch as it does not restrict speech for or against particular *parties*, but rather speech for or against particular *issues*. [It] is perhaps possible to use the term 'impartiality' in the judicial context [to] mean lack of preconception in favor of or against a particular *legal view*. [Impartiality] in this sense may well be an interest served by the announce clause, but it is not a *compelling* state interest, as strict scrutiny requires. [Even] if it were possible to select judges who did not have preconceived views on legal issues, it would hardly be desirable to do so. 'Proof that a Justice's mind at the time he joined the Court was a complete *tabula rasa* in the area of constitutional adjudication would be evidence of lack of qualification, not lack of bias.' [A] third possible meaning of 'impartiality' [might] be described as open-mindedness. [It] may well be that impartiality in this sense, and the appearance of it, are desirable in the judiciary, but we need not pursue that inquiry, since we do not believe the Minnesota Supreme Court adopted the announce clause for that purpose. [In] Minnesota, a candidate for judicial office may not say 'I think it is constitutional for the legislature to prohibit same-sex marriages.' He may say the very same thing, however, up until the very day before he declares himself a candidate, and may say it repeatedly (until litigation is pending) after he is elected. As a means of pursuing the objective of open-mindedness that respondents now articulate, the announce clause is so woefully underinclusive as to render belief in that purpose a challenge to the credulous."

Justice Scalia likewise rejected the suggestion that elected judges might feel special compulsion in later cases to adhere to views they had announced during an election, putting at risk due process for litigants: "[E]lected judges—regardless of whether they have announced any views beforehand—*always* face the pressure of an electorate who might disagree with their rulings and therefore vote them off the bench. [If] it violates due process for a judge to sit in a case in which ruling one way rather than another increases his prospects for reelection, then [the] practice of electing judges is itself a violation of due process." He also downplayed the difference between judicial and legislative elections, noting that "[n]ot only do state-court judges possess the power to 'make' common law, but they have the immense power to shape the States' constitutions as well. Which is precisely why the election of state judges became popular." He concluded that opposition to judicial elections "may be well taken (it certainly had the support of the Founders of the Federal Government), but the First Amendment does not permit it to achieve its goal by leaving the principle of elections in place while preventing candidates from discussing what the elections are about."

Justice O'Connor concurred but wrote separately to express concern that judicial elections undermine the actual and perceived impartiality of state judges. Justice KENNEDY also concurred to argue that "content-based speech restrictions that do not fall within any traditional exception" should be held invalid per se without undergoing the compelling interest and narrow tailoring inquiries required by strict scrutiny. Justice STEVENS dissented, joined by Justices Souter, Ginsburg, and Breyer: "There is a critical difference between the work of the judge and the work of other public officials. In a democracy, issues of policy are properly decided by majority vote; it is the business of legislators and executives to be popular. But in litigation, issues of law or fact should not be determined by popular vote; it is the business of judges to be indifferent to unpopularity." Justice GINSBURG also dissented, joined by Justices Stevens, Souter, and Breyer: "I would differentiate elections for political offices, in which the First Amendment holds full sway, from elections designed to select those whose office it is to administer justice without respect to persons. [Judges] are not political actors. [Thus], the rationale underlying unconstrained speech in elections for political office—that representative government depends on the public's ability to choose agents who will act at its behest—does not carry over to campaigns for the bench."

The Court's cases since White have reaffirmed that strict scrutiny attaches to content-based distinctions on speech. See, for example, the plurality opinion in United States v. Alvarez (2012; p. 1033 above). Recall, however, that this stringent standard of review applies only where the relevant category of speech is protected; where speech falls within an unprotected category, a content-based distinction is permissible if it "reflect[s] the distinction and rationale for the initial nonprotection." Schauer, "Intentions, Conventions, and the First Amendment: The Case of Cross-Burning," 2003 Sup. Ct. Rev. 197 (citing Virginia v. Black (2003; p. 1049 above)). Can these two disparate standards for content-based distinctions be squared?

In **Williams-Yulee v. Florida Bar**, 576 U.S. ___, 135 S. Ct. 1656 (2015), the Court revisited judicial speech in connection with state elections. Chief Justice ROBERTS's opinion upheld the application of Florida's Canon 7C(1), which governs fundraising in judicial elections, to impose sanctions on a judicial candidate's personal solicitation of campaign contributions The Canon, based on a provision in the American Bar Association's Model Code of Judicial Conduct, provides: " 'A candidate, including an incumbent judge, for a judicial office that is filled by public election between competing candidates shall not personally solicit campaign funds, or solicit attorneys for publicly stated support, but may establish committees of responsible persons to secure and manage the expenditure of funds for the candidate's campaign and to obtain public statements of support for his or her candidacy. Such committees are not prohibited from soliciting campaign contributions and public support from any person or corporation authorized by law.' " Most other States, like Florida, prohibit judicial candidates from soliciting campaign funds personally, but allow them to raise money through committees.

The Chief Justice, writing only for a plurality, applied strict scrutiny to Florida's action, asserting that "we hold today what we assumed in Republican Party of Minn. v. White: A State may restrict the speech of a judicial candidate only if the restriction is narrowly tailored to serve a compelling interest." He then continued for a majority of the Court to find that the Florida law was narrowly tailored: "We have emphasized that it is the rare case in which a State demonstrates that a speech restriction is narrowly tailored to serve a compelling interest. But those cases do arise. See Holder v. Humanitarian Law Project (2010; p. 1195 below). [The] Florida Supreme Court adopted Canon 7C(1) to promote the State's interests in 'protecting the integrity of the judiciary' and 'maintaining the public's confidence in an impartial judiciary.' [Judges], charged with exercising strict neutrality and independence, cannot supplicate campaign donors without diminishing public confidence in judicial integrity."

Expressly contrasting the judicial elections case to the mainstream of campaign finance cases (see Chapter 13, Section 3 below), the Chief Justice went on: "A State's interest in preserving public confidence in the integrity of its judiciary extends beyond its interest in preventing the appearance of corruption in legislative and executive elections. [The] role of judges differs from the role of politicians. [The] same is not true of judges. In deciding cases, a judge is not to follow the preferences of his supporters, or provide any special consideration to his campaign donors. [As] in White, therefore, our precedents applying the First Amendment to political elections have little bearing on the issues here."

Rejecting a claim of underinclusivity, Chief Justice Roberts wrote that "[a] State need not address all aspects of a problem in one fell swoop; policymakers may focus on their most pressing concerns. [The] solicitation ban aims squarely at the conduct most likely to undermine public confidence in the integrity of the judiciary: personal requests for money by judges and judicial candidates. [And the] Canon contains zero exceptions to its ban on personal solicitation."

On narrow tailoring, Chief Justice Roberts wrote: "Canon 7C(1) leaves judicial candidates free to discuss any issue with any person at any time. Candidates can write letters, give speeches, and put up billboards. They can contact potential supporters in person, on the phone, or online. They can promote their campaigns on radio, television, or other media. [The] First Amendment requires that Canon 7C(1) be narrowly tailored, not that it be perfectly tailored. The impossibility of perfect tailoring is especially apparent when the State's compelling interest is as intangible as public confidence in the integrity of the judiciary. [The] desirability of judicial elections is a question that has sparked disagreement for more than 200 years. [It] is not our place to resolve this enduring debate."

Justice GINSBURG concurred but did not join the plurality in applying strict scrutiny: "As explained in my dissenting opinion in Republican Party of Minnesota v. White, I would not apply exacting scrutiny to a State's endeavor sensibly to differentiate elections for political offices . . . , from elections designed to select those whose office it is to administer justice without respect to persons."

Justice SCALIA dissented, maintaining that "the Court flattens one settled First Amendment principle after another. [One] need not equate judges with politicians to see that the electoral setting calls for all the more vigilance in ensuring observance of the First Amendment. When a candidate asks someone for a campaign contribution, he tends [also] to talk about his qualifications for office and his views on public issues. This expression lies at the heart of what the First Amendment is meant to protect. In addition, banning candidates from asking for money personally favors some candidates over others—incumbent judges (who benefit from their current status) over non-judicial candidates, the well-to-do (who may not need to raise any money at all) over lower-income candidates, and the well-connected (who have an army of potential fundraisers) over outsiders. This danger of legislated (or judicially imposed) favoritism is the very reason the First Amendment exists. [Among] its other functions, the First Amendment is a kind of Equal Protection Clause for ideas. [The] Court's decision disregards these principles.

"[The court's underinclusiveness] analysis elides the distinction between selectivity on the basis of content and selectivity on other grounds. Because the First Amendment does not prohibit underinclusiveness as such, lawmakers may target a problem only at certain times or in certain places. [The] First Amendment is not abridged for the benefit of the Brotherhood of the Robe."

Justice KENNEDY dissented "to underscore the irony in the Court's having concluded that the very First Amendment protections judges must enforce should be lessened when a judicial candidate's own speech is at issue."

3. ***Speaker restrictions.*** Would Mosley and Carey have come out any differently if the law had limited the antipicketing exception to "unions" rather than speech concerning a labor dispute? Would the "Son of Sam" law have fared better if it had escrowed all proceeds of "memoirs by criminal defendants"? A speaker's identity can sometimes function as a proxy for viewpoint or subject matter. When it does, the Court typically applies the same strict scrutiny to speaker-based restrictions as it applies to other content restrictions.

Speaker restrictions, however, are not always considered the practical equivalent of content restrictions, so long as the ground on which speakers are classified can be described as related to some aspect of their status independent of their beliefs or points of view. For example, the Court declined to find speaker identity a proxy for viewpoint when the government: gave a tax benefit to veterans' groups and not other lobbyists, see Regan v. Taxation with Representation (1983; p. 1323 below) (relating the distinction to veterans' service to the nation); required cable operators to carry the programs of over-the-air broadcasters, but not other video programmers, see Turner Broadcasting v. FCC (1994; p. 1406 below) (relating the distinction to cable's technological chokehold monopoly); enjoined protesters outside abortion clinics but not other entities, see Madsen v. Women's Health Center (1994; p. 1239 below) (relating the distinction to the protesters' past actions that gave rise to the injunction); permitted charitable organizations but not advocacy organizations to solicit funds from federal office workers, see Cornelius v. NAACP (1985; p. 1260 below) (relating the distinction to the function of charitable services); and granted access to public teachers' in-school mailboxes to the incumbent teachers' union but not to its rival, see Perry Education Ass'n v. Perry Local Educators' Ass'n (1983; p. 1258 below) (relating the distinction to service as a collective bargaining representative).

4. ***Communicative impact on the audience.*** Laws barring speech that is deemed likely to cause a certain response in the audience based on its content are typically viewed as skeptically as direct content restrictions. Recall, for example, Forsyth Co. v. Nationalist Movement (1992; p. 997 above), which invalidated a scheme calibrating the price of a parade permit to the expected hostility of the audience response. Likewise, Cohen v. California (1971; p. 998 above) held that a breach-of-peace law could not be applied in order to prevent audience offense. And R.A.V. v. St. Paul (1992; p. 1038 above) found a ban on symbols that caused racial anger or alarm to be impermissibly content-based. Might it be argued that all content-based laws are in a sense aimed at the communicative impact of expression, and presumptively invalid for that reason? If so, laws aimed at audience response are just examples of the general category. See Ely, "Flag Desecration: A Case Study in the Roles of Categorization and Balancing in First Amendment Analysis," 88 Harv. L. Rev. 1482 (1975).

5. ***Content-neutral laws.*** Two types of content-neutral laws have come before the Court on free speech challenge. One type aims at conduct, not speech, but may have the effect of suppressing speech when applied to a "symbolic" or "expressive" version of such conduct. This issue arises in such decisions as United States v. O'Brien (1968; p. 1176 below) (draft-card

burning); Arcara v. Cloud Books (1986; p. 1182 below) (abating as a nuisance a brothel in a bookstore); Clark v. Community for Creative Non-Violence (1984; p. 1232 below) (applying a ban on sleeping in the park to a demonstration against homelessness); and Cohen v. Cowles Media (1991; p. 1541 below) (applying promissory estoppel to a press breach of promise). A pervasive problem in the symbolic conduct cases is when to find the First Amendment triggered at all. Even speakers must obey generally applicable laws; a newscaster is not exempt from the speeding laws merely because she is late for a newscast, nor may she trespass or burgle in pursuit of a hot story. But do speakers sometime merit a constitutionally compelled exemption from content-neutral regulations of conduct? In O'Brien, the Court held that they do, and thus that government may criminally convict a Vietnam War-era draftee who burned his draft card in public in protest, but only because the law barring draft card destruction was closely tailored to serve a "substantial" or "significant" governmental interest and thus met heightened (or intermediate) scrutiny. See p. 1176 below.

A second type of content-neutral law aims at expression, but for reasons unrelated to its content. "Time, place, and manner" regulations of speech in the public forum represent the most common example of this type of content-neutral law. For example, a parade permit requirement, a law limiting the decibel level of amplified sound, and an injunction keeping protestors a certain distance from an abortion clinic entrance all aim at interests in public order, aesthetics, or tranquility and repose—interests that have nothing to do with the content or communicative impact of the speech. The governing standard of review for this type of content-neutral regulation is the same as that for O'Brien-type symbolic conduct regulations: a form of intermediate scrutiny that requires that a law be narrowly tailored or closely related to serving a significant or substantial government interest. Note that, under this test—unlike under the strict scrutiny applied to content-based regulations—the government interest need not be compelling, and the means/ends fit need not be perfect; the state is not obliged to exhaust less restrictive alternatives before it may enact or enforce a content-neutral law.

The Court has used somewhat different language in setting forth the standards of scrutiny applicable to restrictions on symbolic conduct on the one hand and time, place, and manner regulations of speech on the other. In the time, place, and manner context, for example, it has set forth a seemingly additional requirement that a law leave open "ample alternative channels of communication." But the Court has clarified that review in both settings is materially the same—that is, that the O'Brien test "is little if any, different from the standard applied to time, place, and manner restrictions." Clark v. Community for Creative Non-Violence, 468 U.S. 288 (1984; p. 1232 below). Is such consolidation of different kinds of speech restrictions under a single standard of scrutiny appropriate? For one study arguing against such use of intermediate scrutiny as a "default standard" for disparate kinds of speech regulations, see Bhagwat, "The Test that Ate Everything: Intermediate Scrutiny in First Amendment Jurisprudence," 2007 U. Ill. L. Rev. 783.

6. ***Reasons for treating content-based and content-neutral laws differently.*** What First Amendment considerations warrant requiring high standards of justification for content-based regulations, yet less intensive scrutiny of content-neutral ones?

Consider the following possibilities:

a. *Purpose*. Are content-based laws more likely than content-neutral laws to reflect governmental disapproval of the ideas expressed? Government bias in favor of its own viewpoint? Government paternalism toward the listener? Are these improper motivations for a law? For an argument that such concerns with illicit motivation partially explain special scrutiny of content-based laws, see Stone, "Content Regulation and the First Amendment," 25 Wm. & Mary L. Rev. 189 (1983).

If the content-based form of a law is merely the best evidence of the true problem of content-based purpose, then should even content-neutral laws be invalidated whenever such a content-based purpose can be smoked out? Conversely, might some laws that are content-based in form be treated as content-neutral in purpose? Recall that, in Renton v. Playtime Theaters (1986; p. 1089 above), the Court upheld the regulation of sexually explicit speech, even though explicitly drawn by reference to content, because its purpose was found to be prevention of negative "secondary effects" on the surrounding community. For one study suggesting that purpose is the touchstone of the Court's analysis of speech restrictions, and that the Court frequently "designat[es] as content-neutral" speech regulations that "make content distinctions on their face," see McDonald, "Speech and Distrust: Rethinking the Content Approach to Protecting the Freedom of Expression," 81 Notre Dame L. Rev. 1347 (2006).

b. *Effect*. Are content-based laws more likely than content-neutral laws to distort the dialogue that would otherwise take place? Stone, supra, argues as much: "Any law that substantially prevents the communication of a particular idea, viewpoint, or item of information violates the first amendment except, perhaps, in the most extraordinary of circumstances.

Stone's assertion stands not because such a law restricts 'a lot' of speech, but because by effectively excising a specific message from public debate, it mutilates 'the thinking process of the community.' " Do all content-based laws cause such distortion? A law that bars political billboards, for example, has no effect on political leaflets. And yet the presumption against content-based laws extends even to such partial regulations. Should the Court give more consideration to the extent of a content-based law? Moreover, what is the status quo from which "distortion" should be measured? See Baker, "Turner Broadcasting: Content-Based Regulation of Persons and Presses," 1994 Sup. Ct. Rev. 57 ("There is no 'natural' version of public dialogue that the First Amendment could prohibit the government from distorting," given government's existing role in shaping the debate); Sunstein, Democracy and the Problem of Free Speech (1993).

If effect on speech is the problem, might not a content-neutral law do more substantial damage than a content-based law to the permissible quantity, and effective exercise, of speech? For example, judicial invalidation of content-based restrictions might create an incentive for flat bans rather than partial prohibitions, despite their greater impact on the total quantity and diversity of speech. See Redish, "The Content Distinction in First Amendment Analysis," 34 Stan. L. Rev. 113 (1981) ("While governmental attempts to regulate the content of expression undoubtedly deserve strict judicial review, it does not logically follow that equally serious threats to first amendment freedoms cannot derive from restrictions imposed to regulate expression in a manner unrelated to content. [Whatever] rationale one adopts for the constitutional protection of speech, the goals behind that rationale are undermined by *any* limitation on expression, content-based or not.").

c. *Political safeguards.* Are content-neutral laws less likely to require judicial intervention because the political process itself will help protect unpopular speakers against such laws? Consider the case of Lady Godiva, who allegedly rode naked on horseback to Coventry Market to protest an excessive tax. A law prohibiting "nude tax protests" is likely to evince hostility to Lady Godiva's ideas. A law prohibiting "public nudity" generally, in contrast, is less likely to have been passed out of similar hostility. Lady Godiva need not fight passage of such a law by herself; nude sunbathers and commercial purveyors of nude entertainment will be her political allies. Might the impact of this type of content-neutral law on nonspeech interests make it less likely that they will be passed at all? Would the same argument apply to a content-neutral time, place, or manner regulation of speech?

7. ***Total medium bans.*** Is a government ban on the use of a particular medium or format of expression more like a content-based or a content-neutral law? Such laws involve discrimination on neither the basis of viewpoint nor subject matter, yet do single out for special treatment activities of First Amendment concern. Consider the following pairs of regulations: a prohibition on all bookstores in a certain area and a prohibition on all commercial establishments in a certain area, implicitly including bookstores; a prohibition on parades designed to prevent obstruction of traffic and a prohibition on obstructing traffic, including by trucks that take too long to make a delivery and to organizers of parades; a prohibition on soundtrucks designed to prevent excess noise and a prohibition on making excess noise, applied both to jackhammers and soundtrucks; and a prohibition on billboards and a prohibition on all structures higher than a certain height, including billboards. Is the first example in each of these pairs more troublesome than the second? Why? Because the first example singles out speech? Because there is greater reason to trust the political process that generated the second than the first regulation in each pair? Because the regulators are less likely in the second examples to be aiming at unpopular ideas?

Total medium bans have posed difficult questions for the Court that are explored in a number of cases below. The Court struck down various total medium bans in cases of the 1930s and 1940s, focusing on their negative effects on the distribution of speech. See, for example, the invalidation of a total ban on handbills in Schneider v. New Jersey (1939; p. 1214 below); and the invalidation of a ban on door-to-door canvassing in Martin v. City of Struthers (1943; p. 1215 below). These cases in effect treated medium bans as just as suspect under the First Amendment as discrimination against particular ideas. Why? Because a ban on a particular format might have a major effect on the quantity of communication? Because restriction of an entire format might discriminate in effect against those groups who are financially unable to resort to more conventional (and more expensive) means of communication, such as newspapers and the broadcasting media? Modern cases have tended to emphasize the theme of discrimination rather than distribution. Is it tenable to see discrimination as the First Amendment's *only* concern? The Court made clear that it will still invalidate some total medium bans on the ground that they suppress too much speech, without regard to whether they do so selectively. See, for example, City of

Ladue v. Gilleo (1994; p. 1218 below), which involved a ban on residential signs.

CONTENT-NEUTRAL REGULATION AND SYMBOLIC CONDUCT

What if critics of public policies seek to express their views through symbolic *behavior* rather than words: e.g., by burning a draft card or by mutilating or burning the flag? May such critics claim as much protection as would be afforded if their criticism manifested in spoken or printed word? As is clear from R.A.V. v. St. Paul (1992; p. 1038 above), the Court recognizes symbolic conduct as constitutionally protected "speech." Indeed, as early as Stromberg v. California, 283 U.S. 359 (1931), the Court held a state prohibition on displaying a red flag "as a sign, symbol, or emblem of opposition to organized government" unconstitutional on grounds that the law curtailed "the opportunity for free political discussion." In West Virginia Board of Education v. Barnette (1943; p. 1392 below), the Court held that public school children could not be compelled to salute the flag. As made clear in the prevailing opinion in Brown v. Louisiana (1966; p. 1247 below), protecting a public library sit-in, First Amendment rights "are not confined to verbal expression" and "embrace appropriate types of action." See also Tinker v. Des Moines Sch. (1969; p. 1290 below) (holding black armbands as symbolic war protest).

Why should symbolic conduct ever be treated as "speech" within the meaning of the First Amendment? For the argument that treating symbolic expression as speech makes originalist sense "because Framing-era English and American political culture was rich with symbolic expression, used interchangeably with words," including burning effigies, wearing cockaded hats, and raising "liberty poles," see Volokh, "Symbolic Expression and the Original Meaning of the First Amendment," 97 Geo. L.J. 1057 (2009).

In cases such as Stromberg and R.A.V., the challenged law was aimed expressly at symbolic conduct for reason of its symbolism and communicative impact. Such laws are deemed content-based. May a critic also claim First Amendment immunity from a governmental restraint that is not so aimed but that happens to hit his "speech"? The following cases raise the question whether an assertedly content-neutral law that has the effect of prohibiting symbolic conduct should be treated as content-neutral in fact, and even if so, whether a person engaged in symbolic conduct in violation of that law should nonetheless be exempted from it.

United States v. O'Brien

391 U.S. 367, 88 S. Ct. 1673, 20 L. Ed. 2d 672 (1968).

■ CHIEF JUSTICE WARREN delivered the opinion of the Court.

On the morning of March 31, 1966, David Paul O'Brien and three companions burned their Selective Service registration certificates on the steps of the South Boston Courthouse. A sizable crowd, including several [FBI agents], witnessed the event. Immediately after the burning, [O'Brien] stated [that] he had burned his registration certificate because of his beliefs, knowing that he was violating federal law. [For this act, O'Brien was convicted. He stated] to the jury that he burned the certificate publicly to influence others to adopt his antiwar beliefs, as he put it, "so that other people would reevaluate their positions with Selective Service, with the armed forces, and reevaluate their place in the culture of today, to hopefully consider my position."

The indictment upon which he was tried charged that he "willfully and knowingly did mutilate, destroy, and change by burning [his] Registration Certificate" in violation of [§ 462(b)(3) of the Universal Military Training and Service Act (UMTSA) of 1948], amended by Congress in 1965 (adding the words italicized below), so that at the time O'Brien burned his certificate an offense was committed by any person "who forges, alters, *knowingly destroys, knowingly mutilates,* or in any manner changes any such certificate." (Italics supplied.) [The Court of Appeals] held the 1965 Amendment unconstitutional as a law abridging freedom of speech. At the time the Amendment was enacted, a regulation of the Selective Service System required registrants to keep their registration certificates in their "personal possession at all times." Willful violations of regulations promulgated pursuant to [UMTSA] were made criminal by statute. The Court of Appeals, therefore, was of the opinion that conduct punishable under the 1965 Amendment was already punishable under the nonpossession regulation, and consequently that the Amendment served no valid purpose; further, that in light of the prior regulation, the Amendment must have been "directed at public as distinguished from private destruction." On this basis, the court concluded that the 1965 Amendment ran afoul of the First Amendment by singling out persons engaged in protests for special treatment. [We] hold that the 1965 Amendment is constitutional both as enacted and [as applied].

When a male reaches the age of 18, he is required by the [Act] to register with a local draft board. He is assigned a Selective Service number, and within five days he is issued a registration certificate. Subsequently, [he] is assigned a classification denoting his eligibility for induction. [Both] the registration and classification certificates bear notices that the registrant must notify his local board [of] every change in address, physical condition, [etc.]. [The] 1965 Amendment plainly does not abridge free speech on its face. [On its face, it] deals with conduct having no connection with speech. [It] does not distinguish between public and private destruction,[1] and it does not punish only destruction engaged in for the purpose of expressing views. [Cf. Stromberg.] A law prohibiting destruction of Selective Service certificates no more abridges free speech on its face than a motor vehicle law prohibiting the destruction of drivers' licenses, or a tax law prohibiting the destruction of books and records.

[O'Brien nonetheless] first argues that the 1965 Amendment is unconstitutional as applied to him because his act of burning his registration certificate was protected "symbolic speech" within the First Amendment. His argument is that the freedom of expression which the First Amendment guarantees includes all modes of "communication of ideas by conduct," and

---

[1] Compare the comment in the opinion of the Court of Appeals, 376 F.2d at 541: "We would be closing our eyes [if] we did not see on the face of the amendment that it was precisely directed at public as distinguished from private destruction. [In] singling out persons engaging in protest for special treatment the amendment strikes at the very core of what the First Amendment protects."

that his conduct is within this definition because he did it in "demonstration against the war and against the draft." We cannot accept the view that an apparently limitless variety of conduct can be labeled "speech" whenever the person engaging in the conduct intends thereby to express an idea. However, even on the assumption that the alleged communicative element in O'Brien's conduct is sufficient to bring into play the First Amendment, it does not necessarily follow that the destruction of a registration certificate is constitutionally protected activity. This Court has held that when "speech" and "non-speech" elements are combined in the same course of conduct, a sufficiently important governmental interest in regulating the nonspeech element can justify incidental limitations on First Amendment freedoms. To characterize the quality of the governmental interest which must appear, the Court has employed a variety of descriptive terms: compelling; substantial; subordinating; paramount; cogent; strong. [We] think it clear that a government regulation is sufficiently justified if it is within the constitutional power of the Government; if it furthers an important or substantial governmental interest; if the governmental interest is unrelated to the suppression of free expression; and if the incidental restriction on alleged First Amendment freedoms is no greater than is essential to the furtherance of that interest.

We find that the 1965 Amendment [meets] all of these requirements, and consequently that O'Brien can be constitutionally convicted for violating it. [Pursuant to its power] to classify and conscript manpower for military service, [Congress] may establish a system of registration [and] may require such individuals within reason to cooperate in the registration system. The issuance of certificates indicating the registration and eligibility classification of individuals is a legitimate and substantial administrative aid in the functioning of this system. And legislation to insure the continuing availability of issued certificates serves a legitimate and substantial purpose in the system's administration.

O'Brien's argument to the contrary is necessarily premised upon his unrealistic characterization of Selective Service certificates. He essentially adopts the position that such certificates are so many pieces of paper designed to notify registrants of their registration or classification, to be retained or tossed in the wastebasket according to the convenience or taste of the registrant. [However, the registration and classification certificates serve] purposes in addition to initial notification. Many of these purposes would be defeated by the certificates' destruction or mutilation. Among these are [proving that the individual has registered for the draft, facilitating communication between registrants and local boards, demonstrating availability for induction in times of national crisis, and reminding registrants to notify local boards of changes in status]. The many functions performed by Selective Service certificates establish beyond doubt that Congress has a legitimate and substantial interest in preventing their wanton and unrestrained destruction and assuring their continuing availability by punishing people who knowingly and wilfully destroy or mutilate them. And we are unpersuaded that the pre-existence of the nonpossession regulations in any way negates this interest. In the absence of a question as to multiple punishment, it has never been suggested that there is anything improper in Congress' providing alternative statutory avenues of prosecution to assure the effective protection of one and the same [interest].

Equally important, a comparison of the regulations with the 1965 Amendment indicates that they protect overlapping but not identical governmental interests, and that they reach somewhat different classes of wrongdoers. The gravamen of the offense defined by the statute is the deliberate rendering of certificates unavailable for the various purposes which they may serve. Whether registrants keep their certificates in their personal possession at all times, as required by the regulations, is of no particular concern under the 1965 Amendment, as long as they do not mutilate or destroy the certificates so as to render them unavailable. [And] the 1965 Amendment [is] concerned with abuses involving *any* issued Selective Service certificates, not only with the registrant's own certificates. [We] think it apparent that the continuing availability to each registrant of his Selective Service certificates substantially furthers the smooth and proper functioning of the system that Congress has established to raise [armies].

It is equally clear that the 1965 Amendment specifically protects this substantial governmental interest. We perceive no alternative means that would more precisely and narrowly assure the continuing availability of issued Selective Service certificates than a law which prohibits their wilful mutilation or destruction. [Moreover,] both the governmental interest and the operation of the 1965 Amendment are limited to the noncommunicative aspect of O'Brien's conduct. The governmental interest and the scope of the 1965 Amendment are limited to preventing harm to the smooth and efficient functioning of the Selective Service System. When O'Brien deliberately rendered unavailable his registration certificate, he wilfully frustrated this governmental interest. For this noncommunicative impact of his conduct, and for nothing else, he was convicted. The case [is] therefore unlike one where the alleged governmental interest in regulating conduct arises in some measure because the communication allegedly integral to the conduct is itself thought to be harmful. In Stromberg [the "red flag" case], for example, the statute was aimed at suppressing communication [and therefore] could not be sustained as a regulation of noncommunicative conduct. [We] find that because of the Government's substantial interest in assuring the continuing availability of issued Selective Service certificates, because amended § 462(b) is an appropriately narrow means of protecting this interest and condemns only the independent noncommunicative impact of conduct within its reach, and because the noncommunicative impact of O'Brien's act of burning his registration certificate frustrated the Government's interest, a sufficient governmental interest has been shown to justify O'Brien's conviction.

O'Brien finally argues that the 1965 Amendment is unconstitutional as enacted because what he calls the "purpose" of Congress was "to suppress freedom of speech." We reject this argument because under settled principles the purpose of Congress, as O'Brien uses that term, is not a basis for declaring this legislation unconstitutional. It is a familiar principle of constitutional law that this Court will not strike down an otherwise constitutional statute on the basis of an alleged illicit legislative motive. [Inquiries] into congressional motives or purposes are a hazardous matter. When the issue is simply the interpretation of legislation, the Court will look to statements by legislators for guidance as to the purpose of the legislature, because the benefit to sound decision-making in this circumstance is thought sufficient to risk the possibility of misreading Congress' purpose. It is entirely a different matter when we are asked to void a statute that is, under well-settled criteria, constitutional on its face, on the basis of what fewer than a handful of Congressmen said about it. What motivates one legislator to make a speech about a statute is not necessarily what motivates scores of others to enact it, and the stakes are sufficiently high for us to eschew guesswork. We decline to void essentially on the ground that it is unwise legislation which Congress has the undoubted power to enact and which could be reenacted in its exact form if the same or another legislator made a "wiser" speech about it. Reversed.[2]

THE SIGNIFICANCE OF O'BRIEN

1. ***Expression and action.*** Chief Justice Warren assumed arguendo that O'Brien's act was symbolic conduct without deciding as much. In so doing, he cautioned that conduct does not become speech "whenever the person engaging in the conduct intends thereby to express an idea." Was he too cavalier toward O'Brien's symbolic speech claim? See Alfange, "Free Speech and Symbolic Conduct: The Draft-Card Burning Case," 1968 Sup. Ct. Rev. 1. Warren feared that an "apparently limitless variety of conduct" might be labeled "speech." Is that fear of such a "slippery slope" justified, or are there principled ways of distinguishing action from speech? See Emerson, The System of Freedom of Expression (1970) ("To some extent expression and action are always mingled; [the] guiding principle must be to determine which element is predominant. [It] seems quite clear that the predominant element in [the burning of a draft card] is expression (opposition to the draft) rather than action (destruction of a piece of cardboard.")). But see Ely, "Flag Desecration: A Case Study in the Roles of Categorization and Balancing in First Amendment Analysis," 88 Harv. L. Rev. 1482 (1975) ("[B]urning a draft card to express opposition to the draft is an undifferentiated whole, 100% action and 100% expression. [Attempts] to determine which element 'predominates' will therefore inevitably degenerate into question-begging judgments about whether the activity should be protected."); Henkin, "Foreword: On Drawing Lines," 82 Harv. L. Rev. 63 (1968) ("A constitutional distinction between speech and conduct is specious. [I]f it is intended as expression, if in fact it communicates, especially if it becomes a common comprehensible form of expression, it is 'speech.' "). See also Velvel, "Freedom of Speech and the Draft Card Burning Cases," 16 U. Kan. L. Rev. 149 (1968) (arguing that draft-card burning was an especially effective means of protesting the war because it attracted media attention); Nimmer, "The Meaning of Symbolic Speech Under the First Amendment," 21 UCLA L. Rev. 29 (1973) (suggesting that symbolic conduct requires an audience—i.e., both a "communicator and a communicatee"); Baker, "Scope of the First Amendment Freedom of Speech," 25 UCLA L. Rev. 964 (1978).

---

[2] A concurrence by Justice HARLAN stated: "I wish to make explicit my understanding that [the Court's criteria do] not foreclose consideration of First Amendment claims in those rare instances when an 'incidental' restriction upon expression, imposed by a regulation which furthers an 'important or substantial' governmental interest and satisfies the Court's other criteria, in practice has the effect of entirely preventing a 'speaker' from reaching a significant audience with whom he could not otherwise lawfully communicate. This is not such a case, since O'Brien manifestly could have conveyed his message in many ways other than by burning his draft card." Justice DOUGLAS dissented, urging reargument on "the question of the constitutionality of a peacetime draft"; the next year in Brandenburg v. Ohio (p. 978 above), he asserted that O'Brien's conviction was inconsistent with the First Amendment.

2. ***The O'Brien test and the content-based/content-neutral distinction.*** O'Brien set forth a test that has since become canonical in the review of content-neutral laws: they must "further an important or substantial governmental interest" and involve an "incidental restriction on alleged First Amendment freedoms [that] is no greater than is essential to the furtherance of that interest." The latter part of the test has been modified in later cases to make clear that, while a content-neutral law must be closely tailored to its ends, the government need *not* employ the least restrictive alternative. See Ward v. Rock Against Racism (1989; p. 1236 below). O'Brien also set forth an influential definition for distinguishing content-based from content-neutral laws: for a law to be treated as content-neutral, the governmental interest behind the law must be "unrelated to the suppression of free expression." Thus the third of the four factors listed in the O'Brien test on p. 1176 above actually performs a critical switching function at the threshold: in situations where the state interest *is* "related to the suppression of free expression," strict scrutiny is required *unless* the speech is in an unprotected category; but where the state interest is *unrelated* to the suppression of free expression, balancing is the appropriate response. See Ely, "Flag Desecration: A Case Study in the Roles of Categorization and Balancing in First Amendment Analysis," 88 Harv. L. Rev. 1482 (1975).

How can a court tell whether a law is or is not "related to the suppression of free expression"? As Ely explains, "restrictions on free expression are seldom defended on the ground that the state simply didn't like what the defendant was saying: reference will generally be made to some danger beyond the message, such as the danger of riot, unlawful action, or violent overthrow of the government. The constitutional reference must therefore be not to the ultimate interest to which the state points, for that will always be unrelated to expression, but rather to the causal connection the state asserts. If, for example, the state asserts an interest in discouraging riots, the Court should ask why that interest is implicated in the case at bar. If the answer is, as in such cases it will likely have to be, that the danger of riot was created by what the defendant was saying, the state's interest is not unrelated to the suppression of free expression, and the inhibition should be upheld only in the event the expression falls within one of the few unprotected categories." Ely, supra.

How speech-protective was the application of the O'Brien test in O'Brien itself? Ely suggests that the supposedly "substantial" governmental interests identified by the Court were in fact merely "plausible but little more." And the "no greater restriction than essential" criterion was weakly applied: the Court essentially deferred to the government without serious inquiry whether alternative means would serve the government's interest nearly as efficiently at much less cost to speech. See Ely, supra.

3. ***Legislative motivation.*** Should the Court have gone the other way in O'Brien because "the 'purpose' of Congress was 'to suppress freedom of speech' "? See Alfange, supra (suggesting that the legislative history of the 1965 amendment shows with "indisputable clarity" that "the intent of [members of Congress] was purely and simply to put a stop to this particular form of antiwar protest, which they deemed extraordinarily contemptible and vicious—even treasonous—at a time when American troops were engaged in combat"). Chief Justice Warren rejected summarily any inquiry into congressional motive, and noted that statements by members of Congress expressing hostility to draft resisters were offset by the more

authoritative committee reports: while the reports "make clear a concern with the 'defiant' destruction [of draft cards] and with 'open' encouragement to others to destroy their cards, both reports also indicate that this concern stems from an apprehension that unrestrained destruction of cards would disrupt the smooth functioning of the Selective Service System."

Clearly, the Court frequently does inquire into the motivation of executive and administrative decisions. In the equal protection context, see, for example, Arlington Heights v. Metropolitan Housing Corp., 429 U.S. 252 (1977; p. 687 above); and Yick Wo v. Hopkins, 118 U.S. 356 (1886; p. 681 above). In other contexts, such as the religion context, the Court is not shy about looking into even legislative history as a source of possibly impermissible motivation. See, e.g., Church of the Lukumi Babalu Aye v. City of Hialeah, 508 U.S. 520 (1993; p. 1571 below), and Edwards v. Aguillard, 482 U.S. 578 (1987; p. 1660 below). Why then, in O'Brien, was the Court reluctant to inquire into legislative motivation? Are the reasons ones of institutional competence, such as the difficulty of ascertaining any single "real" motivation in a multi-member body where each representative might be voting for different reasons, the inappropriateness of questioning the integrity of a coordinate branch, and the futility of striking down a law that could be reenacted after an assertion of legitimate motives? Doesn't the distinction between content-based and content-neutral laws require some inquiry into legislative ends? Or is the Court suggesting that such an inquiry may take place, so long as it focuses on the objective purpose of the law rather than the subjective motive of particular legislators? On the problem of motivation inquiries, see generally Ely, "Legislative and Administrative Motivation in Constitutional Law," 79 Yale L.J. 1205 (1970); and Brest, "Palmer v. Thompson: An Approach to the Problem of Unconstitutional Legislative Motive," 1971 Sup. Ct. Rev. 95.

4. ***"Incidental" restrictions on expression.*** In O'Brien, the Court employed less-than-strict scrutiny to deal with what it called "incidental limitations on First Amendment freedoms." Was the effect of the law on O'Brien's speech merely "incidental"? Or did the law forbid precisely the action O'Brien engaged in as speech? Should the central question be what was aimed at, as O'Brien suggests, or rather what was hit? See generally Stone, "Content-Neutral Restrictions," 54 U. Chi. L. Rev. 46 (1987).

Should all "incidental" restrictions on speech receive the heightened First Amendment scrutiny required by the O'Brien test? Do some laws have an impact on speech only as a mere byproduct or side effect? A "no parking" zone might preclude one from using a car covered with bumper stickers as a mobile billboard parked before a desired audience. A "no speeding" law might prevent a newscaster from reaching the studio in time to announce the news. Should such laws be subject to more exacting First Amendment review when applied in such circumstances, or need they only satisfy the requirements of minimum rationality?

Consider **Arcara v. Cloud Books, Inc.**, 478 U.S. 697 (1986), which involved a New York law defining places of prostitution, assignation, and lewdness as public health nuisances and providing for the closure of any building found to be such a nuisance. In Arcara, an investigation of an "adult" bookstore found that sexual acts and solicitations to perform sexual acts were occurring on the premises. As a result, the store was ordered closed as a nuisance. The bookstore claimed that this had the effect of preventing the sale of books and other materials that were presumptively protected by the First Amendment. The highest state court, applying the O'Brien test, found that the closure order incidentally burdened speech and that it was unnecessarily broad to achieve its purpose, since an injunction against the illegal activity could achieve the same effect.

The Court reversed that judgment, upholding the closure remedy and holding that it did not warrant even the intermediate scrutiny of the O'Brien standard. Chief Justice BURGER's majority opinion explained that, "unlike the symbolic draft card burning in O'Brien, the sexual activity carried on [here] manifests absolutely no element of protected expression." He continued: "Nor does the distinction drawn by the [law] inevitably single out bookstores or others engaged in First Amendment protected activities for the imposition of its burden. [If] the city imposed closure penalties for demonstrated Fire Code violations or health hazards from inadequate sewage treatment, the First Amendment would not aid the owner of premises who had knowingly allowed such violations to persist." Nor was Chief Justice Burger impressed by the argument that the closure burdened bookselling activities: "The severity of this burden is dubious at best, and is mitigated by the fact that respondents remain free to sell the same materials at another location. In any event, this argument proves too much, since every civil and criminal remedy imposes some conceivable burden on First Amendment protected activities." He added: "[W]e have not traditionally subjected every criminal or civil sanction [to] 'least restrictive means' scrutiny simply because each particular remedy will have some effect [on] First Amendment activities. [Rather,] we have subjected such restrictions to scrutiny only where it was conduct with a significant expressive element that drew the legal remedy in the first place, as in O'Brien, or where a statute based on a nonexpressive activity has the inevitable effect of singling out those engaged in expressive activity, as in Minneapolis Star [(1983; p. 1534 below)]. This case involves neither situation, and we conclude the First Amendment is not implicated by the enforcement of the public health regulation of general application against the physical premises in which respondents happen to sell books." Justice O'Connor's concurrence, joined by Justice Stevens, emphasized that there had been no evidence that the use of a generally applicable regulatory statute was merely a "pretext" for closing down a bookstore.

Justice BLACKMUN, joined by Justices Brennan and Marshall, dissented, arguing: "Until today, this Court has never suggested that a State may suppress speech as much as it likes, without justification, so long as it does so through generally applicable regulations that have 'nothing to do with any expressive conduct.' [When] a State directly and substantially impairs First Amendment activities, such as by shutting down a bookstore, I believe that the state must show, at a minimum, that it has chosen the least restrictive means of pursuing its legitimate objectives. [Petitioner] has not demonstrated that a less restrictive remedy would be inadequate to abate the nuisance. [Because the law] is not narrowly tailored to further the asserted governmental interest, it is unconstitutional as applied."

Was the majority's refusal to apply any First Amendment scrutiny in Arcara justifiable under O'Brien or under general First Amendment principles? Would the opposite result have extended the First Amendment to virtually every law? See Alexander, "Trouble on Track Two: Incidental Regulations of Speech and Free Speech Theory," 44 Hastings L.J. 921 (1993) (arguing that virtually every law, even a marginal tax rate, may be said to have some "incidental" effect on speech, and thus questioning First Amendment review of content-neutral regulation); see also Dorf, "Incidental Burdens on Fundamental Rights," 109 Harv. L. Rev. 1175 (1996).

FLAG DESECRATION

May government bar the burning, mutilation, or physical misuse of the United States flag? The Court considered a series of challenges to efforts to curb such symbolic protests beginning in 1969, but did not squarely reach the central constitutional issue until the flag-burning cases of 1989 and 1990. Is flag desecration "speech" entitled to strong First Amendment protection? What state interests underlie the efforts to protect the flag? Can any of them be described as content-neutral? If not, can any of them be described as compelling?

In **Street v. New York**, 394 U.S. 576 (1969), the Court, in a 5–4 decision, overturned a conviction under a New York law that made it a crime "publicly [to] mutilate, deface, defile, or defy, trample upon, or cast contempt upon either by words or act [any flag of the United States]." Street had burned a flag on a street corner after hearing that civil rights leader James Meredith had been shot by a sniper in Mississippi. He had said to the crowd that gathered, "We don't need no damn flag," and when a police officer stopped and confronted him, he had replied: "Yes, that is my flag; I burned it. If they let that happen to Meredith we don't need an American flag." The Court did not reach the question whether it was constitutional to ban flag burning as a means of political protest, finding instead that, on the record below, the law had been unconstitutionally applied to permit punishment of Street "merely for speaking defiant or contemptuous words about the American flag." Justice HARLAN's majority opinion noted that Street's words had not constituted incitement or fighting words, reiterated that "public expression of ideas may not be prohibited merely because the ideas are themselves offensive to some of their hearers," and held that the conviction could not be justified "on the theory that by making [his] remarks about the flag appellant failed to show the respect for our national symbol which may properly be demanded of every citizen," for the flag-salute cases (see p. 1390 below) had established "the freedom to express publicly one's opinions about our flag, including those opinions which are defiant or contemptuous." Chief Justice Warren and Justices Black, White, and Fortas dissented, each arguing that Street had been punished for his act, not his words, and that the state had constitutional authority to protect the flag from acts of desecration.

In **Smith v. Goguen**, 415 U.S. 566 (1974), the Court, in a 6–3 decision, reversed a appellee's conviction, under a Massachusetts law making it a crime to "publicly mutilate, trample upon, deface or treat contemptuously the flag of the United States," for wearing a small United States flag sewn to the seat of his trousers. Justice POWELL's majority opinion found it unnecessary to reach a variety of First Amendment claims and rested instead on "the due process doctrine of vagueness." Though appellee's behavior seemed to reflect "immaturity" and "silly conduct," Justice Powell observed that "casual treatment of the flag in many contexts has become a widespread contemporary phenomenon." Here, the statutory language "fails to draw reasonably clear lines between the kinds of nonceremonial treatment (of the flag) that are criminal and those that are not." Fair notice standards were not met, given "today's tendencies to treat the flag unceremoniously." Justice Powell emphasized: "Statutory language of such standardless sweep allows policemen, prosecutors, and juries to pursue their personal predilections." Justice WHITE disagreed with the majority's reasoning, though not its result. He defended the constitutionality of flag mutilation laws, but objected that the conviction here "punish[ed] for communicating ideas about the flag unacceptable to the controlling majority." Justice REHNQUIST, joined by Chief Justice Burger, dissented at length, describing the flag as a "unique physical object" and emphasizing the strong state interest in protecting "the physical integrity of a unique national symbol." There was also a dissent by Justice Blackmun, joined by Chief Justice Burger.

And in **Spence v. Washington**, 418 U.S. 405 (1974), the Court, per curiam, overturned a conviction under a Washington statute prohibiting "improper use" of the flag, including the display of any flag to which a "word, figure, mark, picture, design, drawing or advertisement" had been attached. Spence had displayed a United States flag, which he owned, outside the window of his apartment with a large peace symbol made of removable tape affixed to both sides. He testified that he had done so as a protest against the invasion of Cambodia and the killings at Kent State University. The Court found Spence's "pointed expression of anguish [about] the then current domestic and foreign affairs of his government" to be speech within the meaning of the First Amendment and set forth the still-governing test for whether conduct is protected by the First Amendment: "An intent to convey a particularized message was present, and in the surrounding circumstances the likelihood was great that the message would be understood by those who viewed it."

The Court was willing to assume arguendo that the state's asserted interest in "preserving the national flag as an unalloyed symbol of our country" was valid even though it noted that such an interest was "directly related to expression." But it nonetheless found the statute "unconstitutional as applied to appellant's activity. There was no risk that appellant's acts would mislead viewers into assuming that the Government endorsed his viewpoint. To the contrary, he was plainly and peacefully protesting the fact that it did not." Justice REHNQUIST, joined by Chief Justice Burger and Justice White, dissented, arguing that the state's interest in "preserving the flag as 'an important symbol of nationhood and unity' " was a legitimate one.

Does Spence helpfully delineate the contours of protected symbolic conduct? Note the Court's emphasis on two factors: the speaker's intent; and the context indicating that the message would be understood by the audience. Is that a useful approach? Is it adequate? Does it risk the slippery slope Chief Justice Warren feared in O'Brien? What about conduct more ambiguous than that in Spence? For criticism of the Spence standard, see Post, "Recuperating First Amendment Doctrine," 47 Stan. L. Rev. 1249 (1995).

Is there any governmental interest in the flag that is "unrelated to the suppression of free expression" within the meaning of O'Brien? See Ely, "Flag Desecration: A Case Study in the Roles of Categorization and Balancing in First Amendment Analysis," 88 Harv. L. Rev. 1482 (1975) (suggesting that flag misuse laws "do not single out certain messages for proscription," but "*do* single out one set of messages, namely the set of messages conveyed by the American flag, for protection," and that "[o]rthodoxy of thought can be fostered not simply by placing unusual restrictions on 'deviant' expression but also by granting unusual protection to expression that is officially acceptable"). Consider the flag-burning cases of 1989 and 1990, which follow.

Texas v. Johnson

491 U.S. 397, 109 S. Ct. 2533, 105 L. Ed. 2d 342 (1989).

■ JUSTICE BRENNAN delivered the opinion of the Court.

After publicly burning an American flag as a means of political protest, Gregory Lee Johnson was convicted of desecrating a flag in violation of Texas law. This case presents the question whether his conviction is consistent with the First Amendment. We hold that it is not.

I. While the Republican National Convention was taking place in Dallas in 1984, [Johnson] participated in a political demonstration dubbed the "Republican War Chest Tour." [The] purpose of this event was to protest the policies of the Reagan administration and of certain Dallas-based corporations. The demonstrators marched through the Dallas streets, chanting political slogans and stopping at several corporate locations to stage "die-ins" intended to dramatize the consequences of nuclear war. On several occasions they spray-painted the walls of buildings and overturned potted plants, but Johnson himself took no part in such activities. He did, however, accept an American flag handed to him by a fellow protestor who had taken it from a flag pole outside one of the targeted buildings. The demonstration ended in front of Dallas City Hall, where Johnson unfurled the American flag, doused it with kerosene, and set it on fire. While the flag burned, the protestors chanted, "America, the red, white, and blue, we spit on you." After the demonstrators dispersed, a witness to the flag-burning collected the flag's remains and buried them in his backyard. No one was physically injured or threatened with injury, though several witnesses testified that they had been seriously offended by the flag-burning. Of the approximately 100 demonstrators, Johnson alone was charged with a crime. The only criminal offense with which he was charged was the desecration of a venerated object.[1] [He] was convicted, sentenced to one year in prison, and fined $2,000. [The] Texas Court of Criminal Appeals [overturned the conviction.] We affirm.

II. Johnson was convicted of flag desecration for burning the flag rather than for uttering insulting words. This fact somewhat complicates our consideration of his conviction under the First Amendment. We must first determine whether Johnson's burning of the flag constituted expressive conduct, permitting him to invoke the [First Amendment]. [Spence.] If his conduct was expressive, we next decide whether the State's regulation is related to the suppression of free expression. [O'Brien.] If the State's regulation is not related to expression, then the less stringent standard we

---

[1] Tex. Penal Code Ann. section 42.09 (1989) [provided]: "Section 42.09. Desecration of Venerated Object. (a) A person commits an offense if he intentionally or knowingly desecrates: (1) a public monument; (2) a place of worship or burial; or (3) a state or national flag. (b) For purposes of this section, 'desecrate' means deface, damage, or otherwise physically mistreat in a way that the actor knows will seriously offend one or more persons likely to observe or discover his action." [Footnote by Justice Brennan.]

announced in [O'Brien] for regulations of noncommunicative conduct controls. If it is, then we are outside of O'Brien's test, and we must ask whether this interest justifies Johnson's conviction under a more demanding standard.[2] [Spence.] A third possibility is that the State's asserted interest is simply not implicated on these facts, and in that event the interest drops out of the picture.

The First Amendment literally forbids the abridgement only of "speech," but we have long recognized that its protection does not end at the spoken or written word. [In] deciding whether particular conduct possesses sufficient communicative elements to bring the First Amendment into play, we have asked whether "[a]n intent to convey a particularized message was present, and (whether) the likelihood was great that the message would be understood by those who viewed it." [Spence.] [Especially] pertinent to this case are our decisions recognizing the communicative nature of conduct relating to flags. Attaching a peace sign to the flag, Spence; saluting the flag [Barnette (1943; p. 1392 below)]; and displaying a red flag, Stromberg, we have held, all may find shelter under the First Amendment. That we have had little difficulty identifying an expressive element in conduct relating to flags should not be surprising. The very purpose of a national flag is to serve as a symbol of our country. [Pregnant] with expressive content, the flag as readily signifies this Nation as does the combination of letters found in "America." [Texas] conceded for purposes of its oral argument in this case that Johnson's conduct was expressive conduct. [Johnson] burned an American flag as part—indeed, as the culmination—of a political demonstration that coincided with the convening of the Republican Party and its renomination of Ronald Reagan for President. The expressive, overtly political nature of this conduct was both intentional and overwhelmingly apparent [and thus implicates] the First Amendment.

III. The Government generally has a freer hand in restricting expressive conduct than it has in restricting the written or spoken word. It may not, however, proscribe particular conduct because it has expressive elements. [It] is [not] simply the verbal or nonverbal nature of the expression, but the governmental interest at stake, that helps to determine whether a restriction on that expression is valid. Thus, [we] have limited the applicability of O'Brien's relatively lenient standard to those cases in which "the governmental interest is unrelated to the suppression of free expression." [In] order to decide whether O'Brien's test applies here, therefore, we must decide whether Texas has asserted an interest in support of Johnson's conviction that is unrelated to the suppression of expression. If we find that an interest asserted by the State is simply not implicated on the facts before us, we need not ask whether O'Brien's test applies. The State offers two separate interests to justify this conviction: preventing breaches of the peace, and preserving the flag as a symbol of nationhood and national unity. We hold that the first interest is not implicated on this record and that the second is related to the suppression of expression.

---

[2] Although Johnson has raised a facial challenge to [the law], we choose to resolve this case on the basis of his ["as-applied" claim]. Because the prosecution of a person who had not engaged in expressive conduct would pose a different case, and because we are capable of disposing of this case on narrower grounds, we address only Johnson's claim that [the law] as applied to political expression like his violates the First Amendment. [Footnote by Justice Brennan.]

A. Texas claims that its interest in preventing breaches of the peace justifies Johnson's conviction for flag desecration. However, no disturbance of the peace actually occurred or threatened to occur because of Johnson's burning of the flag. [The] only evidence offered [at trial] to show the reaction to Johnson's actions was the testimony of several persons who had been seriously offended by the flag-burning. The State's position, therefore, amounts to a claim that an audience that takes serious offense at particular expression is necessarily likely to disturb the peace and that the expression may be prohibited on this basis. Our precedents do not countenance such a presumption. On the contrary, they recognize that a principal "function of free speech under our system of government is to invite [dispute]." [Terminiello.] [We] have not permitted the Government to assume that every expression of a provocative idea will incite a riot, but have instead required careful consideration of the actual circumstances surrounding such [expression]. [Brandenburg.] To accept Texas' arguments that it need only demonstrate "the potential for a breach of the peace," and that every flag-burning necessarily possesses that potential, would be to eviscerate our holding in Brandenburg. This we decline to do.

[Nor] does Johnson's expressive conduct fall within that small class of "fighting words" that are "likely to provoke the average person to retaliation, and thereby cause a breach of the peace." [Chaplinsky.] No reasonable onlooker would have regarded Johnson's generalized expression of dissatisfaction with the policies of the Federal Government as a direct personal insult or an invitation to exchange fisticuffs. We thus conclude that the State's interest in maintaining order is not implicated on these [facts].

B. The State also asserts an interest in preserving the flag as a symbol of nationhood and national unity. [We are persuaded, as we were in Spence,] that this interest is related to expression in the case of Johnson's burning of the flag. The State, apparently, is concerned that such conduct will lead people to believe either that the flag does not stand for nationhood and national unity, but instead reflects other, less positive concepts, or that the concepts reflected in the flag do not in fact exist, that is, we do not enjoy unity as a Nation. These concerns blossom only when a person's treatment of the flag communicates some message, and thus are related "to the suppression of free expression" within the meaning of O'Brien. We are thus outside of O'Brien's test altogether.

IV. It remains to consider whether the State's interest in preserving the flag as a symbol of nationhood and national unity justifies Johnson's conviction. [Johnson] was not [prosecuted] for the expression of just any idea; he was prosecuted for his expression of dissatisfaction with the policies of this country, expression situated at the core of our First Amendment values. Moreover, Johnson was prosecuted because he knew that his politically charged expression would cause "serious offense." If he had burned the flag as a means of disposing of it because it was dirty or torn, he would not have been convicted of flag desecration under this Texas law: federal law designates burning as the preferred means of disposition of a flag "when it is in such condition that it is no longer a fitting emblem for display," and Texas has no quarrel with this means of disposal. The Texas law is thus not aimed at protecting the physical integrity of the flag in all circumstances, but is designed instead to protect it only against impairments that would cause serious offense to others. Texas concedes as [much]. Whether Johnson's treatment of the flag violated Texas law thus depended on the likely communicative impact of his expressive conduct. [This] restriction on Johnson's expression is content-based. [Johnson's] political expression was restricted because of the content of the message he conveyed. We must therefore subject the State's asserted interest in preserving the special symbolic character of the flag to "the most exacting scrutiny." [Boos.]

Texas argues that its interest in preserving the flag as a symbol of nationhood and national unity survives this close analysis. [The] State's argument is not that it has an interest simply in maintaining the flag as a symbol of *something,* no matter what it symbolizes. [Rather,] the State's claim is that it has an interest in preserving the flag as a symbol of *nationhood* and *national unity,* a symbol with a determinate range of meanings. According to Texas, if one physically treats the flag in a way that would tend to cast doubt on either the idea that nationhood and national unity are the flag's referents or that national unity actually exists, the message conveyed thereby is a harmful one and therefore may be prohibited.

If there is a bedrock principle underlying the First Amendment, it is that the Government may not prohibit the expression of an idea simply because society finds the idea itself offensive or disagreeable. [We] have not recognized an exception to this principle even where our flag has been involved. [Street; Spence.] [Nothing] in our precedents suggests that a State may foster its own view of the flag by prohibiting expressive conduct relating to it. To bring its argument outside our precedents, Texas attempts to convince us that even if its interest in preserving the flag's symbolic role does not allow it to prohibit words or some expressive conduct critical of the flag, it does permit it to forbid the outright destruction of the flag. [Texas's] focus on the precise nature of Johnson's expression [misses] the point of our prior decisions: their enduring lesson, that the Government may not prohibit expression simply because it disagrees with its message, is not dependent on the particular mode in which one chooses to express an idea. If we were to hold that a State may forbid flag-burning wherever it is likely to endanger the flag's symbolic role, but allow it wherever burning a flag promotes that role—as where, for example, a person ceremoniously burns a dirty flag—we would be saying that when it comes to impairing the flag's physical integrity, the flag itself may be used as a symbol [only] in one direction. We would be permitting a State to "prescribe what shall be orthodox" by saying that one may burn the flag to convey one's attitude toward it and its referents only if one does not endanger the flag's representation of nationhood and national unity.

We never before have held that the Government may ensure that a symbol be used to express only one view of that symbol or its referents. Indeed, in Schacht v. United States [398 U.S. 58 (1970)], we invalidated a federal statute permitting an actor portraying a member of one of our armed forces to " 'wear the uniform of that armed force if the portrayal does not tend to discredit that armed force.' " This proviso, we held, "which leaves Americans free to praise the war in Vietnam but can send persons like Schacht to prison for opposing it, cannot survive in a country which has the First Amendment." We perceive no basis on which to hold that the principle underlying our decision in Schacht does not apply to this case. To conclude that the Government may permit designated symbols to be used to communicate only a limited set of messages would be to enter territory having no discernible or defensible boundaries. Could the Government, on this theory, prohibit the burning of state flags? Of copies of the Presidential seal? Of the Constitution? In evaluating these choices under the First Amendment, how would we decide which symbols were sufficiently special to warrant this unique status? To do so, we would be forced to consult our own political preferences, and impose them on the citizenry, in the very way that the First Amendment forbids us to do.

There is, moreover, no indication—either in the text of the Constitution or in our cases interpreting it—that a separate juridical category exists for the American flag alone. [The] First Amendment does not guarantee that other concepts virtually sacred to our Nation as a whole—such as the principle that discrimination on the basis of race [is] odious and destructive—will go unquestioned in the marketplace of ideas. [Brandenburg.] We decline, therefore, to create for the flag an exception to the joust of principles protected by the First Amendment. It is not the State's ends, but its means, to which we object. It cannot be gainsaid that there is a special place reserved for the flag in this Nation, and thus we do not doubt that the Government has a legitimate interest in making efforts to "preserv[e] the national flag as an unalloyed symbol of our country." [Spence.] [To] say that the Government has an interest in encouraging proper treatment of the flag, however, is not to say that it may criminally punish a person for burning a flag as a means of political protest.

[We] are fortified in today's conclusion by our conviction that forbidding criminal punishment for conduct such as Johnson's will not endanger the special role played by our flag or the feelings it inspires. To paraphrase Justice Holmes, we submit that nobody can suppose that this one gesture of an unknown man will change our Nation's attitude towards its flag. [Abrams.] [We] are tempted to say, in fact, that the flag's deservedly cherished place in our community will be strengthened, not weakened, by our holding today. Our decision is a reaffirmation of the principles of freedom and inclusiveness that the flag best reflects, and of the conviction that our toleration of criticism such as Johnson's is a sign and source of our strength. [It] is the Nation's resilience, not its rigidity, that Texas sees reflected in the flag—and it is that resilience that we reassert today. The way to preserve the flag's special role is not to punish those who feel differently about these matters. It is to persuade them that they are wrong. [Precisely] because it is our flag that is involved, one's response to the flag-burner may exploit the uniquely persuasive power of the flag itself. We can imagine no more appropriate response to burning a flag than waving one's own, no better way to counter a flag-burner's message than by saluting the flag that burns, no surer means of preserving the dignity even of the flag that burned than by—as one witness here did—according its remains a respectful burial. We do not consecrate the flag by punishing its desecration, for in doing so we dilute the freedom that this cherished emblem represents. [Affirmed.][3]

---

[3] Justice KENNEDY, who joined Justice Brennan's opinion to make the 5–4 majority here, added a concurrence noting: "Sometimes we must make decisions we do not like. We make them because they are right, right in the sense that the law and the Constitution [compel] the result." He added: "I do not believe the Constitution gives us the right to rule as the [dissenters] urge, however painful this judgment is to announce. [It] is poignant but fundamental that the flag protects those who hold it in contempt. [Johnson's] acts were speech. [So] I agree with the Court that he must go free."

■ CHIEF JUSTICE REHNQUIST, with whom JUSTICES WHITE and O'CONNOR join, dissenting.

In holding this Texas statute unconstitutional, the Court ignores Justice Holmes' familiar aphorism that "a page of history is worth a volume of logic." For more than 200 years, the American flag has occupied a unique position as the symbol of our Nation, a uniqueness that justifies a governmental prohibition against flag burning in the way [Johnson] did here.[4]

[The] American flag, [throughout] more than 200 years of our history, has come to be the visible symbol embodying our Nation. It does not represent the views of any particular political party, and it does not represent any particular political philosophy. The flag is not simply another "idea" or "point of view" competing for recognition in the marketplace of ideas. Millions [of] Americans regard it with an almost mystical reverence regardless of what sort of social, political, or philosophical beliefs they may have. I cannot agree that the First Amendment invalidates the Act of Congress, and the laws of 48 of the 50 States, which make criminal the public burning of the flag.

[But] the Court insists that the [Texas law infringes on] Johnson's freedom of expression. Such freedom, of course, is not absolute. [Here] it may [well] be said that the public burning of the American flag by Johnson was no essential part of any exposition of ideas[, Chaplinsky], and at the same time it had a tendency to incite a breach of the peace. [The] Court could not, and did not, say that Chaplinsky's utterances were not expressive phrases—they clearly and succinctly conveyed an extremely low opinion of the addressee. The same may be said of Johnson's public burning of the flag in this case; it obviously did convey Johnson's bitter dislike of his country. But his act, like Chaplinsky's provocative words, conveyed nothing that could not have been [conveyed] just as forcefully in a dozen different ways. As with "fighting words," so with flag burning, for purposes of the [First Amendment].

[Flag burning] is the equivalent of an inarticulate grunt or roar that [is] most likely to be indulged in not to express any particular idea, but to antagonize others. [The] Texas statute deprived Johnson of only one rather inarticulate symbolic form of protest—a form of protest that was profoundly offensive to many—and left him with a full panoply of other symbols and every conceivable form of verbal expression to express his deep disapproval of national policy. Thus, in no way can it be said that Texas is punishing him because his hearers [were] profoundly opposed to the message that he sought to convey. Such opposition is no proper basis for restricting speech or expression under the First Amendment. It was Johnson's use of this particular symbol, and not the idea that he sought to [convey], for which he was punished. Our prior cases dealing with flag desecration statutes have left open the question that the Court resolves today. [E.g., Street; Spence.]

The Court concludes its opinion with a regrettably patronizing civics lecture, presumably addressed [in part] to the Members of both Houses of Congress [and] the members of the 48 state legislatures that enacted prohibitions against flag burning. [The] Court's role as the final expositor of

[4] At this point, Chief Justice Rehnquist devoted a substantial number of pages to a review of the importance of the flag in American history and literature. He quoted from the poetry of Ralph Waldo Emerson and from Francis Scott Key's "Star-Bangled Banner." Moreover, he printed the full text of John Greenleaf Whittier's "Barbara Fritchie" (including the line " 'Shoot if you must, This old grey head, But spare your country's flag,' She said").

the Constitution is well established, but its role as a platonic guardian admonishing those responsible to public opinion as if they were truant school children has no similar place in our system of government. [Surely] one of the high purposes of a democratic society is to legislate against conduct that is regarded as evil and profoundly offensive to the majority of people—whether it be murder, embezzlement, pollution, or flag burning. [Uncritical] extension of constitutional protection to the burning of the flag risks the frustration of the very purpose for which organized governments are instituted. The Court decides that the American flag is just another symbol, about which not only must opinions pro and con be tolerated, but for which the most minimal public respect may not be enjoined. The government may conscript men into the Armed Forces where they [may] die for the flag, but the government may not prohibit the public burning of the banner under which they fight. I would uphold the Texas statute as applied in this case.

■ JUSTICE STEVENS, dissenting.

[A] country's flag is a symbol of more than "nationhood and national unity." [It is also] a symbol of freedom, of equal opportunity, of religious tolerance, and of goodwill for other peoples who share our aspirations. [The] value of the flag as a symbol cannot be measured. Even so, I have no doubt that the interest in preserving that value for the future is both significant and legitimate. [The] content of respondent's message has no relevance whatsoever to the case. [Moreover, the] case has nothing to do with "disagreeable ideas." It involves disagreeable conduct that, in my opinion, diminishes the value of an important national asset. The Court is therefore quite wrong in blandly asserting that respondent "was prosecuted for his expression of dissatisfaction with the policies of this [country]." Respondent was prosecuted because of the method he chose to express his dissatisfaction with those policies. Had he chosen to spray paint [his] message of dissatisfaction on the facade of the Lincoln Memorial, there would be no question about the power of the Government to prohibit his means of expression. [Though] the asset at stake in this case is intangible, given its unique value, the same interest supports a prohibition on the desecration of the American flag.[5]

TEXAS V. JOHNSON AND ITS AFTERMATH

1. ***The history of the flag as an American symbol.*** Justice Rehnquist predicates his dissent on the argument that "[f]or more than 200

[5] The Court suggests that a prohibition against flag desecration is not content-neutral because this form of symbolic speech is only used by persons who are critical of the flag or the ideas it represents. In making this suggestion the Court does not pause to consider the far-reaching consequences of its introduction of disparate impact analysis into our First Amendment jurisprudence. It seems obvious that a prohibition against the desecration of a gravesite is content-neutral even if it denies some protesters the right to make a symbolic statement by extinguishing the flame in Arlington Cemetery where John F. Kennedy is buried while permitting others to salute the flame by bowing their heads. Few would doubt that a protester who extinguishes the flame has desecrated the gravesite, regardless of whether he prefaces that act with a speech explaining that his purpose is to express deep admiration or unmitigated scorn for the late President. Likewise, few would claim that the protester who bows his head has desecrated the gravesite, even if he makes clear that his purpose is to show disrespect. In such a case, as in a flag burning case, the prohibition against desecration has absolutely nothing to do with the content of the message that the symbolic speech is intended to convey. [Footnote by Justice Stevens.]

years, the American flag has occupied a unique position as the symbol of our Nation, a uniqueness that justifies a governmental prohibition against flag burning." But the American veneration of the flag has not been consistent throughout U.S. history: "before the Civil War the flag was not widely displayed and played only a minor role in the nation's patriotic oratory and iconography." By the outbreak of the war, the flag had become an important enough national symbol that "President James Buchanan's treasury secretary, John Dix, telegraphed to a clerk in New Orleans, 'If anyone attempts to haul down the American flag, shoot him on the spot.' " Such drastic punishment for flag-desecration was carried out at least once during the Civil War, when Union-occupied New Orleans resident William Mumford "was hung for treason [after] a military court found him guilty of pulling down, dragging in the mud, and tearing to shreds an American flag that had been hoisted over the New Orleans mint amid federal reoccupation of the city." The modern flag protection movement arose out of these Civil War-era American nationalist forces. Goldstein, Flag Burning and Free Speech 1–6 (2000).

2. ***Congressional response to Johnson.*** The decision in Johnson elicited considerable public criticism. Soon after the decision, and after outraged floor speeches, the House and Senate passed, by overwhelming votes, resolutions disagreeing with the ruling and pledging to seek means to restore penalties for "such reprehensible conduct." In short order, the battle lines were drawn between those in Congress who wanted the Constitution amended to permit restraints on flag desecration and those who supported new legislation rather than a constitutional amendment. President George H. W. Bush strongly supported the amendment approach, and many of those who agreed with him believed that any new federal law would meet the same fate in the Court as did the Texas law in Johnson. But others (including many liberal Democrats) believed that a carefully drawn statute might be upheld, and that this would forestall the pressure for a constitutional amendment. Several constitutional scholars, including Laurence Tribe, Rex Lee and Geoffrey Stone, testified before Congress that a flag-burning statute might be drafted so as to pass constitutional muster. For a summary of these arguments, see Stone, "Flag Burning and the Constitution," 75 Iowa L. Rev. 111 (1989). The statutory strategy prevailed, and the Flag Protection Act of 1989 was adopted by overwhelming majorities in each House. The bill became law without the President's signature. The Act provided in relevant part: "(a)(1) Whoever knowingly mutilates, defaces, physically defiles, burns, maintains on the floor or ground, or tramples upon any flag of the United States shall be [fined] or imprisoned for not more than one year or both. (2) This subsection does not prohibit any conduct consisting of the disposal of the flag when it has become worn or soiled."

The new law was immediately and publicly violated in order to challenge its constitutionality. In **United States v. Eichman**, 496 U.S. 310 (1990), the Court struck down the 1989 federal law, once again in a 5–4 decision. The Eichman case stemmed from two prosecutions, one in Washington, D.C. and the other in Seattle. In each case, the trial courts dismissed the charges on the ground that the Act was unconstitutional. The Government conceded in Eichman that the flag burning here constituted expressive conduct, but asked the Court to reconsider its rejection in Johnson of the claim that flag burning, like obscenity or "fighting words," was not protected by the First Amendment. Justice BRENNAN's majority opinion replied: "This we decline to do." That left only the question of whether the

Flag Protection Act was "sufficiently distinct" from the Texas law in Johnson to be enforceable here. The Government argued that, unlike the law in Johnson, the new federal law did not "target expressive conduct on the basis of the content of its message," that the federal law was designed to safeguard "the physical integrity of the flag under all circumstances," and that it proscribed "conduct (other than disposal) that damages or mistreats a flag, without regard to the actor's motive, his intended message, or the likely effects of his conduct on onlookers." In rejecting that effort, Justice Brennan emphasized that while the Act "contains no explicit content-based limitation, [it] is nevertheless clear that the Government's asserted *interest* is 'related to the suppression of free expression,' Johnson, and concerned with the content of such expression."

He continued: "Although Congress cast the Flag Protection Act in somewhat broader terms than the Texas statute at issue in Johnson, the Act still suffers from the same fundamental flaw: it suppresses expression out of concern for its likely communicative impact. Despite the Act's wider scope, its restriction on expression cannot be 'justified without reference to the content of the regulated speech.' The Act therefore must be subjected to 'the most exacting scrutiny,' and for the reasons stated in Johnson, the Government's interest cannot justify its infringement on First Amendment rights. We decline the Government's invitation to reassess this conclusion in light of Congress' recent recognition of a purported 'national consensus' favoring a prohibition on flag-burning. Even assuming such a consensus exists, any suggestion that the Government's interest in suppressing speech becomes more weighty as popular opposition to that speech grows is foreign to the First Amendment.

"Government may create national symbols, promote them, and encourage their respectful treatment. But the [Act] goes well beyond this by criminally proscribing expressive conduct because of its likely communicative impact. We are aware that desecration of the flag is deeply offensive to many. But the same might be said, for example, of virulent ethnic and religious epithets, see [Terminiello], vulgar repudiations of the draft, see [Cohen], and scurrilous caricatures, see [Hustler]. 'If there is a bedrock principle underlying the First Amendment, it is that the Government may not prohibit the expression of an idea simply because society finds the idea itself offensive or disagreeable.' Johnson. Punishing desecration of the flag dilutes the very freedom that makes this emblem so revered, and worth revering."

Justice STEVENS's dissent, joined by Chief Justice Rehnquist and Justices White and O'Connor, developed the argument in his Johnson dissent: "[C]ertain methods of expression may be prohibited if (a) the prohibition is supported by a legitimate societal interest that is unrelated to suppression of the ideas the speaker desires to express; (b) the prohibition does not entail any interference with the speaker's freedom to express these ideas by other means; and (c) the interest in allowing the speaker complete freedom of choice of alternative methods of expression is less important than the societal interest supporting the prohibition." He thought that all of these criteria were satisfied here. He emphasized that the Government may "protect the symbolic value of this flag without regard to the specific content of the flag burners' speech. The prosecution in this case does not depend upon the object of the defendants' protest."

3. ***Statute vs. amendment.*** Which would have had more effect on free speech law: the Flag Protection Act if it had been upheld, or a constitutional amendment providing that "Congress and the States shall have power to prohibit the physical desecration of the flag of the United States"? The assumption of many of the reluctant backers of the Flag Protection Act in Congress was that the constitutional amendment would be by far the greater evil. Such an amendment would, for the first time, have amended an original provision of the Bill of Rights. It would also have been only the fifth constitutional amendment to overrule a decision of the Supreme Court. For the contrary argument that a constitutional amendment would have done *less* harm to the fabric of First Amendment doctrine than would a new flag desecration law upheld by the Court, see Michelman, "Saving Old Glory: On Constitutional Iconography," 42 Stan. L. Rev. 1337 (1990).

The decision in Eichman spurred a renewed campaign for a constitutional amendment, but the proposed amendment that reached the floor of both Houses in 1990 fell 34 votes short of the required two-thirds majority in the House and 9 votes short in the Senate. A 1995 version of the proposed amendment fared better, passing by a vote of 312–120 in the House but falling three votes short in the Senate, which voted for the amendment 63–46. Renewed proposals for a flag desecration amendment have continued to circulate in later sessions of Congress.

Consider the application of O'Brien, Texas v. Johnson, and the flag desecration cases in the important War on Terror case below, which involved a statute arguably directed generally at conduct but with provisions that applied to speech.

Holder v. Humanitarian Law Project

561 U.S. 1, 130 S. Ct. 2705, 177 L. Ed. 2d 355 (2010).

■ CHIEF JUSTICE ROBERTS delivered the opinion of the Court.

[The] plaintiffs in this litigation seek to provide support to two [groups designated as foreign terrorist organizations]. Plaintiffs claim that they seek to facilitate only the lawful, nonviolent purposes of those groups, and that applying the material-support law to prevent them from doing so violates the Constitution. In particular, they claim that the statute is too vague, in violation of the Fifth Amendment, and that it infringes their rights to freedom of speech and association, in violation of the First Amendment. We conclude that the material-support statute is constitutional as applied to the particular activities plaintiffs have told us they wish to pursue. We do not, however, address the resolution of more difficult cases that may arise under the statute in the future.

I. This litigation concerns 18 U.S.C. § 2339B, which makes it a federal crime to "knowingly provid[e] material support or resources to a foreign terrorist organization."[1] [The definition of "material support or

[1] In full, 18 U.S.C. § 2339B(a)(1) provides: "UNLAWFUL CONDUCT.—Whoever knowingly provides material support or resources to a foreign terrorist organization, or attempts or conspires to do so, shall be fined under this title or imprisoned not more than 15 years, or both, and, if the death of any person results, shall be imprisoned for any term of years or for life.

resources" in the statute is:] "any property, tangible or intangible, or service, including currency or monetary instruments or financial securities, financial services, lodging, training, expert advice or assistance, safehouses, false documentation or identification, communications equipment, facilities, weapons, lethal substances, explosives, personnel (1 or more individuals who may be or include oneself), and transportation, except medicine or religious materials."

The authority to designate an entity a "foreign terrorist organization" rests with the Secretary of State. [In] 1997, [she] designated 30 groups as foreign terrorist organizations. Two of those groups are the Kurdistan Workers' Party (also known as the Partiya Karkeran Kurdistan, or PKK) and the Liberation Tigers of Tamil Eelam (LTTE). The PKK is an organization founded in 1974 with the aim of establishing an independent Kurdish state in southeastern Turkey. The LTTE is an organization founded in 1976 for the purpose of creating an independent Tamil state in Sri Lanka.

[Plaintiffs] in this litigation are two U.S. citizens and six domestic organizations. [In] 1998, plaintiffs filed suit in federal court challenging the constitutionality of the material-support statute. [Plaintiffs] claimed that they wished to provide support for the humanitarian and political activities of the PKK and the LTTE in the form of monetary contributions, other tangible aid, legal training, and political advocacy, but that they could not do so for fear of prosecution under § 2339B.[2] [As] relevant here, plaintiffs claimed that the material-support statute was unconstitutional [because] it violated their freedom of speech and freedom of association under the First Amendment [by] criminaliz[ing] their provision of material support to the PKK and the LTTE, without requiring the Government to prove that plaintiffs had a specific intent to further the unlawful ends of those organizations. [Plaintiffs also argued that the statute was unconstitutionally vague.]

V. A. We next consider whether the material-support statute, as applied to plaintiffs, violates the freedom of speech guaranteed by the First Amendment. Both plaintiffs and the Government take extreme positions on this question. Plaintiffs claim that Congress has banned their "pure political speech." It has not. Under the material-support statute, plaintiffs may say anything they wish on any topic. They may speak and write freely about the PKK and LTTE, the governments of Turkey and Sri Lanka, human rights, and international law. They may advocate before the United Nations. As the Government states: "The statute does not prohibit independent advocacy or expression of any kind." Section 2339B also "does not prevent [plaintiffs] from becoming members of the PKK and LTTE or impose any sanction on them for doing so." Congress has not, therefore, sought to suppress ideas or opinions in the form of "pure political speech." Rather, Congress has prohibited "material support," which most often does not take the form of speech at all. And when it does, the statute is carefully drawn to cover only

---

To violate this paragraph, a person must have knowledge that the organization is a designated terrorist organization . . . , that the organization has engaged or engages in terrorist activity . . . , or that the organization has engaged or engages in terrorism. . . ." [Footnote by Chief Justice Roberts.]

2 At the time plaintiffs first filed suit, [the statute] provided: "Whoever, within the United States or subject to the jurisdiction of the United States, knowingly provides material support or resources to a foreign terrorist organization, or attempts or conspires to do so, shall be fined under this title or imprisoned not more than 10 years, or both." [Footnote by Chief Justice Roberts.]

a narrow category of speech to, under the direction of, or in coordination with foreign groups that the speaker knows to be terrorist organizations.

For its part, the Government takes the foregoing too far, claiming that the only thing truly at issue in this litigation is conduct, not speech. Section 2339B is directed at the fact of plaintiffs' interaction with the PKK and LTTE, the Government contends, and only incidentally burdens their expression. The Government argues that the proper standard of review is therefore the one set out in [O'Brien]. In that case, [we] applied what we have since called "intermediate scrutiny," under which a "content-neutral regulation will be sustained under the First Amendment if it advances important governmental interests unrelated to the suppression of free speech and does not burden substantially more speech than necessary to further those interests."

The Government is wrong that the only thing actually at issue in this litigation is conduct, and therefore wrong to argue that O'Brien provides the correct standard of review. O'Brien does not provide the applicable standard for reviewing a content-based regulation of speech, [see R.A.V.,] and § 2339B regulates speech on the basis of its content. Plaintiffs want to speak to the PKK and the LTTE, and whether they may do so under § 2339B depends on what they say. [The] Government argues that § 2339B should nonetheless receive intermediate scrutiny because it *generally* functions as a regulation of conduct. That argument runs headlong into a number of our precedents, most prominently [Cohen v. California]. Cohen also involved a generally applicable regulation of conduct, barring breaches of the peace. But when Cohen was convicted for wearing a jacket bearing an epithet, we did not apply O'Brien. Instead, we recognized that the generally applicable law was directed at Cohen because of what his speech communicated—he violated the breach of the peace statute because of the offensive content of his particular message. We accordingly applied more rigorous scrutiny and reversed his conviction.

This suit falls into the same category. The law here may be described as directed at conduct, as the law in Cohen was directed at breaches of the peace, but as applied to plaintiffs the conduct triggering coverage under the statute consists of communicating a message. As we explained in Texas v. Johnson: "If the [Government's] regulation is not related to expression, then the less stringent standard we announced in [O'Brien] for regulations of noncommunicative conduct controls. If it is, then we are outside of O'Brien's test, and we must [apply] a more demanding standard."

B. The First Amendment issue before us is more refined than either plaintiffs or the Government would have it. It is not whether the Government may prohibit pure political speech, or may prohibit material support in the form of conduct. It is instead whether the Government may prohibit what plaintiffs want to do—provide material support to the PKK and LTTE in the form of speech.

Everyone agrees that the Government's interest in combating terrorism is an urgent objective of the highest order. Plaintiffs' complaint is that the ban on material support, applied to what they wish to do, is not "necessary to further that interest." The objective of combating terrorism does not justify prohibiting their speech, plaintiffs argue, because their support will advance only the legitimate activities of the designated terrorist organizations, not their terrorism.

Whether foreign terrorist organizations meaningfully segregate support of their legitimate activities from support of terrorism is an empirical question. When it enacted § 2339B in 1996, Congress made specific findings regarding the serious threat posed by international terrorism. One of those findings explicitly rejects plaintiffs' contention that their support would not further the terrorist activities of the PKK and LTTE: "[F]oreign organizations that engage in terrorist activity are so tainted by their criminal conduct that any contribution to such an organization facilitates that conduct."

Plaintiffs argue that the reference to "any contribution" in this finding meant only monetary support. There is no reason to read the finding to be so limited, particularly because Congress expressly prohibited so much more than monetary support in § 2339B. Congress's use of the term "contribution" is best read to reflect a determination that any form of material support furnished "to" a foreign terrorist organization should be barred, which is precisely what the material-support statute does. [We] are convinced that Congress was justified in rejecting [the view that ostensibly peaceful aid has no harmful effects]. The PKK and the LTTE are deadly groups. "The PKK's insurgency has claimed more than 22,000 lives." The LTTE has engaged in extensive suicide bombings and political assassinations, including killings of the Sri Lankan President, Security Minister, and Deputy Defense Minister. "On January 31, 1996, the LTTE exploded a truck bomb filled with an estimated 1,000 pounds of explosives at the Central Bank in Colombo, killing 100 people and injuring more than 1,400. This bombing was the most deadly terrorist incident in the world in 1996." It is not difficult to conclude as Congress did that the "tain[t]" of such violent activities is so great that working in coordination with or at the command of the PKK and LTTE serves to legitimize and further their terrorist means.

Material support meant to "promot[e] peaceable, lawful conduct," can further terrorism by foreign groups in multiple ways. "Material support" is a valuable resource by definition. Such support frees up other resources within the organization that may be put to violent ends. It also importantly helps lend legitimacy to foreign terrorist groups—legitimacy that makes it easier for those groups to persist, to recruit members, and to raise funds—all of which facilitate more terrorist attacks. "Terrorist organizations do not maintain organizational 'firewalls' that would prevent or deter . . . sharing and commingling of support and benefits." [Money] is fungible, and "[w]hen foreign terrorist organizations that have a dual structure raise funds, they highlight the civilian and humanitarian ends to which such moneys could be put." But "there is reason to believe that foreign terrorist organizations do not maintain legitimate financial firewalls between those funds raised for civil, nonviolent activities, and those ultimately used to support violent, terrorist operations." [There] is evidence that the PKK and the LTTE, in particular, have not "respected the line between humanitarian and violent activities."

The dissent argues that there is "no natural stopping place" for the proposition that aiding a foreign terrorist organization's lawful activity promotes the terrorist organization as a whole. But Congress has settled on just such a natural stopping place: The statute reaches only material support coordinated with or under the direction of a designated foreign terrorist organization. Independent advocacy that might be viewed as promoting the group's legitimacy is not covered.[3]

Providing foreign terrorist groups with material support in any form also furthers terrorism by straining the United States' relationships with its allies and undermining cooperative efforts between nations to prevent terrorist attacks. We see no reason to question Congress's finding that "international cooperation is required for an effective response to terrorism, as demonstrated by the numerous multilateral conventions in force providing universal prosecutive jurisdiction over persons involved in a variety of terrorist acts, including hostage taking, murder of an internationally protected person, and aircraft piracy and sabotage." The material-support statute furthers this international effort by prohibiting aid for foreign terrorist groups that harm the United States' partners abroad.

C. In analyzing whether it is possible in practice to distinguish material support for a foreign terrorist group's violent activities and its nonviolent activities, we do not rely exclusively on our own inferences drawn from the record evidence. [The] State Department informs us that "[t]he experience and analysis of the U.S. government agencies charged with combating terrorism strongly suppor[t]" Congress's finding that all contributions to foreign terrorist organizations further their terrorism. [That] evaluation of the facts by the Executive, like Congress's assessment, is entitled to deference. This litigation implicates sensitive and weighty interests of national security and foreign affairs. [It] is vital in this context "not to substitute . . . our own evaluation of evidence for a reasonable evaluation by the Legislative Branch."

Our precedents, old and new, make clear that concerns of national security and foreign relations do not warrant abdication of the judicial role. We do not defer to the Government's reading of the First Amendment, even when such interests are at stake. [But] when it comes to collecting evidence and drawing factual inferences in this area, "the lack of competence on the part of the courts is marked," and respect for the Government's conclusions is appropriate. [The] Government, when seeking to prevent imminent harms in the context of international affairs and national security, is not required to conclusively link all the pieces in the puzzle before we grant weight to its empirical conclusions.

This context is different from that in decisions like Cohen. In that case, the application of the statute turned on the offensiveness of the speech at issue. Observing that "one man's vulgarity is another's lyric," we invalidated Cohen's conviction in part because we concluded that "governmental officials cannot make principled distinctions in this area." In this litigation, by contrast, Congress and the Executive are uniquely positioned to make principled distinctions between activities that will further terrorist conduct and undermine United States foreign policy, and those that will not.

[We] turn to the particular speech plaintiffs propose to undertake. First, plaintiffs propose to "train members of [the] PKK on how to use humanitarian and international law to peacefully resolve disputes."

---

[3] The dissent also contends that the particular sort of material support plaintiffs seek to provide cannot be diverted to terrorist activities, in the same direct way as funds or goods. This contention misses the point. Both common sense and the evidence submitted by the Government make clear that material support of a terrorist group's lawful activities facilitates the group's ability to attract "funds," "financing," and "goods" that will further its terrorist acts. [Footnote by Chief Justice Roberts.]

Congress can, consistent with the First Amendment, prohibit this direct training. It is wholly foreseeable that the PKK could use the "specific skill[s]" that plaintiffs propose to impart as part of a broader strategy to promote terrorism. The PKK could, for example, pursue peaceful negotiation as a means of buying time to recover from short-term setbacks, lulling opponents into complacency, and ultimately preparing for renewed attacks. [Second,] plaintiffs propose to "teach PKK members how to petition various representative bodies such as the United Nations for relief." The Government acts within First Amendment strictures in banning this proposed speech because it teaches the organization how to acquire "relief," which plaintiffs never define with any specificity, and which could readily include monetary aid. [Finally,] plaintiffs propose to "engage in political advocacy on behalf of Kurds who live in Turkey," and "engage in political advocacy on behalf of Tamils who live in Sri Lanka." [These] proposals are phrased at such a high level of generality that they cannot prevail in this preenforcement challenge.

VI. [The] Preamble to the Constitution proclaims that the people of the United States ordained and established that charter of government in part to "provide for the common defence." As Madison explained, "[s]ecurity against foreign danger is . . . an avowed and essential object of the American Union." [The Federalist No. 41.] We hold that, in regulating the particular forms of support that plaintiffs seek to provide to foreign terrorist organizations, Congress has pursued that objective consistent with the limitations of the First and Fifth Amendments.

■ JUSTICE BREYER, with whom JUSTICES GINSBURG and SOTOMAYOR join, dissenting.

[I] cannot agree with the Court's conclusion that the Constitution permits the Government to prosecute the plaintiffs criminally for engaging in coordinated teaching and advocacy furthering the designated organizations' lawful political objectives. [In] my view, the Government has not made the strong showing necessary to justify under the First Amendment the criminal prosecution of those who engage in these activities. All the activities involve the communication and advocacy of political ideas and lawful means of achieving political ends. [That] this speech and association for political purposes is the *kind* of activity to which the First Amendment ordinarily offers its strongest protection is elementary. [Although] in the Court's view the statute applies only where the PKK helps to coordinate a defendant's activities, the simple fact of "coordination" alone cannot readily remove protection that the First Amendment would otherwise grant.

["Coordination"] with a group that engages in unlawful activity also does not deprive the plaintiffs of the First Amendment's protection under any traditional "categorical" exception to its protection. The plaintiffs do not propose to solicit a crime. They will not engage in fraud or defamation or circulate obscenity. And the First Amendment protects advocacy even of unlawful action so long as that advocacy is not "directed to inciting or producing imminent lawless action and . . . likely to incite or produce such action." [Brandenburg.] Here the plaintiffs seek to advocate peaceful, lawful action to secure political ends; and they seek to teach others how to do the same. No one contends that the plaintiffs' speech to these organizations can be prohibited as incitement under Brandenburg.

[It] is not surprising that the majority, in determining the constitutionality of criminally prohibiting the plaintiffs' proposed activities, would apply, not the kind of intermediate First Amendment standard that applies to conduct, but "a more demanding standard." Indeed, where, as here, a statute applies criminal penalties and at least arguably does so on the basis of content-based distinctions, I should think we would scrutinize the statute and justifications "strictly"—to determine whether the prohibition is justified by a "compelling" need that cannot be "less restrictively" accommodated. [But,] even if we assume for argument's sake that "strict scrutiny" does not apply, [I] doubt that the statute, as the Government would interpret it, can survive any reasonably applicable First Amendment standard. [The] Government does identify a compelling countervailing interest, namely, the interest in protecting the security of the United States and its nationals from the threats that foreign terrorist organizations pose by denying those organizations financial and other fungible resources. I do not dispute the importance of this interest. But I do dispute whether the interest can justify the statute's criminal prohibition. To put the matter more specifically, precisely how does application of the statute to the protected activities before us *help achieve* that important security-related end?

The Government makes two efforts to answer this question. First, the Government says that the plaintiffs' support for these organizations is "fungible" in the same sense as other forms of banned support. [The] proposition that the two very different kinds of "support" are "fungible," however, is not obviously true. There is no obvious way in which undertaking advocacy for political change through peaceful means or teaching the PKK and LTTE, say, how to petition the United Nations for political change is fungible with other resources that might be put to more sinister ends in the way that donations of money, food, or computer training are fungible. [Second,] the Government says that the plaintiffs' proposed activities will "bolste[r] a terrorist organization's efficacy and strength in a community" and "undermin[e] this nation's efforts to delegitimize and weaken those groups." In the Court's view, too, the Constitution permits application of the statute to activities of the kind at issue in part because those activities could provide a group that engages in terrorism with "legitimacy." [But] this "legitimacy" justification cannot by itself warrant suppression of political speech, advocacy, and association. Speech, association, and related activities on behalf of a group will often, perhaps always, help to legitimate that group. Thus, were the law to accept a "legitimating" effect, in and of itself and without qualification, as providing sufficient grounds for imposing such a ban, the First Amendment battle would be lost in untold instances where it should be won. Once one accepts this argument, there is no natural stopping place.

[Nor] can the Government overcome these considerations simply by narrowing the covered activities to those that involve coordinated, rather than independent, advocacy. Conversations, discussions, or logistical arrangements might well prove necessary to carry out the speech-related activities here at issue (just as conversations and discussions are a necessary part of membership in any organization). The Government does not distinguish this kind of "coordination" from any other. I am not aware of any form of words that might be used to describe "coordination" that would not, at a minimum, seriously chill not only the kind of activities the plaintiffs raise before us, but also the "independent advocacy" the Government purports to permit. And, as for the Government's willingness to distinguish independent advocacy from coordinated advocacy, the former is more likely, not less likely, to confer legitimacy than the latter. Thus, other things being equal, the distinction "coordination" makes is arbitrary in respect to furthering the statute's purposes. And a rule of law that finds the "legitimacy" argument adequate in respect to the latter would have a hard time distinguishing a statute that sought to attack the former.

[What] is one to say about [the Government's] arguments—arguments that would deny First Amendment protection to the peaceful teaching of international human rights law on the ground that a little knowledge about "the international legal system" is too dangerous a thing; that an opponent's subsequent willingness to negotiate might be faked, so let's not teach him how to try? What might be said of these claims by those who live, as we do, in a Nation committed to the resolution of disputes through "deliberative forces"? [Whitney.]

[I] believe application of the statute as the Government interprets it would gravely and without adequate justification injure interests of the kind the First Amendment protects. [I] would read the statute as criminalizing First-Amendment-protected pure speech and association only when the defendant knows or intends that those activities will assist the organization's unlawful terrorist actions. [This] reading of the statute protects those who engage in pure speech and association ordinarily protected by the First Amendment. But it does not protect that activity where a defendant purposefully intends it to help terrorism or where a defendant knows (or willfully blinds himself to the fact) that the activity is significantly likely to assist terrorism. Where the activity fits into these categories of purposefully or knowingly supporting terrorist ends, the act of providing material support to a known terrorist organization bears a close enough relation to terrorist acts that, in my view, it likely can be prohibited notwithstanding any First Amendment interest. Cf. [Brandenburg.]

THE IMPLICATIONS OF HUMANITARIAN LAW PROJECT

1. ***The standard of review.*** The majority opinion in Humanitarian Law Project (HLP) purports to apply a distinct standard—"more rigorous scrutiny"—for laws that are generally directed at conduct but are triggered in the particular case by the communication of a message. Was that the standard of review applied by the Court in Cohen v. California (1971; p. 998 above), or referred to in Texas v. Johnson (1989; p. 1186 above)? Is it relevant that in Cohen, the government interest in proscribing speech did not outweigh the First Amendment considerations, whereas in HLP it did? Or was Chief Justice Roberts's heightened standard just strict scrutiny in disguise? The Supreme Court has itself characterized HLP as applying strict scrutiny (albeit only parenthetically), as have several courts of appeals. See McCullen v. Coakley (2014; p. 1244 below); see also United States v. Baumgartner, 581 F. App'x 522, 530 (6th Cir. 2014); Al Haramain Islamic Found., Inc. v. U.S. Dep't of Treasury, 686 F.3d 965, 996 (9th Cir. 2012). If HLP indeed applied strict scrutiny, was its application not highly deferential to the government? As a more basic matter, was the material support statute in HLP generally directed at conduct, as Chief Justice Roberts suggests?

Should it matter that the statute specifically refers to "advice" as a form of material support?

2. ***Prohibitions on counseling.*** What other types of part-conduct, part-speech regulation might be subject to HLP's heightened standard? Several states have passed statutes prohibiting licensed mental health professionals from offering minors the controversial "sexual orientation change efforts" (SOCE) therapy. Since HLP, two federal courts of appeal have upheld such prohibitions, but the courts have disagreed on whether HLP's "more rigorous scrutiny" or O'Brien's "intermediate scrutiny" should apply. Compare King v. Governor of State of N.J., 767 F.3d 216 (3d Cir. 2014) (finding SOCE therapy was "speech" subject to HLP's heightened scrutiny), with Pickup v. Brown, 740 F.3d 1208 (9th Cir. 2013) (holding SOCE therapy is "conduct" subject to O'Brien standard).

3. ***"Material support" and Brandenburg.*** Can the Court's holding in HLP be squared with its decision in Brandenburg v. Ohio (1969; p. 978 above)? Recall that in Brandenburg, the Court held that speech that is not "directed to inciting or producing imminent lawless action and [likely] to incite or produce such action" is protected under the First Amendment. Isn't Chief Justice Roberts's failure even to mention Brandenburg puzzling? Roberts's opinion places great weight on the distinction between "independent" and "coordinated" advocacy; is that difference helpful here?

For his part, Justice Breyer stated in his dissent that the plaintiffs' speech could not be barred as incitement under Brandenburg. The plaintiffs here sought to advocate merely "peaceful, *lawful* action," and Brandenburg protects advocacy of even unlawful behavior, provided it does not amount to incitement. Given this apparent irreconcilability, why does Justice Breyer not state that HLP overrules Brandenburg?

4. ***Deference to congressional findings?*** Whether offering otherwise lawful advice to a terrorist organization constitutes the conduct of material support depends, the Court suggested, on the "empirical question" whether terrorist organizations sequester or separate their lawful from their unlawful activities. On this point, the Court appeared to defer to Congress. Can this approach be reconciled with Justice Brandeis's dissent in Whitney v. California (1927; p. 965 above), where he maintained that the judiciary must not defer to legislative findings of the dangerousness of political speech?

5. ***Material support and the War on Terror.*** After HLP, is there any reason for law enforcement ever to invoke incitement laws to punish speakers who support terrorism? Wouldn't it be easier to charge such speakers with material support of terrorism and then try to show that their speech was not uncoordinated advocacy but intended to support the organization? Consider the defendants in Brandenburg: they were members of the Ku Klux Klan, which certainly acted as a terrorist organization in some (perhaps most) periods of its history. Could their speech have been punished under a properly framed material support statute? If so, then does the Brandenburg tradition of protection for unpopular speech even by members of groups advocating violence still exist in the post-September 11 era?

6. ***Support for domestic organizations.*** The HLP majority was careful to note that its holding was limited to the statute's prohibition on material support for *foreign* terrorist organizations: "We [do] not suggest

that Congress could extend the same prohibition on material support at issue here to domestic organizations." Are there compelling reasons to scrutinize the constitutionality of statutes regulating contributions to domestic terrorist groups more carefully? At least one court of appeals thinks so: In **Al Haramin Islamic Foundation, Inc. v. U.S. Department of Treasury**, 686 F.3d 965 (9th Cir. 2011), the Ninth Circuit held that the government could not constitutionally prohibit an Oregon-based community group, MCASO, from advocating on behalf of a domestic foundation designated by executive order as tied to an international terrorist organization. While the court did not treat the foreign-domestic distinction as dispositive, it was persuaded that the foundation's domestic status undermined the government's interest in prohibiting MCASO's advocacy on its behalf; the court found "little evidence that the pure-speech activities proposed by MCASO on behalf of the domestic branch will aid the larger international organization's sinister purposes." The court thus held that applying the executive's designation to bar MCASO's advocacy did not meet the strict scrutiny required by HLP.

NUDE DANCING

Recall that the Court invalidated a citywide ban on nude entertainment in Schad v. Mt. Ephraim (1981; p. 1084 above) but upheld zoning regulations concentrating or dispersing adult entertainment establishments in Young v. American Mini Theatres (1976; p. 1085 above) and Renton v. Playtime Theatres (1986; p. 1089 above). A 1991 challenge to a ban on public nudity as applied to nude dancing elicited sharp disagreement among the Justices over the applicable standard of review: the plurality found the law content-neutral and reviewed its application under the O'Brien test; Justice Scalia found it content-neutral but subject to more deferential review; and the dissent found it content-based because it aimed at communicative impact.

Barnes v. Glen Theatre, Inc.

501 U.S. 560, 111 S. Ct. 2456, 115 L. Ed. 2d 504 (1991).

■ CHIEF JUSTICE REHNQUIST delivered the opinion of the Court.

Respondents [Kitty Kat Lounge and Glen Theatre] are two establishments in South Bend, Indiana that wish to provide totally nude dancing as entertainment, and individual dancers who are employed at these establishments. The Kitty Kat Lounge, Inc. [ ] sells alcoholic beverages and presents "go-go dancing." Its proprietor desires to present "totally nude dancing," but an applicable Indiana statute regulating public nudity requires that the dancers wear "pasties" and "G-strings" when the dance. Glen Theatre, Inc., suppl[ies] so-called adult entertainment through written and printed materials, movie showings, and live entertainment at an enclosed "bookstore." The live entertainment at the "bookstore" consists of nude and seminude performances and showings of the female body through glass panels. Customers sit in a booth and insert coins into a timing mechanism that permits them to observe the live nude and seminude dancers for a period of time.

[Respondents object to] enforcement of a public indecency statute [providing that] "[a] person who knowingly or intentionally, in a public place, [appears] in a state of nudity [commits] public indecency, a [misdemeanor] and [defining nudity as] showing of the human male or female genitals, pubic area, or buttocks with less than a fully opaque covering [or] the showing of the female breast with less than a fully opaque covering of any part of the nipple." Respondents assert[ed] that [Indiana's] prohibition against complete nudity in public places violated the First Amendment.

[N]ude dancing of the kind sought to be performed here is expressive conduct within the outer perimeters of the First Amendment, though we view it as only marginally so. Indiana, of course, has not banned nude dancing as such, but has proscribed public nudity across the board. Applying the four-part O'Brien test, [we] find that Indiana's public indecency statute is justified despite its incidental limitations on some expressive activity. The public indecency statute is clearly within the constitutional power of the State and furthers substantial governmental interests. It is impossible to discern, other than from the text of the statute, exactly what governmental interest the Indiana legislators had in mind when they enacted this statute, for Indiana does not record legislative history, and the State's highest court has not shed additional light on the statute's purpose. Nonetheless, the statute's purpose of protecting societal order and morality is clear from its text and history. Public indecency statutes of this sort are of ancient origin and presently exist in at least 47 States. Public indecency, including nudity, was a criminal offense at common law. [Public] nudity was considered an act malum in se. Public indecency statutes such as the one before us reflect moral disapproval of people appearing in the nude among strangers in public places. [This] and other public indecency statutes were designed to protect morals and public order. The traditional police power of the States is defined as the authority to provide for the public health, safety, and morals, and we have upheld such a basis for legislation. [Paris Adult; Hardwick.]

[This] interest is unrelated to the suppression of free expression. Some may view restricting nudity on moral grounds as necessarily related to expression. We disagree. It can be argued, of course, that almost limitless types of conduct—including appearing in the nude in public—are "expressive," and in one sense of the word this is true. People who go about in the nude in public may be expressing something about themselves by so doing. But the court rejected this expansive notion of 'expressive conduct' in O'Brien, saying: "We cannot accept the view that an apparently limitless variety of conduct can be labeled 'speech' whenever the person engaging in the conduct intends thereby to express an idea."

■ JUSTICE SCALIA, concurring.

I agree that the judgment of the Court of Appeals must be reversed. In my view, however, the challenged regulation must be upheld, not because it survives some lower level of First Amendment scrutiny, but because, as a general law regulating conduct and not specifically directed at expression, it is not subject to First Amendment scrutiny at all. [Indiana's] statute is in the line of a long tradition of laws against public nudity, which have never been thought to run afoul of traditional understanding of 'the freedom of speech.' Public indecency—including public nudity—has long been an offense at common law. Indiana's first public nudity statute predated by many years the appearance of nude barroom dancing. It was general in scope, directed all public nudity, and not just at public nude expression; and all succeeding statutes, down to the present one, have been the same. Were it the case that Indiana in practice targeted only expressive nudity, while turning a blind eye to nude beaches and unclothed purveyors of hot dogs and machine tools, it might be said that what posed as a regulation of conduct in general was in reality a regulation of only communicative conduct. Respondents have adduced no evidence of that. Indiana officials have brought many public indecency prosecutions for activities having no communicative element.

[The] dissent confidently asserts that the purpose of restricting nudity in public places in general is to protect nonconsenting parties from offense; and argues that since only consenting, admission-paying patrons see respondents dance, that purpose cannot apply and the only remaining purpose must relate to the communicative elements of the performance. Perhaps the dissenters believe that 'offense to others' ought to be the only reason for restricting nudity in public places generally, but there is no basis for thinking that our society has ever shared that Thoreauvian 'you-may-do-what-you-like-so-long-as-it-does-not-injure-someone-else' beau ideal—much less for thinking that it was written into the Constitution. The purpose of Indiana's nudity law would be violated, I think, if 60,000 fully consenting adults crowded into the Hoosier Dome to display their genitals to one another, even if there were not an offended innocent in the crowd. Our society prohibits, and all human societies have prohibited, certain activities not because they harm others but because they are considered, in the traditional phrase, 'contra bonos mores,' i.e., immoral. In American society, such prohibitions have included, for example, sadomasochism, cockfighting, bestiality, suicide, drug use, prostitution, and sodomy. [The] Constitution does not prohibit [such laws] simply because they regulate 'morality.' [See Hardwick; Paris Adult.] The purpose of the Indiana statute, as both its text and the manner of its enforcement demonstrate, is to enforce the traditional moral belief that people should not expose their private parts indiscriminately, regardless of whether those who see them are disedified. Since that is so, the dissent has no basis for positing that, where only thoroughly edified adults are present, the purpose must be repression of communication.

Since the Indiana regulation is a general law not specifically targeted at expressive conduct, its application to such conduct does not in my view implicate the First Amendment. [Virtually] every law restricts conduct, and virtually any prohibited conduct can be performed for an expressive purpose—if only expressive of the fact that the actor disagrees with the prohibition. It cannot reasonably be demanded, therefore, that every restriction of expression incidentally produced by a general law regulating conduct pass normal First Amendment scrutiny, or even [the O'Brien test.] Nor do our holdings require such justification: We have never invalidated the application of a general law simply because the conduct that it reached was being engaged in for expressive purposes and the government could not demonstrate a sufficiently important state interest.

■ JUSTICE SOUTER, concurring.

[The state] assert[s] that the statute is applied to nude dancing because such dancing 'encourages prostitution, increases sexual assaults, and attracts other criminal activity.' This asserted justification for the statute may not be ignored merely because it is unclear to what extent this purpose motivated the Indiana Legislature in enacting the statute. Our appropriate focus is not an empirical enquiry into the actual intent of the enacting legislature, but rather the existence or not of a current governmental interest in the service of which the challenged application of the statute may be constitutional. [In] my view, the interest asserted by petitioners [is] sufficient under O'Brien to justify the State's enforcement of the statute against the type of adult entertainment at issue here.

[This] interest [is] 'unrelated to the suppression of free expression.' [To] say that pernicious secondary effects are associated with nude dancing establishments is not necessarily to say that such effects result from the persuasive effect of the expression inherent in nude dancing. It is to say, rather, only that the effects are correlated with the existence of establishments offering such dancing, without deciding what the precise causes of the correlation actually are.

■ JUSTICE WHITE, dissenting.

The purpose of forbidding people from appearing nude in parks, beaches, hot dog stands, and like public places is to protect others from offense. But that could not possibly be the purpose of preventing nude dancing in theaters and barrooms since the viewers are exclusively consenting adults who pay money to see these dances. The purpose of the proscription in these contexts is to protect the viewers from what the State believes is the harmful message that nude dancing communicates. [The] emotional or erotic impact of the dance is intensified by the nudity of the performers. [The] sight of a fully clothed, or even a partially clothed, dancer generally will have a far different impact on a spectator than that of a nude dancer, even if the same dance is performed. The nudity is itself an expressive component of the dance, not merely incidental 'conduct.'

[This] being the case, it cannot be that the statutory prohibition is unrelated to expressive conduct. Since the State permits the dancers to perform if they wear pasties and G-strings but forbids nude dancing, it is precisely because of the distinctive, expressive content of the nude dancing performances at issue in this case that the State seeks to apply the statutory prohibition. It is only because nude dancing performances may generate emotions and feelings of eroticism and sensuality among the spectators that the State seeks to regulate such expressive activity, apparently on the assumption that creating or emphasizing such thoughts and ideas in the minds of the spectators may lead to increased prostitution and the degradation of women. But generating thoughts, ideas, and emotions is the essence of communication. [Thus] the level of First Amendment protection to be accorded the performances at issue here [should be the] 'exacting scrutiny' [required in Texas v. Johnson.] [Our] cases require us to affirm absent a compelling state interest supporting the statute. [Even] if there were compelling interests, the Indiana statute is not narrowly drawn.

APPLYING BARNES

The Court revisiting the constitutionality of public nudity bans as applied to nude dancing in **City of Erie v. Pap's A.M.**, 529 U.S. 277 (2000). The Pennsylvania Supreme Court, finding no clear precedent in the fragmented Barnes opinions, had employed strict scrutiny to invalidate a municipal nudity ban as applied to the right of an establishment called Kandyland to feature totally nude erotic dancing by women. The state court reasoned that a law was not content-neutral but had sought to "impact negatively on the erotic message of the dance." Reversing, the United States Supreme Court again fragmented in its reasoning, as it had in Barnes. Justice O'CONNOR, writing for the Court in a plurality opinion joined by Chief Justice Rehnquist and Justices Kennedy and Breyer, found that government restrictions on public nudity should be evaluated under the O'Brien test as content-neutral restrictions on symbolic conduct. She rejected any reading of the Erie ordinance as content-based, finding it instead aimed at "combat[ing] the negative secondary effects associated with nude dancing establishments," such as the promotion of "violence, public intoxication, prostitution, and other serious criminal activity." Justice O'Connor found this justification sufficient to satisfy O'Brien, even in the absence of a specific evidentiary record of such secondary effects.

Justice SCALIA, joined by Justice Thomas, concurred in the judgment, reiterating his view in Barnes that a public nudity law such as Erie's is a "general law regulating conduct and not specifically directed at expression," and thus subject to no First Amendment scrutiny at all. He continued: "[E]ven if one hypothesizes that the city's object was to suppress only nude dancing, that would not establish an intent to suppress what (if anything) nude dancing communicates. I do not feel the need, as the Court does, to identify some 'secondary effects' associated with nude dancing that the city could properly seek to eliminate. (I am highly skeptical, to tell the truth, that the addition of pasties and g-strings will at all reduce the tendency of establishments such as Kandyland to attract crime and prostitution, and hence to foster sexually transmitted disease.) The traditional power of government to foster good morals (bonos mores), and the acceptability of the traditional judgment (if Erie wishes to endorse it) that nude public dancing itself is immoral, have not been repealed by the First Amendment."

Justice SOUTER filed an opinion concurring in part and dissenting in part. He agreed that O'Brien was the right test, but insisted that "intermediate scrutiny requires a regulating government to make some demonstration of an evidentiary basis for the harm it claims to flow from the expressive activity, and for the alleviation expected from the restriction imposed." He found the evidentiary record in the case "deficient" under this standard, finding not facts but "emotionalism" in the statements made by city council members. In requiring a better empirical justification for the law in order to satisfy the O'Brien standard, Justice Souter took the unusual step of confessing error about his own prior opinion in Barnes: "Careful readers, and not just those on the Erie City Council, will of course realize that my partial dissent rests on a demand for an evidentiary basis that I failed to make when I concurred in Barnes. I should have demanded the evidence then, too, and my mistake calls to mind Justice Jackson's foolproof explanation of a lapse of his own, when he quoted Samuel Johnson, 'Ignorance, sir, ignorance.'"

Justice STEVENS, joined by Justice Ginsburg, dissented, opposing the plurality's extension of the "secondary effects" test from zoning cases to what he characterized as a "total ban" on a medium of expression. He also criticized the plurality's lenient application of that test: "To believe that the mandatory addition of pasties and a G-string will have any kind of noticeable impact on secondary effects requires nothing short of a titanic surrender to the implausible." He would have found that the Erie ordinance was impermissibly aimed at nude dancing rather than nudity in general, and invalidated it.

Note that, by converging on the secondary effects rationale in Pap's, the Court abandoned as an apparent isolated anomaly the plurality's view in Barnes that morality alone was a good enough content-neutral reason to uphold a regulation of speech under O'Brien review. While the Court once held that morality was a good enough reason to prohibit sex (but recall that Bowers v. Hardwick was later overruled in Lawrence v. Texas, see p. 563 above), it had never otherwise held that morality alone was a sufficient ground for regulating protected speech. But note how thin an empirical record of harm from secondary effects was sufficient for the plurality here to uphold the nudity ban—a point emphasized by Justice Souter in his partial dissent. For criticism of the secondary effects doctrine as it has been applied to prohibitions on nude dancing, see Adler, "Girls! Girls! Girls!: The Supreme Court Confronts the G-String," 80 N.Y.U. L. Rev. 1108 (2005).

For further exploration of the issues in Barnes, see the opinions of Judges Posner (concurring) and Easterbrook (dissenting) in the decision of the Court of Appeals for the Seventh Circuit holding the application of the law unconstitutional below. Miller v. Civil City of South Bend, 904 F.2d 1081 (1990) (en banc). See also Blasi, "Six Conservatives in Search of the First Amendment: The Revealing Case of Nude Dancing," 33 Wm. & Mary L. Rev. 611 (1992).

SPEECH VERSUS CONDUCT IN PRICING

In **Expressions Hair Design v. Schneiderman**, 581 U.S. ___, 137 S. Ct. 1144 (2017), the Court considered a free-speech challenge to New York State law that prohibited merchants from telling customers that they must pay a surcharge on credit-card transactions. In an opinion by Chief Justice ROBERTS, the Court held that the law regulated speech, not conduct, as the Second Circuit had held: "[A] typical price regulation[—for] example, a law requiring all New York delis to charge $10 for their sandwiches—would simply regulate the amount that a store could collect. In other words, it would regulate the sandwich seller's conduct. To be sure, in order to actually collect that money, a store would likely have to put '$10' on its menus or have its employees tell customers that price. Those written or oral communications would be speech, and the law—by determining the amount charged—would indirectly dictate the content of that speech. But the law's effect on speech would be only incidental to its primary effect on conduct. [This law] is different. The law tells merchants nothing about the amount they are allowed to collect from a cash or credit card payer. Sellers are free to charge $10 for cash and $9.70, $10, $10.30, or any other amount for credit. What the law does regulate is how sellers may communicate their prices. A merchant who wants to charge $10 for cash and $10.30 for credit may not convey that price any way he pleases. He is not free to say '$10, with a 3% credit card surcharge' or '$10, plus $0.30 for credit' because both of those displays identify a single sticker price—$10—that is less than the amount credit card users will be charged. Instead, if the merchant wishes to post a single sticker price, he must display $10.30 as his sticker price. Accordingly, [we] cannot accept [the] conclusion that [the law] is nothing more than a mine-run price regulation. In regulating the communication of prices rather than prices themselves, [the law] regulates speech. [The] parties dispute whether [the law] is a valid commercial speech regulation under Central Hudson Gas & Elec. Corp. v. Public Serv. Comm'n of N. Y., and whether the law can be upheld as a valid disclosure requirement under Zauderer v. Office of Disciplinary Counsel of Supreme Court of Ohio. [We] decline to consider those questions in the first instance. Instead, we remand for the Court of Appeals to analyze [the law] as a speech regulation." Does Chief Justice Roberts's opinion telegraph an answer to the question whether the credit-card regulation is commercial speech? And if so, whether the regulation is valid?

SECTION 2. GOVERNMENT POWER TO LIMIT SPEECH IN CONFERRAL OF BENEFITS AS REGULATOR AND EMPLOYER

PUBLIC FORUMS AND PUBLIC PROPERTY

To what extent may government regulate those who want to march in city streets or speak in parks to publicize their views? To what extent does concern with such values as order, quiet, traffic control, and audience sensibilities justify curbs on expression in these contexts? Restraints on speech in public places in the interest of local tranquility did not reach the Court until the late 1930s. Since then, these problems have regularly produced litigation as speakers and demonstrators have sought to use streets, parks, and other public places to publicize their causes, change views and win adherents. Many early cases were stimulated by the "robust evangelism" of the Jehovah's Witnesses. During the fifties, as Harry Kalven remarked, "the story of the streets became a bit quaint." But by the sixties, with the rise of the civil rights and anti-war movements, it became clear "that the story [was] not over." Kalven, "The Concept of the Public Forum: Cox v. Louisiana," 1965 Sup. Ct. Rev. 1. In this era, the proselytizing of the single evangelist selling magazines, ringing doorbells, and speaking at street corners, gave way to a different kind of public speech: sizeable parades in streets, vigils in parks, and protest meetings outside public buildings.

What legal analyses are appropriate in evaluating the claims of those who seek access to public places to air their views? Does the First Amendment guarantee speakers access to the public forum or merely assure them equal access if public spaces are opened to speech at all? May government prohibit noisy parades in residential areas late at night or mass gatherings on heavily traveled streets during rush hour? How far may it go in advancing interests in public safety and order, aesthetic attractiveness, or tranquility, privacy, and repose? Furthermore, should speech in all public places be treated alike? The streets and parks have been treated as the quintessential public forum. Might some other public places—the Senate gallery? courtrooms? libraries? jails? airports?—be so specialized in their function as to justify total exclusion of public speakers? These questions are explored in the cases that follow.

EARLY PUBLIC FORUM CASES

1. ***The First Amendment "right" to a public forum.*** Is government free to exclude any speech it wishes from public places because it "owns" them? Is government in this context equivalent to a private proprietor? This was the view articulated by Justice Holmes when he was a state court judge. In Massachusetts v. Davis, 39 N.E. 113 (Mass. 1895), aff'd, 167 U.S. 43 (1897), the Massachusetts Supreme Judicial Court upheld the conviction of a preacher for speaking on Boston Common without a required permit from the mayor. Justice Oliver Wendell Holmes Jr., then on the Massachusetts court, wrote: "As representative of the public, [the legislature] may and does exercise control over the use which the public may make of such places. [For] the legislature absolutely or conditionally to forbid public speaking in a highway or public park is no more an infringement of the rights of a member of the public than for the owner of a private house to forbid it in his house." The U.S. Supreme Court affirmed, reasoning—at a time before the First Amendment had been held to apply against the states—that "the right to absolutely exclude all right to use, necessarily includes the authority to determine under what circumstances such use may be availed of, as the greater power contains the lesser."

The later Court has not embraced that view. Since the 1930s, the Court has imposed limits on the restrictions government may impose on speech in the "public forum." The origin of the right to speak in a public forum is often traced to a dictum in Justice ROBERTS's opinion in **Hague v. CIO**, 307 U.S. 496 (1939): "Wherever the title of streets and parks may rest they have immemorially been held in trust for the use of the public and, time out of mind, have been used for purposes of assembly, communicating thoughts between citizens, and discussing public questions. Such use of the streets and public places has, from ancient times, been a part of the privileges, immunities, rights and liberties of citizens. The privilege [to] use the streets and parks for communication of views on national questions may be regulated in the interest of all; [but] it must not, in the guise of regulation, be abridged or denied." In answer to Justice Holmes's suggestion that a city is the equivalent of a private proprietor possessing a right to exclude, Justice Roberts suggested that the public has "a kind of First-Amendment easement" of access to the streets and parks for purposes of speech. Kalven, "The Concept of the Public Forum: Cox v. Louisiana," 1965 Sup. Ct. Rev. 1.

2. ***Guaranteed access vs. equal access: is the issue distribution or discrimination?*** Does the First Amendment mandate some guaranteed minimum access to the public forum? Or does it merely require that, if the public forum is opened to speech, it is opened on an evenhanded basis? Both answers appear in different strands of the early cases concerning public forums. One strand suggests that government *must* make some public places available for the expression of ideas. This strand treats the streets and parks as important to the distribution of speech. Just as handbilling is the "poor man's printing press," so too streets and parks have special importance for those who cannot afford to resort to other means of communication. On this view, access to the public forum operates as a compelled subsidy for speech that otherwise might not be heard. Another strand in the early public forum cases focuses on discrimination rather than distribution. On this view, government's obligation is merely to provide *equal* access to public places if it permits access for speech at all. On this view, the danger is not that there will be too little speech, but that the government will pick and choose among

speakers in a biased way. Might the two different approaches point to different outcomes in some cases? How would each approach treat a law banning "radical demonstrations in the park"? How would each approach treat a law banning "all demonstrations in the park"?

For an endorsement of the broader, guaranteed-access view, see Kalven, "The Concept of the Public Forum: Cox v. Louisiana," 1965 Sup. Ct. Rev. 1 ("[I]n an open democratic society the streets, the parks, and other public places are an important facility for public discussion and political process. They are in brief a public forum that the citizen can commandeer."). For a critical reexamination of Kalven's position, see Post, "Between Governance and Management: The History and Theory of the Public Forum," 34 UCLA L. Rev. 1713 (1987) (suggesting that government is subject to greater First Amendment restraints when it acts to govern the general public than when it acts in a "managerial" capacity toward its own institutions). For further discussion of the public forum, see Stone, "Fora Americana: Speech in Public Places," 1974 Sup. Ct. Rev. 233; Cass, "First Amendment Access to Government Facilities," 65 Va. L. Rev. 1287 (1979); Goldberger, "Judicial Scrutiny in Public Forum Cases: Misplaced Trust in the Judgment of Public Officials," 32 Buffalo L. Rev. 175 (1983); and Farber & Nowak, "The Misleading Nature of Public Forum Analysis: Content and Context in First Amendment Adjudication," 70 Va. L. Rev. 1219 (1984).

3. ***Early cases: standardless licensing and the problem of discrimination.*** Several of the Court's early public forum decisions invalidated standardless licensing schemes for conferring too much discretion on public officials to discriminate on the basis of content in regulating access to the public forum. These cases give more support to the equal-access than the guaranteed-access approach. For example, in Lovell v. Griffin (1938; p. 1366 below), the Court invalidated a conviction for leafleting without a license from the city manager on the ground that the licensing scheme vested unfettered discretion in the city manager. Hague v. CIO, the 1939 case containing Justice Roberts's famous dictum, relied on Lovell in holding a Jersey City, New Jersey, ordinance "void upon its face" because access to streets and parks required a permit, and the standards of the ordinance governing issuance of the permit did not adequately curb the possible use of discretion. Thus, a permit could be refused on the "mere opinion [of the head of the police] that such refusal will prevent 'riots, disturbances or disorderly assemblage.' It can thus [be] made the instrument of arbitrary suppression of free expression of views on [national affairs]." That risked "uncontrolled official suppression." Similarly, in Cantwell v. Connecticut (1940; p. 990 above), the Court invalidated a law requiring official approval for the solicitation of contributions to "religious causes."

And in **Saia v. New York**, 334 U.S. 558 (1948), the Court's 5–4 decision held invalid a Lockport, New York, ordinance prohibiting the use of amplification devices without the permission of the police chief. Relying on Lovell, Hague, and Cantwell, Justice DOUGLAS's majority opinion found the ordinance unconstitutional "on its face" for establishing a standardless "previous restraint" on free speech. He stated: "Loud-speakers are today indispensable instruments of effective public speech. The sound truck has become an accepted method of political campaigning. It is the way people are reached. [This] ordinance would be a dangerous weapon if it were allowed to get a hold on our public life. [When] a city allows an official to ban them in his uncontrolled discretion, it sanctions a device for suppression of free communication of ideas. In this case a permit is denied because some persons were said to have found the sound annoying. In the next one a permit may be denied because some people find the ideas annoying. Annoyance at ideas can be cloaked in annoyance at sound. The power of censorship inherent in this type of ordinance reveals its vice." Justice FRANKFURTER dissented, joined by Justices Reed and Burton, arguing that "no arbitrary action or discrimination" had been shown, and that loudspeakers were instruments of "aural aggression" that could intrude into "cherished privacy: [Surely] there is not a constitutional right to force unwilling people to listen." Justice Jackson also dissented.

For later analogues to these early cases emphasizing the dangers of abuse of official discretion over speech, and thus the equal-access rather than the guaranteed-access approach, see, e.g., **Staub v. Baxley**, 355 U.S. 313 (1958) (striking down on its face an ordinance prohibiting the solicitation of membership in dues-paying organizations without a permit from city officials, and holding that First Amendment freedoms may not be made "contingent upon the uncontrolled will of an official"); **Hynes v. Mayor of Oradell**, 425 U.S. 610 (1976) (invalidating as vague an ordinance requiring advance notice to police in writing by "any person desiring to canvass, solicit or call from house to house [for] a recognized charitable [or] political campaign or cause," holding that such an ordinance suffered "from the vice condemned in [Lovell, Cantwell, and Staub]"); **Lakewood v. Plain Dealer Publishing Co.**, 486 U.S. 750 (1988) (invalidating a city ordinance requiring a permit from the mayor in order to place newsracks on public property, holding that it conferred impermissibly "unbridled discretion").

In contrast to these standardless licensing schemes, permit requirements for speech in the public forum have been upheld when they contain some objective criteria that curtail the possibility of discrimination against disfavored content. In **Cox v. New Hampshire**, 312 U.S. 569 (1941), a unanimous Court affirmed the convictions of several Jehovah's Witnesses for violating a state law prohibiting a "parade or procession" upon a public street without first obtaining a permit from local authorities and paying a license fee of not more than three hundred dollars a day. The defendants had marched on busy city sidewalks carrying signs bearing such slogans as "Religion is a Snare and a Racket" and "Serve God and Christ the King." They did not apply for a permit and none was issued.

Writing for the Court, Chief Justice HUGHES stated: "The authority of a municipality to impose regulations in order to assure the safety and convenience of the people in the use of public highways has never been regarded as inconsistent with civil liberties. [The] control of travel on the streets of cities is the most familiar illustration of this recognition of social need. Where a restriction of the use of highways in that relation is designed to promote the public convenience in the interest of all, it cannot be disregarded by the attempted exercise of some civil right which in other circumstances would be entitled to protection. One would not be justified in ignoring the familiar red traffic light because he thought it his religious duty to disobey the municipal [command]. As regulation of the use of the streets for parades and processions is a traditional exercise of control by local government, the question in a particular case is whether that control is exerted so as not to deny or unwarrantedly abridge the right of assembly and the opportunities for the communication of thought and the discussion of public questions immemorially associated with resort to public places.

"In the instant case, we are aided by the opinion of the Supreme Court of the State, [which] defined the limitations of the authority conferred for the granting of licenses. [T]he state court considered and defined the duty of the licensing authority and the rights of the appellants to a license for their parade, with regard only to considerations of time, place and manner so as to conserve the public convenience. The obvious advantage of requiring application for a permit [was] giving the public authorities notice in advance so as to afford opportunity for proper policing. [Moreover,] the license served 'to prevent confusion by overlapping parades, [to] secure convenient use of the streets by other travelers, and to minimize the risk of disorder.' [If] a municipality has authority to control the use of its public streets for parades or processions, as it undoubtedly has, it cannot be denied authority to give consideration, without unfair discrimination, to time, place and manner in relation to the other proper uses of the streets. We find it impossible to say that the limited authority conferred by the licensing provisions of the statute in question as thus construed by the state court contravened any constitutional right.[1] [There] is no evidence that the statute has been administered otherwise than in the fair and non-discriminatory manner which the state court has construed it to [require]."

Consider the following comment: "Of course, Cox v. New Hampshire did no more than to give a general standard for accommodation of the conflicting interests. It did not tell whether certain congested areas or certain times of the day might not always be held unavailable for parading, nor whether the size of some crowds might always be too large. But it seems [to] symbolize the ideal of Robert's Rules of Order for use of the public forum of the streets." Kalven, "The Concept of the Public Forum: Cox v. Louisiana," 1965 Sup. Ct. Rev. 1. But see Baker, "Unreasoned Reasonableness: Mandatory Parade Permits and Time, Place, and Manner Restrictions," 32 Hastings L.J. 711 (1981) (emphasizing the harms of licensing schemes: the loss of " 'spontaneous' demonstrations," the requirement that protestors "bow to the very authorities" they may be criticizing, and the creation of opportunities for subtle official "harassment").

4. ***Early cases: total medium bans and the problem of distribution.*** May government deny access to the public forum for an entire medium of speech, so long as it does so evenhandedly? Is such a total medium ban an impermissible interference with free speech even when the risks of abuse of discretion are absent? In **Schneider v. New Jersey**, 308 U.S. 147 (1939), and consolidated cases from other states, the Court invalidated local ordinances forbidding distribution of leaflets. The cities' central defense was

[1] The Court also sustained the license fee requirement, noting that it was "not a revenue tax, but one to meet the expense incident to the administration of the Act," and thus constitutional. Should municipalities be permitted to impose fees—even very large fees—so long as they are designed to defray the cost of policing? Could such a scheme be attacked as imposing an undue financial burden on the exercise of a constitutional right? See generally Blasi, "Prior Restraints on Demonstrations," 68 Mich. L. Rev. 1481 (1970). See also Goldberger, "A Reconsideration of Cox v. New Hampshire: Can Demonstrators be Required to Pay the Costs of Using America's Public Forums?," 62 Tex. L. Rev. 403 (1983) (arguing that a "proper distribution of costs" would allocate "the costs generated by speech activities to the society as a whole"); Neisser, "Charging for Free Speech: User Fees and Insurance in the Marketplace of Ideas," 74 Geo. L.J. 257 (1985). The Court has never invalidated a content-neutral user fee. Recall, however, the Court's invalidation in Forsyth Co. v. Nationalist Movement (1992; p. 997 above) of a user fee to be calculated according to the anticipated hostility of the audience. Are other advance payment conditions—e.g., insurance requirements—vulnerable to a First Amendment attack?

that flat bans were necessary to prevent littering. Justice ROBERTS, writing for the Court, replied: "Municipal authorities [have] a duty to keep their communities' streets open for movement of people and [property]. So long as legislation to this end does not abridge the constitutional liberty of one rightfully upon the street to import information through speech or the distribution of literature, it may lawfully regulate the conduct of those using the streets. For example, [the] guarantee of freedom of speech or of the press [does not] deprive a municipality of power to enact regulations against throwing literature broadcast in the streets. [But this] Court has characterized the freedom of speech and freedom of press as fundamental personal rights and liberties. [Mere] legislative preferences or beliefs respecting matters of public convenience may well support regulation directed at other personal activities, but be insufficient to justify such as diminishes the exercise of rights so vital to the maintenance of democratic institutions. And so, as cases arise, the delicate and difficult task falls upon the courts to weigh the circumstances and to appraise the substantiality of the reasons advanced in support of the regulation of the free enjoyment of the rights.

"[Although] the alleged offenders were not charged with themselves scattering paper in the streets, their convictions were sustained upon the theory that distribution by them encouraged or resulted in such littering. We are of opinion that the purpose to keep the streets clean [is] insufficient to justify an ordinance which prohibits a person rightfully on a public street from handing literature to one willing to receive it. Any burden imposed upon the city authorities in cleaning and caring for the streets as an indirect consequence of such distribution results from the constitutional protection of the freedom of speech and press."

Note that Schneider accepted that a city's interest in preventing littering and keeping its streets clean is a legitimate and content-neutral local interest, and that distributing leaflets creates a risk of littering. Yet the Court struck down the ban, by applying a variety of strict scrutiny. Invalidating the leaflet ban might impose greater cost on the city in cleaning the streets; yet that was a cost that had to be borne because of the First Amendment. And antilitter laws were available as a less restrictive means. As Kalven stated in "The Concept of the Public Forum," supra: "Leaflet distribution in public places [is] a method of communication that carries as an inextricable and expected consequence substantial littering of the [streets]. It is also a method of communication of some annoyance to a majority of people so [addressed]. Yet the constitutional balance in Schneider was struck emphatically in favor of keeping the public forum open for this mode of communication. [The] operative theory of the Court, at least for the leaflet situation, is that, although it is a method of communication that interferes with the public use of the streets, the right to the streets as a public forum is such that leaflet distribution cannot be prohibited and can be regulated only for weighty reasons." Kalven concluded that Schneider strengthened the case for an assured minimum access right to the streets as a public forum.

Like the decision in Schneider invalidating a flat ban on leafleting, the decision in **Martin v. City of Struthers**, 319 U.S. 141 (1943), invalidated an ordinance prohibiting a medium of communication: here, the distribution of handbills to residences by ringing doorbells or otherwise summoning residents to the door. The City of Struthers, an Ohio industrial community, argued that the law was necessary to protect residents from annoyance and crime; and it emphasized that many of the residents worked night shifts and slept days, making them especially vulnerable to "casual bell pushers" disrupting their sleep. The ordinance was challenged by a Jehovah's Witness who had gone door-to-door to distribute leaflets advertising a religious meeting. In an opinion by Justice BLACK, the Court struck down the ordinance: "While door to door distributors of literature may be either a nuisance or a blind for criminal activities, they may also be useful members of society engaged in the dissemination of ideas in accordance with the best tradition of free discussion. The widespread use of this method of communication by many groups espousing various causes attests its major importance. [Door-to-door] distribution of circulars is essential to the poorly financed causes of little people. Freedom to distribute information to every citizen whenever he desires to receive it is so clearly vital to the preservation of a free society that, putting aside reasonable police and health regulations of time and manner of distribution, it must be fully preserved." Justice Black noted that it would be permissible to make it an offense "for any person to ring the bell of a householder who has appropriately indicated that he is unwilling to be disturbed. [Because the] dangers of distribution [such as annoyance and crime] can so easily be controlled by traditional legal methods, leaving to each householder the full right to decide whether he will receive strangers as visitors, [the] stringent prohibition [here] can serve no purpose but that forbidden by the Constitution, the naked restriction of the dissemination of ideas."

Compare with the decisions in Schneider and Martin the decision in **Kovacs v. Cooper**, 336 U.S. 77 (1949), which upheld a Trenton, New Jersey, ordinance designed to regulate loudspeakers. Kovacs was convicted of violating the ordinance, which banned "any device known as a sound truck, loud speaker or sound amplifier [which] emits therefrom loud and raucous noises and is attached to and upon any vehicle operated or standing [upon] streets or public places." Justice REED's plurality opinion was joined only by Chief Justice Vinson and Justice Burton. He indicated that absolute prohibition of loudspeakers would probably be unconstitutional but found that the ordinance was valid because, as construed by the state court, it applied only to loudspeakers emitting "loud and raucous" noises. He explained: "City streets are recognized as a normal place for the exchange of ideas by speech or paper. But this does not mean the freedom is beyond all control. We think it is a permissible exercise of legislative discretion to bar sound trucks with broadcasts of public interest, amplified to a loud and raucous volume, from the public ways of municipalities. On the business streets, [such] distractions would be dangerous to traffic at all hours useful for the dissemination of information, and in the residential thoroughfares the quiet and tranquility so desirable for city dwellers would likewise be at the mercy of advocates of particular religious, social or political persuasions. We cannot believe that rights of free speech compel a municipality to allow such mechanical voice amplification on any of its streets."

Justice JACKSON concurred in the result even though, unlike Justice Reed, he viewed the ordinance as a flat ban on loudspeakers. He thought the prohibition was justified because loudspeakers conflict "with quiet enjoyment of home and park": loudspeaker regulations were permissible so long as they did not seek "to censor the contents." He agreed with the dissenters that the plurality opinion repudiated Saia. Saia, he noted, "struck down a more moderate exercise of the state's police power" than the one sustained here. In another opinion concurring in the result, Justice FRANKFURTER also voted to sustain the ordinance as a flat ban, in accordance with his Saia dissent. He emphasized that, so long as a city does not seek to censor or discriminate among ideas, "it is not for us to supervise the limits the legislature may impose in safeguarding the steadily narrowing opportunities for serenity and reflection."

Justice BLACK, joined by Justices Douglas and Rutledge, dissented: "The appellant was neither charged with nor convicted of operating a sound truck that emitted 'loud and raucous noises.' The charge [was] that he violated the city ordinance 'in that he [used] a device known as a sound truck.' [This] ordinance wholly bars the use of all loud speakers mounted upon any vehicle in any of the city's public streets. In my view this repudiation of [Saia] makes a dangerous and unjustifiable breach in the constitutional barriers designed to insure freedom of expression. Ideas and beliefs are today chiefly disseminated to the masses of people through the press, radio, moving pictures, and public address systems. [The] basic premise of the First Amendment is that all present instruments of communication, as well as others that inventive genius may bring into being, shall be free from governmental censorship or prohibition. Laws which hamper the free use of some instruments of communication thereby favor competing channels. [Thus,] laws like [this] can give an overpowering influence to views of owners of legally favored instruments of communication.

"There are many people who have ideas that they wish to disseminate but who do not have enough money to own or control publishing plants, newspapers, radios, moving picture studios, or chains of show places. Yet everybody knows the vast reaches of these powerful channels of communication which from the very nature of our economic system must be under the control and guidance of comparatively few people. [It] is no reflection on the value of preserving freedom for dissemination of the ideas of publishers of newspapers [etc.] to believe that transmission of ideas through public speaking is also essential. [Criticism] of governmental action [should] not be limited to criticisms by press, radio, and moving pictures. [And] it is an obvious fact that public speaking today without sound amplifiers is a wholly inadequate way to reach the people on a large scale. Consequently, to tip the scales against transmission of ideas through public speaking [is] to deprive the people of a large part of the basic advantages of the receipt of ideas that the First Amendment was designed to protect." Justice Murphy also dissented.

Would a flat ban on all sound trucks be constitutional? Should it be? Did the various opinions in Kovacs settle the issue? Are the access claims of loudspeaker users entitled to special weight because of the importance of sound trucks (like leaflets) as a form of "poor man's printing press"? Is a ban on loudspeakers justifiable because of a legislative judgment that the particular method of communication is obnoxious? Would a specific ban on all speeches or marches in residential neighborhoods be similarly supportable on grounds of deference to legislative judgment? A ban on all street demonstrations? Would it depend on the available alternative communication channels?

In the decades following these cases, the Court extended the antidiscrimination principle in Schneider, Martin and the Kovacs dissents to invalidate nearly every content-based regulation in the public forum. But the

Court upheld several regulations that challengers sought to characterize as total medium bans, characterizing them instead as "time, place, and manner" regulations that were to be upheld so long as the government could show they were closely tailored to a significant governmental interest. The distributive strand of the Schneider line of cases stayed partially alive in the Court's admonition that time, place, and manner laws must also leave open "ample alternative channels of communication." But such a requirement was less protective of speakers than Justice Roberts's approach in Schneider, which had suggested that "one is not to have the exercise of his liberty of expression in appropriate places abridged on the plea that it may be exercised in some other place."

Schneider and its progeny were never overruled, however, and in 1994, the Rehnquist Court resurrected them in a decision demonstrating that the presumption against total medium bans is, at least in some circumstances, still alive. In **City of Ladue v. Gilleo**, 512 U.S. 43 (1994), the Court unanimously invalidated an ordinance of the City of Ladue, a residential suburb of St. Louis, Missouri, that banned the posting of most signs in order to minimize visual clutter. The ordinance provided for ten exceptions, including signs identifying a home or business, for-sale signs, and on-site signs advertising gasoline. Gilleo challenged the ordinance because it barred her from placing an 8.5- by 11-inch sign in the second story window of her home stating, "For Peace in the Gulf." The district court and the court of appeals invalidated the ordinance on the ground that the selective exemptions rendered it impermissibly content-based. Justice STEVENS wrote for the Court affirming the judgment, but on an expressly different ground. He held that, even assuming that the ordinance and the exemptions were content-neutral, the ordinance banned "too much" speech: "In examining the propriety of Ladue's near-total prohibition of residential signs, we will assume, arguendo, the validity of the City's submission that the various exemptions are free of impermissible content or viewpoint discrimination [because the distinctions are drawn to distinguish signs that are likely to cause more visual clutter from those that are not. Nevertheless,] Ladue has almost completely foreclosed a venerable means of communication that is both unique and important. [Often] placed on lawns or in windows, residential signs play an important part in political campaigns, during which they are displayed to signal the resident's support for particular candidates, parties, or causes. [Our] prior decisions have voiced particular concern with laws that foreclose an entire medium of expression. [Lovell; Martin; Schneider.] Although prohibitions foreclosing entire media may be completely free of content or viewpoint discrimination, the danger they pose to the freedom of speech is readily apparent—by eliminating a common means of speaking, such measures can suppress too much speech.

"Ladue contends, however, that its ordinance is a mere regulation of the 'time, place, or manner' of speech because residents remain free to convey their desired messages by other means, such as hand-held signs, 'letters, handbills, flyers, telephone calls, newspaper advertisements, bumper stickers, speeches, and neighborhood or community meetings.' [We] are not persuaded that adequate substitutes exist for the important medium of speech that Ladue has closed off. Displaying a sign from one's own residence often carries a message quite distinct from placing the same sign someplace else, or conveying the same text or picture by other means. Precisely because of their location, such signs provide information about the identity of the 'speaker.' [Residential] signs are an unusually cheap and convenient form of communication. Especially for persons of modest means or limited mobility, a yard or window sign may have no practical substitute.

"[A] special respect for individual liberty in the home has long been part of our culture and our law; that principle has special resonance when the government seeks to constrain a person's ability to speak there. Most Americans would be understandably dismayed, given that tradition, to learn that it was illegal to display from their window an 8- by 11-inch sign expressing their political views. Whereas the government's need to mediate among various competing uses, including expressive ones, for public streets and facilities is constant and unavoidable, see [Cox v. New Hampshire], its need to regulate temperate speech from the home is surely much less pressing. Our decision that Ladue's ban on almost all residential signs violates the First Amendment by no means leaves the City powerless to address the ills that may be associated with residential signs. We are confident that more temperate measures could in large part satisfy Ladue's stated regulatory needs without harm to the First Amendment rights of its citizens." Justice O'Connor wrote a separate concurrence suggesting that the Court should have decided first whether the ordinance was content-based.

Did the sign ban struck down in Ladue differ in any material respect from the medium bans at issue in Schneider, Martin and Kovacs? How important was it to the holding in Ladue that the ban regulated the use of one's own private home? Should it have mattered whether or not Gilleo herself was advancing "the poorly financed causes of little people"? For pre-Ladue background, see Stone, "Content-Neutral Restrictions," 54 U. Chi. L. Rev. 46 (1987).

Drawing heavily upon early leafleting cases such as Schneider and Martin, the Court in **Watchtower Bible & Tract Society v. Stratton**, 536 U.S. 150 (2002), by a vote of 8–1, invalidated a municipal ordinance's permit requirement for door-to-door activity, reasoning that even though the ordinance was nondiscriminatory, and even though it did not amount to a total medium ban, it inhibited too much speech. The ordinance provided: "The practice of going in and upon private property and/or the private residence of Village residents in the Village by canvassers, solicitors, peddlers, hawkers, itinerant merchants or transient vendors of merchandise or services, not having been invited to do so by the owners or occupants of such private property or residences, and not having first obtained a permit, [for] the purpose of advertising, promoting, selling and/or explaining any product, service, organization or cause, or for the purpose of soliciting orders for the sale of goods, wares, merchandise or services, is hereby declared to be a nuisance and is prohibited."

Justice STEVENS wrote for the Court: "For over 50 years, the Court has invalidated restrictions on door-to-door canvassing and pamphleteering. It is more than historical accident that most of these cases involved First Amendment challenges brought by Jehovah's Witnesses, because door-to-door canvassing is mandated by their religion. [The] Jehovah's Witnesses ['take] literally the mandate of the Scriptures, "Go ye into all the world, and preach the gospel to every creature." Mark 16:15.' Moreover, because they lack significant financial resources, the ability of the Witnesses to proselytize is seriously diminished by regulations that burden their efforts to canvass door-to-door." Justice Stevens noted that cases like Schneider and Martin had established "the historical importance of door-to-door canvassing and pamphleteering as vehicles for the dissemination of ideas." He also noted that dicta in those cases had acknowledged "the interests a town may have in some form of regulation, particularly when the solicitation of money is involved, in preventing the use of door-to-door canvassing as a shield for fraud or crime."

Justice Stevens declined to choose a particular standard of review in assessing the constitutionality of the ordinance: "We find it unnecessary [to] resolve that dispute because the breadth of speech affected by the ordinance and the nature of the regulation make it clear that the Court of Appeals erred in upholding it. [Had the ordinance] been construed to apply only to commercial activities and the solicitation of funds, arguably the ordinance would have been tailored to the Village's interest in protecting the privacy of its residents and preventing fraud. Yet [the] provisions apply to a significant number of noncommercial 'canvassers' promoting a wide variety of 'causes.' [The] ordinance unquestionably applies, not only to religious causes, but to political activity as well. It would seem to extend to 'residents casually soliciting the votes of neighbors,' or ringing doorbells to enlist support for employing a more efficient garbage collector. The mere fact that the ordinance covers so much speech raises constitutional concerns. It is offensive—not only to the values protected by the First Amendment, but to the very notion of a free society—that in the context of everyday public discourse a citizen must first inform the government of her desire to speak to her neighbors and then obtain a permit to do so." In particular, Justice Stevens noted, the permit requirement inhibited both anonymous and spontaneous speech.

But, he continued, "[t]he breadth and unprecedented nature of this regulation does not alone render the ordinance invalid. Also central to our conclusion that the ordinance does not pass First Amendment scrutiny is that it is not tailored to the Village's stated interests. Even if the interest in preventing fraud could adequately support the ordinance insofar as it applies to commercial transactions and the solicitation of funds, that interest provides no support for its application to petitioners, to political campaigns, or to enlisting support for unpopular causes. The Village, however, argues that the ordinance is nonetheless valid because it serves the two additional interests of protecting the privacy of the resident and the prevention of crime. With respect to the former, it seems clear that [a provision allowing] posting of 'No Solicitation' signs, [coupled] with the resident's unquestioned right to refuse to engage in conversation with unwelcome visitors, provides ample protection for the unwilling listener. The annoyance caused by an uninvited knock on the front door is the same whether or not the visitor is armed with a permit. With respect to the latter, it seems unlikely that the absence of a permit would preclude criminals from knocking on doors and engaging in conversations not covered by the ordinance. They might, for example, ask for directions or permission to use the telephone, or pose as surveyors or census takers." Justice BREYER, joined by Justices Souter and Ginsburg, concurred separately to emphasize that an interest in crime prevention could not justify the ordinance because it had not been the village's actual purpose at the time of enactment, and "in the intermediate scrutiny context, the Court ordinarily does not supply reasons the legislative body has not given." Justice Scalia, joined by Justice Thomas, submitted a brief concurrence in the judgment.

Chief Justice REHNQUIST was the lone dissenter: "More than half a century ago we recognized that canvassers, 'whether selling pots or distributing leaflets, may lessen the peaceful enjoyment of a home,' and that 'burglars frequently pose as canvassers, either in order that they may have a pretense to discover whether a house is empty and hence ripe for burglary, or for the purpose of spying out the premises in order that they may return later.' [Martin v. City of Struthers.] These problems continue to be associated with door-to-door canvassing, as are even graver ones. A recent double murder in Hanover, New Hampshire, [of two Dartmouth professors by two teenagers posing as canvassers] illustrates these dangers. [For] over 60 years, we have categorically stated that a permit requirement for door-to-door canvassers, which gives no discretion to the issuing authority, is constitutional. [The] Court today, however, abruptly changes course and invalidates [the] Stratton ordinance [even though it] suffers from none of the defects deemed fatal in [earlier] decisions. The ordinance does not prohibit door-to-door canvassing; it merely requires that canvassers fill out a form and receive a permit. Cf. Martin. The mayor does not exercise any discretion in deciding who receives a permit; approval of the permit is automatic upon proper completion of the form. Cf. Cantwell.

"Just as troubling as the Court's ignoring over 60 years of precedent is the difficulty of discerning from the Court's opinion what exactly it is about the Stratton ordinance that renders it unconstitutional. It is not clear what test the Court is applying, or under which part of that indeterminate test the ordinance fails. [There] is no support in our case law for applying anything more stringent than intermediate scrutiny to the ordinance. The ordinance is content neutral and does not bar anyone from going door-to-door in Stratton. It merely regulates the manner in which one must canvass. [It] is aimed at three significant governmental interests: the prevention of fraud, the prevention of crime, and the protection of privacy. [And it] leave[s] open ample alternatives for expression. [Most] obviously, canvassers are free to go door-to-door after filling out the permit application. And those without permits may communicate on public sidewalks, on street corners, through the mail, or through the telephone. Intermediate scrutiny analysis thus confirms what our cases have long said: A discretionless permit requirement for canvassers does not violate the First Amendment."

THE "TIME, PLACE AND MANNER" TEST

Recall that in Cox v. New Hampshire, (1941; p. 1213 above) Chief Justice Hughes wrote that a government faced with public access claims by speakers is entitled to "give consideration, without unfair discrimination, to time, place and manner in relation to the other proper uses of the streets." What government interests justify such time, place, and manner regulations in the traditional public forum of the streets and parks? How closely must such regulations fit those asserted interests? Should courts defer to legislative and executive judgments on the management of public forums? Or should they scrutinize them independently to make sure government has not, "in the guise of regulation," suppressed too much speech? Should the Court's only concern be content neutrality, or does an emphasis on discrimination or the lack of it obscure underlying problems with the degree of access speakers enjoy? Consider the following decisions elaborating the standard of review for time, place and manner regulations, organized by reference to the asserted government interest.

PUBLIC ORDER AND SAFETY

In **Cox v. Louisiana**, 379 U.S. 536 (1965), the Court invalidated a breach of peace conviction arising from a civil rights demonstration near a courthouse. In the same decision, the Court also overturned Cox's conviction under a Louisiana law prohibiting the obstruction of "the free, convenient and normal use of any public sidewalk, street, [or] other passageway [by] impeding, hindering, stifling, retarding or restraining traffic or passage thereon." Justice GOLDBERG wrote for the Court: "The rights of free speech and assembly, while fundamental in our democratic society, still do not mean that everyone with opinions or beliefs to express may address a group at any public place and at any time. The constitutional guarantee of liberty implies the existence of an organized society maintaining public order, without which liberty itself would be lost in the excesses of anarchy. The control of travel on the streets is a clear example of governmental responsibility to insure this necessary order. A restriction in that relation, designed to promote the public convenience in the interest of all, and not susceptible to abuses of discriminatory application, cannot be disregarded by the attempted exercise of some civil right which, in other circumstances, would be entitled to protection. One would not be justified in ignoring the familiar red light because this was thought to be a means of social protest. Nor could one, contrary to traffic regulations, insist upon a street meeting in the middle of Times Square at the rush hour as a form of freedom of [speech]. Governmental authorities have the duty and responsibility to keep their streets open and available for movement.

"[But we] have no occasion in this case to consider the constitutionality of the uniform, consistent, and nondiscriminatory application of a statute forbidding all access to streets and other public facilities for parades and meetings. Although the statute here involved on its face precludes all street assemblies and parades, it has not been so [applied]. City officials [indicated] that certain meetings and parades are permitted in Baton Rouge, even though they have the effect of obstructing traffic, provided prior approval is obtained. [The] statute itself provides no standards for the determination of local officials as to which assemblies to permit or which to prohibit. [It] appears that the authorities in Baton Rouge permit or prohibit parades or street meetings in their completely uncontrolled discretion. [The] pervasive restraint on freedom of discussion by the practice of the authorities under the statute is not any less effective than a statute expressly permitting such selective [enforcement]. [Such] broad discretion in a public official [permits] the official to act as a censor."

Compare the Court's decision upholding—as a permissible time, place, and manner regulation—the "booth rule" restricting literature distribution and solicitation of funds at the Minnesota State Fair in **Heffron v. International Society for Krishna Consciousness (ISKCON)**, 452 U.S. 640 (1981). Minnesota State Fair Rule 6.05 prohibited the sale or distribution of any merchandise, including printed or written material, except from booths rented to all applicants in a nondiscriminatory manner on a first-come, first-served basis. The rule was challenged by ISKCON, a religious society espousing the views of the Krishna religion. ISKCON asserted that the Rule suppressed the practice of Sankirtan, a religious ritual that enjoins its members to go into public places to distribute or sell religious literature and to solicit donations for the support of the Krishna religion. The highest state court struck down the rule, but Justice WHITE's majority opinion found the restriction permissible. He explained: "[The] First Amendment does not guarantee the right to communicate one's views at all times and places or in any manner that may be desired. [See Cox v. Louisiana.] [T]he activities of ISKCON, like those of others protected by the First Amendment, are subject to reasonable time, place, and manner restrictions. [Cox v. New Hampshire.] We have often approved restrictions of that kind provided that they are justified without reference to the content of the regulated speech, that they serve a significant governmental interest, and that in doing so they leave open ample alternative channels for communication of the information." Under that standard, the Court held the booth rule valid.

Justice White found Rule 6.05 clearly content-neutral, for it applied "evenhandedly to all who wish to distribute and sell written materials or to solicit funds. [Nor] does Rule 6.05 suffer from the more covert forms of discrimination that may result when arbitrary discretion is vested in some governmental authority. The method of allocating space is a straightforward first-come, first-served system." Moreover, it served a "significant governmental interest"—"the need to maintain the orderly movement of the crowd given the large number of exhibitors and persons attending the Fair." (The Fair had an average daily attendance of over 100,000.) "[I]t is clear that a State's interest in protecting the 'safety and convenience' of persons using a public forum is a valid governmental objective. [And the] flow of the crowd and demands of safety are more pressing in the context of the Fair [than in the typical city street or park]." In response to the state court's reasoning that an exemption for the Hare Krishna devotees alone would not defeat the state's interest, Justice White said: "[The] justification for the Rule should not be measured by the disorder that would result from granting an exemption solely to ISKCON. [If the Rule cannot be applied to ISKCON], it is no more valid with respect to the [other] organizations that have rented booths at the Fair. [Intercepting] fair patrons as they move about, [as ISKCON wishes to do], and if success is achieved, stopping them momentarily or for longer periods as money is given or exchanged for literature [could lead to] widespread disorder at the fairgrounds.

Justice White found as well that "alternative forums for the expression [exist] despite the effects of the Rule": "[The] Rule does not prevent ISKCON from practicing Sankirtan anywhere outside the fairgrounds. [It] does not exclude ISKCON from the fairgrounds, nor does it deny that organization the right to conduct any desired activity at some point within the forum. Its members may mingle with the crowd and orally propagate their views [and] may also arrange for a booth and distribute and sell literature and solicit funds from that location on the fairgrounds itself. [Considering] the limited functions of the Fair and the [confined] area within which it operates, we are unwilling to say that [the Rule] does not provide ISKCON and other organizations with an adequate means to sell and solicit on the fairgrounds."

Four Justices were in partial dissent. Justice BRENNAN, joined by Justices Marshall and Stevens, agreed that the limitation of literature sales and funds solicitation to fixed booths was justified, not as a crowd control measure but as an "antifraud measure." But they found the ban on distribution of literature outside of booths "an overly intrusive means of achieving the State's interest in crowd control." Justice Brennan stated his general approach as follows:

"[Once] a governmental regulation is shown to impinge upon basic First Amendment rights, the burden falls on the government to show the validity of its asserted interest and the absence of less intrusive alternatives. See, e.g., [Schneider]. The challenged 'regulation must be narrowly tailored to further the State's legitimate interest.' [The Rule] does not meet this test. [Significantly], each and every fairgoer, whether political candidate, concerned citizen, or member of a religious group, is free to give speeches, engage in face-to-face advocacy, campaign, or proselytize. No restrictions are placed on any fairgoer's right to speak at any time, at any place, or to any person. [Because of the Rule], however, as soon as a proselytizing member of ISKCON hands out a free copy of the Bhagavad-Gita to an interested listener, or a political candidate distributes his campaign brochure to a potential voter, he becomes subject to arrest and removal from the fairgrounds. This constitutes a significant restriction on First Amendment rights.

"In support of its crowd control justification, the State contends that if fairgoers are permitted to distribute literature, large crowds will gather, blocking traffic lanes and causing safety problems. [But] the State has failed to provide any support for these assertions. Relying on a general, speculative fear of disorder, the [State] has placed a significant restriction on respondents' ability to exercise core First Amendment rights. This restriction is not narrowly drawn to advance the State's interests, and for that reason is unconstitutional. [If] the State had a reasonable concern that distribution in certain parts of the fairgrounds—for example, entrances and exits—would cause disorder, it could have drafted its rule to prohibit distribution of literature at those points. If the State felt it necessary to limit the number of persons distributing an organization's literature, it could, within reason, have done that as well. It had no right, however, to ban all distribution of literature outside the booths." Justice Blackmun also concurred in part and dissented in part, favoring the same result as Justice Brennan.

Should the booth rule have been viewed as a total medium ban akin to the bans on distributing literature struck down in Schneider and Martin, rather than as a permissible time, place, or manner regulation? Distribution was prohibited in the open thoroughfares of the fair and confined to the "private" space of rented booths. Should there have been any concern that the rule would have content-differential effects, disadvantaging unpopular speakers who need to approach their audience because their audience is unlikely to come to them? ISKCON ventured such an argument, but Justice White replied in a footnote: "The argument is interesting but has little force. [A preference for listener-initiated exchanges over those originating with the speaker] is inherent in the determination to confine exhibitors to fixed locations, it applies to all exhibitors alike, and it does not invalidate the Rule as a reasonable time, place, and manner regulation."

AESTHETICS

May government limit speech in order to protect the attractive appearance or ambience of its public spaces, even without regard to concerns of public safety? May it prevent visual or aural "pollution"? Is securing beautiful or tranquil surroundings enough of a reason to limit speech? Is there a danger that assertion of such amorphous, intangible interests might conceal improper hostility to the regulated speech? The Court has recognized government aesthetic interests as substantial or significant in a number of cases.

In **Metromedia, Inc. v. San Diego**, 453 U.S. 490 (1981), for example, the Court reviewed a free speech challenge to a San Diego ordinance regulating billboard displays in order "to eliminate hazards to pedestrians and motorists brought about by distracting sign displays" and "to preserve and improve the appearance of the City." Recall that the Court upheld part of the ordinance restricting commercial billboard displays, see p. 1145 above. While the Court struck down the part of a San Diego ordinance restricting noncommercial billboard displays, the opinions of a majority of the Court—the four members of the plurality plus the three dissenters—indicated considerable general willingness to defer to the government's aesthetic interests.

The plurality opinion of Justice WHITE, joined by Justices Stewart, Marshall, and Powell, acknowledged the problems billboards pose "for land-use planning and development," but found San Diego's ordinance impermissibly content-based because it provided a number of exceptions, including exceptions for on-site commercial signs, government signs, temporary political campaign signs, for-sale and for-lease signs, religious symbols, signs telling the time and temperature, historical commemorative plaques, and signs within shopping malls: "[Billboards] combine communicative and noncommunicative aspects. [The] government has legitimate interests in controlling the noncommunicative aspects of the medium, but [the First Amendment forecloses] a similar interest in controlling the communicative aspects." The plurality found that the exceptions unconstitutionally distinguished among subject matters. The exceptions for commercial billboards inverted the usual First Amendment hierarchy "by affording a greater degree of protection to commercial than to noncommercial speech." And "[w]ith respect to noncommercial speech, the city may not choose the appropriate subjects for public discourse. Because some noncommercial messages may be conveyed on billboards throughout the commercial and industrial zones, San Diego must similarly allow billboards conveying other noncommercial messages throughout those zones."

Justice BRENNAN, joined by Justice Blackmun, concurred in the judgment, focusing not on any discrimination in the ordinance but rather on its distributive aspects. Justice Brennan argued that "the *practical* effect of the San Diego ordinance is to eliminate the billboard as an effective medium of communication. [Instead] of relying on the exceptions to the ban to invalidate the ordinance, I would apply the tests [developed] to analyze content-neutral prohibitions of particular media of communication. [Schad; Schneider; Martin.]" Under such a standard, he argued, the city must show "that a sufficiently substantial governmental interest is directly furthered by the total ban, and that any more narrowly drawn restriction, i.e., anything less than a total ban, would promote less well the achievement of that goal." He found the ban unjustified under that standard. He found the evidentiary support for the traffic safety claims weak, and he was especially skeptical of the asserted aesthetic interests: "[B]efore deferring to a city's judgment, a court must be convinced that the city is seriously and comprehensively addressing aesthetic concerns with respect to its environment." (In comparing Justice White's and Justice Brennan's opinions, recall the discussion at p. 1211 above of the discrimination and distribution—or equal-access and guaranteed-access—strands in the early public forum cases.)

Chief Justice BURGER, Justice REHNQUIST, and Justice STEVENS each filed a separate dissent. Chief Justice Burger chided the plurality for undervaluing the importance of local control over local problems. Because ample alternative channels of communications were available, he would not hold the First Amendment to bar San Diego's justifiable and reasonable effort to do something about "what it perceives—and what it has a right to perceive—as ugly and dangerous eyesores thrust upon its citizens." Justice Stevens's dissent disagreed that completely effective alternative channels of communication were available. But he did not see the diminution of communications opportunities as fatal: "The essential concern embodied in the First Amendment is that government not impose its viewpoint on the public or select the topics on which public debate is permissible," and no viewpoint discrimination was presented. Justice Stevens emphasized that a government interest "in securing beautiful surroundings" may sometimes outweigh interests in "uninhibited expression by means of words and pictures in public places." Justice Rehnquist largely agreed with the other dissents.

The Court in Metromedia did not reach the question of the permissibility of a total, content-neutral prohibition of billboards. But the various opinions alluded to such a flat ban in dicta. Justice White, the author of the Metromedia plurality opinion, observed several years later: "A majority of this Court found [in Metromedia] that [aesthetic] considerations *would* be sufficient to justify a content-neutral ban on all outdoor advertising signs, notwithstanding the extent to which such signs convey First Amendment protected messages." Lakewood v. Plain Dealer Publishing Co., 486 U.S. 750, 783 (1988) (White, J., dissenting) (citing the plurality opinion and the dissenting opinions of Burger, C.J., and Rehnquist and Stevens, JJ.) (emphasis added).

Consider in light of Metromedia the following cases involving a ban on the placement of political signs on utility poles and crosswires, and a ban on overnight camping in a public park as applied to anti-homelessness demonstrators. The political sign case arose when Taxpayers for Vincent, a group of supporters of Roland Vincent, a candidate for the Los Angeles City Council, arranged for the production and posting of signs with Vincent's name on them. They attached the signs to utility poles at various locations in Los Angeles by draping them over the cross-arms which support the poles and stapling the cardboard together at the bottom. The signs read: "Roland Vincent—City Council." Acting under a city ordinance, city employees removed all posters attached to utility poles. Most of the signs that were removed were commercial ones, but 48 out of more than 1200 signs removed from public property during the first week of March were "Vincent" signs. This suit challenged the constitutionality of the ordinance. The trial court dismissed the case, but the Court of Appeals reversed. After rejecting an overbreadth challenge, the Supreme Court also rejected Taxpayers' as-applied challenge:

Members of City Council v. Taxpayers for Vincent

466 U.S. 789, 104 S. Ct. 2118, 80 L. Ed. 2d 772 (1984).

▪ JUSTICE STEVENS delivered the opinion of the Court.

Section 28.04 of the Los Angeles Municipal Code prohibits the posting of signs on public property. The question presented is whether that prohibition abridges appellees' freedom of speech within the meaning of the First Amendment. The ordinance prohibits appellees from communicating with the public in a certain manner, and presumably diminishes the total quantity of their communication in the City. [But it] has been clear since this Court's earliest decisions [that] the state may sometimes curtail speech when necessary to advance a significant and legitimate state interest. [The] First Amendment forbids the government from regulating speech in ways that favor some viewpoints or ideas at the expense of [others]. That general rule has no application to this case. For there is not even a hint of bias or censorship in the City's enactment or enforcement of this ordinance.

In [O'Brien] the Court set forth the appropriate [four-step] framework for reviewing a viewpoint neutral regulation of this kind. [In] this case, [Taxpayers] do not dispute that it is within the constitutional power of the City to attempt to improve its appearance, or that this interest is basically unrelated to the suppression of ideas. Therefore the critical inquiries are whether that interest is sufficiently substantial to justify the effect of the ordinance on appellees' expression, and whether that effect is no greater than necessary to accomplish the City's purpose.

[Metromedia] dealt with San Diego's prohibition of certain forms of outdoor billboards. There the Court considered the city's interest in avoiding visual clutter, and seven Justices explicitly concluded that this interest was sufficient to justify a prohibition of billboards. [We] reaffirm the conclusion of the majority in Metromedia. The problem addressed by this ordinance—the visual assault on the citizens of Los Angeles presented by an accumulation of signs posted on public property—constitutes a significant substantive evil within the City's power to prohibit. We turn to the question whether the scope of the restriction on appellees' expressive activity is substantially broader than necessary to protect the City's interest in eliminating visual clutter. The incidental restriction on expression which results from the City's attempt to accomplish such a purpose is considered justified as a reasonable regulation of the time, place, or manner of expression if it is narrowly tailored to serve that interest. [By] banning these signs, the City did no more than eliminate the exact source of the evil it sought to remedy.

It is true that the esthetic interest in preventing the kind of litter that may result from the distribution of leaflets on the public streets and sidewalks cannot support a prophylactic prohibition against the citizens' exercise of that method of expressing his views. In Schneider v. State, the Court held that ordinances that absolutely prohibited handbilling on the streets were invalid. The Court explained that cities could adequately protect the esthetic interest in avoiding litter without abridging protected expression merely by penalizing those who actually litter. Taxpayers contend that their interest in supporting Vincent's political campaign, which affords them a constitutional right to distribute [leaflets] on the public streets of Los Angeles, provides equal support for their asserted right to post temporary signs on objects adjacent to the streets and sidewalks. They argue that the mere fact that their temporary signs "add somewhat" to the city's visual clutter is entitled to no more weight than the temporary unsightliness of discarded handbills and the additional street cleaning burden that were insufficient to justify the ordinances reviewed in Schneider.

The rationale of Schneider is inapposite in the context of the instant case. There, individual citizens were actively exercising their right to communicate directly with potential recipients of their message. The conduct continued only while the speakers or distributors remained on the scene. In this case, appellees posted dozens of temporary signs throughout an area where they would remain unattended until removed. As the Court expressly noted in Schneider, the First Amendment does not "deprive a municipality of power to enact regulations against throwing literature broadcast in the [streets]." A distributor of leaflets has no right simply to scatter his pamphlets in the air—or to toss large quantities of paper from the window of a tall building or a low flying airplane. Characterizing such an activity as a separate means of communication does not diminish the state's power to condemn it as a public nuisance. [With] respect to signs posted by appellees, [it] is the tangible medium of expressing the message that has the adverse impact on the appearance of the landscape. In Schneider, an anti-littering statute could have addressed the substantive evil without prohibiting expressive activity, whereas application of the prophylactic rule actually employed gratuitously infringed upon the right of an individual to communicate directly with a willing listener. Here, the substantive evil—visual blight—is not merely a possible by-product of the activity, but is created by the medium of expression itself. In contrast to Schneider, therefore, the application of [the] ordinance in this case responds precisely to the substantive problem which legitimately concerns the City. The ordinance curtails no more speech than is necessary to accomplish its purpose.

[The challengers argue] that a prohibition against the [posting of signs on public property] cannot be justified on esthetic grounds if it fails to apply to all equally unattractive signs [including those on private property.] [But the] private citizen's interest in controlling the use of his own property justifies the disparate treatment. Moreover, by not extending the ban to all locations, a significant opportunity to communicate by means of temporary signs is preserved, and private property owners' esthetic concerns will keep the posting of signs on their property within reasonable bounds. Even if some visual blight remains, a partial, content-neutral ban may nevertheless enhance the City's appearance.

[A] restriction on expressive activity may be invalid if the remaining modes of communication are inadequate. [E.g., Heffron.] The Los Angeles ordinance does not affect any individual's freedom to exercise the right to speak and to distribute literature in the same place where the posting of signs on public property is prohibited. To the extent that the posting of signs on public property has advantages over these forms of expression, there is no reason to believe that these same advantages cannot be obtained through other means. To the contrary, the findings [indicate] that there are ample alternative modes of communication in Los Angeles. Notwithstanding appellees' general assertions [concerning] the utility of political posters, nothing in the findings indicates that the posting of political posters on public property is a uniquely valuable or important mode of communication, or that appellees' ability to communicate effectively is threatened by ever-increasing restrictions on expression.

Appellees suggest that the public property covered by the ordinance is [a] "public forum." [Appellees'] reliance on the public forum doctrine is misplaced. They fail to demonstrate the existence of a traditional right of access respecting such items as utility poles for purposes of their communication comparable to that recognized for public streets and parks, and it is clear that "the First Amendment does not guarantee access to government property simply because it is owned or controlled by the government." Rather, the "existence of a right of access to public property and the standard by which limitations upon such a right must be evaluated differ depending on the character of the property at issue." Lampposts can of course be used as signposts, but the mere fact that government property can be used as a vehicle for communication does not mean that the Constitution requires such uses to be permitted.[1] Public property which is not by tradition or designation a forum for public communication may be reserved by the state "for its intended purposes, communicative or otherwise, as long as the regulation on speech is reasonable and not an effort to suppress expression merely because public officials oppose the speaker's view." [Perry.] Given our analysis of the legitimate interest served by the ordinance, its viewpoint neutrality, and the availability of alternative channels of communication, the ordinance is certainly constitutional as applied to appellees under this standard.

Finally, [Taxpayers] argue that Los Angeles could have written an ordinance that would have had a less severe effect on expressive activity such as theirs, by permitting the posting of any kind of sign at any time on some types of public property, or by making a variety of other more specific exceptions to the ordinance: for signs carrying certain types of messages (such as political campaign signs), for signs posted during specific time periods (perhaps during political campaigns), for particular locations (perhaps for areas already cluttered by an excessive number of signs on adjacent private property), or for signs meeting design specifications (such as size or color). Plausible public policy arguments might well be made in support of any such exception, but it by no means follows that it is therefore constitutionally mandated, nor is it clear that some of the suggested exceptions would even be constitutionally permissible. [An] assertion that "Jesus Saves," that "Abortion is Murder," that every woman has the "Right to Choose," or that "Alcohol Kills," may have a claim to a constitutional exemption from the ordinance that is just as strong as "[Roland] Vincent—City Council." To create an exception for appellees' political speech and not these other types of speech might create a risk of engaging in constitutionally forbidden content discrimination. [Carey; Mosley.] Moreover, the volume of permissible postings under such a mandated exemption might so limit the ordinance's effect as to defeat its aim of combatting visual blight. Any constitutionally mandated exception to the City's total prohibition against

[1] Any tangible property owned by the government could be used to communicate—bumper stickers may be placed on official automobiles—and yet appellees could not seriously claim the right to attach "Taxpayer for Vincent" bumper stickers to City-owned automobiles. At some point, the government's relationship to things under its dominion and control is virtually identical to a private owner's property interest in the same kinds of things, and in such circumstances, the State, "no less than a private owner of property, has power to preserve the property under its control for the use to which it is lawfully dedicated." [Footnote by Justice Stevens.]

temporary signs on public property would necessarily rest on a judicial determination [that] the City's interests in esthetics are not sufficiently important to justify the prohibition in that category. But [there is] no basis for questioning the substantiality of the esthetic interest [or] for believing that a uniquely important form of communication has been abridged for the categories of expression engaged in by [the challengers].

Therefore, we accept the City's position that it may decide that the esthetic interest in avoiding "visual clutter" justifies a removal of signs creating or increasing that clutter. [We] hold that on this record [the] interests are sufficiently substantial to justify this content neutral, impartially administered [prohibition]. [Reversed.]

■ JUSTICE BRENNAN, with whom JUSTICES MARSHALL and BLACKMUN join, dissenting.

[Because] the Court's lenient approach towards the restriction of speech for reasons of aesthetics [here and in Metromedia] threatens seriously to undermine the protections of the First Amendment, I dissent. [In my view, Los Angeles] has not shown that its interest in eliminating "visual clutter" justifies its restriction of appellees' ability to communicate with the local electorate. [In] deciding this First Amendment question, the critical importance of the posting of signs as a means of communication must not be overlooked. Use of this medium of communication is particularly valuable in part because it entails a relatively small expense in reaching a wide audience, allows flexibility in accommodating various formats, typographies, and graphics, and conveys its message in a manner that is easily read and understood by its reader or viewer. There may be alternative channels of communication, but the prevalence of a large number of signs in Los Angeles is a strong indication that, for many speakers, those alternatives are far less satisfactory. [There] is no proof [e.g.,] that a sufficient number of private parties would allow the posting of signs on their property. A speaker with a message that is generally unpopular or simply unpopular among property owners is hardly likely to get his message across if forced to rely on this medium. [Similarly], the adequacy of distributing handbills is dubious, [for] a message on a sign will typically reach far more people than one on a handbill. [Because] the City has completely banned the use of this particular medium of communication, and because, given the circumstances, there are no equivalent alternative media that provide an adequate substitute, the Court must examine with particular care the justifications that the City proffers for its ban.

[If a] restriction is content-neutral, the court's task is to determine (1) whether the governmental objective advanced by the restriction is substantial, and (2) whether the restriction imposed on speech is no greater than is essential to further that objective. Unless both conditions are met the restriction must be invalidated. [I suggested] in Metromedia [that] courts should exercise special care in addressing these questions when a purely aesthetic objective is asserted to justify a restriction of speech. [I] adhere to that view. [A]esthetic interests are easy for a city to assert and difficult for a court to evaluate. [The] source of those difficulties is the unavoidable subjectivity of aesthetic judgments. As a consequence, [laws] defended on aesthetic grounds raise problems for judicial review that are not presented by laws defended on more objective grounds—such as national security, public health, or public safety. [E.g.,] a reviewing court faces substantial difficulties determining whether the actual objective is related to the suppression of speech. The asserted interest in aesthetics may be only a facade for content-based suppression. [Thus, the real] objective might simply be the elimination of the messages typically carried by the signs. [The] City might easily mask [such an] objective [by] declaring that signs constitute visual clutter.

[Similarly,] when a total ban is justified solely in terms of aesthetics, the means inquiry necessary to evaluate the constitutionality of the ban may be impeded by deliberate or unintended government manipulation. [Once] the government has identified a substantial aesthetic objective and has selected a preferred means of achieving its objective, it will be possible for the government to correct any mismatch between means and ends by redefining the ends to conform with the means. [When] a court reviews a restriction of speech imposed in order to promote an aesthetic objective, there is a significant possibility that the court will be able to do little more than pay lip service to the First Amendment inquiry into the availability of less restrictive alternatives.

The fact that there are difficulties inherent in judicial review of aesthetics-based restrictions of speech does not imply that government may not engage in such activities. [But] because the implementation of these functions creates special dangers to our First Amendment freedoms, there is a need for more stringent judicial scrutiny than the Court seems willing to exercise. In cases like this, where a total ban is imposed on a particularly valuable method of communication, a court should require the government to provide tangible proof of the legitimacy and substantiality of its aesthetic objective. [Statements] of aesthetic objectives should be accepted as substantial and unrelated to the suppression of speech only if the government demonstrates that it is pursuing an identified objective seriously and comprehensively and in ways that are unrelated to the restriction of speech. [In] this case, however, there is no indication that the City has addressed its visual clutter problem in any way other than by prohibiting the posting of signs—throughout the City and without regard to the density of their presence. Therefore, I would hold that the prohibition violates appellees' First Amendment rights.

[A] more limited approach to the visual clutter problem, however, might well pass constitutional muster. I have no doubt, [for example,] that signs posted on public property in certain areas—including, perhaps, parts of Los Angeles—could contribute to the type of eyesore that a city would genuinely have a substantial interest in eliminating. These areas might include parts of the City that are particularly pristine, reserved for certain uses, designated to reflect certain themes, or so blighted that broad gauged renovation is necessary. Presumably, in these types of areas the City would also regulate the aesthetic environment in ways other than the banning of temporary signs. [Similarly,] Los Angeles might be able to attack its visual clutter problem in more areas of the City by reducing the stringency of the ban, perhaps by regulating the density of temporary signs, and coupling that approach with additional measures designed to reduce other forms of visual clutter. In [this] case, I believe that Los Angeles' total ban sweeps so broadly and trenches so completely on appellees' use of an important medium of political expression that it must be struck down as violative of the [First Amendment].

Clark v. Community for Creative Non-Violence

468 U.S. 288, 104 S. Ct. 3065, 82 L. Ed. 2d 221 (1984).

■ JUSTICE WHITE delivered the opinion of the Court.

The issue in this case is whether a National Park Service regulation prohibiting camping in certain parks violates the First Amendment when applied to prohibit demonstrators from sleeping in Lafayette Park and the Mall in connection with a demonstration intended to call attention to the plight of the homeless. We hold that it does [not].

I. The Interior Department, through the National Park Service, is charged with responsibility for the [management] of the National Parks and is authorized to promulgate rules and regulations for the use of the parks in accordance with the purposes for which they were established. The network of National Parks includes the National Memorial-core parks [Lafayette Park and the Mall].[1] Under the regulations involved in this case, camping in National Parks is permitted only in campgrounds designated for that purpose. No such campgrounds have ever been designated in Lafayette Park or the Mall.[2] [Demonstrations] for the airing of views or grievances are permitted in the Memorial-core parks, but for the most part only by Park Service permits. Temporary structures may be erected for demonstration purposes but may not be used for camping.[3]

In 1982, the Park Service issued a renewable permit to respondent Community for Creative Non-Violence (CCNV) to conduct a wintertime demonstration in Lafayette Park and the Mall for the purpose of demonstrating the plight of the homeless. The permit authorized the erection of two symbolic tent [cities]. The Park Service, however, [denied] CCNV's request that demonstrators be permitted to sleep in the symbolic tents. CCNV and several individuals then filed an action to prevent the application of the anti-camping regulations to the proposed [demonstration].[4]

II. We need not differ with the view of the Court of Appeals that overnight sleeping in connection with the demonstration is expressive conduct protected to some extent by the First Amendment. We assume for present purposes, but do not decide, that such is the case, cf. [O'Brien], but this assumption only begins the inquiry. Expression, whether oral or written or symbolized by conduct, is subject to reasonable time, place, and manner restrictions. We have often noted that restrictions of this kind are valid provided that they are justified without reference to the content of the

---

[1] Lafayette Park is a seven-acre square located across Pennsylvania Avenue from the White House. The Mall is a stretch of land running westward from the Capitol to the Lincoln Memorial some two miles away; it includes the Washington Monument as well as a series of pools, trees, lawns, and other greenery. Both park areas are visited by "vast numbers of visitors."

[2] The regulation defined "camping" as "the use of park land for living accommodation purposes such as sleeping activities, or making preparations to sleep." Under the regulations, these activities "constitute camping when it reasonably appears [that] the participants [are] in fact using the area as a living accommodation regardless of the intent of the participants or the nature of any other activities in which they may also be engaging."

[3] The regulations state: "In connection with permitted demonstrations or special events, temporary structures may be erected for the purpose of symbolizing a message or meeting logistical needs such as [first aid facilities]. Temporary structures may not be used outside designated camping areas for [camping activities]."

[4] The District Court had granted summary judgment for the Park Service. The Court of Appeals had reversed by a vote of 6–5 in an en banc decision, finding the regulations invalid as applied. (The eleven judges produced six opinions. See 703 F.2d 586).

regulated speech, that they are narrowly tailored to serve a significant governmental interest, and that they leave open ample alternative channels for communication of the information. It is also true that a message may be delivered by conduct that is intended to be communicative and that, in context, would reasonably be understood by the viewer to be communicative. [Spence.] Symbolic expression of this kind may be forbidden or regulated if the conduct itself may constitutionally be regulated, if the regulation is narrowly drawn to further a substantial governmental interest, and if the interest is unrelated to the suppression of free speech. [O'Brien.]

The United States submits [that] the regulation forbidding sleeping is defensible either as a time, place, or manner restriction or as a regulation of symbolic conduct. We [agree]. [The regulations,] including the ban on sleeping, are clearly limitations on the manner in which the demonstration could be carried out. That sleeping, like the symbolic tents themselves, may be expressive and part of the message delivered by the demonstration does not make the ban any less a limitation on the manner of demonstrating, for reasonable time, place, and manner regulations normally have the purpose and direct effect of limiting expression but are nevertheless valid. Neither does the fact that sleeping, arguendo, may be expressive conduct, rather than oral or written expression, render the sleeping prohibition any less a time, place, or manner regulation. [We] have very little trouble concluding that the Park Service may prohibit overnight sleeping in the parks involved here.

The requirement that the regulation be content neutral is clearly satisfied. [It] is not disputed here that the prohibition on camping, and on sleeping specifically, is content neutral and is not being applied because of disagreement with the message presented. Neither was the regulation faulted, nor could it be, on the ground that without overnight sleeping the plight of the homeless could not be communicated in other ways. The regulation otherwise left the demonstration intact, with its symbolic city, signs, and the presence of those who were willing to take their turns in a day-and-night vigil. Respondents do not suggest that there was, or is, any barrier to delivering to the media, or to the public by other means, the intended message concerning the plight of the homeless. It is also apparent to us that the regulation narrowly focuses on the Government's substantial interest in maintaining the parks in the heart of our capital in an attractive and intact condition, readily available to the millions of people who wish to [enjoy them]. To permit camping [would] be totally inimical to these [purposes].

[It] is evident from our cases that the validity of this regulation need not be judged solely by reference to the demonstration at hand. [Heffron.] Absent the prohibition on sleeping, there would be other groups who would demand permission to deliver an asserted message by camping in Lafayette Park. Some of them would surely have as credible a claim in this regard as does CCNV, and the denial of permits to still others would present difficult problems for the Park Service. With the prohibition, however, [at] least some around-the-clock demonstrations lasting for days on end will not materialize, others will be limited in size and duration, and the purposes of the regulation will thus be materially served. Perhaps these purposes would be more effectively and not so clumsily achieved by preventing tents and 24-hour vigils entirely in the core areas. But the Park Service's decision to permit non-sleeping demonstrations does not, in our view, impugn the camping prohibition as a valuable, but perhaps imperfect, protection to the parks. If the Government has a legitimate interest in ensuring that the National Parks are adequately protected, which we think it has, and if the parks would be more exposed to harm without the sleeping prohibition than with it, the ban is safe from invalidation under the First Amendment as a reasonable regulation on the manner in which a demonstration may be carried out. As in [Taxpayers for Vincent], the regulation "responds precisely to the substantive problems which legitimately concern the [Government]."

[The] foregoing analysis demonstrates that the Park Service regulation is sustainable under the four-factor standard of [O'Brien] for validating a regulation of expressive conduct, which, in the last analysis is little, if any, different from the standard applied to time, place, and manner restrictions.[5] No one contends that aside from its impact on speech a rule against camping or overnight sleeping in public parks is beyond the constitutional power of the Government to enforce. And [there] is a substantial government interest in conserving park property, an interest that is plainly served by, and requires for its implementation, measures such as the proscription of sleeping that are designed to limit the wear and tear on park properties. That interest is unrelated to suppression of expression.

We are unmoved by [view] that the challenged regulation is unnecessary, and hence invalid, because there are less speech-restrictive alternatives that could have satisfied the government interest in preserving park lands. There is no gainsaying that preventing overnight sleeping will avoid a measure of actual or threatened damage to Lafayette Park and the Mall. The Court of Appeals' suggestions that the Park Service minimize the possible injury by reducing the size, duration, or frequency of demonstrations would still curtail the total allowable expression in which demonstrators could engage, whether by sleeping or otherwise, and these suggestions represent no more than a disagreement with the Park Service over how much protection the core parks require or how an acceptable level of preservation is to be attained. We do not believe, however, that either [O'Brien] or the time, place, and manner decisions assign to the judiciary the authority to replace the Park Service as the manager of the Nation's parks or endow the judiciary with the competence to judge how much protection of park lands is wise and how that level of conservation is to be attained. [Reversed.] [Chief Justice Burger filed a separate concurrence suggesting that the activity here was more "conduct" than speech.]

■ JUSTICE MARSHALL, with whom JUSTICE BRENNAN joins, dissenting.

[The] proper starting point for analysis [is] a recognition that the activity in which respondents seek to engage [is] symbolic speech protected by the First Amendment. The majority [so] assumes, without deciding. [Here] respondents clearly intended to protest the reality of homelessness by sleeping outdoors in the winter in the near vicinity of the [White House]. Nor

---

[5] Reasonable time, place, and manner restrictions are valid even though they directly limit oral or written expression. It would be odd to insist on a higher standard for limitations aimed at regulable conduct and having only an incidental impact on speech. Thus, if the time, place, and manner restriction on expressive sleeping, if that is what is involved in this case, sufficiently and narrowly serves a substantial enough governmental interest to escape First Amendment condemnation, it is untenable to invalidate it under O'Brien on the ground that the governmental interest is insufficient to warrant the intrusion on First Amendment concerns or that there is an inadequate nexus between the regulation and the interest sought to be served. We note that only recently, in a case dealing with the regulation of signs, the Court framed the issue under O'Brien and then based a crucial part of its analysis on the time, place, and manner cases. [Taxpayers for Vincent.] [Footnote by Justice White.]

can there be any doubt that in the surrounding circumstances the likelihood was great that the political significance of sleeping in the parks would be understood by those who viewed it. [This] likelihood stems from the remarkably apt fit between the activity in which respondents seek to engage and the social problems they seek to highlight. [It] is true that we all go to sleep as part of our daily regimen and that, for the most part, sleep represents a physical necessity and not a vehicle for expression. But these characteristics need not prevent an activity that is normally devoid of expressive purpose from being used as a novel mode of communication.

[Although] sleep in the context of this case is symbolic speech protected by the First Amendment, it is nonetheless subject to reasonable time, place, and manner restrictions. I agree with the standard enunciated by the majority.[6] [I] conclude, however, that the regulations at issue [here], as applied to respondents, fail to satisfy this standard. [The] majority cites no evidence indicating that sleeping engaged in as symbolic speech will cause *substantial* wear and tear on park property. Furthermore, the Government's application of the sleeping ban in the circumstances of this case is strikingly underinclusive. The majority acknowledges that a proper time, place, and manner restriction must be "narrowly tailored." Here, however, the tailoring requirement is virtually forsaken inasmuch as the Government offers no justification for applying its absolute ban on sleeping yet is willing to allow respondents to engage in activities—such as feigned sleeping—that is no less burdensome.

[By] limiting its concern to whether a given regulation creates a content-based distinction, the Court has seemingly overlooked the fact that content-neutral restrictions are also capable of unnecessarily restricting protected expressive activity. The Court [has] transformed the ban against content-distinctions from a floor that offers all persons at least equal liberty under the First Amendment into a ceiling that restricts persons to the protection of First Amendment equality—but nothing more.[7] [The] Court evidently assumes that the balance struck by officials is deserving of deference so long as it does not appear to be tainted by content discrimination. What the Court fails to recognize is that public officials have strong incentives to overregulate even in the absence of an intent to censor particular views. This incentive stems from the fact that of the two groups whose interests officials must accommodate—on the one hand, the interests of the general public and on the other, the interests of those who seek to use a particular forum for First Amendment activity—the political power of the former is likely to be far greater than that of the latter. [In light of government officials' greater]

[6] I also agree with the majority that no substantial difference distinguishes the test applicable to time, place, and manner restrictions and the test articulated in United States v. O'Brien. [Footnote by Justice Marshall.]

[7] Furthermore, a content-neutral regulation does not necessarily fall with random or equal force upon different groups or different points of view. A content-neutral regulation that restricts an inexpensive mode of communication will fall most heavily upon relatively poor speakers and the points of view that such speakers typically espouse. This sort of latent inequality is very much in evidence in this case, for respondents lack the financial means necessary to buy access to more conventional modes of persuasion. A disquieting feature about the disposition of this case is that it lends credence to the charge that judicial administration of the First Amendment, in conjunction with a social order marked by large disparities in wealth and other sources of power, tends systematically to discriminate against efforts by the relatively disadvantaged to convey their political ideas. In the past, this Court has taken such considerations into account in adjudicating the First Amendment rights of those among us who are financially deprived. See, e.g., [Martin v. Struthers.] [Footnote by Justice Marshall.]

sensitivity to regulatory as opposed to First Amendment interests, [facial] viewpoint-neutrality is no shield against unnecessary restrictions on unpopular ideas or modes of expression, and [here] the Court [should have] subject[ed] the Government's restrictive policy to something more than minimal [scrutiny].

TRANQUILITY, PRIVACY AND REPOSE

1. ***Noise regulations.*** Recall that, in Kovacs v. Cooper (1949; p. 1216 above), the Court upheld a ban on "loud and raucous" sound trucks. In **Ward v. Rock Against Racism**, 491 U.S. 781 (1989), the Court rejected a First Amendment challenge to New York City's regulation mandating the use of city-provided sound systems and technicians to control the volume of concerts at the bandshell in Central Park. The regulation was challenged by a group that claimed that the inability to use its own equipment and technicians in a concert in a public forum interfered with its free expression rights. There was a consensus on the Court that the case involved a "public forum," that the City's interest in limiting excessive noise was substantial, and that the regulation was "content-neutral." The dispute turned on how strictly to interpret the "narrowly tailored means" requirement. Recall that O'Brien had suggested that content-neutral restrictions are valid "if the incidental restriction on alleged First Amendment freedoms is no greater than is essential to the furtherance of that interest." The court of appeals in Ward had read O'Brien to require the "least intrusive means" and found that the city had not shown that it lacked other, less restrictive means of regulating concert volume.

Justice KENNEDY, writing for the Court, explicitly repudiated this view: "[T]he Court of Appeals erred in requiring the city to prove that this regulation was the least intrusive means. [Our] cases quite clearly hold that restrictions on the time, place, or manner of protected speech are not invalid 'simply because there is some imaginable alternative that might be less burdensome on speech. [Lest] any confusion on the point remain, we reaffirm today that a regulation of the time, place, or manner of protected speech must be narrowly tailored to serve the government's legitimate content-neutral interests but that it need not be the least-restrictive or least-intrusive means of doing so. Rather, [narrow] tailoring is satisfied 'so long as [the] regulation promotes a substantial government interest that would be achieved less effectively absent the regulation.' [To] be sure, this standard does not mean that a time, place, or manner regulation may burden substantially more speech than is necessary to further the government's legitimate interests. [So] long as the means chosen are not substantially broader than necessary to achieve the government's interest, however, the regulation will not be invalid simply because a court concludes that the government's interest could be adequately served by some less-speech-restrictive alternative." Applying this deferential standard, and finding that the regulation left open "ample alternative channels of communication," he concluded that it was "a reasonable regulation of the place and manner of expression."

Justice MARSHALL, joined by Justices Brennan and Stevens, dissented, contending that a "least-restrictive-alternative" analysis was built into the "narrowly tailored" requirement. To hold otherwise, he said, was a "serious distortion of the narrow tailoring requirement. [By] holding that the guidelines are valid time, place, and manner restrictions, notwithstanding the availability of less intrusive but effective means of controlling volume, the majority deprives the narrow tailoring requirement of all meaning. [The] majority replaces constitutional scrutiny with mandatory deference. [Under the majority's view, it will be enough] that the challenged regulation advances the government's interest only in the slightest, for any differential burden on speech that results does not enter the calculus. [After] today's decision, a city could claim that bans on handbill distribution or on door-to-door solicitation are the most effective means of avoiding littering and [fraud]."

2. ***Protecting "captive audiences."*** Recall that in Cohen v. California (1971; p. 998 above), the Court held that audiences must simply avert their eyes and ears when they encounter speech that offends them in open public spaces; government may not protect them in advance. The Court likewise held in Consolidated Edison Co. v. PSC (1980; p. 1107 above) and Bolger v. Youngs Drug Products (1983; p. 1140 above), that audiences offended by mail they receive must simply make the "short, regular, journey from mail box to trash can." But the Court held in Rowan v. Post Office (1970; p. 1106 above) that an offended recipient may request that his or her name be removed from mailing lists, and held in FCC v. Pacifica (1978; p. 1100 above) that the federal government may bar indecent radio broadcasts during daytime hours to prevent assault on unwilling listeners who are "captive" in their homes. Are there other contexts in which the Court will permit government to protect the sensibilities of a "captive audience," even from speech upon the public streets and sidewalks? Consider the following cases, which involved targeted residential picketing and abortion clinic protests.

a. *Targeted residential picketing.* Recall that in Carey v. Brown (1980; p. 1165 above), the Court invalidated a law banning all residential picketing except labor picketing, but did not reach the question of the validity of a law "barring all residential picketing regardless of its subject matter." Justice Brennan's majority opinion stated: "We are not to be understood to imply [that] residential picketing is beyond the reach of uniform and nondiscriminatory regulation. For the right to communicate is not limitless. [The] State's interest in protecting the well-being, tranquility, and privacy of the home is certainly of the highest order in a free and civilized society." In **Frisby v. Schultz**, 487 U.S. 474 (1988), the Court narrowly construed and sustained a flat ban on what it called "focused picketing" of a particular residence. A group ranging from 11 to over 40 people picketed, on six occasions within one month, the residence of a doctor who performed abortions. The picketing was orderly and peaceful. Thereafter, the town (a residential suburb of Milwaukee with a population of about 4,300) enacted a flat ban on all residential picketing, barring picketing "on or about the residence [of] any individual." The lower courts enjoined the ordinance, but the Court upheld it. As construed by the Court, the ordinance did not prohibit all residential picketing but only residential picketing that focused on and took place in front of a particular residence.

Justice O'CONNOR's majority opinion in the 6–3 ruling noted that "a public street does not lose its status as a traditional public forum simply because it runs through a residential neighborhood," but nevertheless concluded that the ordinance was valid because it was content-neutral, was "narrowly tailored to serve a significant government interest," and left open "ample alternative channels of communication." Justice O'Connor found the latter requirement "readily" satisfied here, in light of the narrow construction she invoked: the ordinance left protesters free to march through the neighborhood, so long as they did not focus on a particular residence; moreover, they were left free to proselytize door-to-door, and to distribute literature. In addition, there was a "significant government interest": "the protection of residential privacy." She noted that earlier decisions had held that "individuals are not required to welcome unwanted speech into their own homes," citing Pacifica and Kovacs, and added: "There simply is no right to force speech into the home of an unwilling listener."

Turning to the means/end fit, Justice O'Connor found the ordinance "narrowly tailored to protect only unwilling recipients of the communications. [A] complete ban can be narrowly tailored, but only if each activity within the proscription's scope is an appropriately targeted evil. [Taxpayers for Vincent]." She elaborated: "The type of focused picketing [here] is fundamentally different from more generally directed means of communication, that may not be completely banned in residential areas. See, e.g., [Schneider; Martin.] [Here the] picketing is narrowly directed at the household, not the public. The type of picketers banned by the [ordinance] generally do not seek to disseminate a message to the general public, but to intrude upon the targeted resident, and to do so in an especially offensive way. Moreover, even if some such picketers have a broader communicative purpose, their activity nonetheless inherently and offensively intrudes on residential privacy. The devastating effect of targeted picketing on the quiet enjoyment of the home is beyond doubt." She thus rejected the facial challenge to the ordinance.

Justice BRENNAN's dissent, joined by Justice Marshall, accepted that the majority had set forth the appropriate legal test, but argued that the ordinance banned "significantly more speech than is necessary to achieve the government's substantial and legitimate goal." In explaining why the ordinance was not "narrowly tailored," he acknowledged that there were clearly "many aspects of residential picketing that, if unregulated, might easily become intrusive or unduly coercive." Some of these aspects were illustrated here: the trial court had found that the protesters had, for example, warned young children not to go near the house because the physician was a "baby killer," had repeatedly trespassed on his property, and had at least once blocked the exits to his home. Such "intrusive and coercive abuses" could clearly be regulated: "Thus, for example, the government could constitutionally regulate the number of residential picketers, the hours during which a residential picket may take place, or the noise level of such a picket, [to] neutralize the intrusive or unduly coercive aspects of picketing around the home. But to say that picketing may be substantially regulated is not to say that it may be prohibited in its entirety. Once size, time, volume, and the like have been controlled to ensure that the picket is no longer intrusive or coercive, only the speech itself remains, conveyed perhaps by a lone, silent individual, walking back and forth with a sign. Such speech, which no longer implicates the heightened governmental interest in residential privacy, is nevertheless banned by [the ordinance]. Therefore, [it] is not narrowly tailored."

In a separate dissent, Justice STEVENS stated: "[Under this ordinance,] it is unlawful for a fifth-grader to carry [a sign saying 'Get Well Charlie—our Team Needs You'] in front of a residence for the period of time necessary to convey its friendly message to its intended audience. [My] hunch is that the town will probably not enforce its ban against friendly, innocuous, or even brief unfriendly picketing, and that the Court may be right in concluding that its legitimate sweep makes its overbreadth insubstantial. But [the] scope of the ordinance gives the town officials far too much discretion in making enforcement decisions; while [we] await further developments, potential picketers must act at their peril."

b. *Abortion clinic protests.* In **Madsen v. Women's Health Center, Inc.**, 512 U.S. 753 (1994), the Court in part upheld and in part struck down a Florida state court injunction that limited the activities of antiabortion protestors on the public streets outside an abortion clinic. The injunction was aimed largely at protecting the privacy and repose of women seeking to enter and use the abortion clinic's facilities. Chief Justice REHNQUIST, writing for the Court, first found that the injunction was not content-or viewpoint-based simply because it restricted only the speech of antiabortion protesters: "To accept petitioners' claim would be to classify virtually every injunction as content or viewpoint based. An injunction, by its very nature, applies only to a particular group (or individuals) and regulates the activities, and perhaps the speech, of that group." The injunction had been issued because the protestors had violated a previous, narrower injunction against blocking clinic access. "[In] determining content neutrality [we] look to governmental purpose as the primary consideration. Here, the state court imposed restrictions on petitioners [because] they repeatedly violated the court's original order. That petitioners all share the same viewpoint regarding abortion does not in itself demonstrate that some invidious content-or viewpoint-based purpose motivated the issuance of the order. It suggests only that those in the group whose conduct violated the court's order happen to share the same opinion regarding abortions being performed at the clinic."

Having found the injunction content-neutral, Chief Justice Rehnquist nonetheless held that the Ward time, place, and manner test must be applied with special stringency in the context of an injunction, as opposed to a general statute, because "[i]njunctions [carry] greater risks of censorship and discriminatory application than do general ordinances. [When] evaluating a content-neutral injunction, we [must ask] whether the challenged provisions of the injunction burden no more speech than necessary to serve a significant government interest." The majority opinion agreed with the Florida Supreme Court that the injunction served a number of "significant government interests": interests "[in] protecting a woman's freedom to seek lawful medical or counseling services in connection with her pregnancy, [in] ensuring the public safety and order, in promoting the free flow of traffic on public streets and sidewalks, [in] protecting the property rights of all its citizens, [and in vindicating] the State's strong interest in residential privacy, [Frisby], applied by analogy to medical privacy. The [state] court observed that while targeted picketing of the home threatens the psychological well-being of the 'captive' resident, targeted picketing of a hospital or clinic threatens not only the psychological, but the physical well-being of the patient held 'captive' by medical circumstance. We agree [that] the combination of these governmental interests is quite sufficient to justify an appropriately tailored injunction to protect them."

Chief Justice Rehnquist then considered whether each challenged provision of the injunction met the heightened narrow tailoring requirement he had set forth. He upheld the injunction's requirement of a "36-foot buffer zone" around the front of the clinic in which the protestors were barred from "congregating, picketing, patrolling, [or] demonstrating." He emphasized the need for "some deference" to the state court's findings "even under our heightened review": "The state court seems to have had few other options to protect access given the narrow confines around the clinic. The state court was convinced that allowing the petitioners to remain on the clinic's sidewalk and driveway was not a viable option in view of the failure of the first injunction to protect access. And allowing the petitioners to stand in the middle of [the adjacent street] would obviously block vehicular traffic. [Protesters] standing across the narrow street from the clinic can still be seen and heard from the clinic parking lots. On balance, we hold that the 36-foot buffer zone around the clinic entrances and driveway burdens no more speech than necessary to accomplish the governmental interest at stake." He held, however, that the 36-foot buffer zone was invalid as applied to the private property along the side and back of the clinic, as there had been no showing that such speech interfered with clinic access.

He next turned to a portion of the injunction restraining the petitioners from "singing, chanting, whistling, shouting, yelling, use of bullhorns, auto horns, sound amplification equipment or other sounds or images observable to or within earshot of the patients inside the clinic" during the hours of 7:30 a.m. through noon on Mondays through Saturdays. He upheld the provision restricting high noise levels, noting that "[n]oise control is particularly important around hospitals and medical facilities during surgery and recovery periods." But, he held, "[t]he same cannot be said for the 'images observable' provision." Chief Justice Rehnquist reasoned that this restriction burdened "more speech than necessary to achieve the purpose of limiting threats to clinic patients or their families," since it is much easier for the clinic to pull its curtains than for a patient to stop up her ears, and no more is required to avoid seeing placards through the windows of the clinic."

Chief Justice Rehnquist's majority opinion next invalidated a provision of the state court order requiring that the protestors "refrain from physically approaching any person seeking services of the clinic 'unless such person indicates a desire to communicate' in an area within 300 feet of the clinic. The state court was attempting to prevent clinic patients and staff from being 'stalked' or 'shadowed' by the petitioners as they approached the clinic. But it is difficult, indeed, to justify a prohibition on all uninvited approaches of persons seeking the services of the clinic, regardless of how peaceful the contact may be, without burdening more speech than necessary to prevent intimidation and to ensure access to the clinic. Absent evidence that the protesters' speech is independently proscribable (i.e., 'fighting words' or threats), or is so infused with violence as to be indistinguishable from a threat of physical harm, this provision cannot stand."

Finally, the Court invalidated the injunction's prohibition against picketing, demonstrating, or using sound amplification equipment within 300 feet of the residences of clinic staff: "[T]he 300-foot zone around the residences in this case is much larger than the zone provided for in the ordinance which we approved in Frisby. The ordinance at issue there [was] limited to 'focused picketing taking place solely in front of a particular residence.' By contrast, the 300-foot zone would ban 'general marching through residential neighborhoods, or even walking a route in front of an entire block of houses.' [Frisby.] The record before us does not contain sufficient justification for this broad a ban on picketing; it appears that a limitation on the time, duration of picketing, and number of pickets outside a smaller zone could have accomplished the desired result.

"[In] sum, we uphold the noise restrictions and the 36-foot buffer zone around the clinic entrances and driveway because they burden no more speech than necessary to eliminate the unlawful conduct targeted by the state court's injunction. We strike down as unconstitutional the 36-foot buffer zone as applied to the private property to the north and west of the clinic, the 'images observable' provision, the 300-foot no-approach zone around the clinic, and the 300-foot buffer zone around the residences, because these provisions sweep more broadly than necessary to accomplish the permissible goals of the injunction."

Justice STEVENS concurred in part and dissented in part. Unlike the majority, he would have subjected the injunction to more deferential scrutiny, not more stringent scrutiny, than a comparable statute, because an injunction is limited "solely to an individual or a limited group of individuals, who, by engaging in illegal conduct, have been judicially deprived of some liberty." Under that more lenient standard, he would have upheld the 300-foot no-approach zone around the clinic, but would not have reached the question whether the other restrictions were permissible time, place, or manner regulations. Justice Souter also wrote a separate concurrence.

Justice SCALIA, joined by Justices Kennedy and Thomas, concurred in the portions of the majority opinion striking down portions of the injunction, but dissented sharply from the portions upholding the 36-foot buffer zone and the noise prohibition: "[The majority's] appearance of moderation and Solomonic wisdom [is] deceptive." Describing at length a videotape from the record, he concluded that it showed "that a great many forms of expression and conduct occurred in the vicinity of the clinic. [What] the videotape, the rest of the record, and the trial court's findings do not contain is any suggestion of violence near the clinic, nor do they establish any attempt to prevent entry or exit."

Justice Scalia disagreed with the majority's standard of review. He derided the new standard of "intermediate-intermediate scrutiny" as manufactured "for this abortion-related case." He argued instead that restrictions upon speech imposed by injunction generally are "at least as deserving of strict scrutiny as a statutory, content-based restriction," because injunctions likewise lend themselves "to the targeted suppression of particular ideas." He also argued that the particular injunction here was content-based, because it reached all those "acting in concert or participation" with the protestors rather than merely those who had violated the previous order; it thus was, in his view, "tailored to restrain persons distinguished, not by proscribable conduct, but by proscribable views." He found that all the provisions of the injunction failed strict scrutiny, and even failed the majority's test, given the lack of tailoring between the injunction under review and any violation by all of the protestors of the previous injunction or other Florida law. He concluded that "petitioners have a right, not merely to demonstrate and protest at some reasonably effective place, but to demonstrate and protest where they want to and where all other Floridians can, namely, right there on the public sidewalk in front of the clinic. 'One is not to have the exercise of his liberty of expression in appropriate places abridged on the plea that it may be exercised in some other place.' [Schneider.] [What] we have decided seems to be, and will be reported by the media as, an abortion case. But it will go down in the lawbooks, it will be cited, as a free-speech injunction case—and the damage its novel principles produce will be considerable."

In **Schenck v. Pro-Choice Network of Western New York**, 519 U.S. 357 (1997), the Court again reviewed a First Amendment challenge to an injunction against protestors outside an abortion clinic. The injunction, issued by a federal district court after a series of large-scale protests and blockades, banned "demonstrating within fifteen feet from either side or edge of, or in front of, doorways or doorway entrances, parking lot entrances, driveways and driveway entrances of" clinic facilities, or "within fifteen feet of any person or vehicle seeking access to or leaving such facilities." Antiabortion counselors could approach persons entering or exiting clinics in order to make "non-threatening" conversation with them, but if requested to "cease and desist," they had to retreat 15 feet from the people they had been counseling. As construed by the Court, the injunction thus created two kinds of buffer zones: "fixed buffer zones" and "floating buffer zones." Applying the standard set forth in Madsen, Chief Justice REHNQUIST, writing for the Court, struck down the floating buffer zones but upheld the fixed buffer zones:

"We strike down the floating buffer zones around people entering and leaving the clinics because they burden more speech than is necessary to serve the relevant governmental interests. The floating buffer zones prevent defendants—except for two sidewalk counselors, while they are tolerated by the targeted individual—from communicating a message from a normal conversational distance or handing leaflets to people entering or leaving the clinics who are walking on the public sidewalks. [Since] the buffer zone floats, protesters on the public sidewalks who wish (i) to communicate their message to an incoming or outgoing patient or clinic employee and (ii) to remain as close as possible (while maintaining an acceptable conversational distance) to this individual, must move as the individual moves, maintaining 15 feet of separation. But this would be difficult to accomplish [without stepping into the street or into other persons' floating buffer zones]."

In contrast, the Court upheld the fixed buffer zones around clinic doorways, driveways, and driveway entrances, reasoning that such buffer zones were necessary to ensure that people and vehicles trying to enter or exit the clinic property or clinic parking lots could do so. Chief Justice Rehnquist wrote: "As in Madsen, the record shows that protesters purposefully or effectively blocked or hindered people from entering and exiting the clinic doorways, from driving up to and away from clinic entrances, and from driving in and out of clinic parking lots. Based on this conduct [the] District Court was entitled to conclude that the only way to ensure access was to move back the demonstrations away from the driveways and parking lot entrances. [Although] one might quibble about whether 15 feet is too great or too small a distance if the goal is to ensure access, we defer to the District Court's reasonable assessment of the number of feet necessary to keep the entrances clear."

Justice SCALIA, joined by Justices Kennedy and Thomas, dissented from the decision insofar as it upheld fixed buffer zones. He argued that the majority opinion had mischaracterized the zones as intended to preserve unimpeded clinic access, when they were in fact grounded at least in part on the impermissible purpose of protecting listeners from having to hear "unwanted" speech. Justice BREYER dissented from the decision insofar as it struck down the floating buffer zones, arguing that "the preliminary injunction's language does not necessarily create the kind of 'floating bubble' that leads the Court to find the injunction unconstitutionally broad."

In **Hill v. Colorado**, 530 U.S. 703 (2000), the Court reviewed a statute, as opposed to an injunction, challenged for limiting the speech of abortion protestors outside abortion clinics, and upheld it by a vote of 6–3. The statute makes it unlawful within the vicinity of a health care facility for anyone to "knowingly approach" within eight feet of another person, without that person's consent, "for the purpose of passing a leaflet or handbill to, displaying a sign to, or engaging in oral protest, education, or counseling with such other person." Justice STEVENS delivered the opinion of the Court, joined by Chief Justice Rehnquist and Justices O'Connor, Souter, Ginsburg, and Breyer. He found the statute a valid, content-neutral time, place, and manner regulation under the Ward test. It was content-neutral, he wrote, because it regulated not speech but "the places where some speech may occur," it was not adopted because of disagreement with a message, and it was justified by interests in access and privacy that were unrelated to ideas. He declined to find a content basis in the distinction between approaches for "protest, education or counseling" and for other purposes, such as "pure social or random conversation." He concluded that the statute "applies to all 'protest,' to all 'counseling,' and to all demonstrators whether or not the demonstration concerns abortion, and whether they oppose or support the woman who has made an abortion decision. That is the level of neutrality that the Constitution demands." He went on to hold the statute narrowly tailored to important interests in privacy and access and left protestors adequate alternative means of getting their message across. Justice SOUTER filed a concurrence, joined by Justices O'Connor, Ginsburg, and Breyer, emphasizing that the statute addressed "not the content of speech but the circumstances of its delivery," and thus was properly evaluated as content-neutral.

Dissents were filed by Justice SCALIA, joined by Justice Thomas, and by Justice KENNEDY. Justice Scalia argued that the floating buffer zone around oral communication was "obviously and undeniably content-based," because "[w]hether a speaker must obtain permission before approaching within eight feet—and whether he will be sent to prison for failing to do so—depends entirely on what he intends to say when he gets there." He would have applied strict scrutiny, which the statute could not survive: "Suffice it to say that if protecting people from unwelcome communications (the governmental interest the Court posits) is a compelling state interest, the First Amendment is a dead letter. And if forbidding peaceful, nonthreatening, but uninvited speech from a distance closer than eight feet is a 'narrowly tailored' means of preventing the obstruction of entrance to medical facilities (the governmental interest the State asserts) narrow tailoring must refer not to the standards of Versace, but to those of Omar the tentmaker." He accused the Court of distorting First Amendment law in order to "sustain this restriction upon the free speech of abortion opponents": "Does the deck seem stacked? You bet." Justice Kennedy likewise would have found the law content-based, as restrictive of particular topics, and denied that "citizens have a right to avoid unpopular speech in a public forum." He added that the statute interfered with an important First Amendment interest in "immediacy": "Here the citizens who claim First Amendment protection seek it for speech which, if it is to be effective, must take place at the very time and place a grievous moral wrong, in their view, is about to occur. The Court tears away from the protesters the guarantees of the First Amendment when they most need it."

Was Hill unusual in permitting a listener preclearance requirement for speech in the public forum? Note that in cases such as Cohen v. California (1971; p. 998 above), the Court ruled that, in the public forum, speakers may take what initiative they wish toward listeners while offended listeners must simply turn the other cheek. Do Madsen, Schenck, and Hill together establish an exception to that principle for the curtilage of a health facility? Does the law in Hill, by requiring listeners affirmatively to consent to speech, have the likely effect of discriminating in favor of popular or widely accepted messages and against those that are unorthodox or unpopular, where the speaker must initiate contact because the listener will not? Note that, in Heffron v. ISKCON (1981; p. 1222 above), the Court rejected a similar argument against a rule requiring literature distribution and solicitation of funds to be confined to a fixed rented booth at a state fair, noting that the argument that "the regulation is not content-neutral in that it prefers listener-initiated exchanges to those originating with the speaker [is] interesting but has little force." Did Justice Scalia's dissent in Hill find new force in such an argument?

In **McCullen v. Coakley**, 573 U.S. 464 (2014), the Court considered a 2007 Massachusetts statute that went beyond the law in Hill and created a 35-foot buffer zone around abortion-providing facilities during business hours that categorically excluded anyone except persons entering or leaving, facility employees in the scope of their duties, emergency personnel like police and firefighters, and people passing by. The court struck down the law in an opinion by Chief Justice ROBERTS that was joined by Justices Ginsburg, Breyer, Kagan, and Sotomayor. The Court said the law was content-neutral because it "does not draw content-based distinctions on its face. It is true, of course, that by limiting the buffer zones to abortion clinics, the Act has the 'inevitable effect' of restricting abortion-related speech more than speech on other subjects. But a facially neutral law does not become content based simply be-cause it may disproportionately affect speech on certain topics." The Court then held the law to be viewpoint-neutral as well. "There is nothing inherently suspect about providing some kind of exemption to allow individuals who work at the clinics to enter or remain within the buffer zones. In particular, the exemption cannot be regarded as simply a carve-out for the clinic escorts; it also covers employees such as the maintenance worker shoveling a snowy sidewalk or the security guard patrolling a clinic entrance."

Having held that strict scrutiny was unnecessary, Chief Justice Roberts then applied ordinary intermediate scrutiny and found that the law was not narrowly tailored because it burdened "substantially more speech than necessary to further the government's legitimate interests." In particular, the law limited "one-on-one communication" between pro-life activists and women who might be seeking abortions. "Petitioners are not protestors," Chief Justice Roberts wrote. "They seek not merely to express their opposition to abortion, but to inform women of various alternatives and to provide help in pursuing them. Petitioners believe that they can accomplish this objective only through personal, caring, consensual conversations. And for good reason: It is easier to ignore a strained voice or a waving hand than a direct greeting or an outstretched arm." The Court's opinion never directly addressed the status of Hill v. Colorado.

Justice SCALIA, joined by Justices Thomas and Kennedy, concurred only in the judgment and would have found the law to discriminate on the basis of content. He rejected the Court's reliance on facial neutrality. "Every objective indication shows that the provision's primary purpose is to restrict speech that opposes abortion." He also objected to the Court reaching the issue of content neutrality when its decisions truck down the law. Justice Scalia addressed the status of Colorado v. Hill directly: "The provision at issue here was indisputably meant to serve the same interest [as the law in Hill] in protecting citizens' supposed right to avoid speech that they would rather not hear. For that reason, we granted a second question for review in this case (though one would not know that from the Court's opinion, which fails to mention it): whether Hill should be cut back or cast aside. The majority avoids that question by declaring the Act content neutral on other (entirely unpersuasive) grounds. In concluding that the statute is content based and therefore subject to strict scrutiny, I necessarily conclude that Hill should be overruled. [Protecting] people from speech they do not want to hear is not a function that the First Amendment allows the government to undertake in the public streets and sidewalks. One final thought regarding Hill: It can be argued, and it should be argued in the next case, that by stating that 'the Act would not be content neutral if it were concerned with undesirable effects that arise from . . . [l]isteners' reactions to speech,' and then holding the Act unconstitutional for being insufficiently tailored to safety and access concerns, the Court itself has sub silentio (and perhaps inadvertently) overruled Hill. The unavoidable implication of that holding is that protection against unwelcome speech cannot justify restrictions on the use of public streets and sidewalks."

Justice ALITO concurred only in the judgment and wrote to say that the law was not viewpoint-neutral. "Consider this entirely realistic situation. A woman enters a buffer zone and heads haltingly toward the entrance. A sidewalk counselor, such as petitioners, enters the buffer zone, approaches the woman and says, 'If you have doubts about an abortion, let me try to answer any questions you may have. The clinic will not give you good information.' At the same time, a clinic employee, as instructed by the management, approaches the same woman and says, 'Come inside and we will give you honest answers to all your questions.' The sidewalk counselor and the clinic employee expressed opposing viewpoints, but only the first violated the statute."

Was the decision a victory for pro-life or pro-choice activists? What, if anything, does the voting line-up tell you about this question?

INVALID TIME, PLACE, OR MANNER REGULATION

Is time, place, and manner review heightened in theory but toothless in fact? The preceding cases suggest that the Court has generally deferred to government when applying time, place, and manner review. The Court's implementation of the requirement that a regulation be "narrowly drawn to further a substantial governmental interest"—a requirement common to both symbolic expression claims and time, place, and manner challenges—does not involve strict scrutiny, nor serious inquiry into the availability of "less restrictive means" to implement the governmental interest.

As evidence that time, place, and manner review, even under the relatively deferential Ward/CCNV standard, remains more speech-protective than rationality review, consider the different burdens of justification each standard places on the government. Minimal rationality review does not require a showing of actual purpose or empirically sound means/end fit, but rather may be satisfied entirely by conjectural justifications. Rationality review thus permits the government to win dismissal on the pleadings so long as the government can hypothesize a rational relationship to a conceivable government interest. Time, place, and manner review, by contrast, requires government to make an evidentiary showing of substantial ends and means closely tailored to those ends. Arguably, by requiring governments to adduce some empirical evidence that the harms they seek to avoid are material, and that the means they have chosen are superior to obvious alternatives, the test continues to serve a protective First Amendment purpose: even if the government rarely loses a litigated case, it might well avoid enacting or enforcing regulation that could not withstand an evidentiary hearing. On this view, intermediate scrutiny operates as a powerful deterrent even if it is a rarely wielded club.

Moreover, the Supreme Court does occasionally invalidate a challenged time, place, or manner restriction. A leading example is **United States v. Grace**, 461 U.S. 171 (1983). In Grace, the challengers attacked a provision of 40 U.S.C. § 13k that prohibited the "display [of] any flag, banner, or device designed or adapted to bring into public notice any party, organization, or movement" in the U.S. Supreme Court building and on its grounds. One of the challengers sought to distribute to passers-by on the sidewalk leaflets concerning the removal of unfit judges from the bench. The other, Mary Grace, sought to display on the sidewalk a two-and-a-half by four-foot sign on which was inscribed verbatim the text of the First Amendment. The Court held the prohibition invalid as applied to the public sidewalks surrounding the Court building.

Justice WHITE stated: "The sidewalks comprising the outer boundaries of the Court grounds are indistinguishable from any other sidewalks in Washington, D.C., and we can discern no reason why they should be treated any differently. Sidewalks, of course, are among those areas of public property that traditionally have been held open to the public for expressive activities and are clearly within those areas of public property that may be considered, generally without further inquiry, to be public forum property. [There is] no separation, no fence, and no indication whatever to persons stepping from the street to the curb and sidewalks that serve as the perimeter of the Court grounds that they have entered some special type of enclave. [Traditional] public forum property occupies a special position in terms of First Amendment protection and will not lose its historically recognized character for the reason that it abuts government property that has been dedicated to a use other than as a forum for public expression."

Justice White rejected the Government's argument that the ban could be justified as "a reasonable time, place, and manner restriction" on public forum property. He found no sufficient connection with any of the asserted state interests to warrant the restriction. He questioned whether the ban substantially served the purpose of maintaining proper order and decorum within the Court grounds. He also rejected the Government's claim that the restraint was needed lest it "*appear* to the public that the Supreme Court is subject to outside influence or that picketing or marching, singly or in groups, is an acceptable or proper way of appealing to or influencing the Supreme Court": "[We] seriously doubt that the public would draw a different inference from a lone picketer carrying a sign on the sidewalks around the building than it would from a similar picket on the sidewalks across the street." In a separate opinion, Justice MARSHALL argued that the ban should be found "unconstitutional on its face": "[Since] the continuing existence of the statute will inevitably have a chilling effect on freedom of expression, there is no virtue in deciding its constitutionality on a piecemeal basis."

SPEAKER ACCESS TO PUBLIC PLACES OTHER THAN TRADITIONAL PUBLIC FORUMS

In Hague v. CIO (1939; p. 1211 above), Justice Roberts, in speaking of public places which have "immemorially" and "time out of mind" been used for "discussing public questions," mentioned only "streets and parks." And most of the preceding materials involved access to and regulation of streets and parks. What of other public places? In a series of cases, the Court has confronted claims of speakers seeking access to such nontraditional forums as public libraries, jail environs, buses, military installations, mailboxes and federal charitable campaigns. Should an assured minimum-access claim be recognized in these contexts as well? At least an equal-access claim?

The cases that follow consider two different approaches to these questions. One approach, typical in earlier cases such as Brown, Adderley, and Grayned, asks with respect to any public property whether the proposed speech is compatible or not with its other principal uses. On this approach, speech restrictions might theoretically be invalidated in any public space, depending on its particular characteristics. See Stone, "Fora Americana: Speech in Public Places," 1974 Sup. Ct. Rev. 233 (noting that the incompatibility approach turns on functional considerations that bring "streets, parks, public libraries, and other publicly owned places [all] under the same roof"). The second approach, typical of later cases and summarized below in Perry Education Ass'n v. Perry Local Educators' Ass'n, instead uses the characteristics of public property as a ground to classify it in advance as a "public forum," a "designated public forum," or a "nonpublic forum," with different rules applying to each category.

As you read the following materials, consider which approach seems more helpful. How do the governing criteria vary between these approaches? What is the role of tradition or custom in each approach? What is the role of the contemporary function of the property in each approach? What is the role of the compatibility of expressive activities with other uses of the property in each approach? The availability to the First Amendment claimant of alternative forums for expression? The relationship between the subject matter of the protest and the nontraditional forum of protest?

LIBRARIES, JAILS AND SCHOOLS

1. ***Libraries.*** **Brown v. Louisiana**, 383 U.S. 131 (1966), arose from events at a segregated regional public library in Louisiana in 1964. Five

young black men entered the reading room and one of them, Brown, asked branch assistant Reeves for a book. Reeves told Brown that she did not have the book but would request it from the state library and would notify him upon receipt. When Reeves asked the young black men to leave, they refused. Instead, Brown, in protest against the library's "whites only" policy, sat down and the others stood near him. There was no noise or boisterous talking. After about 10 minutes, the sheriff arrived and asked the men to leave; when they did not, he arrested them. Brown and his companions were convicted under Louisiana's breach of the peace statute.

The sharply divided 5–4 decision reversed the convictions. Justice FORTAS's plurality opinion, joined only by Chief Justice Warren and Justice Douglas, stated at the outset that there was no evidence that petitioners had violated the law—"no disorder, no intent to provoke a breach of the peace and no circumstances indicating that a breach might be occasioned by petitioners' actions." But he did not rest exclusively on this due process ground. He added: "We are here dealing with an aspect of a basic constitutional right—the right [of] speech and of assembly, and freedom to petition the Government for a redress of grievances. [These] rights are not confined to verbal expression. They embrace appropriate types of action which certainly include the right in a peaceable and orderly manner to protest by silent and reproachful presence, in a place where the protestant has every right to be, the unconstitutional segregation of public facilities. Accordingly, even if the accused action were within the scope of the [law], [we] would have to hold that the statute cannot constitutionally be applied to punish petitioners' actions in the circumstances of this case. The statute was deliberately and purposefully applied solely to terminate the reasonable, orderly, and limited exercise of the right to protest the unconstitutional segregation of a public facility. Interference with this right, so exercised, by state action is intolerable under our Constitution. [Fortunately], the circumstances here were such that no claim can be made that use of the library by others was disturbed by the demonstration. [Were] it otherwise, a factor not present in this case would have to be considered." Justices Brennan and WHITE each concurred in the judgment. Justice White found that petitioners' actions did not "depart significantly from what normal library use would contemplate."

Justice BLACK dissented, joined by Justices Clark, Harlan and Stewart: "[I]t is incomprehensible to me that a State must measure disturbances in its libraries and on the streets with identical standards. [A] tiny parish branch library, staffed by two women, is not a department store [nor] a bus terminal [nor] a public thoroughfare as in Edwards and Cox v. Louisiana." He continued: "[The plurality's] conclusion that the statute was unconstitutionally applied because it interfered with the petitioners' so-called protest establishes a completely new constitutional doctrine. [The First Amendment] does not guarantee to any person the right to use someone else's property, even that owned by government and dedicated to other purposes, as a stage to express dissident ideas. The novel constitutional doctrine of the prevailing opinion [exalts] the power of private nongovernmental groups to determine what use shall be made of governmental property over the power of the elected governmental officials."

Consider the comment in Kalven, "Upon Rereading Mr. Justice Black on the First Amendment," 14 UCLA L. Rev. 428 (1967): "[I]t remains something of a puzzle how Justice Black, who has been so sympathetic to the 'poor man's printing press' and so tolerant of noise in Kovacs, the intrusion in [Martin v. City of Struthers], the anonymity in [Talley v. California], can be so impatient with this kind of communication. It is as though his strategy of protecting all speech just because it was something other than conduct traps him when he is confronted by conduct which is symbolic."

2. ***Jails.*** In **Adderley v. Florida**, 385 U.S. 39 (1966), in contrast, the Court upheld the convictions of 32 students at Florida A. & M. University in Tallahassee for "trespass with a malicious and mischievous intent" upon the premises of the county jail. They had gone to the jail to protest the arrests of other students the day before and to demonstrate against racial segregation. They did not leave at the county sheriff's request. They did move back from the jail entrance but remained in a driveway normally used by the sheriff's department to transport prisoners to and from the courts several blocks away and by commercial vehicles.

Justice BLACK, writing for the Court, rejected the students' claim that their convictions violated their First Amendment rights. "The sheriff, as jail custodian, had power [to] direct that this large crowd of people get off the grounds. There is not a shred of evidence in this record that this power was exercised [because] the sheriff objected to what was being sung or said by the demonstrators or because he disagreed with the objectives of their protest. The record reveals that he objected only to their presence on that part of the jail grounds reserved for jail uses. There is no evidence at all that on any other occasion had similarly large groups of the public been permitted to gather on this portion of the jail grounds for any purpose. Nothing in the [Constitution] prevents Florida from even-handed enforcement of its general trespass statute against those refusing to obey the sheriff's order to remove themselves from what amounted to the curtilage of the jailhouse. The State, no less than a private owner of property, has power to preserve the property under its control for the use to which it is lawfully dedicated. [The Constitution] does not forbid a State to control the use of its own property for its own lawful nondiscriminatory purpose."

Justice DOUGLAS dissented, joined by Chief Justice Warren and Justices Brennan and Fortas: "[T]he Court errs in treating the case as if it were an ordinary trespass case or an ordinary picketing case. The jailhouse, like an executive mansion, a legislative chamber, a courthouse, or the statehouse itself [Edwards], is one of the seats of government, whether it be the Tower of London, the Bastille, or a small county jail. And when it houses political prisoners or those whom many think are unjustly held, it is an obvious center for protest. The right to petition for the redress of grievances has an ancient history and is not limited to writing a letter or sending a telegram to a congressman; it is not confined to appearing before the local city council, or writing letters to the President or Governor or Mayor. Conventional methods of petitioning may be, and often have been, shut off to large groups of our citizens. Legislators may turn deaf ears; formal complaints may be routed endlessly through a bureaucratic maze; courts may let the wheels of justice grind very slowly. Those who do not control television and radio, those who cannot afford to advertise in newspapers or circulate elaborate pamphlets may have only a more limited type of access to public officials. Their methods should not be condemned as tactics of obstruction and harassment as long as the assembly and petition are peaceable, as these were.

"There is no question that petitioners had as their purpose a protest against the arrest of Florida A. & M. students for trying to integrate public theatres. [There] was no violence; no threat of violence; no attempted jail break; no storming of a prison; no plan or plot to do anything but protest. The evidence is uncontradicted that the petitioners' conduct did not upset the jailhouse routine. [There] was no shoving, no pushing, no disorder or threat of riot. It is said that some of the group blocked part of the driveway leading to the jail entrance. [But] whenever the students were requested to move they did so. If there was congestion, the solution was a further request to move to lawns or parking areas, not complete ejection and arrest."

Does Justice Black in Adderley retreat all the way to Justice Holmes's analogy between the state and the private property owner in Massachusetts v. Davis (1895; p. 1211 above)? Would Justice Black sustain a blanket prohibition of the use of streets and parks for meetings and parades? Or are his broad comments applicable only to such nontraditional forums as jailhouse driveways? Does the holding in Adderley reject any assured access claim beyond the traditional public forum of the streets and parks? Or is there access to nontraditional forums so long as there is no showing of substantial disruption of or interference with the functioning of their primary uses? Is that the message of the Brown case? Can a claim to a nontraditional public forum be adequately analyzed without inquiries as to the availability of adequate alternative forums in which the speaker may reach the desired audience? Should the public forum claimant be required to demonstrate his special interest in the particular location? Was there special justification for the protest near the jailhouse in Adderley? As much as with the library protest in Brown?

3. ***Schools.*** In **Grayned v. Rockford**, 408 U.S. 104 (1972), the Court upheld an ordinance barring a demonstration near a school. Grayned had participated in a demonstration in front of a high school protesting black underrepresentation in activities at the school. The Court affirmed a conviction under an "antinoise" ordinance stating that no person on grounds "adjacent to any [school] building" in which a class is in session "shall willfully make or assist in the making of any noise or diversion which disturbs or tends to disturb the peace or good order of such school session." Justice MARSHALL's majority opinion emphasized that it was "the nature of a place, 'the pattern of its normal activities,'" that determines the reasonableness of time, place, and manner restrictions: "The crucial question is whether the manner of expression is basically incompatible with the normal activity of a particular place at a particular time."

Here, he found the restraint appropriate to the school environment: "Although a silent vigil may not unduly interfere with a public library [Brown], making a speech in the reading room almost certainly would. That same speech should be perfectly appropriate in a park. [Our] cases make clear that in assessing the reasonableness of a regulation, we must weigh heavily the fact that communication is involved [Schneider; Hague]; the regulation must be narrowly tailored to further the State's legitimate interest. Access to the 'streets, sidewalks, parks, and other similar public places [for] the purpose of exercising [First Amendment rights] cannot constitutionally be denied broadly.' In light of these general principles, we do not think that Rockford's ordinance is an unconstitutional regulation of activity around a school. [The] public sidewalk adjacent to school grounds may not be declared off-limits for expressive activity by members of the public. [But] expressive activity may be prohibited if it 'materially disrupts classwork or involves substantial disorder or invasion of the rights of others.' [Tinker (p. 1290 below).] We would be ignoring reality if we did not recognize that the public schools [are] often the focus of significant grievances. [But] schools could hardly tolerate boisterous demonstrators who drown out classroom conversation, make studying impossible, block entrances, or incite children to leave the schoolhouse. [The ordinance] is narrowly tailored to further Rockford's compelling interest in having an undisrupted school session conducive to the students' learning, and does not unnecessarily interfere with First Amendment rights."

BUSES, THEATERS AND MILITARY BASES

Several decisions in the mid-1970s began to foreshadow the Court's later categorizing approach to public property. In these decisions, the nature of the property at issue begins to be more of a focal point than the functional compatibility of speech with its environment:

1. ***Public transportation.*** In **Lehman v. Shaker Heights**, 418 U.S. 298 (1974), the Court upheld a city rule against political advertising on city-owned buses. The city allowed commercial advertising on the buses. A candidate for state assembly who sought unsuccessfully to buy space for campaign advertisements challenged the rule. The Court rejected the challenge in a 5–4 decision. Justice BLACKMUN wrote a plurality opinion joined by Chief Justice Burger and Justices White and Rehnquist: "[It] is urged that the car cards here constitute a public forum protected by the First Amendment, and that there is a guarantee of nondiscriminatory access to such publicly owned and controlled areas of communication 'regardless of the primary purpose for which the area is dedicated.' We disagree. [This situation is] different from the traditional settings where First Amendment values inalterably prevail. Although [our cases have] been jealous to preserve access to public places for purposes of free speech, the nature of the forum and the conflicting interests involved have remained important in determining the degree of protection afforded. [In] much the same way that a newspaper or periodical, or even a radio or television station, need not accept every proffer of advertising from the general public, a city transit system has discretion to develop and make reasonable choices concerning the type of advertising that may be displayed in its [vehicles]."

Justice Blackmun found that the city's distinction between commercial and political advertising was not "arbitrary, capricious, or invidious": "Here, the city has decided that '[p]urveyors of goods and services saleable in commerce may purchase advertising space on an equal basis, whether they be house builders or butchers.' This decision is little different from deciding to impose a 10-, 25-, or 35-cent fare, or from changing schedules or the location of bus stops. Revenue earned from long-term commercial advertising could be jeopardized by a requirement that short-term candidacy or issue-oriented advertisements be displayed on car cards. Users would be subjected to the blare of political propaganda. There could be lurking doubts about favoritism, and sticky administrative problems might arise in parceling out limited space to eager politicians. In these circumstances, the managerial decision to limit car card space to innocuous and less controversial commercial and service oriented advertising does not rise to the dignity of a First Amendment violation."

Justice DOUGLAS, whose vote was needed to forge a majority, concurred in the judgment, emphasizing that transit users were a "captive audience" whom the city could constitutionally protect: "[A] streetcar or bus is plainly not a park or sidewalk or other meeting place for discussion. [It] is only a way to get to work or back home. The fact that it is owned and operated by the city does not without more make it a forum. [If] we are to turn a bus or street car into either a newspaper or a park, we take great liberties with people who because of necessity become commuters and at the same time captive viewers or listeners."

Justice BRENNAN dissented, joined by Justices Stewart, Marshall, and Powell: "[The] city created a forum for the dissemination of information and expression of ideas when it accepted and displayed commercial and public service advertisements on its rapid transit vehicles. Having opened a forum for communication, the city is barred by the [First Amendment] from discriminating among forum users solely on the basis of message content."

Some public transit authorities allow political advertisements generally but maintain rules allowing the exclusion of advertisements that they deem offensive (for example, ads that "demean or disparage" a certain group). Does Lehman's reasoning extend to allow these types of exclusions? Several courts of appeal have struck them down, holding that the respective transit authorities—through accepting political advertising in the first place—had created designated public fora and thus could not exclude advertisements based on their content. See, e.g., United Food & Commercial Workers Union, Local 1099 v. Sw. Ohio Reg'l Transit Auth., 163 F.3d 341 (6th Cir. 1998); N.Y. Magazine v. Metro. Transp. Auth., 136 F.3d 123 (2d Cir. 1998); Planned Parenthood Ass'n/Chi. Area v. Chi. Transit Auth., 767 F.2d 1225 (7th Cir. 1985). But the First and Ninth Circuits have held that accepting some political advertising, even if that advertising features controversial issues, does not transform public-transit advertising space into a designated public forum. See Am. Freedom Defense Initiative v. Mass. Bay Transp. Auth., 781 F.3d 571 (1st Cir. 2015); Seattle Mideast Awareness Campaign v. King County, 781 F.3d 489 (9th Cir. 2015). Those cases allowed the exclusion of controversial advertisements so long as the exclusion was not viewpoint discriminatory, and both courts held that the exclusions at issue were viewpoint-neutral.

What if a transit system excludes *all* advertising, commercial as well as noncommercial? Is a city bus an "anomalous" place for messages? Note that the government property involved here (bus advertising) and in the next note (municipal theater) is property designed for communicative purposes, in contrast to the primary *non*communicative purposes of the public property involved in such contexts as jails. Should that make a difference in the analysis? Even assuming the city could bar all messages on city buses, why could it discriminate against political speech? Doesn't such a subject matter distinction run afoul of Mosley? Is an exception to the Mosley principle justified because the city is running the bus as a business? See generally Wells & Hellerstein, "The Governmental-Proprietary Distinction in Constitutional Law," 66 Va. L. Rev. 1073 (1980) (suggesting that government's "quasi-business interest may adequately support regulation that a court might strike down if applied to the public at large"). Finally, should members of the "captive audience" on the bus have been required, like Cohen's audience, simply to avert their eyes?

2. ***Municipal theaters.*** Contrast Justice BLACKMUN's reluctance to recognize a public forum claim in Lehman with his majority opinion less than a year later in **Southeastern Promotions, Ltd. v. Conrad**, 420 U.S. 546 (1975). There, the Court found that the challenger's First Amendment rights were violated when the municipal board managing city theaters in Chattanooga refused permission to present "the controversial rock musical 'Hair.'" The refusal was based on the ground that the production would not be "in the best interest of the community." Although the alleged obscenity of "Hair" had been the major issue in the lower courts, Justice Blackmun did not reach that question, but rather found that the refusal constituted a prior restraint imposed without sufficient procedural safeguards.

In the course of reaching that conclusion, Justice Blackmun commented that the municipal theaters were "public forums designed for and dedicated to expressive activities. [Petitioner] was not seeking to use a facility primarily serving a competing use. [E.g., Adderley; Brown.] Nor was rejection of the application based on any regulation of time, place, or manner related to the nature of the facility or applications from other users. [E.g., Cox v. New Hampshire.] No rights of individuals in surrounding areas were violated by noise or any other aspect of the production. [Kovacs v. Cooper.] There was no captive audience. See [Lehman; Pollak]. Whether the petitioner might have used some other, privately owned, theater in the city for the production is of no consequence. [That] alone would not justify an otherwise impermissible prior restraint. [Schneider.]"

Justice DOUGLAS, in a concurring opinion, thought the majority's holding did not go far enough: in his view, no prior screening process of any sort was permissible. And he added: "A municipal theater is no less a forum for the expression of ideas than is a public park, or a sidewalk." A dissent by Justice WHITE, joined by Chief Justice Burger, concluded that, whether or not "Hair" was obscene, the city "could constitutionally forbid exhibition of the musical for children" and could "reserve its auditorium for productions suitable for exhibition to all the citizens of the city, adults and children alike." Another dissent, by Justice REHNQUIST, argued that a public auditorium should not be equated with public streets and parks. He feared that the majority had given "no constitutionally permissible role in the way of selection to the municipal authorities" and asked: "May a municipal theater devote an entire season to Shakespeare, or is it required to book any potential producer on a first-come, first-served basis?" He concluded that a city policy not to show attractions "of the kind that would offend any substantial number of potential theater goers" was not "arbitrary or unreasonable."

3. ***Military bases.*** To what extent may a First Amendment claimant gain access to a military base that has been opened up to the general public for some purposes? The per curiam decision in Flower v. United States, 407 U.S. 197 (1972), suggested that military bases might be treated as nontraditional public forums. There, the 7–2 decision reversed a conviction for distributing peace leaflets on a street within the boundaries of an Army base in San Antonio: "Whatever power the authorities may have to restrict general access to a military facility, here the fort commander chose not to exclude the public from the street where petitioner was arrested." But when

the Court confronted the issue more fully four years later, in **Greer v. Spock**, 424 U.S. 828 (1976), the majority interpreted Flower narrowly.

The Spock decision upheld two regulations at Fort Dix, a large Army post in rural New Jersey, that barred political activities on the base: the first prohibited, inter alia, speeches and demonstrations of a partisan political nature; the second, distribution of literature without prior approval of the base commander. Justice STEWART's majority opinion emphasized that the business of a base such as Fort Dix was "to train soldiers, not to provide a public forum," and rejected any claim to a generalized constitutional right to "make political speeches or distribute leaflets" there. He observed that in Spock, unlike in Flower, the military authorities had never "abandoned any claim of special interest" in regulating political activities. Noting "the special constitutional function of the military in our national life," he stated: "The notion that federal military reservations, like municipal streets and parks, have traditionally served as a place for free public assembly and communication of thoughts by private citizens [is] historically and constitutionally false." After using these broad grounds to reject the facial challenges, the majority turned down the as-applied attacks with similar deference to the military. With respect to the ban on speeches and demonstrations, Justice Stewart noted that the regulation had been applied evenhandedly rather than discriminatorily, in accordance with a policy of "keeping official military activities there wholly free of entanglement with partisan political campaigns of any kind"—a policy "wholly consistent with the American constitutional tradition of a politically neutral military establishment under civilian control."

Justice POWELL's concurrence emphasized that access was sought to an "enclave of [the military] system that stands apart from and outside of many of the rules that govern ordinary civilian life in our country." In that context, "our inquiry is not limited to claims that the exercise of First Amendment rights is disruptive of base activity. We also must consider functional and symbolic incompatibility with the 'specialized society separate from civilian society' that has its home on the base." The requirement of prior approval to distribute literature, in his view, was justified not by the public interest in military neutrality, but rather by "the unique need of the military to 'insist upon a respect for duty and a discipline without counterpart in civilian life.' "

Justice BRENNAN's dissent, joined by Justice Marshall, argued that the challengers should be permitted to speak at Fort Dix even if the military installation was not a "public forum." "[The] determination that a locale is a 'public forum' has never been erected as an absolute prerequisite to all forms of demonstrative First Amendment activity. [Because] the permissibility of a certain form of public expression at a given locale may differ depending on whether it is asked if the locale is a public forum or if the form of expression is compatible with the activities occurring at the locale, it becomes apparent that there is need for a flexible approach. Otherwise, with the rigid characterization of a given locale as not a public forum, there is the danger that certain forms of public speech at the locale may be suppressed, even though they are basically compatible with the activities otherwise occurring at the locale." Applying his more flexible test, Justice Brennan concluded that leaflet distribution should be permitted "in those streets and lots unrestricted to civilian traffic," since those areas did not "differ in their nature and use from city streets and lots where open speech long has been protected." Political rallies posed more difficulty because of the "potential for disruption even in unrestricted areas," but not so much as "significantly to impair training or defense, thereby requiring its prohibition." Justice Brennan further argued that the ban was not necessary for military neutrality because no one would associate the speakers' causes with the military, and that allowing speech in unrestricted areas might even enhance neutrality because the military itself is "highly susceptible to politicization," and its isolated members would benefit from "the moderating influence of other ideas."

The Court reaffirmed its view of the special nature of military bases in **United States v. Albertini**, 472 U.S. 675 (1985). That case upheld the exclusion of an individual from Hickam Air Force Base in Hawaii after he had previously been barred for prior unlawful conduct. He sought to enter the base in order to engage in peaceful expressive activity during Hickam's annual open house, when the general public was allowed to enter. Justice O'Connor's majority opinion emphasized that Hickam had not become a public forum merely because the general public had been invited on that day and relied in part on O'Brien in sustaining Albertini's conviction for reentering the base after he had been barred. See also Brown v. Glines, 444 U.S. 348 (1980) (upholding Air Force regulations requiring service members to obtain approval from commanders before circulating petitions on bases). Are these military base cases explainable on the basis of the Court's typical extraordinary deference to military judgments in a range of constitutional contexts? Recall, for example, Rostker v. Goldberg, 453 U.S. 57 (1981; p. 780 above) (finding no sex discrimination in exclusion of women from registration in anticipation of the draft); see also Goldman v. Weinberger (1986; p. 1589 below) (finding no freedom of religion violation in applying an Air Force headgear regulation to bar wearing of yarmulke).

PUBLIC AND NONPUBLIC FORUMS

1. ***The types of forums.*** At one time, commentators assumed that the Court categorized spaces into "traditional, quintessential" public forums, "designated" public forums, and "nonpublic" forums. In traditional public forums, such as streets and parks, content-based exclusions of speech must be necessary to serve a compelling state interest and narrowly drawn to achieve that end. Designated public forums are where the government opens public property for expressive activity. Since the government opens up these forums for expression, only reasonable time, place, and manner restrictions are permissible and content-based restrictions must be narrowly tailored to meet a compelling state interest. Nonpublic forums, like airport terminals, household mailboxes, and open areas in a military base, are public property which is not by tradition or designation a forum for public communication. See Perry Education Ass'n v. Perry Local Educators' Ass'n (1983; below p. 1258).

There was considerable criticism of this classification scheme. See, e.g., Farber & Nowak, "The Misleading Nature of Public Forum Analysis: Content and Context in First Amendment Adjudication," 70 Va. L. Rev. 1219 (1984) ("Classification of public places as various types of forums has only confused judicial opinions by diverting attention from the real First Amendment [issues]—the First Amendment values and governmental interests involved in the case."); Tribe, Constitutional Choices (1985) (criticizing Perry as avoiding "a rigorous analysis of the viewpoint discrimination issue by focusing on the public forum analysis"). For the contrary view, see BeVier, "Rehabilitating Public Forum Doctrine: In Defense of Categories," 1993 Sup. Ct. Rev. 79 (arguing that the central function of the First Amendment is to prevent government distortion of public dialogue, not to enhance the amount of speech, and that "[t]he role of categorical analysis in public forum jurisprudence is to generalize about the kinds of places where denials of access tend systematically to trigger well-founded concerns about deliberate governmental abuse and distortion").

Since then, things have gotten considerably more complicated. First, the Court has been faced with applying forum analysis for non-physical institutional arrangements like the student activities fund in Rosenberger and access to student organization status as in Christian Legal Society v. Martinez (2010; below p. 1277) and cyberspace as in Packingham v. North Carolina (2017; p. 1269). Second, the categories of forum appear to have shifted from "traditional," "designated," and "nonpublic" forum to something else. In Perry Education Ass'n v. Perry Local Educators' Ass'n (1983; below p. 1258), first laying out the three part scheme, Justice White seemed to imply in a footnote that the limited public forum was a type of designated forum. But in a footnote to Christian Legal Society, Justice Ginsburg for the Court distinguished traditional public forum, designated public forum, and limited public forum analysis. Nonpublic forum went unmentioned.

Has the limited public forum been gradually added as a separate category to the original list of three? In Walker v. Texas Division, Sons of Confederate Veterans, (2015; below p. 1270), the Court hinted at the existence of four forum categories. The Walker Court held that words or symbols on specialty license plates were government speech. Justice Breyer, writing for the majority, found that the specialty plates were not a "forum for private speech" and rejected the applicability of traditional, designated, limited, and nonpublic forums. Has the Court displaced the designated public forum, as some commentators have believed based on Justice White's original introduction of the view in Perry? See, e.g., Rohr, "First Amendment Fora Revisited: How Many Categories Are There?", 41 Nova L. Rev. 221, 226 (2017). Or does the Court now use the terms nonpublic forum and limited public forum synonymously, describing a setting governed by the requirement that the government regulation be reasonable and viewpoint neutral? Christian Legal Society suggests the latter: "[T]he Court has permitted restrictions on access to a limited public forum, [w]ith this key caveat: Any access barrier must be reasonable and viewpoint neutral." This description is essentially identical to Justice O'Connor's account of the nonpublic forum in Cornelius, where she wrote that "[c]ontrol over access to a nonpublic forum can be based on subject matter and speaker identity so long as the distinctions drawn are reasonable in light of the purpose served by the forum and are viewpoint neutral." This schema was endorsed in Justice Thomas's dissent in the denial of certiorari in Am. Freedom Def. Initiative v. King Cty., 136 S. Ct. 1022, 1022 (2016), where he wrote that a "limited public forum, [is] also called a nonpublic forum."

Thus, the Court increasingly seems not to speak of the nonpublic forum, and its legal treatment now seems to be the same as the limited public forum. Yet, lower courts continue to struggle to determine "what distinction, if any, exists between a 'designated public forum' and a 'limited public forum.' " Bowman v. White, 444 F.3d 967, 975 (8th Cir. 2006).

2. ***Mailboxes.*** In **U.S. Postal Service v. Council of Greenburgh Civic Ass'ns**, 453 U.S. 114 (1981), the Court rejected a First Amendment challenge to 18 U.S.C. § 1725, which prohibited the deposit of unstamped "mailable matter" in home letter boxes approved by the Postal Service. The statute was challenged by a group of civic associations who asserted that the ban on their delivering messages to local residents by placing unstamped notices and pamphlets in the letter boxes of private homes unduly inhibited their communications with the residents. Justice REHNQUIST, writing for the Court, found the First Amendment challenge without merit. Finding that a letter box "is not traditionally [a] 'public forum,' " he found it unnecessary to apply the principles governing time, place, and manner restrictions on the use of public forums: "property owned or controlled by the government which is *not* a public forum may be subject to a prohibition of speech, leafleting, picketing, or other forms of communication without running afoul of the First Amendment [so long as the government] act[s] reasonably in imposing such restrictions, and the prohibition [is] content-neutral. § 1725 is both a reasonable and content-neutral regulation."

In rejecting the public-forum claim, Justice Rehnquist noted that a "letterbox provided by a postal customer which meets the Postal Service's specifications [becomes] part of the [Service's] nationwide system for the receipt and delivery of mail. [In] effect, the postal customer, although he pays for the physical components of the 'authorized depository,' agrees to abide by the Postal Service's regulations in exchange for the Postal Service agreeing to deliver and pick up his mail. [A] letter box, once designated an 'authorized depository,' does not [undergo] a transformation into a 'public forum' of some limited nature to which the First Amendment guarantees access to all comers." Justice Rehnquist contended that his opinion was consistent with Greer, Adderly, and Shaker Heights, which each "recognized that the First Amendment does not guarantee access to property simply because it is owned or controlled by the government."

Justice BRENNAN, concurring in the judgment, insisted that a letter box *is* a public forum because "the mails and the letter box are specifically used for the communication of information and ideas." But although he disagreed with the majority's mode of analysis, he would have nevertheless held that the law was a reasonable time, place and manner regulation. He noted that the restraint was "content-neutral" and that it advanced "a significant governmental interest—preventing loss of mail revenues." Moreover, there were "ample alternative channels for communication"—for example, placing circulars under doors or attaching them to doorknobs.

Justice MARSHALL dissented. He argued that "[e]ven if the Postal Service were not a public forum, [the] statute advanced in its aid is a law challenged as an abridgment of free expression. [The] question, then, is whether this statute burdens any First Amendment rights enjoyed by appellees. If so, it must be determined whether this burden is justified by a significant governmental interest substantially advanced by the statute." The Postal Service could not meet this standard, he argued, because "the statute's asserted purposes easily could be advanced by less intrusive alternatives, such as a nondiscriminatory permit requirement for depositing unstamped circulars in letter boxes." In any event, he argued, given "its pervasive and traditional use as purveyor of written communication, the

Postal Service [may] properly be viewed as a [public forum]. For the Postal Service's very purpose is to facilitate communication, which surely differentiates it from the military bases, jails, and mass transportation discussed in cases relied on by the Court." Justice STEVENS, in a separate dissent, agreed with Justice Marshall's result, but on the different ground that letter boxes are private property and the law "interferes with the owner's receipt of information that he may want to receive" without adequate justification.

3. ***Teachers' mailboxes.*** In **Perry Education Ass'n v. Perry Local Educators' Ass'n**, 460 U.S. 37 (1983), the Court upheld a provision of a collective bargaining contract giving the incumbent teacher's union, the Perry Education Association (PEA), access to the local interschool mail system and teacher mailboxes, but denying that same access to rival groups, including the Perry Local Educators' Association (PLEA). The Court rejected PLEA's First Amendment challenge. Justice WHITE, writing for the Court, acknowledged that the policy implicated the First Amendment. But, he wrote, "[t]he existence of a right of access to public property and the standard by which limitations upon such a right must be evaluated differ depending on the character of the property at issue." He explained:

"In places which by long tradition or by government fiat have been devoted to assembly and debate, the rights of the state to limit expressive activity are sharply circumscribed. At one end of the spectrum are [streets and parks. Hague v. CIO.] In these quintessential public forums, the government may not prohibit all communicative activity. For the state to enforce a content-based exclusion it must show that its regulation is necessary to serve a compelling state interest and that it is narrowly drawn to achieve that end. The state may also enforce regulations of the time, place, and manner of expression which are content-neutral, are narrowly tailored to serve a significant government interest, and leave open ample alternative channels of communication.

"A second category consists of public property which the state has opened for use by the public as a place for expressive activity. The Constitution forbids a state to enforce certain exclusions from a forum generally open to the public even if it was not required to create the forum in the first place. [E.g., Southeastern Promotions.][1] Although a state is not required to indefinitely retain the open character of the facility, as long as it does so it is bound by the same standards as apply to the traditional public forum.

"Public property which is not by tradition or designation a forum for public communication is governed by different standards. [Greenburgh.] [In] addition to time, place, and manner regulations, the state may reserve the forum for its intended purposes, communicative or otherwise, as long as the regulation on speech is reasonable and not an effort to suppress expression merely because public officials oppose the speaker's view. '[The] State, no less than a private owner of property, has power to preserve the property under its control for the use to which it is lawfully dedicated.' [Greenburgh; Greer; Adderley.]

[1] A public forum may be created for a limited purpose such as use by certain groups [e.g., student groups], or for the discussion of certain subjects [e.g., school board business]. [Footnote by Justice White.]

"The school mail facilities at issue here fall within this third category [of nonpublic forums]. [The] interschool mail system is not a traditional public forum. [On] this point the parties agree. [The] internal mail system [is] not held open to the general public. It is instead PLEA's position that the school mail facilities have become a 'limited public forum' from which it may not be excluded because of the periodic use of the system by private non-school connected groups, and PLEA's own unrestricted access to the system prior to PEA's certification as exclusive representative. Neither of these arguments is persuasive. [The] schools do allow some outside organizations such as the YMCA, Cub Scouts, and other civic and church organizations to use the facilities. This type of selective access does not transform government property into a public forum. [Greer; Lehman.] Moreover, even if we assume that by granting access to [some groups], the school district has created a 'limited' public forum, the constitutional right of access would in any event extend only to other entities of similar character. While the school mail facilities thus might be a forum generally open for use [by] other organizations that engage in activities of interest and educational relevance to students, they would not as a consequence be open to an organization such as PLEA, which is concerned with the terms and conditions of teacher employment.

"[Nor does the] access policy adopted by the Perry schools favor[ ] a particular viewpoint, that of the PEA, on labor relations, [in which case it would] be strictly scrutinized regardless of whether a public forum is involved. There is [no] indication that the school board intended to discourage one viewpoint and advance another. We believe it is more accurate to characterize the access policy as based on the *status* of the respective unions rather than their views. Implicit in the concept of the nonpublic forum is the right to make distinctions in access on the basis of subject matter and speaker identity.

"The differential access provided PEA and PLEA is reasonable because it is wholly consistent with the district's legitimate interest in 'preserv[ing] the property [for] the use to which it is lawfully dedicated.' [Greenburgh.] Use of school mail facilities enables PEA to perform effectively its obligations as exclusive representative of *all* Perry Township teachers. Conversely, PLEA does not have any official responsibility in connection with the school district and need not be entitled to the same rights of access to school mailboxes. [Moreover], exclusion of the rival union may reasonably be considered a means of insuring labor-peace within the [schools]. Finally, the reasonableness of the limitations on PLEA's access to the school mail system is also supported by the substantial alternative channels that remain open for union-teacher communication to take place. These means range from bulletin boards to meeting facilities to the United States mail. During election periods, PLEA is assured of equal access to all modes of communication. [On] government property that has not been made a public forum, not all speech is equally situated, and the state may draw distinctions which relate to the special purpose for which the property is used. [For] a school mail facility, the difference in status between the exclusive bargaining representative and its rival is such a distinction."

Justice BRENNAN dissented, joined by Justices Marshall, Powell, and Stevens: "[Because] the exclusive access provision in the collective bargaining agreement amounts to viewpoint discrimination that infringes the respondents' First Amendment rights and fails to advance any substantial state interest, I dissent. [According] to the Court, the petitioner's status as the exclusive bargaining representative provides a reasonable basis for the exclusive access policy. The Court fundamentally misperceives the essence of the respondents' claims. [This] case does not involve an 'absolute access' claim. It involves an 'equal access' claim. As such it does not turn on whether the internal school mail system is a 'public forum.' In focusing on the public forum issue, the Court disregards the First Amendment's central proscription against censorship, in the form of viewpoint discrimination, in any forum, public or nonpublic. [Addressing] the question of viewpoint discrimination directly, free of the Court's irrelevant public forum analysis, it is clear that the exclusive access policy discriminates on the basis of viewpoint. [The] only reason for [PEA] to seek an exclusive access policy is to deny its rivals access to an effective channel of communication. No other group is explicitly denied access to the mail system. In fact, [many] other groups have been granted access to the system. [The] board has agreed to amplify the speech of [PEA], while repressing the speech of [PLEA] based on [PLEA's] point of view. This sort of discrimination amounts to censorship and infringes the First Amendment rights of the respondents [without] further[ing] any substantial state interest."

Notice that, in a footnote describing the concept of the designated public forum, Justice White wrote that "[a] public forum may be created for a limited purpose such as use by certain groups, or for the discussion of certain subjects." This footnote inaugurated the confusing terminological relation between the "designated public forum" and the "limited public forum." Because it is described in a brief footnote, the limited public forum might seem to be a subset of the designated public forum or interchangeable with it; indeed, several subsequent commentators have treated the two as identical. See, e.g., Laycock, "Theology Scholarships, the Pledge of Allegiance, and Religious Liberty: Avoiding the Extremes but Missing the Liberty," 118 Harv. L. Rev. 155 (2004). Yet Justice White in Perry held that, in a designated public forum, the government "is bound by the same standards as apply to the traditional public forum" which seems discordant with his footnote statement that, in a limited public forum, the government may restrict speech according to subject matter. Perhaps as a result of this discord, the Court has recently described the designated public forum and the limited public forum as distinct and separate categories. See Christian Legal Soc'y v. Martinez (2010; p. 1277 below).

4. ***Charitable campaigns in federal offices.*** **Cornelius v. NAACP Legal Defense & Ed. Fund**, 473 U.S. 788 (1985), was a 4–3 decision (Justices Marshall and Powell did not participate) that upheld the exclusion of political and advocacy groups from the Combined Federal Campaign (CFC), an annual charitable fundraising drive conducted in federal offices during working hours mainly through the voluntary efforts of federal employees. The Executive Order at issue limited the organizations that could participate in CFC to voluntary, tax-exempt, nonprofit charitable agencies that provide direct health and welfare services to individuals; the Order expressly excluded legal defense and political advocacy groups. Justice O'CONNOR's plurality opinion, following the tripartite classification of forums articulated in Perry, found the CFC (not the federal workplace generally) the relevant forum and held that it was a "nonpublic forum," not a "traditional" public forum or a "public forum created by government designation": "[The] government does not create a public forum by inaction or by permitting limited discourse, but only by intentionally opening a non-

traditional forum for public discourse. [Perry.] Accordingly, the Court has looked to the policy and practice of the government to ascertain whether it intended to designate a place not traditionally open to assembly and debate as a public forum. The Court has also examined the nature of the property and its compatibility with expressive activity to discern the government's intent. [Not] every instrumentality used for communication, however, is a traditional public forum or a public forum by designation. [Greenburgh.] [We] will not find that a public forum has been created in the face of clear evidence of a contrary intent, nor will we infer that the government intended to create a public forum when the nature of the property is inconsistent with expressive activity."

Here, Justice O'Connor was not persuaded that the CFC was a "designated" public forum: "The government's consistent policy has been to limit participation in the CFC to 'appropriate' voluntary agencies. [Such] selective access, unsupported by evidence of a purposeful designation for public use, does not create a public forum. [Greer v. Spock.] Nor does the history of the CFC support a finding that the Government was motivated by an affirmative desire to provide an open forum for charitable solicitation in the federal workplace. [It] follows that the Government has the right to exercise control over access to the federal workplace in order to avoid interruptions to the performance of the duties of its employees."

Having determined that the CFC was a "nonpublic forum," Justice O'Connor held the exclusion only to a standard of reasonableness: "Control over access to a nonpublic forum can be based on subject matter and speaker identity so long as the distinctions drawn are reasonable in light of the purpose served by the forum and are viewpoint neutral. [Perry.] Although a speaker may be excluded from a nonpublic forum if he wishes to address a topic not encompassed within the purpose of the forum [Lehman] or if he is not a member of the class of speakers for whose especial benefit the forum was created [Perry], the government violates the First Amendment when it denies access to a speaker solely to suppress the point of view he espouses on an otherwise includible subject." She emphasized: "The Government's decision to restrict access to a nonpublic forum need only be *reasonable;* it need not be the most reasonable or the only reasonable limitation. In contrast to a public forum, a finding of strict incompatibility between the nature of the speech or the identity of the speaker and the functioning of the nonpublic forum is not mandated. [Cf. Perry; Lehman.] [Nor] is there a requirement that the restriction be narrowly tailored or that the Government's interest be compelling. The First Amendment does not demand unrestricted access to a nonpublic forum merely because use of that forum may be the most efficient means of delivering the speaker's message [Greenburgh.]"

Justice BLACKMUN dissented, joined by Justice Brennan. He objected to the majority's holding that, "when the Government acts as the holder of public property other than streets, parks, and similar places, the Government may do whatever it reasonably intends to do, so long as it does not intend to suppress a particular viewpoint." He argued that the CFC was a limited public forum, and that the government's exclusion of "speech that would be compatible with the intended uses of the property" triggered a demand for a "compelling governmental interest." Applying this analysis, he concluded that the asserted justifications "neither reserve the CFC for expressive activity compatible with the property nor serve any other compelling governmental interest." Moreover, he argued that the challenged exclusions were "blatantly viewpoint-based" because "Government employees may hear only from those charities that think that charitable goals can best be achieved within the confines of existing social policy and the status quo." Justice Stevens also submitted a dissent, arguing that the case could be disposed of without using "multitiered analysis" to label the forum, simply on the ground that it discriminated based on viewpoint.

Notice that in Cornelius, Justice O'Connor held that the CFC was a nonpublic forum, while Justice Blackmun would have held that it was a "limited public forum."

5. ***Post office sidewalks.*** Usually, streets and sidewalks are public forums on which speech restrictions demand a strong justification. But **United States v. Kokinda**, 497 U.S. 720 (1990), indicated that use of an area that *appears* to be a sidewalk does not necessarily assure the most careful scrutiny. The Court upheld a Postal Service prohibition of "soliciting" contributions on postal premises. The regulation was applied to soliciting by volunteers for the National Democratic Policy Committee who had set up a table on the sidewalk near the entrance of the Bowie, Maryland, post office in order to collect contributions. As described by the lower court, the post office was a "freestanding" building, with its own sidewalk and parking lot. It was located on a major highway. "A sidewalk runs along the edge of the highway, separating the post office property from the street. To enter the post office, cars enter a driveway that traverses the public sidewalk and enter a parking lot that surrounds the post office building. Another sidewalk runs adjacent to the building itself, separating the parking lot from the building. Postal patrons must use [this] sidewalk to enter the post office. The sidewalk belongs to the post office and is used for no other purpose."

Justice O'CONNOR's plurality opinion, joined by Chief Justice Rehnquist and Justices White and Scalia, began by concluding that the postal "sidewalk" was not the kind of sidewalk that constituted a traditional public forum. Instead, she found that the postal sidewalk was a nonpublic forum and that the postal regulation was constitutional because viewpoint-neutral and reasonable as applied: "Respondents contend that although the sidewalk is on postal service property, because it is not distinguishable from the municipal sidewalk across the parking lot from the post office's entrance, it must be a traditional public forum and therefore subject to strict scrutiny. This argument is unpersuasive. [The] postal sidewalk at issue does not have the characteristics of public sidewalks traditionally open to expressive activity. The municipal sidewalk that runs parallel to the road in this case is a public passageway. The Postal Service's sidewalk is not such a thoroughfare. Rather, it leads only from the parking area to the front door of the post office." Although the postal entryways are open to the public, "that fact alone does not establish that such areas must be treated as traditional public fora." She noted that the Postal Service had not "expressly dedicated its sidewalks to any expressive activity." Instead, the sidewalk was "expressly dedicated to only one means of free communication: the posting of public notices on designated bulletin boards. [To] be sure, individuals and groups have been permitted to leaflet, speak, and picket on postal premises, [but] a practice of allowing some speech activities on public postal property [does] not add up to the dedication of postal property to speech activities. [Cornelius.]"

In finding the restriction "reasonable," Justice O'Connor emphasized what she called "a long-settled principle" that "governmental actions are subject to a lower level of First Amendment scrutiny" when the government is not acting "as lawmaker [but] rather as proprietor." She emphasized that Congress had wanted the Postal Service "to be run more like a business" than had its predecessor, the Post Office Department. Noting that regulation must merely be "reasonable" when Government acts in a proprietary capacity [Lehman], she found that "it is reasonable to restrict access [to] solicitation, because solicitation is inherently disruptive of the Postal Service's business." The plurality also found no impermissible content discrimination in singling out solicitation for special treatment.

Significantly, however, the "reasonableness" standard did not attract a majority of the Court. Justice KENNEDY, who had joined the Court after Cornelius, concurred only in the judgment and specifically distanced himself from the plurality's approach. He suggested that the walkway surrounding a post office "may be an appropriate place for the exercise of vital rights of expression. As society becomes more insular in character, it becomes essential to protect public places where traditional modes of speech [can] take place." However, he found it unnecessary to determine whether the sidewalk was a public or nonpublic forum, because in his view "the postal regulation [meets] the traditional standards we have applied to time, place, and manner restrictions of protected expression," citing Clark and Ward. "Given the Postal Service's past experience with expressive activity on its property, I cannot reject its judgment that in-person solicitation deserves different treatment from alternative forms of solicitation and expression."

Justice BRENNAN, joined by Justices Marshall and Stevens and in part by Justice Blackmun, dissented, criticizing the plurality's distinction between types of sidewalks: "[The plurality] insists, with logic that is both strained and formalistic, that the specific sidewalk at issue is not a public forum. This conclusion is unsupportable. [It] is only common sense that a public sidewalk adjacent to a public building to which citizens are freely admitted is a natural location for speech to occur. [It] is irrelevant that [this] sidewalk [may] have been constructed only to provide access to the [post office]. Public sidewalks, parks, and streets have been reserved for public use as forums for speech even though government has not constructed them for expressive purposes. Parks are usually constructed to beautify a city and to provide opportunities for recreation, rather than to afford a forum for soapbox orators or leafleteers; streets are built to facilitate transportation, not to enable protestors to conduct marches; and sidewalks are created with pedestrians in mind, not solicitors. [That] the walkway at issue is a sidewalk open and accessible to the general public is alone sufficient to identify it as a public forum. [Whatever] the proper application of public forum doctrine to novel situations [such as those in Cornelius and Perry], we ought not unreflectively transfer principles [developed] in those specialized and difficult contexts to traditional forums such as streets, sidewalks, and parks."

Justice Brennan added: "Even if I did not believe that the postal sidewalk is a 'traditional' public forum, I would find that it is a 'limited-purpose' forum from which respondents may not be excluded absent a showing of a compelling interest to which any exclusion is narrowly tailored." He insisted that the regulation could not pass muster under that requirement or the standard applicable to time, place, and manner regulations. He added: "Even if I did not believe that [this] sidewalk was a public forum, I nevertheless could not agree [that] the postal regulation [is] reasonable. [The] Postal Service does not subject to the same categorical prohibition many other types of speech presenting the same risk of disruption as solicitation, such as soapbox oratory, pamphleteering, [or] even flag-burning. [This] inconsistent treatment renders the prohibition on solicitation unreasonable."

6. ***Airport terminals.*** Shifting majorities in **International Society for Krishna Consciousness, Inc. (ISKCON) v. Lee**, 505 U.S. 672 (1992) and its companion case, **Lee v. ISKCON**, 505 U.S. 830 (1992), upheld a ban on the solicitation of money in a public airport terminal, but struck down a ban on the sale or distribution of literature there. The Port Authority operates the three major airports in the New York metropolitan area. It had promulgated rules restricting solicitation and leafleting activities to sidewalks outside the airports' terminals. The Court considered a challenge by ISKCON to these rules. The multiple opinions produced three holdings by different configurations of Justices:

First, by a vote of 5–4, the Court found airport terminals to be *nonpublic forums*. Chief Justice REHNQUIST, writing for the Court on this point, stated that, "given the lateness with which the modern air terminal has made its appearance, it hardly qualifies for the description of having 'immemorially . . . time out of mind' been held in the public trust and used for purposes of expressive activity. [Hague.] [Nor] can we say that [airport] terminals generally have been intentionally opened by their operators to [expressive] activity; the frequent and continuing litigation evidencing the operators' objections belies any such claim. [Airports] are commercial establishments funded by users fees and designed to make a regulated profit," and their purpose is "the facilitation of passenger air travel, not the promotion of expression." Accordingly, "[t]he restrictions here challenged [need] only satisfy a requirement of reasonableness. [Kokinda, Cornelius.]"

Justice KENNEDY's partial concurrence disagreed that airports were nonpublic forums, and was joined on this point by Justices Blackmun, Stevens and Souter: "Our public forum doctrine ought not to be a jurisprudence of categories rather than ideas or convert what was once an analysis protective of expression into one which grants the government authority to restrict speech by fiat." Justice Kennedy's opinion noted the importance of public forums to democracy: "At the heart of our jurisprudence lies the principle that in a free nation citizens must have the right to gather and speak with other persons in public places." He also objected to the majority's deference to the airport authorities' managerial role: "The Court [reintroduces] today into our First Amendment law a strict doctrinal line between the proprietary and regulatory functions of government which I thought had been abandoned long ago. [Compare Davis with Hague; Schneider; Grayned.] [But a] fundamental tenet of our Constitution is that the government is subject to constraints which private persons are not." Finally, he charged that "[t]he Court's analysis rests on an inaccurate view of history. The notion that traditional public forums are property which have public discourse as their principal purpose is a most doubtful fiction. The types of property that we have recognized as the quintessential public forums are streets, parks, and sidewalks. It would seem apparent that the principal purpose of streets and sidewalks, like airports, is to facilitate transportation, not public discourse. [Similarly], the purpose for the creation of public parks may be as much for beauty and open space as for discourse. Thus under the Court's analysis, even the quintessential public forums would appear to lack the necessary elements of what the Court defines as a public forum."

Justice Kennedy urged an alternative approach: "In my view the policies underlying the doctrine cannot be given effect unless we recognize that open, public spaces and thoroughfares which are suitable for discourse may be public forums, whatever their historical pedigree and without concern for a precise classification of the property. [Without] this recognition our forum doctrine retains no relevance in times of fast-changing technology and increasing insularity. In a country where most citizens travel by automobile, and parks all too often become locales for crime rather than social intercourse, our failure to recognize the possibility that new types of government property may be appropriate forums for speech will lead to a serious curtailment of our expressive activity. One of the places left in our mobile society that is suitable for discourse is a metropolitan airport. [If] the objective, physical characteristics of the property at issue and the actual public access and uses which have been permitted by the government indicate that expressive activity would be appropriate and compatible with those uses, the property is a public forum.

"[Under] this analysis, it is evident that the public spaces of the Port Authority's airports are public forums. [First, there are] physical similarities between the Port Authority's airports and public streets. [Airports have] broad, public thoroughfares full of people and lined with stores and other commercial activities. [Second,] the airport areas involved here are open to the public without restriction. [Third,] and perhaps most important, [when] adequate time, place, and manner regulations are in place, expressive activity is quite compatible with the uses of major airports."

Justice SOUTER, joined by Justices Blackmun and Stevens, filed a separate partial concurrence and partial dissent agreeing with Justice Kennedy that airport terminals should be analyzed as public forums: "To treat the class of such forums as closed by their description as 'traditional,' taking that word merely as a charter for examining the history of the particular public property claimed as a forum, has no warrant in a Constitution whose values are not to be left behind in the city streets that are no longer the only focus of our community life. If that were the line of our direction, we might as well abandon the public forum doctrine altogether."

In a second holding, the Court upheld the *solicitation ban* by a vote of 6–3. Chief Justice REHNQUIST again wrote for the Court on this point: "We have on many prior occasions noted the disruptive effect that solicitation may have on business. 'Solicitation requires action by those who would respond: The individual solicited must decide whether or not to contribute (which itself might involve reading the solicitor's literature or hearing his pitch), and then, having decided to do so, reach for a wallet, search it for money, write a check, or produce a credit card.' [Kokinda; see Heffron.] Passengers who wish to avoid the solicitor may have to alter their path, slowing both themselves and those around them. The result is that the normal flow of traffic is impeded. This is especially so in an airport, where [delays] may be particularly costly. [In] addition, face-to-face solicitation presents risks of duress that are an appropriate target of regulation. The skillful, and unprincipled, solicitor can target the most vulnerable, including those accompanying children or those suffering physical impairment and who cannot easily avoid the solicitation. The unsavory solicitor can also commit fraud through concealment of his affiliation or through deliberate efforts to shortchange those who agree to purchase. Compounding this problem is the fact that, in an airport, the targets of such activity frequently are on tight schedules. This in turn makes such visitors unlikely to stop and formally complain to airport authorities. As a result, the airport faces considerable difficulty in achieving its legitimate interest in monitoring solicitation activity to assure that travelers are not interfered with unduly." Noting that "[t]he Port Authority has concluded that its interest in monitoring the activities can best be accomplished by limiting solicitation and distribution to the sidewalk areas outside the terminals," Justice Rehnquist concluded "that the solicitation ban is reasonable."

Justice O'CONNOR, who had joined the majority in finding airports to be nonpublic forums, concurred in the holding that the solicitation ban was constitutional, but wrote separately to emphasize that the fact that "airports are not public fora [does] not mean that the government can restrict speech in whatever way it likes." In her view, some inquiry into a nonpublic forum's "characteristic nature and function" was still required. Even taking into account that an airport is "multipurpose," operating more like "a shopping mall" than like a jail, mailbox, or post office sidewalk, however, she found that "the ban on solicitation is reasonable. Face-to-face solicitation is incompatible with the airport's functioning in a way that the other, permitted activities are not. '[As] residents of metropolitan areas know from daily experience, confrontation by a person asking for money disrupts passage and is more intrusive and intimidating than an encounter with a person giving out information.' [Kokinda.] The record in this case confirms that the problems of congestion and fraud that we have identified with solicitation in other contexts have also proved true in the airports' experience."

Justice KENNEDY provided a sixth vote to uphold the solicitation ban, finding that, even though in his view an airport was a public forum, the solicitation ban satisfied the appropriately heightened scrutiny: "The regulation may be upheld as either a reasonable time, place, and manner restriction, or as a regulation directed at the nonspeech element of expressive conduct. The two standards have considerable overlap in a case like this one. [Solicitation] is a form of protected speech. If the Port Authority's solicitation regulation prohibited all speech which requested the contribution of funds, I would conclude that it was a direct, content-based restriction of speech in clear violation of the First Amendment. The Authority's regulation does not prohibit all solicitation, however; it prohibits the 'solicitation and receipt of funds.' I do not understand this regulation to prohibit all speech that solicits funds. [The] regulation permits expression that solicits funds, but limits the manner of that expression to forms other than the immediate receipt of money.

"So viewed, [the] Port Authority's rule survives our test for speech restrictions in the public forum. In-person solicitation of funds, when combined with immediate receipt of that money, creates a risk of fraud and duress which is well recognized, and which is different in kind from other forms of expression or conduct. [Because] the Port Authority's solicitation ban is directed at these abusive practices and not at any particular message, idea, or form of speech, the regulation is a content-neutral rule serving a significant government interest. [The] regulation does not burden any broader category of speech or expressive conduct than is the source of the evil sought to be avoided. [And] the Port Authority has left open ample alternative channels for the communication of the message which is an aspect of solicitation."

Justice SOUTER, joined by Justices Blackmun and Stevens, dissented from the judgment upholding the solicitation ban, finding the ban not narrowly tailored to preventing coercion because, "[w]hile a solicitor can be insistent, a pedestrian on the street or airport concourse can simply walk away or walk on," and finding it not narrowly tailored to preventing fraud because the Port Authority had available less restrictive alternatives such as prohibiting fraudulent misrepresentations directly and imposing disclosure requirements on solicitors.

In its third holding, by a vote of 5–4, the Court invalidated the *ban on sale or distribution of literature* in the airport terminals. Justice KENNEDY concurred in the judgment on this issue, joined by Justices Blackmun, Stevens, and Souter: "[A] grant of plenary power allows the government to tilt the dialogue heard by the public, to exclude many, more marginal voices. [We] have long recognized that the right to distribute flyers and literature lies at the heart of the liberties guaranteed by the Speech and Press Clauses of the First Amendment. [Schneider.] The Port Authority's rule, which prohibits almost all such activity, is among the most restrictive possible of those liberties. [I] have no difficulty deciding the regulation cannot survive the [stringent] rules applicable to regulations in public forums. The regulation is not drawn in narrow terms and it does not leave open ample alternative channels for communication. The Port Authority's concerns with the problem of congestion can be addressed through narrow restrictions on the time and place of expressive activity." Justice O'CONNOR, concurring in the judgment, provided the fifth vote to invalidate the distribution ban. She stated that the distribution ban was impermissible even under the lenient "reasonableness" test she and the majority viewed as applicable to nonpublic forums: "While the difficulties posed by solicitation in a nonpublic forum are sufficiently obvious that its regulation may 'ring of common-sense,' the same is not necessarily true of leafletting. '[The] distribution of literature does not require that the recipient stop in order to receive the message the speaker wishes to convey; instead the recipient is free to read the message at a later time.' "

Chief Justice REHNQUIST, joined by Justices White, Scalia, and Thomas, dissented from the judgment invalidating the distribution ban: "Leafletting presents risks of congestion similar to those posed by solicitation. The weary, harried, or hurried traveler may have no less desire and need to avoid the delays generated by having literature foisted upon him than he does to avoid delays from a financial solicitation. [Moreover,] those who accept material may often simply drop it on the floor once out of the leafletter's range, creating an eyesore, a safety hazard, and additional clean-up work for airport staff." Thus, he concluded that "the distribution ban, no less than the solicitation ban, is reasonable."

7. ***Non-physical limited public forums.*** In Rosenberger v. Rector (1995; p. 1328 below), the University of Virginia maintained a student activities fund (SAF), funded by mandatory payments of $14 per semester by all students. Qualified student organizations engaged in activities "related to the educational purpose of the University of Virginia" were authorized to submit expenses to the fund for payment. Among these organizations were "student news, information, opinion, entertainment, or academic

communications media groups." The SAF was not available to support "religious activities, philanthropic contributions and activities, political activities, activities that would jeopardize the University's tax-exempt status, those which involve payment of honoraria or similar fees, or social entertainment or related expenses." A student group that published a magazine called "Wide Awake," dedicated to advancing "the Christian perspective," claimed that the SAF challenged the exclusion of religious activities as viewpoint discrimination.

In granting their claim, Justice KENNEDY addressed the question of the limited public forum: "The necessities of confining a forum to the limited and legitimate purposes for which it was created may justify the State in reserving it for certain groups or for the discussion of certain topics. Once it has opened a limited forum, however, the State must respect the lawful boundaries it has itself set. The State may not exclude speech where its distinction is not 'reasonable in light of the purpose served by the forum,' nor may it discriminate against speech on the basis of its viewpoint. Thus, in determining whether the State is acting to preserve the limits of the forum it has created so that the exclusion of a class of speech is legitimate, we have observed a distinction between, on the one hand, content discrimination, which may be permissible if it preserves the purposes of that limited forum, and, on the other hand, viewpoint discrimination, which is presumed impermissible when directed against speech otherwise within the forum's limitations.

"The SAF is a forum more in a metaphysical than in a spatial or geographic sense, but the same principles are applicable. See, e.g., Perry (forum analysis of a school mail system); Cornelius, (forum analysis of charitable contribution program). The most recent and most apposite case is our decision in Lamb's Chapel [1993; p. 1285 below]. There, a school district had opened school facilities for use after school hours by community groups for a wide variety of social, civic, and recreational purposes. The district, however, had enacted a formal policy against opening facilities to groups for religious purposes. Invoking its policy, the district rejected a request from a group desiring to show a film series addressing various child-rearing questions from a 'Christian perspective.' There was no indication in the record in Lamb's Chapel that the request to use the school facilities was 'denied, for any reason other than the fact that the presentation would have been from a religious perspective.' "

In both Perry and Cornelius, the Court analyzed non-physical forums and held that the speech restrictions were permissible and not viewpoint discrimination. In Rosenberger, the Court for the first time held that there was viewpoint discrimination in what Justice Kennedy called a "metaphysical" forum. The Court analogized the non-physical forum to physical space in a school that had been opened "for a wide variety of social, civic, and recreational purposes."

This analogy applies to the internet. The Court first tackled the regulation of online speech in **Reno v. American Civil Liberties Union**, 521 U.S. 844 (1991). Without squarely addressing the traditional forum dichotomy, the Court unanimously held that a provision of the Communications Decency Act prohibiting anyone from knowingly sending minors materials that "depicts or describes, in terms patently offensive as measured by contemporary community standards, sexual or excretory activities or organs" violated the First Amendment. Justice Stevens, writing for the Court, stated that the court was "persuaded that the CDA lacks the precision that the First Amendment requires when a statute regulates the content of speech." He continued: "In order to deny minors access to potentially harmful speech, the CDA effectively suppresses a large amount of speech that adults have a constitutional right to receive and to address to one another. That burden on adult speech is unacceptable if less restrictive alternatives would be at least as effective in achieving the legitimate purpose that the statute was enacted to serve. . . . It is true that we have repeatedly recognized the governmental interest in protecting children from harmful materials. But that interest does not justify an unnecessarily broad suppression of speech addressed to adults. As we have explained, the Government may not reduce the adult population to only what is fit for children. Regardless of the strength of the government's interest in protecting children, the level of discourse reaching a mailbox simply cannot be limited to that which would be suitable for a sandbox."

In **Packingham v. North Carolina**, 582 U.S. ___, 137 S. Ct. 1730 (2017), the Court inched closer to answering whether the internet is a public forum. The Court struck down a North Carolina law prohibiting registered sex offenders from accessing social media sites. Justice Kennedy, writing for the majority, traced the mechanics of the forum doctrine: "A fundamental principle of the First Amendment is that all persons have access to places where they can speak and listen, and then, after reflection, speak and listen once more. The Court has sought to protect the right to speak in this spatial context. A basic rule, for example, is that a street or a park is a quintessential forum for the exercise of First Amendment Rights. Even in the modern era, these places are still essential venues for public gatherings to celebrate some views, to protest others, or simply to learn and inquire. While in the past there may have been difficulty in identifying the important places (in a spatial sense) for the exchange of views, today the answer is clear. It is cyberspace—the vast democratic forums of the Internet in general, and social media in particular." He emphasized that social media facilitates low-cost communication to debate, seek employment, and participate in politics. Yet he cautioned that "While we now may be coming to the realization that the Cyber Age is a revolution of historic proportions, we cannot appreciate yet its full dimensions and vast potential to alter how we think, express ourselves, and define who we want to be. The forces and directions of the Internet are so new, so protean, and so far reaching that courts must be conscious that what they say today might be obsolete tomorrow." Declining to define the internet squarely as a public forum in the analytical sense, Justice Kennedy simply described social media as "the modern public square" that remains a "principal source[ ] for knowing current events, checking ads for employment, speaking and listening."

The remaining ambiguity is evident in Justice Alito's concurrence." Agreeing with the majority that the North Carolina statute "ha[d] a very broad reach and cover[ed] websites that are ill suited for use in stalking or abusing children," he cautioned that "if the entirety of the internet or even just social media sites are the 21st century equivalent of public streets and parks, then States may have little ability to restrict the sites that may be visited by even the most dangerous sex offenders."

Reno and Packingham represent two of the few instances the Supreme Court has addressed the constitutionality of restrictions on internet speech. Lower courts more routinely examine such cases. In **Knight First**

Amendment Institute v. Trump, 302 F. Supp. 3d 541 (S.D.N.Y. 2018), a group of Twitter users blocked by President Trump's personal Twitter account sued that blocking access to the page constituted a violation under the First Amendment. Judge Buchwald held that parts of President Trump's personal Twitter page, specifically the content of the tweets, timeline of the account's tweets, and interactive space of each tweet, were a designated public forum. Judge Buchwald first assessed whether Twitter is amenable to forum analysis. "To potentially qualify as a forum, the space in question must be owned or controlled by the government" and whether the forum analysis is consistent with "the purpose, structure, and intended use" of the space. Finding both in the affirmative, Judge Buchwald then proceeded to classify the Twitter page as a designated public forum. She found that the "interactive space of a tweet" sent by President Trump was not a traditional public forum, given the lack of historical practice of the space being used for public expression. Referring to the Court's decisions in Reno and Packhingham, Judge Buchwald noted that while the Court had analogized the internet to "essential venues of public gatherings of streets and parks, the lack of historical practice is dispositive." Judge Buchwald considered the interactive Twitter space to be a designated public forum, as the account is generally accessible to the public at large such that any person can view his tweets and anyone who wants to follow the account can do so unless the person has been blocked. Finally, Judge Buchwald found that the blocking constituted impermissible viewpoint discrimination.

8. ***License plates.*** In **Walker v. Texas Division, Sons of Confederate Veterans, Inc.**, 576 U.S. ___, 135 S. Ct. 2239 (2015), the Court considered a Texas automotive license plate scheme that gave organizations or individuals the chance to design a particular "specialty plate" by proposing a plate design comprising a slogan, a graphic, or (most commonly) both. If the Texas Department of Motor Vehicles Board approved the design, the State would make it available for display on vehicles registered in Texas. The Texas Division of the Sons of Confederate Veterans proposed a specialty license plate design featuring a Confederate battle flag. The Board rejected the proposal, and the Sons of Confederate Veterans challenged the decision as viewpoint discrimination in a limited public forum.

The Court upheld the State's decision by a vote of 5–4. Justice BREYER wrote for the Court: "When government speaks, it is not barred by the Free Speech Clause from determining the content of what it says. [In] our view, specialty license plates issued pursuant to Texas's statutory scheme convey government speech. Our reasoning rests primarily on our analysis in Pleasant Grove v. Summum [(2009); p. 1287 below]. [First], the history of license plates shows that, insofar as license plates have conveyed more than state names and vehicle identification numbers, they long have communicated messages from the States. [Second], Texas license plate designs are often closely identified in the public mind with the state. Each Texas license plate is a government article serving the governmental purposes of vehicle registration and identification. The governmental nature of the plates is clear from their faces: The State places the name 'TEXAS' in large letters at the top of every plate. [Texas] license plates are, essentially, government IDs. And issuers of ID 'typically do not permit' the placement on their IDs of 'message[s] with which they do not wish to be associated.'

"Indeed, a person who displays a message on a Texas license plate likely intends to convey to the public that the State has endorsed that message. If not, the individual could simply display the message in question in larger letters on a bumper sticker right next to the plate. But the individual prefers a license plate design to the purely private speech expressed through bumper stickers. That may well be because Texas's license plate designs convey government agreement with the message displayed.

"Third, Texas maintains direct control over the messages conveyed on its specialty plates. [The] State has rejected at least a dozen proposed designs. [This] final approval authority allows Texas to choose how to present itself and its constituency. Thus, Texas offers plates celebrating the many educational institutions attended by its citizens. But it need not issue plates deriding schooling. Texas offers plates that pay tribute to the Texas citrus industry. But it need not issue plates praising Florida's oranges as far better. And Texas offers plates that say 'Fight Terrorism.' But it need not issue plates promoting al Qaeda.

"[We] have previously used what we have called forum analysis to evaluate government restrictions on purely private speech that occurs on government property. But forum analysis is misplaced here. Because the State is speaking on its own behalf, the First Amendment strictures that attend the various types of government-established forums do not apply.

"[We] conclude that Texas's specialty license plates are not a nonpublic forum which exists where the government is acting as a proprietor, managing its internal operations. With respect to specialty license plate designs, Texas is not simply managing government property, but instead is engaging in expressive conduct. [The] fact that private parties take part in the design and propagation of a message does not extinguish the governmental nature of the message or transform the government's role into that of a mere forum-provider. [Additionally], the fact that Texas vehicle owners pay annual fees in order to display specialty license plates does not imply that the plate designs are merely a forum for private speech."

Justice ALITO dissented, joined by Chief Justice Roberts and Justices Scalia and Kennedy. He would have found the State to have created a limited public forum in which it could not discriminate based on viewpoint. "Here is a test," he wrote. "Suppose you sat by the side of a Texas highway and studied the license plates on the vehicles passing by. You would see, in addition to the standard Texas plates, an impressive array of specialty plates. (There are now more than 350 varieties.) You would likely observe plates that honor numerous colleges and universities. You might see plates bearing the name of a high school, a fraternity or sorority, the Masons, the Knights of Columbus, the Daughters of the American Revolution, a realty company, a favorite soft drink, a favorite burger restaurant, and a favorite NASCAR driver.

"As you sat there watching these plates speed by, would you really think that the sentiments reflected in these specialty plates are the views of the State of Texas and not those of the owners of the cars?

"[While] all license plates unquestionably contain *some* government speech, [the] State of Texas has converted the remaining space on its specialty plates into little mobile billboards on which motorists can display their own messages. And what Texas did here was to reject one of the messages that members of a private group wanted to post on some of these little billboards because the State thought that many of its citizens would find the message offensive. That is blatant viewpoint discrimination.

"[The] Court badly misunderstands Summum. [Governments] have long used monuments as a means of expressing a government message. [There] is no history of landowners allowing their property to be used by third parties as the site of large permanent monuments that do not express messages that the landowners wish to convey. [And] spatial limitations played a prominent part in our analysis. [These] characteristics [are] not present in Texas's specialty plate program.

"[The] Confederate battle flag is a controversial symbol. [The] Board rejected the plate design because it concluded that many Texans would find the flag symbol offensive. That was pure viewpoint discrimination. [Many] other specialty plates have the potential to irritate and perhaps even infuriate those who see them. Texas allows a plate with the words 'Choose Life,' but the State of New York rejected such a plate because the message '[is] so incredibly divisive.' [Allowing] States to reject specialty plates based on their potential to offend is viewpoint discrimination."

Notice that Justice Thomas joined the Court's majority without explanation. Why? Might his vote be connected to his opinion in Virginia v. Black (2003; p. 1049, above)?

9. ***The special problem of solicitation.*** Is solicitation of funds speech protected by the First Amendment? The Court has held as much in invalidating various restrictions on solicitation. See, e.g., Murdock v. Pennsylvania, 319 U.S. 105 (1943) (flat tax); Hynes v. Mayor of Oradell, 425 U.S. 610 (1976) (licensing requirement); Schaumburg v. Citizens for a Better Environment, 444 U.S. 620 (1980) (overhead limit). In Schaumburg, the Court stated that "charitable appeals for funds [involve] a variety of speech interests—communication of information, the dissemination and propagation of views and ideas, and the advocacy of causes—that are within the protection of the First Amendment." But in Kokinda and ISKCON, the Court readily deferred to government bans on solicitation on public property, suggesting that solicitation causes unique harms. These cases emphasize that solicitation poses greater risk to crowd control than other modes of expression because those solicited must stop and reach for money. They also suggest that solicitation raises a danger of fraud that will be difficult to police except by a prophylactic ban.

Are these problems unique to the settings of "nonpublic forums" such as airports and post office sidewalks? Could a city ban solicitation on all streets and sidewalks? Recall that the Court upheld a solicitation ban throughout the open thoroughfares of the Minnesota State Fair in Heffron v. ISKCON (1981; p. 1222 above), relying on conventional time, place, and manner analysis. Is the solicitation ban in Heffron distinguishable from a citywide solicitation ban because a fair is more enclosed than city streets? Because a citywide ban is broader? Or do the special problems of solicitation emphasized by the Justices in Heffron, Kokinda, and ISKCON suggest that even a citywide ban on in-person solicitation on the streets might be upheld?

Consider in light of these questions the issue of whether begging in public places implicates the First Amendment. Does begging communicate information or advocate a cause? Is it distinguishable for First Amendment purposes from commercial sales? On commercial solicitation, see Breard v. Alexandria, 341 U.S. 622 (1951) (upholding an ordinance barring door-to-door solicitation for magazine subscriptions without the prior consent of the homeowners). Even if it is protected expression, does begging trigger government interests similar to those found sufficient in Kokinda and

ISKCON? For the view that begging is protected speech and that most restrictions on it are unconstitutional, see Hershkoff & Cohen, "Begging to Differ: The First Amendment and the Right to Beg," 104 Harv. L. Rev. 896 (1991). For an argument for government leeway to regulate the public location of begging, see Ellickson, "Controlling Chronic Misconduct in City Spaces: Of Panhandlers, Skid Rows, and Public Space Zoning," 105 Yale L.J. 1165 (1996).

Note that ISKCON, while upholding the airport solicitation ban, invalidated a ban on the *sale* or distribution of literature at airports. Is the sale of literature more like the distribution of leaflets or the solicitation of funds? If sales of charitable literature are allowed in a public place, must sales of other items be granted equal access? What about sales of other expressive items, such as commemorative key rings or message-bearing T-shirts? Would a ban on all peddling in public streets implicate the First Amendment as applied to such sales? Can government draw any lines short of a flat ban without discriminating impermissibly on the basis of the expressive content of the merchandise? Justice Kennedy, who along with Justice O'Connor was one of only two justices to vote for both results in ISKCON, stated in his partial concurrence: "Much of what I have said about the solicitation of funds may seem to apply to the sale of literature, but the differences between the two activities are of sufficient significance to require they be distinguished for constitutional purposes. [The] danger of a fraud arising from such sales is much more limited than from pure solicitation, because in the case of a sale the nature of the exchange tends to be clearer to both parties. [And] the flat ban on sales of literature leaves open fewer alternative channels of communication [as] sales of literature must be completed in one transaction to be workable."

10. ***Candidate debate on public television.*** In **Arkansas Educational Television Commission (AETC) v. Forbes**, 523 U.S. 666 (1998), the Court rejected a free speech challenge to the exclusion of a candidate from a candidate debate televised by a public broadcasting station. The challenge was brought by Ralph Forbes, who had gained enough signatures to run on the ballot as an independent for Arkansas's third congressional district seat, but was regarded by the debate producers as lacking enough popular support to warrant inclusion in the debate along with the Democratic and Republican candidates. Justice KENNEDY, writing the 6–3 decision of the Court, upheld the exclusion, finding that "the candidate debate was subject to constitutional constraints applicable to nonpublic fora under our forum precedents," but that "the broadcaster's decision to exclude the candidate was a reasonable, viewpoint-neutral exercise of journalistic discretion" that satisfied the First Amendment.

Justice Kennedy cautioned that, "having first arisen in the context of streets and parks, the public forum doctrine should not be extended in a mechanical way to the very different context of public television broadcasting," where "broad rights of access for outside speakers would be antithetical, as a general rule, to the discretion that stations and their editorial staff must exercise to fulfill their journalistic purpose and statutory obligations." Thus First Amendment obligations might not apply at all to most public television programming. But the First Amendment does apply in the limited context of publicly televised candidate debates, he wrote, because they are "by design a forum for political speech by the candidates" and have "exceptional significance in the electoral process."

The issue then was whether Forbes's exclusion from the debate was subject to the stricter standards applicable to a designated public forum or the more deferential standards applicable to a nonpublic forum, and Justice Kennedy concluded that nonpublic forum rules applied here: "Under our precedents, the AETC debate was not a designated public forum. To create a forum of this type, the government must intend to make the property 'generally available' to a class of speakers. [Widmar.] [The] government does not create a designated public forum when it does no more than reserve eligibility for access to the forum to a particular class of speakers, whose members must then, as individuals, 'obtain permission,' to use it. [Perry, Cornelius.]" Under this test, he reasoned, "the debate was a nonpublic forum": "Here, the debate did not have an open-microphone format. [AETC] did not make its debate generally available to candidates for Arkansas' Third Congressional District seat. Instead, [AETC] reserved eligibility for participation in the debate to candidates for the Third Congressional District seat (as opposed to some other seat). At that point, [AETC] made candidate-by-candidate determinations as to which of the eligible candidates would participate in the debate." Justice Kennedy suggested that this "distinction between general and selective access furthers First Amendment interests. By recognizing the distinction, we encourage the government to open its property to some expressive activity in cases where, if faced with an all-or-nothing choice, it might not open the property at all." Under the standards applicable to nonpublic forums, the majority found Forbes's exclusion reasonable and viewpoint-neutral: "There is no substance to Forbes' suggestion that he was excluded because his views were unpopular or out of the mainstream. His own objective lack of support, not his platform, was the criterion."

Justice STEVENS dissented, joined by Justices Souter and Ginsburg: "[T]he First Amendment will not tolerate arbitrary definitions of the scope of the forum. [The] dispositive issue in this case [is] not whether AETC created a designated public forum or a nonpublic forum, as the Court concludes, but whether AETC defined the contours of the debate forum with sufficient specificity to justify the exclusion of a ballot-qualified candidate." Justice Stevens analogized AETC's decision to exclude Forbes to the exercise of impermissibly standardless discretion to exclude speakers from the public forum: "No written criteria cabined the discretion of the AETC staff. Their subjective judgment about a candidate's 'viability' or 'newsworthiness' allowed them wide latitude either to permit or to exclude a third participant in any debate. [The] importance of avoiding arbitrary or viewpoint-based exclusions from political debates militates strongly in favor of requiring the controlling state agency to use (and adhere to) pre-established, objective criteria to determine who among qualified candidates may participate."

11. ***Public libraries.*** In **United States v. American Library Ass'n**, 539 U.S. 194 (2003), the Court upheld by a vote of 6–3 the Children's Internet Protection Act (CIPA), under which a public library receiving federal subsidies is required to install filtering software blocking internet access to obscenity, child pornography, or indecent material harmful to minors. In so doing, the Court first rejected the attempted analogy of a public library to a public forum or designated public forum, in a plurality opinion written by Chief Justice Rehnquist and joined by Justices O'Connor, Scalia, and Thomas. (For a different portion of the decision also rejecting a challenge to CIPA as an unconstitutional condition on public funding, see p. 1336 below.)

Chief Justice REHNQUIST wrote: "Public libraries pursue the worthy missions of facilitating learning and cultural enrichment. [To] fulfill their traditional missions, public libraries must have broad discretion to decide what material to provide to their patrons. Although they seek to provide a wide array of information, their goal has never been to provide 'universal coverage.' Instead, public libraries seek to provide materials 'that would be of the greatest direct benefit or interest to the community.' To this end, libraries collect only those materials deemed to have 'requisite and appropriate quality.'

"We have held in two analogous contexts that the government has broad discretion to make content-based judgments in deciding what private speech to make available to the public. In AETC v. Forbes, we held that public forum principles do not generally apply to a public television station's editorial judgments regarding the private speech it presents to its viewers. [The] principles underlying Forbes also apply to a public library's exercise of judgment in selecting the material it provides to its patrons. Just as forum analysis and heightened judicial scrutiny are incompatible with the role of public television stations and the role of the NEA, they are also incompatible with the discretion that public libraries must have to fulfill their traditional missions. Public library staffs necessarily consider content in making collection decisions and enjoy broad discretion in making them.

"[Public] forum principles [are] out of place in the context of this case. Internet access in public libraries is neither a 'traditional' nor a 'designated' public forum. [A] public library does not acquire Internet terminals in order to create a public forum for Web publishers to express themselves, any more than it collects books in order to provide a public forum for the authors of books to speak. It provides Internet access, not to 'encourage a diversity of views from private speakers,' but for the same reasons it offers other library resources: to facilitate research, learning, and recreational pursuits by furnishing materials of requisite and appropriate quality. [The fact that a library] does not review every Web site that it makes available [is not] constitutionally relevant. A library's failure to make quality-based judgments about all the material it furnishes from the Web does not somehow taint the judgments it does make. A library's need to exercise judgment in making collection decisions depends on its traditional role in identifying suitable and worthwhile material; it is no less entitled to play that role when it collects material from the Internet than when it collects material from any other source. Most libraries already exclude pornography from their print collections because they deem it inappropriate for inclusion. We do not subject these decisions to heightened scrutiny; it would make little sense to treat libraries' judgments to block online pornography any differently, when these judgments are made for just the same reason. Moreover, because of the vast quantity of material on the Internet and the rapid pace at which it changes, libraries cannot possibly segregate, item by item, all the Internet material that is appropriate for inclusion from all that is not. While a library could limit its Internet collection to just those sites it found worthwhile, it could do so only at the cost of excluding an enormous amount of valuable information that it lacks the capacity to review. Given that tradeoff, it is entirely reasonable for public libraries to reject that approach and instead exclude certain categories of content, without making individualized judgments that everything they do make available has requisite and appropriate quality.

"[Assuming] the tendency of filtering software to 'overblock' [presents] constitutional difficulties, any such concerns are dispelled by the ease with which patrons may have the filtering software disabled. When a patron encounters a blocked site, he need only ask a librarian to unblock it or (at least in the case of adults) disable the filter. [The] Constitution does not guarantee the right to acquire information at a public library without any risk of embarrassment."

Justices Kennedy and Breyer concurred in the judgment. Justice BREYER wrote: "In ascertaining whether the statutory provisions are constitutional, I would apply a form of heightened scrutiny, examining the statutory requirements in question with special care. The Act directly restricts the public's receipt of information. And it does so through limitations imposed by outside bodies (here Congress) upon two critically important sources of information—the Internet as accessed via public libraries. For that reason, we should not examine the statute's constitutionality as if it raised no special First Amendment concern—as if, like tax or economic regulation, the First Amendment demanded only a 'rational basis' for imposing a restriction. [At] the same time, in my view, the First Amendment does not here demand application of the most limiting constitutional approach—that of 'strict scrutiny.' The statutory restriction in question is, in essence, a kind of 'selection' restriction (a kind of editing). It affects the kinds and amount of materials that the library can present to its patrons. And libraries often properly engage in the selection of materials, either as a matter of necessity (i.e., due to the scarcity of resources) or by design (i.e., in accordance with collection development policies). [To] apply 'strict scrutiny' to the 'selection' of a library's collection (whether carried out by public libraries themselves or by other community bodies with a traditional legal right to engage in that function) would unreasonably interfere with the discretion necessary to create, maintain, or select a library's 'collection' (broadly defined to include all the information the library makes available)."

Under such intermediate scrutiny, in Justice Breyer's view, the law was valid: it "seeks to restrict access to obscenity, child pornography, and, in respect to access by minors, material that is comparably harmful. These objectives are 'legitimate,' and indeed often 'compelling.'" Moreover, he concluded, "software filters 'provide a relatively cheap and effective' means of furthering these goals," and are narrowly tailored because an exception "allows libraries to permit any adult patron access to an 'overblocked' Web site; the adult patron need only ask a librarian to unblock the specific Web site or, alternatively, ask the librarian, 'Please disable the entire filter.' The Act does impose upon the patron the burden of making this request. But it is difficult to see how that burden [could] prove more onerous than traditional library practices associated with segregating library materials in, say, closed stacks, or with interlibrary lending practices that require patrons to make requests that are not anonymous and to wait while the librarian obtains the desired materials from elsewhere. [Given] the comparatively small burden that the Act imposes upon the library patron seeking legitimate Internet, I cannot say that any speech-related harm that the Act may cause is disproportionate when considered in relation to the Act's legitimate objectives."

Justice Stevens and Justice Souter, the latter joined by Justice Ginsburg, dissented, emphasizing the crudeness of filtering software and its likely tendency to "overblock" materials protected by the First Amendment. Justice SOUTER also questioned the assumption made by the plurality and the concurrences that internet filtering software is simply an example of standard selectivity in acquisitions by a library: "The question [is] whether a local library could itself constitutionally impose these restrictions on the content otherwise available to an adult patron through an Internet connection, at a library terminal provided for public use. The answer is no. A library that chose to block an adult's Internet access to material harmful to children (and whatever else the undiscriminating filter might interrupt) would be imposing a content-based restriction on communication of material in the library's control that an adult could otherwise lawfully see. This would simply be censorship. [As] to those who did not qualify for discretionary unblocking, the censorship would be complete and, like all censorship by an agency of the Government, presumptively invalid owing to strict scrutiny in implementing the Free Speech Clause of the First Amendment.

"[The] Court's plurality does not treat blocking affecting adults as censorship, but chooses to describe a library's act in filtering content as simply an instance of the kind of selection from available material that every library [must] perform. Public libraries are indeed selective in what they acquire to place in their stacks, as they must be. There is only so much money and so much shelf space, and the necessity to choose some material and reject the rest justifies the effort to be selective with an eye to demand, quality, and the object of maintaining the library as a place of civilized enquiry by widely different sorts of people. Selectivity is thus necessary and complex, and these two characteristics explain why review of a library's selection decisions must be limited: the decisions are made all the time, and only in extreme cases could one expect particular choices to reveal impermissible reasons (reasons even the plurality would consider to be illegitimate), like excluding books because their authors are Democrats or their critiques of organized Christianity are unsympathetic.

"[But] the Internet blocking here defies comparison to the process of acquisition. Whereas traditional scarcity of money and space require a library to make choices about what to acquire, and the choice to be made is whether or not to spend the money to acquire something, blocking is the subject of a choice made after the money for Internet access has been spent or committed. Since it makes no difference to the cost of Internet access whether an adult calls up material harmful for children or the Articles of Confederation, blocking (on facts like these) is not necessitated by scarcity of either money or space. In the instance of the Internet, what the library acquires is electronic access, and the choice to block is a choice to limit access that has already been acquired. [The] proper analogy therefore is not to passing up a book that might have been bought; it is either to buying a book and then keeping it from adults lacking an acceptable 'purpose,' or to buying an encyclopedia and then cutting out pages with anything thought to be unsuitable for all adults."

12. ***Student organization membership at a public law school.*** Do "limited public forum" principles extend to the setting of membership in public university student organizations? In **Christian Legal Society Chapter of the University of California Hastings College of Law v. Martinez**, 561 U.S. 661 (2010), a public law school established a "Registered Student Organization (RSO)" program that conferred the use of school funds, facilities, and the law school's name and logo on condition that RSOs allow

"all comers" to participate, become members, or seek leadership positions, regardless of their status or beliefs. The parties jointly stipulated in the lower courts that the policy was universally applied to all groups: " 'Hastings requires that registered student organizations allow *any* student to participate, become a member, or seek leadership positions in the organization, regardless of [her] status or beliefs. Thus, for example, the Hastings Democratic Caucus cannot bar students holding Republican political beliefs from becoming members or seeking leadership positions in the organization.' " Under this policy, Hastings declined to grant RSO status to a chapter of the Christian Legal Society (CLS) on the ground that, by requiring members and officers to sign onto a "Statement of Faith" and renounce "unrepentant homosexual conduct," it excluded students based on religion and sexual orientation in violation of the all-comers policy. CLS challenged this denial, claiming that application of the all-comers policy violated its rights to freedom of speech and association.

The Supreme Court rejected the First Amendment challenge by a closely divided 5–4 vote. Justice GINSBURG wrote for the majority, joined by Justices Stevens, Kennedy, Breyer, and Sotomayor. Crucial to her decision was the premise that "Hastings, through its RSO program, [had] established a limited public forum." She explained: "In diverse contexts, our decisions have distinguished between policies that require action and those that withhold benefits. Application of the less-restrictive limited public forum analysis better accounts for the fact that Hastings, through its RSO program, is dangling the carrot of subsidy, not wielding the stick of prohibition." And she found limited public forum principles equally dispositive of CLS's free speech and expressive-association claims.

In a footnote, Justice Ginsburg laid out an account of public forum doctrine and applicable standards of review: "In conducting forum analysis, our decisions have sorted government property into three categories. First, in traditional public forums, such as public streets and parks, 'any restriction based on the content of . . . speech must satisfy strict scrutiny, that is, the restriction must be narrowly tailored to serve a compelling government interest.' Summum. Second, governmental entities create designated public forums when 'government property that has not traditionally been regarded as a public forum is intentionally opened up for that purpose'; speech restrictions in such a forum 'are subject to the same strict scrutiny as restrictions in a traditional public forum.' Id. Third, governmental entities establish limited public forums by opening property 'limited to use by certain groups or dedicated solely to the discussion of certain subjects.' Ibid. As noted in [Summum], '[i]n such a forum, a governmental entity may impose restrictions on speech that are reasonable and viewpoint-neutral.' "

Justice Ginsburg reiterated the standard of scrutiny governing a limited public forum: "Recognizing a State's right to preserve the property under its control for the use to which it is lawfully dedicated, the Court has permitted restrictions on access to a limited public forum, like the RSO program here, with this key caveat: Any access barrier must be reasonable and viewpoint neutral." Applying that standard, she first considered "whether Hastings' policy is reasonable taking into account the RSO forum's function and 'all the surrounding circumstances,' " and answered that question in the affirmative: "[A] college's commission—and its concomitant license to choose among pedagogical approaches—is not confined to the classroom, for extracurricular programs are, today, essential parts of the educational process. [First,] the open-access policy 'ensures that the leadership, educational, and social opportunities afforded by [RSOs] are available to all students.' [Second,] the all-comers requirement helps Hastings police the written terms of its Nondiscrimination Policy without inquiring into an RSO's motivation for membership restrictions. [Third,] the Law School reasonably adheres to the view that an all-comers policy, to the extent it brings together individuals with diverse backgrounds and beliefs, 'encourages tolerance, cooperation, and learning among students.' [These] several justifications [are] surely reasonable in light of the RSO forum's purposes."

Justice Ginsburg next "consider[ed] whether Hastings' all-comers policy is viewpoint neutral," and again answered affirmatively: "In contrast to [Widmar and Rosenberger], in which universities singled out organizations for disfavored treatment because of their points of view, Hastings' all-comers requirement draws no distinction between groups based on their message or perspective. An all-comers condition on access to RSO status, in short, is textbook viewpoint neutral." The majority opinion rejected CLS's argument that the policy is viewpoint-discriminatory in effect because " 'it systematically and predictably burdens most heavily those groups whose viewpoints are out of favor with the campus mainstream,' " finding that such a "differential impact" did not render the policy nonneutral. Justice Ginsburg concluded: "Finding Hastings' open-access condition on RSO status reasonable and viewpoint neutral, we reject CLS' free-speech and expressive-association claims."

Justice STEVENS, joined by Justice Kennedy, concurred to emphasize that "[i]t is critical, in evaluating CLS's challenge [to] keep in mind that an RSO program is a limited forum—the boundaries of which may be delimited by the proprietor. When a religious association, or a secular association, operates in a wholly public setting, it must be allowed broad freedom to control its membership and its message, even if its decisions cause offense to outsiders. [But] the CLS chapter that brought this lawsuit does not want to be just a Christian group; it aspires to be a recognized student organization. The Hastings College of Law is not a legislature. And no state actor has demanded that anyone do anything outside the confines of a discrete, voluntary academic program. [The] RSO forum is [not] an open commons that Hastings happens to maintain. It is a mechanism through which Hastings confers certain benefits and pursues certain aspects of its educational mission. [CLS] excludes students who will not sign its Statement of Faith or who engage in 'unrepentant homosexual conduct.' Other groups may exclude or mistreat Jews, blacks, and women—or those who do not share their contempt for Jews, blacks, and women. A free society must tolerate such groups. It need not subsidize them, give them its official imprimatur, or grant them equal access to law school facilities."

Justice KENNEDY filed a concurrence emphasizing the case's differences from Rosenberger v. Rector (1995; p. 1328 below): "[H]ere the school policy in question is not content based either in its formulation or evident purpose; and were it shown to be otherwise, the case likely should have a different outcome. Here, the policy applies equally to all groups and views. And, given the stipulation of the parties, there is no basis for an allegation that the design or purpose of the rule was, by subterfuge, to discriminate based on viewpoint."

Justice ALITO dissented, joined by Chief Justice Roberts and Justices Scalia and Thomas. The dissent began by vigorously disputing that the stipulation setting forth the all-comers policy truly captured the policy Hastings had applied, arguing that the policy was a pretextual substitute for a prior Nondiscrimination Policy that in practice discriminated against student groups organized around religious viewpoints. The dissent next argued that the case should have been controlled by Healy v. James, 408 U.S. 169 (1972), which invalidated a public college's refusal to recognize a student chapter of Students for a Democratic Society (SDS) because it would not renounce violence.

Reaching the limited public forum principles central to the majority opinion, Justice Alito argued that Hastings' application of its policy is impermissible even if the stipulated all-comers policy were deemed the operative policy and the RSO program were deemed a limited public forum: "Taken as a whole, the regulations plainly contemplate the creation of a forum within which Hastings students are free to form and obtain registration of essentially the same broad range of private groups that nonstudents may form off campus. [The] way in which the RSO forum actually developed corroborates this design. [Hastings] had more than 60 RSOs in 2004–2005, each with its own independently devised purpose. Some addressed serious social issues; others—for example, the wine appreciation and ultimate Frisbee clubs—were simply recreational. Some organizations focused on a subject but did not claim to promote a particular viewpoint on that subject (for example, the Association of Communications, Sports & Entertainment Law); others were defined, not by subject, but by viewpoint. The forum did not have a single Party Politics Club; rather, it featured both the Hastings Democratic Caucus and the Hastings Republicans. There was no Reproductive Issues Club; the forum included separate pro-choice and pro-life organizations. Students did not see fit to create a Monotheistic Religions Club, but they have formed the Hastings Jewish Law Students Association and the Hastings Association of Muslim Law Students. In short, the RSO forum, true to its design, has allowed Hastings students to replicate on campus a broad array of private, independent, noncommercial organizations that is very similar to those that nonstudents have formed in the outside world. The accept-all-comers policy is antithetical to the design of the RSO forum for the same reason that a state-imposed accept-all-comers policy would violate the First Amendment rights of private groups if applied off campus."

13. ***Rights of access to private property.*** Do the principles of the above cases aid in developing claims of access to *private* property? Is there a "private forum" counterpart to the public forum? In Marsh v. Alabama, 326 U.S. 501 (1946), the Court held that Jehovah's Witnesses could claim a constitutional right of access to distribute religious literature in a company-owned town since such a town served a "public function" creating state action. Does such a principle extend to shopping centers? Are shopping centers the modern functional equivalent of the public square?

The 5–4 decision in **Amalgamated Food Employees v. Logan Valley Plaza, Inc.**, 391 U.S. 308 (1968), relied in part on Marsh to hold that a state trespass law could not be applied to enjoin peaceful union picketing of a supermarket in a privately owned shopping center. Justice MARSHALL's majority opinion found that the ban on picketing could not be justified on the ground that picketing constituted an unconsented invasion of private property rights: "The shopping center here is clearly the functional equivalent of the business district of Chickasaw involved in Marsh. [We] see no reason why access to a business district in a company town for the purpose of exercising First Amendment rights should be constitutionally required, while access for the same purpose to property functioning as a business district should be limited simply because the property surrounding the 'business district' is not under the same ownership." Accordingly, Justice Marshall applied public forum principles and found that the state could not "delegate the power, through the use of its trespass laws, wholly to exclude those members of the public wishing to exercise their First Amendment rights on the premises in a manner and for a purpose generally consonant with the use to which the property is actually put."

Logan Valley was "distinguished" in the 5–4 decision in **Lloyd Corp. v. Tanner**, 407 U.S. 551 (1972). In Lloyd, the lower federal courts had relied on Marsh and Logan Valley in holding unconstitutional the application to anti-war leafleteers of a shopping center's ban on the distribution of handbills. The Court reversed, finding the facts in its earlier cases "significantly different." Justice POWELL emphasized that in Logan Valley the First Amendment activity—union picketing of a store—"was related to the shopping center's operations" and the store was "in the center of a large private enclave with the consequence that no other reasonable opportunities" to convey the picketers' message existed. Here, by contrast, the handbilling "had no relation to any purpose for which the center was built and being used" and alternative means of communication were available. He noted, moreover, that "[a]lthough accommodations between [speech and property values] are sometimes necessary, and the courts properly have shown a special solicitude for the [First Amendment], this Court has never held that a trespasser or an uninvited guest may exercise general rights of free speech on property privately owned." Justice MARSHALL's dissent, joined by Justices Douglas, Brennan, and Stewart, objected to the majority's departure from Logan Valley and emphasized the "tremendous need" of the handbillers to have access to the private shopping center.

Even though Lloyd had purported to distinguish Logan Valley, **Hudgens v. NLRB**, 424 U.S. 507 (1976), announced that Lloyd had in effect overruled Logan Valley. Hudgens involved labor picketing of a store in a private shopping center. The picketers were employees of a warehouse maintained by the store owner at a location outside of the shopping center. Justice STEWART's majority opinion concluded that "the constitutional guarantee of free expression has no part to play in a case such as this. [If] the respondent in the Lloyd case did not have a First Amendment right to enter that shopping center to distribute handbills concerning Vietnam, then the respondents in the present case did not have a First Amendment right to enter this shopping center for the purpose of advertising their strike." Justices Marshall and Brennan dissented. On labor speech and the First Amendment generally, see Pope, "The Three-Systems Ladder of First Amendment Values: Two Rungs and a Black Hole," 11 Hast. Const. L.Q. 189 (1984).

14. ***Polling place.*** In **Minnesota Voters Alliance v. Mansky**, 585 U.S. ___, 138 S. Ct. 1876 (2018), the Court struck down a Minnesota law prohibiting individuals from wearing a "political badge, political button, or other political insignia" inside a polling place on Election Day. Chief Justice ROBERTS wrote for the 7–2 Court: "Today, all 50 States and the District of Columbia have laws curbing various forms of speech in and around polling places on Election Day. [The Minnesota] ban applies only in a specific

location: the interior of a polling place. [A] polling place in Minnesota qualifies as a nonpublic forum. It is, at least on Election Day, government-controlled property set aside for the sole purpose of voting. [The] question accordingly is whether Minnesota's ban on political apparel is reasonable in light of the purpose served by the forum: voting. [In] light of the special purpose of the polling place itself, Minnesota may choose to prohibit certain apparel there because of the message it conveys, so that voters may focus on the important decisions immediately at hand. [Although] there is no requirement of narrow tailoring in a nonpublic forum, the State must be able to articulate some sensible basis for distinguishing what may come in from what must stay out. Here, the unmoored use of the term 'political' in the Minnesota law, combined with haphazard interpretations the State has provided in official guidance and representations to this Court, cause Minnesota's restriction to fail even this forgiving test.

"[The] State interprets the ban to proscribe 'only words and symbols that an objectively reasonable observer would perceive as conveying a message about the electoral choices at issue in [the] polling place.' At the same time, the State argues that the category of 'political' apparel is *not* limited to campaign apparel. [Far] from clarifying the indeterminate scope of the political apparel provision, the State's 'electoral choices' construction introduces confusing line-drawing problems. [The] State points to the 2010 Election Day Policy—which it continues to hold out as authoritative guidance regarding implementation of the statute. The first three examples in the Policy are clear enough: items displaying the name of a political party, items displaying the name of a candidate, and items demonstrating 'support of or opposition to a ballot question.' But the next example—'[i]ssue oriented material designed to influence or impact voting,'—raises more questions than it answers. What qualifies as an 'issue'? The answer, as far as we can tell from the State's briefing and argument, is any subject on which a political candidate or party has taken a stance. For instance, the Election Day Policy specifically notes that the 'Please I.D. Me' buttons are prohibited. But a voter identification requirement was not on the ballot in 2010, so a Minnesotan would have had no explicit 'electoral choice' to make in that respect. The buttons were nonetheless covered, the State tells us, because the Republican candidates for Governor and Secretary of State had staked out positions on whether photo identification should be required.

"A rule whose fair enforcement requires an election judge to maintain a mental index of the platforms and positions of every candidate and party on the ballot is not reasonable. Candidates for statewide and federal office and major political parties can be expected to take positions on a wide array of subjects of local and national import. [The] next broad category in the Election Day Policy—any item 'promoting a group with recognizable political views,'—makes matters worse. [The] American Civil Liberties Union, the AARP, the World Wildlife Fund, and Ben & Jerry's all have stated positions on matters of public concern.

"[That] is not to say that Minnesota has set upon an impossible task. Other States have laws proscribing displays (including apparel) in more lucid terms. We do not suggest that such provisions set the outer limit of what a State may proscribe, and do not pass on the constitutionality of laws that are not before us. But we do hold that if a State wishes to set its polling places apart as areas free of partisan discord, it must employ a more discernible approach than the one Minnesota has offered here."

In dissent, Justice SOTOMAYOR, joined by Justice Breyer, wrote that she would have certified the case to the Minnesota Supreme Court for a definitive interpretation of the political apparel ban, likely obviating "the hypothetical line-drawing problems that form the basis of the Court's decision today."

Note that the Court applied the most lenient level of forum analysis—the deferential scrutiny applicable to a nonpublic forum—but still struck down the law as an unconstitutional restriction of speech. What accounts for that decision? In another polling place speech case, Burson v. Freeman (1992; p. 1167), the plurality applied strict scrutiny to a signage ban outside the polling place but still upheld the law. Can the decisions be reconciled?

RELIGIOUS SPEECH ON PUBLIC PROPERTY

The exclusion of religious expression from public spaces would appear to be content discrimination that would normally be impermissible in a traditional or designated public forum, or viewpoint discrimination that would be impermissible even in a nonpublic forum. But is such exclusion dictated by the countervailing constitutional command of the Establishment Clause of the First Amendment? The establishment principles governing these cases are discussed below in Chapter 14. The Establishment Clause has been held to prohibit government from establishing religion not only through coercion but also through symbolic endorsement or financial support. Government bodies have sometimes read the clause to require it to exclude religious speech from forums it has otherwise opened to expression. When these cases have come before the Court, it has consistently held that the Free Speech Clause forbids such discrimination, and that the Establishment Clause does not require it. Consider the following decisions:

In **Widmar v. Vincent**, 454 U.S. 263 (1981), the Court exercised the strict scrutiny it typically applies to content-based exclusions from public places. It held that a state university that makes its facilities generally available for the activities of registered student groups may not constitutionally bar a group desiring to use the facilities for religious worship and discussion. The case arose when the University of Missouri at Kansas City, relying on its policy of prohibiting the use of its facilities "for purposes of religious worship or religious teaching," barred a student religious group from meeting anywhere on its grounds. The Court rejected the University's argument that its interest in promoting the separation of church and state was adequate to survive strict scrutiny.

In explaining the application of free speech principles, Justice POWELL's majority opinion stated: "Through its policy of accommodating their meetings, the University has created a forum generally open for use by student groups. Having done so, the University has assumed an obligation to justify its discriminations and exclusions under applicable constitutional norms. The Constitution forbids a State to enforce certain exclusions from a forum generally open to the public, even if it was not required to create the forum in the first place. The University's institutional mission, which it describes as providing a '*secular* education' to its students, does not exempt its actions from constitutional scrutiny. With respect to persons entitled to be there, our cases leave no doubt that the First Amendment rights of speech and association extend to the campuses of state universities. Here the

[University] has discriminated against student groups and speakers based on their desire to use a generally open forum to engage in religious worship and discussion. These are forms of speech and association protected by the First Amendment. In order to justify discriminatory exclusion from a public forum based on the religious content of a group's intended speech, the University must therefore satisfy the standard of review appropriate to content-based exclusions. It must show that its regulation is necessary to serve a compelling state interest and that it is narrowly drawn to achieve that end. See [Carey.]" Finding that there would be no establishment violation if the university granted access to religious student groups, Justice Powell found no compelling state interest in their exclusion.

In an opinion concurring only in the judgment, Justice STEVENS took issue with the majority's approach: "In my opinion, the use of the terms 'compelling state interest' and 'public forum' to analyze the question presented in this case may needlessly undermine the academic freedom of public universities." He elaborated: "Because every university's resources are limited, an educational institution must routinely make decisions concerning the use of the time and space that is available for extracurricular activities. In my judgment, it is both necessary and appropriate for those decisions to evaluate the content of a proposed student activity. I should think it obvious, for example, that if two groups of 25 students requested the use of a room at a particular time—one to view Mickey Mouse cartoons and the other to rehearse an amateur performance of Hamlet—the First Amendment would not require that the room be reserved for the group that submitted its application first. [Judgments] of this kind should be made by academicians, not by federal judges, and their standards for decision should not be encumbered with ambiguous phrases like 'compelling state interest.' Thus, I do not subscribe to the view that a public university has no greater interest in the content of student activities than the police chief has in the content of a soap box oration on Capitol Hill. A university legitimately may regard some subjects as more relevant to its educational mission than others.

"But the university, like the police officer, may not allow its agreement or disagreement with the viewpoint of a particular speaker to determine whether access to a forum will be granted. If a state university is to deny recognition to a student organization—or is to give it a lesser right to use school facilities than other student groups—it must have a valid reason for doing so." Despite his different approach, Justice Stevens found the University decision unjustified. He explained: "It seems apparent that the policy under attack would allow groups of young philosophers to meet to discuss their skepticism that a Supreme Being exists, or a group of political scientists to meet to debate the accuracy of the view that religion is the 'opium of the people.' If school facilities may be used to discuss anti-clerical doctrine, it seems to me that comparable use by a group desiring to express a belief in God must also be permitted. The fact that their expression of faith includes ceremonial conduct is not, in my opinion, a sufficient reason for suppressing their discussion entirely."

Justice WHITE, the sole dissenter, disagreed with the majority's Establishment Clause and free speech analysis. He objected to the argument that, "because religious worship uses speech, it is protected by the Free Speech Clause of the First Amendment." He added: "This case involves religious worship only; the fact that that worship is accomplished through speech does not add anything to [the challengers'] argument. That argument must rely upon the claim that the state's action impermissibly interferes with the free exercise of respondents' religious practices. Although this is a close question, I conclude that it does not."

In **Lamb's Chapel v. Center Moriches Union Free School District**, 508 U.S. 384 (1993), the Court considered a free speech challenge to a local school district policy that permitted public school facilities to be used after school hours for social, civic, and recreational purposes and by political organizations, but provided that "the school premises shall not be used by any group for religious purposes." The school district twice denied permission to Lamb's Chapel, a local evangelical organization, to show a six-part film series featuring a psychologist who would argue in favor of "Christian family values instilled at an early stage." The district gave as its reason that the series appeared "church related."

The Court unanimously held the district's rule unconstitutional as applied to the Lamb's Chapel film series. Justice WHITE wrote for the Court: "There is no question that the District, like the private owner of property, may legally preserve the property under its control for the use to which it is dedicated. It is also common ground that the District need not have permitted after-hours use of its property for any [expressive] uses." The Church had argued that the schools had been opened after hours to such a wide variety of speech that the district's program should be analyzed as a designated public forum. Justice White declined to reach that issue, holding that, even assuming that the after-hours program was *not* a traditional or designated public forum, the exclusion of the Lamb's Chapel series amounted to impermissible viewpoint discrimination:

"That all religions and all uses for religious purposes are treated alike under [the rule] does not answer the critical question whether it discriminates on the basis of viewpoint to permit school property to be used for the presentation of all views about family issues and child-rearing except those dealing with the subject matter from a religious standpoint. There is no suggestion [that] a lecture or film about child-rearing and family values would not be a use for social or civic purposes otherwise permitted. [Nor] is there any indication [that] the application to exhibit the particular film involved here [would] have been denied for any reason other than [its] religious perspective. In our view, denial on that basis was plainly invalid under [Cornelius:] 'although a speaker may be excluded from a nonpublic forum if he wishes to address a topic not encompassed within the purpose of the forum . . . or if he is not a member of the class of speakers for whose special benefit the forum was created . . . the government violates the First Amendment when it denies access to a speaker solely to suppress the point of view he espouses on an otherwise includible subject.' " As in Widmar, the Court rejected the government's Establishment Clause defense.

Should the reasoning of Lamb's Chapel extend to afterschool use of public school facilities by an evangelical club seeking to engage in prayer and worship as part of its activities? The Court held that it did in **Good News Club v. Milford Central School**, 533 U.S. 98 (2001). The case involved a challenge to a New York local school district's refusal to allow the Good News Club, a private Christian organization, to hold weekly afterschool meetings for elementary school students in order to sing religious songs, hold Bible lessons and memorize scripture. School policy, consistent with Lamb's Chapel, would have allowed speech at afterschool meetings from a religious perspective, but excluded Good News as involving instead "religious instruction."

By a vote of 6–3, the Court held the exclusion unconstitutional under the Free Speech Clause, and rejected the school's establishment defense. Justice THOMAS wrote for the Court, joined by Chief Justice Rehnquist and Justices O'Connor, Scalia, and Kennedy and in part by Justice Breyer. As in Lamb's Chapel, the Court assumed without deciding that the school's afterschool meetings program did not constitute a traditional or designated public forum, but held nonetheless that the exclusion was invalid: "[W]e hold that the exclusion constitutes viewpoint discrimination. Like the church in Lamb's Chapel, the Club seeks to address a subject otherwise permitted under the rule, the teaching of morals and character, from a religious standpoint. [The] only apparent difference between the activity of Lamb's Chapel and the activities of the Good News Club is that the Club chooses to teach moral lessons from a Christian perspective through live storytelling and prayer, whereas Lamb's Chapel taught lessons through films. This distinction is inconsequential."

Justices Stevens filed a dissent, as did Justice Souter joined by Justice Ginsburg. Both dissents argued that the school should have been free to exclude religious uses from the scope of the limited public forum they defined. Justice STEVENS wrote: "Speech for 'religious purposes' may [encompass] religious speech that is simply speech about a particular topic from a religious point of view, [religious] speech that amounts to worship, [or] an intermediate category that is aimed principally at proselytizing or inculcating belief in a particular religious faith. The novel question that this case presents [is] whether a school can, consistently with the First Amendment, create a limited public forum that admits the first type of religious speech without allowing the other two. [As] long as this is done in an even handed manner, I see no constitutional violation in such an effort."

Quoting extensively from the record, Justice SOUTER wrote: "It is beyond question that Good News intends to use the public school premises not for the mere discussion of a subject from a particular, Christian point of view, but for an evangelical service of worship calling children to commit themselves in an act of Christian conversion. The majority avoids this reality only by resorting to the bland and general characterization of Good News's activity as 'teaching of morals and character, from a religious standpoint.' If the majority's statement ignores reality, as it surely does, then today's holding may be understood only in equally generic terms. Otherwise, indeed, this case would stand for the remarkable proposition that any public school opened for civic meetings must be opened for use as a church, synagogue, or mosque."

Should the reasoning in Lamb's Chapel and Good News apply to restrictions on the use of government resources for religious *services*? In **Bronx Household of Faith v. Board of Education of New York City**, 650 F.3d 30 (2d Cir. 2011), the Second Circuit upheld as viewpoint-neutral a school board's prohibition on the after-school use of facilities for "religious worship services." Judge LEVAL distinguished the prohibitions struck down in Lamb's Chapel and Good News because they "categorically excluded *expressions* of religious content," whereas the board's exclusion dealt only with "the conduct of a certain type of *activity*—the conduct of worship services" (emphasis added). And because the Second Circuit had previously found that the facilities were a limited public forum, the viewpoint-neutral prohibition on religious services needed only to be "reasonable in light of the purposes served by the forum." (The court found the prohibition reasonable because the board could have reasonably concluded that allowing religious services in its facilities would run afoul of another First Amendment proscription: the Establishment Clause, a subject taken up in Chapter 14 below.)

In **Capitol Square Review Board v. Pinette**, 515 U.S. 753 (1995), the Court invalidated the denial of permission to the Ku Klux Klan to erect a large Latin cross on Capitol Square, a 10-acre, state-owned plaza surrounding the Statehouse in Columbus, Ohio. The Square was designated a public forum by state law, and several unattended displays had been permitted there. The Court assumed that the Board had denied permission solely on the ground of the cross's religious content and that such a ground for exclusion would violate the Free Speech Clause unless required by the Establishment Clause, which the Court held it was not (see p. 1679 below). Justice SCALIA's plurality opinion stated: "Respondents' religious display in Capitol Square was private expression. Our precedent establishes that private religious speech, far from being a First Amendment orphan, is as fully protected under the Free Speech Clause as secular private expression. Indeed, in Anglo-American history, at least, government suppression of speech has so commonly been directed precisely at religious speech that a free-speech clause without religion would be Hamlet without the prince. [Heffron, Widmar.] It is undeniable, of course, that speech which is constitutionally protected against state suppression is not thereby accorded a guaranteed forum on all property owned by the State. [But] Capitol Square [is] a traditional public forum. Petitioners do not claim that their denial of respondents' application was based upon a content-neutral time, place, or manner restriction. To the contrary, they concede—indeed it is the essence of their case—that the Board rejected the display precisely because its content was religious." The rest of the plurality and the concurring opinions went on to reject the argument that this exclusion was required by the Establishment Clause.

This series of victories for those seeking to engage in religious speech or symbolism on public property came to an end in **Pleasant Grove City v. Summum**, 555 U.S. 460 (2009). A Utah city displayed permanently in a public park various privately donated symbols, including a Ten Commandments monument donated by the Fraternal Order of Eagles. The city, however, denied permission to a religious organization to erect a monument containing the "Seven Aphorisms of Summum." The city explained to the Summum group that monuments in the park were limited to those related to the city's history or donated by groups with longstanding community ties. The Supreme Court unanimously rejected Summum's free speech challenge and upheld the exclusion, holding that, even though a park is undoubtedly a public forum, the display of permanent monuments is "government speech" to which public forum principles are inapplicable.

Justice ALITO wrote the opinion of the Court: "[A]lthough a park is a traditional public forum for speeches and other transitory expressive acts, the display of a permanent monument in a public park is not a form of expression to which forum analysis applies. Instead, the placement of a permanent monument in a public park is best viewed as a form of government speech and is therefore not subject to scrutiny under the Free Speech Clause. [The] Free Speech Clause restricts government regulation of private speech; it does not regulate government speech. Indeed, it is not easy to imagine how government could function if it lacked this freedom. [A] government entity may exercise this same freedom to express its views when it receives assistance from private sources for the purpose of delivering a government-controlled message.

"[There] may be situations in which it is difficult to tell whether a government entity is speaking on its own behalf or is providing a forum for private speech, but this case does not present such a situation. Permanent monuments displayed on public property typically represent government speech. Governments have long used monuments to speak to the public. Since ancient times, kings, emperors, and other rulers have erected statues of themselves to remind their subjects of their authority and power. Triumphal arches, columns, and other monuments have been built to commemorate military victories and sacrifices and other events of civic importance. A monument, by definition, is a structure that is designed as a means of expression. When a government entity arranges for the construction of a monument, it does so because it wishes to convey some thought or instill some feeling in those who see the structure.

"[Just] as government-commissioned and government-financed monuments speak for the government, so do privately financed and donated monuments that the government accepts and displays to the public on government land. It certainly is not common for property owners to open up their property for the installation of permanent monuments that convey a message with which they do not wish to be associated. And because property owners typically do not permit the construction of such monuments on their land, persons who observe donated monuments routinely—and reasonably—interpret them as conveying some message on the property owner's behalf. [While] government entities regularly accept privately funded or donated monuments, they have exercised selectivity. [Government] decisionmakers select the monuments that portray what they view as appropriate for the place in question, taking into account such content-based factors as esthetics, history, and local culture. The monuments that are accepted, therefore, are meant to convey and have the effect of conveying a government message, and they thus constitute government speech.

"In this case, it is clear that the monuments in Pleasant Grove's [park] represent government speech. Although many of the monuments were not designed or built by the City and were donated in completed form by private entities, the City decided to accept those donations and to display them in the Park. [The] City has selected those monuments that it wants to display for the purpose of presenting the image of the City that it wishes to project to all who frequent the Park; it has taken ownership of most of the monuments in the Park, [and] the City has now expressly set forth the criteria it will use in making future selections."

Justice Alito rejected the argument that a monument must have a single meaning, embraced by the government, in order to constitute government speech, noting that the "Imagine" monument to John Lennon in New York City's Central Park or a "Peace" monument may have different meanings for different observers: "[I]t frequently is not possible to identify a single 'message' that is conveyed by an object or structure, and consequently, the thoughts or sentiments expressed by a government entity that accepts and displays such an object may be quite different from those of either its creator or its donor. [By] accepting such a monument, a government entity does not necessarily endorse the specific meaning that any particular donor sees in the monument."

Justice Alito also rejected Summum's proposed analogy of "the installation of permanent monuments in a public park to the delivery of speeches and the holding of marches and demonstrations" in a traditional public forum, noting that "a park can accommodate many speakers and, over time, many parades and demonstrations," but "public parks can accommodate only a limited number of permanent monuments. [Speakers], no matter how long-winded, eventually come to the end of their remarks; persons distributing leaflets and carrying signs at some point tire and go home; monuments, however, endure. They monopolize the use of the land on which they stand and interfere permanently with other uses of public space."

Finally, Justice Alito rejected Summum's proposed analogy to Capital Square v. Pinnette: "[T]hat case involved a very different situation—a request by a private group, the Ku Klux Klan, to erect a cross for a period of 16 days on public property that had been opened up for similar temporary displays, including a Christmas tree and a menorah. Although some public parks can accommodate and may be made generally available for temporary private displays, the same is rarely true for permanent monuments."

The Court did not reach the question whether, if the displays in the park are government speech, the Ten Commandments monument might violate the Establishment Clause. Justice Stevens filed a concurrence, joined by Justice Ginsburg, noting that the city's actions might nonetheless be constrained by the Establishment Clause. Disputing that view, Justice SCALIA filed a concurrence, joined by Justice Thomas, stating: "The city ought not fear that today's victory has propelled it from the Free Speech Clause frying pan into the Establishment Clause fire." Justice BREYER filed a concurrence cautioning that he joined the opinion "on the understanding that the 'government speech' doctrine is a rule of thumb, not a rigid category. Were the City to discriminate in the selection of permanent monuments on grounds unrelated to the display's theme, say solely on political grounds, its action might well violate the First Amendment." And Justice SOUTER concurred only in the judgment, cautioning that, if a monument "has some religious character, the specter of violating the Establishment Clause will behoove [a city] to take care to avoid the appearance of a flat-out establishment of religion, in the sense of the government's adoption of the tenets expressed or symbolized. In such an instance, there will be safety in numbers, and it will be in the interest of a careful government to accept other monuments to stand nearby, to dilute the appearance of adopting whatever particular religious position the single example alone might stand for."

By treating the erection of monuments in the park as a form of government speech, Summum curtailed the possibility that the public park would be treated as a public forum with respect to monuments. The rise of government speech doctrine will be explored immediately below; notice that the doctrine has the effect of avoiding challenging practical problems that might exist if a limited public forum were found.

SPHERES OF GOVERNMENT CONTROL: GOVERNMENT AS EDUCATOR, EMPLOYER AND PATRON

How may government regulate speech when acting as educator, employer, and dispenser of public benefits? In these settings, does government enjoy some of the characteristics of private actors, such that it has greater latitude to control speech? Is the speech of students, employees, and grantees likely to be attributed to government in such settings? Should government be able to regulate or edit its own "message"? The cases below explore this question.

STUDENT SPEECH IN PUBLIC SCHOOLS

Unlike streets and parks and other public "forums," public education is a context in which speech is highly controlled. The classroom is a place of structured dialogue bounded by teacher authority and rules of decorum, and the curriculum itself prescribes which ideas are to be studied and discussed. Yet not every aspect of school is curricular, even inside the classroom. Students socialize outside of class, in the hallways, cafeterias or playing fields. Teachers sometimes share their personal views with students. And students might engage in silent demonstrative conduct even while in class. Does the First Amendment protect student speech in these noncurricular contexts? What should the standard of review be for a restriction on student speech? Should school authorities be given more authority to curtail disruption, or nip it in the bud, than the police enjoy with respect to speakers in the public square? Only in curricular settings or in noncurricular settings too? The following cases explore these questions.

1. ***Black armbands as nondisruptive symbolic conduct.*** In **Tinker v. Des Moines Independent Community School District**, 393 U.S. 503 (1969), the Court held that a public school could not discipline two high school students and one junior high school student for wearing black armbands to school to publicize their objections to the Vietnam War. They were asked to remove their armbands and refused. In accordance with a school policy adopted two days earlier in anticipation of such a protest, the students were suspended until they were ready to return without the armbands. The lower federal court refused to enjoin the disciplinary action.

In reversing, Justice FORTAS's majority opinion stated that "First Amendment rights, applied in light of the special characteristics of the school environment, are available to teachers and students. It can hardly be argued that either students or teachers shed their constitutional rights to freedom of speech or expression at the schoolhouse gate. [The] problem here involves direct, primary First Amendment rights akin to 'pure speech.' The school officials banned and sought to punish petitioners for a silent, passive expression of opinion, unaccompanied by any disorder or disturbance on the part of petitioners. There is here no evidence whatever of petitioners' interference, actual or nascent, with the schools' work or of collision with the rights of other students to be secure and to be let alone. Accordingly, this case does not concern speech or action that intrudes upon the work of the schools or the rights of other students.

"[In] our system, undifferentiated fear or apprehension of disturbance is not enough to overcome the right to freedom of expression. [In] order for the State [to] justify prohibition of a particular expression of opinion, it must be able to show that its action was caused by something more than a mere desire to avoid the discomfort and unpleasantness that always accompany an unpopular viewpoint. [Here, there was no] evidence that the school authorities had reason to anticipate that the wearing of the armbands would substantially interfere with the work of the school or impinge upon the rights of other students. On the contrary, the action of the school authorities appears to have been based upon an urgent wish to avoid the controversy which might result from the expression, even by the silent symbol of armbands, of opposition to this Nation's part in the conflagration in Vietnam.

"It is also relevant that the school authorities did not purport to prohibit the wearing of all symbols of political or controversial significance. The record shows that students in some of the schools wore buttons relating to national political campaigns, and some even wore the Iron Cross, traditionally a symbol of Nazism. The order prohibiting the wearing of armbands did not extend to these. Instead, a particular symbol [was] singled out for prohibition. [In] our system, state-operated schools may not be enclaves of totalitarianism. School officials do not possess absolute authority over their students. Students in school as well as out of school [are] possessed of fundamental rights which the State must respect, just as they themselves must respect their obligations to the State. In our system, students may not be regarded as closed-circuit recipients of only that which the State chooses to communicate. They may not be confined to the expression of those sentiments that are officially approved.

"[This] principle [is] not confined to the supervised and ordained discussion which takes place in the classroom. The principal use to which the schools are dedicated is to accommodate students during prescribed hours for the purpose of certain types of activities. Among those activities is personal intercommunication among the students. [A] student's rights, therefore, do not embrace merely the classroom hours. When he is in the cafeteria, or on the playing field, or on the campus during the authorized hours, he may express his opinions, even on controversial subjects like the conflict in Vietnam, if he does so without 'materially and substantially interfer[ing] with the requirements of appropriate discipline in the operation of the school' and without colliding with the rights of others. [This standard was quoted from Burnside v. Byars, 363 F.2d 744 (5th Cir. 1966) (holding school could not ban "freedom buttons").] But conduct by the student, in class or out of it, which for any reason—whether it stems from time, place, or type of behavior—materially disrupts classwork or involves substantial disorder or invasion of the rights of others is, of course, not immunized by the constitutional guarantee of freedom of speech."

Justice BLACK's dissent charged the majority with taking over from school officials "the power to control pupils." He objected to any view that "students and teachers may use the schools at their whim as a platform for the exercise of free speech—'symbolic' or 'pure.' [I] have never believed that any person has a right to give speeches or engage in demonstrations where he pleases and when he pleases." He argued, moreover, that "the record overwhelmingly shows that the [wearing of the] armbands did exactly what [the school officials] foresaw it would, that is, took the students' minds off their classwork and diverted them to thoughts about the highly emotional subject of the Vietnam War. [One] does not need to be a prophet or the son of a prophet to know that after the Court's holding today some students [will] be ready, able, and willing to defy their teachers on practically all orders. This is the more unfortunate for the schools since groups of students all over the land are already running loose, conducting break-ins, sit-ins, lie-ins, and smash-ins." Justice Harlan also dissented, conceding that the First Amendment applied in school but arguing that impermissible viewpoint discrimination had not been demonstrated.

After Tinker, could a public school prohibit students from wearing all buttons or insignia on their clothing? All "political" buttons or insignia? Could it require students to wear prescribed uniforms? Could it ban the wearing of "gang colors" to prevent outbreaks of violence? Could it stop male students from wearing T-shirts bearing sexist slogans in order to boost female students' self-esteem and academic performance? Could it bar *teachers* from wearing black armbands?

2. ***Coercion in the school setting: the example of the Tinker case.*** Might the vulnerability of minors in the school setting justify special speech protections? Consider the facts of the plaintiffs' Vietnam War protest in Tinker: "Christopher Eckhart [one of the high school student-plaintiffs in Tinker] [was] 'fearful and trembling' as he got out of the car [arriving] at school about eight o'clock went to his locker, and removed his winter coat. [After refusing the principal's request that he remove the armband, Eckhardt was told that] he was 'too young to have opinions' and that 'colleges didn't accept protesters.' [At] this point, [Eckhardt] recalls that [the principal] told him that the 'senior boys were not going to like what [he] was doing' and then he asked him if he 'was looking for a busted nose.' " Johnson, The Struggle for Student Rights 16–17 (1997).

3. ***Book removal from public school libraries.*** In **Board of Education v. Pico**, 457 U.S. 853 (1982), the Court confronted the problem of school authorities' removal of books from school libraries. Members of the school board of Island Trees, New York, obtained from a conservative parents' organization a list of books described as "objectionable" or "improper fare for school students." They found nine of these books in the high school library, and the board ordered all but one of the books to be removed and condemned them as "anti-American, anti-Christian, anti-Semitic, and just plain filthy." They disregarded the recommendation of a staff/parent committee that several more of the books should be retained. The Court held that summary judgment should not have been granted below to the school board, because there remained a genuine issue of material fact: namely, whether the book removal was ideologically or pedagogically motivated. Justice BRENNAN, writing for a plurality including Justices Marshall, Stevens, and (in large part) Blackmun, wrote "Because we are concerned in this case with the suppression of ideas, our holding today affects only the discretion to *remove* books. In brief, we hold that local school boards may not remove books from school library shelves simply because they dislike the ideas contained in those books and seek by their removal to 'prescribe what shall be orthodox in politics, nationalism, religion, or other matters of opinion.' [Barnette (p. 1392 below).] Such purposes stand inescapably condemned by our precedents." Because the key question of intent was disputed in the record, the Court remanded for trial. (The case was abandoned after remand and there was no further hearing on the merits.)." Justice BLACKMUN, concurring in part and concurring in the judgment,

disagreed with the plurality's emphasis on the right to receive information: "[T]he principle involved here is both narrower and more basic than the 'right to receive information' identified by the plurality. I do not suggest that the State has any affirmative obligation to provide students with information or ideas, something that may well be associated with a 'right to receive.'" Justice WHITE, casting the crucial fifth vote, concurred only in the judgment, expressing no view on the constitutional merits. He suggested that the case should have been decided narrowly under routine summary judgment law, thus avoiding "a dissertation on the extent to which the First Amendment limits the discretion of the school board to remove books from the school library."

Chief Justice BURGER dissented, joined by Justices Powell, Rehnquist, and O'Connor. He argued that the schools' role in inculcating fundamental values necessitated "content-based decisions about the appropriateness of retaining materials in the school library and curriculum." Such decisions "express the views of their community; they may err, of course, and the voters may remove them."

Justice REHNQUIST also dissented, joined by Chief Justice Burger and Justice Powell. He urged that the Court "candidly recogniz[e] that the role of government as sovereign is subject to more stringent limitations than is the role of government as employer, property owner, or [educator]": "[Had] petitioners been the members of a town council, I suppose all would agree that [ordinarily] they could not have prohibited the sale of these books by private booksellers within the municipality. But we have also recognized that the government may act in other capacities than as sovereign, and when it does the First Amendment may speak with a different voice. When it acts as an educator, at least at the elementary and secondary school level, the government is engaged in inculcating social values and knowledge in relatively impressionable young people." He continued: "[In] the very course of administering the many-faceted operations of a school district, the mere decision to purchase some books will necessarily preclude the possibility of purchasing others. The decision to teach a particular subject may preclude the possibility of teaching another subject. A decision to replace a teacher because of ineffectiveness may by implication be seen as a disparagement of the subject matter taught. In each of these instances, however, the book or the exposure to the subject matter may be acquired elsewhere. The managers of the school district are not proscribing it as to the citizenry in general, but are simply determining that it will not be included in the curriculum or school library. In short, actions by the government as educator do not raise the same First Amendment concerns as actions by the government as sovereign."

"[Despite] Justice Brennan's suggestion to the contrary, this Court has never held that the First Amendment grants junior high school and high school students a right of access to certain information in school. It is true that the Court has recognized a limited version of that right in other settings, [but] not one of these cases concerned or even purported to discuss elementary or secondary educational institutions. [The] idea [that] students have a right of access, *in the school,* to information other than that thought by their educators to be necessary is contrary to the very nature of an inculcative education." Education consists of the selective presentation and explanation of ideas. The effective acquisition of knowledge depends upon an orderly exposure to relevant information. [Determining] what information *not* to present to the students is often as important as identifying relevant material. [The] libraries of such schools serve as supplements to this inculcative role. Unlike university or public libraries, elementary and secondary school libraries are not designed for free-wheeling inquiry; they are tailored, as the public school curriculum is tailored, to the teaching of basic skills and ideas. [Finally,] the most obvious reason that petitioners' removal of the books did not violate respondents' right to receive information is the ready availability of the books [elsewhere]. The government as educator does not seek to reach beyond the confines of the school. Indeed, following the removal from the school library of the books at issue in this case, the local public library put all nine books on display [and they were] fully accessible to any inquisitive student."

Justice Rehnquist concluded by suggesting that Justice Brennan's distinctions between book acquisition and removal and between good and bad motives were incoherent in relation to the asserted right to receive ideas: "[If] Justice Brennan truly has found a 'right to receive ideas, [the] distinction between acquisition and removal makes little sense. The failure of a library to acquire a book denies access to its contents just as effectively as does the removal of the book from the library's shelf. [If] 'suppression of ideas' is to be the talisman, one would think that a school board's public announcement of its refusal to acquire certain books would have every bit as much impact on public attention as would an equally publicized decision to remove the books. And yet only the latter action would violate the First Amendment under Justice Brennan's analysis. [Moreover,] bad motives and good motives alike deny access to the books removed. If [there truly is] a constitutional right to receive information, it is difficult to see why the reason for the denial makes any difference. Of course Justice Brennan's view is that intent matters because the First Amendment does not tolerate an officially prescribed orthodoxy. But this reasoning mixes First Amendment apples and oranges. The right to receive information differs from the right to be free from an officially prescribed orthodoxy. Not every educational denial of access to information casts a pall of orthodoxy over the [classroom]." He accordingly found the school board's decision "sufficiently related to 'educational suitability' to pass muster under the First Amendment." Justices Powell and O'Connor also filed separate dissents.

Parent-initiated book removal from school curricula and libraries continues to be a frequently litigated issue in the lower courts. Does Pico give adequate guidance? Consider the following comment: "[I]f school boards know that the courts will sometimes get involved, even if only in extreme cases, and [therefore] restrain themselves accordingly, Pico may serve as an effective constitutional limit, even if that limit is poorly defined and mostly symbolic and self-enforced." Yudof, "Library Book Selection and the Public Schools: The Quest for the Archimedean Point," 59 Ind. L.J. 527 (1984).

Pico identified a school library as lying somewhere between the prescribed curriculum, in which student speech may be controlled, and the realm protected by Tinker in which students are free, as public citizens, to engage in voluntary expression and inquiry. Do First Amendment interests attenuate, and government interests increase, as student speech moves closer to the curriculum? Consider the following cases involving speech at a mandatory school assembly and production of a school newspaper in connection with a journalism class.

4. ***Sexual innuendo at a student assembly.*** In **Bethel School District No. 403 v. Fraser**, 478 U.S. 675 (1986), the Court held that the First Amendment did not prevent a school district "from disciplining a high school student for giving a lewd speech at a [school] assembly." Fraser, in nominating a fellow student for student elective office before a high school assembly of approximately 600 students, delivered a speech containing sexual innuendo.[1] During the speech, some students hooted, yelled, and made gestures simulating the sexual activities alluded to in the speech; others appeared bewildered and embarrassed. The school disciplined Fraser under its disruptive-conduct rule by suspending him for two days. He brought an action claiming a violation of his First Amendment rights. The District Court sustained his claim and the Court of Appeals, relying upon Tinker, affirmed. The Court reversed by a vote of 7–2.

Chief Justice BURGER's majority opinion chastised the lower court for ignoring the "marked distinction between the political 'message' of the armbands in Tinker and the sexual content of [Fraser's] speech" here and pointed out that Tinker had emphasized that the armbands worn there did not intrude upon the work of the schools. He pointed out that the "undoubted freedom to advocate unpopular and controversial views in schools and classrooms must be balanced against the society's countervailing interest in teaching students the boundaries of socially appropriate behavior." He added that the inculcation of fundamental societal values was truly the "work of the schools." Accordingly, the school district had acted legitimately in "imposing sanctions upon Fraser in response to his offensively lewd and indecent speech": "Unlike the sanctions imposed [in] Tinker, the penalties imposed [here] were unrelated to any political viewpoint. The First Amendment does not prevent the school officials from determining that to permit a vulgar and lewd speech such as [Fraser's] would undermine the school's basic educational mission. A high school assembly [is] no place for a sexually explicit monologue directed towards an unsuspecting audience of teenage students. Accordingly, it was perfectly appropriate for the school to disassociate itself to make the point to the pupils that vulgar speech and lewd conduct is wholly inconsistent with the 'fundamental values' of public school education."

In an opinion concurring in the judgment, Justice BRENNAN agreed that the school officials' action was not unconstitutional "under the circumstances of this case," but emphasized that Fraser would have been protected had he given the same speech outside of the school environment and might well even have been protected "had he given it in school but under different circumstances, where the school's legitimate interests in teaching and maintaining civil public discourse were less weighty." Justice MARSHALL agreed with Justice Brennan's principles but dissented, relying on the fact that the school board "had not demonstrated any disruption of the educational process." Justice STEVENS also submitted a dissent, arguing that Fraser did not have adequate "reason to anticipate punitive consequences" from his speeches.

---

1 Fraser's speech had included the following passage: "I know a man who is firm—he's firm in his pants, he's firm in his shirt, his character is firm—but most [of] all, his belief in you, the students of Bethel, is firm. Jeff Kuhlman is a man who takes his point and pounds it in. If necessary, he'll take an issue and nail it to the wall. He doesn't attack things in spurts—he drives hard, pushing and pushing until finally—he succeeds. Jeff is a man who will go to the very end—even the climax, for each and every one of you."

5. ***Articles on pregnancy and divorce in a school newspaper.*** **Hazelwood School District v. Kuhlmeier**, 484 U.S. 260 (1988), examined the extent to which educators may exercise editorial control over the contents of a high school newspaper produced as part of a school journalism class and funded by the school. The 5–3 decision upheld a high school principal's deletion of two stories from the school newspaper. One story described three students' experiences with pregnancy; the other discussed the impact of parents' divorce on students at the school. At the outset, Justice WHITE's majority opinion found that the newspaper was not a public forum, either traditionally or by "designation." "Accordingly, school officials were entitled to regulate the contents of [the newspaper] in any reasonable manner. It is this standard, rather than our decision in Tinker, that governs this case." He proceeded:

"The question whether the First Amendment requires a school to tolerate particular student speech—the question that we addressed in Tinker—is different from the question whether the First Amendment requires a school affirmatively to promote particular student speech. The former question addresses educators' ability to silence a student's personal expression that happens to occur on the school premises. The latter question concerns educators' authority over school-sponsored publications, theatrical productions, and other expressive activities that students, parents, and members of the public might reasonably perceive to bear the imprimatur of the school. These activities may fairly be characterized as part of the school curriculum, whether or not they occur in a traditional classroom setting, so long as they are supervised by faculty members and designed to impart particular knowledge or skills to student participants and audiences.

"Educators are entitled to exercise greater control over this second form of student expression to assure that participants learn whatever lessons the activity is designed to teach, that readers or listeners are not exposed to material that may be inappropriate for their level of maturity, and that the views of the individual speaker are not erroneously attributed to the school. Hence, a school may in its capacity as publisher of a school newspaper or producer of a school play 'disassociate itself,' Fraser, [from] speech that is, for example, ungrammatical, poorly written, inadequately researched, biased or prejudiced, vulgar or profane, or unsuitable for immature audiences. A school must be able to set high standards for the student speech that is disseminated under its auspices [and] may refuse to disseminate student speech that does not meet those standards. In addition, a school must be able to take into account the emotional maturity of the intended audience in determining whether to disseminate student speech on potentially sensitive [topics].

"[Accordingly,] we conclude that the standard articulated in Tinker for determining when a school may punish student expression need not also be the standard for determining when a school may refuse to lend its name and resources to the dissemination of student expression. Instead, we hold that educators do not offend the First Amendment by exercising editorial control over the style and content of student speech in school-sponsored expressive activities so long as their actions are reasonably related to legitimate pedagogical concerns. This standard is consistent with our oft-expressed view that the education of the Nation's youth is primarily the responsibility of parents, teachers, and state and local school officials, and not of federal judges. It is only when the decision to censor a school-sponsored publication, theatrical production, or other vehicle of student expression has no valid educational purpose that the First Amendment [requires] judicial intervention to protect students' constitutional rights."

Applying this standard, Justice White held that the principal's deletion of the pregnancy story was "reasonable" because, even though the students mentioned had consented and fictitious names had been used, it was possible that "the students' anonymity was not adequately protected," so that there was a reasonable fear that "the article violated whatever pledge of anonymity had been given to the pregnant students." Moreover, since the article contained discussion of sexual histories and students' use of birth control, it was not unreasonable "for the principal to have concluded that such frank talk was inappropriate in a school-sponsored publication distributed to 14-year-old freshmen and presumably taken home to be read by students' even younger brothers and sisters." Similarly, the deletion of the divorce story was reasonable because a student quoted by name in the article made comments sharply critical of her father, so that the principal could have concluded "that an individual publicly identified as an inattentive parent [was] entitled to an opportunity to defend himself as a matter of journalistic fairness."

Justice BRENNAN's dissent, joined by Justices Marshall and Blackmun, argued that Tinker was controlling and that, under Tinker's standard, there was no valid basis for deleting the stories. In his view, the principal had "violated the First Amendment's prohibitions against censorship of any student expression that neither disrupts classwork nor invades the rights of others, and against any censorship that is not narrowly tailored to serve its purpose." He elaborated: "If mere incompatibility with the school's pedagogical message were a constitutionally sufficient justification for the suppression of student speech, school officials [could convert] our public schools into 'enclaves of totalitarianism' that 'strangle the free mind at its source.' The First Amendment permits no such blanket censorship authority." The Tinker test, he insisted, was adequate to resolve the issue here. After applying it in Fraser, the Court had avoided it here by distinguishing between personal and school-sponsored speech, a distinction unsupported by the precedents. The Court's opinion, he concluded, "denudes high school students of much of the First Amendment protection that Tinker itself prescribed. [The] young men and women of Hazelwood East expected a civics lesson, but not the one the Court teaches them today."

After Hazelwood, could the school restrain publication of the same stories if printed in an "underground" student newspaper funded through private advertisements and sales? Even if distributed on school property? Do Fraser and Hazelwood have any application to a public university setting? For commentary, see Hafen, "Hazelwood School District and the Role of First Amendment Institutions," 1988 Duke L.J. 685 (arguing that Hazelwood indicates that Fraser was "an important transitional case that signaled the Court's [recognition] that broad interpretations of Tinker [had] reduced schools' institutional authority in ways that undermined their educational effectiveness"); and Diamond, "The First Amendment and Public Schools: the Case Against Judicial Intervention," 59 Tex. L. Rev. 477 (1981).

Note that Fraser and Hazelwood emphasize the government's interest in removing its apparent imprimatur of approval from lewd or controversial speech by students in school-sponsored activities. Does this interest in disassociation suggest that government, not the student, will be perceived as the speaker here? Implicit in this view is that government *as speaker* is not constrained by the First Amendment in the same way as it is constrained as sovereign. Do these suggestions in Fraser and Hazelwood vindicate Justice Rehnquist's dissent in Pico? Consider the view that, because "school-sponsored activities are intrinsically and pervasively expressive," such activities should be treated as the equivalent of a "nonforum," in which "government control of student speech [is] shielded from free speech scrutiny." See Brownstein, "The Nonforum as a First Amendment Category: Bringing Order Out of the Chaos of Free Speech Cases Involving School-Sponsored Activities," 42 U.C. Davis L. Rev. 717 (2009). Is it desirable to immunize government from free speech scrutiny altogether when government is "speaking"? Might government distort public dialogue even in its role as speaker or editor?

6. ***Drug-related student speech at a school-sponsored event.*** Under Tinker, Fraser, and Hazelwood, may a public school discipline a student for displaying a 14-foot banner saying "BONG HiTS 4 JESUS" at a school-sponsored event? When the Olympic torch passed through Juneau, Alaska, the local high school principal allowed students to go outside the school to watch. The outing was treated as a school-approved class trip under teacher supervision. When high school senior Joseph Frederick unfurled his banner before the other students (and television cameras), the principal, Deborah Morse, interpreted it as drug-related speech, confiscated it and disciplined Frederick. Juneau school board policy specifically prohibited "any assembly or public expression [that] advocates the use of substances that are illegal to minors." In **Morse v. Frederick**, 551 U.S. 393 (2007), by a vote of 6–3, the Court rejected Frederick's claim that his free speech rights had been violated. Chief Justice ROBERTS wrote for the Court:

"At the outset, we reject Frederick's argument that this is not a school speech. [The] event occurred during normal school hours. It was sanctioned by Principal Morse 'as an approved social event or class trip.' Teachers and administrators were interspersed among the students and charged with supervising them. The high school band and cheerleaders performed. Frederick, standing among other [Juneau] students across the street from the school, directed his banner toward the school, making it plainly visible to most students. Under these circumstances, we agree with the superintendent that Frederick cannot 'stand in the midst of his fellow students, during school hours, at a school-sanctioned activity and claim he is not at school.'

"The message on Frederick's banner is cryptic. It is no doubt offensive to some, perhaps amusing to others. To still others, it probably means nothing at all. Frederick himself claimed 'that the words were just nonsense meant to attract television cameras.' But Principal Morse thought the banner would be interpreted by those viewing it as promoting illegal drug use, and that interpretation is plainly a reasonable one. [The] phrase could be interpreted as an imperative: '[Take] bong hits.' [Alternatively,] the phrase could be viewed as celebrating drug use—'bong hits [are a good thing],' or '[we take] bong hits.' [Frederick does not argue] that the banner conveys any sort of political or religious message. [This] is plainly not a case about political debate over the criminalization of drug use or possession.

"[Our cases] recognize that deterring drug use by schoolchildren is an 'important—indeed, perhaps compelling' interest. Drug abuse can cause severe and permanent damage to the health and well-being of young people. [Student] speech celebrating illegal drug use at a school event, in the presence of school administrators and teachers, thus poses a particular challenge for school officials working to protect those entrusted to their care from the dangers of drug abuse. [The] 'special characteristics of the school environment,' Tinker, and the governmental interest in stopping student drug abuse, [allow] schools to restrict student expression that they reasonably regard as promoting illegal drug use. Tinker warned that schools may not prohibit student speech because of 'undifferentiated fear or apprehension of disturbance' or 'a mere desire to avoid the discomfort and unpleasantness that always accompany an unpopular viewpoint.' The danger here is far more serious and palpable. The particular concern to prevent student drug abuse at issue here, embodied in established school policy, extends well beyond an abstract desire to avoid controversy.

"Petitioners urge us to adopt the broader rule that Frederick's speech is proscribable because it is plainly 'offensive' as that term is used in Fraser. We think this stretches Fraser too far; that case should not be read to encompass any speech that could fit under some definition of 'offensive.' After all, much political and religious speech might be perceived as offensive to some. The concern here is not that Frederick's speech was offensive, but that it was reasonably viewed as promoting illegal drug use. [Reversed.]"

Justice THOMAS concurred, stating his view that there is no constitutional basis to find any free speech rights whatever for students in school. Schools act "*in loco parentis*," Justice Thomas noted, and this doctrine at common law allowed schools to regulate student speech virtually completely: "As originally understood, the Constitution does not afford students a right to free speech in public schools. [Early] public schools gave total control to teachers, who expected obedience and respect from students. And courts routinely deferred to schools' authority to make rules and to discipline students for violating those rules. [I] join the Court's opinion because it erodes Tinker's hold in the realm of student speech, even though it does so by adding to the patchwork of exceptions to the Tinker standard. I think the better approach is to dispense with Tinker altogether, and given the opportunity, I would do so."

Justice ALITO also concurred separately, joined by Justice Kennedy. He emphasized that the majority opinion was narrowly limited to restriction of speech advocating drug use, and "provides no support for any restriction of speech that can plausibly be interpreted as commenting on any political or social issue, including speech on issues such as 'the wisdom of the war on drugs or of legalizing marijuana for medicinal use.'" He also emphasized that the opinion of the Court "does not endorse the broad argument advanced by petitioners and the United States that the First Amendment permits public school officials to censor any student speech that interferes with a school's 'educational mission.' This argument can easily be manipulated in dangerous ways, and I would reject it before such abuse occurs. The 'educational mission' of the public schools is defined by the elected and appointed public officials with authority over the schools and by the school administrators and faculty. As a result, some public schools have defined their educational missions as including the inculcation of whatever political and social views are held by the members of these groups. [The] 'educational mission' argument would give public school authorities a license to suppress speech on political and social issues based on disagreement with the viewpoint expressed. The argument, therefore, strikes at the very heart of the First Amendment." Justice Alito also suggested that, in light of the confined and mandatory environment to which students are subject, schools may regulate speech to nip violence in the bud; by analogy, he suggested, it may regulate speech to prevent drug use, which is also a safety threat to students.

Justice STEVENS dissented, joined by Justices Souter and Ginsburg: "In my judgment, the First Amendment protects student speech if the message itself neither violates a permissible rule nor expressly advocates conduct that is illegal and harmful to students. This nonsense banner does neither, and the Court does serious violence to the First Amendment in [upholding] a school's decision to punish Frederick for expressing a view with which it disagreed. [The] Court's test invites stark viewpoint discrimination. In this case, [the] principal has unabashedly acknowledged that she disciplined Frederick because she disagreed with the pro-drug viewpoint she ascribed to the message on the banner. [And] 'promoting illegal drug use 'comes nowhere close to proscribable 'incitement to imminent lawless action.' Brandenburg. [No] one seriously maintains that drug advocacy (much less Frederick's ridiculous sign) comes within the vanishingly small category of speech that can be prohibited because of its feared consequences.

"Given that the relationship between schools and students 'is custodial and tutelary,' [it] might well be appropriate to tolerate some targeted viewpoint discrimination in this unique setting. And while conventional speech may be restricted only when likely to 'incite imminent lawless action,' it is possible that our rigid imminence requirement ought to be relaxed at schools. But it is one thing to restrict speech that *advocates* drug use. It is another thing entirely to prohibit an obscure message with a drug theme that a third party subjectively—and not very reasonably—thinks is tantamount to express advocacy. Cf. Masses (Hand, J.). [Just] as we insisted in Tinker that the school establish some likely connection between the armbands and their feared consequences, so too [Juneau] must show that Frederick's supposed advocacy stands a meaningful chance of making otherwise-abstemious students try marijuana. [This] is a nonsense message, not advocacy. [Admittedly,] some high school students (including those who use drugs) are dumb. Most students, however, do not shed their brains at the schoolhouse gate, and most students know dumb advocacy when they see it. The notion that the message on this banner would actually persuade either the average student or even the dumbest one to change his or her behavior is most implausible. That the Court believes such a silly message can be proscribed as advocacy underscores the novelty of its position, and suggests that the principle it articulates has no stopping point." Justice Breyer concurred in part and dissented in part, suggesting that the First Amendment question need not be reached as the Court could reverse simply by granting the principal qualified immunity for reasonably thinking the speech was constitutionally proscribable.

Does Morse v. Frederick develop a new exception to Tinker? Note that the majority opinion does not purport to rest the ruling on the Fraser exception for inappropriately vulgar speech in a school setting. Nor does it rest on the Hazelwood exception for speech that is educationally unsuitable and might be wrongly attributed to the school. Indeed, Chief Justice Roberts wrote that "[Hazelwood] does not control this case because no one would reasonably believe that Frederick's banner bore the school's imprimatur." Finally, the ruling does not rest on a categorical exception for *all* drug-related speech; both the majority and Justice Alito's concurrence seem to concede that student discussion of drug reform in civics class would receive Tinker protection. So what is the theory of the decision? Recall that Tinker itself allowed prevention of material disruption of the educational mission. Is drug abuse such a material disruption? Is it a stretch to equate the need to prevent drug use with the need to avert schoolyard violence before it occurs? If so, is the harm sufficiently imminent? Is peer pressure from a sign the equivalent of taunts that provoke a brawl? Does the decision implicitly embrace but water down Tinker's holding that preventing harm to student safety justifies limiting even protected speech? Or is the implicit theory that advocacy of drug use is so worthless in the school context that little justification is required? Finally, was the banner in question "cryptic," as the Court suggested, or "nonsensical," as Justice Stevens had it? Can you make the case that the banner was straightforwardly parodic?

7. ***Public schools and technology.*** To what extent should school officials be able to regulate off-campus speech in an increasingly digital age? The Supreme Court has yet to address the issue, but consider two high-profile Third Circuit en banc decisions, J.S. ex rel. Snyder v. Blue Mountain School District, 650 F.3d 915 (3d Cir. 2011); and Layshock ex rel. Layshock v. Hermitage School District, 650 F.3d 205 (3d Cir. 2011). Both Snyder and Layshock involved students who created fake online profiles of school officials. The Third Circuit found in favor of the students, holding that school officials could not punish students for off-campus expression absent a reasonable forecast that the expression would cause substantial disruption to the school's operation. By contrast, the Ninth Circuit held that a public high school could expel a student for sending instant messages to his classmates "that could be interpreted as a plan to attack the school"; under Tinker, the violent messages "made it reasonable for school officials to forecast a substantial disruption of school activities." Wynar v. Douglas County School Dist., 728 F.3d 1062 (9th Cir. 2013). Should school officials have any authority to regulate students' off-campus speech? If so, how should that authority be cabined?

SPEECH AND ASSOCIATION BY PUBLIC EMPLOYEES AND CONTRACTORS

To what extent does the First Amendment limit governmental power to regulate the behavior of its employees or contractors? Does the government's status as employer or contractor justify regulations and disqualifications because of political expression or association? Is ideological conformity sometimes a bona fide occupational qualification? Does it matter if the expression or association takes place on or off the job?

These would not have been viewed as substantial constitutional questions if Justice HOLMES's views as a state court judge had prevailed. In 1892, he said: "The petitioner may have a constitutional right to talk politics, but he has no constitutional right to be a policeman. There are few employments for hire in which the servant does not agree to suspend his constitutional right of free speech, as well of idleness, by the implied terms of his contract. The servant cannot complain, as he takes the employment on the terms which are offered him." **McAuliffe v. Mayor of New Bedford**, 155 Mass. 216, 29 N.E. 517 (1892).

But the Holmes position has not prevailed: it has long been recognized that, even though there is no "right" to public employment or to a contract, some constitutional restrictions apply when government attempts to discharge employees or contractors for reason of their exercise of constitutionally protected liberties. Why should this be? Because the public sector grew enormously in relation to the private sector in the twentieth century? Because losing one's job can be as coercive as a criminal fine? Because constitutional rights such as the right of free speech are inalienable through bargaining with the government? See generally Van Alstyne, "The Demise of the Right-Privilege Distinction in Constitutional Law," 81 Harv. L. Rev. 1439 (1968); Kreimer, "Allocational Sanctions: the Problem of Negative Rights in a Positive State," 132 U. Pa. L. Rev. 1293 (1984); Epstein, "Foreword: Unconstitutional Conditions, State Power, and the Limits of Consent," 102 Harv. L. Rev. 4 (1988); Sullivan, "Unconstitutional Conditions," 102 Harv. L. Rev. 1413 (1989).

The decisions that follow first explore the question of whether government may discharge or otherwise sanction an employee for statements or other expressive activity. Note the Court's distinction between two categories: where the public employer restricts an employee's First Amendment speech rights *as a citizen* on matters of public concern, and where the restriction applies the public employee's free speech rights *as an employee.* The focus next shifts to the question whether hiring and firing decisions may be based on party affiliation—that is, whether a patronage system violates employee rights of political association. Finally, the materials consider whether rights of speech or association enjoyed by public employees should also extend to independent contractors with the government.

PUBLIC EMPLOYEE SPEECH

In **Pickering v. Board of Education**, 391 U.S. 563 (1968), the Court held that a public school teacher could not constitutionally be dismissed from his job for writing a letter to a newspaper criticizing the school board's handling of revenue measures for the schools and its allocation of financial resources between the schools' educational and athletic programs. Justice MARSHALL's majority opinion "unequivocally" rejected the proposition that "teachers may constitutionally be compelled to relinquish the First Amendment rights they would otherwise enjoy as citizens to comment on matters of public interest in connection with the operation of the public schools in which they work." He relied heavily on decisions from the 1950s and 1960s invalidating efforts to require public employees, especially teachers, to disclose their associations and swear loyalty oaths to the state. (See Chapter 13 below.) But he also noted that "the State has interests as an employer in regulating the speech of its employees that differ significantly from those it possesses in connection with regulation of the speech of the citizenry in general. The problem in any case is to arrive at a balance between the interests of the teacher, as a citizen, in commenting upon matters of public concern and the interest of the State, as an employer, in promoting the efficiency of the public services it performs through its employees."

In the circumstances of the case, Justice Marshall found that the government interests did not outweigh Pickering's speech rights: "[T]he question whether a school system requires additional funds is a matter of legitimate public concern on which the judgment of the school administration, including the School Board, cannot, in a society that leaves such questions to popular vote, be taken as conclusive. On such a question free and open debate is vital to informed decision-making by the electorate. Teachers are, as a class, the members of a community most likely to have informed and definite opinions as to how funds allotted to the operation of the schools should be spent. Accordingly, it is essential that they be able to speak out freely on such questions without fear of retaliatory dismissal. [Pickering's statements were] critical of his ultimate employer but [had not been shown] to have in any way either impeded the teacher's proper performance of his daily duties in the classroom or to have interfered with the regular operation of the schools generally. In these circumstances we conclude that the interest of the school administration in limiting teachers' opportunities to contribute to public debate is not significantly greater than its interest in limiting a similar contribution by any member of the general public." Accordingly, absent any malicious libel of the school board actionable under the New York Times standard, Pickering could not be dismissed.

Givhan v. Western Line Consolidated School District, 439 U.S. 410 (1979), extended the Pickering principle to hold unconstitutional a teacher's dismissal for statements criticizing the school's allegedly racially discriminatory policies in a series of *private* encounters with a school principal. For commentary, see Schauer, " 'Private' Speech and the 'Private' Forum," 1979 Sup. Ct. Rev. 217.

Contrast with Pickering and Givhan the Court's decision in the following case, involving speech by an assistant district attorney critical of her supervisors. The case arose when Sheila Myers, an assistant district attorney in New Orleans, was informed by her boss, longtime New Orleans District Attorney Harry Connick, Sr., that she would be transferred to prosecute cases in a different section of the criminal court. Myers opposed the transfer and expressed her view to several supervisors, including Connick. When one supervisor told her that her concerns were not shared by others in the office, she told him she would do some research and prepared a questionnaire soliciting the views of her fellow staff members concerning office transfer policy, office morale, the need for a grievance committee, the level of confidence in supervisors, and whether employees felt pressured to work in political campaigns. She distributed the questionnaire to 15 assistant district attorneys. One of Connick's first assistants told Connick that Myers was creating a "mini-insurrection" within the office. Connick terminated Myers because of her refusal to accept the transfer and because he found her distribution of the questionnaire an act of insubordination. Myers claimed that her termination violated the Free Speech Clause, and the district court and court of appeals agreed, relying on Pickering. The Court reversed by a vote of 5–4:

———

Connick v. Myers

461 U.S. 138, 103 S. Ct. 1684, 75 L. Ed. 2d 708 (1983).

■ JUSTICE WHITE delivered the opinion of the Court.

[It has long] been settled that a state cannot condition public employment on a basis that infringes the employee's constitutionally protected interest in freedom of expression. [Pickering.] [But the lower courts misapplied Pickering] in striking the balance for respondent. [Connick] contends at the outset that no balancing of interests is required in this case because Myers' questionnaire concerned only internal office matters and that such speech is not upon a matter of "public concern," as the term was used in Pickering. Although we do not agree that Myers' communication in this case was wholly without First Amendment protection, there is much force to Connick's submission. The repeated emphasis in Pickering on the right of a public employee "as a citizen, in commenting upon matters of public concern," was not accidental. This language [reflects] both the historical evolvement of the rights of public employees, and the common sense realization that government offices could not function if every employment decision became a constitutional matter. [Pickering], its antecedents and progeny, lead us to conclude that if Myers' questionnaire cannot be fairly characterized as constituting speech on a matter of public concern, it is unnecessary for us to scrutinize the reasons for her discharge. When employee expression cannot be fairly considered as relating to any matter of political, social, or other concern to the community, government officials should enjoy wide latitude in managing their offices, without intrusive oversight by the judiciary in the name of the [First Amendment].

We do not suggest, however, that Myers' speech, even if not touching upon a matter of public concern, is totally beyond the protection of the First Amendment. [We] in no sense suggest that speech on private matters falls into one of the narrow and well-defined classes of expression which carries so little social value, such as obscenity, that the state can prohibit and punish such expression by all persons in its jurisdiction. For example, an employee's false criticism of his employer on grounds not of public concern may be cause for his discharge but would be entitled to the same protection in a libel action accorded an identical statement made by a man on the street. We hold only that when a public employee speaks not as a citizen upon matters of public concern, but instead as an employee upon matters only of personal interest, absent the most unusual circumstances, a federal court is not the appropriate forum in which to review the wisdom of a personnel decision taken by a public agency allegedly in reaction to the employee's behavior. Our responsibility is to ensure that citizens are not deprived of fundamental rights by virtue of working for the government; this does not require a grant of immunity for employee grievances not afforded by the First Amendment to those who do not work for the state.

Whether an employee's speech addresses a matter of public concern must be determined by the content, form, and context of a given statement, as revealed by the whole record. In this case, with but one exception, the questions posed by Myers to her coworkers do not fall under the rubric of matters of "public concern." We view the questions pertaining to the confidence and trust that Myers' coworkers possess in various supervisors, the level of office morale, and the need for a grievance committee as mere extensions of Myers' dispute over her transfer to another section of the criminal court. Unlike the dissent, we do not believe these questions are of public import in evaluating the performance of the District Attorney as an elected official. Myers did not seek to inform the public that the District Attorney's office was not discharging its governmental responsibilities in the investigation and prosecution of criminal cases. Nor did Myers seek to bring to light [wrongdoing] or breach of public trust on the part of Connick and others. Indeed, the questionnaire, if released to the public, would convey no information at all other than the fact that a single employee is upset with the status quo. While discipline and morale in the workplace are related to an agency's efficient performance of its duties, the focus of Myers' questions is not to evaluate the performance of the office but rather to gather ammunition for another round of controversy with her superiors. These questions reflect one employee's dissatisfaction with a transfer and an attempt to turn that displeasure into a cause celèbre. To presume that all matters which transpire within a government office are of public concern would mean that virtually every remark—and certainly every criticism directed at a public official—would plant the seed of a constitutional case. [The] First Amendment does not require a public office to be run as a roundtable for employee complaints over internal office affairs.

One question in Myers' questionnaire, however, does touch upon a matter of public concern. Question 11 inquires if assistant district attorneys "ever feel pressured to work in political campaigns on behalf of office supported candidates." We have recently noted that official pressure upon employees to work for political candidates not of the worker's own choice constitutes a coercion of belief in violation of fundamental constitutional rights. [see Branti; Elrod, p. 1316 below.] In addition, there is a demonstrated interest in this country that government service should depend upon meritorious performance rather than political service. Given this history, we believe it apparent that the issue of whether assistant district attorneys are pressured to work in political campaigns is a matter of interest to the community upon which it is essential that public employees be able to speak out freely without fear of retaliatory dismissal.

Because one of the questions in Myers' survey touched upon a matter of public concern, and contributed to her discharge, we must determine whether Connick was justified in discharging Myers. Here the District Court again erred in imposing an unduly onerous burden on the state to justify Myers' discharge. The District Court viewed the issue of whether Myers' speech was upon a matter of "public concern" as a threshold inquiry, after which it became the government's burden to "clearly demonstrate" that the speech involved "substantially interfered" with official responsibilities. Yet Pickering unmistakably states [that] the state's burden in justifying a particular discharge varies depending upon the nature of the employee's expression. Although such particularized balancing is difficult, the courts must reach the most appropriate possible balance of the competing interests.

The Pickering balance requires full consideration of the government's interest in the effective and efficient fulfillment of its responsibilities to the public. [Connick's] judgment [was] that Myers' questionnaire was an act of insubordination which interfered with working relationships. When close working relationships are essential to fulfilling public responsibilities, a wide degree of deference to the employer's judgment is appropriate. Furthermore, we do not see the necessity for an employer to allow events to unfold to the extent that the disruption of the office and the destruction of working relationships is manifest before taking action. We caution that a stronger showing may be necessary if the employee's speech more substantially involved matters of public concern. [Also] relevant is the manner, time, and place in which the questionnaire was distributed. [The] fact that Myers, unlike Pickering, exercised her rights to speech at the office supports Connick's fears that the functioning of his office was endangered.

Finally, the context in which the dispute arose is also significant. This is not a case where an employee, out of purely academic interest, circulated a questionnaire so as to obtain useful research. [When] employee speech concerning office policy arises from an employment dispute concerning the very application of that policy to the speaker, additional weight must be given to the supervisor's view that the employee has threatened the authority of the employer to run the office. Although we accept the District Court's factual finding that Myers' reluctance to accede to the transfer order was not a sufficient cause in itself for her dismissal, [this] does not render irrelevant the fact that the questionnaire emerged after a persistent dispute between Myers and Connick and his deputies over office transfer policy.

Myers' questionnaire touched upon matters of public concern in only a most limited sense; her survey, in our view, is most accurately characterized as an employee grievance concerning internal office policy. The limited First Amendment interest involved here does not require that Connick tolerate action which he reasonably believed would disrupt the office, undermine his authority, and destroy close working relationships. Myers' discharge therefore did not offend the First Amendment. [Although] today the balance is struck for the government, this is no defeat for the First Amendment. For it would indeed be a Pyrrhic victory for the great principles of free expression if the Amendment's safeguarding of a public employee's right, as a citizen, to participate in discussions concerning public affairs were confused with the attempt to constitutionalize the employee grievance that we see presented [here]. [Reversed.]

■ JUSTICE BRENNAN, with whom JUSTICE MARSHALL, BLACKMUN, and STEVENS join, dissenting.

[The] Court distorts the balancing analysis required under Pickering by suggesting that one factor, the context in which a statement is made, is to be weighed *twice*—first in determining whether an employee's speech addresses a matter of public concern and then in deciding whether the statement adversely affected the government's interest as an employer. [Moreover,] in concluding that the effect of respondent's personnel policies on employee morale and the work performance of the District Attorney's Office is not a matter of public concern, the Court impermissibly narrows the class of subjects on which public employees may speak out without fear of retaliatory dismissal.

[The Court] suggests that there are two classes of speech of public concern: statements "of public import" because of their content, form and context, and statements that, by virtue of their subject matter, are "inherently of public concern." In my view, however, whether a particular statement by a public employee is addressed to a subject of public concern does not depend on where it was said or why. The First Amendment affords special protection to speech that may inform public debate about how our society is to be governed—regardless of whether it actually becomes the subject of a public controversy. [The] Court misapplies the Pickering test and holds—against our previous authorities—that a public employer's mere apprehension that speech will be disruptive justifies suppression of that speech when all the objective evidence suggests that those fears are essentially [unfounded]. Such extreme deference to the employer's judgment is not appropriate when public employees voice critical views concerning the operations of the agency for which they work. [In] order to protect public employees' First Amendment right to voice critical views on issues of public importance, the courts must make their own appraisal of the effects of the speech.

The Court's decision today inevitably will deter public employees from making critical statements about the manner in which government agencies are operated for fear that doing so will provoke their dismissal. As a result, the public will be deprived of valuable information with which to evaluate the performance of elected officials.

PICKERING AND CONNICK COMPARED

1. ***Public employee political hyperbole.*** In **Rankin v. McPherson**, 483 U.S. 378 (1987), the Court held by a vote of 5–4 that a clerical employee in a county constable's office could not be discharged for remarking, after hearing of the attempted assassination of President Reagan in 1981, "If they go for him again, I hope they get him." Justice MARSHALL's majority opinion held that, even after Connick, the remark constituted speech on a matter of public concern and that the firing violated the First Amendment. He noted that the remark was made in the course of a conversation addressing the policies of the Reagan Administration and added that the "inappropriate or controversial character of a statement is irrelevant to the question whether it deals with a matter of public concern." Having determined that the remark in the context in which it was made did involve a matter of public concern, Justice Marshall balanced the employee's speech interest against the State's interest in the "effective functioning" of government under the Pickering test. He noted that the State "bears a burden of justifying the discharge on legitimate grounds" and commented that the State's interest in content-related sanctions was minimal where the employee "serves no confidential, policymaking, or public contact role." He concluded that there had been no showing that McPherson's statement had interfered with the effective functioning of the office, nor that it was made in a context where it could bring discredit upon the office, and thus that her discharge violated the First Amendment. Justice POWELL concurred, emphasizing that this case involved only "a single, offhand comment" directed to "a co-worker who happened also to be her boyfriend" in a private conversation that was unforeseeably overheard by another co-worker.

Justice SCALIA, joined by Chief Justice Rehnquist and Justices White and O'Connor, dissented. He insisted that "no law enforcement agency is required by the First Amendment to permit one of its employees to 'ride with the cops and cheer for the robbers.'" After disagreeing with the majority's conclusion that this was speech on a matter of public concern, he argued that the employee's statement was, because of the unprotected nature of actual threats, "so near the category of completely unprotected speech" that it could not "fairly be viewed as lying within the 'heart' of the First Amendment's protection." Finding the State's interest in not having such statements made by its employees quite reasonable, he also objected to the Court's distinction between policymaking and nonpolicymaking employees: "Nonpolicymaking employees [can] hurt working relationships and undermine public confidence in an organization every bit as much as policymaking employees. I, for one, do not look forward to the new First Amendment world the Court creates, in which nonpolicymaking employees of the [EEOC] must be permitted to make remarks on the job approving of racial discrimination, nonpolicymaking employees of the Selective Service System to advocate noncompliance with the draft laws, [and] nonpolicymaking constable's deputies to express approval for the assassination of the President."

2. ***Who determines public vs. private concern?*** After Connick, who is to determine whether an employee's speech is on a matter of public or private concern if there is a factual dispute about what was actually said? In **Waters v. Churchill**, 511 U.S. 661 (1994), a nurse sued her public hospital employer for firing her based on a conversation with a co-worker. She claimed the remark was a legitimate complaint about training that could harm patients, but her employer thought was disruptive speech critical of her bosses and unprotected under Connick. A plurality opinion by Justice O'Connor ruled that a public employer does not violate the First Amendment if it fires an employee for what the employer reasonably believed was speech on a matter of private concern. Justice Scalia concurred but would have been even more protective of the employer: he argued that the employer ought not be liable unless it had intentionally—not merely negligently—retaliated against an employee for speech on a matter of public concern. Justice Stevens's dissent argued that an employer ought be absolutely liable if the speech for which the employee was fired was actually on a matter of public concern as objectively determined by a court, regardless of the employer's subjective state of mind.

3. ***The scope of speech on matters of public concern.*** Connick left intact Pickering's broad protection for public employee speech on matters of "public concern." But it left unclear whether an employee had to make any affirmative showing of public interest or importance. Is such speech limited to criticism of governmental policy, as was involved in the letter to the editor in Pickering or in the political hyperbole in McPherson? Or was "matters of public concern" a residual catch-all that included any matter that wasn't an internal employee grievance (that is, a matter of private concern)?

The Court took a broad view of "matters of public concern" in **United States v. National Treasury Employees Union (NTEU)**, 513 U.S. 454 (1995). The case involved a challenge to § 501(b) of the Ethics in Government Act, as amended in 1989 and 1991 to bar a wide range of officers and employees of the federal government from receiving payment of any honorarium "for an appearance, speech or article (including a series of appearances, speeches, or articles if the subject matter is directly related to the individual's official duties or the payment is made because of the individual's status with the Government)." The honorarium ban was challenged by a class of executive branch employees below federal salary grade GS-16. Among the class were a mail handler who had given lectures on the Quaker religion, an aerospace engineer who had lectured on black history, a microbiologist at the Food and Drug Administration who had reviewed dance performances, and a tax examiner who wrote articles about the environment.

Justice STEVENS wrote for the Court, holding the honorarium ban invalid: "Federal employees who write for publication in their spare time have made significant contributions to the marketplace of ideas. They include literary giants like Nathaniel Hawthorne and Herman Melville, who were employed by the Customs Service; Walt Whitman, who worked for the Departments of Justice and Interior; and Bret Harte, an employee of the mint. Respondents have yet to make comparable contributions to American culture, but they share with these great artists important characteristics that are relevant to the issue we confront." Justice Stevens found the case governed by Pickering rather than Connick: "Respondents' expressive activities in this case fall within the protected category of citizen comment on matters of public concern rather than employee comment on matters related to personal status in the workplace. The speeches and articles for which they received compensation in the past were addressed to a public audience, were made outside the workplace, and involved content largely unrelated to their government employment." And he found that the government's "prohibition on compensation unquestionably imposes a significant burden on expressive activity. See [Simon & Schuster.][1]"

Turning to the government's asserted justifications, Justice Stevens stated: "The Government's underlying concern is that federal officers not misuse or appear to misuse power by accepting compensation for their unofficial and nonpolitical writing and speaking activities. This interest is undeniably powerful, but the Government cites no evidence of misconduct related to honoraria in the vast rank and file of federal employees below grade GS-16. [Congress] reasonably could assume that payments of honoraria to [its own Members,] judges or high-ranking officials in the Executive Branch might generate [an] appearance of improper influence. Congress could not, however, reasonably extend that assumption to all federal employees below Grade GS-16, an immense class of workers with negligible power to confer favors on those who might pay to hear them speak or to read their articles."

Justice Stevens also found that the necessity of the total ban to "operational efficiency" was called into "serious doubt" by the fact that honoraria were banned for "a *series* of appearances, speeches, or articles" only if "the subject matter is directly related to the individual's official duties or the payment is made because of the individual's status with the Government." He explained: "Congress' decision to provide a total exemption for all unrelated series of speeches undermines application of the ban to individual speeches and articles with no nexus to Government employment. Absent such a nexus, no corrupt bargain or even appearance of impropriety appears likely. The Government's only argument against a general nexus limitation is that a wholesale prophylactic rule is easier to enforce than one that requires individual nexus determinations. The nexus limitation for series, however, unambiguously reflects a congressional judgment that agency ethics officials [can] enforce the statute when it includes a nexus test. A blanket burden on the speech of nearly 1.7 million federal employees requires a much stronger justification than the Government's dubious claim of administrative convenience. [Such] anomalies in the text of the statute and regulations underscore our conclusion: the speculative benefits the honoraria ban may provide the Government are not sufficient to justify this

[1] This proposition is self-evident even to those who do not fully accept Samuel Johnson's cynical comment: " 'No man but a blockhead ever wrote, except for money.' " J. Boswell, Life of Samuel Johnson LL.D. 302 (R. Hutchins ed. 1952). [Footnote by Justice Stevens.]

crudely crafted burden on respondents' freedom to engage in expressive activities."

Justice Stevens, for the Court, held that the appropriate remedy was facial invalidation of the statutory provision. Justice O'Connor concurred in the judgment in part and dissented in part, arguing that facial invalidation was excessive and that the Court should have invalidated the provision only to the extent it was applied without a nexus provision.

Chief Justice REHNQUIST, joined by Justices Scalia and Thomas, dissented: "The ban neither prohibits anyone from speaking or writing, nor does it penalize anyone who speaks or writes; the only stricture effected by the statute is a denial of compensation. [Unlike] the law at issue in Simon & Schuster, the honoraria ban is neither content nor viewpoint based. As a result, the ban does not raise the specter of Government control over the marketplace of ideas. To the extent that the honoraria ban implicates First Amendment concerns, the proper standard of review is found in our cases dealing with the Government's ability to regulate the First Amendment activities of its employees.

"[Applying] these standards to the honoraria ban, I cannot say that the balance that Congress has struck between its interests and the interests of its employees to receive compensation for their First Amendment expression is unreasonable. The Court largely ignores the Government's foremost interest—prevention of impropriety and the appearance of impropriety—by focusing solely on the burdens of the statute as applied to several carefully selected Executive Branch employees whose situations present the application of the statute where the Government's interests are at their lowest ebb [but who] by no means represent the breadth of the class. [Nor is it necessarily true that] federal employees below grade GS-16 have negligible power to confer favors on those who might pay to hear them speak or to read their articles. [Tax] examiners, bank examiners, enforcement officials, or any number of federal employees have substantial power to confer favors even though their compensation level is below Grade GS-16. [The] Government's related concern regarding the difficulties that would attach in administering a case-by-case analysis of the propriety of particular honoraria also supports the honoraria ban's validity. [Congress] reasonably determined that the prior ethics regime, which required these case-by-case determinations, was inadequate.

"[Unlike] our prototypical application of Pickering which normally involves a response to the content of employee speech, the honoraria ban prohibits no speech and is unrelated to the message or the viewpoint expressed by the government employee. Because there is only a limited burden on respondents' First Amendment rights, Congress reasonably could have determined that its paramount interests in preventing impropriety and the appearance of impropriety in its work force justified the honoraria ban." Chief Justice Rehnquist also objected to the remedy: "One would expect the Court to hold the statute inapplicable on First Amendment grounds to persons such as the postal worker who lectures on the Quaker religion, and others of similar ilk. But the Court, [in] what may fairly be described as an O. Henry ending, holds the statute inapplicable to the entire class before the Court."

In contrast to the broad approach taken in NTEU, however, the Court's per curiam decision in **City of San Diego v. Roe**, 543 U.S. 77 (2004), made clear that there are limits to the scope of matters of public concern on which public employees may make commentary in their capacity as citizens. The case involved a San Diego police officer who made videos of himself stripping off a police uniform and masturbating, including while issuing a traffic ticket, and sold them online on eBay, listing himself in his user profile as in the field of law enforcement. He was terminated from the police force, and alleged that the termination violated his right to free speech. The Court reversed a court of appeals opinion that had deemed his off-duty, off-premises speech protected under Pickering and NTEU: "The Court of Appeals' reliance on NTEU was seriously misplaced. Although Roe's activities took place outside the workplace and purported to be about subjects not related to his employment, the [police department] demonstrated legitimate and substantial interests of its own that were compromised by his speech. Far from confining his activities to speech unrelated to his employment, Roe took deliberate steps to link his videos [to] his police work, all in a way injurious to his employer. [The] present case falls outside the protection afforded in NTEU."

The Court went on to clarify that not all public employee speech that is unrelated to internal workplace grievances under Connick is automatically entitled to Pickering review: "Pickering did not hold that any and all statements by a public employee are entitled to balancing. [In] order to merit Pickering balancing, a public employee's speech must touch on a matter of 'public concern.' [P]ublic concern is something that is a subject of legitimate news interest, that is, a subject of general interest and of value and concern to the public at the time of publication. [Applying] these principles to the instant case, there is no difficulty in concluding that Roe's expression does not qualify as a matter of public concern under any view of the public concern test. He fails the threshold test and Pickering balancing does not come into play."

Garcetti v. Ceballos, 543 U.S. 1186 (2006), further clarified the limited scope of public employee speech on matters of public concern. The case arose in the context of a Los Angeles deputy district attorney who wrote his supervisors a memo stating that an affidavit police had used to obtain a critical search warrant contained serious misrepresentations. He recommended dismissal of a prosecution based on that affidavit. The case was reargued after Justice Alito was confirmed to Justice O'Connor's seat. Writing for a narrowly divided court, Justice KENNEDY, joined by Chief Justice Roberts and Justices Scalia, Thomas, and Alito, rejected the argument that the County's allegedly retaliatory employment actions in the wake of the memo violated the First Amendment: "When a citizen enters government service, the citizen by necessity must accept certain limitations on his or her freedom. [At] the same time, the Court has recognized that a citizen who works for the government is nonetheless a citizen. [The Court's decisions] have sought both to promote the individual and societal interests that are served when employees speak as citizens on matters of public concern and to respect the needs of government employers attempting to perform their important public functions.

"That Ceballos expressed his views inside his office, rather than publicly, is not dispositive. Employees in some cases may receive First Amendment protection for expressions made at work. [The] memo concerned the subject matter of Ceballos' employment, but this, too, is nondispositive. The First Amendment protects some expressions related to the speaker's job. The controlling factor in Ceballos' case is that his expressions were made pursuant to his duties as a calendar deputy. That consideration—the fact that Ceballos spoke as a prosecutor fulfilling a responsibility to advise his supervisor about how best to proceed with a pending case—distinguishes Ceballos' case from those in which the First Amendment provides protection against discipline.

"We hold that when public employees make statements pursuant to their official duties, the employees are not speaking as citizens for First Amendment purposes, and the Constitution does not insulate their communications from employer discipline. [Restricting] speech that owes its existence to a public employee's professional responsibilities does not infringe any liberties the employee might have enjoyed as a private citizen. It simply reflects the exercise of employer control over what the employer itself has commissioned or created. Contrast, for example, the expressions made by the speaker in Pickering, whose letter to the newspaper had no official significance and bore similarities to letters submitted by numerous citizens every day. [Ceballos'] proposed contrary rule [would] commit state and federal courts to a new, permanent, and intrusive role, mandating judicial oversight of communications between and among government employees and their superiors in the course of official business. This displacement of managerial discretion by judicial supervision finds no support in our precedents."

Justice STEVENS filed a dissent arguing that "public employees are still citizens while they are in the office. [It] is senseless to let constitutional protection for exactly the same words hinge on whether they fall within a job description." Justice SOUTER, joined by Justices Stevens and Ginsburg, also dissented, stating: "There is no adequate justification for the majority's line categorically denying Pickering protection to any speech uttered 'pursuant to . . . official duties.' [The] need for a balance hardly disappears when an employee speaks on matters his job requires him to address; rather, it seems obvious that the individual and public value of such speech is no less, and may well be greater, when the employee speaks pursuant to his duties in addressing a subject he knows intimately for the very reason that it falls within his duties. [The] majority is rightly concerned that the employee who speaks out on matters subject to comment in doing his own work has the greater leverage to create office uproars and fracture the government's authority to set policy to be carried out coherently through the ranks. [But] why do the majority's concerns, which we all share, require categorical exclusion of First Amendment protection against any official retaliation for things said on the job?" Justice Souter rejected as a "fallacy" the view that "any statement made within the scope of public employment is [the] government's own speech." He also rejected the view that state and federal statutory protections for "whistleblowers" were sufficient to satisfy the First Amendment.

Justice BREYER filed a separate dissent that, like Justice Souter's, advocated use of the Pickering balancing test in the case, but emphasized "two special circumstances that together justify First Amendment review. First, the speech at issue is professional speech—the speech of a lawyer. Such speech is subject to independent regulation by canons of the profession. Those canons provide an obligation to speak in certain instances. [Second,] the Constitution itself here imposes speech obligations upon the government's professional employee. A prosecutor has a constitutional obligation to learn of, to preserve, and to communicate with the defense about exculpatory and impeachment evidence in the government's possession. [Where] professional and special constitutional obligations are both present, the need to protect the employee's speech is augmented, the need for broad government authority to control that speech is likely diminished, and administrable standards are quite likely available. Hence, I would find that the Constitution mandates special protection of employee speech in such circumstances."

In **Lane v. Franks**, 573 U.S. 228 (2014), the Court applied Pickering and distinguished Garcetti, holding that a government employee's truthful testimony in court outside the scope of his job duties necessarily counts as protected citizen speech. The facts involved an employee of a state community college who fired a no-show employee, then gave testimony at grand jury and trial that led to the fraud conviction of the no-show. Lane, the original employee, was fired in apparent retaliation. Justice SOTOMAYOR wrote for a unanimous Court: "Sworn testimony in judicial proceedings is a quintessential example of speech as a citizen for a simple reason: Anyone who testifies in court bears an obligation, to the court and society at large, to tell the truth. When the person testifying is a public employee, he may bear separate obligations to his employer—for example, an obligation not to show up to court dressed in an unprofessional manner. But any such obligations as an employee are distinct and independent from the obligation, as a citizen, to speak the truth. That independent obligation renders sworn testimony speech as a citizen and sets it apart from speech made purely in the capacity of an employee. [Garcetti] said nothing about speech that simply relates to public employment or concerns information learned in the course of public employment. [The] mere fact that a citizen's speech concerns information acquired by virtue of his public employment does not transform that speech into employee—rather than citizen—speech. The critical question under Garcetti is whether the speech at issue is itself ordinarily within the scope of an employee's duties, not whether it merely concerns those duties."

Justice THOMAS, joined by Justices Scalia and Alito, concurred to observe that the Court had "no occasion to address the quite different question whether a public employee speaks 'as a citizen' when he testifies in the course of his ordinary job responsibilities. For some public employees—such as police officers, crime scene technicians, and laboratory analysts—testifying is a routine and critical part of their employment duties. Others may be called to testify in the context of particular litigation as the designated representatives of their employers."

4. ***Pickering, Connick and school athletic associations.*** Connick and follow-on cases like Ceballos make clear that public employees do not enjoy presumptive protection of speech that interferes with the efficiency of the public entity's internal operations. Does the same principle extend beyond public employees to those who voluntarily join other kinds of public entities or associations? May a school athletic association sanction the speech of a member private school that interferes with the efficient pursuit of its mission? In **Tennessee Secondary School Athletic Ass'n v. Brentwood Academy**, 551 U.S. 291 (2007), the Court gave an affirmative answer to that question. Recall that the Court deemed the Tennessee Secondary School Athletic Association (TSSAA)—a not-for-profit membership corporation organized to regulate interscholastic sports—a "state actor" by virtue of its "entwinement" with the 290 public schools that were among its membership (see p. 877 above). TSSAA also had 55 private

high schools as members, including Brentwood Academy. Since the early 1950's, TSSAA has prohibited high schools from using "undue influence" in recruiting middle school students for their athletic programs. In April 1997, Brentwood's football coach sent a letter to a group of eighth-grade boys inviting them to attend spring practice sessions. That invitation violated TSSAA's antirecruiting rule and the association sanctioned Brentwood. Brentwood claimed the sanction violated its right to speak to prospective recruits.

Justice STEVENS wrote for the Court, which was unanimous in its judgment that TSSAA had not violated Brentwood's free speech rights. He analogized to the public employee line of cases: "Brentwood made a voluntary decision to join TSSAA and to abide by its antirecruiting rule. Just as the government's interest in running an effective workplace can in some circumstances outweigh employee speech rights, see Connick, so too can an athletic league's interest in enforcing its rules sometimes warrant curtailing the speech of its voluntary participants. See Pickering; Umbehr [(1996; p. 1320 below)]. This is not to say that TSSAA has unbounded authority to condition membership on the relinquishment of any and all constitutional rights. As we recently emphasized in the employment context, 'so long as employees are speaking as citizens about matters of public concern, they must face only those speech restrictions that are necessary for their employers to operate efficiently and effectively.' Ceballos. Assuming, without deciding, that the coach in this case was 'speaking as [a] citizen about matters of public concern,' TSSAA can similarly impose only those conditions on such speech that are necessary to managing an efficient and effective state-sponsored high school athletic league.

"That necessity is obviously present here. We need no empirical data to credit TSSAA's common-sense conclusion that hard-sell tactics directed at middle school students could lead to exploitation, distort competition between high school teams, and foster an environment in which athletics are prized more highly than academics. TSSAA's rule discourages precisely the sort of conduct that might lead to those harms, any one of which would detract from a high school sports league's ability to operate 'efficiently and effectively.' For that reason, the First Amendment does not excuse Brentwood from abiding by the same anti-recruiting rule that governs the conduct of its sister schools. To hold otherwise would undermine the principle, succinctly articulated by the dissenting judge at the court of appeals, that 'high school football is a game. Games have rules.' It is only fair that Brentwood follow them."

Justice THOMAS concurred in the judgment, noting that it was "bizarre" to stretch the Pickering line of public employee speech cases to "speech by a private school that is a member of a private athletic association," but that this stretch "was occasioned by the Court when it held that TSSAA, a private organization, was a state actor," a decision he would overrule as erroneous. Was Justice Thomas right? Did Justice Stevens faithfully apply the Connick test here? Does Connick require proof of "necessity" to the efficient operation of the public entity? Was Justice Stevens's application of such "necessity" test in any event quite deferential?

5. ***Targeting error and intent.*** In **Heffernan v. City of Paterson**, 578 U.S. ___, 136 S. Ct. 1412 (2016), the Court addressed a situation in which the government employer targeted an employee's speech based on a mistake of fact. A police officer was targeted for supporting a mayoral candidate, but

in fact he was not supporting the candidate and had merely picked up one of the candidate's signs for his mother. Justice BREYER wrote the opinion for the Court, holding that the First Amendment covered the situation: "In this case a government official demoted an employee because the official believed, but *incorrectly* believed, that the employee had supported a particular candidate for mayor. [When] an employer demotes an employee out of a desire to prevent the employee from engaging in political activity that the First Amendment protects, the employee is entitled to challenge that unlawful action under the First Amendment—[even] if, as here, the employer makes a factual mistake about the employee's behavior. [A] rule of law finding liability in these circumstances tracks the language of the First Amendment more closely than would a contrary rule. Unlike, say, the Fourth Amendment, which begins by speaking of the 'right of the people to be secure in their persons, houses, papers, and effects,' the First Amendment begins by focusing upon the activity of the Government. [We] also consider relevant the constitutional implications of a rule that imposes liability. The constitutional harm at issue in the ordinary case consists in large part of discouraging employees—both the employee discharged (or demoted) and his or her colleagues—from engaging in protected activities. The discharge of one tells the others that they engage in protected activity at their peril. [The] employer's factual mistake does not diminish the risk of causing precisely that same harm."

Justice THOMAS, joined by Justice Alito, dissented, reasoning that Section 1983 "does not provide a cause of action to plaintiffs whose constitutional rights have not been violated."

PUBLIC EMPLOYEE POLITICAL PARTY AFFILIATION

Since the rise of political parties in the early days of the republic, elected officials have engaged in the practice of political patronage: rewarding one's political friends with jobs in or contracts with the government, and declining to so reward one's political enemies. Various statutory devices have been employed over time to check this "spoils system," including state and federal bribery and extortion laws, and the use of merit examinations and civil service protection for rank-and-file government employees. Another device is the federal Hatch Act and the state "mini-Hatch acts," which prohibit active political campaigning by public employees. The decisions that follow rejected challenges to these laws brought by public employees who claimed that they had a free speech right to electioneer. The decisions noted after the Hatch Act challenges review First Amendment challenges by public employees from the other side of the patronage coin: claims by discharged or demoted public officials that they have been turned out by the victorious party solely because of their party affiliation in violation of their rights of free political association.

1. ***The Hatch Act cases.*** In United Public Workers v. Mitchell, 330 U.S. 75 (1947), the Court sustained the constitutionality of § 9(a) of the Hatch Act of 1940, which prohibited federal employees in the executive branch from taking "any active part in political management or in political campaigns." The Court held that "Congress may regulate the political conduct of government employees 'within reasonable limits,' even though the regulation trenches to some extent upon unfettered political action." Justice

Black dissented: "It would hardly seem to be imperative to muzzle millions of citizens because some of them, if left their constitutional freedoms, might corrupt the political process." He suggested that the law actually harmed "the body politic" by "depriving it of the political participation and interest of such a large segment of our citizens."

A Hatch Act challenge likewise failed in **United States Civil Service Commission v. National Ass'n of Letter Carriers**, 413 U.S. 548 (1973). There, the Court rejected a facial overbreadth challenge to § 9(a) and "unhesitatingly reaffirm[ed]" Mitchell: "Neither the right to associate nor the right to participate in political activities is absolute. [P]lainly identifiable acts of political management and political campaigning may constitutionally be prohibited on the part of federal employees." Justice WHITE's majority opinion deferred to the congressional judgment that "partisan political activities by federal employees must be limited if the Government is to operate effectively and fairly, elections are to play their proper part in representative government, and employees themselves are to be sufficiently free from improper influences." He noted that the restrictions were "not aimed at particular parties, groups or points of view, but apply equally to all [covered] partisan activities. [Nor] do they seek to control political opinions or beliefs, or to interfere with or influence anyone's vote at the polls." Applying the Pickering balancing test, he found three government interests substantial enough to outweigh the free speech claims of public employees: ensuring that employees "administer the law in accordance with the will of Congress, rather than [with the] will of a political party," preventing the use of government workers "to build a powerful, invincible, and perhaps corrupt political machine," and ensuring "that Government employees [are] free from pressure [to] vote in a certain way or perform political chores in order to curry favor with their superiors rather than to act out of their own beliefs." Justice DOUGLAS, joined by Justices Brennan and Marshall, dissented: "[No] one could object if employees were barred from using office time to engage in outside activities whether political or otherwise. But it is of no concern of Government what an employee does in his spare time, [unless] what he does impairs efficiency or other facets of the merits of his job."

2. ***Patronage dismissals of public employees.*** In several decisions, the Court has curtailed governmental power to penalize public employees on party allegiance grounds. This development began with **Elrod v. Burns**, 427 U.S. 347 (1976), a 5–3 decision holding that the newly elected Democratic Sheriff of Cook County, Illinois, could not discharge several Republican employees—three process servers, and a juvenile court bailiff and security guard. Justice BRENNAN's plurality opinion, joined by Justices White and Marshall, held that "[t]he cost of the practice of patronage is the restraint it places on freedoms of belief and association. [An] individual who is a member of the out-party maintains affiliation with his own party at the risk of losing his job." He went on to reject three government interests asserted in defense of patronage practices. He doubted that they served "the need to insure effective government and the efficiency of public employees," which could be safeguarded by discharge for good cause, and argued that the lack of an efficiency justification distinguished the case from Mitchell and Letter Carriers. He also denied that wholesale patronage is necessary "for political loyalty" and implementation of the electorate's policy choices; this interest, he argued, could be served by "[l]imiting patronage dismissals to policymaking positions." And he found that patronage was not necessary to the "preservation of the two-party system," which had already survived the

inroads made by civil service merit systems. Justice STEWART's concurrence, joined by Justice Blackmun, concluded more narrowly that "a nonpolicymaking, nonconfidential government employee [cannot be discharged] from a job that he is satisfactorily performing upon the sole ground of his political beliefs."

Justice POWELL, joined by Chief Justice Burger and Justice Rehnquist, dissented, finding strong government interests served by patronage: "[Patronage] hiring practices have contributed to American democracy by stimulating political activity and by strengthening parties. [Patronage] hiring practices also enable party organizations to persist and function at the local level. [In] the dull periods between elections, [precinct] organizations must be maintained; new voters registered; and minor political 'chores' performed for citizens. [It] is naive to think that these types of political activities are motivated at these levels by some academic interest in 'democracy.' [As] every politician knows, the hope of some reward generates a major portion of the local political activity supporting parties." The dissenters found these state interests sufficient to outweigh the limited First Amendment interest in avoiding "the coercion on associational choices that may be created by one's desire [to] obtain [government] employment."

In **Branti v. Finkel**, 445 U.S. 507 (1980), the Court reconsidered patronage systems and expanded the immunity of public employees from patronage dismissals, but left the contours of the broadened constitutional protections somewhat unclear. The new governing rule in Branti invoked criteria differing from Elrod: "the ultimate inquiry is not whether the label 'policymaker' or 'confidential' fits a particular position; rather, the question is whether the hiring authority can demonstrate that party affiliation is an appropriate requirement for the effective performance of the public office involved."

In Branti, two Republican assistant county public defenders successfully challenged their dismissal by the newly named Democratic head of the public defender's office. Justice STEVENS's majority opinion concluded, under his newly formulated standard, that "it is manifest that the continued employment of an assistant public defender cannot properly be conditioned upon his allegiance to the political party in control of the county government." He noted that any policymaking in a public defender's office related to the needs of individual clients, not to any partisan political interests, and that the assistant public defenders' access to confidential information arising out of attorney-client relationships had no bearing on partisan concerns. Accordingly, "it would undermine, rather than promote, the effective performance of an assistant public defender's office to make his tenure dependent on his allegiance to the dominant political party." He conceded that "party affiliation may be an acceptable requirement for some types of government employment," but insisted that the "policymaking or confidential position" criterion did not adequately delineate the proper use of party considerations. He explained: "Under some circumstances, a position may be appropriately considered political even though it is neither confidential nor policymaking in character." (He gave as an example the use of local election judges of different parties to supervise elections at the precinct level.) He added: "It is equally clear that party affiliation is not necessarily relevant to every policymaking or confidential position." (He noted that, for example, a "policymaking" football coach could not be discharged on party affiliation grounds, but that the position of a speechwriting assistant to a governor could properly involve party allegiance if it was to be performed "effectively.") Justice Stevens expressly declined to decide whether a prosecutor, like a public defender, was protected from dismissal on grounds of political party affiliation or loyalty.

Justice POWELL, in the lengthy dissent, objected to the majority's new, "substantially expanded standard for determining which governmental employees may be retained or dismissed on the basis of political affiliation," which he feared would create "vast uncertainty." He noted, for example, that "it would be difficult to say [under the new standard] that 'partisan' concerns properly are relevant to the performance of the duties of a United States Attorney." As in his Elrod dissent, he emphasized that patronage appointments "helped build stable political parties" and that political parties served "a variety of substantial governmental interests." They helped candidates "to muster donations of time and money necessary to capture the attention of the electorate" and thus contribute to the democratic process; moreover, they "aid effective governance after election campaigns end." The majority's approach, he argued, imposed "unnecessary constraints upon the ability of responsible officials to govern effectively and to carry out new policies." Moreover, the "breakdown of party discipline that handicaps elected officials also limits the ability of the electorate to choose wisely among candidates." He concluded: "In sum, the effect of the Court's decision will be to decrease the accountability and denigrate the role of our national political parties."

3. ***Patronage sanctions short of dismissal.*** In Elrod and Branti, then, the First Amendment was held to prohibit patronage dismissals of public employees unless the government could demonstrate that party affiliation was an appropriate requirement for the position involved. Ten years after Branti, the Court confronted the question whether the First Amendment also barred patronage practices other than dismissals. In **Rutan v. Republican Party of Illinois**, 497 U.S. 62 (1990), a divided Court extended Elrod and Branti to decisions about hiring, promotion, transfer, and recalls after layoffs. The case arose from Illinois Republican Governor James Thompson's institution of a hiring freeze, exceptions to which depended on permissions from his office. The challengers claimed that his office operated as a "patronage machine," and that they were denied promotions, transfers, and recalls because they lacked Republican credentials. Justice BRENNAN's majority opinion held that none of these decisions could constitutionally be based on party affiliation and support. Even without being discharged, he found, "[e]mployees who find themselves in dead-end positions due to their political backgrounds [will] feel a significant obligation to support political positions held by their superiors, and to refrain from acting on the political views they actually hold." He held that employees need not show that their treatment amounts to a constructive discharge in order to prevail in their First Amendment claims. Patronage practices even short of dismissal or its equivalent, he held, must be "narrowly tailored to further vital government interests." Justice Stevens concurred separately.

Justice SCALIA dissented, joined by Chief Justice Rehnquist and Justice Kennedy, and in part by Justice O'Connor. Justice Scalia insisted that "Elrod and Branti should be overruled, rather than merely not extended." In his extensive attack on Elrod and Branti, he emphasized the difference in the constitutional restrictions "upon the government in its capacity as lawmaker, i.e., as the regulator of private conduct" and "the restrictions [upon] the government in its capacity as employer." Thus, private citizens "cannot be punished for speech of merely private concern, but government employees can be fired without reason" [Connick], and private citizens "cannot be punished for partisan political activity, but [public] employees can be dismissed and otherwise punished for that reason" [Mitchell; Letter Carriers]. He added, in a section of the dissent not joined by Justice O'Connor: "The provisions of the Bill of Rights were designed to restrain transient majorities from impairing long-recognized personal liberties. They did not create by implication novel individual rights overturning accepted political norms. Thus, when a practice not expressly prohibited by the text of the Bill of Rights bears the endorsement of a long tradition of open, widespread, and unchallenged use that dates back to the beginning of the Republic, we have no proper basis for striking it down. Such a venerable and accepted tradition is not to be laid on the examining table and scrutinized for its conformity to some abstract principle of First Amendment adjudication devised by this Court."

Justice Scalia further objected to the majority's use of a "strict-scrutiny standard." Reiterating that speech restrictions on public employees "are not judged by the test applicable to similar restrictions on speech by non-employees," he noted that the Mitchell case had applied a lenient test of whether the practice could be "reasonably deemed" to further a legitimate goal. He argued that patronage practices satisfied even a less deferential "general 'balancing' test: can the governmental advantages of this employment practice reasonably be deemed to outweigh its 'coercive' effects?" Reiterating Justice Powell's arguments in defense of patronage in his Elrod dissent, Justice Scalia noted that "patronage stabilizes political parties and prevents excessive political fragmentation," both strong governmental interests. He added to Justice Powell's list an additional interest served by patronage: "Patronage, moreover, has been a powerful means of achieving the social and political integration of excluded groups. ['Every] ethnic group that has achieved political power in American cities has used the bureaucracy to provide jobs in return for political support.'" He conceded that "the patronage system entails some constraint upon the expression of views [and] considerable constraint upon the employee's right to associate with the other party." But he denied that patronage really involved "coercion" at all and insisted it did not represent "a significant impairment of free speech or free association."

4. ***The expressive values served in the patronage cases.*** In Elrod, Branti, and Rutan, there arguably were speech interests on both sides. If the out-party employees' free speech and association claims are rejected, they are given an incentive to tailor their views and allegiance to the other party against their true beliefs. If their claims are sustained, however, the expressive and associational rights of members of the in-party are arguably diminished. Moreover, constraints on patronage might even diminish the quantity of political speech on the whole by inhibiting party activism. Did the Court undervalue the interests of the in-party in these cases? Did it undervalue the contributions of patronage to political expression?

Note that the standard of scrutiny in the patronage cases is stricter than the Pickering balancing test. Pickering permits the government to win if it can demonstrate an interest in efficiency in a particular case. Elrod, Branti, and Rutan, in contrast, presume as a general matter that party affiliation is not a justifiable basis for government employment decisions unless the government can demonstrate narrow tailoring to vital "interests." Is it odd to give less constitutional protection in this context to speech, which is an enumerated right, than to association, which is not? Is there a possibility for confusion in applying the two standards if a fact situation involves retaliation for a mixture of both speech and party affiliation?

5. ***Patronage and independent contractors.*** Should the protections granted to public employees in the Pickering and Elrod lines of cases extend to independent contractors with government? On the one hand, contractors might appear less vulnerable than public employees to government coercion of belief and association, as they are less dependent on government work and more likely as a practical matter to support both parties in order to obtain jobs. On the other hand, treating contractors differently from employees might encourage government simply to manipulate job titles and work arrangements so as to increase its power to enforce ideological and partisan fealty. The issue divided the lower courts until settled by two cases decided on the same day.

In **Board of County Commissioners v. Umbehr**, 518 U.S. 668 (1996), a case involving an outspoken trash hauler, the Court extended to independent contractors the protections of the Pickering line of cases. Umbehr had a contract to haul trash for Wabuansee County, Kansas. While under contract, he vocally criticized the three-member governing body of the County. He spoke at the Board's meetings and wrote critical letters and editorials in local newspapers regarding the County's landfill user rates, the Board's meeting practices, and the County's alleged mismanagement of taxpayers' money. The county terminated his contract and Umbehr filed a First Amendment complaint. The Court, by a vote of 7–2, affirmed the court of appeals' reversal of summary judgment for the county.

Justice O'CONNOR wrote for the Court. She reviewed the possible distinctions between public employees and contractors and found them no basis for a departure from the Pickering balancing test: "[I]ndependent contractors work at a greater remove from government officials than do most government employees. [The] Board argues that the lack of day-to-day control accentuates the government's need to have the work done by someone it trusts. [Umbehr,] on the other hand, argues that the government interests in maintaining harmonious working environments and relationships recognized in our government employee cases are attenuated where the contractor does not work at the government's workplace and does not interact daily with government officers and employees. He also points out that to the extent that he is publicly perceived as an independent contractor, any government concern that his political statements will be confused with the government's political positions is mitigated. The Board [retorts] that the cost of fending off litigation, and the potential for government contracting practices to ossify into prophylactic rules to avoid potential litigation and liability, outweigh the interests of independent contractors, who are typically less financially dependent on their government contracts than are government employees. Each of these arguments for and against the imposition of liability has some force. But all of them can be accommodated by applying our existing framework for government employee cases to independent contracts. We [see] no reason to believe that proper application of the Pickering balancing test cannot accommodate the differences between employees and independent contractors." She emphasized that because the case applied only to a terminations, "we need not address the possibility of suits by bidders or applicants for new government contracts."

In **O'Hare Truck Service, Inc. v. City of Northlake**, 518 U.S. 712 (1996), the Court extended to independent contractors the protections of the Elrod line of cases. O'Hare, a tow truck operator who had been on the city's list of available towers, was removed from the list after its owner, John Gratzianna, refused political support and campaign contributions to the mayor and supported the mayor's opponent in the election. Without deciding the case on the merits, the Court held that O'Hare had stated a First Amendment claim. Justice KENNEDY wrote for the Court, which again voted 7–2: "There is no doubt that if Gratzianna had been a public employee whose job was to perform tow truck operations, the city could not have discharged him for refusing to contribute to [the mayor's] campaign or for supporting his opponent. [We] cannot accept the proposition [that] those who perform the government's work outside the formal employment relationship are subject to what we conclude is the direct and specific abridgment of First Amendment rights described in this complaint. [We] see no reason [why] the constitutional claim here should turn on the distinction [between employees and contractors,] which is, in the main, a creature of the common law of agency and torts. Recognizing the distinction in these circumstances would invite manipulation by government, which could avoid constitutional liability simply by attaching different labels to particular jobs."

Justice Kennedy was not convinced that patronage practices are less coercive of independent contractors than employees: "[Perhaps] some contractors are so independent from government support that the threat of losing business would be ineffective to coerce them to abandon political activities. The same might be true of certain public employees, however; they, too, might find work elsewhere if they lose their government jobs. If results were to turn on these sorts of distinctions, courts would have to inquire into the extent to which the government dominates various job markets as employer or as contractor. We have been, and we remain, unwilling to send courts down that path. [Nor are we willing to assume that most independent contractors are] 'political hermaphrodites,' who find it in their self-interest to stay on good terms with both major political parties and so are not at great risk of retaliation for political association." He concluded: "The absolute right to enforce a patronage scheme, insisted upon by respondents as a means of retaining control over independent contractors, [has] not been shown to be a necessary part of a legitimate political system in all instances. [We] decline to draw a line excluding independent contractors from the First Amendment safeguards of political association afforded to employees."

Justice SCALIA, joined by Justice Thomas, dissented from both Umbehr and O'Hare. He first expressed surprise that in O'Hare, despite the addition to the Court of Justice Thomas (who opposes the Elrod line of cases) and the fact that all four Rutan dissenters remained on the Court, the Court had not only declined to overrule Elrod and Branti, but had "extended [them] far beyond Rutan to the massive field of all government contracting." He reiterated that patronage is a longstanding American tradition, and, noting elaborate state and federal laws governing procurement practices, suggested that any answer to the disadvantages of patronage in the contracting context must come from the political process and not the Court. He insisted that political favoritism is an inevitable feature of government: "Government favors those who agree with its political views, and disfavors those who disagree, every day—in where it builds its public works, in the kinds of taxes it imposes and collects, in its regulatory prescriptions, in the design of its grant and benefit programs—in a million ways, including the letting of contracts for government business." And he argued that, even if Elrod and Branti had made any sense, there was no reason to extend them to contractors: "If it is to be possible to dig in our cleats at some point on this [slippery] slope—before we end up holding that the First Amendment requires the City of Chicago to have as few potholes in Republican wards (if any) as in Democratic ones—would not the most defensible point of termination for this indefensible exercise be public employment? A public employee is always an individual, and a public employee below the highest political level (which is exempt from Elrod) is virtually always an individual who is not rich; the termination or denial of a public job is the termination or denial of a livelihood. A public contractor, on the other hand, is usually a corporation; and the contract it loses is rarely its entire business, or even an indispensable part of its entire business."

How far do these cases go in protecting public contractor speech? Suppose that a government contracts out the job of providing security services at a public housing project, and later finds out that the contractor is affiliated with a party that preaches racial supremacy. After O'Hare, may the government terminate the contract?

SPEECH-RESTRICTIVE CONDITIONS ON PUBLIC FUNDS

1. ***Unconstitutional conditions.*** The principle that governmental benefits may not be conditioned on the surrender of First Amendment rights has not been limited to employment. In **Speiser v. Randall**, 357 U.S. 513 (1958), for example, the Court overturned a California requirement that property tax exemptions for veterans would be available only to those who declared that they did not advocate the forcible overthrow of the government. Rejecting California's claim that it could condition the award of a mere "privilege" or "bounty," Justice Brennan's opinion for the Court noted that "to deny an exemption to claimants who engage in certain forms of speech is in effect to penalize them for such speech." The principle has been extended to a variety of government benefits, including both tax benefits and direct grants.

Why should government be constrained not to make speech or silence a condition of a benefit, when it is free not to confer the benefit at all? After all, government is not constitutionally required affirmatively to subsidize the exercise of constitutional rights. This is the conundrum of all so-called "unconstitutional conditions" cases. Unconstitutional conditions problems arise when government offers a benefit on condition that the recipient perform or forego an activity that is generally constitutionally protected from government interference. Such problems have given rise to voluminous commentary. See, e.g., Hale, "Unconstitutional Conditions and Constitutional Rights," 35 Colum. L. Rev. 321 (1935); Van Alstyne, "The Demise of the Right-Privilege Distinction in Constitutional Law," 81 Harv. L. Rev. 1439 (1968); Kreimer, "Allocational Sanctions: the Problem of Negative Rights in a Positive State," 132 U. Pa. L. Rev. 1293 (1984); Epstein, "Foreword: Unconstitutional Conditions, State Power, and the Limits of

Consent," 102 Harv. L. Rev. 4 (1988); Sullivan, "Unconstitutional Conditions," 102 Harv. L. Rev. 1413 (1989).

2. ***Penalties vs. nonsubsidies.*** In the speech context, the Court has attempted to resolve the conundrum by distinguishing denials of benefits that operate as "penalties" on speech from those that operate as mere "nonsubsidies." Under this distinction, government may not use the leverage of a subsidy to induce recipients to refrain from speech they would otherwise engage in with their own resources, but it may refrain from paying for speech with which it disagrees. This distinction is structurally parallel to the distinctions the Court has drawn in the preceding contexts of public space, public education, and public employment. In those contexts, the Court similarly distinguished public forums from nonpublic forums, noncurricular from curricular aspects of public schools, and public employee speech as a citizen on matters of public concern from employee speech on internal matters of labor grievance. In the first category of each pair, the Court views the government as constrained by the First Amendment in much the same manner as if it were regulating the general citizenry, and employs strict or intermediate scrutiny. In the second category of each pair, the Court defers to government with only minimal scrutiny, viewing it as having far more constitutional leeway in its capacity as manager, educator, or boss than it does in its capacity as sovereign regulator. The following pair of cases illustrates the distinction between nonsubsidies and funding penalties on speech.

In **Regan v. Taxation With Representation of Washington (TWR)**, 461 U.S. 540 (1983), the Court unanimously upheld against First Amendment challenge a provision of the Internal Revenue Code (IRC) barring a nonprofit organization that engages in lobbying from receiving tax-deductible contributions. There is no doubt that lobbying, or attempting to influence legislation, is a protected First Amendment activity. The issue in the case was whether lobbying organizations were entitled to the same tax benefits as nonprofit organizations that do not lobby. The Code provides for tax exemptions to two kinds of nonprofit organizations. Nonprofits organized under IRC § 501(c)(3) may not lobby, but taxpayers who contribute to them are permitted to deduct the amount of their contributions on their federal income tax returns. Nonprofits organized under IRC § 501(c)(4) are free to lobby, but contributions to § 501(c)(4) organizations are not tax-deductible to the contributor. Taxation With Representation (TWR) challenged the prohibition against substantial lobbying in § 501(c)(3) because it wanted to use tax-deductible contributions to support its substantial lobbying activities.

Justice REHNQUIST, writing for the Court, accepted that tax-deductibility of contributions to contributors represented a substantial benefit to TWR: "Both tax exemptions and tax deductibility are a form of subsidy that is administered through the tax system. A tax exemption has much the same effect as a cash grant to the organization of the amount of tax it would have to pay on its income. Deductible contributions are similar to cash grants of the amount of a portion of the individual's contributions. The system Congress has enacted provides this kind of subsidy [in the form of tax exemptions] to nonprofit civic welfare organizations generally, and an additional subsidy [in the form of tax deductibility to contributors] to those charitable organizations that do not engage in substantial lobbying. In short, Congress chose not to subsidize lobbying as extensively as it chose to subsidize other activities that nonprofit organizations undertake to promote the public welfare." But Justice Rehnquist rejected the argument that denial of the benefit of tax deductibility violated TWR's First Amendment rights: "TWR is certainly correct when it states that we have held that the government may not deny a benefit to a person because he exercises a constitutional right. But TWR is just as certainly incorrect when it claims that this case fits the [Speiser] model. The Code does not deny TWR the right to receive deductible contributions to support its nonlobbying activity, nor does it deny TWR any independent benefit on account of its intention to lobby. Congress has merely refused to pay for the lobbying out of public moneys. This Court has never held that Congress must grant a benefit such as TWR claims here to a person who wishes to exercise a constitutional right. [Congress] is not required by the First Amendment to subsidize lobbying."

Justice Rehnquist, quoting Speiser, noted that "[t]he case would be different if Congress were to discriminate invidiously in its subsidies in such a way as to '[aim] at the suppression of dangerous ideas.' 'But he held that an exception allowing veterans' organizations to receive tax-deductible contributions even if they lobbied did not constitute content discrimination in violation of this principle. He pointed out that the exemption was based on status, not content: "Veterans have 'been obliged to drop their own affairs to take up the burdens of the nation,' [and our] country has a longstanding policy of compensating veterans for their past contributions by providing them with numerous advantages." In the absence of any viewpoint discrimination, Justice Rehnquist held applicable only a minimal standard of review: "It is not irrational for Congress to decide that tax-exempt charities such as TWR should not further benefit at the expense of taxpayers at large by obtaining a further subsidy for lobbying."

Justice BLACKMUN, joined by Justices Brennan and Marshall, concurred but emphasized that "[t]he constitutional defect that would inhere in 501(c)(3) alone is avoided by § 501(c)(4)," for TWR could simply use its existing § 501(c)(3) organization for its nonlobbying activities while establishing a § 501(c)(4) affiliate to pursue its goals through lobbying. Thus, in the concurring justices' view, "[a] § 501(c)(3) organization's right to speak is not infringed, because it is free to make known its views on legislation through its § 501(c)(4) affiliate without losing tax benefits for its nonlobbying activities."

Contrast with TWR the Court's holding in **FCC v. League of Women Voters**, 468 U.S. 364 (1984). The Public Broadcasting Act of 1967 established the nonprofit Corporation for Public Broadcasting (CPB) to disburse federal funds to noncommercial television and radio stations in support of station operations and educational programming. In League of Women Voters, the Court invalidated, by a vote of 5–4, a provision of the Act forbidding any "noncommercial educational broadcasting station which receives a grant from the Corporation" to "engage in editorializing." Justice BRENNAN, writing for the majority, found the no-editorializing condition to be a penalty on public broadcasters' protected speech, not a mere nonsubsidy of speech as in TWR: "In this case, [unlike] the situation faced by the charitable organization in [TWR], a noncommercial educational station that receives only 1% of its overall income from CPB grants is barred absolutely from all editorializing. Therefore, in contrast to the appellee in Taxation With Representation, such a station is not able to segregate its activities according to the source of its funding. The station has no way of limiting the use of its federal funds to all noneditorializing activities, and, more importantly, it is barred from using even wholly private funds to finance its editorial activity." He noted that the case would be different if Congress permitted "public broadcasting stations, [like] the charitable organization in [TWR, which could lobby through a § 501(c)(4) affiliate], to make known its views on matters of public importance through [a] nonfederally funded, editorializing affiliate without losing federal grants for its noneditorializing broadcast activities."

Having found the editorial ban a penalty on public broadcasters' speech, he also found it impermissibly content-based, even under the less stringent review applicable to broadcasters than other speakers: "Because broadcast regulation involves unique considerations [such as spectrum scarcity], our cases have not followed precisely the same approach that we have applied to other media and have never gone so far as to demand that such regulations serve 'compelling' governmental interests. [But], as our cases attest, [restrictions on broadcaster speech] have been upheld only when we were satisfied that the restriction is narrowly tailored to further a substantial governmental interest, such as ensuring adequate and balanced coverage of public issues." [See Red Lion v. FCC (p. 1545 below).] Under this intermediate standard of scrutiny, he found the government's justifications for the editorial ban inadequate: it was not closely tailored to the goal of protecting public broadcasters from "being coerced, as a result of federal financing, into becoming vehicles for Government propagandizing or the objects of governmental influence," and was far too broad to serve any goal of preventing public broadcasting stations "from becoming convenient targets for capture by private interest groups wishing to express their own partisan viewpoints."

Justice REHNQUIST, joined by Chief Justice Burger and Justice White, wrote a dissent arguing that TWR ought to have been controlling and that the restriction was a permissible nonsubsidy of speech. He wrote that the majority had presented "a scenario in which the Government appears as the 'Big Bad Wolf,' and appellee Pacifica as 'Little Red Riding Hood.' In the Court's scenario, the Big Bad Wolf cruelly forbids Little Red Riding Hood to take to her grandmother some of the food that she is carrying in her basket. [A] truer picture of the litigants, [would show] that some of the food in the basket was given to Little Red Riding Hood by the Big Bad Wolf himself, and that the Big Bad Wolf had told Little Red Riding Hood in advance that if she accepted his food she would have to abide by his conditions. Congress, in enacting [the editorial ban], has simply determined that public funds shall not be used to subsidize noncommercial, educational broadcasting stations which engage in 'editorializing.'" Nor did Justice Rehnquist find any problem in the ban's extension to private as well as public sources of funds: "Given the impossibility of compartmentalizing programming expenses in any meaningful way, it seems clear to me that the only effective means for preventing the use of public moneys to subsidize the airing of management's views is for Congress to ban a subsidized station from all on-the-air editorializing." He therefore rejected the majority's application of intermediate scrutiny: "[W]hen the Government is simply exercising its power to allocate its own public funds, we need only find that the condition imposed has a rational relationship to Congress' purpose in providing the subsidy and that it is not primarily 'aimed at the suppression of dangerous ideas.'" Here, he found, the condition was both rational and viewpoint-neutral: "[I]t is plainly rational for Congress to have determined that taxpayer moneys should not be used to subsidize management's views. [Furthermore,] Congress' prohibition is strictly neutral. In no sense can it be said that Congress has prohibited only editorial views of one particular ideological bent." Justice STEVENS also dissented, finding the ban viewpoint-neutral and justified by "the overriding interest in forestalling the creation of propaganda organs for the Government."

3. ***Abortion-related conditions on family planning subsidies.*** In **Rust v. Sullivan**, 500 U.S. 173 (1991), the Court found a speech-restrictive condition on funds more analogous to the one upheld in TWR than the one struck down in League of Women Voters. In Rust, the Court upheld Health and Human Services Department (HHS) regulations forbidding projects receiving federal family planning funds under Title X of the Public Health Service Act from counseling or referring women for abortion and from encouraging, promoting, or advocating abortion. If the funding recipient engaged in either of these activities, they had to be "physically and financially separate" from the recipient's Title X project. The regulations permitted Title X projects to provide pregnant women with information about childbirth and prenatal care, but advised them to tell any pregnant woman who inquired about abortion that the project does not consider abortion an "appropriate method of family planning." Doctors and Title X grantees did not succeed in their challenge to the regulations under the First Amendment.

The challengers argued that the regulations impermissibly discriminated on the basis of viewpoint because they prohibited discussion of abortion while requiring doctors or counselors to provide information about continuing a pregnancy to term. They relied on the Court's previous statements that, even in the provision of subsidies, government may not "aim at the suppression of dangerous ideas." Chief Justice REHNQUIST, writing for the majority in the 5–4 decision, rejected this argument: "The Government can, without violating the Constitution, selectively fund a program to encourage certain activities it believes to be in the public interest, without at the same time funding an alternative program which seeks to deal with the problem in another way. In so doing, the Government has not discriminated on the basis of viewpoint; it has merely chosen to fund one activity to the exclusion of the other. [This] is not a case of the Government 'suppressing a dangerous idea,' but of a prohibition on a project grantee or its employees from engaging in activities outside of the project's scope. To hold that the Government unconstitutionally discriminates on the basis of viewpoint when it chooses to fund a program dedicated to advance certain permissible goals, because the program in advancing those goals necessarily discourages alternative goals, would render numerous Government programs constitutionally suspect. [When] Congress established a National Endowment for Democracy to encourage other countries to adopt democratic principles, it was not constitutionally required to fund a program to encourage competing lines of political philosophy such as communism and fascism. [Within] far broader limits than petitioners are willing to concede, when the government appropriates public funds to establish a program it is entitled to define the limits of that program."

The challengers also argued that the regulations impermissibly conditioned the receipt of Title X funding on the relinquishment of their right to engage in abortion advocacy and counseling with their own funds. Chief Justice Rehnquist rejected this argument too: "[H]ere the Government is not denying a benefit to anyone, but is instead simply insisting that public funds be spent for the purposes for which they were authorized. The Secretary's regulations do not force the Title X grantee to give up abortion-related speech; they merely require that the grantee keep such activities separate and distinct from Title X activities. Title X expressly distinguishes between a Title X grantee and a Title X project. The grantee, which normally is a health care organization, may receive funds from a variety of sources for a variety of purposes. The grantee receives Title X funds, however, for the specific and limited purpose of establishing and operating a Title X project. The regulations govern the scope of the Title X project's activities, and leave the grantee unfettered in its other activities. [In] contrast, our 'unconstitutional conditions' cases involve situations in which the Government has placed a condition on the recipient of the subsidy rather than on a particular program or service, thus effectively prohibiting the recipient from engaging in the protected conduct outside the scope of the federally funded program. [See League of Women Voters.]" He found it irrelevant that Title X required all Title X projects to raise private matching funds, and that the abortion counseling and advocacy restrictions extended to those funds: "The recipient is in no way compelled to operate a Title X project; to avoid the force of the regulations, it can simply decline the subsidy. [Potential] grant recipients can choose between accepting Title X funds—subject to the Government's conditions that they provide matching funds and forgo abortion counseling and referral in the Title X project—or declining the subsidy and financing their own unsubsidized program. We have never held that the Government violates the First Amendment simply by offering that choice."

Chief Justice Rehnquist cautioned that "[t]his is not to suggest that funding by the Government, even when coupled with the freedom of the fund recipients to speak outside the scope of the Government-funded project, is invariably sufficient to justify Government control over the content of expression." He cited as examples cases upholding speech rights in traditional public forums and academic freedom at public universities. But he found no infringement of any analogous traditional doctor-patient relationship: "Nothing in [the regulations] requires a doctor to represent as his own any opinion that he does not in fact hold. Nor is the doctor-patient relationship established by the Title X program sufficiently all encompassing so as to justify an expectation on the part of the patient of comprehensive medical advice."

Justice BLACKMUN dissented, joined by Justices Marshall and Stevens: "Until today, the Court never has upheld viewpoint-based suppression of speech simply because that suppression was a condition upon the acceptance of public funds. Whatever may be the Government's power to condition the receipt of its largess upon the relinquishment of constitutional rights, it surely does not extend to a condition that suppresses the recipient's cherished freedom of speech based solely upon the content or viewpoint of that speech. [Speiser.] It cannot seriously be disputed that the counseling and referral provisions at issue in the present cases constitute content-based regulation of speech. Title X grantees may provide counseling and referral regarding any of a wide range of family planning and other topics, save abortion. The regulations are also clearly viewpoint based. While suppressing speech favorable to abortion with one hand, the Secretary compels antiabortion speech with the other." Justice Blackmun contended that this viewpoint discrimination distinguished the regulations from those upheld in TWR. He also disagreed with Chief Justice Rehnquist that they constituted mere earmarking of funds to the limited purpose of preconception family planning advice: "[The] majority's claim that the regulations merely limit a Title X project's speech to preventive or preconceptional services rings hollow in light of the broad range of nonpreventive services that the regulations authorize Title X projects to provide [including referral for prenatal or adoption services, physical examinations, and treatment of gynecological problems and sexually transmitted diseases]." He concluded that the regulations should be struck down under strict scrutiny. Justice O'Connor also dissented, but solely on the ground that the regulations exceeded HHS's statutory authority.

4. ***Religion-related conditions on student activity funds.*** The TWR and Rust decisions both stated in dictum that subsidies may not be made selectively so as to "aim at the suppression of dangerous ideas." In **Rosenberger v. Rector & Visitors of University of Virginia**, 515 U.S. 819 (1995), the Court invalidated a funding limitation as viewpoint discrimination. The case arose from a program at the University of Virginia in which mandatory student fees were used to pay the costs of extracurricular activities, including the costs of printing various student-edited publications. The University refused to pay the printing costs of "Wide Awake," a publication of a student group dedicated to advancing "the Christian perspective," under guidelines prohibiting the use of the activities fees for any "religious activity," defined as any activity that "primarily promotes or manifests a particular belief in or about a deity or an ultimate reality." Leaders of the student group claimed that this denial of funding violated their right of free speech. The University argued that it was a permissible nonsubsidy. The Court held, by a vote of 5–4, that Wide Awake's exclusion was forbidden by the Free Speech Clause and was not required by the Establishment Clause. (For the portion of the opinion discussing the Establishment Clause, see p. 1563 below.)

Justice KENNEDY, writing for the Court, found the funding restriction to constitute discrimination on the basis of viewpoint, not subject matter. He analogized the University's action to the school district's exclusion of a religious film series from after-hours use of public school facilities that was invalidated by the Court in Lamb's Chapel (p. 1285 above): "[W]e have observed a distinction between, on the one hand, content discrimination, which may be permissible if it preserves the purposes of [a] limited forum, and, on the other hand, viewpoint discrimination, which is presumed impermissible when directed against speech otherwise within the forum's limitations. The [Student Activities Fund (SAF)] is a forum more in a metaphysical than in a spatial or geographic sense, but the same principles are applicable. [It] is [something] of an understatement to speak of religious thought and discussion as just a viewpoint, as distinct from a comprehensive body of thought. The nature of our origins and destiny and their dependence upon the existence of a divine being have been subjects of philosophic inquiry throughout human history. We conclude, nonetheless, that here, as in Lamb's Chapel, viewpoint discrimination is the proper way to interpret the University's objections to Wide Awake. By the very terms of the SAF prohibition, the University does not exclude religion as a subject matter but selects for disfavored treatment those student journalistic efforts with religious editorial viewpoints. Religion may be a vast area of inquiry, but it also provides, as it did here, a specific premise, a perspective, a standpoint from which a variety of subjects may be discussed and considered. The prohibited perspective, not the general subject matter, resulted in the refusal to make third-party payments, for the subjects discussed were otherwise within the approved category of publications."

The University, relying on TWR and Rust, argued that "content-based funding decisions are both inevitable and lawful." Justice Kennedy found TWR inapposite because it involved no viewpoint discrimination, and Rust inapposite because it, in effect, involved government speech: "[In Rust,] the government did not create a program to encourage private speech but instead used private speakers to transmit specific information pertaining to its own program. We recognized that when the government appropriates public funds to promote a particular policy of its own it is entitled to say what it wishes. When the government disburses public funds to private entities to convey a governmental message, it may take legitimate and appropriate steps to ensure that its message is neither garbled nor distorted by the grantee. It does not follow, however, [that] viewpoint-based restrictions are proper when the University does not itself speak or subsidize transmittal of a message it favors but instead expends funds to encourage a diversity of views from private speakers. [The] distinction between the University's own favored message and the private speech of students is evident in the case before us. [The] University declares that the student groups eligible for SAF support are not the University's agents, are not subject to its control, and are not its responsibility. Having offered to pay the third-party contractors on behalf of private speakers who convey their own messages, the University may not silence the expression of selected viewpoints."

Justice SOUTER dissented, joined by Justices Stevens, Ginsburg, and Breyer: "There is no viewpoint discrimination in the University's application of its Guidelines to deny funding to Wide Awake. [If] the Guidelines were written or applied so as to limit only [Christian] advocacy and no other evangelical efforts that might compete with it, the discrimination would be based on viewpoint. But that is not what the regulation authorizes; it applies to Muslim and Jewish and Buddhist advocacy as well as to Christian. And since it limits funding to activities promoting or manifesting a particular belief not only 'in' but 'about' a deity or ultimate reality, it applies to agnostics and atheists as well as it does to deists and theists. The Guidelines, and their application to Wide Awake, thus do not skew debate by funding one position but not its competitors. As understood by their application to Wide Awake, they simply deny funding for hortatory speech that 'primarily promotes or manifests' any view on the merits of religion; they deny funding for the entire subject matter of religious apologetics." He distinguished Lamb's Chapel as a case in which antireligious perspectives were permitted and only religious perspectives were excluded.

After Rust and Rosenberger, could the government constitutionally condition disbursement of federal Medicaid or Medicare funds to doctors upon their agreement to refrain from prescribing certain especially expensive drugs or courses of treatment? Could it condition federal grants for medical research on researchers' agreement not to publish any results not precleared by the government?

Note that, while Rust v. Sullivan did not make such a distinction, Justice Kennedy in Rosenberger characterized and distinguished Rust as a case about government speech. Rust itself suggested that barring the use of government family funds for abortion counseling did not constitute viewpoint discrimination but rather was a form of subject matter limitation or earmarking. Did he mean to suggest that, when government is speaking through a private recipient of government funds, even viewpoint discrimination is allowed? When government is itself the speaker, it might be argued, viewpoint discrimination is inevitable, and the government has a special interest in not having attributed to it views that are contrary to its preferred policies. A government-sponsored drug treatment program, for example, need not give equal time to a campaign to legalize marijuana. But if government gave out grants for private research "on optimal drug policy," could it rescind the money from a researcher whose data led him to conclude that marijuana should be legalized?

For more commentary on these questions, see Cole, "Beyond Unconstitutional Conditions: Charting Spheres of Neutrality in Government-Funded Speech," 67 N.Y.U. L. Rev. 675 (1992); Fiss, "State Activism and State Censorship," 100 Yale L.J. 2087 (1991); Post, "Subsidized Speech," 106 Yale L.J. 151 (1996); Redish & Kessler, "Government Subsidies and Free Expression," 80 Minn. L. Rev. 543 (1995); Roberts, "Rust v. Sullivan and the Control of Knowledge," 61 Geo. Wash. L. Rev. 587 (1993).

5. ***Conditions on arts funding.*** What leeway does government have to restrict the content of art produced with the support of public subsidies? After a long and heated political debate that began in 1989 with public controversy over the federally subsidized exhibition of homoerotic photographs by Robert Mapplethorpe and religiously controversial photographs by Andres Serrano, this question finally reached the Court in **National Endowment for the Arts (NEA) v. Finley**, 524 U.S. 569 (1998). The case arose from a facial challenge by four individual performance artists and an artists' organization to a 1990 congressional amendment, codified at 20 U.S.C. § 954(d)(1), requiring the Chairperson of the NEA to ensure that "artistic excellence and artistic merit are the criteria by which [grant] applications are judged, taking into consideration general standards of decency and respect for the diverse beliefs and values of the American public." By a vote of 8–1, the Court held the law constitutional on its face. Justice O'CONNOR wrote the opinion of the Court: "Respondents argue that the provision is a paradigmatic example of viewpoint discrimination because it rejects any artistic speech that either fails to respect mainstream values or offends standards of decency. The premise of respondents' claim is that § 954(d)(1) constrains the agency's ability to fund certain categories of artistic expression. The NEA, however, reads the provision as merely hortatory, and contends that it stops well short of an absolute restriction. [It] is clear [that] the text of § 954(d)(1) imposes no categorical requirement. [The] criteria in § 954(d)(1) inform the assessment of artistic merit, but Congress declined to disallow any particular viewpoints. [That] § 954(d)(1) admonishes the NEA merely to take 'decency and respect' into consideration [undercuts] respondents' argument that the provision inevitably will be utilized as a tool for invidious viewpoint discrimination. In cases where we have struck down legislation as facially unconstitutional, the dangers were both more evident and more substantial. [See, e.g., R.A.V. v. City of St. Paul (1992; p. 1038 above).] [Given] the varied interpretations of the criteria [of decency and respect] and the vague exhortation to 'take them into consideration,' it seems unlikely that this provision will introduce any greater element of selectivity than the determination of 'artistic excellence' itself.

"[Any] content-based considerations that may be taken into account in the grant-making process are a consequence of the nature of arts funding. The NEA has limited resources and it must deny the majority of the grant applications that it receives, including many that propose 'artistically excellent' projects. The agency may decide to fund particular projects for a wide variety of reasons, 'such as the technical proficiency of the artist, the creativity of the work, the anticipated public interest in or appreciation of the work, the work's contemporary relevance, its educational value, its suitability for or appeal to special audiences (such as children or the disabled), its service to a rural or isolated community, or even simply that the work could increase public knowledge of an art form.' [It] would be 'impossible to have a highly selective grant program without denying money to a large amount of constitutionally protected expression.' The 'very assumption' of the NEA is that grants will be awarded according to the 'artistic worth of competing applications,' and absolute neutrality is simply 'inconceivable.'

"Respondent's reliance on our decision in Rosenberger is therefore misplaced. In Rosenberger, a public university declined to authorize disbursements from its Student Activities Fund to finance the printing of a Christian student newspaper. We held that by subsidizing the Student Activities Fund, the University had created a limited public forum, from which it impermissibly excluded all publications with religious editorial viewpoints. Although the scarcity of NEA funding does not distinguish this case from Rosenberger, the competitive process according to which the grants are allocated does. In the context of arts funding, in contrast to many other subsidies, the Government does not indiscriminately 'encourage a diversity of views from private speakers.' The NEA's mandate is to make aesthetic judgments, and the inherently content-based 'excellence' threshold for NEA support sets it apart from the subsidy at issue in Rosenberger—which was available to all student organizations that were 'related to the educational purpose of the University,'—and from comparably objective decisions on allocating public benefits, such as access to a school auditorium or a municipal theater [see Lamb's Chapel; Conrad (p. 1285 above)]."

While rejecting the facial challenge to the decency and respect provision, Justice O'Connor held out the possibility that particular applications of such criteria might violate the Free Speech Clause: "Respondents do not allege discrimination in any particular funding decision. [Thus,] we have no occasion here to address an as-applied challenge in a situation where the denial of a grant may be shown to be the product of invidious viewpoint discrimination. If the NEA were to leverage its power to award subsidies on the basis of subjective criteria into a penalty on disfavored viewpoints, then we would confront a different case. We have stated that, even in the provision of subsidies, the Government may not 'aim at the suppression of dangerous ideas,' and if a subsidy were 'manipulated' to have a 'coercive effect,' then relief could be appropriate. [Likewise,] a more pressing constitutional question would arise if government funding resulted in the imposition of a disproportionate burden calculated to drive 'certain ideas or viewpoints from the marketplace.' Unless and until § 954(d)(1) is applied in a manner that raises concern about the suppression of disfavored viewpoints, however, we uphold the constitutionality of the provision."

Justice SCALIA, joined by Justice Thomas, concurred only in the judgment, arguing that there was no need to read § 954(d)(1) as merely hortatory because it was constitutional even if mandatory and clearly viewpoint-based: " 'The operation was a success, but the patient died.' What such a procedure is to medicine, the Court's opinion in this case is to law. It sustains the constitutionality of § 954(d)(1) by gutting it. [By] its terms, [§ 954(d)(1)] establishes content- and viewpoint-based criteria upon which grant applications are to be evaluated. And that is perfectly constitutional.

"[It] is entirely, 100% clear that decency and respect are to be taken into account in evaluating applications. This is so apparent that I am at a loss to understand what the Court has in mind [when] it speculates that the statute is merely 'advisory.' [This] does not mean that those factors must always be dispositive, but it does mean that they must always be considered. [Such] factors need not be conclusive to be discriminatory. To the extent a particular applicant exhibits disrespect for the diverse beliefs and values of the American public or fails to comport with general standards of decency, the likelihood that he will receive a grant diminishes. [The] decisionmaker, all else being equal, will favor applications that display decency and respect, and disfavor applications that do not. This unquestionably constitutes viewpoint discrimination. [If] viewpoint discrimination in this context is unconstitutional, the law is invalid unless there are some situations in which the decency and respect factors do not constitute viewpoint discrimination. And there is none. The applicant who displays 'decency,' that is, 'conformity to prevailing standards of propriety or modesty,' and the applicant who displays 'respect,' that is, 'deferential regard,' for the diverse beliefs and values of the American people, will always have an edge over an applicant who displays the opposite.

"The Court devotes so much of its opinion to explaining why this statute means something other than what it says that it neglects to cite the constitutional text governing our analysis. The First Amendment reads: 'Congress shall make no law . . . abridging the freedom of speech.' To abridge is 'to contract, to diminish; to deprive of.' With the enactment of § 954(d)(1), Congress did not abridge the speech of those who disdain the beliefs and values of the American public, nor did it abridge indecent speech. Those who wish to create indecent and disrespectful art are as unconstrained now as they were before the enactment of this statute. Avant-garde artistes such as respondents remain entirely free to epater les bourgeois;[1] they are merely deprived of the additional satisfaction of having the bourgeoisie taxed to pay for it. It is preposterous to equate the denial of taxpayer subsidy with measures 'aimed at the suppression of dangerous ideas.' One might contend, I suppose, that a threat of rejection by the only available source of free money would constitute coercion and hence 'abridgment' within the meaning of the First Amendment. I would not agree with such a contention, which would

[1] "Which they do quite well. The oeuvres d'art for which the four individual plaintiffs in this case sought funding have been described as follows: Finley's controversial show, 'We Keep Our Victims Ready,' contains three segments. In the second segment, Finley visually recounts a sexual assault by stripping to the waist and smearing chocolate on her breasts and by using profanity to describe the assault. Holly Hughes' monologue 'World Without End' is a somewhat graphic recollection of the artist's realization of her lesbianism and reminiscence of her mother's sexuality. John Fleck, in his stage performance 'Blessed Are All the Little Fishes,' confronts alcoholism and Catholicism. During the course of the performance, Fleck appears dressed as a mermaid, urinates on the stage and creates an altar out of a toilet bowl by putting a photograph of Jesus Christ on the lid. Tim Miller derives his performance 'Some Golden States' from childhood experiences, from his life as a homosexual, and from the constant threat of AIDS. Miller uses vegetables in his performances to represent sexual symbols." [Footnote by Justice Scalia.]

make the NEA the mandatory patron of all art too indecent, too disrespectful, or even too kitsch to attract private support. But even if one accepts the contention, it would have no application here. The NEA is far from the sole source of funding for art—even indecent, disrespectful, or just plain bad art. Accordingly, the Government may earmark NEA funds for projects it deems to be in the public interest without thereby abridging speech.

"Respondents, relying on Rosenberger, argue that viewpoint-based discrimination is impermissible unless the government is the speaker or the government is 'disbursing public funds to private entities to convey a governmental message.' It is impossible to imagine why that should be so; one would think that directly involving the government itself in the viewpoint discrimination (if it is unconstitutional) would make the situation even worse. Respondents are mistaken. It is the very business of government to favor and disfavor points of view on (in modern times, at least) innumerable subjects—which is the main reason we have decided to elect those who run the government, rather than save money by making their posts hereditary. And it makes not a bit of difference, insofar as either common sense or the Constitution is concerned, whether these officials further their (and, in a democracy, our) favored point of view by achieving it directly (having government-employed artists paint pictures, for example, or government-employed doctors perform abortions); or by advocating it officially (establishing an Office of Art Appreciation, for example, or an Office of Voluntary Population Control); or by giving money to others who achieve or advocate it (funding private art classes, for example, or Planned Parenthood). None of this has anything to do with abridging anyone's speech. Rosenberger found the viewpoint discrimination unconstitutional, not because funding of 'private' speech was involved, but because the government had established a limited public forum—to which the NEA's granting of highly selective (if not highly discriminating) awards bears no resemblance. The nub of the difference between me and the Court is that I regard the distinction between 'abridging' speech and funding it as a fundamental divide, on this side of which the First Amendment is inapplicable."

Justice SOUTER alone dissented: "The decency and respect proviso mandates viewpoint-based decisions in the disbursement of government subsidies, and the Government has wholly failed to explain why the statute should be afforded an exemption from the fundamental rule of the First Amendment that viewpoint discrimination in the exercise of public authority over expressive activity is unconstitutional. [Because] 'the normal definition of "indecent" . . . refers to nonconformance with accepted standards of morality' [Pacifica], restrictions turning on decency, especially those couched in terms of 'general standards of decency,' are quintessentially viewpoint based: they require discrimination on the basis of conformity with mainstream mores. [Just] as self-evidently, a statute disfavoring speech that fails to respect America's 'diverse beliefs and values' is the very model of viewpoint discrimination; it penalizes any view disrespectful to [the] ideology, opinions, or convictions of a significant segment of the American public. [It does not matter that § 954(d)(1)] admonishes the NEA merely to take 'decency and respect' into consideration, not to make funding decisions specifically on those grounds. [What] if the statute required a panel to apply criteria 'taking into consideration the centrality of Christianity to the American cultural experience,' or 'taking into consideration whether the artist is a communist,' or 'taking into consideration the political message conveyed by the art,' or even 'taking into consideration the superiority of the white race'? Would the Court hold these considerations facially constitutional, merely because the statute had no requirement to give them any particular, much less controlling, weight? I assume not.

"[The] Government calls attention to the roles of government-as-speaker and government-as-buyer, in which the government is of course entitled to engage in viewpoint discrimination: if the Food and Drug Administration launches an advertising campaign on the subject of smoking, it may condemn the habit without also having to show a cowboy taking a puff on the opposite page; and if the Secretary of Defense wishes to buy a portrait to decorate the Pentagon, he is free to prefer George Washington over George the Third. The Government freely admits, however, that it neither speaks through the expression subsidized by the NEA, nor buys anything for itself with its NEA grants. [When] the Government acts as a patron, financially underwriting the production of art by private artists and impresarios for independent consumption, [this] patronage falls embarrassingly on the wrong side of the line between government-as-buyer or-speaker and government-as-regulator-of-private-speech. [Thus,] Rosenberger [controls] here. The NEA, like the student activities fund in Rosenberger, is a subsidy scheme created to encourage expression of a diversity of views from private speakers. [Given] this congressional choice to sustain freedom of expression, Rosenberger teaches that the First Amendment forbids decisions based on viewpoint popularity. So long as Congress chooses to subsidize expressive endeavors at large, it has no business requiring the NEA to turn down funding applications of artists and exhibitors who [defy] our tastes, our beliefs, or our values."

6. ***Conditions on legal aid funding.*** In **Legal Services Corporation v. Velazquez**, 531 U.S. 533 (2001), the Court, by a vote of 5–4, held invalid as an impermissible viewpoint-based restriction a federal appropriations law barring Legal Services Corporation (LSC) funding of any organization that represented indigent clients in "an effort to amend or otherwise challenge existing" welfare law. The majority, however, declined to address other related federal prohibitions on legal service grantees "participat[ing] [in] litigation, lobbying, or rulemaking, involving an effort to reform a Federal or State welfare system," which the court of appeals had upheld as "prohibit[ing] the type of activity named regardless of viewpoint."

Writing for the Court, Justice KENNEDY, joined by Justices Stevens, Souter, Ginsburg, and Breyer, explained: "[V]iewpoint-based funding decisions can be sustained in instances in which the government is itself the speaker, or instances, like Rust, in which the government 'used private speakers to transmit information pertaining to its own program.' Rosenberger. [Neither] the latitude for government speech nor its rationale applies to subsidies for private speech in every instance, however. [Like] the program in Rosenberger, the LSC program was designed to facilitate private speech, not to promote a governmental message. [The] Government has designed this program to use the legal profession and the established Judiciary of the States and the Federal Government to accomplish its end of assisting welfare claimants in determination or receipt of their benefits. The advice from the attorney to the client and the advocacy by the attorney to the courts cannot be classified as governmental speech even under a generous understanding of the concept. In this vital respect this suit is distinguishable from Rust."

"[The] Government seeks to use an existing medium of expression and to control it, in a class of cases, in ways which distort its usual functioning. [Restricting] LSC attorneys in advising their clients and in presenting arguments and analyses to the courts distorts the legal system by altering the traditional role of the attorneys [and] threatens severe impairment of the judicial function.

"[Moreover,] with respect to the litigation services Congress has funded, there is no alternative channel for expression of the advocacy Congress seeks to restrict. This is in stark contrast to Rust. There, a patient could receive the approved Title X family planning counseling funded by the Government and later could consult an affiliate or independent organization to receive abortion counseling. Unlike indigent clients who seek LSC representation, the patient in Rust was not required to forfeit the Government-funded advice when she also received abortion counseling through alternative channels. Because LSC attorneys must withdraw whenever a question of a welfare statute's validity arises, an individual could not obtain joint representation so that the constitutional challenge would be presented by a non-LSC attorney, and other, permitted, arguments advanced by LSC counsel.

"[Nor is the restriction] necessary to define the scope and contours of the federal program. [Congress] cannot recast a condition on funding as a mere definition of its program in every case, lest the First Amendment be reduced to a simple semantic exercise. Here, notwithstanding Congress' purpose to confine and limit its program, the restriction operates to insulate current welfare laws from constitutional scrutiny and certain other legal challenges. [Arguments] by indigent clients that a welfare statute is unlawful or unconstitutional cannot be expressed in this Government-funded program for petitioning the courts, even though the program was created for litigation involving welfare benefits, and even though the ordinary course of litigation involves the expression of theories and postulates on both, or multiple, sides of an issue. [In] the context of this statute there is no programmatic message of the kind recognized in Rust and which sufficed there to allow the Government to specify the advice deemed necessary for its legitimate objectives. This serves to distinguish [the LSC provision] from any of the Title X program restrictions upheld in Rust, and to place it beyond any congressional funding condition approved in the past by this Court.

"[The] attempted restriction is designed to insulate the Government's interpretation of the Constitution from judicial challenge. The Constitution does not permit the Government to confine litigants and their attorneys in this manner. We must be vigilant when Congress imposes rules and conditions which in effect insulate its own laws from legitimate judicial challenge. Where private speech is involved, even Congress' antecedent funding decision cannot be aimed at the suppression of ideas thought inimical to the Government's own interest. TWR."

Justice SCALIA dissented, joined by Chief Justice Rehnquist and Justices O'Connor and Thomas, taking the view that the LSC measure "defines the scope of a federal spending program. It does not directly regulate speech, and it neither establishes a public forum nor discriminates on the basis of viewpoint. Accordingly, the dissenters would have found the case controlled by Rust: "The LSC Act, like the scheme in Rust, does not create a public forum. Far from encouraging a diversity of views, it has always, 'placed restrictions on its use of funds,' Nor does [the act] discriminate on the basis of viewpoint, since it funds neither challenges to nor defenses of existing welfare law. The provision simply declines to subsidize a certain class of litigation, and under Rust that decision 'does not infringe the right' to bring such litigation. [No] litigant who, in the absence of LSC funding, would bring a suit challenging existing welfare law is deterred from doing so. [Rust] thus controls these cases and compels the conclusion that [the act] is constitutional."

Justice Scalia's dissent further challenged the proposition that "Rust is different because the program at issue subsidized government speech, while the LSC funds private speech": "If the private doctors' confidential advice to their patients at issue in Rust constituted 'government speech,' it is hard to imagine what subsidized speech would *not* be government speech. Moreover, the majority's contention that the subsidized speech in these cases is not government speech because the lawyers have a professional obligation to represent the interests of their clients founders on the reality that the doctors in Rust had a professional obligation to serve the interests of their patients." He concluded by suggesting that the majority had displayed "an improper special solicitude for our own profession."

7. ***Conditions on public library internet access.*** In **United States v. American Library Ass'n**, 539 U.S. 194 (2003), the Court upheld by a vote of 6–3 the Children's Internet Protection Act (CIPA), under which a public library receiving federal subsidies is required to install filtering software blocking internet access to obscenity, child pornography, or indecent material harmful to minors. Writing for a plurality, Chief Justice REHNQUIST, joined by Justices O'Connor, Scalia, and Thomas, first rejected arguments that public library computer terminals are akin to public forums or designated public forums, as libraries are inherently selective in their acquisition of material. (For this portion of the opinion, see p. 1274 above.)

Going on to reject an additional challenge that the restriction was an unconstitutional condition on government funding, Chief Justice Rehnquist stated: "Appellees argue that CIPA imposes an unconstitutional condition on libraries that receive [federal] subsidies by requiring them, as a condition on their receipt of federal funds, to surrender their First Amendment right to provide the public with access to constitutionally protected speech. The Government counters that this claim fails because Government entities do not have First Amendment rights. We need not decide this question because, even assuming that appellees may assert an 'unconstitutional conditions' claim, this claim would fail on the merits. Within broad limits, 'when the Government appropriates public funds to establish a program it is entitled to define the limits of that program.' [Rust.] The same is true here. The [federal subsidy] programs were intended to help public libraries fulfill their traditional role of obtaining material of requisite and appropriate quality for educational and informational purposes. Congress may certainly insist that these 'public funds be spent for the purposes for which they were authorized.' Especially because public libraries have traditionally excluded pornographic material from their other collections, Congress could reasonably impose a parallel limitation on its Internet assistance programs. As the use of filtering software helps to carry out these programs, it is a permissible condition under Rust.

"Appellees mistakenly contend, in reliance on LSC v. Velazquez, that CIPA's filtering conditions '[d]istor[t] the [u]sual [f]unctioning of [p]ublic [l]ibraries.' In Velazquez, the Court concluded that a Government program of furnishing legal aid to the indigent differed from the program in Rust '[i]n th[e] vital respect' that the role of lawyers who represent clients in welfare disputes is to advocate *against* the Government, and there was thus an assumption that counsel would be free of state control. The Court concluded that the restriction on advocacy in such welfare disputes would distort the usual functioning of the legal profession and the federal and state courts before which the lawyers appeared. Public libraries, by contrast, have no comparable role that pits them against the Government, and there is no comparable assumption that they must be free of any conditions that their benefactors might attach to the use of donated funds or other assistance."

In dissent, Justice STEVENS argued: "A federal statute penalizing a library for failing to install filtering software on every one of its Internet-accessible computers would unquestionably violate [the First] Amendment. I think it equally clear that the First Amendment protects libraries from being denied funds for refusing to comply with an identical rule. An abridgment of speech by means of a threatened denial of benefits can be just as pernicious as an abridgment by means of a threatened penalty. [In] an analogous situation, we specifically held that when 'the Government seeks to use an existing medium of expression and to control it, in a class of cases, in ways which distort its usual functioning,' the distorting restriction must be struck down under the First Amendment. [Velazquez.]."

Justice Stevens's dissent distinguished Rust and Finley: "The plurality argues that the controversial decision in [Rust] requires rejection of appellees' unconstitutional conditions claim. But, as subsequent cases have explained, Rust only involved and only applies to instances of governmental speech—that is, situations in which the government seeks to communicate a specific message. The discounts under the [federal subsidy programs] involved in this case do not subsidize any message favored by the Government. As Congress made clear, these programs were designed '[t]o help public libraries provide their patrons with Internet access,' which in turn 'provide[s] patrons with a vast amount of valuable information.' These programs thus are designed to provide access, particularly for individuals in low-income communities, to a vast amount and wide variety of private speech. They are not designed to foster or transmit any particular governmental message.

"[The] plurality's reliance on [Finley] is also misplaced. [Unlike] Finley, the Government does not merely seek to control a library's discretion with respect to computers purchased with Government funds or those computers with Government-discounted Internet access. CIPA requires libraries to install filtering software on *every* computer with Internet access if the library receives *any* discount from the [federal subsidy programs.] This Court should not permit federal funds to be used to enforce this kind of broad restriction of First Amendment rights, particularly when such a restriction is unnecessary to accomplish Congress' stated goal. The abridgment of speech is equally obnoxious whether a rule like this one is enforced by a threat of penalties or by a threat to withhold a benefit." Justice Souter, joined by Justice Ginsburg, filed a separate dissent.

Agency for International Development v. Alliance for Open Society International, Inc.

570 U.S. 205, 133 S. Ct. 2321, 186 L. Ed. 2d 398 (2013).

■ CHIEF JUSTICE ROBERTS delivered the opinion of the Court.

Congress passed the United States Leadership Against HIV/AIDS Act in 2003 after finding that HIV/AIDS had "assumed pandemic proportions, spreading from the most severely affected regions, sub-Saharan Africa and the Caribbean, to all corners of the world, and leaving an unprecedented path of death and devastation." [The] Act "make[s] the reduction of HIV/AIDS behavioral risks a priority of all prevention efforts." [The] President's strategy for addressing such risks must, for example, promote abstinence, encourage monogamy, increase the availability of condoms, promote voluntary counseling and treatment for drug users, and, as relevant here, "educat[e] men and boys about the risks of procuring sex commercially" as well as "promote alternative livelihoods, safety, and social reintegration strategies for commercial sex workers." Congress found that the "sex industry, the trafficking of individuals into such industry, and sexual violence" were factors in the spread of the HIV/AIDS epidemic, and determined that "it should be the policy of the United States to eradicate" prostitution and "other sexual victimization." The United States has enlisted the assistance of nongovernmental organizations to help achieve the many goals of the program. Such organizations "with experience in health care and HIV/AIDS counseling," Congress found, "have proven effective in combating the HIV/AIDS pandemic and can be a resource in . . . provid[ing] treatment and care for individuals infected with HIV/AIDS." Since 2003, Congress has authorized the appropriation of billions of dollars for funding these organizations' fight against HIV/AIDS around the world. Those funds, however, come with two conditions: First, no funds made available to carry out the Leadership Act "may be used to promote or advocate the legalization or practice of prostitution or sex trafficking." [22 U.S.C.] § 7631(e). Second, no funds made available may "provide assistance to any group or organization that does not have a policy explicitly opposing prostitution and sex trafficking, except . . . to the Global Fund to Fight AIDS, Tuberculosis and Malaria, the World Health Organization, the International AIDS Vaccine Initiative or to any United Nations agency." § 7631(f). It is this second condition—the Policy Requirement—that is at issue here.

The Department of Health and Human Services (HHS) and the United States Agency for International Development (USAID) are the federal agencies primarily responsible for overseeing implementation of the Leadership Act. To enforce the Policy Requirement, the agencies have directed that the recipient of any funding under the Act agree in the award document that it is opposed to "prostitution and sex trafficking because of the psychological and physical risks they pose for women, men, and children."

[Respondents] are a group of domestic organizations engaged in combating HIV/AIDS overseas. [They] fear that adopting a policy explicitly opposing prostitution may alienate certain host governments, and may diminish the effectiveness of some of their programs by making it more difficult to work with prostitutes in the fight against HIV/AIDS. They are also concerned that the Policy Requirement may require them to censor their privately funded discussions in publications, at conferences, and in other forums about how best to prevent the spread of HIV/AIDS among prostitutes. [Respondents] sought a preliminary injunction barring the Government from cutting off their funding under the Act for the duration of the litigation, from unilaterally terminating their cooperative agreements with the United States, or from otherwise taking action solely on the basis of respondents' own privately funded speech. The District Court granted such a preliminary injunction, and the Government appealed. While the appeal was pending, HHS and USAID issued guidelines on how recipients of Leadership Act funds could retain funding while working with affiliated organizations not bound by the Policy Requirement. The guidelines permit funding recipients to work with affiliated organizations that "engage [ ] in activities inconsistent with the recipient's opposition to the practices of prostitution and sex trafficking" as long as the recipients retain "objective integrity and independence from any affiliated organization." Whether sufficient separation exists is determined by the totality of the circumstances, including "but not . . . limited to" (1) whether the organizations are legally separate; (2) whether they have separate personnel; (3) whether they keep separate accounting records; (4) the degree of separation in the organizations' facilities; and (5) the extent to which signs and other forms of identification distinguish the organizations. The Court of Appeals summarily remanded the case to the District Court to consider whether the preliminary injunction was still appropriate in light of the new guidelines. On remand, the District Court issued a new preliminary injunction along the same lines as the first, and the Government renewed its appeal.

[The] Policy Requirement mandates that recipients of Leadership Act funds explicitly agree with the Government's policy to oppose prostitution and sex trafficking. It is, however, a basic First Amendment principle that "freedom of speech prohibits the government from telling people what they must say." Were it enacted as a direct regulation of speech, the Policy Requirement would plainly violate the First Amendment. The question is whether the Government may nonetheless impose that requirement as a condition on the receipt of federal funds.

A. [As] a general matter, if a party objects to a condition on the receipt of federal funding, its recourse is to decline the funds. This remains true when the objection is that a condition may affect the recipient's exercise of its First Amendment rights. At the same time, however, we have held that the Government "may not deny a benefit to a person on a basis that infringes his constitutionally protected . . . freedom of speech even if he has no entitlement to that benefit." In some cases, a funding condition can result in an unconstitutional burden on First Amendment rights.

[In] the present context, the relevant distinction that has emerged from our cases is between conditions that define the limits of the government spending program—those that specify the activities Congress wants to subsidize—and conditions that seek to leverage funding to regulate speech outside the contours of the program itself. The line is hardly clear, in part because the definition of a particular program can always be manipulated to subsume the challenged condition. We have held, however, that "Congress cannot recast a condition on funding as a mere definition of its program in every case, lest the First Amendment be reduced to a simple semantic exercise." Velazquez. [Our] decision in Rust v. Sullivan elaborated on the approach reflected in Regan and League of Women Voters. [The] Court stressed that "Title X expressly distinguishes between a Title X *grantee* and a Title X *project*." The regulations governed only the scope of the grantee's Title X projects, leaving it "unfettered in its other activities." "The Title X *grantee* can continue to . . . engage in abortion advocacy; it simply is required to conduct those activities through programs that are separate and independent from the project that receives Title X funds." Because the regulations did not "prohibit[ ] the recipient from engaging in the protected conduct outside the scope of the federally funded program," they did not run afoul of the First Amendment.

B. [Here], we are confident that the Policy Requirement falls on the unconstitutional side of the line. [The] Leadership Act has two conditions relevant here. The first—unchallenged in this litigation—prohibits Leadership Act funds from being used "to promote or advocate the legalization or practice of prostitution or sex trafficking." The Government concedes that § 7631(e) by itself ensures that federal funds will not be used for the prohibited purposes. The Policy Requirement therefore must be doing something more—and it is. [The] Policy Requirement is an ongoing condition on recipients' speech and activities, a ground for terminating a grant after selection is complete. In any event, as the Government acknowledges, it is not simply seeking organizations that oppose prostitution. Rather, it explains, "Congress has expressed its purpose 'to eradicate' prostitution and sex trafficking, and it wants recipients *to adopt* a similar stance." This case is not about the Government's ability to enlist the assistance of those with whom it already agrees. It is about compelling a grant recipient to adopt a particular belief as a condition of funding. By demanding that funding recipients adopt—as their own—the Government's view on an issue of public concern, the condition by its very nature affects "protected conduct outside the scope of the federally funded program." Rust. A recipient cannot avow the belief dictated by the Policy Requirement when spending Leadership Act funds, and then turn around and assert a contrary belief, or claim neutrality, when participating in activities on its own time and dime. By requiring recipients to profess a specific belief, the Policy Requirement goes beyond defining the limits of the federally funded program to defining the recipient.

[The] Government suggests the guidelines alleviate any unconstitutional burden on the respondents' First Amendment rights by allowing them to either: (1) accept Leadership Act funding and comply with Policy Requirement, but establish affiliates to communicate contrary views on prostitution; or (2) decline funding themselves (thus remaining free to express their own views or remain neutral), while creating affiliates whose sole purpose is to receive and administer Leadership Act funds, thereby "cabin[ing] the effects" of the Policy Requirement within the scope of the federal program. Neither approach is sufficient. When we have noted the importance of affiliates in this context, it has been because they allow an organization bound by a funding condition to exercise its First Amendment rights outside the scope of the federal program. See Rust. Affiliates cannot serve that purpose when the condition is that a funding recipient espouse a specific belief as its own. If the affiliate is distinct from the recipient, the arrangement does not afford a means for the *recipient* to express *its* beliefs. If the affiliate is more clearly identified with the recipient, the recipient can express those beliefs only at the price of evident hypocrisy. [The] Government cites but one case to support that argument, Holder v. Humanitarian Law Project. That case concerned the quite different context of a ban on providing material support to terrorist organizations, where the record indicated that support for those organizations' nonviolent operations was funneled to support their violent activities.

[The] Policy Requirement goes beyond preventing recipients from using private funds in a way that would undermine the federal program. It requires them to pledge allegiance to the Government's policy of eradicating prostitution. As to that, we cannot improve upon what Justice Jackson wrote for the Court 70 years ago: "If there is any fixed star in our constitutional constellation, it is that no official, high or petty, can prescribe what shall be orthodox in politics, nationalism, religion, or other matters of opinion or force citizens to confess by word or act their faith therein." Barnette [p. 1392 below].

■ KAGAN, J., took no part in the consideration or decision of this case.

■ JUSTICE SCALIA, with whom JUSTICE THOMAS joins, dissenting.

The Leadership Act provides that "any group or organization that does not have a policy explicitly opposing prostitution and sex trafficking" may not receive funds appropriated under the Act. This Policy Requirement is nothing more than a means of selecting suitable agents to implement the Government's chosen strategy to eradicate HIV/AIDS. That is perfectly permissible under the Constitution. The First Amendment does not mandate a viewpoint-neutral government. Government must choose between rival ideas and adopt some as its own: competition over cartels, solar energy over coal, weapon development over disarmament, and so forth. Moreover, the government may enlist the assistance of those who believe in its ideas to carry them to fruition; and it need not enlist for that purpose those who oppose or do not support the ideas. That seems to me a matter of the most common common sense. For example: One of the purposes of America's foreign-aid programs is the fostering of good will towards this country. If the organization Hamas—reputed to have an efficient system for delivering welfare—were excluded from a program for the distribution of U.S. food assistance, no one could reasonably object. And that would remain true if Hamas were an organization of United States citizens entitled to the protection of the Constitution. So long as the unfunded organization remains free to engage in its activities (including anti-American propaganda) "without federal assistance," refusing to make use of its assistance for an enterprise to which it is opposed does not abridge its speech. And the same is true when the rejected organization is not affirmatively opposed to, but merely unsupportive of, the object of the federal program, which appears to be the case here. (Respondents do not promote prostitution, but neither do they wish to oppose it.) A federal program to encourage healthy eating habits need not be administered by the American Gourmet Society, which has nothing against healthy food but does not insist upon it.

The argument is that this commonsense principle will enable the government to discriminate against, and injure, points of view to which it is opposed. Of course the Constitution does not prohibit government spending that discriminates against, and injures, points of view to which the government is opposed; every government program which takes a position on a controversial issue does that. Anti-smoking programs injure cigar aficionados, programs encouraging sexual abstinence injure free-love advocates, etc. The constitutional prohibition at issue here is not a prohibition against discriminating against or injuring opposing points of view, but the First Amendment's prohibition against the coercing of speech. I am frankly dubious that a condition for eligibility to participate in a minor federal program such as this one runs afoul of that prohibition even when the condition is irrelevant to the goals of the program. Not every disadvantage is a coercion.

But that is not the issue before us here. Here the views that the Government demands an applicant forswear—or that the Government insists an applicant favor—are relevant to the program in question. The program is valid only if the Government is entitled to disfavor the opposing view (here, advocacy of or toleration of prostitution). And if the program can disfavor it, so can the selection of those who are to administer the program. There is no risk that this principle will enable the Government to discriminate arbitrarily against positions it disfavors. It would not, for example, permit the Government to exclude from bidding on defense contracts anyone who refuses to abjure prostitution. But here a central part of the Government's HIV/AIDS strategy is the suppression of prostitution, by which HIV is transmitted. It is entirely reasonable to admit to participation in the program only those who believe in that goal.

According to the Court, however, this transgresses a constitutional line between conditions that operate *inside* a spending program and those that control speech *outside* of it. I am at a loss to explain what this central pillar of the Court's opinion [has] to do with the First Amendment. The distinction was alluded to, to be sure, in Rust, but not as (what the Court now makes it) an invariable requirement for First Amendment validity. That the pro-abortion speech prohibition was limited to "inside the program" speech was relevant in Rust because the program itself was not an anti-abortion program. The Government remained neutral on that controversial issue, but did not wish abortion to be promoted within its family-planning-services program. The statutory objective could not be impaired, in other words, by "outside the program" pro-abortion speech. The purpose of the limitation was to prevent Government funding from providing the *means* of pro-abortion propaganda, which the Government did not wish (and had no constitutional obligation) to provide. The situation here is vastly different. Elimination of prostitution *is* an objective of the HIV/AIDS program, and *any* promotion of prostitution—whether made inside or outside the program—*does* harm the program.

Of course the most obvious manner in which the admission to a program of an ideological opponent can frustrate the purpose of the program is by freeing up the opponent's funds for use in its ideological opposition. To use the Hamas example again: Subsidizing that organization's provision of social services enables the money that it would otherwise use for that purpose to be used, instead, for anti-American propaganda. Perhaps that problem does not exist in this case since the respondents do not affirmatively promote prostitution. But the Court's analysis categorically rejects that justification for ideological requirements in *all* cases, demanding "record indica[tion]" that "federal funding will simply supplant private funding, rather than pay for new programs." This seems to me quite naive. Money is fungible. The economic reality is that when NGOs can conduct their AIDS work on the Government's dime, they can expend greater resources on policies that undercut the Leadership Act. The Government need not establish by record evidence that this will happen. To make it a valid consideration in determining participation in federal programs, it suffices that this is a real and obvious risk.

[The] Court makes a head-fake at the unconstitutional conditions doctrine, but that doctrine is of no help. There is no case of ours in which a condition that is relevant to a statute's valid purpose and that is not in itself unconstitutional (e.g., a religious-affiliation condition that violates the Establishment Clause) has been held to violate the doctrine.

[The] majority cannot credibly say that this speech condition is coercive, so it does not. It pussyfoots around the lack of coercion by invalidating the Leadership Act for "*requiring* recipients to profess a specific belief" and "*demanding* that funding recipients adopt—as their own—the Government's view on an issue of public concern." But like King Cnut's commanding of the tides, here the Government's "requiring" and "demanding" have no coercive effect. In the end, and in the circumstances of this case, "compell[ing] *as a condition* of federal funding the affirmation of a belief," is no compulsion at all. It is the reasonable price of admission to a limited government-spending program that each organization remains free to accept or reject. Section 7631(f) "defin[es] the recipient" only to the extent he decides that it is in his interest to be so defined.

Ideological-commitment requirements such as the one here are quite rare; but making the choice between competing applicants on relevant ideological grounds is undoubtedly quite common. As far as the Constitution is concerned, it is quite impossible to distinguish between the two. If the government cannot demand a relevant ideological commitment as a condition of application, neither can it distinguish between applicants on a relevant ideological ground. And that is the real evil of today's opinion. One can expect, in the future, frequent challenges to the denial of government funding for relevant ideological reasons.

---

8. *Viewpoint and trademark.*

Matal v. Tam

581 U.S. ___, 137 S. Ct. 1744, 198 L. Ed. 2d 366 (2017).

■ JUSTICE ALITO announced the judgment of the Court and delivered the opinion of the Court with respect to Parts I, II, and III–A, and an opinion with respect to Parts III–B, III–C, and IV, in which THE CHIEF JUSTICE, JUSTICE THOMAS, and JUSTICE BREYER join.

[Simon Tam, lead singer of dance-rock band called "The Slants," chose the name to "reclaim" the anti-Asian slur. The members of the ban are Asian-Americans. Tam sought federal registration of the mark "THE SLANTS" from the Patent and Trademark Office (PTO), which denied the application under a Lanham Act provision prohibiting the registration of trademarks that may "disparage . . . or bring . . . into contemp[t] or disrepute" any "persons, living or dead." 15 U. S. C. § 1052(a).]

[We] now hold that this provision violates the Free Speech Clause of the First Amendment. It offends a bedrock First Amendment principle: Speech may not be banned on the ground that it expresses ideas that offend.

I. [Federal] law does not create trademarks. Trademarks and their precursors have ancient origins, and trademarks were protected at common law and in equity at the time of the founding. [For] most of the 19th century, trademark protection was the province of the States. [Under] the Lanham Act, [there] are now more than two million marks that have active federal certificates of registration. [Without] federal registration, a valid trademark may still be used in commerce. And an unregistered trademark can be enforced against would-be infringers in several ways. Most important, even if a trademark is not federally registered, it may still be enforceable under § 43(a) of the Lanham Act, which creates a federal cause of action for trademark infringement. And an unregistered trademark can be enforced under state common law, or if it has been registered in a State, under that State's registration system. Federal registration, however, [(1) serves] as constructive notice of the registrant's claim of ownership of the mark; (2) is prima facie evidence of the validity of the registered mark and of the registration of the mark, of the owner's ownership of the mark, and of the owner's exclusive right to use the registered mark in commerce on or in connection with the goods or services specified in the certificate; and (3) can make a mark incontestable once a mark has been registered for five years.

[At] issue in this case is [what] we will call "the disparagement clause." [When] deciding whether a trademark is disparaging, an examiner at the PTO generally applies a two-part test. The examiner first considers the likely meaning of the matter in question. ["If] that meaning is found to refer to identifiable persons, institutions, beliefs or national symbols," the examiner moves to the second step, asking "whether that meaning may be disparaging to a substantial composite of the referenced group." If the examiner finds that a "substantial composite, although not necessarily a majority, of the referenced group would find the proposed mark . . . to be disparaging in the context of contemporary attitudes," a prima facie case of disparagement is made out, and the burden shifts to the applicant to prove that the trademark is not disparaging. What is more, the PTO has specified that "[t]he fact that an applicant may be a member of that group or has good intentions underlying its use of a term does not obviate the fact that a substantial composite of the referenced group would find the term objectionable."

II. [Before] reaching the question whether the disparagement clause violates the First Amendment, we consider Tam's argument that the clause does not reach marks that disparage racial or ethnic groups [because] racial and ethnic groups are neither natural nor "juristic" persons. Tam's argument is refuted by the plain terms of the disparagement clause. [A] mark that disparages a "substantial" percentage of the members of a racial or ethnic group necessarily disparages many "persons," namely, members of that group.

III. [At] the outset, we must consider three arguments that would either eliminate any First Amendment protection or result in highly permissive rational-basis review. Specifically, the Government contends (1) that trademarks are government speech, not private speech, (2) that trademarks are a form of government subsidy, and (3) that the constitutionality of the disparagement clause should be tested under a new "government-program" doctrine.

A. [Our] cases recognize that "the Free Speech Clause . . . does not regulate government speech." Pleasant Grove City v. Summum. [But] while the government-speech doctrine is important—indeed, essential—it is a doctrine that is susceptible to dangerous misuse. If private speech could be passed off as government speech by simply affixing a government seal of approval, government could silence or muffle the expression of disfavored.

[At] issue here is the content of trademarks that are registered by the PTO. [The] Federal Government does not dream up these marks, and it does not edit marks submitted for registration. Except as required by the statute involved here, an examiner may not reject a mark based on the viewpoint that it appears to express. Thus, unless that section is thought to apply, [registration] is mandatory. [If] an examiner finds that a mark is eligible for placement on the principal register, that decision is not reviewed by any higher official unless the registration is challenged. Moreover, once a mark is registered, the PTO is not authorized to remove it from the register. [In] light of all this, it is far-fetched to suggest that the content of a registered mark is government speech. If the federal registration of a trademark makes the mark government speech, the Federal Government is babbling prodigiously and incoherently.

[The] case on which the Government relies most heavily, Walker, [likely] marks the outer bounds of the government-speech doctrine. Holding that the messages on Texas specialty license plates are government speech, the Walker Court cited three factors distilled from Summum. First, license plates have long been used by the States to convey state messages. Second, license plates "are often closely identified in the public mind" with the State, since they are manufactured and owned by the State, generally designed by the State, and serve as a form of "government ID." Third, Texas "maintain[ed] direct control over the messages conveyed on its specialty plates." [None] of these factors are present in this case.

[If] the registration of trademarks constituted government speech, other systems of government registration could easily be characterized in the same way. [If] federal registration makes a trademark government speech and thus eliminates all First Amendment protection, would the registration of the copyright for a book produce a similar transformation? The Government attempts to distinguish copyright on the ground that it is "the engine of free expression," but as this case illustrates, trademarks often have an expressive content. Trademarks are private, not government, speech.

B. We next address the Government's argument that this case is governed by cases in which this Court has upheld the constitutionality of government programs that subsidized speech expressing a particular viewpoint. These cases implicate a notoriously tricky question of constitutional law. [Unlike] the present case, the decisions on which the Government relies all involved cash subsidies or their equivalent. In Rust v. Sullivan, a federal law provided funds to private parties for family planning services. In National Endowment for Arts v. Finley, cash grants were awarded to artists. And federal funding for public libraries was at issue in United States v. American Library Assn., Inc. [Th]e federal registration of a trademark is nothing like the programs at issue in these cases. The PTO does not pay money to parties seeking registration of a mark.

C. [Finally,] the Government urges us to sustain the disparagement clause under a new doctrine that would apply to "government-program" cases. [But] those cases occupy a special area of First Amendment case law, and they are far removed from the registration of trademarks.

[Potentially] more analogous are cases in which a unit of government creates a limited public forum for private speech. When government creates such a forum, in either a literal or "metaphysical" sense, see *Rosenberger*, some content- and speaker-based restrictions may be allowed. However, even in such cases, what we have termed "viewpoint discrimination" is forbidden.

Our cases use the term "viewpoint" discrimination in a broad sense, and in that sense, the disparagement clause discriminates on the bases of "viewpoint." To be sure, the clause evenhandedly prohibits disparagement of all groups. It applies equally to marks that damn Democrats and Republicans, capitalists and socialists, and those arrayed on both sides of every possible issue. It denies registration to any mark that is offensive to a substantial percentage of the members of any group. But in the sense relevant here, that is viewpoint discrimination: Giving offense is a viewpoint.

IV. [The parties dispute] whether trademarks are commercial speech and are thus subject to the relaxed scrutiny outlined in Central Hudson. We need not resolve this debate [because] the disparagement clause cannot withstand even *Central Hudson* review.

It is claimed that the disparagement clause serves two interests. The first is [that] Government has an interest in preventing speech expressing ideas that offend. [That] idea strikes at the heart of the First Amendment. Speech that demeans on the basis of race, ethnicity, gender, religion, age, disability, or any other similar ground is hateful; but the proudest boast of our free speech jurisprudence is that we protect the freedom to express "the thought that we hate."

The second interest asserted is protecting the orderly flow of commerce. [A] simple answer [is] that the disparagement clause is not "narrowly drawn" to drive out trademarks that support invidious discrimination. [It] applies to trademarks like the following: "Down with racists," "Down with sexists," "Down with homophobes." It is not an anti-discrimination clause; it is a happy-talk clause.

[There] is also a deeper problem with the argument that commercial speech may be cleansed of any expression likely to cause offense. The commercial market is well stocked with merchandise that disparages prominent figures and groups, and the line between commercial and non-commercial speech is not always clear. [If] affixing the commercial label permits the suppression of any speech that may lead to political or social "volatility," free speech would be endangered.

■ JUSTICE KENNEDY, with whom JUSTICE GINSBURG, JUSTICE SOTOMAYOR, and JUSTICE KAGAN join, concurring in part and concurring in the judgment.

[This] separate writing explains in greater detail why the First Amendment's protections against viewpoint discrimination apply to the trademark here. It submits further that the viewpoint discrimination rationale renders unnecessary any extended treatment of other questions raised by the parties.

[In] the instant case, the disparagement clause [identifies] the relevant subject as "persons, living or dead, institutions, beliefs, or national symbols." 15 U. S. C. § 1052(a). Within that category, an applicant may register a positive or benign mark but not a derogatory one. The law thus reflects the Government's disapproval of a subset of messages it finds offensive. This is the essence of viewpoint discrimination.

[To] prohibit all sides from criticizing their opponents makes a law more viewpoint based, not less so. The logic of the Government's rule is that a law would be viewpoint neutral even if it provided that public officials could be praised but not condemned. The First Amendment's viewpoint neutrality principle protects more than the right to identify with a particular side. It protects the right to create and present arguments for particular positions in particular ways, as the speaker chooses. By mandating positivity, the law here might silence dissent and distort the marketplace of ideas.

[The] Court has suggested that viewpoint discrimination occurs when the government intends to suppress a speaker's beliefs, but viewpoint discrimination need not take that form in every instance. The danger of viewpoint discrimination is that the government is attempting to remove certain ideas or perspectives from a broader debate. That danger is all the greater if the ideas or perspectives are ones a particular audience might think offensive, at least at first hearing. An initial reaction may prompt further reflection, leading to a more reasoned, more tolerant position.

[To] the extent trademarks qualify as commercial speech, they are an example of why that term or category does not serve as a blanket exemption from the First Amendment's requirement of viewpoint neutrality. Justice Holmes' reference to the "free trade in ideas" and the "power of . . . thought to get itself accepted in the competition of the market," Abrams v. United States, (dissenting opinion), was a metaphor. In the realm of trademarks, the metaphorical marketplace of ideas becomes a tangible, powerful reality. Here that real marketplace exists as a matter of state law and our common-law tradition, quite without regard to the Federal Government. These marks make up part of the expression of everyday life. [To] permit viewpoint discrimination in this context is to permit Government censorship.

VIEWPOINT DISCRIMINATION

The third part of the majority opinion in Matal v. Tam is the Court's latest word on what constitutes viewpoint discrimination. Writing for the majority, Justice Alito wrote "Our cases use the term 'viewpoint' discrimination in a broad sense, and in that sense, the disparagement clause discriminates on the bases of 'viewpoint.' [ ] To be sure, the clause evenhandedly prohibits disparagement of all groups. It applies equally to marks that damn Democrats and Republicans, capitalists and socialists, and those arrayed on both sides of every possible issue. It denies registration to any mark that is offensive to a substantial percentage of the members of any group. But in the sense relevant here, that is viewpoint discrimination: Giving offense is a viewpoint." See Ned Snow, Denying Trademark for Scandalous Speech, 51 U.C. Davis L. Rev. 2331 (2018); Maura Douglas, *Finding Viewpoint Neutrality in Our Constitutional Constellation*, 20 U. Pa. J. Const. L. 727 (2018).

SECTION 3. OVERBREADTH, VAGUENESS AND PRIOR RESTRAINT

This section turns to a last set of doctrines limiting how government may regulate speech: the doctrines of overbreadth, vagueness, and prior restraint. The flaw in laws invalidated on these grounds is procedural: government went about things the wrong way even if the speaker might constitutionally be restricted if government went about it in a different way.

An overbroad law sweeps in too much speech, a vague law is unclear about what speech it sweeps in, and a prior restraint is premature even if publication might be subsequently punished. These doctrines are accordingly of particular usefulness to a speaker whose own speech might not be protected under the First Amendment under a differently drawn law.

OVERBREADTH

Even if speech is proscribable by a properly drawn law, a speaker may be able to invalidate a law that is overly broad. For example, recall the case of Gooding v. Wilson (1972; p. 988 above), in which the Court invalidated a conviction of an anti-war demonstrator at an induction center who in a scuffle with police said such things as "White son of a bitch, I'll kill you." He was convicted under a Georgia statute prohibiting the use of "opprobrious words or abusive language, tending to cause a breach of the peace." The Court, per Justice Brennan, held that the law swept in too much protected speech along with fighting words proscribable under Chaplinsky: "[It] matters not that the words appellee used might have been constitutionally prohibited under a narrowly and precisely drawn statute. At least when statutes regulate or proscribe speech and when 'no readily apparent construction suggests itself as a vehicle for rehabilitating the statutes in a single prosecution,' [the] transcendent value to all society of constitutionally protected expression is deemed to justify allowing 'attacks on overly broad statutes with no requirement that the person making the attack demonstrate that his own conduct could not be regulated by a statute drawn with the requisite narrow specificity.' [Dombrowski v. Pfister, 380 U.S. 479 (1965).]" Unlike the New Hampshire courts in Chaplinsky, Justice Brennan found, the Georgia courts in Gooding had failed to narrowly construe the opprobrious-words statute to limit its reach to fighting words. Accordingly, the Court voided the statute on its face.

For an example of similar overbreadth reasoning, recall Justice White's concurrence in R.A.V. v. City of St. Paul (1992; p. 1038 above), finding that a law barring racist symbols causing anger or alarm was overbroad because not limited to fighting words. For other examples of overbreadth determinations covered in earlier sections, see Erznoznik v. Jacksonville (1975; p. 1082 above) (ban on nudity in drive-in movies); Schad v. Mt. Ephraim (1981; p. 1084 above) (ban on live entertainment).

1. ***The distinctive features of overbreadth.*** Overbreadth analysis is an exception to two traditional rules of constitutional litigation. First, it results in the invalidation of a law "on its face" rather than "as applied" to a particular speaker. Ordinarily, a particular litigant claims that a statute is unconstitutional as applied to him or her; if the litigant prevails, the courts carve away the unconstitutional aspects of the law by invalidating its improper applications on a case-by-case basis. If a law restricting speech is invalidated as applied to a protected speaker, it is held inapplicable to that speaker, and thus, in effect, judicially trimmed down. Overbreadth analysis, in contrast, does not reach the question whether the *challenger's* speech is constitutionally protected; instead it strikes down the statute entirely, because it might be applied to others not before the Court whose activities are constitutionally protected. When invalidated for overbreadth, a law is

not narrowed, but rather becomes wholly unenforceable until a legislature rewrites it or a properly authorized court construes it more narrowly.

Second, overbreadth is an exception to the usual rules of standing. Ordinarily, challengers to a law are not permitted to raise the rights of third parties and can only assert their own interests. See generally Note, "Standing to Assert Constitutional Jus Tertii," 88 Harv. L. Rev. 423 (1974). In overbreadth analysis, challengers *are* in effect permitted to raise the rights of third parties. But see Monaghan, "Overbreadth," 1981 Sup. Ct. Rev. 1 (arguing that overbreadth involves first-party, not third-party standing, because the litigant's own conduct may only be regulated by a valid rule of law); Monaghan, "Third-Party Standing," 84 Colum. L. Rev. 277 (1984).

The factor that motivates courts to depart from these normal rules of adjudication is the concern with the deterrent or "chilling" effect of the overbroad statute on third parties not courageous enough to bring suit. The Court assumes that an overbroad law's very existence may cause others not before the court to refrain from constitutionally protected speech or expression. An overbreadth ruling is designed to remove that deterrent effect on the speech of those third parties. As Justice Brennan wrote in Gooding, invalidation for overbreadth is "necessary because persons whose expression is constitutionally protected may well refrain from exercising their rights for fear of criminal sanctions provided by a statute susceptible of application to protected expression." See generally Note, "The First Amendment Overbreadth Doctrine," 83 Harv. L. Rev. 844 (1970); Redish, "The Warren Court, the Burger Court, and the First Amendment Overbreadth Doctrine," 78 Nw. U. L. Rev. 1031 (1983); Fallon, "Making Sense of Overbreadth," 100 Yale L.J. 853 (1991). An additional reason to contain overbroad statutes, like vague statutes, is to curb "their potential for selective enforcement" at the discretion of law enforcement officials. See Karst, "Equality as a Central Principle in the First Amendment," 43 U. Chi. L. Rev. 20 (1975).

2. ***The attractiveness of overbreadth analysis.*** Overbreadth analysis has been especially attractive to some Justices because it gives the appearance of judicial modesty. Rather than rewriting a law, it purports to leave alternatives open to the legislature. By holding out the prospect that narrower means may be available to achieve legislative objectives, it conveys the appearance of intervening in legislative policy choices far more marginally than outright "balancing" would. See, e.g., **United States v. Robel**, 387 U.S. 939 (1967), which invalidated as overbroad a federal law making it a crime for members of Communist organizations to be employed in a defense facility, because it swept in passive and active members alike. Chief Justice WARREN's opinion disavowed any substantive "balancing": "[We] have confined our analysis to whether Congress has adopted a constitutional means in achieving its concededly legitimate [goal]. In making this determination we have found it necessary to measure the validity of the means [against] both the goal [and] the First Amendment. But we have in no way 'balanced' those respective interests. We have ruled only that the Constitution requires that the conflict between congressional power and individual rights be accommodated by legislation drawn more narrowly to avoid the conflict."

Is this appearance of judicial modesty deceptive? For an argument that Robel engaged in implicit balancing despite its disavowal, see Gunther, "Reflections on Robel: It's Not What the Court Did but the Way that It Did It," 20 Stan. L. Rev. 1140 (1968). Arguably, overbreadth analysis cannot altogether avoid substantive judgments. In order to decide that a law sweeps in protected as well as unprotected expression, a judgment of overbreadth necessarily must delineate some contours of protected expression. To strike down an excessively broad "means" because it impinges on an "area of protected freedom" presupposes, after all, at least an implicit judgment about what the contours of that "area" are.

A second attraction of overbreadth analysis in the context of state laws is an apparent respect for the values of federalism. In the case of state legislation, only the state courts have authority to construe the statute; the federal courts, including the Supreme Court, may construe federal statutes but must abide by state court construction of state laws. Thus a federal court lacks authority to issue a narrowing construction of an overbroad state law. For a federal court in effect to rewrite a state statute by narrowing it arguably would amount to a quasi-legislative intrusion upon state policymaking prerogatives, whereas a judgment of facial invalidation of an overbroad state statute appears to defer to the state's policymaking role. But is facial invalidation truly a less intrusive exercise of federal judicial power than a narrowing construction would be?

3. ***Criticisms of overbreadth analysis.*** Overbreadth analysis has elicited a number of criticisms, beginning in the Warren Court era. One set of criticisms relates to its departure from usual case and controversy requirements. First, it has been criticized for allowing the Court to act "as if it had a roving commission" to cure unconstitutional provisions. Cox, The Warren Court (1968); see Younger v. Harris, 401 U.S. 37 (1971) (Black, J.) (noting that the federal judicial power to resolve "concrete disputes [does] not amount to an unlimited power to survey the statute books and pass judgment on laws before the courts are called upon to enforce them"). Second, it has been criticized for permitting decisions outside of concrete factual settings and in sterile, abstract contexts. See Bickel, The Least Dangerous Branch (1962). Third, it has been criticized as too speculative. It allows a court to invalidate a law so long as it can hypothesize some impermissible application in circumstances not before it. See, e.g., Gooding v. Wilson, supra (Burger, C.J., dissenting) (criticizing overbreadth for resting on "some insubstantial or imagined potential for occasional and isolated applications that go beyond constitutional bounds"); Younger, supra ("[T]he existence of a 'chilling effect' even in the area of First Amendment rights has never been considered a sufficient basis, in and of itself, for prohibiting state action.").

A second set of criticisms of overbreadth relates to its consequences. Typically, overbreadth analysis assumes that the challenger's behavior is not protected by the First Amendment and is reachable by the state under a more "narrowly drawn" law. Thus the doctrine permits an individual whose own First Amendment rights have not been violated to enjoy a free ride unless and until the appropriate legislature or court redraws the statute. This may well undermine important state interest in the meantime. And there may be various practical obstacles to prompt redrafting by the relevant policymaking bodies. Moreover, it may appear perverse for an unprotected speaker to wield a more powerful weapon against a law than a protected speaker can, since the protected speaker is more likely to be confined to an "as applied" analysis.

4. ***Limits on overbreadth analysis: the requirement of "substantial" overbreadth.*** The above criticisms bore fruit in 1973, when the Court required that overbreadth must be "substantial" before facial

invalidation is appropriate and suggested that overbreadth analysis was less applicable when the challenged statute affected "conduct" rather than "speech." In **Broadrick v. Oklahoma**, 413 U.S. 601 (1973), Justice White—who had dissented from some earlier overbreadth invalidations—wrote for the majority, and Justice Brennan—who had written some of the major overbreadth opinions of the Warren era—wrote for most of the dissenters. Broadrick arose from a challenge to § 818 of Oklahoma's Merit System Act restricting political activities by classified civil servants. Among the challenged provisions of this mini-Hatch Act was one prohibiting employees from "tak[ing] part in the management or affairs of any political party or in any political campaign, except to exercise his right as a citizen privately to express his opinion and to cast his vote." Other provisions more specifically prohibited soliciting for campaign contributions. Appellants, who had campaigned for a superior, challenged § 818 on vagueness and overbreadth grounds. The Court's 5–4 decision rejected those challenges. Justice WHITE's majority opinion devoted most of its focus to overbreadth:

"Appellants assert that § 818 has been construed as applying to such allegedly protected political expression as the wearing of political buttons or the displaying of bumper stickers. But appellants did not engage in any such activity. They are charged with actively engaging in partisan political activities—including the solicitation of money—among their co-workers for the benefit of their superior. Appellants concede [that] § 818 would be constitutional as applied to this type of conduct. [See the Hatch Act cases, p. 1315 above.] They nevertheless maintain that the statute is overbroad and purports to reach protected, as well as unprotected conduct, and must therefore be struck down on its face and held to be incapable of any constitutional application. We do not believe that the overbreadth doctrine may appropriately be invoked in this manner here."

Justice White then proceeded to justify and delineate a "substantial overbreadth" approach: "Embedded in the traditional rules governing constitutional adjudication is the principle that a person to whom a statute may constitutionally be applied will not be heard to challenge that statute on the ground that it may conceivably be applied unconstitutionally to others, in other situations not before the Court. [This principle reflects] the conviction [that] our constitutional courts are not roving commissions assigned to pass judgment on the validity of the Nation's laws. [In] the past, the Court has recognized some limited exceptions to these principles, but only because of the most 'weighty countervailing policies.' [One such exception] has been carved out in the area of the First Amendment. It has long been recognized that the First Amendment needs breathing space and that statutes attempting to restrict or burden the exercise of First Amendment rights must be narrowly drawn and represent a considered legislative judgment that a particular mode of expression has to give way to other compelling needs of society. As a corollary, the Court has altered its traditional rules of standing to permit [litigants] in the First Amendment area to challenge a statute not because their own rights of free expression are violated, but because of a judicial prediction or assumption that the statute's very existence may cause others not before the court to refrain from constitutionally protected speech or expression.

"Such claims of facial overbreadth have been entertained in cases involving statutes which, by their terms, seek to regulate 'only spoken words.' [Gooding v. Wilson.] In such cases, it has been the judgment of this

Court that the possible harm to society in permitting some unprotected speech to go unpunished is outweighed by the possibility that protected speech of others may be muted and perceived grievances left to fester because of the possible inhibitory effects of overly broad statutes. Overbreadth attacks have also been allowed where the Court thought rights of association were ensnared in statutes which, by their broad sweep, might result in burdening innocent associations. Robel.

"[The] consequence of our departure from traditional rules of standing in the First Amendment area is that any enforcement of a statute thus placed at issue is totally forbidden until and unless a limiting construction or partial invalidation so narrows it as to remove the seeming threat or deterrence to constitutionally protected expression. Application of the overbreadth doctrine in this manner is, manifestly, strong medicine. It has been employed by the Court sparingly and only as a last resort. Facial overbreadth has not been invoked when a limiting construction has been or could be placed on the challenged statute. [See, e.g., Cox v. New Hampshire]. Equally important, overbreadth claims, if entertained at all, have been curtailed when invoked against ordinary criminal laws that are sought to be applied to protected conduct.

"It remains a 'matter of no little difficulty' to determine when a law may properly be held void on its face and when 'such summary action' is inappropriate. [But] the plain import of our cases is, at the very least, that facial overbreadth adjudication is an exception to our traditional rules of practice and that its function, a limited one at the outset, attenuates as the otherwise unprotected behavior that it forbids the State to sanction moves from 'pure speech' towards conduct and that conduct—even if expressive—falls within the scope of otherwise valid criminal [laws]. Although such laws, if too broadly worded, may deter protected speech to some unknown extent, there comes a point where that effect—at best a prediction—cannot, with confidence, justify invalidating a statute on its face and so prohibiting a State from enforcing the statute against conduct that is admittedly within its power to proscribe. [To] put the matter another way, particularly where conduct and not merely speech is involved, we believe that the overbreadth of a statute must not only be real, but substantial as well, judged in relation to the statute's plainly legitimate sweep. It is our view that § 818 is not substantially overbroad and that whatever overbreadth may exist should be cured through case-by-case analysis of the fact situations to which its sanctions, assertedly, may not be applied.

"Unlike ordinary breach-of-the-peace statutes or other broad regulatory acts, § 818 is directed, by its terms, at political expression which if engaged in by private persons would plainly be protected by the [First Amendment]. But at the same time, § 818 is not a censorial statute, directed at particular groups or viewpoints. The statute, rather, seeks to regulate political activity in an even-handed and neutral manner. As indicated, such statutes have in the past been subject to a less exacting overbreadth scrutiny. Moreover, the fact remains that § 818 regulates a substantial spectrum of conduct that is as manifestly subject to state regulation as the public peace or criminal trespass. Without question, the conduct appellants have been charged with falls squarely within those proscriptions. Appellants assert that § 818 goes much farther. [They point to] interpretive rules purporting to restrict such allegedly protected activities as the wearing of political buttons or the use of bumper stickers. It may be that such restrictions are impermissible and that

§ 818 may be susceptible of some other improper applications. But, as presently construed, we do not believe that § 818 must be discarded in toto because some persons' arguably protected conduct may or may not be caught or chilled by the statute. Section 818 is not substantially overbroad and is not, therefore, unconstitutional on its face."

The major dissent was by Justice BRENNAN, joined by Justices Stewart and Marshall. Justice Brennan thought the decision a "wholly unjustified retreat from fundamental and previously well-established" principles. The majority had conceded the possibility of some "improper applications," and "that assumption requires a finding that the statute is unconstitutional on its face."

Justice Brennan objected to the majority's "substantial overbreadth" approach: "In the first place, the Court makes no effort to define what it means by 'substantial overbreadth.' We have never held that a statute should be held invalid on its face merely because it is possible to conceive of a single impermissible application, and in that sense a requirement of substantial overbreadth is already implicit in the doctrine. [Whether] the Court means to require some different or greater showing of substantiality is left obscure by today's opinion, in large part because the Court makes no effort to explain why the overbreadth of the Oklahoma Act, while real, is somehow not quite substantial. [More] fundamentally, the Court offers no rationale to explain its conclusion that, for purposes of overbreadth analysis, deterrence of conduct should be viewed differently from deterrence of speech, even where both are equally protected by the [First Amendment]. At this stage, it is obviously difficult to estimate the probable impact of today's decision. If the requirement of 'substantial' overbreadth is construed to mean only that facial review is inappropriate where the likelihood of an impermissible application of the statute is too small to generate a 'chilling effect' on protected speech or conduct, then the impact is likely to be small. On the other hand, if today's decision necessitates the drawing of artificial distinctions between protected speech and protected conduct, and if the 'chill' on protected conduct is rarely, if ever, found sufficient to require the facial invalidation of an overbroad statute, then the effect could be very grave indeed." Justice Douglas dissented separately.

What is the definition of "substantial" overbreadth? How great a ratio of protected to unprotected speech must be covered to qualify? In City Council v. Taxpayers for Vincent (1984; p. 1227 above), Justice Stevens's majority opinion stated: "The concept of 'substantial overbreadth' is not readily reduced to an exact definition. It is clear, however, that the mere fact that one can conceive of some impermissible applications of a statute is not sufficient to render it susceptible to an overbreadth challenge. On the contrary, [there] must be a realistic danger that the statute itself will significantly compromise recognized First Amendment protections of parties not before the Court for it to be facially challenged on overbreadth grounds." For discussion, see Fallon, supra.

Applying Broadrick, the Court found no substantial overbreadth in the New York child pornography law at issue in **New York v. Ferber**, 458 U.S. 747 (1982) (see p. 1095 above). The claim there was that the New York law was "unconstitutionally overbroad because it would forbid the distribution of material with serious literary, scientific or educational value or material which does not threaten the harms sought to be combatted by the State." Justice WHITE wrote for the Court: "We consider this the paradigmatic case of a state statute whose legitimate reach dwarfs its arguably impermissible applications. [While] the reach of the statute is directed at the hard core of child pornography, the [highest New York court] was understandably concerned that some protected expression, ranging from medical textbooks to pictorials in National Geographic, would fall prey to the statute. How often, if ever, it may be necessary to employ children to engage in conduct clearly within the reach of the [law] in order to produce educational, medical or artistic works cannot be known with certainty. Yet we seriously doubt [that] these arguably impermissible applications of the statute amount to more than a tiny fraction of the materials within the statute's reach. [Under] these circumstances, [the law] is 'not substantially overbroad and whatever overbreadth exists should be cured through case-by-case analysis of the fact situations to which its sanctions, assertedly, may not be applied.' [Broadrick.]"

In an opinion concurring in the judgment, Justice STEVENS objected to the majority's quantitative approach. He stated: "My reasons for avoiding overbreadth analysis in this case are more qualitative than quantitative. When we follow our traditional practice of adjudicating difficult and novel constitutional questions only in concrete factual situations, the adjudications tend to be crafted with greater wisdom. Hypothetical rulings are inherently treacherous and prone to lead us into unforeseen errors; they are qualitatively less reliable than the products of case-by-case adjudication. [Moreover,] generally marginal speech does not warrant the extraordinary protection afforded by the overbreadth doctrine."

In contrast, in **Ashcroft v. Free Speech Coalition**, 535 U.S. 234 (2002), the Court found that the Child Pornography Prevention Act of 1996 (CPPA) was unconstitutional for substantial overbreadth. The CPPA had prohibited depictions appearing to portray children engaged in sexual acts, but with no actual children involved in the production process as would make such depictions proscribable under Ferber. (For other portions of the opinion, see p. 1121 above.) Speaking for the Court, Justice KENNEDY applied the overbreadth doctrine to reject the government's argument that the ban on virtual child pornography was justified as a means to enforce the ban on real child pornography: "[T]he Government says that the possibility of producing images by using computer imaging makes it very difficult for it to prosecute those who produce pornography by using real children. [The] argument, in essence, is that protected speech may be banned as a means to ban unprotected speech. This analysis turns the First Amendment upside down."

Dissenting from this part of the Court's decision, Justice O'CONNOR considered the overbreadth too unproven to invalidate the law in its entirety. While she agreed with the Court that "the CPPA's ban on youthful-adult pornography is overbroad," so that films using adult actors to simulate child sexual conduct could not be banned, she found that the challengers had not made out an overbreadth claim against "virtual-child pornography" made with computer-generated images of children: "[Respondents] provide no examples of films or other materials that are wholly computer-generated and contain images that 'appea[r] to be . . . of minors' engaging in indecent conduct, but that have serious value or do not facilitate child abuse. Their overbreadth challenge therefore fails."

Chief Justice REHNQUIST's dissent, joined by Justice Scalia, proposed a narrowing interpretation of the statute that would eliminate the overbreadth problem: "[We] normally do not strike down a statute on First

Amendment grounds 'when a limiting instruction has been or could be placed on the challenged statute.' [Broadrick]. [The] CPPA can be limited so as not to reach any material that was not already unprotected before the CPPA. The CPPA's definition of 'sexually explicit conduct'[1] [should be read to reach] only the sort of 'hard core of child pornography' that we found without protection in Ferber. So construed, the CPPA bans visual depictions of youthful looking adult actors engaged in actual sexual activity; mere suggestions of sexual activity, such as youthful looking adult actors squirming under a blanket, are more akin to written descriptions than visual depictions, and thus fall outside the purview of the statute. [While] potentially impermissible applications of the CPPA may exist, I doubt that they would be 'substantial . . . in relation to the statute's plainly legitimate sweep.' [Broadrick]. The aim of ensuring the enforceability of our Nation's child pornography laws is a compelling one. The CPPA is targeted to this aim by extending the definition of child pornography to reach computer-generated images that are virtually indistinguishable from real children engaged in sexually explicit conduct. The statute need not be read to do any more than precisely this, which is not offensive to the First Amendment."

In **Virginia v. Hicks**, 539 U.S. 113 (2003), the Court unanimously rejected a First Amendment challenge to a public housing development's policy controlling entry to its premises. Aimed at social order and crime control, the policy authorized the Richmond police to serve notice on any person lacking "a legitimate business or social purpose" for being on the premises and to arrest for trespassing any person who returned after having been so notified. Hicks, who was not a resident of the development and who had been charged with damaging property there, returned after being given written notice not to enter, and was charged and convicted of trespass. Although Hicks was not seeking entry in order to engage in any speech, the Virginia Supreme Court found the policy facially void for overbreadth, reasoning that the policy carried with it an "unwritten" rule giving the development manager unfettered discretion to pick and choose which persons might enter the development in order to leaflet or demonstrate. Justice SCALIA wrote for all the Justices, reversing:

"[We] have insisted that a law's application to protected speech be 'substantial,' not only in an absolute sense, but also relative to the scope of the law's plainly legitimate applications, before applying the 'strong medicine' of overbreadth invalidation. [Hicks] has not made such a showing. [Both] the notice-barment rule and the 'legitimate business or social purpose' rule apply to all persons who enter the streets of [the development], not just to those who seek to engage in expression. The rules apply to strollers, loiterers, drug dealers, roller skaters, bird watchers, soccer players, and others not engaged in constitutionally protected conduct—a group that would seemingly far outnumber First Amendment speakers. Even assuming invalidity of the 'unwritten' rule that requires leafleters and demonstrators to obtain advance permission from [the development manager], Hicks has not shown, based on the record in this case, that the [housing authority's] trespass policy as a whole prohibits a 'substantial' amount of protected speech in relation to its many legitimate applications. [Rarely,] if ever, will

[1] Here, Chief Justice Rehnquist quoted CPPA's definition of "sexually explicit conduct" as "visual depictions" of: "actual or simulated . . . sexual intercourse, including genital-genital, oral-genital, anal-genital, or oral-anal, whether between persons of the same or opposite sex; . . . bestiality; . . . masturbation; . . . sadistic or masochistic abuse; . . . or lascivious exhibition of the genitals or pubic area of any person."

an overbreadth challenge succeed against a law or regulation that is not specifically addressed to speech or to conduct necessarily associated with speech (such as picketing or demonstrating)."

5. ***Limits on overbreadth analysis: incapable of a narrowing construction.*** In **Brockett v. Spokane Arcades, Inc.**, 472 U.S. 491 (1985), the Court held that appeals to the "prurient interest" under the Miller test for obscenity (see p. 1062 above) did not encompass "material that provoked only normal, healthy sexual desires," but was limited to materials appealing to a "shameful or morbid interest" in sex. It thus held a Washington obscenity law unconstitutional because it defined "prurient interest" as "that which incites lasciviousness or lust," a definition broad enough to encompass "normal" as well as "shameful" sexual responses. But despite this apparent overbreadth finding, the Court declined to permit an individual whose own rights were violated under the statute to invalidate the law on its face, limiting the challenger to an "as-applied" challenge. Justice WHITE, writing for a 6–2 majority, explained: "[An] individual whose own speech [may] validly be prohibited [is] permitted to challenge a statute on its face because it also threatens others not before the court. [But where, as here,] the parties challenging the statute are those who desire to engage in protected speech that the overbroad statute purports to punish, [there is] no want of a proper party to challenge the [law and it] may forthwith be declared invalid to the extent it reaches too far, but otherwise left intact." Justice BRENNAN, joined by Justice Marshall, dissented, insisting that the law was "substantially overbroad and therefore invalid on its face."

When is such partial validation appropriate? In Brockett, the U.S. Supreme Court could not issue a narrowing construction of the state statute; only the state courts could. But the Court in effect decided that a narrowing construction was readily available to the state courts, as the improper portion of the obscenity definition was easily severable from the rest. Its invalidation of the law as applied in effect cued the state courts as to how to rewrite the law. On the relationship between overbreadth and severability, see Dorf, "Facial Challenges to State and Federal Statutes," 46 Stan. L. Rev. 235 (1994).

In Brockett, the state's otherwise constitutional obscenity statute could be "trimmed of unconstitutional branches," but the Court continues to employ facial invalidation when a statute is "rotten at its very root." Tribe, American Constitutional Law 1029 (2d ed. 1988). For example, the Court has invalidated facially several laws designed to limit charitable solicitation to organizations with low overhead expenses. The 8–1 decision in **Schaumburg v. Citizens for Better Environment**, 444 U.S. 620 (1980), struck down as overbroad an ordinance barring door-to-door and on-street solicitations of contributions by charitable organizations that did not use at least 75% of their receipts for "charitable purposes." "Charitable purposes" were defined to exclude solicitation expenses. Because of that 75% rule, Citizens for a Better Environment (CBE), an environmental group, was denied permission to solicit contributions in Schaumburg, a suburb of Chicago. CBE challenged the law as a free speech violation.

Justice WHITE's majority opinion found that CBE was entitled to a "judgment of facial invalidity if the ordinance purported to prohibit canvassing by a substantial category of charities to which the 75-percent limitation could not be applied consistently with the [First Amendment], even if there was no demonstration that CBE itself was one of these organizations." The organizations to whom the 75% rule could not be applied were found to be those whose "primary purpose is not to provide money or services for the poor, the needy or other worthy objects of charity, but to gather and disseminate information about and advocate positions on matters of public concern." Typically, these organizations use paid employees not only to solicit funds, but also to gather information and advocate positions and thus "would necessarily spend more than 25% of their budgets on salaries and administrative expenses [but] would be completely barred from solicitation in [Schaumburg]." As to such organizations, the ordinance constituted "a direct and substantial limitation of protected activity that cannot be sustained unless it serves a sufficiently strong, subordinating interest that the Village is entitled to protect." Here, Justice White concluded, "the Village's proffered justifications are inadequate."

The Court found that the asserted interests "in protecting the public from fraud, crime and undue annoyance" were "indeed substantial," but were "only peripherally promoted by the 75-percent requirement and could be sufficiently served by measures less destructive of First Amendment interests." With respect to the prevention of fraud, the Court found the 75% rule not a justifiable device for distinguishing charitable from commercial enterprises: organizations primarily engaged in research, advocacy, or publication that use their own paid staffs to carry out these functions could not be labeled as presumptively "fraudulent" or as using the "charitable" label as a cloak for profit making. Under the First Amendment, Schaumburg had to employ more precise measures to separate genuine charitable organizations from profitmaking ones—for example, by prohibiting fraudulent misrepresentations or by requiring financial disclosures. Nor was the Court able to "perceive any substantial relationship" between the 75% rule and the interests in the protection of safety and residential privacy. Organizations devoting more than 25% of their funds to administrative expenses were no more likely "to employ solicitors who would be a threat to public safety than are other charitable organizations." And "householders are equally disturbed by solicitation on behalf of organizations satisfying the 75-percent requirement as they are by solicitation on behalf of other organizations. The 75-percent requirement protects privacy only by reducing the total number of solicitors." Moreover, "[other] provisions of the ordinance, [such as those] permitting homeowners to bar solicitors from their property by posting signs, [suggest] the availability of less intrusive and more effective measures to protect privacy. See [Rowan; Martin]."

In short, the flaw in the statute in Schaumburg was "not simply that it includes within its sweep some impermissible applications, but that in all its applications it operates on a fundamentally mistaken premise that high solicitation costs are an accurate measure of fraud." There was no obvious way for such a statute to be narrowed to a "core of easily identifiable and constitutionally proscribable conduct." In the absence of any conceivable available narrowing construction, facial invalidation was the chosen remedy. In this setting, unlike Brockett, partial invalidation was not an available option.

In **Secretary of State v. Joseph H. Munson Co.**, 467 U.S. 947 (1984), the Court extended Schaumburg to strike down a similar restriction on charitable solicitations despite its provision for a waiver if a charitable organization could demonstrate that the overhead limit "would effectively prevent [it] from raising contributions." The law was challenged by a professional fundraiser who claimed primarily the First Amendment rights of his customers, who were not parties to the action. But the Court, in an opinion by Justice BLACKMUN, found these factors insufficient to distinguish Schaumburg, as the possibility of gaining an exemption was inadequate to prevent the inhibition of protected solicitation.

In Munson, Justice Blackmun distinguished the claim at issue from the type of overbreadth claim in which the challenger's own conduct is unprotected, but the challenge is permitted in order to protect the First Amendment rights of third parties not before the Court. In Schaumburg, he suggested, the term " 'overbreadth' [was] used to describe a challenge to a statute that in *all its applications* directly restricts protected First Amendment activity and does not employ means narrowly tailored to serve a compelling governmental interest" (emphasis added).

Is the latter type of case truly an "overbreadth" case? In Justice Blackmun's interpretation of Schaumburg in Munson, the overhead limit was void "in all its applications" because it drew the wrong sort of line—it used high overhead as a proxy for fraud when such a financial structure might have indicated instead the organization's devotion to education and advocacy. Thus there was no issue whether the overbreadth was substantial or insubstantial in Broadrick's terms; the ratio of impermissible to permissible applications was infinite. Are Schaumburg and Munson simply determinations on the merits that the law amounted to impermissible speaker-based discrimination with content-differential effects? See Monaghan, supra ("[O]verbreadth determinations are simply determinations on the merits of the litigant's substantive constitutional claim."). Recall that the Court frequently invalidates speech-restrictive statutes on their face without any consideration of their overbreadth. See, for instance, Justice Scalia's majority opinion (as opposed to Justice White's concurrence) in R.A.V. v. St. Paul (1992; p. 1038 above). Is overbreadth analysis better reserved for laws that have some constitutional applications?

In Riley v. National Federation of the Blind, 487 U.S. 781 (1988), the Court continued the Schaumburg and Munson line of cases by striking down a state law defining a "reasonable fee" that a professional fundraiser may charge as a percentage of the gross revenues solicited; requiring professional fundraisers to disclose to potential donors the gross percentage of revenues retained in prior charitable solicitations; and requiring professional fundraisers to obtain a license before engaging in solicitation. Justice Brennan's prevailing opinion found this regulatory scheme insufficiently different from those at issue in Schaumburg and Munson to survive First Amendment scrutiny. Justices Scalia and Stevens concurred in part; Chief Justice Rehnquist, joined by Justice O'Connor, dissented, reasoning that the activities of large-scale professional fundraisers were "a far cry indeed" from the grass-roots charitable solicitation protected in cases like Lovell, Martin, and Schneider, and that a limitation of such fundraisers to forego unreasonable fees was not an excessive burden on their speech.

In **Illinois v. Telemarketing Associates, Inc.**, 538 U.S. 600 (2003), the Court clarified the limits of the Schaumburg, Munson, Riley line of cases, holding that these precedents did not preclude enforcement of state antifraud laws against charitable solicitors who make misleading statements about the percentage of funds raised from donors that will go to charitable purposes. The case involved a telemarketing firm retained by a nonprofit organization seeking to raise funds for Vietnam veterans. Their contract provided that the telemarketers would retain 85% of proceeds from donors in Illinois, with the veteran beneficiaries receiving 15%. The Illinois Attorney General charged the telemarketers with fraud for having allegedly made a series of particular false representations to donors that a significant amount of each dollar donated would be paid over to the veterans' organization for its charitable purposes. The Illinois courts dismissed the complaint, holding it precluded by the First Amendment under Schaumburg, Munson, and Riley. Reading those decisions differently, the Supreme Court reversed and allowed the case to proceed. Justice GINSBURG wrote for a unanimous Court:

"The First Amendment protects the right to engage in charitable solicitation. But the First Amendment does not shield fraud. Like other forms of public deception, fraudulent charitable solicitation is unprotected speech. [The] Court's opinions in Schaumburg, Munson, and Riley took care to leave a corridor open for fraud actions to guard the public against false or misleading charitable solicitations. As those decisions recognized, there are differences critical to First Amendment concerns between fraud actions trained on representations made in individual cases and statutes that categorically ban solicitations when fundraising costs run high. Simply labeling an action one for 'fraud,' of course, will not carry the day. [Had] the complaint against Telemarketers charged fraud based solely on the percentage of donations the fundraisers would retain, or their failure to alert potential donors to their fee arrangements at the start of each telephone call, [our precedents] would support swift dismissal. [But fraud actions] targeting misleading affirmative representations about how donations will be used are plainly distinguishable from the measures invalidated in Schaumburg, Munson and Riley. So long as the emphasis is on what the fundraisers misleadingly convey, and not on percentage limitations on solicitors' fees per se, such actions need not impermissibly chill protected speech. [The] gravamen of the fraud action in this case is not high costs or fees, it is particular representations made with intent to mislead."

6. ***Overbreadth and due process.*** What is the effect of a narrowing change in the challenged state law after an overbreadth lawsuit is brought? Ordinarily, an authoritative narrowing construction of an overbroad statute can blunt the effectiveness of an overbreadth attack. The effect of subsequent changes in state law came before the Court in two cases, in 1989 and 1990. The net result of the cases was that a legislative change after the lawsuit was brought could not eliminate an overbreadth challenge, but a *judicial* narrowing of an otherwise overbroad law was effective to eliminate the overbreadth concern.

In **Massachusetts v. Oakes**, 491 U.S. 576 (1989), a law that prohibited the taking of nude and similar photographs of those under the age of 18 was challenged by a man who had been convicted for taking "sexually provocative" photographs of "his partially nude and physically mature 14-year-old stepdaughter." After the highest state court had struck down the law as substantially overbroad, the legislature amended the law to add a "lascivious intent" requirement. As a result, four Justices (Justice O'Connor, joined by Chief Justice Rehnquist and Justices White and Kennedy) refused to reach the overbreadth challenge, insisting that the overbreadth doctrine did not apply to laws no longer in force: "Because it has been repealed, the former version of [the law] cannot chill protected expression in the future." A majority, however, disagreed: Justice SCALIA, joined on this issue by

Justices Blackmun, Brennan, Marshall, and Stevens, rejected the argument that an amendment could foreclose an overbreadth challenge. He explained: "It seems to me strange judicial theory that a conviction initially invalid can be resuscitated by postconviction alteration of the statute under which it was obtained. The overbreadth doctrine serves to protect constitutionally legitimate speech not merely ex post, but also ex ante, that is, when the legislature is contemplating what sort of statute to enact. If the promulgation of overbroad laws was cost free, as the plurality's new doctrine would make it—that is, if no conviction of constitutionally proscribable conduct would be lost, so long as the offending statute was narrowed before the final appeal—then legislatures would have significantly reduced incentive to stay within constitutional bounds in the first place. [In consequence,] a substantial amount of legitimate speech would be 'chilled' as a consequence of the rule the plurality would adopt." (Justice Scalia, joined by Justice Blackmun, found the law not substantially overbroad; only Justice Brennan, joined by Justices Marshall and Stevens, would have struck it down on overbreadth grounds.)

In **Osborne v. Ohio**, 495 U.S. 103 (1990), another child pornography case, Justice WHITE's majority opinion found that a *judicial* narrowing of an otherwise overbroad law *did* end the overbreadth concern. He explained: "Legislators who know they can cure their own mistakes by amendment without significant cost may not be as careful to avoid drafting overbroad statutes as they might otherwise be. But a similar effect will not be likely if a judicial construction of a statute to eliminate overbreadth is allowed to be applied in the case before the Court. This is so primarily because the legislatures cannot be sure that the statute, when examined by a court, will be saved by a narrowing construction rather than invalidated for overbreadth." Accordingly, the statute as construed could be applied "to conduct occurring prior to the construction, provided such application affords fair warning for the defendant." Here, the Court found such "fair warning" yet nevertheless held the conviction a violation of due process because the jury had not been instructed in accordance with the highest state court's subsequent narrowing construction. Do the differing results in these two cases make sense?

7. ***The Court's continued reliance on overbreadth invalidation.*** Later cases made clear that overbreadth analysis survived Broadrick and sometimes offered an attractive alternative to as-applied analysis. In **Houston v. Hill**, 482 U.S. 451 (1987), for example, overbreadth analysis enabled the Court to achieve some degree of agreement where the particular facts were substantially more problematic under the First Amendment than was the statute involved. The case arose from an incident in which Hill, a founding member of the Gay Political Caucus, observed a friend intentionally stopping traffic on a busy street, evidently to enable a vehicle to enter traffic. Two Houston police officers, one of them named Kelley, approached the friend and began speaking with him. Soon after, Hill began shouting to the officers "in an admitted attempt to divert Kelley's attention from [the friend]. Hill first shouted 'why don't you pick on somebody your own size?' After [Officer Kelley] responded '[A]re you interrupting me in my official capacity of a Houston police officer?' Hill then shouted 'Yes, why don't you pick on somebody my size?' " Hill was arrested under a section of the municipal code for "wilfully or intentionally interrupt[ing] a city policeman [by] verbal challenge during an investigation." After Hill was acquitted in a local court, he brought suit to challenge the law, under which he had been arrested

several times and which he was likely to encounter again. The text of the section provided that it was "unlawful for any person to assault, strike or in any manner oppose, molest, abuse or interrupt any policeman in the execution of his duty, or any person summoned to aid in making the arrest."

Justice BRENNAN's majority opinion found the provision overbroad under the Broadrick line of cases. Noting that the provisions dealing with assaulting and striking had been preempted by state law, he found that "the enforceable portion of the ordinance deals not with core criminal conduct, but with speech." He stated that the freedom "verbally to oppose or challenge police action without thereby risking arrest is one of the principal characteristics by which we distinguish a free nation from a police state" and found the ordinance "not narrowly tailored to prohibit only disorderly conduct or fighting words." He added: "Although we appreciate the difficulties of drafting precise laws, we have repeatedly invalidated laws that provide the police with unfettered discretion to arrest individuals for words or conduct that annoy or offend them. The Constitution does not allow such speech to be made a crime." A partial concurrence by Justice POWELL, joined by Justices O'Connor and Scalia, agreed with the overbreadth judgment, but not with its reasoning. He insisted that the view "that the ordinance 'deals not with core criminal conduct, but with speech' [draws] a distinction where none exists." He emphasized, moreover, that there was "no doubt that a municipality constitutionally may punish an individual who chooses to stand near a police officer and persistently attempts to engage the officer in conversation while the officer is directing traffic at a busy intersection." Nevertheless, he concluded that, in the absence of an authoritative limiting construction of the ordinance, it vested excessive discretion in police officers to act against protected speech and was thus unconstitutional.

Overbreadth was also the tool for fashioning agreement in **Board of Airport Commissioners v. Jews for Jesus**, 482 U.S. 569 (1987). At issue was the Board's resolution providing that "if any individual and/or entity seeks to engage in First Amendment activities within the Central Terminal Area at Los Angeles International Airport, said individual and/or entity shall be deemed to be acting in contravention of the stated policy" of the Board. Respondents, who were prevented from distributing religious literature on a pedestrian walkway in the airport, brought an action challenging the resolution. Justice O'CONNOR's opinion relied exclusively on the spectacular overbreadth of the resolution and thus was able to avoid the difficult issues of the constitutionally protected nature of the respondents' behavior and of the then-unsettled "public forum status" of an airport terminal. Speaking for a unanimous Court, she concluded that the resolution was overbroad and hence facially void: "On its face, the resolution [reaches] the universe of expressive activity [and prohibits] *all* protected expression." She noted that it reached "even talking and reading, or the wearing of campaign buttons or symbolic clothing. Under such a sweeping ban, virtually every individual who enters [the airport] may be found to violate the resolution by engaging in some 'First Amendment activit[y].' We think it obvious that such a ban cannot be justified [because] no conceivable governmental interest would justify such an absolute prohibition on speech."

In **United States v. Stevens**, 559 U.S. 460 (2010), the Court facially invalidated as overbroad 18 U.S.C. § 48, which criminalizes the commercial creation, sale, or possession of any visual or auditory depiction "in which a living animal is intentionally maimed, mutilated, tortured, wounded, or killed," if that conduct violates federal or state law where "the creation, sale, or possession takes place," unless the depiction has "serious religious, political, scientific, educational, journalistic, historical, or artistic value." Without deciding whether depictions of extreme animal cruelty might be categorically prohibited by a narrower law, the Court, in a 8–1 opinion by Chief Justice ROBERTS, held the statute invalid as overbroad because " 'a substantial number of its applications are unconstitutional, judged in relation to the statute's plainly legitimate sweep.' " (For the aspects of the decision discussing the speech in relation to other unprotected categories of speech, see p. 1126 above).

In explicating the overbreadth basis for the ruling, the Chief Justice wrote: "We read § 48 to create a criminal prohibition of alarming breadth. [The] text of the statute's ban on a 'depiction of animal cruelty' nowhere requires that the depicted conduct be cruel. [What] is more, the application of § 48 to depictions of illegal conduct extends to conduct that is illegal in only a single jurisdiction. [Views] about cruelty to animals and regulations having no connection to cruelty vary widely from place to place. In the District of Columbia, for example, all hunting is unlawful. Other jurisdictions permit or encourage hunting, and there is an enormous national market for hunting-related depictions in which a living animal is intentionally killed." The Chief Justice rejected the government's argument that the statute was sufficiently narrowed by its exemption for "any depiction that has serious religious, political, scientific, educational, journalistic, historical, or artistic value. And he denied that Miller v. California, on which the "serious value" exception was modeled, had held "that serious value could be used as a general precondition to protecting other types of speech."

Noting that "the markets for crush videos and dogfighting depictions [are] dwarfed by the market for other depictions, such as hunting magazines and videos," covered by § 48, the Chief Justice concluded that "the presumptively impermissible applications of § 48 (properly construed) far outnumber any permissible ones," and thus that the statute was facially invalid for overbreadth.

The sole dissenter, Justice ALITO, disputed the Court's conclusion that § 48 bans a substantial quantity of protected speech. Noting that overbreadth analysis should focus on "a statute's application to real-world conduct, not fanciful hypotheticals," he denied that § 48 even applies to the depictions of hunting on which the majority focused, as hunting is generally legal in all 50 states and any exceptions are not based on the prevention of animal cruelty. He also found the scope of other possible protected speech reached by the statute too trivial to warrant invalidation for substantial overbreadth, noting that "nothing in the record suggests that any one has ever created, sold, or possessed for sale a depiction of the slaughter of food animals or of the docking of the tails of dairy cows that would not easily qualify under the exception" for depictions with serious value.

For portions of the decision declining to denominate depictions of animal cruelty a new, unprotected category of speech, see p. 1126 above.

8. ***"Less restrictive means" analysis and its relation to overbreadth.*** Overbreadth cases typically emphasize the availability of more carefully tailored, narrower means to achieve legislative ends. "Less restrictive means" analysis, however, is not limited to the overbreadth

context. For example, the strict scrutiny applied to content-based laws requires carefully tailored means to "compelling" ends. Does this suggest that overbreadth is simply one application of strict scrutiny? See Monaghan, supra.

VAGUENESS

An "overbreadth" challenge should not be confused with one based on "vagueness," though a challenger will often assert both grounds of invalidity. An unconstitutionally vague statute, like an overbroad one, creates risks of a "chilling effect" upon protected speech and produces rulings of facial invalidity. But a statute can be quite specific—that is, *not* "vague"—and yet be overbroad. Consider a law forbidding "the display of a nude human body on a motion picture screen." A statute can also be vague but not overbroad. Consider a law forbidding "all unprotected speech."

1. ***Vagueness and due process.*** The concept of vagueness under the First Amendment draws on the procedural due process requirement of adequate notice, under which a law must convey "sufficiently definite warning as to the proscribed conduct when measured by common understanding and practices." Jordan v. De George, 341 U.S. 223 (1951). A law will be void on its face for vagueness if persons "of common intelligence must necessarily guess at its meaning and differ as to its application." Connally v. General Constr. Co., 269 U.S. 385 (1926). One of the purposes of this requirement is to ensure fair notice to the defendant. But the ban on vagueness protects not only liberty, but also equality and the separation of executive from legislative power through the prevention of selective enforcement. See Smith v. Goguen (1974; p. 1184 above) ("[We] have recognized [that] the more important aspect of the vagueness doctrine 'is not actual notice,' but the other principal element of the doctrine—the requirement that 'legislatures [set] reasonably clear guidelines for law enforcement officials and triers of fact in order to prevent arbitrary and discriminatory enforcement.' "); see also Kolender v. Lawson, 461 U.S. 352 (1983) (striking down on vagueness grounds a California law "that requires persons who loiter or wander on the streets to provide a 'credible and reliable' identification and to account for their presence when requested by a peace officer"); Papachristou v. Jacksonville, 405 U.S. 156 (1972) (unanimously invalidating as vague a vagrancy ordinance directed at "rogues and vagabonds, or dissolute persons who go about begging," "common drunkards," "common night walkers," "habitual loafers," and "persons wandering or strolling around from place to place without any lawful purpose or object"). See generally Amsterdam, "The Void-for-Vagueness Doctrine in the Supreme Court," 109 U. Pa. L. Rev. 67 (1960); Jeffries, "Legality, Vagueness, and the Construction of Statutes," 71 Va. L. Rev. 189 (1985).

But a finding of First Amendment vagueness has greater bite than a finding of due process vagueness. Like overbreadth challenges, vagueness challenges in the First Amendment context typically produce facial invalidations, while statutes found vague as a matter of due process typically are invalidated "as applied" to a particular defendant. Why might this be? Does it follow from a special concern about the "chilling effect" of vague statutes on protected speech? As Justice Powell wrote in Smith v. Goguen, "Where a statute's literal scope, unaided by a narrowing state court interpretation, is capable of reaching expression sheltered by the First Amendment, the [vagueness] doctrine demands a greater degree of specificity than in other contexts." And as the Court stated in Baggett v. Bullitt, 377 U.S. 360 (1964), which invalidated a loyalty oath for teachers, vague statutes cause citizens to " 'steer far wider of the unlawful zone' [than] if the boundaries of the forbidden areas were clearly marked," causing them to "restrict[ ] their conduct to that which is unquestionably safe. Free speech may not be so inhibited."

2. ***First Amendment vagueness.*** For an example of a decision finding a law impermissibly vague as well as overbroad, consider **Coates v. Cincinnati**, 402 U.S. 611 (1971): An ordinance made it illegal for "three or more persons to assemble [on] any of the sidewalks [and] there conduct themselves in a manner annoying to persons passing by." Justice STEWART's opinion found the ordinance "unconstitutionally vague because it subjects the exercise of the right of assembly to an unascertainable standard, and unconstitutionally broad because it authorizes the punishment of constitutionally protected conduct." On the vagueness point, he stated that the "annoying" criterion meant that "no standard of conduct is specified at all." With respect to overbreadth, he emphasized that the right of assembly could not be restricted "simply because its exercise may be 'annoying' to some people." Such a prohibition "contains an obvious invitation to discriminatory enforcement against those whose association together is 'annoying' because their ideas, their lifestyle or their physical appearance is resented by the majority of their fellow citizens." The majority analyzed the ordinance in Coates "on the face" rather than "as applied." It was able to state all of the facts known to the Court in a portion of a single sentence: the record "tells us no more than that [Coates] was a student involved in a demonstration and the other appellants were pickets involved in a labor dispute." To the four dissenters, that lack of record data was a major factor counseling against a ruling of unconstitutionality. Justice White's dissent argued the law was not vague on its face and added: "Even accepting the overbreadth doctrine with respect to statutes clearly reaching speech, the Cincinnati ordinance does not purport to bar or regulate speech as such."

For an example of a decision rejecting a First Amendment vagueness challenge, recall Grayned v. Rockford (1972; p. 1250 above), where Justice Marshall's opinion found an antinoise ordinance applicable to places adjacent to school buildings not vague because the state courts were likely to interpret the law "to prohibit only actual or imminent interference with the 'peace or good order' of the school." Justice Marshall argued that the ordinance was distinguishable from the ordinance in Coates or general breach of the peace ordinances because it was "written specifically for the school context, where the prohibited disturbances are easily measured by their impact on the normal activities of the school."

3. ***Vagueness and third-party standing.*** Does vagueness, like overbreadth, permit a speaker third-party standing to represent the rights of others not before the Court? It is clear that a litigant may invalidate a law on its face if it is vague in all its possible applications. For example, the Court held in Coates that "no standard of conduct is specified at all." Such a statute has no core of proscribable speech to which it might constitutionally be applied. But what if a litigant's own conduct was unquestionably within the core of the statute's permissible application, and he or she seeks to invalidate

the law because it might be vague to others? See Smith v. Goguen (White, J., concurring) (arguing that anyone of "reasonable comprehension" should have "realize[d] that sewing a flag on the seat of his pants is contemptuous of the flag"); Young v. Am. Mini Theatres (1976; p. 1085 above) (rejecting a vagueness challenge because zoning law was "unquestionably applicable" to the challengers' speech and the Court was "not persuaded" that the law would have a significant chilling effect on other protected speakers).

4. ***Vagueness and subsidies.*** Does the First Amendment prohibition on vagueness extend to vague conditions on public subsidies for speech? In **National Endowment for the Arts v. Finley**, 524 U.S. 569 (1998), the Court unanimously answered that question no. The decision upheld against facial challenge a 1990 amendment to the statutes authorizing arts grants by the National Endowment for the Arts (NEA) that required the Chairperson of the NEA to ensure that "artistic excellence and artistic merit are the criteria by which [grant] applications are judged, taking into consideration general standards of decency and respect for the diverse beliefs and values of the American public." Writing for the Court, Justice O'CONNOR stated: "Under the First and Fifth Amendments, speakers are protected from arbitrary and discriminatory enforcement of vague standards. The terms of the [NEA] provision are undeniably opaque, and if they appeared in a criminal statute or regulatory scheme, they could raise substantial vagueness concerns. It is unlikely, however, that speakers will be compelled to steer too far clear of any 'forbidden area' in the context of grants of this nature. We recognize, as a practical matter, that artists may conform their speech to what they believe to be the decision-making criteria in order to acquire funding. But when the Government is acting as patron rather than as sovereign, the consequences of imprecision are not constitutionally severe." While filing a lone dissent arguing that the provision amounted to unconstitutional viewpoint discrimination, Justice SOUTER agreed that the provision was not unconstitutionally vague: "The necessary imprecision of artistic-merit-based criteria justifies tolerating a degree of vagueness that might be intolerable when applying the First Amendment to attempts to regulate political discussion."

PRIOR RESTRAINT

The Court has frequently reiterated that prior restraint is especially disfavored under the First Amendment: "Any system of prior restraints of expression comes to this Court bearing a heavy presumption against its constitutional validity." Bantam Books, Inc. v. Sullivan, 372 U.S. 58 (1963). That theme has strong historical roots. As noted above in Chapter 11, the licensing system for English presses against which Milton protested played a central role in the development of free speech theories. Blackstone, indeed, argued that prior restraint was the *only* evil to be guarded against, and that subsequent punishment was permissible; and Holmes initially embraced that idea and abandoned it only grudgingly in Schenck. But the question whether there is contemporary justification for greater suspicion of prior restraint than of subsequent punishment is more controversial. The prior restraint concept, like the overbreadth and vagueness doctrines, focuses on the constitutional *means* of restricting speech. Thus, a prior restraint may be struck down even though the particular expression involved could validly be restricted through subsequent criminal punishment or civil liability. In examining these materials, consider especially whether the special hostility to prior restraint is justified, either as a theoretical or a practical matter.

LICENSING

1. ***The concern with administrative discretion.*** What's wrong with licensing? What are the evils of a system that requires preclearance of speech by an official censor? Recall the cases involving standardless licensing of speech in the public forum. Those cases found standardless licensing schemes to confer excessive discretion on public officials, creating the risk of selective and content-discriminatory enforcement. Because of concern with the risks of abuse of discretionary authority, laws granting excessive discretion have been invalidated on their face, apart from any showing that, as applied, the discretion was in fact unconstitutionally abused and without any showing by the challenger that specific protected speech was curtailed.

In **Lovell v. Griffin**, 303 U.S. 444 (1938), the Court invalidated a conviction under an ordinance of the city of Griffin, Georgia, prohibiting the distribution of "circulars, handbooks, advertising, or literature of any kind" within the city "without first obtaining written permission from the City Manager." A Jehovah's Witness distributed religious tracts without applying for a permit. She challenged her conviction on free press and free exercise of religion grounds. Chief Justice HUGHES's opinion for a unanimous Court, in reversing her conviction, stated: "The ordinance is not limited to 'literature' that is obscene or offensive to public morals or that advocates unlawful conduct. [It] embraces 'literature' in the widest sense. The ordinance is comprehensive with respect to the method of distribution. There is thus no restriction in its application with respect to time or place. It is not limited to ways which might be regarded as inconsistent with the maintenance of public order or as involving disorderly conduct, the molestation of the inhabitants, or the misuse or littering of the streets. The ordinance prohibits the distribution of literature of any kind at any time, at any place, and in any manner without a permit from the City Manager.

"We think that the ordinance is invalid on its face. Whatever the motive which induced its adoption, its character is such that it strikes at the very foundation of the freedom of the press by subjecting it to license and censorship. The struggle for the freedom of the press was primarily directed against the power of the licensor. [The] liberty of the press became initially a right to publish '*without* a license what formerly could be published only *with* one.' While this freedom from previous restraint upon publication cannot be regarded as exhausting the guaranty of liberty, the prevention of that restraint was a leading purpose in the adoption of the [First Amendment]. As the ordinance is void on its face, it was not necessary for appellant to seek a permit under it. She was entitled to contest its validity in answer to the charge against [her]."

The reasons for *facially* invalidating licensing laws that grant excessive administrative discretion, as opposed to allowing licensees to challenge abuses of discretion case by case, were elaborated in the 4–3 decision (Chief Justice Rehnquist and Justice Kennedy did not participate) in **Lakewood v. Plain Dealer Publishing Co.**, 486 U.S. 750 (1988). At issue was a local ordinance restricting the placement of newspaper vending racks on public property. Newsracks could be placed on public property only upon an application for and receipt of an annual permit that could be denied for a number of specified reasons including "other terms and conditions deemed necessary and reasonable by the Mayor." Justice BRENNAN's opinion for the Court allowed a facial challenge to the ordinance: "[W]e have [identified] two major First Amendment risks associated with unbridled licensing schemes: self-censorship by speakers in order to avoid being denied a license to speak; and the difficulty of effectively detecting, reviewing, and correcting content-based censorship 'as applied' without standards by which to measure the licensor's action. It is when statutes threaten these risks to a significant degree that courts must entertain an immediate facial attack on the law. Therefore, a facial challenge lies whenever a licensing law gives a government official or agency substantial power to discriminate based on the content or viewpoint of speech by suppressing disfavored speech or disliked speakers."

The Court went on to find these criteria for facial challenges satisfied here: "[The City's scheme is] the sort of system in which an individual must apply for multiple licenses over time, or periodically renew a license. [In addition,] the licensing system [is directed] narrowly and specifically at expression or conduct commonly associated with expression: the circulation of newspapers. Such a framework [establishes] an official charged particularly with reviewing speech, or conduct commonly associated with it, breeding an 'expertise' tending to favor censorship over speech. [Because] of these features in the regulatory system [here], we think that a facial challenge is appropriate, and that standards controlling the Mayor's discretion must be required. Of course, the City may require periodic licensing, and may even have special licensing procedures for conduct commonly associated with expression; but the Constitution requires that [it] establish neutral criteria to insure that the licensing decision is not based on the content or viewpoint of the speech being considered."

Having decided to entertain the facial challenge, the Court had little difficulty in holding the standardless ordinance unconstitutional: "The City asks us to presume that the Mayor will deny a permit application only for reasons related to the health, safety, or welfare of Lakewood [citizens]. This presumes the Mayor will act in good faith and adhere to standards absent from the statute's face. But this is the very presumption that the doctrine forbidding unbridled discretion disallows. The doctrine requires that the limits that the City claims are implicit in its law be made explicit by textual incorporation, binding judicial or administrative construction, or well-established practice. This Court will not write nonbinding limits into a silent state statute."

Justice WHITE, joined by Justices Stevens and O'Connor, dissented. He viewed facial challenges as the exception and not the rule, and an exception that in past cases had been allowed only in those circumstances in which the relevant conduct could not have been prohibited entirely. But where there is no such absolute right to engage in the relevant conduct, he argued, a scheme allowing that conduct under some circumstances but not others should be actionable only if and when it is actually applied in an unconstitutional manner: "[T]he [Lovell] lines of cases would be applicable here if the [City] sought to license the distribution of all newspapers in the City, or if it required licenses for all stores which sold newspapers. These are obviously newspaper circulation activities which a municipality cannot prohibit and therefore, any licensing scheme of this scope would have to pass muster under the [Lovell] doctrine. But—and this is critical—Lakewood has not cast so wide a net. Instead, it has sought to license only the placement of newsracks [on] City property. As I read our precedents, the [Lovell] line of cases is applicable here only if the Plain Dealer has a constitutional right to distribute its papers by means of dispensing devices or newsboxes, affixed to the public sidewalks. I am not convinced that this is the case. [Where] an activity that could be forbidden altogether (without running afoul of the First Amendment) is subjected to a local license requirement, the mere presence of administrative discretion in the licensing scheme will not render it invalid per se. In such a case—which does not involve the exercise of First Amendment protected freedoms—the [Lovell] doctrine does not apply, and our usual rules concerning the permissibility of discretionary local licensing laws (and facial challenges to those laws) must prevail. [The] Court mentions the risk of censorship, the ever-present danger of censorship, and the power of prior restraint to justify the result. Yet these fears and concerns have little to do with this case, which involves the efforts of Ohio's largest newspaper to place a handful of newsboxes in a few locations in a small suburban community. [It] is hard to see how the Court's concerns have any applicability here."

2. ***Procedural safeguards.*** The flaws of a licensing scheme may be corrected as a substantive matter by the provision of objective standards for the licensor to administer. Should procedural safeguards also be required to check abuses of administrative discretion? Some decades ago, the Court's special suspicion of excessive discretion by administrators had especially frequent airings in the context of motion picture licensing, under censorship schemes then widely in use. Beginning with Joseph Burstyn, Inc. v. Wilson, 343 U.S. 495 (1952), the Court scrutinized the statutory standards in film licensing schemes with special care, to avoid abuse of administrative discretion. The Court declined to impose a ban on all prior restraints of films, see Times Film Corp. v. Chicago, 365 U.S. 43 (1961), but repeatedly invalidated particular laws because they lacked adequate specificity, see, e.g., Burstyn (invalidating a ban on a movie as "sacrilegious"). But in the Freedman case in 1965, the Court announced "procedural safeguards designed to obviate the dangers of a censorship system"—safeguards which have proven important in the protection of First Amendment interests in contexts well beyond the obscenity area. On special procedural safeguards in the First Amendment context generally, see Monaghan, "First Amendment 'Due Process,'" 83 Harv. L. Rev. 518 (1970); and Bogen, "First Amendment Ancillary Doctrines," 37 Md. L. Rev. 679 (1978).

Freedman v. Maryland, 380 U.S. 51 (1965), was a successful constitutional challenge to the procedural aspects of a Maryland motion picture censorship law. The challenger exhibited a movie without first submitting the picture to the state censorship board. He was convicted for failure to submit the film for licensing (even though the State conceded that the movie would have been licensed if it had been properly submitted). He argued that the censorship scheme was an invalid prior restraint. He focused particularly on the procedure for an initial decision by the censorship board which, without any judicial participation, effectively barred exhibition of any disapproved film unless and until the exhibitor undertook a time-consuming appeal to the state courts in order to get the censorship agency's decision reversed. The statute did not impose a time limit for completion of judicial review.

The Court, in an opinion by Justice BRENNAN, found the statutory procedure, especially its long time delays for the review process, unconstitutional. Noting that "[risk] of delay is built into the Maryland procedure," Justice Brennan stressed the "heavy presumption" against the validity of prior restraints, noted that a state "is not free to adopt whatever procedures it pleases for dealing with obscenity [without] regard to the possible consequences for constitutionally protected speech," and added: "The administration of a censorship system for motion pictures presents peculiar dangers to constitutionally protected speech. Unlike a prosecution for obscenity, a censorship proceeding puts the initial burden on the exhibitor or distributor. Because the censor's business is to censor, there inheres the danger that he may well be less responsive than a court [to] the constitutionally protected interests in free expression. And if it is made unduly onerous, by reason of delay or otherwise, to seek judicial review, the censor's determination may in practice be final."

The Court proceeded to identify several constitutionally mandated safeguards: "[W]e hold that a noncriminal process which requires the prior submission of a film to a censor avoids constitutional infirmity only if it takes place under procedural safeguards designed to obviate the dangers of a censorship system. First, the burden of proving that the film is unprotected expression must rest on the censor. As we said in Speiser v. Randall, 'Where the transcendent value of speech is involved, due process certainly requires [that] the State bear the burden of persuasion to show that the appellants engaged in criminal speech.' Second, while the State may require advance submission of all films, in order to proceed effectively to bar all showings of unprotected films, the requirement cannot be administered in a manner which would lend an effect of finality to the censor's determination whether a film constitutes protected expression. [Because] only a judicial determination in an adversary proceeding ensures the necessary sensitivity to freedom of expression, only a procedure requiring a judicial determination suffices to impose a valid final restraint. To this end, the exhibitor must be assured [that] the censor will, within a specified brief period, either issue a license or go to court to restrain showing the film. Any restraint imposed in advance of a final judicial determination on the merits must similarly be limited to preservation of the status quo for the shortest fixed period compatible with sound judicial resolution. Moreover, we are well aware that, even after expiration of a temporary restraint, an administrative refusal to license [may] have a discouraging effect on the exhibitor. Therefore, the procedure must also assure a prompt final judicial decision, to minimize the deterrent effect of an interim and possibly erroneous denial of a license. It is readily apparent that the Maryland procedural scheme does not satisfy these criteria [and it therefore constitutes] an invalid previous restraint." A concurrence by Justice DOUGLAS, joined by Justice Black, stated: "I do not believe any form of censorship—no matter how speedy or prolonged it may be—is permissible."

The Freedman standards were relied on in Justice O'Connor's plurality opinion in **FW/PBS, Inc. v. Dallas**, 493 U.S. 215 (1990). The case held that an ordinance requiring the licensing of sexually oriented businesses was an unconstitutional prior restraint in violation of Freedman because there was no "effective limitation on the time within which the licensor's decision must be made" and because the ordinance failed to provide "an avenue for a prompt judicial review." But Justice O'Connor also held that Freedman's requirement that the licensor bear the burden of going to court and the burden of proof was inapplicable where there was no "direct censorship of particular expressive material." Since the licensing board evaluated the business and not each film or book, it was not "passing judgment on the content of any protected speech" and thus a truncated version of the Freedman requirements was sufficient. Justice White (joined by Chief Justice Rehnquist) and Justice Scalia would have upheld the scheme without applying any of the Freedman requirements.

In **Thomas v. Chicago Park District**, 534 U.S. 316 (2002), Justice SCALIA, speaking for a unanimous Court, held that Freedman's procedural requirements did not apply to "a municipal park ordinance requiring individuals to obtain a permit before conducting large-scale events." The ordinance at issue required permits for any " 'public assembly, parade, picnic, or other event involving more than fifty individuals,' " and for any activity featuring amplified sound. Permit applications were to be processed in order of receipt, and the Park District was required to render decisions on applications within 14 days, with the option to extend the decision period by one additional 14-day term. The ordinance enumerated specific grounds for denying an application, and required the District to notify applicants in writing of the reason for denial and suggest alternative times and places if the denial was because of scheduling conflicts for use of the requested venue. Denials were appealable to the Park District superintendent, and applicants could also seek judicial review in state court by common law certiorari.

Justice Scalia wrote: "Freedman is inapposite because the licensing scheme at issue here is not subject-matter censorship but content-neutral time, place, and manner regulation of the use of a public forum. The Park District's ordinance does not authorize a licensor to pass judgment on the content of speech: None of the grounds for denying a permit has anything to do with what a speaker might say. Indeed, the ordinance (unlike the classic censorship scheme) is not even directed to communicative activity as such, but rather to *all* activity conducted in a public park. The picnicker and soccer-player, no less than the political activist or parade marshal, must apply for a permit if the 50-person limit is to be exceeded. And the object of the permit system [is] not to exclude communication of a particular content, but to coordinate multiple uses of limited space, to assure preservation of the park facilities, to prevent uses that are dangerous, unlawful, or impermissible under the Park District's rules, and to assure financial accountability for damage caused by the event.

"We have never required that a content-neutral permit scheme regulating speech in a public forum adhere to the procedural requirements set forth in Freedman. [Such] a traditional exercise of authority does not raise the censorship concerns that prompted us to impose the extraordinary procedural safeguards on the film licensing process in Freedman." Although the specific requirements of Freedman did not apply, the Court recognized the possibility that content-neutral time, place, and manner restrictions might be applied in a discriminatory manner. "Where the licensing official enjoys unduly broad discretion in determining whether to grant or deny a permit, there is a risk that he will favor or disfavor speech based on its content. See Forsyth County [(1992; p. 997 above)]. We have thus required that a time, place, and manner regulation contain adequate standards to guide the official's decision and render it subject to effective judicial review."

The Park District ordinance passed that test: "[Under the ordinance,] the Park District may deny a permit only for one or more of the reasons set forth in the ordinance. [These] grounds are reasonably specific and objective, and do not leave the decision 'to the whim of the administrator.' They provide 'narrowly drawn, reasonable and definite standards' to guide the licensor's determination. And they are enforceable on review—first by appeal to the General Superintendent of the Park District, and then by writ of common-law certiorari in the Illinois courts."

Although the law specified only that the District "may" deny permits on the specified grounds, rather than requiring denial in every instance of violation, the Court did not consider this grant of discretion to be a flaw: "[Granting] waivers to favored speakers (or, more precisely, denying them to disfavored speakers) would of course be unconstitutional, but we think that this abuse must be dealt with if and when a pattern of unlawful favoritism appears, rather than by insisting upon a degree of rigidity that is found in few legal arrangements. [The] prophylaxis achieved by insisting upon a rigid, no-waiver application of the ordinance requirements would be far outweighed [by] the accompanying senseless prohibition of speech (and of other activity in the park) by organizations that fail to meet the technical requirements of the ordinance but for one reason or another pose no risk of the evils that those requirements are designed to avoid."

3. ***Standing to challenge licensing schemes.*** The Court allowed both Lovell and Freedman to challenge the licensing scheme at issue on its face, without their having applied for and been refused a license. As the Court explained in Lovell: "As the ordinance is void on its face, it was not necessary for appellant to seek a permit under it. She was entitled to contest its validity in answer to the charge against [her]." See also Shuttlesworth v. Birmingham, 394 U.S. 147 (1969) (invalidating on its face, as conferring "virtually unbridled and absolute power," a parade permit ordinance authorizing the city commission to deny a permit if "in its judgment the public welfare, peace, safety, health, decency, good order, morals, or convenience require" as much, at the behest of a civil rights marcher who had not sought or obtained a permit).

Thus speakers need not challenge the denial of permission in advance—or even to seek permission—where the claim is that the law is unconstitutional *on its face.* But if the challenge is that a valid permit law is unconstitutionally *applied,* the challengers may not go ahead and hold their meeting or parade if they want to preserve their constitutional defenses. In **Poulos v. New Hampshire**, 345 U.S. 395 (1953), for example, a conviction for holding a meeting in a park without a required permit was sustained without considering the argument that the denial had been arbitrary, because the speakers had not gone to court to challenge the denial of the permission. In Poulos, unlike Lovell, the law requiring a permit was valid on its face; it was the administrative denial of the permit that was claimed to be unconstitutional. Justice REED was unpersuaded by the defendant's objection that "his right to preach may be postponed until a case, possibly after years, reaches this Court for final adjudication of constitutional rights": "Delay is unfortunate, but the expense and annoyance of litigation is a price citizens must pay for life in an orderly society where the rights of the First Amendment have a real and abiding meaning." Has such delay been curtailed as a result of the "careful procedural provisions"—including time requirements—required by Freedman?

4. ***What distinction between prior restraint and subsequent punishment?*** Consider the following arguments that prior restraints are

worse than subsequent punishments: (1) It is easier for an official to restrict speech "by a simple stroke of the pen" than by the more cumbersome apparatus of subsequent punishment and thus prior restraint is likely to restrict more speech. (2) Censors will have a professional bias in favor of censorship, and thus will systematically overvalue government interests and undervalue speech. (3) Censors operate more informally than judges and so afford less procedural safeguards to speakers. (4) Speech suppressed in advance never reaches the marketplace of ideas at all. (5) When speech is suppressed in advance, there is no empirical evidence from which to measure its alleged likely harms; subsequent punishment will thus afford more protection to speech whose bark is worse than its bite. See Emerson, "The Doctrine of Prior Restraint," 20 Law & Contemp. Probs. 648 (1955).

Some of these asserted justifications go to the timing of the restraint. Are such justifications coherent? Doesn't the threat of subsequent punishment, if it is effective, have an equally deterrent effect on speech? Consider the following comment: "The doctrine of prior restraint focuses on the largely irrelevant *timing* of the restraint, to the detriment of attention to those flaws that are the actual source of the objection. It is the identity and discretion of the restrainers and not the timing of the restraint that is important." Schauer, Free Speech: A Philosophical Enquiry 152 (1982). Other justifications above concern the institutional features of administrative licensing schemes. Are such problems cured by the substantive safeguards of objective standards and the procedural safeguards of Freedman? Do they exist at all when the prior restraint is issued not by an executive official but by a judge? Consider the following comment: the only legitimate basis for hostility to interim prior restraints is that "they authorize abridgment of expression prior to a full and fair determination of the constitutionally protected nature of the expression by an independent judicial forum." Redish, "The Proper Role of the Prior Restraint Doctrine in First Amendment Theory," 70 Va. L. Rev. 53 (1984).

In **Kingsley Books, Inc. v. Brown**, 354 U.S. 436 (1957), the Court itself suggested that prior restraints—at least in a scheme with clear standards and speedy judicial hearings—are *not* inevitably more harmful to speech than subsequent punishments. That 5–4 decision sustained a New York procedure, § 22–a, which authorized an injunction to prevent the sale and distribution of allegedly obscene printed matter pending an expedited trial. Kingsley consented to a preliminary injunction and, after trial, his books were found obscene, their further distribution was enjoined, and they were ordered destroyed. Kingsley did not challenge the finding of obscenity, but objected to the injunction as a prior restraint. In sustaining the procedure, Justice FRANKFURTER's opinion stated:

"The phrase 'prior restraint' is not a self-wielding sword. Nor can it serve as a talismanic test. [One] would be bold to assert that the in terrorem effect of [criminal sanctions] less restrains booksellers in the period before the law strikes than does § 22–a. Instead of requiring the bookseller to dread that the offer for sale of a book may, without prior warning, subject him to a criminal prosecution, [the] civil procedure assures him that such consequences cannot follow unless he ignores a court order specifically directed to him for a prompt and carefully circumscribed determination of the issue of obscenity. Until then, he may keep the book for sale and sell it on his own judgment rather than steer 'nervously among the treacherous shoals.'

"[Criminal] enforcement and the proceeding under § 22–a interfere with a book's solicitation of the public precisely at the same stage. In each situation the law moves after publication; the book need not in either case have yet passed into the hands of the public. [In] each case the bookseller is put on notice by the complaint that sale of the publication charged with obscenity in the period before trial may subject him to penal consequences. In the one case he may suffer fine and imprisonment for violation of the criminal statute, in the other, for disobedience of the temporary injunction. The bookseller may of course stand his ground and confidently believe that in any judicial proceeding the book could not be condemned as obscene, but both modes of procedure provide an effective deterrent against distribution prior to adjudication of the book's content—the threat of subsequent penalization."

For further commentary on the distinction between prior restraints and subsequent punishments, see Blasi, "Prior Restraints on Demonstrations," 68 Mich. L. Rev. 1481 (1970); Barnett, "The Puzzle of Prior Restraint," 29 Stan. L. Rev. 539 (1977); Fiss, The Civil Rights Injunction (1978); Blasi, "Toward a Theory of Prior Restraint: The Central Linkage," 66 Minn. L. Rev. 11 (1981); Mayton, "Toward a Theory of First Amendment Process: Injunctions of Speech, Subsequent Punishment, and the Costs of the Prior Restraint Doctrine," 67 Cornell L. Rev. 245 (1982); Jeffries, "Rethinking Prior Restraint," 92 Yale L.J. 409 (1983); and Scordato, "Distinction Without a Difference: A Reappraisal of the Doctrine of Prior Restraint," 68 N.C. L. Rev. 1 (1989).

INJUNCTIONS

Licensing schemes were the paradigmatic prior restraint against which the First Amendment was directed. The institutional weaknesses of a licensing scheme include the fact that an executive official charged with protecting the public from dangerous speech may have excessive zeal for censorship and little incentive to protect speech. But aren't the structural incentives different when a judge is asked to restrain speech? Is not the judge a neutral magistrate who will consider speech interests in the balance? Why, then, extend the doctrine against prior restraints to judicial injunctions restricting speech?

That prior restraints are presumptively forbidden even to judges was made clear in the following case, Near v. Minnesota. A Minnesota law authorized abatement, as a public nuisance, of a "malicious, scandalous and defamatory newspaper, or other periodical." A prosecutor sought to abate publication of "The Saturday Press." The Press had published articles charging in substance "that a Jewish gangster was in control of gambling, bootlegging and racketeering in Minneapolis, and that law enforcing officers and agencies were not energetically performing their duties." The Press especially targeted the chief of police, who was charged with several loosely defined offenses, e.g., "illicit relations with gangsters [and] participation in graft." A state court order "abated" the Press and perpetually enjoined the defendants from publishing or circulating "any publication whatsoever which is a malicious, scandalous or defamatory newspaper." The Supreme Court set aside this state injunction:

Near v. Minnesota ex rel. Olson

283 U.S. 697, 51 S. Ct. 625, 75 L. Ed. 1357 (1931).

■ CHIEF JUSTICE HUGHES delivered the opinion of the Court.

[The] object of the [nuisance abatement] statute is not punishment, in the ordinary sense, but suppression of the offending newspaper. [The] reason for the enactment [is] that prosecutions to enforce penal statutes for libel do not result in "efficient repression or suppression of the evils of scandal." [The] operation and effect of the statute [is] that public authorities may bring the owner or publisher of a newspaper or periodical before a judge upon a charge of conducting a business of publishing scandalous and defamatory matter [and] unless the owner or publisher is able [to prove] that the charges are true and are published with good motives and for justifiable ends, his newspaper or periodical is suppressed and further publication is made punishable as a contempt. This is of the essence of censorship.

The question is whether a statute authorizing such proceedings [is] consistent with the conception of the liberty of the press as historically conceived and guaranteed. In determining the extent of the constitutional protection, it has been generally, if not universally, considered that it is the chief purpose of the guaranty to prevent previous restraints upon publication. The struggle in England, directed against the legislative power of the licenser, resulted in renunciation of the censorship of the press. The liberty deemed to be established was thus described by Blackstone: "The liberty of the press is indeed essential to the nature of a free state; but this consists in laying no *previous* restraints upon publications, and not in freedom from censure for criminal matter when [published]." [The] criticism upon Blackstone's statement has not been because immunity from previous restraint upon publication has not been regarded as deserving of special emphasis, but chiefly because that immunity cannot be deemed to exhaust the conception of the liberty guaranteed by state and federal [constitutions].

[The] protection even as to previous restraint is not absolutely unlimited. But the limitation has been recognized only in exceptional cases. [No] one would question but that a government might prevent actual obstruction to its recruiting service or the publication of the sailing dates of transports or the number and location of troops. On similar grounds, the primary requirements of decency may be enforced against obscene publications. The security of the community life may be protected against incitements to acts of violence and the overthrow by force of orderly government. These limitations are not applicable [here].

The fact that for approximately [150] years there has been almost an entire absence of attempts to impose previous restraints upon publications relating to the malfeasance of public officers is significant of the deep-seated conviction that such restraints would violate constitutional right. Public officers, whose character and conduct remain open to debate and free discussion in the press, find their remedies for false accusations in actions under libel laws providing for redress and punishment, and not in proceedings to restrain the publication of newspapers and periodicals. [The] fact that the liberty of the press may be abused by miscreant purveyors of scandal does not make any the less necessary the immunity of the press from previous restraint in dealing with official misconduct. Subsequent punishment for such abuses as may exist is the appropriate remedy, consistent with constitutional privilege.

The statute in question cannot be justified by reason of the fact that the publisher is permitted to show, before injunction issues, that the matter published is true and is published with good motives and for justifiable ends. If such a statute [is] valid, it would be equally permissible for the legislature to provide that at any time the publisher of any newspaper could be brought before a court, or even an administrative officer, and required to produce proof of the truth of his publication, or of what he intended to publish and of his motives, or stand enjoined. If this can be done, the legislature may provide the machinery for determining in the complete exercise of its discretion what are justifiable ends and restrain publication accordingly. And it would be but a step to a complete system of censorship. [We] hold the statute, so far as it authorized the proceedings in this action, [to] be an infringement of the liberty of the press guaranteed by the [14th Amendment]. [Reversed.]

■ JUSTICE BUTLER joined by JUSTICES VAN DEVANTER, MCREYNOLDS, and SUTHERLAND, dissenting.

[T]he *previous restraint* referred to by [Blackstone] subjected the press to the arbitrary will of an administrative officer. [The] Minnesota statute does not operate as a *previous* restraint on publication within the proper meaning of that phrase. It does not authorize administrative control in advance such as was formerly exercised by the licensers and censors but prescribes a remedy to be enforced by a suit in equity. In this case there was previous publication made in the course of the business of regularly producing malicious, scandalous and defamatory periodicals. The business and publications unquestionably constitute an abuse of the right of free press. [There] is no question of the power of the State to denounce such transgressions. The restraint authorized is only in respect of continuing to do what has been duly adjudged to constitute a nuisance. [It] is fanciful to suggest similarity between the granting or enforcement of the decree authorized by this statute to prevent *further* publication of malicious, scandalous and defamatory articles and the *previous restraint* upon the press by licensers as referred to by Blackstone and described in the history of the times to which he [alludes]. It is well known [that] existing libel laws are inadequate effectively to suppress evils resulting from the kind of [publications] that are shown in this case. The doctrine [of this ruling] exposes the peace and good order of every community and the business and private affairs of every individual to the constant and protracted false and malicious assaults of any insolvent publisher who may have purpose and sufficient capacity to contrive and put into effect a scheme or program for oppression, blackmail or extortion.[1]

---

1. ***Judges and prior restraint.*** Why should an injunction ever be considered a prior restraint? A judicial determination lacks the institutional features that make administrative censorship particularly suspect: it is formal rather than informal, a judge is not in the business of censorship, and

[1] For the history of Near v. Minnesota, see Friendly, Minnesota Rag: The Dramatic Story of the Landmark Supreme Court Case That Gave New Meaning to Freedom of the Press (1981).

it requires some consideration of evidence rather than a mere stroke of the pen. See Redish, "The Proper Role of the Prior Restraint Doctrine in First Amendment Theory," 70 Va. L. Rev. 53 (1984) (suggesting that permanent injunctions issued after trial are far less problematic than nonjudicial administrative licensing schemes, with preliminary injunctions and temporary restraining orders falling in between). Yet the Court in Near and later cases has extended the presumption against prior restraint in the licensing context to judicial restraints as well. For the view that Near was not really about the procedural problem of prior restraint, but rather the substantive problem of seditious libel, see Jeffries, "Rethinking Prior Restraint," 92 Yale L.J. 409 (1983).

2. ***The "collateral bar" rule.*** A frequent explanation for the extension of prior restraint doctrine to injunctions stems from the "collateral bar rule": the rule that an injunction must be obeyed until lifted, and that if it is violated, its unconstitutionality is no defense to a finding of contempt. Perhaps the most famous application of the rule arose in connection with a Good Friday civil rights protest march in Birmingham in 1963, led by several black ministers, including the Rev. Martin Luther King, Jr. The marchers challenged a Birmingham parade permit ordinance that was ultimately found to be unconstitutional. They marched in the face of an ex parte injunction directing compliance with the ordinance without challenging the injunction in court before marching. Indeed, they openly flouted the injunction because they considered it "raw tyranny."

In **Walker v. Birmingham**, 388 U.S. 307 (1967), the Court held, by a vote of 5–4, that the marchers could not defend against contempt charges by asserting the unconstitutionality of the ordinance or the injunction. Justice STEWART, writing for the Court, concluded: "This Court cannot hold that the petitioners were constitutionally free to ignore all the procedures of the law and carry their battle to the streets." The Alabama courts had justifiably relied on the general rule that court orders must be obeyed until "reversed for error by orderly review." Justice BRENNAN's dissent, joined by Chief Justice Warren and Justices Douglas and Fortas, insisted that the Court had elevated a "rule of judicial administration above the right of free expression."

Note that the Court in Walker suggested that the case might have come out differently if the injunction had been "transparently invalid." Does this afford some greater latitude to disobey injunctions? Recall that Lovell, Freedman, and Shuttlesworth were permitted to disobey permit schemes found by the Court to be facially unconstitutional. Why should those bound by an injunction be more restricted? See generally Blasi, "Prior Restraints on Demonstrations," 68 Mich. L. Rev. 1481 (1970).

Moreover, the Court has mitigated the effect of Walker by imposing procedural safeguards limiting the power of courts to issue speech-restrictive injunctions. For example, in **Carroll v. President & Commissioners of Princess Anne**, 393 U.S. 175 (1968), the Court found unconstitutional the ex parte procedure followed in issuing a 10-day temporary restraining order against holding a public rally. Petitioners had held a meeting at which they made "aggressively and militantly racist" speeches to a crowd of both whites and blacks. They announced that they would resume the rally the following night. Before then, local officials obtained the order restraining petitioners and their "white supremacist" National States Rights Party from holding meetings "which will tend to disturb and endanger the citizens of the County." There was no notice to petitioners prior to the issuance of the order.

The rally was cancelled and petitioners (rather than ignoring the injunction as in Walker) challenged the injunction in court. Justice FORTAS's opinion for the Court found no adequate justification for the ex parte nature of the proceedings. In the rare situations where prior restraints were permissible, "the Court has insisted upon careful procedural provisions. [Freedman.] [There] is a place in our jurisprudence for ex parte issuance, without notice, of temporary restraining orders of short duration; but there is no place within the area of basic freedoms guaranteed by the First Amendment for such orders where no showing is made that it is impossible to serve or to notify the opposing parties and to give them an opportunity to participate." Here, procedural care was even more important than in the obscenity context of Freedman: "The present case involves a rally and 'political' speech in which the element of timeliness may be important." Without an adversary hearing, there was "insufficient assurance of the balanced analysis and careful conclusions which are essential in the area of First Amendment adjudication."

PRIOR RESTRAINT AND NATIONAL SECURITY

Recall that in Near, the Court cautioned that the presumption against prior restraint is not absolute: "No one would question but that a government might prevent actual obstruction to its recruiting service or the publication of the sailing dates of transports or the number and location of troops." When, if ever, are concerns of national security sufficient to justify a prior restraint? The following cases explore this question:

New York Times Co. v. United States [The Pentagon Papers Case]

403 U.S. 713, 91 S. Ct. 2140, 29 L. Ed. 2d 822 (1971).

■ PER CURIAM.

We granted certiorari in these cases in which the United States seeks to enjoin the New York Times and the Washington Post from publishing the contents of a classified study entitled "History of U.S. Decision-Making Process on Viet Nam Policy."[1]

---

[1] Portions of that secret Defense Department study (popularly known as the "Pentagon Papers") were published by The New York Times (beginning June 13, 1971) and the Washington Post (on June 18, 1971). The top-secret study reviewed in considerable detail the formulation of American policy toward Indochina, including military operations and diplomatic negotiations. The newspapers obtained this study from Daniel Ellsberg, a former Pentagon official. The government actions to restrain further publication made their way through two district courts and two courts of appeals between June 15 and June 23. The Government claimed that publication would interfere with national security and would undermine the ability to conduct diplomatic negotiations, produce the death of military personnel, and prolong the war. On June 25, the Supreme Court granted certiorari in the Times and Post cases. The cases were argued on June 26 and the decision was issued on June 30, 1971. Restraining orders remained in effect while the decision was pending. (Four Justices—Black, Douglas, Brennan, and Marshall—dissented from the decision to grant certiorari and urged summary action instead, stating that they "would not continue the restraint" on the newspapers.) For insight into the history of the

"Any system of prior restraints of expression comes to this Court bearing a heavy presumption against its constitutional validity." [Bantam Books; see Near.] The Government "thus carries a heavy burden of showing justification for the enforcement of such a restraint." The [District Court] in the New York Times case and the [District Court] and the [Court of Appeals] in the Washington Post case held that the Government had not met that burden. We agree. [The] stays entered June 25, 1971, by the [Second Circuit] are vacated.

■ JUSTICE BLACK, with whom JUSTICE DOUGLAS joins, concurring.

[I] believe that every moment's continuance of the injunctions against these newspapers amounts to a flagrant, indefensible, and continuing violation of the First Amendment. Furthermore, after oral arguments, I agree completely [with] my Brothers Douglas and Brennan. In my view it is unfortunate that some of my Brethren are apparently willing to hold that the publication of news may sometimes be enjoined. Such a holding would make a shambles of the First Amendment. [The] press was protected [by the First Amendment] so that it could bare the secrets of government and inform the people. Only a free and unrestrained press can effectively expose deception in government. [To] find that the President has "inherent power" to halt the publication of news by resort to the courts would wipe out the First Amendment. [The] word "security" is a broad, vague generality whose contours should not be invoked to abrogate the fundamental law embodied in the [First Amendment].

■ JUSTICE DOUGLAS, with whom JUSTICE BLACK joins, concurring.

[The First Amendment] leaves [no] room for governmental restraint on the press. There is, moreover, no statute barring the publication by the press of the material which the Times and Post seek to use. [18 U.S.C. § 793(e), prohibiting "communication" of information relating to the national defense that could be used to the injury of the United States, does not apply to publication.] [I]t is apparent that Congress was capable of and did distinguish between publishing and communication in the various sections of the Espionage Act.[2] So any power that the Government possesses must come from its "inherent power." The power to wage war is "the power to wage war successfully." But the war power stems from a declaration of war. The Constitution by Article I, § 8, gives Congress, not the President, power "to declare War." Nowhere are presidential wars authorized.

[These] disclosures[3] may have a serious impact. But that is no basis for sanctioning a previous restraint on the press. [Near.] [The] Government says that it has inherent powers to go into court and obtain an injunction to

litigation, see Oakes, "The Doctrine of Prior Restraint Since the Pentagon Papers," 15 U. Mich. J.L. Reform 497 (1982).

[2] Justice Douglas added: "The other evidence that § 793 does not apply to the press is a rejected version of § 793. That version read: 'During any national emergency, [the] President may [prohibit] the publishing or communicating of [any] information relating to the national defense which, in his judgment, is of such character that it is or might be useful to the enemy.' During the [1917] debates in the Senate the First Amendment was specifically cited and that provision was defeated."

[3] There are numerous sets of this material in existence and they apparently are not under any controlled custody. Moreover, the President has sent a set to the Congress. We start then with a case where there already is rather wide distribution of the material that is destined for publicity, not secrecy. I have gone over the material listed in the in camera brief of the United States. It is all history, not future events. None of it is more recent than 1968. [Footnote by Justice Douglas.]

protect [national] security. [Near] repudiated that expansive doctrine in no uncertain terms. The dominant purpose of the First Amendment was to prohibit the widespread practice of governmental suppression of embarrassing information. [A] debate of large proportions goes on in the Nation over our posture in Vietnam. The debate antedated the disclosure of the contents of the present documents. The latter are highly relevant to the debate in progress. Secrecy in government is fundamentally anti-democratic, perpetuating bureaucratic errors. Open debate and discussion of public issues are vital to our national health. [The] stays in these cases that have been in effect for more than a week constitute a flouting of the principles of the [First Amendment].

■ JUSTICE BRENNAN, concurring.

The error that has pervaded these cases from the outset was the granting of any injunctive relief whatsoever, interim or otherwise. The entire thrust of the Government's claim throughout these cases has been that publication of the material sought to be enjoined "could," or "might," or "may" prejudice the national interest in various ways. But the First Amendment tolerates absolutely no prior judicial restraints of the press predicated upon surmise or conjecture that untoward consequences may result.[4] Our cases, it is true, have indicated that there is a single, extremely narrow class of cases in which the First Amendment's ban on prior judicial restraint may be overridden. Our cases have thus far indicated that such cases may arise only when the Nation "is at war" [Schenck], during which times "no one would question but that a government might prevent actual obstruction to its recruiting service or the publication of the sailing dates of transports or the number and location of troops." [Near.] Even if the present world situation were assumed to be tantamount to a time of war, or if the power of presently available armaments would justify even in peacetime the suppression of information that would set in motion a nuclear holocaust, in neither of these actions has the Government presented or even alleged that publication of items from or based upon the material at issue would cause the happening of an event of that nature. "The chief purpose of [the First Amendment's] guarantee [is] to prevent previous restraints upon publication." [Near.] Thus, only governmental allegation and proof that publication must inevitably, directly and immediately cause the occurrence of an event kindred to imperiling the safety of a transport already at sea can support even the issuance of an interim restraining order. [Unless] and until the Government has clearly made out its case, the First Amendment commands that no injunction may issue.

■ JUSTICE STEWART, with whom JUSTICE WHITE joins, concurring.

[The] only effective restraint upon executive policy and power in the areas of national defense and international affairs may lie in an enlightened citizenry. [For] this reason, it is perhaps here that a press that is alert, aware, and free most vitally serves the basic purpose of the First Amendment. [Yet] it is elementary that the successful conduct of international diplomacy and the maintenance of an effective national

[4] Freedman v. Maryland and similar cases regarding temporary restraints of allegedly obscene materials are not in point. For those cases rest upon the proposition that "obscenity is not protected by the freedoms of speech and press." Here there is no question but that the material sought to be suppressed is within the protection of the First Amendment; the only question is whether, notwithstanding that fact, its publication may be enjoined for a time because of the presence of an overwhelming [national interest]. [Footnote by Justice Brennan.]

defense require both confidentiality and secrecy. [I] think there can be but one answer to this dilemma, if dilemma it be. The responsibility must be where the power is. [The] Executive must have the largely unshared duty to determine and preserve the degree of internal security necessary to exercise [its] power successfully. [It] is the constitutional duty of the Executive—as a matter of sovereign prerogative and not as a matter of law as the courts know law—through the promulgation and enforcement of executive regulations to protect the confidentiality necessary to carry out its responsibilities in the fields of international relations and national defense. This is not to say that Congress and the courts have no role to play. Undoubtedly Congress has the power to enact specific and appropriate criminal laws to protect government property and preserve government secrets. [But] in the cases before us we are asked neither to construe specific regulations nor to apply specific laws. We are asked, instead, to perform a function that the Constitution gave to the Executive, not the Judiciary. We are asked, quite simply, to prevent the publication by two newspapers of material that the Executive Branch insists should not, in the national interest, be published. I am convinced that the Executive is correct with respect to some of the documents involved. But I cannot say that disclosure of any of them will surely result in direct, immediate, and irreparable damage to our Nation or its people. That being so, there can under the First Amendment be but one judicial resolution of the issues before us. I join the judgments of the Court.

■ JUSTICE WHITE, with whom JUSTICE STEWART joins, concurring.

I concur in today's judgments, but only because of the concededly extraordinary protection against prior restraints enjoyed by the press under our constitutional system. I do not say that in no circumstances would the First Amendment permit an injunction against publishing information about government plans or operations. Nor, after examining the materials the Government characterizes as the most sensitive and destructive, can I deny that revelation of these documents will do substantial damage to public interests. Indeed, I am confident that their disclosure will have that result. But I nevertheless agree that the United States has not satisfied the very heavy burden which it must meet to warrant an injunction against publication in these cases, at least in the absence of express and appropriately limited congressional authorization for prior restraints in circumstances such as these.

The Government's position is simply stated: The responsibility of the Executive for the conduct of the foreign affairs and for the security of the Nation is so basic that the President is entitled to an injunction against publication of a newspaper story whenever he can convince a court that the information to be revealed threatens "grave and irreparable" injury to the public interest; and the injunction should issue whether or not the material to be published is classified, whether or not publication would be lawful under relevant criminal statutes enacted by Congress and regardless of the circumstances by which the newspaper came into possession of the information. At least in the absence of legislation by Congress, based on its own investigations and findings, I am quite unable to agree that the inherent powers of the Executive and the courts reach so far as to authorize remedies having such sweeping potential for inhibiting publications by the press. [To] sustain the Government in these cases would start the courts down a long and hazardous road that I am not willing to travel, at least without congressional guidance and direction.

[Prior] restraints require an unusually heavy justification under the First Amendment; but failure by the Government to justify prior restraints does not measure its constitutional entitlement to a conviction for criminal publication. That the Government mistakenly chose to proceed by injunction does not mean that it could not successfully proceed in another way. [Justice White discussed a number of "potentially relevant" criminal provisions.] It is thus clear that Congress has addressed itself to the problems of protecting the security of the country and the national defense from unauthorized disclosure of potentially damaging information. Youngstown Sheet & Tube Co. v. Sawyer, 343 U.S. 579 (1952) (the Steel Seizure Case). It has not, however, authorized the injunctive remedy against threatened publication. It has apparently been satisfied to rely on criminal sanctions and their deterrent effect on the responsible as well as the irresponsible press. I am not, of course, saying that either of these newspapers has yet committed a crime or that either would commit a crime if they published all the material now in their possession. That matter must await resolution in the context of a criminal proceeding if one is [instituted].[5]

■ JUSTICE MARSHALL, concurring.

[I] believe the ultimate issue in this case [is] whether this Court or the Congress has the power to make law. [I]n some situations it may be that under whatever inherent powers the [Executive may have], there is a basis for the invocation of the equity jurisdiction of this Court as an aid to prevent the publication of material damaging to "national security," however that term may be defined. It would, however, be utterly inconsistent with the concept of separation of powers for this Court to use its power of contempt to prevent behavior that Congress has specifically declined to prohibit. There would be a similar damage to the basic concept of these co-equal branches of Government if when the [executive] had adequate authority granted by Congress to protect "national security" it can choose instead to invoke the contempt power of a court to enjoin the threatened conduct. [In] these cases we are not faced with a situation where Congress has failed to provide the Executive with broad power to protect the Nation from disclosure of damaging state secrets. [See the power to "classify" secret materials in 18 U.S.C. Chapter 37, Espionage and Censorship.] [It] is plain that Congress has specifically refused to grant the authority the Government seeks from this Court. [It] is not for this Court to fling itself into every breach perceived by some Government [official].

■ JUSTICE HARLAN, with whom CHIEF JUSTICE BURGER and JUSTICE BLACKMUN join, dissenting.

[It] is plain to me that the scope of the judicial function in passing upon the activities of the Executive Branch of the Government in the field of foreign affairs is very narrowly restricted. This view is, I think, dictated by the concept of separation of powers upon which our constitutional system

[5] On July 1, 1971—the day after the decision in this case—Attorney General Mitchell commented that the Justice Department "will prosecute all those who have violated federal criminal laws in connection with this matter" and added: "A review of the Court's opinions indicates that there is nothing in them to affect the situation." Daniel Ellsberg and Anthony Russo (the government officials accused of leaking the Pentagon Papers) were subsequently indicted by a grand jury under provisions of federal espionage, theft, and conspiracy laws. Another federal grand jury investigated the involvement of newspapers and reporters. On May 11, 1973, District Judge Matthew Byrne dismissed the Ellsberg-Russo indictment and granted a mistrial based on prosecutorial misconduct, namely that the government had illegally wiretapped the men and lost files pertaining to the taps.

rests. [I] agree that, in performance of its duty to protect the values of the First Amendment against political pressures, the judiciary must review the initial Executive determination to the point of satisfying itself that the subject matter of the dispute does lie within the proper compass of the President's foreign relations power. [Moreover], the judiciary may properly insist that the determination that disclosure of the subject matter would irreparably impair the national security be made by the head of the Executive Department concerned [after] actual personal consideration by that officer. [But] in my judgment the judiciary may not properly go beyond these two inquiries and redetermine for itself the probable impact of disclosure on the national security.

[Even] if there is some room for the judiciary to override the executive determination, it is plain that the scope of review must be exceedingly narrow. I can see no indication in the opinions of [the lower courts] in the Post litigation that the conclusions of the Executive were given even the deference owing to an administrative agency, much less that owing to a co-equal branch of the Government operating within the field of its constitutional prerogative. [Pending] further hearings in each case conducted under the appropriate ground rules, I would continue the restraints on publication. I cannot believe that the doctrine prohibiting prior restraints reaches to the point of preventing courts from maintaining the status quo long enough to act responsibly in matters of such national importance as those involved here.

■ JUSTICE BLACKMUN, dissenting.

I join Justice Harlan in his dissent. [The] First Amendment, after all, is only one part of an entire Constitution. First Amendment absolutism has never commanded a majority of this Court. [E.g., Near; Schenck.] What is needed here is a weighing, upon properly developed standards, of the broad right of the press to print and of the very narrow right of the Government to prevent. Such standards are not yet developed. The parties here are in disagreement as to what those standards should be. But even the newspapers concede that there are situations where restraint is in order and is constitutional. [I] therefore would remand [for the orderly presentation of evidence]. I hope that damage has not already been done. If, however, damage has been done, and if, with the Court's action today, these newspapers proceed to publish the critical documents and there results therefrom "the death of soldiers, the destruction of alliances, the greatly increased difficulty of negotiation with our enemies, the inability of our diplomats to negotiate," to which list I might add the factors of prolongation of the war and of further delay in the freeing of United States prisoners, then the Nation's people will know where the responsibility for these sad consequences rests.

[Chief Justice BURGER's dissent stated that he agreed "generally" with Justices Harlan and Blackmun, but that he was "not prepared to reach the merits." He urged that the temporary restraining orders be extended pending a full trial on the merits. He commented that the cases had been "conducted in unseemly haste" and that "we literally do not know what we are acting on."]

THE SCOPE AND LIMITS OF PENTAGON PAPERS

1. ***Bombmaking instructions.*** Were the principles of Near and the Pentagon Papers case properly applied in **United States v. Progressive, Inc.**, 467 F. Supp. 990 (W.D. Wis. 1979)? There, the district court issued an order enjoining The Progressive, a monthly magazine, from publishing technical material on hydrogen bomb design in an article entitled "The H-Bomb Secret: How We Got It, Why We're Telling It." The author and publisher claimed that the article merely synthesized information available in public documents, insisting that the article would contribute to informed opinion about nuclear weapons and would benefit the nation by demonstrating that open debate was preferable to "an oppressive and ineffective system of secrecy and classification." In issuing the temporary injunction, the district judge distinguished the Pentagon Papers case on three grounds: (1) the documents there had contained only "historical data"; (2) the Government there had not proved that publication affected the national security; and (3) the Government there had failed to establish a statutory basis for injunctive relief.[1]

Although the Government conceded that at least some of the information in the article had been declassified or was in the public domain, it argued that the interest in "national security" permitted it to bar publication of information "originating in the public domain, if when drawn together, synthesized and collated, such information acquires the character of presenting immediate, direct and irreparable harm to the interests of the United States." It submitted affidavits from Cabinet members asserting that publication would increase the risk of thermonuclear proliferation. The district judge accepted the Government's key claims. He noted that the article "contains concepts that are not found in the public realm, concepts that are vital to the operation of the bomb." Moreover, despite the prior declassification of some of the materials in the article, he found that "the danger lies in the exposition of certain concepts never heretofore disclosed in conjunction with one another." Although the district judge conceded that the article probably did not "provide a 'do-it-yourself' guide for the hydrogen bomb," he noted that the article "could possibly provide sufficient information to allow a medium size nation to move faster in developing a hydrogen weapon."

In justifying "the first instance of prior restraint against a publication in this fashion in the history of this country," the district judge explained: "A mistake in ruling against The Progressive [will] curtail defendants' First Amendment rights in a drastic and substantial fashion. [But a] mistake in ruling against the United States could pave the way for thermonuclear annihilation for us all. In that event, our right to life is extinguished and the right to publish becomes moot." He concluded: "Because of this 'disparity of risk,' because the government has met its heavy burden of showing justification for the imposition of a prior restraint, [and] because the Court

[1] For statutory support, the district court relied primarily upon the Atomic Energy Act of 1954, which imposes sanctions on anyone who "communicates, transmits, or discloses [restricted data] with reason to believe such data will be utilized to injure the United States or to secure an advantage to any foreign nation." 42 U.S.C. § 2274(b). The Act also authorizes the Government to seek injunctive relief. 42 U.S.C. § 2280. The trial court ruled that the statute and its definition of "restricted data"—including "all data concerning design, manufacture, or utilization of atomic weapons"—were neither vague nor overbroad "[a]s applied to this case" and that the prohibition against one who "communicates" extended to publication in a magazine.

is unconvinced that suppression of the objected-to technical portions of the [article] would in any plausible fashion impede the defendants in their laudable crusade to stimulate public knowledge of nuclear armament and bring about enlightened debate on national policy questions, the Court finds that the objected-to portions of the article fall within the narrow area recognized by the Court in Near v. Minnesota in which a prior restraint on publication is appropriate."[2] He added: "In view of the showing of harm made by the United States, a preliminary injunction would be warranted even in the absence of statutory authorization because of the existence of the likelihood of direct, immediate and irreparable injury to our nation and its people. New York Times (Justice Stewart)."[3]

2. ***Alternative sanctions.*** Even if it may not restrain the press, may the government seek civil and criminal remedies against former employees who publish secret information? Dicta in the Pentagon Papers case suggested as much. May the government impose employment sanctions as well? Obviously it may fire or demote an employee who divulges secrets. The question of further remedies against a former government employee who had agreed not to disclose confidential government information without authorization came before the Court in **Snepp v. United States**, 444 U.S. 507 (1980). Snepp, a former CIA employee, had agreed not to divulge classified information without authorization and not to publish any information relating to the Agency without prepublication clearance. Without submitting his manuscript for clearance, he published a book about CIA activities in Vietnam. (The Government did not claim that the book contained classified data.) The Court of Appeals held that Snepp could be subjected to punitive damages, but refused to impress a constructive trust on his profits from the book. The Supreme Court's per curiam reversal, decided without oral argument, held that punitive damages were an inappropriate and inadequate remedy and instead imposed a constructive trust on Snepp's profits. The majority's only mention of the First Amendment came in a footnote insisting that "this Court's cases make clear that—even in the absence of an express agreement—the CIA could have acted to protect substantial government interests by imposing reasonable restrictions on employee activities that in other contexts might be protected by the First Amendment. The Government has a compelling interest in protecting both the secrecy of information important to our national security and the appearance of confidentiality so essential to the effective operation of our foreign intelligence service. The agreement that Snepp signed is a reasonable means for protecting this vital interest." A dissent by Justice STEVENS, joined by Justices Brennan and Marshall, objected not only to the Court's extraordinary procedure (deciding without argument an issue raised only in the Government's conditional cross-petition for certiorari, filed to bring the

---

[2] In arguing that the Near exception applied, the district judge pointed to the "troop movements" reference there and added: "Times have changed significantly since 1931 when Near was decided. Now war by foot soldiers has been replaced in large part by war by machines and bombs. No longer need there be any advance warning or any preparation time before a nuclear war could be commenced. In light of these factors, this court concludes that publication of the technical information of the hydrogen bomb contained in the article is analogous to publication of troop movements or locations in time of war and falls within the extremely narrow exception to the rule against prior restraint."

[3] The Government's proceedings against The Progressive were abandoned before full appellate proceedings and a hearing regarding a permanent injunction could take place, because similar information pertaining to nuclear weapons was published independently by others while the litigation was under way.

entire case up in the event the Court granted Snepp's certiorari petition), but also to the Court's fashioning of a "drastic new remedy [to] enforce a species of prior restraint on a citizen's right to criticize his government."

For commentary on Pentagon Papers and related problems, see, for example, Symposium, "National Security and the First Amendment," 26 Wm. & Mary L. Rev. 715 (1985); and Cox, "Foreword—Freedom of Expression in the Burger Court," 94 Harv. L. Rev. 1 (1980). For commentary on Snepp, see Easterbrook, "Insider Trading, Secret Agents, Evidentiary Privileges, and the Production of Information," 1981 Sup. Ct. Rev. 309; Medow, "The First Amendment and the Secrecy State," 130 U. Pa. L. Rev. 775 (1982); and Sunstein, "Government Control of Information," 74 Calif. L. Rev. 889 (1986).

3. ***Prior restraint and WikiLeaks.*** How should Pentagon Papers inform modern-day challenges to government efforts to curb speech on national security grounds? In 2010 and 2011, WikiLeaks—a self-described "not-for profit media organization"—made several high-profile disclosures of classified U.S. materials, including military footage, confidential diplomatic cables, and other sensitive government documents. Predictably, the disclosures precipitated swift and harsh responses from the media and political figures, many of whom sought to distinguish WikiLeaks from the Pentagon Papers.

Does the rationale of the Pentagon Papers case extend to WikiLeaks? Should a prior restraint on expression by such groups be barred only when, as Justice Stewart stated, disclosure would "surely result in direct, immediate, and irreparable damage to our Nation and its people"? Or do the unique circumstances of the WikiLeaks disclosures warrant a different approach? For opposing perspectives, see Benkler, "A Free Irresponsible Press: Wikileaks and the Battle Over the Soul of the Networked Fourth Estate," 46 Harv. C.R.-C.L. L. Rev. 311 (2011) and Bellia, "WikiLeaks and the Institutional Framework for National Security Disclosures," 121 Yale L.J. 1448 (2012). Note that in April 2019, the Department of Justice revealed that it had charged Julien Assange, founder of WikiLeaks, with conspiracy to commit computer intrusion.

PRIOR RESTRAINT AND FAIR TRIAL

In **Nebraska Press Ass'n v. Stuart**, 427 U.S. 539 (1976), the Court considered the permissibility of a prior restraint on the press imposed in the interest of protecting a criminal defendant's right to a fair trial before an impartial jury. The Court reemphasized the high constitutional barriers to prior restraints and held the challenged pretrial restraint unconstitutional.

The state court "gag order," issued in anticipation of a trial in a widely publicized mass murder case, prohibited publication or broadcasting of the accused's confessions or admissions, and of any other facts "strongly implicative" of the accused. In his majority opinion, Chief Justice BURGER found that "the showing before the state court" did not justify the order. Though Chief Justice Burger rejected the priority, "in all circumstances," of the "right to publish" over the "right of an accused," he found a common thread in the prior decisions such as Near and Pentagon Papers: "[P]rior restraints [are] the most serious and least tolerable infringement on First

Amendment rights. A criminal penalty or [a defamation judgment] is subject to the whole panoply of protections afforded by deferring the impact of the judgment until all avenues of appellate review have been exhausted. [A] prior restraint [has] an immediate and irreversible sanction. If it can be said that a threat of criminal or civil sanctions after publication 'chills' speech, prior restraint 'freezes' it at least for the time." Moreover, "the protection against prior restraints should have particular force as applied to reporting of criminal proceedings."

Chief Justice Burger noted that, although the trial judge could reasonably conclude, "based on common human experience, that publicity might impair" the defendant's rights by affecting prospective jurors, that conclusion "was of necessity speculative." Moreover, alternative measures to curb the impact of media publicity might well have been effective: for example, change of venue; postponement of the trial; careful questioning of jurors; jury instructions; sequestration of jurors; and curbing statements by the contending lawyers, the police, and witnesses. Chief Justice Burger also questioned the efficacy of any restraint of the media, in view of the likelihood of rumors in a sensational case. Turning to the terms of the order, he especially objected to the ban on reporting "implicative" information as "too vague and too broad." He concluded that, though there was no doubt about "the gravity of the evil pretrial publicity can work, [the] probability that it would do so here was not demonstrated with the degree of certainty our cases on prior restraint require."

Justices POWELL and WHITE, while joining the majority opinion, each submitted brief concurring statements. Justice Powell emphasized "the unique burden" on a proponent of prior restraint on pretrial publicity. Justice White indicated his "grave doubt [whether] orders with respect to the press such as were entered in this case would ever be justifiable."

In an opinion concurring only in the judgment, Justice BRENNAN, joined by Justices Stewart and Marshall, urged an absolute ban on prior restraints issued in the interest of a fair trial: "I would hold [that] resort to prior restraints on the freedom of the press is a constitutionally impermissible method for enforcing [the right to a fair trial]; judges have at their disposal a broad spectrum of devices for ensuring that fundamental fairness is accorded the accused without necessitating so drastic an incursion on the equally fundamental and salutary constitutional mandate that discussion of public affairs in a free society cannot depend on the preliminary grade of judicial censors." He emphasized that "[c]ommentary and reporting on the criminal justice system is at the core of First Amendment values." Though he recognized pretrial publicity could "destroy the fairness of a criminal trial," he viewed the bar on prior restraints on the press as applicable "no matter how shabby the means by which the information is obtained." He added in a footnote that this did "not necessarily immunize [the press] from civil liability for libel or invasion of privacy or from criminal liability for transgressions of general criminal laws during the course of obtaining that information."

Justice Brennan stressed that, under Near and its progeny, exceptions to the ban on prior restraints were confined to "exceptional cases." He insisted that the narrow national security exception recognized in dicta in Near and Pentagon Papers did not mean, as the highest state court had assumed in this case, "that prior restraints can be justified on an ad hoc balancing approach that concludes that the 'presumption' must be overcome in light of some perceived 'justification.'" Rather, "prior restraints even within a recognized exception to the rule against prior restraints will be extremely difficult to justify; but as an initial matter, the purpose for which a prior restraint is sought to be imposed 'must fit within one of the narrowly defined exceptions to the prohibition against prior restraints.'" And there was no justification here for creating "a new, potentially pervasive exception [for fair trial purposes] to this settled rule of virtually blanket prohibition of prior restraints." He added that "speculative deprivation of an accused's Sixth Amendment right to an impartial jury [is not] comparable to the damage to the Nation or its people that Near and [Pentagon Papers] would have found sufficient to justify a prior restraint on reporting."

In another separate opinion concurring in the judgment, Justice STEVENS stated that he subscribed to "most" of Justice Brennan's opinion, but pointed out some problems he was not yet ready to resolve: "Whether the same absolute protection would apply no matter how shabby or illegal the means by which the information is obtained, no matter how serious an intrusion on privacy might be involved, no matter how demonstrably false the information might be, no matter how prejudicial it might be to the interests of innocent persons, and no matter how perverse the motivation for publishing it, is a question I would not answer without further argument."

Does the Court's special hostility to prior restraint in Nebraska Press underestimate the damage that might be done by other methods of restricting pretrial reporting? Does that emphasis implicitly open the door to other sanctions that may threaten free speech and press to a similar degree, such as subsequent punishment of reporters and orders excluding the press and public from hearings?

CHAPTER 13

BEYOND SPEAKING—COMPELLED SPEECH, ASSOCIATION, MONEY AND THE MEDIA

The Supreme Court has interpreted the right of free speech to entail several associated rights: the right *not* to speak, the right to associate with others for expressive purposes (and *not* to associate), and the right to facilitate speech through the expenditure of money in connection with political campaigns. None of these rights is separately enumerated in the First Amendment, except to the extent that the right of association derives in part from "the right of the people peaceably to assemble, and to petition the Government for a redress of grievances." The right to "freedom of the press," in contrast, is separately enumerated.

These rights are examined in this chapter in turn. Section 1 examines claims that the government may not force one to speak or to serve as a mouthpiece or platform for the speech of others. Section 2 considers what regulations restricting group activities or compelling disclosure about them might violate the First Amendment right of association, or the right against compelled association. Section 3 deals with efforts to regulate the use of money in political campaigns. The "speech" involved here is manifested in funds directed to the support of candidates and causes. Section 4 surveys a series of problems involving the institutional media, considers whether the media are entitled to special protection because "the press" is separately mentioned in the text of the First Amendment, and examines the Court's different treatment of the print and broadcasting media as well as its treatment of cable and the Internet.

SECTION 1. COMPELLED SPEECH: THE RIGHT *NOT* TO SPEAK

Does the right to speak free of government interference entail a right to be free of government compulsion to speak? May government use citizens as mouthpieces for official orthodoxy? May government compel citizens to serve as vehicles for favored expression even if the speech so favored does not express the government's point of view? Any particular point of view? May government compel citizens to provide access to their property for the speech of others? Does it matter whether that property ordinarily has an expressive function? Does it matter why government has sought to compel such access? Does it matter to whom bystanders are likely to attribute the content of the required speech? The following cases examine these questions.

COMPELLED INDIVIDUAL SPEECH

1. ***Citizens as mouthpieces.*** In several cases in the 1940s, members of Jehovah's Witnesses attacked public school regulations requiring students to salute the flag and recite the pledge of allegiance. The challengers claimed that their participation in the exercises amounted to the worship of "graven images" in a manner "forbidden by command of scripture," and thus that the state's requirements violated their rights to the free exercise of religion and to freedom of speech. In the first case, **Minersville School Dist. v. Gobitis**, 310 U.S. 586 (1940), the Court sustained the flag salute requirement by a vote of 8–1. Justice FRANKFURTER found no grounds for a free exercise exemption, then added in his opinion the Court: "[Nor] does the freedom of speech assured by Due Process move in a more absolute circle of immunity than that enjoyed by religious freedom. Even if it were assumed that freedom of speech goes beyond the historic concept of full opportunity to utter and to disseminate views, however heretical or offensive to dominant opinion, and includes freedom from conveying what may be deemed an implied but rejected affirmation, the question remains whether school children [must] be excused from conduct required of all the other children in the promotion of national cohesion. We are dealing with an interest inferior to none in the hierarchy of legal values. National unity is the basis of national security. To deny the legislature the right to select appropriate means for its attainment presents a totally different order of problem from that of the propriety of subordinating the possible ugliness of littered streets to the free expression of opinion through distribution of handbills. [The] case before us must be viewed as though the legislature of Pennsylvania had itself formally directed the flag-salute for the children of Minersville; had made no exemption for children whose parents were possessed of conscientious scruples like those of the Gobitis family; and had indicated its belief in the desirable ends to be secured by having its public school children share a common experience at those periods of development when their minds are supposedly receptive to its assimilation. The precise issue, then, for us to decide is whether the legislatures of the various states and the authorities in a thousand counties and school districts of this country are barred from determining the appropriateness of various means to evoke that unifying sentiment without which there can ultimately be no liberties, civil or religious. To stigmatize legislative judgment in providing for this universal gesture of respect for the symbol of our national life in the setting of the common school as a lawless inroad on that freedom of conscience which the Constitution protects, would amount to no less than the pronouncement of pedagogical and psychological dogma in a field where courts possess no marked and certainly no controlling competence. For ourselves, we might be tempted to say that the deepest patriotism is best engendered by giving unfettered scope to the most crotchety beliefs. But the courtroom is not the arena for debating issues of educational policy. So to hold would in effect make us the school board for the country. That authority has not been given to this Court, nor should we assume it. Except where the transgression of constitutional liberty is too plain for argument, personal freedom is best maintained—so long as the remedial channels of the democratic process remain open and unobstructed—when it is ingrained in a people's habits and not enforced against popular policy by the coercion of adjudicated law. A society which is dedicated to the preservation of these ultimate values of civilization may in self-protection utilize the educational process for inculcating those almost unconscious feelings which bind men together in a comprehending loyalty,

whatever may be their lesser differences and difficulties. That is to say, the process may be utilized so long as men's right to believe as they please, to win others to their way of belief, and their right to assemble in their chosen places of worship for the devotional ceremonies of their faith, are all fully respected. Judicial review, itself a limitation on popular government, is a fundamental part of our constitutional scheme. But to the legislature no less than to courts is committed the guardianship of deeply-cherished liberties."

In his solo dissent, Justice STONE wrote: "The law which is thus sustained is unique in the history of Anglo-American legislation. It does more than suppress freedom of speech and more than prohibit the free exercise of religion, which concededly are forbidden by the First Amendment and are violations of the liberty guaranteed by the Fourteenth. For by this law the state seeks to coerce these children to express a sentiment which, as they interpret it, they do not entertain, and which violates their deepest religious convictions. The guaranties of civil liberty are but guaranties of freedom of the human mind and spirit and of reasonable freedom and opportunity to express them. They presuppose the right of the individual to hold such opinions as he will and to give them reasonably free expression, and his freedom, and that of the state as well, to teach and persuade others by the communication of ideas. The very essence of the liberty which they guaranty is the freedom of the individual from compulsion as to what he shall think and what he shall say, at least where the compulsion is to bear false witness to his religion. If these guaranties are to have any meaning they must, I think, be deemed to withhold from the state any authority to compel belief or the expression of it where that expression violates religious convictions, whatever may be the legislative view of the desirability of such compulsion. We have previously pointed to the importance of a searching judicial inquiry into the legislative judgment in situations where prejudice against discrete and insular minorities may tend to curtail the operation of those political processes ordinarily to be relied on to protect minorities. See United States v. Carolene Products Co., 304 U.S. 144, 152, note 4 [supra, (p. 503)]."

In the aftermath of the Court's holding in Gobitis, Jehovah's Witnesses were targeted for a wave of abuse throughout the country. The ruling "was handed down June 3, 1940, as routed French and British troops [fighting in World War II] were desperately being evacuated from Dunkirk. Many Americans regarded the Witnesses' refusal to recite the pledge as evidence of disloyalty and of their sympathy and even collaboration with the Nazi regime. [For example, in] Richmond, West Virginia, a group of American Legion vigilantes, led by a sheriff's deputy, forced several witnesses to drink large quantities of castor oil, roped them together, then paraded them through the town. Over five hundred taunting citizens followed the procession, which at one point was halted for an impromptu flag salute ceremony . . . the [Jehovah's] Witnesses were [then] marched to the edge of town, where they found their automobiles painted with swastikas and graffiti accusing them of being 'Hitler's spies' and a 'Fifth Column.' Hundreds of other similar events occurred throughout the country. One Deep-South sheriff explained his refusal to intervene when a mob began throwing pieces of wood and rubble at a procession of Jehovah's Witnesses by remarking of the Witnesses that "[t]hey're traitors—the Supreme Court says so. Ain't you heard?" Blasi & Shiffrin, The Story of W. Virginia State Bd. of Educ. v. Barnette 109–11 *in* First Amendment Stories (Garnett & Koppelman eds., 2012).

It was in the backdrop of this religiously motivated violence that the Court would revisit the pledge of allegiance issue in **West Virginia State Bd. of Educ. v. Barnette**, 319 U.S. 624 (1943). Justice JACKSON, who had not been on the Court that decided Gobitis, wrote for the Court in Barnette. Analyzing the issue in terms of free speech rather than free exercise, he held that the state was precluded from making the flag salute and pledge compulsory: "[T]he compulsory flag salute and pledge requires affirmation of a belief and an attitude of mind. It is not clear whether the regulation contemplates that pupils forego any contrary convictions of their own and become unwilling converts to the prescribed ceremony or whether it will be acceptable if they simulate assent by words without belief and by a gesture barren of meaning. [Either way,] the power of compulsion is invoked without any allegation that remaining passive during a flag salute ritual creates a clear and present danger that would justify an effort even to muffle expression. To sustain the compulsory flag salute we are required to say that a Bill of Rights which guards the individual's right to speak his own mind, left it open to public authorities to compel him to utter what is not in his mind."

Having found that the compulsory flag salute implicated freedom of speech, Justice Jackson rejected the argument, relied upon in Gobitis, that the matter should be left to the legislature: "The very purpose of the Bill of Rights was to withdraw certain subjects from the vicissitudes of political controversy, to place them beyond the reach of majorities and officials and to establish them as legal principles to be applied by the courts. One's right to life, liberty, and property, to free speech, a free press, freedom of worship and assembly, and other fundamental rights may not be submitted to vote; they depend on the outcome of no elections. [First Amendment rights] are susceptible of restriction only to prevent grave and immediate danger to interests which the State may lawfully protect."

Finally, he rejected the adequacy of the state's justification that the flag salute promoted national unity: "National unity as an end which officials may foster by persuasion and example is not in question. The problem is whether under our Constitution compulsion as here employed is a permissible means for its achievement. Struggles to coerce uniformity of sentiment in support of some end thought essential to their time and country have been waged by many good as well as by evil men. [Ultimate] futility of such attempts to compel coherence is the lesson of every such effort from the Roman drive to stamp out Christianity as a disturber of its pagan unity, the Inquisition, as a means to religious and dynastic unity, the Siberian exiles as a means to Russian unity, down to the fast failing efforts of our present totalitarian enemies. Those who begin coercive elimination of dissent soon find themselves exterminating dissenters. Compulsory unification of opinion achieves only the unanimity of the graveyard. It seems trite but necessary to say that the First Amendment to our Constitution was designed to avoid these ends by avoiding these beginnings."

He concluded: "[W]e apply the limitations of the Constitution with no fear that freedom to be intellectually and spiritually diverse or even contrary will disintegrate the social organization. To believe that patriotism will not flourish if patriotic ceremonies are voluntary and spontaneous instead of a compulsory routine is to make an unflattering estimate of the appeal of our institutions to free minds. We can have intellectual individualism and the rich cultural diversities that we owe to exceptional minds only at the price of occasional eccentricity and abnormal attitudes. When they are so harmless to others or to the State as those we deal with here, the price is not too great. But freedom to differ is not limited to things that do not matter much. That would be a mere shadow of freedom. The test of its substance is the right to differ as to things that touch the heart of the existing order. If there is any fixed star in our constitutional constellation, it is that no official, high or petty, can prescribe what shall be orthodox in politics, nationalism, religion, or other matters of opinion or force citizens to confess by word or act their faith therein."

Justice BLACK, joined by Justice Douglas, submitted a "statement of reasons for our change of view" since Gobitis. Despite the private urgings of Justice Murphy that he avoid bringing personal matters into his opinion, Justice FRANKFURTER wrote a lengthy dissent, which began: "One who belongs to the most vilified and persecuted minority in history is not likely to be insensible to the freedoms guaranteed by our Constitution. Were my purely personal attitude relevant I should whole-heartedly associate myself with the general libertarian views in the Court's opinion, representing as they do the thought and action of a lifetime. But as judges we are neither Jew nor Gentile, neither Catholic nor agnostic. We owe equal attachment to the Constitution and are equally bound by our judicial obligations whether we derive our citizenship from the earliest or the latest immigrants to these shores. As a member of this Court I am not justified in writing my private notions of policy into the Constitution, no matter how deeply I may cherish them or how mischievous I may deem their disregard. [I]t can never be emphasized too much that one's own opinion about the wisdom or evil of a law should be excluded altogether when one is doing one's duty on the bench. [Of course] patriotism cannot be enforced by the flag salute. But neither can the liberal spirit be enforced by judicial invalidation of illiberal legislation." Justices Roberts and Reed joined Justice Frankfurter in adhering to Gobitis.

Gobitis and Barnette were factually identical cases. Why then did the Court treat Gobitis primarily as a free exercise of religion case, and Barnette primarily as a freedom of speech case? Is there any political or doctrinal significance in the decision to use one framework rather than the other?

2. ***Citizens as mobile billboards.*** The Court relied heavily on Barnette in **Wooley v. Maynard**, 430 U.S. 705 (1977). The case involved a New Hampshire law requiring most automobiles to bear license plates carrying the state motto, "Live Free or Die." Challengers were a married couple, members of Jehovah's Witnesses, who found the motto repugnant to their moral, religious and political beliefs and who covered up the motto on their license plate, a misdemeanor. Chief Justice BURGER's majority opinion stated: "Here, as in Barnette, we are faced with a state measure which forces an individual as part of his daily life—indeed constantly while his automobile is in public view—to be an instrument for fostering public adherence to an ideological point of view he finds unacceptable. In doing so, the State 'invades the sphere of intellect and spirit which it is the purpose of the First Amendment [to] reserve from all official control.' [Barnette.] New Hampshire's statute in effect requires that appellees use their private property as a 'mobile billboard' for the State's ideological message—or suffer a penalty," and this burden was not justified by any sufficiently weighty state interest. Chief Justice Burger emphasized that First Amendment freedom of thought "includes both the right to speak freely and the right to refrain from

speaking at all"; both rights are "complementary components of a broader concept of 'individual freedom of mind.' "

Was the Court correct to analogize the license plate in Wooley to the flag salute in Barnette? Was there a comparable degree of government ventriloquy involved? To whom would passing motorists likely attribute the license plate motto: Maynard or New Hampshire? What is the remedy here: allowing Maynard to cover up the motto? To request a mottoless license plate? Do such remedies themselves involve compelled speech? Consider the following view: "By holding that individuals have a right to refuse this state slogan on their plates while letting the state keep distributing plates bearing the slogan, the Court was forcing those who are most offended by the slogan to come out of the closet. No longer able to just blend in as law abiding citizens whose views nobody could guess from their license plates, now those keeping the 'Live Free or Die' slogan would be marked as having no objection to the sentiment it expressed, while those replacing it would be marked as having affirmatively rejected the slogan." Tribe, "Disentangling Symmetries: Speech, Association, Parenthood," 28 Pepp. L. Rev. 641, 643–44 (2001).

3. ***Compelled disclosure of speaker identity.*** In **Talley v. California**, 362 U.S. 60 (1960), the Court, by a vote of 6–3, invalidated a Los Angeles ordinance that prohibited the distribution of any handbill in the city unless it had printed on it the name and address of the person who prepared, distributed, or sponsored it. The ordinance was challenged by distributors of unsigned handbills urging readers to boycott certain Los Angeles merchants who were allegedly engaging in racially discriminatory employment practices. Holding the ordinance "void on its face," the Court noted that the identification requirement would tend to restrict freedom of expression. Writing for the Court, Justice Black noted that "persecuted groups and sects from time to time throughout history have been able to criticize oppressive practices and laws either anonymously or not at all." The Court rejected the argument that the law was a justifiable "way to identify those responsible for fraud, false advertising and libel," stating that "the ordinance is in no manner so limited."

In **McIntyre v. Ohio Elections Commission**, 514 U.S. 334 (1995), the Court, by a vote of 7–2, invalidated an Ohio election law that, like the law of virtually every state, prohibited the circulation of anonymous leaflets in connection with political campaigns. The law provided: "No person shall write, print, post, or distribute [any] general publication [designed] to promote the nomination or election or defeat of a candidate, or to promote the adoption or defeat of any issue [unless] there appears on such [publication] in a conspicuous place [the] name and residence or business address of [the] person who issues [it]." Margaret McIntyre was fined $100 by the Commission for circulating leaflets opposing a school tax referendum that were either unsigned or signed only "Concerned Parents and Taxpayers."

Justice STEVENS, writing for the Court, reaffirmed Talley and held that "an author's decision to remain anonymous, like other decisions concerning omissions or additions to the content of a publication, is an aspect of the freedom of speech protected by the First Amendment." He noted that "[g]reat works of literature have frequently been produced by authors writing under assumed names," including those written under such pseudonyms as Mark Twain, O. Henry, Voltaire, George Sand, and George Eliot. He noted further that "the Court's reasoning [in Talley] embraced a respected tradition of anonymity in the advocacy of political causes," including the Federalist Papers, written under the pseudonym "Publius," and the papers of the Anti-Federalists, written under such pseudonyms as "Cato," "Brutus," and "the Federal Farmer."

Justice Stevens held the Ohio anonymity requirement invalid even though it was narrower than the blanket ban on anonymous handbilling struck down in Talley. First, he held strict scrutiny to be the appropriate standard: "When a law burdens core political speech, we apply 'exacting scrutiny,' and we uphold the restriction only if it is narrowly tailored to serve an overriding state interest." Next, he found Ohio's proffered interests in increasing voter information and preventing fraud insufficient to satisfy such scrutiny: "[Ohio's] interest in providing voters with additional relevant information does not justify a state requirement that a writer make statements or disclosures she would otherwise omit." And while the state had an undoubtedly legitimate interest in preventing the dissemination of false factual statements in election campaigns, he wrote, "we are not persuaded that they justify [the anonymity ban's] extremely broad prohibition," which "encompasses documents that are not even arguably false or misleading." He suggested that Ohio's direct regulation of falsity in other detailed provisions of its election code was a less restrictive alternative. Finally, he distinguished mandatory disclosure of contributions to political candidates, which the Court had upheld, as "a far cry from compelled self-identification on all election-related writings. A written election-related document—particularly a leaflet—is often a personally crafted statement of a political viewpoint [and] identification of the author against her will is particularly intrusive [because] it reveals unmistakably the content of her thoughts on a controversial issue."

Justice Stevens concluded: "Under our Constitution, anonymous pamphleteering is not a pernicious, fraudulent practice, but an honorable tradition of advocacy and of dissent. Anonymity is a shield from the tyranny of the majority. [Mill, On Liberty.] It thus exemplifies the purpose behind [the] First Amendment: [to] protect unpopular individuals from retaliation—and their ideas from suppression—at the hand of an intolerant society." Justice GINSBURG concurred separately, emphasizing that, in another setting, "a State's interest in protecting an election process 'might justify a more limited identification requirement.' "

Justice THOMAS concurred in the judgment, but argued that the interpretation of the Free Speech and Press Clauses should be determined by reference to "their original meaning," not by the broader principles employed by the majority. Under such an originalist approach, he found McIntyre's leaflets protected by the First Amendment: "There is little doubt that the Framers engaged in anonymous political writing. The essays in the Federalist Papers, published under the pseudonym of 'Publius,' are only the most famous example of the outpouring of anonymous political writing that occurred during the ratification of the Constitution. Of course, the simple fact that the Framers engaged in certain conduct does not necessarily prove that they forbade its prohibition by the government. In this case, however, the historical evidence indicates that Founding-era Americans opposed attempts to require that anonymous authors reveal their identities on the ground that forced disclosure violated the 'freedom of the press.' For example, the earliest and most famous American experience with freedom of the press, the 1735 Zenger trial, [involved] a printer, John Peter Zenger, who refused to reveal the anonymous authors of published attacks on the Crown governor of New York. When the governor and his council could not discover the identity of the authors, they prosecuted Zenger himself for seditious libel. Although the case set the colonies afire for its example of a jury refusing to convict a defendant of seditious libel against Crown authorities, it also signified at an early moment the extent to which anonymity and the freedom of the press were intertwined in the early American mind." He cited as another example the successful Anti-Federalist attack on Federalist editors' policy of refusing to publish anonymous works, which in his view indicated that "both Anti-Federalists and Federalists believed that the freedom of the press included the right to publish without revealing the author's name." He concluded: "While [I] am loath to overturn a century of practice shared by almost all of the States, I believe the historical evidence from the framing outweighs recent tradition."

Justice SCALIA dissented, arguing that, to the contrary, the nearly uniform tradition among the states over the last century trumped the ambiguous textual and historical claims for anonymous leafletting. He objected that the majority had invalidated "a species of protection for the election process that exists, in a variety of forms, in every State except California, and that has a pedigree dating back to the end of the 19th century. Preferring the views of the English utilitarian philosopher John Stuart Mill to the considered judgment of the American people's elected representatives from coast to coast, the Court discovers a hitherto unknown right-to-be-unknown while engaging in electoral politics." He disagreed with Justice Thomas about the inference to be drawn from the history of anonymous pamphleteering: "to prove that anonymous electioneering was used frequently is not to establish that it is a constitutional right." He would have deferred therefore, to the states' longstanding tradition disfavoring anonymity in connection with elections: "Where the meaning of a constitutional text (such as 'the freedom of speech') is unclear, the widespread and long-accepted practices of the American people are the best indication of what fundamental beliefs it was intended to enshrine." Justice Scalia also viewed anonymity more skeptically than the majority, noting that it might well "facilitate[ ] wrong by eliminating accountability." He would have recognized an "exemption from otherwise valid disclosure requirements," if at all, only "on the part of someone who could show a 'reasonable probability' that the compelled disclosure would result in 'threats, harassment, or reprisals from either Government officials or private parties.' "

If the First Amendment as interpreted in McIntyre v. Ohio Elections Commission protects the right to leaflet anonymously, may one who signs a petition to place a referendum on the ballot also claim a right to anonymity? In **Doe v. Reed**, 561 U.S. 186 (2010), the Supreme Court rebuffed such a claim, upholding against First Amendment challenge a requirement of Washington's Public Records Act (PRA) that the names and addresses of those who sign referendum ballot petitions be publicly disclosed. The challenge was brought by supporters of a petition challenging a state law extending certain benefits to same-sex couples.

Writing for an 8–1 majority joined by all but Justice Thomas, Chief Justice ROBERTS explained: "The compelled disclosure of signatory information on referendum petitions is subject to review under the First Amendment. An individual expresses a view on a political matter when he signs a petition under Washington's referendum procedure. In most cases, the individual's signature will express the view that the law subject to the petition should be overturned. [But] that is not to say that the electoral context is irrelevant to the nature of our First Amendment review. [First] Amendment challenges to disclosure requirements in the electoral context [are subject to] 'exacting scrutiny,' which 'requires a "substantial relation" between the disclosure requirement and a "sufficiently important" governmental interest.'" Under that standard, the Chief Justice found disclosure of petition information substantially related to an important interest in "preserving the integrity of the electoral process by combating fraud, detecting invalid signatures, and fostering government transparency and accountability." He accordingly did not reach or resolve the question whether the State had a constitutionally sufficient interest in "providing information to the electorate about who supports the petition."

As the Chief Justice noted, the challengers objected that, "once on the Internet, the petition signers' names and addresses 'can be combined with publicly available phone numbers and maps,' in what will effectively become a blueprint for harassment and intimidation. To support their claim that they will be subject to reprisals, plaintiffs cite examples from the history of a similar proposition in California [i.e., Proposition 8, overturning a decision of the California Supreme Court upholding a constitutional right to gay marriage]." But stating that "typical referendum petitions 'concern tax policy, revenue, budget, or other state law issues,'" he found "no reason to assume that any burdens imposed by disclosure of typical referendum petitions would be remotely like the burdens plaintiffs fear in this case." He concluded: "[W]e must reject plaintiffs' broad challenge to the PRA. In doing so, we note [that] upholding the law against a broad-based challenge does not foreclose a litigant's success in a narrower one" if disclosure could be shown to pose a specific danger of threats, reprisal or harassment.

Justice ALITO concurred, emphasizing the need for potential petition signators to be able to obtain such as-applied exemptions "quickly and well in advance of speaking" and "without clearing a high evidentiary hurdle." He suggested that the petitioners in this case would have a strong argument for an as-applied exemption on remand, given evidence of "widespread harassment and intimidation suffered by supporters of California's Proposition 8." He suggested that any "informational" interest in disclosure attenuates upon proof of risk of harassment, and expressed skepticism about the need for disclosure to prevent electoral fraud, noting that California, which "has had more initiatives on the ballot than any other State save Oregon, [explicitly] protects the privacy of initiative and referendum signatories."

Justice SOTOMAYOR, joined by Justices Stevens and Ginsburg, filed a concurrence emphasizing that the State has strong interests in the integrity of the ballot process and that "the burden of public disclosure on speech and associational rights [is] minimal in this context [as] the process of legislating by referendum is inherently public." She suggested that "any party attempting to challenge particular applications of the State's regulations will bear a heavy burden," and that as-applied exceptions should be available only "when a State selectively applies a facially neutral petition disclosure rule in a manner that discriminates based on the content of referenda or the viewpoint of petition signers, or in the rare circumstance in which disclosure poses a reasonable probability of serious and widespread harassment that the State is unwilling or unable to control."

Justice STEVENS, joined by Justice Breyer, concurred in part and in the judgment, stating that this was "not a hard case" and emphasizing that, unlike in McIntyre, the PRA does not "require that any person signing a petition disclose or say anything." Like Justice Sotomayor, he suggested that as-applied challenges to petition disclosure requirements should be sparingly granted: "For an as-applied challenge to a law such as the PRA to succeed, there would have to be a significant threat of harassment directed at those who sign the petition that cannot be mitigated by law enforcement measures. [Debates] about tax policy and regulation of private property can become just as heated as debates about domestic partnerships. And as a general matter, it is very difficult to show that by later disclosing the names of petition signatories, individuals will be less willing to sign petitions. [I] would demand strong evidence before concluding that an indirect and speculative chain of events imposes a substantial burden on speech."

Justice SCALIA concurred only in the judgment, expressing "doubt whether signing a petition that has the effect of suspending a law fits within 'the freedom of speech' at all" and arguing that "[w]e should not repeat and extend the mistake of McIntyre v. Ohio Elections Comm'n." He would forego "judicial interest-balancing" in this context and hold that "[o]ur Nation's longstanding traditions of legislating and voting in public refute the claim that the First Amendment accords a right to anonymity in the performance of an act with governmental effect." He continued: "When a Washington voter signs a referendum petition subject to the PRA, he is acting as a legislator. [The] exercise of lawmaking power in the United States has traditionally been public. [Voting] was public until 1888 when the States began to adopt the Australian secret ballot. [The] long history of public legislating and voting contradicts plaintiffs' claim that disclosure of petition signatures having legislative effect violates the First Amendment." As to the petitioners' claimed fears of harassment, Justice Scalia replied: "There are laws against threats and intimidation; and harsh criticism, short of unlawful action, is a price our people have traditionally been willing to pay for self-governance. Requiring people to stand up in public for their political acts fosters civic courage, without which democracy is doomed."

Justice THOMAS filed the lone dissent. He would have found the PRA's compelled disclosure requirement unconstitutional because it "severely burdens [and] chills citizen participation in the referendum process" and "there will always be a less restrictive means by which Washington can vindicate its stated interest in preserving the integrity of its referendum process." He explained: "[U]nlike the Court, I read our precedents to require application of strict scrutiny to laws that compel disclosure of protected First Amendment association," meaning that "a disclosure requirement passes constitutional muster only if it is [the] least restrictive means to serve a compelling state interest." Even if the State has a compelling interest in electoral integrity, he argued, it does not need to use the "blunderbuss" approach of public disclosure of referendum signers' names and addresses: it "could put the names and addresses of referendum signers into [an] electronic database that state employees could search without subjecting the name and address of each signer to wholesale public disclosure," "could create a Web site, linked to the electronic referendum database, where a voter concerned that his name had been fraudulently signed could conduct a search using his unique identifier to ensure that his name was absent from the database," or could otherwise enforce existing laws against fraud. And, citing McIntyre, he found constitutionally insufficient any state " 'interest in providing the electorate with relevant information.' " Finding as-applied challenges too time-consuming and cumbersome to protect the speech interests at stake, he would have invalidated the PRA's disclosure requirement on its face.

4. ***Compelled disclosure by providers of professional services.*** The cases above related to the compelled disclosure of citizens in their capacity as general members of the population. Should the analysis of compelled disclosure requirements change when the requirements regulate the speech of professionals? If so, how possible is it to draw a principled scope for who counts as a professional? If not, are all disclosure requirements, even those that relate to professional conduct or food and product safety subject to strict First Amendment scrutiny? Consider these questions in the context of case below.

National Institute of Family and Life Advocates v. Becerra

585 U.S. ___, 138 S. Ct. 2361, 201 L. Ed. 2d 835 (2018).

[The California Reproductive Freedom, Accountability, Comprehensive Care, and Transparency Act (FACT Act) required licensed clinics that primarily serve pregnant women to notify patients that California provides free or low-cost services, including abortions, and to give them a phone number to call. The law also required unlicensed clinics to notify patients that California had not licensed the clinics to provide medical services . Both parts of the law—the licensed and unlicensed notices—were challenged by "crisis pregnancy centers" that aimed to discourage pregnant women from obtaining abortions.]

■ JUSTICE THOMAS delivered the opinion of the Court.

[The] licensed notice is a content-based regulation of speech. By compelling individuals to speak a particular message, such notices alter the content of their speech. Here, for example, licensed clinics must provide a government-drafted script about the availability of state-sponsored services, as well as contact information for how to obtain them. One of those services is abortion—the very practice that petitioners are devoted to opposing.

[Our] precedents have applied more deferential review to some laws that require professionals to disclose factual, noncontroversial information in their "commercial speech." See, e.g., Zauderer v. Office of Disciplinary Counsel of Supreme Court of Ohio [1985; p. 1141]. [And under] our precedents, States may regulate professional conduct, even though that conduct incidentally involves speech. Planned Parenthood of Southeastern Pennsylvania v. Casey [1992; p. 604]. But neither line of precedents is implicated here. [The] licensed notice at issue here is not an informed-consent requirement or any other regulation of professional conduct. The notice does not facilitate informed consent to a medical procedure. [The] licensed notice regulates speech as speech. Outside of the two contexts discussed above, [this] Court's precedents have long protected the First

Amendment rights of professionals. [As] with other kinds of speech, regulating the content of professionals' speech "poses the inherent risk that the Government seeks not to advance a legitimate regulatory goal, but to suppress unpopular ideas or information." ["Professional speech"] is also a difficult category to define with precision. As defined by the courts of appeals, the professional-speech doctrine would cover a wide array of individuals—doctors, lawyers, nurses, physical therapists, truck drivers, bartenders, barbers, and many others. [But] that gives the States unfettered power to reduce a group's First Amendment rights by simply imposing a licensing requirement.

[California has not] identified a persuasive reason for treating professional speech as a unique category that is exempt from ordinary First Amendment principles. We do not foreclose the possibility that some such reason exists. We need not do so because the licensed notice cannot survive even intermediate scrutiny. California asserts a single interest to justify the licensed notice: providing low-income women with information about state-sponsored services. Assuming that this is a substantial state interest, the licensed notice is not sufficiently drawn to achieve it.

If California's goal is to educate low-income women about the services it provides, then the licensed notice is wildly underinclusive. The notice applies only to clinics that have a "primary purpose" of "providing family planning or pregnancy-related services" and that provide two of six categories of specific services. [Such] underinclusiveness raises serious doubts about whether the government is in fact pursuing the interest it invokes, rather than disfavoring a particular speaker or viewpoint. The FACT Act also excludes, without explanation, federal clinics and Family PACT providers from the licensed-notice requirement. [Further,] California could inform low-income women about its services [with] a public-information campaign.

[The] FACT Act unduly burdens protected speech. The unlicensed notice imposes a government-scripted, speaker-based disclosure requirement that is wholly disconnected from California's informational interest. [The] application of the unlicensed notice to advertisements demonstrates just how burdensome it is. [As] California conceded at oral argument, a billboard for an unlicensed facility that says "Choose Life" would have to surround that two-word statement with a 29-word statement from the government, in as many as 13 different languages. In this way, the unlicensed notice drowns out the facility's own message.

[We] express no view on the legality of a similar disclosure requirement that is better supported or less burdensome.

■ JUSTICE KENNEDY, with whom the CHIEF JUSTICE, JUSTICE ALITO, and JUSTICE GORSUCH join, concurring.

[This] separate writing seeks to underscore that the apparent viewpoint discrimination here is a matter of serious constitutional concern. [This] law is a paradigmatic example of the serious threat presented when government seeks to impose its own message in the place of individual speech, thought, and expression. For here the State requires primarily pro-life pregnancy centers to promote the State's own preferred message advertising abortions. This compels individuals to contradict their most deeply held beliefs, beliefs grounded in basic philosophical, ethical, or religious precepts, or all of these. And the history of the Act's passage and its underinclusive application suggest a real possibility that these individuals were targeted because of their beliefs.

■ JUSTICE BREYER, with whom JUSTICE GINSBURG, JUSTICE SOTOMAYOR, and JUSTICE KAGAN join, dissenting.

[The] majority says it applies [heightened] scrutiny to the Act because the Act, in its view, is content based. [This] constitutional approach threatens to create serious problems. Because much, perhaps most, human behavior takes place through speech and because much, perhaps most, law regulates that speech in terms of its content, the majority's approach at the least threatens considerable litigation over the constitutional validity of much, perhaps most, government regulation. Virtually every disclosure law could be considered "content based," for virtually every disclosure law requires individuals "to speak a particular message." Thus, the majority's view, if taken literally, could radically change prior law, perhaps placing much securities law or consumer protection law at constitutional risk, depending on how broadly its exceptions are interpreted.

[The] majority, [perhaps] recognizing this problem, [says] that it does not "question the legality of health and safety warnings long considered permissible, or purely factual and uncontroversial disclosures about commercial products." But this generally phrased disclaimer would seem more likely to invite litigation than to provide needed limitation and clarification. The majority, for example, does not explain why the Act here, which is justified in part by health and safety considerations, does not fall within its "health" category.

[Precedent] does not require a test such as the majority's. [Historically,] the Court has been wary of claims that regulation of business activity, particularly health-related activity, violates the Constitution. Ever since this Court departed from the approach it set forth in Lochner v. New York [1905; p. 489], ordinary economic and social legislation has been thought to raise little constitutional concern. [The] Court has taken this same respectful approach to economic and social legislation when a First Amendment claim like the claim present here is at issue. Even during the Lochner era, when this Court struck down numerous economic regulations concerning industry, this Court was careful to defer to state legislative judgments concerning the medical profession. [In] the name of the First Amendment, the majority today treads into territory where the pre-New Deal, as well as the post-New Deal, Court refused to go.

In Casey [1992; p. 531, above], the Court [considered] a state law that required doctors to provide information to a woman deciding whether to proceed with an abortion. [The Court held that] the statute was constitutional. The joint opinion stated that the statutory requirements amounted to "reasonable measures to ensure an informed choice, one which might cause the woman to choose childbirth over abortion." [The] joint opinion specifically [concluded] that the statute did not violate the First Amendment. [If] a State can lawfully require a doctor to tell a woman seeking an abortion about adoption services, why should it not be able, as here, to require a medical counselor to tell a woman seeking prenatal care or other reproductive healthcare about childbirth and abortion services? As the question suggests, there is no convincing reason to distinguish between information about adoption and information about abortion in this context.

[With respect to the unlicensed clinics, there] is no basis for finding the State's interest "hypothetical." The legislature heard that information-related delays in qualified healthcare negatively affect women seeking to terminate their pregnancies as well as women carrying their pregnancies to term, with delays in qualified prenatal care causing life-long health problems for infants. [The] majority suggests that the Act is suspect because it covers some speakers but not others. [There] is no cause for such concern here. The Act does not, on its face, distinguish between facilities that favor pro-life and those that favor pro-choice points of view. Nor is there any convincing evidence before us or in the courts below that discrimination was the purpose or the effect of the statute. [Finally,] the majority concludes that the Act is overly burdensome. [But] these and similar claims are claims that the statute could be applied unconstitutionally, not that it is unconstitutional on its face.

STATE COMPELLED ACCESS TO PRIVATE FORUMS

1. ***Compelled rights of reply.*** May government compel the press to furnish free coverage of replies by those it has attacked? Two decisions came to opposite answers for the electronic and print media. In **Red Lion Broadcasting Co. v. FCC**, 395 U.S. 367 (1969), discussed further below at p. 1545, the Court upheld against First Amendment challenge the FCC's "fairness doctrine," which required broadcast stations to provide free reply time for individuals subjected to personal attack on the air. The Court relied heavily on the scarcity of the broadcast spectrum as a justification for imposing forced access rights on unwilling media.

In contrast, in **Miami Herald Pub. Co. v. Tornillo**, 418 U.S. 241 (1974), the Court held unconstitutional Florida's "right of reply" law, which granted political candidates a right to equal space to reply to criticism and attacks on their record by a newspaper. The state court had sustained the law because it furthered the "broad societal interest in the free flow of information." Chief Justice BURGER's opinion concluded, however, that the law violated the First Amendment rights of the newspaper by forcing it to publish undesired speech: "[Government] compulsion to publish that which '[newspaper editors believe] should not be published' is unconstitutional. A responsible press is an undoubtedly desirable goal, but press responsibility is not mandated by the Constitution and like many other virtues it cannot be legislated." The fact that the newspaper was not being prevented from giving its own views did not help the defenders of the law: "The Florida statute exacts a penalty on the basis of the content of a newspaper. [Faced] with the penalties that would accrue to any newspaper that published news or commentary arguably within the reach of the right-of-access statute, editors might well conclude that the safe course is to avoid controversy. [Government]-enforced right of access inescapably 'dampens the vigor and limits the variety of public debate.'" And even if there were no such consequences to the law, it would nevertheless be invalid "because of its intrusion into the function of editors": "A newspaper is more than a passive receptacle or conduit for news, comment, and advertising. The choice of material to go into a newspaper, and the decisions made as to limitations on the size and content of the paper, and treatment of public issues and public officials—whether fair or unfair—constitute the exercise of editorial control and judgment."

2. ***Compelled access by speakers to private property.*** In **PruneYard Shopping Center v. Robins**, 447 U.S. 74 (1980), a shopping center, in accordance with its nondiscriminatory policy of barring all expressive activity not directly related to its commercial purposes, had excluded several high school students who sought to solicit signatures for a petition protesting a UN resolution against Zionism. California's highest court interpreted its *state* constitution to guarantee such speakers access to a privately owned shopping center, even though the Supreme Court had rejected such an access right as a matter of federal First Amendment law. PruneYard argued that that interpretation violated its own federal free speech rights. The Court unanimously rejected that argument.

Justice REHNQUIST's opinion for the Court concluded that "state constitutional provisions which permit individuals to exercise free speech and petition rights on the property of a privately owned shopping center to which the public is invited" do not violate the shopping center owner's "First Amendment right not to be forced by the State to use his property as a forum for the speech of others." Although there might be circumstances in which a State could not require an individual "to participate in the dissemination of an ideological message by displaying it on his private property," this was not such a case. Since PruneYard was open to the public, the views expressed in passing out pamphlets or seeking signatures "will not likely be identified with those of the owner." Moreover, "no specific message is dictated by the State to be displayed," so that there was "no danger of governmental discrimination for or against a particular message." And PruneYard could "expressly disavow any connection with a message by simply posting signs in the area where the speakers or handbillers stand." The majority opinion thus found both Wooley and Barnette distinguishable.

Justice POWELL's partial concurrence, joined by Justice White, cautioned that the decision did not constitute "blanket approval for state efforts to transform privately owned commercial property into public forums." He explained that, "even when no particular message is mandated by the State, First Amendment interests are affected by state action that forces a property owner to admit third-party speakers." He noted that "customers might well conclude that the messages reflect the view of the proprietor." Moreover, there might be valid First Amendment objections when speakers sought use of the premises "as a platform for views that [the owner] finds morally repugnant": "To require the owner to specify the particular ideas he finds objectionable enough to compel a response would force him to relinquish his 'freedom to maintain his own beliefs without public disclosure.' Thus, the right to control one's own speech may be burdened impermissibly even when listeners will not assume that the messages expressed on private property are those of the owner." But he found that, "[o]n the record before us, I cannot say that customers of this vast center would be likely to assume that appellees' limited speech activity expressed the views of the PruneYard or of its owner," nor that the owner had any strong ideological disagreement with anything the students or other groups were likely to say. Justices White, Marshall and Blackmun also submitted separate concurrences.

Decided in 1980, PruneYard has gained renewed significance in the era of social media. In lawsuits filed in California state courts, white supremacist and right-wing Twitter users are challenging the platform's ban on their accounts. At least one of these users, see **Johnson v. Twitter, Inc.**, No. 18CECG00078 (Cal. Super. Ct. June 6, 2018), argues that platforms like Twitter are analogous to the shopping center in PruneYard, such that the banning of their account is violative of California's state constitutional guarantee.

As this casebook goes to press, the cases have not been resolved by the California Supreme Court, nor have they reached any federal court. However, they still raise the question of whether Twitter can, for the purposes of First Amendment analysis, be compared to the PruneYard shopping center. Do the nature of the two spaces differ? What about their missions or purposes? Perhaps more fundamentally, is the PruneYard doctrine still vital at all given the following cases that succeeded that 1980 decision?

3. ***Compelled inclusion of third-party speech in private publications.*** After PruneYard, the issue of compelled access again came before the Court in **Pacific Gas & Elec. Co. [PG & E] v. Public Util. Comm'n [PUC]**, 475 U.S. 1 (1986). In upholding a First Amendment claim against state-compelled access, the Court relied on Tornillo and distinguished PruneYard. The case involved a newsletter distributed by PG & E to its customers in the monthly billing envelope. The Commission found that the "extra space" in billing envelopes (i.e., the difference between the maximum weight mailable with a postage stamp and the weight of the monthly bill and any required legal notices) belonged to the ratepayers. The PUC held that PG & E had to allow a private advocacy group called Toward Utility Rate Normalization (TURN), which was typically opposed to PG & E in ratemaking proceedings and elsewhere, to use the extra space four times a year to communicate with PG & E customers. PG & E, a privately owned utility, claimed that requiring it "to include in its billing envelope speech of a third party with which the utility disagrees" violated its First Amendment rights.

The Court sustained this First Amendment claim. Justice POWELL's plurality opinion, joined only by Chief Justice Burger and Justices Brennan and O'Connor, relied heavily on Tornillo in overturning this state-imposed access: "Compelled access like that ordered in this case both penalizes the expression of particular points of view and forces speakers to alter their speech to conform with an agenda they do not set. These impermissible effects are not remedied by the Commission's definition of the relevant property rights. [The] concerns that caused us to invalidate the compelled access rule in Tornillo apply to appellant as well as to the institutional press. [Just] as the State is not free to 'tell a newspaper in advance what it can print and what it cannot,' [the] State is not free either to restrict appellant's speech to certain topics or views or to force appellant to respond to views that others may hold. [Under] Tornillo a forced access rule that would accomplish these purposes indirectly is similarly forbidden. [PruneYard] is not to the contrary. [Notably] absent [there] was any concern that access to this area might affect the shopping center owner's exercise of his own right to speak: the owner did not even allege that he objected to the content of the pamphlets; nor was the access right content-based. PruneYard thus does not undercut the proposition that forced associations that burden protected speech are impermissible."

Justice Powell emphasized that the Commission's order did not "simply award access to the public at large; rather, it discriminates on the basis of the viewpoints of the selected speakers." Among the acknowledged purposes of the access order was the aim "to assist groups [that] challenged [PG & E] in the Commission's ratemaking proceedings in raising funds. [Access] to the envelopes thus is not content-neutral. [Because] access is awarded only to those who disagree with [PG & E's] views and who are hostile to [its] interests, [PG & E] must contend with the fact that whenever it speaks out on a given issue, it may be forced [to] help disseminate hostile views. [PG & E] 'might well conclude' that, under these circumstances, 'the safe course is to avoid controversy,' thereby reducing the free flow of information and ideas that the First Amendment seeks to promote. Appellant does not [have] the right to be free from vigorous debate. But it *does* have the right to be free from government restrictions that abridge its own rights in order to 'enhance the relative voice' of its opponents. [In addition to constituting an impermissible content regulation by favoring some groups rather than others, the] Commission's access order also impermissibly requires appellant to associate with speech with which appellant may disagree. [For] corporations as for individuals, the choice to speak includes within it the choice of what not to say. [Were] the government freely able to compel corporate speakers to propound political messages with which they disagree, this protection [of corporate speech] would be empty, for the government could require speakers to affirm in one breath that which they deny in the next."

Justice MARSHALL concurred only in the judgment, emphasizing two distinctions between this case and PruneYard: PG & E had "issued no invitation to the general public to use its billing envelope for speech or for any other purpose," and the state here had deprived PG & E of control over "the space in [its billing] envelope that [it] would otherwise use for its own speech." Chief Justice Burger, while joining Justice Powell's opinion, submitted a separate concurrence as well.

Justice REHNQUIST, joined by Justices White and Stevens, dissented, emphasizing PG & E's status as a corporation and regulated public utility: "This Court has recognized that natural persons enjoy negative free speech rights because of their interest in self-expression; an individual's right not to speak or to associate with the speech of others is a component of the broader constitutional interest of natural persons in freedom of conscience. [Extension] of the individual freedom of conscience decisions to business corporations strains the rationale of those cases beyond the breaking point. To ascribe to such artificial entities an 'intellect' or 'mind' for freedom of conscience purposes is to confuse metaphor with reality." Even if such a right extended to the institutional media, he argued, it ought not extend to other businesses: "Corporations generally have not played the historic role of newspapers as conveyers of individual ideas and opinion." The dissenters also distinguished Tornillo on the ground that the likelihood of deterrence of speech by PG & E was minimal.

Justice STEVENS added in a separate dissent: "I assume that the plurality would not object to a utility commission rule dictating the format of the bill, even as to required warnings and the type size of various provisos and disclaimers [and] would permit the Commission to require the utility to disseminate legal notices of public hearings and ratemaking proceedings written by it. [Given] that the Commission can require the utility to make certain statements and to carry the Commission's own messages to its customers, it seems but a small step to acknowledge that the Commission can also require the utility to act as the conduit for a public interest group's message that bears a close relationship to the purpose of the billing envelope. An analog to this requirement appears in securities law: the Securities and Exchange Commission requires the incumbent board of directors to transmit proposals of dissident shareholders which it opposes. Presumably the plurality does not doubt the constitutionality of the SEC's requirement under the First Amendment." Justice Blackmun did not participate in the case.

In **Turner Broadcasting System, Inc. v. FCC**, 512 U.S. 622 (1994) (Turner I), the Court considered a claim that compelled access for broadcasters to cable television transmission violates the First Amendment. In Turner, the Court rejected cable operators' argument that sections 4 and 5 of the Cable Television Consumer Protection and Competition Act of 1992, which require cable operators to carry the signals of a specified number of local broadcast television stations, were subject to strict scrutiny under the Court's compelled-speech precedents. Congress enacted the "must-carry" provisions out of concern that "the physical characteristics of cable transmission, compounded by the increasing concentration of economic power in the cable industry, are endangering the ability of over-the-air broadcast television stations to compete for a viewing audience and thus for necessary operating revenues." Cable operators, relying upon Tornillo and PG & E, argued that the must-carry rules interfered with their editorial discretion and forced them to carry unwanted speech in violation of their First Amendment rights.

Justice KENNEDY, writing for the Court, began by acknowledging that "[a]t the heart of the First Amendment lies the principle that each person should decide for him or herself the ideas and beliefs deserving of expression, consideration, and adherence," and that "[g]overnment action [that] requires the utterance of a particular message favored by the Government contravenes this essential right." But he found that the must-carry rules did not fall within this line of precedent because they were content-neutral rather than content-based: "the must-carry rules, on their face, impose burdens and confer benefits without reference to the content of speech. Although the provisions interfere with cable operators' editorial discretion by compelling them to offer carriage to a certain minimum number of broadcast stations, [the] number of channels a cable operator must set aside depends only on the operator's channel capacity, [not] the programming it offers to subscribers." He also rejected the cable operators' argument that "Congress' purpose in enacting [must-carry] was to promote speech of a favored content": "Our review of the Act and its various findings persuades us that Congress' overriding objective in enacting must-carry was not to favor programming of a particular subject matter, viewpoint, or format, but rather to preserve access to free television programming for the 40 percent of Americans without cable. [This] overriding congressional purpose is unrelated to the content of expression disseminated by cable and broadcast speakers." Thus, Justice Kennedy concluded, the must-carry rules, unlike those at issue in Tornillo and PG & E, involved no content-based trigger or penalty. Also unlike the rules in Tornillo and PG & E, must-carry would not "force cable operators to alter their own messages to respond to the broadcast programming they are required to carry. Given cable's long history of serving as a conduit for broadcast signals, there appears little risk that cable viewers would assume that the broadcast stations carried on a cable system convey ideas or messages endorsed by the cable operator."

Having found the compelled access here content-neutral, Justice Kennedy concluded that the appropriate standard of scrutiny was not strict scrutiny as in Tornillo or PG & E, but rather the intermediate scrutiny set forth in United States v. O'Brien and Ward v. Rock Against Racism. He concluded that the must-carry provisions served three important interests unrelated to the suppression of free expression: "(1) preserving the benefits of free, over-the-air local broadcast television, (2) promoting the widespread dissemination of information from a multiplicity of sources, and (3) promoting fair competition in the market for television programming." But, joined on this point only by Chief Justice Rehnquist and Justices Blackmun and Souter, he found the congressional record and the record on summary judgment below insufficient to show must-carry to be narrowly tailored to those interests, and concluded that the case should be remanded. Justice STEVENS provided a fifth vote for remand, even though he stated in a partial concurrence that he would have preferred to affirm the summary judgment for the government: "[a]n industry need not be in its death throes before Congress may act to protect it from economic harm threatened by a monopoly." Justice Blackmun also filed a concurrence.

Justice O'CONNOR, joined by Justices Scalia and Ginsburg and in part by Justice Thomas, dissented in part, arguing that the must-carry rules amounted to impermissibly content-based compulsion of speech: "[L]ooking at the statute at issue, I cannot avoid the conclusion that its preference for broadcasters over cable programmers is justified with reference to content"—for example, by Congress's advertence to the desirable diversity and local affairs focus of broadcast programming. She continued: "[M]y conclusion that the must-carry rules are content based leads me to conclude that they are an impermissible restraint on the cable operators' editorial discretion as well as on the cable programmers' speech. For reasons related to the content of speech, the rules restrict the ability of cable operators to put on the programming they prefer, and require them to include programming they would rather avoid. This, it seems to me, puts this case squarely within the rule of [PG & E and Tornillo.]" Justice GINSBURG also filed a separate partial dissent agreeing that the must-carry rules reflected a content preference and thus required strict scrutiny.

The remand in Turner I led to 18 months of additional factfinding, after which the district court granted summary judgment for the Government and other appellees, concluding that the expanded record contained substantial evidence supporting Congress's predictive judgment that the must-carry provisions furthered important governmental interests in preserving cable carriage of local broadcast stations, and were narrowly tailored to promote those interests. In **Turner Broadcasting System, Inc. v. FCC**, 520 U.S. 180 (1997) (Turner II), the Court affirmed by a vote of 5–4. Justice Kennedy again wrote for the Court. Reiterating the standard of intermediate scrutiny set forth in Turner I, he emphasized the need for deference to Congress: "This is not a case in which we are called upon to give our best judgment as to the likely economic consequences of certain financial arrangements or business structures, or to assess competing economic theories and predictive judgments, as we would in a case arising, say, under the antitrust laws. [The] issue before us is whether, given conflicting views of the probable development of the television industry, Congress had substantial evidence for making the judgment that it did. [We] cannot displace Congress' judgment respecting content-neutral regulations with our own, so long as its policy is grounded on reasonable factual findings supported by evidence that is substantial for a legislative determination."

Under this approach, Justice KENNEDY found that the must-carry requirements were substantially related to important government interests in competition and diversity in video programming. Justice Blackmun had voted with the majority in Turner I, and Justice BREYER, who succeeded him, also joined the majority but concurred separately to note the presence of "important First Amendment interests on both sides of the equation," and to say that he found persuasive the diversity rationale but not the competition rationale. Justice O'CONNOR wrote an extended dissent, joined by all the other dissenters in Turner I. She criticized the majority for applying an "inappropriately lenient level of scrutiny" and "exhibiting an extraordinary and unwarranted deference for congressional judgments," and found even on the new record that "the statute is not narrowly tailored to serve a substantial interest in preventing anticompetitive conduct." For other aspects of Turner see p. 1541 below.

COMPELLED SPEECH, COMMERCIAL SPEECH AND ECONOMIC REGULATION

Federal and state regulatory schemes compel a great deal of speech. Recall Justice Stevens's example, in dissent in PG & E (1986; p. 1404 above), of the SEC requirement that certain materials, including dissident stockholders' proposals, be included in the proxy statements of publicly traded corporations. Consider also the requirement that the Surgeon General's official warnings on the dangers of tobacco be affixed to cigarette packages, and the Food and Drug Administration's many requirements that food content or drug warnings be disclosed on food and drug labels. Most of these regulatory requirements have never been the subject of any serious First Amendment challenge. Consider this traditional deference in the light of Justice Breyer's concern in his National Institute of Family and Life Advocates v. Becerra ("NIFLA") dissent (2018; p. 1399, above) that the Court's reasoning threatened to pull the rug out from under the vast array of economic disclosure regulations. Is it still justified?

What should the limits of this deference to compelled speech in the regulatory context? In **R.J. Reynolds Tobacco Co. v. FDA**, 696 F.3d 1205 (2012), the D.C. Circuit applied intermediate scrutiny and struck down an FDA regulation requiring tobacco companies to display large, graphic warnings on cigarette packaging. Recall that in Virginia Board of Pharmacy (1976; p. 1133 above), the Court suggested that it may be "appropriate to require that a commercial message appear in such a form, or include such additional information, warnings and disclaimers as are necessary to prevent its being deceptive." Are such regulations best understood as infringing speech rights, but justified nonetheless by the government's compelling interest in protecting health and safety?

May the government compel producers to contribute fees to finance generic advertising of their products, even if they object to the advertising?

This issue has now reached the Court three times in connection with various agricultural marketing programs, with inconsistent results.

1. ***Compulsory funding for advertising.*** In **Glickman v. Wileman Bros.**, 521 U.S. 457 (1997), by a vote of 5–4, the Court upheld against First Amendment challenge agricultural marketing orders assessing from California fruit growers the costs of generic advertising of California nectarines, plums, and peaches. The court of appeals had invalidated the assessments, holding that such compelled commercial speech did not satisfy the Central Hudson test (1980; p. 1142 above) because collective generic advertising had not been shown more effective than individual advertising. The Supreme Court reversed.

Justice STEVENS, writing for the Court, found that the assessments did not raise a First Amendment issue at all, but rather "simply a question of economic policy for Congress and the Executive to resolve." He reasoned: "Three characteristics of the regulatory scheme at issue distinguish it from laws that we have found to abridge the freedom of speech protected by the First Amendment. First, the marketing orders impose no restraint on the freedom of any producer to communicate any message to any audience. Second, they do not compel any person to engage in any actual or symbolic speech. Third, they do not compel the producers to endorse or to finance any political or ideological views. Indeed, since all of the respondents are engaged in the business of marketing California nectarines, plums, and peaches, it is fair to presume that they agree with the central message of the speech that is generated by the generic program."

Justice Stevens found that these features distinguished the regulations from those held to have unconstitutionally compelled speech in earlier cases: "The use of assessments to pay for advertising does not require respondents to repeat an objectionable message out of their own mouths, Barnette, require them to use their own property to convey an antagonistic ideological message, Wooley; PG & E v. PUC, force them to respond to a hostile message when they 'would prefer to remain silent,' or require them to be publicly identified or associated with another's message, PruneYard. Respondents are not required themselves to speak, but are merely required to make contributions for advertising. With trivial exceptions [none] of the generic advertising conveys any message with which respondents disagree. Furthermore, the advertising is attributed not to them, but to the California Tree Fruit Agreement."

Justice Stevens concluded that under appropriately deferential scrutiny the assessments were clearly constitutional: "Generic advertising is intended to stimulate consumer demand for an agricultural product in a regulated market. That purpose is legitimate and consistent with the regulatory goals of the overall statutory scheme. [Whether] the benefits from the advertising justify its cost is a question that [involves] the exercise of policy judgments that are better made by producers and administrators than by judges."

Justice SOUTER dissented, joined by Chief Justice Rehnquist and Justice Scalia and in part by Justice Thomas. He would have affirmed the court of appeals, finding that the marketing assessments implicated commercial speech, not mere economic conduct; that they were thus subject to the Central Hudson test generally applicable to commercial speech; and that, under that test, the government's justifications were inadequate. He further argued that the fruit growers' apparent lack of disagreement with the advertising could not be a reason for denying the First Amendment's protection: "[Another ground for] the Court's conclusion that the First Amendment is not implicated here is its assumption that respondents do not disagree with the advertisements they object to subsidizing. But this assumption is doubtful and would be beside the point even if true. [Respondents] do claim to disagree with the messages of some promotions they are being forced to fund: some of the ads promote specific varieties of plums, peaches, and nectarines marketed by respondents' competitors but not by respondents; other ads characterize California tree fruits as a generic and thus fungible commodity, whereas respondents believe that their produce is superior to most grown in California. [In] any event, the requirement of disagreement finds no legal warrant in our compelled-speech cases. [Requiring] a profession of disagreement is [at] odds with our holding [in Hurley] that no articulable message is necessary for expression to be protected. [What] counts here [is] not whether respondents fail to disagree with the generalized message of the generic ads that California fruit is good, but that they do indeed deny that the general message is as valuable and worthy of their support as more particular claims about the merits of their own brands." Justice Thomas also dissented.

2. ***Comprehensive regulation.*** In **United States v. United Foods, Inc.**, 533 U.S. 405 (2001), by contrast, the Court, by a vote of 6–3, found invalid under the First Amendment a federal law mandating that fresh mushroom handlers pay assessments used primarily to fund advertisements promoting mushroom sales. A large mushroom grower objected to being compelled to support generic mushroom advertisements, preferring to be free to convey the message that its brand of mushrooms was superior to those grown by other producers. Writing for the Court, Justice KENNEDY, joined by Chief Justice Rehnquist, and Justices Stevens, Scalia, Souter, and Thomas, sustained the challenge, distinguishing the stone fruit advertising assessment upheld in Glickman on the ground that it involved a comprehensive program of cooperative marketing: "The program sustained in Glickman differs from the one under review in a most fundamental respect. In Glickman the mandated assessments for speech were ancillary to a more comprehensive program restricting marketing autonomy. Here, for all practical purposes, the advertising itself, far from being ancillary, is the principal object of the regulatory scheme. [Here] the statute does not require group action, save to generate the very speech to which some handlers object. [We] have not upheld compelled subsidies for speech in the context of a program where the principal object is speech itself. [The] cooperative marketing structure relied upon by a majority of the Court in Glickman to sustain an ancillary assessment finds no corollary here; the expression respondent is required to support is not germane to a purpose related to an association independent from the speech itself. [For] these and other reasons we have set forth, the assessments are not permitted under the First Amendment."

Justice BREYER dissented, joined by Justice Ginsburg and in part by Justice O'Connor, finding "[t]his case, although it involves mushrooms rather than fruit, [identical] in [all] critical respects" to Glickman: "The Court sees an important difference in what it says is the fact that [Glickman's] fruit producers were subject to regulation (presumably price and supply regulation) that 'displaced competition,' [but] it is difficult to understand why the presence or absence of price and output regulations could make a critical First Amendment difference. [The] advertising here relates directly, not in an incidental or subsidiary manner, to the regulatory program's underlying goal of 'maintaining and expanding existing markets and uses for mushrooms.' [And] compelled payment may be needed to produce those benefits where, otherwise, some producers would take a free ride on the expenditures of others. [Compared] with traditional 'command and control,' price, or output regulation, this kind of regulation—which relies upon self-regulation through industry trade associations and upon the dissemination of information—is more consistent, not less consistent, with producer choice. It is difficult to see why a Constitution that seeks to protect individual freedom would consider the absence of 'heavy regulation,' to amount to a special, determinative reason for refusing to permit this less intrusive program." Justice Breyer found the compelled expression here, like that in Glickman and unlike that in Barnette and Wooley, "incapable of 'engendering any crisis of conscience.' " He found the producers' objections therefore " 'trivial.' "

Justices Breyer, joined on this point only by Justice Ginsburg, would have treated the mushroom regulation as a mere " 'species of economic regulation' " warranting no special First Amendment scrutiny whatsoever: "First, the program does not significantly interfere with protected speech interests. It does not compel speech itself; it compels the payment of money. Money and speech are not identical. [Second], this program furthers, rather than hinders, the basic First Amendment 'commercial speech' objective [by] promot[ing] the dissemination of truthful information to consumers. [Third], there is no special risk of [significant] harm to an individual's conscience [nor] censor[ship of] producer views unrelated to its basic regulatory justification. And there is little risk of harming any 'discrete, little noticed group' [since the] Act excludes small producers, unlike respondent, a large, influential corporation." Justice Breyer cautioned that the Court, "in applying stricter First Amendment standards and finding them violated, sets an unfortunate precedent. That precedent suggests, perhaps requires, striking down any similar program that, for example, would require tobacco companies to contribute to an industry fund for advertising the harms of smoking or would use a portion of museum entry charges for a citywide campaign to promote the value of art." In a final portion of the dissent joined by both Justices O'Connor and Ginsburg, Justice Breyer concluded that, even if the compulsory fee program were subject to First Amendment review under Central Hudson, it should be upheld as serving a substantial government interest in agricultural promotion by means "necessary and proportionate to the legitimate promotional goals that it seeks."

3. ***Compelled speech or compelled subsidy?*** A third free speech challenge to advertising exactions under federal agricultural marketing orders, this time to those used for beef promotion including the slogan "Beef—It's What's for Dinner," made its way to the Court in **Johanns v. Livestock Marketing Association**, 544 U.S. 550 (2005). This time the decision, like that in Glickman and unlike that in United Foods, came down in favor of the government. But the Court expressly disclaimed reliance on Glickman, noting that, while Glickman had found that "compelled support for generic advertising was legitimately part of the Government's 'collectivist' centralization of the market for tree fruit," here, as in United Foods, "there is no broader regulatory system in place that collectivizes aspects of the beef market unrelated to speech, so Glickman is not controlling." Instead, the Court rested its rejection of the free speech challenge on the notion that the beef exaction, like taxation, supported *government* speech. Justice SCALIA wrote the opinion of the Court, which

was joined by Chief Justice Rehnquist and Justices O'Connor, Thomas and Breyer: "In all of the cases invalidating exactions to subsidize speech, the speech was, or was presumed to be, that of an entity other than the government itself. Keller, Abood, United Foods, Southworth. Our compelled-subsidy cases have consistently respected the principle that 'compelled support of a private association is fundamentally different from compelled support of government.' 'Compelled support of government'—even those programs of government one does not approve—is of course perfectly constitutional, as every taxpayer must attest. [We] have generally assumed, though not yet squarely held, that compelled funding of government speech does not alone raise First Amendment concerns."

Applying these principles, Justice Scalia concluded that the beef exactions supported the speech of the government, not of the Beef Board, a nongovernmental entity that was delegated some responsibility over the advertising: "The message of the promotional campaigns is effectively controlled by the Federal Government itself. The message set out in the beef promotions is from beginning to end the message established by the Federal Government. [Congress] and the Secretary have set out the overarching message [and] the Secretary exercises final approval authority over every word used in every promotional campaign." Justice Scalia also rejected the cattle growers' contention "that the beef program does not qualify as 'government speech' because it is funded by a targeted assessment on beef producers, rather than by general revenues": "The compelled-*subsidy* analysis is altogether unaffected by whether the funds for the promotions are raised by general taxes or through a targeted assessment. [The] First Amendment does not confer a right to pay one's taxes into the general fund, because the injury of compelled funding [does] not stem from the Government's mode of accounting. [Here,] the beef advertisements are subject to political safeguards more than adequate to set them apart from private messages." The majority declined to reach the cattle growers' additional argument that "crediting the advertising to 'America's Beef Producers' impermissibly uses not only their money but also their seeming endorsement to promote a message with which they do not agree," reasoning that this compelled-speech as opposed to compelled-subsidy argument was not appropriate on a facial challenge, "[s]ince neither the Beef Act nor the Beef Order *requires* attribution." The opinion noted that such an argument might form the basis for an as-applied challenge if it were established that individual advertisements were attributed to the challengers.

Justice THOMAS concurred, reiterating that he would hold compelled advertising exactions subject to strict First Amendment scrutiny but recognized "that this principle must be qualified where the regulation compels the funding of speech that is the government's own." Justice BREYER filed a concurrence stating that the beef program was analytically indistinguishable from the mushroom program struck down in United Foods, and reiterated his position in dissent from United Foods that the challenged assessments in both cases "involved a form of economic regulation, not speech." Justice GINSBURG concurred only in the judgment: "I resist ranking the promotional messages funded under the [Beef Act], but not attributed to the Government, as government speech, given the message the Government conveys in its own name [urging the American public to limit intake of fatty foods]. I remain persuaded, however, that the assessments in these cases, as in [United Foods and Glickman] qualify as permissible economic regulation."

Justice SOUTER dissented, joined by Justices Stevens and Kennedy: "The ranchers' complaint is on all fours with the objection of the mushroom growers in United Foods, where a similar statutory exaction was struck down as a compelled subsidy of speech prohibited by the First Amendment absent a comprehensive regulatory scheme to which the speech was incidental. [The] Court accepts the [government-speech] defense unwisely. [I] take the view that if government relies on the government-speech doctrine to compel specific groups to fund speech with targeted taxes, it must make itself politically accountable by indicating that the content actually is a government message, not just the statement of one self-interested group the government is currently willing to invest with power. [Because] the Beef Act fails to require the Government to show its hand, I would [hold] the Act unconstitutional. [The] ads are not required to show any sign of being speech by the Government, and [the] tag line, 'funded by America's Beef Producers,' [all] but ensures that no one reading them will suspect that the message comes from the National Government [rather than] the beef producers who stand to profit when beef is on the table. No one hearing a commercial for Pepsi or Levi's thinks Uncle Sam is the man talking behind the curtain. Why would a person reading a beef ad think Uncle Sam was trying to make him eat more steak? [It] means nothing that Government officials control the message if that fact is never required to be made apparent to those who get the message, let alone if it is affirmatively concealed from them." Justice Kennedy also filed a dissent.

4. ***Reconciling Glickman, United Foods and Johanns.*** Can this trilogy of cases be reconciled? All three involved compelled exactions to fund advertising that some producers found unacceptable in content, and all three involved the danger that the reasonable observer would inaccurately associate all producers of the advertised goods with the offending ads. Justice Scalia suggests in Johanns that any objection is eliminated when "government speech" is at stake. But if what's wrong with compelled subsidization of speech is that it violates autonomy, then does forced subsidy of the government's ads differ from forced subsidy of the beef association's ads? For discussion, see Sullivan & Post, "Symposium: Commercial Speech: Past, Present & Future: It's What's For Lunch: Nectarines, Mushrooms, And Beef—The First Amendment And Compelled Commercial Speech," 41 Loy. L.A. L. Rev. 359 (2007). Should it matter whether the objecting farmers assert economic self-interest or ideological objection as the basis for their objection to the compelled exactions? For discussion of whether it would make any difference if "these objectors were small organic farmers objecting to the undifferentiated product descriptions, not because they wanted to differentiate their product as such for self-interested purposes" but rather because they "farm organically for moral and political reasons, from concern for the environment, the health of consumers, or the humane treatment of animals," see Shiffrin, "Symposium: Commercial Speech: Past, Present & Future: Compelled Association, Morality, and Market Dynamics," 41 Loy. L.A. L. Rev. 317 (2007).

Consider the following possible rationalization of the government speech exception in Johanns, based on the view that the central value of free speech is participation in public discourse: "Because the state always speaks for the community as a whole, and never for the personal views of private citizens, the state can never become the personal spokesperson of a citizen, no matter how much money she donates to it. [It] follows that restrictions on donations to the state do not compromise the ability of persons to participate in public discourse. [The] fundamental constitutional question posed by the government speech exception in Johanns is whether the Beef Board advertisements [should] be understood as 'speaking for' the private and particular views of the beef industry, which represents the perspective of one group in the community, or instead as 'speaking for' the official views of the state, which represents the outlook of the whole community." Post, "Compelled Subsidization of Speech: Johanns v. Livestock Marketing Association," 2005 Sup. Ct. Rev. 195.

What other values are at stake in the disagreement over government speech in Johanns? If regulations of the type at issue in Glickman, United Foods, and Johanns are seen as violative of the First Amendment, does this expansion threaten the ability of the government to engage in other types of economic regulation as Justice Breyer's concurrence in Johanns suggests? For the argument that the First Amendment can be used as a resuscitation of Lochner-era economic due process, see Jackson & Jeffries, "Commercial Speech: Economic Due Process and the First Amendment," 65 Va. L. Rev. 1 (1979).

COMPELLED SPEECH AND PRIVATE DISCRIMINATION

Hurley v. Irish-American Gay, Lesbian and Bisexual Group of Boston [GLIB]

515 U.S. 557, 115 S. Ct. 2338, 132 L. Ed. 2d 487 (1995).

[Hurley addressed whether the private organizers of a St. Patrick's Day parade could be required to include a self-proclaimed gay contingent among the parade's marchers. Massachusetts state antidiscrimination law forbids discrimination on the basis of, inter alia, sexual orientation in the admission or treatment of any person in a place of public accommodation. The state courts found the annual Boston St. Patrick's Day parade to be a public accommodation, found GLIB's exclusion from the parade to be based on sexual orientation, and ordered GLIB admitted to the parade. John J. "Wacko" Hurley and other members of the South Boston Allied War Veterans Council, the private organization that customarily organized the parade, protested this forced inclusion as a violation of their First Amendment rights, and the Court sustained their claim.]

■ JUSTICE SOUTER delivered the opinion for a unanimous Court:

The issue in this case is whether Massachusetts may require private citizens who organize a parade to include among the marchers a group imparting a message the organizers do not wish to convey. We hold that such a mandate violates the First Amendment. [We] use the word "parade" to indicate marchers who are making some sort of collective point, not just to each other but to bystanders along the way. [Parades] are [a] form of expression, not just motion. [The] protected expression that inheres in a parade is not limited to its banners and songs, [but extends to its] "symbolism." [A] narrow, succinctly articulable message is not a condition of constitutional protection, which if confined to expressions conveying a "particularized message," would never reach the unquestionably shielded painting of Jackson Pollock, music of Arnold Schonberg, or Jabberwocky verse of Lewis Carroll. [The] South Boston celebration is [expressive:] Spectators line the streets; people march in costumes and uniforms, carrying flags and banners with all sorts of messages (e.g., "England get out of Ireland," "Say no to drugs"); marching bands and pipers play, floats are pulled along, and the whole show is broadcast over Boston television. To be sure, [the Council] is rather lenient in admitting participants. But a private speaker does not forfeit constitutional protection simply by combining multifarious voices, or by failing to edit their themes to isolate an exact message as the exclusive subject matter of the speech. [The] presentation of an edited compilation of speech generated by other persons is a staple of most newspapers' opinion pages, which, of course, fall squarely within the core of First Amendment security [Tornillo], [and the] selection of contingents to make a parade is entitled to similar protection.

Respondents' participation as a unit in the parade was equally expressive. GLIB was formed for the very purpose of marching in it, as the trial court found, in order to celebrate its members' identity as openly gay, lesbian, and bisexual descendants of the Irish immigrants, to show that there are such individuals in the community, and to support the like men and women who sought to march in the New York [St. Patrick's Day] parade. [M]embers of GLIB [the previous year] marched behind a shamrock-strewn banner with the simple inscription "Irish American Gay, Lesbian and Bisexual Group of Boston." GLIB understandably seeks to communicate its ideas as part of the existing parade, rather than staging one of its own.

[Hurley and the Council] disclaim any intent to exclude homosexuals as such, and no individual member of GLIB claims to have been excluded from parading as a member of any group that the Council has approved to march. Instead, the disagreement goes to the admission of GLIB as its own parade unit carrying its own banner. Since every participating unit affects the message conveyed by the private organizers, the state courts' application of the statute produced an order essentially requiring petitioners to alter the expressive content of their parade. [The] state courts' application of the statute had the effect of declaring the sponsors' speech itself to be the public accommodation. Under this approach any contingent of protected individuals with a message would have the right to participate in petitioners' speech, so that the communication produced by the private organizers would be shaped by all those protected by the law who wished to join in with some expressive demonstration of their own. But this use of the State's power violates the fundamental rule of protection under the First Amendment, that a speaker has the autonomy to choose the content of his own message.

[The Council's] claim to the benefit of this principle of autonomy to control one's own speech is as sound as the South Boston parade is expressive. [The] Council clearly decided to exclude a message it did not like from the communication it chose to make, and that is enough to invoke its right as a private speaker to shape its expression by speaking on one subject while remaining silent on another. The message it disfavored is not difficult to identify. Although GLIB's point (like the Council's) is not wholly articulate, a contingent marching behind the organization's banner would at least bear witness to the fact that some Irish are gay, lesbian, or bisexual, and the presence of the organized marchers would suggest their view that people of their sexual orientations have as much claim to unqualified social acceptance as heterosexuals and indeed as members of parade units organized around other identifying characteristics. The parade's organizers may not believe these facts about Irish sexuality to be so, or they may object to unqualified social acceptance of gays and lesbians or have some other reason for wishing to keep GLIB's message out of the parade. But whatever the reason, it boils down to the choice of a speaker not to propound a particular point of view, and that choice is presumed to lie beyond the government's power to control. [Considering] that GLIB presumably would have had a fair shot (under neutral criteria developed by the city) at obtaining a parade permit of its own, respondents have not shown that petitioners enjoy the capacity to "silence the voice of competing speakers."

HURLEY'S REACH

1. ***Public and private forums compared.*** Suppose the parade had been run by the city of Boston rather than the South Boston Allied War Veterans Council. Would GLIB's exclusion have been forbidden by the First Amendment? Would such a parade have amounted to a public forum? A limited public forum? Or not a public forum at all? If the federal government sponsored a parade for military veterans, would it be obliged to include a contingent of avowedly gay former service members? Even if it maintained a policy of excluding homosexuals from the military?

2. ***The limits of Hurley.*** In **Rumsfeld v. Forum for Academic and Institutional Rights (FAIR)**, 547 U.S. 47 (2006), the Court reviewed a First Amendment challenge to the Solomon Amendment, a statute denying federal funding to any institution of higher education that "has a policy or practice [that] either prohibits, or in effect prevents" the military "from gaining access to campuses, or access to students [on] campuses, for purposes of military recruiting in a manner that is at least equal in quality and scope to the access to campuses and to students that is provided to any other employer." A group of law faculties objected to this condition on the ground that the military's "Don't Ask, Don't Tell" policy discriminated on the basis of sexual orientation in violation of the nondiscrimination policies their law schools apply to employers who recruit on campus. Their challenge on free speech, compelled speech, and compelled association grounds was unsuccessful. (For portions of the opinion rejecting FAIR's compelled association claim, see p. 1452 below.)

Writing for a unanimous Court, Chief Justice ROBERTS found that the Solomon Amendment did not amount to an infringement or compulsion of speech and thus required no heightened First Amendment scrutiny: "The Solomon Amendment neither limits what law schools may say nor requires them to say anything. Law schools remain free under the statute to express whatever views they may have on the military's congressionally mandated employment policy, all the while retaining eligibility for federal funds. As a general matter, the Solomon Amendment regulates conduct, not speech. It affects what law schools must *do*—afford equal access to military recruiters—not what they may or may not *say*. [Recruiting] assistance provided by the schools often includes elements of speech. For example, schools may send e-mails or post notices on bulletin boards on an employer's behalf. [This] sort of recruiting assistance, however, is a far cry from the compelled speech in Barnette and Wooley. The Solomon Amendment, unlike the laws at issue in those cases, does not dictate the content of the speech at all, which is only 'compelled' if, and to the extent, the school provides such speech for other recruiters. There is nothing in this case approaching a Government-mandated pledge or motto that the school must endorse."

Having distinguished Barnette and Wooley, the Chief Justice likewise distinguished Hurley and Tornillo: "[A]ccommodating the military's message does not affect the law schools' speech, because the schools are not speaking when they host interviews and recruiting receptions. Unlike a parade organizer's choice of parade contingents, a law school's decision to allow recruiters on campus is not inherently expressive. Law schools facilitate recruiting to assist their students in obtaining jobs. A law school's recruiting services lack the expressive quality of a parade, a newsletter, or the editorial page of a newspaper; its accommodation of a military recruiter's message is not compelled speech because the accommodation does not sufficiently interfere with any message of the school." He also opined that here, as in PruneYard, there was little danger that the military recruiters' speech would be erroneously attributed to the law schools: "Nothing about recruiting suggests that law schools agree with any speech by recruiters, and nothing in the Solomon Amendment restricts what the law schools may say about the military's policies."

3. ***Antidiscrimination law and private commercial transactions.*** Parallel issues were raised in Masterpiece Cakeshop v. Colorado Civil Rights Commission, 584 U.S. ___, 138 S. Ct. 1719 (2018), discussed above (p. 1576), Although the baker raised compelled speech and association claims, the Court resolved the case on the grounds of animus under Lukumi, thereby avoiding the primary claims. If the Court had resolved the case on those grounds, how should the case have been decided? Under the Chief Justice's logic in FAIR, should the compelled baking of a wedding cake for a gay couple be characterized as a mere regulation of conduct? Or should Hurley apply, such that a baker's decision to provide an otherwise available service to a gay couple be seen as "inherently expressive"?

4. ***What standard of scrutiny applies in compelled speech cases?*** Note that the question whether government has compelled a speaker to utter or to be associated with undesired speech is a threshold question. If a law does not compel speech, as the Court found the California constitutional provision upheld in PruneYard did not, then no special First Amendment scrutiny is required; rationality review is sufficient. If a law *does* compel speech, then it is analyzed just as a law forbidding speech would be analyzed. Thus, if a law compels speech of a particular content, as did the laws in Barnette, Wooley, and McIntyre, or compels counterspeech in response to speech of particular content, as did the laws in Tornillo and PG & E, it is treated as content-based and receives strict scrutiny. But if a law compels speech for reasons unrelated to content, as did the must-carry rules in Turner as the majority read them, then, at most, intermediate scrutiny under O'Brien and Ward is required.

What are the other factors that are driving the Court's analysis of compelled speech? In addition to the content neutrality of the provision, the Court has considered the risk of identifying the compelled message with the speaker in PruneYard, the scarcity of available media in Red Lion, and the speaker's ability to convey its own message despite the compelled speech in PG & E. Which of these is most important in the Court's analysis? Which of these factors should be the most important? Consider how these factors reflect underlying free speech values. Should it matter whether disclaimers are available as a practical matter? Justice Souter contrasted Hurley with PruneYard by noting that a shopkeeper can easily disavow leafletters' message but that "disclaimers would be quite curious in a moving parade."

5. ***Compulsion of speech and First Amendment theory.*** Why does compulsion of speech offend free speech values? Because government should not reach into the minds and bodies of speakers and treat them like puppets? Because of concern about enforced adherence to government messages as a form of civic orthodoxy? Note that such justifications cover only cases like Barnette and Wooley, and not cases where government does not script the speaker. What is the core free speech concern in the other cases above? Autonomy from government paternalism?

Note that many of the challengers in the above compelled speech cases are corporations. If the principal value served by the protection from compelled speech is human autonomy, and if corporations lack souls and consciences and thus a capacity for autonomy comparable to that of individuals, then what theory of free speech calls for their protection here? Should corporations like PG & E have a right against compelled speech? A right of free speech at all? Justice Rehnquist's dissent in PG & E notwithstanding, the Court has held that they do. See First National Bank v. Bellotti (1978; p. 1475 below). What alternative rationale might protect corporate rights to speak or not to speak? Might corporate speech be instrumentally valuable in enhancing the free flow of ideas and information to the public, even if it is not intrinsically valuable to any human agent? While such a systemic view might argue against prohibitions of corporate speech, how can it argue against compulsion of corporate speech, which increases the information available to the public? For critical assessments of corporate speech rights, see Bezanson, "Institutional Speech," 80 Iowa L. Rev. 735 (1995); Baker, "Turner Broadcasting: Content-Based Regulation of Persons and Presses," 1994 Sup. Ct. Rev. 57.

If the First Amendment protects a right not to speak, does it also protect a right not to listen? Should objecting listeners be able to exempt themselves from mandatory abortion counseling or mandatory diversity training? For exploration of such a possible right, see Corbin, "The First Amendment Right Against Compelled Listening," 89 Bos. U. L. Rev. 939 (2009).

SECTION 2. FREEDOM OF EXPRESSIVE ASSOCIATION

As early as De Jonge v. Oregon, 299 U.S. 353 (1937), the Court relied on the First Amendment reference to "the right of the people peaceably to assemble" in invalidating a conviction. In NAACP v. Alabama, the 1958 decision that follows, the Court identified an independent constitutional "right of association." The right to associate reflects the notion that individual rights of expression can be made more effectual by collective action. As the Court later summarized in Roberts v. United States Jaycees (1984; p. 1446 below): "An individual's freedom to speak, worship, and to petition the Government for the redress of grievances could not be vigorously protected from interference by the State unless a correlative freedom to engage in group effort toward those ends were not also guaranteed." The Court has tended to view the right of association as dependent on underlying individual rights of expression; there is no right of association in the abstract. See Dallas v. Stanglin, 490 U.S. 19 (1989) (rejecting a freedom of association claim against a Dallas ordinance barring social dancing between teenagers and adults, stating "we do not think the Constitution recognizes a generalized right of 'social association' that includes chance encounters in dance halls").

The Court has reviewed several types of government infringement of the right of expressive association protected by the First Amendment. Most directly, government might simply outlaw an organization or membership in it. The Court has limited such direct restrictions in cases discussed earlier. Recall that the Court in Brandenburg v. Ohio, overruling Whitney, held that one may not be punished simply for assembling with an organization that advocates violent political or industrial reform.

The materials that follow explore several additional government techniques sometimes held to infringe associational liberty. First, government might seek to monitor or intimidate an association by requiring either that the group or an individual member of a group disclose information about group membership in violation of what the Court in NAACP v. Alabama called the right to "privacy in group association." Second, government might restrict activities centrally linked to the purpose of an association, such as meetings or litigation or boycott activities. Third, government might deny governmental benefits or privileges to members of certain associations. Recall that in the Elrod line of cases (p. 1316 above), the Court held that most public jobs may not be conditioned on membership in the victorious political party.

The Court has also held that the right to associate entails a right not to associate, comparable to the right not to speak. It has therefore, for example, invalidated certain compulsory fees exacted from unwilling group members and reviewed laws requiring groups to include unwanted members. These various techniques of interference with associational freedom are examined in turn in the materials that follow.

COMPELLED DISCLOSURE OF MEMBERSHIP

A series of cases in the late 1950s and early 1960s reviewed efforts to inhibit the activities of the National Association for the Advancement of Colored People (NAACP) by requiring disclosure of its membership lists in various contexts. In addition to the cases that follow, see Bates v. Little Rock, 361 U.S. 516 (1960), invalidating a requirement that membership lists be disclosed in connection with an occupational license tax, and Louisiana ex rel. Gremillion v. NAACP, 366 U.S. 293 (1961), restraining enforcement of a statute requiring nonprofit organizations to file membership lists. On these and related cases generally, see Kalven, The Negro and the First Amendment (1965).

NAACP v. Alabama

357 U.S. 449, 78 S. Ct. 1163, 2 L. Ed. 2d 1488 (1958).

[In NAACP v. Alabama, which follows, the Court held unconstitutional Alabama's demand that the NAACP reveal the names and addresses of all of its Alabama members and agents. The State's demand was made in the course of an injunction action brought in 1956 to stop the NAACP from conducting activities in Alabama, on the ground that it had failed to comply with the requirement that foreign corporations qualify before "doing business" in the State. The NAACP, a New York membership corporation, operated in Alabama largely through local affiliates that were unincorporated associations. It considered itself exempt from the State's foreign corporation registration law. While the injunction action was pending, the State moved for the production of a large number of the NAACP's records. The NAACP produced substantially all the data called for, but not its membership lists, as to which it contended that Alabama could not constitutionally compel disclosure. The trial court adjudged the NAACP in contempt and imposed a $100,000 fine. The Supreme Court reversed.]

■ JUSTICE HARLAN delivered the opinion of the Court:

Effective advocacy of both public and private points of view, particularly controversial ones, is undeniably enhanced by group association, as this Court has [recognized] by remarking upon the close nexus between the freedoms of speech and assembly. It is beyond debate that freedom to engage in association for the advancement of beliefs and ideas is an inseparable aspect of the "liberty" assured by the Due Process Clause of the 14th Amendment, which embraces freedom of speech. Of course, it is immaterial whether the beliefs sought to be advanced by association pertain to political, economic, religious or cultural matters, and state action which may have the effect of curtailing the freedom to associate is subject to the closest scrutiny. The fact that Alabama [has] taken no direct action [to] restrict the right of petitioner's members to associate freely does not end inquiry into the effect of the production order. [I]n the domain of these indispensable liberties, whether of speech, press, or association, the decisions of this Court recognize that abridgment of such rights, even though unintended, may inevitably follow from varied forms of governmental [action]. It is hardly a novel perception that compelled disclosure of affiliation with groups engaged in advocacy may constitute [an effective] restraint on freedom of association. [There is a] vital relationship between freedom to associate and privacy in one's associations. [Inviolability] of privacy in group association may in many circumstances be indispensable to preservation of freedom of association, particularly where a group espouses dissident [beliefs].

We think that the production order [must] be regarded as entailing the likelihood of a substantial restraint upon the exercise by petitioner's members of their right to freedom of association. Petitioner has made an uncontroverted showing that on past occasions revelation of the identity of its rank-and-file members has exposed these members to economic reprisal, loss of employment, threat of physical coercion, and other manifestations of public hostility. Under these circumstances, we think it apparent that compelled disclosure of petitioner's Alabama membership is likely to affect adversely the ability of petitioner and its members to pursue their collective effort to foster beliefs which they admittedly have the right to advocate, in that it may induce members to withdraw from the Association and dissuade others from joining it because of fear of exposure of their beliefs shown through their associations and of the consequences of this [exposure].

We turn to the [question] whether Alabama has demonstrated an interest in obtaining the disclosures it seeks from petitioner which is sufficient to justify the deterrent effect which we have concluded these disclosures may well have on the free exercise [of] constitutionally protected right of association. [Such a] "subordinating interest of the State must be compelling." It is important to bear in mind that petitioner asserts no right to absolute immunity from state investigation. [Petitioner] has not objected to divulging the identity of its members who are employed by or hold official positions with it. It has urged the rights solely of its ordinary rank-and-file [members]. Whether there was "justification" in this instance turns solely on the substantiality of Alabama's interest in obtaining the membership lists. [The] exclusive purpose [claimed] was to determine whether petitioner was conducting intrastate business in violation of the Alabama foreign corporation registration statute. [W]e are unable to perceive that the disclosure of the names of petitioner's rank-and-file members has a substantial bearing on the state interest. [W]hatever interest the State may have in obtaining names of ordinary members has not been shown to be sufficient to overcome petitioner's constitutional objections to the production order.[1] [W]e conclude that Alabama has fallen short of showing a controlling justification for the deterrent effect on the free enjoyment of the right to associate which disclosure of membership lists is likely to [have]. Reversed.

COMPELLED DISCLOSURE IN THE CIVIL RIGHTS ERA

1. ***Compelled disclosure and public employment.*** In **Shelton v. Tucker**, 364 U.S. 479 (1960), the Court held unconstitutional an Arkansas statute—Act 10—which required every teacher, as a condition of employment in a state-supported school or college, to file "annually an affidavit listing without limitation every organization to which he has belonged or regularly contributed within the preceding five years." Shelton, who had taught in the Little Rock schools for 25 years, refused to file an affidavit, and his contract was not renewed. In the trial court, the evidence showed that he was not a member of any organization advocating the overthrow of the Government but that he was a member of the NAACP.

Justice STEWART delivered the opinion of the Court: "It is urged [that] Act 10 deprives teachers in Arkansas of their rights to personal, associational, and academic liberty. [I]n considering this contention, we deal with two basic postulates. *First.* There can be no doubt of the right of a state to investigate the competence and fitness of those whom it hires to teach in its schools. [*Second*]. [To] compel a teacher to disclose his every associational tie is to impair that teacher's right of free association. [Such] interference with personal freedom is conspicuously accented when the teacher serves at

[1] Justice Harlan distinguished Bryant v. Zimmerman, 278 U.S. 63 (1928), where the Court had upheld a New York law requiring disclosure of membership lists of any organization requiring an oath as a condition of membership. That law had been challenged by a member of the Ku Klux Klan. One of the distinctions noted by Justice Harlan was that Bryant had rested on "the peculiar character of the Klan's activities, involving acts of unlawful intimidation and violence." Moreover, the KKK, unlike the NAACP here, had refused to give the state "*any* information as to its local activities."

the absolute will of those to whom the disclosure must be made. [The] statute does not provide that the information it requires be kept confidential. [The] record contains evidence to indicate that fear of public disclosure is neither theoretical nor groundless. Even if there were no disclosure to the general public, the pressure upon a teacher to avoid any ties which might displease those who control his professional destiny would be constant and heavy. [The] vigilant protection of constitutional freedoms is nowhere more vital than in the community of American [schools].

The question to be decided here is not whether the State [can] ask certain of its teachers about all their organizational relationships. It is not whether the State can ask all of its teachers about certain of their associational ties. It is not whether teachers can be asked how many organizations they belong to, or how much time they spend in organizational activity. The question is whether the State can ask every one of its teachers to disclose every single organization with which he has been associated over a five-year period. The scope of the inquiry required by Act 10 is completely unlimited. [The Act] requires a teacher [to] list, without number, every conceivable kind of associational tie—social, professional, political, avocational, or religious. Many such relationships could have no possible bearing upon the teacher's occupational competence or fitness. [This] Court has held that, even though the governmental purpose be legitimate and substantial, that purpose cannot be pursued by means that broadly stifle fundamental personal liberties when the end can be more narrowly achieved. The breadth of legislative abridgment must be viewed in the light of less drastic means for achieving the same basic purpose. [The] unlimited and indiscriminate sweep of the statute now before us brings it within the ban of our prior cases. The statute's comprehensive interference with associational freedom goes far beyond what might be justified in the exercise of the State's legitimate inquiry into the fitness and competency of its teachers. Reversed."

Justice FRANKFURTER dissented: "[The] Court strikes down [the law] on the ground that 'many such relationships could have no possible bearing upon the teacher's occupational competence or fitness.' [The selection of teachers] is an intricate affair [and] if it is to be informed, it must be based upon a comprehensive range of information. I am unable to say [that] Arkansas could not reasonably find that the information which the statute requires [is] germane to that selection. [Of course,] if the information gathered [is] used to further a scheme of terminating the employment of teachers solely because of their membership in unpopular organizations, that use will run afoul of the Fourteenth Amendment. It will be time enough, if such use is made, to hold the application of the [law] unconstitutional."

2. ***Compelled disclosure and legislative investigations.*** In **Gibson v. Florida Legislative Investigation Comm.**, 372 U.S. 539 (1963), the Court held that the imprisonment of an NAACP official for failure to comply with a legislative committee's request for a membership list violated the First Amendment. In 1957, an earlier legislative committee had sought the entire membership list of the local NAACP branch. Florida's highest court barred that request but stated that the committee could compel the custodian of the records to bring them to committee hearings and to refer to them to determine whether specific individuals, identified as or suspected of being Communists, were NAACP members. The committee in Gibson was established in 1959 to resume the investigation. Gibson, the President of the Miami branch, was ordered to bring the records pertaining to the identity of

members of and contributors to the Miami and state NAACP organizations. Gibson, relying on the First Amendment, did not bring the records but told the Committee that he would answer questions concerning membership in the NAACP on the basis of his personal knowledge. He was given the names and shown photographs of 14 persons previously identified as being involved in Communist or Communist-front affairs. Gibson said that he could associate none of them with the NAACP. For his failure to produce the records, a state court found him in contempt and sentenced him to six months' imprisonment and a $1200 fine.

Writing for the Court, Justice GOLDBERG struck down the conviction, reasoning that "it is an essential prerequisite to the validity of an investigation which intrudes into the area of constitutionally protected rights of speech, press, association and petition that the State convincingly show a substantial relation between the information sought and a subject of overriding and compelling state interest. Absent such a ['nexus'], the Committee has not 'demonstrated so cogent an interest in obtaining and making public' the membership information sought [as] to 'justify the substantial abridgment of associational freedom which such disclosures will effect.'

[The] record in this case is insufficient to show a substantial connection between the Miami branch of the NAACP and Communist *activities* which [is] an essential prerequisite to demonstrating the immediate, substantial, and subordinating state interest necessary to sustain its right of inquiry into the membership lists. [There] is here merely indirect, less than unequivocal, and mostly hearsay testimony that in years past some 14 people who were asserted to be, or to have been, Communists or members of Communist front or 'affiliated organizations' attended occasional meetings of the Miami branch of the NAACP 'and/or' were members of that branch, which had a total membership of about 1,000. [The] strong associational interest in maintaining the privacy of membership lists of groups engaged in the constitutionally protected free trade in ideas and beliefs may not be substantially infringed upon such a slender showing. [While,] of course, all legitimate organizations are the beneficiaries of these protections, they are all the more essential here, where the challenged privacy is that of persons espousing beliefs already unpopular with their neighbors and the deterrent and 'chilling' effect on the free exercise of constitutionally enshrined rights of free speech, expression, and association is consequently the more immediate and substantial. Reversed."

Justice HARLAN dissented: "[Until] today, I had never supposed that any of our decisions [could] possibly be taken as suggesting any difference in the degree [of] investigatory interest as between Communist infiltration *of* organizations and Communist activity *by* organizations. [The 'nexus' here was sufficient] unless 'nexus' requires an investigating agency to prove in advance the very things it is trying to find out. [I] also find it difficult to see how this case really presents any serious question as to interference with freedom of association. Given the willingness of the petitioner to testify from recollection as to individual memberships in the local branch of the NAACP, the germaneness of the membership records to the subject matter of the Committee's investigation, and the limited purpose for which their use was sought—as an aid to refreshing the witness' recollection, involving their divulgence only to the petitioner himself—this case of course bears no resemblance whatever to [NAACP v. Alabama] or [Bates], [where] the State had sought general divulgence of local NAACP membership lists without any showing of a justifying state interest."

COMPELLED DISCLOSURE OF POLITICAL CAMPAIGN CONTRIBUTIONS

In **Buckley v. Valeo**, 424 U.S. 1 (1976), discussed in full below (see p. 1461), the Court rejected challenges to the disclosure provisions of the Federal Election Campaign Act. The Act required that every political candidate and "political committee" maintain records of the name and address of every person contributing more than $10 in a calendar year and his or her occupation and principal place of business if his contribution exceeded $100, to make such records available for inspection by the Federal Election Commission (FEC), and to file quarterly reports with the FEC disclosing the source of every contribution exceeding $100.

The per curiam opinion stated: "We long have recognized that significant encroachments on First Amendment rights of the sort that compelled disclosure imposes cannot be justified by a mere showing of some legitimate governmental interest. Since [NAACP v. Alabama] we have required that the subordinating interests of the State must survive exacting scrutiny. We also have insisted that there be a 'substantial relation' [Gibson] between the governmental interest and the information required to be disclosed. This type of scrutiny is necessary even if any deterrent effect on the exercise of First Amendment rights arises, not through direct government action, but indirectly as an unintended but inevitable result of the government's conduct in requiring disclosure. [NAACP v. Alabama.]

"Appellees argue that the disclosure requirements of the Act differ significantly from those at issue in Alabama and its progeny because the Act only requires disclosure of the names of contributors and does not compel political organizations to submit the names of their members. [T]he invasion of privacy of belief may be as great when the information sought concerns the giving and spending of money as when it concerns the joining of [organizations]. The strict test established by Alabama is necessary because compelled disclosure has the potential for substantially infringing the exercise of First Amendment rights. But we have acknowledged that there are governmental interests sufficiently important to outweigh the possibility of infringement.

"[The] governmental interests sought to be vindicated by the disclosure requirements are of this magnitude. They fall into three categories. First, disclosure provides the electorate with information 'as to where political campaign money comes [from]' in order to aid the voters in evaluating those who seek Federal office. [Second], disclosure requirements deter actual corruption and avoid the appearance of corruption by exposing large [contributions] to the light of publicity. [Third, such] requirements are an essential means of gathering the data necessary to detect violations of the contribution limitations. [Thus, the] disclosure requirements [directly] serve substantial governmental interests. [It] is undoubtedly true that public disclosure of contributions [will] deter some individuals who otherwise might contribute. In some instances, disclosure may even expose contributors to harassment or retaliation. These are not insignificant burdens on individual rights, and they must be weighed carefully against the interests which Congress has sought to promote by this legislation. [But we agree] that disclosure requirements—certainly in most applications—appear to be the least restrictive means of curbing the evils of campaign ignorance and corruption that Congress found to exist."

The Court also rejected the claim that the disclosure requirements were invalid as applied to minor parties: "[NAACP v. Alabama] is inapposite where, as here, any serious infringement on First Amendment rights brought about by the compelled disclosure of contributors is highly speculative. It is true that the governmental interest in disclosure is diminished when the contribution in question is made to a minor party with little chance of winning an election. [We] are not unmindful that the damage done by disclosure to [the] minor parties [could] be significant. [In] some instances fears of reprisal may deter contributions to the point where the movement cannot survive. [There] could well be a case [where] the threat to the exercise of First Amendment rights is so serious and the state interest furthered by disclosure so insubstantial that the Act's requirements cannot be constitutionally applied. But no appellant in this case has tendered record evidence of [that] sort. [On] this record, the substantial public interest in disclosure identified by the legislative history of this Act outweighs the harm generally alleged. [In any particular case,] [m]inor parties must be allowed sufficient flexibility in the proof of injury to assure a fair consideration of their claim. The evidence offered need show only a reasonable probability that the compelled disclosure of a party's contributors' names will subject them to threats, harassment or reprisals from either government officials or private parties."

Chief Justice BURGER dissented from this portion of Buckley: "[Secrecy] and privacy as to political preferences and convictions are fundamental in a free society. [I] suggest the Court has failed to give the traditional standing to some of the First Amendment values at stake here. Specifically, it has failed to confine the particular exercise of governmental power within limits reasonably required. [Shelton v. Tucker.] [It] seems to me that the threshold limits fixed at $10 and $100 for anonymous contributions are constitutionally impermissible on their face. [To] argue that a 1976 contribution of $10 or $100 entails a risk of corruption or its appearance is simply too extravagant to be maintained. [There] is, in short, no relation whatever between the means used and the legitimate goal of ventilating possible undue influence. Congress has used a shotgun to kill wrens as well as hawks.

"In saying that the lines drawn by Congress are 'not wholly without rationality,' the Court [makes an] abrupt departure from traditional standards; [surely] a greater burden rests on Congress than merely to avoid 'irrationality' when regulating in the core area of the First Amendment. Even taking the Court at its word, the particular dollar amounts fixed by Congress that must be reported to the Commission fall short of meeting the test of rationality when measured by the goals sought to be achieved. Finally, no legitimate public interest has been shown in forcing the disclosure of modest contributions that are the prime support of new, unpopular or unfashionable political causes. There is no realistic possibility that such modest donations will have a corrupting influence, especially on parties that enjoy only 'minor' status. Major parties would not notice them; minor parties need [them].

Flushing out the names of supporters of minority parties will plainly have a deterrent effect on potential [contributors]."

The possibility held out by Buckley—that certain minor parties might, on a proper showing, obtain exemptions from compelled disclosures—was realized in **Brown v. Socialist Workers '74 Campaign Committee**, 459 U.S. 87 (1982). In an opinion by Justice MARSHALL, the Court held, unanimously on this point, that the Socialist Workers Party in Ohio had made a sufficient showing of a "reasonable probability of threats, harassment, or reprisals" so that it could not constitutionally be compelled to disclose information concerning campaign contributions. The Court noted that the Party was "a minor political party which historically has been the object of harassment by government officials and private parties." (The Court also held, over the dissents of Justices O'Connor, Rehnquist, and Stevens, that the same showing also exempted the Party from compelled disclosure of campaign *disbursements.*)

In **McConnell v. Federal Election Comm'n**, 540 U.S. 93 (2003), discussed in full below at p. 1480, the Court upheld against free speech challenge various new provisions of the Bipartisan Campaign Reform Act of 2002 (BCRA), including disclosure provisions. BCRA extended the disclosure requirements upheld in Buckley from hard-money contributions to candidates to expenditures for so-called "electioneering communications," defined as broadcast ads that specifically identify any candidate for federal office within 60 days before an election or 30 days before a primary election. The majority, in an opinion by Justices STEVENS and O'CONNOR, upheld this requirement as closely tailored to the important state interests Buckley had identified in deterring actual or apparent corruption and keeping voters informed. Dissenting from this aspect of the ruling, Justice THOMAS cited his McIntyre concurrence to conclude that "the established right to anonymous speech" may not be abridged in order merely to provide information to voters.

BCRA's disclosure provisions were the only disputed provisions to survive First Amendment challenge in **Citizens United v. Federal Election Commission**, 558 U.S. 310 (2010). By a vote of 5–4, the Court invalidated BCRA's limitations on corporate expenditures for advocacy in electoral campaigns (see p. 1494 below), but, by a vote of 8–1, the Court upheld BCRA's disclaimer and disclosure requirements as applied to *Hillary*, a documentary critical of then-Senator Clinton during her campaign for the presidency, and advertisements for the film. Justice KENNEDY wrote for the Court: "Under BCRA § 311, televised electioneering communications funded by anyone other than a candidate must include a disclaimer that '______ is responsible for the content of this advertising.' The required statement must be made in a 'clearly spoken manner,' and displayed on the screen in a 'clearly readable manner' for at least four seconds. It must state that the communication 'is not authorized by any candidate or candidate's committee; it must also display the name and address (or Web site address) of the person or group that funded the advertisement. Under BCRA § 201, any person who spends more than $10,000 on electioneering communications within a calendar year must file a disclosure statement with the FEC. That statement must identify the person making the expenditure, the amount of the expenditure, the election to which the communication was directed, and the names of certain contributors.

"[We] find the statute valid as applied to the ads for the movie and to the movie itself. [Disclosure] is a less restrictive alternative to more comprehensive regulations of speech. [The] public has an interest in knowing who is speaking about a candidate shortly before an election. [Citizens United] argues that disclosure requirements can chill donations to an organization by exposing donors to retaliation. In McConnell [v. FEC (2003; p. 1480 below)], the Court recognized that § 201 would be unconstitutional as applied to an organization if there were a reasonable probability that the group's members would face threats, harassment, or reprisals if their names were disclosed. [Citizens United,] however, has offered no evidence that its members may face similar threats or reprisals.

"[A] campaign finance system that pairs corporate independent expenditures with effective disclosure has not existed before today. [With] the advent of the Internet, prompt disclosure of expenditures can provide shareholders and citizens with the information needed to hold corporations and elected officials accountable for their positions and supporters. Shareholders can determine whether their corporation's political speech advances the corporation's interest in making profits, and citizens can see whether elected officials are ' "in the pocket" of so-called moneyed interests.' [This] transparency enables the electorate to make informed decisions and give proper weight to different speakers and messages."

Only Justice THOMAS dissented from this portion of the decision, stating: "The disclosure, disclaimer, and reporting requirements in BCRA §§ 201 and 311 [are] unconstitutional. Congress may not abridge the 'right to anonymous speech' based on the 'simple interest in providing voters with additional relevant information.'" He noted that, after California voters passed Proposition 8, a 2008 state ballot proposition that amended California's constitution to overrule a state supreme court decision upholding a right to gay marriage, opponents of Proposition 8 had used information posted on the Internet under California's mandatory disclosure rules to "create[ ] Web sites with maps showing the locations of homes or businesses of Proposition 8 supporters. Many supporters (or their customers) suffered property damage, or threats of physical violence or death, as a result. [The] success of such intimidation tactics has apparently spawned a cottage industry that uses forcibly disclosed donor information to pre-empt citizens' exercise of their First Amendment rights. [These] instances of retaliation sufficiently demonstrate why this Court should invalidate mandatory disclosure and reporting requirements."

Does such anecdotal evidence justify a broader presumption in favor of anonymous political contributions? Who should bear the burden of overcoming the presumption—those who would show good cause for identifying contributors, or those who would show good cause for keeping contributors' identities hidden? Are these contemporary cases consistent with NAACP v. Alabama? Or has the pendulum swung in the opposite direction, rendering NAACP v. Alabama a relic of the Civil Rights Era? Is it possible that disclosure requirements are not only potentially pernicious, as the Civil Rights Era cases demonstrate, but also insufficient to deal with contemporary problems posed by campaign finance regulation?

RESTRICTIONS ON ORGANIZATIONAL ACTIVITY

The Court has also invalidated various direct restraints on characteristic associational activity. For example, in Healy v. James, 408 U.S. 169 (1972), the Court invalidated efforts by Central Connecticut State College to prevent a local chapter of Students for a Democratic Society (SDS), a radical student organization that advocated participatory democracy, racial equality, and antiwar messages, from holding meetings or otherwise organizing on campus, at least in the absence of any demonstrated actual misconduct. More controversial has been the constitutionality of restrictions on such organizational activity as conducting political litigation or boycotts.

Does the government still attempt to place restraints on association? Do contemporary politics raise the same potential for government restraint on association that occurred as a result of the Communist Scare in the 1950s? Or the Civil Rights and Antiwar Movements of the 1960s and 1970s? Consider the following cases.

NAACP v. Button

371 U.S. 415, 83 S. Ct. 328, 9 L. Ed. 2d 405 (1963).

[The Virginia Conference of the NAACP financed litigation aimed at ending racial segregation of the Virginia public schools. NAACP cases were typically not initiated by aggrieved persons applying to the Conference for assistance. Instead, a local NAACP branch usually invited a member of the Conference legal staff to explain to a meeting of parents and children the legal steps necessary to achieve desegregation. The staff member would bring printed forms authorizing NAACP attorneys, rather than any particular lawyer, to represent the signers in desegregation suits.

Virginia prohibited "the improper solicitation of any legal or professional business" and had long banned the solicitation of legal business in the form of "running" or "capping." Before 1956, there was no attempt to apply those regulations to curb the NAACP's activities in sponsoring litigation directed at racial segregation. But in 1956, the laws were amended by adding a Chapter 33 to include, in the definition of "runner" or "capper," an agent for any organization which "employs, retains or compensates" any lawyer "in connection with any judicial proceeding in which it has no pecuniary right or liability." Virginia's highest court held that the NAACP's Virginia activities violated Chapter 33. The Supreme Court reversed and held that the Virginia law was unconstitutional as applied to the NAACP.]

■ JUSTICE BRENNAN delivered the opinion of the Court:

[We] hold that the activities of the NAACP, its affiliates and legal staff shown on this record are modes of expression and association protected by the [First Amendment] which Virginia may not prohibit [as] improper solicitation of legal business. [We reject] the contention that "solicitation" is wholly outside the area of freedoms protected by the First Amendment. [Abstract] discussion is not the only species of communication which the Constitution protects; the First Amendment also protects vigorous advocacy, certainly of lawful ends, against governmental intrusion. [In] the context of NAACP objectives, litigation is not a technique of resolving private differences; it is a means for [achieving] equality of treatment for the members of the Negro community. [It] is thus a form of political expression. Groups which find themselves unable to achieve their objectives through the ballot frequently turn to the courts. [And] litigation may well be the sole practicable avenue open to a minority to petition for redress of grievances. [There] is no longer any doubt that the [First Amendment protects] certain forms of orderly group activity. Thus we have affirmed the right "to engage in association for the advancement of beliefs and ideas." NAACP v. Alabama. [The] NAACP is not a conventional political party, but [for the group] it assists, [association] for litigation may be the most effective form of [political association].

[Under Chapter 33,] a person who advises another that his legal rights have been infringed and refers him to a particular attorney or group of attorneys [for] assistance has committed a [crime]. There thus inheres in the statute the gravest danger of smothering all discussion looking to the eventual institution of litigation on behalf of the rights of members of an unpopular minority. [Such] a vague and broad statute lends itself to selective enforcement against unpopular causes. We cannot close our eyes to the fact that the militant Negro civil rights movement has engendered the intense resentment and opposition of the politically dominant white community of Virginia; litigation assisted by the NAACP has been bitterly fought. In such circumstances a statute broadly curtailing group activity leading to litigation may easily become a weapon of oppression, however evenhanded its terms appear. Its mere existence could well freeze out of existence all such activity on behalf of the civil rights of Negro citizens. [We] have consistently held that only a compelling state interest in the regulation of a subject within [a state's power] can justify limiting First Amendment freedoms. [However] valid may be Virginia's interest in regulating the traditionally illegal practices of barratry, maintenance and champerty, that interest does not justify the prohibition of the NAACP activities disclosed by this record.

■ JUSTICE HARLAN, with whom JUSTICES CLARK and STEWART join, dissenting.

[Litigation,] whether or not associated with the attempt to vindicate constitutional rights, is *conduct*. It is speech *plus*. Although the State surely may not broadly prohibit individuals with a common interest from joining together to petition a court for redress of their grievances, it is equally certain that the State may impose reasonable regulations limiting the permissible form of litigation and the manner of legal representation within its borders.

The interest which Virginia has here asserted is that of maintaining high professional standards among those who practice law within its borders. [A] State's felt need for regulation of professional conduct may reasonably extend beyond mere "ambulance chasing." [Running] perhaps even deeper is the desire of the profession, of courts, and of legislatures to prevent any interference with the uniquely personal relationship between lawyer and client and to maintain untrammeled by outside influences the responsibility which the lawyer owes to the courts he serves. [The] important function of organizations like petitioner in vindicating constitutional rights [is] not substantially impaired by this statute. [This enactment], contrary to the majority's suggestion, [does not] prevent petitioner from recommending the services of attorneys who are not subject to its directions and control. [It] prevents only the solicitation of business for attorneys subject to petitioner's control, and as so limited, should be sustained.

THE MEANING AND IMPLICATIONS OF NAACP V. BUTTON

1. ***Non-constitutional litigation.*** A year after Button, in **Brotherhood of Railroad Trainmen v. Virginia**, 377 U.S. 1 (1964), the Court extended its holding outside the area of litigation involving constitutional rights. The union advised its members to obtain legal advice before making settlements of their personal injury claims, and recommended particular attorneys. The result of its plan was "to channel legal employment to the particular lawyers approved by the Brotherhood." A Virginia court issued an injunction against the union for solicitation and unauthorized practice of law. Justice BLACK's majority opinion concluded that the injunction violated the First Amendment: "The State can no more keep these workers from using their cooperative plan to advise one another than it could use more direct means to bar them from resorting to the courts to vindicate their legal rights." As in the Button case, "the State again has failed to show any appreciable public interest in preventing the Brotherhood from carrying out its plan to recommend the lawyers it selects to represent injured workers. [The] Constitution protects the associational rights of the members of the union precisely as it does those of the NAACP." Justice CLARK's dissent, joined by Justice Harlan, objected that "[p]ersonal injury litigation is not a form of political expression, but rather a procedure for the settlement of damage claims," and thus that Button was distinguishable.

2. ***Group legal services.*** The Button and Trainmen cases in turn provided the basis for setting aside a state order against another variety of allegedly unauthorized practice of law by a union in **United Mine Workers v. Illinois State Bar Ass'n**, 389 U.S. 217 (1967). The union had employed a salaried attorney to assist its members with workmen's compensation claims. Justice BLACK's majority opinion concluded that the state order "substantially impairs the associational rights of the Mine Workers and is not needed to protect the State's interest in high standards of legal ethics." Justice HARLAN dissented. And the Court relied on the Button, Trainmen, and United Mine Workers cases in **United Transportation Union v. State Bar of Michigan**, 401 U.S. 576 (1971), setting aside a broad state court injunction against a union's plan purportedly designed to protect union members from excessive fees by incompetent attorneys in actions under the Federal Employers' Liability Act. Justice BLACK, writing for the Court, emphasized "the basic right to group legal action, a right first asserted in this Court by an association of Negroes seeking the protection of freedoms guaranteed by the Constitution." He added: "The common thread running through our decisions in NAACP v. Button, Trainmen, and United Mine Workers is that collective activity undertaken to obtain meaningful access to the courts is a fundamental right within the protection of the First Amendment. [That] right would be a hollow promise if courts could deny associations of workers or others the means of enabling their members to meet the costs of legal representation." Justices Harlan, White and Blackmun dissented in part.

Were the associational rights concerns protected in the NAACP context of Button equally applicable in the union cases that followed? Would a distinction between "personal injury litigation" and "civil rights litigation" itself have been constitutional? Recall that in Ohralik (1978; p. 1141 above), the right of commercial free speech did not bar regulation of in-person solicitation of clients; but in Primus, the companion case, the Court relied on the Button legacy to protect an ACLU lawyer against solicitation charges for seeking a client to bring a suit against alleged compulsory sterilization. Should the Court have inquired further into (and explicitly relied upon) the State's motives in Button? May reluctance to identify improper motives in cases such as Button have led the Court to give inadequate weight in other cases to "purer" state concerns regarding professional ethics and conflicts of interest?

3. ***Boycotts.*** Does the right of expressive association extend beyond litigation to collective efforts to induce employers or merchants to change their policies through more direct action? Does it extend to picketing or other forms of boycott? The Court has reviewed a number of disputes over labor picketing. In Thornhill v. Alabama, 310 U.S. 88 (1940), the Court held unconstitutional a statute that had been applied to ban all picketing. In Giboney v. Empire Storage & Ice Co., 336 U.S. 490 (1949), however, the Court upheld an injunction barring, as a conspiracy in restraint of trade, a union picket against a wholesale dealer to induce it to refrain from selling to nonunion peddlers. The Court unanimously rejected the argument that the injunction was "an unconstitutional abridgement of free speech because the picketers were attempting peacefully to publicize truthful facts about a labor dispute." Later decisions "established a broad field in which a State, in enforcing some public policy, [could] constitutionally enjoin peaceful picketing in preventing effectuation of that policy." International Brotherhood of Teamsters v. Vogt, Inc., 354 U.S. 284 (1957).

Does the state's power to regulate economic boycotts extend to a boycott motivated by political purposes? This question came before the Court in **NAACP v. Claiborne Hardware Co.**, 458 U.S. 886 (1982). The case (other aspects of which are discussed at p. 981 above) involved an NAACP boycott of white merchants by black citizens in Claiborne County, Mississippi. The boycott, begun in 1966, sought to induce white civic and business leaders to comply with a long list of black citizens' demands for equality and racial justice. The boycott was conducted by largely peaceful means, but it included some incidents of violence as well. In a civil action brought by some of the merchants to recover economic losses allegedly caused by the boycott, a state trial court imposed a judgment for over $1,250,000 on a large group of defendants (including the NAACP). The Mississippi Supreme Court, although not accepting all of the lower court's theories, upheld the judgment of liability on the basis of the common law tort of malicious interference with plaintiffs' businesses. The court found the boycott unlawful because, in its view, the defendants had agreed to use and did use force, violence, and intimidation to coerce nonparticipating blacks to join the boycott, and remanded for a recomputation of damages.

Without dissent (Justice Rehnquist concurred only in the result and Justice Marshall did not participate), the Court reversed, holding "that the nonviolent elements of petitioners' activities are entitled to the protection of the First Amendment" and that, "[w]hile the State legitimately may impose damages for the consequences of violent conduct, it may not award compensation for the consequences of nonviolent, protected activity."

Justice STEVENS, writing for the Court, began by explaining why "the nonviolent elements of petitioners' activities" were entitled to First Amendment protection. He noted that the boycott "took many forms": "The boycott was supported by speeches and nonviolent picketing. Participants repeatedly encouraged others to join in its cause. Each of these elements of the boycott is a form of speech or conduct that is ordinarily entitled to protection under the [First] Amendment. [In] addition, [the names] of boycott violators were read aloud at meetings [and] published in a local black newspaper. Petitioners admittedly sought to persuade others to join the boycott through social pressure and the 'threat' of social ostracism. Speech does not lose its protected character, however, simply because it may embarrass others or coerce them into action." He also noted that "[t]he right to associate does not lose all constitutional protection merely because some members of the group may have participated in conduct or advocated doctrine that itself is not protected."

True, the "presence of protected activity [did] not end the relevant constitutional inquiry": "Governmental regulation that has an incidental effect on First Amendment freedoms may be justified in certain narrowly defined instances. [O'Brien.] A nonviolent and totally voluntary boycott may have a disruptive effect on local economic conditions. This Court has recognized the strong governmental interest in certain forms of economic regulation, even though such regulation may have an incidental effect on rights of speech and association. The right of business entities to 'associate' to suppress competition may be curtailed. Unfair trade practices may be restricted. Secondary boycotts and picketing by labor unions may be prohibited." But, Justice Stevens added, "[w]hile States have broad power to regulate economic activity, we do not find a comparable right to prohibit peaceful political activity such as that found in the boycott in this case. This Court has recognized that expression on public issues 'has always rested on the highest rung of the hierarchy of First Amendment values.' "

Applying these principles, Justice Stevens suggested that the purpose of affecting governmental action was protected by the First Amendment even if there was also an anticompetitive effect: "[A] major purpose of the boycott in this case was to influence governmental action. [The] petitioners certainly foresaw—and directly intended—that the merchants would sustain economic injury as a result of their campaign. [However], the purpose of petitioners' campaign was not to destroy legitimate competition. [The] right of the State to regulate economic activity could not justify a complete prohibition against a nonviolent, politically-motivated boycott designed to force governmental and economic change and to effectuate rights guaranteed by the Constitution itself."

He continued: "[The] fact that such activity is constitutionally protected [imposes] a special obligation on this Court to examine critically the basis on which liability was imposed." Clearly, there were unprotected aspects of the boycott: "The First Amendment does not protect violence. [There] is no question that acts of violence occurred. No federal rule of law restricts a State from imposing tort liability for business losses that are caused by violence and by threats of violence. When such conduct occurs in the context of a constitutionally protected activity, however, 'precision of regulation' is demanded. [NAACP v. Button.] Specifically, the presence of activity protected by the First Amendment imposes restraints on the grounds that may give rise to damage liability and on the persons who may be held accountable for those damages." One such restraint was that petitioners could not be held liable for *all* damages "resulting from the boycott"; "[o]nly those losses proximately caused by unlawful conduct may be recovered."

A second restraint concerned who may be named as a defendant: "The First Amendment [restricts] the ability of the State to impose liability on an individual solely because of his association with another. Civil liability may not be imposed merely because an individual belonged to a group, some members of which committed acts of violence. For liability to be imposed by reason of association alone, it is necessary to establish that the group itself possessed unlawful goals and that the individual held a specific intent to further those illegal aims. 'In this sensitive field, the State may not employ 'means that broadly stifle fundamental personal liberties when the end can be more narrowly achieved.' Shelton v. Tucker." With respect to most of the petitioners, the record failed to show an adequate basis to sustain the judgments against them. Mere participation in the local meetings of the NAACP was "an insufficient predicate on which to impose liability." That would "not even constitute 'guilt by association,' since there is no evidence that the association possessed unlawful aims. Rather, liability could only be imposed on a 'guilt *for* association' theory. Neither is permissible under the First Amendment." Nor could NAACP liability be predicated on any allegedly unlawful conduct by NAACP leader and boycott organizer Charles Evers: "To impose liability without a finding that the NAACP authorized—either actually or apparently—or ratified unlawful conduct would impermissibly burden the rights of political association that are protected by the First Amendment."

Justice Stevens concluded: "The taint of violence colored the conduct of some of the petitioners. They, of course, may be held liable for the consequences of their violent deeds. The burden of demonstrating that it colored the entire collective effort, however, is not satisfied by evidence that violence occurred or even that violence contributed to the success of the boycott. A massive and prolonged effort to change the social, political, and economic structure of a local environment cannot be characterized as a violent conspiracy simply by reference to the ephemeral consequences of relatively few violent acts. Such a characterization must be supported by findings that adequately disclose the evidentiary basis for concluding that specific parties agreed to use unlawful means, that carefully identify the impact of such unlawful conduct, and that recognize the importance of avoiding the imposition of punishment for constitutionally protected activity. The burden of demonstrating that fear rather than protected conduct was the dominant force in the movement is heavy. [The] findings of [the trial court] are constitutionally insufficient to support the judgment that all petitioners are liable for all losses resulting from the boycott."

Does NAACP v. Claiborne Hardware have any application to an economically motivated boycott? In **International Longshoremen's Ass'n v. Allied International, Inc.**, 456 U.S. 212 (1982), decided shortly before Claiborne, the Court rejected a First Amendment claim by a union that refused to unload cargoes shipped from the Soviet Union, as a protest against the Soviet invasion of Afghanistan. The unanimous Court found the protest to be an illegal secondary boycott under federal labor law and rejected the claim that the boycott "was not a labor dispute [but] a political dispute." The Court noted that "conduct designed not to communicate but to coerce merits [little] consideration under the First Amendment." Does Claiborne overrule Longshoremen's? If not, is the distinction between "political" and "economic" purposes justifiable under the First Amendment? For later rulings declining to apply NAACP v. Claiborne Hardware to boycotts stemming from economic rather than political purposes, see Allied Tube & Conduit Corp. v. Indian

Head, Inc., 486 U.S. 492 (1988), and FTC v. Superior Court Trial Lawyers Ass'n, 493 U.S. 411 (1990).

4. ***Material support and terrorism.*** The government's increasing focus on terrorism in recent decades raises novel problems related to the freedom of association. May the government restrict individuals from associating with terrorists even if those individuals do not themselves engage in any violence? Is associating with terrorists different from belonging to a Communist organization? In **Holder v. Humanitarian Law Project**, 561 U.S. 1 (2010), discussed above at p. 1195, the Court addressed a First Amendment challenge on freedom of speech and association grounds to a federal criminal provision which made it unlawful to "knowingly provid[e] material support or resources to a foreign terrorist organization."

Chief Justice ROBERTS delivered the opinion of the Court. "[The] plaintiffs in this litigation seek to provide support to two [organizations that engage in terrorist activity]. Plaintiffs claim that they seek to facilitate only the lawful, nonviolent purposes of those groups, and that applying the material-support law to prevent them from doing so violates the Constitution.

[Plaintiffs] in this litigation are two U.S. citizens and six domestic organizations. [In] 1998, plaintiffs filed suit in federal court challenging the constitutionality of the material-support statute. [Plaintiffs] claimed that they wished to provide support for the humanitarian and political activities of the [Kurdistan Workers' Party (PKK)] and the [Liberation Tigers of Tamil Eelam (LTTE)] in the form of monetary contributions, other tangible aid, legal training, and political advocacy, but that they could not do so for fear of prosecution under § 2339B."

After rejecting the plaintiffs' free speech claim, Chief Justice Roberts turned to the plaintiffs' freedom of association claim: "Plaintiffs' final claim is that the material-support statute violates their freedom of association under the First Amendment. Plaintiffs argue that the statute criminalizes the mere fact of their associating with the PKK and the LTTE, thereby running afoul of decisions like [De Jonge and Keyishian].

The Court of Appeals correctly rejected this claim because the statute does not penalize mere association with a foreign terrorist organization. As the Ninth Circuit put it: 'The statute does not prohibit being a member of one of the designated groups or vigorously promoting and supporting the political goals of the group. . . . What [§ 2339B] prohibits is the act of giving material support. . . .' Plaintiffs want to do the latter. Our decisions scrutinizing penalties on simple association or assembly are therefore inapposite.

Plaintiffs also argue that the material-support statute burdens their freedom of association because it prevents them from providing support to designated foreign terrorist organizations, but not to other groups. [Any] burden on plaintiffs' freedom of association in this regard is justified for the same reasons that we have denied plaintiffs' free speech challenge. It would be strange if the Constitution permitted Congress to prohibit certain forms of speech that constitute material support, but did not permit Congress to prohibit that support only to particularly dangerous and lawless foreign organizations. Congress is not required to ban material support to every group or none at all."

Justice BREYER, joined by Justices Ginsburg and Sotomayor, dissented: "The plaintiffs, all United States citizens or associations, now seek an injunction and declaration providing that, without violating the statute, they can [train on issues of humanitarian and international for peaceful dispute resolution; engage in political advocacy; and teach organization PKK members how to petition representative bodies.] All these activities are of a kind that the First Amendment ordinarily protects.

[That] this speech and association for political purposes is the kind of activity to which the First Amendment ordinarily offers its strongest protection is elementary. [Although] in the Court's view the statute applies only where the PKK helps to coordinate a defendant's activities, [the] simple fact of 'coordination' alone cannot readily remove protection that the First Amendment would otherwise grant. That amendment, after all, also protects the freedom of association. [See NAACP v. Claiborne Hardware Co. and Dejonge]. 'Coordination' with a political group, like membership, involves association.

[The] Government says that the plaintiffs' proposed activities will 'bolste[r] a terrorist organization's efficacy and strength in a community' and 'undermin[e] this nation's efforts to delegitimize and weaken those groups.' In the Court's view, too, the Constitution permits application of the statute to activities of the kind at issue in part because those activities could provide a group that engages in terrorism with 'legitimacy.'

[But] this 'legitimacy' justification cannot by itself warrant suppression of political speech, advocacy, and association. Speech, association, and related activities on behalf of a group will often, perhaps always, help to legitimate that group. Thus, were the law to accept a 'legitimating' effect, in and of itself and without qualification, as providing sufficient grounds for imposing such a ban, the First Amendment battle would be lost in untold instances where it should be won.

[The] 'legitimacy' justification itself is inconsistent with critically important First Amendment case law. Consider the cases involving the protection the First Amendment offered those who joined the Communist Party intending only to further its peaceful activities. In those cases, this Court took account of congressional findings that the Communist Party not only advocated theoretically but also sought to put into practice the overthrow of our Government through force and violence. The Court had previously accepted Congress' determinations that the American Communist Party was a 'Communist action organization.' [Nonetheless,] the Court held that the First Amendment protected an American's right to belong to that party—despite whatever 'legitimating' effect membership might have had—as long as the person did not share the party's unlawful purposes. [See, e.g., Dejonge and Keyishian]. As I have pointed out, those cases draw further support from other cases permitting pure advocacy of even the most unlawful activity-as long as that advocacy is not 'directed to inciting or producing imminent lawless action and . . . likely to incite or produce such action.' [Brandenburg] The Government's 'legitimating' theory would seem to apply to these cases with equal justifying force; and, if recognized, it would have led this Court to conclusions other than those it reached.

[For] the reasons I have set forth, I believe application of the statute as the Government interprets it would gravely and without adequate justification injure interests of the kind the First Amendment protects."

Does Justice Stevens's admonition in NAACP v. Claiborne Hardware Co. that "[t]he right to associate does not lose all constitutional protection merely because some members of the group may have participated in conduct or advocated doctrine that itself is not protected" still hold true for individuals who associate with terrorist organizations? Perhaps Humanitarian Law Project demonstrates that each national security scare adopts new technologies to address the potential threat of civil liberties.

DENIAL OF GOVERNMENT BENEFITS BECAUSE OF ASSOCIATION

Even if government may not outlaw an association, force disclosure of its membership, or restrict its central activities, may it nonetheless use associational ties as a ground for disqualification from government benefits such as jobs and licenses? May government condition such benefits on oaths of loyalty or disavowal of disfavored associations?

The Court has several times relied upon the prohibition on bills of attainder to hold that associational ties may not be the basis for denying a position of public trust. Soon after the Civil War, the Court struck down, as bills of attainder, loyalty oaths directed at former supporters of the Confederacy. See Cummings v. Missouri, 4 Wall. (71 U.S.) 277 (1867) (invalidating denial of the right to preach to those who did not disavow Confederate sympathy), and Ex parte Garland, 4 Wall. (71 U.S.) 333 (1867) (invalidating denial of the right to practice law in federal courts to those who did not disavow Confederate sympathy). The Court has relied on the bill of attainder ban in only one modern case: United States v. Brown, 381 U.S. 437 (1965), holding unconstitutional a federal law making it a crime for a member of the Communist Party to serve as an officer or an employee of a labor union. Chief Justice Warren's majority opinion emphasized that it was not necessary that a bill of attainder name the parties to be punished. He viewed the prohibition "as an implementation of the separation of powers, a general safeguard against legislative exercise of the judicial function, or more simply—trial by legislature."

More commonly, the issue has arisen in connection with First Amendment claims. Such claims typically assert either that membership in an organization is not in itself a sufficient ground to deny a public privilege, or that refusal to discuss or disavow membership is not such a ground. During the Cold War era that followed World War II, for example, loyalty requirements proliferated at all levels of government employment. These programs aimed to prevent Communists and other "subversives" from occupying sensitive government or industrial positions. The Court initially sustained various loyalty programs against constitutional challenge. For example, Adler v. Board of Education, 342 U.S. 485 (1952), upheld a New York law barring from a position as a public school teacher anyone who knowingly became a member of any organization that advocated the violent overthrow of government. In Garner v. Los Angeles Bd. of Public Works, 341 U.S. 716 (1951), the Court upheld a requirement that each city employee take an oath that, within the past five years, he or she had not advocated the overthrow of government by force or violence or belonged to any organization advocating such overthrow, and that the employee disclose whether he or she was or ever had been a Communist Party member. Such requirements were deemed relevant to fitness for the job. The only limitation the Court imposed was a requirement of *knowing* membership. In Wieman v. Updegraff, 344 U.S. 183 (1952), a unanimous Court struck down, on due process grounds, an Oklahoma loyalty oath requiring employees to state that they were not and had not for five years been affiliated with any organization that had been deemed a "Communist front or subversive organization." The Court distinguished Garner and Adler on the ground that, under the Oklahoma law, it did not matter "whether association existed innocently or knowingly."

During these years, the Court also considered a number of cases involving refusals to answer subversion-related questions in the course of bar admission proceedings. In its first encounters with the problem, the Court held on due process grounds that a state could not refuse to admit applicants to the bar on the basis of mere membership in the Communist party. Schware v. Board of Bar Examiners, 353 U.S. 232 (1957); Konigsberg v. State Bar, 353 U.S. 252 (1957). But when the Konigsberg case returned to the Court four years later, the Court upheld the denial of admission on the ground that the applicant had refused, on First Amendment grounds, to answer questions about his political associations and beliefs. **Konigsberg v. State Bar of California** [Konigsberg II], 366 U.S. 36 (1961). Justice HARLAN, writing for the 5–4 majority, emphasized the distinction between refusals to answer relevant questions and substantive grounds for denials of a license. Thus, a state could deny admission for refusing to answer even if affirmative answers would not by themselves have justified exclusion. In response to Konigsberg's claim that questions about his Communist Party membership "unconstitutionally impinged upon rights of free speech and association," Justice Harlan replied: "[We] regard the State's interest in having lawyers who are devoted to the law in its broader sense, [including] its procedures for orderly change, as clearly sufficient to outweigh the minimal effect upon free association occasioned by compulsory disclosure in the circumstances here presented."

In the 1960s, the Warren Court struck down several state-imposed loyalty oaths on "void-for-vagueness" grounds. In **Cramp v. Board of Public Instruction**, 368 U.S. 278 (1961), the Court invalidated a Florida law requiring public employees to swear that they had never "knowingly lent their aid, support, advice, counsel or influence to the Communist Party." Even though the state court had construed the law to include "the element of scienter," Justice STEWART emphasized its "extraordinary ambiguity" and found it "completely lacking [in] terms susceptible of objective measurement." He added that the "vice of unconstitutional vagueness [was] further aggravated [because the law] operates to inhibit the exercise of individual freedoms affirmatively protected by the Constitution." Similarly, in **Baggett v. Bullitt**, 377 U.S. 360 (1964), the Court, in partial reliance on Cramp, invalidated two state loyalty oath requirements, including one obligating state employees to swear that they were not members of a "subversive organization." The majority found the requirements "invalid on their face because their language is unduly vague, uncertain and broad."

In **Elfbrandt v. Russell**, 384 U.S. 11 (1966), the Court finally invalidated a loyalty oath as an infringement of expressive association. Justice DOUGLAS wrote for the Court, holding that Arizona could not impose on an unwilling employee an oath of loyalty to the state and federal constitutions on threat of perjury and discharge if the employee "knowingly and wilfully becomes or remains a member" of subversive organizations. His opinion rested on the danger of guilt by association: "One who subscribes to this Arizona oath and who is, or thereafter becomes, a knowing member of an organization which has as 'one of its purposes' the violent overthrow of the government, is subject to immediate discharge and criminal penalties. Nothing in the oath, the statutory gloss, or the construction of the oath and statutes given by the Arizona Supreme Court purports to exclude association by one who does not subscribe to the organization's unlawful ends. [Thus,] the 'hazard of being prosecuted for knowing but guiltless behavior' is a reality. People often label as 'communist' ideas which they oppose; and they make up our juries."

"[Those] who join an organization but do not share its unlawful purposes and who do not participate in its unlawful activities surely pose no threat, either as citizens or as public employees. Laws such as this which are not restricted in scope to those who join with the "specific intent" to further illegal action impose, in effect, a conclusive presumption that the member shares the unlawful aims of the organization. [This] Act threatens the cherished freedom of association protected by the First Amendment. [A] statute touching those protected rights must be "narrowly drawn." [Legitimate] legislative goals "cannot be pursued by means that broadly stifle fundamental personal liberties when the end can be more narrowly achieved." [Shelton v. Tucker.] [A] law which applies to membership without the "specific intent" to further the illegal aims of the organization infringes unnecessarily on protected freedoms. It rests on the doctrine of "guilt by association" which has no place here. Such a law cannot stand."

Justice WHITE, dissented, joined by Justices Clark, Harlan and Stewart: "[If] the State is entitled to condition employment on the absence of knowing membership, and if an employee obtains employment by falsifying his present qualifications, there is no sound constitutional reason for denying the State the power to treat such false swearing as perjury."

And in **Keyishian v. Board of Regents**, 385 U.S. 589 (1967), the Court again cited the freedom of expressive association as a ground for invalidating a loyalty oath required as a condition of public employment, this time for state university faculty members. Writing for the Court, Justice BRENNAN stated: "[Mere] Party membership, even with knowledge of the Party's unlawful goals, can not suffice to justify criminal punishment. [Legislation that] sanctions membership unaccompanied by specific intent to further the unlawful goals of the organization or which is not active membership violates constitutional limitations. Measured against this standard, [these provisions] sweep overbroadly into association which may not be proscribed. The presumption of disqualification arising from proof of mere membership [cannot be rebutted by] proof of nonactive membership or a showing of the absence of intent to further unlawful aims. [Thus, the provisions] suffer from impermissible 'overbreadth.' They seek to bar employment both for association which legitimately may be proscribed and for association which may not be proscribed consistently with First Amendment rights. Where statutes have an overbroad sweep, just as where they are vague, 'the hazard of loss of substantial impairment of those precious rights may be critical,' [since] those covered by the statute are bound to limit their behavior to that which is unquestionably safe. [Shelton v. Tucker.] We therefore hold [the relevant provisions] invalid insofar as they proscribe mere knowing membership without any showing of specific intent to further the unlawful aims of the [Communist Party]." The Elfbrandt dissenters repeated their dissenting views here.

These decisions did not mean that all oaths of public office were unconstitutional. In **Cole v. Richardson**, 405 U.S. 676 (1972), the Court, by a vote of 4–3, upheld a two-part loyalty oath required of all Massachusetts public employees. The first part required a promise to "uphold and defend the federal and state constitutions"; the second required a promise to "oppose the overthrow of the [government] by force, violence or by any illegal or unconstitutional method." The Court read the "oppose the overthrow" clause as imposing no significantly greater obligation than the "uphold and defend" provision and accordingly concluded that both parts of the oath were constitutional.

And in a trilogy of 5–4 decisions involving challenges to oaths for admission to the bar, Court held that a state may not deny admission to the bar based on the applicant's refusal to answer the question whether she had ever been a member of the Communist Party or any organization "that advocates overthrow of the United States Government by force or violence," see **Baird v. State Bar of Arizona**, 401 U.S. 1 (1971) ("[A] State may not inquire about a man's views or associations solely for the purpose of withholding a right or benefit because of what he believes."); that a state may not refuse bar admission to an applicant for refusing to answer questions about membership in "any organization which advocates the overthrow of the government of the United States by force," and about all other organizations of which he had been a member, see **Application of Stolar**, 401 U.S. 23 (1971) (holding requests for general lists of organizational memberships "impermissible in light of the First Amendment [under Shelton v. Tucker]"); but that a state *could* employ a screening system that asked first, whether the applicant had been a member of any organization he or she knew advocated the overthrow of government by force or violence, and second, if the first answer was affirmative, whether the applicant had the "specific intent to further the aims of such organization," see **Law Students Civil Rights Research Council v. Wadmond**, 401 U.S. 154 (1971) ("[We] are not persuaded that careful administration of such a system as New York's need result in chilling effects upon the exercise of constitutional freedoms."). Is the upshot of these three cases that bar authorities may inquire into an applicant's knowing membership in the Communist Party with the specific intent to advance its ends, and refuse bar admission to one who refuses to cooperate with such a properly narrowed inquiry, but may not refuse admission to one who refuses to answer a question that may disadvantage him or her on the basis of organizational affiliation alone? On the speech implications of moral character requirements for bar admission generally, see Rhode, "Moral Character as a Professional Credential," 94 Yale L.J. 491 (1985).

COMPELLED ASSOCIATION: THE RIGHT NOT TO ASSOCIATE

1. ***Compulsory fees to unions.*** After NAACP v. Alabama clarified that the "right of association" under the First Amendment could not be infringed, claims were made that there was a similar right *not* to associate. Initially, such compelled association claims were brought by individuals who objected to compulsory contributions to organizations—e.g., employees subject to mandatory dues under union shop agreements and lawyers attacking mandatory dues requirements under integrated bar systems.

These cases coincide with an extended period of gradual decline in the power and membership of labor unions. Unions like the American Federation of Labor (AFL) were key to securing workers' rights, like the 40-hour work week, workers' compensation systems, and important labor statutes like the National Labor Relations Act, in the late part of the nineteenth and early twentieth centuries. Today, however, the proper role of unions in American society has become a contentious issue. In particular, public employee unions have come under attack as opponents of unions have sought to curtail their collective bargaining rights and bolster the freedom of non-union employees. Union advocates claim that strong collective bargaining rights, which might entail incidental infringements on the associational rights of employees, are necessary to preserve the gains made on behalf of workers. Opponents argue that these infringements are antithetical to their First Amendment rights of speech and association. Consider the cases that follow in light of this debate.

In **Abood v. Detroit Board of Educ.**, 431 U.S. 209 (1977), the Court confronted a compelled association claim in the context of public employees' unions. Many states allow public-sector unions to negotiate agency-shop agreements that entitle a union to levy fees on employees who are not union members but whom the union represents in collective bargaining. Abood involved public sector employees who were subject to such an agency-shop agreement adopted by a school board and a union pursuant to state law. Under the agreement, every nonunion employee was required to pay to the union "a service fee equal in amount to union dues" as a condition of employment. That scheme was challenged by dissenting employees who objected to having to pay fees for (1) "collective bargaining in the public sector" and (2) "ideological union expenditures not directly related to collective bargaining."

Justice STEWART's majority opinion recognized a right to "refus[e] to associate" and rejected the first challenge but sustained the second. In upholding the exaction of compulsory fees for collective bargaining expenses, Justice Stewart relied in part on earlier cases that had upheld, largely on statutory grounds, the exaction of compulsory dues in the private sector. He found that in the public sector, as in the private sector, the interests in the operation of a collective bargaining system, in assuring labor peace, and in avoiding the risk of "free riders" overcame the objectors' First Amendment interests "in not being compelled to contribute to the costs of exclusive union representation." Justice Stewart concluded, however, that the First Amendment barred requiring dissidents to contribute financially to the support of an ideological cause they found objectionable, and thus a public employee may not be required "to contribute to the support of an ideological cause he may oppose as a condition of holding a job as a public school teacher." The union was free to advance "ideological causes not germane to its duties as collective-bargaining representative," but it had to finance such expenditures with dues only from "employees who do not object to advancing those ideas and who are not coerced into doing so against their will by the threat of loss of governmental employment." He accordingly remanded for development of remedies to prevent "compulsory subsidization of ideological activities by employees who object thereto without restricting the union's ability to require every employee to contribute to the cost of collective-bargaining activities."

Justice POWELL, joined by Chief Justice Burger and Justice Blackmun, concurred in the judgment, arguing that "compelling a government employee to give financial support to a union in the public sector—regardless of the uses to which the union puts the contribution—impinges seriously upon interests in free speech and association protected by the First Amendment," and that the burden should have rested with the State to come forward and demonstrate, as to each union expenditure for which it would exact support from minority employees, that the "compelled contribution is necessary to serve overriding governmental objectives." He objected to the majority's placement of the burden on the dissenting employee to come forward and identify his disagreement in order to obtain a rebate from the union.

Abood appeared to strike a compromise with regard to the constitutionality of union fee charges. Some thirty years later however, the Court began incrementally to weaken the ability of unions to collect such fees in a series of cases that undercut Abood. First, in **Davenport v. Washington Education Ass'n**, 551 U.S. 177 (2007), the Court held that a state law mandating that a union obtain a nonmember's affirmative authorization before using their fees for election-related purposes was constitutional, and that such a requirement was not a violation of the union's own expressive or associational rights. The ruling effectively allowed states to shift the burden of enforcing Abood rights from a dissenting employee to the union.

The Court next decided **Knox v. Serv. Employees Int'l Union (SEIU)**, 567 U.S. 298 (2012), which involved a special assessment on public employees to create a fund for the union's political activities. While the union had sent out a notice for a regular assessment, it failed to send out a new notice for an increase in political expenditures that would have given employees an opportunity to opt out of those fees. Justice ALITO's opinion for the Court held that the special fee assessment violated the First Amendment. In language signaling that Abood's rationale was under attack, he wrote: "The First Amendment creates 'an open marketplace' in which differing ideas about political, economic, and social issues can compete freely for public acceptance without improper government interference. The government may not prohibit the dissemination of ideas that it disfavors, nor compel the endorsement of ideas that it approves. [R.A.V.; Brandenburg; Barnette; Wooley].

[By] allowing unions to collect any fees from nonmembers and by permitting unions to use opt-out rather than opt-in schemes when annual dues are billed, our cases have substantially impinged upon the First Amendment rights of nonmembers. In the new situation presented here, we see no justification for any further impingement. The general rule—individuals should not be compelled to subsidize private groups or private speech—should prevail."

In **Harris v. Quinn**, 573 U.S. 616, 134 S. Ct. 2618 (2014), the Court next declined to extend Abood to what it called "partial public employees," home healthcare personal assistants who belonged to an Illinois union that contracted with the state but were individually answerable to their patient-customers. In a 5–4 opinion for the Court, Justice ALITO declined to overrule Abood, but nevertheless indicated that it was not long for this world. Calling its analysis "questionable on several grounds," he wrote: "Abood failed to appreciate the conceptual difficulty of distinguishing in public-sector cases between union expenditures that are made for collective-bargaining purposes and those that are made to achieve political ends. In the private sector, the line is easier to see. Collective bargaining concerns the union's dealings with the employer; political advocacy and lobbying are directed at the government. But in the public sector, both collective-bargaining and political advocacy and lobbying are directed at the government. [Abood] likewise did not foresee the practical problems that would face objecting nonmembers. Employees who suspect that a union has improperly put certain expenses in the "germane" category must bear a heavy burden if they wish to challenge the union's actions. [Finally,] a critical pillar of the Abood Court's analysis rests on an unsupported empirical assumption, namely, that the principle of exclusive representation in the public sector is dependent on a union or agency shop."

Justice Alito then applied strict scrutiny and dismissed the union's claims as failing to present a compelling state interest. "A union's status as exclusive bargaining agent and the right to collect an agency fee from non-members are not inextricably linked. For example, employees in some federal agencies may choose a union to serve as the exclusive bargaining agent for the unit, but no employee is required to join the union or to pay any union fee. [Any] threat to labor peace is diminished because the personal assistants do not work together in a common state facility but instead spend all their time in private homes, either the customers' or their own. [The] State is not like the closed-fisted employer that is bent on minimizing employee wages and benefits and that yields only grudgingly under intense union pressure.[A] host of organizations advocate on behalf of the interests of persons falling within an occupational group, and many of these groups are quite successful even though they are dependent on voluntary contributions."

In dissent, Justice KAGAN, joined by Justices Ginsburg, Breyer, and Sotomayor, took the view that the collective bargaining agreements in the case "fall squarely within Abood's holding." Abood, she wrote, is not an anomaly. "Our decisions have long afforded government entities broad latitude to manage their workforces, even when that affects speech they could not regulate in other contexts. Abood is of a piece with all those decisions: While protecting an employee's most significant expression, that decision also enables the government to advance its interests in operating effectively—by bargaining, if it so chooses, with a single employee representative and preventing free riding on that union's efforts." Furthermore, Justice Kagan wrote, "The Abood rule is deeply entrenched, and is the foundation for not tens or hundreds, but thousands of contracts between unions and governments across the Nation. Our precedent about precedent, fairly understood and applied, makes it impossible for this Court to reverse that decision."

Then in **Janus v. American Federation of State, County, and Municipal Employees, Council 31**, 585 U.S. ___, 138 S. Ct. 974 (2018), the Court in a 5–4 decision reversed the part of Abood that allowed collection of agency fees. Justice ALITO again, wrote the opinion, joined by Chief Justice Roberts and Justices Kennedy, Thomas and Gorsuch: "Under Illinois law, public employees are forced to subsidize a union, even if they choose not to join and strongly object to the positions the union takes in collective bargaining and related activities. We conclude that this arrangement violates the free speech rights of nonmembers by compelling them to subsidize private speech on matters of substantial public concern.

"[Petitioner] in the present case contends that the Illinois law at issue should be subjected to strict scrutiny. The dissent, on the other hand, proposes that we apply what amounts to rational-basis review. [This] form of minimal scrutiny is foreign to our free-speech jurisprudence, and we reject it here. At the same time, we again find it unnecessary to decide the issue of strict scrutiny because the Illinois scheme cannot survive under even the more permissive standard applied in Knox and Harris.

"In Abood, the main defense of the agency-fee arrangement was that it served the State's interest in 'labor peace.' [We] assume that 'labor peace' [is] a compelling state interest, but Abood cited no evidence that the pandemonium it imagined would result if agency fees were not allowed.

"[The] federal employment experience is illustrative. Under federal law, a union chosen by majority vote is designated as the exclusive representative of all the employees, but federal law does not permit agency fees. Nevertheless, nearly a million federal employees—about 27% of the federal work force—are union members. [Likewise,] millions of public employees in the 28 States that have laws generally prohibiting agency fees are represented by unions that serve as the exclusive representatives of all the employees. Whatever may have been the case 41 years ago when Abood was handed down, it is now undeniable that 'labor peace' can readily be achieved through means significantly less restrictive of associational freedoms than the assessment of agency fees.

"In addition, [Abood] cited the risk of 'free riders' as justification for agency fees. [Petitioner] argues that he is not a free rider on a bus headed for a destination that he wishes to reach but is more like a person shanghaied for an unwanted voyage. [Avoiding] free riders is not a compelling interest. [Many] private groups speak out with the objective of obtaining government action that will have the effect of benefiting nonmembers. May all those who are thought to benefit from such efforts be compelled to subsidize this speech?

"[Those] supporting agency fees contend that the situation here is different because unions are statutorily required to represent the interests of all public employees in the unit, whether or not they are union members. Why might this matter? [It] is simply not true that unions will refuse to serve as the exclusive representative of all employees in the unit if they are not given agency fees. As noted, unions represent millions of public employees in jurisdictions that do not permit agency fees. No union is ever compelled to seek that designation. On the contrary, designation as exclusive representative is avidly sought.

"[There] remains the question whether *stare decisis* nonetheless counsels against overruling Abood. It does not. [*Stare decisis*] applies with perhaps least force of all to decisions that wrongly denied First Amendment rights. Our cases identify factors that should be taken into account in deciding whether to overrule a past decision. [An] important factor in determining whether a precedent should be overruled is the quality of its reasoning. [Abood] was poorly reasoned. [Abood] failed to appreciate the conceptual difficulty of distinguishing in public-sector cases between union expenditures that are made for collective-bargaining purposes and those that are made to achieve political ends. [Abood's] line between chargeable and nonchargeable union expenditures has proved to be impossible to draw with precision. [Objecting] employees also face a daunting and expensive task if they wish to challenge union chargeability determinations. [Developments] since Abood, both factual and legal, have also eroded the decision's underpinnings and left it an outlier among our First Amendment cases.

Abood pinned its result on the unsupported empirical assumption that the principle of exclusive representation in the public sector is dependent on a union or agency shop. But [experience] has shown otherwise. It is also significant that the Court decided Abood against a very different legal and economic backdrop. Public-sector unionism was a relatively new phenomenon in 1977. [Since] then, public-sector union membership has come to surpass private-sector union membership, even though there are nearly four times as many total private-sector employees as public-sector employees. This ascendance of public-sector unions has been marked by a parallel increase in public spending. [Not] all that increase can be attributed to public-sector unions, of course, but the mounting costs of public-employee wages, benefits, and pensions undoubtedly played a substantial role. [Unsustainable] collective-bargaining agreements have also been blamed for multiple municipal bankruptcies. These developments, and the political debate over public spending and debt they have spurred, have given collective-bargaining issues a political valence that Abood did not fully appreciate. Abood is also an anomaly in our First Amendment jurisprudence [when] viewed against our cases holding that public employees generally may not be required to support a political party. [Reliance also] does not carry decisive weight. [It] would be unconscionable to permit free speech rights to be abridged in perpetuity in order to preserve contract provisions that will expire on their own in a few years' time. [Abood also] does not provide a clear or easily applicable standard, so arguments for reliance based on its clarity are misplaced. This is especially so because public-sector unions have been on notice for years regarding this Court's misgivings about Abood."

Justice KAGAN dissented, joined by Justices Ginsburg, Breyer, and Sotomayor: "For over 40 years, Abood struck a stable balance between public employees' First Amendment rights and government entities' interests in running their workforces as they thought proper. [The] Court's decisions have long made plain that government entities have substantial latitude to regulate their employees' speech—especially about terms of employment—in the interest of operating their workplaces effectively. [The] Abood regime was a paradigmatic example of how the government can regulate speech in its capacity as an employer. [The] decision will have large-scale consequences. Public employee unions will lose a secure source of financial support. State and local governments that thought fair-share provisions furthered their interests will need to find new ways of managing their workforces. Across the country, the relationships of public employees and employers will alter in both predictable and wholly unexpected ways. Rarely if ever has the Court overruled a decision [with] so little regard for the usual principles of *stare decisis*. [More] than 20 States have statutory schemes built on the decision. [Reliance] interests do not come any stronger. [And] likewise, judicial disruption does not get any greater.

"[The majority avoids] the key question, which is whether unions without agency fees will be *able to* (not whether they will *want to*) carry on as an effective exclusive representative. And as to that question, the majority again fails to reckon with how economically rational actors behave—in public as well as private workplaces. Without a fair-share agreement, the class of union non-members spirals upward. Employees (including those who love the union) realize that they can get the same benefits even if they let their memberships expire. And as more and more stop paying dues, those left must take up the financial slack (and anyway, begin to feel like suckers)—so they too quit the union. And when the vicious cycle finally ends, chances are that the union will lack the resources to effectively perform the responsibilities of an exclusive representative—or, in the worst case, to perform them at all. The result is to frustrate the interests of every government entity that thinks a strong exclusive-representation scheme will promote stable labor relations.

"In many cases over many decades, this Court has addressed how the First Amendment applies when the government, acting not as sovereign but as employer, limits its workers' speech. [It] must be able, much as a private employer is, to manage its workforce as it thinks fit. A public employee thus must submit to certain limitations on his or her freedom. Garcetti. [When] the government imposes speech restrictions relating to workplace operations, of the kind a private employer also would, the Court reliably upholds them. See, e.g., Connick. Like Pickering, Abood drew the constitutional line by analyzing the connection between the government's managerial interests and different kinds of expression.

"[But] the worse part of today's opinion is where the majority subverts all known principles of *stare decisis*. [Abood] is not just any precedent: It is embedded in the law (not to mention [in] the world) in a way not many decisions are. [Abood is not an outlier because it] coheres with the Pickering approach to reviewing regulation of public employees' speech. [The] majority is likewise wrong to invoke "workability" as a reason for overruling Abood. [As] exercises of constitutional linedrawing go, Abood stands well above average. In the 40 years since Abood, this Court has had to resolve only a handful of cases raising questions about the distinction.

"[One] *stare decisis* factor—reliance—dominates all others here. [The] Court today wreaks havoc on entrenched legislative and contractual arrangements. Over 20 States have by now enacted statutes authorizing fair-share provisions. [Thousands] of current contracts covering millions of workers provide for agency fees. [There] is no sugarcoating today's opinion. [The majority] prevents the American people [from] making important choices about workplace governance. And it does so by weaponizing the First Amendment, in a way that unleashes judges, now and in the future, to intervene in economic and regulatory policy.

[The majority] has overruled Abood because it wanted to. Because, that is, it wanted to pick the winning side in what should be—and until now, has been—an energetic policy debate. [And] maybe most alarming, the majority has chosen the winners by turning the First Amendment into a sword, and using it against workaday economic and regulatory policy. [Speech] is everywhere—a part of every human activity (employment, health care, securities trading, you name it). For that reason, almost all economic and regulatory policy affects or touches speech. So the majority's road runs long. And at every stop are black-robed rulers overriding citizens' choices. The First Amendment was meant for better things."

2. ***Compulsory fees to public universities.*** Should students at a public university have an Abood right to a rebate of the amount of their compulsory student activities fee used to finance student organizations engaging in political or ideological speech to which they object? In **Board of Regents of The University of Wisconsin v. Southworth**, 529 U.S. 217 (2000), the Court held that they do not, and largely rejected a First Amendment challenge to a public university's requirement that students contribute to a student activity fund used in part to support controversial student advocacy organizations. Distinguishing Abood and Keller, Justice KENNEDY wrote for a unanimous Court: "In Abood and Keller the

constitutional rule took the form of limiting the required subsidy to speech germane to the purposes of the union or bar association. [But] the standard of germane speech as applied to student speech at a university is unworkable. [The] speech the University seeks to encourage in the program before us is distinguished not by discernable limits but by its vast, unexplored bounds. To insist upon asking what speech is germane would be contrary to the very goal the University seeks to pursue. It is not for the Court to say what is or is not germane to the ideas to be pursued in an institution of higher learning." He cautioned, though, that "the University must provide some protection to its students' First Amendment interests. [The] proper measure, and the principal standard of protection for objecting students, we conclude, is the requirement of viewpoint neutrality in the allocation of funding support." While upholding the fee program in most respects, he remanded for the lower courts' determination the question whether the University's referendum system for activity funding was adequately viewpoint-neutral. Justice SOUTER, joined by Justices Stevens and Breyer, concurred only in the judgment, cautioning that too rigid an approach to viewpoint neutrality in the university setting might ultimately conflict with principles of academic freedom.

3. ***Compulsory fees for advertising.*** In Glickman, discussed above at p. 1409, writing for the majority, Justice SCALIA analyzed the compulsory fees in the context of compelled association and found the compelled funding for advertising distinct from that involved in the Abood line of cases: "Abood, and the cases that follow it, did not announce a broad First Amendment right not to be compelled to provide financial support for any organization that conducts expressive activities. Rather, Abood merely recognized a First Amendment interest in not being compelled to contribute to an organization whose expressive activities conflict with one's 'freedom of belief.' [In Abood we] found that compelled contributions for political purposes unrelated to collective bargaining implicated First Amendment interests because they interfere with the values lying at the 'heart of the First Amendment.' Here, however, requiring respondents to pay the assessments cannot be said to engender any crisis of conscience. None of the advertising in this record promotes any particular message other than encouraging consumers to buy California tree fruit. Neither the fact that respondents may prefer to foster that message independently in order to promote and distinguish their own products, nor the fact that they think more or less money should be spent fostering it, makes this case comparable to those in which an objection rested on political or ideological disagreement with the content of the message." Moreover, he noted that nothing in the Abood line of cases barred the assessment of fees for nonideological purposes that are " 'germane' to the purpose for which compelled association was justified." Here, he noted, "the generic advertising of California peaches and nectarines is unquestionably germane to the purposes of the marketing orders [and] the assessments are not used to fund ideological activities." Does Glickman limit Abood's holding to organizations with a political message? If so, does this conflict with First Amendment principles of content and viewpoint neutrality? Note that United Foods and Johanns, discussed above at p. 1410, focused primarily on the compelled speech aspects of the cases.

4. ***Compulsory inclusion in membership.*** In **Roberts v. United States Jaycees**, 468 U.S. 609 (1984), the Court rejected an all-male organization's claim that a state antidiscrimination law infringed its freedom of association by requiring it to admit women. At issue was a

Minnesota statute prohibiting sex discrimination in a "place of public accommodation." The law had been applied to the Jaycees, or Junior Chamber of Commerce, a national civic organization which restricted full voting membership to men between the ages of 18 and 35. The Jaycees argued that this restriction on their membership policies interfered with their members' freedom of association.

Justice BRENNAN's opinion for the Court first rejected any claim on the Jaycees' part to a right of intimate association rooted in the liberty clause of the Fourteenth Amendment, given its large and relatively unselective composition. He then proceeded to consider the Jaycees' claim to a right of association protected by the First Amendment. Because the Jaycees engaged in various civic, educational, and related activities, the Court found expressive associational rights "plainly implicated in this case": "There can be no clearer example of an intrusion into the internal structure or affairs of an association than a regulation that forces the group to accept members it does not desire. Such a regulation may impair the ability of the original members to express only those views that brought them together. Freedom of association therefore plainly presupposes a freedom not to associate. Abood." But Justice Brennan did not find that right dispositive here: "The right to associate for expressive purposes is [not] absolute. Infringements on that right may be justified by regulations adopted to serve compelling state interests, unrelated to the suppression of ideas, that cannot be achieved through means significantly less restrictive of associational freedoms." Justice Brennan found this standard satisfied here: "We are persuaded that Minnesota's compelling interest in eradicating discrimination against its female citizens justifies the impact that application of the statute to the Jaycees may have on the male members' associational freedoms."

Crucially, Justice Brennan found the state antidiscrimination law content-neutral both on its face and as applied: "[T]he Minnesota Act does not aim at the suppression of speech, does not distinguish between prohibited and permitted activity on the basis of viewpoint, and does not license enforcement authorities to administer the statute on the basis of such constitutionally impermissible criteria, [nor was it] applied in this case for the purpose of hampering the organization's ability to express its views." Any restriction on associational liberty was merely incidental to Minnesota's interest in preventing sex discrimination. Nor was there any indication that the law imposed "any serious burden on the male members' freedom of expressive association": "The Act requires no change in the Jaycees' creed of promoting the interests of young men, and it imposes no restrictions on the organization's ability to exclude individuals with ideologies or philosophies different from those of its existing members. [Because] Jaycees already invites women to share the group's views and philosophy and to participate in much of its training and community activities, [any] claim that admission of women as full voting members will impair a symbolic message conveyed by the very fact that women are not permitted to vote is attenuated at best." In the absence of a showing far more substantial than that attempted here, "we decline to indulge in the sexual stereotyping that underlies appellee's contention that, by allowing women to vote, application of the Minnesota Act will change the content or impact of an organization's speech."

Justice O'CONNOR's concurring opinion drew a distinction between rights of commercial association and rights of expressive association. As to the former, state regulation should be "readily permit[ted]," but there remained "the ideal of complete protection for purely expressive association." Because the Jaycees, in her view, were primarily commercial, she concurred in rejecting the associational challenge. Justice Rehnquist concurred only in the judgment.

The Court unanimously followed Roberts in **Board of Directors of Rotary International v. Rotary Club**, 481 U.S. 537 (1987). The Court held that application of a California antidiscrimination law that barred exclusion of women from local Rotary clubs did not deny either freedom of intimate, private association or freedom of expressive association. (In a footnote, however, the Court noted that "we have no occasion [to] consider the extent to which the First Amendment protects the right of individuals to associate in the many clubs and other entities with selective membership that are found throughout the country. Whether the 'zone of privacy' established by the First Amendment extends to a particular [club] requires a careful inquiry into the objective characteristics of the particular relationships at issue.") A year later, in **New York State Club Ass'n v. City of New York**, 487 U.S. 1 (1988), the Court unanimously upheld against facial First Amendment challenge a law prohibiting racial, religious, or sex discrimination in any institution, club, or place of accommodation that has more than 400 members, provides regular meal service, and "regularly receives payment from [nonmembers] for facilities and services for the furtherance of trade or business." Justice WHITE's opinion stated that it was "conceivable [that] an association might be able to show that it is organized for specific expressive purposes and that it will not be able to advocate its desired viewpoints nearly as effectively if it cannot confine its membership. [Here,] however, it seems sensible enough to believe that many of the large clubs covered by the [law] are not of this kind." Note also the cursory rejection of a law firm's freedom of association claim in a Title VII sex discrimination case, in Hishon v. King & Spalding, 467 U.S. 69 (1984).

What principle underlies the freedom from compelled association asserted (and rejected) in Jaycees? Under the principles set forth in Jaycees, may a self-styled Male Supremacist Society exclude women? May a self-styled Feminist Separatist Organization exclude men? May the Ku Klux Klan exclude black members? May the NAACP exclude members of the Ku Klux Klan? To what extent must an organization set forth an exclusionary principle publicly in advance in order to maintain a First Amendment right against compulsory inclusion of unwanted members, and how central must such a principle be to its mission? May the exclusion be based upon a fact or status about a person or must it be based upon speech or symbolic conduct that person is likely to engage in? Is there a constitutionally relevant difference between organizations that seek to inculcate values in their members and organizations that serve a more social or commercial purpose? Are courts capable of drawing such lines objectively, or should subjective declarations by the organization be unreviewable? Ex post or only ex ante the exclusion?

Boy Scouts of America v. Dale

530 U.S. 640, 120 S. Ct. 2446, 147 L. Ed. 2d 554 (2000).

[A closely divided Court upheld the First Amendment expressive association right of the Boy Scouts to exclude an otherwise qualified scoutmaster, James Dale, on the ground that he had publicly disclosed his homosexuality. In a 5–4 decision, the Court held that New Jersey may not constitutionally apply its public accommodations law, which bars discrimination on the basis of sexual orientation, to require the Boy Scouts to admit Dale.]

■ CHIEF JUSTICE REHNQUIST delivered the opinion of the Court, in which JUSTICES O'CONNOR, SCALIA, KENNEDY, and THOMAS, joined.

The forced inclusion of an unwanted person in a group infringes the group's freedom of expressive association if the presence of that person affects in a significant way the group's ability to advocate public or private viewpoints. [To] determine whether a group is protected by the First Amendment's expressive associational right, we must determine whether the group engages in "expressive association."

[The] Boy Scouts is a private, nonprofit organization. According to its mission statement: "It is the mission of the Boy Scouts of America to serve others by helping to instill values in young people and, in other ways, to prepare them to make ethical choices over their lifetime in achieving their full potential. The values we strive to instill are based on those found in the Scout Oath—'On my honor I will do my best to do my duty to God and my country and to obey the Scout Law; To help other people at all times; To keep myself physically strong, mentally awake, and morally straight'—and Scout Law—'A Scout is: Trustworthy, Loyal, Friendly, Courteous, Helpful, Kind, Obedient, Cheerful, Thrifty, Brave, Clean, [and] Reverent.'" Thus, the general mission of the Boy Scouts is clear: "[T]o instill values in young people." The Boy Scouts seeks to instill these values by having its adult leaders spend time with the youth members, instructing and engaging them in activities like camping, archery, and fishing. During the time spent with the youth members, the scoutmasters and assistant scoutmasters inculcate them with the Boy Scouts' values—both expressly and by example. It seems indisputable that an association that seeks to transmit such a system of values engages in expressive activity.

Given that the Boy Scouts engages in expressive activity, we must determine whether the forced inclusion of Dale as an assistant scoutmaster would significantly affect the Boy Scouts' ability to advocate public or private viewpoints. This inquiry necessarily requires us first to explore, to a limited extent, the nature of the Boy Scouts' view of homosexuality. The values the Boy Scouts seeks to instill are "based on" those listed in the Scout Oath and Law. Boy Scouts explains that the Scout Oath and Law provide "a positive moral code for living; they are a list of 'do's' rather than 'don'ts.'" The Boy Scouts asserts that homosexual conduct is inconsistent with the values embodied in the Scout Oath and Law, particularly with the values represented by the terms "morally straight" and "clean." Obviously, the Scout Oath and Law do not expressly mention sexuality or sexual orientation. And the terms "morally straight" and "clean" are by no means self-defining. Different people would attribute to those terms very different meanings. For example, some people may believe that engaging in homosexual conduct is not at odds with being "morally straight" and "clean."

And others may believe that engaging in homosexual conduct is contrary to being "morally straight" and "clean." The Boy Scouts says it falls within the latter category.

The New Jersey Supreme Court analyzed the Boy Scouts' beliefs and found that the "exclusion of members solely on the basis of their sexual orientation is inconsistent with Boy Scouts' commitment to a diverse and 'representative' membership . . . [and] contradicts Boy Scouts' overarching objective to reach 'all eligible youth.' " But our cases reject this sort of inquiry; it is not the role of the courts to reject a group's expressed values because they disagree with those values or find them internally inconsistent. The Boy Scouts asserts that it "teach[es] that homosexual conduct is not morally straight," and that it does "not want to promote homosexual conduct as a legitimate form of behavior." We accept the Boy Scouts' assertion.

We must then determine whether Dale's presence as an assistant scoutmaster would significantly burden the Boy Scouts' desire to not "promote homosexual conduct as a legitimate form of behavior." As we give deference to an association's assertions regarding the nature of its expression, we must also give deference to an association's view of what would impair its expression. That is not to say that an expressive association can erect a shield against antidiscrimination laws simply by asserting that mere acceptance of a member from a particular group would impair its message. But here Dale, by his own admission, is one of a group of gay Scouts who have "become leaders in their community and are open and honest about their sexual orientation." Dale was the copresident of a gay and lesbian organization at college and remains a gay rights activist. Dale's presence in the Boy Scouts would, at the very least, force the organization to send a message, both to the youth members and the world, that the Boy Scouts accepts homosexual conduct as a legitimate form of behavior.

Hurley v. GLIB is illustrative on this point. There we considered whether the application of Massachusetts' public accommodations law to require the organizers of a private St. Patrick's Day parade to include among the marchers an Irish—American gay, lesbian, and bisexual group, GLIB, violated the parade organizers' First Amendment rights. We noted that the parade organizers did not wish to exclude the GLIB members because of their sexual orientations, but because they wanted to march behind a GLIB banner. [Here], we have found that the Boy Scouts believes that homosexual conduct is inconsistent with the values it seeks to instill in its youth members. [As] the presence of GLIB in Boston's St. Patrick's Day parade would have interfered with the parade organizers' choice not to propound a particular point of view, the presence of Dale as an assistant scoutmaster would just as surely interfere with the Boy Scout's choice not to propound a point of view contrary to its beliefs.

[Having] determined that the Boy Scouts is an expressive association and that the forced inclusion of Dale would significantly affect its expression, we inquire whether the application of New Jersey's public accommodations law to require that the Boy Scouts accept Dale as an assistant scoutmaster runs afoul of the Scouts' freedom of expressive association. We conclude that it does. [We] recognized in cases such as Roberts that States have a compelling interest in eliminating discrimination against women in public accommodations. But [we] went on to conclude that the enforcement of these statutes would not materially interfere with the ideas that the organization sought to express. [We] have already concluded that a state requirement that the Boy Scouts retain Dale as an assistant scoutmaster would significantly burden the organization's right to oppose or disfavor homosexual conduct. The state interests embodied in New Jersey's public accommodations law do not justify such a severe intrusion on the Boy Scouts' rights to freedom of expressive association. That being the case, we hold that the First Amendment prohibits the State from imposing such a requirement through the application of its public accommodations law.

[That] homosexuality has gained greater societal acceptance [is] scarcely an argument for denying First Amendment protection to those who refuse to accept these views. We are not, as we must not be, guided by our views of whether the Boy Scouts' teachings with respect to homosexual conduct are right or wrong; public or judicial disapproval of a tenet of an organization's expression does not justify the State's effort to compel the organization to accept members where such acceptance would derogate from the organization's expressive message. The judgment of the New Jersey Supreme Court is reversed.

■ JUSTICE STEVENS dissented.

It is plain as the light of day that neither [of the] principles—"morally straight" and "clean"—says the slightest thing about homosexuality. [A] State's antidiscrimination law does not impose a "serious burden" or a "substantial restraint" upon the group's "shared goals" if the group itself is unable to identify its own stance with any clarity. [Dale's] inclusion in the Boy Scouts is nothing like the case in Hurley. His participation sends no cognizable message to the Scouts or to the world. Unlike GLIB, Dale did not carry a banner or a sign; he did not distribute any fact sheet; and he expressed no intent to send any message. If there is any kind of message being sent, then, it is by the mere act of joining the Boy Scouts. Such an act does not constitute an instance of symbolic speech under the First Amendment. [The] only apparent explanation for the majority's holding, then, is that homosexuals are simply so different from the rest of society that their presence alone—unlike any other individual's—should be singled out for special First Amendment treatment. [The harm done by such] atavistic [anti-gay opinions should not] be aggravated by the creation of a constitutional shield for a policy that is itself the product of a habitual way of thinking about strangers.

DALE AND COMPELLED SPEECH AND ASSOCIATION

1. ***Free speech theory and Dale.*** What theory of freedom of speech and association might support the result in Dale? Is the problem that compelled inclusion of Scoutmaster Dale will distort the message that the Boy Scouts will be able to communicate to the outside world as an amplification device for its members? Or is the problem instead that the government is seeking to homogenize all groups in society and assimilate them to shared public values, whereas private expressive associations "provide sites in which the thoughts and ideas of members are formed and in which the content of their expressions is generated and germinated," a function important to a system of expression free from government control? Shiffrin, "What Is Really Wrong With Compelled Association?," 99 Nw. U. L. Rev. 839 (2005).

2. ***Compelled speech and on-campus recruiting.*** Does it follow from Dale that law school faculties should be able to exclude from their on-campus recruiting programs employers they deem to be in violation of their schools' antidiscrimination policies?

In a unanimous decision, the Court rejected such compelled association claims. (For the Court's rejection of related compelled speech claims, see p. 1416 above.) The so-called "Solomon Amendment" (see p. 1416 above) requires equal access for military recruiting on campus as a condition of universities' receiving federal funds. A group of law faculties objected that unwilling association with an employer that discriminates against gay students in violation of their nondiscrimination policies burdened their First Amendment rights, just as the unwanted membership of a gay scoutmaster in a Boy Scout troop did in Dale. Writing for the Court in **Rumsfeld v. Forum for Academic and Institutional Rights (FAIR)**, 547 U.S. 47 (2006), Chief Justice ROBERTS distinguished Dale and found that the Solomon Amendment did not infringe any associational rights belonging to law school faculties: "To comply with the statute, law schools must allow military recruiters on campus and assist them in whatever way the school chooses to assist other employers. Law schools therefore 'associate' with military recruiters in the sense that they interact with them. But recruiters are not part of the law school. Recruiters are, by definition, outsiders who come onto campus for the limited purpose of trying to hire students—not to become members of the school's expressive association. This distinction is critical. Unlike the public accommodations law in Dale, the Solomon Amendment does not force a law school 'to accept members it does not desire.' [A] military recruiter's mere presence on campus does not violate a law school's right to associate, regardless of how repugnant the law school considers the recruiter's message."

Why did the Court not accord deference to FAIR members' own self-defined account of their associational mission, as it did in Dale? For the view that the Court should have accorded greater deference to law school faculties' self-identified mission in the case, see Horwitz, "Three Faces of Deference," 83 Notre Dame L. Rev. 3 (2008) (arguing that the cases either both should have denied deference because "the Boy Scouts do not rise to the level of an occult mystery," or both should have accorded deference because "law school are in a better position than the Court to understand what they do and what would impair them").

FREEDOM OF ASSOCIATION AND POLITICAL PARTY PROCEDURES

1. ***Ballot access.*** The Court has relied upon the First Amendment freedom of association to limit the states' authority to curtail access to ballots by independent candidates and third parties. In **Williams v. Rhodes**, 393 U.S. 23 (1968), the Court held that Ohio's election laws created unduly burdensome obstacles to third-party candidates seeking a place on presidential ballots. Under the Ohio laws, major parties retained their positions on the ballot simply by obtaining 10% of the votes in the last gubernatorial election, while parties newly seeking access to the presidential election had to conduct primaries and to obtain 15%. Justice BLACK's majority opinion stated that these requirements unconstitutionally placed "unequal burdens" on "the right of individuals to associate for the

advancement of political beliefs, and the right of qualified voters [to] cast their votes effectively." He concluded that the state had "failed to show any 'compelling interest' which justifie[d] imposing such heavy burdens" on such "precious freedoms." There were dissents by Justices Stewart and White and by Chief Justice Warren. A concurrence by Justice HARLAN stated that he would rest "entirely" on First Amendment associational rights, not equal protection.

Three years later, a unanimous Court distinguished Williams in rejecting challenges to Georgia's nominating procedures in **Jenness v. Fortson**, 403 U.S. 431 (1971). Unlike Ohio, Georgia permitted write-in votes and allowed independent candidates to appear on the ballots without third-party endorsement if they had filed nominating petitions signed by at least 5% of those eligible to vote in the last election for the office, without any need for an elaborate primary election machinery. Justice STEWART found the scheme more justifiable than that in Williams: "There is surely an important state interest in requiring some preliminary showing of a significant modicum of support before printing the name of a political organization and its candidates on the ballot—the interest, if no other, in avoiding confusion, deception, and even frustration of the democratic [process]." In **Storer v. Brown**, 415 U.S. 724 (1974), and **American Party of Texas v. White**, 415 U.S. 767 (1974), the Court found a set of ballot access barriers to independent candidates and small political parties to be of a magnitude somewhere between Williams and Jenness, and rejected most of the challenges. The majority acknowledged that strict scrutiny was applicable. In Storer, the Court sustained a California provision denying a ballot position to an independent candidate if he or she had registered with a political party within a year prior to the immediately preceding primary election or had voted in that election. In the Texas case, the Court sustained most of that state's provisions regarding independents and minor parties, but invalidated a provision under which only names of major parties were included on absentee ballots.

This line of cases continued to develop in new kinds of equal protection challenges. In **Bullock v. Carter**, 405 U.S. 134 (1972), and **Lubin v. Panish**, 415 U.S. 709 (1974), a unanimous Court invalidated filing fee requirements for candidates. Chief Justice BURGER, writing the prevailing opinion in each case, concluded that the state had not established the "requisite justification" either in its concern about regulating the size of the ballot or in its interest in financing the election, and held "that in the absence of reasonable alternative means of valid access, a State may not, consistently with constitutional standards, require from an indigent candidate filing fees he cannot pay." But in **Clements v. Fashing**, 457 U.S. 957 (1982), Justice Rehnquist's plurality opinion announced that "[n]ot all ballot access restrictions require 'heightened' equal protection scrutiny," and sustained under rationality review two Texas constitutional provisions limiting an incumbent public official's ability to become a candidate for another public office.

Eventually, the Court came to decide ballot access cases entirely on First Amendment, not equal protection grounds. At issue in **Anderson v. Celebrezze**, 460 U.S. 780 (1983), was an Ohio statute that required independent candidates, but not party nominees, to file their nominating petitions by late March in order to be on the November ballot. John Anderson, independent candidate for President in 1980, challenged the statute, claiming that the early filing deadline excessively restricted access to the ballot and impermissibly discriminated against independent candidates. Justice STEVENS's majority opinion upheld Anderson's claim, finding that Ohio's asserted interests in voter education, equal treatment for partisan and independent candidates, and political stability were either illegitimate or too remotely related to the early filing deadline to justify such a substantial barrier to independent candidates. Stating that the ruling rested solely on First Amendment, not equal protection grounds, he set forth the following test: "[A] court [must] first consider the character and magnitude of the asserted injury to the [First Amendment rights]. It then must identify and evaluate the precise interests put forward by the State as justifications for the burden imposed. [Only] after weighing all these factors is the reviewing court in a position to decide whether the challenged provision is unconstitutional."

In **New York State Board of Elections v. Lopez Torres**, 552 U.S. 196 (2008), the Supreme Court rendered a unanimous judgment rejecting a challenge to a New York election law that required parties to select nominees to state trial court judgeships by a convention composed of delegates elected by party members. The challengers sought to compel primary elections for these seats. Justice SCALIA, writing for the Court, found nothing in the First Amendment that would entitle a challenger to so alter a party's selection process: "Respondents' real complaint is [that] the convention process that follows the delegate election does not give them a realistic chance to secure the party's nomination. The party leadership, they say, inevitably garners more votes for its slate of delegates (delegates uncommitted to any judicial nominee) than the unsupported candidate can amass for himself. And thus the leadership effectively determines the nominees. But this says nothing more than that the party leadership has more widespread support than a candidate not supported by the leadership. No New York law compels election of the leadership's slate—or, for that matter, compels the delegates elected on the leadership's slate to vote the way the leadership desires. And no state law prohibits an unsupported candidate from attending the convention and seeking to persuade the delegates to support her.

"Our cases invalidating ballot-access requirements have focused on the requirements themselves, and not on the manner in which political actors function under those requirements. See, e.g., Bullock v. Carter, Williams v. Rhodes, Anderson v. Celebrezze. Here respondents complain not of the state law, but of the voters' (and their elected delegates') preference for the choices of the party leadership." Justices Stevens and Kennedy each concurred separately, expressing doubts about the wisdom of the State's policy.

2. ***Write-in voting.*** In **Burdick v. Takushi**, 504 U.S. 428 (1992), the Court, applying Anderson's flexible standard of review, rejected First Amendment associational claims in upholding Hawaii's prohibition on write-in voting. Justice WHITE's opinion for the Court rejected the idea that all restrictions on the right to vote were subject to strict scrutiny: "[Instead, a] more flexible standard applies. [Anderson]. [Under] this standard, the rigorousness of our inquiry into the propriety of a state election law depends upon the extent to which a challenged regulation burdens First and Fourteenth Amendment rights. [When] those rights are subject to 'severe' restrictions, the regulation must be 'narrowly drawn to advance a state interest of compelling importance.' But when a state election law provision imposes only 'reasonable, nondiscriminatory restrictions' upon the First and

Fourteenth Amendment rights of voters, 'the State's important regulatory interests are generally sufficient to justify' the restrictions." Applying this standard, Justice White found the prohibition on write-in voting constitutionally permissible: "[When] a State's ballot access laws pass constitutional muster, [a] prohibition on write-in voting will be presumptively valid. [In] such situations, the objection [amounts] to nothing more than the insistence that the State record, count, and publish individual protests against the election system or the choices presented on the ballot through the efforts of those who actively participate in the system." Justice KENNEDY, joined by Justices Blackmun and Stevens, dissented, arguing that because "Democratic candidates often run unopposed," a ban on write-in candidates gave dissidents "no way to cast a meaningful vote."

3. ***Fusion tickets.*** In **Timmons v. Twin Cities Area New Party**, 520 U.S. 351 (1997), the Court, by a vote of 6–3, rejected a claim that a state ban on multiparty or "fusion" candidacies violated a party's or candidate's associational rights under the First and Fourteenth Amendments. Chief Justice REHNQUIST, writing for the Court, rejected the argument that such a ban was a "severe burden" on ballot access triggering strict scrutiny: "That a particular individual may not appear on the ballot as a particular party's candidate does not severely burden that party's association rights. [The fusion ticket] ban, which applies to major and minor parties alike, simply precludes one party's candidate from appearing on the ballot, as that party's candidate, if already nominated by another party. Respondent is free to try to convince [a candidate] to be [its], not [another party's], candidate." Nor did the ban prevent a minor party such as respondent "from developing consensual political alliances and thus broadening the base of public participation in and support for its activities." The majority was "unpersuaded [by] the Party's contention that it has a right to use the ballot itself to send a particularized message, to its candidate and to the voters, about the nature of its support for the candidate. Ballots serve primarily to elect candidates, not as fora for political expression."

Accordingly, Chief Justice Rehnquist viewed the fusion ban as among the "lesser burdens" or " 'reasonable, nondiscriminatory restrictions' " that, under Anderson and Burdick, "trigger less exacting review." Under this deferential standard, he concluded that "the burdens Minnesota's fusion ban imposes on the New Party's associational rights are justified by 'correspondingly weighty' valid state interests in ballot integrity and political stability." Specifically, fusion tickets might be used detrimentally to associate party or candidate names with popular slogans and catchphrases, to allow minor parties to hijack another party's popularity to their own use, or to cause "the destabilizing effects of party-splintering and excessive factionalism."

Justice STEVENS dissented, joined by Justice Ginsburg and for the most part by Justice Souter. He found the burden imposed by the fusion ban "significant" rather than minor: "[The] members of a recognized political party unquestionably have a constitutional right to select their nominees for public office and to communicate the identity of their nominees to the voting public. [The] Minnesota statutes place a significant burden on both of those rights. [In] this case [the] burden [is] imposed upon the members of a minor party, but its potential impact is much broader. Fiorello LaGuardia, Earl Warren, Ronald Reagan, and Franklin D. Roosevelt, are names that come readily to mind as candidates whose reputations and political careers were enhanced because they appeared on election ballots as fusion candidates. A statute that denied a political party the right to nominate any of those individuals for high office simply because he had already been nominated by another party would, in my opinion, place an intolerable burden on political expression and association." Nor was Justice Stevens convinced that the fusion ban actually served asserted state interests in "avoiding voter confusion, preventing ballot clutter and manipulation, encouraging candidate competition, and minimizing intraparty factionalism."

4. ***Political party primaries.*** The Court has increasingly found First Amendment freedom of association a limit on state intrusions into political party primary elections. In **Tashjian v. Republican Party**, 479 U.S. 208 (1986), the Court struck down a Connecticut law requiring that the voters in any party primary be registered members of that party. The challenger was the state's Republican Party, which had adopted a party rule permitting independents to vote in its primary. Justice MARSHALL's majority opinion held that the law unconstitutionally interfered with the associational rights of party members to decide for themselves who could vote in their primaries: "The Party's determination of the boundaries of its own association, and of the structure which best allows it to pursue its political goals, is protected by the Constitution." Three years later, in **EU v. San Francisco County Democratic Central Committee**, 489 U.S. 214 (1989), a unanimous Court relied on Tashjian in striking down provisions of California's election law barring political parties from endorsing, supporting or opposing "any candidate for nomination by that party for partisan office in the direct primary election." Justice MARSHALL's opinion applied strict scrutiny and held that the bar on candidate endorsements burdened both the speech and associational rights of the parties, and that California's asserted interest in preserving party stability was not "compelling."

What if the parties prefer to restrict access to their primary elections, rather than to make such access open as in Tashjian? In **California Democratic Party v. Jones**, 530 U.S. 567 (2000), the Court held that the same associational principles dictate deference to the party's choice either way. By a vote of 7–2, the Court struck down a California initiative, Proposition 198, which had changed California's partisan primary election from a closed primary to a blanket primary. Under the new system, any voter could vote for any candidate regardless of party affiliation or registration, and the candidate of each party winning the largest number of votes became the party's nominee. The blanket primary was challenged by the California Democratic Party, the California Republican Party, the Libertarian Party of California, and the Peace and Freedom Party, each of which sought to restrict to its own members primary voting for its candidates.

Writing for the Court, Justice SCALIA rejected the argument that primaries "are wholly public affairs that States may regulate freely," and invalidated the blanket primary system as a violation of parties' right of expressive association under the First Amendment: "Representative democracy in any populous unit of governance is unimaginable without the ability of citizens to band together in promoting among the electorate candidates who espouse their political views. The formation of national political parties was almost concurrent with the formation of the Republic itself. [A] corollary of the right to associate is the right not to associate. [In] no area is the political association's right to exclude more important than in the process of selecting its nominee. [Proposition 198] forces political parties to associate with—to have their nominees, and hence their positions, determined by—those who, at best, have refused to affiliate with the party, and, at worst, have expressly affiliated with a rival.

"[The] evidence in this case demonstrates that under California's blanket primary system, the prospect of having a party's nominee determined by adherents of an opposing party [through cross-over voting] is far from remote—indeed, it is a clear and present danger. [The] record also supports the obvious proposition that these substantial numbers of voters who help select the nominees of parties they have chosen not to join often have policy views that diverge from those of the party faithful. [Even] when the person favored by a majority of the party members prevails, he will have prevailed by taking somewhat different positions—and, should he be elected, will continue to take somewhat different positions in order to be renominated. [After all], the whole purpose of Proposition 198 was to favor nominees with 'moderate' positions. [In] sum, Proposition 198 forces petitioners to adulterate their candidate-selection process—the 'basic function of a political party'—by opening it up to persons wholly unaffiliated with the party. Such forced association has the likely outcome—indeed, in this case the intended outcome—of changing the parties' message. We can think of no heavier burden on a political party's associational freedom. Proposition 198 is therefore unconstitutional unless it is narrowly tailored to serve a compelling state interest."

Applying that standard, Justice Scalia found the state's proffered justifications wanting. He rejected as "inadmissible" any interest in "producing elected officials who better represent the electorate and expanding candidate debate beyond the scope of partisan concerns," or in drawing in "disenfranchised" voters, suggesting that such interests "reduce to nothing more than a stark repudiation of freedom of political association." And he found constitutionally inadequate any supposed government interest in promoting fairness, affording voters greater choice, increasing voter participation, or protecting privacy, by means of the blanket primary device. Even if such interests were compelling, he noted, the state could further them less restrictively by operating a nonpartisan blanket primary, in which voters could pick nominees regardless of party affiliation so long as those nominees did not advance to the general election as any party's nominees.

Justice STEVENS, joined by Justice Ginsburg, dissented, suggesting that "[a] State's power to determine how its officials are to be elected is a quintessential attribute of sovereignty," and that accordingly, "the associational rights of political parties are neither absolute nor as comprehensive as the rights enjoyed by wholly private associations." He insisted that the right not to associate "is simply inapplicable to participation in a [state-run and state-financed primary] election." He also would have given more deference to the state's proffered interests, ranking them "substantial, indeed compelling."

In a later decision concerning political party primaries, the Court ruled, by a vote of 6–3, that Oklahoma's semiclosed primary law did not violate the freedom of political association. The system provided that a political party may invite only its own party members and voters registered as Independents to vote in the party's primary. Under that system, the Libertarian Party of Oklahoma (LPO) was prevented from inviting Republicans and Democrats as well as registered Independents from voting in its primary elections. Writing for the Court in **Clingman v. Beaver**, 544

U.S. 581 (2005), Justice THOMAS upheld this barrier, writing for the Court in an opinion joined by Chief Justice Rehnquist and Justices Scalia, and Kennedy, and in relevant party by Justices O'Connor and Breyer. He distinguished Tashjian as involving more severe burdens on political association: "Connecticut's closed primary limited citizens' freedom of political association [by requiring] Independent voters to affiliate publicly with a party to vote in its primary. That is not true in this case. At issue here are voters who have *already* affiliated publicly with one of Oklahoma's political parties. [These] minor barriers between voter and party do not compel strict scrutiny." Applying a more deferential standard of review, Justice Thomas found reasonable and politically neutral Oklahoma's regulatory interests in preserving the identity of political parties and aiding their efforts at electioneering and party-building.

Justice STEVENS dissented, joined by Justices Souter and Ginsburg: "The Court's decision today diminishes the value of two important rights protected by the First Amendment: the individual citizen's right to vote for the candidate of her choice and a political party's right to define its own mission. No one would contend that a citizen's membership in either the Republican or the Democratic Party could disqualify her from attending political functions sponsored by another party, or from voting for a third party's candidate in a general election. If a third party invites her to participate in its primary election, her right to support the candidate of her choice merits constitutional protection, whether she elects to make a speech, to donate funds, or to cast a ballot. The importance of vindicating that individual right far outweighs any public interest in punishing registered Republicans or Democrats for acts of disloyalty." He would have found the associational interests at stake "virtually identical" to those in Tashjian, and found the state interests so "speculative or simply protectionist" of the parties in power that, "[n]o matter what the standard, they simply do not outweigh the interests of the LPO and its voters."

Eight years after deciding California Democratic Party v. Jones, the Supreme Court reached the opposite result in **Washington State Grange v. Washington State Republican Party**, 552 U.S. 442 (2008). This decision upheld against facial First Amendment challenge a Washington state law (I-872), enacted by voter initiative, providing that candidates must be identified on the primary ballot by their self-designated party preference, that voters may vote for any candidate, and that the two top vote-getters for each office advance to the general election regardless of a party's preference.

Writing for the 7–2 majority, Justice THOMAS, joined by Chief Justice Roberts and Justices Stevens, Souter, Ginsburg, Breyer, and Alito, explained why Jones was not controlling: "[U]nlike the California primary, the I-872 primary does not, by its terms, choose parties' nominees. The essence of nomination—the choice of a party representative—does not occur under I-872. The law never refers to the candidates as nominees of any party, nor does it treat them as such. To the contrary, the election regulations specifically provide that the primary 'does not serve to determine the nominees of a political party but serves to winnow the number of candidates to a final list of two for the general election.' The top two candidates from the primary election proceed to the general election regardless of their party preferences. Whether parties nominate their own candidates outside the state-run primary is simply irrelevant.

"At bottom, respondents' objection to I-872 is that voters will be confused by candidates' party-preference designations. [They] argue that even if voters do not assume that candidates on the general election ballot are the nominees of their parties, they will at least assume that the parties associate with, and approve of, them. This, they say, compels them to associate with candidates they do not endorse, alters the messages they wish to convey, and forces them to engage in counterspeech to disassociate themselves from the candidates and their positions on the issues. We reject each of these contentions for the same reason: They all depend, not on any facial requirement of I-872, but on the possibility that voters will be confused as to the meaning of the party-preference designation. But respondents' assertion that voters will misinterpret the party-preference designation is sheer speculation. [Of course,] it is *possible* that voters will misinterpret the candidates' party-preference designations as reflecting endorsement by the parties. But these cases involve a facial challenge, and we cannot strike down I-872 on its face based on the mere possibility of voter confusion." Finding no heavy burden on party or voter associational rights, the Court found no need for a compelling state interest, and found that, on appropriately deferential review, Washington's "asserted interest in providing voters with relevant information about the candidates on the ballot is easily sufficient to sustain I-872."

Justice SCALIA, joined by Justice Kennedy, dissented, finding Jones materially indistinguishable: "The Court makes much of the fact that the party names shown on the Washington ballot may be billed as mere statements of candidate 'preference.' To be sure, the party is not *itself* forced to display favor for someone it does not wish to associate with, as the Boy Scouts were arguably forced to do by employing the homosexual scoutmaster in Dale, and as the political parties were arguably forced to do by lending their ballot-endorsement as party nominee in Jones. But thrusting an unwelcome, self-proclaimed association upon the party on the election ballot itself is amply destructive of the party's associational rights. An individual's endorsement of a party shapes the voter's view of what the party stands for, no less than the party's endorsement of an individual shapes the voter's view of what the individual stands for. Not only is the party's message distorted, but its goodwill is hijacked. [There] is therefore 'no set of circumstances' under which Washington's law would not severely burden political parties."

Justice Scalia's dissent would have found Washington's law incapable of withstanding the strict scrutiny he thus deemed appropriate: "Even if I were to assume, [that] Washington has a legitimate interest in telling voters on the ballot (above all other things) that a candidate *says* he favors a particular political party, and even if I were further to assume *(per impossibile)* that that interest was a compelling one, Washington would still have to 'narrowly tailor' its law to protect that interest with minimal intrusion upon the parties' associational rights. There has been no attempt to do that here. Washington could, for example, have permitted parties to disclaim on the general-election ballot the asserted association or to designate on the ballot their true nominees. The course the State has chosen makes sense only as an effort to use its monopoly power over the ballot to undermine the expressive activities of the political parties."

5. ***Political gerrymandering.*** In **Vieth v. Jubelirer**, 541 U.S. 267 (2004), discussed above (p. 822), Justice KENNEDY first suggested that political gerrymandering plaintiffs seek recourse under the First

Amendment: "Though in the briefs and at argument the appellants relied on the Equal Protection Clause as the source of their substantive right and as the basis for relief, I note that the complaint in this case also alleged a violation of First Amendment rights. The First Amendment may be the more relevant constitutional provision in future cases that allege unconstitutional partisan gerrymandering. After all, these allegations involve the First Amendment interest of not burdening or penalizing citizens because of their participation in the electoral process, their voting history, their association with a political party, or their expression of political views." Citing Elrod v. Burns and California Democratic Party v. Jones, he further reasoned: "As these precedents show, First Amendment concerns arise where a State enacts a law that has the purpose and effect of subjecting a group of voters or their party to disfavored treatment by reason of their views. In the context of partisan gerrymandering, that means that First Amendment concerns arise where an apportionment has the purpose and effect of burdening a group of voters' representational rights."

Then in **Gill v. Whitford**, 138 S. Ct. 1916 (2018), Justice KAGAN appeared to endorse this argument, and introduced an "associational theory" of harm based on Justice Kennedy's Vieth concurrence to show how "partisan gerrymanders may infringe the First Amendment rights of association held by parties, other political organizations, and their members." Such an associational claim, she wrote, "would occasion a different standing inquiry" because "the gerrymander has burdened the ability of like-minded people across the State to affiliate in a political party and carry out that organization's activities and objects."

To what extent is this First Amendment theory of political gerrymandering of a piece with the Court's prior political free association cases? What are the potential benefits, or downfalls, of prioritizing a First Amendment theory in arguing for the unconstitutionality of political gerrymandering?

SECTION 3. MONEY AND POLITICAL CAMPAIGNS

For a generation since the 1972 Watergate burglary of Democratic campaign headquarters by Republican operatives and the comprehensive federal election campaign regulation that ensued, the Supreme Court has grappled with the question of what First Amendment limits might apply to Congress's and the states' efforts to restrict the flow of money into political campaigns. American elections are expensive because states and congressional districts are relatively large and dispersed, television and radio broadcast advertisements are crucial to reach the electorate in those districts, and the broadcast media are privately owned and charge steeply for such advertisements. The Court's first decision in the area, Buckley v. Valeo, which follows, held that free speech constraints apply with greater force to expenditure limits than to contribution limits, in effect refashioning the statutory scheme that Congress had devised, and setting the template for later cases:

Buckley v. Valeo

424 U.S. 1, 96 S. Ct. 612, 46 L. Ed. 2d 659 (1976).

■ PER CURIAM.

These appeals present constitutional challenges to the key provisions of the Federal Election Campaign Act of 1971 [FECA] and related provisions [as] amended in 1974. [The challenged laws] in broad terms [provide]: (a) individual political contributions are limited to $1,000 to any single candidate per election with an overall annual limitation of $25,000 by any contributor; independent expenditures by individuals and groups "relative to a clearly identified candidate" are limited to $1,000 a year; campaign spending by candidates for various federal offices and spending for national conventions by political parties are subject to prescribed limits; (b) contributions and expenditures above certain threshold levels must [be] publicly disclosed; (c) a system for public funding of Presidential campaign activities is established; [and] (d) a Federal Election Commission is established to administer [the Act].

I. *Contribution and Expenditure Limitations.*

[A.] *General Principles.* The Act's contribution and expenditure limitations operate in an area of the most fundamental First Amendment activities. Discussion of public issues and debate on the qualifications of candidates are integral to the operation of the system of government established by our Constitution. [In] upholding the constitutional validity of the Act's contribution and expenditure provisions on the ground that those provisions should be viewed as regulating conduct not speech, the Court of Appeals relied upon United States v. O'Brien. [We] cannot share the view that the present Act's contribution and expenditure limitations are comparable to the restrictions on conduct upheld in O'Brien. The expenditure of money simply cannot be equated with such conduct as destruction of a draft card. Some forms of communication made possible by the giving and spending of money involve speech alone, some involve conduct primarily, and some involve a combination of the two. Yet, this Court has never suggested that the dependence of a communication on the expenditure of money operates itself to introduce a nonspeech element or to reduce the exacting scrutiny required by the [First Amendment].

Even if the categorization of the expenditure of money as conduct were accepted, the limitations challenged here would not meet the O'Brien test because the governmental interests advanced in support of the Act involve "suppressing communication." The interests served by the Act include restricting the voices of people and interest groups who have money to spend and reducing the overall scope of federal election campaigns. Although the Act does not focus on the ideas expressed by persons or groups subjected to its regulations, it is aimed in part at equalizing the relative ability of all voters to affect electoral outcomes by placing a ceiling on expenditures for political expression by citizens and groups. Unlike [the situation in O'Brien], it is beyond dispute that the interest in regulating the alleged "conduct" of giving or spending money "arises in some measure because the communication allegedly integral to the conduct is itself thought to be harmful." Nor can the Act's contribution and expenditure limitations be sustained [by] reference to the constitutional principles reflected in such decisions as [Kovacs v. Cooper.] [The] critical difference between this case and those time, place and manner cases is that the present Act's contribution and expenditure limitations impose direct quantity restrictions on political communication and association [in] addition to any reasonable time, place, and manner regulations otherwise imposed.[1]

A restriction on the amount of money a person or group can spend on political communication during a campaign necessarily reduces the quantity of expression by restricting the number of issues discussed, the depth of their exploration, and the size of the audience reached.[2] This is because virtually every means of communicating ideas in today's mass society requires the expenditure of money. [The] expenditure limitations contained in the Act represent substantial rather than merely theoretical restraints on the quantity and diversity of political speech. [E.g., the] $1,000 ceiling on spending "relative to a clearly identified candidate" would appear to exclude all citizens and groups except candidates, political parties and the institutional press from any significant use of the most effective means of [communication].

By contrast with a limitation upon expenditures for political expression, a limitation upon the amount that any one person or group may contribute [entails] only a marginal restriction upon the contributor's ability to engage in free communication. A contribution serves as a general expression of support for the candidate and his views, but does not communicate the underlying basis for the support. [At most,] the size of the contribution provides a very rough index of the intensity of the contributor's support for the candidate. A limitation on [contributions] thus involves little direct restraint [on] political communication, for it permits the symbolic expression of support evidenced by a contribution but does not in any way infringe the contributor's freedom to discuss candidates and issues. While contributions may result in political expression if spent by a candidate or an association to present views to the voters, the transformation of contributions into political debate involves speech by someone other than the contributor.

Given the important role of contributions in financing political campaigns, contribution restrictions could have a severe impact on political dialogue if the limitations prevented candidates and political committees from amassing the resources necessary for effective advocacy. There is no indication, however, that the contribution limitations imposed by the Act would have any dramatic adverse effect on the funding of campaigns and political associations. The overall effect of the Act's contribution ceilings is merely to require candidates and political committees to raise funds from a greater number of persons and to compel people who would otherwise contribute amounts greater than the statutory limits to expend such funds on direct political expression, rather than to reduce the total amount of money potentially available to promote political expression. The Act's contribution and expenditure limitations also impinge on protected associational freedoms. [In] sum, although the Act's contribution and

---

1 The nongovernmental appellees argue that just as the decibels emitted by a sound truck can be regulated consistent with the First Amendment, Kovacs, the Act may restrict the volume of dollars in political campaigns without impermissibly restricting freedom of speech. This comparison underscores a fundamental misconception. The decibel restriction upheld in Kovacs limited the *manner* of operating a sound truck but not the *extent* of its proper use. By contrast, the Act's dollar ceilings restrict the extent of the reasonable use of virtually every means of communicating information. [Footnote by the Court.]

2 Being free to engage in unlimited political expression subject to a ceiling on expenditures is like being free to drive an automobile as far and as often as one desires on a single tank of gasoline. [Footnote by the Court.]

expenditure limitations both implicate fundamental First Amendment interests, its expenditure ceilings impose significantly more severe restrictions on protected freedoms of political expression and association than do its limitations on financial contributions.

B. *Contribution Limitations.* [T]he primary First Amendment problem raised by the Act's contribution limitations is their restriction of one aspect of the contributor's freedom of political association. [G]overnmental "action which may have the effect of curtailing the freedom to associate is subject to the closest scrutiny." [NAACP v. Alabama.] Yet, [e]ven a " 'significant interference' with protected rights of political association" may be sustained if the State demonstrates a sufficiently important interest and employs means closely drawn to avoid unnecessary abridgment of associational [freedoms].

It is unnecessary to look beyond the Act's primary purpose—to limit the actuality and appearance of corruption resulting from large individual financial contributions—in order to find a constitutionally sufficient justification for the $1,000 contribution limitation. [To] the extent that large contributions are given to secure political quid pro quos from current and potential officeholders, the integrity of our system of representative democracy is undermined. [The] deeply disturbing examples surfacing after the 1972 election demonstrate that the problem is not an illusory one. [Of] almost equal concern [is] the impact of the appearance of corruption stemming from public awareness of the opportunities for abuse inherent in a regime of large individual financial contributions. [Appellants] contend that the contribution limitations must be invalidated because bribery laws and narrowly-drawn disclosure requirements constitute a less restrictive means of dealing with "proven and suspected quid pro quo arrangements." But laws making criminal the giving and taking of bribes deal with only the most blatant and specific attempts of those with money to influence governmental action. And [Congress] was surely entitled to conclude that disclosure was only a partial measure, and that contribution ceilings were a necessary legislative concomitant to deal with the reality or appearance of [corruption].

[The Court also rejected similar challenges to the $5000 limit on contributions to candidates by "political committees," the limits on volunteers' incidental expenses, and the $25,000 limit on total contributions by an individual during a calendar year.]

C. *Expenditure Limitations.* The Act's expenditure ceilings impose direct and substantial restraints on the quantity of political speech. [It] is clear that a primary effect of these expenditure limitations is to restrict the quantity of campaign [speech]. [While neutral] as to the ideas expressed, [the restrictions] limit political expression "at the core of our electoral process and of the First Amendment [freedoms]."

1. *The $1,000 limitation on expenditures "relative to a clearly identified candidate."* Section 608(e)(1) provides that "[n]o person may make any expenditure [relative] to a clearly identified candidate during a calendar year [which] exceeds $1,000." [Appellants claim] that the provision is unconstitutionally vague. [Unconstitutional vagueness] can be avoided only by reading § 608(e)(1) as limited to communications that include explicit words of advocacy of election or defeat of a candidate.

[We] turn then to the basic First Amendment question—whether § 608(e)(1), even as thus narrowly and explicitly construed, impermissibly burdens the constitutional right of free expression. [T]he constitutionality of § 608(e)(1) turns on whether the governmental interests advanced in its support satisfy the exacting scrutiny applicable to limitations on core First Amendment rights of political expression.

We find that the governmental interest in preventing corruption and the appearance of corruption is inadequate to justify § 608(e)(1)'s ceiling on independent expenditures. First, [the section] prevents only some large expenditures. So long as persons and groups eschew expenditures that in express terms advocate the election or defeat of a clearly identified candidate, they are free to spend as much as they want to promote the candidate and his views. [It] would naively underestimate the ingenuity and resourcefulness of persons and groups desiring to buy influence to believe that they would have much difficulty devising expenditures that skirted the restriction on express advocacy of election or defeat but nevertheless benefited the candidate's campaign. [Second, the] parties defending § 608(e)(1) contend that it is necessary to prevent would-be contributors from avoiding the contribution limitations by the simple expedient of paying directly for media advertisements or for other portions of the candidate's campaign activities. [But] controlled or coordinated expenditures are treated as contributions rather than expenditures under the Act [and are restricted by the valid § 608(b)]. By contrast, § 608(e)(1) limits expenditures for express advocacy of candidates made totally independently of the candidate and his campaign. Unlike contributions, such independent expenditures may well provide little assistance to the candidate's campaign and indeed may prove counterproductive. The absence of prearrangement and coordination of an expenditure with the candidate or his agent not only undermines the value of the expenditure to the candidate, but also alleviates the danger that expenditures will be given as a quid pro quo for improper commitments from the candidate. [While] the independent expenditure ceiling thus fails to serve any substantial governmental interest in stemming the reality or appearance of corruption in the electoral process, it heavily burdens core First Amendment expression.

It is argued, however, that the ancillary governmental interest in equalizing the relative ability of individuals and groups to influence the outcome of elections serves to justify [this expenditure limitation]. But the concept that government may restrict the speech of some elements of our society in order to enhance the relative voice of others is wholly foreign to the First Amendment, which was designed "to secure 'the widest possible dissemination of information from diverse and antagonistic sources,' " and " 'to assure unfettered interchange of ideas.' " [The] First Amendment's protection against governmental abridgment of free expression cannot properly be made to depend on a person's financial ability to engage in public discussion. [We] conclude that § 608(e)(1)'s independent expenditure limitation is unconstitutional under the First Amendment.

2. *Limitation on expenditures by candidates from personal or family resources.* The Act also sets limits on expenditures by a candidate "from his personal funds, or the personal funds of his immediate family, in connection with his campaigns during any calendar year." § 608(a)(1). [The] ceiling on personal expenditures by a candidate in furtherance of his own [candidacy] clearly and directly interferes with constitutionally protected freedoms.

[The] interest in equalizing the relative financial resources of candidates competing for elective office [is] clearly not sufficient to justify the provision's infringement of fundamental First Amendment rights. First, the limitation may fail to promote financial equality among candidates. A candidate who spends less of his personal resources on his campaign may nonetheless outspend his rival as a result of more successful fundraising efforts. Indeed, a candidate's personal wealth may impede his efforts to persuade others that he needs their financial contributions or volunteer efforts to conduct an effective campaign. Second, and more fundamentally, the First Amendment simply cannot tolerate § 608(a)'s restriction upon the freedom of a candidate to speak [on] behalf of his own [candidacy].

3. *Limitations on campaign expenditures.* Section 608(c) of the Act places limitations on overall campaign expenditures by candidates seeking nomination for election and election to federal office. [Presidential] candidates may spend \$10,000,000 in seeking nomination for office and an additional \$20,000,000 in the general election campaign. [Senate campaign expenditures are limited to] the greater of eight cents multiplied by the voting-age population or \$100,000 [in the primary], and in the general election the limit is increased to 12 cents multiplied by the voting-age population or \$150,000. The Act imposes blanket \$70,000 limitations on both primary campaigns and general election campaigns for the House of Representatives. [These limits are subject to adjustments for inflation.]

[No] governmental interest that has been suggested is sufficient to justify [these restrictions] on the quantity of political expression. [The] interest in alleviating the corrupting influence of large contributions is served by [the] contributions limitations and disclosure provisions. [The] interest in equalizing the financial resources of candidates [is not a convincing justification] for restricting the scope of federal election campaigns. [The] campaign expenditure ceilings appear to be designed primarily to serve the governmental interests in reducing the allegedly skyrocketing costs of political campaigns. [But the] First Amendment denies government the power to determine that spending to promote one's political views is wasteful, excessive, or unwise. In the free society ordained by our Constitution it is not the government but the people—individually as citizens and candidates and collectively as associations and political committees—who must retain control over the quantity and range of debate on public issues in a political campaign. [W]e hold that § 608(c) is constitutionally invalid.

In sum, the [contribution limits] are constitutionally valid. These limitations along with the disclosure provisions, constitute the Act's primary weapons against the reality or appearance of improper influence stemming from the dependence of candidates on large campaign contributions. The contribution ceilings thus serve the basic governmental interest in safeguarding the integrity of the electoral process without directly impinging upon the rights of individual citizens and candidates to engage in political debate and discussion. By contrast, the First Amendment requires the invalidation of the Act's independent expenditure ceiling, its limitation on a candidate's expenditures from his own personal funds, and its ceilings on overall campaign expenditures. These provisions place substantial and direct restrictions on the ability of [candidates] to engage in protected political expression, restrictions that the First Amendment cannot [tolerate].

III. *Public Financing of Presidential Election Campaigns*

[Portions of the Act codified at Subtitle H of the Internal Revenue Code provided for a Presidential Election Campaign Fund, financed by taxpayer checkoff on tax returns, that would provide for up to $20 million (indexed for inflation) to finance presidential campaigns by major parties (those that had received more than 25 per cent of the popular vote in the preceding presidential election). It also provided for funding for minor-party campaigns (those receiving 5 to 25 per cent of the vote in the previous election) and new-party campaigns (those receiving less than 5 per cent in the current election) proportional to their share of the vote. Public subsidies for party nominating conventions and matching funds for primary campaigns were also provided. As a condition of receiving a public subsidy, major-party candidates were required to limit their campaign expenditures to the amount of the subsidy and to forego all private contributions except to the extent that the fund was insufficient to provide the full entitlement. Minor-party candidates similarly had to limit their campaign expenditures to the amount of the major-party entitlement and forego private contributions except to the extent needed to make up the difference between that amount and their public funding grant. The Court rejected Spending Clause and equal protection challenges to the funding provisions. In response to the First Amendment challenge, it held:]

Subtitle H is a congressional effort, not to abridge, restrict, or censor speech, but rather to use public money to facilitate and enlarge public discussion and participation in the electoral process, goals vital to a self-governing people. Thus, Subtitle H furthers, not abridges, pertinent First Amendment values.

[In a footnote earlier in the opinion, the Court summarized its holding on the public funding conditions as follows: "For the reasons discussed in Part III, Congress may engage in public financing of election campaigns and may condition acceptance of public funds on an agreement by the candidate to abide by specified expenditure limitations. Just as a candidate may voluntarily limit the size of the contributions he chooses to accept, he may decide to forego private fundraising and accept public funding."]

Affirmed in part and reversed in part.

■ CHIEF JUSTICE BURGER, concurring in part and dissenting [in part].

Contribution and expenditure limits. I agree fully with that part of the Court's opinion that holds unconstitutional the limitations the Act puts on campaign expenditures. [Yet] when it approves similarly stringent limitations on contributions, the Court ignores the reasons it finds so persuasive in the context of expenditures. For me contributions and expenditures are two sides of the same First Amendment [coin]. [Limiting] contributions, as a practical matter, will limit expenditures and will put an effective ceiling on the amount of political activity [that] Government will permit to take place. [The] Court's attempt to distinguish the communication inherent in political *contributions* from the speech aspects of political *expenditures* simply will not wash. We do little but engage in word games unless we recognize that people—candidates and contributors—spend money on political activity because they wish to communicate ideas, and their constitutional interest in doing so is precisely the same whether they or someone else utter the words. [It] is not simply speculation to think that the limitations on contributions will foreclose some candidacies. The limitations will also alter the nature of some electoral contests drastically.

At any rate, the contribution limits are a far more severe restriction on First Amendment activity than the sort of "chilling" legislation for which the Court has shown such extraordinary concern in the past. If such restraints can be justified at all, they must be justified by the very strongest of [state interests].

■ JUSTICE WHITE, concurring in part and dissenting [in part].

I dissent [from] the Court's view that the expenditure limitations [violate] the First Amendment. [The Court] accepts the congressional judgment that the evils of unlimited contributions are sufficiently threatening to warrant restriction regardless of the impact of the limits on the contributor's opportunity for effective speech and in turn on the total volume of the candidate's political communications by reason of his inability to accept large sums from those willing to give. The congressional judgment, which I would also accept, was that other steps must be taken to counter the corrosive effects of money in federal election campaigns. One of these steps is § 608(e) [the expenditure limits]. [It] would make little sense to me, and apparently made none to Congress, to limit the amounts an individual may give to a candidate or spend with his approval but fail to limit the amounts that could be spent on his behalf. Yet the Court permits the former while striking down the latter [limitation]. I would take the word of those who know—that limiting independent expenditures is essential to prevent transparent and widespread evasion of the contribution limits.

[The] Court also rejects Congress' judgment manifested in § 608(c) that the federal interest in limiting total campaign expenditures by individual candidates justifies the incidental effect on their opportunity for effective political speech. [There] is no sound basis for invalidating the expenditure limitations, so long as the purposes they serve are legitimate and sufficiently substantial, which in my view they are. [Expenditure] ceilings reinforce the contribution limits and help eradicate the hazard of corruption. [Moreover,] the corrupt use of money by candidates is as much to be feared as the corrosive influence of large contributions. [I] have little doubt in addition that limiting the total that can be spent will ease the candidate's understandable obsession with fundraising, and so free him and his staff to communicate in more places and ways unconnected with the fundraising function. [It] is also important to restore and maintain public confidence in federal elections. It is critical to obviate or dispel the impression that federal elections are purely and simply a function of money, that federal offices are bought and sold or that political races are reserved for those who have the facility—and the stomach—for doing whatever it takes to bring together those interests, groups, and individuals that can raise or contribute large fortunes in order to prevail at the polls. The ceiling on candidate expenditures represents the considered judgment of Congress that elections are to be decided among candidates none of whom has an overpowering advantage by reason of a huge campaign war chest. [This] seems an acceptable purpose and the means chosen a common sense way to achieve [it].

I also disagree with the Court's judgment that § 608(a), which limits the amount of money that a candidate or his family may spend on his campaign, violates the Constitution. [By] limiting the importance of personal wealth, § 608(a) helps to assure that only individuals with a modicum of support from others will be viable candidates. This in turn would tend to discourage any notion that the outcome of elections is primarily a function of money.

Similarly, § 608(a) tends to equalize access to the political arena, encouraging the less wealthy [to] run for political office. As with the campaign expenditure limits, Congress was entitled to determine that personal wealth ought to play a less important role in political campaigns than it has in the past. Nothing in the First Amendment stands in the way of that [determination].

[In a separate opinion, Justice BLACKMUN dissented from the portion of the decision upholding the contribution restrictions. He found no "principled constitutional distinction" between limits on contributions and limits on expenditures.]

[In another separate opinion, Justice MARSHALL dissented from the invalidation of the limits on the amount a candidate may spend from his own funds. He emphasized the governmental interest "in promoting the reality and appearance of equal access to the political arena," insisting that, even if the wealthy candidate's initial advantage can be overcome, "the perception that personal wealth wins elections may not only discourage potential candidates without significant personal wealth [but] also undermine public confidence in the integrity of the electoral process."]

[Finally, Chief Justice BURGER and Justice REHNQUIST dissented from the portion of the decision upholding the public financing provisions. Justice Rehnquist argued that Congress had "enshrined the Republican and Democratic parties in a permanently preferred position."]

BUCKLEY'S APPROACH AND AFTERMATH

1. ***The level of scrutiny in Buckley: the contribution/expenditure distinction.*** The Court assumed that FECA implicated the First Amendment. What was the speech involved? Is writing a check speech? Is a donor's writing a check speech because it facilitates the candidate's speech? Would price ceilings on book sales implicate the First Amendment? What level of scrutiny did the Court apply in Buckley? Why was any heightened scrutiny appropriate? Because the Act covered political speech at the core of the First Amendment? Because the Act decreased the quantity of speech? Don't all content-neutral regulations decrease the quantity of speech? Why should the quantity restriction here receive stricter scrutiny?

Note that the Court in effect applied less stringent scrutiny to the contribution limits than to the expenditure limits? Why? Do contributions implicate a lesser First Amendment interest than independent expenditures? Do congressional judgments warrant greater deference with respect to contribution limits than to expenditure limits? For commentary on these questions, see Polsby, "Buckley v. Valeo: The Special Nature of Political Speech," 1976 Sup. Ct. Rev. 1; and Sullivan, "Political Money and Freedom of Speech," 30 U.C. Davis L. Rev. 663 (1997).

The Court continued after Buckley to adhere to the distinction between expenditure and contribution limits, reviewing the former more strictly than the latter. From the outset, this distinction was controversial; note that, in Buckley, Justice White would have upheld both types of restriction and Chief Justice Burger and Justice Blackmun would have struck both down as "two sides of the same [coin]." In later decisions, a number of justices likewise argued that the distinction should be eliminated, with some arguing both types of restriction should be invalidated and others suggesting that both should be upheld. Nonetheless, the contribution/expenditure distinction has remained central to the Court's decisions in this area, and over time the Court increasingly formalized the two-tier review applicable to contribution limits on the one hand and expenditure limits on the other.

In **Nixon v. Shrink Missouri Government PAC**, 528 U.S. 377 (2000), for example, the Court reiterated that contribution limits are subject to greater deference than expenditure limits in rejecting a challenge to Missouri's limits on contributions to candidates for state office, brought by a candidate for state auditor who said that a $1075 limit on individual contributions for that office was too low, even if Buckley had upheld a $1000 federal contribution limit, because inflation had since eroded the real value of such a sum. Writing for the 6–3 majority, Justice SOUTER, joined by Chief Justice Rehnquist and Justices Stevens, O'Connor, Ginsburg and Breyer, reiterated that contribution limits need not satisfy strict scrutiny, but will survive if "closely drawn" to a "sufficiently important interest" such as prevention of corruption and the appearance of corruption. He also rejected the challengers' argument that the state must adduce strong empirical evidence of such corruption or its appearance: "The quantum of empirical evidence needed to satisfy heightened judicial scrutiny of legislative judgments will vary up or down with the novelty and plausibility of the justification raised. Buckley demonstrates that the dangers of large, corrupt contributions and the suspicion that large contributions are corrupt are neither novel nor implausible." Justice Souter also rejected the argument that the $1075 was too low in terms of real purchasing power to be constitutional under Buckley: "In Buckley, we specifically rejected the contention that $1,000, or any other amount, was a constitutional minimum below which legislatures could not regulate. [We] asked [instead] whether the contribution limitation was so radical in effect as to render political association ineffective." Justices Stevens and Breyer filed separate concurrences.

Justice KENNEDY dissented, emphasizing that Buckley's "wooden" distinction between contributions and expenditures had led to "adverse, unintended consequences"—specifically, it "has forced a substantial amount of political speech underground, as contributors and candidates devise ever more elaborate methods of avoiding contribution limits, limits which take no account of rising campaign costs. [Soft] money may be contributed to political parties in unlimited amounts, and is used often to fund so-called issue advocacy, advertisements that promote or attack a candidate's positions without specifically urging his or her election or defeat. [Thus] has the Court's decision given us covert speech. This mocks the First Amendment. The current system would be unfortunate, and suspect under the First Amendment, had it evolved from a deliberate legislative choice; but its unhappy origins are in our earlier decree in Buckley, which by accepting half of what Congress did (limiting contributions) but rejecting the other (limiting expenditures) created a misshapen system, one which distorts the meaning of speech." He concluded: "I would overrule Buckley and then free Congress or state legislatures to attempt some new reform, if, based upon their own considered view of the First Amendment, it is possible to do so. Until any reexamination takes place, however, the existing distortion of speech caused by the half-way house we created in Buckley ought to be eliminated. The First Amendment ought to be allowed to take its own course without further obstruction from the artificial system we have imposed. It suffices here to say that the law in question does not come even close to passing any serious scrutiny."

Justice THOMAS likewise dissented, joined by Justice Scalia. He described as a "curious anomaly" the majority's willingness to give less protection to campaign contributions than to other forms of speech (like nude dancing) less central to the political process. He questioned Buckley's contribution/expenditure distinction, stating that "the Constitution leaves it entirely up to citizens and candidates to determine who shall speak, the means they will use, and the amount of speech sufficient to inform and persuade." Finally, he criticized the majority for applying a lower standard of scrutiny to contribution regulations, suggesting that it had "permit[ted] vague and unenumerated harms to suffice as a compelling reason for the government to smother political speech," and argued that the Missouri law should have been subject to strict scrutiny, which it could not survive.

Note the substitution effects described by Justice Kennedy, whereby limitations on political contributions drive political money away from candidates who are accountable at the polls and toward political parties and independent advocacy organizations that are not. Congress later took the view that "soft money" expenditures by parties and "issue ads" by private organizations constitute "loopholes" in the federal election campaign laws and sought to control them by amendments to FECA. These amendments gave rise to constitutional challenges discussed below at p. 1479. For discussion of these substitution effects, see Sullivan, "Against Campaign Finance Reform," 1998 Utah L. Rev. 311 (1998); and Issacharoff & Karlan, "The Hydraulics of Campaign Finance Reform," 77 Tex. L. Rev. 1705 (1999).

In **Randall v. Sorrell**, 548 U.S. 230 (2006), the Court again reiterated the contribution/expenditure distinction, but for the first time found a contribution limit so low that it could not satisfy Buckley's avoidance-of-corruption rationale. Announcing the judgment of the Court, Justice BREYER, joined by Chief Justice Roberts, invalidated Vermont's expenditure limits under Buckley's strict scrutiny, and, joined by Justice Alito, also rejected Vermont's proposed new justification for expenditure limits, namely "that expenditure limits are necessary in order to reduce the amount of time candidates must spend raising money. [In] our view, it is highly unlikely that fuller consideration of this time protection rationale would have changed Buckley's result."

The same three-justice plurality held invalid Vermont's unusually low contribution limits, which allowed any individual to contribute only $400 to a governor's race, $300 to a state senator's race, and $200 to a state representative's race in each election cycle. Justice Breyer wrote: "Since Buckley, the Court has consistently upheld contribution limits in other statutes. [Nonetheless,] as Buckley acknowledged, we must recognize the existence of some lower bound. At some point the constitutional risks to the democratic electoral process become too great. [Contribution] limits that are too low can harm the electoral process by preventing challengers from mounting effective campaigns against incumbent officeholders, thereby reducing democratic accountability. [We] find those danger signs present here. [Vermont's] contribution limits are the lowest in the Nation [and] well below the lowest limit this Court has previously upheld, the limit of $1,075 per election [in Shrink]. [Such] contribution limits are too restrictive. [Taken] together, [Vermont's] substantial restrictions on the ability of candidates to raise the funds necessary to run a competitive election, on the ability of political parties to help their candidates get elected, and on the ability of individual citizens to volunteer their time to campaigns show that the Act is not closely drawn to meet its objectives."

Justice KENNEDY concurred only in the judgment, as did Justice THOMAS in an opinion, joined by Justice Scalia, stating "I continue to believe that Buckley provides insufficient protection to political speech, the core of the First Amendment." Justices Scalia and Thomas would have overruled Buckley insofar as it upheld contribution limits. Justices STEVENS filed a dissent stating that he too would overrule Buckley but in the opposite direction: "I am convinced that holding on expenditure limits is wrong, and that the time has come to overrule it. [I] am firmly persuaded that the Framers would have been appalled by the impact of modern fundraising practices on the ability of elected officials to perform their public responsibilities [and] they surely would not have expected judges to interfere with the enforcement of expenditure limits that merely require candidates to budget their activities without imposing any restrictions whatsoever on what they may say in their speeches, debates, and interviews." Justice SOUTER likewise filed a dissent, joined by Justice Ginsburg and in part by Justice Stevens, stating that he would have upheld Vermont's contribution limits under Buckley and Shrink, and allowed further evidentiary proceedings on whether Vermont's expenditure limits might be justified.

2. ***Government justifications for campaign finance restrictions: the corruption/equalization distinction.*** Buckley found the government interest in avoidance of corruption or the appearance of corruption sufficient to justify contribution limits. What did the Court mean by "corruption"? Not literal bribery, which was already illegal. Disproportionate influence by some over others with respect to legislative decision-making? The Court found the corruption rationale irrelevant to expenditure limits, and rejected as an illegitimate justification for those limits the asserted governmental interest "in equalizing the relative ability of individuals and groups to influence the outcome of elections," finding such an interest "wholly foreign to the First Amendment." Did the Court give adequate weight to the interest in equality as a justification for expenditure limits? Consider the following comments:

a. "We do not think of 'one person one vote' as an example of reducing the speech of some to enhance the relative speech of others. [Why should] superior spending power [be] rightfully mine [if] superior voting power is not [?]" Strauss, "Corruption, Equality, and Campaign Finance," 94 Colum. L. Rev. 1369 (1994).

b. "[In the political process,] ideas and candidates [should] prevail because of their inherent worth, not because [one or the other] side puts on a more elaborate show of support." Wright, "Politics and the Constitution: Is Money Speech?," 85 Yale L.J. 1001 (1976). See also Wright, "Money and the Pollution of Politics: Is the First Amendment an Obstacle to Political Equality?," 82 Colum. L. Rev. 609 (1982).

c. "[Buckley, like Lochner, rests on] a decision to take the market status quo as just and prepolitical, and to use that decision to invalidate democratic efforts at reform." Sunstein, "Free Speech Now," 59 U. Chi. L. Rev. 255 (1992).

d. "[W]hen wealth is unfairly distributed and money dominates politics, then, though individual citizens may be equal in their vote and their freedom to hear the candidates they wish to hear, they are not equal in their own ability to command the attention of others for their own candidates, interests, and convictions. [But] democracy [supposes] that citizens are equals not only as judges but as participants as well." Dworkin, "The Curse of American Politics," N.Y. Rev. of Books, Oct. 17, 1996.

e. "[In a fair constitutional democracy,] each eligible voter should receive the same amount of financial resources for the purpose of participating in electoral politics." Foley, "Equal-Dollars-Per-Voter: A Constitutional Principle of Campaign Finance," 94 Colum. L. Rev. 1204 (1994).

How effectively could campaign finance restrictions advance the goal of equality among speakers in political campaigns, if such a goal were permissible? Is wealth only one basis for political inequality? Would finance reform leave untouched inequality among candidates and their campaigns based on fame, incumbency, and experience in the political arena? Based on the time their supporters were willing to donate to their campaigns? See BeVier, "Campaign Finance Reform: Specious Arguments, Intractable Dilemmas," 94 Colum. L. Rev. 1258 (1994).

Are there any other government interests that might suffice to justify campaign finance restrictions? Might expenditure limits be justified as reducing the diversion of candidates' time to fundraising? (Note that such a justification was rejected in Randall v. Sorrell.) Might they be justified as increasing the responsiveness of elected officials to their constituencies rather than "special interests," or improve the quality of debate by shifting candidates' energies away from expensive but uninformative ads? For commentary on government interests beyond corruption and equalization, see Blasi, "Free Speech and the Widening Gyre of Fund-Raising: Why Campaign Spending Limits May Not Violate the First Amendment After All," 94 Colum. L. Rev. 1281 (1994); Sorauf, "Politics, Experience, and the First Amendment: The Case of American Campaign Finance," 94 Colum. L. Rev. 1348 (1994).

3. ***Public funding of political campaigns.*** Buckley upheld public subsidies for presidential elections, conditioned on the candidates' agreement not to spend above a certain ceiling. Note that such expenditure limits would be unconstitutional if imposed directly. Why wasn't it an unconstitutional condition on the receipt of public funds to impose this ceiling indirectly? The Court gave virtually no discussion to this question in Buckley. Could Congress make any subsidy scheme mandatory rather than voluntary? Would a mandatory public funding scheme violate the First Amendment? Suppose that government offered subsidies in kind, for example by mandating free air time for candidates on the broadcast media. Would such a subsidy violate broadcasters' First Amendment rights, or could such free air time in turn be exacted from broadcasters as a condition of their receipt of a public benefit in the form of a license to a portion of the airwaves? For arguments in favor of public funding, see Raskin & Bonifaz, "The Constitutional Imperative and Practical Superiority of Democratically Financed Elections," 94 Colum. L. Rev. 1160 (1994); see also Powe, "Mass Speech and the Newer First Amendment," 1982 Sup. Ct. Rev. 243.

PARTIES, CORPORATIONS, PACS, SUPER PACS AND POLITICAL MONEY

1. ***Campaign-related expenditures by political parties.*** May political parties expend funds freely in support of or opposition to candidates, so long as they do so independently of a candidate's own campaign? **Colorado Republican Federal Campaign Committee v. FEC**, 518 U.S. 604 (1996) ("Colorado I"), the Court invalidated a provision of FECA imposing dollar limits upon political party "expenditures in connection with the general election campaign of a [congressional] candidate." Justice BREYER, joined in a plurality opinion by Justices O'Connor and Souter, wrote that "the First Amendment prohibits the application of this provision to the kind of expenditure at issue here—an expenditure that the political party has made independently, without coordination with any candidate." He reasoned that "independent expression of a political party's views is 'core' First Amendment activity no less than is the independent expression of individuals, candidates, or other political committees. [We] therefore believe that this Court's prior case law controls the outcome here. We do not see how a Constitution that grants to individuals, candidates, and ordinary political committees the right to make unlimited independent expenditures could deny the same right to political parties." The plurality rejected the government's view that party expenditures on behalf of a candidate's election should be conclusively presumed to be coordinated with the candidate's campaign and thus treated as "contributions" that could be regulated permissibly under Buckley. But in light of its finding that the ads in this case had in fact been independent of any candidate's campaign, the plurality declined to reach the question whether the First Amendment forbids congressional efforts to limit expenditures that were in fact coordinated rather than independent.

Justice KENNEDY, joined by Chief Justice Rehnquist and Justice Scalia, concurred in the judgment and dissented in part. He would have invalidated the party expenditure limits on their face, whether applied to independent or coordinated expenditures. Justice THOMAS, joined by Chief Justice Rehnquist and Justice Scalia in a concurrence in the judgment and partial dissent, also would have invalidated the party spending limits in their entirety on the ground that the anticorruption rationale set forth in Buckley has no application here: "What could it mean for a party to 'corrupt' its candidate or to exercise 'coercive' influence over him? The very aim of a political party is to influence its candidate's stance on issues and, if the candidate takes office or is reelected, his votes. When political parties achieve that aim, [that] is not corruption; that is successful advocacy of ideas in the political marketplace and representative government in a party system." Justice STEVENS, joined by Justice Ginsburg, dissented, arguing that the party expenditure limits were constitutional as to both independent and coordinated expenditures because they served important interests both in avoiding corruption and in "leveling the electoral playing field by constraining the cost of federal campaigns."

The 1996 Colorado Republican decision left open the constitutionality of limits on expenditures by political parties that are coordinated with a candidate's campaign. That question was resolved, in the government's favor, in a second appeal in the same case after remand. In **FEC v. Colorado Republican Federal Campaign Committee**, 533 U.S. 431 (2001) ("Colorado II"), the plurality and the dissenters in Colorado I united to hold, in a 5–4 opinion for the Court by Justice SOUTER, that limits on a party's coordinated expenditures are facially constitutional: "[Parties] are [necessarily] the instruments of some contributors whose object is not to support the party's message or to elect party candidates across the board, but rather [to] use parties as conduits for contributions meant to place candidates under obligation. [A] party is [therefore] in the same position as some individuals and PACs, as to whom coordinated spending limits have already been held valid, Buckley. [We] accordingly apply to a party's coordinated spending limitation the same scrutiny we have applied to the other political actors, that is, scrutiny appropriate for a contribution limit, enquiring whether the restriction is 'closely drawn' to match what we have recognized as the 'sufficiently important' government interest in combating political corruption. Shrink."

Under that standard of intermediate scrutiny, Justice Souter found the limits justified "on the theory that unlimited coordinated spending by a party raises the risk of corruption (and its appearance) through circumvention of valid contribution limits. [Despite] years of enforcement of the challenged limits, substantial evidence demonstrates how candidates, donors, and parties test the limits of the current law, and it shows beyond serious doubt how contribution limits would be eroded if inducement to circumvent them were enhanced by declaring parties' coordinated spending wide open. [Therefore] the choice here is not, as in Buckley and Colorado I, between a limit on pure contributions and pure expenditures. The choice is between limiting contributions and limiting expenditures whose special value as expenditures is also the source of their power to corrupt. Congress is entitled to its choice."

Justice THOMAS dissented, joined by Justices Scalia and Kennedy and in part by Chief Justice Rehnquist. All but the Chief agreed they would overrule Buckley too and apply strict scrutiny to contribution limits. The Chief joined the other three dissenters in concluding that burdens on coordinated expenditures by parties would fail even the intermediate scrutiny applicable to individual contribution limits. Justice Thomas explained: "[T]he Government [has] presented no evidence at all of corruption or the perception of corruption. [The] Court's [alternative] theory [that] the Party Expenditure Provision helps combat circumvention of the limits on individual donors' contributions [is] weak speculation ungrounded in any evidence. [Even] if the Government had presented evidence that the Party Expenditure Provision affects corruption, [there] are better tailored alternatives for addressing the corruption. In addition to bribery laws and disclosure laws, the Government could [treat] contributions that [were 'earmarked] or otherwise directed through an intermediary or conduit to [a] candidate' [as] contributions to the candidate."

2. ***Expenditures by corporations for political speech.*** Should corporations have free speech rights to spend money in political campaigns? In favor of referenda and initiative propositions? In favor of or opposition to candidates? From their own treasuries or only through separate political action committees? Federal election law has long prohibited corporations (since 1907) and labor unions (since 1947) from making contributions from their own treasuries directly to candidates' political campaigns, while allowing them to establish separate, segregated political action committees or "PACs" to support candidates during federal elections.

But in **First National Bank of Boston v. Bellotti**, 435 U.S. 765 (1978), the Court held that the First Amendment prohibits a restriction on corporate expenditures for political speech from their own treasuries to express corporate points of view in state referenda campaigns. By a vote of 5–4, Bellotti invalidated a Massachusetts statute barring any corporation from making contributions or expenditures "for the purpose [of] influencing or affecting the vote on any questions submitted to the voters, other than one materially affecting any of the property, business or assets of the corporation." The law further specified that "[n]o question submitted to the voters solely concerning the taxation of the income, property, or transactions of individuals shall be deemed materially to affect the property, business or assets of the corporation." The challengers in this case (banks and business corporations) were prevented from spending money to oppose a proposed state constitutional amendment to authorize a graduated individual income tax. The state court upheld the statute, holding that the First Amendment rights of a corporation were limited to issues that materially affect its business, property, or assets.

The Supreme Court reversed, with Justice POWELL writing the majority opinion. To begin inquiry with the extent of corporate free speech rights (as the state court had done), he wrote, was to pose "the wrong question": "The proper question [is] not whether corporations 'have' First Amendment rights and, if so, whether they are coextensive with those of natural persons. Instead, the question must be whether [the law] abridges expression that the First Amendment was meant to protect. We hold that it does." In explaining why substantial First Amendment interests were implicated, Justice Powell noted that the expression the challengers wanted to engage in—publicizing their views on a proposed constitutional amendment—lay "at the heart of the First Amendment's protection": "It is the type of speech indispensable to decisionmaking in a democracy. [The] inherent worth of the speech in terms of its capacity for informing the public does not depend on the identity of its [source]." The Constitution and the case law accordingly did not support "the proposition that speech that otherwise would be within the protection of the First Amendment loses that protection simply because its source is a corporation that cannot prove, to the satisfaction of a court, a material effect on its business or property."

Having found the First Amendment implicated, Justice Powell found that the law was content-based and thus required strict scrutiny: "In the realm of protected speech, the legislature is constitutionally disqualified from dictating the subjects about which persons may speak and the speakers who may address a public issue. [Mosley.] If a legislature may direct business corporations to 'stick to business,' it also may limit other corporations—religious, charitable, or civic—to their respective 'business' when addressing the public. Such power in government to channel the expression of views is unacceptable under the First Amendment. Especially where, as here, the legislature's suppression of speech suggests an attempt to give one side of a debatable public question an advantage in expressing its views to the people, the First Amendment is plainly offended."

Under strict scrutiny, Justice Powell found, the law could not survive because it prohibited "protected speech in a manner unjustified by a compelling state interest." The state asserted, first, an interest "in sustaining the active role of the individual citizen in the electoral process and thereby preventing diminution of the citizen's confidence in government." Justice Powell did not find this interest "implicated in this case": he concluded that "there had been no showing that the relative voice of corporations has been overwhelming or even significant in influencing referenda in Massachusetts, or that there has been any threat to the confidence of the citizenry in government." Moreover, he found that the risk of actual or apparent corruption recognized in cases involving candidate elections "simply is not present in a popular vote on a public issue." The "State's paternalism evidenced by this statute" was inconsistent with the First Amendment's emphasis on the people's right to hear.

The state also asserted a second interest in "protecting the rights of shareholders whose views differ from those expressed by management on behalf of the corporation." Justice Powell also rejected this justification, finding that the statute poorly fit it: the statute was underinclusive in that it permitted corporations to lobby for legislation and contribute to candidates, and overinclusive in that it forbade them from spending on referenda even if the shareholders unanimously agreed on their position. Moreover, "The fact that a particular kind of ballot question has been singled out for special treatment undermines the likelihood of a genuine state interest in protecting shareholders. It suggests instead that the legislature may have been concerned with silencing corporations on a particular subject." Justice Powell also questioned the strength of the state interest in protecting shareholders from compulsory support of objectionable causes, noting that "no shareholder has been 'compelled' to contribute anything, [for] the shareholder invests in a corporation of his own volition and is free to withdraw his investment at any time and for any reason."

In a lengthy dissent, Justice WHITE, joined by Justices Brennan and Marshall, wrote that the majority's "fundamental error" was "its failure to realize that the state regulatory interests [are] themselves derived from the First Amendment"—primarily, the value of promoting the free marketplace of ideas by preventing corporate domination. Although Justice White conceded that corporate speech was within the First Amendment, he insisted that corporate speech was "subject to restrictions which individual expression is not." He noted that corporate communications do not further a "principal function of the First Amendment, the use of communication as a means of self-expression, self-realization and self-fulfillment." He added: "Ideas which are not a product of individual choice are entitled to less First Amendment protection." Moreover, "the restriction of corporate speech concerned with political matters impinges much less severely upon the availability of ideas to the general public than do restrictions upon individual speech."

Justice White argued further that the "governmental interest in regulating corporate political communications [raises] considerations which differ significantly from those governing the regulation of individual speech. [T]he special status of corporations has placed them in a position to control vast amounts of economic power which may, if not regulated, dominate not only the economy but also the very heart of our democracy, the electoral process. Although [Buckley] provides support for the position that the desire to equalize the financial resources available to candidates does not justify the limitation upon the expression of support which a restriction upon individual contributions entails, the interest of [the states] which have restricted corporate political activity is quite different. It is not one of equalizing the resources of opposing candidates or opposing positions but rather of preventing institutions which have been permitted to amass wealth as a result of special advantages extended by the State for certain economic purposes from using that wealth to acquire an unfair advantage in the political process. [The] State need not permit its own creation to consume it." Moreover, Justice White found compelling the state's additional interest in "assuring that shareholders are not compelled to support and financially further beliefs with which they disagree."

A separate dissent by Justice REHNQUIST concluded "that the 14th Amendment does not require a State to endow a business corporation with the power of political speech." He emphasized that corporations were created by the state and were limited to rights explicitly or implicitly guaranteed as part of the state-granted charter. He insisted that it could not be readily concluded that "the right of political expression is [necessary] to carry out the functions of a corporation organized for commercial purposes." He explained: "[The] States might reasonably feel that the corporation would use its economic power to obtain further benefits beyond those already bestowed." And he emphasized: "I can see no basis for concluding that the liberty of a corporation to engage in political activity with regard to matters having no material effect on its business is necessarily incidental to the purposes for which the Commonwealth permitted these corporations to be organized." Accordingly, the Massachusetts law provided "at least as much protection as the 14th Amendment requires." He noted that he would uphold the law even if the legislature's actual motive had been to "muzzle corporations on [the tax] issue" in order to increase the chances that the referendum would pass.

3. ***Segregated spending by PACs.*** While barring corporations from contributing directly to candidate campaigns, the federal election laws and the laws of many states have allowed corporations to operate separate, segregated "political action committees" or "PACs" in order to express support for or opposition to political candidates. Might the requirement of operating a separate fund itself burden free speech rights in violation of the First Amendment? In **FEC v. Massachusetts Citizens For Life, Inc. [MCFL]**, 479 U.S. 238 (1986), the Court held that certain nonprofit ideological corporations like MCFL, a grass-roots antiabortion organization, must be permitted to make independent campaign expenditures from their own corporate treasuries. Justice BRENNAN's opinion for the Court held that, as applied to MCFL, a financial segregation requirement is, "while [not] an absolute restriction on speech, a substantial one" that triggers strict scrutiny, and cannot be justified by any interest in preventing corruption (since the expenditures are independent) or by any interest in protecting contributors from the diversion of their funds to causes they do not support (since "individuals who contribute to [MCFL] are fully aware of its political purposes, and in fact contribute precisely because they support those purposes"). Chief Justice REHNQUIST, joined by Justices White, Blackmun, and Stevens, dissented.

Did the MCFL exception from segregated funding requirements apply to any entities beyond nonprofit ideological corporations? The Court rejected an extension of MCFL to an entity serving the interests of for-profit corporations in **Austin v. Michigan Chamber of Commerce**, 494 U.S. 652 (1990). Austin upheld a Michigan restriction that barred corporations from making independent expenditures from general treasury funds on behalf of candidates in political campaigns, even though the restriction was materially identical to the federal restriction invalidated as applied in MCFL.

Justice MARSHALL's majority opinion emphasized the "unique legal and economic characteristics of corporations" that enable them "to use 'resources amassed in the economic marketplace' to obtain 'an unfair advantage in the political marketplace.'" He elaborated: "the political advantage of corporations is unfair because '[t]he resources in the treasury of a business corporation [are] not an indication of popular support for the corporation's political ideas. They reflect instead the economically motivated decisions of investors and customers. The availability of these resources may make a corporation a formidable political presence, even though the power of the corporation may be no reflection of the power of its ideas.'" He held that the state had "articulated a sufficiently compelling rationale" for its restrictions on spending since the law was designed to deal with "the corrosive and distorting effects of immense aggregations of wealth that are accumulated with the help of the corporate form and that have little or no correlation to the public's support for the corporation's political ideas." Justice Marshall held the restriction permissibly applied to the Michigan Chamber of Commerce, reasoning that, unlike MCFL, the Michigan group "was involved in a wide range of activities other than political activity" and "had a large number of members many of whom might not share the Chamber's political goals."

Justice SCALIA dissented, rejecting the majority's view that the corporate form conferred advantages so different in kind from other state benefits as to justify a restriction on political speech and viewing the majority opinion as an attempt to overrule Buckley's rejection of restrictions on political activity in order to equalize speaking power. In another dissent, Justice KENNEDY, joined by Justices O'Connor and Scalia, objected that the majority had upheld "a direct restriction on the independent expenditure of funds for political speech for the first time in the Court's history." He argued that the Court's own distinction between the Michigan Chamber and MCFL was itself a "value-laden, content-based speech suppression that permits some nonprofit corporate groups but not others to engage in political speech." He would have found the Michigan law unable to survive "exacting First Amendment scrutiny": "[In] Buckley and Bellotti, [we] rejected the argument that the expenditure of money to increase the quantity of political speech somehow fosters corruption. The key to the majority's reasoning appears to be that because some corporate speakers are well-supported, [government] may ban all corporate speech to ensure that it will not dominate political debate. The argument is flawed in at least two respects. First, the statute is overinclusive because it covers all groups which use the corporate form, including all nonprofit corporations. Second, it assumes that the government has a legitimate interest in equalizing the relative influence of speakers. [Similar arguments were] rejected in Bellotti."

Was there any way to reconcile Austin with Buckley or Bellotti? Note that Justice Marshall sought to distinguish Austin as implicating an interest in avoiding the distortion of individual speakers' views rather than an interest in equalizing relative speaking power—the interest deemed illegitimate in Buckley. And Austin arose in the context of expenditures on behalf of candidates, not issues in a referendum campaign, as in Bellotti. But if a corporation may make unlimited expenditures on referendum campaigns under Bellotti, why may it not make unlimited independent expenditures in support of political candidates? The tension between Austin on the one hand and Buckley and Bellotti on the other eventually proved too much to sustain, and in Citizens United v. FEC, 558 U.S. 310 (2010), the Court expressly overruled Austin. For the Citizens United decision, see p. 1494 below.

ENACTMENT OF AND CONSTITUTIONAL CHALLENGES TO BCRA

By upholding contribution limits but invalidating expenditure limits, Buckley in effect held that the First Amendment permitted restrictions on the supply of political money, but forbade restrictions on demand. Predictably, as Justice Kennedy noted in Shrink, p. 1469 above, political money found other outlets. Federal election campaigns witnessed a rise in the expenditure of "soft money" by political parties and private interest group "issue advertisements" referencing candidates. Critics called these substitution effects "loopholes" in need of closure, prompting Congress to enact new campaign finance legislation in the Bipartisan Campaign Reform Act of 2002 (BCRA)—commonly called the "McCain-Feingold" law based on its two lead Senate sponsors, Republican John McCain and Democrat Russ Feingold.

1. ***"Soft money."*** Under the Federal Election Campaign Act of 1971 ("FECA") as amended and upheld in Buckley, contributions to federal election campaigns had to be made in limited amounts, had to be fully disclosed, and could not be made directly by certain entities such as unions and corporations. Donations made solely for the purpose of influencing state or local elections, however, were not governed by these disclosure requirements or source and amount limitations. Thus corporations and unions, as well as individuals who had contributed the maximum amounts to federal candidates, could contribute unlimited amounts of what came to be known as "soft money" (as opposed to so-called "hard money" that went directly to candidates) to political parties for activities intended to influence state or local elections. A series of FEC rulings allowed political parties to fund with soft money some mixed state/federal election activities, such as get-out-the-vote drives and generic party advertising. The amount of soft money used in federal campaigns increased each election cycle, accounting for 5% ($21.6 million) in 1984, 11% ($45 million) in 1988, 16% ($80 million) in 1992, 30% ($272 million) in 1996, and 42% ($498 million) in 2000. Advocates of campaign finance restrictions argued that the solicitation of soft money by the national parties for transfer and use by the state parties for de facto federal campaign activity amounted to circumvention of FECA's limitations.

2. ***"Issue advertising."*** In Buckley, the Court construed FECA's disclosure requirements and expenditure limitations "to reach only funds used for communications that expressly advocate the election or defeat of a clearly identified candidate" like "Elect Smith" or "Defeat Doe"—which could be understood as de facto contributions. The use or omission of such so-called "magic words" came to be viewed as determinative of a bright-line test separating regulable "express advocacy," which could be financed using only hard money subject to FECA's source and amount limits, from nonregulable "issue advocacy," which could be funded with soft money donated to the parties or paid for directly by advocacy organizations, corporations, and unions, and aired without disclosing its sponsor. Federal elections

increasingly witnessed a proliferation of issue ads eschewing the use of the magic words and thus in amounts and from sources unregulated by FECA.

3. ***Enactment of the Bipartisan Campaign Reform Act of 2002 (BCRA).*** In response to these trends, Congress enacted BCRA, which amended FECA, the Communications Act of 1934, and other portions of federal law. The law imposed new restrictions on soft money and issue ads that were designed, said its sponsors, to "close loopholes" in existing campaign finance regulation. Portions of the law were challenged immediately on First Amendment grounds by an array of plaintiffs from Republican Senator Mitch McConnell, a leading opponent of the law, to the National Rifle Association, the National Right to Life Committee, the Republican National Committee, the California Democratic Committee and the ACLU. In the 2003 decision in McConnell v. FEC, which follows, the Court upheld both the "soft money" and the "electioneering communications" provisions of BCRA against facial constitutional challenge, but in the 2007 decision in Wisconsin Right to Life, which follows after McConnell, the Court found that the electioneering communications provisions violate the First Amendment as applied to most issue ads:

McConnell v. Federal Election Commission

540 U.S. 93, 124 S. Ct. 619, 157 L. Ed. 2d 491 (2003).

▪ JUSTICE STEVENS and JUSTICE O'CONNOR delivered the opinion of the Court with respect to BCRA Titles I and II. [JUSTICES SOUTER, GINSBURG, and BREYER joined this opinion in its entirety.]

III. [Title I] is Congress' effort to plug the soft-money loophole. The cornerstone of Title I is new FECA § 323(a), which prohibits national party committees and their agents from soliciting, receiving, directing, or spending any soft money. [The] remaining provisions of new FECA § 323 largely reinforce the restrictions in § 323(a). New FECA § 323(b) prevents the wholesale shift of soft-money influence from national to state party committees by prohibiting state and local party committees from using such funds for activities that affect federal elections. [New] FECA § 323(d) reinforces these soft-money restrictions by prohibiting political parties from soliciting and donating funds to tax-exempt organizations that engage in electioneering activities. New FECA § 323(e) restricts federal candidates and officeholders from receiving, spending, or soliciting soft money in connection with federal elections and limits their ability to do so in connection with state and local elections. Finally, new FECA § 323(f) prevents circumvention of the restrictions on national, state, and local party committees by prohibiting state and local candidates from raising and spending soft money to fund advertisements and other public communications that promote or attack federal candidates.

[Like] the contribution limits we upheld in Buckley, § 323's restrictions have only a marginal impact on the ability of contributors, candidates, officeholders, and parties to engage in effective political speech. [For example,] while § 323(a) prohibits national parties from receiving or spending nonfederal money, and § 323(b) prohibits state party committees from spending nonfederal money on federal election activities, neither provision in any way limits the total amount of money parties can spend.

Rather, they simply limit the source and individual amount of donations. [Similarly,] the solicitation provisions of § 323(a) and § 323(e), [leave] open ample opportunities for soliciting federal funds on behalf of entities subject to FECA's source and amount restrictions. [The] fact that party committees and federal candidates and officeholders must now ask only for limited dollar amounts or request that a corporation or union contribute money through its PAC in no way alters or impairs the political message "intertwined" with the solicitation.

[With] these principles in mind, we apply the less rigorous scrutiny applicable to contribution limits to evaluate the constitutionality of new FECA § 323. [New FECA § 323(a)'s restrictions on national party committees] simply effect[ ] a return to the scheme that was approved in Buckley and that was subverted by the creation of the FEC's allocation regime, which permitted the political parties to fund federal electioneering efforts with a combination of hard and soft money. [The] question for present purposes is whether large soft-money contributions to national party committees have a corrupting influence or give rise to the appearance of corruption. Both common sense and the ample record in these cases confirm Congress' belief that they do. [It] is not only plausible, but likely, that candidates would feel grateful for such donations and that donors would seek to exploit that gratitude. The evidence in the record shows that candidates and donors alike have in fact exploited the soft-money loophole, the former to increase their prospects of election and the latter to create debt on the part of officeholders, with the national parties serving as willing intermediaries.

[Our] cases have firmly established that Congress' legitimate interest extends beyond preventing simple cash-for-votes corruption to curbing "undue influence on an officeholder's judgment, and the appearance of such influence." [The] record in the present case is replete [with] examples of national party committees peddling access to federal candidates and officeholders in exchange for large soft-money donations. [Just] as troubling to a functioning democracy as classic quid pro quo corruption is the danger that officeholders will decide issues not on the merits or the desires of their constituencies, but according to the wishes of those who have made large financial contributions valued by the officeholder. [The] best means of prevention is to identify and to remove the temptation. [Accordingly,] we reject the plaintiffs' First Amendment challenge to new FECA § 323(a).

[The Court also upheld Sections 323(b), (d), (e) and (f) as measures that served to prevent circumvention of 323(a) by foreclosing parties from diverting soft money to other conduits and surrogates "and thereby eviscerating FECA." In so doing, the Court applied "substantial deference to the predictive judgments of Congress."]

IV. [Title II] of BCRA [regulates] "Electioneering Communications" and "Independent and Coordinated Expenditures." [Section] 201 comprehensively coins a new term, "electioneering communication," [which] is defined to encompass any "broadcast, cable, or satellite communication" that "(I) refers to a clearly identified candidate for Federal office; (II) is made within (aa) 60 days before a general, special, or runoff election for the office sought by the candidate; or (bb) 30 days before a primary or preference election, or a convention or caucus of a political party that has authority to nominate a candidate, for the office sought by the candidate; and (III) in the case of a communication which refers to a candidate other than President or Vice President, is targeted to the relevant electorate."

[BCRA's] amendments [restrict] corporations' and labor unions' funding of electioneering communications. Plaintiffs challenge the constitutionality of the new term, [arguing] that Buckley drew a constitutionally mandated line between express advocacy and so-called issue advocacy, and that speakers possess an inviolable First Amendment right to engage in the latter category of speech. [That] position misapprehends our prior decisions, for the express advocacy restriction was an endpoint of statutory interpretation, not a first principle of constitutional law. [In] narrowly reading the FECA provisions in Buckley to avoid problems of vagueness and overbreadth, we nowhere suggested that a statute that was neither vague nor overbroad would be required to toe the same express advocacy line. [Nor] are we persuaded, independent of our precedents, that the First Amendment erects a rigid barrier between express advocacy and so-called issue advocacy. [Buckley's] magic-words requirement is functionally meaningless. Not only can advertisers easily evade the line by eschewing the use of magic words, but they would seldom choose to use such words even if permitted. And although the resulting advertisements do not urge the viewer to vote for or against a candidate in so many words, they are no less clearly intended to influence the election.

[Since] our decision in Buckley, Congress' power to prohibit corporations and unions from using funds in their treasuries to finance advertisements expressly advocating the election or defeat of candidates in federal elections has been firmly embedded in our law. The ability to form and administer separate segregated funds [has] provided corporations and unions with a constitutionally sufficient opportunity to engage in express advocacy. [Section] 203 of BCRA [extends] this rule, which previously applied only to express advocacy, to all "electioneering communications." [Because] corporations can still fund electioneering communications with PAC money, it is "simply wrong" to view the provision as a "complete ban" on expression rather than a regulation.

[Plaintiffs] do not contest that the Government has a compelling interest in regulating advertisements that expressly advocate the election or defeat of a candidate for federal office. [Rather,] plaintiffs argue that the justifications that adequately support the regulation of express advocacy do not apply to significant quantities of speech encompassed by the definition of electioneering communications. This argument fails to the extent that the issue ads broadcast during the 30- and 60-day periods preceding federal primary and general elections are the functional equivalent of express advocacy. [The] precise percentage of issue ads that clearly identified a candidate and were aired during those relatively brief preelection time spans but had no electioneering purpose is a matter of dispute between the parties. [Nevertheless,] the vast majority of ads clearly had such a purpose. Moreover, whatever the precise percentage may have been in the past, in the future corporations and unions may finance genuine issue ads during those time frames by simply avoiding any specific reference to federal candidates [or] paying for the ad from a segregated fund. We are therefore not persuaded that plaintiffs have carried their heavy burden of proving that [this section] is [substantially] overbroad.

[Section] 213 of BCRA [forces a political] party that wishes to spend more than $5,000 in coordination with its nominee [to] forgo independent expenditures that make use of magic words[—a] valuable statutory benefit that has been available to parties for many years. To survive constitutional scrutiny, a provision that has such consequences must be supported by a meaningful governmental interest. The interest in requiring political parties to avoid the use of magic words is not such an interest. [Any] claim that a restriction on independent express advocacy serves a strong Government interest is belied by the overwhelming evidence that the line between express advocacy and other types of election-influencing expression is, for Congress' purposes, functionally meaningless. [The] portion of the judgment of the District Court invalidating BCRA § 213 is affirmed.

V. [We] are under no illusion that BCRA will be the last congressional statement on the matter. Money, like water, will always find an outlet. What problems will arise, and how Congress will respond, are concerns for another day. [Affirmed in part and reversed in part.]

Chief Justice REHNQUIST delivered the opinion of the Court with respect to BCRA Titles III and IV. [Justices O'Connor, Scalia, Kennedy, and Souter joined this opinion in its entirety.]

■ CHIEF JUSTICE REHNQUIST, dissenting with respect to BCRA Titles I and V. [JUSTICES SCALIA and KENNEDY joined this dissent in its entirety].

[The] issue presented by Title I is not, as the Court implies, whether Congress can permissibly regulate campaign contributions to candidates, de facto or otherwise, or seek to eliminate corruption in the political process. Rather, the issue is whether Congress can permissibly regulate much speech that has no plausible connection to candidate contributions or corruption to achieve those goals. [Section] 323(a) does not regulate only donations given to influence a particular federal election; it regulates all donations to national political committees, no matter the use to which the funds are put. The Court attempts to sidestep the unprecedented breadth of this regulation by stating that the "close relationship between federal officeholders and the national parties" makes all donations to the national parties "suspect." But a close association with others, especially in the realm of political speech, is not a surrogate for corruption; it is one of our most treasured First Amendment rights. [Under] any definition of "exacting scrutiny," the means chosen by Congress, restricting all donations to national parties no matter the purpose for which they are given or are used, are not "closely drawn to avoid unnecessary abridgment of associational freedoms."

[All] political speech that is not sifted through federal regulation circumvents the regulatory scheme to some degree or another, and thus by the Court's standard would be a "loophole" in the current system.[1] Unless the Court would uphold federal regulation of all funding of political speech, a rationale dependent on circumvention alone will not do. JUSTICE SCALIA, concurring with respect to BCRA Titles III and IV, dissenting with respect to BCRA Titles I and V, and concurring in the judgment in part and dissenting in part with respect to BCRA Title II.

[It] was said by congressional proponents of this legislation, with support from the law reviews, that since this legislation regulates nothing but the expenditure of money for speech, as opposed to speech itself, the

---

[1] BCRA does not even close all of the "loopholes" that currently exist. Nonprofit organizations are currently able to accept, without disclosing, unlimited donations for voter registration, voter identification, and get-out-the-vote activities, and the record indicates that such organizations already receive large donations, sometimes in the millions of dollars, for these activities. [And] who knows what the next "loophole" will be. [Footnote by Chief Justice Rehnquist.]

burden it imposes is not subject to full First Amendment scrutiny. [But in] any economy operated on even the most rudimentary principles of division of labor, effective public communication requires the speaker to make use of the services of others. An author may write a novel, but he will seldom publish and distribute it himself. [To] a government bent on suppressing speech, this mode of organization presents opportunities: [License] printers, and it matters little whether authors are still free to write. Restrict the sale of books, and it matters little who prints them. [What] good is the right to print books without a right to buy works from authors? Or the right to publish newspapers without the right to pay deliverymen? The right to speak would be largely ineffective if it did not include the right to engage in financial transactions that are the incidents of its exercise. [Where] the government singles out money used to fund speech as its legislative object, it is acting against speech as such, no less than if it had targeted the paper on which a book was printed or the trucks that deliver it to the bookstore.

Another proposition which could explain at least some of the results of today's opinion is that the First Amendment right to spend money for speech does not include the right to combine with others in spending money for speech. [But the] freedom to associate with others for the dissemination of ideas—not just by singing or speaking in unison, but by pooling financial resources for expressive purposes—is part of the freedom of speech. [If] it were otherwise, Congress would be empowered to enact legislation requiring newspapers to be sole proprietorships, banning their use of partnership or corporate form.

[The] last proposition that might explain at least some of today's casual abridgment of free-speech rights is [that] the particular form of association known as a corporation does not enjoy full First Amendment protection. Of course the text of the First Amendment does not limit its application in this fashion, even though "[b]y the end of the eighteenth century the corporation was a familiar figure in American economic life." Nor is there any basis in reason why First Amendment rights should not attach to corporate associations—and we have said so. [Bellotti; Button.] People who associate—who pool their financial resources—for purposes of economic enterprise overwhelmingly do so in the corporate form; and with increasing frequency, incorporation is chosen by those who associate to defend and promote particular ideas—such as the American Civil Liberties Union and the National Rifle Association, parties to these cases. [A] candidate should not be insulated from the most effective speech that the major participants in the economy and major incorporated interest groups can generate. But what about the danger to the political system posed by "amassed wealth"? The most direct threat from that source comes in the form of undisclosed favors and payoffs to elected officials—which have already been criminalized, and will be rendered no more discoverable by the legislation at issue here. The use of corporate wealth (like individual wealth) to speak to the electorate is unlikely to "distort" elections—especially if disclosure requirements tell the people where the speech is coming from. The premise of the First Amendment is that the American people are neither sheep nor fools, and hence fully capable of considering both the substance of the speech presented to them and its proximate and ultimate source.

But, it is argued, quite apart from its effect upon the electorate, corporate speech in the form of contributions to the candidate's campaign, or even in the form of independent expenditures supporting the candidate, engenders an obligation which is later paid in the form of greater access to the officeholder, or indeed in the form of votes on particular bills. [If] the Bill of Rights had intended an exception to the freedom of speech in order to combat this malign proclivity of the officeholder to agree with those who agree with him, and to speak more with his supporters than his opponents, it would surely have said so. It did not do so, I think, because the juice is not worth the squeeze. Evil corporate (and private affluent) influences are well enough checked (so long as adequate campaign-expenditure disclosure rules exist) by the politician's fear of being portrayed as "in the pocket" of so-called moneyed interests. The incremental benefit obtained by muzzling corporate speech is more than offset by loss of the information and persuasion that corporate speech can contain.

■ JUSTICE THOMAS, concurring with respect to BCRA Titles III and IV, concurring in the judgment in part and dissenting in part with respect to BCRA Title II, and dissenting with respect to BCRA Titles I and V. [JUSTICE SCALIA joins Parts I, II–A, and II–B of this opinion.]

[Today's] holding continues a disturbing trend: the steady decrease in the level of scrutiny applied to restrictions on core political speech [including] limitations on independent expenditures. A. [BCRA § 214] captures expenditures with "no constitutional difference" from "a purely independent one" [and is thus unconstitutional.] B. As for §§ 203 and 204, the Court rests its decision on another vast expansion of the First Amendment framework described in Buckley, this time of the Court's, rather than Congress', own making. In Austin [the] Court recognized a "different type of corruption" from the " 'financial quid pro quo' ": the "corrosive and distorting effects of immense aggregations of wealth that are accumulated with the help of the corporate form and that have little or no correlation to the public's support for the corporation's political ideas." The only effect, however, that the "immense aggregations" of wealth will have (in the context of independent expenditures) on an election is that they might be used to fund communications to convince voters to select certain candidates over others. Apparently, winning in the marketplace of ideas is no longer a sign that "the ultimate good" has been "reached by free trade in ideas." [It] is now evidence of "corruption." This conclusion is antithetical to everything for which the First Amendment stands. Because Austin's definition of "corruption" is incompatible with the First Amendment, I would overturn Austin and hold that the potential for corporations and unions to influence voters, via independent expenditures aimed at convincing these voters to adopt particular views, is not a form of corruption justifying any state regulation or suppression.

■ JUSTICE KENNEDY, concurring in the judgment in part and dissenting in part with respect to BCRA Titles I and II. [CHIEF JUSTICE REHNQUIST joined this opinion in its entirety, and JUSTICES SCALIA and THOMAS in part; they disagreed, inter alia, that § 323(e) was constitutional.]

The First Amendment guarantees our citizens the right to judge for themselves the most effective means for the expression of political views and to decide for themselves which entities to trust as reliable speakers. [The] majority permits a new and serious intrusion on speech when it upholds § 203, the key provision in Title II that prohibits corporations and labor unions from using money from their general treasury to fund electioneering communications. [The] Government and the majority are right about one thing: The express-advocacy requirement, with its list of magic words, is easy to circumvent. The Government seizes on this observation to defend BCRA § 203, arguing it will prevent what it calls "sham issue ads" that are really to the same effect as their more express counterparts. What the Court and the Government call sham, however, are the ads speakers find most effective. [That] the Government would regulate it for this reason goes only to prove the illegitimacy of the Government's purpose. [We] are now told that "the government also has a compelling interest in insulating federal elections from the type of corruption arising from the real or apparent creation of political debts." [This] rationale has no limiting principle. Were we to accept it, Congress would have the authority to outlaw even pure issue ads, because they, too, could endear their sponsors to candidates who adopt the favored positions. [Section] 203 should be held unconstitutional.

[The] hostility toward corporations and unions that infuses the majority opinion is inconsistent with the viewpoint neutrality the First Amendment demands. [Corporations,] after all, are the engines of our modern economy. They facilitate complex operations on which the Nation's prosperity depends. To say these entities cannot alert the public to pending political issues that may threaten the country's economic interests is unprecedented. Unions are also an established part of the national economic system. They, too, have their own unique insights to contribute to the political debate, but the law's impact on them is just as severe. [The] Court is quite incorrect to suggest that the mainstream press is a sufficient palliative for the novel and severe constraints this law imposes on the political process. The Court should appreciate the dynamic contribution diverse groups and associations make to the intellectual and cultural life of the Nation. It should not permit Congress to foreclose or restrict those groups from participating in the political process by constraints not applicable to the established press.

Federal Election Comm'n v. Wisconsin Right to Life

551 U.S. 449, 127 S. Ct. 2652, 168 L. Ed. 2d 329 (2007).

■ CHIEF JUSTICE ROBERTS announced the judgment of the Court and delivered the opinion of the Court with respect to Parts I and II, and an opinion with respect to Parts III and IV, in which JUSTICE ALITO joins.

Section 203 of the Bipartisan Campaign Reform Act of 2002 (BCRA), makes it a federal crime for any corporation to broadcast, shortly before an election, any communication that names a federal candidate for elected office and is targeted to the electorate. In McConnell v. Federal Election Comm'n, this Court considered whether § 203 was facially overbroad under the First Amendment because it captured within its reach not only campaign speech, or "express advocacy," but also speech about public issues more generally, or "issue advocacy," that mentions a candidate for federal office. The Court concluded that there was no overbreadth concern to the extent the speech in question was the "functional equivalent" of express campaign speech. On the other hand, the Court "assumed" that the interests it had found to "justify the regulation of campaign speech might not apply to the regulation of genuine issue ads." The Court nonetheless determined that § 203 was not facially overbroad. [In] upholding § 203 against a facial challenge, we did not purport to resolve future as-applied challenges. We now confront such an as-applied challenge.

[WRTL is a nonprofit advocacy organization incorporated under § 501(c)(4) that ran several broadcast ads urging constituents to "call Senator Feingold" to protest the Senate's filibuster of judicial nominees and sought a declaratory judgment permitting broadcast of similar ads during the 2004 blackout period.]

III. [Because] BCRA § 203 burdens political speech, it is subject to strict scrutiny. This Court has already ruled that BCRA survives strict scrutiny to the extent it regulates express advocacy or its functional equivalent. So to the extent the ads in these cases fit this description, the FEC's burden is not onerous; all it need do is point to McConnell and explain why it applies here. If, on the other hand, WRTL's ads are *not* express advocacy or its equivalent, the Government [must] then demonstrate that banning such ads during the blackout periods is narrowly tailored to serve a compelling interest. No precedent of this Court has yet reached that conclusion.

The FEC [contends] that McConnell already established the constitutional test for determining if an ad is the functional equivalent of express advocacy: whether the ad is intended to influence elections and has that effect. WRTL and the District Court majority, on the other hand, claim that McConnell did not adopt any test as the standard for future as-applied challenges. We agree. McConnell's analysis was grounded in the evidentiary record before the Court. [The] Court did not explain that it was adopting a particular test for determining what constituted the "functional equivalent" of express advocacy.

[We] decline to adopt a test for as-applied challenges turning on the speaker's intent to affect an election. The test to distinguish constitutionally protected political speech from speech that BCRA may proscribe should provide a safe harbor for those who wish to exercise First Amendment rights. The test should also "reflect our 'profound national commitment to the principle that debate on public issues should be uninhibited, robust, and wide-open.'" A test turning on the intent of the speaker does not remotely fit the bill.

[The] proper standard for an as-applied challenge to BCRA § 203 must be objective, focusing on the substance of the communication rather than amorphous considerations of intent and effect. It must entail minimal if any discovery, to allow parties to resolve disputes quickly without chilling speech through the threat of burdensome litigation. And it must eschew "the open-ended rough-and-tumble of factors," which "invites complex argument in a trial court and a virtually inevitable appeal." In short, it must give the benefit of any doubt to protecting rather than stifling speech.

In light of these considerations, a court should find that an ad is the functional equivalent of express advocacy only if the ad is susceptible of no reasonable interpretation other than as an appeal to vote for or against a specific candidate. Under this test, WRTL's three ads are plainly not the functional equivalent of express advocacy. First, their content is consistent with that of a genuine issue ad: The ads focus on a legislative issue, take a position on the issue, exhort the public to adopt that position, and urge the public to contact public officials with respect to the matter. Second, their content lacks indicia of express advocacy: The ads do not mention an election, candidacy, political party, or challenger; and they do not take a position on a candidate's character, qualifications, or fitness for office.

Looking beyond the content of WRTL's ads, the FEC argue[s] that several "contextual" factors prove that the ads are the equivalent of express advocacy. [For example,] the ads were to be aired near elections but not near actual Senate votes on judicial nominees, [the] ads were run shortly after the Senate had recessed, [and the ads referred to a website that] stated both Wisconsin Senators' positions on judicial filibusters, and allowed visitors to sign up for "e-alerts," some of which contained exhortations to vote against Senator Feingold. [Given] the standard we have adopted for determining whether an ad is the "functional equivalent" of express advocacy, contextual factors of [this] sort should seldom play a significant role in the inquiry.

[Because] WRTL's ads may reasonably be interpreted as something other than as an appeal to vote for or against a specific candidate, we hold they are not the functional equivalent of express advocacy, and therefore fall outside the scope of McConnell's holding.

IV. BCRA § 203 can be constitutionally applied to WRTL's ads only if it is narrowly tailored to further a compelling interest. [That] a compelling interest justifies restrictions on express advocacy tells us little about whether a compelling interest justifies restrictions on issue advocacy. [This] Court has long recognized "the governmental interest in preventing corruption and the appearance of corruption" in election campaigns. McConnell arguably applied this interest—which this Court had only assumed could justify regulation of express advocacy—to ads that were the "functional equivalent" of express advocacy. But to justify regulation of WRTL's ads, this interest must be stretched yet another step to ads that are *not* the functional equivalent of express advocacy. Enough is enough. Issue ads like WRTL's are by no means equivalent to contributions, and the *quid-pro-quo* corruption interest cannot justify regulating them. To equate WRTL's ads with contributions is to ignore their value as political speech.

[One] possible compelling interest recognized by this Court lies in addressing a "different type of corruption in the political arena: the corrosive and distorting effects of immense aggregations of wealth that are accumulated with the help of the corporate form and that have little or no correlation to the public's support for the corporation's political ideas." Austin invoked this interest to uphold a state statute making it a felony for corporations to use treasury funds for independent expenditures on express election advocacy. McConnell relied on this interest in upholding regulation not just of express advocacy, but also its "functional equivalent." These cases did not suggest, however, that the interest in combating "a different type of corruption" extended beyond campaign speech. Quite the contrary. [Accepting] the notion that a ban on campaign speech could also embrace issue advocacy would call into question our holding in Bellotti that the corporate identity of a speaker does not strip corporations of all free speech rights. We hold that the interest recognized in Austin as justifying regulation of corporate campaign speech and extended in McConnell to the functional equivalent of such speech has no application to issue advocacy of the sort engaged in by WRTL.

[Because] WRTL's ads are not express advocacy or its functional equivalent, and because appellants identify no interest sufficiently compelling to justify burdening WRTL's speech, we hold that BCRA § 203 is unconstitutional as applied to WRTL's [ads]. when it comes to defining what speech qualifies as the functional equivalent of express advocacy subject to such a ban [we] give the benefit of the doubt to speech, not censorship.

■ JUSTICE SCALIA, with whom JUSTICES KENNEDY and THOMAS join, concurring in part and concurring in the judgment.[1]

[Austin] was a significant departure from ancient First Amendment principles. In my view, it was wrongly decided. [But] at least Austin was limited to express advocacy, and *nonexpress* advocacy was presumed to remain protected under Buckley and Bellotti, even when engaged in by corporations. [I] recognize the practical reality that corporations can evade the express-advocacy standard. I share the instinct that "what separates issue advocacy and political advocacy is a line in the sand drawn on a windy day." But the way to indulge that instinct consistently with the First Amendment is either to eliminate restrictions on independent expenditures altogether or to *confine* them to one side of the *traditional* line—the express-advocacy line, set in concrete on a calm day by *Buckley*, several decades ago. Section 203's line is bright, but it bans vast amounts of political advocacy indistinguishable from hitherto protected speech.

The foregoing analysis shows that McConnell was mistaken in its belief that as-applied challenges could eliminate the unconstitutional applications of § 203. They can do so only if a test is adopted which contradicts the holding of McConnell—that § 203 is facially valid because the vast majority of pre-election issue ads can constitutionally be proscribed. In light of the weakness in Austin's rationale, and in light of the longstanding acceptance of the clarity of Buckley's express-advocacy line, it was adventurous for McConnell to extend Austin beyond corporate speech constituting express advocacy. Today's cases make it apparent that the adventure is a flop, and that McConnell's holding concerning § 203 was wrong. "*Stare decisis* is not an inexorable command." Overruling a constitutional case decided just a few years earlier is far from unprecedented (citing numerous cases).

■ JUSTICE SOUTER, with whom JUSTICES STEVENS, GINSBURG, and BREYER join, dissenting.

[McConnell's holding] declaring the facial validity of [BCRA's § 203] is effectively, and unjustifiably, overruled today.

[A] century-long tradition of legislation and judicial precedent rests on facing undeniable facts and testifies to an equally undeniable value. Campaign finance reform has been a series of reactions to documented threats to electoral integrity obvious to any voter, posed by large sums of money from corporate or union treasuries, with no redolence of "grassroots" about them. Neither Congress's decisions nor our own have understood the corrupting influence of money in politics as being limited to outright bribery or discrete *quid pro quo;* campaign finance reform has instead consistently focused on the more pervasive distortion of electoral institutions by concentrated wealth, on the special access and guaranteed favor that sap the representative integrity of American government and defy public confidence in its institutions. From early in the 20th century through the decision in McConnell, we have acknowledged that the value of democratic integrity justifies a realistic response when corporations and labor organizations commit the concentrated moneys in their treasuries to electioneering.

[Any] Wisconsin voter who paid attention would have known that Democratic Senator Feingold supported filibusters against Republican presidential judicial nominees, that the propriety of the filibusters was a

[1] Justice Alito concurred separately to note that the Court might be asked to reconsider McConnell if the principal opinion's as-applied standard is found to chill political speech.

major issue in the senatorial campaign, and that WRTL along with the Senator's Republican challengers opposed his reelection because of his position on filibusters. Any alert voters who heard or saw WRTL's ads would have understood that WRTL was telling them that the Senator's position on the filibusters should be grounds to vote against him. Given these facts, it is beyond all reasonable debate that the ads are constitutionally subject to regulation under McConnell. [By refusing] to see and hear what any listener to WRTL's ads would actually consider, [the Chief Justice] thus effectively reinstates the same toothless "magic words" criterion of regulable electioneering that led Congress to enact BCRA in the first place.

MCCONNELL COMPARED WITH WRTL

1. ***Stare decisis.*** Note that Chief Justice Roberts went to considerable lengths in WRTL to distinguish rather than overrule McConnell's holding that the broadcast electioneering provision was facially constitutional. He emphasized that WRTL was an as-applied challenge, and rested on a different factual record. The concurring justices would have overruled McConnell outright on this point, and the dissenting justices lamented that this is the effective result of the decision. Was Chief Justice Roberts's opinion an exercise in judicial moderation? Or was Justice Scalia correct to charge in a footnote that this was "faux judicial modesty" that causes "judicial obfuscation"?

2. ***Regulation or ban?*** The FEC argued that § 203 was narrowly tailored since it left open various alternative means by which an organization like WRTL could have avoided sanction for alleged electioneering. Justice Souter summarized these ostensible alternatives in his dissent: "WRTL could have run a newspaper ad, could have paid for the broadcast ads through its PAC, could have established itself as an MCFL organization free of corporate money, and could have said 'call your Senators' instead of naming Senator Feingold in its ads broadcasted just before the election." Are these alternatives adequate substitutes for the broadcast ads WRTL sought to run?

3. ***For-profit vs. nonprofit corporations.*** All the opinions in WRTL declined to distinguish between for-profit and nonprofit corporations. The decision turns on the nature of the speech rather than the identity of the speaker. But is there greater reason to fear the distorting effect of speech from the corporate treasury of IBM or Google than from the corporate treasury of the National Rifle Association or the ACLU? Would an alternative route to a judgment for WRTL have been to require an exception to the electioneering provision only for nonprofit corporations? An original provision of BCRA proffered by Senators Snowe and Jeffords had taken this approach, but it was superseded by an amendment proposed by the late Senator Wellstone. Did the Court go too far in freeing issue ads by all corporations rather than those engaged in nonprofit advocacy? Is the concern about amassed wealth, gathered for other purposes, greater as to the former than the latter?

4. ***Challenge to BCRA's "Millionaire's Amendment."*** Can expenditures of a wealthy candidate's own money trigger government interest sufficient to justify regulation? In **Davis v. Federal Election Comm'n**, 554 U.S. 724 (2008), the Court invalidated § 319(a) of the

Bipartisan Campaign Reform Act of 2002 (BCRA), the so-called "Millionaire's Amendment," which provided that, when a candidate's expenditure of personal funds exceeded $350,000, he would remain subject to normal contribution limits but his opponent would be permitted to receive individual contributions at treble the normal limit and unlimited coordinated party expenditures. The Court found the law barred by the First Amendment in an opinion by Justice ALITO, joined by Chief Justice Roberts and Justices Scalia, Kennedy and Thomas. Justice Alito wrote:

> "If § 319(a) simply raised the contribution limits for all candidates, Davis' argument would plainly fail. [There is] no constitutional basis for attacking contribution limits on the ground that they are too high. [Section 319(a),] however, does not raise the contribution limits across the board. Rather, it raises the limits only for the non-self-financing candidate and does so only when the self-financing candidate's expenditure of personal funds causes the [$350,000] threshold to be exceeded. We have never upheld the constitutionality of a law that imposes different contribution limits for candidates who are competing against each other, and we agree with Davis that this scheme impermissibly burdens his First Amendment right to spend his own money for campaign speech.
>
> "[Section 319(a)] requires a candidate to choose between the First Amendment right to engage in unfettered political speech and subjection to discriminatory fundraising limitations. Many candidates who can afford to make large personal expenditures to support their campaigns may choose to do so despite § 319(a), but they must shoulder a special and potentially significant burden if they make that choice. Under § 319(a), the vigorous exercise of the right to use personal funds to finance campaign speech produces fundraising advantages for opponents in the competitive context of electoral politics. [Because] § 319(a) imposes a substantial burden on the exercise of the First Amendment right to use personal funds for campaign speech, that provision cannot stand unless it is 'justified by a compelling state interest.' No such justification is present here.
>
> "The burden imposed by § 319(a) on the expenditure of personal funds is not justified by any governmental interest in eliminating corruption or the perception of corruption. [Buckley] reasoned that reliance on personal funds *reduces* the threat of corruption, and therefore § 319(a), by discouraging use of personal funds, disserves the anticorruption interest. [The Government also] maintains that § 319(a)'s asymmetrical limits are justified because they 'level electoral opportunities for candidates of different personal wealth.' Our prior decisions, however, provide no support for the proposition that this is a legitimate government objective. [The] argument that a candidate's speech may be restricted in order to " 'level electoral opportunities' has ominous implications because it would permit Congress to arrogate the voters' authority to evaluate the strengths of candidates competing for office." The majority likewise invalidated the disclosure provisions of Section 319(a) as excessively burdening self-financed candidates' First Amendment rights.

A dissent by Justice STEVENS, joined by Justices, Souter, Ginsburg and Breyer, disagreed with the majority's First Amendment reasoning: "[T]he Millionaire's Amendment represents a modest, sensible, and plainly constitutional attempt by Congress to minimize the advantages enjoyed by wealthy candidates vis-a-vis those who must rely on the support of others to fund their pursuit of public office. [It] cannot be gainsaid that the twin rationales at the heart of the Millionaire's Amendment—reducing the importance of wealth as a criterion for public office and countering the perception that seats in the United States Congress are available for purchase by the wealthiest bidder—are important Government interests. It is also evident that Congress, in enacting the provision, crafted a solution that was carefully tailored to those concerns. [Enhancing] the speech of the millionaire's opponent, far from contravening the First Amendment, actually advances its core principles. If only one candidate can make himself heard, the voter's ability to make an informed choice is impaired." In a portion of Justice Stevens's dissent in which he spoke only for himself, he expressed the view that Justice White's dissent in Buckley had proved correct, and that expenditure limits in general should no longer be subject to strict scrutiny.

In **Arizona Free Enterprise Club's Freedom Club PAC v. Bennett**, 564 U.S. 721 (2011), the Court applied Davis to invalidate, by a vote of 5–4, provisions of the Arizona Citizens Clean Elections Act that allowed candidates for state office who participated in state public financing for elections additional matching funds if expenditures by a privately financed candidate, plus independent expenditures by his supporters, exceeded the publicly financed candidate's initial allotment of public funds. Finding that "[t]he logic of Davis largely controls our approach to this case," Chief Justice ROBERTS wrote for the Court, joined by Justices Scalia, Kennedy, Thomas and Alito, holding that the Arizona scheme burdened a privately financed candidate's speech because "each personal dollar spent by the privately financed candidate results in an award of almost one additional dollar to his opponent." Indeed, the majority found the burden heavier than in Davis because "the benefit to the publicly financed candidate is the direct and automatic release of public money" rather than the mere relaxation of contribution limits, because of the "multiplier effect" on the private candidate if he faced more than one publicly financed opponent, and because "any spending by independent expenditure groups to promote the privately financed candidate's election—regardless whether such support was welcome or helpful—could trigger matching funds." The majority noted that the scheme likewise burdened the speech of groups seeking to make independent expenditures in support of or opposition to candidates.

The majority rejected the State's argument "that the matching funds provision actually results in more speech by 'increas[ing] debate about issues of public concern' in Arizona elections" and that "this promotion of First Amendment ideals offsets any burden the law might impose on some speakers": "[E]ven if the matching funds provision did result in more speech by publicly financed candidates and more speech in general, it would do so at the expense of impermissibly burdening (and thus reducing) the speech of privately financed candidates and independent expenditure groups. This sort of 'beggar thy neighbor' approach to free speech—'restrict[ing] the speech of some elements of our society in order to enhance the relative voice of others'—is 'wholly foreign to the First Amendment.'" The majority also rejected the argument of the United States as amicus in support of Arizona that " '[p]roviding additional funds to petitioners' opponents does not make petitioners' own speech any less effective' and thus does not substantially burden speech": "All else being equal, an advertisement supporting the election of a candidate that goes without a response is often more effective than an advertisement that is directly controverted. And even if the publicly funded candidate decides to use his new money to address a different issue altogether, the end goal of that spending is to claim electoral victory over the opponent that triggered the additional state funding."

Turning to whether the Arizona law could be justified by a compelling state interest, Chief Justice Roberts rejected as illegitimate any state interest in " 'leveling the playing field' in terms of candidate resources": " 'Leveling the playing field' can sound like a good thing. But in a democracy, campaigning for office is not a game. It is a critically important form of speech. The First Amendment embodies our choice as a Nation that, when it comes to such speech, the guiding principle is freedom—the 'unfettered interchange of ideas'—not whatever the State may view as fair." The majority likewise found the burdens imposed by the matching funds provision unjustified "even if [its] ultimate objective [is] to combat corruption," because neither a candidate's expenditure of his own money nor independent expenditures in his support give rise to a threat of corruption or its appearance. Accordingly, the majority concluded, "Arizona's matching funds provision substantially burdens the speech of privately financed candidates and independent expenditure groups without serving a compelling state interest."

Justice KAGAN strongly disagreed in a dissent joined by Justices Ginsburg, Breyer and Sotomayor: "The First Amendment's core purpose is to foster a healthy, vibrant political system full of robust discussion and debate. Nothing in [the] Arizona Citizens Clean Elections Act violates this constitutional protection. To the contrary, the Act promotes the values underlying both the First Amendment and our entire Constitution by enhancing the 'opportunity for free political discussion to the end that government may be responsive to the will of the people.' "

The dissent disagreed with both steps of the majority's analysis. First, Justice Kagan disagreed that the Arizona law burdened speech: "The law has quite the opposite effect: It subsidizes and so produces *more* political speech. [Except] in a world gone topsy-turvy, additional campaign speech and electoral competition is not a First Amendment injury." Noting that the Court has often "distinguished between speech restrictions and speech subsidies" and upheld viewpoint-neutral subsidy schemes, Justice Kagan argued that, because it was viewpoint-neutral, "Arizona's subsidy statute should easily survive First Amendment scrutiny." She continued: "This suit, in fact, may merit less attention than any challenge to a speech subsidy ever seen in this Court. In the usual First Amendment subsidy case, a person complains that the government declined to finance his speech, while bankrolling someone else's. [But] the candidates bringing this challenge [were] never denied a subsidy. Arizona [offers] to support any person running for state office. Petitioners here *refused* that assistance [but argue] that Arizona violated *their* First Amendment rights by disbursing funds to *other* speakers even though they could have received (but chose to spurn) the same financial assistance. Some people might call that *chutzpah*."

Justice Kagan likewise rejected the majority's analogy to the burden on speech struck down in Davis: "In Davis, the candidate's expenditure triggered a discriminatory speech restriction, which Congress could not otherwise have imposed consistent with the First Amendment; by contrast, in this case, the candidate's expenditure triggers a non-discriminatory speech subsidy, which all parties agree Arizona could have provided in the first instance. [Two] great fault lines run through our First Amendment doctrine: one, between speech restrictions and speech subsidies, and the other, between discriminatory and neutral government action. The Millionaire's Amendment fell on the disfavored side of both divides."

The dissent argued, second, that, even if the Arizona law did trigger First Amendment review, it served a compelling interest in preventing corruption or the appearance of corruption in the State's political system. Finding that interest evident from the title of and findings in the statute, and rejecting as unsupported any inference that the State's goal was instead to level the playing field, Justice Kagan concluded that "that interest justifies the matching funds provision at issue because it is [the] thing that makes the whole Clean Elections Act work. [Public] financing has an Achilles heel—the difficulty of setting the subsidy at the right amount. Too small, and the grant will not attract candidates to the program; and with no participating candidates, the program can hardly decrease corruption. Too large, and the system becomes unsustainable, or at the least an unnecessary drain on public resources. But finding the sweet-spot is near impossible because of variation, across districts and over time, in the political system. Enter the matching funds provision, which takes an ordinary lump-sum amount, divides it into thirds, and disburses the last two of these (to the extent necessary) via a self-calibrating mechanism. [If] public financing furthers a compelling interest [then] so too does the disbursement formula that Arizona uses to make public financing effective." Finally, referring to the majority's assertion that "campaigning for office is not a game," Justice Kagan responded, "Truly, democracy is not a game. I respectfully dissent."

5. ***Corporate expenditures and the overruling of Austin.*** After WRTL and Davis, it was unclear what vitality was left to the rationale used in Austin v. Michigan Chamber of Commerce (1990; p. 1477 above) to uphold a requirement that a corporation make independent political expenditures only from a separate, segregated fund or PAC rather than from its own corporate treasury. The majority decision in WRTL sidestepped this issue by holding that Austin did not apply to WRTL's own expenditures. In the case that follows, the Court expressly confronted and overruled Austin, invalidating BCRA's limitations on independent corporate expenditures from corporate treasuries in political campaigns:

Citizens United v. Federal Election Commission

558 U.S. 310, 130 S. Ct. 876, 175 L. Ed. 2d 753 (2010).

■ JUSTICE KENNEDY delivered the opinion of the Court.

[Citizens United] is a nonprofit corporation [with] an annual budget of about $12 million. Most of its funds are from donations by individuals; but, in addition, it accepts a small portion of its funds from for-profit corporations. In January 2008, Citizens United released [a] 90-minute documentary [called "Hillary"] about then-Senator Hillary Clinton, who was a candidate in the Democratic Party's 2008 Presidential primary elections. Hillary mentions Senator Clinton by name and depicts interviews with political commentators and other persons, most of them quite critical of Senator Clinton. Hillary was released in theaters and on DVD, but Citizens United wanted to increase distribution by making it available through video-on-demand. [To] promote the film, it produced two 10-second ads and one 30-second ad for Hillary. Each ad includes a short (and, in our view, pejorative) statement about Senator Clinton, followed by the name of the movie and the movie's Website address. Citizens United desired to promote the video-on-demand offering by running advertisements on broadcast and cable television. [Under] the approach taken in WRTL, Hillary is equivalent to express advocacy. The movie, in essence, is a feature-length negative advertisement that urges viewers to vote against Senator Clinton for President.

[Section 441b] makes it a felony for all corporations—including nonprofit advocacy corporations—either to expressly advocate the election or defeat of candidates or to broadcast electioneering communications within 30 days of a primary election and 60 days of a general election. [Section 441b] is a ban on corporate speech notwithstanding the fact that a PAC created by a corporation can still speak. A PAC is a separate association from the corporation. So the PAC exemption from § 441b's expenditure ban does not allow corporations to speak. Even if a PAC could somehow allow a corporation to speak—and it does not—the option to form PACs does not alleviate the First Amendment problems with § 441b. PACs are burdensome alternatives; they are expensive to administer and subject to extensive regulations. [This] might explain why fewer than 2,000 of the millions of corporations in this country have PACs.

[We] find no basis for the proposition that, in the context of political speech, the Government may impose restrictions on certain disfavored speakers. [The] Court has recognized that First Amendment protection extends to corporations. This protection has been extended by explicit holdings to the context of political speech. [At] least since the latter part of the 19th century, the laws of some States and of the United States imposed a ban on corporate direct contributions to candidates. Yet not until 1947 did Congress first prohibit independent expenditures by corporations and labor unions. [Buckley] did not consider [the] separate ban on corporate and union independent expenditures. [Had that ban] been challenged in the wake of Buckley, however, it could not have been squared with the reasoning and analysis of that precedent. Notwithstanding this precedent, Congress recodified [the] corporate and union expenditure ban [as] § 441b four months after Buckley was decided. Less than two years after Buckley, Bellotti struck down a state-law prohibition on corporate independent expenditures related to referenda issues. [Bellotti] did not address the constitutionality of the State's ban on corporate independent expenditures to support candidates. In our view, however, that restriction would have been unconstitutional under Bellotti's central principle: that the First Amendment does not allow political speech restrictions based on a speaker's corporate identity.

Thus the law stood until Austin [v. Michigan Chamber of Commerce (1990); p. 1477 above]. [To] bypass Buckley and Bellotti, [Austin] identified a new [compelling] governmental interest in preventing "the corrosive and distorting effects of immense aggregations of wealth that are accumulated with the help of the corporate form and that have little or no correlation to the public's support for the corporation's political ideas." [The] Government does little to defend [Austin's antidistortion rationale]. And with good reason, for the rationale cannot support § 441b. [If] the antidistortion rationale were to be accepted, [it] would permit Government to ban political speech simply because the speaker is an association that has taken on the corporate form. [If] Austin were correct, the Government could prohibit a corporation from expressing political views in media beyond those presented here, such as by printing books. [Austin's] antidistortion rationale [also] would produce the dangerous, and unacceptable, consequence that Congress could ban political speech of media corporations. Media corporations are now exempt from § 441b's ban on corporate expenditures. Yet media corporations accumulate wealth with the help of the corporate form, [and] the views expressed by media corporations often "have little or no correlation to the public's support" for those views. [The] law's exception for media corporations is, on its own terms, all but an admission of the invalidity of the antidistortion rationale. And the exemption results in a further, separate reason for finding this law invalid.

Austin [permits] the Government to ban the political speech of millions of associations of citizens. Most of these are small corporations without large amounts of wealth. (96% of the 3 million businesses that belong to the U.S. Chamber of Commerce have fewer than 100 employees [and] more than 75% of corporations whose income is taxed under federal law have less than $1 million in receipts per year). This fact belies the Government's argument that the statute is justified on the ground that it prevents the "distorting effects of immense aggregations of wealth." It is not even aimed at amassed wealth.

[The] Government falls back on the argument that corporate political speech can be banned in order to prevent corruption or its appearance. [The] anticorruption interest is not sufficient to displace the speech here in question. Indeed, 26 States do not restrict independent expenditures by for-profit corporations. The Government does not claim that these expenditures have corrupted the political process in those States. [We] now conclude that independent expenditures, including those made by corporations, do not give rise to corruption or the appearance of corruption. [When] Buckley identified a sufficiently important governmental interest in preventing corruption or the appearance of corruption, that interest was limited to quid pro quo corruption. [Independent] expenditures do not lead to, or create the appearance of, quid pro quo corruption. In fact, there is only scant evidence that independent expenditures even ingratiate. Ingratiation and access, in any event, are not corruption. [Here] Congress has created categorical bans on speech that are asymmetrical to preventing quid pro quo corruption.

[The] Government contends further that corporate independent expenditures can be limited because of its interest in protecting dissenting shareholders from being compelled to fund corporate political speech. This asserted interest, like Austin's antidistortion rationale, would allow the Government to ban the political speech even of media corporations. [The] First Amendment does not allow that power. There is, furthermore, little evidence of abuse that cannot be corrected by shareholders "through the procedures of corporate democracy." Bellotti. [Moreover,] the statute is both underinclusive and overinclusive. [If] Congress had been seeking to protect dissenting shareholders, it would not have banned corporate speech in only certain media within 30 or 60 days before an election. A dissenting shareholder's interests would be implicated by speech in any media at any time. [And] the statute is overinclusive because it covers all corporations, including nonprofit corporations and for-profit corporations with only single shareholders.

Our precedent is to be respected unless the most convincing of reasons demonstrates that adherence to it puts us on a course that is sure error. "Beyond workability, the relevant factors in deciding whether to adhere to the principle of stare decisis include the antiquity of the precedent, the reliance interests at stake, and of course whether the decision was well reasoned." We have also examined whether "experience has pointed up the precedent's shortcomings." [These] considerations counsel in favor of rejecting Austin, which itself contravened this Court's earlier precedents in Buckley and Bellotti. [Austin] was not well reasoned. [Austin is also] undermined by experience since its announcement. Political speech is so ingrained in our culture that speakers find ways to circumvent campaign finance laws. [Corporations,] like individuals, do not have monolithic views. On certain topics corporations may possess valuable expertise, leaving them the best equipped to point out errors or fallacies in speech of all sorts, including the speech of candidates and elected officials. Rapid changes in technology—and the creative dynamic inherent in the concept of free expression—counsel against upholding a law that restricts political speech in certain media or by certain speakers. No serious reliance interests are at stake.

Due consideration leads to this conclusion: Austin should be and now is overruled. We return to the principle established in Buckley and Bellotti that the Government may not suppress political speech on the basis of the speaker's corporate identity. No sufficient governmental interest justifies limits on the political speech of nonprofit or for-profit corporations. [Given] our conclusion we are further required to overrule the part of McConnell that upheld BCRA § 203's extension of § 441b's restrictions on corporate independent expenditures.

■ JUSTICE SCALIA, with whom JUSTICES ALITO and THOMAS join, concurring.[1]

[The dissent] purports to show that today's decision is not supported by the original understanding of the First Amendment, [embarking] on a detailed exploration of the Framers' views about the "role of corporations in society." The Framers didn't like corporations, the dissent concludes, and therefore it follows (as night the day) that corporations had no rights of free speech. [Despite] the corporation-hating quotations the dissent has dredged up, it is far from clear that by the end of the 18th century corporations were despised. If so, how came there to be so many of them? [Even] if we agreed that the Founders disliked founding-era corporations; modern corporations might not qualify for exclusion. Most of the Founders' resentment towards corporations was directed at the state-granted monopoly privileges that individually chartered corporations enjoyed. [Moreover,] at the time of the founding, religious, educational, and literary corporations were incorporated under general incorporation statutes, much as business corporations are today. There were also small unincorporated business associations, which some have argued were the " 'true progenitors' " of today's business

[1] Justice Thomas dissented from the opinion of the Court insofar as it upheld BCRA's disclaimer and disclosure requirements as applied to the Hillary film and advertisements, see p. 1426 above. Chief Justice Roberts, joined by Justice Alito, filed a separate concurrence explaining why they agreed the case warranted a departure from stare decisis.

corporations. Were all of these silently excluded from the protections of the First Amendment?

[The] dissent says that when the Framers "constitutionalized the right to free speech in the First Amendment, it was the free speech of individual Americans that they had in mind." That is no doubt true. All the provisions of the Bill of Rights set forth the rights of individual men and women—not, for example, of trees or polar bears. But the individual person's right to speak includes the right to speak *in association with other individual persons*. Surely the dissent does not believe that speech by the Republican Party or the Democratic Party can be censored because it is not the speech of "an individual American." [The] association of individuals in a business corporation is no different—or at least it cannot be denied the right to speak on the simplistic ground that it is not "an individual American."

[The First] Amendment is written in terms of "speech," not speakers. Its text offers no foothold for excluding any category of speaker, from single individuals to partnerships of individuals, to unincorporated associations of individuals, to incorporated associations of individuals. [To] exclude or impede corporate speech is to muzzle the principal agents of the modern free economy. We should celebrate rather than condemn the addition of this speech to the public debate.

■ JUSTICE STEVENS, with whom JUSTICES GINSBURG, BREYER, and SOTOMAYOR join, dissenting.[2]

[In] the context of election to public office, the distinction between corporate and human speakers is significant. Although they make enormous contributions to our society, corporations are not actually members of it. They cannot vote or run for office. [The] financial resources, legal structure, and instrumental orientation of corporations raise legitimate concerns about their role in the electoral process. Our lawmakers have a compelling constitutional basis, if not also a democratic duty, to take measures designed to guard against the potentially deleterious effects of corporate spending in local and national races.

The majority's approach to corporate electioneering marks a dramatic break from our past. Congress has placed special limitations on campaign spending by corporations ever since the passage of the Tillman Act in 1907. [The] Court today rejects a century of history when it treats the distinction between corporate and individual campaign spending as an invidious novelty born of Austin. [I] am not an absolutist when it comes to *stare decisis*, in the campaign finance area or in any other. No one is. But if this principle is to do any meaningful work in supporting the rule of law, it must at least demand a significant justification, beyond the preferences of five Justices, for overturning settled doctrine. [No] such justification exists in this case. [The] only relevant thing that has changed since Austin and McConnell is the composition of this Court.

[Pervading] the Court's analysis is the ominous image of a "categorical ba[n]" on corporate speech. [This] characterization is highly misleading. [The] statutes upheld in Austin and McConnell [provide] exemptions for PACs, separate segregated funds established by a corporation for political purposes. [A] significant and growing number of corporations avail

[2] The dissenters concurred in part in the opinion of the Court insofar as it upheld BCRA's disclaimer and disclosure requirements as applied to the Hillary film and advertisements, see p. 1426 above.

themselves of this option; during the most recent election cycle, corporate and union PACs raised nearly a billion dollars. [And like] all other natural persons, every shareholder of every corporation remains entirely free under Austin and McConnell to do however much electioneering she pleases outside of the corporate form. The owners of a "mom & pop" store can simply place ads in their own names, rather than the store's. If ideologically aligned individuals wish to make unlimited expenditures through the corporate form, they may utilize an MCFL organization that has policies in place to avoid becoming a conduit for business or union interests. [Moreover,] § 203 functions [like] a time, place, and manner restriction. It applies in a viewpoint-neutral fashion to a narrow subset of advocacy messages about clearly identified candidates for federal office, made during discrete time periods through discrete channels. [The] majority's incessant talk of a "ban" aims at a straw man.

[The] second pillar of the Court's opinion is its assertion that "the Government cannot restrict political speech based on the speaker's . . . identity." [Bellotti.] But the holding in [Bellotti] was far narrower than the Court implies. [Our] First Amendment doctrine has "frowned on" certain identity-based distinctions, particularly those that may reflect invidious discrimination or preferential treatment of a politically powerful group. But it is simply incorrect to suggest that we have prohibited all legislative distinctions based on identity or content. [Campaign] finance distinctions based on corporate identity tend to be less worrisome [because] the "speakers" are not natural persons, much less members of our political community, and the governmental interests are of the highest order. Furthermore, when corporations, as a class, are distinguished from noncorporations, as a class, there is a lesser risk that regulatory distinctions will reflect invidious discrimination or political favoritism.

[A] third fulcrum of the Court's opinion is the idea that Austin and McConnell are radical outliers, "aberration[s]," in our First Amendment tradition. The Court has it exactly backwards. It is today's holding that is the radical departure from what had been settled First Amendment law. [To] the extent that the Framers' views are discernible and relevant to the disposition of this case, they would appear to cut strongly against the majority's position. This is not only because the Framers and their contemporaries conceived of speech more narrowly than we now think of it, but also because they held very different views about the nature of the *First Amendment* right and the role of corporations in society.

Those few corporations that existed at the founding were authorized by grant of a special legislative charter. Corporate sponsors would petition the legislature, and the legislature, if amenable, would issue a charter that specified the corporation's powers and purposes and "authoritatively fixed the scope and content of corporate organization," including "the internal structure of the corporation." Corporations were created, supervised, and conceptualized as quasi-public entities, "designed to serve a social function for the state." [The] individualized charter mode of incorporation reflected the "cloud of disfavor under which corporations labored" in the early years of this Nation. Thomas Jefferson famously fretted that corporations would subvert the Republic. General incorporation statutes, and widespread acceptance of business corporations as socially useful actors, did not emerge until the 1800's. [The] Framers thus took it as a given that corporations could be comprehensively regulated in the service of the public welfare. Unlike our colleagues, they had little trouble distinguishing corporations from human beings, and when they constitutionalized the right to free speech in the *First Amendment*, it was the free speech of individual Americans that they had in mind. While individuals might join together to exercise their speech rights, business corporations, at least, were plainly not seen as facilitating such associational or expressive ends. Even "the notion that business corporations could invoke the First Amendment would probably have been quite a novelty," given that "at the time, the legitimacy of every corporate activity was thought to rest entirely in a concession of the sovereign." In light of these background practices and understandings, it seems to me implausible that the Framers believed "the freedom of speech" would extend equally to all corporate speakers, much less that it would preclude legislatures from taking limited measures to guard against corporate capture of elections.

[The] majority emphasizes Buckley's statement that " '[t]he concept that government may restrict the speech of some elements of our society in order to enhance the relative voice of others is wholly foreign to the First Amendment.' " But this elegant phrase cannot bear the weight that our colleagues have placed on it. [We] made it clear in Austin that a restriction on the way corporations spend their money is no mere exercise in disfavoring the voice of some elements of our society in preference to others. Indeed, we expressly ruled that the compelling interest supporting Michigan's statute was not one of " 'equaliz[ing] the relative influence of speakers on elections,' " but rather the need to confront the distinctive corrupting potential of corporate electoral advocacy financed by general treasury dollars.

[The majority also claims] that Bellotti's holding forbade distinctions between corporate and individual expenditures like the one at issue here. [But Bellotti distinguished] between general corporate speech and campaign speech intended to promote or prevent the election of specific candidates for office. [The] anticorruption interests that animate regulations of corporate participation in candidate elections [do] not apply equally to regulations of corporate participation in referenda. A referendum cannot owe a political debt to a corporation, seek to curry favor with a corporation, or fear the corporation's retaliation. [Bellotti also] involved a *viewpoint-discriminatory* statute, created to effect a particular policy outcome, [and] the law at issue did not make any allowance for corporations to spend money through PACs. [Austin and McConnell,] then, sit perfectly well with Bellotti.

[Having] explained why this is not an appropriate case in which to revisit Austin and McConnell, [I] come at last to the interests that are at stake. [The] majority recognizes that Austin and McConnell may be defended on anticorruption, antidistortion, and shareholder protection rationales. It badly errs both in explaining the nature of these rationales, which overlap and complement each other, and in applying them to the case at hand.

[Corruption] can take many forms. Bribery may be the paradigm case. But the difference between selling a vote and selling access is a matter of degree, not kind. And selling access is not qualitatively different from giving special preference to those who spent money on one's behalf. Corruption operates along a spectrum, and the majority's apparent belief that *quid pro quo* arrangements can be neatly demarcated from other improper influences does not accord with the theory or reality of politics. It certainly does not accord with the record Congress developed in passing BCRA, a record that stands as a remarkable testament to the energy and ingenuity with which corporations, unions, lobbyists, and politicians may go about scratching each other's backs—and which amply supported Congress' determination to target a limited set of especially destructive practices. [When] private interests are seen to exert outsized control over officeholders solely on account of the money spent on (or withheld from) their campaigns, the result can depart so thoroughly "from what is pure or correct" in the conduct of Government, that it amounts to a "subversion . . . of the electoral process." At stake in the legislative efforts to address this threat is therefore not only the legitimacy and quality of Government but also the public's faith therein. [We] have ample evidence to suggest that [the Framers] would have been appalled by the evidence of corruption that Congress unearthed in developing BCRA and that the Court today discounts to irrelevance. It is fair to say that "[t]he Framers were obsessed with corruption," which they understood to encompass the dependency of public officeholders on private interests.

[Even] under the majority's "crabbed view of corruption," the Government should not lose this case. [*Quid pro quo* debts need not] take the form of outright vote buying or bribes, which have long been distinct crimes. Rather, they encompass the myriad ways in which outside parties may induce an officeholder to confer a legislative benefit in direct response to, or anticipation of, some outlay of money the parties have made or will make on behalf of the officeholder. [The] legislative and judicial proceedings relating to BCRA generated a substantial body of evidence suggesting that, as corporations grew more and more adept at crafting "issue ads" to help or harm a particular candidate, these nominally independent expenditures began to corrupt the political process in a very direct sense. The sponsors of these ads were routinely granted special access after the campaign was over; "candidates and officials knew who their friends were."

[The] majority fails to appreciate that Austin's antidistortion rationale is itself an anticorruption rationale, tied to the special concerns raised by corporations. [Corporations] are different from human beings. [Unlike] natural persons, corporations have "limited liability" for their owners and managers, "perpetual life," separation of ownership and control, "and favorable treatment of the accumulation and distribution of assets . . . that enhance their ability to attract capital and to deploy their resources in ways that maximize the return on their shareholders' investments." [Corporations also] have no consciences, no beliefs, no feelings, no thoughts, no desires. Corporations help structure and facilitate the activities of human beings, to be sure, and their "personhood" often serves as a useful legal fiction. But they are not themselves members of "We the People" by whom and for whom our Constitution was established. These basic points help explain why corporate electioneering is not only more likely to impair compelling governmental interests, but also why restrictions on that electioneering are less likely to encroach upon First Amendment freedoms. [The] majority's unwillingness to distinguish between corporations and humans similarly blinds it to the possibility that corporations' "war chests" and their special "advantages" in the legal realm, may translate into special advantages in the market for legislation.

[Interwoven] with Austin's concern to protect the integrity of the electoral process is a concern to protect the rights of shareholders from a kind of coerced speech: electioneering expenditures that do not "reflec[t] [their] support." When corporations use general treasury funds to praise or attack a particular candidate for office, it is the shareholders, as the residual claimants, who are effectively footing the bill. Those shareholders who disagree with the corporation's electoral message may find their financial investments being used to undermine their political convictions. The PAC mechanism, by contrast, helps assure that those who pay for an electioneering communication actually support its content and that managers do not use general treasuries to advance personal agendas.

[In] a democratic society, the longstanding consensus on the need to limit corporate campaign spending should outweigh the wooden application of judge-made rules. The majority's rejection of this principle "elevate[s] corporations to a level of deference which has not been seen at least since the days when substantive due process was regularly used to invalidate regulatory legislation thought to unfairly impinge upon established economic interests." At bottom, the Court's opinion is thus a rejection of the common sense of the American people, who have recognized a need to prevent corporations from undermining self-government since the founding, and who have fought against the distinctive corrupting potential of corporate electioneering since the days of Theodore Roosevelt. It is a strange time to repudiate that common sense.

AFTER CITIZENS UNITED

1. ***The role of corporate speech in politics.*** Citizens United allows unlimited independent political expenditures from corporate treasuries for the support or defeat of political candidates—even if they fund what would be classified as "express advocacy" under the definition in WRTL. The dissent—like many commentators critical of the decision—suggests that corporations should not be as free as individual speakers to speak in support of or opposition to political campaigns and that a "distinctive threat to democratic integrity" is posed "by corporate domination of politics." What is the basis for such arguments? Do the majority and the dissent have competing views of freedom of speech, with the majority favoring a libertarian conception and the dissent favoring an egalitarian conception? For discussion of this possibility, see Sullivan, "The Supreme Court—2009 Term—Comment: Two Concepts of Freedom of Speech," 124 Harv. L. Rev. 143 (2010).

Or do the majority and the dissent divide on whether corporations share relevant characteristics with natural persons? Does the dissent's view depend on the fact that corporations are fictional persons that do not vote? That corporations can use state-conferred powers to amass resources that do not reflect popular support for the speech they engage in? Consider the countervailing view that "restricting corporate speech may impose social costs by reducing the quantity and balance of information made available to voters," and that "restricting corporate political activity could cause laws to be inefficient by permitting noncorporate groups to dominate the political process." Ribstein, "Corporate Political Speech," 49 Wash. & Lee L. Rev. 109 (1992).

Is the dissent's concern rather that shareholders lack sufficient power under existing corporate law to protect themselves from managers who will use corporate money to express views the shareholders disagree with? Shareholders can sell their shares, or try to unseat directors who allow such spending in board elections. Are such methods practical? Consider the view that they are not, and that instead "[t]he answer is to mandate that corporations let stockholders vote annually on whether they want the company to exercise the rights that Citizens United gave them to get into political races. Managers who seek stockholder approval of political activity would explain the actions they intend to take, how those actions would be in stockholders' interests and what the cost will be. If they don't make the case their spending will be voted down." Gilson & Klausner, "That's My Money You're Using," Forbes, Mar. 29, 2010. Would such a mandate itself violate the First Amendment by singling out corporate speakers for special burdens? Does this proposed mandate differ from the notice and opt-in requirements placed on unions in Knox (2012; p. 1441 above)? Is such a mandate necessary given shareholders' wide array of contractual choices? Consider the view that "[e]ven the rare shareholder who cares about corporate speech could choose to invest only in firms that did not engage in political activities or in mutual funds that monitor the political correctness of the corporations in which they invest." Ribstein, supra.

In the wake of Citizens United, are for-profit corporations likely to increase their direct spending on political campaign advocacy? Will the incentives to make money to stay in business or to channel profit to executive compensation or other self-interested ends operate as de facto constraints on the level of corporate political investments? Is there reason to expect that corporate treasury money will instead be pooled in less visible form in the treasuries of trade associations and other advocacy organizations?

Or perhaps corporate managers will engage in an altogether different sort of advocacy. One scholar, drawing on empirical analysis of Supreme Court and appellate decisions, has found that corporations "have increasingly displaced individuals as direct beneficiaries of First Amendment rights." Today, almost half of First Amendment legal challenges benefit business corporations and trade groups. Consider the view that such cases represent a corrosive form of rent seeking: "the use of legal tools by business managers in specific cases to entrench reregulation in their personal interests at the expense of shareholders, consumers, and employees." In addition to the risks to democratic integrity underscored by most critics of Citizens United, as American businesses invest in legal innovation rather than technological innovation this form of corruption could also threaten the productivity of the U.S. economy. Coates, "Corporate Speech and the First Amendment: History, Data, and Implications," 30 Const. Comment. 223 (2015).

2. ***Lower court interpretations of Citizens United.*** In **SpeechNow.org v. Federal Election Comm'n**, 599 F.3d 686 (D.C. Cir. 2010), the D.C. Circuit sitting en banc addressed the question whether FECA's limits on individual contributions to political committees (so-called 527s, named for the provision in Internal Revenue Code) were consistent with the First Amendment. Writing for a unanimous court, Chief Judge SENTELLE assessed the claim of SpeechNow, a First Amendment advocacy organization, that alleged that the FECA restrictions violated the First Amendment: "SpeechNow is an unincorporated nonprofit association registered as a 'political organization' under § 527 of the Internal Revenue Code. [SpeechNow] intends to acquire funds solely through donations by individuals. SpeechNow further intends to operate exclusively through 'independent expenditures.' FECA defines 'independent expenditures' as expenditures 'expressly advocating the election or defeat of a clearly

identified candidate' that are 'not made in concert or cooperation with or at the request or suggestion of such candidate, the candidate's authorized political committee, or their agents, or a political party committee or its agents.'

"[In addition to the donations of its five members] as of August 2008, seventy-five other individuals had indicated on SpeechNow's website that they were interested in making donations. As for expenditures, SpeechNow planned ads for the 2008 election cycle against two incumbent candidates for federal office who, in the opinion of SpeechNow, did not sufficiently support First Amendment rights. These ads would have cost around $12,000 to produce. [SpeechNow] intended to place the ads so that the target audience would view the ads at least ten times, which would have cost around $400,000.

"[Under] FECA, a political committee is 'any committee, club, association, or other group of persons' that receives contributions of more than $1000 in a year or makes expenditures of more than $1000 in a year. 2 U.S.C. § 431(4). Once a group is so designated, contributions to the committee are restricted by 2 U.S.C. § 441a(a)(1)(C) and 441a(a)(3). The first provision limits an individual's contribution to a political committee to $5000 per calendar year; the second limits an individual's total contributions to all political committees to $69,900 biennially.

"[The] First Amendment mandates that 'Congress shall make no law . . . abridging the freedom of speech.' [The] Supreme Court has recognized only one interest sufficiently important to outweigh the First Amendment interests implicated by contributions for political speech: preventing corruption or the appearance of corruption. [The] Court has rejected each of the few other interests the government has, at one point or another, suggested as a justification for contribution or expenditure limits. Equalization of differing viewpoints is not a legitimate government objective. [An] informational interest in 'identifying the sources of support for and opposition to' a political position or candidate is not enough to justify the First Amendment burden. [And] though this rationale would not affect an unincorporated association such as SpeechNow, the Court has also refused to find a sufficiently compelling governmental interest in preventing 'the corrosive and distorting effects of immense aggregations of wealth that are accumulated with the help of the corporate form.' [Citizens United].

"Given this precedent, the only interest we may evaluate to determine whether the government can justify contribution limits as applied to SpeechNow is the government's anticorruption interest. Because of the Supreme Court's recent decision in Citizens United v. FEC, the analysis is straightforward. There, the Court held that the government has no anti-corruption interest in limiting independent expenditures.

"[In Citizens United, the] Court stated, '[W]e now conclude that independent expenditures, including those made by corporations, do not give rise to corruption or the appearance of corruption.' The Court came to this conclusion by looking to the definition of corruption and the appearance of corruption. For several decades after Buckley, the Court's analysis of the government's anti-corruption interest revolved largely around the 'hallmark of corruption,' 'financial quid pro quo: dollars for political favors,' However, in a series of cases culminating in McConnell, the Court expanded the definition to include 'the appearance of undue influence' created by large donations given for the purpose of 'buying access.' [The] Citizens United

Court retracted this view of the government's interest, saying that '[t]he fact that speakers may have influence over or access to elected officials does not mean that these officials are corrupt.' The Court returned to its older definition of corruption that focused on quid pro quo, saying that '[i]ngratiation and access . . . are not corruption.' Therefore, without any evidence that independent expenditures 'lead to, or create the appearance of, quid pro quo corruption,' and only 'scant evidence' that they even ingratiate, the Court concluded that independent expenditures do not corrupt or create the appearance of corruption.

"In its briefs in this case, the FEC relied heavily on McConnell, arguing that independent expenditures by groups like SpeechNow benefit candidates and that those candidates are accordingly grateful to the groups and to their donors. [Whatever] the merits of those arguments before Citizens United, they plainly have no merit after Citizens United.

"In light of the Court's holding as a matter of law that independent expenditures do not corrupt or create the appearance of quid pro quo corruption, contributions to groups that make only independent expenditures also cannot corrupt or create the appearance of corruption. The Court has effectively held that there is no corrupting 'quid' for which a candidate might in exchange offer a corrupt 'quo.'

"Given this analysis from Citizens United, we must conclude that the government has no anti-corruption interest in limiting contributions to an independent expenditure group such as SpeechNow. This simplifies the task of weighing the First Amendment interests implicated by contributions to SpeechNow against the government's interest in limiting such contributions. [All] that matters is that the First Amendment cannot be encroached upon for naught." The court also upheld FECA's organizational and reporting requirements.

What is the combined effect of Citizens United and SpeechNow? First, under Citizens United, unions and corporations may spend unlimited amounts on independent expenditures. SpeechNow added individuals to this list. (Is it surprising that SpeechNow added individuals? Note that the Office of the Solicitor General declined to seek Supreme Court review of the D.C. Circuit's decision.) Second, Citizens United dealt with *spending* by corporations and unions, while SpeechNow addresses *fundraising* by independent expenditure groups. Taken together, these cases affirm both the First Amendment rights of individuals, unions, and corporations to spend unlimited amounts on independent expenditures and the First Amendment rights of independent expenditure groups to fundraise unlimited amounts from each of these parties.

3. ***Citizens United in state courts.*** In **Western Tradition Partnership v. Montana**, 271 P.3d 1 (Mont. 2011), the Montana Supreme Court upheld portions of the Montana Corrupt Practices Act that prohibited independent expenditures by corporations to political campaigns. Attempting to justify why the state law still passed constitutional muster under Citizens United, the court characterized Citizens United as having "applied the long-standing rule that restrictions upon speech are not per se unlawful, but rather may be upheld if the government demonstrates a sufficiently strong interest."

In seeking to prove this sufficiently strong interest, the court then discussed at length the specific history of corporate domination and political contestation in Montana during the early twentieth century. Specifically, this history told the story of how "mining and industrial enterprises controlled by foreign trusts or corporations" dominated the political process, including by engaging in quid pro quo transactions with the Montana Governor and Legislature. To the court, the fact that the state campaign finance law was enacted to counteract these evils helped prove that there was a sufficiently compelling reason for the law, thereby distinguishing Citizens United.

Yet in **American Tradition Partnership, Inc. v. Bullock**, 567 U.S. 516 (2012), the Supreme Court overruled the state court. The short per curiam decision stated plainly that "[t]here can be no serious doubt" that Citizens United applied, such that the Montana state law violates the First Amendment.

Should the Montana Supreme Court have been permitted to take into account the unique political and historical context underlying a state law when calibrating the degree of a compelling state interest? If a state court disagrees with the federal Supreme Court's pronouncements on a constitutional issue, what avenues does it have to express dissent? Imagine that the Montana Supreme Court had first upheld the law as constitutional under the state's free speech provisions, and provided a reasoned explanation for this conclusion Would such an analysis have held any discursive value, even if the court held in the same opinion that it was bound by Citizens United to strike down the law on the basis of the federal constitution? For a discussion of the role that state courts can play in dissenting to federal court pronouncements, and the perspective of California Supreme Court Justice Goodwin Liu, see Liu, State Constitutions and the Protection of Individual Rights: A Reappraisal, 92 N.Y.U. L. Rev. 1307 (2017).

4. ***Political response to Citizens United.*** In the wake of Citizens United, President Obama criticized the decision and invited a legislative response in his State of the Union address, and members of Congress introduced a variety of bills designed to check its impact. Would any of the following proposals be constitutional in light of the Court's decision in Citizens United: A ban on independent political expenditures by corporations more than twenty percent owned by foreign residents? A ban on independent political expenditures by corporations that receive government contracts? A ban on the use of federal bailout money to fund corporate political advertisements? A requirement that CEOs personally appear on camera to say they support a corporate-funded ad? A requirement that publicly traded companies disclose all political expenditures to shareholders and the SEC? After Bennett, discussed above at p. 1492, certain public financing programs are no longer a viable option.

Some critics of Citizens United suggest that such proposed responses do not go far enough; Professor Lawrence Lessig, for example, has urged Congress to consider a proposed constitutional amendment that would provide: "Nothing in this Constitution shall be construed to restrict the power to limit, though not to ban, campaign expenditures of non-citizens of the United States during the last 60 days before an election." Would such an amendment be desirable? If corporations are deemed non-citizens for this purpose, should they also be deemed non-"persons" for purposes of equal protection, due process, and other constitutional guarantees that now apply to them?

Should post-Citizens United elections dampen or stoke the ire around the impact of Citizens United? The 2012 election was the most expensive in history with $6 billion spent over the course of the cycle. Of this, so-called Super PACs spent $546.5 million in the 2012 election, though some reports suggest that Super PAC spending exceeded $858 million. As noted above, President Obama originally decried Citizens United, but he eventually deployed campaign supporters to raise money for pro-Obama Super PACs in his 2012 reelection bid. Confessore, "Result Won't Limit Campaign Money Any More than Ruling Did," N.Y. Times, Nov. 11, 2012. But compare the amount spent by Super PACs to the amount spent by each of the campaigns: $553 million by President Obama's campaign and $360 million spent by Mitt Romney's campaign. Does this suggest that Super PACs are only part of the story of the astronomical increase in campaign spending? Reports also suggest that both candidates spent significant time fundraising, with President Obama holding twice as many fundraising events as campaign rallies and Mitt Romney having only one single public event a day because of a packed fundraising schedule. See Confessore, supra. Does this make the argument that voters are getting more information about the candidates more or less convincing?

5. ***Are some contribution limits invalid?*** In Citizens United, the Court narrowly defined the permissible scope of the government's anti-corruption interest in regulating campaign finance: combating quid pro quo corruption. Although Citizens United dealt exclusively with independent corporate expenditures, might its reasoning be applied to other features of Congress' regulatory scheme? In the case that follows, the Court turned its attention to contribution limits that limited the aggregate amounts that a donor can contribute during an election cycle:

McCutcheon v. F.E.C.

572 U.S. 185, 134 S. Ct. 1434, 188 L. Ed. 2d 468 (2014).

■ CHIEF JUSTICE ROBERTS announced the judgment of the Court and delivered an opinion, in which [JUSTICES] SCALIA, KENNEDY, and ALITO join.

[The] right to participate in democracy through political contributions is protected by the First Amendment, but that right is not absolute. In] a series of cases over the past 40 years, we have spelled out how to draw the constitutional line between the permissible goal of avoiding corruption in the political process and the impermissible desire simply to limit political speech. We have said that government regulation may not target the general gratitude a candidate may feel toward those who support him or his allies, or the political access such support may afford. [Any] regulation must instead target what we have called "quid pro quo" corruption or its appearance. That Latin phrase captures the notion of a direct exchange of an official act for money. [Campaign] finance restrictions that pursue other objectives, we have explained, impermissibly inject the Government into the debate over who should govern. And those who govern should be the last people to help decide who should govern.

The statute at issue in this case imposes two types of limits on campaign contributions. The first, called base limits, restricts how much money a donor may contribute to a particular candidate or committee. 2 U.S.C. § 441a(a)(1).

The second, called aggregate limits, restricts how much money a donor may contribute in total to all candidates or committees. § 441a(a)(3).

This case does not involve any challenge to the base limits, which we have previously upheld as serving the permissible objective of combatting corruption. The Government contends that the aggregate limits also serve that objective, by preventing circumvention of the base limits. We conclude, however, that the aggregate limits do little, if anything, to address that concern, while seriously restricting participation in the democratic process. The aggregate limits are therefore invalid under the First Amendment.

I.B. In the 2011–2012 election cycle, appellant Shaun McCutcheon contributed a total of $33,088 to 16 different federal candidates, in compliance with the base limits applicable to each. He alleges that he wished to contribute $1,776 to each of 12 additional candidates but was prevented from doing so by the aggregate limit on contributions to candidates. McCutcheon also contributed a total of $27,328 to several noncandidate political committees, in compliance with the base limits applicable to each. He alleges that he wished to contribute to various other political committees, including $25,000 to each of the three Republican national party committees, but was prevented from doing so by the aggregate limit on contributions to political committees.

II.B.1. [We] see no need in this case to revisit Buckley's distinction between contributions and expenditures and the corollary distinction in the applicable standards of review. [Because] we find a substantial mismatch between the Government's stated objective and the means selected to achieve it, the aggregate limits fail even under the "closely drawn" test.

III. [The] Government may no more restrict how many candidates or causes a donor may support than it may tell a newspaper how many candidates it may endorse. [The aggregate] limits deny the individual all ability to exercise his expressive and associational rights by contributing to someone who will advocate for his policy preferences. A donor must limit the number of candidates he supports, and may have to choose which of several policy concerns he will advance.

[It] is no answer to say that the individual can simply contribute less money to more people. To require one person to contribute at lower levels than others because he wants to support more candidates or causes is to impose a special burden on broader participation in the democratic process.

IV. [This] Court has identified only one legitimate governmental interest for restricting campaign finances: preventing corruption or the appearance of corruption. We have consistently rejected attempts to suppress campaign speech based on other legislative objectives.

[Moreover], while preventing corruption or its appearance is a legitimate objective, Congress may target only a specific type of corruption—"quid pro quo" corruption. [In] addition to actual quid pro quo arrangements, Congress may permissibly limit the appearance of corruption stemming from public awareness of the opportunities for abuse inherent in a regime of large individual financial contributions to particular candidates.

[Spending] large sums of money in connection with elections, but not in connection with an effort to control the exercise of an officeholder's official duties, does not give rise to such quid pro quo corruption. Nor does the possibility that an individual who spends large sums may garner influence over or access to elected officials or political parties.

[The] definition of corruption that we apply today [has] firm roots in Buckley itself. [The] line between quid pro quo corruption and general influence may seem vague at times, but the distinction must be respected in order to safeguard basic First Amendment rights. [The] dissent laments that our opinion leaves only remnants of FECA and BCRA that are inadequate to combat corruption. Such rhetoric ignores the fact that we leave the base limits undisturbed. Those base limits remain the primary means of regulating campaign contributions—the obvious explanation for why the aggregate limits received a scant few sentences of attention in Buckley.

B. When the Government restricts speech, the Government bears the burden of proving the constitutionality of its actions.

[If] there is no corruption concern in giving nine candidates up to $5,200 each, it is difficult to understand how a tenth candidate can be regarded as corruptible if given $1,801, and all others corruptible if given a dime. And if there is no risk that additional candidates will be corrupted by donations of up to $5,200, then the Government must defend the aggregate limits by demonstrating that they prevent circumvention of the base limits.

The problem is that they do not serve that function in any meaningful way. In light of the various statutes and regulations currently in effect, Buckley's fear that an individual might "contribute massive amounts of money to a particular candidate through the use of unearmarked contributions" to entities likely to support the candidate is far too speculative.

C. [Quite] apart from the foregoing, the aggregate limits violate the First Amendment because they are not closely drawn to avoid unnecessary abridgment of associational freedoms. [Because] the statute is poorly tailored to the Government's interest in preventing circumvention of the base limits, it impermissibly restricts participation in the political process.

1. The Government argues that the aggregate limits are justified because they prevent an individual from giving to too many initial recipients who might subsequently recontribute a donation. [But experience] suggests that the vast majority of contributions made in excess of the aggregate limits are likely to be retained and spent by their recipients rather than rerouted to candidates.

[Likewise, state] parties rarely contribute to candidates in other States. [As] with national and state party committees, candidates contribute only a small fraction of their campaign funds to other candidates. [The] fact is that candidates who receive campaign contributions spend most of the money on themselves, rather than passing along donations to other candidates. In this arena at least, charity begins at home.

2. Importantly, there are multiple alternatives available to Congress that would serve the Government's anticircumvention interest, while avoiding "unnecessary abridgment" of First Amendment rights.

The most obvious might involve targeted restrictions on transfers among candidates and political committees. There are currently no such limits. [Other] alternatives might focus on earmarking. Many of the scenarios that the Government and the dissent hypothesize involve at least implicit agreements to circumvent the base limits—agreements that are already prohibited by the earmarking rules. The FEC might strengthen those rules further by, for example, defining how many candidates a PAC must support in order to ensure that "a substantial portion" of a donor's contribution is not rerouted to a certain candidate.

D. Finally, disclosure of contributions minimizes the potential for abuse of the campaign finance system. [Disclosure] requirements burden speech, but—unlike the aggregate limits—they do not impose a ceiling on speech. For that reason, disclosure often represents a less restrictive alternative to flat bans on certain types or quantities of speech.

With modern technology, disclosure now offers a particularly effective means of arming the voting public with information. [Today], given the Internet, disclosure offers much more robust protections against corruption. [Because] massive quantities of information can be accessed at the click of a mouse, disclosure is effective to a degree not possible at the time Buckley, or even McConnell, was decided.

V. At oral argument, the Government shifted its focus from Buckley's anticircumvention rationale to an argument that the aggregate limits deter corruption regardless of their ability to prevent circumvention of the base limits. [That] new rationale for the aggregate limits—embraced by the dissent—does not wash. [When] donors furnish widely distributed support within all applicable base limits, all members of the party or supporters of the cause may benefit, and the leaders of the party or cause may feel particular gratitude. That gratitude stems from the basic nature of the party system, in which party members join together to further common political beliefs, and citizens can choose to support a party because they share some, most, or all of those beliefs. To recast such shared interest, standing alone, as an opportunity for quid pro quo corruption would dramatically expand government regulation of the political process.

■ JUSTICE THOMAS, concurring in the judgment.

I adhere to the view that this Court's decision in Buckley v. Valeo denigrates core First Amendment speech and should be overruled.

[I] would overrule Buckley and subject the aggregate limits in BCRA to strict scrutiny, which they would surely fail.

■ JUSTICE BREYER, with whom [JUSTICES] GINSBURG, SOTOMAYOR, and KAGAN join, dissenting.

[The] Buckley Court focused upon the same problem that concerns the Court today, and it wrote:

"The overall $25,000 ceiling does impose an ultimate restriction upon the number of candidates and committees with which an individual may associate himself by means of financial support. But this quite modest restraint upon protected political activity serves to prevent evasion of the $1,000 contribution limitation by a person who might otherwise contribute massive amounts of money to a particular candidate through the use of unearmarked contributions to political committees likely to contribute to that candidate, or huge contributions to the candidate's political party. The limited, additional restriction on associational freedom imposed by the overall ceiling is thus no more than a corollary of the basic individual contribution limitation that we have found to be constitutionally valid."

Today a majority of the Court overrules this holding. It is wrong to do so.

II. [The] plurality's first claim—that large aggregate contributions do not give rise to corruption—is plausible only because the plurality defines "corruption" too narrowly. [As] the history of campaign finance reform shows and as our earlier cases on the subject have recognized, the anticorruption interest that drives Congress to regulate campaign contributions is a far broader, more important interest than the plurality acknowledges. It is an interest in maintaining the integrity of our public governmental institutions. And it is an interest rooted in the Constitution and in the First Amendment itself.

Consider at least one reason why the First Amendment protects political speech. Speech does not exist in a vacuum. Rather, political communication seeks to secure government action. A politically oriented "marketplace of ideas" seeks to form a public opinion that can and will influence elected representatives.

[The] First Amendment advances not only the individual's right to engage in political speech, but also the public's interest in preserving a democratic order in which collective speech matters.

[Corruption] breaks the constitutionally necessary "chain of communication" between the people and their representatives. It derails the essential speech-to-government-action tie. Where enough money calls the tune, the general public will not be heard. Insofar as corruption cuts the link between political thought and political action, a free marketplace of political ideas loses its point. That is one reason why the Court has stressed the constitutional importance of Congress' concern that a few large donations not drown out the voices of the many.

[The] "appearance of corruption" can make matters worse. It can lead the public to believe that its efforts to communicate with its representatives or to help sway public opinion have little purpose. And a cynical public can lose interest in political participation altogether.

The upshot is that the interests the Court has long described as preventing "corruption" or the "appearance of corruption" are more than ordinary factors to be weighed against the constitutional right to political speech. Rather, they are interests rooted in the First Amendment itself. They are rooted in the constitutional effort to create a democracy responsive to the people—a government where laws reflect the very thoughts, views, ideas, and sentiments, the expression of which the First Amendment protects. Given that end, we can and should understand campaign finance laws as resting upon a broader and more significant constitutional rationale than the plurality's limited definition of "corruption" suggests.

III. The plurality invalidates the aggregate contribution limits for a second reason. It believes they are no longer needed to prevent contributors from circumventing federal limits on direct contributions to individuals, political parties, and political action committees.

[The] plurality is wrong. Here, as in Buckley, in the absence of limits on aggregate political contributions, donors can and likely will find ways to channel millions of dollars to parties and to individual candidates, producing precisely the kind of "corruption" or "appearance of corruption" that previously led the Court to hold aggregate limits constitutional. Those opportunities for circumvention will also produce the type of corruption that concerns the plurality today. The methods for using today's opinion to evade the law's individual contribution limits are complex, but they are well known, or will become well known, to party fundraisers.

IV. [The] plurality concludes that even if circumvention were a threat, the aggregate limits are "poorly tailored" to address it. The plurality, however, does not show, or try to show, that [its] hypothetical alternatives could effectively replace aggregate contribution limits.

[The] conclusion is simple: There is no "substantial mismatch" between Congress' legitimate objective and the "means selected to achieve it." The Court, as in Buckley, should hold that aggregate contribution limits are constitutional.

V. In the past, when evaluating the constitutionality of campaign finance restrictions, we have typically relied upon an evidentiary record amassed below to determine whether the law served a compelling governmental objective.

[Determining] whether anticorruption objectives justify a particular set of contribution limits requires answering empirically based questions, and applying significant discretion and judgment. To what extent will unrestricted giving lead to corruption or its appearance? What forms will any such corruption take? To what extent will a lack of regulation undermine public confidence in the democratic system? To what extent can regulation restore it?

These kinds of questions, while not easily answered, are questions that Congress is far better suited to resolve than are judges. [Without] further development of the record, however, I fail to see how the plurality can now find grounds for overturning Buckley. The justification for aggregate contribution restrictions is strongly rooted in the need to assure political integrity and ultimately in the First Amendment itself.

---

5. ***Doctrinal reach of anticorruption rationale.*** In **McDonnell v. United States**, 579 U.S. ___, 136 S. Ct. 2355 (2016), the Court had to determine whether the former governor of Virginia had violated the Hobbs Act by taking gifts and cash in exchange for setting up meetings and hosting events. The Court held that McDonnell's actions did not count as "official acts" under the statute. It supported its holding in part on the basis of constitutional avoidance. Chief Justice ROBERTS wrote: "[T]he Government's expansive interpretation of 'official act' would raise significant constitutional concerns. Section 201 prohibits quid pro quo corruption—the exchange of a thing of value for an 'official act. In the Government's view, nearly anything a public official accepts—from a campaign contribution to lunch—counts as a quid; and nearly anything a public official does—from arranging a meeting to inviting a guest to an event—counts as a quo. But conscientious public officials arrange meetings for constituents, contact other officials on their behalf, and include them in events all the time. The basic compact underlying representative government assumes that public officials will hear from their constituents and act appropriately on their concerns—whether it is the union official worried about a plant closing or the homeowners who wonder why it took five days to restore power to their neighborhood after a storm. The Government's position could cast a pall of potential prosecution over these relationships if the union had given a campaign contribution in the past or the homeowners invited the official to join them on their annual outing to the ballgame. Officials might wonder whether they could respond to even the most commonplace requests for assistance, and citizens with legitimate concerns might shrink from

participating in democratic discourse. [None] of this, of course, is to suggest that the facts of this case typify normal political interaction between public officials and their constituents. Far from it. But the Government's legal interpretation is not confined to cases involving extravagant gifts or large sums of money, and we cannot construe a criminal statute on the assumption that the Government will use it responsibly."

SECTION 4. JOURNALISM AND MEDIA

The First Amendment protects not only the "freedom of speech" but also the "freedom of the press." Does that specific reference to the "press" entitle the media to special constitutional protection? Or are press claims more properly analyzed as an aspect of the general freedom of expression guaranteed by the "speech" clause? This section focuses on the constitutional protection of the press. Should the press merit any protections more extensive than those generally available to disseminators of information and opinion? May government compel journalists to divulge information they possess, in aid of such state interests as criminal law enforcement? Does the press enjoy a constitutional right of access to such places as jails and courtrooms in order to obtain newsworthy information? Are the media exempt from tax laws, regulations or civil liability that extend to others? Does it matter whether these laws single out the "press" for special treatment or treat it the same as everyone else? Finally, the Court has read the First Amendment to confer lesser protection on broadcasters than on the print media. Why should this be so? Is such differential treatment still warranted in light of technological change? How should we think about the press and its protections in an age of ubiquitous and diverse media?

Does the Press Clause simply reiterate the Speech Clause or does it provide some protection to the institutional media beyond that enjoyed by other speakers? Consider two alternative views. On the first view, the press occupies a special status as a metaphorical "fourth branch" of government. The most prominent advocate of special significance for the Press Clause was Justice Stewart. He argued that "the Free Press guarantee is, in essence, a *structural* provision of the Constitution. [It] extends protection to an institution. The publishing business [is] the only organized private business that is given explicit constitutional protection. [If] the Free Press guarantee meant no more than freedom of expression, it would be a constitutional redundancy. [It] is [a] mistake to suppose that the only purpose of the constitutional guarantee of a free press is to insure that a newspaper will serve as a neutral forum for debate, a 'market place for ideas,' a kind of Hyde Park Corner for the community. A related theory sees the press as a neutral conduit of information between the people and their elected leaders. These theories, in my view, again give insufficient weight to the institutional autonomy of the press that it was the purpose of the Constitution to guarantee." Justice Stewart also noted that the system of separation of powers "deliberately created an internally competitive system" and argued that the "primary purpose [of the Press Clause was to] create a fourth institution outside the Government as an additional check on the three official branches. [The] relevant metaphor [is that] of the Fourth Estate." In his view, then, the First Amendment protected "the institutional autonomy of the press." Stewart, "Or of the Press," 26 Hast. L.J. 631 (1975).

On the alternative view, the institutional press is just another speaker, with no greater or lesser First Amendment privileges than other nonmedia speakers. Is this view even more plausible in the age of the internet and the blogosphere, where the lines between the institutional press and other sources of information has blurred? For an argument along these lines and contrary to Justice Stewart's, consider dicta in Chief Justice BURGER's concurring opinion in **First National Bank of Boston v. Bellotti**, 435 U.S. 765 (1978): "Because the First Amendment was meant to guarantee freedom to express and to communicate ideas, I can see no difference between the right of those who seek to disseminate ideas by way of a newspaper and those who give lectures or speeches that seek to enlarge the audience by publication and wide dissemination. [I] perceive two fundamental difficulties with a narrow reading of the Press Clause. First although certainty on this point is not possible, the history of the Clause does not suggest that the authors contemplated a 'special' or 'institutional' privilege. [Indeed] most pre-First Amendment commentators 'who employed the term "freedom of speech" with great frequency used it synonymously with freedom of the press.' Those interpreting the Press Clause as extending protection only to, or creating a special role for, the 'institutional press' must either (a) assert such an intention on the part of the Framers for which no supporting evidence is available; (b) argue that events after 1791 somehow operated to 'constitutionalize' this interpretation; or (c) candidly acknowledging the absence of historical support, suggest that the intent of the Framers is not important today.

"To conclude that the Framers did not intend to limit the freedom of the press to one select group is not necessarily to suggest that the Press Clause is redundant. The Speech Clause standing alone may be viewed as a protection of the liberty to express ideas and beliefs, while the Press Clause focuses specifically on the liberty to disseminate expression broadly and 'comprehends every sort of publication which affords a vehicle of information and opinion.' Lovell v. Griffin. Yet there is no fundamental distinction between expression and dissemination. The liberty encompassed by the Press Clause, although complementary to and a natural extension of Speech Clause liberty, merited special mention simply because it had been more often the object of official restraints. [The] second fundamental difficulty with interpreting the Press Clause as conferring special status on a limited group is one of definition. The very task of including some entities within the 'institutional press' while excluding others, whether undertaken by legislature, court or administrative agency, is reminiscent of the abhorred licensing system of Tudor and Stuart England—a system the First Amendment was intended to ban from this country. Further, the officials undertaking that task would be required to distinguish the protected from the unprotected on the basis of such variables as content of expression, frequency or fervor of expression, or ownership of the technological means of dissemination. Yet nothing in this Court's opinions supports such a confining approach to the scope of Press Clause protection.[1] [In short], the First Amendment does not 'belong' to any definable category of persons or entities: it belongs to all who exercise its freedoms."

Chief Justice Burger's disinclination to rest media protections on the Press Clause has been the typical position of the Court. Most press claims

---

1 "Near v. Minnesota, which examined the meaning of freedom of the press, did not involve a traditional institutionalized newspaper but rather an occasional publication (nine issues) more nearly approximating the product of a pamphleteer than the traditional newspaper." [Footnote by Chief Justice Burger.]

have been adjudicated by analysis of the Speech Clause and of general principles of freedom of expression. Would it be preferable to rest any "special status" rights of the press on further elaboration of the Press Clause, or does the press receive adequate protection under the Court's readings of the Speech Clause and the First Amendment generally? Consider these questions in reviewing the materials that follow.

PRESS ACCESS TO GOVERNMENT INFORMATION

Does the First Amendment entitle the press to obtain information the government seeks to withhold? On the view that the press has special institutional responsibility as a watchdog of government, such access rights would appear indispensable. But claims of a special press right of access in general have not fared well, with the exception of the right of access to criminal trials, in the Richmond Newspapers case. What is the proper scope of that newly recognized access? For commentary on press rights of access in order to obtain government information, see BeVier, "An Informed Public, An Informing Press: The Search for a Constitutional Principle," 68 Calif. L. Rev. 482 (1980) (arguing that courts may recognize press rights to publish and disseminate information without also recognizing a right of access to government information); Baker, "Press Rights and Government Power to Structure the Press," 34 U. Miami L. Rev. 819 (1980) (noting a distinction between "offensive" and "defensive" press claims and suggesting that defensive rights of the press against government intrusions are more persuasive than offensive, right-of-access claims); Dyk, "Newsgathering, Press Access, and the First Amendment," 44 Stan. L. Rev. 927 (1992) (arguing for heightened press access to check government).

1. ***Press access to prisons.*** The Court first confronted press demands for access to jails in companion cases, **Pell v. Procunier**, 417 U.S. 817 (1974), and **Saxbe v. Washington Post Co.**, 417 U.S. 843 (1974). In Pell, the majority rejected an attack on a California rule providing that "press and other media interviews with specific individual inmates will not be permitted." And in Saxbe, the Court turned back a challenge to a very similar Federal Bureau of Prisons prohibition of press interviews of individually designated prisoners in most federal prisons. Justice STEWART delivered the majority opinion in each case. Central to his rejection of the journalists' claim was his assertion that, although the First Amendment bars "government from interfering in any way with the free press," it does not "require government to accord the press special access to information not shared by members of the public generally." He explained: "It is one thing to say that a journalist is free to seek out sources of information not available to members of the general public, that he is entitled to some constitutional protection of the confidentiality of such sources, and that government cannot restrain the publication of news emanating from such sources. It is quite another thing to suggest that the Constitution imposes upon government the affirmative duty to make available to journalists sources of information not available to members of the public generally."

Justice POWELL found that approach unduly simplistic. He concluded in Pell that an absolute ban on interviews "impermissibly restrains the ability of the press to perform its constitutionally established function of informing the people on the conduct of their government." Elaborating that position in Saxbe in a lengthy dissent joined by Justices Brennan and Marshall, he stated: "I cannot follow the Court in concluding that *any* governmental restriction on press access to information, so long as it is nondiscriminatory, falls outside the purview of First Amendment concern. [At] some point official restraints on access to news sources, even though not directed solely at the press, may so undermine the function of the First Amendment that it is both appropriate and necessary to require the Government to justify such regulations in terms more compelling than discretionary authority and administrative convenience. [In] seeking out the news the press [acts] as an agent of the public at large." In a separate dissent, Justice DOUGLAS, joined by Justices Brennan and Marshall, similarly rested on the right "of the people": "the public's interest in being informed about prisons [is] paramount." Accordingly, the interview bans were "an unconstitutional infringement on the public's right to know protected by the free press guarantee of the First Amendment."

Press access claims similar to those rejected in Pell and Saxbe resurfaced four years later. But in **Houchins v. KQED, Inc.**, 438 U.S. 1 (1978), the 7-person Court, in an unusual division, sustained a portion of the claim of access to jails. The case arose from an action filed by San Francisco public television station KQED, which sought to gain access to a county jail to investigate allegedly shocking conditions. After the suit was filed, Sheriff Houchins modified his "no-access" policy of barring the general public and the media from Santa Rita and launched a monthly tour program limited to groups of 25 persons. Those on the tour were not permitted to take photographs or interview inmates. The lower court awarded KQED preliminary relief, giving the news media access to the jail "at reasonable times and hours" and authorizing inmate interviews and the use of photographic and sound equipment.

The Court, dividing 3–1–3 (Justices Marshall and Blackmun did not participate in the case), held the order proper in part. Chief Justice BURGER's opinion viewed the case as governed by Pell and Saxbe and found no basis for judicial relief: "[Until] the political branches decree otherwise, [the media have] no right of special access to the [jail] different from or greater than that accorded the public generally." Justice STEVENS's dissent, joined by Justices Brennan and Powell, insisted that Pell was distinguishable because in Pell there had been "substantial press and public access" to the jail; there, the rejected media claim asserted the additional right "to interview specifically designated inmates." He asserted that "the Court has never intimated that a nondiscriminatory policy of excluding entirely both the public and the press from access to information about prison conditions would avoid constitutional scrutiny." He emphasized "the special importance of allowing a democratic community access to knowledge about how its servants were treating [prisoners]." KQED, accordingly, should have prevailed in his view not because of any special press privilege but as an advocate of "the public's right to be informed."

Justice STEWART's decisive concurrence agreed with Chief Justice Burger's basic premises that the press had no special access rights, but differed in applying those principles here: "Whereas [Chief Justice Burger] appears to view 'equal access' as meaning access that is identical in all respects, I believe that the concept of equal access must be accorded more flexibility in order to accommodate the practical distinctions between the press and the general public." That "practical accommodations" approach permitted him to find a basis for limited relief for KQED. Emphasizing the "critical role played by the press in American society," he explained: "[T]erms of access that are reasonably imposed on individual members of the public may, if they impede effective reporting without sufficient justification, be unreasonable as applied to journalists who are there to convey to the general public what the visitors see." Accordingly, the First Amendment "required the Sheriff to give members of the press *effective* access" to all areas open to the public. Simply permitting reporters to sign up for the monthly tours "on the same terms as the public" was inadequate "as a matter of constitutional law." Accordingly, the trial court's order permitting press access "on a more flexible and frequent basis than scheduled monthly tours" was justified in order "to keep the public informed," as was the order permitting the media to bring cameras and recording equipment into the jail.

2. ***Press access to pretrial hearings.*** In **Gannett Co. v. Depasquale**, 443 U.S. 368 (1979), a divided Court rejected a newspaper publisher's attack on an order barring the public, including the press, from a pretrial hearing on suppression of evidence in a murder case. The prevailing opinion held that the press and the public had no independent constitutional right to insist upon access to such pretrial proceedings when the accused, the prosecutor, and the trial judge all had agreed to close the hearing in order to assure a fair trial. Although the Justices focused primarily on the Sixth Amendment provision that, in "all criminal prosecutions, the accused shall enjoy the right to [a] public trial," some comments on First Amendment issues surfaced in most of the opinions. Justice STEWART, writing for the Court, accepted that the Sixth Amendment's public trial guarantee reflected the public as well as the defendant's interest, but held that "our adversary system of criminal justice is premised upon the proposition that the public interest is fully protected by the participants of the litigation," who had agreed to the closure order here. He found nothing in the structure, text or history of the Sixth Amendment to support "any correlative right in members of the public to insist upon a public trial." He found it unnecessary to decide whether there was any First Amendment right to attend criminal trials: "[E]ven assuming, arguendo, that the [First Amendment] may guarantee such access in some situations, a question we do not decide, this putative right was given all appropriate deference by the [trial judge] in the present case."

Justice POWELL's concurring opinion considered the First Amendment issue more fully and concluded, relying on his approach in Saxbe: "Because of the importance of the public's having accurate information concerning the operation of its criminal justice system, I would hold explicitly that petitioner's reporter had an interest protected by the [First Amendment] in being present at the pretrial suppression hearing." But he suggested that a closure motion would be appropriate if "a fair trial for the defendant is likely to be jeopardized by publicity." Applying this standard, Justice Powell found that the First Amendment right of access had been "adequately respected" by the trial judge in this case. Justice REHNQUIST's concurring opinion took a narrower view of the First Amendment. He stated: "Despite the Court's seeming reservation of the [question], it is clear that this Court repeatedly has held that there is no First Amendment right of access in the public or the press to judicial or other governmental proceedings." In his view, the Court had "emphatically" rejected Justice Powell's view "that the First Amendment is some sort of constitutional 'sunshine law' that requires notice, an opportunity to be heard and substantial reasons before a governmental proceeding may be closed to the public and press."

Justice BLACKMUN's partial dissent, joined by Justices Brennan, White and Marshall, derived a public right of access from the Sixth Amendment and argued that states could not exclude the public "from a proceeding within the ambit of the Sixth Amendment's guarantee without affording full and fair consideration to the public's interest in maintaining an open proceeding." Emphasizing the "societal interest in the public trial that exists separately from, and at times in opposition to, the interests of the accused," he argued that a court may not give effect to "an accused's attempt to waive his public trial right" in all circumstances: "[The] public trial interest cannot adequately be protected by the prosecutor and judge in conjunction, or connivance, with the defendant." Justice Blackmun recognized, however, that "the publication of information learned in an open proceeding may harm irreparably, under certain circumstances, the ability of the defendant to obtain a fair trial," and suggested that "limited exceptions to the principle of publicity" would be acceptable if "necessary" in such cases.

3. ***Press access to criminal trials.*** A year after Gannett, the 7–1 decision in **Richmond Newspapers, Inc. v. Virginia**, 448 U.S. 555 (1980), held that, "[a]bsent an overriding interest articulated in findings, the trial of a criminal case must be open to the public." Chief Justice BURGER's opinion announcing the judgment (joined by Justices White and Stevens) stated that the "narrow question" was "whether the right of the public and press to attend criminal trials is guaranteed under [the] Constitution," a question not reached in Gannett. After reviewing the historical practice of having trials "open to all who cared to observe," he concluded that, when the Constitution was adopted, "criminal trials both here and in England had long been presumptively open." He noted the "nexus between openness, fairness, and the perception of fairness" and commented: "To work effectively, it is important that society's criminal process 'satisfy the appearance of justice,' and the appearance of justice can best be provided by allowing people to observe it." Although attendance at trials "is no longer a wide-spread pastime," that merely validated "the media claim of functioning as surrogates for the public" in the modern context. The "unbroken, uncontradicted history" supported his conclusion that "a presumption of openness inheres in the very nature of a criminal trial under our system of justice."

Turning to the constitutional sources for an access claim not explicitly guaranteed, he concluded that "the right to attend criminal trials is implicit in the guarantees of the First Amendment." The First Amendment protections of speech, press, and the right to assemble "share a common core purpose of assuring freedom of communication on matters relating to the functioning of government. Plainly it would be difficult to single out any aspect of government of higher concern and importance to the people than the manner in which criminal trials are conducted." Accordingly, the First Amendment could be read "as protecting the right of everyone to attend trials so as to give meaning to those explicit guarantees"; thus, "the First Amendment guarantees of speech and press, standing alone, prohibit government from summarily closing courtroom doors." He distinguished Pell and Saxbe as involving "penal institutions which, by definition [and tradition], are not 'open' or public places."

Chief Justice Burger conceded that the Constitution did not spell out a "right of the public to attend trials." But he noted that this had not "precluded recognition of important rights not enumerated": "Notwithstanding the appropriate caution against reading into the Constitution rights not explicitly defined, the Court has acknowledged that certain unarticulated rights are implicit in enumerated guarantees. For example, the rights of association and of privacy [as well as] the right to travel appear nowhere in the Constitution or Bill of Rights. Yet these important but unarticulated rights have nonetheless been found to share constitutional protection in common with explicit guarantees." He also noted that the Ninth Amendment had been adopted "to allay the fears of those who were concerned that expressing certain guarantees could be read as excluding others." In short, "fundamental rights, even though not expressly guaranteed, have been recognized by the Court as indispensable to the enjoyment of rights explicitly defined," and "the right to attend criminal trials" could accordingly be found "implicit in the guarantees of the First Amendment."

On the facts of the case, Chief Justice Burger found no "overriding interest articulated in findings" for closing the criminal trial here. The defendant had requested the closure; the prosecution had not objected. The trial judge made no findings to support closure, nor any inquiry "as to whether alternative solutions would have met the need to ensure fairness," such as witnesses' exclusion from the courtroom or their sequestration during the trial. He cautioned: "We have no occasion here to define the circumstances in which all or parts of a criminal trial may be closed to the [public]." A trial judge could impose "reasonable limitations on access to a trial" in the interests of the fair administration of justice. Moreover, "since courtrooms have limited capacity, there may be occasions when not every person who wishes to attend can be accommodated. In such situations, reasonable restrictions on general access are traditionally imposed, including preferential seating for media representatives."

In a brief separate statement Justice WHITE, who joined Chief Justice Burger's opinion, noted that this decision would have been unnecessary if the majority had adopted the dissent's Sixth Amendment position in Gannett. Justice STEVENS, who joined Chief Justice Burger's opinion, also submitted a separate concurrence viewing the Court as recognizing for the first time a broad First Amendment right of access to "newsworthy matter": "the First Amendment protects the public and the press from abridgment of their rights of access to information about the operation of their government, including the Judicial Branch; given the total absence of any record justification for the closure order entered in this case, that order violated the First Amendment."

In an opinion concurring in the judgment, Justice BRENNAN, joined by Justice Marshall, stated: "Because I believe that the First Amendment [secures a] public right of access [to trial proceedings], I agree with those of my Brethren who hold that, without more, agreement of the trial judge and the parties cannot constitutionally close a trial to the public." Justice Brennan relied in part on his "Address," 32 Rutgers L. Rev. 173 (1979), arguing that "the First Amendment embodies more than a commitment to free expression and communicative interchange for their own sakes; it has a *structural* role to play in securing and fostering our republican system of self-government. Implicit in this structural role is not only 'the principle that debate on public issues should be uninhibited, robust, and wide open,' but the antecedent assumption that valuable public debate [must] be informed. The structural model links the First Amendment to that process of communication necessary for a democracy to survive, and thus entails solicitude not only for communication itself, but for the indispensable conditions of meaningful communication."

Applying this approach, he found, perusing materials similar to those relied on by Chief Justice Burger, that, "[a]s a matter of law and virtually immemorial custom, public trials have been the essentially unwavering rule in ancestral England and in our own Nation." Moreover, publicity served several "particular purposes" of the judicial process. He noted, for example, that "judges are not mere umpires, but, in their own sphere, lawmakers—a coordinate branch of *government*. [Thus,] so far as the trial is the mechanism for judicial factfinding, as well as the initial forum for legal decisionmaking, it is a genuine governmental proceeding. It follows that the conduct of the trial is preeminently a matter of public interest. [Popular] attendance at trials, in sum, substantially furthers the particular public purposes of that critical judicial proceeding. In that sense, public access is an indispensable element of the trial process itself." He concluded: "What countervailing interest might be sufficiently compelling to reverse this presumption of openness need not concern us now, for the statute at stake here authorizes trial closures at the unfettered discretion of the judge and parties."

A separate opinion by Justice STEWART concurring in the judgment emphasized that Gannett had left open the First Amendment issues reached here and concluded: "Whatever the ultimate answer to [the First Amendment] question may be with respect to pretrial suppression hearings in criminal cases, the [First Amendment] clearly give[s] the press and the public a right of access to trials themselves, civil as well as criminal. [With] us, a trial is by very definition a proceeding open to the press and to the public. [Even] more than city streets, sidewalks, and parks as areas of traditional First Amendment activity, a trial courtroom is a place where representatives of the press and of the public are not only free to be, but where their presence serves to assure the integrity of what goes on." He added, however, that the access right was not "absolute": "[Much] more than a city street, a trial courtroom must be a quiet and orderly place. Moreover, every courtroom has a finite physical capacity, and there may be occasions when not all who wish to attend a trial may do so. And while there exist many alternative ways to satisfy the constitutional demands of a fair trial, those demands may also sometimes justify limitations upon the unrestricted presence of spectators in the courtroom." Here, reversal was in order because "the trial judge appears to have given no recognition to the right of representatives of the press and members of the public to be present at [the] murder trial."

In still another opinion concurring in the judgment, Justice BLACKMUN reiterated his Sixth Amendment position in Gannett and went beyond: "[W]ith the Sixth Amendment set to one side in this case, I am driven to conclude, as a secondary position, that the First Amendment must provide some measure of protection for public access to the trial. [It] is clear and obvious to me, on the approach the Court has chosen to take, that, by closing this criminal trial, the trial judge abridged [the] First Amendment interests of the public."

Justice REHNQUIST, the sole dissenter, adhered to his position in Gannett and found nothing in the First, Sixth, or Ninth Amendments, or in any other constitutional provision, to prohibit what the state trial judge had done in this case.

What is the scope of Richmond Newspapers? Was it the watershed that Justice Stevens depicted? To what extent should it extend beyond criminal trials to other governmental information and proceedings? For comments on the implications of Richmond Newspapers, see, e.g., Cox, "Foreword—Freedom of Expression in the Burger Court," 94 Harv. L. Rev. 1 (1980), and Lewis, "A Public Right to Know About Public Institutions: The First Amendment as Sword," 1980 Sup. Ct. Rev. 1 (arguing that Richmond Newspapers "put to rest [the] claim that the Press Clause [gives journalists] a distinct and preferred status. As a practical matter it has not been a winning argument anyway. [Most] future cases seeking access to government information will probably be brought by press organizations, but they will be based on the rights of the public.").

4. ***Extension of Richmond Newspapers.*** In **Globe Newspaper Co. v. Superior Court**, 457 U.S. 596 (1982), the Court concluded that the First Amendment had been violated by a Massachusetts law which had been construed to *require* the exclusion of the press and the general public from the courtroom during the testimony of a minor who had allegedly been a victim of a sex offense. The case arose when the Boston Globe unsuccessfully sought access to a state court trial where the defendant had been charged with the rape of three girls who were minors. In upholding the State's mandatory closure rule, the highest state court had distinguished Richmond Newspapers by emphasizing "at least one notable exception" to the tradition of "openness" in criminal trials: "cases involving sexual assault." The mandatory closure law accordingly operated "in an area of traditional sensitivity to the needs of victims."

Justice BRENNAN, writing for the majority, found the law invalid under the principles of Richmond Newspapers. In his view, Richmond Newspapers "firmly established for the first time that the press and general public have a constitutional right of access to criminal trials," even though no such right was "explicitly mentioned [in] the First Amendment." Protecting "the free discussion of governmental affairs" was a major purpose of the Amendment; offering such protection served "to ensure that the individual citizen can effectively participate in and contribute to our republican system of self-government." A "right of access to *criminal trials*" was properly afforded by the First Amendment because "the criminal trial historically has been open to the press and general public" and because "the right of access to criminal trials plays a particularly significant role in the functioning of the judicial process and the government as a whole." This constitutional right of access, though not "absolute," was entitled to protection unless the State showed "that the denial [of access] is necessitated by a compelling governmental interest, and is narrowly tailored to serve that interest." Massachusetts' defense of its law could not survive that strict scrutiny.

Justice Brennan conceded that the first of the two interests put forth by the state—protecting the physical and psychological well-being of minor victims of sex crimes from further trauma and embarrassment—was "a compelling one." But the closure law was not "a narrowly tailored means of accommodating the State's asserted interest: That interest could be served just as well by requiring the trial court to determine on a case-by-case basis whether the State's legitimate concern for the well-being of the minor victim necessitates closure." Nor could the closure law be sustained on the basis of the State's second asserted interest—"the encouragement of minor victims of sex crimes to come forward and provide accurate testimony." In rejecting that argument, Justice Brennan stated: "Not only is the claim speculative in empirical terms, but it is also open to serious question as a matter of logic and common sense. [Even if the law] effectively advanced the State's interest, it is doubtful that the interest would be sufficient to overcome the constitutional attack, for that same interest could be relied on to support an array of mandatory-closure rules designed to encourage victims to come forward: Surely it cannot be suggested that minor victims of sex crimes are the *only* crime victims who, because of publicity, [are] reluctant to come forward and testify."

Justice O'CONNOR concurred only in the judgment. She stated that she did not interpret Richmond Newspapers "to shelter every right that is 'necessary to the enjoyment of other First Amendment rights.' Instead, Richmond Newspapers rests upon our long history of open criminal trials and the special value, for both public and accused, of that openness. [Thus] I interpret neither Richmond Newspapers nor [today's decision] to carry any implications outside the context of criminal trials."

Chief Justice BURGER, joined by Justice Rehnquist, dissented, objecting to the Court's "expansive interpretation" of Richmond Newspapers and "its cavalier rejection of the serious interests supporting Massachusetts' mandatory closure rule." He claimed that Richmond Newspapers had *not* established "a First Amendment right of access to all aspects of all criminal trials under all circumstances." Although that case had emphasized the traditional openness of criminal trials in general, there was "clearly a long history of exclusion of the public from trials involving sexual assaults, particularly those against minors. [It] would misrepresent the historical record to state that there is an 'unbroken, uncontradicted history' of open proceedings in cases involving the sexual abuse of minors"; and such a specific "history of openness" was necessary to invoke Richmond Newspapers.

Chief Justice Burger also found the majority's "wooden application" of strict scrutiny "inappropriate." He emphasized: "Neither the purpose of the law nor its effect is primarily to deny the press or public access to information; the verbatim transcript is made available to the public and the media and may be used without limit. We therefore need only examine whether the restrictions imposed are reasonable and whether the interests of the [State] override the very limited incidental effects of the law on First Amendment rights." To him, it seemed "beyond doubt, considering the minimal impact of the law on First Amendment rights and the overriding weight of the [State's] interest in protecting child rape victims, that the Massachusetts law is not unconstitutional." Moreover, there was adequate justification for making the law mandatory rather than discretionary: "[V]ictims and their families are entitled to assurance [of] protection. The legislature did not act irrationally in deciding not to leave the closure determination to the idiosyncracies of individual judges subject to the pressures available to the media."

In another broad interpretation of Richmond Newspapers, the Court in **Press-Enterprise Co. v. Superior Court**, 464 U.S. 501 (1984), held

Richmond Newspapers applicable to voir dire examination of prospective jurors in a criminal trial—in this instance, a trial involving charges of rape and murder of a teenage girl. Chief Justice BURGER's opinion for the Court rejected a generalized interest in protecting the privacy of prospective jurors, relying extensively on history to show that public jury selection has long been an integral part of public trials. As in both Richmond Newspapers and Globe, however, the Court did not hold the right of public access to this facet of a trial to be absolute: "The presumption of openness may be overcome only by an overriding interest based on findings that closure is essential to preserve higher values and is narrowly tailored to serve that interest. The interest is to be articulated along with findings specific enough that a reviewing court can determine whether the closure order was properly entered." Chief Justice Burger found this standard unmet in this case, especially in light of the trial court's failure to consider alternatives to closure to protect the privacy of prospective jurors. And he suggested a specific alternative: "The jury selection process may, in some circumstances, give rise to a compelling interest of a prospective juror when interrogation touches on deeply personal [matters]. For example a prospective juror might privately inform the judge that she, or a member of her family, had been raped but had declined to seek prosecution because of the embarrassment and emotional trauma from the very disclosure of the [episode]. By requiring the prospective juror to make an affirmative request, the trial judge can ensure that there is in fact a valid basis for a belief that disclosure infringes a significant interest in privacy."

Richmond Newspapers was extended even further in another Press-Enterprise case two years later, **Press-Enterprise Co. v. Superior Court**, 478 U.S. 1 (1986) (Press-Enterprise II). Relying entirely on the First Amendment, the Court held that a newspaper had a right of access to the transcripts of a preliminary hearing in a criminal case, despite the objections of the trial judge, the prosecutor and the defendant, all of whom believed that pretrial publicity would jeopardize the defendant's right to a fair trial. Writing for the Court, Chief Justice BURGER refused to view the right of access and the right to a fair trial as necessarily in tension. Although the defendant clearly had a right to a fair trial, "one of the important means of assuring a fair trial is that the process be open to neutral observers." He went on to conclude that the preliminary hearing in a criminal case should be treated as a trial for First Amendment access purposes: "[T]he First Amendment question cannot be resolved solely on the label we give the event, i.e., 'trial' or otherwise, particularly where the preliminary hearing functions much like a full scale trial." Because of a tradition of access to preliminary hearings of the type at issue here and because public access plays a positive and important role in the functioning of the process (since "the preliminary hearing is often the final and most important step in the criminal proceeding"), there was a presumptive First Amendment right of access here. It followed that access could not be denied in the absence of specific findings that there was a substantial probability of injury to the accused's right to a fair trial and that there were no reasonable alternatives to closure adequate to protect the defendant's rights: "The First Amendment right of access cannot be overcome by the conclusory assertion that publicity might deprive the defendant of [a fair trial]." Justice STEVENS, joined in part by Justice Rehnquist, dissented: "[The] freedom to obtain information that the Government has a legitimate interest in not disclosing [is] far narrower than the freedom to disseminate information. [In] this case, the risk of prejudice to the defendant's right to a fair trial is perfectly obvious," and "that risk is far more significant than the countervailing interest in publishing the transcript of the preliminary hearing sooner rather than later. [I] fear that today's decision will simply further unsettle the law in this area."

5. ***Press interference with judicial proceedings.*** Is the government interest in the administration of justice ever sufficient to justify punishing publication, as opposed to excluding the press from judicial proceedings? In **Landmark Communications, Inc. v. Virginia**, 435 U.S. 829 (1978), the Court invalidated the conviction of a newspaper publisher for printing an accurate report of a pending inquiry by the Virginia Judicial Inquiry and Review Commission that had identified the state judge under investigation. A state law deemed information before the Commission confidential and made disclosure a crime. Chief Justice BURGER, writing for the Court, noted that the information published lay near "the core of the First Amendment" and that the "interests advanced by the imposition of criminal sanctions [were] insufficient to justify the actual and potential encroachments on freedom of speech and of the press." Noting that the operation of judicial inquiry commissions, like the operation of the judicial system itself, was a matter of public interest, he insisted that the State's "legitimate" interests were not "sufficient to justify the subsequent punishment of speech at issue here." The asserted interests were promoting efficient Commission proceedings, protecting the reputation of Virginia's judges, and maintaining the institutional integrity of its courts. In the course of his discussion, Chief Justice Burger commented that "injury to official reputation is an insufficient reason 'for repressing speech that would otherwise be free.' "

In Landmark, the Court relied heavily on a line of cases involving the application of contempt sanctions to publications, even though the state sanctions in Landmark rested on a legislative finding of clear and present danger rather than on the inherent contempt power of the courts. That line of cases began with **Bridges v. California**, 314 U.S. 252 (1941), which reversed contempt convictions in two companion cases. In the first, a newspaper, the Los Angeles Times, was found guilty of contempt for publishing editorials about the pending sentencing of two union members who had previously been convicted of assaulting nonunion workers. One editorial, for example, criticized the defendants as "thugs" and "gorillas," urged the judge to sentence them to San Quentin, and stated that the judge would "make a serious mistake if he grants probation." In the second, union leader Harry Bridges—while a motion for a new trial in a labor dispute was pending—had caused the newspaper publication of his telegram to the Secretary of Labor threatening a strike if the "outrageous" court decision were enforced. The newspaper and Bridges were convicted of contempt. The lower courts had rested their contempt findings on the "tendency" of the publications to interfere with the "orderly administration of justice." Justice BLACK's majority opinion in the 5–4 decision concluded that punishment was permissible only where there was a clear and present danger that justice would be obstructed, and described the clear and present danger standard as "a working principle that the substantive evil must be extremely serious and the degree of imminence extremely high before utterances can be punished." Justice FRANKFURTER's dissent stated: "A trial is not 'a free trade in ideas.' "

In **Pennekamp v. Florida**, 328 U.S. 331 (1946), the Court reaffirmed that the "essential right of the courts to be free of intimidation and coercion [is] consonant with a recognition that freedom of the press must be allowed in the broadest scope compatible with the supremacy of order." In Pennekamp v. Florida, a newspaper involved in an anti-vice crusade published editorials and a cartoon implying that the judges were using legal technicalities to hinder the prosecution of several rape and gambling cases. The newspaper and its associate editor, Pennekamp, were held in contempt and fined by a Florida court. As in Bridges, the Court applied the clear and present danger test and reversed.

In **Craig v. Harney**, 331 U.S. 367 (1947), the Court held that to warrant a sanction, "[t]he fires which [the expression] kindles must constitute an imminent, not merely a likely, threat to the administration of justice. The danger must not be remote or even probable; it must immediately imperil." Craig v. Harney reversed contempt convictions of a newspaper editor who, in an effort to influence an elected lay judge on a pending motion for a new trial in a private lawsuit, published inaccurate reports and unfair criticisms of the judge's action in directing a verdict for a landlord. Justice DOUGLAS's majority opinion commented: "[T]he law of contempt is not made for the protection of judges who may be sensitive to the winds of public opinion. Judges are supposed to be men of fortitude, able to thrive in a hardy climate." One of the dissenters, Justice JACKSON, retorted: "From our sheltered position, fortified by life tenure, [it] is easy to say that this local judge ought to have shown more fortitude in the face of criticism. [Of] course, the blasts of these little papers in this small community do not jolt us, but I am not so confident that we would be indifferent if a news monopoly in our entire jurisdiction should perpetrate this kind of an attack on us."

And in **Wood v. Georgia**, 370 U.S. 375 (1962), the Court invalidated a contempt citation against an elected sheriff in Bibb County, Georgia, who publicly criticized judges who had ordered a grand jury investigation into black voting practices, charging them with an attempt to intimidate black voters and analogizing them to the Ku Klux Klan. Chief Justice WARREN, writing for the Court, held that the state's showing had fallen far short of meeting the clear and present danger standard: "The type of 'danger' evidenced by the record is precisely one of the types of activity envisioned by the [framers of the First Amendment]. Men are entitled to speak as they please on matters vital to them; errors in judgment or unsubstantiated opinions may be exposed, of course, but not through punishment for contempt for the expression. [In] the absence of some other showing of a substantive evil actually designed to impede the course of justice, [his] utterances are entitled to be protected." Justice HARLAN, joined by Justice Clark, dissented, distinguishing Bridges, Pennekamp and Harney on the ground that here the speaker was an elected official and his intended audience a jury rather than a presumably hardier judge.

In Landmark, Chief Justice Burger found the state courts' efforts to distinguish the Bridges line of cases "unpersuasive" and added: "The threat to the administration of justice posed by the speech and publications in Bridges [et al.] was, if anything, more direct and substantial than the threat posed by Landmark's article."

6. ***Press access to sensitive government information.*** In 2010, WikiLeaks, an online news organization that focuses on making sensitive

and classified government documents publicly available, set off a firestorm by releasing hundreds of cables from U.S. embassies and a series of government documents describing the war in Afghanistan known as the Afghan War Diary to established news outlets including the New York Times and the Guardian. Army private Bradley Manning, the source of many of the documents disclosed in 2010, has been charged and tried in military court for giving more than 250,000 documents to WikiLeaks. The United States has not brought charges against the founder and editor-in-chief of WikiLeaks, Julian Assange.

Three years later, a flurry of leaks by former NSA contractor Edward Snowden focused attention once more on the role of the press. Snowden handed over more than 10,000 classified NSA documents to reporters at the Guardian, New York Times, and Washington Post that revealed vast data collection and surveillance programs run by the NSA. Leaked documents also disclosed that the United States had spied on Britain, France, Germany, and China, as well as 114 high-ranking world leaders. The Justice Department charged Snowden, who fled to Russia seeking temporary asylum, with violation of the Espionage Act but did not file charges against the journalists who published the leaks.

Could the U.S. bring charges against Assange or the Snowden journalists consistent with the freedom of the press? For an argument that such a prosecution would violate the freedom of the press and should be protected under First Amendment values, see Yochai Benkler, "A Free Irresponsible Press: Wikileaks and the Battle Over the Soul of the Networked Fourth Estate," 46 Harv. C.R.-C.L. L. Rev. 311 (2011).

Recall Bartnicki v. Vopper (2001; p. 1023 above), in which Justice Stevens wrote for the majority that, "As a general matter, 'state action to punish the publication of truthful information seldom can satisfy constitutional standards.' [And] 'if a newspaper lawfully obtains truthful information about a matter of public significance then state officials may not constitutionally punish publication of the information, absent a need . . . of the highest order.' [We have not] resolve[d] the question 'whether, in cases where information has been acquired *unlawfully* by a newspaper or by a source, government may ever punish not only the unlawful acquisition, but the ensuing publication as well.' " Would the prosecution of Assange or other journalists raise precisely that question? What result?

GOVERNMENTAL DEMANDS FOR INFORMATION FROM THE PRESS

Restraints against publication are not the only sanctions that may confront the press because of information in its possession. The materials that follow arise from situations in which government, typically in the interest of law enforcement, demands that journalists disclose information they have obtained in the course of their newsgathering activities. Can the First Amendment be read to grant to journalists a special immunity from governmental inquiries? The Branzburg case raises that question in the context of grand jury investigations. The Zurcher case involves a claimed press privilege against newsroom searches based on ex parte warrants.

Branzburg v. Hayes

408 U.S. 665, 92 S. Ct. 2646, 33 L. Ed. 2d 626 (1972).

[Branzburg arose from the claims of three journalists: Branzburg, Pappas, and Caldwell. Branzburg, a Louisville reporter, had written articles about drug activities he had observed. He declined to testify before a state grand jury, refusing to identify the persons he had seen possessing marijuana or making hashish. Pappas, a Massachusetts television reporter covering a "civil disorder," was allowed to remain in Black Panther headquarters for several hours on the condition that he disclose nothing. He broadcast no report and refused to tell a grand jury about what had taken place inside the headquarters. Caldwell was a New York Times reporter who had written articles about the Black Panthers after interviewing their leaders. He refused to appear before a federal grand jury investigating "possible violations of a number of criminal statutes" (including those protecting the President against assassination). The trial court issued a protective order stating that he was not required to reveal confidential information unless the government showed "a compelling national interest" in his testimony "which cannot be served by any alternative means." Caldwell thought that limited privilege inadequate, refused to appear, and was sentenced for contempt. Caldwell's conviction was set aside by the Court of Appeals. The Branzburg and Pappas convictions were affirmed by state courts. The reporters sought a conditional privilege that would have barred their mandatory appearance before the grand jury unless the government could demonstrate that they possessed information relevant to a crime and that the information they possessed was unavailable from other sources. The Supreme Court rejected their arguments.]

■ Opinion of the Court by JUSTICE WHITE.

The issue in these cases is whether requiring newsmen to appear and testify before state or federal grand juries abridges the freedom of speech and press guaranteed by the First Amendment. We hold that it does not.

[The journalists] press First Amendment claims that may be simply put: that to gather news it is often necessary to agree either not to identify the source of information published or to publish only part of the facts revealed, or both; that if the reporter is nevertheless forced to reveal these confidences to a grand jury, the source so identified and other confidential sources of other reporters will be measurably deterred from furnishing publishable information, all to the detriment of the free flow of information protected by the First Amendment.

[News] gathering [qualifies] for First Amendment protection; without some protection for seeking out the news, freedom of the press could be eviscerated. But these cases involve no intrusions upon speech or assembly, [and] no penalty, civil or criminal, related to the content of published material, is at issue here. The use of confidential sources by the press is not forbidden or restricted. [No] attempt is made to require the press to publish its sources of information or indiscriminately to disclose them on request. The sole issue [is] the obligation of reporters to respond to grand jury subpoenas as other citizens do and to answer questions relevant to an investigation into the commission of crime. [The Constitution does not protect] the average citizen from disclosing to a grand jury information that he has received in confidence. The claim is, however, that reporters are [exempt].

[The] great weight of authority is that newsmen are not exempt from the normal duty of appearing before a grand jury and answering questions relevant to a criminal [investigation]. The prevailing constitutional view of the newsman's privilege is very much rooted in the ancient role of the grand jury. [I]ts investigative powers are necessarily broad. [The] longstanding principle that "the public has a right to every man's evidence," except for those persons protected by a constitutional, common law, or statutory privilege, is particularly applicable to grand jury proceedings. A [minority] of States have provided newsmen a statutory privilege of varying breadth; [none] has been provided by federal statute.

[We] are asked to [interpret] the First Amendment to grant newsmen a testimonial privilege that other citizens do not enjoy. This we decline to do. [On] the records now before us, we perceive no basis for holding that the public interest in law enforcement and in ensuring effective grand jury proceedings is insufficient to override the consequential, but uncertain, burden on news gathering which is said to result from insisting that reporters, like other citizens, respond to relevant questions put to them in the course of a valid grand jury investigation or criminal trial. This conclusion [does not] threaten the vast bulk of confidential relationships between reporters and their sources. [Only] where news sources themselves are implicated in crime or possess information relevant to the grand jury's task need they or the reporter be concerned about grand jury subpoenas. Nothing before us indicates that a large number or percentage of *all* confidential news sources fall into either category and would in any way be deterred by our [holding].

There remain those situations where a source is not engaged in criminal conduct but has information suggesting illegal conduct by others. Newsmen frequently receive information from such sources pursuant to a tacit or express agreement to withhold the source's name and suppress any information that the source wishes not published. [The] argument that the flow of news will be diminished by compelling reporters to aid the grand jury in a criminal investigation is not irrational, nor are the records before us silent on the matter. But we remain unclear how often and to what extent informers are actually deterred from furnishing information when newsmen are forced to testify before a grand jury. [The] evidence fails to demonstrate that there would be a significant constriction of the flow of news to the public if this Court reaffirms the prior common-law and constitutional rule regarding the testimonial obligations of newsmen. Estimates of the inhibiting effect of such subpoenas on the willingness of informants to make disclosures to newsmen are widely divergent and to a great extent speculative. It would be difficult to canvass the views of the informants themselves; surveys of reporters on this topic are chiefly opinions of predicted informant behavior and must be viewed in the light of the professional self-interest of the interviewees. [Accepting] the fact, however, that an undetermined number of informants not themselves implicated in crime will nevertheless [refuse] to talk to newsmen if they fear identification by a reporter in an official investigation, we cannot accept the argument that the public interest in possible future news about crime from undisclosed, unverified sources must take precedence over the public interest in pursuing and prosecuting those crimes reported to the press by informants and in thus deterring the commission of such crimes in the [future].

We are admonished that refusal to provide a First Amendment reporter's privilege will undermine the freedom of the press to collect and disseminate news. But this is not the lesson history teaches us. [From] the beginning of our country the press has operated without constitutional protection for press informants, and the press has flourished. [It] is said that currently press subpoenas have multiplied, that mutual distrust and tension between press and officialdom have increased, that reporting styles have changed, and that there is now more need for confidential sources. [These] developments, even if true, are treacherous grounds for a far-reaching interpretation of the [First Amendment].

[The] requirements of those cases [e.g., NAACP v. Alabama] which hold that a State's interest must be "compelling" or "paramount" to justify even an indirect burden on First Amendment rights, are also met here. As we have indicated, the investigation of crime by the grand jury implements a fundamental governmental role of securing the safety of the person and property of the [citizen]. If the test is that the government "convincingly show a substantial relation between the information sought and a subject of overriding and compelling state interest" it is quite apparent (1) that the State has the necessary interests in extirpating the traffic in illegal drugs, in forestalling assassination attempts on the President, and in preventing the community from being disrupted by violent disorders endangering both persons and property; and (2) that, based on the stories Branzburg and Caldwell wrote and Pappas' admitted conduct, the grand jury called these reporters as they would others—because it was likely that they could supply information to help the government determine whether illegal conduct had occurred and, if it had, whether there was sufficient evidence to return an indictment.

We are unwilling to embark the judiciary on [the] administration of a constitutional newsman's privilege[, which] would present practical and conceptual difficulties of a high order. Sooner or later, it would be necessary to define those categories of newsmen who qualified for the privilege, a questionable procedure in light of the traditional doctrine that liberty of the press is the right of the lonely pamphleteer [just] as much as of the large metropolitan publisher who utilizes the latest photocomposition methods. [Almost] any author may quite accurately assert that he is contributing to the flow of information to the public, that he relies on confidential sources of information, and that these sources will be silenced if he is forced to make disclosures before a grand jury. [In] each instance where a reporter is subpoenaed to testify, the courts would also be embroiled in preliminary factual and legal determinations with respect to whether the proper predicate had been laid for the reporter's appearance. [In] the end, by considering whether enforcement of a particular law served a "compelling" governmental interest, the courts would be inextricably involved in distinguishing between the value of enforcing different criminal laws. [At] the federal level, Congress has freedom to determine whether a statutory newsman's privilege is necessary and desirable and to fashion standards and rules as narrow or broad as deemed necessary [and], equally important, to re-fashion those rules as experience from time to time may dictate. There is also merit in leaving state legislatures free, within First Amendment limits, to fashion their own standards. [In addition], there is much force in the pragmatic view that the press has at its disposal powerful mechanisms of communication and is far from helpless to protect itself from harassment or substantial [harm].

[Finally,] news gathering is not without its First Amendment protections, and grand jury investigations, if instituted or conducted other than in good faith, would pose wholly different issues for resolution under the First Amendment. Official harassment of the press undertaken not for purposes of law enforcement but to disrupt a reporter's relationship with his news sources would have no justification. Grand juries are subject to judicial control and subpoenas to motions to quash. We do not expect courts will forget that grand juries must operate within the limits of the First Amendment as well as the Fifth.

■ JUSTICE POWELL, concurring in the opinion of the Court.

I add this brief statement to emphasize what seems to me to be the limited nature of the Court's holding. The Court does not hold that newsmen, subpoenaed to testify before a grand jury, are without constitutional rights with respect to the gathering of news or in safeguarding their sources. [As] indicated in the concluding portion of the opinion, the Court states that no harassment of newsmen will be tolerated. If a newsman believes that the grand jury investigation is not being conducted in good faith he is not without remedy. Indeed, if the newsman is called upon to give information bearing only a remote and tenuous relationship to the subject of the investigation, or if he has some other reason to believe that his testimony implicates confidential source relationships without a legitimate need of law enforcement, he will have access to the Court on a motion to quash and an appropriate protective order may be entered. The asserted claim to privilege should be judged on its facts by the striking of a proper balance between freedom of the press and the obligation of all citizens to give relevant testimony with respect to criminal conduct. The balance of these vital constitutional and societal interests on a case-by-case basis accords with the tried and traditional way of adjudicating such questions. In short, the courts will be available to newsmen under circumstances where legitimate First Amendment interests require protection.

■ JUSTICE STEWART, with whom JUSTICES BRENNAN and MARSHALL join, dissenting.

The Court's crabbed view of the First Amendment reflects a disturbing insensitivity to the critical role of an independent press in our society. [While] Justice Powell's enigmatic concurring opinion gives some hope of a more flexible view in the future, the Court in these cases holds that a newsman has no First Amendment right to protect his sources when called before a grand jury. The Court thus invites state and federal authorities to undermine the historic independence of the press by attempting to annex the journalistic profession as an investigative arm of [government].

The reporter's constitutional right to a confidential relationship with his source stems from the broad societal interest in a full and free flow of information to the public. It is this basic concern that underlies the Constitution's protection of a free press. [A] corollary of the right to publish must be the right to gather news. [This right] implies, in turn, a right to a confidential relationship between a reporter and his source. [This] follows as a matter of simple logic once three factual predicates are recognized: (1) newsmen require informants to gather news; (2) confidentiality [is] essential to the creation and maintenance of a news-gathering relationship with informants; and (3) the existence of an unbridled subpoena power [will] either deter sources from divulging information or deter reporters from gathering and publishing information. After today's decision, the potential [source must] choose between risking exposure by giving information or avoiding the risk by remaining [silent].

The impairment of the flow of news cannot, of course, be proved with scientific precision, as the Court seems to demand. [But] we have never before demanded that First Amendment rights rest on elaborate empirical studies demonstrating beyond any conceivable doubt that deterrent effects [exist]. Rather, on the basis of common sense and available information, we have asked, often implicitly, (1) whether there was a rational connection between the cause (the governmental action) and the effect (the deterrence or impairment of First Amendment activity) and (2) whether the effect would occur with some regularity, i.e., would not be de minimis. And in making this determination, we have shown a special solicitude towards the "indispensable liberties" protected by the First Amendment. [Once] this threshold inquiry has been satisfied, we have then examined the competing interests in determining whether there is an unconstitutional infringement of First Amendment freedoms. [E.g., NAACP v. Alabama.] Surely the analogous claim of deterrence here is as securely grounded in evidence and common sense as the claims in [earlier cases], although the Court calls the claim "speculative." [To] require any greater burden of proof is to shirk our duty to protect values securely embedded in the Constitution. [We] cannot escape the conclusion that when neither the reporter nor his source can rely on the shield of confidentiality against unrestrained use of the grand jury's subpoena power, valuable information will not be published and the public dialogue will inevitably be impoverished.

[As our cases hold with respect to witnesses called before legislative investigations, I would hold that,] when a reporter is asked to appear before a grand jury and reveal confidences, [the] government must (1) show that there is probable cause to believe that the newsman has information which is clearly relevant to a specific probable violation of law; (2) demonstrate that the information sought cannot be obtained by alternative means less destructive of First Amendment rights; and (3) demonstrate a compelling and overriding interest in the information. [Both] the "probable cause" and "alternative means" requirements [would] serve the vital function of mediating between the public interest in the administration of justice and the constitutional protection of the full flow of information. These requirements would avoid a direct conflict between these competing concerns, and they would generally provide adequate protection for newsmen. No doubt the courts would be required to make some delicate judgments in working out this accommodation. But that, after all, is the function of courts of law. Better such judgments, however difficult, than the simplistic and stultifying absolutism adopted by the Court in denying any force to the First Amendment in these cases.

■ JUSTICE DOUGLAS, dissenting.

[There] is no "compelling need" that can be shown which qualifies the reporter's immunity from appearing or testifying before a grand jury, unless the reporter himself is implicated in a crime. His immunity in my view [is] quite complete.

JOURNALISTIC PRIVILEGE AFTER BRANZBURG

1. ***The aftermath of Branzburg.*** In response to Branzburg, numerous bills to establish a journalists' privilege were introduced in state legislatures and in Congress. Some forty states and the District of Columbia have enacted "press shield" laws providing at least a qualified free speech privilege against compelled revelation of journalists' anonymous sources. A federal press shield law pending in Congress as of 2010 would bar the compelled disclosure from news providers in federal proceedings of information identifying confidential sources absent a government showing of need and exhaustion and a judicial balancing of the public interest in news gathering and dissemination against the public interest in compelling disclosure (with the burden on the press in criminal cases and on the government in civil cases).

Many lower courts after Branzburg emphasized Justice Powell's concurrence rather than Justice White's opinion for the Court, finding in the concurrence some ground for affording journalists greater-than-normal protection from compulsion to divulge confidential sources. In recent years, however, federal prosecutors have more aggressively demanded confidential source information from journalists in connection with pending criminal investigations, including with respect to leaks of classified or otherwise secret government information, and courts have proved more deferential to the prosecution, reading Branzburg more in line with Justice White's than Justice Powell's opinion. See, e.g., In re Grand Jury Subpoena: Judith Miller, 397 F.3d 964 (D.C. Cir. 2005) (rejecting a claim of journalist privilege against a grand jury subpoena to reveal confidential sources in connection with investigation of possible illegal exposure of an undercover CIA officer's identity).

How should the balance be struck between government need in criminal cases and the press interest in the free flow of information given on a confidential basis? Should courts be permitted to weigh the relative value of the story? Or to look only at the government's need and the extent to which it has exhausted alternative sources? In the Judith Miller case, supra, Judge David Tatel's influential concurrence in the judgment suggested that a court deciding whether to enforce a press privilege in a leak case "must weigh the public interest in compelling disclosure, measured by the harm the leak caused, against the public interest in newsgathering, measured by the leaked information's value." Should courts be permitted thus to balance when leaked information does more harm than good? Are courts institutionally capable of making such judgments?

To what extent is any such balance changed by the rise of the internet? At the time Branzburg was decided, journalism was concentrated in large, organized institutional outlets such as daily newspapers and broadcasting networks. Such organizations adhered to codes and practice of self-regulation such as corroboration and sourcing requirements. With the rise of the internet, news is communicated by a vast array of decentralized sources. Should non-professional "journalists" such as bloggers be permitted to invoke any privilege against disclosure of anonymous sources? How should the scope of any statutory or constitutional reporter's privilege be defined? For discussion, see Papandrea, "Citizen Journalism and the Reporter's Privilege," 91 Minn. L. Rev. 515 (2007).

2. ***Searches of newsrooms pursuant to warrants.*** The Court once more rejected a press claim for special protection from law enforcement demands for information in **Zurcher v. Stanford Daily**, 436 U.S. 547 (1978). In that case, the Court upheld execution of a warrant authorizing a search of a campus newspaper office for photographs of a violent demonstration.[1] The police obtained an ex parte warrant for a search of the Daily's offices for pictures and negatives that might help them to identify the demonstrators. The Daily's civil suit claimed that the police decision to engage in a search rather than proceed by subpoena violated the First Amendment. In rejecting the claim, Justice WHITE's majority opinion emphasized the Fourth Amendment rather than the First. His opinion in 'Zurcher was as skeptical as that in Branzburg about press allegations of chilling effects and risks to confidential sources. His reasoning contained only one sentence suggesting that First Amendment considerations be taken into account in applying Fourth Amendment search warrant criteria in the media context: "[Prior cases insist] that courts apply the warrant requirements with particular exactitude when First Amendment interests would be endangered by the search."

As in Branzburg, Justice POWELL's concurrence built upon a passing remark in the prevailing opinion and elaborated the relevance of First Amendment concerns, stating: "This is not to say that a warrant which would be sufficient to support the search of an apartment or an automobile necessarily would be reasonable in supporting the search of a newspaper office. [While] there is no justification for the establishment of a separate Fourth Amendment procedure for the press, a magistrate asked to issue a warrant for the search of press offices can and should take cognizance of the independent values protected by the First Amendment—such as those highlighted by Mr. Justice Stewart—when he weighs such factors." And he added in a footnote that his separate opinion here, like that in Branzburg, could be read as supporting the view "that under the warrant requirement of the Fourth Amendment, the magistrate should consider the values of a free press as well as the societal interests in enforcing the criminal law." Justice STEWART's dissent argued that warrants to search newspaper offices should issue only when a magistrate finds probable cause to believe that it would be impractical to obtain the evidence by a subpoena. He emphasized that subpoena applications permit the press to obtain an adversary hearing prior to producing the information, by making a motion to quash; ex parte warrants, by contrast, provide "no opportunity to challenge the necessity for the search until after it has occurred and the constitutional protection of the newspaper has been irretrievably invaded."

As a result of legislative efforts that began in the wake of the Stanford Daily decision, Congress adopted the Privacy Protection Act in 1980. 42 U.S.C. § 2000aa. The Act requires state and federal law enforcement officers to use subpoena procedures to obtain documents from persons engaged in the communications industry. Search warrants are permitted only in

---

[1] The division on the Court was strikingly similar to that in Branzburg. Justice Powell once again supplied the critical vote for the majority with a separate concurrence putting a more speech-protective gloss on Justice White's opinion; Justice Stewart once again dissented on First Amendment grounds, this time joined only by Justice Marshall. (Justice Brennan did not participate in the case.) Justice Stevens, who had replaced Justice Douglas since Branzburg, submitted a separate dissent, based on the Fourth Amendment.

exceptional circumstances, such as when there is a fear that the needed materials would be destroyed.

LAWS SINGLING OUT THE PRESS

In the discussion in this section so far, the Court has tended to treat the press on a par with other speakers for First Amendment purposes, and declined to carve out special protections for the institutional media. In one line of cases, however, the Court has suggested that even a content-neutral law requires special scrutiny when it singles out the press, or a small subset of the press, for special treatment. In the case that follows, this result obtained even where the special treatment arguably benefited the press:

Minneapolis Star & Tribune Co. v. Minnesota Comm'r of Revenue

460 U.S. 575, 103 S. Ct. 1365, 75 L. Ed. 2d 295 (1983).

■ JUSTICE O'CONNOR delivered the opinion of the Court.

This case presents the question of a State's power to impose a special tax on the press and, by enacting exemptions, to limit its effect to only a few newspapers.

I. Since 1967, Minnesota has imposed a sales tax on most sales of goods. In general, the tax applies only to retail sales. [As] part of this general system of taxation and in support of the sales tax, Minnesota also enacted a tax on the "privilege of using, storing or consuming in Minnesota tangible personal property." This use tax applies to any nonexempt tangible personal property unless the sales tax was paid on the sales price. Like the classic use tax, this use tax protects the State's sales tax by eliminating the residents' incentive to travel to States with lower sales taxes to buy goods rather than buying them in Minnesota.

The appellant [is] the publisher of a morning [and] an evening newspaper (until 1982) in Minneapolis. From 1967 until 1971, it enjoyed an exemption from the sales and use tax provided by Minnesota for periodic publications. In 1971, however, while leaving the exemption from the sales tax in place, the legislature amended the scheme to impose a "use tax" on the cost of paper and ink products consumed in the production of a publication. Ink and paper used in publications became the only items subject to the use tax that were components of goods to be sold at retail. In 1974, the legislature again amended the statute, this time to exempt the first $100,000 worth of ink and paper consumed by a publication in any calendar year, in effect giving each publication an annual tax credit of $4,000. Publications remained exempt from the sales tax. After the enactment of the $100,000 exemption, 11 publishers, producing 14 of the 388 paid circulation newspapers in the State, incurred a tax liability in 1974. [Appellant] was one of the 11, and, of the $893,355 collected, it paid $608,634, or roughly two-thirds of the total revenue raised by the tax. In 1975, 13 publishers, producing 16 out of 374 paid circulation papers, paid a tax. That year, [appellant] again bore roughly two-thirds of the total receipts from the use tax on ink and paper. [Appellant] instituted this action to seek a refund of the use taxes it paid from January 1, 1974 to May 31, 1975. [The] Minnesota Supreme Court upheld the [tax]. [The Court held that this taxing system violated appellant's First Amendment rights.]

II. Star Tribune argues that we must strike this tax on the authority of Grosjean v. American Press Co., 297 U.S. 233 (1936). Although there are similarities, [we] agree with the State that Grosjean is not controlling. In Grosjean, [Louisiana] imposed a license tax of 2% of the gross receipts from the sale of advertising on all newspapers with a weekly circulation above 20,000. Out of at least 124 publishers in the State, only 13 were subject to the tax. After noting that the tax was "single in kind" and that keying the tax to circulation curtailed the flow of information, this Court held the tax invalid as an abridgment of the freedom of the press. [The argument of the publishers] emphasized the events leading up to the tax and the contemporary political climate in Louisiana. All but one of the large papers subject to the tax had "ganged up" on Senator Huey Long, and a circular distributed by Long and the governor to each member of the state legislature described "lying newspapers" as conducting "a vicious campaign" and the tax as "a tax on lying." [Although] the Court's opinion did not describe this history, it stated, "[The tax] is bad because, in the light of its history and of its present setting, it is seen to be a deliberate and calculated device in the guise of a tax to limit the circulation of information," an explanation that suggests that the motivation of the legislature may have been significant. Our subsequent cases have not been consistent in their reading of Grosjean on this point. [We] think that the result in Grosjean may have been attributable in part to the perception on the part of the Court that the state imposed the tax with an intent to penalize a selected group of newspapers. In the case currently before us, however, there is no legislative history and no indication, apart from the structure of the tax itself, of any impermissible or censorial motive on the part of the legislature. We cannot resolve the case by simple citation to Grosjean. Instead, we must analyze the problem anew under the general principles of the First Amendment.

III. Clearly, the First Amendment does not prohibit all regulation of the press. It is beyond dispute that [government] can subject newspapers to generally applicable economic regulations without creating constitutional problems. Minnesota, however, has not chosen to apply its general sales and use tax to newspapers. Instead, it has created a special tax that applies only to certain publications protected by the First Amendment. Although the State argues now that the tax on paper and ink is part of the general scheme of taxation, the use tax provision is facially discriminatory, singling out publications for treatment that [is] unique in Minnesota tax law.

[By] creating this special use tax, [Minnesota] has singled out the press for special treatment. We then must determine whether the First Amendment permits such special taxation. A tax that burdens rights protected by the First Amendment cannot stand unless the burden is necessary to achieve an overriding governmental interest.

[There] is substantial evidence that differential taxation of the press would have troubled the Framers of the First Amendment. [The] fears of the [Framers] were well-founded. A power to tax differentially, as opposed to a power to tax generally, gives a government a powerful weapon against the taxpayer selected. When the State imposes a generally applicable tax, there is little cause for concern. We need not fear that a government will destroy a selected group of taxpayers by burdensome taxation if it must impose the same burden on the rest of its constituency. When the State singles out the press, though, the political constraints that prevent a legislature from passing crippling taxes of general applicability are weakened, and the threat of burdensome taxes becomes acute. That threat can operate as effectively as a censor to check critical comment by the press, undercutting the basic assumption of our political system that the press will often serve as an important restraint on government. [Differential] treatment, unless justified by some special characteristic of the press, suggests that the goal of the regulation is not unrelated to suppression of expression, and such a goal is presumptively unconstitutional. Differential taxation of the press, then, places such a burden on the interests protected by the First Amendment that we cannot countenance such treatment unless the State asserts a counterbalancing interest of compelling importance that it cannot achieve without differential taxation.

IV. The main interest asserted by Minnesota in this case is the raising of revenue. [Standing alone], however, it cannot justify the special treatment of the press, for an alternative means of achieving the same interest without raising concerns under the First Amendment is clearly available: the State could raise the revenue by taxing businesses generally, avoiding the censorial threat implicit in a tax that singles out the press. Addressing the concern with differential treatment, Minnesota invites us to look beyond the form of the tax to its substance. The tax is, according to the State, merely a substitute for the sales tax, which, as a generally applicable tax, would be constitutional as applied to the press. There are two fatal flaws in this reasoning. First, the State has offered no explanation of why it chose to use a substitute for the sales tax rather than the sales tax itself. [Further,] even assuming that the legislature did have valid reasons for substituting another tax for the sales tax, we are not persuaded that this tax does serve as a substitute. The State asserts that this scheme actually *favors* the press over other businesses, because the same rate of tax is applied, but, for the press, the rate applies to the cost of components rather than to the sales price. We would be hesitant to fashion a rule that automatically allowed the State to single out the press for a different method of taxation as long as the effective burden was no different from that on other taxpayers or the burden on the press was lighter than that on other businesses. One reason for this reluctance is that the very selection of the press for special treatment threatens the press not only with the current *differential* treatment, but with the possibility of subsequent differentially *more burdensome* treatment. Thus, even without actually imposing an extra burden on the press, the government might be able to achieve censorial effects, for "[t]he threat of sanctions may deter [the] exercise of [First Amendment] rights almost as potently as the actual application of sanctions." NAACP v. Button.

A second reason to avoid the proposed rule is that courts as institutions are poorly equipped to evaluate with precision the relative burdens of various methods of taxation. The complexities of factual economic proof always present a certain potential for error, and courts have little familiarity with the process of evaluating the relative economic burden of taxes. In sum, the possibility of error inherent in the proposed rule poses too great a threat to concerns at the heart of the First Amendment, and we cannot tolerate that possibility.[1] Minnesota, therefore, has offered no adequate justification for the special treatment of newspapers.

V. Minnesota's ink and paper tax violates the First Amendment not only because it singles out the press, but also because it targets a small group of newspapers. The effect of the $100,000 exemption [is] that only a handful of publishers pay any tax at [all]. The State explains this exemption as part of a policy favoring an "equitable" tax system, although there are no comparable exemptions for small enterprises outside the press. [Whatever] the motive of the legislature in this case, we think that recognizing a power in the State not only to single out the press but also to tailor the tax so that it singles out a few members of the press presents such a potential for abuse that no interest suggested by Minnesota can justify the [scheme].

VI. We need not and do not impugn the motives of the Minnesota legislature in passing the ink and paper tax. Illicit legislative intent is not the sine qua non of a violation of the First Amendment. We have long recognized that even regulations aimed at proper governmental concerns can restrict unduly the exercise of rights protected by the First Amendment. A tax that singles out the press [places] a heavy burden on the State to justify its action. Since Minnesota has offered no satisfactory justification for its tax on the use of ink and paper, the tax violates the First Amendment. [Reversed.]

■ JUSTICE REHNQUIST, dissenting.

Today we learn from the Court that a State runs afoul of the First Amendment [where] the State structures its taxing system to the advantage of newspapers. [The Court recognizes that Minnesota] could avoid constitutional problems by imposing on newspapers the 4% sales tax that it imposes on other retailers. Rather than impose such a tax, however, the Minnesota legislature decided to provide newspapers with an exemption from the sales tax and impose a 4% use tax on ink and paper; thus, while both taxes are part of one [system], newspapers are classified differently within that system. The problem the Court finds too difficult to deal with is whether this difference in treatment results in a significant burden on newspapers. [Had] a 4% sales tax been imposed, the Minneapolis Star & Tribune would have been liable for $1,859,950 in 1974. The same "complexities of factual economic proof" can be analyzed for 1975. [Had] the sales tax been imposed, as the Court agrees would have been permissible, the Minneapolis Star & Tribune's liability for 1974 and 1975 would have been $3,685,092. The record further indicates that the Minneapolis Star & Tribune paid $608,634 in use taxes in 1974 and $636,113 in 1975—a total liability of $1,244,747. We need no expert testimony from modern day Euclids or Einsteins to determine that the $1,224,747 paid in use taxes is significantly less burdensome than the $3,685,092 that could have been levied by a sales tax. A fortiori, the Minnesota taxing scheme which singles

[1] If a State employed the same *method* of taxation but applied a lower *rate* to the press, so that there could be no doubt that the legislature was not singling out the press to bear a more burdensome tax, we would, of course, be in a position to evaluate the relative burdens. And, given the clarity of the relative burdens, as well as the rule that differential methods of taxation are not automatically permissible if less burdensome, a lower tax rate for the press would not raise the threat that the legislature might later impose an extra burden that would escape detection by the courts. Thus, our decision does not, as the dissent suggests, require Minnesota to impose a greater tax burden on publications. [Footnote by Justice O'Connor.]

out newspapers for "different treatment" has benefited, not burdened, the "freedom of speech, [and] of the press."

[No] First Amendment issue is raised unless First Amendment rights have been [infringed]. [The] State is required to show that its taxing scheme is rational. But in this case that showing can be made easily. [So] long as the State can find another way to collect revenue from the newspapers, imposing a sales tax on newspapers would be to no one's advantage; not the newspaper and its distributors who would have to collect the tax, not the State who would have to enforce collection, and not the consumer who would have to pay for the paper in odd amounts. The reasonable alternative Minnesota chose was to impose the use tax on ink and paper.

[The] Court finds in very summary fashion that the exemption newspapers receive for the first $100,000 of ink and paper used also violates the [First Amendment]. I cannot agree. [The] exemption is in effect a $4,000 credit which benefits all newspapers. Minneapolis Star & Tribune was benefited to the amount of $16,000 in the two years in question; $4,000 each year for its morning paper and $4,000 each year for its evening paper. Absent any improper motive on the part of the Minnesota legislature in drawing the limits of this exemption, it cannot be construed as violating the First Amendment. [There] is no reason to conclude that the State, in drafting the $4,000 credit, acted other than reasonably and rationally to fit its sales and use tax scheme to its own local needs and usages. To collect from newspapers their fair share of taxes under the sales and use tax scheme and at the same time avoid abridging the freedoms of speech and press, the Court holds today that Minnesota must subject newspapers to millions of additional dollars in sales tax liability. Certainly this is a hollow victory for the newspapers and I seriously doubt the Court's conclusion that this result would have been intended by the ["Framers of the First Amendment"]. [Justice White concurred in part and dissented in part; Justice Blackmun joined the majority opinion except for one footnote.]

THE IMPLICATIONS AND LIMITS OF MINNEAPOLIS STAR

1. ***Is the press special?*** The Court in Minneapolis Star Tribune emphasizes the dangers involved in singling out "the press" for special regulatory treatment. Yet, as the preceding materials in this section illustrate, the Court typically has refused to recognize claims of the press to special protection beyond that available to anyone who exercises First Amendment rights by communicating information and opinion. Is the Court's focus on "the press" in Minneapolis Star Tribune therefore superfluous? Is it inconsistent with prior decisions? Or does this case suggest that in some areas the press *will* receive more protection than other claimants under the First Amendment?

If the latter reading is unwarranted and there remains nothing constitutionally special about the press, what was the Court's ground for employing strict scrutiny in Minneapolis Star Tribune? That singling out the press presumptively risks content discrimination, as exemplified by the overt bias of Huey Long in Grosjean? Does Minneapolis Star Tribune suggest that certain subjects—e.g., criticism of government in a broad sense—will receive special protection? Does Minneapolis Star Tribune treat the press as an especially highly protected format of communication? Should it be permissible, by analogy, for zoning regulations to single out bookstores or billboards for special treatment?

2. ***Slippery slopes.*** Although couched in different terms, Justice Rehnquist's objections to the majority's creation of a prophylactic rule to safeguard the press against future abuses of the taxing power raise the perennial problem of the use and misuse of "slippery slope" arguments. The same argument appears in numerous guises, including the search for a "stopping point," the fear of "a foot in the door," the question of "Where do you draw the line?," and the wariness of abuse of power. Regardless of how phrased, the point is the same—if we permit this seemingly innocuous exercise of a power, we are on a slippery slope leading inevitably to much more dangerous exercises of that same power. See generally Schauer, "Slippery Slopes," 99 Harv. L. Rev. 361 (1985).

The contrast between the majority and Justice Rehnquist's dissent makes Minneapolis Star an appropriate vehicle for reconsidering under what circumstances, if any, a currently innocuous exercise of power should be precluded for fear that it will lead to a far less innocuous abuse. Is Court review of every abuse likely? Will such review be timely? If the Court cannot check every abuse, can lower courts serve that function? Can nonjudicial bodies be trusted to follow the spirit as well as the letter of constitutional decisions? But does eagerness to decide cases on the basis of where a currently innocuous policy might lead fly in the face of the Court's reluctance to decide anything other than the case before it? Is a slippery slope argument a variant of an advisory opinion, in the sense that the basis for the decision is a hypothetical scenario that may never occur? Could we not prevent all abuses of power by granting no power whatsoever?

3. ***Antimedia, intramedium and intermedia discrimination.*** In **Arkansas Writers' Project, Inc. v. Ragland**, 481 U.S. 221 (1987), the Court relied on Minneapolis Star in striking down an Arkansas sales tax scheme that exempted newspapers and "religious, professional, trade and sports journals" but not other types of magazines. Part V of Justice O'Connor's opinion in Minneapolis had relied on the existence of discrimination *within* the class of publications, as opposed to distinctions between newspapers and other commodities. This more overt form of content discrimination was the basis for the Court's decision in Ragland. Justice MARSHALL found that the Arkansas exemption not only resembled the $100,000 exemption in Minneapolis Star, but also was even more troublesome because "a magazine's tax status depends entirely on its *content.*" He noted that this type of content-based regulation "does not evade the strictures of the First Amendment merely because it does not burden the expression of particular *views* by specific magazines." Justice SCALIA, joined by Chief Justice Rehnquist, dissented, for reasons paralleling those articulated in Justice Rehnquist's dissent in Minneapolis Star. He argued as well that the selective tax exemption should not be subject to strict scrutiny because it amounted to a subsidy that infringed no one's rights. He commented: "Are government research grant programs or the funding activities of the Corporation for Public Broadcasting subject to strict scrutiny because they provide money for the [study] of some subjects but not others? Because there is no principled basis to distinguish the subsidization of speech in [such an area]—which we would surely uphold—from the subsidization that we strike down here, our decision today places the granting or denial of protection within our own idiosyncratic discretion."

Contrast with Arkansas Writers' Project the decision in **Leathers v. Medlock**, 499 U.S. 439 (1991), upholding a selective sales tax exemption scheme. Arkansas imposed a sales tax on most goods and services, including cable television, but exempted newspapers, magazines and direct satellite broadcast services. Cable operators and subscribers challenged the selective exemption under the First Amendment. The Court rejected the challenge. Justice O'CONNOR, writing for the Court, found Arkansas' tax scheme distinguishable from the ones struck down in Minneapolis Star and Ragland: "[Those] cases demonstrate that differential taxation of First Amendment speakers is constitutionally suspect when it threatens to suppress the expression of particular ideas or viewpoints. Absent a compelling justification, the government may not exercise its taxing power to single out the press. [A] tax is also suspect if it targets a small group of speakers. [Finally,] for reasons that are obvious, a tax will trigger heightened scrutiny under the First Amendment if it discriminates on the basis of the content of taxpayer speech.

"The Arkansas tax at issue here presents none of these types of discrimination. The Arkansas sales tax is a tax of general applicability. It applies to receipts from the sale of all tangible personal property and a broad range of services, unless within a group of specific exemptions. [The] tax does not single out the press. [Furthermore,] there is no indication in this case that Arkansas has targeted cable television in a purposeful attempt to interfere with its First Amendment activities. [Unlike] the taxes involved in Grosjean and Minneapolis Star, the Arkansas tax has not selected a narrow group to bear fully the burden of the tax. The danger from a tax scheme that targets a small number of speakers is the danger of censorship; a tax on a small number of speakers runs the risk of affecting only a limited range of views. The risk is similar to that from content-based regulation: It will distort the market for ideas. [There] is no comparable danger from a tax on the services provided by a large number of cable operators offering a wide variety of programming throughout the State. [This] is not a tax structure that resembles a penalty for particular speakers or particular ideas." Finally, Justice O'Connor rejected cable's argument that the "intermedia discrimination" effected by the tax scheme was impermissible: "Regan v. Taxation with Representation stands for the proposition that a tax scheme that discriminates among speakers does not implicate the First Amendment unless it discriminates on the basis of ideas."

Justice MARSHALL dissented, joined by Justice Blackmun. He would have found that the intermedia discrimination here triggered strict scrutiny no less than the intramedium discrimination struck down in Minneapolis Star and Ragland: "Because cable competes with members of the print and electronic media in the larger information market, the power to discriminate between these media triggers the central concern underlying the nondiscrimination principle: the risk of covert censorship. [By] imposing tax burdens that disadvantage one information medium relative to another, the State can favor those media that it likes and punish those that it dislikes. [We] have previously recognized that differential taxation within an information medium distorts the marketplace of ideas by imposing on some speakers costs not borne by their competitors. Differential taxation across different media likewise 'limits the circulation of information to which the public is entitled,' where, as here, the relevant media compete in the same information market."

In **Turner Broadcasting v. FCC,** 512 U.S. 622 (1994) (Turner I), which held that requirements that cable operators carry broadcast signals were subject only to the level of scrutiny appropriate to content-neutral regulations, the Court found no impermissible discrimination against cable operators or programmers. First, it rejected the cable *operators'* argument "that strict scrutiny applies because the must-carry provisions single out certain members of the press—here, cable operators—for disfavored treatment." Justice KENNEDY wrote for the Court: "Regulations that discriminate among media, or among different speakers within a single medium, often present serious First Amendment concerns. [Minneapolis Star, Arkansas Writers' Project.] It would be error to conclude, however, that the First Amendment mandates strict scrutiny for any speech regulation that applies to one medium (or a subset thereof) but not others. [Leathers.] As Leathers illustrates, the fact that a law singles out a certain medium, or even the press as a whole, 'is insufficient by itself to raise First Amendment concerns.' The taxes invalidated in Minneapolis Star and Arkansas Writers' Project [targeted] a small number of speakers, and thus threatened to 'distort the market for ideas.' But such heightened scrutiny is unwarranted when the differential treatment is 'justified by some special characteristic of' the particular medium being regulated. The must-carry provisions [are] justified by special characteristics of the cable medium: the bottleneck monopoly power exercised by cable operators and the dangers this power poses to the viability of broadcast television. Appellants do not argue, nor does it appear, that other media [that] transmit video programming such as [satellite] are subject to bottleneck monopoly control, or pose a demonstrable threat to the survival of broadcast television. It should come as no surprise, then, that Congress decided to impose the must-carry obligations upon cable operators only. [Moreover,] the regulations are broad-based, applying to almost all cable systems in the country, rather than just a select few. As a result, the provisions do not pose the same dangers of suppression and manipulation that were posed by the more narrowly targeted regulations in Minneapolis Star and Arkansas Writers' Project [and thus] do not call for strict scrutiny."

Second, the Court likewise rejected cable *programmers'* argument that strict scrutiny was called for "because the must-carry provisions favor one set of speakers (broadcast programmers) over another (cable programmers). [Not] all speaker-partial laws are presumed invalid. Rather, [speaker-based] laws demand strict scrutiny when they reflect the Government's preference for the substance of what the favored speakers have to say (or aversion to what the disfavored speakers have to say). [Congress] granted must-carry privileges to broadcast stations on the belief that the broadcast television industry is in economic peril due to the physical characteristics of cable transmission and the economic incentives facing the cable industry. Thus, the fact that the provisions benefit broadcasters and not cable programmers does not call for strict scrutiny under our precedents."

4. ***Laws of general applicability.*** In **Cohen v. Cowles Media Co.**, 501 U.S. 663 (1991), the Court held that the First Amendment did not bar an action in state court for promissory estoppel against a newspaper that breached its promise of confidentiality to a source. Dan Cohen, who worked for the Republican candidate for governor in the 1982 election, leaked to the Minneapolis Star and another paper documents indicating that a Democratic candidate for lieutenant governor had had two criminal charges brought against her. The papers promised him confidentiality, but later made the editorial judgment to identify him as the source in their stories. He was fired

by his employer as a result. Cohen sued the papers for breach of contract and fraud and won $200,000 in compensatory and $500,000 in punitive damages from a jury. The Minnesota Supreme Court found the fraud and contract theories untenable but held that the compensatory damages judgment could be sustained on a promissory estoppel theory, except that it would violate the newspapers' First Amendment rights. The Supreme Court reversed and remanded, finding no First Amendment bar to a promissory estoppel action.

Justice WHITE wrote for the Court: "Respondents [rely on a line of cases holding] that 'if a newspaper lawfully obtains truthful information about a matter of public significance then state officials may not constitutionally punish publication of the information, absent a need to further a state interest of the highest order.' [E.g., Landmark, Fla. Star.] [This] case, however, is not controlled by this line of cases but, rather, by the equally well-established line of decisions holding that generally applicable laws do not offend the First Amendment simply because their enforcement against the press has incidental effects on its ability to gather and report the news. As the cases relied on by respondents recognize, the truthful information sought to be published must have been lawfully acquired. The press may not with impunity break and enter an office or dwelling to gather news. Neither does the First Amendment relieve a newspaper reporter of the obligation shared by all citizens to respond to a grand jury subpoena and answer questions relevant to a criminal investigation, even though the reporter might be required to reveal a confidential source. [Branzburg.] The press, like others interested in publishing, may not publish copyrighted material without obeying the copyright laws. [Zacchini.] Similarly, the media must obey the National Labor Relations Act, Associated Press v. NLRB, 301 U.S. 103 (1937), and the Fair Labor Standards Act, Oklahoma Press Publishing Co. v. Walling, 327 U.S. 186 (1946); may not restrain trade in violation of the antitrust laws, Associated Press v. United States, 326 U.S. 1 (1945); Citizen Publishing Co. v. United States, 394 U.S. 131 (1969); and must pay non-discriminatory taxes, [Murdock; Minneapolis Star.] Accordingly, enforcement of such general laws against the press is not subject to stricter scrutiny than would be applied to enforcement against other persons or organizations.

"There can be little doubt that the Minnesota doctrine of promissory estoppel is a law of general applicability. It does not target or single out the press. Rather, [the] doctrine is generally applicable to the daily transactions of all the citizens of Minnesota. The First Amendment does not forbid its application to the press. [Respondents] and amici argue that permitting Cohen to maintain a cause of action for promissory estoppel will inhibit truthful reporting because news organizations will have legal incentives not to disclose a confidential source's identity even when that person's identity is itself newsworthy. [But] if this is the case, it is no more than the incidental, and constitutionally insignificant, consequence of applying to the press a generally applicable law that requires those who make certain kinds of promises to keep them."

Justice BLACKMUN, joined by Justices Marshall and Souter, dissented. He regarded the lawsuit as penalizing the content of the newspapers' speech and thus as controlled by such cases as Hustler v. Falwell: "There, we found that the use of a claim of intentional infliction of emotional distress to impose liability for the publication of a satirical critique violated the First Amendment. There was no doubt that Virginia's tort of intentional infliction of emotional distress was 'a law of general applicability' unrelated to the suppression of speech. Nonetheless, a unanimous Court found that, when used to penalize the expression of opinion, the law was subject to the strictures of the First Amendment. [As] in Hustler, the operation of Minnesota's doctrine of promissory estoppel in this case cannot be said to have a merely 'incidental' burden on speech; the publication of important political speech is the claimed violation. Thus, as in Hustler, the law may not be enforced to punish the expression of truthful information or opinion."

Justice SOUTER, joined by Justices Marshall, Blackmun and O'Connor, also dissented, finding that, even if the promissory estoppel law did have general applicability, "it [is still] necessary to articulate, measure, and compare the competing interests involved [to] determine the legitimacy of burdening constitutional interests." He emphasized the "importance of the information to public discourse" and argued that "[t]he importance of this public interest is integral to the balance that should be struck in this case. There can be no doubt that the fact of Cohen's identity expanded the universe of information relevant to the choice faced by Minnesota voters in that State's 1982 gubernatorial election, the publication of which was thus of the sort quintessentially subject to strict First Amendment. The propriety of his leak to respondents could be taken to reflect on his character, which in turn could be taken to reflect on the character of the candidate who had retained him as an adviser. An election could turn on just such a factor; if it should, I am ready to assume that it would be to the greater public good, at least over the long run."

Was the newspapers' argument in Cowles Media consistent with the journalists' argument in Branzburg? In Branzburg, the press claimed that any pressure to reveal the names of confidential sources would dry up those sources, reducing the flow of information to the public. In Cowles, the press claimed that it had a First Amendment right to reveal its sources' names, and that this revelation would serve the interest in ensuring the flow of information to the public—an argument Justice Souter endorsed in his dissent. How can both these arguments hold simultaneously? Was the press trying to have its cake and eat it too? For exploration of the issues raised in Cowles, see Levi, "Dangerous Liaisons: Seduction and Betrayal in Confidential Press-Source Relations," 43 Rutgers L. Rev. 609 (1991).

THE FIRST AMENDMENT AND THE BROADCAST MEDIA

To what extent are constitutional restrictions on regulation of the print media applicable to the broadcast media? To what extent may broadcasters be treated differently? That issue has arisen in materials covered earlier. Recall, e.g., FCC v. Pacifica (1978; p. 1100 above), which justified regulation of an indecent radio broadcast on the ground that broadcasting is uniquely intrusive into the home and accessible to children. Recall also the emphasis on the unique nature of broadcasting in Red Lion (1969; p. 1402 above), in which the Court permitted government to enforce rights of access to broadcasting based on the scarcity of the over-the-air spectrum.

In both Pacifica and Red Lion, the Court upheld restrictions upon broadcasters that would have been impermissible if imposed on those seeking to communicate by print or the non-broadcast spoken word. For example, the Court held, in contrast to Pacifica, that offended audiences must simply avert their eyes or ears if they saw Cohen's jacket at a courthouse or received Bolger Drug Products' condom advertisements in the mail. And the Court held, in contrast to Red Lion, that a governmentally imposed right of access violated the First Amendment rights of the Miami Herald newspaper in Tornillo (1974; p. 1402 above). In contrast, the Court allowed government to impose greater access obligations on the broadcast media, rejecting First Amendment challenges beginning with Red Lion.

To understand the cases that follow, it is helpful to consider briefly the background of broadcast regulation. As the Court recounted in Red Lion: "Before 1927, the allocation of frequencies was left entirely to the private sector, and the result was chaos. It quickly became apparent that broadcast frequencies constituted a scarce resource whose use could be regulated and rationalized only by the Government. Without government control, the medium would be of little use because of the cacophony of competing voices, none of which could be clearly and predictably heard." Accordingly, Congress enacted the Radio Act of 1927 and the Communications Act of 1934. As the Court recounted in Turner Broadcasting: "In the Communications Act of 1934, Congress created a system of free broadcast service and directed that communications facilities be licensed across the country in a 'fair, efficient, and equitable' manner. Congress designed this system of allocation to afford each community of appreciable size an over-the-air source of information and an outlet for exchange on matters of local concern. [It] has long been a basic tenet of national communications policy that 'the widest possible dissemination of information from diverse and antagonistic sources is essential to the welfare of the public.' " The 1934 Act created the Federal Communications Commission (FCC) and authorized it to confer licenses on broadcasters and to regulate the broadcast spectrum "as public convenience, interest, or necessity requires." Licenses provide for use but not ownership of a portion of the broadcast spectrum. The Court upheld broadcast licensing in National Broadcasting Co. v. United States, 319 U.S. 190 (1943). For an overview of the tension between broadcasting law and ordinary free speech principles, see Weinberg, "Broadcasting and Speech," 81 Calif. L. Rev. 1101 (1993). For commentary critical of broadcast licensing in particular, see Coase, "The Federal Communications Commission," 2 J. L. & Econ. 1 (1959); Spitzer, "The Constitutionality of Licensing Broadcasters," 64 N.Y.U. L Rev. 990 (1989).

SCARCITY AND ACCESS

1. ***Right-of-reply obligations on the broadcasting media.*** May government safeguard individual reputations by requiring a broadcaster to afford reply time to the target of an attack? When government has sought to vindicate the interest in private reputation by authorizing defamation actions, the Court has sharply curtailed suits against the press. But when the FCC sought to provide rights of access for individuals attacked on the air and imposed requirements that radio and television stations give reply time, the Court sustained the regulations against the claim that they violated the First Amendment rights of the broadcaster. May government regulate the media with the aim of improving the marketplace of ideas?

Red Lion Broadcasting Co. v. FCC, 395 U.S. 367 (1969), rejected broadcasters' First Amendment challenge to the FCC "fairness doctrine," which required licensed broadcast stations to present discussion of public issues, to assure fair coverage for each side, and to provide free reply time in response to certain personal attacks and political editorials. In sustaining those regulations in Red Lion, Justice WHITE's opinion for a unanimous Court reasoned that restricting the editorial discretion of the broadcasting media would "enhance rather than abridge the freedoms of speech and press." He emphasized the "scarcity of broadcast frequencies, the Government's role in allocating those frequencies, and the legitimate claims of those unable without governmental assistance to gain access to those frequencies for expression of their views." He began from the supposition that "differences in the characteristics of news media justify differences in the First Amendment standards applied to them. Just as the Government may limit the use of sound amplifying equipment potentially so noisy that it drowns out civilized private speech, so may the Government limit the use of broadcast equipment." He continued:

"Where there are substantially more individuals who want to broadcast than there are frequencies to allocate, it is idle to posit an unabridgeable First Amendment right to broadcast comparable to the right of every individual to speak, write, or publish. If 100 persons want broadcast licenses but there are only 10 frequencies to allocate, all of them may have the same 'right' to a license; but if there is to be any effective communication by radio, only a few can be licensed and the rest must be barred from the airwaves. It would be strange if the First Amendment, aimed at protecting and furthering communications, prevented the Government from making radio communication possible by requiring licenses to broadcast and by limiting the number of licenses so as not to overcrowd the spectrum.

"[A] license permits broadcasting, but the licensee has no constitutional right to be the one who holds the license or to monopolize a radio frequency to the exclusion of his fellow citizens. There is nothing in the First Amendment which prevents the Government from requiring a licensee to share his frequency with others and to conduct himself as a proxy or fiduciary with obligations to present those views and voices which are representative of his community and which would otherwise, by necessity, be barred from the airwaves. [It] is the right of the viewers and listeners, not the right of the broadcasters, which is paramount. It is the purpose of the First Amendment to preserve an uninhibited marketplace of ideas in which truth will ultimately prevail, rather than to countenance monopolization of that market, whether it be by the Government itself or a private licensee. [It]is the right of the public to receive suitable access to social, political, esthetic, moral, and other ideas and experiences which is crucial here.

"[We cannot] say that it is inconsistent with the First Amendment goal of producing an informed public capable of conducting its own affairs to require a broadcaster to permit answers to personal attacks occurring in the course of discussing controversial issues, or to require that the political opponents of those endorsed by the station be given a chance to communicate with the public. Otherwise, station owners and a few networks would have unfettered power to make time available only to the highest bidders, to communicate only their own views on public issues, people and candidates, and to permit on the air only those with whom they agreed. There is no sanctuary in the First Amendment for unlimited private censorship operating in a medium not open to all.

"It is strenuously argued, however, that if political editorials or personal attacks will trigger an obligation in broadcasters to afford the opportunity for expression to speakers who need not pay for time and whose views are unpalatable to the licensees, then broadcasters will be irresistibly forced to self-censorship and their coverage of controversial public issues will be eliminated or at least rendered wholly ineffective. Such a result would indeed be a serious matter, for should licensees actually eliminate their coverage of controversial issues, the purposes of the doctrine would be stifled. [At] this point, however, as the Federal Communications Commission has indicated, that possibility is at best speculative.

"[It] does not violate the First Amendment to treat licensees given the privilege of using scarce radio frequencies as proxies for the entire community, obligated to give suitable time and attention to matters of great public concern. To condition the granting or renewal of licenses on a willingness to present representative community views on controversial issues is consistent with the ends and purposes of those constitutional provisions forbidding the abridgment of freedom of speech and freedom of the press. In view of the scarcity of broadcast frequencies, the Government's role in allocating those frequencies, and the legitimate claims of those unable without governmental assistance to gain access to those frequencies for expression of their views, we hold the regulations and ruling at issue here are both authorized by statute and constitutional."

Justice White noted in a footnote: "We need not deal with the argument that even if there is no longer a technological scarcity of frequencies limiting the number of broadcasters, there nevertheless is an economic scarcity in the sense that the Commission could or does limit entry to the broadcasting market on economic grounds and license no more stations than the market will support. [A] related argument, which we also put aside, is that quite apart from scarcity of frequencies, technological or economic, Congress does not abridge freedom of speech or press by legislation directly or indirectly multiplying the voices and views presented to the public through timesharing, fairness doctrines, or other devices which limit or dissipate the power of those who sit astride the channels of communication with the general public."

For commentary on the problems raised by Red Lion, see, e.g., Bollinger, "Freedom of the Press and Public Access: Toward a Theory of Partial Regulation of the Mass Media," 75 Mich. L. Rev. 1 (1976); Van Alstyne, "The Mobius Strip of the First Amendment: Perspectives on Red Lion," 29 S.C. L. Rev. 539 (1978); and Krattenmaker & Powe, "The Fairness Doctrine Today: A Constitutional Curiosity and An Impossible Dream," 1985 Duke L.J. 151; Powe, "Or of The [Broadcast] Press," 55 Tex. L. Rev. 39 (1976).

2. ***The limits of Red Lion: technological versus economic scarcity.*** Note that the Red Lion opinion emphasized technological scarcity and expressly declined to reach the broader argument that government may compel access or otherwise regulate speech in order to solve problems of economic scarcity. In Tornillo, Chief Justice BURGER reviewed and rejected, with respect to the print press, arguments for "an enforceable right of access to the press" and the concomitant claim "that Government has an obligation to ensure that a wide variety of views reach the public." Access advocates emphasized the concentration of power in the newspaper business and the

shrinking number of newspapers, noted the disappearance of real opportunity to form competing newspapers by dissidents, and accordingly urged "that the only effective way to insure fairness and accuracy" is "for government to take affirmative action." But the Court in Tornillo was not persuaded: "However much validity may be found in these arguments, at each point the implementation of a remedy such as an enforceable right of access necessarily calls for some mechanism, either governmental or consensual. If it is governmental coercion, this at once brings about a confrontation with the [First Amendment]." For the position of "access advocates," see Barron, "Access to the Press—A New First Amendment Right," 80 Harv. L. Rev. 1641 (1967), and Lange, "The Role of the Access Doctrine in the Regulation of the Mass Media," 52 N. Car. L. Rev. 1 (1973). For reflections on Tornillo, see Powe, "Tornillo," 1987 Sup. Ct. Rev. 345. For a later effort to generalize the holding of Red Lion to broader settings, see Fiss, "Free Speech and Social Structure," 71 Iowa L. Rev. 1405 (1986).

3. ***Repeal of the fairness doctrine.*** The fairness doctrine, despite its validation in Red Lion, was subject to considerable criticism. Broadcasters resisted being treated less protectively than other media. Some observers charged that the doctrine perversely made television and radio blander rather than more diverse because it gave stations an incentive to avoid controversial editorials and pointed attacks. Others criticized it as unadministrable. Above all it was criticized for obsolescence: the expanded capacity of the electromagnetic spectrum and the growth of programming competition from cable and satellite diminished the "scarcity" rationale.

In August 1987, the FCC repealed the fairness doctrine, after an extensive administrative proceeding noting the rise of competition in information services markets and finding that the doctrine "chilled" the First Amendment rights of broadcasters. See Syracuse Peace Council, 2 FCC Rec. 5043 (1987); FCC, Fairness Doctrine Obligations of Broadcast Licensees, 102 F.C.C.2d 142 (1985). In announcing the repeal, then-FCC chairman Mark Fowler stated: "The First Amendment does not guarantee a fair press, only a free press."

4. ***A constitutional right of access to the broadcasting media for editorial advertisements?*** Red Lion held that the First Amendment permitted access obligations to be imposed on broadcasters. But does the First Amendment compel such access? The Court answered this question in the negative three years after Red Lion in **Columbia Broadcasting, Inc. v. Democratic National Comm.**, 412 U.S. 94 (1973). The CBS case originated with complaints filed before the FCC in 1970 by the Democratic National Committee and an anti-war group challenging certain broadcasters' policies of refusing all editorial advertisements. The FCC sustained the broadcasters' position, but the Court of Appeals reversed, holding that "a flat ban on paid public issue announcements is in violation of the First Amendment, at least when other sorts of paid announcements are accepted." The Supreme Court held that, even assuming the broadcasters' refusal amounted to state action, broadcasters were not constitutionally required to accept such advertisements.

Chief Justice BURGER's opinion for the Court rejected the argument that a broad right of access could be drawn from the Red Lion ruling. Instead, he emphasized the statutory indications "that Congress intended to permit private broadcasting to develop with the widest journalistic freedom consistent with its public obligations." He emphasized that even broadcasters have substantial editorial discretion, and concluded: "To agree that debate on public issues should be 'robust, and wide-open' does not mean that we should exchange 'public trustee' broadcasting, with all its limitations, for a system of self-appointed editorial commentators." Chief Justice Burger cautioned against constitutionally mandating an extension of the fairness doctrine: "The Commission's responsibilities under a right-of-access system would tend to draw it into a continuing case-by-case determination of who should be heard and when." Moreover, he noted "the reality that in a very real sense listeners and viewers constitute a 'captive audience.'"

Justice DOUGLAS's concurrence took a far firmer constitutional position on the side of the broadcasters: "My conclusion is that TV and radio stand in the same protected position under the First Amendment as do newspapers and magazines." The Red Lion case, in which he had not participated, curtailed broadcasters' rights unduly, he insisted, since "the First Amendment puts beyond the reach of government federal regulation of news agencies save only business or financial practices which do not involve First Amendment rights." Justice BRENNAN's extensive dissent, joined by Justice Marshall, concluded, in "balancing" the competing interests, that the broadcasters' "absolute ban on editorial advertising" could "serve only to inhibit, rather than to further" robust public debate. He insisted that the fairness doctrine was "insufficient" to provide that kind of debate. He noted not only the interests of broadcasters and of the listening and viewing public, "but also the independent First Amendment interest of groups and individuals in effective self-expression." Drawing on access principles developed in the public forum context, he commented: "[F]reedom of speech does not exist in the abstract. On the contrary, the right to speak can flourish only if it is allowed to operate in an effective forum—whether it be a public park, a schoolroom, a town meeting hall, a soapbox, or a radio and television frequency. For in the absence of an effective means of communication, the right to speak would ring hollow indeed." Accordingly, "in light of the current dominance of the electronic media as the most effective means of reaching the public, any policy that *absolutely* denies citizens access to the airwaves" was unjustifiable.

5. ***A statutory right of access to the broadcasting media for candidates seeking federal elective office.*** Sec. 312(a)(7) of the Communications Act of 1934, as added by the Federal Election Campaign Act of 1971, authorizes the FCC to revoke a broadcaster's license "for willful or repeated failure to allow reasonable access to or to permit purchase of reasonable amounts of time for the use of a broadcasting station by a legally qualified candidate for Federal elective office on behalf of his candidacy." The 6–3 decision in **CBS, Inc. v. FCC**, 453 U.S. 367 (1981), found that this provision created a major new statutory right of access—a right that enlarged the political broadcasting responsibilities of licensees. The Court also held that the FCC's interpretation and application of the provision did not violate broadcasters' First Amendment rights. The controversy originated in October 1979, when the Carter-Mondale Presidential Committee asked each of the three major television networks to sell the Committee a half-hour of early December 1979 air time. The Committee sought to broadcast a documentary on the record of the Carter Administration, to augment President Carter's planned announcement of his candidacy for re-election. All three networks denied the request, relying on their across-the-board rules about political broadcasts. The Committee filed

a complaint, and the FCC ruled that the networks' reasons were "deficient" under the FCC's interpretation of the statute. The FCC concluded that the networks had violated the law by failing to provide "reasonable access." Chief Justice BURGER—who had emphasized "the widest journalistic freedom" for broadcasters in CBS v. DNC (p. 1547 above)—wrote the majority opinion. Justice WHITE's dissent, joined by Justices Rehnquist and Stevens, strongly disagreed with Chief Justice Burger's broad reading of the law and with the Court's endorsement of the FCC standards and their application.

Can CBS v. DNC and CBS v. FCC be reconciled? Are broadcasters better viewed as conduits for speech or as speakers and editors in their own right? Are they both? Do the two CBS decisions simply reflect consistent judicial deference to the expertise of the FCC?

6. ***The standard of review in broadcasting cases.*** Recall that the Court, in **FCC v. League of Women Voters**, 468 U.S. 364 (1984), invalidated 47 U.S.C. § 399, which prohibited "editorializing" by noncommercial educational broadcasting stations receiving public funds from the Corporation for Public Broadcasting. The Court found the law to be content-based, but nonetheless held that the special features of broadcasting dictated applying a standard lower than strict scrutiny. Justice BRENNAN, writing for the Court, stated that regulation of the content of broadcasting would be upheld "only when we [are] satisfied that the restriction is narrowly tailored to further a substantial governmental interest, such as ensuring adequate and balanced coverage of public issues." Because the restriction on expression of editorial opinion was found to lie "at the heart of First Amendment protection," the Court applied its standard carefully and found the government's justifications insufficient to justify the restriction.

7. ***Speaker access to public television.*** **Arkansas Educational Television Comm'n (AETC) v. Forbes**, 523 U.S. 666 (1998), which rejected a free speech challenge to the exclusion of a candidate from a candidate debate televised by a public broadcasting station, raised the question of what First Amendment constraints apply to the exercise of journalistic judgment by public broadcasters. Justice KENNEDY, writing for the majority, suggested that First Amendment obligations of neutrality might not apply at all to most decisions by public broadcasters to exclude speakers: "In the case of television broadcasting, [broad] rights of access for outside speakers would be antithetical, as a general rule, to the discretion that stations and their editorial staff must exercise to fulfill their journalistic purpose and statutory obligations. [Television] broadcasters enjoy the 'widest journalistic freedom' consistent with their public responsibilities. Among the broadcaster's responsibilities is the duty to schedule programming that serves the 'public interest, convenience, and necessity.' Public and private broadcasters alike are not only permitted, but indeed required, to exercise substantial editorial discretion in the selection and presentation of their programming. As a general rule, the nature of editorial discretion counsels against subjecting broadcasters to claims of viewpoint discrimination. Programming decisions would be particularly vulnerable to claims of this type because even principled exclusions rooted in sound journalistic judgment can often be characterized as viewpoint-based. Much like a university selecting a commencement speaker, a public institution selecting speakers for a lecture series, or a public school prescribing its curriculum, a broadcaster by its nature will facilitate the expression of some viewpoints instead of others. Were the judiciary to require, and so to define

and approve, pre-established criteria for access, it would risk implicating the courts in judgments that should be left to the exercise of journalistic discretion. [This] is not to say the First Amendment would bar the legislative imposition of neutral rules for access to public broadcasting. Instead, we say that, in most cases, the First Amendment of its own force does not compel public broadcasters to allow third parties access to their programming." The majority in AETC nonetheless applied a First Amendment requirement of viewpoint neutrality in the particular context of a televised candidate debate, finding it satisfied as Forbes was excluded on the basis of popularity, not platform.

In dissent, Justice STEVENS wrote that a public broadcaster ought to be subject to greater obligations of neutrality than the majority had enforced. Echoing his dissent in FCC v. League of Women Voters (p. 1324 above), he wrote: "Because AETC is owned by the State, deference to its interest in making ad hoc decisions about the political content of its programs necessarily increases the risk of government censorship and propaganda in a way that protection of privately owned broadcasters does not."

THE INFORMATION AGE

The past fifty years have produced rapid changes in media technology and modes of mass communication. Are traditional First Amendment principles applicable to the internet and ever-changing modes of communication? Or are new principles needed to suit changing technologies?

1. ***Cable television and the First Amendment.*** The First Amendment status of cable was long unsettled. The cable industry argued against application of Red Lion or any other lesser standard of protection, reasoning that technological scarcity is not an issue on cable systems. On the other hand, cable is in part a vehicle for broadcasting transmission, and cable systems depend on the grant of municipal franchises, including rights-of-way over streets and utility poles. Government has sometimes taken the position that cable is more like broadcasting than like print media by virtue of these facts, and therefore more regulable.

The Supreme Court put to rest this debate in **Turner Broadcasting v. FCC**, 512 U.S. 622 (1994) (Turner I). In the course of rejecting the cable industry's argument for strict scrutiny of the requirement that it carry certain broadcast signals, the Court rejected any argument for applying Red Lion or extending it by analogy to the cable context. Justice KENNEDY wrote for the Court: "There can be no disagreement on an initial premise: Cable programmers and cable operators engage in and transmit speech, and they are entitled to the protection of the speech and press provisions of the First Amendment. [Leathers.] Through 'original programming or by exercising editorial discretion over which stations or programs to include in its repertoire,' cable programmers and operators 'seek to communicate messages on a wide variety of topics and in a wide variety of formats.' Los Angeles v. Preferred Communications, Inc., 476 U.S. 488 (1986). [The] Government [contends] that regulation of cable television should be analyzed under the same First Amendment standard that applies to regulation of broadcast television. It is true that our cases have permitted more intrusive regulation of broadcast speakers than of speakers in other media. Compare [Red Lion with Tornillo.] But the rationale for applying a less rigorous standard of First Amendment scrutiny to broadcast regulation, whatever its validity in the cases elaborating it, does not apply in the context of cable regulation.

"The justification for our distinct approach to broadcast regulation rests upon the unique physical limitations of the broadcast medium. As a general matter, there are more would-be broadcasters than frequencies available in the electromagnetic spectrum. And if two broadcasters were to attempt to transmit over the same frequency in the same locale, they would interfere with one another's signals, so that neither could be heard at all. The scarcity of broadcast frequencies thus required the establishment of some regulatory mechanism to divide the electromagnetic spectrum and assign specific frequencies to particular broadcasters. In addition, the inherent physical limitation on the number of speakers who may use the broadcast medium has been thought to require some adjustment in traditional First Amendment analysis to permit the Government to place limited content restraints, and impose certain affirmative obligations, on broadcast licensees.

"[Although] courts and commentators have criticized the scarcity rationale since its inception, we have declined to question its continuing validity as support for our broadcast jurisprudence, and see no reason to do so here. The broadcast cases are inapposite in the present context because cable television does not suffer from the inherent limitations that characterize the broadcast medium. Indeed, given the rapid advances in fiber optics and digital compression technology, soon there may be no practical limitation on the number of speakers who may use the cable medium. Nor is there any danger of physical interference between two cable speakers attempting to share the same channel. In light of these fundamental technological differences between broadcast and cable transmission, application of the more relaxed standard of scrutiny adopted in Red Lion and the other broadcast cases is inapt when determining the First Amendment validity of cable regulation.

"[Although] the Government acknowledges the substantial technological differences between broadcast and cable, it advances a second argument for application of the Red Lion framework to cable regulation. It asserts that the foundation of our broadcast jurisprudence is not the physical limitations of the electromagnetic spectrum, but rather the 'market dysfunction' that characterizes the broadcast market. Because the cable market is beset by a similar dysfunction, the Government maintains, the Red Lion standard of review should also apply to cable. While we agree that the cable market suffers certain structural impediments, the Government's argument is flawed in two respects. First, as discussed above, the special physical characteristics of broadcast transmission, not the economic characteristics of the broadcast market, are what underlies our broadcast jurisprudence. Second, the mere assertion of dysfunction or failure in a speech market, without more, is not sufficient to shield a speech regulation from the First Amendment standards applicable to nonbroadcast media. See, e.g., [Austin, MCFL, Tornillo.]"

Accordingly, Justice Kennedy proceeded to use ordinary First Amendment principles—in particular, the distinction between content-based and content-neutral laws—to analyze the must-carry rules. He did, however, find cable's particular characteristics relevant in applying those principles, and thus found cable's "chokehold" monopoly relevant to the determination that the must-carry rules were content-neutral: "When an individual subscribes to cable, the physical connection between the television set and the cable network gives the cable operator bottleneck, or gatekeeper, control over most (if not all) of the television programming that is channeled into the subscriber's home. Hence, simply by virtue of its ownership of the essential pathway for cable speech, a cable operator can prevent its subscribers from obtaining access to programming it chooses to exclude. A cable operator, unlike speakers in other media, can thus silence the voice of competing speakers with a mere flick of the switch. The potential for abuse of this private power over a central avenue of communication cannot be overlooked. The First Amendment's command that government not impede the freedom of speech does not disable the government from taking steps to ensure that private interests not restrict, through physical control of a critical pathway of communication, the free flow of information and ideas."

In **Denver Area Educational Telecommunications Consortium v. FCC**, 518 U.S. 727 (1996), which struck down some but not other cable indecency regulations (see p. 1109 above), the plurality opinion expressly declined to decide whether cable is more analogous to print or to broadcasting. As Justice BREYER explained for the plurality in declining to analogize cable either to a common carrier or to a bookstore: "Both categorical approaches suffer from the same flaws: they import law developed in very different contexts into a new and changing environment, and they lack the flexibility necessary to allow government to respond to very serious practical problems without sacrificing the free exchange of ideas the First Amendment is designed to protect." Justice SOUTER elaborated in concurrence: "All of the relevant characteristics of cable are presently in a state of technological and regulatory flux. [Thus] we should be shy about saying the final word today about what will be accepted as reasonable tomorrow." Justice THOMAS, joined by Chief Justice Rehnquist and Justice Scalia in partial dissent, found the plurality's approach unsatisfactory and would have preferred to state directly that cable's First Amendment protection was equivalent to that of the print press: "Our First Amendment distinctions between media, dubious from their infancy, placed cable in a doctrinal wasteland in which regulators and cable operators alike could not be sure whether cable was entitled to the substantial First Amendment protections afforded the print media or was subject to the more onerous obligations shouldered by the broadcast media. Over time, however, we have drawn closer to recognizing that cable operators should enjoy the same First Amendment rights as the nonbroadcast media. [In] Turner, we stated expressly what we had implied in Leathers: The Red Lion standard does not apply to cable television. [In] Turner, by adopting much of the print paradigm, and by rejecting Red Lion, we adopted with it a considerable body of precedent that governs the respective First Amendment rights of competing speakers. In Red Lion, we had legitimized consideration of the public interest and emphasized the rights of viewers, at least in the abstract. Under that view, 'it is the right of the viewers and listeners, not the right of the broadcasters, which is paramount.' After Turner, however, that view can no longer be given any credence in the cable context. It is the operator's right that is preeminent."

Municipal governments have typically exacted from cable operators the requirement that they dedicate one or more channels to the government as public access channels to be used for public, educational or governmental purposes. Federal legislation governing the cable industry has explicitly permitted such arrangements, and has additionally required that cable operators dedicate a certain number of "leased access" channels for programming from sources unaffiliated with them. Does compulsion to provide public access and leased access channels raise any serious First Amendment issue? Although this issue was not directly presented in Denver Area, Justice Thomas's opinion questioned the constitutionality of requiring public access and leased access channels in the first place: "There is no getting around the fact that leased and public access are a type of forced speech. Though the constitutionality of leased and public access channels is not directly at issue in these cases, the position adopted by the Court in Turner ineluctably leads to the conclusion that the federal access requirements are subject to some form of heightened scrutiny. Following Turner, some commentators have questioned the constitutionality of leased and public access. Such questions are not at issue here." But he argued that even if such access were assumed to be constitutional, cable programmers and viewers had no First Amendment right to insist that any particular programming be shown.

If public access channels are constitutionally created, then do they function as public forums? Justice KENNEDY's opinion in Denver Area took such a view, and thus concluded that government could not authorize content-based discrimination on such channels: "Public access channels meet the definition of a public forum. We have recognized two kinds of public forums. The first and most familiar are traditional public forums, like streets, sidewalks, and parks, which by custom have long been open for public assembly and discourse. 'The second category of public property is the designated public forum, whether of a limited or unlimited character—property that the State has opened for expressive activity by part or all of the public.' Public access channels fall in the second category. Required by the franchise authority as a condition of the franchise and open to all comers, they are a designated public forum of unlimited character. The House Report for the 1984 Cable Act [characterized] public access channels as 'the video equivalent of the speaker's soapbox or the electronic parallel to the printed leaflet. They provide groups and individuals who generally have not had access to the electronic media with the opportunity to become sources of information in the electronic marketplace of ideas.' "

On this view, must a public access channel permit a program by a racist speaker whose speech does not rise to the level of Brandenburg incitement? An indecent program that is not obscene or otherwise proscribed by law? Note Justice Thomas's reply to Justice Kennedy in Denver Area: "Public access channels are [not] public fora. [Cable] systems are not public property. Cable systems are privately owned and privately managed, and [no] case [holds] that government may designate private property a public forum [absent] at least some formal easement or other property interest."

2. ***Net neutrality and the First Amendment.*** Though the questions raised in Turner and Denver Area may seem quaint in the internet age, do they foreshadow potential First Amendment issues with net neutrality policies? The principle of "net neutrality," adopted by the Federal Communications Commission most recently in 2015, requires internet service providers to provide access to all content on the internet so that the internet would remain open to all users and uses. Does net neutrality vindicate the "the right of the public to receive suitable access to social, political, [and] esthetic" ideas that the Court highlighted in Red Lion? Does

it resemble the must-carry provision at stake in Turner? Do internet service providers present the same "potential for abuse of [private power] over a central avenue of communication" as did the cable operators in Turner? Or would the providers' lack of monopoly power—at least in some places—mean that they could prevail on their own First Amendment challenge to such policies?

3. ***The internet and the First Amendment.*** The rapid expansion of the internet presents numerous questions about the parameters of free speech protection and the proper extent of government regulation and control. Proponents of regulation cite the potential for uncontrolled dissemination of pornography, rampant copyright infringement, and the proliferation of harassment and unwanted invasions of privacy. Critics of regulatory frameworks argue that the legislative and judicial response cannot keep pace with the growth of technology; thus, the market should be allowed to develop technological solutions to these problems on its own.

The internet allows individuals to be their own content publishers. An important threshold issue is how to characterize the nature of the speech that occurs in these mediums. A single web page can contain commercial advertisements, political speech, and obscene material. The information can either be contained in the website, or it can take the form of links to other web pages.

On-line postings can also present difficult issues about the responsibility for the content of the postings if found to be libelous or defamatory. Should internet service providers be considered conduits for the distribution of information or publishers with editorial control? What about the companies on whose platforms or sites the communications appear? Who should bear the liability for harassment through threatening postings either to newsgroups or directly to personal e-mail accounts? Does the fact that members of the university community have access to e-mail and campus newsgroups as part of the educational mission of the university alter the level of administrative responsibility (and hence liability) for objectionable conduct perpetuated over the network? Is it constitutionally permissible for a university to restrict students' access to protected material, for example, by prohibiting students from downloading indecent material?

The issue of transmission of obscene as well as indecent material over the internet is complicated by its technological mechanics. How should a court determine the proper forum for evaluating whether a particular transmission is obscene? At the point of origin (the server where the information is stored)? At various points along the message route? At the point where the user downloads the material? See United States v. Thomas, 74 F.3d 701 (6th Cir.1996), cert. denied, 519 U.S. 820 (1996). Whose community standards should be used in evaluating whether a transmission is obscene? The community of internet users? The community where the download occurs? Where the upload occurs? Who will be ultimately liable for the transmission? The individuals who upload the material onto a web site or newsgroup, the individuals who download the material onto their individual hard drives, or the internet service providers through whose servers and networks these transmissions take place?

Should questions about speech on the internet be resolved by finding the most appropriate analogies between existing law on the protection of speech rights and the characteristics of this new medium? For instance, are websites more like bookstores or newspapers? Are internet service providers more like common carriers or do they have some responsibility to regulate the content that passes through their networks? Are online service providers (e.g., Google) more like distributors of information provided by third parties or publishers of content? Are social media platforms public squares or company towns? Is the internet a pervasive and invasive medium like broadcasting (Pacifica) and cable (Denver Area) where content is pushed into the eyes and ears of viewers? Or is the internet best understood as more of a "pull" technology where participants must venture out and subscribe to newsgroups and mailing lists, download data from remote sites, and type in web addresses in order to view particular pages? If this pull interpretation prevails, regulation of speech on the internet may require the development of entirely new analogies and constitutional frameworks. On the other hand, if the internet comes to be dominated by "push" technologies, which allow subscribers to request and receive custom content, analogies to broadcast and cable may appear more applicable. Push services go to favorite web sites, automatically download data, send updates, and push the data directly onto the subscriber's hard drive, thereby alleviating the need for subscribers to venture out onto the web in order to pull the data themselves. Push technologies further complicate the search for parallels to prior methods of constitutional analysis. Just as web pages and bulletin boards give everyone the opportunity to be a publisher, so push technologies promise everyone the opportunity to be his or her own broadcaster. Does this vast communication potential demand the imposition of a regulatory scheme to prevent abuses or does it represent the ultimate free marketplace of ideas where speech can best be countered by more speech?

The Court first addressed such questions in **Reno v. ACLU**, 521 U.S. 844 (1997), reported in full at p. 1111 above. Writing for the Court, Justice STEVENS exhaustively recounted the three-judge district court's findings about the characteristics of the internet, and expressly rejected any analogy between the internet and the broadcasting medium: "[Decisions such as Red Lion v. FCC and FCC v. Pacifica] relied on the history of extensive government regulation of the broadcast medium; the scarcity of available frequencies at its inception; and its 'invasive' nature. Those factors are not present in cyberspace. [The] vast democratic fora of the Internet [have never] been subject to the type of government supervision and regulation that has attended the broadcast industry. Moreover, the Internet is not as 'invasive' as radio or television. The District Court specifically found that 'communications over the Internet do not 'invade' an individual's home or appear on one's computer screen unbidden. Users seldom encounter content 'by accident.' '[Finally,] unlike the conditions that prevailed when Congress first authorized regulation of the broadcast spectrum, the Internet can hardly be considered a 'scarce' expressive commodity. It provides relatively unlimited, low-cost capacity for communication of all kinds, [including] not only traditional print and news services, but also audio, video, and still images, as well as interactive, real-time dialogue. Through the use of chat rooms, any person with a phone line can become a town crier with a voice that resonates farther than it could from any soapbox. Through the use of Web pages, mail exploders, and newsgroups, the same individual can become a pamphleteer. As the District Court found, 'the content on the Internet is as diverse as human thought.' We agree with its conclusion that our cases provide no basis for qualifying the level of First Amendment scrutiny that should be applied to this medium."

In **Packingham v. North Carolina**, 582 U.S. ___, 137 S. Ct. 1730 (2017), discussed above (p. 1269), the Court addressed state exclusion of a sex offender from social media platforms. Acknowledging the limits of the Court's understanding, Justice KENNEDY wrote: "While we now may be coming to the realization that the Cyber Age is a revolution of historic proportions, we cannot appreciate yet its full dimensions and vast potential to alter how we think, express ourselves, and define who we want to be. The forces and directions of the Internet are so new, so protean, and so far reaching that courts must be conscious that what they say today might be obsolete tomorrow."

Does the Court's view of technology demonstrate a valid sense of humility in engaging with changing technology? Or is it unnecessarily fatalistic in forgoing any attempt to impose a comprehensive doctrine? As technological change increasingly leads to the convergence of media, all accessed from a single device, does it any longer make sense to treat First Amendment freedoms as varying by medium?

CHAPTER 14

THE RELIGION CLAUSES: FREE EXERCISE AND ESTABLISHMENT

The role that religion should play in public life has often been a divisive problem in American society. Religious values determine not only where many citizens stand on the issues of abortion, euthanasia, the death penalty, stem-cell research and same-sex marriage, but also whether the government should take a position on these topics at all. The closely related issue of the proper relationship between church and state leads to particularly vitriolic debate: Must religious student groups be allowed to meet on public school grounds? Should courthouses be able to display the Ten Commandments? Although the answers to these questions and others are doctrinally controversial, they lie at the heart of the country's identity—and the country's divisions.

The First Amendment provides that "Congress shall make no law respecting an establishment of religion, or prohibiting the free exercise thereof." The two clauses, commonly referred to as the "Establishment Clause" and the "Free Exercise Clause," have given rise to separate bodies of case law. But this should not obscure the fact that the two clauses are interrelated. They protect overlapping values, yet sometimes exert conflicting pressures. Consider the common practice of exempting church property from taxation. Does the benefit conveyed by government to religion via that exemption constitute an "establishment"? Would the "free exercise" of religion be unduly burdened if church property were not exempted from taxation? Articulating satisfactory criteria to accommodate the potentially conflicting emanations of the two religion clauses is a recurrent challenge in this chapter.

Sections 1 and 2 consider respectively the original history of the religion clauses and the problem of defining religion. Section 3 examines ways in which government may be said to abridge the free exercise of religion. The most direct way is by deliberately prohibiting or disadvantaging a religious sect or its central practices. While such laws are rare in contemporary society, the Court has subjected them to the strictest scrutiny. A harder case is presented when religious objections are raised to the application of general regulations that as applied restrict religious exercise in particular situations. For example, may the Amish claim constitutional exemption from compulsory education laws? The story of the Court's answer to this question has undergone dramatic twists and turns. Such an exemption was denied by the Court for Mormon plural marriage in 1878, the very first time it decided a free exercise case. The principle of non-exemption was reaffirmed in the first flag salute case, Minersville School Dist. v. Gobitis (1940), which itself was repudiated (though not overturned) in West Virginia v. Barnette (1942). In Shebert v. Verner (1963), the Warren Court held free exercise to require some religious exemptions from generally applicable laws. In Employment Division v. Smith (1990), the Rehnquist Court drastically narrowed the scope of such compelled exemptions. Congress sought to reverse Smith by providing for statutory religious exemption claims under the Religious Freedom Restoration Act of 1993, but the Court struck down that law as exceeding Congress's power as applied to state practices in City of Boerne (see p. 902 above). Congress subsequently enacted the Religious Land Use and Institutionalized Persons Act of 2000, which partially restored exemptions in state zoning matters and for prisoners, and the doctrinal trend may now be tending back toward exemptions.

Section 4 focuses on three Establishment Clause issues: the rendering of government financial aid to activities conducted by religious organizations; religion in the public schools; and the use or apparent endorsement of religious teachings or symbols by governmental bodies. Lastly, Section 5 considers how the two clauses may be reconciled: it asks when government is *permitted* to exempt religiously motivated practices from general laws, even if it is not compelled to do so, and whether government ever *must* exempt certain practices despite the fact that the government believes that, in doing so, it would violate the Establishment Clause.

The principal tension in the Establishment Clause cases is among conceptions of government neutrality: Does the clause require a "wall of separation" between church and state? Does it require formal neutrality, whereby government never adverts to religion, for advantage or for disadvantage? Or does it require simply that government treat religious organizations and activities equally, including them in any benefit schemes generally enjoyed by others?

SECTION 1. A BRIEF HISTORY OF THE RELIGION CLAUSES

One of the primary ways in which courts interpret the religion clauses is through the lens of original understanding. Just as controversial as the Supreme Court's jurisprudence interpreting the religion clauses, then, are the historical narratives upon which those interpretations are based. Over the past century, two competing narratives have emerged: The first, "separationism," argues that the Framers intended a secular government and strong divisions between church and state. The second, "nonpreferentialism," asserts that the Framers established a Christian nation and sought only to restrict the national government from preferring one sect over another. This section attempts to set forth a brief, more neutral history of the religion clauses. It then discusses the two narratives constructed by the Court in greater depth, casting doubt on both interpretations.

1. ***The broad outlines of a history of the religion clauses.*** The American movement toward institutional separation of church and state began with the Declaration of Independence in 1776, when the states began the process of drafting new constitutions to replace their colonial charters. In New England, the stronghold of the Congregationalist Church, the states had long collected mandatory taxes to support local ministers, subject to exemptions for religious dissenters who obtained certificates. Rhode Island, founded by dissenter Roger Williams, and Pennsylvania, founded by Quaker

William Penn, never had established churches. In the rest of the country, colonial charters had established the Church of England. Now, throughout the country, the religious minorities of the time—mainly Baptists, Presbyterians, and Quakers—began to advocate for the elimination of state policies requiring them to support churches with their tax dollars.

These dissenters made little headway in New England, but in Virginia, a constitutional convention passed a Declaration of Rights stating that "religion, or the duty which we owe to our Creator, and the manner of discharging it, can be directed only by reason and conviction, not by force or violence; and therefore all men are equally entitled to the free exercise of religion according to the dictates of consciences." The law also freed Virginians from any sort of mandatory church attendance, guaranteed freedom of belief, and exempted them from mandatory tax assessments to support religion.

But some Virginians, including Patrick Henry, were concerned about the potential poverty of ministers and the stability of the state, which was often thought at the time to depend on strong religious institutions. They therefore proposed a new assessment that would tax citizens in support of the ministry of their choice. The proposal faced strong opposition from a coalition that included James Madison, who wrote his famous Memorial and Remonstrance in support of his position. Madison devoted almost the entirety of his argument in the Remonstrance to advocating for religious liberty. He argued that coercion on matters of conscience is wrong because true, meaningful belief is purely voluntary and cannot result from force. Government cannot coerce individuals to make decisions regarding their beliefs, as even the government cannot logically have control over beliefs. Accordingly, the right to liberty of conscience is "in its nature an inalienable right." Government and religion, then, must occupy two separate spheres.

Madison developed these views from his reading of seventeenth-century British philosopher John Locke, who believed that the human conscience should be left free and that consequently religion must occupy a sphere of its own, protected from the coercive power of the state. At the time of the Revolution, many Americans took the further step of arguing that the government must not forcibly collect taxes to support religion against citizens' liberty of conscience.

Madison's opposition to any coerced tax assessment in Virginia succeeded. In 1786 the legislature passed The Virginia Bill for Religious Freedom, originally drafted by Thomas Jefferson in 1779, which enacted: "That no man shall be compelled to frequent or support any religious worship, place or ministry whatsoever, nor shall be enforced, restrained, molested, or burthened in his body or goods, nor shall otherwise suffer on account of his religious opinions or [belief]." Jefferson's preamble to the Bill declared that: "Almighty God hath created the mind free; that all attempts to influence it by temporal punishments or burthens, or by civil incapacitations, tend only to beget habits of hypocrisy and meanness, and are a departure from the plan of the Holy author of our religion, who being Lord both of body and mind, yet chose not to propagate it by coercions on [either]; that to compel a man to furnish contributions of money for the propagation of opinions which he disbelieves, is sinful and tyrannical; that even the forcing him to support this or that teacher of his own religious persuasion, is depriving him of the comfortable liberty of giving his contributions to the particular pastor, whose morals he would make his [pattern]." The Virginia statute, then, focused on protecting religion from the state, not the state from religion. The writings of Madison and his contemporaries are likewise directed at protecting the church from the state. Indeed, many thinkers at this time believed that religious belief actually supported the state by promoting honesty, loyalty and obedience.

By the time the Constitution was ratified, every state constitution guaranteed the liberty of conscience. No such provision, however, appeared in the U.S. Constitution. Madison himself argued that the Bill of Rights was useless: "[E]xperience proves the inefficacy of a bill of rights on those occasions when its controul is most needed. Repeated violations of these parchment barriers have been committed by overbearing majorities in every state." He also argued that the Bill of Rights was unnecessary, urging that, in a country of such size and diversity as the United States, opposed factions would control one another and prevent any single faction from gaining a majority. These structural protections were more efficacious than paper ones: "If there were a majority of one sect, a bill of rights would be a poor protection of liberty." See Finkelman, "James Madison and the Bill of Rights: A Reluctant Paternity," 1990 S. Ct. L. Rev. 301.

Nevertheless, the same religious minorities who had opposed compulsory tax assessments for religion protested the omission of guaranteed liberty of conscience during the ratification debates. Giving into political pressure, Madison spearheaded the effort to amend the Constitution. His draft Bill of Rights provided that "the civil rights of none shall be abridged on account of religious belief or worship, nor shall any national religion be established, nor shall the full and equal rights of conscience be in any manner, or on any pretext, infringed." The House Committee changed the language to read that "no religion shall be established by law, nor shall the equal rights of conscience be infringed." One Connecticut Congressman objected to the first clause of this draft language on the basis that his state's law, which compelled tax assessments for religion but allowed citizens to allocate those assessments to a church of their choice, might be construed as an establishment—a term with an almost universally negative connotation at this time. Madison responded that the Congressman should not be concerned; the Amendment would not apply to the states.

The draft language was then changed to read: "Congress shall make no laws touching religion, or infringing the rights of conscience," and then "Congress shall make no law establishing Religion, or prohibiting the free exercise thereof, nor shall the rights of conscience be infringed." It is unclear why the First Congress deleted the final phrase, but the remaining clauses guaranteed that no one would be compelled to support religion with which he or she disagreed and that Congress could not stop anyone from worshipping as he or she chose. Thomas Jefferson famously described the clauses as "building a wall of separation between Church & State" in his 1802 letter to the Baptists of Danbury, Connecticut.

2. ***The separationist view.*** One major historical interpretation emerging from this evidence is "separationism," which has two components: voluntarism and separatism. Proponents of this view argue that the Founders established a secular state walled off from religion and place particular emphasis on the writings and beliefs of Thomas Jefferson and James Madison.

Separationism was first hinted at by the Supreme Court in the 1878 case of **Reynolds v. United States**, 98 U.S. 145 (1878) (p. 1581, below). Chief Justice WAITE quoted Jefferson's letter to the Danbury Baptist Association, in which he wrote that the Establishment Clause "buil[t] a wall of separation between church and State." The view was later and most famously expounded by Justice BLACK, writing for the Court in **Everson v. Board of Education**, 330 U.S. 1 (1947) (p. 1617, below). Justice Black reviewed historical evidence, once again citing Jefferson to suggest that the Framers favored "a wall of separation":

"A large proportion of the early settlers of this country came here from Europe to escape the bondage of laws which compelled them to support and attend government-favored churches. The centuries immediately before and contemporaneous with the colonization of America had been filled with turmoil, civil strife, and persecutions generated in large part by established sects determined to maintain their absolute political and religious supremacy. With the power of government supporting them, at various times and places, Catholics had persecuted Protestants, Protestants had persecuted Catholics, Protestant sects had persecuted other Protestant sects, Catholics of one shade of belief had persecuted [other Catholics], and all of these had from time to time persecuted Jews. In efforts to force loyalty to whatever religious group happened to be on top and in league with the government of a particular time and place, men and women had been fined, cast in jail, cruelly tortured, and [killed].

"These practices of the old world were transplanted and began to thrive in the soil of the new America. The very charters granted by the English Crown to the individuals and companies designated to make the laws which would control the destinies of the colonials authorized these individuals and companies to erect religious establishments which all, whether believers or nonbelievers, would be required to support and attend. [These] practices became so commonplace as to shock the freedom-loving colonials into a feeling of abhorrence. The imposition of taxes to pay ministers' salaries and to build and maintain churches and church property aroused their indignation. It was these feelings which found expression in the First Amendment. [Virginia provided] able leadership for the movement. The people there, as elsewhere, reached the conviction that individual religious liberty could be achieved best under a government which was stripped of all power to tax, to support, or otherwise to assist any or all religions, or to interfere with the beliefs of any religious individual or group."

Justice RUTLEDGE, who dissented in Everson, nonetheless agreed with Justice Black about the original understanding of the religion clauses. Justice Rutledge's dissent put heavy emphasis on Madison's Remonstrance: "As the Remonstrance discloses throughout, Madison opposed every form and degree of official relation between religion and civil authority. For him religion was a wholly private matter beyond the scope of civil power either to restrain or to support. Denial or abridgment of religious freedom was a violation of rights both of conscience and of natural equality. State aid was no less obnoxious or destructive to freedom and to religion itself than other forms of state interference. 'Establishment' and 'free exercise' were correlative and coextensive ideas, representing only different facets of the single great and fundamental freedom. The Remonstrance, following the Virginia statute's example, referred to the history of religious conflicts and the effects of all sorts of establishments, current and historical, to suppress religion's free exercise. With Jefferson, Madison believed that to tolerate any fragment of establishment would be by so much to perpetuate restraint upon that freedom. Hence he sought to tear out the institution not partially but root and branch, and to bar its return forever."

Consider the following comment on the Black and Rutledge opinions: "What emerges from the Court's examination of history is a pair of fundamental principles [animating] the first amendment: voluntarism and separatism. [Voluntarism means] that the advancement of a church would come only from the voluntary support of its followers and not from the political support of the state. [Separatism means] that both religion and government function best if each remains independent of the other." Tribe, American Constitutional Law § 14–3 (2d ed. 1988). See also Van Alstyne, "Trends in the Supreme Court: Mr. Jefferson's Crumbling Wall—A Comment on Lynch v. Donnelly," 1984 Duke L.J. 770 ("Voluntarism [was] the principle of personal choice. Separatism was the principle of non-entanglement."). But consider also Feldman, Divided By God, 174–75 (2005) ("[T]he period of the framing was not characterized by general religious persecution. [By] contrast, recognition of the extent of Nazi persecution in Europe had indeed produced a shock to reasonable American minds by 1947 and was playing a real part in pushing Black and his colleagues to believe that the federal Constitution should be interpreted to protect religious minorities.").

3. ***The nonpreferentialist view.*** The historical account set forth in Everson by Justices Black and Rutledge has been relied upon as authoritative in many later decisions. But some dispute that account of the history of the religion clauses. One major account suggests that the First Amendment was intended merely to prevent "the establishment of a national church or religion, or the giving of any religious sect or denomination a preferred status." Cord, Separation of Church and State (1982). On this view, government might support religion in general so long as it does not prefer one religion over another. The First Amendment was intended not to protect the government from religion, but to protect religion from government by preventing the government from favoring one religion over another. In addition to the writings of Madison and Jefferson cited by Justice Black, nonpreferentialist scholars point to arguments made by Madison's and Jefferson's contemporaries, who scholars claim sought mainly to protect religious dissenters from government coercion. Although they had different reasons for doing so, then, these dissenters had banded together with Madison and Jefferson to fight for nonpreferentialism and nothing more.

Several Justices have found the nonpreferentialist view persuasive, though it has never commanded a majority of the Court. For example, in **Wallace v. Jaffree**, 472 U.S. 38 (1985) (p. 1646, below), Justice REHNQUIST wrote a dissent taking issue with the "wall of separation" metaphor. He read the history to indicate that Madison did not embrace a strict separationist view of the religion clauses at the time the religion clauses were framed. He emphasized that Madison originally proposed constitutional language barring the establishment of a "*national* religion" and argued that this proposal "obviously does not conform to the 'wall of separation' between church and State idea which latter-day commentators have ascribed to him." Justice Rehnquist concluded: "It seems indisputable from [glimpses] of Madison's thinking, as reflected by actions on the floor of the House in 1789, that he saw the Amendment as designed to prohibit the establishment of a national religion, and perhaps to prevent discrimination among sects. He did not see it as requiring neutrality on the part of government between religion and irreligion. Thus the Court's opinion in Everson—while correct in bracketing Madison and Jefferson together in their exertions in their home State leading to the enactment of the Virginia Statute of Religious Liberty—is totally incorrect in suggesting that Madison carried these views onto the floor of the United States House of Representatives when he proposed the language which would ultimately become the Bill of Rights." Justice Rehnquist also noted that the First Congress had provided for financial aid to sectarian schools in the Northwest Territory and for a presidential proclamation and prayer on the Thanksgiving holiday.

Similarly, concurring in **Rosenberger v. Rector**, 515 U.S. 819 (1995) (p. 1328, above), Justice THOMAS found "much to commend" in the view that "the Framers saw the Establishment Clause simply as a prohibition on governmental preferences for some religious faiths over others." He emphasized that the Virginia assessment that Madison opposed in the Remonstrance was a "Bill Establishing a Provision for Teachers of the Christian Religion." Thus, in Justice Thomas's view, "Madison's objection to the assessment bill did not rest on the premise that religious entities may never participate on equal terms in neutral government programs. [Rather, according] to Madison, the Virginia assessment was flawed because it 'violated that equality which ought to be the basis of every law.' [The] bill singled out religious entities for special benefits. [The] funding provided by the Virginia assessment was to be extended only to Christian sects, and the Remonstrance seized on this defect: 'Who does not see that the same authority which can establish Christianity, in exclusion of all other Religions, may establish with the same ease any particular sect of Christians, in exclusion of all other Sects.' " Justice Thomas also cited Justice Rehnquist's Jaffree dissent for evidence of Madison's nonpreferentialism in the House debates on the First Amendment, and cited "historical examples of [public] funding [of religion] that date back to the time of the founding. To take but one famous example, both Houses of the First Congress elected chaplains, [Congress] enacted legislation providing for an annual salary of $500 to be paid out of the Treasury, [and] Madison himself was a member of the committee that recommended the chaplain system in the House."

In several opinions, Justice SOUTER has sought to refute the nonpreferentialist arguments made by Justices Rehnquist and Thomas, relying in part upon Laycock, " 'Nonpreferential' Aid to Religion: A False Claim About Original Intent," 27 Wm. & Mary L. Rev. 875 (1986). In his concurrence in **Lee v. Weisman**, 505 U.S. 577 (1992) (p. 1648, below), Justice SOUTER wrote: "When James Madison arrived at the First Congress with a series of proposals to amend the National Constitution, one of the provisions read that 'the civil rights of none shall be abridged on account of religious belief or worship, nor shall any national religion be established, nor shall the full and equal rights of conscience be in any manner, or on any pretext, infringed.' Madison's language did not last long. It was [changed] to read that 'no religion shall be established by law, nor shall the equal rights of conscience be infringed' [and then] 'Congress shall make no laws touching religion, or infringing the rights of conscience' [and then] 'Congress shall make no law establishing Religion, or prohibiting the free exercise thereof, nor shall the rights of conscience be infringed.' [The] House [thus] rejected [a] version [that] arguably ensured only that 'no religion' enjoyed an official preference over others, and deliberately chose instead a prohibition extending to laws establishing 'religion' in general. [Indeed, the] Framers repeatedly considered and deliberately rejected such narrow language and instead extended their prohibition to state support for 'religion' in general."

4. ***The interpretations disputed.*** Some commentators have argued that both views are flawed. As an initial matter, both interpretations rely heavily on the writings of Jefferson and Madison. But Jefferson was not even in the country when the First Amendment was voted upon, and Madison, although he spearheaded the congressional effort to pass the Bill of Rights, did not initially believe the Constitution needed to be amended to protect religious freedom.

Commentators also point out that it is not clear that the Founders—at least at the time when they passed the First Amendment—were universally opposed to *any* "entanglement" of the state with religion. Indeed, at the time the First Amendment was passed, both Jefferson and Madison focused on protecting religion from the state. Consider the following argument: "[Jefferson's] focus was on the liberty of conscience and the necessity of individual judgment in finding truth, which he feared that the state might infringe. [At] the same time, Madison and his supporters in opposing [tax assessments supporting religion] and urging religious freedom also had the goal of protecting religion, not the state. [In] America, the establishment of religion by the government came to be seen as posing a fundamental danger to the liberty of conscience by threatening dissenters with the possibility of coercion. The constitutional guarantee of nonestablishment sought to protect conscience from coercion by guaranteeing a division between the institutional spheres of organized religion and government." Feldman, Divided by God 38, 47 (2005).

Nor is it clear that the Founders were concerned solely with nonpreferentialism. First, as noted above, the Founders appear to have been in substantial agreement that all should respect the liberty of conscience. Second, the bill against which Madison wrote his famous Remonstrance was nonpreferentialist in the sense that it treated all religious sects equally: it assessed taxes to support religious establishments, but taxpayers could choose to which religious establishment they directed their payments. Indeed, many of the New England states assessed taxes in similar fashion until 1820 on the ground that religion would fade without mandatory taxation to support it. Despite supporters' protestations to the contrary, dissenters derided the practice as both "establishing" whatever church was dominant and infringing on their liberty. Indeed, as noted above, one Connecticut Congressman objected to draft language of the First Amendment that "no religion shall be established by law" on the basis that his state's law might be construed as an establishment—to which Madison responded only that the Amendment would not apply to the states.

Are these historical debates at all relevant to contemporary interpretation of the religion clauses? Consider Justice BRENNAN's concurrence in Abington School Dist. v. Schempp (p. 1645, below): "A too literal quest for the advice of the Founding Fathers [seems] to me futile and misdirected. [The] historical record is at best ambiguous, and statements can readily be found to support either side of the proposition." Moreover, he added, "[o]ur religious composition makes us a vastly more diverse people than were our forefathers. They knew differences chiefly among Protestant sects. Today the Nation is far more heterogeneous religiously."

5. ***The incorporation of the religion clauses against the states.*** Free exercise of religion, like freedom of speech, is easily understood as the type of "liberty" that might be encompassed by the Fourteenth Amendment and thus applied to the states. The Establishment Clause presents a more difficult case for incorporation—particularly with regard to the nonpreferentialist interpretation of the religion clauses. At the time the First Amendment was adopted, several states, unlike Virginia, had established official churches; under one nonpreferentialist view, one of the motivations of the Establishment Clause was to bar Congress from interfering with state establishments. Thus Cord, supra, argues that the First Amendment was meant to "safeguard the right of freedom of conscience in religious beliefs against invasion solely by the national government [but] to allow the states, unimpeded, to deal with religious establishments and aid to religious institutions as they saw fit." See also Howe, The Garden and the Wilderness (1965). Similarly, Justice Thomas has expressed the view in his opinions that the text and history of the Establishment Clause "resist incorporation" against the states.

Nonetheless, the Court, beginning with Everson, has assumed that the Establishment Clause was incorporated into the Fourteenth Amendment and was therefore applicable to the states—without serious discussion of the federalism problem, or the additional textual difficulty of using the "liberty" of the Fourteenth Amendment as the incorporation route. Justice Brennan sought to fill these gaps in his concurrence in Schempp, supra: "It has been suggested, with some support in history, that [incorporation of the Establishment Clause] is conceptually impossible because the Framers meant the [clause] also to foreclose any attempt by Congress to disestablish the existing official state churches. [But] the last of the formal state establishments was dissolved more than three decades before the Fourteenth Amendment was ratified, and thus the problem of protecting official state churches from federal encroachments could hardly have been any concern of those who framed the post-Civil War Amendments.

"[It] has also been suggested that the 'liberty' guaranteed by the Fourteenth Amendment logically cannot absorb the Establishment Clause because that clause is not one of the provisions of the Bill of Rights which in terms protects a 'freedom' of the individual. The fallacy in this contention [is] that it underestimates the role of the Establishment Clause as a coguarantor, with the Free Exercise Clause, of religious liberty. The Framers did not entrust the liberty of religious beliefs to either clause alone."

SECTION 2. THE DEFINITION OF "RELIGION"

How should religion be distinguished from secular moral or philosophical beliefs? From matters of mere personal preference? How should religious organizations be distinguished from other nongovernmental associations commanding significant loyalty and adherence? These questions can be important in delimiting the scope of religious exemptions or in identifying when government benefits constitute establishments.

Although the Court has never given a definitive meaning to the word "religion" as it appears in the Constitution, it considered the scope of a statutory definition of "religion" in a series of cases arising in the Vietnam era under draft laws that provided for a conscientious objector exemption. Section 6(j) of the Universal Military Training and Service Act of 1948 exempted from combatant military service those persons who were conscientiously opposed to participation in "war in any form" by reason of their "religious training and belief." The latter phrase was defined by the law as a "belief in a relation to a Supreme Being involving duties superior to those arising from any human relation, but [not including] essentially political, sociological, or philosophical views or a merely personal moral code." (A 1967 amendment deleted the statutory reference to a "belief in a relation to a Supreme Being," after the 1966 conviction and three-year sentence that gave rise to Welsh, which follows.)

In **United States v. Seeger**, 380 U.S. 163 (1965), the Court interpreted the statutory term "religion" very broadly. Seeger stated on his selective service form that he preferred to leave the question about his belief in a Supreme Being "open" and that he believed in "goodness and virtue for their own sakes" and had "a religious faith in a purely ethical creed [without] belief in God, except in the remotest sense." Justice CLARK's opinion for the Court found Seeger entitled to the exemption: "[The] test of belief 'in a relation to a Supreme Being' is whether a given belief that is sincere and meaningful occupies a place in the life of its possessor parallel to that filled by the orthodox belief in God of one who clearly qualifies for the exemption. Where such beliefs have parallel positions in the lives of their respective holders we cannot say that one is 'in a relation to a Supreme Being' and the other is not." Justice Clark emphasized "the richness and variety of spiritual life in our country" and noted the writings of modern theologians, whose definitions of God differed from traditional theism. In a concurring opinion, Justice DOUGLAS stated that he "would have difficulties" if he "read the statute differently" from the Court: "For then those who embraced one religious faith rather than another would be subject to penalties; and that kind of discrimination, as we held in [Sherbert], would violate the Free Exercise Clause [and] would also result in a denial of equal protection by preferring some religions over others."

In **Welsh v. United States**, 398 U.S. 333 (1970), Justice BLACK's plurality opinion, joined by Justices Douglas, Brennan and Marshall, found an exemption appropriate even though Welsh had struck the word "religious" on his application: "[V]ery few registrants are fully aware of the broad scope of the word 'religious' as used in § 6(j)." Moreover, Welsh's claim was not barred by the exclusion in § 6(j) of those persons with "essentially political, sociological, or philosophical views or a merely personal moral code." That language, Justice Black concluded, should not be read "to exclude those who hold strong beliefs about our domestic and foreign affairs or even those whose conscientious objection to participation in all wars is founded to a substantial extent upon considerations of public policy. The two groups of registrants that obviously do fall within these exclusions from the exemption are those whose beliefs are not deeply held and those whose objection to war does not rest at all upon moral, ethical, or religious principle but instead rests solely upon considerations of policy, pragmatism, or expediency." Justice HARLAN, concurring in the result, found that § 6(j) must be read as limited to "those opposed to war in general because of theistic beliefs" but that, so read, § 6(j) was unconstitutional: Congress "cannot draw the line between theistic or nontheistic religious beliefs on the one hand and secular beliefs on the other. Any such distinctions are not, in my view, compatible with the Establishment Clause." He concluded that the Court, rather than nullifying the exemption entirely, should extend its coverage to those who, like Welsh, had been unconstitutionally excluded. Justice WHITE's dissent concluded that, whether or not Seeger was an accurate reflection of legislative intent, he could not join a "construction of § 6(j) extending draft exemption to those who disclaim religious objections to war and whose views about war represent a purely personal code arising not from religious training and belief as the statute requires but from readings in philosophy, history, and sociology." And he would have found that the "religious training and belief" requirement did not violate the Establishment Clause even were it not required by the Free Exercise Clause: "It is very likely that § 6(j) is a recognition by Congress of free exercise values. [That] judgment is entitled to respect."

The 8–1 decision in **Gillette v. United States**, 401 U.S. 437 (1971), held that Congress could constitutionally refuse to exempt those who did not oppose all wars but only particular conflicts. One such selective objector, for example, claimed that it was his duty as a faithful Catholic to discriminate between "just" and "unjust" wars, and to refuse to participate in the latter. Justice MARSHALL's majority opinion read the statute to require that "conscientious scruples relating to war and military service must amount to conscientious opposition to participating personally in any war and all war." He found the exemption constitutional as so construed. While "the Establishment Clause forbids subtle departures from neutrality, 'religious gerrymanders,' as well as obvious abuses, [still,] a claimant alleging 'gerrymander' must be able to show the absence of a neutral, secular basis for the lines government has drawn." And that showing had not been made here: "We conclude not only that the affirmative purposes underlying § 6(j) [such as the government's interest in 'fairness'] are neutral and secular, but also that valid neutral reasons exist for limiting the exemption to objectors to all war, and that the section therefore cannot be said to reflect a religious preference." He also found the government's interest sufficient to justify any burden on selective objectors' rights of free exercise. Justice DOUGLAS dissented, emphasizing the "implied First Amendment right" of "conscience" and arguing that the law worked "an invidious discrimination in favor of religious persons and against others with like scruples."

What distinguishes a religious pacifist from a pacifist whose beliefs rest only on "essentially political, sociological, or philosophical views or a merely personal moral code"? A belief in a "supreme being"? Why should that matter? Because it suggests a source of countervailing sovereignty to that of the state? A belief in a transcendent reality? A belief that one's activity will have consequences beyond one's lifetime? Participation in rituals such as prayer? Adherence to a sacred text? The fact that one is born into a religious "way of life" rather than acquiring it through individual choice? Doesn't that leave out converts to a faith? A belief that not all questions in the universe can be answered through human rationality? Why should that matter? Because it disables the religionist from participating fully in rationalist political debate? Is a religious exemption a kind of compensation for the disadvantage religious arguments suffer in secular politics? Is any of these features common to all religions?

Assuming that it is possible to define religion at all, should it be defined the same way for free exercise and establishment purposes? Consider the argument that religion should be defined broadly for free exercise but narrowly for Establishment Clause purposes. See Tribe, American Constitutional Law § 14–6 (1st ed. 1978). Such an approach would allow broad religious exemptions, but would not jeopardize every government action that reflects some arguably religious precept. Thus, for example, Mr. Seeger might receive his draft exemption on the ground that his pacifist beliefs were adequately "religious" for that purpose, but then teach his beliefs in a public school classroom without running afoul of the Establishment Clause. But a dual definition of religion "presents a number of problems, most importantly the first amendment's text." Tribe, American Constitutional Law § 14–6 (2d ed. 1988) (departing from his earlier approach). As Justice Rutledge wrote in his Everson dissent, " 'Religion' appears only once in the Amendment. But the word governs two prohibitions and governs them alike. It does not have two meanings." Might the Seeger problem be solved not by defining "religion" narrowly for Establishment Clause purposes, but rather by defining narrowly what constitutes an "establishment"?

THE LIMITS OF JUDICIAL INQUIRY INTO RELIGIOUS BELIEF

Why insist on an objective definition of religion? Why not allow religion to be subjectively defined by its adherents? One danger is that such a definition might invite fraud, and create the problem of religious "impostors." It might also expand the definition of religion so greatly that courts would respond by curtailing the substantive scope of free exercise protection. Cf. Fallon, "The Linkage Between Justiciability and Remedies—And Their Connections to Substantive Rights," 92 Va. L. Rev. 633, 637 (2006) (arguing that courts balance and adjust justiciability doctrines, available remedies, and the scope of substantive rights in order to avoid "practically intolerable or disturbingly sub-optimal" outcomes). On the other hand, secular inquiry into the truth or falsity of religious beliefs would appear to be a core violation of free exercise and nonestablishment. The Court tried to steer between these difficulties in **United States v. Ballard**, 322 U.S. 78 (1944). The defendants in Ballard were indicted under the federal mail fraud laws. They had solicited funds for the "I Am" movement. Among their representations were the claims that they had been selected as "divine messengers" to communicate the message of the "alleged divine entity, Saint Germain" and that they had, "by reason of supernatural attainments, the power to heal persons of ailments and diseases." Justice DOUGLAS's majority opinion stated that the First Amendment barred submission to the jury of "the truth or verity of respondents' religious doctrines or beliefs," though it did not bar submission to the jury of the question whether the defendants sincerely believed their representations. He commented: "Men may believe what they cannot prove. They may not be put to the proof of their religious doctrines or beliefs. [The] miracles of the New Testament, the Divinity of Christ, life after death, the power of prayer are deep in the religious convictions of many. If one could be sent to jail because a jury in a hostile environment found those teachings false, little indeed would be left of religious freedom." Justice Jackson, dissenting, expressed doubt whether the "sincerity" of beliefs could be examined without evaluating their content: "I do not see how we can separate an issue as to what is believed from considerations as to what is believable." Chief Justice Stone also dissented, joined by Justices Roberts and Frankfurter.

Is the Court's resolution of the difficulty here satisfactory? Can a jury find that defendants knew that their representations were false *without* inquiring into the truth or falsity of the underlying beliefs? Some argue that courts are competent to evaluate a claimant's sincerity because courts regularly consider questions of mental state in other contexts and can evaluate objective evidence such as whether a claimant tries to act in ways consistent with her claimed belief. See, e.g., Adams & Barmore, "Questioning Sincerity: The Role of the Courts After Hobby Lobby," 67 Stan. L. Rev. Online 59 (2014). For an argument that courts must look carefully at a claimant's sincerity in order to prevent fraud and reduce frivolous lawsuits, see Chapman, "Adjudicating Religious Sincerity," 92 Wash. L. Rev. 1185 (2017). Questions of sincerity are particularly relevant regarding groups whose beliefs may be satirical. For instance, the Church of the Flying Spaghetti Monster, or "Pastafarianism," proclaims that a Flying Spaghetti Monster created the universe, and its founder has been an outspoken advocate against teaching creationism and intelligent design in schools. In 2016 a federal judge in the District of Nebraska ruled that Pastafarianism is not a religion, but rather "a parody, intended to advance an argument about science, the evolution of life, and the place of religion in public education." Cavanaugh v. Bartelt, 178 F. Supp.3d 819, 824 (D. Neb. 2016). Consider also the comedian John Oliver's Our Lady of Perpetual Exemption, a church he founded to draw attention to religious organizations' tax-exempt status and sometimes problematic fundraising mechanisms.

Another source of controversy regarding judicial power to decide questions of religious doctrine has been the recurrent effort to draw courts into disputes arising from church schisms. Typically, the posture is that a church splits and both factions claim ownership of existing church property as the genuine "closest continuer" of the church; the court is asked to adjudicate the property dispute, which may entail ruling on which faction is the true church. The normal rule is that courts should try to stay out of internal church disputes. But "marginal judicial involvement" is permissible, so long as the courts do not decide church property disputes by "resolving underlying controversies [of] religious doctrine." The Court has said that courts may apply "[n]eutral principles of law, developed for use in all property disputes," in adjudicating church property controversies, but that the religion clauses preclude determining matters "at the very core of a religion—the interpretation of particular church doctrines and the importance of those doctrines to religion." See Presbyterian Church v. Hull Church, 393 U.S. 440 (1969). The Court has been sharply divided over the application of these guidelines. See, e.g., Jones v. Wolf, 443 U.S. 595 (1979).

While courts may apply "neutral principles of law" to decide church property disputes, there is less clarity about when courts may hear certain tort claims against religious organizations. Resolving some tort cases, such as whether a church negligently supervised a pastor who abused parishioners, could conceivably entangle the court in religion: determining what duty of care a church owes its congregation, or what the relationship between a pastor and a church should look like, could involve questions of religious doctrine. The Supreme Court has never directly addressed tort suits against religious groups, and state courts have split on which tort claims are permissible. See, e.g., Gibson v. Brewer, 952 S.W.2d 239 (Mo. 1997) (en banc) (holding a claim for negligent supervision of clergy would entangle the court in religion); Malicki v. Doe, 814 So.2d 347 (Fla. 2002) (holding a negligent supervision claim was permissible because the church did not claim its supervision of clergy was a religious question).

SECTION 3. THE FREE EXERCISE OF RELIGION

To some extent, claims based on the free exercise of religion overlap with free speech claims. For example, recall the free speech objections raised by members of Jehovah's Witnesses in cases such as Cantwell v. Connecticut, Lovell v. Griffin, Martin v. Struthers and Wooley v. Maynard. But the "free exercise" guarantee raises distinctive problems. *First*, "exercise" implies more than belief or expression; it often implies conduct or action. In many of the cases that follow, the free exercise claimant argues that a general law resting on state interests not related to religion either interferes with behavior dictated by religious belief or compels conduct forbidden by religious belief. Should government have more leeway to regulate conduct than belief? *Second*, the Establishment Clause has no parallel in the Speech Clause. In the religion context, however, it places limits on how far either legislatures or courts can go in exempting religious believers from general regulations, or otherwise accommodating free exercise values. The free exercise cases that follow look first at the question whether government may deliberately disadvantage religion or a particular religion, and second at whether religious practitioners are entitled to exemptions from generally applicable laws that conflict with dictates of their faith.

LAWS DISCRIMINATING AGAINST RELIGION

Free exercise clearly bars outlawing or compelling belief in a particular religious faith. As Chief Justice Burger stated in McDaniel v. Paty, which follows, "The Free Exercise Clause categorically prohibits government from regulating, prohibiting, or rewarding religious beliefs as such." Perhaps because this principle is so basic, free exercise controversies over such attempts at thought control are rare. In Torcaso v. Watkins, 367 U.S. 488 (1961), the Court struck down a Maryland requirement that all holders of public office declare their belief in the existence of God. The decision stated: "Neither the State nor the Federal Government can constitutionally force a person 'to profess a belief or disbelief in any religion,' " nor could they "aid those religions based on a belief in the existence of God as against those religions founded on different beliefs." Torcaso rested principally on the Free Exercise Clause, but also noted by way of analogy the religious test clause of Article VI: "[N]o religious Test shall ever be required as a Qualification to any Office or public Trust under the United States."

In **McDaniel v. Paty**, 435 U.S. 618 (1978), the Court invalidated, under the Free Exercise Clause, a Tennessee provision disqualifying clergy from being legislators or constitutional convention delegates. (Tennessee was the last state to retain the disqualification, once commonplace in state laws.) Chief Justice BURGER's plurality opinion, joined by Justices Powell, Rehnquist and Stevens, found the absolute bar on interference with religious *beliefs* inapplicable, because the state barrier referred to "*status* [as] 'minister' or 'priest' " and ministerial status was "defined in terms of conduct and activity rather [than] belief." The plurality nonetheless applied strict scrutiny to the disqualification's burden on religious practice, and found the State's rationale that it was preventing establishment of religion inadequate to support the ban: "[T]he American experience provides no persuasive support for the fear that clergymen in public office will be less careful of antiestablishment interests or less faithful to their oaths of civil office than their unordained counterparts." Separate concurrences by Justice BRENNAN, joined by Justice Marshall, and by Justice STEWART found that the disqualification did directly burden religious belief and thus was absolutely prohibited under Torcaso, without any further balancing. Justice Brennan wrote: "Clearly freedom of belief protected by the Free Exercise Clause embraces freedom to profess or practice that belief, even including doing so to earn a livelihood." Justice Stewart wrote: "The disability imposed on McDaniel, like the one imposed on Torcaso, implicates the 'freedom to believe' more than the less absolute 'freedom to act.' " (Note that both Torcaso and McDaniel rejected the government's argument that a public job or office is a mere "privilege" to which the state may attach conditions that would otherwise violate the First Amendment.)

Free exercise challenges arise more commonly when laws regulate religious practice or conduct. While previous eras have witnessed various forms of overt discrimination against disfavored religions, modern legislation rarely evinces outright hostility to particular religions or religious practices. Like overt racial bigotry, overt religious prejudice rarely appears on the face of contemporary laws. The Court has proved willing, however, to look behind the face of a statute to discern religiously discriminatory purpose, as illustrated in the Lukumi case, which follows. In Lukumi, the Court unanimously invalidated a city ordinance prohibiting the ritual slaughter of animals, finding that the law, while apparently neutral on its face, actually was targeted against practitioners of the Santería faith and thus violated the Free Exercise Clause:

Church of the Lukumi Babalu Aye v. City of Hialeah

508 U.S. 520, 113 S. Ct. 2217, 124 L. Ed. 2d 472 (1993).

■ JUSTICE KENNEDY delivered the opinion of the Court, except as to Part II–A–2.

[This] case involves practices of the Santeria religion, which originated in the nineteenth century. When hundreds of thousands of members of the Yoruba people were brought as slaves from eastern Africa to Cuba, their traditional African religion absorbed significant elements of Roman Catholicism. The resulting syncretion, or fusion, is Santeria, "the way of the saints." The Cuban Yoruba express their devotion to spirits, called orishas. [The] Santeria faith teaches that every individual has a destiny from God, a destiny fulfilled with the aid and energy of the orishas. The basis of the Santeria religion is the nurture of a personal relation with the orishas, and one of the principal forms of devotion is an animal sacrifice. [According] to Santeria teaching, the orishas are powerful but not immortal. They depend for survival on the sacrifice. Sacrifices are performed at birth, marriage, and death rites, for the cure of the sick, for the initiation of new members and priests, and during an annual celebration. Animals sacrificed in Santeria rituals include chickens, pigeons, doves, ducks, guinea pigs, goats, sheep, and turtles. The animals are killed by the cutting of the carotid arteries in the neck. The sacrificed animal is cooked and eaten, except after healing and death rituals. Santeria adherents faced widespread persecution in Cuba, so the religion and its rituals were practiced in secret. The open practice of Santeria and its rites remains infrequent.

[The Church's] announcement of plans to open a Santeria church in Hialeah[, Florida,] prompted the city council to hold an emergency public session on June 9, 1987. [The] city council adopted Resolution 87–66, which noted the "concern" expressed by residents of the city "that certain religions may propose to engage in practices which are inconsistent with public morals, peace or safety," and declared that "the City reiterates its commitment to a prohibition against any and all acts of any and all religious groups which are inconsistent with public morals, peace or safety." [In] September 1987, the city council adopted three substantive ordinances addressing the issue of religious animal sacrifice. Ordinance 87–52 defined "sacrifice" as "to unnecessarily kill, torment, torture, or mutilate an animal in a public or private ritual or ceremony not for the primary purpose of food consumption," and prohibited owning or possessing an animal "intending to use such animal for food purposes." It restricted application of this prohibition, however, to any individual or group that "kills, slaughters or sacrifices animals for any type of ritual, regardless of whether or not the flesh or blood of the animal is to be consumed." The ordinance contained an exemption for slaughtering by "licensed establishments" of animals "specifically raised for food purposes." [Ordinance] 87–71 [defined] sacrifice as had Ordinance 87–52, and then provided that "it shall be unlawful for any person, persons, corporations or associations to sacrifice any animal within the corporate limits of the City of Hialeah, Florida." The final Ordinance, 87–72, defined "slaughter" as "the killing of animals for food" and prohibited slaughter outside of areas zoned for slaughterhouse use. The ordinance provided an exemption, however, for the slaughter or processing for sale of "small numbers of hogs and/or cattle per week in accordance with an exemption provided by state law." All ordinances and resolutions passed the city council by unanimous vote. Violations [were] punishable by fines not exceeding $500 or imprisonment not exceeding 60 days, or both.

[At] a minimum, the protections of the Free Exercise Clause pertain if the law at issue discriminates against some or all religious beliefs or regulates or prohibits conduct because it is undertaken for religious reasons. Indeed, it was "historical instances of religious persecution and intolerance that gave concern to those who drafted the Free Exercise Clause." [If] the object of a law is to infringe upon or restrict practices because of their religious motivation, the law is not neutral; and it is invalid unless it is justified by a compelling interest and is narrowly tailored to advance that interest.

To determine the object of a law, we must begin with its text, for the minimum requirement of neutrality is that a law not discriminate on its face. [Petitioners] contend that three of the ordinances fail this test of facial neutrality because they use the words "sacrifice" and "ritual," words with strong religious connotations. We agree that these words are consistent with the claim of facial discrimination, but the argument is not conclusive. The words "sacrifice" and "ritual" have a religious origin, but current use admits also of secular meanings. [But] facial neutrality is not determinative. [The] Free Exercise Clause protects against governmental hostility which is masked, as well as overt.

[The] record in this case compels the conclusion that suppression of the central element of the Santeria worship service was the object of the ordinances. [The June 9 resolution aimed at] "certain religions" [and] it cannot be maintained that city officials had in mind a religion other than Santeria. It is [also] a necessary conclusion that almost the only conduct subject to Ordinances 87–40, 87–52, and 87–71 is the religious exercise of Santeria church members. [Ordinance] 87–71 excludes almost all killings of animals except for religious sacrifice, and the primary purpose requirement narrows the proscribed category even further, in particular by exempting Kosher slaughter. Operating in similar fashion is Ordinance 87–52, which prohibits the "possession, sacrifice, or slaughter" of an animal with the "intent to use such animal for food purposes" [but exempts] "any licensed [food] establishment" with regard to "any animals which are specifically raised for food purposes," if the activity is permitted by zoning and other laws. This exception, too, seems intended to cover Kosher slaughter. [Ordinance] 87–40 incorporates the Florida animal cruelty statute. Its prohibition is broad on its face, punishing "whoever . . . unnecessarily . . . kills any animal." The city claims that this ordinance is the epitome of a neutral prohibition. [But the city] deem[s] [k]illings for religious reasons [unnecessary but] deems hunting, slaughter of animals for food, eradication of insects and pests, and euthanasia as necessary. [The city's] application of the ordinance's test of necessity devalues religious reasons for killing by judging them to be of lesser import than nonreligious reasons. Thus, religious practice is being singled out for discriminatory treatment.

[The] legitimate governmental interests in protecting the public health and preventing cruelty to animals could be addressed by restrictions stopping far short of a flat prohibition of all Santeria sacrificial practice. [Counsel] for the city conceded at oral argument that, under the ordinances, Santeria sacrifices would be illegal even if they occurred in licensed, inspected, and zoned slaughterhouses. [With] regard to the city's interest in ensuring the adequate care of animals, regulation of conditions and treatment, regardless of why an animal is kept, is the logical response to the city's concern, not a prohibition on possession for the purpose of sacrifice.

[In Part II–A–2 of Justice Kennedy's opinion, which was joined only by Justices Stevens, Blackmun and O'Connor, he added: "In determining if the object of a law is a neutral one under the Free Exercise Clause, we can also find guidance in our equal protection cases. [Here], as in equal protection cases, we may determine the city council's object from both direct and circumstantial evidence. [Arlington Heights.] [The] minutes and taped excerpts of the June 9 session, both of which are in the record, evidence significant hostility exhibited by residents, members of the city council, and other city officials toward the Santeria religion and its practice of animal sacrifice. The public crowd that attended the June 9 meetings interrupted statements by council members critical of Santeria with cheers and the brief comments of [the Church's leader] with taunts. When [a council member supporting the ordinances] stated that in prerevolution Cuba 'people were put in jail for practicing this religion,' the audience applauded. [One council member said that the] 'Bible says we are allowed to sacrifice an animal for consumption,' [and] continued, 'but for any other purposes, I don't believe that the Bible allows that.' [The] chaplain of the Hialeah Police Department told the city council that Santeria was a sin, 'foolishness,' 'an abomination to the Lord,' and the worship of 'demons.' [This] history discloses the object of the ordinances to target animal sacrifice by Santeria worshippers because of its religious motivation." Resuming his opinion for the Court, Justice Kennedy continued:]

In sum, [the] ordinances had as their object the suppression of religion. The pattern we have recited discloses animosity to Santeria adherents and their religious practices; the ordinances by their own terms target this religious exercise; the texts of the ordinances were gerrymandered with care to proscribe religious killings of animals but to exclude almost all secular killings; and the ordinances suppress much more religious conduct than is necessary in order to achieve the legitimate ends asserted in their defense.

[A] law burdening religious practice that is not neutral or not of general application must undergo the most rigorous of scrutiny. [It] follows from what we have already said that these ordinances cannot withstand this scrutiny. First, even were the governmental interests compelling, [all] four ordinances are overbroad or underinclusive. [The] absence of narrow tailoring suffices to establish the invalidity of the ordinances. [Moreover,] [w]here government restricts only conduct protected by the First Amendment and fails to enact feasible measures to restrict other conduct producing substantial harm or alleged harm of the same sort, the interest given in justification of the restriction is not compelling. [Reversed.]

■ JUSTICE SCALIA, joined by CHIEF JUSTICE REHNQUIST, concurring in part and concurring in the judgment.

I do not join [Part II–A–2] because it departs from the opinion's general focus on the object of the laws at issue to consider the subjective motivation of the lawmakers, i.e., whether the Hialeah City Council actually intended to disfavor the religion of Santeria. [But] it is virtually impossible to determine the singular "motive" of a collective legislative body, and this Court has a long tradition of refraining from such inquiries. [The] First Amendment does not refer to the purposes for which legislators enact laws, but to the effects of the laws enacted: "Congress shall make no law . . . prohibiting the free exercise [of religion]. . . ." This does not put us in the business of invalidating laws by reason of the evil motives of their authors. Had the Hialeah City Council set out resolutely to suppress the practices of Santeria, but ineptly adopted ordinances that failed to do so, I do not see how those laws could be said to "prohibit the free exercise" of religion. Nor, in my view, does it matter that a legislature consists entirely of the pure-hearted, if the law it enacts in fact singles out a religious practice for special burdens. Had the ordinances here been passed with no motive on the part of any councilman except the ardent desire to prevent cruelty to animals (as might in fact have been the case), they would nonetheless be invalid.

[Justice SOUTER filed an opinion concurring in part and in the judgment and Justice BLACKMUN, joined by Justice O'Connor, filed an opinion concurring in the judgment. Both these opinions found this an easy case for invalidation, reasoning that, in Justice Souter's words, Hialeah had enacted "a rare example of a law actually aimed at suppressing religious exercise," and that such a law is nearly always invalid. Justices Souter and Blackmun declined to join all of Justice Kennedy's opinion, however, because it referred in dicta to aspects of Employment Division v. Smith (1997; p. 1593 below) that they found objectionable.]

IDENTIFYING ANTIRELIGIOUS PURPOSE

1. ***Lukumi and religious gerrymanders.*** Justice Kennedy called the law in Lukumi a "religious gerrymander"—that is, "an impermissible attempt to target petitioners and their religious practices." Like drawing a district boundary so as to include or exclude members of a particular race or political party, the Hialeah law was drawn with definitions and exceptions that in practice singled out Santería for adverse treatment.

Hialeah's law was struck down under the Free Exercise Clause. But the Court has also struck down "religious gerrymanders" under the Establishment Clause. For example, in **Larson v. Valente**, 456 U.S. 228 (1982), the Court struck down a Minnesota law imposing registration and reporting requirements for charitable solicitations and exempting some, but not all, religious organizations from the law. The requirements applied only to religious organizations that solicit more than 50% of their funds from nonmembers. The Court found that this scheme violated the "clearest command of the Establishment Clause": "one religious denomination cannot be officially preferred over another." The law was challenged by the Unification Church, which consists of followers of Rev. Sun Myung Moon, on the ground that it preferred traditional over untraditional religions.

In invalidating the 50% rule, Justice BRENNAN's majority opinion applied strict scrutiny and found the law not closely tailored to any government interest in preventing fraudulent or abusive solicitation practices. He emphasized Minnesota's "*selective* legislative imposition of burdens and advantages upon particular denominations," noting that "the provision was drafted with the explicit intention of including particular religious denominations and excluding others." One state senator observed that other lawmakers seemed to have a religious animus toward groups that were included, stating, " 'I'm not sure why we're so hot to regulate the Moonies anyway.' " By contrast, an earlier version of the law was eliminated when "the legislators perceived that [it] would bring a Roman Catholic Archdiocese within the Act." Justice Brennan found that the 50% rule's "capacity—indeed, its express design—to burden or favor selected religious denominations led the Minnesota Legislature to discuss the characteristics of various sects with a view towards 'religious gerrymandering.' "

Note that Larson, like Lukumi, looked behind the facial neutrality of the law to discern a religiously discriminatory purpose. Why was Larson litigated under the Establishment rather than the Free Exercise Clause? Because its selective favoritism toward mainstream religions was more apparent than its selective burdens on unorthodox ones? Because the selective burdens did not fall upon practices central to the free exercise of the Unification faith? Was animal sacrifice more central to Santeria practitioners than solicitation was to Unification Church members? Is solicitation an aspect of the free exercise of religion at all? Should prosecutors, juries and judges be entrusted with deciding such questions?

Conversely, why was Lukumi litigated as a free exercise rather than an establishment case? Justice Kennedy noted several times Hialeah's careful exemption of the kosher slaughter practices used by Orthodox Jews. Did such exemptions for one religious tradition in particular create religious favoritism in violation of the Establishment Clause? Justice Kennedy expressly declined to reach that issue in Lukumi: "We need not discuss whether [the] differential treatment of two religions is itself an independent constitutional violation. Cf. Larson v. Valente. It suffices to recite this feature of the law as support for our conclusion that Santeria alone was the exclusive legislative concern." Does it seem implausible to imagine that Hialeah had "established" Orthodox Judaism, itself a minority faith? The Court has suggested that religious favoritism might violate the Establishment Clause whether it favors mainstream or minority faiths. See Kiryas Joel (1994; p. 1709 below).

2. ***Singling out religion for denial of public funding.*** Lukumi shows that even a law that makes no mention of religion can be found discriminatory against religion. Interestingly, the Court has held that even a law that singles out religion to deny government funding might not be discriminatory. This issue was addressed in Locke v. Davey (2004; below, p. 1696). There, the Court held, in an opinion by Chief Justice Rehnquist, that a Washington state educational scholarship that could not be used to pursue a degree in devotional theology did not unconstitutionally single out religion for disfavor under Lukumi. The Court explained that neither the Washington constitutional provision denying public money for religious instruction nor the program "suggest[ed] animus towards religion." Justice Scalia, in dissent, argued that legislative animus did not matter, a position in keeping with his general rejection of the use of legislative history to establish intent. But the Court distinguished Locke in its decision in Trinity Lutheran Church of Columbia v. Comer (below, p. 1699), when it held Missouri could not deny Trinity Lutheran Church a grant to resurface its school playground—grants the state offered to other secular schools—solely because the organization was a church. To do so, argued Chief Justice Roberts, was to deny Trinity Lutheran its free exercise right.

3. ***Religious or racial animosity?*** The Lukumi case demonstrates that it is not always possible to separate laws motivated by religious animosity from laws motivated by racial, or other, considerations. Such laws often stem from a variety of sources at once. The Church of Lukumi Babalu Aye is a Santería church composed predominately of Cuban-Americans of Afro-Caribbean descent. Much of the opposition to the animal-sacrifice elements of Santería stemmed from the white Cuban population of the Miami area. "Whenever the carcasses of dead animals appeared on beaches or in trash bins, residents blamed the [predominantly Afro-Caribbean] working class. [Cuban] [e]migrees who criticized santería tended to be the white elite, who were embarrassed and resentful of the negative attention." García, Havana USA 96 (1996).

4. ***Expressions of bias and differential results.*** In **Masterpiece Cakeshop v. Colorado Civil Rights Commission**, 584 U.S. ___, 138 S. Ct. 1719 (2018), a Colorado baker, Jack Phillips, told a same-sex couple that he would not create a cake for their wedding celebration because of his religious opposition to same-sex marriages. The couple filed a charge with the Colorado Civil Rights Commission pursuant to the Colorado Anti-Discrimination Act (CADA), which prohibits discrimination based on sexual orientation in a "place of business engaged in any sales to the public and any place offering services . . . to the public." The Colorado Civil Rights Division first found probable cause for a violation and referred the case to the Commission. The Commission then referred the case for a formal hearing before a state Administrative Law Judge, who ruled in the couple's favor.

The case received wide public attention as the first major post-Obergefell clash between religious liberty and marriage equality. Justice

KENNEDY's opinion for a 7–2 Court avoided the major issues of whether the baker was entitled to a religious exemption from Colorado's anti-discrimination law and whether requiring the baker to make a cake would violate his free speech rights. Instead, the Court found a Lukumi violation:

"[Our] society has come to the recognition that gay persons and gay couples cannot be treated as social outcasts or as inferior in dignity and worth. For that reason the laws and the Constitution can, and in some instances must, protect them in the exercise of their civil rights. The exercise of their freedom on terms equal to others must be given great weight and respect by the courts. At the same time, the religious and philosophical objections to gay marriage are protected views and in some instances protected forms of expression. [Nevertheless,] while those religious and philosophical objections are protected, it is a general rule that such objections do not allow business owners and other actors in the economy and in society to deny protected persons equal access to goods and services under a neutral and generally applicable public accommodations law. When it comes to weddings, it can be assumed that a member of the clergy who objects to gay marriage on moral and religious grounds could not be compelled to perform the ceremony without denial of his or her right to the free exercise of religion. This refusal would be well understood in our constitutional order as an exercise of religion, an exercise that gay persons could recognize and accept without serious diminishment to their own dignity and worth. Yet if that exception were not confined, then a long list of persons who provide goods and services for marriages and weddings might refuse to do so for gay persons, thus resulting in a community-wide stigma inconsistent with the history and dynamics of civil rights laws that ensure equal access to goods, services, and public accommodations.

"[The] neutral and respectful consideration to which Phillips was entitled was compromised here, however. The Civil Rights Commission's treatment of his case has some elements of a clear and impermissible hostility toward the sincere religious beliefs that motivated his objection. That hostility surfaced at the Commission's formal, public hearings. [During the Commission's first public meeting,] [one] commissioner suggested that Phillips can believe "what he wants to believe," but cannot act on his religious beliefs "if he decides to do business in the state." A few moments later, the commissioner restated the same position: "[I]f a businessman wants to do business in the state and he's got an issue with the—the law's impacting his personal belief system, he needs to look at being able to compromise." Standing alone, these statements are susceptible of different interpretations. On the one hand, they might mean simply that a business cannot refuse to provide services based on sexual orientation, regardless of the proprietor's personal views. On the other hand, they might be seen as inappropriate and dismissive comments showing lack of due consideration for Phillips' free exercise rights and the dilemma he faced. In view of the comments that followed, the latter seems the more likely.

"[At the Commission's second public meeting,] another commissioner made specific reference to the previous meeting's discussion but said far more to disparage Phillips' beliefs. The commissioner stated: ['Freedom] of religion and religion has been used to justify all kinds of discrimination throughout history, whether it be slavery, whether it be the holocaust, whether it be—I mean, we—we can list hundreds of situations where freedom of religion has been used to justify discrimination. And to me it is one of the most despicable pieces of rhetoric that people can use to—to use their religion to hurt others.' To describe a man's faith as 'one of the most despicable pieces of rhetoric that people can use' is to disparage his religion in at least two distinct ways: by describing it as despicable, and also by characterizing it as merely rhetorical—something insubstantial and even insincere. The commissioner even went so far as to compare Phillips' invocation of his sincerely held religious beliefs to defenses of slavery and the Holocaust. This sentiment is inappropriate for a Commission charged with the solemn responsibility of fair and neutral enforcement of Colorado's antidiscrimination law—a law that protects discrimination on the basis of religion as well as sexual orientation.

"The record shows no objection to these comments from other commissioners. And the later state-court ruling reviewing the Commission's decision did not mention those comments, much less express concern with their content. Nor were the comments by the commissioners disavowed in the briefs filed in this Court. For these reasons, the Court cannot avoid the conclusion that these statements cast doubt on the fairness and impartiality of the Commission's adjudication of Phillips' case. Members of the Court have disagreed on the question whether statements made by lawmakers may properly be taken into account in determining whether a law intentionally discriminates on the basis of religion. See Lukumi (Scalia, J., concurring in part and concurring in judgment). In this case, however, the remarks were made in a very different context—by an adjudicatory body deciding a particular case.

"Another indication of hostility is the difference in treatment between Phillips' case and the cases of other bakers who objected to a requested cake on the basis of conscience and prevailed before the Commission. [On] at least three other occasions the Civil Rights Division considered the refusal of bakers to create cakes with images that conveyed disapproval of same-sex marriage, along with religious text. Each time, the Division found that the baker acted lawfully in refusing service. It made these determinations because, in the words of the Division, the requested cake included 'wording and images [the baker] deemed derogatory.' The treatment of the conscience-based objections at issue in these three cases contrasts with the Commission's treatment of Phillips' objection. The Commission ruled against Phillips in part on the theory that any message the requested wedding cake would carry would be attributed to the customer, not to the baker. Yet the Division did not address this point in any of the other cases with respect to the cakes depicting anti-gay marriage symbolism. Additionally, the Division found no violation of CADA in the other cases in part because each bakery was willing to sell other products, including those depicting Christian themes, to the prospective customers. But the Commission dismissed Phillips' willingness to sell 'birthday cakes, shower cakes, [and] cookies and brownies,' to gay and lesbian customers as irrelevant. The treatment of the other cases and Phillips' case could reasonably be interpreted as being inconsistent as to the question of whether speech is involved, quite apart from whether the cases should ultimately be distinguished."

Justice KAGAN concurred, joined by Justice Breyer: "I write separately to elaborate on one of the bases for the Court's holding. The Court partly relies on the disparate consideration of Phillips' case compared to the cases of [three] other bakers who objected to a requested cake on the basis of conscience. [What] makes the state agencies' consideration [disquieting] is that a proper basis for distinguishing the cases was available—in fact, was obvious. The Colorado Anti-Discrimination Act (CADA) makes it unlawful for a place of public accommodation to deny 'the full and equal enjoyment' of goods and services to individuals based on certain characteristics, including sexual orientation and creed. The three bakers in the cases [brought by William Jack] did not violate that law. Jack requested them to make a cake (one denigrating gay people and same-sex marriage) that they would not have made for any customer. In refusing that request, the bakers did not single out Jack because of his religion, but instead treated him in the same way they would have treated anyone else—just as CADA requires. By contrast, the same-sex couple in this case requested a wedding cake that Phillips would have made for an opposite-sex couple. In refusing that request, Phillips contravened CADA's demand that customers receive 'the full and equal enjoyment' of public accommodations irrespective of their sexual orientation. The different outcomes in the Jack cases and the Phillips case could thus have been justified by a plain reading and neutral application of Colorado law—untainted by any bias against a religious belief. I read the Court's opinion as fully consistent with that view."

Justice GORSUCH concurred, joined by Justice Alito, to disagree with Justice Kagan: "In both cases, the effect on the customer was the same: bakers refused service to persons who bore a statutorily protected trait (religious faith or sexual orientation). But in both cases the bakers refused service intending only to honor a personal conviction. To be sure, the bakers knew their conduct promised the effect of leaving a customer in a protected class unserved. But there's no indication the bakers actually intended to refuse service because of a customer's protected characteristic. We know this because all of the bakers explained without contradiction that they would not sell the requested cakes to anyone, while they would sell other cakes to members of the protected class (as well as to anyone else). So, for example, the bakers in the first case would have refused to sell a cake denigrating same-sex marriage to an atheist customer, just as the baker in the second case would have refused to sell a cake celebrating same-sex marriage to a heterosexual customer. And the bakers in the first case were generally happy to sell to persons of faith, just as the baker in the second case was generally happy to sell to gay persons. In both cases, it was the kind of cake, not the kind of customer, that mattered to the bakers.

Justice GINSBURG dissented, joined by Justice Sotomayor: "The different outcomes the Court features do not evidence hostility to religion of the kind we have previously held to signal a free-exercise violation, nor do the comments by one or two members of one of the four decisionmaking entities considering this case justify reversing the judgment below. [The] bakeries' refusal to make Jack cakes of a kind they would not make for any customer scarcely resembles Phillips' refusal to serve Craig and Mullins: Phillips would *not* sell to Craig and Mullins, for no reason other than their sexual orientation, a cake of the kind he regularly sold to others. When a couple contacts a bakery for a wedding cake, the product they are seeking is a cake celebrating *their* wedding—not a cake celebrating heterosexual weddings or same-sex weddings—and that is the service Craig and Mullins were denied. [Jack,] on the other hand, suffered no service refusal on the basis of his religion or any other protected characteristic. He was treated as any other customer would have been treated—no better, no worse.

"[Statements] made at the Commission's public hearings on Phillips' case provide no firmer support for the Court's holding today. [The] proceedings involved several layers of independent decisionmaking, of which the Commission was but one. [What] prejudice infected the determinations of the adjudicators in the case before and after the Commission? The Court does not say. Phillips' case is thus far removed from the only precedent upon which the Court relies, Lukumi, where the government action that violated a principle of religious neutrality implicated a sole decisionmaking body, the city council."

Does the Masterpiece Cakeshop decision break new ground in identifying antireligious animus? How searching was the Court's inquiry into animus in Masterpiece compared to Lukumi? Has the Court broadened the category of considerations that could count as animus? How much of a role did the allegedly disparate treatment between Phillips and the other bakers' cases play in the Court's decision? Recall that Justice Scalia refused to look to the legislative history of the ordinance in Lukumi, meaning the majority of the Court looked only to the ordinance itself. Can that be reconciled with Justice Kennedy's consideration of adjudicators' motives and statements in Masterpiece? Is his distinction between the adjudicatory versus legislative natures of the proceedings in Masterpiece and Lukumi convincing? Furthermore, were the commissioners' statements genuinely antireligious? For an argument that the Court misread them, see Kendrick & Schwartzman, "The Etiquette of Animus," 132 Harv. L. Rev. 133 (2018).

While the Court left open the questions of whether someone can claim a religious exemption to antidiscrimination laws and whether there is a free speech issue in requiring someone to engage in an arguably artistic project, does the language in Justice Kennedy's opinion provide support for a particular outcome on those questions? How might Justices Kagan and Gorsuch's concurrences be used to argue those issues?

Consider also how Masterpiece Cakeshop fits with another important case from same Term, Trump v. Hawaii, 585 U.S. ___, 138 S. Ct. 2392 (2018), which declined to apply Lukumi analysis to President Donald Trump's allegedly anti-Muslim statements associated with his executive order banning travel from a several majority-Muslim countries. Is there tension between the two decisions? While the majority in Trump v. Hawaii did not directly address the potential establishment violation, Justice Breyer's dissent argued that if the decision to implement the ban were "significantly affected by religious animus," it would violate the First Amendment. Justice Sotomayor, also in dissent, found explicitly that "the primary purpose of the Proclamation is to disfavor Islam and its adherents."

RELIGIOUS EXEMPTIONS

Free exercise claims are more commonly raised against facially neutral laws that are not targeted at a religious practice, but which have a disproportionately adverse impact on religious practitioners. Such laws might either require conduct that is incompatible with religious practice or forbid conduct that is religiously required. The free exercise claimant typically seeks an exemption from, not invalidation of the law. Are religious exemptions ever constitutionally compelled?

The Court's first major decision on free exercise exemptions was **Reynolds v. United States**, 98 U.S. 145 (1878), which upheld application of a federal law making bigamy a crime in the territories to a Mormon claiming that polygamy was his religious duty. As Chief Justice WAITE read the First Amendment, "Congress was deprived of all legislative power over mere opinion, but was left free to reach actions which were in violation of social duties or subversive of good order." He reviewed the traditional condemnation of multiple marriages in modern western society, and cited work by Francis Lieber (better known as the author of the Civil War-era "Lieber Code" on the laws of war) suggesting that "polygamy leads to the patriarchal principle, which, when applied to large communities, fetters the people in stationary despotism, while that principle cannot long exist in connection with monogamy." Chief Justice Waite concluded: "Laws are made for the government of actions, and while they cannot interfere with mere religious belief and opinions, they may with practices. Suppose one believed that human sacrifices were a necessary part of religious worship, would it be seriously contended that the civil government under which he lived could not interfere to prevent a sacrifice? Or if a wife religiously believed it was her duty to burn herself upon the funeral pile of her dead husband, would it be beyond the power of the civil government to prevent her carrying her belief into practice? So here, as a law of the organization of society under the exclusive dominion of the United States, it is provided that plural marriages shall not be allowed. Can a man excuse his practices to the contrary because of his religious belief? To permit this would be to make the professed doctrines of religious belief superior to the law of the land, and in effect to permit every citizen to become a law unto himself. Government could exist only in name under such circumstances."

Cantwell v. Connecticut, 310 U.S. 296 (1940) (p. 990, above), which incorporated the Free Exercise Clause against the states, suggested that religious conduct was not wholly outside the protection of the Free Exercise Clause, even if it was subject to greater regulation than belief. Justice ROBERTS wrote: "[Free exercise] embraces two concepts—freedom to believe and freedom to act. The first is absolute, but in the nature of things, the second cannot be. [In] every case the power to regulate must be so exercised as not, in attaining a permissible end, unduly to infringe the protected freedom."

That same year, in **Minersville School Dist. v. Gobitis**, 310 U.S. 586 (1940) (p. 1390, above), the Court refused to grant a free exercise exemption to Lillian and William Gobitis, Jehovah's Witnesses who had been expelled from a Pennsylvania public school for refusing to salute the flag. In his opinion for the Court, Justice FRANKFURTER wrote: "In the judicial enforcement of religious freedom we are concerned with a historic concept. The religious liberty which the Constitution protects has never excluded legislation of general scope not directed against doctrinal loyalties of particular sects. Judicial nullification of legislation cannot be justified by attributing to the framers of the Bill of Rights views for which there is no historic warrant. Conscientious scruples have not, in the course of the long struggle for religious toleration, relieved the individual from obedience to a general law not aimed at the promotion or restriction of religious beliefs. The mere possession of religious convictions which contradict the relevant concerns of a political society does not relieve the citizen from the discharge of political responsibilities. The necessity for this adjustment has again and again been recognized. In a number of situations the exertion of political authority has been sustained, while basic considerations of religious freedom have been left inviolate. Reynolds. In [previous] cases the general laws in question, upheld in their application to those who refused obedience from religious conviction, were manifestations of specific powers of government deemed by the legislature essential to secure and maintain that orderly, tranquil, and free society without which religious toleration itself is unattainable."

Just three years later, the Court effectively reversed Gobitis, which had been widely criticized, in **West Virginia State Bd. of Educ. v. Barnette**, 319 U.S. 624 (1943) (p. 1392, above), but did so on free-speech grounds, leaving the free exercise holding unchanged. And in **Braunfeld v. Brown**, 366 U.S. 599 (1961), the Court rejected a free exercise challenge to a Pennsylvania Sunday closing law. The challengers were Orthodox Jews whose religion required that they close their stores on Saturdays. They alleged that the Sunday closing laws would place them at such a severe competitive disadvantage as to force them out of business. Chief Justice WARREN's plurality opinion, joined by Justices Black, Clark and Whittaker, rejected the free exercise challenge. Citing Reynolds and Cantwell, Chief Justice Warren emphasized that, unlike the freedom to hold religious beliefs and opinions, the "freedom to act, even when the action is in accord with one's religious convictions, is not totally free from legislative restrictions." He added that the law here did not "make criminal the holding of any religious belief or opinion, nor force anyone to embrace any religious belief. [It simply made] the practice of their religious beliefs more expensive. To strike down [legislation] which imposes only an indirect burden on the exercise of religion, i.e., legislation which does not make unlawful the religious practice itself, would radically restrict the operating latitude of the [legislature]. We are a cosmopolitan nation made up of people of almost every conceivable religious preference. [Consequently,] it cannot be expected, much less required, that legislators enact no law regulating conduct that may in some way result in an economic disadvantage to some religious sects and not to others because of the special practices of the various religions. [If] the State regulates conduct by enacting a general law within its power, the purpose and effect of which is to advance the State's secular goals, the statute is valid despite its indirect burden on religious observance unless the State may accomplish its purpose by means which do not impose such a burden.

"As we pointed out in [McGowan v. Maryland (1961); p. 1665 below, rejecting an Establishment Clause challenge to Sunday closing laws], we cannot find a State without power to provide a weekly respite from all labor and, at the same time, to set one day of the week apart from the others as a day of rest, repose, recreation and tranquility. [To] permit the exemption [sought by the challengers] might well undermine the State's goal of providing a day that, as best possible, eliminates the atmosphere of commercial noise and activity. [E]nforcement problems would be more difficult [and Saturday observers] might well [receive] an economic advantage over their competitors who must remain closed on that day. [Competitors might] assert that they have religious convictions which compel them to close their businesses on what had formerly been their least profitable day. This might make necessary a state-conducted inquiry into the sincerity of the individual's religious beliefs, a practice which a State might believe would itself run afoul of the spirit of constitutionally protected religious guarantees." Justice Frankfurter, joined by Justice Harlan, also rejected the free exercise claim in a separate opinion.

Justice BRENNAN's dissent argued that the law violated the Free Exercise Clause because it "put an individual to a choice between his business and his religion." He argued that the state's interest was "the mere convenience of having everyone rest on the same day. It is to defend this interest that the Court holds that a State need not follow the alternative route of granting an exemption for those who in good faith observe a day of rest other than Sunday. [The Court] conjures up several difficulties with such a system which seem to me more fanciful than real. [The] Court [has] exalted administrative convenience to a constitutional level high enough to justify making one religion economically disadvantageous." Justices Stewart and Douglas also dissented.

Compare with the decision in Braunfeld the Court's decision in the following case, which held that a state must pay unemployment benefits to a Saturday sabbatarian:

Sherbert v. Verner

374 U.S. 398, 83 S. Ct. 1790, 10 L. Ed. 2d 965 (1963).

[Appellant Sherbert, a Seventh-day Adventist, was discharged by her employer "because she would not work on Saturday, the Sabbath Day of her faith." She was unable to obtain other employment because she would not take Saturday work. Her claim for South Carolina state unemployment compensation was denied because the state compensation law barred benefits to workers who failed, without good cause, to accept "suitable work when offered." The highest state court sustained the denial of benefits and the Supreme Court reversed.]

▪ JUSTICE BRENNAN delivered the opinion of the [Court].

[If the state decision is to stand] it must be either because [appellant's] disqualification as a beneficiary represents no infringement by the State of her constitutional rights of free exercise; or because any incidental burden on the free exercise of appellant's religion may be justified by a "compelling state interest in the regulation of a subject within the State's constitutional power to regulate." We turn first to the question whether the disqualification for benefits imposes any burden on the free exercise of appellant's religion. We think it is clear that it does. In a sense the consequences of such a disqualification to religious principles and practices may be only an indirect result of welfare legislation within the State's general competence to enact; it is true that no criminal sanctions directly compel appellant to work a six-day week. But this is only the beginning, not the end, of our inquiry. [Here] not only is it apparent that appellant's declared ineligibility for benefits solely derives from the practice of her religion, but the pressure upon her to forego that practice is unmistakable. The ruling forces her to choose between following the precepts of her religion and forfeiting benefits, on the one hand, and abandoning one of the precepts of her religion in order to accept work, on the other hand. Governmental imposition of such a choice puts the same kind of burden upon the free exercise of religion as would a fine imposed against appellant for her Saturday worship.

[We] must next consider whether some compelling state interest [justifies] the substantial infringement of appellant's First Amendment right. [The] appellees suggest no more than a possibility that the filing of fraudulent claims by unscrupulous claimants feigning religious objections to Saturday work might not only dilute the unemployment compensation fund but also hinder the scheduling by employers of necessary Saturday work. [But] no such objection appears to have been made before the [state courts, and] there is no proof whatever to warrant such fears of malingering or deceit. [Even if] there were such risks, it would plainly be incumbent upon the appellees to demonstrate that no alternative forms of regulation would combat such abuses without infringing First Amendment rights. In these respects, then, the state interest asserted in the present case is wholly dissimilar to the interests which were found to justify the less direct burden upon religious practices in [Braunfeld]. [That statute was] saved by a countervailing factor which finds no equivalent in the instant case—a strong state interest in providing one uniform day of rest for all workers. That secular objective could be achieved, the Court found, only by declaring Sunday to be that day of rest. [Here] no such justifications underlie the determination of the state court that appellant's religion makes her ineligible to receive [benefits].

In holding as we do, plainly we are not fostering the "establishment" of the Seventh-day Adventist religion in South Carolina, for the extension of unemployment benefits to Sabbatarians in common with Sunday worshippers reflects nothing more than the governmental obligation of neutrality in the face of religious differences, and does not represent that involvement of religious with secular institutions which it is the object of the Establishment Clause to forestall. [Nor] do we, by our decision today, declare the existence of a constitutional right to unemployment benefits on the part of all persons whose religious convictions are the cause of their unemployment. This is not a case in which an employee's religious convictions serve to make him a nonproductive member of society. [Our] holding today is only that South Carolina may not constitutionally apply the eligibility provisions so as to constrain a worker to abandon his religious convictions respecting the [day of rest]. [Reversed and remanded.]

■ JUSTICE STEWART, concurring in the result.

[I] think that the guarantee of religious liberty embodied in the Free Exercise Clause affirmatively requires government to create an atmosphere of hospitality and accommodation to individual belief or disbelief. [Yet] in cases decided under the Establishment Clause the Court [has] decreed that government must blind itself to the differing religious beliefs and traditions of the people. With all respect, I think it is the Court's duty to face up to the dilemma posed by the conflict between the [religion clauses].

[I] cannot agree that today's decision can stand consistently with [Braunfeld]. The Court says that there was a "less direct burden upon religious practices" in that case than in this. With all respect, I think the Court is mistaken simply as a matter of fact. The Braunfeld case involved a *criminal* statute [and a drastic impact on the challenger's business]. The impact upon the appellant's religious freedom in the present case is considerably less onerous [than in Braunfeld]. Even upon the unlikely assumption that the appellant could not find suitable non-Saturday employment, the appellant at the worst would be denied a maximum of 22 weeks of compensation payments. I agree with the Court that the possibility of that denial is enough to infringe upon the appellant's constitutional right to the free exercise of her religion. But it is clear to me that in order to reach this conclusion the Court must explicitly reject the reasoning of [Braunfeld]. I think [Braunfeld] was wrongly decided and should be overruled, and accordingly I concur in the result [here].

■ JUSTICE HARLAN, whom JUSTICE WHITE joins, dissenting.

[In] no proper sense can it be said that the State discriminated against the appellant on the basis of her religious beliefs or that she was denied benefits *because* she was a Seventh-day Adventist. She was denied benefits just as any other claimant would be denied benefits who was not "available for work" for personal reasons. With this background, this Court's decision comes into clearer focus. What the Court is holding is that if the State chooses to condition unemployment compensation on the applicant's availability for work, it is constitutionally compelled to *carve out an exception*—and to provide benefits—for those whose unavailability is due to their religious convictions. Such a holding has particular significance in two respects.

First, despite the Court's protestations to the contrary, the decision necessarily overrules [Braunfeld]. Clearly, any differences between this case and Braunfeld cut against the present appellant. *Second,* the implications of the present decision are far more troublesome than its apparently narrow dimensions would indicate at first glance. [The meaning of the holding is that the State] must *single out* for financial assistance those whose behavior is religiously motivated, even though it denies such assistance to others whose identical behavior [is] not religiously motivated. It has been suggested that such singling out of religious conduct for special treatment may violate the constitutional limitations on state action. See Kurland, "Of Church and State and the Supreme Court," 29 U. Chi. L. Rev. 1 (1961). My own view, however, is that at least under the circumstances of this case it would be a permissible accommodation of religion for the State, if it *chose* to do so, to create an exception to its eligibility requirements for persons like the appellant. The constitutional obligation of "neutrality" is not so narrow a channel that the slightest deviation from an absolutely straight course leads to condemnation. [There is] enough flexibility in the Constitution to permit a legislative judgment accommodating an unemployment compensation law to the exercise of religious beliefs such as appellant's. [I] cannot subscribe to the conclusion that the State is constitutionally *compelled* to carve out an exception to its general rule of eligibility in the present case. Those situations in which the Constitution may require special treatment on account of religion are, in my view, few and far between. [Such] compulsion in the present case is particularly inappropriate in light of the indirect, remote, and insubstantial effect of the decision below on the exercise of appellant's religion and in light of the direct financial assistance to religion that today's decision [requires].

LIMITING THE SCOPE OF MANDATORY RELIGIOUS EXEMPTIONS?

In the wake of Sherbert, religious objectors to general regulations repeatedly came to the Court, invoking Sherbert's strict scrutiny in claiming constitutionally mandated exemptions. Although the Court typically adhered to the Sherbert analysis in form, it quite frequently rejected the religious objectors' claims in fact. The major cases in which the free exercise claims succeeded arose in the unemployment compensation context following

Sherbert, and in the education setting following Wisconsin v. Yoder. In other cases, the Court, despite lip service to Sherbert's strict scrutiny standard, in fact exercised a quite deferential variety of review and accordingly refused to carve out exemptions from general regulations.

1. ***Unemployment compensation cases after Sherbert.*** **Thomas v. Review Board**, 450 U.S. 707 (1981), a case factually very close to Sherbert, relied on it to strike down Indiana's denial of unemployment compensation to a Jehovah's Witness who quit his job in a munitions factory because of his religious objections to war. A state court upheld the denial of compensation, because the law denied compensation to all employees who voluntarily left employment for personal reasons without good cause. Chief Justice Burger's majority opinion, however, found the coercive impact here "indistinguishable from Sherbert" and rejected an argument that the grant of benefits to the employee would violate the Establishment Clause. Justice Rehnquist was the sole dissenter, insisting that the majority had read free exercise "too broadly" and had failed "to squarely acknowledge that such a reading conflicts with many of our Establishment Clause cases." He urged that Sherbert be overruled. **Hobbie v. Unemployment Appeals Comm'n**, 480 U.S. 136 (1987), likewise followed Sherbert in upholding the unemployment compensation claim of an employee whose religious beliefs had changed during the course of her employment.

2. ***Compulsory education laws.*** In **Wisconsin v. Yoder**, 406 U.S. 205 (1972), Yoder, a member of the Old Order Amish, was convicted and fined $5 for refusing to send his 15-year-old daughter to school after she had completed the eighth grade, in violation of Wisconsin's requirement of school attendance until age sixteen. The Amish object to high school education because of their "fundamental belief that salvation requires life in a church community separate and apart from the world and worldly influence." They believe that high school exposes their children to worldly influence and emphasizes "intellectual and scientific accomplishments, self-distinction, competitiveness, worldly success, and social life with other students." The Amish society, by contrast, emphasizes "informal learning-through-doing" and "wisdom, rather than technical knowledge; community welfare, rather than competition; and separation [from] contemporary worldly society." Attendance at school through the eighth grade is acceptable to the Amish because it "prepares children to read the Bible [and] to be good farmers and citizens," and because such education does not "significantly expose their children to worldly values." The Wisconsin Supreme Court overturned Yoder's conviction because it violated the Free Exercise Clause. The Court affirmed, with six Justices joining the majority opinion and only one Justice dissenting in part.

Chief Justice BURGER's majority opinion insisted that "a State's interest in universal education" must be strictly scrutinized "when it impinges on fundamental rights and interests" such as the right of free exercise. The State could not prevail unless it showed that its requirement served "a state interest of sufficient magnitude to override the [free exercise claim]." And "only those interests of the highest order and those not otherwise served can overbalance legitimate claims of free exercise. [E.g., Sherbert.]" Applying this analysis, Chief Justice Burger began by asking whether the Amish claim was "rooted in religious belief" (the sincerity of the Amish was conceded), and found it was "not merely a matter of personal preference, but one of deep religious conviction, shared by an organized group, and intimately related to daily living." Compulsory school-attendance laws required the Amish "to perform acts undeniably at odds with fundamental tenets of their religious beliefs" and carried with them "a very real threat of undermining the Amish community and religious practice."

Chief Justice Burger proceeded to reject the State's attempted reliance on the "belief"-"action" distinction: "in this context belief and action cannot be neatly confined in logic-tight compartments." Nor could the case be disposed of because the law was facially nondiscriminatory, for such a regulation might nevertheless "offend the constitutional requirement for governmental neutrality if it unduly burdens the free exercise of religion. [E.g., Sherbert.]" Accordingly exercising the heightened scrutiny demanded by this case as well as Sherbert, the Court examined the interests asserted by the State. Chief Justice Burger noted the State's claim that "some degree of education is necessary to prepare citizens to participate [effectively] in our open political system [and] to be self-reliant and self-sufficient participants in society," but replied that an additional one or two years of formal high school would do "little to serve those interests."

Turning to the State's argument that the Amish position fostered "ignorance," Chief Justice Burger replied that "the Amish community has been a highly successful social unit within our society, even if apart from the conventional 'mainstream.' Its members are productive and very law-abiding members of society." The State also argued that children "may choose to leave the Amish community, and that if this occurs they will be ill-equipped for life." Chief Justice Burger found this argument "highly speculative": "There is nothing in this record to suggest that the Amish qualities of reliability, self-reliance and dedication to work would fail to find ready markets in today's society." Accordingly, the State's interest here "emerges as somewhat less substantial than requiring such attendance for children generally." The Court added that it was "not dealing with a way of life and mode of education by a group claiming to have recently discovered some 'progressive' [process] for rearing children for modern life." In view of the long history of the Amish as a "successful and self-sufficient segment of American society" and their showing of "the adequacy of their alternative mode of continuing informal vocational education in terms of precisely those overall interests that the State advances," a showing that "probably few other religious groups or sects could make, and weighing the minimal difference between what the State would require and what the Amish already accept, it was incumbent on the State to show with more particularity how its admittedly strong interest in compulsory education would be adversely affected by granting an exemption to the Amish. [Sherbert.]" The Court dismissed in a footnote the claim that a mandatory exemption for the Amish would violate the Establishment Clause: "Accommodating the religious beliefs of the Amish can hardly be characterized as sponsorship or active involvement."

Justice DOUGLAS dissented in part, emphasizing the potential conflict of interest between Amish parents and their children. He insisted that the free exercise rights of Amish children had to be reached here. Some Amish children might want to attend high school in order to be able to choose whether to adhere or break with the Amish tradition. (The majority opinion, as well as the concurring notations by Justices Stewart and White, insisted that this issue was not presented by the record.) Justice Douglas also objected to the majority's emphasis on the "law and order record" of the Amish, finding it "quite irrelevant."

3. ***The New Glarus Amish in Yoder v. Wisconsin.*** The Old Order Amish families in Wisconsin v. Yoder were among the least likely groups of people to participate in a precedent-setting legal case. "The Amish feel that 'going to the law' violates their faith's tradition of nonresistance." The great attention brought to the New Glarus community by the Yoder case sparked division between Amish in favor of the litigation and those against it. It also pitted more progressive members of the community against traditionalists. The Amish plaintiffs had "repeatedly argued that [they] would flee the community if the courts ruled against them and thus burdened their religious practice. As it happened, almost all the Amish did leave New Glarus—but after the U.S. Supreme Court ruled *in favor* of their faith. [Far] from preserving their community, the litigation sparked discord that contributed to its disintegration." Peters, The Yoder Case: Religious Freedom, Education, and Parental Rights 2, 6 (2003).

4. ***Denials of free exercise exemption claims between Sherbert and Smith.*** Even though Sherbert and Yoder held that the Free Exercise Clause mandated exemptions from government regulations in certain circumstances, a much larger number of cases during this period rejected such claims. The heightened scrutiny announced by such decisions as Sherbert and Yoder proved quite deferential in fact.

a. **United States v. Lee**, 455 U.S. 252 (1982): Lee, a member of the Old Order Amish, employed several Amish to work on his farm and in his carpentry shop. He objected, on religious grounds, to paying the Social Security tax for his employees, arguing that "the Amish believe it sinful not to provide for their own elderly." Chief Justice BURGER's majority opinion found Yoder distinguishable and rejected Lee's claim. Chief Justice Burger conceded that "there is a conflict between the Amish faith and the obligations imposed by the social security system" and accepted that heightened scrutiny was appropriate. In nevertheless upholding application of the tax law to Lee, he noted that "the State may justify a limitation on religious liberty by showing that it is essential to accomplish an overriding governmental interest"; here, mandatory participation in the Social Security system was indispensable to the fiscal vitality of the system. Chief Justice Burger distinguished Yoder on the ground that here "it would be difficult to accommodate the comprehensive social security system with myriad exceptions flowing from a wide variety of religious beliefs." He also noted that there was "no principled way" to distinguish between general taxes and Social Security taxes, so that, if Lee's claim were granted, a religious opponent to war "would have a similarly valid claim to be exempt from paying [a] percentage of the income tax." "The tax system could not function if denominations were allowed to challenge [it] because tax payments were spent in a manner that violates their religious beliefs."

In a separate opinion concurring only in the judgment, Justice STEVENS criticized the majority for imposing upon the Government "a heavy burden of justifying the application of neutral general laws [to] individual conscientious objectors. In my opinion, it is the objector who must shoulder the burden of demonstrating that there is a unique reason for allowing him a special exemption from a valid law of general applicability." The Amish ought to prevail under strict scrutiny, which he opposed, because an exemption to them would be costless to the government: "[T]he nonpayment of these taxes by the Amish would be more than offset by the elimination of their right to collect benefits. [Since] the Amish have demonstrated their capacity to care for their own, the social cost of eliminating this relatively small group of dedicated believers would be minimal." Nor was there a great risk of myriad similar claims: "[T]he Amish claim applies only to a small religious community within an established welfare system of its own." Nevertheless, he agreed with the majority's result because of the difficulties involved in processing claims to religious exemption from taxes.

b. **Bob Jones University v. United States**, 461 U.S. 574 (1983): This decision rejected a free exercise challenge to IRS denials of tax-exempt status to two educational institutions that practiced racial discrimination in accordance with the religious beliefs upon which they were founded. The IRS claimed that the schools were disqualified as "charities" because their racial policies were "contrary to settled public policy." After finding that the IRS policy was authorized by Congress, Chief Justice BURGER's opinion for the Court rejected the free exercise claim despite formal application of strict scrutiny. Under the Lee standard that "[t]he state may justify a limitation on religious liberty by showing that it is essential to accomplish an overriding governmental interest," the Court found the governmental interest in eradicating racial discrimination in education sufficiently "compelling."

c. **Goldman v. Weinberger**, 475 U.S. 503 (1986): In rejecting a free exercise challenge in this case, involving military service, the Court abandoned any reliance on heightened scrutiny and instead adopted an openly deferential approach. Goldman was an Orthodox Jew, a clinical psychologist in the Air Force, who was disciplined for wearing a yarmulke in violation of uniform dress regulations barring the wearing of headgear indoors. He sought an exemption from the Air Force regulation under the strict scrutiny standard of Sherbert. Justice REHNQUIST's majority opinion answered: "Our review of military regulations challenged on First Amendment grounds is far more deferential than constitutional review of similar [regulations] designed for civilian society. The military need not encourage debate or tolerate protest to the extent that such tolerance is required of the civilian state by the First Amendment; to accomplish its mission the military must foster instinctive obedience, unity, commitment, and esprit de corps." Accordingly, "when evaluating whether military needs justify a particular restriction on religiously motivated conduct, courts must give great deference to the professional judgment of military authorities concerning the relative importance of a particular military interest." In this case, the military judgment was that "the traditional outfitting of personnel in standardized uniforms encourages the subordination of personal preferences and identities in favor of the overall group mission. [The] First Amendment does not require the military to accommodate such practices as the wearing of [the yarmulke] in the face of its view that they would detract from the uniformity sought by the dress regulations."

In a concurring opinion, Justice STEVENS, joined by Justices White and Powell, admitted that Goldman presented "an especially attractive case for an exception" but worried about the application of such an exemption to members of other religious groups who wished to wear, e.g., turbans and dreadlocks. He accordingly insisted on testing the validity of the regulation "as it applied to all service personnel who have sincere religious beliefs." The interest in uniformity was important because it was an interest "in uniform treatment for the members of all religious faiths"; yet the "very strength of [Captain Goldman's] claim creates the danger that a similar claim on behalf of a Sikh or a Rastafarian might readily be dismissed as 'so extreme, so unusual, or so faddish an image that public confidence in his ability to perform his duties will be destroyed.' If exceptions from dress code regulations are to be granted, [inevitably] the decisionmaker's evaluation of the character and the sincerity of the requester's faith—as well as the probable reaction of the majority to the favored treatment of a member of that faith—will play a critical part in the decision. [Yet the] Air Force has no business drawing distinctions between such persons when it is enforcing commands of universal application."

Justice BRENNAN's dissent, joined by Justice Marshall, attacked the majority's "subrational-basis standard—absolute, uncritical 'deference to the professional judgment of military authorities.'" He rejected as "totally implausible" the claim that the "group identity of the Air Force would be threatened" by the wearing of yarmulkes. In response to the Government's fear of "a classic parade of horribles, the specter of a brightly-colored, 'rag-tag band of soldiers,'" he stated: "Although turbans, saffron robes, and dreadlocks are not before us [and] must each be evaluated against the reasons a service branch offers for prohibiting personnel from wearing them while in uniform, a reviewing court could legitimately give deference to dress and grooming rules that have a *reasoned* basis in, for example, functional utility, health and safety considerations, and the goal of a polished, professional appearance. It is the lack of any reasoned basis for prohibiting yarmulkes that is so striking here."

Justice BLACKMUN's dissent stated that the Air Force was justified in considering "the cumulative costs of accommodating constitutionally indistinguishable requests for religious exemptions" and also shared Justice Stevens's concern about discriminating in favor of mainstream religions. He nevertheless joined the dissenters because the "Air Force simply has not shown any reason to fear that a significant number of enlisted [people] would request religious exemptions that could not be denied on neutral grounds such as safety, let alone that granting these requests would noticeably impair the overall image of the service." Justice O'CONNOR's dissent, joined by Justice Marshall, found "two consistent themes" in the precedents: "First, when the government attempts to deny a free exercise claim, it must show that an unusually important interest is at stake, whether that interest is denominated 'compelling,' 'of the highest order,' or 'overriding.' [Sherbert, Yoder, and Lee.] Second, the government must show that granting the requested exemption will do substantial harm to that interest, whether by showing that the means adopted is the 'least restrictive' or 'essential,' or that the interest will not 'otherwise be served.' These two requirements are entirely sensible [and there is no reason why they] should not apply in the military, as well as the civilian, context." Applying these standards here, she stated that she "would require the Government to accommodate the sincere religious belief of Captain Goldman."

After Goldman, Congress enacted a law permitting members of the military to "wear an item of religious apparel while wearing the uniform," unless "the wearing of the item would interfere with the performance [of] military duties [or] the item of apparel is not neat and conservative." 10 U.S.C. § 774.

d. **Bowen v. Roy**, 476 U.S. 693 (1986): The Court by a vote of 8–1 rejected a free exercise challenge to a requirement in the federal AFDC and Food Stamp programs that applicants for welfare benefits be identified by Social Security numbers. The challengers claimed that assignment of a number for their two-year-old daughter, Little Bird of the Snow, would violate their religious beliefs because it would "rob the spirit" of the child. Chief Justice BURGER's majority opinion rejected the claim regarding the *government*'s use of the number by distinguishing free exercise claims with respect to personal conduct from such claims with respect to the government's conduct: "Never to our knowledge has the Court interpreted the First Amendment to require the Government *itself* to behave in ways that the individual believes will further his or her spiritual development. [Free exercise] does not afford an individual a right to dictate the conduct of the Government's internal procedures."

The Court did not rule definitively on the requirement that the *applicant* furnish a Social Security number as a condition of receiving aid, but five Justices indicated that they thought that free exercise warranted an exception here. Chief Justice BURGER, writing on this issue only for himself and Justices Powell and Rehnquist, would have rejected both aspects of the free exercise claim, asserting that scrutiny should be more deferential in the case of a condition on benefits than in the case of "governmental action [that] criminalizes religiously inspired activity or inescapably compels conduct that some find objectionable for religious reasons." Justice WHITE's brief dissent apparently would have granted both aspects of the free exercise claim, finding that the case was controlled by Sherbert and Thomas. Justice O'CONNOR, joined by Justices Brennan and Marshall, disputed Chief Justice Burger's distinction between "conditions" and "compulsion," arguing that the fact that the "underlying dispute involves an award of benefits rather than an exaction of penalties does not grant the Government license to apply a different version of the Constitution." Applying heightened scrutiny, she would have exempted Roy from providing the number. Justices BLACKMUN and STEVENS filed separate partial concurrences, agreeing that free exercise did not bar the government's own use of the Social Security number, but claiming that the record was insufficient to allow consideration of the claims with respect to Roy's furnishing the number. However, Justice Blackmun appended to his concurrence a comment that, if forced to reach the latter issue, he would agree with Justice O'Connor's position. Given Justice Blackmun's comment, and the view of the four dissenters, there was apparently a majority on the Court to uphold a free exercise claim regarding the furnishing of the number.

e. **Lyng v. Northwest Indian Cemetery Protective Ass'n**, 485 U.S. 439 (1988): This was an unsuccessful free exercise challenge to the U.S. Forest Service's plan to build a road through and permit timber harvesting in an area of national forest traditionally used by several Indian tribes as sacred areas for religious rituals. In a 5–3 decision, the Court rejected the free exercise claim. Justice O'CONNOR's majority opinion acknowledged that the challengers' beliefs were "sincere" and that "the Government's proposed actions [would] have severe adverse effects on the practice of their religion," but insisted that the burden was not sufficiently great to trigger any form of heightened scrutiny. Accordingly, the Government did not have to meet a "compelling interest" standard of justification for the project. Relying heavily on Bowen v. Roy (p. 1591 above), she stated: "The building of a road or the harvesting of timber on publicly owned land cannot meaningfully be distinguished from the use of a Social Security number in Roy. In both cases, the challenged Government action would interfere significantly with private persons' ability to pursue spiritual fulfillment according to their own religious beliefs. In neither case, however, would the affected individuals be coerced by the Government's action into violating their religious beliefs; nor would either governmental action penalize the religious activity by denying any person an equal share of the rights, benefits, and privileges enjoyed by other citizens." She acknowledged that "indirect coercion or penalties on the free exercise of religion, not just outright prohibitions, are subject to scrutiny under the First Amendment. [But] this does not and cannot imply that incidental effects of governmental programs, which may make it more difficult to practice certain religions but which have no tendency to coerce individuals into acting contrary to their religious beliefs, require government to bring forward a compelling justification for otherwise lawful actions. The crucial word in the constitutional text is 'prohibit.' "

Justice O'Connor went on to rely heavily on the possibility that many similar claims might impair the operation of government: "[Government] simply could not operate if it were required to satisfy every citizen's religious needs and desires. [The] First Amendment must apply to all citizens alike, and it can give to none of them a veto of public programs that do not prohibit the free exercise of religion. The Constitution does not, and courts cannot, offer to reconcile the various competing demands on Government, many of them rooted in sincere religious belief, that inevitably arise in so diverse a society as ours. That task [is] for the legislatures and other institutions." Thus, though the Government could not forbid the Indian challengers from visiting the area, these rights "do not divest the Government of its right to use what is, after all, *its* land."

Justice BRENNAN, joined by Justices Marshall and Blackmun, dissented. He objected to the majority's limitation of free exercise claims to cases of direct or indirect "coercion": "The constitutional guarantee [draws] no such fine distinctions between types of restraints on religious exercise, but rather is directed against any form of governmental action that frustrates or inhibits religious practice. [I] cannot accept the Court's premise that the form of the Government's restraint on religious practice, rather than its effect, controls our constitutional analysis. [Ultimately,] the Court's coercion test turns on a distinction between governmental actions that compel affirmative conduct inconsistent with religious belief, and those governmental actions that prevent conduct consistent with religious belief. [Such] a distinction is without constitutional significance. The crucial word in the constitutional text, as the Court itself acknowledges, is 'prohibit,' a comprehensive term that in no way suggests that the intended protection is aimed only at governmental actions that coerce affirmative conduct." He accordingly insisted that the Sherbert "compelling interest" standard was appropriate here.

5. ***The Court's methodology in applying Sherbert.*** In the preceding cases, the Court used three techniques to distinguish Sherbert and Yoder. In some cases, it found an overriding government interest in uniformity, for example in the administration of the tax laws. In others, it found that free exercise interests were attenuated and government interests paramount in specialized environments such as the military. And in others, it applied a narrow definition of what constitutes a burden on religious

practice, rejecting free exercise claims seeking to alter "internal" government operations such as the use of Social Security numbers and the development of federal property.

Can these findings be reconciled with Sherbert and Yoder? In particular, can the narrow definition of burdens on free exercise set forth in Roy and Lyng be reconciled with Sherbert? Didn't Sherbert itself compel a change in "internal government operations," and in the use of government "property"? Can government actions even with respect to "internal" operations have negative external effects on religious practitioners? See Williams & Williams, "Volitionalism and Religious Liberty," 76 Cornell L. Rev. 769 (1991) (arguing that the Court undervalues the beliefs of "nonvolitionalist" religions, i.e., those that believe that negative religious consequences can attach even to events over which the religious adherent exercised no personal control). Should the fact that the government had a monopoly over use of a unique worship site have mattered in Lyng? Could the Native American worshippers in Lyng themselves have asserted a countervailing property right? See Lupu, "Where Rights Begin: The Problem of Burdens on the Free Exercise of Religion," 102 Harv. L. Rev. 933 (1988) (arguing that government actions that are comparable to harms actionable at common law should count as burdens on religion, and that in Lyng, the government interfered, in effect, with a prescriptive easement of access to the worship site). In reading the 1990 Smith case, which follows, consider whether the pattern of decisions after Sherbert and Yoder had already abandoned in all but name strict scrutiny of most neutral government regulations challenged as violations of free exercise:

Employment Division, Dept. of Human Resources v. Smith

494 U.S. 872, 110 S. Ct. 1595, 108 L. Ed. 2d 876 (1990).

■ JUSTICE SCALIA delivered the opinion of the Court.

This case requires us to decide whether the Free Exercise Clause [permits] Oregon to include religiously inspired peyote use within the reach of its general criminal prohibition on use of that drug, and thus permits the State to deny unemployment benefits to persons dismissed from their jobs because of such religiously inspired use.

I. Oregon law prohibits the knowing or intentional possession of a "controlled substance," [including] the drug peyote, a hallucinogen derived from [a plant]. Respondents Alfred Smith and Galen Black were fired from their jobs with a private drug rehabilitation organization because they ingested peyote for sacramental purposes at a ceremony of the Native American Church, of which both are members. When respondents applied to petitioner Employment Division for unemployment compensation, they were determined to be ineligible for benefits because they had been discharged for work-related "misconduct". [The Oregon Supreme Court, after a first round of litigation that went up to the Supreme Court, found on remand that respondents' peyote use fell within the prohibition of Oregon's criminal laws, that those laws made no exception for sacramental use of the drug, but that that the ban on sacramental peyote use was invalid under the Free Exercise Clause. Thus, the state court ruled, Oregon could not deny unemployment benefits for engaging in conduct that was constitutionally protected. The Court again granted certiorari.]

II. Respondents' claim for relief rests on our decisions in Sherbert, Thomas, and Hobbie, in which we held that a State could not condition the availability of unemployment insurance on an individual's willingness to forgo conduct required by his religion. As we observed in Smith I, however, the conduct at issue in those cases was not prohibited by law. [Now that it is clear] that Oregon does prohibit the religious use of peyote, we proceed to consider whether that prohibition is permissible under the Free Exercise Clause.

A. [The] free exercise of religion means, first and foremost, the right to believe and profess whatever religious doctrine one desires. [But] the "exercise of religion" often involves not only belief and profession but the performance of (or abstention from) physical acts: assembling with others for a worship service, participating in sacramental use of bread and wine, proselytizing, abstaining from certain foods or certain modes of transportation. It would be true, we think (though no case of ours has involved the point), that a state would be "prohibiting the free exercise [of religion]" if it sought to ban such acts or abstentions only when they are engaged in for religious reasons, or only because of the religious belief that they display. It would doubtless be unconstitutional, for example, to ban the casting of "statues that are to be used for worship purposes," or to prohibit bowing down before a golden calf.

Respondents in the present case, however, seek to carry the meaning of "prohibiting the free exercise [of religion]" one large step further. They contend that their religious motivation for using peyote places them beyond the reach of a criminal law that is not specifically directed at their religious practice, and that is concededly constitutional as applied to those who use the drug for other reasons. They assert, in other words, that "prohibiting the free exercise [of religion]" includes requiring any individual to observe a generally applicable law that requires (or forbids) the performance of an act that his religious belief forbids (or requires). As a textual matter, we do not think the words must be given that meaning. It is no more necessary to regard the collection of a general tax, for example, as "prohibiting the free exercise [of religion]" by those citizens who believe support of organized government to be sinful, than it is to regard the same tax as "abridging the freedom [of] the press" of those publishing companies that must pay the tax as a condition of staying in business. It is a permissible reading of the text, in the one case as in the other, to say that if prohibiting the exercise of religion (or burdening the activity of printing) is not the object of the tax but merely the incidental effect of a generally applicable and otherwise valid provision, the First Amendment has not been offended.

Our decisions reveal that the latter reading is the correct one. We have never held that an individual's religious beliefs excuse him from compliance with an otherwise valid law prohibiting conduct that the State is free to regulate. On the contrary, the record of more than a century of our free exercise jurisprudence contradicts that proposition. [We] first had occasion to assert that principle in [Reynolds], where we rejected the claim that criminal laws against polygamy could not be constitutionally applied to those whose religion commanded the practice. [Subsequent] decisions have consistently held that the right of free exercise does not relieve an individual of the obligation to comply with a "valid and neutral law of general applicability on the ground that the law proscribes (or prescribes) conduct that his religion prescribes (or proscribes)." United States v. Lee (Stevens, J., concurring in judgment). [See also Prince; Braunfeld; Gillette.]

The only decisions in which we have held that the First Amendment bars application of a neutral, generally applicable law to religiously motivated action have involved not the Free Exercise Clause alone, but the Free Exercise Clause in conjunction with other constitutional protections, such as freedom of speech and of the press, see [Cantwell; Murdock]; or the right of parents, acknowledged in Pierce v. Society of Sisters, to direct the education of their children, see Wisconsin v. Yoder. Some of our cases prohibiting compelled expression, decided exclusively upon free speech grounds, have also involved freedom of religion [see Wooley v. Maynard; Barnette.]

[The] present case does not present such a hybrid situation, but a free exercise claim unconnected with any communicative activity or parental right. Respondents urge us to hold, quite simply, that when otherwise prohibitable conduct is accompanied by religious convictions, not only the convictions but the conduct itself must be free from governmental regulation. We have never held that, and decline to do so now. There being no contention that Oregon's drug law represents an attempt to regulate religious beliefs, the communication of religious beliefs, or the raising of one's children in those beliefs, the rule to which we have adhered ever since Reynolds plainly controls.

B. [Respondents] argue that even though exemption from generally applicable criminal laws need not automatically be extended to religiously motivated actors, at least the claim for a religious exemption must be evaluated under the balancing test set forth in Sherbert. Under the Sherbert test, governmental actions that substantially burden a religious practice must be justified by a compelling governmental interest. [We] have never invalidated any governmental action on the basis of the Sherbert test except the denial of unemployment compensation. Although we have sometimes purported to apply the Sherbert test in contexts other than that, we have always found the test satisfied [United States v. Lee; Gillette v. United States]. In recent years we have abstained from applying the Sherbert test (outside the unemployment compensation field) at all. [Roy; Lyng; Goldman.]

Even if we were inclined to breathe into Sherbert some life beyond the unemployment compensation field, we would not apply it to require exemptions from a generally applicable criminal law. The Sherbert test, it must be recalled, was developed in a context that lent itself to individualized governmental assessment of the reasons for the relevant conduct. As a plurality of the Court noted in Roy, a distinctive feature of unemployment compensation programs is that their eligibility criteria invite consideration of the particular circumstances behind an applicant's unemployment. [Our] decisions in the unemployment cases stand for the proposition that where the State has in place a system of individual exemptions, it may not refuse to extend that system to cases of "religious hardship" without compelling reason.

Whether or not the decisions are that limited, they at least have nothing to do with an across-the-board criminal prohibition on a particular form of conduct. [Although] we have sometimes used the Sherbert test to analyze free exercise challenges to such laws, we have never applied the test to invalidate one. We conclude today that the sounder approach, and the approach in accord with the vast majority of our precedents, is to hold the test inapplicable to such challenges. The government's ability to enforce generally applicable prohibitions of socially harmful conduct, like its ability to carry out other aspects of public policy, "cannot depend on measuring the effects of a governmental action on a religious objector's spiritual development." [Lyng.] To make an individual's obligation to obey such a law contingent upon the law's coincidence with his religious beliefs, except where the State's interest is "compelling"—permitting him, by virtue of his beliefs, "to become a law unto himself," Reynolds—contradicts both constitutional tradition and common sense.

The "compelling government interest" requirement seems benign, because it is familiar from other fields. But using it as the standard that must be met before the government may accord different treatment on the basis of race, or before the government may regulate the content of speech, is not remotely comparable to using it for the purpose asserted here. What it produces in those other fields—equality of treatment, and an unrestricted flow of contending speech—are constitutional norms; what it would produce here—a private right to ignore generally applicable laws—is a constitutional anomaly.[1]

Nor is it possible to limit the impact of respondents' proposal by requiring a "compelling state interest" only when the conduct prohibited is "central" to the individual's religion. Cf. [Lyng (Brennan, J., dissenting).] It is no more appropriate for judges to determine the "centrality" of religious beliefs before applying a "compelling interest" test in the free exercise field, than it would be for them to determine the "importance" of ideas before applying the "compelling interest" test in the free speech field. What principle of law or logic can be brought to bear to contradict a believer's assertion that a particular act is "central" to his personal faith? Judging the centrality of different religious practices is akin to the unacceptable "business of evaluating the relative merits of differing religious claims." United States v. Lee (Stevens, J., concurring). [Repeatedly] and in many different contexts, we have warned that courts must not presume to determine the place of a particular belief in a religion or the plausibility of a religious claim. [E.g., Thomas; Ballard.]

If the "compelling interest" test is to be applied at all, then, it must be applied across the board to all actions thought to be religiously commanded. Moreover, if "compelling interest" really means what it says (and watering it down here would subvert its rigor in the other fields where it is applied), many laws will not meet the test. Any society adopting such a system would be courting anarchy, but that danger increases in direct proportion to the society's diversity of religious beliefs, and its determination to coerce or suppress none of them. Precisely because [we] value and protect [religious]

[1] [Just] as we subject to the most exacting scrutiny laws that make classifications based on race or on the content of speech, so too we strictly scrutinize governmental classifications based on religion. But we have held that race-neutral laws that have the *effect* of disproportionately disadvantaging a particular racial group do not thereby become subject to compelling-interest analysis under the Equal Protection Clause, see Washington v. Davis; and we have held that generally applicable laws unconcerned with regulating speech that have the *effect* of interfering with speech do not thereby become subject to compelling-interest analysis under the First Amendment, see Citizen Publishing Co. v. United States, 394 U.S. 131 (1969) (antitrust laws). Our conclusion that generally applicable, religion-neutral laws that have the effect of burdening a particular religious practice need not be justified by a compelling governmental interest is the only approach compatible with these precedents. [Footnote by Justice Scalia.]

divergence, we cannot afford the luxury of deeming *presumptively invalid,* as applied to the religious objector, every regulation of conduct that does not protect an interest of the highest order. The rule respondents favor would open the prospect of constitutionally required religious exemptions from civic obligations of almost every conceivable kind—ranging from compulsory military service [e.g., Gillette] to the payment of taxes [United States v. Lee] to health and safety regulation such as manslaughter and child neglect laws, compulsory vaccination laws, drug laws, and traffic laws; to social welfare legislation such as minimum wage laws, child labor laws, animal cruelty laws, environmental protection laws, and laws providing for equality of opportunity for the races [Bob Jones University]. The First Amendment's protection of religious liberty does not require this.

Values that are protected against government interference through enshrinement in the Bill of Rights are not thereby banished from the political process. Just as a society that believes in the negative protection accorded to the press by the First Amendment is likely to enact laws that affirmatively foster the dissemination of the printed word, so also a society that believes in the negative protection accorded to religious belief can be expected to be solicitous of that value in its legislation as well. It is therefore not surprising that a number of States have made an exception to their drug laws for sacramental peyote use. But to say that a nondiscriminatory religious-practice exemption is permitted, or even that it is desirable, is not to say that it is constitutionally required, and that the appropriate occasions for its creation can be discerned by the courts. It may fairly be said that leaving accommodation to the political process will place at a relative disadvantage those religious practices that are not widely engaged in; but that unavoidable consequence of democratic government must be preferred to a system in which each conscience is a law unto itself or in which judges weigh the social importance of all laws against the centrality of all religious beliefs. [Reversed.]

■ JUSTICE O'CONNOR, concurring in the judgment [joined by JUSTICES BRENNAN, MARSHALL, and BLACKMUN as to Parts I and II of the opinion, but not as to the judgment].

Although I agree with the result the Court reaches, [I] cannot join its opinion. In my view, today's holding dramatically departs from well-settled First Amendment jurisprudence, appears unnecessary to resolve the question presented, and is incompatible with our Nation's fundamental commitment to individual religious [liberty].

II. A. The Court today [interprets] the [Free Exercise] Clause to permit the government to prohibit, without justification, conduct mandated by an individual's religious beliefs, so long as that prohibition is generally applicable. But a law that prohibits certain conduct—conduct that happens to be an act of worship for someone—manifestly does prohibit that person's free exercise of his religion. A person who is barred from engaging in religiously motivated conduct is barred from freely exercising his religion. [The] First Amendment [does] not distinguish between laws that are generally applicable and laws that target particular religious practices. Indeed, few States would be so naive as to enact a law directly prohibiting or burdening a religious practice as such.

[To] say that a person's right to free exercise has been burdened, of course, does not mean that he has an absolute right to engage in the conduct. Under our established First Amendment jurisprudence, we have recognized that the freedom to act, unlike the freedom to believe, cannot be absolute. Instead, we have respected both the First Amendment's express textual mandate and the governmental interest in regulation of conduct by requiring the Government to justify any substantial burden on religiously motivated conduct by a compelling state interest and by means narrowly tailored to achieve that interest.

[The] Court attempts to support its narrow reading of the Clause by claiming that "[w]e have never held that an individual's religious beliefs excuse him from compliance with an otherwise valid law prohibiting conduct that the State is free to regulate." But as the Court later notes, as it must, in cases such as Cantwell and Yoder we have in fact interpreted the Free Exercise Clause to forbid application of a generally applicable prohibition to religiously motivated conduct. [The] Court endeavors to escape from our decisions in Cantwell and Yoder by labeling them "hybrid" decisions, but there is no denying that both cases expressly relied on the Free Exercise Clause, and that we have consistently regarded those cases as part of the mainstream of our free exercise jurisprudence. Moreover, in each of the other cases cited by the Court to support its categorical rule, we rejected the particular constitutional claims before us only after carefully weighing the competing interests. [Prince; Braunfeld; Gillette; Lee.] That we rejected the free exercise claims in those cases hardly calls into question the applicability of First Amendment doctrine in the first place. Indeed, it is surely unusual to judge the vitality of a constitutional doctrine by looking to the win-loss record of the plaintiffs who happen to come before us.

B. [In] my view, [the] essence of a free exercise claim is relief from a burden imposed by government on religious practices or beliefs, whether the burden is imposed directly through laws that prohibit or compel specific religious practices, or indirectly through laws that, in effect, make abandonment of one's own religion or conformity to the religious beliefs of others the price of an equal place in the civil community. [A] State that makes criminal an individual's religiously motivated conduct burdens that individual's free exercise of religion in the severest manner possible. [I] would have thought it beyond argument that such laws implicate free exercise concerns. Indeed, we have never distinguished between cases in which a State conditions receipt of a benefit on conduct prohibited by religious beliefs and cases in which a State affirmatively prohibits such conduct. The Sherbert compelling interest test applies in both kinds of cases. [E.g., Lee; Gillette; Yoder.]

[Legislatures], of course, have always been "left free to reach actions which were in violation of social duties or subversive of good order." [Reynolds.] [But once] it has been shown that a government regulation or criminal prohibition burdens the free exercise of religion, we have consistently asked the Government to demonstrate that unbending application of its regulation to the religious objector "is essential to accomplish an overriding governmental interest" [Lee] or represents "the least restrictive means of achieving some compelling state interest" [Thomas]. To me, the sounder approach—the approach more consistent with our role as judges to decide each case on its individual merits—is to apply this test in each case to determine whether the burden on the specific plaintiffs before us is constitutionally significant and whether the particular criminal interest asserted by the State before us is compelling.

[The] Court today gives no convincing reason to depart from settled First Amendment jurisprudence. There is nothing talismanic about neutral laws of general applicability or general criminal prohibitions, for laws neutral toward religion can coerce a person to violate his religious conscience or intrude upon his religious duties just as effectively as laws aimed at religion. [A] law that makes criminal such an activity therefore triggers constitutional concern—and heightened judicial scrutiny—even if it does not target the particular religious conduct at issue. Our free speech cases similarly recognize that neutral regulations that affect free speech values are subject to a balancing, rather than categorical, approach. See e.g., [O'Brien, p. 1176 above]. [The] Court's parade of horribles not only fails as a reason for discarding the compelling interest test, it instead demonstrates just the opposite: that courts have been quite capable of applying our free exercise jurisprudence to strike sensible balances between religious liberty and competing state interests.

Finally, the Court today suggests that the disfavoring of minority religions is an "unavoidable consequence" under our system of government and that accommodation of such religions must be left to the political process. In my view, however, the First Amendment was enacted precisely to protect the rights of those whose religious practices are not shared by the majority and may be viewed with hostility. The history of our free exercise doctrine amply demonstrates the harsh impact majoritarian rule has had on unpopular or emerging religious groups such as the Jehovah's Witnesses and the Amish. [The] compelling interest test reflects the First Amendment's mandate of preserving religious liberty to the fullest extent possible in a pluralistic society. For the Court to deem this command a "luxury" is to denigrate "[t]he very purpose of a Bill of Rights."

III. The Court's holding today not only misreads settled First Amendment precedent; it appears to be unnecessary to this case. I would reach the same result applying our established free exercise jurisprudence. [In Part III, Justice O'Connor, writing only for herself, found that Oregon had "a compelling interest in prohibiting the possession of peyote by its citizens." The critical question thus was "whether exempting respondents from the State's general criminal prohibition 'will unduly interfere with fulfillment of the governmental interest.' [Lee.]" She concluded: "Although the question is [close,] uniform application of Oregon's criminal prohibition is 'essential to accomplish' its overriding interest in 'preventing the physical harm'" caused by drug use. She rejected the argument that any incompatibility between the general law and an exemption was "belied by the fact that the Federal Government and several States provide exemptions for the religious use of peyote," finding that such other exemptions did not mean that Oregon was "*required*" to grant an exemption by the First Amendment. She added moreover, that the constitutionality of applying Oregon's general criminal prohibition "cannot, and should not turn on the centrality of the particular religious practice at issue."]

■ JUSTICE BLACKMUN, with whom JUSTICES BRENNAN and MARSHALL join, dissenting.

[I] agree with Justice O'Connor's analysis of the applicable free exercise doctrine, and I join parts I and II of her opinion. As she points out, "the critical question in this case is whether exempting respondents from the State's general criminal prohibition 'will unduly interfere with fulfillment of the governmental interest.' " I do disagree, however, with her specific answer to that question.

I. In weighing respondents' clear interest in the free exercise of their religion against Oregon's asserted interest in enforcing its drug laws, it is important to articulate in precise terms the state interest involved. It is not the State's broad interest in fighting the critical "war on drugs" that must be weighed against respondents' claim, but the State's narrow interest in refusing to make an exception for the religious, ceremonial use of peyote. [E.g., Thomas; Yoder.] Failure to reduce the competing interests to the same plane of generality tends to distort the weighing process in the State's favor.

[Oregon] has never sought to prosecute respondents, and does not claim that it has made significant enforcement efforts against other religious users of peyote. The State's asserted interest thus amounts only to the symbolic preservation of an unenforced prohibition. [But] a government interest in ["symbolism"] cannot suffice to abrogate the constitutional rights of individuals. [The] State proclaims an interest in protecting the health and safety of its citizens from the dangers of unlawful drugs. It offers, however, no evidence that the religious use of peyote has ever harmed anyone. [The] carefully circumscribed ritual context in which respondents used peyote is far removed from the irresponsible and unrestricted recreational use of unlawful [drugs]. [Moreover,] just as in Yoder, the values and interests of those seeking a religious exemption in this case are congruent, to a great degree, with those the State seeks to promote through its drug laws. Not only does the Church's doctrine forbid nonreligious use of peyote; it also generally advocates self-reliance, familial responsibility, and abstinence from alcohol.

III. [Finally], although I agree with Justice O'Connor that courts should refrain from delving into questions of whether, as a matter of religious doctrine, a particular practice is "central" to the religion, I do not think this means that the courts must turn a blind eye to the severe impact of a State's restrictions on the adherents of a minority religion. Respondents believe, and their sincerity has *never* been at issue, that the peyote plant embodies their deity, and eating it is an act of worship and communion. Without peyote, they could not enact the essential ritual of their religion. [This] potentially devastating impact must be viewed in light of the federal policy—reached in reaction to many years of religious persecution and intolerance—of protecting the religious freedom of Native Americans. See American Indian Religious Freedom Act, 42 U.S.C. § 1996 ("it shall be the policy of the United States to protect and preserve for American Indians their inherent right of freedom to believe, express, and exercise the traditional religions . . . , including but not limited to access to sites, use and possession of sacred objects, and the freedom to worship through ceremonials and traditional rites"). [The] American Indian Religious Freedom Act, in itself, may not create rights enforceable against government action restricting religious freedom, but this Court must scrupulously apply its free exercise analysis to the religious claims of Native Americans, however unorthodox they may be. Otherwise, both the First Amendment and the stated policy of Congress will offer to Native Americans merely an unfulfilled and hollow promise.

SMITH AND RELIGIOUS EXEMPTIONS

1. ***Smith's story.*** Smith was a Native American who had become a serious alcoholic after a lifetime of harsh treatment by federal authorities. "As a young child he was the unwilling recipient of the U.S. government's policy to deprive American Indians of their native heritage and assimilate them into U.S. society. [As] a young man he lived on the city streets and was unwillingly drafted into the army [only] to come home several years later to a life of alcohol abuse." One day in 1957, after waking up in an alley on some cardboard boxes after a drinking binge, Smith gave up drinking. Smith embraced his Native American heritage and became an alcohol treatment counselor at a Native American alcohol program. The practice of Native American rituals, including the ritual consumption of peyote at issue in the case, was an important part of his recovery from alcoholism. As Smith described his peyote consumption, "I took the medicine—the communion, the sacrament, and I survived. I didn't have to go back to have a relapse." The position from which Smith was fired for peyote use was a counseling position in an alcohol treatment program which required employees to promise they would not drink or use drugs. Long, Religious Freedom and Indian Rights 22–35 (2000).

2. ***The history of religious exemptions.*** The opinions in Smith allude to the text of the First Amendment and the Court's free exercise precedents, but do not discuss whether the Framers might have viewed some religious exemptions as mandatory. In "The Origins and Historical Understanding of Free Exercise of Religion," 103 Harv. L. Rev. 1409 (1990), Michael McConnell traces the historical origins of the Free Exercise Clause, notes that pressure for the Free Exercise Clause came from the evangelical religious movements of the colonial and founding periods, and argues that evangelicals viewed the constitutional guarantee of free exercise as protecting their right actively to fulfill religious obligations without state interference. He concludes that an interpretation of free exercise to mandate religious exemptions was both within the contemplation of the Framers and consistent with then-popular views about religious liberty and limited government. While he concedes that "exemptions were not common enough to compel the inference that the term 'free exercise of religion' necessarily included an enforceable right to exemption," he concludes nonetheless that "the modern doctrine of free exercise exemptions [before Smith] is more consistent with the original understanding than is a position that leads only to the facial neutrality of legislation." In "Free Exercise Revisionism and the Smith Decision," 57 U. Chi. L. Rev. 1109 (1990), McConnell criticizes the Court for failing to undertake in Smith "even a cursory inquiry into the history of the clause." For an alternative view of the same history, see Hamburger, "A Constitutional Right of Religious Exemption: An Historical Perspective," 60 Geo. Wash. L. Rev. 915 (1992), and Hamburger, Separation of Church and State (2002).

In **City of Boerne v. Flores**, 521 U.S. 507 (1997), which held that Congress lacked authority under the civil rights enforcement clauses to enact a statute applying the Sherbert rather than the Smith standard to claims of religious exemption from generally applicable state laws (see p. 902 above), Justices O'Connor and Scalia engaged in a lively colloquy on whether or not historical evidence supported the Smith standard:

Justice O'CONNOR's dissent argued that "the historical evidence casts doubt on the Court's current interpretation of the Free Exercise Clause." She noted that various colonial charters and acts had stated that religious practice should not be interfered with unless it caused some specified public harm: for example, because it was "unfaithfull to the Lord Proprietary, or molest[ed] or conspire[d] against the civil Government" (Maryland Act Concerning Religion, 1649); or was "us[ed] to licentiousness and profaneness [or] to the civil injury, or outward disturbance of others" (Charter of Rhode Island, 1663). "In other words," she argued, "when religious beliefs conflicted with civil law, religion prevailed unless important state interests militated otherwise." Likewise, she noted, early state constitutions quite commonly "guaranteed free exercise of religion or liberty of conscience, limited by particular defined state interests." For example, the New York Constitution of 1777 guaranteed free exercise but provided that it "shall not be so construed as to excuse acts of licentiousness, or justify practices inconsistent with the peace or safety of this State." Other states similarly provided for free exercise subject to the constraints of "the public peace" (New Hampshire) or the "peace or safety of the State" (Maryland, Georgia). Justice O'Connor also cited the Northwest Ordinance of 1787, which established a bill of rights for the Northwest Territory providing that: "No person, demeaning himself in a peaceable and orderly manner, shall ever be molested on account of his mode of worship or religious sentiments."

From this evidence, Justice O'Connor concluded that, "around the time of the drafting of the Bill of Rights, it was generally accepted that the right to 'free exercise' required, where possible, accommodation of religious practice." She suggested that otherwise, "there would have been no need to specify" licentiousness or other justifications for interference. Rather, she argued, "these documents make sense only if the right to free exercise was viewed as generally superior to ordinary legislation, to be overridden only when necessary to secure important government purposes." A particularly protective example, she noted, could be found in James Madison's draft Free Exercise Clause for the Virginia Declaration of Rights, which, though not ultimately adopted, would have provided that "no man [ought] on account of religion to be [subjected] to any penalties or disabilities, unless under color of religion the preservation of equal liberty, and the existence of the State be manifestly endangered."

Justice O'Connor next cited early examples of religious accommodation in the colonies and states. For example, some colonial governments created alternatives to oath requirements to accommodate Quakers and other Protestant sects that did not permit the swearing of allegiance to civil government; some colonies and the Continental Congress exempted Quakers and Mennonites from military service; some states with established churches exempted religious objectors from tithes. From these examples she concluded that state legislatures favored religious accommodations when possible, and that "it is reasonable to presume that the drafters and ratifiers of the First Amendment—many of whom served in state legislatures—assumed courts would apply the Free Exercise Clause similarly."

Finally, Justice O'Connor interpreted the writings of various framers as supporting this interpretation. For example, she read Madison's Memorial and Remonstrance as suggesting that religious duty might prevail over civil law whether that law was directed at religion or was more generally applicable. She concluded: "As the historical sources [show,] the Free Exercise Clause is properly understood as an affirmative guarantee of the right to participate in religious activities without impermissible governmental interference, even where a believer's conduct is in tension with a law of general application."

Justice SCALIA, the author of Smith, wrote a separate concurrence in Boerne disputing Justice O'Connor's historical claims. He argued that "[t]he material that the dissent claims is at odds with Smith either has little to say about the issue or is in fact more consistent with Smith than with the dissent's interpretation of the Free Exercise Clause." As he read the early colonial and state Free Exercise Clauses, they were "a virtual restatement of Smith: Religious exercise shall be permitted so long as it does not violate general laws governing conduct." On his reading, avoiding "licentiousness" or disturbance of public "peace" or "order" simply meant "obeying the laws" or avoiding " 'the occurrence of illegal actions.' " He argued that it was impossible to derive Sherbert's compelling interest test from caveats about mere "peace and order."

Justice Scalia also discounted evidence of early legislative accommodations: "that legislatures sometimes (though not always) found it 'appropriate' to accommodate religious practices does not establish that accommodation was understood to be constitutionally mandated by the Free Exercise Clause." Likewise, as to writings such as Madison's Remonstrance, there was "no reason to think they were meant to describe what was constitutionally required (and judicially enforceable), as opposed to what was thought to be legislatively or even morally desirable."

He concluded that "the most telling point made by the dissent is to be found, not in what it says, but in what it fails to say. Had the understanding in the period surrounding the ratification of the Bill of Rights been that the various forms of accommodation discussed by the dissent were constitutionally required (either by State Constitutions or by the Federal Constitution), it would be surprising not to find a single state or federal case refusing to enforce a generally applicable statute because of its failure to make accommodation. Yet the dissent cites none—and to my knowledge, [none] exists." Accordingly, he found, the "historical evidence does nothing to undermine the conclusion" in Smith that "the people" rather than the Court should decide questions of religious exemption.

3. ***The political economy of religious exemptions.*** In the famous footnote four of the Carolene Products case (p. 503 above), the Court suggested that judicial intervention is appropriate where the political process is unlikely to protect "discrete and insular" minorities. Are religious practitioners "discrete and insular minorities" in need of such judicial protection? Mainstream sects are likely to be able to obtain many exemptions through the political process. Sacramental wine used in Catholic and some Protestant ceremonies, for example, was exempted by statute from Prohibition. Recall too the legislative exemption of the Catholic church from the solicitation restrictions in Larson v. Valente (1982; p. 1575 above). Should the Court presume that members of minority faiths, like racial minorities and political dissenters, are unable similarly to protect their religious practices through the political process and are in need of judicial protection from majority prejudice?

Justice O'Connor took this view in Smith, suggesting that religious minorities are politically powerless and thus in need of judicial solicitude: "[T]he First Amendment was enacted precisely to protect the rights of those whose religious practices are not shared by the majority and may be viewed with hostility. The history of our free exercise doctrine amply demonstrates the harsh impact majoritarian rule has had on unpopular or emerging religious groups." Justice Scalia, in contrast, noted that "a number of States have made an exception to their drug laws for sacramental peyote use," suggesting that even minority faiths may obtain legislative exemptions without resort to the courts. He conceded that "leaving accommodation to the political process will place at a relative disadvantage those religious practices that are not widely engaged in," but viewed that as an "unavoidable consequence of democratic government." Which of these views is more persuasive? Which view is borne out by Congress's passage of RFRA by overwhelming majorities, see p. 1607 below?

Are judges more likely than legislatures to be free of bias or selectivity toward minority religions? One empirical survey found the results of pre-Smith judicial accommodation cases skewed ("Minority religionists bring and lose more cases; majority religionists bring fewer cases and win a larger percentage of them"), and concludes that "Smith had the effect of increasing religious equality because overall it significantly reduced the differential success rates that prevailed under the pre-Smith regime." Krotoszynski, "If Judges Were Angels: Religious Equality, Free Exercise, and the (Underappreciated) Merits of Smith," 102 Nw. L. Rev. 1189 (2008).

Should judicially mandated religious exemptions be required to compensate for a special structural disadvantage the religious suffer in politics—namely, that the Establishment Clause disables them from using religious arguments as a basis for legislation? For such an argument, see Sullivan, "Religion and Liberal Democracy," 59 U. Chi. L. Rev. 195 (1992); Greene, "The Political Balance of the Religion Clauses," 102 Yale L.J. 1611 (1993). For the countervailing view that religion should not enjoy any special exemption from laws that reflect the majority's indifference or neglect, but rather should enjoy exemptions only insofar as similarly situated nonreligious practices would receive them, see Eisgruber & Sager, Religious Freedom and the Constitution (2007) (arguing for a theory of "equal liberty" that "denies that religion is a constitutional anomaly, a category of human experience that demands special benefits and/or necessitates special restrictions").

Is religious argument truly excluded from political debate? For expansive views of its permissibility, see Carter, The Culture of Disbelief (1993); Perry, Love and Power (1991); Perry, "Religious Arguments in Public Political Debate," 29 Loyola L. Rev. 1421 (1996). For a more cautiously approving view, see Greenawalt, Religious Convictions and Political Choice (1988); Greenawalt, "Religious Expression in the Public Square," 29 Loyola L. Rev. 1411 (1996). For arguments for greater restraint on religious participation in politics because the Establishment Clause forbids translation of religious commitments into public policy, see Teitel, "A Critique of Religion as Politics in the Public Sphere," 78 Cornell L. Rev. 747 (1993); Audi, "The Separation of Church and State and the Obligations of Citizenship," 18 Phil. & Pub. Affairs 259 (1989). Consider the following observations on this issue by Justice Scalia in his dissent in Edwards v. Aguillard (1987); p. 1660 below: "Our cases in no way imply that the Establishment Clause forbids legislators merely to act upon their religious convictions. We surely would not strike down a law providing money to feed the hungry or shelter the homeless if it could be demonstrated that, but for the religious beliefs of the legislators, the funds would not have been approved. [We] do not presume that the sole purpose of a law is to advance religion merely because it was supported strongly by organized religions or by adherents of particular faiths. To do so would deprive religious men and women of their right to participate in the political process. [Such] religious activism [resulted, for example,] in the abolition of slavery."

4. ***Smith and constitutional jurisprudence.*** Justice Scalia's opinion for the Court in Smith reflects a strong mistrust of judicial balancing. Indeed, in a footnote, Justice Scalia suggested that "it is horrible to contemplate that federal judges will regularly balance against the importance of general laws the significance of religious practice." He found any judicial inquiry into the significance or "centrality" of a religious practice offensive to free exercise. For elaboration of Justice Scalia's general antipathy toward balancing, see Scalia, "The Rule of Law as a Law of Rules," 56 U. Chi. L. Rev. 1175 (1989). How warranted is Justice Scalia's concern that balancing in the free exercise area will invite subjective or arbitrary judicial discretion? See Marshall, "In Defense of Smith and Free Exercise Revisionism," 58 U. Chi. L. Rev. 308 (1990) ("Exemption analysis threatens free exercise values because it requires courts to consider the legitimacy of the religious claim."). But see McConnell, "Free Exercise Revisionism," supra: "Why is the Free Exercise Clause a particular target? [Unless] Smith is the harbinger of a wholesale retreat from judicial discretion across the range of constitutional law, there should be some explanation of why the problem in this field is more acute than it is elsewhere."

Justice O'Connor, in contrast, endorsed a "balancing, rather than categorical, approach," and argued that courts had adequately protected state interests even though they engaged in balancing under Sherbert, Yoder and their progeny. She favored continued case-by-case determination of "whether the burden on the specific plaintiffs before us is constitutionally significant and whether the particular criminal interest asserted by the State before us is compelling." She denied any need to inquire into the centrality of religious practices. But can the Court determine whether a burden is "constitutionally significant" without making such a centrality inquiry? Is there a danger that courts making such an inquiry will exhibit unconscious bias, viewing minority religions through the lens of mainstream practices?

Was Smith consistent with the doctrine of stare decisis? Note that Justice Scalia sought to distinguish rather than overrule prior cases inconsistent with the deferential rule embraced in Smith. Are these distinctions persuasive? See McConnell, "Free Exercise Revisionism," supra (arguing that the Court's distinction of Yoder and the unemployment compensation cases "appears to have one function only: to enable the Court to reach the conclusion it desired in Smith without openly overruling any prior decisions"). Would candid overrule have been preferable? Did the pre-Smith decisions themselves lack candor? Did Smith simply state the rule immanent in the earlier decisions? Note Justice O'Connor's objection to "judg[ing] the vitality of a constitutional doctrine by looking to the win-loss record of the plaintiffs who happen to come before us."

5. ***A ministerial exemption from antidiscrimination laws?*** Where the Americans with Disabilities Act (ADA) would otherwise permit an action against a religious congregation for employment discrimination against a religious instruction teacher, do the First Amendment Religion Clauses compel a "ministerial" exception to the Act? In **Hosanna-Tabor Evangelical Lutheran Church and School v. Equal Employment**

Opportunity Commission, 565 U.S. 171 (2012), the Supreme Court unanimously answered that question "yes." The EEOC and a teacher brought suit under the ADA against the Hosanna-Tabor Evangelical Lutheran Church and School, alleging that the teacher had been fired in retaliation for threatening to file an ADA lawsuit after the church did not reinstate her after a disability leave. In finding that action foreclosed by both the Free Exercise and Establishment Clauses, Chief Justice ROBERTS wrote for a unanimous Court:

"Until today, we have not had occasion to consider whether [the] freedom of a religious organization to select its ministers is implicated by a suit alleging discrimination in employment. The Courts of Appeals, in contrast, have had extensive experience with this issue, [and have] uniformly recognized the existence of a 'ministerial exception,' grounded in the First Amendment, that precludes application of such legislation to claims concerning the employment relationship between a religious institution and its ministers. We agree that there is such a ministerial exception. The members of a religious group put their faith in the hands of their ministers. Requiring a church to accept or retain an unwanted minister, or punishing a church for failing to do so, intrudes upon more than a mere employment decision. Such action interferes with the internal governance of the church, depriving the church of control over the selection of those who will personify its beliefs. By imposing an unwanted minister, the state infringes the Free Exercise Clause, which protects a religious group's right to shape its own faith and mission through its appointments. According the state the power to determine which individuals will minister to the faithful also violates the Establishment Clause, which prohibits government involvement in such ecclesiastical decisions."

The Chief Justice rejected the EEOC's argument that Employment Division v. Smith precludes recognition of a ministerial exception: "It is true that the ADA's prohibition on retaliation, like Oregon's prohibition on peyote use, is a valid and neutral law of general applicability. But a church's selection of its ministers is unlike an individual's ingestion of peyote. Smith involved government regulation of only outward physical acts. The present case, in contrast, concerns government interference with an internal church decision that affects the faith and mission of the church itself." Based on the record in the case, he held that the teacher qualified as a minister, noting that she had undergone extensive religious training, examination, and certification as a "called" teacher and that her "job duties reflected a role in conveying the Church's message and carrying out its mission." He concluded that, because the teacher "was a minister within the meaning of the exception, the First Amendment requires dismissal of this employment discrimination suit against her religious employer."

Justice THOMAS filed a brief concurrence noting that he would "defer to a religious organization's good-faith understanding of who qualifies as its minister" out of respect for the autonomy of religious decision-making. Justice ALITO, joined by Justice KAGAN, filed a concurrence noting that, given the variety of religious practices protected by the Religion Clauses, the "ministerial" exception should turn on an employee's religious function rather than formal title or any specific process of "ordination": "The 'ministerial' exception should [apply] to any 'employee' who leads a religious organization, conducts worship services or important religious ceremonies or rituals, or serves as a messenger or teacher of its faith. If a religious group believes that the ability of such an employee to perform these key functions has been compromised, then the constitutional guarantee of religious freedom protects the group's right to remove the employee from his or her position."

What do you make of Chief Justice Roberts's suggested distinction under Smith between the "outward act" of ingesting peyote for religious purposes and "government interference with an internal church decision"? For an argument that the religion clauses prohibit the government from interfering with international church affairs—the increasingly influential "church autonomy" theory—see Laycock, "Towards a General Theory of the Religion Clauses: The Case of Church Labor Relations and the Right to Church Autonomy," 81 Colum. L. Rev. 1373 (1981). What else might qualify as an "internal church decision"? Does Hosanna-Tabor carve out a new exception to Smith? If so, what is its nature?

CONSTITUTIONAL LAW BY STATUTE: LEGISLATIVE REPONSES TO SMITH

1. ***The federal Religious Freedom Restoration Act of 1993 and its invalidation.*** After the Court issued the Smith decision, a broad coalition of religious groups began working on legislation that would contain Smith's effects by restoring a range of religious exemptions. The coalition attracted strong bipartisan support in Congress, and in 1993, the Congress overwhelmingly passed and the President signed the Religious Freedom Restoration Act (RFRA), 42 U.S.C. §§ 2000bb et seq. The Act contained formal findings that "laws 'neutral' toward religion may burden religious exercise without compelling justification," and that Smith had "virtually eliminated the requirement that the government justify burdens on religious exercise imposed by laws neutral toward religion." The Act identified as one of its purposes "to restore the compelling interest test as set forth in [Sherbert] and [Yoder]."

The Act, 42 U.S.C. §§ 2000bb–1, provided that: "(a) Government shall not substantially burden a person's exercise of religion even if the burden results from a rule of general applicability, except as provided in subsection (b) of this section. (b) Government may substantially burden a person's exercise of religion only if it demonstrates that application of the burden to the person (1) is in furtherance of a compelling governmental interest; and (2) is the least restrictive means of furthering that compelling governmental interest."

Did Congress have the authority to enact RFRA under § 5 of the Fourteenth Amendment, which permits Congress to "enforce, by appropriate legislation," the substantive guarantees of the Fourteenth Amendment? The Court ruled that it did not in **City of Boerne v. Flores**, 521 U.S. 507 (1997). See p. 902 above. The Boerne decision reasoned that RFRA had rewritten rather than merely enforced the protections of free exercise as the Court had previously interpreted them, exceeding Congress's authority and infringing the prerogatives of the states. At least as to state legislation, RFRA now furnishes no cause of action; but RFRA still binds federal actors.

2. ***The continuing constraints of RFRA on the federal government.*** While Boerne held the application of RFRA to the States to be

beyond Congress' legislative authority under § 5 of the Fourteenth Amendment, it did not invalidate RFRA's application to the federal government. In **Gonzales v. O Centro Espirita Beneficente Uniao do Vegetal**, 546 U.S. 418 (2006), Chief Justice ROBERTS reaffirmed the stringency of RFRA's test for denial of free exercise exemptions in an 8–0 opinion joined by all justices except Justice Alito, who was not yet sitting when the case was heard. The case involved a small religious sect (UDV) that receives communion by drinking a hallucinogenic tea called *hoasca*, brewed from Amazon rainforest plants and containing DMT, a controlled substance under the federal narcotics laws. The Court permitted a suit against the Government to proceed challenging a U.S. Customs interception of a shipment of *hoasca*. The Court held that the Government had failed to demonstrate a compelling interest in barring the tea's sacramental use: "Under the [focused] inquiry required by RFRA and the compelling interest test, the Government's mere invocation of [the] Controlled Substances Act cannot carry the day. It is true, of course, that Schedule I substances such as DMT are exceptionally dangerous. [But] there is no indication that Congress, in classifying DMT, considered the harms posed by the particular use at issue here—the circumscribed, sacramental use of *hoasca* by the UDV. [For] the past 35 years, there has been a regulatory exemption for use of peyote—a Schedule I substance—by the Native American Church. [If] such use is permitted [for] hundreds of thousands of Native Americans practicing their faith, it is difficult to see how those same findings alone can preclude any consideration of a similar exception for the 130 or so American members of the UDV who want to practice theirs."

RFRA engendered greater judicial disagreement—and public controversy—in **Burwell v. Hobby Lobby**, 573 U.S. 682 (2014), a case that raised so many distinct issues it reads like a law school exam. The case arose from the so-called contraceptive mandate derived from the Patient Protection and Affordable Care Act of 2010 (ACA), popularly known as Obamacare. The ACA requires employers with 50 or more full-time employees to offer "a group health plan or group health insurance coverage" that provides "minimum essential coverage." 26 U.S.C. § 5000A(f)(2). In turn, the law requires a group plan to provide "preventive care and screenings" for women without "any cost sharing requirements." 42 U.S.C. § 300gg–13(a)(4). Congress delegated the content of the provision to the Health Resources and Services Administration (HRSA), a part of the Department of Health and Human Services (HHS). HRSA promulgated guidelines under which nonexempt employers are generally required to provide "coverage, without cost sharing" for "all Food and Drug Administration approved contraceptive methods, sterilization procedures, and patient education and counseling." 77 Fed. Reg. 8725.

HHS through the HRSA exempted certain "religious employers" from the contraceptive mandate. That category included "churches, their integrated auxiliaries, and conventions or associations of churches," as well as "the exclusively religious activities of any religious order." When an insurer receives notice that one of its clients has invoked this provision, the issuer must then exclude contraceptive coverage from the employer's plan and provide separate payments for contraceptive services for plan participants without imposing any cost-sharing requirements on the eligible organization, its insurance plan, or its employee beneficiaries. The procedure requires the insurer to bear the cost of these services. Yet HHS determined that this obligation would not impose any net expense on the insurer because its cost would be less than or equal to the cost savings resulting from the services.

Hobby Lobby is a for-profit chain of 500 arts-and-crafts stores with more than 13,000 employees. A closely-held corporation, it is controlled by David and Barbara Green and their children. The firm's statement of purpose says the owners will "honor[ ] the Lord in all [they] do by operating the company in a manner consistent with Biblical principles." Another plaintiff, Conestoga Wood Specialties, is also a for-profit closely held corporation (with 950 employees) controlled by a family who are devout members of the Mennonite Church, which opposes abortion and believes that "[t]he fetus in its earliest stages . . . shares humanity with those who conceived it." As for-profit corporations, Hobby Lobby and Conestoga Wood could not invoke the "religious employers" exemption, and the corporations challenged the contraceptive mandate as applied to them under RFRA.

The Court held 5–4 that Hobby Lobby was entitled to an exception from the regulatory mandate under RFRA. Justice ALITO, joined by Chief Justice Roberts and Justices Scalia, Kennedy, and Thomas, wrote the opinion for the Court. Relying on the Dictionary Act's definition of "person" to include artificial persons, the Court first held that corporations were persons for purposes of RFRA analysis. It then rejected the argument that for-profit corporations were not protected by RFRA on the ground that Braunfeld v. Brown [1961; p. 1582] had considered (and rejected on the merits) the free exercise claims of Sabbath-observant Jewish business owners. The Court further rejected the view that RFRA necessarily encompassed only claims that could have been made under the Free Exercise Clause before Smith.

Next, the Court considered and rejected the argument made by HHS that the sincere beliefs of a for-profit corporation could not be ascertained. Justice Alito wrote: "These cases, however, do not involve publicly traded corporations, and it seems unlikely that the sort of corporate giants to which HHS refers will often assert RFRA claims. HHS has not pointed to any example of a publicly traded corporation asserting RFRA rights, and numerous practical restraints would likely prevent that from occurring. For example, the idea that unrelated shareholders—including institutional investors with their own set of stakeholders—would agree to run a corporation under the same religious beliefs seems improbable. In any event, we have no occasion in these cases to consider RFRA's applicability to such companies. The companies in the cases before us are closely held corporations, each owned and controlled by members of a single family, and no one has disputed the sincerity of their religious beliefs." Justice Alito explained that "the owners of closely held corporations may—and sometimes do—disagree about the conduct of business. And even if RFRA did not exist, the owners of a company might well have a dispute relating to religion. For example, some might want a company's stores to remain open on the Sabbath in order to make more money, and others might want the stores to close for religious reasons. State corporate law provides a ready means for resolving any conflicts by, for example, dictating how a corporation can establish its governing structure."

After finding that the law imposed a substantial burden on the "ability of the objecting parties to conduct business in accordance with their religious beliefs," the Court bracketed the question of compelling government interest and turned to whether HHS had adopted the least restrictive means of furthering the government's interest. It held that HHS had not: "The most straightforward way of doing this would be for the Government to assume the cost of providing the four contraceptives at issue to any women who are unable to obtain them under their health-insurance policies due to their employers' religious objections. This would certainly be less restrictive of the plaintiffs' religious liberty, and HHS has not shown that this is not a viable alternative. HHS has not provided any estimate of the average cost per employee of providing access to these contraceptives, two of which, according to the FDA, are designed primarily for emergency use. Nor has HHS provided any statistics regarding the number of employees who might be affected because they work for corporations like Hobby Lobby [and] Conestoga. [Nor] has HHS told us that it is unable to provide such statistics. It seems likely, however, that the cost of providing the forms of contraceptives at issue in these cases (if not all FDA-approved contraceptives) would be minor when compared with the overall cost of ACA.

"[HHS] contends that RFRA does not permit us to take this option into account because 'RFRA cannot be used to require creation of entirely new programs.' But we see nothing in RFRA that supports this argument, and drawing the line between the 'creation of an entirely new program' and the modification of an existing program (which RFRA surely allows) would be fraught with problems. We do not doubt that cost may be an important factor in the least-restrictive-means analysis, but both RFRA and its sister statute, RLUIPA, may in some circumstances require the Government to expend additional funds to accommodate citizens' religious beliefs. HHS's view that RFRA can never require the Government to spend even a small amount reflects a judgment about the importance of religious liberty that was not shared by the Congress that enacted that law."

Beyond cost, Justice Alito continued, there was a further indication that the government had not adopted the least restrictive means: "In the end, however, we need not rely on the option of a new, government-funded program in order to conclude that the HHS regulations fail the least-restrictive-means test. HHS itself has demonstrated that it has at its disposal an approach that is less restrictive than requiring employers to fund contraceptive methods that violate their religious beliefs. As we explained above, HHS has already established an accommodation for nonprofit organizations with religious objections. Under that accommodation, the organization can self-certify that it opposes providing coverage for particular contraceptive services. If the organization makes such a certification, the organization's insurance issuer or third-party administrator must '[e]xpressly exclude contraceptive coverage from the group health insurance coverage provided in connection with the group health plan' and '[p]rovide separate payments for any contraceptive services required to be covered' without imposing 'any cost-sharing requirements . . . on the eligible organization, the group health plan, or plan participants or beneficiaries.' We do not decide today whether an approach of this type complies with RFRA for purposes of all religious claims. At a minimum, however, it does not impinge on the plaintiffs' religious belief that providing insurance coverage for the contraceptives at issue here violates their religion, and it serves HHS's stated interests equally well."

Justice KENNEDY concurred to insist that "that the Court's opinion does not have the breadth and sweep ascribed to it by the respectful and powerful dissent." Referring to the existing accommodations, Justice Kennedy wrote that "the Government has not met its burden of showing that it cannot accommodate the plaintiffs' similar religious objections under this established framework. RFRA is inconsistent with the insistence of an agency such as HHS on distinguishing between different religious believers—burdening one while accommodating the other—when it may treat both equally by offering both of them the same accommodation."

Justice GINSBURG, joined in full by Justice Sotomayor and partly by Justices Breyer and Kagan, dissented. "In a decision of startling breadth," she began, "the Court holds that commercial enterprises, including corporations, along with partnerships and sole proprietorships, can opt out of any law (saving only tax laws) they judge incompatible with their sincerely held religious beliefs. Compelling governmental interests in uniform compliance with the law, and disadvantages that religion-based opt-outs impose on others, hold no sway, the Court decides, at least when there is a 'less restrictive alternative.' And such an alternative, the Court suggests, there always will be whenever, in lieu of tolling an enterprise claiming a religion-based exemption, the government, i.e., the general public, can pick up the tab. [In] the Court's view, RFRA demands accommodation of a for-profit corporation's religious beliefs no matter the impact that accommodation may have on third parties who do not share the corporation owners' religious faith—in these cases, thousands of women employed by Hobby Lobby and Conestoga or dependents of persons those corporations employ. Persuaded that Congress enacted RFRA to serve a far less radical purpose, and mindful of the havoc the Court's judgment can introduce, I dissent."

Justice Ginsburg explained the background of the contraceptive mandate in the Women's Health Amendment to the ACA. "The genesis of this coverage should enlighten the Court's resolution of these cases," she argued. "While the Women's Health Amendment succeeded, a countermove proved unavailing. The Senate voted down the so-called 'conscience amendment,' which would have enabled any employer or insurance provider to deny coverage based on its asserted 'religious beliefs or moral convictions.' "

Justice Ginsburg then characterized RFRA: "RFRA's purpose is specific and written into the statute itself. The Act was crafted to restore the compelling interest test as set forth in Sherbert v. Verner and Wisconsin v. Yoder, and to guarantee its application in all cases where free exercise of religion is substantially burdened. [In] short, the Act reinstates the law as it was prior to Smith, without 'creat[ing] . . . new rights for any religious practice or for any potential litigant.' 139 Cong. Rec. 26178 (statement of Sen. Kennedy). Given the Act's moderate purpose, it is hardly surprising that RFRA's enactment in 1993 provoked little controversy."

The dissent then addressed the majority's approach to RFRA: "Despite these authoritative indications, the Court sees RFRA as a bold initiative departing from, rather than restoring, pre-Smith jurisprudence. To support its conception of RFRA as a measure detached from this Court's decisions, one that sets a new course, the Court points first to the Religious Land Use and Institutionalized Persons Act of 2000 (RLUIPA), which altered RFRA's definition of the term 'exercise of religion.' RFRA, as originally enacted, defined that term to mean 'the exercise of religion under the First Amendment to the Constitution.' As amended by RLUIPA, RFRA's definition now includes 'any exercise of religion, whether or not compelled by, or central to, a system of religious belief.' That definitional change, according to the

Court, reflects 'an obvious effort to effect a complete separation from First Amendment case law.' The Court's reading is not plausible. RLUIPA's alteration clarifies that courts should not question the centrality of a particular religious exercise. But the amendment in no way suggests that Congress meant to expand the class of entities qualified to mount religious accommodation claims, nor does it relieve courts of the obligation to inquire whether a government action substantially burdens a religious exercise."

Turning to the RFRA analysis, Justice Ginsburg first rejected the idea that a for-profit corporation had rights under the law: "Until this litigation, no decision of this Court recognized a for-profit corporation's qualification for a religious exemption from a generally applicable law, whether under the Free Exercise Clause or RFRA. The absence of such precedent is just what one would expect, for the exercise of religion is characteristic of natural persons, not artificial legal entities. As Chief Justice Marshall observed nearly two centuries ago, a corporation is 'an artificial being, invisible, intangible, and existing only in contemplation of law.' Dartmouth College v. Woodward [1819; p. 637]. Corporations, Justice Stevens more recently reminded [in dissent], 'have no consciences, no beliefs, no feelings, no thoughts, no desires.' Citizens United v. Federal Election Comm'n [2010; p. 1494]. The Court's special solicitude to the rights of religious organizations [is] just that. No such solicitude is traditional for commercial organizations. Indeed, until today, religious exemptions had never been extended to any entity operating in the commercial, profit-making world. The reason why is hardly obscure. Religious organizations exist to foster the interests of persons subscribing to the same religious faith. Not so of for-profit corporations. Workers who sustain the operations of those corporations commonly are not drawn from one religious community. Indeed, by law, no religion-based criterion can restrict the work force of for-profit corporations. The distinction between a community made up of believers in the same religion and one embracing persons of diverse beliefs, clear as it is, constantly escapes the Court's attention. One can only wonder why the Court shuts this key difference from sight. [Had] Congress intended RFRA to initiate a change so huge, a clarion statement to that effect likely would have been made in the legislation."

Justice Ginsburg then challenged the Court's substantial burden analysis: "I agree with the Court that the Green and Hahn families' religious convictions regarding contraception are sincerely held. But those beliefs, however deeply held, do not suffice to sustain a RFRA claim. RFRA, properly understood, distinguishes between factual allegations that [plaintiffs'] beliefs are sincere and of a religious nature, which a court must accept as true, and the legal conclusion . . . that [plaintiffs'] religious exercise is substantially burdened, an inquiry the court must undertake. That distinction is a facet of the pre-Smith jurisprudence RFRA incorporates. Bowen v. Roy. Undertaking the inquiry that the Court forgoes, I would conclude that the connection between the families' religious objections and the contraceptive coverage requirement is too attenuated to rank as substantial. The requirement carries no command that Hobby Lobby or Conestoga purchase or provide the contraceptives they find objectionable. Instead, it calls on the companies covered by the requirement to direct money into undifferentiated funds that finance a wide variety of benefits under comprehensive health plans. [Importantly,] the decisions whether to claim benefits under the plans are made not by Hobby Lobby or Conestoga, but by the covered employees and dependents, in consultation with their health care providers. [It] is doubtful that Congress, when it specified that burdens must be substantial, had in mind a linkage thus interrupted by independent decisionmakers (the woman and her health counselor) standing between the challenged government action and the religious exercise claimed to be infringed."

Justice Ginsburg went on to argue that "the Government has shown that the contraceptive coverage for which the ACA provides furthers compelling interests in public health and women's well being. Those interests are concrete, specific, and demonstrated by a wealth of empirical evidence. To recapitulate, the mandated contraception coverage enables women to avoid the health problems unintended pregnancies may visit on them and their children. The coverage helps safeguard the health of women for whom pregnancy may be hazardous, even life threatening. And the mandate secures benefits wholly unrelated to pregnancy, preventing certain cancers, menstrual disorders, and pelvic pain."

Finally, Justice Ginsburg rejected the Court's least restrictive means analysis: "A least restrictive means cannot require employees to relinquish benefits accorded them by federal law in order to ensure that their commercial employers can adhere unreservedly to their religious tenets." Although the Court suggested that the government pay for the coverage, "the ACA [requires] coverage of preventive services through the existing employer-based system of health insurance 'so that [employees] face minimal logistical and administrative obstacles.' 78 Fed. Reg. 39888. Impeding women's receipt of benefits 'by requiring them to take steps to learn about, and to sign up for, a new [government funded and administered] health benefit' was scarcely what Congress contemplated. [And] where is the stopping point to the 'let the government pay' alternative? Suppose an employer's sincerely held religious belief is offended by health coverage of vaccines, or paying the minimum wage, or according women equal pay for substantially similar work. Does it rank as a less restrictive alternative to require the government to provide the money or benefit to which the employer has a religion-based objection? Because the Court cannot easily answer that question, it proposes something else: Extension to commercial enterprises of the accommodation already afforded to nonprofit religion-based organizations. [I] have already discussed the 'special solicitude' generally accorded nonprofit religion-based organizations that exist to serve a community of believers, solicitude never before accorded to commercial enterprises comprising employees of diverse faiths.

"[Would] the exemption the Court holds RFRA demands for employers with religiously grounded objections to the use of certain contraceptives extend to employers with religiously grounded objections to blood transfusions (Jehovah's Witnesses); antidepressants (Scientologists); medications derived from pigs, including anesthesia, intravenous fluids, and pills coated with gelatin (certain Muslims, Jews, and Hindus); and vaccinations (Christian Scientists, among others)? [The] Court, however, sees nothing to worry about. Today's cases, the Court concludes, are 'concerned solely with the contraceptive mandate.' [But] the Court has assumed, for RFRA purposes, that the interest in women's health and well being is compelling and has come up with no means adequate to serve that interest, the one motivating Congress to adopt the Women's Health Amendment. There is an overriding interest, I believe, in keeping the courts out of the business of evaluating the relative merits of differing religious claims, or the sincerity with which an asserted religious belief is held. Indeed, approving some religious claims while deeming others unworthy of accommodation could be perceived as favoring one religion over another, the very risk the Establishment Clause was designed to preclude. The Court, I fear, has ventured into a minefield by its immoderate reading of RFRA. I would confine religious exemptions under that Act to organizations formed for a religious purpose, engaged primarily in carrying out that religious purpose, and not engaged substantially in the exchange of goods or services for money beyond nominal amounts."

3. ***The continuing constraints of RLUIPA on state governments.*** In 2000, three years after City of Boerne, Congress enacted the Religious Land Use and Institutionalized Persons Act (RLUIPA), which requires a compelling interest for denying free exercise exemptions in a narrower range of contexts than RFRA: prisons and zoning. RLUIPA applies if the substantial burden on religious exercise arises from a federally funded program; if the substantial burden affects interstate commerce; or if "the substantial burden is imposed in the implementation of a land use regulation or system of land use regulations, under which a government makes, or has in place formal or informal procedures or practices that permit the government to make individualized assessments of the proposed uses for the property involved." How may Congress permissibly regulate this final situation consistent with Smith and City of Boerne?

The Court applied RLUIPA in **Holt v. Hobbs**, 574 U.S. ___, 135 S. Ct. 853 (2015). In an opinion by Justice ALITO, a unanimous Court ruled that the Arkansas Department of Correction could not forbid a Muslim prisoner from growing a half-inch beard in accordance with his faith. The Court found that while the Department had a compelling interest in being able to identify prisoners and prevent them from hiding contraband in their hair, it was not clear the policy would actually further those interests, and at the very least it was not narrowly tailored: prisoners with dermatological conditions were permitted to grow short beards, and all prisoners could have more than half an inch of hair on their heads.

4. ***State RFRAs and the changing politics of religious exemptions.*** As evidenced by the overwhelming margins by which RFRA and RLUIPA were passed in Congress, there was a robust political consensus on the importance of religious exemptions not so long ago. This consensus produced legislation at the state as well as the federal level: as of 2019, 21 states had passed RFRAs of their own (including "majority-Democratic states such as Connecticut, Illinois, and Pennsylvania), thereby re-imposing on themselves the constraint that City of Boerne lifted. Other states have developed RFRA-like free-exercise standards through judicial interpretation of their state constitutions.

The early state RFRAs were passed with little opposition. However, two recent judicial developments have dramatically changed the politics of state RFRAs, and of religious exemptions more generally. The first is the Supreme Court's decision to grant a religious exemption from the Affordable Care Act's contraceptive coverage mandate in Hobby Lobby. The second development was the rapid success of the gay-rights movement, culminating in the Supreme Court's decision in Obergefell. As same-sex marriage was legalized in more and more jurisdictions in the run-up to Obergefell, some religious bakers, photographers, and others have argued for a free exercise right to refuse to provide their services in connection with same-sex weddings. In 2013, the New Mexico Supreme Court rejected such an argument in Elane Photography v. Willock, 296 P. 3d 491 (2012), holding that the state Human Rights Act required a Christian wedding photographer to serve a same-sex wedding, despite the state's RFRA, which did not apply to disputes between private parties. After Elane Photography and Hobby Lobby, several state RFRAs were proposed that would have applied to for-profit corporations and disputes between private parties. National controversy erupted over a proposed bill in Arizona, which was ultimately vetoed by the governor, and later one in Indiana, which was passed and signed into law.

The debates over Hobby Lobby and the state RFRAs reflect a notable change in substance and tone from the 1990s and 2000s. Religious exemptions were then primarily about accommodating the beliefs of minority religious groups; now, the discussion of religious exemptions centers around claims by Protestant and Catholic Christians, members of the largest religious groups in America. Many have come to believe that all religious people, even Christians, need protection from a secular state that will otherwise "vilify" those who refuse to assent to "the new orthodoxy," as Justice Alito put it in his Obergefell dissent. On the other side, some liberals have come to see religious exemptions as a way for social conservatives to evade the consequences of political battles that they have lost. For more on the changing politics of religious exemptions, and in particular liberals' waning commitment to exemptions, see Paul Horwitz, The Hobby Lobby Moment, 128 Harv. L. Rev. 154 (2014). For an early version of the liberal case against religious exemptions, see Marci Hamilton, God vs. the Gavel (2005).

SECTION 4. THE ESTABLISHMENT CLAUSE

All interpretations of the Establishment Clause agree that it prohibits the creation of an official church and the mandating of religious conduct. Thus, requiring oaths of fidelity to a faith, or tithes, or other financial support for a church would be paradigmatic violations of the clause. There, however, agreement ends. Modern debates over the scope of the Establishment Clause have centered on what the clause might prohibit beyond official oaths or tithes. Does the Establishment Clause bar official sponsorship of religious tenets or symbols, even if no citizen is coerced to support them? Should psychological "coercion" count? Is government "endorsement" of religion troubling even in the absence of coercion? Must religious entities and functions be excluded from all forms of public financial support? May they be included on an equal footing with other recipients of government largesse? Or should there be an absolute bar on government aid to religious evangelism? This section explores these questions in the context of three kinds of Establishment Clause claims: claims that government has impermissibly provided aid to religion, claims that government has impermissibly allowed religion to intrude into public schools, and claims that government has impermissibly sponsored religious doctrines or symbols.

At the outset, it must be noted that the Court set forth an influential test for Establishment Clause violations in **Lemon v. Kurtzman**, 403 U.S. 602 (1971), that is often referred to in the materials that follow as the "Lemon test." Lemon struck down certain types of financial aid to nonpublic schools. Summarizing past decisions, Lemon held that a statute must meet three criteria in order to withstand Establishment Clause attack: "First, the statute must have a secular legislative purpose; second, its principal or primary effect must be one that neither advances nor inhibits religion; finally, the statute must not foster 'an excessive government entanglement with religion.' "

The Lemon test has been sharply criticized. Several Justices have called for its express repudiation, and commentators have suggested it may be dormant or obsolete. The principal criticisms are: (1) that the "purpose" requirement, taken literally, would invalidate all deliberate government accommodation of religion, even though such accommodation is sometimes required by the Free Exercise Clause, and has sometimes been held permissible under the Establishment Clause even if not constitutionally compelled; (2) that legislative "purpose" is in any case difficult to ascertain in a multimember body, and (3) that the "entanglement" prong contradicts the previous two—*some* administrative "entanglement" is essential to ensure that government aid does not excessively promote religious purposes. Faced with these criticisms, the Court has not formally renounced the Lemon test, but has relied on it less and less in recent cases. The Court's decisions increasingly employ different sets of analytical devices for distinguishing establishments, most particularly the so-called endorsement test first described by Justice O'Connor in her Lynch v. Donnelly concurrence (below, p. 1671) and first applied by the Court's majority in Allegheny County v. ACLU (below, p. 1677). How does the endorsement test differ from Lemon? Is it an improvement? Consider these questions as you read the chapter.

PUBLIC FINANCIAL AID TO RELIGIOUS INSTITUTIONS

In recent decades, sharp Establishment Clause debate has arisen over religious subsidies. The problem is older than the Constitution: Recall that James Madison wrote his 1785 polemic Memorial and Remonstrance Against Religious Assessments, a classic expression of principles of religious liberty, in response to Patrick Henry's proposal to the Virginia legislature that a property tax be imposed to raise funds to be distributed, as the taxpayer directed, to churches for payment of clergy and maintenance of houses of worship. In that document, Madison wrote, "Religion [of] every man must be left to the conviction and conscience of every man," and queried, "Who does not see that the same authority which can establish Christianity, in exclusion of all other Religions, may establish with the same ease any particular sect of Christians, in exclusion of all other Sects? That the same authority which can force a citizen to contribute three pence only of his property for the support of any one establishment, may force him to conform to any other establishment in all cases whatsoever?" Madison, Memorial and Remonstrance Against Religious Assessments, in James Madison: Writings 29 (J. Rakove ed., 1999).

The Court itself did not become fully engaged in deciding issues of financial assistance to religious institutions until the late 1940s. Before that, the issue was of central national importance, but focused on state constitutions. From the 1840s through the 1930s, American Catholics sought state funding for Catholic institutions such as schools, orphanages and hospitals, arguing (with much justification) that equivalent state-supported institutions were de facto Protestant. With rare and typically short-lived exceptions, states refused such funding on the ground that states should not fund "sectarian" (i.e. Roman Catholic) institutions. Struggles over these issues reached a climax in 1875 and 1876, when national Republicans proposed a federal constitutional amendment that would have barred states from funding "sectarian" institutions. Known as the "Blaine Amendment" for presidential aspirant and Republican Congressman James G. Blaine of Maine, the amendment would not have changed the legal landscape much, and was designed to place a wedge between Democratic congressmen and Catholic voters. The federal amendment failed, but in its wake, dozens of states adopted either constitutional amendments or statutes (sometimes called "Baby Blaines") similarly prohibiting funding of sectarian institutions.

The Court's occasional early encounters with the issue were inconclusive. Thus, Bradfield v. Roberts, 175 U.S. 291 (1899)—the Court's first decision in the area—sustained a federal appropriation for the construction of a public ward to be administered as part of a hospital under the control of sisters of the Catholic church; but the Court in Bradfield did not reach the issue of whether aid to religious institutions is permissible, because it held that the hospital was not a religious body. See also Reuben Quick Bear v. Leupp, 210 U.S. 50 (1908) (upholding federal disbursement to Catholic schools of funds held in trust for education of Sioux Indians).

Several decades later, the issue of aid to religious institutions produced the Court's first full-scale examination of constitutional guidelines, in Everson v. Board of Education:

Everson v. Board of Education

330 U.S. 1, 67 S. Ct. 504, 91 L. Ed. 711 (1947).

[This case arose from a challenge to a New Jersey statute that authorized school districts to make rules and contracts to transport children to and from school, "including the transportation of school children to and from school other than a public school, except such school as is operated for profit." Pursuant to that law, a local school board adopted a resolution authorizing reimbursement to parents for money spent to transport their children on public buses. A local taxpayer challenged those payments going to parents of Roman Catholic parochial school students. The highest state court denied relief. The Supreme Court affirmed, but not before setting forth the influential statements that "no tax large or small" may be used to support religion and that there must be a "wall of separation between church and state" (recall the dueling historical accounts given by the majority and dissenters at p. 1558 above):]

■ JUSTICE BLACK delivered the opinion of the Court.

The only contention here is that the state statute and the resolution, insofar as they authorized reimbursement to parents of children attending parochial schools, violate the Federal Constitution [including by] forc[ing] inhabitants to pay taxes to help support and maintain schools which are dedicated to, and which regularly teach, the Catholic Faith. This is alleged to be a use of state power to support church schools contrary to the prohibition of the First Amendment which the 14th Amendment made applicable to the states.

[The] "establishment of religion" clause of the First Amendment means at least this: Neither a state nor the Federal Government can set up a church. Neither can pass laws which aid one religion, aid all religions, or prefer one religion over another. Neither can force nor influence a person to go to or to remain away from church against his will or force him to profess a belief or disbelief in any religion. No person can be punished for entertaining or professing religious beliefs or disbeliefs, for church attendance or non-attendance. No tax in any amount, large or small, can be levied to support any religious activities or institutions, whatever they may be called, or whatever form they may adopt to teach or practice religion. Neither a state nor the Federal Government can, openly or secretly, participate in the affairs of any religious organizations or groups and vice versa. In the words of Jefferson, the clause against establishment of religion by law was intended to erect "a wall of separation between church and State."

We must [not strike down the New Jersey law] if it is within the State's constitutional power even though it approaches the verge of that power. New Jersey cannot consistently with the Establishment Clause of the First Amendment contribute tax-raised funds to the support of an institution which teaches the tenets and faith of any church. On the other hand, other language of the amendment commands that New Jersey cannot hamper its citizens in the free exercise of their own religion. Consequently, it cannot exclude individual Catholics, Lutherans, Mohammedans, Baptists, Jews, Methodists, Non-believers, Presbyterians, or the members of any other faith, *because of their faith, or lack of it,* from receiving the benefits of public welfare legislation. While we do not mean to intimate that a state could not provide transportation only to children attending public schools, we must be careful, in protecting the citizens of New Jersey against state-established churches, to be sure that we do not inadvertently prohibit New Jersey from extending its general state law benefits to all its citizens without regard to their religious belief.

Measured by these standards, we cannot say that the First Amendment prohibits New Jersey from spending tax-raised funds to pay the bus fares of parochial school pupils as a part of a general program under which it pays the fares of pupils attending public and other schools. It is undoubtedly true that children are helped to get to church schools. There is even a possibility that some of the children might not be sent to the church schools if the parents were compelled to pay their children's bus fares out of their own pockets when transportation to a public school would have been paid for by the State. [Similarly,] parents might be reluctant to permit their children to attend schools which the state had cut off from such general government services as ordinary police and fire protection, connections for sewage disposal, public highways and sidewalks. Of course, cutting off church schools from these services, so separate and so indisputably marked off from the religious function, would make it far more difficult for the schools to operate. But such is obviously not the purpose of the First Amendment. That Amendment requires the state to be neutral in its relations with groups of religious believers and non-believers; it does not require the state to be their adversary. State power is no more to be used so as to handicap religions than it is to favor them.

This Court has said that parents may, in the discharge of their duty under state compulsory education laws, send their children to a religious rather than a public school if the school meets the secular educational requirements which the state has power to impose. See Pierce v. Society of Sisters, 268 U.S. 510 (1925). It appears that these parochial schools meet New Jersey's requirements. The State contributes no money to the schools. It does not support them. Its legislation, as applied, does no more than provide a general program to help parents get their children, regardless of their religion, safely and expeditiously to and from accredited schools.

The First Amendment has erected a wall between church and state. That wall must be kept high and impregnable. We could not approve the slightest breach. New Jersey has not breached it here. Affirmed.

■ JUSTICE JACKSON, joined by JUSTICE FRANKFURTER, dissenting.

[The] Court's opinion marshals every argument in favor of state aid and puts the case in its most favorable light, but much of its reasoning confirms my conclusions that there are no good grounds upon which to support the present legislation. In fact, the undertones of the opinion, advocating complete and uncompromising separation of Church from State, seem utterly discordant with its conclusion yielding support to their commingling in educational matters.

■ JUSTICE RUTLEDGE, joined by JUSTICES FRANKFURTER, JACKSON and BURTON, dissenting.

The Amendment's purpose was [to] create a complete and permanent separation of the spheres of religious activity and civil authority by comprehensively forbidding every form of public aid or support for religion. [Does] New Jersey's action furnish support for religion by use of the taxing power? Certainly it does, if the test remains undiluted as Jefferson and Madison made it, that money taken by taxation from one is not to be used or given to support another's religious training or belief, or indeed one's own. [T]he prohibition is [absolute].

Two great drives are constantly in motion to abridge, in the name of education, the complete division of religion and civil authority which our forefathers made. One is to introduce religious education and observances into the public schools. The other, to obtain public funds for the aid and support of various private religious schools. [Both] avenues were closed by the Constitution. Neither should be opened by this Court. The matter is not one of quantity, to be measured by the amount of money expended. Now as in Madison's day it is one of principle, to keep separate [spheres] as the First Amendment drew them, to prevent the first experiment upon our [liberties].

MAINTAINING A "WALL OF SEPARATION"?

1. ***"No tax large or small."*** Everson classically recognizes the tension between antiestablishment and free exercise values. The aid challenged in Everson—provision of free school bus access to parochial school students—was aid directed to individuals (as distinguished from direct aid to the parochial institutions themselves). Since Everson, the Court has often accorded great weight to the identity of the immediate recipient of aid in determining whether an aid program violates the Establishment Clause. Should that be determinative? Madison's Remonstrance objected to sectarian aid even if directed to the church of the taxpayer's choice. The aid program in Everson was also directed to transportation rather than theology. The majority likens the program to the provision of fire, police and sanitation

services to parochial schools. The dissent, on the other hand, rejects this comparison and instead analogizes the Everson aid program to the provision of "textbooks, of school lunches, of athletic equipment, [and] of writing and other materials." Which attempts at classification are more persuasive?

2. ***The "wall of separation."*** In Establishment Clause cases in the years immediately following Everson, the Court repeatedly cited the "wall of separation" metaphor approvingly. Later Courts, however, have been less enthusiastic about the metaphor. In his 1971 majority opinion in Lemon v. Kurtzman, for example, Chief Justice Burger commented: "[We] must recognize that the line of separation, far from being a 'wall,' is a blurred, indistinct, and variable barrier depending on all the circumstances of a particular relationship." And in Lynch v. Donnelly (1984; p. 1671 below), Chief Justice Burger's opinion for the Court called the "wall of separation" metaphor "a useful figure of speech," but went on to say that "the metaphor itself is not a wholly accurate description of the practical aspects of the relationship that in fact exists between church and state."

3. ***Forms of aid: texts, tests, teachers, teaching aids and tuition.*** Everson held, on the one hand, that "[n]o tax in any amount, large or small, can be levied to support any religious activities or institutions," and, on the other hand, that the Establishment Clause does not bar the extension of "general state law benefits to all its citizens without regard to their religious belief." The Court was silent on the issue of aid to parochial education for two decades after Everson. But it returned to the issue in Board of Education v. Allen, 392 U.S. 236 (1968), holding that a state may lend books on secular subjects to parochial school students without violating the Establishment Clause. In Lemon v. Kurtzman, 403 U.S. 602 (1971), better known for its restatement of the three-pronged Establishment Clause test, the Court concluded that the state's reimbursement of nonpublic schools for the cost of teachers' salaries, textbooks, and instructional materials, and its payment of a salary supplement to teachers in nonpublic schools, resulted in excessive entanglement of church and state.

The Court's decisions involving aid to parochial education after Allen and Lemon were far from consistent. In Meek v. Pittenger, 421 U.S. 349 (1975), and Wolman v. Walter, 433 U.S. 229 (1977), for example, the Court held that states may not constitutionally lend instructional materials such as maps, magazines, transparencies, tape recorders and laboratory equipment to parochial school students, despite its holding in Allen that lending *books* to such students is permissible. This aspect of Meek and Wolman was expressly overruled in Mitchell v. Helms (2000; p. 1634 below), which held state loans of textbooks to religious schools constitutionally indistinguishable from state loans of instructional materials, and held such loans permissible. Wolman also held that states may not provide transportation for parochial school students to take field trips, despite its holding in Everson that states *may* provide such students with transportation to and from school. In Levitt v. Committee for Public Education, 413 U.S. 472 (1973), the Court held that states may not reimburse parochial schools for the cost of administering tests that are state-required but teacher-prepared. In Committee for Public Education v. Regan, 444 U.S. 646 (1980), however, the Court held that states *may* subsidize parochial schools for the expense of administering state-prepared examinations. And in Mueller v. Allen (1983; p. 1623 below), the Court upheld a form of financial aid to parents of parochial school students (tax deductions) despite its rejection of a similar type of aid (tuition rebates and tax deductions) in Committee for Public Education v. Nyquist, 413 U.S. 756 (1973). For an effort to find coherence in the parochial education cases, see Tribe, American Constitutional Law 1219–21 (2d ed. 1988).

4. ***Permissible subsidies: general beneficiary class and decentralized choice.*** In attempting to reconcile its decisions in the religious subsidy context, the Court has relied upon several distinctions. First, it has looked at the breadth of the statutory class of beneficiaries: the broader the class, the more likely the Court is to uphold the statute. Is a distinction on the basis of breadth of statutory class a tenable one? The Court has upheld statutes that provide aid to private school students, as opposed to *all* students, on several occasions, presumably because the public school students were already receiving the aid in question. If this reasoning is extended, however, does it not suggest that financial aid to parochial school students is permissible, so long as the statutory class includes all private school students? If this is the case, does the defense that the beneficiary class is a general one require anything more than that parochial school students not receive benefits that students in other schools do not receive?

A second distinction upon which the Court has repeatedly relied is based upon the identity of the initial recipient of the aid. The Court has been far more receptive to programs that channel aid to parochial school students and their parents than it has been to programs that give aid directly to parochial schools. Is this distinction a helpful one? Does it not ignore the economic reality that money is fungible, parochial schools benefit whenever parents of parochial school students benefit, and religious practice benefits anytime a religious institution is relieved of nonreligious costs?

5. ***Other forms of public aid to religion.*** In **McCollum v. Board of Education**, 333 U.S. 203 (1948), the Court struck down a school board's practice of permitting students to attend sectarian classes held in the public schools during school hours by parochial school instructors. Justice Black's majority opinion found two problems: first, public school buildings were used for the purpose of providing religious education, and second, the program afforded "sectarian groups an invaluable aid in that it help[ed] to provide pupils for their religious classes through use of the state's compulsory public school machinery."

Just four years later, however, the Court held in **Zorach v. Clauson**, 343 U.S. 306 (1952), that releasing children during school hours to attend sectarian classes *outside* the public school did *not* violate the Establishment Clause. In his opinion for the Court, Justice DOUGLAS emphasized: "This 'released time' program involves neither religious instruction in public school classrooms nor the expenditure of public funds. All costs, including the application blanks, are paid by the religious organizations.

"[Appellants, taxpayers and residents whose children attend public schools, challenge the law], contending it is in essence not different from the one involved in [McCollum]. Their [argument] reduces itself to this: the weight and influence of the school is put behind a program for religious instruction; public school teachers police it, keeping tab on students who are released; the classroom activities come to a halt while the students who are released for religious instruction are on leave; the school is a crutch on which the churches are leaning for support in their religious training; without the cooperation of the schools this 'released time' program, like the one in

[McCollum], would be futile and ineffective. [The highest state court sustained the law.]

"[No] one is forced to go to the religious classroom and no religious exercise or instruction is brought to the classrooms of the public schools. A student need not take religious instruction. He is left to his own desires as to the manner or time of his religious devotions, if any. There is a suggestion that the system involves the use of coercion to get public school students into religious classrooms. There is no evidence in the record before us that supports that conclusion.

"[Apart] from that claim of coercion, we do not see how New York by this type of 'released time' program has made a law respecting an establishment of [religion]. There cannot be the slightest doubt that the First Amendment reflects the philosophy that Church and State should be [separated]. The First Amendment, however, does not say that in every and all respects there shall be a separation of Church and State. Rather, it studiously defines the manner, the specific ways, in which there shall be no concert or union or dependency one on the other. That is the common sense of the matter. Otherwise the state and religion would be aliens to each other—hostile, suspicious, and even unfriendly. Churches could not be required to pay even property taxes. Municipalities would not be permitted to render police or fire protection to religious groups. Policemen who helped parishioners into their places of worship would violate the Constitution. Prayers in our legislative halls; the appeals to the Almighty in the messages of the Chief Executive; the proclamations making Thanksgiving Day a holiday; 'so help me God' in our courtroom oaths—these and all other references to the Almighty that run through our laws, our public rituals, our ceremonies would be flouting the First Amendment. A fastidious atheist or agnostic could even object to the supplication with which the Court opens each session: 'God save the United States and this Honorable Court.' We would have to press the concept of separation of Church and State to these extremes to condemn the present law on constitutional grounds. [We] are a religious people whose institutions presuppose a Supreme Being. We guarantee the freedom to worship as one chooses. We make room for as wide a variety of beliefs and creeds as the spiritual needs of man deem necessary. We sponsor an attitude on the part of government that shows no partiality to any one group and that lets each flourish according to the zeal of its adherents and the appeal of its dogma. When the state encourages religious instruction or cooperates with religious authorities by adjusting the schedule of public events to sectarian needs, it follows the best of our traditions. For it then respects the religious nature of our people and accommodates the public service to their spiritual needs. To hold that it may not would be to find in the Constitution a requirement that the government show a callous indifference to religious groups. That would be preferring those who believe in no religion over those who do believe. [Government] may not coerce anyone to attend church, to observe a religious holiday, or to take religious instruction. But it can close its doors or suspend its operations as to those who want to repair to their religious sanctuary for worship or instruction. No more than that is undertaken here. [The] constitutional standard is the separation of Church and State. The problem [is] one of degree.

"In the McCollum case the classrooms were used for religious instruction and the force of the public school was used to promote that instruction. Here, [the] public schools do no more than accommodate their schedules to a program of outside religious instructions. We follow [McCollum]. But we cannot expand it to cover the present released time program unless separation of Church and State means that public institutions can make no adjustments of their schedules to accommodate the religious needs of the people. We cannot read into the Bill of Rights such a philosophy of hostility to religion. Affirmed."

In dissent, Justice BLACK maintained that the released-time program constituted public aid to religion: "[Here as in McCollum], the school authorities release some of the children on the condition that they attend the religious classes, get reports on whether they attend, and hold the other children in the school building until the religious hour is over. As we attempted to make categorically clear, the McCollum decision would have been the same if the religious classes had not been held in the school buildings. [New York] is manipulating its compulsory education laws to help religious sects get pupils. This is not separation but combination of [Church and State]."

Justice JACKSON also dissented: "This released time program is founded upon a use of the State's power of coercion, which, for me, determines its unconstitutionality. Stripped to its essentials, the plan has two stages, first, that the State compel each student to yield a large part of his time for public secular education and, second, that some of it be 'released' to him on condition that he devote it to sectarian religious purposes. [If] public education were taking so much of the pupils' time as to injure the public or the students' welfare by encroaching upon their religious opportunity, simply shortening everyone's school day would facilitate voluntary and optional attendance at Church classes. But that suggestion is rejected upon the ground that if they are made free many students will not go to the Church. Hence, they must be deprived of freedom for this period, with Church attendance put to them as one of the two permissible ways of using it. The distinction attempted between [McCollum] and this is trivial, almost to the point of cynicism. [The] wall which the Court was professing to erect between Church and State has become even more warped and twisted than I expected. Today's judgment will be more interesting to students of psychology and of the judicial processes than to students of constitutional law." Justice Frankfurter agreed with Justice Jackson and also filed a separate dissent.

Thirty years later, the Court would articulate a similarly religion-inclusive view of the Establishment Clause in the context of explicitly financial public aid to religion:

Mueller v. Allen

463 U.S. 388, 103 S. Ct. 3062, 77 L. Ed. 2d 721 (1983).

[This case arose from a challenge to Minnesota's income tax law, which permitted its taxpayers to deduct from gross income actual expenses incurred for "tuition, textbooks and transportation" for the education of their dependents attending elementary or secondary schools. The deduction was available for expenses incurred in sending children to public as well as nonpublic schools. The deduction was limited to $500 per child in primary school and $700 per child in secondary school. At the time, about 820,000 children attended Minnesota public schools and about 91,000 attended nonpublic schools; about 95% of the latter group attended religious schools. The Court upheld the deduction:]

■ JUSTICE REHNQUIST delivered the opinion of the Court.

Minnesota allows taxpayers, in computing their state income tax, to deduct certain expenses incurred in providing for the education of their children. The [Court of Appeals] held that the Establishment Clause [was] not offended by this arrangement. We now affirm.

One fixed principle in this field is our consistent rejection of the argument that "any program which in some manner aids an institution with a religious affiliation" violates the Establishment Clause. For example, it is now well-established that a state may reimburse parents for expenses incurred in transporting their children to school [Everson], and that it may loan secular textbooks to all school-children within the state. [Allen.] Notwithstanding the repeated approval given programs such as those in Allen and Everson, our decisions also have struck down arrangements resembling, in many respects, these forms of assistance. See, e.g., [Lemon; Levitt; Meek; Wolman.] In this case we are asked to decide whether Minnesota's tax deduction bears greater resemblance to those types of assistance to parochial schools we have approved, or to those we have struck down. Petitioners place particular reliance on our decision in [Nyquist], where we held invalid a New York statute providing public funds for the maintenance and repair of the physical facilities of private schools and granting thinly disguised "tax benefits," actually amounting to tuition grants, to the parents of children attending private schools. [We] conclude that [the provision here] bears less resemblance to the arrangement struck down in Nyquist than it does to assistance programs upheld in our prior decisions and those discussed with approval in Nyquist.

[We] turn to the specific challenges raised [here] under the Lemon framework. Little time need be spent on the question of whether the Minnesota tax deduction has a secular purpose. [A] state's decision to defray the cost of educational expenses incurred by parents—regardless of the type of schools their children attend—evidences a purpose that is both secular and understandable. An educated populace is essential to the political and economic health of any community, and a state's efforts to assist parents in meeting the rising cost of educational expenses plainly serves this secular purpose of ensuring that the state's citizenry is well-educated. [We] turn therefore to the more difficult but related question whether the Minnesota statute has "the primary effect of advancing the sectarian aims of the nonpublic schools." In concluding that it does not, we find several features of the Minnesota tax deduction particularly significant. First, an essential feature of Minnesota's arrangement is the fact that [the provision] is only one among many deductions [available] under the Minnesota tax laws. Our decisions consistently have recognized that traditionally "[l]egislatures have especially broad latitude in creating classifications and distinctions in tax statutes." [The] Minnesota legislature's judgment that a deduction for educational expenses fairly equalizes the tax burden of its citizens and encourages desirable expenditures for educational purposes is entitled to substantial deference. Other characteristics of [the provision] argue equally strongly for the provision's constitutionality. Most importantly, the deduction is available for educational expenses incurred by *all* parents, including those whose children attend public schools and those whose children attend non-sectarian private schools or sectarian private [schools].

[By] channeling whatever assistance it may provide to parochial schools through individual parents, Minnesota has reduced the Establishment Clause objections to which its action is subject. It is true, of course, that financial assistance provided to parents ultimately has an economic effect comparable to that of aid given directly to the schools attended by their children. It is also true, however, that under Minnesota's arrangement public funds become available only as a result of numerous, private choices of individual parents of school-age children. [All] of our recent cases invalidating state aid to parochial schools [except Nyquist] have involved the direct transmission of assistance from the state to the schools themselves. [Where], as here, aid to parochial schools is available only as a result of decisions of individual parents no "imprimatur of State approval" can be deemed to have been conferred on any particular religion, or on religion generally.

[The] Establishment Clause of course extends beyond prohibition of a state church or payment of state funds to one or more churches. We do not think, however, that its prohibition extends to the type of tax deduction established by Minnesota. The historic purposes of the clause simply do not encompass the sort of attenuated financial benefit, ultimately controlled by the private choices of individual parents, that eventually flows to parochial schools from the neutrally available tax benefit at issue in this case.

Petitioners argue that, notwithstanding [its facial neutrality], in application the statute primarily benefits religious institutions. Petitioners rely [on] a statistical analysis of the type of persons claiming the tax deduction. They contend that most parents of public school children incur no tuition expenses, and that other expenses deductible under [the provision] are negligible in value; moreover, they claim that 96% of the children in private schools in 1978–1979 attended religiously-affiliated institutions. Because of all this, they reason, the bulk of deductions taken [will] be claimed by parents of children in sectarian schools. Respondents reply that petitioners have failed to consider the impact of deductions for items such as transportation, summer school tuition, tuition paid by parents whose children attended schools outside the school districts in which they resided, rental or purchase costs for a variety of equipment, and tuition for certain types of instruction not ordinarily provided in public schools.

We need not consider these contentions in detail. We would be loath to adopt a rule grounding the constitutionality of a facially neutral law on annual reports reciting the extent to which various classes of private citizens claimed benefits under the law. Such an approach would scarcely provide the certainty that this field stands in need of, nor can we perceive principled standards by which such statistical evidence might be evaluated. Moreover, the fact that private persons fail in a particular year to claim the tax relief to which they are entitled—under a facially neutral statute—should be of little importance in determining the constitutionality of the statute permitting such relief.

Finally, private educational institutions, and parents paying for their children to attend these schools, make special contributions to the areas in which they operate. [If] parents of children in private schools choose to take especial advantage of the relief provided by [the law], it is no doubt due to the fact that they bear a particularly great financial burden in educating their children. More fundamentally, whatever unequal effect may be attributed to the statutory classification can fairly be regarded as a rough return for the benefits [provided] to the state and all taxpayers by parents sending their children to parochial schools. In the light of all this, we believe it wiser to decline to engage in the type of empirical inquiry into those persons benefited by state law which petitioners urge. Thus, we hold that the Minnesota tax deduction for educational expenses satisfies the primary effect inquiry of our Establishment Clause cases.

Turning to the third part of the Lemon inquiry, we have no difficulty in concluding that the Minnesota statute does not "excessively entangle" the state in religion. The only plausible source of the "comprehensive, discriminating, and continuing state surveillance" necessary to run afoul of this standard would lie in the fact that state officials must determine whether particular textbooks qualify for a deduction. In making this decision, state officials must disallow deductions taken from "instructional books and materials used in the teaching of religious tenets, doctrines or worship, the purpose of which is to inculcate such tenets, doctrines or worship." [Affirmed.]

■ JUSTICE MARSHALL, with whom JUSTICES BRENNAN, BLACKMUN and STEVENS join, dissenting.

The Establishment Clause [prohibits] a State from subsidizing religious education, whether it does so directly or indirectly. In my view, this principle of neutrality forbids [any] tax benefit, including the tax deduction at issue here, which subsidizes tuition payments to sectarian schools. [Indirect] assistance in the form of financial aid to parents for tuition payments is [impermissible] because it is not "subject [to] restrictions" which " 'guarantee the separation between secular and religious educational functions [and] ensure that State financial aid supports only the former.' " [Nyquist, quoting Lemon.] By ensuring that parents will be reimbursed for tuition payments they make, the Minnesota statute requires that taxpayers in general pay for the cost of parochial education and extends a financial "incentive to parents to send their children to sectarian schools." Nyquist. [That] parents receive a reduction of their tax liability, rather than a direct reimbursement, is of no greater significance here than it was in Nyquist. [It] is equally irrelevant whether a reduction in taxes takes the form of a tax "credit," a tax "modification," or a tax "deduction." What is of controlling significance is not the form but the "substantive impact" of the [financial aid].

[That] the Minnesota statute makes some small benefit available to all parents cannot alter the fact that the most substantial benefit provided by the statute is available only to those parents who send their children to schools that charge tuition. [The] other deductible expenses are de minimis in comparison to tuition expenses. [The] bulk of the tax benefits afforded by the Minnesota scheme are enjoyed by parents of parochial school children not because parents of public school children fail to claim deductions to which they are entitled, but because the latter are simply *unable* to claim the largest tax deduction that Minnesota authorizes. [Parents] who send their children to free public schools are simply ineligible to obtain the full benefit of the deduction except in the unlikely event that they buy $700 worth of pencils, notebooks, and bus rides for their school-age children. Yet parents who pay at least $700 in tuition to nonpublic, sectarian schools can claim the full deduction even if they incur no other educational expenses.

That this deduction has a primary effect of promoting religion can easily be determined without any resort to the type of "statistical evidence" that the majority fears would lead to constitutional uncertainty. [In] this case, it is undisputed that well over 90% of the children attending tuition-charging schools in Minnesota are enrolled in sectarian schools. History and experience likewise instruct us that any generally available financial assistance for elementary and secondary school tuition expenses mainly will further religious education because the majority of the schools which charge tuition are sectarian. Because Minnesota, like every other State, is committed to providing free public education, tax assistance for tuition payments inevitably redounds to the benefit of nonpublic, sectarian schools and parents who send their children to those schools.

[For] the first time, the Court has upheld financial support for religious schools without any reason at all to assume that the support will be restricted to the secular functions of those schools and will not be used to support religious instruction. This result is flatly at odds with the fundamental principle that a State may provide no financial support whatsoever to promote [religion].

RELIGIOUS INCLUSION IN PUBLIC SUBSIDIES: EVERSON VS. MUELLER

1. ***The competing theories in Everson and Mueller.*** If Everson articulated, at least in theory, a separationist view of church and state, Mueller v. Allen articulated an alternative, more inclusionary view. On Everson's strict separationist view, no financial benefit "large or small" could flow from government to religious institutions. In Mueller's more inclusionary view, religious individuals or institutions may receive unlimited government financial aid so long as they do so on the same terms as other comparable beneficiaries. The latter approach would conceive neutrality under the Establishment Clause as requiring equal access for religion, not a wall of separation between church and state. On this view, exclusion of religious participants from the programs of the welfare state may discourage religious choices people would have made in the absence of the state or its programs. Which view of the religion clauses is more persuasive? More administrable? For elaboration of the inclusionary approach and its premises, see McConnell, "Religious Freedom at a Crossroads," 59 U. Chi. L. Rev. 115 (1992); see also Laycock, "Formal, Substantive, and Disaggregated Neutrality Toward Religion," 39 DePaul L. Rev. 993 (1990) (endorsing "substantive neutrality" toward religion that "[n]either encourages nor discourages religious belief or disbelief, practice or nonpractice"). For competing views, see Sullivan, "Religion and Liberal Democracy," 59 U. Chi. L. Rev. 195 (1992); Lupu, "The Lingering Death of Separationism," 62 Geo. Wash. L. Rev. 230 (1994).

2. ***Antecedents to Mueller.*** The Court never embraced completely the separationist view, as the holding, as opposed to the rhetoric, of Everson itself demonstrated. Indeed, a pre-Mueller precursor of the assimilationist view may be found in **Walz v. Tax Commission**, 397 U.S. 664 (1970), which upheld a state tax exemption for "real or personal property used exclusively for religious, educational or charitable purposes." Writing for the Court, Chief Justice Burger noted that the tax exemption conferred "indirect

economic benefit" upon churches, but emphasized that the state had "granted exemption to all houses of religious worship within a broad class of property owned by nonprofit, quasi-public corporations which include hospitals, libraries, playgrounds, scientific, professional, historical and patriotic groups."

Likewise, in another pre-Mueller case, Widmar v. Vincent (1981; p. 1283 above), the Court struck down a state university's ban on the use of its facilities for prayer and religious discussion by student groups. In reaching that conclusion, the Court rejected the university's claim that permitting use of the university forum by the student groups would have violated the Establishment Clause. Justice POWELL's majority opinion found that an "equal access" policy would not violate the Establishment Clause. In applying the "effect" part of the Lemon test, he insisted that any aid to religious groups from a policy of "nondiscrimination against religious speech" would be only "incidental," because "an open forum in a public university does not confer any imprimatur of State approval on religious sects or practices" and the forum "was available to a broad class of non-religious as well as religious speakers": "The provision of benefits to so broad a spectrum of groups is an important index of secular effect." For a holding very similar to Widmar's, see Lamb's Chapel v. Ctr. Moriches Union Free School Dist. (1993; p. 1285 above) (allowing inclusion of religious film in after-hour series at a public school).

3. ***Aid to higher education: a different standard?*** Prior to Mueller, the Court also had found fewer Establishment Clause barriers to financial aid to colleges and universities than to elementary and secondary schools. Although the Court has applied the three-part Lemon test developed in the elementary and secondary school context, the Justices have found it more readily satisfied in higher education cases and have been less prone to find excessive "entanglement" in state supervision schemes. The distinction between the levels of education was first articulated in Chief Justice BURGER's plurality opinion in **Tilton v. Richardson**, 403 U.S. 672 (1971): "There are generally significant differences between the religious aspects of church-related institutions of higher learning and parochial elementary and secondary schools. [C]ollege students are less impressionable and less susceptible to religious indoctrination. [Furthermore], by their very nature, college and postgraduate courses tend to limit the opportunities for sectarian influence by virtue of their own internal disciplines. [Since] religious indoctrination is not a substantial purpose [of] these church-related colleges, [there] is less likelihood than in primary and secondary schools that religion will permeate the area of secular education. This reduces the risk that government aid will in fact serve to support religious activities. Correspondingly the necessity for intensive government surveillance is diminished and the resulting entanglements between government and religion lessened. Such inspection as may be necessary to ascertain that the facilities are devoted to secular education is minimal."

Tilton upheld federal construction grants to church-related colleges. The funds had to be used for facilities devoted exclusively to secular educational purposes. The pattern of Tilton was followed two years later in Hunt v. McNair, 413 U.S. 734 (1973), where a divided Court sustained a construction aid program using state-issued revenue bonds to permit colleges to borrow funds at low interest. In **Roemer v. Maryland Public Works Board**, 426 U.S. 736 (1976), the majority went a step further: it approved annual noncategorical grants to eligible private colleges, including some church-related ones, subject only to the restriction that the funds not be used for "sectarian purposes." Justice BLACKMUN's plurality opinion conceded that the "entanglement" problem (arising from the supervision needed to assure that funds were used only for secular purposes) was more serious in the context of annual grants than with "one-time" aid. He nevertheless found the program permissible.

4. ***Increasing deference to the inclusion of religion in public subsidies.*** Did the principles of Mueller eventually prevail over those in Everson? Did the Court increasingly abandon separationism for a version of substantive neutrality that considered religion capable of inclusion in the public order so long as it was on a par with other social entities? Consider the Court's deference to the inclusion of religion in public subsidies in the following series of cases:

Witters v. Washington Department of Services for Blind, 474 U.S. 481 (1986), held that the "effect" prong of the Lemon test was not violated by a law authorizing payment to a visually handicapped person for vocational rehabilitation services, where the recipient sought to use the funds to pay his tuition at a Christian college in order to prepare himself for a career as a "pastor, missionary, or youth director." The Court was unanimous in supporting that result. Justice MARSHALL's opinion emphasized that the aid program provided "no financial incentive for students to undertake sectarian education" and did not "tend to provide greater or broader benefits for recipients who apply their aid to religious education." Moreover, there was no showing that any "significant portion of the aid expended under the Washington program as a whole will end up flowing to religious education." Justice Marshall's reliance on the small quantity of aid that found its way into religious education, however, did not seem to represent the views of the majority. Concurring opinions by Justices WHITE, POWELL (joined by Chief Justice Burger and Justice Rehnquist) and O'CONNOR all emphasized their reliance on Mueller v. Allen (p. 1623 above). Justice Powell criticized the Court for not relying directly on that case. He insisted that Mueller meant that "state programs that are wholly neutral in offering educational assistance to a class defined without reference to religion do not violate the [effect] part of the [Lemon] test, because any aid to religion results from the private choices of individual beneficiaries."

Bowen v. Kendrick, 487 U.S. 589 (1988): This was a challenge to the Adolescent Family Life Act of 1982, which authorizes federal grants to public and nonpublic organizations, including organizations with ties to religious denominations, for counseling services and research "in the area of premarital adolescent sexual relations and pregnancy." Some of the grants, the Court noted, went "to various organizations that were affiliated with religious denominations and that had corporate requirements that the organizations abide by religious doctrines." The Court, in a majority opinion by Chief Justice REHNQUIST, rejected an on-the-face attack on the Act and remanded the as-applied challenge for further proceedings. Applying the three-part Lemon standard, the Court held that the Act on its face did not violate the Establishment Clause. As to the first prong of Lemon, the Court had no difficulty in concluding that the problem of teenage pregnancy constituted a valid secular purpose. With respect to the "effect" prong, the Court found the issue somewhat more difficult. There were two problems. The first was the specific mention of religious organizations in the law itself.

But since various institutions in the public and private sector were also mentioned, the Court found that any effect of advancing religion was "incidental and remote." Second, the law permits "religious institutions to participate as recipients of federal funds." But again Justice Rehnquist found this permissible: "[This] Court has never held that religious institutions are disabled by the First Amendment from participating in publicly sponsored social welfare programs." Moreover, "nothing on the face of the [law] indicates that a significant proportion of the federal funds will be disbursed to 'pervasively sectarian' institutions." The Court also rejected a claim that the Act necessarily advanced religion because religiously affiliated grantees provided the counseling services: although the Establishment Clause bars government-financed indoctrination into "the beliefs of a particular religious faith," the Court insisted that when aid goes to religiously affiliated institutions that are not "pervasively sectarian," it would not "presume that [it will] be used in a way that would have the primary effect of advancing religion." Finally, the Court did not find a violation of the "excessive entanglement" prong of Lemon, concluding that there was no reason to fear that the monitoring involved here would "cause government to intrude unduly into the day-to-day operations of the religiously affiliated [grantees]." In remanding the as-applied challenge to the trial court, the Court suggested that the validity of the law as applied would turn on such issues as the "pervasive sectarian" nature of the grantees and whether any of the aid was used to finance "specifically religious activit[ies] in an otherwise substantially secular setting."

Justice O'CONNOR's concurrence emphasized that the majority opinion should not read as tolerating "the kind of improper administration that seems to have occurred [here]." She insisted that "*any* use of public funds to promote religious doctrines" was unconstitutional and that "*extensive* violations—if they can be proved in this case—will be highly relevant in shaping an appropriate remedy that ends such abuses." Justice KENNEDY, joined by Justice Scalia, also submitted a concurrence, arguing that a finding that funds went to a pervasively sectarian institution would still not be a sufficient condition for unconstitutionality, but only a preliminary step in determining the way federal funds were used: "The question in an as-applied challenge is not whether the entity is of a religious character, but how it spends its grant."

Justice BLACKMUN, joined by Justices Brennan, Marshall and Stevens, dissented, insisting the law was unconstitutional under the "effect" prong of Lemon. He would have found the law invalid on its face, because the involvement of religious organizations in teaching and counseling create an unacceptable risk that the message would in fact be religious. Although the Court had "recognized that the Constitution does not prohibit the government from supporting secular social-welfare services solely because they are provided by a religiously affiliated organization," he argued, there is "a very real and important difference between running a soup kitchen or a hospital, and counseling pregnant teenagers on how to make the difficult decisions facing them. The risk of advancing religion at public expense, and of creating an appearance that the government is endorsing the medium and the message, is much greater when the religious organization is directly engaged in pedagogy, with the express intent of shaping belief and changing behavior, than when it is neutrally dispensing medication, food, or shelter."

In **Zobrest v. Catalina Foothills School District**, 509 U.S. 1 (1993), the Court, relying on Mueller and Witters, held that the provision of a publicly funded sign language interpreter to a deaf student in a parochial school classroom did not violate the Establishment Clause. The Individuals with Disabilities Education Act and its state equivalent provided for funding such interpreters for hearing-impaired students generally. Writing for the Court, Chief Justice REHNQUIST held that the Establishment Clause did not mandate exclusion from such funding of an otherwise eligible student attending parochial school: "[W]e have consistently held that government programs that neutrally provide benefits to a broad class of citizens defined without reference to religion are not readily subject to an Establishment Clause challenge just because sectarian institutions may also receive an attenuated financial benefit." He emphasized that the Act did not distinguish between public and parochial schools, and found that it thus "creates no financial incentive for parents to choose a sectarian school." He rejected the argument that the Establishment Clause absolutely barred the presence of a public employee on parochial school premises. And he found no danger that the sign language interpreter would personally assist in religious instruction: "Nothing in this record suggests that a sign language interpreter would do more than accurately interpret whatever material is presented to the class as a whole." He concluded: "[Zobrest's] parents have chosen of their own free will to place him in a pervasively sectarian environment. The sign language interpreter they have requested will neither add to nor subtract from that environment, and hence the provision of such assistance is not barred by the Establishment Clause."

Justice BLACKMUN, joined by Justice Souter, dissented, objecting that "[u]ntil now, the Court never has authorized a public employee to participate directly in religious indoctrination. Yet that is the consequence of today's decision." Justice O'Connor, joined by Justice Stevens also dissented, on statutory grounds.

Recall that in **Rosenberger v. Rector and Visitors of The Univ. of Virginia**, 515 U.S. 819 (1995), p. 1328 above, the Court held that the Free Speech Clause required inclusion of an otherwise eligible student-edited evangelical Christian magazine called "Wide Awake" in a public university program that authorized payments from a mandatory Student Activities Fund to outside contractors for the printing costs of a variety of student-authored publications. The Court rejected the contention that such inclusion would violate the Establishment Clause. Justice KENNEDY, writing for the Court, found the Establishment Clause issue similar to that in Widmar: "The governmental program here is neutral toward religion. There is no suggestion that the University created it to advance religion or adopted some ingenious device with the purpose of aiding a religious cause. The object of the [funding program] is to open a forum for speech and to support various student enterprises, including the publication of newspapers, in recognition of the diversity and creativity of student life. [The] neutrality of the program distinguishes the student fees from a tax levied for the direct support of a church or group of churches.

"Government neutrality is apparent [also because the] University has taken pains to disassociate itself from the private speech involved in this case. [There] is no real likelihood that the speech in question is being either endorsed or coerced by the State. [We] do not confront a case where, even under a neutral program that includes nonsectarian recipients, the government is making direct money payments to an institution or group that is engaged in religious activity. [It is undisputed] that no public funds flow directly to [the Christian magazine's] coffers.

"It does not violate the Establishment Clause for a public university to grant access to its facilities on a religion-neutral basis to a wide spectrum of student groups, including groups which use meeting rooms for sectarian activities, accompanied by some devotional exercises. See [Widmar, Lamb's Chapel.] [A] public university may maintain its own computer facility and give student groups access to that facility, including the use of the printers, on a religion neutral, say first-come-first-served, basis. [There] is no difference in logic or principle, and no difference of constitutional significance, between a school using its funds to operate a facility to which students have access, and a school paying a third-party contractor to operate the facility on its behalf. [Any] benefit to religion is incidental to the government's provision of secular services for secular purposes on a religion-neutral basis. [By] paying outside printers, the University in fact attains a further degree of separation from the student publication, for it avoids the duties of supervision, escapes the costs of upkeep, repair, and replacement attributable to student use, and has a clear record of costs. [Moreover,] the student publication is not a religious institution. [It] is instead a publication involved in a pure forum for the expression of ideas."

Justice O'CONNOR wrote a concurrence, noting that "particular features of the University's program—such as the explicit disclaimer, the disbursement of funds directly to third-party vendors, the vigorous nature of the forum at issue, and the possibility for objecting students to opt out—convince me that providing such assistance in this case would not carry the danger of impermissible use of public funds to endorse Wide Awake's religious message." Justice THOMAS likewise concurred, emphasizing the historical pedigree of tax exemptions for religious institutions and arguing that the direct subsidy here posed no greater Establishment Clause problem: "The historical evidence of government support for religious entities through property tax exemptions is [overwhelming]. [Walz.] [This] tradition puts to rest the notion that the Establishment Clause bars monetary aid to religious groups even when the aid is equally available to other groups. A tax exemption in many cases is economically and functionally indistinguishable from a direct monetary subsidy. In one instance, the government relieves religious entities (along with others) of a generally applicable tax; in the other, it relieves religious entities (along with others) of some or all of the burden of that tax by returning it in the form of a cash subsidy. Whether the benefit is provided at the front or back end of the taxation process, the financial aid to religious groups is undeniable. The analysis under the Establishment Clause must also be the same."

Justice SOUTER, joined by Justices Stevens, Ginsburg and Breyer, dissented, arguing that funding Wide Awake would violate the Establishment Clause because it would employ "public funds for the direct subsidization of preaching the word. [If] the Clause was meant to accomplish nothing else, it was meant to bar this use of public money." He criticized the majority for "blanch[ing] the patently and frankly evangelistic character of the magazine." He also found it no defense that the "University's funding scheme is 'neutral,' in the formal sense that it makes funds available on an evenhanded basis to secular and sectarian applicants alike": "Evenhandedness as one element of a permissibly attenuated benefit is, of course, a far cry from evenhandedness as a sufficient condition of constitutionality for direct financial support of religious proselytization, and our cases have unsurprisingly repudiated any such attempt to cut the Establishment Clause down to a mere prohibition against unequal direct aid." He distinguished other cases permitting the inclusion of religious beneficiaries in funding programs: "Witters, Mueller, and Zobrest [explicitly] distinguished the indirect aid in issue from contrasting examples in the line of cases striking down direct aid, and each thereby expressly preserved the core constitutional principle that direct aid to religion is impermissible." He found unconvincing the argument that payment to the third-party printer broke the chain of direct aid: "If this indeed were a critical distinction, the Constitution would permit a State to pay all the bills of any religious institution." He also found unconvincing the argument that the mandatory student fee somehow differed for Establishment Clause purposes from a general tax: "[O]ur cases on direct government aid have frequently spoken in terms in no way limited to tax revenues." He concluded: "The Court is ordering an instrumentality of the State to support religious evangelism with direct funding. This is a flat violation of the Establishment Clause."

The strong trend of deference toward inclusion of religious beneficiaries in public programs in the above cases raised some doubt about two 1985 decisions that had invalidated public educational programs carried out at parochial schools. In **Grand Rapids School District v. Ball**, 473 U.S. 373 (1985), and **Aguilar v. Felton**, 473 U.S. 402 (1985), the Court struck down programs in which public school teachers, paid from public funds, offered supplementary classes such as remedial math and reading in parochial school classrooms, and conducted community education in parochial school buildings.

In **Agostini v. Felton**, 521 U.S. 203 (1997), a case involving the use at private religious schools of public remedial education funds under Title I of the Elementary and Secondary Education Act of 1965, the Court overruled those decisions, declaring Aguilar "no longer good law." Justice O'CONNOR wrote for the 5–4 majority of the Court. She began by noting that, after Aguilar had invalidated the use of public funds to teach publicly funded remedial courses inside parochial school classrooms, the New York school board had resorted to teaching parochial school students "at public school sites, at leased sites, and in mobile instructional units (essentially vans converted into classrooms) parked near the sectarian school," all at significant additional cost. She now rejected Aguilar's and Ball's assumptions: "[First,] we have abandoned the presumption [that] the placement of public employees on parochial school grounds inevitably results in the impermissible effect of state-sponsored indoctrination or constitutes a symbolic union between government and religion. [Zobrest] expressly rejected the notion—relied on in Ball and Aguilar—that, solely because of her presence on private school property, a public employee will be presumed to inculcate religion in the students. Zobrest also implicitly repudiated [the] assumption [that] the presence of a public employee on private school property creates an impermissible 'symbolic link' between government and religion. [Second,] we have departed from the rule relied on in Ball that all government aid that directly aids the educational function of religious schools is invalid. In Witters, we held that the Establishment Clause did not bar a State from issuing a vocational tuition grant to a blind person who wished to use the grant to attend a Christian college and become a pastor, missionary, or youth director. [The] same logic applied in Zobrest. [We] do not see any perceptible (let alone dispositive) difference in the degree of symbolic union between a student receiving remedial instruction in a classroom on his sectarian school's campus and one receiving instruction in a van parked just at the school's curbside. Nor under current law can we conclude that a program placing full-time public employees on parochial campuses to provide Title I instruction would impermissibly finance religious indoctrination. In all relevant respects, the provision of instructional services under Title I is indistinguishable from the provision of sign-language interpreters [in Zobrest]. Both programs make aid available only to eligible recipients. That aid is provided to students at whatever school they choose to attend. [And,] as in Zobrest, Title I services are by law supplemental to the regular curricula. [They] do not, therefore, 'relieve sectarian schools of costs they otherwise would have borne in educating their students.'

"[Where] aid is allocated on the basis of neutral, secular criteria that neither favor nor disfavor religion, and is made available to both religious and secular beneficiaries on a nondiscriminatory basis, [the] aid is less likely to have the effect of advancing religion. [We] therefore hold that a federally funded program providing supplemental, remedial instruction to disadvantaged children on a neutral basis is not invalid under the Establishment Clause when such instruction is given on the premises of sectarian schools."

Justice SOUTER dissented, joined by Justices Stevens, Ginsburg and, in part, Breyer: "[The] flat ban on subsidization antedates the Bill of Rights and has been an unwavering rule in Establishment Clause cases. [The] rule expresses the hard lesson learned over and over again in the American past and in the experiences of the countries from which we have come, that religions supported by governments are compromised just as surely as the religious freedom of dissenters is burdened when the government supports religion. [If] a State may constitutionally enter the schools to teach [remedial education,] it must in constitutional principle be free to assume, or assume payment for, the entire cost of instruction provided in any ostensibly secular subject in any religious school. [Zobrest] is no [sanction] for overruling Aguilar or any portion of Ball. In Zobrest [the] signer could [be] seen as more like a hearing aid than a teacher, and the signing could not be understood as an opportunity to inject religious content in what was supposed to be secular instruction. [In] Zobrest and Witters, it was fair to say that individual students were themselves applicants for individual benefits. [But] under Title I, a local educational agency [may] receive federal funding by proposing programs approved to serve individual students who meet the criteria of need, which it then uses to provide such programs at the religious schools; students eligible for such programs may not apply directly for Title I funds." Justice Ginsburg filed a separate dissent.

In its first major test of the scope of Agostini, **Mitchell v. Helms**, 530 U.S. 793 (2000), the Court upheld against establishment challenge a program that provided publicly funded computers and other teaching aids to public and private elementary and secondary schools, including parochial schools. Justice THOMAS, announcing the judgment of the Court and writing for himself, Chief Justice Rehnquist and Justices Scalia and Kennedy, held that the only issue in the case was whether the program had an impermissibly religious effect, and outlined a comprehensive approach to how neutrality should be assessed in challenges to parochial aid: "As a way of assuring neutrality, we have repeatedly considered whether any governmental aid that goes to a religious institution does so 'only as a result of the genuinely independent and private choices of individuals.' Agostini. [For] if numerous private choices, rather than the single choice of a government, determine the distribution of aid pursuant to neutral eligibility criteria, then a government cannot, or at least cannot easily, grant special favors that might lead to a religious establishment." Justice O'CONNOR, joined by Justice Breyer, filed a separate concurrence only in the judgment, objecting that "the plurality's treatment of neutrality comes close to assigning that factor singular importance in the future adjudication of Establishment Clause challenges to government school-aid programs." Justice SOUTER, joined by Justices Stevens and Ginsburg, dissented: "It is beyond question that the plurality's notion of evenhandedness [as] a practical guarantee of the validity of aid to sectarian schools would be the end of the principle of no aid to the schools' religious mission. [To] the plurality there is nothing wrong with aiding a school's religious mission; the only question is whether religious teaching obtains its tax support under a formally evenhanded criterion of distribution. [In] rejecting the principle of no aid to a school's religious mission the plurality is attacking the most fundamental assumption underlying the Establishment Clause, that government can in fact operate with neutrality in its relation to religion."

5. ***School voucher schemes and parochial schools.*** Mitchell v. Helms gave rise to speculation about the Court's likely reaction to head-on constitutional challenges to voucher schemes that permitted the use of public monies by parents to send their children to religious schools. In the case that follows, the Court finally reached squarely the issue of the constitutionality of such voucher schemes under the Establishment Clause, and found the use of such vouchers permissible:

Zelman v. Simmons-Harris

536 U.S. 639, 122 S. Ct. 2460, 153 L. Ed. 2d 604 (2002).

■ CHIEF JUSTICE REHNQUIST delivered the opinion of the Court.

The State of Ohio has established a pilot program designed to provide educational choices to families with children who reside in the Cleveland City School District. The question presented is whether this program offends the Establishment Clause of the United States Constitution. We hold that it does not.

[There] are more than 75,000 children enrolled in the Cleveland City School District. The majority of these children are from low-income and minority families. Few of these families enjoy the means to send their children to any school other than an inner-city public school. For more than a generation, however, Cleveland's public schools have been among the worst performing public schools in the Nation. [It] is against this backdrop that Ohio enacted [its] Pilot Project Scholarship Program. The program provides financial assistance to families in any Ohio school district that is or has been "under federal court order requiring supervision and operational management of the district by the state superintendent." Cleveland is the only Ohio school district to fall within that category. The program provides [tuition] aid for students in kindergarten through third grade, expanding each year through eighth grade, to attend a participating public or private school of their parent's choosing.

[The] tuition aid portion of the program is designed to provide educational choices to parents who reside in a covered district. Any private school, whether religious or nonreligious, may participate in the program and accept program students so long as the school is located within the boundaries of a covered district and meets statewide educational standards. Participating private schools must agree not to discriminate on the basis of race, religion, or ethnic background, or to "advocate or foster unlawful behavior or teach hatred of any person or group on the basis of race, ethnicity, national origin, or religion." Any public school located in a school district adjacent to the covered district may also participate in the program. Adjacent public schools are eligible to receive a $2,250 tuition grant for each program student accepted in addition to the full amount of per-pupil state funding attributable to each additional student. [Tuition] aid is distributed to parents according to financial need.

[The] program has been in operation within the Cleveland City School District since the 1996–1997 school year. In the 1999–2000 school year, 56 private schools participated in the program, 46 (or 82%) of which had a religious affiliation. None of the public schools in districts adjacent to Cleveland have elected to participate. More than 3,700 students participated in the scholarship program, most of whom (96%) enrolled in religiously affiliated schools. [The] program is part of a broader undertaking by the State to enhance the educational options of Cleveland's schoolchildren in response to the 1995 takeover. That undertaking includes programs governing community and magnet schools.

[The] Establishment Clause of the First Amendment, applied to the States through the Fourteenth Amendment, prevents a State from enacting laws that have the "purpose" or "effect" of advancing or inhibiting religion. There is no dispute that the program challenged here was enacted for the valid secular purpose of providing educational assistance to poor children in a demonstrably failing public school system. Thus, the question presented is whether the Ohio program nonetheless has the forbidden "effect" of advancing or inhibiting religion.

To answer that question, our decisions have drawn a consistent distinction between government programs that provide aid directly to religious schools [Mitchell, Agostini, Rosenberger], and programs of true private choice, in which government aid reaches religious schools only as a result of the genuine and independent choices of private individuals. While our jurisprudence with respect to the constitutionality of direct aid programs has "changed significantly" over the past two decades, our jurisprudence with respect to true private choice programs has remained consistent and unbroken. Three times we have confronted Establishment Clause challenges to neutral government programs that provide aid directly to a broad class of individuals, who, in turn, direct the aid to religious schools or institutions of their own choosing. Three times we have rejected such challenges.

In Mueller, we rejected an Establishment Clause challenge to a Minnesota program authorizing tax deductions for various educational expenses, including private school tuition costs, even though the great majority of the program's beneficiaries (96%) were parents of children in religious schools. [That] the program was one of true private choice, with no evidence that the State deliberately skewed incentives toward religious schools, was sufficient for the program to survive scrutiny under the Establishment Clause. In Witters, we used identical reasoning to reject an Establishment Clause challenge to a vocational scholarship program that provided tuition aid to a student studying at a religious institution to become a pastor. [Finally], in Zobrest, we applied Mueller and Witters to reject an Establishment Clause challenge to a federal program that permitted sign-language interpreters to assist deaf children enrolled in religious schools. [Our] focus again was on neutrality and the principle of private choice, not on the number of program beneficiaries attending religious schools.

[These cases] thus make clear that where a government aid program is neutral with respect to religion, and provides assistance directly to a broad class of citizens who, in turn, direct government aid to religious schools wholly as a result of their own genuine and independent private choice, the program is not readily subject to challenge under the Establishment Clause. A program that shares these features permits government aid to reach religious institutions only by way of the deliberate choices of numerous individual recipients. The incidental advancement of a religious mission, or the perceived endorsement of a religious message, is reasonably attributable to the individual recipient, not to the government, whose role ends with the disbursement of benefits.

[We] believe that the program challenged here is a program of true private choice, consistent with Mueller, Witters, and Zobrest, and thus constitutional. As was true in those cases, the Ohio program is neutral in all respects toward religion. It is part of a general and multifaceted undertaking by the State of Ohio to provide educational opportunities to the children of a failed school district. It confers educational assistance directly to a broad class of individuals defined without reference to religion, i.e., any parent of a school-age child who resides in the Cleveland City School District. The program permits the participation of *all* schools within the district, religious or nonreligious. Adjacent public schools also may participate and have a financial incentive to do so. Program benefits are available to participating families on neutral terms, with no reference to religion.[1]

[There] are no "financial incentives" that "skew" the program toward religious schools. [The] program here in fact creates financial *dis*incentives for religious schools, with private schools receiving only half the government assistance given to community schools and one-third the assistance given to magnet schools. Adjacent public schools, should any choose to accept program students, are also eligible to receive two to three times the state funding of a private religious school. Families too have a financial disincentive to choose a private religious school over other schools. Parents that choose to participate in the scholarship program and then to enroll their children in a private school (religious or nonreligious) must copay a portion of the school's tuition. Families that choose a community school, magnet school, or traditional public school pay nothing.

[We] have repeatedly recognized that no reasonable observer would think a neutral program of private choice, where state aid reaches religious schools solely as a result of the numerous independent decisions of private individuals, carries with it the *imprimatur* of government endorsement.

[1] Later in the opinion Chief Justice Rehnquist noted, "To the extent the scope of Nyquist has remained an open question in light of these later decisions, we now hold that Nyquist does not govern neutral educational assistance programs that, like the program here, offer aid directly to a broad class of individual recipients defined without regard to religion."

[Any] objective observer familiar with the full history and context of the Ohio program would reasonably view it as one aspect of a broader undertaking to assist poor children in failed schools, not as an endorsement of religious schooling in general.

There also is no evidence that the program fails to provide genuine opportunities for Cleveland parents to select secular educational options for their school-age children. Cleveland schoolchildren enjoy a range of educational choices: They may remain in public school as before, remain in public school with publicly funded tutoring aid, obtain a scholarship and choose a religious school, obtain a scholarship and choose a nonreligious private school, enroll in a community school, or enroll in a magnet school. That 46 of the 56 private schools now participating in the program are religious schools does not condemn it as a violation of the Establishment Clause.

[Justice Souter] speculates that because more private religious schools currently participate in the program, the program itself must somehow discourage the participation of private nonreligious schools. But Cleveland's preponderance of religiously affiliated private schools certainly did not arise as a result of the program; it is a phenomenon common to many American cities. Indeed, by all accounts the program has captured a remarkable cross-section of private schools, religious and nonreligious. It is true that 82% of Cleveland's participating private schools are religious schools, but it is also true that 81% of private schools in Ohio are religious schools. [The] constitutionality of a neutral educational aid program simply does not turn on whether and why, in a particular area, at a particular time, most private schools are run by religious organizations, or most recipients choose to use the aid at a religious school. [This] point is aptly illustrated here. The 96% figure upon which respondents and Justice Souter rely discounts entirely (1) the more than 1,900 Cleveland children enrolled in alternative community schools, (2) the more than 13,000 children enrolled in alternative magnet schools, and (3) the more than 1,400 children enrolled in traditional public schools with tutorial assistance. Including some or all of these children in the denominator of children enrolled in nontraditional schools during the 1999–2000 school year drops the percentage enrolled in religious schools from 96% to under 20%.

In sum, the Ohio program is entirely neutral with respect to religion. It provides benefits directly to a wide spectrum of individuals, defined only by financial need and residence in a particular school district. It permits such individuals to exercise genuine choice among options public and private, secular and religious. The program is therefore a program of true private choice. In keeping with an unbroken line of decisions rejecting challenges to similar programs, we hold that the program does not offend the Establishment Clause. [Reversed.]

■ JUSTICE THOMAS, concurring.

Frederick Douglass once said that "education . . . means emancipation. It means light and liberty. It means the uplifting of the soul of man into the glorious light of truth, the light by which men can only be made free." Today many of our inner-city public schools deny emancipation to urban minority students. Despite this Court's observation nearly 50 years ago in Brown v. Board of Education, that "it is doubtful that any child may reasonably be expected to succeed in life if he is denied the opportunity of an education," urban children have been forced into a system that continually fails them.

These cases present an example of such failures. Besieged by escalating financial problems and declining academic achievement, the Cleveland City School District was in the midst of an academic emergency when Ohio enacted its scholarship program. [Today's] decision properly upholds the program as constitutional, and I join it in full.

The Establishment Clause of the First Amendment states that "Congress shall make no law respecting an establishment of religion." On its face, this provision places no limit on the States with regard to religion. [In] the context of the Establishment Clause, it may well be that state action should be evaluated on different terms than similar action by the Federal Government. [Whatever] the textual and historical merits of incorporating the Establishment Clause, I can accept that the Fourteenth Amendment protects religious liberty rights. But I cannot accept its use to oppose neutral programs of school choice through the incorporation of the Establishment Clause. There would be a tragic irony in converting the Fourteenth Amendment's guarantee of individual liberty into a prohibition on the exercise of educational choice.

■ JUSTICE SOUTER, with whom JUSTICES STEVENS, GINSBURG, and BREYER join, dissenting.

The Court's majority holds that the Establishment Clause is no bar to Ohio's payment of tuition at private religious elementary and middle schools under a scheme that systematically provides tax money to support the schools' religious missions. The occasion for the legislation thus upheld is the condition of public education in the city of Cleveland. The record indicates that the schools are failing to serve their objective, and the vouchers in issue here are said to be needed to provide adequate alternatives to them. If there were an excuse for giving short shrift to the Establishment Clause, it would probably apply here. But there is no excuse. Constitutional limitations are placed on government to preserve constitutional values in hard cases, like these.

[The] applicability of the Establishment Clause to public funding of benefits to religious schools was settled in Everson. "No tax in any amount, large or small, can be levied to support any religious activities or institutions, whatever they may be called, or whatever form they may adopt to teach or practice religion." The Court has never in so many words repudiated this statement, let alone, in so many words, overruled Everson. Today, however, the majority holds that the Establishment Clause is not offended by Ohio's Pilot Project Scholarship Program, under which students may be eligible to receive as much as $2,250 in the form of tuition vouchers transferable to religious schools. In the city of Cleveland the overwhelming proportion of large appropriations for voucher money must be spent on religious schools if it is to be spent at all, and will be spent in amounts that cover almost all of tuition. The money will thus pay for eligible students' instruction not only in secular subjects but in religion as well, in schools that can fairly be characterized as founded to teach religious doctrine and to imbue teaching in all subjects with a religious dimension. Public tax money will pay at a systemic level for teaching the covenant with Israel and Mosaic law in Jewish schools, the primacy of the Apostle Peter and the Papacy in Catholic schools, the truth of reformed Christianity in Protestant schools, and the revelation to the Prophet in Muslim schools, to speak only of major religious groupings in the Republic. Can a Court consistently leave Everson on the books and approve the Ohio vouchers? The answer is that it cannot. It is only by ignoring Everson that the majority can claim to rest on traditional law in its invocation of neutral aid provisions and private choice to sanction the Ohio law.

[Although] it has taken half a century since Everson to reach the majority's twin standards of neutrality and free choice, the facts show that, in the majority's hands, even these criteria cannot convincingly legitimize the Ohio scheme. ["Neutrality"] as the majority employs the term is, literally, verbal and nothing more. This, indeed, is the only way the majority can gloss over the very nonneutral feature of the total scheme covering "*all* schools": public tutors may receive from the State no more than $324 per child to support extra tutoring (that is, the State's 90% of a total amount of $360), whereas the tuition voucher schools (which turn out to be mostly religious) can receive up to $2,250. [Likewise,] the majority has confused choice in spending scholarships with choice from the entire menu of possible educational placements, most of them open to anyone willing to attend a public school. [The] majority's view that all educational choices are comparable for purposes of choice thus ignores the whole point of the choice test: it is a criterion for deciding whether indirect aid to a religious school is legitimate because it passes through private hands that can spend or use the aid in a secular school. [The] majority now has transformed this question about private choice in channeling aid into a question about selecting from examples of state spending (on education) including direct spending on magnet and community public schools that goes through no private hands and could never reach a religious school under any circumstance. When the choice test is transformed from where to spend the money to where to go to school, it is cut loose from its very purpose.

[If,] contrary to the majority, we ask the right question about genuine choice to use the vouchers, the answer shows that something is influencing choices in a way that aims the money in a religious direction: of 56 private schools in the district participating in the voucher program (only 53 of which accepted voucher students in 1999–2000), 46 of them are religious; 96.6% of all voucher recipients go to religious schools, only 3.4% to nonreligious ones. Unfortunately for the majority position, there is no explanation for this that suggests the religious direction results simply from free choices by parents. [Evidence shows] that almost two out of three families using vouchers to send their children to religious schools did not embrace the religion of those schools. The families made it clear they had not chosen the schools because they wished their children to be proselytized in a religion not their own, or in any religion, but because of educational opportunity.

[There is] no way to interpret the 96.6% of current voucher money going to religious schools as reflecting a free and genuine choice by the families that apply for vouchers. The 96.6% reflects, instead, the fact that too few nonreligious school desks are available and few but religious schools can afford to accept more than a handful of voucher students. And contrary to the majority's assertion, public schools in adjacent districts hardly have a financial incentive to participate in the Ohio voucher program, and none has. For the overwhelming number of children in the voucher scheme, the only alternative to the public schools is religious. And it is entirely irrelevant that the State did not deliberately design the network of private schools for the sake of channeling money into religious institutions. The criterion is one of genuinely free choice on the part of the private individuals who choose, and a Hobson's choice is not a choice, whatever the reason for being Hobsonian.

[For] perspective on this foot-in-the-door of religious regulation, it is well to remember that the money has barely begun to flow. Prior examples of aid, whether grants through individuals or in-kind assistance, were never significant enough to alter the basic fiscal structure of religious schools; state aid was welcome, but not indispensable. But given the figures already involved here, there is no question that religious schools in Ohio are on the way to becoming bigger businesses with budgets enhanced to fit their new stream of tax-raised income. [The] intensity of the expectable friction can be gauged by realizing that the scramble for money will energize not only contending sectarians, but taxpayers who take their liberty of conscience seriously. Religious teaching at taxpayer expense simply cannot be cordoned from taxpayer politics, and every major religion currently espouses social positions that provoke intense opposition. Not all taxpaying Protestant citizens, for example, will be content to underwrite the teaching of the Roman Catholic Church condemning the death penalty. Nor will all of America's Muslims acquiesce in paying for the endorsement of the religious Zionism taught in many religious Jewish schools, which combines "a nationalistic sentiment" in support of Israel with a "deeply religious" element. Nor will every secular taxpayer be content to support Muslim views on differential treatment of the sexes, or, for that matter, to fund the espousal of a wife's obligation of obedience to her husband, presumably taught in any schools adopting the articles of faith of the Southern Baptist Convention. Views like these, and innumerable others, have been safe in the sectarian pulpits and classrooms of this Nation not only because the Free Exercise Clause protects them directly, but because the ban on supporting religious establishment has protected free exercise, by keeping it relatively private. With the arrival of vouchers in religious schools, that privacy will go, and along with it will go confidence that religious disagreement will stay moderate.

■ JUSTICE BREYER, with whom JUSTICE STEVENS and JUSTICE SOUTER join, dissenting.

I write separately [to] emphasize the risk that publicly financed voucher programs pose in terms of religiously based social conflict. I do so because I believe that the Establishment Clause concern for protecting the Nation's social fabric from religious conflict poses an overriding obstacle to the implementation of this well-intentioned school voucher program.

The principle [of] avoiding religiously based social conflict [ ] remains of great concern. As religiously diverse as America had become when the Court decided its major 20th-century Establishment Clause cases, we are exponentially more diverse today. America boasts more than 55 different religious groups and subgroups with a significant number of members. Major religions include, among others, Protestants, Catholics, Jews, Muslims, Buddhists, Hindus, and Sikhs. And several of these major religions contain different subsidiary sects with different religious beliefs. Newer Christian immigrant groups are "expressing their Christianity in languages, customs, and independent churches that are barely recognizable, and often controversial, for European-ancestry Catholics and Protestants."

Under these modern-day circumstances, how is the "equal opportunity" principle to work—without risking the "struggle of sect against sect"[?] School voucher programs finance the religious education of the young. And, if widely adopted, they may well provide billions of dollars that will do so. Why will different religions not become concerned about, and seek to influence, the criteria used to channel this money to religious schools? Why will they not want to examine the implementation of the programs that provide this money—to determine, for example, whether implementation has biased a program toward or against particular sects, or whether recipient religious schools are adequately fulfilling a program's criteria? If so, just how is the State to resolve the resulting controversies without provoking legitimate fears of the kinds of religious favoritism that, in so religiously diverse a Nation, threaten social dissension?

Consider the voucher program here at issue. That program insists that the religious school accept students of all religions. Does that criterion treat fairly groups whose religion forbids them to do so? The program also insists that no participating school "advocate or foster unlawful behavior or teach hatred of any person or group on the basis of race, ethnicity, national origin, or religion." Ohio Rev. Code Ann. § 3313.976(A)(6). And it requires the State to "revoke the registration of any school if, after a hearing, the superintendent determines that the school is in violation" of the program's rules. § 3313.976(B). As one amicus argues, "it is difficult to imagine a more divisive activity" than the appointment of state officials as referees to determine whether a particular religious doctrine "teaches hatred or advocates lawlessness."

How are state officials to adjudicate claims that one religion or another is advocating, for example, civil disobedience in response to unjust laws, the use of illegal drugs in a religious ceremony, or resort to force to call attention to what it views as an immoral social practice? What kind of public hearing will there be in response to claims that one religion or another is continuing to teach a view of history that casts members of other religions in the worst possible light? How will the public react to government funding for schools that take controversial religious positions on topics that are of current popular interest—say, the conflict in the Middle East or the war on terrorism? Yet any major funding program for primary religious education will require criteria. And the selection of those criteria, as well as their application, inevitably pose problems that are divisive. Efforts to respond to these problems not only will seriously entangle church and state, see Lemon, p. 1615, but also will promote division among religious groups, as one group or another fears (often legitimately) that it will receive unfair treatment at the hands of the government.

THE MEANING AND IMPLICATIONS OF ZELMAN

1. ***The scope of permissible conditions on voucher programs.*** The Cleveland plan permitted public funds to be transferred to religious schools only if they agreed not to discriminate on the basis of race, religion or ethnic background, or to "advocate or foster unlawful behavior or teach hatred of any person or group on the basis of race, ethnicity, national origin, or religion." Are such prerequisites for public funding required by the Establishment Clause? The Equal Protection Clause? Or are they forbidden by the Free Exercise or Free Speech Clauses as unconstitutional conditions on the distribution of public funds?

How far may public values be required to govern the life of religious entities? May the energy of faith-based services be harnessed to the public values of the state without depleting the normative pluralism that religious diversity provides as a check on government in the first place? Are public strings on privatized services a desirable vehicle for liberalizing the private religious realm? Will government's introduction of public values into the religious sphere, in the form of inducements rather than coercion, have a beneficial civilizing and liberalizing influence on religion, helping to curb religious rivalries that tear societies apart and to guide the potentially unruly private religious sector toward ever greater commonality and peace? For suggestions along these lines, see Macedo, "Constituting Civil Society: School Vouchers, Religious Nonprofit Organizations, and Liberal Public Values," 75 Chi.-Kent L. Rev. 417 (2000); Minow, "Public and Private Partnerships: Accounting for the New Religion," 116 Harv. L. Rev. 1229, 1261 (2003). Or are such conditions on religious recipients of public funds a pernicious and colonizing force, likely to homogenize the rich diversity of religious viewpoints and ways of life, leveling all faiths to a bland common denominator and bleeding normative pluralism of its color and vibrancy? See Sullivan, "The New Religion and the Constitution," 116 Harv. L. Rev. 1397 (2003).

Do founding principles of religious liberty offer any guidance on these questions? Consider the view that perhaps "we—and Madison—cannot have it both ways: a multiplicity of politically mobilized but nevertheless distinctive and uncorrupted religious sects that serve as a check on government, combined with a politics of civility, moderation, mutual respect, equal civic status, and significant common ground. [Madison's] philosophy of church-state relations cannot decide for us the constitutionality of school vouchers. But his Memorial and Remonstrance at least should convince us that we cannot resolve this momentous issue in peremptory fashion by giving controlling weight to the features of inclusiveness and parental choice (to uphold a voucher scheme) or the direct subsidization of purely sectarian teaching (to strike it down)." Blasi, Essay, "School Vouchers and Religious Liberty: Seven Questions from Madison's Memorial and Remonstrance," 87 Cornell L. Rev. 783 (2002).

2. ***Implications of Zelman for other forms of religious participation in public programs.*** After Zelman, may government include in a public medical funding scheme a Catholic hospital that denies abortion and contraceptive services on religious grounds? May religious groups use federal housing funds to help build religious worship facilities? May government fund a religious drug treatment contractor that rehabilitates alcoholics and drug addicts through faith and the Word? The federal welfare reform act of 1996 permitted religious entity participation in welfare-to-work programs, and President George W. Bush promoted the inclusion of faith-based organizations in government programs that provide many other kinds of social services. Consider the following view: "The context of Zelman is education, but in principle its approval of indirect funding of services provided by religious entities extends seamlessly to other social services. Formal neutrality and 'true private choice' remain the measure of constitutionality." Lupu & Tuttle, "Zelman's Future: Vouchers, Sectarian Providers, and the Next Round of Constitutional Battles," 78 Notre Dame L. Rev. 917 (2003). See also Esbeck, "A Constitutional Case for Governmental Cooperation with Faith-Based Social Service Providers," 46 Emory L.J. 1, 27 (1997). Does it matter how the funds are distributed—to the provider or the beneficiary? Compare, for example, Freedom from Religion Found., Inc. v. McCallum, 179 F. Supp. 2d 950 (W.D. Wis. 2002) (holding that Wisconsin's direct funding of Faith Works, a faith-based alcohol and drug treatment

program, violates the Establishment Clause), with Freedom from Religion Found., Inc. v. McCallum, 214 F. Supp. 2d 905 (W.D. Wis. 2002) (upholding a voucher-like arrangement whereby the Wisconsin Department of Corrections would refer offenders to Faith Works and pay per offender).

3. ***Continuing barriers to voucher programs.*** Many predicted a rapid proliferation of voucher programs in the immediate wake of Zelman, but this growth failed to materialize. For one explanation of voucher programs' limited political success immediately after Zelman, see James Forman, Jr., The Rise and Fall of School Vouchers: A Story of Religion, Race, and Politics, 54 U.C.L.A. L. Rev. 547 (2007) (citing, among other things, the rise of the "accountability movement" in education and the No Child Left Behind Act).

After Republicans took control of statehouses across the country in the 2010 midterm elections, voucher programs gained renewed popularity, with statewide programs enacted in Louisiana, Indiana, Nevada and Wisconsin. But the constitutions of the latter three states contain "Baby Blaine" amendments, see p. 1616, which prohibit the states from giving financial aid to any sectarian institution. The Florida Supreme Court struck down the nation's first state-wide voucher program in Bush v. Holmes, 919 So. 2d 392 (2006), under the state's Blaine Amendment, and the Colorado Supreme Court issued a similar ruling in 2015. On the other hand, the Wisconsin and Indiana Supreme Courts have heard and rejected Blaine Amendment challenges to the states' voucher programs.

RELIGION IN PUBLIC SCHOOLS

Recall that in McCollum v. Board of Education (p. 1621 above), the Court struck down a school board's practice of permitting students to attend sectarian classes held in public schools during school hours by parochial instructors. The Court stated that the practice not only constituted aid to religion but also was problematic for its use of public school buildings. In Zorach v. Clauson (p. 1621 above), however, the Court upheld a New York City "released time" program that permitted its public schools to release students to go to religious institutions for religious instruction. The Court distinguished Zorach from McCollum on the ground that, in McCollum, "the classrooms were used for religious instruction and the force of the public school was used to promote that instruction." As the materials that follow indicate, the Court has found that additional considerations must be taken into account when addressing Establishment Clause challenges in the context of public schools.

PRAYER IN PUBLIC SCHOOLS

1. ***Teacher-led prayers, Bible readings and moments of silence.*** The Court has consistently struck down school prayer initiated by school officials as a violation of the Establishment Clause. The Court's first encounter with the problem came in **Engel v. Vitale**, 370 U.S. 421 (1962). There, the New York Board of Regents had prepared a "nondenominational" prayer for use in the public schools, which read: "Almighty God, we

acknowledge our dependence upon Thee, and we beg Thy blessings upon us, our parents, our teachers and our Country." A local school board directed that the prayer be recited daily by each class. That practice was challenged by parents of a number of students who claimed that it was "contrary to the beliefs, religions, or religious practices of both themselves and their children." The highest state court upheld the practice, so long as the schools did not compel any student to join in the prayer over a parent's objection. Justice BLACK's majority opinion held the practice "wholly inconsistent with the Establishment Clause." The practice was clearly "a religious activity" and the Establishment Clause "must at least mean that [it] is no part of the business of government to compose official prayers for any group of the American people to recite as a part of a religious program carried on by government."

Justice Black added: "Neither the fact that the prayer may be denominationally neutral, nor the fact that its observance on the part of the students is voluntary, can serve to free it from the limitations of the Establishment Clause, as it might from the Free Exercise [Clause]. Although these two clauses may in certain instances overlap, they forbid two quite different kinds of governmental encroachment upon religious freedom. The Establishment Clause, unlike the Free Exercise Clause, does not depend upon any showing of direct governmental compulsion and is violated by the enactment of laws which establish an official religion whether those laws operate directly to coerce nonobserving individuals or not. This is not to say, of course, that laws officially prescribing a particular form of religious worship do not involve coercion of such individuals. When the power, prestige and financial support of government is placed behind a particular religious belief, the indirect coercive pressure upon religious minorities to conform to the prevailing officially approved religion is plain. But the purposes underlying the Establishment Clause go much further than that. [Its] most immediate purpose rested on the belief that a union of government and religion tends to destroy government and to degrade religion. [Another] purpose [rested upon] an awareness of the historical fact that governmentally established religions and religious persecutions go hand in hand."

Justice STEWART's dissent relied on Zorach in concluding that New York's practice merely recognized "the deeply entrenched and highly cherished spiritual traditions of our Nation"—and that the references to religion and to God in such practices as congressional prayers and official oaths were similarly justified. Justice Douglas concurred separately; Justices Frankfurter and White did not participate.

One year after Engel, the Court extended the principles of that case beyond state-composed prayers. **Abington School District v. Schempp**, 374 U.S. 203 (1963), held that the Establishment Clause prohibits state laws and practices "requiring the selection and reading at the opening of the school day of verses from the Holy Bible and the recitation of the Lord's Prayer by the students in unison." The Pennsylvania law in Schempp provided: "At least ten verses from the Holy Bible shall be read, without comment, at the opening of each public school on each school day. Any child shall be excused from such Bible reading, or attending such Bible reading, upon the written request of his parent or guardian." The Schempp family, members of the Unitarian Church, successfully challenged high school opening exercises involving the recitation of the Lord's Prayer as well as the reading of the Bible verses.

Justice CLARK's opinion for the Court stated: "The wholesome 'neutrality' of which this Court's cases speak [stems] from a recognition of the teachings of history that powerful sects or groups might bring about a fusion of governmental and religious functions or a concert or dependency of one upon the other to the end that official support of the State or Federal Government would be placed behind the tenets of one or of all orthodoxies. This the Establishment Clause prohibits. [The] test may be stated as follows: what are the purpose and the primary effect of the enactment? If either is the advancement or inhibition of religion then the enactment exceeds the scope of legislative power as circumscribed by the Constitution." Applying those principles (which foreshadowed the Lemon test), Justice Clark noted that "it is no defense to urge that the religious practices here may be relatively minor encroachments on the First Amendment. The breach of neutrality that is today a trickling stream may all too soon become a raging torrent." He pointed out that the decision did not bar the "study of the Bible or of religion, when presented objectively as part of a secular program of education." But that was not the case here: these were "religious exercises, required by the State in violation of the command of the First Amendment that the Government maintain strict neutrality, neither aiding nor opposing religion." Justices Douglas, Goldberg and Brennan filed separate concurrences.

Justice STEWART, the sole dissenter, insisted that "religion and government must necessarily interact in countless ways" and that "there are areas in which a doctrinaire reading of the Establishment Clause leads to irreconcilable conflict with the Free Exercise Clause." He elaborated: "The dangers both to government and to religion inherent in official support of instruction in the tenets of various religious sects [see McCollum] are absent in the present cases, which involve only a reading from the Bible unaccompanied by comments which might otherwise constitute instruction. [In] the absence of coercion upon those who do not wish to [participate], such provisions cannot [be] held to represent the type of support of religion barred by the [Establishment Clause]. [W]hether [the exercises] are constitutionally invalid [turns] on the question of coercion. [Certain] types of exercises would present situations in which no possibility of coercion on the part of secular officials could be claimed to exist. [But] a law which provided for religious exercises during the school day and which contained no excusal provision would obviously be unconstitutionally coercive upon those who did not wish to participate. And even under a law containing an excusal provision, if the exercises were held during the school day, and no equally desirable alternative were provided by the school authorities, the likelihood that children might be under at least some psychological compulsion to participate would be great. In a case such as the latter, however, I think we would err if we *assumed* such coercion in the absence of any evidence. Viewed in this light, it seems to be clear that the [record here is] wholly inadequate to support an informed or responsible decision."

The issue of school prayer returned to the Court in **Wallace v. Jaffree**, 472 U.S. 38 (1985). The decision struck down an Alabama law authorizing schools to set aside one minute at the start of each day "for meditation or voluntary prayer." The statute was an amendment of an earlier law which had authorized a one-minute period of silence in all public schools merely "for meditation." Justice STEVENS's opinion for the Court stated that "the individual freedom of conscience protected by the First Amendment embraces the right to select any religious faith or none at all." He found that the law "was not motivated by any clearly secular purpose," thus violating the Lemon test. He noted that the state legislator sponsoring the amendment had said that it was an "effort to return voluntary prayer" to the public schools. He elaborated: "The legislative intent to return prayer to the public schools is, of course, quite different from merely protecting every student's right to engage in voluntary prayer during an appropriate moment of silence during the school day." The earlier law "already protected that right, containing nothing that prevented any student from engaging in voluntary prayer during a silent minute of meditation." Hence, the amendment to that law must have been enacted "to convey a message of State endorsement and promotion of prayer. [The] addition of 'or voluntary prayer' indicates that the State intended to characterize prayer as a favored practice. Such an endorsement is not consistent with the established principle that the Government must pursue a course of complete neutrality toward religion."

Justice O'CONNOR concurred in the result. She did not view all moment-of-silence requirements as unconstitutional. She suggested that the crucial question was whether the state had endorsed religion. "By mandating a moment of silence, the State does not necessarily endorse any activity that might occur during the period," nor "encourage[ ] prayer over other specified alternatives." But in this case, "the purpose and likely effect" of the Alabama amendment was "to endorse and sponsor voluntary prayer in the public schools." Here the state had "conveyed or attempted to convey the message that children should use the moment of silence for prayer." Chief Justice Burger and Justices White and Rehnquist dissented.

2. ***School prayer and "coercion."*** Do the school prayer cases, like the released-time cases (McCollum and Zorach), turn on the principle that coercion into a profession of belief violates the Establishment Clause, and the assumption that the public school setting is inherently coercive? What makes the school setting coercive? The fact that attendance is compulsory? The psychological immaturity of children, and their lack of fully developed faculties of resistance and consent? See Stone, "In Opposition to the School Prayer Amendment," 50 U. Chi. L. Rev. 823 (1983) (noting that children are especially vulnerable to peer pressure).

Why should coercion be a prerequisite to a finding of establishment? The Free Exercise Clause already prohibits coercion into faith or out of it. As Justice Clark noted in Schempp, "the Free Exercise Clause [recognizes] the right of every person to freely choose his own [religious] course, free of any compulsion from the state." Would limiting establishment to cases of "coercion" make the Establishment Clause mere surplusage, redundant of the Free Exercise Clause? What else beyond coercion might the Establishment Clause prohibit? One possibility is religious incentives or inducements that fall short of coercion. See, e.g., Choper, "Religion in the Schools," 47 Minn. L. Rev. 329 (1963) (arguing that the Establishment Clause is violated in public schools when the state engages in "solely religious activity that is likely to result in (1) compromising the student's religious or conscientious beliefs or (2) influencing the student's freedom of religious or conscientious choice"). Why should it not be enough that the school practices are "solely religious"? Why should it also be necessary to demonstrate impact on student beliefs or choice?

Another possibility is suggested by Justice O'Connor's Jaffree concurrence: she argues that the state may not "endorse" religion. Does endorsement cover a broader range of cases than coercion? Why should government have to refrain from religious speech or symbolism if it is not coercing or influencing a citizen to change his or her faith? Justice O'Connor suggested in Jaffree, citing her concurrence in Lynch v. Donnelly (1984; p. 1671 below), that endorsement sends a message of symbolic civic excommunication to nonmembers of the endorsed faith. Why should such a message constitute establishment in the absence of a showing that religious beliefs will be altered as a result? Consider which principle, coercion or endorsement, animates the various opinions in the following case, which invalidated an official prayer at a middle school graduation ceremony.

Lee v. Weisman

505 U.S. 577, 112 S. Ct. 2649, 120 L. Ed. 2d 467 (1992).

[The case arose when the principal of a Providence public middle school invited a rabbi to deliver prayers at the school's graduation ceremony, pursuant to the school district's longstanding custom of inviting members of the clergy for this purpose. The principal advised the rabbi that his prayers should be nonsectarian. The rabbi's invocation read:

> "God of the Free, Hope of the Brave: For the legacy of America where diversity is celebrated and the rights of minorities are protected, we thank You. May these young men and women grow up to enrich it. For the liberty of America, we thank You. May these new graduates grow up to guard it. For the political process of America in which all its citizens may participate, for its court system where all may seek justice we thank You. May those we honor this morning always turn to it in trust. For the destiny of America we thank You. May the graduates of Nathan Bishop Middle School so live that they might help to share it. May our aspirations for our country and for these young people, who are our hope for the future, be richly fulfilled. AMEN."

The rabbi's benediction read:

> "O God, we are grateful to You for having endowed us with the capacity for learning which we have celebrated on this joyous commencement. Happy families give thanks for seeing their children achieve an important milestone. Send Your blessings upon the teachers and administrators who helped prepare them. The graduates now need strength and guidance for the future, help them to understand that we are not complete with academic knowledge alone. We must each strive to fulfill what You require of us all: To do justly, to love mercy, to walk humbly. We give thanks to You, Lord, for keeping us alive, sustaining us and allowing us to reach this special, happy occasion. AMEN."

Deborah Weisman, a student at the school, raised an Establishment Clause challenge to the practice of prayer at the middle school graduation ceremony:]

■ JUSTICE KENNEDY delivered the opinion of the Court.

These dominant facts mark and control the confines of our decision: State officials direct the performance of a formal religious exercise at promotional and graduation ceremonies for secondary schools. Even for those students who object to the religious exercise, their attendance and participation in the state-sponsored religious activity are in a fair and real sense obligatory, though the school district does not require attendance as a condition for receipt of the diploma. [The] controlling precedents as they relate to prayer and religious exercise in primary and secondary public schools compel the holding here that the policy of the city of Providence is an unconstitutional one. [It] is beyond dispute that, at a minimum, the Constitution guarantees that government may not coerce anyone to support or participate in religion or its exercise. [The] State's involvement in the school prayers challenged today violates these central principles.

[We] are asked to recognize the existence of a practice of nonsectarian prayer, prayer within the embrace of what is known as the Judeo-Christian tradition, prayer which is more acceptable than one which, for example, makes explicit references to the God of Israel, or to Jesus Christ, or to a patron saint. [But] though the First Amendment does not allow the government to stifle prayers which aspire to [a civic religion], neither does it permit the government to undertake that task for itself. The First Amendment's Religion Clauses mean that religious beliefs and religious expression are too precious to be either proscribed or prescribed by the State. The design of the Constitution is that preservation and transmission of religious beliefs and worship is a responsibility and a choice committed to the private sphere, which itself is promised freedom to pursue that mission. [The] suggestion that government may establish an official or civic religion as a means of avoiding the establishment of a religion with more specific creeds strikes us as a contradiction that cannot be accepted.

The degree of school involvement here made it clear that the graduation prayers bore the imprint of the State and thus put school-age children who objected in an untenable position. [As] we have observed before, there are heightened concerns with protecting freedom of conscience from subtle coercive pressure in the elementary and secondary public schools. Our decisions in [Engel and Schempp] recognize, among other things, that prayer exercises in public schools carry a particular risk of indirect coercion. [What] to most believers may seem nothing more than a reasonable request that the nonbeliever respect their religious practices, in a school context may appear to the nonbeliever or dissenter to be an attempt to employ the machinery of the State to enforce a religious orthodoxy.

We need not look beyond the circumstances of this case to see the phenomenon at work. The undeniable fact is that the school district's supervision and control of a high school graduation ceremony places public pressure, as well as peer pressure, on attending students to stand as a group or, at least, maintain respectful silence during the Invocation and Benediction. This pressure, though subtle and indirect, can be as real as any overt compulsion. Of course, in our culture standing or remaining silent can signify adherence to a view or simple respect for the views of others. And no doubt some persons who have no desire to join a prayer have little objection to standing as a sign of respect for those who do. But for the dissenter of high school age, who has a reasonable perception that she is being forced by the State to pray in a manner her conscience will not allow, the injury is no less real. There can be no doubt that for many, if not most, of the students at the graduation, the act of standing or remaining silent was an expression of participation in the Rabbi's prayer. That was the very point of the religious exercise. It is of little comfort to a dissenter, then, to be told that for her the act of standing or remaining in silence signifies mere respect, rather than participation. What matters is that, given our social conventions, a reasonable dissenter in this milieu could believe that the group exercise signified her own participation or approval of it.

Finding no violation under these circumstances would place objectors in the dilemma of participating, with all that implies, or protesting. We do not address whether that choice is acceptable if the affected citizens are mature adults, but we think the State may not, consistent with the Establishment Clause, place primary and secondary school children in this position. Research in psychology supports the common assumption that adolescents are often susceptible to pressure from their peers towards conformity, and that the influence is strongest in matters of social convention. To recognize that the choice imposed by the State constitutes an unacceptable constraint only acknowledges that the government may no more use social pressure to enforce orthodoxy than it may use more direct means.

[Although] attendance at graduation [ceremonies] is voluntary, [the argument] that the option of not attending the graduation excuses any inducement or coercion in the ceremony itself [lacks] all persuasion. Law reaches past formalism. And to say a teenage student has a real choice not to attend her high school graduation is formalistic in the extreme. [Everyone] knows that in our society and in our culture high school graduation is one of life's most significant occasions. A school rule which excuses attendance is beside the point. Attendance may not be required by official decree, yet it is apparent that a student is not free to absent herself from the graduation exercise in any real sense of the term "voluntary," for absence would require forfeiture of those intangible benefits which have motivated the student through youth and all her high school years.

[The government argues] that the prayers are an essential part of these ceremonies because for many persons an occasion of this significance lacks meaning if there is no recognition, however brief, that human achievements cannot be understood apart from their spiritual essence. [But this] fails to acknowledge that what for many of Deborah's classmates and their parents was a spiritual imperative was for [her] religious conformance compelled by the State. [The] Constitution forbids the State to exact religious conformity from a student as the price of attending her own high school graduation. [To] say that a student must remain apart from the ceremony at the opening invocation and closing benediction is to risk compelling conformity in an environment analogous to the classroom setting, where we have said the risk of compulsion is especially high.

[We] do not hold that every state action implicating religion is invalid if one or a few citizens find it offensive. People may take offense at all manner of religious as well as nonreligious messages, but offense alone does not in every case show a violation. We know too that sometimes to endure social isolation or even anger may be the price of conscience or nonconformity. But, by any reading of our cases, the conformity required of the student in this case was too high an exaction to withstand the test of the Establishment Clause. The prayer exercises in this case are especially improper because the State has in every practical sense compelled attendance and participation in an explicit religious exercise at an event of singular importance to every student, one the objecting student had no real alternative to avoid. [No] holding by this Court suggests that a school can persuade or compel a student to participate in a religious exercise. That is being done here, and it is forbidden by the Establishment Clause. [Affirmed.]

■ JUSTICE BLACKMUN, with whom JUSTICES STEVENS and O'CONNOR join, concurring.

[The] Court holds that the graduation prayer is unconstitutional because the State "in effect required participation in a religious exercise." Although our precedents make clear that proof of government coercion is not necessary to prove an Establishment Clause violation, it is sufficient. Government pressure to participate in a religious activity is an obvious indication that the government is endorsing or promoting religion.

But it is not enough that the government restrain from compelling religious practices: it must not engage in them either. The Court repeatedly has recognized that a violation of the Establishment Clause is not predicated on coercion. The Establishment Clause proscribes public schools from "conveying or attempting to convey a message that religion or a particular religious belief is favored or preferred," even if the schools do not actually "impose pressure upon a student to participate in a religious activity." [There] is no doubt that attempts to aid religion through government coercion jeopardize freedom of conscience. Even subtle pressure diminishes the right of each individual to choose voluntarily what to believe. [Our] decisions have gone beyond prohibiting coercion, however, because the Court has recognized that "the fullest possible scope of religious liberty" entails more than freedom from coercion. [The] mixing of government and religion can be a threat to free government, even if no one is forced to participate. When the government puts its imprimatur on a particular religion, it conveys a message of exclusion to all those who do not adhere to the favored beliefs. A government cannot be premised on the belief that all persons are created equal when it asserts that God prefers some.

[We] have believed that religious freedom cannot exist in the absence of a free democratic government, and that such a government cannot endure when there is fusion between religion and the political regime. We have believed that religious freedom cannot thrive in the absence of a vibrant religious community and that such a community cannot prosper when it is bound to the secular. And we have believed that these were the animating principles behind the adoption of the Establishment Clause. To that end, our cases have prohibited government endorsement of religion, its sponsorship, and active involvement in religion, whether or not citizens were coerced to conform.

■ JUSTICE SOUTER, with whom JUSTICES STEVENS and O'CONNOR join, concurring.

[Petitioners] rest most of their argument on a theory that [the] Establishment Clause [does] not forbid the state to sponsor affirmations of religious belief that coerce neither support for religion nor participation in religious observance. I appreciate the force of some of the arguments supporting a "coercion" analysis of the Clause. [See] McConnell, "Coercion: The Lost Element of Establishment," 27 Wm. & Mary L. Rev. 933 (1986). But we could not adopt that reading without abandoning our settled law, a course that, in my view, the text of the Clause would not readily permit. Nor does the extratextual evidence of original meaning stand so unequivocally at odds with the textual premise inherent in existing precedent that we should fundamentally reconsider our course.

Over the years, this Court has declared the invalidity of many noncoercive state laws and practices conveying a message of religious endorsement. [For example,] in Wallace v. Jaffree, we struck down a state law requiring a moment of silence in public classrooms not because the statute coerced students to participate in prayer (for it did not), but because the manner of its enactment "conveyed a message of state approval of prayer activities in the public schools." [Our] precedents [cannot] support the position that a showing of coercion is necessary to a successful Establishment Clause claim.

[While] petitioners insist that the prohibition extends only to the "coercive" features and incidents of establishment, they cannot easily square that claim with the constitutional text. The First Amendment forbids not just laws "respecting an establishment of religion," but also those "prohibiting the free exercise thereof." Yet laws that coerce nonadherents to "support or participate in any religion or its exercise," would virtually by definition violate their right to religious free exercise. Thus, a literal application of the coercion test would render the Establishment Clause a virtual nullity. [Without] compelling evidence to the contrary, we should presume that the Framers meant the Clause to stand for something more than petitioners attribute to it.

Petitioners argue from the political setting in which the Establishment Clause was framed, and from the Framers' own political practices following ratification, that government may constitutionally endorse religion so long as it does not coerce religious conformity. [They contend, for example,] that because the early Presidents included religious messages in their inaugural and Thanksgiving Day addresses, the Framers could not have meant the Establishment Clause to forbid noncoercive state endorsement of religion. [But Jefferson] steadfastly refused to issue Thanksgiving proclamations of any kind, in part because he thought they violated the Religion Clauses. [He] accordingly construed the Establishment Clause to forbid not simply state coercion, but also state endorsement, of religious belief and observance. [During] his first three years in office, James Madison also refused to call for days of thanksgiving and prayer, though later, amid the political turmoil of the War of 1812, he did so on four separate occasions. Upon retirement, in an essay condemning as an unconstitutional "establishment" the use of public money to support congressional and military chaplains, he concluded that "religious proclamations by the Executive recommending thanksgivings & fasts are shoots from the same root with the legislative acts reviewed." [To] be sure, the leaders of the young Republic engaged in some of the practices that separationists like Jefferson and Madison criticized. The First Congress did hire institutional chaplains, and Presidents Washington and Adams unapologetically marked days of "public thanksgiving and prayer." [Yet this proves] at worst that [the framers,] like other politicians, could raise constitutional ideals one day and turn their backs on them the next.

[Petitioners] argu[e] that graduation prayers are no different from presidential religious proclamations and similar official "acknowledgments" of religion in public life. But religious invocations in Thanksgiving Day addresses and the like, rarely noticed, ignored without effort, conveyed over an impersonal medium, and directed at no one in particular, inhabit a pallid zone worlds apart from official prayers delivered to a captive audience of public school students and their families. [When] public school officials, armed with the State's authority, convey an endorsement of religion to their students, they strike near the core of the Establishment Clause. However "ceremonial" their messages may be, they are flatly unconstitutional.

■ JUSTICE SCALIA, with whom CHIEF JUSTICE REHNQUIST and JUSTICES WHITE and THOMAS join, dissenting.

[In] holding that the Establishment Clause prohibits invocations and benedictions at public-school graduation ceremonies, the Court—with nary a mention that it is doing so—lays waste a tradition that is as old as public-school graduation ceremonies themselves, and that is a component of an even more longstanding American tradition of nonsectarian prayer to God at public celebrations generally. As its instrument of destruction, the bulldozer of its social engineering, the Court invents a boundless, and boundlessly manipulable, test of psychological coercion.

[From] our Nation's origin, prayer has been a prominent part of governmental ceremonies and proclamations. The Declaration of Independence, the document marking our birth as a separate people, "appealed to the Supreme Judge of the world for the rectitude of our intentions" and avowed "a firm reliance on the protection of divine Providence." In his first inaugural address, after swearing his oath of office on a Bible, George Washington deliberately made a prayer a part of his first official act as President, [offering] "fervent supplications to that Almighty Being who rules over the universe." [Such] supplications have been a characteristic feature of inaugural addresses ever since. [Our] national celebration of Thanksgiving likewise dates back to President Washington. [This] tradition of Thanksgiving Proclamations—with their religious theme of prayerful gratitude to God—has been adhered to by almost every President. The other two branches of the Federal Government also have a long-established practice of prayer at public events. [Congressional] sessions have opened with a chaplain's prayer ever since the First Congress. And this Court's own sessions have opened with the invocation "God save the United States and this Honorable Court" since the days of Chief Justice Marshall.

[The] Court presumably would separate graduation invocations and benedictions from other instances of public "preservation and transmission of religious beliefs" on the ground that they involve "psychological coercion." [But a] few citations of "research in psychology" that have no particular bearing upon the precise issue here cannot disguise the fact that the Court has gone beyond the realm where judges know what they are doing. The Court's argument that state officials have "coerced" students to take part in the invocation and benediction at graduation ceremonies is, not to put too fine a point on it, incoherent.

[The] Court's notion that a student who simply sits in "respectful silence" during the invocation and benediction (when all others are standing) has somehow joined—or would somehow be perceived as having joined—in the prayers is nothing short of ludicrous. [Surely] "our social conventions" have not coarsened to the point that anyone who does not stand on his chair and shout obscenities can reasonably be deemed to have assented to everything said in his presence. [But] let us assume the very worst, that the nonparticipating graduate is "subtly coerced" . . . to stand! Even that [does] not remotely establish a "participation" (or an "appearance of participation") in a religious exercise. [It is] a permissible inference that one who is standing is doing so simply out of respect for the prayers of others that are in progress.

[The] deeper flaw in the Court's opinion does not lie in its wrong answer to the question whether there was state-induced "peer-pressure" coercion; it lies, rather, in the Court's making violation of the Establishment Clause hinge on such a precious question. The coercion that was a hallmark of historical establishments of religion was coercion of religious orthodoxy and of financial support by force of law and threat of penalty. Typically, attendance at the state church was required; only clergy of the official church could lawfully perform sacraments; and dissenters, if tolerated, faced an array of civil disabilities. [Thus,] while I have no quarrel with the Court's general proposition that the Establishment Clause "guarantees that government may not coerce anyone to support or participate in religion or its exercise," I see no warrant for expanding the concept of coercion beyond acts backed by threat of penalty—a brand of coercion that, happily, is readily discernible to those of us who have made a career of reading the disciples of Blackstone rather than of Freud. The Framers were indeed opposed to coercion of religious worship by the National Government; but, as their own sponsorship of nonsectarian prayer in public events demonstrates, they understood that "speech is not coercive; the listener may do as he likes."

The Court relies on our "school prayer" cases, [Engel and Schempp.] But whatever the merit of those cases, they do not support, much less compel, the Court's psycho-journey. [School] instruction is not a public ceremony. [And] we have made clear our understanding that school prayer occurs within a framework in which legal coercion to attend school (i.e., coercion under threat of penalty) provides the ultimate backdrop. [Finally,] our school-prayer cases turn in part on the fact that the classroom is inherently an instructional setting, and daily prayer there—where parents are not present to counter "the students' emulation of teachers as role models and the children's susceptibility to peer pressure," might be thought to raise special concerns regarding state interference with the liberty of parents to direct the religious upbringing of their children. [Voluntary] prayer at graduation—a one-time ceremony at which parents, friends and relatives are present—can hardly be thought to raise the same concerns.

[Given] the odd basis for the Court's decision, invocations and benedictions will be able to be given at public-school graduations next June, as they have for the past century and a half, so long as school authorities make clear that anyone who abstains from screaming in protest does not necessarily participate in the prayers. All that is seemingly needed is an announcement, or perhaps a written insertion at the beginning of the graduation Program, to the effect that, while all are asked to rise for the invocation and benediction, none is compelled to join in them, nor will be assumed, by rising, to have done so. That obvious fact recited, the graduates and their parents may proceed to thank God, as Americans have always done, for the blessings He has generously bestowed on them and on their country. [The] founders of our Republic knew the fearsome potential of sectarian religious belief to generate civil dissension and civil strife. And they also knew that nothing, absolutely nothing, is so inclined to foster among religious believers of various faiths a toleration—no, an affection—for one another than voluntarily joining in prayer together, to the God whom they all worship and seek. [To] deprive our society of that important unifying mechanism, in order to spare the nonbeliever what seems to me the minimal inconvenience of standing or even sitting in respectful nonparticipation, is as senseless in policy as it is unsupported in law.

COERCION VS. ENDORSEMENT

1. ***The Court's division in Lee.*** For decades after the early school prayer decisions, some segments of the religious community had vocally called for them to be overruled, and hoped that the appointment of conservative justices would turn the tide. Lee v. Weisman was a bitter disappointment to them; President Reagan's nominee Justice Kennedy provided the fifth vote to hold once again that establishment principles barred prayer in schools, even where studiously nondenominational. Note the vigorous division on the Court between those who advocate reducing establishment interventions to cases of "coercion," and those who insist that establishment can also occur through "endorsement." Which camp did Justice Kennedy ally with? Did he define "coercion" so loosely that it blurred into "endorsement?" Lee was viewed at the time as a propitious case in which to announce a new, more deferential coercion test; indeed, the Solicitor General filed an amicus curiae brief advocating such a test even though the case did not involve the federal government. As the later cases show, the endorsement test survived this close brush with extinction and continues today. Why is that so, when there were at least nominally five votes for the coercion test in Lee?

2. ***Student-led invocations at school football games.*** Relying on Lee, the Court struck down as facially unconstitutional another version of school prayer in **Santa Fe Independent School District v. Doe**, 530 U.S. 290 (2000). Under the public high school program at issue in the case, which replaced a previous program providing for a student "chaplain" to provide "prayer at football games," the student body was empowered to vote each year on whether to have a student speaker preceding varsity football games who would "deliver a brief invocation and/or message [to] solemnize the event," and on who the student speaker would be.

Writing for the Court, Justice STEVENS, joined by Justices O'Connor, Kennedy, Souter, Ginsburg and Breyer, concluded that "the specific purpose of the policy was to preserve a popular 'state-sponsored religious practice,' that 'invites and encourages religious messages,' which are 'the most obvious method of solemnizing an event.'" He explained that the mere fact that the speech was student-initiated did not make it private student speech rather than official speech: "[T]hese invocations are authorized by a government policy and take place on government property at government-sponsored school-related events. [T]he majoritarian process implemented by the District guarantees, by definition, that minority candidates will never prevail and that their views will be effectively silenced. [While] Santa Fe's majoritarian election might ensure that most of the students are represented, it does nothing to protect the minority; indeed, it likely serves to intensify their offense." Although the chosen speaker was not obligated to deliver a prayer, "the expressed purposes of the policy encourage the selection of a religious message, and that is precisely how the students understand the policy."

He explained: "[The] invocation is [delivered] to a large audience assembled as part of a regularly scheduled, school-sponsored function conducted on school property. The message is broadcast over the school's public address system, [subject] to the control of school officials. [In] this context the members of the listening audience must perceive the pregame message as a public expression of the views of the majority of the student body delivered with the approval of the school administration. [Regardless] of the listener's support for, or objection to, the message, an objective Santa Fe High School student will unquestionably perceive the inevitable pregame prayer as stamped with her school's seal of approval."

Justice Stevens rejected the school district's attempt to distinguish the case from Lee v. Weisman on basis of relative coerciveness: "The District [argues] that attendance at the commencement ceremonies at issue in Lee 'differs dramatically' from attendance at high school football games. [Attendance] at a high school football game, unlike showing up for class, is certainly not required in order to receive a diploma. [There] are some students, however, such as cheerleaders, members of the band, and, of course, the team members themselves, for whom seasonal commitments mandate their attendance, sometimes for class credit. The District also minimizes the importance to many students of attending and participating in extracurricular activities as part of a complete educational experience. [But to] assert that high school students do not feel immense social pressure, or have a truly genuine desire, to be involved in the extracurricular event that is American high school football is 'formalistic in the extreme.' [For] many [students], the choice between whether to attend these games or to risk facing a personally offensive religious ritual is in no practical sense an easy one. The Constitution [demands] that the school may not force this difficult choice upon these students for '[i]t is a tenet of the First Amendment that the State cannot require one of its citizens to forfeit his or her rights and benefits as the price of resisting conformance to state-sponsored religious practice.' Even if we regard every high school student's decision to attend a home football game as purely voluntary, we are nevertheless persuaded that the delivery of a pregame prayer has the improper effect of coercing those present to participate in an act of religious worship. For 'the government may no more use social pressure to enforce orthodoxy than it may use more direct means.' As in Lee, '[w]hat to most believers may seem nothing more than a reasonable request that the nonbeliever respect their religious practices, in a school context may appear to the nonbeliever or dissenter to be an attempt to employ the machinery of the State to enforce a religious orthodoxy.' The constitutional command will not permit the District 'to exact religious conformity from a student as the price' of joining her classmates at a varsity football game."

Chief Justice REHNQUIST, dissenting along with Justices Scalia and Thomas, objected that the majority's decision "bristles with hostility to all things religious in public life. [Respondents] in this case challenged the [program] before it had been put into practice. [The] fact that a policy might 'operate unconstitutionally under some conceivable set of circumstances is insufficient to render it wholly invalid.' [Therefore], the question is not whether the district's policy may be applied in violation of the Establishment Clause, but whether it inevitably will be." Because it was possible for the school district's policy to be applied in nonreligious ways, Chief Justice Rehnquist saw no reason to invalidate the program on its face.

3. ***Student-led prayer in extracurricular school settings.*** By contrast, the Court in the next Term held permissible under the

Establishment Clause the use of school facilities for worship and prayer when led by a private evangelical Christian club as part of an extracurricular afterschool program for elementary school students that was open to other groups such as the Boy and Girl Scouts and the 4-H Club. In **Good News Club v. Milford Central School**, 533 U.S. 98 (2001), the Court held that it was unconstitutional viewpoint discrimination under the Free Speech Clause to exclude such religious speech from a "limited public forum" that had been opened up non-selectively to a wide range of groups (see p. 1283 above). The Court also, by a vote of 6–3, rejected the school's defense that such exclusion was compelled by the Establishment Clause.

Justice THOMAS, writing for the Court, found "unpersuasive" the school's argument that elementary school students would be especially vulnerable to "coercive pressure to participate": "The Good News Club seeks nothing more than to be treated neutrally and given access to speak about the same topics as are other groups. [Allowing] the Club to speak on school grounds would ensure neutrality, not threaten it. [Because] the children cannot attend without their parents' permission, they cannot be coerced into engaging in the Good News Club's religious activities. [Whatever] significance we may have assigned in the Establishment Clause context to the suggestion that elementary school children are more impressionable than adults, we have never extended our Establishment Clause jurisprudence to foreclose private religious conduct during nonschool hours merely because it takes place on school premises where elementary school children may be present. [We] decline to employ Establishment Clause jurisprudence using a modified heckler's veto, in which a group's religious activity can be proscribed on the basis of what the youngest members of the audience might misperceive."

Justice SCALIA concurred, emphasizing that there was no coercion and that endorsement of religion cannot be found in private religious speech expressed in a traditional or designated public forum open to all on equal terms. Justice BREYER concurred in the free speech ruling, but, as to the Establishment Clause defense, noted that children's reasonable perceptions of endorsement would be relevant and that facts relevant to such perceptions required more factual development on remand. Justices STEVENS and SOUTER, each writing in dissent, agreed with Justice Breyer that there should have been a remand on the establishment issue, which the courts below had not reached because they had ruled for the school on the free speech issue. Justice Souter concluded that "there is a good case that Good News's exercises blur the line between public classroom instruction and private religious indoctrination, leaving a reasonable elementary school pupil unable to appreciate that the former instruction is the business of the school while the latter evangelism is not."

RELIGION AND THE PUBLIC SCHOOL CURRICULUM

1. ***The Ten Commandments.*** In **Stone v. Graham**, 449 U.S. 39 (1980), the Court held unconstitutional a Kentucky law that required the posting of a copy of the Ten Commandments, purchased with private contributions, in public school classrooms. In sustaining the law, the state trial court had emphasized that the law's "avowed purpose" was "secular and not religious." The Court reversed summarily, without hearing argument on

the merits. The majority's per curiam opinion concluded that the law had "no secular legislative purpose," even though it required that each display of the Ten Commandments have a notation in small print stating: "The secular application of the Ten Commandments is clearly seen in its adoption as the fundamental legal code of Western Civilization and the Common Law of the United States." The majority viewed the predominant purpose of the posting requirement as "plainly religious," since the Ten Commandments are "undeniably a sacred text in the Jewish and Christian faiths." Even though some of the Commandments address secular matters, "the first part of the Commandments concerns the religious duties of believers."

Justice Rehnquist's dissent insisted that the Court's ruling was "without precedent in Establishment Clause jurisprudence." He noted: "The fact that the asserted secular purpose may overlap with what some may see as a religious objective does not render [the law] unconstitutional." Justice Stewart also dissented on the merits; Chief Justice Burger and Justice Blackmun objected to the summary disposition, arguing that the case should have been given plenary consideration.

2. ***The pledge of allegiance.*** Under the school prayer precedents, is the Establishment Clause violated when teachers in a public school classroom lead students in joint recitation of the Pledge of Allegiance, as modified by Congress in 1954, at the height of anti-communist political fervor, to include the words "one nation *under God*"? In **Elk Grove Unified School District v. Newdow**, 542 U.S. 1 (2004), the court of appeals gave an affirmative answer to that question, but on appeal, the Supreme Court reversed the decision on the ground that the challenger—an atheist father who did not wish his daughter to have to undergo recitation of the Pledge as written at her public elementary school—lacked prudential standing to sue based on state court rulings conferring custody upon the girl's mother.

Chief Justice REHNQUIST, joined by Justice O'Connor and in part by Justice Thomas, concurred in the judgment but would have found standing and reached the merits, finding no Establishment Clause violation. Citing precedents for invoking God in presidential inaugurations from Washington to Wilson, and the motto "In God We Trust" on the national currency, Chief Justice Rehnquist concluded that "our national culture allows public recognition of our Nation's religious history and character." He continued: "I do not believe that the phrase 'under God' in the Pledge converts its recital into a 'religious exercise' of the sort described in Lee. Instead, it is a declaration of belief in allegiance and loyalty to the United States flag and the Republic that it represents. The phrase 'under God' is in no sense a prayer, nor an endorsement of any religion, but a simple recognition of the fact [that] 'from the time of our earliest history our peoples and our institutions have reflected the traditional concept that our Nation was founded on a fundamental belief in God.' Reciting the Pledge, or listening to others recite it, is a patriotic exercise, not a religious one; participants promise fidelity to our flag and our Nation, not to any particular God, faith, or church."

Justice O'CONNOR concurred separately in the judgment, noting that the Pledge did not violate her "endorsement" test: "For centuries, we have marked important occasions or pronouncements with references to God and invocations of divine assistance. Such references can serve to solemnize an occasion instead of to invoke divine provenance. The reasonable observer, [fully] aware of our national history and the origins of such practices, would not perceive these acknowledgments as signifying a government endorsement of any specific religion, or even of religion over non-religion." Justice THOMAS concurred in the judgment as well, but conceded that the court of appeals had acted reasonably under the Court's school prayer precedents, and thus urged "a process of rethinking the Establishment Clause" to avoid such results: "The text and history of the Establishment Clause strongly suggest that it is a federalism provision intended to prevent Congress from interfering with state establishments. Thus, unlike the Free Exercise Clause, which does protect an individual right, it makes little sense to incorporate the Establishment Clause. In any case, I do not believe that the Pledge policy infringes any religious liberty right that would arise from incorporation of the Clause."

3. ***Teaching evolution and creationism.*** In **Epperson v. Arkansas**, 393 U.S. 97 (1968), the Court invalidated the Arkansas version of the Tennessee "anti-evolution" law that gained national notoriety in the Scopes "monkey law" trial in 1927. The Court found the law to be in conflict with the Establishment Clause mandate of "neutrality." The Arkansas law prohibited teachers in state schools from teaching "the theory or doctrine that mankind ascended or descended from a lower order of animals." The highest state court had expressed "no opinion" on "whether the Act prohibits any explanation of the theory of evolution or merely prohibits teaching that the theory is true." On either interpretation, Justice FORTAS's majority opinion concluded, the law could not stand: "The overriding fact is that Arkansas' law selects from the body of knowledge a particular segment which it proscribes for the sole reason that it is deemed to conflict with a particular religious doctrine; that is, with a particular interpretation of the Book of Genesis by a particular religious group. Government in our democracy, state and national, must be neutral in matters of religious theory, doctrine, and practice. It may not be hostile to any religion or to the advocacy of no religion; and it may not aid, foster, or promote one religion or religious theory against another or even against the militant opposite. [The] vigilant protection of constitutional freedoms is nowhere more vital than in the community of American schools. [The] State's undoubted right to prescribe the curriculum for its public schools does not carry with it the right to prohibit, on pain of criminal penalty, the teaching of a scientific theory or doctrine where that prohibition is based upon reasons that violate the First Amendment. In the present case, there can be no doubt that Arkansas has sought to prevent its teachers from discussing the theory of evolution because it is contrary to the belief of some that the Book of Genesis must be the exclusive source of doctrine as to the origin of man. No suggestion has been made that Arkansas' law may be justified by considerations of state policy other than the religious views of some of its citizens. It is clear that fundamentalist sectarian conviction was and is the law's reason for existence. Its antecedent, Tennessee's 'monkey law,' candidly stated its purpose: to make it unlawful 'to teach any theory that denies the story of the Divine Creation of man as taught in the Bible, and to teach instead that man has descended from a lower order of animals.' Perhaps the sensational publicity attendant upon the Scopes trial induced Arkansas to adopt less explicit language. It eliminated Tennessee's reference to 'the story of the Divine Creation of man' as taught in the Bible, but there is no doubt that the motivation for the law was the same: to suppress the teaching of a theory which, it was thought, 'denied' the divine creation of man. Arkansas' law cannot be defended as an act of religious neutrality. Arkansas did not seek to excise from the curricula

of its schools and universities all discussion of the origin of man. The law's effort was confined to an attempt to blot out a particular theory because of its supposed conflict with the Biblical account, literally read."

In separate opinions, Justices BLACK and STEWART explained that they concurred solely on the ground of vagueness. Justice Black criticized the majority for reaching out to "troublesome" First Amendment questions: "It is plain that a state law prohibiting all teaching of human development or biology is constitutionally quite different from a law that compels a teacher to teach as true only one theory of a given doctrine. [A] question that arises for me is whether this Court's decision forbidding a State to exclude the subject of evolution from its schools infringes the religious freedom of those who consider evolution an anti-religious doctrine. If the theory is considered anti-religious, as the Court indicates, how can the State be bound by the Federal Constitution to permit its teachers to advocate such an 'anti-religious' doctrine to schoolchildren? The very cases cited by the Court as supporting its conclusion that the State must be neutral, not favoring one religious or anti-religious view over another. The Darwinian theory is said to challenge the Bible's story of creation; so too have some of those who believe in the Bible, along with many others, challenged the Darwinian theory. Since there is no indication that the literal Biblical doctrine of the origin of man is included in the curriculum of Arkansas schools, does not the removal of the subject of evolution leave the State in a neutral position toward these supposedly competing religious and anti-religious doctrines? [I] am also not ready to hold that a person hired to teach schoolchildren takes with him into the classroom a constitutional right to teach sociological, economic, political, or religious subjects that the school's managers do not want discussed."

In the following case the Court definitively rejected Justice Black's "neutrality" approach, striking down a state law that mandated that the theories of evolution and creation be taught alongside one another, if at all.

Edwards v. Aguillard

482 U.S. 578, 107 S. Ct. 2573, 96 L. Ed. 2d 510 (1987).

■ JUSTICE BRENNAN delivered the opinion of the Court.

The question for decision is whether Louisiana's "Balanced Treatment for Creation-Science and Evolution-Science in Public School Instruction" Act (Creationism Act) is facially invalid as violative of the Establishment Clause. The Creationism Act forbids the teaching of the theory of evolution in public schools unless accompanied by instruction in "creation science." No school is required to teach evolution or creation science. If either is taught, however, the other must also be taught. The theories of evolution and creation science are statutorily defined as "the scientific evidences for (creation or evolution) and inferences from those scientific evidences." Appellees, who include parents of children attending Louisiana public schools, Louisiana teachers, and religious leaders, challenged the constitutionality of the Act. [The] District Court [granted summary judgment to appellees, holding] that the Creationism Act violated the Establishment Clause either because it prohibited the teaching of evolution or because it required the teaching of creation science with the purpose of advancing a particular religious doctrine. The Court of Appeals affirmed. [We affirm.]

[The] Court has been particularly vigilant in monitoring compliance with the Establishment Clause in elementary and secondary schools. [Families] entrust public schools with the education of their children, but condition their trust on the understanding that the classroom will not purposely be used to advance religious views that may conflict with the private beliefs of the student and his or her family. Students in such institutions are impressionable and their attendance is involuntary. The State exerts great authority and coercive power through mandatory attendance requirements, and because of the students' emulation of teachers as role models and the children's susceptibility to peer pressure.

Lemon's first prong focuses on the purpose that animated adoption of the Act. [In] this case, appellants have identified no clear secular purpose for the Louisiana Act. True, the Act's stated purpose is to protect academic freedom. This phrase might, in common parlance, be understood as referring to enhancing the freedom of teachers to teach what they will. The Court of Appeals, however, correctly concluded that the Act was not designed to further that goal. [Even] if "academic freedom" is read to mean "teaching all of the evidence" with respect to the origin of human beings, the Act does not further this purpose. The goal of providing a more comprehensive science curriculum is not furthered either by outlawing the teaching of evolution or by requiring the teaching of creation science. While the Court is normally deferential to a State's articulation of a secular purpose, it is required that the statement of such purpose be sincere and not a sham. It is [clear] that requiring schools to teach creation science with evolution does not advance academic freedom. The Act does not grant teachers a flexibility that they did not already possess to supplant the present science curriculum with a presentation of theories, besides evolution, about the origin of life.

[Furthermore,] the goal of basic "fairness" is hardly furthered by the Act's discriminatory preference for the teaching of creation science and against the teaching of evolution. While requiring that curriculum guides be developed for creation science, the Act says nothing of comparable guides for evolution. Similarly, research services are supplied for creation science but not for evolution. Only "creation scientists" can serve on the panel that supplies the resource services. The Act forbids school boards to discriminate against anyone who "chooses to be a creation-scientist" or to teach "creationism," but fails to protect those who choose to teach evolution or any other non-creation science theory, or who refuse to teach creation science. [Moreover,] the Act fails even to ensure that creation science will be taught, but instead requires the teaching of this theory only when the theory of evolution is taught. Thus we agree with the Court of Appeals' conclusion that the Act does not serve to protect academic freedom, but has a distinctly different purpose of discrediting "evolution by counterbalancing its teaching at every turn with the teaching of creationism. . . ."

[We] need not be blind in this case to the legislature's preeminent religious purpose in enacting this statute. There is a historic and contemporaneous link between the teachings of certain religious denominations and the teaching of evolution. It was this link that concerned the Court in [Epperson]. [The] same historic and contemporaneous antagonisms between the teachings of certain religious denominations and the teaching of evolution are present in this case. The preeminent purpose of the Louisiana legislature was clearly to advance the religious viewpoint that a supernatural being created humankind. The term "creation science" was defined as embracing this particular religious doctrine by those responsible for the passage of the Creationism Act. Senator Keith's leading expert on creation science, Edward Boudreaux, testified at the legislative hearings that the theory of creation science included belief in the existence of a supernatural creator.

[Furthermore,] it is not happenstance that the legislature required the teaching of a theory that coincided with this religious view. The legislative history documents that the Act's primary purpose was to change the science curriculum of public schools in order to provide persuasive advantage to a particular religious doctrine that rejects the factual basis of evolution in its entirety. The sponsor of the Creationism Act, Senator Keith, explained during the legislative hearings that his disdain for the theory of evolution resulted from [his] own religious beliefs. [The] state senator repeatedly stated that scientific evidence supporting his religious views should be included in the public school curriculum to redress the fact that the theory of evolution incidentally coincided with what he characterized as religious beliefs antithetical to his own. The legislation therefore sought to alter the science curriculum to reflect endorsement of a religious view that is antagonistic to the theory of evolution. In this case, the purpose of the Creationism Act was to restructure the science curriculum to conform with a particular religious viewpoint. Out of many possible science subjects taught in the public schools, the legislature chose to affect the teaching of the one scientific theory that historically has been opposed by certain religious sects. As in Epperson, the legislature passed the Act to give preference to those religious groups which have as one of their tenets the creation of humankind by a divine creator.

[Because] the primary purpose of the Creationism Act is to advance a particular religious belief, the Act endorses religion in violation of the First Amendment. We do not imply that a legislature could never require that scientific critiques of prevailing scientific theories be taught. [Teaching] a variety of scientific theories about the origins of humankind to schoolchildren might be validly done with the clear secular intent of enhancing the effectiveness of science instruction. But because the primary purpose of the Creationism Act is to endorse a particular religious doctrine, the Act furthers religion in violation of the Establishment Clause. [Affirmed.]

■ JUSTICE POWELL, with whom JUSTICE O'CONNOR joins, concurring.

I write separately to note certain aspects of the legislative history, and to emphasize that nothing in the Court's opinion diminishes the traditionally broad discretion accorded state and local school officials in the selection of the public school curriculum. [A] religious purpose alone is not enough to invalidate an act of a state legislature. The religious purpose must predominate. [Here,] it is clear that religious belief is the Balanced Treatment's Act's "reason for existence." [Whatever] the academic merit of particular subjects or theories, the Establishment Clause limits the discretion of state officials to pick and choose among them for the purpose of promoting a particular religious belief. The language of the statute and its legislative history convince me that the Louisiana legislature exercised its discretion for this purpose in this [case].

■ JUSTICE SCALIA, with whom CHIEF JUSTICE REHNQUIST joins, dissenting.

[There] is ample evidence that the majority is wrong in holding that the Balanced Treatment Act is without secular purpose. [Senator] Keith and his witnesses testified essentially: (1) [There] are two and only two scientific explanations for the beginning of life—evolution and creation [science]. (2) The body of scientific evidence supporting creation science is as strong as that supporting evolution. In fact, it may be [stronger]. (3) Creation science is educationally valuable. Students exposed to it better understand the current state of scientific evidence about the origin of [life]. (4) Although creation science is educationally valuable and strictly scientific, it is now being censored from or misrepresented in the [public schools]. (5) The censorship of creation science [has] harmful effects. [E.g., it] deprives students of knowledge of one of the two scientific explanations for the origin of life and leads them to believe that evolution is proven [fact]. [We] have no way of knowing, of course, how many legislators believed the testimony of Senator Keith and his witnesses. But in the absence of evidence to the contrary, we have to assume that many of them [did].

[Moreover, the] Louisiana Legislature explicitly set forth its secular purpose ("protecting academic freedom") in the very text of the Act. [If] one adopts the obviously intended meaning of the statutory terms "academic freedom," there is no basis whatever for concluding that the purpose they express is a "sham." [The] legislative history gives ample evidence of the sincerity of the Balanced Treatment Act's articulated purpose. Witness after witness urged the legislators to support the Act so that students would not be "indoctrinated" but would instead be free to decide for themselves, based upon a fair presentation of the scientific evidence, about the origin of life. [It] is undoubtedly true that what prompted the Legislature to direct its attention to the misrepresentation of evolution in the schools (rather than the inaccurate presentation of other topics) was its awareness of the tension between evolution and the religious beliefs of many children. But [a] valid secular purpose is not rendered impermissible simply because its pursuit is prompted by concern for religious [sensitivities].

[Criticizing the Court's inquiry into legislative motivation under the Lemon "purpose" test, Justice Scalia continued:] [W]hile it is possible to discern the objective "purpose" of a statute, [discerning] the subjective motivation of those enacting the statute is, to be honest, almost always an impossible task. The number of possible motivations, to begin with, is not binary, or indeed even finite. To look for the sole purpose of even a single legislator is probably to look for something that does not exist.

Putting that problem aside, however, where ought we to look for the individual legislator's purpose? We cannot of course assume that every member present (if, as is unlikely, we know who or even how many they were) agreed with the motivation expressed in a particular legislator's preenactment floor or committee statement. Quite obviously, "what motivates one legislator to make a speech about a statute is not necessarily what motivates scores of others to enact it." Can we assume, then, that they all agree with the motivation expressed in the staff-prepared committee reports they might have read—even though we are unwilling to assume that they agreed with the motivation expressed in the very statute that they voted for? Should we consider postenactment floor statements? Or postenactment testimony from legislators, obtained expressly for the lawsuit? Should we consider media reports on the realities of the legislative bargaining? All of these sources, of course, are eminently manipulable. Legislative histories can be contrived and sanitized, favorable media coverage orchestrated, and postenactment recollections conveniently distorted. Perhaps most valuable of all would be more objective indications—for example, evidence regarding the individual legislators' religious affiliations. And if that, why not evidence regarding the fervor or tepidity of their beliefs?

Having achieved, through these simple means, an assessment of what individual legislators intended, we must still confront the question (yet to be addressed in any of our cases) how many of them must have the invalidating intent. If a state senate approves a bill by vote of 26 to 25, and only one of the 26 intended solely to advance religion, is the law unconstitutional? What if 13 of the 26 had that intent? What if 3 of the 26 had the impermissible intent, but 3 of the 25 voting against the bill were motivated by religious hostility or were simply attempting to "balance" the votes of their impermissibly motivated colleagues? Or is it possible that the intent of the bill's sponsor is alone enough to invalidate it—on a theory, perhaps, that even though everyone else's intent was pure, what they produced was the fruit of a forbidden tree? Because there are no good answers to these questions, this Court has recognized from Chief Justice Marshall, see Fletcher v. Peck, to Chief Justice Warren, United States v. O'Brien, that determining the subjective intent of legislators is a perilous enterprise.

Given the many hazards involved in assessing the subjective intent of governmental decisionmakers, the first prong of Lemon is defensible, I think, only if the text of the Establishment Clause demands it. That is surely not the case. [In] the past we have attempted to justify our embarrassing Establishment Clause jurisprudence on the ground that it "sacrifices clarity and predictability for flexibility." [I] think it time that we sacrifice some "flexibility" for "clarity and predictability." Abandoning Lemon's purpose test—a test which exacerbates the tension between the Free Exercise and Establishment Clauses, has no basis in the language or history of the amendment, and, as today's decision shows, has wonderfully flexible consequences—would be a good place to start.

DEFINING RELIGION VS. SCIENCE

In Kitzmiller v. Dover Area School District, 400 F. Supp. 2d 707 (M.D. Pa. 2004), a federal district court invalidated a requirement that teachers must read aloud a statement to ninth graders identifying Intelligent Design as an alternative explanation to evolution regarding the origins of life. The court first rejected the requirement under the endorsement test: "The history of the intelligent design (hereinafter ID) movement [and] the development of the strategy to weaken education of evolution by focusing students on alleged gaps in the theory of evolution is the historical and cultural background against which the Dover School Board acted in adopting the challenged ID Policy. [A] reasonable observer, whether adult or child, would be aware of this social context in which the ID Policy arose. [The] concept of intelligent [design], in its current form, came into existence after [Edwards] and [in] addition to the [ID movement] itself describing ID as a religious argument, ID's religious nature is evident because it involves a supernatural designer. [The] evidence at trial demonstrates that ID is nothing less than the progeny of creationism. [Edwards held] that the Constitution forbids teaching creationism as science. [Furthermore, we find that] ID is not science. We find that ID fails on three different levels, any one of which is sufficient to preclude a determination that ID is science. They are: (1) ID violates the centuries-old ground rules of science by invoking and permitting supernatural causation; (2) the argument of irreducible complexity, central to ID, employs the same flawed and illogical contrived dualism that doomed creation science in the 1980's; and (3) ID's negative attacks on evolution have been refuted by the scientific community. [It] is additionally important to note that ID has failed to gain acceptance in the scientific community, it has not generated peer-reviewed publications, nor has it been the subject of testing and research."

The court also held that the requirement failed the Lemon test: "[A] wealth of evidence [reveals] that the District's purpose [in introducing the requirement] was to advance creationism, an inherently religious view, both by introducing it directly under the label ID and by disparaging the scientific theory of evolution, so that creationism would gain credence by default as the only apparent alternative to evolution. [Furthermore, the] effect of Defendants' actions in adopting the curriculum change was to impose a religious view of biological origins into the biology course, in violation of the Establishment Clause."

PUBLIC DISPLAYS OF RELIGIOUS SYMBOLS

Outside the context of the public schools, the Court has been more tolerant of governmental sponsorship of religious symbolism. No justice has seriously questioned, for example, the permissibility of the motto "In God We Trust" on the national currency (on coins since 1864 and paper currency since 1957), or the recitation of the phrase "one nation under God" in the Pledge of Allegiance (added in 1954). What explains this deferential view? That these practices have lost their religious significance over time? That they were civic rather than religious to begin with? That they merely commemorate historical "fact" about the piety of the founding generation? That the nonbelieving observer can readily ignore them? What is the Court's basis for rejecting most Establishment Clause challenges in the following cases?

1. ***Sunday closing laws.*** **McGowan v. Maryland**, 366 U.S. 420 (1961), was one of four companion cases in which the Court rejected claims that Sunday closing laws violated the religion clauses. Chief Justice WARREN wrote the majority opinion. He noted in McGowan that there is "no dispute that the original laws which dealt with Sunday labor were motivated by religious forces." But he concluded: "In light of the evolution of our Sunday Closing Laws through the centuries, and of their more or less recent emphasis upon secular considerations, it is not difficult to discern that as presently written and administered, most of them, at least, are of a secular rather than of a religious character, and that presently they bear no relationship to establishment of religion as those words are used in the [Constitution]. The present purpose and effect of most of them is to provide a uniform day of rest for all citizens; the fact that this day is Sunday, a day of particular significance for the dominant Christian sects, does not bar the State from achieving its secular [goals]. Sunday is a day apart from all others. The cause is irrelevant; the fact exists."

2. ***Legislative prayer.*** In **Marsh v. Chambers**, 463 U.S. 783 (1983), the Court upheld "the Nebraska Legislature's practice of opening each legislative day with a prayer by a chaplain paid by the State." Chief Justice BURGER's majority opinion relied largely on history to sustain the practice despite the fact that the position of chaplain had been held for 16 years by a Presbyterian, that the chaplain was paid at public expense, and that all of the prayers were "in the Judeo-Christian tradition." This was the first case since Lemon in 1971 that did not apply the three-pronged test. Instead, the majority looked at the specific features of the challenged practice in light of a long history of acceptance of legislative and other official prayers. The majority concluded: "Weighed against the historical background, [the allegedly vulnerable] factors do not serve to invalidate Nebraska's practice."

Chief Justice Burger viewed prayer in this context as "unique" in its historical roots: "The opening of sessions of legislative and other deliberative public bodies with prayer is deeply embedded in the history and tradition of this country. From colonial times through the founding of the Republic and ever since, the practice of legislative prayer has coexisted with the principles of disestablishment and religious freedom. In the very courtrooms in which the United States District Judge and later three Circuit Judges heard and decided this case, the proceedings opened with an announcement that concluded, 'God save the United States and this Honorable Court.' The same invocation occurs at all sessions of this Court. [Although] prayers were not offered during the Constitutional Convention, the First Congress, as one of its early items of business, adopted the policy of selecting a chaplain to open each session with prayer. [On] April 25, 1789, the Senate elected its first chaplain; the House followed suit on May 1, 1789. A statute providing for the payment of these chaplains was enacted into law on September 22, 1789. [In] light of the unambiguous and unbroken history of more than 200 years, there can be no doubt that the practice of opening legislative sessions with a prayer has become part of the fabric of our society. [It] is simply a tolerable acknowledgment of beliefs widely held among the people of this country."

Justice BRENNAN, joined by Justice Marshall, filed a lengthy dissent: "Legislative prayer clearly violates the principles of neutrality and separation that are embedded within the Establishment Clause. It is contrary to the fundamental message of Engel and Schempp. It intrudes on the right to conscience by forcing some legislators either to participate in a 'prayer opportunity,' with which they are in basic disagreement, or to make their disagreement a matter of public comment by declining to participate. It forces all residents of the State to support a religious exercise that may be contrary to their own beliefs. It requires the State to commit itself on fundamental theological issues. It has the potential for degrading religion by allowing a religious call to worship to be intermeshed with a secular call to order. And it injects religion into the political sphere by creating the potential that each and every selection of a chaplain, or consideration of a particular prayer, or even reconsideration of the practice itself, will provoke a political battle along religious lines and ultimately alienate some religiously identified group of citizens." Under the Lemon test, he argued, the practice could not be sustained, since the purpose and effect were "clearly religious" and there was also excessive political entanglement.

Justice STEVENS also dissented: "In a democratically elected legislature, the religious beliefs of the chaplain tend to reflect the faith of the majority of the lawmakers' constituents. Prayers may be said by a Catholic priest in the Massachusetts Legislature and by a Presbyterian minister in the Nebraska Legislature, but I would not expect to find a Jehovah's Witness or a disciple of Mary Baker Eddy or the Reverend Moon serving as the official chaplain in any state legislature. Regardless of the motivation of the majority that exercises the power to appoint the chaplain, it seems plain to me that the designation of a member of one religious faith to serve as the sole official chaplain of a state legislature for a period of 16 years constitutes the preference of one faith over another in violation of the Establishment Clause of the First Amendment."

Note that in Marsh, Chief Justice Burger relied heavily on the legislative chaplaincies established by the First Congress as a historical precedent supporting the rejection of the Establishment Clause claim. Was that reliance justified? James Madison, principal author of the religion clauses, was a member of that Congress, but he later stated in correspondence that "it was not with my approbation" that Congress had thus deviated from the " 'immunity of Religion from civil jurisdiction.' " He explained in an essay that " '[t]he law appointing Chaplains establishes a religious worship for the national representatives, to be performed by Ministers of religion, elected by a majority of them, and these are to be paid out of the national taxes. [The] establishment of the chaplainship to Cong[res]s is a palpable violation of equal rights, as well as of Constitutional principles: The tenets of the chaplains elected in [by the Majority] shut the door of worship ag[ain]st the members whose creeds & consciences forbid a participation in that of the majority.' " For an in-depth account of Madison's views on the topic, see Olree, "James Madison and Legislative Chaplains," 102 Nw. U. L. Rev. 145 (2008). For a history of appointments to the congressional chaplaincies, noting controversies sparked by the appointments of Catholic, Unitarian and guest Hindu chaplains and suggesting that such appointments have been more religiously divisive than the Marsh opinion suggests, see Lund, "The Congressional Chaplaincies," 17 Wm. & Mary Bill of Rights J. 1171 (2009).

In **Town of Greece v. Galloway**, 573 U.S. 565 (2014), the Court revisited legislative prayer at a distance of more than thirty years—and upheld it. At issue was the practice in Greece, New York, of asking a series of volunteer clergy to offer prayers at town meetings after the Pledge of Allegiance and roll call. According to the Court's 5–4 opinion by Justice KENNEDY, the town had compiled "a list of willing 'board chaplains.' [The] town at no point excluded or denied an opportunity to a would-be prayer giver. Its leaders maintained that a minister or layperson of any persuasion, including an atheist, could give the invocation. But nearly all of the congregations in town were Christian; and from 1999 to 2007, all of the participating ministers were too. Greece neither reviewed the prayers in advance of the meetings nor provided guidance as to their tone or content. [Some] of the ministers spoke in a distinctly Christian idiom; and a minority invoked religious holidays, scripture, or doctrine."

The Court held that Marsh controlled, though not precisely for the reasons given in the case. "Marsh is sometimes described as 'carving out an exception' to the Court's Establishment Clause jurisprudence, because it sustained legislative prayer without subjecting the practice to any of the formal tests that have traditionally structured this inquiry. The Court in Marsh found those tests unnecessary because history supported the conclusion that legislative invocations are compatible with the

Establishment Clause. [Yet] Marsh must not be understood as permitting a practice that would amount to a constitutional violation if not for its historical foundation. The case teaches instead that the Establishment Clause must be interpreted by reference to historical practices and understandings. That the First Congress provided for the appointment of chaplains only days after approving language for the First Amendment demonstrates that the Framers considered legislative prayer a benign acknowledgment of religion's role in society."

Justice Kennedy rejected the argument that under Marsh, legislative prayer must be nonsectarian. "One of the Senate's first chaplains, the Rev. William White, gave prayers in a series that included the Lord's Prayer, the Collect for Ash Wednesday, prayers for peace and grace, a general thanksgiving, St. Chrysostom's Prayer, and a prayer seeking 'the grace of our Lord Jesus Christ, &c.' The decidedly Christian nature of these prayers must not be dismissed as the relic of a time when our Nation was less pluralistic than it is today. Congress continues to permit its appointed and visiting chaplains to express themselves in a religious idiom. It acknowledges our growing diversity not by proscribing sectarian content but by welcoming ministers of many creeds. [Marsh] nowhere suggested that the constitutionality of legislative prayer turns on the neutrality of its content." However, "[i]n rejecting the suggestion that legislative prayer must be nonsectarian, the Court does not imply that no constraints remain on its content. The relevant constraint derives from its place at the opening of legislative sessions, where it is meant to lend gravity to the occasion and reflect values long part of the Nation's heritage. Prayer that is solemn and respectful in tone, that invites lawmakers to reflect upon shared ideals and common ends before they embark on the fractious business of governing, serves that legitimate function. If the course and practice over time shows that the invocations denigrate nonbelievers or religious minorities, threaten damnation, or preach conversion, many present may consider the prayer to fall short of the desire to elevate the purpose of the occasion and to unite lawmakers in their common effort. That circumstance would present a different case than the one presently before the Court."

Justice Kennedy went on to explain that the fact that the town asked "a predominantly Christian set of ministers to lead the prayer" did not invalidate it. "The town made reasonable efforts to identify all of the congregations located within its borders and represented that it would welcome a prayer by any minister or layman who wished to give one. That nearly all of the congregations in town turned out to be Christian does not reflect an aversion or bias on the part of town leaders against minority faiths. So long as the town maintains a policy of nondiscrimination, the Constitution does not require it to search beyond its borders for non-Christian prayer givers in an effort to achieve religious balancing. The quest to promote a diversity of religious views would require the town to make wholly inappropriate judgments about the number of religions [it] should sponsor and the relative frequency with which it should sponsor each, a form of government entanglement with religion that is far more troublesome than the current approach."

Justice Kennedy rejected the argument that the prayers coerced attendees at town council meetings by exerting "subtle pressure to participate in prayers that violate their beliefs in order to please the board members from whom they are about to seek a favorable ruling." He said that "[t]he inquiry remains a fact-sensitive one that considers both the setting in which the prayer arises and the audience to whom it is directed. [The] principal audience for these invocations is not, indeed, the public but lawmakers themselves, who may find that a moment of prayer or quiet reflection sets the mind to a higher purpose and thereby eases the task of governing. [The] analysis would be different if town board members directed the public to participate in the prayers, singled out dissidents for opprobrium, or indicated that their decisions might be influenced by a person's acquiescence in the prayer opportunity. No such thing occurred in the town of Greece. [Nothing] in the record indicates that town leaders allocated benefits and burdens based on participation in the prayer, or that citizens were received differently depending on whether they joined the invocation or quietly declined. In no instance did town leaders signal disfavor toward nonparticipants or suggest that their stature in the community was in any way diminished." And while some participants might have felt offended, offense "does not equate to coercion. Adults often encounter speech they find disagreeable; and an Establishment Clause violation is not made out any time a person experiences a sense of affront from the expression of contrary religious views in a legislative forum, especially where, as here, any member of the public is welcome in turn to offer an invocation reflecting his or her own convictions."

Finally, Justice Kennedy distinguished Lee v. Weisman [p. 1648, above]: "Nothing in the record suggests that members of the public are dissuaded from leaving the meeting room during the prayer, arriving late, or even, as happened here, making a later protest. [Should] nonbelievers choose to exit the room during a prayer they find distasteful, their absence will not stand out as disrespectful or even noteworthy. And should they remain, their quiet acquiescence will not, in light of our traditions, be interpreted as an agreement with the words or ideas expressed. Neither choice represents an unconstitutional imposition as to mature adults, who presumably are not readily susceptible to religious indoctrination or peer pressure."

Justice KAGAN dissented at length, joined by Justices Ginsburg, Breyer and Sotomayor. Taking Marsh as settled law, she distinguished the facts: "The practice at issue here differs from the one sustained in Marsh because Greece's town meetings involve participation by ordinary citizens, and the invocations given—directly to those citizens—were predominantly sectarian in content. Still more, Greece's Board did nothing to recognize religious diversity: In arranging for clergy members to open each meeting, the Town never sought (except briefly when this suit was filed) to involve, accommodate, or in any way reach out to adherents of non-Christian religions. So month in and month out for over a decade, prayers steeped in only one faith, addressed toward members of the public, commenced meetings to discuss local affairs and distribute government benefits."

Justice Kagan further distinguished Marsh on the ground that the town council was not only a legislative body: "The town hall here is a kind of hybrid. Greece's Board indeed has legislative functions, as Congress and state assemblies do—and that means some opening prayers are allowed there. But [the] Board's meetings are also occasions for ordinary citizens to engage with and petition their government, often on highly individualized matters. That feature calls for Board members to exercise special care to ensure that the prayers offered are inclusive—that they respect each and every member of the community as an equal citizen. But the Board, and the clergy members it selected, made no such effort. Instead, the prayers given in Greece, addressed directly to the Town's citizenry, were more sectarian, and less inclusive, than anything this Court sustained in Marsh. [Still] more, the prayers betray no understanding that the American community is today, as it long has been, a rich mosaic of religious faiths. The monthly chaplains appear almost always to assume that everyone in the room is Christian (and of a kind who has no objection to government-sponsored worship). The Town itself has never urged its chaplains to reach out to members of other faiths, or even to recall that they might be present."

Justice Kagan concluded that "Greece could not do what it did: infuse a participatory government body with one (and only one) faith, so that month in and month out, the citizens appearing before it become partly defined by their creed—as those who share, and those who do not, the community's majority religious belief. In this country, when citizens go before the government, they go not as Christians or Muslims or Jews (or what have you), but just as Americans (or here, as Grecians). That is what it means to be an equal citizen, irrespective of religion. And that is what the Town of Greece precluded by so identifying itself with a single faith."

The "fact-sensitive" inquiry laid out in Town of Greece has led to some disparate outcomes in the lower courts. For instance, after Town of Greece both the Fourth and the Sixth Circuits addressed the question whether the Establishment Clause prohibits county commissioners from offering sectarian prayers (in both cases Christian prayers), when only the commissioners are permitted to offer invocations. In Bormuth v. County of Jackson, 870 F.3d 494 (6th Cir. 2017), the Sixth Circuit ruled the practice was permissible because there is a history of legislator-led prayer; the opportunity to give the prayers was not restricted by religion, but rather depended only on being elected to the office of commissioner; and the prayers did not denigrate non-Christians. The same year, the Fourth Circuit struck down a similar prayer practice in Lund v. Rowan County, 863 F.3d 268 (4th Cir. 2017). The court stated that legislator-led sectarian prayer did not per se violate the Establishment Clause, but that the prayers offered by the commissioners in that case sometimes proselytized and evangelized, thus violating Town of Greece's proscription on denigrating minority faiths and "preach[ing] conversion," and that the local government setting made the risk of coercion greater.

3. ***Public religious displays.*** Clearly, it would violate the Establishment Clause for government to place a Latin cross on the dome of the state capitol. Such symbolism would clearly constitute religious "endorsement." Even under a narrow nonpreferentialist view, government is barred from the symbolic union of a church and the state. The Establishment Clause, at a minimum, prohibits theocracy. But may a government place, or permit others to place, elsewhere on public property a display depicting the birth of Christ at Christmas or a menorah commemorating the Jewish festival of Chanukah? Does such a display implicate the Establishment Clause to the same extent as the cross on the capitol? Will its predominant meaning appear religious? Regardless of the surrounding context? What if private parties finance the display? Will such a display likely be attributed to the government? The following cases consider the constitutionality of such public displays.

Lynch v. Donnelly

465 U.S. 668, 104 S. Ct. 1355, 79 L. Ed. 2d 604 (1984).

■ CHIEF JUSTICE BURGER delivered the opinion of the Court.

[Each] year, in cooperation with the downtown retail merchants' association, the City of Pawtucket, Rhode Island, erects a Christmas display as part of its observance of the Christmas holiday season. The display is situated in a park owned by a nonprofit organization and located in the heart of the shopping district. The display is essentially like those to be found in hundreds of towns or cities across the Nation—often on public grounds—during the Christmas season. The Pawtucket display comprises many of the figures and decorations traditionally associated with Christmas, including, among other things, a Santa Claus house, reindeer pulling Santa's sleigh, candy-striped poles, a Christmas tree, carolers, cutout figures representing such characters as a clown, an elephant, and a teddy bear, hundreds of colored lights, a large banner that reads "SEASONS GREETINGS," and the crèche at issue here. All components of this display are owned by the City. The crèche, which has been included in the display for 40 or more years, consists of the traditional figures, including the Infant Jesus, Mary and Joseph, angels, shepherds, kings, and animals, all ranging in height from 5 inches to 5 feet. In 1973, when the present crèche was acquired, it cost the City $1365; it now is valued at $200. The erection and dismantling of the crèche costs the City about $20 per year; nominal expenses are incurred in lighting the crèche. No money has been expended on its maintenance for the past 10 years. The District Court held that the City's inclusion of the crèche in the display violates the Establishment Clause. [A] divided panel of the [First] Circuit affirmed. [We] reverse.

[There] is an unbroken history of official acknowledgment by all three branches of government of the role of religion in American life from at least 1789. [Our] history is replete with official references to the value and invocation of Divine guidance in deliberations and pronouncements of the Founding Fathers and contemporary leaders. [Long] before Independence, a day of Thanksgiving was celebrated as a religious holiday to give thanks for the bounties of Nature as gifts from God. [Executive Orders] and other official announcements of Presidents and of the Congress have proclaimed both Christmas and Thanksgiving National Holidays in religious terms. [Thus,] it is clear that Government has long recognized—indeed it has subsidized—holidays with religious significance. Other examples of reference to our religious heritage are found in the statutorily prescribed national motto "In God We Trust," which Congress and the President mandated for our currency, and in the language "One nation under God," as part of the Pledge of Allegiance to the [American flag]. [One] cannot look at even this brief resume without finding that our history is pervaded by expressions of religious beliefs such as are found in Zorach. Equally pervasive is the evidence of accommodation of all faiths and all forms of religious expression, and hostility toward [none].

This history may help explain why the Court consistently has declined to take a rigid, absolutist view of the Establishment Clause. [In] our modern, complex society, whose traditions and constitutional underpinnings rest on and encourage diversity and pluralism in all areas, an absolutist approach in applying the Establishment Clause is simplistic and has been uniformly rejected by the Court. Rather than mechanically invalidating all governmental conduct or statutes that confer benefits or give special recognition to religion in general or to one faith—as an absolutist approach would dictate—the Court has scrutinized challenged legislation or official conduct to determine whether, in reality, it establishes a religion or religious faith, or tends to do so. In each case, the inquiry calls for line drawing; no fixed, per se rule can be framed. [In] the line-drawing process we have often found it useful to inquire whether the challenged law or conduct has a secular purpose, whether its principal or primary effect is to advance or inhibit religion, and whether it creates an excessive entanglement of government with religion. [Lemon.] But, we have repeatedly emphasized our unwillingness to be confined to any single test or criterion in this sensitive area.

[In] this case, the focus of our inquiry must be on the crèche in the context of the Christmas season. [Viewed in this context,] there is insufficient evidence to establish that the inclusion of the crèche is a purposeful or surreptitious effort to express some kind of subtle governmental advocacy of a particular religious message. In a pluralistic society a variety of motives and purposes are implicated. [The] crèche in the display depicts the historical origins of this traditional event long recognized as a National Holiday. [The] display is sponsored by the City to celebrate the Holiday and to depict the origins of that Holiday. These are legitimate secular purposes.

[The] District Court found that the primary effect of including the crèche is to confer a substantial and impermissible benefit on religion in general and on the Christian faith in particular. [But we] are unable to discern a greater aid to religion deriving from inclusion of the crèche than from [endorsements] previously held not violative of the Establishment Clause [e.g., in McGowan, Zorach, and Marsh.] The dissent asserts that some observers may perceive that the City has aligned itself with the Christian faith by including a Christian symbol in its display and that this serves to advance religion. We can assume, arguendo, that the display advances religion in a sense; but our precedents plainly contemplate that on occasion some advancement of religion will result from governmental action. [Here,] whatever benefit to one faith or religion or to all religions, is indirect, remote and incidental; display of the crèche is no more an advancement or endorsement of religion than the Congressional and Executive recognition of the origins of the Holiday itself as "Christ's Mass", or the exhibition of literally hundreds of religious paintings in governmentally supported [museums].

[To] forbid the use of this one passive symbol—the crèche—at the very time people are taking note of the season with Christmas hymns and carols in public schools and other public places [would] be a stilted over-reaction contrary to our history and to our holdings. If the presence of the crèche in this display violates the Establishment Clause, a host of other forms of taking official note of Christmas, and of our religious heritage, are equally offensive to the Constitution. The Court has acknowledged that the "fears and political problems" that gave rise to the Religion Clauses in the 18th century are of far less concern today. [Everson.] We are unable to perceive the Archbishop of Canterbury, the Vicar of Rome, or other powerful religious leaders behind every public acknowledgment of the religious heritage long officially recognized by the three constitutional branches of government. Any notion that these symbols pose a real danger of establishment of a state church is farfetched indeed. [Reversed.]

■ JUSTICE O'CONNOR, concurring.

I concur in the opinion of the Court. I write separately to suggest a clarification of our Establishment Clause doctrine. The suggested approach leads to the same result in this case as that taken by the Court, and the Court's opinion, as I read it, is consistent with my analysis.

The Establishment Clause prohibits government from making adherence to a religion relevant in any way to a person's standing in the political community. Government can run afoul of that prohibition in two principal ways. One is excessive entanglement with religious institutions, which may interfere with the independence of the institutions, give the institutions access to government or governmental powers not fully shared by nonadherents of the religion, and foster the creation of political constituencies defined along religious lines. The second and more direct infringement is government endorsement or disapproval of religion. Endorsement sends a message to nonadherents that they are outsiders, not full members of the political community, and an accompanying message to adherents that they are insiders, favored members of the political community. Disapproval sends the opposite message.

[The] central issue in this case is whether Pawtucket has endorsed Christianity by its display of the crèche. To answer that question, we must examine both what Pawtucket intended to communicate in displaying the crèche and what message the City's display actually conveyed. The purpose and effect prongs of the Lemon test represent these two aspects of the meaning of the City's action. [The] proper inquiry under the purpose prong of Lemon, I submit, is whether the government intends to convey a message of endorsement or disapproval of religion. Applying that formulation to this case, I would find that Pawtucket did not intend to convey any message of endorsement of Christianity or disapproval of non-Christian religions. The evident purpose of including the crèche in the larger display was not promotion of the religious content of the crèche but celebration of the public holiday through its traditional symbols. Celebration of public holidays, which have cultural significance even if they also have religious aspects, is a legitimate secular [purpose].

[The] effect prong of the Lemon test [requires] that a government practice not have the effect of communicating a message of government endorsement or disapproval of religion. It is only practices having that effect, whether intentionally or unintentionally, that make religion relevant, in reality or public perception, to status in the political community. Pawtucket's display of its crèche, I believe, does not communicate a message that the government intends to endorse the Christian beliefs represented by the crèche. Although the religious and indeed sectarian significance of the crèche [is] not neutralized by the setting, the overall holiday setting changes what viewers may fairly understand to be the purpose of the display—as a typical museum setting, though not neutralizing the religious content of a religious painting, negates any message of endorsement of that content. The display celebrates a public holiday, and no one contends that declaration of that holiday is understood to be an endorsement of religion. The holiday itself has very strong secular components and traditions. Government celebration of the holiday [generally] is not understood to endorse the religious content of the holiday. [The] crèche is a traditional symbol of the holiday that is very commonly displayed along with purely secular symbols, as it was in Pawtucket.

These features combine to make the government's display of the crèche in this particular physical setting no more an endorsement of religion than such governmental acknowledgments of religion as [printing] "In God We Trust," on coins, and opening court sessions with "God save the United States and this honorable court." Those government acknowledgments of religion serve, in the only ways reasonably possible in our culture, the legitimate secular purposes of solemnizing public occasions, expressing confidence in the future, and encouraging the recognition of what is worthy of appreciation in society. For that reason, and because of their history and ubiquity, those practices are not understood as conveying government approval of particular religious beliefs. The display of the crèche likewise [cannot] fairly be understood to convey a message of government endorsement of [religion].

■ JUSTICE BRENNAN, with whom JUSTICES MARSHALL, BLACKMUN and STEVENS join, dissenting.

[In] my view, Pawtucket's maintenance and display at public expense of a symbol as distinctively sectarian as a crèche simply cannot be squared with our prior cases. [The] City's inclusion of the crèche in its Christmas display simply does not reflect a "clearly secular purpose." [The] nativity scene, unlike every other element of the Hodgson Park display, reflects a sectarian exclusivity that the avowed purposes of celebrating the holiday season and promoting retail commerce simply do not encompass. [The] inclusion of a distinctively religious element like the crèche [demonstrates] that a narrower sectarian purpose lay behind the decision to include a nativity scene.

[The] "primary effect" of including a nativity scene in the City's display [is] to place the government's imprimatur of approval on the particular religious beliefs exemplified by the crèche. [The] effect on minority religious groups, as well as on those who may reject all religion, is to convey the message that their views are not similarly worthy of public recognition nor entitled to public support. [Finally], it is evident that Pawtucket's inclusion of a crèche [does] pose a significant threat of fostering "excessive entanglement."

[The] Court, by focusing on the holiday "context" in which the nativity scene appeared, seeks to explain away the clear religious import of the crèche. [It] blinks reality to claim, as the Court does, that by including such a distinctively religious object as the crèche in its Christmas display, Pawtucket has done no more than made use of a "traditional" symbol of the holiday, and has thereby purged the crèche of its religious content and conferred only an "incidental and indirect" benefit on religion. [Even] in the context of Pawtucket's seasonal celebration, the crèche retains a specifically Christian religious meaning. [It] is the chief symbol of the characteristically Christian belief that a divine Savior was brought into the world and that the purpose of this miraculous birth was to illuminate a path toward salvation and redemption. For Christians, that path is exclusive, precious and holy. But for those who do not share these beliefs, the symbolic re-enactment of the birth of a divine being who has been miraculously incarnated as a man stands as a dramatic reminder of their differences with Christian faith. [To] be so excluded on religious grounds by one's elected government is an insult and an injury that, until today, could not be countenanced by the Establishment Clause.

[The] Court apparently believes that once it finds that the designation of Christmas as a public holiday is constitutionally acceptable, it is then free to conclude that virtually every form of governmental association with the celebration of the holiday is also constitutional. The vice of this dangerously superficial argument is that it overlooks the fact that the Christmas holiday in our national culture contains both secular and sectarian elements. To say that government may recognize the holiday's traditional, secular elements of gift giving, public festivities and community spirit, does not mean that government may indiscriminately embrace the distinctively sectarian aspects of the holiday.

When government decides to recognize Christmas day as a public holiday, it does no more than accommodate the calendar of public activities to the plain fact that many Americans will expect on that day to spend time visiting with their families, attending religious services, and perhaps enjoying some respite from pre-holiday activities. The Free Exercise Clause, of course, does not necessarily compel the government to provide this accommodation, but neither is the Establishment Clause offended by such a step. Cf. [Zorach]. [If] public officials go further and participate in the *secular* celebration of Christmas—by, for example, decorating public places with such secular images as wreaths, garlands or Santa Claus figures—they move closer to the limits of their constitutional power but nevertheless remain within the boundaries set by the Establishment Clause. But when those officials participate in or appear to endorse the distinctively religious elements of this otherwise secular event, they encroach upon First Amendment freedoms. For it is at that point that the government brings to the forefront the theological content of the holiday, and places the prestige, power and financial support of a civil authority in the service of a particular faith.

The inclusion of a crèche in Pawtucket's otherwise secular celebration of Christmas clearly violates these principles. Unlike such secular figures as Santa Claus, reindeer and carolers, a nativity scene represents far more than a mere "traditional" symbol of Christmas. The essence of the crèche's symbolic purpose and effect is to prompt the observer to experience a sense of simple awe and wonder appropriate to the contemplation of one of the central elements of Christian dogma—that God sent His son into the world to be a Messiah. Contrary to the Court's suggestion, the crèche is far from a mere representation of a "particular historic religious event." It is, instead, best understood as a mystical re-creation of an event that lies at the heart of Christian faith. To suggest, as the Court does, that such a symbol is merely "traditional" and therefore no different from Santa's house or reindeer is not only offensive to those for whom the crèche has profound significance, but insulting to those who insist for religious or personal reasons that the story of Christ is in no sense a part of "history" nor an unavoidable element of our national ["heritage"].

[The] Court has never comprehensively addressed the extent to which government may acknowledge religion by, for example, incorporating religious references into public ceremonies, [and] I do not presume to offer a comprehensive approach. Nevertheless, [at] least three principles—tracing the narrow channels which government acknowledgments must follow to satisfy the Establishment Clause—may be identified. First, although the government may not be compelled to do so by the Free Exercise Clause, it may, consistently with the Establishment Clause, act to accommodate to some extent the opportunities of individuals to practice their religion. [That] principle would justify government's decision to declare December 25th a public holiday. Second, our cases recognize that while a particular governmental practice may have derived from religious motivations and retain certain religious connotations, it is nonetheless permissible for the government to pursue the practice when it is continued today solely for secular reasons. [McGowan.] Thanksgiving Day, in my view, fits easily within this principle.

Finally, we have noted that government cannot be completely prohibited from recognizing in its public actions the religious beliefs and practices of the American people as an aspect of our national history and culture. While I remain uncertain about these questions, I would suggest that such practices as the designation of "In God We Trust" as our national motto [and] the references to God contained in the Pledge of Allegiance can best be understood [as] a form of "ceremonial deism," protected from Establishment Clause scrutiny chiefly because they have lost through rote repetition any significant religious content. Moreover, these references are uniquely suited to serve such wholly secular purposes as solemnizing public occasions, or inspiring commitment to meet some national challenge in a manner that simply could not be fully served in our culture if government were limited to purely non-religious phrases. The practices by which the government has long acknowledged religion are therefore probably necessary to serve certain secular functions, and that necessity, coupled with their long history, gives those practices an essentially secular meaning. The crèche fits none of these categories. [By] insisting that such a distinctively sectarian message is merely an unobjectionable part of our "religious heritage," the Court takes a long step backwards to the days when Justice Brewer could arrogantly declare for the Court that "this is a Christian nation." Church of Holy Trinity v. United States, 143 U.S. 457 (1892). Those days, I had thought, were forever put behind us by the Court's decision in [Engel], in which we rejected a similar argument [in defense of the Regents' Prayer].

The American historical experience concerning the public celebration of Christmas, if carefully examined, provides no support for the Court's decision. [Attention] to the details of history should not blind us to the cardinal purposes of the Establishment Clause, nor limit our central inquiry in these cases—whether the challenged practices "threaten those consequences which the Framers deeply feared." [The] intent of the Framers with respect to the public display of nativity scenes is virtually impossible to discern primarily because the widespread celebration of Christmas did not emerge in its present form until well into the [nineteenth century]. [There] is no evidence whatsoever that the Framers would have expressly approved a Federal celebration of the Christmas holiday including public displays of a nativity scene.

[Pawtucket's] action should be recognized for what it is: a coercive, though perhaps small, step toward establishing the sectarian preferences of the majority at the expense of the minority, accomplished by placing public facilities and funds in support of the religious symbolism and theological tidings that the crèche [conveys].

■ JUSTICE BLACKMUN, joined by JUSTICE STEVENS, dissenting.

The crèche has been relegated to the role of a neutral harbinger of the holiday season, useful for commercial purposes, but devoid of any inherent meaning and incapable of enhancing the religious tenor of a display of which it is an integral part. The city has its victory—but it is a Pyrrhic one indeed. The import of [the decision] is to encourage use of the crèche in a municipally sponsored display, a setting where Christians feel constrained in acknowledging its symbolic meaning and non-Christians feel alienated by its presence. Surely, this is a misuse of a sacred symbol.

APPLYING THE ENDORSEMENT TEST

1. ***Holiday displays.*** In **Allegheny County v. American Civil Liberties Union [ACLU]**, 492 U.S. 573 (1989), a majority of the Court held unconstitutional a freestanding display of a nativity scene on the main staircase of a county courthouse. Unlike the display in the Lynch case, the crèche belonged to a Catholic organization and was not surrounded by figures of Santa Claus or other Christmas decorations. But a different majority in the same case upheld the display of a Jewish Chanukah menorah placed next to a Christmas tree and a sign saying "Salute to Liberty" in the City-County Building, a block away from the courthouse. The menorah was owned by a Jewish group, but stored, erected, and removed annually by the city.

In the course of reaching these holdings, the Court, by a 5–4 majority, adopted Justice O'Connor's "no endorsement" analysis as a general approach to Establishment Clause adjudication. Justice BLACKMUN, joined by Justices Brennan, Marshall, O'Connor and Stevens, noted: "In recent years, we have paid particularly close attention to whether the challenged governmental practice either has the purpose or effect of 'endorsing' religion. [Of course,] the word 'endorsement' is not self-defining. [But whether] the key word is 'endorsement,' 'favoritism,' or 'promotion,' the essential principle remains the same. The Establishment Clause, at the very least, prohibits government from appearing to take a position on questions of religious belief or from 'making adherence to a religion relevant in any way to a person's standing in the political community.' [Lynch (O'Connor, J., concurring).]"

Justice KENNEDY, joined by Chief Justice Rehnquist and Justices White and Scalia, rejected the majority's "endorsement" analysis, viewing it as reflecting "an unjustified hostility toward religion." The dissent argued for a narrower test of establishment: "government may not coerce anyone to support or participate in any religion or its exercise; and it may not, in the guise of avoiding hostility or callous indifference, give direct benefits to religion in such a degree that it in fact 'establishes a [state] religion or religious faith, or tends to do so.' [Lynch.] [But] non-coercive government action within the realm of flexible accommodation or passive acknowledgement of existing symbols does not violate the Establishment Clause unless it benefits religion in a way more direct and more substantial than practices that are accepted in our national heritage." He also objected that Justice O'Connor's endorsement test disregarded history: "Few of our traditional practices recognizing the part religion plays in our society [such as Thanksgiving Proclamations and legislative prayer] can withstand scrutiny under a faithful application of this formula." Finally, he argued, the "endorsement" approach was "unworkable in practice": it "threatens to trivialize constitutional adjudication [by embracing] a jurisprudence of minutiae" governing the detailed context of governmental displays.

Justice O'CONNOR, joined by Justices Brennan and Stevens, defended the endorsement test against Justice Kennedy's attack and criticized his proposed narrower test: "An Establishment Clause standard that prohibits only 'coercive' practices or overt efforts at government proselytization, but fails to take account of the numerous more subtle ways that government can show favoritism to particular beliefs or convey a message of disapproval to others, would not, in my view, adequately protect the religious liberty or respect the religious diversity of the members of our pluralistic political community. Thus, this Court has never relied on coercion alone as the touchstone of Establishment Clause analysis. To require a showing of coercion, even indirect coercion, as an essential element of an Establishment Clause violation would make the Free Exercise Clause a redundancy."

A 5–4 majority of the Court found the crèche display here unconstitutional. Justice BLACKMUN, joined by Justices Brennan, Marshall, O'Connor and Stevens, noted that "here, unlike in Lynch, nothing in the context of the display detracts from the crèche's religious message." The display in Lynch, for example, was accompanied by Santa's house, reindeer and a talking wishing well; here, the crèche "stands alone." To the majority, the crèche conveyed an essentially religious message and constituted an endorsement of Christian doctrine. Justice KENNEDY, joined by Chief Justice Rehnquist and Justices White and Scalia, dissented from this holding. In his view, the crèche display was a permissible, noncoercive accommodation of religious faith: "The crèche [is a] purely passive symbol[ ] of [a] religious holiday. Passersby who disagree with [its] message are free to ignore [it], or even to turn their backs, just as they are free to do so when they disagree with any other form of government speech." Justice Kennedy conceded that "[s]ymbolic recognition or accommodation of religious faith may violate the Clause in an extreme case, [such as] the permanent erection of a large Latin cross on the roof of city hall." But the crèche here, in his view, represented no similar "effort to proselytize on behalf of a particular religion."

By a vote of 6–3, however, the Court upheld the display of the menorah. Justice BLACKMUN, writing here only for himself, found that the menorah, while "a religious symbol," conveyed a message that was "not exclusively religious." He emphasized that it stood next to a Christmas tree and a sign saluting liberty and thus had "an 'overall holiday setting' that represents both Christmas and Chanukah—two holidays, not one." He acknowledged that a simultaneous endorsement of Judaism and Christianity would still violate the Establishment Clause, but insisted that government may acknowledge both Christmas and Chanukah as secular holidays. Moreover, he argued, "the relevant question [is] whether the combined display of the tree, the sign, and the menorah has the effect of endorsing both Christian and Jewish faiths, or rather simply recognizes that both Christmas and Chanukah are part of the same winter-holiday season, which has attained a secular status in our society. [The] latter seems far more plausible and is also in line with Lynch." Justice O'CONNOR agreed that the menorah display was constitutional but criticized Justice Blackmun for obscuring the religious nature of the menorah and the holiday of Chanukah. She added: "One need not characterize Chanukah as a 'secular holiday' or strain to argue that the menorah has a 'secular dimension' in order to conclude that [the] display does not convey a message of endorsement of Judaism or of religion in general." She concluded that the joint display as a whole "conveyed a message of pluralism and freedom of belief during the holiday season" and was therefore permissible.

Justice BRENNAN, joined by Justices Marshall and Stevens, dissented with respect to the menorah, finding that it was "indisputably a religious symbol, used ritually in a celebration that has deep religious significance." He concluded that government may not "promote pluralism by sponsoring or condoning displays having strong religious associations on its property." Justice STEVENS, joined by Justices Brennan and Marshall, also dissented with respect to the menorah, arguing that the Establishment Clause "should be construed to create a strong presumption against the display of religious symbols on public property. There is always a risk that such symbols will offend nonmembers of the faith being advertised as well as adherents who consider the particular advertisement disrespectful."

Are the distinctions drawn in Allegheny between the crèche and the menorah display persuasive? Which matters more, the location or the surrounding elements? Is it fair to criticize the opinion as more about "interior decorating" than law? Or does the Court's focus on the perceptions of the reasonable observer capture accurately the concerns animating the Establishment Clause?

2. ***Ku Klux Klan cross.*** In **Capitol Square Review Board v. Pinette**, 515 U.S. 753 (1995), the Court held that the Free Speech Clause compelled the city of Columbus, Ohio, to permit the Ku Klux Klan to erect a large unattended Latin cross on a public square adjacent to the Statehouse, and that the Establishment Clause did not forbid it. Having found that the Free Speech Clause otherwise barred content-based discrimination against the cross because the setting was a public forum (see p. 1283), the Court held, by a vote of 7–2, that permitting the cross equal access to public property along with other unattended private symbols would not, as the city argued, violate the Establishment Clause, even assuming that the Klan cross was an entirely religious and not political symbol (Justice Thomas alone would have treated it as the latter). The Court was divided on the appropriate Establishment Clause analysis, but there were still five votes—those of the concurring and dissenting justices—for applying the "endorsement" test.

While Justice SCALIA wrote for seven Justices on the result, he wrote only for a four-Justice plurality in his reasoning. Joined by Chief Justice Rehnquist and Justices Kennedy and Thomas, he acknowledged that the endorsement test had been applied in previous cases but would not have applied it here. He would have paid no attention to what any observer would have thought, reasonably or otherwise, about whether the Christian symbolism of the Klan cross ought to be attributed to the city government of Columbus: "Petitioners argue [that], because an observer might mistake private expression for officially endorsed religious expression, [permitting the cross would violate the Establishment Clause.] [Petitioners] rely heavily on Allegheny County and Lynch, but each is easily distinguished. In Allegheny County we held that the display of a privately-sponsored crèche on the 'Grand Staircase' of the Allegheny County Courthouse violated the Establishment Clause. That staircase was not, however, open to all on an equal basis, so the County was favoring sectarian religious expression. [In] Lynch we held that a city's display of a crèche did not violate the Establishment Clause because, in context, the display did not endorse religion. [The] case neither holds nor even remotely assumes that the government's neutral treatment of private religious expression can be unconstitutional. [What] distinguishes Allegheny County and [Lynch] is the difference between government speech and private speech. Petitioners assert, in effect, that that distinction disappears when the private speech is conducted too close to the symbols of government [and thus] private speech can be mistaken for government speech. That proposition cannot be accepted, at least where, as here, the government has not fostered or encouraged the mistake. [It] has radical implications for our public policy to suggest that neutral laws are invalid whenever hypothetical observers may—even reasonably—confuse an incidental benefit to religion with state endorsement." The plurality would have adopted instead a per se rule: "Religious expression cannot violate the Establishment Clause where it (1) is purely private and (2) occurs in a traditional or designated public forum, publicly announced and open to all on equal terms."

Justice O'CONNOR wrote a concurrence joined by Justices Souter and Breyer, and Justice SOUTER wrote a concurrence joined by Justices O'Connor and Breyer. The three concurring Justices expressly reaffirmed Justice O'Connor's endorsement test. Justice O'Connor wrote: "I part company with the plurality on a fundamental point: I disagree that 'it has radical implications for our public policy to suggest that neutral laws are invalid whenever hypothetical observers may—even reasonably—confuse an incidental benefit to religion with State endorsement.' On the contrary, when the reasonable observer would view a government practice as endorsing religion, I believe that it is our duty to hold the practice invalid. The plurality today takes an exceedingly narrow view of the Establishment Clause that is out of step both with the Court's prior cases and with well-established notions of what the Constitution requires. The Clause is more than a negative prohibition against certain narrowly defined forms of government favoritism; it also imposes affirmative obligations that may require a State, in some situations, to take steps to avoid being perceived as supporting or endorsing a private religious message."

The concurring Justices would have required Columbus to exclude the cross from the public square if they had thought its message would be attributed to the city, but they did not view such attribution as likely in the circumstances of this case. Justice O'Connor emphasized that the cross was in the public square rather than upon a government building: "In this case, I believe, the reasonable observer would view the Klan's cross display fully aware that Capitol Square is a public space in which a multiplicity of groups, both secular and religious, engage in expressive conduct [and] able to read and understand an adequate disclaimer. [On] the facts of this case, therefore, I conclude that the reasonable observer would not interpret the State's tolerance of the Klan's private religious display in Capitol Square as an endorsement of religion." Justice Souter noted that the Klan, in support of its application, had stated that the cross would be accompanied by a disclaimer, "legible 'from a distance,' explaining that the cross was erected by private individuals 'without government support,' " and stressed that the city could easily have required the Klan to affix a sign to the cross disclaiming any government endorsement of the Christian faith.

Justices STEVENS and GINSBURG each filed a dissent. Justice Stevens wrote that "the Constitution generally forbids the placement of a symbol of a religious character in, on, or before a seat of government." In his view, "the Establishment Clause prohibits government from allowing, and thus endorsing, unattended displays that take a position on a religious issue.

If the State allows such stationary displays in front of its seat of government, viewers will reasonably assume that it approves of them. [A] reasonable observer would likely infer endorsement from the location of the cross erected by the Klan in this case. Even if the disclaimer at the foot of the cross (which stated that the cross was placed there by a private organization) were legible, that inference would remain, because a property owner's decision to allow a third party to place a sign on her property conveys the same message of endorsement as if she had erected it herself." Justice Ginsburg emphasized that the disclaimer offered here was inadequate, deferring the question whether a disclaimer could ever dispel the Establishment Clause problem.

3. ***Coercion, endorsement, acknowledgment and the Lemon test.*** Do the religious symbolism cases from Lynch to Allegheny and Pinette retain any continuing analytic role for the three-part Lemon test? Or did the Court in these cases effectively adopt a different three-part test: coercion and endorsement are impermissible under the Establishment Clause, but mere acknowledgment of religion is not? On this analysis, the school cases are treated as instances of coercion, even if it means stretching that concept quite far to embrace even psychological coercion. The crèche in Allegheny is invalidated as endorsement. But Sunday closings, legislative prayer, and crèches or menorahs in secularized contexts each count as mere government acknowledgments of religion, comparable to religious allusions in holiday proclamations, on the currency, in the Pledge of Allegiance, and in the art on the walls of public museums. Are such holdings sufficiently respectful toward religion? See Kurland, "The Religion Clauses and the Burger Court," 34 Cath. U. L. Rev. 1 (1984) (arguing that the Court's treatment of the crèche in Lynch "further detracts from the religious significance of the Christmas holiday, [which] every year [pays] more homage to Mammon than to God").

Can the endorsement test be objectively administered, or will it always tend to be administered from the perspective of members of majority faiths? See Van Alstyne, "Trends in the Supreme Court: Mr. Jefferson's Crumbling Wall—A Comment on [Lynch]," 1984 Duke L.J. 770 (suggesting that Lynch reflected "religious ethnocentrism"); Tushnet, "The Constitution of Religion," 18 Conn. L. Rev. 701 (1986) ("Judges will always be broadly representative of the general population, and will be susceptible to all the distortions of interpretation that membership in the majority entails."). Can the endorsement test be consistently administered? Why is a crèche less of an endorsement when surrounded by reindeer and talking wishing wells than when it is standing alone? For commentary favorable toward the endorsement test, see Beschle, "The Conservative as Liberal: The Religion Clauses, Liberal Neutrality, and the Approach of Justice O'Connor," 62 Notre Dame L. Rev. 151 (1987) and Marshall, " 'We Know It When We See It': The Supreme Court and Establishment," 59 S. Cal. L. Rev. 495 (1986). For commentary critical of the test, see Smith, "Symbols, Perceptions, and Doctrinal Illusions: Establishment Neutrality and the 'No Endorsement' Test," 86 Mich. L. Rev. 266 (1987).

4. ***The Ten Commandments.*** Recall that the Court in Stone v. Graham invalidated the posting of the Ten Commandments in a public school classroom. Is the posting or placement of the Ten Commandments in other public settings more permissible? Less coercive? Less likely to appear to be an endorsement? Several prominent public controversies over Ten Commandments displays culminated in a pair of cases decided by the Court at the end of Justice O'Connor's last full Term on the Court. Justice Breyer

provided the decisive vote yielding opposite outcomes in the two cases. On what grounds does he distinguish the two Ten Commandment displays for Establishment Clause purposes? What test does the Court apply in the cases that follow? Does the Lemon test make a comeback?

McCreary County v. ACLU of Kentucky

545 U.S. 844, 125 S. Ct. 2722, 162 L. Ed. 2d 729 (2005).

■ JUSTICE SOUTER delivered the opinion of the Court [in which JUSTICES STEVENS, O'CONNOR, GINSBURG, and BREYER joined].

I. [In] the summer of 1999, petitioners McCreary County and Pulaski County, Kentucky (hereinafter Counties), put up in their respective courthouses large, gold-framed copies of an abridged text of the King James version of the Ten Commandments, including a citation to the Book of Exodus. [In] each county, the hallway display was "readily visible to . . . county citizens who use the courthouse to conduct their civic business." [In] November 1999, respondents American Civil Liberties Union of Kentucky sued the Counties in Federal District Court. Within a month, [the] legislative body of each County authorized a second, expanded display, by nearly identical resolutions reciting that the Ten Commandments are "the precedent legal code upon which the civil and criminal codes of . . . Kentucky are founded." [After] the District Court [ordered] that the "display . . . be removed from [each] County Courthouse," [the] Counties [installed] another display in each courthouse, [consisting] of nine framed documents of equal size, one of them setting out the Ten Commandments explicitly identified as the "King James Version" at Exodus 20:3–17. Assembled with the Commandments are framed copies of the Magna Carta, the Declaration of Independence, the Bill of Rights, the lyrics of the Star Spangled Banner, the Mayflower Compact, the National Motto, the Preamble to the Kentucky Constitution, and a picture of Lady Justice.

II. [Despite] the intuitive importance of official purpose to the realization of Establishment Clause values, the Counties ask us to abandon Lemon's purpose test, or at least to truncate any enquiry into purpose here. [They argue] true "purpose" is unknowable, and its search merely an excuse for courts to act selectively and unpredictably in picking out evidence of subjective intent. The assertions are [unconvincing.] Governmental purpose is a key element of a good deal of constitutional doctrine. [In] Establishment Clause analysis [an] understanding of official objective emerges from readily discoverable fact, without any judicial psychoanalysis of a drafter's heart of hearts. The eyes that look to purpose belong to an " 'objective observer,' " one who takes account of the traditional external signs that show up in the " 'text, legislative history, and implementation of the statute,' " or comparable official act. [The] Counties [want] an absentminded objective observer, not one presumed to be familiar with the history of the government's actions and competent to learn what history has to show. The Counties' position just bucks common sense: reasonable observers have reasonable memories, and our precedents sensibly forbid an observer "to turn a blind eye to the context in which [the] policy arose."

III. We take Stone v. Graham (1980; p. 1657 above), as the initial legal benchmark, our only case dealing with the constitutionality of displaying the

Commandments. Stone recognized that the Commandments are an "instrument of religion." [The] display rejected in Stone had two obvious similarities to the first one in the sequence here: both set out a text of the Commandments as distinct from any traditionally symbolic representation, and each stood alone, not part of an arguably secular display. Stone stressed the significance of integrating the Commandments into a secular scheme to forestall the broadcast of an otherwise clearly religious message and for good reason, the Commandments being a central point of reference in the religious and moral history of Jews and Christians. They proclaim the existence of a monotheistic god (no other gods). They regulate details of religious obligation (no graven images, no sabbath breaking, no vain oath swearing). And they unmistakably rest even the universally accepted prohibitions (as against murder, theft, and the like) on the sanction of the divinity proclaimed at the beginning of the text. [The] Counties' solo exhibit here did nothing more to counter the sectarian implication than the postings at issue in Stone. [When] the government initiates an effort to place this statement alone in public view, a religious object is unmistakable.

[In the] second display, unlike the first, the Commandments were not hung in isolation, [but] include[d] the statement of the government's purpose expressly set out in the county resolutions, and underscored it by juxtaposing the Commandments to other documents with highlighted references to God as their sole common element. The display's unstinting focus was on religious passages, showing that the Counties were posting the Commandments precisely because of their sectarian content. That demonstration of the government's objective was enhanced by serial religious references and the accompanying resolution's claim about the embodiment of ethics in Christ. Together, the display and resolution presented an indisputable, and undisputed, showing of an impermissible purpose.

[After] the Counties changed lawyers, they mounted a third display, without a new resolution or repeal of the old one. The result was the "Foundations of American Law and Government" exhibit, which placed the Commandments in the company of other documents the Counties thought especially significant in the historical foundation of American government. [The] extraordinary resolutions for the second display passed just months earlier were not repealed or otherwise repudiated. Indeed, the sectarian spirit of the common resolution found enhanced expression in the third display, which quoted more of the purely religious language of the Commandments than the first two displays had done. No reasonable observer could swallow the claim that the Counties had cast off the objective so unmistakable in the earlier displays. [He] would probably suspect that the Counties were simply reaching for any way to keep a religious document on the walls of courthouses constitutionally required to embody religious neutrality.

[We] do not decide that the Counties' past actions forever taint any effort on their part to deal with the subject matter. We hold only that purpose needs to be taken seriously under the Establishment Clause and needs to be understood in light of context; an implausible claim that governmental purpose has changed should not carry the day in a court of law any more than in a head with common sense. [Nor] do we have occasion here to hold that a sacred text can never be integrated constitutionally into a governmental display on the subject of law, or American history. We do not forget, and in this litigation have frequently been reminded, that our own courtroom frieze was deliberately designed in the exercise of governmental authority so as to include the figure of Moses holding tablets exhibiting a portion of the Hebrew text of the later, secularly phrased Commandments; in the company of 17 other lawgivers, most of them secular figures, there is no risk that Moses would strike an observer as evidence that the National Government was violating neutrality in religion.

IV. [The dissent] puts forward a limitation on the application of the neutrality principle, with citations to historical evidence said to show that the Framers understood the ban on establishment of religion as sufficiently narrow to allow the government to espouse submission to the divine will. [But] the dissent's argument for the original understanding is flawed from the outset by its failure to consider the full range of evidence showing what the Framers believed. [There] is also evidence supporting the proposition that the Framers intended the Establishment Clause to require governmental neutrality in matters of religion, including neutrality in statements acknowledging religion. [Jefferson] refused to issue Thanksgiving Proclamations because he believed that they violated the Constitution. And Madison [criticized] Virginia's general assessment tax not just because it required people to donate "three pence" to religion, but because "it is itself a signal of persecution. It degrades from the equal rank of Citizens all those whose opinions in Religion do not bend to those of the Legislative authority." The fair inference is that there was no common understanding about the limits of the establishment prohibition, and the dissent's conclusion that its narrower view was the original understanding stretches the evidence beyond tensile capacity.

[While] the dissent fails to show a consistent original understanding from which to argue that the neutrality principle should be rejected, it does manage to deliver a surprise [in saying] that the deity the Framers had in mind was the God of monotheism, with the consequence that government may espouse a tenet of traditional monotheism. This is truly a remarkable view. [It] apparently means that government should be free to approve the core beliefs of a favored religion over the tenets of others, a view that should trouble anyone who prizes religious liberty. Certainly history cannot justify it; on the contrary, history shows that the religion of concern to the Framers was not that of the monotheistic faiths generally, but Christianity in particular, a fact that no member of this Court takes as a premise for construing the Religion Clauses.

[We] are centuries away from the St. Bartholomew's Day massacre and the treatment of heretics in early Massachusetts, but the divisiveness of religion in current public life is inescapable. This is no time to deny the prudence of understanding the Establishment Clause to require the Government to stay neutral on religious belief, which is reserved for the conscience of the individual. [Affirmed.]

■ JUSTICE O'CONNOR, concurring.

[Given] the history of this particular display of the Ten Commandments, the Court correctly finds an Establishment Clause violation. The purpose behind the counties' display is relevant because it conveys an unmistakable message of endorsement to the reasonable observer. It is true that many Americans find the Commandments in accord with their personal beliefs. But we do not count heads before enforcing the First Amendment. Nor can we accept the theory that Americans who do not accept the Commandments' validity are outside the First Amendment's protections. [It] is true that the

Framers lived at a time when our national religious diversity was neither as robust nor as well recognized as it is now. They may not have foreseen the variety of religions for which this Nation would eventually provide a home. They surely could not have predicted new religions, some of them born in this country. But they did know that line-drawing between religions is an enterprise that, once begun, has no logical stopping point. [The] Religion Clauses, as a result, protect adherents of all religions, as well as those who believe in no religion at all.

■ JUSTICE SCALIA, with whom CHIEF JUSTICE REHNQUIST and JUSTICE THOMAS join, and with whom JUSTICE KENNEDY joins as to Parts II and III, dissenting.

I. On September 11, 2001 I was attending in Rome, Italy an international conference of judges and lawyers, principally from Europe and the United States. That night and the next morning virtually all of the participants watched, in their hotel rooms, the address to the Nation by the President of the United States concerning the murderous attacks upon the Twin Towers and the Pentagon, in which thousands of Americans had been killed. The address ended, as Presidential addresses often do, with the prayer "God bless America." The next afternoon I was approached by one of the judges from a European country, who, after extending his profound condolences for my country's loss, sadly observed "How I wish that the Head of State of my country, at a similar time of national tragedy and distress, could conclude his address 'God bless ______.' It is of course absolutely forbidden." That is one model of the relationship between church and state—a model spread across Europe by the armies of Napoleon, and reflected in the Constitution of France, which begins "France is [a] . . . secular . . . Republic." Religion is to be strictly excluded from the public forum. This is not, and never was, the model adopted by America. George Washington added to the [Presidential oath] the concluding words "so help me God." The Supreme Court under John Marshall opened its sessions with the prayer, "God save the United States and this Honorable Court." The First Congress instituted the practice of beginning its legislative sessions with a prayer. [The] day after the First Amendment was proposed, the same Congress that had proposed it requested the President to proclaim "a day of public thanksgiving and prayer, to be observed, by acknowledging, with grateful hearts, the many and signal favours of Almighty God." [And] of course the First Amendment itself accords religion (and no other manner of belief) special constitutional protection.

These actions of our First President and Congress and the Marshall Court were not idiosyncratic; they reflected the beliefs of the period. Those who wrote the Constitution believed that morality was essential to the well-being of society and that encouragement of religion was the best way to foster morality. [Nor] have the views of our people on this matter significantly changed. Presidents continue to conclude the Presidential oath with the words "so help me God." Our legislatures, state and national, continue to open their sessions with prayer led by official chaplains. The sessions of this Court continue to open with the prayer "God save the United States and this Honorable Court." Invocation of the Almighty by our public figures, at all levels of government, remains commonplace. Our coinage bears the motto "IN GOD WE TRUST." And our Pledge of Allegiance contains the acknowledgment that we are a Nation "under God." With all of this reality (and much more) staring it in the face, how can the Court possibly assert that " 'the First Amendment mandates governmental neutrality between . . . religion and nonreligion,' " and that "manifesting a purpose to favor . . . adherence to religion generally," is unconstitutional?

[Besides] appealing to the demonstrably false principle that the government cannot favor religion over irreligion, today's opinion suggests that the posting of the Ten Commandments violates the principle that the government cannot favor one religion over another. That is indeed a valid principle where public aid or assistance to religion is concerned, or where the free exercise of religion is at issue, but it necessarily applies in a more limited sense to public acknowledgment of the Creator. If religion in the public forum had to be entirely nondenominational, there could be no religion in the public forum at all. One cannot say the word "God," or "the Almighty," without contradicting the beliefs of some people that there are many gods, or that God or the gods pay no attention to human affairs. Historical practices [demonstrate] that there is a distance between the acknowledgment of a single Creator and the establishment of a religion. [The] three most popular religions in the United States, Christianity, Judaism, and Islam—which combined account for 97.7% of all believers—are monotheistic. All of them, moreover (Islam included), believe that the Ten Commandments were given by God to Moses, and are divine prescriptions for a virtuous life. Publicly honoring the Ten Commandments is thus indistinguishable, insofar as discriminating against other religions is concerned, from publicly honoring God. Both practices are recognized across such a broad and diverse range of the population—from Christians to Muslims—that they cannot be reasonably understood as a government endorsement of a particular religious viewpoint.[1]

[Justice Stevens asserts] that I would "marginalize the belief systems of more than 7 million Americans" who adhere to religions that are not monotheistic. Surely that is a gross exaggeration. The beliefs of those citizens are entirely protected by the Free Exercise Clause, and by those aspects of the Establishment Clause that do not relate to government acknowledgment of the Creator. [Justice Stevens] fails to recognize that in the context of public acknowledgments of God there are legitimate competing interests: On the one hand, the interest of that minority in not feeling "excluded"; but on the other, the interest of the overwhelming majority of religious believers in being able to give God thanks and supplication as a people, and with respect to our national endeavors. Our national tradition has resolved that conflict in favor of the majority.

II. [As] bad as the Lemon test is, it is worse for the fact that, since its inception, its seemingly simple mandates have been manipulated to fit whatever result the Court aimed to achieve. Today's opinion is no different. In two respects it modifies Lemon to ratchet up the Court's hostility to religion. First, the Court justifies inquiry into legislative purpose, not as an end itself, but as a means to ascertain the appearance of the government action to an " 'objective observer.' " [Under] this approach, even if a government could show that its actual purpose was not to advance religion,

[1] This is not to say that a display of the Ten Commandments could never constitute an impermissible endorsement of a particular religious view. The Establishment Clause would prohibit, for example, governmental endorsement of a particular version of the Decalogue as authoritative. Here the display of the Ten Commandments alongside eight secular documents, and the plaque's explanation for their inclusion, make clear that they were not posted to take sides in a theological dispute. [Footnote by Justice Scalia.]

it would presumably violate the Constitution as long as the Court's objective observer would think otherwise. [Second,] the Court replaces Lemon's requirement that the government have "a secular . . . purpose," with the heightened requirement that the secular purpose "predominate" over any purpose to advance religion. [The] new demand that secular purpose predominate contradicts Lemon's more limited requirement, and finds no support in our cases. In all but one of the five cases in which this Court has invalidated a government practice on the basis of its purpose to benefit religion, it has first declared that the statute was motivated entirely by the desire to advance religion. See Santa Fe, Wallace, Stone, Epperson. [I] have urged that Lemon's purpose prong be abandoned, because [even] an exclusive purpose to foster or assist religious practice is not necessarily invalidating. But today's extension makes things even worse.

III. [Even] accepting the Court's Lemon-based premises, the displays at issue here were constitutional. To any person who happened to walk down the hallway of the McCreary or Pulaski County Courthouse during the roughly nine months when the Foundations Displays were exhibited, the displays must have seemed unremarkable—if indeed they were noticed at all. The walls of both courthouses were already lined with historical documents and other assorted portraits; each Foundations Display was exhibited in the same format as these other displays and nothing in the record suggests that either County took steps to give it greater prominence.

[On] its face, the Foundations Displays manifested the purely secular purpose that the Counties asserted before the District Court: "to display documents that played a significant role in the foundation of our system of law and government." That the Displays included the Ten Commandments did not transform their apparent secular purpose into one of impermissible advocacy for Judeo-Christian beliefs. [When] the Ten Commandments appear alongside other documents of secular significance in a display devoted to the foundations of American law and government, the context communicates that the Ten Commandments are included, not to teach their binding nature as a religious text, but to show their unique contribution to the development of the legal system. [The] acknowledgment of the contribution that religion in general, and the Ten Commandments in particular, have made to our Nation's legal and governmental heritage is surely no more of a step towards establishment of religion than was the practice of legislative prayer we approved in Marsh v. Chambers, and it seems to be on par with the inclusion of a crèche or a menorah in a "Holiday" display that incorporates other secular symbols, see Lynch, Allegheny.

[In] any event, the Court's conclusion that the Counties exhibited the Foundations Displays with the purpose of promoting religion is doubtful. [If] the Commandments have a proper place in our civic history, even placing them by themselves can be civically motivated—especially when they are placed, not in a school (as they were in the Stone case upon which the Court places such reliance), but in a courthouse. [The] first displays did not necessarily evidence an intent to further religious practice; nor did the second displays, or the resolutions authorizing them; and there is in any event no basis for attributing whatever intent motivated the first and second displays to the third.

Van Orden v. Perry

545 U.S. 677, 125 S. Ct. 2854, 162 L. Ed. 2d 607 (2005).

■ CHIEF JUSTICE REHNQUIST announced the judgment of the Court and delivered an opinion, in which JUSTICES SCALIA, KENNEDY, and THOMAS join.

[The] 22 acres surrounding the Texas State Capitol contain 17 monuments and 21 historical markers commemorating the "people, ideals, and events that compose Texan identity." The monolith challenged here stands 6-feet high and 3-feet wide. It is located to the north of the Capitol building, between the Capitol and the Supreme Court building. Its primary content is the text of the Ten Commandments.

[This case presents] us with the difficulty of respecting both faces [of the Establishment Clause]. Our institutions presuppose a Supreme Being, yet these institutions must not press religious observances upon their citizens. One face looks to the past in acknowledgment of our Nation's heritage, while the other looks to the present in demanding a separation between church and state. Reconciling these two faces requires that we neither abdicate our responsibility to maintain a division between church and state nor evince a hostility to religion by disabling the government from in some ways recognizing our religious heritage.

[Whatever] may be the fate of the Lemon test in the larger scheme of Establishment Clause jurisprudence, we think it not useful in dealing with the sort of passive monument that Texas has erected on its Capitol grounds. Instead, our analysis is driven both by the nature of the monument and by our Nation's history. [In] this case we are faced with a display of the Ten Commandments on government property outside the Texas State Capitol. Such acknowledgments of the role played by the Ten Commandments in our Nation's heritage are common throughout America. We need only look within our own Courtroom. Since 1935, Moses has stood, holding two tablets that reveal portions of the Ten Commandments written in Hebrew, among other lawgivers in the south frieze. Representations of the Ten Commandments adorn the metal gates lining the north and south sides of the Courtroom as well as the doors leading into the Courtroom. Moses also sits on the exterior east facade of the building holding the Ten Commandments tablets.

[Of course,] the Ten Commandments are religious—they were so viewed at their inception and so remain. The monument, therefore, has religious significance. According to Judeo-Christian belief, the Ten Commandments were given to Moses by God on Mt. Sinai. But Moses was a lawgiver as well as a religious leader. And the Ten Commandments have an undeniable historical meaning, as the foregoing examples demonstrate. Simply having religious content or promoting a message consistent with a religious doctrine does not run afoul of the Establishment Clause.

There are, of course, limits to the display of religious messages or symbols. For example, we held unconstitutional a Kentucky statute requiring the posting of the Ten Commandments in every public schoolroom. Stone v. Graham. [Neither] Stone itself nor subsequent opinions have indicated that Stone's holding would extend to a legislative chamber. The placement of the Ten Commandments monument on the Texas State Capitol grounds is a far more passive use of those texts than was the case in Stone, where the text confronted elementary school students every day. [Texas] has treated her Capitol grounds monuments as representing the several strands in the State's political and legal history. The inclusion of the Ten

Commandments monument in this group has a dual significance, partaking of both religion and government. We cannot say that Texas' display of this monument violates the Establishment Clause of the First Amendment. [Affirmed.]

■ JUSTICE SCALIA, concurring.

I join the opinion of the Chief Justice because I think it accurately reflects our current Establishment Clause jurisprudence. [I] would prefer to reach the same result by adopting an Establishment Clause jurisprudence that is in accord with our Nation's past and present practices, and that can be consistently applied—the central relevant feature of which is that there is nothing unconstitutional in a State's favoring religion generally, honoring God through public prayer and acknowledgment, or, in a nonproselytizing manner, venerating the Ten Commandments.

■ JUSTICE THOMAS, concurring.

[This] case would be easy if the Court were willing to abandon the inconsistent guideposts it has adopted for addressing Establishment Clause challenges, and return to the original meaning of the Clause. I have previously suggested that the Clause's text and history "resist incorporation" against the States. If the Establishment Clause does not restrain the States, then it has no application here, where only state action is at issue.

Even if the Clause is incorporated, or if the Free Exercise Clause limits the power of States to establish religions, our task would be far simpler if we returned to the original meaning of the word "establishment" than it is under the various approaches this Court now uses. The Framers understood an establishment "necessarily [to] involve actual legal coercion." There is no question that, based on the original meaning of the Establishment Clause, the Ten Commandments display at issue here is constitutional. In no sense does Texas compel petitioner Van Orden to do anything. The only injury to him is that he takes offense at seeing the monument as he passes it on his way to the Texas Supreme Court Library. He need not stop to read it or even to look at it, let alone to express support for it or adopt the Commandments as guides for his life. The mere presence of the monument along his path involves no coercion and thus does not violate the Establishment Clause.

■ JUSTICE BREYER, concurring in the judgment.

[If] the relation between government and religion is one of separation, but not of mutual hostility and suspicion, one will inevitably find difficult borderline cases. And in such cases, I see no test-related substitute for the exercise of legal judgment. That judgment is not a personal judgment. Rather, as in all constitutional cases, it must reflect and remain faithful to the underlying purposes of the Clauses, and it must take account of context and consequences measured in light of those purposes. [The] case before us is a borderline case. [On] the one hand, the Commandments' text undeniably has a religious message, invoking, indeed emphasizing, the Deity. On the other hand, focusing on the text of the Commandments alone cannot conclusively resolve this case. Rather, to determine the message that the text here conveys, we must examine how the text is used. And that inquiry requires us to consider the context of the display.

In certain contexts, a display of the tablets of the Ten Commandments can convey not simply a religious message but also a secular moral message (about proper standards of social conduct). And in certain contexts, a display of the tablets can also convey a historical message (about a historic relation between those standards and the law)—a fact that helps to explain the display of those tablets in dozens of courthouses throughout the Nation, including the Supreme Court of the United States. Here the tablets have been used as part of a display that communicates not simply a religious message, but a secular message as well. The circumstances surrounding the display's placement on the capitol grounds and its physical setting suggest that the State itself intended the latter, nonreligious aspects of the tablets' message to predominate. And the monument's 40-year history on the Texas state grounds indicates that that has been its effect.

The group that donated the monument, the Fraternal Order of Eagles, a private civic (and primarily secular) organization, while interested in the religious aspect of the Ten Commandments, sought to highlight the Commandments' role in shaping civic morality as part of that organization's efforts to combat juvenile delinquency. [The] physical setting of the monument, moreover, suggests little or nothing of the sacred. The monument sits in a large park containing 17 monuments and 21 historical markers, all designed to illustrate the "ideals" of those who settled in Texas and of those who have lived there since that time. [If] these factors provide a strong, but not conclusive, indication that the Commandments' text on this monument conveys a predominantly secular message, a further factor is determinative here. As far as I can tell, 40 years passed in which the presence of this monument, legally speaking, went unchallenged (until the single legal objection raised by petitioner). [Those] 40 years suggest more strongly than can any set of formulaic tests [that] the public visiting the capitol grounds has considered the religious aspect of the tablets' message as part of what is a broader moral and historical message reflective of a cultural heritage.

This case, moreover, is distinguishable from instances where the Court has found Ten Commandments displays impermissible. The display is not on the grounds of a public school, where, given the impressionability of the young, government must exercise particular care in separating church and state. This case also differs from McCreary County, where the short (and stormy) history of the courthouse Commandments' displays demonstrates the substantially religious objectives of those who mounted them, and the effect of this readily apparent objective upon those who view them. That history there indicates a governmental effort substantially to promote religion, not simply an effort primarily to reflect, historically, the secular impact of a religiously inspired document. And, in today's world, in a Nation of so many different religious and comparable nonreligious fundamental beliefs, a more contemporary state effort to focus attention upon a religious text is certainly likely to prove divisive in a way that this longstanding, pre-existing monument has not.

[At] the same time, to reach a contrary conclusion here, based primarily upon on the religious nature of the tablets' text would, I fear, lead the law to exhibit a hostility toward religion that has no place in our Establishment Clause traditions. Such a holding might well encourage disputes concerning the removal of longstanding depictions of the Ten Commandments from public buildings across the Nation. And it could thereby create the very kind of religiously based divisiveness that the Establishment Clause seeks to avoid.

■ JUSTICE STEVENS, with whom JUSTICE GINSBURG joins, dissenting.

The sole function of the monument on the grounds of Texas' State Capitol is to display the full text of one version of the Ten Commandments.

The monument is not a work of art and does not refer to any event in the history of the State. It is significant because, and only because, it communicates the following message: "I AM the LORD thy God. Thou shalt have no other gods before me. Thou shalt not make to thyself any graven images. Thou shalt not take the Name of the Lord thy God in vain. Remember the Sabbath day, to keep it holy. Honor thy father and thy mother, that thy days may be long upon the land which the Lord thy God giveth thee. Thou shalt not kill. Thou shalt not commit adultery. Thou shalt not steal. Thou shalt not bear false witness against thy neighbor. Thou shalt not covet thy neighbor's house. Thou shalt not covet thy neighbor's wife, nor his manservant, nor his maidservant, nor his cattle, nor anything that is thy neighbor's."

Viewed on its face, Texas' display has no purported connection to God's role in the formation of Texas or the founding of our Nation; nor does it provide the reasonable observer with any basis to guess that it was erected to honor any individual or organization. The message transmitted by Texas' chosen display is quite plain: This State endorses the divine code of the "Judeo-Christian" God.

I. [At] the very least, the Establishment Clause has created a strong presumption against the display of religious symbols on public property. [Government's] obligation to avoid divisiveness and exclusion in the religious sphere is compelled by the Establishment and Free Exercise Clauses, which together erect a wall of separation between church and state. [The] wall that separates the church from the State does not prohibit the government from acknowledging the religious beliefs and practices of the American people, nor does it require governments to hide works of art or historic memorabilia from public view just because they also have religious significance. This case, however, is not about historic preservation or the mere recognition of religion. The monolith displayed on Texas Capitol grounds cannot be discounted as a passive acknowledgment of religion, nor can the State's refusal to remove it upon objection be explained as a simple desire to preserve a historic relic. This Nation's resolute commitment to neutrality with respect to religion is flatly inconsistent with the plurality's wholehearted validation of an official state endorsement of the message that there is one, and only one, God.

II. When the Ten Commandments monument was donated to the State of Texas in 1961, it was not for the purpose of commemorating a noteworthy event in Texas history, signifying the Commandments' influence on the development of secular law, or even denoting the religious beliefs of Texans at that time. To the contrary, the donation was only one of over a hundred largely identical monoliths, and of over a thousand paper replicas, distributed to state and local governments throughout the Nation over the course of several decades. This ambitious project was the work of the Fraternal Order of Eagles, a well-respected benevolent organization whose good works [including combating juvenile delinquency] have earned the praise of several Presidents. [When] Cecil B. DeMille, who at that time was filming the movie The Ten Commandments, heard of the judge's endeavor, he teamed up with the Eagles to produce the type of granite monolith now displayed in front of the Texas Capitol and at courthouse squares, city halls, and public parks throughout the Nation.

[Though] the State of Texas may genuinely wish to combat juvenile delinquency, and may rightly want to honor the Eagles for their efforts, it cannot effectuate these admirable purposes through an explicitly religious medium. The State may admonish its citizens not to lie, cheat or steal, to honor their parents and to respect their neighbors' property; and it may do so by printed words, in television commercials, or on granite monuments in front of its public buildings. [The] message at issue in this case, however, is fundamentally different from either a bland admonition to observe generally accepted rules of behavior or a general history lesson.

The reason this message stands apart is that the Decalogue is a venerable religious text. [For] many followers, the Commandments represent the literal word of God as spoken to Moses and repeated to his followers after descending from Mount Sinai. The message conveyed by the Ten Commandments thus cannot be analogized to an appendage to a common article of commerce ("In God we Trust") or an incidental part of a familiar recital ("God save the United States and this honorable Court"). Thankfully, the plurality does not attempt to minimize the religious significance of the Ten Commandments. Attempts to secularize what is unquestionably a sacred text defy credibility and disserve people of faith.

[Moreover,] the Ten Commandments display projects not just a religious, but an inherently sectarian message. There are many distinctive versions of the Decalogue, ascribed to by different religions and even different denominations within a particular faith; to a pious and learned observer, these differences may be of enormous religious significance. In choosing to display this version of the Commandments, Texas tells the observer that the State supports this side of the doctrinal religious debate. [Even] if, however, the message of the monument, despite the inscribed text, fairly could be said to represent the belief system of all Judeo-Christians, it would still run afoul of the Establishment Clause by prescribing a compelled code of conduct from one God, namely a Judeo-Christian God, that is rejected by prominent polytheistic sects, such as Hinduism, as well as nontheistic religions, such as Buddhism. [Today] there are many Texans who do not believe in the God whose Commandments are displayed at their seat of government. Many of them worship a different god or no god at all. Some may believe that the account of the creation in the Book of Genesis is less reliable than the views of men like Darwin and Einstein. [Recognizing] the diversity of religious and secular beliefs held by Texans and by all Americans, it seems beyond peradventure that allowing the seat of government to serve as a stage for the propagation of an unmistakably Judeo-Christian message of piety would have the tendency to make nonmonotheists and nonbelievers "feel like [outsiders] in matters of faith, and [strangers] in the political community."

III. The plurality relies heavily on the fact that our Republic was founded, and has been governed since its nascence, by leaders who spoke then (and speak still) in plainly religious rhetoric. [The] speeches and rhetoric characteristic of the founding era, however, do not answer the question before us. [When] public officials deliver public speeches, we recognize that their words are not exclusively a transmission from the government because those oratories have embedded within them the inherently personal views of the speaker as an individual member of the polity. The permanent placement of a textual religious display on state property is different in kind; it amalgamates otherwise discordant individual views into a collective statement of government approval.

The plurality's reliance on early religious statements and proclamations made by the Founders is also problematic because those views were not espoused at the Constitutional Convention in 1787 nor enshrined in the Constitution's text. Thus, the presentation of these religious statements as a unified historical narrative is bound to paint a misleading picture. [Notably] absent from their historical snapshot is the fact that Thomas Jefferson refused to issue the Thanksgiving proclamations that Washington had so readily embraced [and] Madison more than once [stated] unequivocally that with respect to government's involvement with religion, the " 'tendency to a usurpation on one side, or the other, or to a corrupting coalition or alliance between them, will be best guarded against by an entire abstinence of the Government from interference, in any way whatever, beyond the necessity of preserving public order, & protecting each sect against trespasses on its legal rights by others.' " These seemingly nonconforming sentiments should come as no surprise. Not insignificant numbers of colonists came to this country with memories of religious persecution by monarchs on the other side of the Atlantic.

[Many] of the Framers understood the word "religion" in the Establishment Clause to encompass only the various sects of Christianity. [For] nearly a century after the Founding, many accepted the idea that America was not just a religious nation, but "a Christian nation." The original understanding of the type of "religion" that qualified for constitutional protection under the Establishment Clause likely did not include those followers of Judaism and Islam who are among the preferred "monotheistic" religions Justice Scalia has embraced in his McCreary County opinion. The inclusion of Jews and Muslims inside the category of constitutionally favored religions surely would have shocked Chief Justice Marshall and Justice Story. [Justice Scalia's] inclusion of Judaism and Islam is a laudable act of religious tolerance, but it is one that is unmoored from the Constitution's history and text, and moreover one that is patently arbitrary in its inclusion of some, but exclusion of other (e.g., Buddhism), widely practiced non-Christian religions. [Such a] reading of the First Amendment [would] eviscerate the heart of the Establishment Clause. It would replace Jefferson's "wall of separation" with a perverse wall of exclusion—Christians inside, non-Christians out. It would permit States to construct walls of their own choosing—Baptists inside, Mormons out; Jewish Orthodox inside, Jewish Reform out. A Clause so understood might be faithful to the expectations of some of our Founders, but it is plainly not worthy of a society whose enviable hallmark over the course of two centuries has been the continuing expansion of religious pluralism and tolerance.

[It] is our duty, therefore, to interpret the First Amendment's command that "Congress shall make no law respecting an establishment of religion" not by merely asking what those words meant to observers at the time of the founding, but instead by deriving from the Clause's text and history the broad principles that remain valid today. [The] principle that guides my analysis is neutrality. The basis for that principle is firmly rooted in our Nation's history and our Constitution's text. I recognize that the requirement that government must remain neutral between religion and irreligion would have seemed foreign to some of the Framers. [Fortunately,] we are not bound by the Framers' expectations—we are bound by the legal principles they enshrined in our Constitution. The Establishment Clause [forbids] Texas from displaying the Ten Commandments monument.

■ JUSTICE O'CONNOR, dissenting.

For essentially the reasons given by Justice Souter, as well as the reasons given in my concurrence in McCreary County, I respectfully dissent.

■ JUSTICE SOUTER, with whom JUSTICES STEVENS and GINSBURG join, dissenting.

[A] governmental display of an obviously religious text cannot be squared with neutrality, except in a setting that plausibly indicates that the statement is not placed in view with a predominant purpose on the part of government either to adopt the religious message or to urge its acceptance by others. [A] pedestrian happening upon the monument at issue here needs no training in religious doctrine to realize that the statement of the Commandments, quoting God himself, proclaims that the will of the divine being is the source of obligation to obey the rules. [To] ensure that the religious nature of the monument is clear to even the most casual passerby, the word "Lord" appears in all capital letters (as does the word "am"), so that the most eye-catching segment of the quotation is the declaration "I AM the LORD thy God." [Nothing] on the monument [detracts] from its religious nature. [The] government of Texas is telling everyone who sees the monument to live up to a moral code because God requires it, with both code and conception of God being rightly understood as the inheritances specifically of Jews and Christians.

The monument's presentation of the Commandments with religious text emphasized and enhanced stands in contrast to any number of perfectly constitutional depictions of them, the frieze of our own Courtroom providing a good example, where the figure of Moses stands among history's great lawgivers. While Moses holds the tablets of the Commandments showing some Hebrew text, no one looking at the lines of figures in marble relief is likely to see a religious purpose behind the assemblage or take away a religious message from it. Only one other depiction represents a religious leader, and the historical personages are mixed with symbols of moral and intellectual abstractions like Equity and Authority. Since Moses enjoys no especial prominence on the frieze, viewers can readily take him to be there as a lawgiver in the company of other lawgivers.

[Texas] says that the Capitol grounds are like a museum for a collection of exhibits. [The] Government of the United States does not violate the Establishment Clause by hanging Giotto's Madonna on the wall of the National Gallery. But 17 monuments with no common appearance, history, or esthetic role scattered over 22 acres is not a museum, and anyone strolling around the lawn would surely take each memorial on its own terms without any dawning sense that some purpose held the miscellany together more coherently than fortuity and the edge of the grass. One monument expresses admiration for pioneer women. One pays respect to the fighters of World War II. And one quotes the God of Abraham whose command is the sanction for moral law. The themes are individual grit, patriotic courage, and God as the source of Jewish and Christian morality; there is no common denominator.

[Our] numerous prior discussions of Stone have never treated its holding as restricted to the classroom. Nor can the plurality deflect Stone by calling the Texas monument "a far more passive use of [the Decalogue] than was the case in Stone, where the text confronted elementary school students every day." Placing a monument on the ground is not more "passive" than hanging a sheet of paper on a wall when both contain the same text to be read by anyone who looks at it. The problem in Stone was simply that the State was putting the Commandments there to be seen, just as the monument's inscription is there for those who walk by it. To be sure, Kentucky's compulsory-education law meant that the schoolchildren were forced to see the display every day, whereas many see the monument by choice, and those who customarily walk the Capitol grounds can presumably avoid it if they choose. But [a] state capitol building [is] the civic home of every one of the State's citizens. If neutrality in religion means something, any citizen should be able to visit that civic home without having to confront religious expressions clearly meant to convey an official religious position that may be at odds with his own religion, or with rejection of religion.

How convincing is Justice Breyer's distinction between the Ten Commandments exhibit in McCreary County and the monument on the Texas capitol grounds in Van Orden? How much does, or should, a monument's age affect what a reasonable observer would think of it? Is the Court's approach to religious monuments simply "we know it when we see it," or is there a workable legal standard that incorporates age, history and physical context? These issues arose in oral argument in in The American Legion v. American Humanist Association (No. 17-1717, February 27, 2019), a challenge to a 93-year-old, 40-foot-tall cross-shaped World War I memorial that sits on public land in the middle of a road and is maintained by the government.

SECTION 5. RECONCILING THE RELIGION CLAUSES

As this chapter illustrates, the two religion clauses are sometimes in tension. Some accommodations may appear to have the effect of establishing religion, and a fastidious application of establishment principles might burden free exercise. In the face of these frictions, how much leeway should government have to "accommodate" free exercise concerns, when the Free Exercise Clause does not compel such accommodation? And how much leeway should government have to refuse accommodations on establishment grounds before free exercise compels an exemption? Although several of the above cases deal with these issues, this section addresses them explicitly. It first asks what values might serve to reconcile the clauses. The section then explores, in the words of Chief Justice Rehnquist, how much "play in the joints" there is between the two clauses.

VALUES RECONCILING THE RELIGION CLAUSES

Some commentators have suggested that the two religion clauses can be harmonized by recognizing that "establishment" and "free exercise" serve a single value—protecting the individual's freedom of religious belief and practices, with "free exercise" barring the curbing of that freedom through penalties and "establishment" barring inhibitions on individual choice that arise from governmental aid to religion. Yet viewing the clauses as protecting that single goal does not eliminate the potential tensions. If either the anti-penalties or anti-rewards theme is taken as an absolute, the competing theme will be unduly denigrated: if all penalties are barred, undue benefit to religion may result; if all benefits are barred, undue burdens on religion may be the consequence. Identifying a single "freedom" value, then, does not eliminate the need for accommodation.

Would "neutrality" be a better reconciling theme? Can the religion clauses be read as making the Constitution "religion-blind"? Philip Kurland proposed as a unifying principle that "the freedom and separation clauses should be read as a single precept that government cannot utilize religion as a standard for action or inaction because these clauses prohibit classification in terms of religion either to confer a benefit or to impose a burden." Kurland, "Of Church and State and the Supreme Court," 29 U. Chi. L. Rev. 1 (1961). This view would limit government decisionmaking to secular criteria and would forbid any deliberate accommodation of religion. The Court has never embraced such a strict "neutrality" approach, as the materials below demonstrate. For critical commentary on Kurland's position, see Choper, "The Religion Clauses of the First Amendment: Reconciling the Conflict," 41 U. Pitt. L. Rev. 673 (1980); Pfeffer, "Religion-Blind Government," 15 Stan. L. Rev. 389 (1963).

As another possibility, consider the view that the two clauses might be reconciled by a broad view of permissible accommodation. On this view, free exercise compels some accommodation of religion, establishment forbids other accommodation of religion, and between these two areas lies a broad zone where religious accommodation by government is neither forbidden nor required. This was the view expressed by Justice HARLAN in dissent from **Sherbert v. Verner**, 374 U.S. 398 (1963), which held that free exercise compelled the grant of unemployment benefits to a person who lost her job because she observed Saturday as her sabbath. Justice Harlan expressly noted his disagreement with Kurland that all religious accommodations were forbidden. He viewed a religious exemption from the definition of voluntary unemployment as constitutionally permissible but not compelled: "[There] is, I believe, enough flexibility in the Constitution to permit a legislative judgment accommodating an unemployment compensation law to the exercise of religious beliefs such as appellant's. [But] I cannot subscribe to the conclusion that the State is constitutionally compelled to carve out an exception to its general rule of eligibility in the present case. Those situations in which the Constitution may require special treatment on account of religion are, in my view, few and far between." Consider whether Justice Harlan's view has prevailed in the cases that follow.

FUNDING FOR RELIGIOUS EDUCATION AND INSTITUTIONS

1. In **Locke v. Davey**, 540 U.S. 712 (2004), the Court upheld the State of Washington's refusal, in accordance with its state constitutional ban on the appropriation of public money for "any religious worship exercise or instruction," to allow student recipients of its Promise Scholarship Program to "use the scholarship at an institution where they are pursuing a degree in devotional theology." Although the court of appeals held that Washington's action impermissibly "singled out religion for unfavorable treatment," the Court reversed.

In his opinion for the Court, Chief Justice REHNQUIST stated: "[There] are some state actions permitted by the Establishment Clause but not required by the Free Exercise Clause. [There] is no doubt that the State could, consistent with the [Establishment Clause], permit Promise Scholars to pursue a degree in devotional theology. The question before us, however, is whether Washington, pursuant to its own constitution, [can] deny them such funding without violating the Free Exercise Clause. [The religion clauses] are frequently in tension. Yet we have long said that 'there is room for play in the joints' between them. In other words, there are some state actions permitted by the Establishment Clause but not required by the Free Exercise Clause.

"[Davey] contends that under the rule we enunciated in Lukumi (1993; p. 1571 above), the program is presumptively unconstitutional because it is not facially neutral with respect to religion. [This] would extend the Lukumi line of cases well beyond not only their facts but their reasoning. [In] the present case, the State's disfavor of religion (if it can be called that) [imposes] neither criminal nor civil sanctions on any type of religious service or rite. [The] State has merely chosen not to fund a distinct category of instruction.

"[Because] the Promise Scholarship Program funds training for all secular professions, Justice Scalia contends the State must also fund training for religious professions. But training for religious professions and training for secular professions are not fungible. Training someone to lead a congregation is an essentially religious endeavor. And the subject of religion is one in which both the United States and state constitutions embody distinct views—in favor of free exercise, but opposed to establishment—that find no counterpart with respect to other callings or professions. That a State would deal differently with religious education for the ministry than with education for other callings is a product of these views, not evidence of hostility toward religion.

"[There are] few areas in which a State's antiestablishment interests come more into play. Since the founding of our country, there have been popular uprisings against procuring taxpayer funds to support church leaders, which was one of the hallmarks of an 'established' religion. [Most] States that sought to avoid an establishment of religion around the time of the founding placed in their constitutions formal prohibitions against using tax funds to support the ministry. That early state constitutions saw no problem in explicitly excluding only the ministry from receiving state dollars reinforces our conclusion that religious instruction is of a different ilk.

"Far from evincing the hostility toward religion which was manifest in Lukumi, we believe that the entirety of the Promise Scholarship Program goes a long way toward including religion in its benefits. The program permits students to attend pervasively religious schools, so long as they are accredited. [And] under the Promise Scholarship Program's current guidelines, students are still eligible to take devotional theology courses. [In] short, we find neither in the history or text of Article I, § 11 of the Washington Constitution, nor in the operation of the Promise Scholarship Program, anything that suggests animus towards religion. Given the historic and substantial state interest at issue, we therefore cannot conclude that the denial of funding for vocational religious instruction alone is inherently constitutionally suspect. Without a presumption of unconstitutionality, Davey's claim must fail. The State's interest in not funding the pursuit of devotional degrees is substantial and the exclusion of such funding places a relatively minor burden on Promise Scholars. If any room exists between the two Religion Clauses, it must be here."

Justice SCALIA, joined by Justice Thomas, dissented: "The [Lukumi] opinions are irreconcilable with today's decision, which sustains a public benefits program that facially discriminates against religion. [When] the State makes a public benefit generally available, that benefit becomes part of the baseline against which burdens on religion are measured; and when the State withholds that benefit from some individuals solely on the basis of religion, it violates the Free Exercise Clause no less than if it had imposed a special tax.

"That is precisely what the State of Washington has done here. It has created a generally available public benefit, whose receipt is conditioned only on academic performance, income, and attendance at an accredited school. It has then carved out a solitary course of study for exclusion: theology. No field of study but religion is singled out for disfavor in this fashion. [The] Court's reference to historical 'popular uprisings against procuring taxpayer funds to support church leaders,' is therefore quite misplaced. That history involved not the inclusion of religious ministers in public benefits programs like the one at issue here, but laws that singled them out for financial aid. [One] can concede the Framers' hostility to funding the clergy specifically, but that says nothing about whether the clergy had to be excluded from benefits the State made available to all.

"[The] interest to which the Court defers is not fear of a conceivable Establishment Clause violation, budget constraints, avoidance of endorsement, or substantive neutrality. [It] is a pure philosophical preference: the State's opinion that it would violate taxpayers' freedom of conscience not to discriminate against candidates for the ministry. This sort of protection of 'freedom of conscience' has no logical limit and can justify the singling out of religion for exclusion from public programs in virtually any context. The Court never says whether it deems this interest compelling (the opinion is devoid of any mention of standard of review) but, self-evidently, it is not.

"[The] other reason the Court thinks this particular facial discrimination less offensive is that the scholarship program was not motivated by animus toward religion. The Court does not explain why the legislature's motive matters, and I fail to see why it should. [We] rejected the Court's methodology in McDaniel v. Paty. The State [there] defended [its clergy-disqualification] statute as an attempt to be faithful to its constitutional separation of church and state, and we accepted that claimed benevolent purpose as bona fide. Nonetheless, because it did not justify facial discrimination against religion, we invalidated the restriction.

"[What next?] Will we deny priests and nuns their prescription-drug benefits on the ground that taxpayers' freedom of conscience forbids medicating the clergy at public expense? This may seem fanciful, but recall that France has proposed banning religious attire from schools, invoking interests in secularism no less benign than those the Court embraces today. When the public's freedom of conscience is invoked to justify denial of equal treatment, benevolent motives shade into indifference and ultimately into repression."

Justice THOMAS filed a separate dissent noting that in his view, "the study of theology does not necessarily implicate religious devotion or faith."

2. ***Vouchers and establishment vs. free exercise.*** Recall that in Zelman v. Simmons-Harris (2002; p. 1635, above), the Court held that the

Establishment Clause permits inclusion of religions schools in public education funding schemes. After Locke and Zelman, is it fair to say that the Establishment Clause permits but the Free Exercise Clause does not compel the inclusion of parochial schools in voucher schemes? Are these positions consistent?

FUNDING FOR RELIGIOUS ENTITIES

Trinity Lutheran Church of Columbia, Inc. v. Comer

581 U.S. ___, 137 S. Ct. 2012, 198 L. Ed. 2d 551 (2017).

■ ROBERTS, C. J., delivered the opinion of the Court, except as to footnote 3.

The Missouri Department of Natural Resources offers state grants to help public and private schools, nonprofit daycare centers, and other nonprofit entities purchase rubber playground surfaces made from recycled tires. Trinity Lutheran Church applied for such a grant for its preschool and daycare center and would have received one, but for the fact that Trinity Lutheran is a church. The Department had a policy [based on Article I, Section 7 of the Missouri Constitution] of categorically disqualifying churches and other religious organizations from receiving grants under its playground resurfacing program. The question presented is whether the Department's policy violated the rights of Trinity Lutheran under the Free Exercise Clause of the First Amendment.

II. [The] parties agree that the Establishment Clause [does] not prevent Missouri from including Trinity Lutheran in [its] Program. That does not, however, answer the question under the Free Exercise Clause, because we have recognized that there is "play in the joints" between what the Establishment Clause permits and the Free Exercise Clause compels.

III. A. [The] Department's policy expressly discriminates against otherwise eligible recipients by disqualifying them from a public benefit solely because of their religious character. [Such] a policy imposes a penalty on the free exercise of religion that triggers the most exacting scrutiny. [Like] the disqualification statute in McDaniel, the Department's policy puts Trinity Lutheran to a choice: It may participate in an otherwise available benefit program or remain a religious institution. Of course, Trinity Lutheran is free to continue operating as a church, just as McDaniel was free to continue being a minister. But that freedom comes at the cost of automatic and absolute exclusion from the benefits of a public program for which the Center is otherwise fully qualified. And when the State conditions a benefit in this way, [the] State has punished the free exercise of religion. [It] is true the Department has not criminalized the way Trinity Lutheran worships or told the Church that it cannot subscribe to a certain view of the Gospel. But [as] the Court put it more than 50 years ago, "[i]t is too late in the day to doubt that the liberties of religion and expression may be infringed by the denial of or placing of conditions upon a benefit or privilege." Sherbert.

B. [The] Department [argues] that the free exercise question in this case is instead controlled by our decision in Locke v. Davey. It is not. [Davey] was not denied a scholarship because of who he was; he was denied a scholarship because of what he proposed to do—use the funds to prepare for the ministry. Here there is no question that Trinity Lutheran was denied a grant simply because of what it is—a church.

The Court in Locke also stated that Washington's choice was in keeping with the State's antiestablishment interest in not using taxpayer funds to pay for the training of clergy; in fact, the Court could "think of few areas in which a State's antiestablishment interests come more into play." [Here] nothing of the sort can be said about a program to use recycled tires to resurface playgrounds.

[The] Department emphasizes Missouri's similar [tradition] of not furnishing taxpayer money directly to churches. But Locke took account of Washington's antiestablishment interest only after determining [that] the scholarship program did not "require students to choose between their religious beliefs and receiving a government benefit." [In] this case, there is no dispute that Trinity Lutheran is put to the choice between being a church and receiving a government benefit. The rule is simple: No churches need apply.[1]

C. Under [the "most rigorous" scrutiny] standard, only a state interest "of the highest order" can justify the Department's discriminatory policy. Yet the Department offers nothing more than Missouri's policy preference for skating as far as possible from religious establishment concerns. In the face of the clear infringement on free exercise before us, that interest cannot qualify as compelling.

■ JUSTICE THOMAS, with whom JUSTICE GORSUCH joins, concurring in part.

[This] Court's endorsement in Locke of even a "mild kind" of discrimination against religion remains troubling. But because the Court today appropriately construes Locke narrowly, see Part III-B, ante, and because no party has asked us to reconsider it, I join nearly all of the Court's opinion.

■ JUSTICE GORSUCH, with whom JUSTICE THOMAS joins, concurring in part.

[I] offer only two modest qualifications.

First, the Court leaves open the possibility a useful distinction might be drawn between laws that discriminate on the basis of religious status and religious use. Respectfully, I harbor doubts about the stability of such a line. Does a religious man say grace before dinner? Or does a man begin his meal in a religious manner? Is it a religious group that built the playground? Or did a group build the playground so it might be used to advance a religious mission? The distinction blurs in much the same way the line between acts and omissions can blur when stared at too long, leaving us to ask (for example) whether the man who drowns by awaiting the incoming tide does so by act (coming upon the sea) or omission (allowing the sea to come upon him).

[Second] and for similar reasons, I am unable to join the footnoted observation, n. 3, that "[t]his case involves express discrimination based on religious identity with respect to playground resurfacing." Of course the footnote is entirely correct, but I worry that some might mistakenly read it

[1] [Footnote 3 to the opinion of the Court]: This case involves express discrimination based on religious identity with respect to playground resurfacing. We do not address religious uses of funding or other forms of discrimination.

to suggest that only "playground resurfacing" cases, or only those with some association with children's safety or health, or perhaps some other social good we find sufficiently worthy, are governed by the legal rules recounted in and faithfully applied by the Court's opinion. [And] the general principles here do not permit discrimination against religious exercise—whether on the playground or anywhere else.

■ JUSTICE BREYER, concurring in the judgment.

[I] find relevant, and would emphasize, the particular nature of the "public benefit" here at issue. The Court stated in Everson that "cutting off church schools from" such "general government services as ordinary police and fire protection . . . is obviously not the purpose of the First Amendment." Here, the State would cut Trinity Lutheran off from participation in a general program designed to secure or to improve the health and safety of children. I see no significant difference. [I] would leave the application of the Free Exercise Clause to other kinds of public benefits for another day.

■ JUSTICE SOTOMAYOR, with whom JUSTICE GINSBURG joins, dissenting.

[This] case is about nothing less than the relationship between religious institutions and the civil government—that is, between church and state. The Court today profoundly changes that relationship by holding, for the first time, that the Constitution requires the government to provide public funds directly to a church.

[This] is a case about whether Missouri can decline to fund improvements to the facilities the Church uses to practice and spread its religious views. [The] Court has repeatedly warned that [payments] from the government to a house of worship would cross the line drawn by the Establishment Clause. [The] Establishment Clause does not allow Missouri to grant the Church's funding request because the Church uses the Learning Center, including its playground, in conjunction with its religious mission. [The] Court may simply disagree with this account of the facts and think that the Church does not put its playground to religious use. If so, its mistake is limited to this case. But if it agrees that the State's funding would further religious activity and sees no Establishment Clause problem, then it must be implicitly applying a rule other than the one agreed to in our precedents. [Such] a break with precedent would mark a radical mistake.

[Even] assuming the absence of an Establishment Clause violation and proceeding on the Court's preferred front—the Free Exercise Clause—the Court errs. It claims that the government may not draw lines based on an entity's religious "status." But we have repeatedly said that it can. [The] play in the joints between the Free Exercise and Establishment Clauses gives government some room to recognize the unique status of religious entities and to single them out on that basis for exclusion from otherwise generally applicable laws. [The] State need not, for example, fund the training of a religious group's leaders, those "who will preach their beliefs, teach their faith, and carry out their mission." It may instead avoid the historic "antiestablishment interests" raised by the use of "taxpayer funds to support church leaders." Locke.

Missouri has decided that the unique status of houses of worship requires a special rule when it comes to public funds. [Missouri's] decision, which has deep roots in our Nation's history, reflects a reasonable and constitutional judgment. [The] use of public funds to support core religious institutions can safely be described as a hallmark of the States' early experiences with religious establishment. Every state establishment saw laws passed to raise public funds and direct them toward houses of worship and ministers. And as the States all disestablished, one by one, they all undid those laws. [In] Locke, this Court expressed an understanding of, and respect for, this history.

[Like] the use of public dollars for ministers at issue in Locke, turning over public funds to houses of worship implicates serious anti-establishment and free exercise interests. [As] was true in Locke, a prophylactic rule against the use of public funds for houses of worship is a permissible accommodation of these weighty interests. The rule has a historical pedigree identical to that of the provision in Locke. [Today,] thirty-eight States have a counterpart to Missouri's Article I, § 7.10. The provisions, as a general matter, date back to or before these States' original Constitutions. That so many States have for so long drawn a line that prohibits public funding for houses of worship, based on principles rooted in this Nation's understanding of how best to foster religious liberty, supports the conclusion that public funding of houses of worship "is of a different ilk." Locke.

[The Court also] suggests that this case is different because it involves "discrimination" in the form of the denial of access to a possible benefit. But in this area of law, a decision to treat entities differently based on distinctions that the Religion Clauses make relevant does not amount to discrimination.

At bottom, the Court creates the following rule today: The government may draw lines on the basis of religious status to grant a benefit to religious persons or entities but it may not draw lines on that basis when doing so would further the interests the Religion Clauses protect in other ways. Nothing supports this lopsided outcome.

---

1. ***Footnote 3 and secular use.*** Much of the discussion around Trinity Lutheran has focused on footnote 3: "This case involves express discrimination based on religious identity with respect to playground resurfacing. We do not address religious uses of funding or other forms of discrimination." Only Chief Justice Roberts and Justices Kennedy, Alito, and Kagan signed on; Justices Thomas and Gorsuch did not. Commentators have pointed to this plurality footnote as a way in which the Court has left itself the option of letting states decline to provide funds when the activity involved seems more "religious" than playground resurfacing. How important to the Court's reasoning is the secular nature of the funds' use? What other things could count as "secular" uses of money? Could a church be eligible for a state grant program that helps weatherproof buildings if the church wants to use the funds to renovate its sanctuary, as opposed to a related school? How do you weigh Justice Sotomayor's argument that the church conceives of the school as part of its religious mission?

2. ***Locke v. Davey after Trinity Lutheran.*** The Court did not overrule Locke; instead, it distinguished the case by saying Locke addressed the religious *use* of funds, while the issue in Trinity Lutheran involved the church's *status* as religious. How convincing is this distinction? Is Justice Gorsuch correct that status and use are not coherent categories? Trinity Lutheran is the first case in which the Court has required the government to give money directly to a religious organization. How much of Locke's reasoning still stands after Trinity Lutheran? Is there still room for play in

the joints between the religion clauses, or does Trinity Lutheran narrow the gap between what the Establishment Clause permits and the Free Exercise Clause requires? For an analysis of Trinity Lutheran's consideration of, and potential effect on, Locke and other areas of religion clauses jurisprudence, including vouchers, see Laycock, "Churches, Playgrounds, Government Dollars—And Schools?", 131 Harv. L. Rev. 133 (2017).

LEGISLATIVE ACCOMMODATION OF RELIGION

1. ***Accommodation.*** Statutory accommodations in the interest of free exercise values present recurrent problems of tension between the goals of the Free Exercise and Establishment Clauses. Statutory exemptions are widespread in legislation in such areas as social security and labor. Recall that, in Sherbert, Justice Harlan's dissent argued that legislators have broad discretion to promote free exercise values by enacting statutory accommodations. By what standards should statutory accommodations of religious practices be judged? Might some legislative accommodations amount to the impermissible establishment of religion? The following cases explore this question.

2. ***Accommodation vs. delegation.*** One clear limit on religious accommodation is that government may not, consistent with the Establishment Clause, delegate to a religious entity the power to exercise civic authority. **Larkin v. Grendel's Den, Inc.**, 459 U.S. 116 (1982), struck down a Massachusetts law that gave churches and schools the power to veto the issuance of liquor licenses to restaurants within 500 feet of the church or school buildings. By a vote of 8–1, the Court balked at the notion that governmental authority could so be conferred on religious organizations. Chief Justice BURGER's majority opinion conceded a church's "valid interest in being insulated from certain kinds of commercial establishments, including those dispensing liquor," but concluded that the delegation of a veto power to churches had the effect of "advancing religion," impermissible under the Lemon standards. He added that "the mere appearance of a joint exercise of legislative authority by Church and State provides a significant symbolic benefit to religion in the minds of some." Moreover, turning to the "entanglement" prong of the Lemon test, he found that the law "enmeshes churches in the exercise of substantial governmental powers contrary to our consistent interpretation of the Establishment Clause." Justice REHNQUIST, the sole dissenter, argued that because the state could have banned all liquor establishments within 500 feet of a church, the Constitution did not prevent the state from electing a less drastic alternative of allowing each church to decide whether it wished to be "unmolested by activities at a neighboring bar."

3. ***Permissible statutory accommodations and their limits.*** Title VII of the Civil Rights Act of 1964, which forbids employment discrimination on the basis of, inter alia, race, gender or religion, requires employers to make reasonable accommodations to the religious practices of employees. (For an interpretation of the statutory "reasonable accommodation" requirement, see Trans World Airlines v. Hardison, 432 U.S. 63 (1977).) The Court has never questioned the permissibility of that accommodation provision. But **Estate of Thornton v. Caldor, Inc.**, 472 U.S. 703 (1985), struck down a Connecticut law providing: "No person who states that a

particular day of the week is observed as his Sabbath may be required to work on such day. An employee's refusal to work on his Sabbath shall not constitute grounds for his dismissal." The law was the result of a substantial revision of the state's Sunday closing laws; under the revision, many businesses were allowed to remain open on Sundays. Chief Justice BURGER's opinion for the Court held that this mandatory, absolute deference to the Sabbath observer constituted an impermissible establishment of religion because the statute clearly advanced "a particular religious practice." The law gave employees an "absolute and unqualified right" not to work on their Sabbath. "The State thus commands that Sabbath religious concerns automatically control over secular interests at the workplace; the statute takes no account of the convenience or interests of the employer or those of other employees who do not observe a Sabbath. [Moreover], there is no exception when honoring the dictates of Sabbath observers would cause the employer substantial economic burdens or when the employer's compliance would require the imposition of significant burdens on other employees required to work in place of the Sabbath observers. Finally, the statute allows for no consideration as to whether the employer has made reasonable accommodation proposals. This unyielding weighting in favor of Sabbath observers over all other interests contravenes a fundamental principle of the Religion Clauses." Justice O'CONNOR, joined by Justice Marshall, filed a concurring opinion in which she sought to distinguish the exception here from that in Title VII. To her, the crucial distinctions were the exclusive religious orientation and absolute character of the Connecticut law: "[A] statute outlawing employment discrimination based on race, color, religion, sex, or national origin has the valid secular purpose of assuring employment opportunity to all groups in our pluralistic society. Since Title VII calls for reasonable rather than absolute accommodation and extends that requirement to all religious beliefs rather than protecting only the Sabbath observance, I believe an objective observer would perceive it as an anti-discrimination law rather than an endorsement of religion or a particular religious provision."

In **Corporation of Presiding Bishop v. Amos**, 483 U.S. 327 (1987), the Court upheld a different provision of Title VII, this one accommodating religious employers rather than employees. Title VII generally prohibits discrimination in employment on the basis of religion, but exempts religious organizations. The exemption, 42 U.S.C. § 702, provides that the antidiscrimination provision "shall not apply [to] a religious corporation [with] respect to the employment of individuals of a particular religion to perform work connected with a carrying on by such corporation [of] its activities." An employee of the Mormon Church who had been discharged from his job as a janitor at a gymnasium run by the Church for failing to qualify as a church member claimed that his firing on the basis of religion violated the Act. The Church claimed that its action was permitted by the exemption in § 702. The employee in turn claimed that if § 702 were "construed to allow religious employers to discriminate on religious grounds in hiring for nonreligious jobs," it violated the Establishment Clause.

Without dissent, the Court rejected the Establishment Clause attack on § 702. Justice WHITE's opinion defended the constitutionality of the general principle underlying the exemption: "We find unpersuasive the District Court's reliance on the fact that [§ 702] singles out religious entities for a benefit. Although the Court has given weight to this consideration in its past decisions [e.g., Mueller; Nyquist] it has never indicated that statutes that give special consideration to religious groups are per se invalid. That would run contrary to the teaching of our cases that there is ample room for accommodation of religion under the Establishment Clause. Where [government] acts with the proper purpose of lifting a regulation that burdens the exercise of religion, we see no reason to require that the exemption come packaged with benefits to secular entities." Justice White insisted that the exemption was "in no way questionable under the Lemon analysis." Under its "purpose" prong, the law need not be "unrelated to religion"; rather, "Lemon's 'purpose' requirement aims at preventing the [governmental] decisionmaker [from] abandoning neutrality and acting with the intent of promoting a particular point of view in religious matters." Nor did the exemption violate the "effect" prong: "A law is not unconstitutional simply because it *allows* churches to advance religion. [For] a law to have forbidden 'effects,' [it] must be fair to say that the *government itself* has advanced religion through its own activities and influence."

Justice BRENNAN, joined by Justice Marshall, concurred in the judgment. He emphasized that "religious organizations have an interest in autonomy in ordering their internal affairs" and must be free to discriminate on a religious basis with respect to religious activities. He was willing to uphold the extension of the exemption to nonreligious activities because distinguishing religious from nonreligious activities would necessitate "ongoing government entanglement in religious affairs," which in turn would have a chilling effect on free exercise. Justice O'CONNOR also concurred only in the judgment, emphasizing her "endorsement" approach set forth in Lynch v. Donnelly. She urged the Court to recognize that laws such as this *do* advance religion, but that the Constitution permits such advancement unless the government's purpose was to endorse religion and "the statute actually conveys a message of endorsement." Justice BLACKMUN also concurred in the judgment, indicating substantial agreement with Justice O'Connor's opinion.

Two years later, however, in **Texas Monthly, Inc. v. Bullock**, 489 U.S. 1 (1989), the Court refused to accept an "accommodation" argument in the context of a tax exemption available only to religious publications. The decision struck down a Texas law exempting from the sales tax "[p]eriodicals that are published or distributed by a religious faith and that consist wholly of writings promulgating the teaching of the faith and books that consist wholly of writings sacred to a religious faith." Justice BRENNAN's plurality opinion, joined by Justices Marshall and Stevens, held that the statute violated the Establishment Clause, relying heavily on the fact that the exemption was not available to any similarly situated nonreligious publication. He thus distinguished such cases as Mueller and Widmar, for in each of these the benefit to religious organizations was one also available to secular organizations: "In all of these cases, [we] emphasized that the benefits derived by religious organizations flow to a large number of nonreligious groups as well. Indeed were those benefits confined to religious organizations, they could not have appeared other than as state sponsorship of religion. [How] expansive the class of exempt organizations or activities must be to withstand constitutional assault depends upon the State's secular aim in granting a tax exemption." For example, if the State chose "to subsidize, by means of a tax exemption, all groups that contributed to the community's cultural, intellectual, and moral betterment, than the exemption for religious publications could be retained." The plurality distinguished the Amos case on the ground that there, but not here, granting the exemption "prevented potentially serious encroachments on protected religious freedoms," since in most cases the payment of a sales tax would not violate the religious tenets of a religious organization.

Justice BLACKMUN, joined by Justice O'Connor, concurred in the judgment. He stressed the inevitable tension between free exercise and Establishment Clause values and insisted that the plurality had gone too far in preferring the latter over the former. He therefore would hold only that "a tax exemption *limited* to the sale of religious literature by religious organizations violates the Establishment Clause." The exemption here constituted a "preferential support for the communication of religious messages. Although some forms of accommodating religion are constitutionally permissible, this one surely is not." Justice White also concurred in the judgment.

Justice SCALIA, joined by Chief Justice Rehnquist and Justice Kennedy, dissented. He argued that the decision would invalidate many religiously targeted tax exemptions, e.g., for church-owned residences for members of the clergy, motor vehicles owned by religious organizations, and meals served at church functions. He relied heavily on Walz, arguing that its sustaining of a tax exemption for religious property did not depend on the availability of a similar exemption for property owned by nonreligious charitable organizations. More broadly, he rejected the conclusion in both the plurality and the concurring opinions that "no law is constitutional whose 'benefits [are] confined to religious organizations' except, of course, those laws that are unconstitutional *unless* they contain benefits confined to religious organizations. Our jurisprudence affords no support for this unlikely proposition." He added that the Court had "often made clear that '[t]he limits of permissible state accommodation of religion are by no means coextensive with a noninterference mandated by the Free Exercise Clause.'" Although it was "not always easy to determine when accommodation slides over into promotion, and neutrality into favoritism," the "withholding of a tax upon the dissemination of religious materials is not even a close case." He argued that where an exemption "comes so close to being a constitutionally required accommodation, there is no doubt that it is at least a permissible one."

Three years after Widmar, Congress enacted the Equal Access Act of 1984, 28 U.S.C. § 4071. The Act extended the access rights recognized for university students in Widmar to secondary school students. The Act provided, inter alia: "It shall be unlawful for any public secondary school which receives Federal financial assistance and which has a limited open forum to deny equal access [to] any students who wish to conduct a meeting within that limited open forum on the basis of the religious, political, philosophical or other content of the speech at such meetings." The Senate Report accompanying the bill contained a finding that high school students are capable of understanding the difference between student-initiated religious speech and state-sponsored religious activity. In **Board of Education v. Mergens**, 496 U.S. 226 (1990), the Court interpreted the Act broadly and rejected the argument that the law violated the Establishment Clause by mandating school sponsorship of religious organizations. The Court held that the school officials' denial of a request for formation of a student Christian club violated the Act and that the application of the law here did not violate the Establishment Clause. There was no majority opinion on the Establishment Clause analysis. Justice O'CONNOR's plurality opinion, joined by Chief Justice Rehnquist and Justices White and Blackmun, found that requiring the school to recognize the religious club did not violate the three-pronged Lemon test. On the "effect" issue, she stated: "Because the Act on its face grants equal access to both secular and religious speech, we think it clear that the Act's purpose was not to 'endorse or disapprove of religion,' Wallace v. Jaffree (quoting Lynch v. Donnelly, O'Connor, J., concurring). [There] is a crucial difference between *government* speech endorsing religion, which the Establishment Clause forbids, and *private* speech endorsing religion, which the Free Speech and Free Exercise Clauses protect. We think that secondary school students are mature enough and are likely to understand that a school does not endorse or support student speech that it merely permits on a nondiscriminatory basis."

Justice KENNEDY, joined by Justice Scalia, concurred only in the judgment on the Establishment Clause issue. He rejected Justice O'Connor's endorsement test and argued instead that the Establishment Clause is violated only where government either gives such direct benefits to a religion that it has the effect or tendency of establishing a state religion, or "coerce[s] any student to participate in a religious activity." He found no such "coercion" here. Justice MARSHALL's concurrence in the judgment, joined by Justice Brennan, emphasized that the Act as applied could be sustained only if a school took special steps to disassociate itself from religious speech and "to avoid appearing to endorse [a religious group's] goals." He insisted that the plurality approach dismissed "too lightly the distinctive pressures created by [the school's] highly structured environment." Justice STEVENS, the sole dissenter, relied solely on statutory grounds, arguing that the Act's requirements were triggered only if other "controversial or partisan" groups were granted access, which was not the case here.

In **Cutter v. Wilkinson**, 544 U.S. 709 (2005), the Court rejected an Establishment Clause defense raised by prison officials against prisoners' attempts to enforce section 3 of the Religious Land Use and Institutionalized Persons Act of 2000 (RLUIPA), which provides: "No government shall impose a substantial burden on the religious exercise of a person residing in or confined to an institution," unless the burden furthers "a compelling governmental interest," and does so by "the least restrictive means." Congress enacted the statute in reaction to the Court's ruling in Employment Division v. Smith (1990; p. 1593 above), which held that the Free Exercise Clause did not require religious exemptions from generally applicable laws, and to the Court's invalidation in City of Boerne v. Flores (1997; p. 902 above), as exceeding Congress's civil rights enforcement authority, of the Religious Freedom Restoration Act, which had attempted to correct Smith by providing statutory religious exemptions across the board.

In Cutter, the Court held unanimously that that the much narrower exemption provisions of RLUIPA on their face qualified as a permissible accommodation of religion. Justice GINSBURG wrote the opinion of the Court: "Just last Term, in Locke v. Davey, the Court reaffirmed that 'there is room for play in the joints between' the Free Exercise and Establishment Clauses, allowing the government to accommodate religion beyond free exercise requirements, without offense to the Establishment Clause. [We] hold that § 3 of RLUIPA fits within the corridor between the Religion Clauses: On its face, the Act qualifies as a permissible legislative accommodation of religion that is not barred by the Establishment Clause. Foremost, we find RLUIPA's institutionalized-persons provision compatible with the Establishment Clause because it alleviates exceptional government-created burdens on private religious exercise. Kiryas Joel, Amos. Furthermore, the Act on its face does not founder on shoals our prior decisions have identified: Properly applying RLUIPA, courts must take adequate account of the burdens a requested accommodation may impose on nonbeneficiaries, see Thornton, and they must be satisfied that the Act's prescriptions are and will be administered neutrally among different faiths, see Kiryas Joel. [RLUIPA] protects institutionalized persons who are unable freely to attend to their religious needs and are therefore dependent on the government's permission and accommodation for exercise of their religion.

"We do not read RLUIPA to elevate accommodation of religious observances over an institution's need to maintain order and safety. Our decisions indicate that an accommodation must be measured so that it does not override other significant interests. [We] have no cause to believe that RLUIPA would not be applied in an appropriately balanced way, with particular sensitivity to security concerns. [Lawmakers] supporting RLUIPA were mindful of the urgency of discipline, order, safety, and security in penal institutions. They anticipated that courts would apply the Act's standard with 'due deference to the experience and expertise of prison and jail administrators in establishing necessary regulations and procedures to maintain good order, security and discipline, consistent with consideration of costs and limited resources.' [Should] inmate requests for religious accommodations become excessive, impose unjustified burdens on other institutionalized persons, or jeopardize the effective functioning of an institution, the facility would be free to resist the imposition. In that event, adjudication in as-applied challenges would be in order." Justice THOMAS filed a concurrence reiterating his position that the Establishment Clause is best interpreted in accord with its original meaning as a federalism provision limiting Congress's but not the states' choices of religious policy.

4. ***Accommodation and public officials.*** Soon after the Court's decision in Obergefell (p. 583 above), a Kentucky county clerk named Kim Davis entered the national spotlight when she began refusing to issue marriage licenses to any couple in order to avoid issuing them to same-sex couples, which she believed would be contrary to her Christian faith. Several couples brought suit against Davis, and a federal district court ordered her to resume issuing marriage licenses. Davis refused to comply even after the Supreme Court denied her request for a stay of the order, and the district judge ordered her jailed for contempt of court. After five days, the judge ordered Davis released on the condition that she not interfere with her deputies issuing marriage licenses. However, Davis was not required to sign the licenses herself, as she had previously done.

Meanwhile, North Carolina enacted a law that permitted public officials to recuse themselves from performing all duties related to marriage ceremonies due to a sincerely held religious objection. Several clerks in North Carolina have invoked the law to avoid issuing marriage licenses to same-sex couples. The statute granted public officials an absolute right to recuse themselves, subject to no balancing test that might take into account the inconvenience to the state or to couples seeking marriage licenses. Does this unqualified accommodation run afoul of the Court's decision in Estate of Thornton v. Caldor, supra 1703?

5. ***Accommodation and religious gerrymandering.*** May a legislature accommodate a religious community by gerrymandering a school

district to keep its students isolated from other students in a distinctive religious community? The Court answered that question negatively in **Board of Education of Kiryas Joel v. Grumet**, 512 U.S. 687 (1994). The case involved a community of ultra-orthodox Jews, the Satmar Hasidim, living in the town of Kiryas Joel, New York, which was named for Grand Rebbe Joel Teitelbaum, the founder of the sect. The boundaries of the town had been drawn carefully under New York's general village incorporation law to exclude all but Satmars, but the town was part of the broader Monroe-Woodbury school district.

The Satmar children in the community attended religious schools with the exception of schoolchildren with special needs. Those children were originally educated by the state in a special annex to one of the private religious schools in Kiryas Joel. But after the then-governing decision in Aguilar v. Felton (1985; p. 1633 above, overruled in 1997 by Agostini v. Felton, p. 1633 above), the special needs children were sent to public schools. Parents of most of these children soon withdrew them from the secular public schools, citing "the panic, fear and trauma [the children] suffered in leaving their own community and being with people whose ways were so different." The Satmar community then turned to the state legislature, which passed a law designating Kiryas Joel as its own school district in order to create a special needs school that would not include students other than Satmar orthodox Jews. In signing the bill into law, Governor Mario Cuomo called it "a good faith effort to solve the unique problem" of providing special education services to the village. By a vote of 6–3, the Court invalidated the special law creating the new school district.

Justice SOUTER, writing for the Court, found the law carving out the separate school district to serve the Satmar community to violate the Establishment Clause under Larkin v. Grendel's Den, which "teaches that a State may not delegate its civic authority to a group chosen according to a religious criterion. [It] is [not] dispositive that the recipients of state power in this case are a group of religious individuals united by common doctrine, not the group's leaders or officers. Although some school district franchise is common to all voters, the State's manipulation of the franchise for this district limited it to Satmars, giving the sect exclusive control of the political subdivision. In the circumstances of this case, the difference between thus vesting state power in the members of a religious group as such instead of the officers of its sectarian organization is one of form, not substance. [If] New York were to delegate civic authority to 'the Grand Rebbe,' Larkin would obviously require invalidation (even though under McDaniel the Grand Rebbe may run for, and serve on his local school board), and the same is true if New York delegates political authority by reference to religious belief. [There is a difference] between a government's purposeful delegation on the basis of religion and a delegation on principles neutral to religion, to individuals whose religious identities are incidental to their receipt of civic authority." He looked behind the facial neutrality of the state law to find a legislative history indicating the state's intent to draw "boundary lines of the school district that divide residents according to religious affiliation."

Justice O'CONNOR concurred in part and in the judgment, emphasizing the particularity of the accommodation here: "Accommodations may [justify] treating those who share [a deeply held] belief differently; but they do not justify discriminations based on sect. A state law prohibiting the consumption of alcohol may exempt sacramental wines, but it may not exempt sacramental wine used by Catholics but not by Jews." She argued that a more generally drafted statute might survive Establishment Clause challenge: "A district created under a generally applicable scheme would be acceptable even though it coincides with a village which was consciously created by its voters as an enclave for their religious group." Justice KENNEDY concurred in the judgment, objecting to New York's "religious gerrymandering," which drew "political boundaries on the basis of religion."

Justice SCALIA, joined by Chief Justice Rehnquist and Justice Thomas, dissented: "The Court today finds that the Powers That Be, up in Albany, have conspired to effect an establishment of the Satmar Hasidim. I do not know who would be more surprised at this discovery: the Founders of our Nation or Grand Rebbe Joel Teitelbaum, founder of the Satmar. The Grand Rebbe would be astounded to learn that after escaping brutal persecution and coming to America with the modest hope of religious toleration for their ascetic form of Judaism, the Satmar had become so powerful, so closely allied with Mammon, as to have become an 'establishment' of the Empire State. And the Founding Fathers would be astonished to find that the Establishment Clause—which they designed 'to insure that no one powerful sect or combination of sects could use political or governmental power to punish dissenters,' has been employed to prohibit characteristically and admirably American accommodation of the religious practices (or more precisely, cultural peculiarities) of a tiny minority sect." He distinguished Larkin v. Grendel's Den on the ground that here there was no delegation to a religious entity, and emphasized the facial neutrality of the law. He found no basis for finding a religious preference here, nor for presuming that New York would not be "as accommodating toward other religions (presumably those less powerful than the Satmar Hasidim) in the future."

What distinguishes the act of incorporation originally creating Kiryas Joel in an area occupied exclusively by Satmar Hasidim from the New York State Legislature's act designating the town as a school district to accommodate special needs children? What implications, if any, does Kiryas Joel have for other accommodations? What Establishment Clause values underlay Justice Souter's opinion?

APPENDIX

TABLE OF JUSTICES

Two sets of dates are given for each Justice, indicating his entire life as well as his years on the Supreme Court; but only the term of office is indicated for each President. The Presidents who made no appointments to the Supreme Court are not included in the table. They were Presidents William H. Harrison (Mar.–Apr. 1841), Zachary Taylor (1849–1850), Andrew Johnson (1865–1869), and Jimmy Carter (1977–1981).

The symbol * and the figure (1) designate the Chief Justices. The other figures trace lines of succession in filling vacancies among the Associate Justices. For example, by following the figure (2) it can be seen that Justice Rutledge was succeeded by Justice Thomas Johnson, he by Justice Paterson, he in turn by Justice Livingston, etc.

Appointed by President Washington, Federalist from Virginia (1789–1797)

*(1) Jay, John (1745–1829). Fed. from N.Y. (1789–1795). Resigned.

(2) Rutledge, John (1739–1800). Fed. from S.C. (1789–1791). Resigned without ever sitting.

(3) Cushing, William (1732–1810). Fed. from Mass. (1789–1810). Died.

(4) Wilson, James (1724–1798). Fed. from Pa. (1789–1798). Died.

(5) Blair, John (1732–1800). Fed. from Va. (1789–1796). Resigned.

(6) Iredell, James (1750–1799). Fed. from N.C. (1790–1799). Died.

(2) Johnson, Thomas (1732–1819). Fed. from Md. (1791–1793). Resigned.

(2) Paterson, William (1745–1806). Fed. from N.J. (1793–1806). Died.

*(1) Rutledge, John (1739–1800). Fed. from S.C. (1795). [Unconfirmed recess appointment.]

(5) Chase, Samuel (1741–1811). Fed. from Md. (1796–1811). Died.

*(1) Ellsworth, Oliver (1745–1807). Fed. from Conn. (1796–1800). Resigned.

Appointed by President John Adams, Federalist from Massachusetts (1797–1801)

(4) Washington, Bushrod (1762–1829). Fed. from Pa. and Va. (1798–1829). Died.

(6) Moore, Alfred (1755–1810). Fed. from N.C. (1799–1804). Resigned.

*(1) Marshall, John (1755–1835). Fed. from Va. (1801–1835). Died.

Appointed by President Jefferson, Republican from Virginia (1801–1809)

(6) Johnson, William (1771–1834). Rep. from S.C. (1804–1834). Died.

(2) Livingston, [Henry] Brockholst (1757–1823). Rep. from N.Y. (1806–1823). Died.

(7) Todd, Thomas (1765–1826). Rep. from Ky. (1807–1826). Died.

Appointed by President Madison, Republican from Virginia (1809–1817)

(5) Duvall, Gabriel (1752–1844). Rep. from Md. (1811–1835). Resigned.

(3) Story, Joseph (1779–1845). Rep. from Mass. (1811–1845). Died.

Appointed by President Monroe, Republican from Virginia (1817–1825)

(2) Thompson, Smith (1768–1843). Rep. from N.Y. (1823–1843). Died.

Appointed by President John Quincy Adams, Republican from Massachusetts (1825–1829)

(7) Trimble, Robert (1777–1828). Rep. from Ky. (1826–1828). Died.

Appointed by President Jackson, Democrat from Tennessee (1829–1837)

(7) McLean, John (1785–1861). Dem. (later Rep.) from Ohio (1829–1861). Died.

(4) Baldwin, Henry (1780–1844). Dem. from Pa. (1830–1844). Died.

(6) Wayne, James M. (1790–1867). Dem. from Ga. (1835–1867). Died.

*(1) Taney, Roger B. (1777–1864). Dem. from Md. (1836–1864). Died.

(5) Barbour, Philip P. (1783–1841). Dem. from Va. (1836–1841). Died.

Appointed by President Van Buren, Democrat from New York (1837–1841)

(8) Catron, John (1778–1865). Dem. from Tenn. (1837–1865). Died.

(9) McKinley, John (1780–1852). Dem. from Ky. (1837–1852). Died.

(5) Daniel, Peter V. (1784–1860). Dem. from Va. (1841–1860). Died.

Appointed by President Tyler, Whig from Virginia (1841–1845)

(2) Nelson, Samuel (1792–1873). Dem. from N.Y. (1845–1872). Resigned.

Appointed by President Polk, Democrat from Tennessee (1845–1849)

(3) Woodbury, Levi (1789–1851). Dem. from N.H. (1845–1851). Died.

(4) Grier, Robert C. (1794–1870). Dem. from Pa. (1846–1870). Resigned.

Appointed by President Fillmore, Whig from New York (1850–1853)

(3) Curtis, Benjamin R. (1809–1874). Whig from Mass. (1851–1857). Resigned.

Appointed by President Pierce, Democrat from New Hampshire (1853–1857)

(9) Campbell, John A. (1811–1889). Dem. from Ala. (1853–1861). Resigned.

Appointed by President Buchanan, Democrat from Pennsylvania (1857–1861)

(3) Clifford, Nathan (1803–1881). Dem. from Me. (1858–1881). Died.

Appointed by President Lincoln, Republican from Illinois (1861–1865)

(7) Swayne, Noah H. (1804–1884). Rep. from Ohio (1862–1881). Resigned.

(5) Miller, Samuel F. (1816–1890). Rep. from Iowa (1862–1890). Died.

(9) Davis, David (1815–1886). Rep. (later Dem.) from Ill. (1862–1877). Resigned.

(10) Field, Stephen J. (1816–1899). Dem. from Cal. (1863–1897). Resigned.

*(1) Chase, Salmon P. (1808–1873). Rep. from Ohio (1864–1873). Died.

Appointed by President Grant, Republican from Illinois (1869–1877)

(4) Strong, William (1808–1895). Rep. from Pa. (1870–1880). Resigned.

(6) Bradley, Joseph P. (1803–1892). Rep. from N.J. (1870–1892). Died.

(2) Hunt, Ward (1810–1886). Rep. from N.Y. (1872–1882). Resigned.

*(1) Waite, Morrison (1816–1888). Rep. from Ohio (1874–1888). Died.

Appointed by President Hayes, Republican from Ohio (1877–1881)

(9) Harlan, John Marshall (1833–1911). Rep. from Ky. (1877–1911). Died.

(4) Woods, William B. (1824–1887). Rep. from Ga. (1880–1887). Died.

Appointed by President Garfield, Republican from Ohio (Mar.–Sept. 1881)

(7) Matthews, Stanley (1824–1889). Rep. from Ohio (1881–1889). Died.

Appointed by President Arthur, Republican from New York (1881–1885)

(3) Gray, Horace (1828–1902). Rep. from Mass. (1881–1902). Died.

(2) Blatchford, Samuel (1820–1893). Rep. from N.Y. (1882–1893). Died.

Appointed by President Cleveland, Democrat from New York (1885–1889)

(4) Lamar, Lucius Q.C. (1825–1893). Dem. from Miss. (1888–1893). Died.

*(1) Fuller, Melville W. (1833–1910). Dem. from Ill. (1888–1910). Died.

Appointed by President Harrison, Republican from Indiana (1889–1893)

(7) Brewer, David J. (1837–1910). Rep. from Kan. (1889–1910). Died.

(5) Brown, Henry B. (1836–1913). Rep. from Mich. (1890–1906). Resigned.

(6) Shiras, George (1832–1924). Rep. from Pa. (1892–1903). Resigned.

(4) Jackson, Howell E. (1832–1895). Dem. from Tenn. (1893–1895). Died.

Appointed by President Cleveland, Democrat from New York (1893–1897)

(2) White, Edward D. (1845–1921). Dem. from La. (1894–1910). Promoted to chief justiceship.

(4) Peckham, Rufus W. (1838–1909). Dem. from N.Y. (1895–1909). Died.

Appointed by President McKinley, Republican from Ohio (1897–1901)

(10) or (8) McKenna, Joseph (1843–1926). Rep. from Cal. (1898–1925). Resigned.

Appointed by President Theodore Roosevelt, Republican from New York (1901–1909)

(3) Holmes, Oliver Wendell (1841–1935). Rep. from Mass. (1902–1932). Resigned.

(6) Day, William R. (1849–1923). Rep. from Ohio (1903–1922). Resigned.

(5) Moody, William H. (1853–1917). Rep. from Mass. (1906–1910). Resigned.

Appointed by President Taft, Republican from Ohio (1909–1913)

(4) Lurton, Horace H. (1844–1914). Dem. from Tenn. (1909–1914). Died.

(7) Hughes, Charles E. (1862–1948). Rep. from N.Y. (1910–1916). Resigned.

*(1) White, Edward D. (1845–1921). Promoted from associate justiceship. (1910–1921). Died.

(2) Van Devanter, Willis (1859–1941). Rep. from Wyo. (1910–1937). Retired.

(5) Lamar, Joseph R. (1857–1916). Dem. from Ga. (1910–1916). Died.

(9) Pitney, Mahlon (1858–1924). Rep. from N.J. (1912–1922). Retired.

Appointed by President Wilson, Democrat from New Jersey (1913–1921)

(4) McReynolds, James C. (1862–1946). Dem. from Tenn. (1914–1941). Retired.

(5) Brandeis, Louis D. (1856–1941). Dem. from Mass. (1916–1939). Retired.

(7) Clarke, John H. (1857–1945). Dem. from Ohio (1916–1922). Resigned.

Appointed by President Harding, Republican from Ohio (1921–1923)

*(1) Taft, William H. (1857–1930). Rep. from Conn. (1921–1930). Resigned.

(7) Sutherland, George (1862–1942). Rep. from Utah (1922–1938). Retired.

(6) Butler, Pierce (1866–1939). Dem. from Minn. (1922–1939). Died.

(9) Sanford, Edward T. (1865–1930). Rep. from Tenn. (1923–1930). Died.

Appointed by President Coolidge, Republican from Massachusetts (1923–1929)

(8) Stone, Harlan F. (1872–1946). Rep. from N.Y. (1925–1941). Promoted to chief justiceship.

Appointed by President Hoover, Republican from California (1929–1933)

*(1) Hughes, Charles E. (1862–1948). Rep. from N.Y. (1930–1941). Retired.

(9) Roberts, Owen J. (1875–1955). Rep. from Pa. (1930–1945). Resigned.

(3) Cardozo, Benjamin N. (1870–1938). Dem. from N.Y. (1932–1938). Died.

Appointed by President Franklin D. Roosevelt, Democrat from New York (1933–1945)

(2) Black, Hugo, L. (1886–1971). Dem. from Ala. (1937–1971). Retired.

(7) Reed, Stanley F. (1884–1980). Dem. from Ky. (1938–1957). Retired.

(3) Frankfurter, Felix (1882–1965). Ind. from Mass. (1939–1962). Retired.

(5) Douglas, William O. (1898–1980). Dem. from Conn. and Wash. (1939–1975). Retired.

(6) Murphy, Frank (1893–1949). Dem. from Mich. (1940–1949). Died.

(4) Byrnes, James F. (1879–1972). Dem. from S.C. (1941–1942). Resigned.

*(1) Stone, Harlan F. (1872–1946). Promoted from associate justiceship (1941–1946). Died.

(8) Jackson, Robert H. (1892–1954). Dem. from N.Y. (1941–1954). Died.

(4) Rutledge, Wiley B. (1894–1949). Dem. from Iowa (1943–1949). Died.

Appointed by President Truman, Democrat from Missouri (1945–1953)

(9) Burton, Harold H. (1888–1964). Rep. from Ohio (1945–1958). Retired.

*(1) Vinson, Fred M. (1890–1953). Dem. from Ky. (1946–1953). Died.

(6) Clark, Tom C. (1899–1977). Dem. from Tex. (1949–1967). Retired.

(4) Minton, Sherman (1890–1965). Dem. from Ind. (1949–1956). Retired.

Appointed by President Eisenhower, Republican from New York (1953–1961)

*(1) Warren, Earl (1891–1974). Rep. from Cal. (1953–1969). Retired.

(8) Harlan, John Marshall (1899–1971). Rep. from N.Y. (1955–1971). Retired.

(4) Brennan, William J., Jr. (1906–1997). Dem. from N.J. (1956–1990). Retired.

(7) Whittaker, Charles E. (1901–1973). Rep. from Mo. (1957–1962). Retired.

(9) Stewart, Potter (1915–1985). Rep. from Ohio (1958–1981). Retired.

Appointed by President Kennedy, Democrat from Massachusetts (1961–1963)

(7) White, Byron R. (1917–2002). Dem. from Colo. (1962–1993). Retired.

(3) Goldberg, Arthur J. (1908–1990). Dem. from Ill. (1962–1965). Resigned.

Appointed by President Lyndon B. Johnson, Democrat from Texas (1963–1969)

(3) Fortas, Abe (1910–1982). Dem. from Tenn. (1965–1969). Resigned.

(6) Marshall, Thurgood (1908–1993). Dem. from N.Y. (1967–1991). Retired.

Appointed by President Nixon, Republican from California (1969–1974)

*(1) Burger, Warren E. (1907–1995). Rep. from Minn. and Va. (1969–1986). Resigned.

(3) Blackmun, Harry A. (1908–1999). Rep. from Minn. (1970–1994). Retired.

(2) Powell, Lewis F., Jr. (1907–1998). Dem. from Va. (1972–1987). Retired.

(8) Rehnquist, William H. (1924–2005). Rep. from Ariz. (1972–1986). Promoted to chief justiceship.

Appointed by President Ford, Republican from Michigan (1974–1977)

(5) Stevens, John Paul (1920–____). Rep. from Ill. (1975–2010). Retired.

Appointed by President Reagan, Republican from California (1981–1989)

(9) O'Connor, Sandra Day (1930–____). Rep. from Ariz. (1981–2006). Retired.

*(1) Rehnquist, William H. (1924–2005). Promoted from associate justiceship. (1986–2005). Died.

(8) Scalia, Antonin E. (1936–2016). Rep. from D.C. (1986–2016). Died.

(2) Kennedy, Anthony M. (1936–____). Rep. from Cal. (1988–2018). Retired.

Appointed by President Bush, Republican from Texas (1989–1993)

(4) Souter, David H. (1939–____). Rep. from N.H. (1990–2009). Retired.

(6) Thomas, Clarence (1948–____). Rep. from Ga. (1992–____).

Appointed by President Clinton, Democrat from Arkansas (1993–2001)

(7) Ginsburg, Ruth Bader (1933–____). Dem. from N.Y. (1993–____).

(3) Breyer, Stephen G. (1938–____). Dem. from Mass. (1994–___).

Appointed by President George W. Bush, Republican from Texas (2001–2009)

*(1) Roberts, John G., Jr. (1955–____). Rep. from D.C. (2005–____).

(9) Alito, Samuel, A., Jr. (1950–____). Rep. from N.J. (2006–____).

Appointed by President Obama, Democrat from Illinois (2009–2017)

(4) Sotomayor, Sonia M. (1954–____). Dem. from N.Y. (2009–____).

(5) Kagan, Elena (1960–____). Dem. from Mass. (2010–____).

Appointed by President Trump, Republican from New York (2017–____)

(8) Gorsuch, Neil M. (1967–____). Rep. from Colo. (2017–____).

(2) Kavanaugh, Brett M. (1965–____). Rep. from D.C. (2018–____).

INDEX

References are to Pages